THE OXFORD COMPANION TO

# THE SUPREME COURT
# OF THE UNITED STATES

# THE OXFORD COMPANION TO
# THE SUPREME COURT
# OF THE UNITED STATES

EDITOR IN CHIEF

**Kermit L. Hall**

EDITORS

James W. Ely, Jr.

Joel B. Grossman

William M. Wiecek

New York   Oxford   □   OXFORD UNIVERSITY PRESS   □   1992

Oxford University Press

Oxford   New York   Toronto
Delhi   Bombay   Calcutta   Madras   Karachi
Kuala Lumpur   Singapore   Hong Kong   Tokyo
Nairobi   Dar es Salaam   Cape Town
Melbourne   Auckland   Madrid

and associated companies in
Berlin   Ibadan

Copyright © by Oxford University Press, Inc. 1992

Published by Oxford University Press, Inc.,
200 Madison Avenue, New York, NY 10016

Library of Congress Cataloging-in-Publication Data
The Oxford companion to the Supreme Court of the United States
Kermit L. Hall, editor in chief;
James W. Ely, Jr., Joel B. Grossman, William M. Wiecek, editors.
p. cm.   Includes bibliographical references and index.
ISBN 0-19-505835-6
1. United States. Supreme Court—Encyclopedias.   I. Hall, Kermit.
KF8742.A35093   1992   347.73'26'03—dc20
[347.3073503]   92-3863

All photographs are courtesy of the collection of the
Supreme Court of the United States.


9 8 7 6 5 4 3 2 1
Printed in the United States of America
on acid-free paper

# Contents

# Introduction

The Supreme Court of the United States is at once the least and the most accessible branch of the federal government. Unlike the executive and legislative departments, its members are appointed rather than elected, and once appointed they serve during good behavior, a virtual grant of life tenure. While the justices hear arguments of cases in open court, they make their decisions in a secret conference, one so closed to the outside world that we have knowledge of its operations only through the usually fragmentary notes kept by the justices. When in conference to debate and decide cases, the justices are alone with each other, excluding even their trusted law clerks.

Yet for all of its secrecy, the Court must ultimately explain most of its decisions through written opinions. The almost five hundred volumes of *United States Reports,* the official reporter of the Supreme Court, provide mute testimony to the Niagara of words that has cascaded from the high court in the past two centuries. In seeking to explain itself, of course, the Court fulfills its ultimate responsibility—to provide, as the inscription above the main entrance of the Supreme Court Building indicates, "Equal Justice Under Law." Because the Court is the highest tribunal for all cases and controversies arising under the Constitution or laws of the United States, it functions as the preeminent guardian and interpreter of the Constitution. The editors of *The Oxford Companion to the Supreme Court of the United States* have taken as their chief task the illumination of the way in which the Court performs this crucial role.

Chief Justice Charles Evans Hughes once declared that the Court is "distinctly American in concept and function." Few other courts in the world have the same scope of power to interpret their national constitutions; none has done so for anything approaching the more than two centuries the Court has been hearing and deciding cases. As Alexis de Tocqueville observed in *Democracy in America,* "I am unaware that any nation on the globe has hitherto organized a judicial power in the same manner as the Americans. . . . A more imposing judicial power was never constituted by any people."

Given the influence that the Court has exercised over American life during the past two centuries, its story is more than just facts and figures, more than just justices and cases. Its story has been, instead, the history of the country itself. Once again, Tocqueville captured the significance of the Court when he observed that "scarcely any political question arises in the United States that is not resolved, sooner or later, into a judicial question." Through the decisions of the Supreme Court, the law has become an extension of political discourse. Anyone seeking to understand the Court must, at the same time, come to terms with the political, social, and economic forces that have generated so much of its work.

We think of the Supreme Court as a legal institution, and certainly it is that. The editors of the *Companion,* however, have also approached the Court as a hybrid political, social, economic, and cultural institution, one that speaks through the law but whose decisions shape and at the same time are shaped by the social order of which it is a part. Hence, the *Companion* is meant to capture the drama of the Court, both in its reaction to the social pressures that bear upon it and in its internal struggles over the Constitution's meaning. In most instances, moreover, the two—external pressures and internal conflict—have been closely related. Recall, for example, the battle between Chief Justice Roger B. Taney and Associate Justice Benjamin R. Curtis over the constitutional basis of slavery in the *Dred Scott* case (1857). Their legal disagreement about whether persons of African descent could be citizens of the United States mirrored the larger struggle between North and South on the eve of the Civil War. In this volume, we have sought to humanize the high court, to place the justices and their decisions within the general framework of American history and life, and to illuminate the practice as well as the theory of "Equal Justice Under Law."

This book provides a comprehensive guide to the history and current operation of the Supreme Court. It does so through an alphabetical organization that comprises several broad categories of entries. Biographical entries explore the personal and professional careers of all of the justices, the nominees who were rejected by the Senate, the most prominent lawyers who have argued before the Court, and many other figures important in the Court's history. Biographical sketches of the justices, such as those about John Marshall and Oliver Wendell Holmes, Jr., include information about their family origins, educations, important formative influences, and occupations, and concentrate on the subjects' legal and judicial careers, the reasons for their attainment of coveted positions on the high court, and the contributions that they made to constitutional law once on the bench.

Another category of entries treats concepts that are central either to the Court's operation or to the meaning of American constitutionalism—including such protean topics as due process of law, separation of powers, and equal protection of the law. Such entries define a concept and trace its historical origins and development; explore the role the concept plays in the Court's operation; discuss the current understanding attached to the concept by lawyers, judges, and scholars; and investigate the meaning of the concept generally in American history and legal culture.

A special emphasis of the volume is on explaining the way in which the justices conduct the day-to-day operations of the Court—its processes, practices, and procedures. Thus, institutional entries cover, in historical perspective, such topics as the office of the chief justice, the judicial clerks, the assignment and writing of opinions, and the justices' workloads. In addition, a number of articles focus on the physical surroundings of the Court, including buildings that have historically housed the Court, and the architecture of the current Supreme Court building. Interesting, as well, are brief pieces on such subjects as the Supreme Court press room and library, the justices' chambers, and the paintings and sculpture adorning the Supreme Court building.

More than four hundred entries in yet another category examine the Court's decisions, from the great case of *Marbury* v. *Madison* (1803), which established the power of the justices to review the constitutionality of acts of Congress, to *Pollock* v. *Farmers' Loan & Trust* (1895), which declared the federal income tax unconstitutional, to *Baker* v. *Carr* (1962), which required that legislative districts be apportioned on the basis of "one person, one vote." The editors have selected the most historically significant of these cases, ones that shed light not just on the evolution of constitutional law but also on the nation's underlying social, cultural, and political dynamics. These entries, therefore, typically provide background information on the case, explain the way in which the justices decided the case, explore any disagreement among the justices about the legal doctrines and public values at stake, and offer insights into what impact the decision has had—on the law and on American life.

Also included in the volume are broad, interpretive entries designed to further two goals. First, a wide range of essays sums up developments in important substantive and procedural areas in which the Court's decisions have had a vital effect on the life of the nation. For example, there are informative treatments of substantive topics ranging from abortion, affirmative action, censorship, education, employment discrimination, and gender, to libel, obscenity and pornography, race and racism, religion, and school prayer; and of procedural topics ranging from cameras in the courtroom and coerced confessions to the insanity defense, right to counsel, self-incrimination, and trial by jury. These essays fashion coherent overviews of major bodies of the Court's work, and are among the most important in the *Companion* because they explore the dynamic relationship between the Court and the society of which it is a part, and the ways in which social demands are mediated into legal responses.

Second, there are four sweeping chronological essays that together form the entry "History of the Court." These articles provide an overview of crucial developments during the entire course of the Court's and the nation's history: Establishment of the Union (1789–1865); Reconstruction, Federalism, and Economic Rights (1866–1920); The Depression and the Rise of Legal Liberalism (1921–1954); and Rights Consciousness in Contemporary Society (1955–1990). Taken as a whole, the "History of the Court" entry explains the process of social demand and legal response that has been such an integral feature of the Court's history, and traces the Court's evolution as the nation's most important body to interpret the Constitution. Also included in the volume is a wide array of articles on historical subjects of particular significance in the history of the Court, including pieces on slavery, Reconstruction, World Wars I and II, the Vietnam War, the civil rights movement, Progressivism, and many more.

A final category of entries explains vocabulary and phrases. These articles are of two kinds: basic technical terms (what is a "writ of mandamus"?) and famous words and phrases associated with the Court (such as the phrase "separate but equal" used in *Plessy* v. *Ferguson* [1896] or "with all deliberate speed" formulated in *Brown* v. *Board of Education II* [1955]).

In creating this volume, the editors wished to make authoritative information about the Court available and accessible to a wide range of readerships, including students, general readers, scholars in law, history, political science, and related disciplines, and professionals in a variety of areas—lawyers, judges, journalists, public servants, and others. There was, and continues to be, a great deal of writing about the Court, but much of it is both highly technical in nature and not readily available to an extended readership, being stored in monographs and in technical publications in specialized libraries. The editors have sought to fill this need for a widely available, authoritative reference source on all aspects of the Court. In the end, almost three hundred contributors have brought to the volume the far-ranging insights and expertise of many disciplines, their ranks including lawyers, judges, journalists, and scholars. They were encouraged to make their presentations fully accessible to a general readership, by offering historical and interpretive background to their subjects, and by avoiding the use of arcane legal terminology.

Within the covers of this volume, there are subjects and perspectives of interest to a diverse array of readers. For nonspecialists, areas of particular note are the volume's extensive offerings on the internal operations and history of the Court; its wealth of biographical information on all of the justices and other major historical figures; its definitions of basic legal and constitutional terminology; its coverage of the process by which justices are selected, nominated, and confirmed (including an entry on the important Senate Judiciary Committee); and its wide-ranging treatment of historical subjects like the famous court-packing incident of 1937, the history of the Japanese Relocation cases, and the role of the Court in dealing with issues such as racial segregation and affirmative action. The broadly formulated interpretive entries described above should be of substantial interest to both general and more specialized readers. Readers with a specialized or technical interest in the Court should note in particular the volume's thorough coverage of the Court's major decisions, as well as its discussions of the Court in relation to important aspects of constitutional law, both substantive and procedural. Some of the essays in the *Companion* are technical in nature; after all, a comprehensive treatment of the Court implies coverage of matters such as the Court's stance on the "Takings" Clause of the Constitution, and the issue of reciprocal tax immunities—perspectives of interest to lawyers, judges, and other specialists.

The editors hope that all readers will benefit from the efforts to cast subjects in broad terms, to do more than present the law. Throughout, contributors have sought to interpret the Court as a symbol of the values of American culture and as an institution whose behavior affects our daily lives. The essay "Contraception," for example, reviews the ways in which the Court's decisions have influenced the most intimate social relations. The essay "First Amendment" assesses the scope of freedom that Americans enjoy in expressing their political ideas. Other entries highlight a variety of cultural perspectives on the Court— including possibilities for understanding the Court's place in American popular culture through movies, plays, and novels. We hope that the *Companion* serves all of its readers well.

### How to Use the Companion

The *Companion* is organized alphabetically with several kinds of cross-references. These cross-references form a carefully planned pattern of articles designed to guide the reader to topics of related interest and from there to topics of general interest. For example, a reader interested in judicial self-restraint would find references leading to a discussion of cases and controversies, the doctrines of standing, ripeness, and mootness, and ulti-mately to the article on judicial review. There are also two indexes—one for all cases mentioned in the volume and the other for topics, proper names, and concepts—and several appendixes. Each element of the *Companion* is meant to complement the others and to facilitate the user's search for information.

Entries in the *Companion* are arranged in alphabetical order on a letter-by-letter rather than a word-by-word basis. Hyphens and spaces between words are ignored, but punctua-tion marks such as commas and semicolons are taken into account; thus "Johnson, Thomas" precedes "Johnson and Graham's Lessee v. McIntosh." In most instances, this system is straightforward enough. The entry "Cohens v. Virginia," for example, precedes "E. C. Knight v. United States"; however, "Cohens v. Virginia" also precedes "Cohen v. California," since the letter "s" in Cohen**s** comes alphabetically before the "v" in "Cohen **v.**" Entry terms that are this closely linked alphabetically are relatively rare. In addition, entries on cases in which the United States is involved as a plaintiff are listed under the name of the other party. For example, the case *United States* v. *Robel* is found as the entry "Robel, United States v." The same holds true for ex parte cases, such as "Siebold, Ex parte."

Each case included as an entry opens with standard information. After the name of the case, readers will find the official *United States Reports* citation—for example, the case of *Kent* v. *Dulles* can be found at 357 U.S. 116, meaning that the case appeared in volume 357 of *United States Reports* and that it begins on page 116. The year the case was decided follows in parentheses. The article opening goes on to provide the date or dates argued (in *Kent* it was 10 April 1958) and decided (16 June 1958); the justices' vote (5 to 4); who wrote for the Court (Justice Douglas); who, if anyone, joined with a concurring opinion; and who dis-sented (Justices Clark, Burton, Harlan, and Whittaker).

The *Companion* relies on several cross-referencing schemes to facilitate its use. At the highest level of organization are blind entries. Blind entries appear within the alphabetical range of headwords, and, for synonyms, related subjects, and inverted terms, refer the reader to the actual entry term under which the topic is discussed. For example, the blind entry "Pentagon Papers Case" refers the reader to the case's official title, *New York Times* v. *United States* (1971). In some instances, a blind entry will send the user to another entry that discusses the concept as part of a larger topic. For example, "Peremptory Challenge" appears as a blind entry that directs the reader to the entry, "Due Process, Procedural."

Within the body of an article, cross-references may also be denoted by insertion of an asterisk. Topics marked in this way will be found elsewhere in the volume as separate entries. For example, in the entry "Boyd v. United States" the terms Fourth and Fifth Amend-ments and privacy are preceded by asterisks, meaning that the reader may wish to look up the entries "Fourth Amendment," "Fifth Amendment," and "Privacy." In some instances, an item marked with an asterisk may not exactly match the form of the entry term. For example, the concept of substantive due process of law is mentioned several times in the *Companion*, but the entry term for this article is inverted as "Due Process, Substantive." When a cross-reference is being made to this entry in another article, the phrase appears as "substantive *due process," which then leads the reader alphabetically to "Due Process, Substantive." Note as well that there is a separate entry titled "Due Process, Procedural." When the use of an asterisk is not feasible, or when doing so would be misleading or unclear, the cross-reference is made parenthetically. For example, in the essay on Justice Joseph P. Bradley, there is a discussion of the doctrine of "affected with a public interest." There is no entry in the *Companion* that specifically treats this term, but it is discussed at length in the entry for the case *Munn* v. *Illinois* (1877), which has thus been placed after the term as a parenthetical cross-reference. Finally, at the end of many entries there are cross-references that direct the user to related or expanded discussions found in other entries. For example, following the entry "Abington School District v. Schempp," a case involving the issue of prayer in public schools, the reader will find a cross-reference to "Religion," an extended essay on the entire subject of the Supreme Court's treatment of religion.

Two other items follow at the end of each entry. Many entries list bibliographical references that users may find helpful if they wish to learn more about the topic in question; longer essays are typically supported by the most bibliographical material. Every effort has been made to include in the bibliographies nontechnical literature that is readily available in a good public library. We have given special attention to books because they are, on balance, usually more accessible than are specialized journals in law, history, and political science. The second item, which either follows the end of the bibliography or, if there is none, the text, is the name of the article's author. To find all articles in the *Companion* by a particular contributor, readers may consult the topical index.

Appendixes have been placed at the end of the *Companion* to provide additional material that does not readily fit in any one entry but that is important to understanding the history and current operation of the Court. These appendixes include tables indicating the succession of justices; the number of days that particular seats on the Court have been left vacant; the presidents who appointed the justices; the Senate votes (when votes were taken) to confirm or reject nominees; and the length of service of each justice. Where appropriate these lists also include persons who were nominated for a position on the high court but who, for a variety of reasons, never served. An additional appendix includes a list of trivia and firsts (for example, what justice served the longest? who was the first woman admitted to the bar of the Supreme Court?) and of traditions (why are the justices seated in a particular way?).

In addition to the cross-references and appendixes, the analytical power of the *Companion* is enhanced by two indexes. The first is an index of every case mentioned in the *Companion* along with its proper citation. In the instance of Supreme Court cases the citation is to *United States Reports* rather than the nominative reports, such as Dallas, Cranch, and Wheaton. The reader interested in learning more about these nominative reporters, who published the Court's decisions until 1874, should turn to the entry "Reporters, Supreme Court." The only exception to the use of *United States Reports* occurs when cases recently decided were available at the time of publication only through the unofficial *Supreme Court Reports, Lawyers' Edition*, or *U.S. Law Week*. The decisions of lower federal courts are cited in *Federal Cases*, for reports in the district and circuit courts up to 1880; the *Federal Supplement*, for district cases since 1880 and circuit cases from 1880 to 1932; and the *Federal Reporter*, for circuit court and U.S. Court of Appeals decisions since 1932. When citing state cases, the editors have relied on the official reports, which are issued by the courts themselves as the authoritative text of their decisions, rather than the widely used but unofficial reports of the West Publishing Company (National Reporter System) and Lawyers Co-operative Publishing Company (*American Law Reports*). Some states, of course, have ceased issuing their own reports and have instead adopted the National Reporter System as their official reporter. The case index covers more than just the cases listed as entries; it encompasses *all* of the cases mentioned anywhere in the volume. Hence, even if a case is not covered as an entry, it may well appear somewhere in the volume, and the case index is the best way to determine if it does.

The *Companion* also has a topical index that directs readers to concepts, persons, places, and institutions mentioned in the text. For example, a user interested in learning about all of the references made to religion that fall outside of the entry "Religion" can turn to the index, which will direct the user not only to cases involving religion but to the use of the concept of religion by the Court. The topical index supplements and reinforces the system of cross-references employed in the main body of the work, and provides access to detailed points of information that are not themselves the subjects of independent entries.

## Acknowledgments

The *Companion* is the work of many people. A separate list of contributors provides the names and institutional affiliations of the approximately three hundred persons whose scholarship, learning, and erudition made this volume possible. We are grateful for the strong support that our colleagues in many disciplines have given to this project.

Along the way, we received excellent help from the Curator's Office of the United States Supreme Court. The entire office performed magnificently, but special thanks are due to its director, Gail Galloway, and to her assistants, Priscilla Goodwin and Lois Long. They not only furnished access to the Supreme Court photograph files but also provided information on the traditions, history, and development of the Court. We are also grateful for the assistance of the staff of the Supreme Court Library and the Supreme Court Historical Society, all of whom gave generously of their time not only to the editors but also to several of the authors. Eric Rise and Timothy Huebner, history graduate students at the University of Florida, in addition to contributing to this volume, also skillfully performed a number of research tasks. Rosalie Sanderson of the Legal Information Center at the University of Florida was helpful in untold ways, as was the entire staff. The editors also thank the library staffs at the University of Wisconsin, the Syracuse University College of Law, and the Vanderbilt University Law School. Delores Keith, Cassie Chism, Danny Payne, Gwen Reynolds, and Betty Donaldson at the University of Florida College of Law's secretarial pool provided expert support.

The idea for the *Companion* was the inspiration of Linda Halvorson Morse at Oxford University Press. She demonstrated, along with her assistant Nancy Davis, patience and considerable insight into the problems of organizing a reference work of this kind. Throughout the past three years she has provided a watchful eye and a supportive presence to help keep the editors headed in the right direction. We wish especially to thank Jeffrey Edelstein, the editor assigned to shepherd the *Companion* to publication. He was a model of decorum, patience, and diplomacy: a perfect blend of hardnosed editor, careful organizer, and sympathetic listener. We and the authors have been fortunate to have such fine support; despite the best efforts of all of these persons, the shortcomings that remain are our own.

15 *May* 1992

Kermit L. Hall
*Editor in Chief*

James W. Ely, Jr.
Joel B. Grossman
William M. Wiecek
*Editors*

# Directory of Contributors

**Henry J. Abraham**
James Hart Professor of Government and
  Foreign Affairs, University of Virginia

**Shirley S. Abrahamson**
Justice, Wisconsin Supreme Court

**David Adamany**
President and Professor of Political Science,
  Wayne State University

**Dean Alfange, Jr.**
Professor of Political Science, University of
  Massachusetts, Amherst

**Francis A. Allen**
Professor of Law and Huber C. Hurst Eminent
  Scholar, University of Florida

**Noel J. Augustyn**
Assistant Director, Court Programs,
  Administrative Office of the United States
  Courts

**Lawrence H. Averill**
Professor of Law, University of Arkansas at
  Little Rock

**Judith A. Baer**
Associate Professor of Political Science, Texas
  A&M University

**Gordon E. Baker**
Professor of Political Science, University of
  California, Santa Barbara

**Richard Allan Baker**
Director, Historical Office, United States Senate

**Thomas E. Baker**
Professor of Law, Texas Tech University

**Gordon Morris Bakken**
Professor of History, California State
  University, Fullerton

**David C. Baldus**
Joseph B. Tye Professor of Law, University of
  Iowa

**Howard Ball**
Dean, College of Arts and Sciences, and
  Professor of Political Science and Public
  Administration, University of Vermont

**William C. Banks**
Professor of Law, Syracuse University

**Randy E. Barnett**
Norman and Edna Freehling Scholar and
  Professor of Law, Illinois Institute of
  Technology, Chicago-Kent College of Law

**Alice Fleetwood Bartee**
Professor of Political Science, Southwest
  Missouri State University

**Lawrence Baum**
Professor of Political Science, Ohio State
  University

**Maurice Baxter**
Professor of History, Indiana University

**Craig Becker**
Associate Professor of Law, University of
  California, Los Angeles

**Hugo Adam Bedau**
Austin Fletcher Professor of Philosophy, Tufts
  University

**Michal R. Belknap**
Professor of Law, California Western School of
  Law

**Martin H. Belsky**
Professor of Law, Albany Law School, Union
  University

**Herman Belz**
Professor of American Constitutional History,
  University of Maryland, College Park

**Michael Les Benedict**
Professor of History, Ohio State University

**Loren P. Beth**
Professor Emeritus of Political Science,
  University of Georgia

**Robert H. Birkby**
Professor of Political Science, Vanderbilt
University

**Susan Low Bloch**
Professor of Constitutional Law, Georgetown
University

**Maxwell Bloomfield**
Professor of History and Law, Catholic
University of America

**Theodore Y. Blumoff**
Professor of Law, Mercer University

**Philip Bobbitt**
Counselor on International Law, United States
Department of State

**David J. Bodenhamer**
Professor of Legal History and Director, POLIS
Research Center, Indiana University—
Purdue University at Indianapolis

**Edgar Bodenheimer**
Professor Emeritus of Law, University of
California, Davis (deceased)

**Lee C. Bollinger**
Dean and Professor of Law, University of
Michigan Law School

**Daan Braveman**
Associate Dean and Professor of Law, Syracuse
University College of Law

**R. Randall Bridwell**
Strom Thurmond Professor of Law, University
of South Carolina

**John Brigham**
Professor of Political Science, University of
Massachusetts, Amherst

**Stanley C. Brubaker**
Associate Professor of Political Science, Colgate
University

**Jon W. Bruce**
Professor of Law, Vanderbilt University

**Patrick J. Bruer**
Assistant Professor of Political Science,
University of North Carolina at Chapel Hill

**Augustus M. Burns III**
Associate Professor of History, University of
Florida

**Gregory A. Caldeira**
Professor of Political Science, Ohio State
University

**Bruce A. Campbell**
Professor of Law, University of Toledo

**Mark W. Cannon**
McLean, Virginia

**Bradley C. Canon**
Professor of Political Science, University of
Kentucky

**Norman L. Cantor**
Professor of Law, Rutgers University, Newark

**Lincoln Caplan**
Staff Writer, The New Yorker Magazine

**Lief H. Carter**
Professor of Political Science, University of
Georgia

**Bill F. Chamberlin**
Joseph L. Brechner Eminent Scholar of
Freedom of Information and Director,
Brechner Center for Freedom of Information,
University of Florida

**Eric A. Chiappinelli**
Associate Professor of Law, University of Puget
Sound

**Kevin M. Clermont**
Flanagan Professor of Law, Cornell Law School

**Morris L. Cohen**
Librarian (Retired) and Professor of Law, Yale
Law School

**Peter J. Coleman**
Professor Emeritus of History, University of
Illinois at Chicago

**Stephen A. Conrad**
Professor of Law, Indiana University,
Bloomington

**Beverly Blair Cook**
Professor Emerita of Political Science,
University of Wisconsin, Milwaukee

**Richard C. Cortner**
Professor of Political Science, University of
Arizona

**Robert J. Cottrol**
Associate Professor of Law, Rutgers University,
Camden

**Barbara Craig**
Associate Professor of Government, Wesleyan
University

**Charles G. Curtis, Jr.**
Partner, Foley & Lardner, Madison, Wisc.

**Michael Kent Curtis**
Associate Professor of Law, Wake Forest
University

**George Dargo**
Professor of Law, New England School of Law

**Thomas Y. Davies**
Associate Professor of Law, University of
Tennessee, Knoxville

**Sue Davis**
Associate Professor of Political Science,
University of Delaware

**Raymond T. Diamond**
Associate Professor of Law, Tulane University

**Michael B. Dougan**
Professor of History, Arkansas State University

**Donald A. Downs**
Associate Professor of Political Science,
University of Wisconsin, Madison

**Robert E. Drechsel**
Professor of Journalism and Mass
Communication, University of Wisconsin,
Madison

**Mary L. Dudziak**
Professor of Law, University of Iowa

**Gerald T. Dunne**
Professor Emeritus of Law, St. Louis University

**Walter Ehrlich**
Professor of History and Education, University
of Missouri—St. Louis

**Theodore Eisenberg**
Professor of Law, Cornell Law School

**Ward E. Y. Elliott**
Professor of Government, Claremont KcKenna
College

**Richard E. Ellis**
Professor of Constitutional and Political
History, State University of New York at
Buffalo

**James W. Ely, Jr.**
Professor of Law and History, Vanderbilt
University

**Leon D. Epstein**
Hilldale Professor Emeritus of Political Science,
University of Wisconsin, Madison

**Nancy S. Erickson**
Attorney, Brooklyn, N.Y.

**Daryl R. Fair**
Professor of Political Science, Trenton State
College

**Richard H. Fallon, Jr.**
Professor of Law, Harvard Law School

**Malcolm M. Feeley**
Professor of Law and Director, Center for the
Study of Law and Society, University of
California, Berkeley

**David Fellman**
Vilas Professor Emeritus of Political Science,
University of Wisconsin, Madison

**Martha A. Field**
Professor of Law, Harvard Law School

**Paul Finkelman**
Visiting Associate Professor, Brooklyn Law
School

**Peter G. Fish**
Professor of Political Science and Law, Director
of Undergraduate Studies in Political
Science, Duke University

**Owen M. Fiss**
Alexander M. Bickel Professor of Public Law,
Yale Law School

**William E. Forbath**
Professor of Law, University of California, Los
Angeles

**Tony Freyer**
University Research Professor of History and
Law, University of Alabama

**Eric T. Freyfogle**
Professor of Law, University of Illinois at
Urbana-Champaign

**Charles Fried**
Carter Professor of General Jurisprudence,
Harvard Law School

**Steven F. Friedell**
Professor of Law, Rutgers University, Camden

**Gerald E. Frug**
Professor of Law, Harvard Law School

**Richard Y. Funston**
Associate Vice-President and Academic
Council, San Diego State University

**Tim Gallimore**
Assistant Professor of Journalism, University of
Missouri—Columbia

**Gail Galloway**
Curator, Supreme Court of the United States

**Richard A. Gambitta**
Associate Professor of Political Science,
University of Texas at San Antonio

**Bryan A. Garner**
Adjunct Professor of Law, Southern Methodist
University

**Patrick M. Garry**
Fellow, Gannett Foundation Media Center,
Columbia University

**Gerard W. Gawalt**
Specialist in Early American History, Library of
Congress

**Frederick Mark Gedicks**
Professor of Law, Brigham Young University

**James L. Gibson**
Distinguished University Professor of Political Science, University of Houston

**Donald Gifford**
Dean and Professor of Law, West Virginia University College of Law

**William Gillette**
Professor of History, Rutgers University

**James J. Gobert**
Professor of Law, University of Essex, England

**Sheldon Goldman**
Professor of Political Science, University of Massachusetts, Amherst

**Leslie Friedman Goldstein**
Professor of Political Science, University of Delaware

**Stephen E. Gottlieb**
Professor of Law, Albany Law School, Union University

**William Crawford Green**
Associate Professor of Government, Morehead State University

**Kent Greenawalt**
University Professor, Columbia University Law School

**Linda Greenhouse**
Supreme Court Correspondent, The New York Times

**Erwin N. Griswold**
Former Dean, Harvard Law School; Attorney, Jones, Day, Reavis & Pogue, Washington, D.C.

**Michael Grossberg**
Associate Professor of History and Law, Case Western Reserve University

**Joel B. Grossman**
Professor of Political Science and Law, University of Wisconsin, Madison

**Joan R. Gundersen**
Professor of History and Women's Studies, California State University, San Marcos

**Kermit L. Hall**
Dean, Henry Kendall College of Arts and Sciences, and Professor of History and Law, University of Tulsa

**Richard F. Hamm**
Assistant Professor of History, State University of New York at Albany

**William H. Harbaugh**
Langbourne M. Williams Professor Emeritus of American History, University of Virginia

**Christine B. Harrington**
Associate Professor of Politics, New York University

**Geoffrey C. Hazard, Jr.**
Sterling Professor of Law, Yale Law School

**Francis Helminski**
Legal Counsel, Mayo Clinic

**Beth M. Henschen**
Associate Professor of Political Science, Loyola University of Chicago

**Herbert Hill**
Professor of Afro-American Studies and Industrial Relations, University of Wisconsin, Madison

**Charles F. Hobson**
Editor, Papers of John Marshall, Institute of Early American History and Culture, College of William and Mary

**Michael Hoeflich**
Dean and Professor of Law, Syracuse University College of Law

**Peter Charles Hoffer**
Professor of History, University of Georgia

**Wythe Holt**
University Research Professor of Law, University of Alabama

**Ari Hoogenboom**
Professor of History, Brooklyn College and Graduate School and University Center, City University of New York

**Herbert Hovenkamp**
Ben V. and Dorothy Willie Professor of Law, University of Iowa

**J. Woodford Howard, Jr.**
Thomas P. Stran Professor of Political Science, Johns Hopkins University

**Timothy S. Huebner**
Doctoral Candidate in American Legal History, University of Florida

**N. E. H. Hull**
Associate Professor of Law, Rutgers University, Camden

**Dennis J. Hutchinson**
Associate Professor in the University and Senior Lecturer in Law, University of Chicago

**Harold M. Hyman**
William P. Hobby Professor of History, Rice University

**Stanley Ingber**
James Madison Chair in Constitutional Law, Drake University

**Robert M. Ireland**
Professor of American Constitutional and Legal History, University of Kentucky

**Robert J. Janosik**
Associate Professor of Politics, Occidental College

**Carol E. Jenson**
Professor of History, University of Wisconsin, La Crosse

**Herbert A. Johnson**
Ernest F. Hollings Professor of Constitutional Law, University of South Carolina

**John W. Johnson**
Professor of History, University of Northern Iowa

**Alan R. Jones**
Parker Professor of History, Grinnell College

**Carolyn C. Jones**
Professor of Law, University of Connecticut

**James E. Jones, Jr.**
Nathan P. Feinsinger Professor of Labor Law, University of Wisconsin, Madison

**Craig Joyce**
Associate Professor of Law, University of Houston

**Ronald C. Kahn**
Professor of Politics, Oberlin College

**Laura Kalman**
Professor of History, University of California, Santa Barbara

**John P. Kaminski**
Director, Center for the Study of the American Constitution, University of Wisconsin, Madison

**Yale Kamisar**
Henry King Ransom Professor of Law, University of Michigan, Ann Arbor

**Kenneth L. Karst**
David G. Price and Dallas R. Price Professor of Law, University of California, Los Angeles

**Irving R. Kaufman**
Judge, U.S. Court of Appeals for the Second Circuit (*deceased*)

**Paul Kens**
Assistant Professor of Political Science, Southwest Texas State University

**Drew L. Kershen**
Professor of Law, University of Oklahoma

**Douglas W. Kmiec**
Professor of Constitutional Law, University of Notre Dame

**Joseph F. Kobylka**
Associate Professor of Political Science, Southern Methodist University

**Donald P. Kommers**
Professor of Law and Government, University of Notre Dame

**Alfred S. Konefsky**
Professor of Law, State University of New York at Buffalo

**Milton R. Konvitz**
Professor Emeritus of Law and Industrial and Labor Relations, Cornell University

**J. Morgan Kousser**
Professor of History and Social Science, California Institute of Technology

**Samuel Krislov**
Professor of Political Science, University of Minnesota, Twin Cities

**Philip B. Kurland**
William R. Kenan Distinguished Service Professor, University of Chicago

**Stanley I. Kutler**
E. Gordon Fox Professor of American Institutions, University of Wisconsin, Madison

**David E. Kyvig**
Professor of History, University of Akron

**Wayne R. LaFave**
David C. Baum Professor of Law and Center for Advanced Study Professor of Law, University of Illinois at Urbana-Champaign

**Jacob W. Landynski**
Professor of Political Science, Graduate Faculty, New School for Social Research

**William Lasser**
Associate Professor of Political Science, Clemson University

**Susan E. Lawrence**
Associate Professor of Political Science, Rutgers University

**William E. Leuchtenburg**
William Rand Kenan, Jr., Professor of History, University of North Carolina at Chapel Hill

**Sanford Levinson**
W. St. Garwood and W. St. Garwood, Jr., Regents Chair in Law, University of Texas at Austin

**Gregory Leyh**
Clerk, Judge Richard F. Suhrheinrich, U.S. Court of Appeals for the Sixth Circuit

**Jonathan Lurie**
Professor of History and Adjunct Professor of Law, Rutgers University

**Stewart Macaulay**
Malcolm Pitman Sharp Professor of Law, University of Wisconsin, Madison

**Thomas C. Mackey**
Assistant Professor of American History, University of Louisville

**Harold G. Maier**
David Daniels Allen Distinguished Professor of Law, Vanderbilt University

**Diane C. Maleson**
Professor of Law, Temple University

**John Anthony Maltese**
Assistant Professor of Political Science, University of Georgia

**Earl M. Maltz**
Professor of Law, Rutgers University, Camden

**Robert F. Martin**
Professor of United States History, University of Northern Iowa

**Karen J. Maschke**
Assistant Professor of Political Science, University of Georgia

**Albert R. Matheny**
Associate Professor of Political Science, University of Florida

**Lynn Mather**
Professor of Government, Dartmouth College

**Mari J. Matsuda**
Associate Professor of Law, University of Hawaii, Honolulu

**James May**
Professor of Law, American University

**Michael W. McCann**
Associate Professor of Political Science, University of Washington

**Thomas R. McCoy**
Professor of Law, Vanderbilt University

**Forrest McDonald**
Distinguished Research Professor, University of Alabama

**G. Roger McDonald**
Lecturer in Government, John Jay College of Criminal Justice, City University of New York

**Gary L. McDowell**
Bradley Visiting Scholar, Harvard Law School

**Marian C. McKenna**
Professor of American Constitutional History, University of Calgary

**William McLauchlan**
Associate Professor of Political Science, Purdue University

**R. Michael McReynolds**
Director, Textual Reference Division, National Archives

**Wallace Mendelson**
Professor Emeritus of Government, University of Texas at Austin

**Philip L. Merkel**
Associate Professor of Law, Western State University

**Roy M. Mersky**
Elton M. Hyder and Martha Rowan Hyder Centennial Professor of Law and Director of Research, University of Texas at Austin

**Keith C. Miller**
Ellis and Nelle Levitt Professor of Law, Drake University

**Elizabeth B. Monroe**
Assistant Professor of History, Indiana University—Indianapolis

**Ralph James Mooney**
Professor of Law, University of Oregon

**Jeffrey B. Morris**
Visiting Associate Professor of Law, Tuoro College

**Paul L. Murphy**
Regents' Professor of American History, University of Minnesota, Twin Cities

**A. E. Keir Nash**
Professor of Political Science, University of California, Santa Barbara

**R. Kent Newmyer**
Professor of History, University of Connecticut

**Gene R. Nichol**
Dean and Professor of Law, University of Colorado School of Law

**Marlene Arnold Nicholson**
Professor of Law, DePaul University

**Donald G. Nieman**
Professor of History, Clemson University

**Jill Norgren**
Professor of Government, John Jay College of Criminal Justice, City University of New York

**Sheldon M. Novick**
Scholar in Residence, Vermont Law School

**David M. O'Brien**
Professor of Government, University of
   Virginia

**Karen O'Connor**
Professor of Political Science, Emory University

**Robert M. O'Neil**
University Professor and Director, Thomas
   Jefferson Center for the Protection of Free
   Expression, University of Virginia

**Timothy J. O'Neill**
Tower-Hester Associate Professor of Politics,
   Southwestern University

**Susan M. Olson**
Associate Professor of Political Science,
   University of Utah

**Peter Onuf**
Mary Ball Washington Professor of American
   History, University of Virginia

**John V. Orth**
Reef C. Ivey II Research Professor of Law,
   University of North Carolina at Chapel Hill

**Ellen Frankel Paul**
Deputy Director, Social Philosophy and Policy
   Center, and Professor of Political Science,
   Bowling Green State University

**J. W. Peltason**
President, University of California

**Barbara A. Perry**
Assistant Professor of Government, Sweet
   Briar College

**H. W. Perry, Jr.**
Associate Professor of Government, Harvard
   University

**Leo Pfeffer**
Attorney, Central Valley, N.Y.

**Richard Polenberg**
Goldwyn Smith Professor of American History,
   Cornell University

**Mary Cornelia Aldis Porter**
Professor Emerita of Political Science, Barat
   College

**Robert Post**
Professor of Law, University of California,
   Berkeley

**H. Jefferson Powell**
Professor of Law, Duke University

**Walter F. Pratt, Jr.**
Associate Professor of Law, University of Notre
   Dame

**Stephen B. Presser**
Professor of Law, Northwestern University

**Kathryn Preyer**
Professor Emerita of History, Wellesley College

**C. Herman Pritchett**
Professor Emeritus of Political Science,
   University of California, Santa Barbara

**Steven Puro**
Associate Professor of Political Science and
   Public Policy, St. Louis University

**David M. Rabban**
Thomas Shelton Maxey Professor of Law,
   University of Texas at Austin

**Robert J. Rabin**
Professor of Law, Syracuse University

**Michael L. Radelet**
Associate Professor of Sociology, University of
   Florida

**Fred D. Ragan**
Professor of History, East Carolina University

**J. H. Reichman**
Professor of Law, Vanderbilt University

**Inez Smith Reid**
Attorney, Laxalt, Washington, Perito & Dubuc,
   Washington, D.C.

**Eric W. Rise**
Doctoral Candidate in U.S. Legal History,
   University of Florida

**Donald L. Robinson**
Professor of Government and Sylvia Dlugasch
   Baumer Professor of American Studies,
   Smith College

**Donald M. Roper**
Associate Professor of History, State University
   of New York, College at New Paltz

**Gerald N. Rosenberg**
Assistant Professor of Political Science and
   Lecturer in Law, University of Chicago

**Norman L. Rosenberg**
Professor of History, Macalester College

**Ronald D. Rotunda**
Professor of Law, University of Illinois at
   Urbana-Champaign

**Robert A. Rutland**
Research Fellow, University of Tulsa

**John Paul Ryan**
Director, Commission on College and
   University Nonprofessional Legal Studies,
   American Bar Association

**Lucy E. Salyer**
Assistant Professor of History, University of New Hampshire

**Thomas O. Sargentich**
Professor of Law, American University

**Judith K. Schafer**
Associate Director, Murphy Institute of Political Economy, Tulane University

**Frederick Schauer**
Frank Stanton Professor of the First Amendment, John F. Kennedy School of Government, Harvard University

**John M. Scheb II**
Associate Professor of Political Science, University of Tennessee, Knoxville

**Harry N. Scheiber**
Associate Dean, School of Law, and Professor of Law and History, University of California, Berkeley

**John R. Schmidhauser**
Professor of Political Science, University of Southern California

**Benno C. Schmidt, Jr.**
President, The Edison Project, Whittle Communications

**Robert G. Seddig**
Professor of Political Science, Allegheny College

**Robert A. Sedler**
Professor of Law, Wayne State University

**John E. Semonche**
Professor of American Constitutional and Legal History, University of North Carolina at Chapel Hill

**Jeffrey M. Shaman**
Professor of Law, DePaul University

**Charles H. Sheldon**
Professor of Political Science, Washington State University

**E. Lee Shepard**
Senior Archivist, Division of Manuscripts and Archives, Virginia Historical Society

**Suzanna Sherry**
Professor of Law, University of Minnesota, Twin Cities

**Stephen A. Siegel**
Professor of Law, DePaul University

**Jerold L. Simmons**
Professor of Constitutional History, University of Nebraska at Omaha

**Christopher Slobogin**
Professor of Law, University of Florida

**Elliot E. Slotnick**
Associate Professor of Political Science, Ohio State University

**Rodney A. Smolla**
Arthur B. Hanson Professor of Law and Director, Institute of Bill of Rights, College of William and Mary

**Aviam Soifer**
Professor of Law, Boston University

**Rayman L. Solomon**
Associate Dean, Northwestern University School of Law

**Harold J. Spaeth**
Professor of Political Science, Michigan State University

**Peter W. Sperlich**
Professor of Political Science, University of California, Berkeley

**Howard T. Sprow**
Professor Emeritus of Law, Albany Law School, Union University

**Robert J. Steamer**
Professor Emeritus of Political Science, University of Massachusetts, Boston

**Barbara C. Steidle**
Assistant Provost and Associate Professor of History, Michigan State University

**Robert David Stenzel**
Attorney, New York, N.Y.

**William B. Stoebuck**
Professor of Law, University of Washington

**Geoffrey R. Stone**
Dean and Harry Kalven Professor of Law, University of Chicago Law School

**James B. Stoneking**
Attorney, Bordas & Bordas, Wheeling, W. Va.

**Rennard Strickland**
Professor of Law and Director, Center for the Study of American Indian Law and Policy, University of Oklahoma

**Michael F. Sturley**
Professor of Law, University of Texas at Austin

**Erwin C. Surrency**
Professor of Law and Director, Law Library, University of Georgia

**Martha Swann**
Assistant Professor of Political Science, Catawba College

**Mary K. Bonsteel Tachau**
Professor of History, University of Louisville

**Susette M. Talarico**
Sandy Beaver Professor of Political Science and
    Director, Criminal Justice Studies, University
    of Georgia

**Abigail M. Thernstrom**
Adjunct Professor, School of Education, Boston
    University

**Michael E. Tigar**
Joseph D. Jamail Centennial Chair in Law,
    University of Texas School at Austin

**Mark V. Tushnet**
Professor of Law, Georgetown University

**Reed Ueda**
Associate Professor of History, Tufts University

**Melvin I. Urofsky**
Professor of History, Virginia Commonwealth
    University

**Sandra F. VanBurkleo**
Assistant Professor of Legal and Constitutional
    History, Wayne State University

**Stephen Vaughn**
Associate Professor of History of
    Communications, University of Wisconsin,
    Madison

**John R. Vile**
Professor of Political Science, Middle Tennessee
    State University

**Samuel Walker**
Professor of Criminal Justice, University of
    Nebraska, Omaha

**Thomas G. Walker**
Professor of Political Science, Emory University

**David Warrington**
Assistant Librarian for Special Collections,
    Harvard Law School Library

**Stephen L. Wasby**
Professor of Political Science, State University
    of New York at Albany

**Carol Weisbrod**
Professor of Law, University of Connecticut

**William M. Wiecek**
Chester Adgate Congdon Professor of Public
    Law and Legislation and Professor of
    History, Syracuse University

**Robert A. Williams**
Professor of Law, University of Arizona

**John W. Winkle III**
Associate Professor of Political Science,
    University of Mississippi

**Christopher Wolfe**
Associate Professor of Political Science,
    Marquette University

**Stephen B. Wood**
Professor of Political Science, University of
    Rhode Island

**John R. Wunder**
Professor of History and Director, Center for
    Great Plains Studies, University of
    Nebraska—Lincoln

**Tinsley E. Yarbrough**
Professor of Political Science, East Carolina
    University

**Mark G. Yudof**
Dean and John Jeffers Research Chair in Law,
    University of Texas at Austin School of Law

**Nicholas S. Zeppos**
Associate Professor of Law, Vanderbilt
    University

**Abington School District v. Schempp,** 374 U.S. 203 (1963), argued 27–28 Feb. 1963, decided 17 June 1963 by vote of 8 to 1, Clark for the Court, Brennan, Douglas, and Goldberg concurring, Stewart in dissent. *Schempp* was essentially a rerun of the Court's decision the previous term in *\*Engel v. Vitale* (1962). In the earlier case the Court identified a constitutional violation and struck the offending legislation; in *Schempp* it reasserted its logic and result as if to say, "We meant what we said." *Schempp* repeats both the *Engel* holding— the Establishment Clause forbids public schools from sponsoring religious practices akin to prayer—and its coalition of justices. This time, however, Justice Tom C. *Clark (Presbyterian) wrote for the majority and the Court's religious diversity—Arthur *Goldberg (Jewish) and William *Brennan (Catholic)—was made manifest in separate concurring opinions.

*Schempp* came in the wake of a hostile response to *Engel,* which raged throughout the summer of 1962 and into the Court's next term. Representative L. Mendell Rivers accused the Court of "legislating—they never adjudicate—with one eye on the Kremlin and the other on the NAACP." Cardinal Spellman said it had struck "at the very heart of the Godly tradition in which America's children have for so long been raised." Representative Frank Becker called *Engel* "the most tragic [ruling] in the history of the United States," and offered an amendment to reverse this (and, later, the *Schempp*) decision (see CONSTITUTIONAL AMENDING PROCESS). According to the Gallup Poll, 76 percent of Americans supported this approach. All told, 150 such amendments were offered by 111 members of Congress, with Becker's coming to a vote but losing in the House of Representatives.

The *Schempp* decision actually decided two cases: itself and *Murray v. Curlett* (1963). The former was brought by the Schempps—a non-Jewish family sought out by the ACLU, which argued the case—who objected to a Pennsylvania law requiring that ten verses of the Bible be read at the opening of each public school day. The latter was brought by Madalyn Murray and her son William, professed atheists, who attacked a Baltimore statute providing for the "reading, without comment, of a chapter in the Holy Bible and/or the use of the Lord's Prayer" in opening exercises in city schools. Both of these cases saw the same type of *amicus curiae group participation as in *Engel,* with separationists opposing the prayers and accommodationists supporting them.

Justice Clark's majority opinion was light on history and long on the importance of religion in American life. Its conclusion, however, was the same as that tendered the year before: the Constitution forbids state establishment of religion, prayer is religion, and thus prayer in public schools is constitutionally impermissible. For the first time, a "test" for Establishment Clause questions was formally articulated by the Court. To pass constitutional muster, legislation must have "a secular legislative purpose and a primary effect that neither advances nor inhibits religion" (p. 222). The fact that the religious material here was not, like that in *Engel,* composed by the state, was constitutionally inconsequential; the "wall of separation" was real and was to be kept high.

The concurring opinions were unexceptional,

save for the religious affiliations of the justices who wrote them and their somewhat self-consciously apologetic tone; it was as if they sought to reassure the nation that the Court's posture was not antireligious. Most noteworthy was Brennan's seventy-four page opus reviewing the history of the First Amendment—and judicial and legislative glosses on it—which concluded that government may neither foster nor promote religion.

Justice Potter *Stewart's dissent reasserted themes he initially voiced in *Engel*. Charging the majority with hostility (not neutrality) to religion, he would have upheld the practices as a legitimate accommodation. In addition, Stewart noted that the separationist doctrine enunciated by the Court in the two prayer cases posed a difficult interpretive conundrum: if states sought to protect free exercise rights (say, by paying military chaplains to minister to the needs of troops in battle zones) they could run afoul of the Establishment Clause by pursuing policies that were primarily (if not solely) religious in purpose. He contended that his approach, stressing the pre-eminence of free exercise values, would avoid this dilemma.

(See also RELIGION.)

Joseph Kobylka

**Ableman v. Booth; United States v. Booth,** 21 How. (62 U.S.) 506 (1859), argued 19 Jan. 1859, decided 7 Mar. 1859 by vote of 9 to 0; Taney for the Court. In the spring of 1854, Benjamin S. Garland, a slaveowner from Missouri, went to Wisconsin seeking to recapture a runaway slave. Joshua Glover had escaped two years earlier and found work in a mill outside Racine. The slaveowner invoked the Fugitive Slave Act of 1850 and filed a complaint before the United States commissioner in Milwaukee, who promptly issued a warrant for Glover's arrest. A deputy marshal, with the assistance of the slaveowner, forcibly entered Glover's cabin, knocked him down, and carried him off bound and handcuffed to the Milwaukee jail.

A boisterous public meeting condemned the capture, resolved "the slave catching law of 1850 disgraceful and . . . repealed," and dispatched one hundred men to Milwaukee to secure Glover's release. In the meantime, Sherman M. Booth, an abolitionist and editor of an antislavery newspaper, obtained a writ of *habeas corpus for Glover from a local county court judge. The federal marshal and the county sheriff refused to produce the prisoner on the theory that he was properly in federal custody and could not be released through a state court habeas proceeding. However, a crowd broke into the jail and rescued Glover, who was never recaptured. Soon thereafter, Booth and others were indicted and convicted for violating federal law by aiding and abetting the rescue.

This was the dramatic start of a long jurisdic-

tional confrontation between state and federal authority. Federal prosecution of Booth produced repeated defiance by Wisconsin judges of federal authority, even that of the United States Supreme Court. At one point, the judges of the Wisconsin Supreme Court, in an attempt to forestall federal review, ordered their clerk to make no return to the writ of error issued by the United States Supreme Court and to enter no order in the case. Judges and legislators battled over state habeas corpus jurisdiction versus federal judicial authority. (See JUDICIAL POWER AND JURISDICTION; FEDERALISM.)

The conflict culminated with Chief Justice Roger B. *Taney's unanimous opinion in the companion cases of *Ableman* v. *Booth* and *United States* v. *Booth* (1859), though his decision did not end the struggle. Taney condemned the Wisconsin Supreme Court's stance, arguing it "would subvert the very foundations of this Government" (p. 525). His opinion echoed the broad nationalism of famous decisions of John *Marshall's era, such as *McCulloch* v. *Maryland* (1819). It is ironic that *Ableman* v. *Booth's* assertion of sweeping national power issued from the pen of a chief justice known for his strong states' rights views. Moreover, Taney's opinion in dictum expressed the unanimous view that the 1850 Fugitive Slave Act was "in all its provisions, fully authorized by the Constitution of the United States" (p. 526). When Booth was subsequently reindicted in a federal court in 1860, the Wisconsin Supreme Court still split evenly over whether Booth might be entitled to a writ of habeas corpus despite the mandate of the United States Supreme Court. The Wisconsin legislature condemned Taney's decision as "despotism" and called for "positive defiance" by the states. Only the *Civil War settled the issue.

Perhaps because of its connection to *slavery and to Taney, widely reviled for his *Dred *Scott opinion two years earlier, *Ableman* v. *Booth* is seldom invoked as precedent. *Ableman* v. *Booth* clearly established the lack of state judicial authority to issue writs of habeas corpus to remove someone from federal custody, yet the question was relitigated after the Civil War. *Tarble's Case* (1872) reached the same result and has become the standard citation for the supremacy of federal jurisdiction. Actually though, until *Ableman* v. *Booth* the law was not clear. A leading treatise on habeas corpus published in 1858 supported the position of the Wisconsin Supreme Court.

Many people considered *Ableman* v. *Booth* a frightening extension of *Dred Scott*. There were other contemporaneous conflicts over the authority of federal judges in the context of slavery, but antislavery forces saw *Ableman* v. *Booth* as the end of hope for constitutional argument against the Slave Power. The strong constitutional resistance expressed by the Wisconsin judges and the repeated calls by legislators and citizens of Wisconsin for forceful opposition provided a paradoxical mirror image of secessionist arguments advanced simultaneously in the South.

(See also FUGITIVE SLAVES; SLAVERY; STATE SOVEREIGNTY AND STATES' RIGHTS.)

□ Robert M. Cover, *Justice Accused: Antislavery and the Judicial Process* (1975).                     Aviam Soifer

**Abortion.** The prominence of the Supreme Court in the controversy over reproductive choice would not have surprised Alexis de Tocqueville, who observed in *Democracy in America* that "there is hardly a political question in the United States which does not sooner or later turn into a judicial one" (Meyer, ed., 1969, p. 270). It was not until the latter half of the nineteenth century that criminal sanctions against abortion became widespread, and not until the latter half of the twentieth century that the notion of a constitutional right to sexual autonomy took hold in the public mind. That development guaranteed that abortion would turn into a judicial question.

As part of the *police power over public health and morals, abortion laws have traditionally been the province of state governments. In early American history, abortion was so dangerous— more deadly than childbirth, which was life-threatening itself—that lawmakers who regulated sexual activity in minute detail saw no need to make abortion a crime. When medical advances made abortion safer in the nineteenth century, some states forbade abortion primarily to protect pregnant women. Other early anti-abortion laws were essentially elements of state *obscenity statutes, often called "little Comstock laws." These laws, similar to the 1873 federal Comstock Act, included contraceptives and abortifacients among the forbidden "obscene" materials. Early in the twentieth century, reformers like Margaret Sanger began to promote birth control, as a means of limiting family size, especially for the poor. By 1960, forty-eight states had legalized birth control.

The decriminalization of birth control enhanced individual freedom by increasing women's control over their fertility, but *contraception did not ensure reproductive self-determination for women. Sexual intercourse could occur without a woman's consent—for example, rape— and, therefore, without her being able to take precautions. Traditional family law obliged wives to submit to their husband's sexual demands. Further, existing methods of female contraception were unreliable (see FAMILY AND CHILDREN; MARRIAGE).

Since women still found themselves confronted with unwanted pregnancies, access to abortion was necessary for reliable fertility control. But abortion has always been a more controversial issue than contraception. For those who consider fetuses persons, abortion is the equivalent of homicide. And even some who are not convinced that fetuses are full human beings

have difficulty accepting the idea of legal abortion. While both men and women use contraception, only women get pregnant and can abort. The idea that women have equal rights with men is a relatively new notion. Moreover, society's cultural idea of womanhood has traditionally been bound up with motherhood. The choice of abortion is made by a woman who, at least at that specific point in time, does not want a child—and this possibility challenges widely accepted notions of the role of women.

As late as the 1960s, abortion was still illegal everywhere in the United States, except to save the mother's life. The revitalization of feminism in the late 1960s gave greater impetus to the struggle for the right to abortion. A portent of changing opinions was the 1962 Model Penal Code, in which the American Law Institute recommended that abortion be legal in certain circumstances: for example, when the pregnancy resulted from rape or when the baby was likely to suffer from a serious defect. The abortion controversy heated up in the state legislatures in the late 1960s and early 1970s. Fourteen states adopted some or all of the ALI recommendations between 1965 and 1970. New York, Alaska, and Hawaii repealed their abortion laws outright.

*Griswold* v. *Connecticut* (1965) disposed of the last surviving laws against birth control and established a constitutional right to a realm of *privacy. The Court ruled that the right to use contraceptives lay within a protected "zone of privacy" created by "penumbras," emanating from several provisions of the *Bill of Rights. Many legal scholars found this argument a less than persuasive justification for the judicial creation of a right nowhere mentioned in the Constitution, but the ruling established a right whose content would be defined and expanded by later decisions.

In 1973, the Court extended the right of privacy to the choice of abortion. In *Roe* v. *Wade*, a majority of seven justices ruled that the "right of privacy . . . is broad enough to encompass a woman's decision whether or not to terminate her pregnancy" (p. 153). Justice Harry *Blackmun's majority opinion emphasized "the detriment that the state would impose upon the pregnant woman" and "the distress, for all concerned, associated with an unwanted child" (p. 159). But many critics (on all sides of the abortion issue) consider his opinion unpersuasive or poorly grounded. It fails to build a logical bridge between *Roe* and *Griswold*. *Roe* contains no argument that abortion is sufficiently similar to birth control to justify its inclusion within the protected zone of privacy. The Court's resolution of the legal status of the fetus provoked still more criticism. Blackmun observed that no societal consensus existed that fetuses are human beings and that American law did not recognize the unborn as persons. But the state did have an interest in "potential human life." The state could also restrict abortion when necessary to protect the health of the mother. Each of these interests became strong enough to justify restrictions at different stages of pregnancy: maternal health at the end of the third month; potential life at the end of the sixth (when, according to medical authorities at the time, the fetus was viable outside the womb). Therefore, the constitutional right to choose abortion was a limited one. In the first trimester, the state had no power to restrict abortion; beginning with the second trimester, the state might regulate, but could not prohibit, abortion; and in the third trimester, the state might forbid abortion except when necessary for the mother's life or health.

*Roe* has become one of the most controversial decisions in the history of the Supreme Court. *Roe* was welcomed enthusiastically by supporters of reproductive freedom. But *Roe* also led to the formation of the "Right-to-Life" movement. Even many Americans who opposed restrictions on abortion thought that the Court had usurped a power belonging to the elected branches of government. Critics pointed to the absence of textual authority in the Constitution and demanded that the people, through their elected representatives, decide what abortion laws they wanted and whether or not the word "person" in the *Fourteenth Amendment included the unborn.

Efforts to counter *Roe* v. *Wade* have continued from 1973 to the present. A constitutional amendment was proposed that defined "person" to include the unborn. But neither this "human life amendment," nor a bill that attempted the same result through a federal law, emerged from Congress. However, Congress and many state legislatures repeatedly passed laws negating, or at least narrowing, the decision. These statutes attempt to put various kinds of obstacles in the way of women who seek abortions. When the statutes were challenged in the courts, judges distinguished between obstacles to the choice of abortion and refusals to facilitate it, invalidating most of the former while upholding the latter.

Some statutory obstacles to abortion are direct: for example, a spousal consent requirement for a married woman or parental consent for a minor. A Missouri law containing both these requirements was the first post-*Roe* law to reach the Court. *Planned Parenthood* v. *Danforth* (1976) decisively rejected both provisions. Parental consent requirements have proved problematic, though. Because parental consent is necessary before a minor can get medical treatment, and the constitutional rights of minors are not as extensive as those of adults, the Supreme Court upheld a parental notification requirement (*H.L.* v. *Matheson*, 1981), and has sustained laws requiring consent from either a parent or a judge (e.g., *Bellotti* v. *Baird*, 1979; *Planned Parenthood* v. *Ashcroft*, 1983; *Ohio* v. *Akron Center for Reproductive Health*, 1990). In 1990, the Court upheld a

Minnesota statute requiring consent from both parents or a judge (*Hodgson* v. *Minnesota*).

Some laws established obstacles designed not so much to impede the choice of abortion as to discourage it. The Court struck down most of these. Among them were laws prohibiting the use of certain abortion techniques, requiring a physician to counsel the patient, mandating a waiting period, or requiring that some or all abortions be performed in hospitals (the vast majority of elective abortions take place in clinics). Several decisions between 1976 and 1986 overturned these provisions, either on grounds of vagueness and unreasonableness or because, as Justice William J. *Brennan wrote in *Thornburgh* v. *American College of Obstetricians and Gynecologists* (1986), "the states are not free, under the guise of protecting maternal health or potential life, to intimidate women into continuing pregnancies" (p. 759). Some provisions, such as the requirement that a doctor obtain the woman's written consent and a requirement for fetal testing at the patient's expense, were sustained.

The Court has upheld laws that embodied government's refusal to support a woman's choice of abortion, such as those denying the use of public funds for abortions. The first "Hyde Amendment," a limitation on the expenditure of Medicaid funds, was enacted in 1976. It and similar state laws, all of which make exceptions for abortions necessary to save the mother's life, have all been upheld by the same 6-to-3 vote.

In *Harris* v. *McRae*, Justice Potter *Stewart declared that "although government may not place obstacles in the path of a woman's exercise of her freedom of choice, it need not remove those not of its own creation. *Indigency falls in the latter category" (p. 316). Justices Brennan, Thurgood *Marshall, and Blackmun have consistently maintained that these laws make safe abortions unavailable for poor women to obtain, thus creating a double standard of constitutional rights. But Stewart's view has prevailed. The federal government and forty-one states now permit the use of public funds for abortions only when the mother's life is in danger. *Rust* v. *Sullivan* (1991) further limited poor women's access to abortion by upholding regulations forbidding clinics receiving federal funds, like Planned Parenthood, from even advising clients that abortion is an available choice.

In the 1990s, constitutional doctrine with respect to abortion is unstable. Interaction between Court, lawmakers, interest groups, and the people is a dynamic process. Constituencies press lawmakers to respond to a court decision; lawmakers enact legislation that sends a message to the Court; the Court reviews these new laws; attentive publics react to the new decision; legislators pass new laws; and the Court reviews them. Meanwhile, biennial elections change the composition of the executive and legislative branches and, indirectly, of the Court.

The anti-abortion movement showed its electoral strength in 1980, when Ronald *Reagan won the presidency and the Republicans won a majority in the Senate. Reagan promised to appoint justices who would vote to overrule *Roe*. His administration politicized the process of judicial selection to an unprecedented degree (see SELECTION OF JUSTICES). When Chief Justice Warren *Burger retired in 1986, Reagan elevated William *Rehnquist, one of the dissenters in *Roe*, to that office. The other Reagan appointees, Sandra Day *O'Connor, Antonin *Scalia, and Anthony *Kennedy, evince varying degrees of opposition to the right to abortion.

The *Roe* consensus had begun to unravel even before the emergence of the Rehnquist Court. For example, a dissent by Justice O'Connor in the 1983 case of *Akron* v. *Akron Center for Reproductive Health* insisted that the *Roe* trimester framework "is clearly on a collision course with itself" (p. 458). O'Connor discussed medical advances since 1973 that had made late abortion safer and had kept alive infants born before the seventh month of pregnancy. "Just as improvements in medical technology will inevitably move *forward* the point at which the State may regulate for reasons of maternal health, different technological improvements will move *backward* the point of viability" (p. 463). Medical experts agree with O'Connor that the trimester framework is obsolescent.

*Webster* v. *Reproductive Health Services* (1989) eliminated the trimester framework and represented a significant retreat from abortion rights. In upholding a Missouri law that declared that life began at conception, forbade the use of any public funds and facilities for abortions, and required viability testing in abortions after twenty weeks, the Court sustained restrictions similar to those it had invalidated in *Akron* and *Thornburgh*. *Webster* stopped short of overturning *Roe* v. *Wade* outright—but only by one vote. Justice O'Connor, who supported the restrictions on the choice of abortion, refused to join the other four members of the majority in an outright reversal. Chief Justice Rehnquist's charge that "the dissent accuses us . . . of cowardice," Justice Scalia's sarcastic prediction that "the outcome of today's case will doubtless be heralded as a triumph of judicial statesmanship," and Justice Blackmun's "fear for the integrity of, and public esteem for, this Court" typify the reaction to *Webster* within and outside the judiciary. The courts have never been detached from politics, but in *Webster*, the Court politicized itself to an unprecedented degree; no opinion, and no public reaction, made any distinction between result and doctrine. Students of the Supreme Court's role in American politics might conclude that this episode illustrates the dangers of the Court's attempting to resolve political disputes. But we might just as plausibly conclude that the real lesson of *Webster* is the danger of any efforts by elected officials to remove constitutional rights once courts have recognized them.

Meanwhile, the development of RU-486, an abortion-inducing drug, may well eventually render both the constitutional and political controversy obsolescent. But the Food and Drug Administration has not approved this drug for use or testing in the United States, and the anti-abortion movement promises to devote its energies to preventing such a move.

(See also DUE PROCESS, SUBSTANTIVE; FUNDAMENTAL RIGHTS.)

□ John Hart Ely, *Democracy and Distrust* (1980). Kristin Luker, *Abortion and the Politics of Motherhood* (1984). Rosalind P. Petchesky, *Abortion and Woman's Choice* (1983). Eva Rubin, *Abortion, Politics, and the Courts* (1987). Laurence H. Tribe, *Abortion: The Clash of Absolutes* (1990).
Judith A. Baer

**Abrams v. United States,** 250 U.S. 616 (1919), argued 21 Oct. 1919, decided 10 Nov. 1919 by vote of 7 to 2; Clarke for the Court, Holmes in dissent. On 23 August 1918, Jacob Abrams, a Russian immigrant and an anarchist, was arrested in New York City along with several of his comrades, among them Molly Steimer, Hyman Lachowsky, and Samuel Lipman. They had written, printed, and distributed two leaflets, one in English and one in Yiddish, which condemned President Woodrow Wilson for sending American troops to fight in Soviet Russia. The Yiddish leaflet also called for a general strike to protest against the government's policy of intervention. Abrams and the others were indicted under the Sedition Act of 16 May 1918, which made it a crime to "willfully utter, print, write, or publish any disloyal, profane, scurrilous, or abusive language" about the United States' form of government, or to "wilfully urge, incite, or advocate any curtailment of production" of things "necessary or essential to the prosecution of the war . . . with intent by such curtailment to cripple or hinder the United States in the prosecution of the war." Tried in October 1918, before federal district court judge Henry DeLamar Clayton, Jr., they were found guilty and sentenced to 15- to 20-year prison terms.

In March 1919, while Abrams and the others were out on bail, the Supreme Court upheld the convictions of antiwar socialists under the 1917 Espionage Act (*Schenck* v. *U.S.*) and under the 1918 Sedition Act (*Debs* v. *U.S.*). Both decisions were unanimous, and both were written by Oliver Wendell *Holmes, who reasoned in *Schenck* that "[t]he question in every case is whether the words used are used in such circumstances and are of such a nature as to create a clear and present danger that they will bring about the substantive evils that Congress has a right to prevent" (p. 52).

Justice John H. *Clarke's majority decision in *Abrams* closely followed Holmes's reasoning. The leaflets created a clear and present danger, Clarke said, because they had been distributed "at the supreme crisis of the war" and amounted to "an attempt to defeat the war plans of the Government" (p. 623). Moreover, he continued, even if the anarchists' primary purpose and intent had been to aid the Russian Revolution, the general strike they advocated would have necessarily hampered prosecution of the war with Germany.

But by the time the Court ruled in *Abrams*, Holmes had modified his view. Disturbed by the repression resulting from antiradical hysteria and influenced by the views of several friends and acquaintances—including Harvard Law School professor Zechariah *Chafee, federal district judge Learned *Hand, and political theorist Harold J. Laski—Holmes edged toward a more libertarian interpretation of the clear and present danger standard. Consequently, his dissent in the *Abrams* case, joined by Louis D. *Brandeis, refined the standard in crucial ways.

Congress, Holmes now declared, "constitutionally may punish speech that produces or is intended to produce a clear and imminent danger that will bring about forthwith certain substantive evils that the United States constitutionally may seek to prevent" (p. 627). Holmes denied that "the surreptitious publishing of a silly leaflet by an unknown man" (p. 628) created such a danger, and he denied, too, the existence of the requisite intent, since Abrams' "only object" was to stop American intervention in Russia. Holmes reasoned that the First Amendment protected the expression of all opinions "unless they so imminently threaten immediate interference with the lawful and pressing purposes of the law that an immediate check is required to save the country" (p. 630).

The Supreme Court would wrestle with reformulations of the clear and present danger standard for fifty years, until, in *Brandenburg* v. *Ohio* (1969), it substituted a direct incitement test. What endures in Holmes's *Abrams* dissent is his eloquent discussion of the connection between freedom of speech, the search for truth, and the value of experimentation: "when men have realized that time has upset many fighting faiths, they may come to believe even more than they believe in the very foundations of their own conduct that the ultimate good desired is better reached by free trade in ideas—that the best test of truth is the power of the thought to get itself accepted in the competition of the market, and that truth is the only ground upon which their wishes safely can be carried out. That at any rate is the theory of our Constitution. It is an experiment, as all life is an experiment" (p. 630).

(See also CLEAR AND PRESENT DANGER TEST; ESPIONAGE ACTS; FIRST AMENDMENT SPEECH TESTS; SPEECH AND THE PRESS; WORLD WAR I.)

□ Richard Polenberg, *Fighting Faiths: The Abrams Case, the Supreme Court, and Free Speech* (1987).
Richard Polenberg

**Abstention Doctrine,** one of a number of policies adopted by the Supreme Court that allow the federal judiciary to refrain from ruling on constitutional questions. Often called the "Pullman" abstention doctrine because it was adopted by the Court in *Railroad Commission of Texas* v. *Pullman Co.* (1941), the doctrine is applicable when two conditions are met. First, a state statute that has not yet received a definitive interpretation by the state supreme court must be challenged in federal court on constitutional grounds. Second, the statute must be sufficiently unclear so that an authoritative construction by the state judiciary may resolve the constitutional issue. Under such circumstances the federal courts, without permanently relinquishing jurisdiction, may choose to abstain from issuing a constitutional ruling until the state's highest court determines the statute's meaning. Federal judges have a great deal of discretion in invoking the doctrine and may choose not to do so, for example, when the statute on its face violates fundamental liberties.

The primary purpose of Pullman abstention is to reinforce principles of *federalism. It is based on the proposition that federal courts should not intervene in state affairs unless absolutely necessary. If an interpretation by a state court may potentially resolve a dispute, then it is preferable to permit the state judiciary to act before the federal courts interfere. The notion of generally limiting federal court involvement in state affairs has existed since the beginning of the republic, with Congress making reference to it as early as 1793.

(See also FEDERAL QUESTIONS; STATE CONSTITUTIONS AND INDIVIDUAL RIGHTS; STATE COURTS.)
Thomas G. Walker

**Academic Freedom.** American professors had fought for academic freedom since the nineteenth century, but the term itself did not appear in a United States Supreme Court decision until 1952. Justice William O. *Douglas invoked it then, dissenting in *Adler* v. *Board of Education*. The majority, laboring in the shadow of the Cold War and McCarthyism (see COMMUNISM AND COLD WAR), had upheld New York's Feinberg law, which prohibited employment of teachers in public institutions if they belonged to "subversive organizations," as identified by the New York Board of Regents.

Constitutional recognition of academic freedom was foreshadowed by *Meyer* v. *Nebraska* (1923) and *Pierce* v. *Society of Sisters* (1925). In *Meyer*, the Court invalidated a state law that prohibited teaching foreign languages to students before the ninth grade. In *Pierce*, the Court struck down an Oregon statute that required parents to send their children aged eight through sixteen to public schools. Both cases rested upon the substantive *due process rights of private schools, as well as upon parents' right to control the sort of education their children receive.

Since *Adler*, however, two recurring questions have arisen: (1) does "academic freedom" imply an enhanced immunity from censorship and regulation, or does the phrase simply describe a cluster of rights available to all; and (2) whom does "academic freedom" make free to do what?

**Measure of Academic Freedom.** *Adler* held that teachers' freedom of speech and association may be curtailed as a condition of public employment. This premise has since been rejected: public employees, including teachers, have at least the same rights of expression as others (*\*Keyishian v. Board of Regents*, 1967). *Adler* also held that teachers' associational freedom could be curtailed because they have contact with impressionable "young minds" (p. 493). This premise has also been discarded.

Although its decisions are sometimes ambiguous, the Court has continued to speak of academic freedom as identifying rights of expression uniquely valuable to teachers and schools. In *Sweezy v. New Hampshire* (1957), the Court upheld a Marxist professor's refusal to answer state investigators' questions about his teaching and political views at the University of New Hampshire. Chief Justice Earl *Warren rejected *Adler's* rationale and identified freedom of thought and expression as essential to an academic institution. Justice Felix *Frankfurter, concurring, spoke both of the need to protect the "ardor and fearlessness of scholars" and of the institutional independence of universities (pp. 262–263).

In *\*Barenblatt v. United States* (1959), the Court by a 5-to-4 margin refused to insulate academics from congressional inquiry into their political beliefs and associations. But in later cases invalidating teacher loyalty oaths, it decried the chilling effect of coerced political conformity on teachers. In the oath cases, the Court clearly united free expression and procedural fairness values in describing a zone of autonomy that merits the description "academic freedom." As the majority said in *Keyishian*: "[A]cademic freedom . . . is a special concern of the First Amendment, which does not tolerate laws that cast a pall of orthodoxy over the classroom" (p. 603).

**Different Sorts of Academic Freedom.** Teachers were the first beneficiaries of the Court's expanding conception of academic freedom. In *Epperson v. Arkansas* (1968), the Court struck down a criminal statute that forbade teachers from teaching the theory of *evolution, holding that the state's undoubted power to control the curriculum is delimited by the First Amendment.

The scope of protected speech may, however, be narrower when the teacher criticizes school officials. In *Pickering v. Board of Education* (1968), the Court held that the First Amendment prohibited firing a teacher who had publicly questioned school board policies. Although the Court invoked academic freedom, it made clear that a teacher is also an employee, and that disruptive speech, even on a matter of public concern, could be the basis for termination. *Mt. Healthy City School District Board of Education v. Doyle* (1977) reaffirmed school authorities' power by permitting termination of a teacher whose speech dealt with public issues, if the employer could show independent grounds for discharge.

In *Board of Regents v. Roth* (1972), the Court held that the Due Process Clause does not require a university to state reasons and provide a hearing when it does not renew a nontenured teacher's contract. The teacher can claim a hearing only if she makes a credible showing that the nonrenewal would stigmatize her in searching for new employment.

The Court has been more hesitant to recognize student claims to academic freedom. While the wave of *civil rights protest that began in 1960 was led by college students, the cases that reached the Supreme Court did not arise in academic settings, and the Court's decisions in those cases did not deal with academic freedom.

*Lower federal courts developed due process and First Amendment standards that restrained public schools and colleges from expelling or disciplining students because they had engaged in nonviolent protest. In *\*Tinker v. Des Moines School District* (1969), the Court invalidated a school district's suspension of high school students who had worn black armbands in protest against the *Vietnam War. But at the same time, administrators on college campuses sought to stem the threat of disruption by curbing student speech and denying campus access to radical student organizations. In *Healy v. James* (1972), Justice Lewis *Powell addressed this conflict, holding that a public university may enforce reasonable rules governing the time, place, and manner of student expression. It may deny campus access to provably disruptive groups. But it may not base its actions upon the content of the views students wish to express, even if those views are "abhorrent" (p. 188).

Justice Frankfurter, concurring in *Sweezy*, had stressed the independence of universities from governmental control. His stress upon institutional freedom to choose students, teachers, and curriculum harks back to an older tradition of university autonomy, and has been echoed in the Court's more recent decisions.

There is an obvious tension here, for judicial reluctance to intervene in school or university decisions can mean judicial abdication in the face of claims by students or teachers that the institution is inhibiting their rights to self-expression or fairness. In *Minnesota State Board for Community Colleges v. Knight* (1984), the Court rejected any First Amendment basis for professors' participation in academic governance.

In contrast, *\*Regents of the University of California v. Bakke* (1978) invoked institutional academic freedom to permit the University of California's medical school to take race into account in its admissions policy, while striking down the specific race-conscious policy the University had adopted. *Board of Education* v. *Pico* (1982) recognized a school board's discretionary power over curriculum and book selection but held that the board could not bow to community pressure to remove "objectionable" books from school library shelves. *Pico* affirmed institutional autonomy, but only if the institution functions free from improper pressure to censor.

The Court's opinions will no doubt continue to waver between individual-oriented and institutional theories of academic freedom. The hard task facing future Courts will be to see that deference to institutional autonomy does not mean surrender to institutional censorship or caprice.

(See also EDUCATION; FIRST AMENDMENT.)

□ "Academic Freedom," symposium in *Texas Law Review* 66 (1988): 1247–1659. Edmund L. Pincoffs, ed., *The Concept of Academic Freedom* (1972).        Michael E. Tigar

**Access to Trials.** See RICHMOND NEWSPAPERS, INC. V. VIRGINIA.

**Actual Malice,** a burden of proof imposed on public officials and public figures suing for defamation and falsity, requiring them to prove with clear and convincing evidence that an offending story was published with knowing falsehood or reckless disregard for the truth. The Supreme Court said in *New York Times Co.* v. *Sullivan* (1964) that the *First Amendment required proof of actual malice in order to protect a wide open and robust debate about government affairs. Proof of falsity and negligence are not sufficient to establish actual malice. The Court said in *Garrison* v. *Louisiana* (1964) that the proof of actual malice requires plaintiffs to establish that defamatory statements were made with a "high degree of awareness of their probable falsity." Actual malice usually requires proof of a combination of factors including dependence on an unreliable source and failure to check factual assertions in the face of substantial reasons to doubt their accuracy. Findings that can contribute to actual malice include minimal deadline pressures, inconsistencies within a story, a failure to check important sources, evidence that journalists knew information contrary to what was published, a desire to increase circulation, and political motivations. The Court has said that actual malice is distinct from common-law malice, which requires proof of hatred or ill will. In *Masson* v. *New Yorker Magazine Inc.* (1991), the Court reaffirmed its commitment to the principles of actual malice but said that use of the term "actual malice" can be confusing and that judges therefore should use the phrases "knowledge of falsity" and "reckless disregard as to the truth" when giving jury instructions. Since public officials and public figures have been required to

prove actual malice, they have rarely won *libel suits.

(See also SPEECH AND THE PRESS.)

                                    Bill F. Chamberlin

**Adair v. United States,** 208 U.S. 161 (1908), argued 29–30 Oct. 1907, decided 27 Jan. 1908 by vote of 7 to 2; Harlan for the Court, McKenna and Holmes in dissent. The Erdman Act of 1898 was enacted to prevent disruption of interstate commerce by labor disputes. It protected union members by prohibiting yellow dog contracts and the discharge or blacklisting of employees for union activity. An employer who discharged an employee for union membership challenged the constitutionality of the statute. Writing for the majority, Justice John Marshall *Harlan posited equal bargaining power between employer and employee. He held the law to be an unreasonable invasion of personal liberty and property rights guaranteed by the due process clause of the Fifth Amendment. Relying on *Fourteenth Amendment precedents, Harlan grafted the substantive conception of due process and freedom of contract onto the Fifth Amendment. He also found the act to be outside the scope of congressional *commerce power. Ignoring the statute's legislative history, he asserted there was "no legal or logical connection" between union membership and interstate commerce (p. 178).

Justice Joseph *McKenna in dissent called for judicial realism, whereas Justice Oliver Wendell *Holmes echoed the position of restraint he had espoused in *Lochner* v. *New York* (1905): the legislature was the proper arbiter of public policy and could reasonably limit freedom of contract.

Conservatives extolled *Adair* for condemning "class legislation," while Roscoe Pound thought it epitomized "mechanical jurisprudence," the use of "technicalities and conceptualizations" to defeat the ends of justice. The precedent supported invalidation of state laws providing similar protections for unions (*Coppage* v. *Kansas*, 1915) until the New Deal era revolutionized labor-management relations.

(See also CONTRACT, FREEDOM OF; DUE PROCESS, SUBSTANTIVE; FIFTH AMENDMENT.)

                                    Barbara C. Steidle

**Adams, John Quincy** (b. Braintree [now Quincy], Mass., 11 July 1767; d. Washington, D.C., 21 Feb. 1848), lawyer, president of the United States, 1825–1829. The son of John and Abigail Adams, John Quincy Adams graduated from Harvard College in 1787, read law with Theophilus Parsons, and passed the bar in July 1790. In mid-1794, President George *Washington commissioned him minister to Holland. In 1803, the Massachusetts legislature sent him to the United States Senate; a year later, he was admitted to the Supreme Court bar. After arguing for the defendant in *Fletcher* v. *Peck* (1810), Adams accepted an ill-paid post as ambassador to Russia; shortly afterward, he turned down President James *Madison's more lucrative appointment as associate justice of the Supreme Court. In 1817, Adams became secretary of state; in 1824 he was elected president of the United States.

Following Andrew *Jackson's victory in 1828, Adams was elected to the House of Representatives, where he opposed *nullification, the imposition of a gag rule, and annexation of Texas. In 1841, abolitionists persuaded him to defend the right to freedom of fifty-three Africans before the Supreme Court in *United States* v. *The Amistad* (1841). Justice Joseph *Story termed Adams's argument "extraordinary, for its power [and] bitter sarcasm." After resuming his House seat, Adams doggedly pressed the antislavery cause; in 1842, he introduced a bogus petition advocating the dissolution of the union to cordon off slavery, for which he was rewarded with threats of expulsion from the House. On 21 February 1848, during the House roll call, Adams suffered a cataclysmic stroke. He died two days later.

Sandra F. VanBurkleo

**Adamson v. California,** 332 U.S. 46 (1947), argued 15–16 Jan. 1947, decided 23 June 1947 by a vote of 5 to 4; Reed for the Court, Frankfurter concurring, Black, Douglas, Murphy, and Rutledge in dissent. *Adamson* reflected the intense debate over whether the *Fourteenth Amendment's *Due Process Clause incorporates specific provisions of the *Bill of Rights, thus making them applicable to state criminal proceedings. The question was whether the prosecution's calling the jury's attention to the defendant's refusal to testify violated the *Fifth Amendment's ban on *self-incrimination. The majority reiterated the holding of *Palko* v. *Connecticut* (1937) that the Fourteenth Amendment "does not draw all the rights of the federal Bill of Rights under its protection," but incorporates only those that are so fundamental that they are "implicit in the concept of ordered liberty" (p. 54). It upheld the conviction because the prosecutor's comments did not result in an "unfair trial."

Justice Hugo *Black argued in dissent that the due process clause should be read to guarantee that "no state could deprive its citizens of the privileges and protections of the Bill of Rights" and therefore argued that the Fourteenth Amendment incorporates "the full protection of the Fifth Amendment's provision against compelling evidence from an accused to convict him of a crime" (p. 75). The Court has never adopted Black's "total incorporation" approach. It has, however, incorporated nearly all the individual components of the Bill of Rights under a doctrine called "selective incorporation." Thus, in *Griffin* v. *California* (1965) the Court held that the Fourteenth Amendment does not permit state prose-

cutors to call the jury's attention to a defendant's failure to testify.

(See also DUE PROCESS, PROCEDURAL; INCORPORATION DOCTRINE.)

Thomas Y. Davies

**Adkins v. Children's Hospital,** 261 U.S. 525 (1923), argued 14 Mar. 1923, decided 9 Apr. 1923 by vote of 5 to 3; Sutherland for the Court, Taft and Holmes in dissent, Brandeis not participating. Reflecting widespread popular acceptance of laissez-faire economics, the Supreme Court in the 1890s fashioned the liberty of contract doctrine, which affirmed the constitutional right of private parties to enter contractual arrangements. This doctrine curtailed the power of government to interfere with contractual freedom through regulatory legislation. The landmark *Adkins* decision exemplified the Court's commitment to laissez-faire principles and the liberty of contract.

At issue in *Adkins* was a 1918 federal law establishing a minimum wage for women in the District of Columbia. The announced purpose of the act was to protect the health and morals of women from detrimental living conditions caused by inadequate wages. Felix *Frankfurter, a future Supreme Court justice, appeared as counsel in support of the legislation. He sought to justify the measure as a valid exercise of the police power to ameliorate the handicaps experienced by women in the marketplace. Children's Hospital, on the other hand, contended that the statute was a price-fixing law that unconstitutionally interfered with the liberty of contract for employment.

Justice George *Sutherland, speaking for the majority, invalidated the minimum wage law as a violation of the liberty of contract guaranteed by the *due process clause of the *Fifth Amendment. Although Sutherland recognized that the terms of contracts could be regulated in certain situations, he stressed that "freedom of contract is . . . the general rule and restraint the exception" (p. 546). Distinguishing wage laws from measures limiting the hours of labor, he reasoned that the minimum wage law arbitrarily cast upon employers a welfare function that belonged to society at large. In view of the *Nineteenth Amendment and changes in the legal position of women, Sutherland further maintained that women could not be subjected to greater restrictions on their liberty of contract than men. He argued that the minimum wage law disregarded the "moral requirement implicit in every contract of employment" that the value of labor and wages should be equivalent (p. 558). In short, wages must be ascertained by the operation of the free market. (See LABOR.)

In a forceful dissent, Chief Justice William Howard *Taft asserted that lawmakers could limit the freedom of contract under the *police power to regulate the maximum hours or minimum wages of women. He cautioned that the justices should not strike down regulatory statutes simply because they deem particular economic policies to be unwise. Justice Oliver Wendell *Holmes questioned the constitutional basis of the liberty of contract doctrine. Noting that "pretty much all law consists in forbidding men to do some things that they want to do," Holmes pointed out that the Court had sustained many laws that limited contractual freedom (p. 568). He argued that legislators might reasonably conclude that fixing minimum wages for female employees would improve their health and morals.

The *Adkins* decision was a striking expression of laissez-faire constitutionalism. It demonstrated the Court's conviction that wage and price determinations were at the heart of the free market economy and must be secured against unwarranted legislative interference. During the 1920s and early 1930s the Supreme Court frequently cited *Adkins* for a broad interpretation of the liberty of contract doctrine. In particular, the justices invoked *Adkins* to overturn several state minimum wage laws.

As a consequence of the Great Depression and the political triumph of the *New Deal, the Supreme Court in 1937 abandoned laissez-faire constitutionalism and permitted both federal and state governments to play a major role in directing economic life. The Court's new outlook was revealed in *West Coast Hotel* v. *Parrish* (1937), in which the justices narrowly upheld a Washington minimum wage law for women and minors and overruled *Adkins*. The decision in *West Coast Hotel* marked the effective end of the liberty of contract doctrine as a constitutional norm. (See also CONTRACT, FREEDOM OF.)

□ Joel Francis Paschal, *Mr Justice Sutherland: A Man Against the State* (1951).          James W. Ely, Jr.

**Administration of Federal Courts.** The Supreme Court throughout history has figured importantly in administering the federal judicial system, a role involving the Court in legislation, adjudication, and administration. Concern for systemic independence and administrative integrity figured in *Northern Pipeline Construction Co.* v. *Marathon Pipe Line Co.* (1982) rejecting congressional vesting of judicial power in non–*Article III judges bereft of tenure and compensation protection. Approved in *Wayman* v. *Southard* (1825) and reaffirmed in *Mistretta* v. *United States* (1989) have been congressional delegations of administrative and rulemaking duties " 'necessary and proper . . . for carrying into execution all the judgments which the judicial department has [the] power to pronounce' " (p. 22).

The nineteenth-century Court marginally supervised systemwide administration. Congress in 1922 delegated extensive oversight responsibilities in the highly decentralized system to the Judicial Conference of the United States, the judiciary's administrative policy-making institution chaired by the chief justice. The 1939 act establishing an Administrative Office of the United States Courts supportive of and supervised by the conference largely severed the Supreme Court itself from administration of the lower courts. That act also created circuit councils endowed with power, affirmed in *Chandler* v. *Judicial Council* (1970), to issue orders promoting regional administration and, after 1980, to investigate judges' misbehavior preliminary to impeachment.

Early congressional grants to the Court of piecemeal authority to prescribe rules of practice and procedure in the lower courts became broad delegations beginning in 1934 for civil procedure rules. Important rules were spawned in the course of adjudication; most emerged from a Court-appointed advisory committee until 1958, when the Judicial Conference assumed drafting responsibilities. Justices' *dissents to the Court's nonadjudicatory rulemaking persisted until intense congressional opposition to some rules resulted in reform of the process in 1988.

Peter G. Fish

**Administrative Assistant to the Chief Justice.** In order to assist Chief Justice Warren E. *Burger in his nonjudicial responsibilities, Congress in 1972 created the position of administrative assistant to the chief justice. With the assistance of a small staff, the administrative assistant carries out the tasks assigned by the *chief justice. These usually include recruiting new staff and officers of the Court, conducting research for speeches and publications by the chief justice, and generally solving problems involving the Court's *staff. The administrative assistant also serves as a liaison between the chief justice and other institutions and organizations, including the Congress, the executive branch, state courts, research centers, bar associations, law schools, and private associations, and assists the chief justice in carrying out his responsibilities to the Judicial Conference, the Federal Judicial Center, and the Smithsonian Institution.

Occupants of the Office of Administrative Assistant have been Mark W. Cannon, a political economist and public administrator; Noel J. Augustyn, an official of the Association of American Law Schools; Lawrence H. Averill, Jr., a law school dean; and Robb M. Jones, a litigator with an interest in communications.   Mark W. Cannon

**Administrative Office of U.S. Courts.** See ADMINISTRATION OF FEDERAL COURTS.

**Administrative State.** With deceptive simplicity the Constitution divides governmental power among three branches. Article I confers the legislative power on a Congress, composed of the Senate and House of Representatives. Article II confers the executive power on the president. *Article III confers the judicial power on the

Supreme Court and such inferior federal courts as Congress chooses to establish (see JUDICIAL POWER AND JURISDICTION). The Constitution leaves little doubt over which of these three branches has the primary policy-making role. The cursory descriptions of power conferred on the president and the judiciary stand in marked contrast to the grants of power to Congress. Article I, section 8 of the Constitution confers upon Congress no fewer than seventeen specific grants of power, ranging from the limited power to provide for the punishment of counterfeiting, to the generous authority to tax, spend money, regulate commerce, and raise and support armies. Additionally, Congress is given the power to make all laws necessary and proper for carrying out its other specific powers.

If this attention to the powers of Congress reflected the framers' vision of how power might be shared in our constitutional system, that vision bears little resemblance to the structure of modern American government. While the Constitution in the twentieth century was undergoing a radical transformation in the area of civil liberties and individual rights, it underwent an equally fundamental change in the basic structure of our governmental system (see HISTORY OF THE COURT; RIGHTS CONSCIOUSNESS IN CONTEMPORARY SOCIETY). To be sure, Congress continues to exercise broad policy-making power. But law in the post–New Deal era is increasingly made through the administrative agencies. Law promulgated by the agencies now occupies an importance equal to statutory law in regulating every aspect of American society. In this transformation the Supreme Court has played a central role. The Court continues to be a key player in shaping and controlling the balance of power in the administrative state.

The administrative agencies' uncertain fit in our constitutional system is apparent from the commingling of functions in them. Thus, while Article I empowers Congress to legislate, Article II empowers the president to execute the law, and Article III empowers the courts to adjudicate, administrative agencies exercise all three constitutional powers in one entity. For example, the National Labor Relations Board (NLRB)—the agency empowered by statute to regulate union activities—is authorized to promulgate rules that are indistinguishable from legislative enactments. The NLRB also exercises executive power, in the broadest sense of carrying out legislative policies, as well as exercising particular functions long recognized as quintessentially executive, such as making prosecutorial decisions. Finally, the NLRB exercises judicial functions in adjudicating disputes between unions and employers.

It is not clear from the Constitution that this transference of governmental power to the agencies is constitutional. Indeed, the text may suggest just the opposite. The Constitution confers all legislative powers on the Congress and all

judicial power on the judiciary. Agencies exercise functions seemingly reposed in the other branches of government. The most fundamental challenge to the administrative state focused on whether this delegation of power is permissible. The Court's affirmative answer to this question represents one of the most important developments in constitutional history.

Prior to the New Deal the Court consistently upheld the delegation of governmental power. In *Field* v. *Clark* (1892) the justices sustained Congress's delegation of power to the president to impose a retaliatory tariff on foreign goods. The statute empowered the president to impose the tariff upon a determination that American goods were subject to "unequal and unreasonable" duties in the foreign country. The retaliatory tariff was to remain in effect for so long as the president deemed "just" (p. 680). While acknowledging that Congress could not delegate legislative power to the president, the Court nonetheless upheld the statute. The Court reasoned that Congress had defined the statutory goal and statutory sanction, with the president responsible only for the finding of the required contingency—that is, that foreign countries subjected American goods to "unequal and unreasonable rates."

Subsequently, the Court upheld even more sweeping delegations of authority to the president and his subordinates. In *United States* v. *Grimaud* (1911) the justices sustained a statute authorizing the secretary of agriculture to adopt regulations to protect the public forests. Characterizing the secretary's power as merely filling up the details of the statute, the Court concluded that the statute did not transgress constitutional boundaries. In *J. W. Hampton Jr. & Co.* v. *United States* (1928) the Court sustained a tariff act that allowed the president to adopt a set of customs duties. Clearly, the Court had gone beyond *Field* v. *Clark* to authorize wholesale lawmaking by the executive branch.

This judicial tolerance for transferring lawmaking power to the president and his delegates was challenged in the New Deal (see HISTORY OF THE COURT: THE DEPRESSION AND THE RISE OF LEGAL LIBERALISM). Responding to the Great Depression, Congress adopted a number of measures that transferred substantial lawmaking power to the executive branch. The Court invalidated these measures on delegation grounds. In *Schechter Poultry Corp.* v. *United States* (1935) and *Panama Refining Co.* v. *Ryan* (1935), the Court struck down the provisions of the National Industrial Recovery Act authorizing the president to adopt "fair" codes of competition for virtually all aspects of the American economy.

*Schecter Poultry* and *Panama Refining* marked the last time the Court invalidated congressional measures on the basis that they improperly delegated legislative power. Indeed, the inhospitable judicial environment of the mid-1930s did little to deter Congress from continuing to place governmental power in the hands of administrative agencies. Although other delegations did not attain the breadth of the New Deal measures invalidated in *Schecter Poultry* and *Panama Refining*, the Court soon adopted a more accepting position on the delegation question. In *American Power & Light Co.* v. *SEC* (1946) the Court sustained the power of the Securities and Exchange Commission to regulate the restructuring of public corporations. In *Yakus* v. *United States* (1944) the Court upheld the Emergency Price Control Act of 1942, which authorized the Office of Price Administration to fix the prices of commodities and rents.

Many of the New Deal regulatory programs authorized agencies to adjudicate disputes between the government and a private party or between two private parties. Constitutional challenges were raised to this exercise of adjudicative power by agency officials. Parties forced to try their claims before an employee of the agency argued that such a scheme violated the command of Article III vesting the judicial power of the United States in an independent federal judiciary. The Supreme Court consistently rejected this objection to the structure of administrative government. In *Crowell* v. *Benson* (1932) the Court upheld the authority of the deputy commissioner of the U.S. Employee's Compensation Commission to adjudicate a dispute between an employer and its employee over an award of workmen's compensation. In *Commodity Futures Trading Commission* v. *Schor* (1985) the justices reaffirmed the power of Congress to delegate adjudicative power to administrative agencies. The Court, relying on *Crowell* v. *Benson*, upheld the Commodity Future Trading Commission's authority to adjudicate a contract dispute between a securities broker and his customer.

In light of the post–New Deal cases, some have suggested that there are virtually no judicially enforceable limits on transfers of lawmaking powers to administrative agencies. The Court's two most recent delegation cases—*Mistretta* v. *United States* (1989), upholding the delegation to the Sentencing Commission to establish guidelines for criminal sentencing, and *Skinner* v. *Mid-America Pipeline* (1989), upholding the delegation of authority to the secretary of transportation to assess a tax on users of pipelines—generally support this position. Yet it would be a mistake to suggest that the Court remains unconcerned about the transfers of lawmaking power to administrative agencies. In *Industrial Union Department, AFL-CIO* v. *American Petroleum Institute* (1980), the Court invalidated a regulation of the Occupational Safety and Health Administration (OSHA) limiting the amount of benzene, a known carcinogen, in the workplace. The Court concluded that the regulation exceeded the scope of the authority granted by Congress to OSHA. The Court rejected OSHA's reading of its statutory mandate, cautioning that such a broad delegation of authority might well be an unconstitutional delegation. The Court—to the surprise of many commentators—cited *Schecter Poultry* and *Panama Refining* with approval. The Court's decision in *Industrial Union Department* illustrates that while the delegation doctrine may not be applied to invalidate transfers of power to the agencies, concerns about entrusting excessive power to unelected agency officials influence the Court's interpretation of the statutes defining the scope of an agency's authority.

The Court's general acceptance of delegation of lawmaking power to administrative agencies has undoubtedly encouraged Congress to rely upon agencies to make policy. In the 1930s alone Congress again sought solutions to pressing problems either by creating new agencies, or by expanding the regulatory responsibilities of existing agencies. This pattern of congressional behavior, however, should not be understood as a lack of legislative interest in the subject matter. Indeed, the opposite conclusion could be drawn. Congress often chooses to delegate in the most sensitive political areas—for example, the environment or labor-management relations—precisely because interest group pressure is so intense that a workable legislative solution is politically impossible. Thus, despite the transfer of power to agencies, Congress remains concerned about the course of action agencies pursue under their broad mandates.

As if to underscore the point, Congress searches for mechanisms that allow it to continue to exercise control over the agencies. By far the most controversial control mechanism was the *legislative veto. Under a legislative veto, agency actions would be nullified if one house of Congress (the one-house veto) or both houses (the two-house veto) adopted a resolution of disapproval. Proponents of the legislative veto touted it as a useful device for allowing Congress to continue to play a role in supervising agency actions. By contrast, opponents feared that legislative vetoes placed greater power in the hands of influential members of Congress, and, without adequate procedures or judicial oversight, left Congress largely unrestrained in supervising administrative agencies.

In *Immigration and Naturalization Service* v. *Chadha* (1983) the Court, speaking through Chief Justice Warren *Burger, invalidated the legislative veto. The Court concluded that the legislative veto violated the precise requirements Article I of the Constitution sets forth for the exercise of legislative power. Specifically, the one-house veto contravened the requirement that legislative power be exercised by a bicameral legislature and the involvement of the president. Similarly, the two-house veto violated the Article I requirement that all legislative measures be presented to the president for veto.

While the Court has shared concerns over

policing administrative agencies, the decision in *Chadha* reflects the Court's determination that the abuses associated with the legislative veto outweighed its effectiveness as a control mechanism. Of particular concern was the role of special interest groups that, unsuccessful before the agency, could return to Congress and block the agency's initiative through a legislative veto.

The invalidation of the legislative veto does not leave Congress without other means of influencing agency action. Through oversight hearings, appropriations measures, statutory enactments, or informal "jaw-boning" of regulators, Congress retains ample means for shaping the regulatory efforts of agencies. Congress may also seek to influence policy by controlling the personnel charged with running the agency. In this context the Court has had to referee disputes between Congress and the president, who historically has insisted on plenary power to control the appointment and removal of agency policy-makers (see APPOINTMENT AND REMOVAL POWER).

The Court's first major decision in this area was *Myers* v. *United States* (1926). In *Myers* the president discharged a postmaster of the United States. The postmaster challenged the discharge, claiming that under the statute creating his position he could be removed only with the consent of the Senate. The Court held the statute unconstitutional. Chief Justice William Howard *Taft's opinion reasoned that it is unconstitutional for Congress to interfere with the president's power to remove agency officials executing the law.

The breadth of *Myers* was uncertain. The Court's opinion suggested that any limits on the president's power to appoint or remove agency officials would be unconstitutional. But the case also seemed to turn on the Senate's reservation of a role for itself in removal. In *Humphrey's Executor* v. *United States* (1935), the Court gave *Myers* the latter, more narrow interpretation. *Humphrey's Executor* involved removal of a commissioner of the Federal Trade Commission by President Franklin D. *Roosevelt. The commissioner's estate sued for back pay (he having died), claiming that Congress had limited the president's power to remove only for good cause. The Court upheld this limitation, rejecting the view that the president has unfettered power to remove agency officials. The Court distinguished *Myers* on the basis that Congress reserved no direct role for itself in removal.

*Humphrey's Executor* proved to be a particularly important precedent for the structure of the administrative state. The decision allowed Congress to delegate power not simply to Cabinet officers who serve at the will of the president, but to so-called "independent agencies" as well. These independent agencies—multimember commissions with bipartisan members who serve fixed, staggered terms and are not removable at will by the president—exercise significant lawmaking power in the administrative state. *Humphrey's Executor* permits Congress to insulate these agencies from direct presidential control. Scholars have disagreed over whether this political independence is either possible or indeed desirable. After all, presidential control provides some means for ensuring that agencies do not operate outside the influence of popularly elected officials.

The Court has not retreated from the holding of *Humphrey's Executor*. In *Bowsher* v. *Synar* (1986) the Court, in an opinion by Chief Justice Burger, struck down the Balanced Budget Emergency Deficit Control Act (1985), popularly known as the "Gramm-Rudman-Hollings Act." The Court declared unconstitutional the placing of the budget cutting power in the comptroller general of the United States, a presidential appointee removable by a joint resolution of Congress. Adhering to *Myers*, the Court concluded that Congress could play no role in the removal of an executive officer. The Court, however, left undisturbed the holding of *Humphrey's Executor*.

Any doubts about the continued vitality of *Humphrey's Executor* were laid to rest in *Morrison* v. *Olson* (1988), which concerned the constitutionality of the independent counsel provisions of the Ethics in Government Act (1978). The act—passed in response to President Richard *Nixon's summary termination of Watergate prosecutor Archibald Cox—authorizes a special panel of federal judges to appoint an independent counsel who is to investigate alleged criminal activities of high-level executive branch officials. The independent counsel could be removed by the president but only for malfeasance in office. High-level Department of Justice officials subject to an inquiry by an independent counsel challenged the constitutionality of the act. The Court, under Chief Justice William *Rehnquist, upheld the act. Finding *Humphrey's Executor* controlling, the Court concluded that Congress may limit the president's power to remove executive officials who—like the independent counsel—were concededly performing core executive branch functions.

The Court's reaffirmation and indeed expansion of *Humphrey's Executor* in *Morrison* left in place a large part of the constitutional edifice upon which the administrative state has been built. At the same time, *Morrison* as well as the Court's decision in *Mistretta* v. *United States* (1989) reflect a judicial tolerance for further innovations in congressional structuring of administrative agencies. Much of the Court's administrative law jurisprudence defines the reach of congressional and presidential power in the administrative agencies. In *Morrison* and *Mistretta* the Court approved of judicial involvement in the functioning of agencies. In *Morrison* the Court sustained the appointment of the independent counsel by a panel of federal judges, and in *Mistretta* the Court upheld the service of federal judges on the Sentencing Commission.

One of the major concerns in the administrative state has been to assure that agencies remain accountable and subject to controls. The Court's separation of powers cases reflect efforts by both Congress and the president to assume primacy in performing this checking function. Each branch seeks to justify its roles by claiming that it represents the will of the people through the electoral process. The Supreme Court has also assumed an important role in checking administrative agencies. By interpreting the Constitution, the statutory grant of power to the agency, or the basic statute governing all agencies—the Administrative Procedure Act (APA)—the Court enforces procedural and substantive limits on the agencies. The Court's supervisory role is at once understandable and paradoxical: understandable because *Marbury v. Madison (1803) established the Court as the ultimate arbiter of constitutional disputes; paradoxical, however, because concerns about the political accountability and control of the agencies had now become the business of a life-tenured unelected Court.

Because the Court is limited by Article III of the Constitution to deciding *"cases" or "controversies" the Court performs this checking function in the context of judicial review of agency actions. *Judicial review can be authorized by the APA or by a specific statute. The Court's review of agency decisions is broad, covering constitutional law, statutory law, and questions of fact. In the area of judicial review of agency action, debate over the Court's role has largely mirrored the larger controversy about the Court's role in a democratic government. How active a role should the Court play in reviewing agency decisions?

Many of the Court's early post–New Deal decisions reflected a willingness to defer to agency decisions. For example, in National Labor Relations Board v. Hearst Publications, Inc. (1944) the Court left undisturbed the NLRB's decision that newspaper vendors were "employees" entitled to the protection of the labor laws. The Court cautioned that these sorts of determinations were largely left to the expert agency and only rarely should be set aside by the court. In Universal Camera Corp. v. NLRB (1951) the Court set forth a similar deferential standard for agency factual determinations.

The Court's deferential attitude reflects a particular view about the role of the agency in American government. During the New Deal, agencies were viewed as experts, above politics, bringing forth studied solutions to problems of social or economic policy. The Court naturally deferred to such expertise. Eventually, however, this perspective was challenged. Scholars and government officials realized that agency claims of being expert and apolitical were overstated. Focus returned to the reason for the initial delegation to an agency. Congress did so not only because of time constraints, lack of interest, or

expertise, but because the problems were often politically intractable. Thus, the political clashes avoided by Congress were played out again in the context of the agency's decision-making process. Agency decisions were not simply the result of applied expertise, but were in reality political decisions.

The Court has responded to this in two ways. First, it has explicitly acknowledged that Congress may delegate to an agency to avoid having to make a political choice, thus leaving the agency to resolve the clash among the competing interest groups. In Chevron U.S.A. Inc. v. Natural Resources Defense Council Inc. (1984), the Court upheld the Environmental Protection Agency's interpretation of the Clean Air Act Amendments of 1977. The Court recognized that Congress had specifically avoided resolution of the issue and that the decision was to be made by a politically accountable agency and not by the Court.

The Court's second response to the explicitly political nature of agency decision-making has been to ensure that agency decisions are the result of reasoned elaboration and fair process. These requirements are part of the Court's review under the "arbitrary and capricious" standard of the APA. The Court guarantees that interested parties have meaningful access to the process, that the agency considers the views of interested parties, and that the agency elaborates an explanation for its choice. By doing so the Court permits the agency the ultimate course of regulatory action but attempts to make that process a rational one. For example, in Motor Vehicle Manufacturers Association v. State Farm Automobile Insurance Co. (1983), the Court invalidated the Department of Transportation's rescission of a rule requiring passive restraints (e.g., automatic seatbelts or airbags) in automobiles. The Court held that while the agency ultimately was allowed to choose the means for accomplishing automobile safety, any choice must be the result of full and adequate consideration of reasonable alternatives.

As vital as the Court's role in supervising agencies has been, Congress on occasion seeks to eliminate judicial second-guessing of agency decisions. Congress, for example, may wish to avoid the delays associated with judicial review. The APA contemplates that Congress may choose to preclude judicial review. This option for eliminating judicial oversight has caused tension between competing goals. The Court seeks to honor Congress's decision to preserve agency autonomy. Yet the Court also wishes to preserve the judicial supervision deemed essential in the administrative state.

To accommodate these dual concerns the Court has narrowly read statutes precluding review to preserve the essential aspects of judicial review. In Traynor v. Turnage (1988) the Court reviewed a Veterans Administration (VA) regulation denying educational benefits to victims of alcoholism. The Court narrowly interpreted the statute precluding judicial review of the VA's benefits decisions. The Court read the statute as precluding judicial review only of cases involving individual benefits determinations applying established statutory standards to a particular set of facts. The Court preserved for itself the power to review the agency's decision on a question of statutory interpretation, reflecting its concern about abdicating to the agency pure questions of law that mark the boundaries of agency authority.

The Court's preservation of its reviewing role is even more pronounced where constitutional issues are raised. In *Webster* v. *Doe* (1988), the Court held that a former agent of the Central Intelligence Agency could obtain judicial review of the constitutionality of his discharge. The Court conceded that the national security concerns implicated in the case argued for a narrow judicial role. Yet the Court was unwilling to remove entirely from judicial scrutiny the question of agency compliance with the Constitution. The Court's decision in *Webster* v. *Doe* again reflects the influence of *Marbury* v. *Madison* in the administrative state. The Court's ultimate authority to interpret the Constitution, established in *Marbury*, strongly argues for a judicial role to guarantee agency conformity with the constitution. Congress has the authority to limit judicial review of agency action. But against the backdrop of *Marbury* v. *Madison* the Court in *Webster* v. *Doe* stressed that only if Congress speaks in the clearest of terms would the Court assume a congressional intent to preclude judicial review of constitutional claims. Even then, the Court stated that such a decision would raise serious constitutional questions.

The Court has largely left unexamined the constitutionality of precluding judicial review over claims that the agency has acted unconstitutionally, primarily because the issue has never been squarely presented. The Court's constitutional concerns are not directly tied to any specific constitutional text but rather to more basic concerns about the structure of the Constitution. The Court views the Constitution as the supreme law of the land, enforced primarily by the Court. Administrative agencies, like other governmental entities, must act within the Constitution as interpreted by the Court. To eliminate judicial review would be to abandon the idea of the Constitution as law. These rule-of-law concerns are particularly acute given the uncertain constitutional status of administrative agencies. Indeed, the judicial tolerance for the very idea of delegation of lawmaking power to agencies may depend on the ability of the Court to ensure agency conformity to the Constitution.

The Court has developed doctrines that prevent undue judicial interference with agency operations. Two such doctrines are exhaustion of administrative remedies and the need for final agency action. The rule of exhaustion requires an aggrieved person to pursue all avenues of relief within the agency before seeking judicial review. For example, in *Myers* v. *Bethlehem Shipbuilding Corp.* (1938) a corporation sought to enjoin a hearing scheduled by the NLRB. The corporation claimed that its business did not involve interstate commerce and thus could not be constitutionally regulated by the NLRB. The Court dismissed the action, emphasizing that all claims must first be pursued before the agency. The Court reached a similar result in *Federal Trade Commission* v. *Standard Oil Co.* (1980). There the Federal Trade Commission initiated an administrative proceeding against the oil industry alleging unfair pricing practices during the oil shortage of the 1970s. The oil companies filed suit claiming that the FTC had not met the agency's internal standards for the initiation of agency action. The Court ordered dismissal of the oil companies' lawsuit. The Court stressed that judicial review could occur only after the agency issued its final decision in the case.

In the context of judicial review of agency action, the Court has frequently been called upon to define the appropriate procedure to be used by the agencies in the exercise of their lawmaking powers. Most importantly, the Court must decide whether the agency's procedure conforms to the requirements of procedural due process. Agencies often proceed by adopting rules or regulations, which like statutes are of general application and future effect. Typically the rules are promulgated after notice to the public and the opportunity to submit written comments. In *United States* v. *Florida East Coast Ry. Co.* (1973) the Court held that due process is satisfied if prior to the adoption of a rule the agency gives notice to the public and an opportunity for interested parties to file written comments. The agency need not conduct a trial-type hearing—for example, discovery, oral testimony, cross-examination, a decision based on evidence presented.

When the agency enforces a law against a particular individual, the Court requires more elaborate procedures. Agencies wield tremendous power over individuals. They may terminate Social Security benefits, withhold a license for industrial development, or bring a penal action against an individual or business. In such actions, the Court has held that due process requires individual notice and opportunity to be heard (see DUE PROCESS, PROCEDURAL). This notice and hearing must generally occur before the agency takes action. Thus, for example, in *Brock* v. *Roadway Express* (1987) the Department of Labor ordered a trucking company to reinstate a discharged truck driver who allegedly was fired for filing safety complaints against the company. The Court held that before the agency could order reinstatement the company must be given some opportunity to be heard to give its version of the incident and to refute the agency's evidence. In *Cleveland Board of Education* v. *Loudermill* (1985) the

Court held that a public employer must give an employee notice and opportunity to be heard before the employee is discharged.

In measuring agency procedures against the requirements of due process the Court has recognized an agency's need to act summarily when faced with an emergency situation, postponing notice and hearing until after the agency acts. In *Ewing* v. *Mytinger & Casselberry, Inc.* (1950), the Court allowed the Food and Drug Administration to seize a misbranded drug without allowing the drug manufacturer prior notice and opportunity for hearing. Even when prior notice and opportunity to be heard must be afforded, the Court has rarely required that the proceeding be a trial-type hearing with oral testimony and cross-examination. In *Mathews* v. *Eldridge* (1976) the Court held that Social Security disability benefits could be terminated prior to a trial-type hearing so long as the individual was given some opportunity to contest the agency's determination.

The Court's role in the administrative state has been that of both facilitator and skeptic. The Court assumed leadership in the constitutional evolution that integrated the administrative agency into our constitutional structure. The Court's acceptance of the delegation of lawmaking powers to administrative agencies is now settled, yet it remains an important factor in the growth of the administrative state. Having allowed the establishment of the administrative state, the Court has assumed a role in supervising the agencies. In this role the Court tries to avoid unduly interfering with the operation of the president and Congress, which supervise, staff, and fund the administrative agencies. But the Court is unwilling to remove itself entirely from a supervisory role. As in virtually every other area of law, the Court tends to equate judicial review with the very idea of the rule of law. So long as the principle of judicial review announced in *Marbury* v. *Madison* continues to have vitality, the Court's role in the administrative state will remain firmly established.

(See also DELEGATION OF POWERS; LABOR; SEPARATION OF POWERS.)

□ Walter Gellhorn, Clark Byse, Peter L. Strauss, Todd Rakoff, Roy A. Schotland, *Administrative Law: Cases and Comments*, 8th ed. (1987). Richard A. Harris and Sidney M. Milkis, *The Politics of Regulatory Change* (1989). Theodore J. Lowi, *The End of Liberalism: Ideology, Policy, and the Crisis of Public Authority* (1969). Richard B. Stewart, "The Reformation of American Administrative Law," *Harvard Law Review* 88 (1975): 1667–1813. Peter L. Strauss, *An Introduction to Administrative Justice in the United States* (1989). Cass R. Sunstein, "Constitutionalism After the New Deal," *Harvard Law Review* 101 (1987): 421–510. Cass R. Sunstein, *After the Rights Revolution* (1990).

Nicholas S. Zeppos

**Admiralty and Maritime Law.** *Article III, section 2 of the United States Constitution empowers the federal judiciary to hear "all Cases of admiralty and maritime Jurisdiction." This jurisdiction is nowhere defined in the Constitution or in any act of Congress. The federal courts have therefore been required to determine the territorial scope and the types of cases that are included within it, as well as the kinds of relief that can be granted. Congress has on occasion broadened the admiralty jurisdiction of the federal courts, and so far the Supreme Court has upheld the constitutionality of these efforts.

The framers of the Constitution conferred admiralty and maritime jurisdiction on the federal courts because of the vital importance that international and interstate shipping had to the new nation. Both in times of war and in times of peace the national interest in an orderly resolution of disputes involving shipping transcended any local interest. Prior to 1875, when federal courts were granted full *federal question jurisdiction, the grant of admiralty jurisdiction was the only basis that federal trial courts had for hearing cases that arose between citizens of the same state.

Before the *Civil War, the Supreme Court was often severely divided about the proper scope of federal admiralty jurisdiction. Opponents pointed to the jurisdiction of the High Court of Admiralty in England, which was limited to disputes arising solely on the seas, such as collisions, salvage, and seamen's claims for wages. The English Admiralty Court had virtually no jurisdiction over maritime *contracts. Those who sought to limit the federal courts' admiralty jurisdiction were concerned about federal encroachment on the power of the states. But most of the Court's decisions gradually expanded the jurisdiction to include cases over marine insurance contracts, bills of lading, and charter parties—matters vital to the the shipping industry.

Justice Joseph *Story was a leading nineteenth-century proponent of expansive federal admiralty jurisdiction. His circuit court decision in *De Lovio* v. *Boit* (1815) rejected the applicability of the English precedents and broadly asserted that the admiralty jurisdiction extended to all contracts "which relate to the navigation, business, or commerce of the sea." This position was consistent with Story's views in the famous Supreme Court case of *Swift* v. *Tyson* (1842) that federal courts are not bound by state court determinations of common law in commercial law cases. If a federal court was to be an effective commercial court, Story and others believed that it had to have the power to declare the law in commercial cases and in admiralty cases, which were intimately tied to commercial dealings. A majority of the Court generally adopted Story's broad view.

In England, the jurisdiction of the High Court of Admiralty was limited geographically to cases arising on the sea or within the ebb and flow of the tide. Initially the Supreme Court adopted this rule in *The Thomas Jefferson* (1825). The rule became unsatisfactory as steamboat traffic on the rivers and Great Lakes subtantially increased. In *The *Genesee Chief* v. *Fitzhugh* (1852) the Court overruled *The Thomas Jefferson*. The Court held that the Constitution's grant of admiralty jurisdiction extended to cases arising on internal rivers and lakes, provided only that those waterways be navigable, that is, capable of carrying interstate or international commercial traffic.

When a case is solely within the federal court's admiralty jurisdiction there is no right to a *trial by jury. *State courts have concurrent jurisdiction as to most admiralty matters. Most admiralty claims are not within the federal court's exclusive jurisdiction because of the famous "Saving to Suitors" clause in section 9 of the *Judiciary Act of 1789. In its current formulation, this clause saves to suitors "in all cases all other remedies to which they are otherwise entitled." The clause embodies the intention of the framers of the Constitution. In the nineteenth century, it was generally understood that the state courts would apply state law to admiralty cases, that federal courts having admiralty jurisdiction would apply general admiralty law, and that federal courts having diversity jurisdiction in admiralty cases would apply *federal common law. But following the decision of the Court in *Southern Pacific Co. v. Jensen* (1917), state and federal courts must apply the same law to an admiralty case. That law is usually admiralty law, although state law may be applied to some matters, such as environmental pollution and the regulation of local pilots, where the states are thought to have a strong interest.

There are some admiralty cases in which federal jurisdiction is exclusive, however. Foremost among these is the admiralty *in rem* suit, which rests on the fiction that the ship is the defendant. To exercise *in rem* jurisdiction, a plaintiff may actually have a United States marshal seize a vessel. Although rarely tried in this century, prize cases, those brought to condemn an enemy ship or cargo, can also be heard only in federal court. Though it has been traditionally thought that salvage cases are similarly not triable in state court, a few state courts have heard such cases in recent years, and a number of scholars have argued that the "Saving to Suitors" clause empowers state courts to hear salvage cases when the plaintiff sues *in personam.

There are also some powers seemingly necessary to an admiralty court that have been traditionally thought to be outside admiralty jurisdiction. Chief among these is the power to grant equitable relief (see INJUNCTIONS AND EQUITABLE REMEDIES). The early approach of the Court, summarized in an 1890 case, *The Eclipse*, was that a court of admiralty jurisdiction had no power to grant equitable relief. The origins of this doctrine are unclear. It may have been grounded in the notion that courts of equity act *in personam*, that is, they order individuals to do something or to refrain from doing something, whereas courts of admiralty traditionally acted *in rem*. Or the doc-

trine may have developed out of a concern for state powers in the federal system and a desire to limit the power of the federal courts. In any event, lower federal courts made exceptions to it in cases where equitable relief was incidental to other relief that the federal court was empowered to grant. And in *Swift & Co. Packers v. Compania Colombiana Del Caribe, S.A.* (1950), the Supreme Court expanded these exceptions to allow a federal court to set aside a fraudulent transfer by the owner of a vessel that had been attached as security for a maritime claim. More recently, some lower courts have jettisoned entirely the earlier doctrine and will now grant equitable relief in any admiralty case where such relief is appropriate.

Although the general lines of admiralty and maritime jurisdiction have been worked out satisfactorily, there remain a number of anomalies. Contracts to repair a vessel are maritime, while contracts to build a vessel are not, owing to the Court's 1858 decision in *People's Ferry Co. v. Beers*, which rested on the now-discredited notion that all contracts made on land and that were to be performed on land must be considered nonmaritime. Lower courts have held that contracts to sell a vessel are nonmaritime even though contracts to charter a vessel are maritime. Most surprisingly, courts have held, following the Supreme Court's 1854 decision in *Minturn v. Maynard*, that a general agency contract to manage all aspects of a vessel's business is treated as being nonmaritime. In 1991 the Supreme Court overturned *Minturn v. Maynard* and reiterated that federal courts have admiralty jurisdiction to protect maritime commerce (*Exxon Corp. v. Central Gulf Lines, Inc.*).

These limited views of the Court's admiralty jurisdiction with respect to contracts are in sharp contrast to its traditional approach to maritime *tort cases, where the Court has asserted jurisdiction over any wrong done on the water regardless of its importance to commercial shipping. Lower courts exercised jurisdiction when swimmers were struck by surfboards, when airplanes crashed in territorial waters, and in similar matters. But in 1972 the Court adopted a more restrictive approach for tort cases, requiring that to be within the admiralty jurisdiction a tort must "bear a significant relationship to traditional maritime activity" (*Executive Jet Aviation, Inc. v. City of Cleveland*, p. 268). But in a subsequent 5-to-4 decision, the Court held that collisions between pleasure craft on navigable waters were within the admiralty jurisdiction (*Foremost v. Richardson*, 1982). Lower federal courts have struggled to apply these decisions to other types of cases. Although there was initially some disagreement, all appellate courts that have decided the issue now hold that claims by shipyard workers against manufacturers of asbestos for injuries caused by exposure to that product are nonmaritime. On the other hand lower courts are receptive to hearing injury claims by seamen and passengers even when there is nothing uniquely maritime about the tort.

The Supreme Court has largely defined the meaning of the Constitution's grant of admiralty jurisdiction. In addition, the Supreme Court and the lower federal courts have played a significant role in developing the law relating to commercial shipping in this country. As a result, the federal courts have fulfilled their mission of advancing the federal interest in the uniform resolution of disputes involving maritime commerce.

(See also JUDICIAL POWER AND JURISDICTION; LOWER FEDERAL COURTS.)

□ Steven F. Friedell, *Benedict on Admiralty,* 7th rev. ed. (1988). Grant Gilmore and Charles L. Black, Jr., *The Law of Admiralty,* 2d ed. (1975). Thomas J. Schoenbaum, *Admiralty and Maritime Law* (1987).      Steven F. Friedell

## Admission to Practice Before the Bar of the Court.

From 1853 through the early 1990s, nearly 225,000 attorneys have been admitted to practice before the bar of the Supreme Court. No admissions records exist for the period between 1790 and 1853. Prior to 1925, no written applications were required for admission, and attorneys were admitted on oral motion by bar members. The number of living members of the Supreme Court bar is not known.

Between four thousand and five thousand attorneys are annually admitted to practice before the bar. Each of them must have been admitted to practice previously in the highest court of a state, territory, possession, or the District of Columbia for at least three years. The applicant must be free from any adverse disciplinary action and must be of good moral and professional character. As evidence of these qualifications, the applicant must provide a personal statement, a certificate from an official of the *state court to which he is admitted and a statement of two sponsors who are members of the Supreme Court bar and who know but are not related to the applicant.

Based upon this documentation, the clerk notifies the applicant of his acceptance. Upon paying the required fee ($100 in 1990), the applicant may then be admitted by taking the oath of admission either before a notary public or in open Court, swearing that he will conduct himself uprightly and according to law and will support the Constitution of the United States.

Noel J. Augustyn

## Advance Sheets.

After the *slip decisions, advance sheets are the next preliminary form of publication of decisions from a particular court or jurisdiction. Each of these paperback volumes contains a group of decisions in roughly chronological order. The contents of several such pamphlets (anywhere from three to six) are combined to make up a single bound volume, usually retaining the same page numbers as in the advance sheet. Since judges can make changes in their opinions before the bound volume is published, minor differences in the pagination may occur. Advance sheets are issued for both official and unofficial reports and are typically discarded after the bound volume appears.

(See also REPORTING OF OPINIONS.)

Morris L. Cohen

**Advertising, Bar.** See BAR ADVERTISING.

**Advisory Opinions.** President George *Washington sought an advisory opinion (a practice then common in *state courts) from the Supreme Court on 18 July 1793 concerning the obligations of the 1778 Franco-American Treaty. The French minister's insistence that the treaty allowed him to commission privateers in the United States seemed in conflict with Washington's recent Proclamation of Neutrality. Concerned about the imminent departure from an American port of the *Little Sarah* as a French privateer, Washington sought the Court's advice on twenty-nine issues related to the treaty.

Chief Justice John *Jay, in a letter requesting a delay until the full court could meet, noted that the justices saw "much difficulty" in replying. On 8 August 1793, the justices by letter formally declined to provide the requested advice, citing problems related to *separation of powers. Jay stated that the justices were "judges of a court in the last resort" and should not decide matters unless brought to the courts by actual litigation. This refusal reinforced the attorney general's role as presidential legal adviser as well as the court's independence of the executive.

Although later justices were tempted to provide advisory opinions concerning circuit duty and internal improvements, they refrained, using actual litigation as the forum for issuing legal opinions. Unofficially, justices have occasionally issued legal advice to the executive or legislative branches. Observers, however, have usually considered such informal measures unfortunate partisan activities. Some state constitutions do permit their Supreme Courts to issue advisory opinions.

(See also CASES AND CONTROVERSIES; JUSTICIABILITY.)

Joan R. Gundersen

**Affected with a Public Interest.** See COMMERCE POWER; MUNN V. ILLINOIS; POLICE POWER.

**Affirmative Action** is a term of general application referring to government policies that directly or indirectly award jobs, admission to universities and professional schools, and other social goods and resources to individuals on the basis of membership in designated protected groups, in order to compensate those groups for past discrimination caused by society as a whole. For political as well as prudential reasons reflecting racial sensitivities, public justification of affirmative action has tended to describe it as a logical extension of equality of opportunity for individuals. In fact, affirmative action embodies ideas that are philosophically antithetical to the principle of *equal protection of the laws that is the basis of equality of opportunity. The essential difference is that affirmative action policies are designed to benefit persons on the basis of membership in a group, rather than according to individual qualifications and experience. Affirmative action focuses on the results of the procedures used by public and private organizations measured with respect to racial balance, rather than on the existence of procedures that assure equal treatment of individuals irrespective of race, ethnicity, or sex. It can therefore be described as a civil rights policy premised on the concept of group rather than individual rights, which seeks equality of result rather than equality of opportunity.

As a general description of civil rights policy, affirmative action comprehends such matters as school desegregation, voting rights, housing sales and rentals, university admissions, the activities of federally funded agencies, and public and private employment. In each of these areas there have been judicial decisions asserting the principles of group rights and equality of result that define affirmative action. The historical development and rationale of the policy are best illustrated, however, in employment discrimination law. Before the adoption of the *Civil Rights Act of 1964, employers were permitted to select employees according to race or any other consideration, unlike the situation in voting or public education where racial discrimination was arguably unconstitutional. Accordingly, affirmative action in employment involved declaring practices that were lawful when they occurred unlawful, in order to justify awarding economic benefits to members of groups that were seen as victims of societal discrimination.

Affirmative action in employment originated in the 1960s in the policies of administrative agencies enforcing Title VII of the Civil Rights Act and Executive Orders Nos. 10925 and 11246 regulating federal contractors. In the 1970s the Supreme Court played a major role in rationalizing and legitimating the new race-conscious approach to civil rights. In general the Court proceeded on the theory that racial discrimination was by definition class discrimination and was essentially the same phenomenon regardless of where or in what form it appeared. The Court assumed that measures used in school desegregation and voting rights cases to remedy the effects of past discrimination, which took account of race and insisted on specific degrees of racial balance, could be applied in employment despite the substantially different nature of the activities involved. In the 1980s, the Supreme Court decisively protected and legalized affirmative action

preferences in employment against the attempt of the executive branch to reorient civil rights policy in the direction of impartial individual rights and equality of opportunity.

Affirmative action challenges the traditional liberal principle that individuals have rights in respect of which they are entitled to be protected equally without regard to race or other irrelevant personal characteristics. The guarantee of these rights where government acts upon individuals establishes equality before the law, the principal meaning of equality of opportunity. To deny an individual his or her rights or treat the individual differently because of race is to discriminate. In contrast to this view, which may be referred to as the *disparate treatment theory of discrimination, affirmative action postulates the *disparate impact theory of discrimination. This theory asserts that discrimination is a statistical racial disparity resulting from employment practices or other social institutional activity that can not be justified as essential or necessary to business enterprise or the activity in question. According to this view, unlawful discrimination is not an intentional denial of rights motivated by racial prejudice. It is the social effects of legitimate social and economic practices measured by a standard of racial inclusiveness or proportional representation.

The disparate impact concept of discrimination was initially employed in school desegregation and voting rights cases, where courts held that racially neutral policies were unlawful because they had the effect of excluding African-Americans. In *Gaston County* v. *U.S.* (1969), for example, the Supreme Court decided that a racially neutral literacy test was discriminatory on the ground that past school segregation denied African-Americans equal educational opportunity, thereby preventing them from developing their intellectual ability in a way that would enable them to pass the test. In employment affirmative action based on the disparate impact theory was anticipated in seniority desegregation cases, in which courts held that racially integrated departmental classifications continued the effects of past (lawful) discrimination and were hence unlawful under Title VII.

In the landmark decision in *Griggs* v. *Duke Power Company* (1971), the Supreme Court adopted the disparate impact concept of discrimination as the theoretical framework for enforcing Title VII. The Court held unanimously that an aptitude test and high school graduation requirement used by a company to select employees were unlawful because they had a disparate racial impact. The company had practiced racial discrimination before the enactment of Title VII, and its introduction of testing as a selection device at the time the act went into effect might have been judged intentionally discriminatory against African-Americans. The Court did not find intentional discrimination, however. Declaring that Title VII was directed at the consequences of employment practices and that Congress intended that the posture and condition of the job-seeker be taken into account, Chief Justice Warren *Burger said practices that operated to exclude African-Americans were illegal unless shown to be related to job performance, or justified by "business necessity."

*Griggs* was broadly applied by the *lower courts to strike down employment practices shown to have a disparate racial impact. Affirmed in *Albemarle Paper Company* v. *Moody* (1975), the disparate impact theory of Title VII enforcement provided a strong incentive for private and public employers, who were brought under Title VII coverage in 1972, to engage in race-conscious hiring to avoid discrimination charges based on statistics of racial imbalance. Concurrently federal executive agencies, acting under regulations of the Office of Federal Contract Compliance, required employers to submit written affirmative action plans specifying goals and timetables to correct "underutilization" of minority groups and women.

Most large employers, who were covered by both Title VII and the contract compliance program, responded as expected by engaging in preferential practices. As affirmative action plans were put into effect, white male employees began to file discrimination suits charging unlawful practices under the Civil Rights Act. In the late 1970s three reverse discrimination cases in the Supreme Court challenged the emerging structure of affirmative action under the disparate impact theory.

In *Regents of the University of California* v. *Bakke* (1978), the Supreme Court considered a medical school affirmative action plan that assigned sixteen of one hundred places in its entering class to members of minority groups. Bakke, whose qualifications were superior to those of most of the minority admittees, claimed that the plan violated his statutory and constitutional right to equal protection of the laws. In an artfully contrived compromise for which Justice Lewis *Powell was the sole spokesman, the Court in effect handed down two decisions. It decided, 5 to 4, that the affirmative action plan was an illegal quota that denied Bakke's right not to be discriminated against because of race. Justice Powell declared, however, that race-conscious policies adopted as a remedy for proven discrimination, which by 1978 had assumed considerable proportions in employment, were permissible under the Civil Rights Act and the Constitution. Joining with a different group of justices to form a pro–affirmative action majority, Powell, in what amounted to a second decision, held that race was a legitimate factor that could be considered in a state university's admission policy, on the theory that it advanced the *First Amendment value of "diversity."

Although *Bakke* struck down an absolute

quota, it protected the evolving structure of affirmative action in higher education and in agencies subject to the nondiscrimination requirements imposed on federally funded activities under Title VI of the Civil Rights Act. In *United Steelworkers of America* v. *Weber* (1979), the Court broadened the scope of affirmative aciton under Title VII. It rejected a reverse discrimination claim by a white male employee against a joint labor union and employer affirmative action plan that imposed a 50 percent racial quota under contract compliance pressure and the threat of Title VII discrimination charges. For the 5-to-4 majority, Justice William *Brennan said the quota was a form of private and voluntary affirmative action that, although it could not be required by government officials enforcing Title VII, was permitted under the law in order to "eliminate manifest racial imbalance in traditionally segregated job categories." Whereas in previous quota cases preferential measures were ordered by lower courts as a remedy for unlawful discrimination, the Supreme Court in *Weber* approved a quota without requiring a finding of illegal practices. It protected race-conscious policies that employers and unions were forced to adopt under the disparate impact theory of discrimination and the concept of underutilization in contract compliance.

The Supreme Court further expanded affirmative action in *Fullilove* v. *Klutznick* (1980). At issue was the constitutionality of a provision in the Public Works Employment Act of 1977 requiring that 10 percent of all federal grants awarded by the Department of Commerce be given to minority business enterprises. Rejecting a white contractor's charge of discrimination, the Court decided, 6 to 3, to uphold the law as an exercise of congressional power under the *Fourteenth Amendment to prohibit public contracting practices that perpetuated the effect of past discrimination. Although several justices used remedial rhetoric, the Court did not require a finding of unlawful discrimination as a predicate for racial preference. Directed against societal discrimination, the decision sanctioned broad congressional authority to legislate racial preferences that in reality rested on the principle of proportional racial representation under the disparate impact theory of discrimination.

In the 1980s the Reagan administration tried to stop the spread of affirmative action. Although enforcing Title VII under the disparate impact theory and seeking remedies for victims of unlawful practices, the Department of Justice challenged the legality of quotas whether imposed by judicial decree or adopted "voluntarily" by employers. It argued that preferential treatment for members of a minority group who were not themselves victims of discrimination, in order to redress societal discrimination against the group as a whole at the expense of innocent nonminority individuals rather than the employer who might have discriminated, violated the non-discrimination requirements of Title VII and exceeded the scope of judicial authority under the act. The Justice Department's litigation policy forced the Supreme Court, after years of avoiding the issue, to decide on the legality of Title VII quota remedies.

In a series of decisions in the mid-1980s, the Supreme Court reaffirmed the legality of quotas and defined the scope of race-conscious affirmative action. In *Local 28 Sheet Metal Workers International Association* v. *Equal Employment Opportunity Commission* (1986), the Court approved, 5 to 4, a lower court quota order that imposed a 29 percent membership goal on a union found in violation of Title VII. For the Court, Justice Brennan declared that quota or "race-conscious class relief" was appropriate where an employer or union "has engaged in persistent or egregious discrimination, or where necessary to dissipate the lingering effects of pervasive discrimination" (p. 445). In *Local 93 International Association of Firefighters* v. *City of Cleveland* (1986), the Court upheld a *consent decree between the city and a class of minority employees that provided for promotion quotas. Justice Brennan's majority opinion viewed the consent decree as a form of voluntary affirmative action that did not infringe the rights of nonminority employees. And in *United States* v. *Paradise* (1987), the Court affirmed, 5 to 4, the constitutionality of a 50 percent promotion quota ordered as a remedy for egregious discrimination by a state police department. Describing the standards for adopting an affirmative action plan, Justice Brennan said the quota order was flexible, temporary, and fair to white employees because it merely postponed their advancement rather than dismiss them.

From its inception in the 1960s, the underlying logic of the disparate impact theory of discrimination was to induce employers to engage in preferential practices as though they were doing it voluntarily, rather than under the threat of discrimination suits based on statistical disparities. The effectiveness of the policy further required protecting employers against reverse discrimination charges when they took affirmative action, without admitting to past discrimination that would have opened them to Title VII suits by minority group individuals. In *Johnson* v. *Santa Clara County* (1987), the Supreme Court confirmed this fundamental rationale. It rejected a white male employee's claim of discrimination against a public employer's *gender-based preference under a voluntary affirmative action plan. Clarifying and going beyond *Weber,* the Court dispensed with the idea that affirmative action is a remedy for unlawful discrimination. For the majority, Justice Brennan said the use of race or sex as a consideration in job selection was justified by "the existence of a 'manifest imbalance' that reflected an underrepresentation of women 'in traditionally segregated job categories' " (p.

617). In *Johnson* the Court acknowledged that affirmative action is a prospective policy based on the idea of group rights that aims at achieving racial and gender balance, under the idea of proportional representation that is inherent in the disparate impact theory of discrimination.

While broadly approving race-conscious measures, the Court placed some limits on affirmative action. In *Firefighters Local Union No. 1794* v. *Stotts* (1984), the Court decided, 6 to 3, that a judicial order modifying a consent decree to protect black affirmative action hires from being laid off under a seniority agreement exceeded judicial authority under Title VII. In *Wygant* v. *Jackson Board of Education* (1986), the Court held, 5 to 4, that an affirmative action plan that protected minority employees against layoff and caused the layoff of more senior white teachers violated the equal protection clause of the Constitution. These decisions reflected the solicitude for seniority rights evident in *Teamsters* v. *U.S.* (1977), where the Supreme Court overruled a line of precedents conferring benefits to blacks under the present-effects doctrine, and held that intent to discriminate must be proved in order to find a seniority system unlawful.

Having protected affirmative action against the Reagan administration's antiquota policy, the Supreme Court in 1989 appeared to shift course by modifying the evidentiary rules for proving discrimination under the disparate impact theory. Easing the burden on employers defending against discrimination charges, the Court limited the tendency toward quotas inherent in the disparate impact concept and merged the disparate impact and disparate treatment ideas in a unified theory of employment discrimination. In *Ward's Cove Packing Company* v. *Atonio* (1989), the Court stated that in a disparate impact case the burden of proof remained on the plaintiff throughout the trial, as in a disparate treatment case. It held further that a simple statistical comparison of racial percentages between skilled and unskilled jobs was insufficient to make a prima facie case. And it said that in defending against a disparate impact charge, the employer was required to show only that its practices served legitimate business purposes, not that they were essential or indispensable.

The Court further tightened the rules of affirmative action in *Richmond* v. *J. A. Croson Company* (1989). In a 6-to-3 decision, it struck down a city-ordered 30 percent quota for minority contractors as an unconstitutional violation of the rights of white contractors. Applying for the first time the standard of *strict scrutiny review to a benign racial classification, the Court held that the set-aside was defective because it was not justified by a showing of past discrimination in public contracting.

In 1990, the Court continued its zig-zag course on affirmative action by approving preferential treatment in the broadcasting industry. In *Metro

*Broadcasting Inc.* v. *Federal Communications Commission*, the Court declared, 5 to 4, that an FCC policy favoring minority broadcasters, which Congress through the appropriations process had required the agency to maintain, was substantially related to achieving the important governmental objective of broadcast diversity. Affirming congressional power to legislate racial preferences under the standardless appropriations power (in contrast to the more limited legislative power under the Fourteenth Amendment), the Court focused on the future benefits rather than the remedial justification of affirmative action.

*Metro Broadcasting*, like *Johnson*, reflected the tendency of supporters of affirmative action to view group rights and equality of result as principles of public policy needed to overcome societal discrimination. Despite the reservations about the disparate impact theory of discrimination expressed by the Supreme Court in *Ward's Cove*, as the struggle to define the meaning of equality continued in the 1990s, affirmative action remained solidly entrenched in the policies of the civil rights bureaucracy. With the passage of the *Civil Rights Act of 1991, Congress overturned *Ward's Cove* and other recent decisions that had limited the scope of federal civil rights protections, thereby reaffirming the national commitment to the principles of affirmative action.

(See also EMPLOYMENT DISCRIMINATION; RACE AND RACISM.)

Herman Belz

**Agriculture** is not a concept the Supreme Court uses to decide cases. Rather, agriculture is a context from which cases arise.

From 1790 to 1860, through disputes involving agricultural lands, the Court rendered decisions establishing the sovereignty (*Fremont* v. *United States*, 1854) and private ownership of the American land base (*United States* v. *Noe*, 1859). Litigation between inventors of agricultural implements gave rise to early interpretations of the Constitution's patents clause (*Seymour* v. *McCormick*, 1854).

After the Civil War, agricultural products were the basis of a flourishing commerce. As this commerce grew, state legislatures passed statutes governing elevators, railroads, and packers. These measures stirred profound debate in the Supreme Court from 1873 to 1940. One set of justices believed that states had constitutional authority through their *police power to protect the public's health, safety, and welfare. These justices accepted state statutes licensing livestock butchers (*Slaughterhouse Cases*, 1873) or grain storage (*Payne* v. *Kansas*, 1918). They also approved regulation of rates charged by elevators (*Munn* v. *Illinois*, 1877) and minimum and maximum retail prices for milk (*Nebbia* v. *New York*, 1934). Another set of justices believed that these state statutes contravened the *Fourteenth Amendment's due process, equal protection,

and *privileges and immunities clauses. These justices invoked the Fourteenth Amendment to protect American citizens from state monopoly franchises (*Slaughterhouse Cases*, 1884), confiscatory rate regulations (*Brass* v. *North Dakota*, 1894), and differential licensing standards among agricultural processors (*Frost* v. *Oklahoma Corporation Commission*, 1929). Although the context shifted from agricultural commerce after 1940, the debate about the interplay between state police power and the Fourteenth Amendment persisted (see COMMERCE POWER).

The Supreme Court often addressed matters of agriculture when determining congressional authority over American commerce. The justices have held that states can protect their internal agriculture from contagious diseases (*Missouri, Kansas & Texas Railway Co.* v. *Haber*, 1898; *Mintz* v. *Baldwin*, 1933) but that they cannot isolate themselves from interstate trade and competition (*Lemke* v. *Farmers' Grain Co.*, 1922; *Baldwin* v. *G.A.F. Seelig, Inc.*, 1935). Simultaneously, as a government of delegated powers, Congress can only regulate interstate commerce. In the process of defining agricultural interstate commerce, the Court made several of its most momentous rulings.

Initially, the Supreme Court perceived agriculture susceptible to federal power when it was in the stream of commerce between states (*Stafford* v. *Wallace*, 1922) but not before it entered that stream (*Illinois Central Railroad Co.* v. *McKendree*, 1905). As the Depression deepened in 1933, however, the Court had to reevaluate its position in light of the National Industrial Recovery Act (NIRA) and Agricultural Adjustment Act (AAA). Both laws expanded federal power over commerce through administrative agencies. In *Schechter Poultry Corporation* v. *United States* (1935) and *United States* v. *Butler* (1936), the Supreme Court ruled the two laws unconstitutional.

In *Schechter*, the Supreme Court expressed concern that Congress delegated legislative power to administrative agencies without proper standards for bureaucratic action (see DELEGATION OF POWERS). Congress responded by enacting the second Agricultural Adjustment Act in 1938. The Court upheld the new law because Congress had set substantive standards to govern the Department of Agriculture (*Mulford* v. *Smith*, 1939). Moreover, in a series of cases beginning in 1936 (*St. Joseph Stock Yards Co.* v. *United States*) and ending in 1941 (*United States* v. *Morgan*), the Court developed doctrines of procedural fairness to govern the Department of Agriculture's administrative actions.

In *Butler*, the Court ruled that an agricultural tax to bring production in line with demand unconstitutionally invaded state power over intrastate commerce. By early 1942, however, the Court upheld federal regulation of intrastate milk directly affecting interstate commerce (*United*

*States* v. *Wrightwood Dairy*). Later in 1942, the Court, in *Wickard* v. *Filburn*, adopted the expansive substantial economic effect test to determine when Congress can control intrastate commerce. *Wickard* remains the leading constitutional case approving sweeping federal power to govern American agriculture through the Commerce Clause.

Today, agriculture rarely provides the context for important Supreme Court decisions. Agriculture provided the context for the state action exemption to federal antitrust laws (*Parker* v. *Brown*, 1943), for the definition of investment contracts under securities law (*Securities and Exchange Commission* v. *Howey Co.*, 1946), and a major case determining the extent of federal common law (*United States* v. *Kimbell Foods, Inc.*, 1979). Aside from these three cases, however, the Supreme Court harvest from agricultural cases is complete.

(See also CAPITALISM.)

Drew L. Kershen

**Akron v. Akron Center for Reproductive Health, Inc.,** 462 U.S. 416 (1983), argued 30 Nov. 1982, decided 15 June 1983 by vote of 6 to 3; Powell for the Court, O'Connor, with White and Rehnquist, in dissent. The Court invalidated a number of restrictions imposed by the city of Akron, Ohio, on abortion: a ban on performing second-trimester abortions in clinics rather than hospitals, a requirement that physicians provide detailed information about abortions to women before they signed consent forms, and a twenty-four-hour waiting period between giving consent and having an abortion. The Court said that the hospital requirement increased the cost of abortions without a significant increase in the woman's safety, that the information specified by the ordinance was designed to persuade the woman not to have an abortion rather than to inform her about the procedure, and that the waiting period increased costs by requiring two trips and was unnecessarily inflexible.

Justice Sandra Day *O'Connor wrote her first major abortion opinion in this case. She criticized the trimester approach adopted in *Roe* v. *Wade* as rigid and likely to come under strain as medical technology pushed the time of viability back into the second trimester or even earlier. She proposed that regulations of abortion be permitted unless they placed an "undue burden" on a woman's decision. For her, neither the hospitalization nor the waiting period did so, because abortions were available in local hospitals and the waiting period was "a small cost to impose to ensure that the woman's decision is well-considered in light of its certain and irreparable consequences on fetal life" (p. 474).

(See also ABORTION; PRIVACY.)

Mark V. Tushnet

**Albemarle Paper Co. v. Moody,** 422 U.S. 405 (1975), argued 14 Apr. 1975, decided 25 June 1975 by vote of 7 to 1; Stewart for the Court, Marshall, Rehnquist, and Blackmun concurring, Burger dissenting in part, Powell not participating. This case and *United Papermakers and Paperworkers* v. *Moody* were decided in the same opinion and dealt with two important issues under Title VII of the *Civil Rights Act of 1964: (1) the standards a district court should use in deciding back pay awards to employees who suffered monetary loss because of racial discrimination; and (2) the requirements placed upon an employer to establish that preemployment tests that have a discriminatory effect are sufficiently "job related" to survive a legal challenge.

The plaintiffs in *Moody* consisted of present and former African-American employees of Albemarle Paper Company's mill in Roanoke Rapids, North Carolina. They charged that the company's seniority system perpetuated the overt segregation that existed in the plant's departmental job assignment system prior to 2 July 1965 (the effective date of Title VII), and they sought injunctive and back pay relief.

The Court found that tests used by the company were not sufficiently job related to be valid under Title VII and held that the trial court should have enjoined the use of the tests and awarded back pay. In deciding the issue of back pay awards, the Court ruled that such awards should follow closely upon a finding of discrimination and that ordering back pay was an appropriate incentive to employers to comply with Title VII. It concluded that the certainty of the remedy would best effectuate the statute. In all essential aspects this holding continues to provide a major form of relief under Title VII.

(See also EMPLOYMENT DISCRIMINATION; RACE AND RACISM; SEGREGATION, DE FACTO.)

Herbert Hill

**Albertson v. Subversive Activities Control Board,** 382 U.S. 70 (1965), argued 18 Oct. 1965, decided 15 Nov. 1965 by vote of 8 to 0; Brennan for the Court, White not participating. The Internal Security Act, passed over President Truman's veto in 1950 and generally known as the *McCarran Act, sought to expose the Communist party in the United States by the device of compulsory registration. The statute ordered communist organizations to register with the attorney general; the Subversive Activities Control Board (SACB) was created to administer the registration process. Registered organizations were required to disclose the names of their officers and the source of their funds. Members of registered organizations were subject to various sanctions, including denial of passports and the right to work in defense plants. The Supreme Court upheld the registration requirements in *Communist Party* v. *Subversive Activities Control Board* (1961) but postponed any decision on the constitutionality of the sanctions until they were actually enforced.

As anticipated, the Communist party refused to register. The attorney general then asked the SACB to order individual party members to register. Albertson and others refused, claiming that registration, with resulting penalties, amounted to self-incrimination in violation of the *Fifth Amendment. The Supreme Court unanimously agreed. While the statute purportedly granted immunity from prosecution for the act of registration, the Court held that registration could in fact be used as evidence in criminal prosecutions, or to supply investigatory leads.

The SACB was no more successful in other cases. The ban on defense plant employment was struck down in United States v. *Robel (1967). With this record of futility, the Nixon Administration allowed the SACB to die in 1973.

(See also COMMUNISM AND COLD WAR; SELF-INCRIMINATION; SUBVERSION.)

C. Herman Pritchett

**Alienage and Naturalization.** The constitutional law of alienage and naturalization reflects broader themes in American political, economic, and social history. The French Revolution, for an early example, took place just after ratification of the Constitution of 1787, and produced fears of foreign meddling in domestic affairs. The Alien and Sedition Acts of 1798, passed by Federalists over strong Jeffersonian-Republican opposition, gave the president broad power to detain or expel aliens. The government made no arrests under the Alien Act, and President Thomas *Jefferson pardoned the few Republican editors jailed under the *Sedition Act. Yet fear inspired by these laws prompted the Virginia and Kentucky Resolutions—classic statements of states' rights—and provided ammunition for the Jeffersonians in the election of 1800 (see STATE SOVEREIGNTY AND STATES' RIGHTS).

In the late nineteenth century, economic pressures resulting from industrial development combined with fear of foreign political ideas and powerful nativist sentiments to produce a backlash against aliens and immigration. The *Fourteenth Amendment's *Equal Protection Clause became the centerpiece in the constitutional law of alienage. It limited, if unevenly, the powers of the states to base classifications on citizenship, while the federal government's constitutional prerogatives over aliens and the naturalization process remained substantial (see FEDERALISM). Recent alienage cases deal with eligibility for governmental benefits, public sector employment, and due process issues, and reflect the rise of the welfare state.

Since alienage and naturalization alike deal with the status of noncitizens, it is useful to begin by briefly considering the constitutional law of citizenship. To define alienage as the lack of citizenship raises the question of how the Consti-

tution establishes who is a citizen. While the Constitution requires that representatives and senators be citizens and that the president be a "natural born citizen," the document provides no definition of United States citizenship.

The requirement that the president be a "natural born" citizen implies that the framers recognized the principle of jus soli. According to this doctrine—literally meaning "right of land or ground"—citizenship results from birth within a national territory. This contrasts with jus sanguinis, or right of blood, according to which citizenship derives from descent. Citizenship based on an ascriptive characteristic like place of birth was medieval and in conflict with modern principles of liberal political theory. Birthright citizenship, however, offered several practical advantages: it established a clear basis for *property rights; it promoted immigration; it avoided jurisdictional conflicts; and it eased fears of massive expatriation in wartime.

Only after the *Civil War, however, did the principle of jus soli become constitutional law. In *Scott v. Sandford (1857), Chief Justice Roger B. *Taney wrote that the slave Dred Scott, who had been taken by his master from the slave state of Missouri to the free state of Illinois and into Wisconsin Territory, could not sue for his freedom in federal court since no one of African descent, freeman or slave, could be a citizen of the United States (see SLAVERY). To reverse Dred Scott, the Fourteenth Amendment (1868) declared: "All persons born or naturalized in the United States, and subject to the jurisdiction thereof, are citizens of the United States and of the State wherein they reside."

The Fourteenth Amendment not only defined citizenship but also gave aliens constitutional rights. This is because the Fourteenth Amendment's *due process and equal protection clauses apply not just to citizens, but to all persons. In the *Slaughterhouse Cases (1873), Justice Samuel F. *Miller observed that the Civil War Amendments (the *Thirteenth, Fourteenth, and *Fifteenth) were enacted primarily to secure the rights of the newly freed slaves (although only the Fifteenth speaks in race-specific terms). Miller added, however, that these amendments did not necessarily apply to African-Americans alone. Miller wrote that, for example, the Thirteenth Amendment would not allow slavery to develop in the western territories under the "Chinese coolie Labor system" (p. 72).

Justice Miller rightly noted the problems of the "Chinese coolie." The federal government had initially welcomed Chinese immigration, beginning with the California Gold Rush of 1848. These immigrants provided labor to build the transcontinental railroad. With the line completed in 1869, a wave of European immigrants flooded the West and labor was no longer scarce. Chinese aliens became victims of harsh and sometimes violent discrimination.

A case from San Francisco, *Yick Wo v. Hopkins* (1886), testing an overtly neutral law designed to exclude Chinese laundries, became a constitutional landmark. Taking up Justice Miller's remarks in the *Slaughterhouse Cases,* a unanimous Supreme Court ruled that the equal protection clause of the Fourteenth Amendment applied to aliens. The *Yick Wo* holding was especially significant since federal law prohibited Chinese aliens from becoming citizens.

In order to analyze the civil rights of aliens after *Yick Wo*, it is useful to distinguish the scope of federal power versus state authority. While aliens have used the Fourteenth Amendment to nullify state regulations, the Supreme Court has recognized broad federal authority over noncitizens.

Consider first the cases in which the states have enacted laws based on alienage. While the states have police powers to regulate health, safety, welfare, and morals, *Yick Wo* held that these powers were subject to the federal equal protection clause. In *Truax v. Raich* (1915), for instance, the Court invalidated a state law that required 80 percent of workers in most businesses to be citizens. This law had the impermissible effect of freezing aliens out of the marketplace. Yet court decisions did not always favor aliens. Just a year earlier, in *Patsone v. Pennsylvania* (1914), the justices upheld a state law forbidding aliens to hunt game. Justice Oliver Wendell *Holmes—a proponent of the "rational man" test in his *Lochner v. New York* (1905) dissent—wrote for a unanimous court that a state could "reasonably" restrict aliens as a class in order to preserve natural resources for citizens (see RULE OF REASON). Similarly, the Court upheld state laws limiting the right of Japanese aliens to own or rent land in *Terrace v. Thompson* (1923).

With some irony, the *Japanese Exclusion Cases* led to expanded equal protection rights for aliens. *Korematsu v. United States* (1944) upheld the emergency relocation, after Pearl Harbor, of persons of Japanese ancestry living on the West Coast. Though he accepted the military's reasons for this extreme action, Justice Hugo L. *Black wrote that racial classifications were "inherently suspect" and must be subject to the "most rigid scrutiny" (see STRICT SCRUTINY; SUSPECT CLASSIFICATIONS). While the classification at issue was racial, Black emphasized that even citizens like Korematsu—let alone aliens—could be subject to race-based exclusion during a wartime emergency (see RACE AND RACISM). Though never overruled, *Korematsu's* approval of racially discriminatory treatment in emergencies has surely been displaced by more recent developments in equal protection law.

During the 1970s, the Burger Court applied *Korematsu's* "strict scrutiny" to state regulations affecting aliens. Under this test, reversing the normal presumption that a challenged law is constitutional, the state bears the burden of proof to show that a law employing a "suspect classifica-

tion" serves compelling governmental interest. The cases deal chiefly with access to governmental benefits and public employment.

In *Graham v. Richardson* (1971), the Court held that alienage, like race, was a suspect classification and applied strict scrutiny in ruling that a state could not deny welfare benefits to aliens. Arizona's interest in preserving limited funds for its citizens (a rationale that parallels *Patsone*) did not justify limiting benefits. In *In re Griffiths* (1973), also applying strict scrutiny, the Court held that states may not prohibit resident aliens from practicing law.

Two years later, in *Sugarman v. Dougall* (1973), the Court created an important category of exceptions to *Graham*. The opinion by Justice Harry *Blackmun held that a state could not make aliens ineligible for certain state civil service jobs. *Dictum, however, suggested that aliens could be barred from elective and even some nonelective posts in state government. Blackmun wrote that aliens could be kept from positions that involve the formulation, execution, or review of broad public policy since these political functions "go to the heart of representative government." In *Foley v. Connelie* (1978), however, the Court only used ordinary scrutiny to uphold a New York regulation that prevented aliens from becoming state troopers, since law officers exercise considerable discretion in enforcing public policy. To apply the high hurdle of strict scrutiny to every alienage classification, Chief Justice Burger wrote in *Foley*, would "obliterate all the distinctions between citizens and aliens, and thus depreciate the historic values of citizenship" (p. 295). Where the state's vital public functions are involved, a state need show only a rational basis for an alienage classification. A majority followed *Foley's* political functions analysis to uphold alienage restrictions for public school teachers in *Ambach v. Norwick* (1979) and for deputy probation officers in *Cabell v. Chavez-Salido* (1982). But the Court rejected similar eligibility requirements for notaries public in *Bernal v. Fainter* (1984).

In *Plyler v. Doe* (1982), the Court applied yet another equal protection standard—intermediate or heightened scrutiny—to alienage classifications. Unlike the cases discussed so far, in which the noncitizens involved were legally in the country, *Plyler* dealt with the children of illegal aliens. Texas had allowed its school districts to deny a free public education to the children of "illegals." While a Court majority rejected Texas's argument that illegal aliens are not "persons" covered by the Fourteenth Amendment, it refused to apply strict scrutiny. By a 5-to-4 vote, it invalidated the Texas law using the intermediate standard of equal protection review. Justice Lewis F. *Powell wrote a pivotal concurring opinion that emphasized the special circumstances of the case—the involuntary presence of the alien children in the country and the importance of the governmental benefit involved.

Unlike invidious racial classifications, which are inherently suspect, the state may thus enact some laws that draw distinctions between aliens and citizens. With respect to aliens legally in the country who are denied important benefits, *Graham* establishes a presumption that alienage classifications are suspect and liable to strict scrutiny. *Foley*, however, recognizes an exception to this rule: states need show only a rational basis for excluding aliens from public functions vital to representative government. With respect to illegal aliens, the picture is less clear. *Plyler* applies an intermediate standard of review, but the narrow and divided nature of that ruling makes it difficult to generalize beyond the facts of the case.

While state power to classify aliens is variable, the cases involving federal law have a single theme: the national government's power over aliens is substantial. Again, cases involving Chinese aliens in the late nineteenth century state key principles. In one of the *Chinese Exclusion Cases, Chae Chan Ping* v. *United States* (1889), the Supreme Court said that congressional power to restrict entry of aliens into the United States was a fundamental attribute of national sovereignty. Thus, Congress could enforce a ban on immigration from Asia. In *Fong Yue Ting* v. *United States* (1893), the Court similarly gave Congress a free hand to set criteria for deportation.

Congress exercised those prerogatives early when it passed the Alien and Sedition Acts in 1798. Yet just as Congress did not broadly exercise its commerce powers until the latter part of the nineteenth century, it did not enact limitations on immigration until the 1890s. Significant antagonism existed toward southern and eastern European immigrants that led to further restrictions on aliens during this era. The assassination of President William McKinley by Leon Czolgosz in 1901 fueled fears of aliens, anarchism, and violence. By 1903, Congress had passed laws making anarchism grounds for deportation and exclusion from entry into the country. *World War I and the "Red Scare" after the Bolshevik Revolution precipitated greater intolerance and repression directed against radicals of all kinds, many of whom were aliens. In 1917 and 1918, Congress passed immigration laws that allowed the federal government to deport aliens for political reasons and even to revoke the citizenship granted to naturalized aliens who had been associated with anarchism.

Since the Supreme Court has broadly endorsed congressional authority over aliens, there are fewer cases challenging federal as opposed to state laws based on alienage. In 1976, however, the Burger Court ruled that the Civil Service Commission could not enforce a rule making aliens ineligible for the federal civil service. Justice Powell's opinion for the five-person majority in *Hampton* v. *Mow Sun Wong* (1976) rejected the view that the federal government's power over aliens is plenary. For example, noncitizens

have due process rights in deportation hearings (*Wong Yang Sung* v. *McGrath*, 1950); and the *Fourth Amendment's ban on unreasonable searches and seizures applies to investigation of illegal aliens by immigration authorities, though with flexibility regarding "border searches" (*United States* v. *Brignoni-Ponce*, 1975). Yet the Court ultimately rejected the Commission's regulation on due process grounds and avoided taking up any equal protection issues. The limited scope of the *Fifth Amendment's equal protection component, based on *Bolling* v. *Sharpe* (1954), in federal alienage cases became evident in a case decided along with *Hampton*. In *Mathews* v. *Diaz* (1976), the Court unanimously ruled that Congress had to show only a rational basis for denying Medicare benefits to aliens living in the country for at least five years.

Naturalization, the process by which persons become citizens other than by birth, also reflects broad federal authority. Congressional power over aliens rests in part on Article I's grant of power to establish a uniform rule of naturalization. In 1790, Congress provided that a free white alien who had lived in the United States for two years could be naturalized by any common law court, given evidence of good character and willingness to uphold the Constitution. These basic requirements—residence, moral fitness, and fidelity to constitutional principles—remain the core requirements for naturalization today. Yet Congress retains broad power to define these standards, as underscored in *United States* v. *MacIntosh* (1931). Congress has required literacy as a condition of naturalization and allowed denial of citizenship on the grounds of moral turpitude (drunkenness, gambling, prostitution, or polygamy) or prior criminal activity.

In *Osborn* v. *Bank of the United States* (1824), Chief Justice John *Marshall maintained that there was no difference between a naturalized and a native-born citizen. Yet, since passage of the Naturalization Act of 1906 there has been one significant exception to this rule. A naturalized citizen may be stripped of citizenship if there is evidence of bad faith or fraud in the naturalization process. In *Schneiderman* v. *United States* (1943), however, the Court placed a heavy burden of proof on the government in order to denaturalize a citizen. It was not enough to establish Schneiderman's failure to support the Constitution (a statutory requirement for naturalization) by proving that he had been a member of the Communist party when he became a citizen (see COMMUNISM AND COLD WAR). The Court required clear, unequivocal, and convincing evidence of disloyalty in order to revoke citizenship.

Alienage and naturalization reflect two themes in the history of American civil rights policy. First, the history of alienage law underscores the fragility of civil rights in times of real or perceived emergency and demonstrates the interaction of economic, political, and social forces in the definition of those rights. From the Alien and Sedition Acts, to the anti-Asian restrictions of the late nineteenth century, to the repression of the Red Scare and the anticommunism of the post–World War II era, threats to security—economic or political—have stimulated efforts to limit the scope of civil rights for citizens and aliens alike (see SUBVERSION). Second, as with the perennial civil rights problem in American society—race relations—alienage cases reflect the contours of American *federalism. Federal power to regulate alienage and naturalization is an attribute of sovereignty and is substantial. Where functions broadly considered vital to representative government are not involved, the Fourteenth Amendment limits state authority to classify persons on the basis of citizenship.

(See also CITIZENSHIP.)

□ Thomas Alexander Aleinikoff and David A. Martin, *Immigration: Process and Policy* (1985). "Developments in the Law: Immigration Policy and the Rights of Aliens," *Harvard Law Review* 96 (1983): 1286–1465. Charles Gordon and Harry Rosenfield, *Immigration Law and Procedure* (1984). Elizabeth Hull, *Without Justice For All: The Constitutional Rights of Aliens* (1985).                    Patrick J. Bruer

**Alien and Sedition Acts.** See SEDITION ACT OF 1798.

**Alien Land Laws.** The rights of aliens to own real property in the United States are not absolute nor are they protected by the Constitution. Since 1776, American courts and legislatures have confronted this issue.

The first Supreme Court case to grapple with alien rights to realty was *Fairfax's Devisee* v. *Hunter's Lessee* (1813). Denny Fairfax, a British citizen, inherited Virginia land. During the Revolutionary War, Virginia wished to prevent enemy aliens from gaining rights to real property, and it conveyed Fairfax's inheritance to a Virginia citizen, David Hunter. Although the Supreme Court upheld Fairfax's right to inherit the land, it did so only because Virginia had not correctly followed escheat procedures. If Virginia had drafted its statute correctly, it could have denied Fairfax's claim. This narrow holding allowed state legislatures and Congress to restrict alien rights.

Many states restricted the ability of aliens to own land. Some required evidence of prospective American *citizenship; others limited the amount of property. Most of these restrictions occurred from 1850 to 1920 in the American West. States and *territories prohibited Chinese and Japanese from owning farm and mineral lands as a means of discouraging Asian immigration.

The federal government also restricted aliens. In 1887 Congress passed a statute preventing future aliens from owning or leasing real estate in federal territories. Mineral and timber lands were also carefully controlled.

Challenges to legislation restricting alien land

ownership have generally failed. Courts have upheld the right of legislatures to restrict alien rights to property. Most of these restrictions have been repealed, but they can be reinstituted at any time.

(See also ALIENAGE AND NATURALIZATION; PROPERTY RIGHTS.)

                    John R. Wunder

**All Deliberate Speed.** Of the many equivocal signals sent by Chief Justice Earl *Warren's opinion for the Court in *Brown* v. *Board of Education II* (1955), the phrase came to symbolize the Court's hesitancy about desegregation and became a rationalization for those resisting change. The phrase was placed in the opinion at the insistence of Justice Felix *Frankfurter, who thought, inaccurately, that the formulation originated with Justice Oliver Wendell *Holmes in his interpretation of nineteenth-century equity practice. The original source was a poem, "The Hound of Heaven," by the nineteenth-century Catholic devotional writer Francis Thompson (1859–1907). The Court shunned further reliance on the notion in *Griffin* v. *County School Board of Prince Edward County* in 1964 and repudiated the phrase in *Green* v. *County School Board of New Kent County* in 1968. That same year, Justice Hugo *Black criticized the Court's use of the phrase during a television interview—at the time an unprecedented off-the-bench criticism of a governing opinion by a sitting justice.                    Dennis J. Hutchinson

**Allegheny County v. ACLU Greater Pittsburgh Chapter,** 492 U.S. 573 (1989), argued 22 Feb. 1989, decided 3 July 1989 by votes of 5 to 4 (to strike) and 6 to 3 (to uphold), Blackmun announced the judgment, O'Connor concurring in part, Brennan and Stevens concurring in part and dissenting in part, Kennedy concurring in judgment in part and dissenting in part. The Supreme Court's policy of the early 1980s favoring religious accommodation was manifest in *Lynch* v. *Donnelly* (1984). There, against a challenge brought by the *American Civil Liberties Union, it upheld a publicly sponsored Christmas display by a 5-to-4 vote. Apllying the three-part "test" enunciated in *Lemon* v. *Kurtzman* (1971) (see LEMON TEST), the Court held that in the context of a larger display— which included a Santa, reindeers, and talking wishing wells—a creche had a secular purpose, did not have a primary effect advancing or inhibiting religion, and did not excessively entangle church and state. In *Allegheny*, the Court refused to extend *Lynch* to approve a seasonal display that focused predominantly on religious symbols.

Justice Harry *Blackmun announced the judgment of the Court in an opinion joined only by Justice Sandra Day *O'Connor. He held that the context contemplated by *Lynch* was the display itself, not that of the general holiday season. Thus, a creche—unadorned by other, more secular objects—could not constitutionally be placed in the public display of a country courthouse. A menorah, however, could occupy a similar setting, so long as it was in a context—surrounded by secular symbols—that emphasized the diversity of the holiday. Brennan, Marshall, and Stevens would have struck both displays; Rehnquist, White, Scalia, and Kennedy would have upheld them.

(See also RELIGION.)

Joseph F. Kobylka

**Allgeyer v. Louisiana,** 165 U.S. 578 (1897), submitted 6 Jan. 1897, decided 1 Mar. 1897 by vote of 9 to 0; Peckham for the Court. In *Allgeyer* v. *Louisiana* the Supreme Court for the first time ruled a state law unconstitutional for depriving a person of the right to make contracts. The case arose in Louisiana, which like other states prohibited businesses from operating within its jurisdiction unless they met certain conditions. To enforce this policy, Louisiana made it illegal for Louisianans to enter into certain insurance contracts by mail with companies operating outside the state. Allgeyer & Co. was prosecuted for entering into such an insurance contract with a New York company.

The Court had earlier held that insurance was not interstate commerce and so could not rule the Louisiana law unconstitutional for invading national jurisdiction. Instead, the Court held that the contract was effected in New York and lawful under New York. The Court then held that the Due Process Clause of the *Fourteenth Amendment guaranteed the right to enter into lawful contracts.

*Allgeyer* v. *Louisiana* became the key case establishing the doctrine of "liberty of contract." Although the opinion itself only declared that the right to make lawful contracts was a liberty protected by the Due Process Clause, the courts developed the principle that freedom of contract was the rule and restraint the exception, the reasonability of which states had to justify. Employers regularly cited this principle to challenge legislation regulating terms of employment—setting maximum working hours or minimum wages, for example. Until the mid-1930s such challenges often were successful.

(See also CONTRACT, FREEDOM OF; DUE PROCESS, SUBSTANTIVE.)

Michael Les Benedict

**American Bar Association Committee on Federal Judiciary.** The American Bar Association (ABA) Standing Committee on Federal Judiciary is the principal nongovernmental actor in the federal judicial selection process. The ABA Committee was formally established in 1946 following earlier unsystematic efforts by the organized bar to influence federal judicial selection. The role of the committee has varied greatly during different administrations, although its influence has generally been greatest when a Republican occupies the presidency. Early on, the committee sometimes generated names for judgeships. Its contemporary role, however, has been limited to evaluating candidates submitted to it for review. At times, such as during the Eisenhower and most of the Nixon years, the ABA's advice was sought as a screening mechanism for candidates prior to their actual nomination. Similarly, President Gerald Ford sought the ABA's views on fifteen candidates before nominating John Paul *Stevens to the Supreme Court. More routinely, however, the committee reviews candidates after they have been formally nominated and its findings are presented during the Senate confirmation process.

The Committee is currently composed of fifteen members chosen by the ABA president to represent the regions of the country in a manner that mirrors the regional structure of the federal bench. The primary responsibility for investigating a nominee falls upon the committee member representing the area in which a vacancy arises. Such an arrangement invites controversy since the committee's deliberations inevitably focus on the recommendations of one individual.

Currently, candidates for Supreme Court vacancies are rated "well qualified," "not opposed," or "not qualified." A unanimous finding of "well qualified," as occurred in the appointment of Anthony *Kennedy, clearly facilitates confirmation. When the Committee's endorsement is more ambiguous, such as in the nomination of Robert *Bork, significant trouble is foreshadowed for nominee. Votes of "not qualified" for Supreme Court nominees are rare and, indeed, none (including the ill-fated candidacies of Clement *Haynsworth, G. Harrold *Carswell, and Robert Bork) have been labeled "not qualified" by a committee majority.

Committee ratings of *lower federal court nominees (district and courts of appeal) utilize a scale of "well qualified," "qualified," "qualified/not qualified," (indicating a split vote), and "not qualified." Since presidential administrations enjoy numerous appointment opportunities to the lower courts, analysts often make comparative assessments of an administration's recruitment success on the basis of how many of its nominees attained the ABA's highest ratings and how few were found to be "not qualified." Unlike Supreme Court nominees (who are unambiguously the candidates of the president), lower court nominees are often associated with local political factors.

The role of the committee has been controversial since its inception. Questions have been raised about the virtual monopoly enjoyed by the ABA as an institutionalized, nongovernmental voice in the staffing of critical judgeship positions. Further, since the ABA has historically been viewed as representative of the most successful, conservative elements of the bar, questions have been raised about possible bias in the committee's judgments. Indeed, research conducted on the Carter administration revealed that positive ABA ratings were strongly associated with a nominee's white male status, age, and years of legal experience. ABA ratings also appeared to favor candidates who attended elite law schools, pursued traditional practices, and enjoyed relatively higher incomes prior to nomination. During the Reagan administration some criticism of the committee's operation came from conservative interests, such as the Washington Legal Foundation, which claimed that the committee was obstructing conservative nominees and aiding in opposition to them. Thus, nearly a half century after its creation, the ABA Standing Committee on Federal Judiciary is an important, albeit controversial element in federal judicial selection. It remains in a state of flux reflecting the contemporary political environment as well as the expectations raised and opportunities created by the presidential administration of the moment.

(See also APPOINTMENT AND REMOVAL POWER; SELECTION OF JUSTICES.)

Elliot E. Slotnick

**American Civil Liberties Union** (ACLU), a private voluntary organization dedicated to the defense of individual rights under the Constitution. The ACLU's program includes litigation, public education, and lobbying. ACLU attorneys offer free legal assistance to individuals who believe that their civil liberties have been violated.

Founded in January 1920, the ACLU was the successor to the National Civil Liberties Bureau, established in 1917 to defend *conscientious objectors and fight the suppression of civil liberties during *World War I. The distinctive feature of the ACLU has been its self-proclaimed nonpartisan defense of civil liberties. The ACLU has defended the free speech rights of unpopular groups such as communists, Nazis, and the Ku Klux Klan to protect the principle of free speech as such and not because it supports the content of the speech in question, a distinction seldom perceived by the ACLU's critics.

The ACLU's agenda has continued to evolve. In the early 1920s the organization concentrated on defending the *First Amendment rights of political radicals and *labor union organizers. The 1926 case of *Scopes* v. *State* catapulted the ACLU to national prominence. The ACLU's challenge to a Tennessee law prohibiting the teaching of *evolution added the issues of *academic freedom and separation of church and state to its agenda. By the 1930s the ACLU's program included defense of the free exercise of *religion, particularly in a series of important Jehovah's Witnesses cases, challenges to *censorship in the arts, support for the civil rights of racial minori-

ties (see RACE AND RACISM), and advocacy of judicial protection of the rights of criminal suspects (see DUE PROCESS, PROCEDURAL).

In the 1960s the ACLU's conception of civil liberties expanded to include the rights of women (see GENDER), students, prisoners, poor people, homosexuals, and other "victim groups." The ACLU raised constitutional challenges to existing criminal *abortion laws, *capital punishment, and in 1970, to the *Vietnam War. At the same time, its position on First Amendment issues evolved in a more "absolutist" direction to include opposition to all forms of censorship and any form of government aid to religion (see FIRST AMENDMENT ABSOLUTISM).

The ACLU has won many Supreme Court cases that have produced important constitutional doctrines. One historian estimated that the ACLU participated in 80 percent of the recognized "landmark" cases from 1925 to the present. In *Gitlow* v. *New York* (1925), the ACLU helped persuade the Court that the Due Process Clause of the *Fourteenth Amendment incorporated the protections of the First Amendment (see INCORPORATION DOCTRINE). ACLU lawyers successfully argued *Stromberg* v. *California* (1931), *Powell* v. *Alabama* (1932), *DeJonge* v. *Oregon* (1937), and *Hague* v. *CIO* (1939). They also argued *Hirabayashi* v. *United States* (1943) and *Korematsu* v. *United States* (1944), which unsuccessfully challenged the evacuation and internment of the Japanese-Americans during *World War II. In the post–World War II period the ACLU participated in most of the leading cases in the areas of church and state (e.g., *Engel* v. *Vitale,* 1962), censorship (e.g., *Jacobellis* v. *Ohio,* 1964), and criminal procedure (e.g., *Miranda* v. *Arizona,* 1966). It also joined the *NAACP in the major civil rights cases, including *Brown* v. *Board of Education* (1954).

The ACLU's legal program traditionally relied on the pro bono services of cooperating attorneys who filed *amicus briefs raising points of constitutional law. In the 1960s the ACLU increasingly provided direct representation to its clients and made greater use of paid staff attorneys. In the 1970s the ACLU created a series of "special projects" devoted to particular issues such as reproductive rights, prisoners' rights, and women's rights. The projects were funded by foundation grants and employed full-time staff. By 1980 the ACLU brought an estimated six thousand court cases annually, with most handled by volunteer cooperating attorneys on behalf of ACLU affiliates. In the Supreme Court, it filed *briefs in about thirty cases per year, appearing before the Court more often than any other organization except the United States government.

The ACLU's position on civil liberties issues has generated enormous controversy over the years, with criticisms coming from several directions. Conservative anticommunists accused the ACLU of supporting *communism because of its defense of the First Amendment rights of communists. Religious fundamentalists attacked the ACLU as "Godless" or "anti-Christian" because of its position on separation of church and state. The ACLU's opposition to censorship and restrictions on *contraception and abortion produced a long history of conflict with the Catholic church. Because of its defense of the rights of criminal suspects, conservatives attacked the ACLU for being the "criminals' lobby." Left-wing critics accused the ACLU of failing to oppose vigorously anticommunist measures during the Cold War and have occasionally attacked it for defending Nazis or other extreme right-wing groups.

Beginning in the 1970s, conservatives accused the ACLU of abandoning its traditional role as a nonpartisan defender of civil liberties in favor of a liberal political agenda, citing the ACLU's challenge to the constitutionality of the Vietnam War and its support for the *impeachment of President Richard *Nixon in the Watergate affair. Conservative legal scholars argued that the ACLU's position on a constitutional right to *privacy and, in particular, the right to an abortion, was not supported by the text or history of the Constitution. Generally, these critics claimed that the ACLU and liberal judges had substituted their personal political values for the *original intent of the framers of the Constitution. The ACLU replied that its conception of civil liberties was supported by the structure and purposes of limited government established by the Constitution and the *Bill of Rights.

Organizationally, by the 1980s the ACLU consisted of a national office and a network of affiliates and chapters in all fifty states. Affiliates were bound by the policies adopted by the national board of directors but exercised a high degree of autonomy in developing their own programs. Several affiliates employed their own full-time attorneys and lobbyists. Membership in the ACLU grew from about one thousand in 1920 to more than 275,000 in 1990. The ACLU national office includes a legal staff and public education department, a legislative office in Washington with eleven staff counsel, and persons working on ten special projects.

(See also SPEECH AND THE PRESS.)

□ Charles Lamm Markmann, *The Noblest Cry: A History of the American Civil Liberties Union* (1965). Samuel Walker, *In Defense of American Liberties: A History of the ACLU* (1990). Samuel Walker

**American Communications Association v. Douds,** 339 U.S. 382 (1950), argued 10–11 Oct. 1949, decided 8 May 1950 by vote of 5 to 1; Vinson for the Court, Frankfurter concurring in part, Jackson concurring and dissenting, Black in dissent; Douglas, Clark, and Minton not participating. This case involved the constitutionality of cold war–era anticommunist legislation. The Supreme Court upheld section 9(h) of the Taft-Hartley Act (1947), which required officers of labor unions to sign affidavits indicating that they were not Communist party members or supporters and did not believe in unlawful overthrow of the U.S. government. Unions whose officers did not sign affidavits were unable to seek relief before the National Labor Relations Board for unfair labor practices.

The Court did not rest its judgment on a threat to national security, but on a threat to interstate commerce. The majority found that the statute fell within the broad scope of Congresses' *commerce power because the Communist party could reasonably be expected to engage in political strikes that were disruptive of the national economy. The Court recognized that the statute had a chilling effect on political rights protected by the *First Amendment. Nevertheless, it ruled that the First Amendment was not violated because that statute protected the public from harmful conduct—political strikes—not harmful ideas. The Court then applied the *clear and present danger test as a simple balancing test and concluded that Congress's interest in protecting the nation from political strikes outweighed the burden the act placed on the rights of union members.

Although *Douds* has not been specifically overturned, it is dubious authority. The statute replacing section 9(h) was struck down by the court in *United States* v. *Brown* (1965).

(See COMMUNISM AND COLD WAR; LABOR; SPEECH AND THE PRESS.)

Mary L. Dudziak

**American Indians.** See NATIVE AMERICANS.

**American Insurance Company v. Canter,** 1 Pet. (26 U.S.) 511 (1828), argued 8, 10, 11 Mar. 1828, decided 15 Mar. 1828 by vote of 7 to 0; Marshall for the Court. Questions of *federalism were among the most difficult confronting the early Supreme Court. One of them was the appropriate division of *admiralty and maritime jurisdiction between federal superior courts for the Florida territory and certain lesser courts that Congress had authorized the territory itself to establish. The *American Insurance Company* case involved an appeal by a libellant in admiralty from a salvage award by a local court in the Florida territory. The larger questions presented by the case included the power of Congress to acquire and govern territories and the source of that power; the division of jurisdiction between federal and local courts; the scope of the admiralty and maritime jurisdiction conferred by *Article III; and the sources of law in the territories.

For a unanimous Court, Chief Justice John *Marshall affirmed the award by the local court, explaining that when Congress had granted federal superior courts in the territory partial Article III jurisdiction, it had not conferred on them the full measure of federal judicial power. The Constitution extended such power to, *inter* *alia,* cases arising under the federal Constitution, laws, or treaties; and admiralty and maritime cases. Thus admiralty suits were not among those arising under the "laws and constitution of the United States" but were instead "as old as navigation itself; and the law admiralty and maritimes, as it has existed for ages, is applied by our courts to the cases as they arise" (p. 544). Marshall also stated that Congress derived plenary power to acquire and govern territories from the territories clause of Artice IV, a position ignored by Chief Justice Roger B. *Taney in the *Dred *Scott Case* (1857).

(See also LOWER FEDERAL COURTS; TERRITORIES AND NEW STATES.)

Ralph James Mooney

## Americans United for the Separation of Church and State.
In 1947 a group of political, religious, and educational leaders, fearful that advocates of parochial school education were mounting a drive for public financial subsidies, formed Americans United for Separation of Church and State. Known today simply as Americans United, AU believes that the principle of separation of church and state is a cornerstone of religious liberty. Today AU represents more than 52,000 individuals as well as 3,000 churches and religious groups.

Although viewing its primary task as educational, over the years AU has participated in a variety of church-state litigation. AU sponsors cases, prodives counsel, and submits *amicus curiae briefs. Since 1971, AU has been involved in some fifteen cases before the Supreme Court as well as dozens in lower courts.

AU has challenged government aid in any form to parochial schools, contending that their educational programs are infused with the sectarian beliefs of their sponsoring church. The most significant suits in which AU has participated are *Lemon v. Kurtzman* (1971), providing the basic doctrine to date for Establishment Clause analysis, and *Flast v. Cohen* (1968), establishing standing for federal taxpayers contesting the use of federal funds on Establishment Clause grounds. Generally, AU has been successful in cases where government aid directly finances school activities, as in *Aguilar v. Felton* (1985) and *School District of the City of Grand Rapids v. Ball* (1984), but less successful when the support is funnelled through the child's family as a tax credit, only indirectly benefitting the school, as in *Mueller v. Allen* (1983).

(See also EDUCATION; RELIGION.)

Stanley Ingber

## Amicus Brief.
An amicus curiae ("friend of the court") *brief is filed by someone not a party to the case but interested in the legal doctrine to be developed there because of the relevance of that doctrine for their own preferred policy or later litigation. Amicus curiae almost invariably align themselves with one of the parties, making them primarily friends of the parties despite the "friend of the court" label. Amicus briefs are potentially important because they can bring to the court's attention legal arguments and perspectives different from the parties' views. Such briefs may, for example, help the justices see the effects of potential rulings. An amicus curiae is usually an organization, although it may be an individual.

Few amicus briefs are filed in the federal district courts or in the U.S. courts of appeals (see LOWER FEDERAL COURTS). In the Supreme Court, where most are filed, some are submitted in connection with petitions for *certiorari. The presence of many interested organizations may alert the Court to a case's importance, making the grant of review more likely. Most amicus briefs, however, are filed after the Court has accepted a case for review. In the Supreme Court, amicus briefs can be filed by private parties only with permission. If either party refuses permission, the Court itself may grant it. Under the Court's rules, neither the United States government, through the *solicitor general, nor state governments need obtain such permission. At times the Court invites an organization or agency—most often the solicitor general—to submit their views in a case. When a party has abandoned support for a position it argued in the lower courts, the Supreme Court may appoint an amicus to argue that position. It did this in *Bob Jones University* v. *United States* (1983), appointing William Coleman to argue that racially discriminatory private schools should not receive tax exemptions, after the Reagan administration had abandoned that argument.

Organizations seek to file amicus briefs for several reasons. The most obvious is to attempt to influence the Court's rulings. However, some amicus submissions are to "show the flag," with a group's leaders wishing to show the membership that the organization is active. An organization lacking financial resources or legal staff to provide support for litigation starting at the trial stage finds an amicus brief a far less expensive way of participating in a case. However, some conservative public-interest law firms, even when they could afford greater trial-level participation, have tended to participate through amicus briefs, using them to attempt to offset liberal organizations' amicus views.

The Supreme Court's receptivity to amicus briefs has varied over time, although the Court now seems to welcome them. In controversial cases, like *Webster v. Reproductive Health Services* (1989), there have been more than sixty amicus briefs. The extent to which amicus briefs make a difference in the Court's decisions is not known. At times they do appear to have had an effect. For example, in *Terry v. Ohio* (1968), the amicus brief of Americans for Effective Law Enforcement may have convinced the Supreme Court to appreciate the danger to police that could be avoided by *stop-and-frisk measures. In *Mapp v. Ohio (1961), the argument in an *American Civil Liberties Union amicus brief that improperly seized evidence should be excluded from criminal trials provided a basis for the Court's extension of the *exclusionary rule in state cases. Some skeptics, however, say that justices pay little heed to amicus briefs, perhaps not even reading them. A more serious problem is that the briefs are generally not subject to the give-and-take of the adversary system because they are filed in the Supreme Court on a common date and thus do not respond to each other. The assertions they contain are also not tested through dispute between lawyers, since an organization filing an amicus brief is seldom allowed to participate in *oral argument. Stephen L. Wasby

**Amicus Curiae,** literally "a friend of the court," is a designation given to an individual or an organization, other than a party's counsel, who files a legal brief with the Court. Although such individuals or organizations have a political or ideological interest in the outcome of the case, the person(s) filing the brief cannot have a direct, personal stake in the dispute. In recent years, *amicus briefs have been most effective in civil liberties cases, involving such issues as school desegregation, employment discrimination, and abortion. Timothy S. Huebner

**Antecedents to the Court.** English history, American colonial experience, and the operation of the national government under the Articles of Confederation provide the background for the U.S. Supreme Court authorized by *Article III of the Federal Constitution.

***English Antecedents.*** By the time of English colonization of North America there were three *common-law courts: Common Pleas, King's Bench, and Exchequer. The first exercised general *civil jurisdiction; the second was a criminal trial court, with certain appellate authority over Common Pleas; and the third, originating as a revenue collection agency, determined controversies to which the Crown was a party. A fourth court, the High Court of Chancery, provided a system for giving equitable relief to parties that were precluded from recovery by the strict rules of common law, and it has been said that the court's authority was based upon the king's obligation to do justice to his subjects.

These four courts formed the basis for colonial court systems, and variations between colonial systems resulted from assigning jurisdiction to courts of a different name or combining types of jurisdiction within one or more courts. After 1686 a number of colonies adopted the jurisdictional pattern established by Sir Edmund Andros for the Dominion of New England. This placed the jurisdiction of Common Pleas, King's Bench, and

Exchequer into a single common-law court, usually called a Supreme Court of Judicature, or a Supreme Judicial Court. In Massachusetts, Pennsylvania, and some other jurisdictions the functions of a chancery court were performed by the common-law courts; but it was usually the case that chancery powers were exercised by a separate chancery court, in most cases composed of the colonial governor and members of his council. American colonial legal systems drew heavily upon the English court system for their concepts of jurisdiction, but they also tended to combine types of jurisdiction that for historical reasons remained separate in England. The Supreme Court of the United States, exercising both common-law and equity jurisdiction, represents a continuance of this American trend (see JUDICIAL POWER AND JURISDICTION.)

Separate from the English common-law and chancery courts was the High Court of Admiralty (established ca. 1360), which decided civil disputes that occurred on the high seas, punished crimes and piracy, and in time of war exercised prize jurisdiction (necessary to award an enemy vessel and its cargo to the capturing crew). American colonial admiralty courts (formally established ca. 1696) performed these functions under the appellate control of the English High Court of Admiralty.

In England judges of the common-law courts had traditionally gone on circuit to try cases (called "nisi prius" or "assize" jurisdiction), with the entry of judgment and decision of difficult points of law being reserved to the whole bench of their courts after completion of the circuit. Most American colonies adopted some form of this "nisi prius" jurisdiction, which continued in state practice after the War for Independence. The United States Supreme Court, as originally established by the *Judiciary Act of 1789, was involved in the trial of cases in the federal circuit courts. One or more Supreme Court justices were assigned to a circuit, covering a number of adjacent states, and presided over trials with the assistance of district judges (see CIRCUIT RIDING). Although technically this was not trial at nisi prius as practiced in England, it was similar in utilizing appellate court judges for the trial of cases throughout the nation. After the 1802 Judiciary Act (see JUDICIARY ACTS OF 1801 AND 1802) the Supreme Court was empowered to decide questions certified by the federal circuit court when the judges of that court could not agree; this was a close parallel to nisi prius practice in England.

***English Imperial Administration.*** Colonial and early state practice and court organization drew much from English models, and the U.S. Supreme Court reflects a similar inheritance, particularly in regard to its authority within the federal judicial system. However, the Supreme Court also functioned within a federal system that presented many of the same administrative challenges as did the British Empire on the eve of the American Revolution (see FEDERALISM).

Central to English/British imperial administration was the function of the Privy Council, a group of royal advisers that since Tudor times (1485–1603) exercised general administrative supervision over the realm and that since ancient times had exerted appellate judicial authority over the dominions of the Crown (that is, lands owing allegiance to the Crown, but not forming part of the realm of England). In regard to the American colonies, the Privy Council was responsible for reviewing colonial legislation and disallowing, in the monarch's name, such legislation that was repugnant to the law of England. Within certain jurisdictional amounts, the decrees and judgments of colonial courts were also subject to appellate review before the Privy Council. These functions, coupled with general administrative supervision of colonial governments, put the Privy Council in a position to control colonial initiatives, to ensure compliance with international law, and to shape colonial economic policies to English priorities.

*Admiralty cases decided in American colonial vice-admiralty courts were subject to appellate review in the English High Court of Admiralty, and in a limited number of instances, to Privy Council review. This insured that maritime cases, the interpretation of international law, and the exercise of prize jurisdiction would remain within the control of the home government at Whitehall.

Conflicting *land grants at times threatened to generate hostilities between American colonial governments, or between those who held titles from differing colonies. The Privy Council established boundary commissions to arbitrate the dispute and report their findings to the Council, which would then officially establish the new boundary. The procedure was made part of the Articles of Confederation (put into effect in 1781), and formed a basis for the Federal Constitution's grant of boundary jurisdiction to the United States Supreme Court.

*Federal question jurisdiction in the United States Supreme Court, particularly in matters of international law and treaty rights, mirrors the function of the Privy Council and High Court of Admiralty in coordinating colonial initiatives with the diplomacy and public policy of the mother country. Other federal question issues arise when state laws or court decisions conflict with federal constitutional or statutory law. The Supremacy Clause (Art. VI) of the federal Constitution mandates that the federal provisions supercede state law. In this regard the U.S. Supreme Court performs functions similar to those of the Privy Council when it disallowed colonial laws deemed repugnant to the "Law of England." The standards of appellate review are quite different since the Privy Council was not bound by a written constitution in making its determinations.

One of the essential functions of the Privy Council was the control of colonial economic activity, thus assuring that the benefit of trade accrued to the mother country. In the federal Constitution the United States Supreme Court by virtue of the Commerce Clause of the Constitution (Art. I, sec. 8) has similar authority designed to discourage state mercantilism and to insure uniform rules in interstate and foreign commerce. While the Privy Council maintained economic control over colonies, federal authority under the Constitution exists to create and police a common market among the American states.

*Early State Constitutions.* Since the generation that fought the American Revolution preferred legislative to executive or judicial authority, many of the early state constitutions placed legislative tribunals at the head of their court systems. Composed of judges, members of both houses of the legislature, and perhaps some representative of the executive branch, these appellate courts proved to be cumbersome agencies for the review of cases litigated in the judicial courts. The establishment of the United States Supreme Court in the federal Constitution represents a clear preference for the doctrine of *separation of powers; it also demonstrates renewed confidence in the ideal of an independent judiciary that had been a point of public debate in the years preceding the Revolution.

Some state constitutions contained provisions for constitutional review of legislative acts either before their effective date or thereafter. Under New York's 1777 constitution, a Council of Revision, composed of the governor, the chancellor, and the justices of the Supreme Court, exercised a suspensive veto over legislation. The legislative act could become law only if it was repassed by a two-thirds vote of both houses of the legislature. Pennsylvania's 1776 constitution established a board of censors to draw public attention to the defects of statutes and the misfeasance of state officers. The Virginia Plan, as presented to the Philadelphia Constitutional Convention, proposed that the federal legislature be empowered to review and disallow state legislative acts; that proposal was defeated, but the supremacy clause was inserted in Article VI, creating the strong inference that the United States Supreme Court should exercise judicial review in aid of federal supremacy.

*Articles of Confederation.* Although drafting of the Articles was completed in 1776, rivalry between the states over western land claims delayed ratification until 1781. Judicial authority under the articles was limited to boundary disputes, conflicting land claims based on disputed boundaries, and admiralty, maritime, and prize jurisdiction to review decisions of state admiralty courts.

Boundary claims were adjudicated by mixed arbitration tribunals under Article IX of the Articles of Confederation. These followed Privy

Council procedures and were utilized to resolve a dispute between Connecticut and Pennsylvania over lands in the northeastern corner of the latter state (1782) and a similar disagreement between New York and Massachusetts concerning western New York (1784). Article III, section 2 of the Federal Constitution gives this power to the Supreme Court of the United States. Also within that section is the authorization to decide the adverse claims of private parties claiming land under the grants of two American states.

Before the Articles of Confederation were ratified admiralty jurisdiction was exercised by a committee of Congress that reviewed the decisions of state admiralty courts. In 1781 a Court of Appeals in Cases of Prize and Capture was established; it disposed of more than one hundred cases in the two years of its existence. When the Supreme Court of the United States began its sessions, the official records of the Court of Appeal were deposited with the Supreme Court clerk.

*Ratification of the Constitution.* Discussion of the federal Constitution, both at the Philadelphia Convention and in the ratifying conventions of the various states, indicated that the establishment of a separate federal judicial system was the cause of much concern. There was fear of trials being conducted at distant and inconvenient locations. Many participants in the conventions expressed fear about the lack of jury trial protections in the text of Article III. These, and many other objections, were the product of American legal traditions that dated back to the days of Puritan persecution in England (1620–1648) and abuses of jury trial in Restoration England (1660–1688). The years immediately prior to the War for Independence heightened American interest in procedural protections, and many state constitutions contained guarantees similar to those finally included in the Bill of Rights amendments.

*Conclusion.* The United States Supreme Court can trace its institutional development far into the history of Anglo-American law, and its functions parallel those of earlier judicial bodies in England, in the British empire, in the early American colonies and states, and in the Articles of Confederation government. At the same time the historical antecedents of the Court suggest that it is very much the product of the American historical experience, both within specific states and colonies, and also in the broader scope of imperial relations.

(See also HISTORY OF THE COURT: ESTABLISHMENT OF THE UNION.)

□ Julius Goebel, Jr., *History of the Supreme Court of the United States*, vol. 1, *Antecedents and Beginnings to 1801* (1971). S. C. F. Milsom, *Historical Foundations of the Common Law* (1969). Theodore F. T. Plucknett, *A Concise History of the Common Law* (1969). Joseph H. Smith, *Appeals to the Privy Council from the Colonial Plantations* (1950).                                      Herbert A. Johnson

**Antelope, The,** 10 Wheat. (23 U.S.) 66 (1825), argued 26 Feb.–3 Mar. 1825, decided 16 Mar. 1825, Marshall for the Court, with the justices divided in various and sometimes conjectural ways on the issues presented; no dissents. *The Antelope* raised for the first time in the Supreme Court the question of the legitimacy of the international slave trade. In 1822, Justice Joseph *Story on circuit had held in *United States* v. *La Jeune Eugenie* that trade was illegal and "repugnant to the general principles of justice and humanity," that is, *natural law. *The Antelope* revisited this question under the following facts. A privateer raided North Atlantic shipping, capturing the slaver *The Antelope*. The captors and slaves were seized by an American revenue cutter and brought for disposition before Justice William *Johnson on circuit, who ordered the slaves apportioned by lottery among American, Spanish, and Portuguese claimants.

In the Supreme Court on appeal by various claimants, Chief Justice John *Marshall conceded that the slave trade was "contrary to the law of nature," but held that it had nevertheless been sanctioned by "the usages, the national acts, and the general assent" both of colonizing nations and of the peoples of western Africa, and therefore "claimed all the sanction which could be derived from long usage and general acquiescence" (pp. 66, 115, 121). His disposition of the case, however, had the effect of remitting approximately 120 of the slaves, as "American," to "repatriation" to the American Colonization Society's colony in modern-day Liberia, and approximately 30, as "Spanish" (i.e., the property of Spanish claimants), to *slavery in Florida.

William M. Wiecek

**Antidrummer Statutes.** See COMMERCE POWER.

**Antitrust** law consists of a body of statutes, judicial decisions, and enforcement activities designed to check business activities posing a threat to free-market competition. The core antitrust concern with competition reflects a fundamental belief that economic questions generally are best determined in the American economy through a process of independent, competitive decision making by profit-seeking firms striving to serve consumers who seek maximum satisfaction through their choices among market alternatives. Antitrust law aims to protect economic competition by prohibiting collusive, exclusionary, and monopolistic practices that restrain competition and thereby pose a danger of increased prices and reduced output, quality, and innovation. In so doing, it contrasts with other forms of economic regulation that directly prescribe the number, rates, and service offerings of particular firms, for example, in "natural monopoly" settings where economies of scale are thought to preclude active multifirm competition.

***Basic Provisions and Long-run Patterns.*** Antitrust law originated in reaction to tremendous economic changes in late nineteenth- and early twentieth-century America. Since that time, federal antitrust developments have dominated the field, although state antitrust efforts also were prominent prior to World War I and have regained significance in recent years. Federal antitrust law is founded on three main enactments. Section 1 of the Sherman Act of 1890, the most important of these acts, focuses on group behavior in broadly banning "[e]very contract, combination . . . or conspiracy" in restraint of interstate or foreign trade or commerce; Section 2 primarily targets the activities of individual firms in its prohibition of monopolization and attempted monopolization. The Clayton Act of 1914 specifically addresses the competitive dangers arising from price discrimination, "tying" arrangements, exclusive dealing, mergers, and interlocking directorates. The Federal Trade Commission Act of 1914 sweepingly empowers the administrative agency it establishes to police "unfair methods of competition."

Violations of the \*Sherman Antitrust Act are punishable by substantial criminal penalties. In addition, private parties as well as the United States Department of Justice can seek injunctive relief against threatened violations of either the Sherman or Clayton Acts (see INJUNCTIONS AND EQUITABLE REMEDIES). The Federal Trade Commission is authorized to issue cease and desist orders ultimately enforceable through the federal courts to remedy breaches of either the Clayton Act or Federal Trade Commission Act. The United States and private parties also can collect three times the amount of the actual damages they have suffered as a result of conduct prohibited by the Sherman or Clayton Acts. Under "parens patriae" legislation passed in 1976, individual states can seek treble damages on behalf of natural persons residing within their borders who have been injured by Sherman Act violations.

Although grounded in legislative enactments, substantive antitrust doctrine since its inception has developed primarily through Supreme Court interpretation of federal antitrust statutes. Indeed, the centrality of the Court's doctrinal role and the widespread belief that these measures are fundamental to the maintenance of the American free enterprise system often have prompted suggested parallels between constitutional and antitrust jurisprudence.

Over time, antitrust enforcement and interpretation repeatedly have changed course, reflecting larger changes and patterns in American economic, political, and intellectual life. Ever since the first antitrust acts were passed, moreover, the nature and purpose of antitrust law have been the subject of recurring debate. Some jurists, scholars, and enforcement officials have conceived of antitrust law's protection of competition solely or primarily as a means to enhance economic efficiency and the overall maximization of social wealth. Others have placed greater stress on such ends as fairer wealth distribution, the preservation of individual business opportunity, and the protection of political freedom from potential threats posed by increased concentrations of private economic power. In recent years, even as such disagreements have continued, antitrust law has placed sharply increased emphasis on neoclassical economic perspectives stressing the promotion of economic efficiency. Today this trend prevails with respect to all four of the main types of conduct addressed by antitrust law: horizontal agreements among competitors, single-firm activities directed toward the acquisition or maintenance of monopoly power, vertical arrangements among firms in a supplier-purchaser relationship, and mergers.

***Origins and Early Development.*** Late nineteenth-century antitrust legislation and case law built upon earlier English and American responses to monopolies and restraints of trade. Early English and American restrictions on anticompetitive private behavior chiefly were contained in common-law precedents on contracts, combinations, and conspiracies in restraint of trade. These precedents varied significantly among state jurisdictions and over time; no uniform body of American \*common law existed when the first antitrust laws were enacted.

As American markets expanded geographically in the post–Civil War decades, new technological innovations repeatedly boosted productivity in excess of demand, contributing to a sharp intensification of competitive rivalry in many lines of business (see HISTORY OF THE COURT: RECONSTRUCTION, FEDERALISM, AND ECONOMIC RIGHTS). These developments prompted large numbers of late nineteenth- and early twentieth-century American businesses to seek greater security and higher returns through various forms of multifirm combination. At first turning primarily to loose arrangements such as simple cartels, American businesses increasingly embraced tighter, more fully integrated combinations such as trusts, holding companies, and mergers beginning in the 1880s. As a series of major new trusts appeared in the later years of that decade, public concerns, which earlier had centered on disturbing railroad practices, shifted to focus more broadly on predatory business behavior, cartelization, and industrial concentration in general, prompting a burst of new antitrust activity at the state level. The perceived practical and legal limitations of state efforts, however, soon led to mounting popular pressure for new federal antitrust legislation, resulting in adoption of the Sherman Act in 1890.

In the debates preceding passage of the act, congressmen expressed strong support for the protection of competition and concerns to safeguard economic opportunity, fair consumer prices, efficiency, and political liberty. Scholars long have differed as to which of these values Congress primarily or even exclusively sought to promote. In late nineteenth-century thinking, however, these goals and values typically were thought to be largely complementary so that most congressmen may well have hoped to serve all of these ends simultaneously.

Neither the statute itself nor the congressional debates provided any detailed guidance as to the practical application of the Act's general language. Congress generally sought to incorporate the traditional common-law restraint of trade approaches of the *state courts, doing so without any understanding of what those doctrines had become by 1890. Congress intended to delegate significant authority to the federal courts to develop more precise doctrine. Passage of the act was an important symbolic affirmation of the basic ideal of competitive free markets, and the statute's enforcement provisions went substantially beyond earlier common-law doctrines providing merely for the legal unenforceability of restrictive trade agreements.

The first decade after passage of the act saw only limited federal enforcement, partly as a result of the Supreme Court's restrictive reading of congressional commerce-clause authority in its rejection of a challenge to a monopolistic merger of sugar refineries in *United States* v. *E. C. Knight Co.* (1895), the Court's first consideration of the statute. Within a few years, however, the Court strongly supported the application of the act in a variety of other contexts, beginning with cases against railroad cartels in the late 1890s. A dramatic acceleration in the growth of overall economic concentration as a result of a major new wave of mergers in the late 1890s and early 1900s heightened public apprehension and led to increased federal enforcement efforts under Presidents Theodore Roosevelt and William Howard *Taft. These efforts produced a number of Supreme Court victories, climaxing in the Court's decisions in *Standard Oil Co.* v. *United States* (1911) and *United States* v. *American Tobacco Co.* (1911). In those cases, the Court ordered the dissolution of two of the greatest industrial combinations of the day to remedy violations of the Sherman Act, although doing so in a way that did not effectively dissipate the concentrated economic power established by those combinations.

During these years, the Supreme Court debated the proper general standard of Sherman Act analysis. Initially dominant was Justice Rufus W. *Peckham's rejection of any defense of "reasonableness" for challenged restraints and his view that the act condemned any agreement directly and immediately restraining competition and therefore trade in interstate or foreign commerce. Chief Justice Edward D. *White was the chief proponent of the alternative *"rule of reason" position that ultimately triumphed in the

Court's *Standard Oil* and *American Tobacco* opinions. The Peckham and White standards contained substantial ambiguities. Chief Justice White's "rule of reason" opinion in *Standard Oil*, for example, itself contemplated that certain types of agreements, because of their inherent nature, could be summarily condemned as anticompetitive without any extended inquiry into reasonableness. This aspect of the opinion foreshadowed the Court's subsequent, more extensive development of the central, but often troubled, antitrust distinction between activities condemnable "per se" and those to be judged only after a more lengthy "rule of reason" examination of purposes, market power, effects, and possible less restrictive alternatives available to achieve particular legitimate ends.

The Supreme Court's affirmation of a "rule of reason" approach revitalized political controversy over antitrust law. This subject became a main focus of the three-way presidential race between Theodore Roosevelt, William Howard Taft, and Woodrow Wilson in 1912. Following Wilson's election, efforts to buttress the Sherman Act resulted in the 1914 passage of the Clayton and Federal Trade Commission Acts.

During World War I and the 1920s, concern over anticompetitive and monopolistic behavior substantially declined as Americans came to accept the increased level of economic concentration established during the Progressive Era, associating it with heightened economic prosperity (see WORLD WAR I; PROGRESSIVISM). In these years, federal officials and the Supreme Court continued to condemn nakedly anticompetitive arrangements such as price fixing but encouraged other forms of cooperation among competing businesses such as the sharing of general data on business conditions.

*From the New Deal to the 1970s.*  Public confidence in business and in the health of American markets collapsed with the stock market crash of 1929. Yet the federal government in the early years of President Franklin D. *Roosevelt's *New Deal turned not to renewed antitrust enforcement but instead to expanded business cooperative efforts under the National Industrial Recovery Acct. The Supreme Court held that act to be unconstitutional in *Schechter Poultry Corporation* v. *United States* (1935), however, and later New Deal efforts proceeded in a very different direction. Spurred by a new economic downturn in 1937, concerns over the consequences of contemporary cartelization in Europe, and growing economic scholarship criticizing concentrated markets as typically productive of troublesome economic performance, federal antitrust activity soon expanded many times over. The intensified antitrust efforts begun in the later 1930s did not result in any significant rollback of the levels of economic concentration established in the early years of the twentieth century. They did, however, set the stage for a continued, bipartisan commitment in the succeeding decades to a much higher level of antitrust activity than had prevailed before the New Deal.

In this setting of expanded enforcement, antitrust case law grew substantially. In numerous decisions through the early 1970s the Supreme Court strongly supported the vigorous application of federal antitrust law, repeatedly displaying substantial skepticism toward cooperative business agreements, single-firm activities promoting market preeminence, and mergers. While continuing to acknowledge that certain types of cooperation among competitors, such as general data dissemination or reasonably limited joint ventures, could improve efficiency and competitive performance in particular circumstances, the Supreme Court greatly increased its use of summary, per se rules to condemn such collective agreements as price fixing, output limitation, market division, and concerted refusals to deal.

In the area of vertical restrictions, the Court similarly continued its long-established per se condemnation of resale price maintenance restrictions imposed by manufacturers on dealers and announced new similar treatment for manufacturer-imposed restrictions on dealers' geographic territories or customers. At the same time, the Court also established a strict "partial" per se test condemning most tying arrangements whereby the purchase of a desired good is conditioned on the simultaneous purchase of a second, different item as well. While the Court proved to be somewhat more sympathetic toward exclusive dealing agreements requiring a purchaser to deal solely in a particular manufacturer's brand, it declared such arrangements to be unlawful whenever they threatened to "foreclose" any substantial share of market sales.

The Court strongly endorsed the landmark court of appeals monopolization opinion in *United States* v. *Aluminum Co. of America (Alcoa)* (2d Cir., 1945), which exhibited considerable suspicion of the legitimacy of dominating market power in general and stressed the social and political as well as economic importance of antitrust law. While requiring both dominant market power and its acquisition or maintenance through wrongful conduct distinguishable from competition on the merits as elements of Sherman Act monopolization, the *Alcoa* decision limited the range of conduct deemed to be mere skill, foresight, and industry to a very narrow ambit. Supreme Court opinions in subsequent years continued this two-element test but otherwise left monopolization doctrine in a state of considerable confusion.

Supreme Court merger decisions in the post–New Deal decades initially departed from these trends, permitting very large acquisitions under the Sherman Act. The Clayton Act's original 1914 ban on anticompetitive mergers rarely was invoked because it applied only to stock and not asset acquisitions and did not extend beyond horizontal mergers to reach vertical and conglomerate acquisitions. Renewed economic, social, and political concerns for rising economic concentration in the 1940s, however, prompted Congress to amend the act to close these loopholes in 1950, leading the Court to reverse its approach to mergers by the 1960s. The Court then greatly limited the range of permissible merger activity, for example, condemning horizontal mergers creating companies with combined market shares as low as 5 percent. Exhibiting strong concerns for even early market trends toward increasing concentration, the Court acted to protect smaller competitors endangered by the creation of new, more efficient merged entities even where such protection sacrificed new cost savings and lower consumer prices potentially obtainable through the mergers the Court condemned.

*Recent Law.* Since the middle 1970s, foreign import activity has heightened the competitiveness of many American markets, and sentiment supporting government regulation in general has declined. In this context, antitrust enforcement and interpretation have changed dramatically through an increasing, sometimes controversial, incorporation of new economic perspectives stressing the efficiency-enhancing potential of diverse types of horizontal and vertical agreements, single-firm activities, and mergers that previously were viewed with considerable suspicion or hostility in antitrust law.

The Supreme Court in recent years has continued to invoke per se rules for certain types of horizontal and vertical agreements, even retaining this approach for maximum price fixing and vertical resale price maintenance despite substantial criticism contending that such arrangements can promote competition. Generally, however, the Court has expanded its use of the more extended rule of reason analysis and has reduced the frequency and scope of per se treatment. For instance, in its landmark decision in *Continental T.V., Inc.* v. *GTE Sylvania, Inc.* (1977), the Court overturned its decade-old per se condemnation of nonprice vertical restrictions on dealers. The Court found that such "intraband" restraints often generated more than offsetting increases in interbrand competition. For example, "intraband" restraints induced more aggressive promotional efforts by dealers who wanted to reap the benefits of their own promotional efforts by restricting the intensity of intraband rivalry and eliminating "free riders" who costlessly took advantage of other dealers' expensive promotional activity.

The Court's expanding rule of reason evaluation of horizontal agreements similarly has reflected increasing sensitivity to developing economic scholarship. Although stressing that Sherman Act analysis focuses narrowly on whether a challenged restraint promotes or suppresses competition, the Court nevertheless has looked not simply to whether any business rivalry has been tempered but also to whether any such effects have been offset by new gains in efficiency, such as the reduction of transaction costs and increases in output.

In its limited treatment of monopolization issues, the Court has contributed to continuing controversy over the extent of any obligation to cooperate with smaller rivals and the legality of various practices raising rivals' costs. The Court has held that a dominant firm may not severely disadvantage a smaller competitor by discontinuing a long established cooperative marketing arrangement, at least in the absence of any plausible efficiency justification (*Aspen Skiing Co. v. Aspen Highlands Skiing Corp.*, 1985). In recent years, lower courts have taken the lead in developing monopolization doctrine, allowing dominant firms substantial room for product innovations, further enhancing their market position and evolving new tests keyed to particular categories of firm costs for identifying unlawful predatory pricing. Practical concerns raised in prior years by large-scale monopolization litigation have eased. The government has not initiated any new major monopolization cases following its dismissal in 1982 of its multiyear suit against the International Business Machines Corporation and the simultaneous settlement of its suit against the American Telephone and Telegraph Company. The latter resulted in the largest divestiture in antitrust history, separating the company's long distance service from its local operating companies.

In the middle 1970s, the Supreme Court also substantially altered its previous restrictive approach to mergers, requiring a more thorough economic assessment of the likely competitive impact of particular acquisitions before mergers could be declared unlawful (e.g., *United States* v. *General Dynamics Corp.*, 1974). Much of the change in the antitrust treatment of mergers, however, has resulted from more recent changes in federal enforcement policy. While still reflecting concern that particular mergers may increase single-firm market power or the risks of multifirm collusion, the revised merger guidelines adopted by the Department of Justice emphasized the potential economic benefits of merger activities and established much higher thresholds for antitrust challenges than had prevailed in earlier Supreme Court case law and department philosophy.

*Conclusion.* Although the major developments discussed here have dominated antitrust law since the late nineteenth century, antitrust analysis also has focused on such other important issues as the scope of various exceptions to antitrust coverage, including exceptions for restraints attributable to state rather than private decision making and for First Amendment protected activities. Today, in the midst of ongoing debate over general goals and specific doctrine,

the meaning of antitrust law's protection of competition continues to evolve as the Sherman Act enters its second century and as American economic, intellectual, and political contexts continue to change.

(See also CAPITALISM.)

□ Phillip Areeda and Donald Turner, *Antitrust Law: An Analysis of Antitrust Principles and Their Application* (1978). Robert Bork, *The Antitrust Paradox: A Policy at War with Itself* (1978). Ernest Gellhorn, *Antitrust Law and Economics* (1986). Earl Kintner, *Federal Antitrust Law* (1980). James May, "Antitrust in the Formative Era: Political and Economic Theory in Constitutional and Antitrust Analysis, 1880–1918," *Ohio State Law Journal* 50 (1989): 257–395. E. Thomas Sullivan and Jeffrey L. Harrison, *Understanding Antitrust and Its Economic Implications* (1988). Hans Thorelli, *The Federal Antitrust Policy: Origination of an American Tradition* (1955). James May

**Apodaca v. Oregon,** 406 U.S. 404 (1972), argued 1 Mar. 1971, reargued 10 Jan. 1972, decided 22 May 1972 by vote of 5 to 4; White for the plurality, Blackmun concurring, Powell concurring in the judgment, Douglas, Brennan, Stewart, and Marshall in dissent.

Until 1970 it was assumed that juries consisted of twelve members and that unanimous votes were required. *Williams* v. *Florida* (1970), however, permitted state juries of fewer than twelve members. *Apodaca*, a companion case to *Johnson* v. *Louisiana* (1972), held that the *Sixth Amendment jury trial guarantee, applied to the states by the *Fourteenth Amendment, does not require a unanimous jury verdict in noncapital state criminal cases.

The plurality was unable to decide whether Congress, when it passed the Sixth Amendment in 1789, had intended to freeze the size of the jury at twelve. On balance it decided that the right to *trial by jury was primarily designed to protect against corrupt or overzealous prosecutors or judges and therefore "perceive[d] no difference between juries required to act unanimously and those permitted to convict or acquit by votes of 10–2 or 11–1" (p. 411). *Johnson* permitted conviction by a 9-to-3 vote.

Justice Lewis *Powell, whose concurrence provided the controlling vote, believed that the Sixth Amendment did require unanimity but that the Fourteenth Amendment did not apply all elements of the Sixth Amendment to the states: the states could employ nonunanimous juries, but the federal courts could not. The dissenters argued that a nonunanimous verdict in either state or federal courts was inconsistent with the constitutional requirement that a criminal jury's decision be "beyond a reasonable doubt." Thus, while separate majorities held that the Sixth Amendment required unanimous jury verdicts and that the Fourteenth Amendment incorporated the Sixth in its entirety, the net result was that the states may employ nonunanimous juries. *Apodaca* and *Johnson* still govern, but few states have adopted the jury nonunanimity rule in criminal cases. The Court subsequently raised doubts about the statistical assumptions on which *Apodaca* was based in *\*Ballew* v. *Georgia* (1978).                                 Stephen E. Gottlieb

**Appeal.** A litigant dissatisfied with the outcome of a lawsuit may exercise certain rights of appeal. To appeal means to have a lower court proceeding reviewed by a superior court. The party taking an appeal, known as the "appellant" or *\**"petitioner," argues through written briefs and oral arguments that errors committed by the lower court were sufficiently serious to invalidate the outcome. The opposing party, known as the "appellee" or "respondent," argues that the lower court acted correctly and that its decision should stand.

Appeals courts are staffed by multiple judges and are interested only in whether prejudicial errors have been committed in a lower court. They are not concerned with new findings of fact. Consequently, the appeals court makes its decision based on an examination of the lower court record, written briefs, and oral arguments, not on newly introduced evidence or testimony. Depending upon whether any "reversible errors" are found, an appeals court may affirm, vacate, modify, or reverse the lower court ruling. Decisions are announced by written opinions following deliberation among the judges.

Appeals are either obligatory or discretionary. An obligatory appeal is one in which the appellant has the right to have the case reviewed and decided on its merits. In a discretionary appeal there is no obligation for the appeals judges to give the case such a full review. The Supreme Court historically has heard both obligatory and discretionary appeals, but the *Judicial Improvements and Access to Justice Act of 1988 made the Court's *appellate jurisdiction almost exclusively discretionary.                        Thomas G. Walker

**Appellate Jurisdiction.** The U.S. Supreme Court's task of reviewing *state and *lower federal court decisions to determine whether they are consistent with the Constitution and laws of the United States is complicated by technical requirements that govern the presentation of cases to the Court. Each term the Court grants full review to only about 160 out of the four to five thousand cases that parties seek to have reexamined.

The Constitution and federal statutes divide the Supreme Court's jurisdiction into two main categories: *original, the power to hear cases as an initial matter; and *appellate. The original jurisdiction, which includes suits between states and actions against ambassadors, is rarely invoked. In addition to the provisions relating to original jurisdiction, *Article III of the Constitution provides that "the Supreme Court shall have appellate Jurisdiction, both as to Law and Fact,

with such Exceptions, and under such Regulations as the Congress shall make." Congress thus has broad powers to determine the nature and scope of the Supreme Court's power to review cases.

Appellate cases reach the Court after either a lower federal court or state court has passed on the matter. Statutory provisions govern the three main avenues of review: writ of *certiorari, *appeal, and certification of specific questions. In charting this thicket of rules, it is simplest to consider federal appellate procedure first, followed by an analysis of state court review.

*Review of Federal Cases.* Certiorari jurisdiction may encompass any civil or criminal case decided by a federal district or appellate court. Any party may petition the Supreme Court to exercise plenary review of a final decision in the case. If at least four of the nine Supreme Court justices believe the case merits a hearing, the Court will issue a writ of certiorari—or "grant cert"—and schedule the case for full briefing and oral argument. The decision whether to grant or deny a cert petition is wholly discretionary, with special attention given to resolving conflicts among the federal *courts of appeals, federal district courts, and/or state courts on important legal principles or issues of law.

Less frequently, a party may invoke the Supreme Court's "appeal" jurisdiction. In theory, appeal jurisdiction is mandatory when the requirements for its invocation are met. In practice, "obligatory" appeal jurisdiction actually operates similarly to certiorari. Any losing party at the court of appeals level may seek review of certain decisions that rely on federal law to invalidate statutes. Unless, however, four justices note "probable jurisdiction," indicating that the Court in fact has the power to hear the dispute and the matter warrants further review, even "appeal" cases are summarily disposed of by order, without a full hearing. In this way, supposedly mandatory consideration of a crushing volume of cases is avoided.

Appeal of right from a federal appellate court will occur when a state statute is struck down as contrary to federal law or when, in civil proceedings to which the United States government is a party, a federal statute is held unconstitutional. The limitation that the Court may hear only claims that are federal in nature further circumscribes review. Consequently, although a lower federal court may have passed on both state and federal claims in one case, the Supreme Court cannot rule on the purely state issues, preventing complete case review. Under these circumstances, certiorari provides the only avenue through which the entire case may be scrutinized.

Direct appeals of district court decisions are infrequent. Generally, jurisdiction exists only for appeals from a district court decision holding an act of Congress unconstitutional in a case where the United States is a party and for appeals from final decisions of three-judge district courts (a provision rendered largely irrelevant after Congress's abolition of almost all these courts in 1976).

Finally, in extremely rare cases, a United States court of appeals may certify an issue of great public importance for immediate review by the Supreme Court. Consideration of certified questions is mandatory, but a variety of technical grounds allow the Court to dismiss the certification as improper. Unlike appeals and cert petitions, the circuit court alone, and not the parties, decides when an issue deserves to be certified.

*Review of State Court Decisions.* The other major category of cases considered by the Supreme Court under its appellate jurisdiction consists of state court determinations. Although the Constitution does not expressly grant the Supreme Court power to review state court decisions, from the birth of the republic many believed that such oversight was necessary to ensure the supremacy of federal law. This power, which potentially threatens federal court domination over the states, has been strictly circumscribed to accommodate notions of *federalism. Statutory provisions divide the Court's jurisdiction over state cases into appeal and certiorari jurisdiction roughly paralleling federal case organization. Mandatory appeals are limited to those circumstances where a state court finds a federal law invalid or where it upholds a state law against a federal challenge. Certiorari is available for state court decisions that implicate federal law.

Statutes limit certiorari or appeal review of state court decisions to *federal questions decided in final judgments of the state's highest tribunal. Additionally, if a state decision is sustained by adequate nonfederal grounds—that is, if the result is entirely supportable on the basis of purely state-law holdings adopted by the state court—the Supreme Court may not hear the case even to review any federal-law determination. This requirement ensures that scarce judicial resources are not spent in issuing essentially advisory opinions. If it is unclear which basis the state court relied on, the Court will assume that the decision turned on federal law and may assert jurisdiction.

So complex is the interplay and overlap between the Supreme Court's obligatory and discretionary powers of review that an improvidently raised appeal is automatically treated as a petition for certiorari. Recent efforts have aimed at eliminating all appeals as a matter of right and rendering the appellate jurisdiction of the Supreme Court wholly discretionary. The Supreme Court awaits further legislation that would streamline its appellate jurisdiction and relieve it of its ever-increasing workload. Until then, the Court will have to endure the crush of cases as best it can and remain creative in its jurisdictional

jurisprudence so that it can continue to hear and resolve the most crucial legal questions.

(See also JUDICIAL REVIEW.)

□ Leah Brilmayer, *An Introduction to Jurisdiction in the American Federal System* (1986). Robert Stern et al., *Supreme Court Practice,* 6th ed. (1986).

Irving R. Kaufman

**Appointment and Removal Power.** The Constitution of the United States contains two references to the appointment and removal power. Article II, section 2, provides that the president, "by and with the advice and consent of the Senate, shall appoint Judges of the Supreme Court." *Article III, section 1, states that "the Judges, both of the supreme and inferior courts, shall hold their offices during good behavior." Appointment and removal are linked because the framers' concern about judicial independence determined, in part, the limitations upon executive authority contained in each of these clauses. This concern for judicial integrity, competence, and independence was founded in the experience of British colonial policy in the decade preceding the Revolutionary War. According to Gordon Wood, British judicial appointment policy had become one of "strengthening the court (monarchical) interest" and "advancing to the most eminent stations men without education, and of dissolute manners, . . . sporting with our persons and estates, by filling the highest seats of justice with bankrupts, bullies, and blockheads . . ." (Wood, 1969, pp. 78, 145). Ironically, between 1776 and 1787 the mode of judicial selection became an issue in the regional and institutional conflicts that divided convention delegates. Ultimately, the framers did not provide any criteria, professional or otherwise, for the choices of justices, although the delegates did discuss the need for well-qualified jurists.

Institutional power and regional influence overshadowed judicial qualifications in the Convention discussions. Just as support for state legislative judicial appointment authority waned after the revolution, the initial effort to place appointment of the justices in the "national legislature" failed. Conversely, Federalist efforts at placing judicial selection solely under the authority of the president also failed. Selection by the Senate alone also was defeated, although from 13 June to 7 September 1787 a majority of the delegates supported this alternative. The present scheme of presidential nomination and appointment with the advice and consent of the Senate was adopted in the closing days of the Convention.

The necessity of accommodating regional and cultural differences modified nationalistic Federalist ideology. While President George *Washington chose sound Federalists for the Supreme Court, he and his successors carefully distributed the judicial seats regionally, as required by political necessity and by the provisions of the *Judiciary Act of 1789, which assigned the justices to circuit duties within the region from which they were chosen (see CIRCUIT RIDING). Thus the entire Congress rather than the Senate alone initially had some influence, albeit indirect, over presidential selection by linking circuit duty to Supreme Court service, judicial selection to a regional distribution pattern, and the size of the Court's membership to the number of circuits. This relationship was maintained by Congress for over a century. Additional manifestations of congressional assertiveness took the form of proposed constitutional amendments in the nineteenth century either to provide the House of Representatives a role equal to that in the Senate (1808) or to eliminate the president's role and place selection entirely in the two legislative chambers (1818 and 1867, 1868). Of much greater importance to the selection process was the relative influence of senatorial advice and consent upon successive presidential nominations.

The Senate's practice of defeating nominees because of their political and ideological positions began during the presidency of George Washington. John *Rutledge's public opposition to the Federalist-sponsored Jay Treaty with Great Britain was the real reason for his defeat, but many senators chose his alleged eccentric behavior as the ostensible reason, thus establishing a tradition of masking partisan objections behind a veneer of fitness qualifications. The Senate has rejected some nominees for lack of ability or probity. President Ulysses S. Grant's nomination of his corrupt attorney general George H. *Williams, is illustrative.

Contemporary debate over the significance of Robert *Bork's defeat has centered upon whether the Senate introduced novel partisan and ideological considerations. Yet any assessment of such factors must also include an examination of presidential behavior. The historical and contemporary record indicates no significant change. When partisan and ideological differences placed presidents and senators in opposition over judicial nominations, the outcome was determined most frequently on the basis of the relative political strength, tenacity, and strategic ability of the contenders. Thus is is not surprising that John *Tyler, who completed a term of a deceased president, was denied the opportunity to fill two long-vacant justiceships. The denial was not because of his succession to the presidency, but his political weakness. Similarly, even presidents who had gained large electoral majorities have been thwarted as lame ducks. Lyndon Johnson's attempt to elevate Justice Abe *Fortas to chief justice and Ronald *Reagan's Bork nomination provide twentieth-century examples. But the constitutional framework also contributes to the relationship of president and senate in a determinative manner (see NOMINEES, REJECTION OF).

The central institutional factor is the constitutional limitation on arbitrary removal, the guarantee of terms during good behavior. In a frequently cited analysis completed in the late 1950s, Robert Dahl concluded that "the policy views dominant on the Court are never long out of line with the policy views dominant among the lawmaking majorities of the United States" (Dahl, 1957, p. 293). Dahl's indication that a president could anticipate a new Supreme Court appointment every twenty-two months was based on sound averaging but was of little comfort to presidents who had no opportunity to appoint (Andrew Johnson and Jimmy Carter) or who had below average opportunities (*Jefferson, *Madison, Monroe, John Quincy *Adams, Taylor, Fillmore, Pierce, Buchanan, McKinley, Wilson, Coolidge, Lyndon Johnson, and Ford).

Removal has not been available to thwarted Presidents. Eight articles of *impeachment were adopted by the House of Representatives in 1804 against Justice Samuel *Chase, but the Senate acquitted him. The failure of that early attempt at establishing judicial partisanship as a basis of removal meant in practice that health and personal inclination were the only limits on a justice. As a result, the tension between presidential desire to make judicial appointments consistent with an individual president's policy preferences and judicial inclination to remain on the Supreme Court becomes especially great after periods of fundamental electoral change such as critical elections (see PARTY SYSTEM). Death and severe illness have been the inexorable involuntary factors that have concluded judicial careers.

Throughout the Court's history, an overwhelming number of members have either voluntarily left the Court during a presidential administration of their own political party or remained on the Court as long as possible. The major twentieth-century exception, Chief Justice Earl *Warren's 1968 announcement of retirement after President Johnson decided against another run for the presidency, underscored the generally unspoken assumption. Subsequent attacks on Warren by Republican senators and vice-presidential candidate Spiro Agnew were followed, after the November 1968 election, by District of Columbia Circuit Judge John A. Danaher's December announcement that he would retire after 20 January 1969, so that president-elect Nixon could fill the vacancy. Danaher believed that it was entirely fitting for him to return the vacancy to the Republican Party.

In sum, presidential choice is limited by tenure during good behavior and, assuming good health, the extent to which justices prefer to remain on the Court. Despite several dramatic senatorial rejections, (Judge John J. *Parker, Justice Fortas, and, as a result, Judge Homer *Thornberry, and Judges Bork and *Ginsberg), the proportion of Senate rejections by vote or forced withdrawals has diminished in the twentieth century in comparison to the nineteenth century (see NOMINATIONS, CONTROVERSIAL).

One major long-term problem related to both the presidential and the senatorial roles in the selection of justices has been the availability of basic information about nominees. From the era of the Robber Barons until the advent of public hearings by the *Senate Judiciary Committee, there were recurrent attempts by Populist and Progressive senators to show the alleged influence by corporate interests in Supreme Court selections through public disclosure of the communications received by a president. Conversely, the Senate maintained its procedure of handling all nominations in closed sessions until 1929. The *Brandeis (1916) and *Stone (1925) nominations were the only exceptions before the adoption of Senator Robinson's 1929 rule change, which provides that nomination sessions are public unless made closed by majority vote.

Senate Judiciary Committee practice changed in 1939 when nominees, beginning with Felix *Frankfurter, were questioned by the committee. Such questioning obviously provided greater opportunities for critics of presidential nominees to either embarass a president or contribute to the defeat of the nominee. Senator Strom Thurmond's shouted taunt "Mallory! Mallory! I want that name to ring in your ears" to Justice Fortas dramatized the extent to which doctrinal issues are often openly invoked by protagonists and opponents in Supreme Court nomination controversies. The basic question is whether senatorial opponents are willing to be as candid about the doctrinal or ideological basis of their opposition as Thurmond's South Carolina colleague was in the Fortas controversy. Senator Fritz Hollings flatly argued that a vote to confirm Fortas as chief justice was tantamount to approving his brand of judicial philosophy. Ironically, most intense conflicts over the ideological or doctrinal basis of nomination support or rejection are characterized by lack of candor on the part of the major contestants. For example, most Senate opponents of Bork denied rejection on liberal doctrinal grounds, just as President Reagan and Attorney General Meese denied employing a conservative "litmus" test to screen potential judicial nominees.

An additional and very important dimension of selecting Supreme Court members involves the special role of the American Bar Association. At least as early as the administration of President Herbert Hoover, the ABA was granted an important informal role in the nomination and appointment process. Because the ABA's key committees frequently opposed New Deal legislation, the then conservative organization was out of favor during Franklin D. *Roosevelt's presidency. After years of informal but highly visible advice, the American Bar Association House of Delegates in 1952 asked the platform committees of both the Democratic and Republican parties to adopt planks requiring the president to consult with the *American Bar Association Committee on Federal Judiciary (which had been created in 1946). President Eisenhower did so and in subsequent years the ABA committee increased its influence. The high point in presidential-ABA relationship was reached under President Nixon, when the ABA's reputation was involved in behalf of the president's nominee, Clement *Haynsworth. During the decades of ABA influence in the Supreme Court selection process, it was initially criticized for bias against liberal candidates and for conservative ones. After the Bork nomination controversy, conservatives bitterly denounced the ABA committee. Regardless of whether the charges of bias came from liberals or conservatives, there has always been a serious underlying constitutional question about the appropriateness of the extraordinary delegation of executive constitutional power to a small private organization.

(See also SELECTION OF JUSTICES.)

▢ Robert A. Dahl, "Decision-Making in a a Democracy: The Supreme Court as a National Policy Maker," *Journal of Public Law* 6 (1957): 279–295. Paul A. Freund, "Appointment of Justices: Some Historical Perspectives," *Harvard Law Review* 101 (1988): 1146–1163. John R. Schmidhauser, *Judges and Justices, the Federal Appellate Judiciary* (1979). Gordon Wood, *The Creation of the American Republic, 1776–1787* (1969).               John R. Schmidhauser

**Aptheker v. Secretary of State,** 378 U.S. 500 (1964), argued 21 Apr. 1964, decided 22 June 1964 by vote of 6 to 3; Goldberg for the Court, Clark, Harlan, and White in dissent. The Passport Act of 1926 authorized the secretary of state to grant passports, required for foreign travel, to American citizens. Under pressure of the Cold War following World War II, the State Department adopted a policy of refusing passports to American communists or persons whose travel abroad would prejudice the interests of the United States. This policy generated widespread controversy, and many persons were denied passports who asserted they were not communists. In *Kent v. Dulles* (1958) the Supreme Court ruled that the right of American citizens to travel across national frontiers was a part of the "liberty" protected by the *Fifth Amendment, and that the secretary of state was not authorized by the Passport Act to promulgate regulations denying passports.

Another statute was available, however. The Internal Security Act of 1950 (see MCCARRAN ACT) required all "communist-action" organizations to register with the attorney general and denied passports to members of such organizations. The registration provisions were upheld by the Supreme Court in *Communist Party v. Subversive Activities Control Board* (1961). But the State Department's effort to resume passport denials under this authorization was rejected in *Aptheker v. Secretary of State* (1964), involving two leading members of the American Communist party. Justice Arthur *Goldberg recognized that the right to travel was not absolute but held that the language of the Internal Security Act was too broad, taking no account of individual communists' degree of activity in the organization or the purposes of their travel. However, restrictions on travel to particular countries or specific areas were subsequently upheld in *Zemel* v. *Rusk* (1965).

(See also COMMUNISM AND COLD WAR; SUBVERSION; TRAVEL, RIGHT TO.)

C. Herman Pritchett

**Architecture of the Supreme Court Building.** Chief Justice William Howard *Taft liked to think of the Constitution as the "Ark of the Covenant," and the judiciary as a priestly class guarding its sacred principles. When Taft became chairman of the Supreme Court Building Commission created by Congress in 1928, he selected his friend Cass *Gilbert to design a suitably impressive edifice for the Court's first permanent home. Gilbert was a logical choice for the assignment. A leading exponent of neoclassicism in American architecture, he had been greatly influenced in his early career by the famous "White City" exhibit at the Chicago World's Fair of 1893. The buildings on display there had all been imposing white structures, whose classical façades and ornamentation created a make-believe world of antiseptic beauty. With its evocation of past imperial grandeur, the Beaux-Arts version of classicism soon captured the imagination of an expansionist America and became the official style of federal buildings for the next half century.

Working within this tradition, Gilbert designed a monumental temple of justice that symbolized the power and legitimacy of the modern Court. The site—a square-block area on East Capitol Street across from the Capitol grounds—largely determined the size of the new building, since it had to balance the other massive buildings of the Capitol group, including the adjacent Library of Congress. On this site Gilbert proposed to erect a majestic structure of white marble, consisting of a tall, navelike central section flanked by two low symmetrical wings. The center contained the courtroom; and, with its great columned hall and ornate portico, resembled the Greek Parthenon, which Gilbert used as his model. To enhance a visitor's sense of solemnity, the architect set the building far back on the lot, leaving room in front for a spacious marble plaza and a grand stairway of fifty-three steps leading up to the central entrance doors (see figure 1).

The effect is undeniably impressive, and intimidating as well. Two huge marble blocks flank the stairway, and support large sculptures by James E. Fraser. On the right a seated male figure representing the "Authority of Law" holds a tablet inscribed "Lex" in his left hand, while a sheathed sword at his side indicates the availability of government force to execute the laws. The corresponding sculpture on the left is titled "Contemplation of Justice," and features a classically draped female figure who embodies the spirit of equity, as opposed to strict law. In her right hand she holds a small statue of "Justice" balancing the scales, while a lawbook rests near her left hand. Like guardian sculptures outside some ancient tomb, Fraser's giant creations evoke the feelings of apprehension and awe that laymen tend to associate with the expounders of black-letter law.

At the top of the steps a double row of Corinthian columns supports a triangular pediment designed by Robert Aitken. Aitken's frieze combines allegorical symbols and figures from American history to celebrate the concept of ordered liberty; or, as the legend immediately below the group panel proclaims, "Equal Justice Under Law." In the center the Goddess of Liberty sits enthroned, with the scales of justice on her lap; on either side a Roman soldier, representing "Order" and "Authority," respectively, strikes a protective pose. Two other figures on each side represent "Council," while a recumbent figure, "Research," fills out each end of the triangle. The toga-clad councillors on the right bear a marked resemblance to Charles Evans *Hughes, who succeeded Taft as chief justice in 1930, and Aitken himself; those on the left are likenesses of Cass Gilbert and the lawyer-statesman Elihu Root. For his Research figures Aitken chose to portray John *Marshall and William Howard Taft as young students.

The complementary pediment on the east side of the building bears an inscription devised by Chief Justice Hughes: "Justice, the Guardian of Liberty." In his frieze sculptor Herman A. MacNeil pays tribute to the civilizing effects of legal authority. A trio of ancient lawgivers—Moses, flanked by Confucius and Solon—occupies the center of the panel, which otherwise features alleogorical figures intended to symbolize beneficent aspects of judicial dispute resolution.

Inside the building the appeal to tradition and authority intensifies. Beyond the massive bronze entrance doors, which slide into a wall recess during the hours when the building is open to the public, monolithic columns of white marble support the coffered ceiling of the Great Hall. This spacious corridor, which serves as a foyer for the courtroom at its farther end, displays busts of all the Court's deceased chief justices, either in wall niches or on alternating pedestals. Like the columns, the floor, and the walls, the busts are of white marble, and help to establish a mood of reverence as one approaches the red-curtained doorway of the courtroom.

Substantially larger than its predecessors in the Capitol, the Court *Chamber provides seating for about three hundred persons. The ele-

Figure 1. *Supreme Court Building*

vated justices' bench along the east wall dominates the room. It was traditional in design until 1972, when the Court approved its conversion into a "winged" or semihexagonal shape, to facilitate communication between the justices during oral arguments (see figures 2a and 2b). Behind the bench a row of marble columns and a backdrop of heavy red curtains add a touch of real dignity, while Adolph Weinman's friezes along the upper walls remind spectators of the necessity and grandeur of legal authority. Pursuant to Gilbert's design, the justices enter the courtroom through a private corridor, parting the curtains dramatically to take their seats as each session begins.

The rest of the main floor contains the justices' chambers, auxiliary offices, and *conference and *robing rooms. While the Court met in the Capitol, the justices had no private offices because of a shortage of available space. Gilbert was careful to remedy this deficiency by providing each justice with a suite of three rooms—one for personal use, and the others to accommodate law clerks and secretaries. Anticipating that a justice might wish to destroy documents unobtrusively on occasion, he also furnished each jurist's pri-

vate chamber with a working fireplace. The scale of the building left ample room for the expansion of office space, and retired justices sometimes continue to occupy their chambers.

Throughout their workday the justices remain screened from contact with the public. In the crowded Capitol they once had to put on their robes in full view of the courtroom audience; and when they secured an adequate robing room, they still had to parade across a corridor sometimes filled with sightseers in order to reach the courtroom. Taft considered such exposure detrimental to judicial dignity; and Gilbert accordingly devised physical arrangements to safeguard the Court's privacy. The justices thus park their cars in the basement of the building and take a private elevator up to a corridor on the main floor that is closed to the public. The corridor in turn gives access to all judicial chambers, as well as a conference room, a robing room, and the courtroom. The justices may similarly ascend to a private dining room and library reading room on the second floor. Such elaborate security contributes to a mystique of the Court as a group of detached sages who are impervious to popular pressures.

Figure 2a. *Supreme Court Bench, original design*

Figure 2b. *Supreme Court Bench, current "winged" design*

The Court's main *library occupies the entire third floor. Its handsome, oak-paneled reading room offers exceptional research facilities for the justices' clerks, members of the Supreme Court bar, members of Congress, and lawyers representing federal agencies. Taft had been particularly concerned about the absence of adequate storage space in the Capitol for the Court's accumulating records and archives. Gilbert therefore made generous provision for records rooms, with temperature and humidity controls to ensure the preservation of historic documents. At Taft's suggestion, he also set aside two rooms on the ground floor for the use of the press (see PRESS ROOM).

Gilbert's architectural sketches were approved by the Supreme Court Building Commission in 1929, and Congress appropriated $9,740,000 for construction purposes. Eventually the Commission returned $93,532.03 of unused funds. Construction did not begin in earnest until 1931, and the building finally opened its doors to the public on Monday, 7 October 1935.

(See also BUILDINGS, SUPREME COURT; SCULPTURE IN THE SUPREME COURT BUILDING.)

□ Lois Craig and the Staff of the Federal Architecture Project, *The Federal Presence: Architecture, Politics, and Symbols in United States Government Building* (1977). Alpheus Thomas Mason, *William Howard Taft: Chief Justice* (1965). Catherine Hetos Skefos, "The Supreme Court Gets a Home," *Supreme Court Historical Society Yearbook* (1976): 25–36.          Maxwell Bloomfield

**Argersinger v. Hamlin,** 407 U.S. 25 (1972), argued 6 Dec. 1971, reargued 28 Feb. 1972, decided 12 June 1972 by vote of 9 to 0; Douglas for the Court; Brennan, Stewart, Burger, Powell, and Rehnquist concurring.

Argersinger was charged with carrying a concealed weapon, an offense punishable by imprisonment up to six months, a thousand-dollar fine, or both. Indigent, he was tried without counsel by a judge, found guilty, and sentenced to ninety days in jail. Argersinger then filed a *habeas corpus action in the Florida Supreme Court alleging that he was deprived of his *Sixth Amendment right to counsel. The Florida court rejected his claim.

The U.S. Supreme Court reversed. It extended *Gideon v. Wainwright* (1963), holding that "absent a knowing and intelligent waiver, no person may be imprisoned for any offense, whether classified as petty, misdemeanor, or felony, unless he was represented by [appointed or retained] counsel at his trial" (p. 37). In concurrence, Justice Lewis F. *Powell expressed concern that the majority's decision would substantially burden the already congested criminal justice system and would allow those fined rather than imprisoned to present equal protection challenges.

Seven years later in *Scott v. Illinois* (1979), the Court clarified its *Argersinger* decision, holding

that defendants charged with offenses where imprisonment is authorized but not actually imposed do not have a Sixth Amendment right to counsel. The Court also noted that despite concerns when *Argersinger* was decided, the decision had proved "reasonably workable" (p. 373).

(See also COUNSEL, RIGHT TO.)

Susan E. Lawrence

**Arizona v. Fulminante,** 111 S.Ct. 1246 (1991), argued 10 Oct. 1990, decided 26 Mar. 1991 by vote of 5 to 4; Rehnquist for the Court, White in dissent. For many decades, the "rule of automatic reversal" governed *coerced confession cases. Under this rule, if a coerced or "involuntary" confession had been erroneously admitted at the trial, the conviction had to be reversed regardless of how much untainted evidence of guilt remained to support the conviction. In *Fulminante*, however, the Court held that an erroneously admitted coerced confession was subject to "harmless-error" analysis.

Noting that confessions obtained in violation of *Massiah v. United States* (1964) and *Miranda v. Arizona* (1966) had already been subject to "harmless-error" analysis, the Court emphasized that "the evidentiary impact" of a coerced confession and its effect upon the trial was indistinguishable from that of a confession inadmissible for any other reason. The erroneous admission of a coerced confession may often be "devastating" to a defendant, but that may be said of any inadmissible confession. There is nothing inherent in a confession obtained in violation of *Massiah or Miranda* that gives it a lesser impact on a jury than a coerced confession.

The dissenters argued that because a coerced confession is a constitutional error of great magnitude it should be treated differently than confessions inadmissible on other grounds. They emphasized that the methods used to extract coerced confessions offend a fundamental principle: "ours is an accusatorial and not an inquisitorial system" (p. 1256).          Yale Kamisar

**Arlington Heights v. Metropolitan Housing Development Corp.,** 429 U.S. 252 (1977), argued 13 Oct. 1976, decided 11 Jan. 1977 by vote of 7 to 1; Powell for the Court, Marshall and Brennan concurring in part and dissenting in part, White in dissent; Stevens not participating. The case originated in an attempt by the Metropolitan Housing Development Corp. (MHDC), a nonprofit developer, to build racially integrated low- and moderate-income housing in the Chicago suburb of Arlington Heights. The village Board of Trustees denied MHDC's rezoning petition, thus preventing it from building. MHDC then brought suit in federal district court alleging that the denial was racially discriminatory in violation of both the *Fourteenth Amendment of the U.S. Constitution and federal law. The district court upheld the village's decision but was reversed by the U.S. Court of Appeals for the Seventh Circuit.

In the Supreme Court the crucial issue was the standard for proving racial discrimination under the Fourteenth Amendment; the decision focused on the difference between a racially disproportionate impact and racially discriminatory intent. The Court, following *Washington v. Davis* (1976), rejected a showing only of racially disproportionate impact. It held that proof of racially discriminatory intent or purpose was necessary to make out a constitutional violation. Examining the historical background of the zoning decision, the sequence of events leading up to it, and the official minutes, the Court held that the original plaintiffs had failed to prove that racial discrimination was a motivating factor in the village's decision. The court of appeals' decision was reversed and remanded for consideration of the statutory claim.

The decision has been criticized for giving insufficient direction as to what counts as proof of discriminatory purpose and for maintaining high barriers for overcoming housing discrimination, both locally and nationally. When the case was argued, only 27 (.04 percent) of the village's 64,000 residents were African-American. The village estimates that in 1989 that number only had risen to approximately 300 (.4 percent) of its more than 75,000 residents.

(See also DISCRIMINATORY INTENT; EQUAL PROTECTION; RACE AND RACISM; ZONING.)

Gerald N. Rosenberg

**Arms, Right to Bear.** See SECOND AMENDMENT.

**Article III.** The story of Article III, the judiciary article of the Constitution, is in many ways the story of American constitutionalism itself. The tale has a beginning but no end, and it is fraught with tensions, uncertainties, and ambivalences.

Article III of the Constitution defines and delimits the "judicial Power of the United States." Intended to guarantee an independent federal judiciary, its first section provides that federal judges shall enjoy tenure during good behavior. Section 2 enumerates the categories of cases in which a federal court either may or must have jurisdiction. Section 3 defines the crime of treason.

Although Article III purposely establishes the judicial branch as the coequal of the legislative and executive branches established by Articles I and II, the framers' plans for judicial power were beset with ambivalence. At the Constitutional Convention, all agreed that there should be "one Supreme Court," and Article III provides in mandatory terms for that tribunal's establishment. But the framers, some of whom feared that federal courts would intrude excessively on the states' lawmaking prerogatives, divided sharply over whether there should be any *lower federal courts at all. The dispute ended in a compromise,

under which Article III grants Congress the power to create lower federal courts but does not require it to do so. It is a corollary of this so-called Madisonian Compromise that the jurisdiction of the lower federal courts is subject to congressional limitation.

Even the Constitution's provision for Supreme Court power is surprisingly laconic and apparently compromised. Article III subjects the Court's *appellate jurisdiction to "such Exceptions, and under such Regulations as the Congress shall make."

To some commentators and critics, it is also striking that Article III nowhere provides expressly for the power of *judicial review—the courts' power to assess the constitutionality of state and federal legislation. Alexander *Hamilton, in The *Federalist, no. 78, argued for the existence of this extraordinary power. But because Article III never mentions judicial review explicitly, the debate over the framers' intent is perennial.

Viewed solely as a text, Article III thus determines very little. It affords the potential for what in fact has developed: perhaps the most powerful judicial system in the history of the world. But the words of Article III are also consistent with a relatively insignificant federal judiciary, possibly without the power of judicial review, and with the federal courts' jurisdiction delimited by Congress to protect claimed congressional and executive prerogatives.

*Case or Controversy Requirement.* By universal acknowledgement, the founding genius of expansive judicial power under Article III was the fourth chief justice of the United States, John *Marshall. Among his political and jurisprudential triumphs, Marshall authored the 1803 opinion in *Marbury v. Madison that established the authority of the federal courts to engage in judicial review.

At the time that it was introduced, judicial review was breathtaking as a matter of comparative politics, and it remains controversial. The continuing locus of concern involves the question of how, rather than whether, the courts should exercise this extraordinary power. The debate, which has filled countless pages, has tended to organize itself around different polarities at different times: "strict constructionists" have contended with *"judicial activists"; those who would limit the judicial role to enforcing "the framers' intent" have disputed with proponents of a "living constitution" (see ORIGINAL INTENT). But the lines of division have never been wholly clear, perhaps because there is so large a core of shared assumptions among the professed antagonists. All agree that, as an apparent anomaly in a fundamentally democratic society, judicial review must be carefully structured and duly restrained if it is not to subvert other fundamental presuppositions of the constitutional scheme. In addition, courts must assure themselves of the functional requisites of effective judicial decision making.

The principal conceptual device for defining the judicial role and ensuring its effective exercise emerges from the text of Article III, which limits federal judicial power to the decision of *"Cases" and "Controversies." In defining those terms, the courts have developed what are frequently known as *justiciability doctrines.

One set of justiciability doctrines serves largely to protect judicial independence from the legislative and executive branches. Especially during the early years of the republic, both Congress and the president showed some disposition to enlist the federal courts as their advice-giving assistants. Sensing that judicial independence, prestige, and power were at stake, the justices of the Supreme Court quickly established two principles of continuing validity. Article III prohibits the issuance of *"advisory opinions" by Article III courts. In addition, it requires that judicial decisions possess "finality," or immunity from executive revision.

Other Article III justiciability doctrines aim to establish the functional requisites of sound judicial decision making. The most important of these, the *standing doctrine, establishes that no one can bring a lawsuit unless he or she has personally suffered a judicially cognizable injury. This requirement ensures a concrete set of facts to focus issues for judicial resolution. The standing doctrine's demand for concrete litigants also promotes the adversarial presentation of issues as a means of illuminating judicial decision makers. *Mootness and *ripeness doctrines, which govern the timing of a lawsuit, serve similar interests.

A third and final purpose of Article III justiciability doctrines is that of judicial self-limitation. Reflecting an intuition that judicial review is permanently and even appropriately precarious in a substantially democratic constitutional order, the Supreme Court has created the *political question doctrine. Although deeply contestable, this doctrine reflects a core notion that some questions of constitutional stature must be viewed as entrusted to the political branches and thus as outside the judicial competence. The Court has also held that the standing doctrine has an explicitly "prudential" dimension, developed to keep the Article III courts from deciding questions that are more suitable for decision by politically accountable decision makers.

All of the Article III justiciability doctrines are fuzzy at their edges, if not at their cores, and both their definitions and their applications have evolved over American judicial history. Within the modern era, a self-confident Supreme Court headed by Chief Justice Earl *Warren eroded the political question, standing, and mootness doctrines to decide questions of deep political significance in cases in which other governmental institutions betrayed insensitivity to constitutional concerns.

The signal case of *Baker v. Carr (1962) held that the political question doctrine did not bar suits challenging the apportionment of state legislatures; it ultimately led to the "one person, one vote" rule (see REAPPORTIONMENT CASES). *Flast v. Cohen (1968), upholding a taxpayer's standing to challenge the lawfulness of government expenditures under the *First Amendment's Establishment Clause, sought to permit effective judicial policing of the constitutional bounds between church and state (see RELIGION).

Retrenching from decisions such as these, the Burger and Rehnquist Courts have imposed a new stringency at least on the standing component of the case or controversy requirement. The Court's recent stiffening of justiciability doctrines does not lack for historical precedent. To appreciate this development, however, is only to grasp how the scope of *judicial power varies with the prevailing conception of what constitutes a justiciable case or controversy under Article III.

***Sovereign Immunity and Public Rights.*** Beyond the case or controversy requirement that is rooted in the text of Article III, two extratextual concepts have limited the role of the Article III courts under the separation of powers doctrine. The first is *sovereign immunity—a traditional doctrine, transplanted from English to American soil, holding that the sovereign cannot be sued without its consent. In a series of cases tracing as far back as *Cohens v. Virginia (1821), the Supreme Court has affirmed that the Constitution, although it nowhere mentions this doctrine and although Article III provides for federal jurisdiction in cases to which the United States is a party, presupposes the sovereign immunity of the United States.

Beyond the doctrine of sovereign immunity, a sundry category of so-called public rights cases has also been viewed as lying beyond the historically intended scope of Article III. The concept of a public right is notoriously vague, shifting, and elusive; it is as often employed to avoid as to advance analysis. But core historical examples can be identified. These include disputes arising from coercive exercises of government power outside of the criminal law, such as the seizure of alleged contraband, and claims of entitlement to governmentally provided benefits. Although capable of being assigned to Article III courts, public rights cases have not been understood to require judicial resolution, and have often been assigned by Congress to decision makers who lack Article III's safeguards of adjudicatory independence. These non–Article III adjudicators have included administrative agencies, officials of the executive branch, and judges of so-called legislative courts who serve for a term of years rather than enjoying the tenure during good behavior guaranteed to the Article III judiciary.

*Congressional Control of Federal Jurisdiction.*
Although permitted by Article III to define the
jurisdiction of the lower federal courts and to
make exceptions to the jurisdiction of the Supreme Court, Congress has generally exercised
its power in uncontroversial ways. Perhaps the
most significant statutes affecting the Supreme
Court's jurisdiction, mandated by practical necessity, have authorized the Court to choose which
cases to decide. At the foundation of the republic,
the number of appeals was sufficiently small so
that the Supreme Court could decide all of the
cases in which its jurisdiction was lawfully invoked. Today, the volume is so large that the
Court could no longer function in this way, and it
generally selects those cases that it regards as
most interesting and important (see JUDICIAL
IMPROVEMENTS AND ACCESS TO JUSTICE ACT).

The most perplexing question surrounding
Congress's Article III power to define the federal
courts' jurisdiction involves the use of that power
to insulate arguably unconstitutional action from
federal judicial review. Although old Supreme
Court cases suggest otherwise, Professor Henry
Hart, in a famous commentary that relies on the
structure and spirit of the constitutional plan,
terms it "preposterous" that the Article III power
to control jurisdiction could be relied on to nullify
constitutional rights. Despite a raging academic
debate, there are few if any modern cases in
which Congress has actually enacted legislation
with this purpose or effect. As recently as 1979,
however, the Senate passed a bill that would
have stripped the federal courts of jurisdiction in
cases brought to challenge the constitutionality of
voluntary prayer in public schools and buildings
(see SCHOOL PRAYER AND BIBLE READING). The
House rejected the measure.

*Article III and Federalism.* As the framers
well appreciated, the scope of federal jurisdiction under Article III implicates state political
power. The most important question is well
settled. In *Martin v. Hunter's Lessee* (1816), the
Supreme Court held that it has the authority to
review the decisions of *state courts, including
state supreme courts. As much as any decision
in the *United States Reports, Martin v. Hunter's
Lessee* helped to establish a workable scheme of
American *federalism. Justice Oliver Wendell
*Holmes once remarked that the federal republic
could have survived without the federal courts
exercising judicial review of acts of Congress.
But it could not have survived, he said, without
federal judicial review of state laws and executive action.

Although *Martin v. Hunter's Lessee* established
a vital federal authority, state judicial prerogatives are amply protected by the 1875 holding of
*Murdock v. Memphis* that the Supreme Court will
not second-guess state courts' decisions of state
law. The conjunction of *Murdock* with *Martin v.
Hunter's Lessee* means that state courts are the
ultimate expositors of state law, while the federal

Supreme Court has the last word on questions of
federal law.

The scope of Article III judicial authority remains clouded, however, by the traditional doctrine of state sovereign immunity. In the early
case of *Chisholm v. Georgia* (1793), the Supreme
Court held that Article III deprived the states of
sovereign immunity when sued by citizens of
another state in federal court. But *Chisholm* was
met with a firestorm of adverse reaction, which
culminated in the oddly worded *Eleventh
Amendment to the Constitution of the United
States. Though clearly intended to protect the
states from federal judicial power under Article
III in some way, the Eleventh Amendment makes
no explicit reference to sovereign immunity, and
it contains no literal barrier to federal suits to
enforce the Constitution and laws of the United
States.

After an early period of narrow constructions,
the Supreme Court, in its 1890 decision in *Hans v.
Louisiana,* ruled that the Eleventh Amendment
bars all unconsented suits brought by citizens
against the states in federal courts, including
suits to enforce the Constitution. But the *Hans*
principle is functionally unworkable; as the framers had recognized in authorizing the federal
judicial power under Article III to be coextensive
with substantive federal authority, the supremacy of federal law requires a federal enforcement
mechanism. Bowing to this truth, the subsequent
history of Eleventh Amendment jurisprudence is
substantially one of creating and defining a series
of exceptions to *Han's* broad holding and broader
dicta. Among the most important exceptions, the
Supreme Court held in *Ex parte *Young* (1908) that
the Eleventh Amendment does not bar suits for
*injunctions against state officials. The Court has
held more recently, in *Pennsylvania v. Union Gas
Co.* (1989), that the Eleventh Amendment does
not apply to suits against the states that are
expressly authorized by Congress.

Also mediating the relationship between the
Article III federal courts and state political authority are various doctrines founded on the traditional concept of "equitable discretion." These
judge-made doctrines call upon federal trial
courts to "abstain" from deciding certain kinds of
cases that implicate important state interests at
least until a state court has pronounced on
relevant state-law issues. The *abstention doctrines are motivated by two kinds of concerns.
One involves the functional interest in an efficient allocation of business between the state and
federal judiciaries. The other reflects a largely
political interest in curbing perceived "judicial
activism" by the lower federal courts.

After a period of erosion under the politically
liberal Warren Court, abstention doctrines are
now in a position of ascendency. Judicially defined and managed, abstention doctrines constitute an important exception to John Marshall's
assumption that federal courts must exercise the

jurisdiction conferred on them by Congress under Article III. Abstention doctrines also illustrate the interaction between evolving and contestable conceptions of appropriate federalism and the scope of federal judicial power under Article III.

*Legislative Courts and Administrative Agencies.* Although Article III provides that "the judicial Power of the United States" shall be vested in judges who enjoy tenure during good behavior and protection against reduction in salary, this stricture has not been stringently construed. Beginning with military courts (see MILITARY JUSTICE), and with the early appointment of territorial judges to terms of years, Congress has provided for a miscellaneous assortment of cases—most but not all of which have involved public rights—to be tried before federal adjudicators who are not "Article III judges." This longstanding but problematic practice took on new importance with the burgeoning of administrative agencies, many of which are authorized to pursue a mix of rule-making and adjudicative activities (see ADMINISTRATIVE STATE).

Although hard to square with the letter of Article III, the concept of administrative adjudication received a reasonable jurisprudential foundation in the pathbreaking case of *Crowell* v. *Benson* (1932). *Crowell* can be read to rely on the notion that exercise of the federal judicial power through appellate review of agency action is both necessary and sufficient to reconcile administrative adjudication with Article III's requirement that "the judicial Power of the United States" be vested in life-tenured judges.

Surprisingly, the Supreme Court revisited the problem of administrative adjudication in 1982, in *Northern Pipeline Construction Co.* v. *Marathon Pipe Line Co.*, as if oblivious to the entrenched status of administrative adjudication in a host of statutory schemes. Although the case before it involved a narrow question about the permissible powers of non–Article III bankruptcy courts, the plurality opinion painted with a broad brush. The Court's inclination in *Northern Pipeline*, and apparently in subsequent cases, has been to limit the permissibility of administrative adjudication to a set of historically defined exceptions to Article III's apparently simple textual norm that the federal judicial power, if vested at all, must be vested in Article III courts. The principal effect of the Court's stance is to legitimate administrative adjudication in public rights cases—a classification whose ancient but troublesome lineage was noted above—but generally not elsewhere.

The Court's approach is unfortunate. The public rights category has always lacked clear definition, and the Court's recent cases have only exacerbated its vagaries. The public rights doctrine also threatens both individual rights and the constitutional *separation of powers. For example, the public rights category has traditionally included most noncriminal cases to which the

government is a party. In light of the enormous power of modern government, and the significance of government action for private well-being, it is deeply troubling for the Supreme Court to imply acceptance of the historic notion that public rights cases lie beyond the necessary reach of the Article III judicial power.

Although seemingly disregarded for the short term, *Crowell* v. *Benson* suggests an alternative. *Crowell's* appellate review requirement would establish an accommodation between the value of independent adjudication that is enshrined in Article III, which would be vindicated through appellate review, and the functional imperative of administrative adjudication within the modern administrative state. An appellate review approach could also be adapted to preserve an important but manageable role for the Article III courts even in public rights cases.

□ Akhil Amar, "A Neo-Federalist View of Article III: Separating the Two Tiers of Federal Jurisdiction," *Boston University Law Review* 65 (1985): 205–272. Paul M. Bator, Daniel J. Meltzer, Paul J. Mishkin, and David L. Shapiro, *Hart & Wechsler's The Federal Courts and the Federal System*, 3d ed. (1988). Erwin Chemerinsky, *Federal Jurisdiction* (1989). Richard H. Fallon, Jr., "The Ideologies of Federal Courts Law," *Virginia Law Review* 74 (1988): 1141–1251. Richard H. Fallon, Jr., "Of Legislative Courts, Administrative Agencies, and Article III," *Harvard Law Review* 101 (1988): 915–999. Martin H. Redish, *Federal Jurisdiction: Tensions in the Allocation of Federal Judicial Power*, 2d ed. (1990). Richard H. Fallon, Jr

**Ashwander v. Tennessee Valley Authority,** 297 U.S. 288 (1936), argued 19–20 Dec. 1935, decided 17 Feb. 1936 by vote of 8 to 1; Hughes for the Court, Brandeis concurring, McReynolds in dissent. Claiming that the Tennessee Valley Authority Act was unconstitutional, minority shareholders of a utility company sought to annul their board's agreement to purchase electricity from the T.V.A. The Court upheld the act and found Congress had authority to construct dams for national defense and improve interstate commerce. The sale of electricity—a byproduct—was authorized by Article IV, section 3 of the Constitution, granting the federal government power to sell property it lawfully acquires.

Justice Louis *Brandeis believed the constitutional question should never have been addressed because the case involved a simple internal dispute among shareholders. He maintained that the Court should avoid making decisions on the constitutionality of legislation, and the case is rememberd for his list of guidelines—the "Ashwander rules": (1) The Court will not determine the constitutionality of legislation in nonadversary proceedings; (2) it will not anticipate a question of constitutional law; (3) it will not formulate a rule of constitutional law broader than needed; (4) it will not rule on constitutionality if there is another ground for deciding the case; (5) it will not determine a statute's validity unless the person complaining has been injured by it; (6) it will not invalidate a statute at the instance of persons who have taken advantage of its benefits; and (7) the Court will always ascertain whether any reasonable interpretation of a statute will allow it to avoid the constitutional issue.

(See also COMMERCE POWER; JUDICIAL REVIEW.)

Paul Kens

**Assembly and Association, Freedom of.** The "right of the people peaceably to assemble" is specifically guaranteed in Article I of the *Bill of Rights and it has been incorporated as incumbent upon the states via the *Fourteenth Amendment (see INCORPORATION DOCTRINE). But there is not mentioned either in the Constitution of the United States nor in that of the several states any specific right of association. Yet the latter is clearly a derivative and/or a component of the former, and as the judiciary began to develop and expand *First Amendment rights in the twentieth century, especially after *World War II, there was little doubt that a right of association was viewed as part-and-parcel of the right of assembly. Given what Alexis de Tocqueville accurately, if bemusedly, recognized 150 or more years ago as the American mania for joining organizations, such a marriage of rights was a natural development. Neither right is an "absolute" (see FIRST AMENDMENT ABSOLUTISM), and considerable litigation continues to reach the highest tribunals in the land. Both have been accorded generally liberal interpretations, but because both involve expressive conduct rather than pure speech, restrictions are bound to be as necessary as they are controversial (see FIRST AMENDMENT BALANCING; FIRST AMENDMENT SPEECH TESTS).

Thus, in the realm of the freedom to assemble, lines have been drawn by all three branches of the government with respect to assertions of the exercise of the right vis-à-vis the public streets, parades, processions, the public parks, at or near private homes, in both public and private shopping centers, picketing, and the communications industry. And the lines have proved to be vexatious, for almost any exercise of the right of peaceable assembly connotes the exercise of "speech plus"—a melange of speech mixed with conduct. The right of association poses similarly complex questions, although it is perhaps less obviously characterized by the "conduct" syndrome than assembly. However, problems arising from membership in organizations, such as the basic right to join with others in the pursuit of certain aims, be they private, public, political, social, or economic, have frequently reached the courts. Exclusions from quasi-private organizations or clubs on the basis of *race, *religion, *gender, or similar group characteristics have been the subject of much recent litigation. Lines between the "public" and "private" character of organizations have become increasingly blurred

in the eyes of the judiciary (see PRIVATE DISCRIMINATORY ASSOCIATIONS). A few specific illustrations of the Supreme Court's posture in assembly and association cases serve to underscore the endemic problems in drawing viable, lasting lines.

In the case of the right to assemble peaceably, the Court has repeatedly pointed out that the First Amendment does not "afford the same kind of freedom" to communicate conduct as to that which it extends to "pure speech" (e.g., *Cox v. Louisiana*, 1965, p. 555). There is no doubt that peaceful picketing, for example, is a vital and protected prerogative of freedom of assembly. But picketing that applies physical force to those who might wish to exercise their equal rights of freedom of expression by disregarding the picket line, or certain kinds of picketing violative of a picketee's *property rights or utterly unrelated to his or her "operations," or picketing in derogation of secondary boycott statutes, is not privileged (e.g., compare and contrast *Thornhill v. Alabama*, 1940, with *Giboney v. Empire Storage and Ice Co.*, 1949; or *Amalgamated Food Employees Union v. Logan Valley Plaza*, 1968, with *Lloyd Corporation v. Tanner*, 1972). In *Frisby v. Schultz* (1988), the Court ruled that when picketers concentrate on a single household rather than an entire neighborhood, the government may forbid such picketing in order to protect the homeowner's *privacy. To prevent the clogging of sidewalks and public streets, licenses may be required for public parades and processions (*Cox v. New Hampshire*, 1941). And the Court has differentiated between demonstrations in front of a legislature (*Edwards v. South Carolina*, 1963) and on the premises of a jail (*Adderley v. Florida*, 1966), upholding the former and rejecting the latter.

In the associational sphere, the Cold War period of the 1950s and 1960s saw numerous cases reaching the Supreme Court. Many of them involved claims of associational freedom for communists and other allegedly subversive organizations (see SUBVERSION). While mindful of government authority to guard against proscribed subversive activity (e.g., *Dennis v. United States*, 1951, and *Barenblatt v. United States*, 1959), the Court ultimately and pointedly rejected a doctrine of "guilt by association" and focused on individual rather than group action and responsibility (e.g., *Yates v. United States*, 1957, and *DeGregory v. New Hampshire*, 1966) (see COMMUNISM AND COLD WAR). But in a series of cases involving harassment of the *NAACP by state legislative investigating bodies, it made clear that groups that themselves are neither engaged in subversive or other illegal or improper activities, nor demonstrated to have any substantial connections with such activities, are entitled to be protected in their rights of free and private association (e.g., *NAACP v. Alabama*, 1958, and *Gibson v. Florida Legislative Committee*, 1963).

The 1980s brought sundry challenges to the

exclusivist practices of clubs and associations that, invoking the right of freedom of association, would discriminate on grounds of applicants' gender and race. Here the Court developed a consistent policy of upholding laws and ordinances that bar such discrimination, especially when the organizations are sizeable and nonexclusive (e.g., *Roberts v. U.S. Jaycees*, 1984, and *Rotary International* v. *Rotary Club of Duarte*, 1987) or when private clubs above a certain size (four hundred in New York City) provide regular meal service for members and guests and have members' dues paid by nonmembers, such as employers (*New York State Club Association* v. *City of New York*, 1988).

☐ M. Glenn Abernathy, *The Right of Assembly and Association*, 2d rev. ed. (1981). David Fellman, *The Constitutional Right of Association* (1963).          Henry J. Abraham

**Attainder, Bills of.** During the sixteenth and seventeenth centuries the British Parliament often employed enactments called bills of attainder to inflict the death penalty on persons deemed guilty of seditious acts, such as attempting to overthrow the government. In addition to the death sentence, a bill of attainder usually carried with it a "corruption of blood," which meant that the attainted party's property could not pass to his heirs. If the bill imposed a punishment short of death, such as banishment, confiscation of goods, or loss of the right to vote, it was called a bill of pains and penalties. These two kinds of bills were not restricted to England. During the American Revolution, the legislatures of many states enacted bills of attainder or bills of pains and penalties against persons deemed guilty of disloyalty to the American cause.

Article I, section 9, clause 3 of the U.S. Constitution forbids the federal government from passing bills of attainder. The same prohibition is imposed on the states by Article I, section 10, clause 1. The U.S. Supreme Court decided at an early time, without argument, that these two clauses covered bills of pains and penalties as well as bills of attainder proper. Although this conclusion is not compelled by the language of the Constitution, it becomes entirely persuasive when the purpose of the prohibition is considered. Both bills of attainder and bills of pains and penalties are legislative acts that inflict punishment without a judicial trial. Regardless of whether the punishment decreed is death or something less than death, such enactments violate principles deeply embedded in the constitutional structure. The Constitution separates the judicial power from the legislative power (see SEPARATION OF POWERS). Legislative bodies are supposed to enact general rules, applicable to all persons or certain classes of people, which grant rights to them or impose duties, prohibitions, or disabilities on them. It is the function of the judicial branch to decide, under structured proce-

dures containing safeguards against error and abuse of power, whether a specific person is entitled to a right, or subject to a duty, prohibition, or disability established by the legislatures. Bills of attainder and bills of pains and penalties are thoroughly at odds with these principles. They inflict punitive sanctions in disregard of judicial methods of proof designed to insure fairness in fact-finding. The history of bills of attainder has also shown that their passage was often induced by popular passion or motivated by unproved suspicions.

In the context of the bill of attainder clauses of the Constitution, the concept of punishment has not been restricted by the courts to the typical sanctions employed by the system of criminal justice, such as *capital punishment, imprisonment, punitive fines, and confiscation of property. The bill of attainder clauses have been broadly construed to include deprivations of rights, civil or political, disqualification from office, and legislative bars to participation in specific employments or professions. Essential to a finding of attainder is a determination by the court that it was the legislature's intent to punish rather than to regulate for a legitimate political purpose.

Traditionally, most bills of attainder designated the persons subjected to punishment by name. In some cases, however, legislatures imposed punishment on groups whose individual members could be ascertained without much difficulty. For example, a federal statute made it a crime for members of the Communist party to serve as officers of a *labor union. The purpose of the statute was to protect the national economy by minimizing the danger of political strikes. The Court in *United States* v. *Brown* (1965) invalidated the statute as a bill of attainder. Since not all members of the Communist party were likely to incite political strikes, and since noncommunist agitators might also engage in such conduct, the decision whether the activities of a particular person presented the danger to be guarded against should have been left to the judicial branch. The Supreme Court suggested that Congress could validly enact a general rule barring persons expected to initiate political strikes from union office instead of imputing the undesirable trait to specific persons, namely members of the Communist party (see COMMUNISM AND COLD WAR).

☐ Laurence H. Tribe, *American Constitutional Law*, 2d ed. (1988), pp. 641–656.          Edgar Bodenheimer

**Automobile Searches.** The inherent conflict in police work between apprehending suspects and protecting individual rights is perhaps most acute in automobile searches. Since *Carroll* v. *U.S.* (1925), the Supreme Court has not required a warrant to search an automobile on the theory that it is impractical to secure a warrant and preserve evidence that is, or shortly might be, in transit. In articulating an "automobile exception" to the Fourth Amendment warrant requirement, Chief Justice William Howard *Taft argued that individual *privacy considerations would still be protected by requiring police to demonstrate that they had probable cause to believe contraband was inside the vehicle.

The scope of this exception has increased substantially during the 1980s, following the general trend of search and seizure doctrine. Specifically, the relative weight given to the core elements of the automobile exception has shifted to favor governmental interests (police safety and preservation of evidence) over individual freedom from unwarranted intrusions (warrantless search and seizure). Indeed, it can be argued that the courts have abandoned the "balancing test" (government interests versus individual *privacy interests) in this area altogether. In *United States* v. *Ross* (1982), for example, the Court ruled that automobiles could be searched without a warrant if the police had probable cause to believe they contained contraband or weapons. In *California* v. *Carney* (1985), the Court further held that mobile homes capable of traveling on a public highway were not to be excluded from the automobile exception, even though the home in question, which operated as a center for the exchange of drugs and sex, was located in a parking lot. Both cases exemplify how the Court has moved away from Chief Justice Taft's earlier concern with the inherit mobility of automobiles to the view that individuals have limited expectations of privacy in their automobiles.

(See also FOURTH AMENDMENT; SEARCH WARRANT RULE, EXCEPTION TO.)

Christine B. Harrington

# B

**Badger, George Edmund** (b. New Bern, N.C., 17 Apr. 1795; d. Raleigh, N.C., 11 May 1866), unconfirmed appointee to the U.S. Supreme Court. Badger attended Yale University (1810–1811), studied law with John Stanley, and was admitted to the North Carolina bar in 1815. President William Henry Harrison appointed Badger secretary of the Navy. Badger retained this post on the succession of John Tyler but with other members of the cabinet resigned in protest over Tyler's opposition to the creation of a national bank.

From 1846 until 1854 Badger represented North Carolina in the U.S. Senate. He advocated reform of the Supreme Court docket and calendar and proposed salary increases for the justices. Following inaction on the nomination of Edward A. *Bradford, President Millard Fillmore on 10 January 1853 nominated Badger to the Supreme Court to fill a vacancy. Badger's residency outside the fifth circuit aroused criticism from Alabama, Mississippi, and Louisiana senators, who preferred resident candidates. In a rare rejection of one of its own, the Senate postponed action on the nomination on 11 February 1853 by a vote of 26 to 25. At the outbreak of the Civil War, Badger was elected to the North Carolina secession convention and after some hesitancy voted for the ordinance of secession.

(See also NOMINEES, REJECTION OF.)

Elizabeth B. Monroe

**Bad Tendency Test,** a test used to analyze free speech issues that derived from the English *common law of *libel synthesized by Blackstone before the American Revolution. This test mea-

sured the legality of speech by its tendency to cause an illegal action. Scholars frequently attacked the bad tendency test as a vestige of English law that could not be reconciled with the democratic principles of the *First Amendment, but federal and *state courts at all levels typically applied it to restrict expression without viewing the First Amendment as requiring that speech be treated differently from other categories of attempts or crimes.

Two Supreme Court decisions written by Justice Oliver Wendell *Holmes in the decade before *World War I illustrate the bad tendency test in operation. Upholding the contempt conviction of an editor who did not have an opportunity to prove truth as a defense, Holmes observed in *Patterson* v. *Colorado* (1907) that newspaper criticism of judicial behavior in pending cases, even if accurate, "tends to obstruct the administration of justice" (p. 462). In *Fox* v. *Washington* (1915), a state statute itself incorporated the bad tendency test by defining as a misdemeanor the publication of written matter "having a tendency to encourage or incite the commission of any crime, breach of the peace or act of violence" (p. 275). Writing for a unanimous Court, Holmes reasoned that an article entitled "The Nude and the Prudes," which encouraged a boycott against anyone interfering with nude bathing, "by indirection but unmistakably" encouraged violations of laws against indecent exposure (p. 277). Holmes emphasized that speech would be punished for its bad tendency even without an explicit statutory prohibition.

The Supreme Court, through Justice Holmes, continued to apply the bad tendency test in the trilogy of *Espionage Act cases commonly thought to inaugurate the modern First Amendment tradition in 1919. The Espionage Act punished attempts to cause insubordination in the military and obstruction of recruitment. Attorneys for the defendants argued that the First Amendment protection for discussion of government policies prohibited juries from using inferences about the tendency of antiwar speech as the basis for finding criminal intent to commit these crimes. Following the analysis of his prewar opinions, Holmes summarily rejected this argument without fully addressing it. "If the act (speaking, or circulating a paper), its tendency and the intent with which it is done are the same," Holmes wrote in *Schenck v. United States (1919), "we perceive no ground for saying that success alone warrants making the act a crime" (p. 52). Holmes expressed the bad tendency test metaphorically in Frohwerk v. United States (1919) by observing that "a little breath would be enough to kindle a flame" (p. 209). And in Debs v. United States (1919), Holmes concluded that a jury could find that the antiwar speeches of Eugene Debs, the recent socialist candidate for president, "had as their natural tendency and reasonably probable effect to obstruct the recruitment service" even if the relationship between the words and the crime had been indirect and incidental (p. 216). Evaluating the tendency of language as evidence of the speaker's intent, Holmes added, is a principle "too well established and too manifestly good sense to need citation of the books" (p. 216).

The Supreme Court majority continued to use the bad tendency test to reject First Amendment claims throughout the 1920s. However, Justices Holmes and Louis *Brandeis, beginning with their dissent in *Abrams v. United States in the fall of 1919, relied on the words "clear and present danger," a phrase Holmes used casually and interchangeably with the bad tendency test in Schenck, to construct a First Amendment test that provided greater protection for speech by requiring a more immediate connection between speech and crime. In their frequent dissents, Holmes and Brandeis repeatedly claimed that speech cannot constitutionally be punished for its indirect, remote, or possible tendency.

By Herndon v. Lowry in 1937, the Supreme Court majority adopted a rigorous version of the *clear and present danger test while rejecting the "vague and indeterminate" standard of "dangerous tendency" as a "dragnet" that violates the First Amendment (pp. 256, 263). Dissenting four years later in Bridges v. California, Justice Felix *Frankfurter pointed out that the phrase clear and present danger "itself is an expression of tendency and not of accomplishment, and the literary difference between it and 'reasonable tendency' is not of constitutional dimension" (p. 295). Ironically, though cases like Herndon and Bridges required a much closer connection between speech and crime than the old bad tendency test, subsequent reformulations of clear and present danger, especially in affirming the convictions of Communist party leaders in *Dennis v. United States (1951), diluted the immediacy requirement to make the two tests quite similar. (See also SPEECH AND THE PRESS.)

□ David M. Rabban, "The First Amendment in Its Forgotten Years," Yale Law Journal 90 (January 1981): 514–595.                                David M. Rabban

**Bail.** When a person has been arrested and charged with the commission of a crime, there is inevitably an interval of time before trial. Bail relates to the defendant's right to freedom during this interval. It involves a pledge of money, property, or a "signature bond" as security that one will be available for trial when requested to appear. Failure of the defendant to appear may result in the forfeiture of the bail. The person who puts up the money is also known as the bail.

The right to bail is deeply rooted in English law and practice. That bail must be in a reasonable amount was established by Parliament with the enactment in 1689 of the Bill of Rights, which declared that "excessive bail ought not to be required." This principle was incorporated into the Eighth Amendment of the U.S. Constitution, which decrees that "excessive bail shall not be required." Most state constitutions also forbid excessive bail.

The purpose of bail is to free the accused during the period of time before trial, while at the same time requiring sufficient surety to make it reasonably certain that he will present himself for trial or punishment as ordered. A competent court or magistrate accepts the undertaking that the bail will pay to the state a specified sum that will be forfeited if the accused fails to make the required appearance.

There are compelling reasons why persons accused of crime should be allowed to be free on bail, after arrest and before trial. The right to bail implements the basic presumption of innocence that the law assumes for every person charged with crime. An accused is presumed to be innocent until actually convicted, and like all innocent people does not belong in jail.

Furthermore, to allow a person accused of crime to go free on bail permits unhampered preparation of a defense. The defendant retains one's job and thus is able to provide family support and contribute to the cost of a lawyer. There is also a chance to put personal affairs in order, and an opportunity to cooperate more meaningfully with counsel. Many studies of pretrial detention show that prolonged detention seriously increases the chances of conviction.

For the federal courts, the underlying law requiring bail is found in the Bail Reform Acts of 1966 and 1984, and in rule 46 of the Federal Rules of Criminal Procedure. Each state has a body of statutes and court decisions that also define the right to bail in state courts (see FEDERALISM). The 1966 Bail Reform Act created a presumption favoring pretrial release. However, the 1984 act, reflecting different priorities, emphasized the need to protect community safety and authorized judges to refuse bail to persons who pose a grave danger to others. This is known as preventive detention. The 1984 act was upheld by the Supreme Court in *United States* v. *Salerno* (1987). The Court ruled that preventive detention was not a punishment for dangerous individuals but an attempt to address the serious problems of crimes committed by persons who have been released on bail.

The judge or magistrate fixing bail must take into account the nature and circumstances of the offense charged, the weight of the evidence against the accused, family and community ties, employment stability, financial resources, character and mental condition, and any previous record of appearance at court proceedings. Most importantly, in assessing the danger of fleeing from the court's jurisdiction, the judge must make an assessment of the accused's ties to the community. After conviction, the defendant usually has a right to appeal, but bail after conviction is not a matter of right, since the presumption of innocence can no longer be claimed.

Forfeiture of bail does not give the accused any immunity from being tried for the offense in question. Bail is designed to secure appearance at trial and submission to the judgment of the court. It is not designed as a satisfaction for the offense.

The judge or magistrate dealing with bail necessarily exercises a large discretion. The judge's decision will not be set aside by a reviewing court unless there is a strong proof of an abuse of that discretion. The judge is ordinarily in the best position to evaluate the facts of the crime.

Until recently bail bonds were furnished by private bail bondsmen who collected a 10 percent fee from the defendant in return for posting bond. They had extraordinary powers to capture those who "jumped bail" and did not appear in court as required. Widely viewed as a source of corruption, the bondsman system has been replaced in some states by a bail system run by the courts themselves. Based on the assumption that the sole purpose of bail is to assure the defendant's appearance in court, bail reform efforts have stressed the likelihood that most persons will appear as required. Wherever possible a defendant—one with a job and strong ties to the community, and not charged with a serious violent crime—can be released on his or her own recognizance. Alternatively, a signature bond can be posted, which requires no cash down payment but which must be paid if the defendant fails to appear. Beyond that, if bail money is deemed necessary, the defendant can obtain it from the court by posting a small down payment; most of that down payment is returned upon

appearance. This makes bail affordable to most people and eliminates the profit motive of the private bondsman. The work of the Vera Institute in New York City in the 1960s was the catalyst for the bail reform movement. A shift in public attitudes away from defendants' rights and toward reducing crime has slowed but not halted bail reform.

(See also DUE PROCESS, PROCEDURAL; EIGHTH AMENDMENT.)

David Fellman

**Bailey v. Drexel Furniture Co.,** 259 U.S. 20 (1922), argued 7–8 Mar. 1922, decided 15 May 1922 by vote of 8 to 1; Taft for the Court, Clarke, without opinion, in dissent. Immediately following the unexpected invalidation of the first federal child labor law in 1918, Congress sought another way to protect dependent and exploited children in the workplace. With the two houses again virtually unanimous, the Child Labor Tax law was enacted (1919), its justification resting upon contemporary precedents, notably Chief Justice Edward D. *White's opinion in *McCray* v. *United States* (1904), which sustained the imposition of confiscatory excises to end the production of offending articles.

While White lived, the Court did not render a decision in the first child labor tax case, *Atherton* v. *Johnston* (1922), but, following his death, the new chief justice, William Howard *Taft, massed the bench in *Bailey* to invalidate the Child Labor Tax. His opinion sought to distinguish *McCray* and the other cases in which the Court had legitimated using the taxing power for regulatory purposes. The constitutionally sanctioned regulatory measures, he asserted, had involved "only . . . incidental restraint and regulation," while the stigmatized statute imposed a penalty whose "prohibitory and regulatory effect" was palpable (pp. 36–37). As in *Hammer* v. *Dagenhart* (1918), the Court found in *Bailey* that Congress had exceeded its authority and invaded the states' internal affairs.

Although Taft's distinction lacked merit, the lone dissenter, Justice John H. *Clarke, failed to challenge it. With the coming of the *New Deal, this distinction began to erode but Congress relied primarily thereafter upon the *commerce power to protect the social and economic welfare of the country.

(See also FAMILY AND CHILDREN; LABOR; POLICE POWER; TAXING AND SPENDING CLAUSE.)

Stephen B. Wood

**Baker v. Carr,** 369 U.S. 186 (1962), argued 19–20 Apr. 1961, set for reargument 1 May 1961, reargued 9 Oct. 1961, decided 26 Mar. 1962 by vote of 6 to 2; Brennan for the Court, Stewart and Clark concurring, Frankfurter and Harlan in dissent, Whittaker not participating. After serving for fifteen years on the Supreme Court, Chief Justice Earl *Warren, himself the author of the Court's opinion in the celebrated school desegregation case, *Brown v. Board of Education (1954), called Baker v. Carr "the most vital decision" during his service on the Court, and the apportionment revolution it inaugurated as the most important achievement of his Court. Baker v. Carr did not establish the "one-person, one vote principle"—that was first announced in *Gray v. Sanders (1963) and was confirmed with respect to congressional and legislative districts in *Wesberry v. Sanders (1964) and *Reynolds v. Sims (1964). But Baker v. Carr opened the federal courts to urban interests that had been unable to force state legislators to reapportion state legislatures or to redistrict congressional seats to reflect the urbanization of the United States, or to secure any redress of their grievances either from Congress or their respective state courts.

Warren might have exaggerated the importance of the case, but it clearly inaugurated a decade of lawsuits, at the end of which the political map of the nation had been redrawn. Some have termed this a revolution in redistributing political power, although there is continuing controversy as to whether the realignment of legislative districts that clearly did transfer legislative votes from the rural to the urban and suburban populations has had significant policy consequences.

Baker v. Carr was initiated in Tennessee in 1959 when a number of plaintiffs from Memphis, Nashville, and Knoxville brought an action before the federal district court in Nashville against Joseph Cordell Carr, the Tennessee secretary of state, and George McCanless, the attorney general. The Tennessee Constitution required the General Assembly to apportion the members of the General Assembly among the state's ninety-five counties after each decennial census. But the last time it had done so was in 1901, and even then it had failed to give city voters a fair share of seats. The Tennessee courts had been equally unsympathetic and declined to intervene.

The Baker plaintiffs, pointing out that the federal courts were the only forum that offered any promise of relief, asked for a *declaratory judgment that the Tennessee apportionment act was unconstitutional and an *injunction to prevent state officers from conducting any more elections under it. The three-judge district court, following established precedent, dismissed the complaint on the grounds that the relief requested and the legal wrongs alleged were not within the scope of judicial power conferred on federal courts by *Article III of the Constitution and the federal statutes implementing that article. Furthermore, said the district court, even if the Courts had jurisdiction, the questions presented to it were nonjusticiable, that is, they were "political questions" unsuited for judicial inquiry and adjustment.

On direct appeal to the Supreme Court, *amicus briefs were filed by various urban-based groups, and most importantly, by *Solicitor General Archibald Cox in behalf of the recently inaugurated Kennedy administration. As Justice Tom *Clark pointed out in his concurring opinion, Baker v. Carr was one of the "most carefully considered" Supreme Court decisions of modern times. The Court heard three hours of oral argument on 19 and 20 April 1961, three times more than it gives to most cases, and then held the case for another three hours of argument at the opening of the 1961 term. And as Justice Clark commented, Baker was considered "over and over again by us in Conference and individually" (p. 258).

The Court announced its decision on 26 March 1962 in five opinions taking up 163 pages. The opinions were unusually sharp toned for their day. Justice Clark, for example, characterized Justice Felix *Frankfurter's 64-page dissent as "bursting with words that go through so much and conclude with so little."

Justice William *Brennan, speaking for the Court, carefully avoided explicit discussion of the merits of the case. There was little doubt that the majority felt that Tennessee had acted unconstitutionally, but it limited its holding to questions of jurisdiction, standing, and justiciability. Justice Brennan distinguished between the two grounds relied upon by the district court—jurisdiction and nonjusticiability—pointing out that in instances of nonjusticiability, consideration of the cause is not wholly and immediately foreclosed; rather, the Court's inquiry necessarily proceeds to the point of deciding whether the duty asserted can be judicially identified and its breach judicially determined, and whether protection for the right can be judicially molded. Where jurisdiction is lacking, however, the case goes no further.

Justice Brennan quickly concluded that the subject matter was within the jurisdiction of federal courts, and that the plaintiffs had a sufficient interest in the weight of their votes to have standing. More difficult to decide was whether the question presented was justiciable. In revisiting the doctrine of political questions, first announced by Chief Justice Roger B. *Taney in *Luther v. Borden (1849), Justice Brennan asserted that political questions chiefly relate to *separation of powers issues (which raise questions about relations among coequal branches of the national government) and thus call for judicial deference. In contrast, *federalism questions (which raise issues about the consistency of a state's action with the federal Constitution) do not call for such judicial deference. "Prominent on the surface of any case held to involve a political question," he wrote, "is found a textually demonstrable constitutional commitment of the issue to a coordinate political department; or a lack of judicially discoverable and manageable standards for resolving it; or the impossibility of deciding without an initial policy determination of a kind clearly for nonjudicial discretion; or the

impossibility of a court's undertaking independent resolution without expressing lack of respect due coordinate branches of government; or
an unusual need for unquestioning adherence to
a political decision already made; or the potentiality of embarrassment from multifarious pronouncements by various departments on one
question" (p. 217). He also distinguished between questions such as those presented by
*Luther* v. *Borden*, arising under the *Guarantee
Clause of Article IV, where "judicially manageable standards are lacking," and those arising
under the *Equal Protection Clause, where standards are "well developed and familiar" (p. 226).

Perhaps the most difficult obstacle for the
majority was the one precedent of *Colegrove* v.
*Green* (1946). In *Colegrove* the Court had refused to
force the Illinois legislature to correct the inequities in the state's congressional apportionment
that had given Illinois both the largest and
smallest congressional districts in the United
States, one nine times the size of the other.
Colegrove was a 3 to 3 to 1 decision (Justice
Robert *Jackson had been absent as the U.S.
prosecutor at the Nuremberg War Crimes Tribunal, and no one had as yet been appointed to
replace the recently deceased Chief Justice Harlan F. *Stone). Justice Frankfurter, speaking for
the Court, but with the concurrence of only two
other justices, coined the phrase *political
thicket, which has come to be the recognized
shorthand warning against federal courts intervening in political questions where they allegedly
have neither commission nor competence to
decide. Justice Brennan, however, dismissed Justice Frankfurter's opinion as "the minority opinion," arguing that four of the seven sitting judges
in *Colegrove* had found no constitutional obstacles
to federal courts reviewing the constitutionality
of legislative apportionments.

Although in *Baker* the Court limited its holding
to jurisdictional matters, it did not restrict its
holding to situations such as in Tennessee where
the legislature had failed to comply with its own
constitution. Justice Brennan made it clear that
any legislature that failed to reapportion its
districts in such a fashion as to reflect in some
way population equality was in jeopardy of
violating the Equal Protection Clause. His opinion thus called into question the constitutionality
of legislative apportionment in practically every
state in the Union. "We conclude," wrote Justice
Brennan, "that the complainant's allegations of
denial of equal protection present a justiciable
constitutional cause of action upon which appellants are entitled to a trial and a decision" (p. 237).

Justices William O. *Douglas, Tom Clark, and
Potter *Stewart, while joining the opinion of the
Court, wrote separate *concurrences. To Justice
Douglas the issues were uncomplicated: it was a
voting rights case and voting rights have long
been within the protection of federal courts.
Justice Clark took issue with Justice Harlan's

dissenting opinion, which contended that the
Court's decision would mean that the Equal
Protection Clause required "mathematical equality among voters." (In this, Justice Clark was a
poor prophet, for that is what before too long
became the controlling standard.) Rather, Justice
Clark concluded that all that had to be decided
was that Tennessee's apportionment is a "crazy
quilt without rational basis" (p. 254). Unless the
federal courts provided relief, he claimed, there
could be no remedy for what he believed to be a
patent violation of the Equal Protection Clause.

Justice Stewart wrote to emphasize that the
Court had only decided three things and no
more: that federal courts possessed jurisdiction
of the subject matter, that the appellants had
standing to challenge the Tennessee apportionment statutes, and that reapportionment was a
justiciable issue.

Justice Frankfurter, in the last opinion he
would write before retiring from the Court, was
obviously distressed by the short shrift given to
his *Colegrove* opinion and by what he alleged to be
the Court's "massive repudiation of the experience of our whole past in asserting destructively
novel judicial power demands" (p. 251). He
reiterated his *Colegrove* view that the federal
courts should not intervene in the "essentially
political conflict of forces by which the relation
between population and representation has time
out of mind been and now is determined" (p.
267). He predicted that the injection of the courts
into this clash of political forces in political
settlements could undermine their authority. As
in *Colegrove*, Frankfurter told those aggrieved by
the Tennessee legislature that the remedy "must
come through an aroused popular conscience
that sears the conscience of the people's representatives" (p. 270). The Court, he contended, was
being asked to "choose among competing bases
of representation—ultimately, really, among competing theories of political philosophy" (p. 300)
and that was not an appropriate issue for judges.
He pointed out that representation according to
population is not, in our history or Constitution,
enshrined as the only standard or the standard by
reference to which the reasonableness of apportionment plans may be judged.

Justice John M. *Harlan, in his dissenting
opinion, went to the merits. He contended that
even if federal courts had jurisdiction—which he
did not think to be the case—there is no federal
constitutional requirement that state legislatures
must be structured so as to reflect equally the
voice of every voter. There is nothing in the
federal Constitution, said Justice Harlan, to prevent Tennessee, if it so wishes, from giving rural
voters more electoral weight than urban ones.
Moreover, he warned that "the majority has
wholly failed to reckon with what the future may
hold in store" when federal courts try to determine what is and what is not a constitutional
apportioning policy (p. 339).

In an extended appendix, Justice Harlan set out to prove the inadequacy of arithmetical formulas as measures of the "irrational rationality" of Tennessee's apportionment. The disparity in electoral strength among the various counties in Tennessee, he argued, may be accounted for by various economic, political, and geographic considerations. It is a constitutionally permissible decision to preserve the electoral strength of the rural interests, notwithstanding shifts in population.

It did not take long for other states to go through the door opened by *Baker* v. *Carr.* In one year, thirty-six states had become involved in reapportionment lawsuits. During the next several years the Court rounded out the reapportionment revolution. Justices Harlan and Frankfurter proved to be inaccurate prophets about the difficulties that the courts would have in finding appropriate judicial standards. The judges quickly retreated from the "rationality test"—that apportionment plans were to be evaluated in terms of whether or not they had any rational basis—to what many think to be a simplistic but nonetheless more manageable standard of mathematical strict equality—*one person, one vote. Within a short time the Court had concluded that no factors—not geographical districts, nor a desire to keep governmental units intact, nor a federal compromise in which one chamber would represent population and the other governmental units such as counties—but strictly equal population districts would pass constitutional muster. The Court, in a series of cases, moved from a requirement of "substantial equality among districts" to "precise mathematical equality" to a distinction between congressional districts where strict equality is required, and state legislative districts where some tolerance is allowed to permit consideration of other appropriate factors.

(See also FAIR REPRESENTATION; JUSTICIABILITY; POLITICAL QUESTIONS; REAPPORTIONMENT CASES.)

□ Jack W. Peltason, *Federal Courts in the Political Process* (1955). Jack W. Peltason, *Fifty-Eight Lonely Men: Southern Federal Judges and School Desegregation* (1971). Jack W. Peltason, *Understanding the Constitution,* 12th ed. (1991).
J. W. Peltason

**Bakke Decision.** See REGENTS OF THE UNIVERSITY OF CALIFORNIA V. BAKKE.

**Baldwin, Henry** (b. New Haven, Conn., 14 Jan. 1780; d. Philadelphia, Pa. 21 Apr. 1844; interred Greendale Cemetery, Meadville, Pa.), associate justice, 1830–1844. Born of aristocratic stock, Baldwin received an LL.D. degree from Yale University in 1797. Thereafter, he studied in Philadelphia with Alexander J. *Dallas. Having gained admission to the bar, Baldwin set out for Ohio, but he settled in Pittsburgh, where he quickly gained social and political prominence. Throughout western Pennsylvania he became

*Henry Baldwin*

known for his intelligence, indefatigability, and ribald sense of humor.

After the death of his first wife, he married Sally Ellicott, and they established a second home in Crawford County, Pennsylvania, from which he was elected to the U.S. House of Representatives in 1816. Reared as a Federalist, Baldwin was often at odds with rural Jeffersonian Republican party regulars. Ill health forced Baldwin's resignation in 1822, but six years later, he energetically supported Andrew *Jackson's presidential candidacy.

With the death of Justice Bushrod *Washington in 1829, Jackson nominated Baldwin to the Supreme Court, passing over Pennsylvania Chief Justice John Bannister Gibson and Horace Binney of Philadelphia. Baldwin was confirmed with only two dissenting votes.

Baldwin's views on major constitutional issues were generally consistent over his fourteen-year tenure. He supported unobstructed interstate commerce, sought to preserve states' rights, and regarded slaves as private property. When federal power was pitted against state sovereignty, Baldwin argued against expansion of the former. The vehemence of this position first appeared in a dissent in *Ex parte Crane* (1831), in which he objected to the extension of federal court jurisdiction to issue writs of *mandamus.

In constitutional interpretation, Baldwin was a moderate, eschewing the extremes of autonomous *state sovereignty and expanded federal supremacy. Baldwin in 1837 published an extended pamphlet, *A General View of the Origin and*

*Nature of the Constitution and Government of the United States . . .* , in which he presented a "full explanation of what may be deemed my peculiar views of the constitution" (p. 1). He placed himself in a middle category between the extremes, writing that he belonged among those "willing to take the Constitution . . . as it is, and to expound it by the accepted rules of interpretation" (p. 37). He believed that by exercising political sensitivity the Supreme Court could arbitrate disputes over which powers belonged to the federal government and which to the states. Baldwin's key votes between 1830 and 1844 reveal him as a moderate, pro-Northern justice in cases dealing with the role of corporations, federal-state relations, and slavery.

Baldwin's abrasive individualism ran counter to and helped to break down the consensual nature of the Marshall Court. In 1831, for example, he dissented seven times, violating a longstanding norm of Court unanimity. Sociable and well liked early in his career, Baldwin grew increasingly eccentric and, on occasion, violent. He may have suffered from an obsessive-compulsive syndrome, exacerbated in his final years by financial problems. He died, penniless, of paralysis in 1844.           Robert G. Seddig

**Ballard v. United States,** 329 U.S. 187 (1946), argued 5 Oct. 1946, decided 9 Dec. 1946 by vote of 5 to 4; Douglas for the Court, Jackson concurring in the result; Frankfurter, Vinson, Jackson, and Burton in dissent. Edna W. Ballard appealed her conviction for fraudulent use of the mails by challenging the practice of the federal courts in California of systematically excluding women from juries. The charges stemmed from her leadership of the "I Am" movement, whose teachings included the claims that she, her son, and her husband were spiritually in touch with Saint Germain and that the Ballards had performed hundreds of miracle cures.

Federal law then required that federal court juries had to have the same qualifications as those of the highest state court of law. California law did make women eligible for jury duty, but as a matter of systematic state practice, the California state courts did not summon women to serve. Federal courts in California followed the state practice.

The Supreme Court reversed Ballard's conviction, reasoning that the totality of federal statutes on the subject of juries reflected a design to make them fair cross sections of the community and truly representative of it. Since California law made women eligible jurors, they were part of the "community" from which federal juries must draw a cross section. All-male federal juries in such states were inconsistent with the congressional scheme. Although the case technically turned on how best to interpret the statutory mandate of Congress, the reasoning about the desirability of having a fair cross section of the

community for jury service was later used in *Taylor* v. *Louisiana* (1975) to explain the meaning of the *Sixth Amendment phrase *"trial by jury." (See also GENDER.)

Leslie Friedman Goldstein

**Ballew v. Georgia,** 435 U.S. 223 (1978), argued 1 Nov. 1977, decided 21 Mar. 1978 by vote of 9 to 0; Blackmun for the Court, Stevens, White, and Powell concurring. Pursuant to state law, Ballew was tried and convicted of a misdemeanor by a jury of five persons. He had filed a pretrial motion to impanel a jury (or at least six), arguing that a five-person jury would deprive him of his *Sixth and *Fourteenth Amendment rights to trial by jury. Ballew was sentenced to one year imprisonment and a fine of two thousand dollars. The Georgia courts rejected Ballew's appeal but the Supreme Court ruled in his favor.

*Ballew* is the Court's most recent ruling on the proper size of state criminal juries. The Anglo-American trial jury for centuries had been a body of twelve, deciding unanimously. However, *Williams* v. *Florida* (1970) had caused considerable uncertainty regarding this matter. *Williams* held that a state criminal jury of six was permissible but did not indicate what the smallest constitutionally adequate jury might be. *Colegrove* v. *Battin* (1973) increased the uncertainty by authorizing six-person federal civil juries. And the Court compounded the problem by approving nonunanimous majority verdicts for state criminal juries in *Johnson* v. *Louisiana* (1972) and *Apodaca* v. *Oregon* (1972). *Ballew* answered this question by establishing six as the minimum.

Justice *Blackmun's opinion reviewed the many empirical studies, inspired by *Williams,* on the effects of six-person juries and then held that a criminal jury of five was unable to fulfill the constitutional purposes and functions of a jury. While this holding was consistent with the evidence, it did not fairly regard it. Though Justice Blackmun declared that the studies cited had raised "significant questions about the wisdom and constitutionality of a reduction below six" (p. 232), none, in fact, was an investigation of five-person juries. Rather, what these studies had shown was that six- and twelve-person juries were not functionally equivalent. The functional equivalence of six- and twelve-person juries was the foundation and chief claim of *Williams*. If the Court had truly relied on them, it would have been obligated to overturn *Williams* instead of reaffirming it.

As a result of *Ballew* and the other cases herein cited, juries with as few as six members may now be employed in federal civil cases and in both civil and criminal cases in state courts.

(See also TRIAL BY JURY.)

Peter W. Sperlich

**Bank of Augusta v. Earle,** 38 U.S. 519 (1839), argued 30 Jan.–1 Feb. 1839, decided 9 Mar. 1839 by vote of 8 to 1; Taney for the Court, Baldwin concurring, McKinley in dissent. This case marked the first time the Supreme Court ruled on the powers of a state over a *corporation chartered in another state. Three banks chartered outside of Alabama bought bills of exchange in that state and sued the makers of the bills when the makers refused to pay the bills on the grounds that foreign banks were not authorized to do business in Alabama.

The banks argued that a foreign corporation had a constitutional right to do business in any state and that an adverse ruling would invalidate millions of dollars of financial transactions, causing the current depression to worsen. The makers of the bills contended that a state could exclude a foreign corporation from doing business within its boundaries and that Alabama had done so.

The Supreme Court adopted a middle ground, holding that a state could exclude a foreign corporation from doing business or could impose reasonable conditions on that business, but that the exclusion or conditions must be clearly stated. Since Alabama had not expressly prohibited foreign banks from dealing in bills of exchange, the Court ruled for the banks and thereby avoided the financial disorder that had been predicated for a contrary holding. The principles of the case continue to be good law, although the Supreme Court has ruled that a state may not, through its regulation of foreign corporations, impose an undue burden on interstate commerce.

(See also CAPITALISM; PRIVATE CORPORATION CHARTERS.)

Robert M. Ireland

**Bank of the United States v. Deveaux,** 5 Cranch (9 U.S.) 61 (1809), argued 10–11 Feb. 1809, decided 15 Mar. 1809 by vote of 6 to 0; Marshall for the Court, Livingston not participating. The Constitution gives federal courts jurisdiction over cases between citizens of different states (this is known as *diversity jurisdiction). Deveaux involved the issue of whether a corporation can sue or be sued in a federal court under diversity jurisdiction and, if so, how the citizenship of the corporation is to be determined for diversity purposes. The Bank of the United States sued Deveaux, a Georgia tax collector, in federal court to recover property he had seized when the bank refused to pay a Georgia tax. Deveaux argued that the federal court had no jurisdiction because the bank as a corporation was not a citizen for purposes of diversity of *citizenship jurisdiction and, in the alternative, that if the bank was a citizen, there was no diversity since some of its shareholders resided in Georgia. The Court held that a corporation was a "citizen" for purposes of diversity jurisdiction but that there was no diversity in this case because the citizenship of the corporation was to be determined by

the citizenship of its shareholders, some of whom resided in the same state as the defendant. Later, Marshall and other members of the Court reportedly expressed regret over the decision because it severely limited the right of corporations to sue or be sued in federal court and thereby diminished federal judicial power. But *Deveaux* remained valid until it was overruled in *Louisville Railroad Co.* v. *Letson* (1844), which held that the citizenship of a corporation for diversity purposes was that of the state that chartered it.

(See also JUDICIAL POWER AND JURISDICTION; LOWER FEDERAL COURTS.)

Robert M. Ireland

**Bankruptcy and Insolvency Legislation.** When the framers of the Constitution provided in Article I, section 8, that Congress be empowered to established "uniform Laws on the subject of Bankruptcies throughout the United States," they sought to promote a national economy based on interregional and international trade in agricultural products and manufactured goods. A national bankruptcy law was essential to that goal. Although some states, mainly in the North, had insolvency and bankruptcy systems of their own, the Constitution implied that Congress had exclusive jurisdiction in that field. Confirmation of that view can be found in section 10 of Article I, which prohibits state laws impairing the obligation of contracts, the essential feature of any bankruptcy law.

*Early Bankruptcy Law.* The first national bankruptcy law did not come until 1800. Unpopular with the Jeffersonians and restricted in its coverage, it was shortly repealed. The same fate befell the bankruptcy laws of 1841 and 1867, leaving the way open for the states to retain or to create their own insolvency and bankruptcy systems.

But could such laws be constitutional? It took the Court almost forty years to give the states definitive guidelines to follow. Three issues had to be resolved. Did the Constitution give Congress exclusive authority in the bankruptcy field? If not, could state laws discharge debts, thereby impairing the obligation of contracts? And could such discharges, if constitutional, apply to debts contracted in another state?

These questions did not reach the Court until 1819, suggesting that lenders and borrowers alike generally had no quarrel with state relief laws, seeing them as mutually beneficial and in the public interest. In *Sturges* v. *Crowninshield,* Chief Justice John *Marshall spoke for the Court, striking down New York's insolvency law of 1811. Absent a national bankruptcy law, the states could create their own systems, but they could not discharge debt contracts. The next day the Court also struck down a Louisiana relief law in *McMillan* v. *McNeill,* a case involving a debt contracted in South Carolina. Taken together, these two rulings left state authority confused and uncertain. Did the Court intend to confer bankruptcy powers on the states but deny them the essential power of discharge? Or did it intend to restrict discharges to contracts entered into after the passage of the law (one of the issues in the *Sturges* case) and to contracts between parties within the state (the central issue in *McMillan*)?

The Court finally clarified state authority in *Ogden v. Saunders* (1827) by allowing the states to create their own bankruptcy systems in the absence of a national law. Discharges could be granted only to loans made after the passage of the statute, making the possibility of bankruptcy relief an implied feature of the debt contract. Interstate debts could not be discharged.

This clarification of state authority did not produce a flood of bankruptcy legislation. For example, Massachusetts did not begin discharging debts until 1838. Rhode Island, which had created a bankruptcy system by petition and private bill in 1756, abandoned that process following the *Sturges* decision in 1819 and did not reenter the bankruptcy field until 1896.

There are four principal explanations for the reluctance of the states to enact full relief laws. First, legislators worried that a bankruptcy law would discourage lending, encourage recklessness and fraud, and reduce business morality. Second, despite the *Ogden* decision, many continued to argue that state bankruptcy laws were unconstitutional and favored the enactment of a national law. Third, policy makers found it extremely difficult to frame a law acceptable to borrowers and lenders alike, one that would be easy to apply and that would not be open to fraud and chicanery. They also wanted a law that would return to the creditors as much as possible. Experience had shown that receivers and attorneys often gutted the insolvent's estate, leaving almost nothing for distribution to lenders. Fourth, some states evaded the constitutional issue by enacting stay and other relief laws during financial panics, as in 1819, 1837, and 1857, realizing that they would be thrown out by the courts, but knowing that debtors and creditors would in the meantime enjoy a breathing space in which to put their affairs in order.

**The 1898 System.** By the end of *Reconstruction and with the experience of the disastrous bankruptcy law of 1867 behind them, leading politicians, lawyers, judges, and businessmen came to a consensus that a workable and permanent national relief system was urgently required. That did not happen until 1898, primarily because of the difficulties in drafting legislation acceptable to such a broad spectrum of interests. The law that finally emerged reflected a series of compromises on virtually every point of substance and procedure and was, as a consequence, seriously flawed. It survived into the 1970s primarily because no political agreement could be reached on fundamental reform. Essentially, the law gave both debtors and creditors the right to initiate bankruptcy proceedings; it denied bankruptcy relief to fraudulent insolvents; and it allowed the states to protect certain assets from attachment.

There were three principal difficulties with the 1898 system. Although the Supreme Court issued rules for the guidance of the courts, jurisdiction lay in the district courts, which, in effect, delegated authority to separate bankruptcy courts. These inadequately staffed courts suffered from enormous caseloads and officers unqualified to deal with so complex a field of law (see LOWER FEDERAL COURTS). Second, district judges, by the nature of their functions, were generalists and had neither the time nor the skills to provide close supervision. Third, the referees in bankruptcy, later called judges, were unsalaried, being paid instead by fees for service, which raised questions about their impartiality. Also troublesome was the combination, in such judges, of both administrative and judicial functions. Finally, appeals from their rulings lay with the very district judges who had appointed them. The system worked, but to the complete satisfaction of few.

**Bankruptcy Reform.** Congress corrected some of these defects by statute and a sympathetic Supreme Court by repeated changes in the rules of procedure, but it became increasingly clear that the whole system needed overhauling. What may have suited business needs in 1898 was totally outmoded by the 1960s. The public also became alarmed at the magnitude of some corporate failures, such as the Penn Central collapse in 1970, and at the prospect of widespread municipal bankruptcies, as New York City's financial crisis of the 1970s demonstrated. An extended period of public debate culminated in the Bankruptcy Reform Act of 1978, which established the Bankruptcy Court as a separate judicial entity charged with the administration of the new law.

The underlying thrust of the new system reveals how far public policy has shifted from the punitive principles of the eighteenth century to the rehabilitative ones of the late twentieth. There are many instances in which insolvent individuals are in such desperate plight that they need to be discharged from all their past debts, and insolvent corporations so bereft of assets that they need to be closed down. Nonetheless, the main business of the bankruptcy courts is providing individuals with a breathing space in which to get their affairs in order and failing corporations with reorganization so that they can work their way back to solvency.

Several additional observations can be made. First, the new bankruptcy code has been used by some corporations, most notably Texas Air Corporation, to rescind labor contracts. Second, the uniformity requirement in the bankruptcy clause of the Constitution has caused some difficulty. In *Railway Labor Executives Association* v. *Gibbons* (1982), the Court ruled that statutes protecting the rights of employees could not deal with the problems of a single railroad. Uniformity might not be required in the case of geographically isolated railroads because of the problems presented, but the Rock Island liquidation had to be incorporated in uniform legislation dealing with comparable major railroad bankruptcies if it were to meet the constitutional test.

Third, as highly technical as bankruptcy law may have become in the twentieth century, judges have nevertheless been forced by the breadth and complexity of the issues presented to become generalists. They deal, for example, with questions as diverse as Fifth Amendment rights, international law, the rules of evidence, and innovative financial instruments.

Fourth, for this reason much of the debate over the bankruptcy bill focused on the quality of judicial appointments. Should judges have lifetime tenure "during good behavior" or should they be appointed by and serve at the pleasure of district or appeals court judges? Congress voted for a compromise between these extremes—presidential appointments for fourteen-year terms. The Supreme Court struck down that provision in *Northern Pipeline* v. *Marathon Pipe Line* (1982), declaring that the judge's tenure violated the provisions of *Article III, section 1, of the Constitution.

Congress responded with difficulty, finding agreement impossible until 1984. Amendments then made bankruptcy judges once more adjuncts to the district courts, serving without limited tenure. Congress also restricted the use of bankruptcy proceedings to modify labor contracts and imposed some limitations on the rights of individuals to bankruptcy relief.

Finally, the Court has accepted the proposition, in *Granfinanciera, S. A.* v. *Nordberg* (1989), that parties accused of fraud in bankruptcy proceedings are entitled, in accordance with the *Seventh Amendment, to a *jury trial, but it has not decided whether bankruptcy courts can hold such trials.

(See also CAPITALISM; CONTRACTS CLAUSE.)

□ Peter J. Coleman, *Debtors and Creditors in America: Insolvency, Imprisonment for Debt, and Bankruptcy, 1707–1900* (1974). Martin A. Frey, Warren L. McConnico, and Phyllis Hurley Frey, *An Introduction to Bankruptcy Law* (1990). Charles Warren, *Bankruptcy in United States History* (1935).                Peter J. Coleman

**Bar Admission.** See ADMISSION TO PRACTICE BEFORE THE BAR OF THE COURT.

**Bar Advertising.** In *Bates* v. *State Bar of Arizona* (1977), the Supreme Court decided that lawyer advertising was commercial speech protected by the *First Amendment. States cannot prohibit all lawyer advertising, but the Court left open the boundaries of permissible regulation for case-by-case development. Regulators of lawyers have tried to retain maximum control, while entrepreneurial lawyers have continued to challenge

these efforts. This has provoked many Supreme Court decisions. States may prohibit clearly misleading advertising but not potentially misleading techniques when the information could be presented accurately. States may ban in-person solicitation but not personal letters to potential clients. States may not ban newspaper advertisements giving legal advice, but they may require that advertising of contingent-fee services disclose that clients must pay the costs of unsuccessful lawsuits. Lawyers may assert on letterheads that they are certified by the National Board of Trial Advocacy, a private group.

Despite rhetoric and advocacy in the guise of social science, the impact of lawyer advertising is unclear. Proponents such as the Federal Trade Commission assert that advertising lowers prices, promotes efficiency, and increases access to justice. However, bar association leaders argue that lawyers, who are forced to offer services at advertised prices, will cut the quality of their work. The major Federal Trade Commission study of lawyer advertising rests on a questionable sample and ignores all indications in its own data that advertising regulation has little impact on lowering fees.

A few lawyers have used expensive television ads, but these lawyers had to pay to reach many viewers who had no need for legal services. Most lawyers have advertised in less costly telephone-directory Yellow Pages. Many lawyers advertise a free initial consultation, and this may attract clients who fear high fees. Few lawyers unqualifiedly advertise particular services for specified fees. Without such specific advertising, prices are unlikely to drop. Moreover, potential clients may be skeptical of cut-rate lawyering. Debate about lawyer advertising may divert attention from ways of avoiding or solving problems without lawyers. Many routine services sometimes advertised at low prices could be performed by paralegal workers, other professionals, or client self-help.

(See also COMMERCIAL SPEECH.)

                Stewart Macaulay

**Barber Shop.** Located on the ground floor of the Supreme Court building, the barber shop contains a single black-and-white barber's chair and related hair-cutting equipment. The Court employs one barber. Male Court employees can obtain a haircut there, but the shop is not open to the public.                Francis Helminski

**Barbour, Philip Pendleton** (b. Orange County, Va., 25 May 1783; d. Washington, D.C., 25 Feb. 1841; interred Frascati, Orange County), associate justice, 1836–1841. The son of a politically active Virginia planter, Thomas Barbour, and the socially well-connected Mary Pendleton Thomas, Barbour enjoyed a prominent political and judicial career by adhering to strict construction of the Constitution, states' rights, and southern particularism. (See STATE SOVEREIGNTY AND STATES' RIGHTS.)

Barbour was locally educated and apprenticed to a Virginia lawyer. After less than a year as a law clerk, Barbour embarked in 1800 on a legal career in Kentucky. He returned to Virginia in 1801 and attended the College of William and Mary before beginning to practice law in Orange County. Noted for his intelligence, family connections, and a fluid, powerful oratorical style, Barbour flourished in the county and state courts. In 1804 he married Frances Johnson, a local planter's daughter.

Inspired by the political careers of his father and older brother James, Barbour in 1812 successfully sought a seat in the Virginia House of Delegates. The Barbour brothers, both states' rights Republicans, bounded upon the national stage in 1814, when James was elected to the U.S. Senate and Philip won a seat in the House of Representatives.

Barbour was a bulwark for the strict constructionist Democrats throughout his eight terms in Congress (1814–1825 and 1827–1830). His staunch defense of Andrew *Jackson in 1819 and his efforts in 1827 to strip the Bank of the United States of every vestige of government agency earned him the confirmed support of President Jackson and an 1830 appointment to the District Court for Eastern Virginia. He endangered his relationship with Jackson by opposing Martin Van Buren for the 1832 vice-presidential nomination but then rescued his career and probably guaranteed his nomination to the U.S. Supreme Court by withdrawing as the southern rights candidate in favor of Van Buren, the regular party nominee.

Barbour's nomination to the Supreme Court had been feared by constitutional nationalists since Jackson's first term, but their attention was diverted in 1836 by the simultaneous nomination of Roger *Taney as chief justice. The March 1836 confirmation of Barbour, "the pride of the Democracy of Virginia" (Thomas Ritchie, Richmond Enquirer, 24 March 1836), was welcomed by Democrats, who were eagerly awaiting a philosophically narrow Court. National Republicans and Whigs, however, were shocked at Barbour's appointment.

During his short tenure on the Supreme Court, Barbour strongly supported state sovereignty and the extension of state legislative powers in critical cases such as *New York v. Miln (1837), *Charles River Bridge v. Warren Bridge (1837), *Briscoe v. Bank of Kentucky (1837), and *Holmes v. Jennison (1840).

Barbour wrote a dozen opinions, but his only important majority opinion was New York v. Miln. This case presented the Court with a clear choice between the application of a state's *police powers, the federal government's power to regulate commerce, and individuals' rights to pursue their own pecuniary interests. (See FEDERALISM.) In

*Philip Pendleton Barbour*

the Miln decision, Barbour wrote, "That a state has the same undeniable and unlimited jurisdiction over all persons and things, within its territorial limits as any foreign nation; where that jurisdiction is not surrendered or restrained by the constitution of the United States. That, by virtue of this, it is not only the right, but the bourden and solemn duty of a state, to advance the safety, happiness and prosperity of its people, and to provide for the general welfare, by any and every act of legislation, which it may deem to be conducive to these ends" (p. 139).

In a notable concurring opinion in Holmes v. Jennison, Barbour extended his argument that the relations of states to foreign countries are not defined by the constitution and added that in the absence of legislation the state governor has absolute authority.

Daniel *Webster, no friend of Barbour's judicial and political philosophies, presented a reasonable and balanced view of the judge in an 1837 letter: "Barbour, I really think is honest & conscientious; & he is certainly intelligent; but his fear, or hatred, of the powers of this government is so great, his devotion to State rights so absolute, that perhaps [a case] could hardly arise, in which he would be willing to exercise the power of declaring a state law void" (C. M. Wiltse et al, eds., The Papers of Daniel Webster, vol. 4, 1980, p. 192).

Barbour's sudden death on 25 February 1841 cut short a potentially influential tenure on the Court.

□ P. P. Cynn, "Philip Pendleton Barbour," in John P. Branch Historical Papers of Randolph-Macon College, vol. 4 (1913), pp. 67–77. Charles D. Lowery, James Barbour, A Jeffersonian Republican (1984).                     Gerard W. Gawalt

**Barenblatt v. United States,** 360 U.S. 109 (1959), argued 18 Nov. 1958, decided 8 June 1959 by vote of 5 to 4; Harlan for the Court, Black, joined by Warren and Douglas, in dissent, Brennan also dissenting. This decision signaled a retreat from *Watkins* v. *United States* (1957), which had placed limits on the ability of congressional committees to inquire into political beliefs and associations. *Watkins* and similar decisions provoked concerted efforts in Congress to curb the Court's authority, which, although unsuccessful, nevertheless persuaded a majority to be more circumspect for a time in protecting the rights of alleged subversives. *Barenblatt* upheld the conviction for contempt of Congress of a witness who had refused to testify before the House Committee on Un-American Activities about his beliefs and his membership in a communist club at the University of Michigan.

The Court dismissed Barenblatt's *First Amendment claim through a "balancing of interests" (see FIRST AMENDMENT BALANCING). It defined the government's interest as national self-preservation despite the fact that the only evidence concerning the club was that its members held abstract intellectual discussions. At the same time, it treated the First Amendment interest as essentially irrelevant. The Court also found that the House committee had made clear the pertinency of its questions, contrary to *Watkins,* where the Court held that pertinency had not been made clear, even though the committee's explanation had been essentially the same in both cases. Although *Barenblatt* has never been explicitly overruled, the Court has since displayed far less reluctance to reverse convictions of uncooperative witnesses before such committees on constitutional grounds.

(See also ASSEMBLY AND ASSOCIATION, FREEDOM OF; COMMUNISM AND COLD WAR; CONGRESSIONAL POWER OF INVESTIGATION.)

□ Dean Alfange, Jr., "Congressional Investigations and the Fickle Court," *University of Cincinnati Law Review* 30 (Spring 1961): 113–171. Dean Alfange, Jr.

**Barnes v. Glen Theatre, Inc.,** 111 S.Ct. 2456 (1991), argued 8 Jan. 1991, decided 21 June 1991 by vote of 5 to 4; Rehnquist for the Court, White, joined by Marshall, Blackmun, and Stevens, in dissent. In this case the Supreme Court upheld an Indiana statute that prohibited the knowing or intentional appearance in public in a condition of nudity; as applied in this case it required female dancers to wear "pasties" and a "G-string" when performing. Respondents were two South Bend establishments that provided totally nude dancing as entertainment. In *Schad v. Borough of Mount Ephraim* (1981), the Court had ruled that barroom-type nude dancing, which was expressive conduct, merited some *First Amendment protection. But the ordinance in *Schad* covered all live entertainment, making it both more content-

specific than Indiana's statute and overbroad by being applicable to other forms of protected expression. Indiana's statute prohibited all forms of public nudity, not simply live entertainment.

The Court treated Indiana's law as *"time, place, and manner" measure that regulated the incidental effects of speech. Such regulation is valid if it satisfies a four-part test developed in *United States* v. *O'Brien* (1968): if it is "within the constitutional power of the government; if it furthers an important or substantial governmental interest; if the governmental interest is unrelated to the suppression of free expression; and if the incidental restriction on alleged First Amendment freedoms is no greater than is essential to the furtherance of that interest" (pp. 376–377).

Justice William *Rehnquist concluded that the Indiana law met this test. Most importantly and controversially, he maintained that the measure was "unrelated to the suppression of free expression" because "the perceived evil that Indiana seeks to address is not erotic dancing, but public nudity" (pp. 2461, 2463). The breadth of Indiana's statute saved it in this regard.

Justice Byron *White's dissent was directed primarily to this key contention. Because the dancers' nudity is itself an important expressive component of their dance, "it cannot be said that the statutory prohibition is unrelated to expressive conduct" (p. 2474).

(See also SPEECH AND THE PRESS.)

Donald A. Downs

**Barron v. Baltimore,** 7 Pet. (32 U.S.) 243 (1833), argued 11 Feb. 1833, decided 16 Feb. 1833 by vote of 7 to 0; Marshall for the Court. A wharf owner sued the city of Baltimore for economic loss occasioned by the city's diversion of streams, which lowered the water level around his wharves. He claimed that the city took his property without *just compensation in violation of the *Fifth Amendment. This presented the question whether the Fifth Amendment restrained the states. After surveying the history of the *Bill of Rights, Chief Justice John *Marshall concluded that the first ten amendments restrained only the federal government, thus requiring Americans to look to state constitutions for protection of their civil and political liberties. The opinion marked a retreat from Marshall's earlier nationalism, one impelled by the changing composition of the Court and the growth of states' rights sentiment. The Court reaffirmed the holding of *Barron* in *Permoli* v. *New Orleans* (1845).

With the ratification of the *Fourteenth Amendment in 1868, the application of the Bill of Rights to the states again became an issue. In *Hurtado* v. *California* (1884), the Court held that the Fourteenth Amendment was a limit on state power. Not until the twentieth century incorporation cases, beginning with *Gitlow* v. *New York* (1925) did *Barron* lose its authoritative status. Today almost all of the guarantees of the Bill of Rights have been incorporated as restraints on the states.

(See also INCORPORATION DOCTRINE; STATE CONSTITUTIONS AND INDIVIDUAL RIGHTS; STATE SOVEREIGNTY AND STATES' RIGHTS.)

David J. Bodenhamer

**Bates v. State Bar of Arizona,** 433 U.S. 350 (1977), argued 18 Jan. 1977, decided 27 June 1977 by vote of 5 to 4; Blackmun for the Court; Burger, Powell, and Rehnquist in dissent. In *Bates* the Supreme Court struck down state legal ethics codes that prohibited lawyers from advertising. Two young lawyers, John Bates and Van O'Steen, sought to create a test case by placing a newspaper advertisement indicating that they offered "legal services at very reasonable fees" and listing some of the fees they charged. The Board of Governors of the State Bar recommended that the two lawyers be suspended. The Arizona Supreme Court upheld the decision but reduced the punishment to censure.

In the U.S. Supreme Court the attorneys attacked the Arizona rule on two grounds: that it violated the *Sherman Antitrust Act by creating a restraint of trade, and that it violated the *First Amendment by restraining the right of free speech. The Supreme Court rejected the *antitrust claim, but held that their First Amendment rights of speech, together with the right of the public consumers of legal services to receive their message, outweighed any adverse effects on professionalism that advertising might have (see COMMERCIAL SPEECH). The Court subsequently limited the First Amendment right in *Ohralik* v. *Ohio State Bar Association* (1978), where it sanctioned a policy of totally barring in-person solicitation of clients.

*Bates* opened up the practice of law to greater competition and made possible the growth of legal clinics that provide routine legal needs of the middle and lower middle class. One empirical study in Arizona found that, after *Bates*, the average cost of these legal services declined. The case, along with *Goldfarb* v. *Virginia State Bar* (1975), which prohibited bar-sponsored fee schedules, signaled the end to total self-regulation of the bar, which the leadership of the American legal profession has decried.

(See also BAR ADVERTISING.)

Rayman L. Solomon

**Batson v. Kentucky,** 476 U.S. 79 (1986), argued 12 Dec. 1985, decided 30 Apr. 1986 by vote of 7 to 2; Powell for the Court, White, Marshall, O'Connor, and Stevens (with Brennan) concurring, Burger and Rehnquist in dissent. Batson, a black man, was tried for second-degree burglary and the receipt of stolen goods. The judge conducted the voir dire examination of the potential jurors, excused some of them for cause, and then permitted prosecution and defense to exercise their peremptory challenges—six and nine re-

spectively. The prosecutor's exercise of the peremptories removed all four black persons on the panel. Batson moved for a discharge of the jury, asserting that the removal of all of the black panelists violated his *Sixth and *Fourteenth Amendment rights to a jury drawn from a cross section of the community as well as his Fourteenth Amendment right to the *equal protection of the laws. The trial judge denied the motion and Batson was convicted on both counts. The Supreme Court of Kentucky denied Batson's appeal and affirmed the verdict. The U.S. Supreme Court reversed.

Ruling in favor of Batson, the Court placed substantial limits on the prosecutor's use of peremptory challenges. Overruling *Swain* v. *Alabama* (1965) in part, the Court applied the equal protection principle to the exercise of peremptory challenges. For all practical purposes, it thereby transformed peremptory challenges into challenges for cause, even if the holding refers to a lesser (but undefined) standard to sustain a disputed peremptory challenge than would be required to support a challenge for cause. The *Batson* Court's claim that it did not "undermine the contribution the [peremptory] challenge generally makes to the administrations of justice" (pp. 98–99) is entirely unconvincing.

The thrust of *Batson* is not toward color-blind but color-conscious law, applying a racial test to the prosecutor's use of peremptory challenges. The ultimate effect of *Batson* may even be the de facto introduction of racial quotas for trial juries since the racially disproportionate use of peremptories now may be attacked as constitutionally improper. Given the lack of standards for a successful rebuttal, the only safe use of peremptories will be racially proportionate to venire and/or community makeup.

The Court failed to distinguish between the selection of the jury venire (where *representativeness* is the chief concern) and the selection of the jury (where *impartiality* must be the primary consideration). The Court also failed to distinguish between general and particular jury fitness. A person's general fitness to be a juror (to be included in the venire) is, indeed, not a matter of race. A person's suitability to serve on a particular jury, however, may well be related to race. It is not difficult to imagine a crime that so offends a particular social group that it must be feared that all of its members lack the impartiality of the proper juror. When exercising peremptory challenges, attorneys must be able to act upon this fear. To hold otherwise is to forfeit at least the *appearance* of jury impartiality. Given that the *facts* of jury impartiality cannot be known with certainty, the appearance of impartiality becomes a matter of extraordinary importance. All this the Court did not recognize (p. 97).

The use of peremptory challenges typically brings into conflict the goals of jury impartiality and jury representativeness. Until *Batson*, this conflict was resolved in favor of impartiality, that is, the Court agreed that the essential nature of a peremptory challenge was found in its exercise without explanation, judicial inquiry, or control by the court. *Batson* overturned *Swain* but pretended otherwise by taking the position that jury selection can meet both goals. Only Justice Thurgood *Marshall freely admitted that he regarded representativeness as more important than impartiality, and that this reevaluation, in fact, pointed toward the abolition of the traditional peremptory challenge.

*Batson* was limited in three ways. It applied only to the prosecution, only to criminal trials, and only to challenges in which the excluded juror was of the same race as the defendant. In *Edmonson* v. *Leesville Concrete* (1991), however, the Court held that a private litigant in a civil case could not exclude prospective jurors because of their race. The majority concluded that there was sufficient interaction between a court and the jury selection process to satisfy the *"state action" requirement. While this decision did not explicitly also extend the *Batson* principle to either private defense lawyers or public defenders in criminal cases, the logic of *Edmonson* makes this result forseeable if not inevitable. In *Powers* v. *Ohio* (1991), the Court held that white defendants are entitled to new trials if convicted by juries from which blacks had been improperly excluded because of their race. Thus it now appears that *any* racial exclusion in jury selection is likely to be held constitutionally unacceptable. In addition, there appears to be a substantial chance that the Court will apply the extended *Batson* principles to gender-based exclusions from jury service.

(See also DUE PROCESS, SUBSTANTIVE; RACE AND RACISM; TRIAL BY JURY.)

Peter W. Sperlich

**Beard, Charles Austin** (b. near Knightstown, Ind., 27 Nov. 1874; d. New Haven, Conn., 1 Sept. 1948), constitutional historian and political scientist. The son of William Beard, a farmer and banker, Beard received his Ph.D. from Columbia University in 1904. He served on the faculties of history and public law at Columbia until 1917, when he resigned to protest the university's decision not to reappoint several faculty members critical of United States involvement in World War I.

Beard was the foremost Progressive historian of *judicial review and public law. In *The Supreme Court and the Constitution* (1912), he argued unequivocally that the delegates to the Philadelphia Convention had intended to clothe the justices with power to declare acts of Congress unconstitutional. Beard, like most Progressive writers on the Supreme Court, took his intellectual cues from *sociological jurisprudence, which treated the Constitution not as divine revelation but as a political testament. The justices who interpreted it were, according to Beard, subject to human emotions and failings. In 1913, Beard published his most famous work, *An Economic Interpretation of the Constitution,* in which he asserted that the framers of the Constitution were actuated more by a concern for property rights than by either principles of political science or concern for the public good. Although recent scholarship has criticized Beard's faulty methodology and economic determinism, his work continues to enjoy currency in universities and public schools.

(See also HISTORY, COURT USES OF.)

Kermit L. Hall

**Belle Terre v. Boraas,** 416 U.S. 1 (1974), argued 19–20 Feb. 1974, decided 1 Apr. 1974 by vote of 7 to 2; Douglas for the Court, Brennan and Marshall in dissent. Appellees owned a house in the small Long Island village of Belle Terre, New York. They leased it to six unrelated college students and were subsequently cited for violating a *zoning ordinance that limited occupancy in one-family dwellings to traditional family units or to groups of not more than two unrelated people. Excluded from the ordinance were lodging, boarding, fraternity, and multiple-dwelling houses.

The owners of the house plus three of the tenants brought suit challenging the ordinance. Among their claims was the contention that the ordinance violated their constitutional right of *privacy. The Court rejected that argument and upheld the ordinance, saying that it bore a rational relationship to a permissible state objective. "A quiet place where yards are wide, people few, and motor vehicles restricted are legitimate guidelines in a land-use project addressed to family needs," Justice William O. *Douglas wrote. "The *police power is not confined to elimination of filth, stench, and unhealthy places" (p. 9).

Justice Thurgood *Marshall dissented on the grounds that the ordinance unnecessarily burdened appellees' *First Amendment freedom of association and their constitutional right to privacy. Marshall argued that because of that infringement of fundamental rights, a mere rational basis test was not enough to sustain the ordinance. Rather, he argued that the ordinance could "withstand constitutional scrutiny only upon a clear showing that the burden imposed is necessary to protect a compelling and substantial governmental interest" (p. 18).

(See also ASSEMBLY AND ASSOCIATION, FREEDOM OF.)

John Anthony Maltese

**Benton v. Maryland,** 395 U.S. 784 (1969), argued 12 Dec. 1968, reargued 24 Mar. 1969, decided 23 June 1969 by vote of 7 to 2; Marshall for the Court, Harlan and Stewart in dissent. The issue in *Benton* was whether the Due Process Clause of the *Fourteenth Amendment prohibits a state from subjecting a person to *double jeopardy.

The Court had confronted that precise issue thirty years earlier in *Palko* v. *Connecticut* (1937), where it ruled that the double jeopardy standard of the *Fifth Amendment did not apply to the states. Rejecting the doctrine of incorporation, *Palko* applied the principle that the Fourteenth Amendment's Due Process Clause incorporates only those rights that are "implicit in the concept of ordered liberty" (p. 324).

In *Benton* the Court overruled *Palko* in part, holding that the double jeopardy prohibition applies to the states through the Fourteenth Amendment. Most significantly, the Court rejected the *Palko* notion that states can deny rights to criminal defendants so long as the denial is not shocking to a universal sense of justice. Instead, the Court ruled that states must extend those guarantees in the *Bill of Rights that are fundamental to the American scheme of justice.

With respect to the guarantee against double jeopardy, the Court observed that its origins can be traced to English *common law, which was adopted in our country's jurisprudence. Every state has some form of the prohibition in its constitution or common law. Accordingly, the guarantee against double jeopardy is clearly among those rights that are deeply ingrained in the American system and thus made applicable to the states through the Fourteenth Amendment.

(See also DUE PROCESS, PROCEDURAL; INCORPORATION DOCTRINE.)

Daan Braveman

**Berman v. Parker,** 348 U.S. 26 (1954), argued 19 Oct. 1954, decided 22 Nov. 1954 by vote of 9 to 0; Douglas for the Court. A Washington, D.C., urban renewal statute allowed the city to condemn land and sell it to private developers, who would redevelop it according to the renewal plan. The plan included not only slum eradication but also beautification projects. A landowner challenged the statute, mainly on the ground that, under the *Takings Clause of the *Fifth Amendment, the condemnation was not "for public use." The owner argued unsuccessfully that there was no public use because the land was to be sold to a private developer and for the purpose of beautification. The Supreme Court upheld the statute.

The decision is important in two ways. First, it established that aesthetics are a legitimate public purpose, for which government may regulate and condemn land. This principle has encouraged increased governmental intervention to achieve aesthetic and environmental goals. Second, *Berman* made clear that the phrase "public use" in the Takings Clause did not mean that land condemned had to remain in government ownership or be used physically by the public. The Court seemed to hold that *eminent domain might be used to advance any goal that government could pursue under any of its powers.

Subsequent decisions have confirmed this broad understanding of Berman. Thus, under the Takings Clause, "public use" means only public purpose.

(See also PROPERTY RIGHTS; PUBLIC USE DOCTRINE.)

William B. Stoebuck

**Betts v. Brady,** 316 U.S. 455 (1942), argued 13–14 Apr. 1942, decided 1 June 1942 by vote of 6 to 3; Roberts for the Court, Black in dissent. After indictment for robbery, Betts asked the trial court to appoint an attorney to assist in his defense. The trial judge refused; Betts represented himself and was convicted. While incarcerated, Betts filed *habeas corpus petitions. Lower courts rejected these petitions, and Betts filed a *certiorari petition with the U.S. Supreme Court.

At issue before the Court was Betts's claim that the trial court's refusal to extend the right to counsel to noncapital felonies constituted a violation of the *Sixth Amendment provision as incorporated by the *Fourteenth Amendment (see INCORPORATION DOCTRINE). In his opinion for the Court, Justice Owen J. *Roberts rejected Betts's claim, concluding that most states did not require appointment of counsel for fair trials and that the circumstances of his case did not suggest that such assistance was necessary. The Court distinguished Betts's situation from that of an earlier Court decision, *Powell v. Alabama (1932), where young African-American defendants were charged with a capital offense and where the Court concluded that appointed counsel was essential for a fair trial.

Justice Hugo *Black was joined in dissent by Justices William O. *Douglas and Frank *Murphy. Black emphasized that Betts's petition would have been granted had he been a defendant in federal criminal proceedings, that the petitioner was entitled to the procedural protection provided by the federal Constitution, and that the right to counsel was fundamental to criminal due process.

*Betts v. Brady* was ultimately overruled by *Gideon v. Wainwright (1963), where the minority position in Betts was unanimously adopted by the Court.

(See also COUNSEL, RIGHT TO; DUE PROCESS, PROCEDURAL.)

Susette M. Talarico

**Bible Reading in Public Schools.** See SCHOOL PRAYER AND BIBLE READING.

**Bickel, Alexander** (b. Bucharest, Romania, 17 Dec. 1924; d. New Haven, Conn., 7 Nov. 1974), scholar and law professor. Bickel arrived in the United States with his parents in 1938. He graduated Phi Beta Kappa from the City College of New York in 1947 and *summa cum laude* from Harvard Law School, where he had served as an editor of the *Harvard Law Review* in 1949. During the U.S.

Supreme Court's 1952 term, Bickel became clerk to Justice Felix *Frankfurter, who influenced Bickel's intellectual commitment to judicial restraint in constitutional law. He assisted Frankfurter in drafting a memorandum ordering that *Brown v. Board of Education (1954) be reargued to explore the historical intent of the framers of the Fourteenth Amendment with respect to school segregation and the character of judicial remedies available for it. The order also assured the splintered Court time to seek consensus. In August 1953 Bickel completed a study of the congressional debates on the Fourteenth Amendment, concluding that the framers left open the way for future congressional or judicial action to abolish school segregation. His memorandum laid the groundwork for the Court's conclusion in Brown that historical investigation could not ground its decision on school segregation.

From 1956 until his death, Bickel taught at Yale Law School, becoming Chancellor Kent Professor of Law and Legal History in 1966 and Sterling Professor of Law in 1974. In 1957 he edited The Unpublished Opinions of Mr. Justice Brandeis; these eleven *Brandeis draft opinions emphasize *judicial self-restraint, Bickel's own central constitutional tenet.

The theme of judicial restraint emerged more forcefully in Bickel's most influential book, The Least Dangerous Branch: The Supreme Court at the Bar of Politics (1963). Bickel denied that judicial action is either a mechanical interpretation of constitutional words or a willful assertion of judges' values. Instead he maintained that judicial action should be the principled process of enunciating and applying enduring values embodied in, but not sharply defined by, the Constitution. Bickel maintains that identifying those values requires both historical understanding and constitutional analysis. Judges should not affirm unprincipled legislative actions because that would confer constitutional legitimacy on those laws. Nor should they make principled decisions that cannot gain public support, for the courts lack power to enforce their decrees. Hence, judges must act on principle but may do so only when their decisions can gain acceptance. While awaiting public readiness for principled decisions, the Court must avoid constitutional adjudication by refusing to take cases, by employing jurisdictional doctrines to avoid decision, or by basing decisions on the vagueness of laws, statutory construction, or other grounds that are not constitutional barriers to subsequent legislative action.

None of Bickel's other six monographs had the influence of The Least Dangerous Branch. The Supreme Court and the Idea of Progress (1970) contains Bickel's rejection of the activism and doctrines of the Warren Court, which he accuses of promoting equality at the expense of other values also embedded in the Constitution and society. Bickel criticizes the activist justices' "belief that progress,

called history, would validate their course" (pp. 13]14), pointing out that "history has little tolerance for any of [the Court's] reasonable judgments that have turned out to be wrong" (p. 11). Bickel maintains that the Court's "noblest enterprise—school desegregation—and its most popular enterprise—reapportionment—not to speak of school prayer cases and those concerning aid to parochial schools, are headed toward obsolescence and in large measure abandonment" (p. 178).

Bickel's vision of judicial restraint was likewise evident in his representation of the New York Times in the so-called Pentagon Papers Case of 1971 (see *New York Times Co. v. United States). Bickel rejected the argument that *prior restraint of newspaper publication of classified government documents is always unconstitutional. Rather, he argued that the government had failed to rebut a heavy presumption against prior restraints and that such restraints should be grounded in congressional legislation rather than assertions either of inherent governmental power or executive responsibilities. Three of the six justices who rejected the government's claim for injunctive relief incorporated one or both of Bickel's arguments in their opinions.

Bickel was also an essayist, publishing more than a hundred articles in the New Republic, the New York Times, and other newspapers and magazines on constitutional issues and Supreme Court cases. His often distinctive views—for example, his defense of President *Nixon's order to dismiss Archibald Cox as Watergate special prosecutor—had a wide audience and were influential in shaping the opinion of the public as well as that of the legal profession.

(See also CONSTITUTIONAL INTERPRETATION; HISTORY, COURT USES OF; LEAST DANGEROUS BRANCH.)

□ John Moeller, "Alexander Bickel: Toward A Theory of Politics," Journal of Politics 47 (February 1985): 113–139.
David Adamany

**Bigelow v. Virginia,** 421 U.S. 809 (1975), argued 18 Dec. 1974, decided 16 June 1975 by vote of 7 to 2; Blackmun for the Court, Rehnquist, joined by White, in dissent. In February 1971 the Virginia Weekly of Charlottesville published an advertisement for the Women's Pavilion, a New York City for-profit organization that assisted women in obtaining *abortions. The Weekly's editor, Jeffrey C. Bigelow, was prosecuted for violating a Virginia statute that made it a misdemeanor to publish or "encourage or prompt the procuring of abortion." Bigelow argued that the statute was unconstitutionally overbroad and a violation of his free press rights under the *First Amendment. But the Virginia courts declared the statute a proper consumer protection measure, and, relying on U.S. Supreme Court precedent, held that Bigelow lacked standing to raise the overbreadth issue because the "commercial" nature of the advertisement rendered it unprotected by the First Amendment.

In 1942 the Supreme Court had held that *"commercial speech" was unprotected because it was more like an economic inducement than the exposition of ideas (*Valentine* v. *Chrestenson*). But the expansion of First Amendment freedoms in the intervening decades, and the fact that the Supreme Court had recently made abortion a constitutionally protected right (*Roe* v. *Wade*, 1973), compelled Justice Harry *Blackmun (the author of *Roe*) and the Court to reconsider the commercial speech doctrine. The Court thus ruled that the *Weekly's* advertisement merited First Amendment protection because it conveyed truthful information about a matter of significant public interest.

*Bigelow* set the stage for the Court's decision the next year formally to give some constitutional protection to commercial speech (*Virginia State Board of Pharmacy* v. *Virginia Citizens Consumer Council*, 1976). Today commercial speech is considered a "quasi-protected" category of expression.

(See also SPEECH AND THE PRESS.)

Donald A. Downs

**Bill of Rights.** The Bill of Rights is commonly viewed as consisting of the first ten articles of Amendments to the Constitution of the United States of America. There are still some, however, who regard only the first eight articles as the Bill of Rights, viewing the Ninth and Tenth as general statements depicting constitutional structural divisions of power rather than specific, identifiable guarantees on behalf of the individual versus the state. The *Ninth commands that the "enumeration in the Constitution of certain rights shall not be construed to deny or disparage others retained by the people." It has become an increasingly visible and highly controversial source of powers and limitations upon powers only during the past two decades—particularly because of its judicial utilization in the realms of sexual orientation and contact and abortion. The *Tenth, which quickly became a focal point in the adjudication of the parameters of the Constitution's division of powers between the national government and the states, mandates that the "powers not delegated to the United States by the Constitution, nor prohibited by it to the States, are reserved to the States respectively, or to the people." It has been, and surely will continue to be, the source of a substantial amount of litigation before the federal courts.

But it is the first eight amendments that the public normally regards as the Bill of Rights, and with considerable justification. Although specifics may not be readily "citable" by the average citizen, the spirit of the Bill of Rights is deeply engrained in our collective consciousness. Comprising a mere 413 words, the Bill of Rights is roughly divided between substantive and procedural rights. The suggested dichotomy is not a hard-and-fast line, but generally speaking the *First Amendment, comprising the quintet of guarantees involving religion, speech, press, assembly, and petition, addresses substantive rights, whereas the contents of the six following amendments depict much more obviously procedural rights (see DUE PROCESS, PROCEDURAL). For example, the *Fourth Amendment's stipulated safeguards against "unreasonable searches and seizures" spell out in remarkable detail the obligations to be met by both the executive branch's enforcement personnel and, second, in a good many cases, hearing and adjudicating appeals arising from their activities. The *Sixth Amendment, to cite another frequently litigated one, provides, among its components, for rights of notification of the nature of an accusation and for the procuring of both favorable and unfavorable witnesses as well as for the "assistance of counsel" for the defense, which the Supreme Court in *Gideon* v. *Wainwright* (1963) has interpreted as a basic constitutional guarantee even for those who cannot afford to hire a lawyer (see COUNSEL, RIGHT TO). And the *Fifth Amendment, to point to another basic procedural guarantee, contains, among others, the fundamental proviso against compulsory *self-incrimination.

The English *common law, colonial charters, legislative enactments, and a variety of events in the thirteen colonies were the chief elements contributing to the basic rationale for the call for a Bill of Rights as an internal element of the nascent U.S. Constitution. It was, however, no easy task. Much opposition abounded—initially and perhaps surprisingly embraced by the leading Virginia Founding Fathers. They believed that a Bill of Rights was simply unnecessary: that the states, after all, had their own bills of rights; that the body of the Constitution, as it finally surfaced at the conclusion of the Constitutional Convention's deliberations, contained ample safeguards against national (federal) mischief; that the Constitution was itself a bill of rights; that in fact it was unnecessary in a constitutional republic founded upon popular sovereignty and inalienable natural rights; and that the new federal government had, in any case, only limited and enumerated powers.

Largely through the efforts of George Mason, Thomas *Jefferson, and James *Madison, the Bill of Rights was born. Framed in its ultimate form chiefly by Madison, it was submitted to the First Congress for approval in April 1789. Much of it was based on George Mason's "Declaration of Rights" for Virginia's Constitution of 1776—a sixteen-provision document that remains part and parcel of Virginia's present constitution. Serving as its effective floor leader in the national House of Representatives was Congressman James Madison. George Mason, it might be noted, along with Virginia's Patrick Henry, had voted against ratification of the United States Constitution in the Virginia Constitutional Convention largely, although not exclusively, because of the absence of a Bill of Rights. On 25 September 1789, by the required two-thirds majority in both of its chambers, Congress sent twelve amendments to the states for ratification as the Bill of Rights, but the first two proved to be sharply controversial and failed to be ratified (one called for a fixed schedule of apportionment for the House of Representatives; the other dealt with altering the pay of members of Congress).

Fully alive now to the need for its approval, Jefferson had written to Madison in March 1789 that "[t]he Bill of Rights is necessary because of the legal check which it puts into the hands of the judiciary." What he meant was a legal check against the national government—he was not worried greatly about the states since most of them had their own bills of rights, comprising restrictions that the framers considered comfortably satisfactory (see STATE CONSTITUTIONS AND INDIVIDUAL RIGHTS). The central government, however, was a different matter, and there is no doubt that the overriding reason for the Virginians' authorship and sponsorship of the federal Bill of Rights was to place demonstrably far-reaching restraints on the fledgling central government. Indeed, the very first phrase of what became Article I of the approximately twenty-five assorted rights to be found in the Bill of Rights reads: "Congress shall make no law. . . ." Although the noun *Congress* reappears nowhere in the remainder of the eight articles, the latter was unquestionably intended to be applicable against the national government only. Certainly that was the understanding with which most of the states ratified the Bill of Rights. Madison, however, would soon come to believe that, once having become the law of the land, it ought to be applied against the states as well as against the national government, a contention echoed for somewhat more self-interested reasons by elements of the propertied community.

It would fall to Chief Justice John *Marshall, another renowned Virginian, to be the first to adjudicate the question, in *Barron* v. *Baltimore* (1833). As was true of the vast majority of Marshall's opinions, he spoke for a unanimous tribunal in ruling that the Bill of Rights applied only against the national government, emphatically not against the states. His holding commenced a history of litigation on the question of the Bill of Rights' applicability that, arguably, has never really been wholly settled. But, to all intents and purposes, it was the *due process and *equal protection clauses of the *Fourteenth Amendment that provided the Court, largely due to the intellectual leadership of Justice Hugo L. *Black in the 1940s, 1950s, and 1960s, with the perceived tools to refashion constitutional law so as to apply the Bill of Rights to the states. This process has been variously known as "incorporation," "absorption," or "nationalization" (see INCORPORATION DOCTRINE). Although the justifiability of this process has remained controversial to this day, it has *ipso facto* taken place with but few exceptions.

Where do we stand today in terms of the current constitutional law of the Bill of Rights and its application or incorporation to the states? Justice Black has triumphed—but not quite. Not quite because five of the enumerated rights in the Bill of Rights are still "out," that is, not incorporated—although they are relatively insignificant. Yet ironically and intriguingly, "not quite" also because the Court, led by Justice William O. *Douglas in the 1950s and 1960s, and after Douglas's departure notably by Justices William *Brennan and Thurgood *Marshall until their retirements, has at least partially adopted a position advanced by Justices Frank *Murphy and Wiley *Rutledge in the key case of *Adamson* v. *California* in 1947. There the Court held that if the verbiage of the Bill of Rights guarantees did not suffice to attain "justice" as they believed it to require, then the Court's resort to other, implied or inherent, provisions of the Constitution, and even *natural law, might be invoked—what some have called "incorporation plus." That policy, which Justice Black derided as "going upstairs" or which Justice Oliver Wendell *Holmes referred to as resorting to a "brooding omnipresence in the sky," was anathema to the libertarian Alabaman, who was a principled, devoted, consistent literalist. If it was not written down in the Constitution, it could not be utilized; but if it was spelled out, Black viewed the literal commands of any provision as absolutist, especially the First Amendment's quintet of rights, which Justice Benjamin *Cardozo had pronounced as being "the matrix, the indispensable condition, of nearly every other form of freedom."

When Hugo Black joined the Court in 1937, only those rights subsequently listed in Justice Cardozo's T-square of fundamental and nonfundamental rights as fundamental, which he had created in *Palko* v. *Connecticut* (1937) earlier that year, had been incorporated, or would soon be by virtue of his dichotomous classification. Once he had planted his feet firmly on the highest bench in the land, Justice Black commenced on the odyssey that would become his lasting epitaph. Under his leadership, he would steer the Court to triumphant "selective incorporation," that is, application to the fifty states—although frequently only by 5-to-4 or 6-to-3 votes—the following major Bill of Rights safeguards, all of which the states are thus now constitutionally bound to follow (in addition, of course, to those already applied earlier, notably all of the First Amendment's safeguards except the separation clause):

1947: separation of church and state (9 to 0)
1948: public trial (7 to 2)

1961: "unreasonable"—but not "reasonable"—searches and seizures (6 to 3)
1962: cruel and unusual punishments (7 to 2)
1963: counsel in all criminal cases (7 to 2)
1964: self-incrimination (5 to 4)
1965: certain "unspecified" additional rights contained in the Ninth Amendment (7 to 2)
1966: trial by an "impartial" jury (8 to 1)
1967: a "speedy" trial (9 to 0)
1968: trial by jury in all criminal cases (7 to 2)
1969: double jeopardy (6 to 2)

As the Supreme Court concluded its 1990–1991 term—its fifth term under Chief Justice William H. *Rehnquist, no further provisions of the Bill of Rights had been incorporated since the double *jeopardy clause in 1969. Those provisions that remain "out" include: (1) grand jury indictment—a segment of the Fifth Amendment; (2) trial by a jury in civil cases—an aspect of the *Seventh Amendment; (3) the excessive *bail and fines prohibitions of the *Eighth Amendment (although there is some difference of opinion among the justices as to whether the excessive bail provision has been incorporated [e.g., *Browning-Ferris v. Kelco Disposal, 1989]); (4) the so-called right to bear arms in the *Second Amendment; and (5) the *Third Amendment's safeguards against involuntary quartering of troops in private homes. There appears to be no immediate likelihood that any of these provisions will be incorporated. What is crucial is the increasing recognition and acceptance, both on and off the bench, that if there is anything at all "national" in scope and application under the United States Constitution, it is our fundamental civil rights and liberties.

Generally protected by judicial guardianship—a guardianship that is by no means confined to the federal Supreme Court—the meaning of the Bill of Rights seems fundamentally secure if unlikely to be expanded much in the foreseeable future. Under the Supremacy Clause of Article VI, *state courts cannot interpret the Bill of Rights (or the Constitution generally) differently than the U.S. Supreme Court. But a number of state supreme courts—in many hundreds of opinions since 1969—have in fact interpreted their own constitutions more liberally than the federal constitution to provide additional protections for their citizens. The Supreme Court has found this to be acceptable provided that the enhanced rights are grounded entirely and exclusively in state law or state constitutions (e.g., Michigan v. Long, 1983). States do not, however, have the authority to reduce civil rights and liberties from what the federal constitution requires.

□ Hugo Lafayette Black, A Constitutional Faith (1968). Irving Brant, The Bill of Rights: Its Origin and Meaning (1965). Learned Hand, The Bill of Rights (1958). Robert Allen Rutland, The Birth of the Bill of Rights, 1776–1791, rev. ed. (1983).                    Henry J. Abraham

**Black, Hugo Lafayette** (b. Harlan, Ala., 27 Feb. 1886; d. Bethseda, Md., 25 Sep. 1971, interred Arlington Cemetery, Arlington, Va.), associate justice, 1937–1971. Black's humble origins as the son of a storekeeper in rural Clay County, Alabama, offered little basis for optimism about his future career. His two-year undergraduate law program at the University of Alabama and brief tenure as a Birmingham police court judge were equally discouraging. But his intelligence and sheer determination—traits inherited largely from his beloved mother—enabled Black to overcome the tremendous odds his background posed. By the early 1920s he was elected to the first of two terms in the U.S. Senate; and in August 1937 he became Franklin D. *Roosevelt's first appointee to the Supreme Court, a position he held for thirty-four years until his retirement in September 1971, a week before his death.

Black's rise to the nation's highest court was as controversial as it was remarkable. Birmingham's business leaders considered the populist Democrat, whose clients had included labor unions, a "Bolshevik," yet as defense counsel in a notorious murder trial he had appealed to racial and religious bigotry to win his client's acquittal, and in 1923 he had joined the Ku Klux Klan. He resigned his Klan membership in 1926 at the beginning of his first Senate campaign and said in later years that he had joined the "Invisible Empire" largely because many Alabama jurors were also members. He won election to the Senate with KKK support, however, and remained politically indebted to the organization until the early 1930s. As an ardent New Dealer, on the other hand, Black alarmed even President Roosevelt with his attacks on privilege and his support for a thirty-hour workweek. His heavy-handed Senate investigations of government ties to big business later led to charges that he was bullying the business community.

The controversy that surrounded Black's career followed him to the Supreme Court. When his Klan membership became public knowledge shortly after his appointment to the bench, the revelation created a national furor (see NOMINATIONS, CONTROVERSIAL). Anticipating the rhetoric of southern segregationists by nearly two decades, one group condemned 4 October 1937, the Justice's first day on the bench, as "Black Day." The liberal voting record Black forged largely allayed those initial doubts, but certain civil libertarians were never entirely comfortable with his stewardship and would find especially offensive his 1944 decision for the Court in *Korematsu v. United States, upholding *World War II sanctions against Japanese-Americans. Nor were such concerns alleviated by his defense of Korematsu in a 1967 newspaper interview in which he remarked, "They all look alike to a person not a Jap."

An exceptionally tenacious, wily defender of positions he thought important, Black often an-

*Hugo Lafayette Black*

tagonized those justices with whom he most frequently differed, especially Robert *Jackson and Felix *Frankfurter. When Black refused to recuse himself from a case involving the Jewell Ridge Coal Company and a miners' union even though his former law partner was the union's lawyer, Jackson bitterly criticized his colleague. Later, when Jackson served as an American prosecutor of Nazi war criminals at Nuremberg, he became convinced that Black was attempting in his absence to undermine his chances to replace Harlan Fiske *Stone as chief justice, and Jackson dispatched a remarkable fifteen-hundred-word cable to Congress, accusing Black of "bullying tactics" and worse. After that incident the two resumed outwardly cordial relations, but Jackson remained resentful of Black, convinced that Black had worked to deny him the Court's center seat. (See JACKSON-BLACK FEUD.)

Frankfurter, on the other hand, was relatively assiduous in maintaining cordial relations with the wily Alabaman. Even after his retirement from the bench, Frankfurter wrote Black flattering letters and applauded his refusal to extend *First Amendment protection to participants in *sit-in demonstrations. Frankfurter's jurisprudential ally John M. *Harlan II enjoyed warm relations with Black, but Frankfurter's papers indicate that he regularly fed Jackson, Harlan, and others unflattering gossip regarding their colleague. And those who corresponded with Frankfurter apparently had no inhibition about referring to Black as a "skunk."

Black was not merely one of the Court's most controversial members, however; he was also one of its intellectual leaders. He embraced a

positivist conception of the judicial role and of *constitutional interpretation that many, including justices whose voting patterns closely resembled his own, considered outmoded and unworkable. As a New Deal senator, Black had been appalled at the Court's use of substantive *due process and at its expansive construction of the *Tenth Amendment to place a laissez faire gloss on the Constitution's text. He went to the bench determined to restrict the reach of judicial discretion. The jurisprudence that that commitment produced emphasized an interpretivist approach to constitutional meaning and the belief that notions of reasonableness, fairness, social utility, and related noninterpretivist considerations were an appropriate interpretive guide only when the text and the historical record proved unavailing. Black's view was that such penumbral situations rarely arise, and he exhibited a preference for relatively fixed constructions limiting the scope of judicial discretion. (See INTERPRETIVISM AND NONINTERPRETIVISM.)

His positivist jurisprudence permeated Black's approach to specific constitutional questions. He rejected, for example, judicial power to review the reasonablenesss of state controls over interstate commerce, insisting that the Constitution's text had given Congress, not the courts, the *commerce power. But he did not invariably defer to congressional, presidential, or state authority. He rejected, for example, any congressional power to strip persons of their citizenship, and for him the issue was simple: the Constitution's text gave Congress authority to grant, not deny, that status. When President Truman asserted an inherent executive power to seize the nation's steel mills as a means of averting inflationary pressures and a threat to war production, Black required only thirteen paragraphs to explain what he saw as clear differences between executive and lawmaking power, as well as his view that constitutional and statutory texts, not considerations of national interest, dictated the reach and limits of presidential power.

Elements of Black's positivism were most clearly reflected, however, in his construction of important civil liberties guarantees. His literalist, absolutist interpretation of the First Amendment was part and parcel of that jurisprudence (see FIRST AMENDMENT ABSOLUTISM). The amendment's language stipulates that "Congress shall make no law" abridging the freedoms it guarantees. For Black—a self-styled "backward country fellow"—those words meant what they said, sophisticated efforts to distinguish "speech" and "freedom of speech" notwithstanding. He thus opposed controls over *obscenity, *libel, and "subversive" speech as well as the *clear and present danger test, balancing (see FIRST AMENDMENT BALANCING), and other nonabsolutist measures of governmental authority. At the same time, he opposed extension of the amendment's provisions to picketing and other forms of "speech-plus" or to *"symbolic speech," and he recognized broad governmental power over access to public and private property, rejecting any notion that the amendment granted people freedom to express their views wherever they happened to be, and largely insisting only that regulations regarding access be evenhanded and clearly worded.

While Black's First Amendment absolutism provided the clearest illustration of his literalism, his views regarding the relationship of the *Bill of Rights to the *Fourteenth Amendment and his conception of due process as an independent constitutional guarantee may best demonstrate both his reliance on historical intent where language proves an elusive guide to constitutional meaning and his commitment to restricting the scope of judicial discretion. As he extensively explained in his dissent in *Adamson v. California (1947), his study of the Fourteenth Amendment's adoption had convinced him that its framers intended its first section, taken as a whole, to incorporate the Bill of Rights, thus making those precious guarantees fully binding on the states as well as the national government (see INCORPORATION DOCTRINE). Although, as the Court's spokesman in Chambers v. Florida (1940) and a few other cases, he seemed to equate due process with "fair" proceedings, he generally limited the meaning of that potentially limitless guarantee to the requirement, originally embraced in the English Magna Carta, that government proceed according to the "law of the land," that is, according to existing laws and procedures, in taking away a person's life, liberty, or property. Through his total-incorporation thesis and relatively fixed approach to due process, he gave the Fourteenth Amendment a construction that was not only consistent with his reading of the historical record but also limiting on the reach of judicial discretion.

Neither the language nor history of *equal protection, the amendment's other potentially open-ended guarantee, permitted the sort of fixed construction Black preferred. With the exception of the *strict scrutiny he accorded malapportioned governmental bodies and certain discriminatory criminal procedures, however, he confined equal protection's meaningful bite—and thus the scope of judicial latitude—largely to the guarantee's historical racial context. He refused, for example, to give the poll tax or other varieties of discrimination based on wealth or birth status the strict review to which he and the other members of the Warren Court subjected discrimination based on race, color, or national origin (see POLL TAXES).

During much of his career, Black's postivist jurisprudence carried him in "liberal-activist" directions, but for Black the Constitution had a "ceiling" as well as a "floor." The *Fourth Amendment, for example, guaranteed protection only against "unreasonable" searches or seizures, and

the Justice was reluctant to read broad restrictions on governmental power into so flexible a term, as evidenced by his vacillation on the *exclusionary rule. He refused, moreover, to extend the amendment's protection of "persons, houses, papers, and effects" to eavesdropping, especially since he found it impossible to conceive of an eavesdropping warrant that could satisfy the requirement that it "particularly" describe the things to be seized. Nor was he willing to use a penumbra doctrine, substantive due process, the *Ninth Amendment, or any other *"natural law" device to create rights not reflected in the Constitution's text or the intent of its framers. When a majority embraced a broad right of marital *privacy in the controversial *Griswold v. Connecticut (1965), for example, he vigorously dissented, charging that the amendment process, not judicial inventiveness, was the appropriate medium of constitutional change. In conference, he assumed the same stance in opposing judicial recognition of the *abortion right that the Court would embrace after his death.

Judicial and scholarly critics have probably subjected Hugo Black's judicial and constitutional views to more systematic scrutiny than accorded the thinking of any other jurist. During the early years of Black's tenure, Charles Fairman, Wallace Mendelson, and other admirers of Felix Frankfurter regularly attacked Black's "expansive" First Amendment jurisprudence and incorporation thesis as well as what they considered to be the ultimate futility of his resorts to literalism and historical intent. During the last decade of his life, however, the justice's votes and opinions became increasingly "conservative-restraintist" in direction and tone. Not only did he dissent in Griswold and reject extension of the Fourth Amendment to eavesdropping; in numerous contexts he endorsed broad governmental power over demonstrative speech and the uses of property, vehemently rejected the expansion of procedural safeguards beyond the specifics of the Bill of Rights, challenged the notion that the First Amendment reaches shopping centers and other privately owned places of public accommodation (much less school classrooms), and dissented from the Warren Court's expansive interpretations of equal protection. Such thinking produced another group of scholarly critics, who rejected his repeated avowals of doctrinal consistency across his career.

Certain elements of Black's thinking are obviously vulnerable to criticism. While modern scholarship has more frequently supported than attacked his incorporation thesis, for example, his reading of the record underlying the Fourteenth Amendment's adoption is certainly open to challenge. His attempts to distinguish protected speech from unprotected speech-related conduct and direct from indirect burdens on First Amendment freedoms can be faulted, too, even though a majority of the Court has also traditionally drawn such distinctions. Black's papers and those of his contemporaries abound with evidence, however, that he was remarkably consistent both in his conception of the judicial function and in his approach to specific issues throughout his long tenure. It is arguable that Black developed a workable, if imperfect, jurisprudence that reflected both plausible readings of language and history and regard for the dangers of unrestrained judicial power—a jurisprudence that struck an acceptable balance between the necessity for judicial review and equally compelling principles of majoritarian democracy.

(See also HISTORY OF THE COURT: THE DEPRESSION AND THE RISE OF LEGAL LIBERALISM.)

□ Howard Ball, *The Vision and the Dream of Hugo L. Black: An Examination of a Judicial Philosophy* (1975). Gerald T. Dunne, *Hugo Black and the Judicial Revolution* (1977). Virginia Van der Veen Hamilton, *Hugo Black: The Alabama Years* (1977). Tinsley E. Yarbrough, *Mr. Justice Black and His Critics* (1988).                    Tinsley E. Yarbrough

**Black, Jeremiah Sullivan** (b. Stony Creek, Pa., 10 Jan. 1810; d. York, Pa., 19 Aug. 1883), U.S. attorney general, unconfirmed nominee to the Supreme Court, and Supreme Court reporter. Black studied law with Chauncey Forward and was admitted to the bar on 3 December 1830. In 1842 he was appointed president judge of the Court of Common Pleas of Pennsylvania. In 1851 Black was elected to the Pennsylvania Supreme Court and by lot was chosen chief justice. In 1854 he was reelected to the Supreme Court. His principal contribution on the bench lay in the construction of corporate charters.

In 1857 President James Buchanan appointed Black U.S. attorney general. While in that office Black prosecuted frauds associated with California land titles, causing the U.S. Supreme Court to reverse many district court decisions. Black consistently enforced federal laws relating to the slave trade and the return of fugitive slaves. He also helped establish the administration position on secession and enforcement of federal laws. Late in Buchanan's term Black served briefly as secretary of state. On 5 February 1861 Buchanan nominated Black to fill a vacancy on the Supreme Court, but on 21 February the Senate rejected the nomination.

Between late 1861 and 1864 Black served as Supreme Court reporter and prepared the well-respected *Black's Reports* (two volumes). He then resumed private practice, arguing against the federal government's violations of civil rights in *Ex parte \*Milligan* (1866) and *Ex parte \*McCardle* (1869). He also served as Samuel Tilden's counsel before the commission that investigated the 1876 presidential election.

(See also NOMINEES, REJECTION OF; REPORTERS, SUPREME COURT.)

Elizabeth B. Monroe

**Black Monday.** On "Black Monday," 27 May 1935, the Supreme Court handed down three separate unanimous (9 to 0) opinions that struck down key provisions of the \*New Deal recovery plan. More importantly, these decisions appeared to signal the beginning of a Supreme Court attack on the reform measures President Franklin D. \*Roosevelt had devised to lead the country out of the Depression. In *Louisville Bank* v. *Radford* (1935), the Court declared unconstitutional the Frazier-Lemke Act, which provided mortgage relief to bankrupt farmers. In *\*Humphrey's Executor* v. *United States* (1935), the Court denied the president the power to replace at will members of independent regulatory agencies thus thwarting his ability to bring the agencies in line with administration regulatory policies. In the most dramatic and famous case that day, *\*Schechter Poultry Corp.* v. *United States* (1935), the so-called sick chicken case, the Court declared the National Recovery Act unconstitutional, holding that Congress could not delegate such sweeping powers to an executive body. It also held that the Schechters' poultry business was intrastate, not interstate, commerce and thus not subject to federal regulation. It was the latter that worried President Roosevelt because the three liberal justices—Louis D. \*Brandeis, Benjamin \*Cardozo and Harlan Fiske \*Stone—voted against the government's position. If the Court were to apply this approach across the board to regulatory issues, it would frustrate New Deal efforts. Roosevelt called a press conference the next day in which he vehemently denounced the Court for relegating the country to "the horse-and-buggy definition of interstate commerce."

Black Monday had two major consequences. First, it forced President Roosevelt to abandon the corporatist approach of the NRA and caused the administration to pursue more radical reform measures such as income tax reform, which attacked business and the wealthy. Second, Roosevelt began to plan his attack on the Supreme Court that, following further Supreme Court defeats in 1936, led to the \*court-packing plan of 1937. The controversy surrounding that proposal eventually led to the Supreme Court's reversal of its position on the scope of congressional power to regulate interstate commerce and thus allowed New Deal programs to pass constitutional muster, although FDR failed in his efforts to change the method of nominating federal judges.

Rayman L. Solomon

**Blackmun, Harry Andrew** (b. Nashville, Ill., 12 Nov. 1908), associate justice, 1971–. Blackmun grew up in St. Paul, Minnesota, where his father owned a small store. He was educated at Harvard College, where he majored in mathematics, and at Harvard Law School. His early interest in medicine was reflected in his service as counsel for the Mayo Clinic. In 1959, President Dwight D. Eisenhower appointed him to the U.S. Court of

*Harry Andrew Blackmun*

Appeals for the Eighth Circuit, to fill the seat vacated by John Sanborn, for whom Blackmun had clerked.

The "third man" after the defeated nominations of judges Clement *Haynsworth and G. Harrold *Carswell, Blackmun was appointed to the Supreme Court by President Richard *Nixon. He was at the time a little-known federal judge, and it was thought he would bring to the Court the same values as his friend Chief Justice Warren E. *Burger, playing his part in Nixon's effort to reorient the Court in a conservative ideological direction. Initially, Blackmun's voting was quite close to Burger's—something Burger may have taken for granted—and they were sometimes referred to as the "Minnesota Twins." He was quiet, even diffident, and a slow writer, which limited his influence within the Court. As he became more sure of himself, however, he moved away from Burger toward the liberal end of the Court, becoming outspoken and explicit in his efforts to keep an increasingly conservative Court on center.

Blackmun's early opinions reflected conservatism, support for law enforcement, and a general deference to government and social institutions. Later he came to demonstrate a growing skepticism about those institutions' effectiveness in relation to the common person. By the mid-1980s, Justice Blackmun, giving a high level of support for civil liberties claims, had become a regular voting partner of Justices William J. *Brennan and Thurgood *Marshall. His judicial transformation manifested itself even on matters of criminal procedure, where his initial conservatism had lasted longest. He questioned the

Court's search-and-seizure positions and disagreed with the Court's haste in upholding death-penalty convictions, thus bringing his votes into line with his early statement, in *Furman* v. *Georgia* (1972), of "distance, antipathy, and . . . abhorrence" for the death penalty, which for him "violated childhood's training and life's experience" (p. 405).

Blackmun made a number of major contributions to Supreme Court jurisprudence. He was a key player on the question of whether Congress, through the Commerce Clause, could impose requirements on state and local governments, and he wrote for the Court in *Garcia* v. *San Antonio Metropolitan Transit Authority* (1985) in holding local governments subject to minimum wage requirements, saying that their representation in Congress provided states and localities with adequate protection (see COMMERCE POWER). He also showed he could be the states' friend by allowing them to impose nondiscriminatory, properly apportioned franchise taxes and by supporting state economic policy making if it was not narrowly parochial.

His changing views on judicial *federalism paralleled his changes on civil liberties. At first he was unwilling to let state courts provide greater federal constitutional protection than did the U.S. Supreme Court, and he took a restrictive view of federal courts' use of *habeas corpus to redress state defendants' claims. Later, however, Blackmun wished to make habeas more available for those pressing federal constitutional claims, and he also gave a broad reading to title 42, section 1983 of the U.S. Code, the primary federal civil rights statute. In his Madison Lectures at New York University Law School in 1984, Blackmun argued strongly that federal courts should work actively to uphold individuals' federal rights asserted in section 1983 cases.

Blackmun's major civil liberties contributions concerned *commercial speech, aliens' rights, and *abortion. On the question of *First Amendment protection for "commercial speech" such as lawyer advertising, he opposed the states' paternalistic position of denying access to information that advertising would provide and argued that consumers ought to have more, not less, information. He took the side of aliens denied welfare benefits without satisfying long residence requirements or barred from holding public jobs (see ALIENAGE AND NATURALIZATION). His key opinions opposed states' denying aliens the right to be civil servants, public school teachers, or probation officers; however, he was willing to allow a ban on their being police officers.

Blackmun's best-known contributions are his abortion opinions, particularly those for the Court in *Roe* v. *Wade* and *Doe* v. *Bolton* (1973), in which, respectively, the justices invalidated criminal penalties for performing abortions and established the basic trimester framework for evaluating whether and when the state could impose restrictions on a woman's freedom to obtain an abortion. He was strongly committed to any woman's right to obtain an abortion and reacted strongly against the Court's upholding the government's refusal to provide Medicaid funding of abortions. The strength of his commitment continued through the many cases in which the Court dealt with states' efforts to limit abortion and was nowhere clearer than in his dissent in *Webster* v. *Reproductive Health Services* (1989). There he attacked his colleagues for dismantling *Roe* v. *Wade* and for "cast[ing] into darkness the hopes and visions of every woman who had come to believe that the Constitution guaranteed her the right to exercise some control over her unique ability to bear children," creating "inevitable and brutal consequences" with the government again able to intrude improperly into women's lives (pp. 3077–3078).

When Blackmun took his seat on the Supreme Court, few would have expected him to be a spokesperson for those on whom the hand of government weighed heavily. His service on the Court signifies the possibility, and actuality, that a justice can change views when confronted with situations that call deeply held beliefs into question. Blackmun will also remain the symbol of one of the nation's most divisive issues— abortion. However, he stands out most as a thoughtful justice representing centrism laced with compassion.          Stephen L. Wasby

**Blair, John, Jr.** (b. Williamsburg, Va., 1732; d. Williamsburg, 31 Aug. 1800; interred Bruton Parish churchyard, Williamsburg), associate justice, 1789–1795. The son of John and Mary Munro Blair, John Blair studied law at the Middle Temple in London in 1755–1756 after graduating from William and Mary College with honors in 1754. In 1756 he returned to Virginia and commenced a successful law practice before the General Court in Williamsburg. From 1765 to 1770 he served in the House of Burgesses, where he opposed Patrick Henry's Stamp Act resolutions in 1765, but favored economic boycotts of English imports in 1769–1770. Although he served as clerk of the Governor's Council from 1770 to 1775, he supported the revolutionary movement. A joint session of the legislature elected him to the newly constituted state General Court in 1777 and in 1779 he was chosen chief justice of that tribunal. In 1780 the legislature elected him chancellor of the High Court of Chancery. He also served as a member of Virginia's first Court of Appeals, which was organized in May 1779. While on the latter tribunal he and one other judge declared in *Commonwealth of Virginia* v. *Caton et al.* (1782) that the court had the power to declare invalid an unconstitutional act of the legislature, one of the first expressions of judicial review.

Perhaps because of Blair's distinguished judicial service and his support, as a delegate to the

*John Blair, Jr.*

Philadelphia and ratifying conventions, of the new Constitution, George Washington, on 24 September 1789, nominated him to be one of the original six members of the United States Supreme Court. The Senate confirmed him two days later. Justice Blair's most significant opinion came in *Chisholm* v. *Georgia* (1793), delivered seriatim in support of the Court's ruling that *Article III, section 2 of the United States Constitution entitled a citizen of one state to sue another state in a federal circuit court. The strongest point in Blair's opinion dealt with the assertion that Article III only contemplated that a state would appear in federal court as a plaintiff. Clearly that argument failed, he wrote, when one understood that Article III also conferred jurisdiction on the federal judiciary in controversies between two states, one of which had to be a defendant. (See JUDICIAL POWER AND JURISDICTION.) Georgia refused to appear before the Court or to honor its decision. Congress subsequently proposed and the states ratified the *Eleventh Amendment to the Constitution, which overruled *Chisholm* v. *Georgia*.

Blair participated in perhaps his most significant opinion while sitting on the United States Circuit Court (required of Supreme Court justices until after the Civil War). In *Hayburn's Case* (1792), Blair and his two colleagues (James *Wilson and Richard *Peters) became the first federal judges to hold an act of Congress unconstitutional when they ruled that a federal statute requiring circuit courts to act as pension commissions violated the *separation of powers doctrine and the spirit of judicial independence.

Much of what little other business the Supreme Court transacted during Blair's tenure concerned technical rulings on *admiralty and prize law, with which he was in accord. Pleading failing health, he resigned from the Court on 25 October 1795 and retired to his home in Williamsburg. His wife, Jean Balfour, had died four years earlier.                    Robert M. Ireland

**Blatchford, Samuel** (b. New York, N.Y., 9 Mar. 1820; d. 7 July 1893, Newport, R.I.; interred Greenwood Cemetery, Brooklyn, N.Y.), associate justice, 1882–1893. Samuel Blatchford is remembered for his quiet tenacity and close attention to the intricacies of *patent and *admiralty law. Blatchford was an unassuming centrist who played a pivotal role on the Court in the early 1890s. He wrote the important majority opinion that marked the first clear use of substantive *due process, but two years later he also wrote the majority opinion that proclaimed that federal judges ought to use this new constitutional scrutiny of state regulations only in severely limited circumstances.

Blatchford, the son of Richard M. Blatchford, a prominent Whig lawyer and legislator, and Julia Ann Mumford, entered Columbia University when he was thirteen years old and graduated at the head of his class in 1837. He read law in the office of Governor William H. Seward and served as Seward's private secretary before joining his father's prestigious Manhattan legal practice in 1842. After Samuel married Caroline Appleton of Lowell, Massachusetts, in 1844, he moved to Auburn, New York, where he joined Seward's law practice and served in several state legal posts. In 1854, he returned to New York City to practice law and was soon offered, but declined, an appointment to the state supreme court.

Blatchford built a considerable reputation for diligence not only as a lawyer but also as the publisher of admiralty decisions and the decisions of the Circuit Court of the United States for the Second Circuit. Andrew Johnson in 1867 appointed Blatchford a federal district judge in the Southern District of New York and President Rutherford B. Hayes in 1878 elevated him to the circuit court. When Ward Hunt resigned from the Supreme Court in 1882, President Chester A. Arthur failed to convince either Roscoe *Conkling (whom the Senate had confirmed) or Senator George F. Edmunds of Vermont to accept the post. Arthur then appointed Blatchford, who was quickly confirmed, taking his seat on 13 April 1882.

In his two best known opinions, Blatchford held that it made a constitutional difference whether state legislatures made regulatory decisions themselves or delegated power to do so to agencies or commissions. In *Chicago, Milwaukee and St. Paul Railway Co. v. Minnesota (1890), his majority opinion explained that the Constitution required the Court to strike down a Minnesota law that established an independent commission

*Samuel Blatchford*

with the final say as to whether railroad rates were "equal and reasonable" (see RULE OF REASON). This decision had great significance because it clearly departed from the Court's earlier deference to state economic regulation, as in *Munn v. Illinois (1877), in which the business being regulated was said to be "affected with the public interest." In *Budd v. New York (1892), Blatchford again wrote for a divided Court. This time, however, his opinion upheld state power to regulate businesses, such as grain elevators, at least when the state legislature itself set rates.

Many observers argued that the distinction Blatchford attempted did not make sense, and certainly should not make a constitutional difference. Owing in part to the rise of populism, a severe economic depression, and the charged atmosphere of the early 1890s, Blatchford's attempt to find and hold a solid center was strained at best. This may help explain the relatively restrained praise for Blatchford after his death. Seymour D. Thompson, the outspoken editor of the *American Law Review,* proclaimed, "It is no great disparagement of him to say that he was probably a better reporter than judge." During the Court's formal memorial service Attorney General Richard Olney said of Blatchford, "If he was not brilliant, he was safe."

However, Blatchford's lawyerly enthusiasm for procedural detail contributed to his significant civil liberties decision extending the *Fifth Amendment privilege against self-incrimination in *Counselman v. Hitchcock (1892). Blatchford's ruling for a unanimous Court emphasized that the Fifth Amendment protected Counselman from giving evidence that could be used in "any criminal case," including a grand jury proceeding. Blatchford was explicit about moving beyond prior federal and state law, as he relied on the spirit and principle of constitutional guarantees.

Despite Counselman and a few other votes by Blatchford in favor of civil liberties, Blatchford attracted slight public notice; he was most noteworthy for his businesslike approach and his orderly, prosperous, and placid career.

□ Aviam Soifer, "The Paradox of Paternalism and Laissez-Faire Constitutionalism: United States Supreme Court, 1888–1921," Law and History Review 5 (Spring, 1987): 249–279.                    Aviam Soifer

**Blue Laws.** See SUNDAY CLOSING LAWS.

**Bolling v. Sharpe,** 347 U.S. 497 (1954), argued 10–11 Dec. 1952, reargued 8–9 Dec. 1953, decided 17 May 1954 by vote of 9 to 0; Warren for the Court. Chief Justice Earl *Warren held that the Due Process Clause of the Fifth Amendment implicitly forbade most racial discrimination by the federal government just as the *Equal Protection Clause of the *Fourteenth Amendment restricts states. Having just held in *Brown v. Board of Education (1954) that states could not segregate public schools on the basis of race, Warren wrote that "to impose a lesser duty" in the District of Columbia—where the *Fifth Amendment covered congressional action—would be "unthinkable" (p. 500) but many scholars accused Warren of begging the question.

(See also EDUCATION; RACE AND RACISM.)
                              Dennis J. Hutchinson

**Bork, Robert Heron** (b. Pittsburgh, Pa., 1 Mar. 1927), federal appellate judge and unsuccessful nominee for the U.S. Supreme Court. Following a distinguished career in private law practice, on the faculty of Yale Law School, and as U.S. *solicitor general (1973–1977), Bork was appointed to the U.S. Court of Appeals, District of Columbia Circuit, by President Ronald *Reagan in 1982. On 1 July 1987, Reagan nominated him for the Supreme Court vacancy created by the retirement of Lewis *Powell. After an unusually lengthy hearing, the *Senate Judiciary Committee rejected the nomination, 9 to 5; the full Senate defeated it by a vote of 58 to 42 on 23 October 1987. Bork resigned from the court of appeals in February 1988 and became a resident scholar at the American Enterprise Institute.

Bork's nomination sparked intense interest-group activity, including unprecedented efforts to mobilize grassroots opposition. Bork's legal competence and personal integrity were indisputable, and debate focused on his conservative

political and legal views, particularly those relating to the constitutional right to *privacy and the *First Amendment. Broader political factors also contributed to his defeat: The Iran-Contra scandal had weakened the Reagan administration, and it failed to mobilize its resources effectively in Bork's behalf. The Democrats controlled the Senate, and even southern Democrats, becoming more responsive to their black constituents, who widely opposed Bork, failed to support the nomination. Liberals saw this vacancy as crucial because of Justice Powell's swing vote in many civil rights and liberties cases and because of his support of *Roe v. Wade (1973).

(See also NOMINATIONS, CONTROVERSIAL; NOMINEES, REJECTION OF.)
                              Susan M. Olson

**Boudinot, Elias** (b. Philadelphia, Pa., 2 May 1740; d. Burlington, N.J., 24 Oct. 1821), lawyer and statesman. Boudinot, a distinguished New Jersey politician and statesmen of the Revolutionary era, was the first lawyer admitted to the Supreme Court bar. Of Huguenot descent, he was licensed as an attorney in 1760 and gained the high professional rank of sergeant-at-law in 1770. For many years Boudinot was a trustee of Princeton University, and he held numerous public and private offices. Contemporaries found him a well-tempered and tolerant man.

Boudinot was active in New Jersey colonial politics as a conservative Whig, but he joined a committee of correspondence and slowly embraced the ideals of the Revolution. In 1777 the Continental Congress appointed Boudinot commissary-general of prisoners, a post he filled conscientiously, even contributing $30,000 of his own money for prisoners' care. He had a close political and personal relationship with George Washington.

Boudinot was elected to the Continental Congress in 1777 and served until 1784. During his last two years of service, he was president of the congress, and from 1783 he also served as secretary of foreign affairs. He was a signatory of the 1783 peace treaty with Great Britain.

After the Revolution, Boudinot became a Federalist and helped secure the Constitution's ratification in New Jersey. Three terms in the House of Representatives were followed by ten years as director of the U.S. Mint. On 5 February 1790, Boudinot became the first member of the Supreme Court bar. Later president of the American Bible Association, he filled his last years with religious study.                    Francis Helminski

**Bowers v. Hardwick,** 478 U.S. 186 (1986), argued 31 Mar. 1986, decided 30 June 1986 by vote of 5 to 4; White for the Court, Blackmun and Stevens in dissent. In this case, the Supreme Court refused to extend the constitutional right of *privacy to protect acts of consensual homosexual sodomy performed in the privacy of one's own home. The narrow majority led by Justice Byron *White differentiated this case from earlier right-to-privacy decisions, saying that those decisions were limited to circumstances involving "family, marriage, or procreation"—things that bore "no connection" to homosexual activity (p. 191). Indeed, White claimed that the right to privacy was limited to the reach of those previous cases. He further claimed that the proposition that "any kind of private sexual conduct between consenting adults is constitutionally insulated from state proscription is unsupportable" (p. 191). To argue that the right to engage in such conduct is a fundamental right " 'deeply rooted in this Nation's history and tradition' or 'implicit in the concept of ordered liberty' is, at best, facetious," White wrote (p. 194). He pointed out that until 1961 all fifty states had outlawed sodomy and that twenty-four states and the District of Columbia continued to do so in 1986. He then rejected Hardwick's claim that such laws lack a rational basis.

White also differentiated the *Hardwick* case from *Stanley* v. *Georgia* (1969), arguing that *Stanley* should be understood as a *First Amendment case that was not relevant to the issues raised in *Hardwick*. Although *Stanley* protected individuals from prosecution for possessing and reading obscene materials in the privacy of their homes, White stressed that it did not offer blanket protection to otherwise illegal conduct simply because it occurs in the home.

The present case evolved out of the arrest of Michael Hardwick, a gay Atlanta bartender, for performing oral sex with another man in his own bedroom. They were discovered by a police officer who had come to serve a warrant on Hardwick for not paying a fine for drinking in public. The officer was given permission to enter the house by another tenant who did not know whether Hardwick was at home. Under Georgia law, sodomy (defined as "any sexual act involving the sex organs of one person and the mouth or anus of another") was a felony that could bring up to twenty years in prison.

Although the district attorney did not prosecute, he did not drop the charge. Hardwick then brought a civil suit challenging the law's constitutionality in federal court. The defendant was Georgia's attorney general, Michael J. Bowers. The district court granted Bowers' motion to dismiss, but a divided panel of the Court of Appeals for the Eleventh Circuit reversed on the grounds that the Georgia statute violated Hardwick's fundamental rights. The Supreme Court then granted Bowers's petition for *certiorari. Since the only claim before the Court dealt with homosexual sodomy, it expressed no opinion about the constitutionality of the Georgia statute as applied to acts of heterosexual sodomy.

Justice Lewis *Powell was the crucial swing vote in the case. It appears that at conference he tentatively agreed to provide the fifth vote for striking down the Georgia statute, but then later changed his mind. Powell felt that a prison sentence for sodomy would create a serious *Eighth Amendment issue that could be used to strike down the statute, but Hardwick had not been prosecuted. Thus, Powell was unable to apply the Eighth Amendment issue to this case, and he was apparently uncomfortable with using the right of privacy to strike down the statute. In October 1990, Powell told law students at New York University that he had "probably made a mistake" in ultimately voting the way he did. Nonetheless, he maintained that *Hardwick* was "a frivolous case" since no one had been prosecuted.

Had Powell not changed his vote, Justice Harry *Blackmun would have written the majority opinion. Instead, White wrote the majority opinion, Powell added a carefully worded concurrence that pointed out the Court's inability to address the Eighth Amendment issue, and Blackmun wrote a harsh dissent. When the decision was handed down, both White and Blackmun took the unusual step of reading detailed portions of their opinions from the bench.

Blackmun strongly criticized the majority opinion, saying that the case was no more about a "fundamental right to engage in homosexual sodomy" than *Stanley* v. *Georgia* was about a fundamental right to watch obscene movies. Rather, he concluded, "this case is about 'the most comprehensive of rights and the right most valued by civilized men,' namely, 'the right to be let alone' " (p. 199). Blackmun also took issue with the majority's refusal to consider whether the Georgia statute ran afoul of the Eighth or *Ninth Amendments or the *Equal Protection Clause of the *Fourteenth Amendment. "The Court's cramped reading of the issue before it makes for a short opinion," Blackmun concluded, "but it does little to make for a persuasive one" (pp. 202–203).

(See also HOMOSEXUALITY.)

John Anthony Maltese

**Bowsher v. Synar,** 478 U.S. 714 (1986), argued 23 Apr. 1986, decided 7 July 1986 by vote of 7 to 2; Burger for the Court, Stevens, joined by Marshall, concurring, White and Blackmun in dissent. In this decision, the Supreme Court struck down a key provision of the Balanced Budget and Emergency Deficit Control Act of 1985. The statute provided that there should be progressive annual cuts in the federal budget deficit. The contested provision stated that the cuts would be specified by the comptroller general if Congress could not agree on them.

The constitutional challenge rested on the fact that the comptroller general is regarded as a legislative branch officer who is removable only by joint resolution of both houses of Congress. The majority concluded that the specification of budget cuts was an executive function and that to vest such a function in a legislative branch officer violated the principle of separation of powers.

Justice John Paul *Stevens, concurring in the judgment, concluded that the comptroller general's function should be seen as legislative in nature. He reasoned that a legislative action could not be taken by a single legislative officer but instead must be adopted by both houses of Congress and presented to the president for approval or veto (see *Immigration and Naturalization Service v. Chadha, 1983).

The majority concluded that a "legislative action" consists of the adoption of general legal standards, whereas an "executive action" consists of acting pursuant to statute. This sequential definition of the separation of powers is formalistic and, as Justice Stevens's concurrence shows, subject to different interpretations. Nonetheless, Bowsher reinforces the idea that the separation of powers should be given some bright-line meaning despite the difficulties of doing so in an era of complex government.

(See also SEPARATION OF POWERS.)

Thomas O. Sargentich

**Boyd v. United States,** 116 U.S. 616 (1886), argued 11, 14 Dec. 1885, decided 1 Feb. 1886 by vote of 9 to 0; Bradley for the Court, Miller concurring. Boyd was the first decision of the Supreme Court to give extensive consideration to the relationship between the *Fourth and *Fifth Amendments. Although later opinions have restricted its expansive interpretation of the two amendments, Boyd remains a landmark in the development of protections for the right to *privacy.

The case concerned an allegation that E. A. Boyd & Sons had imported plate glass without paying the duty required by the 1874 customs act. As authorized by the act, the United States attorney obtained a court order that the Boyds produce their invoices for the glass. The case was a civil proceeding, involving no criminal charges. The Boyds contended that the compulsory production of records violated their rights under the Fourth Amendment prohibiting unreasonable searches and seizures and the Fifth Amendment protecting freedom from compulsory *self-incrimination.

The entire Court upheld the Boyds' arguments, with the exception of two justices who declined to accept the Fourth Amendment argument. Justice Joseph P. *Bradley, writing for the Court, relied on over two centuries of English and American legal history to support his conclusion that the two amendments protected the privacies of individual life from governmental intrusion. He rejected arguments that the amendments applied only in criminal proceedings and when there had been a physical invasion of property. Accordingly, he concluded that a section of the customs statute was unconstitutional because it authorized the compulsory production

of records. Bradley also anticipated the *exclusionary rule by holding that the admission of the invoices into evidence was unconstitutional.

Walter F. Pratt, Jr.

**Bradford, Edward Anthony** (b. Connecticut, 1814; d. Paris, France, 22 Nov. 1872), unconfirmed nominee to the Supreme Court. Bradford graduated from Yale College and studied law at Harvard. He moved to Louisiana in 1836 and became a prominent New Orleans lawyer.

On 16 August 1852 President Millard Fillmore nominated Bradford to the Supreme Court to fill the vacancy caused by the death of Justice John *McKinley. The Democratic majority in the Senate failed to act upon the nomination before the end of the session. Subsequently, Fillmore nominated George E. *Badger (U.S. Senator from North Carolina) and William C. *Micou (a New Orleans attorney), although the vacancy remained for Fillmore's successor to fill. Bradford and Micou were soon to be associated in a law firm with Judah P. Benjamin, U.S. Senator from Louisiana, later attorney general, secretary of war, and secretary of state of the Confederate States of America.

(See also NOMINEES, REJECTION OF.)

Elizabeth B. Monroe

**Bradley, Joseph P.** (b. Albany County, N.Y., 14 Mar. 1813; d. Washington, D.C., 22 Jan. 1892; interred North Reformed Church Cemetery, Newark, N.J.), associate justice, 1870–1892. Oldest of eleven children born to a subsistence farmer, Bradley was a self-made man, achieving success in professional life through hard work and native ability. Largely self-taught before he entered Rutgers College at age twenty, Bradley read law after graduation and was admitted to the New Jersey bar in 1839 at the relatively advanced age of twenty-six. Quickly accepted in legal circles, he married Mary Hornblower, daughter of William *Hornblower, the chief justice of New Jersey. Bradley specialized in providing legal services for railroads, eventually becoming general counsel for the corruption-ridden Camden and Amboy Line, in which post he seemed to keep his own hands clean. Originally a Whig, Bradley became an early and enthusiastic Republican. When in January 1870 President Ulysses S. Grant received advance intelligence of the Supreme Court's impending invalidation of the Legal Tender Act, he moved swiftly to fill two vacancies with appointees who could be counted on to convert the minority in support of the act into a majority. The pragmatic Bradley was an obvious choice for one seat; the other went to William *Strong. Once on the Court, the two dutifully voted to overturn the year-old precedent and uphold the Legal Tender Act. (See LEGAL TENDER CASES.)

In 1877 Bradley accepted the thankless task of serving on the electoral commission created to determine the winner of the disputed presiden-

*Joseph P. Bradley*

tial election of 1876. On a commission equally balanced between Democrats and Republicans, Bradley was assigned the role of swing man. Although apparently pulled in both directions, he closed ranks with his fellow Republicans and declared Rutherford B. Hayes president-elect. As if in support of Hayes's conciliatory policy toward the South, Bradley later authored the opinion of the Court in the notorious *Civil Rights Cases* (1883), invalidating key provisions of the Civil Rights Act of 1875. Opposed, as he put it, to "running the *slavery argument into the ground," Bradley declared the newly freed blacks to be no longer "the special favorite of the laws." (pp. 24–25). In the troublesome cases concerning southern state indebtedness that plagued the Court from 1883 to 1890, Bradley again displayed his powerful grip on political realities and his penchant for blunt language and unsubtle legal reasoning. While leading the Court, in *McGahey v. Virginia* (1890), to hold Virginia to the obligation of its contracts with bondholders on the basis of a provision making interest on the bonds an offset to state taxes, he simultaneously led it, in *Hans v. Louisiana* (1890), to a fateful expansion of a state's immunity from suit in federal court, thereby freeing most other southern states from legal accountability. *Hans*, still a landmark in federal jurisdiction, holds that states may not be sued in federal court by their own citizens, a result seemingly based on a reading of the constitutional grant of power in *Article III, as explained by the history of the *Eleventh Amendment. In Bradley's view the 1793 decision in *Chisholm v. Georgia* created such a "shock of surprise" that the Constitution had

been immediately amended to restore in part the original understanding (p. 11). In *Hans* the Court completed the process.

Joining the Court soon after the ratification of the *Fourteenth Amendment, Bradley participated in many early cases concerning its meaning. Dissenting in the *Slaughterhouse Cases* (1873), he argued that the *Privileges and Immunities Clause protects economic enterprise from unreasonable state interference, but during the same term he turned a deaf ear to a feminist plea for protection. When Myra Bradwell challenged her exclusion from the practice of law in Illinois, Bradley filed a separate concurring opinion rejecting her claim (see *Bradwell v. Illinois*, 1873). Proposing to write Victorian mores into the Constitution, he declared it "the law of the Creator" that woman's destiny is limited to "the noble and benign offices of wife and mother" (p 141). (See also GENDER.) Returning to the economic issue, Bradley contributed largely to Chief Justice Morrison *Waite's opinion of the Court in the *Granger Cases* (1877), apparently supplying the key concept of property "affected with a public interest" (see *Munn v. Illinois*, 1877).

Described in old age by a colleague as full of "vinegar," Bradley was distinguished by a seasoned willingness to face facts and make hard, and hard-headed, decisions.

□ Charles Fairman, "Mr. Justice Bradley," in *Mr. Justice,* edited by Allison Dunham and Philip B. Kurland (1956).
John V. Orth

**Bradwell v. Illinois,** 16 Wall. (83 U.S.) 130 (1873), argued 18 Jan. 1873, decided 15 Apr. 1873 by vote of 8 to 1; Miller for the Court, Bradley, Field, and Swayne concurring, Chase in dissent. Myra Bradwell (1831–1894), who had studied law with her attorney husband, James B. Bradwell, founded and published the *Chicago Legal News,* the leading midwestern legal publication. An Illinois statute provided that any adult "person," of good character and having the requisite training, was eligible for admission to the bar. The Illinois Supreme Court denied her admission, however, because she was a woman. Bradwell then sought a writ of error from the U.S. Supreme Court, claiming that her right to practice law was one of the privileges protected by the *Fourteenth Amendment.

The Court's majority upheld the action of the Illinois court on the grounds that the *Privileges and Immunities Clause of the Fourteenth Amendment, having been given its first (and extremely restrictive) interpretation only the day before in the *Slaughterhouse Cases* (1873), did not embrace the right to practice a profession. *Bradwell v. Illinois* thus confirmed the narrow view of the clause that has characterized the Court's approach to it ever since. But the decision is best remembered for dicta in Justice Joseph P. *Bradley's concurrence. He stated: "The paramount destiny and mission of woman are to fulfill the noble and benign offices of wife and mother. This is the law of the Creator" (p. 141). It was not until almost one hundred years later that the Court began to use the Fourteenth Amendment to overturn sex discriminatory state laws, and then it used the "equal protection" clause of that amendment rather than the "privileges and immunities" clause (*Reed v. Reed, 1971).

(See also BAR ADMISSION; GENDER.)

Nancy S. Erickson

**Brandeis, Louis Dembitz** (b. Louisville, Ky., 13 Nov. 1856; d. Washington, D.C., 5 Oct. 1941; ashes interred in portico of University of Louisville Law School), lawyer and associate justice, 1916–1939. Born to prosperous immigrants from Bohemia, Louis Brandeis grew up in an atmosphere of bourgeois German culture and constant talk about current events. Anticipating the depression of 1873, Brandeis's father, Adolph, closed down his wholesale grain business and took the family on an extended three-year tour of Europe. During that time Louis attended the *Annen-realschule* in Dresden, and while he did not care for the overly strict discipline, he later said that there he learned to think rigorously. Returning to the United States in 1875, he entered the Harvard Law School, then undergoing the great case-study reform introduced by its dean, Christopher Langdell. Brandeis excelled at the law school, stayed on for a year of graduate work, and then began practice with a friend of his family in St. Louis.

Lonely and unhappy, he returned in one year to Boston to open a practice with his law school friend, Samuel Warren. The partnership prospered, and in time became one of the city's larger commercial firms. Brandeis was one of the new breed of lawyers responding to the demands of the industrial revolution, whom clients consulted prior to taking action to make sure they were not running afoul of the law. Brandeis developed a reputation as a lawyer who knew more about his clients' businesses than they did, a master of facts, and a courtroom advocate to be feared by opponents. By the 1890s, at a time when most lawyers in the United States made less than five thousand dollars yearly, Brandeis earned more than fifty thousand dollars.

An altruistic streak drove him to join the company of progressive reformers then seeking to ameliorate the harsher aspects of industrial life. He started first in Boston, fighting corrupt streetcar franchises, then tackled the insurance companies, and devised the plan for savings bank life insurance. Brandeis was the first to do this work without a fee, a practice that many of his contemporaries viewed as eccentric.

In 1908 Brandeis argued in defense of a state ten-hour law for women in *Muller v. Oregon,* and introduced the *"Brandeis brief," a paradigm of what legal reformers at the time called *"sociological jurisprudence." Devoting only two pages to

*Louis Dembitz Brandeis*

legal precedent, he spent more than one hundred pages detailing the latest studies about the effects of long hours on working women. This effort to educate the judiciary in the social and economic effects of legislation became the model for later defenses of reform measures.

Brandeis set out his philosophy as a lawyer and reformer in a speech to the Harvard Ethical Society in 1905, later reprinted and widely distributed under the title "The Opportunity in the Law." There Brandeis charged that lawyers too often supported only the large corporations, to the detriment of the public. "Instead of holding a position of independence, between the wealthy and the people, prepared to curb the excesses of either," he charged, "able lawyers have, to a large extent, allowed themselves to become adjuncts of large corporations." Brandeis called on other lawyers to speak for the people and to be independent, a value he prized more highly than any other in his personal as well as his professional life.

By 1912 Brandeis had achieved a national reputation as "the people's attorney" and he helped Woodrow Wilson craft the basic arguments of Wilson's New Freedom. Brandeis, who believed bigness to be antithetical to democracy, suggested that the solution to the trust problem should not be regulation of monopoly, as Theodore Roosevelt argued, but regulation of competition, so that all business could compete on a fair playing field (see CAPITALISM). In 1914 Brandeis undertook another, and for him a new reform, Zionism, and for the next seven years headed the American Zionist movement.

Wilson had originally thought of making Brandeis his solicitor general, an idea that the business wing of the Democratic party quickly killed. Brandeis understood the politics involved and did not allow them to interfere in his close relationship with the president. In late January 1916 Wilson nominated Brandeis to the Supreme Court to succeed Joseph R. *Lamar, and in doing so triggered a four-month confirmation battle, in which conservative forces within American industry and the bar fought furiously to defeat the nomination. Wilson stood by Brandeis, and reform groups of all varieties also backed the nomination, which the Senate finally approved in June.

His twenty-three years on the high court are in some ways a continuation of the type of law he had practiced for more than three decades. He showed himself to be the finest legal craftsman to sit on the Court in the twentieth century. But the advocate had to give way to the jurist, and he demonstrated most of the time a mastery of his own individual beliefs and in doing so defined the idea of judicial restraint.

As an advocate, Brandeis had attempted to instruct judges in the facts behind reform measures, and this practice he continued on the bench, although usually in dissent. When, for example, the Court in Burns Baking Co. v. Bryan (1924) struck down a Nebraska statute establishing a standard weight for a loaf of bread, Brandeis amassed evidence to show why the legislature had considered the measure necessary. He and his clerks would labor over his opinions, and then would say, "The opinion is now convincing. What can we do to make it more instructive." Friends sometimes wished, as Harold Laski put it, that Brandeis opinions read a little less like Brandeis briefs.

Brandeis in dissent could be a powerful advocate, especially for causes he favored. But he also believed that the judiciary had no business second-guessing the legislature, nor striking down laws simply because the judges did not agree with their underlying philosophy. When Oklahoma during the Depression enacted a licensing scheme that granted ice companies local monopolies, the Court struck it down. One might have expected Brandeis to vote with the majority, but he dissented, and eloquently pleaded with his brethren to allow states to experiment with different plans, no matter how wise or foolish. "If we would guide by the light of reason," he declared in *New State Ice Co. v. Liebmann (1932), "we must let our minds be bold." Thus, during the 1930s, Brandeis voted in most instances to uphold New Deal legislation, even though he privately opposed much of it on grounds that big government constituted as much of a menace to democracy as big business.

Although Brandeis believed that judges should defer to the legislature in matters of economic policy, he took a different tack when governmental laws or policies affected individual liberties. Shortly after *World War I the Court heard a series of cases involving prosecutions under the *Espionage Act of 1917 as well as state sedition laws. In the first case, *Schenck v. U.S. (1919), Oliver Wendell *Holmes approved such restrictions under a *"clear and present danger test." Although Brandeis voted with the majority, he felt uncomfortable, and soon afterwards he and Holmes began dissenting. In the first case in which he wrote the dissenting opinion, Schaefer v. U.S. (1920), Brandeis set about the task of converting the Holmes test into a constitutional rule to protect speech rather than permit its restriction. (See SPEECH AND THE PRESS.)

In his dissenting opinion in another 1920 case, Gilbert v. Minnesota, Brandeis suggested that the liberty guaranteed by the Fourteenth Amendment went beyond property rights to include personal freedoms as well, the first time that a justice had suggested that the *Fourteenth Amendment might apply the *Bill of Rights against the states. Within a few years the Court in *Gitlow v. New York (1925) accepted this idea in regard to freedom of speech. Through the process of *incorporation the Court gradually expanded the idea to most of the other protections of the first eight amendments.

Brandeis, however, went far beyond the conservatives who sat on the Taft and Hughes Courts in his advocacy of free speech, and he penned one of the most eloquent defenses of free expression in his concurring opinion in *Whitney v. California (1927). The men who won our independence, he declared, "believed that freedom to speak as you will and to speak as you think are indispensable to the discovery and spread of political truth. . . . To courageous, self-reliant men, with confidence in the power of free and fearless reasoning applied through the processes of popular government, no danger flowing from speech can be deemed clear and present, unless the incidence of the evil apprehended is so imminent that it may befall before there is opportunity for full discussion. . . . Such, in my opinion, is the command of the Constitution" (p. 376).

Although the word *"privacy" is not found in the Constitution, Brandeis had long believed privacy one of the most precious rights. He and Samuel Warren had written a pioneering law review article on the subject in 1890, and he returned to the theme in his dissent in *Olmstead v. U.S. (1928). The Court had held that wiretapping did not constitute a violation of the *Fourth Amendment, and Brandeis objected to this invasion of privacy. "The makers of our Constitution," he declared, "conferred, as against the government, the right to be let alone—the most comprehensive of rights and the right most valued by civilized men" (p. 478). Ultimately, the Court adopted the idea of a constitutionally protected right of privacy in *Griswold v. Connecticut (1965).

Although Brandeis, like Holmes, came to be known as a dissenter, he wrote 454 of his 528 opinions for the Court. Most of these are far shorter and less fact-crammed than his dissents, since he knew that he had to tailor his writing to reflect the views of at least four other justices. Brandeis understood, however, the value of elaboration in his dissents, for there he laid the groundwork for the future. As he once told Felix *Frankfurter, "my faith in time is great."

Brandeis had an almost mystic faith in the Court, and he revered it as an institution. He believed that the Court and in fact the federal courts as a whole should have limited jurisdiction, since in a federal system they should deal only with those issues that truly went beyond the concerns of the states. The bulk of litigation should take place in the *state courts, and he objected to the old rule of *Swift v. Tyson (1842) that allowed federal courts to ignore state law in favor of a *federal common law. This had led commercial litigants to remove their cases to federal courts, where they could evade many state commercial restrictions. Brandeis objected to this practice continuously, and finally won over the Court in *Erie Railroad Co. v. Tompkins (1938), which forced federal courts to follow state rules and did away with forum shopping.

Publicly Brandeis held to a strict standard of judicial behavior, refusing to comment on the work of the Court or even accept an honorary degree. Recent scholarship, however, has shown that he played an extraordinarily active role in the political affairs of his time, often using as a surrogate Professor Felix Frankfurter of the Harvard Law School. Especially during the *New Deal, Brandeis consulted often with members of the administration and even with President Franklin D. *Roosevelt. While there is no evidence that his off-the-court activities had any affect on his judicial behavior, it violated both his own professed rules of judicial restraint as well as what we would now consider acceptable conduct by a Supreme Court justice.

Aside from this, Brandeis's reputation as one of the great justices in Supreme Court history is secure. His defense of freedom of speech and the right to privacy were adopted and expanded by later courts. His advocacy of *judicial self-restraint and deference to the legislative branches in matters of economic policy also won out, and he lived to see the Court move away from the use of substantive *due process to strike down reform measures. His use of facts and nonlegal materials to understand the impact of law upon society and economics has now become commonplace. But perhaps more than anything else, his craftsmanship as a judge in defining and elucidating the law set a standard for all who followed.

□ Alpheus T. Mason, Brandeis: A Free Man's Life (1946). Bruce A. Murphy, The Brandeis/Frankfurter Connection (1982). Philippa Strum, Louis D. Brandeis: Justice for the People (1984). Melvin I. Urofsky and David W. Levy, eds., Letters of Louis D. Brandeis, 5 vols. (1971–1978).
Melvin I. Urofsky

**Brandeis Brief.** As counsel in *Muller v. Oregon (1908), Louis D. *Brandeis, then a well-known attorney and social activist, submitted a lengthy *brief supporting the constitutionality of an Oregon statute that limited the hours per day that women could work in laundries and other industries. The Brandeis brief led to important changes in legal analysis and Supreme Court litigation.

The Muller brief devoted a mere two pages to discussion of legal issues; the remaining 110 pages presented evidence of the deleterious effects of long hours of labor on the "health, safety, morals and general welfare of women." This evidence was culled from medical reports, psychological treatises, statistical compilations, and conclusions of various legislative bodies and public committees by Brandeis's sister-in-law, Josephine Goldmark, and several of her colleagues from the National Consumers' League. Surprisingly, the conservative David J. *Brewer, who wrote for the majority in Muller, noted the contribution of the brief favorably.

The Brandeis brief was unprecedented. Brandeis used it to demonstrate that there was a reasonable basis for the Oregon statute. In several prior decisions, most notably *Lochner v. New York (1905), conservative Supreme court justices were only too willing—as Brandeis and other Progressives complained—to impose their own beliefs about what constituted reasonable legislation. The Muller brief's analysis was consonant with the fact-oriented *"sociological jurisprudence" of the Progressive era. It forced the Court to consider data that state legislators employed in drafting reform laws.

The success of the Brandeis brief led to subsequent efforts by Brandeis and other lawyers to support of a wide range of economic legislation. Even lawyers representing interests opposed to Progressive regulation used the Brandeis techniques to attack such laws. The Brandeis brief has also seen service in contexts far removed from economic regulation and thus has become a staple of litigation before the Supreme Court. (See also GENDER, PROGRESSIVISM.)
John W. Johnson

**Brandenburg v. Ohio.** 395 U.S. 444 (1969), argued 27 Feb. 1969, decided 9 June 1969 by unanimous vote; per curiam decision. Brandenburg v. Ohio was decided in the context of the significant expansion of *First Amendment freedoms in the 1960s. It was the final step in the Supreme Court's tortuous fifty-year development of a constitutional test for speech that advocates illegal action.

Clarence Brandenburg was convicted of violating an Ohio *criminal syndicalism statute for advocating racial strife during a televised Ku Klux

Klan rally. The statute was identical to one previously upheld by the Supreme Court in *Whitney* v. *California* (1927). The Court fashioned a test that was significantly more protective of dangerous speech than the previous *"clear and present danger" test employed in previous cases. *Whitney* was overturned.

In its various incarnations, the old clear and present danger test had permitted the punishment of speech if it had a "tendency" to encourage or cause lawlessness (*Schenck* v. *U.S.*, 1919), or if the speech was part of a broader dangerous political movement, like the communist party (*Dennis* v. *U.S.*, 1951). (See COMMUNISM AND THE COLD WAR.) The *Brandenburg* test, however, allowed government to punish the advocacy of illegal action only if "such advocacy is directed to inciting or producing imminent lawless action and is likely to incite or produce such action" (p. 447).

By requiring an actual empirical finding of imminent harm, this test protects the advocacy of lawlessness except in unusual instances. But government may still punish speech that is demonstrably dangerous. The test is also distinctly more objective than the old danger test. *Brandenburg* is the lynchpin of the modern doctrine of free speech, which seeks to give special protection to politically relevant speech and to distinguish speech from action.

(See also FIRST AMENDMENT; SPEECH AND THE PRESS.

Donald A. Downs

**Branzburg v. Hayes; In re Pappas; United States v. Caldwell,** 408 U.S. 665 (1972), argued 22–23 Feb. 1972, decided 29 June 1972 by vote of 5 to 4; White for the Court, Stewart, Brennan, Marshall, and Douglas in dissent. Social unrest during the early 1970s prompted an increased grand jury interest in information collected by investigative reporters who often claimed *First Amendment privilege to protect the confidentiality of sources.

Paul Branzburg of the *Louisville Courier-Journal* moved to quash a Kentucky grand jury subpoena that sought additional information about his story on the manufacture of hashish. Television journalist Paul Pappas refused to answer a Massachusetts grand jury's questions about his coverage of the Black Panthers. A Northern District of California federal grand jury held *New York Times* reporter Earl Caldwell in comtempt for refusing to appear to answer questions about the Black Panthers. A Ninth Circuit Court of Appeals later reversed the ruling.

The U.S. Supreme Court, in a sharply divided vote, decided against a special First Amendment privilege for the press. Justice Byron *White relied on common law and case law to hold that a reporter's responsibility to a grand jury did not differ from any other citizen. The grand jury, he said, was entitled to "everyman's evidence" (p.

688). White concluded that only legislatures could establish additional protection for reporters' testimonial privilege.

Justice Potter *Stewart, dissenting for himself, William *Brennan, and Thurgood *Marshall, argued that protecting the confidentiality of sources was essential to newsgathering. He thus would have required the showing of a compelling interest before a grand jury could obtain privileged information from reporters. Justice William O. *Douglas also dissented vigorously and emphasized the importance of the public's access to information.

The *Branzburg* case prompted spirited discussion and a movement for shield laws to protect the press. A number of states added statutes or modified those in place, but shield proponents were unable to persuade Congress to pass a national privilege protection law. Nearly twenty years later in *Cohen* v. *Cowles Media* (1991), White again wrote for a majority of five to deny a claim of a special press privilege. The Court held that the First Amendment does not protect a newspaper from litigation if an editor, asserting the public's right to information, breaks a reporter's promise of confidentiality to a source.

(See also GRAND JURIES; SPEECH AND THE PRESS.)

Carol E. Jensen

**Breedlove v. Suttles,** 302 U.S. 277 (1937), argued 16–17 Nov. 1937, decided 6 Dec. 1937 by vote of 9 to 0; Butler for the Court. This case involved a challenge to the Georgia poll tax by a white male citizen who claimed that it denied his right to equal protection of the laws under the *Fourteenth Amendment and his *Nineteenth Amendment right not to be discriminated against in voting on account of sex. The law required a tax of one dollar per year before registering to vote but exempted persons under 21 and over 60, blind persons, and females who did not register to vote. The Supreme Court unanimously upheld the law and rejected the claim. Observing that the Equal Protection Clause does not require absolute equality, Justice Pierce *Butler asserted that it was reasonable to limit the poll tax in the manner of the statute. He explained that it would be impossible to make the tax universal because many people were too poor to pay. He said further that women were naturally entitled to special considerations that permitted the state to discriminate in their favor. The Nineteenth Amendment challenge failed because it would have made the amendment in effect a limitation on the state taxing power.

(See also EQUAL PROTECTION; POLL TAXES; VOTE, RIGHT TO.)

Herman Belz

**Brennan, William Joseph, Jr.** (b. Newark, N.J., 25 Apr. 1906), associate justice, 1956–1990. Justice Brennan played a singular role in the constitu-

*William Joseph Brennan, Jr.*

tional revolution of the past two generations. The architect of many of the Warren Court's landmark decisions in the late 1950s and 1960s, he subsequently emerged as the leading proponent on the Burger and Rehnquist Courts of giving the Constitution a broad construction to promote individual liberty and equality. He continued up through his retirement in 1990 to engineer significant extensions of constitutional doctrine in some areas, while in others writing in passionate dissent against decisions he viewed as undermining the Warren Court's legacy. Brennan's judicial philosophy remains the subject of spirited controversy, but his supporters and critics agree that he ranks as one of the great justices in the nation's history.

Brennan, an Irish-Catholic Democrat, was appointed to the Court by President Dwight D. Eisenhower, a Republican, in the midst of Eisenhower's 1956 reelection campaign. Although Eisenhower in later years viewed his selection of Brennan as one of his worst mistakes, Brennan's performance should not have come as a surprise. The second of eight children born to parents who had immigrated to the United States in the 1890s, Brennan grew up in a struggling middle-class family and was a first-hand witness to suffering and social unrest in Newark, New Jersey. By his own account, the most influential person in Brennan's life was his father, a coal shoveler in a local brewery who later became a prominent labor leader and municipal reformer. The elder Brennan passed his activist social philosophy on to his son and pushed him to achieve excellence. William junior was an honors graduate of the Wharton School of the University of Pennsylvania and ranked high in his class at Harvard Law

School, which he completed through scholarships and odd jobs after his father's death.

Brennan practiced law with a prominent New Jersey firm in the 1930s. He joined the Army during World War II, served as a labor troubleshooter for the undersecretary of war, and was awarded the Legion of Merit. Brennan returned to private practice after the war, was a leader of the New Jersey court reform movement in the late 1940s, and within a three-year period progressed through the state judiciary from the trial bench to the state supreme court. He advocated the rights of criminal defendants and, in speeches around the state, bluntly compared McCarthy-era excesses to the Salem witch trials (see COMMUNISM AND COLD WAR). (Senator McCarthy cast the lone dissenting vote when the Senate subsequently confirmed President Eisenhower's nomination of Brennan.)

Notwithstanding his junior rank, Brennan quickly became one of the Supreme Court's most influential members. He authored a forceful restatement of federal judicial supremacy in *Cooper* v. *Aaron* (1958), the Court's response to southern "massive resistance" to desegregation orders. His opinion in *Baker* v. *Carr* (1962) opened the door to the *"reapportionment revolution" of the 1960s and 1970s and the rule of *"one person, one vote" in legislative districting; Chief Justice Earl *Warren later described the decision as the most important of his tenure. And in *New York Times* v. *Sullivan* (1964), Brennan led the Court in extending the protections of the *First and *Fourteenth Amendments to criticism of public officials, imposing sharp restrictions in libel cases to promote "the principle that debate on public issues should be uninhibited, robust, and wide-open" (p. 270). Brennan repeated this pathbreaking performance in numerous other areas—authoring eminent opinions that, for example, restricted loyalty oaths and government regulation of pornography, recognized a broad freedom of association, supported curbs on prayer in public schools, and expanded the availability of *habeas corpus and other federal judicial remedies for constitutional violations. (See ASSEMBLY AND ASSOCIATION, FREEDOM OF.)

Several factors account for Brennan's early prominence on the Court. He quickly joined what was oft-described as the Court's "liberal" wing, which, after Justice Arthur *Goldberg's appointment to the Court in 1962, commanded a solid majority receptive to expansive claims of individual rights and federal powers. At the same time, Brennan frequently took a more cautious approach than his "liberal" colleagues; indeed, an analysis of voting patterns shows he was squarely at the Warren Court's center and the justice least likely to be in dissent. Brennan tended more than others to avoid absolutes in favor of a "balancing" of competing interests, which in turn put him in a better position to forge majority consensus.

For example, Brennan in the *Sullivan* case rejected the view of Justices Hugo *Black, William O. *Douglas, and Arthur Goldberg that criticism of public officials' conduct should be absolutely immune from libel suits under the First Amendment, instead fashioning a privilege for such criticism that could be overcome through proof of *"actual malice," which he defined as deliberate or reckless disregard of the truth. Similarly, Brennan's opinion in *Schmerber* v. *California* (1966) held, over the dissents of Chief Justice Warren and Justices Black, Douglas, and Abe *Fortas, that the *Fifth Amendment's privilege against self-incrimination applies only to "testimonial" or otherwise "communicative" evidence and thus does not prohibit the forcible extraction of blood samples from suspected drunken drivers.

Brennan's pivotal position also resulted from his superb personal, tactical, and intellectual abilities. Although he disparaged references to his role as a "coalition builder," the historical record demonstrates otherwise. As Chief Justice Warren said of Brennan, "[f]riendly and buoyant in spirit, a prodigious worker and a master craftsman, he is a unifying influence on the bench and in the conference room" (Warren, "Mr. Justice Brennan," *Harvard Law Review* 80 [Nov. 1966]: 1–2). Brennan became Warren's closest colleague; the two met weekly before court conferences to discuss cases and plan strategy. Frequently a majority would agree upon an outcome while fragmenting on the appropriate analysis; in these situations Warren repeatedly turned to Brennan to build a decisional framework for the Court's result. Brennan's opinions were scholarly and closely reasoned; he displayed remarkable patience and skill in revising his drafts to accommodate his colleague's concerns and thereby reach a (sometimes fragile) majority consensus.

These abilities served Brennan well as the composition of the Court began to change at the end of the 1960s and into the 1970s. Although Brennan found himself in the minority with increasing frequency, he continued to play a significant leadership role on the Burger Court (and, to a lesser extent, on the Rehnquist Court until his retirement because of declining health in 1990). He authored several opinions recognizing broad remedies against municipalities and federal, state, and local officials for violations of federal law. Brennan was similarly influential in the First Amendment area. His opinions in *Elrod* v. *Burns* (1976) and *Rutan* v. *Republican Party of Illinois* (1990) sharply curtailed patronage practices as infringing the freedom of political association; *Texas* v. *Johnson* (1989) and *U.S.* v. *Eichman* (1990) invalidated on identical 5-to-4 votes laws that made it a crime to desecrate the United States flag. The opinions in the latter two cases, joined by two Reagan appointees, were vintage Brennan, emphasizing in *Johnson* the "special place reserved for the flag in this Nation" while under-

scoring the rights of political protest: "We do not consecrate the flag by punishing its desecration, for in doing so we dilute the freedom that this cherished emblem represents" (p. 420). Brennan similarly continued to attract occasional majorities to his views on the strict separation of church and state (see RELIGION).

Perhaps Brennan's greatest achievements in these later years were in the *equal protection area. He successfully advocated heightened judicial scrutiny of *gender-based classifications in *Craig* v. *Boren* (1976) and became the Court's most vocal advocate of gender equality, openly supporting the proposed Equal Rights Amendment. He similarly played a major role in sustaining the constitutionality of *affirmative action measures designed to counteract the societal effects of past racial and ethnic discrimination.

But Brennan frequently was in caustic dissent, particularly in cases involving those suspected or convicted of crime. His isolation from the Court became most pronounced on the death penalty, which Brennan (along with Justice Thurgood *Marshall) believed in all instances to be *cruel and unusual punishment prohibited by the *Eighth and *Fourteenth Amendments (see CAPITAL PUNISHMENT). His dissents railed against what he viewed to be the brutality of the death penalty, the arbitrariness by which it was administered, and its use against minorities, youth, and the retarded.

Brennan's critics argue that, perhaps more than any other justice, he epitomized an unrestrained federal judiciary that had arrogated unto itself the ultimate control over virtually every facet of daily life, thus demeaning the right of citizens to govern themselves through representative democracy (see JUDICIAL SELF-RESTRAINT). Judges like William Brennan, the argument continues, frequently exercise this power on the basis of their own policy preferences rather than the language or original intent of any particular constitutional provision.

Brennan commented in the *South Texas Law Review* (1986) that such arguments are "little more than arrogance cloaked as humility." He maintained that the Constitution, as amended by the *Bill of Rights and the *Reconstruction Era Amendments, is fundamentally a charter embodying "a sparkling vision of the supremacy of the human dignity of every individual"; the Court's duty is to protect this value as "transcendent, beyond the reach of temporary political majorities." In doing so, the Court's interpretation and application of the Constitution's broadly worded guarantees must constantly evolve. "Current Justices read the Constitution in the only way that we can: as twentieth-century Americans. . . . [T]he genius of the Constitution rests not in any static meaning it might have had in a world that is dead and gone, but in the adaptability of its great principles to cope with current problems and current needs" (pp. 433, 435–438).

One of the most notable examples of the way Brennan applied these principles, occasionally in conflict with justices who otherwise shared his philosophy, was in the area of government benefits. The Fifth and Fourteenth Amendments provide that a person's *"property" cannot be deprived without due process of law. In the twentieth century a variety of relationships with government have arisen that in no sense can be described as traditional "property"—welfare, subsidies, tax exemptions, licenses, grants, and other forms of public benefits. Brennan's opinion in *Goldberg v. Kelly (1970), which analogized welfare to "property" for constitutional purposes, launched what has been called the "modern procedural due process revolution" by requiring fair procedures for granting and revoking government benefits, even though such benefits are not themselves constitutionally required. Brennan authored other landmark opinions holding that such benefits cannot be administered in ways that would penalize the exercise of constitutional rights; for example, *Shapiro v. Thompson (1969) held, over the dissents of Chief Justice Warren and Justice Black, that laws requiring lengthy residence as a condition of welfare assistance unconstitutionally burden citizens' rights of interstate movement.

Brennan's theory of an evolving Constitution is further illustrated by his efforts to curb government intrusions on individual *"privacy"—a word nowhere mentioned in the Constitution. His opinion in *Eisenstadt v. Baird (1972), which struck down a law making it a crime to give contraceptives to unmarried women, emphasized that the unwritten "right to privacy" protects "the decision whether to bear or beget a child" (p. 453). His reasoning provided the foundation for the Court's curb on *abortion regulations the following year in *Roe v. Wade (1973). Brennan also stressed privacy rights in his dissents from court decisions upholding increasingly sophisticated police investigative techniques, periodically invoking the horrors of the totalitarian technological society portrayed in George Orwell's 1984.

A leading advocate of a strong federal judiciary, Brennan nevertheless urged others to move even further in protecting individual rights. His opinion in *Katzenbach v. Morgan (1966) recognized a broad congressional authority under section 5 of the Fourteenth Amendment to extend constitutional guarantees beyond the lines drawn in court decisions. *United Steelworkers v. Weber (1979) upheld voluntary affirmative action programs in the private sector. And as he increasingly found himself in dissent, Brennan in the mid-1970s began calling upon *state courts to "step into the breach" by interpreting their own state constitutions more expansively than the federal Constitution was currently being construed. In opinions, articles, and speeches he urged, with increasing success, that state courts

should "thrust themselves into a position of prominence in the struggle to protect the people or our nation from governmental intrusions on their freedoms"(Brennan, "State Constitutions and the Protection of Individual Rights," *Harvard Law Review* 90 [Jan. 1977]: 489, 503). It is an ironic comment on the man and his changing times that Brennan, a former state supreme court justice who cemented his place in history as an architect of federal judicial supremacy, emerged late in his career as a leading advocate of independent state judiciaries (see STATE CONSTITUTIONS AND INDIVIDUAL RIGHTS).

□ Vincent Blasi, ed., *The Burger Court: The Counter-Revolution That Wasn't* (1983). William J. Brennan, Jr., *An Affair with Freedom: A Collection of His Opinions and Speeches Drawn From His First Decade as a United States Supreme Court Justice,* edited by Stephen J. Friedman (1967). Edward V. Heck, "Justice Brennan and the Heyday of Warren Court Liberalism," *Santa Clara Law Review* 20 (Fall 1980): 841–887. Bernard Schwartz, *Super Chief: Earl Warren and His Supreme Court—A Judicial Biography* (1983).

Charles G. Curtis, Jr., and Shirley S. Abrahamson

**Brewer, David Josiah** (b. Smyrna, Asia Minor [modern Turkey], 20 Jan. 1837; d. Washington, D.C., 28 Mar. 1910; interred Mt. Muncie Cemetery, Leavenworth, Kans.), associate justice, 1890–1910. David Josiah Brewer was born of Congregational missionary parents in Asia Minor and then raised in privilege. After attending Wesleyan and Yale universities and Albany Law School, Brewer moved to Kansas in the late 1850s to begin his professional career. There he served on the Supreme Court of Kansas (1870–1884) and the Eighth Federal Circuit Court (1884–1889). In 1890 President Benjamin Harrison appointed him to the U.S. Supreme Court. Brewer was twice married: to Louise R. Landon of Burlington, Vt., in 1861, and after her death, to Emma Miner Mott of Washington, D.C., in 1901.

Today Brewer is largely forgotten, partly because at various points his tenure overlapped with three titans of the law—his uncle, Stephen J. *Field, John Marshall *Harlan, and Oliver Wendell *Holmes. Nevertheless, it was Brewer, along with Rufus W. *Peckham, who served as the intellectual leader of a bloc of justices—largely appointed by Grover Cleveland, a Democrat, and Benjamin Harrison, a Republican—that dominated the Supreme Court at the turn of the century. That group included Chief Justice Melville W. *Fuller, who described Brewer as "one of the most lovable of them all."

Brewer's overriding purpose was to affirm the idea of limited state interference with the economy. He marveled at the abundance that *capitalism had produced and defended inequalities in the distribution of wealth as inevitable and just.

In re *Debs (1895), Brewer wrote a unanimous opinion for the Court upholding an injunction against the Pullman strike of 1894 on the theory that Eugene Debs and his followers were obstructing the free flow of commerce among the states (see COMMERCE POWER). In *Reagan* v. *Farmers' Loan and Trust Co.* (1894), Brewer set aside a regulation of the Texas Railroad Commission limiting railroad rates because no return was coming to the investors. He thereby limited *Munn* v. *Illinois* (1877) and in that respect showed a philosophical link with his uncle Field, who originally dissented in that case and was adamant on the protection of *property rights.

Brewer was not, however, altogether blinded by his devotion to capitalism, and he was not opposed to the use of state authority when business power threatened the market. In *Northern Securities* v. *United States* (1904), for example, he provided the decisive vote to sustain Theodore Roosevelt's effort to set aside a merger between two corporate barons of the day, James Hill and J. P. Morgan.

Moreover, for a man so committed to the market and the system of liberties it implied, Brewer evidenced an instinctive concern for the disfranchised. Although he joined Peckham's opinion in *Lochner* v. *New York* (1905), which invalidated a statute establishing maximum hours for bakers, he wrote the opinion for a unanimous Court in *Muller* v. *Oregon* (1908), upholding a similar statute for women working in laundries. Brewer also passionately protested the treatment of the Chinese, on both substantive and procedural grounds. He dissented from Holmes's opinions in *United States* v. *Sing Tuck* (1904) and *United States* v. *Ju Toy* (1905), which denied resident Chinese access to the federal courts to try their claims of *citizenship, and from Harlan's opinion in the *Japanese Immigrant Case* (1903), which undermined a Japanese alien's claim for due process in deportation proceedings. He also dissented in *Fong Yue Ting* v. *United States* (1893), which involved the use of a pass system for resident Chinese under the Geary Act of 1892. Brewer complained: "In view of this enactment of the highest legislative body of the foremost Christian nation, may not the thoughtful Chinese disciple of Confucius ask, why do they send missionaries here?" Brewer also spoke out against the colonialism that swept the nation in the years immediately following the Spanish American War in 1898. "To introduce government by force over any portion of the nation," he said, "is to start the second quarter of the second century of our life upon principles which are the exact opposite of those upon which we have hitherto lived."

Like most justices of his time, Brewer's record is mixed on the rights of blacks. In *Berea College* v. *Kentucky* (1908), he upheld a state statute prohibiting private schools and colleges from providing instruction on an integrated basis; in *Hodges* v. *United States* (1906), he ruled that the federal government lacked power to prosecute a gang of whites who forced blacks off a job in Arkansas

*David Josiah Brewer*

(see RACE AND RACISM). The *Berea* decision rested on Brewer's view of the totality of a state's power over corporations, entities, or institutions that it helped create; he thought there would be serious constitutional doubts if the Kentucky statute were applied to individuals. The *Hodges* decision reflected the allocation of power between the states and the national government effectuated by the *Civil Rights Cases* of 1883. In a critical decision concerning voting discrimination, *Giles* v. *Harris* (1903), Brewer, along with Harlan, dissented from an opinion of Holmes that confessed an inability or unwillingness of the federal courts to provide relief against the massive program of racial disfranchisement against African-Americans then sweeping the South (see VOTE, RIGHT TO).

Brewer's special gift was his conception of the judge's role, which he both propounded and exemplified. He feared the popular movements of his day, which he saw as a threat to civilization, but unlike Holmes, who harbored similar sentiments, Brewer did not believe that the judge was to sit as a spectator while history unfolded; Brewer believed a judge's duty was to remind the people of their highest ideals, to lead rather than to acquiesce. He recognized that there was nothing that a judge could do to stop the inevitable triumph of the masses, but still believed that it was the judge's obligation to try. "It is one thing," Brewer once said, "to fail of reaching your ideal. It is an entirely different thing to deliberately turn your back on it."

□ Owen M. Fiss, "The Fuller Court," in *Encyclopedia of the American Constitution*, edited by Leonard Levy, Kenneth L. Karst, and Dennis J. Mahoney (1986), vol. 2, pp.

816–823. Arnold M. Paul, *Conservative Crisis and the Rule of Law: Attitudes of Bar and Bench, 1887–1895* (1960).

Owen M. Fiss

**Bricker Amendment.** See CONSTITUTIONAL AMENDING PROCESS.

**Briefs.** A brief is a written statement setting forth the factual background and legal contentions of a party in appellate litigation.

It is chiefly through written briefs that counsel persuade the Supreme Court. Justice Oliver Wendell *Holmes, for example, was influenced rarely by oral argument—usually, instead, by the record and the briefs. That is not surprising, since oral argument is fleeting, whereas briefs are permanent. A brief may be referred to in the seclusion of chambers, before and after argument. Whether in forming a justice's initial impression of the case, or in answering questions about a party's position during the writing of an opinion, the briefs alone speak for the parties.

Not always have advocates briefed the Court. It was not until 1821 that the Supreme Court rules first required all parties to submit written briefs:

After the present term, no cause standing for argument will be heard by the Court, until the parties shall have furnished the Court with a printed brief or abstract of the cause containing the substance of all the material pleadings, facts, and documents, on which the parties rely, and the points of law and fact intended to be presented at the argument. (19 U.S. [6 Wheat.], v, rule XXX, Feb. term 1821)

Half a century later, the rule on briefing was amended and expanded (14 Wall. xi), and it has undergone several changes in this century, but the crucial parts remain the same: (1) a succinct statement of the case and of the questions involved; and (2) the argument, specifically citing the authorities relied upon (see RULES OF THE COURT).

Today's Supreme Court rules emphasize that a brief should be what its very name suggests: "A brief must be compact, . . . concise, and free from burdensome, irrelevant, immaterial, and scandalous matter" (rule 24.6). It was not just an abstract fear of lawyerly verbosity but experience that demanded such a rule. Early in the twentieth century, when there were no page limits on briefs, Justice John H. *Clarke complained of briefs with more than a thousand pages. Under the current rule 24.6, such a brief would be "disregarded and stricken by the Court" (e.g., *Huffman* v. *Pursue*, 1974).

Experienced advocates today put what they need into fewer than fifty pages. In the mid-1970s, Chief Justice Warren *Burger suggested a fifty-page limit, and in 1980 the revised rules established that limit.

Most of the briefs submitted to the Court are not written by advocates experienced in Supreme Court practice, and the justices must contend with the "diffuseness" that Chief Justice Charles Evans *Hughes lamented. In many dozens of cases every year, lawyers reveal in their briefs little awareness of what the Court finds persuasive. In short, the average written argument is inadequate.

Too many advocates approach briefing just with a view of getting the facts and the law down on the page. They fail in imagination and tight analytical rigor. As a result, briefs are too often uninteresting as well as unpersuasive. And an inadequate brief hurts a party's chances of prevailing. In a 1942 article in the *ABA Journal* on appellate briefing, Justice Wiley B. *Rutledge advised: "[M]ake your briefs clear, concise, honest, balanced, buttressed, convincing and interesting. The last is not the least. A dull brief may be good law. An interesting one will make the judge aware of this" (p. 255).

That an unfocused brief may lose the case, even with good law behind it, may shock some. Given the great burdens upon the Court's time, however, an effective brief concisely brings home the nub of why the case ought to occupy the justices' attention.

Though the rules about briefing have become more and more specific with time, the qualities that go into a good brief have remained the same. In the early nineteenth century, Justice Joseph *Story described the "eloquence of the bar"— written as well as oral—as "plain, direct, and authoritative. . . . It forbids declamation, and efflorescence of style" (*Selections from the Works of Joseph Story*, 1839, pp. 186–187, 188).

(See also OPINIONS, ASSIGNMENT AND WRITING OF; ORAL ARGUMENT.)

□ Robert L. Stern and Eugene Gressman, *Supreme Court Practice*, 6th ed. (1986).

Bryan A. Garner

**Briscoe v. Bank of the Commonwealth of Kentucky,** 11 Pet. (36 U.S.) 257 (1837), argued 28 Jan., 1 Feb. 1837, decided 11 Feb. 1837 by vote of 6 to 1; McLean for the Court, Story in dissent. With the death of John *Marshall in 1835, the Supreme Court's orientation shifted away from his nationalist outlook. *Briscoe* v. *Bank of Kentucky* manifested this change in the field of banking and currency in the first full term of the court's new chief justice, Roger B. *Taney. Article I, section 10 of the Constitution prohibited states from using money "bills of credit," but the precise meaning of a "bill of credit" remained unclear. In *Craig* v. *Missouri* (1830) the Marshall Court had held, by a vote of 4 to 3, that state interest-bearing loan certificates were invalid under the constitutional prohibition. However, in the *Briscoe* case, the Court upheld the issuance of circulating notes by a state-chartered bank even when the Bank's stock, funds, and profits belonged to the state, and where the officers and directors were appointed by the state legislature. The Court narrowly defined a "bill of credit" as a note issued by the state, on the faith of the state, and designed to circulate as money. Since the notes in question were redeemable by the bank and not by the state itself, they were not "bills of credit" for constitutional purposes. By validating the constitutionality of state bank notes, the Supreme Court completed the financial revolution triggered by President Andrew *Jackson's refusal to recharter the Second Bank of the United States and opened the door to greater state control of banking and currency in the antebellum period.

(See also CAPITALISM.)

George Dargo

**Bronson v. Kinzie,** 42 U.S. 311 (1843), submitted without oral argument, decided 23 Feb. 1843 by vote of 6 to 1; Taney for the Court, McLean in dissent, Story and McKinley not participating. *Bronson* exemplified the Supreme Court's determination to protect private contracts from infringement by state legislation. At issue were two 1841 Illinois statutes that limited mortgage foreclosure sales and gave mortgagors expanded rights to redeem foreclosed property. These measures were retroactive, applying to mortgages made before the acts were passed. Prior to passage of the statutes, John H. Kinzie had mortgaged his property to Arthur Bronson. Bronson sought to foreclose the mortgage free of the legislative restrictions.

Chief Justice Roger B. *Taney held that this legislative attempt to modify the terms of the existing mortgage was an unconstitutional impairment of the obligation of *contract. Taney agreed that a state could alter the remedies available to enforce past as well as future contracts. He nonetheless emphasized that such changes could not materially impair the rights of creditors. In broad language Taney extolled the virtue of the *Contract Clause: "It was undoubtedly adopted as a part of the Constitution for a great and useful purpose. It was to maintain the integrity of contracts, and to secure their faithful execution throughout this Union" (p. 318). In dissent, Justice John *McLean argued that the statutes simply modified the remedy for the enforcement of contracts.

The Court long adhered to the *Bronson* rule, invalidating state laws that interfered with contractual rights in the guise of regulating remedies. The decision was effectively superseded, however, by *Home Building and Loan Association v. Blaisdell* (1934), in which the justices ruled that contracts were subject to the reasonable exercise of state *police power.

James W. Ely, Jr.

**Brown, Henry Billings** (b. South Lee, Mass., 2 Mar. 1836; d. Bronxville, N.Y., 4 Sep. 1913; interred Elmwood Cemetery, Detroit, Mich.), associate justice, 1890–1906. Brown was the son of a prosperous New England businessman. He graduated from Yale University, read law, and received some formal legal training at Yale and

*Henry Billings Brown*

Harvard. Migrating to the Great Lakes port of Detroit, Michigan, in 1859, Brown specialized in admiralty law. He married the daughter of a wealthy lumber trader, and an inheritance from his father-in-law made Brown's family financially independent. Following brief service as a Republican appointee to the county circuit court, he enjoyed a flourishing practice. Brown also taught law, unsuccessfully sought nomination for Congress, and delivered occasional papers and addresses. He shared private practice with duties as assistant U.S. attorney and in 1875 was appointed to the U.S. District Court for the Eastern District of Michigan. On that bench Brown became nationally known for his admiralty opinions. Benjamin Harrison in 1890 appointed him to the U.S. Supreme Court, a goal Brown had cultivated through political and social contacts. He remained on the Court until failing eyesight forced his retirement.

A generally moderate justice, Brown was highly protective of *property rights and was reluctant to extend criminal procedural protections and civil liberties. His concurrence with the Court's opinion in *Lochner v. New York* (1905), which struck down a maximum work hours law, showed his general unwillingness to support the *police power when it seriously interfered with business. A social Darwinist, he emphasized individual responsibility for economic decisions and personal conduct, no matter how harsh the consequences for the individual. He did, however, vote to uphold the federal income tax in *Pollock v. Farmers' Loan & Trust Co.* (1895), showing some flexibility under changing social conditions. As a judge, he employed a rather mechanical jurisprudence, strictly applying precedent to facts in a formulaic manner.

A usually careful, cautious legal technician and a capable justice, Brown had no transcendent judicial philosophy; he has been markedly forgotten, or when remembered, vilified for authoring the Court's opinion in *Plessy* v. *Ferguson* (1896), a 7-to-1 decision upholding state-mandated racially segregated railway cars. *Plessy's* *separate but equal doctrine provided a constitutional foundation for discriminatory "Jim Crow" laws in the United States until the mid-twentieth century.

Brown, a privileged son of the Yankee merchant class, was a reflexive social elitist whose opinions of women, African-Americans, Jews, and immigrants now seem odious, even if they were unexceptional for their time. Brown exalted, as he once wrote, "that respect for the law inherent in the Anglo-Saxon race." Although he was widely praised as a fair and honest judge, *Plessy* has irrevocably dimmed his otherwise creditable career. Though some may argue that Brown bears personal guilt for the racial evils *Plessy* helped make possible, others respond that Brown was a man of his day, noting that the decades of de jure discrimination that came after *Plessy* merely reflected the *Zeitgeist*.

Warmly regarded for his amiable character, Brown inspired real personal fondness in acquaintances. His diaries suggest a likable, modest, but ambitious man, personally conservative, frequently depressed, disinclined to sustained hard work, and often self-doubting.

□ Robert J. Glennon, Jr., "Justice Henry Billings Brown: Values in Tension," *University of Colorado Law Review* 44 (1973): 553–604.                    Francis Helminski

**Browning-Ferris Industries v. Kelco Disposal, Inc.,** 492 U.S. 257 (1989), argued 18 Apr. 1989, decided 26 June 1989 by vote of 7 to 2; Blackmun for the Court, O'Connor and Stevens dissenting in part. In *Browning-Ferris Industries,* the Court considered whether the Excessive Fines Clause of the *Eighth Amendment applies to punitive damage awards in civil cases between private parties. The issue arose in a case involving the waste disposal business in Burlington, Vermont. Plaintiffs sued Browning-Ferris Industries (BFI) alleging that the company had attempted to drive them out of that business. The jury found for the plaintiffs and judgment was entered for more than $150,000 in treble compensatory damages and $6 million in punitive damages. On appeal to the Supreme Court, BFI argued that the punitive damages award was excessive and violated the Eighth Amendment, which reads: "Excessive bail shall not be required, nor excessive fines imposed, nor cruel and unusual punishments imposed."

The Court held that the Eighth Amendment does not apply to awards of punitive damages in cases between private parties. Although the Eighth Amendment received little debate in the First Congress, the word "fine" was understood to mean a payment to a sovereign. The "undisputed purpose and history" of that amendment confirm the conclusion that it places no limits on the amount of punitive damages that can be awarded to private parties. Rather, the amendment restricts the government's power to punish and deter individuals.

The Court left open two related issues. First, it did not decide whether the Excessive Fines Clause applies in civil cases brought by the government. Second, because the question was not properly presented, the Court did not decide whether the *Due Process Clause limits a court's power to award punitive damages.

Daan Braveman

**Brown's Indian Queen Hotel.** Located on Pennsylvania Avenue near Capitol Hill, the Indian Queen became Washington's most prestigious hotel when it opened in 1820. Here, or in one of the boardinghouses in the neighborhood, the members of the Marshall Court lived during Court terms, sharing meals and conversation in an atmosphere that encouraged consensus. (See also COLLEGIALITY.)

Maxwell Bloomfield

**Brown v. Board of Education,** 347 U.S. 483 (1954), argued 9 Dec. 1952, reargued 8 Dec. 1953, decided 17 May 1954 by vote of 9 to 0; Warren for the Court (*Brown I*); 349 U.S. 294 (1955), reargued, on the question of relief, 11–14 April 1954, decided 31 May 1955 by vote of 9 to 0; Warren for the Court (*Brown II*). With a brisk, nontechnical and unexpectedly unanimous opinion running only ten pages, Chief Justice Earl *Warren ignited a legal and social revolution in race relations and constitutionalism. "*Brown* was the beginning," Alexander M. *Bickel later wrote—the beginning not only of substantive changes in the American social structure but also in the nature and expectations of how the Supreme Court interpreted the Constitution.

*Background.* The decisions—on the merits (*Brown I*) and on relief (*Brown II*)—culminated a litigation campaign by the *National Association for the Advancement of Colored People (NAACP) and its legal arm, the *Legal Defense and Education Fund, Inc., that began twenty years earlier. Beginning in the mid-1930s, the NAACP brought suits first at the state and then at the federal level challenging, on constitutional grounds, the legal regime of "Jim Crow"—state-imposed racial segregation in public accommodations and in education (see SEGREGATION, DE JURE). The goal was to abolish Jim Crow and to spur substantive improvement in public education for African-Americans. The primary obstacle facing the NAACP was *Plessy* v. *Ferguson* (1896), in which the Supreme Court had held 7 to 1 that state-imposed racial segregation in public facilities was not "unreasonable" and therefore did not violate the *Equal Protection Clause of the *Fourteenth Amendment.

The initial steps in the strategy did not confront *Plessy* frontally but sought to undermine it. When the Supreme Court invalidated Missouri's out-of-state tuition program for African-American law students in 1938 (*Missouri ex rel. Gaines* v. *Canada*), everyone knew that the legal superstructure of Jim Crow was vulnerable. Successive decisions by the Court, largely involving cases brought by the NAACP, continued the erosion of Jim Crow in public transportation and in *education.

The biggest break occurred in 1948, when the United States attorney general, for the first time, signed an *amicus curiae brief in a race case (*Shelley* v. *Kraemer*), which signaled the federal government's symbolic support for the NAACP strategy. The Court held racially *restrictive covenants unconstitutional in that case, but the watershed did not come until two years later in 1950, when the Court invalidated segregation in graduate schools (*McLaurin* v. *Oklahoma State Board of Regents*) and in law schools (*Sweatt* v. *Painter*). The Court's opinions in both cases noted the inequality of facilities created by Jim Crow, but disapproved, for the first time, the "intangible" but genuine harms of racial segregation—such as inability of blacks to associate with white colleagues and the consequent limitation to their education. Unbeknownst outside the Court, many of the justices concluded privately in 1950 that *McLaurin* and *Sweatt* sealed the fate of Jim Crow and of *Plessy* itself.

The stumbling block in the *Brown* litigation, which affected more than a dozen states and the District of Columbia, and their millions of school children, and which was in progress when the 1950 cases were decided, was the scope of relief. When *Brown* was first argued in 1952, the Court internally was divided not so much on the merits but on how, and at what pace, to order relief. The Court remained at loggerheads over the issue during the summer of 1953 when fate intervened. Chief Justice Fred *Vinson, who wrote *Sweatt* and *McLaurin* but hesitated to require massive desegregation, died suddenly. His replacement, Earl Warren, responded to the situation by convincing his colleagues to decide the merits in one opinion and to defer the question of relief to a second opinion following reargument. At the time, Warren's greatest achievement was thought to be massing a Court unanimous in both vote and opinion; to do so, he had to convince at least two justices, Robert H. *Jackson (concurrence) and Stanley F. *Reed (dissent), to suppress opinions that they were then preparing. The Court's ultimate unanimity was publicly applauded and was said to buttress the wisdom of the result.

*Opinions.* Warren later revealed in his memoirs that he wrote *Brown I* in a short, non-accusatory and nontechnical style so that it could be understood by laymen and even be reprinted widely in the public press. The opinion elided all of the hard questions: the evidence of the historical understanding of the Equal Protection Clause (see HISTORY, COURT USES OF)—upon which the parties had been directed to focus their reargument—was deemed "inconclusive"; *Plessy*'s claim that segregation caused no harm was refuted by modern social science data (including highly controversial works cited in *Footnote 11); and *Plessy* itself was disingenuously circumscribed ("In the field of public education, *separate but equal has no place" [p. 494]). Warren tried to show that the Court had incrementally chipped away at *Plessy* in the preceding cases and, in a larger sense, that the logic of *Plessy* had self-destructed over time, as African-Americans became more successful in various fields, and as education became more central to American life. Indeed, *Brown* self-consciously avoided questioning the entire structure of Jim Crow in all of its applications but focused exclusively on segregated education and on its harm to those separated because of their race.

If *Brown I* contained moral clarity without explicit doctrinal foundation, *Brown II*—rendered one year later—lacked both. The NAACP urged desegregation to proceed immediately, or at least within firm deadlines. The states claimed both were impracticable. The Court, fearful of hostility and even violence if the NAACP views were adopted, embraced a view close to that of the states—but with insistence that progress begin soon. Nonetheless, the opinion equivocated on every line and essentially returned the problem to the courts where the cases began for appropriate desegregative relief—with, in the phrase that soon was condemned for its invitation to recalcitrance, *"all deliberate speed." A Court admirably unanimous on the merits in 1954 became ambiguously, indeed emptily, unanimous on the key issue of relief in 1955.

*Brown II* imposed substantial costs on all concerned. The burden of producing multimillion-student desegregation plans was placed on the plaintiffs and the NAACP, who were undermanned, thinly financed, and targets of hostility. The justices had privately hoped that the Department of Justice, which had participated in all of the *Brown* arguments, would energetically support the plaintiffs, but President Eisenhower chronically avoided the issue and promised no more than "to obey the law of the land." School districts were caught in a political whipsaw between a handful of reform-minded residents who wished to make desegregation work and the vast majority who resisted change and saw the issue as fuel for their own devices. Southern congressional leaders and regional governors were especially outspoken in their defiance of the decisions.

The Court itself suffered symbolically to some

extent. If *Brown I* was a clarion call, *Brown II*'s ambivalence implicitly diminished the moral imperative of the first decision. As organized resistance, especially in Congress, and less organized resistance at the grass roots, mounted, the Court retreated and did not hear another case involving segregation for more than three years after *Brown II*. Then, in *Cooper* v. *Aaron* (1958), the Court's opinion on the Little Rock, Arkansas, school crisis of 1957–1958, spoke more to the importance of the Court's own power than to the substantive issue of *equal protection of the laws.

*Aftermath.* Between *Brown II* and *Cooper* v. *Aaron*, the Court refused to hear further cases involving segregation and the scope of *Brown* but issued a series of controversial *per curiam decisions based solely on requests for review of lower court decisions. The Court invalidated segregated state parks, beaches and bath houses, golf courses, and even public transportation. The final decision (*Gayle* v. *Browder,* 1956), was tinged with irony, because it effectively overruled *Plessy*—a step the Court found unnecessary to take in *Brown* and that the per curiam order did not even admit was in issue. The reasonless per curiam orders prompted many legal scholars to warn that the Court was acting more out of conviction than principle and urged the justices to explain their actions, both to refute southern charges of willfulness and to provide guidance for future cases involving racial issues in nonsegregation situations. *Bolling* v. *Sharpe* (1954), the companion case to *Brown* from the District of Columbia, provided the rudimentary doctrinal apparatus to meet the need, but the Court eschewed the opportunity.

Because *Brown II* provided so little guidance, either as to relief or as to the precise doctrinal foundation of *Brown I,* the Court put itself in the position of reexplaining, and effectively remaking, the basic principle in every successive segregation case. After reaffirming *Brown* against gubernatorial resistance in 1958 at Little Rock, the Court turned a doctrinal and substantive corner with *Green* v. *County School Board of New Kent County* in 1968 when it held that compliance with *Brown II* required not simply abolition of state-imposed segregative practices but the effective desegregation of formerly segregated schools. After *Green,* busing for racial balance was inevitable, which the Court confirmed in *Swann* v. *Charlotte-Mecklenburg County Board of Education* (1971).

On one level, *Brown* was remarkably ineffectual. By 1964, a decade after the first decision, less than 2 percent of formerly segregated school districts had experienced any desegregation. As *Brown* was applied outside the original jurisdictions where segregation was imposed or permitted by law, local resistance became even more fierce and sustained. Yet *Brown* was a potent catalyst for ambitious social change, both in Congress, where the aspirations of *Brown* helped prompt the *Civil Rights Act of 1964 and the *Voting Rights Act of 1965 among others, and in the federal courts themselves, where the decision's bold moral hopes and impatience with formal doctrinal obstacles encouraged a generation of lawyers and activists to improve society under the rubric of constitutional exegesis. Inspired by *Brown,* lawyers and judges breathed new life into not only the Equal Protection Clause of the Fourteenth Amendment but also its *Due Process Clause (in both its procedural and its more controversial substantive senses). (See DUE PROCESS, SUBSTANTIVE.) The Court itself was emboldened in part by the experience of *Brown* to expand federal protection for state defendants in criminal proceedings and to strengthen the protection of the *First Amendment to critics of first state and then of the federal government during the decade following *Brown.* For example, the constitutional doctrine of "freedom of association," which was created by the Court in *NAACP v. Alabama* (1958), was directly related to school desegregation: state officials tried to compel the publication of the organization's membership lists in part to discourage support for desegregating schools.

Earl Warren's opinion for the Court in *Brown I* made the decision seem inevitable, and today, as Warren said in the companion case, a contrary result seems unthinkable. Yet the outcome was the product of a lengthy process that involved more than the NAACP and critical maneuvers inside the Court during the 1953 term. In many respects, the seeds for *Brown* were sown in the early 1930s, when the justices were presented with case after case in which black criminal defendants in the South were victimized by police, judges, and all-white juries. The stark reality of Jim Crow, and its routine brutality, impelled the Court to begin the process of dismantling Jim Crow piecemeal well before the NAACP strategy hit full stride during *World War II. The courage of African-American servicemen during the war, and President Harry Truman's willingness to make civil rights a national issue in 1948—with a presidential commission and at the Democratic Convention as well as in *Shelley* v. *Kraemer*—provided the important symbolic presence of national support that helped to steel the Court's will to move from protection of African-American individuals to African-Americans as a class, and, inevitably, as a social movement. Whatever the consequences borne out by the case law, *Brown* remains a potent symbol of the aspiration for the Constitution and the values it enshrines.

(See also RACE AND RACISM.)

□ Alexander M. Bickel, *The Least Dangerous Branch* (1962). Charles L. Black, Jr., "The Lawfulness of the Segregation Decisions," *Yale Law Journal* 69 (1960): 421–430. Dennis J. Hutchinson, "Unanimity and Desegregation," *Georgetown Law Journal* 68 (1979): 1–96. Richard

# 96 □ Brown v. Maryland

Kluger, *Simple Justice* (1975). Philip B. Kurland, "*Brown v. Board of Education* Was the Beginning," *Washington University Law Quarterly* (1979): 309–405. Gerald Rosenberg, *The Hollow Hope* (1990). Mark Tushnet, *The NAACP's Legal Strategy Against Segregated Education, 1925–1950* (1987).
— Dennis J. Hutchinson

**Brown v. Maryland,** 12 Wheat. (25 U.S.) 419 (1827), argued 28 Feb. and 1 Mar. 1827, decided 12 Mar. 1827 by vote of 6 to 1; Marshall for the Court, Thompson in dissent. In *Brown v. Maryland*, importers of foreign goods challenged a state law that required all persons who sold such goods to purchase a license. They alleged that it violated the ban on import taxes in Article I, section 10 of the Constitution, as well as interfered with federal authority over interstate and foreign commerce. Chief Justice John *Marshall sustained both contentions. He formulated the "original package" doctrine, which held that the taxing power of a state does not extend to imports from abroad so long as they remain in the original package. Only after the goods became mixed with the general property in the state could the state treat them as it did all domestic goods for sale. Marshall held a license tax on the importer to be indistinguishable from a tax on the import itself. Roger B. *Taney, who succeeded Marshall as *chief justice, had argued the case as counsel for the state of Maryland, but he later wrote that he believed the case had been correctly decided.

Marshall hinted that the *Brown* decision applied to domestic imports from a sister state, but in *Woodruff* v. *Parham* (1869) the Court held that the original package rule did not apply to goods moving in interstate commerce. In 1976 the Court further diluted the *Brown* doctrine when in *Michelin Tire Corporation* v. *Wages* it decided that a state might assess a value-based property tax upon a foreign import stored in a warehouse awaiting sale. To exempt a foreign import from a uniform state property tax, declared the Court, would accord it preferential treatment.

(See also COMMERCE POWER; TAXING AND SPENDING CLAUSE.)
— Robert J. Steamer

**Brown v. Mississippi,** 297 U.S. 278 (1936), argued 10 Jan. 1936, decided 17 Feb. 1936 by vote of 9 to 0; Hughes for the Court. In *Brown* v. *Mississippi*, the Supreme Court reversed the convictions of three African-American Mississippi tenant farmers for the murder of a white planter. At the trial, the prosecution's principal evidence was the defendants' confessions to police officers. During the trial, however, prosecution witnesses freely admitted that the defendants confessed only after being subjected to brutal whippings by the officers. The confessions were nevertheless admitted into evidence; the defendants were convicted by a jury and sentenced to be hanged; and the convictions were affirmed by the Mississippi Supreme Court on appeal.

Aided by financial contributions from the *National Association for the Advancement of Colored People and the Commission on Interracial Cooperation, ex–Mississippi governor Earl Leroy Brewer appealed the convictions to the U.S. Supreme Court, which the Court unanimously reversed under the Due Process Clause of the *Fourteenth Amendment. Although reaffirming the fact that the *Self-Incrimination Clause of the *Fifth Amendment did not apply to the states, Chief Justice Charles Evans *Hughes nevertheless held that a criminal conviction based upon confessions elicited by physical brutality violated the fundamental right to a fair trial mandated by the Due Process Clause. *Brown* began a line of cases involving the methods by which confessions were elicited from criminal defendants, that culminated with *Miranda* v. *Arizona* (1966).

(See also COERCED CONFESSIONS; DUE PROCESS, PROCEDURAL.)
— Richard C. Cortner

**Buchanan v. Warley,** 245 U.S. 60 (1917), argued 10–11 Apr. 1916, decided 5 Nov. 1917 by vote of 9 to 0; Day for the Court. In this case the Supreme Court considered the constitutionality of a Louisville, Kentucky, ordinance that required residential segregation by race. Enacted in 1914, the law prohibited blacks and whites from living in houses on blocks where the majority of houses was occupied by persons of the other race. In a case designed to test a type of legislation then appearing in several upper south states, a contract for the sale of property was arranged between a white seller and a black purchaser. In a unanimous decision the Supreme Court declared the law unconstitutional.

Justice William R. Day said the Civil Rights Act of 1866 and the *Fourteenth Amendment secured the right of blacks to acquire property without state legislation discriminating against them solely because of color. More generally, the Court asked whether a white man could be denied the right to dispose of his property to a purchaser solely because the purchaser was black. Although acknowledging that race hostility was a problem that the law to some extent was bound to recognize, Justice Day stated that its solution "cannot be promoted by depriving citizens of their constitutional rights and privileges" (p. 81). Day concluded that the law violated the rights of both whites and blacks to dispose of their property and directly violated the Fourteenth Amendment prohibition of interference with property rights, except by due process of law (See DUE PROCESS, PROCEDURAL). The Court distinguished *Plessy* v. *Ferguson* (1896) and *Berea College* v. *Kentucky* (1908) as approving reasonable regulations of Fourteenth Amendment rights under the *separate but equal rule. This decision placed limits on the movement to segregate blacks and showed that protection of property rights could have the effect of securing civil rights.

(See also HOUSING DISCRIMINATION; PROPERTY RIGHTS; RACE AND RACISM; SEGREGATION, DE JURE.)

Herman Belz

**Buckley v. Valeo,** 424 U.S. 1 (1976), argued 16 Nov. 1975, decided 30 Jan. 1976 by varying votes on specific questions; opinion was unsigned, Burger, Blackmun, Rehnquist, White, and Marshall all dissented in part, Stevens not participating. Rarely has the Court recast congressional legislation in so many substantial particulars as it did in this case in ruling on the several provisions of the Federal Election Campaign Act (FECA) of 1971, as amended in 1974, and on relevant provisions of the Revenue Act of 1971, as amended in 1974. As the *per curiam opinion indicates, different majorities of the eight participating justices decided the various challenges raised by candidates and others seeking to prevent the new campaign legislation from taking effect in the 1976 election.

The Court invalidated a provision of the law that permitted Congress to choose a majority of voting members of the Federal Election Commission (FEC) created to administer and enforce the FECA. Holding that this arrangement violated the Appointments Clause that empowered only the president to nominate such officers, the Court effectively told Congress to rewrite this portion of the FECA (which it promptly did) in order to maintain the FEC's considerable powers. The powers themselves were upheld, as were the FECA's detailed disclosure and reporting requirements.

More complicated were the Court's holdings on the *First Amendment challenges to FECA restrictions of contributions and expenditures in federal elections. It upheld the several contribution limits (for example, the thousand-dollar maximum that each individual can contribute to a congressional or presidential candidate in each election campaign) on the ground that they are appropriate legislative weapons against improper influence stemming from the dependence of candidates on large contributions. On the other hand, expenditure limits were invalidated as substantial and direct restrictions on political expression in violation of the First Amendment. The Court thus erased Congress's attempt to fix not only overall limits on a candidate's expenditures, but also the limits on how much others could spend relative to a candidate (apart from direct contributions to the candidate) and the limits on how much candidates could spend from their own or their family's funds.

Invalidation of the last of these limits illustrates the nature of the Court's distinction between contributions and expenditures. Using millions of one's own dollars in a campaign, though effectively substituting for large contributions

from others, does not corrupt or even seem to corrupt the candidate. Nevertheless, unwealthy opponents might well regard the Court-granted freedom of a rich candidate to spend millions from family wealth as an especially unfair advantage because they could not now, under the law, so readily compensate by finding a few very large contributors. A larger and more significant legal loophole was created by the Court's invalidation of the provision for limiting how much individuals and groups could spend to help candidates. These expenditures need only be "independent" of the candidate and the candidate's campaign committee in order to be unlimited as contributions to candidates are not.

In contrast to its mixed response to Congress's regulations of private campaign finance, the Court fully upheld the new provisions for public funding of presidential campaigns. These provisions include income tax check-off funds for parties to conduct presidential nominating conventions, for presidential primary candidates (on a matching basis), and for presidential general election candidates (on a virtually full-funding basis). Such funding, the Court held, is within Congress's power to spend under the *General Welfare Clause, and it does not violate either the First Amendment or the *Fifth Amendment's Due Process Clause. The latter issue arose because the arrangement for distributing funds was more likely to help major parties and their candidates than minor parties, new parties, or independents. But the Court interpreted the law as allowing sufficient opportunity for minor parties and their candidates to qualify for public funds, even though at lower levels.

One last element of judicial law-making should be noted. In upholding public funding, the Court also ruled that it is constitutionally valid to require, as Congress had done, that a presidential candidate must agree to an expenditure ceiling as a condition for receiving such funding. A ceiling thus voluntarily accepted does not fall under the Court's general prohibition of expenditure ceilings. Accordingly, if Congress or state legislatures should want to fix expenditure ceilings for candidates for other offices, the constitutional means to do so is to provide public funds along with the ceilings. But the Court made clear, in *Federal Election Commission* v. *National Conservative Political Action Committee* (1985), that such ceilings cannot be applied to those spending independently to help a publicly funded candidate.

(See also ELECTIONS; FINANCING POLITICAL SPEECH; SPEECH AND THE PRESS.)

Leon D. Epstein

**Buck v. Bell,** 274 U.S. 200 (1927), argued 22 Apr. 1927, decided 2 May 1927 by vote of 8 to 1; Holmes for the Court, Butler in dissent without opinion. Gifted with the ability to express himself in tersely developed phrases, Justice Oliver Wendell *Holmes provided some of his most quoted expressions in *Buck* v. *Bell* (1927). Upholding in an 8-to-1 opinion a Virginia law that provided for sterilization, Holmes not only continued a long held disposition to allow states the full sweep of their police powers but also laced his opinion with the prejudices shared by a nation.

The case had its beginnings in the Progressive Era (see PROGRESSIVISM) with Albert Priddy, superintendent of the State Colony for Epileptics and Feeble-Minded at Lynchburg, Virginia. Enthusiastically endorsing the drive for race improvement through eugenical sterilization, Priddy practiced sterilization with the encouragement of the colony's board of directors. Since the legislation did not clearly sanction sterilization, a court in 1918 warned Priddy of his personal liability and he discontinued the operation.

State budget problems coincided with Priddy's efforts to get unequivocal legislation. With Aubrey Strode representing Priddy and the eugenical community, the 1924 assembly enacted a statute that provided for release, after sterilization, of individuals who otherwise might require permanent institutionalization. The law outlined procedures to be followed, including approval of the institution's board, appointment of a guardian, a hearing, and appeals to the courts.

Carrie Buck became caught in the web of events in 1924. A victim of rape, Carrie became pregnant. The family with which the eighteen-year-old lived had her committed to the colony, once the revised Binet-Simon I.Q. test revealed her mental age as nine. Her mother, Emma, who had been found to have a mental age of less than eight years, was also confined in the colony. After the birth of her daughter, Vivian, on 28 March 1924, Priddy recommended that Carrie be sterilized because she was feebleminded and a "moral delinquent." Concluding that Vivian inherited the same condition from her mother who had in turn inherited it from her mother, Priddy had a perfect test case. The colony board accepted his recommendation and retained attorneys, Strode to represent the colony and Irving Whitehead, former member of the colony's board and friend of Strode, to represent Carrie.

The trial in the county circuit court took place on 18 November 1924. Strode presented eight witnesses and an expert's disposition to prove Carrie's feeblemindedness. Describing the Buck family as part of the "shiftless, ignorant, and worthless class of anti-social whites" in the South, the court heard that Vivian, the third generation, was "not quite normal."

Whitehead called no witness to dispute either the "experts" or the allegations made about Carrie and her family. He could have challenged the charge of Carrie's illegitimacy and emphasized her church attendance and rather average school record. Whitehead failed in his defense because he intended to fail. The end he sought

appears to have been the same as that sought by Priddy and Strode.

Now named *Buck* v. *Bell*, because John H. Bell had replaced Priddy at the colony, Whitehead in 1925 appealed the case to the United States Supreme Court. Strode's brief argued that due process had been afforded and that state police powers allowed its officers to protect and decide for persons such as Carrie Buck. Whitehead countered that the law discriminated against those confined to institutions and that a state could not surgically deprive persons of their "full bodily integrity." If allowed to do so, he warned, new classes, even "races" might be brought within the scope of the law and the "worst forms of tyranny practiced" in a "reign of doctors . . . inaugurated in the name of science."

Holmes rejected the argument for equal protection in his May 1927 opinion, noting that the law "indicates a policy, applies it to all within the lines and seeks to bring [others] within the lines . . . so fast as its means allow" (p. 208). Accepting eugenical arguments, he felt procedural guarantees had been "scrupulously" followed. Holmes contended that if the nation could call upon its "best citizens" for their lives during war it could demand a "lesser" sacrifice of those who "sap the strength" of society (p. 207). Prevention of procreation by degenerates would benefit society because "[t]hree generations of imbeciles are enough" (p. 207).

After the Court's ruling, Carrie was sterilized in October 1927. Numerous states passed similar laws and Nazi Germany gave the fullest sweep to the movement. This case provides a strong argument for careful scrutiny, especially at the local level, of ideas grounded upon popular notions of science.

(See also DUE PROCESS, PROCEDURAL; POLICE POWER.)

□ Paul A. Lombardo, "Three Generations, No Imbeciles: New Light on *Buck* v. *Bell*," *New York Law Review* 60 (April 1985): 30–62. Fred D. Ragan

**Budd v. New York,** 143 U.S. 517 (1892), argued 17–18 Nov. 1891, decided 29 Feb. 1892 by vote of 6 to 3; Blatchford for the Court, Brewer, Field, and Brown in dissent. *Budd* v. *New York* was an appeal from a decision of the New York Court of Appeals, *People* v. *Budd* (1889), which had upheld the constitutionality of a New York statute regulating rates charged by grain elevators, the same issue that had been resolved in *Munn* v. *Illinois* (1877). Conservative critics of *Munn* urged its repudiation in light of the doctrine of substantive *due process that had grown ever more potent since 1877 and that had recently triumphed in Justice Samuel *Blatchford's majority opinion in *Chicago, Milwaukee & St. Paul Railway Co.* v. *Minnesota* (1890).

But in *Budd* Justice Blatchford reaffirmed *Munn*, upholding the legitimacy of regulating grain elevators as businesses affected with a public interest. Rate regulation of such enterprises did not deny their owners due process of law in violation of the *Fourteenth Amendment. Because regulation was confined to the territorial jurisdiction of New York, Blatchford found no violation of the Commerce Clause of Article I, section 8, either (see COMMERCE POWER).

All this was too much for Justice David J. *Brewer, dissenting. Brewer denounced the basic doctrine of *Munn* as "radically unsound" (p. 548) and trumpeted his clarion of *laissez-faire constitutionalism. "The paternal theory of government is to me odious," Brewer wrote (p. 551). Though never explicitly overruled, *Munn* and *Budd* suffered an erosion of their authority through the *New Deal.                    William M. Wiecek

**Budget of the Court.** When the Supreme Court first met in February 1790, it placed negligible burdens on the federal budget. There were only six justices earning salaries of $4,000 for the chief justice and $3,500 for the associates. The Court had no permanent headquarters, but met in a second floor room of the Royal Exchange Building in New York City. There were no law *clerks or other supporting personnel. Congress had not even provided a law *library. Over the years the operations of the Supreme Court expanded as its authority and caseload grew. Since 1935 the Supreme Court has had a permanent home in a majestic marble building across the street from the Capitol in Washington (see BUILDINGS, SUPREME COURT). Nine justices now hold office and they are supported by a full range of staff members to help the Court carry out its duties. The financial needs of the Court have correspondingly increased, but it remains today a rather inexpensive institution relative to the other federal agencies.

The Supreme Court is dependent upon Congress for its funding and must submit to the legislature an annual budget request. The budgetary process starts more than a year prior to the beginning of the fiscal year for which funds are being requested. In the spring and summer months of each year the Court formulates budget requests and justifications. The Office of the *Marshal of the Court, principally through its director of the budget, oversees the budget formulation process. The final requested amounts must be approved by the Court and submitted to the Office of Management and Budget. The Supreme Court's requests, along with those of all other federal departments and agencies, are incorporated into the budget proposals the president submits to Congress. Unlike its authority over other agency requests, OMB is expressly prohibited by law from making any modifications in the level of funding requested by the judiciary.

Congressional action begins in the late winter months and often extends well into the summer. The requests from the judiciary are initially sent to the appropriate House and Senate Appropriations Subcommittees, where the proposals are given careful scrutiny. In addition to the requests of the Supreme Court, separate proposals are submitted by five other major judicial entities (the *Court of Appeals for the Federal Circuit, the Court of International Trade, the District Courts and *Circuit Courts of Appeals, the Administrative Office of the United States Courts, and the Federal Judicial Center). When the subcommittees consider the Supreme Court's financial needs, two justices delegated by the chief justice as well as several administrative officers of the Court are normally present to answer questions and justify requested funding levels. Full committee review of subcommittee recommendations and floor approval in each house is necessary before an appropriations bill is passed and sent to the president.

In recent years the Supreme Court has been quite successful in its annual quest for funding. During the 1980s, the justices received approval from Congress for about 97 percent of the funds requested. This success rate is largely a result of the respect the Congress has for the Court and the very reasonable requests the justices submit. For the 1990 fiscal year, the Supreme Court received $22 million in appropriated funds, an amount that constituted less than 1.3 percent of all funds allocated to the various units of the federal judiciary. While the proportions of the budget allocated to specific expenditures can vary significantly from year to year, about 70 percent of the funds are needed to cover salary and benefit costs for personnel. About one-fifth of the budget is used for the care of the Supreme Court building and grounds. The remaining funds cover operational expenses, of which printing, equipment, communications, and utilities are the largest categories. Prior to 1935, the Supreme Court's funds were administered through the Justice Department. In that year, however, the Court was authorized to manage its own budgetary allocations. The marshal of the Court, as its chief financial officer, executes the institution's fiscal management responsibilities.

(See also ADMINISTRATION OF FEDERAL COURTS; BUREAUCRATIZATION OF THE COURT.)
                    Thomas G. Walker

**Buildings, Supreme Court.** Until October 1935, when the Supreme Court moved into its own building, it had always shared space with other governing institutions. The Court held its first session in February 1790, on the second floor of the Royal Exchange Building in New York City. The lower house of the state legislature used the large vaulted room for its meetings during the morning hours, while the Court sat in the afternoon. With no cases on the docket in the February and August terms, the Court met only a few days to handle routine administrative matters, including the admission of attorneys to its bar. Judicial concentration was not encouraged by the presence of a nearby market, although the city attempted to decrease the noise of passing wagons by blocking off the immediate area of the Exchange (see figure 1).

In December 1790 Philadelphia became the new seat of government, pursuant to an act of Congress. The Court found temporary quarters in the State House, occupying a room on the first floor that had long been used by the supreme court of Pennsylvania. As a courtroom, this handsome Georgian chamber left little to be desired, except for winter stoves, which the legislature refused to provide. With no cases yet to be heard, the Court completed its February term in only two days. It reconvened in October 1791 in a more permanent location, the newly constructed city hall.

Located on the east side of the State House Square, Philadelphia's city hall housed local courts and municipal offices, while offering limited accommodations to the federal judiciary. For the next nine years the Court shared a comfortable room on the first floor with the Mayor's Court. In case of a schedule conflict, which occurred in 1796, the justices had to vacate the room and move upstairs to the chambers of the Common Council. Congress and the president, in contrast, occupied buildings of their own.

As the construction of a permanent national capital on the banks of the Potomac got underway, the judicial branch aroused little public interest. Pierre Charles L'Enfant's original plan for the city of Washington had reserved a site for the Court midway between the Capitol and the White House, but no construction had begun when the government moved from Philadelphia in 1800. Congress finally permitted the Court to use a committee room on the first floor of the Capitol, only one wing of which had yet been completed.

In this small, unfinished chamber, described by architect Benjamin Latrobe as "meanly furnished, very inconvenient," the Court met from 1801 until 1808. During that time it occasionally shared space with the district and circuit courts of the District of Columbia and endured distracting noise from the crowds milling around in the corridor outside. In 1808 the Capitol underwent major repair and remodeling, as the floor of the Senate chamber was raised one story above its original level. To escape the resulting din, the Court moved to another room, which normally housed the Library of Congress; and in 1809 it sat for a time in a nearby tavern.

When the justices reconvened for the February 1810 term, they occupied a new chamber that had been specially designed for their use by Latrobe. Located directly beneath the Senate chamber in what was now the basement of the Capitol, this semicircular courtroom boasted a handsome vaulted ceiling that supported the floor above (see figure 2). The Court had little time to enjoy its new surroundings, however, thanks to the War of 1812. British troops invaded Washington and burned the Capitol in the summer of 1814, forcing the Court to seek alternative accommodations once again.

For two years the justices met in a rented house on Capitol Hill, before returning to a dingy makeshift chamber in the still unrestored Capitol. Finally, in 1819, they were able to reoccupy their courtroom, where they remained for the next forty years. The room had some attractive features: The justices sat behind individual mahogany desks on a slightly raised platform; below them was a railed enclosure for the bar, from

Figure 1. *Royal Exchange Building, New York City*

Figure 2. *Old Supreme Court Chamber*

Figure 3. *Old Senate Chamber*

which several steps ascended to an encircling visitors' gallery. But the courtroom was also small, damp, and poorly lighted, and the justices had to share it, as before, with some lower federal courts.

In the late 1850s two new wings were added to the Capitol to accommodate an overgrown House and Senate. The Court then moved upstairs to the old Senate chamber, while its basement courtroom became a law library. The change of quarters in 1860 gave the Court some needed space and a more impressive forum for its deliberations. Contemporary visitors praised the beauty of the renovated chamber, with its soft brown carpet, its row of green marble columns behind the justices, and its benches fitted with red velvet cushions for spectators (see figure 3). Across the corridor, in rooms formerly used by the Senate, was the judicial robing room and offices for the Court's clerks, marshal, and reporter. In 1866 Congress further provided a comfortable conference room for the justices on the ground floor, near the library.

Despite these improvements, serious problems remained. The justices had to parade across an often crowded public corridor to enter and leave the courtroom; the offices of the Court's employees were small and crowded, and no chambers were available for the justices themselves; and there was a critical lack of space for the expansion of the Court's library and the preservation of its increasing records. In light of these unpromising conditions, Chief Justice William Howard *Taft began vigorous lobbying efforts in 1925 to secure for the Court a separate building under its exclusive control.

Congress responded favorably to Taft's initiatives and approved the site he recommended: a plot on East Capitol Street adjoining the Library of Congress and facing the Capitol grounds. As chairman of the building commission, Taft further supervised the architectural design of the structure by Cass *Gilbert. When completed in 1935, the Supreme Court Building—a grandiose temple of white marble, with a central portico and matching wings—effectively symbolized the power and independence of the judicial branch. (For ill., see ARCHITECTURE OF THE SUPREME COURT BUILDING.)

(See also CHAMBERS; PAINTINGS IN THE SUPREME COURT BUILDING; SCULPTURE IN THE SUPREME COURT BUILDING.)

□ Catherine Hetos Skefos, "The Supreme Court Gets a Home," *Supreme Court Historical Society Yearbook* (1976), pp. 25–36. Charles Warren, *The Supreme Court in United States History*, 2 vols. (1922). Maxwell Bloomfield

**Bunting v. Oregon,** 243 U.S. 426 (1917), argued 18 Apr. 1916, reargued 12 June 1916, reargued 19 Jan. 1917, decided 9 Apr. 1917 by vote of 5 to 3; McKenna for the Court, White, Van Devanter, and McReynolds in dissent, Brandeis recused. A 1913 Oregon law established a ten-hour day for all workers, men as well as women, in mills, factories, and manufacturing establishments, and required time-and-a-half pay for overtime. Bunting, a foreman in a mill, required an employee to work thirteen hours but did not pay the overtime and was convicted of violating the law. The National Consumers' League secured the services of Louis *Brandeis to defend the law, but before the case came up for argument, he was appointed to the Court. Felix *Frankfurter took over the case and submitted a massive *"Brandeis brief" laden with facts showing that long hours were detrimental to workers' health.

The Court was badly split on this issue, primarily because some of the justices saw the overtime requirement as a wage regulation, the first step toward statutorily established minimum rates; the case had to be reargued twice. Finally a bare majority agreed that the time-and-a-half provision did not constitute a wage regulation but a penalty designed to discourage overtime work.

In his opinion, Justice Joseph *McKenna indicated that the Court need not pass on the wisdom of the act but should accept the judgment of the Oregon legislature that a ten-hour maximum was necessary or useful for preserving the health of employees. The fact that the law did not apply to all workers but only to those in certain industries, did not constitute discrimination that violated the Due Process Clause. Three members of the Court dissented without opinion.

(See also DUE PROCESS, SUBSTANTIVE; POLICE POWER.)

Melvin I. Urofsky

**Bureaucratization of the Court.** The Supreme Court consists of nine jurists who, at least in theory, after meaningful collegial deliberation interpret the Constitution based on their individual philosophies, wisdom, and legal scholarship without delegating significant work to supporting personnel. During the Court's first several decades this was indeed the case. The Court met for relatively short terms and its docket was manageable; indeed, justices lived together in the same boarding house. The justices were able to conduct their business without significant assistance. Gradually, however, a bureaucracy developed to aid them in both administrative chores and judicial responsibilities. At first this occurred on a somewhat informal basis with part time and often unofficial administrators assuming Court duties. Today, the Court's bureaucracy of more than three hundred employees has become fully institutionalized and quite professional.

Historically, the Court has enjoyed the support of four major administrative officials authorized by Congress: the clerk, reporter of decisions, marshal, and librarian. Each is chosen by the Court and heads an office staffed at appropriate personnel levels. The first clerk was appointed in 1790, just three days into the Court's history. For several years he performed all of the Court's administrative duties, but remained somewhat independent, being paid from filing fees and allowed to engage simultaneously in other professional activities. Today, the clerk is responsible for administering the judicial business of the Court; this includes receiving all papers filed by attorneys, managing the calendar and docket, maintaining Court records, supervising admissions to the Supreme Court bar, and instructing attorneys on proper Court procedure. (See CLERK, OFFICE OF THE; CLERKS OF THE COURT.)

The position of reporter of decisions was authorized by Congress in 1817, replacing the informal practice of private individuals publishing Supreme Court opinions and profiting from their sale. Today's reporter is responsible for editing, summarizing, printing, and distributing the Court's opinions (see REPORTERS, SUPREME COURT). The *marshal of the Court was created by Congress in 1867 to provide security and carry out the orders of the Court. Previously these duties were executed by the marshal of the District of Columbia District Court. Today the marshal has a wide array of responsibilities, including supervision of the Court's police force, maintaining the building and grounds, enforcing order during public sessions, and managing the Court's fiscal affairs.

The librarian began official duties in 1887. Before Congress authorized this position, the Court's library holdings were supervised initially by the clerk and then later by the marshal (see LIBRARY). In addition to these traditional administrative offices, the Court added a *public information officer in 1935, an *administrative assistant to the chief justice in 1972, and a *curator in 1974.

The justices are assisted in their judicial duties by law clerks assigned to their individual offices. In 1882, the first law clerk was hired by Justice Horace *Gray at his own expense when Congress initially refused to appropriate funds for the employment of clerks. Each associate justice is now entitled to hire as many as four law clerks, and the chief justice five. The clerks are chosen from among the recent graduates of the nation's top law schools often after serving as clerks in the courts of appeals. They normally serve for one year. Clerks evaluate *certiorari applications, do research and initial writing, draft opinions, critique legal arguments, and perform other duties as assigned by their justice (see CLERKS OF THE JUSTICES).

Additional assistance with judicial matters is provided by the Legal Office, established in 1973 to act as house counsel for the Court. Staffed by two attorneys appointed by the chief justice, who serve at least four years, the Legal Office advises the Court on various legal matters, including questions of jurisdiction and procedure, *original jurisdiction cases, and extraordinary or emergency matters that affect the Court or individual justices (see LEGAL COUNSEL, OFFICE OF).

The growth in administrative staff has generally been considered necessary, as the Court's case filings have more than tripled since 1950. The expansion of the judicial support staff, on the other hand, has been the subject of substantial criticism. The law clerks, for example, have been accused of becoming too influential in the Court's decision making, a charge over which there is still controversy. An additional concern had been that the increased numbers of law clerks and the emergence of the Legal Office may be converting the Court from a council of nine deliberating jurists into the equivalent of a system of independent but interacting law firms. To some critics, this detracts from the Court's uniqueness and its strength as a political and legal institution.

Thomas G. Walker

**Bureaucratization of the Federal Judiciary.** The *Judiciary Act of 1789, which gave birth to the federal courts, created a simple three-tiered judicial system staffed by six Supreme Court justices and thirteen district court judges. Over the years, the judiciary grew as the nation expanded. By 1990, with ninety-four district courts and twelve regional circuit courts, staffed by 743 judges as well as a number of more specialized tribunals, the federal court system became a complex operation with an annual budget in excess of $1.7 billion. Inevitably, such growth has spawned an administrative bureaucracy.

The emergence of administrative structures, however, was slow in developing. The judiciary operated in a very decentralized fashion. There existed no central arm of the judicial branch to exercise administrative or policy-making authority. The Department of Justice, a unit of the executive branch, performed all administrative functions that were necessarily national in scope.

Concerned about the court system's lack of integration, Chief Justice William Howard *Taft lobbied Congress for the creation of a single agency to aid in communication, coordination, and policy making for the judiciary. Congress responded in 1922 by establishing the Judicial Conference of Senior Circuit Judges. The conference, chaired by the *chief justice, consists of the chief judges of each circuit, the chief judge of the Court of International Trade, and an elected district judge from each circuit. Now known as the Judicial Conference of the United States, it has evolved into the judiciary's central policy-making organ and is the court system's primary liaison with Congress. The conference formally meets twice annually, but functions throughout the year through a system of some twenty-five committees that focus on matters of special administrative and policy concern.

In response to heated political battles between the judiciary and the executive branch over the administration of the courts, Congress in 1939 created the Administrative Office of the United States Courts and in so doing granted the judiciary its administrative independence. With an annual budget in 1990 of $34 million, the administrative office provides the fiscal, clerical, and management services necessary for the national operation of the federal courts.

In 1967, congress added a third unit to the national judicial bureaucracy, the Federal Judicial Center. This organization carries out training, research, and development programs for the courts. It has been particularly effective in sponsoring seminars and continuing education programs for newly appointed and veteran judges and in conducting research on methods of improving the administration of justice.

The judiciary's centralized bureaucratic machinery focused almost exclusively on administrative matters until 1984, when because of growing concern over disparities in criminal sentences, Congress created the United States Sentencing Commission. The commission was empowered to promulgate mandatory sentencing guidelines. This was the first agency in the judicial bureaucracy to exercise a degree of control over the actual decisions of federal judges. The commission's constitutional validity was upheld by the Supreme Court in *Mistretta v. United States (1989).

In spite of the centralizing influence of these bureaucratic units, the lower federal courts remain localized, and the norm of judicial independence remains well entrenched. Each of the twelve circuits has authority to handle matters of circuit administration and policy. The primary decision-making entity is the Circuit Council, a body whose membership includes both court of appeals and district court judges. The councils exercise wide ranging authority over the federal courts of the circuit and make recommendations to the Judicial Conference when problems extend beyond the region, or when a congressional response is required. Within each council rests the authority to monitor judicial conduct and to take appropriate action when disability occurs or discipline is required. These powers were approved by the Supreme Court in Chandler v. The Judicial Council of the 10th Circuit (1970) and later codified with passage of the Judicial Councils Reform and Judicial Conduct and Discipline Act of 1980.

Rapid increases in litigation have necessitated the creation of additional administrative positions for the lower federal courts. Since 1971, each circuit has been authorized to appoint a circuit executive, a professional judicial administrator who, at the council's directive manages the circuit's nonjudicial operations. At both the court of appeals and district court levels there is support personnel to assist in the processing of judicial business, including court clerks, marshals, magistrates, staff attorneys, law clerks, and clerical staff. These expansions in the judiciary's administrative apparatus have prompted some observers to caution against an excessively

bureaucratized judiciary, a condition under which judges must devote greater amounts of time to managing staff and caseload and less to their essential judicial duties. Such a situation may lead to an increasingly impersonal and inflexible judiciary in which the processing of cases takes priority over the quality of the justice rendered.

(See also ADMINISTRATION OF FEDERAL COURTS; COURTS OF APPEALS; LOWER FEDERAL COURTS; WORKLOAD.)

□ Peter Graham Fish, *The Politics of Federal Judicial Administration* (1973).          Thomas G. Walker

**Burger, Warren Earl** (b. St. Paul, Minn., 17 Sept. 1907), chief justice, 1969–1986. Burger, the fifteenth chief justice, was a self-made man. Of Swiss and German ancestry, he grew up in modest circumstances. While selling insurance during the day Burger attended school in the evening: two years at the University of Minnesota and four at St. Paul College of Law (now William Mitchell College of Law), where he graduated in 1931 *magna cum laude.*

Burger practiced law with Boyesen, Otis & Faricy in St. Paul from 1931 to 1953, primarily handling corporate, real estate, and probate matters. He was also involved in civic and political activities, most notably as a backer of Minnesota governor Harold Stassen's presidential bids. Burger served as Stassen's floor manager in the 1948 and 1952 Republican conventions, where he won the respect of national Republican leaders. When Dwight Eisenhower became president in 1953, Attorney General Herbert Brownell named Burger assistant attorney general in charge of the Claims Division (later the Civil Division).

From 1956 to 1969 Burger served on the U.S. Court of Appeals for the District of Columbia Circuit, among America's most influential courts. As circuit judge he attracted national attention from bench and bar for his judicial administration and for his jousts with the civil libertarians on that talented but badly divided court. Moderately conservative in most matters, Burger led the wing of the court that opposed extending the rights of criminal defendants and modernizing the insanity defense, preferring instead to give considerable leeway to police, prosecution, and trial judges.

Burger's appointment as chief justice by Richard *Nixon became possible after Lyndon Johnson's nominee, Associate Justice Abe *Fortas, failed to win confirmation. By the time Nixon focused attention upon the vacancy (May 1969), Fortas had resigned from the Court following accusations of improprieties. Burger was chosen because of his judicial experience, his opposition to Warren Court criminal procedure decisions, his criticism of judicial activism, and because his career was free of ethical blemishes.

Contrary to expectations, while Burger was

*Warren Earl Burger*

chief justice, the Supreme Court consolidated most of the major initiatives of the Warren Court (such as civil rights and reapportionment), although the pace of change became more moderate. The Court recognized new rights and opened to judicial exploration such areas as *gender discrimination, *abortion, *affirmative action, and welfare rights. Burger was among the least enthusiastic of the justices regarding these trends but was at the forefront when the Court reversed direction in the criminal area, cut back access of litigants to the federal courts, and demonstrated more sensitivity to traditional principles of *federalism than had Warren's Court.

Among twentieth-century chief justices, Burger appears to have been considerably less successful in guiding the other justices to jurisprudential results he favored than either Earl *Warren or William Howard *Taft had been. His colleagues William J. *Brennan, Jr., and William H. *Rehnquist were far more influential with their fellow justices, and Lewis *Powell, Jr., in a different way, left a greater imprint upon constitutional jurisprudence. Burger was unable to take advantage of his allies within the Court, the relatively quiescent political environment, or the absence for much of his tenure of problems caused by aging or cantankerous justices. Within the Court, he appears to have been more pugnacious than conciliatory. Throughout his tenure, there were leaks to the press—some clearly from his colleagues—indicating dissatisfaction with his leadership. He does not seem to have been successful in managing the conference of the justices, and individual statements of opinion proliferated to an extent not seen since

before 1800. Burger himself was less willing than any chief justice except Harlan F. *Stone to suppress his own dissents to preserve the appearance of harmony.

As a judge Burger was not of the first rank, but his work was much better than contemporary critics allowed and not recognizably different in craftsmanship from that of most of his colleagues. Not a man given to inner agonies, Burger usually was quite clear as to what he thought the law was. His opinions were generally short, fact-oriented, straightforward, and clearly written.

Burger's opinions of greatest importance are those dealing with *separation of powers. His opinion for the unanimous Court in *United States v. *Nixon* (1974) rejected Nixon's claim of *executive privilege and ordered him to turn over tapes of conversations with aides for use in a criminal trial but also recognized a presumptive privilege for presidential conversations. Generally, Burger's approach to separation of powers was formalistic, stressing the separateness of each branch and the supremacy of each within its own assigned sphere. He wrote the opinion in *Immigration and Naturalization Service v. Chadha* (1983), invalidating the *legislative veto. His final opinion, *Bowsher v. Synar* (1986), held the Gramm-Rudman-Hollings budget-cutting law to be unconstitutional because it gave executive functions to the comptroller-general, who is removable by Congress.

Personally critical of the media and extremely sensitive to press criticism, Burger wrote a number of important opinions upholding *First Amendment claims. Among them were *Nebraska Press Association v. Stuart* (1976), where the Court held that the protection against prior restraints makes the use of "gag" orders in a criminal trial a last resort, and *Miami Herald Publishing Co. v. Tornillo* (1974), which invalidated a Florida statute requiring newspapers that had assailed the character of a political candidate to afford free space to the candidate for reply. However, Burger rejected the view that the First Amendment guarantees the press a right of access to sources of information broader than that accorded to members of the general public, the right not to divulge sources to a grand jury, or immunity from police searches. (See also SPEECH AND THE PRESS.)

Burger was by no means antagonistic to the civil rights heritage of the Warren Court, but he was far more cautious in employing judicial power to force integration. He spoke for a unanimous Court in *Swann v. Charlotte-Mecklenburg Board of Education* (1971), which affirmed a district court order to redraw attendance zones and to bus students to achieve a racial mix at each school approximating the racial composition of the entire district. In *Bob Jones University v. United States* (1983), he rejected a Reagan administration position by holding that the Internal Revenue Service has the authority to deny tax exemptions to private schools—even schools run by religious organizations—that discriminate on the basis of race. On the other hand, writing for a closely divided court in *Milliken* v. *Bradley* (1974), he held that even though the Detroit school system was unconstitutionally segregated, the judiciary had no power to order an integration plan that would include suburban schools absent proof that interdistrict segregation was the product of race-conscious *gerrymandering. No enthusiast where affirmative action was concerned, Burger still wrote the opinion in *Fullilove* v. *Klutznick* (1980) upholding congressional power to require 10 percent of the funds in a public works job bill to be set aside for awards to minority businesses.

The nonjudicial aspects of the office of chief justice were well suited to Burger's abilities and temperament, and to this dimension of his role he brought enormous energy, forcefulness, tenacity, and the willingness to risk controversy. Like Taft, Burger saw his office as a place to promote reform in the administration of justice, and, like Taft, he was a conservative reformer, primarily concerned with the traditional agenda of limiting high costs and long delays. Burger also saw his office as a "bully pulpit" from which to call attention to the problems of *state courts. He had much to do with the founding of the Institute for Court Management, the National Center for State Courts, and the annual Brookings Seminars at which leaders of the three branches meet to discuss problems of judicial reform. He pressed hard but with limited success for reforms in the corrections process but made somewhat more headway in pressing for upgrading the quality of trial attorneys.

During Burger's tenure, new technologies, from copying machines to computers, were installed in the Court's offices, its personnel practices were overhauled, and a small central legal staff was created. The Court was also made more accessible to scholars and the public. Burger was unsuccessful in persuading Congress either to create a temporary national court of appeals to offer some relief to the Supreme Court or to increase federal appellate capacity (see JUDICIAL POWER AND JURISDICTION). Although the time spent on these efforts and the ceremonial aspects of his office may have undermined Burger's leadership on the Court, no one could gainsay the deep commitment he brought to his work, his profound desire to measure up to his predecessors, or the fondness felt for him by his staff.

(See also CHIEF JUSTICE, OFFICE OF THE; HISTORY OF THE COURT: RIGHTS CONSCIOUSNESS IN CONTEMPORARY SOCIETY.)

□ Vincent Blasi, ed., *The Burger Court: The Counter-Revolution That Wasn't* (1983). Bernard Schwartz, *The Ascent of Pragmatism: The Burger Court in Action* (1990).
Jeffrey B. Morris

**Burr, Aaron** (b. Newark, N.J., 6 Feb, 1756; d. New York, N.Y., 14 Sept. 1836), lawyer and statesman. Graduating from the College of New Jersey (later Princeton) in 1772, Burr studied law with Tapping Reeve. During the Revolutionary War, he compiled an impressive record as a Continental Army officer. After the war Burr settled in New York City and embarked on a successful career as a lawyer and politician. A shrewd and opportunistic political strategist, Burr founded the Jeffersonian Republican party of New York and secured that state for the party in 1800—an achievement that earned him a place on the ticket with Thomas *Jefferson. He served one term as vice president, in which capacity he presided over the impeachment trial of Justice Samuel *Chase (1805). After his duel with Alexander *Hamilton (1804), in which Hamilton was killed, Burr faced political ruin. An obscure military expedition down the Ohio River ultimately led to his arrest on a charge of treason for attempting to detach the western country from the United States. *United States* v. *Burr*, tried before Chief Justice John *Marshall on circuit in 1807, was an episode in the larger story of the Marshall Court's struggle to preserve judicial independence. Though under intense pressure from the Jefferson administration to convict, Marshall rendered a landmark opinion narrowly construing the Constitution's definition of treason, leaving the jury no choice but to acquit. After a four-year exile in Europe, Burr returned to New York City and resumed the practice of law. His last years were clouded by the death of his daughter and chronic indebtedness.
Charles F. Hobson

**Burton, Harold Hitz** (b. Jamaica Plain, Mass., 22 June 1888; d. Washington, D.C., 28 Oct. 1964; interred Highland Park Cemetery, Cleveland, Oh.), associate justice, 1945–1958.

During the October 1954 term, the Court's law *clerks voted on the one justice they would choose to preside if they themselves were on trial. Out of a Court that included Earl *Warren, Hugo *Black, Felix *Frankfurter, and William O. *Douglas, they overwhelmingly selected Harold Burton. His service on the Court was dedicated to producing painstakingly crafted opinions, most resting on narrow grounds, designed to appeal to as many of his colleagues as possible.

Burton was raised in Boston where his father was dean of the faculty at the Massachusetts Institute of Technology. He graduated *summa cum laude* from Bowdoin College in 1909, where he had been active in athletics. He received the LL.B. from the Harvard Law School in 1912, married Selma Florence Smith, and moved to Cleveland, where he practiced law. Serving in the army in World War I, he rose to the rank of captain and received the Purple Heart.

Burton was elected to the Ohio legislature in 1929 after a failed attempt to win appointment to a vacancy on the United States District Court for

*Harold Hitz Burton*

the Northern District of Ohio. He also served as the chief legal official of Cleveland from 1929 to 1932. He was elected mayor of Cleveland in 1935 and was reelected twice. As mayor, his principal achievement was coping with high unemployment and inadequate welfare funds. In 1940 Burton easily won both the Republican nomination and the general election to the United States Senate. In his service in the Senate Burton exhibited a mildly conservative, predominantly moderate stance.

After the October 1944 term of the Court ended, Justice Owen J. *Roberts announced his retirement, giving President Harry Truman, a Democrat, his first opportunity to make a high court appointment. The president was under considerable pressure to name a Republican to the vacancy. President Franklin D. *Roosevelt had only appointed Democrats to the Court (with the exception of Stone's elevation to chief justice); no Republican had been named for over a decade. Truman selected Burton not only because he thought well of him but also because the governor of Ohio, a Democrat, was likely to appoint a member of his own party to Burton's Senate seat. Burton was confirmed within a day of his nomination; the *Senate Judiciary Committee heard no testimony and the full Senate approved the appointment unanimously.

During his thirteen terms Justice Burton staked out a moderate position on a highly fractured Court. In segregation cases he was a leading member favoring the extension of constitutional protection for African-Americans, while in other cases he tended to favor more often Justice Frankfurter's doctrines of restraint. For example,

in civil liberties and national security cases he usually voted to uphold government authority against claims of individual rights (see FIRST AMENDMENT; SPEECH AND THE PRESS). In business cases he mostly voted in an economically conservative fashion, often against labor union power and in favor of narrow construction of *antitrust laws.

Shortly after the October 1958 term began, Parkinson's disease compelled Justice Burton's resignation. His health slowly deteriorated and he died six years later.

□ Mary Frances Berry, *Stability, Security, and Continuity: Mr. Justice Burton and Decision-Making in the Supreme Court, 1945–1958* (1978).          Eric A. Chiappinelli

**Burton v. Wilmington Parking Authority,** 365 U.S. 715 (1961), argued 21, 23 Feb. 1961, decided 17 Apr. 1961 by vote of 6 to 3; Clark for the Court; Harlan, Frankfurter, and Whittaker in dissent. In this case the Court addressed the vexing if not logically inscrutable problem, judged pivotal to the success of the *civil rights movement at the time, of defining the meaning of state action under the *Fourteenth Amendment. The city built a public parking garage within which it leased space to a restaurant. A Delaware statute provided that a restaurant was not obliged to serve persons whose reception would be offensive to the major part of its customers. An African-American who was refused service claimed discrimination in violation of the Fourteenth Amendment. The Supreme Court held, 6 to 3, that a sufficient degree of state action was present to constitute a denial of the equal protection of the laws. Justice Tom C. *Clark for the majority emphasized that the state owned and operated the building in which the incident occurred and hence had a responsibility to prevent it. The state's inaction under the circumstances made it a party to the discrimination, rendering it unlawful. The decision did little to clarify the state action problem. Justice Clark limited the scope and precedential value of the decision in stating that "to fashion and apply a precise formula for recognition of state responsibility under the *Equal Protection Clause is an 'impossible task,' " and in observing: "Only by sifting facts and weighing circumstances can the nonobvious involvement of the State in private conduct be attributed its true significance" (p. 722). The dissenters urged that the case be remanded to the *state court for clarification of its decision upholding the restaurant in relation to the state law under which the restaurant acted.

(See also RACE AND RACISM; STATE ACTION.)
          Herman Belz

**Business of the Court.** The business of the Supreme Court has not been static but rather has registered broad socio-economic and political changes. Major shifts in the amount and nature of the Court's business have also prompted jurisdictional reforms and institutional changes. The modern Supreme Court has virtually complete discretion over which and what kinds of cases it grants review and decides by written opinions. The expansion of the Court's discretionary jurisdiction enables it not only to manage its caseload but also to set its substantive agenda as well. As a result, the Court is no longer primarily concerned with resolving disputes per se or even with correcting the errors of lower courts. Instead, it addresses issues of national importance involving primarily constitutional and statutory interpretation.

The Court's caseload or docket has grown phenomenally during the course of its history. In its first decade (1791–1800), the Court had little business, fewer than 100 cases. The docket, however, steadily grew in the late nineteenth century and continued to do so in the twentieth century. Whereas in 1920 there were only 565 cases on the docket, that number rose to more than 1,300 by 1950, more than 2,300 by 1960, and more than 4,200 by 1970. By 1990, the Court's docket exceeded 6,000 cases.

The ebb and flow of cases largely reflects changes in congressional legislation, governmental regulation, and broader socio-economic and political trends. The Court's own decisions, though, may sometimes invite an increase in its docket. For example, rulings on the constitutional rights of indigents significantly contributed to an increase in the filing of unpaid, or *in forma pauperis*, petitions. The Court's rulings basically constitutionalized the congressionally established practice of giving every citizen the right to file a suit without payment of court filing fees upon taking an oath of indigency. Since the 1930s and 1940s, much of the increase in the Court's docket has been the result of a rise in the number of unpaid petitions. The filing of unpaid petitions steadily increased from 59 in 1935, to more than 1,000 in 1960, to almost half of the Court's docket in the 1980s and early 1990s. Of the more than 2,200 unpaid petitions filed each year, the largest category comes from "jailhouse lawyers" and indigent prisoners claiming some constitutional violation or deprivation.

During the first half of the nineteenth century the Court's caseload grew largely because of population growth, territorial expansion, and the incremental development of federal regulation. The *Civil War and *Reconstruction, both great sources of legal conflict, and the late nineteenth-century business boom, dramatically swelled the docket even further. No less importantly, Congress greatly expanded the jurisdiction of all federal courts. In particular, federal jurisdiction was extended to include civil rights, *habeas corpus appeals, questions of federal law decided by state courts, and all suits over five hundred dollars arising under the Constitution or federal legislation (see FEDERAL QUESTIONS).

By the 1870s the Court confronted a growing backlog of cases. In response, Congress first raised the jurisdictional amount in diversity cases (cases between citizens of different states) to two thousand dollars. In the Evarts Act, or Circuit Court of Appeals Act of 1891, Congress provided immediate (if not long-lasting) relief by creating *Circuit Courts of Appeals (see JUDICIARY ACT OF 1891). These courts were given final jurisdiction over most appeals, with the exception of certain civil cases and cases involving capital or otherwise infamous crime. The *Courts of Appeals generally had final say in *admiralty and diversity suits, criminal prosecutions, and revenue and patent law violations. But, the Evarts Act preserved access to the Court by providing, instead of a mandatory right of *appeal, for petitions for writs of *certiorari that the Court could refuse to grant. The Evarts Act thus for the first time gave the Court some power of discretionary review, the power to deny cases review.

In the early twentieth century, the Court's docket grew again, partially because of further population increases. Economic changes brought more *bankruptcy cases, and later, *World War I brought a rash of disputes over war contracts and suits against the government. A large measure of the Court's congested docket was nonetheless the result of expanding congressional legislation and administrative regulations. Congress directly added to the Court's docket by expanding the opportunities for both government and special-interest groups to appeal directly to the Court. Direct and mandatory review was extended, for instance, to government appeals from dismissals of federal criminal prosecutions. Individuals and businesses challenging administrative decisions under antitrust and interstate commerce laws and the Federal Employer's Liability Act (FELA) and *injunctions issued by three-judge federal district courts were also given the right of appeal to the Supreme Court.

The Supreme Court once again could not stay abreast of its caseload. Congress initially responded in a piecemeal fashion. It slightly enlarged the Court's discretionary jurisdiction by eliminating mandatory rights of appeal in narrow though important areas, such as under FELA. Then, owing to a campaign waged by Chief Justice William H. *Taft for further relief, Congress passed "the Judges' Bill," or *Judiciary Act of 1925, which basically established the jurisdiction of the modern Court. That act replaced many provisions for mandatory review of appeals with discretionary review of petitions by writs of *certiorari*, thus enabling it largely to set its own agenda and to decide only cases of national importance.

Along with Congress's expansion of the Court's discretionary jurisdiction in the Judiciary Act of 1925, the justices committed themselves to the informal *"rule of four" to decide which petitions would be reviewed. During their weekly private conferences to discuss cases on the docket, at least four justices must agree that a case merits hearing *oral arguments and full consideration by the Court. Still, the justices continued to feel burdened by having to decide mandatory appeals. Accordingly, in 1928 the Court began requiring the filing of a jurisdictional statement, explaining the circumstances of an appeal, the questions presented, and why the Court should grant review. This requirement allowed the justices to screen appeals just like petitions for certiorari and to decide them summarily without hearing oral arguments and handing down written opinions in each case.

The Court's caseload dramatically increased yet again after *World War II. In response the number of law *clerks assigned to each justice was increased from two to three to four, and the number of secretaries grew as well. The justices also delegated more responsibility for screening cases to their law clerks. In 1972 a so-called *cert pool was created in which eight of the justices collectively have their law clerks divide (randomly) all paid and unpaid cases and write memos on each, recommending whether or not they should be granted review. The justices and their own law clerks then review the memos and cases. Each justice then decides whether a case should be put on the *discuss list for the justices' weekly conference. Only those few cases deemed worthy of consideration (about 30 percent) are discussed by the justices. In these ways, the Court has attempted to expedite the processing of its caseload.

In the 1970s, Congress provided further incremental relief by eliminating many statutory provisions for mandatory review of appeals, particularly those from three-judge courts. Although the number of mandatory appeals coming to the Court declined in the 1980s, the justices pushed for Congress to eliminate most of the remaining statutes requiring the Court to review cases involving *lower federal and *state courts, invalidation of federal and state laws. Finally, Congress in 1988 passed the *Judicial Improvements and Access to Justice Act. The legislation eliminated virtually all of the Court's nondiscretionary appellate jurisdiction. The only mandatory appeals that the Court must now review are those that involve reapportionment cases, the Civil Rights and Voting Rights Acts, some *antitrust matters, and the Presidential Election Campaign Fund Act. From the more than five thousand cases annually on its docket, the Court currently grants review to about 3 percent, or fewer than 150 cases; more than 95 percent of the cases on the docket are simply denied review.

The business of the Court in the twentieth century bears only a family resemblance to that in the nineteenth century. In the last century, the Court did not have the power to set its own agenda, nor did its docket include the kinds of major issues of public policy that currently arrive.

The business of the Court evolves (more or less quickly) in response to technological developments and socio-economic changes. In the nineteenth century, for example, the Court's docket did not include issues of personal *privacy raised by the possibility of electronic surveillance and computer data banks, or controversies over *abortion and the patentability of organic life forms (see PATENT).

During its first decade, more than 40 percent of the business coming to the Court consisted of admiralty and prize cases. About 50 percent raised issues of *common law, and the remaining 10 percent matters such as equity, including one probate case. Not until the chief justiceship of John *Marshall (1801–1835) did the Court fully assert its power of *judicial review. Still, only a tiny fraction of its business raised important issues of public policy.

By the late nineteenth century, the Court's business had gradually changed in response to economic and political developments in the country. The number of admiralty cases dwindled to less than 4 percent by 1882. Almost 40 percent of the Court's rulings still dealt with either disputes at common law or questions of jurisdiction and procedure in the federal courts. More than 43 percent of the Court's business, however, involved interpreting newly enacted congressional statutes. Less than 4 percent raised issues of constitutional law. The decline in admiralty and common-law litigation in the late nineteenth century and the concomitant increase in cases involving statutory interpretation reflected the impact of the Industrial Revolution, greater governmental regulation, and more litigation attacking the regulation of social and economic relations (see ADMINISTRATIVE STATE).

The trend toward more litigation challenging governmental regulations and raising questions of constitutional and statutory interpretation continued into the twentieth century. By the 1980s about 47 percent of the cases granted review and decided by written opinions involved matters of constitutional law. Another 38 percent dealt with the interpretation and application of congressional legislation. The remaining 15 percent resolved issues of administrative law, taxation, patents, and claims.

Since the nationalization of the *Bill of Rights and the revolution in criminal law forged by the Warren Court (1954–1969), a large portion of the constitutional cases annually taken involve the rights of the accused and the *equal protection of the laws. By contrast, in the late nineteenth and early twentieth century the Court's plenary docket included a large number of cases involving economic liberty, land legislation, and taxation (see CONTRACT, FREEDOM OF; DUE PROCESS, SUBSTANTIVE; PROPERTY).

The federal government, and in particular the *solicitor general, has not surprisingly come to play a larger role in determining the business of the Court. Since the creation of the office in 1870, the *solicitor general has assumed responsibility for screening all prospective appeals and petitions by agencies of the federal government (except the *Interstate Commerce Commission) and for deciding which should be taken to the Court. Government litigation now figures prominently in the work of the Court. From the mid-1950s through the 1980s, for example, the Court on average granted 71 percent of the government's cases each year, whereas less than 6 percent of all others were granted. In addition, the Court grants more than 90 percent of the government's requests to participate in other cases by filing *amicus briefs.

Depending on the Court's composition and direction, special-interest groups may also more or less successfully influence the business of the Court by raising important issues of public policy; for example, business organizations and corporations attacking government regulations in the late nineteenth century; the Jehovah's Witnesses' claims of freedom of religion and speech in the 1930s; the *American Civil Liberties Union (ACLU) and the *National Association for the Advancement of Colored People (NAACP) fighting racial discrimination in the 1950s and 1960s; women's rights organizations and consumer and environmental protection groups in the 1970s; and conservative public interest law firms in the 1980s. The Court's rulings in turn may further encourage or discourage such interest-group litigation. The ACLU, for example, won 90 percent of the cases it appealed in the last year of the Warren Court (1969). By contrast, in the mid-1970s the ACLU's win rate plunged below 50 percent and, like some other liberal public interest law firms, it became more and more reluctant to take cases to the Burger Court (1969–1986) and to the Rehnquist Court (1986–).

In historical perspective, as Felix *Frankfurter and James Landis observed in their classic book *The Business of the Supreme Court* (1927), the Court gradually became a tribunal of constitutional and statutory law owing to the increasing and changing nature of its caseload. "The function of the [modern] Supreme Court," in Chief Justice Taft's words, is "not the remedying of a particular litigant's wrong, but the consideration of cases whose decision involves principles, the application of which are of wide public or governmental interest, and which should be authoritatively declared by the final court" (Taft, 1925, p. 2).

The changing character and amount of business before the Court contributed to an expansion of its discretionary jurisdiction and other institutional changes. The Court can now choose which cases and issues it wants to hear from a very large docket. This enables it to participate in a broad range of public policy matters. Although more than half of the cases on its docket involve indigents' claims and issues of criminal procedure, relatively few are granted review. Cases raising other issues of constitutional law have a better chance of being selected, as do those involving governmental regulations and litigation brought by the solicitor general. The modern Court, regardless of its composition, thus selects and decides primarily cases and controversies of national importance for the governmental and political process.

(See also JUDICIAL POWER AND JURISDICTION; WORKLOAD.)

☐ Samuel Estreicher and John Sexton, *Redefining the Supreme Court's Role* (1986). William P. McLauchlan, *Federal Court Caseloads* (1984). David M. O'Brien, *Storm Center: The Supreme Court in American Politics*, 2d ed. (1990). William Howard Taft, "The Jurisdiction of the Supreme Court under the Act of February 13, 1925," *Yale Law Journal* 35 (1925): 1–12.    David M. O'Brien

**Busing.** See DESEGREGATION REMEDIES.

**Butchers' Benevolent Association of New Orleans v. Crescent City Livestock Landing and Slaughterhouse Co.** See SLAUGHTERHOUSE CASES.

**Butler, Charles Henry** (b. New York, N.Y., 18 June 1859; d. Washington, D.C., 9 Feb. 1940), Supreme Court reporter of decisions, 1902–1916. Butler was the grandson of former U.S. attorney general Benjamin F. Butler. He attended Princeton University with the class of 1881, but left before graduating. After studying law in his father's office, Butler was admitted to the New York bar in 1882. He practiced in New York until 1902, serving in 1898 as the legal expert for the Fairbanks-Herschell Commission, which fixed the permanent boundary between Alaska and Canada. In 1902, he became reporter of decisions of the U.S. Supreme Court, producing volumes 187 to 241 of the *U.S. Reports*. While Supreme Court reporter, Butler also served as a delegate to the Hague Peace Conference in 1907. Butler resigned as reporter in 1916 and practiced law in Washington, D.C., until late in his life.

Butler authored *A Century at the Bar of the Supreme Court of the United States* (1942), a chatty, anecdotal account of the Court and his work as reporter. In it, he described his relations with the justices as delightful and congenial, his salary as comfortable, and his reporter's duties as neither difficult nor all-consuming. Butler eventually found his tasks monotonous, however, and disliked the position's relative anonymity—for example, he wrote of once being introduced at a meeting as "Head Stenographer of the Supreme Court."

Princeton awarded Butler an honorary M.A. in 1912. He published several works concerning U.S. relations with Spain and Cuba and other questions of international law.

(See also REPORTERS, SUPREME COURT.)
Francis Helminski

**Butler, Pierce** (b. Pine Bend, Minn., 17 Mar. 1866; d. Washington, D.C., 16 Nov. 1939; interred Calvary Cemetery, St. Paul, Minn.), associate justice, 1923–1939. Butler came to the Supreme Court after an active career. Raised in rural Minnesota and educated in a one-room school, Butler went on to graduate from Carleton College and gain admission to the Minnesota bar in 1888. He briefly served as state's attorney for Ramsey County before establishing a thriving St. Paul law firm that specialized in representing railroads, including those of local magnate James J. Hill. Although Butler served as a special prosecutor in several *antitrust cases, most of his work involved defending railway interests against governmental regulation. He also played an active role in educational issues, gaining a reputation as a staunch opponent of "radical" professors at the University of Minnesota.

Butler's ascension to the Supreme Court in 1923 was marked by political maneuvering and controversy (see SELECTION OF JUSTICES). A Democrat and a Roman Catholic, Butler's legal conservativism also attracted powerful Republicans, especially Chief Justice William Howard *Taft and Justice Willis *Van Devanter, a former railroad lawyer himself. After President Warren G. Harding, another Republican, selected Butler for the Court, the nominee attracted close scrutiny. Minnesota's senator Hendrik Shipstead charged that Butler's stance toward the *academic freedom of university professors showed that he was "not judicial in mind or attitude"; the nominee's hometown paper, the *St. Paul Dispatch*, countered, "Why should any but a 100 per cent American sit on the bench of the highest court?" Roman Catholic and business groups backed Butler, while labor and progressive organizations opposed him with equal conviction. Yet, despite the lengthy debates, only eight senators ultimately voted against his confirmation.

Controversy followed Butler onto the Court. Taft considered him a reliable supporter of basic constitutional values, and Butler spoke eloquently of the need to protect individual liberties. "Abhorrence, however, great, of persistent and menacing crime will not excuse transgression in the courts of the legal rights of the worst offenders," he wrote. And in *Olmstead v. United States* (1928), in a memorable dissent, he condemned the use of wiretaps. But in *First Amendment cases, Butler's concern for liberty seemed to pale before his animus against dissenters. In another of his famous opinions, dissenting in *Near v. Minnesota* (1931), he supported the constitutionality of a *prior-restraint law from his native Minnesota (see SPEECH AND THE PRESS).

More typically, Butler attracted criticism, both from contemporaries and later constitutional scholars, for his opposition to welfare-state measures (see ADMINISTRATIVE STATE). In most cases involving railroads and utilities, for example, Butler invariably lined up against state regula-

*Pierce Butler*

tions. During the 1930s, political foes dismissed him as simply one of the "Four Horsemen," the reactionary quartet who fought a rearguard judicial action against President Franklin D. *Roosevelt's *New Deal. Butler voted against the constitutionality of every New Deal measure that came before the Court in the 1930s. Opposing Roosevelt to the end, Pierce Butler died, at the age of seventy-three, while still a member of the Court.

□ David J. Danelski, *A Supreme Court Justice Is Appointed* (1964).                    Norman L. Rosenberg

**Butler, United States v.,** 297 U.S. 1 (1936), argued 9–10 Dec. 1935, decided 6 Jan. 1936, by vote of 6 to 3; Roberts for the Court, Stone, Brandeis, and Cardozo in dissent. The Agricultural Adjustment Act of 1933 represented a major *New Deal effort to ameliorate the depression in agriculture and raise farm prices by limiting production. Farmers who agreed to reduce crop acreage received benefit payments, the funds coming from a tax levied on the first processor of the commodities involved. Butler, a processor, refused to pay the tax. The circuit court of appeals upheld Butler, and the government appealed.

By a vote of 6 to 3 in *United States v. Butler* (1936) the Supreme Court declared the tax unconstitutional. Justice Owen J. *Roberts's opinion for the majority, characterized by Leonard Levy as "monumentally inept," undertook a preliminary explanation of the Court's limited role in deciding constitutional questions. The judicial duty was simply "to lay the Article of the Constitution which is invoked beside the statute which is challenged and to decide whether the latter squares with the former" (p. 62). This simplistic explanation of the process of *constitutional interpretation has been generally considered unrealistic.

Roberts did, however, settle a long-standing dispute concerning the taxing power of Congress. Article I, section 8, authorizes Congress to levy taxes "to pay the debts and provide for the common defense and general welfare of the United States. . . ." James *Madison contended that "general welfare" purposes were limited to authorizations elsewhere in the Constitution, whereas Alexander *Hamilton held that this language amounted to an independent power to tax and spend, provided only that the "general welfare" was served. Accepting Hamilton's view, Roberts determined that the processing taxes were justified under the General Welfare Clause.

Roberts's support for the spending power was irrelevant, however, for he immediately transferred the argument to an entirely new issue. Whether the spending was for national rather than local welfare was of no consequence, because the statutory plan to regulate and control agricultural production invaded the reserved powers of the states and so was invalid under the *Tenth Amendment.

Justices Harlan F. *Stone, Louis D. *Brandeis, and Benjamin N. *Cardozo dissented. In a scathing rebuttal Stone called Roberts's ruling "a tortured construction of the Constitution" (p. 87). But the most widely noted language in Stone's dissent was his warning against judicial arrogance: "Courts are not the only agency of government that must be assumed to have capacity to govern. . . . [T]he only check upon our own exercise of power is our own sense of self-restraint" (p. 79). These words were widely read as a rebuke to the Court's conservatives who had been declaring New Deal statutes unconstitutional.

As a threat to other New Deal programs, the Roberts opinion was soon a dead letter. The tax provisions of the Social Security Act were upheld in *Steward Machine Co. v. Davis (1937), and the agricultural program struck down in Butler was reenacted by Congress under the commerce power and upheld in *Mulford v. Smith (1939) and *Wickard v. Filburn (1942).

In retrospect, the principal positive contribution of the Butler majority is the principle, as restated by Chief Justice Warren E. *Burger in *Fullilove v. Klutznick (1980), that the power to provide for the general welfare "is an independent grant of legislative authority, distinct from other broad congressional powers" (p. 247). Otherwise, the opinion by Roberts is valueless. Justice Felix *Frankfurter in International Association of Machinists v. Street (1961) spoke of "the severely criticized, indeed rather discredited case of United States v. Butler" (p. 807). The most enduring feature of the decision is Stone's dissent; his plea for judicial self-restraint has been invoked on many subsequent occasions by Court

minorities, both liberal and conservative. In *Shapiro v. Thompson (1969) Justice John M. *Harlan cited the Butler fiasco in warning his colleagues that cases come to the Court with "an extremely heavy presumption of validity" (p. 675).

(See also GENERAL WELFARE; JUDICIAL SELF-RESTRAINT; TAXING AND SPENDING POWER.)

C. Herman Pritchett

**Butz v. Economou,** 438 U.S. 478 (1978), argued 7 Nov. 1977, decided 29 June 1978 by vote of 5 to 4; White for the Court, Rehnquist for the minority, which concurred in part and dissented in part. After successfully aborting a complaint against him filed by the secretary of agriculture and subordinates, Economou, a commodities dealer, sued these officials for $32 million claiming they had proceeded against him because he was a critic of department policies. The government sought to quash the suit claiming absolute immunity was conferred in accordance with Spalding v. Vilas (1896) and Barr v. Matteo (1959). The court of appeals reversed the district court's dismissal.

Justice *White's careful opinion denied absolute immunity and somewhat disingenuously asserted that neither Spalding nor Barr granted such immunity where a claim of violation of a constitutional right was involved. Spalding had found a common-law exemption of high federal officials from "suits where they were carrying out duties imposed . . . by law" even if allegations of personal animosity were involved (p. 495). The plurality opinion in Barr v. Mateo was similarly sweeping, involving a press release by a government official containing substantial errors. But White noted these cases dealt with the scope of the officials' authority, not the harm of an alleged unconstitutional action.

Conceding the value to decision-making of all immunity from litigation, White argued that immunity is such a departure from the rule of law that it must be carefully measured. Judges and prosecutors and others in the executive branch in judgelike positions needed the immunity. Other executive officials were only entitled to the "qualified good-faith immunity" that previous decisions had extended to state officials. Immunity exists for mere error, so long as the official acted without malice or knowledge of illegality and reasonably could have believed the actions lawful and constitutional. But where the official knew, or should have known, of an unconstitutional deprivation of rights, immunity should be controlled.

Rehnquist's minority opinion suggests the majority standards exposed officials excessively to frivolous suits since ingenious lawyers would have no difficulty in recasting claims in constitutional terms. In Harlow v. Fitzgerald (1982) the Court rejected a claim by President Richard Nixon's aides of absolute immunity, but modified the Economou standard by eliminating the subjective test that required a hearing of evidence as to the decision maker's attitudes, conduct, and such. The remaining test—that the official has immunity unless no reasonable decision maker could deem the action lawful—facilitates summary judgment on frivolous complaints.

Samuel Krislov

**Byrnes, James Francis** (b. Charleston, S.C., 2 May 1879; d. 9 Apr. 1972, Columbia, S.C.; interred Trinity Cemetery, Columbia), associate justice, 1941–1942. A self-taught South Carolina lawyer, Byrnes was the son of James F. Byrnes and Elisabeth E. McSweeney, a dressmaker. He studied at St. Patrick's parochial school, worked as a court stenographer and reporter, and read law in his spare time.

"Jimmy" Byrnes served as a Democratic member of the House of Representatives (1911–1925) and from 1931 to 1941 as a member of the U.S. Senate. Byrnes was a crucial Southern advocate of the *New Deal, particularly effective in behind-the-scenes negotiations in support of President Franklin D. *Roosevelt's policies. He also earned the president's gratitude in working for a compromise in the wake of the ill-advised *court-packing bill. Byrnes counseled against pressing for a vote on the bill because several decisions of 1937 revealed a new alignment on the Court and because of the resignation of Justice Willis *Van Devanter. Byrnes allegedly asked, "Why run for a train after you've caught it?"

In June 1941 Roosevelt nominated Byrnes to fill the seat vacated by Harlan Fiske *Stone who had been appointed chief justice. During his one term on the Court, Byrnes wrote only sixteen majority opinions. He wrote no concurring or dissenting opinions. His brief Supreme Court service is remembered principally for his decision in *Edwards* v. *California* (1941), which struck down a California law that made it a crime to bring indigents into the state. In his opinion for the five-member majority, Byrnes argued that California's "anti-Okie" law placed an unacceptable burden upon interstate commerce. Among Byrnes's other majority opinions was a decision limiting the right to strike on board ship, a decision exempting a New York teamsters' strike from provisions of a federal anti-racketeering law, and a decision striking down a Georgia law that made it a criminal offense not to fulfill a labor contract (see LABOR).

At President Roosevelt's request, Byrnes left the Court in October 1942 to serve as the director of economic stabilization. Less than a year later

*James Francis Byrnes*

he accepted another presidential appointment to head the new War Mobilization Board. An able administrator, Byrnes made the most of this post, becoming popularly known as "assistant president." Shortly after Roosevelt's death, the new president, Harry S. Truman, nominated his good friend and former Senate colleague to become secretary of state. After two years in Truman's cabinet, Byrnes resigned and returned to South Carolina. In 1951 he was elected overwhelmingly governor of the Palmetto State. As a Southern governor in the 1950s, Byrnes was a racial moderate: he supported segregation in schools and public facilities but successfully pushed for a bill to suppress the Ku Klux Klan (see SEPARATE BUT EQUAL DOCTRINE).

Byrnes was clearly more comfortable and effective in his positions as a legislator, administrator, and executive than as a justice. Of South Carolina's many noted political figures, only John C. Calhoun and Strom Thurmond held as many important governmental positions or had as significant a national stature as had James F. Byrnes. Appropriately, Byrnes's autobiography is titled *All in One Lifetime.*

John W. Johnson

# C

**Calder v. Bull,** 3 Dall. (3.U.S.) 386 (1798), argued 8 and 13 Feb. 1798, decided 8 Aug. 1798 by vote of 4 to 0; seriatim opinions by Chase, Paterson, Iredell, and Cushing, Ellsworth and Wilson not participating. *Calder* v. *Bull* was one of the Supreme Court's first decisions involving constitutional limitations on governmental power. The Connecticut legislature enacted a resolution granting a new hearing in a probate trial. The Calders, disappointed heirs, challenged this action as a violation of the ban in Article I, section 10, on ex post facto laws. Justices William *Paterson, James *Iredell, and William *Cushing accepted the legislature's action because before Independence the legislature had functioned as the state's highest appellate court and was thus merely continuing to act in that capacity (Connecticut had not yet adopted a new constitution).

Assuming that the legislature's resolution was a "law" within the meaning of the Ex Post Facto Clause, Justices Samuel *Chase, Paterson, and Iredell agreed that the clause was addressed only to laws imposing retroactive punishment (by creating criminal sanctions for actions that were legal when carried out or increasing the punishment set for a particular offense and applied retrospectively) and thus was inapplicable in civil disputes. Chase and Paterson, in addition, rested their rejection of the Calders' argument on the grounds of textual interpretation. Citing such sources as Blackstone, *The *Federalist,* and the constitutions of other states, they concluded that the expression "ex post facto" was a technical legal term that, long before the Revolution, had come to apply only to laws imposing or increasing criminal punishment, and the Constitution's

makers must have "understood and used the words in their known and appropriate signification" (p. 397). Both justices buttressed this reading of the clause by noting its close proximity to provisions such as the impairment of *Contracts Clause that would be redundant if "ex post facto" were extended to cover civil legislation.

Alone among the justices, Chase raised and then rejected another possible ground for invalidating the Connecticut resolution: its incompatibility with "the very nature of our free Republican governments" (p. 388). In a long and rambling paragraph Chase denied "the omnipotence of a state Legislature" even in the absence of express constitutional limits on its power. Using language reminiscent of Locke, Chase insisted that "the great first principles of the social compact" determined what actions of a legislature could be regarded as "a rightful exercise of legislative authority" (pp. 387–388). He went on to list a number of actions that could not be deemed legitimate regardless of the absence of any express constitutional prohibition; among them were ex post facto laws in the technical, criminal sense and "a law that takes property from A and gives it to B" (p. 388). Chase avoided applying these fundamental principles in *Calder* v. *Bull* itself, if indeed he even meant to suggest that judges were entitled to enforce them against the legislature, on the ground that whatever rights the losing heirs might have had to the property had not yet vested when the legislature acted and thus were still subject to interference by law.

Iredell appears to have interpreted Chase's opinion to assert a power in courts to pronounce a statute "void, merely because it is, in [the judges'] judgment, contrary to the principles of natural justice" (p. 399). Observing that persons of intelligence and good will disagree about the dictates of natural justice, Iredell denied that judicial invalidation of a statute on such a basis could express anything but a difference of opinion, and he expressly limited the exercise of judicial review to the enforcement of express limitations on legislative power.

The subsequent career of *Calder v. Bull* has been controversial. Early nineteenth-century critics attacked its limitation of the Ex Post Facto Clause to criminal statutes. Justice William *Johnson appended a long note to the report of an 1829 case, *Satterlee* v. *Mathewson,* arguing with considerable force that *Calder's* actual holding rested on the characterization of the Connecticut legislature's action as judicial rather than legislative in nature, and criticizing the *Calder* justices' use of legal authority. In the modern era, the case has been the subject of widely varying interpretations. Some scholars maintain that *Calder* is direct evidence of an "original understanding" that courts would enforce unwritten fundamental-law limitations on governmental power, while others insist that the case reflected the transition from the Revolutionary era's political rhetoric of social compact and natural rights to the textbound *interpretivism of the later Marshall Court. Whatever they may have meant originally by their remarks, Chase's invocation of constitutional principles transcending the constitutional text and Iredell's insistence on the textual nature of judicial review continue to play a role in the debate over the legitimacy of the Supreme Court's jurisprudence.

(See also EX POST FACTO LAWS; HIGHER LAW; JUDICIAL REVIEW; NATURAL LAW.)

□ Suzanna Sherry, "The Founders' Unwritten Constitution," *University of Chicago Law Review* 54 (1987): 1127–1177.                                    H. Jefferson Powell

**California, United States v.,** 332 U.S. 19 (1947), argued 13–14 Mar. 1947, decided 23 June 1947 by vote of 6 to 2; Black for the Court, Reed and Frankfurter in dissent, Jackson not participating. The United States sued California to determine whether the federal or the state governments owned or had paramount rights in and power over the submerged lands lying between the low-water mark and the three-mile limit. At stake were huge royalties and rights from gas and oil deposits. Until this time the federal government had not claimed ownership, nor had it denied it, but had left control over the submerged coastal lands to the states.

The Court held that the federal government had full power and dominion over the submerged lands, and Justice Hugo *Black rejected the states' claims that the thirteen colonies had separately acquired ownership of the three-mile strip at the time they achieved independence.

The federal government had always had dominion over coastal waters, even if it chose not to exercise that power or if it had delegated it to the states.

Justice Felix *Frankfurter took the states' claims of historic ownership more seriously and arugued that no evidence existed to show that the Constitution or the states ratifying it had intended the federal government to have dominion, which implies ownership, of the coastal strip.

Several years later Congress reversed the rulings in this and two other offshore oil cases by quit-claiming the coastal strips to the states in the Submerged Lands Act (1953).

(See also ENVIRONMENT; PROPERTY RIGHTS; PUBLIC LANDS; STATE SOVEREIGNTY AND STATES' RIGHTS; TIDELANDS OIL CONTROVERSY.)

Melvin I. Urofsky

**California v. Acevedo,** 111 S.Ct. 1982 (1991), argued 8 Jan. 1991, decided 30 May 1991 by vote of 6 to 3; Blackmun for the Court, Scalia concurring, Stevens in dissent. Until the 1991 *Acevedo* case was decided, two different rules governed the search of closed containers found in a motor vehicle. In *United States* v. *Ross* (1982), the Court held that if the police had probable cause to search an entire vehicle for contraband and came upon a closed container in the course of the automobile search, they could open the container without first obtaining a warrant. On the other hand, in *Arkansas* v. *Sanders* (1979) the justices had held that if probable cause focused exclusively on a particular closed container whose presence in a vehicle was purely fortuitous, the police had to obtain a search warrant before opening it.

In *Acevedo* the Court eliminated the warrant requirement for closed containers set forth in the *Sanders* case and adopted "one clear-cut rule" for all searches of closed containers found in an automobile. There is no difference, the Court concluded, whether the search of a vehicle coincidentally turns up a container, or the search of a container coincidentally turns up in a vehicle.

A number of commentators predicted that the reasoning of *Acevedo* would apply (or be extended) to closed containers outside vehicles. Indeed, in *Acevedo* Justice Antonin *Scalia concurred in the result on the ground that the validity of the search of a closed container anywhere, so long as it occurs outside a home, should not depend upon whether the police could have obtained a warrant.

(See also FOURTH AMENDMENT; SEARCH WARRENT RULE, EXCEPTIONS TO.)

Yale Kamisar

**Cameras in Courtrooms.** Public policy and legal doctrine have changed in recent years toward greater acceptance of cameras in the courtroom. Aversion to cameras emerged in the late 1930s following the highly photographed trial of Bruno

Hauptmann for the kidnapping and murder of the infant son of Charles Lindbergh. Shocked by the media disruption and sensational coverage of the trial, the American Bar Association recommended in 1937 that all courtroom photography be eliminated. Congress then enacted rule 53 of the Federal Rules of Criminal Procedure, prohibiting all photography or broadcasting of federal criminal cases. Most states followed suit, so that by 1962 all except Texas and Colorado forbade cameras in courtrooms.

In *Estes* v. *Texas* (1965) the Supreme Court overturned the conviction of Billy Sol Estes, holding that camera disruptions during the trial violated Estes' due process rights. Four justices of the five-member majority found that televising trials, at least under then-existing technology, was inherently unconstitutional. The fifth justice took a narrower view based on the specific circumstances of the *Estes* case and refrained from endorsing a blanket prohibition against all broadcasting of state trials.

During the 1970s, television broadcasters lobbied for greater access to courtrooms. Some states responded by experimenting with televised trials, using judicial guidelines to protect defendants' rights.

The Supreme Court revisited the cameras question in *Chandler* v. *Florida* (1981) and unanimously upheld Chandler's burglary conviction despite the fact that parts of his trial were televised over his objections. Chief Justice Warren *Burger, writing for the Court, held that states should be free to develop their own procedures for broadcasting trials and that such television coverage was not an inherent violation of due process. The Court stated that it was not overturning *Estes* but instead was reading the earlier decision in its narrower sense, as not banning all broadcasting of state trials. The shift from *Estes* to *Chandler* can be explained largely by improvements in the technology of broadcasting that made it less disruptive, by a move toward parity for broadcasting and print media in the right of courtroom access (cf. *Richmond Newspapers* v. *Virginia*, 1980), by the Burger Court's predisposition toward defederalizing criminal procedure, and by the retirement of the original five justices from the *Estes* majority. In *Chandler* the Court declined to endorse explicitly the broadcasting of trials, but many states read the 1981 decision as an invitation to open their courtrooms to television.

By 1990, forty-five states had changed their rules to allow (on either an experimental or permanent basis) some televised coverage of courtroom proceedings. In contrast, the long-standing ban on cameras in federal courtrooms has remained intact. Criminal cases in the federal courts continue to be off limits to broadcasting because of rule 53 of the Federal Rules of Criminal Procedure. However, beginning in July 1991, civil cases in six of the ninety-four federal district courts and two of the thirteen federal *courts of appeals were broadcast under a three-year experiment authorized by the U.S. Judicial Conference.

Perhaps the Supreme Court will reexamine the ban on live coverage of its own proceedings. Chief Justices Earl *Warren and Warren Burger were both adamantly opposed to television coverage of the Court. They argued that it would destroy the dignity of the proceedings and distort the appellate process, believing that only brief or sensational portions would be selected for broadcast. Those favoring broadcasting point in contrast to the educative functions of television, and to the need, as they see it, to open the Court to the public.

In a related constitutional issue, KQED, a public TV station in California, has sought to televise on a delayed basis an execution. In June 1991, federal district judge denied KQED's request. That decision is now on appeal.

(See also DUE PROCESS, PROCEDURAL; SPEECH AND THE PRESS.)

Lynn Mather

**Campbell, John Archibald** (b. Washington, Ga., 24 June 1811; d. Baltimore, Md., 12 March 1889; interred Green Mount Cemetery, Baltimore), associate justice, 1853–1861. John Campbell was the son of a well-to-do and politically active Georgia landowner and lawyer of Scotch-Irish descent. Reflecting his family's intellectual ability, Campbell enrolled at the University of Georgia at the age of eleven and graduated three years later with top honors. He began studying law in 1828 and was admitted to the Georgia bar the same year. Moving to Alabama in 1830, Campbell became involved in politics, serving in the state legislature from Montgomery in 1836 and from Mobile in 1842. His law practice also prospered and he was acclaimed for his arguments before the U.S. Supreme Court.

The death of fellow Democrat and native Alabaman justice John McKinley on 19 July 1852 provided Campbell the opportunity to join the Supreme Court himself. Lame-duck Whig president Millard Fillmore could not satisfy the Democrat-controlled Senate, despite sending three nominations. Consequently, the vacancy remained unfilled by the inauguration of Franklin Pierce, 4 March 1853. In an unprecedented display of judicial clout (and presidential impotence), the Court requested the president to nominate Campbell. On 25 March 1853, the forty-one-year-old Campbell received the Senate's unanimous confirmation.

A states' rights Jacksonian Democrat, Campbell was nonetheless a moderate on the *slavery issue. He commanded wide respect not only of the Court and Senate, but also of the public, possessing a hard-earned reputation based on dedication, talent, and unswerving integrity.

While on the Court, Campbell often delivered powerful and eloquent dissents. In *Dodge* v.

*John Archibald Campbell*

*Woolsey* (1856), for example, he opposed the Court's enlargement of federal jurisdiction over state-chartered corporations. The state legislatures, he said, should regulate matters within the states, for they are the truer voice of the states' citizens. Accordingly, the Court should exercise judicial restraint by strictly construing the Constitution.

As the nation became polarized during the late 1850s, Campbell's position became increasingly untenable. His moderate stance on slavery alienated Southerners, while his proslavery opinion in the *Dred *Scott* case outraged many Northerners. By 1860, Campbell found himself in the unenviable position of a moderate seeking accommodation between irreconcilable factions. He believed free labor would gradually and peacefully displace the less efficient "peculiar institution." Secession though possible was therefore unwise and unnecessary.

Nevertheless, when war came and Alabama seceded, Campbell resigned from the Court on 26 April 1861, ever loyal to his home state. He served the Confederacy as assistant secretary of war, hoping somehow to bring about peace. But following Appomattox he was thrown into prison at Fort Pulaski for four months.

Upon his release at the order of President Andrew Johnson, Campbell went to New Orleans, where he established a prosperous law practice. His skill brought him before the Supreme Court time and again. In the *Slaughterhouse Cases* (1873), Campbell ably contended that the Due Process Clause of the Fourteenth Amendment prevented state governmental encroachment upon economic liberty. Although his argu-

ment failed in a 5-to-4 decision, the Court reversed itself some twenty years later.

Tony Freyer

**Cantwell v. Connecticut,** 310 U.S. 296 (1940), argued 29 Mar. 1940, decided 30 May 1940, by vote of 9 to 0; Roberts for the Court. In *Lovell* v. *City of Griffin* (1938), the Supreme Court sustained the free speech rights of Jehovah's Witnesses without discussing the claim of free exercise of religion. In *Cantwell* v. *Connecticut,* however, the Court relied on that clause to uphold the Witnesses' practices.

*Cantwell* dealt with a Witness who went from door to door asking the resident if he or she would like to hear a record or accept a pamphlet. Both materials included an attack on the Catholic religion—and this in an overwhelmingly Catholic neighborhood. The Jehovah's Witness was convicted for failing to obtain the required approval by the secretary of public welfare.

The Court adjudged the conviction invalid, expressing what would become a universal rule of law. A state may regulate the times, the places, and the manner of soliciting contributions and holding meetings on its streets, but cannot forbid them altogether. The *First Amendment provided for both a freedom to believe and to act.

(See also ASSEMBLY AND ASSOCIATION, FREEDOM OF; RELIGION; SPEECH AND THE PRESS; TIME, PLACE, AND MANNER RULE.)

Leo Pfeffer

**Capitalism.** In a capitalist economic system a large proportion of productive assets are held by private owners and most decisions about how goods are produced and distributed are made by the market rather than government command. Capitalism thus suggests a system of economic regulation that involves a minimum of state involvement. Nonetheless, even the most purely capitalistic of economic systems contains some governmental supervision and interference. The government must establish the basic institutional regimes, such as contract law, that define the workings and domain of markets. The government must also legislate to correct instances of "market failure," or situations where the unregulated market does not work well. Most importantly, in any democratic political system a large number of interest groups continually petition all levels of government for laws that bias the market processes in their favor. Perhaps the Supreme Court's most important function as regulator of capitalism is to define the appropriate constitutional limit of governmental interference with individual, market-driven decision making.

The relationship between the Supreme Court and American capitalism is both indirect and complex, for two quite different reasons. First, capitalism envisions an economic system with minimal direct government regulation, and courts in any event are not the government's primary business regulators. Second, most market regulation has historically been the prerogative of the states, and the Supreme Court resolves disputes mainly involving questions of federal law (see FEDERALISM).

Notwithstanding these limitations, the Supreme Court has occupied a central position in the development of American capitalist institutions since the beginning of the nineteenth century. Through most of that time its principal function has been to protect the market from various regulatory incursions by different levels of government. The Constitution's framers envisioned a regime in which most decisions about the allocation of goods and services in the American economy should be private. The *Contracts Clause, the Commerce Clause, the Due Process Clause, and the *Takings Clause of the *Fifth Amendment are strong examples of that commitment. Through its interpretation of these clauses, other parts of the Constitution, and a wide array of federal and state statutes and *common-law rules, the Supreme Court has defined the balance between individual prerogative and the independence of markets, on the one hand, and sovereign power to interfere on the other.

Until the late 1930s the prevailing economic ideology on the Supreme Court was that of the classical political economists, who also had a strong bias in favor of the "unregulated" market. The result was a general judicial hostility toward state and federal regulation. A far-reaching revolution in economic theory in the 1930s was followed, however, by a Supreme Court that was much less trusting of markets and more tolerant of regulatory intervention than it had previously been.

Although the Supreme Court has had a prominent presence in the history of American capitalism, the word "capitalism" does not appear often in Supreme Court opinions. Further, nearly all the references before 1950 are pejorative, appearing in *First Amendment cases involving the right of left-wing groups to make statements attacking capitalism as an institution. In Debs v. United States (1919), for instance, the defendant attacked capitalism as a cause of war. In addition, Justice Louis D. *Brandeis used the term occasionally in dissenting opinions in which he spoke about the evils of uncontrolled capitalism.

The historical relationship between the Supreme Court and American capitalism has developed through several controversies concerning the proper scope of federal and state regulatory power.

**The Business Corporation.** American capitalism as we know it today would be unthinkable without the giant, multistate business corporation, a creature whose development was facilitated by a series of Supreme Court decisions stretching across the nineteenth century (see PRIVATE CORPORATION CHARTERS). The Court both adopted and expanded the common law's

view that the business corporation is a "person" entitled to many of the same constitutional protections given to natural persons. Chief Justice John *Marshall had clung to the traditional English view of Sutton's Hospital Case (1613) that a corporation was incapable of suing and being sued in its own name. Rather, the suit must name all the shareholders individually. Marshall's view was rejected by his own Court in Bank of United States v. Dandridge (1827). Thereafter, corporations could freely sue and be sued in federal court. Likewise, the Court held in *Bank of the United States v. Deveaux (1809) that a corporation was not a "citizen" under the Constitution but should be treated merely as a collection of its individual shareholders. As a result, the requirement that federal jurisdiction over a dispute did not exist unless plaintiff and defendant were from different states was not satisfied unless every shareholder in the dispute was from a different state than the party on the opposite side (see JUDICIAL POWER AND JURISDICTION). Deveaux was overruled in Louisville, Cincinnati & Charleston Railroad Co. v. Letson (1844), in which the Court held that a corporation should be deemed a citizen of the incorporating state. The result was to increase federal protection of corporations substantially. Under the Letson rule more disputes between corporations and out-of-state parties could be heard by the federal courts.

The Court recognized the American business corporation as a "person" for federal constitutional purposes in *Santa Clara County v. Southern Pacific Railroad (1886). Although liberals attacked the Santa Clara decision as exhibiting a Court bias in favor of big business, the decision's importance should not be exaggerated. In fact, Santa Clara was a sensible mechanism for permitting the corporation as an entity, rather than its shareholders as numerous individuals, to assert the corporation's constitutional claims. The Court's rationale in Santa Clara and its progeny was that a corporation was nothing more than an association of the stockholders who owned it. Giving the corporation itself the constitutional claim was more efficient than giving it to the shareholders themselves. After Santa Clara, individual shareholders could assert the constitutional rights of the corporation only if they brought a stockholders' derivative suit designed to force the corporation to defend its own rights.

One of the most important doctrines facilitating the growth of the multistate business corporation during the late nineteenth century was the evolving view that the states lacked the power to exclude "foreign" corporations, that is, corporations chartered in a different state, from doing business within their borders. The traditional view had been to the contrary. In *Bank of Augusta v. Earle (1839), the Supreme Court held that corporations of one state could do business in another state, but only subject to that state's permission and regulation. As late as the 1880s the Supreme Court permitted states to exclude foreign corporations from doing business directly within their borders. However, in *Welton* v. *Missouri* (1876) it held that the Commerce Clause forbade states from excluding the products made by out-of-state corporations. Under *Welton* a corporation chartered in New Jersey, for example, could not build a plant in New York without New York's consent, but New York did not have the power to exclude the products of New Jersey corporations, if the goods could legally be sold by New York's own corporations. The Court gradually narrowed a state's power to exclude foreign corporations from manufacturing within its borders as well, finally holding in *Western Union Telegraph Co.* v. *Kansas* (1910) that a corporation is a "person" within the jurisdiction of a state where it is doing business and could not be expelled except for violations of state law.

During the nineteenth century the Supreme Court frequently became involved in matters of corporate finance, the extent of limitations on corporate liability, and the scope of a corporation's power under its charter. Most such decisions were diversity jurisdiction cases, brought under the common law, but at a time when the federal courts were entitled to develop their own body of common-law rules. The result was substantial federal doctrine regulating the inner workings of the nineteenth-century corporation, its finances, and its dealings with outsiders. For example, in *Sawyer* v. *Hoag* (1873) the Court adopted the "trust fund" doctrine, which held that if a corporation's stated paid-in capital was larger than the amount the shareholders had actually paid in, the shareholders themselves could be liable for the shortfall. The doctrine was designed to protect creditors from "watered" stock. Likewise, the Court often considered the question whether corporate activities were *ultra vires*, or unauthorized by the corporate charter—generally adopting a narrower view than that prevailing in the states. For example, in *Thomas* v. *West Jersey Railroad* (1879) the Court struck down as *ultra vires* an effective merger of two railroads when one leased all its track to the other.

The Supreme Court gradually relaxed the strict rule preventing corporations from doing business not authorized in their charters, particularly if the additional business was "necessary or convenient" to the corporation's authorized business. For example, in *Jacksonville, Mayport, Pablo Railway & Navigation Co.* v. *Hooper* (1896), the Court permitted a railroad to acquire a hotel in order to accommodate railroad passengers. The result was increased judicial approval of corporate vertical integration, a phenomenon that characterized much of the corporate growth at the turn of the century.

An unanticipated result of the use of business-purposes statutes to challenge corporate mergers was that mergers of competitors were generally legal. For example, a corporation authorized to manufacture and distribute fuel oil, such as Standard Oil Company, could legally acquire a competing refinery, for that acquisition would not involve the corporation in unauthorized business. However, if Standard attempted to acquire a shoe factory, the acquisition would have been challenged as outside the scope of Standard's charter. As a result, mergers of competitors—usually the most damaging to competition—were generally legal, while "conglomerate" mergers, whose competitive consequences are generally negligible, were forbidden. Consequently, American merger policy gradually ceased to be the prerogative of corporate law and entered the domain of *antitrust laws, discussed below.

In *Briggs* v. *Spaulding* (1891), the Court adopted a broad version of the "business judgment" rule, thereby giving corporate directors expansive power to make decisions without concern about liability suits from stockholders. This and other decisions served to separate the ownership of the American business corporation from its management. The eventual result was a cry for more intensive regulation.

During the *New Deal era the Supreme Court gradually accommodated more intensive state and federal regulation of the business corporation. For example, in *Federal Trade Commission* v. *F. R. Keppel & Bros.* (1934), the Court held that the Federal Trade Commission had the power to reach "unfair" business practices even if such practices were not anticompetitive under antitrust laws.

More recently, the Supreme Court has exhibited a strong tendency to relax certain aspects of corporate regulation and return to the market. For example, in several decisions including *Chiarella* v. *United States* (1980) and *Basic, Inc.* v. *Levinson* (1988), it has developed the concept that the market for corporate securities generally operates efficiently; as a result, corporate managers and other insiders have no special obligation to provide information to buyers and sellers of their corporation's securities, although they may have a general duty to provide information about impending mergers directly affecting the value of the corporation's shares. Furthermore, the Court held in *Dirks* v. *Securities and Exchange Commission* (1983) that at least some people should be able to profit from secret information about corporate illegality by buying and selling of the corporation's stock. Such transactions encourage the discovery of this information. The fact that such trading may be "unfair" to people who do not have the information is not as important as the fact that permitting such trades makes the market work more efficiently.

***Limits on Regulatory Power.*** Classical nineteenth-century political economy contained a strong bias in favor of the free market and against regulation. This bias appeared not only in substantive legal rules but also in various procedural and jurisdictional restrictions designed to limit state authority to regulate. One of the most important, but often overlooked, devices that the Supreme Court has used to protect American capitalism from political interference lies in legal rules confining state authority to the state's own territory and federal authority to activities clearly in the flow of interstate commerce.

The Supreme Court held in *Gibbons v. Ogden* (1824) that the Constitution's Commerce Clause forbade a state from giving a steamboat company a monopoly on the route between ports in two different states (see COMMERCE POWER). Although nothing in the federal Constitution prevented a state from creating monopoly rights as a basic matter, *Gibbons* effectively limited the scope of such rights to intrastate activities. In *Wabash, St. Louis & Pacific Railway Co. v. Illinois* (1886), the Supreme Court held that a state could not impose rate regulation on railroad traffic if any part of the railroad's route lay outside the state. The decision in *Pennoyer v. Neff* (1878) reflected the Court's view that state courts had little power to obtain jurisdiction over people located outside the state.

Perhaps the most important limitation on state regulatory power in the nineteenth century was the rule in *Swift v. Tyson* (1842) that, in federal-court controversies between citizens of different states, the federal judge was not bound to follow state law but could refer to a "general" common law. Justice Joseph *Story's purpose in *Swift* was unambiguous: interstate markets would work efficiently only if they were governed by a body of uniform rules on which entrepreneurs could rely. If one state engaged in parochial rule-making—for example, to protect its debtors from out-of-state creditors—merchants would lose confidence in the interstate commercial market. *Swift* itself applied the doctrine of the "holder in due course" to interstate transactions: a third party who acquired commerical paper in good faith could assert the obligation even if the underlying transaction between the original parties was invalid. Although *Swift* covered only common-law rules, later decisions such as *Watson v. Tarpley* (1855) applied the *Swift* doctrine to state statutes. The result was the creation of a uniform system of debtor-creditor rules in federal court, long before such transactions were comprehensively regulated by federal statute.

The Court also limited the states' power to apply their substantive law to activities that occurred outside the state. For example, the Court in *Allgeyer v. Louisiana* (1897) substantially undermined state power to regulate out-of-state insurance companies. Similarly, in *New York Life Insurance Co. v. Dodge* (1918) the justices reduced the power of a state to apply its unique contract law to contracts that had been executed in a different state. Importantly, however, the general common law was not considered "regulatory" but rather as a body of universal rules that courts need only recognize. As a result, a state could apply the general common law to interstate transactions even if the state lacked the power to regulate the same transaction by statute, as the Court held in *Western Union Telegraph Co. v. Call Publishing Co.* (1901). This practice was consistent with the Court's general position that the common law, if properly applied, did not interfere with markets but rather facilitated them.

The nineteenth-century Supreme Court's hostility toward state regulation also showed up in severe limitations on state administrative agencies. For example, in *Chicago, Milwaukee & St. Paul Railway Co. v. Minnesota* (1890), the Court struck down a state statute that gave a regulatory agency final authority to set railroad rates. Only in the 1920s did the Supreme Court become tolerant of railroad rate-making by regulatory agencies rather than courts or legislatures.

The Supreme Court was also hostile toward regulatory incursions by the federal government and limited federal power to transactions that clearly involved interstate commerce, narrowly defined. For example, in *United States v. *E. C. Knight Co.* (1895) the Court held that the federal antitrust laws could not be applied to a multistate manufacturing trust because manufacturing was not deemed part of interstate commerce. Likewise, in *Hammer v. Dagenhart* (1918) it struck down a federal child-labor statute because the labor itself was performed within a single state. It was not sufficient that the goods produced by the labor were destined to be shipped in interstate commerce.

The New Deal signaled a dramatic change in the Supreme Court's philosophy concerning the jurisdictional power to regulate of both states and the federal government. The *Swift* decision was overruled by *Erie Railroad Co. v. Tompkins* (1938). In *International Shoe* (1945) the Court greatly expanded state court jurisdiction over outsiders. The limitations on a state's power to apply its substantive law to transactions occurring elsewhere were relaxed in *Watson v. Employers Liability Assurance Corp.* (1954). On the other hand, in *National Labor Relations Board v. Jones & Laughlin Steel Corp.* (1937), the justices greatly expanded federal power to regulate labor relations, provided the employer had any substantial interstate business. *Hammer*, the 1918 child-labor decision, was expressly overruled by the Court in *United States v. *Darby* (1941). Since the Court's decision in *Wickard v. Filburn* (1942), federal power to regulate has extended to highly localized activities where the "effect" on interstate commerce seems to be all but trivial. One result, not entirely fortunate, is that many activities are now simultaneously subject to federal and state regulation, and the two levels do not necessarily have consistent policies.

**Monopolies.** In the history of American capitalism, *monopoly* has two quite different meanings. Historically, a monopoly was an exclusive right given to a private entrepreneur by the sovereign.

Throughout the nineteenth century the Supreme Court was repeatedly involved in questions about state power to create monopolies, thus denying to others the right to participate in a particular area of economic activity. A second conception of monopoly, discussed below, involved the Supreme Court as ultimate interpreter of the federal antitrust laws.

Aside from the *Gibbons* case noted earlier, the Supreme Court's first important brush with a state-created monopoly was the famous decision in *Charles River Bridge* v. *Warren Bridge* (1837). Taking a strictly classicist approach, Chief Justice Roger B. *Taney held that, although a state had the basic power to confer monopoly privileges on a business corporation, such rights would not be implied. As a result, a bridge corporation could not obtain an injunction against the construction of a competing bridge unless the corporation's charter expressly gave it a monopoly privilege.

Even the basic doctrine that the state had the power to create monopolies was challenged in the *Slaughterhouse Cases* (1873), where a bitterly divided Court approved a corporate charter that gave one corporation the exclusive right to operate a public slaughterhouse in New Orleans. Specifically, the Court found that no clause of the recently enacted *Thirteenth and *Fourteenth Amendments took the power to create monopolies away from the states. The *Slaughterhouse* grant has been widely described as a product of the worst kind of special interest legislation; however, it was really a quite sensible mechanism for dealing with an important public health problem that arose when small slaughterhouses deposited animal waste into the Mississippi River, which constituted New Orleans' supply of drinking water (see POLICE POWER). As a basic premise, both *Charles River Bridge* and *Slaughterhouse* remain good law. States have the power to grant monopoly charters to corporations such as public utilities, but monopolies will not ordinarily be implied where the legislative grants are silent.

**Liberty of Contract.** Classical political economy was committed to the belief that people should be able to contract freely for what they want, provided that the subject matter of the contract was not independently illegal. One version of this view was expressly written into the Constitution, in the Contract Clause, and became one of the most important vehicles for the protection of the capitalist system in the first half of the nineteenth century. A second, quite different version of freedom of *contract was not expressly written into the Constitution but was created by the Supreme Court around the beginning of the twentieth century in the doctrine of substantive due process.

Both branches of liberty of contract doctrine reflected hostility against legislation that interfered with private economic decision making. "Liberty of contract" was the nineteenth century's equivalent of "public choice" theory—a

theory about why legislatures are much worse at allocating society's resources than are economic markets. This hostility can be seen in the Supreme Court's attitude toward the political process, for example, its conclusion in *Marshall* v. *Baltimore & Ohio Railroad Co.* (1853) that legislatures were enslaved to special interests, whose lobbyists "subject the State government to the combined capital of wealthy corporations, and produce universal corruption." These "speculators in legislation" would "infest the capital of the Union and of every State, till corruption shall become the normal condition of the body politic" (pp. 334–335).

*The Contract Clause.* The states were forbidden by the Contract Clause from impairing the obligation of previously created contracts. The clause was never interpreted to regulate the subject matter of prospective contracts; rather, it was used to prevent states from changing the terms of contracts that had been previously created.

During the Marshall period the Court developed two distinct branches of Contract Clause jurisprudence. A "private" branch generally prevented states from interfering with previous contracts between private parties and was principally a limitation on state power to pass debtor-relief statutes. For example, the Court in *Sturges* v. *Crowninshield* (1819) held that a state could not limit a creditor's recovery to a debtor's existing property, excluding attachment of future wages. The decision in *Ogden* v. *Saunders* (1827), from which Chief Justice Marshall dissented, upheld state insolvency statutes provided they were applied only to debts created after the statute was passed. (See BANKRUPTCY AND INSOLVENCY LEGISLATION.) Later Supreme Courts generally followed the Marshall-era policy of according strict protection to previously created private agreements. For example, in *Bronson* v. *Kinzie* (1843) the Supreme Court held that a state could not create a statutory right of redemption on foreclosed property and apply it to mortgages created before the statute was passed. And in *Gelpcke* v. *Dubuque* (1864) the Supreme Court forbade a state from invalidating municipal bonds issued by one of its own cities to out-of-state creditors. Not until the New Deal, when constitutional classicism was in its death throes, did the Supreme Court deviate substantially from this course. For example, in *Home Building and Loan Association* v. *Blaisdell* (1934), the justices sustained a depression-era statute placing a moratorium on mortgage foreclosures.

The "public" branch of Contract Clause jurisprudence historically limited a state's power to renege on its own contractual obligations. In the seminal decision in *Fletcher* v. *Peck* (1810), the Supreme Court held that a state could not revoke its previously given land grant. In *Dartmouth College* v. *Woodward* (1819), the Court extended the Contract Clause to cover corporate charters. After that, most Supreme Court decisions in the "public" branch considered the scope of a state's power to amend the previously granted charters of business corporations. The public branch of Contract Clause jurisprudence revealed a great tension in Supreme Court liberty of contract analysis. On the one hand, corporate charters were contracts, and belief in the sanctity of contract was nothing less than an article of faith. On the other, in the early nineteenth century the states had seen fit to give corporations a wide array of monopoly privileges, tax exemptions, and other special prerogatives. These were generally abhorrent to classical political economy's view that the market alone should govern the fortunes of its entrepreneurial participants. The question now was whether to permit the states to renege on some of the promises, thus restoring the fairness and balance of the market but, in the process, undermining the sanctity of the contract as corporate charter. The general answer was that even liberty of contract should be subordinated to the greater good of preserving the market.

In the *Charles River Bridge* case, previously mentioned, the Supreme Court held that the Contract Clause did require implication of a monopoly provision in a corporate charter that did not expressly confer monopoly privileges. From that point on the Supreme Court generally gave the states broad power over their corporations, holding, for example, in the *Railroad Commission Cases* (1886) that a corporate charter that permitted a railroad to charge "reasonable" rates nevertheless permitted a state agency to determine what rates were reasonable. After about 1850, the Contract Clause was no longer a substantial impediment to state power to limit corporate prerogative.

*Substantive Due Process.* The Fourteenth Amendment doctrine of substantive due process was a product of a uniquely American version of classical political economy. In England, where land was scarce, labor restive, and social and economic mobility quite restricted, classicism's strict preference for the market had given way by 1850 to much more interventionist views of the role of the state. Economists such as John Stuart Mill and, later, Alfred Marshall supported some state-imposed redistribution of wealth. But the United States after the Louisiana Purchase (1803) held an abundance of undeveloped land and experienced both rapid economic growth and apparent high mobility for those who were ambitious. Within the classical vision, every laborer could quite easily become a landowner or entrepreneur—never mind that this did not include slaves or, in most states, women. As a result, Adam Smith's historical reverence for the unrestrained market persisted in the United States long after it was tempered in England. This belief was constitutionalized in substantive due process, a doctrine that developed in state courts in the 1880s but passed quickly to the Supreme Court as well. The Supreme Court justices may not have read the classical political economists directly, but they were quite familiar with Thomas M. *Cooley's thoroughly classical *Treatise on the Constitutional Limitations Which Rest upon the Legislative Power of the States of the American Union* (1868), which provided the intellectual foundation for substantive due process as a constitutional doctrine. (See DUE PROCESS, SUBSTANTIVE.)

Substantive due process, unlike Contract Clause doctrine, regulated not merely the sanctity of preexisting contracts but also the right of people to enter into various kinds of contracts. The era was hardly a period of "dry formalism," as Roscoe Pound and other Progressive critics suggested (see PROGRESSIVISM), but rather of great judicial creativity. For example, in *In re *Debs* (1895) the Court cut from new cloth the doctrine that the executive branch has the power to protect interstate commerce from labor disputes, even though Congress had not passed a statute authorizing the executive's action. And in *Ex parte *Young* (1908) Justice Rufus *Peckham held that the *sovereign immunity provision of the *Eleventh Amendment did not apply when a private party sought to enjoin a state official from enforcing an unconstitutional statute, because the official is "stripped of his official or representative character" (p. 160). In this case, the statute was a railroad rate regulation alleged to violate liberty of contract.

The most controversial of the Supreme Court's substantive due process decisions was *Lochner v. New York* (1905), which struck down a statute that forbade bakers of loaf bread from working more than ten hours per day or sixty hours per week. Clearly, Peckham held, the statute took away a baker's liberty to agree with his employer about how many hours he wished to labor. Using the same reasoning, the Court struck down statutes that regulated product quality. For example, in *Jay Burns Baking Co.* v. *Bryan* (1924) it upset a statute requiring standardized weights for bread, and in *Weaver v. Palmer Bros.* (1926) it rejected a statute regulating the quality of bedding materials.

One of the most frequent targets of substantive due process analysis was rate regulation. Many forms of rate regulation were legal. Even during the height of substantive due process, a state could regulate the prices charged by a corporation if the power to regulate was set in the corporate charter. The charter itself was a contract, and liberty of contract reigned supreme. Further, in the important decision in *Munn v. Illinois* (1877), which preceded the substantive due process era, the Supreme Court extended the power over rates to unincorporated firms as well, provided that they operated in areas "affected with a public interest." These included enterprises that traditionally had been accorded monopoly protection or the eminent domain power, such as shipping lines, wharfs, common carriers and, in the case of *Munn*, grain elevators.

Later in the substantive due process period the

Court made clear that the states lacked a general power to regulate rates; further, the prerogative of deciding what kinds of industries were affected with the public interest belonged to the courts. Perhaps the most famous decision involving price regulation was *Adkins v. Children's Hospital* (1923), which overturned a Washington, D.C., minimum-wage law that applied only to women. The Supreme Court, using language borrowed from the classical political economists, concluded that there is a "moral requirement" of "just equivalence" between the price to be charged for labor and the value the employer places upon it (p. 558).

One of the markets consistently found to be affected with the public interest was the railroads, and the Supreme Court generally upheld state and later federal regulation of railroad rates. However, in *Smyth v. Ames* (1898) it held that such regulation must provide the railroad with a reasonable return on its investment. To this day, the rule basically survives that rate regulation is generally permissible but that regulation that deprives a private entrepreneur of a reasonable competitive profit is an unconstitutional taking of property.

Progressive-era critics were fond of drawing the Supreme Court majority during this period as a probusiness, antilabor group of mediocre intellectuals. But that view both underestimates the justices' intellects and overestimates their favoritism toward business. They were classicists, committed to the unregulated market. As such, they were just as quick to condemn probusiness regulatory legislation as wage-and-hour legislation. Progressive critics began with the premise that virtually all regulation was in the public interest and then focused their critique of the Court almost exclusively on protective labor legislation. In fact, however, the Court struck down equal numbers of statutes that were the product of regulatory "capture" by special interest groups within the business class. For example, in *Louis K. Liggett Co. v. Baldridge* (1928) it condemned a statute that required the licensing of pharmacists, designed mainly to protect druggists from cost-cutting new competitors. In *New State Ice Co. v. Liebmann* (1932) it upset a statute that conditioned entry into the business of manufacturing ice on the applicant's demonstration of "necessity" and inadequacy of existing facilities—certainly another device for protecting those in a particular industry from competition.

Even during the heyday of substantive due process, the Supreme Court did not condemn all regulatory legislation. In general, such legislation was justified if the Court perceived some kind of undesirable effects that the unregulated market was imposing on society in general. For example, in *Muller v. Oregon* (1908) the Court upheld a ten-hour law similar to that condemned in *Lochner*, but which applied only to women (see GENDER). In his famous *Brandeis brief of social science

data, Louis D. Brandeis argued to the Court that women occupy a special position as the bearers of society's future children and that women were generally unable to represent their own interests responsibly in the contracting process. The Supreme Court accepted these sexist, paternalistic arguments. Likewise, in *Euclid v. Ambler Realty Co. (1926) the Supreme Court upheld comprehensive land-use planning and *zoning, largely on the argument that high density and unplanned development could impose large costs on other members of the community through increased traffic, noise, congestion, and demand for public services.

In a single year, 1937, substantive due process ended even more quickly than it had begun. This was largely a result of the famous *court-packing plan of the Roosevelt administration and Justice Owen J. *Roberts's change of mind on the subject of minimum-wage legislation in *West Coast Hotel Co. v. Parrish* (1937), which overruled *Adkins*.

**The Court as Regulator of Competition.** One of the Court's most important roles as facilitator of American capitalism has resulted from its position at the top of the complex hierarchy of institutions that regulate the competitive process. Competition is regulated by courts and administrative agencies of both state and federal governments. The Supreme Court oversees all of these to some degree (see ADMINISTRATIVE STATE).

Before 1890, when the *Sherman Antitrust Act was passed, business competition was regulated mainly through the common law of trade restraints. The Supreme Court's supervisory role in that regime was the same as it was over other common-law decision making. The Court was the final arbiter of federal law, as well as of the "general" common law applied in diversity of citizenship cases.

In most instances, the Supreme Court's interpretation of the common law of trade restraints did not deviate noticeably from the generally accepted common law. For example, in *Oregon Steam Navigation Co. v. Winsor* (1873) it upheld a ten-year covenant not to compete given as part of the sale of a steamship route, on the theory that the covenant was reasonable because it (1) was ancillary to the sale of a business; (2) was restricted to a reasonable length of time; and (3) covered only the geographic area served by the route itself. But in *Central Transportation Co. v. Pullman's Palace Car Co.* (1890) the Court condemned a noncompetition covenant contained in a ninety-nine-year lease of railroad sleeping cars because the period of protection was unreasonably long. The court also adopted common-law rules that were completely tolerant of business mergers, and even of price fixing, provided the price-fixers did not use coercion or intimidation against others who attempted to undercut their prices. But in *Gibbs v. Consolidated Gas Co.* (1889) it held that price fixing of an article of "public necessity," in this case illuminating gas, should be illegal even though price fixing in ordinary items might be protected by liberty of contract.

The Supreme Court's position on price fixing changed remarkably with the passage of the Sherman Antitrust Act in 1890. In its first substantive antitrust decision, *United States* v. *Trans-Missouri Freight Association* (1897) it condemned a price-fixing and traffic-pooling arrangement among a group of railroads. The Supreme Court was unpersuaded by the economic argument, adopted by the lower court, that railroads were a network industry in which packages could reliably be transferred from one line to another only if there was a common scheme for scheduling and setting rates. It also rejected the argument that railroads were a peculiar industry containing a very high percentage of fixed costs and that rate competition was inherently ruinous—a phenomenon that eventually resulted in federal rate regulation. After *Trans-Missouri*, price fixing by competitors has been almost uniformly illegal in the United States, unless an industry is exempted by federal or sometimes state legislation. In *Loewe* v. *Lawlor* (1908) the Court held that agreements among laborers to insist on a certain wage was subject to the Sherman Act, at least when accompanied by enforcement practices such as picketing and boycotts. In the Supreme Court's mind, the labor union was just another kind of cartel. The result of *Loewe* was the rise of the federal labor *injunction—a powerful union-busting device until New Deal labor legislation largely exempted labor unions from antitrust law. The new legislation, which greatly increased labor union bargaining power, was upheld by the Supreme Court in *National Labor Relations Board v. Jones & Laughlin Steel Corp.* (1937).

The Supreme Court also used the antitrust laws to develop an American merger policy dictated by principles of competition rather than corporate structure. In *Addyston Pipe & Steel Co.* v. *United States* (1899) it approved then-Judge William Howard *Taft's lower court ruling that price "fixing" that is merely ancillary to the combination of businesses into a single enterprise should not be treated as harshly as naked price fixing by firms that continue to hold themselves out as competitors. In *Northern Securities Co.* v. *United States* (1904), however, the Court condemned a merger that eliminated all competition between two transcontinental railroads, and in *United States* v. *Union Pacific Railway Co.* (1912) it held that the federal antitrust law could condemn a merger even though the merger was entirely legal as a matter of state corporation law. From that point on considerations of competition became the dominant concern of federal merger policy, and state corporation law became largely secondary or irrelevant. The Supreme Court's principal concern in merger cases became the protection of consumers from high prices that might result from monopoly or collusion.

In 1950, however, Congress amended the antitrust laws to reflect a much greater concern with the fortunes of small businesses forced to compete with large firms. The result was a twenty-year interlude, from the 1960s into the early 1980s, during which the Supreme Court encouraged lower courts to condemn mergers that made the postmerger firm more efficient, on the theory that such mergers would injure competitors of the merging firms. Only in the 1970s and 1980s did the Court begin to return to a more explicitly consumer-oriented merger policy.

Between naked price fixing at one end and simple mergers at the other lay an array of business combinations and practices that may contain some attributes of both. Beginning in 1911 with the decisions in *Standard Oil* v. *United States* and *United States* v. *American Tobacco Co.*, the Court began to fashion a *rule of reason for evaluating the great majority of these practices. The rule of reason required a court to examine the history and development of a particular practice, its likely effects on competition, and any efficiency rationales that the practice might have. The Court later used this approach in *Maple Flooring Manufacturers Association* v. *United States* (1925) to approve such things as an agreement of competitors to exchange information about prices but not to charge a particular price. However, in *Eastern States Retail Lumber Dealers' Association* v. *United States* (1914), it condemned concerted boycotts directed against competitors under the per se rule.

The Supreme Court also became heavily involved in business decisions about how products should be distributed. For example, in *Dr. Miles Medical Co.* v. *John D. Park & Sons Co.* (1911), the Court condemned resale price maintenance, that is, agreements under which suppliers specify the price at which their products are to be resold. The rule that resale price maintenance is illegal per se survives until this day, although it has been made subject to numerous exceptions, both transient and permanent, by Congress and the Supreme Court itself.

The Supreme Court's position on nonprice restraints, such as clauses in which manufacturers specify the territories in which retailers can resell products, has been far less consistent. But the Court decided in *Continental T.V.* v. *GTE Sylvania* (1977) that vertical nonprice restrictions should be governed by the rule of reason. Under that rule most such restrictions are legal.

*Takings.* The constitutional doctrine developed most recently by the Supreme Court to limit state power to interfere with markets is the Fifth Amendment clause providing that private property may not be "taken" without payment of just compensation. The Court first applied the *Takings Clause to the states in *Chicago, Burlington and Quincy Railroad Co.* v. *Chicago* (1897). In *Pennsylvania Coal Co.* v. *Mahon* (1922) the Court, speaking through Justice Oliver Wendell *Holmes, struck down a state statute that required owners of underground coal mines to support the surface property even if the mining company owned a preexisting legal right to cause surface subsidence. Since the 1970s the Supreme Court has looked closely at state and local regulatory legislation that had a severely negative impact on the value of private property or that forced the private-property owner to accept the intrusion of unwanted objects or persons.

*Conclusion.* The governance of American capitalism was undoubtedly the primary activity of the Supreme Court in the nineteenth century. During that period the Court was heavily influenced by classical political economy, and this interest shows up in the Court's strong bias in favor of the unregulated market. In the twentieth century the mixture of decisions has changed somewhat, but overseeing the regulation of economic markets continues to be among the Supreme Court's most important obligations. As regulator of capitalism the Supreme Court has frequently been doctrinaire and has often overruled itself when underlying ideology changed. Unquestionably, however, the Court has been a stabilizing influence on an economy that would have been far less robust had it been subject to every vagary of changing political power.

(See also LABOR; PROPERTY RIGHTS.)

☐ Lawrence M. Friedman, *A History of American Law,* 2d ed. (1985). Kermit L. Hall, *The Magic Mirror: Law in American History* (1989). Morton J. Horwitz, *The Transformation of American Law: 1780–1860* (1978). Herbert Hovenkamp, *Enterprise and American Law, 1836–1937* (1991). J. Willard Hurst, *The Legitimacy of the Business Corporation in the Law of the United States, 1780–1970* (1970). Arthur Selwyn Miller, *The Supreme Court and American Capitalism* (1968).          Herbert Hovenkamp

**Capital Punishment** penalizes those convicted of certain classes of crimes by killing them. While many societies practice capital punishment, a substantial majority of developed countries have abolished the death sentence in this century. Although outlawed in some states, capital punishment was legal in thirty-eight states in 1991. Sanctioned methods of execution in the United States include death by electrocution, poison gas, hanging, firing squad, and lethal injection, the last now the most common. Across human history, however, beheading has probably been the most frequent mode of dispatch. The word *capital* comes directly from the Latin *capitalis,* "of the head."

Historical interpretations of the Constitution leave little doubt about capital punishment's legality. The *Eighth Amendment, applied to the states through the *Fourteenth Amendment, prohibits inflicting *cruel and unusual punishments, but no Supreme Court majority has interpreted that phrase to prohibit all forms of capital punishment in all circumstances. Historically the phrase "cruel and unusual" referred to punishments

that were far more serious than the offense involved, to torture, and to forms of execution that prolonged the pain of dying. The *Fifth and Fourteenth Amendments implicitly sanction capital punishment by stating that one cannot "be deprived of life . . . without due process of law."

However, interpretative approaches that stress the evolving character of constitutional norms have enabled the Supreme Court to address the complex moral and empirical questions associated with capital punishment. Since *Furman v. Georgia* (1972), which nullified all death sentences imposed without statutory guidelines, decisions have debated the following criticisms of capital punishment:

1. It is hypocritical to punish heinous crimes by means of a heinous crime—the deliberate taking of another human life.

2. Research does not confirm the claim that capital punishment is an effective general deterrent. Studies instead tend to confirm the old English story about pickpockets working the crowds attending the hangings of pickpockets.

3. Once inflicted, the death penalty's irreversibility prevents correcting those instances in which the criminal justice system convicts the wrong person. While absolute truth on such matters is unattainable, there are strong suspicions that some innocent persons have received the death sentence.

4. Administration of capital punishment in law and practice is inconsistent with retributive theories of punishment, for under such theories we would punish by death all those convicted of premeditated murder but would punish no other crime in this manner. Furthermore, the logic of retribution entails punishing cruelly and unusually those who murdered in this fashion, but the Eighth Amendment forbids just this retributive logic.

5. Data on those who receive the death penalty show that the criminal justice system does not apply it in proportion to the seriousness of the crime. Rather, it appears to be imposed on a randomly selected subset of those convicted of capital offenses. Prosecutorial discretion in charging and the discretionary practice of plea bargaining virtually assure this randomness. As this randomness suggests, no definitive study has isolated a strong racial bias in death sentencing. However, aggregate data convincingly show that the death penalty is more frequently imposed on those who victimize whites than those who victimize blacks.

6. As a class, paroled murderers show lower recidivism rates for their crimes than do most classes of felons. There is no evidence that the death penalty, as opposed to long-term imprisonment, is an effective specific deterrent. Murderers on death row are more likely to engage in violent crimes within prison than are those serving life terms.

On the other hand, sociological theory at least

since Émile Durkheim (1858–1917) has posited that setting absolute outer limits on deviance is a necessary component of group identification and survival. Justice Oliver Wendell *Holmes may have sensed this truth when he wrote, in *The Common Law* (1881), "The first requirement of a sound body of law is that it should correspond with the actual feelings and demands of the community, whether right or wrong" (1938 ed., p. 41). Public opinion continues to support the death penalty. (In fact, polls taken a few months after *Furman* showed a substantial jump in public approval of the death penalty.) Additionally, modern models of social interaction suggest that parties must occasionally threaten to take irrational and extreme actions in order to strengthen their capacity to negotiate resolutions of conflict peacefully. Finally, the precise effects of the death penalty versus less harsh punishments are impossible to measure because due process of law prohibits conducting controlled experiments.

From 1930 until the late 1960s, when the Court began systematically remanding all death sentences, 87 percent of all executions had been for murder and 12 percent for rape. Kidnapping, treason, espionage, and aircraft piracy, the other crimes made capital in the United States, accounted for the remaining 1 percent. Today, virtually all death sentences are imposed for intentional homicide.

In *Gregg* v. *Georgia* (1976) the Supreme Court ended the moratorium initiated in *Furman*. *Gregg* required legislatures to create statutory sentencing standards to guide sentencing bodies. A companion case, *Woodson* v. *North Carolina*, held unconstitutional a statutorily mandated death penalty. The Eighth Amendment, it said, required consideration of individual aggravating and mitigating circumstances. Continued litigation concerning the specifics of these decisions, however, prevented virtually all executions during the next six years.

By April 1991, statutes in thirty-eight states and the federal government permitted capital punishment. Since *Gregg,* approximately 145 people had been executed in sixteen states, led by Texas (39) and Florida (27). Twelve of these sixteen states lay below the Mason-Dixon line. More than 2,400 convicts were on death row at that time.

Since *Gregg*, the Court has required a separate penalty trial before imposing the death penalty. In this phase the jury considers aggravating and mitigating information not admissible at trial. The search for precise definitions of such key concepts as proportionality of punishment and mental competence, however, generated a seemingly endless series of *habeas corpus petitions and delays. Most recently, Chief Justice William H. *Rehnquist's efforts to streamline the appeals process and remove obstacles to implementing the death sentence led to the ruling, in *Butler* v. *McKellar* (1990), that defendants cannot appeal

"reasonable good-faith interpretations of existing precedents made by state courts even though they are shown to be contrary to later decisions" (p. 1217).

A conservative Court majority now seems determined to turn over the development of capital punishment policies and procedures to state legislatures and courts. Since many state judges face at least potential electoral challenges, conventional political processes seem likely to play the major role in shaping future death penalty policies.

(See also RACE DISCRIMINATION AND THE DEATH PENALTY.)

☐ Hugo Adam Bedau, ed., *The Death Penalty in America* (1982). Errol Morris, *The Thin Blue Line* (film, 1987).
Lief H. Carter

**Capitol, Supreme Court in the.** See BUILDINGS, SUPREME COURT.

**Cardozo, Benjamin Nathan** (b. New York City, 24 May 1870; d. Port Chester, N.Y., 9 July 1938; interred Cypress Hills Cemetery, Long Island, N.Y.), associate justice, 1932–1938. The son of Albert Cardozo and Rebecca Washington, Benjamin Cardozo was born into a community of persecuted Spanish and Portuguese Jews established in New Amsterdam in 1654. Governor Peter Stuyvesant attempted to expel them but was overruled by the Dutch West India Company. Cardozo's family produced distinguished patriots including Emma Lazarus, whose words once adorned the Statue of Liberty.

Cardozo was educated at Columbia College and Law School and practiced law in New York City. He was a member of the New York Court of Appeals from 1914 and chief judge from 1926 until his appointment to the United States Supreme Court in 1932.

While on the New York Court of Appeals, Cardozo became America's most celebrated state common law judge. In tort law he is most renowned for expanding the class of persons to whom a legal duty is owed. *MacPherson* v. *Buick* (1916) has become the fountain of products liability and *Ultramares Corporation* v. *Touche* (1931) similarly expanded the law of fraud to protect third parties. In contract law Cardozo was most closely associated with efforts to instill fairness into ambiguous contracts rather than permitting contracts to fail and entrap one of the parties. Cardozo understood that intentions are often unexpressed, indeed unformed, and must often be presumed. He substituted a presumption of mutually cooperative behavior for a presumption of purely competitive behavior (*Jacob and Youngs* v. *Kent,* 1921).

His method of reaching these decisions made Cardozo the standard bearer for a movement that came to dominate American legal thought. While serving on the Court of Appeals he was invited to

*Benjamin Nathan Cardozo*

deliver the Storrs Lectures at Yale, which became his classic statement of the proper judicial decision-making process, *The Nature of the Judicial Process* (1921). Cardozo argued for what he described as sociological jurisprudence, rooted in a sophisticated understanding of positivist jurisprudence and expressed with elegance and clarity. He led both bench and bar to interpret law guided by its purpose and function rather than as purely conceptual or "formal." As he wrote later in *Carter v. Carter Coal Co.* (1936), "a great principle of constitutional law is not susceptible of comprehensive statement in an adjective" (p. 327).

Cardozo's appointment to the Supreme Court was urged with unique unanimity on President Herbert Hoover. Cardozo, however, moved from a leader on the New York court to a dissenter for most of his career in Washington. Like Oliver Wendell *Holmes whom he succeeded, he joined Justices Louis D. *Brandeis and Harlan Fiske *Stone insisting on deference to Congress and the states. They succeeded in redefining constitutional law in a series of cases beginning in 1937 just before Cardozo's death. He delivered the opinions in *Steward Machine Co. v. Davis* (1937) and *Helvering v. Davis* (1937) in which the Court, reversing itself on the nature of *federalism, upheld the power of Congress under the taxing and spending clauses to enact provisions of the Social Security Act.

Prior law had been based on a set of judicially defined mutually exclusive rights and powers (see SEPARATION OF POWERS). Deference to other branches of government required rethinking every aspect of constitutional law. After 1937 both

rights and powers would be understood as concurrent and overlapping. Concurrent and overlapping rights and powers leave boundaries undefined. Cardozo led the way in substituting a new constitutional rationale for the now absent boundaries. He contributed to that redefinition most memorably in *Palko v. Connecticut* (1937), in which Cardozo's formula, "the essence of a scheme of ordered liberty" (p. 325), became the basis for the *incorporation of most of the Bill of Rights into the *Fourteenth Amendment and eventuated in making those provisions applicable to the states. In a related area, Cardozo wrote for a deeply divided Court in *Nixon v. Condon* (1932), one of the early *white primary cases, that a state may not authorize a committee of a political party to exclude members of a racial minority from a party primary.

Cardozo's opinions, like those of Holmes and Brandeis, are cited for the authority of the author and the clarity of his pen. He is remembered in innumerable current opinions of members of the Supreme Court for his attention to justice, his emphasis on the purpose of law, and for his majestic description of the relationship between policy and precedent in his books and opinions.

□ Felix Frankfurter, "Mr. Justice Cardozo and Public Law," *Columbia Law Review* 39 (1939): 88–118, *Harvard Law Review* 52 (1939): 440–470, *Yale Law Journal* 48 (1939): 458–488. Warren A. Seavey, "Mr. Justice Cardozo and the Law of Torts," *Columbia Law Review* 39 (1939): 20–55, *Harvard Law Review* 52 (1939): 372–407, *Yale Law Journal* 48 (1939): 390–425. Stephen E. Gottlieb

**Carroll v. United States,** 267 U.S. 132 (1925), argued 4 Dec. 1923, rescheduled 28 Jan. 1924, reargued 14 Mar. 1924, decided 2 Mar. 1925 by vote of 6 to 2; Taft for the Court, McReynolds and Sutherland in dissent. George Carroll and John Kiro were convicted of transporting liquor in an automobile in violation of the Volstead Act (National Prohibition). Federal officers acknowledged that they were not following Carroll and Kiro at the time of arrest but that when they saw them, they suspected that they were carrying prohibited liquor and decided to give chase. The Supreme Court considered the constitutionality of the car search that yielded the evidence and specifically reviewed Carroll and Kiro's claim that since there was no basis to search the car, the resulting evidence should have been excluded from trial.

The Court rejected their claim and recognized the car search exception to the warrant requirement for the first time. Detailing the legislative history of the National Prohibition Act, Chief Justice William H. *Taft concluded for the majority that Congress intended to distinguish the need for a search warrant in private dwellings from searches conducted in automobiles or other moving vehicles. Furthermore, Taft emphasized that such a distinction was consistent with Fourth

Amendment guarantees and other Supreme Court decisions and argued that "the right to search and the validity of the seizure are not dependent on the right to arrest" (p. 158).

Justice James *McReynolds was joined in dissent by Justice George *Sutherland. He argued that there was insufficient cause to stop the vehicle without a warrant, that the mere suspicion that existed was ill founded, and that the Volstead Act did not authorize arrest or seizure on simple suspicion. McReynolds noted that without explicit statutory authorization, the common-law tradition that distinguished between arrest without warrant in the case of felonies and misdemeanors should apply. He concluded, then, that the "validity of the seizure under consideration depends on the legality of the arrest," and supported Carroll's contention that his *Fourth (and *Fifth) Amendment rights had been violated (p. 169).

The Court has continued the position first articulated in *Carroll* that although the *privacy interests in an automobile have constitutional protection, its mobility justifies less sweeping protection and therefore exemption from more customary warrant requirements. Later Court decisions have not extended this exception to any or all movable containers (e.g., *United States* v. *Chadwick*, 1977), although the Court has continued to apply less stringent protection for automobiles than stationary objects.

(See also SEARCH WARRANT RULE, EXCEPTIONS TO.)

Susette M. Talarico

**Carswell, George Harrold** (b. Irwinton, Ga., 22 Dec. 1919), federal judge and rejected nominee for U.S. Supreme Court. After five years in private practice and another five years as U.S. attorney, Carswell was appointed to the U.S. District Court for Northern Florida by President Dwight Eisenhower in 1958. In 1969 President Richard *Nixon elevated him to the Fifth Circuit Court of Appeals. Six months later, on 19 January 1970, Nixon nominated Carswell for the Supreme Court vacancy created by the resignation of Abe *Fortas, after the Senate had rejected Nixon's first nominee, Clement *Haynsworth. The Senate also rejected Carswell, 51 to 45, on 8 April 1970. Two weeks later Carswell resigned from the federal bench to run in the Florida Republican primary for the U.S. Senate. He lost that election and returned to Tallahassee to practice law.

The Carswell nomination was attacked on both political and professional grounds. He was criticized for racial remarks in a 1948 campaign speech, for his courtroom treatment of African-Americans, and for helping a municipal golf course evade desegregation while he was U.S. attorney. Prominent lawyers and law professors criticized his judicial record, noting that his reversal rate as district judge was among the highest in his circuit. Republican senator Ro-

man Hruska of Nebraska, who was floor manager for the nomination, did not help Carswell with his comment, cited in the *Congressional Record*, that even the mediocre are "entitled to a little representation."

(See also NOMINATIONS, CONTROVERSIAL; NOMINEES, REJECTION OF.)

Susan M. Olson

**Carter v. Carter Coal Co.,** 298 U.S. 238 (1936), argued 11, 12 Mar. 1936, decided 18 Mar. 1936 by vote of 5 to 4; Sutherland for the Court, Cardozo, Brandeis, and Stone in dissent, Hughes dissenting in part. The *Carter* case arose in the vortex of controversy surrounding President Franklin D. *Roosevelt's *New Deal efforts to curb the disastrous effects of the Depression. The critical issue before the Court involved competing visons of *federalism and the appropriate allocation of power between state and federal government. Much New Deal legislation was premised on the belief that the *commerce power granted Congress extensive authority to regulate labor relations, commercial activities, agriculture and the like. The idea was diametrically opposed to the vision of the commerce power embraced by a majority of the Supreme Court. The *Carter* decision was viewed by many as yet another example of Court intransigence that led ultimately to Roosevelt's unsuccessful *court-packing plan.

The Bituminous Coal Conservation Act of 1935 sought to stem overproduction and ruinous competition. Wages were so appalling in the coal industry that *labor unrest and strikes, sometimes accompanied by violence, had become endemic. The act created local boards to set minimum prices for coal and also provided for collective bargaining to achieve acceptable wage and hour agreements. Congress based its authority for the law squarely on its ability to regulate interstate commerce.

Justice George *Sutherland's majority opinion brushed aside the bare recitation of the direct effect of coal mining on the economy. He drew what was for him a critical distinction. Although Congress's motives might be laudable, the Commerce Clause and the *Tenth Amendment worked in tandem to define the appropriate spheres of state and federal governments. Since the powers of Congress are rigidly enumerated in the Constitution, it cannot cede its powers to others. Sutherland acknowledged that such a system was cumbersome, but he argued that the benefits of preserving the boundaries between states and the federal government were central to the integrity of the constitutional system. Congress, in short, had overstepped its constitutional limits. In a sentence reminiscent of a seduction he said, "Every journey to a forbidden end begins with the first step; and the danger of such a step by the government in the direction of taking over the powers of the states is that the end of the journey may find the states so despoiled of their powers, or—what may amount to the same thing—so relieved of the responsibilities which possession of the powers necessarily enjoins, as to reduce them to little more than geographical subdivisions of the national domain" (p. 866). Sutherland also drew on the distinction between items of production and things in commerce. Congress may regulate once goods enter into commerce or when there is a direct effect on commerce. Since he found no direct effect on commerce and since the coal was still in the production phase, only the states could constitutionally regulate coal mining.

Justice Benjamin *Cardozo in dissent had a more pragmatic view of the situation. In response to the majority's direct/indirect test he said that "a great principle of constitutional law is not susceptible of comprehensive statement in an adjective" (p. 327).

*Carter* represents the twilight of the Tenth Amendment and states' rights. One year later, in *National Labor Relations Board* v. *Jones & Laughlin Steel Corp.* (1937), the Court adopted Cardozo's minority position. The Commerce Clause became the basis for a massive restructuring of the federal-state relationship.

(See also DELEGATION OF POWERS; STATE SOVEREIGNTY AND STATES' RIGHTS.)

Diane C. Maleson

**Cases and Controversies.** The framers of the Constitution provided, in *Article III, section 2, that federal courts were to have jurisdiction only of "Cases" and "Controversies." These two words are the origin of a body of law that imposes important restraints on the power of the federal judiciary. Federal courts may consider only issues that are presented in an adversary context. They may not answer merely hypothetical or abstract questions: their power is limited by law to questions that arise out of an actual dispute. The most widely cited reason for that requirement is to ensure full development of cases. When parties contend in a real dispute, each side is permitted to be zealously represented and the court may consider the legal issues against the backdrop of real facts.

A second aspect of the cases or controversies requirement relates not to the power of courts but to their willingness to decide certain kinds of cases. The framers constructed a government comprising three distinct branches—legislative, executive, and judicial—and made each branch dominant in its own sphere. Federal courts therefore approach cases that involve conflicts within or between branches cautiously. A refusal by the legislative or executive branch to comply with a court decision would be a blow to public confidence in the court system. Federal courts therefore have usually declined to become involved in so-called *political question cases, citing the cases or controversies limitation to justify abstention. Since *Baker* v. *Carr* (1962), however,

the polticial questions doctrine has ceased to inhibit federal courts in cases involving questions of *federalism, such as reapportionment or the reach of the *Tenth Amendment.

(See also COLLUSIVE SUITS; JUDICIAL POWER AND JURISDICTION; JUDICIAL REVIEW; SEPARATION OF POWERS.)

James B. Stoneking

**Catron, John** (b. Pennsylvania, 1786; d. Nashville, Tenn., 30 May 1865; interred Mt. Olivet Cemetery, Nashville), associate justice, 1837–1865. Although the exact location and date of his birth have not been determined, John Catron was probably born in Pennsylvania in 1786; his family moved to Virginia when he was a child. Catron's parents were poor German immigrants, and his early life was one of considerable hardship and little formal education. Catron grew to adulthood in Kentucky, where he married Mary Childress in 1807. In 1812 he and his wife moved to Tennessee and built a home in the western foothills of the Cumberland Mountains. Catron served under General Andrew *Jackson in the War of 1812 and, after cessation of hostilities, returned to Tennessee to seek his fortune as a lawyer. Little is known about Catron's legal training, but in 1815 he was admitted to the Tennessee bar. Initially, Catron established a general private practice, although he also served as a part-time public prosecutor. He moved to Nashville in 1818 and soon became one of the leaders of the Davidson County bar. In 1824 he was appointed to the highest state tribunal, the Court of Errors and Appeals, and in 1831 was elevated to chief justice.

As a state jurist, Catron wrote a number of

*John Catron*

## 130 □ Censorship

colorful opinions dealing with such matters as gambling and dueling, which he detested, and *slavery, which he supported. When the Tennessee legislature abolished the Court of Errors and Appeals in 1834, Catron returned to private practice. A loyal Jacksonian Democrat, Catron managed Martin Van Buren's 1836 presidential campaign in Tennessee. On his last day in office, President Jackson rewarded Catron with a nomination to the United States Supreme Court, and Catron was sworn in as associate justice on 1 May 1837.

Throughout his twenty-eight-year tenure on the Supreme Court, Catron was a stalwart defender of states' rights (see STATE SOVEREIGNTY AND STATES' RIGHTS) and of the "peculiar institution" of slavery. Catron joined the Court's decision in the landmark case of *Cooley v. Board of Port Wardens (1852), where the justices upheld the power of state governments to regulate local aspects of interstate commerce. Catron also concurred in Dred *Scott v. Sandford (1857), in which the Court struck down the Missouri Compromise of 1820 in which Congress had banned slavery in certain federal territories.

Despite his views on slavery and states' rights, Catron did not support southern secession. When the Supreme Court completed its term in the spring of 1861, Catron returned to Tennessee hoping to prevent the state from leaving the Union. After secession, Catron still attempted to hold federal court in Tennessee but was eventually persuaded to leave the state lest he face difficulties with Confederate authorities. Catron was, however, able to continue his "circuit riding" duties in Kentucky and Missouri, where he cooperated with the military's detention of civilian Confederate sympathizers by refusing to grant writs of *habeas corpus.

His staunch unionism notwithstanding, Catron dissented from the Supreme Court's decision in the *Prize Cases (1863), in which the Court upheld President Abraham *Lincoln's unprecedented order for a naval blockade of southern ports shortly after the outbreak of hostilities. Catron lived just long enough to see the Union maintained by General Lee's surrender. He died in Nashville on 30 May 1865, survived only by his wife. John M. Scheb II

**Censorship.** The Supreme Court has found censorship to be an especially intolerable restriction on freedom of expression. The term *censorship* might encompass almost any restriction on the dissemination or content of expression, but most fundamentally it means *prior restraint*—any government scheme for screening either who may speak or the content of what people wish to say before the utterance. Although the Court has never held prior restraint to be inherently unconstitutional, it has emphasized that "any system of prior restraints of expression comes to this Court bearing a heavy presumption against its constitu-

tional validity" (*Bantam Books, Inc.* v. *Sullivan*, 1963, p. 70).

The Court first directly addressed the constitutionality of prior restraint in *Near v. Minnesota* (1931). In question was a Minnesota law that allowed judges to eliminate as a public nuisance any "malicious, scandalous and defamatory" newspaper or periodical (see LIBEL). A state court had declared a newspaper, the *Saturday Press*, to be a public nuisance after it had attacked public officials with allegations of corruption, laziness, and illicit contact with gangsters. Much of the material seemed anti-Semitic. The state court issued an order forever prohibiting the editors "from producing, editing, publishing, circulating, having in their possession, selling or giving away any publication whatsoever which is a malicious, scandalous or defamatory newspaper" either under the title of the *Saturday Press* or any other title (p. 706). Violation of the order would constitute contempt of court.

By a margin of 5 to 4, the U.S. Supreme Court found the statute to be an unconstitutional form of censorship, because before a banned newspaper could publish again, the editors would have to satisfy a judge as to the new publication's good character. Chief Justice Charles Evans *Hughes for the majority concluded that prior restraint would be constitutional only in extreme circumstances, for example, if a newspaper were about to publish the location of troops in wartime. Speaking for dissenters, Justice Pierce *Butler protested that the Minnesota law did not constitute a classic form of censorship because the newspaper had published nine issues before being suppressed. He noted that the law "does not authorize administrative control in advance such as was formerly exercised by the licensers and censors" (p. 735).

In subsequent cases, the Court disapproved of administrative licensing of speech where the licenser can make decisions based on the context of the would-be speaker's expression. For example, in *Lovell v. Griffin (1938) the Court held unconstitutional an ordinance banning distribution of literature without permission of the city manager, where the manager had carte blanche to grant or deny permits. Likewise, the Court in *Joseph Burstyn, Inc. v. Wilson* (1951) found unconstitutional a New York scheme under which exhibition licenses could be denied to motion pictures found to be "sacrilegious." Nor would the Court allow the postmaster general to revoke *Esquire* magazine's second-class mailing privileges on grounds that the publication was not contributing sufficiently to the public good and welfare (*Hannegan* v. *Esquire, Inc.*, 1946). The Court struck down *injunctions prohibiting newspapers from publishing articles based on the Pentagon Papers, classified documents that had been leaked to the press (*New York Times Co. v. United States*, 1971). And it held that judges could not prohibit journalists from publishing material potentially prejudicial to a criminal defendant when such material was obtained in open court (*Nebraska Press Association* v. *Stuart,* 1976).

On the other hand, the Court is likely to allow licensing systems that minimize administrative discretion, regulate the *time, place, and manner of expression without regard to its content, and are guided by clear and specific standards (*Cox* v. *New Hampshire,* 1941; *Poulos* v. *New Hampshire,* 1953). The Court has allowed government censorship of obscene movies, but only if stringent procedures are followed, including prompt *judicial review (*Freedman* v. *Maryland,* 1965). The Court has also granted public elementary and secondary schools broad power to censor student publications (*Hazelwood School District* v. *Kuhlmeier,* 1988). It has also concluded that the federal government has broad power to require many government employees to submit to censorship of their speech and writing even after they leave government employment and even when unclassified material is involved (*Snepp* v. *United States,* 1980). Further, the Court has held that people who disobey court orders restraining expression may be punished for contempt even if the restriction is likely to be found unconstitutional (*Walker* v. *City of Birmingham,* 1967).

The *Near* decision itself has been invoked to justify prior restraint, which has led critics to complain that the Court has provided no clear theory or standards for determining when prior restraint is permissible. In the *Pentagon Papers Case,* justices on both sides of the decision used *Near* to support their positions—some for the proposition that prior restraint is presumptively unconstitutional, but others for the proposition that exceptional circumstances can justify prior restraint. And when, in 1979, a federal district court issued an injunction prohibiting *The Progressive* magazine from publishing an article purporting to explain how to build a hydrogen bomb, the judge concluded that the article was analogous to the types of exceptional circumstances listed in *Near* (*United States* v. *The Progressive*). (The injunction was lifted after similar material was published elsewhere and the government dropped the case.)

In recent years, spirited scholarly debate has arisen over the question of whether the evil of prior restraint might be overstated. Some have argued that judicially imposed restraints are less serious than administrative censorship, that freedom of expression may be served better by the use of prior restraint than by severely punishing expression after the fact. Fear of severe subsequent punishment, they assert, may have a far greater "chilling effect" on speech than narrowly focused, judicially supervised prior restraint.

The Supreme Court appears thus far not to have been swayed by such argument. It appears to remain committed to the view that censorship, whether imposed by administrators or by judges, is presumptively unconstitutional and

the most deplorable way of restricting freedom of expression.

(See also FIRST AMENDMENT; SPEECH AND THE PRESS.)

□ "Near v. Minnesota, 50th Anniversary," symposium in *Minnesota Law Review* 66 (1981):1–208. Martin H. Redish, "The Proper Role of the Prior Restraint Doctrine in First Amendment Theory," *Virginia Law Review* 70 (1984):53–10u.                Robert E. Drechsel

**Center Chair.** In recent journalistic usage "center chair" refers to the chief justice of the United States, who occupies the center seat of the bench of the Supreme Court.                William M. Wiecek

**Certification,** the process through which a U.S. court of appeals (and, until recently, the U.S. Court of Claims) can certify questions of law at issue in a case to the Supreme Court for binding instructions. Although counsel in a few cases have attempted unsuccessfully to invoke the certification procedure, only a lower court is permitted to certify questions to the Supreme Court. Moreover, only questions of law about which the lower court entertains doubt, not questions of fact, can be certified. Such cases thus form a very small part of the Supreme Court's caseload, averaging only about one each term in recent decades. One of the rare illustrations of the procedure's use arose in 1963, when the Court of Appeals for the Fifth Circuit certified to the Supreme Court the question whether Mississippi's governor and lieutenant governor were entitled to a *jury trial on criminal contempt citations growing out of their attempts to prevent the admission of James Meredith, a black man, to the University of Mississippi at Oxford. In *United States* v. *Barnett* (1964) the Court held that the Mississippi officials were subject to summary proceedings. (The circuit court cleared them the following year, citing "changed circumstances and conditions.") In 1968, the Court was to hold that defendants in serious criminal contempt cases are entitled to jury trials. (See also COURTS OF APPEALS; LOWER FEDERAL COURTS.)
                Tinsley E. Yarbrough

**Certiorari, Writ of,** the primary means by which a case comes before the United States Supreme Court. Litigants who seek review by the Supreme Court petition the Court for the writ, and if granted, the case comes before the Court for disposition. The party seeking review is known as the *petitioner, and the opposing party is the respondent.

The Supreme Court, like any court, must have jurisdiction before it can decide a case. Its jurisdiction is determined by *Article III of the Constitution and by congressional statute. Certiorari jurisdiction, given to the Court by Congress, accounts for the vast majority of cases. In addition to certiorari, there are four other ways a case can come before the court: by *original jurisdiction, on *appeal, by *certification, or by an extraordinary writ. The last two are rarely used. Appeals and cases of original jurisdiction have mandatory review in the Supreme Court whereas the decision to grant certiorari, or "cert," is solely at the discretion of the justices. Article III of the Constitution identifies the cases that qualify for original jurisdiction, and Congress has established categories of cases that qualify as appeals. The terminology can be a bit confusing because the word *appeal* is commonly and generically used to mean taking a case to a higher court for review. Technically, however, when a case is "on appeal" before the U.S. Supreme Court, it means that Congress has mandated review for this type of case. Since 1988, however, most categories of appeals have been eliminated. Therefore, except for cases of original jurisdiction, which usually constitute about one or two cases a year, and a few other extraordinary types of cases, most cases today are before the Supreme Court on a writ of certiorari.

The Court has not always had broad discretion in case selection. Before 1925 most of its docket consisted of cases for which review was obligatory. The workload had grown to such an extent, however, that on 13 February 1925, an act known as the "Judges' Bill" was passed. The most ardent supporter of the legislation was Chief Justice William Howard *Taft. The act greatly expanded the Court's certiorari jurisdiction, which meant that its docket was to become largely discretionary. By the 1970s, certiorari accounted for about 90 percent of the Court's workload. Appeals constituted about 10 percent of the Court's docket until the 1988 legislation effectively eliminated most categories of appeals (see JUDICIAL IMPROVEMENTS AND ACCESS TO JUSTICE ACT). Even prior to 1988, however, the Court often finessed its appellate jurisdiction by "dismissing" appeals by not giving them full review.

Of the approximately five thousand cases a year for which review by the Supreme Court is sought, fewer than 5 percent are granted cert. If a case is denied cert, the decision below stands, and with a few exceptions, there are no further avenues of review. As a matter of law, a denial of cert. has no meaning other than that the particular case will not be reviewed. It does not mean that the Court believes that the case has been correctly decided in the court below, nor may lawyers cite a denial of cert as evidence of the Court's position on the issue. Some observers, however, argue that a denial of cert can be read to mean something more, which of course it may, although the Court continues to disavow such a position.

The justices have been intentionally vague as to what makes a case "certworthy." Rule 10 of the "Rules of the Supreme Court of the United States" purports to offer criteria, but it is of little help:

A review on writ of certiorari is not a matter of right, but of judicial discretion, and will be granted only when there are special and important reasons therefor. The following, while neither controlling nor fully measuring the Court's discretion, indicate the character of reasons that will be considered.

With one exception, the criteria that follow the statement offer little guidance as to what the Court really looks for when selecting a case. In short, the rule is almost a tautology: cases are important enough to be reviewed by the justices when the justices think they are important. Or as Justice Frank *Murphy put it, "Writs of certiorari are matters of grace" (Wade v. Mayo, 1948, p. 680). The one criterion in rule 10 that is helpful in determining whether or not a case will be deemed "certworthy" is when federal *circuit courts of appeals are in conflict over an issue. Though a "circuit split" does increase the likelihood that a case will be reviewed, it does not guarantee review. It is not always obvious when circuit courts are in conflict. Moreover, the Court often prefers to wait for additional courts of appeals to weigh in on a matter before it decides to resolve it. Nevertheless, the justices do see resolving conflicts among the circuit courts as one of their primary responsibilities.

Deciding what to decide is one of the most important functions performed by the Supreme Court. Given the difficulty of access to the Court, understanding how and why one case is selected and another rejected is important both in determining how the Court works and how access is achieved. Agenda setting has both behavioral and normative implications. To the extent that there has been scholarly interest in agenda setting beyond jurisdictional and procedural questions, it has mostly been by political scientists. They have focused much of their research on trying to determine factors that increase the likelihood of review. Results have been mixed, although there seems to be credible evidence to suggest that the likelihood of review is enhanced if there is a genuine conflict among circuit courts of appeal; or, if the United States is the petitioning party in the case; or if an *amicus brief is filed urging a grant. Likewise, it has been demonstrated that a justice's vote on certiorari is related to his or her later vote on the merits, that is, the decision to affirm or reverse the decision below. Despite these insights from research, it is still very difficult to predict grants of certiorari in individual cases.

Until recently, little was known about the certiorari decision process. Actually, there are nine separate processes because each justice handles cert. differently, but these are primarily individual variations on two basic routines. In some chambers, the justice and law clerks do all of their own cert. work. The clerk reads the petition and writes a memo to the justice. The clerk notes the important issues, analyzes the case, and recommends a grant or denial. Eight justices, however, are members of the *cert pool. When petitions arrive at the Court, they are divided randomly among the justices in the pool. One clerk writes a memo for all pool chambers. Upon receipt of the pool memo, clerks will then "mark-up" (annotate) the pool memo for their individual justices. Each justice reads the memo and makes a tentative decision on how to vote on cert.

Prior to the conference, the chief justice circulates a *"discuss list." This list contains all the cases thought worthy of discussion at conference. Any justice can add any case to this list. Cases that do not make the discuss list—about 70 percent—are automatically denied cert. In *conference, most cases receive very little discussion. The chief justice announces the case and the justices simply vote, in order of *seniority, to grant or deny the case. If any justice feels that a case merits discussion, the justices speak and vote in order of seniority. For some time, scholars thought votes were taken in reverse order, but even if this once was the case, it is not so now.

If four justices vote in favor, cert. is granted. This *"rule of four" is an informal rule of long standing developed and adhered to by the justices. Cert. votes are not made public. Some justices have recorded cert votes and left them in their private papers, but usually it is impossible to know how the justices voted. From time to time, a justice will feel strongly enough about a case to note publicly a dissent from the denial of certiorari. This may be accompanied by an opinion outlining why the case should have been taken. Some justices, however, disapprove of any public airing of cert. votes and refuse to write dissents from denials. Dissents from denial of cert are uncommon except that Justices William *Brennan and Thurgood *Marshall always noted that they would grant cert. in cases involving the death penalty because they believed *capital punishment is unconstitutional.

(See also JUDICIAL POWER AND JURISDICTION; WORKLOAD.)

□ Gregory A. Caldeira and John R. Wright, "Organized Interests and Agenda Setting in the U.S. Supreme Court," *American Political Science Review* 82 (December 1988): 1109–1127. H.W. Perry, Jr., "Agenda Setting and Case Selection," in *American Courts: A Critical Assessment,* edited by John B. Gates and Charles A. Johnson (1990), pp. 235–253. H. W. Perry, Jr., *Deciding to Decide: Agenda Setting in the United States Supreme Court* (1991).
H. W. Perry, Jr.

**Cert Pool.** With thousands of petitions for writs of *certiorari to consider each term, the Supreme Court justices have long relied on their law *clerks' help to identify "certworthy" cases. Beginning in 1972, Chief Justice Warren *Burger and Justices Byron *White, Harry *Blackmun, Lewis *Powell, and William H. *Rehnquist pooled the efforts of their clerks: one clerk writes a single "pool memo" on each case for all the participating

justices. The number of justices in the cert pool grew to six when Justice Sandra Day *O'Connor joined the Court in 1981; the number remained at six for the rest of the 1980s, with Justices Antonin *Scalia and Anthony *Kennedy participating; and the number grew to eight when Justice David *Souter joined the Court in 1990 and Justice Clarence *Thomas joined the Court in 1991.

The mechanics of the cert pool are straightforward. An administrator in the *chief justice's chambers systematically allocates the cases on each conference list among the participating justices. Each justice's law clerks then divide the cases assigned to that justice's chambers among themselves. With eight justices in the pool and four clerks in most chambers, a clerk generally writes four pool memos each week. The finished memos go to the administrator, who checks them for technical errors and distributes them to the participating justices.

The format for pool memos is well established. The heading identifies the case and provides basic information about it (such as the lower court and judges). Section 1 provides a brief summary of the case—often only a sentence or two. Section 2 describes the facts and the lower-court decision. Section 3 summarizes the parties' contentions. Section 4 analyzes the case and evaluates the contentions. Section 5 recommends a disposition. The memo concludes with additional information that might be helpful (such as the existence of a response), the date, and the name of the clerk who wrote the memo. Within this format, there is tremendous variation. A complicated case may require a thirty-page memo; a frivolous case may take only two pages.

When a pool memo arrives in chambers, one of the justice's own law clerks reviews it. Often the reviewing clerk simply agrees with the memo's recommendation, but in some cases the clerk will examine the original papers, do additional research, or even write a separate memorandum solely for his or her own justice.

Critics object that the cert pool reduces the number of people who screen each case. Supporters observe, however, that clerks writing pool memos take a close look at each assigned case. This one close look is arguably better than the eight cursory reviews that might well have occurred under the old system.
Michael F. Sturley

**Chafee, Zechariah, Jr.** (b. Providence, R.I., 7 Dec. 1885; d. Cambridge, Mass., 8 Feb. 1957), educator, lawyer, writer, and civil libertarian. Chafee was the father of modern free speech law in the United States. A member of a comfortable New England family, he worked in the family's iron business for three years before entering the Harvard Law School. He immersed himself in sociological jurisprudence, and when he returned to teach, he took over Roscoe *Pound's third-year equity course. Pound's interest in injunctions against *libel intrigued Chafee, who prominently explored all pre-1916 federal cases on the subject, concluding that free speech law was clearly in need of modernization. This development was strengthened in 1917 and 1918 by congressional enactment of wartime espionage and sedition laws. (See ESPIONAGE ACTS.) Their frequently arbitrary enforcement persuaded Chafee of the importance of clarifying the speech and press provisions of the First Amendment, something he set out to do in a controversial 1920 book, *Freedom of Speech*. He argued for a healthy openness of expression even in wartime, with speech curtailed only when the public safety was seriously imperiled. Chafee appreciated the views set forth by Judge Learned *Hand in the *Masses* case of 1917, where Hand had attempted to establish that the test for suppressing expression was "neither the justice of its substance, nor the decency or propriety of its temper, but the strong danger it would cause injurious acts."

Few people in positions of power shared Chafee's confidence in the open democratic process. Thus, his criticism of Oliver Wendell *Holmes's initial *"clear and present danger" construct in *Schenck* v. *United States* (1919) was itself criticized by conservative leaders. Nonetheless, Chafee persisted, setting out to persuade Holmes that the true test for free speech should be the power of the expression to get itself accepted in the competition of the marketplace of ideas. Accepting Chafee's argument, Holmes incorporated it in his dissent in *Abrams* v. *United States* (1919), hoping to set a national policy that would encourage a search for truth yet maintain a balance of social and individual interests.

Chafee was highly critical of the Court's restrictive opinion and its unwillingness to accept Holmes's view. Such criticism led to an unsuccessful move by conservative alumni to oust Chafee from the Harvard Law School.

Chafee's later involvement with the Supreme Court was at once peripheral and direct. A generation of young civil libertarians in the 1920s embraced his First Amendment views. This had a liberalizing effect on Holmes's and Brandeis's dissents, not only in *Abrams*, but in *Gitlow* v. *New York* (1925) and *Whitney* v. *California* (1927). Indeed, Brandeis used *Freedom of Speech* extensively in preparing his influential concurring opinion in *Whitney*, an opinion that contained the last and most speech-protective of the two justices' various restatements of the danger test. Eventually, the Court majority used the test in the 1930s and 1940s to void local ordinances against the distribution of leaflets and contempt of court by newspapers. Similarly Chafee viewed the 1937 *DeJonge* v. *Oregon* decision as an important broadening of the protection of freedom of assembly. As coauthor of the brief that the American Bar Association's Committee on the Bill of Rights submitted in that case, he later used it to attack the repressive anti-union behavior of Mayor Frank Hague of Jersey City (see *Hague* v. *CIO*,

1939). The ABA Committee participated as amicus curiae in subsequent civil liberties cases, with Chafee as a major draftsman. He later described his Committee service as "one of the most absorbing and fruitful things I have ever done." When he chaired the Committee, he threw himself into the early 1940s cases involving the Jehovah's Witnesses' refusal to have their children participate in a compulsory flag salute. When the Committee decided in *West Virginia State Board of Education* v. *Barnette* (1943) to seek reversal of the *Minersville School District* v. *Gobitis* case of 1940, Chafee drafted the brief. The Court ultimately accepted its logic in reversing the earlier upholding of the salute. Making an eloquent plea for freedom of religion and freedom of expression, he was particularly pleased to see Justice Robert *Jackson's opinion couple the *preferred freedoms concept with the clear and present danger test to protect the individual against arbitrary actions by the state.

In 1947, Chafee left the Committee, after being named to the United Nations Subcommission on Freedom of Information and the Press. There, as in his service to the Committee, he nudged the organization, as he had the Supreme Court, into a newly assumed role of champion of free expression. In his later days, Chafee taught and wrote widely in the area of human rights. His 1956 book, *The Blessings of Liberty*, portentously stressed the dangers of economic inequality to the full operation of the marketplace process, and advocated the elimination of arbitrary obstacles to full free expression.

(See also FIRST AMENDMENT; SPEECH AND THE PRESS.)

Paul L. Murphy

**Chambers.** As long as the Supreme Court met in the Capitol or other space-sharing location, Congress provided no private offices for the justices. They maintained chambers in their homes, and received small federal allotments for furniture, books, and maintenance expenses. In 1886 Congress authorized the hiring of a secretary or law *clerk for each justice, but only in 1919 did it fund both positions.

Working conditions improved when the Court moved into its own building in October 1935. Each justice now occupies a suite of three rooms on the main floor, with private access to adjacent chambers, *conference and *robing rooms, and the courtroom.

(See also BUILDINGS, SUPREME COURT.)

Maxwell Bloomfield

**Champion v. Ames,** 188 U.S. 321 (1903), argued 15–16 Dec. 1902, decided 23 Feb. 1903 by vote of 5 to 4; Harlan for the Court, Fuller in dissent. Known as the *Lottery Case, Champion* v. *Ames* raised crucial questions regarding the extent of congressional power over interstate commerce and the existence of a federal equivalent of the state police power. These issues were central to the *Progressives' attempts to make federal authority commensurate with the nation's emerging needs.

Champion challenged the constitutionality of an 1895 statute designed to suppress the lottery traffic in interstate commerce under which he had been indicted. The majority focused on two major issues: whether lottery tickets were subjects of commerce and the scope of the interstate commerce power. Justice John Marshall *Harlan ruled the tickets were items of real value, whose carriage across state lines was indeed interstate commerce. Defining the commerce power in extensive terms that recognized congressional authority to prohibit certain transportation and to meet expanding needs, he held the lottery act constitutional.

The minority opinion differed on definitions and the scope of power. It equated lottery tickets with contracts and negotiable instruments, which were not considered objects of traffic; denied that the tickets were intrinsically injurious; and maintained that federal exercise of the police power violated the *Tenth Amendment. Despite Harlan's guarded language, both proponents and opponents viewed the decision as establishing a de facto federal police power, and national protective legislation increased rapidly. However, the focus on the injuriousness of the product provided a measure of flexibility that permitted the Court to retrench as progressivism waned.

(See also COMMERCE POWER; POLICE POWER.)

Barbara C. Steidle

**Chaplinsky v. New Hampshire,** 315 U.S. 568 (1942), argued 5 Feb. 1942, decided 9 Mar. 1942 by vote of 9 to 0; Murphy for the Court. While distributing religious pamphlets for Jehovah's Witnesses, Chaplinsky attracted a hostile crowd. When a city marshal intervened, Chaplinsky denounced him as a "racketeer" and a "Fascist" and called other officials "agents of Fascists." The Court upheld Chaplinsky's conviction for violating a state law against offensive and derisive speech or name-calling in public.

Justice Frank *Murphy advanced a "two-tier theory" of the *First Amendment. Certain "well-defined and narrowly limited" categories of speech fall outside the bounds of constitutional protection. Thus, "the lewd and obscene, the profane, the libelous," and (in this case) insulting or "fighting" words neither contributed to the expression of ideas nor possessed any "social value" in the search for truth (pp. 571–572).

This two-tier approach retains importance for those who believe that carefully crafted controls over certain categories of speech (such as pornography, commercial advertising, or abusive epithets) do not violate First Amendment guarantees. Although the Court continues to cite *Chaplinsky's* position on "fighting words" approv-

ingly, subsequent cases have largely eroded its initial, broad formulation; libelous publications and even verbal challenges to police officers have come to enjoy some constitutional protection. *Chaplinsky* remains the last case in which the Court explicitly upheld a conviction only for "fighting words" directed at public officials.

(See also SPEECH AND THE PRESS; UNPROTECTED SPEECH.)

Norman L. Rosenberg

**Charles River Bridge v. Warren Bridge,** 11 Pet. (36 U.S.) 420 (1837), argued 7–11 Mar. 1831, reargued 19–26 Jan. 1837, decided 12 Feb. 1837 by vote of 4 to 3; Taney for the Court, McLean, Story, and Thompson in dissent. To provide the public better access from Charlestown to Boston, the Massachusetts legislature in 1785 incorporated the Proprietors of the Charles River Bridge to build a bridge connecting Boston to its northern hinterland via Charlestown and authorized the proprietors to collect tolls on the bridge. In 1828 the legislature authorized Charlestown merchants to build the new Warren Bridge and to collect tolls for its use until they had been reimbursed, when their bridge would revert to the state and become free.

The Charles River Bridge proprietors sought an *injunction to halt construction of the new bridge, asserting that the Warren Bridge charter violated both the Massachusetts constitutional guarantee of "life, liberty and property" and the Contracts Clause of the U.S. Constitution, which prevented state impairment of contracts. After the Supreme Judicial Court of Massachusetts affirmed denial of the injunction the Charles River Bridge proprietors sought a writ of *error from the U.S. Supreme Court. In 1831 the Court heard arguments, but the justices' divergent views on the protection of vested property rights, as well as illnesses and vacancies on the bench, delayed decision. In 1837 the case was reargued before a court dominated by Democratic appointees.

Daniel *Webster and Warren Dutton, appearing for the Charles River Bridge, relied on Contracts Clause and vested-rights arguments. According to them the Warren Bridge charter violated the state's contract obligation to the Charles River Bridge proprietors by effectively destroying their exclusive property in tolls, which was the essence of the original grant.

John Davis and Simon Greenleaf for the Warren Bridge proprietors argued that the Charles River Bridge had not been granted an exclusive right to the line of travel. When the Charles River Bridge proprietors accepted an extension of their charter, they acknowledged the state's ability to make competing grants. The grant to the Warren Bridge was within the legislature's authority.

Chief Justice Roger B. *Taney's majority opinion and Justice Joseph *Story's dissent presented contrasting views of legal principles, government responsibility, and economic progress—views that reflected their different political affiliations. They disagreed on matters of judicial interpretation of charters, the powers of the states, and the relative importance of the rights of the community and the rights of the individual.

Taney, one of Andrew *Jackson's recent Democratic appointees, held that the legislature, representing the sovereign power of the people, had granted the privilege to build a bridge and collect tolls to the Charles River Bridge proprietors. Taney reasoned that the legislative grants should be construed narrowly to protect the public interest. Narrow construction disposed of any implied exclusive rights to the line of travel; the legislature's later authorization of a competing grant did not destroy the proprietors' property in tolls. While Taney declared that the "rights of private property must be sacredly guarded" (p. 548), he asserted that "the object and end of all government is to promote the happiness and prosperity of the community . . . ; and it can never be assumed, that the government intended to diminish its power of accomplishing the end for which it was created" (p. 547).

Justice Story insisted in dissent that the Charles River Bridge charter was a form of contract granted for valuable consideration. The proprietors had offered to build the bridge to further the public good and the legislature had conferred the right to collect tolls. Where valuable consideration was received, courts should construe public contracts in favor of the grantee. Story's broad construction of the bridge charter inferred an exclusive grant to collect tolls along the line of travel. "If the government means to invite its citizens to enlarge the public comforts and conveniences, . . . there must be some pledge that the property will be safe; . . . and that success will not be the signal of a general combination to overthrow its rights, and to take away its profits" (p. 608).

The decision of the majority recognized that demand for improved technologies would lead to their rapid adoption. It warned that older corporations would "awaken from their sleep" (p. 552) and called upon the courts to protect vested property rights. Fearing this threat to the millions of dollars ventured in new enterprises, Taney fashioned his opinion to justify creative destruction of old property in order that new ventures might prosper.

(See also CAPITALISM; CONTRACTS CLAUSE; PROPERTY RIGHTS.)

☐ Stanley I. Kutler, *Privilege and Creative Destruction: The Charles River Bridge Case* (1971).     Elizabeth B. Monroe

**Chase, Salmon Portland** (b. Cornish, N.H., 13 January 1808; d. New York, N.Y., 7 May 1873; interred Spring Grove Cemetery, Cincinnati), chief justice, 1864–1873. After being raised an orphan, Salmon P. Chase graduated from Dart-

*Salmon Portland Chase*

mouth (1823) and then read law in Washington, D. C., where he began practice in 1829. Moving to Cincinnati, Chase was thrice married (1834–1846), his wives predeceasing him, and the father of six children. He compiled *The Statutes of Ohio* (1835), defended in courts runaway slaves and their abettors, and was Ohio's senator (1849), then governor (1855–1861).

An early Republican critic of the 1850 Fugitive Slave law and an advocate of "freedom national" constitutionalism, Chase emerged as a would-be presidential candidate in 1860. The nomination and the election went to Abraham *Lincoln and Chase then became treasury secretary. He ably administered wartime tax, greenback, and banking laws, commerce with occupied Southern areas, rebels' confiscated properties including slaves, and educational, agricultural, and industrial experiments for displaced bondsmen. Chase influenced Lincoln and Congress toward military emancipation in wartime state reconstruction, toward nationwide emancipation by constitutional amendment, and, by early 1865, toward equal legal and political rights for African-Americans. Succeeding Roger B. *Taney as chief justice in 1864, Chase tried but failed to convince either President Andrew Johnson or most of the justices that the *Thirteenth Amendment incorporated the *Declaration of Independence and *Bill of Rights against national and state officials as well as private persons. He also failed in his argument that the amendment created a new *federalism of interstate diversity in laws and rights but of intrastate, race- and gender-blind equality (see RACE AND RACISM).

Republican congressmen sharing his perceptions enacted the 1866 Civil Rights law, providing federal alternatives to racially prejudiced state justice in matters of private rights as well as public law. On circuit in Maryland, Chase in *In re Turner* (1867) entertained a former slave's plea for discharge from her work contract with her former master turned employer. Affirming the constitutionality of the Civil Rights Act, Chase held that the Thirteenth Amendment clothed black citizens with full federal rights to litigate and testify, that private contracts existed only with state sanction, and that Turner's private contract, whose terms were inferior to contracts given to white apprentices, reduced her to involuntary servitude.

Encouraged by President Johnson, the white South resisted such policies. Overturning vetoes, Congress's various Military Reconstruction laws required biracial electorates to ratify the *Fourteenth and *Fifteenth Amendments before Southern states rejoined the Union. However, although Lincoln had appointed four other justices along with Chase, the chief justice was unable to form a majority on race equality. In *Ex parte *Milligan* (1866), for example, Chase joined three other dissenters in opposing the Court's holding that Congress could impose military justice. The 5-to-4 Test Oath decisions, *Ex parte Garland* and *Cummings* v. *Missouri* (1867), voided federal and state loyalty requirements for officeholders and licensed professionals as punitive *ex post facto laws, bills of attainder, and denials of presidential pardons for rebels. Chase and the other dissenters insisted that the oaths were proper qualifications and questioned federal court jurisdiction. These decisions prevented the democratization of Southern officialdom and political leadership, impelling Congress toward military reconstruction.

Chase retained influence among the justices though not consistent leadership, a condition evident when Mississippi and Georgia petitioned the Court to enjoin Military Reconstruction. Chase, for a unanimous Court, in *Mississippi* v. *Johnson* (1867) and *Georgia* v. *Stanton* (1868), declined to politicize injunctions. In *Ex parte *McCardle* (1869), a racist Mississippi editor arrested by military authorities for incendiary articles appealed to the Court based on the 1867 Habeas Corpus Act, key jurisdictional portions of which Congress had repealed (see JUDICIAL POWER AND JURISDICTION). The Court affirmed Congress's power over its *appellate jurisdiction, but Chase noted that as well the 1867 law did not touch the Court's independent *habeas corpus power. In *Texas* v. *White* (1869), Chase reasserted basic Republican constitutional principles that the Union and states were indissoluble, holding that Congress and not the Court had the sole authority to recognize state governments.

Chase presided ably over the impeachment trial of Andrew Johnson in early 1868. Ever ambitious, Chase sought unsuccessfully to become a presidential nominee (see EXTRAJUDICIAL

ACTIVITIES). On the bench, his influence over his fellow justices oscillated. He dissented from their validation of prewar slave-purchase contracts, in *Osborn* v. *Nicholson* (1873), their rejection of Thirteenth and Fourteenth Amendment claims by a qualified white woman to practice law, in *Bradwell* v. *Illinois* (1873) and, above all, from their *Slaughterhouse* decision (1873). The last consigned the fate of blacks seeking federally protected access to job markets to the very white state authorities who oppressed them, by limiting the Thirteenth Amendment to the abolition of formal *slavery and reducing the Fourteenth Amendment's *Privileges or Immunities Clause to inconsequentiality. Although a frequent dissenter, Chase helped "his" Court to exercise a full measure of governance by avoiding dangerous policy confrontations.

(See also CHIEF JUSTICE, OFFICE OF THE.)

□ Frederick J. Blue, *Salmon P. Chase: A Life in Politics* (1987). David Donald, ed., *Inside Lincoln's Cabinet: The Civil War Diaries of Salmon P. Chase* (1954).
Harold M. Hyman

**Chase, Samuel** (b. Somerset County, Md., 17 Apr. 1741; d. Baltimore, Md., 19 June 1811; interred St. Paul's Cemetery, Baltimore), associate justice, 1796–1811. Samuel Chase was the most brilliant of the Supreme Court justices to sit before Chief Justice John *Marshall, and was, in some ways, a more impressive figure than the great chief justice himself. Chase signed the *Declaration of Independence, served in the Revolutionary War Congress, and was a noted judge on the Maryland bench as well as the federal judiciary, but he is today remembered chiefly as having been the only Supreme Court justice ever to have been impeached. He is usually dismissed by most American historians as nothing but a rabid partisan. He was, study of Chase's opinions reveals, one of the most important political and legal theorists at work in the early republic, and there is still much that can be learned from his work.

In his most widely quoted Supreme Court opinion, *Calder* v. *Bull* (1798), Chase explored what might be regarded as the *natural law basis for the federal Constitution of 1789. In that case he explained that there were some supraconstitutional principles that circumscribed any legislature, whether or not such principles had been explicitly spelled out in the written fundamental law. Chase gave only two examples in his opinion: making a person judge and party in his or her own case, and taking A's property and giving it to B without any compensation to A. But his work has been taken to have established the doctrine now referred to as "substantive *due process," the reading into the *Fifth or *Fourteenth Amendment's Due Process Clause guarantees of particular rights or liberties not expressly found elsewhere in the Constitution, rights or liberties generally drawn from some sort of conception of natural law theory.

This sort of approach to constitutional law, recently favored by many advocates of "liberal" constitutional theory, has always been opposed in our history by judicial conservatives, who have maintained that "strict construction" or *"original intent" is a more certain guide to appropriate constitutional interpretation. Curiously, however, Chase is also one of the founders of the "strict constructionist" approach. In one of his most notable opinions while riding circuit, *United States* v. *Worrall* (1798), Chase became the only late eighteenth-century Federal judge to reject the theory of the "federal common law of crimes," the doctrine that the federal government, as a matter of self-defense, could punish crimes such as bribery or *seditious libel even before Congress prohibited such particular conduct by means of a specific statute (see FEDERAL COMMON LAW). Chase's view on this point was eventually upheld by the Supreme Court in the early nineteenth century.

Riding on circuit, Chase also established in his opinions the principle of *judicial review to declare unconstitutional acts of Congress void, the principle later famously brought to national attention in Marshall's opinion in *Marbury* v. *Madison* (1803). Marshall was reported to be in the audience during one occasion when Chase discussed judicial review on circuit in Virginia and to have adopted some of Chase's language (which was itself probably borrowed from Alexander *Hamilton's *Federalist*, no. 78) for use in *Marbury*.

Chase was a political as well as a judicial conservative and found himself impeached by the Jeffersonians as a result of having presided over several criminal trials and proceedings in which he sought to implement the Adams administration's attempts to silence what it believed to be destructive and dangerous attacks on the government by rebels and mendacious critics. Chase also unsuccessfully sought to convince John Marshall that some of the Jeffersonian usurpations should be ruled unconstitutional and reversed. The event that triggered his impeachment occurred during the early years of Jefferson's administration, however, when Chase delivered to a Baltimore grand jury a charge critical of the Jeffersonians' abolition of several federal judgeships and their conduct in the Maryland legislature. Chase warned that such conduct violated constitutional guarantees of an independent judiciary as well as political principles that insisted that law be undergirded with morality, and morality with religion. Chase's grand jury charge borrowed heavily from the philosophy of Edmund Burke, with whom Chase had spent a fortnight on a trip to England, and warned that unthinking Democratic Jeffersonian advocates of the "rights of man" were plunging the country in the direction of mobocracy.

*Samuel Chase*

Jefferson and his followers sought to silence Chase by the *impeachment proceedings, and the best lawyers among the Adams Federalists immediately enlisted in Chase's defense, agreeing to work for no fees. At Chase's trial before the Senate in 1805, the impeachment charges were effectively shown to be little more than politically motivated calumny. With the votes of some Jeffersonians in his favor, Chase's opponents failed to muster the needed two-thirds majority of the Senate to convict him, and Chase was acquitted. John Marshall played a rather disappointing role at the trial, refusing to do much in Chase's defense, and even suggesting, contrary to his reputation as a great defender of judicial review, that perhaps Congress ought to be the only arbiter of the constitutionality of its own acts.

Historians usually point to the failure of the Senate to remove Chase as a victory for judicial independence and as having established the precedent that a judge could not be removed merely as a result of the stating of political views from the bench. More correctly, however, the proceeding ought to be seen as establishing the principle that it was dangerous for a judge, such as Chase, to articulate political philosophy, particularly one at odds with the prevailing democratic ethos of the Jeffersonians. The trouble Chase was confronted with must have had much to do in convincing John Marshall that he should seek to have the judiciary portrayed as somehow different from and above "politics" and led to the convenient constitutional-law fiction that there are "objective" answers to constitutional questions. In our own time, when this view is no longer tenable, and, in particular, as conservatives search for a reasoned constitutional philosophy emphasizing responsibilities over rights, the

Burkean beliefs of Chase might be due for an impressive resurgence. There is even a chance that future scholars will begin to accord Chase the recognition he deserves and raise the man most now only perceive as a rabid partisan to his proper place in the judicial pantheon, one very possibly at the level of Marshall himself.

□ Robert Bork, *The Tempting of America: The Political Seduction of the Law* (1990). Stephen Presser, "The Original Misunderstanding: The English, the Americans, and the Dialectic of Federalist Constitutional Jurisprudence," *Northwestern University Law Review* 84 (1989): 106–185. Stephen B. Presser

**Checks and Balances.** See SEPARATION OF POWERS.

**Cherokee Cases,** collective name of two companion cases of the 1830s: *Cherokee Nation v. Georgia*, 5 Pet. (30 U.S.) 1 (1831), argued 5 Mar. 1831, decided 18 Mar. 1831 by vote of 4 to 2; Marshall for the Court, Johnson and Baldwin concurring, Thompson in dissent; and *Worcester v. Georgia*, 6 Pet. (31 U.S.) 515 (1832), argued 20 Feb. 1832, decided 3 Mar. 1832 by vote of 5 to 1; Marshall for the Court, Baldwin in dissent. The *Cherokee Cases* evolved out of attempts by Georgia to assert jurisdiction over Cherokee lands within the state that were protected by treaty. In *Cherokee Nation v. Georgia*, Chief Justice John *Marshall held that the Supreme Court had no jurisdiction to hear a Cherokee request to enjoin Georgia's effort. He defined Cherokees as a "domestic, dependent nation," rather than a sovereign nation for *Article III purposes, and as being wards of the federal government (p. 2).

The Court modified *Cherokee Nation* one year later in *Worcester v. Georgia*. A Congregational missionary had been convicted of failure to have a license Georgia required to live in Cherokee country. The Court held the Georgia laws void because they violated treaties, the *contract and *commerce clauses of the Constitution, and the sovereign authority of the Cherokee nation. Georgia refused to acknowledge the proceeding.

Marshall no longer considered the *Cherokee Nation* case controlling, although he did not overrule it. Instead he emphasized the concept of "nation," as opposed to "domestic" or "dependent." He held that Indian nations were a distinct people with the right to retain independent political communities. President Andrew *Jackson, however, refused to enforce the Court's ruling and supported the removal of the Cherokees to Indian Territory. Many Cherokees perished during their exodus, known since as the "Trail of Tears."

(See also JUDICIAL POWER AND JURISDICTION; NATIVE AMERICANS; RACE AND RACISM; STATE SOVEREIGNTY AND STATES' RIGHTS.)
John R. Wunder

**Chicago, Burlington & Quincy Railroad Company v. Chicago,** 166 U.S. 226 (1897), argued 6, 9 Nov. 1896, decided 1 Mar. 1897 by vote of 7 to 1; Harlan for the Court, Brewer in dissent, Fuller not participating.

In this case the Court unanimously held that the *Fourteenth Amendment's Due Process Clause compelled the states to award just compensation when it took private property for public use. (Justice Brewer concurred on this point while dissenting from other parts of the judgment.) The case, which came to the Court as an appeal from a ruling of the Illinois Supreme Court upholding a jury award of one dollar when a street was opened across a railroad track, was among the earliest instances in which the Court applied the due process concept to protect substantive property rights. It was an important step in the Court's development of due process limits on state control of economic liberties. Yet *Chicago B. & Q. R.R. v. Chicago* remains good law despite its relation to the doctrine of laissez-faire constitutionalism. In contemporary constitutional law, the case stands as an early example of the doctrine that the Fourteenth Amendments's Due Process Clause incorporates the specific guarantees of the Bill of Rights (see INCORPORATION DOCTRINE).

In a dissenting opinion, Justice David J. *Brewer agreed that the Due Process Clause required the states to pay compensation when private property was taken, but argued that the jury verdict provided only nominal, rather than just, compensation to the railroad.

(See also DUE PROCESS, SUBSTANTIVE; JUST COMPENSATION; PROPERTY RIGHTS; TAKINGS CLAUSE.)
Stephen A. Siegel

**Chicago, Milwaukee & St. Paul Railway Co. v. Minnesota,** 134 U.S. 418, argued 13, 14 Jan. 1890, decided 24 Mar. 1890 by vote of 6 to 3; Blatchford for the Court, Miller concurring, Bradley, Gray, and Lamar in dissent. When the Court in *Munn v. Illinois* (1877) upheld legislative power to control railroad rates, it also ruled that governmentally set rates were not subject to *judicial review. This ruling was an application of the traditional principle that the Court determined the Constitution's allocation of power among branches of government but did not supervise the discretionary exercise of those powers. Yet in *Chicago, M. & St.P. Ry. v. Minnesota*, the Court voided legislation that did not permit judicial review of rates set by the state's Railroad and Warehouse Commission. This was the first case in which the Court adopted a modern approach to the constitutional arrangements of the regulatory state. Implicit in the Court's ambiguous opinion was the fundamental tenet of contemporary administrative law: due process requires *judicial review of administrative agency procedures and decisions to determine their fidelity to constitutional norms. In particular, the Court asserted the power to judge the reasonableness of utility rates. With this decision, the Court began to review not only whether a particular branch of government had authority to act but also the reasonableness of the procedures through which officials act and the reasonableness of the decisions themselves.

(See DUE PROCESS, SUBSTANTIVE; PROPERTY RIGHTS.)

Stephen A. Siegel

**Chief Justice, Office of the.** The Constitution established the Supreme Court but mandated only that its chief justice preside over presidential *impeachment trials. Actual creation of the office awaited passage of the *Judiciary Act of 1789. The nature, functions, and powers of the chief justiceship remained undefined. The office was thereafter shaped not only by custom and statutory accretion but also by each of the sixteen chief justice's personality and perception of his role.

Chief justices perform the traditional judicial function as titular leaders: they preside over the Court's public and closed proceedings. Court-related managerial and public relations duties devolve on them as have extensive responsibilities for administering the entire federal judiciary. Finally, the office offers opportunities for statesmanship in the broadest sense.

*Presiding Officer.* The chief justice's most conspicuous customary duty is that of presiding over Supreme Court proceedings and serving as circuit justice for his allotted circuit (see CIRCUIT COURTS OF APPEALS). Opening and closing Court sessions, making announcements, admitting lawyers, and enforcing sartorial standards and etiquette on attorneys are duties within the chief justice's province. Foremost among them is that of controlling the flow of proceedings.

Behind closed doors, the chief justice chairs Court *conferences on case selection and on argued cases. Although his vote counts merely as one of nine, his titular position affords a special opportunity for leadership. Success depends on a combination of effective task and social leadership skills. Professional and managerial expertise characterize the former while the latter is marked by a capacity for promoting intracourt harmony. Charles Evans *Hughes possessed both talents as did John *Marshall and Earl *Warren. Harlan Fiske *Stone, however, fell short on both. William Howard *Taft, the prototypical social leader, was emulated by Warren *Burger.

The chief justice plays a pivotal role in shaping the Court's agenda when he presides over the screening of cases for plenary review. From Taft's to Burger's tenure, when the function was diffused among the associate justices and their law clerks, the chief justice enjoyed deference in his selection of cases from the increasingly large number of *pro se petitions filed. The chief justice opens discussion of previously argued cases. He frames the issues, presents at length the salient

facts and law, and states his conclusions. Discussion proceeds in order of descending seniority followed, in the Hughes era, by voting in reverse order of seniority, a system conducive to strategic voting on the chief justice's part. A single-step process subsequently emerged wherein each justice speaks and votes in descending order of seniority.

If in the majority, the chief justice enjoys the critical power of assigning authorship of the Court's opinion. A product of Marshall's adoption of Lord Mansfield's style, the unified opinion enhances institutional visibility and the power of the assignor. Assignment criteria have included administrative, professional, and strategic/political considerations. The chief justice may exercise the prerogative of his office and assign authorship to himself, characteristic behavior in important constitutional cases. In their capacity as jurist-presiding officer, great chief justices have materially enhanced the prestige and authority of the office they occupied.

*Court Manager and Guardian.* Chief justices perform a variety of Court management duties. Routine interactions with associate justices and staff are interspersed with others of far-reaching importance. Melville *Fuller, Taft, Hughes, and Burger all dealt gracefully in easing off the bench a disabled colleague. Internal administration involves the chief justice with the Court's bureaucracy and its heads: *clerk, *marshal, *reporter of decisions, librarian, and nonstatutory officers. Budget estimates are traditionally the chief justice's responsibility as is their presentation to congressional appropriations committees by his designatees. Chief justices differ in their degrees of interest in management of the Supreme Court building. Both Taft and Burger saw their office as mandating vigorous action on the subject. Burger directly intervened in personnel matters and in regulations affecting the *library and the law clerks (see CLERKS OF THE JUSTICES). The chief justice's expanding administrative functions caused enlargement of his personal staff, most significantly by the addition of an *administrative assistant to the chief justice in 1972.

Chief justices act as public advocates and defenders of the Court. They press the institution's interests before coordinate branches of the national government and the public. Salmon *Chase and Fuller led successful legislative campaigns for ameliorating the Court's burgeoning post–Civil War docket by relieving justices of their *circuit duties. Taft boldly promoted the *Judiciary Act of 1925, which gave the Court considerable control over its docket. Burger followed suit without success in pressing for establishment of a new tier in the judicial hierarchy—a National Court of Appeals. Chief Justice William H. *Rehnquist was instrumental in the passage of the long-awaited 1988 act intended to improve the administration of justice by further reducing the Court's mandatory appeal jurisdiction (see

JUDICIAL IMPROVEMENTS AND ACCESS TO JUSTICE ACT).

Nurturing the status of colleagues and Court falls to the chief justice, who is expected to defend the members in matters of protocol and salary parity. On the chief justice also devolves the duty of visibly protecting judicial independence. Marshall in *Marbury* v. *Madison* (1803) utilized the judicial function to achieve this end. Hughes employed extrajudicial commentary in spearheading public refutation of the 1937 *"court-packing" plan. Warren adopted a publicist strategy in attacking a quiet Court-curbing constitutional amendment campaign.

*Third Branch Chieftain.* Taft's chief justiceship marked a watershed in the dimensions of the office. Commissions issued to John *Jay through Morrison *Waite denoted each as "chief justice of the Supreme Court of the United States." But Fuller, commissioned in 1888, became the first "chief justice of the United States," a title given significance by Taft.

Taft's efforts spawned creation in 1922 of the *Judicial Conference of the United States, composed of *lower federal court judges and chaired by the chief justice. He regarded the conference as integrating federal judicial administration and thereby strengthening the courts' capabilities. Under Hughes the conference was augmented in 1939 by the Administrative Office of the United States Courts, bulwarking the judicial branch against executive threats to judicial independence. A research and continuing education capacity was added at Warren's behest in 1967 with the opening of the Federal Judicial Center. Its functions conformed well with his desire to facilitate judicial caseflow without constricting access to the lower courts (see ADMINISTRATION OF FEDERAL COURTS).

As conference chairman, the chief justice stands first among unequals and controls an institutional structure that potentially facilitates transmutation of judicial issues into administrative issues. He presides over the biannual meetings, manages the agenda, votes, and appoints committees. The last assumed importance after 1957, when Congress expanded conference membership. Committee composition enables the chief justice to attempt to shape policy, as attested by Rehnquist's 1988 appointment of an ad hoc Committee on Federal *Habeas Corpus in Capital Cases to study filings in federal courts of multiple postconviction challenges to state criminal proceedings. Tapped judges, most of them nonmembers of the conference, covet their committee appointments and their association with the chief justice. Strategies of social leadership further enhance the chief justice's success in using the conference process.

Other levers of power are available to the chief justice through the Administrative Office. Its director is formally selected by the Court but the justices defer to the candidate favored by the

chief justice, who chairs the conference that supervises and directs the agency. As chairman of the Federal Judicial Center's Governing Board, he may influence the appointment of the center's director, inspire reports, and reach out to newly commissioned judges attending the center's educational programs.

The chief justice has statutory responsibilities for personnel management in the lower courts. The 1922 act empowered him to assign consenting judges to and from any circuit. Subsequent legislation permitted assignments to specific panels and to special courts. Exercise of this administrative power has excited controversy on grounds of its capacity for influencing substantive results. This allegation was made about Taft's transfer of "dry" judges to "wet" districts during Prohibition and Burger's conservative appointments to the Foreign Intelligence Surveillance Court.

The act of 1922 fundamentally altered the relationship between courts and Congress. Thereafter, the chief justice transmitted to Congress the judiciary's conference-approved legislative program. Transmittal, however, is merely a first step. Taft and Hughes personally testified before congressional committees in promoting conference measures. Subsequent development of the conference committee system reduced the necessity for the chief justice's presence, but did not end it. Taft and Frederick *Vinson extensively lobbied individual legislators as did Burger in opposing the 1978 bankruptcy act and Rehnquist in advocating the 1989 judicial compensation act.

As the visible symbol of the federal judiciary, the chief justice as publicist seeks to mobilize public support for the judiciary's legislative programs. A variety of organizational affiliations provide him with ample opportunities. Warren and Burger labored fruitlessly for a "State of the Judiciary" address to a joint session of Congress. But beginning in 1970 the American Bar Association's annual meetings have afforded a surrogate forum. Additional elements of the communications network enable the chief justice to reach professional elites with his program and to stimulate their endorsements.

Burger's conception of the scope of responsibilities associated with the office included calls for reforming the administration of justice in the states, reforms compatible with his view on the proper relationships between federal courts and state institutions. Modernization of state judicial systems facilitated by creation of the National Center for State Courts would improve their capacities for fairly adjudicating the rights of citizens and reducing the need for intrusive federal court supervision. His state penal reform proposals were aimed at decreasing federal court entanglement with prison administration and de-emphasizing criminal procedural niceties and postconviction remedies.

*Statesman.* Supreme Court members from the earliest days served as all-purpose public servants. To this role the chief justice essentially transfers the credibility of his office, its authority, prestige, and association with the highest symbols of law—reason, probity, and commitment to justice. The high status of the office has encouraged Congress to impose extrajudicial duties. Incumbents from John *Jay to Marshall served on the Sinking Fund Commission authorized in 1790. The commission model endured when Congress established in 1846 the Smithsonian Institute and its Board of Regents headed by Roger Taney, the first of the chief justices to hold the position of chancellor. Except for international arbitration duties, volition nurtured by presidential invitations accounts for most extrajudicial activities undertaken by chief justices. Constitutionally barred only from membership in Congress, Jay and Marshall served simultaneously, albeit briefly, as chief justice and secretary of state. Important special missions in foreign diplomacy attracted Jay and Oliver *Ellsworth. Others from Jay through Burger have acted as presidential advisers. Some advised on matters fraught with partisan politics and even broke ethical constraints as did Vinson in his counseling of President Harry Truman on the constitutionality of seizing investor-owned steel mills, an issue which he subsequently adjudicated in *Youngstown Sheet & Tube Co. v. Sawyer (1952). Modern presidents have called upon chief justices to head presidential commissions. Warren reluctantly chaired the controversial investigation of the assassination of President John Kennedy. Few have perceived the office as a stepping stone to the presidency. Salmon Chase stands alone as one who harbored serious presidential aspirations.

Elapse of two centuries have vastly altered the office of chief justice. Once largely judicial in nature punctuated by important statesmanship duties, the office has become characterized by substantial administrative functions that clearly differentiate its incumbent from those of the associate justices as well as from all other federal judges. It is an office endowed with multiple levers of power wherein judicial issues can be transformed into administrative questions. Depending on the role perceptions and skills of the incumbent, the contemporary office affords resources for attaining important public policy goals.

(See also EXTRAJUDICIAL ACTIVITIES; OPINIONS, ASSIGNMENT AND WRITING OF.)

☐ Peter G. Fish, *The Office of Chief Justice* (1984). Walter F. Murphy, *Elements of Judicial Strategy* (1964). David M. O'Brien, *Storm Center: The Supreme Court in American Politics*, 2d ed. (1990). Robert J. Steamer, *Chief Justice: Leadership and the Supreme Court* (1986).　Peter G. Fish

**Child Labor.** See HAMMER V. DAGENHART.

**Children.** See FAMILY AND CHILDREN.

**Chimel v. California,** 395 U.S. 752 (1969), argued 27 Mar. 1969, decided 23 June 1969 by vote of 6 to 2 (with one vacancy); Stewart for the Court, Harlan concurring, White and Black in dissent. If the police have lawfully arrested a person for some criminal offense, how extensive a warrantless search may they make incident to that arrest? The Supreme Court answered this question in many different ways over a span of about sixty years. These responses ranged all the way from search of the person of the arrestee only to search of the person and the entire premises where the arrest was made. *Chimel* adopted a position between these extremes and has become the Court's major statement on the limits of a warrantless search pursuant to a lawful arrest.

To appreciate *Chimel*, it is important to understand the prior state of the law announced in *Harris* v. *United States* (1947) and *United States* v. *Rabinowitz* (1950). The *Harris-Rabinowitz* rule had these characteristics: (1) the scope of a permissible search was not limited to the person or areas the arrestee might reach to destroy evidence or obtain a weapon and thus appeared to cover the entire premises where the arrest was made; (2) it was never made clear whether such a warrantless search was permissible only if there was probable cause evidence of the crime would be found on the premises; and (3) the search was limited in its intensity and length by the items being sought.

*Chimel* involved a warrantless search of the defendant's home, incident to his arrest there, for the fruits of a burglary. The Court, in overruling *Harris* and *Rabinowitz*, first stated that the person of an arrestee may be searched so as to deprive him of weapons by which he could resist arrest or escape and also to prevent his concealment or destruction of evidence. The Court then continued: "And the area into which an arrestee might reach in order to grab a weapon or evidentiary items must, of course, be governed by a like rule. A gun on a table or in a drawer in front of one who is arrested can be as dangerous to the arresting officer as one concealed in the clothing of the person arrested. There is ample justification, therefore, for a search of the arrestee's person and the area 'within his immediate control'— construing that phrase to mean the area from within which he might gain possession of a weapon or destructible evidence" (p. 763).

The *Chimel* dissenters offered this rationale for retaining the *Harris-Rabinowitz* rule: (1) warrantless arrests are generally upheld without regard to whether there was time to get a warrant; (2) this is so because there is very often a risk of flight making acquisition of a warrant impracticable; (3) police will thus often make arrest without either an arrest or search warrant, and the arrest itself creates "exigent circumstances," as if police then leave to get a warrant "there must almost always be a strong possibility that confederates of the arrested man will in the meantime remove the items for which the police have probable cause to search" (p. 774); (4) thus, if after arrest the police have "probable cause to believe that seizable items are on the premises" (p. 773), they should be permitted to make an emergency search without a search warrant.

Empirical data, however, indicates that in a substantial number of cases arrests are not made under circumstances requiring immediate action to prevent escape. The "exigent circumstances" referred to by the *Chimel* dissenters often will have been unnecessarily created by the police themselves by not having a search warrant in hand at the time of the arrest. This is evident from the facts of *Chimel*. The burglary for which the defendant was arrested occurred a month earlier; the police knew he had not fled in the interim but continued to reside and work in the area; the police obviously felt there was no emergency because they obtained an arrest warrant and delayed serving it for several days; and no explanation was offered as to why the police could not have obtained a search warrant at the same time.

(See also DUE PROCESS, PROCEDURAL; FOURTH AMENDMENT; SEARCH WARRANT RULE, EXCEPTIONS TO.)

□ David E. Aaronson and Rangeley Wallace, "A Reconsideration of the Fourth Amendment's Doctrine of Search Incident to Arrest," *Georgetown Law Journal* 64 (1975): 53–84. Wayne R. LaFave

**Chinese Exclusion Cases,** a series of disputes settled by the Supreme Court during the 1880s and 1890s: *Chew Heong* v. *United States*, 112 U.S. 536 (1884), argued 30 Oct. 1884, decided 8 Dec. 1884 by vote of 7 to 2, Harlan for the Court, Field and Bradley in dissent; *United States* v. *Jung Ah Lung*, 124 U.S. 621 (1888), argued 9 Jan. 1888, decided 13 Feb. 1888 by vote of 6 to 3, Blatchford for the Court, Harlan in dissent; *Chae Chan Ping* v. *United States* (also recorded as *The Chinese Exclusion Case*), 130 U.S. 581 (1889), argued 28 Mar. 1889, decided 13 May 1889 by vote of 9 to 0, Field for the Court; and *Fong Yue Ting* v. *United States*, *Wong Quan* v. *United States*, and *Lee Joe* v. *United States*, 149 U.S. 698 (1893), argued 10 May 1893, decided 15 May 1893 by vote of 6 to 3, Gray for the Court, Brewer, Field, and Fuller in dissent. These decisions refined congressional legislation designed to prevent Chinese immigration.

In 1882 Congress passed the first of a series of Chinese Exclusion Acts prohibiting Chinese laborers and miners from entering the United States. An 1884 amendment required all Chinese laborers who lived in the Unites States before 1882 and who left the country with plans to return to have a reentry certificate. Six years later, the Scott Act (1888) became law. This statute prohibited Chinese laborers abroad or who planned future travels from returning. Over twenty thousand Chinese were stranded. The Scott Act did allow merchants and teachers to

return if they had proper papers. This loophole began the "paper names" industry whereby Chinese created new identities to return.

Congress passed a second exclusionary act, known as the Geary Act (1892). This law continued the ban on Chinese laborers and added the denial of bail to Chinese in *habeas corpus proceedings and the requirement for all Chinese to have identification certificates or face deportation. The McCreary Act (1893) further defined laborers to include merchants, laundry owners, miners, and fishers. Finally, the Chinese Exclusion Act of 1902 permanently closed the door on all Chinese immigration.

The government of China, Chinese living in the United States, and Chinese-Americans challenged the constitutionality of these anti-Chinese laws. The first case to reach the Supreme Court was *Chew Heong* v. *United States* (1884). In this case a Chinese laborer who resided in the United States in 1880 but left in 1881 was denied reentry in 1884 because he did not have a certificate. In a habeas corpus proceeding, he was denied a writ by Justice Stephen *Field; on appeal Justice John *Harlan led a divided Court in a reversal of Field's decision. Harlan determined that Chew Heong had befallen a statutory glitch, leaving before the 1882 act and returning after the 1884 amendments. Field and Justice Joseph *Bradley dissented.

In 1888 the Court decided *United States* v. *Jung Ah Lung*. The defendant, a Chinese laborer, had been an American resident before 1882, and he had left to return to China in 1883 with a reentry certificate. When Jung tried to return in 1885, he did not have his certificate and was denied reentry. He sued for a writ of habeas corpus, which was issued. Once again a divided Court, this time led by Justice Samuel *Blatchford, upheld the challenge of the Chinese to the enforcement of the Exclusion Act of 1882 as amended in 1884. The government argued that Chinese challenges through writs of habeas corpus were not allowed. Had the Court accepted this argument, Chinese rights would have been seriously curtailed. Once again Justice Field dissented, but he was gaining followers, including Justice Harlan.

After *Jung Ah Lung*, Congress passed the Scott Act, and the Supreme Court was quickly asked its interpretation in *Chae Chan Ping* v. *United States* (1889). Under the Scott Act, reentry certificates were abolished. Instead, an outright prohibition of reentry was established. Chae, a San Francisco Chinese laborer, left the United States to visit China before the Scott Act was passed but after the 1884 amendment. Although he had a reentry certificate, he was prevented from reentry and denied a writ of habeas corpus. The Supreme Court in an opinion written by Justice Field unanimously found the Scott Act constitutional.

The final Chinese attempt to challenge the Exclusion Acts came in 1893. In 1892 Congress renewed the Exclusion Act of 1882 for another ten years, and it added a new requirement that all Chinese laborers had to have certificates of residence or face deportation. Three Chinese were subsequently found guilty of not having residence papers, and they appealed. In the 1893 cases the Court completed the closing of the door to Chinese immigration and the restriction of basic freedoms to Chinese-Americans by holding that Congress had the power retroactively to require Chinese to have residential certificates and allowing those without certificates to be deported.

After initially offering narrow holdings to protect Chinese reentry to the United States, the Supreme Court eventually succumbed to the anti-Chinese hysteria of the era and ratified far-reaching restrictions on basic rights for Chinese under American law.

(See also IMMIGRATION.)

□ Milton R. Konvitz, *The Asian and the Asiatic in American Law* (1946). John R. Wunder

**Chisholm v. Georgia,** 2 Dall. (2 U.S.) 419 (1793), argued 5 Feb. 1793, decided 18 Feb. 1793 by vote of 4 to 1; seriatim opinions by Jay, Cushing, Wilson, and Blair, Iredell in dissent. The first great case decided by the Court, *Chisholm* presented a conflict between federal jurisdiction and state sovereignty. The plaintiff, a citizen of South Carolina and the executor of a South Carolina merchant, sued the state of Georgia for the value of clothing supplied by the merchant during the Revolutionary War. Georgia refused to appear, claiming immunity from the suit as a sovereign and independent state. The Constitution (*Article III, sec. 2) extended federal judicial power to controversies between "a State and Citizens of another State" (see CASES AND CONTROVERSIES). The Court entered a default judgment against Georgia. The opinions of James *Wilson and John *Jay were ringing declarations of the nationalist view that sovereignty resided in the people of the United States "for the purposes of Union" and that as to those purposes Georgia was "not a sovereign state" (p. 457). *Chisholm* roused old Antifederalist fears of "consolidation" while raising the prospect of creditors flocking to the federal courts. The immediate consequence of the decision was action by Congress ultimately leading to the *Eleventh Amendment (1798), which took away jurisdiction in suits commenced against a state by citizens of another state or of a foreign state. This was the first instance in which a Supreme Court decision has been superseded by constitutional amendment. (See also FEDERALISM; REVERSALS OF COURT DECISIONS BY AMENDMENT; STATE SOVEREIGNTY AND STATES' RIGHTS.) Charles F. Hobson

**Chisom v. Roemer,** 111 S.Ct. 2354 (1991), argued 12 Apr. 1991, decided 20 June 1991 by vote of 6 to 3; Stevens for the Court, Scalia, joined by Rehnquist and Kennedy, in dissent, Kennedy in dissent. **Houston Lawyers' Association v. Attorney General of Texas,** 111 S.Ct. 2376 (1991), argued 22 Apr. 1991, decided 20 June 1991 by vote of 6 to 3; Stevens for the Court, Scalia, joined by Rehnquist and Kennedy, in dissent. The 1982 amendments to the *Voting Rights Act of 1965 amended section 2 to make clear that practices that result in the denial or abridgement of voting rights, even if not the product of discriminatory intent, are unlawful. The amendments extended section 2's protection beyond the *Fifteenth Amendment that, under *Mobile v. Bolden (1980), proscribes only intentional discrimination in voting. *Chisom* holds that section 2's "results test" applies to state judicial elections.

For purposes of electing two of Louisiana's seven Supreme Court justices, Orleans Parish, in which black voters constituted a majority, was combined into a multimember district with three parishes in which white voters constituted a majority. The five other justices were elected in single-member districts. Black Orleans Parish voters alleged that the multimember district denied their voting rights, but the question arose whether section 2 applies to judicial elections. The Supreme Court noted that section 2, prior to its amendment in 1982, was regarded as applying to judicial elections, and that *Clark* v. *Roemer* (1991) had held that section 5 of the Voting Rights Act, which requires certain states to submit for approval changes in voting procedures with federal authorities, applies to judicial elections. The Court held that the use of the word "representatives" in section 2 did not reflect Congress's desire to limit section 2 to legislators and executive officials. *Houston Lawyers' Association* held that section 2 applies to the election of trial judges.

(See also VOTE, RIGHT TO.)

Theodore Eisenberg

**Choate, Joseph Hodges** (b. Salem, Mass., 24 Jan. 1832; d. New York, N.Y., 14 May 1917), lawyer and diplomat. In the best tradition of the legal profession, Choate was far more than a superb advocate and a witty after-dinner speaker. As a Republican reformer, he roused public support against both the Tweed Ring and Tammany Hall. Dedicated to public service, he was a founder of the Metropolitan Museum of Art and the American Museum of Natural History and an active participant in charitable enterprises. And as ambassador to England from 1899 to 1905, he helped forge a new era in Anglo-American relations. Such achievements are representative of his distinguished extralegal career.

During the 1880s and 1890s, Choate appeared frequently before the Supreme Court. He was unsuccessful in fighting state liquor prohibition in *Mugler* v. *Kansas* (1887) and anti-Chinese legislation in *Fong Yue Ting* v. *United States* (1893)

(see CHINESE EXCLUSION CASES), but he successfully defended both the claims of the New York Indians in *New York Indians* v. *United States* (1898) and Stanford University, the beneficiary of the will of Leland Stanford, from challenges by the federal government in *United States* v. *Stanford* (1896). His most colorful winning argument came in *\*Pollock* v. *Farmers' Loan & Trust Co.* (1895), when he attacked the federal *income tax of 1894: "The act . . . is communistic in its purposes and tendencies, and is defended here upon principles as communistic, socialistic—what should I call them—populistic as ever have been addressed to any political assembly in the world" (p. 532).

John E. Semonche

**Church and State.** See RELIGION.

**Circuit Courts of Appeals.** Congress established the federal circuit courts in the *Judiciary Act of 1789 and divided the country into three circuits, each of which contained several states. The circuit courts performed both trial and appellate functions and, until 1869, were staffed by federal district court judges and by U.S. Supreme Court justices riding circuit. The difficulty of travel to many of the circuits made *circuit riding a hardship, and the practice fell into disuse by the 1840s. The district judges were thus left to conduct business of both the districts and circuits, which made appellate duties impossible. Congress attempted to remedy the situation in the *Judiciary Act of 1869 by creating a circuit judgeship in each of the then nine circuits.

As the jurisdiction of the federal courts expanded, the business of both the circuit and district courts increased, and the circuit judges attended mostly to trial work. This put pressure on the Supreme Court, as appellate review was either unavailable in the circuit courts or judges were reviewing their own work. Congress attempted a remedy in the Evarts Act in 1891 (see JUDICIARY ACT OF 1891), which established the United States circuit courts of appeals and transferred all appellate work to them. Congressional traditionalists, however, refused to abolish the old circuit courts and they retained original trial jurisdiction over capital cases, tax cases, and diversity cases where the amount in controversy exceeded the district court's limit. Congress increasingly became convinced that the circuit courts were dispensable, and in a 1911 statute it made the district courts the exclusive federal trial courts. The circuit courts ceased to exist on 1 January 1912. The circuit courts of appeal were renamed the *courts of appeal in 1948.

(See also JUDICIAL POWER AND JURISDICTION; LOWER FEDERAL COURTS.)

Rayman L. Solomon

**Circuit Riding.** The *Judiciary Act of 1789 required that the justices of the Supreme Court serve also as judges of the *circuit courts. The justices complained that circuit riding caused serious physical hardships and diverted them from more important duties in the nation's capital. The southern circuit, for example, required travel of nearly 1,800 miles, twice a year, in a country that had poor roads or, in some places, none at all. The early justices even agreed to take a reduction in salary if Congress would appoint separate circuit judges. Congress, however, believed that circuit riding transformed the justices into republican schoolmasters, who brought federal authority and national political views to the distant states. Through their charges to juries in early criminal cases, for example, the circuit-riding justices impressed on the citizenry the authority of the remote national government. Circuit riding also exposed the justices to local political sentiments and legal practices.

Congress in 1801 abolished circuit riding on grounds of efficiency, but a year later a new Jeffersonian Republican majority restored the practice, obliging each justice to hold circuit court along with a district court judge. Gradually, however, improved communications, increasing business in the nation's capital, and the strengthening of American nationhood following the *Civil War rendered circuit riding anachronistic. Congress in the *Judiciary Act of 1869 established a separate circuit court judiciary, although the justices retained nominal circuit riding duties until the Circuit Court of Appeals Act of 1891 (see JUDICIARY ACT OF 1891). Congress officially ended the practice in 1911.

(See also CIRCUIT COURTS OF APPEALS.)

Kermit L. Hall

**Citation,** a term that has several meanings in American practice. It can be a writ or order, analogous to a summons, that is issued by a court commanding a person to appear before that court. Or it may refer to the way in which opinions of the Supreme Court are cited. The proper form for citing opinions to the offical reports and the two unofficial reporters is: *Brown* v. *Board of Education,* 347 U.S. 483, 74 S.Ct. 686, 98 L.Ed. 873 (1954). The antecedent number refers to the volume in *United States Reports, Supreme Court Reporter,* and *Lawyers' Edition,* respectively, while the subsequent number is the page on which the report begins.

(See also REPORTERS, SUPREME COURT.)

William M. Wiecek

**Cities.** See MUNICIPAL CORPORATIONS.

**Citizenship.** In giving meaning to citizenship, the Supreme Court has often had to look beyond the "four corners" of the Constitution. With no definition of citizenship in the framers' text, the Court until after the *Civil War decided its citizenship cases using a mix of ideas drawn from international law and *natural law. The most famous antebellum attempt to define the limits of citizenship—*Dred *Scott* v. *Sandford* (1857)—ultimately provided a rare occasion on which the amendment process reversed a constitutional decision of the Supreme Court. Since 1868, when the *Fourteenth Amendment defined United States citizenship, the Court's decisions have been more concerned with safeguarding citizenship against unjust deprivation than with elaborating the content of U.S. citizenship.

The Constitution referred to but did not define U.S. citizenship. Article I required that representatives and senators be citizens of the United States. Article II further said that the president must either be a citizen of the United States "at the time of Adoption" or be a "natural born" citizen. Article III gave federal courts jurisdiction in cases involving citizens, among others. Article IV provided that "citizens of each state" would have "all Privileges and Immunities of Citizens in the Several States."

What, then, would make a person a United States citizen? The framers' stipulation that the president be a "natural born" citizen is an implicit rule of *jus soli*. According to this ancient doctrine—the term means "right of land or ground"—citizenship results from birth within a territory. This contrasts with *jus sanguinis*, or right of blood, by which nationality derives from descent. Citizenship based on place of birth was a feudal remnant, in tension with principles of liberal theory that rest political legitimacy on a foundation of consent. Birthright citizenship, however, offered several practical advantages: it helped clarify *property rights; it promoted *immigration; it avoided jurisdictional conflicts; and it eased fears of massive expatriation in wartime.

Not until the slavery crisis did the principle of *jus soli* become an explicit part of the Constitution—in spite of what the Supreme Court had ruled. Chief Justice Roger B. *Taney's opinion in *Dred Scott* denied that a person of African descent could be a citizen of the United States. The Fourteenth Amendment exploded this decision by declaring that "All persons born or naturalized in the United States, and subject to the jurisdiction thereof, are citizens of the United States and of the State wherein they reside."

The Fourteenth Amendment did not settle the matter entirely in favor of birthright citizenship. In *Elk* v. *Wilkins* (1884), for example, the Supreme Court ruled that *Native Americans born in the United States were not automatically citizens. As members of tribes, they were not wholly "subject to the jurisdiction" of the federal government. Congress, however, later reversed the result of the *Wilkins* decision.

One of many Supreme Court cases arising out of late nineteenth-century discrimination against persons of Chinese ancestry, *United States* v. *Wong Kim Ark* (1898), broadly interpreted *jus soli*. The Fourteenth Amendment's rule of citizenship by birth within U.S. territory made Wong Kim Ark a citizen, even though the parents could not legally be naturalized.

Once defined in 1868, citizenship became an operative term in four more amendments. In particular, the citizen's right to vote could not be denied because of *race (Fifteenth Amendment); *gender (Nineteenth Amendment); failure to pay a *poll tax (Twenty-fourth Amendment) or age (Twenty-sixth Amendment). Though the Supreme Court has had many cases requiring interpretation of these amendments, the concept of citizenship per se has not been at the core of these disputes.

Despite the place of citizenship in several amendments, what is notable is the remarkably limited scope of citizenship in the Supreme Court's work. This is so since, while one must be a citizen to vote or hold federal office, most of the Constitution's key rights and liberties do not extend to citizens only. No less than the entire *Bill of Rights applies to "the people"—citizen and the noncitizen alike.

The Supreme Court's interpretation of the Equal Protection Clause appears to diminish the constitutional consequence of citizenship. Beginning in 1971, the Court began to apply *"strict scrutiny" to state laws affecting aliens. Under this test, the state must show that laws drawing distinctions based on citizenship serve compelling governmental interests. In *Graham* v. *Richardson* (1971), for example, the Court ruled that states could not deny welfare benefits to noncitizens based simply on their alien status. Two years later in *Sugarman* v. *Dougall* (1973), the Court created an important category of exceptions to the rule of *Graham*, holding that certain important public sector jobs may be set aside for a state's citizens. The Court's continued reliance on *Graham*, however, casts doubt on citizenship classifications drawn by the states.

Other decisions, however, have stressed the unique, valued, and protected position of citizenship. *Schneiderman* v. *United States* (1943), for instance, dealt with denaturalization. Schneiderman became a United States citizen in 1927. Since he was a member of the Communist party from 1924 and, after naturalization, became active in party leadership, the government moved to have his citizenship stripped. The government argued that Schneiderman's political conduct—though he had never been arrested—failed to show the attachment to constitutional principles which Congress required for naturalization. In ruling for Schneiderman, the Supreme Court held that a naturalized person could not lose citizen status without the clearest justification, construing the facts and law as far as is reasonably possible in the citizen's favor. In *Trop* v. *Dulles* (1958), the Court affirmed the importance of citizenship by holding that a citizen by birth could not be expatriated for desertion from the military in wartime. Chief Justice Earl *Warren wrote for a four-person *plurality that loss of citizenship would amount to *cruel and unusual punishment banned by the *Eighth Amendment.

The Supreme Court's decisions have tended to reflect the Constitution's own ambivalence about citizenship. Despite its status as fundamental law, the Constitution did not explicitly define criteria for membership in the political community it created. The Court's antebellum attempt to fill this void broke apart on the fault line of slavery. While the Court has upheld birthright citizenship and has erected high barriers to deprivation of citizenship, its equal protection decisions have tended to underscore the Constitution's tendency toward a narrow conception of citizenship closely tied to voting and office holding.

(See also ALIENAGE AND NATURALIZATION; EQUAL PROTECTION; PRIVILEGES AND IMMUNITIES.)

□ Joseph H. Carens, "Who Belongs? Theoretical and Legal Questions about Birthright Citizenship in the United States," *University of Toronto Law Journal* 37 (1987): 413–443. Peter Schuck and Rogers Smith, *Citizenship Without Consent: Illegal Aliens in American Politics* (1985).
Patrick J. Bruer

**Civil Law** has two distinct meanings. As used within the American legal system, "civil law" is noncriminal law such as the law of property, commercial law, administrative law, and the rules governing procedure in civil cases. But "civil law" also refers to a body of law distinct from *common law, and that is the sense of the term that is treated here.

Civil law is the legal tradition that derives from *Roman law. The civil-law tradition developed on the continent of Europe and spread throughout the world as a byproduct of the European expansion that took place from the fifteenth through the twentieth century. Some of the countries whose legal systems are based on the civil-law tradition are France, Germany, Italy, Spain, all of Latin America, and Japan. Most nations of eastern Europe, including the Soviet Union, were civil-law jurisdictions prior to the communist era, and with the collapse of the communist bloc they may revert to that tradition. While legal systems within the civil-law tradition differ among themselves, they are so closely related that legal scholars refer to them as members of a single civil-law "family."

Civil-law systems differ from common-law systems in the substantive content of the law, the operative procedures of the law, legal terminology, the manner in which authoritative sources of law are identified, the institutional framework within which the law is applied, and the education and structure of the legal profession.

Thus, for example, in common-law systems, the law of contracts requires consideration for a promise, but consideration has no true analogue in civil law. In common-law systems before the statutory reforms of the mid-twentieth century, a seller's warranty had to be expressed in a contract of sale; it could not be implied. But in civil-law systems, buyers have always had remedies based upon the seller's implied warranty that the goods sold possessed qualities that the buyer could presume. Other differences can be found in the law of property, the law of *torts (delicts), family law, and other areas of substantive law.

Civil-law systems depend heavily upon written codes of private law, such as the French Civil Code (*Code Napoléon*) of 1804 and the German *Bürgerliches Gesetzbuch* (the "B.G.B.") of 1900, as primary sources for authoritative statements of the law. Judicial decisions are less important than they are in common-law jurisdictions. While a line of judicial decisions establishing a particular legal proposition (Fr., *jurisprudence constante*) does carry substantial weight, the common-law rule of binding precedent (Lat., *stare decisis*) is not recognized in traditional civil-law systems.

Because post–Roman civil law developed in the medieval universities of Italy and France rather than in courts of law as in England, the civil law gives greater authority to the writings of legal academicians and scholars than does the common law, which continues to emphasize the law in practice as it is developed case by case in written decisions of appellate courts.

Within the United States and its territories, only three jurisdictions are considered civil-law systems—Louisiana, Puerto Rico, and Guam—but because of the strong influence of common law in these jurisdictions, they are really "mixed systems" of civil and common law. Under the Supreme Court's ruling in *Erie* v. *Tompkins* (1938), Louisiana courts are the final authority on matters involving issues of civil law under the Louisiana Code of 1870. Similarly, courts in Puerto Rico and Guam have responsibility for the development of the civil law in those island jurisdictions.

Civil law is usually of tangential concern to the U.S. Supreme Court. The justices of the Supreme Court are products of the American common-law tradition, and, with few exceptions, they have not been familiar with civil-law sources or methods. Nevertheless, with the growth of international private law, the expanding commercial importance of the European Community and Japan, and increasing contacts among legal practitioners and legal elites across national boundaries, the Supreme Court will have to come to terms with the civil law, the most widespread and important legal tradition in the modern world.

□ John E. C. Brierly and René David, *Major Legal Systems in the World Today: An Introduction to the Competitive Study of Law*, 3d ed. (1985). John H. Merryman, *The Civil Law Tradition: An Introduction to the Legal Systems of Western Europe and Latin America* (1969).
George Dargo

**Civil Liberties.** See HISTORY OF THE COURT: RIGHTS CONSCIOUSNESS IN CONTEMPORARY SOCIETY.

**Civil Rights Act of 1964.** The broad underlying purpose of the Civil Rights Act of 1964 was to eliminate the pervasive discrimination against racial minorities that had long existed in American society. The two most important provisions of the act are Title II and Title VII, which provide federal administrative and judicial remedies against racial and other group-based kinds of discrimination in public accommodations and in employment, respectively. The Supreme Court has interpreted the act with reference to its broad underlying purpose and has resolved the major substantive and remedial questions under the act in such a way as to maximize the protection afforded to racial minorities.

The Court has ensured that racial minorities will have full access to all public facilities by broadly defining a "place of public accommodation" within the meaning of Title II to include facilities such as a "family restaurant" (*Katzenbach* v. *McClung*, 1964), a recreational area (*Daniel* v. *Paul*, 1969), and a community swimming pool (*Tillman* v. *Wheaton-Haven Recreation Association*, 1973). As a result of this expansive interpretation, no person, because of race, can be excluded from any facility that is open to the public as a whole.

The Court likewise has interpreted Title VII with a view toward improving significantly the employment opportunities for racial minorities at all levels and in the workplaces of all employers. Most importantly, the Court has held that Title VII reaches not only intentional employment discrimination, but also employment practices that have a discriminatory effect on racial minorities and other protected groups. (*Griggs* v. *Duke Power Co.*, 1971). The focus on racially discriminatory effect, or to use the legal phrase, "racially *disparate impact*," has resulted in the invalidation of many tests and other employment requirements that are not job related and that would deny employment opportunities to racial minorities (see DISCRIMINATORY INTENT).

The Court has also upheld the use of judicially imposed affirmative hiring and promotional remedies to overcome the present consequences of the employer's past racial discrimination. These remedies have been imposed in a large number of class actions against major employers and have had the effect of providing minorities with a fair share of the jobs in the workforces of these employers (see AFFIRMATIVE ACTION).

At the same time, the Court has held that Title VII does not prevent an employer from undertaking "voluntary, race-conscious efforts to abolish traditional patterns of racial segregation and hierarchy" in the employer's workforce (*United Steelworkers* v. *Weber*, 1971). The employer may adopt hiring, training, and promotional programs that give a limited preference to racial minorities in order to open up employment opportunities in the occupations that traditionally had been closed to them.

Not all of the Court's decisions interpreting Title VII, however, have been favorable to the claims of racial minorities. In dealing with the matter of seniority, the Court has been constrained by the language of section 703(h) of the act, which protects "bona fide seniority systems" from court interference. Thus, courts cannot require an out-of-line seniority layoff in order to maintain minority hiring gains under a court order directed toward remedying the employer's illegal racial discrimination (*Firefighters Local Union No. 1784* v. *Stotts*, 1984). And in the last few years, when dealing with the myriad procedural and remedial questions arising under Title VII, the Court's decisions have generally favored the interests of employers in resisting discrimination claims. For example, the Court has held that discrimination claimants have the burden of proving that an employment practice having a discriminatory effect on racial minorities is not job-related (*Ward's Cove Packing Co.* v. *Atonio*, 1989). The *Civil Rights Act of 1991*, however, blunted the full force of the *Ward's Cove* decision.

These limitations aside, the Court's interpretation of Title VII, when viewed in perspective, has provided racial minorities and other protected groups with a very significant legal weapon in their quest for equal employment opportunity in the economy. The Court's interpretation of the Civil Rights Act of 1964 has moved the United States in the direction of eliminating the pervasive racial discrimination that for so long had been a prominent feature of American life.

(See also EMPLOYMENT DISCRIMINATION; RACE AND RACISM.)

☐ Barbara Lindermann Schlei and Paul Grossman, *Employment Discrimination Law*, 2d ed. (1983).

Robert A. Sedler

**Civil Rights Act of 1991.** In 1991 Congress amended the *Civil Rights Act of 1964* in an effort to strengthen federal civil rights laws, to provide for damages in *employment discrimination* cases, and to clarify provisions of the 1964 act relating to *"disparate impact"* actions. After months of political debate over civil rights issues, a compromise measure gained bipartisan support in Congress, and President George Bush signed the act into law on 21 November 1991.

In large part, Congressional action on civil rights was in response to recent attempts by the Rehnquist Court to weaken the scope of federal civil rights protections. In *Ward's Cove Packing Co.* v. *Atonio* (1989), for example, the Court held that plaintiffs suing for discrimination in employment needed to demonstrate that the application of a specific employment practice had created the "disparate impact" under attack. If plaintiffs met this burden of proof, the employer could then justify the discriminatory practice by proving that it was a "business necessity." The Civil Rights Act of 1991 reversed this decision by eliminating the claim of "business necessity" as a defense against intentional discrimination. Moreover, in *Patterson* v. *McLean Credit Union* (1989) the Court, by narrowly interpreting a provision of the Civil Rights Act of 1866 that prohibited discrimination in making contracts, had refused to extend the law's protection to an employee's claim of posthiring racial harassment. The 1991 legislation, however, explicitly broadened the language of the 1866 law to include such actions. Finally, although the Court had granted wide latitude to those desiring to challenge affirmative action policies in the courts in *Martin* v. *Wilks* (1989), the Civil Rights Act narrowed the opportunities for such litigation. In short, the 1991 law reversed recent attempts by the Court to limit the scope of civil rights protections by clarifying and expanding previous legislation.

(See also RACE AND RACISM; REVERSAL OF COURT DECISIONS BY CONGRESS.)

Timothy S. Huebner

**Civil Rights Cases,** 109 U.S. 3 (1883), submitted on the briefs 7 November 1882, argued 29 March 1883, decided 15 October 1883 by vote of 8 to 1; Bradley for Court, Harlan in dissent. Few decisions better illustrate the Supreme Court's early inclination to interpret narrowly the Civil War Amendments than the *Civil Rights Cases.* There the Court declared unconstitutional provisions of the Civil Rights Act of 1875 that prohibited racial discrimination in inns, public conveyances, and places of public amusement. The decision curtailed federal efforts to protect African-Americans from private discrimination and cast constitutional doubts on Congress's ability to legislate in the area of Civil Rights, doubts that were not completely resolved until enactment of the *Civil Rights Act of 1964.*

The *Civil Rights Cases* presented two conflicting views of the *Thirteenth and *Fourteenth Amendments. The conservative view saw the amendments in narrow terms: the Thirteenth Amendment simply abolished *slavery; the Fourteenth granted the freed people *citizenship and a measure of relief from state discrimination. The more radical view believed the amendments helped secure to the freed people and others all rights of free people in Anglo-American legal culture. Moreover, the amendments gave the national government authority to protect citizens against both state and private deprivations of rights.

Justice Joseph P. *Bradley's majority opinion rejected the more radical interpretation of the new amendments. He held that the Fourteenth Amendment only prohibited state abridgement of individual rights. In Bradley's view the 1875 Civil Rights Act was an impermissible attempt by Congress to create a municipal code regulating the private conduct of individuals in the area of racial discrimination. He asserted in dicta that even private interference with such rights as

voting, jury service, or appearing as witnesses in state court were not within the province of Congress to control. An individual faced with such interference had to look to state government for relief. Bradley also rejected the contention that the Thirteenth Amendment allowed Congress to pass the 1875 legislation, declaring that denial of access to public accommodations did not constitute a badge or incident of slavery. In his view such a broad construction of the Thirteenth Amendment would make the freed person "the special favorite of the laws."

In his dissent, Southerner and former slaveholder Justice John Marshall *Harlan rejected the majority's narrow construction of the Civil War Amendments. Asserting that the decision rested on grounds that were "narrow and artificial," Harlan argued that the Thirteenth Amendment gave Congress broad powers to legislate to insure the rights of freed people (p. 26). He contended that the freedom conferred by the Thirteenth Amendment went beyond the simple absence of bondage. It encompassed freedom from the incidents of slavery, including all "badges of slavery" (p. 35).

Along with the decision in the *Slaughterhouse Cases* (1873), which effectively stripped the Fourteenth Amendment's *Privileges or Immunities Clause of significant meaning, and U.S. v. *Cruikshank* (1876), which upheld congressional efforts to protect blacks and others against private deprivations of constitutional rights, the *Civil Rights Cases* fashioned a Fourteenth Amendment jurisprudence considerably less protective of individual rights than many of its framers had envisioned. The extent to which the Court's narrow reading of Fourteenth Amendment protections helped usher in and foster the era of extensive segregation in southern and other states is open to debate. But the Supreme Court's decision in the *Civil Rights Cases* largely mandated the withdrawal of the federal government from civil rights enforcement. That withdrawal would not be reversed until after World War II.

In 1964 Congress again passed legislation prohibiting discrimination in public accommodations. Ironically the Bradley opinion, which expressly did not rule on whether or not the Constitution's Commerce Clause provided a basis for congressional legislation in this area, played a role in the drafting of the 1964 statute (see COMMERCE POWER). The 1964 act's public accommodations provision was based on the Commerce Clause.

(See also RACE AND RACISM.).

□ Eugene Gressman, "The Unhappy History of Civil Rights Legislation," *Michigan Law Review* 50 (1952): 1323–1358. Robert J. Cottrol

**Civil Rights Movement.** The American struggle for racial equality can hardly be placed within clear temporal boundaries. It obviously includes the brilliant writings of Frederick Douglass, the courage of Harriet Tubman, the stirring speeches of Sojourner Truth, the hesitant proclamations of Abraham Lincoln, the advocacy of W. E. B. DuBois, the calm spirit of Jackie Robinson, and the post–World War II litigation efforts of Thurgood Marshall. And since, in Martin Luther King's language, the *Declaration of Independence has always represented a "declaration of intent rather than of reality," the unfulfilled quest for equality will test the nation's best efforts for generations to come.

Still, it is not inappropriate to characterize the period from the mid-1950s until about 1970 as a unique watershed in the civil rights stuggle in the United States. When the seamstress Rosa Parks refused to step to the back of an Alabama bus on 1 December 1955—thus inspiring the successful Montgomery bus boycott—a decade and a half of civil rights protests were sparked that forever changed the American social fabric. Mrs. Parks explained that her refusal was "a matter of dignity; I could not have faced myself and my people if I had moved." The young preacher whom the boycott brought to prominence, Martin Luther King, Jr., believed that the civil rights movement was an attack on "man's hostility to man." Encouraging widespread boycotts, freedom rides, and sit-ins to protest segregation, King stressed that one who breaks an unjust law openly and with a willingness to accept the penalty expresses "the very highest respect for the law."

It is clear that the protest movement, which began in the Deep South and spread to the nation at large, had a dramatic impact upon American institutions—particularly, American legal institutions. The role of the Supreme Court—as advocate, prophet, protector, and product of the civil rights struggle—constitutes one of the most fascinating chapters of the Court's history.

It makes sense to begin with *Brown v. Board of Education (1954). The ruling, handed down at the beginning of Chief Justice Earl *Warren's tenure, determined that in the field of "public education, the doctrine of separate-but-equal has no place" (p. 495). Warren's painstaking and successful effort to forge a united front to overturn *Plessy v. Ferguson was surely the greatest of his many judicial accomplishments. The opinion, which drew on Warren's own sense of fair play and opportunity, emphasized that separating children "of similar age and qualifications solely because of their race generates a feeling of inferiority as to their status in the community that may affect their hearts and minds in a way unlikely ever to be undone" (p. 494). Brown was thus a bold move—even if it was a belated one, designed to rid the legal system of a court-created impediment to equality.

The Brown decision gave impetus to the demonstrations that began across the South in 1955. Robert L. Carter, former general counsel of the

*National Association for the Advancement of Colored People, has written that the desegregation ruling altered the status of blacks, who were no longer supplicants "seeking, pleading, begging to be treated as full-fledged members of the human race." Rather they were entitled to equal treatment under the law; the constitution promised no less. Therefore, Brown's indirect consequences were dramatic. But most of the work—for both the Court and the civil rights activists—lay ahead.

Brown's demand for a unitary public school system presented massive implementation problems. The Court's remedial decision, Brown II (1955), called for the dismantling of segregated schools under a cautious charge of *"all deliberate speed." If recalcitrant local school officials sought to move slowly, though, civil rights protestors did not. For the entire decade of the 1960s the Supreme Court faced a series of trespass, contempt, and breach of the peace convictions arising from protests for racial equality. The Court regularly demonstrated a strong solicitude for these cases that, on one level, could have been seen as mere matters of local law enforcement practice, unfit for Supreme Court attention. Actually though, the justices repeatedly bent traditional principles of review to offer protection to a protest movement of tremendous historical moment.

In Boynton v. Virginia (1960), for example, the Supreme Court reversed a black law student's trespass conviction for refusing to leave the white section of a restaurant operated by a private company in the Richmond Trailways Bus Terminal. Boynton had been arrested under Virginia's trespass statute rather than any overt segregation provision. His lawyers at trial had failed to challenge the conviction under the Interstate Commerce Act, which made discrimination in certain aspects of interstate transportation illegal. Despite these difficulties, the Court ruled that under the Commerce Act the terminal and the restaurant stood in the place of the bus company in the performance of its transportation obligations (see COMMERCE POWER). Although the courts below made no findings of fact, the Supreme Court ruled that "the evidence in this case shows such a relationship and situation here" (p. 461). Under normal concepts of appellate review, the Court would have demanded that the Interstate Commerce Act defense have been preserved at trial.

The following year, in Garner v. Louisiana (1961), a unanimous Court reversed the disturbing-the-peace convictions of sixteen blacks who refused to leave a "whites-only" lunch counter. After searching the record, the justices concluded that there was no evidence to support the breach of peace claims—reaching what could be seen as a local law conclusion that mere presence could not constitute a valid disturbance. In Peterson v. City of Greenville (1963) the justices reversed another group of sit-in cases under the theory that the trespass convictions were not the result of mere private discrimination. Stretching the *"state action" doctrine significantly, the Court concluded that well-publicized statements of local public officials indicating that sit-ins would not be permitted brought the case under the purview of the *Fourteenth Amendment (see SIT-IN DEMONSTRATIONS).

The willingness, evidenced in *Peterson*, to apply constitutional mandate to what had traditionally been regarded as mere private conduct was continued throughout the 1960s. In *Burton* v. *Wilmington Parking Authority* (1961) the Court extended the state action concept to embrace a private restaurant's refusal to serve a black customer. The establishment in question was located in a parking garage owned by a local government entity under a complex leasing arrangement that allowed the parking authority to benefit from the restaurant's practices. In *Griffin* v. *Maryland* (1964), a trespass conviction in a private amusement park was reversed because the park employee making the arrest was also a deputy sheriff. This dual status gave the seizure a sufficiently public character to be deemed action of the state, and thus subject to constitutional stricture. The justices in *Robinson* v. *Florida* (1964) found enough public coercion in a set of state health regulations requiring segregated toilets to overturn a restaurant owner's private segregation policy.

The *First Amendment principles of vagueness and overbreadth were given new vigor during this period as well. A multitude of convictions arising from marches against segregation were reversed in *Edwards* v. *South Carolina* (1963). In this case, college students were arrested after a peaceful assembly on the grounds of a state capitol. The Court ruled that the breach of the peace statute, as construed, was so vague that it permitted the abrogation of First Amendment protected expression. In *Cox* v. *Louisiana* (1965) the justices held a Louisiana obstructing-public-passages statute as unnecessarily broad and overturned a sentence of twenty-one months in jail for engaging in a peaceful demonstration.

Expanding First Amendment protections in another direction, the Supreme Court also reached out in the mid-1960s to protect directly the primary litigation arm of the civil rights movement, the NAACP. In *NAACP* v. *Button* (1963), the justices invalidated an effort by the Virginia legislature to outlaw as solicitation of legal business the litigation strategy of the NAACP *Legal Defense and Education Fund. And six months later, in *Gibson* v. *Florida Legislative Investigation Committee* (1963), the Court shielded the organization itself from being forced to disclose its membership to a state legislative committee.

There were exceptions to the Court's generous treatment of civil rights activitist. The convictions of thirty-two Florida A&M University students, arrested for protesting on the grounds of a jailhouse, were upheld in *Adderley* v. *Florida* (1966). And in *Walker* v. *City of Birmingham* (1967) the justices sustained contempt convictions of Martin Luther King, Jr. and others for marching in violation of a seemingly unconstitutional court order. It may be that the Court was, by the late 1960s, becoming impatient with the growing militancy of civil rights demonstrators. But it is also true that in the early part of the decade the Court seemed to be passing on more than the merits of isolated trespass convictions. Indeed, the protestors won almost all of their cases in the highest court. The justices' near constant involvement in cases reflected a concern that the civil rights movement should not be worn down by local prosecutions.

It is indisputable, then, that the Supreme Court contributed significantly to the success of the civil rights movement in the 1960s. Martin Luther King, for example, acknowledged that the Court's determination that local laws requiring segregation on Montgomery's buses were unconstitutional greatly rejuvenated his watershed communitywide boycott. Nonetheless, it is not too difficult to carry a reciprocal claim that the civil rights movement—over the longer course—contributed even more substantially to the development of the Supreme Court.

Some of the constitutional initiatives of the civil rights era have faded. The great stretches of the state action doctrine between 1960 and 1972, for example, were dramatically pared back. Ambitious civil and voting rights statutes passed in 1964, 1965, and 1968 diminished the need for constitutional intervention in nonpublic discrimination (see CIVIL RIGHTS ACT OF 1964; VOTING RIGHTS ACT OF 1965). Intrusive jurisdictional principles, designed to allow significant federal intervention into unconstitutional *state court processes, have also been overruled as a sense of emergency has waned. Still, large areas of modern constitutional jurisprudence are deeply rooted in the civil rights/protest era. If the Supreme Court was forced to discard traditional principles of deference toward other government decision makers in oder to assist a fragile civil liberties movement, the effect has been long-term and beneficial.

*Brown* and its progeny, both within the federal courtrooms and outside them, have helped to transform the Supreme Court into a meaningful institution for the protection of civil and political rights. For example, litigation involving flag burning drew strength from the earlier civil rights movement. In 1969, a conviction arising from the burning of a flag by an African-American man protesting the shooting of James Meredith was reversed in *Street* v. *New York*. Voting rights decisions like *Harper* v. *Virginia Board of Elections* (1966), striking down the use of the poll tax, and *Gomillion v. Lightfoot (1960), requiring the racially equitable composition of political districts, have spawned a vital jurisprudence of political equality.

These changes, however, pale in comparison to the effect that *New York Times v. Sullivan (1964) has had on freedom of expression in the United States. In the Sullivan case, the Supreme Court reversed a $500,000 libel judgment awarded to the police commissioner of Montgomery, Alabama. State courts had found that a group of civil rights activists and the New York Times had damaged the commissioner's reputation and brought him into public contempt. Prior to the Sullivan decision in 1964, statements found to be libelous by state courts were, without more, deemed outside the protection of the First Amendment. Realizing the significant threat to democratic processes resulting from such a strong chill on a citizen's ability to criticize government officials, the Court ruled in Sullivan that the free speech guarantee requires significant federal judicial oversight of state libel decisions. Sullivan held that public officials are prevented from recovering damages for a defamatory falsehood relating to official conduct unless *"actual malice"—that is, wreckless disregard for the truth—is shown.

The ruling in New York Times v. Sullivan is the centerpiece of the American law of freedom of expression. The decision is not infrequently characterized as the most important free speech ruling in Supreme Court history. Not only has the Sullivan principle given far wider berth to the discussion of public affairs, it began the erosion of a categorical First Amendment jurisprudence that had the result of leaving many key forms of expression outside the First Amendment's purview. Not only libel, but commercial speech, offensive speech, profane speech, provocative utterances, and sexually explicit expression have received more protection in the past two decades as the result of the process that New York Times v. Sullivan initiated (see OBSCENITY AND PORNOGRAPHY).

And what of Brown v. Board of Education itself? The desegregation ruling unleashed, over the course of the next two decades, a cascade of previously unembraced civil liberties protections. They were unimaginable without Brown's earlier path clearing. An institution previously rendered silent by its battles with the *New Deal and the revelations of legal realism was effectively resurrected. During the Warren era, the judiciary's reemergence was accomplished primarily on behalf of egalitarianism. Substantially broadening the participatory base of our democracy, the Warren Court shook the dust from old tools of judicial activism in an effort to realize more fully the goal of equal dignity for all. The result, in no small degree, was the development of an institution that views its primary responsibility as the protection of individual liberties against majority intrusion.

(See also HISTORY OF THE COURT: RIGHTS CONSCIOUSNESS IN CONTEMPORARY SOCIETY; RACE AND RACISM.)

☐ Catherine A. Barnes, Journey from Jim Crow (1983). Derrick A. Bell, Race, Racism and American Law (1980). Robert L. Carter, "The Warren Court and Desegregation," Michigan Law Review 67 (1968): 237–248. Jack Greenberg, "The Supreme Court, Civil Rights, and Civil Dissonance," Yale Law Journal 77 (1968): 1520–1544. Martin Luther King, Stride Towards Freedom (1958).
Gene R. Nichol

**Civil War.** Constitutional history of the Civil War period underscores the principal characteristics of the Supreme Court as a coordinate branch of government in the context of nineteenth-century political culture. As the war signaled the end of three decades of Democratic rule and the start of a long period of Republican dominance, so it marked the transition from the *state sovereignty doctrines of the Taney Court to the constitutional nationalism of the Chase Court. The process of change that accelerated these political and jurisprudential trends was dramatically illustrated in the withdrawal from the federal government of southern members of Congress and the resignation from the Supreme Court of Justice John A. *Campbell of Alabama.

Changes in the membership of the Supreme Court at the start of the Civil War permitted the effects of the political realignment that put Abraham *Lincoln in the White House to be registered in constitutional law more rapidly than is usually the case following critical elections in American political history. Problems arising from the war encouraged the Court to refrain from judicial activist policy-making at the expense of the political branches. Military exigencies caused most of the major constitutional questions that arose to be resolved by the executive and Congress and induced in the justices a more deferential attitude toward political officers than might otherwise have prevailed (see WAR).

Three vacancies existed on the Supreme Court at the start of President Abraham Lincoln's administration. Justice Peter V. *Daniel died in 1860 and President James Buchanan's nomination of a Democratic successor was blocked by Republicans in the Senate in February 1861. Justice John *McLean died on 4 April 1861, and on 25 April Justice Campbell resigned. Lincoln appointed Noah H. *Swayne, an Ohio Republican, in January 1862, Republican Samuel F. *Miller of Iowa in July, and Illinois Republican David *Davis, a state judge, in October. When Congress created a tenth judicial circuit (thereby increasing the size of the Court to ten justices) in 1863, Lincoln named Stephen J. *Field of California, a Democrat and ardent Unionist, to the high bench. These appointments produced a more politically balanced Court, consisting of six antebellum Democrats (Samuel *Nelson, Nathan *Clifford, James

M. *Wayne, Robert C. *Grier, John *Catron, and Roger B. *Taney), and four wartime appointees sympathetic to the Republican administration. The composition of the Court remained stable until Chief Justice Taney died in October 1864 and was replaced by Salmon P. *Chase, secretary of the treasury under Lincoln.

The war raised constitutional questions that were inappropriate for judicial resolution because of their military and political nature. Confiscation, emancipation, taxation and fiscal policy, *conscription, and treason were among these issues. Yet the judiciary's traditional concern for individual liberty and *property rights provided the basis for limited Supreme Court involvement in matters relating to internal security policy and to the politically sensitive question of the legal nature of the war.

President Lincoln's suspension of the privilege of the writ of *habeas corpus in April 1861 presented an issue of government infringement of civil liberties that could reasonably be brought before the judicary. The executive and Congress provided for the nation's internal security without benefit of any Supreme Court opinion on the constitutionality of the measures adopted. Before the government's policy was put in place, however, Chief Justice Taney attempted to control the actions of the executive branch by invalidating Lincoln's suspension of the writ of habeas corpus. Taney questioned the president's action in Ex parte Merryman in May 1861.

John Merryman was a pro-Confederate Maryland political leader, who was arrested under authority of Lincoln's suspension of habeas corpus in May 1861 for participating in the destruction of railroad bridges. He petitioned Chief Justice Taney, presiding judge of the circuit court at Baltimore, for a writ of habeas corpus. Taney issued the writ, but the military commander to whom it was addressed refused to produce Merryman. The chief justice then issued a writ of attachment ordering the military commander to be apprehended. He was again rebuffed. Holding a session at chambers as chief justice of the U.S. Supreme Court (rather than presiding over a session of the circuit court), Taney on 28 May 1861 declared Merryman entitled to his freedom. In an unusual move, he filed an opinion condemning Merryman's arrest as an arbitrary and illegal denial of civil liberty (see MILITARY TRIALS AND MARTIAL LAW).

Taney stated that military detention of civilians like Merryman was unconstitutional because only Congress had authority to suspend the writ of habeas corpus. He based this conclusion on the fact that the provision authorizing suspension of the writ appears in Article I of the Constitution, dealing with the powers of the legislative branch. In a broader constitutional analysis, Taney described the president as a mere administrative officer charged with faithful enforcement of the laws. According to the chief justice, this

amounted to a constitutional duty not to execute the laws on the president's own authority or initiative, but rather to act in support of the judicial authority by executing the laws "as they are expounded and adjudged by the co-ordinate branch of the government, to which that duty is assigned by the Constitution." Taney sent a copy of his opinion to Lincoln, who in his 4 July 1861 message to Congress justified his action suspending the writ of habeas corpus on the basis of his constitutional oath to take care that the laws be faithfully executed. The president reasoned further that the Constitution did not expressly state who can order suspension of the writ and that the framers did not intend that in an emergency no action should be taken to protect the public safety by suspending habeas corpus until Congress could be assembled. Lincoln prevailed in the contest with Taney.

The Supreme Court at other times deferred to the government's internal security policy, even when executive action exceeded habeas corpus suspension, as in Ex parte Vallandigham in 1864. In April 1863, General Ambrose Burnside issued an order prohibiting in the area of his command any declarations of sympathy for the enemy. He also declared that persons who helped the enemy would be tried under military authority. Former Democratic representative Clement L. Vallandigham condemned the order and urged resistance to it. He was arrested, tried, and convicted by a military commission. Burnside imposed a prison sentence, which President Lincoln commuted into banishment beyond Confederate lines. Removing to Canada, Vallandigham petitioned a federal circuit court in Ohio for a writ of habeas corpus, but since he was no longer in custody, no basis existed for Supreme Court review of the lower court's denial of the petition. Vallandigham then applied to the Supreme Court for a writ of *certiorari to review directly the decision of the military commission.

With Chief Justice Taney not participating in the case, the Court denied the petition for certiorari. Justice Wayne's opinion for a unanimous Court asserted that the Court lacked jurisdiction under the *Judiciary Act of 1789, because a military commission was not a court whose decisions could be reviewed by the Supreme Court. He noted that the Constitution defined the *original jurisdiction of the Court in a way that precluded review of the case. Although the disposition of the case was favorable to the government, the Court did not reach the issue of the constitutionality of military trial of civilians in circumstances like those surrounding the arrest of Vallandigham.

While generally refraining from decisions having an impact on military or war-related policies, the Supreme Court handed down a major decision determining the legal nature of the conflict. This question was presented in the *Prize Cases (1863), where the issue was the legality of the navy's capture of ships bound for Confederate ports under the blockade ordered by President Lincoln in April 1861. If a state of war recognized by international law existed, the blockade was legal and the captures legitimate. If a war did not exist when the executive imposed the blockade, the captures were illegal. In March 1863, the Supreme Court decided 5 to 4 that the blockade was legal. According to Justice Grier's majority opinion, a state of war existed in April 1861 that justified resort to a blockade. Grier wrote that although the conflict began as an insurrection against the federal government and without a formal declaration, it was nonetheless a war—a civil war. He observed that the Civil War was a fact of which the Supreme Court was bound to take notice. Turning to the Constitution, he pointed out that although neither Congress nor the executive could declare war on a state, the president was authorized by statutes of 1795 and 1807 to call out the militia and use military force to suppress insurrection against the United States. Grier stated that it was for the president as commander in chief to decide whether in suppressing an insurrection it was justifiable to treat the opponents as belligerents (see PRESIDENTIAL EMERGENCY POWERS). He furthermore contended that the Supreme Court must be governed by the president's decision. Grier concluded that the proclamation of the blockade was evidence that a state of war existed.

The *Prize Cases* recognized broad executive power to respond to military attack on the United States. Of more immediate practical import was the Court's holding that persons in the seceded states could be treated both as rebels and enemies, or as a belligerent party. The Court did not, however, acknowledge or confer executive authority unilaterally to declare and carry on a war indefinitely without legislative approval.

Justice Nelson wrote a *dissenting opinion joined by Justices Clifford, Catron, and Taney. Nelson argued that war did not exist when Lincoln ordered the blockade because Congress had not exercised its exclusive power to declare war. He said that whether war existed was a legal question unaffected by material facts and realities. When Congress on 13 July 1861 authorized the executive to declare the existence of a state of insurrection, war began and the blockade was legal. Before that date the conduct of hostilities by the United States was a "personal war" of President Lincoln.

During the Civil War the Supreme Court decided many nonmilitary questions. California land disputes arising out of Mexican rule were prominent on its docket, as well as cases dealing with contracts, partnership, bankruptcy, usury, patent rights, and other commercial matters. A few cases illustrated continuity with earlier trends in constitutional law, despite changes in the Court's membership.

In *Gelpcke* v. *Dubuque* (1864), the Court over-

ruled an Iowa supreme court decision holding that a city's nonpayment of municipal bonds, issued for a railroad that was never built, was constitutional under the state constitution. Although not expressly stated, the effective basis of the Court's decision seemed to be the *Contract Clause of the Constitution. The case also may have illustrated the Court's belief that it could shape a *federal common law of commerce, as in *Swift* v. *Tyson* (1842).

The Supreme Court also ruled against state power in *People ex rel. Bank of Commerce* v. *Commissioner of Taxes* (1863). In this case the Court considered a New York tax on bank stock, including federal government securities that were otherwise exempt from *state taxation. Although Congress in 1862 passed an act declaring stocks, bonds, and other U.S. securities exempt from state taxes, the Court struck down the state tax on constitutional grounds. Yet the Court declined to decide the constitutionality of the Legal Tender Act of 1862. In *Roosevelt* v. *Meyer* (1863), it inexplicably held that it lacked jurisdiction to review a New York state court ruling favorable to the Legal Tender Act. It is not clear whether this decision, which was overruled in 1872, reflected unwillingness to tackle the controversial issue of national currency policy or was instead a flawed legal analysis of the Judiciary Act of 1789. (See LEGAL TENDER CASES.)

The December 1864 term of the Supreme Court marked the end of the Taney era. While Congress debated and rejected a proposal to place a marble bust of the late Chief Justice Taney in the Supreme Court room in the Capitol, the Court under Chief Justice Chase disposed of a series of cases involving the illegal slave trade. In February 1865, John S. Rock was sworn in as the first African-American attorney to be admitted to the bar of the Supreme Court. This event signified the emergence of racial equality as a major constitutional issue in the judicial history of the *Reconstruction period that would soon engage the Court's attention.

(See also HISTORY OF THE COURT: ESTABLISHMENT OF THE UNION.)

□ David P. Currie, *The Constitution in the Supreme Court: The First Hundred Years 1789–1888* (1985). David M. Silver, *Lincoln's Supreme Court* (1956). Carl B. Swisher, *History of the Supreme Court of the United States*, vol. 5, *The Taney Period 1836–64* (1974). Charles Warren, *The Supreme Court in United States History*, 2 vols. (1926).

Herman Belz

**Clark, Tom Campbell** (b. Dallas, Tex., 23 Sep. 1899; d. New York City, N.Y. 13 June 1977; interred Restland Memorial Park, Dallas), associate justice, 1949–1967. Tom Clark grew up in Dallas, Texas, in a family of lawyers. After military service in World War I, Clark graduated from the University of Texas in 1921 and its law school in 1922. He and a brother worked in his

*Tom Campbell Clark*

father's law firm for a few years; subsequently, he was appointed civil district attorney of Dallas.

Clark's career shifted from Texas to Washington, when he joined the Justice Department in 1937 as a special assistant. During World War II he briefly coordinated the Japanese-American relocation; later, he headed the Anti-Trust and Criminal Divisions. In 1945 shortly after Franklin D. *Roosevelt's death, President Harry Truman appointed him attorney general. Clark's unusual rise through the ranks of the Justice Department was aided by the sponsorship of Texas politicians and by his own political support for Harry Truman's contested vice-presidential candidacy in 1944.

On the death of Justice Frank *Murphy in July 1949, Truman nominated Tom Clark to replace him. His nomination was widely expected, but not so widely applauded. Charges of cronyism from the press and criticism of his zeal for national security from civil liberties groups helped fuel three days of Senate debate prior to his confirmation by a vote of 73 to 8.

Clark's years on the Supreme Court were marked by independence, the authorship of key opinions in criminal justice and *religion cases, and a growing interest and involvement in the improved administration of justice. His political independence was put to the test relatively soon after appointment; in 1952, he was one of six justices in *Youngstown Sheet and Tube Co. v. Sawyer (1952) to strike down President Truman's seizure of the nation's steel mills during the Korean War, provoking derisive and bitter reaction from Truman. He also showed ideological independence, floating between the Court's conservative and liberal blocs. Though Clark regularly and vigorously sided with the government in loyalty and national security cases (prompting historian Richard Kirkendall to view him as a cold war zealot on the bench), he also authored opinions of the Court in leading cases restricting the power of government.

In *Mapp v. Ohio (1961), Clark wrote his most significant opinion: a controversial decision prohibiting, in state criminal trials, the use of evidence obtained through unreasonable search and seizure. This *exclusionary rule still stands today (see FOURTH AMENDMENT). Clark also penned key decisions in religion cases, including *Abington School District v. Schempp (1963), which banned recitation of the Lord's prayer and Bible reading in public schools, and U.S. v. Seeger (1965), a Vietnam-era case that broadened the opportunity for young men to attain *conscientious objector status based upon religious belief. In Mapp and Schempp, Clark crafted majority opinions for a nonunanimous, highly divided Court.

In later years Clark became a champion for judicial reform. He was a tireless writer and public speaker who worked with legal organizations to stimulate improvements in court procedures, rule making, and in-service judicial education. He continued this work after his retirement from the Court, helping to establish the Federal Judicial Center and serving as its first director.

The public career of Tom Campbell Clark spanned more than forty years, highlighted by his eighteen years on the Supreme Court. He was the most successful of President Truman's four Court appointees and, though frequently characterized as an "average" justice, Clark left a substantial legacy.

□ Richard Kirkendall, "Tom C. Clark," in The Justices of the United States Supreme Court 1789–1969, edited by Leon Friedman and Fred L. Israel, vol. 4 (1969), pp. 2665–2695. Alvin T. Warnock, Associate Justice Tom C. Clark: Advocate of Judicial Reform (Ph.D. diss., 1972).

John Paul Ryan

### Clark Distilling Co. v. Western Maryland Railway Co.,

242 U.S. 311 (1917), argued 10–11 May 1915, ordered for reargument 1 Nov. 1915, reargued 8–9 Nov. 1916, decided 8 Jan. 1917 by vote of 7 to 2; White for the Court, Holmes and Van Devanter in dissent. Responding to Anti-Saloon League complaints that it was impossible to enforce state prohibition laws in the face of a flood of interstate liquor shipments, Congress in February 1913 enacted the Webb-Kenyon Act forbidding the shipment of intoxicating liquor into a state in violation of its laws. President William H. *Taft vetoed the act as unconstitutional, on the basis of a series of Court rulings that the Commerce Clause required common carriers to accept interstate shipments of liquor as not subject to state law until after received by the consignee. Congress immediately overrode Taft's

veto, and shortly West Virginia obtained an *injunction against the Western Maryland Railway and the Adams Express Companies to prevent them from carrying liquor into West Virginia in violation of its law against manufacture, sale, or possession of intoxicating liquors. The Clark Distilling Company sued Western and Adams to compel the carriers to accept shipments of liquor that had been ordered for personal use, which was not explicitly forbidden, and deliver them in West Virginia.

Anti-Saloon League general counsel Wayne Wheeler defended the Webb-Kenyon law before the Supreme Court because the Justice Department declined to do so. The Court held that while the unquestionable power of the government to regulate interstate commerce in intoxicating liquors did not have to be fully or uniformly exercised, it did extend to prohibiting interstate commerce in violation of state law. This validation of the Webb-Kenyon Law bolstered temperance forces on the eve of the 1917 congressional battle over adoption of the *Eighteenth Amendment.

(See also COMMERCE POWER; STATE SOVEREIGNTY AND STATES' RIGHTS.)

David E. Kyvig

*John Hessin Clarke*

**Clarke, John Hessin** (b. New Lisbon, Oh., 18 Sep. 1857; d. San Diego, Ca., 22 Mar. 1945; interred Lisbon Cemetery, Lisbon, Oh.), associate justice, 1916–1922. John Hessin Clarke was the only son of John and Melissa Hessin Clarke, both Irish Protestants. After attending local schools and graduating from Western Reserve College in 1877, Clarke studied law with his father, passed the Ohio bar examinations with honors, and began to practice law in his hometown in 1878. Clarke soon moved to Youngstown, where he gained renown as a trial lawyer and as part owner of the *Youngstown Vindicator*. He never married. He moved to Cleveland in 1897 and became counsel to railroads and other corporate clients. Clarke joined the reformers around Cleveland Mayor Tom L. Johnson but clashed with Johnson about taxes on railroad property and other reforms affecting his clients.

By 1903, Clarke had become a mainstream Democratic progressive and twice unsuccessfully sought a U.S. Senate seat from Ohio. He advocated direct election of senators, home rule for cities, municipal ownership of railways, and disclosure of campaign expenditures. In 1914, Clarke received the endorsement of reform Democrats for a third Senate campaign but instead accepted Woodrow Wilson's appointment as a federal district judge in the Northern District of Ohio. Clarke's friend Newton D. Baker in July 1916 helped convince Wilson to appoint Clarke to the Court when Charles Evans *Hughes resigned to run for president.

Former president William Howard *Taft joined conservative newspapers in attacking the appointments of Louis D. *Brandeis and *Clarke in 1916, claiming the pair represented a new school of constitutional construction that threatened the nation's legal fabric. When Taft joined Brandeis and Clarke as chief justice in 1921, however, their relationships were quite cordial. Yet James *McReynolds, whose animosity toward Brandeis is well known, was so nasty to Clarke that his attitude helped prompt Clarke's resignation. McReynolds refused to sign the official letter expressing regret at Clarke's departure.

During his time on the Court, Clarke voted consistently as a Wilson Progressive and usually sided with Brandeis. Yet Clarke went further than Brandeis in supporting legislative power. Clarke wrote the majority opinion in *Abrams* v. *United States* (1919), upholding the conviction and lengthy prison sentences of six agitators under the *Espionage Act of 1918. His dissents in *Hammer* v. *Dagenhart* (1918) and *Bailey* v. *Drexel Furniture Co.* (1922) affirmed respectively that congressional power was broad enough to reach child labor through either the Commerce Clause or the taxing power. Clarke's respect for legislative enactments extended to the states' *police power and to vigorous federal *antitrust enforcement.

Clarke is remembered primarily for his resignation from the Court. (See RESIGNATION AND RETIREMENT.) He had served for five terms and was in good physical health at the age of sixty-five when he announced in 1922 that he had decided to devote himself to seeking America's entry into the League of Nations. As with Arthur *Goldberg's decision to resign in 1965, Clarke found that his quest for world peace only led to his own relative obscurity. By 1927, Clarke realized that the United States would not enter the League of Nations, and he retired from public life, although he reemerged briefly to back Franklin D. *Roosevelt's *court-packing scheme in 1937.

□ David M. Levitan, "The Jurisprudence of Mr. Justice Clarke," *Miami Law Quarterly* 7 (December 1952): 44–72.
                                        Aviam Soifer

**Class Actions.** The class action has developed in the twentieth century as a way of managing complex, multiparty litigation. It may be traced to the "bill of peace," a proceeding that originated in England's equity courts in the seventeenth century. The bill of peace was used when the parties to a dispute were too numerous to be easily managed and when all parties shared a common interest in the issues. It permitted the case to be tried by representative parties, with the judgment rendered binding all. This was more efficient than trying each case individually and was more consistent with equity's goal of doing complete justice (see INJUNCTIONS AND EQUITABLE REMEDIES).

American courts continued to use the bill of peace. Its most eloquent spokesman was Justice Joseph *Story. In his *Equity Jurisprudence* (1836) and his *Equity Pleadings* (1838), Story stated that the purpose of the bill of peace was to promote finality. Law courts could only try issues between the plaintiff and the defendant in a particular case. Equity courts possessed a "power to bring all the parties before them, . . . at once to proceed to the ascertainment of the general right, . . . and then to make a decree finally binding upon all the parties." The bill of peace provided a way to resolve multiparty disputes quickly and effectively.

The effectiveness of the bill of peace and the class action that evolved from it was limited in two ways. First, the procedure applied only in equity cases. To remedy that, it was broadened in 1938 by adoption of rule 23 of the Federal Rules of Civil Procedure to include all cases in law as well as equity. Second, some doubt was expressed in early federal cases whether a judgment could bind unnamed parties. This uncertainty remained until 1966, when rule 23 was amended to make it clear that unnamed parties were bound.

Modern rules have defined three kinds of class actions. The first is appropriate where separate litigation might adversely affect members of the class or the defendant in one of two ways. First, the defendant might have inconsistent standards of conduct imposed in piecemeal litigation. Second, multiple suits might "impair or impede" the class members (usually plaintiffs) from protecting their various interests. In the second kind of class action, a class seeks an injunction or some form of declaratory relief. In the third category, a class action is available where questions common

to the class predominate over questions peculiar to each plaintiff, and a class action is superior to other proceedings as a means of resolving the controversy among the parties. For this third variety of class action only, rule 23 permits individual members of the class to opt out of litigation if they do not wish to be bound by the results of the class action.

Class actions have become commonplace today, especially as a vehicle for social and economic reform. Many of the leading civil rights cases, for example, were commenced by class action. The class action is also used to promote consumer protection. It is frequently used in *antitrust cases and to combat consumer fraud, price fixing, and other commercial abuses. It is also widely utilized in mass *tort cases, where numerous plaintiffs are injured at the hands of a single defendant. The Dalkon Shield, Agent Orange, and asbestos cases are prominent examples.

□ Stephen Yeazell, *From Medieval Group Litigation to the Modern Class Action* (1987).          James B. Stoneking

**Classic, United States v.,** 313 U.S. 299 (1941), argued 7 Apr. 1941, decided 26 May 1941 by vote of 5 to 3; Stone for the Court, Douglas in dissent. Two Supreme Court decisions before *World War II allowed white Democrats in the one-party South to disfranchise black citizens by denying them primary ballots. *Newberry v. United States* (1921) concluded that Congress lacked power under Article I, section 4 of the Constitution to regulate party primaries. *Grovey v. Townsend* (1935) held that a state party convention's exclusion of African-Americans from primary participation constituted private rather than *state action and, therefore, the *Fourteenth and *Fifteenth Amendments did not apply.

The newly created Civil Rights Division of the Justice Department brought this successful test case establishing federal authority to redress corruption and discrimination in the state electoral process. The government charged the Louisiana election commissioners with willfully altering and falsely counting congressional primary election ballots in violation of federal civil rights statutes.

The Supreme Court overruled *Newberry* to hold that Congress's power under Article I, section 4 to regulate "elections" includes the power to regulate primaries when state law makes the primary an integral part of the procedure for choosing candidates for federal office. The Court also reasoned that Article I, section 2 guarantees citizens the right to *vote in congressional primaries and to have their votes properly counted; moreover, this right is protected against interference by individual as well as state action. While *Grovey* was not mentioned, the reasoning in *Classic* undercut the rationale of that decision to make inevitable its overruling in *Smith v. Allwright* (1944), which held that primary elections for either federal or state office were subject to the Constitution.

(See also RACE AND RACISM; WHITE PRIMARY.)

Thomas E. Baker

**Clear and Present Danger Test.** The words "clear and present danger," first used as a casual phrase by Justice Oliver Wendell *Holmes, became an important test for determining whether speech is protected by the *First Amendment. Holmes introduced this phrase in *Schenck v. United States, a 1919 opinion for a unanimous Court upholding against First Amendment challenges the convictions of socialists who had distributed antiwar circulars to men accepted for military service in *World War I. In explaining why the defendants could constitutionally be punished for violating the prohibition in the 1917 *Espionage Act against obstruction of recruitment, Holmes wrote, "The question in every case is whether the words used are used in such circumstances and are of such a nature as to create a clear and present danger that they will bring about the substantive evils that Congress has a right to prevent" (p. 52). Relying on the prevailing *bad tendency test he himself had applied in previous cases involving speech, Holmes reasoned that in the circumstances of war these circulars had a tendency to obstruct recruitment. In *Frohwerk v. United States* and *Debs v. United States,* two companion unanimous decisions that also invoked the bad tendency of antiwar speech in affirming convictions under the Espionage Act, Holmes did not mention clear and present danger.

Even though Holmes used the phrase clear and present danger only in *Schenck* and relied on the bad tendency test in all three opinions, Zechariah *Chafee, Jr., then a young professor at Harvard Law School, soon wrote a law review article claiming that Holmes intended the clear and present danger test to make "the punishment of words for their bad tendency impossible." As Justices Holmes and Louis *Brandeis rapidly became more sensitive to the value of free speech during the "Red Scare" following the war, they found it useful to rely on Chafee's misconstruction of clear and present danger in *Schenck* to express their developing views without repudiating their prior decisions. From the dissent by Holmes in *Abrams v. United States* (1919) through the concurrence by Brandeis in *Whitney v. California* (1927), Holmes and Brandeis elaborated the meaning of clear and present danger in ways that transformed it into a First Amendment test providing substantial protection for dissident speech. Most significantly, they infused an immediacy requirement into the clear and present danger test that precluded punishment of speech unless imminently threatened an illegal act. Brandeis's concurrence in *Whitney*, moreover, belatedly responded to the majority's assertion in *Gitlow v. New York* (1925) that both the bad tendency test and the clear and present danger variant apply only "in those cases where the statute merely

prohibits certain acts involving the danger of substantive evil, without any reference to language itself" (p. 670). A statute that itself defines speech as criminal, Brandeis insisted in *Whitney,* is also subject to *judicial review under the clear and present danger test.

The Supreme Court majority continued throughout the 1920s to apply the traditional bad tendency test and did not refer to clear and present danger when it first overturned convictions on First Amendment grounds in the early 1930s. From the late 1930s to the early 1950s, many majority decisions did rely on the clear and present test previously developed by Holmes and Brandeis to protect speech in a wide variety of contexts, and the Court never referred to clear and present danger in decisions that denied First Amendment claims. Yet at the height of cold war fear about a communist conspiracy, the Court in *Dennis v. United States* (1951) removed the immediacy requirement and accepted Judge Learned *Hand's reformulation of the clear and present danger test: "whether the gravity of the 'evil,' discounted by its improbability, justifies such invasion of free speech as is necessary to avoid the danger" (p. 510). Applying this new standard, the Court upheld the convictions of eleven Communist party leaders for conspiring to advocate the violent overthrow of government (see COMMUNISM AND COLD WAR).

Since the *Dennis* decision, the Supreme Court has largely ignored but has not entirely abandoned the clear and present danger test while developing different doctrines to analyze a proliferating range of First Amendment issues. The clear and present danger test may have resurfaced in the Court's 1969 *per curiam opinion in *Brandenburg v. Ohio,* which reversed the conviction of a Ku Klux Klan leader under a state statute prohibiting the advocacy of *criminal syndicalism. In an abrupt holding accompanied by scant and unconvincing analysis of prior decisions, the Court declared that "the constitutional guarantees of free speech and free press do not permit a State to forbid or proscribe advocacy of the use of force or of law violation except where such advocacy is directed to inciting or producing imminent lawless action and is likely to incite or produce such action" (p. 447). Several scholars have interpreted this passage, although it does not contain the phrase clear and present danger, as combining the immediacy requirement derived from the Holmes-Brandeis opinions with a further requirement that speech constitute an incitement to illegal action. The Court has not subsequently elaborated its analysis in *Brandenberg* and has applied it only infrequently, leaving its meaning uncertain, particularly in contexts other than subversive advocacy.

(See also SPEECH AND THE PRESS.)

□ David M. Rabban, "The Emergence of Modern First Amendment Doctrine." *University of Chicago Law Review* 50 (Fall 1983): 1205–1355.            David M. Rabban

**Clerk, Office of the.** The *Clerk of the Court is responsible for the Court's administrative business. The office was established by the Court's first formal rule in February 1790. To date, only nineteen clerks have served the Court.

The first clerk, John Tucker, was responsible for the Court's library, courtroom, employees, salaries, and the justices' lodgings. The current clerk, William K. Suter (1991–), manages the Court's dockets and calendars; receives, records, and distributes all case motions and documents; advises counsel on Court rules and procedures and supervises a large staff. A computer system was installed in 1975 to help carry out the clerk's many duties.

(See also BUREAUCRATIZATION OF THE COURT; STAFF OF THE COURT, NONJUDICIAL.)

Martha Swann

**Clerks of the Court.** The clerk of the Court, one of the Supreme Court's four statutory officers, is responsible for the day-to-day administrative management of the Court's caseload. Since the office was established by the Court's first formal rule, on 2 February 1790, only nineteen individuals have served as clerk of the Court.

The first clerk, John Tucker, was selected during the Court's first session and given responsibility for the Court's library, courtroom, and employees, as well as for collecting justices' salaries and finding local lodgings for the justices. Many of the clerk's early duties were later taken over by the court *reporter, the *marshal of the Court, and, more recently, by the *administrative assistant to the chief justice.

Four of the following nineteen individuals to serve as clerk of the Court held that position for more than twenty-five years: John Tucker (1790–1791); Samuel Bayard (1791–1800); Elias B. Caldwell (1800–1825); William Griffith (1826–1827); William T. Carroll (1827–1863); D. W. Middleton (1863–1880); J. H. McKenney (1880–1913); James D. Maher (1913–1921); William R. Stansbury (1921–1927); C. Elmore Cropley (1927–1952); Harold B. Willey (1952–1956); John T. Fey (1956–1958); James R. Browning (1958–1961); John F. Davis (1961–1970); E. Robert Seaver (1970–1972); Michael Rodak, Jr. (1972–1981); Alexander Stevas (1981–1985); Joseph F. Spaniol, Jr. (1985–1991); and William K. Suter (1991–).

Over the two centuries since the first clerk was selected, the clerk's duties have greatly expanded to include maintaining the Court's dockets and calendars; receiving, recording, and distributing to the justices all motions, petitions, statements and *briefs filed in all cases; collecting all filing fees; preparing and maintaining the *order list and journal (which contain all the Court's formal judgments and mandates); preparing the Court's formal judgments and mandates; handling the preparation of all *in forma pauperis briefs; obtaining certified case records from *lower federal courts; supervising the Supreme Court bar (including the admission and disbarment of attorneys who wish to practice before the Court); and providing procedural advice to any counsel or litigants who need assistance in complying with the Court's rules.

The clerk often works closely with other Court personnel to carry out the Court's business. The clerk participates in monthly meetings with the other officers of the Supreme Court to discuss current Court business under the direction of the administrative assistant. Along with the marshal, the clerk participates in the Court's formal opening ceremonies before oral arguments begin. After the justices have made their decisions and the Court's written opinions are printed, a final copy goes to the clerk for safekeeping and to the reporter of decisions. When case decisions are announced by the Court, the clerk's office notifies the information officer, who then distributes copies of each new opinion to the press.

The clerk and his assistant, the chief deputy clerk, currently have a twenty-six member staff to help handle the ever-increasing paperwork; prepare the Court's calendars; and check, record, and sort all the incoming cases for review. Of the over 5,100 annual cases the clerk's office is currently processing, only 150 to 180 are accepted for oral arguments.

In spite of the computer system installed in 1975 to help monitor the clerk's records, every motion and thousands of briefs must still be entered and processed by hand. The Office of the Clerk operates a word-processing and data-management system, which is programmed and maintained by the relatively new Data System Office. The justices' chambers have a separate computer network for opinion-writing tasks, one that now produces a camera-ready document (see COMPUTER ROOM).

The clerk's office was entirely self-supporting during its first hundred years. The clerk's salary and those of his assistants, as well as all operating expenses, were paid out of the filing fees the office collected. From 1800 to 1883, the clerks were paid considerably more than the justices. In 1883, Congress required the Court to be strictly accountable for its funds. Filing fees, docket fees, and administrative fees are collected by the clerk's office and go into the U.S. General Treasury Fund. The salaries of all Court personnel, as well as the Court's expenses, are now appropriated by Congress. In 1988, the salary of the clerk was set at $75,000.

(See also CLERK, OFFICE OF THE; STAFF OF THE COURT, NONJUDICIAL.)

Martha Swann

**Clerks of the Justices** are the justices' personal assistants and among the most important of the Supreme Court's support staff. The law-clerking institution began in 1882, when Justice Horace *Gray hired a recent Harvard Law School graduate. Gray had begun hiring clerks when he was chief justice of the Massachusetts Supreme Court in 1875, and he continued this practice at the U.S.

Supreme Court, where he paid their salaries himself. The 1922 Appropriation Act allowed each justice to employ one clerk at an annual salary of up to $3,600, and in 1924 Congress made law clerk positions at the Court permanent.

Gray's half-brother, John Chipman Gray, a Harvard Law School professor, initially selected Harvard honor graduates for one-year terms at the Court, working with Justice Gray and his successor, Oliver Wendell *Holmes. When John Chipman Gray retired, Felix *Frankfurter provided Holmes with Harvard graduates. Gradually, other justices adopted the practice. Justice Louis D. *Brandeis, like Gray, hired recent Harvard Law School graduates. Justice Harlan F. *Stone selected clerks from his alma mater, Columbia University Law School.

Selection processes varied between 1900 and 1945. Many justices hired students and recent graduates of law schools in Washington, D.C., occasionally retaining clerks for long periods of time. Justice Pierce *Butler employed one clerk from 1923 until 1939; Justice Owen J. *Roberts kept another clerk from 1930 to 1945. Sometimes older attorneys in Washington, D.C., law firms clerked for the Court. Occasionally the Justice Department selected clerks from among its younger employees with the understanding that they would return to the department when their tenure at the Court ended.

Justices often retained the law clerks of their predecessors or hired friends and family of other justices. When Charles Evan *Hughes replaced Chief Justice William H. *Taft, he retained Taft's law clerk and personal secretary. Chief Justice Melville W. *Fuller's first law clerk, James S. Harlan, who had read law in Fuller's Chicago law office from 1884 to 1888, was the son of Justice John Marshall *Harlan. Fuller also employed Justice William R. *Day's son, Stephen, as a clerk. Two of Day's sons clerked for their father. Harlan's first clerk was his son, John Maynard Harlan.

Some justices have expected their clerks to agree with them philosophically and to share their habits. Justice James C. *McReynolds frequently insisted that his clerks be single and not smoke or chew tobacco. McReynold's strong language and offensive behavior made it quite difficult for friends to find clerks willing to work for him.

As the Court's caseload increased, so did the number of law clerks. Today, each justice may have as many as seven assistants: four law clerks, two secretaries, and one messenger. Chief Justice William H. *Rehnquist and Justice John Paul *Stevens usually hire only three law clerks. Retired senior justices, like Warren *Burger and Lewis F. *Powell, may hire one secretary and one law clerk at government expense.

Justices have total control in selecting their clerks; each usually receives between 250 to 350 applications annually. While most law clerks work at the Court for only one year, many justices retain a clerk from the previous term to act as a "senior clerk" within the chambers. Not until the mid-1970s were women regularly selected: as of 1970, only three women had clerked at the Court; by 1986, that number had risen to seventy-one.

Most clerks have attended prestigious law schools (including Harvard, Yale, Stanford, New York University, the University of Virginia, and the University of Chicago), have graduated at the top of their class, and have clerked in a *lower federal court for at least one year. Upon leaving the court, many clerks work for large national law firms. Some move to the Justice Department, often working in the *solicitor general's office. Several former clerks have become law school professors. Thirty-two former clerks have become judges, including three who have become U.S. Supreme Court justices: William Rehnquist clerked for Robert H. *Jackson; John Paul Stevens clerked for Wiley B. *Rutledge, and Byron R. White clerked for Fred M. *Vinson.

Clerks' duties include reading, analyzing, and preparing memoranda for the justices (see, e.g., CERT POOL). After joining the Court in late summer, they assist justices in the two-stage case selection process through the fall. Clerks review case records, research questions of law, categorize essential information in all incoming cases, and summarize petitions. In ruling on cases to be selected for review, justices often rely on their clerks' summaries and recommendations. During the spring, after the Court has reached its decisions, clerks assist the justices in the preparation of written opinions.

In spite of the valuable assistance law clerks render the Court, their actions have not escaped criticism. The annual turnover of clerks leads to a lack of institutional memory at the Court. Chief Justice Burger created the Office of *Legal Counsel in 1973 to provide a measure of continuity for both the chief justice and the Court that the revolving-door law clerk system could not provide.

The law clerks undeniably contribute to the decision-making and opinion-writing process, but the extent of their contributions has been a matter of some debate by outsiders. Justices have often praised their clerks, but have also been quick to point out that they themselves, not the clerks, decide cases.

The clerks and their justices form close, personal relationships. Clerks naturally are privy to confidential information. Preserving the confidentially of the justices' working habits, personal opinions, and attitudes toward peers was an honored tradition—at least until the 1979 publication of The Brethren, by Bob Woodward and Scott Armstrong, a book about the Court based on interviews with former law clerks and other court personnel.

Because of their position, clerks have a uniquely "inside" view of the Court and the justices, as well as access to private information in opinion drafts, internal memoranda, and discussions. The clerks' duty to be discreet is not well defined, but the justices certainly expect them to uphold that duty. Regardless of the possible problems, the Court clearly could not manage its current caseload without the valuable assistance law clerks provide.          Martha Swann

**Clifford, Nathan** (b. Rumney, N.H., 18 Aug. 1803; d. Cornish, Maine, 25 July 1881; interred Evergreen Cemetery, Portland, Maine), associate justice, 1858–1881. Clifford is remembered for his role in *Hepburn* v. *Griswold* (1870), the decision that declared the Legal Tender Act unconstitutional (see LEGAL TENDER CASES). He should also be recognized, however, for his contributions to technical legal subjects. He edited an influential series of reports (cited by his name) that contained his opinions and those of other federal circuit judges.

Clifford's education was obtained by his own efforts, and his formal schooling was limited. He studied law under Josiah Quincy, a prominent New Hampshire lawyer, and he was admitted to the New Hampshire bar in May 1827. Soon after, he moved to Maine. In 1830 he was elected to the Maine legislature, where he served three two-year terms, the last as speaker of the House. A Democrat, he then served two terms in the U.S. House of Representatives. In 1846, after an interval of private law practice, Clifford was appointed U.S. attorney general by President James K. Polk. Polk later named him ambassador to Mexico. After Clifford had returned to Portland, Maine, to resume private law practice, President James Buchanan in 1857 nominated him to succeed Justice Benjamin R. *Curtis on the U.S. Supreme Court. His nomination to the Court was opposed by Republicans because of his southern sympathies, but the Senate narrowly confirmed him by a vote of 26 to 23.

Clifford wrote no major constitutional opinions during his tenure. On circuit, he held in *Collector* v. *Day* (1871) that the federal government could not tax the salary of a state officer—a decision later affirmed by the full Court (see TAX IMMUNITIES). His greatest constitutional decision was in *Loan Association* v. *Topeka* (1874), where he wrote the majority opinion holding that the Court could declare unconstitutional any statute of Congress on grounds other than a stated constitutional provision (see JUDICIAL REVIEW).

The opinion of Clifford's that caused the most controversy was *Johnson* v. *Dow* (1879), involving a judgment by default, rendered by the courts of Louisiana during the federal occupation against a military commander for the taking of property. After the war, the owner brought suit in the federal court of Maine against the former military commander, then a resident of Maine, based on the judgment of the Louisiana court. Under the federal practice of the time, an appeal to the Supreme

*Nathan Clifford*

Court required a split opinion of the two judges on the *circuit court. Clifford wrote the opinion supporting the validity of the judgment of the Louisiana court, which the Supreme Court reversed on the grounds that Louisiana was under military occupation when the decision was rendered (see MILITARY TRIALS AND MARTIAL LAW).

Clifford's other decisions involved technical subjects. His decision in *Leon* v. *Galceran* (1870) held that *admiralty jurisdiction was not exclusive where the *common law could provide a remedy—a decision of historic importance in that it helped to blur the distinction between the common law and admiralty. His opinion in *Lawrence* v. *Dana* (1869) was an important contribution to the law of *copyright infringement. Later scholars have described his opinions unflatteringly as "dreary" and "tedious," but he was usually concise and orderly in his legal arguments (see OPINIONS, STYLE OF). His contemporaries on the bench recognized his learning and his steady judicial temperament.

In 1877 Clifford chaired the electoral commission established to settle the disputed presidential election of 1876. He vigorously supported the Democratic aspirant, Samuel Tilden, but the commission ultimately decided in favor of the Republican, Rutherford B. Hayes (see EXTRAJUDICIAL ACTIVITIES). Clifford suffered a stroke in 1880, but he continued to attempt to perform his duties when it was clear to everyone except himself that he was unable to do so (see DISABILITY OF JUSTICES). He died in 1881.

□ Philip G. Clifford, *Nathan Clifford, Democrat* (1922).
                                          Erwin C. Surrency

**Coerced Confessions** by criminal suspects are generally regarded as inadmissible in court proceedings because of the privilege against compulsory self-incrimination included in the *Fifth Amendment. The adoption of this protection in the United States, first in the form of an evidentiary rule and eventually in a constitutional amendment, reflected the founding fathers' abhorrence of the use of torture. Through most of the nation's history, Supreme Court review of criminal convictions alleged to have been obtained by coerced confessions drew on *Fourteenth Amendment due process protections (see DUE PROCESS, PROCEDURAL). When the Supreme Court incorporated the Fifth Amendment privilege against self-incrimination and applied this provision to the states in 1964 (*Malloy v. Hogan), coerced confession claims were reviewed against that provision of the *Bill of Rights (see INCORPORATION DOCTRINE).

Prior to the *Malloy* decision and other cases in the Warren Court's "due process revolution," the Court relied on the voluntariness test in reviewing claims of coerced confessions. One of the earliest cases of this genre was *Brown v. Mississippi* (1936), where the Court presumed a confession involuntary because of the brutal treatment accorded the accused. In this case a law enforcement officer went to Brown's home and led him to the house of a murder victim. There Brown was hanged from a tree, though not until dead, and later tied to a tree and whipped severely. Several days later, Brown was arrested and beaten again until he eventually confessed to the murder in question. Concluding that "the rack and torture chamber may not be substituted for the witness stand," the Court ruled that physically coerced confessions violated that Due Process Clause of the Fourteenth Amendment (pp. 285–286).

Since that time the Court has moved beyond a concern with physical coercion and concluded that prolonged interrogation (*Ashcraft v. Tennessee*, 1944), threats (*Lynumm v. Illinois*, 1963), and deceit (*Spano v. New York*, 1959) also constitute coercion that may invalidate criminal confessions. The Court has also argued that delays in suspect appearances before judicial officers might also contribute to coerced confessions (*McNabb v. United States*, 1943; *Mallory v. United States*, 1957), although the so-called McNabb-Mallory rule was only applied to federal courts and was later overshadowed by the Court's decision in *Miranda v. Arizona* (1966).

In an effort to supplement the voluntariness test, the Court has advanced other means for insuring that defendant confessions are the result of "free and unconstrained choice" (*Culombe v. Connecticut*, 1961, p. 602). The most prominent is the Court's emphasis on right to *counsel. In a series of decisions in the 1960s the Supreme Court expressed dissatisfaction with the voluntariness test and its lingering ambiguity and replaced that standard with requirements that drew on Fifth and *Sixth Amendment protections. In *Massiah v. U.S.* (1964), for example, the Court argued that the right to counsel attaches once a person is formally charged or adversary proceedings initiated, while in *Escobedo v. Illinois* (1964), the Court concluded that that right applies even before judicial or adversarial processes have started. In the aforementioned *Miranda* decision (1966), the Court not only ruled that the privilege against compulsory self-incrimination applies to police interrogation but also specified that defendants were entitled to counsel in those situations.

Contrasting objectives underlie these Supreme Court decisions. The justices have ruled that coerced confessions can be excluded because they constitute unreliable evidence, restrain freedom of choice, or deter undesirable police conduct. These objectives are not all realized in a given case. For example, in *Ashcraft v. Tennessee* (1944), the six-justice majority apparently did not reject the confession because it was unreliable—evidence suggested that the defendant was in fact responsible for the offense—but because it thought that thirty-six hours of continous interrogation constituted unacceptable police conduct. Similarly, in *Miranda*, the Court explicitly reviewed the history of police misconduct in criminal interrogation and made no secret of its intention to advance a deterrent in the warnings requirement.

The tension that results from competing objectives is illustrated in *Arizona v. Fulminante* (1991). A five-justice majority concluded that coerced confessions can be regarded as "harmless error" and may not automatically invalidate a criminal conviction. Writing for the majority, Chief Justice Willian H. *Rehnquist argued that there is a difference between due process violations that are structurally defective and those that simply reflect trial error. Other evidence obtained independently of the confession can be used to sustain a conviction in which case the coerced confession is judged harmless beyond a reasonable doubt. The Supreme Court's decision in *Fulminante* overturned a 1967 decision, *Chapman v. California*, and constitutes something of a departure from the Court's longstanding reluctance to recognize the constitutional validity of coerced confessions.

(See also SELF-INCRIMINATION.)

Susette M. Talarico

**Cohens v. Virginia**, 6 Wheat. (19 U.S.) 264 (1821), argued 13 Feb. 1821, decided 3 Mar. 1821 by vote of 6 to 0; Marshall for the Court. Philip and Mendes Cohen sold lottery tickets in Virginia under the authority of an act of Congress for the District of Columbia. The Cohens appealed their conviction for violating the state statute, which had banned such lotteries. Virginia asserted that the *Eleventh Amendment precluded the Supreme Court from hearing the case and that section 25 of the *Judiciary Act of 1789 did not apply.

The *Cohens* case reflected the effort by several states, including Virginia, to challenge John *Marshall's opinion in *McCulloch* v. *Maryland* (1819). Marshall seized on *Cohens*, which some historians believed was contrived, to reemphasize federal judicial power. He asserted that the Constitution made the Union supreme and that the federal judiciary was the ultimate constitutional arbiter. While the states could interpret their own laws, any federal question must ultimately be resolved, as section 25 provided, only by the federal courts. The Eleventh Amendment did not prevent federal courts from deciding properly a legitimate federal question, even where a state was the appellee.

Marshall avoided Virginia noncompliance by holding that the lottery statute applied only in the District of Columbia, but Virginia states' rights advocates nonetheless blasted his judicial nationalism.

(See also JUDICIAL POWER AND JURISDICTION.)

Kermit L. Hall

**Cohen v. California,** 403 U.S. 15 (1971), argued 22 Feb. 1971, decided 7 June 1971 by vote of 5 to 4; Harlan for the Court, Blackmun in dissent, joined by Burger and Black, and White in part. In April 1968 Paul Robert Cohen wore a jacket bearing the words "Fuck the Draft" in a Los Angeles courthouse. He was arrested and subsequently convicted for violating a California statute prohibiting any person from "disturb[ing] the peace . . . by offensive conduct." The Supreme Court had to decide whether Cohen's speech was punishable because it fit one of the "exceptions" to free speech protected by the *First Amendment.

The Court conceded that Cohen's expletive was "vulgar," but it concluded that his speech was nonetheless protected by the First Amendment. It was neither an "incitement" to illegal action nor "obscenity." Nor did it constitute "fighting words" (personally abusive epithets), for it had not been directed at a person who was likely to retaliate or at someone who could not avoid the message. Therefore, the conviction could be justified only by the state's desire to preserve the cleanliness of discourse in the public sphere. The Court refused to permit the state such a broad power, holding that no objective distinctions can be made between vulgar and nonvulgar political speech, and that the emotive aspects of speech are often as important as the purely cognitive. "It is . . . often true," Justice Harlan wrote, "that one man's vulgarity is another's lyric . . . words [which] are often chosen as much for their emotive as their cognitive force" (pp. 25–26).

By expanding the constitutional foundation for protecting provocative and potentially offensive speech, *Cohen* has become a landmark decision.

(See also SPEECH AND THE PRESS; UNPROTECTED SPEECH.)

Donald A. Downs

**Cohen v. Cowles Media Co.,** 111 S.Ct. 2513 (1991), argued 27 Mar. 1991, decided 24 June 1991 by vote of 5 to 4; White for the Court, Blackmun and Souter in dissent. During the 1982 Minnesota gubernatorial race, Dan Cohen, a campaign adviser to the Republican candidate, leaked damaging information about the Democratic candidate to reporters from the Minneapolis and St. Paul newspapers after they promised not to identify him as their source. Editors at the two papers, over the objection of the reporters, broke the promise of confidentiality and identified Cohen. Cohen was fired from his job and he sued the papers for fraudulent misrepresenation and breach of contract.

A trial court awarded Cohen $200,000 in compensatory damages and $500,000 in punitive damages. The Minnesota Court of Appeals said Cohen failed to establish a fraud claim and reversed the punitive damages award. It upheld the finding of breach of contract and the compensatory damages award. But the Minnesota Supreme Court reversed the compensatory damages award, holding that enforcement of confidentiality under contract law would violate the newspapers' rights because identifying Cohen amounted to an editorial decision protected under the *First Amendment.

The Supreme Court reversed, holding that the First Amendment does not forbid the general application of Minnesota's contract law to the press even if it has incidental effects on news gathering and reporting. Justice Byron *White wrote that the newspapers' First Amendment claim was "constitutionally insignificant" and that contract law "requires those who make certain kinds of promises to keep them" (p. 2519). The Court directed the Minnesota Supreme Court to reconsider whether Cohen's claim could be upheld under an oral contract doctrine or if Minnesota's Constitution could be interpreted to shield the press from Cohen's claim.

Justices Harry *Blackmun and David *Souter dissented, saying the First Amendment prohibits the use of generally applicable laws to burden societal interest in truthful political speech without a compelling state interest. Souter argued separately that laws of general applicability "may restrict First Amendment rights just as effectively as those directed specifically at speech itself" (p. 2522).

The decision could be significant. Anonymous sources may dry up. In addition, shield law protection for reporters may be diminished because of the Court's position that confidentiality promises are a matter of contract law and not a First Amendment immunity to gather and report the news.

(See also SPEECH AND THE PRESS.)

Tim Gallimore

**Coker v. Georgia,** 433 U.S. 584 (1977), argued 28 Mar. 1977, decided 29 June 1977 by vote of 7 to 2;

White for the plurality, Brennan and Marshall concurring, Powell concurring in part and dissenting in part, Burger and Rehnquist in dissent. While serving sentences for murder, rape, kidnapping, and aggravated assault, Coker escaped from a Georiga prison and, while committing an armed robbery, raped a woman. He was convicted of these crimes and received the death sentence for rape. The jury, under Georgia's bifurcated trial procedure and following the statutory guidelines approved in *Gregg* v. *Georgia* (1976), found that two aggravating circumstances existed: the petitioner had prior capital felony convictions and the rape was committed in the course of committing another capital felony, armed robbery. The Georgia Supreme Court reviewed the sentence for comparability and affirmed it. The U.S. Supreme Court reversed.

Justice Byron *White's plurality opinion held that the *Eighth Amendment's proscription of *cruel and unusual punishments prohibited punishments that are grossly disproportionate to the crime. Such penalties are a purposeless and needless imposition of pain and suffering. White noted that Georgia was the only state to impose the death penalty for rape of an adult woman and that Georgia juries themselves rarely called for the death penalty in rape cases. White repeatedly emphasized that the death penalty, the deliberate taking of a human life, was proportional only to the crime of first degree murder. Justice Lewis *Powell concurred only to the extent that the crime was not committed with excessive brutality and that the victim did not sustain serious or lasting injury.

The result highlights the tensions inherent in *Gregg* and *Woodson* v. *North Carolina* (1976). If civilized standards require highly individualized sentencing, then the very reasons for rejecting mandatory sentencing should validate jury findings in some cases that certain persons with long histories of criminal behavior deserve the death sentence. Coker's record did not contradict such a finding in his case.

(See also CAPITAL PUNISHMENT.)

Lief H. Carter

**Cold War.** See COMMUNISM AND COLD WAR.

**Colegrove v. Green,** 328 U.S. 549 (1946), argued 7–8 Mar. 1946, decided 10 June 1946 by vote of 4 to 3; Frankfurter for the Court, Black in dissent, Jackson not participating (Stone's death left one vacancy). Qualified voters challenged the apportionment of congressional districts in Illinois as lacking appropriate compactness and equality. A three-judge district court dismissed the case and Justices Felix *Frankfurter, Stanley *Reed, and Harold *Burton affirmed that action. These justices branded apportionment a political question and reasoned that invalidation of Illinois districts might, in requiring statewide elections, create an evil greater than that remedied. Such party contests should be resolved by the state legislature subject to congressional supervision. Justice Wiley B. *Rutledge concurred in the result, convinced that the short time between a judicial judgment and the impending election made an equitable remedy difficult. Justice Hugo *Black, joined by William *Douglas and Frank *Murphy, believed the failure to reapportion the Illinois districts since 1901 denied the *equal protection of the laws and of the guarantee in Article I of the right to *vote for congressional representatives.

Weakened by the close division of the justices and by the continuing inaction of state legislatures, the Court declared in *Baker* v. *Carr* (1962) that apportionment issues were cognizable under the *Fourteenth Amendment's Equal Protection Clause. This action set the stage for later decisions requiring approximate equality of electoral districts.

(See also POLITICAL QUESTIONS; REAPPORTIONMENT CASES.)

John R. Vile

**Coleman v. Miller,** 307 U.S. 433 (1939), argued 10 Oct. 1938, reargued 17–18 Apr. 1939, decided 5 June 1939 by vote of 7 to 2; Hughes for the Court, Butler and McReynolds in dissent. The Court faced three issues: (1) could the lieutenant-governor of Kansas break a tie in the state senate in favor of the proposed Child Labor Amendment; (2) could the state ratify an amendment it had previously rejected; and (3) could a state ratify an amendment thirteen years after Congress proposed it with no time limit? The court was "equally divided" (p. 447) on the first issue and thus left standing the Kansas Supreme Court's judgment sanctioning the lieutenant governor's participation. Citing congressional promulgation of the *Fourteenth Amendment, the Court held that the latter two issues were political questions for Congress to decide. Concurring Justices Hugo *Black, Owen *Roberts, Felix *Frankfurter, and William *Douglas wanted to entrust all amending issues to Congress. The dissenters, citing *Dillon* v. *Gloss* (1921), argued that Kansas's ratification was untimely. Addressing similar issues in the companion case, *Chandler* v. *Wise*, the majority dismissed an action against Kentucky's governor, declaring his certification of the state's ratification conclusive.

*Coleman* muddied the amending process and introduced the ambiguous precedent of the Fourteenth Amendment. Subsequent decisions concerning political questions could limit *Coleman's* reach. Thus, in *Idaho* v. *Freeman* (1981), a U.S. district court sanctioned a state's rescission of ratification of the proposed Equal Rights Amendment after Congress extended the amendment's original seven-year deadline.

(See also CONSTITUTIONAL AMENDING PROCESS; JUDICIAL POWER AND JURISDICTION; POLITICAL QUESTIONS.)

John R. Vile

**Collector v. Day,** 11 Wall. (78 U.S.) 113 (1871), argued 3 Feb. 1871, decided 3 Apr. 1871 by vote of 8 to 1; Nelson for the Court, Bradley in dissent. *Collector v. Day* was one in a line of cases involving intergovernmental *tax immunities, and, as such, traced its origins to the latter part of Chief Justice John *Marshall's opinion in *McCulloch v. Maryland* (1819), which held that a state could not tax an instrumentality of the federal government. Following this reasoning, the Court had held in *Dobbins v. Erie County* (1842) that a state could not tax the income of a federal officer. *Collector v. Day* was the reciprocal of *Dobbins,* holding that the federal government could not tax the income of a state judge. Justice Samuel *Nelson relied on the *Tenth Amendment and on doctrines of dual sovereignty to hold that the state and federal governments were independent of each other and that the states retained all aspects of sovereignty not delegated to the federal government (see DUAL FEDERALISM). Consequently, he reasoned, the federal government could not tax essential instrumentalities of the states. The *Day* doctrine was weakened by the Court's decision in *Helvering v. Gerhardt* (1938) and finally explicitly overruled in *Graves v. O'Keefe* (1939).

William M. Wiecek

**Collegiality.** The unique structural characteristic of a collegial body such as the Supreme Court is the equality of formal authority of the members. Tension exists between the individual responsibility created by the collegial structure and the necessity for cooperation to produce collective decisions. Cooperation and the appearance of unity serve to increase power and respect for a collegial institution. Chief Justice John *Marshall arranged accommodations in one boardinghouse to foster fellowship and developed the single opinion of the Court to create a symbol of judicial solidarity (see SERIATIM OPINIONS). Later chief justices emphasized individual responsibility. Contemporary justices freely exhibit the individualism inherent in the collegial structure.

However, effective collective action requires the cooperative participation of every justice. Collegiality does not mandate unanimity but does demand loyalty to the institution and civil treatment of colleagues. Evidences of the justices' strong commitment to the Court are long tenures, unanimity in cases that threaten institutional integrity, and resolution of internal difficulties without appeals for external intervention. Although vigorous debates and biting opinions reveal their differences over law and policy, the hostility exhibited by James *McReynolds toward certain colleagues and the public competition between Robert H. *Jackson and Hugo L. *Black were aberrant (see JACKSON-BLACK FEUD). Justices have maintained cordial relations across ideological lines and warm friendships have developed between some pairs with shared values. The justices have traditionally treated incapacitated

brethren generously, sharing circuit and opinion writing duties and shielding them from public notice. Court practices remind the justices of their mutual dependence, equal power, and personal esteem, for example, the handshakes before conference initiated by Chief Justice Melville W. *Fuller, the holding of a case until each justice has determined his or her vote, and the luncheons, letters, or gifts for significant personal occasions.

Other structural characteristics and changes in the Court's environment have affected the requirements of collegiality. The Court has remained a small group in size; therefore, skillful chief justices can satisfy individuals and harmonize Court functioning. However, the growth of the federal court system and the Court bureaucracy has diverted the chief justice's attention to other duties (see BUREAUCRATIZATION OF THE FEDERAL JUDICIARY). In the nineteenth century short court terms, circuit duties and home offices limited contacts among justices. Longer Court terms and a separate building have brought justices into proximity. Conversely, heavy workloads, personal staffs, and new office technologies have focused their energies upon individual rather than collective decision-making. Resolution of the tensions between equal authority and collective duty requires different strategies in the late twentieth century, when the Court has become a powerful institution and the justices work in relative isolation.

(See also CHIEF JUSTICE, OFFICE OF THE; WORKLOAD.)

Beverly B. Cook

**Collusive Suits.** In the Constitution, *Article III confines the jurisdiction of federal courts to *cases and controversies. This limitation has spawned a body of case law on jurisdiction over moot or premature cases (see MOOTNESS), *political questions, and problems of the plaintiff's *standing. Included in this family of jurisdictional problems are collusive or feigned cases— litigation brought by "friendly" parties having no antagonistic interest, who seek to secure an opinion on the constitutionality of a statute by concocting a *test case.

Beginning in 1850, the Supreme Court has sternly discountenanced such cases, stating in *Lord v. Veazie* that a collusive suit "was in contempt of the court, and highly reprehensible" (p. 255; see CONTEMPT POWER OF THE COURT). The constitutional requirement mandates "a necessity in the determination of real, earnest and vital controversy between individuals" (*Chicago & Grand Trunk Railway Co. v. Wellman,* 1892, p. 345). Despite this constraint, some of the Court's leading constitutional decisions began as collusive suits, including *Hylton v. United States* (1796), *Fletcher v. Peck* (1810), the *Income Tax Cases* (1895, see *Pollock v. Farmers' Loan & Trust Co.*), and *Carter v. Carter Coal Co.* (1936). The disastrous consequences of some of these decisions demonstrate the wisdom of the ban on collusive suits.

Federal courts vigilantly review the status of parties in suits before them to prevent fraud, to ensure fairness to other parties and the legislatures that enacted challenged legislation, and to prevent the manufacture of diversity jurisdiction for purposes of getting into a federal court.

(See also JUDICIAL POWER AND JURISDICTION.)

James B. Stoneking

**Columbus Board of Education v. Penick,** 443 U.S. 449 (1979), argued 24 Apr. 1979, decided 2 July 1979 by vote of 7 to 2; White for the Court, Burger and Stewart concurring, Powell and Rehnquist in dissent. Notwithstanding the intervening decisions of *Milliken* v. *Bradley* (1974) and *Pasadena City Board of Education* v. *Spangler* (1976), which cast doubt on the Court's continuing desire to uphold large urban school desegregation plans, the Court reaffirmed the basic principles of *Swann* v. *Charlotte-Mecklenburg* (1971) and *Keyes* v. *Denver School District No. 1* (1973). It reiterated that proof of purposeful segregation in a substantial portion of an urban school district created a strong presumption that the school board had practiced systemwide segregative intent and had tolerated systemwide segregative effects—or both—thus warranting wholesale district-wide relief. Contrary evidence of the board's objectives was viewed with skepticism. Even where current racial imbalance in the schools could be shown to have been caused by innocent behavior on the part of the board, as long as the system was infected with segregative intent when *Brown* v. *Board of Education* (1954) was decided, the school board remained liable to dismantle the dual system if it had not taken substantial steps since then to do so.

Justice Lewis *Powell reiterated the view he expressed in *Keyes* that the de facto/de jure distinction (see SEGREGATION, DE FACTO; SEGREGATION, DE JURE) made no sense. Justice William *Rehnquist filed a lengthy dissent complaining of the Court's unwarranted intrusion into local education policy making and, in effect, of the Court's entire post–*Green* v. *County School Board of New Kent County* (1968) case law.

(See also DESEGREGATION REMEDIES; RACE AND RACISM.)

Dennis J. Hutchinson

**Comity** is the courtesy one jurisdiction gives by enforcing the laws of another jurisdiction. Comity is granted out of respect, deference, or friendship, rather than as an obligation. In American constitutional law comity has arisen in two ways. Historically important, although less common in the modern era, was the failure of comity in interstate relations. In the modern context comity is usually an issue that involves the federal courts' willingness (or unwillingness) to

rule on a state law in the absence of decision by a state court on the same issue.

In the antebellum period the status of slaves brought to free states raised particularly troublesome comity questions. Before 1830, courts in Louisiana, Kentucky, Mississippi, and Missouri gave comity to free-state and emancipated slaves who had lived or sojourned in a nonslaveholding jurisdiction. In *Commonwealth* v. *Aves* (1836), the Supreme Judicial Court of Massachusetts freed a Louisiana slave brought to Massachusetts by a visitor. In reaching this decision the court rejected arguments that Massachusetts ought to give comity to the slave laws of Louisiana. On the eve of the *Civil War some northern border states did allow masters to travel through their jurisdictions with slaves as a matter of comity; similarly, some southern states continued to recognize the free status gained by a slave who had lived in the North (see SLAVERY).

But, the trend was clearly against comity. In *Strader* v. *Graham* (1851) and *Dred *Scott* v. *Sandford* (1857), the Supreme Court held that slave states were under no obligation to grant comity to free-slave laws but the Court was ambiguous about whether northern states were obligated to grant comity to southern laws regulating slavery. Symbolic of this denial of comity was *Mitchell* v. *Wells* (1859). In that case, Mississippi's highest court refused to acknowledge the freedom of a slave whose owner had taken her to Ohio, where he legally manumitted her. In *Lemmon* v. *The People* (1860), New York's highest court upheld the free status of slaves brought to New York City by a traveler who was merely changing ships for a direct boat to Louisiana.

Differences in state divorce laws have also led to denials of interstate comity. Despite claims that a divorce proceeding was an "act or judicial proceeding" that all other states were obligated to enforce under the Constitution's *"Full Faith and Credit" provision in Article IV, various states have refused to recognize divorces granted under laws more lenient than their own (see FAMILY AND CHILDREN). In most areas of law, however, interstate comity has worked smoothly. Thus, states usually allow visitors to drive cars with drivers' licenses from other states, usually recognize *marriages and adoptions in other states, and often grant professional licenses to migrants or visitors, as a matter of reciprocity and comity.

The concept of comity has also led to the modern doctrine of *abstention, which stems from the notion that the state and federal courts are equally obligated to enforce the United States Constitution. Justice Sandra Day *O'Connor noted in *Brockett* v. *Spokane Arcades, Inc.* (1985): "[T]his Court has long recognized that concerns for comity and federalism may require federal courts to abstain from deciding federal constitutional issues that are entwined with the interpretation of state law . . . [W]here uncertain questions of state law must be resolved before a federal constitutional question can be decided, federal courts should abstain" from reaching a decision on federal issues "until a state court has addressed the state questions" (pp. 27–28).

Similarly, on grounds of comity and pursuant to federal law, the Supreme Court has generally refused to allow federal courts to intervene in pending cases in state courts absent a showing of bad faith harassment. As it noted in *Younger v. Harris* (1971), comity is "a proper respect for state functions, a recognition of the fact that the entire country is made up of a Union of separate state governments, and a continuance of the belief that the National Government will fare best if the States and their institutions are left free to perform their separate functions in their separate ways. This, perhaps, for lack of a better and clearer way to describe it, is referred to by many as 'Our Federalism,' and one familiar with the profound debates that ushered our Federal Constitution into existence is bound to respect those who remain loyal to the ideals and dreams of 'Our Federalism' " (p. 44).

(See also FEDERALISM; FEDERAL QUESTIONS.)

□ Paul Finkelman, *An Imperfect Union: Slavery, Federalism, and Comity* (1981). Paul Finkelman

**Commerce Power.** A strong impetus for calling the Constitutional Convention of 1787 was the need for national controls over the nation's commerce, which had become chaotic as many states had erected barriers to interstate trade in an effort to protect business enterprise for its own citizens. Thus, little discussion surrounded the adoption of clause 3 in Article I, section 8 of the Constitution, which empowered Congress "to regulate Commerce with foreign nations, among the several States, and with the Indian Tribes." Unlike the rules governing domestic commerce, those dealing with the Indian tribes and with foreign nations have occasioned relatively minor controversy over the years. Court decisions have upheld virtually all legislation dealing with *Native Americans, including the prohibition of the sale of intoxicating liquors on tribal reservations. Similarly, congressional power over foreign commerce has been held to be complete and exclusive, including authority to set tariffs, regulate shipping, aviation, communications, and to prohibit imports and establish embargoes against unfriendly foreign countries.

However, the phrase, "to regulate Commerce . . . among the several States," generated more litigation between 1789 and 1950 than any other clause in the Constitution and eventually became the single most important source of national power. Chief Justice John *Marshall set the stage for the future commercial development of the nation in *Gibbons v. Ogden* (1824) when, in the Supreme Court's initial interpretation of the Commerce Clause, he spoke in broad, expansive language in holding New York's grant of a

monopoly of steam navigation on its waters to be in conflict with a federal statute. Marshall maintained that commerce was not simply traffic but "intercourse" and included navigation (pp. 189–190). Moreover, the federal power, said Marshall, is "complete in itself" and "acknowledges no limitations, other than are prescribed in the Constitution" (pp. 196–197). The word "among," Marshall went on, means "intermingled with" and thus commerce among the states does not stop at state boundaries but "may be introduced into the interior" (p. 194). Nevertheless Marshall recognized state autonomy, declaring that the clause did not comprehend that commerce which is completely within a state and "which does not extend to or affect other states" (p. 194). Thus he rejected exclusive national authority over all internal commerce. Maintaining the same constitutional posture in *Willson v. Blackbird Creek Marsh Co.* (1829), Marshall observed that the Commerce Clause in its "dormant state" without supporting federal law was not a bar to state regulations of navigable waterways.

*Conflicts with State Powers.* Until the passage of the Interstate Commerce Act of 1887 and the *Sherman Antitrust Act of 1890, the national government rarely resorted to the Commerce Clause as authority for national regulations of any kind. Thus, litigation reaching the Court for roughly the first century after the adoption of the Constitution involved allegations that state regulatory laws constituted unconstitutional burdens on interstate commerce.

Before the *Civil War, rulings growing out of such conflicts approached sheer confusion until the justices arrived at a formula in *Cooley v. Port Wardens of Philadelphia* in 1852. Upholding a state regulation of harbor pilots, the Court adopted the doctrine of *"selective exclusiveness." In brief, the doctrine states that when the subject matter of the commerce requires a national uniform rule, only Congress may regulate; if, however, the commerce is of a local nature and Congress has not acted, the states may regulate. While the Court finally had a formula to buttress its decisions—and the *Cooley* case has never been overruled—as the justices soon realized, it could not be applied automatically.

Application of the *Cooley* rule by the Supreme Court frequently triggered action by Congress. For example, when the railroad industry was in its infancy, the states began to protect the public from exploitation by enacting regulatory measures including the fixing of rates. In *Peik v. Chicago and Northwestern Railway Co.* (1877), the Supreme Court upheld a Wisconsin law fixing rates on common carriers operating within the state. Even though the state's regulations might indirectly affect carriers outside its borders, unless Congress intervened, the states were free to act. Within ten years the Court reversed its position, holding in *Wabash, St. Louis & Pacific Railway Co. v. Illinois* (1886) that if a railroad was a part of an interstate network, a state might not regulate rates even for the part of the line that lay within its borders. Hence the railroads would be totally unregulated unless Congress filled the breach. It did so with the passage of the Interstate Commerce Act of 1887.

In a series of cases between 1887 and 1914 the Court upheld the authority of the Interstate Commerce Commission to oversee rates on interstate railroads and, in the *Shreveport Rate Cases* (1914), it approved the commission's power to order intrastate lines to charge the same rates as those levied on interstate carriers. The Court observed that wherever the "interstate and intrastate transactions of carriers are so related that the government of the one involves the control of the other, it is Congress and not the State, that is entitled to prescribe the final and dominant rule" (pp. 351–352).

In the first case to arise under the Sherman Antitrust Act, *United States* v. *E. C. Knight Co.* (1895), the government attempted to dissolve a monopoly of sugar processing, charging the American Sugar Refining Company with illegally restraining trade across state lines. The fact that an article was manufactured for export to another state, said the Court, did not make it part of interstate commerce. Within a few years, however, the justices began to retreat from a rigid transportation/manufacturing distinction when in *Swift & Co.* v. *United States* (1905) they agreed unanimously that a price-fixing arrangement among meat packers, although done locally, was indeed a restraint on commerce. Promulgating the *"stream of commerce" theory, Justice Oliver Wendell *Holmes, writing for the Court, emphasized that the movement of cattle from one state to another for meat processing and subsequent shipment of meat to other parts of the country constituted a "typical, constantly recurring course," a current or stream of commerce, and the effect of local price-fixing upon interstate commerce was not "accidental, secondary, remote or merely probable" (pp. 396, 399). By the end of the 1920s the Court had relied on this doctrine to uphold an increasing number of national regulatory measures over business enterprise.

**National Police Power.** As the nation expanded and problems began to spill over state borders, pressures increased for congressional action to deal with matters that could no longer be effectively handled at the state level. Since the Constitution nowhere permitted Congress to legislate in behalf of the public health, morals, safety, or welfare, it could do so only by indirection, by relying on a specified power that might be tied to the regulatory measure. It was the Commerce Clause that became the primary vehicle for such regulations. In *Champion* v. *Ames* (1903), the Supreme Court constructed a new theory to uphold a federal statute that prohibited the transport of lottery tickets across state lines. Heretofore Congress could protect the free flow

of commerce by keeping the channels free from obstruction but under the new theory articles not harmful to the commerce and harmful intrinsically, but injurious in their general effects, might be prohibited.

From the lottery case it was but a short step to other national police measures such as the *Mann Act of 1910, which made it a crime to transport women across state lines for immoral purposes (upheld in *Hoke* v. *United States,* 1913) and the Automobile Theft Act of 1915, which made it a federal offense knowingly to drive a stolen automobile across a state line (upheld in *Brooks* v. *United States,* 1925). By barring the use of the channels of interstate commerce to immoral transactions and criminal activities, Congress was able to protect the public from evils that were beyond the competence of the individual states. But in 1918 the Supreme Court once again adhered to the distinction between manufacturing and commerce. With the purpose of outlawing child labor Congress enacted a statute in 1916 prohibiting the shipment in interstate commerce of products made in factories or mines by children under the age of fourteen. In *Hammer* v. *Dagenhart* (1918), the Court declared that Congress had exceeded its authority. It was permissible to prohibit harmful transactions or adulterated food and drugs from commerce, but it was another matter to prohibit goods, harmless in themselves, that posed no obstruction to commerce. The evil of child labor, declared the Court, involved manufacturing, not commerce, was local in nature, and was thus an inappropriate subject for congressional cognizance.

**The New Deal.** After the decision in the *Dagenhart* case Congress refrained for some fifteen years from regulating local business activity, but with the near collapse of the nation's economy in the early thirties and the subsequent election of an administration dedicated to economic recovery, the Congress, pursuing the initiative of President Franklin D. *Roosevelt, resurrected the Commerce Clause. In a series of laws the president and Congress attempted to bring some order to what had been industrial chaos, but until 1937 a majority of the justices maintained the distinction between commerce and manufacturing, between activities that had a direct versus an indirect effect on commerce. As a result much of the early New Deal legislation was consigned to oblivion. The National Industrial Recovery Act of 1933, for example, which authorized the president to establish industrial codes of fair competition including the regulation of wages and hours, was declared unconstitutional in *Schechter Poultry Corporation* v. *United States* (1935), in part because the code attempted to regulate intrastate commerce.

After suffering several defeats at the hands of a conservative Supreme Court, President Roosevelt proposed to increase the size of the Court, popularly called the *"court-packing plan," which would have moderated the conservatism by adding justices of the president's political and constitutional persuasion. Although the plan was defeated, the threat of interference with judicial integrity may have had the desired effect on judicial propensities, for beginning in 1937 a majority of the justices discarded much of the earlier doctrines restrictive of expansion of national power based on the Commerce Clause.

In a series of cases the Court abandoned all the old distinctions between manufacturing and commerce, between direct and indirect effects and burdens. Among the most prominent were *National Labor Relations Board v. Jones & Laughlin Steel Corporation (1937), sustaining the National Labor Relations Act of 1935, a law that guaranteed collective bargaining to all employees engaged in the production of goods for interstate commerce; United States v. *Darby Lumber Company (1941), upholding the Fair Labor Standards Act of 1938, which barred the use of interstate commerce to goods made by workers who were not paid a minimum wage of forty cents an hour and guaranteed a forty-hour work week, specifically overruling Hammer v. Dagenhart; and *Wickard v. Filburn (1942), upholding the Agricultural Adjustment Act of 1938, which regulated agricultural production affecting interstate commerce.

Commerce Power Today. During the fifty years following the post–New Deal era Congress expanded national regulation into myriad aspects of the national life, using the Commerce Clause as the constitutional base, all with the Supreme Court's approval. One of the most significant areas of national intervention was that of racial discrimination. In 1964 Congress enacted a *Civil Rights Act banning racial discrimination in hotels, motels, restaurants, theaters, and motion picture houses throughout the country, now based on the Commerce Clause rather than the *Fourteenth Amendment. In *Heart of Atlanta Motel, Inc. v. United States (1964) and *Katzenbach v. McClung (1964), the Supreme Court found that racial discrimination had a deleterious effect on interstate commerce and was a proper object for congressional attention.

In *National League of Cities v. Usery (1976), the Court struck down legislation based on the Commerce Clause for the first time in forty years when it held that the minimum wage–maximum hour requirements of the amended Fair Labor Standards Act of 1938 could not be extended to state and local government employees. Such requirements, said the Court, involved a congressional intrusion into an "attribute of state sovereignty" (p. 845). Less than a decade later the Court overruled the Usery case in *Garcia v. San Antonio Metropolitan Transit Authority (1985).

□ Edward S. Corwin, The Commerce Power Versus States Rights (1936). Richard A. Epstein, "The Proper Scope of the Commerce Clause," Virginia Law Review 73 (1987): 1387–1455. Felix Frankfurter, The Commerce Clause Under

Marshall, Taney and Waite (1937). R. S. Myers, "The Burger Court and the Commerce Clause: An Evaluation of the Role of State Sovereignty," Notre Dame Law Review 60 (1985): 1056–1093. — Robert J. Steamer

**Commercial Speech.** The Supreme Court has developed a separate level of First Amendment protections for commercial advertising. Under the commercial speech doctrine, as it has evolved over the last half century, commercial speech receives a lesser degree of protection than does noncommerical speech. Nonetheless, despite the somewhat vague and inconsistent growth of the commercial speech doctrine, an overall trend toward greater protection for commercial speech has emerged in the Court's opinions.

The Court first articulated a commercial speech doctrine in Valentine v. Chrestensen (1942), in which it ruled that commercial advertising was unprotected under the First Amendment. During the 1970s, however, the Court began to protect commercial speech that did more than simply propose a commercial transaction and that contained material of public interest.

In the landmark case on commercial speech, Virginia State Board of Pharmacy v. Virginia Citizens Consumer Council (1976), the Court declared unconstitutional a statute banning the advertisement of prescription drug prices. The Court reasoned that such advertisements conveyed vital information to consumers and that a free-enterprise economy depended upon a free flow of commercial information. However, as the Court suggested, deceptive or misleading advertising, even if not false, did not serve any social interests and could be regulated.

The Virginia Pharmacy opinion, as well as subsequent case law, expressed the Court's utilitarian view of commerical speech. For instance, in *Bates v. State Bar of Arizona (1977), holding that state restrictions on lawyer advertising are unconstitutional, the Court recognized the consumers' need for the particular information but acknowledged that false, deceptive, or misleading advertising could be regulated. In looking at the content of the speech and its contribution to the marketplace of ideas, the Court has demonstrated its willingness to protect only such speech that furthered the social interest in the free flow of information. Thus, under the commercial speech doctrine, audience interests has taken priority over speaker's interests.

This approach also guided the Court in Central Hudson Gas v. Public Service Commission of New York (1980), where it announced a four-part test for determining whether regulations impermissibly infringed upon the First Amendment right of commercial speech. In overturing a statute banning certain advertising by utilities, the Court stated that the First Amendment's application to commercial speech rests upon the informational function of advertising: thus, commercial messages that do not accurately inform the public about lawful activity may be regulated. Under the analysis in *Central Hudson*, the Court must decide first, whether the expression concerns lawful activity and is not misleading; second, whether the asserted governmental interest is substantial; third, whether the regulation directly advances the governmental interest; and fourth, whether less restrictive means of advancing the governmental interest exist.

A comparison of this test with the traditional First Amendment analysis demonstrates that commercial speech receives a lesser degree of protection than that conferred upon noncommercial speech. For instance, there is no requirement under traditional First Amendment analysis that the underlying activity be lawful or that the speech not be false or misleading. In addition, with noncommercial speech cases, the governmental interest must be "compelling" rather than just "substantial." Furthermore, the *Central Hudson* requirement that the regulation must be no more extensive than necessary to serve the asserted governmental interest is easier to satisfy than the least restrictive alternative test imposed on regulations concerning noncommercial speech. The Court clarified this difference in *Board of Trustees* v. *Fox* (1989), holding that a regulation restricting commercial speech need only be a reasonable means of accomplishing the governmental objection. To apply a more rigid standard, the Court said, would be inconsistent with the subordinate position of commerical speech under the First Amendment.

More so than in noncommercial speech cases, the content of the speech and the governmental interest in controlling that speech play important roles in determining the application of the First Amendment to commercial speech. Despite these limitations, the Supreme Court in *Peel* v. *Attorney Registration and Disciplinary Committee of Illinois* (1990) declared that truthful advertising relating to a lawful activity was entitled to First Amendment protection.

(See also FIRST AMENDMENT; SPEECH AND THE PRESS.)

Patrick M. Garry

**Common Carriers.** English common law traditionally has characterized public transportation businesses as "common carriers"—a subcategory of "common callings." Such businesses were distinguished from ordinary ones in that their services were available to the general public. In addition, the quality and cost of those services were of special significance to social and economic life. Under the *common law, the courts imposed three distinctive obligations upon common carriers: (1) they had a duty to serve all who applied for their services, (2) unreasonableness in their rates of charge and operations was prohibited, and (3) they were held to liability standards far stricter than those applied in general business law.

In the United States, until the Interstate Commerce Act (1887) and its many amendments largely displaced this field of judge-made law in the regulation of national commerce, the Supreme Court was the final arbiter of questions regarding carriers' legal obligations and immunities. In *New Jersey Steam Navigation Co.* v. *Merchants' Bank of Boston* (1848) the Court established the rules, for example, as to whether carriers on land or water could contract away their strict liability for negligence. It also decided upon the reach of the "duty to serve" concept in *Parrot* v. *Wells Fargo* (1872), a case involving dangerous cargo. After enactment of federal transportation laws, moreover, the Court engaged in statutory interpretation that determined the extent to which Congress had intended to displace the traditional common law in areas such as the carrier's negligence (*Adams Express* v. *Croninger*, 1912).

In *Munn* v. *Illinois* (1877), the Court imported into constitutional law the common-law distinction between ordinary businesses and those burdened with special obligations to the public. The *Munn* doctrine designated grain warehouses and railroads as businesses "affected with a public interest." Hence they were subject to public regulation of rates and operating practices beyond what might be imposed by the states upon merely "ordinary" businesses. For more than sixty years the Court reviewed the validity of state regulatory legislation by applying this doctrine. In *Nebbia* v. *New York* (1934), the Court abandoned the *Munn* formula, leaving to the legislatures the decision as to what business activities warranted exercise of the regulatory power over their rates and practices.

(See also INTERSTATE COMMERCE COMMISSION.)

□ Jurgen Basedow, "Common Carriers: Continuity and Disintegration in U.S. Transportation Law," *Transportation Law Journal* 13 (1983): 1–42, 16–188. Harry N. Scheiber, "The Road to *Munn*: Eminent Domain and the Concept of Public Purpose in the State Courts," *Perspectives in American History* 5 (1971): 327–402.

Harry N. Scheiber

**Common Law** is the body of judge-made law that was administered in the royal courts of England (King's Bench, Common Pleas, Exchequer, and Exchequer Chamber)—in contrast with other bodies of English law administered in different courts, such as equity (see INJUNCTIONS AND EQUITABLE REMEDIES), *admiralty, canon law, and the customary law of the borough and manorial courts. William Blackstone described the common law as the general customary law of the realm as interpreted by the royal judges, the "living oracles" of the law. The phrase "common law" is sometimes used in contradistinction to *"civil law," which describes the code-based legal systems of continental Europe (and nations influenced by Europe) that descend ultimately from *Roman law.

The common law was received in the American colonies and adopted as the basis of American legal systems after the Revolution in the state and federal constitutions. The Supreme Court is a *common-law court. The Court early held, however, that there is neither a *federal common law of crimes (*United States* v. *Hudson and Goodwin*, 1812) nor a federal civil common law (*Wheaton* v. *Peters*, 1834). In American practice, the common law is one of two legal systems (the other being equity), now merged in all jurisdictions including the federal, that are the basis of the American legal order.                    William M. Wiecek

**Common-Law Court.** The Supreme Court is a common-law court that operates in a system that has little *federal common law. Yet its common-law nature is important to the Court's functioning as a constitutional arbiter. *Common law is a system of law made not by legislatures but by courts and judges. Although often called "unwritten law," the phrase actually refers only to the source of law, which is presumed to be universal custom, reason, or *natural law. In common law, the substance of the law is to be found in the published reports of court decisions. Two points are critical to the workings of a common-law system. First, law emerges only through litigation about actual controversies. Second, *precedent guides courts: holdings in a case must follow previous rulings, if the facts are identical. This is the principle of *stare decisis*. But subsequent cases can also change the law. If the facts of a new case are distinguishable, a new rule can emerge. And sometimes, if the grounds of a precedent are seen to be wrong, the holding can be overruled by later courts.

When the Constitution was drafted, American society was infused with common-law ideas. Common law originated in the medieval English royal courts. By 1776, it had been received in all the British colonies. The revolutionary experience heightened Americans' adherence to common law, especially to the idea that the principles embodied in the common law controlled the government. While there is no express provision in the Constitution stating that the Supreme Court is a common-law court, *Article III divides the jurisdiction of federal courts into law (meaning common law), equity, and *admiralty. The Philadelphia Convention of 1787 rejected language that would limit federal jurisdiction to matters controlled by congressional statute. Thus the Constitution implicitly recognizes the Supreme Court as a common-law court, as does the *Seventh Amendment in the *Bill of Rights.

The Constitution left open the question whether there was a federal common law. The Supreme Court first held, in *United States* v. *Hudson and Goodwin* (1812), that there is no federal common law of crimes, and then, in *Wheaton* v. *Peters* (1834), that there is no federal civil common law. But in *Swift* v. *Tyson* (1842), the Court permitted *lower federal courts to decide commercial law questions on the basis of "the general principles and doctrines of commercial jurisprudence" (p. 19), thus opening the door to later growth of a general federal common law. A century later, the Court put a stop to this development in *Erie Railroad* v. *Tompkins* (1938) by declaring *Swift* unconstitutional. (Yet, at the same time, it acknowledged the existence of bodies of specialized federal common law, such as, for example, judicial development of a body of *labor law under federal statutes governing labor relations.) Today, federal courts must generally follow state substantive law, including state common law.

Despite the lack of a federal common law, the Supreme Court relies on common law in interpreting the Constitution. For example, it refuses to render *advisory opinions, waiting instead for litigants to bring issues before it. Precedent shapes the Court's power of *judicial review; because of it, any ruling of the Court is a precedent for similar cases. Thus if one state's law is held unconstitutional, all similar statutes in other states are unconstitutional, a point the Court was obliged to underscore forcibly in *Cooper* v. *Aaron* (1958) in the face of intransigent southern resistance to the Court's holding in *Brown* v. *Board of Education* (1954).

□ Karl Llewellyn, *The Common-Law Tradition: Deciding Appeals* (1960).                    Richard F. Hamm

**Communism and Cold War.** Communism became a central concern of the Supreme Court during the most frigid phase of the international confrontation between the United States and the Soviet Union. The cold war arose out of American unwillingness to accept Russian domination of Central and Eastern Europe after *World War II. By 1947 the United States had committed itself to the containment of the Soviet Union. Because American policy makers equated communism with Soviet imperialism, implementation of this strategy involved not only the erection of a military fence around the USSR but also efforts to reduce the appeal of domestic Communist parties in European, and later Third World, nations by providing them with economic assistance. The anticommunist rhetoric of government leaders, such as President Harry Truman, aroused concern about communism in this country. Although American Communists were few in numbers and posed little real threat to national security, political demagogues, such as Senator Joseph R. McCarthy, exploited this issue relentlessly, thereby creating a Red Scare.

This anticommunist hysteria inspired a variety of governmental actions intended to thwart espionage and *subversion. These included congressional enactment of the Internal Security Act of 1950 and the Communist Control Act of 1954, criminal prosecutions and deportations of radicals, development of loyalty-security programs, official designation of certain organizations as subversive, loyalty oath requirements, and free-wheeling investigations by several congressional committees, the most notorious of which was the House Committee on Un-American Activities (known by the acronym HUAC). Many of these governmental actions imperiled individual rights, generating issues that eventually came before the Supreme Court.

In cases of this type the Vinson Court generally upheld the challenged governmental action. Thus, in *American Communications Association v. Douds* (1950), it affirmed the constitutionality of a provision of the Taft-Hartley Act that required *labor union officials to file affidavits disavowing membership in the Communist party. In *Dennis v. United States* (1951), it rejected a *First Amendment attack on the *Smith Act by Communist leaders convicted of violating that law.

At about the time that Vinson died in 1953, international tensions began to ease. An armistice brought an end to the Korean War. In 1955 President Eisenhower met with the new Soviet leadership at a Geneva summit conference. At home, anticommunist hysteria abated. Indicative of the changing atmosphere was the Senate's censure of McCarthy in December 1954.

By 1956 the decisions of the Warren Court were also beginning to reflect the country's new mood. In *Peters v. Hobby* (1955) and *Cole v. Young* (1956), the Court reinstated federal employees discharged under the loyalty-security program. It also overturned the conviction of a Communist leader for violation of a state sedition law and threw out an order requiring the Communist party to register with the Subversive Activities Control Board. On "Red Monday" (17 June 1957), the Court, in *Watkins v. United States* (1957), overturned the *contempt conviction of a man who had refused to answer some questions asked him by HUAC and, in *Sweezy v. New Hampshire* (1957), imposed constitutional constraints on investigations conducted by state legislatures. In *Service v. Dulles* (1957) it ordered the federal government to reinstate an alleged security risk, and in *Yates v. United States* (1957) it reversed the Smith Act convictions of California Communist leaders.

These decisions outraged many conservative members of Congress, who mounted a drive to negate their effects through legislation. Senator William Jenner introduced a bill to take away the Supreme Court's appellate jurisdiction in five types of loyalty and subversion cases. His proposal failed, in considerable part because the Supreme Court retreated from the positions it had taken on Red Monday. In *Barenblatt v. United States* (1959) and *Uphaus v. Wyman* (1959), it rendered decisions on similar issues that contrasted sharply with *Watkins* and *Sweezy*, and in *Scales v. United States* (1961), it upheld a Smith Act conviction for membership in the Communist party. The Court's change of direction occurred

because Justices Felix *Frankfurter and John M. *Harlan switched from supporting civil liberties claims to backing governmental actions taken to combat communism. This reversal proved to be only temporary, for after Frankfurter's retirement in 1962, the Court proceeded to invalidate a host of legal leftovers from the cold war era.

(See also ASSEMBLY AND ASSOCIATION, FREE-DOM OF; SPEECH AND THE PRESS.)

□ Michal R. Belknap, *Cold War Political Justice: The Smith Act, the Communist Party and American Civil Liberties* (1977). David Caute, *The Great Fear: The Anti-Communist Purge under Truman and Eisenhower* (1978).
Michal R. Belknap

## Communist Party v. Subversive Activities Control Board,

367 U.S. 1 (1961), argued 11–12 Oct. 1960, decided 5 June 1961 by vote of 5 to 4; Frankfurter for the Court, Warren, Black, Douglas, and Brennan in dissent. The Internal Security Act, passed over President Truman's veto in 1950 and generally known as the *McCarran Act, sought to expose the Communist party in the United States by the devices of compulsory registration. The statute ordered communist organizations to register with the attorney general; the Subversive Activities Control Board (SACB) was created to administer the registration process. Registered organizations were required to disclose the names of their officers and the source of their funds. Members of registered organizations were subject to various sanctions, including denial of passports and the right to work in defense plants.

The SACB promptly identified the American Communist party as a "communist action organization" and ordered it to register, which the officers of the party refused to do. After eleven years of litigation, including one remand by the Supreme Court to the board because of the possibility that the record was tainted by perjured testimony, the Court finally upheld the registration provisions of the act in *Communist Party v. SACB* (1961). But it postponed any decision on the constitutionality of the statutory sanctions until they were actually enforced.

When passports were subsequently denied to party members, this action was held to be an unconstitutional violation of the right to *travel in *Aptheker v. Secretary of State* (1964). In *Albertson v. SACB* (1965) the Court ruled that compulsory registration of party members violated the *Fifth Amendment. *United States v. *Robel* (1967) voided the ban on party members working in defense plants. Other provisions of the McCarran Act remained in effect and were the subject of much controversy, but the SACB was allowed to die in 1973 by failure to appropriate funds.

(See also ASSEMBLY AND ASSOCIATION, FREE-DOM OF; COMMUNISM AND COLD WAR; SUBVERSION.)

C. Herman Pritchett

**Compensation.** See JUST COMPENSATION.

**Compulsory Process.** Under the *common law parties to a law suit and others who possess information about it have a duty to come forward and cooperate with the court when ordered to do so. This duty is reinforced by inherent powers of the courts to compel the appearance of witnesses and parties. Typically the device used to compel appearance is the *subpoena, but courts can also issue warrants of arrest or attachment if needed. Courts have a variety of sanctions at their disposal to secure compliance to orders compelling appearance, including the power of *contempt, which can result in fines and/or imprisonment.

The *Sixth Amendment regards compulsory process as a *fundamental right for the accused in criminal proceedings. It provides in part that the accused in a criminal prosecution has a right "to have compulsory process for obtaining witnesses in his favor," that is to have a court compel the appearance of witnesses who will benefit them. This guarantee was one of several provisions in the Sixth Amendment designed to reject earlier English practices that did not permit persons accused of felonies or treason to introduce witnesses in their own defense. In *Washington* v. *Texas* (1968), the Sixth Amendment right of compulsory process was made applicable to the states via the *Due Process Clause of the *Fourteenth Amendment (see INCORPORATION DOCTRINE).

Malcolm M. Feeley

**Computer Room.** Located next to the print shop on the ground floor, the computer room connects the Supreme Court's microcomputer system. Computers were installed in the Court in the 1970s and are used for preparing and typesetting opinions, for docket tracking, and for storage of the Court's bar records, library databases, and historical collections catalogs.    Francis Helminski

**Concurrent Power.** American *federalism was a unique solution to the problem of dividing power between the government of a whole nation and the governments of the parts of that nation. Central to the acceptance of that solution was the determination, after considerable compromise, of the institution that would serve as the final arbiter of federal-state relations. As that arbiter, the U.S. Supreme Court has on a number of occasions defined the scope and limitations of the exercise of concurrent power by the legislatures of the states and the Congress of the United States. Justice John *McLean's opinion in the *Passenger Cases* (1849) provides a standard nineteenth-century definition: "The general government and a State exercise concurrent powers in taxing the people of the State. The objects of taxation may be the same, but the motives and policy of the tax are different, and the powers are distinct and independent" (p. 283). McLean chose to limit state power, holding a New York

state tax on immigrant passengers an unconstitutional "regulation of foreign commerce, [a power] exclusively vested in Congress" (p. 284). Similarly, the Fugitive Slave Clause (Art. IV, sec. 2) was defined as an exclusively federal responsibility in *Prigg* v. *Pennsylvania* (1842), as was sedition when the federal government alone was involved (see also FUGITIVE SLAVES). State and federal courts share concurrent jurisdiction in a great many categories of law not denied to the states by *Article III or by explicit congressional limitation, and the Supreme Court has the continuing responsibility for defining that jurisdiction.

(See also JUDICIAL POWER AND JURISDICTION.)

John R. Schmidhauser

**Concurring Opinions** are written by justices who agree with the outcome or the decision in a case, but disagree with the logic or the reasons for that decision. In short, although the outcome is acceptable to the concurring justice, the explanation for that result requires a separate opinion that outlines different reasons for the result.

A concurring opinion may clarify the outcome in the case and strengthen the result. Certainly it explicates the reasoning of the individual justice or justices. This is advantageous to the justice, and it may provide some comfort to the future litigant who relies on that separate opinion rather than the majority opinion for *precedent. Such an opinion may also assist the development of legal doctrine if the majority opinion is unclear or confusing. However, a concurrence can also detract from the impact of the majority opinion, and even the threat of preparing such an opinion can cause the majority opinion writer to adjust the majority opinion to accommodate the position of the possible concurring justice.

Traditionally, justices were reluctant to invest their time and energies in such opinions since the result in the case was acceptable to them. However, recently there is an impression that justices are concurring with separate opinions more frequently. There has been some increase in the numbers and the ratio of majority opinions to concurring opinions at times during the past two decades, but these figures are not any higher now than several decades ago.

The potential problem, which began to surface more frequently in the past two decades, is the absence of any majority opinion. This is the extreme consequence of concurring opinions, as more and more members of the majority write a separate opinion. Such a proliferation of opinions leads to a lack of clear precedent and borders on the practice of *seriatim opinions rendered by the Supreme Court when it began functioning in 1789. This approach, however, has not been predominant.

(See also PLURALITY OPINIONS.)

William McLauchlan

**Condemnation.** See INVERSE CONDEMNATION.

**Conference, The,** a private meeting of the justices of the Supreme Court of the United States. During the Court's annual term, beginning in October, the justices meet as a group twice each week to screen petitions for review of new cases, to deliberate cases currently on the Court's docket, and to transact miscellaneous Court business.

At the sound of a buzzer, the justices assemble in the Court's panelled Conference Room, under a portrait of Chief Justice John *Marshall. After a handshake, each justice takes a preassigned seat around a long table with the *chief justice at one end, the senior associate justice at the other, and the remaining justices along the sides. No clerks, secretaries, or visitors are permitted behind the closed doors once a conference has begun.

In recent years, conferences have been scheduled for Wednesday afternoons, during which the justices deliberate the four cases orally argued the previous Monday. Typically, the Court meets again for a full-day session on Friday to discuss the eight cases argued on Tuesday and Wednesday. This schedule has varied, however, throughout history. In the Court's early years, conferences were scheduled in the evening or on weekends, often in the boarding houses or hotels shared by justices while in residence in Washington. Until 1955, the Court conferred on Saturdays to discuss all cases argued the previous week.

While meeting times have varied, the basic agenda of a typical conference session has remained constant for some time. The chief justice presides, allowing a brief period for consideration of the petitions for hearing (*certiorari petitions) on the Court's *"discuss list." This list includes all petitions deemed worthy of full-dress treatment by any justice. If four justices agree to review a case, it is then scheduled for briefing and oral argument. The chief justice initiates discussion of a petition with a statement as to why he feels it is worthy of consideration on the merits. In order of seniority on the Court, the eight associate justices may then comment.

In addition to this ongoing work with certiorari petitions throughout the regular term, the Court added a series of several late September daylong meetings in the 1970s. These meetings are exclusively for the purpose of considering certiorari petitions that accumulate during the Court's summer recess.

Following discussion of matters relating to the Court's docket and of any miscellaneous items and motions awaiting the attention of the justices, the chief justice moves on to the deliberation of the cases argued before the Court in the previous few days. Customarily, the chief justice frames the discussion of a case with a review of its facts and mention of its history and of relevant legal precedent. In descending order of seniority, the remaining justices present their views.

In the past, a vote was taken after the newest justice to the Court spoke, with the justices voting in order of ascending seniority largely, it was said, to avoid pressure from long-term members of the Court on their junior colleagues. By contrast, recent practice suggests that the initial comments of each justice carry an indication of that individual's vote, making a separate vote unnecessary in most instances. After everyone has spoken, the chief justice announces his vote tally before moving on to the next case.

Since the justices jealously guard the secrecy of their conferences, no formal records of these meetings are kept. However, many of the justices maintain personal notes summarizing the discussions to assist recall of particular conferences. Court-watchers have been able to reconstruct the general tenor of past conferences by tapping these notes as they are made public, frequently years after the justice's death. Researchers also have been aided by occasional off-the-bench remarks and publications of justices.

These judicial materials suggest that the atmosphere of conferences can vary considerably, depending on the attitudes and style of the presiding chief justice, the personalities of the associate justices, and the complexity and emotional content of the case at hand. Overall, conference notes suggest that the justices are generally both cordial and frank. But the occasional acrimonious interchange over a particularly divisive case justifies Chief Justice William *Rehnquist's assessment of the conference mechanism as a "relatively fragile instrument."

Rehnquist has made it clear that he prefers a businesslike conference in which each justice speaks in turn, uninterrupted. In his *The Supreme Court: How It Was, How It Is* (1987), the chief justice notes, "the true purpose of the conference discussion of argued cases is not to persuade one's colleagues through impassioned advocacy to alter their views, but instead by hearing each justice express his own views to determine therefrom the view of the majority of the Court." (p. 295).

Other twentieth-century chief justices have adopted contrasting styles during their stewardships of the Court's conferences. During the 1930s, for example, the respect accorded to Chief Justice Harlan Fiske *Stone's formidable memory, analytic skills, and managerial talents allowed him to tightly control discussion and to move the group along at a brisk tempo. However, some of his associate justices at times complained that the Stone style discouraged important interchanges. Between 1953 and 1969, Chief Justice Earl *Warren's personal disposition and desire for consensus typically encouraged a more unstructured discussion of agenda items. In any event, the unlimited give-and-take that commonly occurred in the nineteenth century has disappeared with the growing case load faced by the modern Court.

Although the conference remains a critical stage in the Court's decision-making process, the limited opportunity for extended discussion of

*Conference Room*

cases at conference has increased the importance of subsequent, informal judicial interaction. A justice's thinking about a case, and even his or her vote, may change in the ensuing weeks and months, while opinions and memoranda are drafted and informal discussions continue. During that period, the justices may negotiate for the wording of passages in a yet-to-be-published opinion or suggest a new approach to the legal issues presented by a case. In sum, the deliberation that began at conference continues in a variety of informal ways until the Court announces its decision in a case, often many months later.

(See also DECISION-MAKING DYNAMICS.)

□ David M. O'Brien, *Storm Center: The Supreme Court in American Politics* (1986). Bob Woodward and Scott Armstrong, *The Brethren: Inside the Supreme Court* (1979).
Robert J. Janosik

**Confessions, Coerced.** See COERCED CONFESSIONS.

**Confirmation Process.** See APPOINTMENT AND REMOVAL POWER; NOMINATIONS, CONTROVER-

SIAL; SELECTION OF JUSTICES; SENATE JUDICIARY COMMITTEE.

**Conflict of Interest.** See EXTRAJUDICIAL ACTIVITIES; JUDICIAL ETHICS.

**Congress, Arrest and Immunity of Members of.** The framers of the Constitution recognized the fundamental necessity of protecting members of Congress from arbitrary arrest. Article I, section 6 provides that members "shall in all Cases, except Treason, Felony and Breach of the Peace, be privileged from Arrest during their Attendance at the Session of their respective Houses and in going to and returning from the same." That clause also extended to members' immunity against being "questioned in any other Place" for "Speech or Debate in either House."

Today the provision of this clause protecting members against arrest is virtually obsolete. It was intended to apply only to arrests in civil suits, a practice common in the late eighteenth century, but no longer followed. The clause does not protect members against service of process in either civil or criminal cases, in the latter instance because of members' lack of privilege in cases involving "treason, felony and breach of the peace."

Members enjoy immunity from legal action resulting from the pursuit of legitimate legislative activity. In *Gravel v. United States* (1972) and *Doe v. McMillan* (1973) the Supreme Court sharply defined this activity (see SPEECH AND DEBATE CLAUSE) to exclude protection from liability for publication of defamatory or national security classified materials outside the halls of Congress. In *United States v. Brewster* (1972) the Court decided that the clause offered no protection to members charged with taking a bribe, for the subject of the action is the bribe, rather than the legislative objective the bribe was intended to promote.

(See also SEPARATION OF POWERS.)

Richard A. Baker

**Congress, Qualifications of Members of.** The Constitution sets forth only three qualifications for membership in Congress: U.S. *citizenship, residency in the state represented, and a minimum age. The framers set the citizenship requirement at seven years for members of the House of Representatives and nine years for senators. Representatives must be at least twenty-five years old to take their oath of office, while senators must be thirty. (Contrary to earlier interpretations, both bodies now recognize that a person may stand for election prior to reaching the required age or term of citizenship.) On several occasions early in the nineteenth century, members-elect were admitted before attaining the specified minimum age. When Kentucky's Henry Clay took his Senate oath in 1806 at the age of twenty-nine years and eight months, he allegedly told those who asked about the constitutionality of this action to "propound that question to my constituents."

During the *Civil War, Congress added an additional membership qualification. All members-elect were required to take an oath that they had never been disloyal to the government of the United Staes. Several persons were excluded in the years following the war for refusing to ascribe to that oath (see TEST OATHS). After World War I, the House twice denied a seat to Socialist Victor Berger on grounds of disloyalty but later admitted him when the Supreme Court reversed his espionage conviction (see SUBVERSION). Finally in 1969, the Supreme Court ruled in *Powell v. McCormack* that the Constitution's requirements for membership were exclusive. In the *Powell* case, the Court decided that although the Constitution gives Congress the right to judge the qualifications of its members, it must exercise that right within the Constitution's express provisions. Richard A. Baker

**Congressional Power of Investigation.** Congress is a legislative body, but it must have procedures that enable it to acquire information. Further-more, Congress must keep a critical eye on those who administer the laws it enacts and who spend the money it appropriates. The business of Congress is not to govern the country, but rather to see to it that those who do govern perform their functions properly. To perform its legislative functions effectively, Congress must have the power to investigate. While the Constitution is silent on this subject, the courts have had little difficulty in concluding that the power to investigate is a necessary corollary of Congress's other powers, particularly in view of the *implied powers provisions of Article I, section 8, clause 18.

In the leading decision on this subject, *McGrain v. Daugherty* (1927), Justice Willis *Van Devanter noted that in legislative practice the power to secure needed information by means of investigations "has long been treated as an attribute of the power to legislate. It was so regarded in the British Parliament and in the Colonial legislatures before the American Revolution; and a like view has prevailed and been carried into effect in both houses of Congress and in most of the state legislatures" (p. 161).

However broad the congressional power to investigate may be, it is necessarily subject to recognized limitations. In *Quinn v. United States* (1955), Chief Justice Earl *Warren pointed out that the investigatory power "cannot be used to inquire into private affairs unrelated to a valid legislative purpose" and that this power does not "extend to an area in which Congress is forbidden to legislate." He added that "the power to investigate must not be confused with any of the powers of law enforcement," which are assigned by the Constitution to the executive and the judiciary (p. 155). Warren stressed above all that the legislative power of investigation is subject to the specific individual guarantees of the *Bill of Rights, notably the *Fifth Amendment privilege against compulsory *self-incrimination.

These expressed limitations on the legislative investigating power are not as impressive as they may seem to be at first glance. It is abundantly clear that the powers of Congress, including the power to propose constitutional amendments on almost any subject, are broad enough to justify almost any investigation. Furthermore, when Congress authorizes an investigation, a legislative purpose is presumed by the courts. Witnesses who refuse to testify are subject to punishment for contempt, and members of Congress are not subject to liability (e.g., for slander) under the *Speech and Debate Clause of the Constitution.

Recent years have seen widespread criticism of congressional investigating committees, mainly on the ground that their purpose is not always to provide information for legislation but rather to subject individuals to public exposure, as in cases involving allegations of disloyalty. The courts have usually ruled that the fact that an investigation may expose someone to public calumny is incidental and does not invalidate the inquiry.

Legislative committees operate on the fiction that the destruction of a person's reputation is not technically punishment, from which it follows that most of the rights guaranteed to defendants accused of crime by the Constitution do not apply to persons who are being investigated by legislative committees. For example, the rule of *double jeopardy does not apply to investigation procedures. A person cleared by one investigating committee in regard to allegations of subversive activity may be investigated further on the same charges. Other allegations leveled against legislative investigating committees relate to their taste for guilt by mere association and the denial of such elementary rights as the right to the full benefit of *counsel and the right to prior notice of precise charges (see DUE PROCESS, PROCEDURAL). Clearly, the right most consistently sustained by the courts has been the privilege against compulsory self-incrimination. Even if the privilege is pleaded in an evasive way to avoid public odium, courts protect the witness from any effort to compel admission of criminal activity, as in Emspak v. United States (1955). In *Watkins v. United States (1957), the Court ruled that the investigatory power of Congress was limited by the free speech guaranty of the *First Amendment.

□ Alan Barth, Government by Investigation (1955). Robert K. Carr, The House Committee on Un-American Activities (1952). Will Maslow, "Fair Procedure in Congressional Investigations: A Proposed Code," Columbia Law Review 54 (1954): 839–892.                              David Fellman

**Congressional Power to Enforce Amendments.**
Once ratified, constitutional amendments become the law of the land, equal in authority to provisions in the original Constitution itself. Just as some clauses in the original constitutional text grant powers to Congress, so too, have some amendments expanded congressional authority. Eight amendments include specific congressional enforcement provisions.

The enforcement provisions of the *Thirteenth through *Fifteenth Amendments have received most attention. Given the legacy of the Dred *Scott case (1857) and other antebellum rulings involving the rights of African-Americans, the authors of the Civil War Amendments feared that the judiciary might prove laggard in enforcing civil rights legislation enacted during *Reconstruction (1865–1877). The Supreme Court confirmed these fears in the *Civil Rights Cases of 1883 when it voided the Civil Rights Act of 1875, which prohibited discrimination in places of public accommodation (see RACE AND RACISM; SEGREGATION, DE JURE). The Court limited congressional remedial power under the Fourteenth Amendment to cases of *state action rather than the actions of private individuals. This restrictive reading of the Fourteenth Amendment reinforced the Court's narrow interpretation of the

Fourteenth Amendment's *Privileges or Immunities Clause in the *Slaughterhouse Cases (1873). Consequently, when Congress enacted civil rights legislation in the 1960s, such as the *Civil Rights Act of 1964 prohibiting discrimination in places of public accommodation, it relied upon its power under the Interstate Commerce Clause (see COMMERCE POWER).

In the 1960s, however, new attention focused on the enforcement provisions of the Civil War Amendments. In section 4(e) of the *Voting Rights Act of 1965, Congress provided that those who had completed the sixth grade in an American Spanish-speaking school would be exempt from state-mandated literacy tests (see VOTE, RIGHT TO). Although the Court had previously upheld literacy tests against equal-protection challenges, it ruled in *Katzenbach v. Morgan (1966) that Congress had authority to prohibit such exams under section 5 of the Fourteenth Amendment. Speaking for the Court, Justice William *Brennan likened congressional powers under section 5 to those exercised under the Necessary and Proper Clause. If Congress had a rational basis for believing that eliminating literacy tests could promote *equal protection, it could legislate accordingly. Similarly, in *South Carolina v. Katzenbach (1966) the Court sanctioned remedial mechanisms adopted by Congress—including suspension of literacy tests, assignment of federal registrars, and the prohibition of new state electoral schemes without the approval of the U.S. attorney general—under section 2 of the *Fifteenth Amendment. In a related vein, *Jones v. Alfred H. Mayer Co. (1968) enforced provisions of the Civil Rights Act of 1866 that protected the rights of African-Americans to buy property without being subject to discrimination (see HOUSING DISCRIMINATION). Some justices in United States v. *Guest (1966) were willing to use section 5 of the Fourteenth Amendment to punish conspiracies against civil rights, whether or not they were accompanied by state action.

The Court has generally agreed that Congress has power under the enforcement clauses to remedy and perhaps even forestall violations of rights already recognized by the courts. There is less agreement about the extent of the powers of Congress, particularly through use of its unique fact-finding capabilities, to identify and protect new substantive rights. Moreover, no case has definitively clarified the scope of congressional enforcement provisions. *Oregon v. Mitchell (1970) suggested that the Court might view Congress's enforcement powers restrictively. Justice John M. *Harlan expressed concern in his *dissent in Katzenbach v. Morgan that Congress might employ its enforcement powers to narrow the Fourteenth Amendment's guarantees, but Justice Brennan responded "that Congress's power under Section 5 is limited to adopting measures to enforce the guarantees of the Amendment; section 5 grants Congress no power to restrict, abrogate or dilute these guarantees" (p. 651). This logic has been likened to a constitutional one-way ratchet.

Even if Brennan's interpretation is accepted, justices may disagree over the impact of congressional enforcement legislation. Laws proposed to restrict judicially mandated busing to achieve racial balance might, for example, be seen as an enlargement or restriction of equal protection. Similarly, dispute has centered on congressional authority to enforce a bill proposed by Senator Jesse Helms attempting to reverse the Court's decision in *Roe v. Wade* (1973) by declaring that human life begins at conception and enjoys due process protection from that point forward.

(See also CONSTITUTIONAL AMENDING PROCESS; CONSTITUTIONAL AMENDMENTS.)

☐ Jesse H. Choper, "Congressional Power to Expand Judicial Definitions of the Substantive Terms of the Civil War Amendments," *Minnesota Law Review* 67 (1982): 299–341. — John R. Vile

**Congressional Rules.** See POLITICAL QUESTIONS.

**Conkling, Roscoe** (b. Albany, N.Y., 30 Oct. 1829; d. New York, N.Y., 18 Apr. 1888), lawyer and senator; declined a confirmed nomination to the U.S. Supreme Court. Conkling studied law in the offices of Spencer & Kurnan in Utica, New York, and became a member of the New York bar in 1850. Eight years later, he was elected to the House of Representatives, where he served until 1867, with the exception of the 1863–1865 term. Elected to the Senate in 1866, he became the undisputed leader of the Republican party in New York through the judicious use of federal patronage. He was reelected to the Senate in 1872 and 1878.

Conkling's friendship with President Ulysses S. Grant induced Grant to offer Conkling nomination as chief justice of the Supreme Court to fill the vacancy caused by the death of Salmon P. *Chase in November 1873. Conkling declined this offer. In 1881 Conkling lost a bitter struggle with President James A. Garfield for control of federal patronage in New York. He resigned his Senate seat in protest two weeks later. After Garfield's death, President Chester A. Arthur on 24 February 1882 nominated Conkling as associate justice of the Supreme Court. The Senate confirmed Conkling on 2 March 1882 by a vote of 39 to 12. Five days later, however, Conkling formally declined the position. The *New York Times* suggested that the reason was that the position paid too little money and did not carry any patronage.

Conkling moved to Manhattan and resumed the private practice of law. He established a reputation in a short time and reportedly made a fortune. He died in New York City on 18 April 1888. — Judith K. Schafer

**Conscientious Objection.** A conscientious objector refuses to participate in *war because of ethical, moral, or religious principles. Congress and the Supreme Court have struggled to accommodate such beliefs to two public interests: first, the power of the national government to raise an army; and, second, the *First Amendment prohibition on an establishment of religion and its related guarantee of free exercise of religion. According to the Court in *United States* v. *Seeger* (1965), these First Amendment provisions acquire special meaning because of "the richness and variety of spiritual life in our country" and because "over 250 sects inhabit our land" (p. 174). Conscientious objection issues are presented when the government raises an army by conscription, or when someone who has enlisted in the military undergoes a change of views and becomes opposed to participation in war.

The 1917 Draft Act required all able-bodied males to serve but provided that members of any "well-recognized religious sect or organization" whose creed forbade "members to participate in war in any form" would be assigned to noncombatant service. Draft-age objectors claimed that this provision violated the Establishment Clause because it excluded honest believers who were not members of historic "pacifist churches," such as the Society of Friends, and infringed on free exercise of religion. The Supreme Court tersely rejected both claims in the *Selective Draft Law Cases* (1918).

The Court revisited the issue in *United States* v. *MacIntosh* (1931), holding that the Constitution does not require Congress to exclude conscientious objectors from military service. Five justices held that the naturalization statute could be construed to require MacIntosh to declare his unqualified willingness to bear arms. In dissent Chief Justice Charles Evans *Hughes argued that the statute did not require an oath that the applicant bear arms and that respect for religious conviction and our national history of tolerance for conscientious objection counselled the Court to construe the statute favorably to the applicant.

When Congress passed the Selective Training and Service Act of 1940, it relied upon Chief Justice Hughes's analysis and provided a conscientious objector exemption that included anyone who was conscientiously opposed to "war in any form" by reason of "religious training and belief," regardless of whether that belief was part of the dogma of an established church. The draft statutes from 1948 through 1967 further defined religious training and belief as limited to belief "in relation to a Supreme Being."

Despite statutory changes, the Supreme Court's views on conscientious objection have remained consistent since *World War II in draft cases and those arising in the military. The Court has never qualified its view that there is no constitutional right to exemption from draft registration or military service and has upheld the requirement that those who obtain conscientious objector status may be compelled to do alternative civilian service. It has, however, continued to construe statutory exemptions broadly.

The Court in *Clay* v. *United States* (1971) evaluated conscientious objector claims under a three-part test: is the belief "religious," is the claimant opposed to "war in any form," and is he or she sincere (p. 700). A religion-based claim may include even views that are not theistic, as in *Seeger*, where the registrant had "a belief in and devotion to goodness and virtue for their own sakes" and renounced "belief in God, except in the remotest sense" (p. 166).

In *Gillette* v. *United States* (1971), the Court held that opposition to war in any form excluded those who object only to particular wars, even if the objection is religious in character. However, an objector need not be a complete pacifist. Willingness to fight in self-defense is not disqualifying, nor is a belief in theocratic war directed by a supernatural being, the justices concluded in *Sicurella* v. *United States* (1955).

The issue of sincerity has proved troublesome, because officials charged with administering conscientious objector provisions have often been hostile to claimants and have masked their political disagreements behind vague assertions that the claimant seemed insincere. The Court took pains in *Witmer* v. *United States* (1955) to require that denial of a claim as insincere be supported by objective, nonspeculative evidence.

(See also RELIGION.)

□ Michael E. Tigar, "The Rights of Selective Service Registrants," in *The Rights of Americans*, edited by Norman Dorsen (1971), pp. 499–517.　　Michael E. Tigar

**Conscription** may be simply described as the power of the state to raise and maintain armed forces. Athough commonly associated with federal authority, during the American Revolution initial American efforts to raise an army involved local militias on a temporary multistate basis. The Continental army did consist of paid enlistees, but they were recruited largely by the colonies, now newly established states, which retained the ability to conscript and tax—two prerequisites not granted to the Confederation Congress. Most of the military was made up of volunteers, with terms lasting from a few weeks to approximately six months. While several states resorted to the draft, substitutes could be hired and frequently were. The need to resolve possible conflicts between the ideal of the volunteer citizen soldier and a professional standing army (with related issues of *state sovereignty, taxation, and a national government) dissipated with the end of the war when, in 1784, Congress discharged the entire Continental army, with the exception of eighty-three soldiers to protect military supplies.

The *Civil War generated large numbers of volunteers, but when it became clear that casualties would be heavy, portending an extended conflict, both North and South resorted to con-

scription. In 1862, the Confederacy made all healthy, white males between the ages of eighteen and thirty-five eligible for three years of service, and those already in the army were required to stay for the duration of the conflict, whether their enlistment term ended or not. The North followed suit, but the draft met with much evasion, resistance and, on several occasions, actual rioting. The constitutionality of conscription during the Civil War never reached the Supreme Court, in large measure because President Abraham *Lincoln suspended the writ of *habeas corpus, thus blocking *state courts from the release of draft resisters and other protesters.

The decision of President Woodrow Wilson to rely primarily on conscription rather than volunteers in 1917 for military service during *World War I made a legal challenge to the draft necessary if only to ensure that it received judicial sanction from the Supreme Court. This it did when Chief Justice Edward *White, on behalf of a unanimous bench, upheld the Draft Act (*Arver et al.* v. *United States*, 1918) and relegated state authority over the militias to a very limited level, subordinate to the federal government. Effectively raising military forces for both *World War II and the Korean Conflict, by 1968 the draft reflected the collapse of consensus that accompanied the *Vietnam War. In 1973, it was eliminated, and replaced with an all volunteer armed force—a decision resulting from political rather than military consideration. Registration for a national draft continues, however, and conscription remains readily available, now causing ambivalence rather than the antagonism of an earlier era.

(See also WAR.)

□ John Whiteclay Chambers II, *To Raise an Army: The Draft Comes to Modern America* (1987). Stephen M. Kohn, *Jailed for Peace: The History of American Draft Law Violators, 1658–1985* (1986).　　Jonathan Lurie

**Consent Decree,** a final judgment of a court entered by agreement of the parties. A consent decree terminates litigation but binds only the parties, not persons who were not parties to the litigation.　　William M. Wiecek

**Constitutional Amending Process.** Article V of the Constitution provides for a two-step amending process with two alternatives. Amendments may be proposed by two-thirds majorities in both houses of Congress or by a special convention called at the request of two-thirds of the state legislatures. Amendments are then ratified by three-fourths of the state legislatures or by special state conventions, depending on congressional specification. Despite thousands of proposals in the nation's history, only thirty-three have been approved by Congress, and only twenty-six have been ratified. To date, no convention for proposing amendments has been called. Only one amendment—the *Twenty-first, repealing national alcholic prohibition as established by the *Eighteenth—has been ratified by state conventions. The amending process has been used in four instances—the *Eleventh, *Fourteenth, *Sixteenth, and *Twenty-sixth—to overturn or modify judicial decisions (see REVERSAL OF COURT DECISIONS BY AMENDMENT).

A formal amending mechanism is a New World invention and logical complement to a written Constitution where constitutional reforms cannot simply be enacted by the legislative branch. Having just been through a revolution, the former colonists were aware of the need for peaceful alternatives that provided for necessary changes. Hence, a number of early state constitutions provided for amending mechanisms, some entrusting such power to the legislature and others to special conventions. Under the Articles of Confederation, however, state unanimity was required, and this wooden provision was subsequently bypassed by the Constitutional Convention that met in 1787.

Delegates to the Constitutional Convention generally agreed on the need for an amending mechanism, but they differed over who should institute changes and by what majorities. The result was a mechanism that entrusted Congress with the role of proposing amendments and the states with the task of ratifying them. The alternate convention mechanism was included in case Congress proved unresponsive to perceived needs. James *Madison defended the amending process in The *Federalist as a federal mechanism that guarded "equally against that extreme facility, which would render the Constitution too mutable, and that extreme difficulty, which might perpetuate its discovered faults" (Rossiter, ed., 1961, p. 278).

Article V contained two entrenchment clauses. One, designed to safeguard the provision permitting the importation of slaves for twenty years, is no longer in force (see SLAVERY). The second proviso, prohibiting states from being deprived of their equality in the Senate without their consent, is presumably still valid. Questions about whether there were additional unstated limits on the substance of amendments surfaced in connection with amendments *Fifteen through Twenty-one, but the Court rejected the *state sovereignty arguments in such cases as the National Prohibition Cases (1920) and United States v. Sprague (1931). More recently, some scholars have argued that courts might have power to void amendments that would take away certain fundamental guarantees of rights, but, since no such amendments have been adopted, this theory, which critics believe could set the judicial branch above the people, remains untested.

Most amendments have been ratified relatively quickly—the average is about two and a half years—but the Constitution specifies no time limits. In *Dillon v. Gloss (1921), the Court ruled that ratification should be soon enough to express a contemporary consensus of the states. While the Court had settled this and other issues (such as the determination in Hollingsworth v. Virginia, 1798, that the president's signature was not needed for amendments and in Hawke v. Smith, 1920, that a state could not predicate ratification on approval by a popular referendum), the much criticized opinion in *Coleman v. Miller (1939) subsequently stated that issues surrounding amendments were *political questions," appropriate for legislative resolution only. Amendments *Twenty through *Twenty-two contained seven-year limits within their texts. The proposed Equal Rights Amendment, by contrast, contained this same limit in its authorizing resolution. In a highly debated move, proponents subsequently extended the ratification deadline by thirty-nine additional months.

The notion of contemporary consensus, in contrast to more formal models that would limit scrutiny to the simple words of the Constitution, suggests that states might rescind ratification of pending amendments, just as they currently can approve amendments they previously rejected. In Idaho v. Freeman (1981) a U.S. district court sanctioned a state's attempt to rescind ratification of the Equal Rights Amendment after its deadline was extended by Congress. A similar controversy arose during ratification of the Fourteenth Amendment. Though Congress counted the rescinding states, their votes were unnecessary for ratification. Allowing states to rescind would make rescinding amendments parallel to ratifying them and would better guarantee a contemporary consensus. Such a procedure would also introduce greater uncertainty into an already arduous process.

Many questions about the amending process have centered on the unused convention mechanism. Most nineteenth-century petitions called for general conventions whereas most twentieth-century calls have been for single issue concerns like *income tax limitation in the 1950s, reapportionment in the 1960s (see FAIR REPRESENTATION), prayer in school (see SCHOOL PRAYER AND BIBLE READING), busing, federal deficit limitations, or *abortion in the 1970s and 1980s. The proposal for a convention to reverse the Court's stance on apportionment fell but one state short, and the balanced budget convention also came quite close. Congressional legislation has been proposed on the convention issue but never passed, thus leaving numerous unanswered questions.

Two prominent issues, presumably left to congressional judgment, are how long petitions for amendments should remain in force and how similar in content they should be to constitute a valid call for a convention. These issues are complicated by controversy over whether a convention can or cannot be limited to a single issue, with proponents of conventions generally arguing that they can and opponents that they cannot. Those who believe a convention can be limited tend to rely on legislative and/or judicial control or on oaths to be taken by members of a convention, while those thinking a convention cannot be limited generally agree that a convention would set its own agenda. Despite widespread fears of a "runaway" convention, a convincing case can be made that there are adequate legal and political safeguards—including the requirement for subsequent state ratification—against such a contingency.

Recently, it has been argued that the provisions in Article V are not exclusive and that amendments might also be proposed and/or adopted by referendum or other means. There is little evidence, however, that the framers intended for there to be unstated means of formal constitutional change.

Alterations have been proposed that would make the amending process easier and/or more democratic. The adoption of only twenty-six amendments in more than two hundred years underscores the difficulty of the current process, although periods of reform during which clusters of amendments have been ratified also demonstrate that such changes often spring from strong currents of social, economic, and political change.

(See also CONSTITUTIONAL AMENDMENTS.)

□ Walter Dellinger, "The Legitimacy of Constitutional Change: Rethinking the Amending Process," *Harvard Law Review* 97 (December 1983): 386–432. Alan P. Grimes, *Democracy and the Amendments to the Constitution* (1978). Kermit L. Hall, Harold M. Hyman, and Leon V. Sigal, eds. *The Constitutional Convention as an Amending Device* (1981). John R. Vile

**Constitutional Amendments.** All twenty-six amendments that have become the law of the land have been proposed by two-thirds majorities in both houses of Congress and ratified by three-fourths of the states. In some instances, the framers of these amendments aimed them directly at the Court; in most cases, however, the amendments have themselves fueled the justices' *workload. Taken together with the high court's interpretation of them, these amendments are a barometer of the social, economic, and political change within the constitutional system.

The first ten constitutional amendments have been the most protean source of judicial interpretation. The first eight guaranteed individual liberties, and the ninth and tenth were adopted as assurances that nondelegated powers would remain with the states and the people. None of the ten amendments altered the structure of the new government, but the first eight gave recourse to the courts in cases where individuals thought their rights were being violated. Initially, the Court had little directly to do with the *Bill of Rights, since its provisions were held to apply

only against the national government. Indeed, in *Barron* v. *Baltimore* (1833), the justices decided as much. After the *Fourteenth Amendment specified that states could not deprive any person of "due process of law," however, the Court began increasingly to look to the provisions in the Bill of Rights as guides to the meaning of this Due Process Clause. Guarantees once applied only to the national government were gradually "absorbed" or "incorporated" into the Fourteenth Amendment and applied to the states (see INCORPORATION DOCTRINE). Thus, in *Gitlow* v. *New York* (1925), the Court ruled that freedom of *speech (formerly guaranteed only by the *First Amendment) might now be considered to be protected against state invasion as well. The Court has subsequently heard a myriad of state cases involving such controversial issues as the regulation of *obscenity, sedition laws, advertising by attorneys (see BAR ADVERTISING), and *symbolic speech acts such as picketing, wearing arm bands, flag burning, and the like.

The nineteenth-century Supreme Court became involved with constitutional amendments in other ways. The *Eleventh Amendment was arguably less important for what it did than for the fact that it established the amending mechanism as a way of reversing judicial decisions and restricting judicial jurisdiction (see REVERSALS OF COURT DECISIONS BY AMENDMENT). This amendment was ratified in 1798 in reaction to *Chisholm* v. *Georgia* (1793), in which the Court, contrary to some Federalist interpretations during debates over ratification of the U.S. Constitution, but arguably in accord with the literal words of Article III, had accepted a suit instituted against Georgia for payment of a debt by a citizen of another state. Narrowly interpreted by the Marshall Court, this amendment was construed more expansively after the Civil War and was later again interpreted more restrictively.

Perhaps the most notable nineteenth-century collision between the Court and the amending process involved the great constitutional debate over the extension of *slavery into the *territories. In *Scott* v. *Sandford* (1857), the Court denied congressional power to exclude slavery in such areas and further declared that blacks were not and could not become citizens of the United States. But three amendments adopted after the *Civil War overturned the Court's most infamous decision. The *Thirteenth Amendment prohibited involuntary servitude except as punishment for crimes. The Fourteenth Amendment declared that "[a]ll persons born or naturalized in the United States and subject to the jurisdiction thereof, are citizens. . . ." Three provisions in this section extended to such citizens the *"privileges or immunities" of *citizenship as well as *"due process" and *"equal protection" of the law against state action.

The guarantees of the Fourteenth Amendment were in tension with the federal system, and a series of Court decisions demonstrated anew the complex relationship between change effected by amendment and change brought about by judicial interpretation. Cases narrowly interpreting the Fourteenth Amendment included the *Slaughterhouse Cases* (1873), restricting the Privileges or Immunities Clause, the *Civil Rights Cases* (1883), limiting protection against discrimination to cases of *"state action," and *Plessy* v. *Ferguson* (1896), sanctioning state-mandated segregation as long as facilities were equal (see SEPARATE BUT EQUAL DOCTRINE). The Privileges or Immunities Clause was damaged beyond repair; the Equal Protection Clause would later gain new life when, in *Brown* v. *Board of Education* (1954), the Court overturned *Plessy* and when *Baker* v. *Carr* (1962) opened the door to application of equal protection analysis to legislative apportionment (see REAPPORTIONMENT CASES). Similarly, the Due Process Clause—increasingly applied at the end of the nineteenth century to the protection of industries (legally recognized as "persons") against regulations—became the mechanism in the twentieth century by which most of the guarantees in the Bill of Rights, once applicable only to the national government, were now applied to the states as well.

The last of the three Civil War Amendments, the *Fifteenth Amendment, ratified in 1870, was designed to prevent citizens' voting rights from being abridged on the basis of color. The adoption of *grandfather clauses, *poll taxes, literacy tests, and *white primaries effectively nullified this amendment well into the second half of the twentieth century. About this time, however, it came to serve as the basis of such cases as *Smith* v. *Allwright* (1944)—outlawing the all-white primary—and others (see VOTE, RIGHT TO).

The four amendments ratified from 1913 through 1920 were products of the Progressive movement (see PROGRESSIVISM). The *Sixteenth Amendment was the third to overturn a Supreme Court decision. Legalizing the *income tax after the Court had declared in *Pollock* v. *Farmers' Loan & Trust Company* (1895) that this tax was void, the amendment presented the opportunity both to put government programs on a solid financial footing and to redistribute income. This latter possibility, with its overtones of socialism, appears to have motivated the *Pollock* decision more than constitutional language that was ambiguous. While the *Seventeenth Amendment, which provided for the direct election of senators, did not stir litigation, the far more controversial *Eighteenth did. Nonetheless, the justices willingly acceded to the constitutional prohibition on alcohol in the *National Prohibition Cases* (1920) and in *U.S.* v. *Sprague* (1931) and allowed expansion of prohibiton legislation already in force during *World War I. The new amendment spawned a number of important cases, including *Carroll* v. *United States* (1925) and *Olmstead* v. *United States* (1928), both related to searches and seizures (see

FOURTH AMENDMENT). The only amendment ever formally repealed—by the *Twenty-First Amendment ratified in 1933 by state conventions, rather than, as all other amendments to date, by state legislatures—the Eighteenth Amendment is more frequently remembered for the widespread disobedience it spawned and the boost it gave to organized crime, than for its more "noble" motives. The *Nineteenth Amendment, ratified in 1920, extended voting rights to women. The amendment had been preceded by years of suffragette acvtivity and marks America's greatest expansion of the franchise. Like the earlier prohibition amendment, the Nineteenth Amendment was accepted in *Leser* v. *Garnett* (1922) as a legitimate exercise of the amending power.

Not all efforts in the Progressive era to overcome Supreme Court decisions were successful. A proposed child labor amendment was both prompted by judicial decisions, like *Hammer* v. *Dagenhart* (1918) and *Bailey* v. *Drexel Furniture Co.* (1922), declaring such national laws to be unconstitutional, and mooted by a subsequent judicial reversal of this stance in *United States* v. *Darby Lumber Co.* (1941).

The Court has also figured prominently in determining the exact scope of constitutional amendments, often doing through judicial authority what the Congress refused to do in the amending process. For example, the *Twenty-fourth Amendment overturned the poll tax in federal elections, but it was the Supreme Court's decision in *Harper* v. *Virginia Board of Elections* (1966) that abolished the tax on the state level. The Congress and the states retain significant power to broaden constitutional protections beyond what the Court is willing to do. The *Twenty-sixth Amendment extended the right to vote to eighteen year olds after the Court declared in *Oregon* v. *Mitchell* (1970) that congressional legislation by itself could only extend the vote in national elections, and not in state and local contests.

Two proposals have failed in recent years—the Equal Rights Amendment that would have prohibited discrimination on the basis of sex and an amendment that would have granted congressional representation to the District of Columbia. Debate over the Equal Rights Amendment was particularly vigorous, and the amendment failed despite a questionable thirty-nine-month extension of the original seven-year ratification proposed by Congress. Ironically, one argument raised against the amendment was that increasingly liberal judicial decisions such as *Reed* v. *Reed* (1971) and *Frontiero* v. *Richardson* (1973) had made it unnecessary. The decision liberalizing *abortion in *Roe* v. *Wade* (1973) also raised concerns about how such an amendment might be interpreted by the Court (see GENDER).

The judiciary can alter constitutional understandings through interpretation, but courts are subject to the amending check. Among proposed amendments in recent years that have been directed to modify or reverse court decisions are proposals concerning state legislative apportionment, *school prayer and Bible reading, school busing, abortion, and flag burning. The Eleventh, Fourteenth, Sixteenth, and Twenty-sixth Amendments, while sometimes producing results that would have surprised their authors, show that such attempts can be successful. Although amendments serve as authoritative statements of popular will, they are, by comparison to judicial interpretations, extremely difficult to adopt; this difficulty exerts pressure on the courts to adapt constitutional interpretations to changing times. While there are obvious structural changes that can only be effected by amendment, debates on and off the bench about the proper extent of judicial interpretation demonstrate the perpetual tension and constant interplay that will always exist between formal constitutional amendment and judicially initiated changes in constitutional intepretation.

(See also CONSTITUTIONAL AMENDING PROCESS.)

□ Alan P. Grimes, *Democracy and the Amendments to the Constitution* (1978). J. W. Peltason, *Understanding the Constitution*, 12th ed. (1991). United States Senate, Subcommittee on the Constitution, Committee on the Judiciary, *Amendments to the Constitution: A Brief Legislative History* (1985). Clement E. Vose, *Constitutional Change: Amendment Politics and Supreme Court Litigation Since 1900* (1972).                    John R. Vile

**Constitutional Interpretation** is both the process by which the American Constitution is construed and the study of that process. The latter is principally an academic activity, while the former art is practiced daily by government officials and private lawyers. Because the American Constitution proscribes any acts by government that are inconsistent with the Constitution, every legal question depends on an interpretation of the Constitution, since no claim is enforceable unless that enforcement is compatible with the Constitution. Let us first look at how judges and practitioners interpret the Constitution and then survey what academics have said about that practice.

*Judicial Interpretation.* For the many centuries preceding the adoption of the American Constitution, the constitutive rules of political society were not construed along legal lines. Other ways prevailed of giving meaning to the rules that determined what government might legitimately do: theological, conventional, hereditary, strategic. Although it is usually taken for granted, it is in fact significant that the ways in which the American Constitution may be legitimately interpreted are similar to the ways in which lawyers and judges construe legal documents. This in part is a consequence of the fact that the United States Constitution is a written constitution (indeed the first modern written constitution). The important American innovation was not the writing per se, however, but rather the political theory whereby the state was objectified and made a mere instrument of the sovereign will that lay in the people. Thus the distinction between the sovereign and the organs of state, which seemed so absurd to minds before the eighteenth century, was an indispensable premise for a comprehensive, written constitution that conveyed limited powers.

By this means, the United States put the power of the state under law. A written constitution made constitutional interpretation along customary legal modes of thinking feasible. It is possible to have a limited government without a written constitution (Great Britain, for example); and it is possible to have a written constitution and unlimited government (the former Soviet Union, for example). But a limited government, put under the written constraints of a superior legal instrument, will inevitably introduce the modalities of legal reasoning and argument into decisions affecting the legitimate power of the State.

One way of understanding the centrality of having a text to construe is to look at the role of texts in other legal contexts. One might say that a written constitution is like a trust agreement. It specifies what powers the trustees are to have and it endows these agents with certain authority delegated by the settlors who created the trust. Because the American Revolution and the *Declaration of Independence severed sovereignty from the state and put it in the hands of the people, the "trustees" in the constitutional scheme (the government) are not identical with the "settlor" (the sovereign) and therefore are not at liberty to alter the trust agreement and change the limits of their own authority. From this agreement must come decisions about the extent of that authority. And thus a written constitution is not only a set of rules; it is a way of creating rules. Like the trust agreement, the governing text will constrain the agents that it creates only if the methods of interpretation compel such constraints. When Thomas *Jefferson wrote that "Our peculiar security is in the possession of a written constitution," he meant that the constraints manifest in a written charter would act as safeguards against a governmental usurpation of powers that belonged to the People. Because Jefferson as principal drafter of the Declaration of Independence believed that the state was the creation of sovereign power, not the other way around, he insisted on a written Constitution and a written *Bill of Rights. The phrase "inalienable rights" that appears in the Declaration means that the people cannot alienate—that is, sell or trade—their rights because to do so would render the people less than sovereign.

By relying on a written instrument to perfect the constitutional understanding, the framers of the Constitution introduced the habits and style of Anglo-American legal argument into the politics of the State. This determined the foundation for constitutional interpretation in the United States. Since the Constitution was the supreme law, its terms had to govern; since it was a comprehensive law, it would be implicated in every legal decision; since it was written law, it had to be construed, both to give it supreme effect and to apply it in situations not explicitly anticipated in the text. And because it was law, this was to be done according to the prevailing methods of legal construction. The ways in which Americans interpret the Constitution could have been different; indeed, the forms of constitutional discourse are very different in other societies. For Americans, however, these ways have taken the forms of common-law argument, largely those forms prevailing at the time of the drafting and ratification of the U.S. Constitution. Thus the methods hitherto used to construe deeds, wills, contracts, and promissory notes, methods familiar to the mundane subjects of the *common law, became the methods of constitutional construction once the state itself was put under law.

These methods of reasoning and ways of making arguments determine the ways in which constitutional propositions are characterized as valid from a legal point of view. These methods might be divided or recategorized in different ways, but the following six forms or modalities of constitutional argument are widely accepted: (1) *historical*—relying on the intentions of the framers and ratifiers of the Constitution (see ORIGINAL INTENT; HISTORY, COURT USES OF); (2) *textual*—looking to the meaning of the words of the Constitution alone, as they would be interpreted by an average contemporary American today; (3) *structural*—inferring structural rules from the relationships that the Constitution mandates; (4) *doctrinal*—applying rules generated by precedent; (5) *ethical*—deriving rules from those moral commitments of the American ethos that are reflected in the Constitution; and (6) *prudential*—seeking to balance the costs and benefits of a particular rule. A modality is the way in which a proposition is characterized as true. To clarify these approaches, let us undertake a somewhat more formal statement of each form of argument, illustrated by some examples.

*History.* May a state validly enforce a law that makes it a crime to procure an abortion? Constitutional arguments from a historical perspective are: the framers and ratifiers of the Due Process Clause of the *Fourteenth Amendment intended to prohibit such legislation because the ratification debates of the period demonstrate a concern to protect previously disfranchised persons from debasement by the state; or the framers and ratifiers did not intend to do so because blacks, not women, and voting, not the intimate acts of private persons, were the subjects of their debates; or we cannot ascertain what their intention was regarding the state's coercive power to compel women to bear children because the debates, while broad in subject matter are fragmentary in detail. Arguments that rely on this interpretive modality might also approach the abortion question as follows. Did the framers and ratifiers of the Fourteenth Amendment intend to countenance extant state laws forbidding abortions? Because these statutes were unmentioned in the debates, were they thus tacitly tolerated? Or did they intend to overturn them by means of the amendment? Or are their intentions unclear? Because the framers made general references to an evolving standard of protection from state intrusion, did they mean to delegitimate such statutes? Or is the historical record simply unclear as to those anti-abortion laws that were on the statute books at the time of ratification? In any case, determinations of constitutionality will be made on the basis of historical evidence about the intentions of the framers and ratifiers of the relevant clauses of the Constitution.

Often the historical approach is confused with textual argument because historical argument usually refers to a specific text of the Constitution. Historical or "originalist" approaches to construing the text, however, are distinctive in their reference to what a particular provision is supposed to have meant to the ratifiers. These approaches seek to determine what the original purpose of a provision was to those who endowed it with legal authority. When Chief Justice Roger B. *Taney in *Dred *Scott* v. *Sandford* (1857) construed the scope of the *diversity jurisdiction in *Article III in order to determine whether a slave could seek freedom through a diversity suit before a federal court, he wrote:

We must inquire who, at that time [1787–1788], were recognized as the citizens of a state, whose rights and liberties had been outraged by the English government; and who declared their independence, and assumed the powers of Government to defend their rights by force of arms. . . . We refer to these historical facts for the purpose of showing the fixed opinions concerning that race, upon which the statesmen of that day spoke and acted. (pp. 407–409)

*Dred Scott* demonstrates the limitations of historical argument. Although the decision—which denied diversity jurisdiction to slave litigants and repudiated the Missouri Compromise—is regarded with shame by many constitutional scholars, there is nothing erroneous about Taney's historical argument. Perhaps, however, the framers and ratifiers did not intend that their contemporary opinions on every subject should govern every subsequent argument. More importantly, it is anachronistic and presumptuous to assume that we can determine what the framers and ratifiers of a particular provision, drafted a century or two before the present, would have preferred to happen in a world they could no more anticipate than we can successfully imagine theirs. We assume that Jefferson would be opposed to the intrusiveness and scope of the federal government today because he opposed Federalist policies so vehemently in his own day. But it is not clear whether he would have opposed the expansion of federal authority to eradicate the effects of *slavery, an evil he also opposed but despaired of ever correcting. We do not assume that Alexander *Hamilton would have opposed the World War I alliance with France simply because he opposed such an alliance in 1792. This sort of question is frequently encountered in more familiar private-law contexts: should a court construe the intentions of a long-dead testator whose will that endows a "Christian college for women" to admit men of other faiths? The interpretive method is the same.

*Text.* One of the constitutional questions in the *Dred Scott* case—who are the "citizens" for purposes of diversity jurisdiction (see CITIZENSHIP)—provides an example for the textual modality. The text of the Constitution provides that "The judicial Power shall extend . . . to Controversies . . . between Citizens of different States . . ." (Art. III, sec. 2). Does this text of the Constitution, to the average person, appear to declare that a former slave can bring suit in federal court (because the text's use of the word *citizen* is not qualified by race)? Or does the text appear to deny this jurisdiction (because the text's use of the word *citizen* rather than *person* implies a distinction by race)? Or is the language simply too vague to say whether a suit between a black American in one state and his former employer, a white American resident in another state, is a "controversy . . . between Citizens of different States"? The current meaning of those words is different from what Taney found them to mean to the framers and ratifiers of 1789.

Textual approaches are not, however, inevitably more progressive than originalist approaches. Sometimes the text can be a straitjacket, confining the judge within language that would have been different if its drafters had foreseen later events. Is twentieth-century wiretapping prohibited by the *Fourth Amendment, which guarantees "[t]he right of the people to be secure in their persons, houses, papers, and effects, against unreasonable searches and seizures"? Chief Justice William Howard *Taft engaged in textual argument in a case where federal prohibition officers obtained incriminating information by intercepting telephone conversations of defendants:

The amendment itself shows that the search is to be of material things—the person, the house, his papers or his effects. The amendment does not forbid what was done here for there was no seizure. The evidence was secured by the sense of hearing and that only. There was not entry of the houses. The language of the amendment cannot be extended and expanded. (*Olmstead* v. *United States*, 1928, p. 464)

Textual argument is associated with the dominant figure of the postwar Supreme Court, Justice Hugo *Black, and his frequently voiced assertion that the Constitution contained various "absolutes." Black cited the *First Amendment's provision that "Congress shall make no law . . . abridging the freedom of speech" as an example of a textual absolute on the grounds that if he read such a provision to the average citizen, it would be interpreted to mean "no law" whatsoever could constitutionally be applied to abrogate speech (see SPEECH AND THE PRESS). To the objections that such an interpretation would strike down virtually all *obscenity laws and a great many *defamation, conspiracy, and anti-incitement statutes, Black simply interposed the text without further argument. Some texts, Black allowed, did not state their prohibitions quite so categorically. The *Eighth Amendment's bar against *cruel and unusual punishments, for example, does not specify what such punishments are; but, argued Black, whatever they may be determined to be, they are absolutely prohibited because that is what the language would mean to an ordinary American today. Textual argument is thus often juxtaposed against judicial balancing tests that would concede, for example, that a particular punishment is cruel but that require the circumstances and necessity of the punishment to be taken into account.

The demands of textual argument for a clear and explicit text are responsible for the constitutional doctrine of *"incorporation" by which a Black-led Supreme Court absorbed the texts of much of the Bill of Rights into the Fourteenth Amendment's otherwise-vague prohibitions against the states.

*Structure.* Can a Congressional committee issue a subpoena for the disclosure of the president's working notes and diaries? Structural modes of argument would argue that the institutional relationships promulgated by the Constitution provide such power because Congress must have full information in order to fulfill its statutory function; or deny it because the president must be able to preserve the integrity of his deliberations free from the self-consciousness that follows from the anticipation of private debate that will be made public; or speak equivocally because in some contexts the need for public information outweighs the damage to the executive process of policy formulation. Many celebrated examples of this form of argument can be found. The 1980s were particularly notable for the Court's focus on structural issues, as in *Morrison* v. *Olson* (1988), upholding the appointment of a special prosecutor despite her ambivalent status as an executive officer with responsibilities to the judicial branch; *Bowsher* v. *Synar* (1986), striking down an attempt to use an officer responsive to the legislative branch in an executive role; and, most importantly, *Immigration and Naturalization Service* v. *Chadha* (1983), which struck down the *legislative veto. But structural argument is not a recent invention. (See SEPARATION OF POWERS.)

The second part of *McCulloch v. Maryland (1819), the principal foundation case for constitutional analysis, relied almost wholly on structural approaches. In determining whether a Maryland tax on the federally chartered Bank of the United States could be enforced, Chief Justice John *Marshall refused to specify what particular text supported his argument and explicitly rejected reliance on historical arguments, preferring instead to state the rationale on inferences from the structure of federalism. A federal structure could not be maintained, he concluded, if the states, whose officials are elected by a state's constituency, could tax the agencies of the federal government present in a state and thereby levy a tax on a nationwide constituency. By taxing a federal agency the state would be able to manipulate directly the choices made by the federal government—effectively prohibiting some choices by making them expensive—without the check of being answerable to affected constituents. The constitutional structure would not tolerate such a practice even though the text and the ratification debates did not explicitly condemn it.

Structural arguments are less intuitively obvious than arguments from the text or history of the Constitution. Arguments in this modality usually follow a pattern: first, an uncontroversial statement about a constitutional structure is introduced; second, a relationship is inferred from this structure; third, a factual assertion about the world is made; finally, a conclusion is drawn that provides the rule in the case.

Thus in *National League of Cities v. Usery (1976), Justice William H. *Rehnquist addressed the question whether a state may be required to observe federal minimum wage laws. He reasoned: (1) the Constitution sets up a federal system, that is, a system in which some things are committed to state determination (structure) (see FEDERALISM); (2) if the federal government could control all such determinations, we would cease to have a federal system (relationship); (3) determining how much to pay certain state employees would effectively manipulate all other state choices and thus be incompatible with a federal system (conclusion).

*Prudence.* Can a state require mandatory testing for the AIDS virus antibodies? One might argue that it is wise because an epidemic can only be controlled by public health measures; or that it is unwise because of the distress caused to those who will falsely test positive and because the intrusiveness of testing an overwhelmingly virus-free population outweigh the benefits of locating a few victims; or that it is unclear on the present facts whether or not it is wise to permit such testing because the efficacy of the tests and the scope of the epidemic are subject to inconclu-

sive debate. These questions propose an evaluation from a *prudential* point of view.

In the first half of the twentieth century, the prudential mode of constitutional argument was associated with doctrines that sought to protect the political position of the courts, though it had long been a staple of constitutional argument in the other branches. Justice Louis *Brandeis, most notably in his concurrence in *Ashwander v. Tennessee Valley Authority* (1936), introduced prudential argument on this limited basis into judicial opinions. The national crises of depression and world war provided reason for the courts to consider the practical effects of constitutional doctrine as elements in the rationales underpinning doctrine. One such case arose when, in the depths of the midwestern farm depression, the Minnesota legislature passed a statute providing a moratorium from foreclosure for those unable to pay a mortgage. On its face, this statute seemed to vindicate the fears of the framers that state legislatures would compromise the national credit market by enacting debtor relief statutes and also seemed to violate the *Contracts Clause of Article I that was the textual product of such concerns. Nevertheless the Court upheld the statute, observing that an emergency existed in Minnesota that furnished a proper occasion for the exercise of the reserved power of the state to protect the vital interests of the community (*Home Building and Loan Association v. Blaisdell*, 1934). The Court recognized the political expediency of the state's action and acquiesced in it. Another national crisis provided the background of *Bowles v. Willingham* (1944). Congress enacted the Emergency Price Control Act, providing for administrative actions to freeze or reduce rents for housing adjacent to defense establishments. The Court upheld the statute in frankly prudential language:

Congress was dealing here with conditions created by activities resulting from a great war effort. A nation which can demand the lives of its men and women in waging of that war is under no constitutional necessity of providing a system of price control on the domestic front which will assure each landlord a "fair return" on his property . . . Congress . . . has done all that due process under the war emergency requires. (p. 519)

The prudential approach is not confined to problems a nation encounters in emergencies. Prudential argument is based on facts, as these play into political and economic policies. From a prudential point of view, the legal rule to be applied is derived from a calculus of costs and benefits, after the facts are taken into account. Often this calls for a balancing of costs and benefits since more than one policy will be at stake.

*Doctrine.* When a judge states that a neutral, general principle derived from the case law construing the Constitution should apply (that a particular precedent is on "all fours" with the instant case), or that it does not apply (the present case is one of "first impression") or that it may apply (the precedents are divided, with authority for competing positions), such arguments are made in a doctrinal mode. Doctrinal arguments are not confined to arguments originating in judicial or administrative case law; there are also precedents from other institutions, such as the practices of earlier presidents or Congress.

This mode of argument is the stuff of common-law legal reasoning. First-year law courses are devoted to its mastery and it is not unique to constitutional law. Consider as an example the question: to what extent can a state constitutionally provide financial aid to parochial schools? Suppose, for example, that parochial school students whose schools are not on the route of free public school buses are given a cash allowance by the state to provide for their transportation. Does this offend the Establishment Clause of the First Amendment because the state is bearing costs that would otherwise be born by church members? A judge confronting such a case might begin, not by reading the text of the First Amendment that states a rule in rather general terms, but by turning to precedent to find similar cases providing authoritative decisions. In the area of Establishment Clause jurisprudence a great deal of constitutional doctrine has been developed in numerous cases. The standards these cases develop and apply can be stated as legal rules. The case "on point," whose facts are similar in relevant aspects, is *Everson v. Board of Education* (1947), which sustained the power of local authorities to provide free transportation for children attending church-related schools. In *Everson* the Supreme Court treated the provision of transportation as a form of public welfare legislation, noting that it was being extended by the state "to all its citizens without regard to their religious belief" (p. 16). The majority reasoned that transportation benefited the child in the same way as did police protection at crossings near the church school, fire protection for the school building, connections to the building for sewage disposal, and public highways and sidewalks by which one traveled to a parochial school. Based on the rationale of this case, subsequent courts have developed a three-pronged test to separate the merely incidental benefits of general social expenditures such as these from programs that attempted to assist parochial education directly: does the state program have a secular purpose; is its principal effect neither to advance nor inhibit *religion; does the administration of the program excessively entangle the state in religious affairs?

Applying this test to the illustrative question, the judge might write: "*Everson* can be distinguished from the instant case because the program in *Everson* provided transportation common to all students, whereas here only some students, the parochial ones, are given cash

allowances. While doubtless the legislature had a secular purpose in mind, the effect of these allowances was in fact to make the parochial schools more attractive to parents than their secular counterparts and thereby advance the cause of religious institutions. Moreover, the oversight required of the state to ensure that the allowances are in fact spent on providing a system of parochial school transportation intrudes the administrative apparatus of the state into the affairs of the church schools. This can only lead to interference with budgets and an insistence on allocations for transportation that will excessively entangle the state in the administration of church affairs. Accordingly, the program must be held unconstitutional."

Or the judge might write: "*Everson*, which also involved public transportation to parochial school students, governs this case. Here as there, the state's program provides aid to students and their parents and not—as in cases that have applied *Everson* and struck down state assistance in this area—direct assistance to church-related schools. Its secular purpose, to provide school transportation at greater efficiency and less cost to the state than expanding its own bus fleets, is apparent. Like school lunches, public health services, and secular textbooks, the transportation provided here confers a benefit on the parochial student that is at parity with what the secular student receives. Thus its effect is neither to advance nor inhibit religion, but rather to avoid exacting a penalty from the parochial student. Finally, whatever state management is required to administer the program will be limited to the oversight of transportation; such involvement as there may be need not, therefore, excessively entangle the state in those religious matters with regard to which it has no role."

In either case, the judge has applied a rule derived from the relevant case law. The rule is neutral as to the parties; that is, it applies equally to Catholic, Jewish, and atheist claimants and does not vary depending on who is bringing or defending the suit. And the rule is general; that is, it applies to all cases in which the state is giving assistance to religious institutions and is not confined to the facts of the original case that gave birth to the rule.

The commitment to neutral, general principles does not mean that cases cannot be overruled. A particular precedent may be overruled because it does not comport with a persuasive reading of the cases on which it itself relied, or those from a competing line of doctrine originating in wholly distinct facts but progressively encroaching on the area of its operation. More significantly, doctrinal argument is not confined to the application of *stare decisis*, that is, the strict adherence to cases previously decided, because one of the assumptions of American doctrinalism is that the Supreme Court may reverse *precedent. This would appear to follow from the family of modalities—that provide alternative legal rules—and the supremacy of the Constitution to the acts of government (including its judicial branch). The Court is empowered, indeed obligated, to overrule itself when it is persuaded that a particular precedent wrongly construed the Constitution.

*Ethos.* The modality of ethical argument denotes an appeal to those elements of the American ethos that are reflected in the Constitution. The fundamental American constitutional ethos is the idea of limited government, which presumes that all residual authority remains in the private sphere. Thus when we argue that a particular constitutional conclusion is required, permitted, or forbidden by the American ethos that has allocated certain decisions to the individual or to private institutions, we are arguing in an ethical mode.

Ethical arguments arise as a consequence of the fundamental constitutional arrangement by which rights, in the American system, are defined as those choices beyond the power of government to compel. This contrasts with some European constitutions that define rights affirmatively.

Structural and ethical arguments share some similarities. Each is essentially an inferred set of arguments. Like structural arguments, ethical arguments do not depend on the construction of any particular piece of text but rather on the necessary relationships that can be inferred from the overall arrangement expressed in the text. Structural argument infers rules from the powers granted to governments; ethical argument, by contrast, infers rules from the powers denied to government. The principal error regarding ethical argument is the assumption that any statute or executive act is unconstitutional if it causes effects that are incompatible with some preferred elements of the American ethos. Such an assumption equates ethical argument, a constitutional form, with moral and political argument generally. The American constitutional ethos is largely confined to the reservation of powers not delegated to a limited government.

A hypothetical example shows the basic pattern of ethical argument. Suppose a state judge offers a choice of a thirty-year prison sentence or impotence-inducing medical treatment to a convicted sex offender. The defendant accepts the latter option and is released on probation on terms that require that this pledge be fulfilled by systematic drug-induced impotence. If the probationer were to cease taking the prescribed drug and his probation revoked, a constitutional challenge to the terms of his probation might take this form:

1. There is no express constitutional power in federal courts to implement a program of eugenics. Indeed the reservation to the individual of the decision whether to have children is deeply rooted in the American belief in the integrity of the individual conscience, which is reflected in several parts of the Constitution.

2. Moreover, eugenics programs are not an appropriate means ancillary to any express power that is allocated to government; therefore there is no federal power to assume this otherwise private authority.

3. Those means denied the federal government are also denied the states.

4. The hypothetical sentence would compel a man to comply with a eugenics scheme that rendered him ineligible to procreate.

The element of the American ethos at stake is the reservation to individuals and families of the freedom to make certain kinds of decisions. Similar arguments are found in cases in which a state attempted to bar schools from teaching foreign languages (*Meyer* v. *Nebraska,* 1923); in which a state passed a compulsory education act requiring every school-age child to attend public school, which implicitly outlawed private schools (*Pierce* v. *Society of Sisters,* 1925); in which a local *zoning ordinance intended to exclude communes was applied to prohibit a grandmother from living with her grandchildren (*Moore* v. *East Cleveland,* 1977); in which parents sought to end the artificial nutrition of their severely brain-injured daughter (*Cruzan* v. *Director, Missouri Department of Health,* 1990); and in which a man allegedly suffering from delusions (but concededly harmless) was confined to a mental hospital for almost twenty-five years without treatment (*O'Connor* v. *Donaldson,* 1975). Each of these examples can be stated in the form of an ethical argument. For example, the *Pierce* arguments could be framed thus: (1) there is no express constitutional power to monopolize education; (2) a statute outlawing private education is not an appropriate means associated with any express power (such as regulating commerce or providing for armed forces); (3) the decision to educate one's children privately or parochially or publicly is reserved to the family; (4) a statute compelling attendance exclusively at public schools amounts to a scheme to coerce families into a particular educational choice and destroy private education.

***Academic and Political Commentary.*** Commentary on these modes of constitutional argument by scholars and critics constitute the field of constitutional interpretation outside the courts and legislatures. From the mid-1950s onward, the interpretation of the American Constitution has assumed a central place in American public life. Racial segregation, abortion, the powers of the presidency, and the legitimacy of the courts have all been made to turn on these methods of construction. At the same time, constitutional interpretation has become a rich academic field in its own right, attracting the attention of scholars in collateral disciplines, such as history, political science, and philosophy.

In retrospect, one can see that the seminal

works in the academic field were Charles Black's *Structure and Relationship in Constitutional Law* (1969) and Alexander *Bickel's *The Least Dangerous Branch* (1962). Black's remarkable study isolated one particular form of argument, the structural, and established criteria for making and assessing such arguments. Bickel did much the same for prudential argument, tracing its lineage to Justice Louis D. *Brandeis and demonstrating a family of related judicial techniques. John Hart Ely's *Democracy and Distrust* (1980) was the first sustained effort to answer the countermajoritarian objection to *judicial review (the argument that overturning a legislative decision by a court amounts to a reversal of democratic, majoritarian choices) by relying on one of the classic forms of argument as preeminent. Ely divided the forms of argument into the interpretivist, that is, historical, textual and structural forms, and noninterpretivist, that is, ethical, prudential, and doctrinal forms (see INTERPRETIVISM AND NONINTERPRETIVISM). Paul Brest, in an important series of articles and an influential casebook, wrote about interpretation as argument and isolated some of the paradigmatic forms of argument. *Constitutional Fate* (1982), by Philip Bobbitt, identified and described the six forms of argument described here. Bobbitt argued that there could be no hierarchy of arguments. He maintained that the countermajoritarian objection was fundamentally nonsensical since legitimacy was conferred not by majoritarianism but by following accepted conventional forms, which could not be genuinely applied in the absence of judicial review. Laurence Tribe's *Constitutional Choices* (1985) asserted that judicial review was inevitable. In *Red, White, and Blue* (1988) Mark Tushnet collected the various objections to each of the paradigmatic forms and evaluated these from a prudential point of view, loosely associated with the Critical Legal Studies movement. At the same time, questions of interpretation had come to the forefront of literary criticism, and the influence of semiotics, especially the school of deconstruction associated with Jacques Derrida, Paul de Man, Michel Foucault and others, was felt in the field of constitutional interpretation.

In the political arena, attention also was focused on the methods of constitutional interpretation. The inspiring but methodologically problematic opinion in *Brown* v. *Board of Education* (1954) invited such scrutiny. Perhaps the most influential member of the judiciary, Judge Learned *Hand, implicitly criticized Chief Justice Earl *Warren's opinion in lectures published as *The Bill of Rights* (1958). With this controversy, the countermajoritarian objection was revived and with it the debate about the proper methods of constitutional interpretation. Controversial Warren Court human rights and criminal process cases in the 1960s fueled this controversy, which erupted with new vehemence when the Supreme Court decided the abortion case *Roe* v. *Wade*

(1973). The debate was framed in terms of the legitimacy of judicial review itself rather than in terms of its various methods. By the 1980s, debate over method had begun to predominate. Most critics of the Court were willing to admit that there was a proper role for judicial scrutiny of legislative and executive acts for their constitutionality; the focus of debate was the acceptable methods to be employed in that scrutiny.

Edwin Meese, attorney general of the United States in the later Reagan administration, and Justice William *Brennan presented contrasting views of what scrutiny was legitimate for courts to undertake. In Meese's view, judicial review was confined to "strict construction" of the Constitution. He held that only historical, textual, and structural arguments provide a legitimate basis by which to evaluate statutes and practices for their constitutionality. Judicial review on any other basis amounts to a usurpation of democratically delegated power. Justice Brennan took a more expansive view, stressing the prudential and ethical modalities of judicial review.

Nowhere was this conflict more clearly and dramatically presented than in the Senate hearings on the nomination of Robert *Bork to the Supreme Court (see SENATE JUDICIARY COMMITTEE). The nominee repeatedly refused to criticize the outcomes in various controversial cases, including *Roe* v. *Wade*, and limited his assessments to the arguments brought forth by the Court in support of those holdings. "The judge's authority [in a constitutional democracy] derives entirely from the fact that he is applying the law and not his personal values." To the question of how a judge should go about finding the law, Bork testified that the only legitimate way "is by attempting to discern . . . the intentions of . . . those . . . who ratified our Constitution and its various amendments. The judge's responsibility is to discern how the framers' values, defined in the context of the world they knew, apply in the world we know. If a judge abandons intention as his guide, there is no law available to him and he . . . goes beyond his legitimate power." Repeatedly Bork denied that there was "any legitimate method of constitutional reasoning" that would support controversial holdings that he opposed, but he was scrupulous about not criticizing them as policy. His objections were interpretive and thus went to the legitimacy of the arguments on which the Court relied; consistent with his views of the judge's role, he did not evaluate controversial decisions on political grounds. His rejection by the Senate may be taken as an affirmation of the legitimacy of the decisions that, as Bork argued, cannot be rationalized on strict constructionist grounds.

There has long been a certain association between particular forms of argument and specific political points of view. Jefferson and his followers were strict constructionists in their day, holding that such a set of modalities tended to restrain the scope of federal power by confining the domain of federal judicial review. Each of the various forms of argument can be used to construct an ideology, a set of political and practical commitments whose values are internally consistent and externally distinct from those of competing ideologies constructed around other modalities. Some persons believe that one particular modality represents the only legitimate means of interpreting the constitution (e.g., historical argument) since it is verifiable by a resort to materials (e.g., the evidence of the intentions of the framers) that are legitimated according to a particular political theory of interpretation. This has led some commentators to argue that the modalities of argument are no more than instrumental, rhetorical devices to be deployed in the service of the political ideologies of which they are a subsidiary part. Other critics have concluded that the modalities must be ranked in priority. In either case, some standard external to constitutional interpretation is imported into the decision making.

According to the latter argument, everyone agrees that the Constitution is law. Therefore, the Constitution does not merely mean what particular people want it to mean. If it did, it would not be law. The problem is that it is not always clear what the Constitution means, how it is to be applied/interpreted. Reasonable people disagree about what it means. Some think that a Constitution that guarantees "the equal protection of the laws" requires race-conscious *affirmative action policies in order to remove the effects of past and present discrimination (a prudential argument); others think that a state that engages in affirmative action is violating that same guarantee (a textual argument). In hard cases, two or more legitimate modalities will conflict. Since the Constitution itself does not direct how it is to be interpreted—does not say which modality to be used—those who interpret the Constitution have to look to something other than the various legitimating forms of argument. This means that the interpretation of the Constitution must inevitably be based on principles that are external to the words of the Constitution itself. Those principles have to be created rather than found; the Constitution does not contain instructions for its own interpretation.

This does not mean that the Constitution could mean anything at all, that it is "indeterminate" regarding its appropriate interpretation. Sometimes the resort to interpretive principles admits of only one answer. Additionally, what the Supreme Court thinks, and what it will say about questions not yet decided but likely to arise soon, can be predicted with some accuracy. Moreover, some interpretations are better than others, that is, only some correspond to the various legitimating modalities. Some interpretations of ambiguous provisions will produce an unacceptable increase in judicial discretion (prudential); others

will leave politically weak groups at the mercy of the state (structural); others will make liberty too fragile (ethical); others will be insufficiently respectful of the claims of original intent (historical). So constitutional interpretation is not indeterminate even though it does not always yield unique answers.

How shall we choose, however, among good interpretations? What is the legal basis for this and why is it legitimate? Perhaps importing an external standard to govern such choices—say, a preference for liberty or equality or efficiency, which would allow us to justify our decisions—sacrifices their legitimacy, since it requires a rule that is not generated by the legitimating modalities of argument. Perhaps we cannot, in fact, give good reasons that explain our choice of one legitimate outcome over a different, equally legitimate outcome if, by "good" reasons, we mean legitimate reasons. This, at any rate, is the most important question confronting the field of constitutional interpretation.

(See also JUDICIAL REVIEW.)

□ Alexander Bickel, *The Least Dangerous Branch: The Supreme Court at the Bar of Politics* (1962). Charles Black, *Structure and Relationship in Constitutional Law* (1969). Philip Bobbitt, *Constitutional Fate* (1982). Philip Bobbitt, *Constitutional Interpretation* (1991). Paul Brest and Sanford Levinson, *Processes of Constitutional Decision-Making*, 2d ed. (1983). John Hart Ely, *Democracy and Distrust* (1980). Learned Hand, *The Bill of Rights* (1958). Laurence Tribe, *Constitutional Choices* (1985). Mark Tushnet, *Red, White, and Blue: A Critical Analysis of Constitutional Law* (1988).
Philip Bobbitt

**Constitutionalism** is a form of political thought and action that seeks to prevent tyranny and to guarantee the liberty and rights of individuals on which free society depends. This definition, drawn mainly from English and American political history, may be compared with a more formalistic view that regards constitutionalism as the conduct of politics in accordance with a constitution. The import of this definition depends on the meaning of constitution, a term that has been variously interpreted in western political thought. During the American Revolution, Americans conceived of a constitution as the permanent, binding, and paramount political law of the polity. Although this theoretical innovation did not end all controversy over the meaning of the concept, it generally caused constitutionalism to be defined thereafter as the forms, principles, and procedures of limited government.

Constitutionalism addresses the perennial problem of how to establish government with sufficient power to realize a community's shared purposes, yet so structured and controlled that oppression will be prevented. In the absence of any means of assuring statesmanship in rulers, two approaches to the problem of government have been employed. One approach proceeds through the ordering of political and governmental institutions. From ancient to modern times the idea of the mixed regime, juxtaposing properly balanced institutions of monarchy, aristocracy, and democracy, and the social orders they represent, illustrates this way of limiting government. A second approach to the problem is through the rule of law. Historical examples of this tradition are the Roman idea that the law of nature provides a standard of justice for evaluating the legitimacy of government enactments and the English practice, beginning with Magna Carta, of subjecting the monarchical power to legal limits and *common-law rules protecting the liberty and property of subjects.

Although analytically distinct, these approaches are historically related in the institutional arrangements and practices that provide the basis for defining constitutionalism. In modern political science a constitution is an authoritative text possessing legal force that prescribes the structure and principles of limited government. The constitutional text is normative, stipulating how government shall be organized, the ends it may pursue, and the means to be employed in pursuit of those ends. In premodern political thought constitution had a descriptive connotation, referring to the ordering of the polity or the way institutions had evolved and assumed their present form. It is important to note that this concept of constitution was also thought to have a normative aspect. The English writer Lord Bolingbroke, for example, defined the English constitution in the early eighteenth century as "that assemblage of laws, institutions, and customs, derived from certain fixed principles of reason, directed to certain fixed objects of public good, that compose the general system, according to which the community hath agreed to be governed." Bolingbroke said a good government exists when the administration of affairs is wisely pursued "and with a strict conformity to the principles and objects of the constitution."

In Roman and medieval times the word *constitutio, constitutiones*, of which constitution is a transliteration, referred to enactments, decrees, or regulations of a ruler or sovereign. (In Latin, *constituere* means "to cause to stand," or "to fix, set, or make" a thing.) It has been suggested that the enactments of the Roman emperor implied the idea of limited government insofar as they collectively defined the scope of state action. Subsequently "constitution" was superseded by "statute" with respect to government enactments providing rules of action for the community.

The word *constitution* entered political discourse as a term describing the structure of the polity or the arrangement of governmental institutions in the seventeenth century. This usage was analogous to that employed in describing the constitution of the human body. Although in the nineteenth century the term *constitution* was proposed as a translation of the Greek word *politeia*, before that time *politeia* was translated as government, regime, or policy. The tradition of political science deriving from Aristotle did not require use of the word *constitution*.

A form of American constitutionalism began in the seventeenth century as voluntary associations of settlers founded colonies under royal charters conferring on a person or corporate group governmental powers for specific purposes. As the basis of local government, the colonists wrote and adopted covenants, compacts, combinations, ordinances, fundamental orders, and other instruments of mutual consent. Through these documentary agreements they constituted themselves as a political community, defined their purposes, affirmed the principles of a way of life, specified the rights of citizens, and organized governmental institutions.

In the imperial conflicts of the 1760s and 1770s, Americans gained a new understanding of what the constitution of a free state was and how it functioned to guarantee liberty. They rejected the idea that a constitution described the governmental order of the polity. American critics of English policy argued that a constitution was a deliberately framed agreement among the people that imposed effective limits on government in order to protect community and individual liberty. If Parliament was a component of the English constitution and could change the fundamental law by its enactments, they concluded, then England did not have a real constitution. The important distinction was that although a constitution conferred power, it was not the simple equivalent of a mandate to legislate or govern. The Massachusetts General Court in 1768 pointed the direction of modern American constitutionalism in declaring: "in all free States the Constitution is fixed; & as the supreme Legislative derives its Power & Authority from the Constitution, it cannot overleap the Bounds of it, without destroying its own foundation."

During the Revolution Americans wrote constitutions of liberty, the distinctive feature of which was their legal superiority to legislative enactments and other sources of ordinary law. This supremacy was more theoretical than actual in the early years of written constitutions, when state legislatures framed the documents and often exercised power despite their provisions. Constitutions took on greater authority when popularly elected conventions wrote them and the people ratified them. The Massachusetts constitution of 1780 and the New Hampshire constitution of 1784 were modeled in this way. In employing the constitutional convention device the framers of the federal Constitution established it as the norm for modern constitutionalism.

Unlike the state constitutions, which expressed the idea of forming political communities out of the state of nature, the original U.S. Constitution contained no bill of rights and only a brief preamble stating the nation's basic principles and ends. In effect the *Declaration of Independence is the preamble to the Constitution. Accordingly, the framers wrote a document that was less a social compact for a cohesive, like-minded community than a contractual specification of the powers, duties, rights, and responsibilities among the diverse people that constituted the American Union. Reacting against state encroachments on liberty and property, the framers emphasized protection of individual rights rather than promotion of virtue and community consensus.

In the political context of the 1780s, the founders' constitutional reforms signified the creation of energetic government to fill the vacuum of power under the Articles of Confederation. In the perspective of western political thought, the Constitution of 1787 marks the emergence of modern constitutionalism as a political theory combining limited government for the protection of individual rights with the principles of the people as constituent power.

Constitutionalism requires that the primary rules for the conduct of government be impartially maintained against the demands of political passion, interest, ideology, and ambition. It is remarkable therefore that the founders provided for enforcement of the Constitution by the political branches of the government as well as by the judiciary. Each of the coordinate departments was responsible for applying and interpreting the provisions of the constitutional document that defined or regulated the performance of its duties and responsibilities.

Asserted by Presidents Andrew *Jackson and Abraham *Lincoln in the nineteenth century, the departmental theory of constitutional decision making has never been effectively repudiated or expunged from the American political tradition. Yet it has in the twentieth century been obscured by the legalistic approach to constitutional interpretation, institutionalized in judicial review, which confers a monopoly of power on the judiciary with respect to the settlement of constitutional disputes. In *Marbury v. Madison (1803), Chief Justice John *Marshall asserted the power of *judicial review in judiciary cases concerning individual rights, while adhering to the departmental theory in regard to *political questions or public policy matters. In later cases dealing with *federalism and the *Contract Clause, however, Marshall employed a legalistic method of constitutional decision making based on the application of common-law rules of interpretation to the text of the Constitution. In this approach the Constitution became supreme ordinary law susceptible to judicial adaptation and emendation in a way that blurred the distinction between questions of a judiciary nature and policy matters properly subject to determination by the political branches of government. The Constitution was transformed from fundamental political principles into supreme ordinary law. A consequence was the steady expansion of judicial power into the sphere of public policy making. By the

beginning of the twentieth century, constitutionalism in the United States was considered to be mainly a body of legal doctrines and rules that enabled the courts to play an active role in government and politics.

Constitutionalism in twentieth-century America continued to be largely juridical and increasingly policy oriented. Limited government constitutionalism, grounded in natural rights principles and protective of entrepreneurial liberty and property, persisted until 1937. Political demands for a more socially responsive rule of law that were first asserted in the Progressive period came to fruition in the *New Deal era. The consequence was a general questioning of the nineteenth-century view of limited government and the expansion of government activism in social and economic regulation.

From 1937 until the 1980s, the Supreme Court generally approved governmental activism as a means of guaranteeing positive liberty or the provision of material support as the basis of individual autonomy and self-expression. To some extent the idea of liberty against government (negative government) persisted as the Court nationalized the *Bill of Rights as limitations on the states. In other respects the Court confirmed the activist government tradition by transforming civil rights into group- and class-based claims to public benefits and entitlements.

The expansion of government under the concept of positive liberty raised the question whether the Constitution was the binding political law that limited government, or a rhetorical abstraction or symbol used by government officials, including the Supreme Court, to justify policy decisions. Did the Constitution control the government, or did the government control the Constitution?

From the eighteenth century to the mid-twentieth century, the essential element in modern constitutionalism was the doctrine of limited government under a written fundamental law. Postmodern constitutionalism in the second half of the twentieth century challenged this outlook by creating activist government to achieve social justice and positive liberty. Tension between these two conceptions of constitutionalism was a prominent feature of American politics as the third century of constitutional government began in the 1990s.

□ Gerhard Casper, "Changing Concepts of Constitutionalism: 18th to 20th Century," *Supreme Court Review* (1989): 311–332. Donald S. Lutz, *The Origins of American Constitutionalism* (1988). Sylvia Snowiss, "From Fundamental Law to Supreme Law of the Land: A Reinterpretation of the Origins of Judicial Review," *Studies in American Political Development* 2 (1987): 1–67. Gerald Stourzh, "*Constitution*: Changing Meanings of the Term from the Early Seventeenth to the Late Eighteenth Century," in *Conceptual Change and the Constitution*, edited by Terence Ball and J. G. A. Pocock (1988), pp. 35–54.

Herman Belz

**Contempt Power of Congress.** Legislative contempt or contempt of Congress refers to Congress's power to penalize an act of disrespect, disobedience, or interference with the legislative process. There is no explicit grant of this power in the Constitution, although Congress has assumed it since 1795. In *Anderson v. Dunn* (1821), which dealt with an attempt to bribe members, the Supreme Court held that the legislative contempt power was inherent in "a deliberate assembly, clothed with the majesty of the people" (p. 228). The courts will overturn a congressional finding only when the matter is deemed beyond the cognizance of Congress—that is, almost never.

The inherent contempt power, time consuming and of uncertain scope, has not been the favored procedure since 1857, when Congress enacted a contempt statute providing for a regular criminal process in the *lower federal court with prescribed penalties. Bribery of members today is a separate criminal offense and the contempt statute is used primarily against witnesses who refuse to cooperate.

From 1945 to 1957, the House Committee on Un-American Activities held approximately 230 public hearings and subpoenaed more than 3,000 persons, of whom 135 were cited for contempt for refusal to testify or cooperate with the committee (see COMMUNISM AND COLD WAR). HUAC's authority to investigate the domestic activities of the Communist Party was upheld in *Barenblatt v. United States* (1959). But the Court has required Congress to adhere to constitutional procedural safeguards, including the privilege against *self-incrimination, the prohibition on unreasonable searches and seizures, and the general requirements of notice and an opportunity to be heard. The Court has thus guarded against the abuse of summary legislative contempt findings.

(See also SEPARATION OF POWERS.)
Thomas E. Baker

**Contempt Power of the Courts.** A contempt of court is disobedience to a court's order or disrespect to its authority, either in or out of court. Despite the silence of the Constitution on this subject, an inherent power of contempt, derived from *common law, has been deemed necessary to insure that federal courts are able to enforce their judgments and orders. The *Judiciary Act of 1789 conferred power on federal courts to punish contempts, and they retain that power today.

A civil contempt is the refusal to obey an order in a civil case. Usually the person is ordered into custody or is fined progressively, or both, until the contempt is purged by compliance—for example, by testifying or producing a document. A criminal contempt is an act that cannot be purged, and for which punishment is imposed to vindicate the authority and dignity of the court. A person who commits a criminal contempt may be charged under a statute for a separate crime and

separately tried, or may be summarily held in contempt without the rights afforded a criminal defendant.

Procedurally, constitutional rulings have narrowed the authority of the judge to act summarily and have required due process safeguards (see DUE PROCESS, PROCEDURAL). Substantively, the *First Amendment is the most important limit on the contempt authority. In *Nebraska Press Association v. Stuart* (1976), for example, the Court applied the *clear and present danger test to reverse a "gag order" restraining publication of material disclosed before trial that implicated a criminal defendant (see PRETRIAL PUBLICITY AND THE GAG RULE).

(See also LOWER FEDERAL COURTS.)
Thomas E. Baker

**Contraception.** The Supreme Court's involvement in defining the constitutional right to obtain and use contraceptives has been limited until the relatively recent past. In 1927, however, the Court upheld the constitutionality of one contraceptive practice. *Buck v. Bell* (1927) involved the forced eugenic sterilization of a woman in a state mental institution who was considered to be genetically "unfit." Justice Oliver Wendell *Holmes, writing for the Court, found that none of her rights were violated and that sterilization was "better for all the world" (p. 207) than childbearing by persons with poor genes. In *Skinner v. Oklahoma* (1942), the Court limited the permissible scope of forced sterilizations, overturning an Oklahoma law providing for compulsory sterilization as a punishment for repeat offenders of certain crimes. The Court held that the right to procreate was a fundamental liberty protected by the Constitution. *Skinner* was decided on equal protection grounds and did not reverse *Buck v. Bell*. Although at odds with present privacy jurisprudence, *Buck* has never been overruled.

Legal restriction on the sale and use of birth control dates back to Congress's passage in 1873 of the Comstock Act, which made sending contraceptives or information about them through the mails or in interstate commerce a crime. Many states passed their own statutes restricting the sale or use of birth control. During the first half of the twentieth century, the *lower federal courts and some *state courts narrowly construed bans on birth control so that by the 1940s, in most jurisdictions, prescription of contraceptives by medical professionals was legal. In the states of Connecticut and Massachusetts, however, birth control bans continued. These statutes kept birth control clinics closed for years, interfering with access to effective birth control methods by low-income women.

The Supreme Court had opportunities to review the constitutionality of birth control bans on a number of occasions but dismissed cases on *standing grounds, *Tileston v. Ullman* (1943), or for want of a substantial *federal question, *Gard-*

ner v. *Massachusetts* (1938). In *Poe* v. *Ullman* (1961), the Court denied review of a *declaratory judgment action challenging the Connecticut law because it believed that the statute was not being enforced.

After Planned Parenthood of Connecticut opened a birth control clinic, the clinic's executive director and medical director were arrested for violating the state law. Their conviction was appealed to the U.S. Supreme Court in *Griswold* v. *Connecticut* (1965). The Court struck down the law, finding that married persons have a constitutionally protected privacy right to use contraceptives. This right of marital privacy was "older than the *Bill of Rights" (p. 486). Although not explicitly mentioned in the Constitution, it was implicitly protected, for it lay "within the zone of privacy created by several fundamental constitutional guarantees" (p. 485).

*Griswold*'s holding centered on privacy in marital relations. The right to privacy in the use of birth control was extended to unmarried persons in *Eisenstadt* v. *Baird* (1972). Justice William J. *Brennan wrote that "[i]f the right of privacy means anything, it is the right of the *individual*, married or single, to be free from unwarranted governmental intrusion into matters so fundamentally affecting a person as the decision whether to bear or beget a child" (p. 453). This right was extended to minors when, in 1977, a plurality struck down a ban on distribution of contraceptives to persons under the age of sixteen because minors, as well as adults, had privacy rights (*Carey* v. *Population Services International*, 1977).

Also in *Carey*, the Court overturned a New York law permitting only pharmacists to distribute nonprescription contraceptives because the statute burdened the fundamental right to decide whether to bear a child, without serving any compelling state interests. It struck down the statute's total ban on advertising contraceptives on the ground that it suppressed *commercial speech in violation of the *First Amendment. The Court expanded First Amendment protection of the advertising of contraceptives when it struck down a federal ban on mailing unsolicited advertisements for contraceptives: *Bolger* v. *Youngs Drug Product Corp.* (1983).

The right to privacy developed in the birth control cases served as the basis for the Court's ruling that women have a privacy right to obtain an *abortion in *Roe* v. *Wade* (1973). Although the Court has recently retreated somewhat in its protection of abortion rights (e.g., *Webster* v. *Reproductive Health Services*, 1989), the right to obtain and use contraceptives remains firmly, and broadly, protected.

(See also DUE PROCESS, SUBSTANTIVE; FAMILY AND CHILDREN; GENDER; PRIVACY.)

□ C. Thomas Dienes, *Law, Politics, and Birth Control* (1972).  Mary L. Dudziak

**Contract.** The Supreme Court has had little impact on contract law, a fact largely attributable to structures and attitudes within the federal system that seek to preserve the states as separate law-making authorities (see FEDERALISM). The Court has played a more significant role in other areas of commercial law, such as *admiralty and *bankruptcy, for which there are constitutional provisions assigning responsibility to the national government. There is no comparable provision for contracts. Thus, with few exceptions, contract law has been viewed as within the purview of the states.

Some parts of the Constitution do, however, relate tangentially to contract law. Here the Court has had a significant impact, but one that affects the structures of government rather than the substance of contract law. For example, because the Constitution and national laws are supreme (Art. VI, sec. 2), the Court is the final arbiter of disputes originating in procurement contracts to which the federal government is a party.

The other two relevant provisions of the Constitution are the *Contracts Clause (Art. I, sec. 10, cl. 1) and the *Due Process Clauses of the *Fifth and *Fourteenth Amendments. The Court early applied the Contracts Clause, which prohibits states from interfering with the obligation of contracts, in *Fletcher* v. *Peck* (1810) and *Dartmouth College* v. *Woodward* (1819). In both cases the Court declared state laws unconstitutional as interferences with the obligation of contracts. In the process, the Court gave such a broad definition to "contract" that for most of the nation's history private individuals have had great freedom to form their own contracts. Only under the pressures of the Great Depression did the Court retreat and allow states to modify contracts, and then only to declare a temporary moratorium on making mortgage payments in *Home Building & Loan Association* v. *Blaisdell* (1934).

In *Lochner* v. *New York* (1905) and *Adkins* v. *Children's Hospital* (1923), the Court also excepted important areas from state intervention when it used the Due Process Clauses to protect "freedom of contract" in striking down regulations of conditions of employment such as wages and hours (see CONTRACT, FREEDOM OF). But beyond ensuring a wide range for individual action in shaping contractual relations, the Court again had little to do with the doctrine of contract law.

The only significant exceptions to the Court's general inefficacy with respect to contract law occurred during the second half of the nineteenth century. The Court's influence on commercial law in general peaked in the half-century following *Swift* v. *Tyson* (1842), a decision that held that federal courts could decide questions of commercial law in accord with general principles, without being restricted to the decisions of the state in which the case arose. Thus, for half a century or so, the Court's search for a uniform *federal common law coincided with similar interests in uniformity that originated in the growing commercial economy. In the end, however, the Court proved unable to satisfy the calls for a uniform national law.

Even at the peak of its influence on contract law, the Court tended to hear major issues only occasionally—for the simple reason that the Supreme Court is a court of limited jurisdiction. *State courts, by contrast, are courts of general jurisdiction, which can hear and decide any issue (see JUDICIAL POWER AND JURISDICTION). By the end of the nineteenth century, therefore, a number of organizations began to look elsewhere for uniformity. In light of the contemporaneous view that Congress's powers over commerce were limited, the only path to uniformity was for each state legislature to adopt the same act. Moreover, the Court itself backed away from a federal common law when it reversed *Swift* in *Erie Railroad v. Tompkins* (1938). In the years since *Erie* the Court has regularly declined to hear contract cases, thereby continuing its minimal impact on the substantive law.　　　　Walter F. Pratt, Jr.

**Contract, Freedom of,** sometimes termed "liberty of contract," was a private-law concept imported into constitutional jurisprudence in the heyday of substantive due process. The term, credited to Justice Rufus *Peckham in *Lochner v. New York* (1905), was popularized a generation previously by Justice Stephen J. *Field. The doctrine holds that parties capable of entering into a contract and giving their consent to its terms ought not to be curbed by the state, save to protect the health, welfare, and morals of the community or to prevent criminal activities.

Gilded-age judges incorporated the freedom of contract doctrine into the Constitution by reading the *Fifth and *Fourteenth Amendment bars upon deprivation of liberty or property without *due process of law to extend to employment contracts. In a series of cases, the Supreme Court declared that states could not deprive citizens of a state the right to make contracts out of the state (*Allgeyer v. Louisiana,* 1897) or to set maximum hours for bakers (*Lochner*). Moreover, the federal government could not prevent an employer from dismissing an employee upon the grounds of union membership (*Adair v. U.S.,* 1908). The Court retreated from this position on employment contracts in *Muller v. Oregon* (1908) and *Bunting v. Oregon* (1917), but in the 1920s the tide of opinion on the Court again flowed in favor of freedom of contract. Its high-water mark was *Adkins v. Children's Hospital* (1923), overturning minimum wage provisions in the District of Columbia.

Freedom of contract doctrine reified extra-constitutional theories of the value of labor. The doctrine was a centerpiece of laissez-faire jurisprudence. Judicial faith in the *natural laws of economics—the free market ideology of "classical" economists—provided another foundation for freedom of contract.

In the main, freedom of contract favored powerful employers. The language of *Lochner* and *Adair* gave little hint of political partisanship or class bias, but judges were well aware of the consequences of the doctrine in the workplace. Although federal courts usually deferred to the *police power of states, from its inception freedom of contract was a much-controverted doctrine. Justice Oliver Wendell *Holmes rebuked the majority in *Lochner* that "the Fourteenth Amendment does not enact Mr. Herbert Spencer's Social Statics" (p. 75). Theodore Roosevelt hammered at *Lochner* and *Adair* in his 1912 campaign for the presidency. Freedom of contract was largely abandond in the late 1930s, part of a broader pattern of judicial deference to legislatures on economic questions.

(See also DUE PROCESS, SUBSTANTIVE; LABOR; LAISSEZ-FAIRE CONSTITUTIONALISM; POLICE POWER.)

　　　　Peter Charles Hoffer

**Contracts Clause.** Article I, section 10, clause 1 of the Constitution provides that "No State shall . . . pass any Law impairing the Obligation of Contracts." On its face an absolute limitation on state power, the meaning of this clause has varied greatly in Supreme Court interpretation. In the early years of the nation, the Contracts Clause dominated the Supreme Court's case docket, and the Court's interpretations constrained *state action, especially actions seeking to redistribute wealth. In modern times, the Court has all but forgotten the clause as a consequence of its substantial deference to state legislative judgment in economic matters.

The Contracts Clause fits neatly alongside constitutional prohibitions against state passage of *ex post facto laws and bills of *attainder. These provisions ensure the general application of the law in a manner that allows citizens a fair opportunity to adjust and plan their affairs.

At the Constitutional Convention, the Contracts Clause was introduced late in the proceedings by Massachusetts delegate Rufus King. King modeled the clause after a similar provision in the *Northwest Ordinance of 1787, which had been adopted just six weeks earlier by the Congress of the Articles of Confederation. At the convention and during subsequent ratification debates, the objection was put forward that the clause would unduly constrain the states, precluding them from acting in times of emergency. James *Madison admitted this "inconvenience," but thought the "utility" of the clause outweighed these concerns. James *Wilson of Pennsylvania noted that the unforeseen circumstance was still within the legislative power since the clause prohibited "retrospective interferences only."

Because at the time the Constitution was written there was much concern with debtor relief laws, it has sometimes been suggested that the clause was singularly aimed at precluding this type of legislation. The general language of the clause, however, and its early application by the Supreme Court easily refute this limiting characterization. There was perhaps no greater proponent of the clause than Chief Justice John *Marshall, who applied the clause broadly to public as well as private contracts. Thus, in *Fletcher v. Peck (1810), Marshall denied the Georgia legislature power to revoke previous public land grants. Marshall conceived of the clause's protection as absolute, so even allegations that the prior grants had been tainted with fraud were not enough to justify an impairment. His opinion in *Sturges v. Crowninshield (1819) firmly rejected social-welfare arguments in favor of abrogating contracts in order to discharge the debts of insolvent debtors in *bankruptcy. In *Dartmouth College v. Woodward (1819), Marshall ruled that a corporate charter could be impaired as much by adding additional provisions to the charter or contract as by nullifying existing provisions. Marshall's expansive reading of the clause, however, was not enough to convince the Court to disregard the framers' original understanding and apply it to laws that operate prospectively; the Court rejected this interpretation in *Ogden v. Saunders (1827).

While the Marshall period hewed closely to the text and history of the Constitution, its application of the clause to all public contracts caused difficulty. This problem surfaced in *Stone v. Mississippi (1880), where the state sought to prohibit the sale of lottery tickets by a corporate entity that had a charter to conduct a lottery. To retroactively apply this prohibition to the corporate charter would seemingly run afoul of the clause as previously interpreted, but to deny the state the lottery prohibition would restrict the exercise of *police power over health, safety, and morals. The Stone Court resolved the dilemma by articulating the reserved power doctrine that no state can contract away its police power. Since the nineteenth-century conception of police power was limited to matters of health and safety, and did not cover modern redistributions of wealth, the Stone reservation constituted no more than a correction of Marshall's expansive reading of the clause.

Then, however, the clause fell into eclipse. From the *Civil War until the 1930s, there was little need for the Court to rely upon the clause to negate overzealous state economic regulation since this objective was accomplished under substantive economic *due process. Because it possessed a much weaker constitutional pedigree, however, substantive due process fell of its own weight during the Great Depression, when the freedom of *contract policy it espoused went out of fashion.

The decline of the Contracts Clause is frequently associated with *Home Building & Loan Association v. Blaisdell (1934). In Blaisdell, the Court upheld a Minnesota statute that extended the period of redemption for mortgage default. The Court's justification was entirely pragmatic. In the face of economic emergency, and given the temporary nature of the mortgage relief provided by the statute, the Court construed the clause "in light of our whole experience and not merely in view of what was said a hundred years ago" (p. 443). "Public needs," said the Court, required that the "reservation of the reasonable exercise of the protective power of the State [be] read into all contracts" (p. 444). The Court tried to check the decline of the clause in a series of cases following Blaisdell, finding no pervasive emergency. The ever-broadening conceptions of police power, however, eventually transformed the absolute prohibition of the clause into a matter to be balanced with reasonable judgment.

Following United States Trust v. New Jersey (1977), where the Court invalidated an abrogation of a covenant in a public bond contract, there was speculation that the clause might have regained some of its prior importance. Yet the test applied in U.S. Trust bore little resemblance to the text of the Constitution. Writing for the Court, Justice Harry *Blackmun stated that contractual impairments might be upheld if they were "reasonable and necessary to serve an important public purpose" (p. 25). Curiously, that ill-defined standard was to be applied more rigorously where state law impaired public, rather than private, contracts. Nevertheless, with rare exception, the Contracts Clause has been routinely subordinated to the modern Court's substantial deference to state legislative judgment in matters of economics. In *Keystone Bituminous Coal Association v. DeBenedictis (1987), Justice John Paul *Stevens stated, "It is well-settled that the prohibition against impairing the obligation of contracts is not to be read literally" (p. 502).

Douglas W. Kmiec

**Cooley, Thomas McIntyre** (b. near Attica, N.Y., 6 Jan. 1824; d. Ann Arbor, Mich., 12 Sep. 1898), treatise writer and jurist. Cooley was an important figure in the growth of the University of Michigan and its law school. Elected to the Michigan Supreme Court in 1864, he served with distinction there for twenty years. In 1887 President Grover Cleveland appointed Cooley to the newly created *Interstate Commerce Commission (ICC). Though Cooley was disappointed in not being nominated to the U.S. Supreme Court, he had no inclination for private law practice.

In 1868, Cooley published the influential Treatise on the Constitutional Limitations which Rest upon the Legislative Power of the States of the American Union. His discussion of due process in that treatise and his denial that individuals could arbitrarily be "deprived of liberty in particulars of primary importance to his or their 'pursuit of happiness' " have been interpreted as an authoritative source for judicial protection of *property rights, as well as a source for the doctrine of liberty of contract (see CONTRACT, FREEDOM OF).

Such a laissez-faire interpretation misses the persistence of democratic values in Cooley's writings, as his opinions for the Michigan Supreme Court indicate. Cooley was troubled by the growing concentration of corporate power in the late nineteenth century. His suspicion of any kind of arbitrary power, coupled with his democratic values, made him an ambivalent critic of the collusion between corporate and legislative power. On the ICC, he sought to umpire relations between railroads and the federal government. Cooley's conservatism reflected a nostalgia for the simpler Jeffersonian world of preindustrial America.                    Alan R. Jones

**Cooley v. Board of Wardens of the Port of Philadelphia,** 12 How. (53 U.S.) 299 (1852), argued 9–11 Feb. 1852, decided 2 Mar. 1852 by vote of 6 to 2; Curtis for the Court, Daniel concurring, McLean and Wayne in dissent, McKinley absent. A Pennsylvania statute provided that any vessel entering or leaving the port of Philadelphia was required to pay one-half the usual pilotage fee if its master chose not to employ a local pilot. The fee went into a fund for the relief of infirm pilots and pilots' widows and orphans. The fee affected interstate and international commerce flowing into Philadelphia and was challenged as an interference with Congress's power to regulate such commerce.

The Taney Court had previously been unable to resolve Commerce Clause issues presented in *New York v. Miln (1837), the *License Cases (1847), and the *Passenger Cases (1849) because of complications posed by issues of *slavery and *federalism that lay under the surface of all Commerce Clause cases of the era. The Court had either evaded such questions or, in trying to resolve them, had splintered confusingly. In *Cooley,* the Court was finally able to achieve a coherent resolution of a Commerce Clause issue. Justice Benjamin R. *Curtis defined the question in terms of the subject matter of regulation rather than the nature of the commerce power, with some subjects being national in scope and others, like pilotage laws, local. Though this formula failed to enlist the support of states'-rights enthusiasts such as Justice Peter V. *Daniel and nationalists such as Justices John *McLean and James M. *Wayne, its pragmatism has proved enduring. *Cooley* ranks with *Gibbons v. Ogden (1824) as one of the most important Commerce Clause cases of the nineteenth century.

(See also COMMERCE POWER.)
                        Donald M. Roper

**Cooperative Federalism** is an amorphous constitutional concept that was first used in the *New Deal era to refer, among other things, to federal grant-in-aid programs that established national regulatory programs administered by the states and funded by Congress. Intended to replace the concept of competitive, divided-sovereignty federalism, the idea of cooperative federalism served as a euphemism for centralization of policy making in the national government at the expense of states' rights and autonomous state policy making.

Since the 1930s, the Supreme Court has given broad constitutional approval to grant-in-aid programs, the primary form of cooperative federalism. In *Garcia v. San Antonio Metropolitan Transit Authority (1985), the Court pointed to cooperative federalism programs and the vast sums of money they brought to the states as evidence of the constitutional vitality of states' rights. Consistent with *Garcia's* understanding of cooperative federalism as a centralizing doctrine, the Court in *South Carolina v. Baker (1988) eliminated one of the last vestiges of divided-sovereignty federalism by upholding a congressional tax on interest income from unregistered state and local bonds. This decision ended the ancient rule of intergovernmental *tax immunity that had long signified the existence of reciprocally limiting spheres of national and state authority.

(See also DUAL FEDERALISM; FEDERALISM.)
                        Herman Belz

**Cooper v. Aaron,** 358 U.S. 1 (1958), argued 28 Aug. and 11 Sept. 1958, decided 12 Sept. 1958 by vote of 9 to 0; Warren for the Court. In *Brown v. Board of Education (1954) the Court decided unanimously to invalidate racial segregation in the public schools and discard the *separate but equal doctrine articulated in *Plessy v. Ferguson (1896). In holding that in the field of public education "separate" could never be "equal," the Court gave new meaning to the Equal Protection Clause of the *Fourteenth Amendment. Yet the ambiguous enforcement standard formulated in *Brown II* (1955) encouraged unanticipated defiance throughout the South.

In accordance with the first *Brown* decision, the city of Little Rock, Arkansas, school board established a plan for desegregation starting in September 1957 at Central High School. The day before desegregation was to begin, Governor Orval Faubus, claiming that public disturbances were imminent, ordered the Arkansas National Guard to prevent the entrance of nine black students. For three weeks, Faubus, President Dwight Eisenhower, the Little Rock school board, the city's black community, the *NAACP, rabid segregationists, and the local federal district court were embroiled in intractable confrontation. After the federal district court found the governor's assertions concerning impending disorder groundless, Faubus withdrew the guard, but when the "Little Rock nine" entered Central a few rabble-rousers galvanized the crowd outside, forcing the students' withdrawal. The next day President

Eisenhower dispatched combat-ready paratroopers, who enforced the federal court's original desegregation order.

At the end of the school year, in order to end the tension, Little Rock school officials asked for and received from the federal district court a two-and-a-half year delay in implementing desegregation. The NAACP appealed the case, *Cooper* v. *Aaron*, to the Supreme Court.

The *Cooper* case was the first significant legal test of the enforcement of *Brown*. The issues were: whether a good faith postponement of a desegregation program due to anticipated racial unrest would violate the constitutional rights of black students, and whether the governor and legislature of a state were bound by decisions of the U.S. Supreme Court. In an unprecedented action all nine members of the Court signed the opinion. They held, first, that even postponing plans for desegregation in good faith and the interest of preserving public peace would violate black students' rights under the Equal Protection Clause. Thus no delay was allowed. Second, governors and state legislatures were bound under the Supremacy Clause of the Constitution to uphold decisions of the Supreme Court just as they were bound by oath to uphold the Constitution itself. "No state legislative, executive, or judicial officer," the Court said, "can War against the Constitution without violating his undertaking to support it" (p. 18). No governor has the right to annul judgments of the federal courts.

The *Cooper* decision, however, initially fostered rather than discouraged southern resistance. Even during the dramatic dispatch of paratroopers, Eisenhower did not defend the *Brown* decision, which he personally opposed, creating the distinct impression that he would implement desegregation only under extreme circumstances. Yet neither the American public nor the Court knew the complete truth. In the September trial of Faubus involving his use of the national guard to prevent desegregation, the Justice Department declined to introduce evidence that demonstrated conclusively that prior to and during the crisis the Justice Department, school officials, a federal judge, and Faubus himself engaged in surreptitious contacts to negotiate an end to the confrontation in a manner that ultimately proved to be politically advantageous to the governor. The Justice Department even attempted, clandestinely and unsuccessfully, to persuade the NAACP to withdraw its suit on behalf of the nine black students.

Thus, notwithstanding the strong language of the *Cooper* decision, the federal judiciary faced massive southern resistance virtually alone until the sit-in cases and Martin Luther King, Jr.'s nonviolent *civil rights movement, coupled with the support of Presidents Kennedy and Johnson, stimulated passage of the *Civil Rights Act of 1964. That act endorsed *Brown* by name, and authorized the attorney general to intervene directly in school desegregation suits. Most important, Title VI, which cut off federal funds to institutions practicing racial discrimination, was used by the Department of Health, Education, and Welfare to compel compliance by threatening to withhold federal school funds.

(See also DESEGREGATION REMEDIES; EQUAL PROTECTION; INTERPOSITION; RACE AND RACISM.)

Tony Freyer

**Copyright.** The Constitution empowers Congress "[t]o promote the Progress of Science . . . by securing for limited Times to Authors . . . the exclusive Right to their . . . Writings. . . ." Long described simply as the law of literary property, today copyright law affords to creators not only of most literary, musical, and artistic works, but also of architectural works and computer software and databases, a limited monopoly on the use of the products of their minds—a powerful incentive to create.

The foundational decision was *Wheaton* v. *Peters* (1834), in which the Supreme Court held that copyright exists primarily to benefit the public rather than the creator and may be conditioned on compliance with statutory formalities. Other early cases sensibly defined the Constitution's requirements concerning "Writings" (*Burrow-Giles* v. *Sarony*, 1884), and "Authors" (*Bleistein* v. *Donaldson Lithographing*, 1903). In *Baker* v. *Selden* (1879), the Court created the vital distinction between nonprotectible ideas and their protectible expressions.

The Court's most doubtful decisions have resulted from reluctance to protect rights in works embodied by means of new technologies (e.g., *White-Smith* v. *Apollo*, 1908), and, more recently, works exploited by others, without authorization, through such technologies (e.g., *Sony* v. *Universal City Studios*, 1984). Such results, said Justice Oliver Wendell *Holmes (concurring in *White-Smith*), "give to copyright less scope than its national significance and the ground on which it is granted seem . . . to demand" (p. 19).

But the landmark opinion in *Feist* v. *Rural Telephone* (1991), announcing as a fundamental principle that copyright rewards the originality rather than the effort of the creator, promises new fidelity to copyright history and current legislative intent.

Craig Joyce

**Coram Nobis** (Lat., "before us") is a writ addressed to a court, calling attention to errors of fact that would vitiate a judgment already given. It has been abolished in federal practice by rule 60(b) of the Federal Rules of Civil Procedure.

William M. Wiecek

**Corporations.** Corporation law has traditionally been the domain of state legislatures and state courts, although nothing in the Constitution prohibits a federal role in corporate governance. The influence of the United States Supreme Court on corporation law until recently has therefore been decidedly secondary to that of the state courts, especially those of Delaware and New York. Nevertheless, before World War II, several Supreme Court decisions had momentous consequences for the place of corporations in American society. Since 1950, the Court has come to exercise an ever-expanding influence on corporation law, due partly to the impact of securities regulation on corporate affairs, and partly to an increasing nationalization of corporation law.

*Dartmouth College v. Woodward* (1819) marked the debut of the private profit-making corporation because it extended the protection of the *Contracts Clause of Article I, section 10 of the Constitution to corporate charters, treating them as contracts between the state and entrepreneurs. *Dartmouth College* prevented arbitrary state interference with charters, thereby giving some security to investors. *Charles River Bridge v. Warren Bridge* (1837) contributed a salutary counterpoise to *Dartmouth College* because of Chief Justice Roger B. *Taney's insistence that states could reserve a right to amend the charter when they issued it. Taney refused to read implied grants of monopolies into charters, thereby establishing a creative balance between the demands of investors and the need for state regulatory power. In *McCulloch v. Maryland* (1819), Chief Justice John *Marshall upheld the power of Congress to charter banking corporations as one of the *implied powers that Alexander *Hamilton had identified in his 1791 arguments on the constitutionality of the bill to charter the first Bank of the United States.

For a century after *Charles River Bridge*, the Supreme Court had little direct involvement with the law of corporations, except for the offhand dictum of Chief Justice Morrison R. *Waite in *Santa Clara County v. Southern Pacific Railroad* (1886) that corporations were "persons" within the meaning of the *Fourteenth Amendment's *Equal Protection Clause. The Court's various substantive *due process and freedom of *contract decisions between 1890 and 1937 strengthened the hand of corporations in their dealings with employees, unions, consumers, and state legislatures. Another instance of constitutional protection for the corporate entity came in *First National Bank v. Bellotti* (1978), where the Court extended the *First Amendment's protection to corporate political speech.

The expansion of various bodies of federal law after World War II has had an extensive impact on corporations. Because federal courts have exclusive jurisdiction of cases under the Securities Exchange Act of 1934 and concurrent jurisdiction with state courts over nearly all the remainder of federal securities statutes, the Supreme Court has had an immeasurable influence on the securities-regulation domain of corporation law (e.g., the definition of insider trading in cases like *Chiarella v. United States*, 1980). In *J. I.*

*Case Co. v. Borak* (1964), a proxy solicitation case, the Supreme Court created the implied private right of action and the role of "private attorney general," greatly enhancing the enforceability of federal securities statutes. In a bankruptcy case, *Taylor v. Standard Gas & Electric Co.* (1939), the Court invented the so-called Deep Rock doctrine, which subordinated the debt claims of a corporate shareholder to the claims of outside creditors.

Extensive criticism of state regulatory law, especially Delaware's, led to demands for federal corporation law, statutory, administrative, common law, or a combination of all three, in the 1960s and 1970s. The Supreme Court emphatically rebuffed attempts to accomplish this through expansion of the SEC's rule 10b-5 prohibition of fraud in *Santa Fe Industries v. Green* (1977), thus reaffirming the primacy of the states in all aspects of corporate governance except securities regulation.

While eschewing responsibility for the law of corporations directly, the Court has considerably affected the development of that law in cases involving the rights of corporations or those who deal with them.

(See also CAPITALISM; PRIVATE CORPORATION CHARTERS.)

□ Robert C. Clark, *Corporate Law* (1986).

William M. Wiecek

**Corrigan v. Buckley,** 271 U.S. 323 (1926), argued 8 Jan. 1926, decided 24 May 1926 by vote of 9 to 0; Sanford for the Court. This case involved a *restrictive covenant formed by white property owners in the District of Columbia in 1921 to prevent the sale of property to black citizens. Subsequently a white owner made a contract to sell her property to a black person, provoking a suit to enforce the covenant and stop the sale. Federal courts in the District of Columbia upheld enforcement of the covenant. In a unanimous decision, the Supreme Court in effect affirmed this outcome by dismissing the suit for lack of jurisdiction. Justice Edward T. *Sanford disposed of the constitutional argument raised against the covenant by noting that the *Fifth Amendment limited the federal government, not individuals; the *Thirteenth Amendment, in matters other than personal liberty, did not protect the individual rights of blacks; and the *Fourteenth Amendment referred to state action, not the conduct of private individuals. The Court observed that while the Civil Rights Act of 1866 conferred on all persons and citizens the legal capacity to make contracts and acquire property, it did not prohibit or invalidate contracts between private individuals concerning the control or disposition of their own property. Justice Sanford furthermore denied, without elaboration, that judicial enforcement of the restrictive covenant was tantamount to government action depriving persons of liberty and property without *due process of law. Sanford's statement was regarded in the next two decades as having settled the question whether judicial enforcement of racial covenants was state action under the Fourteenth Amendment. The decision temporarily closed the door to racial integration in housing that had been pried open in *Buchanan v. Warley (1917). In *Shelley v. Kraemer (1948) the Court held such covenants valid between the parties to the agreement, but judicially unenforceable as a form of state action prohibited by the Equal Protection Clause of the Fourteenth Amendment.

(See also JUDICIAL POWER AND JURISDICTION; RACE AND RACISM; STATE ACTION.)

Herman Belz

**Corwin, Edward Samuel** (b. near Plymouth, Mich., 19 Jan. 1878; d. Princeton, N.J., 29 Apr. 1963), political scientist and authority on American constitutional law and history. Corwin received his Ph.D. from the University of Pennsylvania in 1905 and joined the faculty of Princeton University, where he helped to organize the department of politics and taught jurisprudence until 1946.

Corwin emerged as the twentieth century's foremost academic commentator on the presidency, constitutional law, and the Supreme Court. Like Charles *Beard, Corwin emphasized the historical context of constitutional law, giving special attention to the evolution of the concepts of *due process, *vested rights, *higher law, and judicial review. Corwin's analysis of the last of these made him a sharp critic of the high court during the *New Deal, when the justices overturned several important pieces of recovery legislation. His Twilight of the Supreme Court (1934) upheld the New Deal's emphasis on strong presidential and congressional powers in time of crisis. Although Corwin subsequently modulated some of his harshest judgments about the Court, he remained skeptical of judicial power throughout his career. His best known work was The Constitution and What It Means Today (1920), which, updated by others, remains in print. This, more than any other single book, gave the American public a clear introduction to the high court's interpretation of the Constitution. Throughout his writing, Corwin repeatedly stressed one fundamental theme: the development of liberty against government.

(See also HISTORY, COURT USES OF; JUDICIAL REVIEW.)

Kermit L. Hall

**Counsel, Right to.** The Sixth Amendment to the Constitution dictates that "[i]n all criminal prosecutions, the accused shall . . . have the Assistance of Counsel for his defence." For the better part of American history, this guarantee assured that those persons who could afford counsel would have one. Over time the Supreme Court has interpreted this Sixth Amendment provision in an expansive way, first by adding requirements to provide counsel and second by specifying the stages where counsel is required.

The Court began to expand the class of defendants entitled to legal counsel in criminal cases with its decision in *Powell v. Alabama (1932), where it ruled that defendants in state capital cases were entitled to legal assistance. Six years later in *Johnson v. Zerbst, the Court ruled that the Sixth Amendment required the appointment of counsel for all felony defendants in federal courts. In a break from this expansive pattern, the Court rejected a similar mandate for state felony courts in *Betts v. Brady (1942), where it held that the appointment of counsel for indigents in state felony cases should be dictated by the circumstances of the case. Betts was overruled twenty-one years later in one of the Supreme Court's most important decisions, *Gideon v. Wainwright (1963). The Court ruled that counsel is required for defendants in all state felony cases. This guarantee was extended to misdemeanors in *Argersinger v. Hamlin (1972) and Scott v. Illinois (1979), although the Court concluded that misdemeanor courts are not required to appoint counsel where imprisonment is possible but not specified.

Related to the Court's requirement of counsel for indigents are the specifications regarding the stages in criminal procedure where counsel is required. The Sixth Amendment holds that the assistance of counsel is required in all criminal prosecutions. In several twentieth-century decisions the Court has interpreted this to include arraignment, trial, and sentencing. Specifically, the right to counsel is mandated for lineups (U. S. v. *Wade, 1967), for pretrial arraignments (Hamilton v. Alabama, 1961), for preliminary hearings (Coleman v. Alabama, 1970), for trials (Gideon v. Wainwright, Argersinger v. Hamlin, Scott v. Illinois), for sentencing (Mempa v. Rhay, 1967), and at first, automatic appeals (Douglas v. California, 1963). The right to counsel mandated by the Court for police interrogations in the famous *Miranda v. Arizona decision of 1966 derived from the *Fifth Amendment's privilege against *self-incrimination, and not the Sixth Amendment's guarantee. In contrast to these expansive holdings, the Court has declined to extend the right to counsel to *grand jury processes (U.S. v. Mandujano, 1976), or to postconviction procedures beyond sentencing. The latter includes probation and parole revocation proceedings that do operate under some due process norms (Gagnon v. Scarpelli, 1973; Morrissey v. Brewer, 1972).

Recent holdings have considered the constitutionality of self-representation (Faretta v. California, 1975) where the Court, in effect, accepted the idea that "fools" may choose to represent themselves and also the quality of legal representation. The central holding on this last point is Strickland v. Washington (1984), where the Court ruled that the Sixth Amendment right to counsel can be infringed by incompetent counsel. Here defendants must establish that counsel's performance was deficient, that that performance prejudiced the case, and that were it not for that deficiency, the defendant would have been acquitted.

In spite of the Supreme Court's expansive interpretation of the Sixth Amendment right to counsel, several issues remain. The Court has offered no standards related to *indigency nor has it required any particular system for public assistance. In spite of this silence, it is clear that the Supreme Court's decisions relative to right to counsel constitute important precedents for criminal procedure. The assistance of counsel, more than any other dimension of due process, evokes general American support for fair play and reflects the centrality of attorneys in the adversarial tradition of countries with common law.

(See also DUE PROCESS, PROCEDURAL; SIXTH AMENDMENT.)

Susette M. Talarico

**Counselman v. Hitchcock,** 142 U.S. 547 (1892), argued 9–10 Dec. 1891, decided 11 Jan. 1892 by vote of 9 to 0; Blatchford for the Court. In *Counselman,* the Court considered the constitutionality of a federal statute granting a witness immunity from a criminal prosecution based on evidence obtained from the witness in a judicial proceeding. Notwithstanding this statute, Charles Counselman, claiming the *Fifth Amendment privilege against self-incrimination, refused to answer certain questions before a federal grand jury. Confined for *contempt of court, Counselman sought a writ of *habeas corpus. The Court upheld his refusal to testify. It held that the privilege against self-incrimination could be exercised not only by an accused person in a criminal case but also by a witness in any investigation, including *grand jury proceedings. It also ruled that the federal immunity statute did not compel the appellant to testify, because its scope of protection was not as broad as that afforded by the privilege against self-incrimination. The statute prevented the direct use of appellant's testimony in any federal proceeding but did not prohibit the use of his testimony to search for other evidence to be used against him.

There was broad language in *Counselman* that a valid immunity statute must afford a person compelled to testify absolute protection from prosecution for any offense to which the testimony relates. In *Kastigar v. United States* (1972), however, the Court held that an immunity statute need not safeguard a person compelled to testify against a prosecution based on evidence obtained independently of the compelled testimony.

(See also DUE PROCESS, PROCEDURAL; FIFTH AMENDMENT IMMUNITY; SELF-INCRIMINATION.)

Edgar Bodenheimer

**Court Curbing.** The American system of government embodies the principle of separation of powers under which three distinct branches are entrusted with overlapping authority, each having what James *Madison, writing in The *Federalist,* no. 51, called "a will of its own. . . ." As possibly the weakest branch of government, with no popular electoral base to support it, the judicial branch may be even more vulnerable to political challenge by the other two. Moreover, with its power to declare state and federal laws unconstitutional, the Supreme Court may often find itself in conflict with the other two branches, or with the states (see JUDICIAL REVIEW).

There are a variety of mechanisms by which the Court may be curbed. Most obviously, amendments to the Constitution can be proposed by Congress and ratified by the states to reverse or modify unpopular decisions (see REVERSAL OF COURT DECISIONS BY AMENDMENT). Very early in the nation's history, the *Eleventh Amendment (ratified 1798) overturned the Court's decision in *Chisholm v. Georgia* (1793) and restricted the jurisdiction of the Court, albeit over a relatively narrow set of cases—those brought against a state by citizens of other states or nations. The *Fourteenth Amendment (ratified 1868) overturned the unpopular Dred *Scott decision (1857) and extended citizenship rights to all native-born and naturalized Americans, while the *Sixteenth Amendment (ratified 1913) reversed the Court's decision in *Pollock v. Farmers' Loan & Trust Co.* (1895) and permitted imposition of a national income tax. The *Twenty-sixth Amendment (ratified 1971) subsequently modified the Court's decision in *Oregon v. Mitchell* (1970) by extending the right to *vote to eighteen year olds in state as well as in federal elections. To date, such amendments have—with the possible exception of the Eleventh—been aimed at specific decisions rather than at the Court's authority as a whole, but constitutional amendments have been proposed from time to time since the 1820s that would have weakened judicial power by requiring that justices be elected to fixed terms, mandating an extraordinary judicial vote to void legislation, or permitting Congress to override judicial decisions. The chief obstacle to curbing the Court by constitutional amendment is its extreme difficulty, as the ratification of a mere twenty-six amendments in more than two hundred years of American constitutional history shows.

Congress is not, of course, bound to follow the amendment route in cases involving statutory, as opposed to constitutional, interpretations. Accordingly, there are numerous instances in American history where Congress has reversed such judicial interpretations, clarifying its earlier language or indicating that the Court had taken too narrow or broad a view of stated legislative purposes. Even in cases of constitutional interpretation, the Court is sometimes more engaged in an ongoing dialogue with the political branches than in asserting judicial power to interpret the Constitution with finality.

The Supreme Court is not immune from political and institutional restraints. Though the Court is at the top of a judicial hierarchy, *lower federal courts and *state courts sometimes resist its doctrinal innovations, as do law enforcement officers and others responsible for implementing judicial decisions (see IMPACT OF COURT DECISIONS). Many of the Court's justices have been convinced that their role in a democratic republican system requires deference to legislative decisions and the exercise of judicial restraint. Justices are, moreover, appointed by the president with the advice and consent of the Senate (see SELECTION OF JUSTICES.) Presidents are aware that their choices will influence the future ideological direction of the Court, though many have found that it is difficult to predict the stances that an appointee, once on the Court, will take.

In addition to these well-established restraints on the judicial branch, there is greater controversy over other mechanisms by which the electoral branches might curb the Court. The Constitution nowhere establishes the number of Supreme Court justices, for example, Congress could increase the number of justices and thus give the appointing president increased power to influence its decisions. The last change in the number of Supreme Court justices, however, was in 1869. Moreover, the twentieth century's most publicized attempt to "pack the Court"— Franklin Roosevelt's proposal in 1937 to add one justice, up to fifteen, for every justice who stayed on the Court over the age of 70—received such an overwhelming rebuff from Congress as an assault on judicial independence that it is unlikely to be proposed again (see COURT-PACKING PLAN).

Among the most controversial proposals to curb the Court have been plans aimed at legislatively restricting the jurisdiction of the Supreme Court and/or other federal courts over certain topics or classes of cases in which its decisions have proved to be unpopular (see JUDICIAL POWER AND JURISDICTION). This possibility is suggested by the language in *Article III, section 1 of the United States Constitution vesting the judicial power "in one supreme Court, and in such inferior Courts as the Congress may from time to time ordain and establish" and by Article III, section 2, granting *appellate jurisdiction to the Court "both as to Law and Fact, with such Exceptions, and under such Regulations as the Congress shall make." In a Reconstruction case, Ex parte *McCardle (1869), the Court sanctioned such a congressional action, refusing to decide a case over which Congress had withdrawn jurisdiction. Controversy continues to surround the original purpose of Article III, however, and the scope of McCardle is uncertain, especially in light of the Supreme Court's decision in United States v. Klein (1872). In that case, the Court rejected a congressional attempt to restrict the Court's jurisdiction over cases in which claimants relied on a presidential *pardon. The Court ruled that this was an improper attempt to prescribe rules of evidence inevitably working in the government's favor as well as being an unconstitutional intrusion on the president's pardoning power.

Some scholars are concerned that restriction on jurisdiction could undermine the supremacy of the Constitution proclaimed in Article VI, produce discordant constitutional interpretations, and deny *due process to litigants. At the very least, there are almost surely limits that would prohibit Congress from altering jurisdiction so as to treat claimants before the Court in a discriminatory fashion.

There was rarely a time when the Supreme Court had no enemies, and proposals for curbing the Court can be found throughout American history. In a survey of court-curbing movements focusing on congressional bills, Stuart Nagel identified seven such periods from 1802 through 1959. He considered four as relatively successful. Though no comparable study has been made since Nagel's, the late 1970s and early 1980s constitute another period of court-curbing attempts. Court-curbing proposals are noticeably more frequent when the Court is perceived as having made controversial or unpopular decisions. Such proposals may be tied to times of political crisis and partisan conflicts and often have a strong regional base.

The earliest court-curbing period occurred in 1802–1804 and reflected conflict between the newly elected Democratic Republican president, Thomas *Jefferson, and leading Federalists. Republicans reacted to Federalist attempts to stack the judicial branch with new officeholders before relinquishing power in 1801. Disputes over this attempt produced the Court's celebrated announcement of the power of judicial review in *Marbury v. Madison (1803). Jeffersonian Republicans repealed the *Judiciary Act of 1801, which had expanded the number and jurisdiction of federal courts. Attacks on the Court waned, however, after the unsuccessful attempt in the Senate to convict Justice Samuel *Chase, who had been *impeached in 1804 because of his intemperate Federalist partisanship on the bench. The failure of the Chase impeachment discouraged resort to impeachment as a court-curbing device.

The next round of court curbing occurred between 1823 and 1831. The Marshall Court had antagonized state and local interests by asserting its jurisdiction over a number of cases involving appeals from the states—for example, *Martin v. Hunter's Lessee (1816) and *Cohens v. Virginia (1821)—and by invalidating state economic regulatory statutes, most notably in *McCulloch v. Maryland (1819), which struck down Maryland's tax on a branch of the Bank of the United States. Attempts to modify or repeal section 25 of the *Judiciary Act of 1789 failed in 1831, however, and the Court retreated from the aggressive nationalism that had characterized its decisions through 1824.

After the Court's notorious *Dred Scott* decision of 1857, which helped ignite the *Civil War, through 1869, the Court encountered hostility to some of its decisions as war was followed by attempts at congressional *Reconstruction. The Fourteenth Amendment reversed *Dred Scott* and prepared the way for a new federal-state relationship. In *Ex parte McCardle*, the Court declined to jeopardize its reputation by a struggle with Congress over jurisdiction.

The periods 1893–1897 and 1922–1924 were characterized by the federal judiciary's assertion of power over economic matters and its dogma of freedom of *contract. In the earlier period, Populists condemned the Court's decision in *Pollock v. Farmers' Loan & Trust Co.* (1895), prohibiting Congress from levying an unapportioned income tax, and its decision limiting application of the *Sherman Antitrust Act in *United States* v. *E. C. Knight Co.* (1895). These and other decisions supportive of laissez-faire economics, epitomized by *Lochner v. New York* (1905) and its progeny, provoked the second round of attacks on the Court, led by *Progressive spokesmen, from 1922 to 1924. Both periods led to President Roosevelt's 1937 court-packing plan, which attempted to curb judicial invalidation of *New Deal programs. Though Roosevelt's effort failed, the Court has since given minimal scrutiny to legislation involving economic matters and has focused instead on civil rights and civil liberties issues.

These latter issues can also cause controversy, as demonstrated by the period 1955–1959. Reactions to *Brown v. Board of Education* (1954), which overturned *Plessy v. Ferguson* (1896) and mandated an end to the doctrine of *separate but equal in race relations, and to decisions curtailing the scope of state and national internal security laws led to calls for the impeachment of Chief Justice Earl *Warren (see COMMUNISM AND COLD WAR; SUBVERSION). Legislation such as the "Jenner Bill" (named after Senator William Jenner of Indiana), which would have restricted federal courts' jurisdiction in areas such as internal security, where the Court's decisions had been controversial, ultimately came to nought.

In the 1970s and 1980s, there have been numerous attempts to restrict judicial decisions relating to prayer (*Engel v. Vitale*, 1962) and Bible reading (*Abington School District v. Schempp*, 1963) in public schools (see RELIGION), school busing as a means to achieve racial balance (*Swann v. Charlotte-Mecklenburg Board of Education*, 1971), and *abortion (*Roe v. Wade*, 1973). Statutory attempts to restrict judicial jurisdiction have so far failed, as have proposed constitutional amendments. Bills attempting to exercise congressional enforcement powers under the Fourteenth Amendment by declaring that busing violates

equal protection or that human life begins at the moment of conception have also failed.

The Supreme Court has shown its resilience throughout American history, sometimes modifying or reversing its course, but never abandoning its authority as a coordinate branch of government. Justices are appointed and confirmed by the political branches, and the Court depends for enforcement of its decisions on them as well, so the Court cannot long remain out of line with the mainstream of public life. The tenure during good behavior and salary protections for the justices were designed to give the Court independence from most partisan controversies. Threats to curb the Court serve as continuing reminders both of the Court's vital place in the American governmental scheme and of the limits of its authority.

(See also CONSTITUTIONAL AMENDING PROCESS; CONSTITUTIONAL AMENDMENTS; POLITICAL PROCESS; SEPARATION OF POWERS.)

□ Louis Fisher, *Constitutional Dialogues* (1988). Edward Keynes with Randall K. Miller, *The Court vs. Congress* (1989). Walter F. Murphy, *Congress and the Court* (1962). Stuart S. Nagel, "Court-Curbing Periods in American History," *Vanderbilt Law Review* 18 (1965): 925–944.
John R. Vile

**Court-Packing Plan.** In February 1937 President Franklin D. *Roosevelt sent to Congress a bill to change the composition of the federal judiciary. This "court-packing bill," as it was promptly dubbed, was FDR's attempt to expand the membership of the Supreme Court so that he could nominate justices who would uphold the constitutionality of *New Deal legislation. The court-packing struggle constitutes a critical episode in Roosevelt's presidency and one of the bitterest clashes between the judiciary and the executive in American history.

The appointment of conservative justices in the 1920s created a majority on the Supreme Court that held a restrictive view of federal regulatory power. In his 1932 election campaign, Roosevelt denounced the Court as too Republican. He feared that the justices would threaten many reform measures needed to deal with the depression.

Despite cases in which the Court upheld reform legislation, the president received a shock on the so-called *Black Monday, 27 May 1935, when the Court delivered three unanimous opinions that struck down key provisions of the New Deal recovery plan. In *Louisville Bank v. Radford*, the Court declared unconstitutional an act that provided mortgage relief to farmers. In *Humphrey's Executor v. United States*, the Court denied the president the power to replace members of independent regulatory agencies, thus thwarting his ability to bring the agencies in line with administration regulatory policies (see APPOINTMENT AND REMOVAL POWERS). And in *Schechter

*Poultry Corporation* v. *United States* the Court struck down the National Industrial Recovery Act, holding that Congress could not delegate such sweeping powers to an executive body (see DELEGATION OF POWERS). The Court also held that the Schechters' poultry business was intrastate commerce and thus not subject to federal *commerce power. Roosevelt was troubled because the three liberal justices—Louis D. *Brandeis, Benjamin N. *Cardozo and Harlan F. *Stone—voted against the government's position. If the Court were to apply this approach to all regulatory issues, it would cripple the New Deal. At a press conference the next day Roosevelt denounced the Court for reverting to "the horse-and-buggy definition of interstate commerce."

FDR avoided a direct confrontation with the Court during 1936 because he wanted to prevent giving Republicans a campaign issue in the presidential election that year. But the Courtt invalidated several more New Deal programs, including the Agricultural Adjustment Act and the National Bituminous Coal Act, and a popular New York minimum-wage statute (*U.S.* v. *Butler*, 1936; *Carter* v. *Carter Coal Co.*, 1936; *Morehead* v. *New York ex rel. Tipaldo*, 1936). The liberal justices in these cases dissented, and Chief Justice Charles Evans *Hughes had often sided with them, thus leaving Justice Owen *Roberts as the swing vote.

Following his landslide electoral victory, Roosevelt instructed his attorney general, Homer Cummings, to come up with a plan to provide a court majority that would uphold the constitutionality of his regulatory program. They rejected constitutional amendment as too slow a process and instead drew up a statute that would add one justice for every Supreme Court justice over age seventy, up to a total of six, as well as up to forty-four lower court judges. FDR's rationale was that the older justices could not handle the volume of work, and the new justices would improve the courts' efficiency.

The court-packing plan was a bombshell when Roosevelt announced it on 5 February 1937; a political firestorm ensued. Republicans, the leaders of the organized bar, southern and moderate Democrats, and newspaper editors condemned the proposal. Even the liberal Supreme Court justices denounced the plan. Roosevelt, however, remained firm and appeared to have the votes in Congress.

In March, however, a 5-to-4 majority upheld a Washington minimum wage law that was almost identical to the one struck down the previous year (*West Coast Hotel Co.* v. *Parrish*), as well as the constitutionality of the National Labor Relations Board (*NLRB* v. *Jones & Laughlin Steel Corp.*). Justice Owen Roberts' shift, which journalists called the "switch in time that saved nine," doomed the court-packing legislation because Americans believed that FDR achieved his goals without tampering with tradition. Addi-

tionally, Justice Willis *Van Devanter announced that he would retire, providing Roosevelt five sympathetic votes even without Roberts. The president, however, would not abandon his plan. The sudden death of Senate floor leader Joe Robinson ended any hope the president's legislation had.

Roosevelt lost the legislative battle, but won the war. His reforms were thereafter upheld by the Supreme Court. The ramifications on the court-packing controversy were significant. It shook the New Deal coalition that FDR had created, costing him the support of some Democrats, many in the middle class, and some Republicans as well. It augured an end to the social and economic reforms Roosevelt had begun. It reinforced the American people's understanding that law and politics should be separated, and that although the Supreme Court was not wholly above politics, it must not be converted into a political institution.

□ William E. Leuchtenburg, "The Origins of Franklin D. Roosevelt's 'Court-Packing' Plan," in *The Supreme Court Review* (1966) pp. 347–400. William E. Leuchtenburg, "Franklin D. Roosevelt's Supreme Court 'Packing' Plan," in *Essays on the New Deal*, edited by Harold M. Hollingsworth and William F. Holmes (1969), pp. 69–115.                                    Rayman L. Solomon

**Court Reporters.** See REPORTERS, SUPREME COURT.

**Courts of Appeals.** The United States courts of appeals are the intermediate courts in the federal judicial system. They hear *appeals from the U.S. district courts and are reviewed by the U.S. Supreme Court. There are currently thirteen circuits, which are divided geographically. All but two are composed of three or more states. The courts of appeals are presided over by judges who are nominated by the president and confirmed by the Senate, as provided for in Article II of the Constitution. There are approximately 175 judgeships divided among the circuits, with the largest number being twenty-eight on the Ninth Circuit (the west coast) and the smallest being six on the First Circuit (New England). A litigant may appeal a final judgment from the district court as a matter of right. The parties can not introduce new evidence after the district court judgment; the grounds for appeals are claimed procedural errors or errors of law committed by the district judge. After an appeal is filed, the case is briefed by both parties, and counsel are often allowed *oral argument before a panel of three judges. The court typically takes the case under advisement and then issues a written opinion several months later. There are a variety of decisional possibilities including affirmance, reversal, (in whole or in part, and with various directions to the district court) or dismissal. Judges may write the majority opinion, submit dissents, or write separately, concurring in the result but disagreeing with the majority's reasoning. On rare occasions an opinion may be controversial enough that the entire court (*en banc*) rehears an appeal and issues a new opinion. The courts of appeals have experienced steady increases in their caseload, especially in the 1980s, when the increase has been approximately 3 percent per annum. More than forty thousand cases were docketed in 1989.

The courts of appeals marked their centennial in 1991. The Evarts Act of 1891, which established the present federal appellate system, capped almost three decades of lawyers' and legislative reformers' attempts to correct abuses in the process of review by the circuit courts of appeals (see JUDICIARY ACT OF 1891). The reformers also sought to relieve the overburdened Supreme Court by channeling appeals through the newly created courts. Congress allowed the Supreme Court to decide what cases it would hear by making review in some cases dependent on the Court granting a writ of *certiorari, which is a discretionary writ. During the past century the Supreme Court's certiorari jurisdiction has expanded most notably in the *Judiciary Act of 1925, until its mandatory jurisdiction was almost completely eliminated by 1988 legislation (see JUDICIAL IMPROVEMENTS AND ACCESS TO JUSTICE ACT). As the Supreme Court's discretionary jurisdiction expanded, the courts of appeals' importance grew. One pre-1988 study revealed that decisions of the courts of appeals remained final in 98.6 percent of the cases heard.

Additionally, the courts of appeals have gained prominence because of the substance of their caseload. For their first twenty-five years these courts decided mostly private-law appeals. Diversity cases (suits between citizens of different states), *bankruptcy, *patent, and *admiralty made up most of the work of the *lower federal courts. However, as federal regulation increased through the creation of federal administrative agencies, first during the Progressive Era, then during the *New Deal, and finally during the 1960s and 1970s, the role of the courts of appeals changed. Appeals from these agencies went directly to the courts of appeals, thus making them the supervisors of the regulators. Other developments that increased the policy-making importance of these courts were the increased scope of federal prosecutions, especially those dealing with civil rights crimes, drugs, racketeering, and political corruption. Also adding to their importance were the post-1954 use of federal courts to oversee state laws regarding school *desegregation and *abortion, as well as federal policing of state institutions such as prisons, mental hospitals, and reapportionment of state legislatures. Because the ability of the Supreme Court to review decisions of lower federal courts is constrained, decisions of courts of appeals remain final in most cases.    Rayman L. Solomon

**Cox v. New Hampshire,** 312 U.S. 569 (1941), argued 7 Mar. 1941, decided 31 Mar. 1941 by vote of 9 to 0; Hughes for the Court. Beginning in the late 1930s the Jehovah's Witnesses, complaining that a variety of police laws denied them religious freedom, set out to test such legislation. Initially successful, the sect received a mild judicial rebuff in *Cox v. New Hampshire.* A Manchester city ordinance required every parade or procession upon a public street to obtain a license and pay a fee. A group of Jehovah's Witnesses marched single file through the streets carrying placards to advertise a meeting without the licence or fee. They were arrested. Cox, their leader, argued that the defendants did not have a parade. They also claimed that the ordinance was invalid under the *Fourteenth Amendment for depriving them of their freedom to worship, freedom of speech and press, and freedom of assembly. The ordinance, they contended, vested unreasonable arbitrary power in the licensing authority and was vague and indefinite.

A unanimous Supreme Court upheld the measure as a reasonable *police regulation designed to promote the safe and orderly use of the streets. The Court made clear that it was treating the licence requirement as a traffic regulation and that the conviction was not for conveying information or holding a meeting.

The loss was a temporary setback to the Witnesses' program. *Cox* initiated a long line of cases establishing the right of government to make reasonable regulations concerning the time, place, and manner of speech, so long as those regulations were not used to prevent speech or to favor some speakers over others.

(See also ASSEMBLY AND ASSOCIATION, FREEDOM OF; RELIGION; SPEECH AND THE PRESS.)

Paul L. Murphy

**Coyle v. Smith,** 221 U.S. 559 (1911), argued 5–6 Apr. 1911, decided 29 May 1911 by vote of 7 to 2; Lurton for the Court, McKenna and Holmes in dissent without opinion. In an enabling act providing for the admission of Oklahoma to statehood, Congress stipulated that Guthrie would be the temporary capital until 1913. Accepting this provision, Oklahoma was admitted into the Union on an equal footing with the original states in 1907. Three years later, the Oklahoma legislature provided for the removal of the capital to Oklahoma City. When a suit challenging the action was instituted, the Oklahoma courts upheld the act of the state legislature.

The question was whether Congress, in its acknowledged discretion to admit new states, could impose conditions that would bind the state after its admission. Drawing upon a tradition stretching back to the *Northwest Ordinance of 1787, the majority found the restrictions that Congress placed on Oklahoma invalid and upheld the state's right to locate its capital where it chose. Congressional discretion to admit a state was not subject to *judicial review, but once the national legislature had acted the new states were entitled to all the governmental powers that the older ones enjoyed. Although the majority justices could find no constitutional language imposing such a check on congressional power, they did not hesitate to read the unwritten tradition of state equality into the Constitution itself.

(See also TERRITORIES AND NEW STATES.)

John E. Semonche

**Craig v. Boren,** 429 U.S. 190 (1976), argued 5 Oct. 1976, decided 20 Dec. 1976 by vote of 7 to 2; Brennan for the Court, Blackmun, Powell, Stevens, and Stewart (as to result) concurring, Burger and Rehnquist in dissent. The Court announced for the first time that sex-based classifications were subjected to *stricter scrutiny under the Equal Protection Clause of the *Fourteenth Amendment than was provided by the rational basis or "ordinary scrutiny" test. As stated by Justice William J. *Brennan, the constitutional standard that would have to be met for a statute classifying by gender is that it "must serve important governmental objectives and must be substantially related to those objectives" (p. 197). This standard appeared to be somewhat less rigorous than the *strict scrutiny test applied to "suspect" classifications such as race. Brennan claimed that (although the Court had never before mentioned it) this was the test that had applied to gender discrimination ever since *Reed v. Reed (1971). (The period 1971–1976, coincided with a nearly successful effort at the congressional and state level to add an Equal Rights Amendment to the Constitution.)

The Oklahoma law at issue in Craig allowed females aged 18–20 to purchase beer of 3.2% alcohol. Males could not purchase beer until age 21. The law was challenged by two underage men, Mark Walker and Curtis Craig, joined by a female beer vendor, Carolyn Whitener. By the time the case was argued at the Supreme Court, both men had turned 21, so the woman's standing proved decisive (see STANDING TO SUE).

Oklahoma defended the statute as a prophylactic against drunk driving, offering statistics showing that arrests of males 18–20 outnumbered those of females of similar age by a factor of ten for "drunk" driving (2 percent vs. .18 percent), by a factor of eighteen for "driving under the influence," and by a factor of ten for public drunkenness.

Brennan ruled for the Court that, while enhancing traffic safety did demonstrate an important government interest, the statistical evidence offered by Oklahoma did not meet the other half of the test: the *gender line drawn by the state did not "substantially" further the government's goal. Also, explaining that the *Twenty-first Amendment did not alter otherwise applicable *equal protection standards, he rejected the state's argument that the extra legislative power

secured by that amendment should cause this statute to be sustained.

Justice Harry *Blackmun concurred in the result and in all of the opinion except the discussion of the Twenty-first Amendment. Justice Lewis *Powell concurred but stated that he would have preferred a rule that said gender classifications must bear a "fair and substantial relation" to the object of legislation. Justice John Paul *Stevens concurred but suggested that rather than three differing degrees of equal protection scrutiny the Court should apply the rule that states must govern impartially. For him the requirement of impartiality entailed measuring the importance of the government interest, the degree to which any classification furthers that interest, and the degree of obnoxiousness of the classification. While this law did further traffic safety somewhat, and while that was an important goal, he felt that the offensiveness of a gender-based law outweighed these two considerations here.

Justice Potter *Stewart argued that the rationality test employed in Reed v. Reed still was the appropriate test for gender discrimination, but that this statute did not satisfy even that minimum standard and thus was unconstitutional.

Justice William *Rehnquist dissented, objecting both to the introduction of a new level of scrutiny and to its application to male plaintiffs, since males were not in need of special solicitude from the Court. He argued that rationality was the correct test and that the statistical evidence easily satisfied that standard. Chief Justice Warren *Burger expressed general agreement with Rehnquist's dissent but argued that the Court should not have taken the case, because, he said, it should never have extended standing to Ms. Whitener, a mere saloon-keeper.

Leslie Friedman Goldstein

**Craig v. Missouri,** 4 Pet. (29 U.S.) 410 (1830), argued 2–3 Mar. 1830, decided 12 Mar. 1830 by vote of 4 to 3; Marshall for the Court, Johnson, Thompson, and McLean dissenting. Craig demonstrated the transitional character of the late Marshall Court. The question presented was whether a Missouri statute authorizing loan certificates issued by the state violated Article I, section 10's ban on bills of credit. Arguing for Missouri, Senator Thomas Hart Benton, a leading critic of judicial nationalism, urged the Court to uphold the statute as a legitimate exercise of state sovereignty. He also argued that section 25 of the *Judiciary Act of 1789, under which the case came up to the Supreme Court, was unconstitutional, an argument that strengthened those in Congress working for its repeal.

Speaking for a bare majority, Chief Justice John *Marshall struck down the statute, grounding his reading of the constitutional prohibition of state paper money in the history of the Confederation. He also reaffirmed the Court's jurisdiction under section 25, contending as he had done in *Cohens

v. *Virginia* (1821) that the justices had no discretion in taking jurisdiction. Justices William *Johnson, Smith *Thompson, and John *McLean dissented, finding enough latitude in the wording of the statute to exempt it from the operation of the constitutional bar.

Just seven years later, the dissenters won the day in *Briscoe* v. *Bank of Kentucky* (1837), when the Court, now under Chief Justice Roger B. *Taney, upheld a variant currency scheme, by which a state bank's notes served as a circulating medium.

(See also CAPITALISM.)

R. Kent Newmyer

**Cranch, William** (b. Weymouth, Mass., 17 July 1769; d. Washington, D.C., 1 Sep. 1855), second Supreme Court reporter, 1801–1815. Like his predecessor Alexander *Dallas, Cranch became reporter more by chance than premeditation. The son of Abigail Adams's sister, Cranch moved to Washington as legal agent for a land speculation syndicate and was ruined by its collapse. He was rescued by his well-placed uncle, President John Adams. Appointed assistant judge of the new District of Columbia Circuit Court in 1801, Cranch survived the Republicans' purge of "midnight judges" in 1802 and served fifty-four years, becoming chief judge in 1805.

Meanwhile, the Supreme Court arrived in Washington from Philadelphia, and Cranch began reporting its decisions, motivated less by money than by a desire to bequeath the nation the gift of useful *precedents. Law reporting as a private venture, however, remained difficult and unremunerative. Although the justices often furnished what opinion notes they had, both the justices and the bar complained of inaccuracies in Cranch's product. Also, while the number of cases reported annually had quadrupled since Dallas's time, many concerned maritime matters of little interest to potential purchasers.

Burdened by the expense of producing his *Reports*, Cranch fell increasingly behind schedule. He left the reportership in 1815, and his last three volumes were so tardy that Chief Justice John *Marshall attributed them to his successor, Henry *Wheaton. Still, Cranch had kept "the chain of cases . . . complete," a result he rightly characterized to Dallas at the outset as "important to the stability of our national jurisprudence."

(See also REPORTERS, SUPREME COURT.)

Craig Joyce

**Creation Science.** See EVOLUTION AND CREATION SCIENCE.

**Criminal Syndicalism Laws,** statutes making it a crime to defend, advocate, or set up an organization committed to the use of crime, violence, sabotage, or other unlawful means to bring about a change in the form of government or in industrial ownership or control. Twenty states enacted such laws between 1917 and 1920. Their target was a radical labor organization known as the Industrial Workers of the World. Since the IWW was strongest in the West, criminal syndicalism laws appeared first in that region. The prototype was a 1917 Idaho statute. Some states, such as California, prosecuted a number of radicals for *criminal syndicalism during the post–*World War I Red Scare, and there were also prosecutions under these statutes during the *labor troubles of the 1930s. Thereafter, they fell into disuse.

In *Whitney* v. *California* (1927), the Supreme Court upheld the constitutionality of a criminal syndicalism law. Justice Louis *Brandeis attacked the majority's position in an opinion regarded as the classic statement of the *"clear and present danger" test for the protection of free speech (see SPEECH AND THE PRESS). The Court first reversed a criminal syndicalism law in *Fiske* v. *Kansas* (1927). In a broader ruling in *DeJonge* v. *Oregon* (1937), the justices held that it was a violation of the *First Amendment for a state to punish someone for participating in a peaceful meeting sponsored by an organization that advocated criminal syndicalism. Finally, in *Brandenburg* v. *Ohio* (1969), the Court struck down an Ohio criminal syndicalism law, overruled *Whitney,* and imposed narrow First Amendment restrictions on the punishment of speech advocating violence or unlawful action.

(See also SUBVERSION.)

Michal R. Belknap

**Crittenden, John Jordan** (b. near Versailles, Ky., 10 Sep. 1787; d. Frankfort, Ky., 26 July 1863), lawyer, statesman, and unconfirmed nominee for the Supreme Court. Crittenden prepared for college at Kentucky seminaries, read law with George Bibb, graduated from William and Mary College in 1806, and was admitted to the Kentucky bar in 1807. In 1812, voters sent him to the state assembly; in 1817, he was elevated to the U.S. Senate, where he remained until the Panic of 1819 compelled his return to Kentucky.

After 1824, Crittenden was a staunch supporter of Henry Clay and John Quincy *Adams; the latter made him U.S. district attorney for Kentucky in 1827. On the eve of Andrew *Jackson's election, Adams nominated Crittenden as an associate justice of the Supreme Court, but the Senate declined to consider the appointment. President William Henry Harrison appointed him attorney general in 1841. In that capacity, he helped avert war with Britain during the McLeod trial, but resigned after John *Tyler became president. After 1842, he sat in the Senate as a Whig and later served as attorney general under President Millard Fillmore. In 1853, he returned to the Senate. There, Crittenden decried disunionism as well as President James Buchanan's position on the Lecompton Constitution, but he also opposed radical abolition, defending the merits of 1820 Missouri Compromise. Crittenden helped to found the Constitutional Union Party in 1858, and later opposed the Emancipation Proclamation.                                      Sandra F. VanBurkleo

**Crow Dog, Ex Parte,** 109 U.S. 557 (1883), argued 20 Nov. 1883, decided 17 Dec. 1883 by a vote of 9 to 0; Matthews for the court. Crow Dog, a Brule Sioux, was tried, convicted, and sentenced to death for the murder of another Sioux, who was known as Spotted Tail, in a Dakota territorial court. He sought release on a writ of *habeas corpus, arguing that tribal and not federal law should apply because territorial courts lacked jurisdiction over crimes committed by one Indian against another in Indian country (see TERRITORIES AND NEW STATES).

Sioux tribal law required that Crow Dog, as punishment for murder, must support Spotted Tail's dependent relatives but did not subject him to execution. Crow Dog contended that he was not subject to the criminal laws of either Dakota Territory or the United States. The United States maintained that federal criminal jurisdiction over Indian country was acquired under the Sioux Treaty of 1868 interpreted in connection with general federal Indian statutes.

The Supreme Court held that the Dakota territorial court was without jurisdiction. Crow Dog was governed in his relationship with other reservation Indians solely by the tribal laws of the Brule Sioux and was responsible only to the tribal law enforcement authorities. The Court regarded exclusive tribal jurisdiction over tribal members as a surviving attribute of tribal sovereignty despite treaty language that appeared to subject the Sioux to the laws of the United States.

The *Crow Dog* decision did not deny the power of Congress to legislate over Indian affairs or to curtail the scope of Indian self-government. But the Court declared that Congress had not done so in any clear fashion and thus found no congressional intent to limit Indian self-government. The Court stated that the tribes retained their right of "self-government [and] the maintenance of order and peace among their own members" (p. 568). Unless this power is limited by explicit legislation or surrendered by the tribe, Indian tribes retain exclusive judicial jurisdictions over reservation Indian affairs. Thus today most tribes operate their own tribal court systems. Except to the extent mandated by the Indian Civil Rights Act (1968), the structure and procedure of such courts is determined by the tribes themselves (see INDIAN BILL OF RIGHTS).

The decision in *Crow Dog* prompted action by nineteenth-century reformers who wanted Indians to be absorbed into the mainstream of American life. One goal of the assimilationists was to have the same laws applied to Indians as applied to all other citizens and to outlaw the Indians' own "heathenish" laws and customs. The fact that Crow Dog could not be executed for murder

shocked them and their congressional supporters. Congress appended to the Appropriation Act of 3 March 1885, an Indian section known as "The Major Crimes Act" specifying seven crimes over which the federal courts were authorized to exercise jurisdiction. Thus, within two years, in reaction against *Crow Dog,* Congress enacted new legislation making it a federal crime for one Indian to murder another within Indian country. Today, there are fourteen enumerated offenses under the amended Indian Major Crimes Act.

Despite legislation aimed at reversing its specific outcome, *Crow Dog* remains a major precedent in Native American affairs. *Crow Dog* affirms that treaties and statutes are interpreted in favor of retained tribal self-government and property rights (see TREATIES AND TREATY POWER). Doubts and ambiguities in treaties and statutes are to be resolved in Indians' favor and federal Indian laws are interpreted liberally toward carrying out their protective purposes. *Crow Dog* established that federal protection of tribal self-government has never depended on any particular tribal social structure or political organization.

*Crow Dog* articulated the fundamental constitutional principle that federal laws do not preempt tribal authority unless Congress's intent to do so is clear. Congressional intent to include tribes within the scope of laws applying generally to persons, groups, corporations, or associations must be firmly established because of Indian tribes' unique status. The broad concepts of tribal self-government articulated in *Crow Dog* continue as a basic constitutional guide in modern Indian law.

(See also NATIVE AMERICANS.)
                                      Rennard J. Strickland

**Cruel and Unusual Punishment.** For nearly a century after the establishment of the United States, the *Eighth Amendment's prohibition of cruel and unusual punishments was virtually a dead letter. The Supreme Court did concede that torture and punitive "atrocities," such as burning at the stake, crucifixion, or breaking on the wheel, would be cruel and unusual (*Wilkerson v. Utah,* 1879). But other forms of punishment actually authorized by statute—hanging, shooting, electrocution—were not (*In re Kemmler,* 1890). The Court's criterion seems to have been whether a punishment would have been considered cruel and unusual in 1791, when the *Bill of Rights was ratified.

In 1910 the Court in *Weems* v. *United States* invalidated a territorial statute derived from Spanish law that imposed *cadena temporal*—twelve to twenty years chained in prison—for knowingly entering a false statement in the public record. Because this penalty was excessive and disproportionate to the crime, the Court ruled that it was cruel and unusual. Against a narrow historic reading of the Eighth Amendment, the Court observed, "[A] principle to be vital must be capable of wider application than the mischief which gave it birth" (p. 373). Yet the criteria implied by this broader reading of the clause have remained obscure. Recently, the Court has held that the death penalty for rape (*Coker v. Georgia, 1977) and for kidnapping (Eberheart v. Georgia, 1977) was cruel and unusual because "grossly disproportionate to the offense." In 1958 the Court ruled that expatriation, which is denial of an offender's very "right to have rights," violated the clause (*Trop v. Dulles). Punishments, the Court said, must comport with "the basic concept of human dignity at the core" of the clause (p. 100). In the Court's first application of the clause to invalidate a state penal law, it struck down imprisonment for the status offense of narcotics addiction (*Robinson v. California, 1962).

The question whether *capital punishment was cruel and unusual was not considered until 1972. In *Furman v. Georgia, a divided Court held that the death penalty as then typically administered for murder and rape was so "arbitrary" and "freakish" as to be cruel and unusual. However, four years later, in the wake of newly enacted capital statutes in three dozen states, the Court declared that the death penalty as such was not a cruel and unusual punishment (*Gregg v. Georgia, Proffitt v. Florida, Jurek v. Texas, 1976). The Court was influenced not only by popular support for the death penalty but also by new statutory guidelines intended to make the choice of sentence (death or imprisonment) more rational. The Court did hold, however, that a mandatory death penalty for murder, which sought to avoid arbitrariness by sacrificing "individualized" sentencing, was cruel and unusual (*Woodson v. North Carolina, 1976). Such a punishment may not be employed even for a prisoner convicted of murder while serving a life term for murder (Sumner v. Shuman, 1987).

The Court has yet to decide whether the death penalty for nonhomicidal crimes, such as treason and espionage, is a cruel and unusual punishment. Legislative repeal of traditional corporal punishments has so far mooted any decision on their constitutional status.

□ Larry C. Berkson, *The Concept of Cruel and Unusual Punishment* (1975).                H. A. Bedau

**Cruikshank, United States v.,** 92 U.S. 542 (1876), argued 30–31 Mar. and 30 Apr. 1875, decided 27 Mar. 1876 by vote of 9 to 0; Waite for the Court, Clifford concurring. The *Cruikshank* case arose after an armed white force in Reconstruction Louisiana killed more than one hundred black men over a disputed gubernatorial election. Three white men involved in the 1873 Colfax Massacre were found guilty of violating section 6 of the Enforcement Act of 1870, which forbade conspiracies to deny the constitutional rights of any citizen. The convicted defendants appealed on the grounds that the indictments were faulty.

The case came before a Supreme Court that had evinced a growing concern about congressional efforts to broaden federal power. Emphasizing the distinctions between the rights of federal and state citizens, the Court found the indictments deficient because they did not allege the denial of federal rights (see CITIZENSHIP). The right to assemble (see ASSEMBLY AND ASSOCIATION, FREEDOM OF) and to bear arms in the *First and *Second Amendments, respectively, only protected citizens from congressional interference. The right to *due process and *equal protection in the *Fourteenth Amendment limited actions by states, not those by individuals (see STATE ACTION). Finally, interference with the right to vote was not an actionable offense because the indictment did not allege that the defendants' actions were motivated by the victims' race.

The Court concluded that punishment for the offenses committed in the Colfax Massacre lay with the state. Unfortunately, the likelihood that southern states would prosecute such offenses was small. The *Cruikshank* opinion encouraged violence in the Reconstruction South and is one of several Supreme Court decisions that marked the nation's retreat from Reconstruction.

(See also RACE AND RACISM; RECONSTRUCTION; VOTE, RIGHT TO.)

Lucy E. Salyer

**Cruzan v. Director, Missouri Department of Health,** 110 S.Ct. 2841 (1990), argued 6 Dec. 1989, decided 25 June 1990 by vote of 5 to 4; Rehnquist for the Court, Brennan, joined by Marshall, Blackmun, and Stevens, in dissent. In June 1990, the U.S. Supreme Court issued its first pronouncement concerning the constitutional interests of dying medical patients. The case dealt with the fate of Nancy Cruzan, a woman mired in a permanently unconscious state in the wake of an automobile accident in which she sustained severe brain injuries. Her parents sought judicial authorization to act on their daughter's behalf to end the artificial nutrition maintaining Nancy's existence. Nancy had previously made informal oral declarations indicating she would not have wished to be maintained in a permanently vegetative state. The Missouri Supreme Court had ruled, however, that there was inadequate evidence to establish the now-incompetent patient's preferences. In the absence of "clear and convincing" evidence of the patient's will, the Missouri court refused to permit a guardian's determination to withdraw life-preserving medical treatment. The parents appealed to the U.S. Supreme Court, contending that Nancy's constitutional right to reject unwanted medical treatment had been violated.

By a 5-to-4 margin, the Supreme Court rejected this challenge. Chief Justice William *Rehnquist's majority opinion ruled both that a

# 210 □ Cummings v. Missouri

state may confine terminal decisions on behalf of incompetent patients to instances when the patient has previously expressed such a preference and that the state may demand clear evidence of the patient's wishes. These precautions were reasonable, the majority declared, in order to safeguard against potential abuses. Missouri could legitimately be concerned about subjective, "quality of life" decisions being made on behalf of incompetent patients. The Court was dubious that family members—in the absence of clear prior expressions—would make precisely the decision the patient would want.

While the Supreme Court rejected the constitutional challenge, the *Cruzan* decision contains much encouragement for the advancement of patient rights to shape medical intervention in natural dying processes. The majority was willing to assume that a competent patient has a constitutionally based liberty right to reject life-preserving medical treatment. Moreover, the Court did not draw any distinction between artificial nutrition and other forms of medical technology. Likewise, no distinction was drawn between a patient facing unavoidable, imminent death and one whose life might be preserved for years. Finally, the Court appears to have endorsed giving full recognition to a patient's prior expressions even after the patient has lost competence. This increases the incentive for people to make advance directives governing their medical handling in the event of later incompetence.

The *Cruzan* decision does nothing to disrupt the policies regarding incompetent medical patients that prevail in most states. Most states allow guardians to make medical decisions—including rejection of life-preserving intervention—on behalf of incompetent patients even without clear prior expressions. Some states authorize a "substituted judgment" standard, which allows consideration of informal patient declarations as well as other indices of the patient's preferences. Some states allow guardians to secure withdrawal of life-preserving care where such a decision promotes the "best interests" of the patient. A "best interests" determination includes consideration of a patient's previous informal declarations. *Cruzan* makes clear that nothing in the Constitution prevents states from continuing to use such standards.

Norman L. Cantor

**Cummings v. Missouri,** 71 U.S. 277 (1867), argued 15, 16, 19, and 20 Mar. 1866, decided 14 Jan. 1867 by vote of 5 to 4; Field for the Court, Miller in dissent. **Ex parte Garland,** 71 U.S. 333, argued 13–15 Mar. 1866, decided 14 Jan. 1867 by vote of 5 to 4; Field for the Court, Miller in dissent. These cases challenged the constitutionality of retrospective loyalty oaths established during the *Civil War. Cummings* involved a Missouri regulation requiring persons in various occupations to swear that they had not aided or sympathized

with the rebellion; *Garland* concerned a federal statute compelling attorneys who practiced in federal courts to swear that they had not supported the Confederacy.

Writing for 5-to-4 majorities in both cases, Justice Stephen J. *Field noted that although the laws did not impose fines or imprisonment, they were punitive measures because they prevented former rebels from practicing their occupations. Therefore, he held that they violated the Constitution's ban on bills of *attainder and *ex post facto laws. They were bills of attainder, Field explained, because they subjected a designated class to punishment without a trial; they were ex post facto laws because they imposed punishment for acts that had not been criminal when committed or inflicted additional punishment for acts that had been. Speaking for the four Republicans on the Court, Justice Samuel *Miller denied that the measures inflicted punishment and therefore that they were bills of attainder or ex post facto laws. They were, he contended, regulations to assure that practitioners in various professions possessed the qualifications—including the moral character—essential to serve the public.

The Court has never repudiated these decisions, and in *U.S. v. Brown* (1965) it invoked them to strike down a federal law excluding former Communists from serving as officers of labor unions.

(See also TEST OATHS.)

Donald G. Nieman

**Cumming v. Richmond County Board of Education,** 175 U.S. 528 (1899), argued 30 Oct. 1899, decided 18 Dec. 1899 by vote of 9 to 0; Harlan for the Court. Three years after its decision in *Plessy v. Ferguson,* the Supreme Court refused to enforce the "equal" part of the *"separate but equal" doctrine. *Cumming,* the Court's first decision on racial discrimination in schools, has never been explicitly overruled, nor has anyone ever satisfactorily explained why the Court, and especially the erstwhile racial egalitarian Justice John Marshall *Harlan, concluded that *Cumming* did not present a "case of clear and unmistakable disregard of rights" (p. 545).

Pressured by black voters and facing an explicit "separate but equal" state law, the school board of Augusta, Georgia, in 1879 established the first public high school for African-Americans in the state. Ware High School thrived until 1897, when, reportedly at the suggestion of a black private school principal, the school board closed it, claiming that the money was needed for black primary education. Black parents sued.

Because the state law was so clear, local Judge Enoch Callaway did not reach the constitutional issue. Callaway's injunction was overturned by Georgia Supreme Court Justice Thomas J. Simmons, who hardly bothered to say why. On further appeal, former Reconstruction Congressman and Senator George F. Edmunds argued that if a school board supported high schools for whites, the Equal Protection Clause of the *Fourteenth Amendment at least required it to offer blacks a high school.

Citing no lower court decisions, most of which went against him, Justice Harlan announced that plaintiffs had to prove that the board's decision had been motivated solely by a "hostility to the colored population because of their race" (pp. 544–545), a nearly impossible standard. Fortunately, most judges in subsequent cases ignored the opinion.

(See also EDUCATION; EQUAL PROTECTION; RACE AND RACISM; SEGREGATION, DE JURE.)

J. Morgan Kousser

**Curator, Office of the.** The chief justice in 1973 established the office of the curator to record and preserve the history and memorabilia of the Supreme Court. The office has accumulated an extensive collection of historic and contemporary photographs, prints, films, and videos, as well as manuscripts and memorabilia related to the justices. Its holdings also include decorative and fine arts and historic furnishings.

The collections form the basis of the two exhibits the curatorial staff produce each year. These exhibits, in the lower Great Hall, interpret many facets of the Court's history. A movie exploring the history and role of the Court is shown continuously in the exhibit hall.

The staff maintains files on hundreds of research topics related to the Court and responds to a high volume of information requests from the public, scholarly community, and justices. The office frequently assists with publications and documentaries and provides illustrative materials to editors, publishers, and producers.

The more than 700,000 yearly visitors to the Court benefit from hourly lectures in the courtroom given by the curatorial staff. Private and congressional tours are provided and international visitors, sponsored by federal agencies, participate in special tours of the building followed by briefings.

The curator is a nonstatutory officer of the Court. The first person to hold the position was Catherine Hetos Skefos. Gail Galloway has been curator since 1976. The staff includes a collections and exhibits coordinator, photograph collections coordinator, visitor programs coordinator, curatorial assistant, and secretary. The office hires from four to six interns every three months to assist with tours and projects.

Gail Galloway

**Curtis, Benjamin Robbins** (b. Watertown, Mass., 4 Nov. 1809; d. Newport, R.I., 15 Sept. 1874; interred Mt. Auburn Cemetery, Cambridge, Mass.), associate justice, 1851–1857. Curtis was the son of a Massachusetts ship captain who died on a sea voyage when Curtis was a child. Curtis

*Benjamin Robbins Curtis*

graduated from Harvard in 1829 and from the law school there in 1832. Shortly thereafter he established a law practice in Boston and became a Whig in politics. It was on the recommendation of then Secretary of State Daniel Webster that President Millard Fillmore appointed Curtis to the high court in 1851.

On the Court, Curtis became known for his participation in two major cases. The first was *Cooley* v. *Board of Wardens* (1852), in which he enunciated the doctrine of *selective exclusiveness (see COMMERCE POWER). In this commerce clause case, Curtis held for the Court that where the object of regulation is such as to require a uniform national rule, the power to legislate is reserved exclusively to Congress; but where a uniform national rule is not required, the states are constitutionally free to enact their own regulation, unless and until Congress legislates.

Curtis's other major opinion was a dissent in *Dred *Scott v. Sandford* (1857). Curtis repudiated Chief Justice Roger B. *Taney's opinion for the Court by relying upon facts to show that at the time of the ratification of the Constitution, there were African-American citizens in several states, northern and southern (see RACE AND RACISM). There being no federal *citizenship clause in the Constitution, Curtis reasoned, the states must have created federal citizens automatically by having conferred state citizenship. Thus, Scott, despite being of African ancestry, could be a citizen within the meaning of *Article III of the Constitution.

With respect to congressional control of *slavery in federal territories, Curtis cited no fewer than fourteen separate instances in which Congress had legislated with respect to slavery in the territories prior to the Missouri Compromise.

Thus, he concluded that by settled practice Congress had had the power to enact the Compromise, and Scott's residence in the areas governed by that congressional legislation had made him a free man.

The rancor engendered by the *Dred Scott* decision so strained Curtis's relations with his fellow justices that he resigned. He returned to his Boston law practice and, after the Civil War, argued several significant cases before the Court.

His greatest legal contribution, however, came as one of the defense counsels in the impeachment trial of President Andrew Johnson. In that case—and perhaps contrary to the intent of the founders—Curtis was able to convince the Senate that impeachment was exclusively a judicial not a political proceeding, a trial of and not a vote of confidence in the president.

Curtis died at the age of sixty-four; having been married three times, he was the father of twelve children. In his short tenure on the Supreme Court he gave promise of being a great justice. Whether he would have realized that potential had he remained on the Court will never be known. But today the *Cooley* Rule is the law of the land, and *Dred Scott* is not.

□ Richard H. Leach, *Benjamin R. Curtis: Case Study of a Supreme Court Justice* (Ph.D. diss., Princeton University, 1951).                     Richard Y. Funston

**Curtiss-Wright Export Corp., United States v.,**
299 U.S. 304 (1936), argued 19–20 Nov. 1936, decided 21 Dec. 1936 by vote of 7 to 1; Sutherland for the Court, McReynolds in dissent, Stone not participating. The powers of the federal government in foreign affairs are derived principally from inferences based on the history and structure of the Constitution, rather than from specific constitutional language. In *Curtiss-Wright*, the Supreme Court relied on just such inferences to conclude not only that the foreign affairs power vested in the national government as a whole, but that the president of the United States had "plenary" powers in the foreign affairs field not dependent upon congressional delegation.

Congress, acting by joint resolution, had authorized the president to place an embargo on arms shipments to countries at war in the Chaco region of South America. Acting pursuant to the resolution, President Franklin *Roosevelt proclaimed such an embargo. When Curtiss-Wright Export Corp. was indicted for violating the embargo, it defended itself on the grounds that the embargo and the proclamation were void because Congress had improperly delegated legislative power to the executive branch by leaving what was essentially a legislative determination to the president's "unfettered discretion."

The Court ruled that the joint resolution and the president's actions were not based on unconstitutional delegation of nonenumerated powers because of "fundamental differences" in national power with respect to internal and to external affairs. Key language from the Court's dictum explaining this conclusion has become a basis for broad executive branch claims to inherent presidential power in foreign affairs (see INHERENT POWERS).

Justice George *Sutherland argued that the powers of sovereignty in foreign affairs did not depend upon express grants in the Constitution. The foreign affairs power had been transmitted immediately from Great Britain to the united colonies as an essential element of nationhood upon the success of the Revolution. Although many scholars have refuted Justice Sutherland's "springing sovereignty" analysis on historical grounds, there is general agreement that the foreign affairs power resides exclusively in the national government.

A more controversial question is raised by the presumptive identity between national power and executive power over foreign affairs that the Court's language and holding suggest. The opinion concluded that if sovereign power resided in the federal government, the power to deal with foreign nations must reside in the executive branch. Consequently, no allocation of specific powers, other than the general conferral of executive power in Article II of the Constitution, was necessary to empower the president to act in foreign affairs matters.

Despite the controversy surrounding it, the *Curtiss-Wright* decision is one of the Supreme Court's most influential. Most cases involving executive branch-legislative branch conflicts involve *political questions that the courts refuse to adjudicate. Therefore, the sweeping language of *Curtiss-Wright* is regularly cited to support executive branch claims of power to act without congressional authorization in foreign affairs, especially when there is no judicial intervention to interpret the meaning of that text.

The Court's characterization of the president's power as "plenary" has been cited as legal sanction for executive branch initiatives in foreign affairs that often result in Congress being faced with a *fait accompli*. The *Curtiss-Wright* opinion has been cited to support the president's power to enter into executive agreements with foreign nations, claims of executive privilege in national security and other matters, as well as much of the executive branch activity during the *Vietnam War. *Curtiss-Wright* was also cited to attack the constitutionality of the 1973 *War Powers Act, requiring the president under certain conditions to withdraw combat troops committed abroad if not authorized by Congress.

The Court has not recognized the full scope of executive power suggested by Justice Sutherland's sweeping language. Congressional authorization may be necessary to legitimize many executive acts. In *Regan v. Wald* (1984), for example, the Supreme Court cited *Curtiss-Wright* in upholding the constitutionality of the president's regulations restricting travel to Cuba expressly on the ground that they had been authorized by Congress. On the other hand, in *Federal Energy Administration* v. *Algonquin SNG, Inc.* (1976), the Court validated presidential restrictions on oil imports based on very broad congressional language delegating apparently unlimited regulatory authority to the executive branch.

(See also DELEGATION OF POWERS; FOREIGN AFFAIRS AND FOREIGN POLICY.)

Harold G. Maier

**Cushing, Caleb** (b. Salisbury, Mass., 17 Jan. 1800; d. Newburyport, Mass., 2 Jan. 1879), lawyer, attorney general, diplomat, and unconfirmed nominee for chief justice of the Supreme Court. Cushing attended Harvard Law School and became a member of the Massachusetts bar. In 1834 he was elected to Congress as a Whig, serving four terms. Although Cushing was against *slavery, he believed that it was more important to preserve the Union than to abolish slavery. He became alienated from the Whig party when he sided with President John *Tyler against Henry Clay. The Senate repeatedly rejected Tyler's attempt in 1843 to name Cushing secretary of the treasury. His shifts of party affiliation—from Whig to Democrat in 1841 and from Democrat to Republican in 1861—can be explained by his devotion to the Union, although many saw him as a political chameleon.

In 1844 Tyler sent Cushing to China to negotiate an important commercial agreement with that country. President Franklin Pierce appointed him attorney general in 1852. Cushing expanded the duties of that office, handling pardons, extraditions, and judicial appointments, matters formerly managed by the State Department. Cushing was the first attorney general to adhere to the residence requirement, abandoning his private law practice while in office.

President Ulysses S. Grant nominated Cushing as chief justice of the Supreme Court on 9 January 1874. His age and his political record hurt him in the Senate. When it became obvious that he would not be confirmed, Grant withdrew his name at Cushing's request on 14 January. Partisan motives deprived the country of a chief justice who was honest, learned in the law, and devoted to the Union.

After serving as ambassador to Spain from 1874 to 1877, Cushing retired to Newburyport, where he died on 2 January 1879.

(See also NOMINEES, REJECTION OF.)

Judith K. Schafer

**Cushing, William** (b. Scituate, Mass., 1 Mar. 1732; d. Scituate, 13 Sep. 1810; interred in family graveyard, Scituate), associate justice, 1789–1810. The son and grandson of judges of the Superior Court of the province of Massachusetts Bay, Cushing took his A.B. at Harvard College in 1751 and received an M.A. from Yale in 1753 and

*William Cushing*

the same degree from Harvard in 1754. After reading law with the eminent Boston lawyer Jeremiah Gridley, he became a member of the Boston bar in 1755 upon Gridley's recommendation. The first years of his practice were difficult, despite being admitted in 1758 as an attorney to the superior court. Although he lived with his father at Scituate, he earned such a scant livelihood that in 1760 he moved to the northern frontier village of Pownalborough (now Dresden, Maine) where, as the only lawyer in the newly created county of Lincoln, he was appointed both justice of the peace and judge of probates. When his father retired from the superior court in 1772, he arranged for his son to succeed him as an associate justice. Cushing in 1774 married Hannah Phillips.

Forced by the rising conflict between the Colonies and the Crown to declare his allegiance to the patriot cause, Cushing alone of the royal appointees continued on the court after it was reorganized in October 1775 by the revolutionary council. He represented Scituate in the convention that drafted the Massachusetts Constitution of 1780. As chief justice (he succeeded John Adams in 1777), he presided over *Commonwealth* v. *Jennison* (1783), the case that in effect abolished slavery in the state, and in 1787 he tried the leaders of Shay's Rebellion. A strong advocate of the Constitution, he acted as vice president of the state convention that narrowly ratified the document in February 1788.

The first associate justice that *George Washington appointed, William Cushing served on the Supreme Court for twenty-one years. His age and his increasingly ill health, coupled with the rigors of *circuit riding, so taxed his strength that he wrote only nineteen opinions. The most important of these were *Chisholm v. Georgia (1793), where he concurred with the majority that a state could be sued by a citizen of another state (see ELEVENTH AMENDMENT); *Ware v. Hylton (1796), in which he wrote that a treaty is of equal force with the Constitution and hence cannot be violated by state laws; and *Calder v. Bull (1798), where in a two-sentence opinion characteristic of his propensity for brevity and perhaps for oversimplification, he agreed that the Constitution forbids *ex post facto laws in criminal cases but not in civil ones. In January 1795, following the Senate's rejection of John *Rutledge to be chief justice, that body confirmed President Washington's recommendation that Cushing be appointed to the post. After holding the commission for a week, Cushing declined because of ill health. He continued on the bench as an associate justice until his death, the last of Washington's original appointees.

□ *The Documentary History of the Supreme Court of the United States, 1789–1800*, vol. 1 (1985), pp. 28–29, 101–103.　　　　　　　　　　　　　　David R. Warrington

# D

**Dallas, Alexander James** (b. Kingston, Jamaica, 21 June 1759; d. Philadelphia, Pa., 16 Jan. 1817), first Supreme Court reporter, 1791–1800. Dallas's reportership was purely an entrepreneurial venture. Even before the Court's 1791 arrival in Philadelphia, he had published reports of state cases in periodicals and in a single bound volume. Hence 1 *Dallas*, now 1 *United States Reports*, contains no Supreme Court matter. Three more volumes followed, chronicling the Court's first decisions, from August term 1791 through its final activities in Philadelphia in August term 1800.

We owe much to Dallas for recognizing the need for Supreme Court reports, thereby in theory making the decisions of the new nation's highest court available to judges, lawyers, and citizens. Apart from his *Reports*, the Court's rulings could be known only through correspondence, word of mouth, and occasional newspaper accounts.

The execution of Dallas's self-appointed task was marked, however, by delay, expense, omission, and questionable accuracy. In fairness, he faced formidable obstacles. Lack of government funding forced selective reporting, reflecting purchasers' unwillingness to finance fuller reports. Likewise, because the Court had no requirement of written decisions and Dallas's practice precluded constant attendance at its proceedings, he often relied on others' notes.

The results were uneven. Five years elapsed between *Chisholm* v. *Georgia* (1793), the last Supreme Court decision recorded in 2 *Dallas*, and publication of that volume; between Dallas's retirement as reporter and publication of 4 *Dallas*,

seven years passed. Buyers complained of the volumes' price. Barely half of the Court's dispositions during its first decade were reported, and accounts of many cases, including *Ware* v. *Hylton* (1796), contain matter clearly not the justices' own.

Dallas left things better than he found them, but both he and the Court were disappointed in comparing aspiration with accomplishment. "I have found such miserable encouragement for my Reports," he wrote upon relinquishing the reportership, "that I have determined to call them all in, and devote them to the rats in the State-House."

(See also REPORTERS, SUPREME COURT.)

Craig Joyce

**Dames & Moore v. Regan,** 453 U.S. 654 (1981), argued 24 June 1981, decided 2 July 1981 by vote of 9 to 0; Rehnquist for the Court, Stevens concurring in part, Powell concurring in part and dissenting in part. This decision upheld certain actions taken by President Jimmy Carter in January 1981 to settle the controversy resulting from the seizure of American personnel as hostages at the American Embassy in Tehran, Iran, in 1979. To secure the hostages' release, the United States agreed with Iran to terminate legal proceedings in U.S. courts involving claims by U.S. nationals against Iran, to nullify attachments against Iranian property entered by U.S. courts to secure any judgments against Iran, and to transfer such claims from U.S. courts to a newly created arbitration tribunal. These agreements were implemented by executive orders.

The Court upheld these presidential actions

against challenges that they were unauthorized by law. The Court concluded that the International Emergency Economic Powers Act (IEEPA) authorized the president to nullify the attachments and to transfer Iranian assets. It also approved the suspension of claims filed in U.S. courts even though no specific statutory provision authorized that step. In so doing the Court relied on inferences drawn from related legislation, a history of congressional acquiescence in executive claims settlement practices, and past decisions recognizing broad executive authority.

This decision has been criticized for applying a too-undemanding standard to the question of presidential power, in particular by relying on inferences from statutes that do not directly deal with certain subjects at hand and, especially, on legislative acquiescence in executive activity. On any view, this decision is an important recognition of broad presidential power in foreign relations.

(See also FOREIGN AFFAIRS AND FOREIGN POLICY; PRESIDENTIAL EMERGENCY POWERS.)

Thomas O. Sargentich

**Danbury Hatters' Case.** See LOEWE V. LAWLOR.

**Daniel, Peter Vivian** (b. Stafford County, Va., 24 Apr. 1784; d. Richmond, Va., 31 May 1860; interred Hollywood Cemetery, Richmond), associate justice, 1841–1860. The personification of Jeffersonian Republicanism, agrarianism, and strict constructionism in a rapidly changing antebellum America, Daniel spent most of his eighteen years on the U.S. Supreme Court dissenting from the majority opinions of his fellow justices.

Born into a prominent Virginia family, Daniel attended the College of New Jersey briefly before settling in Richmond to read law with former attorney general and founding father Edmund Randolph. Two years after being admitted to the Virginia bar in 1808, Daniel married Randolph's daughter Lucy. He gained election to the Virginia House of Delegates from Stafford County in 1809. Three years later the assembly elevated him to the Privy Council, the governor's advisory body, where for much of his twenty-three-year tenure he served as lieutenant governor.

As an attorney in Richmond, Daniel enjoyed modest success. Politically active, he was admitted to the Richmond Junto, through which he organized and led the Old Dominion's Jacksonian Democrats. In recognition of his party loyalty and support of the bank war, Andrew *Jackson in 1836 appointed Daniel judge of the U.S. District Court for Eastern Virginia.

When Associate Justice Philip P. *Barbour died suddenly in February 1841, outgoing president Martin Van Buren hurriedly seized the opportunity to nominate his friend Daniel to the Court. Despite the efforts of Whig senators to thwart this move, Daniel was confirmed about midnight of 2–3 March 1841.

*Peter Vivian Daniel*

Selected more for his political faithfulness than his legal ability or judicial stature, Daniel joined the Court in December 1841 unswervingly opposed to banks, corporations, and economic consolidation of any sort, an extreme defender of states' rights, limited government, and the institution of *slavery, and consumed with a hatred for anything northern. As a justice, he consistently opposed the expansion of federal regulatory or jurisdictional authority and resisted the doctrine of federal exclusiveness under the commerce clause (see COMMERCE POWER; LICENSE CASES [1847]; PASSENGER CASES [1849]).

Fearful of the growing power of corporations, Daniel declared such chartered bodies to be artificial persons and thus not entitled to standing in federal courts on the basis of diversity of citizenship (see STANDING TO SUE). In his strongly worded dissent in *Planters' Bank of Mississippi v. Sharp* (1848), he opposed application of the *contracts clause to corporate charters, arguing that contracts remained subject to the *police power of the states.

Daniel's majority opinion in *West River Bridge Co. v. Dix* (1849) held that a state must have the power, under the doctrine of *eminent domain, to condemn any property, whether corporate or unincorporated, for public use. He also joined the majority in Dred *Scott v. Sandford* (1857), in which his concurring opinion declared that freed black slaves, because they had been originally held as property, could not be citizens.

Highly principled but markedly out of step with the legal and constitutional developments of his day, Daniel was doomed to stand his ground with carefully articulated but extreme opinions that ultimately left little mark on American constitutional law.

(See also STATE SOVEREIGNTY AND STATES' RIGHTS.)

□ John P. Frank, *Justice Daniel Dissenting: A Biography of Peter V. Daniel, 1784–1860* (1964).          E. Lee Shepard

**Darby Lumber Co., United States v.,** 312 U.S. 100 (1941), argued 19–20 Dec. 1940, decided 3 Feb. 1941 by vote of 9 to 0; Stone for the Court. The Fair Labor Standards Act (often called the Wages and Hours Act), adopted in 1938, was the last major piece of New Deal legislation. The statute provided for the setting of minimum wages and maximum hours for all employees in industries whose products were shipped in interstate commerce and made violation of the wages and hours standards unlawful. The act applied to all employees "engaged in commerce or in the production of goods for commerce."

The Constitution authorizes Congress "to regulate commerce . . . among the several states." In the classic case of *Gibbons* v. *Ogden* (1824) the Supreme Court gave a broad reading to the federal *commerce power, and regulation of commerce has been a major congressional concern. Around the beginning of the twentieth century Congress began to explore use of the Commerce Clause as a kind of national *police power. An act forbidding the interstate transportation of lottery tickets was upheld in *Champion* v. *Ames* (1903). The Pure Food and Drug Act of 1906 prohibited the introduction of impure food and drugs into the states by interstate commerce. The *Mann Act (1910), forbidding the transportation of women in interstate commerce for the purpose of prostitution and debauchery, was upheld in *Hoke* v. *United States* (1913).

This technique of closing the channels of commerce to achieve social welfare purposes was then utilized by Congress in the federal Child Labor Act of 1916. The statute prohibited transportation in interstate commerce for products of commercial operations where children under fourteen years of age had been employed and where certain dangerous conditions had prevailed. The Supreme Court called a halt to such use of the commerce power in the famous case of *Hammer* v. *Dagenhart* (1918), where a bare majority held the Child Labor Act unconstitutional as an infringement on powers reserved to the states under the *Tenth Amendment. The Court's argument was based on the concept of *dual federalism—that powers delegated to the national government by the Constitution are nevertheless limited by the reserved powers of the states. In a noteworthy dissent to the *Hammer* decision, Justice Oliver Wendell *Holmes rejected this view, arguing that use of a power specifically conferred on Congress by the Constitution "is not made

any less constitutional because of the indirect effects that it may have" (p. 277).

When the Fair Labor Standards Act came before the Supreme Court in *United States* v. *Darby*, it was upheld unanimously. Because Congress in adopting the act had exercised its undoubted power over the movement of goods across state lines, there would have been little need for discussion of the constitutional issue except for the decision in *Hammer* v. *Dagenhart*. Justice Harlan F. *Stone, writing for the Court, had to dispose of that roadblock. Invoking "the powerful and now classic dissent of Mr. Justice Holmes," Stone wrote, "The conclusion is inescapable that *Hammer* v. *Dagenhart* was a departure from the principles which have prevailed in the interpretation of the Commerce Clause both before and since the decision and that such vitality, as a precedent, as it then had has long since been exhausted. It should be and now is overruled" (pp. 115–116).

While the constitutionality of the Wages and Hours Act was ratified by *Darby*, problems with respect to the coverage of the act remained, for the statute had failed to invoke the total power of Congress over commerce. Rather, it was made applicable to employees engaged "in commerce" or "in the production of goods for commerce." Consequently there was much confusion as to whether specific employees were covered by the act. A noteworthy controversy arose over the applicability of the federal statute to state employees. In *Maryland* v. *Wirtz* (1968) the Court rejected a contention that enforcing the act's standards against state employees violated state sovereignty. But eight years later the Court accepted that contention. In *National League of Cities* v. *Usery* (1976) the Court by vote of 5 to 4 overruled *Wirtz*, rehabilitated *Hammer* v. *Dagenhart*, and held that federal wage and hour standards for state and municipal employees were unconstitutional. In turn, *Usery* was reversed nine years later in *Garcia* v. *San Antonio Metropolitan Transit Authority* (1985).

(See also LABOR.)

C. Herman Pritchett

**Dartmouth College v. Woodward,** 4 Wheat. (17 U.S.) 518 (1819), argued 10–12 Mar. 1818, decided 2 Feb. 1819 by vote of 5 to 1; Marshall for the Court, Washington and Story concurring separately, Duvall in dissent without opinion. In 1816, New Hampshire's newly elected Jeffersonian-Republican governor, William Plumer, and the Republican-dominated legislature determined to transform Dartmouth College by ousting what they regarded as a self-perpetuating Federalist hierarchy among the college's trustees and replacing it with trustees appointed through the political process. They therefore enacted statutes that revised the royal charter of 1769 that created the college, changing the institution to a "University," altering the procedures of internal control, and imposing external, public restraints on the governance of the school. The college's extant trustees determined to contest the constitutionality of this action.

When the case reached the United States Supreme Court for argument in 1818, the college's lawyers, led by Daniel *Webster, directed their arguments to the meaning and impact of the *Contract Clause of the Constitution (Article I, section 10), contending that the New Hampshire legislature, in amending the original charter of the college, had passed a law "impairing the Obligation of Contracts." Webster argued that in effect the state legislature had "take[n] away from one . . . rights, property, and franchises, and give[n] them to another" (p. 558). He asserted that the Contract Clause should be interposed as a constitutional barrier to state activity of this kind.

Chief Justice John *Marshall responded in his characteristically facile manner. Though the Court had previously decided Contract Clause cases, Marshall, for the first time, extended the prote .ion of the Contract Clause to a corporate charter. Since the college insisted that it was entitled to constitutional protection from the legislative acts, Marshall had to analyze the relationship between the Contract Clause and the legal status of the college. He found that the college charter was a contract and that the college under the charter was a private and not a public corporation. This last point was important because the New Hampshire state courts had construed the college to be a public, and not a private entity, and therefore subject to the state's regulatory power. If the college were held to be private, the state could not interfere with its *vested rights, particularly its property rights of acquisition, management, or control, because the Contract Clause, according to Marshall, was directed at acts affecting private property. The Contract Clause prevented the state from impairing the obligations of the original contract between the college and the state (as successor to the colonial government under the original royal grant). When a charter or an act of incorporation is found to be a contract between a state and a private party, it is protected from legislative interference. Only Justice Joseph *Story's concurring opinion modified the sweep of Marshall's statements, suggesting that legislatures could retain certain prerogatives by including "reservation" clauses in corporate charters that allowed legislatures to alter or amend the charter.

By construing the Contract Clause as a means of protecting corporate charters from state interventions, Marshall derived a significant constitutional limitation on state authority. As a result, various forms of private economic and social activity would enjoy security from state regulatory policy. Marshall thus encouraged, through constitutional sanction, the emergence of the relatively unregulated private, autonomous economic actor as the major participant in a liberal political economy that served the commonwealth by promoting enlightened self-interest.

(See also PRIVATE CORPORATION CHARTERS; PROPERTY RIGHTS.)

☐ G. Edward White, *History of the Supreme Court of the United States*, vols. 3–4, *The Marshall Court and Cultural Change, 1815–35* (1988). Alfred S. Konefsky

**Davis, David** (b. Sassafras Neck, Md., 9 Mar. 1815; d. Bloomington, Ill., 26 Jun. 1886; interred Evergreen Cemetery, Bloomington), associate justice, 1862–1877. The son of a physician and plantation owner, Davis was born on the Eastern Shore of Maryland in 1815. As a boy Davis attended New Ark Academy for two years, where he read Cicero and Horace in Latin. At thirteen Davis entered Kenyon College in Ohio. After graduation he studied law and clerked for two years in the office of Henry W. Bishop in Lenox, Massachusetts. It was here that he met his first wife, Sarah Woodruff Walker, whom he married in 1838. (Sarah died in 1879.) In an effort to advance his career, Davis in 1835 entered the New Haven Law School, which had a tenuous association with Yale Law School. Davis studied at New Haven for less than a year.

Davis then headed west and opened a law office in Pekin, Illinois, in 1835. He was soon induced by a friend, Jesse W. Fell, to purchase Fell's legal practice in Bloomington, Illinois, where he moved in the fall of 1836 and remained a resident for the rest of his life. It was during this period that Davis met another Illinois attorney, Abraham *Lincoln, whose friendship and political association would profoundly impact his life and career.

Davis had an abiding interest in politics and ran unsuccessfully for the state senate in 1840. In 1844, running as a Whig, Davis won a seat in the Illinois house. Three years later Davis was elected to the Illinois constitutional convention, where he championed the cause of judicial reform. Elected circuit judge in 1848, Davis served on the Illinois bench until his appointment to the U.S. Supreme Court in 1862.

In Illinois Davis and Lincoln were members of an itinerant bar that held court in several counties in the central part of the state during the late 1840s and early 1850s. The association between the two grew closer when Davis actively supported Lincoln's 1854 bid to become a U.S. senator. When Lincoln secured the Republican presidential nomination in 1860, his tireless campaign manager was David Davis. In 1862 Lincoln appointed Davis to the Supreme Court.

Davis's tenure on the Supreme Court was made notable by his majority opinion in *Ex parte* *Milligan* (1866). In *Milligan,* the Court held that the military trial and conviction of a man found guilty of paramilitary activity in support of the

*David Davis*

Confederacy was illegal, in part because Indiana, the place of Milligan's activities, was not the site of war and civil courts were available to try the case. Davis took pride in the Court's decision not to acquiesce to the interests of the executive and legislative branches.

In 1877 Davis resigned from the Supreme Court and served one term in the U.S. Senate, where from 1881 to 1883 he served as president pro tem. A loyal friend and trusted adviser to Lincoln, Davis was an industrious, pragmatic, and independent lawyer and judge. His significance should be measured not only by his carefully drafted opinion in *Milligan* but perhaps more by his contribution to the election of President Lincoln.

□ Willard L. King, *Lincoln's Manager David Davis* (1960).
Gregory Leyh

**Davis, John Chandler Bancroft** (b. Worcester, Mass., 29 Dec. 1822; d. Washington, D.C., 27 Dec. 1907), diplomat, historian of law, and Supreme Court reporter of decisions, 1883–1902. Davis held an impressive succession of positions before ending his career as the U.S. Supreme Court's reporter of decisions. The son of Massachusetts governor John Davis, he attended Harvard but was suspended in 1840. His A.B. degree was finally awarded to him in 1847. After studying law, Davis became secretary of the American legation at London in 1849 and for a time was its acting chargé d'affaires. He then practiced law in New York and was the American correspondent for the London *Times*. Suffering from ill health, Davis gave up his law practice in 1862. Recovered from his illness, his

career resumed with election to the New York Assembly in 1868. President Ulysses S. Grant soon appointed him assistant secretary of state, a post Davis held until 1871. He resigned to become American secretary to the joint High Commission with Great Britain, which set a mechanism for settlement of claims from Confederate depredations on the high seas. Davis prepared the United States' case before the resulting arbitration tribunal at Geneva. He was later arbitrator between Great Britain and Portugal in a dispute over African possessions. He became minister to Germany in 1874 and was appointed to the Court of Claims in 1877.

Davis finished his public service as the U.S. Supreme Court reporter of decisions from 1883 to 1902, editing volumes 108 through 186 of the *United States Reports. At the Court, he classified historical items in the Office of the *Clerk. Davis authored various works on diplomacy and history and was awarded an honorary LL.D. by Columbia University in 1887.

(See also REPORTERS, SUPREME COURT.)
Francis Helminski

**Davis, John William** (b. Clarksburg, W. Va., 13 Apr. 1873; d. Charleston, S.C., 24 Mar. 1955), lawyer and solicitor general, 1913–1918. Member of Congress from 1910 to 1913, ambassador to the Court of St. James's from 1918 to 1921, and Democratic candidate for president in 1924, Davis was preeminently an appellate lawyer. During his five years (1913–1918) as *solicitor general of the United States during the Wilson administration and three decades as the head of the Wall Street law firm of Davis, Polk, Wardwell, Sunderland & Kiendl, he argued more cases in the Supreme Court than any attorney to that time. Davis's conception of the law was wholly traditional. He believed devoutly in stare decisis (see PRECEDENT), states' rights (see STATE SOVEREIGNTY AND STATES' RIGHTS), and strict constructionism, and he regarded *property rights and human liberty as inseparable. He became a founding member of the anti–New Deal Liberty League in 1934, and he attacked the *New Deal in half a dozen arguments before the Supreme Court. In 1952, as counsel for the steel industry in *Youngstown Sheet and Tube Co. v. Sawyer, Davis successfully challenged the constitutionality of the Truman administration's seizure of the industry. In the epic *Brown v. Board of Education* (1954), he unsuccessfully defended school segregation. "Somewhere, sometime," he declared in oral argument, "to every principle [e.g., segregation] comes a moment of repose."

A man of gentle wit and superior learning, Davis was esteemed by the bar; his grace and quiet elegance charmed almost everyone he touched.

□ William H. Harbaugh, *Lawyer's Lawyer: The Life of John W. Davis* (1973).
William H. Harbaugh

**Davis v. Bandemer,** 478 U.S. 109 (1986), argued 7 Oct. 1985, decided 30 June 1986: for justiciability by vote of 6 to 3, White for the Court, O'Connor, Burger, and Rehnquist in dissent; against merits by vote of 7 to 2, White for the Court, Powell and Stevens in dissent. Two central issues were posed in this case, in which Democrats contended that Indiana state legislative district lines were drawn by Republicans for partisan advantage: (1) is political gerrymandering justiciable? (see JUS-TICIABILITY) and, if so, (2) did the districting in Indiana violate the Constitution's *Equal Protection Clause? In a complex division, the Court answered yes (6–3) to the first question and no (7–2) to the second. The plurality opinion, upholding both outcomes, was written by Justice Byron *White for himself, William *Brennan, Thurgood *Marshall, and Harry *Blackmun. Lewis *Powell and John Paul *Stevens would have upheld a district court decision that responded positively to both questions. The three remaining justices, Sandra Day *O'Connor, Warren *Burger, and William *Rehnquist, would have reversed the lower court's judgment invalidating the Indiana districting on the ground that political gerrymandering claims were nonjusticiable.

The plurality opinion concluded that political gerrymandering is subject to judicial scrutiny, but only where there is "continued frustration of the will of a majority of the voters or a denial to a minority of voters of a fair chance to influence the political process" (p. 133). The opinion found no evidence that Indiana's 1981 redistricting consigned the opposition party to seemingly perpetual minority status throughout the decade regardless of voting trends.

*Davis* v. *Bandemer* drew widespread attention. Ironically, *amicus curiae briefs were filed by the Republican National Committee supporting Indiana's Democrats and by California's Democratic congressional delegation in support of the Republican redistricting—in both instances reflecting concerns outside Indiana. Some legislative and congressional redistrictings after the 1990 census were expected to trigger appeals to the Supreme Court to apply the 1986 ruling's guidelines.

(See also FAIR REPRESENTATION; GERRYMANDERING.)

Gordon E. Baker

**Davis v. Beason,** 133 U.S. 333 (1890), argued 9–10 Dec. 1889, decided 3 Feb. 1890 by vote of 9 to 0; Field for the Court. *Davis* v. *Beason* interpreted free exercise of religion narrowly and inconsistently. Idaho had enacted a territorial statute denying the vote to those who advocated or practiced plural marriage or belonged to an organization that did. Samuel B. Davis and a number of nonpolygamous Mormons, after trying unsuccessfully to vote in the 1888 election, sued. The Idaho court treated their disfranchisement solely as a *political question. On appeal, the U.S. Supreme Court upheld the statute as within the territorial powers of the legislature to set voter qualifications. The justices held that religion was a matter of belief, which was constitutionally protected but that conduct was outside the purview of the *First Amendment. The Court then defined polygamy as conduct rather than religious belief. Using the Idaho statute as a soapbox for a diatribe on polygamy, Justice Stephen J. *Field concluded that "crime is not the less odious because sanctioned by what any particular sect may designate as religion" (p. 345). The preservation of a monogamous family unit was more important to American society than religious liberty for believers in polygamy. "Religion" was defined solely as having reference to one's view of relations with the creator and to the obligations they imposed.

(See also RELIGION; VOTE, RIGHT TO.)

Paul L. Murphy

**Day, William Rufus** (b. Ravenna, Ohio, 17 Apr. 1849; d. Mackinac Island, Mich., 9 Jul. 1923; interred West Lawn Cemetery, Canton, Ohio), associate justice, 1903–1922. Day's formative years were molded by the political environment of post–Civil War Republican party politics in Ohio. Educated at the University of Michigan, Day also spent one year in law school there. His pre-Court career included a number of roles: trial attorney in Canton, Ohio; personal confidant of President William McKinley; United States secretary of state (1898); and judge on the United States Sixth Circuit Court of Appeals (1899–1903). Following McKinley's assassination, President Theodore Roosevelt elevated Day to the U.S. Supreme Court in an effort to bolster his support with the Ohio wing of the Republican party.

During a nineteen-year career on the Court, Day was overshadowed by prominent jurists such as Oliver Wendell *Holmes and Louis D. *Brandeis. Nevertheless, he played a significant role as a swing justice between the Court's liberal and conservative blocs, a role well suited to his finely developed social skills.

The major constitutional issues before the Court during Day's tenure involved, on the one hand, federal power under the Commerce Clause with its corollary issue of federal *antitrust policy (see COMMERCE POWER), and on the other hand, the scope of state *police powers under the *Tenth Amendment. Day has often been identified as a states' rights advocate who, while finding extensive powers for state progressive experimentations, narrowly construed national power under the Commerce Clause (see STATE SOVEREIGNTY AND STATES' RIGHTS). This interpretation is based primarily on his landmark opinion in *Hammer* v. *Dagenhart* (1918) declaring the 1916 Federal Child Labor Act unconstitutional. Day's opinion defined commerce to exclude manufactured goods that were harmless in and of themselves. The impact of *Hammer* lasted until 1941

*William Rufus Day*

and overshadowed Day's other opinions, which sanctioned federal power to reach interstate traffic of impure food, drugs, and liquor and to prosecute trusts and monopolies that wielded a potential power to restrain trade. Day fully endorsed the use of national power through the *Sherman Antitrust Act of 1890. In *United States* v. *Union Pacific Railway Company* (1912), for example, he championed a vigorous exercise of federal police power against giant combinations including railroads, steel industries, lumber companies, and trusts.

Day preferred state to national regulation, however. He gave a liberal, expansive construction to state *police powers to enact laws and safety requirements for plants and railroads. His two famous dissents in *Lochner* v. *New York* (1905) and *Coppage* v. *Kansas* (1915) demonstrated his belief that state promotion of public welfare could override individual claims of liberty of contract and right to work (see CONTRACT, FREEDOM OF). Day also championed *progressivism in *Green* v. *Frazier* (1920), which sanctioned state taxation to create state-owned public services. He limited state powers to discriminate on the basis of race, however. Day struck down a city residential *zoning ordinance excluding African-Americans and a state law requiring railroads to provide segregated cars. (See RACE AND RACISM.)

Moving from the ideology of nineteenth-century liberalism's laissez faire into the twentieth-century's acceptance of the welfare state, Day ultimately became a moderate liberal, upholding governmental power over economic and moral evils.          Alice Fleetwood Bartee

**Dead List.** See DISCUSS LIST.

**Death Penalty.** See CAPITAL PUNISHMENT; RACE DISCRIMINATION AND THE DEATH PENALTY.

**Debs, In re,** 158 U.S. 564 (1895), argued 25–26 Mar. 1895, decided 27 May 1895 by vote of 9 to 0; Brewer for the Court. By refusing to grant a writ of *habeas corpus to Eugene Debs, president of the American Railway Union, the Supreme Court sanctioned the use of injunctions against striking labor unions. During the depression of the 1890s, the Pullman company, while still paying dividends, reduced its workers' pay literally to the starvation level. The laborers went on strike and were soon adopted by the newly formed American Railway Union. The union pursued a strategy of boycotting railroads using Pullman cars. Members refused to handle trains with the cars; if dismissed by the road, then all the company's union members would strike. This plan was a direct challenge to the General Managers Association, a group of twenty-six Chicago railroads. Claiming that their contracts required them to use Pullman cars, they provoked strikes throughout the Midwest and nation by firing trainmen who refused to handle Pullman cars. Contending that the strikers were interfering with interstate commerce and the mails, the association urged federal intervention. Attorney General Richard *Olney, fearing the violence of a large strike, came to the association's aid. While wanting to send in the army, Olney settled initially for lesser measures. He created more than five thousand special deputies to preserve order, prepared a case of criminal conspiracy against the union leaders, and sought an injunction in federal *circuit court that would prohibit interference with the railroads' businesses. Not surprisingly, these actions and the activities of strikebreakers provoked rioting. To suppress violence, blown out of proportion by an alarmist press, the government sent in troops.

The federal circuit court, reasoning that the strike was a combination in restraint of interstate commerce, granted a sweeping injunction. The decree applied to the leaders of the union, all those who combined with them, and any persons whomsoever. It commanded such individuals to cease hindering the railroads, including by means of persuading employees, from carrying the mails and engaging in interstate commerce. Within a week of his arrest for criminal conspiracy, Debs and his fellow officers were again arrested for contempt of court for violating this injunction. While they were in jail the strike folded and the new union crumpled. Though the criminal trial collapsed, the contempt of court charge netted Debs six months' imprisonment. He sought release by writ of habeas corpus to the Supreme Court, arguing that he was tried for a criminal act in a court of equity and thus denied his constitutional right of *trial by jury.

Justice David J. *Brewer, speaking for a unanimous Supreme Court, rejected Debs's plea. Refusing to rest the decision on the narrow ground of a conspiracy in restraint of trade, he based the ruling on broad principles. Brewer asserted that the government of the United States, though a government of enumerated powers, had full attributes of sovereignty, within those powers. It could forcibly remove any obstructions to commerce or the mails, either by military power or through an appeal to the federal courts' equity power. He labeled the union's action to be a public nuisance, which like a private nuisance was subject to equity jurisdiction. That Debs's acts violated the criminal law did not bar equitable relief. The actions also threatened the *property rights of the railroads, which were protected under equity jurisdiction. Therefore, no matter what occurred on the criminal side of the law, the equity side could also be utilized. To preserve their authority in such equity proceedings courts needed the power to punish through *contempt. Thus, Brewer rejected the argument that Debs had been denied a jury trial. Brewer touted the use of federal tribunals as a better method than armed force in settling labor troubles; it met the potential mob violence not with force but with the rule of law. For the next thirty years, corporations faced with labor troubles turned to the Federal courts; the Pullman injunction proved the model for many others. Not until the *New Deal era did such labor injunctions fade away.

(See also COMMERCE POWER; INJUNCTIONS AND EQUITABLE REMEDIES; LABOR; LOWER FEDERAL COURTS.)

Richard F. Hamm

**Decision-making Dynamics.** Within the Supreme Court, as within any other institution, individuals interact within a matrix of formal rules, informal customs, and norms of behavior. The Court's internal dynamics are affected by justices' ideologies, their views of the judicial role, and other cross-cutting factors. Informal customs and norms are the most important of these factors, as there are few formal rules to tell the justices how to deal with each other.

Ideology obviously affects the results the justices reach, particularly in nonunanimous cases, but it is hardly the only factor affecting the Court's decision making. Friendships among the justices, perhaps more a function of personality than of politics, cut across ideological lines. More important is the justices' often-shared view of the Court's role in the American governmental system, which leads to considerable unanimity both in decisions as to which cases to review and in actual decisions on cases.

The *chief justice, although technically only the first among equals, can play an important role in the Court's decision-making dynamics, particularly in helping the Court to function smoothly and cohesively. The "chief" can be extremely effective—Earl *Warren was nicknamed "Super-chief"—or, like Harlan Fiske *Stone and perhaps

Warren *Burger, can lack the ability to hold the Court together or to affect its dynamics as either its task leader or social leader.

The process of reaching the decision to grant or deny review has undergone some change. Because photocopying now allows all justices to have the same *certiorari documents, the chief justice's role in those cases has decreased. Less change has occurred with respect to the process of deciding cases accepted for review. In the past, after their discussion of a case, the justices voted in reverse order of seniority; that is, the most junior first, after their discussion, which is held in descending order of seniority. Nowadays they often dispense with a formal vote. After the discussion, someone is assigned (by the chief justice if he is in the majority) to write the opinion of the Court; the opinion writer then circulates the draft opinion for agreement or comment. When justices circulate *concurring opinions, or *dissents, they may persuade the justice writing the opinion of the Court to change that opinion; votes may also change. That all justices participate in this process produces a different dynamic from a procedure, used in some *state courts, in which cases are assigned to a judge in advance of oral argument.

The Court's dynamics crucially affect the Court's ability to reach a decision and to obtain agreement on an "opinion of the Court." Whenever the Court is badly fractured, leaving a *plurality opinion in which a majority agrees on a result but not on the reasoning used to reach it, the justices fail to give guidance to the lower courts or to lawyers seeking to advise clients. When the public sees the Court as badly split, the Court's legitimacy may be questioned; certainly the notion that the justices find the law rather than make it is difficult to maintain when the Court is regularly divided 5 to 4. Moreover, justices' shrill criticism of each other, in opinions and off-the-bench speeches, however much it may prove that the members of the high court are human, also serves to tarnish its legitimacy.

(See also CLERKS OF THE JUSTICES.)

Stephen L. Wasby

**Declaration of Independence.** In one vibrant paragraph of the Declaration of Independence, Thomas *Jefferson managed to compress both a résumé of American constitutional theory that justified the struggle for independence and a précis of a revolutionary, republican theory of government. "All men are created equal"; they enjoy "unalienable Rights" (this repudiated arguments by Thomas Hobbes and William Blackstone that people surrender their natural rights when they leave the state of nature); these rights include "Life, Liberty and the pursuit of Happiness" (a liberal and literary improvement on John Locke's triad of life, liberty, and property); governments exist to protect those rights; governments are created by "the consent of the governed" (the compact theory); the people retain the right "to alter or to abolish" government when it violates its ends, "and to institute new Government" to secure the people's "Safety and Happiness" (the commonwealth theory). In their totality, these concepts provided a comprehensive statement of popular sovereignty.

The remainder of the Declaration consisted of a indictment arraigning King George III with thirty offenses, some constitutional, some legal, and some merely matters of policy. The indictment omitted counts drafted by Jefferson that condemned the slave trade, at the insistence of South Carolina and Georgia delegates, who were determined that self-government and unalienable rights in America were to remain the prerogatives of white men exclusively.

The Declaration was drafted by Thomas *Jefferson, with only minor participation by a committee that included John Adams, Benjamin Franklin, Roger Sherman, and Robert Livingston, pursuant to a resolution of the Second Continental Congress. It was adopted by Congress on 4 July 1776. Jefferson himself belittled the originality of his work, stating that, though he penned the Declaration without consulting other sources, it contained nothing novel in the way of political thought. In this, he was correct: the basic theory of the Declaration was derivative of the thought of Locke and reflected English Whig theory as it had evolved in the preceding century and a half. George Mason had anticipated much of the substance of Jefferson's ideas in his draft of the Virginia Declaration of Rights (12 June 1776), though the literary grace and felicity of Jefferson's Declaration eclipsed the ponderous lawyer's couplets and triplets of the Virginia Declaration.

The constitutional and legal status of the Declaration of Independence is curiously ambiguous. John Hancock (in his capacity as president of the Second Continental Congress) and James *Madison both considered it to be, in Madison's words, "the fundamental Act of Union of these States." Reflecting that view, Congress has placed it at the head of the United States Code, under the caption, "The Organic Laws of the United States of America." The Supreme Court has infrequently accorded it binding legal force, for example, in resolving questions of alienage (*Inglis* v. *Trustees of Sailor's Snug Harbour*, 1830). Yet lawyers generally, and the Supreme Court in particular, have been reluctant to treat the Declaration as part of American organic law, or even to accord it the restricted status of the Preamble to the Constitution. Conservatives like Daniel *Webster denied that there is a constitutionally recognized right of revolution, and those state supreme courts that have addressed the issue in the twentieth century have adopted Webster's view. Reformers, such as antebellum abolitionists, insisted that the Declaration was part of the constitutional order, while their opponents, including John C. Calhoun, denigrated its authority and

validity. The adoption of the *Thirteenth and *Fourteenth Amendments allayed the urgency of that question by incorporating concepts of equality, freedom, and citizenship into the operative constitutional text.

Nevertheless, the Declaration of Independence endures as the basic statement of the principles of American government. Abraham *Lincoln invoked its authority in the supreme crisis of the union, and it remains today the foundation of our constitutional order.

(See also NATURAL LAW.)

□ Carl Becker, *The Declaration of Independence* (1922).
William M. Wiecek

**Declaratory Judgments.** Parties bringing actions in courts usually seek active relief, such as an award of money damages or an injunction. Modern courts, however, can also give passive relief that merely defines legal relations through declaratory judgments.

The traditional, restrictive view of the judicial process limited courts to active relief. Moreover, the U.S. Supreme Court, in *Willing* v. *Chicago Auditorium Association* (1928), implied that a special barrier to declaratory relief lay in the Constitution's limiting the federal judicial power to *cases and controversies. But a practical need for declaratory relief might exist where a dispute has not progressed far enough to authorize active relief or where an aggrieved person does not yet choose to seek active relief; for example, a party to a contract might justifiably want to determine whether certain behavior would be or is a breach. In the 1930s, the Court reversed its previous direction, encouraging and then upholding congressional enactment of the Federal Declaratory Judgment Act of 1934.

So today a federal court may in its discretion give a declaratory remedy in a case that has ripened beyond an abstract question into an actual controversy and that is otherwise within its jurisdiction. Although a *state court might be more permissive or restrictive regarding declaratory relief, most states follow the federal approach.

(See also DECISION-MAKING DYNAMICS; INJUNCTIONS AND EQUITABLE REMEDIES).
Kevin M. Clermont

**Defamation.** See LIBEL.

**DeJonge v. Oregon,** 299 U.S. 353 (1937), argued 9 Dec. 1936, decided 4 Jan. 1937 by vote of 8 to 0; Hughes for the Court, Stone not participating. The Court overturned the conviction of Dirk DeJonge, who had been prosecuted under Oregon's *criminal syndicalism law for helping to conduct a meeting in Portland organized by the Communist party to protest police shootings of striking longshoremen and raids on workers' homes and halls. Despite the party affiliations of

DeJonge and the other organizers, no more than 15 percent of those at the meeting were Communists. One lecturer discussed the Young Communist League, and DeJonge tried to sell some party publications, but no one advocated criminal syndicalism or unlawful conduct, and the meeting was completely orderly. The principal evidence against DeJonge was party literature found elsewhere that tended to establish that the Communist party promoted criminal syndicalism. The Oregon Supreme Court held that a person could be convicted under the statute for doing nothing more than participating in a wholly innocent meeting called by the party. In reversing the Oregon court's decision, Chief Justice Charles Evans *Hughes declared, "[P]eaceable assembly for lawful discussion cannot be made a crime" (p. 365). The Oregon criminal syndicalism law had deprived DeJonge of the rights to free speech and peaceable assembly guaranteed by the Due Process Clause of the *Fourteenth Amendment.

(See also ASSEMBLY AND ASSOCIATION, FREEDOM OF; FIRST AMENDMENT; SPEECH AND THE PRESS.)

Michal R. Belknap

**Delegation of Powers.** An often-repeated proposition of Anglo-American law is that delegated authority cannot be redelegated. In the case of the Supreme Court, the doctrine of nondelegation purportedly derives from the Constitution, although admittedly without any basis in the constitutional text. The usual argument for the invalidity of delegation of powers turns on the concept of *separation of powers, that is, the forbidding of certain general powers to one or another of the general branches of government. Actually, there are few specific constitutional provisions for the separation of powers. There *are* provisions for checks and balances among the three branches of government, however. Separation of powers would create monopolies of certain powers in particular branches; checks and balances forbids such monopolies and, in fact, generally requires the joinder of two branches before governmental action is validated. Thus, the legislature cannot enact a law without presidential approval or, if the president disapproves, a two-thirds overriding vote of each house; the judicial branch cannot pass judgment except within legislatively defined limits specified by statute; no one may expend moneys except those appropriated by the legislature and according to the terms specified by the legislature.

The Court has adhered to a limited concept of separation of powers not unlike that prescribed by the Massachusetts Constitution of 1780. Within this judicially recognized doctrine of separation of powers it has spoken of a *non*delegation of powers by one branch to another. In cases such as *Field* v. *Clark* (1892) the issue has usually involved delegation of legislative power to the executive branch. But the doctrine applies to the

other branches as well. Congressional authority has often been shared with or delegated to another branch of government, but, as under most constitutional doctrines, the question has not been whether the executive branch is exercising *any* legislative power but whether it is exercising too much legislative power. "How much is too much?"—is the question that tries the capacities of the justices.

It should be noted that the Supreme Court, for all the lip service it has paid to the so-called doctrine of invalid delegation, has only once in its history struck down legislation as unconstitutional on this ground. In the mid-1930s, when the Court was rapidly disabling *New Deal legislation, the Court concluded in three cases (*Panama Refining Co.* v. *Ryan*, 1935; *Schechter Poultry Corp.* v. *United States*, 1935; *Carter* v. *Carter Coal Co.*, 1936) that Congress had improperly provided for delegation of legislative power. But the holdings in these New Deal cases could not have been based on a theory of separation of powers, because, as the majority said in *Carter*, this was delegation "in its most obnoxious form, for it is not even delegation to an official or an official body, presumptively disinterested, but to private persons whose interests may be and are adverse to the interests of others in the same business" (p. 311).

The concept of invalid delegation of legislative power is phoenixlike in its appearance in American judicial history, burning fiercely from time to time, turning to ash, then reviving. It was thought to have been ultimately disposed of in *Yakus* v. *United States* (1944). In that case, Congress had granted price-fixing powers to the Office of Price Administration during *World War II without specifying any standards for guidance except that the prices fixed be "fair and equitable." The statute was sustained despite the challenge of invalid delegation, a doctrine not seriously raised again for a generation. The Court had already decided, in *United States* v. *Curtiss-Wright Export Corp.* (1936), that the "invalid delegation doctrine" had less bite in the area of foreign affairs than in domestic law.

Every branch of government of necessity exercises some rule-making, enforcement, and adjudicative powers. Since no totally pure system of separation of powers can exist, the problem of delegation is likely to arise in each of the three branches. Thus, while the Constitution gives the exclusive power to *impeach government officials to Congress, it leaves criminal prosecution of such officials to law enforcement, that is, to the executive branch. Where the official suspected of wrongdoing is in a sufficiently influential position, it is sometimes thought necessary to go outside the administration for prosecution to ensure a fair and unbiased proceeding. Congress has provided for appointment of a special prosecutor under such circumstances. Once again, problems of invalid delegation of authority arise. The special prosecutor is an executive-branch official, so under what circumstances can the president be prevented from discharging him or her? That question arose during the Watergate scandal of the early 1970s but did not receive judicial resolution. A decade and a half later, in *Morrison v. Olson* (1988), a case that arose out of the Iran-Contra scandal, the Court held that the special prosecutor arrangement was a valid delegation of power.

Thus, in *Morrison* the doctrine of invalid delegation reappeared, only to be rejected once again. Though objection was made to empowering the appointment of a special prosecutor who could not be removed even by the president except for "good cause shown," the displacement of ordinary, attorney general–supervised processes and the consequent delegation of executive power were sustained. The following year, when a challenge was made to the promulgation of sentencing guidelines in criminal cases by appointees of the president, replacing the judicial power that had previously been exercised, the "invalid delegation" rubric was again found inadequate (*Mistretta v. United States*, 1989).

Invalid delegation is spoken of as a constitutional question, but it is more likely to be used as a standard of statutory construction than one of constitutional validity. It adds one more device to the judicial arsenal for shaping national legislation closer to the Court's predilections and almost never serves as a rule of decision.

Philip B. Kurland

**DeLima v. Bidwell.** See INSULAR CASES.

**Dennis v. United States,** 341 U.S. 494 (1951), argued 4 Dec. 1950, decided 4 June 1951 by vote of 6 to 2; Vinson for the Court, Black and Douglas in dissent, Clark not participating. In *Dennis* the Supreme Court affirmed the convictions of eleven Communist party leaders for violation of the *Smith Act. In the process the Court significantly modified the so-called *clear and present danger test.

The section of the statute at issue in *Dennis* made it a crime to teach or advocate the violent overthrow of any government in the United States, to set up an organization to engage in such teaching or advocacy, or to conspire to teach, advocate, or organize the violent overthrow of any government in the United States. Although the Smith Act was designed to combat the Communist party, because that organization was closely tied to the Soviet Union and because the United States and the U.S.S.R. were allies during *World War II, the government refrained from using the new law against Communists for several years. In the late 1940s, however, Soviet-American relations deteriorated. President Harry Truman, a Democrat, sought to rally public support for an anti-Soviet foreign policy by characterizing this conflict as a struggle between communism and freedom, and Republicans re-

sponded by castigating him for ignoring the threat posed by domestic communism. Under intense political pressure to prove that the Truman administration was not soft on communism, Justice Department lawyers obtained indictments on 20 July 1948 charging the members of the Communist party's national board with violation of the Smith Act's conspiracy provisions.

A 1949 trial before federal district judge Harold Medina, conducted amid mounting anticommunist hysteria, ended with the conviction of all eleven defendants. This tumultuous, nine-month-long proceeding featured judicial bias, which manifested itself in questionable rulings on the admission and exclusion of evidence, as well as the employment of dubious tactics by both the prosecution and the defense. The convicted Communists appealed their convictions to the Second Circuit Court of Appeals, but it unanimously affirmed them. Judge Learned *Hand's opinion rebuffed defense attacks on the impartiality of the judge and jury, on the prosecution's use of informant witnesses, and on Medina's conduct of the trial. It also rejected the Communists' contention that the Smith Act was unconstitutional.

The Supreme Court granted *certiorari only on that issue. Hence, the justices did not have before them a complete record of what had gone on at the trial and did not realize how unimpressive the prosecution's evidence had been. Even if he had known these things, Chief Justice Fred *Vinson, who seldom displayed much sympathy for civil liberties claims, probably would have voted to affirm. He believed the government had to protect itself from Communists and that it dared not wait until their preparations for its overthrow had reached the point of rebellion. The clear and present danger test precluded punishing speech unless it posed an immediate threat of a serious substantive evil. Consequently, Vinson employed a modified version of that principle (now known as the "grave and probable danger" rule), which Judge Hand had developed. "In each case," Vinson wrote, courts "must ask whether the gravity of the 'evil' discounted by its improbability, justifies such invasion of free speech as is necessary to avoid the danger" (p. 510). This rule afforded far less protection to freedom of expression than had the clear and present danger test.

Only three other justices endorsed Vinson's opinion. Unable to accept what the chief justice had done to the clear and present danger test, Robert *Jackson insisted that it was inapplicable to conspiracies, such as communism, but that the convictions could be sustained because the defendants were guilty of conspiring to overthrow the government. Felix *Frankfurter also concurred, suppressing his distaste for the Smith Act because of his commitment to the principle of *judicial self-restraint. Both Hugo *Black and William O. *Douglas filed vigorous dissents. The Justice Department interpreted *Dennis* as authorization for an all-out attack on the Communist party. The Court's subsequent ruling in *Yates v. United States* (1957) thwarted this assault, but *Yates* neither held the Smith Act unconstitutional nor overruled the 1951 decision. Although *Dennis* is inconsistent with more recent rulings, the Supreme Court has never repudiated its grave and probable danger rule.

(See also COMMUNISM AND COLD WAR; FIRST AMENDMENT SPEECH TESTS; SPEECH AND THE PRESS.)

□ Michal R. Belknap, *Cold War Political Justice: The Smith Act, the Communist Party and American Civil Liberties* (1977). Michal R. Belknap

**Desegregation Remedies.** *Brown* v. *Board of Education II* (1955) held that desegregation should occur "with all deliberate speed." Initially some southern courts and school boards interpreted *Brown* to require only the elimination of race as a basis for deciding which schools children should attend (see SEGREGATION, DE JURE). That interpretation, described as "desegregation not integration," was in some tension with the Supreme Court's concern that school boards have time to respond to the administrative and other difficulties that it foresaw.

Immediately after *Brown* a variety of desegregation methods were adopted by some school boards. These included "freedom of choice" plans, in which parents selected the schools their children would attend, with the predictable result that white parents chose the previously white schools and black parents, concerned about their children's safety, often chose the previously black schools; and "one grade a year" plans, in which schools were desegregated one grade at a time, starting either in first grade or in twelfth grade. In addition, some southern legislatures engaged in a program of "massive resistance," making no effort whatever to comply with *Brown* v. *Board of Education* and preventing local boards from doing so.

The Supreme Court intervened in the process of desegregation only once between 1955 and 1963, chastising the governor of Arkansas for interfering with the desegregation of the schools in Little Rock (*Cooper* v. *Aaron*, 1958). Starting in 1963 the Court began to insist that the time for "all deliberate speed" had passed. Although it did not question pure freedom of choice plans, it invalidated a system under which those who were members of a minority race in a school could transfer to a school in which they would be part of the majority, thereby preventing whites from resegregating schools (*Goss* v. *Board of Education*, 1963).

With the passage of the *Civil Rights Act of 1964*, enforcement of *Brown* became more vigorous. The Department of Health, Education, and Welfare developed guidelines to determine when schools had desegregated and were therefore entitled to federal financial assistance. The department began to enforce these guidelines with some vigor, and the courts began to use them as measures of appropriate desegregation remedies.

In 1968 the Supreme Court in *Green* v. *County School Board of New Kent County* invalidated freedom of choice plans, saying that school boards had to adopt desegregation plans that "promise[d] realistically to work *now*" (p. 438). By this time, residential segregation in most urban school districts and in many rural ones had become so pronounced that simply establishing neighborhood schools would not eliminate racial disparities in individual schools (see SEGREGATION, DE FACTO). In 1971 the Supreme Court in *Swann* v. *Charlotte-Mecklenburg Board of Education* upheld a district judge's order requiring that children attend schools away from their neighborhood to achieve a rough racial balance in all the schools in the district.

Busing remedies were extremely unpopular among whites and some blacks, particularly because in many instances more black children were bused than whites and because many schools remained racially identifiable even after busing. In the South, however, busing in rural districts had been common as a result of school consolidations, and resistance to busing was substantially weaker than resistance to desegregation itself had been. In the North, however, where desegregation litigation was coming to a head in the 1970s, resistance to desegregation occurred simultaneously with resistance to busing and was encouraged to some degree by expressions of opposition to the courts by President Richard *Nixon and Vice President Spiro Agnew.

The Supreme Court did little in the area of desegregation remedies through the 1970s and 1980s, concentrating instead on specifying the circumstances under which northern districts could be required to desegregate and those in which districts could be held to have done enough to be free of further obligations to desegregate. *Milliken* v. *Bradley* (1977) held that federal courts could order educational improvements, such as remedial reading programs, as part of a desegregation remedy, and in 1990 the Court held that they could bar states from imposing barriers to tax increases to finance such improvements (*Missouri* v. *Jenkins*, 1990).

(See also RACE AND RACISM.)

□ J. Harvie Wilkinson, *From Brown to Bakke: The Supreme Court and School Integration, 1954–1978* (1979). Mark V. Tushnet

**Dictum.** See OBITER DICTUM.

**Dillon v. Gloss,** 256 U.S. 368 (1921), argued 22 Mar. 1921, decided 16 May 1921 by vote of 9 to 0; Van Devanter for the Court. This case involved a conviction for transporting intoxicating liquors in violation of the Volstead Act. Dillon raised two issues. First, he challenged the provision requiring ratification of the *Eighteenth Amendment within seven years. Second, he argued that the . law under which he was charged was not effective until one year after the Eighteenth Amendment was proclaimed by the secretary of state (and hence after his arrest) rather than one year after its ratification. On the first issue, Justice Willis *Van Devanter decided that Congress could set a reasonable deadline so that ratification was "sufficiently contemporaneous . . . to reflect the will of the people in all sections at relatively the same time period" (p. 375). On the second issue, the Court ruled that the amendment's date of consummation, not its proclamation, was controlling.

The Eighteenth Amendment was the first to specify a deadline within its text. When the Equal Rights Amendment was proposed, the deadline was placed in an accompanying authorizing resolution that, in a debated move, Congress later extended. Deadlines within the texts of amendments are presumably self-enforcing. Without distinguishing internal from external deadlines, Dillon v. Gloss ruled that ratifications must be contemporaneous and left to the judgment of Congress. *Coleman v. Miller (1939) reinforced and widened Dillon in declaring that the ratification issue was a *political question for congressional resolution.

(See also CONSTITUTIONAL AMENDING PROCESS.)

John R. Vile

**Disability of Justices.** Holding office during "good behavior" (Art. III, sec. 1), the justices are not removable by *impeachment when physically and/or mentally disabled. Incapacitated members impair the Court's work. But light pre–Civil War caseloads, the dominance of Chief Justice John *Marshall, and the multimember nature of the bench limited their impact on the Court. More deleterious was the effect of disabled justices on the work of the circuit courts prior to the creation in 1869 of separate circuit judgeships. (See JUDICIARY ACT OF 1869.)

Absenteeism because of disability prevented a statutorily mandated Supreme Court quorum in 1811, and the justices prematurely adjourned the term. The absence in 1834 of cancer-ridden William *Johnson and deaf octogenarian Gabriel *Duvall combined with a promised 3-to-2 split on three landmark cases prompted an outvoted Marshall to continue them. Marshall ruled that resolution of constitutional questions would ordinarily require the concurrence of a majority of the Court's authorized membership. A strategy of granting continuances was followed by the Taney Court with enfeebled John *McKinley and by the Taft Court with mentally confused Joseph *McKenna. But if a justice sat for *oral arguments on a case and subsequently became incapaci-

tated, absentee conference votes cast through peer proxies were permitted.

Judicial disability burdens the decisional process when opinion assignments are redistributed to favor incapacitated justices, overloading healthy members and particularly the *chief justice. Chief Justice William Howard *Taft dealt with McKenna and Mahlon *Pitney; Charles Evans *Hughes worked with a faltering ninety-year-old Oliver Wendell *Holmes; and Warren Burger assisted stroke victim William O. *Douglas. Dysfunctional behavior of a disabled justice may directly impair the Court's work. McKenna's temper tantrums, Henry *Baldwin's violent rages, and senile Stephen J. *Field's exaggerated irritability roiled the Court. Irrational judicial performances surfaced when a mentally and physically incapacitated Robert *Grier's confused waffling in Hepburn v. Griswold (1870) delayed the closely divided Court's decision invalidating the Legal Tender Act (see LEGAL TENDER CASES). Nor could either befogged Nathan *Clifford or McKenna be relied upon to execute their opinion assignments responsibly.

Disabled justices have clung to their seats for financial considerations (William *Cushing), for the social status derived by family members from their official position (Grier, Salmon *Chase), and because of political antipathy toward the president who would name their successor (Duvall, Clifford, Ward *Hunt, Taft, Douglas).

The pitiful condition of four members of the Civil War Court and a growing caseload captured congressional attention. The still fresh memory of aged Chief Justice Roger *Taney's physical infirmity induced Congress to act in 1868, four years after his death. It then authorized devolution of a disabled chief justice's powers and duties to the senior associate justice. The next year saw enactment of a Supreme Court pension bill to encourage timely and voluntary departure. Aimed especially at Grier, the 1869 act permitted resignation at the salary then received for justices who had attained age seventy and had served at least ten years. Further enhancement of this option occurred in 1937 when Congress extended to the justices the privilege of retirement rather than resignation. The former status allowed retention of the judicial office, the salary of which was protected by the Constitution's compensation clause as stipulated in Booth v. United States (1934). Postretirement salary increases became applicable to the pay of retired justices in 1944. In 1954 Congress lowered the minimum retirement age to sixty-five after fifteen years of service and in 1984 established a flexible age-service eligibility schedule.

With leverage afforded by the 1869 act, peers proved willing and able to persuade Grier, Field, McKenna, and Holmes to avail themselves of the congressional beneficence. But excluded from the act's scope were disabled justices who had not attained the requisite age and duration of service. For egregious cases, Congress extended the act, conditional on prompt acceptance, to specific and otherwise ineligible physically disabled justices: Hunt (1882), William *Moody (1910), Pitney (1922). Not until 1939 did Congress enact general legislation making available to physically disabled justices, regardless of age, retirement at half pay for service of less than ten years and at full salary for service of more than ten years. Under its terms, sixty-one-year-old Charles *Whittaker retired in 1962 having certified himself as permanently disabled after five years on the bench.

Physical infirmity and eligibility for retirement benefits markedly increases the probability of departure. Peer influence and media publicity about health and performance may hasten the event. But no additional justice, senior in commission, may be appointed to pressure a disabled jurist as with afflicted lower court judges. In the absence of a constitutional amendment, retirement is voluntary, not mandatory.

(See also RESIGNATION AND RETIREMENT.)

Peter G. Fish

**Discriminatory Intent.** In *Washington v. Davis (1976), the Supreme Court held that the Equal Protection Clause was violated only by government actions that were taken with an intent to injure the group adversely affected. In *Personnel Administrator of Massachusetts v. Feeney* (1979), the Court explained that such intent was present when the government took the challenged action "because of" and not merely "in spite of" an adverse impact on the affected group. These cases rejected the argument that *equal protection required that the government refrain from actions that have a disparate negative impact on minority groups. The Court's majority believed that a disparate-impact test would require substantial modifications in many government policies that dealt with general social problems— policies that, given the nature of U.S. society, necessarily have a disparate impact on minority groups. In addition, the idea of "intent" fits well with the idea that the Equal Protection Clause was meant to eliminate actions based on prejudice, which is ordinarily thought of as a willingness—that is, an intention—to inflict injury on others. Determining discriminatory intent can be difficult, however, because legislation may result from mixed motives or from decisions by political coalitions in which some members have discriminatory intent and others do not. The Court suggested that statements about intent might be particularly revealing where the nondiscriminatory reasons for the policy appeared weak. The distinction between disriminatory intent and disparate impact was weakened by the acknowledgement, in Village of *Arlington Heights v. Metropolitan Development Corp. (1977), that disparate impact can provide evidence of discriminatory intent, particularly when it is accompanied by

evidence that the government departed from its ordinary practices in adopting the challenged policy. (See also HOUSING DISCRIMINATION; RACE AND RACISM.)

Mark V. Tushnet

**Discuss List,** the chief administrative device by which the Supreme Court manages its caseload. The list is also one of numerous small ways in which the *chief justice influences the agenda of the Court. Too many cases now arise each year for the justices to consider and decide every dispute. The Court possesses a variety of mechanisms to select the cases that it wishes to hear. Some of these mechanisms are authorized by federal law; others have developed within the Court. The discuss list, one of the internal mechanisms, emerged when the number of cases had increased beyond the ability of the justices to discuss every request that they review a lower court's decision.

The Court initially followed the practice of having the chief justice distribute a "dead list"— cases that did not merit discussion before being denied review. After *World War II, however, the Court changed to a more restrictive practice. The chief justice now circulates a "discuss list" of cases he deems worthy of discussion; any justice may add a case to the list. Each case presented to the Court is still reviewed in each justice's chambers, but only those cases on the discuss list are talked about at the justices' regular conference. Approximately 30 percent of the filed cases reach the discuss list. The remaining requests for review are rejected, without further consideration.

Walter F. Pratt, Jr.

**Disparate Impact.** Title VII of the *Civil Rights Act of 1964 prohibits overt and purposeful discrimination in employment. In *Griggs v. Duke Power Co. (1971), the Court held that the act "proscribes not only overt discrimination but also practices that are fair in form but discriminatory in operation" (p. 850). As modified and restricted by *Ward's Cove Packing Co. v. Atonio (1989), the employee has the initial burden of proving that a facially neutral employment practice has a discriminatory effect. If the employer can furnish evidence of a valid business justification for the practice, the employee then bears the burden of showing that alternative practices, "without a similarly undesirable effect, would also serve the employer's legitimate interest(s)" (*Albemarle Paper Co. v. Moody, 1975, p. 425).

Outside of the employment context, disparate impact (such as de facto school segregation or allegedly discriminatory voting districts) violates the Constitution only if it is shown to be intentional. However, section 2 of the *Voting Rights Act (as amended in 1982) permits a claim of discrimination without a showing of intent.

(See also EMPLOYMENT DISCRIMINATION; RACE AND RACISM.)

Joel B. Grossman

**Disparate Treatment** in employment is explicit facial discrimination on account of an individual's race, color, religion, sex, or national origin. It is prohibited by Title VII of the *Civil Rights Act of 1964. Although proof of an employer's discriminatory motive is not required, evidence of an employer's subjective intent to discriminate is required. Title VII does, however, permit an employer to discriminate "in those certain instances where religion, sex, or national origin is a bona fide occupational qualification (BFOQ) reasonably necessary to the normal operation of that particular business or enterprise." The BFOQ exception has been strictly construed and is rarely granted. (See also EMPLOYMENT DISCRIMINATION.)                Elaine J. Grant

**Dissent.** Strictly speaking, dissent represents disagreement with the outcome of a case and with the Supreme Court's treatment of the parties involved. If the Court affirms the decision of a *lower federal court, for instance, a dissent disagrees with the decision to affirm. But a justice who dissents does not simply disapprove of the majority's legal reasoning; that justice also disapproves of the treatment of the parties. The Supreme Court decides cases by majority rule, and the views of justices who disagree with the majority have no legal force. Nonetheless, dissent is a regular and important feature of the Court's decisions.

When a justice dissents, that justice will almost always write a dissenting opinion or join in a colleague's dissenting opinion. Such an opinion offers a rationale for disagreement with the outcome in the case. A dissenting opinion should be distinguished from a *concurring opinion, which agrees with the outcome but expresses a rationale for the outcome that differs in some way from that of the majority opinion.

Some complications arise in practice. For example, a justice might disagree with the outcome of a case—but only in part. If the Court overturns the convictions of two criminal defendants, for instance, a dissenter might argue that only one of the convictions should have been reversed. An opinion reflecting partial disagreement usually is labeled "concurring in part and dissenting in part." In this and other respects, however, the justices are not entirely consistent in their labeling of opinions.

*Functions of Dissent.*  Through dissent, a justice expresses and justifies disagreement with the Court's decision. Supreme Court decisions involve important matters, and they are frequently the result of hard-fought battles among the justices. It is understandable, therefore, that justices would wish to make known their belief that the majority was wrong and the reasons for this belief. It is also understandable that many dissenting opinions express strong criticism of the Court's decision and that a few even ridicule the decision. In *Holland* v. *Illinois* (1990), for instance, Justice Thurgood *Marshall referred to "the majority's selective amnesia with respect to our cases in this area" and added that its suggestion concerning one claim by a litigant could "only be described as staggering" (p. 818).

A dissenting opinion is often the product of the battle itself. If a justice voted in the minority in the original conference discussion of a case, that justice may write an opinion to try to win colleagues over and thus obtain a majority; in most cases, that effort is unsuccessful. In another instance, a justice might be assigned the Court's opinion but then be unable to retain a majority. In either case, an opinion that was written for another purpose can be adapted to become a dissenting opinion.

Dissenting opinions can have substantial impact outside the Court. By casting doubt on the Court's decision, a dissenting justice may hope to influence the ways that lower courts respond to the decision. Alternatively, the dissenter may encourage Congress to take action to limit or overturn the decision (see REVERSALS OF COURT DECISIONS BY CONGRESS).

Sometimes the dissenter hopes to influence the Court itself. While the Supreme Court generally adheres to its own *precedents, it is not rare—and has become increasingly common—for it to overturn precedents. It is even more common for the Court to modify precedents in deciding related issues. A dissenter can hope to exert sufficient persuasive force to influence the Court's decisions in the future. It is usually difficult, however, to determine whether a shift in the Court's position reflects influence from an earlier dissent. Justice Hugo *Black dissented against the Court's holding in *Betts* v. *Brady* (1942) that indigent state criminal defendants were not ordinarily entitled to a free attorney. Twenty-one years later he was able to write the Court's opinion in *Gideon* v. *Wainwright* (1963) reversing the *Betts* decision. But even here the reversal was probably due primarily to changes in the Court's membership and in societal conditions rather than to the belated persuasiveness of Black's 1942 opinion.

*Prevalence of Dissent.*  Only a minority of Supreme Court decisions today are unanimous; dissenting votes and opinions are a routine part of the Court's work. The frequency of dissent can be ascribed to two conditions. First, the cases that the Court accepts seldom are "easy" in the sense that one outcome is clearly dictated by the law. As a result, justices with different policy preferences are likely to reach different conclusions. Second, the justices generally feel that it is entirely appropriate to express openly their disagreements with Court decisions.

In recent terms, the number of dissenting opinions has sometimes exceeded the number of decisions. But the high levels of dissent that exist today represent a recent phenomenon in the history of the Court. For most of that history, dissents were unusual. According to the data in Albert Blaustein and Roy Mersky's *The First One Hundred Justices* (1978), however, the 1942 term was the first in which the justices wrote as many as one dissenting opinion per three decisions.

One reason for this change is that the Court only gained significant power to determine which cases it would hear in 1891 and did not obtain its present nearly complete power over its agenda until 1925 (see JUDICIARY ACT OF 1925). These jurisdictional changes allowed the Court to cull out most of the "easy" cases brought to it— cases that would tend to produce unanimous decisions—and thus created the potential for higher rates of dissent.

That potential has been realized chiefly because of changes in norms concerning dissent. Chief Justice John *Marshall (1803–1835), with his firm control over the Court, helped to create a tradition of suppressing disagreement in the interest of unanimity. That tradition remained strong as late as the first few decades of the twentieth century. Even those justices who were renowned for their dissents, such as Oliver Wendell *Holmes (1902–1932) and Louis D. *Brandeis (1915–1939), actually cast dissenting votes only occasionally.

The elevation of Justice Harlan Fiske *Stone to *chief justice in 1941 was the key factor in the change in Court norms concerning dissent, according to Thomas Walker, Lee Epstein, and William Dixon (1988). As an associate justice, Stone had chafed under the strong leadership of Chief Justice Charles Evans *Hughes (1930–1941), who gave a high priority to achieving unanimity. As chief, Stone was quite tolerant of dissent and himself dissented at a far higher rate than any previous chief justice. His colleagues responded by increasing their own propensities to dissent (and to write concurring opinions as well). The overall increase in dissent was dramatic; the ratio of dissenting opinions to decisions during Stone's five terms as chief justice was about three times as high as it had been in the preceding five terms.

Although Stone's tenure as chief was relatively brief, the acceptance of dissent that marked his leadership had a permanent effect. Rates of dissent remained very high by historical standards under his successor, Fred M. *Vinson (1946–1953), and since then have remained consistently far above the level that characterized the Court's history before 1941.

The continuation of high dissent rates since the 1940s is noteworthy in light of the growth in the Court's caseload. During Stone's tenure as chief justice, the Court received an average of a little more than one thousand cases per term; in the 1980s, the average was more than four thousand. Increasingly, the justices have complained about the burdens of handling so many cases. Dissent—or at least the writing of dissenting opinions— might have been expected to

decline as justices sought a means to reduce their workload. The absence of such a decline reflects in part the increased number of law *clerks (now four) provided to each justice; the clerks enhance the ability of justices to write separate opinions. It has been suggested that the Court's workload actually encourages dissent, in that the justices have become too busy to take the time necessary to compromise their differences. Whether or not this is true, it is clear that the Court's norms concerning dissent have changed fundamentally. While the interest in maximizing consensus in decisions has not disappeared altogether, it survives only in attenuated form. For the most part, justices feel free to cast dissenting votes when they disagree with the position of the majority, and their voting behavior has become a more accurate reflection of their personal policy preferences.

*Impact of Dissent.* The traditional norm limiting dissent reflected a belief that dissent could have undesirable effects, a belief that has not disappeared. Most important, it is thought that departures from unanimity detract from the authority attached to decisions of the Court, and the practical impact of this lost authority might be to increase noncompliance with decisions. Even in an era of frequent dissent, at least some justices seem to share this view, and it can influence their behavior under special circumstances. Chief Justice Earl *Warren worked long and skillfully to achieve a unanimous decision in *Brown v. Board of Education* (1954), largely because he shared with some of his colleagues the belief that division within the Court would encourage resistance to a decision that required desegregation of southern public schools.

The belief that dissent encourages noncompliance is supported by the fact that critics of decisions frequently use dissents to buttress their positions. Moreover, it seems logical that disagreement within the Court detracts from the authority of a decision. But the impact of dissent on responses to the Court's decisions has not been established empirically, in part because of the difficulty of measuring that impact. If dissent does affect responses, it seems likely that its impact is marginal; the policy preferences and self-interest of those who respond to decisions are probably far more powerful factors. It is worth recalling that the Court's unanimity in *Brown* proved insufficient to prevent overwhelming noncompliance with that ruling in the Deep South, because southern officials had strong reasons to oppose desegregation.

It is possible that dissent has eroded the Court's authority, not so much in individual decisions but more generally. As justices regularly cast doubt on the correctness of Court decisions, the cumulative effect may be to increase skepticism about the Court's right to bind other institutions in the legal system with its interpretations of the law. The validity of this hypothesis is probably impossible to determine, but it is plausible.

Even if dissent were proved to have a negative effect on the Court's impact, however, it seems unlikely that the rate of dissent would decline. Frequent dissent and its justification in opinions have become well-established features of the Supreme Court, and the justices would find it very difficult to return to the earlier era in which dissent was exceptional.

(See also OPINIONS, ASSIGNMENT AND WRITING OF.)

□ Stephen C. Halpern and Kenneth N. Vines, "Institutional Disunity, The Judges' Bill and the Role of the U.S. Supreme Court," *Western Political Quarterly* 30 (1977): 471–483. Maurice Kelman, "The Forked Path of Dissent," in *The Supreme Court Review 1985,* edited by Philip B. Kurland, Gerhard Casper, and Dennis J. Hutchinson (1986), pp. 227–298. Thomas G. Walker, Lee Epstein, and William J. Dixon, "On the Mysterious Decline of Consensual Norms in the United States Supreme Court," *Journal of Politics* 50 (1988): 361–389.

Lawrence Baum

**Diversity Jurisdiction** permits a federal court to hear a case involving questions of state law if the opposing parties are citizens of different states. A *corporation is considered a citizen of the state in which it is incorporated and the state in which it maintains its principal place of business. Litigants must also satisfy a "jurisdictional amount" set by Congress; since 1989 only diversity cases involving amounts in controversy greater than fifty thousand dollars may be filed in federal court.

Supporters of diversity jurisdiction advance three justifications for its continued importance. First, access to the federal courts permits out-of-state litigants to escape the prejudice of local judges and juries. Second, some litigants believe that federal courts are superior to *state courts, permitting them access to the tribunal most likely to deliver the highest quality of justice (see LOWER FEDERAL COURTS.). Finally, diversity jurisdiction fosters national economic development (see CAPITALISM). The ability of the federal courts to fashion a uniform law of commerce in the nineteenth century, for example, stimulated investment in areas where the state law regarding commercial activity was uncertain or inhospitable to speculation.

Opponents of diversity jurisdiction counter that these concerns are now irrelevant. The professionalization of state judiciaries has reduced parochialism and increased the quality of justice. The Supreme Court's decision in *Erie Railroad* v. *Tompkins* (1938), which required federal tribunals to apply state law in diversity cases, halted the federal courts' ability to administer uniform economic development. Furthermore, diversity jurisdiction needlessly crowds the federal docket with cases involving exclusively state law and impairs the ability of federal judges to

resolve important federal issues (see BUSINESS OF THE COURT). Nevertheless, efforts to abolish diversity jurisdiction have failed to gain wide acceptance (although in 1978 the House of Representatives approved a bill abolishing diversity jurisdiction). However, the *Judicial Improvements and Access to Justice Act (1988), which raised the jurisdictional amount from ten thousand to fifty thousand dollars, represented a compromise between abolitionists and those who favored a wide choice of judicial forums.

(See also JUDICIAL POWER AND JURISDICTION.)

Eric W. Rise

**Dobbins v. Erie County,** 16 Pet. (41 U.S.) 435 (1842), argued 14 Feb. 1842, decided 4 Mar. 1842 by vote of 9 to 0; Wayne for the Court. In *Dobbins,* the captain of a United States revenue cutter stationed in Pennsylvania challenged the validity of that state's taxation on the income derived from his office. The United States Supreme Court, reviewing a decision by the Pennsylvania Supreme Court upholding the validity of the tax, unanimously reversed, holding that "the unconstitutionality of such taxation by a state as that now before us may be safely put—though it is not the only ground—upon its interference with the constitutional means which have been legislated by the government of the United States to carry into effect its powers to lay and collect taxes, duties, imposts, etc., and to regulate commerce" (p. 449). (See TAXING AND SPENDING CLAUSE; COMMERCE POWER.) *Dobbins'*s classic formulation of the principle that the state governments cannot lay a tax upon the constitutional means employed by the federal government to execute its constitutional powers was implicitly overruled by the Supreme Court's 1939 decision in *Graves* v. *New York.*

*Dobbins* was an important case in a line of nineteenth-century Supreme Court precedents, beginning with Chief Justice John *Marshall's opinion in *McCulloch* v. *Maryland,* (1819), interpreting the doctrine of intergovernmental immunities broadly. This doctrine holds that the federal and state governments possess some degree of reciprocal immunity from each other's taxing and regulatory powers. It has been sharply curtailed in its scope since the mid-1930s by the Court. *Dobbins* thus is no longer good law.

(See also TAX IMMUNITIES.)

Robert A. Williams

**Dodge v. Woolsey,** 18 How. (59 U.S.) 331 (1856), argued 6 Feb. 1856, decided 8 Apr. 1856 by vote of 6 to 3; Wayne for the Court, Campbell, Catron, and Daniel in dissent. In 1845 the Ohio legislature enacted a general banking act, which authorized any bank chartered thereunder to pay the state 6 percent of its annual profits in lieu of any taxes imposed by the state. In 1851 Ohio adopted a new state constitution that in effect repealed the *tax immunity in the statute of 1845. In 1853 the legislature increased the tax on banks beyond that allowed in the statute of 1845. John W. Woolsey, a citizen of Connecticut and a shareholder of a Cleveland bank, sought an *injunction from a federal circuit court to prevent George C. Dodge, Cuyahoga County, Ohio, treasurer, from collecting the tax on the bank, claiming the tax unconstitutionally impaired the obligation of a contract. The "contract" was the relationship between the state and any corporation chartered under the 1845 act.

The Supreme Court upheld the injunction on the ground that the tax provision in the 1845 statute constituted a contractual obligation of the state, which it had impaired by the constitution of 1851 and the statute of 1853. Justice John A. *Campbell wrote a dissenting opinion in which he denounced the arrogance of corporations and argued that the Supreme Court was unconstitutionally encroaching upon the rights of a sovereign state. Subsequent decisions of the Court, while attempting to distinguish Woolsey, severely confined the holding in that case by ruling that for a tax exemption to be valid it would have to be contained in a specific corporate charter and not in a general statute.

(See also CAPITALISM; CONTRACTS CLAUSE.)

Robert M. Ireland

**Dombrowski v. Pfister,** 380 U.S. 499 (1965), argued 25 Jan. 1965, decided 26 Apr. 1965 by vote of 5 to 2; Brennan for the Court, Harlan, joined by Clark, in dissent, Black and Stewart not participating. Dombrowski, an officer of the Southern Conference Educational Fund, sought an *injunction against the governor of Louisiana, law enforcement officers, and the chairman of the state's Legislative Joint Committee on Un-American Activities for prosecuting or threatening to prosecute his organization under several state *subversion statutes. Dombrowski alleged that the statutes violated the *First Amendment and that he and his civil rights colleagues were subjected to continuous harassment, including arrests without intent to prosecute and seizures of necessary internal documents.

A three-judge federal court dismissed the complaint, holding that Dombrowski had not demonstrated the required irreparable injury and that this was a case for invocation of the "abstention doctrine" to permit the state courts to interpret the statutes consistent with the federal Constitution.

The Supreme Court reversed. Justice William *Brennan's opinion held that the statutes clearly violated the First Amendment. Further, he argued that the continuous threats of prosecution, seizure of records, and harassment sufficiently chilled free expression to justify federal court intervention. Injunctive relief in these circumstances was clearly appropriate as an exception to the general rule against federal court intervention in state criminal prosecutions. In *dissent, Justice John *Harlan argued that permitting federal court

intervention, even under these circumstances, was a significant and unwarranted departure from the principle of *comity and a threat to the integrity of the federal system.

Dombrowski, seen by civil rights lawyers as a loophole in the traditional principle of nonintervention, unleashed a torrent of lawsuits seeking federal court protection against state prosecutions. The loophole, however, proved only temporary; the Supreme Court closed it substantially in *Younger v. Harris (1971).

(See also ABSTENTION DOCTRINE; CIVIL RIGHTS MOVEMENT; JUDICIAL POWER AND JURISDICTION; LOWER FEDERAL COURTS.)

Charles H. Sheldon

**Double Jeopardy.** The Double Jeopardy Clause of the *Fifth Amendment states: "nor shall any person be subject for the same offence to be twice put in jeopardy of life or limb." The principle is one of the oldest in Western civilization, having roots in ancient Greek and Roman law. Nevertheless, the clause is one of the least understood in the *Bill of Rights, and the Supreme Court has done little to remove the confusion.

The Court decided relatively few double jeopardy cases until after 1969, when, in *Benton v. Maryland, it held that the Fifth Amendment's double jeopardy provision is incorporated in the *Fourteenth Amendment and applies to the states as well as the federal government (see INCORPORATION DOCTRINE).

As a general proposition, the Double Jeopardy Clause applies only to criminal cases and consists of three separate constitutional protections. First, it protects against a second criminal prosecution for the same offense after acquittal. Second, it protects against a subsequent prosecution for the same offense after conviction. Finally, it protects against multiple punishments for the same offense.

The simplicity of these general statements masks the real confusion resulting from their application. As Judge Monroe McKay observed, terms like "acquittal," "multiple punishments," and "same offense" prompt "the most vehement disagreement among the Justices" (McKay, 1983, pp. 1–2). The Court has struggled to give meaning to these terms.

Difficulties arise in determining when a new prosecution is for the "same offense." The issue is presented when the same criminal act or transaction violates two separate statutes. In Grady v. Corbin (1990), the Court explained that in such circumstances the critical inquiry should focus on the conduct the prosecution will attempt to prove in the second prosecution, not the evidence that it will use to prove that conduct. For example, if someone has an automobile accident and is convicted of driving while intoxicated, that person cannot then be prosecuted for criminally negligent homicide arising from the same accident if the state intends to use the drunk driving conviction to prove the homicide charge. On the other hand, the homicide prosecution will not be barred if the state uses other conduct (such as driving too fast) to prove the homicide charge.

The Court has also developed rather complicated rules to resolve the issue of whether a defendant has been "put twice in jeopardy." The protection of the clause applies only in instances where jeopardy "has attached." In a case tried by a judge rather than by a jury, jeopardy attaches after the first witness has been sworn to testify. In a case tried by a *jury, jeopardy attaches after the jury has been empaneled. Finally, where a defendant enters a plea, jeopardy attaches when the court accepts the plea.

There are, however, a number of exceptions to these propositions. If the first prosecution resulted in a mistrial, a subsequent prosecution is permitted if the defendant consented to the mistrial or if there was "manifest necessity" for the mistrial. Manifest necessity would be found, for example, where a mistrial was declared because the indictment contained a defect that would have been a basis for reversing a conviction.

Similarly, a new prosecution is permitted if a conviction is reversed on appeal. If the defendant is then reconvicted, however, a higher sentence may be imposed at the second trial. A jury verdict of not guilty, however, may not be appealed by the prosecutor and bars a second prosecution. The rules are more complex when a judge, rather than a jury, decides the case. Generally, a dismissal or acquittal by a judge bars reprosecution for the same offense. However, if the dismissal was requested by the defendant and was for a reason that would prevent prosecution, the prosecutor may appeal. If the dismissal is reversed, the defendant may be prosecuted again.

Finally, double jeopardy does not prevent a separate sovereignty from prosecuting again for the same offense. In *Heath* v. *Alabama* (1985), the Supreme Court held that federal prosecution is not barred by a previous state prosecution for the same offense.

Commentators have argued that the continuing confusion surrounding double jeopardy results from the Court's failure to articulate the precise values served by the clause. At least five different values have been suggested: (1) preventing the government from using its superior resources to wear down an innocent defendant, (2) preserving the integrity of jury verdicts, (3) protecting the defendant's interest in finality, (4) limiting excessive prosecutorial discretion in charging individuals, and (5) preventing imposition of sentences not authorized by the legislature. A coherent, sound approach to double jeopardy will not be developed until the Court identifies the values embedded in the Double Jeopardy Clause.

□ Monroe McKay, "Double Jeopardy: Are the Pieces the Puzzle?" *Washburn Journal* 23 (1983): 1–23.
Daan Braveman

**Douglas, William Orville** (b. Maine, Minn., 16 Oct. 1898; d. Washington, D.C., 19 Jan. 1980; interred Arlington National Cemetery, Arlington, Va.), associate justice, 1939–1975. Born into crushing poverty and crippled by polio in youth, Douglas worked his way through college and law school, quickly became a distinguished legal scholar, was named third chairman of the Securities and Exchange Commission (SEC) and then, as associate justice, served longer than any other member in the history of the Supreme Court. A rugged outdoorsman and individualist who delighted, especially in later years, in flouting convention, Douglas became a spokesman for personal freedom on and off the Court. Unlike Hugo L. *Black, Felix *Frankfurter, or William J. *Brennan among his contemporaries, Douglas left little theoretical legacy after his retirement but is remembered, with both affection and anger, as a symbol of the constitutional values he came to espouse (see JUDICIAL ACTIVISM).

*Early Career.* Douglas was born in Minnesota but spent most of his childhood in or near Yakima, Washington. His father, a Presbyterian home minister, died when Douglas was six and left his family virtually penniless. As therapy for polio, Douglas took to making solitary hikes in the foothills of the Cascades, which he later reported to be the source of his lifelong love of the outdoors as well as of his devotion to solitude. He worked his way through Whitman College, where poverty forced him to live in a tent one term. After graduating from Whitman in 1920 and teaching school for two years, he "hopped a freight and rode east," as he later recalled (with some embellishment), to attend Columbia Law School, from which he graduated near the top of his class after working almost full-time tutoring and doing odd jobs.

He coveted a clerkship with Associate Justice Harlan Fiske *Stone, which customarily went to a top Columbia graduate, and when another graduate was selected, Douglas settled uneasily for a Wall Street law firm job that he later claimed to have hated. After two years at what is now Cravath, Swaine & Moore, Douglas left Wall Street to teach, first at Columbia Law School (1927–1929) and then, after a faculty rift over selection of Columbia's new dean, at Yale (1929–1934), where he became one of that law school's youngest chaired professors. His specialty was corporate law, including agency, bankruptcy, and reorganization. Although never closely identified with the American *legal realist movement, which then flourished at both Columbia and Yale, Douglas was strongly influenced by its leading figures. He came to see legal doctrines not as autonomous but as devices that could be manipulated for social good or ill. Always restless, Douglas, like several prominent legal scholars, went to Washington to work in the *New Deal, and he soon became a member (1936) and then chairman (1937) of the SEC, where he pressed for reform and battled the governors of the New York Stock Exchange over its operation. All the while, he developed close friendships—galvanized, he said, at poker games—within the Roosevelt administration and its inner circle, especially with Harold Ickes, the secretary of the interior.

*Service on the Court.* When Louis D. *Brandeis retired as associate justice in February 1939, President Franklin D. *Roosevelt made clear that he wished to appoint a Westerner but that he viewed Douglas, who had been mentioned as a possible candidate, as an Easterner from Yale. While friends, especially Jerome Frank and Thomas Corcoran, lined up western political support, Douglas privately curried favor with influential political insiders. Then, just as his chances rose, his loyalty to the New Deal became supsect, so he made a fiery speech condemning the financial community and confirming his reformist brand of New Dealism. Within a week, Roosevelt offered Douglas Brandeis's seat, and he was confirmed 4 April 1939 by 62-to-4 vote (the four dissenters labeling him a reactionary tool of Wall Street). At forty-one, Douglas was the second-youngest Supreme Court appointee in history and the youngest in 128 years; only Joseph *Story, at thirty-two, was younger.

The Supreme Court that Douglas joined was in transition, both personally and philosophically. Black, Stanley *Reed, and Frankfurter had all been appointed since 1937, so Douglas—with the holdover Stone—provided a solidly pro–New Deal outlook. Over the next two years, during which three more Roosevelt appointees were added, the Court consolidated the post–1937 judicial imprimatur on the remaining New Deal programs that were in litigation. Black and Douglas played central roles, providing arguments for sustaining or interpretatively expanding late New Deal legislation, especially in the areas of *labor law and control of markets (see PROPERTY).

Despite his later reputation as a civil libertarian, Douglas's most important and enduring work during World War II concerned regulation of business. His greatest achievements, still essentially undisturbed, are *FPC* v. *Hope Natural Gas* (1944), which established standards for reviewing agency rate-making, and *United States* v. *Socony-Vacuum Oil Co.* (1940), which held that a combination to fix prices was illegal per se without further inquiry into the reasonableness of the activity. Although Douglas did not coin the "per se" test, he firmly established its authority and permanently changed antitrust analysis of price fixing. Perhaps his most pervasive influence was in the administration of *bankruptcy law, where he wrote definitive opinions on most aspects of the field. Douglas explained his judicial philosophy in business cases as a function of his predecessor's views, and many of his opinions quote Brandeis's opinions and nonjudicial works. In later life he would also trace the origins of his views to Thorstein Veblen and even to an

*William Orville Douglas*

influential preparatory school teacher, but, fully formed, his theoretical outlook was entirely his own.

During World War II, liberal members of the Court, particularly Black and Douglas, were caught between clashing symbols: while seeking to protect civil liberties in increasingly dark times, they also wished to support the war effort of the president who appointed them. Both justices initially supported compulsory flag-salute laws (*Minersville* v. *Gobitis,* 1940), quickly repented publicly (*Jones* v. *Opelika,* 1942), and enthusiastically joined reversal of the first decision in *West Virginia* v. *Barnette* (1943). Both dissented from a highly restrictive reading of treason law, and Douglas filed a jingoistic dissent (*Cramer* v. *United States,* 1945). Both supported the constitutionality of the exclusion of Japanese from the West Coast during wartime, with Black speaking for the Court and Douglas concurring—although there is evidence that Douglas's vote vacillated until almost the last minute (*Korematsu* v. *United States,* 1944).

After the war, Black and Douglas found their voice and began to write opinion after opinion upholding civil liberties claims, particularly of free speech. Douglas's most controversial opinion for the Court at the time was *Terminiello* v. *Chicago* (1949), in which a speaker's conviction for insulting a hostile mob was reversed. To hold otherwise, he wrote, "would lead to standardization of ideas either by legislatures, courts, or dominant political or community groups" (p. 5). Black and Douglas filed spirited dissents in *Dennis* v. *United States,* the 1951 decision upholding convictions of American Communist party members for conspiracy to teach and advocate overthrow of the government.

In most cases, Douglas wrote or voted silently in support of theories developed and advanced by Black. Douglas's most famous civil liberties opinion for the Court was *Griswold v. Connecticut* (1965), in which he identified a constitutional right to *privacy emanating from the "penumbras" of rights enshrined in the *First, *Third, *Fourth, *Fifth and *Ninth amendments. Although the theory in fact owed much to Justice Brennan, Douglas was identified with the approach, which, critics remarked unkindly, revealed that his constitutional views were more shadow than substance.

Black dissented in *Griswold* and again two years later in *Harper v. Virginia Board of Elections*, in which Douglas's opinion for the Court invalidated *poll taxes. During much of Black's last decade on the Court, 1961–1971, the two former allies were in opposite camps as Black sought limiting principles for his theories and Douglas sought to extend his views to their logical conclusion. During the same period, Douglas's analytical habits came under sharper scholarly attack for their tendentiousness, especially in tax cases, or simply for sloppiness. Douglas, ever the rebel, seemed to relish the criticism and appeared to bait his antagonists—larding his opinions, for example, with quotations from Walt Whitman and Vachel Lindsay (*Papachristou v. Jacksonville*, 1972), or staking out the most extreme positions, such as claiming that trees have legal standing to bring lawsuits (*Sierra Club v. Morton*, 1972, dissent). Douglas's record, especially from the mid-1960s onward, displays positions that often appear to be casual, even in areas that he obviously cared about. To take the most startling example, the author of *Papachristou*, which invalidated a vagrancy ordinance in lyrical terms, also wrote to uphold *zoning ordinances preserving traditional lifestyles (*Belle Terre v. Boraas*, 1974). To the end of his career, many critics charged that Douglas too often took positions simply to be in the center of the action, with his last-minute stay in 1953 of the Rosenbergs' execution representing the most distasteful incident of this kind.

Douglas's motivation in that case is not free from doubt, but it is clear that his personal style changed dramatically in the early 1950s, when he divorced his wife of twenty-nine years and embarked on annual globe-trotting expeditions that routinely led to popularly targeted books about his travels. He was remarried three times, the last time, when he was sixty-six, to a woman of twenty-two. The combination of his sensational private life, maverick views, and personalization of his ideology led in April 1970 to a call by then-House Minority Leader Gerald R. Ford for Douglas's *impeachment. His puckishness temporarily suppressed, Douglas mounted a feverish defense, and the charges were rejected eight months later by a House judiciary subcommittee. Vindicated, Douglas reverted to form.

On 31 December 1974, Douglas suffered a debilitating stroke. He was partially paralyzed and never recovered his full capacities. He was absent for much of the rest of that Supreme Court term, and though he returned to the Court the following term, he was at far less than full strength. On 12 November 1975, he submitted a letter of retirement to President Ford after serving longer (by more than two years) than any other justice in history.

*Legacy.* Unlike Black and Frankfurter, who left competing theoretical legacies, or Brennan, who provided creative doctrinal dexterity, Douglas's intellectual legacy as a justice is slight. While sitting, Douglas's plain eloquence supported the causes of the day but now seems time-bound, just as his voluminous occasional writing—more than thirty books and hundreds of articles—seems ephemeral.

Douglas's historical significance now seems to rest on his symbolism as the personification of individualism and on his advocacy for the powerless. Yet the symbol is muddied by his own paradoxical complexity: his record is riddled with contradiction, both substantively and personally (the great humanitarian was notorious for abusing staff and for indulging his conceits). Part of the tension may have been due to his restiveness on the Court, which could not contain his vast energy and which provided less of a forum than he sometimes wished. He was a plausible vice-presidential candidate in 1944 and flirted with a wildcat run for the Democratic presidential nomination in 1948. After his national political possibilities were finally foreclosed in 1948, he devoted more of his time to nonjudicial pursuits, which were aimed at reaching a wide audience interested in both legal and nonlegal—especially environmental—issues.

Douglas allowed himself to be a hero to professionals and laypeople alike, and at times even appeared to cultivate the role. He wished to be remembered for his faith in the individual, in the Constitution, and in the sanctity of the environment. His lasting monument, which touched him deeply, was designation by Congress of the parkland along the C & O Canal, a favorite walking trail in Washington, as the William O. Douglas National Park.

(See also HISTORY OF THE COURT: THE DEPRESSION AND THE RISE OF LEGAL LIBERALISM and RIGHTS CONSCIOUSNESS IN CONTEMPORARY SOCIETY.)

□ Vernon L. Countryman, *The Judicial Record of Justice William O. Douglas* (1974). William O. Douglas, *Go East, Young Man* (1974). William O. Douglas, *The Court Years, 1939–1975* (1980). James F. Simon, *Independent Journey* (1980). Melvin I. Urofsky, ed., *The Douglas Letters* (1987).

Dennis J. Hutchinson

**Downes v. Bidwell.** See INSULAR CASES.

**Draft.** See CONSCRIPTION.

**Dred Scott Case.** See SCOTT V. SANDFORD.

**Dual Federalism,** a concept that derives from the view that the Constitution was a "compact" made by the sovereign states and the people of those states for the limited purpose of giving the new national government a range of explicitly enumerated powers. The states otherwise retained all the authority of sovereign polities. The states were co-equals with the national government because in their own "spheres" of authority—in exercise of their "reserved" powers—they were as fully supreme as the national government was in its sphere. Many, in the founding period and now, consider the *Tenth Amendment an expression of this view; others deny that it should be viewed as derogatory of federal supremacy, especially in light of the *Fourteenth Amendment, adopted in 1868.

Even constitutional nationalists such as Alexander *Hamilton and John *Marshall were willing to acknowledge rhetorically the concept of states' sovereignty in their own spheres. But they never accepted that a state's consent might be withdrawn nor interposition of state authority or outright secession permitted. Southern proslavery interests had a powerful stake in dual federalism, and the decisions of the Taney Court fulfilled their expectations on most counts (see SLAVERY).

Despite the outcome of the *Civil War and adoption of the postwar amendments, the Court continued to rely on doctrines based on dual federalism as instruments for invalidating federal regulatory legislation, as in the child labor case *Hammer* v. *Dagenhart* (1918), in which the Court sustained the inviolability of the states' reserved powers (see LABOR).

Dual federalism virtually disappeared from the Court's formal jurisprudence, however, as the result of the *New Deal "constitutional revolution," especially the expanded view of federal *commerce power. Since *World War II, the only application of the Tenth Amendment as a limitation on congressional regulatory power in areas "belonging to the states" has been in *National League of Cities* v. *Usery* (1976), a decision on wage and hour legislation that was reversed in *Garcia* v. *San Antonio Metropolitan Transit Authority* (1985).

(See also FEDERALISM; STATE ACTION; STATE SOVEREIGNTY AND STATES' RIGHTS.)

Harry N. Scheiber

**Due Process, Procedural.** The concept of due process derives from the Magna Carta (1215), the great charter of English liberties whereby the nobles limited the king's authority. Its phrase "law of the land" was transformed over the years to "due process of law," a phrase included in 1692 in a Massachusetts statute. The *Fifth Amendment of the Constitution (ratified 1791) requires that the federal government not deprive any person of "life, liberty, or property without due process of law." The same language is included in the *Fourteenth Amendment (ratified 1868) as a constraint on the states.

The central aim of due process doctrine is to assure fair procedure when the government imposes a burden on an individual. The doctrine seeks to prevent arbitrary government, avoid mistaken deprivations, allow persons to know about and respond to charges against them, and promote a sense of the legitimacy of official behavior.

Procedural due process does not prevent the government ultimately from making a deprivation. The notion of *substantive *due process does place substantive limits on official power, whereas procedural due process is concerned solely with the manner in which the government acts. This distinction appears in *Londoner* v. *Denver* (1908) and *Bi-Metallic Investment Co.* v. *State Board of Equalization* (1915). Taken together, these cases distinguish between the situation in which government singles out an individual for a deprivation based on the facts of a case, which triggers procedural due process requirements, and a broad rule affecting large numbers of people, which does not. In the former cases, the government must provide the procedural protections of notice and hearing; as the Supreme Court held in *Grannis* v. *Ordean*, (1914), "[t]he fundamental requisite of due process of law is the opportunity to be heard" (p. 394).

A governmental deprivation of an individual's property will implicate due process. *Property has a *common-law meaning, including land and personal property. In the 1970s, the Court articulated a "new property" concept, which includes government-provided benefits, licenses, or statuses (such as that of public employee) that have value, are relied upon by individuals, and can be called statutory, regulatory, or contractual entitlements. A statutory benefit such as welfare (*Goldberg* v. *Kelly,* 1970), a driver's license (*Bell* v. *Burson,* 1971), the expectation of continued employment as a tenured professor (*Board of Regents* v. *Roth,* 1972), and the status of a civil servant protected from at-will dismissal (*Arnett* v. *Kennedy,* 1974), are examples of such "new property" interests. The Court held in *Roth* that the mere hope or unilateral expectation of some property interest is not enough.

The term "liberty" has its own history. In the Fourteenth Amendment, "liberty" has been held to incorporate major protections of the *Bill of Rights. "Liberty" also has an independent meaning in, for example, the criminal context. Basic freedom from incarceration, as well as a parolee's interest in staying on parole (*Morrissey* v. *Brewer,* 1972), are liberty interests. Liberty in the civil context includes certain personal interests in *privacy, which were recognized in a series of substantive due process cases, notably *Roe v. Wade* (1973). In civil cases involving procedural claims, several interests have been recognized as "liberty"—such as the interest in parental status (*Lassiter* v. *Department of Social Services*, 1981) or a school child's interest in being free from corporal punishment (*Ingraham* v. *Wright*, 1977).

The Court in *Cleveland Board of Education* v. *Loudermill* (1985) separated the issue of whether due process is triggered from the question of how much process is "due." A court is to weigh the extent of an individual's interest in additional procedure, as well as its value and cost. *Mathews* v. *Eldridge* (1976) held a post-termination evidentiary hearing to be sufficient due process in a disability-benefit termination case. *Mathews* gives courts much leeway. Sometimes, a fairly full, trial-type hearing is required. At other times, a court simply requires basic notice and opportunity to speak.

The many due process cases that come before the federal courts—involving prisons, schools, social security, and public employment, among other areas—testify to the continuing centrality of this area of law and the undiminished controversy surrounding it. Increasingly, two opposing visions dominate: a personal participation model, which stresses dignitary values and greater procedure, and a bureaucratic model, which stresses efficient and cost-effective decision-making. This tension is likely to persist.

Thomas O. Sargentich

**Due Process, Substantive.** The constitutional doctrine of substantive due process can be traced back to the English idea of a fundamental but unwritten constitution and flows forward to modern constitutional guarantees of *privacy. Though its antecedents include basic notions of republican government and individual *civil rights, our modern notions of substantive due process are founded upon Justice Stephen J. *Field's dissent in the *Slaughterhouse Cases* (1873). Behind the spare language of the Due Process Clause of the *Fourteenth Amendment that barred Louisiana's statutory conferring of a monopoly upon a single slaughterhouse, Field discerned inalienable individual liberties:

Clearly among these must be placed the right to pursue a lawful employment in a lawful manner, without other restraint than such as equally affects all persons. . . . The equality of right, with exemption from all disparaging and partial enactments, in the lawful pursuits of life, throughout the whole country, is the distinguishing privilege of citizens of the United States. (pp. 97, 109–110)

*Free-Labor Ideology.* Field brought to his dissent the powerful free-labor ideology of the victorious Republican party. Before the *Civil War, he had been a leading Republican jurist and judge; after the war he transformed this notion of equality into constitutional opinions. In his dis-

sent in the *Slaughterhouse Cases* and in *Munn* v. *Illinois* (1877), Field clung to his own personal version of this free-labor ideology. He admitted that states had the right to regulate the economic activity of public enterprises, like the grain elevator companies in *Munn*, when that regulation was evenhanded and served a genuine public need. But regulation of public businesses and private enterprises had no natural stopping place; it might, Field wrote in *Munn*, "justify an intermeddling with the business of every man in the community, so soon, at least, as his business became generally useful" (p. 141).

Though not a major theme in substantive due process scholarship, which instead focuses on the doctrine as a defense of property, it is apparent that Field's concern was the protection of free-labor ideology. Ironically, Field's antebellum Republican views better fit the Gilded Age than they did the *Reconstruction era. His view of the Due Process Clause gained ground in the almost entirely reconstituted Court of the late 1880s and 1890s. Field was never as comfortable with giant corporations as newer members of the Court, such as Justices David *Brewer and Rufus *Peckham, but his ideal of liberty of enterprise became the orthodoxy of the Court in the late nineteenth century. Field's concurrence in *Butcher's Union Co.* v. *Crescent Co.* (1884), a direct descendent of the *Slaughterhouse Cases*, expressed this vision: the "liberty of the individual to pursue a lawful trade or employment" was a "common right," one of the "certain principles of morality . . . without which society would be impossible, . . . [one of the] certain inherent rights [that] lie at the foundation of all action." "[U]pon them alone," Field wrote, "can free institutions be maintained" (p. 756).

For the Court, substantive due process was the wedge by which states were barred from abridging freedom of *contract and liberty of enterprise. Substantive due process would take on a life of its own, but at its heart it remained a vision not of constitutional law but of a good society whose free marketplaces were managed by a benevolent, invisible hand. Equality of opportunity would be undermined by class legislation. Too much state intervention would pervert and destroy the natural relationships by which the United States had become an economic giant. One may say with much truth that freedom of contract theory was as responsible for the formulation and continuing vitality of substantive due process as substantive due process was for the legitimation of freedom of contract.

The Court expanded its jurisdiction by holding the states to a substantive due process standard (see JUDICIAL POWER AND JURISDICTION). Potentially, every state regulatory statute had to pass muster as a valid exercise of health, welfare, morals, or *police power. Most went untouched, but whenever a statute was found unconstitutional under substantive due process review a furor invariably ensued. In *Allgeyer* v. *Louisiana* (1897), the Court overturned a Louisiana law requiring all corporations doing business with Louisiana residents to pay fees to the state. In *Lochner* v. *New York* (1905), the Court found a maximum-hours statute unconstitutional. In *Adair* v. *U.S.* (1908) the Court voided a federal law barring dismissals of interstate *common carrier workers because they were members of unions. In *Coppage* v. *Kansas* (1915) the Court invalidated a state law barring *yellow dog contracts. In *Adkins* v. *Children's Hospital* (1923) the Court struck down the minimum-wage-setting powers of a District of Columbia employment commission. The Court relied on substantive due process grounds to void price regulation in nonpublic industries and licensing of nonpublic enterprises, and the prevention of German-language teachers and parochial school teachers from earning a living at their trade (see FIRST AMENDMENT).

*The Reasonableness Standard.* Throughout these cases, the Court asked itself whether the state economic regulations were reasonable— that is, did they fit the legitimate objectives of state intervention in the economy. The public/private enterprise distinction Chief Justice Morrison *Waite employed in *Munn* was one attempt to elucidate a standard of reasonableness, as was the Court's weighing of evidence on the health of bakers in *Lochner*. The alternative—simple and uniform deference to the popularly elected representatives in state legislatures and Congress— was unpalatable to the majority in these substantive due process cases. The search for an appropriate and supple test of reasonableness—a *rule of reason—in substantive due process cases nevertheless bedeviled the Court.

Meanwhile, progressive critics of substantive due process, notably James Thayer, Louis D. *Brandeis, Roscoe Pound, and Theodore Roosevelt, accused the Court of setting itself up as a "super legislature" (see PROGRESSIVISM). The same criticisms were voiced even more stridently by a new generation of reformers in support of *New Deal programs. Recognizing that the line between public enterprises and private business and *labor had become blurred in an *administrative state and conceding that the legislatures had far greater ability to find and weigh facts than did the courts, Progressives on the Supreme Court, including Chief Justice Charles Evans *Hughes and Justices Owen J. *Roberts, Harlan Fiske *Stone, and Benjamin N. *Cardozo, began to lead the Court away from the freedom of contract version of substantive due process.

In *Nebbia* v. *New York* (1934), the Court, speaking through Roberts, found that a New York statute establishing a commission to fix milk prices was a reasonable health and welfare measure. The Court could only ask that state regulation not be unreasonable or arbitrary and that the

regulation have a real relation to the object of the legislation. Free market forces had failed to accommodate themselves to the needs of the community. There was nothing sacred about commodity prices that would prevent their regulation in the public interest.

The Court tackled minimum wage laws, the second major object of the Court's scrutiny under the regime of substantive due process, in *West Coast Hotel Co.* v. *Parrish* (1937). A much-divided Court, with the majority clinging to a strict version of substantive due process, validated a Washington State minimum wage law for women. Chief Justice Hughes wrote that the "Constitution does not speak of freedom of contract" (p. 391). Hughes signaled that Field's logic of free labor, which laissez-faire advocates had gilded with their own ideal of free markets, no longer influenced the majority of the Court. He did not strike at the doctrine of substantive due process per se, but at the freedom of contract faith hidden within the older economic version of substantive due process. As Hughes wrote, "The liberty safeguarded [by the Due Process Clause] is liberty in a social organization which requires the protection of law against the evils which menace the health, safety, morals and welfare of the people" (p. 391). The state could protect the liberty of a class of workers who were in an unequal bargaining position and were relatively defenseless against inadequate wages. The state could insure liberty as well as curtail it, a conception quite opposite Field's and one more appropriate to the New Deal than the antebellum free-labor ideology. After *West Coast Hotel*, economic due process review went into an eclipse from which it has not emerged.

If economic due process cases no longer absorbed a major portion of the Court's energies, substantive due process challenges to state and municipal regulations thrived in a new setting. Though recent Courts have generally observed a deferential policy toward state economic regulations, it has exempted from that approach state laws that discriminated against groups unable to gain the ear of the legislature, groups discriminated against by reason of race, gender, or other suspect categorization, and groups whose private lives were unduly invaded by the state (see SUSPECT CLASSIFICATIONS).

*Challenges to Segregation.* In particular, the deferential approach to state economic regulations was not extended to state restrictions on the right to *vote in primary elections or state-sponsored or state-condoned segregation of education, public facilities, or employment (see SEGREGATION, DE JURE). These decisions remade private worlds as well as public places, ending widespread patterns of segregation. Critics of *Brown* v. *Board of Education* (1954) claimed that its sweeping language had no textual basis in the Constitution and, like economic due process, it merely rested upon the external, private social and philosophical beliefs of the justices. Given the great differences in the regional, political, and educational background of the justices on the *Brown* Court, their unanimity could not have arisen from a consensus of personal values, but the critics are right in one respect: *Brown* and its sister cases do reflect deeply felt aspirations that reach behind the text of the Constitution.

*Privacy.* Beginning in the 1960s, a new class of "social" substantive due process suits issues arrived on the Court's docket. These tracked our society's heightened concern for expressive individualism and the right to practice distinct family and personal lifestyles. The "new" social substantive due process rested on the recently articulated freedom of personal choice and *privacy that the justices found in the "penumbras" of the *Bill of Rights in *Griswold v. Connecticut* (1965), and imposed upon the states through the Due Process Clause of the Fourteenth Amendment. The right to exercise those choices in the private spaces of one's life sustained the legality of *abortion in *Roe v. Wade* (1973) but did not protect homosexuals or adulterers from prosecution (see HOMOSEXUALITY), permit policemen to violate departmental personal-appearance regulations, deny states the right to collect and store information on drug prescriptions, or prevent state and local governments from releasing employees without explanation. In this group of cases the deferential policy of the Court proved that the freedom of contract doctrine is alive and well, for the government employer and the dismissed employee were hardly equal in bargaining power, particularly when the employee could not force the employer to divulge the reasons for the dismissal.

Despite the Court's retreat, under Chief Justice William H. *Rehnquist, from earlier social due process decisions, substantive due process retains its protean ability to adapt constitutional law to changing social mores. In tandem with claims based on the *Equal Protection Clause, due process challenges to state laws restricting individual choice will continue to make their way to the Supreme Court.

(See also CAPITALISM; FUNDAMENTAL RIGHTS.)

□ Lawrence Friedman, *The Republic of Choice, Law, Authority, and Culture* (1990). Herbert Hovenkamp, "The Political Economy of Substantive Due Process," *Stanford Law Review* 40 (1988): 379–447. William E. Nelson, *The Fourteenth Amendment* (1988). Michael J. Phillips, "Another Look at Economic Substantive Due Process," *Wisconsin Law Review* (1987): 265–324.

Peter Charles Hoffer

**Due Process Revolution.** See HISTORY OF THE COURT: RIGHTS CONSCIOUSNESS IN CONTEMPORARY SOCIETY; WARREN, EARL.

**Duncan v. Kahanamoku,** 327 U.S. 304 (1946), argued 7 Dec. 1945, decided 25 Feb. 1946 by vote of 6 to 2; Black for the Court, Murphy and Stone concurring, Burton and Frankfurter in dissent, Jackson absent. The *Duncan* case is often associated with the Japanese exclusion cases (*Hirabayashi* v. *United States*, 1943; *Korematsu* v. *United States*, 1944; and *Ex parte Endo*, 1944) because it involved wartime curtailment of fundamental civil liberties under the aegis of military authority.

After the attack on Pearl Harbor by Japanese naval forces on 7 December 1941, Hawaii's territorial governor, Joseph B. Poindexter, acting under the authority of the territorial Organic Act of 1900, suspended the writ of *habeas corpus, placed Hawaii under martial law, and relinquished civilian gubernatorial and judicial authority to U.S. Army General Walter C. Short. On the next day, General Short created military tribunals that had power to try civilians for offenses against federal or territorial law and for violation of orders of the military government he had established. He closed all civil courts. This regime of military authority was terminated in October 1944.

In an appeal by two civilians tried by military tribunals, Justice Hugo *Black, in a cautiously circumscribed opinion, held that the Organic Act's authorization of martial law did not include the power to supplant civilian courts with military tribunals. Black drew extensively on English and American history to support civilian supremacy over the military. But he carefully avoided constitutional issues raised by the creation of military government, confining himself to statutory construction.

(See also MILITARY TRIALS AND MARTIAL LAW.)

William M. Wiecek

**Duncan v. Louisiana,** 391 U.S. 145 (1968), argued 17 Jan. 1968, decided 20 May 1968 by vote of 7 to 2; White for the Court, Black, Douglas, and Fortas concurring, Harlan, joined by Stewart, in dissent. Duncan was convicted of misdemeanor battery without benefit of a jury and sentenced to sixty days in jail and a fine of $150. The crime was punishable by a maximum of two years in prison and a $300 fine. Duncan was denied a jury trial because the Louisiana Constitution required juries only in capital cases or where imprisonment at hard labor could be imposed. His appeal to the United States Supreme Court claimed a *Sixth Amendment right to a jury trial, although the Court had not yet incorporated that portion of the *Bill of Rights into the *Fourteenth Amendment.

According to the majority, the test for selective incorporation was whether the right under consideration was "fundamental." In earlier cases a right qualified as fundamental only if a civilized system could not be imagined without it. However, under the new and prevailing test, if history indicated that a procedural right found in the Bill of Rights was an integral part of the "Anglo-American regime of ordered liberty," it was deemed fundamental (see FUNDAMENTAL RIGHTS).

Justice Byron *White's opinion argued that the right to trial by jury had enjoyed such an uninterrupted history and, consequently, was to be incorporated "bag and baggage" into the due process clause of the Fourteenth Amendment and thus applied to the states. Duncan's conviction was reversed. The Court also denied Louisiana's claim that this was a petty offense that did not require a jury trial. The majority admitted that some minor offenses may not require a jury trial but left these petty offenses undefined. Justice Hugo *Black, joined by William *Douglas, concurred, arguing again the correctness of his total incorporation *dissent in *Adamson v. California (1947). Justice Abe *Fortas concurred but expressed grave doubts about imposing the federal model onto the states. Justice John *Harlan, joined by Potter *Stewart, dissented because he feared a further loss of state prerogatives.

(See also DUE PROCESS, PROCEDURAL; INCORPORATION DOCTRINE; TRIAL BY JURY.)

Charles H. Sheldon

**Duplex Printing Co. v. Deering,** 254 U.S. 443 (1921), argued 22 Jan. 1920, decided 3 Jan. 1921 by vote of 6 to 3; Pitney for the Court, Brandeis, Holmes, and Clarke in dissent. In response to growing public pressure to control the unprecedented concentrations of economic power that developed after the Civil War, Congress enacted the *Sherman Antitrust Act (1890). It proscribed "unlawful restraints and monopolies" in interstate commerce as well as conspiracies to erect them. Soon thereafter federal judges began to employ the measure to combat efforts to unionize workers and to deny labor its traditional self-help weapons. To counteract this "government by *injunction," Congress included in the Clayton Act (1914) provisions that sought to preclude application of antitrust legislation against organized labor.

The Supreme Court reached the issue in Deering, a six-judge majority holding that the Clayton Act did not insulate labor unions engaged in illegal activities, such as the conduct of a secondary boycott. Justice Mahlon *Pitney asserted that the machinist union's coercive action constituted an unlawful conspiracy to "obstruct and destroy" (p. 460) the interstate trade of complainant, a company with which they were not "proximately or substantially concerned" (p. 472). Writing for the three dissenters, Justice Louis D. *Brandeis charged the majority with ignoring law and reality: the injunction imposed by the Court deprived labor of forms of a collective action Congress had tried "expressly" to legalize (p. 486).

For more than a decade, the majority's narrow interpretation of the nation's antitrust legislation sanctioned judicial application of injunctions against workers seeking to organize to advance their interests. With the dramatic transformation of opinion brought about by the Great Depression, Congress included in the Norris-LaGuardia Act (1932) provisions to exempt organized labor from antitrust injunctions, and the Supreme Court legitimated this fundamental *New Deal legislation.

(See also ANTITRUST; LABOR.)

Stephen B. Wood

**Duvall, Gabriel** (b. Prince Georges County, Md., 6 Dec. 1752; d. Prince Georges County, 6 March 1844; interred at family estate, Glen Dale, Prince Georges County); associate justice, 1811–1835. Although he held the office for almost twenty-five years, Duvall is one of the least important justices ever to serve on the U.S. Supreme Court. Born into an affluent Huguenot family in Maryland, Duvall was well educated, trained in the law, and admitted to the bar in 1778. He married Mary Bryce on 24 July 1787, and after her death three years later he married Jane Gibbon on 5 May 1795; she died in 1834.

Duvall strongly supported the movement for independence and for the next quarter of a century held a number of important state positions. He was selected to be a delegate to the Constitutional Convention in Philadelphia in 1787, but for unknown reasons, he declined to serve. In 1796 he became chief justice of the General Court of Maryland. He also was a supporter of Thomas *Jefferson during the 1790s, serving in Congress and helping to organize the

*Gabriel Duvall*

state for the Democratic-Republicans in the election of 1800. In 1802 Jefferson appointed him the first comptroller of the United States Treasury.

President James *Madison appointed Duvall to the Supreme Court in 1811 as a replacement for Samuel *Chase, also from Maryland. In his constitutional decisions, Duval invariably supported John *Marshall and Joseph *Story, even following the chief justice in his dissent in *Ogden v. Saunders (1827). The only important case in which Duvall did not go along with Marshall was in *Dartmouth College v. Woodward (1819), but his reasons are unknown; the record only indicates that he dissented without an opinion. He did, however, write knowledgeable and able opinions in a number of minor cases involving commercial and maritime law.

Duvall had strong antislavery leanings (see SLAVERY). He disagreed with a Supreme Court ruling in Mima Queen and Child v. Hepburn (1813), which excluded hearsay evidence from a case in which two blacks claimed they were free. Duvall argued "that the reason for admitting hearsay evidence upon a question of freedom is much stronger than in the case of pedigrees or in controversies relative to the boundaries of land. It will be universally admitted that the right to freedom is more important than the right to property" (pp. 298–299).

In his old age, Duvall, who was sickly and deaf, was something of an embarrassment to the Court. Despite his condition he delayed his resignation for nearly a decade until it became clear that President Andrew *Jackson intended Roger B. *Taney, a fellow Marylander, to be Marshall's successor as chief justice (see DISABILITY OF JUSTICES).

□ Irving, Dillard, "Gabriel Duvall," in The Justices of the United States Supreme Court (1780–1969), edited by Leon Friedman and Fred L. Israel, vol. 1 (1969), pp. 419–429.

Richard E. Ellis

# E

**E. C. Knight Co., United States v.,** 156 U.S. 1 (1895), argued 24 Oct. 1894, decided 21 Jan. 1895 by vote of 8 to 1; Fuller for the Court, Harlan in dissent. In early 1892, the American Sugar Refining Company, the corporate successor to the Sugar Trust, acquired all of the stock of its leading competitors. The company thereby secured control of almost all sugar refining in the United States, and the federal government soon filed a civil challenge under the newly enacted *Sherman Antitrust Act of 1890.

In its first decision interpreting the act, the Supreme Court affirmed the lower court's dismissal of the government's suit. Chief Justice Melville W. *Fuller declared that the key question was whether a monopoly of manufacturing could be suppressed under the Sherman Act. He stressed the power of each state to protect the lives, health, property, and morals of its citizens, and noted that this power encompassed the regulation of practical monopolies within the state's borders. In Fuller's view, while the Constitution granted Congress exclusive authority to regulate activities that constituted commerce among the several states, activities not belonging to interstate or foreign commerce fell exclusively within the jurisdiction of state *police power.

The Court conceded that the ability to control the manufacture of an article involved simultaneous control over the article's subsequent disposition in interstate commerce and further agreed that combinations to control manufacturing might tend to restrain interstate trade. The Court declared, however, that this was an insufficient basis for congressional regulation because these were not direct but merely indirect or incidental effects on interstate commerce. The Court insisted upon a sharp distinction between manufacturing and commerce and stated that a producer's intention to distribute its products in other states subsequent to their manufacture provided no basis for the exercise of congressional Commerce Clause power. If indirect effects on interstate commerce could justify a federal challenge to the sale of manufacturing stock and the acquisition of refineries, the Court declared, Congress would have sweeping power to regulate the details of not only manufacturing but of "every branch of human industry" (p. 14) whenever ultimate interstate distribution was contemplated. The states simultaneously would be denied any police power authority over these matters within their own borders. The Court declared that Congress had framed the Sherman Act in the light of these "well-settled principles" (p. 16) and that the government's suit therefore exceeded the scope of the act.

Justice John Marshall *Harlan dissented. He believed that the Sherman Act constitutionally could reach combinations like the one challenged in this case. Harlan declared that such dominating combinations had the object and ability to control not only manufacturing but also the price at which manufactured goods were sold in interstate commerce and therefore should be deemed to affect interstate commerce directly. Accordingly, he believed, Congress could seek to remove such combinations because they constituted unreasonable restraints of interstate trade. In Harlan's view, if Congress was not empowered to deal with such threatening interstate combinations, Americans would be left unprotected because individual states would not have sufficient power to control them effectively.

Scholars have differed concerning the origins and impact of the Court's decision. Some scholars, for example, see the decision as largely the product of a politically conservative Court majority fearful of extensions of federal government power. In recent years, an increasingly prominent alternative view has been that the majority genuinely sought to preserve substantial state regulatory authority over the in-state operations of corporations in the ultimately unrealized expectation that the states would use those powers effectively to block monopolistic combinations.

Some maintain that the Court's decision helped pave the way for the great merger waves that began in the late 1890s, which dramatically increased the levels of economic concentration in the United States. Yet the Court strongly supported the application of the Sherman Act in a series of other major cases soon after the *Knight* case was decided. Doctrinally, the Court's limited conception of the scope of federal commerce authority, and particularly its direct-indirect effects test, retained validity until the late 1930s, when it was finally rejected by the Court in favor of a much more expansive view of federal power.

(See also ANTITRUST; COMMERCE POWER.)

□ Charles W. McCurdy, "The *Knight* Sugar Decision of 1895 and the Modernization of American Corporation Law, 1869–1903," *Business History Review* 53 (1979): 304–342.                                    James May

**Edelman v. Jordan,** 415 U.S. 651 (1974), argued 12 Dec. 1973, decided 25 Mar. 1974 by vote of 5 to 4; Rehnquist for the Court, Douglas, Brennan, and Marshall (joined by Blackmun) in dissent. As interpreted by the Supreme Court, the *Eleventh Amendment generally prohibits suits against a state in the federal courts, without its consent, by citizens of that state or of other states. *Edelman* v. *Jordan* concerns the scope of exceptions to that prohibition.

John Jordan filed a *class-action lawsuit against several Illinois state and county officials (in effect, against the state), arguing that they were administering federal aid under aged, blind, or disabled programs in violation of the *Fourteenth Amendment and of federal regulations by initiating payments later than was required by federal law. A federal district court found the state rules to violate federal regulations and ordered retroactive payments to individuals whose rights had been violated.

On appeal, the state officials argued that ordering retroactive payments was barred by the Eleventh Amendment. The court of appeals ruled against them, but the Supreme Court reversed its decision. The Court held that participation by Illinois in the federal program did not constitute a waiver of its Eleventh Amendment immunity to suits. It also held that a 1908

decision, *Ex parte *Young,* which allowed suits against states to obtain *injunctions affecting their future policies, did not extend to suits for retroactive payments by a state. The dissenters attacked both these holdings.

The impact of *Edelman* has been limited by more recent decisions that allow Congress to overcome the immunity of states from lawsuits through its powers to enforce the Fourteenth Amendment (*Fitzpatrick* v. *Bitzer,* 1976) and to regulate commerce (*Pennsylvania* v. *Union Gas Co.,* 1989). Because of the breadth of those powers, these decisions significantly narrow state immunity.

(See also STATE SOVEREIGNTY AND STATES' RIGHTS.)

Lawrence Baum

**Edmonson v. Leesville Concrete Co.,** 111 S.Ct. 2077 (1991), argued 15 Jan. 1991, decided 3 June 1991 by vote of 6 to 3; Kennedy for the Court, O'Connor, Rehnquist, and Scalia in dissent.

Extending its decision in *Batson* v. *Kentucky* (1986), the Court held that potential jurors could not be peremptorily excluded from a federal jury on the basis of race in civil as well as criminal trials. Such exclusion, the Court held, violates the excluded juror's *Fifth Amendment rights. An opposing litigant has third-party standing to raise the excluded juror's rights in the opposing litigant's behalf. The *equal protection component of the Fifth Amendment applies even though the exclusion is effectuated by a private attorney or private party and not by the state itself. "If a government confers on a private body the power to choose the government's employees or officials," Justice Anthony *Kennedy held, "the private body will be bound by the constitutional mandate of race-neutrality" (p. 2085).

The dissenters, led by Justice Sandra Day *O'Connor, argued that "[n]ot everything that happens in a courtroom is *state action," and that the peremptory exclusion of civil jurors "is fundamentally a matter of private choice" not covered by the Fifth and *Fourteenth Amendments (p. 2089).

(See also DUE PROCESS, PROCEDURAL; RACE AND RACISM; TRIAL BY JURY.)

William Lasser

**Education.** The first compulsory education law was enacted in Massachusetts in 1852. For the next century public education was almost entirely governed by state statutes and constitutional provisions. Few disputes resulted in litigation, and those that did generally were resolved by state courts on relatively narrow grounds. The involvement of the United States Supreme Court in public school litigation was rare, accelerating only in the period after the Supreme Court's landmark decision in *Brown* v. *Board of Education* in 1954.

***Compulsory Schooling and Socialization.*** The constitutional framework for modern education cases was established in *Pierce* v. *Society of Sisters* (1925), *Meyer* v. *Nebraska* (1923), and *Farrington* v. *Tokushige* (1927). In *Pierce* the Court held that Oregon could not constitutionally require all parents of school-age children to send their offspring to public schools. Relying on substantive *due process and the natural rights of parents to raise their children, the Court, while recognizing the legitimacy of compulsory attendance laws, held that the private school alternative may not be abolished. *Pierce* has never been repudiated by the Court, though some commentators argue that it would rest today more persuasively on *First Amendment grounds. They maintain that a state monopoly over elementary and secondary education would present a danger of indoctrinating youth to particular beliefs, thereby undermining the ability of citizens to formulate and articulate their own points of view. The *"Pierce* compromise" requires the state to allow parents to choose private schools, but it does not require the state to defray the additional costs of such schooling.

*Meyer* and *Farrington* shed additional light on *Pierce*. In those cases, the Court held that the states may not regulate private education in such an intrusive manner as to convert private schools into public schools in all but name. The state must allow private schools a reasonable latitude in shaping the curriculum.

The Court has recognized only one limited exception to the proposition that all children may be required to attend public school or a reasonably regulated private school. In *Wisconsin* v. *Yoder* (1972) the Court held that a Wisconsin law, requiring all children to attend public or private school until age sixteen, violated the First Amendment's Free Exercise Clause as applied to Amish parents and children (see RELIGION). The Amish believed that public high schools introduced their children to modern values that were antithetical to their religious beliefs. Balancing this free exercise claim against the state's interests in preparing all children for adult *citizenship, nurturing economic self-sufficiency, and stamping out ignorance, the Court held that minimal education after age fourteen (or the eighth grade) was sufficient to achieve the state's objectives.

Taken together these cases stand for the proposition that there are constitutional limits to the state's role in socializing children in private and public schools. With respect to private schools, the Court has held that state support of parochial schools violates the Establishment of Religion Clause of the First Amendment unless the funding has a clear secular purpose, the primary effect is not to advance religion, and there is no excessive entanglement between church and state (*Lemon* v. *Kurtzman*, 1971; *Committee for Public Education & Religious Liberty* v. *Nyquist*, 1973). While parents have the constitutional right to seek to inculcate religion in private schools, state

financial support of that inculcation violates the constitutional ban on establishment of religion.

The application of the Establishment Clause to a multitude of state efforts to channel funds to parochial schools has been chaotic. For example, in *Wolman* v. *Walter* (1977) the Court disapproved of public funding for transportation for field trips and the loan of instructional materials although it had previously approved the provision of funds for bus fares and the loaning of textbooks (*Everson* v. *Board of Education*, 1947; *Board of Education* v. *Allen*, 1968). In *Committee for Public Education and Religious Liberty* v. *Regan* (1980), the Court permitted state subsidies to private religious schools for particular secular programs (testing and taking attendance), while in *Mueller* v. *Allen* (1983) Justice William H. *Rehnquist suggested that benefits to parents of children in public and private schools (tax deductions for tuition, transportation, and textbook expenses) did not impermissibly advance religion despite the *Nyquist* decision.

In the public sphere, the Court has held that it is unconstitutional for public schools to seek to indoctrinate students to religion, though teachers may teach about religion in its historical and social context. *School prayer and some forms of moments of silence are not permissible (*Abington School District* v. *Schempp*, 1963; *Wallace* v. *Jaffree*, 1985), and a state may not require the teaching of creationism or a balanced curriculum between creationism and evolution (*Epperson* v. *Arkansas*, 1968; *Edwards* v. *Aguillard*, 1987). In this context, the Establishment Clause acts as a substantive limitation on the messages that public schools may convey to students. Conversely, lower courts have held that curricula and textbooks emphasizing secular values do not constitute an unconstitutional establishment of a religion or a violation of the Free Exercise Clause (*Smith* v. *Board of School Commissioners*, 1987; *Mozert* v. *Hawkins County Board of Education*, 1987).

***Student Rights.*** There are numerous Supreme Court cases, mostly decided under the speech clause of the First Amendment, bearing on the question of the constitutional limits on socialization in public schools. The earliest case is *West Virginia Board of Education* v. *Barnette* (1943), in which the Court held that students may not be compelled to salute the flag and to affirm beliefs that they do not hold. Public school officials have a legitimate interest in educating students to their citizenship responsibilities and the political culture (*Ambach* v. *Norwick*, 1979), but *Barnette* limits the means of accomplishing these objectives.

In 1969 the Court, reacting to the assertion of students' civil rights during the Vietnam era protests, held in *Tinker* v. *Des Moines Independent Community School District* that "state-operated schools may not be enclaves of totalitarianism" (p. 511). Students may engage in expressive activities on campus so long as school authorities cannot reasonably forecast that "substantial disruption" of school activities will result (p. 513). The students' right of expression is limited by the state's legitimate interest in carrying on its educational functions.

The *Tinker* standard is not applicable to vulgar or offensive speech (*Bethel School District* v. *Fraser*, 1986). And, while *Tinker* protects the personal expression of students, it does not protect their speech within curricular activities—for example, the articles they write as staff members of a school newspaper operated as a part of the curriculum (*Hazelwood School District* v. *Kuhlmeier*, 1988). *Tinker* also does not apply to the expressive activities of the school itself. For example, a majority of the justices appear to embrace the proposition that library books may be removed for good faith educational reasons, including efforts to eliminate vulgar or obscene books, but school officials may not do so if their purpose is to impose an official orthodoxy or ideology (*Board of Education* v. *Pico*, 1982).

*Due Process Protections.* The Supreme Court has afforded due process protection (e.g., hearings) to suspended or expelled students and held that the *Fourth Amendment limits the methods that school officials may use to gather evidence of infractions (*Goss* v. *Lopez*, 1975; *New Jersey* v. *T.L.O.*, 1985). Due process guarantees, however, run only to disciplinary sanctions and not to academic decisions such as grades (*Board of Curators* v. *Horowitz*, 1979; *Regents of University of Michigan* v. *Ewing*, 1985). (See DUE PROCESS, PROCEDURAL.)

*Equality of Opportunity.* In *Brown* v. *Board of Education* (1954), the *Equal Protection Clause of the *Fourteenth Amendment was construed as forbidding the deliberate assignment of students by race to segregated public schools (see SEGREGATION, DE JURE; SEPARATE BUT EQUAL). Once such discrimination has been found there is an obligation to take affirmative steps to eliminate the vestiges of such discrimination and to establish a unitary school system (*Green* v. *County School Board of New Kent County*, 1968). Neighborhood assignment of school children, resulting in continued segregation of the races, is impermissible if it is still tainted by prior acts of discrimination (*Swann* v. *Charlotte-Mecklenburg Board of Education*, 1971). Unless there is evidence of interdistrict violations, the *desegregation remedy is limited to the specific school district implicated in the wrongs, and metropolitan remedies are not permissible (*Milliken* v. *Bradley*, 1974). The typical remedy seeks to achieve racial balance in the schools in the district. The district must comply, in good faith, with the desegregation order for a reasonable period of time before the decree may be dissolved (*Oklahoma City Board of Education* v. *Dowell*, 1991).

The Court has construed the Equal Protection Clause as placing a substantial burden of proof on school authorities to demonstrate the necessity of discrimination by sex or gender (*Mississippi University for Women* v. *Hogan*, 1982). This constitutional approach is bolstered by Title IX of the Education Amendments Act of 1972, prohibiting many forms of sex discrimination in public schools.

In *San Antonio Independent School District* v. *Rodriguez* (1973), the Court held that education is not a fundamental interest under the Equal Protection Clause and that discrimination based on the wealth of the school district in which a student attends school is not a suspect classification. It upheld state school financing plans that result in unequal expenditures per student because of the varying local property tax bases of school districts. A denial of all educational opportunities, based on an absolute inability to afford a tuition charge made by a school district, however, is a violation of equal protection (*Plyler* v. *Doe*, 1982).

(See also FUNDAMENTAL RIGHTS; POLICE POWER.)

□ Tyll van Geel, *The Courts and American Education Law* (1987). Richard Kluger, *Simple Justice* (1977). Mark G. Yudof, *When Government Speaks* (1983). Mark G. Yudof, David L. Kirp, and Betsy Levin, *Educational Policy and the Law*, 3d ed. (1992).                          Mark G. Yudof

**Edwards v. California**, 314 U.S. 160 (1941), argued 28 Apr. 1941, reargued 21 Oct. 1941, decided 24 Nov. 1941 by vote of 9 to 0; Byrnes for the Court, Douglas and Jackson concurring. The Supreme Court has long recognized a constitutional right to travel, even though the source of the right remains obscure. The Court upheld this right, even though further obscuring its source, in *Edwards* v. *California*.

In *Edwards*, the Court relied on the Commerce Clause of Article I, section 8 to invalidate a California statute, popularly known as the "Okie Law" (see COMMERCE POWER). The statute prohibited a person from bringing any nonresident indigent person into California. The Court held that the transportation of persons constituted commerce within the meaning of the clause. The Court suggested in dicta that it would not accept stereotypical judgments about the poor as justification for laws discriminating against them. Justice Robert H. *Jackson, concurring, urged the Court to hold that interstate travel is a privilege of U.S. *citizenship and that the statute violated the *Privileges and Immunities Clause of the *Fourteenth Amendment. Jackson argued that a person's property status should not be used by a state to qualify one's rights as a citizen of the United States.

The legacy of *Edwards* is twofold. First, it strengthened the constitutional right of travel. Second, it foreshadowed later court decisions that voided statutes discriminating against the poor.

(See also INDIGENCY; TRAVEL, RIGHT TO.)

Patrick M. Garry

246 □ Edwards v. South Carolina

**Edwards v. South Carolina,** 372 U.S. 229 (1963), argued 13 Dec. 1962, decided 25 Feb. 1963 by vote of 8 to 1; Stewart for the Court, Clark in dissent. *Edwards* was a \*"time, place, and manner" case in which the Supreme Court, reversing the convictions of civil rights demonstrators, established the principle that the Due Process Clause of the \*Fourteenth Amendment, which incorporates the provisions of the \*First Amendment, does not permit a state to make criminal the peaceful expression of unpopular views.

Approximately two hundred African-American high school and college students walked in groups of fifteen from a church in Columbia, South Carolina, to the grounds of the state capitol, an area normally open to the public. Their purpose in visiting this traditional public forum was to protest discrimination against blacks and to seek repeal of the laws that produced unequal treatment. Three dozen law enforcement officers were on the capitol grounds when the demonstrators arrived. They informed the students of their right to be peacefully present there. For the better part of an hour, the demonstrators walked through the grounds in an orderly fashion carrying placards expressing their pride in being black and their opposition to \*segregation. During this time, a crowd of two hundred to three hundred curious, but nonhostile, onlookers gathered at the periphery of the capitol grounds. Police protection at all times was adequate to meet any foreseeable possibility of disorder.

Nonetheless, the police informed the students that they would be arrested if they did not disperse within fifteen minutes. The students commenced to sing "The Star Spangled Banner" and other patriotic and religious songs. When fifteen minutes expired, the students were arrested and their conviction for common law breach of the peace was upheld by the South Carolina Supreme Court.

(See also ASSEMBLY AND ASSOCIATION, FREE-
DOM OF; RACE AND RACISM; SPEECH AND THE PRESS.)

Harold J. Spaeth

**Eichman, United States v.,** 496 U.S. 310 (1990), argued 14 May 1990, decided 11 June 1990 by vote of 5 to 4; Brennan for the Court, Rehnquist, White, Stevens, and O'Connor in dissent. *United States* v. *Eichman* involved two consolidated appeals by the United States in cases in which appellees had been prosecuted for publicly burning American flags in violation of the 1989 Flag Protection Act. This law prohibited the knowing mutilation, defacement, physical defilement, burning of, or trampling on any American flag. Two U.S. district courts ruled the act unconstitutional, based on the Supreme Court's ruling in *Texas* v. *Johnson* (1989). *Johnson* had declared unconstitutional a Texas statute that prohibited knowing desecration of venerated objects in a manner that "the actor knows will seriously

offend one or more persons" (p. 400). Texas had applied the statute to a person who had burned an American flag during a protest at the Republican national convention in Dallas in 1984. Indeed, Congress passed the Flag Protection Act in order to give the Supreme Court an opportunity to reconsider its *Johnson* ruling.

In *Johnson,* Justice William \*Brennan found Texas's statute invalid because Texas's interest in preserving the flag as a symbol of nationhood was integrally related to the state's disagreement with the message conveyed. The law became operative "only when a person's treatment of the flag communicates some message" (pp. 12–13). This basis for state action violated the central \*First Amendment tenet that political speech may not be abridged simply because of its content, however controversial. Texas's law went beyond a mere \*"time, place, and manner" regulation, which is directed at only the "incidental effects" of expressive conduct, such as excessive noise or unsafe conduct, rather than the message, per se. Accordingly, the Supreme Court applied the strictest standard of review to the law, rather than the more deferential standard that governs restrictions relating only to incidental effects. (*U.S.* v. *O'Brien,* 1968).

In *Eichman,* however, the government contended that the Flag Protection Act was not directed at offensive expressive conduct, but rather at all forms of flag mistreatment. The law did not single out "offensive" forms of mistreatment, as had Texas's law. Thus, the United States maintained that the act should not be subject to the most exacting constitutional scrutiny.

The Supreme Court disagreed: "Although the Flag Protection Act contains no explicit content-based limitation on the scope of prohibited conduct, it is nevertheless clear that the Government's asserted interest is 'related to the suppression of free expression' " (p. 2408). Justice Brennan intimated that a majority of the Court would construe virtually any law directed at forms of flag desecration as constitutionally suspect, for such laws are inescapably linked to government's disapproval of the message conveyed.

In dissent, Justice John Paul \*Stevens maintained that the Flag Protection Act and similar laws are consistent with the First Amendment. First, they leave protestors with ample alternative means of conveying their ideas, so the impact on free \*speech is minimal. Second, they are more neutral concerning the specific content of speech than the majority alleged. "The flag uniquely symbolizes the ideas of liberty, equality, and tolerance . . . the message thereby transmitted [by the flag] does not take a stand upon our disagreements, except to say that those disagreements are best regarded as competing interpretations of shared ideals" (p. 2411).

*Eichman* reaffirmed the Court's commitment to protecting extremely provocative expression.

Donald A. Downs

**Eighteenth Amendment.** The only amendment to the Constitution to be repealed subsequently, the Eighteenth Amendment prohibited "the manufacture, sale, or transportation of intoxicating liquors within, the importation thereof into, or the exportation thereof from the United States and all territory subject to the jurisdiction thereof for beverage purposes." Commonly referred to as national prohibition, the Eighteenth Amendment was adopted by bipartisan majorities in excess of two-thirds in each house of Congress in December 1917, ratified by three-fourths of the states as of 16 January 1919, put into effect on 17 January 1920, and, after more than a decade of controversy, overturned by equally lopsided margins when the *Twenty-first Amendment was ratified on 5 December 1933.

National prohibition was the product of a century-long, broad-based temperance crusade. After voluntary abstinence campaigns sharply reduced American alcohol consumption, antebellum temperance advocates sought legal bans on liquor to extend the benefits of abstinence. During the 1850s a dozen states briefly adopted prohibition laws. From the 1880s to *World War I, local option laws and statewide prohibition spread. Encouraged by this success, a coalition of church groups, feminists, social and political reformers, and businessmen, all of whom believed in the benefits of a dry society, began calling for a total, seemingly permanent national solution, constitutional prohibition.

Senators, reluctant to vote for the prohibition amendment but afraid to vote against it, required ratification within seven years. They calculated that this innovation would thwart ratification but were proved mistaken: forty-four state legislatures ratified within thirteen months. By 1922 every state but Rhode Island had ratified. A 1919 Ohio referendum overturning ratification was invalidated by the Supreme Court in *Hawke* v. *Smith* (1920) but fostered an impression that the amendment lacked popular support.

Opponents also bore responsibility for another distinctive feature of the amendment: a one-year delay in its taking effect to cushion the blow to the liquor industry. Nevertheless, prohibition devastated the previously legal manufacturing, distribution, and retail liquor business, the seventh largest industry in the country. In two centuries of constitutional development only the *Thirteenth Amendment, ending *slavery, had a greater impact on *property rights.

The Eighteenth Amendment specified that state and federal governments would have *concurrent power to enforce prohibition. In 1919 Congress, overriding Woodrow Wilson's veto, adopted the Volstead Act to provide for federal enforcement and define as intoxicating any beverage containing more than .5 percent alcohol. The ban on beer and wine was unexpected and controversial. In the *National Prohibition Cases* (1920), the Supreme Court quickly rejected a variety of challenges to the constitutionality of the amendment. Thereafter the Court sought to aid its implementation by treating *concurrent power expansively in *United States* v. *Lanza* (1922), upholding warrantless automobile searches in *Carroll* v. *United States* (1925), restricting medicinal liquor prescriptions in *Lambert* v. *Yellowley* (1926), and permitting telephone surveillance by means of off-premises wiretapping in *Olmstead* v. *United States* (1928). Nevertheless, popular resistance and organized opposition to national prohibition grew until, in 1933, the Twenty-first Amendment repealed what Herbert Hoover once called "an experiment noble in motive."

(See also CONSTITUTIONAL AMENDMENTS.)

□ Jack S. Blocker, Jr., *American Temperance Movements: Cycles of Reform* (1989).           David E. Kyvig

**Eighth Amendment.** Adopted in 1791 as part of the *Bill of Rights, the Eighth Amendment was inspired by language from the English Bill of Rights (1689). It declares: "Excessive *bail shall not be required, nor excessive fines imposed, nor *cruel and unusual punishments inflicted." These three clauses provide the only substantive federal constitutional limits on the severity of permissable sanctions in criminal justice.

The Court has done little to interpret "excessive fines," declaring that it would overrule a lower court only if the fine was "so grossly excessive as to amount to a deprivation of property without due process of law" (*Waters-Pierce Oil Co.* v. *Texas (No. 1)*, 1909, p. 86).

Regarding "excessive bail," the Court has ruled that bail must not be so heavy as to exceed the capacity of the defendant to pay; yet it may be set sufficiently high as to guarantee a person's appearance for trial at a later date (*Stack* v. *Boyle*, 1951). Recently the Court has upheld statutes allowing trial judges to jail an arrestee without bail if the arrestee is believed to be dangerous to certain persons even though he or she has not yet been convicted of any crime (*U.S.* v. *Salerno*, 1987).

The clause prohibiting "cruel and unusual punishments" has been by far the most important of the three constraints imposed by the Eighth Amendment. Since *Weems* v. *U.S.* (1910), the Court has held several different kinds of punishments to be objectionable under this clause, including *capital punishments for certain nonhomicidal crimes and even for murder if "arbitrarily" administered.

(See also CONSTITUTIONAL AMENDMENTS.)

H. A. Bedau

**Eisenstadt v. Baird,** 405 U.S. 438 (1972), argued 17–18 Nov. 1971, decided 22 Mar. 1972 by vote of 6 to 1; Brennan for the Court, Burger in dissent, Powell and Rehnquist not participating. This case expanded the right of privacy articulated in *Griswold* v. *Connecticut* (1965).

*Griswold* had invalidated a Connecticut law banning the use of *contraceptives by married couples (see MARRIAGE). *Eisenstadt* held that a Massachusetts ban on the distribution of contraceptives to unmarried individuals was equally unpermissible. "If the right of privacy means anything," Justice William Brennan wrote, "it is the right of the *individual,* married or single, to be free from unwarranted governmental intrusion into matters so fundamentally affecting a person as the decision whether to bear or beget a child" (p. 453).

Massachusetts law made it a felony for anyone to distribute contraceptives to unmarried persons. The law allowed contraceptives to be distributed only to married couples and only by registered doctors and pharmacists. The Court held that the distinction between married and unmarried persons violated the *Equal Protection Clause of the *Fourteenth Amendment and that the statute was not a legitimate health measure since it was both discriminatory and overbroad and since other laws already regulated the distribution of unsafe drugs.

At issue was William Baird's conviction for giving away Emko Vaginal Foam to a woman after a lecture on birth control and overpopulation at Boston University. Baird was not an authorized distributor of contraceptives. Justice Byron *White concurred, arguing that a legitimate health interest would have been raised if Baird had not distributed a form of contraception requiring a prescription. Chief Justice Warren *Burger dissented, saying that a legitimate health interest already existed.

(See also PRIVACY.)

John Anthony Maltese

**Elections.** The American political system is one of representative democracy. Such a government requires a process, held at more or less regular intervals, through which the populace may choose its representative policy-makers. Elections constitute the mechanism by which government is held publicly accountable, thus assuring that the will of the people is carried out. The franchise offers a forum for public participation in political decision-making, legitimizing the state's authority to make policy and exercise coercive power. Without the right to the franchise, all other rights are illusory, subject only to the whim of those who control governmental power.

The Constitution, by its own terms, mandates popular elections only for members of Congress. Article I, section 2 provides that members of the House of Representatives shall be elected by the people of the respective states. The *Seventeenth Amendment, ratified in 1913, provides similarly for the election of senators. Other amendments have expanded the scope of the polity generally. The *Fifteenth Amendment prohibits the states from impairing the franchise on the basis of race, color, or previous condition of servitude. The

*Nineteenth Amendment forbids discrimination in electoral qualification based on sex, and the *Twenty-fourth Amendment prevents the state from imposing "any poll or other tax" as a condition of voting for a federal office (see POLL TAX). The *Twenty-sixth Amendment effectively grants the right to vote to all eligible citizens at eighteen years of age. As a constitutional matter, the president is not elected popularly but, according to Article II, section 1, by an electoral college made up of state delegations equal in number to the sum of each state's senators and representatives and elected on the basis of state law.

During the modern era, the issue of reapportionment and the impact of the Fourteenth Amendment have led to the constitutionalization of virtually all elections (see REAPPORTIONMENT CASES). Until the 1960s, courts were reluctant to interfere in the political task of apportionment. Because the first half of the twentieth century had witnessed great changes in the distribution of the population, epitomized by a migration from rural to urban communities, the judicial finding that apportionment was a nonjusticiable *"political question" allowed political intransigence to leave unrectified enormous disparities in the number of voters in different districts. The effect was an extreme dilution of the impact of the franchise in urban communities, significantly the residence of an increasing proportion of the nation's ethnic and racial minorities.

In *Baker* v. *Carr* (1962), a case that Chief Justice Earl Warren would later recollect as the most significant decision during his judicial tenure, the Court held *justiciable a Fourteenth Amendment attack on legislative malapportionment. Only two years later in *Reynolds* v. *Sims* (1964), it declared the right to vote a *"fundamental right" under the Fourteenth Amendment and adopted a "one man, one vote" standard for constitutional apportionment (see ONE PERSON, ONE VOTE). Many of the critics who had heralded the Court's opinion in *Baker* blasted the *Reynolds* decision, which allowed for only majority-rule elections, as bad political theory. "Madisonian democracy," unlike majoritarian democracy, they argued, was to be based on interest politics—the complex politics of group bargaining that considered the measure of intensity surrounding an issue, the lobbying ability of various groups, the effect of party loyalties, and the rights of minority groups. Unwilling to enter this political morass, the Court chose instead a simple head-counting procedure that required little beyond a cold statistical record. Representation was to be closely based upon population unless a legitimate state objective demanded otherwise.

Early reapportionment cases left unclear the types of legislatures covered by the one person, one vote rule, the degree of mathematical equality required among districts, and the types of state policy that could justify deviations from mathematical equality. The Court did make clear that its equal population rule applied to both houses of a bicameral state legislature (*Maryland Committee for Fair Representation* v. *Tawes*, 1964) and that the burden of justifying deviations from the equal population standard lay with the state (*Lucas* v. *Forty-Fourth Colorado General Assembly*, 1964). Some were dismayed that the Court would hold unconstitutional the very accommodation of majoritarianism and territoriality enshrined in the Constitution's formulation of Congress. The *Reynolds* Court, however, rejected the federal legislative analogy, stressing that while the states had once been fully sovereign, subdivisions such as counties and cities had—and were—not.

For some time the relevance of the mathematical equality rule to local governments remained unclear. Finally, in *Avery* v. *Midland County* (1968) and, more explicitly, in *Hadley* v. *Junior College District* (1970), the Court extended the *Reynolds* rule to any election—whether federal, state, or local—where the "government decides to select persons by a popular election to perform governmental functions" (p. 56). It further refused to distinguish for purposes of the apportionment rule between elections for "legislative" and those for "administrative" officials. However, *Hadley* excepted from its holding the election of functionaries "whose duties are . . . far removed from normal governmental activities and . . . disproportionately affect different groups" (p. 56). Since *Hadley*, this exception for specialized local bodies has been applied only twice, both cases involving election of water district members. The Court found the districts' activities "so disproportionately" affected landowners as to release them from the demands of the *Reynolds* rule. Although this determination may be justified in the first of the two cases, *Salyer Land Co.* v. *Tulare Lake Basin Water Storage District* (1973), where the district's primary purpose was to provide for the acquisition, storage, and distribution of water for farming in the surrounding river basin, it is not as clearly appropriate in the second, *Ball* v. *James* (1981), in which the water district also generated and supplied electricity for hundreds of thousands of state residents—landowners and nonlandowners alike.

Even where the one person, one vote principle holds, courts must still consider how far an apportionment scheme may deviate from precise mathematical equality before it violates the Constitution. *Reynolds* emphasized that states were responsible to make an honest and good faith effort to construct districts "as nearly of equal population as is practicable" (p. 577). This strict equality standard has been unwaveringly applied in cases involving state apportionment of congressional districts. In *Kirkpatrick* v. *Preisler* (1969), for example, the Court struck down a districting plan where the discrepancy between the most and the least populous district was under 6 percent. Even such slight deviations were permissible only if they were unavoidable

despite good faith efforts to achieve absolute equality.

The *Kirkpatrick* decision did not clearly distinguish between state legislative and congressional districts. However, beginning with *Mahan* v. *Howell* (1973), the Court has made clear that there is considerably more leeway in apportioning state legislatures. In *Brown* v. *Thomson* (1983), for example, population disparities ranging up to 10 percent were deemed *de minimis*, not requiring state justification. Even disparities of more than 10 percent have been upheld when justified as furthering the goals of compactness, contiguity, and the preservation of political subdivisions. Although county and other political subdivision lines may be considered irrelevant to the determination of congressional districts because persons in Congress are not primarilly concerned with legislation that affects specific counties within a state, the same cannot be said of the actions of state legislators. States, therefore, may have greater legitimate reasons for wishing to keep voter groups in county or other political subdivisions when voting for state legislative positions and may also wish to guarantee representation to small counties so as to assure them legislative input on matters effecting them in unique ways.

Legislative districts, although mathematically consistent with Fourteenth Amendment standards, may still be attacked as a violation of *equal protection if they appear to obstruct fair representation by diluting the voting strength of an identifiable racial or ethnic minority or, perhaps, a particular political association. Two distinct apportionment practices most often have been questioned. First, apportionment plans sometimes provide that the residents of certain districts are to elect more than one representative. Such multimember or "at large" district plans may comply with the equal population rule, yet still function to exclude or submerge particular minority groups. The "winner-take-all" character of most elections creates the possibility that a specific majority will elect all of the representatives from a multimember district, whereas the outvoted minority might have been able to elect some representatives if the district had been broken down into several single member districts. The decision to use multimember districts can thus serve to eradicate the political voice of a minority. Second, apportionment plans often rely on *gerrymandering—the drawing of district lines so as to delimit the voting power of cognizable groups of voters. A majority might attempt to abridge or dilute the voting power of a minority by grouping minority voters disproportionately in one or a few districts, thus limiting minority impact to specific designated areas.

Despite recognizing the risk these practices pose to voter minorities, the Court in *Whitcomb* v. *Chavis* (1971) refused to hold multimember districts per se unconstitutional. Two years later, however, in *White* v. *Regester* (1973) the justices upheld a district court decision invalidating two multimember districts. The Court found that the plaintiffs had adequately proven, through an amalgam of historical and contemporary evidence, that African- and Mexican-Americans had been invidiously excluded from effective participation in political life. Left ambiguous was whether a claim of vote dilution could succeed under either the Fourteenth or Fifteenth Amendments without proving discriminatory intent. In 1980, *Mobile v. Bolden resolved this ambiguity by requiring specific proof of discriminatory intent for lawsuits brought under section 2 of the *Voting Rights Act of 1965.

Quickly, Congress, concerned that *Bolden's* evidentiary requirement might seriously retard the Voting Rights Act's effort to prevent racial discrimination in the franchise, amended section 2 to restore a predominantly effects standard. As amended, claimants need prove only that the challenged practice results in a denial of equal opportunity to participate in the political process and to elect candidates of their choice. The Court, interpreting the amended section 2 in *Thornburg v. Gingles* (1986), set forth a detailed legal standard for adjudicating such claims. Minority voters must demonstrate that the apportionment scheme "operates to minimize or cancel out their ability to elect their preferred candidates" (p. 48). This claim can be proved by showing that a "bloc voting majority [is] usually . . . able to defeat candidates supported by a politically cohesive, geographically insular minority group" (p. 49). The standard requires a court to find that significant racial bloc voting exists that has led to minorities suffering "substantial difficulty" in electing their preferred representative. Although proof of intent is not required, the evidentiary mandates remain complex. The Supreme Court recently has decided in *Chisom v. Roemer* (1991) that the Voting Rights Act's provisions encompass state judicial elections.

Much of the judicial involvement in the election process since *Baker* has been motivated by a felt need to protect minority ethnic and racial groups from legislative discrimination and ensure them a voice and presence in our legislative halls. Given the nation's history, such a concern is justifiable. The Court, however, has not appeared equally willing to confront vote dilution claims brought by members of political or ideological groups. Initially, the Court viewed political gerrymandering as simply politics as usual. Presumably, any legislative majority will choose, among otherwise equally acceptable districting maps, the one that gives the incumbent party the best chance to retain its majority position. Courts, thus, appeared unenthused about entering the thicket of political gerrymandering that might compel judges to determine the "proper balance" between rival political parties in the legislature.

Still, if one dominant political party can draw legislative districts so as to dilute greatly the representation of the minority party, individuals would have their voting power limited because of their political beliefs and associations. Since the legislature cannot grant or withhold other benefits on such a basis without violating both the guarantees of equal protection and freedom of association, so limiting the effective franchise is difficult to defend.

In *Davis v. Bandemer* (1986), the Court recognized this apparent inconsistency and ruled that claims of political gerrymandering were also justiciable under the *Equal Protection Clause. A majority, however, was not able to agree on the appropriate standard for deciding such claims. The most to be gleaned from the fractured Court opinions is that the mere disadvantaging of a political party in one or two elections is likely to be insufficient to constitute a successful constitutional attack.

*Bandemer,* like *Baker,* merely opens courts to hear claims of improper gerrymandering. However, behind *Baker* loomed the one person, one vote rule soon articulated in *Reynolds.* No comparable simple standard of review in the *Bandemer* context is readily apparent. Lower courts have been left with little guidance. One thing is clear: courts are likely to become even more deeply entangled in the political process as elections become more fully constitutionalized and thereby nationalized.

(See also FAIR REPRESENTATION; POLITICAL PARTIES; POLITICAL PROCESS; VOTE, RIGHT TO.)

□ Walter L. Carpeneti, "Legislative Apportionment: Multimember Districts and Fair Representation," *University of Pennsylvania Law Review* 120 (1972): 666–700. Armand Derfner, "Racial Discrimination and the Right to Vote," *Vanderbilt Law Review* 26 (1973): 523–584. "Developments in the Law—Elections," note in *Harvard Law Review* 88 (1975): 1111–1339. Ward E. Y. Elliott, *The Rise of Guardian Democracy: The Supreme Court's Role in Voting Rights Disputes, 1845–1969* (1975).

Stanley Ingber

**Eleventh Amendment** restricts the power of federal courts to hear suits against states brought by citizens of other states or by aliens. One of only two constitutional amendments adopted explicitly to repudiate a Supreme Court decision—the other being the *Sixteenth Amendment—the Eleventh Amendment overturned *Chisholm v. Georgia* (1793), which upheld the right of a citizen of one state to sue another state in an original action in the Supreme Court (see REVERSALS OF COURT DECISIONS BY AMENDMENT). Proposed by Congress on 4 March 1794, the amendment was ratified by the legislatures of the necessary three-fourths of the states by 7 February 1795 but was not formally declared part of the Constitution until a presidential message to Congress on 8 January 1798. Although the latter date is that traditionally given for the adoption of the Eleventh Amendment, it is now recognized that the president has no role in the process of amendment, so 1795 is gaining recognition as its effective date.

Despite its brevity—a mere forty-three words—the Eleventh Amendment has been cited as authority for an elaborate and perplexing body of jurisdictional rules. Although its obvious effect was to amend the Constitution, the Court in *Hans* v. *Louisiana* (1890) interpreted it as restating rather than altering the original understanding. Reconceptualized as a constitutional recognition of state *sovereign immunity, the Eleventh Amendment has been used to justify decisions extending far beyond its actual language.

The Eleventh Amendment denies federal courts the power to decide suits against states brought by two classes of plaintiffs: "Citizens of another State" and "Citizens or Subjects of any Foreign State." Although referring only to suits "in law or equity," the amendment (and its associated doctrine of state sovereign immunity) was held in *Ex parte New York* (1921) to apply as well to suits in *admiralty jurisdiction. In the landmark federal jurisdiction case *Hans* v. *Louisiana*, the Court extended the reach of the amendment by holding that citizens could not sue their own states in federal court. In *New Hampshire* v. *Louisiana* (1883), the Court held that one state could not sue another when it represented not its own interests but those of its citizens. Finally, in *Monaco* v. *Mississippi* (1934) the Court denied federal jurisdiction over suits against states brought by foreign sovereigns. In general, then, states cannot be sued in federal court by citizens of any state (their own included), by foreigners, or by foreign nations. In contrast, federal courts are open to suits against states brought by the United States or by other American states representing their own interests. In addition, state immunity to suit does not extend to political subdivisions of states, such as counties and towns, or to certain governmental entities.

Because restrictions on federal judicial power may threaten important national goals, the Eleventh Amendment and state sovereign immunity are subject to a number of significant exceptions. States may waive the amendment and consent to suit—this despite the general rule that parties may not confer jurisdiction on a court. Furthermore, Congress may create private causes of action against states by virtue of its enforcement powers under the *Fourteenth and *Fifteenth Amendments, pursuant to its powers under the Commerce Clause (see COMMERCE POWER), and perhaps in other cases. By far the most important restriction on state immunity, however, is the possibility of suit against state officers, which is in effect often a suit against the state itself. In the landmark case of *Ex parte* *Young* (1908), this exception to the Eleventh Amendment was explicitly approved when a state attempts unconstitutional action. Difficulties nonetheless remain: suits against state officers in which the remedy for past wrongs would be paid for out of the state treasury are still barred under the amendment (*Edelman* v. *Jordan,* 1974).

Complex, even inconsistent, the law of the Eleventh Amendment and state sovereign immunity seems ripe for restatement and simplification. The holding in *Hans* v. *Louisiana,* in particular, has been challenged, and the suggestion has been made that the amendment be confined to cases within *diversity jurisdiction, leaving the national courts open to suits against states by plaintiffs raising *federal questions. Some scholars have even suggested a return to a literal reading of the Eleventh Amendment. Until the law is renovated, however, citizens with grievances against states are confined to political action or lawsuits within the exceptions mentioned above.

(See also CONSTITUTIONAL AMENDMENTS; JUDICIAL POWER AND JURISDICTION.)

□ John V. Orth, *The Judicial Power of the United States: The Eleventh Amendment in American History* (1987).

John V. Orth

**Elfbrandt v. Russell,** 384 U. S. 11 (1966), argued 24 Feb. 1966, decided 18 Apr. 1966 by vote of 5 to 4; Douglas for the Court, White, Clark, Harlan, and Stewart in dissent. The issue in this case was the constitutionality of a loyalty oath for Arizona state employees. A legislative gloss interpreting the oath made it a violation knowingly to be a member of the Communist party or any other organization having as its purpose the violent overthrow of the state government. A violation would subject the employee to discharge and to prosecution for perjury. A school teacher contended that she did not understand the gloss since the statute provided no opportunity for a hearing. The state supreme court upheld the statute. On *certiorari, the U.S. Supreme Court remanded the case for consideration in light of *Baggett* v. *Bullitt* (1964). Again the state supreme court upheld the statute, and certiorari was again granted.

The legislative gloss, the Court said, could be interpreted to condemn a member of an organization that had both legal and illegal purposes even though that person did not subscribe to the illegal purposes. This, the Court concluded, interfered with the freedom of association guaranteed by the *First and *Fourteenth Amendments. Persons who do not share an organization's unlawful purposes and do not participate in its unlawful activities pose no threat as citizens or as public employees. Previously, in *Wieman* v. *Updegraff* (1952) and *Garner* v. *Board of Public Works* (1951), the Court had held that loyalty oath statutes may punish only employees who know of the unlawful purpose of the organization; in *Elfbrandt* the Court added that the employee must have a specific intent to further this purpose.

(See also ASSEMBLY AND ASSOCIATION, FREEDOM OF.)

Milton R. Konvitz

**Ellsworth, Oliver** (b. Windsor, Conn., 29 Apr. 1745; d. Windsor, 26 Nov. 1807; interred Old Cemetery, Windsor), chief justice, 1796–1800. Oliver Ellsworth came from a prominent and well-connected Connecticut family, the son of Captain David Ellsworth and Jemima Leavitt. Although he started college at Yale he completed his education at Princeton, graduating in 1766. He first studied for the ministry but turned to the law and was admitted to the bar in 1771. He quickly gained a reputation for being one of the most able lawyers in New England and soon was prosperous in his own right. He married Abigail Wolcott in 1771. Entering politics, he strongly supported the movement for independence and in the years immediately following 1776 he held a variety of local offices, serving in the Continental Congress between 1776 and 1783. In this capacity he was a member of the court of appeals, which reviewed the decisions of state admiralty courts, and he helped to overrule a Pennsylvania decision in the case of Gideon Olmstead and the British sloop *Active* that led eventually to the important case of *United States* v. *Peters* (1809). In 1785 he became a judge of the Connecticut Supreme Court.

Ellsworth vigorously supported the movement to create a stronger central government in the federal convention in 1787. In this capacity he helped to engineer an agreement between the large and small states that has become known as the Great Compromise. It arranged for a two-house national legislature with proportional representation in the lower house according to population and for each state to have two senators in the upper house.

Ellsworth was elected to serve in the first United States Senate. He supported Alexander *Hamilton's financial measures and his various pro-British policies. Ellsworth also was the main author of the *Judiciary Act of 1789 that implemented the vague and undeveloped *Article III of the United States Constitution (see JUDICIAL POWER AND JURISDICTION).

George *Washington appointed Ellsworth to the United States Supreme Court in 1796. He held the post for a little over three years and did not have much of an impact on the Court's development. Illness forced him to curtail his activities and then a decision to accept a diplomatic assignment, while remaining chief justice, further limited his participation in the business of the Court. He generally favored expanding the authority of the federal courts, and he extended various common law procedures in appeals to equity and admiralty cases. As *chief justice he tried, not entirely successfully, to initiate the policy of the Supreme Court's handing down *per curiam opinions, or single decisions, for the entire Court as opposed to *seriatim, or separate opinions by individual justices.

While abroad as a part of a special diplomatic mission to end the undeclared naval war with

*Oliver Ellsworth*

France, Ellsworth resigned the chief justiceship, citing ill health.

□ William G. Brown, *The Life of Oliver Ellsworth* (1905). Julius Goebel, Jr., *History of the Supreme Court of the United States*, vol. 1, *Antecedents and Beginnings to 1801* (1971).
Richard E. Ellis

**Elrod v. Burns,** 427 U.S. 347 (1976), argued 19 Apr. 1976, decided 28 June 1976 by vote of 5 to 3; Brennan for the Court, Stewart and Blackmun concurring, Burger, Powell, and Rehnquist in dissent, Stevens not participating. Five members of the Court, in two separate opinions, imposed a *First Amendment barrier to time-honored party patronage practices. In Cook County, Illinois, a newly elected Democratic sheriff sought to discharge noncivil service employees who were Republican appointees of a previous Republican sheriff. The Supreme Court affirmed a court of appeals judgment for injunctive relief (see INJUNCTIONS AND EQUITABLE REMEDIES). Although unprotected by civil service laws, the employees were not in policymaking positions, were assumed to be performing their duties satisfactorily, and were being discharged solely because they were Republicans occupying positions now meant for Democrats. Dismissals in these circumstances, the Court declared, severely restrict political belief and association as protected by the First Amendment. More controversially, it also held that such restrictions are not outweighed by any contribution of patronage to the democratic process. Government could serve asserted vital purposes by less restrictive means than patronage dismissals.

Justice William *Brennan's *plurality opinion seemed to challenge the patronage system so broadly as to raise doubts about even the validity of government hiring of party supporters. Unwilling to join that broad a challenge, Justices Potter *Stewart and Harry *Blackmun concurred only with reference to the unconstitutionality of discharging nonconfidential, nonpolicymaking employees. In dissent, Justice Lewis *Powell wrote an especially strong defense of patronage. It contributed sufficiently, Powell said, so that the state's interest in preserving it is greater than the burden on First Amendment rights.

In *Branti* v. *Finkel* (1980), *Elrod* was extended to protect Republican assistant public defenders from dismissal by a new Democratic public defender. Ten years later, the Court invoked the principles of *Elrod* and *Branti* to invalidate patronage practices in promotions, transfers, recalls from layoffs, and hiring in its decision in *Rutan* v. *Republican Party of Illinois* (1990).

(See also ASSEMBLY AND ASSOCIATION, FREEDOM OF; POLITICAL PARTIES.)

Leon D. Epstein

**Eminent Domain** is the power of a government to compel owners of real or personal property to transfer it, or some interest in it, to the government. Eminent domain has long been regarded as an inherent power of both the federal and state governments. State governments have delegated this power to their political subdivisions, such as cities and counties. The federal and state governments have also to some extent delegated the power to private corporations that perform quasi-public functions, such as railroads and utility companies.

For several centuries before the American Revolution, the English parliament exercised the power of eminent domain for public projects. The American colonies also used the power, mostly for roads and bridges. The *Takings Clause of the *Fifth Amendment placed constitutional limitations upon the exercise of the eminent domain power by requiring the payment of *just compensation. The Supreme Court determined that the *Bill of Rights applied to only the federal government in *Barron* v. *Baltimore* (1833). However, in *Chicago, Burlington & Quincy Railroad* v. *Chicago* (1897), the Supreme Court ruled that the Fifth Amendment's just compensation requirement constituted an element of *due process guaranteed by the *Fourteenth Amendment. In addition, nearly all state constitutions contain similar limitations.

Eminent domain compels owners to sell to the government for public purposes. But under the Constitution an owner will receive the fair market value of the property. Thus, a compromise is struck whereby needed public projects may be carried out, but owners are made whole.

William B. Stoebuck

**Employment Discrimination.** The United States did not begin the deliberate elimination of race and gender discrimination in employment until 1964. Before then, there were few legal prohibitions against discrimination in the workplace. The *Equal Protection Clause of the *Fourteenth Amendment does not extend to private employers or *labor unions because of the *state-action doctrine, and state statutes outlawing employment discrimination appeared only sporadically. As a result, race and gender discrimination by employers and unions went largely unredressed. In the wake of the *civil rights movement and the assassination of President John F. Kennedy, Congress enacted the comprehensive *Civil Rights Act of 1964, which included a separate Title VII outlawing employment discrimination. The act prohibits employers from discriminating against employees on the basis of race, color, religion, sex, or national origin. It established an agency, the Equal Employment Opportunities Commission, which is empowered to help the individual complainant seek redress under the statute.

Because the primary assault on employment discrimination has been legislative, the Supreme Court has not taken the initiative in that area, as it has in combatting school segregation. The Court has, however, played a major role in shaping the meaning of Title VII and has imposed limits on the use of *affirmative action programs.

Perhaps the Court's most important decision involving Title VII was *Griggs* v. *Duke Power Co.* (1971). In striking down a testing and education requirement imposed by an employer, the Court developed the *disparate-impact doctrine, which holds that an employer's practice may violate Title VII even if the employer did not intend to discriminate. Under this approach, an employment practice, such as a test, that disqualifies a greater proportion of minority employees must be eliminated unless the employer can demonstrate that it is necessary for sound business operations. Although the Court attempted to limit the scope of *Griggs* in *Ward's Cove Packing Co.* v. *Atonio* (1989), which placed a much heavier burden on the plaintiff by requiring the employee to demonstrate that the challenged practice actually caused the claimed discriminatory impact, Congress overrode this decision by passing the *Civil Rights Act of 1991. This measure, which clarified and expanded previous congressional legislation on civil rights, eliminated the claim of "business necessity" as a defense against intentional discrimination, thus making it easier for plaintiffs to win employment discrimination suits than under *Ward's Cove*.

Employers and unions often establish affirmative action programs to achieve greater minority representation in the workplace. *United Steelworkers of America* v. *Weber* (1979) held this permissible under Title VII, as long as the program is designed to correct a societal pattern of discrimination, is temporary, and does not unduly limit the possibility of advancement for nonminority employees. The decision affirmed the congressional policy of encouraging private efforts to comply with the objectives of Title VII.

Affirmative action programs of public employers, and programs put into place under judicial supervision, involve state action and thus implicate the greater constraints of the Constitution. In these situations, the Court will not permit preferential employment treatment for minority employees unless there is a prior finding that the employer has discriminated, and affirmative relief is limited to those workers who have been the specific victims of prior discrimination. The Court has also been reluctant to grant affirmative relief to minority workers at the expense of innocent nonminority employees. Thus, in *Wygant* v. *Board of Education* (1986), the Court refused to uphold a contract provision that called for recently hired minority teachers to remain on the job while more senior nonminority employees were placed on layoff. The multiple opinions in this *plurality decision demonstrate that the Court was divided on the issues of what degree of proof of discrimination is required before a remedial program may be upheld and how narrowly the remedial arrangement must be tailored to avoid an impact on nonminority employees.

The Court revived three *Reconstruction era Civil Rights Acts in a 1976 decision by holding that they apply to private employment. Actions under these statutes have certain procedural advantages and offer the possibility of punitive damages. The Court substantially cut back the reach of these statutes, however, in *Patterson* v. *McLean Credit Union* (1989) by holding that a claim of racial harassment in the workplace is not actionable under one of them, section 1981 of Title 42. The Court reasoned that while that section prohibits racial discrimination in the making and enforcing of contracts, it does not apply to subsequent conduct that occurs as part of the employment relationship.

Congress in 1990 enacted the Americans with Disabilities Act, which prohibits almost all employers from discriminating against handicapped workers. Until the passage of this act, restrictions against handicap discrimination applied to only some workplaces, under state law and under a federal statute limited to federal employers and contractors doing business with the federal government. One of the most difficult issues under these statutes is whether the employer is required to make accommodations, such as job modifications, that make performance easier. In its one opportunity to consider this question, under the Federal Rehabilitation Act, the Court in *Southeastern Community College* v. *Davis* (1979) took a restrictive view, holding that the employer was not required to admit a hearing impaired person to a nursing program, nor make substan-

tial modifications to enable her to complete her training.

(See also EQUAL PROTECTION; GENDER; RACE AND RACISM.)

□ Barbara Schlei and Paul Grossman, *Employment Discrimination,* 2d ed. (1983).                    Robert J. Rabin

**Engel v. Vitale,** 370 U.S. 421 (1962), argued 3 Apr. 1962, decided 25 June 1962 by vote of 7 to 1; Black for the Court, Douglas concurring, Stewart in dissent, White not participating. The Supreme Court did not work from a blank slate when it first faced the constitutionality of governmentally sponsored prayers in public schools. In *Everson* v. *Board of Education of Ewing Township* (1947), *Illinois ex rel. McCollum* v. *Board of Education* (1948), and *Zorach* v. *Clauson* (1952), it had held the Establishment Clause of the First Amendment to require a "wall of separation" between church and state. The height of this "wall," however, was unclear. *Everson* and *Zorach* allowed public accommodation of religious practices, but *McCollum* struck them down. Additionally, during this period the Court declined to hear *Doremus* v. *Board of Education* (1952)—a case squarely raising the constitutionality of Bible reading in public schools. Nine years later, in *Engel* v. *Vitale* (1962), it took up a similar question.

Not only was the Court's slate cluttered with legal precedents, but it also contained the badge of modern constitutional litigation: substantial interest group presence. Pushing the strong separationist line it had drawn since *Everson,* the *American Civil Liberties Union joined the parents of ten public school students in a suit claiming that a state-authored prayer—"Almighty God, we acknowledge our dependence upon Thee, and we beg Thy blessings upon us, our parents, our teachers and our Country"—was an unconstitutional establishment of religion. Supporting the ACLU position were *amicus curiae briefs filed by the American Ethical Union, the American Jewish Committee (joined by the Anti-Defamation League of B'nai B'rith), and the Synagogue Council of America (joined by the National Community Relations Advisory Council). (See AMICUS BRIEF.)

Essentially, the separationist argument boiled down to this: any state support given to religion, either direct or indirect, violates the Constitution. In support of this contention, these litigants offered legal precedents and a history of the religion clauses that drew heavily from the writings of Thomas *Jefferson (the "wall" metaphor was initially his) and James *Madison. Particular emphasis was placed on the latter's "Memorial and Remonstrance against Religious Assessments."

Although they had the numerical edge, separationist groups were not the only organized litigators involved in *Engel.* Sharing oral argument with counsel for the school board was Porter R. Chandler, an attorney frequently called "the Cardinal's lawyer" because of his close association with the Archdiocese of New York. Chandler appended himself to the case by intervening on behalf of parents and children in the school district. Appearing as amicus curiae in support of the prayer were the Board of Regents of the State of New York and twenty state attorneys general. Essentially, they contended that the prayer, because it created no Establishment Clause problems, facilitated free exercise values, was not coercive, and involved no expenditure of public monies.

The majority opinion of Justice Hugo *Black sided with separationist interests. He held that use of public schools to encourage prayer was "a practice wholly inconsistent with the Establishment Clause" (p. 424). Drawing solely on British and American history to support this judgment, Black cited no precedent to reach this conclusion. Seemingly as an afterthought, he commented that the Constitution did not require that all religious values be purged from public life, but merely that schools could not sponsor them.

Justice Potter *Stewart tendered the sole dissent, charging the majority with misconstruing the meaning of the First Amendment's religious clauses. His reading of them led him to two conclusions: government cannot coerce one's religious beliefs—the Free Exercise Clause was preeminent, and the Establishment Clause simply forbids governmental establishment of an official church. Though unpersuasive to others on the Court at this time, the second line of argument was to be given new life by Justice William *Rehnquist in his *Wallace v. Jaffree (1985) dissent.

(See also RELIGION.)

Joseph F. Kobylka

**Entitlements.** See PROPERTY RIGHTS.

**Environment.** Until the 1960s, control of private property in the United States was based on centuries-old *common-law doctrines in each state and by a few local and state statutory restrictions. With limited exceptions, these doctrines and local restrictions allowed a property owner to use and even abuse his property. If the government or private individuals desired to preclude activities that injured the environment or natural resources, they could do so only by purchase of property or a property use.

Harmful activities could be successfully challenged in *state courts only on a case by case basis, by those individuals who could show a specific duty owed to them and a breach of that duty that resulted in a specific injury (Bartel v. Ridgefield Lumber Co., 1924). Broader controls on land use or pollution were only upheld if consistent with local governments' inherent *police powers to enact *zoning regulations or to abate public nuisances (*Euclid v. Amber Realty Co., 1926; Georgia v. Tennessee Copper Co., 1907).

Few attempts were made to impose national conservation or protection standards. Federal legislation was permissible only if based on a specific grant of power to Congress. The general power of the federal government over interstate commerce was not considered a sufficient basis for national environmental controls (see COMMERCE POWER). Thus, control over migratory birds was upheld under the power of Congress to pass legislation to implement a *treaty (*Missouri v. Holland, 1920). Prevention of discharges of pollutants was only allowable if necessary to protect navigable waters (United States v. Republic Steel Corp., 1960).

Beginning in the mid-1960s, increasing public concern about the environment, and the inability of traditional legal doctrines to deal with ecological problems, led to a new aggressive, and primarily federal, statutory environmental law focus. The Supreme Court frequently has been called upon to consider this new environmental law framework.

There are now comprehensive federal statutes designed to protect the air, water, oceans, and public lands of America. States have also enacted new programs designed to complement and sometimes expand federal requirements.

The primary constitutional limit on local or federal governmental power to establish these rules and regulations is the *Fifth Amendment's mandate that "private property may [not] be taken for public use without *just compensation" (the *Takings Clause). Until recently, the Supreme Court accepted extensive restrictions of the use of property as being within the traditional police powers of government. These were not takings. No compensation was required. So long as the owner retained some reasonable use of his or her property, considered within the context of the overall impact of a regulatory scheme, there was no constitutional violation, and no need for payment (*Penn Central Transportation Co. v. New York, 1978). Such property owners, the Court said, were merely being asked to share the burdens, as well as the benefits of government (Agins v. City of Tibouron, 1980).

More recently, the Court has shown a willingness to apply the Takings Clause to regulatory action (see REGULATORY TAKINGS). Restrictions on activities analogous to a nuisance would still be considered appropriate exercises of police power (*Keystone Bituminous Coal Association v. DeBenedictis, 1987). Other restrictions for general land use control or aesthetics, however, would now be more carefully scrutinized. In *Nollan v. California Coastal Commission (1987), the Court said that such regulations would be a taking unless they "substantially advance a legitimate state interest" and bore a close nexus or tie to that interest (p. 834). Even a temporary restriction, later removed or invalidated, may still be a taking, entitling the owner to compensation (*First English Lutheran Church v. County of Los Angeles, 1987).

Another possible limit on federal environmental laws might be the exclusive powers of a state, under the *Tenth Amendment. However, in *Hodel* v. *Indiana* (1981), the Supreme Court has now indicated that the federal government has broad power, under the Commerce Clause, to establish environmental controls, even if in conflict with traditional state power over land and utilities. At one time, the Court also indicated that there might be, in addition to specific federal statutes, a broad *federal common law of nuisance that would apply to pollution. However, it later decided that this federal common law has been displaced by comprehensive federal legislation as to almost all aspects of environmental law (*Milwaukee* v. *Illinois*, 1981).

Similarly, the Supreme Court stated in *Vermont Yankee Nuclear Power Corp.* v. *Natural Resources Defense Council* (1978) that while the National Environmental Policy Act of 1969 establishes "significant substantive [environmental] goals for the Nation," it, in fact, only imposes responsibilities that are "essentially procedural" (p. 557). Other statutes call for clean air and clean water by certain dates. But the Court has been unwilling to apply these broad policy statements. Rather, its focus has been limited to the specific requirements of specific laws.

The Court also appears unwilling to promote the broad congressional policy goal of environmental protection by relaxing procedural limitations established by general administrative law. This can be illustrated by cases dealing with federal preemption, *standing, *delegation of powers, and *appellate review. Under the Constitution, federal law is supreme and supplants any inconsistent state or local laws. This doctrine of federal preemption has led the Court to declare state and local laws invalid that interfere with comprehensive federal environmental laws and regulations (*Burbank* v. *Lockheed Air Terminal*, 1973).

Many federal environmental statutes, however, contain specific "nonpreemption" provisions that authorize states to enact complementary laws. The Court has narrowly interpreted these provisions, however, and often restricted states from applying state statutes and state common law in areas where there are comprehensive federal laws and regulations (*Exxon Corp.* v. *Hunt*, 1986; *International Paper Co.* v. *Ouillette*, 1987).

Many federal statutes include specific provisions providing for "citizen" standing to implement environmental protections. Early cases indicated that the Supreme Court would interpret these provisions broadly to allow for suits with, at best, an attenuated chain of causation of the challenged action to injury. (*United States* v. *Students Challenging Regulatory Agency Procedures*, 1973). More recent cases, however, have returned to the more traditional administrative law standard requiring a showing of direct injury (*Duke Power Co.* v. *Carolina Environmental Study*

*Group, Inc.*, 1978; *Lujan* v. *National Wildlife Federation*, 1990). Still, the Court continues to take a slightly more liberal view of standing in environmental cases. For example, it has held that such direct injury need not be economic but can also include injury to a plaintiff's physical environment, including aesthetic considerations (*Sierra Club* v. *Morton*, 1972).

Environmental statutes are written in very general terms, leaving broad discretion to regulatory agencies. Early Supreme Court cases indicated that the Court would take a "hard look" at agency attempts to implement environmental laws (*Citizens to Preserve Overton Park* v. *Volpe*, 1971). More recently, however, the Court has limited its review and has accorded broad discretionary powers to agencies. The Court relies on the expertise of the regulatory agency and usually accepts that agency's interpretation of statutory language. It has instructed lower courts that only arbitrary and capricious action, or actions clearly beyond statutory authority, are to be invalidated (*Vermont Yankee Nuclear Power Corp.* v. *Natural Resources Defense Council*, 1978).

The Supreme Court, of course, retains its broad inherent power to determine if there is imminent environmental harm and to enjoin harmful activities if such harm is shown. Under this equity power, it weighs the costs and benefits of relief and, as with other regulatory issues, often relies on the expertise of the federal agency responsible for a particular environmental risk (*Amoco Petroleum Co.* v. *City of Gamble*, 1987). Congress can limit this judicial power, but only, the Court has said, by explicit language (*Weinberger* v. *Romero-Barcelo*, 1982). For example, the Endangered Species Act specifically precludes activities that threaten an endangered species. The snail darter is an endangered species and no action, such as construction of a dam, may be taken that would threaten it. In *Tennessee Valley Authority* v. *Hill* (1978), the Court said that, in such circumstances, it cannot defer to agencies or independently weigh the costs and benefits of preserving the snail darter compared to construction of a dam. Only Congress can create exceptions to an absolute rule.

For more than twenty years, the Supreme Court has been quite tolerant of the new environmental law, and especially of the comprehensive national laws implemented broadly by federal agencies. In recent years, however, the Court has seemed more willing to consider restrictions on the environmental policy agenda. It is not yet certain what impact this new judicial policy will have on environmental law generally.

(See also PROPERTY RIGHTS.)

□ Martin H. Belsky, "Environmental Policy Law in the 1980s: Shifting Back the Burden of Proof," *Ecology Law Quarterly* 12 (1984): 1–88. William Rodgers, *Environmental Law* (1978). William H. Rodgers, Jr., *Environmental Law*, 3 vols. (1986).                    Martin H. Belsky

**Equal Protection.** The Equal Protection Clause of the Fourteenth Amendment, adopted in 1868, expressed the commitment of the victorious Republican forces after the *Civil War to include in the Constitution some protection for the equal rights of the newly emancipated slaves. Discussions of equality in 1868 did not sharply distinguish among the protections afforded by the *Due Process Clause, the *Privileges and Immunities Clause, and the Equal Protection Clause. The focus of the concern for equality was on the rights of African-Americans, but the framers of the equal protection clause deliberately drafted it to provide protection for the equal rights of all persons. In recent years this has meant that the clause provides protection for the rights of noncitizens, but shortly after the adoption of the amendment the most important result of the use of the general term "person" was to assure that corporations would be protected against invasions of their rights by state legislatures (*Santa Clara County v. Southern Pacific Railroad Co., 1886).

By its terms, the Equal Protection Clause covers action only by state governments. *Bolling v. Sharpe (1954), one of the desegregation cases that involved the District of Columbia schools, held that discrimination by Congress could violate the Due Process Clause of the *Fifth Amendment. The Court has in general applied the same standards of equal treatment to action by Congress as it has to action by state legislatures.

Ideas of equality prevalent in the 1860s distinguished between civil, political, and social rights. One reason the Fourteenth Amendment was adopted was to ensure that the Civil Rights Act of 1866 could not be repealed. That act protected equality with respect to civil rights, understood as including the right to own *property and make contracts and to appear as a witness in court to protect those rights. Equality with respect to civil rights meant equal status in the legal relations of the private economy, coupled with the right to enforce that equal status. Equality with respect to political rights was more controversial at the outset, with many supporters of equal civil rights opposed to equal voting rights for African-Americans. The adoption of the *Fifteenth Amendment largely abated any concern over equal political rights for a time, but concern about equal social rights persisted well into the twentieth century. Social rights were those arising from the personal, noneconomic interactions among people, and there was general agreement in 1868 that the federal government ought not attempt to guarantee equality in that domain.

The distinction between civil, political, and social rights became blurred in the late nineteenth century, as the national commitment to equal rights of some sort for African-Americans faded. The Supreme Court held that statutes explicitly denying African-Americans the right to sit on juries violated the Constitution's promise of equality (*Strauder v. West Virginia, 1880) and

also held that the Constitution was violated when administrators used a law that did not overtly refer to race to impose disabilities only on members of a racial minority (*Yick Wo v. Hopkins, 1886). However, the Court construed some federal civil rights statutes narrowly and held that Congress lacked power under section 5 of the Fourteenth Amendment to enact a law barring places of public accommodation from discriminating on the basis of race because, in the Court's view, that was an effort to require equality in social rights (*Civil Rights Cases, 1883). When the Court upheld a statute requiring railroads to segregate their passengers by race (*Plessy v. Ferguson, 1896), it effectively abandoned the effort to assure civil equality for African-Americans through the Constitution, for in the terms used in 1868 the statute denied the equal right of African-Americans to enter into a contract on nondiscriminatory terms that the railroads were willing to offer.

Until the 1940s the Equal Protection Clause was rarely invoked to invalidate legislation, occasionally being used to restrict the ability of states to regulate business. Concern about the racist policies of Nazi Germany, and about the incompatibility of racial discrimination with the values the allied powers were defending during *World War II, led to a revitalization of the Equal Protection Clause. The Court suggested that it would apply the Constitution with special care in cases involving disabilities imposed on "discrete and insular minorities" (*Footnote Four, United States v. Carolene Products, 1938). And in the course of upholding the internment of Japanese-Americans during the war, it stated that classifications affecting racial minorities had to survive *"strict scrutiny" (*Korematsu v. United States, 1944), which the Japanese relocation measures did, the only instance in modern times when a race-discriminating government action has. The final element of the revival of the Equal Protection Clause occurred when the Court invalidated a statute requiring the sterilization of violent recidivists but not recidivists in white-collar crime, on the ground that classifications affecting fundamental interests had to be strictly scrutinized (*Skinner v. Oklahoma, 1942).

During the 1950s the Supreme Court overturned numerous statutes requiring segregated public facilities and began to explore the broader implications of the doctrine it had begun to develop in the prior decade. Cases like *Shapiro v. Thompson (1969), invalidating a requirement that recipients of public assistance reside in a state for a year before they became eligible for assistance, suggested that the Court was about to treat poverty as a classification that entailed strict scrutiny (see INDIGENCY). The Court under Chief Justice Warren *Burger pulled back from the broader suggestions in these cases and ultimately held that strict scrutiny was appropriate only in cases involving traditional racial minorities and fundamental interests that were themselves spelled out in the Constitution (*San Antonio School District v. Rodriguez*, 1973).

Formally, the problem of equal treatment arises when the government treats one group differently from another in the pursuit of some social goal. Ordinarily not all members of the disadvantaged group will contribute to the evil that the government is trying to avert, and some members of the favored group will contribute to that evil. Classifications are therefore typically both "overinclusive" and "underinclusive." The problem for equal protection law is to specify what degree of lack of correspondence between the social goal and the classification used is permissible under what circumstances.

Equal protection law can be described in two ways. First, the Court distinguishes between statutes that themselves utilize racial or other *"suspect" classifications, and statutes that, though stated in nonracial terms, nonetheless have a *"disparate impact" on racial minorities. If the statutes use racial terms, they must survive "strict scrutiny," which means that the legislature must be attempting to promote extremely important social goals, and the use of the racial category must be almost essential if those goals are to be served. The fit between the social goal and the classification must be extremely close. In contrast, if the statutes are "facially neutral" in not using racial terms, the fact that they have a disparate impact in practice does not automatically lead to strict scrutiny. Only if the unfair impact on minorities is deliberately intended by the legislature will the Court demand strict scrutiny; otherwise the legislation must simply be using a classification that is a rational method of accomplishing social goals that the legislature believes important.

The second description of equal protection law treats the distinction between "strict scrutiny" and "rational relationship" differently. On this view the Court has identified several types of classifications. Some, such as racial classifications, call for strict scrutiny, where the fit between social goal and classification must be extremely close, while others, such as those basing government action on the ability of people to pay for services or on their participation in certain aspects of the private economy, are social and economic legislation where the legislature must merely be rational in using the classification to serve its goals. In the latter cases the fit between social goal and classification can be quite loose; the legislature can regulate many people who do not contribute to the evil it is trying to avert, and it can fail to regulate a great many people who do contribute to that evil. Groups who are entitled to "strict scrutiny," the Court has suggested, are "discrete and insular minorities" who have historically faced extensive unjustifiable discrimination, who are unable to remove themselves from the category, and who have been the subject of

such prejudice that they are unable to protect their interests in the legislative process.

There is, however, a third group of classifications that calls for *"intermediate" scrutiny. The doctrinal formulations of intermediate scrutiny have varied, as have the groups that elicit it. The prototypical case involves a classification based on *gender, but the Court has sometimes used heightened or intermediate scrutiny in cases involving aliens and extramarital children (see ALIENAGE AND NATURALIZATION). Intermediate scrutiny typically means that the Court will look somewhat skeptically on the claim that using a gender or similar classification is necessary to serve important social goals, but it will not demand the extraordinarily high levels of justification that it seeks in cases involving strict scrutiny. Using intermediate scrutiny the Court invalidated gender segregation in nursing schools (*Mississippi University for Women v. Hogan*, 1982) and various provisions of the federal social security statutes that had the effect of providing smaller benefits for the survivors of women who contributed to the social security funds than for survivors of men who contributed exactly the same amount (e.g., *Califano v. Goldfarb*, 1977). It upheld a requirement that only men register for the draft, at least when women are not eligible by statute for combat duty (*Rostker v. Goldberg*, 1981).

Analysts have had difficulty reconciling the Court's results with the doctrinal formulations it uses. For example, the Court explicitly refrained from requiring either strict or intermediate scrutiny in a case involving discrimination against the mentally retarded, but it nonetheless found unconstitutional a city's attempt to bar a residential group home for the mentally retarded (*City of Cleburne v. Cleburne Living Center*, 1985). Justice Thurgood *Marshall has criticized the Court for pretending that its equal protection analysis uses rigid categories, in which only a few *"suspect" classifications or *fundamental rights spelled out elsewhere in the Constitution receive special protection. Rather, he has argued, it has adjusted the degree of justification it demands according to a sensitive calculus that takes into account questions of degree. These questions include how important the interest affected is, whether or not that interest is specifically protected by the Constitution, and how similar the affected group is to groups that have historically been the subjects of unjustifiable discrimination.

*Plyler v. Doe* (1982) illustrates the contrast between Marshall's approach and the prevailing one. The Court, by a 5-to-4 vote, held unconstitutional a Texas statute barring the children of illegal aliens from the public schools. The dissenters argued that aliens, and their children, were not a "suspect" class calling forth strict scrutiny and that public *education, because it was not specifically protected by the Constitution, was not a fundamental interest. Thus, according to the dissenters, the denial of public education to these children had to satisfy only the "rationality" requirement. For them, the statute was a rational response to the problem of illegal immigration; if parents know that their children will be unable to attend free public schools, they may find immigration less attractive. The majority said that although the parents of the children might have some control over their own status, the children themselves did not; thus, the classification implicated a status that was, from the children's point of view, immutable. Further, the absolute denial of public education might indeed itself violate the Constitution. Justice Marshall's analysis would not require the Court to go through the process of identifying a suspect class and a fundamental interest. It would be enough for him that the children of illegal aliens resemble groups that have received special protection in the past and that the availability of public education is an important dimension of government activity.

Commentators generally agree that Marshall's analysis makes more sense of the Court's actual behavior, and that a more flexible approach than the Court's is appropriate to deal with the varied problems of classification that the Court confronts. The Court's analysis of *affirmative action issues seems to many to be insensitive to the complex normative problems those cases present, no matter how the cases are resolved. Nonetheless, the Court has steadfastly adhered to its "two- or three-tiered" approach in the face of this criticism.

(See also FOURTEENTH AMENDMENT; RACE AND RACISM.)

□ Michael Kent Curtis, *No State Shall Abridge: The Fourteenth Amendment and the Bill of Rights* (1986). Gerald Gunther, "Foreword: In Search of Evolving Doctrine on a Changing Court: A Model for a Newer Equal Protection," *Harvard Law Review* 86 (1972): 1–48. Kenneth W. Simons, "Overinclusion and Underinclusion: A New Model," *UCLA Law Review* 36 (1989): 447–528.
Mark V. Tushnet

**Equitable Remedies.** See INJUNCTIONS AND EQUITABLE REMEDIES.

**Erie Railroad Co. v. Tompkins,** 304 U.S. 64 (1938), argued 31 Jan. 1938, decided 25 Apr. 1938 by vote of 8 to 0; Brandeis for the Court; Butler, McReynolds, and Reed concurring; Cardozo not participating. The *Judiciary Act of 1789 provided that "the laws of the several states . . . shall be regarded as rules of decision in trials at common law" in federal courts (sec. 34). This provision, which in modern times is known as the Rules of Decision Act, requires federal courts to follow state substantive law in cases where the federal courts have jurisdiction because the parties are citizens of different states, but does not define the sources of state law. In *Swift v. Tyson (1842),

Justice Joseph *Story construed the phrase "laws of the several states" to include statutes and the law of real property but to exclude "contracts and other instruments of a commercial nature," which federal courts could construe in the light shed by the "general principles and doctrines of commercial jurisprudence" [p. 19]. Story thus called into being a general federal common law in the field of commercial law. His words transformed what had merely been an ambiguity into an enigma.

Standing alone, *Swift* would not have severely distorted the federal system. But after the *Civil War, the notion of a general federal common law underwent a seemingly limitless expansion beyond the commercial law ambit of *Swift*, extending to municipal bonds, civil procedure, *corporations, *torts, real property, and workers' compensation. At the same time, the power of the federal courts was expanding exponentially, and federal courts were using doctrines of substantive *due process and liberty of contract (see CONTRACT, FREEDOM OF) to annul federal and state economic regulation. Conservatives extolled these substantive developments and the concomitant expansion of federal courts' *diversity jurisdiction as vital to the protection of eastern investors' interests in the southern and western states, while progressives denounced the resort to federal courts by large corporations seeking to avoid state regulatory policies (see PROGRESSIVISM). A particularly notorious example of this occurred in the *Black & White Taxicab* case of 1928, where federal courts invoked a *Swift*-derived "general law" to enable a corporation to avoid state antitrust legislation. Disturbed by such use of federal judicial power, progressives determined to eradicate *Swift*.

Their opportunity came in *Erie*, which overruled *Swift*. Writing for the Court, Justice Louis D. *Brandeis declared that "there is no federal general common law" (p. 78). He found *Swift* to be inconsistent with the intentions of the legislators who drafted the Rules of Decision Act. In an action unique in the history of the Court, Brandeis held one of its decisions, *Swift*, unconstitutional, presumably as an intrusion on rights reserved to the states by the *Tenth Amendment.

*Erie* did not eliminate the notion of a federal common law, however. On the same day that he handed down his *Erie* opinion, Brandeis also acknowledged the existence of specialized bodies of federal common law. Nor did *Erie* resolve the enigma of *Swift*. Since 1938, the Court has attempted without much success to articulate guidelines that would achieve "the twin aims of the *Erie* rule: discouragement of forum-shopping and avoidance of inequitable administration of the laws" (*Hanna v. Plummer*, 1963, p. 468). Justice William J. *Brennan suggested an approach that balances state and federal policy interests (*Byrd v. Blue Ridge Rural Electric Cooperative, Inc.*, 1958), while Chief Justice Earl *Warren in *Hanna* sought to protect the Federal Rules of Civil Procedure from being overriden by state law through use of an analytical algorithm that traces the rules' validity to their statutory source, the Rules Enabling Act of 1934, and thence to the Constitution itself. The debate engendered by *Swift* and *Erie* will persist as the Court continues to define the contours of judicial *federalism in the United States.

(See also FEDERAL COMMON LAW; FEDERALISM; JUDICIAL POWER AND JURISDICTION.)

☐ John H. Ely, "The Irrepressible Myth of Erie," *Harvard Law Review* 87 (1974): 693–740.     William M. Wiecek

**Ernst, Morris Leopold** (b. Uniontown, Ala., 23 Aug. 1888; d. New York, N.Y., 21 May 1976), lawyer and author. Ernst, a New York attorney with a broad practice, stands out as a fighter against *censorship, an advocate of reproductive freedom, and a successful litigant before the Supreme Court in *First Amendment cases. As general counsel for the *ACLU from 1929 to 1954, he guided that body's litigation program. Coming to public attention when he won the famous *Ulysses* case in 1933 in a lower federal court, his defense of James Joyce's novel turned the tide against censorship and led to legal victories upholding the general sale of sexually oriented literature. He also brought the first legal challenge to the Connecticut Birth Control law in a lower court in 1940, the law that the Supreme Court ultimately threw out in *Poe v. Ullman* (1961) and *Griswold v. Connecticut* (1965).

As attorney for the American Newspaper Guild, he assisted in the first case carried through the courts to sustain the constitutionality of the National Labor Relations Board, thereby establishing the rights of newsmen to organize. He directed the legal strategy in *Hague v. CIO* (1939), gaining an *injunction against Jersey City mayor Frank Hague's denial of First Amendment freedoms, especially freedom of *assembly. His virulent anticommunism led him to support the unsuccessful Mundt-Nixon bill in 1948 that embraced his strategy of forced disclosure for dealing with communists.

(See also SPEECH AND THE PRESS.)

Paul L. Murphy

**Error, Writ of.** At *common law, a writ of error lay from an appellate to an inferior court, commanding the latter to send up the record of a case for review of alleged errors of law (not of fact). Review was limited to errors that appeared on the face of the record. The writ of error figured prominently in Supreme Court jurisdiction until the twentieth century, having been established in section 25 of the *Judiciary Act of 1789 as the procedural vehicle for review of *state court decisions involving *federal questions. The functions of the writ of error were transferred to *certiorari and appeal by federal legislation of

1916 and 1928, respectively, and the writ is obsolete in federal practice today. (See also APPELLATE JURISDICTION.)     William M. Wiecek

**Escobedo v. Illinois,** 378 U.S. 438 (1964), argued 29 Apr. 1964, decided 22 June 1964 by vote of 5 to 4; Goldberg for the Court, Harlan, Stewart, White, and Clark in dissent. When Danny Escobedo, a murder suspect, was taken to the police station and put in an interrogation room, he repeatedly asked to speak to the lawyer he had retained. Escobedo's lawyer soon arrived at the station house and repeatedly asked to see his client. Despite the persistent efforts of both Escobedo and his lawyer, the police prevented them from meeting. The police also failed to advise Escobedo of his right to remain silent. In response to accusations that he had fired the fatal shot, Escobedo made some incriminating remarks and then confessed to the crime.

Even though Escobedo had been interrogated before adversary proceedings had commenced against him (compare *Massiah v. United States, 1964), the Supreme Court threw out his confession. Because of the accordionlike quality of Justice Arthur *Goldberg's opinion for the narrow majority, a great deal of confusion resulted. At some places the opinion seemed to say that a person's right to *counsel is triggered once he becomes the "prime suspect" or once the investigation shifts from the "investigatory" to the "accusatory" stage and begins to "focus" on him. (Because this reading of the opinion threatened to cripple police interrogation, it alarmed many members of the bench and bar). At other places, however, the opinion seems to limit the case's holding to the specific facts preceding Escobedo's confession.

Two years later *Escobedo* was shoved offstage by the equally controversial case of *Miranda v. Arizona* (1966). *Miranda* shifted from a "prime suspect," or "focal point," test to a "custodial interrogation" standard, moving from *Escobedo*'s right-to-counsel rationale to one grounded primarily in the privilege against *self-incrimination. Thus, although *Miranda* maintained the momentum in favor of suspects' rights generated by *Escobedo*, it largely displaced that case's rationale.

(See also DUE PROCESS, PROCEDURAL.)

Yale Kamisar

**Espionage Acts** prohibit not only spying but also a variety of other activities, including certain kinds of expression. Consequently, they have often been at issue in *First Amendment litigation before the Supreme Court. Congress enacted the first such law during *World War I, amid concern about spies and the subversive activities of foreign agents. The Espionage Act of 15 June 1917 was an omnibus measure that not only punished the unauthorized obtaining, receiving, and communicating of national defense information but also contained provisions dealing with foreign ships in American ports, the seizure of arms intended for export, passports, search warrants, and even the counterfeiting of government seals. One section made it a crime, whenever the United States was at war, to make or convey false reports with the intent to interfere with military operations or promote the success of America's enemies; to cause or attempt to cause disobedience or disloyalty in the armed forces; and to obstruct willfully the recruiting services. Another title barred from the mails all written matter that violated the statute.

The following year Congress imposed further restrictions on expression in an amendment to the Espionage Act, commonly known as the Sedition Act. In 1940 it amended the law again, raising the penalties for violation of many of its provisions. A Korean War addition to the Espionage Act authorized seizure of unlawfully exported arms. The 1954 Espionage and Sabotage Act proscribed transmitting national defense information with the intent to injure the United States or aid a foreign nation, as well as the destruction of war material.

Only a few sections of these espionage acts have come before the Supreme Court. In *Gorin* v. *United States* (1941), the Court held that the government could convict someone for furnishing national defense information to a foreign country without proving that the defendant's actions had actually benefitted the other nation or harmed the United States. The case of convicted atomic spies Julius and Ethel Rosenberg was before the Supreme Court several times in the early 1950s. The only decision that involved the substance of the Espionage Act was *Rosenberg* v. *United States* (1953), holding that the death penalty provisions of the statute had not been superseded by the Atomic Energy Act of 1946 (see CAPITAL PUNISHMENT).

Most of the Court's Espionage Act decisions have involved the few provisions limiting expression, and most of those rulings were rendered in cases arising out of the widespread repression of radicalism and dissent that accompanied American participation in World War I. The federal government employed the original 1917 law and its Sedition Act amendments against German-Americans, socialists, members of the Industrial Workers of the World, and supporters of the Bolshevik Revolution in Russia. When the postmaster general used it to exclude the socialist *Milwaukee Leader* from the mails, the Supreme Court ruled in *Social Democratic Publishing Co.* v. *Burleson* (1921) that the *postal power gave him the authority to do so.

The Court also reviewed several of the 1,050 criminal convictions the government obtained under the Espionage Act. It upheld them all. Despite the fact that provisions of both the original Espionage Act and the Sedition Act appeared to violate the First Amendment, the

justices consistently rejected constitutional attacks on those laws and their application. In the most famous of these cases, *Schenck* v. *United States* (1919), Justice Oliver Wendell *Holmes formulated the *"clear and present danger" test, under which expression can be punished only if it creates an obvious and immediate threat of some substantive evil. Holmes nonetheless sustained the Espionage Act conviction of some Philadelphia socialists for sending out a leaflet urging draftees to assert their constitutional rights. He declared that many things that might be said in time of peace did not enjoy constitutional protection when the nation was at war.

During *World War II, however, there was far less repression of dissent. Federal prosecutors seldom used those provisions of the Espionage Act that limited expression, and consequently the Supreme Court heard few cases of this type. In *Hartzel* v. *United States* (1944), it overturned a rare conviction on grounds that the prosecution had failed to prove that the defendant intended to bring about the consequences prohibited by the statute and that his activities created a clear and present danger. Since World War II the Supreme Court has decided no Espionage Act cases of this type.

(See also COMMUNISM AND COLD WAR; SUBVERSION.)

□ Zechariah Chafee, Jr., *Free Speech in the United States* (1941).                    Michal R. Belknap

**Establishment Clause.** See RELIGION.

**Euclid v. Ambler Realty Co.,** 272 U.S. 365 (1926), argued 27 Jan. 1926, reargued 12 Oct. 1926, decided 22 Nov. 1926 by vote of 6 to 3; Sutherland for the Court, Van Devanter, McReynolds, and Butler in dissent. During the first quarter of the twentieth century, many municipalities, including Euclid, Ohio, enacted comprehensive *zoning schemes. These zoning ordinances were challenged on various constitutional grounds, and *state courts disagreed as to their constitutionality. The zoning ordinance enacted by the Euclid village council is noteworthy because litigation over its validity reached the Supreme Court. In *Euclid* v. *Ambler Realty Co.*, the justices concluded that zoning was a constitutional exercise of the *police power, thereby laying the foundation for virtually universal implementation of this form of land use regulation.

In 1922, Euclid was a community of fewer than ten thousand citizens located in the Cleveland metropolitan area and in the path of urban expansion. The village council adopted a comprehensive zoning ordinance dividing the town into use districts, area districts, and height districts. These districts or zones overlapped, so that development of each parcel of land in the community was restricted as to use, area, and height. The use limitations, the controversial feature of the ordinance, were cumulative in nature. With a few minor exceptions, single-family dwellings were the only structures permitted in the most restrictive use zone (U-1). Progressively more intensive uses were permitted in five other use zones (U-2 through U-6), with virtually all types of residential, commercial, and manufacturing use permitted in the least restrictive zone (U-6).

Ambler Realty Co. owned a large, unimproved tract of land in Euclid. It apparently was holding this sixty-eight-acre parcel for investment, planning to sell it for industrial development. A considerable portion of the property was zoned U-6 and thus could be used for industrial purposes. However, the rest of the property was zoned U-2 or U-3, thereby being significantly restricted and substantially reduced in value.

Ambler Realty Co. filed suit in federal district court challenging the validity of the Euclid zoning ordinance on *due process, *equal protection, and *taking grounds. The court ruled in favor of the landowner, finding that its property had been taken without *just compensation, and granted an *injunction prohibiting the village from enforcing the ordinance.

The Supreme Court reversed the lower court's decision, sustaining the constitutionality of zoning as a means of regulating private land use. The Court initially noted that zoning only could be justified as an exercise of the *police power to promote the public welfare. Drawing an analogy to nuisance law, the Court concluded that a zoning arrangement must be viewed in a given context. The Court focused on the prohibitory aspects of the Euclid ordinance, particularly the exclusion of commercial enterprises and apartment buildings from certain residential zones, and found a rational relationship between these restrictions and the health, safety, and general welfare of the citizens of the municipality. It noted a number of factors that established this nexus, including the minimization of traffic hazards and the reduction of noise. The Court stressed that it was upholding the zoning ordinance in its "general scope." It, however, recognized the possibility that an ordinance might be unconstitutional as applied to a specific parcel.

The *Euclid* decision established the legal foundation for zoning. Over time, local governments throughout the country employed this system of land use control with, of course, numerous variations. Nevertheless, as anticipated in *Euclid*, landowners soon attacked zoning ordinances as they applied to particular parcels. One such case reached the Supreme Court shortly after *Euclid*. In *Nectow v. City of Cambridge* (1928), the Court ruled in favor of the landowner, holding that application of the zoning ordinance to the parcel greatly reduced the land's value without enhancing the public welfare.

Having established the constitutionality of comprehensive zoning and demonstrated that a zoning ordinance valid in its general terms might be unconstitutional in application, the Supreme Court essentially withdrew from the zoning scene, leaving subsequent battles to be fought primarily in state courts. Since 1970, however, the Court has reentered the picture and rendered numerous decisions regarding various land use regulation techniques. Nonetheless, the Court has shown no inclination to reconsider its landmark decision in *Euclid*.

(See also PROPERTY RIGHTS.)

☐ Daniel R. Mandelker, *Land Use Law*, 2d ed. (1988; supp., 1991).                                        Jon W. Bruce

**Evans v. Abney,** 396 U.S. 435 (1970), argued 12–13 Nov. 1969, decided 29 Jan. 1970, by vote of 6 to 2; Black for the Court, Douglas and Brennan in dissent, Marshall not participating. *Evans* is one of a series of Supreme Court decisions that have considered racially discriminatory land-use covenants and other, privately created, racial land-use limits. *Evans* dealt with a public park in Macon, Georgia, which was open only to white residents in accordance with restrictions placed on the park by the donor of the property in 1911. In *Evans v. Newton* (1966), the Court decided that the city could not operate this all-white park without violating the Equal Protection Clause. Upon remand, Georgia courts decided that, in light of the clearly expressed discriminatory intent of the donor, the only suitable way to carry out the donor's wish was to return the property to his heirs.

In *Evans v. Abney* the Court upheld this action even though the effect was to close the park to blacks. Georgia courts reached their decision by relying on racially neutral, well-settled principles for the interpretation of wills. In accord with these interpretive principles, the donor's intent was best carried out, not by eliminating the racial restrictions, but by ending the park. The effect of the action, the Court noted, was not racially discriminatory because both whites and blacks lost access to the park land.

In reaching this conclusion the Court distinguished the case from its landmark ruling, *Shelley v. Kraemer* (1948), in which the Court announced that a state court violated the Equal Protection Clause when it enforced a privately created racial land-use covenant.

(See also EQUAL PROTECTION; INHERITANCE and ILLEGITIMACY; PROPERTY RIGHTS; RACE AND RACISM; RESTRICTIVE COVENANTS.)

Eric T. Freyfogle

**Everson v. Board of Education of Ewing Township,** 330 U.S. 1 (1947), argued 20 Nov. 1946, decided 10 Feb. 1947 by vote of 5 to 4; Black for the Court, Jackson, Frankfurter, Rutledge, and Burton in dissent. *Everson* involved a New Jersey statute that authorized boards of education to reimburse parents, including those whose children went to Catholic parochial schools, for the cost of bus transportation to and from school. To Arch Everson, a local resident and taxpayer, this practice violated the Establishment Clause.

At first reading it would seem that all the Court's members agreed with Everson. Justice Hugo *Black, speaking for the Court, concluded that with the period of early settlers, the American people believed that individual religious liberty could be best achieved by a government that was stripped of all power to tax, to support, or otherwise to assist any or all religions. In 1785–1786 Thomas *Jefferson and James *Madison led a successful fight against a tax to support Virginia's established church. A major part of the fight was the latter's great "Memorial and Remonstrance." In it Madison argued that a true religion did not need the support of law; that no person, either believer or nonbeliever, should be taxed to support a religious institution of any kind; that the best interest of a society required that the minds of men always be wholly free; and that cruel persecutions were the inevitable result of government-established religions. The "Memorial" led to the rejection of the tax measure and to the enactment of Jefferson's famous Virginia Bill for Religious Liberty.

At this point it would seem that Justice Black had made an incontrovertible case for a judgment of unconstitutionality. But for him, and four others, the net result was just the opposite. We must not, he said, strike down New Jersey's statute because it reaches the verge of its power or deprives its citizens of benefits because of their religion. The First Amendment requires the state to be neutral in its relation with groups of religious and nonbelievers, it does not require the state to be their adversary. State power is no more to be used to handicap than to favor religions. The state contributes no money to the parochial schools. It does not support them. Its legislation, as applied, does no more than provide a general program to help parents get their children, regardless of their religion, safely and expeditiously to and from accredited schools. New Jersey has not in the slightest breached a wall between church and state. Its statute is therefore constitutional.

While a minority of the Court—Justices Wiley *Rutledge, Felix *Frankfurter, Robert H. *Jackson and Harold *Burton—agreed with the basic premise expressed by Justice Black, they disagreed with the idea that it was not to be applied in *Everson*.

*Everson* remains good law. More importantly, however, the case held that the religion clauses of the First Amendment are made applicable to the states by the *Fourteenth Amendment, and it set out a standard by which the religion clauses were to be interpreted. The heart and soul of the *Everson* opinion, which has been and still is

invoked in full or part is that neither the state or federal government can set up a religion.
(See also EDUCATION; RELIGION.)

Leo Pfeffer

**Evolution and Creation Science.** The term *evolution* is used to describe the theory of the long, gradual development of the earth and its species. The terms *creationism* and *creation science* are used in both legal and general discussion to identify an opposing theory, which holds that the earth was created within the specific time stated in Genesis and that the species were created at once and did not evolve from lower to higher orders. Implicit in the debate over these two versions of the creation of the universe is the debate over the status of the Bible and revelation as a source of human knowledge.

While much energy was devoted in the nineteenth century to the reconciliation of evolutionary theory and the traditional claims of Christianity, it was in the twentieth century that litigation became the special forum for the debate. This litigation has particularly focused on public school *education. The first well-known instance was the Scopes trial of the 1920s, known often as the "monkey trial." A Tennessee teacher was criminally charged with teaching evolution in the public schools in violation of a state statute. The attorneys included Clarence Darrow as defense counsel and William Jennings Bryan as special prosecutor. The dramatic trial is better remembered than the appellate decision in *Scopes* v. *State* (1926), which upheld the constitutionality of the statute forbidding the teaching of evolution.

Uncertainty about the legal issue marked the next period. Supreme Court Justice Felix *Frankfurter, dissenting in *West Virginia Board of Education* v. *Barnette* (1943), questioned whether the Supreme Court should define the limits within which states could experiment with school curricula. Frankfurter urged what is generally referred to as judicial restraint (see JUDICIAL SELF-RESTRAINT). He saw the substantive issue, deriving from deeply held opposing beliefs and religious and philosophic sensibilities, as necessarily complex. "The religious consciences of some parents may be offended by subjecting their children to the Biblical account of creation," Frankfurter wrote, "while another state may offend parents by prohibiting a teaching of biology that contradicts such Biblical account" (p. 659).

The Supreme Court has entered the controversy in litigation directly testing the constitutionality under the *First Amendment of particular state statutes dealing with creation science and evolution. In *Epperson* v. *Arkansas* (1968), the Court held invalid an Arkansas statute that banned the teaching of evolution in the public schools as inconsistent with the First Amendment prohibition of an establishment of *religion. The court's theory was that public school education must not be tailored to the principles or prohibitions of any religious sect. In *Edwards* v. *Aguillard* (1987), the Supreme Court held invalid Louisiana's Creationism Act, which forbade the teaching of evolution in the public schools unless accompanied by instruction in creation science as an establishment of religion. This ruling centered on the point that the statute had no clear secular purpose but was rather intended to discredit evolutionism. In dissent, Justice Antonin *Scalia argued that the Louisiana statute had a secular purpose, the protection of academic freedom.

The issues in the argument over creation science are as complex as any involving religious belief and the public order. The controversies raise, from the point of view of the creationist, issues of a "hidden curriculum," behind apparently neutral teaching. Seemingly neutral presentation may have a tendency to subvert particular values and ideologies. Modern science instruction tends to stress the value of truth based on human reason and experiment and, to that extent, denigrates truth derived from revelation. From the point of view of those opposed to creationism, the dispute concerns reason and unreason, the historic struggle between science and religion, and the power of religious groups to control public discourse.

□ Stephen Carter, "Evolutionism, Creationism and Treating Religion as a Hobby," *Duke Law Journal* 6 (1987): 977–996. Laurie Godfrey, ed., *Scientists Confront Creationism* (1983). Carol Weisbrod

**Exclusionary Rule,** the name commonly given to the principle that evidence obtained by the government in violation of a defendant's constitutional right may not be used against him. A defendant may prevent the prosecution from using evidence against him by making a "motion to suppress" before trial asking the judge to rule that the evidence is inadmissible. Physical evidence, confessions, or line-up identifications are all subject to exclusion if obtained in violation of a defendant's constitutional right. The term "exclusionary rule" usually refers, however, to suppression of physical evidence that has been seized by the police in violation of a defendant's *Fourth Amendment right not to be subjected to an unreasonable search or seizure. The Burger and Rehnquist Courts have substantially curtailed the degree to which the exclusionary principle actually operates as a "rule." This curtailment reflects a fundamental redefinition of the character and purpose of the rule.

*"Principled" Origin.* The exclusionary rule was created in *Weeks* v. *United States* (1914), in which the Supreme Court prohibited the federal government from using certain documents in a prosecution for sending lottery tickets in the mail because the documents had been seized in an unconstitutional warrantless search of Weeks's home. Justice William *Day's opinion for a unanimous Court concluded that the trial court's decision to allow the documents to be used in the defendant's trial was "a denial of the constitutional rights of the accused" and that the trial court had no authority to allow unconstitutionally seized evidence to be admitted at trial (p. 398).

The *Weeks* Court was writing on a nearly blank slate regarding the law of search and seizure. Like the other provisions of the *Bill of Rights, the Fourth Amendment does not spell out the consequences if the right that it announces is violated. Prior to *Weeks*, a violation of a defendant's Fourth Amendment rights was inconsequential, so a defendant had no reason to challenge the constitutionality of a police search. Thus, courts had no occasion to spell out Fourth Amendment standards, and search law remained undeveloped. Only when the exclusionary rule was created was the Court presented with opportunities to announce Fourth Amendment search standards.

The *Weeks* opinion does not explain the theoretical basis for the exclusionary principle in detail. Read in the context of the formalist jurisprudence of the time, however—especially as reflected in the Court's decision in *Boyd* v. *United States* (1886)—it is clear that the exclusionary principle derives from the constitutional concept of limited governmental power. *Weeks* posits that a search that exceeds the constitutional authority of law enforcement officials must be deemed null and void and treated accordingly. If the government had no authority to seize the evidence, then a court—another branch of government—had no "right" to retain the evidence for use in a trial either. In keeping with the principled nature of the *Weeks* rationale, exclusion was the rule for unconstitutionally seized evidence in the federal courts for several decades. As Justice Oliver Wendell *Holmes wrote in *Silverthorne Lumber Co.* v. *United States* (1920), the point of the exclusionary principle was that unconstitutionally seized evidence "shall not be used at all" (p. 392). The only significant limitation on the rule's operation in the years following *Weeks* was a *"standing" requirement, developed by lower federal courts, which prevented a defendant from challenging a search that did not violate his own personal *privacy (for example, a defendant cannot usually challenge the constitutionality of a search of another person's house, even if that search produced evidence that incriminated the defendant).

*Extension to State Proceedings.* At the time of *Weeks*, the *Bill of Rights was construed to apply only to the federal government, and *Weeks* explicitly stated that its rule did not apply to searches by state police officers. In the years following *Weeks*, a number of *state courts considered whether to create state exclusionary rules on their own. Some did; more did not. The arguments in the state debates over the rule mirrored the debate over *Weeks* itself. Critics of the rule said it served no purpose—suppression of evidence didn't really punish the offending police officer—but its operation was costly to society because criminals were released. As Justice (then New York judge) Benjamin *Cardozo put it: "the criminal goes free because the constable has blundered" (*People* v. *Defore*, N.Y., 1926). Critics of the rule suggested that alternative remedies for arbitrary searches—such as suits for damages or administrative sanctions against the offending police officers—would be more effective than the rule. Defenders of the rule expressed doubts regarding the availability or efficacy of these alternatives and argued that the rule was the only practical way to give meaning to the *privacy right protected by the Fourth Amendment.

The issue of whether the *Weeks* rule should be applied to the states was reopened when the Court began to construe the degree to which the Fourteenth Amendment's *Due Process Clause protected the rights of defendants in state criminal cases. In *Wolf* v. *Colorado* (1949), Justice Felix *Frankfurter wrote for a 5-to-4 majority that, although the concept of due process does include some degree of protection from arbitrary government searches, that protection is not as extensive as the standards of the Fourth Amendment. Therefore, he concluded that the states were not required to apply the *Weeks* rule; rather they were free to address the problem of arbitrary police searches through any of a variety of alternative remedies.

After *Wolf*, a *"silver platter" doctrine allowed evidence seized by state officers to be admitted in federal trials, even though the searches violated Fourth Amendment standards. A decade later a 5-to-4 majority of the Court rejected the "silver platter" doctrine in *Elkins* v. *United States* (1960). Justice Potter *Stewart's majority opinion asserted that the protections provided by the Fourth and *Fourteenth Amendments against unreasonable searches were equivalent, thus repudiating the basis for *Wolf's* refusal to extend the exclusionary rule to the states. In the very next term, in *Mapp* v. *Ohio* (1961), five justices voted that the states were required to apply the *Weeks* exclusionary rule. Justice Tom *Clark's *plurality opinion reiterated the *Weeks* position that the rule is part of a defendant's Fourth Amendment right, but he also argued that the rule was needed because the states had not developed any meaningful alternative remedies for arbitrary searches in the decade since *Wolf*.

*Mapp's* application of the rule to state prosecutions had the effect of extending Fourth Amendment protections to a much larger and more diverse set of defendants than the white-collar criminals or tax evaders often found in federal prosecutions. Perhaps for that reason, *Mapp* generated far more political controversy than *Weeks* had. In particular, *Mapp* was denounced by police administrators and politicians for "handcuffing" the police.

*Deterrence Rationale.* Much of the controversy over *Mapp* focused on the practical effects of the rule. Defenders of the decision such as Professor Yale Kamisar argued that it had finally caused police departments to begin to train officers about search standards. Critics of the rule such as Professor Dallin Oaks responded that the rule could not affect police behavior because suppression of evidence did not directly punish offending officers. They also argued that the rule was not constitutionally required but was really only a judge-made, instrumental policy aimed at deterring future police misconduct. Because the critics believed that the rule failed as a deterrent, they argued that it should be abandoned as soon as another remedy for unconstitutional searches could be put in place. Thus, what has come to be known as the "deterrence rationale" for the exclusionary rule paradoxically opened up possibilities for attacking, limiting, or even abolishing it.

The deterrence rationale took on increased importance when President Richard *Nixon named four justices to the Court—including Chief Justice Warren *Burger, an outspoken critic of the rule—who were inclined to favor law enforcement interests. In *United States* v. *Calandra* (1974), the Court fundamentally redefined the rule's purpose, substituting the deterrence rationale for the previous principled formulation of the rule in *Weeks*. Justice Lewis *Powell's opinion for the six-justice majority repudiated the idea that the exclusionary rule was a constitutional right of a defendant who was the victim of an unconstitutional search. It was, he said, merely a prophylactic measure rather than a constitutional rule. Powell asserted that violation of the Fourth Amendment by an unconstitutional search is "fully accomplished" when the search ends and that the admission of unconstitutionally seized evidence in a later trial "work[s] no new Fourth Amendment wrong" (p. 354). Instead, Powell declared that "the rule's prime purpose is to deter future unlawful police conduct" (p. 347).

Powell's *Calandra* opinion also reasoned that because the rule was intended only to deter, the test for whether it should be applied in a particular setting should be to weigh the "deterrent benefits" of applying the rule against the social "costs" of its operation. In *Calandra*, the Court decided that the exclusionary rule would not be applied to evidence in grand jury proceedings because exclusion in that setting would not produce any significant increment of deterrence.

Although *Calandra* only limited the rule's operation, the adoption of a "costs and benefits" approach was widely thought to have positioned the Court to abolish the exclusionary rule on the ground that it generally failed as a deterrent. As it turned out, however, persuasive empirical data about the rule's effectiveness as a deterrent proved to be unavailable. In a pair of 1976 decisions, *Stone* v. *Powell* and *United States* v.

*Janis*, the Court substituted speculation for the unobtainable data, and announced that henceforth it would assume that the rule is effective as a deterrent when evidence is excluded from the prosecutor's case in chief at trial, but that it was doubtful that exclusion in other settings would create any significant "incremental deterrent effect" (*Stone* v. *Powell*, p. 493).

Although the Court had decided not to abolish the rule entirely (it may be significant that no alternative means of enforcing search standards has ever emerged), this approach to the rule's deterrent effect allowed the Court to curtail sharply the scope of its application. The Court has invoked "costs and benefits analysis" to admit unconstitutionally seized evidence in civil cases and in deportation hearings, in addition to *grand jury proceedings; it has also allowed unconstitutionally seized evidence to be used liberally to impeach a defendant's testimony at trial (which may effectively prevent defendants who have succeeded in having evidence suppressed from testifying); and it has also limited review of state court search rulings through federal *habeas corpus proceedings. Meanwhile, lower courts have invoked "costs and benefits" logic to admit unconstitutionally seized evidence in sentencing and probation or parole revocation hearings—among the most common proceedings in criminal prosecutions.

*Exceptions.* The Burger and Rehnquist Courts have also limited the operation of the rule by creating several new exceptions that allow the prosecutor unlimited use of unconstitutionally seized evidence, even in his or her case in chief at trial. One exception, announced in *Nix* v. *Williams* (1984), allows the use of unconstitutionally seized evidence if, hypothetically, the police would have "inevitably discovered" the evidence even if the unconstitutional search had not occurred (p. 441). The Court created another exception (commonly but inaccurately called a "good-faith exception") in *United States* v. **Leon* (1984), which allows the use of evidence that was seized in a search conducted pursuant to an unconstitutionally issued search warrant. There the Court reasoned that a defective warrant is the fault of the magistrate who issued it rather than the police officers who searched; thus suppressing the evidence would not affect police conduct. A parallel exception, created in *Illinois* v. *Krull* (1987), allows the use of evidence seized by police who conducted a search pursuant to an unconstitutional statute.

The exclusionary rule today is a shadow of that envisioned in *Weeks*. Ironically, the "deterrence rationale" has been invoked to permit so many uses of unconstitutionally seized evidence that the rule's efficacy as a deterrent may well be diminished. Certainly, unconstitutionally seized evidence can often be used to the government's advantage. It also appears that the rule is less "costly" than has often been assumed. A 1983

study by Thomas Davies that was discussed in the *Leon* opinions estimates that only between 0.6 and 2.35 percent of all felony arrests are "lost" at any stage in the arrest disposition process (including trials and appeals) because of the operation of the exclusionary rule. The rate of lost arrests is somewhat higher in drug and other possessory offenses, but much lower in violent crimes. Thus, the continuing debate over exclusion would appear to be fueled as much by the ideological commitments of the participants as by the effects the rule now exerts on the criminal justice system.

□ Thomas Y. Davies, "A Hard Look at What We Know (and Still Need to Learn) About the 'Costs' of the Exclusionary Rule," *American Bar Foundation Research Journal* (1983): 611–690. Yale Kamisar, "Does (Did) (Should) the Exclusionary Rule Rest on a 'Principled Basis' Rather than an 'Empirical Proposition'?" *Creighton Law Review* 16 (1983): 565–667. Dallin H. Oaks, "Studying the Exclusionary Rule in Search and Seizure," *The University of Chicago Law Review* 37 (1970) 665–757. Potter Stewart, "The Road to *Mapp* v. *Ohio* and Beyond: The Origins, Development and Future of the Exclusionary Rule in Search and Seizure Cases," *Columbia University Law Review* 83 (1983): 1365–1404.     Thomas Y. Davies

**Executive Agreements.** Under the Constitution, treaties with other countries require consent of two-thirds of the Senate. The framers, by requiring congressional approval of state agreements or compacts, clearly intended joint action of the national executive and legislature to make binding international obligations.

Executive agreements, unmentioned in the text, are alternatives made by the president alone. They are so ubiquitous in American foreign relations—and sometimes so controversial—that one should distinguish various forms. The vast bulk are authorized by statute or treaty. Starting early with postal relations, these cover many complex subjects such as copyrights, foreign aid, and trade. If the subject is within Congress's broad powers, the Supreme Court accepts the delegation of legislative power and the Senate bypass. Most disputes concern agreements rooted in the president's independent powers as national negotiator and commander in chief. Starting modestly with President James Monroe's agreement to limit arms on the Great Lakes in 1817, a device used mainly for temporary or detailed arrangements later became an instrument for major foreign policies. Armistices, for example, ended fighting in the Spanish-American War and World War I. The Boxer protocols and other agreements recognized special interests in China.

President Franklin D. *Roosevelt converted executive agreements into primary instruments of foreign relations. He approved the Litvinov Agreement recognizing the Soviet Union in 1933 and the destroyer bases deal of 1940. During World War II, Roosevelt and Truman made secret agreements with allies at Cairo, Yalta, and Potsdam affecting most of the world. Postwar alliances and a global economy spawned thousands of executive agreements, more than 2,800 in the Reagan administration alone.

Military agreements of the commander in chief such as armistices raise few problems of principle. Secret arrangements committing troops and treasure, such as Yalta or the bombing of Cambodia, aroused great hostility. Constitutional challenges center on the domestic effects and proper scope of sole executive agreements. The Supreme Court has never flatly equated executive agreements with treaties as internal law, but *United States* v. *Belmont* (1937) and *United States* v. *Pink* (1942) rejected arguments that Congress must authorize or approve executive agreements internally. The Court upheld the Litvinov assignment of Russian assets here as an incident of national supremacy, presidential authority to recognize foreign governments, and "a modest implied power" of the country's "sole organ" in international relations (*U.S.* v. *Pink*, p. 229). Thus, presidents may override conflicting state laws without consulting senators, traditional guardians of state interests. Whether sole executive agreements, like treaties, supersede existing federal statutes is doubtful but unsettled.

The issue of scope is whether the Constitution limits the subject matter of executive agreements. On one side, given the framers' design of shared powers to check foreign adventures, critics charge that making major policies by executive agreement rather than by treaty dangerously evades constitutional controls by changing labels. On the other side, given the need for speed, secrecy, and concentrated decision in foreign affairs, not to mention the difficulties and delays of consultation exposed by the League of Nations debacle, defenders claim that executive agreements are essential to modern statecraft.

Political practice largely determines these issues. Justices usually defer to political branches in matters of foreign affairs (*Dames & Moore* v. *Regan*, 1981). A major attempt to require congressional implementation of executive agreements as internal law collapsed in 1954 when a substitute for the proposed Bricker Amendment failed Senate passage by one vote (see CONSTITUTIONAL AMENDING PROCESS). The sheer volume of agreements involved, unclear criteria for appropriate uses of treaties and agreements, and realization that Congress by legislation can repeal treaties domestically, all affected the result. The Supreme Court's decision in *Reid* v. *Covert* (1957) also relaxed fears by voiding an executive agreement that permitted criminal trials of civilian dependents of American personnel in military courts abroad. Often cited is Justice Hugo *Black's ringing *plurality opinion that all agreements are subordinate to the Constitution and the *Bill of Rights.

Secret arrangements for military bases in Spain and in the *Vietnam War aroused other attempts to limit executive agreements in the 1970s. The Case Act (1972) requires the secretary of state to transmit to Congress any international agreement made other than by treaty. But this has been circumvented. Presidents Nixon, Ford, and Carter made secret agreements regarding South Vietnam, Sinai, and disarmament, respectively, which they labeled "arrangements" or "accords" and did not report. The Iran-contra scandal illustrates other hazards of compliance. Executive agreements are striking examples of expanding presidential power, reminders that form follows function in constitutional development.

(See also FOREIGN AFFAIRS AND FOREIGN POLICY; TREATIES AND TREATY POWER.)

□ Louis Henkin, *Foreign Affairs and the Constitution* (1972).                    J. Woodford Howard, Jr.

**Executive Immunity.** The Constitution provides no exemption for the presidency from the legal processes of other branches. Congress alone is blessed with such a protection, but that shield, the *Speech and Debate Clause, is strictly limited to legislative functions. It has been assumed, however, that the president enjoys some shield from both judicial and congressional control. If presidents were obligated to justify legally each contestable action of the executive branch, they would be subject to intolerable control and inspection by a supposedly coordinate branch and would be burdened by countless impediments to effective action. Even if criminal charges are brought against a president, there are several conceptual problems: what if the president should grant himself a *pardon or give himself immunity from local prosecution? These possibilities have led some authorities to argue that *impeachment must always precede criminal judicial proceedings against a president.

Presidents have generally claimed absolute immunity, meaning that, except for impeachment proceedings, they can personally ignore all other processes of law. Most of the early executive immunity cases involved the role of presidents as witnesses or potential witnesses and such a role is not usually vital to the process of another branch. Thus, in *Marbury* v. *Madison* (1803) neither President Thomas *Jefferson nor Secretary of State James *Madison (the nominal defendant) appeared in Court even through an attorney. In Aaron *Burr's 1806 trial for treason, Jefferson was permitted by Chief Justice John *Marshall, riding circuit, to reply to questions all in written form.

The high-water mark of presidential immunity was *Mississippi* v. *Johnson* (1867), where the Supreme Court refused to hear an argument for an *injunction against presidential enforcement of a statute. The decision's strong language against judicial direction of presidential power as "an absurd and excessive extravagance" has generally been assumed to deny judicial authority of this type, though the opinion expressly reserves the question of whether a president may be forced to perform the rather small number of ministerial duties of that office (p. 499). In any event, the language of *Mississippi* v. *Johnson* is construed by critics of presidential authority like Raoul Berger as merely arguing the prudence of judicial abnegation and not as setting constitutional limits.

Throughout U.S. history presidents have worked out accommodations with both Congress and the courts. As a result, both strong advocates of immunity and of the competing principle that no one is above the law can claim ample precedent depending on how they interpret precisely the same events. Presidents Abraham *Lincoln and Theodore Roosevelt voluntarily appeared before congressional committees, and President Ulysses S. Grant voluntarily sent a deposition in a congressional investigation (see CONGRESSIONAL POWER OF INVESTIGATION). In response to a committee summons, ex-president John *Tyler testified, and former president John Quincy Adams sent a deposition. However, former president Harry S. Truman chose to ignore a subpoena from the House Un-American Activities Committee.

Both incumbent and former cabinet members and other high officials have cooperated freely with congressional committees, and committees have generally accommodated their schedules. Courts proceed routinely against high presidential appointees, though they are accorded qualified immunity in civil matters, as in *Butz* v. *Economou* (1978).

Courts have been quite circumspect with both ex-presidents and sitting chief executives. Supreme Court opinions have emphatically asserted the rule of law—and the Court's prerogative "to say what the law is"—but, as noted in *Marbury*, the Burr case, and *Mississippi* v. *Johnson*, judges in fact usually accept very nominal compliance, and constitutional authorities have generally interpreted Court accommodations as claiming little or no authority over the president in an official capacity.

The issue in *United States* v. *Nixon* (1974) was quite different. President Richard *Nixon was suspected of knowledge of an illegal break-in at Democratic party headquarters and of being involved in a coverup to protect the perpetrators. (He was in fact an unindicted co-conspirator, not publicly identified nor proceeded against because of legal doubts about indicting a sitting president.) Nixon had in his possession tapes of conversations likely to be able to resolve the issue, and the prosecutor was able to identify the conversations sought with great particularity. Under such circumstances presidential immunity is at a minimum. Because criminal proceedings were never instituted against Nixon, the issue of presidential answerability on criminal charges remained poorly defined, in contrast to the

considerable clarification of the nature and limits of *executive privilege that were this case's result.

The controlling statement of presidential immunity is found in *Nixon* v. *Fitzgerald* (1982), a case decided by a narrow 5-to-4 vote with two concurrences by Chief Justice Warren *Burger. The majority held that a president could not be personally sued for dismissing a federal employee, even though it was alleged that the dismissal was retaliation for the employee's "whistle-blowing" cooperation with a congressional committee. The "singular importance" of the president's duties requires freedom from private lawsuits for decisions taken within the "outer perimeter" of the office (p. 755). Basing its argument ambiguously on both constitutional and functional grounds, Justice Lewis *Powell's plurality opinion reserved the question whether Congress could define and delimit executive immunity. Burger's concurrence argued that there is a sweeping constitutional underpinning for absolute immunity.

The four dissenters argued that the decision removed the president from the rule of law, a view denied by both Powell and Burger, who pointed out that the possibility of other kinds of criminal and civil proceedings remained open. The dissenters also argued that the Court was inconsistent in view of its support of the qualified immunity test of *Butz* v. *Economou* for other executive-branch employees. This test was followed in the companion case of *Harlow* v. *Fitzgerald* (1982), which was decided by a vote of 8 to 1. If adequate protection could be given such officials by granting selective immunity in most instances and absolute immunity only in highly specific functional circumstances, why could not such an approach be used for the president?

Obviously, the majority believed, as Burger asserted in his dissent in *Harlow*, that an approach that would treat the president, cabinet members, and presidential subordinates "on the same plane constitutionally" would be egregiously wrong (p. 828). Indeed, Burger argued that presidential aides—as direct instruments of the president—are entitled to *more* constitutional protection than cabinet members, on analogy with congressional aides.

(See also INHERENT POWERS; SEPARATION OF POWERS.)

Samuel Krislov

**Executive Privilege.** Until about 1960 "executive privilege" was referred to as "presidential discretion to withhold information" or some similar term. Because there is no textual underpinning in the Constitution for the claim to executive privilege, which presidents have based on notions of *separation of powers, critics as diverse as former Undersecretary of State George Ball and legal historian Raoul Berger have labeled it "a constitutional myth." Still, the issue has been contested since George *Washington's administration, and it is difficult to see why this matter is different from issues such as presidential removal power or the *congressional power of investigation. Given the sparseness of language in many provisions of the Constitution, principles often emerge from a combination of litigation and custom.

Until recent decades, when executive privilege controversies have arisen more frequently, presidential discretion to withhold information was seldom differentiated from the presidential claim of discretion not to appear—*executive immunity—and in real-life situations the two are often intertwined. Theoretically, both claims of executive prerogative affect relations with courts and legislature, but executive control of prosecution tends to minimize problems at the judicial level while the rise of routine investigations in Congress has thrust questions of executive privilege to the forefront. Until this century virtually all disputes were resolved by mutual accommodation, but in recent years the judiciary has increasingly become the decision maker. Of course, most matters are still resolved by the practical politics of the situation.

Several core notions are hidden behind the label of executive privilege. First, presidents have insisted that they have a need for confidential, candid advice from subordinates and that too-easy public revelation of that advice will destroy these vital relationships. This need was acknowledged by Chief Justice John *Marshall in *Marbury v. Madison (1803) and has historically been tenderly treated both by Congress and the courts. Any claim to an absolute privilege seems undercut by ex-presidents' and ex-subordinates' growing propensity to write kiss-and-tell memoirs immediately upon leaving office. Second, presidents sometimes claim executive privilege by virtue of reasons of state, insisting that military and foreign-affairs secrets should not be divulged. Both courts and congressional committees have developed techniques of limited, in camera, inspection of secret materials by trusted congressional leaders or judges, but there are limits to this as well. Third, the claim is sometimes based on practical necessity, as when, for example, the identities of spies or informers may need to be protected. The validity of the argument from practical necessity is historically well founded: the issue first arose when President Washington withheld information on the Jay treaty from the House of Representatives, and congressional leader James *Madison recognized that the untimely disclosure of otherwise pertinent information could jeopardize national interests.

Since the Eisenhower administration, presidents have repeatedly pressed for an absolute privilege—but they have suffered an almost uniform record of rebuffs in the courts. Nevertheless, strong conditional privilege rights have been established. Both politically and legally the executive has had to accommodate to the functional claims of the other branches, which have their own valid needs to obtain information.

At one extreme, such needs arise during the process of confirmation of presidential subordinates. The Senate's power to reject a nomination makes it imperative for the president to share even the most confidential information in some way if the Senate insists. When a congressional committee (authorized by the entire chamber) litigates to obtain information, the courts have insisted upon the judiciary's right to decide and frame the conditions of the investigation. In general, courts are highly deferential to executive claims; even the series of cases involving President Richard *Nixon tended to acknowledge the normal presumption that the executive withholding was correct and the burden of proof was on the party challenging such a decision. In criminal matters the courts will accept executive claims, but if a defendant makes a reasonable showing that confidential material might significantly affect the case the court may force the government to choose between confidentiality and giving up the prosecution. Where the officeholder is the criminal defendant the claim of confidentiality is at its weakest. Under the decisions in United States v. *Nixon (1974) and *Nixon v. Administrator of General Services (1977), the courts must weigh the advantages and disadvantages of disclosure, but clearly officeholders do not have the last word about confidentiality involving colleagues, and least of all about themselves. The case for executive privilege is strongest in private civil suits, although even there the courts retain the last word.

(See also APPOINTMENT AND REMOVAL POWER; FOREIGN AFFAIRS AND FOREIGN POLICY.)

Samuel Krislov

**Exhaustion of Remedies** is a judicially created doctrine that often requires a litigant to seek relief elsewhere before bringing an action in federal court. A state prisoner, for example, normally may not obtain federal *habeas corpus without exhausting state remedies. Similarly, a federal court will frequently deny judicial relief if the plaintiff has not exhausted available administrative remedies.

The Court recognized the habeas corpus version of the doctrine in Ex parte Royall (1886); in 1948 Congress codified it in section 2254(b) of the Judicial Code. Since then, the Court has focused on such issues as how a prisoner satisfies the exhaustion requirement, which claims must be presented to *state courts, and whether a state may waive the requirement.

The leading case in the administrative context is Myers v. Bethlehem Shipbuilding Corp. (1938), where the Court imposed an unqualified exhaustion requirement. The Court has nevertheless recognized many exceptions. In Patsy v. Board of Regents (1982), for example, the Court held that the requirement does not apply in federal civil rights actions. In *Mathews* v. *Eldridge* (1976), the Court held that the plaintiffs need not exhaust a remedy that they challenged as inadequate. Indeed, there are so many exceptions, and the cases are so difficult to reconcile, that exhaustion of administrative remedies is a confusing maze for even the most sophisticated observer.

In habeas corpus cases, the Court has explained that the exhaustion of remedies doctrine is based on notions of *comity, and the concerns are similar to those faced in *abstention doctrine cases. In administrative cases, the doctrine is closely related to the doctrines of finality and *ripeness.                          Michael F. Sturley

**Ex Parte** (Lat., "on behalf of"), phrase that generally refers to action taken without notice to the adverse party or participation by that party in the hearing. When the phrase is used in the title of a case (e.g., *Ex parte* *Young*, 1908) it indicates that the action was taken on behalf of the person named in the case's caption.    William M. Wiecek

**Ex Post Facto Laws** are statutes that make an act punishable as a crime when such an act was not an offense when committed. Article I, section 10, clause 1 of the Constitution provides that no state shall pass any ex post facto law; Article I, section 9, clause 3 imposes the same prohibition upon the federal government. The Supreme Court early determined that these clauses prohibit laws with retroactive effect only in the field of criminal law and do not apply to statutes dealing with civil matters. Nonetheless, retroactive laws in the civil area may under certain circumstances violate the *Contract or *Due Process Clauses of the Constitution. The ban on ex post facto laws operates solely as a restraint on legislative power and has no application to changes in the law made by judicial decision.

Besides preventing the enactment of laws making acts criminal that were not criminal when committed, the Ex Post Facto Clauses also render invalid the retroactive application of laws that, while not creating new offenses, aggravate the seriousness of a crime. Moreover, a statute that prescribes a greater punishment for a crime already committed violates the clauses. A law that alters the rules of evidence so as to make it substantially easier to convict a defendant is likewise prohibited by the Constitution.

Edgar Bodenheimer

**Ex Rel.** (Lat., *ex relatione*, "on the relation of"). When this phrase appears in the title of a case, it indicates that the case was brought by the attorney general in the name of the state but at the behest of a private party having an interest in the subject of the suit.    William M. Wiecek

**Extrajudicial Activities.** The participation of justices in activities outside the normal duties of the judicial office has been an issue throughout the institutional life of the Supreme Court. Such extrajudicial activities have occurred in two broad subject matter categories. The first, and the focus of greatest scholarly as well as public interest, involves the acceptance of a position of national or international consequence that is clearly not within the scope of the regular duties of the judicial office. The second, which generally stimulates little interest outside of legal circles, involves private activities undertaken in addition to the regular duties of a justice. These public and private extrajudicial activities have often provoked distinct types of praise or criticism. But both have been the targets of one recurring attack. Put simply, any outside obligation may drain attention and energy that should be devoted to the significant burdens of the judicial office. This criticism has often been expressed by members of the Court and was stressed by Chief Justices William Howard *Taft and Harlan Fiske *Stone in the twentieth century.

The desirability and legitimacy of extrajudicial activities was debated occasionally at the Constitutional Convention of 1787. For future opponents of such activities, the convention's rejection of a proposal for the judicial sharing of presidential *veto power over legislation was deemed definitive of the opinion of the framers of the Constitution. But a close examination of Convention opinion about judicial involvement in nonjudicial matters suggests considerable flexibility on the issue. James *Madison proposed creation of a Council of Revision consisting of the president "and a convenient number of the National Judiciary" to review acts of Congress. Supporters of Madison argued that lawmaking would benefit from use of judicial ability. Some opponents, conversely, suggested that judges should not participate in policy making because judges lacked knowledge of public policy matters. Other opponents of the Council of Revision rejected formal judicial participation in what became the presidential veto, but supported ad hoc extrajudicial activities on the ground that judicial talent and legal ability would be valuable to the other branches.

Immediately after the adoption of the Constitution in 1789, Congress and the president assigned or recommended extrajudicial tasks for members of the Supreme Court. The first ten years of the Supreme Court was a seminal era regarding the theory and practice of extrajudicial activity. In theory, the principle of *separation of powers would provide a clear definition. But in practice, the earliest justices did not make a definitive ruling on the issue despite the variety of interpretations given in *Hayburn's Case (1792). Congress specified the judges of the federal circuit courts as the evaluators of injured Revolutionary War veterans' pension qualifications. Since, under the *Judiciary Act of 1789, there were no separate circuit judges, the federal district judges and justices of the Supreme Court were to fulfill these responsibilities while on circuit court duty (see CIRCUIT RIDING). The statute required the circuit judges to examine not only the documents determining Revolutionary War military service but also the wounds to determine the seriousness of the injury, a duty not commonly deemed judicial. The findings were to be reported to the secretary of war who could review the determination of the circuit judges and send a report to Congress recommending rejection of the judges' findings. The subsequent letters from the judges of the three federal circuits declining to fulfill these tasks noted the nonjudicial nature of the duties, the lack of a constitutional basis for such assignment to the circuit judges, and the subjection of the judges' findings to review by a nonjudicial cabinet officer. The objections were grounded in separation of powers theory.

Despite this rejection, the earliest justices participated in a number of presidentially or congressionally requested extrajudicial tasks that were beyond the scope of judicially deciding *cases or controversies. One 1790 law required judges to determine, after investigation, the validity of fine or forfeiture remission claims by persons guilty of unintentional customs violations. Like the rejected veterans' pension procedure, the judges were required by statute to report their findings to a cabinet officer, in this instance the secretary of the treasury. Another 1790 law required judges to evaluate petitions from seamen regarding the safety of their ships. The judges were to designate maritime experts to examine the vessels and, on the basis of their report, determine whether the ships were fit to proceed on their intended voyage. A 1795 act placed the task of determining whether aliens met the naturalization requirements established by Congress upon the judges (see ALIENAGE AND NATURALIZATION).

Acquiescence in these tasks did not, however, extend to all congressionally or presidentially assigned tasks. Presidential requests for advice from the justices began with George *Washington and have been repeated through two centuries. Two examples from Washington's era illustrate the complexity of the issue. Then as now, requests for advice from the justices about the problems of the federal judicial system poised no separation of powers problems. Thus, Washington's 1790 request for advice on the operation of the federal court system was answered readily with a critical appraisal including the accurate observation that judging at two interrelated court levels was "unfriendly to impartial justice." Conversely, when Washington requested the justices to accept a role as permanent advisers on matters of international law, the justices declined on several grounds, separation of powers chief among them. The prospect of obligating future justices to this advisory role and the possibility that an *advisory opinion would harden into an actual judicial position were also concerns. Notwithstanding the reservations clearly expressed in these early positions, Chief Justices John *Jay and Oliver *Ellsworth both accepted important diplomatic tasks that not only detracted from their regular judicial obligations but also thrust them, especially the former, into heated political controversy.

Beginning in the first decade of the Supreme Court, members of the Court were called upon to fill a wide range of ad hoc public positions of the Court. The most visible and controversial were the diplomatic missions of Chief Justices Jay and Ellsworth noted above. The rigors of transatlantic travel and the mission severely affected Ellsworth's health, leading to his retirement. Congress also imposed upon Jay duties as a sinking fund commissioner and as an inspector of coins minted by the United States, tasks he performed intermittently, indicating that judicial duties were paramount.

Chief Justice John *Marshall was nominally engaged in these previously established ex officio duties, but was not called upon to engage in new tasks. Only three other justices participated in public missions prior to the *Civil War. Associate Justice Henry *Baldwin took part in an investigation of General Andrew *Jackson's campaign against the Seminole Indians. On the eve of the Civil War Justices Samuel *Nelson and John Archibald *Campbell served as intermediaries to the Confederacy to avert the outbreak of hostilities.

Public extrajudicial roles became more frequent after the Civil War. Appointed by President Ulysses S. Grant in 1871, Nelson served on a Geneva Commission to arbitrate U.S. claims against Great Britain for permitting the building and refitting of Confederate men-of-war. The selection of five Supreme Court members to the 1876 Electoral Commission that ultimately settled the Hayes-Tilden presidential contest on strictly partisan lines did not enhance the Court's reputation. Justice Stephen J. *Field was a member of a California Commission on the Revision of State Statutes. In the late nineteenth century, Chief Justice Melville W. *Fuller and Justice David J. *Brewer served as boundary arbitrators in a dispute between Venezuela and British Guiana and Justice John Marshall *Harlan served as an arbitrator in the Fur Seal Arbitration proceedings. In 1911, Justice Charles Evans *Hughes served on a commission to set second class postal rates. In the 1920s, Justice William R. *Day served on an American-German war claims commission. In 1930, Chief Justice Hughes chaired a special tribunal to settle a border dispute between Guatemala and Honduras. Willis *Van Devanter was an arbitrator in an American-British dispute over the seizure of the vessel *I'm Alone*. Justice Owen J. *Roberts served on a Mexican claims commission and during World War II in the investigation of the Pearl

Harbor preparedness issue. After the war, President Harry Truman appointed Justice Robert H. *Jackson prosecutor in the Nuremberg War Trials. President Lyndon B. Johnson persuaded Chief Jutice Earl *Warren to chair the commission investigating the assassination of President John F. Kennedy. The enduring ex officio extrajudicial roles of the chief justice have been chairing the board of trustees of the National Gallery of Art and serving as chancellor of the Board of Regents of the Smithsonian Institution.

In contrast to the type of extrajudicial tasks assigned by congressional legislation or presidential assignments, a wide range of public and private activities have been generated by individual justices. These included the practice of providing advice to presidents or, occasionally, to members of Congress as well as outright lobbying efforts. Most examples of such activity were not publically known and so did not stimulate adverse criticism. Several instances, however, did become public and aroused partisan or professional concerns. Early nineteenth-century examples include Justice Joseph *Story's communication to President Madison regarding the nationalization of state militia, William *Johnson's lobbying efforts for improved harbor fortifications for Charleston, South Carolina, and Justice Thomas *Todd's consultations with congressional war hawks. Joseph Story made extensive contacts with executive officials and members of Congress including Attorney General William Pinkney and Daniel *Webster in order to push for judicial legislation and occasionally provided draft statutes to his legislative contacts. Many other members of the Court privately advised or consulted with presidents and members of Congress. Some, such as John Marshall, engaged in writing anonymous political letters to newspapers. Usually advice to presidents remained private but Justice John *Catron's to President James Buchanan on the outcome of the *Dred *Scott* decision became an open political issue as did Justice Abe *Fortas's advice to President Lyndon B. Johnson on the Vietnam War, the Detroit riots, and other domestic issues.

Several justices have sought presidential nominations while on the Supreme Court. In the nineteenth century Justice John *McLean and Chief Justice Salmon P. *Chase both unsuccessfully pursued the presidency. The only justice actually to win a nomination, Justice Charles Evans Hughes, lost the general election but returned to the Court as chief justice. Hughes, however, had observed the proprieties and had resigned from the Court before running. Members of the Court have, on a number of occasions, sought to influence the selection of new members by recommendations to a president or by holding a seat until a president of their own party or ideological inclination took office. Republican Chief Justice Earl Warren's mode of resignation—

an announced delay until President Johnson's selection of his successor—precipitated a firestorm of conservative and Republican resistance, in part because Warren provided an opportunity for a president of the opposite party to chose his successor when the Republican Party hoped for victory in 1968. President Johnson's nominee, Justice Abe Fortas, became the center of the most extensive reexamination of the propriety of extrajudicial activities in modern times. His presidential consultations noted above, his acceptance of a $15,000 fee for a law school seminar lecture, and his involvement in executive statutory proposals all contributed to his withdrawal as nominee. Subsequently, the disclosure of his financial relationship with the private foundation of indicted financier Louis W. Wolfson led to his resignation from the Supreme Court (see FORTAS RESIGNATION).

The disclosure of Fortas's financial arrangement with Wolfson underscores a dimension of extrajudicial activity that rarely receives media attention. This includes matters relating to personal finances or combined money earning. Joseph Story, for example, taught classes at Harvard University Law School and also served as a bank officer in Salem. Justice Samuel *Blatchford edited and sold collections of decisions of the federal circuit on which he served in the nineteenth century.

One of the most interesting modern examples of extensive but discreet extrajudicial activity was that of Associate Justice Louis *Brandeis. For more than two decades, Brandeis engaged in extensive efforts to guide American domestic policy toward the fulfillment of a number of progressive goals and to steer American foreign policy toward favorable responses to Zionist objectives. A number of biographers agreed that Brandeis's extrajudicial activities conducted through a surrogate, future justice Felix *Frankfurter, violated the very institutional proprieties both justices publically extolled. Brandeis privately financed Frankfurter for approximately two decades, facilitating a continuous effort to influence domestic and foreign policy occasionally in areas highly likely to come before the federal courts.

Extrajudicial activity, whether arising out of the private activities of individual justices or from congressional statutes or presidential appointments, raises two fundamental questions. Depending upon the circumstances, one question involves conflict of interest or conflict of principle. A justice may *recuse himself if a real or potential conflict of interest is self-defined or may, albeit rarely, be challenged by an attorney to step down. Conflicts of principle may occur where separation of powers issues are inherent in the situation. Appearance of potential conflict of interest or potential bias received attention in the nineteenth and early twentieth centuries because of the close association of some members of the Court, such as Stephen J. Field, with powerful corporate leaders. A more contemporary issue involves membership in private clubs that discriminate on the basis of *race, ethnicity, *religion, or *gender.

The second question, noted earlier, has received increasing attention in the twentieth century when the overall caseload of the Supreme Court has steadily grown. Chief Justices Edward D. *White, Taft, and Stone, expressed strong concern over the serious effect of taking justices away from the constant task of keeping up with the heavy caseload of the Court.

(See also JUDICIAL ETHICS.)

□ Walter J. Cibes, Jr., "Extrajudicial Activities of the United States Supreme Court, 1790–1960" (Ph.D. diss., Princeton University, 1975). Alpheus Thomas Mason, "Proprieties," in *Harlan Fiske Stone: Pillar of the Law* (1956), pp. 698–722. Bruce Allen Murphy, *The Brandeis-Frankfurter Connection* (1982). Russell Wheeler, "Extrajudicial Activities of the Early Supreme Court," in *1973 Supreme Court Review*, pp. 123–158.

John R. Schmidhauser

# F

**Fairfax's Devisee v. Hunter's Lessee,** 7 Cranch (11 U.S.) 603 (1813), argued 27–28 Feb. 1812, decided 15 Mar. 1813 by vote of 3 to 1; Story for the plurality, Johnson dissenting, Marshall, Washington, and Todd absent. *Fairfax's Devisee* was the prelude to the great constitutional confrontation between Virginia jurists and the United States Supreme Court that culminated in *\*Martin v. Hunter's Lessee* (1816). It implicated the politically sensitive questions of state wartime confiscation of Loyalist property, state obligations under the unpopular Jay Treaty of 1794, and the authority of the Supreme Court over decisions of state supreme courts under section 25 of the *\*Judiciary Act of 1789. The Virginia Supreme Court of Appeals upheld title to property on the Northern Neck derived from state confiscation. On a writ of *error, Justice Joseph *Story, writing for himself and only two other justices, virtually voided the state confiscation act and upheld the claim derived from a Loyalist's title. On remand, the Virginia Supreme Court of Appeals refused to honor the mandate of the Supreme Court; it held section 25 unconstitutional; and Judge Spencer Roane denounced the "centripetal" tendencies of power to accumulate in the federal government. This set the stage for *Martin* v. *Hunter's Lessee.* (See also JUDICIAL POWER AND JURISDICTION.)

William M. Wiecek

**Fairness Doctrine.** See SPEECH AND THE PRESS.

**Fair Representation** was the phrase Chief Justice Earl *Warren used to respond to Justice Felix *Frankfurter's warning that courts should stay out of the *political thicket of *reapportionment cases. The phrase comes from *\*Reynolds v. Sims* (1964), where Warren declared "fair and effective representation for all citizens" to be "the basic aim of legislative apportionment" (pp. 565–566).

Although fair and effective representation in governmental bodies (*Gaffney v. Cummings,* 1973) is a goal to be achieved under the Constitution, what it consists of is not readily obvious. In fact, debate over this very point was perhaps the most contentious issue of the Constitutional Convention.

In *Reynolds* v. *Sims* the Court established that population is "the criterion for judgment in legislative apportionment controversies" (p. 567). Despite considerable criticism that this simplisticly ignores many other valid bases for representation, and that even the Court's insistence upon mathematical equality leads to unfair and ineffective representation, the Court has persisted in using population as the almost exclusive standard for judging fair and effective representation. It has supplemented this, however, by holding that even with equal population districts, racial *gerrymandering is unconstitutional; in more recent times, it has also declared partisan gerrymandering unconstitutional. (The Court has been unable to define the term "partisan gerrymandering" with precision.)

Fair and effective representation has thus come to serve as a shorthand conclusion for those who support judicial supervision of how representation is effected, whereas concern about the "political thicket" is identified with those who have apprehensions about judicial intervention in these controversial and difficult matters.

(See also VOTE, RIGHT TO.)

J. W. Peltason

**Fair Value Rule.** Adopted as a constitutional standard by the Supreme Court in *Smyth* v. *Ames* (1898), the fair value rule was an attempt to protect regulated industries against confiscatory rates. Under this rule a utility was entitled to receive a "fair return" on the "fair value" of investments employed for public service. Fair value was defined as the current value of the company's assets. In theory the fair value rule provided the equivalent of a competitive market return. The rule, however, was difficult to administer because it required courts to make a complex assessment of the present value of utility assets. The fair value rule was abandoned by the Supreme Court in 1944.

James W. Ely, Jr.

**Family and Children.** "Issues involving the family . . . are among the most difficult that courts have to face, involving as they often do, serious problems of policy disguised as questions of constitutional law" (pp. 624–625), declared Justice Potter *Stewart in *Parham* v. *J.R.* (1979). Stewart's declaration revealed the tensions that have accompanied the Supreme Court's increasing involvement in American family life. Family cases coming before the court pit state and federal regulations against challenges by husbands and wives, mothers and fathers, sons and daughters, and various other family claimants. The disputes have compelled the justices both to devise ever more intricate legal doctrines to govern families and to articulate their conceptions of family responsibilities and roles. Their decisions reveal a broad judicial commitment to the family yet deep disagreements over how to implement that commitment. As a result, family cases have become some of the most controversial and contentious on the Supreme Court's docket.

That was not always the case. For most of its history, the Court avoided extensive involvement with family disputes. Under nineteenth-century conceptions of *federalism, states had the primary responsibility for family laws. Rules for *marriage, divorce, childrearing, *inheritance, and other family issues were the province of the state. The Supreme Court endorsed state jurisdiction over the family in a number of decisions, most notably in *Maynard* v. *Hill* (1888). The Court's main contribution was to clarify issues of *comity, that is, it determined the responsibility of one state to enforce the rules of another in disputes over marriage or child custody. Generally, the justices encouraged states to grant *full faith and credit to the family rules of other jurisdictions. In addition, the Court got involved in specific controversies such as the fight against polygamy, in which the justices refused to defer to marriage laws of Utah endorsing the practice.

In general, the Court's endorsement of state family regulation encouraged an array of local and regional differences in American family law. These variations ranged from bans on interracial marriages to limits on the inheritance rights of illegitimate children.

In the twentieth century, the states continued to structure family life, but the Court assumed an even greater supervisory role culminating in a set of national family law standards. Significant federal judicial involvement in family disputes began in a series of parental rights cases in the 1920s. In *Meyer* v. *Nebraska* (1923) and *Pierce* v. *Society of Sisters* (1925), the Court upheld the right of a parent to direct his or her child's *education. The decisions endorsed parental authority by asserting that families existed in a constitutionally protected private realm of society. *Prince* v. *Massachusetts* (1944) widened the Court's commitment to family privatism by declaring that there is a realm of family life that the state cannot enter without substantial justification. Through shifting determinations of such justifications, the Court has granted families autonomy from state regulations as protections of liberty guaranteed by the *Fourteenth Amendment. In the years after World War II, such constitutional protection became the basis of the court's growing involvement with the nation's families.

A series of interrelated developments encouraged the Court to act. American families underwent significant changes. Divorces increased dramatically; women entered the permanent labor force in growing numbers; *contraception and *abortion became available family limitation practices; and alternative family arrangements from foster homes to *homosexual unions challenged existing definitions of families. These and many other changes transformed family life and created growing controversies and an escalating number of lawsuits. Indeed, as at times of social tension in the past, the family became a battleground for contests spawned by social change. Unlike the past, though, the federal government, and especially the Supreme Court, became one of the primary arenas of that struggle. The federal government's role in family life had increased dramatically with the creation of programs like Social Security and Aid to Families with Dependent Children. The civil rights revolution also sparked new concerns about national family policies and a new sense of rights consciousness among family members. Similarly, an expanding sense of *privacy encouraged new assertions of family autonomy over decisions about pregnancy and childrearing. Consequently, many of the endemic tensions in American family law that had plagued *state courts in the nineteenth century emerged to bedevil the Supreme Court in the twentieth.

Beginning in the 1960s, the Court's construction of family law rules became more and more extensive. As the range of family matters under its scrutiny increased, the family beliefs, commitments, and disagreements of the justices became more evident. The Court often split over whether to defer to state policies or to enlarge individual rights. Both the range and limits of the Court's family jurisprudence indicates its new role in the nation's households. In almost every area of family life, the Court issued rulings that significantly altered the balance of power within the family and between family members and the state. At the same time, the justices struggled over the extent and character of these changes. Decisions on four issues illustrate the results: parents and children; illegitimacy; family *privacy; and family definition.

The Court has redefined the legal relationship of parent and child. It has created new balances between state and parental control over socialization as well as between the rights of children and parents. The cases also exhibited the persistent tension in family law over whether the court should support the rights of individual family members or those of the family as a unit. The overlapping claims and rights of families made these troubling issues. The Court responded to them in part by continuing the policy of supporting parental rights. In *Wisconsin v. Yoder (1972), it granted constitutional sanction to Amish parents who withdrew their children from school in violation of compulsory school laws. Yet for the first time, children received constitutionally protected rights they could assert against the state and even against their parents. In re *Gault (1967) launched the expansion of juvenile rights. In granting youths coming before juvenile courts procedural rights such as the right to *counsel, the Court declared the young had rights similar to those of adults. It extended them in cases like *Tinker v. Des Moines Independent Community School District (1969) by giving students political rights, since the young had rights they do not leave "at the schoolhouse gate" (p. 506). At the same time, the Court ruled that minors could act independently of their parents by seeking abortions and by gaining protections against abuse and neglect. However, the Court refused to grant minors rights as extensive as those of adults. Parents retained considerable authority over their offspring. In Parham, which supported the right of parents to commit their children to mental institutions, Chief Justice Warren *Burger used the kind of language often heard in family cases: "[O]ur jurisprudence historically has reflected Western civilization concepts of the family as a unit with broad parental authority over minor children" (p. 602). The Court, in short, rearranged the balance of rights and duties between parents, children, and the state by using the *Due Process and *Equal Protection Clauses to create a series of newly protected family rights.

Similarly, the Court tackled the age-old problem of illegitimacy by giving new rights to these star-crossed children and their biological parents.

Anglo-American law had long tried to protect the family created by marriage by refusing to grant illegitimate children full family rights. Challenges to the policies stressed their unfairness and raised concerns about child dependency in an era of rising illegitimacy. Drawing on the Equal Protection Clause, the Court created a new set of national illegitimacy rules beginning with Levy v. Louisiana (1968). In Levy, the justices overturned a law denying illegitimate children the same rights as legitimate offspring to recover for the wrongful death of their mother. The decision highlighted a judicial dedication to the primacy of individual rights evident throughout the Court's family law cases. In other decisions, the court increased the inheritance and support rights of illegitimates. Equally dramatic, in Stanley v. Illinois (1972), the Court expanded the rights of unwed, biological fathers by granting them hearings before state agencies could remove their children on charges of parental unfitness. Later cases extended those rights as well. And yet, neither illegitimate children nor unwed fathers won rights as extensive as their legitimate and married peers. The Court narrowed but retained the law's longstanding moral commitment to matrimony by limiting the rights of illegitimate children and their parents. (See also INHERITANCE AND ILLEGITIMACY.)

Quite to the contrary, the Court greatly expanded its conception of family privacy. A series of decisions had long upheld the right of individuals to wed and procreate, but those rights had always been balanced against state regulations on marriage and birth. *Griswold v. Connecticut (1965) fundamentally shifted the balance by granting family privacy constitutional protection. In overturning a birth control ban, the ruling initiated a series of decisions that protected the right to make private choices free from state interference in a range of matters. The Court ruled that the state could not deprive persons of the right to marry or to take away their ability to have children, nor forbid the use of contraception or abortion. As before, the newly expanded private realm of family life was not entirely immune from state regulation. The Court shifted the balance toward individual choice and against state regulation by knocking down state laws dating back to the mid-nineteenth century. The decisions also documented the reemergence of persistent family law themes such as the interconnection of *gender and family issues evident in the clash of fetal versus women's rights, and the class dimension of legal rules revealed in rulings upholding the right of states to bar public funding of abortion. Equally significant, the family privacy cases demonstrated how contentious family law cases could be as they thrust the Court into the center of political controversy.

Finally, the Court was forced to define the family itself in constitutional terms. New family forms, federal policies, and legal rules spurred debate over what sort of families warranted constitutional protection. Over the years, the justices had issued a stream of statements in support of the family. The meaning of that commitment became clearer in decisions like *Moore v. East Cleveland* (1977) upholding the right of extended, biologically related families to live together in defiance of local *zoning ordinances limiting family size. Equally telling was *Belle Terre v. Boraas* (1974) in which the Court endorsed a zoning law limiting the number of unrelated people who could live together. It refused to accept a communal arrangement of college students as a family in conformance with the law. Other decisions limited the rights of foster families and refused to accept as families alternative family arrangements such as homosexual unions and cohabiting couples. In these cases, the Court reiterated a longstanding state and federal judicial commitment to the "traditional" family, especially to the primacy of blood ties, and an aversion to granting alternative family arrangements legal protection. As in decisions involving illegitimate children, unwed fathers, and poor women seeking state-funded abortions, class and moral commitments of the Court emerged in these decisions. The dual system of family law that had long dominated state rules and rulings—a set of liberationist rules for the middle and upper classes and those in traditional arrangements, and a set of repressive rules for the lower classes, the dependent, and cultural minorities—now appeared in national family jurisprudence.

By the 1990s the Supreme Court had issued extensive rulings on family life. The cases spilled over into issues ranging from religion to gender equity. And the disputes were so intense that they generated apocalyptic statements from the justices and intense debate among the public. Despite their inconsistencies and contradictions, the Court's rulings had redefined the legal and constitutional basis of the American family. Significantly, the Court had become a major source of national family policies. Its decisions helped structure American family life on everything from birth to death.

□ Robert A. Burt, "The Constitution of the Family," *Supreme Court Review* (1979), 329–395. Michael Grossberg, *Governing the Hearth, Law and the Family in Nineteenth Century America* (1985). Robert H. Mnoonkin et al., *In the Interests of Children, Advocacy, Law Reform, and Public Policy* (1985). Eva Rubin, *The Supreme Court and the American Family* (1986).          Michael Grossberg

**Fay v. Noia,** 372 U.S. 391 (1963), argued 7–8 Jan. 1963, decided by vote of 6 to 3; Brennan for the Court, Harlan, Clark, and Stewart in dissent. The relationship between the national government and the states is the central problem of American *federalism. This is illustrated in examining how the state and federal courts interact with respect to the administration of criminal justice. The

availability of federal *habeas corpus to persons who have been convicted of crime in *state courts is such an issue.

Since the enactment of the *Judiciary Act of 1789, all federal courts have been authorized to grant writs of *habeas corpus to federal prisoners. Not until the adoption of the Judiciary Act of 1867, however, was federal habeas corpus made available to state as well as federal prisoners in all cases where a violation of a federal right was alleged.

*Fay v. Noia* is a notable example of the expansion of the rights of state prisoners through a federal habeas corpus proceeding. Noia had been convicted in a New York court of a felony murder. The question arose whether he could gain federal habeas corpus relief after he was denied state post-conviction relief because the time had lapsed for a review by a state appellate court. The bone of contention was the admissibility of a confession that in the case of two confederates had been held to have been coerced. As construed by the Supreme Court, the Due Process Clause of the *Fourteenth Amendment prohibits the use in any state court of coerced confessions.

The U.S. District Court for the Southern District of New York denied Noia relief, holding that under the federal habeas corpus statute a state prisoner could be granted the writ only if the applicant had exhausted the remedies available in the state courts. The federal court of appeals reversed the district court, holding that "exceptional circumstances" were present that excused compliance with the state rule relating to appeals. This court held that a state remedy was no longer available to Noia at the time the federal habeas proceeding was commenced; the state had conceded that Noia's confession had been coerced, relying entirely on his failure to take a timely appeal from his original conviction to a state appellate court.

The Supreme Court agreed with the court of appeals. The Court majority refused to apply the rule that state procedural defaults constitute an adequate and independent state ground for barring a direct review by the Supreme Court of the original conviction. It held that the rule relating to direct review should not be extended to limit the power granted to federal courts by the federal habeas corpus statute. In other words, because of the crucial importance of the writ of habeas corpus, Noia's failure to make a timely appeal in the state courts was not an intelligent and understanding waiver of his right to seek federal relief.

Justice William *Brennan asserted that there is no higher duty than to maintain unimpaired the right to seek the writ, whose "root principle is that in a civilized society, government must always be accountable to the judiciary for a man's imprisonment . . ." (p. 402).

There was another important procedural issue in this case. A long line of court decisions and a federal statute had established the proposition that after a state prisoner has been convicted in a state trial court, before seeking a federal writ, he must first exhaust all available state remedies. Normally, a prisoner had to exhaust appeals to state appellate courts, which usually meant review by the state supreme court. The U.S. Supreme Court in *Darr* v. *Burford* (1950) held that state remedies were not exhausted until a defendant had also attempted to secure a review of the highest state court action in the U.S. Supreme Court by means of the writ of *certiorari. The Court, of course, denies more than 90 percent of the applications for certiorari and almost never gives reasons for doing so. In *Fay* v. *Noia*, the Court abandoned the position it had taken in *Darr*, holding that a petition to the Supreme Court for certiorari is not a "state remedy." The justices condemned the *Darr* rule as unduly burdensome, since most petitions for certiorari clogged the Court's calendar and needlessly consumed time.

(See also DUE PROCESS, PROCEDURAL; EXHAUSTION OF REMEDIES.)

□ David Fellman. *The Defendant's Rights Today* (1976), chap. 5. David Fellman

**Federal Common Law.** When written federal constitutional or statutory law does not provide the answer to a particular issue presented in a case, a federal judge may decide either that state laws control or that the court should devise a rule of federal common law to govern, in state and federal courts, at least until Congress replaces it with a statutory rule. In *Swift* v. *Tyson* (1842) the court established a federal commercial law.

Sometimes judges make federal common law to govern specific issues, as when they fill a gap in a federal statutory scheme (*Clearfield Trust Co.* v. *United States*, 1943). Sometimes the Supreme Court interprets an enactment to direct judges to create federal rules throughout a substantive area. For example, the Supreme Court has interpreted *Article III's grant of *admiralty and maritime jurisdiction to give courts power to create a body of federal admiralty law.

A central issue is how judges are to be confined to making law only when consistent with congressional or constitutional intent. To date, the system has relied primarily on *judicial self-restraint; judges are to make federal common law only when important federal interests require it. There is uneasiness with such an open-ended approach, yet no workable alternative has been found. Because state law may apply if judges do not make a federal rule, the exercise of restraint in developing federal common law contributes to a healthy *federalism.

Federal common law is often misunderstood because of the famous statement in *Erie Railroad* v. *Tompkins* (1938) that "there is no federal general common law" (p. 78). Nonetheless, federal common law is an important part of our

tradition of case-by-case adjudication, allowing the judiciary to resolve unforeseen issues fairly; federal common law shows no sign of diminishing in importance.

(See also COMMON LAW; JUDICIAL POWER AND JURISDICTION.)

Martha A. Field

**Federalism.** The proper balance of state and national powers in the American federal system, wrote Woodrow Wilson in 1911, is not a matter that can be settled "by the opinion of any one generation." Changes in the social and economic condition of society, in the electorate's perception of issues needing to be addressed by government, and in the prevailing political values, Wilson declared, require each successive generation to treat federal-state relationships as "a new question," subject to full and searching reappraisal.

The Supreme Court has only rarely admitted to considering such a pragmatic view of the basis on which the boundary lines ought to be drawn demarcating the limits of national power and the proper realm of the states' authority. On the contrary, even when the justices have broken new doctrinal ground or moved away from earlier positions on matters of the highest importance in law and policy, their rhetoric typically has referred to the letter—and, ineluctably, also to "the spirit"—of the Constitution. They have sought for consistency of principle, even when they are most obviously engaged in a process of transforming the working legal rules under the rubric of established principle. They have tended to speak of the issue of federalism not as "a new question," as Wilson urged, but as an old and in vital respects a timeless formulation.

*Judicial Authority and Federal Structure.* The need for concern with consistency of principle was recognized well by the justices from the start of the Court's history. As Justice James *Iredell declared only a few years after adoption of the 1787 Constitution, "the judicial system under the authority of the union is of a higher and more important nature than it is in most governments." This was so, Iredell wrote, because the judiciary was not only to rule upon disputes but was also "established as a great constitutional guard of the constitution itself, since it is to carry into effect no laws but such as the constitution authorized" (see JUDICIAL POWER AND JURISDICTION). The judicial system would serve to check the legislative power in this republican government; in this sense, it was a place where the individual could turn for protection of liberty. The other side of such judicial power was, of course, the guarding of the Constitution from excessive claims from the states impinging on the center. It was this view of the principled questions associated with judicial power and the definition of federal boundaries that was expressed 120 years later by the justices in *Hammer* v. *Dagenhart*

(1918). The Court held that it had "no more important function than that which devolves upon it the obligation to preserve inviolate the constitutional limitations upon the exercise of authority, [both] federal and state . . ." (p. 276).

Another side of the Court's decisions in cases bearing on federalism addresses the intensely practical function of maintaining a "balance" of national and state powers that will permit the government to operate effectively—or, at moments of high crisis, even to survive. For all its vaunted concern for the abstract questions of constitutional principle, *"original intent," and what are often termed the "political values of federalism," the Court perforce has been concerned with the government's capacity. In his charge to the federal grand jury in New York in 1790, Chief Justice John *Jay gave expression to this important aspect of the federal judiciary's role. If the new Constitution were to be effective as well as just, Jay declared, it was essential to "provide against Discord between national and State Jurisdictions, to render them auxiliary instead of hostile to each other; and so to connect both as to leave each sufficiently independent, and yet sufficiently combined."

In certain periods of the nation's history, the Court has provided strong intellectual leadership in the development of constitutional federalism—either in a progressive mode, encouraging of policy innovation and change, or else in a conservative mode, providing vital doctrinal support to political groups that wanted to use federalism as a bulwark against movements for change. In other periods, the Court has been notably reticent, keeping issues of federalism and boundary-setting fairly well isolated from other types of questions brought before it. On one unique occasion, in Dred *Scott v. Sandford (1857), the Court plunged unnecessarily into the most explosive area of contemporary politics in a way that caused its most notorious "self-inflicted wound."

In whichever of these modes it has operated at given times, the Court, when it has spoken on issues of federalism, has done so with uniquely definitive authority to frame policy questions in constitutional and legal terms; and in so doing, it has effectively elevated these issues to new levels of discourse, always running some risk of escalating existing controversies to a new level of intensity as well. As illustrated by such instances as the Court's inability to get President Andrew *Jackson to enforce the terms of its decision in *Worcester v. Georgia (1832), it is one thing for the Court to pronounce a "definitive" constitutional resolution to a controversial question, but it is quite another thing to command assent to its mandates. For this reason the Supreme Court's role as "umpire of the federal system" has often been a source of ideological tension—and occasionally of high political drama—in the course of the nation's history.

*Context of Antebellum Federalism.* From the founding period to the Civil War, the Supreme Court's deliberations on matters of federalism were consistently subject to a number of distinctive configuring pressures. The first of such pressures was the legacy of the American Revolution with respect to distrust of centralized power. The Revolution had been fought in the name of American home rule; from the outset of the crisis, the issues of self-governance, republicanism, and *natural rights had all been debated in terms of liberation from a too-powerful authority at the center, in London, being used arbitrarily against American interests and political communities. This experience with excessive centralization of power was part of the American political consciousness not only in 1776 but throughout the antebellum era. Hence, when the specter of "consolidation" was raised in constitutional discourse, including argument before the Supreme Court, it was a powerful and troubling image— one that had to be reckoned with by nationalists who sought to define and protect the new national government's authority. Posed against it, however, also as part of the Revolutionary era's legacy, was the understood need for a central government that could command respect in international relations and could maintain domestic stability.

A second pressure on the Court derived from the ambiguities that were part of the legacy of the ratification debates. In the debate over the Constitution, there was agreement on all sides that the national government was to be one of limited powers—limited because they were "enumerated" powers, given to that government by the people through the ratification process in the states. There was a striking lack of agreement, however, on the extent to which enumeration meant that a survival of "sovereignty" in the states, as constituent units within the larger system, ensured certain elements of state jurisdiction against any encroachments by the central government (see CONCURRENT POWER). "Consolidation" was a repugnant alternative to federalism in the rhetoric of the early Republic; but different political elements had different views of how far centralization might legitimately go before it became a dangerous variety of "consolidation," threatening individual liberty and legitimate pursuit of local concerns with a stifling conformity imposed from the center. The result of the Convention's labors in 1787 had been, as James *Madison would write, "a novelty and a compound," in its new federal aspects that perpetuated the states as political units yet established a national government that acted directly upon the people rather than, as in the Confederation period, only upon the states. But where, and even how, to mark out the spheres of authority and the extent to which the states had what Madison termed "an inviolable sovereignty" in residual areas of authority remained controversial questions. The Supreme Court, even at its most nationalistic moments, could not escape easily from this legacy of ambiguity.

The third pressure derived from the fact that the potential for disruption or dissolution of the Union—secession by disaffected states, declaring their right to resume independent sovereign existences as constitutional polities—remained until the *Civil War a serious possibility (see NULLIFICATION).

Fourth among these pressures unique to the antebellum era from 1789 to 1861 was the fact that the states were manifestly competent—as a practical matter—to perform a wide range of governmental functions whose effective pursuit in a later era would require much greater centralization of authority and governmental effort. The system of a highly decentralized federalism in which the national government could without danger to the Republic undertake only relatively few areas of governance exclusively—and in the other areas of governance primarily or even exclusively to the states—meant that the Court would face the possibility of volatile charges of "reaching" beyond what even pragmatic considerations required whenever it denied state authority.

Finally, cutting through all these pressures on the court, was the question of *slavery in the South. No issue bearing on federalism and the national government's proper role could ever escape the implications of doctrine and policy for the future of the slave system controlled by the state governments. Just as all of politics was infused by the slavery question, so was all of constitutional law. Neither "state rights" nor "consolidation" was a concept separable from race relations and the maintenance of the slave system in antebellum governance.

*Judicial Nationalism and Dual Federalism.* In its first four decades—as might be expected in a nation-building period when both the British threat (which materialized in the War of 1812) and the strength of state loyalties, with their decentralizing potential, posed serious dangers to the new Republic—the Court's line of decisions was principally important for its contributions to shoring up the new national government's authority (see HISTORY OF THE COURT: ESTABLISHMENT OF THE UNION). To be certain, its nationalism was neither militant nor even uncompromising; and so significant concessions to the claims of the states were made. One was the decision in *United States* v. *Hudson and Goodwin* (1812) that the federal judiciary did not have a *common-law jurisdiction over crimes; its jurisdiction in the criminal area was restricted according to statutory authority (see FEDERAL COMMON LAW). A second was the adoption of rulings in a variety of cases that assured the *state courts of their unquestioned authority to construe their own state constitutions and statutes as well as to perpetuate many important rules of common law in regard to

estates, property, trespass, and *torts. The Court's position in this regard was affirmed in broad terms in *Elmendorf* v. *Taylor* (1825).

Third, the Court—even at the height of the Court's enthusiasm for broad construction in a nationalist mode, in the era of Chief Justice John *Marshall's leadership—provided a rhetorical legacy that in later years, when enthusiasm for state rights reigned supreme, would lend support to the doctrines of *"dual federalism." Thus in the case of *Cohens* v. *Virginia* (1821), a powerfully nationalizing decision, Marshall himself conceded that "these States . . . are members of one great empire—for some purposes sovereign, and for some purposes subordinate" (p. 412). Then, in *Gibbons* v. *Ogden* (1824), even while broadly asserting national power over commerce, Marshall made explicit reference to the state police powers as embracing elements of authority "not surrendered to the general government" (p. 203)—a concept that he broadened in a subsequent decision, *Willson* v. *Blackbird Creek Marsh Co.* (1829), to provide the basic doctrine of the dormant *commerce power. Similarly, in *Weston* v. *Charleston* (1829), the Court established a doctrine that proved long lived in future jurisprudence—the immunity of state agencies against the federal taxing power (the obverse side of *McCulloch* v. *Maryland* [1819] and its immunizing of federal instrumentalities from state taxation). (See TAX IMMUNITIES.)

The most important "decentralizing" decision with respect to the role of the states in the nation's governance, however, was *Barron* v. *Baltimore* (1833), in which the Court decided that the *Bill of Rights amendments had never been intended to apply as checks upon the state governments. Thus the hand of the federal courts was stayed; not until a much later time would they mobilize their constitutional authority—and then mainly through application of the *Fourteenth Amendment—to provide judicial protection for individuals and groups against state governmental threats to the great liberties embraced in the first eight amendments.

The impact of these decisions favoring the sovereignty of the states paled in significance against the countertrend of the first four decades. This was the Court's movement toward nationalism and a broad construction of the enumerated powers granted to the national government in the Constitution. The principal instruments for recognizing broad discretionary authority in Congress and the federal courts themselves included the Supremacy Clause, the Commerce Clause, and the *Contract Clause. Asserting in *Cohens* v. *Virginia* (1821) that "no government ought to be so defective in its organization, as not to contain within itself, the means of securing the execution of its own laws" (p. 387), Marshall indicated the Court's readiness to find authority to enforce—in this instance, through review of state decisions that presumed to pass on the constitutionality of an act of Congress—wherever the Constitution provided the authority to act in the first place. In *McCulloch* v. *Maryland*, striking down Maryland's attempted taxation of the Bank of the United States, the Court mobilized the Supremacy Clause to give unstinted notice of its intent to read broadly authority to act. "The government of the Union," Marshall declared for the Court, "though limited in its powers, is supreme within its sphere of action. . . . It is the government of all, its powers are delegated by all; it represents all, and acts for all" (p. 404).

This magisterial view of the government "of all" carried over to commerce and contract decisions in which the Court boldly deployed its own judicial authority to review state legislation and thereby constrain and limit *state action. Application of these clauses of the Constitution to protect recipients of land grants or other *property from the state legislature (as in *Fletcher* v. *Peck*, 1810), or to throw a blanket of Contract Clause protection over the incorporeal elements of corporate franchises (in *Dartmouth College* v. *Woodward*, 1819), or to assure freedom of navigation on internal waters and a free internal market for movement of goods in commerce in *Gibbons* v. *Ogden* was a powerful move by the Court (see CAPITALISM). For the nation's mercantile and investor interests, the Court thereby provided the very type of nationalization of rights that the Court declined to extend to civil rights and liberties in *Barron* v. *Baltimore*.

In the latter part of the antebellum era, from 1836 until the Civil War, the Court significantly altered its posture with regard to the juridical nature of American federalism. Led by Chief Justice Roger B. *Taney in this period, the Court moved strongly to shore up the doctrines of a "dual federalism," based on the notion of the state and national governments as coequals—each operating in its own sphere, autonomous within that sphere. The first move in this direction came in *Charles River Bridge* v. *Warren Bridge* (1837), when the Court's new majority declared that state governments enjoyed wide discretionary authority to advance and protect rights of the public as against the claims of corporations (see PRIVATE CORPORATION CHARTERS). No charter should be given a broad construction, and thereby afforded sweeping protection under the Contract Clause against regulation or new competition. The Court's concern now was to assure that the states would retain "the rights reserved to [them]" by the Constitution—that is, "the power over their own internal policy and improvement, which is so necessary to their well being and prosperity" (p. 552).

The Court further narrowed the effectiveness of the Contract Clause limitation on state action by ruling in *West River Bridge* v. *Dix* (1848) that when the states exercised the *eminent domain power to take property, challenges to the propriety of such *takings or to the compensation to the former owners of property taken were the exclusive concern of the state's own agencies; the federal courts would not intervene. In this and later eminent domain cases, the Court declined to make the state governments subject to judicial supervision.

Whereas the holdings of the Court in the *Charles River Bridge* and *West River Bridge* cases greatly reduced the range of Contract Clause barriers to the states' authority, a series of Commerce Clause cases beginning with *New York* v. *Miln* (1837) and culminating with *Cooley* v. *Board of Wardens* (1852) did similar damage to another key doctrinal buttress of the Marshall Court's nationalism (see PASSENGER CASES; LICENSE CASES). Some subjects of regulatory authority in commerce, the Court declared in *Cooley*, demanded "a single uniform rule," but others "as imperatively demand[ed] that diversity, which alone can meet the local necessities of navigation" (p. 318). (See SELECTIVE EXCLUSIVENESS.) In the *Miln* decision, the Court had declared that in its own sphere "the authority of a State is complete, unqualified, and exclusive." It referred to the "undeniable and unlimited jurisdiction" of the state in that sphere (p. 138). In the *Passenger Cases* (1849), the justices disagreed, but the majority view revealed the further implications of this new jurisprudence of the nation and states as coequals, reasserting that state powers sprang from their sovereignty and were not dependent on the sufferance of Congress.

These decisions not only reflected but also reinforced the tendencies in Jacksonian-era politics to enshrine the doctrines of state sovereignty and a limited practical role in policy-making for the national government. The Court's new version of federalism also reflected vividly, however, the Jacksonians' dilemma of how to continue accommodating the demands of the southern slave states—above all, that their "peculiar institution" be safely kept behind the ramparts of that "inviolable sovereignty" that would assure perpetuation of the bondage of blacks under white society's complete control. Although southern states' righters bitterly denounced nationalist decisions of the Marshall era—most especially the *McCulloch* supremacy doctrine—in no case directly dealing with slavery did either the Marshall or the Taney Court ever reach a conclusion in law that explicitly curbed, or even indirectly challenged, the slaveowners' control over their slaves. The *Dred Scott* decision, only the second in the Court's history to overturn a congressional statute, fecklessly overreached to extend the mantle of protection over the institutions of slavery and interests of the slave states. Ironically, then, the Taney Court, so dedicated to doctrines of state sovereignty and dual federalism, proved quite ready to support sweeping congressional powers to restrict procedural rights of defendants in cases brought under the national Fugitive Slave Law of 1850 (see FUGITIVE

SLAVES). As the sectional crisis ominously unfolded in the 1850s, moreover, the Court in *Ableman* v. *Booth* (1859) and other cases unhesitatingly put down all efforts by state legislatures, courts, and officials to interfere with enforcement of the fugitive acts on grounds that the status of persons of whatever color or prior condition of servitude came within the "exclusive sphere" of state authority when present within that state's borders.

Insofar, however, as the Taney Court otherwise promoted nationalistic doctrines—and it did so in several important areas of law, despite its absorption in the main task of advancing dual federalism—it presented only a mild challenge to politically controversial exercises of state authority and decentralized governance. One such area concerned the extent of the federal courts' admiralty jurisdiction; in the *Genesee Chief* v. *Fitzhugh* (1852), the Court upheld congressional expansion of that jurisdiction far beyond what English precedent and the Court's earlier doctrines had permitted, so as to include all major navigable waters. National power was also extended by the Court in regard to uniformity of rules applicable in commercial cases brought in federal courts. Thus, in *Swift* v. *Tyson* (1842), a rare victory for Justice Joseph *Story in his losing struggle to maintain Marshall's principles against the tide of change exemplified by Taney, the Court did declare that certain elements of uniformity were essential.

The Taney Court also was responsible for developing a generous definition of "diversity of citizenship," so as to open the federal courts to suits involving *corporations domiciled in various states (see DIVERSITY JURISDICTION). Occasionally decisions on corporate activity cut both ways, notably in *Bank of Augusta* v. *Earle* (1839), in which the Court ruled that under comity principles there was a presumption that "foreign" (that is, out-of-state) corporations could do business in a state unless that state had explicitly adopted a policy of exclusion. Advancing a nationalist view by encouraging the open internal market for movement of capital and doing business, the decision did, however, leave the way open in theory for a complete exclusion of "foreign" firms—a policy not likely to be resorted to in the real world of business and politics.

When the guns sounded at Fort Sumter in 1861, the doctrines of interstate *comity, the niceties of rules of construction in federal commercial law, and similar traditional concerns of the Court became irrelevancies overnight. These great constitutional questions—what legitimate claims the Union might impose upon states seeking to dissociate and what protection might the Constitution forever require to sustain slavery in this nation as nearly the last remaining stronghold of that institution in a world claiming modern enlightenment—would be settled not by jurists but instead by the Union armies.

*Post–Civil War Jurisprudence: Federalism, Conservatism, and Centralization.* If ever the Court was faced with federal-state relationships as "a new question," it was in the Civil War and *Reconstruction years. In its famous dictum in *Texas* v. *White* (1869) that "[t]he Constitution, in all its provisions, looks to an indestructible Union, composed of indestructible States" (p. 725), the Chase Court enshrined the Radical Republicans' view of federalism. This was the epitaph for the "compact theory" that so long had been championed by states' rights advocates in the antebellum era. Under this theory, the Court not only held the State of Texas to its obligations to creditors, the immediate issue, but expressed a doctrine as to the Union that had lent constitutional sanction to a wide range of extraordinary wartime emergency powers mobilized by President Abraham *Lincoln. This doctrine would also validate Congress's use of federal military forces to administer its Reconstruction program (see PRESIDENTIAL EMERGENCY POWERS).

Though the indivisibility of the Union was a settled question, other major issues remained on the Court's agenda in the post–Civil War era and through the first three decades of the twentieth century. Crucial among these issues was the rising industrialization of the nation, along with the emergence of a corporate structure that had become well established as the prototype of advanced capitalism by the early 1900s (see HISTORY OF THE COURT: RECONSTRUCTION, FEDERALISM, AND ECONOMIC RIGHTS). The giant national economy, stressed by the successive impacts of new technologies and the ways in which older regions were challenged by the velocity of accelerating economic change, manifestly could not be brought under effective public regulation without a strong degree of centralization of power. How much centralizing the Constitution approved, and the extent to which even the authority of the state governments were subject to constitutional limitations, remained vital questions.

No less momentous for the future of the nation and its federal system was the Court's response to the post–Civil War Amendments—especially the *Fourteenth, which many of its congressional authors clearly had intended to effect a fundamental change in the balance of state and national power.

In ways reminiscent of the Marshall Court's mobilization of contract, commerce, and supremacy doctrines to limit the autonomy of the states, the Court in the late nineteenth century created a formidable arsenal of doctrines that expanded national authority while placing curbs on the reach of state power. Commerce Clause jurisprudence continued to be of central importance. In *Pensacola Telegraph Co.* v. *Western Union* (1877), the Court invalidated a state law that conflicted with congressional regulations of the new electric telegraph industry. "Within the scope of its powers," the Court forthrightly declared, the national government "operates on every foot of territory under its jurisdiction. It legislates for the whole nation, and is not embarrassed by State lines" (p. 10). By striking down state railroad rate regulations that impinged on interstate operations, the Court in *Wabash, St. Louis, and Pacific Railway* v. *Illinois* (1886) gave new life to the concept of the "dormant commerce power" of Congress: even in the absence of national legislation, state action that burdened interstate commerce would not be tolerated. The latter decision undoubtedly served as a trigger for Congress to step in with major legislation, in this instance the 1887 Interstate Commerce Act (see INTERSTATE COMMERCE COMMISSION). Once Congress occupied a legislative field, the door was opened for the Court to engage in statutory interpretation that would find specific congressional intent to "preempt" the entire area and thus foreclose types of state regulation that might otherwise have passed a constitutional test. In the 1890s, the expanded formal authority that Congress thus enjoyed lent impetus to its legislation for national regulation of lotteries, the liquor traffic, and commerce in game taken in violation of state laws. The Pure Food and Drug Act of 1906 heralded a qualitative change in the character of federal intervention, since this law relied for enforcement upon a large bureaucratic force of agency experts doing inspections in the field.

The post–Civil War Court also built on the earlier doctrine of a federal commercial common law to develop a more expansive notion of a "general jurisprudence" that could be invoked to overturn state court decisions that upheld bond repudiation. The justices' deployment of new doctrines as negative checks on state action went forward apace from that foundation. Thus by 1900, gradually accepting most of Justice Stephen *Field's property-minded theories and leaning upon the jurisprudence of Thomas *Cooley and other conservatives, the Court had developed a full-blown doctrine of "implied limitations" expressed in a variety of modes. Ironically the concept of "business affected with a public interest," derived from *Munn* v. *Illinois* (1877), in which the Court had upheld strong regulatory interventions by the states. But over time, the drawing of the boundary between "ordinary" businesses, which the Court ruled could not be regulated, and those in the "affected" category became a means of immunizing many forms of enterprise from state control. Another major doctrine that provided for limitations on state authority was "liberty of contract," which obtained its fullest expression in 1905 in *Lochner* v. *New York* (see CONTRACT, FREEDOM OF). A third was the notion of "public purpose" limits upon use of the taxation power of the states; it became linked with a conservative move by the Court to curb the range of federal taxation as well (see DUE PROCESS, SUBSTANTIVE). In addition, the Supreme

Court upheld uses of the federal equity power in labor disputes, often over the objections of state officials in the locations affected or even against the thrust of state legislation (see LABOR).

Of course, the Court's activism in all these respects constituted an exercise of centralized power that profoundly affected the balance of the federal system (see JUDICIAL ACTIVISM). This does not mean either that the Court always disfavored the states or that it consistently supported the uses of national power that Congress chose to pursue. As to the states, for example, the Court did uphold a broad discretionary authority for them to develop their natural resources through various uses of the eminent domain power, the ordering of their water law on highly diverse lines, and even the adoption of a variety of regulatory measures such as public health enforcement. The Court declined to extend an activist federal judicial censorship over the states' efforts to cope with some of the leading challenges of economic development and the attainment of new goals in the areas of public health and welfare. (Indeed, the high courts of many states invoked "due process" doctrine and principles of *vested rights even more rigorously than did the federal justices to strike down legislative initiatives.) Similarly, the Supreme Court declined to extend federal procedural guarantees in the criminal justice area, so that state and local authorities continued to enjoy wide discretion in their police operations, court houses, and jails (see DUE PROCESS, PROCEDURAL). Only in regard to property takings did the Court depart from *Barron* v. *Baltimore*, ruling as early as 1897 that the Fourteenth Amendment "incorporated" the takings provisions of the *Fifth (see INCORPORATION DOCTRINE).

As to the permissible range of congressional authority, the Supreme Court began to give close scrutiny to national legislation that it regarded as exceeding constitutional authority; thus, in 1879 it struck down an act of Congress protecting trademarks, and in 1883 it rendered the Civil Rights Acts virtually unenforceable. In the next decade, the Court virtually eviscerated the *Sherman Antitrust Act by ruling that control of manufacturing was not authorized by the Commerce Clause powers, resulting in a significant delay in effective enforcement; and in *Pollock* v. *Farmers' Loan & Trust Co.* (1895), the Court found unconstitutional a federal income tax.

The culmination of this line of conservative decision-making was the 1918 decision in *Hammer* v. *Dagenhart*, which overturned an act of Congress that would have banned the products of child labor from interstate commerce. This decision crystallized the conservative majority's successful reformulation of "dual federalism" for the Court. Insisting that enumeration of powers in the Constitution must be read literally—and be measured against the guarantees of "local power . . . reserved to the States in the Tenth

Amendment"—the majority provided a lecture on constitutional principle that John C. Calhoun would have found quite acceptable: "the powers not expressly delegated to the National Government are reserved, . . . [and] the power of the States to regulate their purely internal affairs by such laws as seem wise to the local authority is inherent and has never been surrendered to the general government" (pp. 275–276). It would be the Court itself, of course, that would determine on a case-by-case basis that affairs were "purely internal" in their character, and thus were in an exclusively state-controlled sphere of authority.

**Constitutional Transformation: The New Deal Era.** The potential of dual federalism and the other conservative doctrines for crippling the national government in a dire emergency would be fully realized, at least for a short interval, when the Great Depression struck and the early *New Deal legislation came before an often-divided but generally hostile Court. In *United States* v. *Butler,* (1936), the Court overturned the New Deal's agricultural control program on *Tenth Amendment and dual federalism grounds, reasserting the delegated powers doctrine of the *Dagenhart* decision and trumpeting the sacredness of "reserved rights of the states." In a parallel move, the conservative majority deployed its now cramped and restrictive version of the commerce power to rule that, like agriculture, mining and manufacturing did not constitute commerce, hence could not be reached by congressional regulations. In the decision striking down one of the keystones of the early New Deal—the National Industrial Recovery Act—*Schechter Poultry* v. *U.S.* (1935), the Court declaimed with horror against the heresy that the Commerce Clause might be construed as "reach[ing] all enterprises and transactions which could be said to have an indirect effect upon interstate commerce." Such a doctrine, the justices contended, would permit federal power to "embrace practically all the activities of the people;" and in such event, "the authority of the State over its domestic concerns would exist only by sufferance of the federal government" (p. 546).

By gutting the New Deal's economic program in 1935–1936, the Court invited the "Court fight" that ensued, as President Franklin D. *Roosevelt moved to "pack" the Court so that it would cease to lay what he termed its "dead hand" on desperately needed programs that enjoyed broad popular support reflected in the election statistics (see COURT-PACKING PLAN). But the drama of the Court fight somewhat obscured another side of this political drama—the fact that the Court was already sending mixed signals. So far as state regulatory power (as opposed to congressional authority) was concerned, the Court indicated in two decisions in 1934 that a sea change in constitutional doctrine was possible. Thus, in *Nebbia* v. *New York,* it abandoned the distinction defining business "affected with a public inter-est." This knocked over one of the great props of due process and extended the range of permissible activity for the states. Similarly with the decision in *Home Building and Loan Association* v. *Blaisdell* (1934), in which a majority upheld a state moratorium on payments of mortgages, the Court set aside brusquely the entire heritage of Contract Clause limits on the states on grounds that emergency conditions warranted it. Little wonder that Chief Justice Charles Evans *Hughes expressed worry that the the the Court's recent decisions were something like "excursion tickets," good for a day, instead of being enduring and reliable doctrines of basic law.

As Roosevelt was able to appoint New Dealers to the high court, the justices maintained a more consistent course on the line begun in 1937. Quickly there occurred what has been termed a "constitutional revolution" in doctrine, largely completed by 1941; it was in good part a revolution in the principles of constitutional federalism (see HISTORY OF THE COURT: THE DEPRESSION AND THE RISE OF LEGAL LIBERALISM). The Commerce Clause as a limitation on congressional regulatory power was entirely discarded; even by 1941 it had become (as the Court reaffirmed in *American Power & Light* v. *SEC* (1946) "as broad as the economic needs of the nation" required (p. 104). Similarly, the Tenth Amendment as emblematic of limits on the reach of federal regulatory authority was now renounced as "but a truism"—a provision merely "declaratory," and so of no limiting effect (*U.S.* v. *Darby,* 1941, p. 124).

The dimensions of the expanded national role, with Congress occupying one area of responsibility after another that had formerly been exclusively state concerns, was truly transforming in the 1930s. The constitutional revolution was only the formal expression of a fundamentally changed balance of state and national power. The Social Security program, begun in 1935, was the first of the social "entitlement" programs of national scope—the foundation stone of the modern national welfare system. *Agriculture became a federally managed sector; the Wagner Act nationalized labor-industrial relations policy; and for the first time in American history Congress enacted wages and hours legislation for the general work force—a measure upheld by the Court in a stark abandonment of the doctrines it had formerly maintained, thus validating federal preemption of a key regulatory area. In addition, a vast array of new regulatory functions and agencies similarly preempted vital segments of regulation affecting communications, transportation, and finance. Taken together with the relief, employment, experimental community, medical and other social programs of the New Deal, these initiatives amounted to a massive centralization of agenda setting, financing, and administrative decision making (see ADMINISTRATIVE STATE).

In large measure, government in the United States had become unitary rather than truly federal in the sense that there was any perceptible constitutional limit on nationalization of authority. The Court's decisions as to congressional authority under the spending power and the taxing power, taken together with new Commerce Clause doctrine, amounted to a broad—virtually plenary—federal police power. The states survived as constitutional and political entities, to be sure; and the Court renounced the federal commercial *common law in *Erie Railroad Co. v. Tompkins (1938). But more generally, the extent and importance of the states' autonomous powers (relative to those of the federal government) had been dramatically attenuated. Subsequent flourishing of the states, as evidenced by administrative reforms, expanded functions, and greater efficiency, meant that the federal system was more vibrant and delivered services more effectively than before in many areas; but it did not reverse this fundamental shift toward centralized government—the New Deal era's great legacy.

*New Deal Legacy: Extensions, Revisions, and Reversals.* Many, perhaps most, of the fundamentally important—and politically most controversial—decisions of the Supreme Court since the New Deal have implicated vital questions of the federal-state balance (see HISTORY OF THE COURT: RIGHTS CONSCIOUSNESS IN CONTEMPORARY SOCIETY). The unifying theme in nearly all these decisions has been the reconsideration of the Fourteenth Amendment's proper reach. In the line of desegregation cases that centered on *Brown v. Board of Education (1954), the Warren Court placed the most traditionally local of all governmental institutions, the public school, under the close scrutiny of the federal judiciary; and the *"separate but equal" doctrine that had long immunized the states from significant regulation from the center in matters of segregation, now was abandoned by the Court as a misguided element of law.

Declaration of broad principle in *Brown* was to have been followed, as the Court declared (and believed would happen), by compliance with "all deliberate speed." The actual result was dramatically different. School desegregation required dispatch of federal troops and marshals to school grounds and university campuses to set integration in motion in the South (see EDUCATION; DESEGREGATION REMEDIES; SEGREGATION, DE JURE). It required the federal district courts to undertake continuous supervision of school board policies and their implementation. This new role for the federal judges—undertaken in only one comparable capacity previously, in supervising railroad bankruptcies—became the model of a new "institutional reform" or "institutional management" function. As the reach of the Fourteenth Amendment was extended in subsequent years, down to the present, to affect other areas of state and local government where discriminatory practices were found—in violation either of the Constitution itself or of the federal civil rights statutes enacted beginning in the 1960s—prisons and jails, law enforcement officers, voting officials, and even state judicial bodies came under varying degrees of unprecedented close supervision.

In the *Reapportionment Cases of the 1960s, the Court extended the *"equal protection" doctrine to create a new set of constitutional imperatives ending the long-entrenched system of patent inequalities in representation. Bitterly resisted by Justices John M. *Harlan and Felix *Frankfurter in dissent, the Court in *Baker v. Carr (1962) abandoned the view that state representational process and structure constituted a *"political question" beyond the proper jurisdiction of the federal courts (see FAIR REPRESENTATION). Again, application of the new doctrines often required institutional supervision of reapportionment and district boundaries.

Much of the modern expanded activism in other areas—its revisions of constitutional interpretation as well as its statutory interpretations, especially with respect to acts of Congress deemed preemptive of state powers—similarly invaded the once-sacred legal preserves of the states. So it was, for example, with decisions regarding church and state, academic freedom, censorship, syndicalism laws, and other *First Amendment questions; and, equally, with decisions in the fields of *privacy, beginning with *Griswold v. Connecticut (1965), striking down a state law banning dispensing of contraceptive devices; decisions affecting *gender and age discrimination in the job market; and that most vexed and passionate of issues in the 1980s and early 1990s, the *abortion rights question. In all respects, these decisions centered on the basic affirmative requirements of state action or else on the limits of how far state regulation of behavior might properly go.

As the "Warren Court Revolution"—a revolution in doctrines affecting individual and group claims to rights—ran its course, there was also concomitant expansion of the liability of state and local officials for violations of civil rights as the Supreme Court opened the doors of the federal courts to such suits on a progressively broader basis, much to the discomfiture of conservative jurists and politicians who claimed to want to restore a system based on dual federalism, with the states largely secure from such intensive federal oversight. Withal, the achievement of uniform national minimum standards by the process of "incorporating" the Bill of Rights to place limits on state action by way of the Fourteenth Amendment, has been the most important single transforming force in American federalism in the last half century (see INCORPORATION DOCTRINE).

In the Burger Court and Rehnquist Court years, there has been significant pulling back from some of the most assertive nationalist doctrines that have so transformed the federal-state balance. As early as 1971, Justice Hugo L. *Black wrote for a majority in *Younger* v. *Harris* that when a state defendant applied for relief on civil rights grounds from a federal court, there must be "a proper respect for state functions, a recognition of the fact that the entire country is made up of a Union of separate state governments" (p. 44). In language reminiscent of traditional dual federalism, Black declared that "the National Government will fare best if the States and their institutions are left free to perform their separate functions in their separate ways" (p. 44). In the ensuing two decades, an increasingly conservative Court has frequently invoked this language with reverence to reduce the level and intensity of federal courts' interference with state judicial review of police and other functions. Similarly, the Court in the 1980s and 1990s has significantly restored some of the discretion of state and local police in the enforcement of criminal law, hedging and even threatening to abandon some of the Warren Court's *Fourth Amendment decisions and doctrines on right to *counsel. Even the Burger and Rehnquist Courts' majorities, however, have granted that in the interpretation of its own *state constitution, the judiciary of a state is free to hold its own government's officials to a higher standard in areas such as free speech or search and seizure than the Supreme Court's interpretation of similar provisions of the U.S. Constitution would require.

Some classic issues of state sovereignty have also centered on efforts by the Court's new conservative justices to restore the force of the Tenth Amendment as a substantive limitation on Congress's commerce powers. Thus in *National League of Cities* v. *Usery* (1976), invalidating an act of Congress that applied wage and hours limitations to state and local government employees, the Court for the first time in forty years overturned an act of Congress regulating economic relationships. "The states as states" must be protected against such intrusions of federal authority, the majority declared; but that sway proved only temporary, as a shift of one justice's vote led to abandonment of the *Usery* doctrine only a few years later, in *Garcia* v. *San Antonio Transit Authority* (1985). In this decision, Justice Harry A. *Blackmun wrote for the Court that "political safeguards" of the states' interests that were integral to political process—especially the representation of states on an equal basis in the Senate—were protection enough (p. 565). The dissenters in *Garcia* served notice, however, that the issue might well be revisited when new justices should be appointed in future years.

Meanwhile, the Reagan administration—building on strident criticisms of the Warren Court for "activism" and excessively liberal Fourteenth Amendment doctrines—pursued a course of demanding a return to *"judicial self-restraint," to "law and order" principles of crimi-

nal justice, and to reduction of the federal judiciary's role in mandating due process reforms of state and local agencies.

The main drift of the Court in the early 1990s, reflecting the new appointments of justices by Presidents Ronald *Reagan and George Bush, was toward curtailing the reach of federal power where Warren Court doctrines had extended them for protection of women and of minorities that had been subjected to discrimination. Ironically, the conservative Court also validated highly intrusive extensions of discretionary federal administrative authority in matters such as abortion counseling and mandatory medical sustenance of impaired newborn infants—matters in which the justices shared the national government's views on a conservative "social agenda"—even though this sometimes meant invading areas formerly controlled by the states.

Historically, the political values associated with federalism have been invoked with equal zeal by Marshall Court nationalists and their antebellum state rights opponents, by Radical Republicans in the Civil War era and the champions of substantive due process in the *Lochner* era, and by the Progressives and liberals on the one side and their various conservative protagonists on the other in the modern era. These political values include the notion of government responsible to the electorate at the grass roots, fostering of diversity of interests and ideas and policies, and support of human dignity and freedoms. The Supreme Court's successive formulations and revisions of federalism doctrine have reflected how the process of constitutional ordering expresses the competition of basic values in the marketplace of political ideas. They also reflect how pursuit of such values as individual dignity have sometimes required the imposition of national standards and curbing of state prerogatives. But the Court also has maintained a concern, perforce, with making government effective—with squaring the mandates of a constitutional federalism with the need for government to respond to changing social and economic conditions, emergencies of war and peacetime, and evolving political ideals. Maintenance of terms on which the Union will function as "a nation of states" has thus been at the very heart of the Court's historical importance in American governance.

(See also STATE SOVEREIGNTY AND STATES' RIGHTS.)

□ Jesse H. Choper, *Judicial Review and the National Political Process: A Functional Reconsideration of the Role of the Supreme Court* (1982). Kermit L. Hall, ed., *Federalism: A Nation of States—Major Historical Interpretations* (1987). Harold M. Hyman, *A More Perfect Union: The Impact of the Civil War and Reconstruction on the Constitution* (1973). Paul L. Murphy, *The Constitution in Crisis Times, 1918–1969* (1972). Harry N. Scheiber, "American Federalism and the Diffusion of Power," *University of Toledo Law Review* 9 (1978): 619–680. Harry N. Scheiber, "Federalism and Legal Process: Historical and Contemporary Analysis of the American System," *Law and Society Review* 10 (1980): 663–72. Harry N. Scheiber and Malcolm M. Feeley, eds., *Power Divided: Essays on the Theory and Practice of Federalism* (1988). Bernard Schwartz, *From Confederation to Nation: The American Constitution, 1837–1877* (1973).                    Harry N. Scheiber

**Federalist, The.** America's most significant political treatise, *The Federalist Papers* have assumed a special place in legal scholarship. Originally written as eighty-five essays under the pseudonym "Publius," the essays were published in New York City newspapers between 27 October 1787 and 28 May 1788. The early essays were reprinted widely in newspapers and the entire series was published in two volumes in March and May 1788. Alexander *Hamilton and James *Madison were the principal authors, while John *Jay wrote five essays.

The *Federalist* was published to persuade the people of New York to elect delegates who would ratify the proposed Constitution in the forthcoming state convention. Publius attempted to clarify and justify various provisions of the Constitution and to explain why other provisions, such as a *bill of rights, had been omitted. Americans, Publius argued, had a rare opportunity to create their own form of government through reason and choice rather than relying on chance or force, which had dictated previous constitutions. Demonstrating the necessity of union and the insufficiency of the Articles of Confederation, Publius showed that the Constitution created a republican form of government that was strong, but that was restrained by checks and balances. This government would safeguard liberty and *property and restore respect for America abroad.

Though two-thirds of the delegates elected to the New York convention opposed an unamended Constitution, Publius provided the raw material from which other political writers and orators drew. While responding to specific Antifederalist arguments, *The Federalist* also offered a unified conceptualization of the principles upon which the new Constitution rested. This philosophical underpinning, based on history, recent experience, and reason, demonstrated why this republican government could survive, where so many others had failed.

Refuting the strongly held belief, often attributed to Montesquieu, that republics could survive only in small territories occupied by homogeneous populations, Madison in number 10 argued that republics could thrive best in large territories where many diverse factions continually vied with each other. Occasionally factions would unite in favor of specific policies, but these coalitions would be short lived. Through the persistent struggles of these factions, the liberty of both majorities and minorities would be maintained. The enlarged republic would also provide better leadership by enlarging the pool of qualified individuals from which each representative would be chosen.

The three branches of the federal government were to be separate, each serving as a check upon the other. Although not totally separate, the viability of each branch was guaranteed by giving it sufficient power to defend itself against the actions of the other branches. Furthermore, when any branch overstepped its constitutionally defined role, the other branches could act to check the abuse.

Publius also contended that the new Constitution safeguarded liberty by allocating power between the central and state governments. This new American federalism established spheres of power and some concurrent powers for each level of government. Publius maintained that the Constitution created a central government with limited powers. The powers of Congress and the president were specified. All other powers were implicitly left to the states or to the people. If representatives violated their mandate, the people could replace them through the frequent and free elections guaranteed by the Constitution. If the president or the federal judiciary violated their trust, Congress could impeach and, upon conviction, remove them from office.

Since its first appearance, *The Federalist* has assumed an honored place in American jurisprudence. Scholars, lawyers, and jurists have cited it as an authority. Too often, however, Publius has been taken at face value without an understanding of the context of the original debate over the ratification of the Constitution. Knowledge of this contemporary debate reveals that Publius was sometimes bested by his opponents; that the views espoused by Publius sometimes differed from the arguments made by Hamilton and Madison in the Constitutional Convention; and that a large portion of the American people and the delegates to the state ratifying conventions did not agree with *The Federalist*. Nevertheless, from the beginning of government under the Constitution, Americans have relied on *The Federalist* as the most authoritative source for understanding the intent of the framers (see ORIGINAL INTENT).

(See also FEDERALISM; SEPARATION OF POWERS.)

☐ Jacob E. Cooke, ed., *The Federalist* (1961). John P. Kaminski and Richard Leffler, eds., *The Response to The Federalist* (1990).                    John P. Kaminski

**Federal Justice Center.** See ADMINISTRATION OF FEDERAL COURTS.

**Federal Questions.** The Constitution, in *Article III, section 2, empowers federal courts to adjudicate "all Cases, in Law and Equity, arising under this Constitution, the Laws of the United States, and Treaties made . . . under their Authority." An act of Congress grants jurisdiction to the federal courts in almost identical language. The jurisdiction thus provided has come to be known as federal question jurisdiction. Yet judicial interpretation has made clear (1) that some disputes in which the sole legal question is one of state law can be heard in federal courts under federal question jurisdiction and (2) that some disputes centering on a controverted issue of federal law cannot be heard in federal court under the statutory grant. What constitutes a federal question is thus not completely clear.

During the first quarter-century after the adoption of the Constitution in 1787, proponents of national power sometimes argued that "Laws of the United States" included all the laws of the several states. This argument, if it had been accepted, would have made cognizable in federal court all *common-law cases now thought of as within the exclusive domain of the states, such as questions of *tort, *contract, and *property (see FEDERAL COMMON LAW). A scattering of federal court decisions that seemed to adopt this position with regard to criminal law was soundly rejected by the Supreme Court in 1812 in United States v. *Hudson and Goodwin.

However, in 1824, in *Osborn v. Bank of the United States and a companion case, the Supreme Court established a broad interpretation of the constitutional language. In a suit against a federally chartered entity (the bank) that involved only ordinary issues of contract law and where no issue of federal law was controverted, the Court permitted federal question jurisdiction because of the strong federal interests involved. Since some states vigorously opposed a national bank and desired to tax it out of existence, the bank could rationally conclude that in such states only a federal court would provide a fair forum.

The 1824 ruling was based on an act of Congress, the federal bank's charter. Except for a brief interlude in 1801–1802, no statute granted federal question jurisdiction to the national courts as a general matter until 1875. The *Judiciary Act of 1875, essentially still on the books, has not been construed as broadly as the constitutional "arising under" language has been. For example, the Court made it clear in Merrell Dow Pharmaceuticals v. Thompson (1986) that only the most important of federal interests would allow a case like Osborn—a federal interest contained in a state-created cause of action—to constitute a federal question under the statute. The Court today believes that, given the crowding of federal dockets and the principles of *federalism it finds embedded in the Constitution, *state courts should normally hear state-created causes of action.

Even where a controverted issue of federal law is at stake, the Court has ruled that only important, or "substantial," federal issues constitute federal questions under the statute. Further, in a longstanding (but criticized) ruling reaffirmed in Franchise Tax Board v. Construction Laborers Vacation Trust (1983), the substantial federal question must appear in the plaintiff's well-pleaded complaint; that is, it must not only be raised by the plaintiff but also be an issue that belongs to the plaintiff's case. This doorkeeping rule, seemingly unrelated to the constitutional reasons for the existence of federal question jurisdiction, has the potential to exclude genuinely important federal issues from federal court, particularly where the plaintiff has sued in state court and the defendant wishes to raise a substantial federal issue and then to remove the case to federal court.

The federal question statute has also been broadly construed. The most important example is that state law issues, as well as other issues normally outside federal jurisdiction, can be brought into federal court under "pendent jurisdiction" by appending them to even marginally substantial federal issues arising from the same facts. Many find it difficult to understand why the constitutional word "Cases" does not include important federal issues raised by the defendant as well as those raised by the plaintiff.

(See also JUDICIAL POWER AND JURISDICTION.)

□ Paul M. Bator et al., Hart and Wechsler's The Federal Courts and the Federal System, 3d ed. (1988).

Wythe Holt

**Federal Rules of Civil Procedure.** See DUE PROCESS, PROCEDURAL.

**Federal Rules of Criminal Procedure.** See DUE PROCESS, PROCEDURAL.

**Federal Tort Claims Act.** "The King can do no wrong" was a maxim brought to America from England. It reflected the concept of *sovereign immunity. In America, the notion of executive, or governmental, immunity was translated into statutes and incorporated into the jurisprudence of the new nation. One could not sue a state or one of its subdivisions, or the federal government, unless permission was given to so proceed in the courts. Obviously this led to unfairness and inequity for persons who were tortiously injured by agents of government.

The Federal Tort Claims Act, Title VI of the Legislative Reorganization Act of 1946, was passed by the Congress in an effort to reduce the adverse impact of the doctrine of sovereign immunity. Additionally, it was designed to eliminate the practice of congresspersons introducing private relief bills for constituents who had been injured owing to government negligence. In it, the government gave its general consent to be sued in civil tort actions in federal court. It required a federal district court judge, sitting without a jury, to render judgment in these cases "under circumstances, where the United States government, if a private person, would be liable to the claimant for such damage loss, injury or death in accordance with the law of the place where the act or the omission took place." However, it placed the burden of proof on the plaintiff in a *tort action; it also contained thirteen exceptions to governmental liability.

In 1953, in *Dalehite* v. *United States,* the Supreme Court interpreted the "discretionary function" exception in such a way that effectively ruled out most substantive tort actions against the government. In 1950, the justices created another exception to the FTCA when, in *Feres* v. *U.S.* (1950), they concluded that one injured while on active duty in the military could not sue the government under the FTCA. Given these and other precedents and little or no reaction to the Court's statutory interpretations by the Congress, the FTCA has not been a major benefit to persons injured or killed because of negligent actions of federal employees.          Howard Ball

**Feiner v. New York,** 340 U.S. 315 (1951), argued 17 Oct. 1950, decided 15 Jan. 1951 by vote of 6 to 3; Vinson for the Court, Frankfurter concurring, Black, Douglas, and Minton in dissent. On the evening of 8 March 1949 college student Irving Feiner stood atop a wooden box on a street corner in Syracuse, New York, and harangued a mixed-race crowd of seventy-five to eighty people. Feiner excoriated President Harry Truman, the American Legion, and local officials, and he urged blacks to take up arms and fight for equal rights. The crowd became unruly, some of its members supporting Feiner and some opposing him. One man threatened violence. A policeman asked Feiner three times to get down off the box. When he refused, the officer arrested him for violation of a New York statute that made it a crime to use offensive, threatening, abusive, or insulting language with intent to provoke a breach of the peace. Feiner contended that his arrest and conviction violated his *First Amendment right to freedom of expression, but the Supreme Court disagreed. Chief Justice Fred *Vinson took the position that because the arrest was necessary to preserve order in the face of a *clear and present danger to public safety, it was constitutional. In a strong dissent Justice Hugo *Black argued that Feiner was being sent to the penitentiary because the views he had expressed on matters of public interest were unpopular. *Feiner* v. *New York* exemplifies the conservative, pro-government position generally taken by the Vinson Court in free speech cases.

(See also SPEECH AND THE PRESS.)
                                        Michael R. Belknap

**Feist Publications, Inc. v. Rural Telephone Service Company, Inc.,** 111 S.Ct. 1282 (1991), argued 9 Jan. 1991, decided 27 Mar. 1991 by vote of 9 to 0; O'Connor for the Court, Blackmun concurring. Rural published a local white-pages telephone directory. Feist resorted Rural's listings and included them in a regional directory overlapping Rural's service area. Rural claimed *copyright

infringement. The Supreme Court held Rural's copyright invalid.

*Feist*'s importance lies in its reaffirmation of copyright's historic character as the law of authorship and its rejection of the latter-day heresy that *copyright also protects works, or portions of works, which are the product not of authorship but of "industrious collection" (or "sweat of the brow"). In short, "copyright rewards originality, not effort" (p. 1297).

In so deciding, the Court relied on the Copyright Clause of the Constitution, which authorizes Congress to grant exclusive rights in creative works only to their "Authors," and the Court's own precedents, including *Harper & Row* v. *Nation Enterprises* (1985), which reinforced prior rulings that no one can claim authorship in facts or other nonoriginal matter. In addition, the Court found that the current Copyright Act limits protection in compilations like Rural's directory to the compiler's originality in selecting or arranging preexisting data or other materials.

*Feist*'s impact upon claims of copyright protection in so-called low authorship works beyond directories—from certain computer databases to page numbers in law reports and statutory compilations—may be great. Whether Congress can legislate noncopyright protection in these instances, for example, via the Commerce Clause, remains to be seen (see COMMERCE POWER). But by jealously guarding the public domain against appropriation by would-be copyright owners of matter that they have not authored, *Feist* at least assures more careful consideration of such claims by Congress and the courts.                              Craig Joyce

**Female Suffrage.** See NINETEENTH AMENDMENT.

**Field, Stephen Johnson** (b. Haddam, Conn., 4 Nov. 1816; d. Washington, D.C., 9 Apr. 1899; interred Rock Creek Cemetery, Washington), associate justice, 1863–1897. Field was the sixth of nine children born to Submit Dickinson, a descendant of a long line of New England Puritans, and David Dudley Field, a strict Congregationalist minister who brought up his children to be pious Puritans. The family moved to Stockbridge, Massachusetts, when Stephen was still a baby. At thirteen he was sent to Turkey with his sister, whose husband was a missionary, and spent several years traveling in the Greek islands and residing in Athens, an experience that greatly broadened his outlook. As a seventeen-year-old youth he entered Williams College, where he was deeply influenced by the teachings of Mark Hopkins and from which he graduated at the top of his class in 1837. He read law in the New York office of his brother, David Dudley Field, who was fast becoming one of America's leading lawyers, and with whom he practiced law until 1848. Stephen also spent a year traveling in Europe with his father and other family members. Thus far, however, he had shown none of the leadership qualities that were to become so prominent later in his life.

A craving for excitement led him to voyage to California during the Gold Rush year of 1849. Instead of prospecting, however, he quickly entered legal practice and politics, becoming the equivalent of mayor-plus-judge in Marysville; he also became wealthy through real estate speculation and fees. Field emerged as a colorful and controversial character in the unsettled days of the little community, making enemies whose hostility would follow him even to the Supreme Court. Elected to the California state legislature in 1850, he was the major contributor to the civil and criminal laws it passed in 1851, which were widely copied in the western states. He served only one year, however, before being defeated in a race for the state senate in 1851. Turning his attention wholly to the practice of law, he quickly became one of the state's leading lawyers, and he was elected to the state supreme court in 1857.

In his six years on the state court Field achieved an enviable reputation, which traveled beyond the state's boundaries. He did not, however, cease to acquire enemies, both political and personal. Despite this, when Congress created a tenth Supreme Court seat, Field was the logical appointee. He was not only a well-regarded lawyer and judge but also a strong Unionist (although a Democrat). A California appointment was thought to be particularly useful both politically and legally, for it might help to cement the new state to the Union and it would provide the Court with a member familiar with the distinctive characteristics of California mining and land law. He took his seat on the Court in December 1863.

Field sat on what was to become one of the strongest Supreme Courts in history. There has never been a quadrumvirate that has surpassed in ability that of Field, Samuel F. *Miller, Joseph P. *Bradley, and John Marshall *Harlan. Each was stubborn, dogmatic, and intellectually arrogant, however—a situation that led to a high level of disagreement and dissent. No great case decided during Field's tenure was without a strong dissent, which greatly reduced the value of the Court's decisions as *precedents. And, in fact, most of that Court's rulings have been reversed or modified over time.

Field's philosophy as a judge was dictated by an attachment to an ideal of inalienable rights that, however, did not have specifically to appear in the Constitution. He was, in other words, strongly result-oriented: if he felt that a claimed right was inalienable he could find a place in the Constitution for it (usually the *Fourteenth Amendment in state cases). His opinions are thus studded with dogmatic assertions that in many cases are not strongly supported by any constitutional provision.

Increasingly through the 1870s and 1880s Field

*Stephen Johnson Field*

came to believe in a rather extreme version of an inalienable right of *property, protected from interference by the states by the Due Process Clause of the *Fourteenth Amendment. This theory, known as "substantive due process" because it looks at substantive rights (especially the right to hold and use property) rather than process, was probably first suggested to Field when John A. *Campbell used it in arguing for the rights of Louisiana butchers in the *Slaughterhouse Cases (1873). Certainly he used it in his dissent in that case and enlarged on it in another dissent in *Munn v. Illinois (1877). In the latter case he argued that Illinois could not regulate the prices charged by grain elevators. In both cases there is a strong *natural law flavor to Field's arguments, which most of the justices shared to some extent; but the Californian had to campaign for twenty years before the Court's majority would accept the doctrine of substantive due process, and the Court would never carry it to the extent that Field probably would have wished. (See DUE PROCESS, SUBSTANTIVE.)

Field was thus the leader of the Court's movement toward reading laissez faire into the Constitution—a movement that reached its apogee in Harlan's opinion in *Smyth v. Ames (1898), Rufus *Peckham's opinion in *Lochner v. New York (1905), and in various decisions of the Taft Court in the 1920s (see LAISSEZ-FAIRE CONSTITUTIONALISM). Not content with providing such protection for the burgeoning large corporations of the day, Field went on to attempt to build bulwarks against federal action as well. A notorious example is his concurring opinion in *Pollock

v. *Farmers' Loan & Trust Co.* (1895), in which he made plain his fear that a federal *income tax would be but the first movement in a slide into communism. He also participated in the decision limiting the power of the federal government to break up monopolies (*United States* v. *E. C. Knight Co.*, 1895), and of the Interstate Commerce Commission to prescribe railroad rates (*Cincinnati, New Orleans & Texas Pacific Railway* v. *ICC*, 1896). Using various arguments, he also argued against state regulation of railroads (e.g., in *Stone* v. *Wisconsin*, 1876), although he was often in the minority in such cases. In none of these areas were his arguments solidly grounded in the Constitution; he was reduced to hortatory statements based on the theory that private property is almost always to be protected: that is, that property is an inalienable right.

Like most judges, Field was not entirely consistent in his record of voting to protect private corporations. Notably, he was often ready to find them—especially railroads—liable for compensation to injured or killed workers under the common law "fellow servant" doctrine. Here he was, again, often at odds with the Court majority (see, e.g., *Baltimore & Ohio Railroad* v. *Baugh*, 1893).

Theories of economics and finance were freely used by both sides in the much-debated *Legal Tender Cases*, which involved the constitutionality of the issuance of paper money by the federal government. Field wrote at great length to prove that there was an inalienable right to the use of gold and silver as currency and thus that there was no constitutional power to force Americans to accept paper money as legal tender (*Knox* v. *Lee*, 1871). Nevertheless the five-justice majority ruled the law to be valid, reversing an earlier decision. Field repeated much the same arguments—but this time as a minority of one—in 1884 in *Juilliard* v. *Greenman*.

On the California Supreme Court and later as a U.S. circuit court judge, Field applied the idea of inalienable rights to the Chinese, who were discriminated against by California law. This made him politically unpopular in the Golden State, and it may be because of this that he slowly gave up his "extreme" opinions against anti-Chinese state or local enactments (see, e.g., *Barbier* v. *Connolly*, 1885). His record on the Chinese cases shows a good deal of inconsistency, which he never bothered to explain or even acknowledge.

Despite the Fourteenth Amendment's plain purpose to protect African-Americans from state discrimination, Field showed no tendency to give effect to its provisions. Indeed, he went so far as to claim, in a dissenting opinion, that the amendment did not even secure for African-Americans the right to serve on juries (*Ex parte Virginia*, 1880). In the frequent cases in which the Court majority refused to use the amendment to protect African-Americans' rights, Field merely went along with the majority, writing no opinions. Where then was his doctrine of inalienable rights? The civil rights cases illustrate the major difficulty with such doctrines—that of definition. In Field's case it became obvious that the rights of private property were more inalienable than the right to equal protection under the law. Each judge had to define the word "right" for himself, and the Constitution disappeared in the process.

Field, true to his beliefs, did not retire from politics when he ascended the supreme bench. He served as a Democratic member of the electoral commission that decided the Hayes-Tilden presidential election in 1876, voting down the line for the Democrat Tilden. When Hayes was declared the victor, Field manifested his disagreement by refusing to accompany the rest of the Court to the inauguration. Urged on by his brothers, the Californian became a more or less open candidate for the presidency in 1880, but, due partly to old and new enmities made in California, he failed badly at the nominating convention. Nevertheless, he remained a storm center in California politics for some years. He also, apparently, expected that President Grover Cleveland would appoint him chief justice when Morrison *Waite died in 1888, since he was the only Democrat on the bench and he felt that Cleveland owed him some political debts. Cleveland felt otherwise and appointed an outsider, Melville *Fuller; Field never forgave the president. (See EXTRAJUDICIAL ACTIVITIES.)

The events leading to the killing, in California, of Judge David S. *Terry, by Deputy Marshall David Neagle, are too complex to summarize. Neagle shot Terry in an apparent attempt to protect Field's life. In a celebrated case that reached the Supreme Court itself, Neagle's act was upheld as being pursuant to his duty to the United States (*In re *Neagle*, 1890). It was another example of Field's tendency to appear at the center of controversy, whether legal, political, or personal.

Because he was intent on remaining on the Court longer than the thirty-three-year record then held by John *Marshall, Field refused to step down even when diplomatically asked to do so by Justice Harlan at the insistence of the other justices. Field had done less and less Court work through the 1890s, and by the time of his retirement was practically useless to his colleagues. An element in his decision not to resign earlier was his extreme dislike of both Presidents Cleveland and Harrison: he did not want either of them to appoint his successor. After his retirement in 1897 he became increasingly feeble, turned back to the religion he had largely ignored during most of his life, and died after a brief illness in 1899.

Field was undoubtedly a chief contributor to the development of Fourteenth Amendment jurisprudence, especially that of the Due Process Clause. If he turned that provision to uses that were neither intended by the amendment's framers nor required by its words, he was at least in tune with his times and with the felt needs of an industrializing society. Substantive due process was, it is true, dropped by later, more liberal Courts, which did not share Field's attachment to the rights of private property; but these same liberals were to find the doctrine useful in developing noneconomic inalienable rights such as the right to personal *privacy used to justify the right to *abortion. Field, in his grave, may find a certain ironic satisfaction in the attempts of his critics to define very different inalienable rights by calling on the same natural law approach he used in constitutional interpretation. And who is to say whether Field or William O. *Douglas chose rights that are truly inalienable?

☐ Howard Jay Graham, "Justice Field and the Fourteenth Amendment." *Yale Law Journal* 52 (September 1943): 851–889. Robert Green McCloskey, *American Conservatism in the Age of Enterprise* (1951), chap. 4. Carl Brent Swisher, *Stephen J. Field, Craftsman of the Law* (1930). G. Edward White, *The American Judicial Tradition* (1976), chap. 4.                                    Loren P. Beth

**Fifteenth Amendment.** The framers of the Fifteenth Amendment, ratified in 1870, intended that it would enfranchise most black American males. Actually, African-Americans had voted in several states in the North for almost a century. After the American Revolution, some free blacks met the property and other restrictive suffrage qualifications. As these requirements were gradually abolished, blacks did not share the widening franchise because whites distrusted blacks and Democratic politicians wanted to prevent blacks from voting for their opponents. So in several northern states blacks lost the right to vote as more whites gained it. For example, in 1846 New York under its new constitution retained property qualifications for blacks while eliminating them for whites.

By the end of the *Civil War in 1865 *slavery was virtually abolished. The right of blacks to vote became a controversial question. In March 1867, under the First Military Reconstruction Act, the Thirty-Ninth Congress enfranchised black males in ten southern states as a requirement for readmission of those states. But elsewhere in the former slave states, Democratic state governments blocked Negro enfranchisement. The only exception was Tennessee, which Republicans controlled. In most of the North, especially the lower North where most blacks lived, blacks could not vote and whites rejected any change. Blacks, however, voted in New England (except Connecticut) and in four midwestern states.

The stimulus for the Fifteenth Amendment came from the election returns of 1868. Although Republican presidential candidate Ulysses S. Grant won 73 percent of the electoral vote, he won only 52 percent of the popular vote. Without the southern black voter, Grant would have lost the popular, though not the electoral, vote. In

state after state Grant and the Republicans won by precarious margins. Democrats also gained seats in Congress. And in the South during 1868, white Democrats resorted to violence and intimidation in order to prevent black Republicans from voting. Such disfranchisement of blacks in the South, defeats in state referenda on suffrage throughout the North, and close calls in many elections convinced Republicans that something had to be done by the Fortieth Congress before Democrats arrived in force in the new Congress and in the statehouses.

Republican congressmen in early 1869 believed it was necessary to enfranchise adult black males as a counterweight against a resurgent Democratic party. Just as political need impelled Congress to mandate black voting for the South by federal law two years earlier, so now Congress found it expedient to inaugurate African-American voting in the northern and border states by means of a constitutional amendment. Republicans in Congress also wished to advance the cause of equal rights and impartial justice. The idealistic motive reinforced the pragmatic one. In addition, Republicans had an important secondary objective. They sought an unrepealable amendment to the Constitution to safeguard black voting in the South by banning racial discrimination in the exercise of the franchise. Though Republican congressmen agreed on these goals, they were divided over details in framing the Fifteenth Amendment and anxious about its chances for ratification. They abandoned a guarantee of officeholding by blacks as well as abolition of state literacy, property, and nativity tests for suffrage because they deemed such far-reaching reform politically impossible. Thus the amendment reflected more the limited pragmatic instincts of moderate Republicans and practical radicals than the idealistic views of some radical Republicans.

The struggle for ratification during 1869 and early 1870 followed party lines: Republicans supported the amendment and Democrats opposed it. The fight for ratification was fiercest in the lower North, where party division was closest and where the press and politicians regarded the potential African-American voter as the balance of power. Despite Republican control of most state legislatures, the struggle for ratification was intense and the outcome remained uncertain until almost the very end. But national party pressure, congressional and presidential intervention, hard work, and good timing paid off. The amendment was formally ratified on 30 March 1870. Since military Reconstruction had made the franchise a reality in the South, and because some northern states permitted black voting, the practical effect of the amendment was to open the ballot in seventeen northern and border states.

Republicans regarded the Fifteenth Amendment as the crowning achievement of Reconstruction. Northern blacks retained the franchise permanently. But blacks in the border states during the 1870s and later gradually lost the vote by force and fraud. As retreat from Reconstruction gained momentum throughout the nation during the 1870s and the three decades that followed, most southern blacks also lost the vote. Meanwhile, northern whites became apathetic about the fate of the freedmen in the South. The federal government, necessarily the ultimate guarantor of the Fifteenth Amendment, failed to enforce the right to vote at the ballot box and in the courts. With repression in the South, indifference in the North, and inaction in Washington, the Fifteenth Amendment went unenforced.

The Fifteenth Amendment became much less significant than the *Fourteenth Amendment in its constitutional meaning and practical importance. Often federal courts interpreted the Fifteenth Amendment narrowly. The United States Supreme Court put state and local elections off limits to federal election enforcement in *United States* v. *Reese* (1876); literacy tests and *poll taxes, designed to disfranchise blacks, were upheld in *Williams* v. *Mississippi* (1898). The amendment reached its nadir in *James* v. *Bowman* (1903) when the Court emasculated the amendment by denying federal authority under it to prosecute a nonofficial who by bribery prevented some Kentucky blacks from voting in a congressional election. Even later, when Justice Oliver Wendell *Holmes in *Nixon* v. *Herndon* (1927) found authority to invalidate a *white primary of the Democratic party, he based his decision not on the Fifteenth Amendment but on the Fourteenth.

The Court, however, poured new meaning into the virtually empty vessel of the Fifteenth Amendment in *Smith* v. *Allwright* (1944) by reaching the same result as in *Nixon,* but on the basis of the Fifteenth, not the Fourteenth, Amendment. Although the Fourteenth Amendment continued to be of supreme importance in laying the constitutional foundation of the Second Reconstruction, the Supreme Court no longer treated the Fifteenth Amendment as a historical curiosity and constitutional irrelevancy. When Congress passed the *Voting Rights Act in 1965, it revolutionized the politics of the South by spurring enfranchisement of black Southerners. Thus, the most durable achievement of the Second Reconstruction owed its constitutional underpinning to the Fifteenth Amendment of the First Reconstruction. After almost a century, the Fifteenth Amendment was once again bearing fruit.

(See also CONSTITUTIONAL AMENDMENTS; RACE AND RACISM; RECONSTRUCTION; VOTE, RIGHT TO.)

□ Ward, E. Y. Elliott, *The Rise of Guardian Democracy: The Supreme Court's Role in Voting Rights Disputes, 1845–1969* (1974). William Gillette, *The Right to Vote: Politics and the Passage of the Fifteenth Amendment* (1969). William Gillette, *Retreat from Reconstruction, 1869–1879* (1979).
William Gillette

**Fifth Amendment.** Adopted in 1791 as part of the *Bill of Rights, the Fifth Amendment of the Constitution contains a number of important clauses that protect individuals against governmental authority. Many of these guarantees pertain to the procedures governing the prosecution of criminal offenses. Thus, the Fifth Amendment requires that "No person shall be held to answer for a capital, or otherwise infamous crime" without presentment or indictment by a *grand jury. The amendment also prevents a person from being tried twice for the same offense (see DOUBLE JEOPARDY), and from being compelled "to be a witness against himself" in any criminal case.

In addition to these safeguards against abuses of criminal law, the Fifth Amendment provides that no person shall be "deprived of life, liberty, or property, without due process of law." Drawn from Magna Carta, the Due Process Clause places procedural limitations on the exercise of governmental power by insisting that officials follow established procedures (see DUE PROCESS, PROCEDURAL). Some commentators also argued that the Due Process Clause went beyond procedural regularity, and placed substantive limitations on the unreasonable use of government authority.

To the framers of the Constitution and Bill of Rights *property rights were closely associated with personal liberty. Underscoring this identification of property ownership with liberty, the Fifth Amendment declares: "nor shall private property be taken for public use, without just compensation." The *Takings Clause significantly protects property owners by limiting the power of *eminent domain under which government can seize private property. Hence, the Fifth Amendment protects individuals against both arbitrary punishment and confiscation of property.

Provisions similar to those in the Fifth Amendment are included in the constitutions of nearly all states (see STATE CONSTITUTIONS AND INDIVIDUAL RIGHTS). The Fifth Amendment was long held not to apply to the states, but the Supreme Court in *Chicago, Burlington & Quincy Railroad Co.* v. *Chicago* (1897) ruled that the *just compensation requirement was an essential element of due process as guaranteed by the *Fourteenth Amendment. Several of the important criminal procedural provisions were subsequently made effective to state proceedings. In *Malloy* v. *Hogan* (1964) the justices determined that the privilege against *self-incrimination was incorporated into the Due Process Clause and applicable to the states. Likewise, the Court incorporated the double jeopardy prohibition in *Benton* v. *Maryland* (1969).

Although all of the above-mentioned rights are protected by the Fifth Amendment, the amendment is often regarded as synonymous with the privilege against self-incrimination. When we say that a person "takes the Fifth Amendment," this is a shorthand way of saying that the person asserted the privilege to avoid testifying against himself or herself. Although according to the constitutional text the privilege applies only "in any criminal case," it has from the beginning been held to bar compelling any testimony that might lead to a criminal prosecution or that might eventually be used in a criminal prosecution of the person required to speak.

*Origins.* Traces of a privilege against incriminating oneself can be found in English law as early as the twelfth century. It seems to have arisen in controversies between the king and the church. The ecclesiastical courts followed an inquisitorial approach, examining people about a wide variety of alleged offenses. A bishop, by virtue of his office (*ex officio*), could require someone to take an oath (called an *ex officio* oath) in the ecclesiastical courts to tell the truth to the full extent of his or her knowledge. In the King's courts, however, *accusatorial* procedure was slowly developing—that is, the prosecuting officer had to develop evidence that the accused was free to respond to or not.

By the sixteenth century, the idea was expressed in the Latin maxim *Nemo tenetur prodere se ipsum* ("No one should be required to accuse himself"). Although frequently voiced, the maxim does not seem by any means to have reflected the practice of the period. In the prerogative courts, such as the Star Chamber and the High Commission, it was apparently standard practice not only to make suspected persons give evidence against themselves but even to use torture to make sure that the accused would speak. Indeed, the development of the privilege may to a considerable extent have resulted from the struggle to eliminate torture as a standard prosecutorial practice.

By the latter half of the seventeenth century, there were many occasions when the privilege was recognized by English courts as part of the *common law. It is still a matter of common law in England but is so deeply embedded in the common law that it is an established part of the English Constitution.

*Introduction to America.* The early English settlers in North America brought the privilege with them as a part of their legal heritage. In Pennsylvania, for example, William Bradford was summoned in 1689 before the provincial governor and council. Bradford had printed the charter of the province so that people could read their rights, and the governor demanded that Bradford admit to his action. Bradford responded, "Governor, it is an impracticable thing for any man to accuse himself; thou knows it very well."

Little is heard about self-incrimination during the eighteenth century, perhaps because the privilege was generally recognized in the Colonies as a part of English common law. The privilege was included in the Virginia Bill of Rights of 1776, drafted by George Mason, and it made its way in various forms into the constitutions of many of the original states. When the Constitution was being considered for ratification by the states, a number of state conventions proposed amendments specifically requesting the addition of the privilege against self-incrimination. The privilege was included in the proposals made by the First Congress that in 1791 became the Bill of Rights.

*Justification.* Many efforts have been made to explain why the privilege is a desirable or essential part of our basic law. The Supreme Court in *Twining* v. *New Jersey* (1908) suggested, for example, that the privilege was designed to protect the innocent and to further the search for truth. In *Tehan* v. *United States ex rel. Shott* (1966) the Court explained that "the basic purposes that lie behind the privilege against self-incrimination . . . relate . . . rather to preserving the integrity of a judicial system in which even the guilty are not to be convicted unless the prosecution 'shoulder the entire load' " (pp. 415–416). It may well be that the basic function of the privilege, as foreshadowed by its history, is to serve as a guard against the use of torture or those kinds of police practices that involve physical and psychological intimidation and are colloquially known as "the third degree." Indeed, the privilege against self-incrimination is one of the great landmarks in the struggle to fashion a more civilized society.

Two major decisions in the twentieth century have helped to effectuate the privilege as a protection against improper police conduct. In *McNabb* v. *United States* (1943), the Court held that a confession could not be used as evidence at trial when it was obtained after an "unnecessary delay" in presenting a suspect for arraignment after arrest. In *Miranda* v. *Arizona* (1966) the Court held that the prosecution may not use a statement taken from a person held in custody unless, prior to any questioning, the person is "warned that he has a right to remain silent, that any statement he does make may be used as evidence against him, and that he has a right to the presence of an attorney, either retained or appointed" (pp. 444–445). Although the defendant may waive these rights, such a waiver must be made voluntarily and knowingly. Moreover, no questioning can be performed if the person "indicates in any manner and at any stage of the process that he wishes to consult with an attorney before speaking" (p. 445).

Despite the breadth of these rulings, the Court has not pressed the privilege to a logical extreme. For example, a person engaged in an illegal business may be prosecuted for not filing an income tax return, despite his contention that the return would be self-incriminating. In *California* v. *Byers* (1970), the Court sustained the constitutionality of a state hit-and-run statute requiring the driver involved in an accident to stop and give his name and address. However, statutes requiring a person to register as a member of the Communist party, for example, or for occupational tax as a gambler have been held invalid.

*Meaning of the Privilege.* It is not true that a claim of privilege amounts to a confession of guilt. As the Supreme Court said in *Burdick* v. *United States* (1915), "If it be objected that . . . [a defendant's] refusal to answer was itself an implication of crime, we answer, not necessarily in fact, and not at all in theory of law" (p. 94). But this is often misunderstood by the press and the public. In modern times most problems about the privilege have arisen during investigations by legislative committees and not in court proceedings. During the redbaiting McCarthy era of the early 1950s, persons who claimed the privilege before legislative committees were often referred to as "Fifth Amendment Communists" (see CONGRESSIONAL POWER OF INVESTIGATION). They were subjected to serious practical penalties, losing their jobs or becoming unemployable (see COMMUNISM AND COLD WAR). Nevertheless, the better judgment of the American people strongly supports the privilege. It is generally understood that an innocent person may honestly fear a risk of prosecution because of circumstances over which he or she has no control. Further, witnesses who might be willing to answer many questions are often advised to claim the privilege in order to avoid the risk that they may inadvertently waive the privilege simply as a result of giving answers to some of the questions.

*Limitations on the Privilege.* The Fifth Amendment privilege is not applicable after a person has been convicted and the decision has become final, since the constitutional provision against *double jeopardy protects one from further prosecution. Similarly, a witness cannot claim the privilege if the statute of limitations has run out or if he or she has received a *pardon. Also, a statute may grant transactional immunity, protecting a witness who has been compelled to testify about an offense against prosecution for that offense, regardless of what other evidence may be produced. Such a statute was sustained by the Supreme Court in *Brown* v. *Walker* (1896), and such statutory provisions have become part of our constitutional fabric.

In 1970, Congress adopted a statute providing for "use immunity." Use immunity differs from transactional immunity in that it does not prevent *any* prosecution but only protects a witness against the use of the compelled testimony and any evidence obtained through a lead provided by the compelled testimony. It does not prevent subsequent prosecution for the offense when the prosecution is based on independent evidence shown to be available to the prosecutor before the use immunity was granted or on evidence that is otherwise wholly independent from the evidence the witness was required to give. The constitutional validity of this statute was sustained in *Kastigar* v. *United States* (1972).

Many difficult questions arise under use-immunity statutes. A number of these were involved in the prosecutions arising from the Iran-Contra scandal, in which leading figures were compelled to testify before a congressional committee after a grant of use immunity (see FIFTH AMENDMENT IMMUNITY).

*Conclusion.* The Fifth Amendment has now been in effect for two hundred years. It continues to generate controversy, and this is particularly true in times of stress, when such safeguards are most needed. The privilege against self-incrimination has served the country well, representing a basic moral value in our constitutional structure. It has long played a central role in protecting the individual against the collective power of the state, and it is important as a symbol of our fundamental concern for human rights. Thoughtful people have from time to time proposed that the privilege should be restricted, yet there seems to be little doubt that in the future, as in the past, the basic value of the Fifth Amendment will be recognized and preserved.

□ Henry J. Friendly, "The Fifth Amendment Tomorrow: The Case for Constitutional Change," *University of Cincinnati Law Review* 37 (1968): 671–726. Erwin N. Griswold, *The Fifth Amendment Today* (1955). Leonard W. Levy, *Origins of the Fifth Amendment: The Right Against Self-Incrimination* (1968). Edmund Morgan, "The Privilege against Self-Incrimination," *Minnesota Law Review* 34 (1949): 1–45.
Erwin N. Griswold

**Fifth Amendment Immunity.** The Fifth Amendment guarantees that "no person . . . shall be compelled in any criminal case to be a witness against himself." Sometimes called the Great Right, the privilege against *self-incrimination originated in objections to the inquisitorial practices of sixteenth-century English church and royal courts, especially the Court of Star Chamber. By the end of the 17th century, *common law incorporated the principle that no man was bound to accuse himself or to answer any questions about his actions. Many early *state constitutions included this guarantee, and nineteenth-century *state courts extended its protection to confessions obtained both within and outside the courtroom.

An early federal circuit case, *United States* v. *Burr* (1807), incorporated many of the common-law requirements as part of the Fifth Amendment right: an individual must assert the right; the court will judge the validity of the claim; and the answer must incriminate directly or be an essential link in a chain of evidence leading to incrimination. The Supreme Court, in *Boyd* v. *United States* (1886) and *Counselman* v. *Hitchcock* (1892), expanded the right to all criminal cases as well as to civil cases where testimony might lead to criminal prosecution.

Federal standards have governed this privilege since *Malloy* v. *Hogan* (1964), when the Court incorporated the right against self-incrimination into the *Due Process Clause of the *Fourteenth

Amendment (see INCORPORATION DOCTRINE). *Miranda v. Arizona (1966) required law officers to inform suspects of their Fifth Amendment right to silence in clear and unequivocal terms. The privilege, however, is not absolute: it offers no protection against compulsory fingerprinting, physical examination, voice recordings, reenactment of a crime, or sobriety tests, among other things; it does not apply when a defendant voluntarily testifies on his own behalf; and it may be overcome by a grant of transactional or use immunity (see *Kastigar v. United States, 1972).

(See also FIFTH AMENDMENT.)

David J. Bodenhamer

**Fighting Words.** See CHAPLINSKY V. NEW HAMP-SHIRE; UNPROTECTED SPEECH.

**Finality of Decision.** By statute (Title 28, section 1257 of the U.S. Code), the Supreme Court has jurisdiction to review "[f]inal judgments or decrees rendered by the highest court of a State in which a decision could be had." Section 1257 makes review possible when the validity of a federal law is drawn in question, when a state statute is drawn in question for being repugnant to some federal law, or when a claim is made under some federal law. This jurisdiction rests on a *federal question: a controlling issue of federal law.

The Constitution does not expressly authorize the Supreme Court to review decisions of the *state courts. Today this authority is taken for granted, but it has not always been so. As Charles Alan Wright explains in Federal Courts: "It is unusual for the court of one sovereign to have appellate jurisdiction over the courts of other sovereigns, but federalism itself is—or was when the Constitution was adopted—an unusual system, and the Supremacy Clause is a sufficient basis on which to rest the appellate jurisdiction over state court decisions" (p. 736).

Section 25 of the *Judiciary Act of 1789 generally authorized the Supreme Court to review state court decisions that invalidated a federal statute or treaty or ruled against a claim based on federal law. Between 1790 and 1815, the Court reviewed seventeen cases from state courts. Its authority was directly challenged when the Virginia Court of Appeals refused to obey a mandate of the Supreme Court on the ground that section 25 was unconstitutional. Justice Joseph *Story wrote the opinion refuting the Virginia court in the famous decision of *Martin v. Hunter's Lessee (1816). Chief Justice John *Marshall, who had not participated in that decision, reaffirmed the constitutionality of section 25 and the authority of the Supreme Court to review state court judgments in *Cohens v. Virginia (1821). Chief Justice Roger B. *Taney rebuffed the last serious challenge to this orthodoxy in *Ableman v. Booth (1859), a dramatic pre–Civil War decision sustaining the Fugitive Slave Act (see FUGITIVE SLAVES).

To satisfy section 1257, a state court decision must be "final" in two ways. First, procedurally the decision must be one that is not subject to further review in any higher state court. A decision need not have been by the state supreme court but only by "the highest court of a state in which a decision might be had." For example, the U.S. Supreme Court reviewed a decision of the police court of Louisville, Kentucky, in Thompson v. City of Louisville (1960), since there was no further review possible in the state courts.

Second, the Court in Catlin v. United States (1945) has defined a judgment or decree to be functionally final if it "ends the litigation on the merits and leaves nothing for the court to do but execute the judgment" (p. 233). Finality depends on the interpretation of the federal statute, section 1257, and the Court has developed a pragmatic approach to treat some categories of judgments as sufficiently final to allow for review.

The requirement of finality serves several ends. These were highlighted by Justice William O. *Douglas in North Dakota State Board of Pharmacy v. Snyder's Drug Stores, Inc. (1973): "(1) it avoids piecemeal review of state court decisions; (2) it avoids giving advisory opinions in cases where there may be no real 'case' or 'controversy' in the sense of Art. III [see CASES AND CONTROVERSIES]; (3) it limits federal review of state court determinations of federal constitutional issues to leave at a minimum federal intrusion in state affairs" (p. 159).

The requirement of finality thus is not merely a technical abstraction, but a requirement based on important underlying principles of judicial efficiency and federalism. Considerations of federalism pull in opposite directions: interests of *comity would suggest that the Supreme Court set a high threshold of finality to show respect for sovereign state courts; however, the Supreme Court necessarily also has a special role in preserving uniformity and supremacy in federal law. It is thus often necessary for the Court to make adjustments between state judicial sovereignty and federal supremacy.

(See also FEDERALISM.)

□ Robert L. Stern, Eugene Gressman, and Stephen M. Shapiro, Supreme Court Practice, 6th ed. (1986). Charles Allen Wright, Federal Courts, 4th ed. (1983).

Thomas E. Baker

**Financing Political Speech.** The funding of political campaigns represents a serious dilemma of representative democracy. The antidemocratic ramifications of financial contributions to candidates, including the potential for corruption of public officials, have been apparent for many years. In the early 1900s Congress first enacted campaign-finance restrictions. They were riddled with loopholes, however, and went with virtually unenforced.

The first meaningful reform of campaign finance was the Federal Election Campaign Act of 1971, which contained effective disclosure requirements. The information gleaned through this legislation regarding the amounts, sources, and uses of campaign funds helped expose the abuses of Watergate and in turn created the impetus for further reforms, which were enacted in the 1974 amendments to the statute.

In *Buckley v. Valeo* (1976), the Supreme Court considered the constitutionality of the sweeping reforms contained in the 1974 amendments. In a lengthy *per curiam opinion, the Court rejected challenges to the requirements for disclosure of campaign contributions and expenditures, to limitations on contributions, and to public subsidies for presidential candidates. The Court did, however, invalidate limitations on total campaign expenditures, expenditures of candidates' own funds, and expenditures made independently by supporters, holding that such restrictions violated the *First Amendment. In reaching this result, the Court rejected the argument that campaign funding was primarily conduct rather than speech. Thus it purported to apply the "rigorous standard of review" applicable to First Amendment challenges. It appears, however, that the Court actually applied different standards of review to the various restrictions; the methodology ranged from extreme deference to Congress to near-absolutist First Amendment analysis.

The restrictions the Court upheld were found to further government interests in preventing the reality or appearance of corruption or improper influence. However, the Court rejected the government's interest in equalizing the political influence of the less affluent as a basis for restrictions, asserting that the concept was "wholly foreign to the First Amendment" (p. 48). Perhaps reflecting the internal inconsistencies in *Buckley*, the Court has subsequently fluctuated between extreme deference to Congress and rigid First Amendment strict scrutiny. Despite such oscillation, some consistent themes have emerged from the post-*Buckley* cases. The Court has been more tolerant of limitations on contributions than those on expenditures, in part because it has viewed the First Amendment burdens caused by contribution limitations to be less severe. Reasoning, however, that only candidate elections involve a danger of corruption of public officials, the Court has invalidated restrictions on both contributions and expenditures in referendum elections. Also, it has usually applied more deferential review to statutes limiting political funding by corporations than to statutes restricting individuals.

The theoretical underpinnings of *Buckley* and its progeny are often inconsistent, as exemplified by the recent case of *Austin v. Michigan State Chamber of Commerce* (1990). The majority upheld a state statute, similar to federal restrictions, that prohibited corporations from making expendi-

tures in support of political candidates except from funds voluntarily contributed to the corporation's political action committee. For the majority, Justice Thurgood *Marshall reasoned that the statute reduced corruption by preventing the influence of immense aggregations of corporate wealth on the election. Asserting that the wealth of the Michigan Chamber of Commerce was not necessarily accumulated from persons who supported the organization's political ideas, the Court distinguished *FEC v. Massachusetts Citizens for Life* (1986), in which it had found the application of a similar federal statute unconstitutional.

The dissents asserted that the majority's new definition of corruption was no different than the equalization rationale that had been rejected in *Buckley* and subsequent cases. But the majority purported to confine its reasoning to the corporate setting, thereby distinguishing *Austin* from *Buckley*. The Court asserted that there was a compelling government interest in assuring that the economic advantages granted by the state to corporations did not give them an unfair advantage in electoral politics. (This same argument had been rejected in 1978, when the Court in *First National Bank of Boston v. Bellotti* invalidated bans on expenditures by corporations in ballot-measure elections.)

*Austin* may open up possibilities for further reforms that legislators had previously considered constitutionally foreclosed. As political-funding scandals and the spiraling costs of campaigns focus more attention on the campaign-financing morass, this case, which suggests a shift toward greater attention to political equality, could be an important precedent.

(See also POLITICAL PROCESS.)

□ Robert E. Mutch, *Campaigns, Congress, and Courts: The Making of Federal Campaign Finance Law* (1988). "The Supreme Court's Meandering Path in Campaign Finance Regulation," symposium in *University of Virginia Journal of Law and Politics* 3 (1987): 509–565.
Marlene A. Nicholson

**First Amendment.** More than a constitutional guarantee against government interference with the freedom of *speech and the press or a guarantee of the separation of church and state, the First Amendment is also one of the nation's foremost normative and cultural symbols. More than any other provision of the *Bill of Rights, the First Amendment reflects vital attributes of the American character. It is known by virtually all citizens, who may not be able to recite its precise phrasing but who understand that because of it people are free to speak their minds, practice their religious beliefs, and never be subject to a state-imposed *religion.

***Early Free-Speech Cases.*** Most citizens probably do not realize, however, that the origins of most of what the First Amendment actually means today—in the sense of what it specifically prohibits government from doing—lie in Supreme Court decisions made in this century. Indeed, the Supreme Court's first significant decision interpreting the amendment's Free Speech Clause did not come until 1919, with *Schenck v. United States*—and it was not a particularly auspicious beginning. Schenck was the general secretary of the Socialist party. Along with another member of the party's executive board, he was convicted under the *Espionage Act of 1917 for having distributed some fifteen thousand leaflets arguing, in "impassioned language," that the *conscription law during *World War I was immoral and unconstitutional and that people should resist. Though the leaflet confined itself to peaceful measures, the Court upheld the conviction, finding no constitutional violation.

Even more surprising, the Court's opinion was authored by Justice Oliver Wendell *Holmes, the justice who today is most credited with having led the first battle in this century for greater sensitivity to the values of freedom of speech. Holmes did announce his famous *clear and present danger test of the limit of freedom of speech in *Schenck,* saying that the question in every case was "whether the words used are used in such circumstances and are of such a nature as to create a clear and present danger that they will bring about the substantive evils that Congress has a right to prevent" (p. 47). It was, Holmes said, a "question of proximity and degree," but he added that even the most stringent protection of free speech would not protect a person who falsely shouted fire in a theater and caused a panic (p. 52). This latter sentiment controlled the Court's decision in the *Schenck* case.

Within a year, however, Holmes began to change course. In *Abrams v. United States* (1919) Holmes joined forces with Justice Louis D. *Brandeis in dissenting from a decision upholding the convictions of five Russian aliens who had called for a general strike in protest against President Woodrow Wilson's decision to send American troops to Russia. In one of his most stirring opinions, Holmes eloquently argued for the importance to society of a constitutional commitment to wide-open debate, even for "these poor and puny anonymities," whose beliefs he labeled a "creed of ignorance and immaturity" (p. 629). In a famous passage, Holmes set forth a major theory of free speech:

But when men have realized that time has upset many fighting faiths, they may come to believe even more than they believe the very foundations of their own conduct that the ultimate good desired is better reached by free trade in ideas—that the best test of truth is the power of the thought to get itself accepted in the competition of the market, and that truth is the only ground upon which their wishes safely can be carried out. That at any rate is the theory of our Constitution. (p. 630)

*Social Function of Free Speech.* The future embraced the Holmes of *Abrams* rather than the Holmes of *Schenck.* First Amendment jurisprudence over the past seven decades has provided extraordinary protection to radical, even extremist, speech—though it should be noted that the McCarthy era was an exception to this general progression of widening constitutional protection for speech (see COMMUNISM AND COLD WAR). For the contemporary world, the best example of the legacy of Holmes's dissent in *Abrams* is a well-known case from 1978 involving a group of neo-Nazis who claimed a right to march in the Chicago suburb of Skokie, Illinois, home to some forty thousand Jews and several thousand survivors of concentration camps. Both the Illinois Supreme Court and the U.S. *Court of Appeals held, in two separate cases arising out of that dispute, that the proposed march was protected speech under Supreme Court precedents, despite the reprehensible ideas of the speakers.

Modern First Amendment theory also relies heavily on Holmes's idea that freedom of speech is justified by the importance society places on the search for truth. This conception of the importance of free speech is rooted in classical writings of Western civilization, such as John Milton's *Aeropagitica* and John Stuart Mill's *On Liberty.* A significant variation on this rationale of truth-seeking, and one especially prominent in contemporary writings about free speech, is that open discussion is vital to a democratic system of government.

A third rationale for free speech is that it reflects a social commitment to the value of individual freedom or autonomy. More recent writings have begun to explore still-broader social functions of free speech, seeing in the extraordinary protection of harmful speech acts (such as the Nazi demonstration in Skokie) the effort to reinforce certain desired character traits within the society, including tolerance and self-restraint in dealing with bad behavior generally.

It is important to recognize, however, that the modern principle of freedom of speech and press encompasses a wide range of doctrines that extend well beyond the simple question of subversive advocacy that Holmes and the Court initially dealt with in *Schenck* and *Abrams.* Today an elaborate set of cases, with subtle and intricate rules and distinctions, govern the First Amendment.

*Content-Neutral Regulations.* A major distinction is drawn between state regulations that seek to control speech because the ideas communicated are "dangerous" or "offensive" and regulations that are neutral with regard to the content of the speech but limit its *time, place, or manner. Content regulations are generally prohibited by the First Amendment; only a few exceptions—for example, for *obscenity and fighting words—are constitutionally allowed. In cases involving time, place, and manner regulations, the courts balance the free-speech interest in open discussion against the neutral state interest in conflict with the speech. But in a long line of cases the Supreme

Court has developed the First Amendment right to use certain state property—most notably streets and parks—as a *public forum for speech. Courts rarely permit *prior restraints against speech, either in the form of general licensing schemes or in the form of *injunctions against speaking. Hecklers are generally not permitted to exert a "veto" over speech by creating a threat of violence and disorder; the state is obliged to protect, not stop, the controversial speaker.

*Libel.* Since *New York Times Co.* v. *Sullivan* (1964), where the Court specifically held that *libel actions brought by a public official against the press were prohibited by the First Amendment absent a showing of *actual malice, a large body of case law has developed governing the First Amendment and the press. Within this case law is a complex set of First Amendment decisions approving an extensive system of public regulation of the newer media of radio and television.

*Religion.* The First Amendment's *religion clauses have also provided fertile ground for litigation and the development of labyrinthine rules. Two fundamental principles are involved. The first is that there shall be no "establishment of religion." Here the central idea has been seen as maintaining a "wall of separation" between the state and the exercise of religion. Everyone agrees that the Establishment Clause of the First Amendment forbids the creation of a single "official" religion. The problems arise when government acts in such a way as to "aid" religion or particular religions. Some aid, such as police and fire protection, must be permitted. But what about financial subsidies to parochial schools, or to the parents who send their children to such schools? It is here that the courts have had to evaluate numerous government programs and schemes. A body of constitutional decisions and rules has evolved that has two primary characteristics: the rules forbid most, but not all, forms of such "aid," and they appear to lack logical coherence. There has also been a backlash of claims, led by Chief Justice William H. *Rehnquist, that the "wall of separation" metaphor does not represent the *original intent of the framers and that it unduly favors "separationist" over "accommodationist" interpretations.

The other fundamental principle is that, as with the right of freedom of speech and press, there shall be constitutional protection for the "free exercise" of religious belief and practices. Regarding this principle the problems have been fewer in number, but those that have arisen have been highly complex. In one example, the well-known case of *Wisconsin* v. *Yoder* (1972), Amish parents resisted a state requirement that all children receive a formal high-school *education. The Amish objected that public schooling inculcated values in their children inconsistent with the Amish religion. Wisconsin answered that insuring minimum education for all children was

its legitimate prerogative and responsibility. The Supreme Court ruled in favor of the parents, finding the special interests of the members of the Amish faith paramount under the Free Exercise Clause.

The idea of separation of church and state has become a major—and controversial—principle in American society. Fearing the divisiveness that might arise from official involvement in religious affairs, the Court has in general sought to drive a wedge between the official and the religious. (See also SPEECH AND THE PRESS.)

□ Lee C. Bollinger, *Images of a Free Press* (1991).
Lee C. Bollinger

**First Amendment Absolutism.** Among the several attempts to draw a line between constitutionally and legally appropriate application of the quintet of *First Amendment guarantees—separation of church and state, free exercise of *religion, freedom of *speech and the press, freedom of peaceable *assembly, and the right to petition the government for redress of grievances—a claim to an "absolutist" right of their exercise has perhaps been the most sweeping and the most dramatic. Associated most closely with the views Justice Hugo L. *Black, the absolutist stance requires a reading of First Amendment rights that permits no "balancing" (see FIRST AMENDMENT BALANCING) of individual and societal rights but instead insists that the enumerated First Amendment guarantees are absolute in and of themselves and that they cannot be infringed by any governmental action that would inhibit their exercise.

As Black intoned again and again, the First Amendment command that "Congress shall make no law . . . abridging the freedom of speech or of the press" means precisely that neither Congress nor, by later implication, the several states have the authority to make *any* law that would "abridge" those stated prerogatives. To proffered demurrers, usually beginning "But, Mr. Justice," Black's instant if gentle response would be, "But, nothing." Lifting the ten-cent copy of his beloved Constitution from his pocket, he would ask his questioner to read the words of the First Amendment. When the latter would reach the phrase "no law," Black would utter a soft "thank you" and observe that the language at issue required an absolutist interpretation as to the exercise of the precious constitutional guarantees involved—that, if the issue dealt with expression qua expression, there simply could be no limitation placed upon it.

To qualify for absolute protection, however, the claimed First Amendment right had to be "speech," "press," "peaceable assembly," or bona fide "religion." If it was not, it was not entitled to absolutist privileges and thus could be subjected to permissible governmental regulation. Here, then, appeared the controversial line that Black and his followers would attempt to draw, giving rise to a chorus of criticism. For example, "speech" and "press" connoted absolute rights—but "conduct," however, did not. The latter could thus properly be controlled by governmental action, within the limits of *due process of law. Hence, while speaking and printing are, in the eyes of absolutists, immune to governmental strictures—including what others might consider libelous or slanderous statements or obscenities, be they visual or spoken— "conduct" is not similarly protected.

Such activities as public demonstrations, certain types of public assemblies, and flag defacing (*Street* v. *New York*, 1969) were subject to regulation in Black's view—a position that is still utilized by some judges and justices. For some jurists flag-burning constitutes an exercise of freedom of speech (*Texas* v. *Johnson*, 1989; *United States* v. *Eichman*, 1990), but to others (Black certainly would have been among them) such an activity is clearly proscribable conduct. Black and his supporters found a peaceable demonstration in front of a legislative hall to be a valid exercise of a First Amendment right (*Edwards* v. *South Carolina*, 1963) but rejected the First Amendment claims of those who had demonstrated in the front lobby of a jail (*Adderly* v. *Florida*, 1966) and on a crowded street (*Cox* v. *Louisiana*, 1965), where the demands of law and order were seen as justifying restraints by the authorities.

Slander and *libel laws, in Black's view, were utterly unconstitutional on their face, for they inhibit the freedom to speak and write. The same reasoning governed the showing of films or the printing of books: for the First Amendment absolutist, *censorship is simply incompatible with the amendment's guarantees. Yet such symbolic expressive manifestations as wearing black armbands in public schools as a protest against the *Vietnam War (*Tinker* v. *Des Moines School District*, 1969) and an anti-draft expletive emblazoned on a leather jacket worn by a young man in a courthouse (*Cohen* v. *California*, 1971) were viewed by Black, in dissent, as conduct subject to regulation or even prohibition (see NONVERBAL EXPRESSION).

Although First Amendment absolutism continues to be embraced by jurists as well as pundits and though the liberal jurisprudence of the modern Supreme Court may have reached a "near-absolutist" level of protection for most forms of expression, the doctrine itself does not command majority support. Deceptive in its simplicity and arguably appealing in its generosity to the exercise of individual freedoms, absolutism has necessarily been subjected to balancing between individual and societal prerogatives and responsibilities.

□ Henry J. Abraham, *Freedom and the Court: Civil Rights and Liberties in the United States*, 5th ed. (1988).

Henry J. Abraham

**First Amendment Balancing.** Notwithstanding the specific guarantees of the *First Amendment and, by implication, that of the *Fourteenth, the quintet of rights enumerated in its language are not regarded as absolute, despite Justice Hugo *Black's ardent advocacy of such an approach (see FIRST AMENDMENT ABSOLUTISM). Accordingly, a "balancing" between individual and societal rights seems a logical compromise between those who would brook no governmental regulation of First Amendment rights, whatsoever, and those who readily support stern, sometimes draconian, measures on the grounds of *national security or law and order. In general, the judicial branch has endeavored to draw a viable line between protected constitutional rights and permissible government regulation.

Unless one rejects utterly any regulatory governmental authority, First Amendment balancing, by whatever name, is an obvious necessity. The difficulty, however, is in determining a constitutionally and legally viable line, particularly since many First Amendment claims are inherently controversial and polycentric. To note but a few recurring ones: Where does, where should, the judiciary draw the line between assertions of a right to engage in free exercise of *religion, even if that would extend to the refusal to provide medical aid to minor children, and a perceived governmental responsibility to protect their lives (*Commonwealth of Pennsylvania* v. *Cornelius*, 1956)? Or, in the always contentious realm of the separation of church and state (the Establishment Clause), may Louisiana require the teaching of "creationism" to balance that of "evolution" in its public school curriculum (*Edwards* v. *Aguillard*, 1987; see EVOLUTION AND CREATION SCIENCE)? Or, to what extent, if any at all, may a trial judge impose "gag" orders against the press, sharply restricting pretrial coverage (*Nebraska Press Association* v. *Stuart*, 1976; see PRETRIAL PUBLICITY AND THE GAG RULE)? Or, may Georgia forbid the printing or publication of the name of a rape victim, whose parents invoked *privacy considerations where the name was inadvertently left in the public record (*Cox Broadcasting Corp.* v. *Cohn*, 1975)? The judiciary "balanced" personal and governmental rights and obligations in each of the above cases—and in each, except the last, it sided with the individual claimants as against asserted governmental prerogatives.

To an "absolutist" such as Justice Black, "balancing" is anathema: it flies into the face of the literal commands of the amendment, as he always saw it. For him, "balancing," as he wrote in *A Constitutional Faith* (1968), three years prior to his death, "should be used only where a law is aimed at conduct and indirectly affects speech; a law directly aimed at curtailing speech and political persuasion can, in my opinion, never be saved through a balancing process" (p. 61). Arguably, he met the issue most squarely with his dissenting opinion in *Barenblatt* v. *United States* (1959), the legislative investigation case at the height of the cold war. A Vassar College instructor, Lloyd Barenblatt, had refused to answer certain questions put to him by the House Un-American Activities Committee. For his refusal, he was convicted, fined, and sentenced to six months in prison. Speaking for the 5-to-4 Court majority, Justice John M. *Harlan upheld the Committee's authority against First Amendment claims of freedom of expression and association, concluding that "the balance between the individual and governmental interests here at stake must be struck in favor of the latter" (p. 134). (See ASSEMBLY AND ASSOCIATION, FREEDOM OF.) In a bitter dissenting opinion, Justice Black argued that to apply the Court's balancing test under the circumstances at issue is to read the First Amendment to say: "Congress shall pass no law abridging freedom of speech, press, assembly and petition, unless Congress and the Supreme Court reach the joint conclusion that on balance the interest of the Government in stifling these freedoms is greater than the interest of the people in having them exercised" (p. 143).

Yet there is little doubt that the judicial role encompasses the need to continue to engage in balancing. To what extent the latter tilts toward a "liberal" or "conservative" construction of the First Amendment often depends upon value judgments.

(See also SPEECH AND THE PRESS.)

□ Henry J. Abraham, *Freedom and the Court*, 5th ed. (1988). Henry J. Abraham

**First Amendment Speech Tests.** All judicial line-drawing between individual and societal rights and obligations involves a degree of "balancing" (see FIRST AMENDMENT BALANCING). But, subsumed under the general notion of balancing, a number of tests have surfaced. These tests were not really articulated by the Supreme Court until the end of *World War I; very little litigation on the free-speech front reached the high tribunal until then. Not counting "balancing" as a specific test per se, a handful of speech tests may be identified. In roughly chronological order, they are (1) the "clear and present danger" test, (2) the "bad tendency" test, (3) the "public versus private speech" test, and (4) the "clear and present danger plus imminence" test—with the last now widely recognized as the controlling Court doctrine.

Authorship of the *clear and present danger doctrine belongs to Justice Oliver Wendell *Holmes, with an assist from Judge Learned *Hand and active support from Justice Louis D. *Brandeis. Initially developed by Holmes in *Schenck* v. *United States* (1919), the case grew out of activities engaged in by Schenck and some colleagues that were designed to hamper the government's wartime effort. Convicted under

the *Espionage Act of 1917, Schenck appealed on *First Amendment freedom-of-speech grounds. Speaking for a unanimous Court, Holmes pointed out that in ordinary times the defendants' activities would have been constitutionally protected, but that the character of every act depends upon the circumstances in which it is done. Holmes added, "The most stringent protection of free speech would not protect a man in falsely shouting fire in a theatre and causing a panic. . . . The question in every case is whether the words used are used in such circumstances and are of such a nature as to create a clear and present danger that they will bring about the substantive evils that Congress has a right to prevent" (p. 52).

But six years later, in *Gitlow* v. *New York* (1925), the new doctrine was modified by adopting a "kill the serpent in the egg" approach, which came to be known as the *bad tendency test. The New York State Criminal Anarchy Act of 1902 prohibited numerous subversive activities, including the "advocacy, advising, or teaching" of the overthrow of New York's government. Gitlow published and distributed a pamphlet entitled *Left Wing Manifesto* and was convicted for violation of the statute. With Holmes and Brandeis in bitter dissent, Justice Edward T. *Sanford, for the Court, contended that the danger from the utterances at issue could not reasonably be required to be measured in "the nice balance of a jeweler's scale," that a "single revolutionary spark may kindle a fire," and that the state may thus "suppress the threatened danger in its incipiency" (p. 669).

In *Dennis* v. *United States* (1951), eleven top members of the Communist party had been tried and convicted under the *Smith Act of 1940 by a lower federal court. Although he claimed to be utilizing the clear and present danger test, Chief Justice Fred M. *Vinson, in upholding the conviction, adapted the formula to ascertain "whether the gravity of the 'evil' discounted by its improbability" would justify governments limits on *speech (p. 510). This leaned more toward the bad tendency test and provoked passionate dissents by Justices Hugo *Black and William O. *Douglas.

The "public versus private speech" test was prominently articulated by the philosopher and educator Alexander Meiklejohn in the second quarter of the twentieth century. To Meiklejohn, "public" speech comprises any expression concerning public policy and/or public officials and is entitled to absolute protection in the interests of a self-governing, free, democratic society, based on the First Amendment and the *Privileges or Immunities Clause of the *Fourteenth Amendment. An example would be the advocacy of a violent change of our form of government. "Private" speech, on the other hand, pertains to speech that concerns only private individuals in their personal, private concerns, and it can accordingly be regulated or restricted, but only under the *due process of law safeguards of the *Fifth and Fourteenth Amendments. Perhaps surprisingly, one of Meiklejohn's examples is the realm of the visual arts.

Fourth is the clear and present danger *plus imminence* test. Suggested as early as 1927 by Brandeis and Holmes in the former's concurring opinion in *Whitney* v. *California,* it became Court doctrine some four decades later in *Brandenburg* v. *Ohio* (1969). In it, the Court made clear that mere abstract advocacy of the use of force or of law violation was no longer legally or constitutionally punishable *"except* where such advocacy is directed to inciting or producing *imminent* lawless action and is likely to produce such action" (p. 444).

(See SPEECH AND THE PRESS.)

□ Alexander Meiklejohn, *Free Speech and Its Relation to Self-Government* (1948). Henry J. Abraham

### First English Evangelical Lutheran Church of Glendale v. County of Los Angeles, 482 U.S. 304 (1987), argued 14 Jan. 1987, decided 9 June 1987 by vote of 6 to 3; Rehnquist for the Court, Stevens in dissent. *First Lutheran* is the Supreme Court's landmark pronouncement that a land-use regulation can amount to a taking of property, with compensation therefore due the owner, even if the regulation is withdrawn upon a successful judicial challenge. The First English Evangelical Church owned buildings that were destroyed by a flood. After the flood a new county ordinance prohibited all construction in a flood plain area that included the church's land. California courts decided that the church could seek compensatory damages for the alleged taking only if (1) the ordinance was first declared an unlawful taking, and (2) the county then chose not to rescind the ordinance. The Court, in effect, reversed the second component of this state court ruling. The justices announced that invalidation and withdrawal of an excessive ordinance are not adequate remedies; the local government must, in addition, pay compensation for the excessive interferences with property rights that occur prior to the date that the offending ordinance is withdrawn (see JUST COMPENSATION).

Although the Court announced that compensation is due for temporary takings, it did not explain when in the land-use regulatory process a taking occurs. Nor did the Court intimate how damages might be calculated. The Court did suggest that no taking occurs "in the case of normal delays in obtaining building permits, changes in zoning ordinances, variances, and the like" (p. 321). Justice John Paul Stevens in dissent argued that the ruling would unduly inhibit local land-use regulatory processes because regulators, facing uncertain liability, might refrain from legitimate land-use planning. After the case was remanded, lower courts decided that the flood plain ordinance did not effect a taking.

(See also TAKINGS CLAUSE.)

Eric T. Freyfogle

### First Monday in October. Congress in 1916 advanced the convening of the Supreme Court from the second Monday in October, fixed in 1873, to the first (beginning in 1917). This measure, drafted by Justice James C. *McReynolds, was intended to expand the Court's capacity for handling its growing docket.

First Mondays are solemn ceremonial occasions. The *chief justice opened the proceedings at noon until 1961 and thereafter at ten o'clock. Tributes are offered to retired and deceased colleagues and court officers. New justices take their judicial oaths, *solicitors general are presented, and attorneys are admitted to the Court's bar. Fidelity to the rule of law is symbolized by the presence of members of the executive and legislative branches, as in 1962 when President John F. Kennedy and Vice President Lyndon B. Johnson attended during the then-raging Mississippi racial crisis. Other symbolically significant First Mondays have been signaled by the presence of the first black page (1954), the first black justice (1967), and the first woman justice (1981).

Little business is transacted in the usually brief proceedings. Circuit allotments are reported, and arguments on motions are presented. The most important event is the release of a lengthy *orders list of dispositions of *certiorari petitions. Civil rights litigation shook the placid First Monday tradition in 1958, when Justice Felix *Frankfurter filed his concurring opinion in *Cooper* v. *Aaron.* The Court in 1964 heard arguments on the public accommodations section of the new *Civil Rights Act. Similar opening day oral arguments occurred intermittently thereafter. A politically symbolic but defunct First Monday tradition, which lasted from 1917 until *World War II, was adjournment for a White House visit. Peter G. Fish

### First National Bank of Boston v. Bellotti, 435 U.S. 765 (1978), argued 9 Nov. 1977, decided 26 Apr. 1978 by vote of 5 to 4; Powell for the Court, Burger concurring, White, Brennan, Marshall, and Rehnquist in dissent. Reversing the highest court of Massachusetts, a bare majority of the Supreme Court held unconstitutional the portion of a state statute that banned corporations from spending to influence the outcome of a ballot referendum concerning a graduated *income tax. Such corporate expenditure is protected by the *First Amendment no less than anyone else's expenditure in the exercise of the right to free speech. The Court thus added another constitutional barrier to the major obstacles already erected by *Buckley* v. *Valeo* (1976) against legislative efforts to restrict campaign expenditures (see FINANCING POLITICAL SPEECH).

Banks and other corporations, like individuals,

are free to spend their funds to advocate or oppose public policies submitted for voter consideration. They could still, however, be constitutionally prohibited, as they are by federal and many state laws, from contributing money to candidates for elective office. And, it turned out, corporations could also be prohibited from spending on behalf of a candidate independently of a candidate's campaign (*Austin* v. *Michigan Chamber of Commerce,* 1990).

In *Bellotti,* the Court appears to follow its distinction in *Buckley* between campaign expenditures and campaign contributions to candidates. Expenditures are entitled to a constitutional protection not afforded to contributions that might be thought, when large, to corrupt elected officials. *Bellotti* is significant in extending the protection of expenditures to outlays of corporate funds. Justices Byron *White and William *Rehnquist, in vigorous dissenting opinions, separately dispute this result, contending that states should have the power to determine the potential harm of corporate campaign expenditures.

(See also ELECTIONS; POLITICAL PROCESS; SPEECH AND THE PRESS.)

Leon D. Epstein

**Fiscal and Monetary Powers.** Article I, section 8 of the Constitution authorizes Congress "To lay and collect Taxes, Duties, Imposts and Excises, to pay the Debts and provide for the common Defence and general Welfare of the United States." Other provisions of this article, however, declare that no tax can be laid on exports, require that direct taxes be apportioned among the states according to population, and demand that all duties, imposts, and excises apply uniformly throughout the United States.

Before 1895, the Court's precedent suggested that only taxes on real estate and poll (or capitation) taxes were direct taxes subject to the requirement of apportionment. In *Pollock* v. *Farmers' Loan & Trust Co.* (1895), however, the Court struck down the Income Tax Act of 1894 as an unapportioned direct tax because it taxed income that derived from real estate and personal property. This opinion ultimately prompted the 1913 adoption of the *Sixteenth Amendment, giving Congress the power to impose *income taxes without apportionment.

In the twentieth century, questions of congressional tax authority have mainly centered on the regulatory impact of taxation. The Supreme Court has classified only certain taxes as regulatory measures requiring a constitutional basis beyond the power to tax. Indicating a reluctance to inquire into congressional motives, the Court, in cases such as *McCray* v. *United States* (1904), for example, has not considered a federal tax to be a regulation if the impact on disfavored activity arises merely from the magnitude of the tax imposed. The Court has declared other statutes to be regulatory, however, when taxation has

been triggered by the violation of new standards of conduct announced along with the tax, as in *Bailey* v. *Drexel Furniture Co.* (1922). Classification of a tax as a regulatory measure now has much less practical significance than it once did because of the expansive interpretation the Supreme Court has given to the scope of federal regulatory power since the 1930s. The Court has, however, indicated in *Marchetti* v. *United States* (1968) and similar cases that a tax measure may be unconstitutional if it infringes on a specific constitutional prohibition, such as the *Fifth Amendment's protection against *self-incrimination.

Controversy regarding the limits of congressional spending power under Article I, section 8, has centered on the meaning of the General Welfare Clause and the legitimacy of conditional grants to the states. The Court resolved the former question in *United States* v. *Butler* (1936). In that case the Court endorsed Alexander *Hamilton's view that the clause grants an additional substantive power to spend, limited only by the requirement that such spending further the *general welfare of the United States rather than some merely local interest. Where this requirement has been met, the Court in cases such as *South Dakota* v. *Dole* (1987) has approved federal grants to the states conditioned on state activity in furtherance of a federal regulatory objective, whether or not that objective was one that Congress could achieve directly. The chief limitation on congressional authority is the requirement that such power not be used to induce the states to engage in activity that would itself be unconstitutional, such as invidious discrimination against some of its citizens.

Article I, section 8 authorizes Congress to borrow funds and to coin money and regulate its value. The Constitution neither expressly grants nor precludes congressional power to establish a national banking system, to emit bills of credit that can be used to pay debts to the national government, to promote a paper-money currency by making such bills of credit legal tender for all public and private debts or to control the value of that currency. By the 1930s the Supreme Court found all these to be *implied powers. The Court, for example, upheld an implied congressional power to charter a national bank in *McCulloch* v. *Maryland* (1819) and held that a state could not constitutionally tax such an institution. In the *Legal Tender Cases* (1871), the Court declared that Congress had authority to make U.S. Treasury notes legal tender. In the *Gold Clause Cases* (1935) the Court supported congressional power to control the value of such currency by upholding congressional invalidation of "gold clauses" (requiring payment in gold) in private contracts.

□ John E. Nowak, Ronald D. Rotunda, and J. Nelson Young, *Treatise on Constitutional Law: Substance and Procedure* (1986), pp. 340–366. Laurence H. Tribe, *American Constitutional Law,* 2d ed. (1988), pp. 318–323.

James May

**Flag Burning.** See EICHMAN, UNITED STATES V.; SYMBOLIC SPEECH; TEXAS V. JOHNSON.

**Flast v. Cohen,** 392 U.S. 83 (1968), argued 12 Mar. 1968, decided 10 June 1968 by vote of 8 to 1; Warren for the Court, Douglas, Stewart, and Fortas concurring separately, Harlan in dissent. A group of taxpayers sued to enjoin the allegedly unconstitutional expenditure of federal funds for the teaching of secular subjects in parochial schools. A federal court decided that they lacked standing to sue as taxpayers under *Frothingham* v. *Mellon* (1923), but the Supreme Court reversed and held that, under certain limited circumstances, taxpayers could sue in federal courts to challenge federal expenditures.

Chief Justice Earl *Warren's opinion rejected the contention that *Frothingham* articulated a constitutional requirement that absolutely barred taxpayer suits. Rather, he said, *Frothingham* was more deeply rooted in policy considerations that permitted greater discretion to federal judges to entertain such suits. Taxpayer suits would be permitted if the petitioner was a proper and appropriate party to invoke federal judicial power. Standing to sue would be measured by a two-part test: first, a taxpayer could challenge the constitutionality only of the exercise of congressional power under the *Taxing and Spending Clause of Article I, section 8. It would not be enough merely to challenge "incidental" expenditures under Congress's enumerated powers; second, the taxpayer must show that the challenged enactment is prohibited by a specific constitutional limitation on Congress's taxing and spending power and not merely by a general limitation on its powers, such as the *Tenth Amendment.

Flast satisfied both requirements. She challenged an expenditure under the Taxing and Spending Clause alleging it violated the establishment and free exercise clauses of the *First Amendment. Frothingham would have met the firxt nexus, but not the second. She had challenged the Maternity Act of 1921, which was enacted under the Taxing and Spending Clause; but she claimed only that it violated Congress's general legislative powers, the *Due Process Clause of the *Fifth Amendment, and the *Tenth Amendment. Thus in *Flast* the Court was able to distinguish *Frothingham* without overruling it.

Justice William O. *Douglas, urging the widest latitude for "private attorneys general" to sue (and thus broad taxpayer access to the courts), argued that *Frothingham* was incompatible with the spirit if not the holding in *Flast,* and should be overruled. In dissent, Justice John M. *Harlan conceded that *Frothingham* was too rigid and should be modified but contended that *Flast* went too far and would open the courts to abuse that strained the judicial function.

*Flast* was central to the Warren Court's liberal activist philosophy of increasing public access to federal courts and making them more receptive to public law litigation. But it remained unclear how far the decision went in removing traditional barriers to such litigation. Warren formally declined to speculate on whether "the Constitution contains other specific limitations" on the taxing and spending power (p. 105). But *Flast* was widely seen as an invitation to litigants to seek redress of their constitutional grievances in the federal courts without having to demonstrate the traditional personal injury or harm. A flood of taxpayer lawsuits, many challenging the legality of the war in *Vietnam, followed.

In *United States* v. *Richardson* (1974), and *Valley Forge Christian College* v. *Americans United for Separation of Church and State* (1982), the more conservative Burger Court closed the door again to taxpayer suits, at least for cases that did not meet *Flast's* specific test. Speaking in the latter case, Justice William H. *Rehnquist firmly rejected the *Flast* philosophy: "Implicit [in *Flast*] is the philosophy that the business of the federal courts is correcting constitutional errors, and that 'cases and controversies' [required by Article III] are at best merely convenient vehicles for doing so and at worst nuisances that may be dispensed with. . . . This philosophy has no place in our constitutional scheme" (p. 489).

(See STANDING TO SUE.)

Joel B. Grossman

**Fletcher v. Peck,** 6 Cranch (10 U.S.) 87 (1810), argued 15 Feb. 1810, decided 16 March 1810 by vote of 4 to 1; Marshall for the Court, Johnson dissenting in part; Cushing and Chase not participating. In *Fletcher* v. *Peck* the Supreme Court employed the *Contracts Clause of the Constitution as an instrument of judicial nationalization. In 1794, after notorious bribery involving virtually every member of the Georgia legislature, two U.S. senators, and many state and federal judges (including Justice James *Wilson of the Supreme Court), the Georgia legislature authorized the sale of thirty-five million acres in the Yazoo area (present-day Alabama and Mississippi) to four land companies for 1.5 cents per acre. Corrupted legislators were defeated at the polls and in 1796, the legislature rescinded the Yazoo grant, invalidating all property rights derived from it. In the meantime, however, purchasers under the 1794 statute sold off millions of acres. One of the purchasers under this later sale, Robert Fletcher, brought what amounted to a collusive suit against his seller, John Peck, for breach of warranty of title, the ultimate objective being to invalidate the legislative rescission.

*Fletcher* v. *Peck* presented Chief Justice John *Marshall with a dilemma. He had to uphold the original legislative grant, corrupted by bribery, in order to reassure investors who took land under state grants, while voiding the later, untainted statute. He therefore proceeded cautiously. The only question before the Court, Marshall said, was title; to remedy political corruption, citizens should resort to the polls, not to the courts. Having sidestepped the corruption issue, Marshall deftly took up the constitutional issues. Could legislatures deprive bona fide investors of the lands they had acquired under the corrupt grant? Each buyer, said Marshall, had procured "a title good at law, he is innocent, whatever may be the guilt of others, and equity will not subject him to the penalties attached to that guilt. All titles would be insecure, and the intercourse between man and man would be very seriously obstructed, if this principle be overturned" (pp. 133–134).

Marshall held the rescinding act an unconstitutional abridgment of the obligation of lawful contracts under the Contract Clause. Equally important, he tied the rights protected by that clause to the *natural law doctrine of *vested rights: when an agreement was "in its nature a contract, when absolute rights have vested under that contract, a repeal of the law cannot divest those rights" (p. 134). He concluded that "either by principles which are common to our free institutions, or by the particular provisions of the constitution of the United States" (p. 139), a state legislature could not enact legislation that impaired contracts or disturbed land titles supposedly acquired in good faith.

*Fletcher v. Peck* provoked public outcry, particularly from proponents of states' rights who accused the Court of pandering to speculators and of imposing a doctrinal strait-jacket on frontier legislatures. Marshall's opinion did in fact support land speculators and protected the titles of some unscrupulous investors as well as bona fide purchasers of western lands. But Marshall considered contractual rights and obligations essential to the American experiment in self-rule. Thus, *Fletcher's* legacy was complex: it was a benchmark in Marshall's campaign to protect the law of property and contracts from legislative interference, an early statement about the need to separate politics from law, and an example of judicial receptivity to the needs of investors in an age of capital scarcity. At the same time, it reflected the Court's commitment to the security of contracts and *property rights as protected under the Constitution.

□ C. Peter Magrath, *Yazoo: Law and Politics in the New Republic* (1966).　　　Sandra F. VanBurkleo

**Fletcher v. Rhode Island** See LICENSE CASES.

**Florida v. Bostick,** 111 S.Ct. 2382 (1991), argued 26 Feb. 1991, decided 18 June 1991 by vote of 6 to 3; O'Connor for the Court, Marshall in dissent. What constitutes a "seizure" within the meaning of the *Fourth Amendment? Police practices need not be "reasonable"—indeed, are not regulated by the Fourth Amendment at all—unless they are considered "searches" or "seizures." In this case, which involved a growing antidrug police tactic

known as "working the buses" (randomly approaching a bus passenger and asking him for identification and to grant permission to search his luggage), the Court took a narrow view of what constitutes a "seizure."

Police boarded an interstate bus on which Bostick was a passenger, asked for his identification, and questioned him. Bostick later claimed that an illegal "seizure" had occurred because a reasonable person in those circumstances would not have felt free to leave; moreover, he had done nothing to arouse suspicion. Bostick contended the illegal seizure tainted and invalidated his subsequent "consent" to search his luggage (a search that turned up cocaine).

The Florida Supreme Court agreed. It excluded the cocaine and banned the use of bus-boarding tactics. But the U.S. Supreme Court held that the state court had committed error when it adopted a flat rule prohibiting the police from boarding buses and approaching passengers at random as a means of drug interdiction.

The Court noted that Bostick's movement was restricted by a factor independent of police conduct—by his being a passenger on a bus. (If he had left the bus, Bostick would have risked being stranded and losing whatever luggage he had locked away in the luggage compartment.) Under such circumstances, the Court pointed out, the appropriate inquiry is not whether a reasonable person would feel free to leave but whether he or she would feel free to "terminate the encounter" or to "ignore the police presence" (p. 2387). Although the Court remanded the case to the state court for further findings on this issue, it broadly hinted that Bostick had not been "seized" within the meaning of the Fourth Amendment.

(See SEARCH WARRANT RULE, EXCEPTIONS TO.)
　　　　　　　　　　　　　　　　Yale Kamisar

**Footnote Eleven** (of *Brown v. Board of Education*). In 1954 the Supreme Court ruled in *Brown* v. *Board of Education* that racial segregation in public schools violated the *Equal Protection Clause of the *Fourteenth Amendment. The decision was based on two propositions: that segregated schools were inherently unequal and that the very act of racial segregation generated a feeling of inferiority that had a detrimental effect on the mental and emotional well-being of minority schoolchildren. In support of the latter proposition, the Court, in Footnote Eleven (p. 495), cited works by prominent psychiatrists, psychologists, sociologists, and anthropologists describing the harmful social and psychological effects of segregation.

Critics of the Court's decision in *Brown* complained that the justices had relied on imprecise data from the social sciences to forge constitutional doctrine. Some of the critics agreed with the Court's decision outlawing segregation but argued that the nonlegal materials cited provided too flimsy a basis for such an important ruling. Supporters of the Court's method pointed out, first, that the decision did not rest solely on material from the social sciences but also that such material was in fact vital in helping the Court deal with social issues. In *Brown*, the Court recognized that the social sciences could provide information pertinent to the issue of racial segregation, and it used that information to render an informed decision.

(See also RACE AND RACISM; SEPARATE BUT EQUAL; SOCIAL SCIENCE.)

Jeffrey M. Shaman

**Footnote Four** (of *United States* v. *Carolene Products Co.*), 304 U.S. 144 (1938), *Carolene Products* case argued 6 April 1938, decided 25 April 1938; Stone for himself, Hughes, Brandeis, and Roberts, Cardozo and Reed not participating, McReynolds in dissent, Butler concurring separately, Black not concurring in the part of Stone's opinion containing the footnote. (Thus only four justices concurred in the footnote.)

What is probably the most renowned footnote in Supreme Court history appeared in a case that would otherwise be forgotten. In the *Carolene Products* case, the Court applied the presumption of constitutionality to uphold a law passed by Congress regulating commerce, but included its famous Footnote Four, which contained three paragraphs:

There may be narrower scope for operation of the presumption of constitutionality when legislation appears on its face to be within a specific prohibition of the Constitution, such as those of the first ten amendments, which are deemed equally specific when held to be embraced within the Fourteenth. . . .

It is unnecessary to consider now whether legislation which restricts those political processes which can ordinarily be expected to bring about repeal of undesirable legislation, is to be subjected to more exacting judicial scrutiny under the general prohibitions of the Fourteenth Amendment than are most other types of legislation. . . .

Nor need we enquire whether similar considerations enter into the review of statutes directed at particular religions, . . . or national, . . . or racial minorities . . . ; whether prejudice against discrete and insular minorities may be a special condition, which tends seriously to curtail the operation of those political processes ordinarily to be relied upon to protect minorities, and which may call for a correspondingly more searching judicial inquiry. . . .                (pp. 152–153)

The *Carolene Products* footnote suggests the appropriateness of applying different degrees of judicial scrutiny to different types of legislation. It appeared one year after the Court had abandoned its previous position of *judicial activism in defense of the economic rights of businesses and employers. Typically in such cases, the Court had rigidly scrutinized legislation affecting *property rights to determine whether it served a legitimate public purpose and was reasonable in

its terms. After 1937 the Court embraced instead a posture of deference to the policy judgments of Congress and state legislatures. It presumed the constitutionality of such laws, and declined to consider whether they were wise, necessary, or desirable. Justice Harlan Fiske *Stone's footnote, written in the most tentative terms, suggested that there might be situations in which the presumption of constitutionality should be less stringently applied.

Each of the footnote's three paragraphs identified one possible justification for a less strict application of the presumption of constitutionality. The first paragraph suggested that the presumption might be lessened when the challenged legislation appeared to violate a specific constitutional prohibition. As originally conceived, the footnote did not include this paragraph, which was added at the behest of Chief Justice Charles Evans *Hughes, apparently to explain the evident inconsistency between his opinions for the Court in *West Coast Hotel Co.* v. *Parrish* (1937), employing the presumption in order to uphold legislation limiting freedom of *contract, which is not specifically guaranteed in the Constitution, and *Near v. Minnesota* (1931), declining to employ the presumption in the case of legislation that abridged the *First Amendment guarantee of freedom of the press. The difficulty with this paragraph is that, unless constitutional prohibitions are absolutes, the rights they protect may validly be abridged under certain circumstances, and the paragraph does not explain why courts and not legislatures should make the policy judgments as to when the circumstances justifying abridgment exist.

The second and third paragraphs, originally composed by Stone's law clerk, Louis Lusky, escape this difficulty. They identify instances where the democratic process may be obstructed and imply that courts need not defer to legislative judgments arrived at through a flawed process from which some groups may have been excluded. The second paragraph suggests that greater scrutiny may be appropriate in reviewing legislation restricting effective participation in the political process, such as by limiting the rights to vote, to express political viewpoints, to organize politically, or to assemble (see ASSEMBLY AND ASSOCIATION, FREEDOM OF; VOTE, RIGHT TO). Since the presumption of constitutionality rests on the assumption that it is unnecessary as well as improper for courts to review the wisdom or desirability of legislation because bad laws may be repealed through the political process, employment of the presumption loses its fundamental justification when the persons or groups adversely affected by a law find themselves denied effective access to that process.

The third paragraph suggests that, for like reasons, the presumption may be inappropriate for laws that affect "discrete and insular minorities"—powerless groups hated or feared by the majority of society. Because prejudice against religious, national, or racial minorities may skew the political process and distort its functioning, more intensive judicial scrutiny may be called for when laws are targeted at such minorities. Clearly much legislation existed at that time, particularly at the state level, that reflected majority prejudice against African-Americans, Asians (e.g., laws preventing aliens of Asian ancestry from owning land or pursuing certain occupations), and unpopular religious groups, such as the Jehovah's Witnesses. Members of these groups, precisely because they were the victims of intense prejudice, were incapable of using the political process to protect themselves. The third paragraph reflected an awareness that an even-handed but *pro forma* application of the presumption of constitutionality could leave these groups at the mercy of an intolerant majority, and it provided a theoretical basis for future judicial activism in defense of powerless minorities. Recognition of the need for special judicial protection for such groups is the footnote's greatest strength and the principal reason for its continued vitality.

(See also BILL OF RIGHTS; FUNDAMENTAL RIGHTS; INCORPORATION DOCTRINE; PREFERRED FREEDOMS DOCTRINE; STRICT SCRUTINY.)

Dean Alfange, Jr.

**Foreign Affairs and Foreign Policy.** Of the three branches of the federal government, the judiciary has least to say on the subjects of foreign affairs and foreign policy. While the Constitution empowers justices to try cases involving foreign ambassadors and to enforce *treaties as supreme law of the land, the Supreme Court has made no important foreign policies and usually defers to Congress and presidents regarding foreign relations. Indeed, as the nation rose as a superpower, courts legitimated the concentration of national and executive authority far more often than they limited it.

The Constitution does govern foreign-policy makers, but their sources of authority are broader and their limits are less restrictive in foreign than in domestic affairs. The landmark decision *United States v. *Curtiss-Wright Export Corp.* (1936) declared, first, that powers of external sovereignty derived from nationhood rather than the Constitution and, second, that presidents have "very delicate, plenary and exclusive power . . . as the sole organ of the Federal government in the field of international relations" (p. 320). However flawed as history, *Curtiss-Wright* undergirds claims of executive hegemony over foreign policy. It implies that states have no foreign powers to surrender and that in the realm of relations with foreign countries presidents may do anything that the Constitution or statutes do not expressly forbid.

The Court has consistently championed a national monopoly in foreign policy. *Federalism is irrelevant externally; state lines disappear. From the initial peace treaty with Britain in 1783, to the United States' recognition of the Soviet Union in 1933, to President Jimmy Carter's transfer of Iranian assets in 1981, no treaty or executive agreement has been nullified for invading state reserved powers or private property. An early *environment case challenging federal protection of migratory birds, *Missouri v. Holland* (1920), reaffirmed broad *implied power to implement treaties domestically. Even *executive agreements prevail over state law.

*Separation of powers mostly limits the Court itself. Broadly speaking, most foreign policy decisions are beyond *judicial review. The prime rationale is the fuzzy *political question doctrine: that courts cannot consider subjects belonging by law, function, or prudence to political branches. Territorial boundaries, recognition of governments, termination of hostilities, abrogation of treaties, the legality of the *Vietnam War, are all controversial instances of this judicial self-abrogation. Barriers against excessive *delegation of powers by the legislative branch also are minimal.

Individual rights attract greater judicial scrutiny. Easing fears of unfettered executive power after *World War II, *Reid v. Covert* (1957) affirmed that at least some protections of the *Bill of Rights shield citizens under American control abroad. The Court ruled that the *Fifth and *Sixth Amendments prohibit U.S. military trials of civilian dependents accompanying service personnel overseas for crimes committed in peacetime (see MILITARY TRIALS AND MARTIAL LAW). Citizens also enjoy a constitutional right of foreign *travel (*Kent v. Dulles,* 1958), though the justices did uphold travel bans on former CIA agents and a ban on Americans traveling to Cuba. The *Fourth Amendment applies neither to wiretapping of foreign agents in the U.S. nor to searches and seizures by American drug agents in foreign homes of nonresident aliens arrested in the United States. (*United States v. Verdugo-Urquidez,* 1990).

The Constitution thus intermittently follows the flag. The primary controls on foreign-policy makers are political, not judicial. Adapting internal law to international facts of life, the Supreme Court has validated more than it has restrained the government's organic growth into an increasingly unitary state dominated by executive leadership in world affairs. Ironically, the Supreme Court's main influence abroad may derive from the example it sets as a domestic constitutional court enforcing federalism and individual rights. Since World War II many nations and some supranational organizations have adopted the American model of written covenants, a bill of rights, and judicial review to police allocations of power and, especially, to advance human rights.

(See also INHERENT POWERS; NATIONAL SECU-
RITY; PRESIDENTIAL EMERGENCY POWERS; WAR
POWERS.)

□ Edward S. Corwin, *The President: Office and Powers*
(1957). Louis Fisher, *Constitutional Conflicts Between Congress and the President* (1985). Michael J. Glennon, *Constitutional Diplomacy* (1990). Louis Henkin, *Foreign Affairs
and the Constitution* (1972).      J. Woodford Howard, Jr.

**Fortas, Abe** (b. Memphis, Tenn., 19 June 1910; d.
Washington, D.C., 5 Apr. 1982; cremated), associate justice, 1965–1969. The son of immigrant
Jews, Fortas won scholarships to Southwestern
College and Yale Law School. Arriving in New
Haven during the heyday of legal realism, Fortas
learned to treat law as a tool of social policy and
became the protégé of Thurman Arnold and
William O. *Douglas. Fortas served as editor in
chief of the *Yale Law Journal* and stood second in
his class when he graduated in 1933.

Fortas became a New Dealer and joined the Agricultural Adjustment Administration. In 1935,
he married Carolyn Agger, and the couple moved
to New Haven so she could attend Yale Law
School. Fortas taught there and commuted to
Washington to work with Douglas at the Securities and Exchange Commission until she graduated. In 1939, Fortas joined the Department of
Interior and made himself indispensable to the
department's irascible secretary, Harold Ickes. As
under secretary during World War II, Fortas
supported land reform, opposed the imposition
of martial law in Hawaii and fought the internment of Japanese-Americans. Critics questioned
his tactics, but few doubted his efficacy.

With other New Dealers, Fortas realized his
expertise in interpreting governmental regulations could prove lucrative at war's end. Fortas
established a law firm in Washington with Thurman Arnold and Paul Porter and began representing the corporate interests New Dealers had once
attacked. Yet few lawyers more vigilantly protected civil liberties during the postwar Red Scare
than Fortas, who defended Owen Lattimore and
other victims of McCarthyism. Later, he successfully argued two landmark pro bono cases: *Dur-
ham* v. *United States* (1954), which updated the
legal definition of insanity, and *Gideon* v. *Wainwright* (1963), which established a right to counsel
in all state felony cases. A brilliant legal strategist,
Fortas was a great courtroom advocate and was
considered a "lawyer's lawyer." As managing
partner of Arnold, Fortas & Porter, Fortas was
disliked by many associates who found him cold,
but he built it into one of Washington's most
successful firms and was earning nearly $175,000
annually by 1964.

By that time he had become one of President
Lyndon B. Johnson's most trusted advisers. The
loud, crude politician and the quiet lawyer who
loved chamber music seemed an odd couple, but
Fortas had successfully defended Johnson in his

*Abe Fortas*

disputed 1948 primary election for senator and
proved his loyalty repeatedly afterwards. To
reward his friend, Johnson engineered Arthur
*Goldberg's departure from the Court in 1965 and
offered Fortas the vacancy. Fortas initially demurred. Both he and Agger, who had joined his
firm, feared the salary cut; and the firm needed
him. But Fortas wanted the job, and Johnson
insisted he take it.

As a justice, Fortas shared the Warren Court
majority's commitment to expanding civil liberties and civil rights. His two most important
opinions involved children: *In re *Gault* (1967)
extended to juvenile offenders many due process
protections previously reserved for adults and in
*Tinker* v. *Des Moines Independent Community
School District* (1969), Fortas insisted on students'
right to engage in nondisruptive protest and to
express their opposition to the *Vietnam War by
wearing black armbands to school. With his
support, the Court issued *Miranda* v. *Arizona*
(1966), upheld the *Voting Rights Act of 1965,
invalidated the *poll tax, and insisted on legislative reapportionment. He sided with the Court's
majority against big business and wrote one of
the Warren Court's most radical antitrust opinions, *U.S.* v. *Arnold, Schwinn and Company* (1967).
Unlike the majority, however, Fortas despised
the press and sought unsuccessfully to subordinate *First Amendment freedoms to the right to
*privacy in his dissent in *Time, Inc.* v. *Hill* (1967).
Fortas was capable of writing well-crafted opinions, such as *Epperson* v. *Arkansas* (1968), in which
he struck down a state statute prohibiting the
teaching of evolution. More frequently, however,

his opinions reflected a concern for social policy over legal precedent. His tendency to interpret the *Due Process Clause as a broad guarantee of fairness enraged Hugo *Black, but most of his brethren applauded his activism.

Like Black, however, they were dismayed by Fortas's continuing closeness to Johnson. Because he was restless in the cloistered environs of the Court and could not resist Johnson's entreaties, Fortas became involved in the divisive issues that destroyed his friend's presidency. He strongly advocated American intervention in Vietnam and advised Johnson to send troops into riot-torn Detroit (see EXTRAJUDICIAL ACTIVITIES).

When Chief Justice Earl *Warren resigned in 1968, Johnson nominated Fortas for the position. Senators used Fortas's confirmation hearings as a forum for claiming that the Warren Court's protection of individual rights had aided criminals and damaged the state. Though Fortas downplayed his relationship with Johnson and noted that justices had long counseled presidents, opponents also charged that Fortas had violated the principle of *"separation of powers." Johnson, who had announced he would not seek reelection, could do little for Fortas. The nomination was already doomed when senators learned that Fortas, who was dissatisfied with his salary, had accepted fifteen thousand dollars raised by Paul Porter from the justice's friends and former clients for teaching a summer course at American University, an arrangement many considered improper. Republicans and conservative southern Democrats launched a filibuster, and the nomination was withdrawn at Fortas's request.

A year later Fortas's financial dealings came under renewed scrutiny when *Life* magazine revealed that he had accepted an honorarium for serving on a charitable foundation headed by a former client. Fortas resigned from the Court in disgrace (see FORTAS RESIGNATION). When his old firm refused to take him back, he opened a small firm, where he again established a flourishing practice combining corporate law with pro bono work. He did not have the time or temperament to become a great justice, but he was a great lawyer.

□ Laura Kalman, *Abe Fortas* (1990). Bruce Murphy, *Fortas: The Rise and Ruin of a Supreme Court Justice* (1988).
Laura Kalman

**Fortas Resignation.** On 5 May 1969, *Life* magazine revealed that in 1966, Justice Abe *Fortas had accepted a twenty-thousand-dollar honorarium for becoming a consultant to a charitable foundation headed by his former client, Louis Wolfson, which he had returned after Wolfson had been twice indicted. The article suggested that Fortas might have given Wolfson legal advice and noted that Wolfson had dropped Fortas's name "in strategic places."

In the dramatic days that followed, Fortas issued an obfuscatory statement that satisfied no one. The media hounded him. Liberals deserted him. The Nixon administration, which wanted Fortas's seat for a conservative, worked to force him off the bench. Soon after Fortas resigned on 14 May, the public learned that while he had indeed returned the money mentioned in the *Life* article, the foundation had initially agreed to pay Fortas twenty thousand dollars annually for life and the same amount annually to his wife should she survive him.

Justices commonly supplemented their salaries by accepting honoraria for serving on foundation boards, and Fortas did not give Wolfson legal advice or seek preferential treatment for him. But Fortas's relationship with Wolfson seemed suspect, and the American Bar Association declared it contrary to the provision in the canon of judicial ethics that a judge's conduct must be free of the appearance of impropriety. Fortas's actions led the association to revise its canon of judicial ethics in an attempt to deter judges from accepting income for outside activities by requiring that they report it publicly.

(See also RESIGNATION AND RETIREMENT.)
Laura Kalman

**Four Horsemen,** phrase employed during the mid-1930s to describe Pierce *Butler, Willis *Van Devanter, George *Sutherland, and James *McReynolds, four justices of the Supreme Court who consistently opposed *New Deal economic and social legislation. Originally employed by critics of these justices, the term evoked the legendary Four Horsemen of the Apocalypse.
James W. Ely, Jr.

**Fourteenth Amendment.** With the end of the *Civil War and the abolition of *slavery by the *Thirteenth Amendment (ratified 1865), the Confederate states sought readmission to the Union and to Congress. Under Article I, section 2 of the Constitution, a slave had been counted as three-fifths of a person for purposes of representation. Because of the abolition of slavery, southern states expected a substantial increase in their representation in the House of Representatives. The Union, having won the war, might lose the peace.

*Reconstruction.* In 1865–1866, southern states and localities enacted Black Codes to regulate the status and conduct of the newly freed slaves. The codes deprived blacks of many basic rights accorded to whites, including full rights to own property, to testify in court in cases in which whites were parties, to make *contracts, to *travel, to preach, to assemble, to speak, and to bear arms. To Republicans, the Black Codes were only the latest southern attack on individual rights. Before the war, southern states had suppressed fundamental rights, including free *speech and press, in order to protect the institution of slavery. Though the Supreme Court had ruled in 1833 that guarantees of the Bill of Rights did not limit the states (*Barron* v. *Baltimore*), many Republicans thought state officials were obligated to respect those guarantees. The Court in *Dred *Scott* v. *Sandford* (1857) had held that blacks, including free blacks, were not citizens under the Constitution and therefore were entitled to none of the rights and privileges it secured. Republicans also rejected *Dred Scott* and thought the newly freed slaves should be citizens entitled to all the rights of citizens (see CITIZENSHIP).

The Fourteenth Amendment was proposed by Congress in 1866 and ratified by the states in 1868. It reflected Republican determination that southern states should not be readmitted to the Union and Congress without additional guarantees. Section 1 made all persons born within the nation citizens both of the United States and of the states where they resided (thereby reversing *Dred Scott*) and prohibited states from abridging *privileges or immunities of citizens of the United States and from depriving persons of *due process of law or *equal protection of the laws. Section 2 reduced the representation of any state that deprived a part of its male population of the right to *vote, an indirect attempt to protect the voting rights of blacks. Other sections protected the federal war debt, prohibited payment of the Confederate debt, and disabled from holding office those who had sworn to uphold the Constitution but who had engaged in rebellion. Section 5 empowered Congress "to enforce, by appropriate legislation," the preceding sections.

*Early Interpretation.* The first major interpretation of the Fourteenth Amendment's effect came in the *Slaughterhouse Cases* (1873), in which the Court held that the basic civil rights and liberties of citizens remained under control of state law. The Court limited the privileges and immunities of citizens of the United States referred to in the amendment to relatively narrow rights such as protection on the high seas and the right to travel to and from the nation's capital. The *Slaughterhouse Cases* drastically curtailed the protection afforded by the amendment against state violations of fundamental guarantees of liberty. One reason for the majority's narrow construction of the amendment was its fear that a more expansive reading would threaten the basic functions of state governments, both by federal judicial action and through enforcement by federal statutes that might displace large areas of state law (see FEDERALISM).

Contrary to the expectations of some of the amendment's framers, the Supreme Court held that it did not overrule *Barron* v. *Baltimore* (1833) to require states and local governments to respect the guarantees of the *Bill of Rights. The Court also held that because the amendment provided that "no state shall" deprive persons of the rights it guaranteed, Congressional legislation protecting blacks and Republicans from Ku Klux Klan violence exceeded the power of the federal government. In the *Civil Rights Cases* (1883) the Court nullified provisions of the 1875 Civil Rights Act guaranteeing equal access to public accommodations. It held that the amendment reached only *state action, not purely private action.

In *Plessy* v. *Ferguson* (1896) the Court held that state-mandated racial segregation of railway cars did not violate the amendment's Equal Protection Clause (see SEGREGATION, DE JURE). In 1908 it upheld a state statute requiring segregation of private colleges (*Berea College* v. *Kentucky*). Justice John Marshall *Harlan registered eloquent but lonely *dissents to the Court's decisions sanctioning state-imposed segregation. The Court also held, in *Bradwell* v. *Illinois* (1873) and *Minor* v. *Happersett* (1875), respectively, that the amendment did not protect the right of women to practice law or to vote (see GENDER).

Although the Court first embraced a narrow reading of the amendment, it gradually expanded its protection of corporate and *property interests. In 1886 the Court declared that a corporation was a "person" for purposes of the Fourteenth Amendment (*Santa Clara County* v. *Southern Pacific Railroad Co.*). By 1897 it had begun reading the amendment as protecting freedom of *contract, finding in *Allgeyer* v. *Louisiana* that a state statute restricting out-of-state insurance companies violated due process. In *Lochner* v. *New York* (1905) it held that a law limiting bankers to a sixty-hour week violated the liberty of contract secured by the amendment's *Due Process Clause.

*Liberty Protections.* After the constitutional crisis of 1937 (see COURT-PACKING PLAN), the Court repudiated its decisions striking down economic regulation. But while the amendment shrank as a protection of economic interests, it grew as a protection of other liberty interests. Much of this modern growth has resulted from extension of the Bill of Rights to the states. Since *World War II, the *Equal Protection Clause has emerged from obscurity. Under it, the Court has subjected racial discrimination to increasingly *strict (usually fatal) scrutiny. In *Brown* v. *Board of Education* (1954) the Court found that segregated *education denied minority schoolchildren the equal protection of the laws.

In *Reynolds* v. *Sims* (1964) the Court found that malapportioned state legislative districts also violated the Equal Protection Clause (see REAPPORTIONMENT CASES). Other discrimination, such as that against aliens, was also subjected to strict judicial scrutiny and struck down (see ALIENAGE AND NATURALIZATION). While state legislation restricting *fundamental rights is subject to strict judicial scrutiny, economic regulation is usually measured by a more relaxed test that merely requires the court to find some rational purpose for the classification, which it usually does. Discrimination based on sex or illegitimacy has been scrutinized less strictly than discrimination based on race but more strictly than purely economic regulation.

By a broader reading of what constituted state action, the Court has reached a wide range of action once considered private and therefore outside the protection of the Fourteenth Amendment. In *Shelley* v. *Kraemer* (1948) the Court outlawed judicial enforcement of racially *restrictive covenants in housing (see HOUSING DISCRIMINATION). In *United States* v. *Guest* (1966) six justices in dicta indicated that congressional power under the Fourteenth Amendment could reach racially motivated private violence.

Another major area of expansion of the Fourteenth Amendment was in the application of the Bill of Rights to the states. As early as 1908, in *Twining* v. *New Jersey*, the Court suggested that some Bill of Rights guarantees might limit the states through the Due Process Clause. In *Gitlow* v. *New York* (1925) the Court began to apply guarantees of speech, press, assembly, religion, and counsel to the states. The guarantees applied to the states were those the Court considered essential to ordered liberty (*Palko* v. *Connecticut*, 1937). A majority of the Court thought that many rights in the Bill of Rights—*trial by jury and the privilege against *self-incrimination, for example—did not meet that test. The *incorporation of the Bill of Rights accelerated under the Warren Court. By 1969 most Bill of Rights guarantees had been incorporated as limits on state power.

In addition to applying the Bill of Rights to the states, the Court found other fundamental rights, though not specifically set out in the Constitution, were entitled to protection under the Due Process Clause. These included a right to *privacy that embraced the right of married couples to use birth-control devices (*Griswold* v. *Connecticut*, 1965) and the right of women to obtain an *abortion (*Roe* v. *Wade*, 1973). The abortion decision has been subjected to severe political attack (see also CONTRACEPTION). Recently the Court has questioned the rationale of the privacy decisions. In 1986, in *Bowers* v. *Hardwick*, the Court held the right to privacy did not protect consenting adults from prosecution for homosexual conduct under state sodomy laws (see HOMOSEXUALITY). The decision criticized prior privacy cases as having "little or no textual support in the constitutional language" and suggested that they were of questionable legitimacy (p. 191).

By 1968 the Warren Court's decisions, particularly in areas of criminal procedure, provoked political criticism. President Richard *Nixon's appointees to the Court, followed by those of Presidents Ronald *Reagan and George Bush have espoused a narrower view of guarantees of liberty, particularly as they affect the rights of the accused. So the Fourteenth Amendment remains, as it has been through most of its history, a center of controversy, and it continues both to mirror and to shape changes in American society.

(See also RACE AND RACISM; RECONSTRUCTION; SPEECH AND THE PRESS.)

□ Michael Kent Curtis, *No State Shall Abridge: The Fourteenth Amendment and the Bill of Rights* (1986). William E. Nelson, *The Fourteenth Amendment: From Political Principle to Judicial Doctrine* (1988). Laurence H. Tribe, *American Constitutional Law*, 2d ed. (1988).

Michael Kent Curtis

**Fourth Amendment.** Millions of arrests and searches are carried out by police each year in the United States. In addition, numerous administrative inspections are made pursuant to regulatory legislation. The Fourth Amendment, with its ban on "unreasonable searches and seizures," is the constitutional provision that, more directly than any other, governs police and administrative investigations. It is designed to preserve the most cherished values of a free society by striking a fair balance between society's demand for order and public safety, on the one hand, and the individual's need for security and privacy, on the other.

*Origins.* Unlike other provisions in the *Bill of Rights, the Fourth Amendment is rooted mainly in American, rather than English, history. It signified the determination of Americans to prevent the recurrence of a specific historical grievance, the high-handed search measures in the American colonies preceding the Revolution.

In order to stem rampant smuggling to which the colonists resorted in evasion of laws that restricted trade to areas within the empire, vast powers of search were conferred on British customs officials. The Writ of Assistance, a general search warrant authorized by Parliament, granted them virtually unlimited discretion to search and was valid for the lifetime of the sovereign. This writ was usually not directed at the perpetrators of particular acts. Casting its net widely, it required neither *probable cause nor description of persons and premises nor even a magistrate's authorization of a particular search. The Fourth Amendment, in contrast, places control of the warrant process in the hands of a judge who acts as a buffer between the police and the citizen, so that the crucial determinations of probable cause and the allowable scope of the search are made by an independent authority.

Despite its apparent comprehensiveness, the amendment actually tells us very little about how to deal with numerous search situations. Its history teaches us a preference, wherever feasible, for a search under warrant over a judicially unsupervised police action. The text requires a standard of probable cause, and particularity of description of persons and premises. It does not define probable cause, an enormously flexible term, not does it even define a search.

*Interpretation.* The Supreme Court has at times tightly construed the text or hewed closely to the history of the amendment. At one point it insisted that electronic eavesdropping did not fall within the amendment's ambit, nor was the home protected against warrantless administrative inspection. Eavesdropping, it said, did not require entry onto premises, and the "search" was for the intangible human voice, rather than of the "persons, houses, papers, and effects" specified in the text. So, too, administrative inspections were carried out to safeguard the public, not to gather evidence of crime; and the origins of the amendment spoke more closely to the security interest of the citizen—protection against unbridled law enforcement—than to the *privacy interest in keeping out a health inspector. Only after the Court pried the animating spirit of the amendment from the anchors of text and history, did it hold that these new forms of search are indeed subject to the warrant requirements. The citizen must be able to invoke the protection of the Constitution against new contrivances of science that pose an even greater threat to security than the physical search. Moreover, it would be paradoxical to construe the amendment to provide greater protection to criminal suspects than to law-abiding citizens who merely wish to secure their privacy against government.

The great dilemma of interpretation concerns the relationship between the amendment's two clauses. The first clause bans "unreasonable searches," the second states the conditions for issuance of a warrant. Three possible interpretations emerge; all have found sanction at one time or another in Court decisions. The most obvious is to consider the warrant clause as explanatory of the reasonableness clause. A reasonable search is one conducted under a warrant issued by a magistrate; an unreasonable, and therefore unconstitutional, search is one that is not. This interpretation has been followed in most of the Court's cases. In Justice Potter *Stewart's words, "searches conducted outside the judicial process are *per se* unreasonable under the Fourth Amendment—subject only to a few specifically established and well-delineated exceptions" (*Katz v. United States,* 1967, p. 357).

A second interpretation reinforces the first, by holding that some searches may be so contrary to civilized standards that they are unreasonable even under warrant. Thus the Court in 1886 proscribed the search and seizure of private papers, though authorized by judicial process, and in 1921 it limited the search power to contraband and the fruits and instrumentalities of crime, banning the seizure of "mere evidence." These restrictions no longer apply. More recently, the Court has refused to allow surgical removal on a warrant of a bullet embedded in a suspect's body (*Winston v. Lee,* 1985).

The third interpretation treats the two clauses as separable: the reasonableness of a search is not dependent on the existence of a warrant but on what Justice Sherman *Minton called, "the facts and circumstances—the total atmosphere of the case" (*United States v. Rabinowitz,* 1950). For two decades preceding 1969 this view of the amendment, advocated by Justice Hugo *Black, held sway, and under it the Court sanctioned extensive warrantless searches of the premises where arrests were made. While the Court currently gives official sanction to the first interpretation, at times this seems lip service, for there appears to be considerable sentiment to return to a freefloating and less warrant-dependent reasonableness standard.

Either of the first two interpretations is faithful to the amendment's purpose. The third is not. A standard of reasonableness divorced from warrant requirement is really no standard at all, for it allows determination of probable cause in nonexigency situations to be made by police. Like the general warrant, it gives wide-ranging discretion to officers. Why should the drafters have bothered with strict warrant requirements after having, in effect, negated them by authorizing "reasonable" warrantless searches in the first clause?

Even under the view that a reasonable search is one conducted under warrant, exceptions have always been allowed. Exigent circumstances, where delay in procuring a warrant would defeat the purpose of the search constitute the most significant. Among exigencies so far identified are: (1) the "incidental" search of an arrestee and the immediate area within his reach, so as to safeguard the arresting officer and prevent destruction of evidence (*Chimel v. California,* 1969); (2) stop and search of a moving vehicle and its contents on probable cause (*United States v. *Ross,* 1982; see AUTOMOBILE SEARCHES); (3) "hot pursuit" of a felon into premises that he has entered (*Warden v. Hayden,* 1967); and (4) *"stop and frisk" of suspects who may be dangerous (*Terry v. Ohio,* 1968). These are only examples; any true emergency—say, a cry for help or a shot coming from behind closed doors, or the need to procure evidence from a burning building—will justify warrantless entry by the police.

A warrant is also not required in a number of other situations, such as where consent to the search is given or where an officer lawfully on premises obtains a "plain view" of contraband. Customs searches at an international border likewise do not require warrants for they are considered incidents of national sovereignty, as is the opening of international mail. While there is agreement on these exceptions, their application often creates knotty problems. For instance, who besides the suspect is entitled to consent to a search? (a spouse is, a landlord is not).

The amendment covers arrest (seizure of the person) as well as search, but there is a crucial difference. An outdoor felony arrest is always viewed as an exigency not requiring a warrant. However, entry into a person's house in order to make an arrest requires a warrant, barring a demonstrated exigency (*Payton v. New York, 1980).

"Probable cause" is an especially elusive concept. Generally speaking, it means (in the case of arrest) evidence that would lead a careful person to believe that the suspect has committed a specific offense or (in the case of search) that evidence related to the crime is present in the place to be searched. The surest way to establish probable cause is through the personal knowledge of the officer, or through an informant who is either another police officer or any law-abiding citizen. Informants with criminal records, on whom police must often rely, present difficult questions of veracity.

Homes and businesses are equally protected against warrantless police searches and administrative inspections. In the case of an inspection, probable cause is satisfied by a showing that the inspection is necessary; reason to believe that a violation has occurred is not required. For some businesses, such as those dealing in liquor or guns, no justification whatever is required; they can be inspected at any time without a warrant because historically they have been subject to "pervasive regulation."

*Enforcement.* The most creative—and controversial—feature of the Court's Fourth Amendment jurisprudence is the rule requiring exclusion of evidence seized in violation of constitutional standards. To suppress evidence merely because of the wrongful manner of its acquisition rather than because of its doubtful reliability (as with *coerced confessions), is something unique to American law; it has no precise counterpart in the law of any other country.

This *exclusionary rule appeared embryonically in *Boyd v. United States (1886). It was made explicit for the federal courts in *Weeks v. United States (1914), and finally extended to state prosecutions in *Mapp v. Ohio (1961). The reasons both for and against the rule can be equally compelling. The Court considered it vital in order to preserve constitutional standards, since there seem to be no viable alternatives to deter breaches of the amendment. Conversely, a successful invocation of the rule will usually set a guilty person free. The officer's misdeeds thus become society's burden. The theory behind the rule is that exclusion removes the incentive for unlawful searches by making them unprofitable. Studies indicate, however, that many, perhaps most, searches are made not to procure evidence, but to harass criminals and keep them off balance. The deterrent effect of the rule is thus not nearly as clear-cut as the Court had supposed.

Supporters of exclusion argue the long-range benefits to society of reduced police misconduct. Opponents point to the immediate cost of allowing undoubted criminals to go free. The precise extent of the costs is unclear. The percentage of failed prosecutions as a result of exclusion is small in some jurisdictions, but many cases are never brought to trial because the evidence would, if challenged, be suppressed. One may ask: if exclusion is indeed infrequent, does this not indicate general police compliance with the law, and no need for an exclusionary rule? But perhaps it is the rule that makes the police conscious of the Fourth Amendment's commands and abrogation might undo its constraint.

The rule operated rigidly through the years. The evidence was excluded no matter how major the crime or how minor the infraction of law. Responding to heated criticism, both on and off the bench, the Court in the post-Warren era has retreated, calibrating the rule by refusing to order exclusion in situations where its deterrent effect on the police would probably be limited. The most prominent case is United States v. *Leon (1984), which ruled that "good faith" reliance by police on a defective judicial warrant does not require exclusion. This development may portend a good faith rule even for warrantless searches or, possibly, the eventual abandonment of the rule altogether.

*The Amendment and the Court.* The status of the Fourth Amendment has waxed and waned in different periods of the Court's history. The initial phase of Fourth Amendment interpretation, which began with Boyd in 1886, was marked by liberal construction and the formulation of the exclusionary rule. The Prohibition era brought a more tolerant attitude toward law enforcement procedures; most notably, warrantless vehicle searches were sustained, the scope of incidental searches was widened, and eavesdropping was held to be beyond the amendment's protection. Under the Warren Court, the amendment regained its lost stature. The Court brought eavesdropping under the aegis of the amendment, imposed the exclusionary rule on the states, tightened probable cause standards, and required warrants for some regulatory searches. It also freed the amendment from the property concepts to which it had been linked by holding that what counted, in invoking the amendment's protection, was not a property interest in the area or thing searched, but rather a person's expectation of privacy, one that society would recognize as reasonable. "For the Fourth Amendment protects people, not [only] places" (Katz v. United States, p. 351).

The Fourth Amendment's lodestar is a judicially issued warrant based on probable cause; exigent circumstances have traditionally permitted a warrantless search but, again, on probable cause. Under the Burger and Rehnquist Courts, the warrant requirement has increasingly been narrowed—evidently in response to the plague of drugs—and probable cause has frequently been replaced by a lesser "reasonable suspicion" standard. Ironically, reasonable suspicion was initially formulated by the Warren Court in *Terry* to allow police to "stop and frisk" suspects. The decision was specifically limited to threatening street situations in which the suspect might be armed. The Court reasoned that, in the case of temporary detentions and surface searches for weapons, rather than full-fledged arrests and searches for evidence, a more lenient standard than probable cause should apply. This standard has now, however, replaced probable cause to permit investigative "stops" in some situations in which there is no immediate apprehension of public danger; for example, someone suspected of past criminal activity. Moreover, the reasonable suspicion standard itself has been diluted to "some minimum level of objective justification." Police may now seize a person on the nebulous basis of an anonymous tip that weds accurate predictions of innocent behavior (e.g., leaving an apartment, carrying a briefcase, driving a car toward a particular location) with allegations of crime (*Alabama* v. *White*, 1990).

Nor has the Court found much justifiable expectation of privacy. It has ruled that a homeowner has no reasonable interest in privacy from aerial surveillance, illogically equating police observation of a fenced-in backyard from an altitude of one hundred feet with the tiny invasion of privacy incurred from ordinary airplane flights. So, too, regardless of "No Trespassing" signs, warrantless entry is allowed into privately owned open fields, since they are accessible to the public. And one does not have a reasonable expectation of privacy in bags of garbage left for collection outside the curtilage of the home. More remarkably, the Court held that a "pen register" may be used to record numbers dialed from a telephone, and that the government may be granted access to personal bank records, without needing to show special justification, because by sharing this information with a telephone company or bank, the individual has forfeited a reasonable expectation of privacy. Since the telephone and checkbook are indispensable adjuncts to daily life in contemporary society, the Court's conclusion seems utterly unrealistic.

Ultimately, interpretation of the amendment depends on the significance one assigns to the values it safeguards. Because its protection is so often claimed by those least worthy of it, it is easy to relegate the amendment to a secondary position in the Bill of Rights. It was designed, however, to protect society as a whole against the bane of general searches and seizures, behind which the framers saw the specter of lawless government. In Justice Louis *Brandeis's timeless words, the Fourth Amendment "conferred, as against the government, the right to be let alone—the most comprehensive of rights and the right most valued by civilized men" (*Olmstead* v. *United States*, 1928, p. 478).

(See also SEARCH WARRANT RULE, EXCEPTIONS TO.)

□ David Fellman, *The Defendant's Rights Today* (1976). Wayne R. LaFave, *Search and Seizure*, 3 vols. (2d ed., 1987). Jacob W. Landynski, *Search and Seizure and the Supreme Court* (1966). Nelson B. Lasson, *The History and Development of the Fourth Amendment to the United States Constitution* (1937).                     Jacob Landynski

**Framers of the Constitution.** See HISTORY OF THE COURT: ESTABLISHMENT OF THE UNION; ORIGINAL INTENT.

**Frankfurter, Felix** (b. Vienna, 15 Nov. 1882; emigrated to U.S. 1894; d. Washington, D.C., 21 Feb. 1965; interred Mt. Auburn Cemetery, Cambridge, Mass.), associate justice, 1939–1962. Small in stature, wiry in youth, of boundless enthusiasm for liberal causes and indefatigable political energy before and after his appointment to the Supreme Court, Felix Frankfurter was the most controversial justice of his time. Though he denied having any party affiliation, and served under both Democratic and Republican administrations, his politics were openly progressive. Justice Louis *Brandeis, whom Professor Frankfurter aided with research and other services, called Frankfurter the most useful lawyer in America. Despite, or perhaps because of this accolade, Professor Frankfurter was feared by conservatives and corporate spokesmen as a dangerous radical. Seated on the Court, Frankfurter acted with restraint, mixing deference to popularly elected executive and legislative branches of government and reasoned, precise elucidations of the rights of minorities, causing some scholars to accuse Frankfurter of changing his stance on many issues. Frankfurter himself lamented that a judge could not write his personal preferences into the law, though Frankfurter decried some of his brethren for just such license (see JUDICIAL ACTIVISM.) Accused by Senator Patrick McCarran of being a friend of known communists, Frankfurter was in war and peace a patriot.

The essence of this most complex man was a sense of intellectual commitment. Frankfurter was first and foremost a teacher in the rabbinic style. He welcomed complexities, balanced truths, entertained questions, and understood puzzles. He brought to law a sense of history, comparison, and respect for law's sister disciplines. In front of his classes at Harvard Law School, in his chambers at Court, he demanded reasoned discourse. The job of the teacher was to speak, not to be silent; hence his many thoughtful and fulsome concurrences and dissents and his lectures to the conference that his brethren sometimes resented. The Supreme Court itself he conceptualized as a tutor to the lower courts and Congress. Opinions were part of a continuing dialogue within the hierarchy of courts. Like a good teacher, the Court had to choose among cases, seeking those that best made its points, hearing only those cases that were ripe for

*Felix Frankfurter*

decisions and whose parties had suffered real injuries that the courts could remedy.

Frankfurter's vision of his role on the court thus was the culmination of a vision of himself. He always believed that he rose in the world from an immigrant lad of twelve who spoke no English to Supreme Court justice through intellectual achievement, and his opinion had much factual support. His intellectual curiosity, precociousness, and diligence, marked his stay at the City College of New York and at Harvard Law School, where he graduated first in his class. He was a brilliant scholar, speaker, and negotiator in the public service. Whether ferreting out corporate wrongdoers as assistant to the federal attorney for the Southern District of New York, or as Woodrow Wilson's labor troubleshooter in the dangerous years of 1916–1918, Frankfurter demonstrated that intellect could solve practical problems and make the world a fairer place. A professor from 1913 until 1939, he loved Harvard Law School as the most egalitarian place on earth—an aristocracy of talent and intellect. During his quarter century of service on its faculty he became the friend and tutor of two generations of government servants, in class, on the walkways around Langdell Hall, and in his own home inculcating in students a love of the law and of service to government. No person was a better mentor, friend, or ally, but every friendship, no matter how high or how low the status of the recipient, was cemented with ideas. His law clerks, many of whom went on to distinguished government and academic careers, remembered with fondness and awe the justice's appetite for intellectual discourse, new ideas, for sheer pleasure as well as use.

In his memoirs he admitted as well his skill in courting people whose views he supported. These contacts, assiduously cultivated and loyally maintained, were not sinister or cynical. Instead, he genuinely sought mentors and in his turn nurtured and placed many younger lawyers and law scholars. Indeed, it can be argued that he was the model of the modern mentor. Early in his career he developed an affection for Henry L. Stimson, whose disinterested public spiritedness, personal courage, and work habits Frankfurter admired. Frankfurter also attached himself to Justice Oliver Wendell *Holmes, whose intellectual appetites were as voracious as the younger man's, and to Justice Louis Brandeis, whose social conscience needed a strong right arm unencumbered by the restraints that a justice of the Supreme Court felt. Brandeis helped defray medical expenses in the Frankfurter household and Frankfurter carried on research and political advocacy for the justice throughout the 1920s and 1930s. Frankfurter also courted Franklin Delano *Roosevelt, a courtship that made the professor one of the President's most trusted and most avid advisers. Frankfurter, who introduced the course in administrative law in American law schools, used his connection to Roosevelt to place many of his former students, so-called hot dogs, in the *New Deal. Frankfurter himself continued to advise Roosevelt. Indeed, even after his appointment to the Court, Frankfurter was a constant visitor to the White House.

Frankfurter's zeal as a teacher on and off the Court rested on his personal faith that policy must be based on reasoned balancing of interests by political leaders. His opinions in *First and *Fourteenth Amendment cases rested on precise calculations of balancing. Frankfurter conceived claims in terms of group interests—here he betrayed the influence of the early work of Roscoe *Pound, work that attracted him to the faculty at Harvard Law School—rather than individual rights. He was never a formalist, a literal reader of the Constitution or of statutes, much less of judicial precedents. He balanced the many sources of law just as he balanced the claims of interest groups and of agencies of government. Frankfurter added to the balance conditions external to the Court. For example, he joined in *Korematsu v. United States (1944) and maintained his commitment to the flag salute requirement in *West Virginia State Board of Education v. Barnette (1943) because the United States was engaged in a war with a horrific foe, and the claims of government, based upon any reasonable construction, must trump individual rights, unless those rights were essential to the broader historical framework of republican constitutionalism.

More than some abstract and rigid set of "ordered liberties" Frankfurter insisted that the Constitution rested upon an historical evolution of basic notions. Its terms resonated with multiple overlapping meanings that the judge must discern and apply in each case. He was unwilling, thus, to follow Justice Hugo *Black's theory of the wholesale *incorporation of the *Bill of Rights in the Fourteenth Amendment. Not only did Black's formulation violate Frankfurter's understanding of the historical origins of the amendments to the Constitution, Frankfurter suspected that Black's theory was a screen for blatantly political aims.

Not that Frankfurter was apolitical once he reached the Court; quite the opposite was true. Frankfurter believed that the political process was a vital part of the evolution of law but that the Court should defer to the politics of elected assemblies. He did his own politicking in person, through intermediaries, and through the mails. Frankfurter also believed that the High Court must educate public opinion on constitutional issues. Although his opinions often deferred to the prior decisions of elected state judges and legislatures and the Congress, he always explained why deference should be paid. He never hid or dismissed the policy considerations behind such deference. To this extent he was one of the "progressive pragmatists" who transformed law teaching in the 1910s and 1920s from the inculcation of a set of formulae to the open-ended study of public values. His own commitment to deference was an early part of his jurisprudence, perhaps the influence of the theories of Holmes and Brandeis.

Frankfurter's strong attachment to coordinate *federalism, expressed in his dissents in *Mapp v. Ohio (1961) and *Baker v. Carr (1962), was of a piece with his deference to popularly elected assemblies. An aroused citizenry could do what no court might venture, and the court must not squander its always limited and precious reserve of political influence by entering into *political questions (see JUDICIAL SELF-RESTRAINT).

On the bench, Frankfurter was a formidable adversary and a fulsome ally. He was ever trying to build majorities around his positions, an echo of his political organizing efforts over the preceding two decades. Initially close to younger progressive justices like Hugo Black, William O. *Douglas, Frank *Murphy, and Wiley *Rutledge, Frankfurter found himself increasingly estranged from the liberal wing of the court. In part the estrangement was owing to Frankfurter's pro-government stance in the Flag Salute cases, a stance that he maintained throughout his tenure. When the integrity of the courts or the bar was threatened by government, Frankfurter joined his liberal brethren. This philosophy came to have a shape distinct from deference in the work of Frankfurter proteges and students at Harvard Law School. "Process jurisprudence," filled out in the writings of Henry Hart and Albert Sacks at Harvard Law School, was Frankfurter's inspiration. Its central principle was a rational, balanced, system-conserving restraint. The courts

could not save the world, but neither would they stand by when government threatened the process of adjudication itself. The doctrines of mootness, ripeness, standing, and a "second look" in constitutional questions—reasons for avoiding reaching constitutional questions—that Brandeis pioneered and Frankfurter popularized fit perfectly into this jurisprudence.

On the Court, no one had more concern for legal craftsmanship than Frankfurter. He never forgot his origins, how far he had come, and thus never lost his respect for his office. This, perhaps more than anything else, explains why Frankfurter privately criticized the opinion of Douglas, whom Frankfurter believed to be brilliant but lazy, and Black, whose commitment to abstract first principles and correct political outcomes Frankfurter lamented. Frankfurter's strongest allies on the court were craftsmen like Robert H. *Jackson and John M. *Harlan. In his last years Frankfurter reconciled with Black. In their opinions on the bench and in their personal lives both men rediscovered their initial affinities.

Both men believed, for example, that desegregation was constitutional, and must come. (See BROWN V. BOARD OF EDUCATION.) Both men feared the practical consequences of an immediate desegregation order. Both men worked behind the scenes to fashion rules that would allow localities to move toward desegregation in a lawful manner. They joined, thus, in rejecting legal segregation of housing, political primaries, and schools and other public facilities.

Before he died, Frankfurter asked that a Jewish prayer be recited at his death. This was the Kaddish, not mentioning death but extolling the glory and the justness of God. Frankfurter remarked, in explanation, that he was born a Jew and wished to die a Jew. Though not conventionally religious in adulthood, he came from an Orthodox Jewish family—indeed his father had trained as a rabbi in Vienna—and Frankfurter spoke Yiddish and Hebrew before he spoke English. Throughout his career, he was a Zionist and a supporter of secular Jewish causes.

The rabbinical scholarship of the Talmud speaks of obligations, not of rights. The Jew is commanded to do justice, love mercy, and walk humbly with God. The way to understand these and the many other mitzvot (God's laws) is study—study of law. Frankfurter's belief in duty, the duty of one individual to another, of the government to individuals, of individuals to government, is all of a piece with Jewish law. Process jurisprudence is a philosophy of obligations.

Frankfurter's most controversial opinions, in *Minersville School District v. Gobitis (1940), for example, upholding the suspension from public school of Jehovah's Witnesses for their unwillingness to salute the flag, an action they claimed violated their right to free exercise of *religion, and his dissent in *Everson v. Board of Education of

*Ewing Township* (1947), in which the majority of the Court upheld a state law permitting state funds to underwrite religious education, fit the ideal of a law of obligation. No one was entitled to special treatment, special exemptions, or special subsidies under the law. Frankfurter's opinions on labor union practices in strikes and controversial concurrence in *Cooper v. Aaron* (1958) restated this theme: the obligations of law precede and create rights.

If one concedes that this rabbinic fidelity to law lay deep in Frankfurter's consciousness, his life and career no longer appear marked by contradiction. He labored in fidelity to the great principle of obligation. He owed public service and patriotic devotion to the land that had adopted him, the school that entrusted him to teach, and to his fellow citizens who allowed him to hold high office. Throughout his life, he honored the obligation to teach, to study, and to live by law, and he exalted this principle on the eve of his passing. He died three years after suffering a debilitating stroke, leaving his widow, the former Marion A. Denman.

□ Leonard Baker, *Brandeis and Frankfurter, A Dual Biography* (1984). Bruce Allen Murphy, *The Brandeis/Frankfurter Connection* (1982). Michael E. Parrish, *Felix Frankfurter and His Times: The Reform Years* (1982). James F. Simon, *The Antagonists: Hugo Black, Felix Frankfurter, and Civil Liberties in Modern America* (1989). Mark Silverman, *Constitutional Faiths: Felix Frankfurter, Hugo Black, and the Process of Judicial Decision Making* (1984).

Peter Charles Hoffer

**Frank v. Mangum,** 237 U.S. 309 (1915), argued 25–26 Feb. 1915, decided 19 Apr. 1915 by vote of 7 to 2; Pitney for the Court, Holmes in dissent. In one of the most sensational murder cases of the era, Leo Frank, one of the owners of the National Pencil Factory in Atlanta, was accused of killing a thirteen-year-old female employee. In a clear miscarriage of justice, Frank was convicted and sentenced to death. An atmosphere of violence surrounding the courtroom had led the trial judge to ask that the defendant and his counsel not be present when the verdict was returned. As the jurors were being polled, their voices were drowned out by the cheers of the crowd outside.

After the failure of numerous motions and state appeals, Frank's lawyers sought a writ of *habeas corpus in the federal district court; its denial brought the case to the Supreme Court. Counsel argued that mob intimidation had deprived Frank of *due process of law. Justice Mahlon *Pitney, for the majority, saw any trial impropriety cleansed by the Georgia appellate process, but Justice Oliver Wendell *Holmes, in dissent, condemned the trial and the intimidation of the jury.

Although the Court during this time period liberally used the Due Process Clause of the *Fourteenth Amendment to supervise state action concerning property, it hesitated in finding a similar federal supervisory power over state criminal proceedings. Such reluctance would dissipate as early as *Moore v. Dempsey* (1923), but this was much too late to save Leo Frank, who was lynched after Georgia's courageous governor had commuted the sentence to life imprisonment.

John E. Semonche

**Freedom of _____.** See under latter part of term.

**Free Exercise Clause.** See RELIGION.

**Freund, Ernst** (b. New York, N.Y., 30 Jan. 1864; d. Chicago, Ill., 20 Oct. 1932), educator, lawyer, writer, and social reformer. Freund, a son of German immigrants, has been called the "father of American administrative law." He influenced the Supreme Court through his highly influential treatise *Police Power: Public Policy and Constitutional Rights* (1904) and through his strong views on the desirable breadth of freedom of speech. Educated in universities at Berlin and Heidelberg, he practiced law in New York and became professor of administrative law and municipal corporations at Columbia University, where he also earned a Ph.D. in political science. Moving to the University of Chicago, he joined its new law school faculty in 1903 and took a prominent part in founding its school of social service, teaching courses in social legislation, and calling for a science of legislation. This prompted later scholars, impressed with his commitment to keeping legal enactments abreast of human relations, to see him as a prominent forerunner of *sociological jurisprudence. Indeed, Louis *Brandeis, writing in 1934, claimed that Freund, as much as Roscoe Pound, was the founder of that movement.

His *Police Power* came immediately to the notice of the bench and bar, and the Supreme Court cited its exposition of the restrictions placed on legislative power by the *Fourteenth Amendment. In it Freund defined the *police power as the power of government to promote the public welfare by restraining and regulating the use of property. He also addressed the conditions that called for restraint and regulation. These included especially: peace and security from crime, public safety and health, public order and comfort, and public morals. He also dealt with the control of dependent classes, seeking to protect them against fraud and exploitation. He argued that government should not impose particular burdens on individuals or corporations but should also not grant special privileges or monopolies. Legislative discrimination should be justified by legitimate differences of status based on logical social distinctions.

Freund was a theoretical defender of free speech in the Progressive Era who distinguished the legitimate substantive due process defense of free speech from the excessive substantive due process defense of laissez faire, based on legal formalism that ignored real world conditions (see

PROGRESSIVISM). For him, the Fourteenth Amendment Due Process Clause gave the courts the power to protect "the fundamental rights of the individual," which included the freedom of the individual to enter into legal relations with others and of appealing in any manner to public opinion or sentiment. He stressed the *First Amendment's role in guaranteeing the most ample freedom of discussion of public affairs (including freedom of pursuit in art, literature, and science). Speech had a clear social utility. (See SPEECH AND THE PRESS.) For example, he felt the outcome of the Court's rule in Debs v. United States (1919), in particular, was dangerously unsound, illustrating most clearly in the arbitrariness of the whole idea of limited provocation. Such a view led Justice Oliver Wendell *Holmes, in his dissent in *Abrams v. United States (1919), to modify his position and embrace a more nearly Freundian view of the First Amendment.

During his later years, Freund prepared widely used guides on legislative drafting for the ABA, and in his Administrative Powers over Persons and Property (1928), he warned against the growth of government powers, arguing for a type of regulation that combined respect for individual rights with a growing sense of the social obligations of property, while recognizing the paramount claims of public interest. Always a fastidious, probing, and diverse scholar (his many pamphlets ranged from English history, administrative law and labor law, to immigration and illegitimacy), his legal realism stressed sound empirical work and the utility of social research in making the law responsive to human needs.

Paul L. Murphy

**Frontiero v. Richardson,** 411 U.S. 677 (1973), argued 17 Jan. 1973, decided 14 May, 1973 by vote of 8 to 1; Brennan for plurality, Powell, Burger, Blackmun, and Stewart concurring; Rehnquist in dissent. This case presented a constitutional challenge to a federal law that awarded a salary supplement in the form of an extra housing allowance and extra medical benefits to every married male in the "uniformed services" of the United States. A married female in the military, however, received the supplement only if she could prove she paid more than half of her husband's living costs. The suit was brought by Sharron Frontiero, an Air Force lieutenant who paid slightly under half of her husband's living costs. Her challenge relied on the *equal protection concept implied in the *Fifth Amendment Due Process Clause.

Frontiero's lawyers argued that while there might be some reason for the differential treatment, that should not be enough to sustain the statute, because gender discrimination like race discrimination should be viewed as constitutionally "suspect" and upheld only if the government proves "compelling" justification. This argument had been tried two years earlier in *Reed v. Reed

(1971) but the Court's opinion had ignored it, relying instead on the the rational basis test to strike down the statute. In Frontiero the justices exhumed and dissected Reed.

Justice William *Brennan's opinion for the plurality of four argued that the Reed result made no sense under the rational basis test. The statute in that case had preferred males to females as estate administrators; there was some reason for this, since males in 1971 were more conversant than females with the world of business. Brennan insisted that Reed's result implied that gender classifications are, like race, suspect and therefore demand strict scrutiny, which requires proof that the classification is "necessary for attaining a compelling government interest." They argued that this test is appropriate for four reasons: (1) sex like race is an "immutable" accident of birth, which is generally irrelevant to the purpose of a statute; (2) like race it has long been the basis of invidious discrimination in the United States; (3) like race it is a highly visible trait; and (4) Congress, by proposing the Equal Rights Amendment (E.R.A.) and sending it to the states for ratification, had endorsed the idea that sex classifications are "inherently invidious" (p. 687) or "suspect" (p. 688). Respect for a "co-equal branch of government" thus counseled treating sex as a suspect classification.

Justice Lewis *Powell agreed that the classification was unconstitutional, but argued to the contrary that respect for other branches of government and for the constitutional amending process counseled delay in making gender a suspect classification, for that change was precisely the point of the E.R.A. (At the time of this decision, thirty states of the required thirty-eight had ratified the E.R.A., and six years remained of the initial seven-year ratification period.) Powell reminded the Court that Reed had struck down the sex discrimination in question without invoking strict scrutiny and insisted that the Reed standard would "abundantly" support Frontiero's challenge as well. Stewart's lone concurrence avoided all these issues and was simply a one-sentence statement that the law challenged here worked an "invidious discrimination" and thus unconstitutional on the authority of Reed.

Justice William *Rehnquist's dissent simply cited as its foundation the reasoning of the district court judge, whose opinion had employed the rational basis test and had argued that the savings accrued in not requiring married servicemen to document actual financial dependency of their wives, when more than a million cases were involved and when only a small fraction was likely to be ineligible for the benefit, amply satisfied the test. Judge Rives mentioned in a footnote that Reed, too, had employed the rational basis test.

Thus, although the Court upheld Frontiero's claim and invalidated the law by an 8-to-1 vote, there was no majority for establishing sex as a *suspect classification. That issue was not explicitly addressed again by the Supreme Court until *Craig v. Boren (1976), in which the justices adopted a test somewhere between strict scrutiny and the rational basis test, known variously as "heightened" or "intermediate" scrutiny.

(See also GENDER; INTERMEDIATE SCRUTINY; STRICT SCRUTINY.)

Leslie Friedman Goldstein

**Frothingham v. Mellon,** 262 U.S. 447 (1923), argued together with **Massachusetts v. Mellon,** 3–4 May 1923, decided 4 June 1923 by a vote of 9 to 0; Sutherland for the Court. Frothingham and the state of Massachusetts brought suit against the U.S. secretary of treasury to invalidate the Federal Maternity Act of 1921. Under this statute the federal government would contribute funds to the states for the purpose of "promoting the welfare and hygiene of maternity and infancy." Participating states were required to comply with federal regulations and match federal appropriations.

Massachusetts claimed the federal plan usurped authority reserved to the states by the *Tenth Amendment. Frothingham argued that the use of federal appropriations to carry out the plan resulted in a taking of her property without *due process of law. The Court did not address either of these substantive complaints but rejected the cases for want of *jurisdiction. Frothingham's case depended upon whether she had the required standing to challenge this statute in court. Her only claim to that status was that she was a federal taxpayer. Reasoning that her interest in any federal appropriations act was remote, the Court ruled that she did not have standing. To obtain standing, it ruled, a taxpayer must not only present a claim that the statute is invalid but also must show that some immediate personal injury was sustained. Here there was no *case or controversy. This rule against taxpayer standing remained until it was modified in *Flast v. Cohen (1968).

(See also FEDERALISM; STANDING TO SUE; STATE SOVEREIGNTY AND STATES' RIGHTS.)

Paul Kens

**Fugitives From Justice.** Article IV of the Articles of Confederation provided for the rendition of fugitives from justice on "demand of the Governor" of the state from which they fled. Article IV, section 2 of the Constitution contained almost identical language. This clause contemplated a direct state-to-state rendition procedure, but following a dispute between Virginia and Pennsylvania, Congress adopted a combined extradition and *fugitive slave law in 1793 that set out procedures for extradition cases.

Extradition has usually been pro forma, except when requisitions have been technically inadequate or when people have been accused of politically charged crimes. Before the *Civil War

northern governors refused to extradite people accused of helping slaves escape from the South, while southern governors refused to extradite Southerners accused of kidnapping free blacks and enslaving them. These cases led to controversies between many southern (Virginia, Georgia, Missouri, and Kentucky) and northern (Pennsylvania, Maine, New York, Illinois, and Ohio) states. In *Kentucky v. Dennison (1861), the Supreme Court ruled that the federal government had no power to force a state governor to extradite a fugitive.

Modern refusals to extradite have usually been politically motivated. In 1950 Michigan's Governor G. Mennen Williams refused to extradite one of the "Scottsboro boys" who escaped from an Alabama prison. In the 1970s California's Governor Edmund G. Brown, Jr., refused to extradite an American Indian activist wanted in South Dakota. In Puerto Rico v. Branstad (1987), the Supreme Court overturned Dennison, ruling that state governors had no discretion in extradition cases. This destroyed a basic principle of *federalism that had existed since 1787.

Paul Finkelman

**Fugitive Slaves.** In colonial America the interjurisdictional return of runaway slaves was sporadic, despite occasional agreements on the matter, such as that in the New England Confederation of 1643. In Somerset v. Stewart (1772), the Court of King's Bench ruled that any slave who came to England, either by the voluntary action of his master or by running away, might claim his freedom because there was no positive law establishing *slavery in England. This precedent was part of the American *common law when some of the newly independent American states began to abolish slavery during the Revolution. Pennsylvania's Gradual Emancipation Act of 1780 allowed for the recapture of fugitive slaves, as did similar laws passed in other states. The Articles of Confederation, however, did not obligate states to return fugitive slaves. The *Northwest Ordinance of 1787 prohibited slavery in the Northwest Territory but also provided that a fugitive slave "may be lawfully reclaimed and conveyed to the person claiming his or her labor or service."

Late in the Constitutional Convention of 1787, South Carolina's Pierce *Butler proposed a clause to "require fugitive slaves and servants to be delivered up like criminals." The next day, without any further debate or recorded dissent, the delegates adopted what became the Fugitive Slave Clause, providing that runaways could not be emancipated in the states to which they escaped but were to "be delivered up on Claim of the party to whom such service or labour may be due." The framers seemed to contemplate enforcement of the clause by state and local governments or through individual action. The location of the clause in Article IV, alongside other clauses dealing with interstate relations, supports this analysis.

In the Fugitive Slave Law of 1793 Congress spelled out procedure for the return of runaways. The law allowed masters or their agents capturing fugitives to bring them to any magistrate, state or federal, to obtain a "certificate of removal" and then to take the runaway back to the state where the slave owed service. The law provided fines for those who interfered with the rendition process and preserved masters' rights to seek damages from those who knowingly helped fugitive slaves.

Before the 1830s many northern states passed personal-liberty laws to protect their free black populations from kidnapping or mistaken seizure. These statutes also provided state procedures to facilitate the return of bona fide fugitives. The northern states balanced protection of their free black population from kidnapping against compliance with their constitutional obligation to return runaway slaves. Until 1842 the constitutionality of both the state laws and the federal law remained in doubt. However, in *Jack* v. *Martin* (1835), New York's highest court declared the federal law unconstitutional but remanded the runaway slave Jack to his owner because the court believed New York was obligated to enforce the Fugitive Slave Clause of Article IV. A year later, in an unpublished opinion, Chief Justice Joseph Hornblower of New Jersey declared the federal law of 1793 unconstitutional and also declared the black man in question free.

In *Prigg* v. *Pennsylvania* (1842), U.S. Supreme Court Justice Joseph *Story held that the 1793 law was constitutional and that state personal-liberty laws interfering with the rendition process were not. Story characterized the Fugitive Slave Clause as a "fundamental article" of the Constitution necessary for its adoption, even though the history of the clause, which Story knew, shows that this was not true (p. 541). Story urged state officials to continue to enforce the 1793 law but stated that they could not be required to do so. A number of states soon passed new personal-liberty laws prohibiting their officials from acting under the federal law.

In *Jones* v. *Van Zandt* (1847), the Supreme Court upheld a particularly harsh interpretation of the 1793 law in a civil suit for the value of slaves who had escaped from Kentucky to Ohio, where Van Zandt offered them a ride in his wagon. Van Zandt's attorneys, Salmon P. *Chase and William H. Seward, unsuccessfully argued that in Ohio all people were presumed free and thus Van Zandt had no reason to know he was transporting runaway slaves.

As part of the Compromise of 1850, Congress revised the 1793 Fugitive Slave Act, creating more arbitrary rendition procedures and harsher penalties. Under this statute, accused fugitives could not testify on their own behalf or benefit from *trial by jury. In reaction to state refusals to participate in the rendition process, the 1850 law

provided federal commissioners, appointed in every county in the country, to enforce the law. They received five dollars if they decided that the black person before them was not a slave but were paid ten dollars if they found in favor of the claimant. Popular opposition to the law increased after the publication of Harriet Beecher Stowe's highly successful fictional attack on slavery, *Uncle Tom's Cabin* (1852).

The 1850 law led to riots, rescues, and recaptures in Boston, Massachusetts; Syracuse, New York; Christiana, Pennsylvania; Oberlin, Ohio; Racine, Wisconsin; and elsewhere. Federal prosecutions of rescuers often failed. In Christiana more than forty men were indicted for treason after a group of fugitives fought their would-be captors and killed a slaveowner. The defendants were released when U.S. Supreme Court Justice Robert *Grier, on circuit, ruled in *United States* v. *Hanway* (1851) that opposition to the Fugitive Slave Act did not constitute treason. After these incidents the act was a dead letter in much of the North. In *Ableman* v. *Booth* (1859), stemming from the Racine rescue, the Supreme Court affirmed the constitutionality of the 1850 law and the supremacy of the federal courts.

Peaceful enforcement of the 1850 law was sometimes possible, especially along the Ohio River and the Mason-Dixon line. Some removals required a show of federal force and the use of troops. Under the 1850 act, more than nine hundred fugitives were returned between 1850 and 1861. Southerners estimated, however, that as many as ten thousand slaves escaped during that period.

Ultimately the Fugitive Slave Clause and the two statutes passed to enforce it did little to protect southern property but did much to antagonize sectional feelings. Southerners saw the North as unwilling to fulfill its constitutional obligation. Northerners believed the South was trying to force them to become slave catchers and, in the process, to undermine civil liberties in the nation.

(See also COMITY; FUGITIVES FROM JUSTICE; STATE SOVEREIGNTY AND STATES' RIGHTS.)

☐ Paul Finkelman, "*Prigg* v. *Pennsylvania* and Northern State Courts: Anti-Slavery Use of a Pro-Slavery Decision," *Civil War History* 24 (March 1979): 5–35. Paul Finkelman, *An Imperfect Union: Slavery, Federalism, and Comity* (1981). Thomas D. Morris, *Free Men All: The Personal Liberty Laws of the North, 1780–1861* (1974).
                                                                    Paul Finkelman

**Fuller, Melville Weston** (b. Augusta, Maine, 11 Feb. 1833; d. Sorrento, Maine, 4 Jul. 1910; interred Graceland Cemetery, Chicago, Ill.), chief justice, 1888–1910. Of an old New England family, Fuller grew up surrounded by lawyers. Because of his parents' divorce, he was raised in the household of his maternal grandfather, the chief justice of the Maine Supreme Judicial Court. After graduat-

*Melville Weston Fuller*

ing from Bowdoin College in 1853, Fuller read law in his uncles' law offices and briefly attended the Harvard Law School, an experience that later earned him the distinction of being the first chief justice with significant academic legal training. In 1855 he was admitted to the bar in Maine but soon left the state, apparently because of a disappointment in romance. Settling in Chicago, Fuller engaged in a moderately successful law practice. He married in 1858, but his wife died six years later. An active Democrat, he enthusiastically supported Stephen Douglas against Abraham *Lincoln. Fuller served in the Illinois Constitutional Convention in 1861 and for one term (1863–1864) in the state House of Representatives. Although close to Copperhead circles during the Civil War, Fuller was never actively disloyal. In 1866 he married Mary Ellen Coolbaugh, securing a boost to business, since his new father-in-law headed the largest bank in Chicago. Thereafter Fuller withdrew from politics and devoted himself to making money from his burgeoning law practice and real estate investments.

Increasingly known as a lawyer's lawyer, he specialized in appellate work, particularly in commercial cases, appearing regularly before the United States Supreme Court. On the death of Chief Justice Morrison *Waite in March 1888, President Grover Cleveland decided to appoint an Illinoisan in hopes of bettering the Democrats' chances in the November election. When the president's first choice declined the post, Cleveland quickly turned to Fuller, who shared his views in favor of sound money and against protective tariffs.

On the Court Fuller showed himself a convivial colleague and competent administrator rather than a judicial leader, his slender stock of jurisprudential ideas suiting him for little else (see CHIEF JUSTICE, OFFICE OF THE). Himself a man of property, Fuller often appeared to the common man as the defender of wealth, most notably in his opinions for the Court in both rounds of *Pollock v. Farmers' Loan & Trust Co. (1895), invalidating the federal *income tax on the questionable ground of the prohibition against direct taxes unless proportioned to state population (see PROPERTY). The result was eventually overturned by the *Sixteenth Amendment. In the same term as the income tax case Fuller also penned the majority opinion in United States v. *E. C. Knight Co. (1895), the prosecution of the Sugar Trust under the *Sherman Antitrust Act. Finding in favor of the trust, Fuller held that manufacture for sale is not commerce, a dubious interpretation that was to be steadily eroded by later decisions. In commercial law, Fuller's specialty, he led the Court in Leisy v. Hardin (1890) to adopt his version of the "original package" doctrine, holding that imported goods still in the original package were not subject to state regulation. As applied in Leisy, this invalidated a key part of the Iowa prohibition law. The doctrine survived, but its specific application was promptly eliminated by legislation ending federal protection of interstate traffic in liquor. In In re Rahrer (1891), Fuller wrote the opinion upholding the constitutionality of that statute.

Fuller believed that the *Fourteenth Amendment worked "no revolutionary change"; in consequence he could preside comfortably over a Court that turned a blind eye to racial injustice. On other civil rights issues he was unpredictable, dissenting in United States v. *Wong Kim Ark (1898), which held that the children of Chinese immigrants born in this country were American citizens, and again in Downes v. Bidwell (1901), one of the *Insular Cases, which held that the newly acquired island territories were not covered by the Constitution. Concerning the rights of labor, Fuller was also unpredictable, writing the opinion of the Court in the Danbury hatters' case, *Loewe v. Lawlor (1908), which held the Sherman Antitrust Act applicable to labor unions, while consistently limiting the fellow-servant rule, which insulated employers from liability for many injuries to employees (see LABOR).

Enjoying the limelight and the break from judicial routine, Fuller accepted appointment to the Venezuelan Boundary Commission in 1897 and served on the Permanent Court of Arbitration at The Hague from 1900 (see EXTRAJUDICIAL ACTIVITIES).

□ Willard L. King, *Melville Weston Fuller* (1950).
John V. Orth

**Full Faith and Credit.** Article IV, section 1, of the Constitution provides that "Full Faith and Credit shall be given in each State to the public Acts, Records and judicial Proceedings of every other State; And the Congress may by general Laws prescribe the Manner in which such Acts, Records and Proceedings shall be proved, and the Effect thereof." This provision was designed to unify the nation by binding together its several states.

Dispute exists as to whether, as an original matter, the clause was intended to provide merely that public records, including judgments, could be admitted into evidence in other states, or whether it was intended to give such records conclusive legal effect in other states. The Constitutional Convention did not resolve this issue. Congress soon clarified matters by legislation, however. In 1790, it enacted a statute providing for the manner in which acts of legislatures and records of judicial proceedings of the states would be authenticated. In addition, Congress provided that "the said records and judicial proceedings shall have such faith and credit given to them in every court of the United States, as they have by law or usage in the courts of the State from whence the said records are or shall be taken." In 1804, Congress enacted another statute requiring that full faith and credit be given to the records and judicial proceedings of the territories of the United States.

The Supreme Court held in *Mills* v. *Duryee* (1813) and *Hampton* v. *McConnell* (1818) that a judgment rendered in one state or territory generally has conclusive effect in other states or territories. The court in the original state must have had jurisdiction, and the requirements of due process must have been satisfied. Also, the original judgment must have been on the merits and it must have been final. When there have been inconsistent judgments in other states, the last-in-time rule provides that the latest judgment gets full faith and credit.

The constitutional provision does not specifically address the recognition of state court judgments in federal courts or federal court judgments in state courts. But the Supreme Court held in *Stoll* v. *Gottlieb* (1938) and *St. John* v. *Wisconsin Employment Relations Board* (1951) that federal courts must grant full faith and credit to state court judgments, and vice versa.

Courts distinguish between the recognition of judgments under the Full Faith and Credit Clause and the enforcement of judgments. The method of enforcing a judgment must be determined under the law of the state where enforcement is sought. Moreover, the Full Faith and Credit Clause does not apply to the judgments of foreign countries, which are governed by principles of *comity (Hilton* v. *Guyot,* 1895).

The clause speaks not only of judgments and records, but also public acts, or statutes. The 1790 act however, spoke only of judgments and records, presumably because it would be difficult to establish general principles about when one state should be compelled to apply another's law. In 1948, Congress revised Title 28 of the United States Code, which contains the full faith and credit legislation, requiring that full faith and credit be given not only to records and judgments but also to acts. The exact scope of this provision remains in doubt, as courts have not construed it definitively.

(See also FEDERALISM.)

Thomas O. Sargentich

**Fullilove v. Klutznick,** 448 U.S. 448 (1980), argued 27 Nov. 1979, decided 2 July 1980 by vote of 6 to 3; Burger for the Court, Marshall, Brennan, and Blackmun concurring, Stewart, Rehnquist, and Stevens in dissent. In the Public Works Employment Act of 1977, Congress provided for a 10 percent "set aside" for minority business enterprises (MBEs). This was the first federal statute containing an explicitly race conscious classification since the Freedman's Bureau Act of 1866.

The MBE provision was challenged by a group of nonminority contractors, which argued that the provision violated the "equal protection component" of the *Fifth Amendment's Due Process Clause recognized in *Bolling* v. *Sharpe* (1954). A federal district court dismissed the suit and the Court of Appeals for the Second Circuit affirmed the lower court's action.

Six justices of the Supreme Court voted to uphold the set-asides, although they differed sharply in their reasoning. One plurality (*Burger, *Powell, and *White) deferred to the unique status accorded congressional judgments on racial issues by Article I's spending and commerce clauses and the *Fourteenth Amendment's Enforcement Clause (section 5). Congress need not "act in a wholly 'color-blind' fashion" (p. 482), and the set-asides were a "reasonably necessary means of furthering the compelling governmental interest in redressing the discrimination that affects minority contractors" (p. 515). Chief Justice Warren Burger's opinion accepted the government's contention that Congress had acted with due deliberation and knowledge even though there had been no specific legislative hearings or deliberations on the set-aside. The 1977 act did not appear out of nowhere; Congress had been struggling with the plight of MBEs for years, and its members were familiar with the discriminatory practices of the construction industry. The evidentiary and justiciability restraints that hobble judicial action do not apply to Congress. It may act to eradicate social evils where a court must wait for a case challenging constitutional or statutory violations. Furthermore this was not an inflexible quota; it was temporary in duration, limited in coverage, and selective in enforcement.

A second plurality (*Marshall, *Brennan, and *Blackmun) relied on the rationale developed by

Brennan in *Regents of the University of California v. Bakke* (1978). Since the set-asides did not elevate any individual or group to a status of racial superiority, the stringent test of equal protection applied to invidious racial distinctions was inapposite. However, the risk that even so well-intentioned a program might impose unfair burdens on innocent third parties necessitated judicial scrutiny more demanding than the traditional equal protection test. The set-aside provision, in the opinion's judgment, withstood this heightened scrutiny (see INTERMEDIATE SCRUTINY).

The three dissenters were not persuaded. For Potter *Stewart and William *Rehnquist, the MBE set-asides were a return to the discredited *Plessy v. Ferguson* (1896) rule of preferences "based on lineage"—of a "government of privileges based on birth" (p. 531). Government endorsement of racial classifications, even when these classifications are drawn to advance salutary rather than invidious objectives, perpetuates the socially divisive belief that race should count. Rather than celebrating the plenary powers granted to Congress, Stewart and Rehnquist argued that if "a law is unconstitutional, it is no less unconstitutional just because it is a product of the Congress of the United States." In their opinion, only courts of equity acting in proceedings that identify specific victims and victimizers possess the "dispassionate objectivity" and "flexibility" necessary to "mold a race conscious remedy" consistent with the Constitution's command of strict race neutrality (p. 527).

John Paul *Stevens's dissent emphasized the absence of hearings on the MBE provision or any legislative findings of discriminatory practices. He questioned whether the program would distribute compensation "in an even handed way" (p. 539) and not, as is often the case, to the least disadvantaged members of the group. And he questioned whether non-black minority groups, which in his judgment lacked the discriminatory history of blacks that warranted special treatment, could or should qualify for special treatment.

*Fullilove*'s impact was substantial. The ruling encouraged minority set-aside programs at the national level (e.g., the Highway Improvement Act of 1982 and the International Security and Development Assistance Authorizations Act of 1983) and at the state, and local levels. The state and local versions, however, have not weathered judicial scrutiny. In *Richmond v. J. A. Croson Co.* (1989), the Court held that the special dispensation for color-conscious preferences accorded Congress did not extend to other governmental entities.

(See also AFFIRMATIVE ACTION; EQUAL PROTECTION; RACE AND RACISM.)

☐ Drew S. Days III, "Fullilove," *Yale Law Journal* 96 (January 1987): 453–485.          Timothy J. O'Neill

**Fundamental Fairness Doctrine.** See DUE PROCESS, PROCEDURAL.

**Fundamental Rights.** Because individual liberty lies at the core of the American constitutional system, more rights are protected under law in the United States than in other societies. Under such conditions, not all rights will be considered equal, but a hierarchy of valued liberties will emerge. The freedoms that Americans deem the most important are denominated *fundamental rights.*

The justices of the Supreme Court have defined fundamental rights to be those without which neither liberty nor justice would exist. They are freedoms essential to the concept of ordered liberty, inherent in human nature, and consequently inalienable (*Palko v. Connecticut,* 1937). As such, these are rights that should prevail if in conflict with governmental authority or other, less valued, liberties.

The specific rights that fall under the definition of fundamental rights have varied over the country's history. During the nation's first century, for example, freedom of *contract and other rights of *property were considered fundamental. With the decline of economic substantive *due process, however, these property rights lost their primacy. In the twentieth century, personal liberties have taken on fundamental status. Through the process of selective incorporation, the Supreme Court has determined that with only a few exceptions the provisions of the *Bill of Rights meet the definition of fundamental liberties and are constitutionally immune from encroachment by state and local governments as well as federal. In recent years, the right to *privacy and protections against various forms of discrimination have increasingly been seen as fundamental.

Thomas G. Walker

**Furman v. Georgia,** 408 U.S. 238 (1972), argued 17 Jan. 1972, decided 29 June 1972 per curiam by vote of 5 to 4; Stewart, White, Douglas, Brennan, and Marshall each concurred separately; Burger, Blackmun, Powell, and Rehnquist dissented jointly and separately. The Supreme Court, for the first time, struck down the death penalty under the *cruel and unusual punishment clause of the *Eighth Amendment. A jury in Georgia had convicted Furman for murder, and juries in Georgia and Texas had convicted two other petitioners for rape. All three juries imposed the death penalty without any specific guides or limits on their discretion. The Supreme Court in *McGautha v. California* (1971) had previously held that such guidelines were unnecessary. All three petitioners were African-American. Three justices for the majority found that jury discretion produced a random pattern among those receiving the death penalty and that this randomness was cruel and unusual.

Two justices found capital punishment a per se violation of the Constitution.

More specifically, Justice William O. *Douglas concluded that death was disproportionately applied to the poor and socially disadvantaged; he virtually equated the Eighth Amendment with *equal protection values. Justice Potter *Stewart argued that the failure of the legislature to call for a mandatory death sentence, coupled with the infrequent imposition and execution of death sentences, in practice made the penalty cruel and unusual in the same way that being struck by lightning is cruel and unusual. White insisted that the infrequency of execution prevented the penalty from serving as an effective deterrent and from consistently meeting social needs for retribution. For White the penalty's social irrationality made it cruel and unusual.

Justices William *Brennan and Thurgood *Marshall both concluded that the death penalty was per se cruel and unusual. Brennan found the punishment degrading to human dignity, arbitrarily severe, and unnecessary. Marshall attacked the penalty most directly, finding it excessive, unnecessary, and offensive to contemporary values.

The dissenters argued that the courts should not challenge legislative judgments about the desirability and effectiveness of punishments. They also pointed to opinion polls showing general public support for the penalty.

*Furman* halted all executions in those thirty-nine states that sanctioned the death penalty. More than six hundred people waited on death row at the time. *Furman* also seemed to create three Eighth Amendment options: mandatory death sentences for crimes carefully defined by statute, development of guidelines to standardize jury discretion, and outright abolition. Of these, outright abolition was least likely, since a majority of the justices acknowledged the validity of the retributive motive in punishment and only two condemned the penalty per se. But, like life and death themselves, the course of the law has taken unforseen turns.

In *Gregg* v. *Georgia* (1976), the Court embraced a form of guided jury discretion, although the guidelines do not systematically reduce randomness. Juries sitting in the penalty phases of capital trials as prescribed by *Gregg* consider unique aggravating and mitigating circumstances in each case. This trend has effectively overruled *Furman*'s holding because juries, even when they operate under statutory guidelines, consider unique circumstances. This process inevitably perpetuates inconsistencies in sentencing, but the Court no longer finds these inconsistencies constitutionally unacceptable.

(See also CAPITAL PUNISHMENT).

Lief H. Carter

# G

**Gag Rule.** See PRETRIAL PUBLICITY AND THE GAG RULE.

---

**Garcia v. San Antonio Metropolitan Transit Authority,** 469 U.S. 528 (1985), argued 19 Mar. 1984, reargued 1 Oct. 1984, decided 19 Feb. 1985 by vote of 5 to 4; Blackmun for the Court, joined by Brennan, White, Marshall, and Stevens; Powell in dissent, joined by Burger, Rehnquist, and O'Connor; Rehnquist filed a separate dissent; O'Connor filed a separate dissent, joined by Powell and Rehnquist.

*Garcia* reversed the Supreme Court's 1976 decision in *National League of Cities* v. *Usery.* That decision had restricted Congress's power to regulate the states "as states"; *Garcia* removed virtually all federalism-based constitutional limitations on congressional power under the *Commerce Clause.

*Garcia* involved the application of the maximum hours and minimum wage provisions of the Fair Labor Standards Act to a city-owned and -operated public transportation system. Under the rule established in *National League of Cities,* as summarized by the Court in *Hodel* v. *Virginia Surface Mining and Reclamation Association* (1981), the economic activities of the states or of their political subdivisions could be regulated by Congress only if four tests were met. First, the statute at issue had to regulate the states "as States." Second, the statute must address "matters that are indisputably attribute[s] of *state sovereignty"; third, such regulation must "directly impair" the states' ability to "structure integral operations in areas of traditional governmental functions." Finally, "the nature of the federal interest" must be substantial enough to "justify state submission" (p. 264). Despite a number of attempts to clarify the meaning of these tests, no clear lines had been established at the time of *Garcia.*

On the surface, *Garcia* seemed to present the question of whether operating a municipal transportation system was a "traditional" or "essential" state function under the *National League of Cities* rule, and whether the federal regulation of such a system interfered with an attribute of state sovereignty. In previous cases, federal courts had held that licensing ambulance drivers, operating a municipal airport, and disposing of solid wastes were protected from federal regulation under *National League of Cities,* while regulating traffic on public roads, operating a mental health facility, and providing in-house domestic services for the aged and handicapped were not protected. Instead of making such a determination in *Garcia,* Justice Harry *Blackmun gave up, and overruled *National League of Cities* altogether.

Blackmun's frustration with the Court's inability to arrive at meaningful and clear distinctions under the *National League of Cities* precedent is evident throughout his opinion. The distinctions drawn in prior cases, he declared, were "elusive at best"; such distinctions were "unworkable," "illusory," and not susceptible to "reasonably objective" measurement. The emphasis on traditional governmental functions, moreover, was unfairly biased against state activities that were innovative or unorthodox.

Rejecting all such attempts, Blackmun held that the protection of the states' interests in the federal system was left not to the courts but to the other institutions of government, particularly Congress. "The structure of the Federal Government itself was relied on to insulate the interests of the States," he wrote (p. 551). "The Framers chose to rely on a federal system in which special restraints on federal power over the States inhered principally in the workings of the National Government itself, rather than in discrete limitations on the objects of federal authority" (p. 552). Specifically, Blackmun cited the representation of the states in the Senate, and noted the many federal laws that operated to the benefit of the states.

Four justices dissented. Among other arguments, the dissenters challenged Blackmun's assertion that the federal government adequately represents state interests. "Members of Congress are elected from the various States," wrote Justice Lewis *Powell, "but once in office they are Members of the Federal Government" (pp. 564–565). The dissenters pointed out the significance of the Seventeenth Amendment, which provided for the direct election of Senators, and invoked *Marbury* v. *Madison* and the doctrine of judicial supremacy to counter the majority's conclusion that the Court should play no role in the supervision of congressional regulation of the states.

Most significantly, the dissenters indicated a hope that *Garcia* would itself be overruled some day. Justice William *Rehnquist, in a brief but painful dissent, expressed confidence that the *National League of Cities* principle, now repudiated, "will . . . in time command the support of a majority of this Court" (p. 580). "The Court today surveys the battle scene of federalism and sounds a retreat," added O'Connor. "I share Justice Rehnquist's belief that this Court will in time again assume its constitutional responsibility" (pp. 580, 589).

(See also COMMERCE POWER; FEDERALISM.)

William Lasser

**Gault, In re,** 387 U.S. 1 (1967), argued 6 Dec. 1966, decided 15 May 1967 by vote of 8 to 1; Fortas for the Court, Black and White concurring, Harlan concurring in part and dissenting in part; Stewart in dissent. From the turn of the century until the 1960s, the assumptions of juvenile justice had drawn inspiration from the reform ideology of the *Progressives. State intervention into the juvenile's life was justified as *parens patriae*, that is, a protective, paternal interest in the welfare of a wayward or otherwise distressed child. This approach led to a nationwide institutional distinction between the adversary process of adult criminal adjudication and the flexible and informal decision making created for juvenile proceedings. Separate legislative codes and correctional alternatives were established for juveniles whose behavior would have been considered criminal if they were adults.

The growing problem of juvenile misconduct and a popular perception that the juvenile justice system was failing both society and its clientele called into question the assumptions of that system and attracted the attention of both scholars and government officials. Following the Supreme Court's landmark rulings that brought unprecedented procedural reforms to federal and state criminal justice systems, it seemed inevitable that the justices would also place the nation's juvenile justice system under the scrutiny of constitutional due process.

The Court first signaled its interest in the area in *Kent* v. *United States* (1966), a 5-to-4 decision that rejected a cursory waiver of Kent's juvenile status so that he might be tried as an adult. The majority used the occasion to speculate that a juvenile—faced with incarceration in an informal juvenile proceeding, yet unprotected by the due process guarantees afforded adults under the constitution—might encounter "the worst of both worlds" (p. 556). Developing this theme boldly a year later, Justice Abe *Fortas's opinion in *Gault* attacked the entire juvenile justice system, with only Justice Potter *Stewart disagreeing on the merits of the case.

At issue was the commitment of fifteen-year-old Gerald Gault to Arizona's State Industrial School until his majority (a maximum of six years), following his adjudication as a "delinquent child" for making an obscene phone call to a neighbor while on probation for another juvenile offense. Had Gault been tried as an adult, his maximum punishment would have been a fifty-dollar fine or two months incarceration. What made Gault's case significant was that, despite the severity of his punishment, Arizona law afforded him virtually no "due process" at all—no offical notice of his precipitous hearings (he was committed within a week of the offense), no notification that counsel could be present at the hearings, no opportunity to confront or cross-examine the woman who complained about the phone call, and no protection against self-incrimination. His questionable admission about taking part in the phone call became the primary basis for the commitment.

Fortas took the opportunity to question broadly the wisdom of *parens patriae* as the guiding principle of juvenile adjudication. He then tailored a careful holding that extended many (but not all) of the rights of adult criminal defendants, under the *Due Process Clause of the *Fourteenth Amendment, to those juveniles subject to a deprivation of liberty upon adjudication of delinquency. Included were adequate and timely notice of charges and hearings, notice of the right to counsel at adjudication, the right to confront and cross-examine witnesses, and the protection against self-incrimination. Justice Fortas argued that the extension of these protections would not interfere fundamentally with the distinctive informality and flexibility of juvenile adjudication.

The majority opinion was controversial both on the Court and off. Justices Hugo *Black and John M. *Harlan used the case as an occasion to continue their ongoing debate about the proper interpretation of "due process" as it applied to the states—a debate that grew more heated in a subsequent juvenile justice case, In re *Winship (1970). Justice Stewart dissented primarily on the ground that the majority's decision ran the risk of making the juvenile process identical to the adult criminal process, thus recreating the problem that the Progressives had attacked at the turn of the century.

Gault and its practical consequences for juvenile justice (particularly the decision's emphasis on procedural compliance and its injection of defense counsel into the system) have produced considerable controversy, although the case remains the constitutional landmark for juvenile adjudication. Critics have attacked the decision as part of the larger "due process revolution" of the 1960s, charging that the Warren Court majority placed too much faith in the efficacy of procedural remedies to accomplish substantive reforms in criminal justice. Particularly with regard to Gault, critics complain that an overemphasis on due process, on the one hand, diverts attention from the larger substantive issue of the system's fundamental capacity to develop appropriate remedies for delinquent behavior and, on the other hand, adds to the case management woes of the already overburdened juvenile courts.

(See also DUE PROCESS, PROCEDURAL; JUVENILE JUSTICE.)

☐ John R. Sutton, Stubborn Children: Controlling Delinquency in the United States, 1640–1981 (1988). Stanton Wheeler and Leonard S. Cottrell, Jr., Juvenile Delinquency: Its Prevention and Control (1966).

Albert R. Matheny

**Geduldig v. Aiello,** 417 U.S. 484 (1974), argued 26 Mar. 1974, decided 17 June 1974 by vote of 6 to 3; Stewart for the Court, Brennan in dissent. Pregnancy was the topic of two important Supreme Court decisions in its 1973 term. In January, Cleveland Board of Education v. LaFleur (1974) effectively ended mandatory maternity leaves. Anyone who thought that LaFleur signaled a new judicial sensitivity to women's rights was quickly disillusioned by Geduldig, decided in June.

Carolyn Aiello was one of three state employees who challenged California's disability benefits system. This plan, financed by salary deductions, excluded from coverage any hospitalization resulting from a normal pregnancy. The workers claimed that the denial of pregnancy benefits constituted sex discrimination and therefore violated the Equal Protection Clause of the *Fourteenth Amendment.

The Supreme Court upheld the law, although it had already been amended to include pregnancy. Justice Potter *Stewart pointed out that LaFleur had relied, not on equal protection, but on *due process, and was therefore not a *precedent to be followed. California's policy benefits, he said, bore the required rational relationship to the state's legitimate goal of reducing costs. And the law did not discriminate against women; instead, it merely distinguished between pregnant women and all other (i.e., nonpregnant) persons: "There is no risk from which men are protected and women are not" (pp. 496–497). Justice William *Brennan disagreed, writing in his dissent that policy distinctions based on "physical characteristics inextricably linked to one sex" denied equal protection (p. 501). The Pregnancy Discrimination Act of 1978 enacted the dissenters' view by requiring equal treatment for pregnant employees.

(See also EMPLOYMENT DISCRIMINATION; EQUAL PROTECTION; GENDER; PREGNANCY, DISABILITY, AND MATERNITY LEAVES.)

Judith A. Baer

**Gelpcke v. Dubuque,** 1 Wall. (68 U.S.) 175 (1864), argued 15 Dec. 1863, decided 11 Jan. 1864 by vote of 8 to 1; Swayne for the Court, Miller in dissent, Taney not participating. The competition of northern cities before the *Civil War for rail traffic resulted in imprudent bond issues, with consequent defaults and repudiations. Dubuque, Iowa, promoters issued bonds in amounts that exceeded the debt limit specified in the state constitution. A reform-minded state supreme court reversed earlier holdings sustaining the validity of the bonds. The bondholders appealed to the U.S. Supreme Court, arguing that federal courts, under *Swift v. Tyson (1842), could construe state constitutions when state supreme court precedent was inconsistent. In Leffingwell v. Warren (1862), the Supreme Court had stated that it was obliged to follow the most recent state supreme court holdings construing state constitutions.

Yet in Gelpcke v. Dubuque, Justice Noah *Swayne rejected the latest Iowa Supreme Court construction. Federal judges were not bound by *state courts' oscillations, Swayne asserted. "We shall never immolate truth, justice, and the law, because a State tribunal has erected the altar and decreed the sacrifice," he wrote (pp. 206–207). Justice Samuel Freeman *Miller (an Iowan) dissented, arguing that only state judges should have final authority to construe the state's constitution and laws.

Investors, law writers, and legal academics praised Gelpcke. Critics charged that it deepened animosities between federal judges and the elected state courts and that it throttled urban development. In its disdain for state judicial authority, Gelpcke was a precursor of substantive *due process.

(See also CAPITALISM; JUDICIAL POWER AND JURISDICTION.)

Harold M. Hyman

**Gender.** As early as 31 March 1776, Abigail Adams wrote to her husband John, who was attending the Second Continental Congress, urging him to "remember the Ladies, and be more generous and favourable to them than your ancestors" (Butterfield et al., 1975, p. 21). Adams's admonitions to her husband had little impact on either the Articles of Confederation or the Constitution. Not until 1920 was the *Nineteenth Amendment added to the Constitution, offering women that most basic element of *citizenship—suffrage. And, in the 1990s, despite long years of a concerted drive by women's rights groups to have an amendment guaranteeing equal rights ratified, the Constitution continues to afford women less protection from discrimination than men.

The Supreme Court is often looked upon as ahead of its time, or at least *public opinion, in the expansion of rights of minorities. This has not been the case with the rights to women. Instead, as a general rule, the Court has lagged behind societal mores and realities when it has dealt with issues of concern to women.

*Colonial Period to the Civil War Amendments.* During the colonial period, suffrage was largely determined by local custom and usage. While there are few records of women voting, it is clear that some did, especially large landowners. Once individual states began to draft written constitutions, however, female suffrage evaporated. Women were also excluded by the gradual shift from gender-neutral property-owning requirements to near universal male suffrage. This emphasis on male suffrage also fostered the codification of many of the practices Abigail Adams had denounced as contributing to second-class citizenship for women.

Recognition of their inferior legal status, however, did not come to women overnight. In 1848, in what is widely hailed as the first major step toward female equality under the Constitution, a women's rights convention was held in Seneca Falls, New York. Eight years earlier, in 1840, two women active in the American abolitionist movement had traveled to London for the annual meeting of the International Anti-Slavery Society. After a long and arduous journey, Elizabeth Cady Stanton and Lucretia Mott were denied seating on the floor of the convention solely because they were women. Forced to take places in the rear of the balcony, they could not help but begin to see parallels between their status and that of the slaves they were trying to free (see SLAVERY). They resolved to call a meeting to discuss women's second-class status but the antislavery movement and issues in their own lives kept them from sending out the call to Seneca Falls until 1848.

At Seneca Falls, and at a later meeting held in Rochester, New York, a series of resolutions and a Declaration of Sentiments were drafted calling for expanded rights for women in all walks of life.

Both documents reflected dissatisfaction with contemporary moral codes, divorce and criminal laws, and the limited opportunities for women to obtain an education, participate in the church, and enter careers in medicine, law, and politics. While these issues continue to dominate the field of sex discrimination law today, none of the participants at Seneca Falls or subsequent conventions for women's rights saw the Constitution as a potential source of rights for women. Women's rights activists did, however, eventually see the need to amend the Constitution to achieve the right to *vote.

While women continued to press for changes in state laws to ameliorate their inferior legal status, they also continued to be active in the abolitionist movement. During the *Civil War most women's rights activists concentrated on the war effort and abolition. Many who had been present at Seneca Falls or active in subsequent efforts for women's rights joined the American Equal Rights Association (AERA), an association dedicated to abolition and woman suffrage. AERA members saw the issues of slavery and women's rights as inextricably intertwined, believing that suffrage would be granted when the franchise was extended to newly freed slaves.

Even the AERA, however, soon abandoned the cause of female suffrage with its support of the proposed *Fourteenth Amendment. When a majority of its members agreed "Now is the Negro's hour," key women's rights activists including Stanton and Susan B. Anthony were outraged. They were particularly incensed by the text of the proposed amendment, which introduced the word *male* into the Constitution for the first time. Although Article II of the Constitution does refer to the president as "he," the use of the word *male* to limit suffrage was infuriating to many women. Not only did Stanton and Anthony argue that women should not be left out of any attempt to secure fuller rights for freed slaves, but they were concerned that the text of the proposed amendment would necessitate the passage of an additional amendment to enfranchise women. How right they were. Soon after passage of the Fourteenth Amendment, the *Fifteenth Amendment was added to the Constitution in order to enfranchise black males previously ineligible to vote. Feverish efforts to have the word *sex* added to the amendment's list of race, color, or previous condition of servitude as improper limits on voting were unsuccessful. Women once again were told that the rights of blacks must come first.

Passage of the Fifteenth Amendment, and the AERA's support of it, led Anthony and Stanton to found the National Women's Suffrage Association (NWSA) in 1869. Its relatively radical demands for the reform of family and standards of dress, as well as its support of a well-known supporter of free love, Victoria Woodhull, led many to deride its more conservative demand for suffrage via a national *constitutional amendment.

**Litigating for Suffrage.** The National Women's Suffrage Association's advocacy of controversial reforms led to a severe image problem for both the association and its goals. In 1869, to lend credibility to its cause as well as to short-circuit the possiblity of a long battle for a universal suffrage amendment, Francis Minor, an attorney and the husband of a prominent NWSA member, put forth his belief that women, as citizens, were entitled to vote under the existing provisions of the Fourteenth Amendment. Minor saw the NWSA's possible resort to the courts as means to gain favorable publicity for the organization. Victoria Woodhull's presentation to Congress in 1871, urging it to pass enabling legislation to give women the right to vote under the Fourteenth Amendment, provided the impetus for renewed efforts.

Minor, along with Susan B. Anthony, quickly seized on the enthusiasm that Woodhull's suggestions created. Minor urged that test cases be brought to determine if the courts would obviate the need for additional legislative action. A number of legal scholars and judges had publicly agreed with Minor's arguments, and, moreover, in rejecting Woodhull's request for enabling legislation, the House of Representatives had noted that if a right to vote was vested by the Constitution, that right could be established in the courts without further legislation. More importantly, the newly appointed chief justice, Salmon P. *Chase, had suggested that women test the parameters of the Constitution to determine if they were already enfranchised by its provisions.

Despite Chase's encouragement, prior references to women by the Supreme Court had generally accepted a limited role for them. In *Dred *Scott v. Sandford (1857), for example, Chief Justice Taney noted, "Women and minors, who form a part of the political family, cannot vote" (p. 422). Ignoring this discouraging language, NWSA initiated several *test cases hoping to have at least one heard by the Supreme Court. Somewhat fittingly, the only one to reach the Supreme Court was *Minor v. Happersett, (1875), which involved both Minors as coplaintiffs, since married women had no legal right to sue in their own names.

Unfortunately for NWSA, before *Minor* could be appealed to the Supreme Court, the justices heard another case challenging gender discrimination under the Fourteenth Amendment. *Bradwell v. Illinois (1873) involved a challenge to the Illinois Supreme Court's refusal to admit Myra Bradwell to the practice of law because she was a woman. Bradwell's lawyer based her claim on the amendment's clause concerning *privileges or immunities. Because Bradwell's lawyer was cognizant of the suffrage test cases, in his argument he rejected the notion that women were enfranchised under the same provisions. He carefully differentiated the practice of a

chosen profession from the right to *vote, putting the Court on notice that not even all women were in agreement over the scope and reach of the Fourteenth Amendment. Despite the care he took to dissociate his client from NWSA's tactics, the Court ruled 8 to 1 against Bradwell's petition.

The majority opinion in *Bradwell*—the first pronouncement from the Supreme Court on the issue of gender—was based on two grounds. First, because Bradwell was suing as a citizen of Illinois, the Privileges or Immunities Clause of Article IV, section 2 of the Constitution was held inapplicable to her claim and to apply only to matters involving U.S. citizenship. Second, since admission to the bar of any state was not one of the privileges and immunities of U.S. citizenship, the Fourteenth Amendment did not secure that right.

Far more damaging to women's rights, however, was a concurrence written by Justice Joseph P. *Bradley, which is often referred to as the promulgation of the "Divine Law of the Creator." Writing for himself and two other justices, Bradley observed "a wide difference in the respective sphere and destinies of man and woman" and went on to insist that the "natural and proper timidity and delicacy which belongs to the female sex evidently unfits it for many of the occupations of civil life. . . . The paramount destiny and mission of woman are to fulfil the noble and benign offices of wife and mother. This is the law of the Creator" (p. 141).

Two years later, in *Minor v. Happersett* (1875), the Court again ruled against a claim for expanded woman's rights. The Court rejected the argument that the judiciary was empowered to read into the Fourteenth Amendment the right of suffrage as a natural privilege and immunity of citizenship. Writing for a unanimous Court, the newly appointed chief justice, Morrison R. *Waite, argued that the states were not inhibited by the Constitution from committing "that important trust to men alone" (p. 178). Nevertheless, the Court stressed that women were "persons" and might even be "citizens" within the meaning of the Fourteenth Amendment.

All of the gender discrimination cases heard by the Supreme Court during this era involved construction of the Privileges or Immunities Clause, and not the Due Process and *Equal Protection Clauses, of the Fourteenth Amendment. In The *Slaughterhouse Cases (1873), argued and decided shortly after *Bradwell*, the Supreme Court had meticulously examined the Fourteenth Amendment. In addition to limiting the constitutional significance of the Privileges or Immunities Clause, the court concluded that the Equal Protection Clause "is so clearly a provision for [the Negro] that a strong case would be necessary for its application to any other" (p. 81). Although the Fourteenth Amendment would be revived as a potential tool for women's rights soon after the beginning of the twentieth century, at the end of the nineteenth century women had yet to win a favorable decision against sex discrimination from the Supreme Court. While women were gaining greater rights within the *family through passage of married women's property acts in various states and were beginning to gain entry into institutions of higher education, the Court stuck rigidly to its interpretation that the Equal Protection Clause of the Fourteenth Amendment was intended primarily to protect African-Americans (i.e., African-American males) from discrimination, and it held fast to traditional notions concerning women's proper role in society.

***Litigating to Protect Women.*** Although the *Slaughterhouse Cases* did not provide a useful precedent for women seeking to practice law or to vote, the Court's opinion planted the seeds for judicial adoption of a very broad state *police power to enact laws to protect the public health, welfare, safety, and morals. This view was accepted in several subsequent cases. In *Mugler v. Kansas* (1887), however, in sustaining a law prohibiting intoxicating beverages, the Court built on the *Slaughterhouse* dissents of Justices Bradley and Stephen *Field, announcing that it was ready to examine the *substantive* reasonableness of such legislation. According to Justice John Marshall *Harlan, when state laws involving "the public morals, the public health, or the public safety" were at issue, the Court would "look to the substance of things" so as not to be "misled by mere pretenses" (p. 661). Ten years later, in *Allgeyer v. Louisiana* (1897), the Court for the first time invalidated a state statute on substantive *due process grounds. And, in *Lochner v. New York* (1905), the Court similarly invalidated a law regulating the work hours of bakers.

Until then the Court had rarely looked to the substance of legislation in addressing its validity. The Court's earlier readings of the Due Process Clause of the Fourteenth Amendment (or the *Fifth Amendment, where federal legislation was involved) had only guaranteed that legislation be passed in a fair manner, even though it might have an arbitrary or discriminatory impact (see also DUE PROCESS, PROCEDURAL). In *Lochner*, however, state laws would fail *unless* the provisions at issue were deemed reasonable under "common knowledge." Thus, the Court refused to accept New York's claim that a ten-hour maximum-hour law for bakers was reasonable to ensure the health of the bakers. Instead, the Court found that it unreasonably interfered with the employers' and employees' freedom of *contract protected by the Fourteenth Amendment, and found no "common knowledge" to justify such actions by New York (see DUE PROCESS, SUBSTANTIVE).

The importance of common knowledge cannot be understated in chronicling the Court's treatment of the issue of gender. Often, "common knowledge" has substituted for the personal views of the individual justices. As Bradley's "Divine Law of the Creator" opinion had made

quite clear, that view could easily lead to restrictions on the rights of women.

In the early 1900s, concern about the health, welfare, and morals of women led activists, particularly those closely allied with the growing suffrage movement, to press for state laws to upgrade the status of working women (see POLICE POWER). Large numbers of women had begun to enter the *labor force out of necessity. Most were confined to low-paying jobs in substandard conditions, a circumstance highlighted by the 1911 Triangle Shirtwaist Factory fire in New York City, in which many young female workers lost their lives. Even before that time, however, efforts had begun to improve the working conditions of women and children. And, whether out of civic concern or moral outrage, beginning in the 1890s, resolutions were adopted annually at suffrage conventions calling for improved conditions for women workers.

The organization most responsible for change, and for the Court's again addressing issues of gender, was the National Consumers' League (NCL). Through the work of its national staff and numerous affiliates, the NCL secured maximum-hour or other restrictions on night work for women in eighteen states. Its leaders therefore immediately recognized how much they had at stake when the Supreme Court decided to review *Muller v. Oregon* (1908), a case challenging the constitutionality of an Oregon law that prohibited the employment of women for more than ten hours a day. (Muller, the owner of a small laundry, had been convicted of violating the statute.) When *Muller* was accepted for review and oral argument, the NCL went to work immediately. Its general secretary quickly asked Louis D. *Brandeis, the brother-in-law of one of the organization's most active members and already a famous progressive lawyer, to take the case. Brandeis did so under one condition—that he have sole control of the litigation, a condition to which Oregon gladly acceded, thus allowing the NCL to represent it in court.

Numerous *state court decisions involving protective legislation for women, as well as the Supreme Court's recent decision in *Lochner*, made it clear to Brandeis that a victory could be forthcoming only by presenting information, or "common knowledge," that could persuade the Court that the dangers to women working more than ten hours a day made them more deserving of state protection than the bakers in *Lochner*, and by proving that there was something different about women that justified an exception to the freedom of contract doctrine enunciated in *Lochner*. Brandeis and the NCL would not challenge the Supreme Court's right, under substantive due process, to make that judgment.

NCL researchers compiled information about the possible detrimental effects of long work hours on women's health and morals, as well as on the health and welfare of their children, including their unborn children. Brandeis stressed women's differences from men and the reasonableness of the state's legislation. In fact, his brief had but three pages of strictly legal argument as against 110 pages of sociological data culled largely from European studies of the negative effects of long hours of work on women's health and reproductive capabilities. The information presented by Brandeis was not all that much different (except in quantity) from that presented on behalf of New York in *Lochner*, yet the Court appears to have been keenly persuaded by the contents of what has been come to be called the *Brandeis brief.

In holding that the Oregon law was permissible, the Court unanimously concluded that "woman's physical structure and the performance of maternal functions place her at a disadvantage in the struggle for subsistence" (p. 211). Such a condition meant the state had an interest in protecting women's health through appropriate legislation.

*Muller's* impact was immediate. State courts began to hold other forms of protective legislation for women constitutional, whether or not they involved the kind of ten-hour maximums at issue in *Muller*. Thus, eight-hour maximum work laws in a variety of professions, outright bans on night work for women, and minimum-wage laws for women were routinely upheld under the *Muller* rationale. Much of this Court-sanctioned governmental protection, however, worked to keep women out of high-paying evening jobs or positions that they desperately needed to support their families.

The NCL's efforts to protect women from unscrupulous employers, were victorious in the Supreme Court in several additional cases, but then ran into trouble in the early 1920s. In *Stettler v. O'Hara* (1917), a lower court decision upholding Oregon's minimum-wage law for women was appealed to the Supreme Court. Forces opposed to governmental interference in contractual rights feared that a decision supporting additional protective legislation would open the floodgates of governmental regulation. Stettler's lawyers argued that a labor agreement between an employer and an employee could not be disturbed by the government. Because the Fourteenth Amendment forbade the state from denying any individual liberty without due process of law, they argued that freedom of *contract was protected by the Amendment. The Court had once been amenable to this kind of argument, as attested by the decision in *Lochner*.

Building on the Court's far-ranging discussion of women and their physical, social, and legal differences from men, Brandeis, presenting the state's case, structured his arguments similarly to those offered in *Muller*, arguing the importance of a living wage to the health, welfare, and morals of women. Before the Court could decide the case, however, a vacancy occurred on the Court and

Brandeis himself was appointed to fill it. *Stettler* was then reargued in 1917; with Justice Brandeis not participating, the Court divided 4 to 4, thus sustaining the lower court's decision.

The next NCL-sponsored case, *Bunting* v. *Oregon* (1917), thus attracted a significant amount of attention. Felix *Frankfurter, Brandeis's hand-picked successor as counsel for the NCL, use the same kind of arguments Brandeis had used in *Muller* and *Stettler*. In a 5-to-3 decision (with Brandeis again not participating) the Court extended *Muller* to uphold an Oregon statute that established maximum hours for all factory and mill workers.

Although the NCL was victorious in these two cases, it had not anticipated the impact that the controversy within the suffrage movement over protective legislation would have on pending litigation. During the early twentieth century, women had come together to lobby for passage and then ratification of the Nineteenth Amendment. Once it was ratified, attempts were made to secure other rights for women. Women in the more radical branch of the suffrage movement, represented by the National Woman's Party (NWP), proposed the addition of an equal rights amendment to the Constitution. Progressives and those in the NCL were horrified because they believed that an equal rights amendment would immediately invalidate the protective legislation they had lobbied so hard to enact.

When *Adkins* v. *Children's Hospital* (1923) came to the Court, the NWP was ready. *Adkins* involved the constitutionality of a Washington, D.C., minimum-wage law for women. The NWP filed an *amicus curiae brief urging the Court to rule that, in light of the Nineteenth Amendment, women should be viewed on a truly equal footing with men. The division among women concerning equal rights and protective legislation was now exposed to public view. It was a debate that was to be resurrected again and again, both in the Court and in public discourse to the present day.

In *Adkins* the Court ruled 5 to 4 that minimum-wage laws for women were unconstitutional, thus resurrecting *Lochner*, which most observers thought had been overruled *sub silentio* in *Bunting*. The Court was unwilling to overrule *Muller* and thus simply distinguished it because it involved maximum hours and not wages. Nevertheless, the justices clearly believed that the Nineteenth Amendment conferred more rights upon women than just the right to vote. In noting their newly emancipated status, the Court undoubtedly was responding at least in part to the pro-equality arguments offered by the National Women's Party.

*Adkins*, unlike *Muller*, was decided by the narrowest of majorities. But it stood as valid law and as a ringing endorsement of the doctrine of freedom of contract regarding minumum-wage laws for women until 1937 (although the Court continued to uphold state maximum-hour provisions). In *West Coast Hotel v. Parrish* (1937), the Court finally abandoned its endorsement of substantive due process, explicitly overruled *Adkins*, and upheld Washington State's minimum-wage laws for women. By *United States v. *Darby Lumber Co.* (1941), the Court had completely abandoned substantive due process (and an equally insidious and excessively narrow view of the power of Congress under the Commerce Clause) when it upheld the validity of the federal Fair Labor Standards Act, which prescribed maximum hours and minimum wages for all workers (see COMMERCE POWER). In hammering the last nail in the coffin of substantive due process, the Court also appeared to be escaping from the constitutional need to establish a difference between men and women.

While the Court was enunciating a view that men and women were equal as permissible objects of regulation, clearly they were not. Most states continued to bar or limit night work for women. And while a separate minimum wage for women could no longer be valid, employer practices of clustering women into certain positions at far lower wages than those paid to men continued to exist.

No new cases involving women's rights came to the Supreme Court until 1948. The NCL had obtained what it wanted, and the coalition of women's groups that had pressed for suffrage had largely disintegrated. Women were urged to support the war effort and, after the war ended, to return home—to their traditional roles as wives and mothers. Thus, few groups were left to press for women's rights either in the legislatures or through the courts. The National Woman's Party did continue to press for equal rights and, in fact, was able to get a proposed equal rights amendment introduced into every session of Congress after 1923, but it chose to stay out of litigation until the 1970s.

*New Attempts To Expand Rights.* In *Goesaert v. Cleary* (1948) and *Hoyt v. Florida* (1961) the Court again made it clear that women were not guaranteed additional rights under the Fourteenth Amendment or elsewhere in the Constitution. Although the Fourteenth Amendment is a pledge of protection against state discrimination, over the years the Court has generally applied a two-tiered level of analysis to claims advanced under its provisions. Classifications based on race or national origin are considered *suspect classifications and are entitled to be judged by the severe test of *strict scrutiny. As such they are presumed invalid unless the government can show that they are "necessary to a compelling state interest" and that there were no less-restrictive alternative ways to achieve those goals. In contrast, when the Court applies the less stringent level of ordinary scrutiny, which until 1976 included all other legislative classifications, a state must show only a conceivable or reasonable basis for its action.

Until 1971, the Court routinely applied this minimal rationality test to claims involving discrimination against women. In *Goesaert*, for example, it sustained a statute that prohibited women from dispensing drinks from behind a bar unless they were the wives or daughters of male bar owners. Thus, forty years after *Muller*, the Court once again justified differential treatment of women by deferring to the state's special interest in women's social and "moral" problems. Under the reasonableness test, all that needed to be shown was some rational basis for the law.

In *Hoyt* the Supreme Court accepted sex-role stereotypes as sufficient reason to uphold a Florida statute that required men to serve on juries while women could merely volunteer for jury service (see TRIAL BY JURY). When Hoyt was convicted by an all-male jury of second-degree murder for killing her husband with a baseball bat, she argued that the conviction violated her rights to equal protection of the laws and her *Sixth Amendment right to be judged by a jury of her peers. The Supreme Court disagreed, holding that the Florida statute was not an arbitrary and systematic exclusion of women. Justice John M. Harlan concluded:

Despite the enlightened emancipation of women from the restrictions and protections of bygone years, and their entry into many parts of community life formerly considered to be reserved to men, woman is still regarded as the center of home and family life. (pp. 61–62)

It was not until the dawn of the current women's movement that judicial perspectives on what constitutes reasonable discrimination against women began to change. In 1966, the *National Organization for Women (NOW) was founded. Soon after, a plethora of other women's rights groups were created. Most of these groups renewed the call for passage of an equal rights amendment (ERA) to the Constitution. While significant lobbying was carried out on that front, some groups, cognizant of the successes that the National Association for the Advancement of Colored People had in securing additional rights for African-Americans through the courts, began to explore the feasibility of a litigation strategy designed to seek a more expansive interpretation of the Fourteenth Amendment. Although prior forays into the courts had ended unfavorably, some believed that the times had changed enough for the justices (or some of the justices) to recognize that sex-based differential treatment of women was unconstitutional. Many believed that the status of women and the climate for change was sufficiently positive to convince even a conservative Court that some change was necessary.

The *American Civil Liberties Union (ACLU), long a key player in the expansion of constitutional rights and liberties, led the planning for a comprehensive strategy to elevate sex to suspect-classification status. Its first case was *Reed v. Reed (1971). Ruth Bader Ginsburg, a member of the ACLU board, argued the case before the Supreme Court. Her enthusiasm and interest in the expansion of women's rights via constitutional interpretation led the ACLU to found the Women's Rights Project (WRP).

At issue in Reed was the constitutionality of an Idaho statute that required that males be preferred to otherwise equally qualified females as administrators of estates for those who died intestate. NOW, the National Federation of Business and Professional Women, and the Women's Equity Action League all filed *amicus curiae briefs urging the Court to interpret the Fourteenth Amendment as prohibiting discrimination against women on account of sex. Democratic senator Birch Bayh of Indiana, a major sponsor of the ERA, wrote one of the briefs, in which he attempted to apprise the Court of the glaring legal inequities faced by women and to link those inequities, at least in part, to the Court's own persistent refusal to expand the reach of the Equal Protection Clause to gender discrimination. Judicial decisions such as Goesaert and Hoyt, which allowed states to discriminate against women on minimally rational grounds, had made it clear to women's rights activists that a constitutional amendment was necessary if women were ever to enjoy full citizenship under the Constitution. But Reed was a critical first step.

Chief Justice Warren *Burger, writing for a unanimous Court in Reed, held that the Idaho statute that provided "different treatment . . . to the applicants on the basis of their sex . . . establishes a classification subject to scrutiny under the Equal Protection Clause" (p. 75). With these simple words, the Supreme Court for the first time concluded that sex-based differentials were entitled to some sort of scrutiny under the Fourteenth Amendment. But what type of scrutiny? According to Burger, who quoted Royster Guano v. Virginia (1920), the test was whether the differential treatment was "reasonable, not arbitrary" and rested "upon some ground of difference having a fair and substantial relation to the object of the legislation, so that all persons similarly circumstanced will be treated alike" (p. 76). The Court then found that the state's objective of reducing the workload of probate judges was insufficient justification to warrant this kind of sex-based statute. In fact, according to the Court, this was "the very kind of arbitrary legislative choice forbidden by the Equal Protection Clause" (p. 76).

This major breakthrough heartened women's rights activists. It also encouraged the WRP to launch a full-blown test case strategy like that pursued by the NAACP *Legal Defense and Education Fund that had culminated successfully in *Brown v. Board of Education (1954). WRP attorneys jumped at the opportunity to assist the Southern Poverty Law Center of Alabama with

the next major sex-discrimination case to come before the Supreme Court, *Frontiero v. Richardson (1973). At issue in Frontiero was the constitutionality of a federal statute that, for the purpose of computing allowances and fringe benefits, required female members of the armed forces to prove that they contributed more than 50 percent of their dependant husbands' support. Men were not required to make any such showing about their wives.

By an 8-to-1 vote, the Court struck down the statute, which gave male members of the armed forces potentially greater benefits than females. More importantly, though, only a plurality of four justices voted to make sex a suspect classification entitled to the strict scrutiny standard of review. While four other justices agreed that the statute violated the Equal Protection Clause, they did not agree that sex should be made a suspect classification. In fact three of them specifically noted the pending ratification of the ERA as a reason to wait—to allow the political process to guide judicial interpretation. This was to be the high-water mark of efforts to include sex, along with race, in the category of suspect classifications.

In *Craig v. Boren (1976) Justice William J. *Brennan, author of the plurality opinion in Frontiero, formulated a different test, known as *"intermediate" or "heightened" scrutiny, to apply to sex-discrimination cases. The case involved a challenge to an Oklahoma law that prohibited the sale of 3.2-percent beer to males under the age of twenty-one and females under the age of eighteen. In determining whether this kind of gender-based differential violated the Equal Protection Clause, Brennan wrote that "classifications by gender must serve important governmental objectives and must be substantially related to achievement of those objectives" (p. 197). He also specifically identified two governmental interests that would not justify sex discrimination: neither administrative convenience nor "fostering 'old' notions of role typing" (p. 198) would any longer be considered constitutionally adequate rationalizations of sex classifications. Shedding many of the stereotypes that had been at the core of Muller, Hoyt, and Goesaert, the Court specifically noted that there was no more place for "increasingly outdated misconceptions concerning the role of females in the home rather than in the 'marketplace and world of ideas' " (pp. 198–199). This new intermediate standard of review was subsequently used to invalidate a wide range of discriminatory practices including some Social Security, welfare, and workmen's compensation programs, alimony laws, age of majority statutes and jury service exemptions.

This is not to say that stereotypes do not still exert influence on the Court. In *Rostker v. Goldberg (1981), for example, the Court considered congressional combat restrictions sufficient to rationalize the exclusion of women from the new draft registration requirements of the Military

Selective Service Act (see CONSCRIPTION). A majority of the Court accepted the government's position that the statutory exclusion of women from combat positions combined with the need for combat-ready troops were sufficiently important justifications to meet the burden of the intermediate standard of review. It did not bother to consider the validity of the combat restrictions themselves. And, in *Michael M. v. Superior Court of Sonoma County* (1981), the Court held that California's statutory rape law, which applied only to males, did not violate the Equal Protection Clause. Justice William H. *Rehnquist noted that the state's concern about teenage pregnancy was a sufficiently strong state interest to justify the statute. Moreover, Rehnquist's opinion pointedly did not apply intermediate scrutiny.

In late 1981 the Court was joined by its first female member, Sandra Day *O'Connor. It was not long before she and the other justices were faced with another sex-based claim made under the Fourteenth Amendment. *Mississippi University for Women* v. *Hogan* (1982) involved a state policy that restricted enrollment in one state-supported nursing school to females. Writing for a five-member majority, O'Connor noted that when the purpose of a statute was to "exclude or 'protect' members of one gender because they are presumed to suffer from an inherent handicap or to be innately inferior, the objective itself is illegitimate" (p. 725). As one commentator noted, "she out-Brennaned Justice Brennan." For example, O'Connor went even further than Brennan (long the Court's foremost liberal) by suggesting in a footnote that sex might best be treated by the Court as a suspect classification.

O'Connor's strong opinion in *Hogan* again brought to four the number of justices on the Court who apparently favored some sort of strict standard of review for sex-based classifications. It is unlikely, however, that sex will soon be measured, at least formally, with anything more than heightened scrutiny. The elevation of William Rehnquist to chief justice, the appointments of Justices Antonin *Scalia, Anthony *Kennedy, David *Souter, and Clarence *Thomas could have a long-term impact on the direction the Court takes in considering sex-discrimination claims. Too, as additional justices retire, it is unlikely that they will be replaced with strong proponents of even a heightened standard of review. A change of but one justice in *Hogan* would have allowed Mississippi to continue its maintenance of an all-female nursing school. Given the likelihood that most, if not all, members of the current Court would probably find that deliberate maintenance of an all-black public school violates the Equal Protection Clause of the Fourteenth Amendment, the contrast is clear: race is a suspect classification, sex is not.

Recognizing the fragile nature of even the middle tier of review and the Court's uneven application of its standards, women's rights groups again are seeking passage of an equal rights amendment to the Constitution. Most see such an amendment as the only way to guarantee that women will ever be recognized as fully equal under the Constitution. Some see passage of an amendment as especially important given the kinds of sex-based discrimination cases that the Court is likely to address in the future. Although most of these involve challenges under Title VII of the *Civil Rights Act of 1964 and its prohibition against discrimination in employment, Court watchers fear that without the force of an equal rights amendment to overshadow interpretation of the law, the Court's decisions could grow increasingly adverse to women's full equality. In spite of the absence of an ERA, however, even the Rehnquist Court has revealed a reluctance to go back to pre-*Reed* days, when sex-discrimination claims never found a favorable audience with the Court. Its decisions clearly have added to a climate that frowns on blatant discrimination. Given the increasingly conservative nature of the Court, however, and the increasingly complex patterns of discrimination that are being presented to it, it is unlikely that the scope of constitutional protections for women will grow unless other societal changes take place. The active-combat roles played by women in the Gulf War in early 1991, for example, could prompt the Court to uphold a new challenge to the discriminatory provisions of the Military and Selective Service Act previously held constitutional in *Rostker*.

Fewer and fewer constitutional cases involving sex discrimination come before the Court each year, perhaps because women's rights groups are using their time and money to fend off challenges to *Roe v. Wade* (1973) and to keep *abortion legal. Moreover, most of the "easy" cases have been decided, and there is fairly uniform application of the intermediate standard of review in the lower courts. Thus, most gender cases that the Court now chooses to hear involve employment discrimination and the scope of bona fide occupational qualifications permissible under Title VII. During its 1990 term, for example, the Court heard arguments in *International Union, UAW v. Johnson Controls, Inc.* (1991), which involved a company fetal-protection policy that required women in certain hazardous positions be sterilized as a condition of their employment. Many women's rights activists argued that a judicial finding in support of the company policy would inevitably lead to the exclusion of women in all types of lucrative positions and to the resurrection of the paternalism of *Muller v. Oregon*. Their fears, however, proved to be unfounded. In *Johnson Controls* the Court ruled unanimously that the company's policies did not constitute bona fide occupational qualifications and thus violated Title VII. Many commentators now take this as an omen that the Court will continue to build on existing precedents and not retreat to earlier decisions more "protective" of women. Nevertheless, it is likely that the Court's decision regarding fetal-protection policies will spur continued litigation in this area as more cases come to the Court presenting issues that involve women's reproductive capabilities and the "special treatment" some employers would like to give their female workers on account of that status. The consensus evidenced by the Court, however, leaves women's rights activists far more optimistic than they were just a short time ago.

□ L. H. Butterfield et al., eds. *The Book of Abigail and John* (1975). Ellen Carol DuBois. *Feminism and Suffrage: The Emergence of an Independent Women's Movement in America 1848–1869* (1978). Sara M. Evans. *Born for Liberty: A History of Women in America* (1989). Susan M. Hartmann. *From Margin to Mainstream: American Women and Politics since 1960* (1989). Herma Hill Kay. *Sex-Based Discrimination: Text, Cases and Materials*, 3d ed. (1988). Naomi B. Lynn, ed. *Women, Politics and the Constitution* (1990). Karen O'Connor. *Women's Organizations' Use of the Courts* (1980). Wendy Williams. "Sex Discrimination: Closing the Law's Gender Gap," in *The Burger Years*, edited by Herman Schwartz (1987) pp. 109–124.

Karen O'Connor

**General Welfare.** Congress is granted authority under Article I, section 8 of the Constitution to "pay the debts and provide for the common Defence and general Welfare of the United States." The meaning of this *Taxing and Spending Clause provoked controversy as early as 1792. One interpretation is that it gives Congress broad power to legislate in the public interest. Such a view is inconsistent with the concept of a limited constitution, however. A second view, promoted by Alexander *Hamilton, suggested that Congress's power to tax and spend for the general welfare was additional to its other powers. A third view, represented by Thomas *Jefferson and James *Madison, argued that the phrase was simply a summary or general description of the specific powers and that it gave Congress no additional power.

The Supreme Court had no opportunity to interpret this clause until 1936, in *United States* v. *Butler.* In striking down the Agricultural Adjustment Act of 1933, Justice Owen *Roberts, writing for the majority, held with Hamilton's view, saying that the Taxing and Spending Clause was indeed a separate grant of power to Congress. Because the Court could determine for itself whether a particular tax or expenditure was in the general welfare of the country, however, Roberts read the clause as limiting Congress's reach to matters of "national, as distinguished from local welfare." The limitation proposed by *Butler* remained hypothetical, however, since the Court struck down the statute in question on other grounds.

In any event, the expansion of congressional power under the Commerce Clause has rendered the question almost moot since Congress's authority, in practical terms, now reaches most of the concerns that might come under the rubric of "general welfare" (see COMMERCE POWER).

William Lasser

**Genesee Chief v. Fitzhugh,** 12 How. (53 U.S.) 443 (1852), argued 2, 5, 6 Jan. 1852, decided 20 Feb. 1852 by vote of 8 to 1; Taney for the Court, Daniel in dissent. In *Genesee Chief* the Supreme Court expanded the scope of federal admiralty jurisdiction to encompass navigable fresh water lakes and rivers. The Supreme Court in an 1825 admiralty decision, *The Thomas Jefferson,* had adopted the traditional English rule restricting admiralty jurisdiction to tidal waters. Congress, however, desired to promote trade on interior waterways and enacted a statute in 1845 extending the jurisdiction of the federal courts to certain cases arising on the Great Lakes. The Supreme Court, in an opinion by Chief Justice Roger B. *Taney, sustained the 1845 act and overruled its earlier decision. Taney emphasized that the English rule was unsuitable in the United States, with its network of navigable rivers and lakes. He concluded that admiralty jurisdiction depended upon "the navigable character of the water, and not upon the ebb and flow of the tide" (p. 457). In dissent, Justice Peter V. *Daniel maintained that federal admiralty power was determined by the English practice at the time the Constitution was ratified.

The decision in *Genesee Chief* significantly encouraged commerce and navigation. By rejecting the tidal waters doctrine, the Supreme Court allowed Congress to regulate shipping on inland lakes and rivers by uniform admiralty principles. Moreover, the ruling exemplified the Court's willingness to accommodate legal doctrine to the emergence of new technology. The invention of the steamboat had revolutionized travel on inland waterways and rendered the tidal waters rule obsolete.

(See also ADMIRALTY AND MARITIME LAW.)

James W. Ely, Jr.

**Geofroy v. Riggs,** 133 U.S. 258 (1890), argued 23 Dec. 1889, decided 3 Feb. 1890, by vote of 9 to 0; Field for the Court. T. L. Riggs, a U.S. citizen, died intestate, leaving as heirs family members who included both American and French nationals. The French descendants claimed, as part of their inheritance, property located in Washington, D.C. But the American heirs argued that the local law of Maryland, which the Federal District had incorporated, prohibited the descent of real estate to aliens. The issue was: could French aliens inherit from a U.S. citizen land situated in a U.S. territorial jurisdiction such as the District of Columbia?

After losing in the *lower federal court the aliens appealed to the Supreme Court. Their argument was that a provision of an 1853 treaty between the United States and France permitted the descent of real estate to French nationals in "all states" whose local law so permitted. In addition, though it made no specific reference to Frenchmen, another treaty of 1800 governing Washington, D.C., had displaced the property law incorporated from Maryland. The Americans countered, however, that the District of Columbia was not a "state" within the meaning of the 1853 treaty.

Justice Stephen *Field's opinion held that for purposes of the treaty a "state" was any political entity with an established government, including Washington, D.C. Reasoning that the American litigants' interpretation of the treaty would result in discriminatin against aliens and jeopardize reciprocity between the United States and France, the Court held that the French heirs could inherit property in the District of Columbia.

The decision expanded the right to transfer property and the rights of aliens primarily in Washington, D.C. But the precedent also applied if ambiguity existed in a particular state's law.

(See also ALIENAGE AND NATURALIZATION; INHERITANCE AND ILLEGITIMACY; PROPERTY RIGHTS; TREATIES AND TREATY POWER.)

Tony Freyer

**Gerrymandering,** named for a salamander-shaped district devised by Massachusetts Governor Elbridge Gerry in 1812, is the practice of drawing the boundaries of a political district to the advantage or disadvantage of some person, party, or other group. Every winner-take-all district is somewhat gerrymandered in this sense, but common usage confines the term to districts that are blatantly discriminatory or exotically shaped.

Apart from the landmark *Gomillion v. Lightfoot (1960), the Supreme Court has ducked gerrymandering controversies for want of acceptable, enforceable standards. In Gomillion the city of Tuskegee, Alabama, had drawn up an "uncouth, 28-sided figure" excluding almost every black from voting in the city, while keeping every white voter within the city's boundaries. The Supreme Court voided the new boundaries. Its action opened the way for *Baker v. Carr (1962) and decades of wrestling with a new "fundamental principle" of the Constitution requiring "equal representation for equal numbers" (see REAPPORTIONMENT CASES). Courts have freely applied this principle to equalize the population of districts, but they have been cautious about applying it to gerrymanders, which govern the effective, outcome-affecting votes of different groups within a jurisdiction.

Four leading cases—Wright v. Rockefeller (1964), *United Jewish Organizations of Williamsburgh v. Carey (1977), *Davis v. Bandemer (1986), and Badham v. Eu (1988)—illustrate the Court's caution. Wright and United Jewish Organizations both involved racial gerrymanders, con-

centrating African-American and Puerto Rican populations in New York City into "racial boroughs." Had the minority voters been divided among adjacent districts, they could have had majorities in more than one district.

In Wright, the African-American plaintiffs wanted to achieve more effective voting power for blacks through deconcentration; the black incumbent, however, sided with the defendants and argued that it was better to have one strong, safe black seat than two weak, marginal ones. The Court declined to intervene against the obvious racial gerrymander, claiming that there was no evidence of racial discrimination. In United Jewish Organizations, the U.S. attorney general had ordered the state to create two new nonwhite-majority districts by dismembering a Hasidic Jewish district. The Jewish plaintiffs objected to the explicit racial quotas, which they argued cost them voting power, but the Court ruled that the quotas did not constitute discrimination against the Jews. As in Wright, the evidence of discrimination was strong but the rules for interpreting it were uncertain (see RACE AND RACISM).

Davis and Badham were both partisan districting cases, where the "in" party, by gerrymandering, had given itself half again as many seats per vote as the "out" party. The Court in Davis declared that egregious gerrymandering that would "consistently degrade a voter's . . . influence on the political process" (p. 132) would violate the *Equal Protection Clause, but it did not find Indiana's suppression of Democrats, in one house in one election, egregious enough to be a constitutional violation. Though Badham involved several successive elections and a pro-Democrat, pro-incumbent gerrymandering so tight that virtually no legislative district changed party hands, the Court declined to hear the case.

Liberals often support judicial action against racial gerrymanders, which are largely designed to deprive African-Americans and Latinos of voting strength, but not against partisan ones, which have very often robbed Republicans of district majorities. Conservatives divide between noninterventionists, who argue that courts should not intervene without clear standards, and activists, who argue that any kind of intervention, by the initiative process (if available) or by the judiciary is preferable to waiting for state legislators to revamp their own districts (see JUDICIAL ACTIVISM).

California has provided extreme examples both of gerrymandering and of attempts to control it. Many Californians have concluded that gerrymandering, besides producing safe seats and stable one-party rule, has also polarized and insulated the legislature and rendered it less responsive to changes in public opinion. They have turned to initiatives, clumsy as they are, to get results. Many initiatives have been tried against gerrymandering, but none has yet succeeded. It seems inevitable that initiatives will continue to be put forward—either until gerrymandering is curbed or until the public comes to see it and its attendant problems as unavoidable facts of life.

(See also ELECTIONS; FAIR REPRESENTATION.)

□ Ward Elliott, *The Rise of Guardian Democracy* (1975).
Ward E. Y. Elliott

**Gertz v. Robert Welch, Inc.,** 418 U.S. 323 (1974), argued 14 Nov. 1973, decided 25 June 1974 by vote of 5 to 4; Powell for the Court, Blackmun concurring, Burger, Douglas, Brennan, and White in dissent. *Gertz v. Robert Welch, Inc.* arose in 1969 when *American Opinion* magazine, a publication of the John Birch Society, attacked Elmer Gertz, an attorney who was representing clients in a suit for civil damages against a policeman who had earlier been convicted of second-degree murder. *American Opinion* falsely stated that Gertz had been responsible for framing the policemen in his murder trial, that Gertz had a criminal record, and that he was a "Leninist" and a "Communist-fronter." Gertz sued for defamation.

In 1964 the Supreme Court had held in *New York Times Co. v. Sullivan* that plaintiffs who were public officials could not recover damages for defamation unless they could demonstrate that the defamation had been published with " 'actual malice'—that is, with knowledge that it was false or with reckless disregard of whether it was false or not" (pp. 279–280). In the aftermath of *New York Times* there was considerable uncertainty about the range of application of this revolutionary rule of actual malice. The Court's opinion in *Gertz* was to resolve this uncertainty by establishing a doctrinal structure that would remain stable for the next decade.

The Supreme Court held that the *First Amendment required public figures and public officials to demonstrate *actual malice but that all other *libel plaintiffs, like Elmer Gertz, need only prove some degree of "fault." *Gertz* also held that the First Amendment prohibited the recovery of punitive or presumptive damages in the absence of actual malice, although it specifically held that mental anguish was a compensable form of "actual" damage.

An important weakness of *Gertz* is that it never explained why the Constitution should preempt *common-law defamation doctrine as applied to all cases involving private plaintiffs. In 1985, in *Dun & Bradstreet, Inc. v. Greenmoss Builders*, the Court began to cut back the application of the *Gertz* rules so that they would only pertain to defamations which, although about private plaintiffs, were also about matters of "public concern."

(See also SPEECH AND THE PRESS.)
Robert C. Post

**Gibbons v. Ogden,** 9 Wheat. (22 U.S.) 1 (1824), argued 4–9 Feb. 1824, decided 2 Mar. 1824 by vote of 6 to 0; Marshall for the Court, Johnson concurring. It was thirty-five years after ratification of the Constitution before the Supreme Court decided a case related to the clause empowering Congress to regulate interstate and foreign commerce (Article I, sec. 8). In *Gibbons v. Ogden* (1824), Chief Justice John *Marshall delivered an opinion that was a classic statement of nationalism. Over the years, it became a source of extensive authority for Congress to address new problems in the regulation of the national economy. Judges and lawyers would analyze it to explain the distribution of powers between nation and states in the American federal system (see FEDERALISM).

The case arose during the early days of the steamboat. In 1807, Robert Fulton, the most successful of the many inventors seeking a practical steam-propelled craft, ran his boat up the Hudson River at the speed prescribed by a New York law and thereby acquired a monopoly of steam navigation on the state's waters. Ambitious interlopers challenged this monopoly, which led to lively litigation. One line of cases involved Aaron Ogden, who held a state-required Fulton-Livingston license, and Thomas Gibbons, who held a federal coasting license and ran competing boats between New Jersey and Manhattan. The New York courts repeatedly upheld the monopoly against such competition (*Livingston v. Van Ingen*, 1812, and *Gibbons v. Ogden*, 1820). By 1824 the dispute reached the U.S. Supreme Court on appeal.

Daniel *Webster made the principal argument for Gibbons. He set out the options for interpreting the Constitution in matters concerning state and national powers over interstate commerce: (1) exclusive national power; (2) fully concurrent state and national powers (see CONCURRENT POWER); (3) partially concurrent state power not reaching "higher branches" of that commerce; and (4) supremacy of a national statute over a contrary state statute. In arguing for the first of these, Webster construed commerce broadly and warned against a tangle of conflicting local policies. One of Ogden's counsel, Thomas Emmet, insisted that states had frequently legislated on many interstate matters and ought to have fully concurrent power over commerce between states.

Marshall spoke for the entire Court, except William *Johnson, who filed a concurring opinion. Marshall plainly preferred the exclusive option. He defined commerce expansively, far beyond mere exchange of goods, to include persons and new subjects such as the steamboat. Nevertheless, he held back from deciding the case on exclusivity grounds, probably because of the possible impact such a broad reading of federal power might have on slaveholding states, nervous as they were about federal authority (see SLAVERY). But Justice Johnson, a South Carolinian who was a fervent nationalist on this question, adopted that option. In the actual holding, Marshall construed Gibbons's federal license to nullify the New York grant of monopoly. He saw a conflict of congressional and state statutes, thus selecting the narrowest strategy and postponing a more comprehensive ruling.

Lawyers and judges explored this question in several cases over the next quarter-century and finally arrived at a compromise formula that acknowledged a partially concurrent state power over interstate commerce. In *Cooley v. Board of Wardens* (1852), the Taney Court decided that some subjects of commerce required a uniform rule and national uniformity, while others permitted a degree of state action. However, *Cooley's* general formulation left many specifics unclear (see SELECTIVE EXCLUSIVENESS).

During its conservative periods, the Court expressed hostility to both national and state regulatory powers. For example, in the late nineteenth century, both state railroad regulation and national antitrust reform suffered from narrow and tortured readings of the Commerce Clause. This judicial negativism persisted until the 1930s, albeit with respectful citations to *Gibbons*. After the constitutional revolution that began in 1937, the Court read the steamboat case differently to permit almost unlimited federal power, whether for regulating the economy or, as in Marshall's time, for stimulating its growth. Entirely new uses for the *commerce power, notably protection of *civil rights, have emerged. At the same time, the Court has allowed a broad field for state legislation, no doubt much broader than Chief Justice Marshall would have favored.

□ Maurice G. Baxter, *The Steamboat Monopoly: Gibbons v. Ogden, 1824* (1972).                 Maurice G. Baxter

**Gideon v. Wainwright,** 372 U.S. 335 (1963), argued 15 Jan. 1963, decided 18 Mar. 1963 by vote of 9 to 0; Black for the Court, Douglas, Clark, and Harlan concurring. Clarence Earl Gideon was charged with breaking and entering a poolroom with intent to commit a misdemeanor, a felony under Florida law. Being without funds, Gideon requested that counsel be appointed for him; the Florida trial court refused and Gideon conducted his own defense "about as well as could be expected from a layman" (p. 337). The jury returned a verdict of guilty. Gideon filed a *habeas corpus petition in the Florida Supreme Court claiming that his federal constitutional rights had been abridged by the trial court's refusal to appoint counsel for him; the Florida Supreme Court denied relief and Gideon appealed *in forma pauperis* to the U.S. Supreme Court.

The Court appointed Abe *Fortas, a prominent lawyer who later served as a justice, to argue Gideon's case and address whether *Betts v. Brady* (1942) should be overruled. *Betts* had held that, in *state courts, the *Fourteenth Amendment's Due Process Clause only required that appointed counsel be provided to indigents in special circumstances. However, the Court had not upheld a single denial of right to counsel under the *Betts* rule since its 1950 decision in *Quicksal v. Michigan*. The Court was looking for an opportunity to overrule *Betts*, and *Gideon* provided that opportunity.

A unanimous Court overruled *Betts* and held that the Sixth Amendment, as applied to the states by the Fourteenth Amendment, required that counsel be appointed to represent indigent defendants charged with serious offenses in state criminal trials. At his retrial, Gideon was represented by appointed counsel who uncovered new defense witnesses and discredited prosecution witnesses; a new jury acquitted Gideon.

In overruling *Betts*, Justice Hugo *Black, for the majority, argued that the Court was "returning to . . . old precedents, sounder we believe than the new" (p. 334). In *Powell v. Alabama* (1932), the Court had held that when an indigent defendant is charged with a capital offense in a state court and is incapable of making his own defense, *due process requires that counsel be appointed for him. It noted that "the right to be heard would be of little avail if it did not comprehend the right to be heard by counsel" (p. 68). In *Johnson v. Zerbst* (1938), the Court declared a right to appointed counsel in federal criminal cases. By 1942, thirty-five states required that counsel be appointed to represent indigents in serious noncapital as well as capital cases. Indeed, in *Gideon* twenty-two states filed an amicus curiae brief urging reversal of *Betts* and only three states, including Florida, argued that *Betts* should be upheld.

*Gideon* was widely interpreted as applying only to felony cases; but, in *Argersinger v. Hamlin* (1972), the Court extended the right to appointed counsel to misdemeanors when the defendant is sentenced to imprisonment. In another case decided the same day as *Gideon*, *Douglas v. California*, the Court held that the *Equal Protection Clause conferred a right to appointed counsel for first appeals of right. In subsequent years, *Gideon* spawned two lines of cases. One series of cases deals with the Sixth Amendment right to counsel and at what stages of the criminal justice process the defendant must be allowed the benefit of counsel. Another line of cases acknowledges that the right to counsel implies the right to effective counsel and attempts to develop standards for determining when that right had been denied.

Today, most large cities and some states have public defender offices that provide counsel to indigents in criminal cases. In other regions, trial court judges appoint private attorneys to represent indigent defendants. A 1984 Department of Justice survey reported that two-thirds of the nation's population is served by public defenders. Various studies have shown that a defendant's chance of being convicted is not significantly affected by whether he is represented by a public defender or private counsel, although defendants who proceed without counsel are significantly more likely to be convicted. *Gideon*, along with *\*Mapp v. Ohio* (1961), marked the beginning of the Court's "due process revolution," which resulted in the constitutionalization of state criminal procedure and a series of only partially successful attempts to convince the Court to extend due process guarantees to civil and quasi-legal proceedings.

(See also COUNSEL, RIGHT TO; SIXTH AMENDMENT.)

□ Anthony Lewis, *Gideon's Trumpet* (1964).

Susan E. Lawrence

**Gilbert, Cass** (b. Zanesville, Ohio, 24 Nov. 1859; d. Brockenhurst, England, 19 May 1934), architect of the Supreme Court Building. Gilbert grew up in St. Paul, Minnesota, and studied architecture for a year at the Massachusetts Institute of Technology. After serving as an assistant to Stanford White in New York City, Gilbert designed municipal and business buildings, churches, residences, railway stations, bridges, and the Minnesota, West Virginia, and Arkansas state capitols. Among his most noted works during the turn-of-the-century period are the United States Custom House, the Federal Court Building, and the Woolworth Building, all in New York City. The Woolworth Building, at sixty-six stories, was the tallest building in the world at its 1913 completion and remained so for almost two decades. His other designs include the Treasury Annex and U.S. Chamber of Commerce buildings in Washington, D.C., and the Detroit and St. Louis public libraries. The Supreme Court Building was under construction at the time of his death during a visit to England in 1934. The structure was completed under the supervision of his son, Cass Gilbert, Jr.

The senior Gilbert was a traditionalist, and chose to take no part in the modern functionalist movement that became preeminent in architecture early in the twentieth century. His eclectic designs, especially for public buildings such as the Supreme Court, combine tasteful solidity, grandeur, and a scale appropriate to their importance. Although some architectural critics now find his works uninviting and unoriginal, he was much honored in his lifetime. Gilbert is generally considered one of the most capable architects the United States has produced.

(See also ARCHITECTURE OF THE SUPREME COURT BUILDING.)

Francis Helminski

**Ginsburg, Douglas Howard** (b. Chicago, Ill. 25 May 1946), federal appellate judge and unsuccessful nominee for the U.S. Supreme Court. After eight years as a Harvard law professor and three years in the Reagan administration Justice Department and Office of Management and Budget, Ginsburg was appointed by President Ronald *\*Reagan to the U.S. Court of Appeals for the District of Columbia in 1986. Less than a year later, on 29 October 1987, Reagan announced that he was nominating Ginsburg to the Supreme Court vacancy created by the retirement of Lewis *\*Powell, Jr., after the Senate had rejected the nomination of Robert *\*Bork. Ginsburg withdrew his nomination on 7 November 1987, before it was formally submitted to the Senate, and returned to the D.C. court of appeals, where he still serves.

Ginsburg's nomination occurred in the wake of the tremendous ideological conflict generated by Bork's defeat. Conservative Republicans prevailed over moderates, and Ginsburg was nominated quickly, before the usual background checks had been completed. Allegations of a financial conflict of interest during his work for the administration and of a misrepresentation of his amount of courtroom experience were soon raised. Conservative support dwindled rapidly following the disclosure, later admitted, that Ginsburg had smoked marijuana while on the Harvard law faculty.

(See also NOMINEES, REJECTION OF.)

Susan M. Olson

**Gitlow v. New York,** 268 U.S. 652 (1925), argued 12 Apr. 1923, reargued 23 Nov. 1923, decided 8 June 1925 by vote of 7 to 2; Sanford for the Court, Holmes and Brandeis in dissent. The landmark *Gitlow* case marks the beginning of the "incorporation" of the First Amendment as a limitation on the states. This process, which continued selectively over the next fifty years, resulted in major changes in the modern law of civil liberties, affording citizens a federal remedy if the states deprived them of their *\*fundamental rights. Ironically, however, the Court rejected Gitlow's free speech claim. At the time the ruling's significance was largely doctrinal.

Benjamin Gitlow was a member of the left-wing section of the Socialist party. He was convicted for violating the New York Criminal Anarchy Law of 1902, which made it a crime to advocate the violent overthrow of the government. Specifically, he had been arrested during the 1920 Red Scare for writing, publishing and distributing sixteen thousand copies of a pamphlet called *Left-wing Manifesto* that urged the establishment of socialism by strikes and "class action . . . in any form." He was also charged with being an "evil disposed and pernicious person," with a "wicked and turbulent disposition," who tried to "excite discontent and disaffection." At his trial, the famed attorney Clarence Darrow sought to frame the entire issue as one of freedom of speech on the grounds that the *Left-wing Manifesto* advocated nothing but urged abstract doctrine. The New York court, however, ruled that communists had to be held responsible for the potential danger of their abstract concepts and upheld the conviction.

The Supreme Court used the case as an occasion to examine the concept that the speech and press protections of the First Amendment should be extended to the states. Gitlow's brief, prepared by the brilliant *ACLU lawyer Walter H. *Pollak, argued persuasively that liberty of expression was a right to be protected against state abridgment. This, he contended, was established by the authoritative determination of the meaning of liberty as used in the *Fourteenth Amendment and by implicit declarations with respect to the related right of free assembly. The Court was impressed. Justice Edward T. *Sanford, speaking for the majority, agreed that "for present purposes, we may and do assume that freedom of speech and of the press . . . are among the fundamental personal rights and 'liberties' protected by the due process clause of the Fourteenth Amendment from impairment by the States" (p. 666). He nonetheless sustained the New York law and upheld Gitlow's conviction. "[A] state may punish utterances endangering the foundations of organized government and threatening its overthrow by unlawful means," Sanford wrote, (p. 667). Gitlow's pamphlet, while not immediately inciting criminal action, could be viewed as a "revolutionary spark" that might at some later time burst into "sweeping and destructive conflagration" (p. 669).

Justice Oliver Wendell *Holmes wrote a famous dissent in which Justice Louis D. *Brandeis concurred. He disagreed with the majority's ruling that words separated from action could be punished. Holmes declared, "The only difference between the expression of an opinion and an incitement in the narrower sense is the speaker's enthusiasm for the result. Eloquence may set fire to reason. But whatever may be thought of the redundant discourse before us, it had no chance of starting a present conflagration" (p. 673). This view, which called for punishment of action, not expression, under the *clear and present danger doctrine, was to be embraced by the Supreme Court in the 1960s.

The Gitlow decision launched "incorporation" of the First Amendment. It was not until *Stromberg v. California (1931), however, that the Court actually ruled a state law unconstitutional on First Amendment free speech grounds.

(See also INCORPORATION DOCTRINE; SPEECH AND THE PRESS.)

Paul L. Murphy

**Goldberg, Arthur Joseph** (b. Chicago, Ill., 8 Aug. 1908; d. Washington, D.C., 19 Jan. 1990; interred Arlington National Cemetery), associate justice, 1962–1965. Born of Russian immigrant parents, the youngest of eight children, Goldberg was reared and educated in Chicago and graduated from Northwestern University Law School in 1929 at the head of his class. He married Dorothy Kurgans in 1931. Except for army service (1942–1944), Goldberg practiced labor law in Chicago

*Arthur Joseph Goldberg*

until 1948, when he became general counsel of the United Steelworkers and the Congress of Industrial Relations. Goldberg was largely responsible for the AFL-CIO merger of 1955 and was recognized as one of the formost labor mediators of the 1950s. President John F. Kennedy appointed him secretary of labor in 1961, and when Justice Felix *Frankfurter resigned from the Court in 1962, Kennedy appointed Goldberg to the "Jewish seat" because he knew what to expect from him.

Goldberg's tenure on the Court was significant, particularly considering its brevity. There was a marked contrast between Frankfurter's adherence to judicial restraint (see JUDICIAL SELF-RESTRAINT) and Goldberg's belief that the Court should protect a "permanent minority" that had been excluded from the political process. Thus, a four-justice minority was transformed into a five-member majority, and Goldberg's negotiating skill often held it together. In this capacity, his formula called for balancing state interest against individual rights and liberties, with close scrutiny applied to the state.

Goldberg's best-known opinions are that for the Court in *Escobedo v. Illinois (1964), and his concurrence in *Griswold v. Connecticut (1965). Escobedo was an important step toward adaption of the doctrine of *Miranda v. Arizona (1966), by ruling a defendant had a right to remain silent in the absence of his attorney. In Griswold, the Court invalidated a Connecticut anti–birth control law, and in the absence of a violation of a specific constitutional provision, Goldberg maintained that the right to marital *privacy was a *"fundamental right" protected by the *Ninth Amendment. While *Escobedo* was largely abandoned by the Court in *Kirby* v. *Illinois* (1972), *Griswold* was followed by the Court in *\*Roe* v. *Wade* (1973), including Goldberg's concurring opinion.

Also important was Goldberg's ruling in *Gibson* v. *Florida Legislative Investigation Committee* (1963) that the right of association (see ASSEMBLY AND ASSOCIATION, FREEDOM OF) could be infringed only if Florida "convincingly" showed a "compelling state interest," and in *\*Aptheker* v. *Secretary of State* (1964), that legislation revoking passports had to be precisely drawn, since traveling abroad was a liberty protected by the *Fifth Amendment. At least two of his dissents had important results. His dissent in *United States* v. *Barnett* (1964) helped reduce the use of criminal *contempt for punishment by federal judges; and his protest in *Rudolph* v. *Alabama* (1963) against denial of *certiorari in a case of *capital punishment for rape signaled the constitutional war over capital punishment.

In the summer of 1965, President Lyndon Johnson manuevered Goldberg off the bench to create a vacancy for Abe *Fortas. Appointed United Nations representative, Goldberg found the position unsatisfactory, and resigned in 1968. He also made an ignominious run for governor of New York in 1970 but should best be remembered during his twenty-four-year post-Court career for his continuing advocacy of human rights.

□ Stephen J. Friedman, "Arthur J. Goldberg," in *The Justices of the United States Supreme Court 1789–1969,* edited by Leon Friedman and Fred L. Israel, vol. 4 (1969), pp. 2977–3011.                     Donald M. Roper

**Goldberg v. Kelly,** 397 U. S. 254 (1970), argued 13 Oct. 1969, decided 23 Mar. 1970 by vote of 6 to 3; Brennan for the Court; Black, Burger, Stewart in dissent. The procedure in New York City for the termination of welfare payments required seven-day notice and gave the welfare recipient the right to submit a written statement of protest. It did not, however, afford an evidentiary hearing before termination of benefits. The Court held that procedural *due process under the *Fourteenth Amendment required that welfare recipients be afforded an evidentiary hearing before termination of benefits.

The right to submit only a written statement, or affording a posttermination evidentiary hearing, did not meet requirements of due process. The pretermination hearing need not be, however, in the nature of a judicial or quasi-judicial trial. But the recipient must be afforded an opportunity to confront and cross-examine witnesses, to retain an attorney if so desired, and to present oral evidence to an impartial decision maker, whose conclusion must rest solely on legal rules and evidence adduced at the hearing.

While the state has an interest in conserving fiscal and administrative resources, this interest is outweighed by the interest of the recipient in uninterrupted receipt of public assistance, which is not mere charity but a means to promote the *general welfare. The governmental interests that prompt the provision of welfare prompt as well its uninterrupted provision to those eligible to receive it. Welfare benefits, the Court said, "are a matter of statutory entitlement for persons qualified to receive them" (p. 262). The Court thus injected the concept of "entitlement" into the concept of *property right protected by the Due Process Clause.                     Milton R. Konvitz

**Gold Clause Cases** (1935), common collective name for three companion cases of the New Deal era: *Norman* v. *Baltimore & Ohio Railroad Co.,* 294 U.S. 240; *Nortz* v. *United States,* 294 U.S. 317; and *Perry* v. *United States,* 294 U.S. 330. All three argued 8–11 Jan. 1935, decided 18 Feb. 1935 by votes of 5 to 4; Hughes for the Court, McReynolds in dissent in each case. As part of the New Deal program to conserve gold reserves during the economic emergency of the Great Depression, Congress in 1933 abrogated the clauses in private and public contracts stipulating payment in gold. Consequently, such obligations could be paid in devalued currency. In these three cases, bondholders challenged this action as a breach of the obligation of *contract and a deprivation of property without *due process.

Speaking for the Court, Chief Justice Charles Evans *Hughes sustained the power of Congress to regulate the monetary system. He ruled that the gold clauses in private contracts were merely provisions for payment in money. Further, Hughes concluded that Congress could override private contracts that conflicted with its constitutional authority over the monetary system. With respect to the gold clauses in government bonds, however, Hughes found that Congress had unconstitutionally impaired its own obligations. However, he determined that the bondholders could only recover nominal damages for breach of contract and thus could not sue in the Court of Claims. In a bitter dissenting opinion, Justice James C. *McReynolds charged that the congressional action portended confiscation of property and financial chaos. He extemporaneously declared that "this is Nero at his worst."

Although the Supreme Court in effect permitted Congress to impair existing contracts, the *Gold Clause Cases* reaffirmed comprehensive congressional power over monetary policy. Moreover, as a practical matter, enforcement of the gold clauses would have had a deleterious impact on the depressed national economy.

(See also CONTRACTS CLAUSE.)

James W. Ely, Jr.

**Goldfarb v. Virginia State Bar,** 421 U.S. 773 (1975), argued 25 Mar. 1975, decided 16 June 1975 by vote of 8 to 0; Burger for the Court, Powell not participating.

The Goldfarbs were unable to find a lawyer

who would perform a real estate title examination for a fee less than that prescribed in a minimum fee schedule published by the Fairfax County [Virginia] Bar Association and enforced by the Virginia State Bar. They alleged that the fee schedule constituted price fixing, in violation of section 1 of the *Sherman Antitrust Act.

The Supreme Court found that the bar association's activities constituted a classic case of price fixing. The fee schedule established a rigid price floor; every lawyer contacted by the petitioners adhered to it; no lawyer would charge less. Moreover, ethics opinions issued by the Virginia bar threatened disciplinary action for regularly charging less than the suggested minimum fee. Since only attorneys licensed to practice in Virginia could legally examine a title, consumers had no alternative but to pay the prescribed fee.

The Court also held that because a substantial portion of the funds used for purchasing homes in Fairfax County came from outside Virginia, interstate commerce was sufficiently affected to bring this action under the Sherman Act (see COMMERCE POWER). It rejected the contention that Congress never intended to include "learned professions" within the meaning of "trade or commerce" in section 1 of the Sherman Act. Moreover, the Court held that such anticompetitive activities were not exempt from the Sherman Act as "state action."

In holding that minimum fee schedules violate federal *antitrust law, Goldfarb opened the door to price competition in legal services. Perhaps the greatest immediate impact of the Court's decision was the development of low-cost legal clinics that handle relatively routine matters such as wills and divorces.                    Beth M. Henschen

**Goldwater v. Carter,** 444 U.S. 996 (1979), decided 13 Dec. 1979 by vote of 6 to 3 (certiorari granted, vacated, and remanded with directions to dismiss the complaint); Rehnquist, Burger, Stewart, Powell, Stevens, and Marshall concurring, Brennan, White and Blackmun in dissent. Senator Barry Goldwater and other members of Congress challenged President Jimmy Carter's termination of the Mutual Defense Treaty with Taiwan without consulting or securing the prior approval of the Senate. Article II, section 2, clause 2 of the Constitution states that the president has the power to make treaties, provided that two-thirds of the Senate concur. However, the Constitution does not address the question of how a treaty may be abrogated.

The Supreme Court summarily reversed a *court of appeals decision holding that the president had authority to terminate a treaty without congressional approval. Justice William *Rehnquist, in a concurring opinion joined by Chief Justice Warren *Burger and Justices Potter *Stewart and John Paul *Stevens, argued that this was a nonjusticiable political question because it involved the "authority of the President in the conduct of our country's foreign relations . . . specifically a treaty commitment to use military force in the defense of a foreign government if attacked" (pp. 1002–1004). The Court was "asked to settle a dispute between coequal branches of government, each of which has resources available to protect and assert its interests, resources not available to private litigants outside the judicial forum" (p. 1004). Justice Lewis *Powell concurred separately, arguing that the issue was not "ripe" for judicial decision since Congress had not yet confronted the president about the treaty (see RIPENESS AND IMMEDIACY).

In dissent, Justice William *Brennan argued that the political question doctrine does not apply when the Court merely examines whether a particular branch has been "constitutionally designated as the repository of political decision-making power" (p. 1007). This was a constitutional law question, he said, that falls within the competency of the courts. Addressing the merits of the case, Brennan argued that since abrogation of the Taiwan Defense Treaty was related to the president's decision to recognize the government of mainland China, and since the president alone has the power to recognize foreign governments, he had the authority to abrogate the treaty.

(See also FOREIGN AFFAIRS AND FOREIGN POLICY; POLITICAL QUESTIONS; TREATIES AND TREATY POWER.)

Joel B. Grossman

**Gomillion v. Lightfoot,** 364 U.S. 339 (1960), argued 18–19 Oct. 1960, decided 14 Nov. 1960 by vote of 9 to 0; Frankfurter for the Court, Douglas and Whittaker concurring. Black voters charged that an Alabama law, changing the city boundaries of Tuskegee in such a way as to exclude all but four or five black voters without eliminating any white ones, was unconstitutional. A federal district court dismissed the complaint and the Court of Appeals for the Fifth Circuit affirmed. The Supreme Court reversed unanimously.

That the Supreme Court would in 1960 strike down this obvious race-based denial of constitutional rights is not so unusual. What is interesting is that Justice Felix *Frankfurter had to find a way to skirt his own *Colegrove v. Green (1946) holding that questions relating to legislative apportionment are nonjusticiable *"political questions" and thus outside the scope of federal judicial power. Frankfurter felt strongly that federal courts should not enter the reapportionment battlefield, but he was equally passionately against racial discrimination. To reconcile these two values, he keyed his Gomillion decision to *Fifteenth Amendment rather than to *Fourteenth Amendment grounds. "The appellants in Colegrove," he wrote, "complained only of a dilution of the strength of their votes as a result of legislative inaction over the course of many years. The petitioners here complain that affirmative legislative action deprives them of their votes. . . . When a legislature thus singles out a readily isolated segment of a racial minority for special discriminatory treatment, it violates the Fifteenth Amendment. . . . [A]part from all else, these considerations lift this controversy out of the so-called 'political' arena and into the conventional sphere of constitutional litigation" (pp. 346, 347).

Justices William O. *Douglas and Charles *Whittaker, concurring separately, would have struck down Alabama's action as a violation of the Fourteenth Amendment.

*Gomillion's* opening of federal courts to charges of racial *gerrymandering reflected no softening in Frankfurter's views that courts should stay out of legislative apportionment issues, but it did encourage urban interests to keep pressing federal courts for relief. A few days after *Gomillion*, the Court noted probable jurisdiction in *Baker* v. *Carr* (1962), which did directly raise the *justiciability of *reapportionment cases.

(See also, RACE AND RACISM; VOTE, RIGHT TO.)
J. W. Peltason

**Gompers v. Buck's Stove & Range Co.,** 221 U.S. 418 (1911), argued 27 and 30 Jan. 1911, decided 15 May 1911 by vote of 9 to 0; Lamar for the Court. When workers struck the Bucks Stove Company, the American Federation of Labor organized a boycott of the company's products. The manufacturer secured an *injunction against the boycott, from which the union planned an appeal. Before it could do so the company sought a criminal *contempt citation against Samuel Gompers and two other union leaders, claiming that they had violated the injunction by publishing the company's name on its "Unfair" and "We don't patronize" lists in *The American Federationist.* The defendants appealed the citation, claiming that what they printed in the paper was protected *speech under the *First Amendment, an argument the Court completely ignored. While he reversed the criminal contempt citation on a technicality, Justice Joseph *Lamar's opinion made it clear that the Court sided with employers in their battles against labor. Lamar cited approvingly one case after another to demonstrate that the courts frowned on any action, including speech, that injured *property rights.

(See also LABOR.)
Melvin I. Urofsky

**Good Faith Exception.** See LEON, UNITED STATES V.

**Graham v. Richardson,** 403 U.S. 365 (1971), argued 22 Mar. 1971, decided 14 June 1971 by vote of 9 to 0; Blackmun for the Court, Harlan specially concurring. This Supreme Court case established the doctrine that alienage, like race, is a suspect

classification under the *Fourteenth Amendment. Aliens are such, said the Court, because they are a discrete and politically powerless minority. As a result, governmental classifications based on alienage are subject to *strict scrutiny; to pass muster constitutionally, they must be closely related to a compelling governmental interest.

In this case, Arizona regulations conditioning the receipt of welfare benefits either on U.S. citizenship or residence within the United States for a specified number of years failed to meet this test and thereby violated the Equal Protection Clause. The states in question justified their regulations on the basis of their special public interest in favoring their own residents over aliens in the dispersal of limited public resources.

In voiding the state residency requirements, the Supreme Court provided an alternative basis for its decision: the Constitution grants the federal government authority to admit aliens and the conditions under which they may reside in the United States. State laws disabling aliens, as in *Graham*, may interfere with overriding federal policies and thereby violate the Supremacy Clause.

Decisions subsequent to *Graham*—such as *Foley* v. *Connelie* (1978) and *Ambach* v. *Norwick* (1979)—have intimated that federal classifications based on alienage may demand lesser scrutiny while those of the states will be scrutinized under the Supremacy, rather than the Equal Protection, Clause. The Court has also held that a denial of essential services such as Medicare would be scrutinized more carefully than barriers to other programs. But it did uphold the ineligibility of non–permanently resident aliens for the Medicare Supplemental Medical Insurance Program in *Mathews* v. *Diaz* (1976).

(See also ALIENAGE AND NATURALIZATION; EQUAL PROTECTION; SUSPECT CLASSIFICATIONS.)
Harold J. Spaeth

**Grandfather Clause,** an exemption of current rights-holders and sometimes their descendants from a new regulation or legal qualification. More specifically, the phrase refers to the release of men eligible for the suffrage in 1867, and their legal progeny, from literacy or property requirements for voting established by six southern states in the late nineteenth and early twentieth centuries. This transparently racist attempt to circumvent the *Fifteenth Amendment actually derived from a law that preserved the rights of some black voters. The grandfather of the grandfather clause was a Connecticut law of 1818 that disfranchised all African-Americans in the future but allowed those currently eligible to continue to *vote. In 1857 Massachusetts, in a nativist reaction against the massive influx of Irish immigrants during the potato famine, instituted a literacy test for the franchise but excused any man already registered.

In a widely circulated pamphlet published in 1879, aristocratic South Carolina lawyer Edward McCrady, Jr., proposed that the South copy the Massachusetts literacy test, including the 1857 date, to ensure that older white illiterates would remain enfranchised. If the 1857 date was legal in Massachusetts in 1857, he apparently reasoned, it was legal in South Carolina in 1879. Other southern disfranchisers added lineage to McCrady's racist exemption or modified it to allow illiterate ex-soldiers, including Confederates and their sons and grandsons, to vote. The Supreme Court invalidated the Oklahoma grandfather clause in *Guinn v. United States* (1915), holding that it violated the Fifteenth Amendment.

(See also RACE AND RACISM.)

J. Morgan Kousser

**Grand Juries.** The American grand jury has its origin in English law. The earliest manifestation appears to have developed toward the end of the tenth century, when leading citizens were summoned to court to report what crimes had been committed in their communities. A more direct antecedent is the Clarendon jury of inquest of 1166, which was established in each community by Henry II as an accusatory body of twelve "good and lawful men." It reported all offenses that had been (or were said to have been) committed in the venue to a group of knights who, in turn, reported the accusations to visiting royal officers (justices). The reports of the juries of inquest became the key instrument for initiating criminal proceedings. When *trail by jury replaced oath-taking, battle, and ordeal (after the Fourth Lateran Council in 1215), jurors were drawn initially from among the members of the jury of inquest.

Grand and *petit juries became distinct entities by the middle of the fourteenth century. The modern form of the grand jury dates from 1368, when Edward III appointed twenty-four men to an inquisitorial and accusatory board in each English county. It required another three hundred years (the *Colledge* and *Shaftesbury* cases of 1681) before the grand jury gained the function that is now regarded as its prime virtue and justification: the protection of citizens from unwarranted, malicious, and political prosecutions.

The grand jury came to the American colonies as part of English law. As conflicts developed with the mother country, the colonists made use of the grand jury's protective functions by, for example, refusing to authorize prosecutions sought by the crown. The most famous example was the *Zenger* case of 1735. The American grand jury served as an instrument of resistance, as a revolutionary organizing body, and as an arm of democratic self-government. The *Fifth Amendment to the Constitution of the United States mirrors colonial esteem by providing that "no person shall be held to answer for a capital or otherwise infamous crime, unless on a presentment or indictment of a grand jury."

The U.S. Supreme Court, in *Wood v. Georgia* (1962), stated that the grand jury always

has been regarded as a primary security to the innocent against hasty, malicious and oppressive persecution; it serves the invaluable function in our society of standing between the accuser and the accused . . . to determine whether a charge is founded upon reason or was dictated by an intimidating power or by malice and personal ill will. (p. 390)

In *United States v. Calandra* (1974) the Court also affirmed extraordinary powers and a wide procedural latitude for the grand jury. It guaranteed that the proceedings of grand juries be secret in *United States v. Procter & Gamble Co.* (1958). In *In re Horowitz* (1973) the Court affirmed the grand jury's extensive powers to compel the appearance of witnesses, their testimony under oath, and their production of documents. The Court held in *Branzburg v. Hayes* (1972) that not even newspaper reporters' sources of information are immune from the grand jury's *subpoena power.

Persons appearing before the grand jury enjoy few procedural rights. The public prosecutor is not obligated to present exculpatory evidence, and the witness has no right to do so. The accused cannot confront and cross-examine his accusers. No warnings are required regarding *self-incrimination (*United States v. Wong*, 1977). The likelihood of a criminal prosecution need not be pointed out (*United States v. Washington*, 1977). Witnesses can be granted immunity against their will. This may be "transactional" immunity (*Brown v. Walker*, 1896), but it is more likely to be the considerably more hazardous "use" immunity (*Kastigar v. United States*, 1972). The protection against *double jeopardy does not apply to grand jury proceedings. Hearsay evidence may be taken into account and the *exclusionary rule does not apply (*United States v. Calandra*). Although a witness may ask leave to step outside for consultation, he has no right to be advised by his attorney in the grand jury room (*United States v. Mandujano*, 1976). Interestingly, the Court has not extended the right to a grand jury hearing and indictment to state proceedings (*Hurtado v. California*, 1884). Fewer than one-half of the states now use grand juries; the majority authorize prosecutions by way of preliminary hearings before a magistrate.

The qualifications for grand jury service generally include *citizenship, the ability to read and write English, mental soundness, and minimum age and residency requirements. The size of most federal grand juries is twenty-three. Sixteen grand jurors constitute a quorum; twelve must agree to issue an indictment. The term of service typically is from three to eighteen months but can be extended. The Federal Jury Selection and Service Act of 1968 requires grand jurors to be drawn at random from a fair cross-section of the community, without attention to race, color, religion, sex, national origin, or economic status. (See also FIFTH AMENDMENT IMMUNITY.)

□ LeRoy Clark, *The Grand Jury* (1972). Marvin E. Frankel and Gary P. Naftalis, *The Grand Jury: An Institution on Trial* (1977). Richard D. Younger, *The People's Panel: The Story of the Grand Jury* (1963). Peter W. Sperlich

**Granger Cases.** See CHICAGO, BURLINGTON & QUINCY RAILROAD CO. V. CHICAGO; MUNN V. ILLINOIS.

**Graves v. New York ex rel. O'Keefe,** 306 U.S. 466 (1939), argued 6 Mar. 1939, decided 27 Mar. 1939 by vote of 7 to 2; Stone for the Court, Hughes and Frankfurter concurring, Butler and McReynolds in dissent. Until this case, there had been an explicit immunity of state employees from federal taxation and federal employees from state taxes, going back to the 1871 decision in *Collector* v. *Day.* This immunity had been reinforced in the famous Income Tax Cases (see *\*Pollock* v. *Farmers' Loan & Trust,* 1895), in which the Court had held that a tax on income was a tax on the source of that income.

New York imposed an income tax on a New York resident employed by the Federal Home Owners Loan Corporation, who paid the tax and then appealed on the basis of intergovernmental tax immunity. The Court held that nothing in the Constitution required such an immunity, nor did any act of Congress specifically grant immunity to federal employees. The Court thus concluded that salaries of federal employees were subject to regular state taxes.

Justice Harlan Fiske \*Stone's opinion specifically overruled *Collector* v. *Day* and other cases supporting immunity as well as the doctrine that a tax on income constitutes a tax on the source of that income.

Later in the year Congress enacted the Public Salary Tax Act, specifically extending federal income taxes to state employees and also consenting to state taxes on the incomes of federal employees, although under the ruling in this case such consent was no longer necessary. (See also TAX IMMUNITIES.) Melvin I. Urofsky

**Gray, Horace** (b. Boston, Mass., 24 March 1828; d. Nahant, Mass., 15 Sept. 1902; interred Mt. Auburn Cemetery, Cambridge, Mass.), associate justice, 1882–1902. Energized by temporary family financial reverses, Gray studied law at Harvard and was admitted to the Massachusetts bar in 1851. From 1853 to 1861 he gained visibility as the reporter of the decisions of the Supreme Judicial Court. In 1864 Gray became the youngest man ever appointed to the Massachusetts Supreme Court; nine years later he became its chief justice.

Gray was a prodigious worker and legal

*Horace Gray*

scholar. His manner was formal and unyielding, and he did not hesitate to instruct lawyers upon proper behavior and dress. While on the Massachusetts court Gray employed recent Harvard Law School graduates, recommended by his half-brother Professor John Chipman Gray, as his temporary law clerks. (Louis D. \*Brandeis served in this capacity from 1879 to 1881.) Gray continued this practice on the U.S. Supreme Court, and in time it became the rule in the American judiciary.

Massachusetts Senator George F. Hoar, a former classmate, claimed credit for Gray's appointment to the U.S. Supreme Court, but the nomination had such considerable support that the candidacy seemed irresistible. President James Garfield died before he could act upon it, and the formal nomination came with his successor, Chester A. Arthur. In Washington, Gray found new stature and also a wife, when on 4 June 1889 he married Jane Matthews, the daughter of his recently deceased colleague, Stanley Matthews.

The Supreme Court that Gray joined in early 1882 was in transition, moving from a steadfast defense of the federal structure to a greater willingness to find new reservoirs of national power in the Constitution (see FEDERALISM). Gray's reputed nationalism rests on *Juilliard* v. *Greenman* (1884) and *Fong Yue Ting* v. *United States* (1893) in which he saw no constitutional limits on congressional authority, respectively, to issue paper money and to deal with resident aliens. However, despite a reluctance to dissent, he opposed the Court's development of substantive *due process as a limitation on *state action, its search for avenues of escape from the confines of the *Eleventh Amendment, and its commerce clause inroads on state police power. He saw one of his dissents vindicated when Congress passed legislation allowing states to prohibit the shipment of liquor into their jurisdiction.

Of all the decisions in which Gray played a central role, the most notable was *United States* v. *Wong Kim Ark* (1898). Congress had declared Chinese ineligible for naturalization but held that their children born in the United States were citizens. Using Anglo-American common law as his guide, he interpreted the *Fourteenth Amendment as commanding that *citizenship be made a birthright, no matter the claimant's race or national origin.

Gray's heavy-handed, drawn-out opinions that often turned into scholarly historical essays took substantial time to construct, and in his later years his vigor and capacity for work diminished. When a stroke left him partially paralyzed, he resigned contingent on the appointment of his successor. He died before the confirmation of Oliver Wendell *Holmes, who at the time held the same judicial post vacated by Gray twenty years earlier.

□ Elbridge B. Davis and Harold A. Davis, "Mr. Justice Gray: Some Aspects of His Judicial Career," *American Bar Association Journal* 41 (May 1955): 421–424, 468–471.

John E. Semonche

**Gray v. Sanders,** 372 U.S. 368 (1963), argued 17 Jan 1963, decided 18 Mar. 1963 by vote of 8 to 1; Douglas for the Court, Stewart and Clark concurring, Harlan in dissent. Concerned with inequality of voting power, *Gray* v. *Sanders* proved to be the jurisprudential steppingstone between *Baker* v. *Carr* (1962) and the 1964 legislative *reapportionment cases.

*Gray* involved a challenge to Georgia's system that decided primary elections for statewide and congressional offices by county units in a pattern severely weighted against urban areas. Candidates who won the popular vote could, and at times did, lose the election. The Georgia statute had survived several earlier appeals to the Supreme Court, but the decision in *Baker* v. *Carr* triggered a fresh one.

Invoking the *Equal Protection Clause of the *Fourteenth Amendment, the Supreme Court upheld a federal district court's invalidation of the Georgia county unit system but set aside as "inapposite" the lower tribunal's suggested alternative analogous to the national Electoral College.

The Supreme Court declared *Gray* v. *Sanders* to be a voting rights case without implications for

legislative representation—a point stressed by concurring Justices Potter *Stewart and Tom C. *Clark. Yet Justice William O. *Douglas, speaking for the Court, concluded on a broader note that was to be sounded in subsequent reapportionment cases: "The conception of political equality from the Declaration of Independence, to Lincoln's Gettysburg Address, to the *Fifteenth, *Seventeenth, and *Nineteenth Amendments can mean only one thing—one person, one vote" (p. 381).

In dissent, Justice John M. *Harlan found the record inadequate to prove invidious effects in a matter profoundly touching the barrier between federal judicial and state legislative authority. To Harlan, *Gray* seemed one more judicial step into the forbidden *"political thicket."

(See also FAIR REPRESENTATION; VOTE, RIGHT TO.)

Gordon E. Baker

**Greenberg, Jack** (b. Brooklyn, N.Y., 22 Dec. 1924), lawyer. Greenberg joined the *NAACP *Legal Defense Fund (LDF) as a staff counsel in 1949 and became director-counsel in 1961 when Thurgood *Marshall was appointed a judge on the Court of Appeals for the Second Circuit. Some supporters of the LDF criticized Greenberg's promotion on the ground that Robert Carter, an African-American who had been associated with the NAACP since 1945, should have become director. Greenberg guided the LDF during the period of substantial implementation of the desegregation decisions in the Deep South, coordinated the group's challenge to the death penalty (see CAPITAL PUNISHMENT), and instituted a substantial program of employment discrimination litigation under Title VII of the *Civil Rights Act of 1964. He retired from the LDF in 1984 to become a professor at Columbia Law School, then dean of the college at Columbia University.

Mark V. Tushnet

**Green v. Biddle,** 8 Wheat. (21 U.S.) 1 (1823), argued 16 Feb. 1821, decided 5 Mar. 1821 by vote of 6 to 0; Story for the Court, Washington absent. Motion for rehearing 12 Mar. 1821, reargued 8–11 Mar. 1822; decided 27 Feb. 1823 by vote of 4 to 0; Washington for the Court, Johnson concurring, Livingston, Todd, and Marshall absent. The decisions in *Green* v. *Biddle* were the Court's most important effort after *Fletcher* v. *Peck* (1810) to expand the Contracts Clause to encompass public as well as private agreements—in this case, the Virginia-Kentucky compact of 1792.

The compact provided that the validity of Kentucky land titles was to be "determined by the laws now existing," that is, Virginia's. Kentucky, however, enacted a system of Occupying Claimant Laws, providing that actual settlers, if ejected by nonresident titleholders, could secure compensation for improvements and crops. Litigation testing the validity of Kentucky's 1792 and

1812 occupant laws went up to the Supreme Court on a certificate of division from the federal circuit court in a case brought against an occupant by John Green of Virginia. Justice Joseph *Story delivered an opinion in 1821 holding the Occupying Claimant Laws unconstitutional as a violation of the Contracts Clause of Article I, section 10 and inconsistent with the Compacts Clause in the same section.

Story's opinion encountered a storm of political opposition led by Kentucky's two powerful senators, Henry Clay and Richard Johnson. In the face of this resistance, the Story opinion was "withdrawn," to be replaced by an 1823 opinion for three justices by Bushrod *Washington, joined by William *Johnson's concurring opinion. (Chief Justice John *Marshall was absent, Brockholst *Livingston mortally ill, and Thomas *Todd "indisposed.") Washington's opinion held the Virginia-Kentucky compact to be a contract and as such inviolate under the Contracts Clause, but impaired by the Kentucky statutes. Kentucky again resisted vehemently and continued to enforce its land claims statutes, while the furor in Congress over the authority of the Supreme Court continued unabated.

(See also CONTRACTS CLAUSE.)

Sandra F. VanBurkleo

**Green v. County School Board of New Kent County,** 391 U.S. 430 (1968), argued 3 Apr. 1968, decided 27 May 1968 by vote of 9 to 0; Brennan for the Court. Characterized by the Court simply as a case about the appropriate scope of a school *desegregation remedy under *Brown v. Board of Education II (1955), Green was a watershed in the definition—or redefinition—of the substantive right enshrined in Brown I.

Virginia was one of four states whose racially segregated school systems were constitutionally challenged in the litigation collectively styled by the name of the lead case, Brown v. Board of Education I. For a decade after Brown II Virginia disingenuously handled compliance with Brown on a statewide basis by a State Pupil Assignment Law, which substantially impeded desegregation. Under threat of losing federal monies in 1965, the law was scrapped and the New Kent County school board adopted a "freedom-of-choice plan," which essentially allowed students in the rural, residentially integrated district to choose which of two schools they wished to attend—the formerly all-black Watkins School or the formerly all-white New Kent School. After three years of the new plan, no whites had elected to attend Watkins and only 115 blacks attended New Kent; 85 percent of blacks in the system still attended Watkins. The plaintiff black school children argued that the "freedom-of-choice plan" in practice operated to perpetuate the racially dual school system formerly mandated by state law.

Writing for the Court, Justice William J. *Brennan framed the decisive issue in the case as whether the "freedom-of-choice plan" complied with Brown II. In an opinion that purported to be carefully limited, Brennan noted that "[w]e do not hold that a 'freedom-of-choice' plan might of itself be held unconstitutional . . . but [only] that in desegregating a dual system a plan utilizing 'freedom of choice' is not an end in itself" (pp. 439–440). The appropriate end to the Court was a plan that "promise[d] realistically to convert promptly to a system without a 'white' school and a 'Negro' school, but just schools" (p. 442).

The Court's underlying rationale was that a variety of factors, not necessarily found as fact by the trial court in Green but identified in federal studies, made "freedom of choice" unlikely to work—fear of hostility or retaliation to those electing to change schools, undue influence by public officials and private parties, ancillary effects of poverty, and unequal facilities between schools. Because of such factors, the Court concluded that freedom of choice was likely to fail to accomplish what Brown II required, the disestablishment of a dual system.

Green is the most significant school case decided after Brown II. Under a narrow reading of both Brown opinions, formerly state-segregated school systems could discharge their constitutional obligations by removing legally imposed attendance assignments based on race. Indeed, for a brief period, the *National Association for the Advancement of Colored People (NAACP), which had brought Brown and its precursors, urged its local affiliates after Brown II to request "freedom of choice plans."

In the face of southern "massive resistance" to desegregation, and later of white flight first to private schools and then simply away from areas populated by black families, the NAACP changed its strategy to press for the type of relief sought, and eventually approved, in Green. The thrust of Brown was thus recast as one directed at the effects of dual systems instead of at their basis. The consequence was that compliance with Brown, at least in formerly state-segregated (de jure) systems, could soon only be demonstrated by schools with racial composition reflecting the school-age population. As white flight accelerated, only busing could achieve Green's objective. NAACP counsel conceded during oral argument in Green that the new remedy paradoxically required the states and the Court to sanction what Brown notionally condemned—racially based pupil assignments. On a less conspicuous level, Green also diverted the emphasis in school desegregation from equality of educational opportunity to numerical congruity in school attendance.

(See also EDUCATION; RACE AND RACISM.)

Dennis J. Hutchinson

**Gregg v. Georgia,** 428 U.S. 153 (1976), argued 31 Mar. 1976, decided 2 July 1976 by a vote of 7 to 2;

Stewart announced the decision in an opinion joined by Powell and Stevens; White, Burger, Rehnquist, and Blackmun concurring; Brennan and Marshall in dissent. With two companion cases from Florida and Texas, the Supreme Court reaffirmed the constitutionality of the death penalty in the wake of *Furman* v. *Georgia* (1972). The justices in *Gregg* upheld statutes that guide judge and jury when imposing the death penalty. The Court rejected claims that *capital punishment was unconstitutional per se but implied strongly that mandatory death penalty statutes would violate the *Eighth Amendment's proscription of *cruel and unusual punishment. *Woodson* v. *North Carolina* (1976) decided the same day, specifically outlawed the mandatory death sentence.

Gregg had been convicted of two counts of armed robbery and two counts of murder. The Georgia death penalty statute provided guidelines for the jury to follow in the sentencing stage of a bifurcated trial. The statute required the jury to find beyond a reasonable doubt and to specify in writing that at least one of ten specified aggravating circumstances existed before it could impose the death penalty. The aggravating circumstances included whether the accused (1) created a great risk of death to more than one person in a public place; (2) acted as either the agent of or the principal for another in the commission of a murder; (3) had a prior conviction for a capital felony; (4) had escaped from custody; or (5) had killed a firefighter or a criminal justice system officer in the performance of that officer's duties. The Georgia Supreme Court had previously struck down as insufficiently clear and objective an aggravating circumstance in which the offender had "a substantial history of serious assaultive criminal convictions."

The Georgia statute also required consideration of such mitigating circumstances as the offender's youth, cooperation with the police, and emotional state at the time of the offense. And it provided mandatory review of death sentences by the Georgia Supreme Court to consider whether (1) the sentence was influenced by passion, prejudice, or any other arbitrary factor; (2) the evidence supported the finding of an aggravated circumstance; and (3) the penalty was excessive or disproportionate in relation to similar cases and defendants.

The trial judge in *Gregg* advised the jury that it could recommend the death sentence or life imprisonment for each count and that it was free to consider mitigating as well as aggravating circumstances. Specifically, he instructed the jury that it could not impose the death sentence unless it found beyond a reasonable doubt that the murders were committed in one or more of the three applicable aggravating circumstances, that is, during the commission of other capital crimes, for the purpose of receiving the victim's property, or that the crime was outrageously

heinous. The jury found the first two of these aggravating circumstances and imposed the death penalty on all counts. The Georgia Supreme Court found that the sentences for murder did not result from prejudice or other arbitrary factors and that they were not excessive in relation to the crime. But it reversed the sentences for robbery on the ground that the death penalty was rarely imposed for armed robbery in Georgia.

For the Supreme Court, Justice Potter *Stewart declared that the Eighth Amendment incorporated a "basic concept of human dignity." He found the death penalty was not cruel and unusual per se. The *Fifth and *Fourteenth Amendments' due process clauses imply it. More important, the concept of dignity is consistent with the purposes of deterrence and of retribution. In light of evolving standards of decency, the penalty, according to Stewart, is constitutional when it is proportional to the severity of the crime (not arbitrary) and is not a wanton infliction of pain. Legislatures need not prove that the death penalty deters, nor need they select the least severe penalty possible. Legislative choices of penalties thus carry a heavy presumption of validity. Stewart also emphasized that constitutional acknowledgment and public acceptance of the death penalty strengthen its presumptive validity and that retribution is a valid legislative consideration.

The Georgia statute, according to Stewart, effectively prevents arbitrary and disproportionate death sentences (1) because the bifurcated procedure allows full exploration of the evidence relating to the penalty; (2) because the sentencing body must make specific factual findings to support the result; and (3) because state supreme court review insures comparability and proportionality among defendants who receive the death penalty. Stewart rejected the argument that prosecutorial discretion, *plea bargaining and executive clemency, which introduce elements of randomness that comparability studies will not detect, made the death penalty arbitrary and hence in violation of the Eighth Amendment. He also endorsed Georgia's requirement that the sentencing body consider a broad scope of evidence and argument before determining the sentence.

Justice Byron *White, joined by Warren *Burger and William *Rehnquist, stated that Gregg had failed in his burden of showing that the Georgia Supreme Court had not in this case insured against discriminatory, freakish, or wanton administration of the death penalty. Nor had he demonstrated that the Georgia Supreme Court could not adequately do so in any and all cases. White also insisted that rational considerations, for example, the strength of evidence and the likelihood that the jury would in fact impose the penalty, determine the prosecutor's discretionary decision whether to seek the death penalty. Therefore, limited prosecutorial discretion did not make the penalty unconstitutionally arbitrary.

Basic criticisms of the reasoning in *Gregg* focus on the plurality's failure to connect persuasively its initial claim that the Eighth Amendment embodies a basic concept of human dignity with its conclusion that sentences may consider a wide range of information in deciding whether to apply the penalty. If, in other words, human dignity stands as an independent moral criterion for deciding when a punishment is cruel and unusual, then the plurality should have read into the amendment the specific moral and factual conditions that aggravate and mitigate the case for capital punishment.

By failing to do so, the Supreme Court gave little guidance to legislatures attempting to draft a death penalty statute with respect to (1) the criteria for choosing aggravating and mitigating circumstances; (2) the breadth of discretion sentencing bodies should retain once the circumstances are known; and (3) how the sentencing body will in practice determine whether a given circumstance does or does not exist. Indeed, without settling such matters it is difficult to see how an appellate court on mandatory review can determine that the requirement for comparability has been met, except by resorting to gross statistical comparisons. Such comparisons would violate the Court's requirement that juries take account of mitigating circumstances. A mandatory death penalty applied in narrowly defined circumstances would apparently achieve proportionality more effectively, but *Woodson v. North Carolina* struck down mandatory sentences precisely because they would not permit considering mitigating circumstances.

It is equally difficult to square the autonomous human dignity standard with the plurality's endorsement of retribution and deterrence. Penological evidence does not support the proposition that the death penalty serves effectively as either a general or a specific deterrent, and retribution lies too close to vengeance to accept as an unquestioned component of human dignity. Yet the plurality made no serious attempt to defend deterrence or retribution on either rational or human-dignity grounds. Similarly, the obvious randomizing tendencies introduced by prosecutorial discretion, plea bargaining, and executive clemency cried out for a human-dignity defense, but the plurality dismissed this difficulty without serious discussion. In short, *Gregg* failed to specify conditions and procedures for restricting in practice the arbitrariness it condemned. Justices William *Brennan and Thurgood *Marshall noted these points in dissent.

□ Hugo Adam Bedau, ed., *The Death Penalty in America* (1982). Welsh S. White, *The Death Penalty in the Eighties: An Examination of the Modern System of Capital Punishment* (1987).                                    Lief H. Carter

**Grier, Robert Cooper** (b. Cumberland County, Pa., 5 Mar. 1794; d. Philadelphia, Pa., 25 Sep. 1870; interred West Laurel Hill Cemetery, Bala-Cynwyd, Pa.) associate justice, 1846–1870. The eldest of the eleven children of the Rev. Isaac Grier and Elizabeth Cooper, Grier grew up in Lycoming County, Pennsylvania, and then Northumberland, where his father farmed, preached, and taught school. Educated in his boyhood by his Presbyterian father, Grier enrolled as a junior at Dickinson College and graduated in 1812. After his father's death in 1815, Grier, at age twenty-one, assumed control of his father's academy and began studying law. Admitted to the Pennsylvania bar in 1817, he practiced in Bloomsburg and Danville, supported his mother, and provided for the education of his ten brothers and sisters. In 1829 he married the wealthy Isabella Rose.

In 1833 Grier was appointed judge of the Allegheny County district court. The appointment was something of a political accident, and his elevation to the supreme bench was equally accidental. Henry Baldwin, the "Pennsylvania Justice," had died in 1844, and Presidents John *Tyler and James K. Polk had been unable to find a successor until Polk nominated the noncontroversial (and almost unknown) Grier.

During his twenty-three years on the Court Grier occupied a middle ground. In the *License Cases* (1847), he upheld the states' *police power even when it interfered with interstate commerce, but he drew the line in the *Passenger Cases* (1849), which involved two states levying taxes on ship masters. The eventual solution, found in the decision in *Cooley v. Board of Wardens* (1852) and known as *"selective exclusiveness," met with Grier's approbation (see COMMERCE POWER).

In *Marshall* v. *Baltimore and Ohio Railroad Co.* (1853), Grier upheld the Court's jurisdiction in a *diversity of citizenship case involving corporations, but found the contract contrary to the public interest: lobbyists were "a compact corps of venal solicitors" (p. 335). Usually he supported states' rights, notably in *Woodruff v. Trapnall* (1850) and *Waring* v. *Clarke* (1847).

Grier identified with the southern wing of the Court in *slavery cases. In 1847 he irritated Pittsburgh abolitionists in his charge to the jury in a *fugitive slave case. In *Moore* v. *Illinois* (1852) he found constitutional sanction for *double jeopardy for those who aided runaways. But he refused to consider armed opposition to the Fugitive Slave Act as treason since it did not amount to levying war.

In *Dred *Scott v. Sandford* (1857) Grier played a minor role. Initially Grier wished to avoid the question of *citizenship for blacks, but the consensus broke down. Determined that the Court's vote not be strictly sectional, Justice John *Catron enlisted President James Buchanan to lobby Grier, who willingly promised his full support for Chief Justice Roger *Taney's opinion and indicated the direction the opinion would take. In his inaugural address of 4 March 1857, Buchanan disingenuously mentioned the case. When the decision was announced two days later, northern critics furiously charged *Taney with tipping off the president, although Grier was the real culprit.

Although known as a "doughface," a northern man with southern principles, Grier remained a committed Unionist. On the circuit in *United States* v. *William Smith* (1861), he instructed the jury that the Confederate government had no recognized legal existence, a view repeated that in the *Prize Cases* (1863), which sustained President Abraham *Lincoln's blockade and war policy. Grier was less supportive in other areas. He questioned the validity of the *income tax; opposed on circuit the confiscation of a newspaper; and interpreted narrowly the uses of paper money.

Grier opposed Radical *Reconstruction. In *Ex parte *Milligan* (1866) Grier sided with Justice David *Davis's extreme opinion and leaked the vote to Attorney General Orville Browning. He voted against test oaths in *Cummings* v. *Missouri* (1867) and *Ex parte *Garland* (1867) and opposed the delay in deciding *Ex parte *McCardle* (1869), which allowed time for Congress to remove the court's jurisdiction (see JUDICIAL POWER AND JURISDICTION). In *Texas* v. *White* (1869), he argued eloquently that the conquered Republic of Texas was politically not a state.

Grier's health declined seriously after 1867. In conference on the *Legal Tender Cases* (1870–1871), his mind and votes wandered. Justice Stephen Johnson *Field led a delegation urging his retirement, and Grier complied.

*Robert Cooper Grier*

Grier was a large, ruddy man given to trout fishing. He was at once a natural-born vulgarian—coarse and harsh—and an above-average writer with interests in Greek and Latin.

□ Don E. Fehrenbacher, *The Dred Scott Case; Its Significance in American Law and Politics* (1978). David M. Silver, *Lincoln's Supreme Court* (1957).     Michael B. Dougan

**Griffin v. California,** 380 U.S. 609 (1965) argued 9 Mar. 1965, decided 28 Apr. 1965 by vote of 7 to 2; Douglas for the Court, Stewart and White in dissent. The *Fifth Amendment's privilege against *self-incrimination, which binds the federal government, applies equally to the states through the *Due Process Clause of the *Fourteenth Amendment. The issue in this case was whether a state violates this privilege when it allows prosecutors and judges to comment adversely on a defendant's failure to testify in a criminal proceeding. In holding that it does, the Supreme Court said that such a practice makes the defendant pay a price for refusing to speak. He pays a price for his silence because the comments of the prosecutor or judge invite jurors to disregard the presumption of innocence to which he is constitutionally entitled. Even an innocent or honest person may have many reasons—timidity is one of them—for not taking the witness stand in his own defense. Needless to say, however, the privilege protects the guilty as well.

Allowing judges or jurors to draw inferences of guilt from the silence of the accused, remarked the Court, is a remnant of the inquisitorial system of criminal justice. Because the American system is accusatorial, the Fifth and Fourteenth Amendments must be construed to forbid comment on the defendant's failure to testify by either the prosecutor or the court. There is of course no way of keeping a jury from drawing an adverse inference from silence even in the absence of such commentary. But as the Court said, "[w]hat it may infer when the court solemnizes the silence of the accused into evidence against him is quite another [matter]" (p. 614). *Griffin* overruled *Adamson* v. *California* (1947).     Donald P. Kommers

**Griffin v. County School Board of Prince Edward County,** 377 U.S. 218 (1964), argued 30 Mar, 1964, decided 25 May 1964 by vote of 9 to 0; Black for the Court, Clark and Harlan concurring. Instead of complying with the mandate of *Brown* v. *Board of Education II* (1955) to eliminate racial assignments to public schools, the Prince Edward County, Virginia, Board of Education, pursuant to state law, closed its public schools and provided tuition grants and tax credits to private schools attended only by white children. Justice Hugo *Black's opinion for the Court impatiently swept aside plausible procedural defenses of the policy and announced that "[t]he time for mere 'deliberate speed' has run out" (p. 234), that the district court was empowered to enjoin further use of grants and credits, that the court could superintend the board's taxing and appropriation powers, and even that it could order the public schools reopened. On the final point, Justices Tom *Clark and John M. *Harlan "disagree[d]" without explanation—marking the first time since well before *Brown* that even partially dissenting views had been expressed in the Court with respect to litigation involving segregation and the *Fourteenth Amendment.

Of greater significance was the Court's unequivocal rejection of tactics designed to forestall compliance with *Brown II*. After *Griffin*, affected school districts appeared to choose between either desegregating their racially dual systems or acquiescing in white flight to private academies. (See also ALL DELIBERATE SPEED; DESEGREGATION REMEDIES; RACE AND RACISM.)

Dennis J. Hutchinson

**Griggs v. Duke Power Co.,** 401 U.S. 424 (1971), argued 14 Dec. 1970, decided 8 Mar. 1971 by vote of 8 to 0; Burger for the Court, Brennan not participating. *Griggs* is recognized as the most significant case in the development of *employment discrimination law under Title VII of the *Civil Rights Act of 1964. It provided new definitions of job discrimination that had far-reaching consequences.

The district court found that prior to the effective date of Title VII, the company discriminated on the basis of race in the hiring and assigning of workers at its facility in Draper, North Carolina. The company's longstanding practice was to hire blacks into an all-black labor classification where the highest paying job paid less than the lowest paying job in the all-white departments. Job promotion was based upon racial lines of progression within segregated departments. On 2 July 1965, the date on which Title VII became effective, the company established a new policy of requiring applicants for jobs in the traditional white classifications, including those who wished to transfer from other departments, to score acceptable grades on two aptitude tests in addition to fulfilling the requirement of a high school education. The district court held that the earlier practices "were beyond the reach" of Title VII and that the new tests were not intentionally discriminatory.

The Supreme Court overruled and held in favor of the black plaintiffs. It noted the systemic nature of employment discrimination and that Title VII was intended to eliminate such patterns of discrimination; thus the act required the removal of all barriers perpetuating the benefits that white employees obtain at the expense of blacks. Ostensibly neutral practices are unlawful, according to the Court, if they operate to maintain the effects of past discrimination.

The Court held further that intent or discriminatory purpose is irrelevant; it is conse-quences that matter. Tests used for hiring and promotion must be job related and validated under Equal Employment Opportunity Commission guidelines.

Finally the Court held invalid practices, however neutral in intent, that caused a *disparate impact upon a group protected by the act. The *Griggs* disparate impact concept was based on the Court's construction of section 702 (a) (2) of Title VII and has been successfully invoked in many contexts. Although Title VII law has continued to evolve and the burden of proof had shifted to plaintiffs, the basic holdings of *Griggs* remain valid.

In *Ward's Cove Packing Co.* v. *Atonio* (1989), the Court in a 5-to-4 decision revised the standards governing proof of discrimination in Title VII disparate impact cases. Under the standard established in *Griggs*, the burden was upon the employer to prove that any disparate impact caused by his practices was justified by business necessity. Under the standards required in *Ward's Cove*, the burden of proof remains with the plaintiff at all times. In *Price Waterhouse* v. *Hopkins* (1989), the Court shifted the burden of proof, holding that a disparate treatment plaintiff must demonstrate by direct evidence that employment practices substantially depended on illegitimate criteria. The *Civil Rights Act of 1991 altered the burden once again.

(See also RACE AND RACISM.)

Herbert Hill

**Griswold v. Connecticut** 381 U.S. 479 (1965), argued 29 Mar. 1965, decided 7 June 1965, by vote of 7 to 2; Douglas for the Court, Goldberg, Harlan, and White concurring, Black and Stewart in dissent. *Griswold* is a curious but important case in American constitutional history. It concerned an "uncommonly silly law" (as Justice Potter Stewart called it) that was technically difficult to challenge on constitutional grounds, as evidenced by the divergent positions of the justices concurring with the majority position. These opinions not only made *Griswold* one of the most significant decisions of the 1965 term but fueled controversies both about the general character of constitutional lawmaking and about specific rights that have continued decades later.

*Evolution of the Dispute.* A Connecticut statue of 1879 made it a crime for any person to use any drug, article, or instrument to prevent conception. This statute had been challenged twice before, in 1943 (*Tileston* v. *Ullman*), where the Supreme Court held that the plaintiff lacked *standing, and in 1961 (*Poe* v. *Ullman*), where the Court determined that the controversy was not ripe because the plaintiff had not been prosecuted (see RIPENESS AND IMMEDIACY).

By 1965, however, the Court determined to resolve the constitutionality of the statute. Suit was initiated by two members of the Planned Parenthood League of Connecticut. Its executive director and medical director had been convicted of violating the statute by giving information, instruction, and medical advice to married persons regarding means of preventing conception (see CONTRACEPTION). The conviction was affirmed by the Supreme Court of Errors of Connecticut.

On appeal, the United States Supreme Court reversed by a 7-to-2 margin. The majority determined that: (1) the appellants had standing to raise the constitutional rights of people with whom they had a professional relationship; and (2) the statute was invalid because it infringed on the constitutionally protected right to "privacy" of married persons.

*Implied Rights: The New Substantive Due Process?* The majority holding in *Griswold* to a large extent was positioned within post-1937 constitutional theory. It protected basic constitutional rights and applied them against the states in conventional fashion under the *Fourteenth Amendment, and it mandated a stricter scrutiny for laws that interfere with *"fundamental personal rights" than for those that regulate economic relations (see DUE PROCESS, SUBSTANTIVE). The Court's more controversial step of applying this logic to fundamental rights—here, of privacy—not expressly enumerated in the *Bill of Rights likewise was hardly unprecedented. The Court previously had affirmed the unwritten rights to teach one's child a foreign language (*Meyer* v. *Nebraska*, 1923), to send one's children to private schools (*Pierce* v. *Society of Sisters*, 1925), to procreate (*Skinner* v. *Oklahoma*, 1942), to resist certain invasions of the body (*Rochin* v. *California*, 1952), and to travel abroad (*Aptheker* v. *Secretary of State*, 1964). What made *Griswold* a landmark case was the Court's willingness to explicitly justify at length this practice of investing such unenumerated rights with full constitutional status.

It is on this point that the justices were most divided. Indeed, four different lines of justification in defense of unenumerated fundamental rights were outlined by supporters of the majority decision. Justice William O. *Douglas, writing for five members of the Court, referred to rights that are implicit in, or peripheral to, other express guarantees in the *Bill of Rights. In his famous words, "specific guarantees . . . have penumbras, formed by emanations from those guarantees that help give them life and substance" (p. 484). Just as the Court earlier had found that *First Amendment rights to freedom of speech implied a peripheral "right to freedom of association," he reasoned, so do the First, *Third, *Fourth, *Fifth, and *Ninth Amendments imply "zones of privacy" that form the basis for the general privacy right affirmed in this case.

Justice Arthur *Goldberg, joined by Chief Justice Earl *Warren and Justice William *Brennan, staked out a more expansive approach to justifying the right of privacy. Although he found

merit in the penumbra and emanations argument of Douglas, Goldberg argued further that "liberty protects those personal rights that are fundamental, and is not confined to the specific terms of the Bill of Rights." The *Fourteenth Amendment may not incorporate all of the first eight amendments, Goldberg acknowledged. However, the specific "language and history of the Ninth Amendment" provide strong support for judicial *incorporation of additional rights "so rooted in the traditions and conscience of our people as to be ranked fundamental" in our constitutional legacy (p. 487).

Justices John M. *Harlan and Byron *White advanced positions that, by contrast, severed altogether the link between the Fourteenth Amendment and the Bill of Rights. Harlan rejected the *incorporation doctrine as a historically groundless and ineffective check on judicial discretion, while reproaching the "letter or penumbra" logic of Douglas as overly restrictive of future rights development. Instead, he affirmed a commitment to due process and liberty that "stands . . . on its own bottom," constrained only by the forces of history and cultural values that bind the court. By this logic, the Connecticut statute violated basic values "implicit in the concept of ordered liberty" (p. 500). Justice White rooted his argument in a similarly expansive interpretation of Fourteenth Amendment due process guarantees but focused his attention on the terms of strict scrutiny by which the Court should balance fundamental rights of individuals with compelling state interests in such cases.

The dissents by Justices Hugo *Black and Potter *Stewart expressed the same disdain for the Connecticut statute as had the majority. However, both denied that the state law infringed upon any fundamental constitutional right. In their view, such a right—whether rooted in the "implied rights" theories of Douglas and Goldberg or, in the "natural justice" positions of Harlan and White—lacked specific constitutional authorization and represented an arbitrary exercise of judicial power that threatened the American system of government (see JUDICIAL SELF-RESTRAINT). "Use of any such broad, unbounded judicial authority would make of this Court's members a day-to-day constitutional convention," argued Black. This would amount to a "great unconstitutional shift of power to the courts which . . . will be bad for the courts and worse for the country" (p. 520).

Scholarly debate has amplified these disagreements among members of the Court. In particular, many critics of the decision have elaborated Black's charge that the majority was simply offering a new and unwarranted version of the old "substantive *due process" doctrine. Why, critics asked, is it less dangerous for Supreme Court justices to impose their personal preferences on legislators and society in matters of personal rights than in matters of economic relations? If the old *Lochner* logic was wrong, why is this new form of "Lochnerizing" not wrong as well? Moreover, are judges any more qualified to determine one form of rights than another? And is the legitimacy of a "government of laws" no less undermined by unrestrained, arbitrary judicial policy-making in one sphere than in another?

Defenders of the majority have ranged even more widely in their arguments than did the justices. Some supporters have emphasized the decision's solid groundings in past judicial practice, theoretical logic, and constitutional text. Indeed, both Douglas and Goldberg explicitly declined the invitation to follow in the substantive due process tradition. "We do not sit as a super-legislature to determine the wisdom, need, and propriety of laws that touch economic problems, business affairs, or social conditions," wrote Douglas. The law in question, by contrast, "operates directly on an intimate relation of husband an wife" that long has received constitutional protection (p. 482).

Other supporters of the majority instead have affirmed Justices Harlan and White's unabashed rejection of formalist illusions about textual constraints upon judicial action. They argue that legal interpretation is always discretionary, and that textual constraints on judges are far less important than cultural and political forces. Moreover, many scholars have defended the Court's zealous defense of personal rights as both within its institutional capacities and functionally necessary to maintaining liberty in our modern corporate society. Such arguments were sufficiently compelling that all nine justices, including Stewart, by 1973 had accepted the Court's role in giving the Fourteenth Amendment's Due Process Clause a substantive content that exceeds the Bill of Rights, although considerable differences remained about how and when that authority should be exercised.

***Privacy Rights: Subsequent Case Law and Theoretical Disputes.*** Controversies over the constitutional grounding of unenumerated rights have been paralleled by controversies over the range of practices and relations that such rights protect. Indeed, the majority in *Griswold* was far more expansive about legal justifications for a right of privacy than about its theoretical content and reach. And while the Court recognized that commitments to privacy have deep roots in American society and its laws, that legacy has provided a vague guide for determining the substantive scope of privacy rights in modern social relations. Not surprisingly, questions regarding conceptual coherence have continued to surround the doctrine.

Critics query whether the logic of "privacy" extends to all social relations—including the sale of contraceptives to unmarried individuals (*Carey v. Population Services International*, 1977), relations among *homosexuals (*Bowers* v. Hardwick, 1986), and women's choices regarding abortion (*Roe v. Wade*, 1973). For example, is it really privacy that is most infringed by regulations restricting the sale and distribution of contraceptives? Do regulations of sales concern privacy more than those on solicitation, which was treated primarily as matter of free speech in *Bolger* v. *Youngs Drug Product Corp.* (1983).

Moreover, the privacy doctrine has been increasingly attacked from both ends of the political spectrum. On the one hand, the doctrine as applied to abortion since *Roe* has continued to provoke the outrage of conservatives over both the expansion of judicial authority and its resulting protections for allegedly immoral individual actions. Ironically, conservatives have rejected the privacy doctrine because it limits state intervention into the lives of citizens.

On the other hand, the privacy doctrine has been assailed from the political left for advancing a far too truncated and archaic liberal understanding of freedom. Critics on the left condemn the *Griswold* decision for limiting the privacy protection for contraception use to persons bound in conventional marriage relations. This shield for contraception use was extended a few years later to unmarried persons in *Eisenstadt* v. *Baird* (1972), but the Court's repeated denial of protection for homosexual relationships has revealed privacy limits as a challenge to traditional norms regarding sexuality (*Bowers*). Moreover, while the privacy logic has been useful to limit at least some unwanted state intervention in intimate sexual matters, it has also been employed to preclude a positive state role in educating citizens and providing funding essential for the exercise of rights to use birth control and receive an abortion. Some critics thus argue for the need to replace the privacy logic with a more affirmative conception of autonomy rights that is more consistent with the goals of equality and empowerment.

***Legacy.*** The legacy of the privacy rights doctrine thus points to the perennial problem of Court efforts to deal with changing social needs, values, and interests though invocation of traditional norms long supportive of quite different relationships. The right of privacy affirmed in *Griswold* still stands, but clearly is jeopardized by increasingly restrictive Court rulings on protections for abortion, its most important doctrinal application.

(See also ABORTION; PRIVACY.)

□ Rhonda Copelon, "Beyond the Liberal Idea of Privacy: Toward A Positive Right of Autonomy," in *Judging the Constitution: Critical Essays on Judicial Lawmaking*, edited by Michael W. McCann and Gerald L. Houseman, (1989), pp. 287–316. Allan Dionisopolous and Craig Ducat, eds., *The Right to Privacy: Essays and Cases* (1976). Louis Henken, "Privacy and Autonomy," *Columbia Law Review* 74 (1974): 1410–1433. "Symposium on the *Griswold* Case and the Right of Privacy," *Michigan Law Review* 64 (1965): 197–282.　　　Michael W. McCann

**Grosjean v. American Press Co.,** 297 U.S. 233 (1936), argued 14 Jan. 1936, decided 10 Feb. 1936, by vote of 9 to 0; Sutherland for the Court. The Court unanimously invalidated a license tax on the business of selling advertising (in the amount of 2 percent of the gross receipts from such sales) imposed by Louisiana in 1934 on all newpapers with a circulation of more than twenty thousand copies per week. The tax was challenged as an abridgment of freedom of the press and as a violation of *equal protection. It was noted by counsel that only thirteen of the 163 newspapers in the state had sufficient circulation to be required to pay it, and twelve of those thirteen were actively opposed to the Huey Long administration, at whose instigation the tax was enacted.

The Court considered only the free press challenge. It equated the license tax to the "taxes on knowledge" imposed on newspapers and advertising by Parliament in the eighteenth century, whose purpose was not to raise revenue but to reduce the circulation of newspapers and thus limit public access to criticisms of the Crown. The obviously similar motivation of the Louisiana legislature was plainly crucial to the Court's conclusion here. The tax was held unconstitutional because it was hostile to the press. It applied only to "a selected group of newspapers" (p. 251) and was "a deliberate and calculated device in the guise of a tax to limit the circulation of information" pertaining to public affairs (p. 250).

The year after *Grosjean,* the Court made clear that newspapers are not exempt from nondiscriminatory general taxation. In *Giragi v. Moore* (1937), it dismissed without opinion a claim for such an exemption. The Court has since categorically declared that newspapers are subject to all forms of nondiscriminatory economic regulation, including taxation (*Minneapolis Star & Tribune Co. v. Minnesota Commissioner of Revenue,* 1983).

(See also FIRST AMENDMENT; SPEECH AND THE PRESS; TAXING AND SPENDING POWER.)

Dean Alfange, Jr.

**Grove City College v. Bell,** 465 U.S. 555 (1984), argued 29 Nov. 1983, decided 28 Feb. 1984 by vote of 6 to 3; White for the Court, Powell concurring in part and dissenting in part, Brennan, joined by Marshall and Stevens, concurring in part and dissenting in part. In this case the Court found that Title IX of the Education Amendments of 1972 prohibited gender discrimination in colleges and universities that receive federal funds. Grove City College's enrollment of students who received Basic Educational Opportunity Grants from the federal government was found sufficient to trigger Title IX, although the college, as a matter of principle, received no other federal funds. But the sanction of Title IX—the cut-off of federal funds—was limited to the discriminatory program and could not be applied to any other programs at the school. Thus, under the Court's

ruling a university that discriminated against women could continue to receive federal funding so long as specific discriminatory programs did not.

Reaction to *Grove City* was immediate. Civil rights and women's groups were outraged by the decision. So too were many members of Congress who saw this case as a prime example of the weakening of the Reagan administration's civil rights commitment. *Grove City* originally had been filed by the Justice Department under the Carter Administration. It took the position that Grove City College was not in compliance with Title IX because all programs needed to comply in order for a school to have funding eligibility. However, when the case reached the Supreme Court the Reagan adminstration Justice Department retreated from that position to one urging only a limited cutoff of funding.

In 1987, over the veto of President Ronald *Reagan, Congress enacted the Civil Rights Restoration Act to overturn *Grove City.* The bill specified that Title IX applies to any college or university if any part of the institution receives federal assistance. Thus, all of the university's federal funds are now at risk even if there is proven discrimination in only one program.

(See also EDUCATION; GENDER.)

Karen O'Connor

**Groves v. Slaughter,** 15 Pet. (40 U.S.) 449 (1841), argued 12, 13, 15–18 Feb. 1841 and decided 10 Mar. 1841 by vote of 5 to 2; Thompson delivered the judgment of the Court but wrote only for himself and Wayne; Taney, McLean, and Baldwin concurring only in the result; McKinley and Story in dissent; Catron was absent for illness and Barbour had just died. *Groves v. Slaughter* involved explosive problems arising out of the relationship among *slavery, the interstate slave trade, federal *commerce power, and state *police power. Mississippi by 1832 constitutional amendments prohibited the introduction of slaves into the state for sale, but did not enact legislation enforcing the prohibition. A purchaser defaulted on notes given for imported slaves, and the seller contended that the state constitutional prohibition was void because of conflict with the federal commerce power.

Justice Smith *Thompson's opinion avoided the constitutional issues by holding that the constitutional prohibition was not self-executing. But Justice John *McLean insisted on delivering a concurring opinion filled with crypto-abolitionist dicta, which provoked Chief Justice Roger B. *Taney and Justice Henry *Baldwin to deliver counterconcurrences refuting McLean's points with proslavery dicta (see OBITER DICTUM). Taney and Baldwin both insisted that state control over slavery and African-Americans was exclusive of all federal power. The inability of the Court to cohere on, or even to evade, constitutional questions implicated by interstate commerce and slavery was symptomatic of deep divisions among the justices, which in turn reflected the emerging sectional controversy over slavery in the country.                    William M. Wiecek

**Grovey v. Townsend,** 295 U.S. 45 (1935), argued 11 Mar. 1935, decided 1 Apr. 1935 by vote of 9 to 0; Roberts for the Court. In 1923 Texas prohibited blacks from participating in the Democratic primaries in the state, but in *Nixon v. Herndon (1927) the Supreme Court ruled this law violated the *Equal Protection Clause of the *Fourteenth Amendment. The Texas legislature then authorized the party's executive committee to prohibit blacks from voting in party primaries, but in *Nixon v. Condon (1932) the Court ruled that this still constituted impermissible *state action because the party executive committee was a creation of the legislature. Even before the Court decided the *Grovey* case, the Texas Democratic Party took steps to protect their whites-only primary system. In May 1932 a convention of Texas Democrats limited party membership to whites. R. R. Grovey, a black resident of Houston, sued the county clerk for refusing to give him a ballot for a Democratic primary election. Justice Owen *Roberts ruled that the party convention's decision to exclude blacks from the Democratic primary was not state action because the party was a voluntary association of its members, who had acted in their private capacity to exclude blacks. Roberts reached this conclusion despite his acknowledgment that the state regulated primaries in a variety of ways, including a requirement that sealed ballot boxes be turned over to county clerks after each primary election. In the absence of state action, Roberts found that the white primary was constitutional when authorized by a party convention without any encouragement from the state legislature. This holding was later specifically reversed in *Smith v. Allwright* (1944).

(See also EQUAL PROTECTION; RACE AND RACISM; VOTE, RIGHT TO; WHITE PRIMARY.)

Paul Finkelman

**Guarantee Clause.** Article IV, section 4 of the Constitution reads: "The United States shall guarantee to every State in this Union a Republican Form of Government." By inserting these words in the Constitution, the framers, fearful of aristocratic or mobocratic threats to representative government, sought to preserve republican ideals and institutions in the states.

The Supreme Court's first major interpretation of the Guarantee Clause emerged out of the Dorr Rebellion, in which Thomas Dorr and his followers challenged the legitimacy of the established government of Rhode Island. In *Luther v. Borden (1849), Chief Justice Roger B. *Taney held that the power to assess either the legitimacy or the republican character of a state government rested with Congress, not the courts. Such questions,

he argued, were "political" in nature and thus lay beyond the scope of the Court's power (see POLITICAL QUESTIONS). Taney's reluctance to assert judicial power in *Luther* affected the constitutional development of the Guarantee Clause for the next century. During the *Reconstruction period, for example, Republicans in Congress understood this interpretation of the clause to acknowledge congressional authority to prescribe the terms of Reconstruction.

Not until the reapportionment controversies of the 1960s did the Guarantee Clause again emerge at the center of constitutional debate (see REAPPORTIONMENT CASES). In *Baker v. Carr (1962), proponents of reapportionment argued that it was the duty of the courts to guarantee republican governments in the states by invalidating legislative malapportionment. The Supreme Court, however, avoided a reinterpretation of the Guarantee Clause and instead decided that malapportionment violated the *Equal Protection Clause. Although the justices did not overturn Taney's decision that Guarantee Clause cases presented nonjusticiable political questions, the Court nevertheless narrowed the number of cases they would exclude from their jurisdiction under the political question doctrine.

(See also JUDICIAL POWER AND JURISDICTION.)

William M. Wiecek and Timothy S. Huebner

**Guest, United States v.,** 383 U.S. 745 (1966), argued 9 Nov. 1965, decided 28 Mar. 1966 by vote of 9 to 0; Stewart for the Court, Clark concurring, Harlan and Brennan concurring and dissenting; **United States v. Price,** 383 U.S. 787 (1966), argued and decided on same dates as *Guest,* also by vote of 9 to 0; Fortas for the Court. These cases arose from incidents of violence connected with the modern *civil rights movement. *Guest* resulted from the Klan-style murder of Lemuel Penn, an African-American Washington, D.C., educator, in Georgia; *Price* stemmed from the murders of three civil rights workers in Neshoba County, Mississippi. In its rulings, the Court gave broad readings to two Reconstruction-era civil rights statutes—one forbidding conspiracies to interfere with rights "secured" by the Constitution and federal law, the other punishing violations, under color of law, of rights "secured or protected" by U.S. law. *Guest* came close, moreover, to rejecting the holding of the *Civil Rights Cases (1883) that Congress's power to enforce the *Fourteenth Amendment extended only to state, not private, action.

In overturning a federal district judge's dismissal of most counts of an indictment against eighteen defendants in *Price,* Justice Abe *Fortas concluded that the first of these Reconstruction-era statutes reached Fourteenth Amendment rights in addition to the privileges of national *citizenship it had traditionally covered and further held that private citizens acting in concert with local police could be tried for violating the other statute's "under color of law" provisions. In *Guest*, Justice Potter *Stewart reversed the dismissal of charges against six defendants, two of whom had already been acquitted in state court of Lemuel Penn's murder. Stewart upheld a count of the indictment charging an interference with interstate travel as a privilege of national citizenship. Since another count of the indictment charged false reports to police as part of the defendants' conspiracy to intimidate African-Americans in the equal utilization of public facilities, Stewart was also able to reinstate that count without challenging the precedent created in the *Civil Rights Cases*. In separate opinions, however, three justices agreed that Congress had authority to punish private interferences with Fourteenth Amendment rights.

(See also RACE AND RACISM; STATE ACTION.)

Tinsley E. Yarbrough

**Guinn v. United States,** 238 U.S. 347 (1915), argued 17 Oct. 1913, decided 21 June 1915 by vote of 8 to 0: White for the Court, McReynolds recused. To convince poor and illiterate whites to support literacy and property qualifications for voting, southern Democrats in the late nineteenth and early twentieth centuries included escape clauses in their suffrage restriction laws. The least subtle of these was the *grandfather clause, which allowed anyone to register to vote if he had been eligible in 1867, before the *Fifteenth Amendment was ratified, or it he were a legal descendant of such a man. Some representatives of the southern upper class opposed this as too transparent an attempt to evade the Constitution, or because they wished to disfranchise the white, as well as the black, lower class.

Accordingly, restrictionists limited the time for qualifying under the grandfather clause in the five Old South states that adopted it, beginning with Louisiana in 1898. In September 1910, however, Oklahoma passed a literacy test with a permanent grandfather clause. Fearing political oblivion if his party lost its African-American support, Republican U.S. District Attorney John Emory brought criminal charges under the 1870 Ku Klux Klan Act against two election officials. The state's Democratic party provided the opposing counsel. Only after President William Howard *Taft determined that he needed the votes of

African-American delegates to win renomination at the Republican convention in 1912 did the Justice Department embrace this thoroughly political suit.

In *Williams* v. *Mississippi* (1898), the Supreme Court had refused to throw out Mississippi's notoriously discriminatory voting barriers because the lawyer for the African-American plaintiffs, Cornelius J. Jones, had offered evidence only of the intent of the delegates to the Mississippi Constitutional Convention. Presented with evidence of effect as well as of intent by attorney Wilford H. Smith in *Giles* v. *Harris* (1903), the Court, through "liberal" Justice Oliver Wendell *Holmes, declared the whole matter a *"political question." Yet in *Guinn* and two companion cases, the Court received no evidence of either intent or effect, sidestepped precedent, and joined Louisiana-bred Chief Justice Edward D. *White's opinion declaring the statute a prima facie violation of the Fifteenth Amendment.

There were two main reasons why the Court decided the case in this manner. First, *Guinn* had no practical effect. In all the ex-Confederate states, the grandfather clauses had already lapsed, and Oklahoma continued administrative discrimination without further legal challenge. Second, the grandfather clause was a symbolic embarassment that even the president of the Louisiana Constitutional Convention of 1898 had termed "ridiculous." The decision in *Guinn* was neither inevitable nor particularly progressive.

(See also RACE AND RACISM; VOTE, RIGHT TO.)

J. Morgan Kousser

**Gymnasium.** The Supreme Court gymnasium is a brightly lit, low-ceilinged, white room containing a full basketball court. It is sometimes called the "highest court in the land" because of its location on the top floor of the Supreme Court building. The space, which also holds exercise equipment, had originally been planned for library expansion but was converted to its present use in the 1940s. A single locker-room with shower is adjacent; different hours for its use are assigned for male and female court employees. Basketball games are forbidden while the Court is in session, since the dribbling can be heard in the courtroom directly below.

Francis Helminski

# H

**Habeas Corpus.** The "Great Writ" of habeas corpus is available so that a judge may inquire into the legality of any form of loss of personal liberty. Detention, or loss of personal liberty, may occur at all levels of government, and may take various forms: incarceration in some sort of jail or penitentiary pursuant to a court judgment, detention in a police station after an arrest, commitment in a mental institution, service in the armed forces, detention on the basis of quarantine regulations, or restraint by private authority, as in the case of spouses or the custody of minors.

Habeas corpus has certain important characteristics. For one thing, there is no statute of limitations regarding access to it, since the right of personal freedom from illegal restraint never lapses. Neither does one failure to secure the *writ forbid later application, which means that the usual doctrine regarding the finality of court judgments (*res judicata*) does not apply to habeas corpus. In recent decisions, the Supreme Court has expressed its disapproval of multiple application for the writ. Furthermore, unlike other legal actions, a relative or friend may petition for the writ in behalf of a person unable to apply on his or her own behalf. Called "the most important human right in the Constitution," Chief Justice Salmon P. *Chase described it in *Ex parte Yerger* (1868) as "the best and only sufficient defense of personal freedom" (p. 95).

The historical roots of the Great Writ are not clear, but it is usually ascribed to section 39 of Magna Carta (1215). During the Middle Ages the writ had various uses. For example, it could be used to compel a person to appear in court to give testimony. As a remedy against the Crown (that is

to say, the government), its availability dates from the end of the fifteenth century. The essential elements of the writ as it is now generally understood were spelled out by Parliament in the Habeas Corpus Act of 1679. In the American colonies the writ was available as part of the *common law. After independence, habeas corpus was guaranteed in most of the early *state constitutions. The U.S. Constitution, in Article I, section 9, forbids suspension of the writ "unless when in Cases of Rebellion or Invasion the public Safety may require it." The very first statute enacted by the First Congress, the *Judiciary Act of 1789, empowered all federal courts "to grant writs of habeas corpus for the purpose of an inquiry into the cause of commitment." All states have similar statutes.

The writ orders the person who is responsible for the detention—for example, the warden or jailer—to produce the petitioner (that is, the body, or *corpus*) quickly, in court, so that a judge may decide the lawfulness of the detention. Neither federal nor state habeas corpus statutes attempt to define just what constitutes an unlawful detention; they merely provide for a procedure by which a judge may look into the matter. However, as Justice William J. *Brennan pointed out in *Fay v. Noia* (1963),

Although in form the Great Writ is simply a mode of procedure, its history is inextricably intertwined with the growth of fundamental rights of personal liberty. For its function has been to provide a prompt and efficacious remedy for whatever society deems to be intolerable restraints. Its root principle is that in a civilized society, government must always be accountable to the judiciary for a man's imprisonment: if the imprisonment cannot be shown to conform with the fundamental requirements of law, the individual is entitled to his immediate release. (pp. 401–402)

While historically the writ was mainly concerned with jurisdictional matters, legislative bodies and courts have gradually broadened its reach.

Congress in 1867 enacted a habeas corpus statute that authorized the writ whenever any person is restrained or deprived of liberty in violation of any federal right, that is, any right guaranteed by the Constitution, acts of Congress, or treaties. The *Due Process Clause of the *Fourteenth Amendment has been construed to secure the right to a fair hearing, thus providing a very broad ground for granting the writ. A state prisoner is not eligible to apply to a federal judge for habeas corpus until first exhausting all remedies available under state law. Similarly, a member of the armed forces may not sue for the writ in a federal court until the remedies provided for in the military court system have been exhausted (see EXHAUSTION OF REMEDIES).

President Abraham *Lincoln suspended habeas corpus at the beginning of the *Civil War, but Chief Justice Roger B. *Taney protested that only Congress may do so (Ex parte Merryman, 1861). Soon afterward, however, Congress validated the President's suspension. Pursuant to statute, later presidents invoked limited suspensions in 1871 and 1905. A presidential suspension in Hawaii in 1941, however, which was performed without statutory authorization, was ruled illegal by the Supreme Court in *Duncan v. Kahanamoku (1946).

The granting of habeas corpus writs by federal courts to state prisoners has been resented by many state authorities. Perhaps this explains why, in *Stone v. Powell (1976), the Supreme Court, by a vote of 6 to 3, held that where a state prisoner has had a chance to litigate a *Fourth Amendment search and seizure claim fully and fairly in the *state courts, that prisoner is not also entitled to consideration by a federal habeas corpus court if the allegation that evidence was received by an illegal search and seizure was introduced at the prisoner's trial. The Court majority argued that the possible deterrent effect on unlawful police conduct was outweighed by the detriment to the criminal justice system resulting from the reexamination by the federal court of an issue already settled by the state courts. In dissent, Justice Brennan protested that this ruling portended "substantial evisceration of federal habeas corpus jurisdiction" (p. 503). Subsequent decisions have not, however, seemed to justify this dire prophecy.

☐ David Fellman, *The Defendant's Rights Today* (1976).
David Fellman

## Hague v. Congress of Industrial Organizations,

307 U.S. 496 (1939), argued 27–28 Feb. 1939, decided 5 June 1939 by vote of 5 to 2; Roberts for the Court, Stone and Hughes concurring, McReynolds and Butler in dissent, Frankfurter and Douglas not participating. The problem of state attempts to control public meetings first came before the Supreme Court in *Hague* v. *CIO*. The case involved the constitutionality of a Jersey City municipal ordinance requiring permits from a "director of public safety" for the conduct of public meetings and for the distribution of printed material in streets, parks, and other public places. Mayor Frank "I am Law" Hague had used the ordinance particularly against labor union activities. With support from the *American Civil Liberties Union an *injunction was sought against Hague's systematic denial of *First Amendment rights. The injunction ordered the city to stop evicting union organizers and to cease interfering with meetings and the distribution of literature.

Upholding the injunction in a plurality opinion, the Supreme Court found the ordinance unconstitutional but the justices disagreed in their reasoning. Justice Owen *Roberts, for the Court, defined the streets and parks as public forums protected by the First Amendment as a part of the privileges, immunities, rights and liberties of citizens. Stone, concurring, felt that the ordinance violated the right of U.S. citizens peaceably to assemble as guaranteed by the Fourteenth Amendment's *Due Process Clause.

The ruling was significant in opening public areas like streets and parks to free public discussion of ideas, no matter what the subject. Such use, the Court ruled, could be regulated, but not arbitrarily denied or abridged because the authorities did not favor the ideas being discussed. The ruling proved a boon to the labor movement, and was popular as the curtailment of the arbitrariness of local officials.

(See also ASSEMBLY AND ASSOCIATION, FREEDOM OF; LABOR; SPEECH AND THE PRESS.)
Paul L. Murphy

## Hall v. Decuir,

95 U.S. 485 (1878), argued 17 Apr. 1877, decided 14 Jan. 1878 by vote of 9 to 0; Waite for the Court, Clifford concurring. In *Hall* v. *DeCuir*, the Court overturned a Louisiana Supreme Court decision that had awarded damages authorized by a Louisiana statute to Josephine DeCuir, a black woman, who had been refused admission to a steamship's stateroom reserved for whites during her voyage between New Orleans and Hermitage, Louisiana. The Court's opinion by Chief Justice Morrison R. *Waite held that the statute burdened interstate commerce because the steamship also traveled between Louisiana and Mississippi. Waite held that the statute regulated interstate commerce, something within the exclusive province of Congress. In the absence of congressional action, states could not require carriers engaged in interstate commerce to offer integrated facilities even for trips that took place solely within state bound-

aries. Waite did not consider whether Congress might have intended, through inaction, to permit the states to control some aspects of interstate commerce incidentally in the exercise of their *police power over intrastate activities, a power later acknowledged in the *Shreveport Rate Cases (1914).

The concurring opinion by Justice Nathan *Clifford demonstrated the Court's concern with preserving racial custom. It included a defense of what would later be termed the *"separate but equal" doctrine. The Court inconsistently held in *Louisville, New Orleans & Texas Railway Co. v. Mississippi (1890), that a state statute requiring segregation in intrastate commerce did not run afoul of Congress's commerce power. It was not until after *World War II that the Court recognized the illogic of these holdings and relied on the Hall precedent to void state legislation mandating intrastate segregation, because of its impact on interstate commerce.

(See also COMMERCE POWER; RACE AND RACISM.)

Robert J. Cottrol

**Hamilton, Alexander** (b. Nevis, British West Indies, 11 Jan. 1757; d. New York, N.Y. 12 July 1804), lawyer and statesman. Though best known for his achievements as the first secretary of the Treasury, Hamilton contributed significantly to the establishment and interpretation of the Constitution. He, along with James *Madison and John Dickinson, parlayed the 1786 Annapolis commercial convention into the Constitutional Convention of 1787. He attended the latter as a delegate from New York and signed the finished document. He wrote well over half of the celebrated *Federalist Papers, including those essays analyzing the federal judiciary, and in no. 78 he formulated the definitive justification of *judicial review. In 1788 he also led the successful campaign for the Constitution's ratification in New York.

Early in 1791 President George *Washington asked Hamilton for an opinion on the proposed Bank of the United States, and Hamilton responded with the classical statement of loose construction: "If the end be clearly comprehended within any of the specified powers, & if the measure have an obvious relation to that end, and is not forbidden by any particular provision of the constitution—it may safely be deemed to come within the compass of the national authority" (McDonald, 1979, p. 207). That doctrine prevailed throughout the Supreme Court tenure of Chief Justice John *Marshall; indeed, Marshall's opinion in *McCulloch v. Maryland (1819) reflected Hamilton's logic and echoed his words.

After he retired from the Treasury to resume private law practice in 1795, Hamilton became involved in a major Supreme Court case. Virginians challenged the federal carriage tax of 1794 as a direct tax not proportioned among the states according to population as required by Article I, section 2. Hamilton, on request of Attorney General William Bradford, argued the case for the government and persuaded the Court that the carriage tax was an excise tax needing only to be uniform throughout the states. This case, *Hylton v. United States (1796), was the first in which the Supreme Court ruled upon the constitutionality of an act of Congress.

In that same year Hamilton wrote an advisory legal opinion that influenced another major decision. After the Georgia legislature canceled its Yazoo land grants, investors requested Hamilton's legal opinion. He argued that the *Contract Clause applied to *contracts between a state and individuals as well as between individuals. Grants being contracts, Georgia's rescinding act was unconstitutional. When litigation reached the Supreme Court in *Fletcher v. Peck (1810), the Court followed Hamilton's reasoning.

One of Hamilton's last cases, argued before the Supreme Court of New York, was pivotal to freedom of speech. Under the *common law, truth was not a defense in cases of *seditious libel. In Croswell v. People (1804) Hamilton argued that truth should be a defense. He lost the case but swayed those members of the state legislature who heard him. They soon enacted his position into law, thus establishing a legal foundation for the ideal of a free and responsible press (see SPEECH AND THE PRESS).

(See also CONSTITUTIONAL INTERPRETATION.)

□ Forrest McDonald, *Alexander Hamilton* (1979).

Forrest McDonald

**Hammer v. Dagenhart,** 247 U.S. 251 (1918), argued 15–16 Apr. 1918, decided 3 June 1918 by vote of 5 to 4; Day for the Court, Holmes, McKenna, Brandeis, and Clarke in dissent. As the Progressive movement (see PROGRESSIVISM) coalesced early in the twentieth century, Congress increasingly used the *commerce power and *taxing and spending power for *police power purposes, enacting regulatory legislation to ameliorate social problems deemed national in character. Prominent among these problems was concern for children working outside their homes, who were dependent, often exploited, nearly always powerless to effect the conditions under which they labored. As it became increasingly apparent that state legislation could not effectively establish national regulatory standards, reformers turned to Congress, seeking federal legislation that would abolish child labor. In 1916, in what became recognized as the climax of the Progressive movement, substantial majorities in the House and the Senate enacted the Keating-Owen Child Labor Act, which utilized the commerce power to bar goods made by children from interstate commerce.

Because the Supreme Court had repeatedly legitimated national police power enactments, notably in such seemingly decisive holdings as *Champion* v. *Ames* (1903), *Hipolite Egg Company* v. *United States* (1911), and *Hoke* v. *United States* (1913), it was widely expected that the Supreme Court would build upon this precedential foundation in its decision in *Hammer* v. *Dagenhart*. The earlier opinions seemed to establish the principle that Congress could use its power over commerce to prohibit interstate transportation as the national welfare dictated. Congress had authority, *Hoke* had declared, "to occupy, by legislation, the whole field of interstate commerce" (p. 320).

However, a five-justice majority on a bitterly divided bench rejected this constitutional justification and recurred to a line of reasoning thought to have been repudiated earlier in the century. Justice William Rufus *Day's opinion rested upon the distinction between manufacture and commerce enunciated in *United States* v. *E. C. Knight Co.* (1895): the congressional "power is one to control the means by which commerce is carried on, which is directly the contrary of the assumed right to forbid commerce" (pp. 269–270). He condemned the Keating-Owen law as having reached an area of regulation wholly within the ambit of the states and exerting power not warranted in the Constitution. While conceding that child laborers needed protection, Day charged Congress with action destructive to *federalism. "[T]he far-reaching result," if Congress was not stopped, he asserted, was that "all freedom of commerce will be at an end . . . and thus our system of government be practically destroyed" (p. 276). This resort to the *grand peur* was characteristic of the doctrines of constitutional *laissez faire* to which the majority now returned.

Writing with uncharacteristic passion, Justice Oliver Wendell *Holmes fashioned one of the most notable dissenting opinions in the Court's history. He excoriated the majority for intruding their personal judgments "upon questions of policy and morals" (p. 280). "I should have thought," Holmes wrote, "that if we were to introduce our own moral conceptions where, in my opinion, they do not belong, this was preeminently a case for upholding the exercise of all its powers by the United States" (p. 280). To Holmes, one analytical proposition was indisputable: the congressional prohibition applied only at the point where an offending state sought to transport its commercial products across its borders into national commerce. "Regulation means the prohibition of something" (p. 277), he argued, and he enumerated the line of constitutional development, stretching back to *Veazie Bank* v. *Fenno* (1869), in which the Court had lent sanction to national regulation of the kind embodied in the Keating-Owen law. "The power to regulate commerce and other constitutional powers could not be cut down or

qualified," he asserted, as a consequence of their "indirect effects" (p. 278).

Holmes's revulsion at what he considered the majority's defiance of the democratic will mirrored the consternation evident throughout the country. Congress swiftly responded by enacting the second federal child labor law, using the taxing power to apply against manufacturers the same regulatory standards embodied in the Keating-Owen law (see TAXING AND SPENDING CLAUSE). Even though the Court overturned this statute in *Bailey* v. *Drexel Furniture Co.* (1922), the minority was vindicated two decades later, following the Constitutional Revolution in 1937, when a unanimous bench in *United States* v. *Darby Lumber Co.* (1941) adopted and, indeed, went beyond the constitutional principles set forth in what Justice Harlan Fiske *Stone characterized as Holmes's "powerful and now classic dissent" (p. 115).

(See also LABOR; STATE REGULATION OF COMMERCE.)

☐ Stephen B. Wood, *Constitutional Politics in the Progressive Era* (1968). Stephen B. Wood

**Hand, Billings Learned** (b. Albany, N.Y., 27 Jan. 1872; d. New York, N.Y., 18 Aug. 1961), federal judge. Learned Hand enjoyed one of the longest tenures on the federal bench of any judge in this century. President William Howard *Taft, seeking to improve the federal bench, appointed Hand to the district court in New York in 1909 upon the recommendation of Charles Burlingham. In 1924 Calvin Coolidge elevated Hand to the *Court of Appeals for the Second Circuit; Hand served as chief judge of that court from 1939 until his nominal retirement in 1951, but he continued to carry a heavy load as a senior judge until his death.

Twice Hand came close to appointment to the Supreme Court. In the 1920s he was considered for every vacancy on the high court, but then Chief Justice William Howard Taft, still bitter at Hand's having backed Theodore Roosevelt's Bull Moose ticket in 1912, blocked his appointment. Then in the early 1940s Felix *Frankfurter lobbied incessantly to have Hand appointed, but Franklin D. *Roosevelt wanted younger men and also resented Frankfurter's heavy-handed tactics.

Hand's reputation lies less in constitutional law, since at that time relatively few constitutional cases came before the Second Circuit, than in private law and statutory interpretation, in which he set high standards for clarity of expression and judicial craftsmanship. Yet his voice was also important in the ongoing debate over *judicial activism and the expansion of constitutional liberties.

Like his good friend Felix Frankfurter, Hand believed that judges had a limited role to play, a philosophy that, like Frankfurter, he derived from his studies with James Bradley *Thayer at the Harvard Law School, from which he graduated in 1896. He would later claim that Thayer and others had taught him that the highest satisfaction a lawyer or a judge could derive came from knowing a job had been done in a craftsman-like manner. Hand did not see judicial restraint as an abdication of responsibility, nor as an intellectually sterile enterprise. Within modest parameters judges had important work to do, exploring the underlying questions of law and creating legal rules appropriate to the times. Larger questions of policy, however, should be left to the elected branches (see JUDICIAL SELF-RESTRAINT).

Hand constantly expressed his dissatisfaction with the activist wing of the Court headed by Hugo *Black and William O. *Douglas, and in the Holmes lectures at Harvard in 1958 he questioned the propriety of judges enlarging the meaning of the *Bill of Rights. Years earlier he had attacked the majority decision in *Lochner v. New York (1905) for imposing conservative personal values in place of legislative wishes, and he now applied that same reasoning to the Warren Court. Like Frankfurter, Hand believed that the extent of Bill of Rights protection, as well as its enforceability, should be left to the legislature.

Hand believed strongly in free speech, and in 1917 handed down a highly controversial opinion in Masses Publishing Co. v. Patten, in which he argued that the *First Amendment protected all speech short of direct incitement to illegal action. When the Supreme Court issued its first rulings in the wartime speech cases, Holmes's *clear and present danger test in *Schenck v. United States (1919) fell far short of Hand's standard. Hand criticized the Holmes test as too vague and assumed that the Court had implicitly rejected the Masses criterion.

This explains why, despite his lifelong commitment to free speech, Hand confirmed the conviction of eleven communist leaders in United States v. *Dennis (1950), a case in which the clear and present danger test was watered down to allow the government to prosecute people for conspiring to teach the overthrow of the government, a far cry from the Masses test. But Hand in this case was carrying out what he saw as his role as a judge—adherence to *precedent and deference to the elected branches of government; privately he still adhered to the Masses test. Eventually the Supreme Court moved away from Schenck and Dennis, and in *Brandenburg v. Ohio (1969) adopted what many commentators believe is essentially Learned Hand's approach.

□ Kathryn Griffith, *Judge Learned Hand and the Role of the Federal Judiciary* (1973).          Melvin I. Urofsky

**Harlan, John Marshall** (b. Boyle County, Ky., 1 June 1833; d. Washington, D.C., 14 Oct. 1911; interred Rock Creek Cemetery, Washington, D.C.), associate justice, 1877–1911. Raised in privileged circles on the border between North and South, Harlan had much in common with his namesake, the great chief justice from Virginia. Of a slaveowning family, himself briefly a slaveowner, Harlan was personally acquainted with the South's "peculiar institution." A fervent believer in the Constitution, Harlan also looked to law and the institutions of government to preserve the Union, notwithstanding social differences. Yet Harlan was to carry the Marshall tradition into a very different world. An almost exact contemporary of chief Justice Melville *Fuller, under whom Harlan served for twenty-three years, he was forced to confront the issues raised by the near breakup of the Union: the emancipation of the slaves and the constitutional amendments that consolidated the North's victory.

*Early Career.* Harlan's father, a staunch Whig and close friend of Henry Clay, was a successful lawyer and electable politician, serving successively as United States congressman, Kentucky secretary of state, state legislator, and state attorney general. Completing his education by a stay at Centre College in Danville, Kentucky, the young Harlan then studied law at Transylvania University and in his father's law office. Admitted to the Kentucky bar in 1853, he seemed destined to follow his father in a career as a Whig lawyer-politician, but the deaths of Clay and Daniel *Webster the previous year had deprived the party of enlightened leadership in troubled times. Trying demagogic nativism, Whigs like the senior and junior Harlan became Know-Nothings, a gambit that was ultimately doomed but that brought the younger Harlan his first elective office as county judge in 1858. The years as an active Know-Nothing also piled up a host of recorded racist and states' rights speeches that were later to embarrass their author.

The secession crisis in 1861 revealed Harlan's true colors: Union blue. Commissioned a lieutenant colonel in the United States Army, he speedily raised a company of infantry volunteers. The senior Harlan's sudden death in 1863 caused Col. Harlan to resign his commission and take over his father's unfinished business. Characteristically, the young veteran plunged promptly into politics; running as a Constitutional Unionist (the Whigs' new party), he was elected state attorney general. At war's end the Unionists faded as a political force and Harlan cast in his lot with the Republicans. In his professional career the move was reflected in his law partnership with Benjamin Bristow, soon to be Grant's secretary of the treasury. Despite Harlan's best efforts—he ran twice for governor—the Kentucky Republicans failed to thrive. It was his good fortune, however, to head the Kentucky delegation to the Republican national convention in 1876, when his timely swing to Rutherford B. Hayes secured the outcome. After the contested presidential election and the ordeal of the scrutiny by the Electoral Commission, Hayes was declared the victor. The new president moved quickly to settle unfinished business and named a commission of five, including Harlan, to report on which of two rival Louisiana state governments was legitimate. In keeping with the president's policy of ending *Reconstruction, the commission advised in favor of the Democrats, despite the fact that the same returning board that had certified the Hayes electors had also certified the state Republican candidates. On inauguration Hayes had inherited a Supreme Court vacancy caused by Justice David *Davis's precipitate resignation (apparently to avoid service on the Electoral Commission; see EXTRAJUDICIAL ACTIVITIES). Consistent with his policy of reconciliation, Hayes was determined to name a Southerner. Admirably qualified and politically deserving, the forty-four-year-old Harlan was the obvious choice.

*Service on the Court.* Although his tenure on the Court was long, almost as long as Marshall's, and despite the fact that he wrote often and at length, Harlan's reputation at his death thirty-four years later seemed unlikely to exceed those of his colleagues, Justices Joseph P. *Bradley, Stephen J. *Field, and Samuel F. *Miller—even, perhaps, that of the lackluster Chief Justice Fuller. In his defense of private property he was if anything more zealous than other judges of the Gilded Age, being particularly stern in his refusal to countenance state or municipal debt repudiation (see PROPERTY). What has brought him the interest and respect of posterity was not, however, his conventional views but rather what he wrote in certain of his dissents (see DISSENT). So frequent and vigorous were Harlan's disagreements with the majority on everything from civil rights and *due process to the federal *income tax and *antitrust law that he was joshingly said by his colleagues to suffer from "dissent-ery." To many he seemed to be no more than "an eccentric exception," which is what Justice Felix *Frankfurter called him in *Adamson* v. *California* (1947; p. 62), but because important aspects of his dissents were to gain majorities years after his death, he came to be seen as a twentieth-century liberal born too soon.

What has secured Harlan's modern reputation more than anything else, perhaps, is his position on the civil rights of the newly freed African-Americans, a position all the more compelling coming from a former slaveowner and speechifying Know-Nothing. Alive to all the ironies, Harlan was pleased to write his blistering dissent in the *Civil Rights Cases* (1883) with the very pen and inkwell that Chief Justice Roger *Taney had used when composing the opinion of the Court in *Dred *Scott* v. *Sandford* (1857). While the majority struck down key provisions of the Civil Rights Act of 1875, Harlan maintained that segregation in public accommodation was a "badge of slavery" that Congress could constitutionally outlaw under the enforcement section of the *Thirteenth Amendment. His own approach to statutory construction was in striking contrast to the major-

*John Marshall Harlan*

ity's crabbed reading: "It is not the words of the law but the internal sense of it that makes the law: the letter of the law is the body; the sense and reason of the law is the soul" (p. 26). He scathingly contrasted the Court's post-Reconstruction reluctance to recognize national power to defend the civil rights of ex-slaves with its pre–Civil War zeal "for the protection of slavery and the rights of the master of fugitive slaves" (p. 53). In the notorious case of *Plessy* v. *Ferguson* (1896), upholding Jim Crow laws, Harlan again dissented. Crashing through the argument in favor of *separate but equal treatment for African-Americans, he passionately urged the Court to take judicial notice of what "every one knows": "The thing to accomplish was, under the guise of giving equal accommodation for whites and blacks, to compel the latter to keep to themselves" (p. 557). In the latter-day civil rights movement, associated with *Brown* v. *Board of Education* (1954), which overruled *Plessy,* Harlan's dissents were seen as a more honorable past than that of the Court's majority.

In another area of posthumous vindication, *Fourteenth Amendment law, Harlan's dissents again pointed the way of the future. While the majority consistently ruled that the amendment's protection against state action was not necessarily that detailed by the *Bill of Rights against federal action, Harlan stoutly maintained the view that " 'due process of law,' within the meaning of the national Constitution, does not import one thing with reference to the powers of the States, and another with reference to the powers of the general government" (*Hurtado* v. *California,* 1884, p. 541). Beginning with scattered cases in the 1920s and developing into a steady stream of holdings in the 1950s and 1960s, the so-called *incorporation theory, that is, that the Fourteenth Amendment incorporates most of the Bill of Rights, steadily became law (see STATE ACTION).

On another topic, the federal income tax, Harlan's vindication came by way of constitutional amendment rather than judicial volte-face. Dissenting in *Pollock v. Farmers' Loan & Trust Co. (1895), which invalidated the federal income tax on the dubious ground of the constitutional provision against direct taxes not proportioned to state population, Harlan berated the majority for overturning precedent and engaging in judicial legislation. Again pointing to the reality involved, he acidly observed that "the practical effect of the decision today is to give to certain kinds of property a position of favoritism and advantage" (p. 685). The *Sixteenth Amendment overturned Pollock in 1913, two years after Harlan's death.

But Harlan's prophetic spirit was by no means infallible. The same preference for the simple solution that limits judicial discretion, which brought him prematurely to the incorporation theory, led Harlan to resist the majority's reading of the *rule of reason into the *Sherman Antitrust Act in *Standard Oil Co. v. United States (1911); his very last published opinion, in United States v. American Tobacco Co. (1911), denounced the doctrine as usurping the functions of Congress. It was this view on the heated issue of "trust busting" that won him contemporary popularity. On questions of substantive due process—to what extent the Constitution limits the power of government to regulate the economy—Harlan was unpredictable. He wrote the opinion of the Court in *Smyth v. Ames (1898), striking down a Nebraska statute setting railroad rates on the ground that it violated the Due Process Clause of the Fourteenth Amendment by not allowing the companies a "fair return" on the "fair value" of their property; the effect, whether intended or not, was to place the work of all state railroad commissions under court surveillance. By contrast, in *Lochner v. New York (1905), which invalidated New York's eight-hour-day law for bakers, Harlan dissented, a dissent overshadowed by Oliver Wendell *Holmes's more trenchant statement. By contrast again, in *Adair v. United States (1908), which invalidated a federal law prohibiting "yellow dog" (antiunion) contracts on interstate railroads, Harlan wrote for the majority, over Holmes's ringing dissent. "The employer and employee have equality of right," Harlan unrealistically explained, "and any legislation that disturbs that equality is an arbitrary interference with the liberty of contract, which no government can legally justify in a free land" (p. 175). (See LABOR; CONTRACT, FREEDOM OF.)

*Character and Legacy.* Cases such as the latter led Holmes to deny that Harlan shone "either in analysis or generalization." "He had a powerful

vise," Holmes wrote, "the jaws of which couldn't be got nearer than two inches to each other." Even with respect to race relations Harlan's prophetic vision reached only so far. His justly famous dissent in Plessy includes this unqualified affirmation: "Our Constitution is color-blind, and neither knows nor tolerates classes among citizens" (p. 559), a doctrine that cannot be squared with modern *affirmative action programs.

Because he unsparingly pointed out the real-world consequences of many judicial decisions, Harlan was criticized by the formalist legal scholars of his day for including extraneous matter in his dissents. Confident in his convictions, he regularly risked breaches in judicial decorum: reading his dissent in the Income Tax Case, he pounded his fist on the desk and wagged his finger in the faces of the chief justice and Justice Field. Charles Evans *Hughes once remarked to Frankfurter that he had heard even worse: in the days of Bradley and Harlan the justices "actually shook fists at one another." Justice David J. Brewer, a close friend, described the source of Harlan's certitude: "He retires at eight with one hand on the Constitution and the other on the Bible, safe and happy in a perfect faith in justice and righteousness." At Harlan's memorial service Attorney General George W. Wickersham candidly conceded: "He could lead but he could not follow. . . . His was not the temper of a negotiator." A more emollient temperament might have left Harlan in the minority less often, although it is unlikely, given his strong-willed colleagues. More likely, his doughtiness enabled him to persevere in often solitary dissent, expressing with realism some of the best instincts of his day.

Despite his active participation in judicial life Harlan also taught constitutional law at Columbian (now George Washington) University from 1889 until his death. In 1893 he served on the Bering Sea Arbitration Tribunal, which settled a dispute between the United States and the British Empire over Alaskan fur-seal fisheries. Harlan had married Malvina F. Shanklin in 1856 and fathered six children; his grandson John Marshall *Harlan II was also a justice of United States Supreme Court.

(See also DUE PROCESS, SUBSTANTIVE; JUDICIAL REVIEW; RACE AND RACISM.)

□ Henry J. Abraham, "John Marshall Harlan: A Justice Neglected," Virginia Law Review 41 (1955): 871–891. Floyd Barzilia Clark, The Constitutional Doctrines of Justice Harlan (1915). Alan F. Westin, "Mr. Justice Harlan," in Mr. Justice, edited by Allison Dunham and Philip B. Kurland, rev. ed. (1964). G. Edward White, The American Judicial Tradition: Profiles of Leading American Judges (1976), chap. 6, "John Marshall Harlan I: The Precursor."

John V. Orth

**Harlan, John Marshall II** (b. Chicago, Ill., 20 May 1899; d. Washington, D.C., 29 Dec. 1971; cremated and interred Emmanuel Episcopal Ceme-

tery, Weston, Conn.), associate justice, 1955–
1971. John M. Harlan, which he preferred to be
called to distinguish himself from his more illustri-
ous grandfather, the first Justice John Marshall
*Harlan, was born and reared a patrician, despite
the financial difficulties his father regularly confronted. His father, John Maynard Harlan, a controversial and colorful lawyer and reform Republican politician, was a Chicago alderman and unsuccessful mayoral candidate who railed against
the city's traction (streetcar) interests and their
grip on local officials. Ultimately, however, the
frustration of failed campaigns and the resulting
strains on the elder Harlan's law practice took
their toll, and he made his peace with the traction
interests, becoming their counsel on a lucrative
retainer.

The financial security his new clients provided, as well as the family's impeccable social
connections, placed the Harlans at the center of
Chicago society. But the young Marshall was to
spend little of his life in Chicago. At an early age
he was enrolled in a Canadian boarding school,
and the family spent summers at the elder Justice
Harlan's Quebec summer home. In Canada, John
excelled in academics and sports. After a final
year of preparatory education at the Lake Placid
School in New York, he enrolled at Princeton in
the class of 1920. He compiled an outstanding
record at Princeton, where he was president of
the student newspaper, then attended Oxford on
a Rhodes scholarship.

On his return from England, Harlan obtained a
position with Root, Clark, Buckner & Howland,
one of New York City's most prestigious firms.
The firm's chief litigator, Emory Buckner, quickly
became young Harlan's mentor and the most
significant influence on the development of his
professional career. Buckner first insisted that his
charge, whose studies in jurisprudence at Oxford
had hardly equipped him for an American law
practice, enroll at New York Law School, where
he completed the two-year program in a year; he
won admission to the bar in 1924. Under
Buckner's watchful eye, Harlan honed the litigator's skills, becoming a master of careful preparation and attention to detail—a "lawyer's lawyer"
in the eyes of his contemporaries. The elder
attorney also provided his young associate with
his first taste of public service. When Buckner in
1925 became U.S. attorney for New York's Southern District, Harlan and other promising young
lawyers—"Buckner's Boy Scouts," the press
dubbed them—joined his staff, and Harlan soon
became his mentor's chief assistant, vigorously
enforcing the prohibition law both personally
detested. In the late 1920s, when Buckner became
a special state attorney general prosecuting the
Queens borough president on charges of municipal graft, Harlan was again the elder attorney's
top assistant. By that early point in his adult life,
moreover, he had become second only to
Buckner as their firm's principal trial advocate.

*John Marshall Harlan II*

In the 1930s, as Buckner's health began to
decline, Harlan increasingly assumed leadership
of Root, Clark's litigation team. In his first major
case, he successfully defended heirs to the estate
of the eccentric New York millionairess Ella
Wendel from more than two thousand claimants.
By the end of the decade, moreover, he was chief
advocate for numerous major corporate clients.
When a state judge overruled the appointment of
the controversial British philosopher Bertrand
Russell to the faculty of the City College of New
York, Harlan also represented the college board
in an unsuccessful appeal of the court's decision.

By the outbreak of World War II, Harlan was
well past the usual age of military service. Even
so, he was anxious to have a role in the conflict.
When he was offered the opportunity to head the
Army Air Corps' operations analysis section in
England, he enthusiastically accepted. Harlan's
team—consisting of a diverse group of scientists
and skilled lawyers—made numerous recommendations to the military authorities, improving the Eighth Bomber Command's record from
an abysmal 5-percent rate of successful air strikes
to an impressive 65-percent success rate. Toward
the end of his tour, he also served on a committee
planning the postwar occupation of Germany.

Following the war, Harlan returned to his law
firm and an impressive array of corporate clients.
By the early 1950s, he was considered one of the
nation's foremost litigators in *antitrust and related actions. In a lengthy Chicago trial, for
example, he successfully defended the Du Pont
brothers and a number of their corporate interests from antitrust charges growing out of the

defendants' grip on General Motors and the United Rubber Company.

Even before the trial judge had reached a decision in the Du Pont case, however, Harlan's career had taken a new and permanent direction. While never extremely active in Republican politics, Harlan had held positions in a number of GOP campaigns. More importantly, his circle of New York friends included Governor Thomas E. Dewey, for whom he had served briefly as chief counsel to the New York Crime Commission, and the governor's close associate Herbert Brownell. When Brownell became President Dwight Eisenhower's attorney general and a vacancy opened on the U.S. *Court of Appeals for the Second Circuit, Brownell offered Harlan the post. And Harlan—whose public service lineage included not only his grandfather but also an uncle who had been an interstate commerce commissioner and an aunt who had served as secretary to the wives of several Republican presidents—accepted.

Harlan's tenure on the Second Circuit was brief, his caseload confined largely to tax matters and other mundane issues. The one notable exception was United States v. Flynn (1954), in which a three-judge appeals panel, speaking through Harlan, upheld the *Smith Act convictions of twelve Communists. The reading Harlan gave the *clear and present danger test in the case was so deferential to government that a critical commentator was reminded of the archaic English law of constructive treason.

Such a decision, of course, hardly tarnished the judge's reputation with the Eisenhower administration. When Brownell approached Harlan about the circuit judgeship, he had indicated that tenure on the lower court could give his friend the prior judicial experience the Eisenhower administration, following Earl *Warren's appointment as chief justice, was insisting that Supreme Court nominees possess. It was hardly surprising, then, that when Justice Robert H. *Jackson, another New Yorker, died in October 1954, Harlan was Brownell's candidate. Confirmation of the nomination would be delayed in the Senate nearly five months as segregationists and other conservatives used the occasion for attacks on the Court and Harlan's nominal membership in the Atlantic Union Council, which critics decried as an organization of "one worlders" and a threat to American sovereignty. But the appointment was never in doubt with the Senate voting 71 to 11, with 14 abstaining.

On the bench, Harlan quickly joined the restraintist voting bloc headed by Felix *Frankfurter, whom the new justice had met years before through Emory Buckner, one of Frankfurter's closest friends. Harlan also developed a jurisprudence that closely resembled Frankfurter's. A fundamental element of his thinking was a belief that the political processses and principles of *federalism and *separation of powers were ultimately more effective safeguards of individual liberty than specific constitutional guarantees, as well as the corollary view that judicial constructions of the latter must give due regard to the importance of the former in a free society. Harlan's regard for the "passive virtues" did not mean, of course, that he invariably rejected civil liberties claims. His opinion for the Court in *NAACP v. Alabama (1958) was the first to include freedom of association within the scope of *First and *Fourteenth Amendment guarantees (see ASSEMBLY AND ASSOCIATION, FREEDOM OF); his dissent in Poe v. Ullman (1961) embraced a right of *privacy four years before a majority did; and, in his final term, he spoke for the Court in *Cohen v. California (1971), rejecting governmental power to cleanse the public's vocabulary of vulgar speech. While extremely deferential to government assertions of national security claims—as evidenced especially by his last-term dissent in the Pentagon Papers Case (New York Times Co. v. United States, 1971)—his constructions of the Smith Act in *Yates v. United States (1957) and *Scales v. United States (1961) made successful prosecution of subversive advocacy and membership an exceedingly difficult undertaking. In the main, however, his voting patterns reflected deference to governmental power, especially assertions of state authority. In *Barenblatt v. United States (1959) and related cases, for example, he rejected Justice Hugo *Black's absolutist construction of the First Amendment, embracing instead a balancing approach to the amendment's reach, and one according government wide latitude. In the criminal procedure field, moreover, he rejected the *Miranda restrictions on police interrogation of suspects and extension of the *Fourth Amendment *exclusionary rule to state cases.

Harlan also became a *common-law jurist with a firm regard for *precedent. When able, in good conscience, to distinguish a precedent, he naturally took advantage of the situation, as in the reapportionment field, where each extension of the *one person, one vote principle seemed, to his mind, distinguishable from earlier decisions (see REAPPORTIONMENT CASES). The failure of the Court to muster a majority definition of obscenity after 1957, moreover, meant no binding precedent in that intractable field, thus enabling Harlan to continue espousing his view that federal obscenity controls should be narrowly confined while states were given broad authority (see OBSCENITY AND PORNOGRAPHY). Normally, however, Harlan scrupulously honored even those precedents with which he most strenuously disagreed.

Harlan was sensitive to the creative role judges can play through their interpretive function. He believed, however, that adherence to *abstention and related doctrines of self-restraint, rather than attempts to confine judges within the constraints of what, to him, was a generally elusive quest for literally or historically intended meaning, was the proper avenue for restraining judicial power (see JUDICIAL SELF-RESTRAINT). Along similar lines, he favored narrow constitutional interpretations closely tied to the facts of the case at issue and thus limited in their potential for expansion to other contexts. A prime reason for his refusal, in *Griffin* v. *Illinois* (1956), to go along with the Court in holding that indigent defendants are entitled to free trial transcripts or comparable assistance in appealing their convictions was his concern about such a decision's potential impact. His opposition to one person, one vote was motivated by similar considerations, as was his rejection of the Warren Court's expansive reading of the *equal protection guarantee and to the incorporation of the *Bill of Rights into the Fourteenth Amendment (see INCORPORATION DOCTRINE). And while the flexible, evolving conception of due process that he embraced could be used to expand indefinitely the scope of constitutional rights, as his jurisprudential adversary Justice Black argued, in Harlan's hands that vague guarantee was typically accorded a narrow meaning, and one strictly confined to the circumstances of the particular case (see DUE PROCESS, SUBSTANTIVE). In *Boddie* v. *Connecticut* (1971), for example, he invoked due process in overturning filing fee requirements for indigents seeking to initiate divorce proceedings. His opinion made it clear, however, that his position was based on the absolute monopoly states possessed over the granting of a divorce, thus making extension of the ruling to other civil proceedings unlikely.

Finally, Harlan was a leading proponent of the "Wechslerian ideal"—the view, espoused by law professor Herbert Wechsler, that judicial decisions must be truly principled, based on analysis and reasons transcending the immediate result of specific cases. Like Wechsler, Harlan believed that judicial decisions should be based on "neutral" principles, not appeals to "justice" or social utility. He was particularly concerned, moreover, that the Court avoid the appearance of favoritism toward particular groups and causes. The Harlan Papers at Princeton reveal, for example, that in a 10 October 1956 memorandum to his colleagues relating to *Hood* v. *Board of Trustees*, a school desegregation case, he contended that the Court should adhere to traditional limitations on its powers as much in cases "where a lower court has gone *against* colored folk as it does . . . where the decision has been in their favor." In later years, he continued to urge his colleagues to refrain from extending any group or cause special protection simply out of a well-meaning but shortsighted desire to do "justice."

Among those only vaguely aware of his record, Harlan is unfortunately perceived largely as Felix *Frankfurter's shadow. Arguably, however, Harlan was a more eloquent, balanced, scholarly, and ultimately effective defender of their restraintist positions than Frankfurter himself. More critically, Frankfurter left the Court in 1962, at the beginning of the most "liberal-activist" period in the Warren Court's history. It might fairly be said, therefore, that Harlan, not Frankfurter, was the most significant critic of Warren Court trends.

□ Norman Dorsen, "The Second Mr. Justice Harlan: A Constitutional Conservative," *New York University Law Review* 44 (April 1969): 249–271. "Mr. Justice Harlan: A Symposium," *Harvard Law Review* 85 (December 1971): 369–391. David L. Shapiro, ed, *The Evolution of a Judicial Philosophy* (1969). J. Harvie Wilkinson III, "Justice John M. Harlan and the Values of Federalism," *Virginia Law Review* 57 (October 1971): 1185–1221. Tinsley E. Yarbrough, *John Marshall Harlan: Great Dissenter of the Warren Court* (1992).                      Tinsley E. Yarbrough

**Harper v. Virginia State Board of Elections,** 383 U.S. 663 (1966), argued 25–26 Jan. 1966, decided 24 Mar. 1966 by vote of 6 to 3; Douglas for the Court, Black and Harlan, joined by Stewart, in dissent. The *Twenty-fourth Amendment (1964) to the U.S. Constitution banned poll taxes as a condition for voting in national elections. *Harper* challenged the $1.50 Virginia annual poll tax as a precondition for voting in state elections. A three-judge U.S. District Court followed *Breedlove* v. *Suttles* (1937) and dismissed the claim.

On appeal the Supreme Court overruled *Breedlove* in part and held that state requirements for fees or taxes that limit the right to vote are unconstitutional. Justice William O. *Douglas, writing for the majority, argued that the political franchise is a *fundamental right that cannot be denied because of lack of wealth, property, or economic status. Such standards constitute invidious discrimination that violates the *Equal Protection Clause of the *Fourteenth Amendment. He also suggested that lack of wealth—or indigency—might be regarded as a *suspect classification requiring *strict scrutiny. *Harper* extends the *Reynolds* v. *Sims* (1964) principle that all voters must have an equal opportunity to participate in state elections.

The dissenters claimed that there was a rational basis for the Virginia poll tax and that states should have broad constitutional leeway under the Equal Protection Clause to establish voter qualifications. Both argued that property qualifications and poll taxes are part of the constitutional framework.

The impact of *Harper* was limited. Only three states used poll taxes (Alabama, Texas, and Mississippi) as a condition of voting at that time. And Douglas's suggestion that wealth be regarded as a suspect classification was rejected by *Dandridge* v. *Williams* (1970) and *San Antonio Independent School District* v. *Rodriguez* (1973).

(See also POLL TAXES; VOTE, RIGHT TO.)

Steven Puro

**Harrison, Robert H.** (b. Charles County, Md., 1745; d. Charles County, 20 April 1790.), lawyer and judge. The eldest son of Richard and Dorothy Hanson Harrison, little is known of Harrison's early life and legal education. He began law practice in Alexandria, Virginia, where he enjoyed success, numbering among his clients George *Washington, with whom he also established a close and lasting friendship. For much of the Revolutionary War he served as Washington's secretary, resigning in March 1781 to accept appointment as chief judge of the General Court of Maryland, a position he held until his death.

Probably because of Harrison's loyal friendship and solid reputation among the legal circles of Maryland, Washington on 24 September 1789 nominated him as one of his original six appointments to the Supreme Court and the Senate confirmed the nomination two days later. Harrison declined the appointment because of failing health, but Washington persuaded him to reconsider and intending to accept the position, Harrison began a journey to New York City on 14 January 1790. One week later a sudden illness forced him to terminate his trip and to decline irrevocably the appointment to the Court. He had also recently declined appointment as chancellor of Maryland.

Harrison's record as chief justice of the General Court of Maryland contains no hints about what he might have done as an associate justice of the United States Supreme Court. The reported cases of his tenure concerned narrow questions of real estate law or other issues that were of no relevance to the significant business of the Supreme Court.                         Robert M. Ireland

**Harris v. McRae,** 448 U.S. 297 (1980), argued 21 Apr. 1980, decided 30 June 1980 by vote of 5 to 4; Stewart for the Court, Brennan, joined by Marshall and Blackmun, and Stevens in dissent. *Harris* upheld the constitutionality of the Hyde Amendment, a law that barred the use of federal Medicaid funds for abortions except where the life of the mother would be endangered or in cases of rape or incest. The Court held that the right to choose abortion protected by *Roe* v. *Wade* (1973) did not require the government to subsidize that choice. According to the Court, *Roe* meant that the government could not put obstacles in the path of choice. The inability of poor women to purchase medical services, including abortions, without government assistance, said the Court, was not an obstacle the government had created. The dissenters argued that the government did burden the woman's choice of abortion as against childbirth by providing medical assistance when she chose the latter but not when she chose the former.

Critics of *Harris* argue that the only reason the government has for refusing to pay for abortions is that it believes that abortions are immoral, a belief that under *Roe* v. *Wade* may not be the basis for government action, and that the decision sanctions a two-class system of the availability of abortions. Defenders reply that abortion is not one of those situations, rare in our society, in which the government has the duty to alleviate the burdens, which are many, that result from the unequal distribution of wealth in a market-oriented economy.

(See also ABORTION; GENDER; INDIGENCY; PRIVACY.)

Mark V. Tushnet

**Harris v. New York,** 401 U.S. 222 (1971), argued 17 Dec. 1970, decided 24 Feb. 1971 by vote of 5 to 4; Burger for the Court, Brennan, joined by Douglas and Marshall, in dissent, Black in dissent without opinion. Decided after Warren *Burger and Harry *Blackmun were appointed to the Supreme Court by President Richard *Nixon, *Harris* was the first case to limit *Miranda* v. *Arizona* (1966). At his trial Harris testified in his own defense, denying that a bag sold to an undercover agent contained heroin. During police interrogation, however, which occurred without Harris being given the *Miranda* warnings, Harris had told a different story. To impeach his credibility, the prosecution cross-examined Harris about his answers during police questioning. On appeal, Harris's counsel argued that *Miranda* prohibited reference to those answers when it said: "[S]tatements merely intended to be exculpatory by the defendant are often used to impeach his testimony at trial. . . . These statements are incriminating in any meaningful sense of the word and may not be used without the full warnings and effective waiver . . ." (p. 477).

The Court limited the *Miranda* exclusion to evidence presented in the prosecution's case-in-chief and permitted use of answers given without warnings for impeachment purposes when defendants chose to testify. Burger wrote that while *Miranda* can be read as prohibiting the use of an uncounseled statement for any purpose, such a reading was unnecessary to its logic and thus not controlling. *Miranda*, he maintained, was not a license to use perjury with no risk of being confronted with prior inconsistent statements.

(See MIRANDA WARNINGS.)        Bradley C. Canon

**Hawaii Housing Authority v. Midkiff,** 467 U.S. 229 (1984), argued 26 Mar. 1984, decided 30 May 1984 by vote of 8 to 0; O'Connor for the Court, Marshall not participating. *Midkiff* stands as the Supreme Court's most important explanation of the requirement that any governmental taking of private property must be for a "public use," as set forth in the *Fifth Amendment. The case involved a challenge to a Hawaii statute that attempted to undercut a landowning oligopoly that had long tied up land titles in the state. The contested statute gave lessees of single family homes the right to invoke the government's power of *eminent domain to purchase the property that they leased, even if the landowner objected. The challengers claimed that such a condemnation was not a taking for a public use because the property, once condemned by the state, was promptly turned over to the lessee.

In *Midkiff* the Court virtually eliminated public use as a limit on when governments can condemn property. A public use is present, the Court held, even when the property is immediately turned over to private hands and is never used by the public. The requirement is satisfied whenever the taking is rationally related to some conceivable public purpose; it is the purpose of the taking, not the use of the property, that is important. This meant, the Court said, that the condemnation power is equal in breadth to the *police power. The Court also held that courts should defer to legislative determinations of whether a purpose is a public one unless the determination is without reasonable foundation.

(See also PROPERTY RIGHTS; PUBLIC USE DOCTRINE; TAKINGS CLAUSE.)

Eric T. Freyfogle

**Hayburn's Case,** 2 Dall. (2 U.S.) 409 (1792). *Hayburn's Case* was an early and ambiguous precedent that raised issues of *judicial review and *justiciability. In 1792, Congress enacted legislation that required the United States Circuit Courts to hear disability pension claims by veterans of the War for Independence and to certify their findings to the secretary of war. Five of the then-six justices of the Supreme Court (*Jay, *Cushing, *Wilson, *Blair, and *Iredell), sitting as judges of the three *circuit courts, tendered opinions in the form of letters to President George *Washington declining to serve in that capacity. All agreed that the statute imposed nonjudicial duties on the courts and thus violated the principle of *separation of powers. All objected to the *implied power of the secretary of war (an officer of the executive branch) to revise or to refuse to honor the courts' reports. Two of the letters objected to Congress's power to decline to make appropriations to support the courts' findings. Congress in the next session revised the claims procedure to obviate the constitutional difficulties. Despite its ambiguities Hayburn's case is regarded as an early assertion of the power of federal courts to hold statutes enacted by Congress unconstitutional and to refuse to enforce them. The case also anticipated problems of *justiciability because of its concern for the finality of judicial determinations. (See also JUDICIAL POWER AND JURISDICTION.)

William M. Wiecek

**Haynsworth, Clement Furman, Jr.** (b. Greenville, S.C., 30 Oct. 1912; d. Greenville, 22 November 1989), federal appellate judge and rejected nominee for the Supreme Court. Following some twenty years of private law practice in South Carolina, Haynsworth was appointed to the U.S. Court of Appeals for the Fourth Circuit by President Dwight Eisenhower in 1957. He became chief judge in 1964. On 18 August 1969,

President Richard *Nixon nominated Haynsworth for the vacancy created when Abe *Fortas resigned from the Supreme Court. After eight days of hearings and a 10 to 7 vote in favor of Haynsworth in the *Senate Judiciary Committee, the full Senate rejected the nomination by a vote of 55 to 45 on 21 November 1969. Haynsworth returned to the court of appeals and continued to serve there as a senior judge after 1981 until his death in 1989.

In the confirmation debate, Haynsworth was charged with voting in two cases involving subsidiaries of companies in which he owned stock and with buying a company's stock between the decision and announcement of the decision in a case involving that company. Senators who had emphasized Fortas's ethical improprieties felt obligated to take these charges seriously. For many senators, however, the ethics charges masked opposition on ideological grounds. The *NAACP and AFL-CIO opposed Haynsworth as insufficiently supportive of civil rights and labor litigants. Furthermore, the nomination debate occurred in the context of liberal-conservative tension over Representative Gerald Ford's proposal to impeach Supreme Court Justice William O. *Douglas and the Nixon administration's efforts to slow southern school desegregation.

(See also NOMINATIONS, CONTROVERSIAL; NOMINEES, REJECTION OF.)

Susan M. Olson

**Head Money Cases,** 112 U.S. 580 (1885), argued 19–20 Nov. 1884, decided 8 Dec. 1885 by vote of 9 to 0; Miller for the Court. This case arose after Congress moved to assume greater control over *immigration in the Immigration Act of 1882. Until that point, states had regulated the entry of immigrants. Though the states tended to be liberal in their admission of immigrants, concern about the potential financial burden of indigent immigrants prompted the biggest ports to impose head taxes or bonds upon ship captains to provide a fund for needy immigrants. In the *Passenger Cases* (1849) and *Henderson* v. *Mayor* (1876), the Supreme Court had struck down such regulations as an infringement on the federal *commerce power. To alleviate the states' financial responsibility, Congress in the act of 1882 imposed a federal head tax of fifty cents per immigrant, which was given to the states for the support of immigrants in distress.

Shippers challenged the constitutionality of the federal head tax, principally on the grounds that it was not applied uniformly throughout the United States nor did it raise revenue for the common defense and *general welfare of the country. The Supreme Court rejected such arguments, reiterating its earlier holdings that immigration was a form of foreign commerce over which Congress had plenary power. The head tax was a "mere incident of the regulation of commerce" (p. 595) not an exercise of the *taxing power. The money collected was closely related to the government's legitimate interest in regulating immigration. The *Head Money Cases* helped to consolidate federal control over immigration and also helped to broaden congressional power to impose taxes in carrying out other constitutional powers.

Lucy E. Salyer

**Headnotes** are syllabuses, or summaries, found at the beginning of court decisions. They identify major facts and holdings in a case and give references to pages where specific points may be found. The *reporter of decisions of the Supreme Court now generally issues headnotes on the same day that cases are released to the public with the aim of increasing the accuracy by which such cases are interpreted and reported. In two cases, however, *United States* v. *Detroit Timber and Lumber Company* (1905) and *Burbank* v. *Ernst* (1914), the Court has affirmed that headnotes have no independent legal force or standing. Thus, in *Detroit Timber,* the Court referred to headnotes as "simply the work of the reporter . . . prepared for the convenience of the profession in the examination of the records" (p. 337). Reference to this case and its comments on headnotes is now stated in a note at the top of the first page of *slip opinions released by the Court. Commercial publishers of cases sometimes include their own headnotes to decisions to clarify major points of law. Like headnotes prepared by the clerk of the court, these have no independent legal authority.

John R. Vile

**Heart of Atlanta Motel v. United States,** 379 U.S. 241 (1964), argued 5 Oct. 1964, decided 14 Dec. 1964 by vote of 9 to 0; Clark for the Court, Black, Douglas, and Goldberg concurring. *Heart of Atlanta Motel* was the major constitutional test of the public accommodations provisions (Title II) of the *Civil Rights Act of 1964 as well as an important reaffirmation of Congress's broad powers under the Commerce Clause. A motel owner in Atlanta, whose motel served mostly transient interstate travelers, refused to serve blacks as required by the act. He claimed that Congress had exceeded its Commerce Clause authority to regulate private businesses and also that the act was invalid under the *Fifth Amendment's Due Process Clause and the *Thirteenth Amendment.

A three-judge U.S. district court upheld Title II and permanently enjoined the motel from discriminating on account of race. The Supreme Court unanimously affirmed. Justice Tom *Clark, citing *Gibbons* v. *Ogden* (1824) and a long line of cases upholding Congress's plenary power to regulate under the Commerce Clause, held that Congress could regulate both interstate commerce and intrastate activities that affected commerce as part of its "national *police power" to legislate against moral wrongs.

Congress employed the Commerce Clause as primary authority for the act because the *Civil Rights Cases* (1883), as then interpreted, prohibited it from enforcing the *Fourteenth Amendment against privately owned restaurants and hotels. Justices William O. *Douglas and Arthur *Goldberg, however, claimed that the statute could have been upheld under section 5 of the Fourteenth Amendment as well.

In *Katzenbach* v. *McClung* (1964), a companion case that tested the act's applicability to a small, essentially intrastate restaurant ("Ollie's Barbecue"), the Court found that even though the restaurant's customers were local, it purchased much of its food and supplies through interstate commerce and thus was also covered. Taken together the two cases provided a major impetus to congressional efforts to legislate on behalf of civil rights.

(See also COMMERCE POWER; RACE AND RACISM.)

Steven Puro

**Heightened Scrutiny.** See INTERMEDIATE SCRUTINY.

**Helvering v. Davis,** 301 U.S. 619 (1937), argued 5 May 1937, decided 24 May 1937 by vote of 7 to 2; Cardozo for the Court, Butler and McReynolds in dissent. In this case the Court sustained the old-age benefits provisions of the Social Security Act of 1935. Writing for the majority, Justice Benjamin *Cardozo adopted an expansive view of the federal taxing and spending power. He judged the old age benefits provisions of the Social Security Act constitutional pursuant to Article I, section 8 of the Constitution.

In response to the claim that the *Tenth Amendment prohibited Congress's use of the taxing and spending power to raise revenue for a purpose traditionally reserved to the states, Cardozo pointed out that the Social Security Act was born in response to a "nation-wide calamity" that was unsolvable without a concerted federal effort (p. 641). If some states funded programs and some did not, Cardozo speculated, indigents would flock to the funding states just as industry would flee those states to avoid the requisite new payroll taxes.

Only a few days before the Court handed down its decision in *Helvering,* Justice Willis *Van Devanter announced his retirement. After waiting impatiently for more than four years, President Franklin *Roosevelt finally had a Supreme Court nomination. This welcome prospect, coupled with the new voting stance of Justice Owen *Roberts, meant that the president's much criticized *court-packing plan was no longer necessary. As South Carolina Senator James F. Byrnes queried, "Why run for a train after you've caught it?"

(See also TAXING AND SPENDING CLAUSE.)

John W. Johnson

**Hepburn v. Griswold.** See LEGAL TENDER CASES.

**Higher Law.** Throughout the Supreme Court's history, higher-law concepts have played a role in debate over the limits of governmental power. Higher law, understood as an unwritten law binding government or providing a standard by which to judge positive (i.e., written) law, was a familiar if complex idea for late eighteenth-century Americans. From their English legal heritage, Americans derived the notion that an idealized "ancient constitution" or tradition of the *common law set limits to the sovereign's prerogative and, perhaps, even to the legislative power of Parliament. Especially when taken out of context, Sir Edward Coke's famous remark, in *Dr. Bonham's Case*, that if a statute were "against common right and reason . . . the common law will controul it and adjudge such act to be void" suggested both the existence of higher law and its paramount authority in courts of law (p. 118a). The most common form of higher-law argument in the late colonial and Revolutionary periods involved the invocation of unwritten "rights" variously conceived as divinely ordained, derived from English tradition, or "natural." The *Declaration of Independence as well as many of the early state declarations of rights continued this practice of asserting the existence of rights derived from higher-law sources, and early state judicial opinions referred with some frequency to such sources.

During the Supreme Court's first few decades, the justices referred on occasion to higher-law ideas. The only extended discussion of the role of higher law occurred in 1798, in *Calder* v. *Bull*, where Justice Samuel *Chase expressly denied "the omnipotence of a state legislature" even in the absence of express constitutional restrictions. "Vital principles in our free Republican governments" or derived from "the social compact"—in particular those safeguarding personal security and property—would "overrule an apparent and flagrant abuse of legislative power" regardless of the absence of any written provision forbidding that abuse (pp. 387–388). In the same case, though, Justice James *Iredell rejected the power of courts to declare a statute void merely because it offended the judges' sense of "natural justice." Between them, Chase and Iredell foreshadowed the future of higher-law argument in the Supreme Court. The Court eventually accepted Iredell's strictures against the direct invocation of higher law to overturn legislation. By the time of Chief Justice John *Marshall's death in 1835, the Court had abandoned the direct invocation of higher law almost entirely.

The demise of higher-law rhetoric in the opinions of the Court did not spell the end of higher-law argument. Politically, higher law flourished: antislavery activists and their foes, the opponents of state regulation of *property, and the opponents of state extensions of property rights to women all found the language of higher law useful when the written law seemed unfavor-able. Attacking the geographical extension of *slavery by the Compromise of 1850, Senator William H. Seward brushed aside the argument that the Constitution sanctioned the compromise with the retort that Congress was subject to a "higher law" than the Constitution, and that this higher law forbade cooperation with slavery. The availability of higher-law rhetoric to both Seward and the defenders of slavery illustrated the rhetoric's strength and weakness—its lack of any definite meaning.

The sorts of argument associated with higher law in the eighteenth century remain alive, and controversial, in the opinions of the Supreme Court. A century ago, the Court protected property and freedom of *contract on implicit higher-law grounds, but it did so as a matter of legal doctrine by interpreting the Due Process Clauses of the *Fifth and *Fourteenth Amendments. More recently, the Court's *privacy decisions, also interpretations of due process, suggest the claim of early higher-law exponents that courts should invalidate acts of flagrant injustice regardless of any constitutional provision expressly forbidding them. Substantive *due process will no doubt remain controversial; it seems equally clear that its barely concealed inheritance from notions of higher law will continue to influence the decisions of the Court.

(See also JUDICIAL REVIEW; NATURAL LAW.)

▫ Edward S. Corwin, *The "Higher Law" Background of American Constitutional Law* (1955). Leslie F. Goldstein, "Popular Sovereignty, the Origins of Judicial Review, and the Revival of Unwritten Law," *Journal of Politics* 48 (1986): 51–71.　　　　　　　　　　H. Jefferson Powell

**Hirabayashi v. United States,** 320 U.S. 81 (1943), argued 10 and 11 May 1943, decided 21 June 1943 by vote of 9 to 0; Stone for the Court, Douglas and Murphy concurring in separate opinions with the result; Rutledge concurring in a separate opinion with the Court's opinion. At the beginning of World War II officials expressed concern about the presence of approximately 112,000 Japanese-Americans on the West Coast. At the urging of General John L. DeWitt of the Western Defense Command and numerous state and national officials, President Franklin D. *Roosevelt on 19 February 1942 signed Executive Order no. 9066, empowering the secretary of war to create "military areas" from which civilians might be excluded (see SUBVERSION). On 18 March Roosevelt established the War Relocation Authority for the purpose of interning all West Coast Japanese-Americans. Congress unanimously passed legislation implementing these executive orders.

General DeWitt subsequently imposed an 8:00 P.M. to 6:00 A.M. curfew for West Coast Japanese-Americans, prohibited Japanese-Americans from moving out of his defense command, and then prohibited Japanese-Americans from remaining within his command. They could neither leave their homes nor stay in them; instead they had to report to civilian control, or assembly, centers. From these centers the Japanese-Americans were evacuated to "relocation camps," where most remained until 1945.

Gordon Hirabayashi, an American-born citizen of Japanese ancestry and a senior at the University of Washington, intentionally violated the curfew and the order to report to a civilian control center. Hirabayashi believed if he obeyed the curfew and exclusion order "he would be waiving his rights as an American citizen" (p. 81). Convicted on both counts, the court sentenced him to concurrent three-month sentences. On appeal the Supreme Court upheld the conviction for the curfew violation, and because of the concurrent sentences, refused to consider the constitutionality of the order to report to assembly center.

Speaking for the Court, Chief Justice Harlan F. *Stone argued that Congress and the president could consitutionally impose a curfew under the "power to wage war successfully" (p. 93). (See PRESIDENTIAL EMERGENCY POWERS.) The big question, however, was whether Japanese-Americans, as a group, could be singled out for the curfew.

Stone noted that Japanese immigrants were ineligible for United States *citizenship, that under Japanese law American-born children of Japanese immigrants were considered to be citizens of Japan and that "social, economic and political conditions" in the nation had "in large measure prevented their assimilation as an integral part of the white population" (p. 96). He pointed out that large numbers of Japanese-American children had been "sent to Japanese language schools" and that some of these schools were "generally believed to be sources of Japanese nationalistic propaganda . . ." (p. 97). There had, Stone observed "been relatively little social intercourse between them and the white population" (p. 98).

Stone felt "Congress and the Executive could reasonably have concluded that these conditions have encouraged the continued attachment of members of this group to Japan and Japanese institutions" and that "those charged with . . . the national defense" could "take into account" these factors in "determining the nature and extent of the danger of espionage and sabotage, in the event of an invasion or air raid attack" (pp. 98–99). The Court could not "reject as unfounded" the military and congressional judgment "that there were disloyal members of that population, whose number and strength could not be precisely and quickly ascertained" (p. 99).

Stone agreed that "racial discriminations are in most circumstances irrelevant" but argued that "in dealing with the perils of war, Congress and the Executive" could take "into account those facts which are relevant to measures for our national defense . . . which may in fact place

citizens of one ancestry in a different category from others" (p. 100). In upholding the curfew, Stone specifically declared that the Court was not considering whether more drastic measures would be permissible.

Although a unanimous decision, Justices William O. *Douglas, Wiley *Rutledge, and Frank *Murphy qualified their support and sought to narrow the scope of the decision. Murphy's concurrence reads more like a *dissent. He noted that this was "the first time" the court had ever "sustained a substantial restriction of the personal liberty of citizens of the United States based on the accident of race or ancestry." Murphy believed the internment bore "a melancholy resemblance to the treatment accorded to members of the Jewish race in Germany and in other parts of Europe" and went "to the very brink of constitutional power" (p. 111).

(See also RACE AND RACISM; WORLD WAR II.)

□ Roger Daniels, *Concentration Camps, North America* (1981). Roger Daniels, *The Decision to Relocate the Japanese-Americans* (1986). Peter Irons, *Justice At War* (1983).
Paul Finkelman

**History, Court Uses of.** Criticism of the Supreme Court's use of history to decide constitutional and statutory cases is common in legal literature. The reproach is understandable; at times the Court has elevated to legal truth contradictory conclusions drawn from the same historical data. Despite repeated controversy focused on its method and use of history, the Court continues to consult historical sources to resolve legal issues. When it does so, it tends to borrow desultorily, sometimes seeking and finding a determinate answer, sometimes appearing to find but not really seeking a determinate answer, and sometimes not even appearing to seek, or seeking but not finding, a historically derived answer. And the Court's use of history is always instrumental, divorced from the story the historian ventures to tell.

*Whose History?* The difficulty and controversy the Court faces when it turns to history are illustrated by *Home Building & Loan Association* v. *Blaisdell* (1934). The case asked whether the Minnesota legislature could, consistent with the constitutional *injunction against state impairment of *contracts, place a temporary moratorium on mortgage foreclosures to save homeowners' properties during the Great Depression. Justice George *Sutherland's dissent, using traditional primary and secondary historical sources, made a convincing case that the provision was intended to prevent states from giving debtors relief during times of hardship. "A constitutional provision," he argued, "does not admit of two distinctly opposite interpretations" (pp. 448–449). What it meant a hundred years before, it meant in 1934: the state law violated the clause. Writing for a five-member majority, Chief Justice

Charles Evans *Hughes did not directly refute Sutherland's historical analysis. Rather, he deemed it largely irrelevant:

It is no answer . . . to insist that what the provision . . . meant to the vision of [a century ago] it must mean to the vision of our time. . . . It was to guard against such a narrow conception that Chief Justice Marshall uttered the memorable warning—"We must never forget that it is a *constitution* we are expounding . . . a constitution intended to endure for ages . . . to be adapted to the various *crises* of human affairs." (pp. 442–443)

The majority found in the Court's own historiography, in *McCulloch* v. *Maryland* (1819), sufficient grounds for refutation.

Any first-year law student who has completed a basic course in constitutional law uncovers almost immediately the apparent sleight-of-hand that produced the desired result. The quote from *McCulloch* was inapposite, at least on its facts. Chief Justice John *Marshall's exegesis addressed *congressional* authority to regulate pursuant to its express powers; *Blaisdell* dealt with *state* authority to circumvent an express constitutional limitation.

Yet both Hughes and Sutherland had history and the constitution on their side, a conclusion that raises far more questions than it answers. Whose history counts? What would the framers have wanted the Depression-era Court to do in the face of a threat of massive foreclosures? Did they even intend future Courts to be bound by their vision? What normative theory would require subsequent Courts to be so bound, even if we assume the framers wanted the *Blaisdell* Court to be bound? All those questions separate the Court's use of history from the historian's.

*Textual Authority and Judicial Imagination.* Despite the problematic nature of its endeavor, at one level the Court must use a historical approach. Whether construing a statute or interpreting the Constitution, the Court must always profess devotion to textual authority. Justice Owen *Roberts, writing in *United States* v. *Butler* (1936), elevated the authority of text beyond the limits of logic. Taking an approach totally at odds with Hughes's reasoning, Roberts explained that when a statute is challenged as beyond legislative authority, the Court's only task is "to lay the article of the Constitution which is invoked beside the statute which is challenged and to decide whether the latter squares with the former" (p. 62). Roberts's opinion reflects a radically austere, ahistorical, and ultimately indefensible description of the judicial role. The bare constitutional language authorizing Congress to tax and spend (see TAXING AND SPENDING CLAUSE) could not possibly determine the issue in *Butler*. (And, in fact, Roberts himself used historical sources in the course of the opinion.) Nonetheless, the Court must perceive and project itself as a faithful interpreter of received text, perhaps especially when it breaks from text and embraces

historical sources to support its interpretation. Any description of itself divorced from textual command subjects the Court to the charge of becoming a "super legislature" threatening majoritarian will. Public confidence in the Court and continuity in constitutional doctrinal development require the Court to root its decisions in the text and statements of those who created it.

The Court cannot escape critical denunciation, at least in part, because of the epiphenomenon generated by two interactive processes: the interface between the need for textual authority and the notion of autonomous text, on the one hand, and, on the other, the Court's ongoing role within the development of constitutional doctrine. Together the processes practically ensure the continuation of critical scrutiny.

The idea of autonomous historical texts that contain original authority to which scholars pledge allegiance is incompatible with good history. The historian R. G. Collingwood pointed out in his essay "The Historical Imagination" that truth is not what text says. Rather, the historian constantly cross-examines text for credibility in a process that is dependent in large part on idiosyncratic experience, inference, and interpolation. Being idiosyncratic, the historian's creation necessarily demands personal responsibility for an inherently discretionary exercise.

Consider by comparison the constraints that operate on the judiciary at the intersection of textual authority and autonomy. Beyond the need to acknowledge efforts at fidelity to higher authority, justices are politically foreclosed from taking personal responsibility for the decision reached in the same way that the historian must acknowledge his or her discretionary efforts. The justice simply cannot admit that the judicial decision depends upon constructive imagination. Folded within this distinction is irony. Whereas the historian is relatively free to discard authority for defensible reasons, the Court rarely even asks the antecedent question of what authority the framers' conception of text is entitled to. When it risks the question and eschews traditional historical authority, as in *Blaisdell*, the result is inevitably controversial. But if we decide as a purely descriptive matter that justices, although politically and institutionally prohibited from acknowledging discretionary constitutional interpretation, in fact *must* personally choose the outcome of a case worth litigating to the Supreme Court, the justices lay open to the charge of usurpers or hypocrites.

*Judges as History-Makers.* The justice, to a much greater extent than the historian, is a player in history. Historians do interact with their materials; that is the point of Collingwood's description of the cross-examination process, of "constructive history." The Court goes beyond merely reconstructing the past; it canonizes the past and immediately affects the future of the litigants before it and the Constitution it interprets.

Through its decisions and resulting precedents, the Court makes history as it decides it. Its expression of fidelity to textual autonomy reveals the Court as duplicitous: it usually purports merely to transmit received wisdom, but it cannot escape an active, generative role in creating the wisdom it transmits.

Other distinctions between the historian and justice help account for frequently shoddy judicial history. Where the historian selects problems that pique intellectual curiosity, the justice's problems come without (very much) luxury of choice. This fact alone means that justices cannot escape decision-making, despite scarce time or resources. And the justice, unlike the historian who narrates a story with nuance and doubt, must find a single truth, at least for the immediate problem. Although justices enjoy discretion in selecting and defining the issues for which *certiorari is granted, and in describing the controlling facts that constitute the issue, they cannot equivocate as to the very issue they resolve.

Moreover, the justice lacks the comfort of the temporal existence afforded the historian's conclusions. Historians' errors are quickly corrected by the audience to which like-minded scholars appeal. And even without colleagues motivated by his or her error, the historian's creation is temporary: "settled facts" remain static only until reinvestigated at the whim of another. The Court, though theoretically free at any time to revisit settled issues, is constrained by the doctrine of *precedent, as well as by sociopolitical forces such as the need to plan and defend institutional stability. The Court acts as a final decider. "We are not final because we are infallible," Justice Robert *Jackson wrote in Brown v. Allen (1953), "but we are infallible only because we are final" (p. 540).

The climate that envelopes the Court ensures that criticism will occur. Regardless of how it uses history, the Court is always a participant in the interpretive process that it purports to shepherd as a neutral. But all the Court's uses of history occur within a larger system that imposes inconsistent demands. If this description is correct, the best we can hope for is integrity—judicial candor in explicating the values the justices bring to the task before them.

(See also CONSTITUTIONAL INTERPRETATION; INTERPRETIVISM AND NONINTERPRETIVISM.)

□ Theodore Y. Blumoff, "The Third Best Choice: An Essay of Law and History," Hastings Law Journal 41 (1990): 537–576. Robert F. Nagel, "The Formulaic Constitution," Michigan Law Review 84 (1985): 165–212. Michael J. Perry, "The Authority of Text, Tradition, and Reason: A Theory of Constitutional Interpretation," Southern California Law Review 58 (1985): 551–602.
Theodore Y. Blumoff

**History of the Court.** [*This entry treats the historical development of the Supreme Court from its origins to the present. The material has been divided chronologi-*cally as follows:* Establishment of the Union (1789–1865), Reconstruction, Federalism, and Economic Rights (1866–1920), The Depression and the Rise of Legal Liberalism (1921–1954), *and* Rights Consciousness in Contemporary Society (1955–1990). *Each essay treats the major developments on the Court within the context of social change during specific eras.*]

### ESTABLISHMENT OF THE UNION

When the Constitutional Convention met in Philadelphia in 1787, it was unclear whether the government that would emerge from its deliberations would include a national court system or a supreme court. All the delegates acknowledged that a national government more powerful than that operating under the Articles of Confederation had to be empowered with some kind of lawmaking capability and that national laws would have to be enforced by some court system. But delegates committed to state power and suspicious of national authority considered the existing *state courts fully capable of enforcing national laws. Nationalists like James *Madison, on the other hand, envisioned a national judiciary that would not only enforce national law but supervise the state judiciaries as well.

*Creating Judicial Power.* The convention delegates reconciled these divergent views in several ways in *Article III of the Constitution: they created a Supreme Court, giving it original and appellate jurisdiction but subjecting it to whatever "Exceptions" and "Regulations" Congress might choose to make. The convention permitted but did not require the creation of *lower federal courts. The framers defined the "judicial Power of the United States" in terms of nine categories of jurisdiction over parties or causes, and they provided the protection of tenure during good behavior and undiminished pay for federal judges (see JUDICIAL POWER AND JURISDICTION).

The First Congress fleshed out the skeletal authorizations of Article III in the *Judiciary Act of 1789, creating a Supreme Court of six judges and a three-tiered federal judicial structure. Congress established a United States district court in each state, plus circuit courts, consisting of the district judge and two justices of the Supreme Court on circuit, that had both *original and *appellate jurisdiction (see CIRCUIT RIDING). In the act's celebrated section 25, Congress conferred on the Supreme Court appellate jurisdiction over *federal questions arising in state-court litigation, thus creating a potent guarantee of national power that became a focus of contention not resolved until the Civil War.

In the first decade of its existence, the Supreme Court was held in low esteem by most Americans—Congress had originally neglected even to supply it with a chamber; the *chief justiceship went begging for nominees more than once. Yet in this unpromising atmosphere, the fledgling

Court managed to establish precedents of lasting importance. It began to define the contours of federal judicial power, vis-à-vis both the other branches (the problem of *separation of powers) and the states (the problem of *federalism).

One of the most vital tasks facing the early Court was to define what the judicial function was for the federal courts. In *Hayburn's Case (1792), various federal judges declined to act in their official judicial capacity as claims commissioners resolving controversies over veterans' pensions. Chief Justice John *Jay, on circuit, instructed Congress that the political branches could "constitutionally assign to the judicial any duties but such as are properly judicial" (p. 410). In 1793, the Court, speaking through Jay, declined to render *advisory opinions on questions President George *Washington asked it concerning interpretation of the 1778 Franco-American treaty. In a letter to Washington of 8 August, Jay referred to the "lines of separation drawn by the Constitution between the three departments of government" and advised the president that the justices were "judges of a court in the last resort." Finally, in 1796 the Court implicitly claimed the power of *judicial review—that is, the power to declare an act of Congress unconstitutional. In *Hylton v. United States, three of the justices sitting en banc upheld a federal carriage tax as not being a "direct Tax" under Article I, section 9—and in so doing implicitly assumed the power of passing on the question of constitutionality.

As the Court established its role vis-à-vis Congress and the president, it also attempted to extend its authority over the states. But the mixed results that greeted this effort—as demonstrated in *Chisholm v. Georgia—cautioned that questions of federalism would prove much more problematic than questions of the separation of powers. The Constitution granted the Court jurisdiction over controversies "between a State and Citizens of another State," so when citizens of South Carolina brought suit against Georgia under the Supreme Court's original jurisdiction (because a state was a party) in a contractual claim for goods supplied during the Revolutionary War, the Court's assumption of jurisdiction seemed unexceptionable. But this implicated the extremely sensitive questions of confiscation and debt-repudiation by the states during the war and seemed to contradict assurances made by Federalists during the ratification struggle that no state would be sued without its consent. The *Eleventh Amendment, withdrawing such jurisdiction, was immediately proposed and ratified, cautioning the Court that the states would jealously protect their interests against the federal judiciary.

If spokesmen for state power expected that the Court would timorously avoid other confrontations in the future, they were soon disappointed. In *Ware v. Hylton (1796) the justices returned to the touchy subject of state debt-repudiation,

voiding a 1777 Virginia statute that sequestered debts owed by citizens of the newly independent state to British creditors on the grounds that it conflicted with the Treaty of Paris (1783). Justice Samuel *Chase, writing for the Court, not only voided the statute for incompatibility with treaty obligations but also hinted that, the treaty aside, the statute was void under *higher-law principles. Despite noisy criticism, the Ware result was not overturned by amendment, but the states remained sullenly hostile to the Court when its power impinged on what they saw as their sovereignty (see STATE SOVEREIGNTY AND STATES' RIGHTS).

The early Court began exploring the theoretical bases of judicial review. Justice William *Paterson, in a grandiloquent jury charge on circuit in Van Horne's Lessee v. Dorrance (1795), asserted that state legislatures were subordinated to "the principles of the social contract, or of the constitution" (p. 312). He and his colleagues returned to the question in *Calder v. Bull (1798), an appeal from a Connecticut statute that set aside a probate decree and granted a rehearing. The Court declined to void the statute on *ex post facto grounds, but Chase asserted in sweeping dicta that "vital principles in our free republican governments" would void state legislation even if no specific principle of the state constitution forbade it (p. 388). (See OBITER DICTUM). Justice James *Iredell demurred from this reliance on *natural law, arguing that "the ideas of natural justice are regulated by no fixed standard" and provided judges with no legitimate and universally accepted criteria for holding state statutes unconstitutional (p. 399).

From a nationalist's point of view, the 1789 Judiciary Act was defective in several respects. It conferred only a fraction of the *federal-question jurisdiction authorized by the Constitution, and it imposed onerous cricuit-riding responsibilities on the justices, some of whom were becoming aged and infirm and all of whom had better things to do than ride circuits a thousand miles away from the national capital. Determined to ensconce their political ideology in the federal courts after they were repudiated at the polls in 1800, Federalists enacted the *Judiciary Act of 1801, which conferred full federal-question jurisdiction and enlarged both diversity and *removal jurisdiction. It expanded the federal judiciary by creating six new circuit courts staffed by their own judges, thus eliminating the burden of riding circuit. Jeffersonian Republicans, outraged at this eleventh-hour power grab, repealed the 1801 act within a year, and Chief Justice John Marshall prudently upheld the constitutionality of the repeal in *Stuart v. Laird (1803).

**The Marshall Court.** Though the accomplishments of the Court in its first decade were significant, they had really not secured the place of the judiciary in American government. That was left to Chief Justice John *Marshall, who was appointed in 1801 and served until his death in 1835. The generation of Marshall's tenure seems divided, in retrospect, into two periods. The first, lasting until 1824, was a time of expansive constitutional interpretation, when Marshall and his colleagues boldly elevated the stature and power of the Supreme Court and the federal judiciary generally. The second period, the decade after 1824, was by contrast a period of contraction and compromise.

*Expansion of the Court's Power, 1801–1824.* In order to assure the Court's position as a coequal partner with Congress and the president in the tripartite structure of the federal government, it was necessary for Marshall to establish the power of *judicial review: the authority to determine that an act of Congress or the executive branch was a violation of the Constitution. Alexander *Hamilton had claimed this power for the federal courts in The *Federalist no. 78, but the power was not conceded by the American legislatures as the new century dawned.

Drawing extensively on *Federalist* 78, Marshall conjured up the doctrine of judicial review in *Marbury* v. *Madison* (1803). Adroitly criticizing the new administration of President Thomas *Jefferson yet leaving the Court invulnerable to political attack, Marshall reprimanded Secretary of State James Madison for refusing to deliver a justice of the peace commission to William Marbury. He went on to hold that the Supreme Court lacked power to provide the relief that Marbury sought, a writ of *mandamus, because the 1789 Judiciary Act, which authorized it, unconstitutionally granted to the Court a power not authorized by the Constitution.

Marshall justified this result by holding that when the Court is asked to determine whether a statute is unconstitutional, it merely determines which of two laws, statute and Constitution, is of controlling authority. Implicit in this reasoning was the crucial assumption that the Constitution is a law, to be administered by courts like any other law. But that idea produced *Marbury's* central ambiguity: when exercising the power of judicial review, does the Court perform a unique function of monitoring the conformity of the other branches to the constitutional mandate, or is it merely doing what courts normally do—that is, applying a law to resolve a dispute? That ambiguity persists into the present. Marshall also suggested a distinction that has assumed great significance in the twentieth century between the "ministerial" responsibilities of the other branches, which courts could force them to perform, and "political" or discretionary powers, which courts cannot compel (see POLITICAL QUESTIONS).

The political implications of Marshall's assertion of power were not lost on Jefferson. They confirmed for him the suspicion he had borne since his election that a Federalist-dominated judiciary would deprive him of the fruits of the Republican victory in what he called "the Revolution of 1800." Repeal of the 1801 Judiciary Act was one response; another was the powerful threat of impeaching obnoxious federal judges. Jeffersonian Republicans began their political assault on the federal judiciary with the successful but meaningless *impeachment of District Judge John Pickering, who at his trial in the Senate was found to be insane. Jefferson's party then impeached Samuel Chase of the Supreme Court, who on circuit had presided over prosecutions under the *Sedition Act of 1798 with unbecoming zeal and severity. Later, in some *grand jury charges, Chase had delivered intemperate and antidemocratic political harangues about the "mobocracy" that would be grossly improper by modern standards. But Jeffersonians could not muster the necessary two-thirds vote in the Senate to convict Chase, thus leaving the judiciary immune from impeachment used exclusively as a political weapon by a dominant party determined to purge the federal bench of its opponents.

The president was further frustrated by the failure of the treason prosecution of his erstwhile vice president, Aaron *Burr, in 1807. The motives behind Burr's mysterious 1806 military expedition on the Ohio River remain obscure. But Jefferson zealously pursued his political enemy by an indictment for treason, only to be frustrated by Marshall, sitting as chief judge on circuit in Virginia. In *United States* v. *Burr* (1807) Marshall construed the treason clause of Article III in a way that erected a high threshold for all treason prosecutions, preventing resort to such prosecutions used as a political device and burying Jefferson's attempt to import the doctrine of "constructive treason" into American law.

The Marshall Court exerted a major influence on economic development in the United States. In *Fletcher* v. *Peck* (1810) it gave a broad reading to the *Contracts Clause of Article I, which for most of the century provided the doctrinal basis for the courts' supervision of legislative regulation. *Fletcher* involved a state conveyance of lands that the Georgia legislature subsequently rescinded on the grounds that the grant was contaminated by bribery. Marshall construed the original grant to be a *contract, thus extending the reach of the clause to contracts where the state itself was a party and to contracts already executed. It is questionable whether the framers anticipated either reading of the clause. Nevertheless, *Fletcher* was the first in a line of cases that made the Contracts Clause an inhibition on state legislative power.

Marshall expanded the clause in *Dartmouth College* v. *Woodward* (1819) to protect corporate charters from rescission or modification by the state. In *Terrett* v. *Taylor* (1815), Justice Joseph *Story had devised a major new concept in American law, that of the *private corporation. Before the nineteenth century, the corporation served chiefly as a vehicle for public enterprises such as municipalities, charitable institutions, transportation facilities (roads, bridges, ferries), and trading companies. Purely private, profit-oriented enterprise was carried on under other forms, such as partnerships. But on the eve of the Industrial Revolution, a new legal entity was needed to permit entrepreneurs to amass capital without the double risk imposed by the partnership form—unlimited individual liability for enterprise debts and the termination of the enterprise by the death or withdrawal of a partner. The corporation avoided those risks, but investors sought assurances that the legislature would not subsequently modify corporate charters to their disadvantage. Story attempted to provide that guarantee in *Terrett*, but he did so only on the vague higher-law principles of *Calder* v. *Bull*.

In the *Dartmouth College* case, Marshall shifted the protection for corporations to a more certain textual base, the Contracts Clause, holding that the clause prohibited states from subsequently modifying the terms of the "contract" between them and investors, namely, the corporate charter. *Dartmouth College* has been hailed, somewhat extravagantly, as the midwife of corporate *capitalism in the United States. The case was also significant in that Marshall dropped *Calder*'s higher-law concepts completely from the Court's jurisprudence, thenceforth relying solely on some specific clause of the Constitution. This approach gave the Court's expanding role in supervising legislatures a more secure and legitimate foundation.

A different kind of corporation—a bank—provided the subject of one of the Marshall's Court's most influential decisions, *\*McCulloch* v. *Maryland* (1819). Marshall again relied on arguments originally made by Alexander Hamilton and elevated them to the status of constitutional doctrine. When Congress originally chartered the Bank of the United States in 1791, President George Washington sought his cabinet's advice as to whether Congress had constitutional authority to do so. Thomas Jefferson, Washington's secretary of state, argued that it did not, articulating for the first time the strict-constructionist arguments that have assumed such a prominent place in present-day constitutional debate. Hamilton, the secretary of the treasury confidently claimed the authority for Congress, holding it to be implied from other express powers granted Congress in Article I, such as the power to raise armies, which necessarily implied a power to pay them and to handle the funds in any way not explicitly prohibited by the Constitution.

After Congress chartered the second Bank of the United States in 1816, southern and western states reacted to it with vociferous hostility because they believed that the bank inhibited the growth of capital in their regions and that it engaged in fraudulent and speculative fiscal practices. Accordingly, they either forbade its operations in their jurisdictions or taxed it prohibi-

tively. The bank appealed a Maryland tax to the Supreme Court, raising again the question that Jefferson and Hamilton had debated in 1791. In *McCulloch*, Marshall adopted Hamilton's arguments, upholding Congress's power to charter a bank despite the absence of express warrant in the Constitution. The power could be implied, Marshall held, and Congress had wide latitude under the "necessary and proper" clause of Article I to effect its enumerated powers. He did concede, though, that Congress could not enact legislation on the mere "pretext" of exercising its enumerated powers (see IMPLIED POWERS).

Marshall then went on to hold that the states could not constitutionally levy a tax on an instrumentality of the federal government, observing that "the power to tax involves the power to destroy" (p. 431). This holding, subordinating state regulatory power to the supervision of the federal courts, provoked a vigorous denunciation from Virginia political and judicial leaders. The reaction demonstrated to thoughtful observers such as Madison how widely the North and South were diverging from each other in their constitutional theory.

The Constitution of 1787 was a sheaf of compromises, the most fundamental involving the nature of the Union it created. One view, later expressed by Jefferson and Madison in the Virginia and Kentucky Resolutions of 1798 and 1799, held that the states remained substantially sovereign, creating a national government of limited and delegated powers while reserving to themselves all residual powers of sovereignty. The textual basis of this position was the *Tenth Amendment. The contrasting position maintained that, as Marshall put it in *McCulloch*, "the government of the Union, though limited in its powers, is supreme within its sphere of action" (p. 405). The textual source for this view was the Supremacy Clause of Article VI.

These differing emphases clashed before the Court in at least two other major decisions besides *McCulloch*: *\*Martin* v. *Hunter's Lessee* (1816) and *\*Cohens* v. *Virginia* (1821). Arguments before the Court were supplemented by anonymous newspaper polemics written by Marshall and Chief Judge Spencer Roane of the Virginia Supreme Court of Appeals, tracing in prolix argument the implications of the Constitution's basic ambiguity concerning federalism. In *Martin*, Justice Story held that section 25 of the 1789 Judiciary Act was constitutional and that therefore decisions of state supreme courts could be appealed to the United States Supreme Court. Because the case involved lands in Virginia's Northern Neck and was appealed from Roane's court, Virginians condemned the Supreme Court, Story's reasoning, and section 25. Three years later, *McCulloch*, with its assertion of federal supremacy, inflamed their resentments further. So when Marshall, in *Cohens*, reaffirmed Story's highly nationalist position, the Virginians, defending the state-sovereignty position of 1798–1799, demanded repeal of section 25 or a constitutional amendment that would subordinate the Court's authority to state power.

A related conflict over national power came before the Court in the last great case of the Marshall Court's expansive phase, *Gibbons* v. *Ogden* (1824). Marshall there relied on a strained and expansive reading of a federal coastal licensing statute to strike down a New York statute that granted monopoly of an interstate ferry route. The constitutional basis of his position was the Commerce Clause of Article I, here given its earliest—and an extremely broad—interpretation. *Gibbons* is the origin of the pervasive federal regulatory power under the Commerce Clause that has dominated the Court's assumptions about federalism since 1937 (see COMMERCE POWER).

In addition to its implications for federalism, *Gibbons* and its state-court antecedents (e.g., *Livingston* v. *Van Ingen*, 1812) also reflected a controversy about the future of American economic development. On one side were protagonists of monopoly, like New York's Chief Justice James Kent (later joined by Story), who believed that the law had to encourage investors with exclusive and monopolistic grants to entice their risk capital into promoting development. Other jurists, like New York's Chancellor John Lansing, took the opposing view, believing that competition and not monopoly was the surest guarantor of economic advance. Though it struck down a monopoly, Marshall's *Gibbons* opinion did not really endorse the latter view.

*The Marshall Court's Retreat, 1824–1835.* Even during the expansive phase of his tenure, Marshall had respected the constraints that political realities imposed on the scope of the Court's action. For example, he went along with Justice William *Johnson's opinion in *United States* v. *Hudson and Goodwin* (1812) denying federal courts common-law criminal jurisdiction, a prudent approach given the sensitivity of this issue. In line with this view, the Court held in *Wheaton* v. *Peters* (1834) that there was no general *federal common law. But a number of events that occurred after the War of 1812 forced on Marshall a more inhibited approach to questions involving federal judicial power. The depression of 1819 coincided with the Missouri Controversy, which brought in its train a series of crises to the internal security of the slave states. The southern states' affirmation of the postulates announced in the Virginia and Kentucky Resolutions and their hostility to federal jurisdiction forced on Marshall the concessions to state authority that characterized his later years.

Insolvency legislation provides a good example of the Court's retreat in the 1820s. Article I of the Constitution empowers Congress to enact *bankruptcy legislation, and it prohibits states from impairing the obligation of contracts. These clauses came together in *Sturges* v. *Crowninshield* (1819), when Marshall held that the Bankruptcy Clause did not imply an exclusive federal power. It did not prevent the states from enacting bankruptcy laws, but the Contracts Clause did prohibit insolvency laws that applied to contracts made before their passage. This left a question open: could state insolvency laws apply to debts contracted *after* their enactment? In *Ogden* v. *Saunders* (1827), the Court held that such application of insolvency laws to future contracts did not impair the obligation of contracts, a necessary concession to state power. Marshall, for almost the only time in his tenure of thirty-four years, dissented.

And so it went throughout his last decade. Dogged by the movement to repeal section 25, Marshall prudently threw concession after concession to his political enemies. In *Willson* v. *Blackbird Creek Marsh Co.* (1829), a mere five years after *Gibbons*, Marshall held that state legislation that authorized the damming of a navigable waterway was not invalid, even though it impinged on a route of interstate commerce. And when Marshall's prudence lapsed, political retaliation reminded him of the limits of the Court's power. The *Cherokee Cases* (*Cherokee Nation* v. *Georgia*, 1831, and *Worcester* v. *Georgia*, 1832) demonstrated that when the states enjoyed the sympathetic support of the political branches of the federal government, the Supreme Court was impotent in its isolation. Marshall had attempted to extend some measure of protection to *Native Americans from the hostility and rapacious land-hunger of Georgia whites, to no avail. President Andrew Jackson may never have uttered the perhaps-apocryphal remark attributed to him—"The Chief Justice has made his decision; now let him enforce it"—but the president's sentiment expressed the wisdom of Hamilton's observation in *Federalist* 78 that the Court would always require the support of the political branches because it controlled neither army nor treasury. The most significant Marshall concession to state power came in *Barron* v. *Baltimore* (1833), where Marshall held that the *Bill of Rights was a limitation only on the federal government, not on the states.

*The Taney Court.* Historians have long discredited the contemporary idea that Roger B. *Taney's accession to the chief justiceship signaled a revolutionary change in the values and direction of the Supreme Court. Modern scholars have emphasized the continuities between the Marshall and Taney Courts: both were dedicated to the ideals of limited government as a security for individual liberty; both respected the need for effective authority in the federal and state governments to ward off the evils of enfeebled governance; both valued the opportunities that capitalism provided and were determined to use the law to remove impediments to realizing those opportunities; neither sought to disturb the social order in any significant way; and both expanded and used federal judicial power. But the Court of 1837 was undoubtedly different from its predecessor of 1801. For one thing, it now consisted of nine justices. Five of them were Democrats appointed by President Andrew *Jackson: Taney, John *McLean, Henry *Baldwin, James M. *Wayne, and Philip P. *Barbour. Four members of the Court, including Taney, were from slaveholding states, while only one, McLean, could reasonably be suspected of harboring antislavery leanings. Conservatives, including Story, James Kent, and the anti-Jacksonian Whig press, saw portents of revolution in the new Court and its chief justice, mainly because of three major opinions in Taney's maiden term.

The most far-reaching of these was *Charles River Bridge v. Warren Bridge (1837), which bundled together a remarkable array of constitutional questions, including the power of a state legislature to control economic development, the place of monopolies in American economic life, the impact of technological change on the law, and the role of the Supreme Court in supervising state public policy. The Massachusetts legislature chartered a bridge company, giving it the power to collect tolls but saying nothing about an exclusive right to carry traffic over the Charles River. A generation later, responding to the need for increased traffic-carrying capacity between Boston and its northern hinterland, the legislature chartered another bridge, which was eventually to become a free bridge, thus destroying the value of the original bridge's charter. The old bridge insisted that its charter contained an implied monopoly and that creation of a new free bridge destroyed the *vested rights it enjoyed in that monopoly.

Taney, for the Court, rejected that argument, relying on a course of reasoning that Marshall had laid out seven years earlier in *Providence Bank v. Billings (1830). Remaining securely within the constitutional boundaries of the Dartmouth College case, Marshall and Taney held that extraordinary privileges, such as an exemption from taxation or monopoly of a bridge site, may not be read into a corporate charter by implication (see STATE TAXATION). The state legislature may grant such privileges if it wishes, but it must do so explicitly. Any other rule, Taney warned, would permit older and obsolete technologies to impede material progress. Story dissented, insisting that the effect of Taney's instrumentalist opinion was to discourage investors by frustrating their expectations. The Court's position implicitly endorsed the competitive, rather than the monopoly, model of economic development that had been at issue in the Gibbons case.

Judicial Statesmanship. Taney's most enduring legacy is found in cases that involved the scope of federal judicial power. This would have surprised his contemporary conservative critics, who knew him only as the ghost-author of Jackson's Bank veto message of 1832. Taney, then the attorney general, had there maintained that the Supreme Court's opinion on a constitutional question, such as the power of Congress to charter a bank, was not binding on the other branches of government, which enjoyed a coordinate authority to resolve constitutional questions for themselves. (This view would be later echoed by other presidents, most notably Abraham *Lincoln, who found certain Supreme Court holdings irksome.)

Throughout his twenty-seven-year tenure on the Court, Taney strove to establish a balance between state regulatory power and the authority of the federal courts, seeking to enhance both. One of his early opinions, *Bank of Augusta v. Earle (1839), demonstrated this tendency of his judicial statesmanship. The issue presented was whether a corporation could do business within any state other than the one that chartered it. Taney held that a corporation might do business in any state consenting to its presence. That consent would be implied unless the state took some positive steps to exclude foreign corporations. Taney thus avoided the evils of making corporations the protégés of federal courts, which would have heightened state animosities toward both courts and companies, and of imposing an unnecessary inhibition on interstate enterprise by the federal system.

In *Louisville Railroad Co. v. Letson (1844) the Taney Court discarded an undesirable jurisdictional doctrine originating in *Bank of the United States v. Deveaux (1809), which had held that for diversity purposes, all the shareholders of a corporation that was a party to a suit in a federal court must be diverse from the other party. Especially where a corporation was the other party, this effectively shut the doors of federal courts to corporate litigants, an unnatural constraint on federal jurisdiction that became less desirable as interstate business expanded. In Letson, the Court scuttled Deveaux by holding that, for diversity purposes, a corporation is deemed a citizen only of the state in which it was incorporated. This expanded the jurisdiction of federal courts and opened their doors to corporations seeking to flee the more hostile environment of state courts presided over by elected judges.

Taney expanded the political-question doctrine in *Luther v. Borden (1849), one of his longest-lived opinions. Arising out of the Dorr Rebellion of 1842 in Rhode Island, Luther v. Borden raised the question whether federal courts had any role in enforcing the clause of Article IV that empowered the federal government to "guarantee to every State in this Union a Republican Form of Government" (see GUARANTEE CLAUSE). Taney held that they did not, such issues presenting political questions allocated by the Constitution to Congress or the president for resolution. The political-question doctrine remains today one of the most influential monitors of federal jurisdiction, reflecting the creative spirit of Taney's jurisprudence.

The Supreme Court under Taney did not hesitate to strike down an exercise of state power that it deemed pernicious, as it did in *Gelpcke v. Dubuque (1864), the last major case of Taney's tenure. The case arose when out-of-state bondholders faced state repudiation of public indebtedness. The Court refused to be bound by a state supreme court construction of state constitutional provisions when it believed that the state court's reading deprived investors of rights protected by the federal Constitution.

One of the most salient characteristics of the Taney Court, and one of the few that set it off from its predecessor, was its keen sensitivity to the impact of technological change on the law. *Charles River Bridge* displayed that sensitivity; so did *West River Bridge v. Dix (1848), in which the Court ratified the doctrine of *eminent domain and permitted a state to revoke a bridge franchise on payment of *just compensation. In *Genesee Chief v. Fitzhugh (1852), the Court repudiated another Marshall Court precedent that had confined the *admiralty jurisdiction of federal courts to tidal waters. Though this early ruling conformed to English admiralty doctrine, it was out of place in the geographic setting of the United States, with its vast river systems and the Great Lakes, "inland seas" as Taney called them. In place of the tidewater doctrine, Taney adopted the navigability test for federal admiralty jurisdiction, thus extending federal judicial authority throughout the inland waterways. Both decisions reflected the impact of a new technology, the external-combustion engine, on law. Eminent domain facilitated the expansion of railroads, while *Genesee Chief* mirrored the influence of steam navigation.

*Commerce Clause Decisions.* A concomitant of technological change was the expansion of interstate commerce, and that in turn posed the question of how far federal courts should encourage and monitor the national market. The enigmatic case of *Swift v. Tyson (1842) presented the Court with an opportunity to expand its supervision of the economy and thus to extend federal power considerably. Section 34 of the 1789 Judiciary Act made state law the rule of decision in federal courts in diversity cases. The question presented in *Swift* was whether state law included decisional law, that is, the *common law evolved by the state courts. Story, writing for a unanimous Court, held that in commercial law cases it did not, the federal courts being free to select rules of substantive law from "the general principles and doctrines of commercial jurisprudence" (p. 2). Story hoped thereby to encourage the development of a uniform body of national commercial law, with federal courts assuming a leading role in discovering and declaring its substantive content. Over the next century, *Swift*

proved to be the basis for an ever-widening expansion of federal jurisdiction, until it was repudiated as unconstitutional by Justice Louis D. *Brandeis in *Erie Railroad v. Tompkins (1938).

Cases involving the Commerce Clause provide a striking contrast with the creativity and statesmanship displayed by the Taney Court in other areas. Antebellum Commerce Clause cases, with one exception, present a record of frustration and confusion. The Court got off to a compromised start in one of the other major opinions of Taney's first term, *Mayor of *New York v. Miln (1837), which upheld the validity of a state law requiring the captain of a vessel carrying immigrants to provide a manifest containing information about them, the state's purpose being to exclude diseased and insane foreigners. Justice Barbour upheld the state's authority on the basis of its "exclusive" *police power, the general authority of a sovereign to regulate for the health, safety, welfare, and morals of its people. But this holding evaded rather than resolved the question of the exercise of the police power when it conflicted with an actual or dormant regulation of interstate commerce by Congress. The Court proved unable to provide usable Commerce Clause doctrine in the *License Cases (1837) and the *Passenger Cases (1849), which presented similar questions. The justices produced nine opinions in the former, eight in the latter, a sure sign of profound doctrinal confusion and unhealthy instability.

*The Slavery Question.* The cause of this instability, usually hidden behind the facade of opinions, was *slavery. The southern justices, led by Taney, feared that an acknowledgment of a broad federal commerce power might threaten certain aspects of slavery, notably the interstate trade in slaves. There is no evidence that in doing so the southern justices were motivated by the conclusion of modern historians that the interstate slave trade was essential to the vitality and even the long-term existence of slavery in both the old and new slave states. The Southerners' attention was fixated on another problem, the worldwide movement to abolish slavery and the threat that movement posed for the internal security of slavery at home. Thus they bristled at suggestions that Congress could exercise any authority, even indirect or benign, over any aspect of slavery. Most Commerce Clause cases presented just such a possibility.

The Court did achieve one breakthrough in this area, however, in *Cooley v. Board of Wardens (1852), by redefining the problem and temporarily distancing itself from the specter of abolition. *Cooley* involved pilotage fees levied in the port of Philadelphia, which were attacked as an interference with interstate and foreign commerce. Justice Benjamin R. *Curtis upheld the fees on the basis of a distinction between subjects of regulation that were inherently local (and thus appropriate for *state regulation of commerce) and those that were national in scope, which were reserved to Congress. Vague though this formula was, *Cooley* provided the basis for subsequent allocations of authority between states and Congress in questions of commerce regulation (see SELECTIVE EXCLUSIVENESS).

Slavery proved to be the cancer of the Constitution. The framers had incorporated protections for slavery, direct and indirect, in ten provisions of the Constitution, but they assumed that the federal government would have no responsibilities concerning it, except for the one specified matter of the international slave trade. The Marshall Court, sensing the danger and probable futility of becoming involved in slavery matters, managed to avoid rendering any significant decisions on the subject. Taney and several of his colleagues not only lacked the prudence of their predecessors but were determined to mold public law to protect slavery and suppress all threats to its security and expansion. The result was the greatest disaster the Supreme Court has ever inflicted on the nation.

The conflict over slavery intensified after 1830. Demonstrating the validity of Alexis De Tocqueville's dictum that sooner or later all political controversies in America end up in the courts, both sides in the controversy began litigating—in both state and federal courts—legal questions involving the peculiar institution. The first major issues to come before the Supreme Court were *fugitive slaves and personal liberty laws, in *Prigg* v. *Pennsylvania* (1842). The lineup of opinions in *Prigg* was confusing; even today scholars debate what the case really determined, and a dictum by Story, who wrote for the Court on several points, is often wrongly taken to be the holding of the Court. Nevertheless, the result in *Prigg* was the invalidation of existing state laws that interfered with procedures under the 1793 federal Fugitive Slave Act for the capture and rendition of fugitive slaves. Taking advantage of a loophole suggested by Story in a dictum, however, several northern states quickly enacted new personal liberty laws that avoided the vices defined in *Prigg;* these generally prohibited the use of state officials and facilities in fugitive recaptures.

The problem of fugitive slaves returned to the Court in different guise in *Jones* v. *Van Zandt* (1847), in which Justice Levi *Woodbury, a New Hampshire Democrat, sustained the constitutionality of the Fugitive Slave Act and its provision for civil penalties against persons who assisted in the liberation of a fugitive. Woodbury extolled the slavery clauses of the Constitution as "sacred compromises." He also dismissed antislavery suggestions that a judge must refuse to enforce an immoral law on the positivist grounds that a judge swears to uphold the law as given, not to disregard law because it offends his moral views.

The slavery controversy entered an intensified and terminal phase with enactment of the Compromise of 1850 and the Kansas-Nebraska Act of 1854. The violent political reactions to those two efforts to impose a legislative solution on the slavery crisis led some to seek a judicial resolution instead. Taney was eager to oblige. *Dred *Scott v. Sandford* (1857) came to the Supreme Court from a decision of a federal circuit court in Missouri in a protracted freedom suit holding a Missouri African-American, Dred Scott, his wife, and their two daughters to be slaves under Missouri law, despite having been taken by their owner to a free state and a territory designated free under the Northwest Ordinance of 1787. By the time it reached the Supreme Court, *Dred Scott* had become politicized, for it raised the question of Congress's power to control the spread of slavery into the *territories. Not only counsel on both sides, but most of the justices of the Supreme Court as well, sought a final judicial determination of the question, in the fatuous expectation that a pronouncement by the Court could quell the entire slavery controversy. All nine justices wrote opinions in the case, but Taney's must be taken as that of the Court; McClean and Curtis dissented.

Taney began with a procedural question that had far-reaching substantive implications: could a person of African descent, whether slave or free, be a "citizen" for purposes of the grant of diversity jurisdiction in Article III? If that question were answered in the negative, then Scott's suit was not within the jurisdiction of federal courts and ought to have been dismissed (see CITIZENSHIP). But with the recklessness that characterized his handling of all slavery questions, Taney refused to end discussion at that point; he gratuitously went on to extrapolate from his discussion of the meaning of "citizen" the historically unfounded conclusions that blacks could never become members of the national body politic (though he conceded with distaste that a misguided state might make them into citizens.) It was here that he uttered the statement that drove his reputation into obloquy: blacks were "regarded as beings of an inferior order, and altogether unfit to associate with the white race, either in social or political relations; and so far inferior, that they had no rights which the white man was bound to respect" (p. 407).

Taney then went on to consider the power of Congress over slavery in the territories. If Congress could not prohibit slavery in the territories, then a slave could not be made free by being taken into a territory, as Scott had been, even if Congress had purported to abolish slavery there. Taney held that Congress lacked such power, thereby depriving the Republican party of the central plank in its platform. At three points in his poorly reasoned opinion, Taney endorsed the extremist constitutional position that had been evolved by John C. Calhoun and his acolytes since 1837: Congress not only could not abolish slavery in the territories; it had to protect and promote it there. He also suggested in passing that the *Fifth Amendment's Due Process Clause protected the rights of slaveowners in the territories. Many have seen this as the sudden appearance of substantive *due process, but this is reading more into Taney's brief and offhand allusion than he intended. Taney also gratuitously rejected the constitutional validity of the northern wing of the Democratic party, encapsulated in the slogan "Popular Sovereignty," by holding that Congress could not authorize a territorial government to abolish slavery (see TERRITORIES AND NEW STATES).

The *Dred Scott* decision touched off a political firestorm, but Taney remained obstinately indifferent to the damage he had done to the Court's reputation and to the process of constitutional adjudication. Two years later, in *Ableman v. Booth* (1859), he upheld the constitutionality of the Fugitive Slave Act of 1850 in dictum. He condemned the efforts of the Wisconsin Supreme Court to free an abolitionist held under that statute as well as its disregard of an order of the U.S. Supreme Court. A case coming to the Supreme Court from the New York Court of Appeals, *Lemmon v. The People* (1860), might have provided it with an opportunity of forcing slavery into the free states as it had forced it into the territories (a possibility predicted by Abraham Lincoln in 1858), but the coming of the war aborted that possibility.

The Court played only a peripheral role during the *Civil War, not because it was abashed by the reaction to *Dred Scott* but because the Court's significance in resolving great questions of public policy normally recedes when the United States is immersed in total *war, as also happened in *World War I and *World War II. It did, however, by a 5-to-4 margin, uphold the legitimacy of Lincoln's response to secession in the *Prize Cases* (1863). Apart from that, the Court's wartime role was marked by a salutary sense of the limits of its influence, as the great constitutional questions of the day were being resolved at the cannon's mouth. Few foresaw that war's end would bring with it as great an expansion of judicial power as Marshall had accomplished in his first two decades.

□ David P. Currie, *The Constitution in the Supreme Court: The First Hundred Years, 1789–1888* (1985). Don E. Fehrenbacher, *The Dred Scott Case: Its Significance in American Law and Politics* (1978). Julius Goebel, Jr., *History of the Supreme Court of the United States*, vol. 1, *Antecedents and Beginnings to 1801* (1971). Charles G. Haines, *The Role of the Supreme Court in American Government and Politics, 1789–1835* (1944). George L. Haskins and Herbert A. Johnson, *History of the Supreme Court of the United States*, vol. 2, *Foundations of Power: John Marshall, 1801–15* (1981). R. Kent Newmyer, *Supreme Court Justice Joseph Story: Statesman of the Old Republic* (1985). Carl B. Swisher, *History of the Supreme Court of the United States*, vol. 5, *The Taney Period, 1836–1864* (1974). Charles Warren, *The Supreme Court in United States History*, rev. ed. (1931). G. Edward White, *History of the Supreme Court of the United States*, vols. 3–4, *The Marshall Court and Cultural Change, 1815–35* (1988).
William M. Wiecek

### RECONSTRUCTION, FEDERALISM, AND ECONOMIC RIGHTS

From 1789 to 1865 the Supreme Court's most compelling concerns had been to establish its own constitutional authority, to establish the scope of the powers of the national government, and to define the relations between the national and the state governments. By the end of the *Civil War in 1865, the Court's authority as expositor of the Constitution was well accepted. Moreover, the war itself established the national character of the central government and the apparent breadth of its powers. The proslavery record of the Court, however, especially its disastrous decision in Dred *Scott v. Sandford* (1857), had weakened its authority (see SLAVERY). It seemed quite possible that the now-dominant Republican party would challenge the Court's claim to review national legislation. At the same time, the Civil War and *Reconstruction precipitated a potentially revolutionary change in the federal system. Finally, tremendous economic and social changes, associated with the rise of modern American industrialism, took place in the decades following the Civil War. These raised constitutional issues about *property rights and government regulation that would come to dominate the Supreme Court's agenda.

*Reconstruction.* After the Civil War, Americans faced the difficult problem of how to reconstruct both the Union and the individual southern states. Despite significant opposition on the part of northern Democrats aided by President Andrew Johnson, who succeeded Abraham *Lincoln, the Republican party was able to maintain control of the national government. Republicans were deeply committed to protecting the basic rights of the newly freed slaves and of white southern unionists. Closely related was a determination that unreconstructed Confederates not be permitted to resume control of the southern states. But these commitments had to be reconciled with the general desire for a speedy restoration of the Union, for generosity to rebels who demonstrated renewed loyalty, and for the maintenance of a balanced federal system.

Republicans determined to establish a program to secure these goals before they restored southern states to normal relations in the Union. Ultimately, Congress passed a Reconstruction Act (1867) that declared the Johnson-authorized governments provisional and placed them under military authority until Congress recognized new governments to be established by constitutional conventions and subsequent elections.

These decisions raised the profound constitutional question of the status of the southern states and people upon the close of the war. White Southerners, northern Democrats, and President

Johnson were convinced that Republicans were abrogating the rights of the southern states and unconstitutionally subjecting the southern people to military government. As northern Democrats and Johnson lost the political struggle to the Republicans, white southerners appealed to the Supreme Court.

They had some hope of success, because in *Ex parte *Milligan* (1866) five of the justices opined that Congress could suspend the privilege of *habeas corpus and authorize *military trials—a key element of military supervision of the South—only when ordinary courts were closed by invasion or insurrection. Moreover, in *Cummings v. Missouri* (1867) and *Ex parte Garland* (1867) the justices by 5-to-4 margins had signaled their distaste for the Republican program by ruling that *test oaths could not be used to bar former rebels from practicing their professions. The "test oath" laws made the ability to take an oath of past loyalty a test for admission to the bar, clergy, or other influential professions.

These decisions led to charges that the Court was continuing its old proslavery ways. Leading Republicans in Congress proposed to strip the Court of the power to review national laws or to require two-thirds majorities to rule federal laws unconstitutional. But in *Mississippi* v. *Johnson* (1867) and *Georgia* v. *Stanton* (1868) the Court refused requests from the Johnson-organized state governments for *injunctions restraining the president and his secretary of war from enforcing the Reconstruction Acts (see JUDICIAL REVIEW).

The Court exercised judicial restraint again in *Ex parte *McCardle* (1869), in which southerners challenged the Reconstruction Act's provision for military trials and the constitutionality of the Reconstruction Act in general. Although several justices wanted to speed the decision, the majority refused, allowing Congress to repeal the legal provision under which the case had been brought. The Court then agreed that the repeal had destroyed its jurisdiction, even though the case had been pending.

The Court's discretion helped to restore its moral authority as a neutral expositor of law. But despite their concerns, most Republicans never intended to attack the Court as an institution. On the contrary, they recognized that it would be a crucial instrument for carrying out their program to provide federal protection for civil and political rights.

*The Republican Program.* There were two aspects to the Republican Reconstruction program. First, Republicans tried to reshape the southern states in such a way that the state governments would themselves provide *equal protection for the rights of citizens. Rejecting radical proposals to redistribute property, take over education, and reduce the states to territories directly subject to congressional control, Republicans relied primarily on giving black men the right to *vote through

the Reconstruction Act and the *Fifteenth Amendment to the Constitution, ratified in 1870. If politically empowered, black Southerners would be able to demand protection in their rights in exchange for their votes, Republicans believed.

The second element of the Republican Reconstruction program was to pass national laws and constitutional amendments barring states from depriving citizens of basic rights and mandating their equal protection. The Civil Rights Act of 1866 defined as citizens everyone born in the United States except untaxed *Native Americans, who were still subject to tribal government (see CITIZENSHIP). It then declared that every citizen was entitled to the same basic rights (which it listed) as white citizens, notwithstanding any law, ordinance, rule, or custom to the contrary. The Civil Rights Act of 1875 barred discrimination in inns, transportation, and amusement places. The *Thirteenth Amendment, ratified in 1866, abolished slavery. The Fourteenth, ratified in 1868 declared all persons born in the United States and subject to its jurisdiction to be citizens of the Court. It forbade states from abridging the *privileges or immunities of United States citizens; from depriving any person of life, liberty, or property without *due process of law; and from denying any person equal protection of the laws. The Fifteenth Amendment, as already noted, barred both the states and the United States from making racial discriminations in voting rights. Each amendment authorized Congress to pass appropriate legislation to enforce it, and the Republicans did so immediately upon their ratification.

Potential in these laws and amendments was a radical change in the federal system. The primary responsibility for protecting the ordinary rights of citizens had always lain with the states; the national government had never been able to enforce the few provisions in the pre–Civil War Constitution that guaranteed civil liberties against state invasion. If the states themselves did protect rights equally obeying the mandates of the new laws and constitutional amendments, then the practical change in the federal system would be minimal. But if they refused, Congress would have to enforce them. In that case Reconstruction would mark a revolutionary change in the federal system, with the national government passing laws forcing the states to fulfill their constitutional responsibilities and perhaps directly assuming the job itself. Therefore, the more successfully the Republicans completed the first part of their program, the less radical would be the practical effect on federalism of the second.

The form of the Fourteenth and Fifteenth Amendments indicated the leading role Republicans expected the courts to take in their enforcement. Republicans framed them on the pattern of limitations that Article I, section 10 of the Constitution had placed on state authority to impair the obligation of *contracts, regulate interstate or foreign commerce, and other matters—limitations that the federal courts had vigorously enforced before the war and that Article VI of the Constitution obligated the state courts to enforce as well.

Moreover, in a series of laws culminating in the *Removal Act of 1875, Republicans authorized parties to remove cases to federal courts when they could not secure federally guaranteed rights in the *state courts. In fact, the 1875 act authorized the removal to the federal courts of any case arising under the federal Constitution, laws, or treaties, and for the first time gave the lower federal courts original jurisdiction in all such cases.

Republicans hoped that further national legislation would be unnecessary because more direct national enforcement would threaten the balance of the federal system, something most Republican policy-makers themselves did not desire and something that might cost them political support. But when black voters placed Republicans in control of the governments of most of the southern states, the great majority of southern whites refused to accept their legitimacy. They resisted with terror and violence. When southern Republican governments proved unable to protect their citizens, the Republican Congress and President Ulysses S. Grant were reluctantly forced to protect them by direct legislation.

Congress passed laws making it illegal to conspire to violate rights secured by the Constitution and laws of the United States. At first the Republicans aimed the laws at people acting under the color of state authority, but finally they had to direct the laws at terrorism carried out by private citizens. The Force Act of 1871—often called the Ku Klux Klan Act—authorized President Grant to suspend the privilege of habeas corpus and use troops to suppress violence. Grant regularly sent federal troops to keep the peace during election campaigns, at the request of state authorities or United States marshals and district attorneys.

Republican legislation after 1870 made the revolution in federalism that had been potential in the Civil War Amendments real. A vocal and influential minority of Republican leaders insisted that these laws went beyond the powers delegated by the amendments, arguing they were aimed at *state action alone. Democrats took an even narrower view of their meaning. By the mid-1870s enough northerners were alienated by the course of events to threaten Republican control of the national government. As a consequence, Republicans ended their most dramatic efforts to intervene in the South, allowing southern Democrats to regain control of their state governments through violence and fraud.

*Dual Federalism.* At first the federal courts seemed to sustain a broad interpretation of the power the Civil War Amendments had delegated

to the national government to protect civil and political rights. However, by the time cases reached the Supreme Court, many Americans had begun to worry that national efforts to protect rights were undermining the federal system. In 1872 the Supreme Court heard its first case testing a Reconstruction law, *Blyew* v. *United States.* The Court's decision demonstrated its concern that congressional legislation might alter the federal system too radically. Blyew and an accomplice had been convicted in federal court of murdering blacks in Kentucky. Kentucky had indicted them, but federal marshals removed them from state hands and brought them to trial in the federal district court because Kentucky did not allow blacks to testify in cases to which they were not parties. The Court ruled that only the state and the defendant were parties in a criminal case and that therefore Kentucky's indictment of Blyew raised no issues under the Civil Rights Act. Congress, the justices held, could not have intended that the federal courts take jurisdiction of any case in which a party alleged that a black witness might give evidence.

This concern reflected the general understanding of *federalism that most Americans shared in the nineteenth century. No matter where they drew it, nearly all agreed that there was some line separating state from federal jurisdiction and marking an area where state authority was supreme. Ordinary criminal law enforcement, health and safety regulations, and the day-to-day relations of local citizens all were on the state side of that line. Although the majority of the justices of the Supreme Court after the Civil War identified with the Republican party, they made clear that they adhered to this traditional understanding, which scholars call *dual federalism. In cases such as *Texas* v. *White* (1869), the justices affirmed that the national and state governments were equally soveriegn and supreme in their own spheres, with neither subject to the other within those spheres. In *Collector* v. *Day* (1871) the Court held that the Constitution imposed implied limitations on national authority to legislate within state jurisdiction, even when carrying out expressly delegated powers.

Like other Republicans, most of the justices were committed to the principle that in carrying out these responsibilities the states must not invade the liberty of citizens or discriminate against citizens on racial grounds. But the *Blyew* case had raised the specter that the national government would enforce that policy by replacing state law enforcement in general—in this case replacing the state's murder prosecution with its own. Since the enforcement sections of the Civil War Amendments gave the broadest latitude to congressional power, authorizing all legislation "appropriate" to carry out their provisions, the prospect was very real. According to the principle firmly established in the great case of *McCulloch* v. *Maryland* (1819), any federal laws that "are plainly adapted" to achieving a purpose authorized by the Constitution were "appropriate" and thus constitutional (p. 421).

The first dispute to directly test the meaning of the Fourteenth Amendment before the Supreme Court raised the problem starkly. It did not involve the rights of blacks at all. Instead, the *Slaughterhouse Cases (1873) involved Louisiana butchers who claimed that a health law regulating the slaughtering of animals deprived them of their right as citizens to freely practice their occupations. Nothing could have been better calculated to demonstrate to the justices the far-reaching potential of the Fourteenth Amendment. Even if the justices ruled that the law was a reasonable exercise of the state's *police power, it would encourage future Fourteenth Amendment challenges to ordinary state laws simply by considering the issue. It would, the majority of the justices said, make the Court "a perpetual censor upon all legislation of the states" that could be construed to violate someone's civil rights (p. 78).

To avoid the result, the majority of the justices arrived at a tortured construction of the Privileges or Immunities Clause of the Fourteenth Amendment. The amendment barred the states only from depriving persons of those privileges or immunities they held as United States citizens, as distinct from those they held as state citizens. Ordinary rights, such as those to follow one's occupation, make contracts, and dispose of property were associated with state citizenship and were not the subject of the Fourteenth Amendment. The judges in effect avoided a result that Republicans had not intended when they passed the Fourteenth Amendment by construing an important section of it in a way they had not intended either. The result of this opinion, never reversed, was virtually to eliminate the Privileges or Immunities Clause as protection for civil liberty.

The *Slaughterhouse* decision did not make clear just what were the "privileges or immunities of citizens of the United States." Some federal law-enforcement officials maintained that they must include those specified in the *Bill of Rights, since those were the privileges Americans had held in their relationship to the government of the United States. In *Hurtado v. California (1884) the Court interpreted the meaning of the amendment's Due Process Clause in a way that clearly precluded it from protecting any of the liberties specified in the Bill of Rights.

The justices manifested a similar concern for maintaining the federal system in cases involving federal prosecutions of criminal conspiracies to deprive persons of their constitutional rights. They sustained the Ninth Circuit Court's vigorous defense of the rights of Chinese against discriminatory legislation in California and Nevada. The justices also firmly sustained national power to prosecute any state officer, even a

judge, who violated Fourteenth or Fifteenth Amendment rights or laws governing federal elections; they rejected arguments that prosecution of state officials violated the basic tenet of dual federalism—that the state and national governments were equally sovereign and that neither could be subjected to the other. The justices dismissed dual-federalist objections and sustained Congress's power to authorize the *removal of cases from state to federal courts when parties could not secure equal rights there. But the Court drew the line when the federal government tried to prosecute private citizens who did not act under state authority. Replacing state enforcement of ordinary laws with federal enforcement posed too great a threat to the federal system.

*The Court Restricts Reconstruction Reforms.* In a series of cases, the justices tried to work out a position that both preserved the federal system and saved national power to protect the fundamental civil and political rights of the former slaves. To preserve traditional federalism the Court posited the state-action doctrine of the Fourteenth Amendment, articulated with particular clarity in the *Civil Rights Cases (1883). The amendment did not authorize the national government to protect rights directly, the justices held. The government could act only against state action that deprived rights. The Court's language has been taken to mean that only positive state actions are subject to the amendment. The Thirteenth Amendment, which was not framed in terms of state action, did authorize Congress to protect basic rights of freedom against violation from any source. But only the most fundamental of rights came under that protection. Despite its apparent state-action language, the Fifteenth Amendment did invest people with a positive right to vote without racial discrimination, and Congress could enforce that right against anyone who violated it whether under color of state authority or not. Finally, the nature of the federal system implied that Congress had plenary authority over federal *elections, and it could pass any law whatsoever to protect their integrity.

All this suggested rather broad congressional power to protect civil and political rights, but the actual decisions in which these positions were taken badly undermined the Republican Reconstruction program. Ironically, Republicans had avoided framing Reconstruction statutes in such a way as to specifically protect blacks from discrimination. The Court therefore declared several provisions of the Enforcement Acts unconstitutional because they failed to specify that private individuals could be prosecuted only if they deprived people of rights on account of their race or previous condition of servitude. Likewise, the Court found indictments wanting for failing to specify such racial motivations. In the political climate of the times, the decisions were perceived to be virtual endorsements of southern violence and signs of hostility to Reconstruction in general.

Likewise, the *Civil Rights Cases*, while articulating grounds under which Congress could protect fundamental rights under the Thirteenth Amendment, ruled the Civil Rights Act of 1875 unconstitutional. Observers naturally noted its trenchant articulation of the state-action doctrine and the apparent endorsement of racial discrimination more than its reservation of power to Congress.

Finally, after Congress narrowly failed to pass a tough, new law to enforce the Fifteenth Amendment in 1890, new justices on the Supreme Court did take overtly racist constitutional positions. In *Plessy* v. *Ferguson* (1896) the Court sustained state-required segregation of government and other public facilities in an opinion that not only found the laws constitutional but that seemed to endorse them. Although the decision found *separate-but-equal facilities to conform to the Equal Protection Clause of the Fourteenth Amendment, the Court for decades ignored the equality part of the separate-but-equal doctrine and never applied it to laws mandating segregation of private business. In *James* v. *Bowman* (1903) the Court applied the state-action doctrine to the Fifteenth Amendment (see SEGREGATION, DE JURE).

In sum, the Supreme Court's effort to preserve both the federal system and national power to protect rights proved a failure, and it has generally been condemned by historians and legal scholars, who have often failed to recognize the degree to which the effort was made. Beginning in the 1910s, the Court began a slow process of ruling unconstitutional state laws that too overtly violated the Civil War Amendments. Not until the middle of the twentieth century would it reverse the crippling decisions of the 1890s and 1900s.

*Federalism and Economic Change.* From its founding, the United States had always been a commercial nation. The Constitution itself was framed and ratified by men who believed that commercial success required stronger central government. But between the Civil War and the first decade of the twentieth century, commercial activity expanded and changed radically. A great revolution in transportation, precipitated by the application of steam engines to sea and land travel, created a national, and to some degree international, marketplace.

American agricultural products, always exported in large amounts, came into competition with newly opened European and Asian agricultural regions. Prices declined for many crops and economic pressure on farmers intensified, especially in the West and South, where farm debt was highest. Local manufacturers, no longer isolated, had to meet competitors from around the nation, although a system of protective tariffs kept international competitors out of American markets.

Companies sought to survive price competition by increasing output while reducing production costs. Both goals were accomplished by the application of technology to manufacturing. Not only did new industrial technology increase the amount one worker could produce, it simplified jobs, permitting the substitution of low-paid unskilled and semiskilled labor for highly skilled craftsmen.

Huge industrial concerns began to replace small producers. In 1900 nearly eleven million people worked in manufacturing, mining, construction, and transportation, with another three million in trade and finance, outnumbering those in *agriculture by some three million.

The nationalization of the economy led the federal government to take a larger role in promoting and regulating it. Congress established a protective tariff to shelter American industries from international competition in their home market, created a national banking system, and regulated both the amount of currency in circulation and its distribution. It subsidized railroad and canal building, the improvement of harbors, the establishment of rural roads and stage lines, and the operation of international steamship companies. In 1887 Congress established the *Interstate Commerce Commission to regulate railroads, and in 1890 it passed the *Sherman Antitrust Act to combat overconcentration of economic power. It came under pressure to set an example in *labor relations by establishing an eight-hour day for government employees. Slowly, it began to exercise a national police power through regulation of interstate and foreign commerce and by barring the importation of undesirable goods and banning their distribution through the mail or interstate commerce. Some of these activities came under attack in the courts for going beyond the powers the Constitution delegated to the national government.

*State Regulation.* Economic and social changes also put pressure on state governments, which had to provide services to a growing, more urban population and faced demands from various groups to help cope with problems that grew out of the economic transition. Like the national government, state governments had always responded to demands to help develop American transportation and industry, but in a simpler society the free market had seemed to provide adequate regulation, with individuals protecting their own interests through freely made contracts. The triumphant antislavery movement had embodied this understanding, granting to black Americans the same ability to protect their interests as whites.

The fervor of the antislavery struggle recommitted most Americans to this system just as economic change made its effectiveness questionable. The traditional system had been based on a equality of power between contracting parties that the growth of big business destroyed. Yet many objected to demands for government regulation to protect farmers, workers, and others from the sometimes devastating effects of the change, or to protect consumers in general from the growing power of producers and transportation companies. Such regulations smacked of "class legislation"—the use of government power to benefit one person or class in the community at the expense of another. Shocked by the proliferation of demands for such legislation—by farmers, by workers, by blacks in the South and immigrants in the cities of the North—many Americans perceived a concentrated "socialistic" or "agrarian" demand for the redistribution of property. In response, they insisted that government had no right to redistribute wealth. The free market distributed rewards justly, they maintained, and the government must not intervene; it must follow the "let-alone" principle—what political economists call "laissez faire."

Moreover, since the national companies, especially the railroads and insurance industry, were controlled by northeastern financial interests, southerners and westerners viewed excess profits and rates that favored eastern over local merchants as exactions, unfairly transferring wealth from one region of the country to another. Some state regulations were designed to bring these "alien" forces under a degree of local control and prevent the worst abuses. In turn, the owners and managers of the regulated industries complained of local bias.

Nonetheless, state governments often responded to demands for regulations. At the behest of farmers and small businessmen many states passed so-called Granger laws (named after the farmers' organization, the Patrons of Husbandry, or Grange). These laws created commissions to regulate the practices and rates charged by railroads and grain warehouses. They created safety bureaus to set working conditions in mines and dangerous industries. They barred contracts that called for payment in company scrip; they set maximum working hours; and they forbade the employment of women and children in certain capacities. As labor began to organize, some states banned yellow dog contracts, which made employment dependent on an agreement not to join a union.

Defeated in the legislatures, businessmen often turned to the courts—and ultimately the Supreme Court—for succor, arguing that such legislation violated constitutional protections of liberty, unfairly oppressed out-of-state corporations, or infringed on interstate commerce. The Court had to deal with the beginnings of the modern regulatory state in the framework of a federal system; it had to decide not only what the Constitution permitted government to do, but which government had the constitutional authority to do it.

The problem of adjusting constitutional doctrines of federalism to the modern national economy proved particularly difficult. The Court was committed to preserving the traditional federal system, yet it was extremely sensitive to the pressure on local governments to discriminate against outside economic interests on behalf of their own. Likewise, the justices were aware of the economic burdens that a myriad of conflicting local regulations placed upon national businesses.

The Court took a firm line when western and southern state and local governments tried to escape paying the principle and interest on bonds issued to subsidize railroad building or to avoid fulfilling guarantees to pay off railroad company bonds when a company defaulted. The issue arose as many railroads failed to complete their lines or went bankrupt in the hard times of the late 1860s and the 1870s. If the states succeeded in repudiating the debts, eastern and foreign bondholders would be the losers. Local governments alleged that many of the bonds were secured or issued fraudulently. State courts ruled guarantees of railroad bonds null and void because legislatures had lacked the constitutional authority to issue them. But in a line of cases stemming from *Gelpcke* v. *Dubuque* (1864) the Court protected the out-of-state investors, holding that such repudiation violated the Constitution's obligation-of-contracts clause.

The Court likewise protected representatives of out-of-state corporations from special taxes and discriminatory license fees. The key cases were *Welton* v. *Missouri* (1876) and *Robbins* v. *Taxing District of Shelby County* (1887). The first overturned a law requiring licenses to sell goods produced out of state, the second overturned a law requiring a license of all traveling salesmen. Similarly, the Court overturned freight taxes levied on interstate commerce.

The federal courts also took a generous view of the Removal Act of 1875, permitting almost any out-of-state corporation to remove a case from the state to the federal courts on an allegation of bias. At the same time, out-of-state corporations became more and more likely to take advantage of new laws to bring cases in federal rather than state courts. All this led to a significant increase in the business of the Supreme Court and the other federal courts, which ultimately forced Congress to restructure the federal judiciary in the Circuit Court of Appeals Act of 1891 (see JUDICIARY ACT OF 1891). That law created federal *circuit courts of appeals with final jurisdiction in many areas, subject only to the Supreme Court's certification by writ of *certiorari that it accepted an appeal.

Yet the justices also tried to maintain states' authority to regulate businesses within their boundaries. In *Paul* v. *Virginia* (1869), for example, they declared that the insurance business involved state rather than interstate commerce. They then reaffirmed the old rule that states could bar companies incorporated elsewhere from doing business within their boundaries. The Court sustained state taxes challenged on the ground that they inhibited interstate commerce. It sustained state temperance and prohibition legislation against challenges that it trespassed on the interstate *commerce power reserved to Congress.

The Court at first sustained state efforts to regulate interstate railroads. In *Munn v. Illinois (1877) it upheld the far-reaching authority states granted to their railroad commissions. By the 1880s, however, the Court decided that such authority was incompatible with the national transportation system that had developed. It began to overturn various health, safety, and civil-rights laws that states had applied to interstate transportation companies. In *Wabash, St. Louis & Pacific Railway Co. v. Illinois (1886), it limited state power over railroads in general, precipitating the creation of the Interstate Commerce Commission in 1887.

Supreme Court and Federal Regulation. While it sustained state regulatory power, the Supreme Court plainly was troubled when the national government used its delegated powers to secure ends normally considered within the police powers of the states. The crucial question was whether the *Tenth Amendment, which reserves to the states or people all powers not delegated to the United States, precluded the national government from using delegated powers, such as that over interstate commerce, as means to secure undelegated ends. Such a construction lay at the heart of dual federalism, because it meant that there was a line separating state and national sovereignty that the national government could not cross. Therefore the Supreme Court quickly ruled unconstitutional a national law barring adulteration of kerosene with dangerous naphtha in United States v. DeWitt (1869). The Court held that states alone had the authority to pass such a safety regulation.

The Court's clearest and most controversial articulation of the dual-federalist position came in United States v. *E. C. Knight Co. (1895), when the national government brought suit under the Sherman Antitrust Act to break up a sugar refining company that controlled about 90 percent of all the sugar refined in the United States. The Court interpreted the Sherman Act to apply only to trading activities, not to production. Otherwise, the Court said, the act would infringe upon the exclusive right of the states to regulate local business.

Yet the Court sustained congressional use of the *postal and commerce powers to promote good morals, perhaps because it viewed these laws as augmenting similar state regulations rather than as competing with them. Thus in Ex parte Jackson (1878) the Court sustained the Comstock Act (1873), which barred pornography from the mail. In *Champion v. Ames (1903) it sustained a law banning the sale of lottery tickets through interstate commerce.

Property Rights. As the justices wrestled with questions of federalism and the economy, they also had to grapple with what property rights the Constitution secured against government regulation in general. The courts had a long heritage of protecting such rights. In the early years of the Republic judges had agreed that laws occasionally wrongfully deprived individuals of *vested rights—that is, property rights to which they had become fully entitled and that were not dependent on any contingent event. All agreed that governments could not simply confiscate property, for example. Particularly troubling were state laws that seemed to transfer a right to property from one person to another, or one group of people to another. By the 1840s it was quite common for state courts to hold that such legislative acts violated state constitutional provisions stating that one could be deprived of property only according to "the law of the land" or according to "due process of law."

At the same time, the definition of property expanded dramatically. Originally limited to material things, "property" also came to refer to the commerical use one could make of them. Thus government limitations on the use of property, as well as physical *takings, could be considered confiscation. This new conception of property increased the instances in which government regulations might be challenged as violations of vested rights. Nonetheless, before the Civil War, courts had ruled few regulations unconstitutional for violating property rights. States had a police power to regulate property rights for the benefit of the health, safety, and morals of the community, and so long as challenged laws served such a purpose, courts had held that they did not deprive persons of property without due process.

The Supreme Court had indicated a similar understanding of the meaning of "due process of law" in dicta in Scott v. Sandford (1857). The Constitution's Due Process Clause, however, appeared in the Bill of Rights, which according to *Barron v. Baltimore (1833) limited only the federal government, not the states. Therefore, although limitations were able to secure relief when state legislation could be construed to impair the obligation of a contract, before the Civil War they could not appeal to the Supreme Court to overturn other state laws that deprived them of property without due process.

The ratification of the Fourteenth Amendment, which included both a Due Process Clause and a clause protecting privileges or immunities of citizenship, seemed to present the Court with the jurisdiction it had lacked. The Fourteenth Amendment was ratified just as demands grew for increased government action to cope with economic change and as opponents of such activity argued it amounted to class legislation that deprived them of property without due process of law. Litigants soon began to challenge various laws as violations of the the Fourteenth Amendment.

Fearful of disrupting the traditional balance of the federal system, the Court at first rejected the invitation to use the Fourteenth Amendment to limit state authority in the *Slaughterhouse Cases*. However, the four dissents in that decision encouraged further attempts. Almost immediately railroad companies made a concerted effort to overturn the Granger laws, insisting that the maximum rates set by the state railroad commissions amounted to confiscation of their property for the benefit of the shippers. Once again a narrowly divided Court refused to intervene. In *Munn* v. *Illinois* (1877) the justices reasoned that some businesses, such as inns, mills, warehouses, and roads, had traditionally been "affected with a public interest" and therefore were subject to broad government regulation.

But conflict over economic regulation grew more intense in the 1880s and 1890s, which were punctuated by strikes and labor-related violence. The People's party, or Populists, gained widespread support in the early 1890s by calling for government action to remedy the inequities of the new industrial system. In 1896 the Democratic party seemed to endorse the calls for radical reform, entering the presidential election on a platform of inflating the currency to help southern and western debtors at the expense of northeastern and urban financial interests.

These proposals challenged conservatives' conceptions of constitutional liberty, and the Court came under ever-greater pressure to limit how far government could go in regulating property rights. Even as it sustained state economic regulations in the 1870s and 1880s, the Court explicitly reserved the power to rule truly confiscatory laws unconstitutional. Finally, as Populist strength grew, the justices became convinced that the Court must serve as the bulwark of property rights against threatened radical legislation. In the 1890 Minnesota Rate Case—*Chicago, Milwaukee & St. Paul Railway Co.* v. *Minnesota*—the Court ruled a railroad commission law unconstitutional because it provided for no judicial review of the reasonability of the rate. An unreasonably low rate would be confiscatory and unconstitutional. Implicitly, the justices were imposing on the courts an obligation to determine what rate was reasonable (see RULE OF REASON). In *Reagan* v. *Farmers' Loan & Trust Co.* (1894) and *Smyth* v. *Ames* (1898) the Court finally held particular state-imposed rates unconstitutional. From that time forward shippers regularly appealed rate decisions to the courts, which often overturned them.

The Court similarly constricted the authority of the new federal Interstate Commerce Commission. In a series of decisions in the 1890s it denied that the law creating the commission had empowered it to set rates; the Court also limited the ICC's investigative powers. The Court ruled that Congress could not establish a *income tax in *Pollock* v. *Farmers' Loan & Trust Co.* (1895). The opinion concentrated on technicalities of constitutional languages, but the underlying concern was that the tax applied only to those who made more than a certain income, once more raising the specter of class legislation. With these decisions, the Court accepted the argument that various provisions of the Constitution incorporated the moral and economic principle of laissez faire and that government could not interfere with the free market's distribution of economic wealth and power. The decision in the E. C. Knight Case, limiting the government's power to fight trusts, confirmed the perception. Meanwhile, the Court sustained the power of government to intervene to break strikes that affected interstate commerce or mail delivery. Although the justices had limited the scope of the Sherman Antitrust Act's application to business, it sustained its application to labor unions (see ANTITRUST).

The Court also began to scrutinize state police regulations more closely for signs that they infringed on property rights. In *Allgeyer* v. *Louisiana* (1897) the Court declared that the individual's liberty to make contracts was one of the liberties that government could not infringe without due process of law. This placed at risk any regulations that limited the outcomes of free negotiations to set prices, wages, work conditions, or any other economic relationship. In the classic case of *Lochner* v. *New York* (1905) a divided Court applied this principle of "liberty of contract" to overturn a law limiting the working day of bakers to ten hours. Such an interference with freedom of *contract was constitutional only if the Court could be convinced that such a law served some general community interest in health, safety, or morals. Otherwise the substance of the law, no matter how fairly enforced, violated due process of law—a notion legal scholars call "substantive *due process." In 1908 the Court in *Adair* v. *United States* ruled unconstitutional a federal law that barred interstate transportation companies from requiring workers to promise not to join unions as a condition of employment.

These cases were signals for a wholesale assault on regulations of the workplace in the state and federal courts. For a law to pass muster as a constitutional police regulation, courts had to be satisfied that it served their constricted view of the *general welfare rather than the economic interest of some favored group. The courts, state and national, had become committed to *"laissez-faire constitutionalism"—reading the Due Process Clause, the *Contracts Clause, the tax clauses, and other parts of the Constitution to incorporate laissez-faire principles.

*Progressivism.* The Courts came under bitter attack for their narrow view of what legislation served the general welfare. Social reformers, farmer and labor groups, economists, and large numbers of academics and intellectuals insisted that the complexities of the modern industrial state necessitated wide-ranging government activity that did, in fact, serve the general welfare. They called for a "general-welfare state" rather than a "laissez-faire state." The decision of what was in the general interest should be left to democratic decision in the state legislatures and Congress, they insisted. Courts should exercise *judicial self-restraint and rule unconstitutional only those laws that unambiguously and without doubt violated the words of the Constitution. They should make themselves aware of the practical, social purpose of law and decide cases in light of those purposes, rather than engage in formalistic legal reasoning that ignored the real world. Oliver Wendell *Holmes became the spokesman for such views on the Supreme Court, filing a celebrated, trenchant dissent in *Lochner* v. *New York*.

In the first decades of the twentieth century, the so-called Progressive era, these ideas swept the nation. State legislatures and Congress passed wide-ranging regulations to protect consumers from dangerous products, to combat vice, to control business practices, to improve working conditions, and to render more equal the economic power of business, labor, and consumers (see PROGRESSIVISM).

Many Progressives proposed action to limit the power of state and federal judges, but judges, too, came to see that Progressive legislation served the general welfare and generally sustained them against constitutional challenges. The Supreme Court ratified the expanded jurisdiction of the federal government, unequivocally recognizing a national police power in *Champion* v. *Ames* and *McCray* v. *United States* (1904). The national power to regulate interstate commerce and to levy taxes, the justices held, was plenary and absolute. It could be used to serve the health and safety of the community—by regulating what passed through interstate commerce or banning transportation of undesirable goods entirely, or by levying prohibitively high taxes to suppress undesirable products. That such laws had the character of police regulations, traditionally within state jurisdiction, did not affect their constitutionality as regulations of interstate commerce. Thus the Court seemed to abandon the key tenet of dual federalism. In response, the federal government passed numerous interstate commerce regulations designed for other general-welfare purposes.

Likewise the Court abandoned its cramped interpretation of the Sherman Antitrust Act. It allowed federal health and safety regulation of local businesses at the source or terminus of what it now saw as a *stream of commerce, and it sustained government regulations governing almost every aspect of employment in interstate transportation companies.

Prodded by legal briefs that included sociological data, first submitted by Louis D. *Brandeis in *Muller* v. *Oregon* (1908), the justices expanded their understanding of what legislation might serve the general welfare (see BRANDEIS BRIEF). In that case, the Court sustained legislation setting maximum hours women might work in public laundries, accepting the principle that the general welfare was served when legislation took into account the special circumstances of dangerous or unhealthy occupations and vulnerable workers, such as women and children (see GENDER). The Court also sustained workmen's compensation laws, which required employers to contribute to a fund to protect workers against the economic consequences of accidents. In general the Court accepted a broad range of laws that interfered with "liberty of contract."

The Court's progressivism culminated in decisions sustaining pervasive economic controls imposed by Congress during *World War I. National defense was so clearly related to the public welfare that the Court sustained price and rent controls and other rigorous wartime regulations of the American economy (see also WAR).

As most Americans endorsed a return to "normalcy" after war's end, however, the Supreme Court also retreated from Progressivism. In the child-labor cases of *Hammer* v. *Dagenhart* (1918) and *Bailey* v. *Drexel Furniture Company* (1922), the Court revived dual-federalist limitations on the national interstate commerce and taxing powers, holding that neither could be used to suppress child labor. Regulation of employment of companies not engaged in transportation was within state, not federal, jurisdiction. Then, in *Adkins* v. *Children's Hospital* (1923), the Court ruled that a minimum wage for women interfered with liberty of contract in a way that could not be justified as serving the general welfare. The Court seemed to have revived dual federalism and laissez-faire constitutionalism. The resulting confusion would not be resolved until the constitutional crisis precipitated when the Court applied these principles to the *New Deal.

□ Michael Les Benedict, "Preserving Federalism: Reconstruction and the Waite Court," *Supreme Court Review* (1978): 39–79. Michael Les Benedict, "Laissez Faire and Liberty: A Re-Evaluation of the Meaning and Origins of Laissez-Faire Constitutionalism," *Law and History Review* 3 (1985): 293–331. Loren P. Beth, *The Development of the American Constitution, 1877–1917* (1971). Charles Fairman, *History of the Supreme Court of the United States*, vols. 6–7, *Reconstruction and Reunion, 1864–88* (1971, 1987). Robert J. Kaczorowski, *The Politics of Judicial Interpretation: The Federal Courts, Department of Justice and Civil Rights, 1866–1876* (1985). Stanley I. Kutler, *Judicial Power and Reconstruction Politics* (1968). John J. Semonche, *Charting the Future: The Supreme Court Responds to a Changing Society, 1890–1920* (1978). William F. Swindler, *Court and Constitution in the Twentieth Century: The Old Legality, 1889–1932* (1969). Michael Les Benedict

The United States entered the decade of the 1920s with a probusiness mentality. The free-enterprise system would provide Americans with the highest standard of living in the history of the world, and most Americans did not want to do anything to threaten that system. On the Supreme Court, the decade also began with the conservative majority sensitive to real or perceived threats to *property rights and less concerned about individual liberties. In the three decades that followed, however, the Court's agenda turned completely around, and by 1954 the question of property rights had receded to a relatively unimportant place on the Court's docket. Instead, the judiciary had taken the lead in extending constitutional protections of life and liberty to all of the nation's citizens.

During the Progressive era, the Supreme Court had shown itself surprisingly receptive to the protective legislation passed by the states and Congress to ameliorate the harshest aspects of industrial life (see PROGRESSIVISM). Although in the most famous of these cases *Lochner v. New York (1905), a 5-to-4 majority struck down a state working-hours law, that case was really an aberration from the generally positive record of the Court.

**The Taft Court.** By the end of *World War I, however, a distinctly conservative tone had set in, despite the appointment of the liberals Louis D. *Brandeis and John H. *Clarke to the bench, as evidenced in the first child-labor case, *Hammer v. Dagenhart (1918). This conservative cast took a distinctly stronger tone with the appointment of William Howard *Taft as *chief justice in 1921.

The Court during the decade that Taft occupied the *center chair is a study in contradictions. On the one hand, it took an uncompromisingly probusiness stance and steadfastly opposed both state and federal efforts to regulate the economy; on the other, it showed a clear sympathy for individual liberties.

*Probusiness Decisions.* Given the makeup of the Court, its tilt in favor of business is hardly surprising. Taft strongly believed in the sanctity of property rights and assumed that the Court should play a major role in sustaining a constitutional system that upheld those rights. Taft found a strong ally in Justice James C. *McReynolds, the near-reactionary former attorney general whose *antitrust sentiment had led President Woodrow Wilson to mistakenly assume that McReynolds was a progressive. Taft used his political influence with the Harding administration to secure the appointment of George *Sutherland, Pierce *Butler, and Edward *Sanford to the bench. Together with Justices Willis *Van Devanter and Mahlon *Pitney, whom Taft had appointed when was president, they made a comfortable majority to strike down legislation that attempted to regulate business. Only Justices Oliver Wendell *Holmes and Brandeis opposed this view; Justice Clarke had resigned from the Court in 1922 to take up the work of the League of Nations.

The environment of the 1920s strongly favored business, so much so that Calvin Coolidge could say that "the business of America is business." Industry expanded enormously in the postwar decade and in doing so significantly raised the American standard of living. By the time Herbert Hoover ran for president in 1928, he could confidently predict that poverty would soon disappear from American life. Just let businessmen alone, and the free enterprise economy would do the rest (see CAPITALISM).

The conservative majority on the Court shared this sentiment. It practically emasculated the Federal Trade Commission in *FTC* v. *Curtis Publishing Co.* (1923), in which Justice McReynolds dismissed the FTC's factual investigation and held that courts could reexamine evidence *de novo*. A business could thus stymie the FTC by claiming that it had not evaluated the evidence properly and then tie up the agency in court for years. The Court had similarly tied the hands of state regulatory agencies in *Southwestern Bell Telephone Co.* v. *Public Service Commission of Missouri* (1923).

The antilabor bias that had marked the Court for more than three decades continued unabated during the 1920s, even though labor leaders believed they had won a significant victory in the Clayton Antitrust Act of 1914. Section 6 of that act had specifically declared that *labor did not constitute a commodity or an article of commerce and that the *antitrust laws should not be used to hinder unions seeking legitimate objectives. Section 20 directly responded to the widespread use of *injunctions against unions, prohibiting federal courts from issuing injunctions in labor disputes "unless necessary to prevent irreparable injury to property, or to a property right."

Despite the clear intent of the law, the Taft Court found a way around it. In *Duplex Printing Press Co.* v. *Deering* (1921), Justice Pitney interpreted the law not to apply to secondary boycotts and held that injunctions could therefore be issued not only against the immediate parties to the labor disputes but also against anyone trying to help the unions. This decision came immediately after *Truax* v. *Corrigan* (1921), in which the Court voided a state anti-injunction statute. The two decisions are indicative of what some scholars have labeled *dual federalism, a gray area in which neither the states nor the federal government could operate. As a result, both state and federal courts continued to issue injunctions in labor disputes as if the Clayton Act had never been passed, and the matter was not settled until Congress passed the Norris-LaGuardia Anti-Injunction Act in 1932, when the depression had undermined the influence of business interests.

Protective legislation also fared poorly in the

Taft Court. After the first child-labor case, in which the Court had said that Congress could not regulate child labor under the Commerce Clause, Congress had passed a second bill, utilizing its taxing powers, which up to that time had been considered practically unlimited (see COMMERCE POWER). Nonetheless, in *Bailey v. Drexel Furniture Co. (1922), the Court struck down the second Child Labor Act on the grounds that Congress could not use the taxing power to achieve an end forbidden it under the Commerce Clause (see TAXING AND SPENDING CLAUSE).

But the one decision that epitomized the probusiness attitude of the Court in this era was *Adkins v. Children's Hospital (1923), which led even some conservatives to protest. In striking down a District of Columbia minimum-wage statute for women, Justice Sutherland resurrected the Lochner doctrine and reaffirmed the supremacy of freedom of *contract in economic affairs. By this time the nation believed, based on several court decisions going back to *Muller v. Oregon (1908), that states and the federal government could protect women under the *police power. Sutherland, however, held that the *Nineteenth Amendment had emancipated women and that they no longer needed special protection (see GENDER). This proved too much even for Taft, who could hardly be described as a liberal, and who issued one of his rare dissents, claiming that Congress had the power to pass such legislation and that the courts should not interpose their views concerning the wisdom of such legislation.

Following Adkins, the Court found approximately 140 state laws unconstitutional, most on the grounds that they violated the rights of property and contract guaranteed by the *Due Process Clause of the *Fourteenth Amendment. Even where there had been a clear line of precedent supporting regulatory legislation, the Court reinterpreted it in a probusiness manner. Thus in *Wolff Packing Co. v. Court of Industrial Relations (1923), Taft struck down a state experiment in labor relations by taking a narrow view of "business affected with a public interest." But practically no enterprise would fit into this category, a conclusion reinforced in *Tyson v. Banton (1927) and Ribnik v. McBride (1928), when the Court voided state efforts to control ticket and employment agencies, both of which, it said, had no relation to public interest regardless of what the state had decided.

It is hardly surprising that throughout the decade the National Association of Manufacturers passed resolutions praising the Supreme Court as the "indispensable interpreter of our written Constitution" and the protector of property from the "babel voices of the mob." So long as the nation continued to be prosperous it appeared that business could do no wrong, and the Court, despite powerful protests from Justices Holmes and Brandeis, would make sure that government did not interfere with business.

*Civil Liberties*. One might have expected that a Court so overwhelmingly probusiness and antilabor would have been indifferent if not actually hostile to civil rights and civil liberties. There are some cases that support this view, such as the infamous *Buck v. Bell (1927), in which Holmes upheld a state compulsory sterilization law on the grounds that "three generations of imbeciles are enough" (p. 207). The Court that had shown little concern for freedom of *speech in the postwar years a decade later upheld government investigation through wiretaps in *Olmstead v. United States (1928). Yet the story is not simple. The clash between tradition and modernism going on in the larger society had its reflex within the Court, which during the 1920s took the first steps toward a modern jurisprudence of civil rights and civil liberties.

Although reformers won few victories during the 1920s, the reform spirit remained alive in Congress and the states through the efforts of people like Wisconsin senator Robert M. La Follette, New York senator Robert Wagner, and labor reformer Florence Kelley. The spirit of legal reform, at least in the academies, also showed itself far from dead. Legal scholars at Yale and Columbia established the foundations of "legal realism," which would revolutionize legal thinking in the years to come.

Holmes, in his Lowell Lectures on the *common law in 1881, had suggested that all sorts of nonlegal matters affected the law even more than abstract logic. During the early part of the century, advocates of *"sociological jurisprudence" had used this insight in an effort to get courts to take economic and social facts into account; the most famous example was the brief Brandeis submitted in the Muller case to support the Oregon working-hours law (see BRANDEIS BRIEF).

The legal realists went even further, seeing law not as fixed but as constantly in flux, responding to changing social conditions. Moreover, as Karl Llewellyn and others argued, one had to look not at legal rules but at how law actually came to be, and this involved a wide variety of social, economic, and even psychological factors. Judges did not "discover" law; they made it, and the courts provided the creative response necessary to keep law abreast of the times.

The realists found some allies on the bench, such as Learned *Hand and Benjamin N. *Cardozo, but on the Supreme Court they looked especially to Brandeis. Although we often talk about "Holmes and Brandeis" dissenting, Holmes is remembered mostly for his wit, style, and ability to sum up an argument in a pithy epigram while Brandeis, in his lengthy dissents, provided the analysis of the law and, especially, the facts and conditions surrounding a law that would influence future jurisprudence.

Brandeis led the way, for example, in his *dissent in Gilbert v. Minnesota (1920), a speech case in which he suggested for the first time that the liberties protected by the Fourteenth Amendment might include civil liberties as well as property rights. That argument began to take on substance when Justice McReynolds, in *Meyer v. Nebraska* (1923), struck down a state law forbidding the teaching of foreign languages in elementary school. Liberty, McReynolds declared, went beyond freedom from bodily restraint to include "those privileges long recognized at common law as essential to the orderly pursuit of happiness by free men" (p. 399). (See EDUCATION.)

Two years later, McReynolds again spoke for a unanimous Court in *Pierce v. Society of Sisters* (1925) in striking down an Oregon law, inspired by the Ku Klux Klan, that had the clear intent of driving Catholic schools out of business. McReynolds found the right to educate one's children to be another liberty protected by the Fourteenth Amendment. This decision led the *American Civil Liberties Union to challenge a New York Criminal Anarchy Act on the grounds that it violated free speech.

Ever since *Barron v. Baltimore* (1833) the *Bill of Rights had been held to apply only to the federal government and not to the states. Brandeis's suggestion that the Fourteenth Amendment somehow "incorporated" the provisions of the first eight amendments, making them applicable to the states as well as to the federal government, bore fruit in *Gitlow v. New York* (1925). Although a 7-to-2 majority of the Court upheld the New York statute, Justice Sanford noted that "for present purposes we may and do assume that freedom of speech and of the press—which are protected by the *First Amendment from abridgement by Congress—are among the fundamental personal rights protected by the due process clause of the Fourteenth Amendment from impairment by the States" (p. 666). It would be several years before the full impact of this holding would be felt, and it would then trigger a major jurisprudential debate over the extent to which the Fourteenth Amendment incorporated other rights (see INCORPORATION DOCTRINE).

The Taft Court, however, began this process of "nationalizing" rights in an area that had traditionally been left entirely to the discretion of the states, criminal law. In *Moore v. Dempsey* (1923), Holmes ruled that a federal court should hear the appeal of five African-Americans, convicted of first-degree murder by an Arkansas state court, where the constant threat of mob violence had tainted the proceedings. And in the infamous Scottsboro case, *Powell v. Alabama* (1932), Justice Sutherland specifically applied the *Fifth Amendment right to a fair trial to the states (see TRIAL BY JURY).

Not all of the Taft Court decisions furthered civil rights or civil liberties. In *Corrigan v. Buckley* (1926), the justices unanimously refused to invalidate racially *restrictive covenants as violative of due process. The justices also showed little concern for other racial groups, upholding a

variety of state and federal restrictions on Asians and aliens. For instance, the Court in *United States v. Schwimmer* (1929) sustained the denial of a citizenship application because of the applicant's pacifist views.

Even though the Court extended the reach of the First Amendment, a majority showed little concern for the actual protection of free speech. In one of the most famous cases of the decade, *Whitney v. California* (1927), the majority upheld the conviction of Anita Whitney under the California *Criminal Syndicalism Act for helping to organize a communist party in that state. Justice Brandeis concurred in the result on technical grounds, but his opinion remains one of the strongest defenses of freedom of speech ever penned by a member of the Court, setting out for the first time the idea of free speech as an essential requisite for active *citizenship in a republic.

Brandeis also claimed that the Constitution protected *privacy in his dissent in the wiretapping case, *Olmstead v. United States*. Chief Justice Taft's opinion for the majority declared that, since there had been no actual physical intrusion into the house, wiretapping did not violate the *Fourth Amendment. This elicited a short dissent from Holmes, who called wiretapping a "dirty business," and a longer and well-reasoned scholarly analysis from Justice Butler, generally considered a conservative. But Brandeis, in dissent, evoked the spirit of the Fourth Amendment, which he declared protected Americans in their right to be let alone, "the most comprehensive of rights, and the right most valued by civilized man" (p. 478). Wiretapping remained legally permissible, although Congress outlawed the use of wiretap service in federal courts in 1934. Not until *Berger v. New York* (1967) did the Court overrule *Olmstead* and adopt the Brandeis view. Two years before that, in *Griswold v. Connecticut* (1965), the Court recognized privacy as a constitutionally protected right.

**The Hughes Court.** The mixed record of the Court during the Taft years left no clear legacy to its successors, although its hesitant first steps in incorporating the Bill of Rights and establishing national standards would lead the way to one of the great jurisprudential developments of the twentieth century. But the underlying context of the Taft Court—the probusiness attitude of the nation—collapsed in late 1929. When Charles Evans Hughes took Taft's place in the center chair, he and the Court faced a variety of new challenges generated by the depression and Franklin D. *Roosevelt's *New Deal efforts to deal with the economy.

The Hughes Court retained a solid bloc of four conservative judges—McReynolds, Van Devanter, Sutherland and Butler—opposed to any and all efforts by the government to regulate business. The smaller bloc of liberals would have permitted the states and the federal government greater leeway in responding to the crisis. This group consisted of Justices Brandeis, Harlan Fiske *Stone, and the widely respected Benjamin N. Cardozo, who had taken Holmes's place in 1932. In the middle of this spectrum were Hughes and Justice Owen J. *Roberts, appointed to the Court by Herbert Hoover in 1930, either one of whom would give the Four Horsemen, as the conservative bloc came to be known, a majority in opposing reform legislation.

*New Deal under Fire.* State efforts to regulate business reached the Court in *New State Ice Co. v. Liebmann* (1932). Oklahoma had attempted to stabilize the ice market by requiring new entrants to secure a certificate of convenience. The majority struck down the bill as exceeding the state's power and denied that ice-making affected the public interest. Justice Brandeis's dissent is notable for several reasons. First, he painstakingly explored the various economic factors that had led the state to pass the legislation. Second, he called on his fellow justices to practice *judicial self-restraint and not interpose their views in place of the action of duly elected legislators. And then, in a most eloquent manner, he spoke of the nature of *federalism and the advantages of having individual states serve as social laboratories in the face of an overwhelming national crisis.

Onlookers believed that perhaps this message had gotten through, because soon afterwards the Court did uphold two state laws aimed at ameliorating the effects of the depression. It sustained a Minnesota mortgage moratorium in *Home Building and Loan Association v. Blaisdell* (1934) and a New York price-fixing statute in *Nebbia v. New York* (1934). These decisions, both reached by bare 5-to-4 majorities, did not bode well for the New Deal, which unlike any reform movement that preceded it tried to manage as well as reform the economy. President Roosevelt compared the depression to war and proposed drastic and innovative legislation to deal with the crisis. Without getting into the question of whether the New Deal actually relieved the depression, one can say that conservatives bitterly opposed the government's efforts to regulate the economy and especially its efforts to help labor and other underprivileged groups. One can also say that the American people, as evidenced in the 1936 election, overwhelmingly supported the New Deal. They agreed with Roosevelt's philosophy that something had to be done—and that if one measure did not work, something else should be tried. The New Deal can be seen, in part, as the legislative analogue of legal realism, with its emphasis not on abstract theory but on fact: that is, did a program work or not.

This pragmatism left the conservative bloc on the Court aghast, and beginning in 1935 it struck down state and federal laws one after another. It voided the oil regulation section of the National Recovery Administration in *Panama Refining Co.*

v. *Ryan,* the highly praised Railroad Retirement Act of 1934 in *Retirement Board v. Alton Railroad Co.,* and then, on *Black Monday, 27 May 1935, it invalidated the National Industrial Recovery Act in *Schechter Poultry Corp. v. United States,* the Frazier-Lemke Mortgage Act in *Louisville Joint Stock Land Bank v. Radford,* and severely restricted the president's power to remove members of independent regulatory commissions in *Humphrey's Executor v. United States* (see APPOINTMENT AND REMOVAL POWER). Soon after, it voided New York's model minimum-wage law in *Morehead v. New York ex rel. Tipaldo* (1936), struck down the Agricultural Adjustment Act in *United States v. *Butler* (1936), and invalidated the Guffy-Snyder Coal Act in *Carter v. Carter Coal Co.* (1936).

Not all of these were 5-to-4 decisions. In some cases Chief Justice Hughes joined with the conservatives to make it a 6-to-3 vote. In a few instances, such as the case involving the NRA, even the liberals believed the statute so badly drawn that they also voted to invalidate. And the administration did win a few decisions. By narrow votes the Court sustained the New Deal's abandonment of the gold standard in the *Gold Clause Cases* and also upheld the Tennessee Valley Authority in *Ashwander v. Tennessee Valley Authority* (1936).

*Court-Packing Plan.* Despite these few victories, the administration believed that it could not get its reform measures past the Court, and, shortly after his landslide victory in the 1936 election, Roosevelt unveiled his *court-packing plan, which would have added up to six justices on the high court and forty-four on the lower benches. Although Roosevelt claimed that he only wanted to alleviate a crowded docket, the transparency of the scheme doomed it. Chief Justice Hughes, joined by Justices Brandeis and Van Devanter, wrote a letter to the *Senate Judiciary Committee denying that the Court had fallen behind in its work. An increase in justices, instead of making the Court more efficient, would only cause delays because of "more judges to hear, more judges to confer, more judges to discuss, more judges to be convinced and to decide."

Conservatives opposed the plan, but so did many liberals and moderates who perceived the plan as an attack on the independence of the judiciary. Moreover, if a liberal president could pack the Court now, then a conservative could do the same in the future. After months of bitter debate, the Senate finally voted the measure down on 28 July 1937.

By then, however, the president might well have believed that even if he had lost the battle, he had won the war. In *West Coast Hotel Co. v. Parrish* (1937), decided in the midst of the court-packing battle, the Court sustained a Washington State minimum-wage law in a case practically identical to *Morehead.* This time Justice Roberts voted to sustain the measure, leading wags to claim that "a switch in time saves nine." Actually, the case had been heard and decided—but not announced—before Roosevelt's message. Roberts, who always hewed to a narrow definition of judging, never explained his vote, but his papers indicate clearly that in the earlier case, counsel had not asked the Court to overrule the *Adkins* holding and that he therefore felt bound to decide *Morehead* in light of *Adkins*. In the later case the lawyers did ask the Court to reconsider *Adkins;* Roberts did, found it wanting, and in *West Coast Hotel* voted to overrule it.

After *West Coast Hotel* the Court sustained every New Deal measure that came before it. Moreover, with the retirement of Justice Van Devanter, Roosevelt now had the opportunity of naming men sympathetic to the New Deal, which he proceeded to do. In 1938 he appointed Hugo *Black and Stanley *Reed; in 1939 Felix *Frankfurter and William O. *Douglas joined the bench; and in the next few years Frank *Murphy, Robert H. *Jackson and Wiley *Rutledge came on board. Instead of the cramped and narrow interpretation of federal powers that the Four Horsemen had espoused, the Roosevelt Court adopted a far more expansive view of the commerce and *taxing powers. By the time the Court decided *Wickard v. Filburn* (1942), it had expanded the affecting commerce doctrine so that almost any activity could be so defined.

One might well look at the court-packing fight as a marker to delineate the changing agenda of the Supreme Court. Prior to 1940, the bulk of the Court's cases, and the controversy surrounding them, dealt with economic matters—the balancing of property rights against legislatively determined public welfare. With the transformation of the Court following 1937, economic matters played an increasingly smaller and less important role on the Court's agenda. As Brandeis had urged, so long as the legislature had the power, judges should defer to the wisdom of the elected branches and not interpose their own policy views. Although the Court continues to hear economic cases, it has established a rule of great deference to the legislature, sustaining economic regulations if at least a rational basis can be put forward to explain the legislative policy.

The Court also extended a far greater tolerance to state legislation, reviving the nineteenth-century rule of *Cooley v. Board of Wardens* (1852) that in areas where the federal government had not asserted its commerce power the states could exercise their own authority (see SELECTIVE EXCLUSIVENESS). And, once again following Brandeis's assertion that in a federal system national courts should wherever possible follow local law, the Court did away, at least temporarily, with *federal common law doctrines in *Erie Railroad Co. v. Tompkins* (1938). By the eve of *World War II, the Supreme Court stood poised to go down a new path, one that would constitute the bulk of its agenda for the rest of the century, namely,

marking out how far the Constitution protected individual rights and liberties.

*Incorporation Doctrine.* The question of rights, of course, had never been totally absent from the docket, but beginning in the 1920s, with the idea of incorporation, it took on a new immediacy. Starting in the late 1930s, more and more cases testing the reach of constitutional liberties came before the Court, triggering one of the major jurisprudential debates in its history.

In 1937 the Court heard *Palko v. Connecticut, in which the defendant in a state criminal prosecution claimed that the Fourteenth Amendment applied the Fifth Amendment's guarantee against *double jeopardy to the states. Justice Cardozo said that it did not and put forward a theory of "selective incorporation." The Fourteenth Amendment did, he said, incorporate all the provisions of the First Amendment, since freedom of expression is "the matrix, the indispensible condition" (p. 327) for nearly every other form of freedom. (The Press Clause had been incorporated earlier in *Near v. Minnesota, 1931). But as for the Second through Eighth Amendments, the Court should apply only those that are "of the very essence of a scheme of ordered liberty" and so deeply rooted in American traditions as to be considered fundamental (p. 325).

*World War II.* Over the next ten years, Justice Black, who voted with the majority in *Palko*, grew increasingly uncomfortable with selective incorporation because he believed it left too much discretion in the hands of justices. He finally reached the point he was seeking a decade later, in his dissent in *Adamson v. California* (1947), where he put forward the idea of "total incorporation." All the guarantees of the first eight amendments, Black said, applied to the states as well as to the federal government.

The chief opponent of Black's view, and the main defender of selective incorporation, was Justice Frankfurter, who also argued for judicial deference to legislatures. Frankfurter exercised a great deal of influence on the Court in the 1940s and early 1950s, but as the Court's agenda moved from economic matters to individual liberties, his notion of deference began to strike some of his colleagues as judicial abdication.

*Flag-Salute Cases.* The debate began in earnest during the early years of World War II with several *religion cases. Jehovah's Witnesses brought a number of suits charging that various regulations, while not aimed specifically at them, nonetheless impinged on their free exercise of religion. The most famous of these were the flag-salute cases, which showed how some members of the Court came to realize that rights cases called for a different judicial attitude than economic regulation.

In the first flag-salute case, *Minersville School District v. Gobitis* (1940), Frankfurter spoke for an 8-to-1 majority in holding that a school could require children to salute the flag, since the necessity for inculcating patriotism was of sufficient importance to justify a relatively minor infringement on religious belief. The courts, he declared, should defer to legislative wisdom in these matters.

Only Justice Stone dissented, but as reports began filtering in of attacks on Witnesses, and as the Court heard other cases regarding Witness beliefs, several justices changed their minds, and in *West Virginia State Board of Education v. Barnette (1943), the Court declared that the state could not impinge on the First Amendment by compelling the observance of rituals.

*Japanese-American Internment.* The flag-salute cases arose in the context of a nation at *war, and both the Roosevelt administration and the Court seemed determined to avoid the infringements on civil liberties that had occurred during World War I. For the most part, the Court maintained its regard for civil liberties during the war; the one exception proved to be the worst blot on the Court's record in this century, the Japanese internment cases.

Following Pearl Harbor, anti-Japanese fear on the West Coast led the Roosevelt administration to order all persons of Japanese descent, whether Issei (Japanese nationals) or Nisei (American-born citizens), relocated to internment camps. The military also imposed a curfew on Japanese-Americans and set rules that made it impossible for them to stray on the West Coast without violating the law.

Within the Court the justices disagreed seriously on the constitutionality of the internment, but they also realized the problem of invalidating an executive program that the commander in chief had said was vital to the war effort. Stone, whom Roosevelt had elevated to chief justice following Hughes's retirement in 1941, managed to talk the dissenters into going along with the program for the sake of the war, and the Court unanimously upheld the curfew in *Hirabayashi v. United States (1943), although Justices Murphy, Douglas, and Rutledge entered concurring opinions that practically amounted to dissents.

In *Korematsu v. United States (1944) the majority sustained the detention without addressing the central issue of whether singling out a particular race violated the *Equal Protection Clause. Justice Black's opinion glossed over this question and focused on the president's *war powers. This time Justices Murphy, Roberts, and Jackson entered vigorous dissents, stating bluntly that Japanese-Americans had been singled out because of race. By then the tide of war had shifted, and in the fall the Court ordered the release of a Japanese-American woman whose loyalty had been firmly established in *Ex parte Endo* (1944). (See RACE AND RACISM.)

Ever since, there has been a general condemnation of the internment program as well as of the Court's condoning it. Perhaps it is too much to expect judges to remain free of the wartime passions that grip the rest of the nation, but there is a certain irony in comparing Stone's famous *footnote four in the *Carolene Products* case, which called for a "more exacting judicial scrutiny" in cases touching on race, and his opinion in *Hirabayashi,* which condemned discrimination in general and then approved it in this case.

Stone, as it turned out, proved to be less than ideal as chief justice. He had earned a solid reputation as a good jurist and a liberal in the sixteen years he had been an associate justice, and at Frankfurter's suggestion Roosevelt had elevated the Republican Stone to the center chair as a gesture of wartime unity. Stone's misfortune was to preside over one of the most cantankerous courts in the nation's history. Justice Frankfurter's effort to gain intellectual dominance over his colleagues ran into the twin obstacles of Justices Hugo Black and William O. Douglas, who soon came to epitomize *judicial activism and the expansion of individual liberties just as Frankfurter stood for judicial restraint and minimalism. Frank Murphy may have been one of the most liberal persons ever to sit on the bench, while the more conservative Owen Roberts and Robert Jackson tended to side with Frankfurter. By 1943 most of the decisions the Court handed down had multiple opinions.

*The Vinson Court.* Chief Justice Stone died of a cerebral hemorrhage in April 1946, and Fred *Vinson took his place that fall, but, before he did so, a truncated Court turned down the first challenge to malapportioned legislatures in a number of states (see FAIR REPRESENTATION). With Justice Jackson at the Nuremburg trials, Justice Frankfurter spoke for a 4-to-3 majority in *Colegrove v. Green (1946), holding that apportionment constituted a *political question and was therefore nonjusticiable. The case highlighted the differing philosophies on the bench, with Frankfurter warning the Court to avoid what he called the *political thicket and to accept whatever inequities resulted from malapportionment as an inevitable cost of the federal system. Justice Black, joined by Justices Douglas and Murphy, anticipated the philosophy of the Warren Court era, and argued that such a blatant violation of *equal protection could certainly be handled by the courts—and that in fact the judiciary had a responsibility to do so (see also REAPPORTIONMENT CASES).

Chief Justice Vinson only presided over the Court for seven years, yet during that time the Court underwent a significant transformation. Although the Court would not decide the school desegregation cases until 1954, the judicial battle for civil rights began to pick up steam in the postwar years. The Court also had to deal with the question of internal security and how such programs affected freedom of speech. The increasing willingness of minorities to litigate also led the Court to examine how far the doctrine of incorporation extended.

*Cold War.* Although the Soviet Union had been an ally during World War II, the onset of the cold war in 1946 immediately revived all the old fears about communism (see COMMUNISM AND COLD WAR). The exposure of spy rings, the communist takeover of eastern Europe and China, and the demand by rightist demagogues forced the Truman administration to implement a massive loyalty program (see SUBVERSION). The attorney general issued a list of organizations suspected of communist sympathies, and at the same time Congress began a series of committee hearings that culminated in Senator Joseph McCarthy's investigations into alleged communism in the State Department and the army.

These programs all raised significant issues about freedom of speech and association. Although Justice Frankfurter personally detested McCarthyism and the whole atmosphere of the Red Scare, his philosophy of judicial restraint, which reached the height of its influence during these years, made the Court powerless to defend these basic First Amendment rights.

The government indicted twelve leaders of the Communist party of the United States under the 1940 *Smith Act and charged them with conspiring to teach or advocate the forceful overthrow of the government and with belonging to an organization that advocated such an overthrow. The indictment thus departed from what had been accepted doctrine—that one could only be charged with those words or actions presenting a *clear and present danger to society. A jury found the twelve guilty, and on appeal the high Court upheld the convictions in *Dennis* v. *United States* (1951). Chief Justice Vinson wrote the majority opinion, which interpreted the clear and present danger test so as to allow the government to move against any doctrine it held potentially subversive. Only Black and Douglas dissented, pointing out that the convictions represented prosecutions for beliefs and thus threatened the entire notion of freedom of thought. Here again, one sees the Court caught up in the same hysteria as the general population, and utilizing the notion of judicial deference to avoid dealing with critical issues. Not until the mid-1950s, after the waning of Senator McCarthy's power, did the Court finally begin to assert a positive view of freedom of speech.

The war against communism, this time the "police action" in Korea, also led to a major decision on *separation of powers. In April 1952, to avert a strike of steelworkers, President Harry S. Truman invoked his powers as commander in chief and ordered the seizure of the nation's steel mills. The steel companies complained not that the government had no power to seize their mills, but that in this instance the wrong branch of government had acted—that only Congress, not the president, could authorize the seizure.

Although most commentators believed that a Court composed entirely of Roosevelt and Truman appointees would reject such a claim, in fact the Court invalidated the president's action by a 6-to-3 vote in *Youngstown Sheet & Tube Co.* v. *Sawyer* (1952). Justice Black's majority opinion flatly denied that the president had any authority, either by express provision of the Constitution or by the implied powers of commander in chief to act as he had done; he needed specific congressional authorization. The decision represented one of the few setbacks to growing executive authority that had begun in 1933 (see PRESIDENTIAL EMERGENCY POWERS).

*Bill of Rights Cases.* The Vinson Court also wrestled with the problems of civil liberties and the extent to which the *Bill of Rights should apply to the states. Although Justice Cardozo had said that the entire First Amendment should be incorporated, the Court had avoided interpreting the religion clauses, and had decided the wartime Jehovah's Witness cases on speech rather than religion grounds. The Court explicitly extended the Establishment Clause to the states in *Everson* v. *Board of Education* (1947). In a strange opinion, Justice Black depicted a high "wall of separation" that must divide church and state, and then he approved a New Jersey statute that allowed school districts to reimburse parents for transporting their children to parochial schools. Four justices dissented, not from Black's reasoning, but from the result, and elicited one of the great lines in the Court's literature, Justice Jackson's comment that "the case which irresistibly comes to mind as the most fitting precedent is that of Julia who, according to Byron's reports, 'whispering "I will ne'er consent"—consented' " (p. 19). Black eventually took an absolutist position, and his later votes opposed any involvement between church and state.

The Vinson Court, however, was still feeling its way in this corner of First Amendment jurisprudence, and it sent somewhat confusing signals in two cases involving *released time, in which students received religious instruction during school hours. In *Illinois ex rel. McCollum* v. *Board of Education* (1948), the Court struck down a released-time program in which ministers came into the schools and taught religious education classes during school hours. The uproar over this decision led the Court to retreat somewhat in *Zorach* v. *Clauson* (1952). There Justice Douglas, who also later took an absolutist position on the First Amendment, noted, "We are a religious people whose institutions presuppose a Supreme Being" (p. 313). He therefore upheld a program where the students left school during regular hours to receive religious instruction off school grounds.

The Vinson Court also began to explore how far the rights accorded to accused persons under the Fourth, Fifth, and *Sixth Amendments applied to the states. The right to *counsel had been one of the first rights nationalized in *Powell* v. *Alabama* (1932), but ten years later the Court had refused to extend that right to noncapital cases in *Betts* v. *Brady* (1942). Rather, a majority ruled that courts should determine on a case-by-case basis if lack of counsel deprived the accused of a fair trial. During the Vinson years Justice Frankfurter managed to keep a majority in favor of the *Betts* rule, but in nearly every case the Court found special circumstances to warrant providing the defendant with a lawyer. Not until *Gideon* v. *Wainwright* (1963) did the Court finally extend the Sixth Amendment to noncapital cases.

Justice Frankfurter also prevailed in preventing the Court from applying the *exclusionary rule to the states, although in *Wolf* v. *Colorado* (1949) he did apply the Fourth Amendment protections regarding search and siezure to the states. Federal courts since 1919 had refused to admit evidence seized in violation of the Fourth Amendment, a rule designed to make sure police did not violate constitutional guidelines. Dissenters in *Wolf* claimed that without such a prophylactic measure, state police would not be scrupulous regarding warrant and search requirements. This prophecy proved correct, and the Court finally extended the exclusionary rule to the states in *Mapp* v. *Ohio* (1961).

*Civil Rights.* Undoubtedly, the most important judicial struggle to occur after the war involved African-Americans' fight for civil rights. The promise of equality in the *Reconstruction amendments, especially the Equal Protection Clause, had long been blighted. In *Plessy* v. *Ferguson* (1896), the Court had approved racial segregation and the so-called *separate but equal doctrine. The Equal Protection Clause itself had fallen into disuse, derided by Holmes as the "last resort" in a constitutional argument.

The Court had taken its first hesitant step against racial segregation in *Missouri ex rel. Gaines* v. *Canada* (1938), where Chief Justice Hughes had startled the South by declaring that if the southern states wanted to keep segregated schools, then it had to make them equal as well (see SEGREGATION, DE JURE). That same year Justice Stone called for heightened scrutiny of race discrimination in his *Carolene Products* footnote. Justice Douglas breathed life back into the Equal Protection Clause in *Skinner* v. *Oklahoma* (1942). But undoubtedly it was the experience of black soldiers in the war, as well as President Truman's desegregation of the armed services, that gave the *civil rights movement an unstoppable momentum.

In 1948 two cases reached the Court dealing with *restrictive covenants, which denied blacks access to housing in white neighborhoods. In *Shelley* v. *Kraemer*, the Court made these covenants unenforceable in *state courts, since enforcement of racial discrimination would constitute the type of state action forbidden by the Fourteenth Amendment. In a companion case, *Hurd* v. *Hodge*, Chief Justice Vinson applied the same rule to the District of Columbia. In *Sipuel* v.

*Board of Regents of the University of Oklahoma* (1948) the Supreme Court required Oklahoma to provide Ada Sipuel, whom it had denied admission to the state law school, with an equal legal education. A few years later Oklahoma again tried to get around the rules; after admitting a black man to its graduate program in education, it made him sit in the hall outside the classroom and at separate tables in the library and dining hall. For a unanimous bench, Vinson held in *McLaurin* v. *Oklahoma State Regents* (1950) that this treatment violated the Equal Protection Clause. Although the Court had not indicated any willingness to reverse *Plessy,* in *McLaurin* and other cases it had hinted at its growing unease with the separate-but-equal doctrine. In *Sweatt* v. *Painter* (1950), for example, the Court recognized that a black Texas law school did not compare in quality with the University of Texas, and for the first time implied that separate might, in fact, never be equal.

In 1952 the Court granted *certiorari in five cases all addressed to the issue of racial segregation in public schools. Chief Justice Vinson died before the Court decided the cases, and it fell to his successor, Earl *Warren, appointed by President Dwight Eisenhower in 1953, to hand down what is arguably the Court's most important decision of the twentieth century, *Brown* v. *Board of Education* (1954). Recent research has indicated that despite earlier descriptions of the Court as seriously divided over desegregation, in fact nearly all of the justices were prepared to overrule *Plessy.* The problem, which Warren solved by splitting the decision from the implementation, was how to go about the task.

*Brown* in many ways represents a logical culmination of much that had occurred in the previous three decades. The Court under Taft and Hughes had focused primarily on economic issues but had begun to explore the problems of individual liberty in a modern society. By the time Warren came to the Court, economic issues had taken a back seat to the problems of equality. The conservatives who decided *Adkins* v. *Children's Hospital* (1923) had derided the fact-laden brief Felix Frankfurter had submitted in defense of a minimum-wage law as irrelevant to judicial inquiry, but the Court that decided *Brown* paid attention to the evidence submitted by the *National Association for the Advancement of Colored People that segregation inflicted emotional harm on black schoolchildren.

Critics of the Court in the 1920s and 1930s demanded that judges be restrained and that they defer to the legislatures in determining policy. Justice Frankfurter carried this philosophy onto the Court with him, but by 1953 it had given way to the demand that courts take the lead in determining the extent to which the Constitution protected individual liberties. The legal realists, who in the 1920s had argued that judges not only reflected the attitudes of society but should consciously take those attitudes into consideration in their decision making, might well have applauded the changes that had taken place during these years (see JUDICIAL ACTIVISM).

□ Leonard Baker, *Back to Back: The Duel between FDR and the Supreme Court* (1967). Michal R. Belknap, *Cold War Political Justice: The Smith Act, the Communist Party, and American Civil Liberties* (1977). Richard C. Cortner, *The Supreme Court and the Second Bill of Rights* (1981). Richard Kluger, *Simple Justice: The History of Brown v. Board of Education and Black America's Struggle for Equality* (1976). Paul L. Murphy, *The Constitution in Crisis Times, 1918–1969* (1972). William E. Nelson, *The Fourteenth Amendment: From Political Principle to Judicial Doctrine* (1988). C. Herman Pritchett, *Civil Liberties and the Vinson Court* (1954). G. Edward White, *The American Judicial Tradition*, rev. ed. (1988). Melvin I. Urofsky

RIGHTS CONSCIOUSNESS IN
CONTEMPORARY SOCIETY

In the second half of the twentieth century Americans have become very conscious of their "rights." There is much talk about both gaining rights and protecting existing rights. The current ethos holds that there should be access to law to assert claims about those rights, especially through the Supreme Court. Although judicial rulings have been only one factor in the development of this new "rights consciousness," critics complain that decisions by the courts over the past several decades have contributed to a litigation explosion and "hyperlexis"—that is, excessive law. Whether we have in fact become "over-lawyered" and "overjudged," the fact remains that the Supreme Court has been at the heart of the growth of the rights consciousness.

*"Rights Consciousness."* The general awareness of rights to be claimed or asserted against others, particularly the government, is what we mean by "rights consciousness." People are certainly aware that they possess "rights" that the government and other citizens should not abridge. They may express their belief in these rights at a high level of generality and often misunderstand the content of the rights they actually have, overestimating their scope. But even if members of the public do not understand the precise content and scope of their rights, they have become more willing to seek recognition and expansion of those rights and to assert an entitlement to them.

A general sense of awareness of the direction in which the Supreme Court is heading in expanding or contracting rights may inspire greater or lesser optimism about these rights. Yet regardless of whether members of the public understand the Supreme Court's message, the *lower federal courts are quite likely to hear the Court's signals encouraging them to take positions supportive of rights claims; thus the lower courts, too, play a role in the content of "rights consciousness."

Rights consciousness may have either a general or a specific focus. The right involved may be quite different, such as the right against being compelled to incriminate oneself (see SELF-INCRIMINATION). Belief in another specific right, the right to *counsel, led one convicted felon, Clarence Gideon, to appeal his conviction, and that appeal was the Supreme Court's vehicle for enunciating, in *Gideon v. Wainwright* (1963), an indigent's right to an attorney at felony trials. A general right such as the right to *privacy first articulated by the Supreme Court in the *contraception case of *Griswold v. Connecticut* (1965) and central to consideration of the defeated nomination of Judge Robert *Bork to the Supreme Court, may find applications far beyond the case in which it was originally identified. The right to privacy, for example, has played a part in cases dealing with a woman's right to choose *abortion (*Roe v. Wade*, 1973) and consenting adults' protection against arrest and prosecution under state sodomy laws (*Bowers v. Hardwick*, 1986; see also HOMOSEXUALITY).

Another general right is the right to be treated fairly. Because so many rights are related to the procedures by which life, liberty, or property are obtained or removed, the right to *due process of law is among those about which people often are conscious. Indeed, although modified by later rulings in which the justices were deferential to law enforcement agencies and particularly to prison administrators, a "due process revolution," including rulings requiring hearings before termination of welfare benefits (*Goldberg v. Kelly*, 1970) and before suspending or expelling students from school for disciplinary reasons (*Goss v. Lopez*, 1975), led people to be more willing to challenge treatment by executive agencies and to demand more protections from abuse by bureaucrats.

Due process rights are but one cluster of rights the Supreme Court has articulated. Two others are to be found in the *First Amendment: freedom of expression, including freedom of *speech and the press, freedom to *petition, and the corollary right to free *assembly and association; and rights associated with *religion, specifically the freedom to practice one's religion and the right not to have another religion imposed on one (or "established" by the government). Rights of criminal defendants constitute another major cluster, which includes pretrial rights, such as the protection against improper searches and against being forced to incriminate oneself to the police, and rights at trial, such as the right to have an attorney and the right to a *speedy, public trial, with a properly selected jury (see TRIAL BY JURY). There is also a cluster of *citizenship rights, such as the right to *vote and a general expectation that the government will treat one without regard to one's race, sex, religion, or national origin.

One can distinguish between rights clearly stated in the Constitution, such as freedom of speech and the press and the right to the free exercise of religion, and "new," or derivative, rights recognized or created by the Supreme Court. Among the latter are the right of association, inferred from the First Amendment's freedom of speech guarantee, and the right of privacy, originally derived from the "penumbras" of specifically named portions of the *Bill of Rights and from the *Ninth Amendment (which states that nonenumerated rights may exist) but now based in the liberty protected by the Due Process Clause of the *Fourteenth Amendment.

*Individual versus Group Rights.* Debate about some of these rights has been with us for many decades; issues of freedom of speech and religion have been prominent throughout the nation's history. Controversy about *slavery brought about the *Civil War, and issues of racial equality again came to the fore of the nation's agenda in the mid-twentieth century, leading people to become conscious not only of *individual* rights but also far more conscious of *group* rights (see RACE AND RACISM).

Concern about the rights of *labor unions to organize workers had brought attention to the constitutional right of association, but until the *civil rights movement of the 1950s and 1960s, people still tended to think of rights primarily in terms of the individual. Particularly after the Court's landmark rulings mandating equal treatment regardless of race in schools and public facilities, the need to consider remedies for *segregation and racial discrimination (and whether those remedies could be race-conscious) focused attention more on an individual's position as a member of a group—and thus on group rights. This shift in attention was part of a change in concern from rights as protection against the government to rights as a way of changing social relations; the emphasis on greater equality—not only on "equality before the law" or "equality of opportunity" but specifically on "equality of results"—has clearly done just that.

The extension of civil-rights consciousness from African-Americans to other groups— women, Latinos, the disabled, and gay men and lesbians—also increased group rights concerns. Attention to group matters was furthered by recognition of institutional racism and sexism, that is, the notion that discrimination is not only a matter of overt discriminatory acts against individuals but includes neutral-seeming mechanisms that are discriminatory in their effects on whole categories of people. When people of a specific racial or gender grouping focused on their common attributes or background, as in the "consciousness-raising" groups in the women's movement, it was only a short step to raise the consciousness of others both inside the grouping (for example, other women) or outside it. Similarly, if welfare recipients looked at their economic situation as resulting from structural conditions they had in common, they would be more likely to be conscious of their rights and to assert them (as was done by the Welfare Rights Organization) than to attribute their indigency to personal failure.

The Supreme Court has made it difficult to maintain this group emphasis. Particularly in recent years, the Court has reinforced an individualistic focus through adoption of a "perpetrator perspective" in which, before someone can be held liable for violating an individual's rights, that person (or entity) must be found to have *intended* such a violation; examples can be found in cases on *employment discrimination (*Washington* v. *Davis,* 1976) and voting rights (*Mobile* v. *Bolden,* 1980). Adoption of a "victim perspective" in discrimination cases, with consideration given to the institutional or cultural disadvantages faced by all those in a discriminated-against grouping, would not only lead more readily to adoption of race- or sex-conscious remedies but would also reinforce a group-rights consciousness.

*Seeking Rights.* Rights consciousness may be accompanied by action to achieve the rights thought to exist. Although appeals for legislative change and other types of political activism have been more frequently employed in recent years in the pursuit of rights, litigation has often been used in the effort to secure statements of these rights and their effective application. Because Supreme Court rulings supportive of rights provide evidence of litigation's effectiveness, they can be said to have created "litigation consciousness" as much as rights consciousness.

Trying to get the Supreme Court to pay greater heed to claims that rights should be enforced, groups have long used litigation to press their rights agendas; from time to time, those efforts have led to favorable results. The *American Civil Liberties Union (ACLU) has often raised freedom of expression and church-state issues and criminal procedure questions. The *NAACP *Legal Defense Fund (LDF) and other groups based on the LDF model, such as the Mexican-American Legal Defense Fund (MALDEF), have pressed for elimination of segregation and discrimination in *housing, *education, jobs, and voting. The LDF has also led the battle in the courts against the death penalty (see CAPITAL PUNISHMENT), and comparable organizations in the women's movement have focused on abortion or reproductive rights. Conservatives, too, have developed such litigating entities to make their views of rights heard. This growth in litigation capacity and greater attention to seeking goals through litigation has enhanced the Supreme Court's ability to exercise leadership with respect to rights, because better-developed legal arguments, expanding the boundaries of existing rights doctrine, are presented to the justices. With that ammunition and their discretion to control the Court's docket, the justices can craft the judicial opinions necessary to express support for rights.

***The Supreme Court's Roles.*** It is difficult to determine whether the Supreme Court's rulings after 1953, when Earl *Warren became chief justice, were more the cause of the growing consciousness of rights or the result of a preexisting, underlying societal rights consciousness. To say that the Court has created rights consciousness is implicitly to adopt the general view that the Warren Court led public opinion, influencing rights consciousness and at times moving that consciousness beyond where it had been. It is important not to ignore the fact that the Warren Court also responded to demands made on it by those already concerned about rights.

One can certainly find instances where the Court, instead of following, led the way. In graduate-education cases before *Brown* v. *Board of Education* (1954)—such as *Sweatt* v. *Painter* (1950)—the Court sent a signal to the NAACP that an outright attack on the *separate but equal doctrine was in order. The *Brown* litigation was certainly responsive to that signal. The Warren Court's criminal-procedure cases also provide examples of the Court moving farther than litigants sought—in fact, most such cases were brought to the Court not by groups pursuing broad rights agendas but by defense lawyers seeking only to reverse their clients' criminal convictions. The *Mapp* v. *Ohio* (1961) *exclusionary-rule case came to the Court as an *obscenity case, but the Court transformed it into a vehicle to apply the exclusionary rule to the states.

When its rulings reaffirm rights previously recognized or recognize new rights, particularly those of underrepresented minorities, the Court can be said to be fulfilling one of its roles in American democracy—countering majoritarian tendencies by upholding minority rights. The Court can, however, play other, somewhat more limited, roles with respect to rights. One is the role of legitimator, a role the Court played in the *Civil Rights Act of 1964 (*Heart of Atlanta Motel* v. *United States,* 1964) and the *Voting Rights Act of 1965 (*South Carolina* v. *Katzenbach,* 1966); in those cases it upheld Congress's actions and generally made clear that it would defer to congressional leadership in civil rights matters.

The Court has also legitimated others' efforts to gain and protect rights. For example, it invalidated southern efforts after *Brown* v. *Board of Education* to immobilize the NAACP through state requirements that the organization reveal its membership lists (*NAACP* v. *Alabama,* 1956) and through charges of barratry leveled against the NAACP because it advised people of their constitutional rights to equal treatment (*NAACP* v. *Button,* 1963). The Court's revival of the *Reconstruction-era civil rights statutes (as in, e.g., *United States* v. *Guest,* 1966; *United States* v. *Price,* 1966; and *Jones* v. *Alfred H. Mayer Co.,* 1968) also facilitated private citizens' complaints about deprivations of their rights.

One does not have to look far to find instances in which the Court's reaction to claims of rights has reflected the larger society's concerns. Given Americans' inclination, noted by Alexis de Tocqueville, to transform most social and economic and political problems into legal ones, the Court's agenda of course reflects the societal agenda. Starting in the late nineteenth century, imperatives of economic growth were translated into "liberty of contract" doctrine, that is, freedom from government regulation of business, including its relations with its employees; this helped create the core of the Court's agenda through the mid-1930s (see CONTRACT, FREEDOM OF).

After *World War II, a new elite consensus on the economic and social-welfare functions of government, coupled with the desire to portray the virtues of "democracy" in its battle against *communism, shifted the agenda of rights issues to matters such as free speech, although, in another reflection of elite concerns, the amount of speech allowed by the Supreme Court was far from unlimited. *Brown* v. *Board of Education,* although portrayed at the time as radical and often as an instance in which the court led public opinion, is another example of the justices lending their authority to a preexisting social movement and responding to concerns of political elites. Elites, more liberal than the general public, felt that after the World War II fight against Nazi ideology, segregated education was inappropriate and made the United States "look bad" in the postwar competition with the Soviet Union. Thus *Brown* was not only an effort by the Court to deal with the plight of African-American students and to raise the nation's consciousness of racial discrimination but also a "cold war imperative."

The Warren Court, in turning its attention to rights, adopted an increasingly liberal rights agenda including freedom of speech and the press, separation of church and state, equality for minorities, the rights of criminal defendants, and more recently, *gender equality. However, after Barry Goldwater, George Wallace, and Richard *Nixon attacked the Warren Court's criminal-procedure decisions in their "law 'n order" presidential campaigns, the liberal rights agenda was displaced by a more conservative one, which had several components: opposition to continuing school *desegregation remedies such as busing; opposition to abortion; support of the "rights of whites" and opposition to *affirmative action; renewed interest in the rights of *property, which could not be taken without *just compensation; greater concern for the rights of those who practice religion; and, in criminal matters, increased attention to the interests of law enforcement and the victims of crime, and support for the death penalty. The Burger Court's rulings on this agenda illustrate both that newly appointed justices reflect public opinion and that the justices' response to public opinion may move the

Court *away* from protection for rights claimed by liberals and toward deference to the majority. We see this in the Court's early-1970s decisions limiting the rights of criminal defendants and its late-1980s rulings responsive to complaints of disgruntled white males or white females that affirmative action programs produce "innocent" white victims of "reverse discrimination," particularly when layoffs of whites result (*Wygant* v. *Board of Education*, 1986).

**The Court's Attention to Rights.** Contemporary rights consciousness can be traced directly to the post–World War II period, but it also has an older history. This older past is rooted in a set of rights, asserted primarily by business interests in the late nineteenth century, relating to freedom from government regulation. A more immediate prelude to postwar rights consciousness can be seen in the Court's World War II battles over the rights of Jehovah's Witnesses to distribute their literature and to refuse to salute the flag and in negative reaction to the Court's upholding the relocation of Japanese-Americans (*Korematsu* v. *United States*, 1944). The genesis of the Court's more recent attention to rights can be seen in Justice Harlan *Stone's *Footnote Four in the *Carolene Products* case (1938), indicating that the Court would look with *stricter scrutiny at statutes affecting political rights and the rights of insular minorities.

After the early years of the cold war, the Warren Court not only gave greater attention to rights claims but also ultimately sustained a high proportion of those claims across a wide range of subjects. Along with the *school-prayer cases and the *one person, one vote *reapportionment cases of the early 1960s came the "revolution" in which criminal procedure was nationalized. The specific protections of the *Fourth, *Fifth, *Sixth, and *Eighth Amendments were extended to state criminal defendants and increased due process was required in dealing with criminal defendants. The Court began this "revolution" by outlawing use of improperly seized evidence in state criminal trials (*Mapp* v. *Ohio*, 1961). It continued by requiring appointed counsel for indigents at felony trials (*Gideon* v. *Wainwright*, 1963), protecting against improperly obtained confessions in the period before trial (*Escobedo* v. *Illinois*, 1964; *Miranda* v. *Arizona*, 1966), and extending the right to a jury trial to the states (*Duncan* v. *Louisiana*, 1968). The effect of a *set* of rulings was particularly evident in these cases: whatever the impact of these rulings might have been individually, their cumulative effect was a generally heightened rights consciousness. To be sure, *Mapp* by itself would have affected our collective consciousness, but the steady drumbeat of decisions over several years had a magnified effect.

The Burger Court continued to devote much of its docket to rights issues and initially supported some new claims of rights—for women (including abortion), for prisoners disciplined for violat-

ing regulations, and for mental patients, in the context of involuntary civil commitment. Contrary to expectations, the Burger Court did not directly overrule even the most-criticized of the Warren Court criminal-procedure rulings—*Miranda* and *Mapp*. However, the new majority did refuse to extend those rulings and undercut advances in other areas, such as rights for welfare beneficiaries.

The Burger Court's record of support for rights was nonetheless higher than the Court's record in the pre-Warren Court period. This is particularly evident if one recognizes that rights claims made to the Burger Court were more difficult than those presented earlier. General claims, such as whether the criminal procedure provisions of the Bill of Rights should be extended to the states, had been answered by the Warren Court. Succeeding rights claims, pressing well beyond liberal Warren Court rulings, were less likely to be upheld. However, because the Burger Court chose to operate within the Warren Court's precedents, the result was a more generous approach to rights than an earlier Court would have demonstrated.

The modern Supreme Court's sustained attention to rights has made it easy to assume that the Court has always paid considerable attention to rights issues. As is clear both from history and from the current mobilization of a new conservative majority, however, it has only been in this century that the Supreme Court has given attention to civil liberties and civil rights.

The Court can signal that greater attention should be paid to rights, but it can also convey a contrary message, so situations in which the Court was especially *unheedful* of rights must also be taken into account. Patriotism during the early part of World War II led the Court initially to uphold a compulsory flag-salute for schoolchildren over the claims of religious minorities (*Minersville School District* v. *Gobitis*, 1940), although it soon changed its mind (*West Virginia Board of Education* v. *Barnette*, 1943). Concern for the success of the war effort led the court to ignore the racist motivations behind restrictions on the freedom of Japanese-Americans on the West Coast when it upheld government actions in the *Hirabayashi* (curfew) and *Korematsu* (relocation) cases in 1943 and 1944. Concern in the 1940s and 1950s over the presence of communists in government led to a growing indifference to government employees' due process rights when their loyalty was challenged or they were thought to be security risks, and to communists' free speech rights. The Court initially upheld loyalty-security programs for the most part, and upheld convictions for conspiring to teach the advocacy of overthrow of the government (*Dennis* v. *United States*, 1951). When, in the mid-1950s, the Court began to criticize aspects of anticommunist efforts, congressional attacks on the Court led it to retreat. Many of these decisions were, however, eventually modified or overturned. In the late 1980s, concern about drugs likewise led to a diminished concern about search and seizure rights in criminal cases and about privacy rights in the context of employment.

**The Court's Impact on Rights Consciousness.** In the 1950s and early 1960s, the Court was "the only game in town" for the achievement of civil rights. The Warren Court's actions, beginning with its outlawing of segregation in public education in *Brown*, placed rights on the national legal and political agenda, where they have remained ever since. *Brown* by itself, however, was not enough to establish a broad rights consciousness. It took the Warren Court's unusually high support of rights claims in a multitude of areas to crystallize contemporary rights consciousness. Yet even if the Court had handed down no more *race relations rulings, *Brown* would have had a great effect on minorities' consciousness of their rights. This was so because it discarded "separate but equal," the constitutional basis for segregation created in *Plessy* v. *Ferguson* (1896), leading people to assert their rights to the desegregated education to which they felt equal opportunity entitled them. This occurred despite the Court's first calling for desegregation to proceed "with all deliberate speed" (*Brown* v. *Board of Education II*, 1955) and then disengaging itself from enforcement by deciding very few school desegregation cases until 1968, except when it intervened in cases of extreme resistance.

The Court did provide support for restaurant and library sit-ins and related demonstrations by accepting many cases and reversing many convictions on a variety of technical grounds (see SIT-IN DEMONSTRATIONS). By avoiding pronouncing major new doctrine, however, the Court did not provide much leadership on the question of access to public accommodations. Instead, Congress, responding to the sit-ins, passed the public accommodations provision (Title II) of the 1964 Civil Rights Act—which the Court then upheld in *Heart of Atlanta Motel*. Likewise, after striking down the *white primary (*Smith* v. *Allright*, 1944), the Court did not directly promote the assertion of the right to vote without racial discrimination; it was Congress that responded to major events, such as the 1965 civil rights march from Selma to Montgomery, Alabama, by passing important new legislation. Here again the Court's role was largely one of legitimation, when it affirmed Congress's right to enact such legislation (*South Carolina* v. *Katzenbach*, 1966). After Congress passed the Civil Rights Act of 1964 and Voting Rights Act of 1965, the Court reentered the fray—but not as a leading actor, although it was still important when, as in *Jones* v. *Mayer*, it restored life to *Reconstruction-era civil rights laws as a weapon against discrimination in housing by private individuals.

That little immediate desegregation occurred in the deep South in response to *Brown* and that it did not take place until the other branches had acted, reflects the oft-noted phenomenon of "law in action" versus "law on the books." Although civil rights activists undertook their more direct action in part because of Court-stimulated rights consciousness, they also took to the streets because many of them felt that litigation was taking too long to achieve rights. A widespread sense of injustice played a much larger role than specific Court rulings in stimulating effective opposition to racial discrimination. The recent retreats by a more conservative Court have led some to a different interpretation—that the Court is still contending with the legacy of slavery and is moving us back toward the pre-*Brown* situation, with minorities' economic situation getting worse, not better.

**Rights by Reaction.** Sometimes, the supposed beneficiaries of Supreme Court rulings granting rights have been prompted to develop rights consciousness by the negative reaction of opponents to these rulings. If a Court ruling upholding a claimed right is readily complied with by those who earlier interfered with the right, the consciousness of those who had gained the right might not be stimulated as much as if those who opposed the right continue in their obstruction. Conflict is an essential dynamic of change. Part of the rights consciousness deriving from *Brown* may have resulted from the South's massive resistance to school desegregation. Likewise, the concerted efforts to overturn the school-prayer rulings created greater awareness of the rights involved in those rulings than if school officials had promptly stopped prayers from being recited in class. The strenuous, even apoplectic, reaction to rulings like *Mapp* and *Miranda* by the law enforcement community—often reflected in films and the media—also served to make people, both inside and outside that community, far more aware of the rulings than if there had been a quieter, even if disgruntled, response.

Consciousness of what might be called "rights in opposition" also can result from the Court's actions. Race relations and abortion provide examples. Affirmative-action programs, along with judicially imposed race-conscious remedies for racial discrimination found to violate Titles VI and VII of the 1964 Civil Rights Act, led to disaffection by white males who felt entitled to positions or promotions gained by minorities or women. This disaffection, along with a more general fear of quotas, in turn led to increased consciousness of whites' "rights" to equal treatment in employment, and to "reverse discrimination" lawsuits such as *Regents of University of California* v. *Bakke* (1978). Conversely, when the Court handed down rulings in 1989 limiting its own earlier job-discrimination rulings (e.g., *Ward's Cove Packing Co.* v. *Atonio*, 1989), there was renewed "rights consciousness" in the minority community, leading to efforts to pass additional civil rights statutes to overturn those decisions (see CIVIL RIGHTS ACT OF 1991).

Prior to *Roe* v. *Wade* (1973), with opposition to abortion institutionalized in restrictive statutes, those opposing abortion did not need to be active. When *Roe* invalidated those laws, it changed the landscape of rights permanently, just as *Brown* did for racial equality. *Roe* prompted formation of the "right to life" movement by those opposed to abortion and galvanized those opposed to the Equal Rights Amendment. Each subsequent ruling striking down restrictions on abortion further stimulated antiabortion activity, long before "prochoice" elements organized effectively. When *Webster* v. *Reproductive Health Services* (1989) and *Hodgson* v. *Minnesota* (1990) appeared to invite the states to impose greater limits on the right to an abortion, it stimulated prochoice forces to direct political action to prevent such restrictions, thus illustrating that rights consciousness is formed not only by rulings sustaining rights but also by rulings that seem to withdraw them. Likewise, the Court in *Grove City College* v. *Bell* (1984), which limited the reach of federal antidiscrimination rules applying to recipients of federal funds, stimulated renewed consideration of the rights to be enforced through this mechanism and ultimately led to enactment by Congress of the Civil Rights Restoration Act. The public may well react more negatively to a threat to remove an existing right than it will to the denial of a new right (see REVERSAL OF COURT DECISIONS BY CONGRESS).

*Rights Consciousness, Action, and Results.* Rights consciousness may lead to the assertion of rights, through litigation or legislative efforts, but it does not always result in immediate action. There may be no apparent need to implement those rights. Those who became more aware of segregation in schools, and therefore of a right to an equal education, often saw school segregation as a southern problem requiring no implementation in the North. Thus, little attention was directed to more subtle forms of de facto *segregation resulting from regulation or practice, to inequality of education, or to unequal spending among schools depending on the schools' racial composition. When efforts were made to implement *Brown* against segregated schools in the North, concern about a theoretical "right to equal education" was replaced, even among many liberal Democrats, by opposition to school desegregation or at least to those measures, such as busing, that would make it effective. The Supreme Court's requirement that intentional discrimination based on race be proved provided an essential (and "neutral") legal tool to those resisting further desegregation (see DISCRIMINATORY INTENT).

If formal pro–civil rights actions have been only symbolic, how much change has resulted? Effectuation of rights in legislation may allow most of those *not* discriminated against to think that discrimination has ended. This is part of a more general problem in which legislation, whether intended as symbolic or not, is in the end only that, largely because of the faulty assumption that law will be implemented effectively by the executive branch and followed fully and without complaint. The belief that statutes or judicial decisions are self-enforcing also helps to explain why, beyond NAACP-initiated district-by-district litigation, rights consciousness stimulated by *Brown* did not at first result in action by its intended minority beneficiaries. When people realized that *Brown* was not being enforced, it became a basis for protest, indicating a possible lag between creation of rights consciousness and actions stemming from it. If a landmark ruling like *Brown* becomes part of our broader consciousness, the likelihood that people will work to bring it into actuality is increased. In fact, one may say that *Brown* probably had more of a short-term effect in giving African-Americans the impetus to fight for their rights, both with regard to school desegregation and other civil rights as well, than it did on elementary school desegregation itself.

*Litigation and Rights.* Successful litigation is widely imitated. Often it stimulates further litigation to expand those rights already won in addition to ensuring their enforcement. Seeking rights through the Supreme Court may, however, carry a limited payoff. Some rulings are not favorable to desired rights claims and may even undermine rights thought to have been won. In addition, if rights sought by differing groups are in conflict, what may be victory for one can be a defeat for another. For example, those who seek to ban pornography as endangering women, a position arising directly from consciousness of women's rights, find themselves at odds with more traditional liberals who ardently protest any limitations on freedom of expression. There is also the continuing question whether mere formal legal rights, to which most attention has been paid, can ever be dispositive: the formal equality of African-Americans or Latinos with whites, critics say, cannot supply quality education in the ghetto and barrio, and may even distract attention from the quest for effective education and economic well-being. A belief that formal legal victories can effectively redress social and economic inequality may actually induce acceptance and quiescence and mitigate against real reform efforts.

Focusing on rights as achievable only through the courts may hinder political mobilization to gain those rights. This is a result of what we might call the "myth of rights," that is, the idea that there *are* rights that courts declare, that the courts *will* declare them, and that these declared rights will be easily *implemented*. All three components of this formulation are questionable. The criticism, by activists who took to the streets, of the NAACP's reliance on litigation can be stated this way: overreliance on the courts, with attendant enforcement difficulties, distracts from the development of necessary political (electoral or legislative) strategies and actions. Some interest groups outside the civil liberties and civil rights arenas have been careful to use a combination of legislation and litigation to achieve rights rather than relying heavily, if not solely, on litigation. They have, for example, used court cases to attract public attention to their causes and to raise funds, and they have obtained important information through litigation, information they then use to stimulate legislative activity.

An important aspect of reliance on litigation is the key role of lawyers. When litigation is felt to be the central means for achieving rights, lawyers—mostly white and male—tend to be in charge; they tend to define the problems and set the parameters. Lawyer's central role makes it difficult to raise others' consciousness about rights. When people's rights consciousness has been raised, turning to litigation to achieve those rights may put the group members or activists in the back seat. Within certain groups—for example, those seeking greater rights for the mentally ill—where consciousness of rights has been a device used to build a sense of community, tensions between group members and lawyers have been considerable; the group members wish to retain control of "their movement" and not to have it become, in their view at least, the lawyers' plaything. And if the courts are seen as unwilling to provide the rights being sought, achievement of effective action in the community is viewed as better than negative national precedents from the Supreme Court. Rights consciousness may thus lead away from the courts, and particularly away from the Supreme Court, with litigation seen as a possibly self-defeating strategy.

The Supreme Court, particularly during the Warren era, has shown that it can stimulate greater consciousness of rights. The Court, however, can also produce rulings limiting rights. Whatever its direction, the Court may have an effect in producing rights consciousness because rulings affirming rights may stimulate pursuit of rights when negatively received, and consciousness of other rights may develop among those opposing the Court's rulings. For all this, we must be careful not to overestimate the Supreme Court's effect on rights consciousness. A number of factors limit such effects, including the way in which people view their own situations and the extent to which they assume that the Court's rulings will be routinely enforced.

□ Kristin Bumiller, The Civil Rights Society: The Social Construction of Victims (1988). Alan David Freeman, "Legitimizing Racial Discrimination Through Antidiscrimination Law: A Critical Review of Supreme Court Doctrine," Minnesota Law Review 62 (1978): 1049–1119. Lawrence M. Friedman, Total Justice (1985). Stuart Scheingold, "Constitutional Rights and Social Change: Civil Rights in Perspective," in Judging the Constitution: Critical Essays on Judicial Lawmaking, edited by Michael

W. McCann and Gerald L. Houseman (1989), pp. 73–91. Stuart A. Scheingold, The Politics of Rights: Lawyers, Public Policy, and Political Change (1974).        Stephen L. Wasby

**Hoar, Ebenezer Rockwood** (b. Concord, Mass., 21 Feb. 1816; d. Concord, 31 Jan. 1895), jurist, attorney general, congressman, and rejected nominee for the U.S. Supreme Court. A grandson of Roger Sherman, Hoar graduated from Harvard Law School in 1835. After practicing law for five years, he won a seat in the Massachusetts senate. During the campaign he stated his strong antislavery convictions.

In 1849 he was appointed judge of the Court of Common Pleas in Massachusetts, a position he resigned to resume private practice in 1855. In 1859 he became an associate justice of the Supreme Judicial Court of Massachusetts. He left the bench to become President Ulysses S. Grant's attorney general in 1869. When Congress created nine new circuit judgeships, Hoar's insistence that these positions be filled by persons of integrity and ability earned him the animosity of many senators, who considered these positions opportunities for political patronage (see JUDICIARY ACT OF 1869). President Grant nominated Hoar for a seat on the Supreme Court on 15 December 1869; a bitter fight over his confirmation raged for seven weeks. The Senate rejected his nomination on 3 February 1870 by a vote of 33 to 24. His high professional standards, refusal to play party politics, and advocacy of a civil service system lost for the nation a justice of uncompromising integrity.

Hoar resigned his position as attorney general in 1870 at Grant's request, as Grant felt it politically expedient to appoint a person from the South to the post. He served a single term in Congress (1873–1875) after which he resumed his private law practice and retired from public life. Hoar died on 31 January 1895.

(See also NOMINEES, REJECTION OF.)
                                                Judith K. Schafer

**Hodgson v. Minnesota**, 110 S.Ct. 2926 (1990), argued 29 Nov. 1989, decided 25 June 1990 by vote of 5 to 4 on one issue and 5 to 4 on another; Stevens announced judgment of Court on the first issue in an opinion joined by Brennan, Marshall, Blackmun, and O'Connor, from which Rehnquist, White, Scalia, and Kennedy dissented; O'Connor concurring in result on second issue with Rehnquist, White, Scalia, and Kennedy. Hodgson, the Court's first confrontation with the abortion issue after its decision in *Webster* v. *Reproductive Health Services* (1989), indicated that substantially greater restrictions on abortions were constitutionally permissible. The case involved a statute requiring minors seeking abortions to notify both parents; a minor who obtained a court's determination that she was mature or that an abortion without notice to the parents was in her best interests could have an abortion.

A majority of the Court held that the two-parent notification requirement was unconstitutional; it was not a reasonable method of assuring proper parental involvement in the abortion decision, given the large numbers of families in which the minor seeking abortion did not reside with both parents, often because the absent parent was physically abusive. The dissenters argued that a legislature could properly act with the majority of families in mind; in most families, notification of both parents would promote desirable consultation.

A different majority of the Court held that permitting minors to invoke a judicial "bypass" in lieu of parental notification was constitutional because it was "an expeditious and efficient means" to identify cases where notification of both parents would not be sound. The dissenters objected to requiring that minors disclose intimate personal details to a judge. Further, experience with the procedure showed that permission to obtain an abortion was almost never denied; however, obtaining permission burdened the minor's choice because of delays in scheduling hearings and difficulties in locating judges in rural areas who would make the necessary findings.

*Hodgson* was the first case in which Justice Sandra Day *O'Connor voted to hold a restriction on the availability of abortions unconstitutional. The two-parent notification requirement was quite unusual, however, and the implications of *Hodgson* may be quite limited.

(See also ABORTION; PRIVACY.)

Mark V. Tushnet

**Holden v. Hardy,** 169 U.S. 366 (1898), argued 21 Oct. 1897, decided 28 Feb. 1898 by vote of 6 to 2; Brown for the Court, Brewer and Peckham in dissent, Field retired. To challenge his conviction for violating a Utah statute that prohibited employment of workers in mines for more than eight hours a day, Albert F. Holden initiated this *habeas corpus proceeding against the sheriff, Harvey Hardy. Holden contended that the statute deprived him of freedom to contract with employees and violated three provisions of the *Fourteenth Amendment: *privileges or immunities, due process, and *equal protection. The Supreme Court rejected these arguments, treating them as a single contention.

Justice Henry Billings *Brown accepted the importance of freedom of contract. He emphasized, however, that the right was subject to limitation by a state's *police power to protect the health, safety, or morals of its citizens. The Fourteenth Amendment, in his view, was not intended to inhibit severely the evolution of the states' exercise of powers to protect their citizens, because law was "to a certain extent a progressive science" (p. 385). Obscured by that sweeping pronouncement was Brown's pivotal conclusion

that there was a reasonable basis in fact to support the legislature's judgment about the danger of mining. In spite of the opinion's recognition of state power, the real import of the decision lies in the implication that the Court would assess the reasonableness of any regulatory statute (see RULE OF REASON). The significance became apparent when the Court subsequently struck down a statute regulating the hours worked by bakers in *Lochner* v. *New York* (1905). Thus, in spite of its apparent support for state experimentation, *Holden* actually foreshadowed a period of active judicial supervision of economic legislation.

(See also CONTRACT, FREEDOM OF; DUE PROCESS, SUBSTANTIVE; LABOR.)

Walter F. Pratt, Jr.

**Holding,** a statement of law in a judicial opinion that is necessary to the resolution of the legal problem presented in the case. It is contrasted with a dictum, which is a gratuitous statement of opinion in a decision not necessary to the result in the case (see OBITER DICTUM). William M. Wiecek

**Holmes, Oliver Wendell** (b. Boston, Mass., 8 Mar. 1841; d. Washington, D.C., 6 Mar. 1932; interred Arlington National Cemetery, Arlington, Va.), associate justice, 1902–1932. Holmes was born in Boston to a family of moderate means. His father, for whom he was named, was a physician and *littérateur* who supplemented the income from a meager Boston medical practice with lectures on anatomy at the Harvard Medical School and lectures on literary subjects to general audiences. The elder Holmes was a gifted conversationalist and a compulsive writer of light verse; in 1856, when his son was just entering college, Dr. Holmes began writing a series of essays and poems, collectively titled *The Autocrat of the Breakfast Table,* for *The Atlantic Monthly;* his work became immensely popular in Great Britain and the United States. Like his father, the younger Holmes was intensely talkative, with a light, combative manner and a knack for verse rhythms and imagery.

Mrs. Holmes, born Amelia Lee Jackson, the daughter of a prominent Boston lawyer and judge, Charles Jackson, married late and devoted herself to her husband and three children, of whom the future Supreme Court justice was the first. Holmes—tall, thin, lantern-jawed—resembled his mother more than his short, round-faced father, and he was deeply affected by her. He was her favorite, and he acquired a secure self-confidence as a result. He also received from his mother a powerful sense of duty and a talent for strong, warmly affectionate friendships. With his sense of duty came an unyielding adherence to the factual, a sharp skepticism for all but the self-evident, and a near-mystical acceptance of whatever in life seemed irrevocably given.

*Influences.* Holmes attended private schools and Harvard College, but the principle influences on his intellectual development were outside the classroom. He acquired early, as an article of faith, belief in a pre-Darwinian doctrine of evolution compounded of the theories of Thomas Malthus and German Romanticism. In later life, Holmes said that the great figures of his youth, other than his father, were John Ruskin, Thomas Carlyle, and Ralph Waldo Emerson. He probably absorbed their ideas as much from conversation in his father's house, where Emerson and other literary figures were occasional callers, as from his reading. Emerson passed on the "ferment" of philosophical inquiry to Holmes, partly by encouraging his combative independence of mind.

In his undergraduate essays Holmes announced the need for a "rational" explanation of duty, a sort of scientific substitute for religion, which he sought in an evolutionary, "scientific" account of both history and philosophy.

The other great influence on his youth was a revival of chivalry then sweeping over the United States and Great Britain, partly inspired by the poems and novels of Alfred, Lord Tennyson and Sir Walter Scott. Like many of his contemporaries Holmes acquired a lifelong commitment to courtly ideals and conduct. Chivalry was the code of duty for which he sought—and, ultimately, believed he had found—scientific justification.

*Early Career.* Holmes enlisted in the federal army in July 1861, shortly after the Civil War had broken out; he obtained a commission as a lieutenant and served for two years in the Twentieth Massachusetts Volunteer Infantry at Ball's Bluff, the Peninsula campaign, and Antietam. In those two years he was wounded three times, twice almost fatally, and suffered from dysentery. Exhausted and reluctant to assume a command for which he had little aptitude, in the winter of 1863–1864 Holmes accepted a post as aide to General Horatio Wright (and then to General John Sedgwick) of the Sixth Corps. In the relative leisure of winter quarters he turned to philosophical writing, in notebooks he later destroyed, developing his combat experience into a materialist, evolutionary philosophy steeped in the conflict of rival nations and races and governed by the rules of chivalry.

He served through the Wilderness campaign and the siege of Vicksburg, and then, exhausted and telling himself that his duty lay in pursuing his philosophy, he left the army before the war's end and returned home to Boston.

Holmes attended Harvard Law School and in the summer of 1866, to complete his education, traveled to Great Britain and the Continent. He made a sort of debut in London polite society, was invited to a great many homes, and made lasting friendships. One of the most important was with Leslie Stephen, who greatly reinforced Holmes's interest in rationalist philosophy, evolution, and

*Oliver Wendell Holmes*

chivalry. Throughout his life, Holmes returned to England during the summer social season whenever he could, and kept up an energetic and extensive correspondence with British friends between visits.

On his return to Boston Holmes entered a clerkship and was admitted to the bar in 1867. He briefly gave up practice and attempted a career as an independent scholar, editing the twelfth edition of James Kent's *Commentaries on American Law* (1873), writing dozens of brief articles and reviews for the newly formed *American Law Review* and also occasional poetry. Elements of his later thought were formed in these years, but he did not put them into systematic form.

In 1872 he married a childhood friend, Fanny Dixwell, and joined a Boston law firm, Shattuck, Holmes, and Munroe, which had a busy commercial and admiralty practice. Fanny Holmes became seriously ill with rheumatic fever shortly after their marriage, and Holmes devoted himself to her care and to his law practice for several years. They never had children.

*Scholarship.* Holmes gradually returned to scholarly work in his spare hours, and in 1876, with "Primitive Notions in Modern Law," he began a series of essays that presented a systematic analysis of the *common law. He completed the series, somewhat hastily, and presented the essays as the Lowell Lectures in Boston in November and December 1880. They were published as a book, *The Common Law*, in 1881, a few days before Holmes's fortieth birthday.

*The Common Law*, often called the greatest work of American legal scholarship, became one of the founding documents of the *sociological and, then, the realist schools of jurisprudence, and it had a considerable impact on tort and contract law in both the United States and Great Britain. It marked the beginning of empirical studies of judges' behavior and formed the basis of Holmes's later work on the Supreme Court.

In Holmes's view, acquired in twelve years of law practice, judges decided cases first and found reasons afterward. Their actual grounds of decision were based on the "felt necessities" of their time as much as on precedent or purely logical calculation. Consciously or unconsciously, judges expressed the wishes of their class. Law therefore was both an instrument and a result of natural selection. If law was simply an instrument to accomplish certain material ends, it seemed to follow that the law should concern itself solely with external behavior, and Holmes argued that he could discern in the developing common law a trend toward complete reliance on "external standards" of behavior rather than subjective states of mind or personal culpability.

Holmes had labored unsuccessfully, like his predecessors, to make sense of the tangled mass of legal rules of behavior. In 1880, however, he seems to have seen a new organizing principle. The question in every case, Holmes realized, was whether liability would be imposed. His general organizing principle then became clear: liability would be imposed when the breach of a rule of conduct resulted in injuries that an ordinary person would have foreseen. The injuries, and not the breach as such, were the central motive of policy; the law was founded on a policy of avoiding unjustified harms. (It was this insight that later made possible an economic analysis of the law.)

In *The Common Law* Holmes argued that law had evolved from more primitive origins toward this still partly unconscious "external standard" and that law would continue to evolve toward a fully self-conscious instrument of social purpose. Holmes's book itself, presumably, was an important step in this evolution toward self-awareness.

**Service on the Massachusetts Court.** After *The Common Law* appeared, Holmes taught for a single semester at Harvard Law School and then accepted appointment to the Supreme Judicial Court of Massachusetts, where he served for twenty years, becoming chief justice in 1899.

Holmes wrote more than a thousand opinions for the Massachusetts court, most of them deciding common law questions or construing statutes in light of the common law, relentlessly working through the thesis of *The Common Law*. Holmes generally avoided writing opinions in constitutional cases, but when obliged to state a view he almost without exception expressed deference to the legislature. His opinions and letters of the time make clear that he based this deference on the English constitutional principle that the legislature was omnipotent, a principle modified in

the United States only to the extent that written constitutions contained clear limitations on legislative authority. This was the reasoning of Thomas M. *Cooley's famous treatise, *Constitutional Limitations*, a book Holmes had favorably reviewed and had used when teaching, but it would have been a natural enough conclusion from his own approach to jurisprudence.

In the 1890s, Holmes made one last major addition to his system to ideas. In "Privilege, Malice, and Intent," published in 1894, Holmes discussed libel and slander cases in which liability was based, at least in part, on the defendant's state of mind—*actual malice—rather than on an external standard of foreseeable harm. In these cases, Holmes argued, a common-law privilege to do harm, like the privilege accorded to truthful speech, was based on a social policy favoring freedom of speech, but the privilege would be withdrawn when used for a malicious purpose. Holmes maintained that a general policy of avoiding unjustified harms was the basis of the privilege as well as the defense of actual malice, which accordingly were consistent with the thesis of *The Common Law*. He would later incorporate this theory into his opinions on the *First Amendment. In 1896, he applied the theory in dissenting opinions in which he argued that a privilege should be extended to trade unions to organize and picket peacefully so long as these activities were carried on without malice.

Holmes strongly suggested that in English and American cases in which unions' right to conduct strikes or boycotts had been denied, judges had typically been biased by class prejudice. He argued forcefully that it was the duty of a judge to decide cases fairly, even if the result appeared dangerous to his class interests.

This argument seemed consistent with Holmes's theory that judges were instruments of the dominant force in society, but he never adequately explained the seeming contradiction of his Darwinist views, which he continued to affirm.

**Service on the Supreme Court.** On 11 August 1902, President Theodore Roosevelt nominated Holmes to the U.S. Supreme Court. He took his seat on 8 December 1902, and thereupon seemed to come into his own. After thirty-five years of trying to extract philosophical principles from the most meager materials, petty disputes and sordid crimes, he for the first time was addressing great questions of public life and national policy. With a new self-confidence, he developed opinion writing into an art with a very personal stamp; while his opinions were often difficult to follow and were criticized for over brevity and obscurity, they often achieved a unique beauty and power.

Holmes served on the Supreme Court for thirty years, under four chief justices. Through his longevity and his talent for getting cases assigned to him he wrote 873 opinions for the Court, more than any other justice. He wrote proportionately fewer *dissents than many justices, but as these were particularly forceful and well written they are the best-known of his opinions. A handful of his dissents, especially in substantive *due process' and free *speech cases, are now cited as precedent.

The Court in those years believed it had the power to base decisions on general principles of common law. Holmes, although he had done more to elucidate such general principles than anyone else, doubted whether they were a "brooding omnipresence in the sky" and insisted the Court must refer to the law of some actual jurisdiction. His views prepared the way for the decision after his death, in *Erie Railroad v. Tompkins* (1938), that there was no general *federal common law.

When construing statutes, the Court did not yet consult "legislative history," and Holmes's readings of statutes were carefully limited to the four corners of the statutes themselves. Where meanings of terms were not clear he consulted the common law, in accordance with the canon that if words had an established meaning in common law, Congress was assumed to have used them in that sense.

*Antitrust Cases.* Thus, in a famous line of dissents, Holmes insisted that that *Sherman Antitrust Act, by its plain language, did not prevent former competitors from merging, as at common law such mergers were not "combinations in restraint of trade." On similar grounds he argued that the Sherman Act did not prohibit retail price maintenance agreements or forbid trade associations in which price and production data were exchanged. In these opinions Holmes insisted that the majority read their own unstated economic views into the statute. Holmes was at pains to expose these "inarticulate premises," and in the process he expressed his own views of economics in compressed form.

Holmes believed that the Sherman Antitrust Act was an "imbecile statute" that, he said in a letter, aimed "at making everyone fight and forbidding anyone to be victorious." Dissenting from the Court's opinion that retail price maintenance agreements violated the Sherman Act, Holmes said that the Court majority's apparent policy was mistaken: competition within a sector of industry had little effect on price, and accordingly their reason for applying the Sherman Act failed even on policy grounds. Similary, while upholding trade unions' right to organize and strike, he maintained that higher wages would be obtained by unions only at the cost of other workers. (See also ANTITRUST.)

The basis for these views was his often-expressed conviction that the "stream of products," by which he apparently meant something like the gross national product, was fixed at any one time and that any increase was quickly absorbed by the growth of population. He believed further that the share withdrawn by the wealthy capitalist class for its own consumption was minuscule in comparison to the total (see CAPITALISM). If essentially all the wealth in society was consumed by the large mass of its citizens, it seemed to follow by an iron logic that workers competed with each other, not with capitalists, for a larger share of the national product and that prices reflected not costs or competition but the share of the product that consumers were willing to give to any one commodity. Proposals for economic reform, redistribution of wealth, and enhanced competition, therefore seemed to him equally wrong. He insisted that the only hope for improved living conditions lay in eugenics and population control—"taking life in hand"—a view brutally expressed in his opinion in *Buck v. Bell,* upholding Virginia's compulsory sterilization law.

*Constitutional Cases.* Holmes's most important opinions concerned constitutional law. Holmes believed that the Constitution, too, should be construed in light of the common law. The general terms of the Constitution—freedom of speech, due process of law—were to be understood as embodying "relatively fundamental principles of right" found in the common law (see FUNDAMENTAL RIGHTS). As that law was changing, so too were the meanings of constitutional terms evolving: as he wrote, "A word is not a crystal, transparent and unchanging, but the skin of a living thought." Fundamental principles were to be viewed from the perspective of centuries, a perspective from which universal suffrage was a recent innovation, and property rights were by no means fixed or eternal.

To Holmes the fundamental guarantees revolved around fairness in judicial proceedings. He objected to the unrestrained investigations of the *Interstate Commerce Commission, which seemed to compel *self-incrimination. He refused to accept a procedure of empty forms when African-American and Jewish defendants were tried in lynch-mob settings in the South. He insisted on the right of the federal courts to intervene in state proceedings by writ of *habeas corpus. He wrote opinions limiting the power of courts to punish *contempt summarily, without trial. But when a lynch mob defied the Court's *habeas corpus decree, he managed the criminal contempt trial, the only criminal trial ever held in the Supreme Court (*United States v. Shipp,* 1906).

Holmes was much more deferential to the states and to the other branches of government with regard to substantive guarantees of the Constitution. In his first opinion for the Court, *Otis v. Parker* (1902), he embraced the doctrine of "substantive due process" but gave it sharply narrowed scope. Substantive due process was the doctrine that the guarantee of due process of law extended by the *Fifth and *Fourteenth Amendments ensured more than a fair hearing in court. It was held to ensure that legislation also met some minimum requirements, but the Court had not very clearly articulated what those requirements were. In *Otis* Holmes identified them as "relatively fundamental principles of right" of the common law. His opinions over the years elucidated these fundamental principles, which were essentially those rights recorded in the *Bill of Rights, which Holmes called evolving institutions "transplanted from English soil" (*Gompers* v. *United States*, 1914, p. 610).

Although the term "substantive due process" has been discredited, Holmes's opinions and dissents presage the modern view that the due process guarantee in the Fourteenth Amendment "incoporates" the Bill of Rights and makes it applicable to the states (see INCORPORATION DOCTRINE). Holmes did not take an expansive view of these rights. He had grown up in a world in which the right to *vote was still limited to men of property, and his views of the power of government were formed in the Civil War. Although he had nearly given his life in the Abolitionist cause and was nearly free of racial prejudice as anyone of his time in public life, he repeatedly avoided any defense of the right of African-Americans to vote. In *Bailey* v. *Alabama* (1911) and *United States* v. *Reynolds* (1914), he dissented from the Court's decision that southern statutes making it a crime for tenant farmworkers to break their contracts were a form of *peonage. He did not believe that wiretaps were unreasonable searches and seizures forbidden by the *Fourth Amendment, and he expressly rejected a right of *privacy based on the Fourth and Fifth Amendments.

If Holmes took a narrow view of *civil rights, he took a similarly restrained approach to rights of *property. He believed that property rights were created by legislatures and could be undone pretty much at will, the only question usually being whether compensation was owed when the government destroyed a form of property. His opinion in *Pennsylvania Coal Co.* v. *Mahon* (1922) gave the modern formulation of when such compensation is due.

Dissenting in *Lochner* v. *New York* (1905), perhaps his most famous opinion, Holmes argued for the right of New York's legislature to enact a statute limiting the labor of bakery workers to ten hours per day. Holmes said that the majority of the Court, in striking down the statute as a violation of due process, had based their opinion on an inarticulate "major premise," an economic theory that was plainly not a fundamental principle of right. "The Fourteenth Amendment does not enact Mr. Herbert Spencer's *Social Statics*," Holmes famously remarked (p. 75). This dissent is often cited as if it were critical of the whole method of substantive due process, but, as others have noted, Holmes was simply saying that economic principles were not fundamental principles of law.

*Free Speech Cases.* Of all Holmes's opinions the most important and the most controversial were in cases concerning the First Amendment's guarantee of freedom of speech. During *World War I the federal government had prosecuted thousands of men and women who opposed or resisted mobilization. The first of these cases to come to the Court concerned speeches and leaflets that the government claimed were intended to obstruct the draft, in violation of the Espionage Act. In the first such case (*Schenck* v. *United States*, 1919) Holmes, writing for a unanimous Court, said that Congress had the power to forbid speeches and publications that threatened to interfere with the draft. Freedom of speech was not absolute: someone could legitimately be punished for falsely crying fire in a theater and causing a panic. As Congress could make it a crime to obstruct the draft, so it might also punish speech that posed a *clear and present danger of having this forbidden result. Holmes then applied this standard to affirm a series of convictions for obstructing the draft, including the conviction of Eugene Debs, the Socialist candidate for President, for a speech critical of the war and of the draft.

Holmes's opinion in *Schenck* was generally approved at the time, but the Court never cited the clear and present danger standard except to uphold convictions, and it gradually came to be identified with the prosecutor's view. Modern commentators have criticized the *Schenck* opinion for giving too little protection to speech.

Holmes himself, however, strenuously objected to this one-sided use of his opinion, and in a second group of cases decided in 1919 he dissented. It appeared to Holmes that, in this second group of cases, the federal government had broadened its campaign of prosecutions to include political dissidents as well as draft resisters and that these new defendants were being convicted for their socialist and anarchist ideas, not for any acts intended or likely to harm the war effort. In *Abrams* v. *United States* (1919), the first of these cases to be decided, Holmes restated the clear and present danger test in terms drawn from his 1894 article "Privilege, Malice, and Intent." The defendants in *Abrams* had thrown leaflets from a garment factory window; neither by the external standard of foreseeability nor by the test of actual intent, Holmes said, did the defendants' acts pose a clear and present danger to the war effort.

Holmes went on to give his statement of the policy that he believed underlay the privilege afforded by the Constitution to honest expressions of opinion that posed no clear and present danger: "The best test of truth is the power of the thought to get itself accepted in the competition of the market, and that truth is the only ground upon which our wishes safely can be carried out [in law]" (p. 630). Political dissent was to be freely allowed; it was precisely those ideas that challenged and tested the principles of American society in the free competition of discourse that were to be most jealously protected.

*Legacy.* Holmes's constitutional opinions fit into a coherent view of the American system evolved from his own experiences and his studies of the common law. Holmes believed that the law of the English-speaking peoples was an experiment in peaceful evolution in which a fair hearing in court substituted for the violent combat of more primitive societies. In the American federal system, a refinement of this experiment, the states provided "insulated chambers" for experiments in law and political economy; these experiments were to be tolerated so long as they were conducted in accordance with the rules for making fair decisions. Experiments, even in socialism, were not foreclosed by any principle fundamental to the law. Nor did Holmes believe that any religious or ethical precepts were fundamental.

To Holmes, life was a continual clash of groups—nations, races, classes—representing great conflicting principles, struggling for survival in a world of limited resources. The Constitution required only that the domestic struggle be fair and peaceful. The task of the judge was to choose fairly between contending forces. Political truth was to be worked out in the competition of the marketplace and not imposed by armies or police.

The inconsistency in Holmes's idea of the judge's role became more marked as he grew older. His Darwinist, quasi-scientific system called for judges to serve, in the end, the survival of their own class or nation. Yet in the chivalrous system of law Holmes described, the judge must set aside his personal loyalties and views, deciding cases fairly even when that would mean death to the existing order.

Holmes's self-denying sense of duty, his loyalty to the future of humanity rather than its present order, apparently was founded on faith in something outside the evolutionary system of law. It could not be reconciled with Holmes's system and indeed seemed to contradict it. As he grew older, Holmes's sense of duty came to predominate, so that his opinions seemed to be the impersonal voice of duty itself.

His health failed in the summer of 1931, and on 12 January 1932 he submitted his resignation to President Herbert Hoover. He died of pneumonia at his Washington, D.C., home in the early hours of 6 March 1935.

□ Alexander M. Bickel and Benno C. Schmidt, Jr., *The Judiciary and Responsible Government, 1910–1921* (1984). George A. Bruce, *The Twentieth Regiment of Massachusetts Volunteer Infantry, 1861–1865* (1906). Oliver Wendell Holmes, Jr., "Privilege, Malice, and Intent," *Harvard Law Review* 8 (1894): 1–14. Mark DeWolfe Howe, ed., *Touched with Fire: Civil War Letters and Diary of Oliver Wendell Holmes, Jr., 1861–1864* (1946). Mark DeWolfe Howe, *Justice Oliver Wendell Holmes: The Shaping Years, 1841–1870* (1957). Mark DeWolfe Howe, comp., *The Occasional Speeches of Justice Oliver Wendell Holmes* (1962). Mark DeWolfe Howe, *Justice Oliver Wendell Holmes: The Proving Years, 1870–1882* (1963). Max Lerner, *The Mind and Faith of Justice Holmes: His Speeches, Essays, Letters and Judicial Opinions* (1943). Sheldon M. Novick, *Honorable Justice: The Life of Oliver Wendell Holmes* (1989).

Sheldon M. Novick

**Holmes v. Jennison,** 14 Pet. (39 U.S.) 540 (1840), argued 24–25 Jan. 1840, dismissed 4 Mar. 1840 by vote of 4 to 4; Taney for himself, Story, McLean, and Wayne; opinions in disagreement by Thompson, Baldwin, Barbour, and Catron; McKinley absent. Silas H. Jennison, governor of Vermont, ordered George Holmes, a resident of Quebec, arrested and sent back to Canada to be tried for murder even though the United States had no extradition treaty with Canada. The Vermont Supreme Court refused to issue a writ of *habeas corpus. Dividing 4 to 4 over the question, the U.S. Supreme Court dismissed the case for want of jurisdiction (see JUDICIAL POWER AND JURISDICTION).

Chief Justice Roger B. *Taney affirmed the Court's jurisdiction as well as the exclusive power of the federal government to govern foreign relations. Because of that exclusive power, Taney reasoned, a state governor had no authority to surrender fugitives to a foreign country. Four justices disagreed, believing that the Court lacked jurisdiction over denial of habeas corpus by a state court. Justice Smith *Thompson, however, implied in his opinion that Governor Jennison had no authority to order Holmes's surrender. Because five of the eight justices sitting on the case denied Jennison's authority, the Vermont Supreme Court ordered Holmes released even though the U.S. Supreme Court had refused, because of the tie vote, to take jurisdiction of the case. Taney's language in favor of the exclusive right of the federal government over foreign relations stands as the most notable and enduring feature of this case. Nationalists such as Joseph *Story applauded Taney's reasoning, while states-rightists such as James Buchanan deplored it.

(See also FOREIGN AFFAIRS AND FOREIGN POLICY; FUGITIVES FROM JUSTICE.)

Robert M. Ireland

## Home Building and Loan Association v. Blaisdell, 290 U.S. 398 (1934), argued 8 and 9 Nov. 1933, decided 8 June 1934 by vote of 5 to 4; Hughes for the Court, Sutherland, Butler, McReynolds, and Van Devanter in dissent. The Court's decision in *Home Building and Loan Association* v. *Blaisdell* was important not only because it upheld a critical state law passed during the Great Depression but also because it revealed the sharp divisions on the high court over the proper response to the economic crisis.

The legislation at issue was the 1933 Minnesota Mortgage Moratorium Law. The act authorized a Minnesota state court, when called upon by a beleaguered debtor, to consider exempting property from foreclosure "during the continuance of the emergency and in no event beyond May 1, 1935." The law was passed by a legislature especially mindful of the problems of farmers facing mortgage foreclosures.

This particular case arose as a result of the desire of Mr. and Mrs. John H. Blaisdell, who had received a mortgage on a house and lot from the Home Building and Loan Association, to avoid foreclosure and to extend their mortgage redemption period. A Minnesota district court sided with the Blaisdells on the condition that certainly monthly installments be paid in a timely fashion. The Supreme Court of Minnesota affirmed the ruling. The Loan Association appealed to the U.S. Supreme Court, maintaining that the Moratorium Law was in conflict with the *Contracts Clause in Article I, section 10 of the Constitution and the *due process and *equal protection clauses of the *Fourteenth Amendment. The Contract Clause argument proved especially crucial. The Loan Association maintained that the clause's language—"No State shall enter into any . . . Law impairing the Obligation of Contracts . . ."—prohibited Minnesota from altering the contractual relationship between the Blaisdell's and the Loan Association.

Chief Justice Charles Evans *Hughes and Justice Owen J. *Roberts joined with the liberals and ruled the Moratorium Law constitutional by a vote of 5 to 4. Hughes wrote the majority opinion. He submitted that "while emergency does not create power, emergency may furnish the occasion for the exercise of power" (p. 426). In what has been called the most important Contract Clause case since *Charles River Bridge v. Warren Bridge (1837), Hughes stated that the Contract Clause was not absolute and that a state always possessed the authority to safeguard the vital interests of its citizens. Hughes found a "growing appreciation . . . of the necessity of finding ground between individual rights and public welfare." The chief justice concluded that the "question is no longer merely that of one party to a contract against another but of the use of reasonable means to safeguard the economic structure upon which the good of all depends" (p. 442).

For the four conservative dissenters, Justice George *Sutherland argued that the Contract Clause should be interpreted literally. He refused to acknowledge that emergencies could justify state authorized modification of contracts. Sutherland predicted that if the Court allowed the Minnesota Moratorium Act to stand, it could well be the harbinger of greater invasions of the sanctity of contracts. And, if the Contract Clause was so interpreted, Sutherland lamented, all constitutional restrictions on legislative prerogative might collapse. Essentially, Sutherland threw down the constitutional gauntlet. Again and again over the next three years, the Four Horsemen would saddle up and ride out to attempt to thwart state and national attempts to come to terms with the hardships imposed by the Great Depression.                     John W. Johnson

**Homosexuality.** The Supreme Court has protected some aspects of sexual autonomy within the context of a constitutional right of *privacy. It has recognized an individual's right to use contraceptives in *Griswold v. Connecticut (1965) and *Eisenstadt v. Baird (1972) and upheld and a woman's right to decide whether or not to terminate her pregnancy in *Roe v. Wade (1973). In *Bowers v. Hardwick (1986), the Court refused to construe the right of privacy to protect consensual homosexual activity by adults in their own homes. At that time, twenty-four states plus the District of Columbia outlawed sodomy. The 5-to-4 majority in Hardwick held that such laws had a rational basis. In his majority opinion, Justice Byron *White maintained that the right to privacy did not confer a general right to sexual autonomy but was limited to questions of marriage, family, and procreation, concluding that homosexual activity bore no connection to any of those. In a strong dissent, Justice Harry *Blackmun insisted that the majority had addressed issues not before it. Gay rights groups denounced Hardwick as their equivalent of the Dred *Scott case.

Despite increasing litigation in the 1970s and 1980s, efforts to secure more expanded constitutional protection for homosexuals have been largely unsuccessful. In addition to the privacy claim rejected in Hardwick, advocates have suggested that constitutional protection of the rights of homosexuals could be derived from the *First, *Eighth, and *Ninth Amendments as well as from the *Equal Protection Clause of the *Fourteenth Amendment. Justice Lewis *Powell, concurring in Hardwick, suggested that imprisonment for private consensual sexual conduct would raise a serious Eighth Amendment issue. Still, the Eighth Amendment ban on *cruel and unusual punishment would provide only limited protection to homosexuals.

The most direct concern of many lesbians and gay men is not imprisonment but the discrimination that they face on a regular basis at the workplace, in securing housing, and in gaining custody of their children. Although some courts have granted First Amendment protection for such activities as public acknowledgement of one's homosexuality, advocacy of gay rights, and even some forms of symbolic speech, the Supreme Court has been reluctant to extend broad First Amendment protection to homosexuals. For instance, it has consistently denied *certiorari in cases concerning the dismissal of schoolteachers because of their known homosexual status.

The Court's recognition of homosexuality as a *suspect classification under the *Equal Protection Clause of the Fourteenth Amendment would provide more expansive constitutional protection. Some argue that homosexuals as a group meet the criteria established for suspect classification, but the Supreme Court has not agreed. In *Hardwick* the Court concluded that conduct that is a defining characteristic of homosexuality is not constitutionally protected and may be criminalized. The Court has been reluctant to create new suspect classes, and federal civil rights statutes that bar discrimination do not specifically address the issue of sexual orientation (see DISCRIMINATORY INTENT).

□ "The Constitutional Status of Sexual Orientation: Homosexuality as a Suspect Classification," note in *Harvard Law Review* 98 (1984): 1285–1309.

John Anthony Maltese

**Hornblower, William Butler** (b. Paterson, N.J., 13 May 1851; d. Litchfield, Conn., 16 Jun. 1914), corporate lawyer and rejected nominee for the U.S. Supreme Court. Hornblower was involved in corporate practice in New York City after his graduation from Columbia Law School in 1875. On 19 September 1893, President Grover Cleveland nominated him to fill a vacancy on the Supreme Court. A year earlier, Hornblower, as a member of a committee of the New York City Bar Association, had conducted an investigation into an election irregularity, leading to the defeat of Isaac H. Maynard in a contest for a seat on the New York Court of Appeals. Maynard's powerful ally and friend Senator David B. Hill of New York retaliated by leading a successful campaign to defeat Hornblower's nomination; the nomination was rejected by a vote of 30 to 24 on 15 January 1894. When another vacancy occurred on the Court in 1895, Cleveland again considered Hornblower for the position, but Hornblower declined because of the financial sacrifice a Supreme Court seat entailed.

Hornblower took a seat on the New York City Court of Appeals on 30 March 1914 but resigned one week later because of ill health. He died shortly thereafter.

(See also NOMINEES, REJECTION OF.)

Judith K. Schafer

**Housing Discrimination** is one of the most virulent and intractable forms of discrimination. It occurs when purchase or rental of housing is denied to otherwise qualified individuals because of their *race, ethnicity, *gender, *religion, marital status, or disability. The Court's contribution to ending housing discrimination was sporadic at first; it became more consistent over time as the *civil rights movement expanded and both the executive branch and the Congress acted to combat discrimination. However, the Court has focused mostly on *discriminatory intent and on action that is not neutral on its face and has generally refrained from invalidating actions where only a showing of a discriminatory impact has been made.

The Court's earliest positive contribution to ending housing segregation came in *Buchanan v.

*Warley* (1917), in which the Court, applying the *Fourteenth Amendment for the first time in a housing discrimination case, struck down a city ordinance requiring neighborhood racial segregation in housing.

In 1926, the Court, in *Corrigan v. Buckley* (1926), appeared to support the constitutionality of *restrictive covenants, which were clauses in deeds restricting the conveyance of real property to members of certain racial, religious, or ethnic groups. In *Shelley v. Kraemer* (1948), however, the Court held that judicial enforcement of restrictive covenants constituted discriminatory state action prohibited by the Fourteenth Amendment. In a companion case, *Hurd v. Hodge* (1948), the Court relied on the Civil Rights Act of 1866 to reach a similar conclusion. The final blow to restrictive covenants came in *Barrows v. Jackson* (1953), in which the Court prohibited the granting of damages for the breach of a restrictive covenant. Thus, by 1953 the Court had removed the legal enforceability of restrictive covenants.

In the 1950s and much of the 1960s, the Court refrained from hearing housing discrimination cases. In 1967 it returned to the problem when it held unconstitutional an amendment to the California constitution, adopted by referendum, prohibiting the state from acting in any way to prevent racial discrimination in the sale or lease of property. In *Reitman v. Mulkey* (1967), the Court held that the amendment, in the California environment of state laws prohibiting such discrimination, violated the *Fourteenth Amendment by implicating the state in private racial discrimination. Similarly, in *Hunter v. Erickson* (1969), the Court struck down an amendment to the Akron, Ohio, city charter that blocked implementation of a fair housing ordinance.

When Congress finally acted to ban most housing discrimination in Title VIII of the 1968 Civil Rights Act, the Court upheld the effort. In *Jones v. Alfred H. Mayer Co.* (1968), the Court gave an expansive reading to laws prohibiting housing discrimination. The appellee refused to sell a house to the Joneses on the ground that the husband was African-American. The Court held that the 1866 Civil Rights Act barred all racial discrimination in housing, private as well as public. The Court followed this up with another expansive reading, this time of Title VIII of the 1968 Civil Rights Act. In *Trafficante v. Metropolitan Life Insurance Co.* (1972), a unanimous Court broadly construed standing requirements to allow current tenants in a large apartment complex to sue their landlord on behalf of minority applicants (see STANDING TO SUE). The Court also upheld the standing and a claim of discrimination by municipality and four of its residents who alleged that local realtors were destroying integration by racial steering in *Gladstone v. Village of Bellwood* (1979).

The Court has been more circumspect about allegations that facially nondiscriminatory *zoning has supported housing discrimination. In *Warth* v. *Seldin* (1975), the Court denied standing to various parties who alleged that the zoning plan of a Rochester, New York, suburb effectively prohibited the construction of low-income, integrated housing. Similarly, in *Village of *Arlington Heights* v. *Metropolitan Housing Development Corp.* (1977), the Court upheld zoning that effectively prevented low-cost integrated housing from being built. In *James* v. *Valtierra* (1971) and *City of Eastlake* v. *Forest City Enterprises, Inc.* (1976), the Court upheld a state requirement for referendum approval of subsidized housing projects and zoning changes, respectively; though the discriminatory impact of such actions was conceded.

The Court has decided a number of cases involving community wide attempts to keep certain kinds of people out. For example, in *Village of *Belle Terre* v. *Boraas* (1974), the Court upheld a local ordinance limiting occupancy to nuclear families, against a *First and Fourteenth Amendment challenge by a group of unrelated students. Three years later however, in *Moore* v. *City of East Cleveland* (1977), the Court struck down a similar ordinance that was used to prohibit a grandmother from living with her grandson. And in *City of Cleburne* v. *Cleburne Living Center* (1985), it struck down a municipality's attempt to bar a group home for the mentally retarded.

Housing discrimination has not been eliminated by Court action, however. In February 1985, a nationwide study found massive racial segregation in public housing projects sheltering nearly ten million people. The U.S. Commission on Civil Rights noted that in the 1970s housing segregation seemed to worsen as whites fled to suburbs that blacks could not afford or were kept out of by active discrimination. While part of the reason may be the failure of the executive branch to implement existing laws, judicial action has had little impact. Court decisions have resulted in little appreciable change in housing discrimination.

□ Robert G. Schwemm, *Housing Discrimination Law* (1983; supp. 1986). Clement E. Vose, *Caucasians Only* (1967). Gerald N. Rosenberg

**Houston, Charles Hamilton** (b. Washington, D.C., 3 Sept. 1895; d. Washington, D.C., 22 Apr. 1950), lawyer and educator. Houston attended Amherst college and Harvard Law School, where he became the first African-American member of the *Harvard Law Review* in 1921. In 1924 he joined his father's law practice and the law faculty at Howard University, where he was academic dean from 1929 to 1935. As dean, Houston transformed the law school from a traditional part-time operation into a full-time school with a focus on civil rights law. Houston inspired many of his students, including Thurgood *Marshall, to devote substantial parts of their careers to civil

rights law. Houston also worked closely with the *National Association for the Advancement of Colored People, and in 1935 he joined the staff of the NAACP in New York as its counsel. Initially Houston was paid from a grant from the American Fund for Public Service, which agreed to support a lawyer to plan litigation challenging segregation in education, transportation, and voting. Houston concentrated on segregation in universities and won the first major case in this campaign in *Missouri ex rel Gaines* v. *Canada* (1938). Houston left his position at the NAACP in 1939, returning to Washington because of illness and family obligations. He remained active as an adviser to the NAACP, and his legal practice included much civil rights work. His challenge to the exclusion of African-Americans from labor unions persuaded the Supreme Court to adopt the rule that unions had a "duty of fair representation" to all workers even if they excluded those workers from membership (*Steele* v. *Louisville & Nashville Railroad Co.*, 1944). Mark V. Tushnet

**Houston, East and West Texas Railway Co. v. United States.** See SHREVEPORT RATE CASES.

**Howard, Benjamin Chew** (b. Baltimore County, Md., 5 Nov. 1791; d. Baltimore, Md., 6 Mar. 1872), Supreme Court reporter of decisions, 1843–1861. One of the nominative reporters, Howard served the Court during the years preceding the *Civil War. He published volumes 1 through 24 of Howard's Reports (42–65 of U.S. Reports). Howard's father, John Eager Howard, had been a Revolutionary officer. His maternal grandfather, Benjamin Chew, was president of the Pennsylvania Court of Errors and Appeals before the Revolution. Howard earned his A.B. in 1809 and his A.M. in 1812, both from Princeton. His subsequent law studies were interrupted by the War of 1812, during which he organized troops and fought in battle against the British. He was admitted to the Maryland bar about 1816. A Democrat, Howard served at various times on the Baltimore City Council and in both chambers of the Maryland legislature. Elected to four terms in Congress, he chaired the House Foreign Relations Committee from 1835 to 1839.

Howard's long association with Chief Justice Roger *Taney apparently gained him the reporter's position in 1843, although nothing suggests that he sought the job or intrigued before the summary discharge of his precedessor, Richard *Peters. Howard's reports were praised as clear, thorough, and well written, although Justice Peter V. *Daniel accurately complained on one occasion that his name had been omitted before a dissenting opinion.

After serving as a delegate to the Wartime Peace Conference in February 1861, Howard resigned between terms of the Court in 1861 to run, unsuccessfully, as Democratic candidate for governor of Maryland. In 1869, Princeton awarded him an LL.D.

(See also REPORTERS, SUPREME COURT.)

Francis Helminski

**Hoyt v. Florida,** 368 U.S. 57 (1961), argued 19 Oct. 1961, decided 12 Mar. 1961 by vote of 9 to 0; Harlan for the Court, Warren (with Black and Douglas) concurring. Gwendolyn Hoyt killed her husband with a baseball bat during a marital dispute over his adultery. She had offered to forgive and take him back, but his refusal provoked the homocide. She pleaded "temporary insanity" (see INSANITY DEFENSE) and was convicted of second-degree murder by an all-male jury.

Florida law provided that no female could serve on a jury unless she had specifically requested to be put on the jury list. Because men did not have to make these efforts, the law naturally produced a disproportionate number of male to female jurors, which resulted in many all-male juries. (Of ten thousand persons on her local jury list of eligibles, only ten were women.) Hoyt claimed that this statute denied her *equal protection of the law because women jurors would have been more empathetic than men in assessing her defense of temporary insanity.

The majority rejected her claim on the grounds that Florida's exemption of women from jury duty was not arbitrary. Rather, it was a reasonable accommodation of community beliefs that women's social role was to serve family life in the home. The concurrence reasoned simply that Florida was making a good faith effort to let those women who wanted to do so serve on juries. Both groups ignored the implication of *Ballard v. U.S. (1946) that women need to be included if juries are to represent a fair cross-section of the community. *Hoyt* was effectively overruled by *Taylor v. Louisiana (1975).

(See also GENDER; TRIAL BY JURY.)

Leslie Friedman Goldstein

**Hudson & Goodwin, United States v.** 7 Cranch (11 U.S.) 32 (1812), submitted without oral argument, decided 13 Feb. or 14 March 1812 by unknown vote. In this case the Supreme Court put an end to a decade-long dispute between Republicans and Federalists by denying the existence of a federal common law of crimes. That ruling remains good law today.

Barzillai Hudson and his codefendant George Goodwin were indicted in federal court in 1806 and 1807 for common-law *seditious libel, for publishing a report that President Thomas *Jefferson had conspired with Napoleon Bonaparte. Federal courts had for some time been upholding common-law convictions, but Republicans— who had won both the Congress and the presidency for the first time in 1800—had long insisted that federal courts had no constitutional power to create or enforce common-law crimes. The dis-

pute over the common law of crimes had its roots in the most fundamental disagreement between Republicans and Federalists: Republicans generally denied that any branch of the federal government had any power not explicitly granted by the Constitution.

By 1812, when the *Hudson* case reached the Supreme Court, Republican appointees comprised a majority. The Court dismissed the indictments, holding that no federal court could exercise common law jurisdiction in criminal cases. The majority opinion, authored by Justice William *Johnson, rested on the Republican principle that federal courts derive their powers solely from the Constitution and the Congress and have no residual jurisdiction. No dissents are recorded, but it is probable that Chief Justice John *Marshall and Justices Bushrod *Washington and Joseph *Story dissented.

(See also FEDERAL COMMON LAW.)

Suzanna Sherry

**Hudson v. Palmer,** 468 U.S. 517 (1984), argued 7 Dec. 1983, decided 3 July 1983 by vote of 5 to 4; Burger for the Court, O'Connor concurring, Stevens, joined by Brennan, Marshall, and Blackmun, concurring in part and dissenting in part. The Supreme Court held in this case that prison inmates do not have a right to *privacy in their prison cells that would entitle them to *Fourth Amendment protection against unreasonable searches. Palmer was an inmate at the Bland Correctional Center in Bland, Virginia. Hudson, an officer at the center, along with another corrections officer, conducted a "shake-down" search of Palmer's locker and cell. The officers found a ripped pillowcase in the trashcan and Palmer was charged with destroying state property. Palmer brought suit under section 1983 of the civil rights statutes (Title 42 of the U.S. Code) alleging that Hudson had conducted the search solely to harass him and further that Hudson had destroyed some of his noncontraband property in violation of the due process protections of the *Fourteenth Amendment.

Chief Justice Warren *Burger wrote for the majority that, under *Katz v. United States (1967), there was no reasonable expectation of privacy in a prison cell; therefore the Fourth Amendment protection against unreasonable searches and siezures did not apply. The Court also dismissed Hudson's due process claim on the basis of *Parratt v. Taylor (1981), which held that a state employee's negligent deprivation of an inmate's property does not violate the Due Process Clause if the state makes a meaningful postdeprivation remedy available.

(See also DUE PROCESS, PROCEDURAL; SEARCH WARRANT RULE, EXCEPTIONS TO.)

Daryl R. Fair

**Hughes, Charles Evans** (b. Glen Falls, N.Y., 11 Apr. 1862; d. Cape Cod, Mass., 27 Aug. 1948;

had a knack for picking legal talent for the emerging elite corporate bar of New York. Hughes attained much-needed financial rewards through his association with Carter. He also met and married the great love of his life, Carter's daughter Antoinette.

Hughes became a partner, but overwork and poor health soon drove him to a teaching position at Cornell Law School. He basked in the intellectual stimulation of teaching and in a happy home life with Antoinette and their two small children. Financial pressures and guilt-inducing letters from his father-in-law ended the Cornell idyll. Hughes reentered practice and made a minor fortune and major reputation as a leader of the corporate bar.

Hughes became a nationally known figure in the muckraking, trustbusting age as a result of his role as the studious head of the New York "gas inquiry." His independence, diligence, and capacity for sorting through the endless financial tangle of ratemaking and pricegouging won him a following in the press and the public. He next took on an investigation of corruption in the insurance industry. Hughes's reputation as an independent-minded Republican led to his election as governor of New York in 1906. Although corporate interests comprised both his former clients and his campaign supporters, Hughes showed independence in his two terms as governor, supporting creation of a Public Service Commission with strong powers to regulate corporate activity.

***Service as Associate Justice.*** President William Howard *Taft's nomination of Hughes to the Supreme Court was uncontroversial. Hughes shared the bench with the formidable Oliver Wendell *Holmes and developed an intellectual camaraderie with him, although they often disagreed. In *Bailey* v. *Alabama*, (1911), Hughes wrote the majority opinion declaring unconstitutional a state statute that, in effect, enforced *peonage. Holmes dissented. This case represents the contrasting ideology of Hughes, the conservative reformer, and Holmes, the unsentimental defender of legislative prerogative. Hughes, although a conservative, was more likely to use the power of the bench to engage in moderate social reform. In *Frank* v. *Mangum*, (1915), Holmes and Hughes joined as dissenters, decrying the "lynch law" trial of a Jew accused of murdering a young southern woman, during a time of antisemitic mob violence. Neither Hughes nor Holmes would tolerate baldfaced lawlessness.

As an associate justice, Hughes sat on the Court during a period of emerging challenges to economic legislation. Hughes voted to uphold congressional powers to regulate commerce, and he dissented in *Coppage* v. *Kansas* (1915), which forbade the prolabor Kansas legislature from outlawing the *yellow dog contract. Hughes, who started his public career as a reformer, was capable of rejecting employer arguments that

*Charles Evans Hughes*

interred Woodlawn Cemetery, New York, N.Y.), associate justice, 1910–1916; chief justice, 1930–1941. It was said of Charles Evans Hughes that no one ever slapped him on the back and called him Charlie. The stern, hardworking, religious Hughes was known for intelligence and integrity rather than conviviality.

Hughes's father, David Charles Hughes, emigrated to the United States from Wales and became a preacher. A Methodist, he converted to the Baptist church to marry a Baptist minister's daughter, Mary Connelly. The Dutch-descended Connellys traced their American roots to before the Revolution. David and Mary Hughes shared a devotion to their religion, and to their prized only child, Charles. Educated mostly at home by his adoring parents, Charles was a precocious child; he began reading when he was three years old, studied in several languages, and could recite from the classics by the time he was nine. Throughout his life, he was known for intelligence and a photographic memory. Attempts to enroll the adultlike child in various schools failed, as boredom or ill health returned him to home study. His parents were of modest means and passed on to Charles humility and respect for education, hard work, and religion.

***Early Career.*** Hughes entered Madison University (now Colgate University) at age fourteen and later transferred to Brown. He went on to graduate first in his class at Columbia Law School and breezed through the New York bar examination with a record high score. He was admitted to practice in 1884, at the age of twenty-two. He worked for the firm of Chamberlin, Carter, and Hornblower, where he had earlier served as an unpaid clerk. Walter S. Carter, the senior partner, protective labor legislation interfered with freedom of *contract (see DUE PROCESS, SUBSTANTIVE; LABOR).

Hughes' national reputation made him an obvious choice to run for president against the popular incumbent Woodrow Wilson. Hughes was nominated by the Republicans, and on 10 June 1916 he resigned from the Court to commence his unsuccessful campaign. After the close election, he promptly returned to a successful private practice and to active participation in the civic affairs of the period.

From 1921 to 1925, Hughes served as secretary of state under Presidents Warren G. Harding and Calvin Coolidge. He pushed for U.S. participation in the League of Nations, advocated international reduction of arms, promoted the World Court, and supported various international efforts to fend off another world war. In 1925, suffering from overwork, Hughes resigned his cabinet post to resume private practice. He briefly served on the International Court of Justice before his 1930 appointment by President Herbert Hoover to serve as chief justice of the United States.

***Service as Chief Justice.*** Hughes led the Court in what were perhaps its most significant days since the time of Chief Justice John *Marshall. The Great Depression and the gradual economic recovery, along with President Franklin D. *Roosevelt's effort to coerce the court into supporting his policies through the *court-packing plan, marked Hughes's tenure. Hughes also managed the court during the period when the great Justice Holmes was failing in health and when the strongminded liberal, Louis *Brandeis shared the bench with stubborn, conservative old-timers. Hughes was said to possess a diplomacy that limited acrimony and promoted efficiency in the beleagured Court.

Substantively, Hughes was a moderate, capable of activism when, in his view, the Constitution so compelled. Hughes supported civil liberties, generally voting in favor of free speech rights, as in *Stromberg v. California (1931) and Herndon v. Lowry (1937).

Hughes also supported the rights of the accused in the infamous Scottsboro Boys cases, in which African-American youths were sentenced to death on dubious rape charges (see *Powell v. Alabama, 1932). Hughes looked realistically at the facts when racial discrimination was probable. A true believer in the sanctity of the legal process, he was outraged by the flagrantly racist practices common in the criminal justice system of his time. In cases such as *Brown v. Mississippi (1936), in which authorities had obtained confessions by torturing African-American defendants, Hughes responded with angry denunciation (see RACE AND RACISM).

When the *New Deal legislation hit the courts, Hughes again voted as an independent-minded, moderate reformer. In *Schechter Poultry Co. v. United States (1935), he opposed the National Recovery Act as too broad an allocation of power, although at other times he had supported state and federal regulatory powers, as in *Home Building & Loan Association v. Blaisdell (1934).

Roosevelt grew dismayed at the Court's repeated rejection of legislation designed to combat the depression. After his reelection in 1936 by a resounding landslide, Roosevelt proposed a bill—known as the *court-packing plan—to add judges to the Court. After the announcement of Roosevelt's plan, the Court handed down progovernment decisions in *West Coast Hotel Co. v. Parrish (1937), with Hughes writing for the majority, and *National Labor Relations Board v. Jones & Laughlin Steel Corp. (1937), which sustained the National Labor Relations Act.

In spite of his support for government economic regulation in the past, Hughes was now seen by some as capitulating to Roosevelt's threats. Hughes maintained that nothing in his legal analysis had changed. Roosevelt withdrew his controversial plan.

Hughes was determined to retire before his capacities faded, and he resigned on 1 July 1941. In his retirement years he enjoyed time with his family, and he organized records of his career for the benefit of historians. He died in 1948.

□ Samuel Hendel, *Charles Evans Hughes and the Supreme Court* (1951). Merlo Pussey, *Charles Evans Hughes,* 2 vols. (1951).                    Mari J. Matsuda

**Humphrey's Executor v. United States,** 295 U.S. 602 (1935), argued 1 May 1935, decided 27 May 1935 by vote of 9 to 0; Sutherland for the Court. In 1933, President Franklin D. *Roosevelt removed a conservative member of the Federal Trade Commission, William E. Humphrey. Humphrey contested his removal in the U.S. Court of Claims, a suit carried on by the executor of his estate after his death.

In *Myers v. U.S., Chief Justice William Howard *Taft had affirmed presidential removal of a postmaster and in *obiter dictum stated that the president's removal power extended even to members of independent regulatory commissions. But in *Humphrey's Executor* Justice George *Sutherland, speaking for a unanimous Court, held that a president may remove a commissioner only for cause and that an unqualified removal power violated the *separation of powers. Sutherland distinguished *Myers* by asserting that a commissioner, unlike a postmaster, was not an executive officer but an official who acts quasi-legislatively and quasi-judicially.

Sutherland's opinion has been praised for liberating commissioners from fear of political reprisal but denounced for denying that a commissioner is a member of the executive branch, for hampering a president seeking to develop a coherent economic program, and for failing to acknowledge that Roosevelt had reason to believe he was acting in compliance with existing precedent. More angered by *Humphrey* because of its implication that he had willfully violated the Constitution than by the more important ruling in *Schechter Poultry Corp.* v. *U.S.* handed down that same day, Roosevelt was determined to seek ways to curb the Court, a course that led to his ill-fated *court-packing plan of 1937. Unlike other decisions hostile to the *New Deal, *Humphrey's Executor* has not been reversed, and its principle was expanded in *Wiener* v. *U.S.* (1958).

(See also APPOINTMENT AND REMOVAL POWER.)

William E. Leuchtenburg

**Hunt, Ward** (b. Utica, N.Y., 14 June, 1810; d. Washington, D.C., 24 Mar. 1886; interred Forest Hill Cemetery, Utica), associate justice, 1873–1882. The son of Montgomery Hunt and Elizabeth Stringham, Hunt attended Hamilton and later Union College, graduating in 1828. After completing legal studies at Litchfield Law School he was admitted to the New York bar in 1831 and entered a partnership with Judge Hiram Denio.

After serving a term in the New York assembly (1838) he was elected mayor of Utica (1844) and helped organize the Republican party in New York. His ambitions, however, were for judicial office.

In 1865, after several unsuccessful attempts, he was finally elected to the New York Court of Appeals, succeeding Denio. With the backing of Samuel Hoar and Roscoe *Conkling, Hunt was viewed by President Ulysses S. Grant as the ideal candidate to succeed Justice Samuel *Nelson to a seat on the U.S. Supreme Court. Hunt was

*Ward Hunt*

appointed late in 1872 and confirmed within a week. Of the three appointees to the high court in Grant's first term, only Hunt voted consistently to uphold the liberal legislation passed to implement the Civil War amendments. Otherwise, his name is not associated with any outstanding decision or judicial doctrine. He was nonetheless hard-working when in good health, and his opinions, while not brilliant, were clearly written and well researched.

Two of his opinions deserve special mention. The first was a U.S. circuit court case in which Hunt presided at the trial of Susan B. Anthony, who claimed the right to vote under the *Fourteenth Amendment. In his opinion Hunt distinguished between the rights of citizens of the states and of the United States, following the reasoning in the *Slaughterhouse Cases* (1873). He dismissed Anthony's claim and directed the jury to find her guilty under the Enforcement Act of 1870. In *United States* v. *Reese* (1876) Hunt registered one of his rare dissents. Writing for the majority, Chief Justice Morrison R. *Waite gave a narrow interpretation of voting rights under the *Fifteenth Amendment. Hunt, in his dissent, argued that the Enforcement Act of 1870 in its first two sections applied directly to cases of wrongful refusal of the right to vote because of discrimination based on race, while the third and fourth sections made it a punishable offense to deny the right of any citizen to vote. He concluded with the somber observation that the majority opinion brought to "an impotent conclusion" the vigorous amendments on the subject of *slavery (p. 253).

Failing health caused Hunt to miss a number of court sessions in 1877, and a month after the Court adjourned in December 1878 he suffered a disabling stroke. Because he had served for less than the ten years required to make him eligible for a pension, however, he failed to resign his seat. David B. *Davis, his former colleague on the bench, who was by then a senator from Illinois, introduced a special retirement bill for Hunt, and he resigned his seat the day the bill passed (27 Jan. 1882).

Rated by scholars in a 1971 survey as only "average" among all Supreme Court justices, Hunt was a politically loyal Grant appointee. He wrote the opinion of the Court in 149 cases and authored four dissents, and he dissented without opinion in eighteen cases. Hunt was twice married—in 1837 to Mary Ann Savage of Salem, New York, by whom he had two children, and in 1853 to Maria Taylor of Albany. He never recovered from the paralytic stroke, which affected his right side, and he remained an invalid until his death in Washington on 24 March 1886.

□ Stanley Kutler, "Ward Hunt," in *Justices of the United States Supreme Court, 1789–1969*, edited by Leon Friedman and Fred Israel, vol. 1 (1969), pp. 1221–1229.

Marian C. McKenna

**Hurtado v. California,** 110 U.S. 516 (1884), argued 22–23 Jan. 1884, decided 3 Mar. 1884 by vote of 8 to 1; Matthews for the Court, Harlan in dissent. This case involved a provision in the constitution of California that authorized prosecutions for felonies by information, after examination by a magistrate, without indictment by a *grand jury. The defendant, on the basis of information filed by district attorney, was tried for murder and sentenced to death. He argued on appeal that proceeding by information in capital cases violated the *Due Process Clause of the *Fourteenth Amendment, asserting that this clause incorporated the *Fifth Amendment requirement of grand jury indictment in federal capital cases, thus making it binding upon the states (see CAPITAL PUNISHMENT.) The Supreme Court rejected the argument, holding that the Due Process Clause of the Fourteenth Amendment could not logically encompass the specific procedural guarantees of the Fifth Amendment.

The defendant also contended that due process signified those settled usages and modes of proceeding existing in the common and statute law of England before the settlement of the American colonies, unless unsuited to colonial conditions. He claimed that proceeding by information in capital cases was not authorized by English or colonial law. The Court disagreed, holding that other procedures may be consonant with due process. The test that the Court adopted was that any legal proceeding, whether sanctioned by age or newly devised, which preserved the fundamental principles of liberty and justice lying at the base of American political institutions, must be deemed to constitute due process. In the Court's opinion, the California procedure did not violate these principles.

(See INCORPORATION DOCTRINE.)

Edgar Bodenheimer

**Hustler Magazine v. Falwell,** 485 U.S. 46 (1988), argued 2 Dec. 1987, decided 24 Feb. 1988 by vote of 8 to 0; Rehnquist for the Court, White concurring, Kennedy not participating. In a parody that appeared in *Hustler* magazine the prominent fundamentalist evangelist Reverend Jerry Falwell was depicted as a drunk in an incestuous sexual liaison with his mother in an outhouse.

A jury in the U.S. District Court for the Western District of Virginia found that the parody was not libelous, because no reasonable reader would have understood it as a factual assertion that Falwell had engaged in the described activity. Nevertheless, the jury awarded $200,000 in damages on a separate count of "intentional infliction of emotional distress," a cause of action that did not require that a false statement of fact be made.

The Supreme Court overturned the jury verdict and held that a public figure or official may not recover for intentional infliction of emotional distress arising from a publication unless the publication contains a false statement of fact that was made with *actual malice (knowledge of falsity or reckless disregard for truth or falsity). That the material might be deemed outrageous and that it might have been intended to cause severe emotional distress were not enough to overcome the *First Amendment. Vicious attacks on public figures, the Court noted, are part of the American tradition of satire and parody, a tradition of speech that would be hamstrung if public figures could sue them anytime the satirist caused distress.

(See also LIBEL; SPEECH AND THE PRESS.)

Rodney A. Smolla

**Hutchinson v. Proxmire,** 443 U.S. 111 (1979), argued 17 Apr., 1979, decided 26 June 1979 by vote of 7 to 1 to 1; Burger for the Court, Stewart concurring in part and dissenting in part, Brennan in dissent. This case explored the scope of protection afforded members of Congress by the Constitution's Speech and Debate Clause (Art. 1, sec. 6). In addition, the Court revisited the question of who was a "public figure" when determining the standard of proof in *libel claims.

The case centered on the "Golden Fleece Award" bestowed by Senator William Proxmire on federal agencies he judged guilty of wasteful spending. An award was given to several agencies funding the research of Dr. Ronald Hutchinson, a psychologist developing an objective measure of aggression through experimentation on monkeys. Proxmire announced the award on the floor of the Senate, while noting it in a press release, his newsletter, media interviews, and other settings. Claiming "emotional anguish," Hutchinson sued Proxmire for defamation, asserting that his reputation had been damaged, his contractual relations interfered with, and his *privacy invaded.

The Court narrowly viewed protected legislative acts under the Speech and Debate Clause. Immunity did not extend to newsletters, press releases, and activities not essential to the Senate's deliberations. Such activities did not fall under the Senate's informing function since they involved views and actions of one member and not collective chamber activity. Further, Hutchinson was not a "public figure," since he was thrust into the limelight by Proxmire's actions and did not personally seek it. Consequently, following *New York Times v. Sullivan (1964), a lesser standard of proof than *actual malice could prevail for Hutchinson. Justice William *Brennan dissented from this narrow view of privileged legislative acts. A legislator's criticism of governmental expenditures, whatever its form, he argued, was protected by the Speech and Debate Clause.

(See also SPEECH AND DEBATE CLAUSE.)

Elliot E. Slotnick

**Hylton v. United States,** 3 Dall. (3 U.S.) 171 (1796), argued 23–25 Feb. 1796, decided 8 Mar. 1796 by vote of 3 to 0; seriatim opinions by Iredell, Paterson, and Chase.

In 1794, Congress levied a carriage tax on passenger vehicles. The U.S. government sued Daniel Hylton in the federal circuit court of Virginia for nonpayment of the required duty. Hylton claimed that the levy was a "direct tax" within the meaning of Article I, section 8 of the Constitution, which prohibits Congress from levying direct taxes not apportioned according to the population of the several states. The controversy touched the sensitive question of the revenue-raising power of the new national government. The circuit court was divided on the question, but Hylton confessed to judgment (admitted liability) in order to test the constitutionality of the tax by an appeal to the Supreme Court. The three justices who heard the case—Samuel *Chase, William *Paterson, and James *Iredell—unanimously agreed that the carriage levy was an indirect tax and, therefore, not proscribed by Article I. The Court's view on the tax issue remained the law until the *Income Tax Cases of 1895 (see *Pollock v. Farmers Loan & Trust Co.). Hylton was also significant because it implicitly raised the issue of the Supreme Court's power of *judicial review. While the members of the Hylton court never addressed that issue directly, the justices appeared to assume that they had the power to nullify unconstitutional acts of Congress. Justice Chase declared that if the Court did have such power, however, he would exercise it only "in a very clear case" (p. 175). Not until Chief Justice John *Marshall's celebrated opinion in *Marbury v. Madison (1803) did the Supreme Court finally explain its power of judicial review under the Constitution.

(See also TAXING AND SPENDING CLAUSE.)

George Dargo

# I

**IFP.** See IN FORMA PAUPERIS.

**Illegitimacy.** See INHERITANCE AND ILLEGITIMACY.

**Illinois ex rel. McCollum v. Board of Education,** 333 U.S. 203 (1948), argued 8 Dec. 1947, decided 8 Mar. 1948 by vote of 8 to 1; Black for the Court, Reed in dissent. *McCollum* v. *Board of Education* was one of the Supreme Court's early examinations of the part of the *First Amendment that forbids establishment of *religion. The Court decided that public schools could not allow religious teachers to offer religious instruction within school buildings. The tenor of the majority and concurring opinions was strictly separationist, suggesting a high wall between the state and religious activities.

The Illinois school board allowed students to receive religious instruction, Protestant, Catholic, or Jewish, for thirty or forty-five minutes in each school week. The instructors received no public funds but were subject to approval by the superintendent of schools. Students whose parents did not request religious instruction went elsewhere in the building; those enrolled for religious instruction were required to attend.

Justice Hugo *Black, whose opinion for the Court in *Everson* v. *Board of Education* (1947), had applied the Establishment Clause against state agencies and endorsed broadly separationist guidelines, wrote for the Court again in *McCollum.* His opinion treated the school district's program as a plainly impermissible public aid to religion. A concurring opinion by Justice Felix *Frankfurter, joined by four other justices, em-phasized a historical trend against commingling sectarian and secular instruction in public schools and noted that almost two million students were in *"released time" programs of one kind or another. Justice *Reed's dissent argued that the Establishment Clause should be interpreted more narrowly to permit such incidental assistance to religion by the state. *McCollum's* practical impact on "released time" programs was sharply circumscribed by the Court's next case on the subject, *Zorach* v. *Clauson* (1952).

Kent Greenawalt

**Immigration.** The largest international transfer of population in modern history to the United States has introduced fifty million newcomers since the early nineteenth century. The Supreme Court has assumed an important role in defining the proper relationship of the federal government to immigration. Its decisions established the legal basis of the modern system for regulating immigration.

In the antebellum era, the federal government did little to supervise immigration. Coastal states with large ports, such as Massachusetts, New York, Pennsylvania, and Maryland, established mechanisms to monitor and process the accelerating influx of immigrants. New York, for example, passed laws requiring ships' masters to report the name, occupation, birthplace, age, and condition of passengers and to pay a small head-tax on each of them. Coastal states established immigration boards, staffed by amateur volunteers, to execute these new laws. State lawmakers hoped that these measures would reduce the admission of potential indigents, diseased and insane people, and other custodial cases.

The New York laws were challenged in *New York v. Miln* (1837). The defendant, a ship's master, argued that the New York laws obstructed interstate and foreign commerce. The Supreme Court, however, sustained the laws as a legitimate exercise of the state's *police power. Justice Philip P. *Barbour stated that it was

as competent and necessary for a State to provide precautionary measures against the moral pestilence of paupers, vagabonds, and possibly convicts, as it is to guard against the physical pestilence which may arise from unsound or infectious articles imported, or from a ship, the crew of which may be laboring under an infectious disease. (pp. 142–143)

This conclusion affirmed the right of state governments to set criteria for the admission of immigrants and to reject those who did not fit those standards (see STATE SOVEREIGNTY AND STATES' RIGHTS). The problem of controlling immigrants was complicated by the intrusive problem of southern insistence on plenary state powers to control the ingress of free or enslaved blacks, abolitionists, and antislavery propaganda (see SLAVERY).

The Supreme Court reversed its position more than a decade later in the decision known as the *Passenger Cases* (1849). The Court found that state laws imposing taxes on immigrants infringed on the power of Congress "to regulate Commerce with foreign Nations" granted by Article I, section 8 of the Constitution (see COMMERCE POWER; STATE TAXATION). This decision placed the immigration of free persons under the sole purview of Congress, with the exception of health and safety questions within the domain of state competence.

The Supreme Court went beyond this decision in 1875. In *Henderson* v. *Mayor of New York*, the Court held that all immigration laws of the seaboard states were unconstitutional because they usurped the exclusive power vested in Congress to regulate foreign commerce. In response to *Henderson*, states abolished their immigration commissions and port authorities. The entire burden of orienting foreigners and turning away the incapacitated fell to private, philanthropic organizations. Overwhelmed by the strain that immigration put on their resources, charity workers petitioned Congress to have the federal government assume the duties of regulating the influx. (By the 1880s, more than half a million immigrants a year were disembarking in American ports).

In the 1880s, Congress began to bring immigration under direct federal control for the first time. It could no longer rely on volunteerism or informal processes to manage this powerful social force. In 1891 Congress established the first federal administrative agency for the regulation of immigration in the Treasury Department. Congress later refined and strengthened the control of immigration. Statutes that restricted immigration according to increasingly stringent standards of admissibility—terminating the period of free and unlimited immigration by the early twentieth century—were made possible by the Supreme Court's position that the exclusive constitutional power to regulate immigration resided in Congress.

Reed Ueda

**Immigration and Naturalization Service v. Chadha,** 462 U.S. 919 (1983), argued 22 Feb. 1982, reargued 7 Dec. 1982, decided 23 June 1983 by vote of 7 to 2; Burger for the Court, Powell concurring, White in dissent, Rehnquist in dissent. Born in Kenya of Indian parents and holding a British passport, Jagdish Chadha had come to the United States to study in the mid-1960s. When his student visa expired, neither Great Britain nor Kenya would let him return so Chadha applied for permanent residency in the United States. After a lengthy hearing process his application to stay was approved by the Immigration and Naturalization Service (INS). Then, two years later the U.S. House of Representatives voted to "veto" the INS decision and Chadha faced deportation.

The *legislative veto was a simple concept, originally "invented" by Congress in the 1930s as a way to retain some control over power delegated to the president to reorganize executive branch agencies. In the wake of the Vietnam War and the Watergate scandal, the legislative veto became especially attractive as a tool for controlling presidential excesses (see DELEGATION OF POWERS).

At the same time it became apparent that the legislative veto might be a means for exercising congressional control over administrative regulations. By the mid-1970s a tidal flood of regulations to implement all the environmental, consumer, and other social legislation that had passed over the previous decade was pouring out of Washington bureaucracies. Legislative vetoes offered members of Congress a way to respond to the complaints of powerful business and industrial interests subject to these regulations. Public interest groups that had fought long and hard to get legislation passed to accomplish their goals were faced with the prospect of losing regulation by regulation. Alan Morrison, chief litigator for consumer activist Ralph Nader, seized the opportunity to strike out at the legislative veto by taking over Chadha's case.

Department of Justice attorneys in both the Carter and Reagan administrations joined the case on behalf of the immigration service arguing with Morrison against the constitutionality of the legislative veto. Congress was forced to intervene to defend the constitutionality of its legislative veto. Chadha's small case had turned into a battle of Titans: Congress versus the president.

Chief Justice Warren *Burger wrote the Court's opinion. The Constitution provides, Burger pointed out, "a single, finely wrought and exhaustively considered procedure" (p. 951) for exercise of the legislative power of the federal government. "Explicit and unambiguous provisions of the Constitution prescribe and define the respective functions of the Congress and of the Executive in the legislative process" (p. 945). Any actions taken by either house of Congress if "they contain matter which is properly to be regarded as legislative in character and effect" must conform with the constitutionally designed legislative process that includes bicameral passage and presentment to the president (p. 952). He then went on to spell out what the Court meant. "Legislative in character and effect" includes any action that has the "purpose and effect of altering the legal rights, duties, and relations of persons outside the legislative branch" (p. 952). Legislative vetoes represent efforts by one or both houses of Congress to subvert the "step-by-step, deliberate and deliberative process" (p. 959) for legislation set out in the Constitution and are thus unconstitutional.

In one fell swoop the Court in *Chadha* effectively overturned more congressional enactments than it had previously over its entire history. In Justice Lewis *Powell's opinion the case should have been decided on far narrower grounds based on a balancing of the legislative veto's utility against its potential for intrusion into another branch's rightful domain. When Congress finds that a particular person does not satisfy the statutory criteria for permanent residence in this country, it has assumed, Powell argued, a judicial function, in violation of *separation of powers. That, according to Powell, was the only issue raised by this case, and the only issue that should have been decided.

In a vehement dissent, Justice Byron *White defended the legislative veto as "an important if not indispensable political invention that allows the president and Congress to resolve major constitutional policy differences, assures the accountability of independent regulatory agencies, and preserves Congress'[s] control over lawmaking" (p. 972). White's opinion attacked the rigidity of the majority's application of the constitutional lawmaking process as "irresponsible" in its failure to recognize the reality of the modern administrative state where much "law" is made outside the presentment clause process by unelected bureaucrats (p. 974).

It is too soon to tell whether *Chadha* foreshadows a Supreme Court intention to apply constitutional requirements strictly to police the struggle of power between the branches. *Bowsher* v. *Synar*, the 1986 challenge to the Gramm-Rudman-Hollings deficit reduction law, gives some evidence that the Court might be leaning in this direction, but two more recent decisions *Morrison* v. *Olson*, the 1988 challenge to the special prosecutor law, and *Mistretta* v. *U.S.*, the 1989 challenge to the sentencing commission law, may presage a Court retreat from a strict reading of separation of powers requirements.

☐ Barbara Hinkson Craig, *Chadha: The Story of an Epic Constitutional Struggle* (1988). Louis Fisher, "Judicial Misjudgments About the Lawmaking Process: The Legislative Veto Case," *Public Administration Review, Special Issue* (November 1985): 705–711.          Barbara Craig

**Immunity.** See CONGRESS, ARREST AND IMMUNITY OF MEMBERS OF; EXECUTIVE IMMUNITY; FIFTH AMENDMENT IMMUNITY; JUDICIAL IMMUNITY FROM CIVIL DAMAGES; PRIVILEGES AND IMMUNITIES.

**Impact of Court Decisions.** The Supreme Court's decisions potentially affect many people and in fact have considerable effects. The extent to which the Court does have impact—direct and indirect, short-run and long-term—indicates its importance in the American political system (see POLITICAL PROCESS). The extent of compliance, when people intentionally conform behavior to the dictates of a Court ruling, may indicate the legitimacy accorded the Court by those potentially affected. Likewise, people's noncompliance, their refusal to follow a Supreme Court ruling and their evasion of the ruling—giving it technical obedience but avoiding its spirit or rationale—is a way in which the public, unable to vote on acceptance of the Court's rulings, holds the Court accountable.

The terms *impact* and *compliance*, although theoretical concepts, point to important aspects of what the Court is able to accomplish. Compliance, for example, cannot occur unless people know of a ruling, indicating the importance of how they learn about judicial rulings. Sometimes people, giving credence to the Court, try to do what they believe the Court ultimately will require; this is anticipatory compliance. Impact is broader than compliance. It includes effects not only of decisions mandating certain action but also the effects of permissive rulings, those that do not require adoption of certain policy, such as one allowing six-person rather than the traditional twelve-person juries (see TRIAL BY JURY). And there are effects not only from individual rulings but also from sets of rulings, in which the Court reinforces its initial pronouncements, as it did repeatedly after approving the right to an *abortion. The Court can have impact not only when it issues a ruling with full opinion but also by refusing to review a case—in a way, by not acting. There are many factors playing a part in the Court's impact. One is the self-interest of those affected; another is the state of public opinion and of existing policy; and a third is the extent to which officials attempt to implement the Court's rulings.

Since the nation's beginning, the Supreme Court has shaped American life. Chief Justice John *Marshall's decisions, for example, helped develop a strong central government and national economy. Somewhat later, the Court spurred sectional division with *Scott v. Sandford (1857) and helped solidify racial separation with *Plessy v. Ferguson (1896) (see RACE AND RACISM). The Court's decisions have a potential effect on many people. At times, the Court's decrees are carried out: school prayers cease and criminal suspects are warned of their rights. But at other times, noncompliance results: school prayers continue to be said and improper searches do not abate. Some rulings are welcomed and willingly enforced; many others are carried out with indifference. Particularly if we look beyond such controversial topics as school prayer and search and seizure, there is a high degree of compliance with the Court's rulings. However, resistance has led to overturning the Court's rulings, most dramatically when the Constitution itself is amended, as it was to eliminate *slavery (*Thirteenth Amendment) and to allow an *income tax (*Sixteenth) and the vote for eighteen-year-olds (*Twenty-sixth). (See CONSTITUTIONAL AMENDING PROCESS.) After the Court interprets a statute, legislators frequently rewrite the laws to retain their earlier intent. Thus, as a policy maker, the Court does not have the final word: the law is "what the Court says it is" but only after all others have had their say.

Court rulings can sweep broadly in their effects—on Congress, whose internal operations and districts were affected by the Court and many of whose legislative outputs have been invalidated; on the presidency, where the impact has generally been to legitimate the president's actions, particularly in time of *war and with respect to *foreign affairs; on the states, where the greatest effect has occurred because the Court has been far more willing to strike down state than national legislation; on the economy; on public opinion; and on civil liberties and civil rights.

Impact is not simply a matter of the Court speaking and others responding. Responses reach the Court through its awareness of its surroundings or because people bring cases challenging those responses, producing a continuing dialogue between the Supreme Court and other political actors. A visible example is the appearance before the Court of legislation regulating abortion and the Court's frequent rulings on the subject. Resistance to the Court's rulings, as in efforts to limit availability of abortion, may be seen as illegitimate—because we should obey the Supreme Court's rulings as "the law of the land." However, if the Supreme Court is to be at least somewhat responsive to those it will affect, resistance and the new cases it spawns help make the Court aware of its effects. It is also true that the Court's legitimacy may increase the extent to which its decisions are followed.

(See also SEPARATION OF POWERS.)

Stephen L. Wasby

**Impeachment** is the procedure by which members of the federal judiciary, who hold their office for tenure during good behavior, can be removed from office if guilty of "treason, bribery, or other high crimes and misdemeanors." The articles of impeachment, or accusations of misconduct, are drafted by the House of Representatives and determined by majority vote; the trial is before the Senate, with a two-thirds vote needed for conviction. The Constitution also stipulates that conviction in a case of impeachment can only involve removal from office and disqualification from holding future office but does not prevent the guilty party from being held further accountable under the law in regular courts of law. Finally, the presidential *pardoning power is excepted in cases of impeachment.

Although the concept of impeachment has deep roots in English and American colonial history, the matter of exactly what kind of behavior can make a federal judge liable to removal by impeachment has remained a matter of debate. Only one Supreme Court Justice, Samuel *Chase in 1805, has been subjected to this procedure, and his acquittal played an important role in narrowing the impeachment provisions in the Constitution to criminal behavior. Chase, a native of Maryland, was an important and controversial member of the Revolutionary generation. A signer of the *Declaration of Independence, he was combative, irascible, aggressive, and overbearing. With some reluctance, because Chase lacked a judicial temperament, President George *Washington appointed him to the Supreme Court in 1796. Nevertheless, Chase had a first-rate legal mind and he was one of the most significant members of the pre–John *Marshall Court. He also was an extreme Federalist partisan and vigorously enforced the *Sedition Acts, which had been passed during the administration of John Adams to allow the prosecution of Republican editors and politicians, especially in the cases of Thomas Cooper, John Fries, and James T. Callender (see SEDITIOUS LIBEL).

The Republicans emerged victorious from the election of 1800. Not only did Thomas *Jefferson become president, but they captured control of both houses of Congress. Many Republicans, led by John Randolph of Virginia, favored a direct assault on the national judiciary, which they viewed as the last stronghold of unchecked Federalist power. But Jefferson, who wished to conciliate and absorb the defeated Federalist party, was more cautious. He preferred to pursue a policy of live and let live. However, when Jefferson received reports of the activities of John Pickering, an abusive, partisan, and alcoholic district court justice from New Hampshire, who most likely also was insane and who refused to resign his position, he went along with impeachment proceedings. Even so, many Republicans balked at the idea of impeaching and convicting an insane man for high crimes and misdemeanors; neither the Constitution nor the laws of the United States made provision for the removal of a civil officer who was not in his right mind. In the end, however, most Republican senators, responding to pressure from the White House, voted guilty, since the only alternative was to leave Pickering in his present position. In so doing, they gave a liberal definition to the impeachment provision of the Constitution, which in turn played into the hands of those more aggressive Republicans who argued that the process of impeachment should be considered in effect as a mode of removal and not simply as a punishment for criminal activity. Support for this interpretation of the impeachment process came from a number of eighteenth-century English and American colonial precedents in which impeachment had indeed been used as a way of removing one's political opponents from office.

Pickering was the first federal judge to be removed by impeachment, and the significance of this became clear on the day of his conviction, when Randolph moved, in the House of Representatives, for impeachment proceedings against Chase. At first, Jefferson favored this development, because Chase continued to use his position on the bench for partisan purposes. But it soon became clear that Randolph and his allies intended to redefine the impeachment process so that it would be a way of removing political opponents from office. If they convicted Chase they intended to go after other Federalist members of the Supreme Court, including William *Paterson and John Marshall. Jefferson was unwilling to proceed this far and he opted not to go along with the effort, withdrawing his support for the impeachment proceedings against Chase.

In the ensuing trial before the Senate, which took place in February and early March 1805, Chase, aided by a battery of skilled lawyers, vigorously defended himself. He effectively argued that he had not violated established judicial norms, that what he did was not criminal, and that his various rulings were justifiable, especially at a time in American history when courtroom procedures, particularly in political trials, had not been clearly spelled out and what was considered proper behavior by a judge was open to dispute. On the other hand, Randolph, who was not a trained lawyer, botched the prosecution. This, along with Jefferson's refusal to enforce party regularity in the final vote, prevented the Republicans from obtaining the two-thirds majority necessary to convict.

The results of Chase's trial supported the views of those more moderate Republicans who argued that the grounds for impeachment should be criminal rather than political. This view has prevailed down to the present. Although various *lower federal court judges have been impeached, convicted, and removed from office, this has occurred only in clear-cut cases. For members of the Supreme Court the threat of

impeachment has been mainly rhetorical and ephemeral. Since Jefferson, all presidents and most members of Congress have generally eschewed the impeachment process as too cumbersome and partisan.

To be sure, from time to time, individuals and even groups have called for the impeachment of particular Supreme Court justices for espousing controversial or unpopular points of view. Perhaps the most well-known expression of this attitude was the campaign to impeach Chief Justice Earl *Warren. Instituted by the John Birch Society in the early 1960s, the campaign distributed pamphlets and erected numerous billboards but had no appreciable effect on judicial behavior. In a similar vein, Gerald Ford, a socially conservative congressman, introduced a resolution sponsored by 110 representatives, calling for the impeachment of Justice William O. *Douglas in 1970. Ford asserted that an impeachable offense was whatever the House and Senate wanted it to be, but no formal action was ever taken on his resolution. The threat of impeachment may also have been a factor in forcing Justice Abe *Fortas to resign in 1969 when some Republicans charged him with the breaking of the law by accepting a retainer fee from a foundation. More significantly, while the justices of the Supreme Court have often had strong points of view (*states' rights and nationalist views before the Civil War, views for and against government regulation of the economy, and liberal and conservative views on various social issues after the Civil War), they have avoided becoming spokesmen for particular political parties or causes and have refrained from anything that might be termed criminal activities.

The Supreme Court has not dealt with the impeachment issue extensively. Mention of the impeachment process by the justices has been mostly incidental to the discussion of other issues, such as the right to *trial by jury or the reach of the *pardon power.

□ Raoul Berger, *Impeachment: The Constitutional Problem* (1973).                                                                   Richard E. Ellis

**Implied Powers.** One of the basic axioms of constitutional law is that Congress may take no action that is not authorized by the Constitution. The most obvious source of congressional authority is the enumeration of specific powers in Article I, section 8. The doctrine of implied powers allows Congress to exercise authority that is implied by these specific grants of power.

The textual justification for the doctrine of implied powers is Article I, section 8, paragraph 18, which provides that Congress shall have authority to "make all Laws which shall be necessary and proper for carrying into Execution the [enumerated] Powers." The scope of this Necessary and Proper Clause was a subject of heated debate in the late eighteenth and early nineteenth centuries. Thomas *Jefferson argued that the clause gave Congress authority only to enact measures absolutely necessary to implementation of the enumerated powers; Alexander *Hamilton, by contrast, contended that the clause empowered Congress to adopt any measure having a natural relationship to the subjects specifically mentioned. The dispute was settled by Chief Justice John *Marshall in *McCulloch v. Maryland (1819). There, finding that Congress had authority to charter a bank, the Supreme Court clearly adopted the Hamiltonian view: "Let the end be legitimate, let it be within the scope of the constitution, and all means which are appropriate, which are plainly adapted to that end, which are not prohibited, but consistent with the letter and spirit of the constitution, are constitutional" (p. 421). Thus, the doctrine of implied powers became firmly established as a significant source of federal authority.          Earl M. Maltz

**Impoundment Powers.** Thomas *Jefferson informed Congress in 1803 that he had not spent a fifty-thousand-dollar appropriation for gunboats because of the "peaceful turn of events." From that modest beginning, Richard *Nixon in 1973 claimed an "absolutely clear" constitutional right to impound funds.

Jefferson's precedent was rarely invoked, but after *World War II, Presidents Harry S. Truman, Dwight D. Eisenhower, and John F. Kennedy used it to control defense spending and to resist interest-group legislation that had been logrolled through Congress. President Lyndon Johnson based his impoundments on his attorney general's opinion that "an appropriation act in itself does not constitute a mandate to spend." But Nixon escalated impoundment use, particularly to pursue his own policy agenda. Congressional inertia signaled benign acquiescence. When Nixon vetoed amendments to the Federal Water Pollution Act of 1972, Congress overrode his veto, but Nixon announced he still would not spend the money. What had been more or less a stylized game, whereby Congress satisfied its special constituencies and allowed the president discretion, now became a clear constitutional conflict. The House briefly considered Nixon's impoundments as impeachable offenses, but the idea was dropped as "a temporary abrasion" of power (see IMPEACHMENT). More realistically, Congress itself had been an accomplice. In the Budget and Impoundment Act of 1974, Congress attempted to stifle impoundments but again proved unwilling to enforce its own assertions of power.

Lower courts twice rejected Nixon's attempts to use discretionary power for spending on congressional programs. In Train v. City of New York (1975), the Supreme Court held that the president had no authority to withhold funds provided by Congress in the Clean Water Act of 1972. The Court ruled that Congress had man-

dated public expenditures for waste-treatment plants, but the decision turned on statutory construction and avoided a specific constitutional ruling. Still, certain constitutional principles were inherent in the ruling, including Congress's right to authorize spending, a presidential obligation to execute the laws, and the judiciary's right to compel presidential action.

(See also INHERENT POWERS.)

Stanley I. Kutler

**In Camera.** Hearings in camera (Lat., "in the chamber") are held either in a justice's private chambers or in a courtroom from which spectators have been excluded, the purpose being to protect privacy, confidentiality, or secrets.

William M. Wiecek

**Income Tax.** Questions involving federal income taxes provoked extraordinary controversy throughout the nineteenth century, most strikingly in the 1890s. The controversy ended only with the passage of the *Sixteenth Amendment in 1913.

Federal income taxes raised two types of constitutional issues. First, the Supreme Court had to decide, for constitutional purposes, whether an income tax was a "direct tax" or an "indirect tax." This distinction was critical, since the Constitution commanded that direct taxes had to be apportioned among the several states "in proportion to the Census." If an income tax were considered a direct tax, it would be unconstitutional since it could not be apportioned. Second, even if an income tax were considered an indirect tax, it still needed to be "uniform" and had to fulfill a variety of other constitutional requirements. The latter requirement was interpreted to apply only to geographic uniformity and was held not to require that a tax be uniform as applied to different individuals with different income levels.

The Supreme Court upheld the *Civil War income tax, holding in *Springer v. United States (1881) that such a tax was indirect and need not be apportioned. The Springer Court followed a 1796 precedent, *Hylton v. United States, which had upheld a carriage tax on the grounds that it was an indirect tax. The fact that a carriage tax could not be apportioned convinced the Court to declare the tax indirect; Justice James *Iredell held that "the Constitution contemplated [no tax] as direct, but such as could be apportioned" (p. 181). In Springer, the Court held that the only direct taxes contemplated by the Constitution were "capitation taxes . . . and taxes on real estate" (p. 586).

In 1895, the income tax issue arose again, this time in a period of extreme political tension. In the midst of the populist movement, conservatives seized upon the tax issue as a question of great moral importance. "The act of Congress which we are impugning before you is communistic in its purposes and tendencies," argued Joseph *Choate before the Supeme Court in *Pollock v. Farmers' Loan & Trust Co. (1895; p. 537). Failure to strike down the tax, Choate told the justices, would endanger "the very keystone of the arch upon which all civilized government rests" (p. 534). The Court's first decision in Pollock, in April 1895, produced a deadlock on the key issues, with the justices divided 4 to 4 on whether the income tax was a direct tax per se and thus unconstitutional. (Justice Howell *Jackson, who was ill, did not participate.)

The Court then held another set of hearings, and two weeks later produced a 5-to-4 decision striking down the tax on the grounds that income taxes were, per se, direct taxes. Surprisingly, Jackson was in the minority, meaning that one of the four justices who had voted to uphold the tax in the first Pollock decision had switched his vote. The political consequences of the Court's decision were significant. It energized the conservative wing of the Democratic party, providing the key momentum for the conservatives' subsequent takeover of the party at the 1896 convention.

Confusion on whether an income tax was or was not a direct tax continued even after Pollock. In Flint v. Stone (1911) the Court upheld a tax on the income of corporations as an indirect tax on the privilege of doing business in the corporate form. Finally, in 1913, the states ratified the Sixteenth Amendment, explicitly granting to Congress the power "to lay and collect taxes on incomes, from whatever source derived, without apportionment among the several States, and without regard to any census or enumeration."

Only technical questions remained—concerning, for example, the definition of income under the Sixteenth Amendment. Federal taxing power, of course, remains subject to other constitutional requirements, including *due process, *equal protection, and other guarantees.
(See also TAXING AND SPENDING CLAUSE.)

William Lasser

**Income Tax Case.** See POLLOCK V. FARMERS' LOAN & TRUST CO.

**Incorporation Doctrine.** By the incorporation doctrine, the United States Supreme Court has held that most, but not all, guarantees of the federal *Bill of Rights limit state and local governments as well as the federal government through the *Due Process Clause of the *Fourteenth Amendment. States have been required to respect freedom of *speech, press, and *religion, and most of the other guaranties. They have not been required to provide jury trials in civil cases or indictment by *grand jury, however (see SECOND AMENDMENT; THIRD AMENDMENT).

Whether the guarantees that are "incorporated" apply to the states just as they apply to the federal government has been the subject of

judicial controversy. Usually the guarantees have the same operation in each case. With reference to the *First Amendment, a historical and functional argument could be made (based on statements by the framers of the original Constitution) for a more nearly absolute prohibition at the federal level (of sedition or *obscenity laws, for example). Such an argument has not prevailed in the courts.

The incorporation doctrine has a curious and intensely controversial history. Until 1866 the rule, established by the Supreme Court in 1833 in the case of *Barron v. Baltimore, was that guarantees of the federal Bill of Rights limited only the federal government, not state governments.

From the 1830s until the *Civil War southern states made speech and publication critical of *slavery a crime. A number of leading Republicans viewed these statutes as violations of the rights of American citizens protected by the First Amendment and by other provisions of the Constitution. After the Civil War and before the ratification of the Fourteenth Amendment, Republicans complained that southern states were denying African-Americans, Republicans, and loyalist citizens basic rights to free speech and press, to due process, and to bear arms.

The Fourteenth Amendment made all persons born in the United States citizens and provided that no state should abridge the *privileges or immunities of citizens or deny due process or *equal protection to any person (see CITIZENSHIP). Several of the amendment's framers suggested that privileges or immunities of citizens of the United States included rights in the Bill of Rights. In 1866, no senator or representative explicitly contradicted them on this point and a number suggested the amendment protected the constitutional rights of American citizens. Yet most congressmen did not address the point and others made remarks that some have read as inconsistent with application of the Bill of Rights to the states.

In the *Slaughterhouse Cases (1873), the Court considered whether Louisiana could grant a monopoly on slaughtering animals. The majority held it could and in the process deprived the Privileges or Immunities Clause of any significant meaning. Later decisions held one after another of the guarantees of the Bill of Rights did not limit the states. Then, first the guarantee that private *property would not be taken for *public use without *just compensation (*Chicago, Burlington and Quincy Railroad Co. v. Chicago, 1897) and later free speech and press (*Gitlow v. New York, 1925) were construed to be limits on the states.

So the Court began to incorporate particular Bill of Rights guarantees selectively as limits on the states. In 1937, in *Palko v. Connecticut, with little attention to section one of the Fourteenth Amendment, the Court explained that some privileges and immunities in the Bill of Rights were so fundamental that the states were required to respect them under the Due Process Clause; other Bill of Rights privileges and immunities were less important, so states were free to disregard them.

Then in 1947, in *Adamson* v. *California,* Justice Hugo *Black, speaking for four dissenting justices, argued that the Fourteenth Amendment required the states to respect all rights specified in the Bill of Rights. Though his view did not prevail, the Court later overruled a number of prior cases (including *Palko*) and applied almost all guarantees of the Bill of Rights to the states.

In the 1980s, Edwin Meese, then attorney general, and others criticized the incorporation doctrine as inconsistent with the intent of the Framers of the Constitution. So far these attacks have not been successful.

(See also FEDERALISM; STATE ACTION.)

□ Michael Kent Curtis, *No State Shall Abridge: The Fourteenth Amendment and the Bill of Rights* (1986). William Nelson, *The Fourteenth Amendment: From Political Principle to Judicial Doctrine* (1988).        Michael Kent Curtis

**Independent and Adequate State Grounds Doctrine.** The Supreme Court first enunciated the independent and adequate state grounds doctrine in *Murdock* v. *Memphis* (1875). It later stated succinctly in *Fox Film Corp.* v. *Muller* (1935) the grounds for the doctrine: "the settled rule [is] that where the judgment of a state court [that has been appealed to the United States Supreme Court under Title 28, section 1257 of the U.S. Code, the present version of section 25 of the 1789 Judiciary Act] rests upon two grounds, one of which is federal and the other non-federal in character, our jurisdiction fails if the non-federal ground is independent of the federal ground and adequate to support the judgment" (p. 210). The basis of the rule is obvious in principle, but difficult in application. Assume a case appealed from a state supreme court under section 1257 that has two bases of decision, one resting on an interpretation of federal law and the other on an interpretation of state law. If the United States Supreme Court reversed for error in the federal ruling, on remand the *state court would merely reaffirm the original result based on the state ruling. In such a case, the United States Supreme Court's action would in effect be an *advisory opinion; it would provide an unnecessary ruling on a constitutional issue in disregard of Justice Louis D. *Brandeis's caution in *Ashwander* v. *T.V.A.* (1936); it would be a waste of both courts' time; and it would cause unnecessary annoyance to the state judiciary. More recently, the doctrine has been central to the growing role of *state courts in deciding issues of individual rights. (See also STATE CONSTITUTIONS AND INDIVIDUAL RIGHTS.)        William M. Wiecek

**Indian Bill of Rights (1968).** The Indian Civil Rights Act, popularly known as the "Indian Bill of Rights," was adopted as Title II of the Civil Rights Act of 1968. The most important provisions limit the power of tribal governments by applying portions of the federal *Bill of Rights to Indian tribes, thus limiting tribal sovereignty.

The Supreme Court had held in *Talton* v. *Mayes* (1896), that Indian tribal governments were not subject to restraints placed on the federal and state governments by the Constitution and the Bill of Rights. The Indian Bill of Rights extends ten restrictions derived from the U.S. Bill of Rights and other parts of the Constitution. These comprise: freedoms of *speech, press, *assembly, petition, and *religion; security against unreasonable searches and seizures, accompanied by the requirement of a *search warrant; freedom from *double jeopardy; guarantees against *self-incrimination, excessive *bail and fines, and *cruel and unusual punishment; prohibition of taking private property without *just compensation; in modified form, the criminal-procedure protections of the *Sixth Amendment; the *due process and *equal protection clauses; prohibition of *bills of attainder and *ex post facto laws; and guarantee of a six-person criminal jury trial (see TRIAL BY JURY). Congress deliberately chose to limit its incursion into tribal sovereignty by omitting certain other securities, such as the right to a republican form of government (see GUARANTEE CLAUSE), the ban on religious establishments, the requirement of free *counsel for indigent criminal defendants, the right to jury trial in civil cases, (see CIVIL LAW) and the *privileges and immunities clauses.

In *Santa Clara Pueblo* v. *Martinez* (1978), the Court upheld Congress's authority to impose the Indian Bill of Rights but held that federal enforcement authority is limited to *habeas corpus jurisdiction on behalf of persons in tribal custody. The Court held that Congress had not limited the tribes' immunity from suit, so the act cannot be enforced directly against them. Thus, the Indian Bill of Rights is primarily enforceable in tribal forums.

(See also NATIVE AMERICANS.)
        Rennard J. Strickland

**Indigency.** During the 1950s and 1960s, the Warren Court initiated a massive expansion of the rights of many underprivileged segments of American society, including racial and ethnic minorities. Using the *Equal Protection Clause of the *Fourteenth Amendment, the Court applied *"strict scrutiny" to statutes that discriminated against "discrete and insular minorities" or by drawing *"suspect classifications." Such statutes had to be justified by a compelling state interest, rather than merely supported by a rational basis. This heightened scrutiny for laws further disadvantaging the already disadvantaged led many scholars to speculate that the Court might soon expand its protection to the indigent. Like racial minorities, the indigent seemed to suffer disproportionately in a political system in which they lacked the power to influence legislators. Thus, they might be considered a "discrete and insular minority," entitled to greater judicial protection.

In a number of cases the Court appeared to be moving in that direction. In *Gideon v. Wainwright (1963) the Court held that indigent criminal defendants were constitutionally entitled to a state-appointed lawyer in felony prosecutions, and in Griffin v. Illinois (1956) it held that such defendants were entitled to a free trial transcript for purposes of appeal (see COUNSEL, RIGHT TO). In *Shapiro v. Thompson (1969), the Court removed some state-created obstacles to obtaining welfare benefits. It held that the constitutionally protected right to interstate travel prohibited states from imposing long residency requirements for welfare eligibility (see TRAVEL, RIGHT TO). In *Harper v. Virginia State Board of Elections (1966) the Court invalidated state *poll taxes that disenfranchised the poor. All of these cases, however, involved rights that the Court labeled "fundamental" (such as voting), and thus the Court did not confront the question whether laws depriving indigents of nonfundamental rights should be subject to strict scrutiny.

In 1970 the Supreme Court put an end to the speculation. In Dandridge v. Williams (1970) plaintiffs challenged a state law that provided for incrementally smaller increases in welfare payments for each child born to a family, with no additional increase granted after four children. The Court refused to apply strict scrutiny to the statute and upheld it as a rational method of conserving state financial resources. The Court has since adhered firmly to the position that poverty alone is not a suspect classification. It has upheld laws that create large financial differentials among school districts depending on the wealth of the district (*San Antonio Independent School District v. Rodriguez, 1973), laws that deny public funding to indigent women seeking *abortions (*Harris v. McRae, 1980), and state failures to provide counsel to indigent defendants beyond one level of appeal (Ross v. Moffit, 1974). All of these laws were subjected only to minimal scrutiny and upheld as rationally related to a legitimate state interest. No heightened scrutiny was applied (see INTERMEDIATE SCRUTINY).

The Court has remained somewhat sensitive to the plight of the poor in two instances, however. First, where fundamental rights are involved, the Court may still apply heightened scrutiny to policies that deprive the poor of such rights. For example, in Boddie v. Connecticut (1971), the Court invalidated a filing fee for divorce, and in Zablocki v. Redhail (1978), the Court struck down a law that restricted remarriage of those with children to parents who could show that the children would not become a financial burden on the state. Both cases implicated the fundamental right of *marriage.

The Court has also indicated that it might be wary of upholding laws that create or perpetuate a permanent underclass. In *Plyler v. Doe (1982) the Court invalidated a Texas law that prohibited children of illegal aliens from attending free public schools. Although the Court found neither a *suspect classification nor a fundamental right—and purported, therefore, to apply only minimal scrutiny—the law was struck down as a violation of equal protection. The majority opinion by Justice William J. *Brennan noted that the law "raised the specter of a permanent caste" of the underclass (pp. 218–219). It is unclear whether the Plyler approach will survive, however. Plyler was decided by a slim 5-to-4 majority, and since the case was decided, three of the justices in the majority have retired. Their successors have not yet indicated any views on the Plyler approach.

In summary, the Court is generally unsympathetic to any constitutional challenges to laws that classify on the basis of wealth or burden the indigent.

(See also FUNDAMENTAL RIGHTS.)

Suzanna Sherry

**In Forma Pauperis.** *Appeals that come before the Supreme Court from litigants who cannot afford to pay court costs are known as in forma pauperis petitions. In the 1930s the Court began to receive in forma pauperis petitions in significant numbers and by the 1988 term more than half of all cases received by the Court were petitions by indigent defendants. In the early 1980s the Court began to require indigent petitioners to provide documentation that they could not afford to pay the court costs. Against the objections of four justices the Court also began to deny motions to proceed in forma pauperis without first having determined whether the *certiorari petitions merited plenary review.

Most in forma pauperis petitions come from criminal defendants. When the court agrees to review in forma pauperis petitions from federal defendants it usually does so in order to resolve an intercircuit conflict and/or to decide an issue of statutory law. On the other hand, state petitions from indigent defendants that are granted review tend to be challenges to the state court's rejection of a constitutional claim. Regardless of the nature of the claim, all in forma pauperis petitions have a much lower chance of being granted review than do paid petitions. Approximately 1 percent of in forma pauperis petitions was granted review during the Court's 1988 term compared to 10 percent of the paid petitions.

(See also PAID DOCKET.)

Karen J. Maschke

**Inherent Powers.** The concept of inherent powers depends on a distinction between powers that are explicitly spelled out in the Constitution or in statutes, and those that a government, or an individual officer of government, possesses implicitly, whether owing to the nature of sovereignty or to a permissive interpretation of the language of the Constitution.

In the American constitutional system, the existence of inherent powers has always been a contested point. Those opposed to the notion of inherent powers argue that the government and all its officers derive their authority from the Constitution, whose terms contain all the powers that the people intended to grant. Justice Hugo *Black took this position in his opinion for the Court in *Youngstown Sheet and Tube Co. v. Sawyer (1952): "The president's power, if any, . . . must stem either from an act of Congress or from the Constitution itself" (p. 585). Any powers not granted by the Constitution are, in the words of the *Tenth Amendment, "reserved to the States respectively, or to the people."

The argument in favor of inherent powers is usually advanced on behalf of the president. It derives either from the language of the vesting clauses of Articles I and II of the Constitution, or from the role of the chief executive as commander of the armed forces and as the official primarily responsible for the maintenance of law and order, or from the status of the president as head of a sovereign nation.

The vesting clause of Article I gives to Congress "all legislative power herein granted," whereas the corresponding clause in Article II says merely that "the executive power" is vested in the president. In his argument before the Supreme Court in the Steel Seizure Case, the *solicitor general claimed that "this clause [that is, the vesting clause of Article II] constitutes a grant of all the executive powers of which the Government is capable" (p. 640). Subsequent language in Article II specified certain presidential responsibilities but was not meant to be exhaustive. Supporters of executive power have maintained that the difference in the vesting clauses was indicative of the framers' understanding that the executive power, unlike the legislative, was incapable of enumeration.

Abraham *Lincoln used the president's command over the military as part of the justification for his actions at the start of the *Civil War. As commander in chief of the armed forces, sworn to preserve the Constitution, Lincoln said that his actions, "whether strictly legal or not, were ventured upon under what appeared to be a popular demand and a public necessity." He implied that it was the president's responsibility to discern that demand and that necessity, and to meet it.

In declaring independence in 1776, the United States immediately became a sovereign power, and its government assumed all the powers and responsibilities of an independent nation under international law. In 1789, the newly ratified Constitution became "the supreme Law of the Land." It distributed certain powers to Congress, the president, and the Supreme Court. It did not,

however, circumscribe the nation's standing as a sovereign entity, nor did it intend to prevent the federal government from doing what was necessary to sustain that status.

The locus classicus of this argument is Justice George *Sutherland's opinion in United States v. *Curtiss-Wright Export Corp. (1936). Sutherland insisted that the powers of the federal government were different in external and internal affairs. In internal affairs, he wrote, its powers were "specifically enumerated in the Constitution." Here the Constitution took, from the "general mass of legislative powers then possessed by the states," those the framers thought best to vest in the federal government (p. 316). But "since the states . . . never possessed international powers," these must have come from another source. They came, argued Sutherland, as a result of the separation from Great Britain, to the "colonies in their collective and corporate capacity as the United States of America" (p. 316). These powers, he argued, by their very nature belong to the president, who has confidential sources of information, who alone can keep secrets and act with dispatch.

Thus, concluded Sutherland, when the Constitution specifically delegates a power in the field of foreign relations to another branch (as when it gives Congress power to declare war, or makes *treaties subject to the consent of the Senate), it is making an exception. As a rule, the executive is the "sole organ of the federal government in the field of international relations," and his powers must be construed expansively (p. 320). The argument against inherent powers responds by rejecting the distinction between external and internal affairs, noting that the president is bound, without distinction, to "take care that the laws be faithfully executed."

The Supreme Court generally tries to find authority for governmental acts in the Constitution, but it has also been reluctant to insist on narrow interpretations of the executive powers granted by the Constitution, particularly in the field of foreign relations. In his opinion for a unanimous court in *Dames & Moore v. Regan (1981), Justice William *Rehnquist noted that President Jimmy Carter's actions in terminating the hostage crisis with Iran went beyond the mandate of the laws. Yet "where, as here, the settlement of claims has been determined to be a necessary incident to the resolution of a major foreign policy dispute . . . , and where, as here, we can conclude that Congress acquiesced in the President's action, we are not prepared to say that the President lacks the power to settle such claims" (p. 688). The Court seemed to confirm that the president had inherent powers but that they were conditioned by the interactions of the political branches of the government.

(See also FOREIGN AFFAIRS AND FOREIGN POLICY; SEPARATION OF POWERS; WAR POWERS.)

Donald L. Robinson

**Inheritance and Illegitimacy.** Illegitimate children, as the law classifies those born out of wedlock, have long faced barriers to full family membership. Limited inheritance has remained the most significant legal penalty for those born outside legally recognized families. For property-conscious common lawyers, inheritance cemented domestic bonds by creating a common interest in preserving the family heritage and resources. Denying inheritance rights to illegitimates represented an attempt to discourage birth out of wedlock and promote the legitimate family. In recent years as the Supreme Court has become more involved in these issues, inheritance has continued to be the most serious legal penalty facing these star-crossed children.

Like most family policies, until recently, illegitimacy fell under the jurisdiction of the states and was rooted in traditional English law. Labeled *filius nullius*, the child of no one, English law had denied illegitimates the rights derived from family membership. Where legitimate children had the right to the family name, could inherit property, and had a right to food and *education, illegitimate children could not inherit from either parent or other relations and had no right to the family name or even the custody, guardianship, or support of either parent. Beginning with Thomas *Jefferson's path-breaking 1785 Virginia statute, American laws eased the penalties of illegitimacy by granting first mothers and then fathers some custody and guardianship rights as well as support responsibilities. Acting out of a child-centered attempt to cease punishing children for parental mistakes and to protect taxpayers from supporting these children, such changes became widespread and altered the status of illegitimate children. But inheritance remained more limited than other changes and one of the most litigated questions in the law of illegitimacy. Illegitimate children gained the right to inherit from their biological mothers in most states, but state codes split on whether these children could share in the estates of their mother's other kin. Bars to claims on paternal estates remained in most jurisdictions. The resistance to inheritance rights produced a patchwork of contradictory codes and decisions that revealed a continuing fear that inheritance rights for illegitimates would undermine paternal property rights and the family itself.

The Supreme Court's involvement in these issues has echoed the state experience. Beginning with *Stevenson's Heirs* v. *Sullivan* (1820), in which the Court interpreted the pioneering Virginia statute to mean that children born out of wedlock could not inherit from their siblings and that mothers could not claim the estates of their illegitimate children, the justices have been reluctant to grant inheritance rights to illegitimates. Judicial reticence emerged most vividly after 1968. The court used the *Equal Protection Clause to challenge the legal restrictions of illegitimacy in a se-

ries of path-breaking cases such as *Levy* v. *Louisiana* (1968), which granted illegitimate children the right to recover for the wrongful death of their mother, and *Stanley* v. *Illinois* (1972), which extended new custody rights to the fathers of illegitimate children. In an era of rising concern about illegitimacy, these and other decisions labeled many of the legal penalties imposed on these children as unfair constitutional violations that undermined child welfare by limiting their claims for support. But in *Labine* v. *Vincent* (1971), the court refused to extend their challenge to inheritance. A 5-to-4 majority upheld the right of states to restrict inheritance rights and rebuffed claims that illegitimacy was a *suspect classification and should not be used as a classifying device. Writing for the majority, Justice Hugo *Black accepted the right of states to distinguish between legitimate and illegitimate children and to use inheritance penalties on those born out of wedlock to promote the legally recognized family.

Inheritance thus continues to be the outer limit of reform in the legal rights of illegitimate children. It reveals the continued policy appeal of this age-old legal classification. The persistent restriction is one answer in the long-running debate over whether American family laws should be used to promote individual rights or protect the legitimate family. Like state courts before it, the Supreme Court's recognition of the constitutionality of inheritance restrictions on children born out of wedlock represents a continuing determination that the interests of illegitimate children should be sacrificed to a majoritarian vision of the society's larger interests in protecting the family.

(See also FAMILY AND CHILDREN; PROPERTY RIGHTS.)

□ Michael Grossberg, *Governing the Hearth, Law and the Family in Nineteenth Century America* (1985).

Michael Grossberg

**Injunctions and Equitable Remedies.** By the fourteenth century, England possessed two distinct and somewhat rival court systems, known popularly as "law" and "equity" courts. Law courts were characterized by their development of the *common law, use of juries (see TRIAL BY JURY), reliance on common-law pleading and the *writ system, and a rigid formality in their approach to resolving legal conflicts. Equity courts adopted a more flexible approach to cases and provided for broad remedies. A party suing in a law court was limited to a recovery of money as compensation for injury or damage. By contrast, one who sued in an equity court could choose from an array of coercive remedies, including injunctions to require or prohibit conduct, to require the specific performance of a contract, or to order the division of jointly owned property. These and other equitable remedies provided a flexibility lacking in the law courts.

America's court system drew heavily on its English origins. One of the principal tasks of the framers of the Constitution was to define the "judicial power" of the new federal courts. They stated simply that that power should "extend to all Cases in Law and Equity," thus empowering federal courts to provide all the remedies developed in England's equity courts. The development of equity in the states had been controversial throughout the colonial period, but after the Revolutionary period all states provided for equity courts, either as separate bodies or unified with law courts (see STATE COURTS).

In the federal courts, equitable remedies have been used aggressively during the past century to enforce federal law against the states. Previously, however, equity was not a significant element in judicial *federalism, for two reasons. First, the *Eleventh Amendment provided that federal courts could not take jurisdiction of "any suit in law or equity" against a suit brought by citizens of other states or nations. Second, there was little federal law to be enforced. Few of the Constitution's provisions apply, on their face, to the states. Furthermore, in the landmark case of *Barron v. Baltimore (1833), Chief Justice John *Marshall held that the *Bill of Rights did not apply to the states. Thus, only a few state statutes were struck down by federal courts in the first century of the nation's history.

**Decline of State Immunity.** This changed dramatically after ratification of the *Fourteenth Amendment. During the rapid economic expansion and industrial development after the *Civil War, federal courts frequently struck down state laws that tended to stifle economic growth, using the Due Process Clause of the Fourteenth Amendment. It was necessary, however, to overcome the states' constitutional immunity from suit (see DUE PROCESS, SUBSTANTIVE).

Ex parte *Young (1908) provided the Supreme Court an opportunity to revise the scope of state immunity from suit under the Eleventh Amendment. In 1907, the Minnesota legislature had enacted a statute reducing certain in-state rail rates. Railroads contended that the statute deprived them of property in violation of the Due Process Clause, and they sought an injunction in a federal court to prevent the statute's enforcement. One of the named respondents was Edward Young, the attorney general of Minnesota. The federal judge issued a temporary injunction, and Young was cited for contempt when he attempted to enforce the statute in a Minnesota court anyway. The Supreme Court concluded that the suit against Young was not barred by the Eleventh Amendment. Justice Rufus *Peckham for the 8-to-1 majority held that if a state officer attempts to enforce an unconstitutional statute he is "stripped of his official . . . character" and becomes personally subject to liability (p. 160). This is an utterly—and doubly—illogical holding. First, under the *state action doctrine enunci-

ated in the *Civil Rights Cases (1883), federal power under the Fourteenth Amendment reaches only "acts done under State authority," not private acts. Thus if the state attorney general was being enjoined in his private character, the injunction would not inhibit the exercise of *state* power. Second, it is impossible to know whether a statute is unconstitutional until after the case has been decided on its merits. The upshot of Young, therefore, was that a suit need only *allege* a statute's unconstitutionality to override state immunity. Despite such inconsistencies, however, Young's result remains today an essential weapon in the federal judicial armory for supervising the actions of the states.

Most constitutional attacks on state legislation after Young were aimed at economic reform laws. Such statutes were meant by lawmakers to improve the lot of industrial workers in a variety of ways: restricted hours, workplace improvements, minimum wages, elimination of child labor, and so on (see LABOR). Federal judges enjoined such statutes so often that political progressives demanded that federal equity powers be curtailed. Several statutes partially accomplished this, among them the Johnson Act of 1934, which prohibited federal injunctions against state regulation of utility rates, and the Tax Injunction Act of 1934, and federal legislation mandated that only three-judge panels be able to issue injunctions against state employees.

**Broadening Use of Injunctions.** These developments were soon overshadowed, however. In *Gitlow v. New York (1925), the Court stated for the first time that the *Bill of Rights applied to the states. Free *speech, the Court concluded, was a form of "liberty" that was protected from state encroachment under the Fourteenth Amendment's Due Process Clause. Gitlow heralded a new era in constitutional law. Over the next thirty years, the Court selectively made provisions of the Bill of Rights enforceable against the states. With this expanded constitutional activism came a broadened use of injunctions (see INCORPORATION DOCTRINE).

Two examples illustrate the extent to which injunctions have been used as an instrument to enforce federally secured rights and to restrain state power. The first concerns the apportionment of legislative bodies. *Baker v. Carr (1962) involved a challenge to malapportionment of state legislatures. Baker expressly overruled precedents holding that malapportionment cases presented nonjusticiable *political questions and concluded that *equal protection of the laws was denied if state election districts were not fairly apportioned.

Two years later, in *Reynolds v. Sims (1964), the Court considered the kinds of remedies that were available in apportionment cases. Reynolds stated that lower courts were to rely on the principles of equity to fashion a proper remedy. If an equal protection violation was found, federal judges were to proceed cautiously to provide the state an opportunity to correct the infirmity. If a proper apportionment was not completed in a timely way, federal courts could enjoin further elections under the state's flawed apportionment plan. Beyond that, federal judges could develop their own temporary apportionment plan and actually implement it to remedy the violation (see REAPPORTIONMENT CASES).

Another example of the use of federal injunctions may be found in the school desegregation cases. In the landmark case of *Brown v. Board of Education I* (1954), the Court ruled that the maintenance of separate public schools for white and black students violated equal protection. In the followup to that case, *Brown v. Board of Education II* (1955), the Court made it clear that the objective of *Brown* was to eliminate dual school systems "with *all deliberate speed*" (p. 301). To that end, the federal courts were specifically instructed to apply historic principles of equity and devise appropriate equitable remedies. Lower courts were first authorized to redraw school-district lines, and in some cases even ignore municipal, county, and other political boundaries. Courts were also authorized to order busing of students between districts to insure that desegregation was accomplished (see DESEGREGATION REMEDIES).

These apportionment and desegregation cases are representative but not exhaustive. Federal injunctions are now an indispensable tool to uphold the constitutional rights of individuals. To accomplish this federal courts rely on the muscle and flexibility that characterize all of equity's remedies.

***Criminal Cases.*** In contrast with the wideranging use of federal injunctions in civil matters, federal judges are constrained to use equitable remedies sparingly in criminal cases, even when criminal prosecutions trench on federally secured rights. In *Younger v. Harris* (1971), a defendant was indicted for violation of a California law that criminalized certain forms of political speech. The defendant sought an injunction from a federal court. On appeal to the Supreme Court, Justice Hugo *Black found that issuance of the injunction was improper. He held that the principles of equity required that federal courts not interfere in the state's criminal case and that use of an injunction failed to respect state authority in the American federal system.

It has always been one of the basic principles of equity that an equitable remedy may be used to prevent irreparable injury. If a criminal case has been initiated in a state court, *Younger* stated, a defendant is free to litigate fully his constitutional claims there. An injunction should generally be unnecessary so long as the state has provided a substantively and procedurally fair opportunity to defend against criminal prosecution. Black also held that *judicial self-restraint was necessary so as not to intrude on the lawful activities of the states. A proper division of responsibility be-

tween state and federal authorities, which Black referred to as "Our Federalism," has played an important role in America's history and must be preserved. *Younger* thus forbade the use of injunctions against states in criminal cases except in unique circumstances (see ABSTENTION DOCTRINE).

*Younger* runs counter to the trend in civil cases. Equitable remedies have historically been used aggressively against the states. *Younger* and its progeny hold that federal courts must refuse equitable relief against a state's criminal justice system. The resultant tension is not destructive to the federal system or symptomatic of some flaw in the law. To the contrary, it is an inherent part of the American system of jurisprudence, representing the intersection of two conflicting objectives. Federal courts have a duty to enforce federal law, while at the same time respecting the independence of state court systems. *Younger* represents an attempt to strike a proper balance between these two interests.

(See also JUDICIAL POWER AND JURISDICTION; LOWER FEDERAL COURTS.)

□ Peter C. Hoffer, *The Law's Conscience: Equitable Constitutionalism in America* (1990). William H. Holdsworth, *A History of English Law*, 7th ed. (1956). Laurence H. Tribe, *American Constitutional Law*, 2d ed. (1986).

James B. Stoneking

**In Personam Jurisdiction.** The Supreme Court has consistently held that in order for a court to take jurisdiction of a cause, the *Fifth or *Fourteenth Amendments' *due process clauses require that it have jurisdiction over the person of the defendant as well as subject-matter jurisdiction over the cause itself. In the early case of *Pennoyer v. Neff* (1878), Justice Stephen J. *Field asserted twin fundamental principles derived from the *Tenth Amendment: "[E]very State possesses exclusive jurisdiction and sovereignty over persons and property within its territory" and "no State can exercise direct jurisdiction and authority over persons or property without its territory" (p. 722). The first of these has been generally reaffirmed in *Burnham v. Superior Court* (1990), upholding so-called tag service on a person physically present in a state's territory.

Revolutions in communications and transportation, the ensuing growth of the interstate market, and the preeminence of the corporation in the American economy soon rendered Field's position insufficient. In *International Shoe Co. v. Washington* (1945), the Court modernized concepts of in personam jurisdiction by requiring that a person have "minimum contacts with [a state] such that the maintenance of the suit does not offend 'traditional notions of fair play and substantial justice' " (p. 316). States quickly exploited this new standard by enacting "long-arm" statutes extending the jurisdiction of their courts to out-of-state parties who had the requisite minimum contacts, defined in terms of contractual or tortious activity having an impact in the state. The Supreme Court upheld jurisdiction exercised under such statutes in *Burger King Corp. v. Rudziewicz* (1985).

(See also JUDICIAL POWER AND JURISDICTION; STATE COURTS.)

William M. Wiecek

**In Re** (Lat., "in the matter of"), phrase used to designate cases lacking formally adversarial parties. It refers to the *res* (Lat., "thing") that is the subject of the litigation, such as an estate or a physical object.

William M. Wiecek

**In Rem Jurisdiction** refers to one of three kinds of jurisdiction that federal and *state courts assert, the others being *in personam and quasi–in rem. In rem jurisdiction was traditionally conceived of as extending to things (that is, physical objects or real property) located within the forum jurisdiction and was thus construed in the classic case of *Pennoyer* v. *Neff* (1877). However, as Massachusetts Chief Justice Oliver Wendell *Holmes pointed out, all proceedings are really against persons. In rem jurisdiction differs from quasi–in rem in that in the former, the *res* (Lat., "thing") is thought of as being itself the object of the litigation, while in the latter, the *res* is merely attached to satisfy a potential judgment in litigation involving something other than the thing attached.

Assertion of in rem and quasi–in rem jurisdiction in the twentieth century became complicated by the rise in importance of intangible *property, such as trusts, as well as by the mobility of property, which presented baffling metaphysical problems of *situs*. Responding to this complexity, the Supreme Court in *Shaffer* v. *Heitner* (1977) held that assertion of in rem and quasi–in rem jurisdiction must meet the same due process requirements as assertion of in personam jurisdiction under *International Shoe Co.* v. *Washington* (1945), which required that the defendant have minimum contacts with the forum jurisdiction (see DUE PROCESS, PROCEDURAL).

William M. Wiecek

**Insanity Defense,** the principal legal doctrine permitting consideration of mental abnormality in assessing criminal liability. The roots of the defense stretch back to Greece before the birth of Christ. In the English-speaking world, written evidence of cases in which pardons were granted on the ground of "madness" exist from medieval England. In the United States, the insanity defense has always been an accepted part of criminal law doctrine. Nonetheless, the defense has been controversial, because it allows those who commit heinous crimes to escape criminal punishment (although those who are acquitted are still usually committed to a hospital for an indeterminate period).

The Supreme Court has proceeded cautiously in this area, directing most of its attention to the proper formulation of the test for insanity. In modern times, "insanity" has been defined as a mental impairment that either impedes a person's ability to understand the wrongfulness of his or her act (the "cognitive" prong) or to control the act (the "volitional" prong). In *Leland* v. *Oregon* (1952), the Court held that, if a state chooses to adopt the defense, the Constitution does not mandate use of a test any broader than the historical M'Naghten formulation (a test devised by the English House of Lords in 1843 that focuses solely on "cognitive" impairment). The Court indicated that, given the state of knowledge at the time, a "volitional" excuse was not constitutionally necessary.

Two later Court decisions, although not directly relevant to the insanity defense, bolstered this aspect of *Leland*. In *Robinson* v. *California* (1962), the justices held that the *Eighth Amendment (which bars *"cruel and unusual punishment") prohibits punishing someone merely for being addicted to heroin. In *Powell* v. *Texas* (1968), five members of the Court interpreted this holding to mean that "the chronic alcoholic with an irresistible urge to consume alcohol should not be punishable for drinking or for being drunk" (p. 549). But the majority in *Powell* also held that one could be punished for being drunk in public. Thus, analogously, while a state would be forbidden from punishing a person merely for being mentally ill (assuming this condition were "irresistible"), it would not be barred by *Robinson* or *Powell* from punishing a mentally ill person for committing a crime.

Further evidence that the Court may not find the insanity defense to be an essential aspect of criminal liability comes from its treatment of the burden of proof relating to the defense. *Leland* also held that the state may require the defendant to prove insanity beyond a reasonable doubt. Almost two decades later, the Court called into question this portion of *Leland* when it held in *In re *Winship* (1970) that the prosecution must prove beyond a reasonable doubt "every fact necessary to constitute proof of the crime with which [the defendant] is charged" (p. 364). But in *Rivera* v. *Delaware* (1976), the Court later dismissed, for want of a substantial *federal question, an *appeal of a conviction under an instruction placing the burden of proving insanity on the defendant by a preponderance of the evidence.

Christopher Slobogin

**Insolvency Legislation.** See BANKRUPTCY AND INSOLVENCY LEGISLATION.

**Insular Cases.** The *Insular Cases* are a group of some fourteen decisions of the period 1901–1904 that involve the application of the Constitution and *Bill of Rights to overseas territories (see TERRITORIES AND NEW STATES). The cases arose after the United States acquired island territories through the treaty ending the Spanish-American War (1898). The nation's determination to become a world power, as evidenced by the war and the acquisition of foreign territories, received overwhelming popular endorsement in the presidential election of 1900. The *Insular Cases* translated the political dispute into the vocabulary of the Constitution, with the Supreme Court eventually echoing the popular sentiment.

Two competing positions lay behind the arguments before the Court. One opinion, largely racially motivated, was that the people of the new territories were unfit to become citizens—a conclusion that foreclosed the possibility of statehood and relegated the people to permanent territorial status (see CITIZENSHIP; RACE AND RACISM). The other view was the century-old tradition that all territory would eventually become states.

The *Insular Cases* presented three questions of constitutional law and statutory construction: (1) whether the national government had the power to acquire territories by treaty; (2) whether certain statutes applied to territories; and (3) whether the Bill of Rights applied automatically to any territory upon acquisition by the United States. In *De Lima v. Bidwell* (1901) the Court confirmed that the nation had the power to acquire territory, pointing for support to the long history of acquisitions.

The Court also considered whether duties could be imposed on goods shipped between Puerto Rico and the United States. For goods imported into the United States, the Court avoided the constitutional question by relying upon language in the Dingley Tariff Act (1897), which imposed tariffs on "all articles imported from foreign countries." In *De Lima*, Justice Henry Billings *Brown wrote for the Court that Puerto Rico ceased to be "foreign" once ceded to the United States by treaty. Hence, the statute did not apply to Puerto Rico.

The Court could not, however, avoid the constitutional question for goods exported to Puerto Rico. So long as the United States military governed there, exports could be taxed under the war powers of Congress (*Dooley v. United States*, 1901). Once the special powers of the military ended, however, any imposition of tariffs seemed to violate the Constitution's requirement that duties be "uniform throughout the United States" (Art. I, sec. 8). In *Downes v. Bidwell* (1901) Brown reiterated that Puerto Rico was not "foreign"; but he reasoned that it was also not part of "the United States," a term that meant only the states themselves. Justice Edward D. *White and three other justices concurred but rejected Brown's constitutional categories as being too restrictive of the nation's powers in world affairs. White concluded that constitutional limitations applied to a territory only after Congress had taken action to "incorporate" the territory into the United States. Chief Justice Melville W. *Fuller rejected White's nebulous category between foreign and incorporated, reasoning that once a territory came under the nation's sovereign power, it became part of "the United States."

Later cases, involving the Bill of Rights, revealed a movement away from Brown's position to White's, which is still the prevailing view. Brown continued to find modest restrictions in the Constitution itself. For example, he held in *Hawaii v. Mankichi* (1903) that, in the absence of congressional action, only those rights that were "fundamental in their nature" would apply (p. 218). Justice White agreed with the conclusion that there was no requirement for indictment by a grand jury or a unanimous jury. But he again concluded that because Congress had not incorporated Hawaii into the United States, no part of the Bill of Rights applied.

A majority of the Court finally accepted the incorporation doctrine in *Dorr v. United States* (1904). Justice William R. *Day noted that the natives of the Philippines were not fit for *jury trials and that Congress need not accord them that right until it chose to incorporate the islands.

The cases present myriad justifications and tortured reasoning. Their clear import is that the justices wanted to allow the president and Congress the greatest possible freedom in world affairs. Many people thought that the opinions reflected the election results, since in the election of 1900 the voters had soundly rejected the Democrats' call to repudiate the acquisitions of overseas territories. But the cases show more than a politically savvy Court; they also anticipate the later debate over the application of the Bill of Rights to the states, when *"incorporation" and *"fundamental rights" would again be operative phrases. The Court's opinions therefore represent tentative, early arguments in what would become half a century of debate about the reach of the Bill of Rights.

☐ James E. Kerr, *The Insular Cases: The Role of the Judiciary in American Expansionism* (1982).        Walter F. Pratt, Jr.

**Insurance Rates, Equality and.** A multi-billion-dollar industry insures Americans' lives, health, homes, and property against risks such as injury, illness, and death. Insurees make regular payments, called "premiums," to insurers. When an event that is insured against— hospitalization, theft, fire, a car accident— occurs, the insured submits a claim to the insurance company. After reviewing the claim, the company pays the expenses if it determines that the policy applies to the situation. Individuals may buy private insurance policies (most property insurance is bought in this way) or they may belong to group life, health, and retirement plans, usually through their employers. Group plans may be funded by a combination of employee and employer contributions.

The insurance industry is subject to government regulation, mostly by the states, but it is a private enterprise. The insurer, therefore, sets the amount of both premiums and benefits. It is at this point that questions about equality arise. Group insurance plans do not permit close assessment of individual risks, so better risks always subsidize poorer risks: for example, an employee with two dependents pays the same for health insurance as does an employee with seven dependents.

Private insurance policies generally determine premiums on the basis of assessments of the risks presented by the individual buying the policy and the property being insured. For example, young, single men typically pay higher automobile insurance premiums than do other car-owners because they represent the segment of the population most often involved in automobile accidents. Redlining, the practice of refusing to insure property in neighborhoods the companies considered unsafe, was once common. Redlining gave rise to suspicions of race discrimination when the neighborhoods involved were predominantly African-American or Latino (see HOUSING DISCRIMINATION). Retirement plans have often discriminated on the basis of sex. Since women, on the average, live longer than men, insurers anticipated that the interval between retirement and death would be longer for women, obligating them to pay out more money to their female insurees than to males. Companies developed two ways of dealing with this predictable expense. The first was to charge women higher premiums; the second, to pay them lower benefits.

Is it fair to discriminate against individuals on the basis of statistically accurate generalizations about groups to which they belong? The courts' answer to that question has depended on the affected group. Courts have viewed age discrimination as presenting few, if any, difficulties. A Pennsylvania case sustained the practice of charging young, single men higher auto-insurance rates against an *equal protection challenge. The practice of redlining has become less common because of the increasing publicity given to its racial overtones. Sex discrimination has been the subject of several court cases and of efforts, so far unsuccessful, to enact federal legislation prohibiting it.

The U.S. Supreme Court has never ruled that discriminatory insurance laws are unconstitutional per se. It has never needed to reach that question, since Title VII of the *Civil Rights Act of 1964 prohibits sex discrimination in employment. It is not surprising, therefore, that two cases have rendered sex discrimination illegal. What may be surprising is that the decisions were neither unanimous nor retroactive.

*Los Angeles Department of Water and Power v. Manhart* (1978) invalidated a group plan requiring women to pay higher premiums; *Arizona Governing Committee v. Norris* (1983) did the same for lower benefits for women. Since the pension plan invalidated in *Manhart* was funded partly from employee contributions, a male employee's take-home pay was higher than that of a woman earning the same salary. Chief Justice Warren *Burger and Justice William H. *Rehnquist agreed with the city's justification for the plan: that longevity was a factor justifying the different treatment of male and female workers. The other seven justices, however, disagreed. "Even a true generalization about the class," wrote Justice John Paul *Stevens, could not justify a policy that treats "individuals as simply components of a racial, religious, sexual, or national class" (p. 708).

The dissenters picked up an additional vote in *Norris*, but not because of the difference between forcing women to make higher contributions while they were working and paying them lower benefits when they retired. Instead, Justice Harry *Blackmun joined Burger and Rehnquist in dissent because Arizona, unlike Los Angeles, allowed its retirees to buy private insurance with state funds. The majority, however, insisted that the state had simply "offered a range of discriminatory benefits, rather than only one, [which] provides no basis whatever for distinguishing *Manhart*" (p. 708).

(See also GENDER; RACE AND RACISM.)

□ Judith A. Baer, *Equality under the Constitution: Reclaiming the Fourteenth Amendment* (1991). Claire Sherman Thomas, *Sex Discrimination and the Law* (1982).
Judith A. Baer

**Intergovernmental Tax Immunity.** See TAX IMMUNITIES.

**Intermediate Scrutiny** is the standard under the Equal Protection Clause that federal courts use to assess the constitutionality of government action based on sex (see GENDER) and illegitimacy (see INHERITANCE AND ILLEGITIMACY). Also known as heightened or semisuspect scrutiny, the standard requires that governmental action be "substantially" related to an "important" governmental interest. As such, it differs from the other two standards that the Supreme Court has formulated to determine whether governmental classifications under the Equal Protection Clause pass constitutional muster: *strict scrutiny, which controls race and state efforts to regulate aliens, and minimum scrutiny, which applies to social and economic classifications, as well as to those based on age, sexual orientation, and physical and mental handicaps. The latter merely requires that governmental action "reasonably" relate to a "legitimate" governmental interest, while strict scrutiny requires governmental action to relate "closely" to a "compelling" governmental interest.

Intermediate scrutiny formally dates from 1976, in the Court's decision in *Craig v. Boren*. Its addition to the two other levels of scrutiny has complicated definitional matters by requiring courts to distinguish among reasonable, substantial, and close relationships, and to determine as well the weight of the governmental interest at stake.

(See also EQUAL PROTECTION.)

Harold J. Spaeth

**International Union v. Johnson Controls, Inc.,** 111 S.Ct. 1196 (1991), argued 10 Oct. 1990, decided 20 Mar. 1991 by vote of 9 to 0; Blackmun for the Court, White, joined by Rehnquist and Kennedy, concurring in part and concurring in the judgment, Scalia concurring in the judgment. In this landmark sex discrimination case, several unions and women employees brought a *class action suit under Title VII of the *Civil Rights Act of 1964, as amended by the Pregnancy Discrimination Act of 1978. The suit challenged the "fetal protection policy" of Johnson Controls, a battery-manufacturing company that, since 1982, had barred fertile women from high-paying jobs involving exposure to lead.

Reversing both the district court and the *court of appeals, which had ruled in favor of the company, the Supreme Court held that the fetal protection policy was not facially neutral because it did not apply to males as well as females despite evidence that lead exposure also harms the male reproductive system. Since this was a policy of *"disparate treatment," it could be justified under Title VII only as a bona fide occupational qualification (BFOQ). However, the Court held that since pregnant employees must be treated the same as other employees unless they differ in their ability to do the work, and since there was no showing here of such a disability, the BFOQ exception was not justifiable. The company's main concern was not with whether the female employees could do the job, but with whether lead exposure would harm their unconceived fetuses. However important this may be, the Court said, the health of a fetus is not essential to the business of battery manufacturing and thus cannot qualify as a BFOQ. The Court also rejected the company's claim that its policy was justified by a fear of *tort liability. Justice Byron *White, joined by Chief Justice William *Rehnquist and Justice Anthony *Kennedy, agreed that the Johnson Controls policy was discriminatory, but disagreed that the BFOQ defense was so narrow that it could never justify a sex-specific fetal protection policy.

(See also GENDER.)

Joel B. Grossman

**Interposition** implied that the states have a right to interpose their authority to protect their citizens from the unconstitutional measures of the federal government. In 1798 Virginia proposed interposition to resist the *Sedition Act. In the 1830s South Carolina asserted its rights to nullify a federal tariff but backed down when threatened

with military force by President Andrew *Jackson. Later Senator John C. Calhoun argued for interposition to prevent the delivery of mail in the South containing abolitionist propaganda.

In the 1850s many Northerners urged interposition, in the form of personal liberty laws and court actions, to prevent enforcement of the Fugitive Slave Act of 1850 (see FUGITIVE SLAVES). In 1854 the Wisconsin Supreme Court declared the 1850 law unconstitutional and released the abolitionist Sherman Booth from federal custody. In overturning this decision, Chief Justice Roger B. *Taney declared, in *Ableman v. Booth (1859), that such "propositions are new in the jurisprudence of the United States" and that the Supreme Court had the final authority to interpret the meaning of the Constitution (p. 514). Secession was the most dramatic form of interposition, and it was met with an equally dramatic and forceful response by President Abraham *Lincoln .

After *Brown v. Board of Education (1954), some southern states fought school desegregation with "massive resistance," a form of interposition. In *Cooper v. Aaron (1958), which involved the integration of schools in Little Rock, Arkansas, the federal courts cited Ableman v. Booth to reaffirm the principle that the Supreme Court had final authority to interpret the meaning of the Constitution. Interposition is now a relic of constitutional theory that died in the *Civil War but was briefly and futilely resurrected in the 1950s and 1960s by diehard segregationists.

(See also NULLIFICATION; STATE SOVEREIGNTY AND STATES' RIGHTS.).

Paul Finkelman

**Interpretivism and Noninterpretivism.** The distinction between interpretivism and noninterpretivism lies at the heart of the contemporary debate over the nature and extent of *judicial power under the Constitution. Must the Supreme Court be bound to the text of the Constitution and the intentions behind that text or may it go beyond the "four corners" of the document to ascertain its meaning? The debate over interpretivism and noninterpretivism is closely tied to the role of *original intent in constitutional and legal interpretation.

Interpretivism and noninterpretivism should not be confused with the more traditional distinction between strict construction and loose construction. Strict and loose construction are both forms of "interpretivism," where the only question is *how* to read the Constitution, loosely or strictly. The idea of noninterpretivism, on the other hand, raises the question of *whether* to read the Constitution in the sense of being bound by its text and the meaning behind that text.

The more extreme noninterpretivists, such as Michael Perry and Ronald Dworkin, for example, believe that it is not only appropriate but necessary for judges to infuse the Constitution with contemporary conceptions of justice; the inquiry is not so much what the Constitution means as what it should mean. The objective of noninterpretivism is to render the Constitution a morally evolutionary document untied to either the text strictly speaking or the original intention and meaning behind that text.

Critics charge that such a view reduces the written Constitution to nothing more than judicial opinion and that interpretivism is the sole legitimate approach under a written Constitution deemed to be lasting unless changed by formal amendment. Interpretivists, in the strictest sense, argue that not only the literal text but the original intention behind that text must govern every judicial decision; more moderate interpretivists seek to be guided more by the text than the original intention as such. Thus, as Robert *Bork has argued, even though the framers of the *Fourth Amendment's prohibition of unreasonable searches and seizures could not have had electronic eavesdropping in mind, the prohibition logically extends that far.

In fact, most judges fall between the polar extremes of interpretivism and noninterpretivism, seeking some pragmatic position for the resolution of the cases and controversies that come before them.

(See also CONSTITUTIONAL INTERPRETATION.)

Gary L. McDowell

**Interstate Commerce Commission.** Although the Constitution (Article I, section 8) gave Congress the power to regulate interstate commerce, Congress neglected to regulate railroads until 1887, when it passed the Interstate Commerce Act (ICA) establishing the Interstate Commerce Commission (ICC). Prior to this federal action, individual states established railroad commissions, some of which regulated railroad rates to eliminate rampant discrimination. The Supreme Court declared state rate regulation constitutional in *Munn v. Illinois (1877), when it ruled that in the absence of federal legislation state legislatures could regulate interstate railroads. State regulation, however, made rates even more chaotic, and the Court in *Wabash, St. Louis and Pacific Railway Co. v. Illinois (1886) concluded that interstate transportation charges could only be regulated by Congress.

Although the Supreme Court in effect forced the creation of the ICC, the Court retained the authority to oversee rail rates. In 1890 it declared that due process demanded that rates set by a state commission be subject to judicial review; in *Smyth v. Ames (1898) the Court decided that railroads were constitutionally entitled to a fair return on their property (see DUE PROCESS, SUBSTANTIVE). The Court also denied that the ICC had implicit rate-making authority. Even when agreeing with the ICC the Court often restricted the powers of the agency. In U.S. v. Trans-Missouri Freight Association (1897) the Court decided that

rate and tonnage agreements among railroads restrained trade and violated the *Sherman Antitrust Act rather than the antipooling section of the ICA. The Court also destroyed the ICC's power to prevent the long-short-haul abuse in ICC v. Alabama Midland Railway (1897).

During the Progressive Era the Supreme Court responded to the temper of the times and helped make the ICC a powerful regulatory agency (see PROGRESSIVISM). After the Hepburn Act (1906) gave the ICC power to set rates, opponents of regulation were disappointed when the Court refused to exercise a broad *judicial review of rates. Regarding rate setting as an administrative function, the Court determined only that the ICC had power to set rates, not whether it exercised that power with wisdom. The Court also, in the Minnesota Rate Cases (1913), allowed the ICC to regulate intrastate rates that discriminated against interstate commerce, elevating the ICC over the conflicting laws and regulations of state legislatures and commissions. Still reflecting the Progressive spirit the Court in Dayton-Goose Creek Railway v. U.S. (1924) urged the ICC to play a positive, creative role in building an adequate rail system and agreed that the railroads should be put "more completely than ever under the fostering guardianship and control" of the ICC (p. 478).

But when the ICC refused to lead, the Court did not appear dismayed. It even objected to occasional attempts by the ICC to take the initiative. In 1931 the Court blocked a rare effort by the ICC to prevent the cheating of bondholders in a railroad reorganization scheme, and in 1933 it reversed the ICC's only order to a railroad to build an extension line. Since the ICC failed to coordinate transportation in the 1920s the agency was largely bypassed in the crises of depression and war during the 1930s and 1940s.

In the post–World War II years the ICC failed to cope with the nation's transportation problems. By the 1960s the Court tried to clarify the ICC's hazy but crucial minimum-rate policy, which determined whether railroads, trucks, or barges would carry freight between competing points. The ICC tended to preserve existing relationships and avoid destructive intermodal competition. The Court, however, forced the ICC to allow more competition even when rates failed to cover fully distributed costs but at least covered out-of-pocket costs. Subsequently, the Court protected a low-cost mode of transportation by insisting that a rate be based on fully distributed costs. Having moved the ICC to foster intermodal competition as long as it was not predatory and having nudged it in the direction of a more rational rate system, the Supreme Court remained aloof in the 1970s and 1980s while the nation allowed the ICC to atrophy and turned to the panaceas of mergers and deregulation to cure its transportation malaise.

(See also ADMINISTRATIVE STATE; COMMERCE POWER.)

□ Ari Hoogenboom and Olive Hoogenboom, *A History of the ICC: From Panacea to Palliative* (1976).

Ari Hoogenboom

**Interstate Compacts.** As a vestige of the power to make treaties enjoyed by sovereign nations, the Constitution (Art. I, sec. 10) permits states, with the consent of Congress, to enter into an agreement or compact with another state. From 1789 to 1920, thirty-six interstate compacts were made, primarily dealing with boundaries and cessions of territory. In the next three decades sixty-five compacts were made on matters such as protection of the environment and the use of natural resources, crime control, transportation, utility regulation, tobacco production, and sundry local issues that transcended state boundaries. Since the 1950s, interstate cooperation has become institutionalized by permanent commissions in all the states and the Council of State Governments, which study narrowly conceived and technical problems that might be handled through interstate compacts. The hope of many students of *federalism in the 1930s that interstate cooperation and uniform state legislation could provide an alternative to consolidation of policy making in the national government has not been realized. Nevertheless, interstate compacts are a means by which states retain control over some local issues and preserve a modicum of power in an increasingly centralized polity.

The most important Supreme Court decision on this subject was *Virginia* v. *Tennessee* (1893). The Court held that the assent of Congress was not required to agreements having no tendency to increase the political powers of the states or to encroach on the supremacy of the national government.

Herman J. Belz

**Inverse Condemnation** is a cause of action that can be brought by a property owner when a governmental entity allegedly has taken property without initiating any formal *eminent domain proceedings. The action is based on the Just Compensation Clause of the *Fifth Amendment to the Constitution, which declares: "nor shall private property be taken for public use, without just compensation." In *Chicago, Burlington & Quincy Railroad Co.* v. *Chicago* (1897), the United States Supreme Court held that the constitutional requirement that just compensation be paid when property is taken for a *public use applies to the states as well as to the federal government by operation of the *Fourteenth Amendment's Due Process Clause (see DUE PROCESS, SUBSTANTIVE).

Inverse condemnation suits may also be based on the just compensation provisions contained in *state constitutions. Many of these state constitutional provisions parallel the language of the federal constitution's just compensation clause. Many, however, go further and require compensation not only when a taking occurs but also when property is merely "damaged" by governmental activity.

Property owners are constitutionally entitled to bring inverse condemnation actions even in the absence of legislation authorizing such litigation. Congress and several states, however, have enacted legislation providing specific procedures for such actions.

Over the last three decades, the nature and frequency of inverse condemnation litigation has changed markedly and has become the focus of considerable controversy. A dramatic expansion of state and federal property regulation has focused increasing attention on the question of relief for the adverse impacts of regulatory activity. When the term "inverse condemnation" initially gained prominence in the 1960s, it generally referred to redress for takings as a result of physical invasions of land—for example through flooding as a result of government public works projects. During the 1960s, however, a number of prominent land use scholars urged that the just compensation clause should be interpreted more broadly to support "reverse" or "inverse" condemnation actions by persons injured by stringent forms of regulation, even in the absence of physical interference with their property. In the 1970s, numerous inverse condemnation actions began to appear asserting such claims.

These ongoing developments sparked considerable scholarly debate. At the same time, the Supreme Court, after a long absence from the field of land use regulation, finally returned to the takings issue in a series of cases beginning in the 1970s. The Court's opinions to date, however, have not fully clarified the standards for granting relief in inverse condemnation litigation.

For compensation to be awarded, the plaintiff must demonstrate a "taking" of "property" for a "public purpose." The Supreme Court has interpreted the third of these elements quite broadly. Neither the federal nor a state government constitutionally can take an individual's property simply to give it to another private person for the latter's private benefit. In such a case, the Just Compensation Clause would not come into play because no valid taking would have occurred. However, in addition to equitable relief, the property owner in such an instance could bring an action under Title 42, section 1983 of the U.S. Code to recover money damages for injury resulting from a due process violation.

A finding of no public purpose is quite rare. Almost any governmental activity will meet this test as long as it may further some public health, safety, or general welfare purpose (see POLICE POWER). In the leading case of *Berman* v. *Parker* (1954), the Supreme Court declared that non-offending commercial property could be taken to be resold to private developers for use in implementation of a pubic plan to redevelop areas of a city blighted by substandard housing. More recently, the Court in *Hawaii Housing Authority* v.

*Midkiff* (1984) approved state legislation that provided for the compensated taking of residential real estate and its subsequent transfer to the lessees of the property. The Court concluded that this legislation did not merely serve the private interests of the lessees but rationally addressed social and economic problems resulting from perceived evils of land oligopoly in Hawaii.

Inverse condemnation actions can be brought to challenge alleged takings of forms of property besides real estate. The Court has held, for example, that intangible interests such as trade secret rights in health and safety data constitute property that can be taken.

The greatest confusion has arisen not over the public use requirement or the relevant definition of property but over the question of the appropriate standards for finding that a taking has occurred. Government action can be found to be a taking in a wide variety of circumstances. In addition to formal appropriation of property, a taking can be found, for example, where a governmental authority physically invades or destructively interferes with a claimant's property. Flooding of neighboring land as a result of government activity and frequent low-level airplane overflights greatly impairing the usefulness of a claimant's land are prominent examples of government actions that have been found to constitute takings on this basis.

The most difficult questions, however, have arisen with regard to "regulatory takings." In his seminal opinion for the Supreme Court in the case of *Pennsylvania Coal Co. v. Mahon* (1922), Justice Oliver Wendell *Holmes conceded that governmental authorities have substantial police power authority to regulate the use of property without paying compensation to affected owners. However, he noted the essential similarity between the formal taking of property through eminent domain proceedings and the severe reduction of the value of private property sometimes resulting from police power regulation. Accordingly, Justice Holmes extended the traditional definition of "takings" by declaring that when the diminution in value resulting from regulation "reaches a certain magnitude, in most if not in all cases there must be an exercise of eminent domain and compensation to sustain the act" (p. 413). In short, he stated, "if regulation goes too far it will be recognized as a taking" (p. 415).

Justice Holmes's opinion in *Pennsylvania Coal* set the stage for concentrated judicial and scholarly efforts ever since to distinguish between noncompensable regulatory activity and regulation whose impact is so severe as to amount to a taking requiring the payment of just compensation.

The Supreme Court repeatedly has stressed that takings claims must be decided in light of the basic purpose of the just compensation clause "to bar Government from forcing some people alone to bear public burdens which, in all fairness and justice, should be borne by the public as a whole" (*Armstrong* v. *United States,* 1960, p. 49). The Court, however, has not yet adopted any single test for determining when fairness demands a finding that a compensable taking has occurred. Decisions have sometimes emphasized the diminution in value factor stressed by Justice Holmes. But recent Supreme Court takings analyses usually have looked to multiple factors. The general standard most frequently invoked by the Supreme Court since the late 1970s has been the three-part formulation announced in *Penn Central Transportation Co.* v. *New York City* (1978). In that decision the Court stressed as relevant factors the character of the governmental activity under challenge, the "economic impact of the regulation on the claimant and, particularly, the extent to which the regulation has interfered with distinct investment-backed expectations" (p. 124).

At other times the Court has suggested other general standards for determining the existence of a taking, including a two-part test announced in the 1980 case of *Agins* v. *City of Tiburon* (1980). In that case, the Court declared that the application of a *zoning ordinance "effects a taking if the ordinance does not substantially advance legitimate state interests . . . or denies an owner economically viable use of his land" (p. 260). The *Penn Central* and *Agins* standards have been variously interpreted and applied by the Court.

Judicial analyses of takings challenges have tended to be highly fact-specific inquiries. The character and impact of the governmental activity continue to be critical issues. The Court, for example, has viewed all permanent physical invasions as particularly serious intrusions. Accordingly, it has declared that any permanent physical occupation by the government or by authorized third parties constitutes a taking regardless of its actual public benefit or economic impact on the owner (*Loretto* v. *Teleprompter Manhattan CATV Corp.*, 1982). On the other hand, the Supreme Court, *lower federal courts, and *state courts generally have been reluctant to find a compensable "taking" on the basis of regulatory activity not involving any physical invasion and have done so only in extreme cases where the owner has been deprived of virtually any economically viable use of the affected land.

Judicial analyses of takings claims also focus prominently on the circumstances prompting the government's activity. Even though governmental action may have a severe impact, no compensation will be required if a court finds that the government acted to mitigate a "nuisancelike" or "noxious" use of the claimant's property that the claimant had no legitimate right to maintain.

Over the last decade, inverse condemnation commentary and case law have not been confined to these basic questions of public purpose, property, and the definition of a "taking." A major additional focus has been the related question of the remedy to be granted when a taking is found. Some scholars and state court decisions in the 1980s adopted the view that when a taking is found the government should be allowed either to discontinue the activity in question or to initiate formal *eminent domain proceedings to acquire the affected property in return for the payment of fair compensation. These scholars and judges contended, however, that the governmental actor should not be required to pay compensation for the impact of the activity up to the time that the court declared it to constitute a taking. This view reflected concern for the increased financial liability that otherwise might be placed on government bodies and the potential inhibition of government regulatory activity that might result if such "temporary takings" were deemed to be compensable.

During the 1980s, the Supreme Court agreed to review a number of cases that raised the issue of compensation for temporary takings. In *San Diego Gas & Electric Co.* v. *San Diego* (1981), Justice William *Brennan dissented in an influential opinion that presaged the decision ultimately reached by the Supreme Court six years later. Justice Brennan concluded that both fairness and the Just Compensation Clause demanded monetary relief for the period beginning when the taking first took effect and ending when the regulation was rescinded. Three other justices joined in Justice Brennan's dissent. Justice William *Rehnquist indicated in a separate opinion that he agreed with much of Justice Brennan's opinion.

A majority of the Court finally endorsed this emerging position on the temporary takings issue when the Court squarely decided the issue in the case of *First English Evangelical Lutheran Church of Glendale* v. *Los Angeles* (1987). In that case, a temporary flood control ordinance prevented building construction on the plaintiff's land. The Court found it unnecessary to decide whether a taking actually had occurred because it found that the California courts had held that no recovery would be allowable for the period prior to a finding of a taking even if the plaintiff had been deprived of all economic use of the property. Relying on cases where temporary appropriations of private property had been deemed to be compensable takings, the Court declared that temporary regulatory takings similarly required monetary redress. The Court majority, however, took pains to distinguish compensable temporary takings from normal delays resulting from applications for variances, building permits, "and the like" (p. 321).

The ultimate impact of the *First English* decision remains to be seen. In a dissenting opinion, Justice John Paul *Stevens expressed concern that the Court's holding would spark an explosion of litigation with undesirable inhibiting effects on the activities of local government. He also cautioned that not every government activity that would be deemed a taking if permanent should be deemed automatically to be a temporary taking if in effect for an interim period. Finally, he found untenable the Court majority's suggested distinction between temporary takings and other "normal delays" as a result of government administrative activities.

The issue of precisely when governmental activity constitutes a "taking" continues to be a subject of considerable scholarly and judicial debate. While it is now clear that regulatory activity can become so stringent as to be a taking and that even temporary takings must be compensated, there continues to be considerable uncertainty as to what governmental activity can be successfully challenged through an inverse condemnation suit for just compensation.

(See also JUST COMPENSATION; PROPERTY RIGHTS; TAKINGS CLAUSE.)

□ Gus Bauman, "The Supreme Court, Inverse Condemnation and the Fifth Amendment: Justice Brennan Confronts the Inevitable in Land Use Controls," *Rutgers Law Journal* 15 (1983): 15–99. Frank I. Michelman, "Property, Utility and Fairness: Commentaries on the Ethical Foundations of 'Just Compensation' Law," *Harvard Law Review* 80 (1967): 1165–1258. Andrea L. Peterson, "The Takings Clause: In Search of Underlying Principles. Part I-A Critique of Current Takings Clause Doctrine," *California Law Review* 77 (December 1989): 1299–1363. Laurence H. Tribe, *American Constitutional Law,* 2d ed. (1988), 575–578, 587–604.
James May

**Iredell, James** (b. Lewes, England, 5 Oct. 1751; d. Edenton, N.C., 20 Oct. 1799; interred Gov. Samuel Johnston's private burial ground, Hayes, N.C.); associate justice, 1790–1799. The son of Francis and Margaret McCulloch Iredell, James Iredell was reared in England. Upon his father's illness and ensuing poverty, Iredell sailed to North Carolina in 1768 to become comptroller of His Majesty's Customs at Edenton, a position purchased for him by his mother's wealthy relatives. His official responsibilities allowed him time to study law, which he did under the tutelage of Samuel Johnston, whose sister, Hannah, he married on 18 July 1773. They had three children. He commenced law practice in December 1770, a vocation that he pursued until his appointment to the United States Supreme Court. He also served in various public offices during that period, including collector of the Port of Edenton (1774–1776), judge of the North Carolina Superior Court (1777–1778), and attorney general of North Carolina (1779–1781). He eagerly supported the revolutionary movement.

Impressed by Iredell's eloquent and energetic efforts in behalf of the ratification of the Constitution and desirous to appoint a North Carolinian to a prominent position in the federal government, President George *Washington nominated Iredell to the Supreme Court on 8 February 1790 and the Senate unanimously confirmed him two days later. Despite the fierce nationalism that he

*James Iredell*

had displayed during the debate over the new Constitution, some of Iredell's most notable moments on the Court were as a dissenter in the defense of states' rights (see STATE SOVEREIGNTY AND STATES' RIGHTS). When he sided with the majority, which was often, he sometimes did so for reasons independent of his colleagues. Iredell dissented in *Chisholm* v. *Georgia* (1793), which held that a state could be sued without its consent in a federal court under *Article III, section 2 of the Constitution. His dissent argued that English *common law was binding on the question and that this law did not give a citizen the right to sue a sovereign state without its consent. The final sentence of his dissent hinted broadly at the firestorm of protest that would greet the majority's ruling and cause it eventually to be rescinded.

Because he had been a member of the circuit court that had tried the case, Iredell did not participate in *Ware* v. *Hylton* (1796), which held that the treaty with Great Britain of 1783 invalidated Virginia's confiscation of a debt owed to a British creditor. He did, however, read his circuit court opinion, which argued that the treaty with Great Britain did not apply retroactively to a debt that had been confiscated in 1777. His opinion in *Calder* v. *Bull* (1798), which supported the Court's ruling that the *Ex Post Facto Clause applied only to criminal cases, represented one of the earliest and most eloquent statements in support of *judicial self-restraint. His opinion in *Hylton* v. *United States* (1796), which endorsed the Court's upholding of a federal carriage tax, included a very succinct and practical definition of the term "direct tax."

The physically taxing duties of riding his federal judicial circuit contributed to his death in 1799 (see CIRCUIT RIDING). Had he lived a longer life and continued to serve on the Court during the period of John *Marshall, his brilliant legal mind, states rights *federalism, and penchant for *dissent might have undermined the chief justice's campaign for judicial unanimity and constitutional nationalism.                Robert M. Ireland

# J

Jackson, Andrew (b. Waxhaw, S.C., 15 Mar. 1767; d. near Nashville, Tenn., 8 June 1845), president of the United States, 1829–1837. During his two terms, President Andrew Jackson made six appointments to the high court, more than any other president except George *Washington, William Howard *Taft, and Franklin D. *Roosevelt. Though Jackson took account of such traditional criteria as geography and public service, he calculated the political gain to be realized through his selections. In nominating John *McLean of Ohio, a presidential aspirant popular in the West, Jackson extracted from him a promise not to seek the presidency in return for a place on the Court. Jackson thereby shelved a potential rival. Politics also figured in Jackson's other Court nominations. In 1830 he selected Henry *Baldwin, a Pennsylvania congressman who had helped deliver that state to Jackson in 1828. James M. *Wayne (1835), Philip P. *Barbour (1836), and John *Catron (1837) had also rendered valuable political service to the president. Jackson's most controversial nominee, however, was Roger B. *Taney of Maryland. Taney as secretary of the treasury had played a crucial role in Jackson's attack on the Second Bank of the United States. Senate Whigs and disaffected Democrats thwarted Taney's first nomination in 1835. Jackson refused to make another appointment, however, and when Chief Justice John *Marshall died on 6 July 1835, the president had not one but two positions to fill. In December he nominated Philip P. Barbour, a strong states' rights Democrat from Virginia, to replace Gabriel *Duvall and Taney to fill Marshall's post. The Senate agreed to the selections only after three months of wrangling.

Jackson's appointees dominated American constitutional development down to the Civil War, and some historians even argue that they, especially Taney in Dred *Scott (1857), contributed to the war's coming. Yet like most of the justices that he appointed, Jackson's view of the Court and constitutional law blended states' rights and nationalism. He was pragmatic though assertive; he pushed his criticism of the Court when it was effective and backed off when it was not. He was also determined to use his office to shape the nation's destiny without being encumbered by the other branches. Jackson used the appointment process to impress his political views on the Court but also claimed that as the tribune of the people he was obliged to interpret the Constitution as he understood it. In his veto of the act rechartering the Second Bank of the United States in 1832, Jackson argued for strict construction of the Constitution and asserted a departmental theory of constitutional interpretation. He held that each of the branches of government had the right and duty to interpret the Constitution independently of the other branches. No previous president, not even Thomas *Jefferson, had ever gone so far in claiming that the Court's opinions could be ignored.

Yet Jackson's hostility to the Court had limits. He allegedly remarked, following the Supreme Court's decision in Worcester v. Georgia (1832), that "John Marshall had made his decision, now let him enforce it" (see CHEROKEE CASES). Jackson did not make that statement (although he did nothing to stop Georgia from defying the Court's decision) and he never asserted an inherent prerogative to disregard judicial decisions. He merely wanted equality among the branches of government in matters of constitutional interpretation. (See SELECTION OF JUSTICES; JUDICIAL POWER AND JURISDICTION.)

□ Henry J. Abraham, *Justices and Presidents: A Political History of Appointments to the Supreme Court,* 2d ed. (1985).
Kermit L. Hall

**Jackson, Howell Edmunds** (b. Paris, Tenn., 8 Apr. 1832; d. Nashville, Tenn., 8 Aug. 1895; interred Mt. Olivet Cemetery, Nashville), associate justice, 1893–1895. The first native Tennessean to serve on the United States Supreme Court, Howell E. Jackson was, by all accounts, a serious child and an excellent student, and at the age of eighteen he graduated from West Tennessee College. After several years of tutoring and a year of law school at Cumberland University, Jackson embarked on a legal career. In 1858 he formed the partnership of Currin and Jackson in Memphis. The partnership was short lived, however, owing to Tennessee's secession from the Union in 1861. Personally opposed to secession, Jackson nevertheless accepted an official position with the Confederate government. After the Civil War, Jackson returned to Memphis and resumed the practice of law in partnership with B. M. Estes. In 1874 he removed to Jackson, Tennessee, where he established a practice that regularly brought him before the Tennessee Supreme Court.

Although a Whig before the Civil War, Jackson joined the Democratic party and in 1875 secured a judgeship on the provisional Court of Arbitration for West Tennessee. When this tribunal was abolished two years later, Jackson sought unsuc-

cessfully to win a seat on the Tennessee Supreme Court. He then shifted his energies to the state legislature, and in 1880 he was elected to the state House of Representatives. Within a matter of months Jackson ran successfully for the United States Senate.

In Washington, Jackson earned a reputation as one of the hardest-working members of Congress. More important in terms of his judicial future, Jackson developed close friendships with President Grover Cleveland and with Republican Senate colleague Benjamin Harrison, who succeeded Cleveland as president in 1889. In 1887 Jackson left the Senate to take a position on the United States *Court of Appeals for the Sixth Circuit, at the request of President Cleveland. Seven years later, despite the difference in their party affiliations, President Harrison nominated Jackson to the United States Supreme Court. The Senate confirmed him without opposition.

Howell Jackson took his seat on the Supreme Court on 4 March 1893. Because of failing health, his tenure on the Court was only two and a half years and illness prevented him from participating in many important constitutional decisions. He did, however, manage to participate in *Pollock* v. *Farmers' Loan and Trust Company* (1895), in which the Court (dividing 5 to 4) struck down a federal *income tax law, notwithstanding Jackson's vigorous dissenting opinion. In Jackson's view, the Court's decision in *Pollock* was "the most disastrous blow ever struck at the constitutional power of Congress" (p. 704). Congress regained its power to levy an income tax when the *Sixteenth Amendment was ratified in 1913.

When the Supreme Court finished its term in late spring of 1895, a seriously ill Justice Jackson returned to his home at West Meade, just outside Nashville. There he passed away on 8 August 1895.
John M. Scheb II

**Jackson, Robert Houghwout** (b. Spring Creek, Pa., 13 February 1892; d. Washington, D.C., 9 October 1954; interred Maple Grove Cemetery, Jamestown, N.Y.), associate justice, 1941–1954. Born in Pennsylvania, Jackson and his family moved to Frewsburg, New York, when he was five years old; there Jackson's father owned and operated a hotel and livery stable. After graduation from high school in 1910, Jackson went to work as a clerk in Jamestown in the law office of Frank Mott—a figure in Democratic circles. Jackson spent a year (1911) at Albany Law School and then returned to his clerkship in Mott's office. He passed the bar in November of 1913. Accordingly, he is the last member of the Supreme Court to have qualified for the bar by "reading law" in an office rather than through graduation from law school. For the next twenty years, Jackson built and maintained a thriving and highly remunerative general practice. He married Irene Gerhardt on 24 April 1916.

Before he entered the practice of law, Jackson

*Howell Edmunds Jackson*

became enmeshed in politics as a Democratic state committeeman—a Democrat in a Republican area. Following Woodrow Wilson's victory in 1912, Jackson worked closely with Franklin D. *Roosevelt, then assistant secretary of the navy, on problems of federal patronage. With Roosevelt in the governor's chair from 1928 through 1932, Jackson again surfaced as an informal adviser. He stumped throughout New York for Roosevelt's presidential campaign in 1932 and then went to Washington in February 1934 as general counsel of the Bureau of Internal Revenue. After climbing up the ladder through various legal positions in the Treasury and later the Department of Justice, Roosevelt in 1938 named him *solicitor general.

Jackson in 1952 described his tenure as solicitor general as the happiest period of his public life. The litigation of the United States proceeded at an orderly pace and Jackson placed many important matters before the Court. At the time of Jackson's appointment to the solicitor generalship, Roosevelt had discussed with Jackson the possibility of a seat in the cabinet as attorney general or on the Supreme Court, but the two had decided it best to place Frank *Murphy as attorney general. Early in 1940, FDR moved Murphy from Justice to the Supreme Court and Jackson into the cabinet as attorney general. Jackson's tenure as attorney general proved brief.

Roosevelt in June 1941 named Jackson to the Supreme Court. Once again, FDR had dangled higher office—the chief justiceship—before Jackson and then decided to elevate Harlan F. *Stone. Contrary to the expectations of many observers, once on the Supreme Court Jackson did not coalesce with New Dealers such as William O. *Douglas; instead, he adopted a position of strong nationalism together with an attachment to *judicial self-restraint. During his tenure as associate justice, Jackson's judicial philosophy and voting behavior paralleled the moderate conservatism of Justice Felix *Frankfurter.

On the issue of federalism, a crucial one for the survival of the *New Deal, Jackson charted a course that firmly committed him to national over state power (see FEDERALISM). For example, in *Edwards v. California (1941), the Court invoked the federal *commerce power to strike down California's "Okie law." Jackson concurred and argued that the right of entry into any state is a "privilege" of U.S. *citizenship. "If national citizenship means less than this, it means nothing" (p. 183). In *Wickard v. Filburn (1942), Jackson wrote the majority opinion in which the Court upheld the Agricultural Adjustment Act of 1938 and thereby ended the last vestiges of *dual federalism.

Jackson showed a subtle understanding of the importance of the values in the *First Amendment. In *West Virginia Board of Education v. Barnette (1943), for example, he wrote for the majority in striking down a mandatory flag-

Robert Houghwout Jackson

salute; "if there is any fixed star in our constitutional constellation, it is that no official, high or petty, can prescribe what shall be orthodox in politics, nationalism, religion, or other matters of opinion" (p. 642). Much the same concern emerged in United States v. *Ballard (1944) in which he dissented from a decision to uphold a conviction on mail fraud against an offbeat religion: "I would dismiss the indictment and have done with this business of judicially examining other people's faiths" (p. 95).

During World War II, and especially after the Nuremberg Trials, Jackson began to see the need to balance freedom and public order. In *Terminiello v. Chicago (1949), in which the Court reversed a conviction for breach of peace, Jackson chided the majority for a "doctrinaire" view that might "convert the Bill of Rights into a suicide pact" (p. 37). Despite the threat to the First Amendment, Jackson supported federal measures to deal with domestic communism in cases such as *Dennis v. United States (1951) and *American Communications Association v. Douds (1950).

In May 1945, President Harry Truman asked Jackson to serve as chief counsel for the United States in the prosecution of Nazi war criminals. He encountered many difficulties at Nuremberg, but he and others amassed persuasive evidence against the defendants.

Jackson returned to the Court in the fall of 1946. In the meantime, Chief Justice Stone had died. At the death of Stone, rumors about successors swirled around Washington. The names of Jackson and Justice Hugo *Black figured prominently on this list. Allies of the two mobilized against each other. Ultimately, both Black and Jackson threatened to resign if the president nominated the other. This highly public controversy embarrassed Black and Jackson and the Court (see JACKSON-BLACK FEUD). President Truman instead chose Fred *Vinson as chief justice.

Near the end of the 1953 term, a serious heart attack felled Jackson. Nonetheless, he took part in *Brown v. Board of Education (1954). In the fall of 1954, he once again took his chair as the term began but he died a few days later.

□ Eugene Gerhart, America's Advocate: Robert H. Jackson (1958). Alfred E. Kelly, "Jackson, Robert Houghwout." In Dictionary of American Biography: Supplement Five, 1951–1955, edited by John A. Garraty (1977). Glendon Schubert, Dispassionate Justice: A Synthesis of the Judicial Opinions of Robert H. Jackson (1969).

Gregory A. Caldeira

**Jackson-Black Feud.** The Supreme Court's unique role of final constitutional umpire has depended in part on maintaining a public image of impartiality. Following Chief Justice Harlan F. *Stone's death in 1946, a bitter feud between Justices Hugo L. *Black and Robert H. *Jackson tested this image.

The feud had its origins with the debate among the liberal justices appointed by President Franklin D. *Roosevelt over the limits of *judicial self-restraint, particularly the interpretation of the Fair Labor Standards Act (FLSA) of 1938. One of the later New Deal's most controversial measures, the act established federal control of minimum wages and maximum hours for employees who produced goods for interstate trade.

In United States v. *Darby Lumber Co. (1941) the Court upheld FLSA unanimously. By 1944, however, Roosevelt's liberal justices were severely divided over whether the act should apply to the underground travel by miners to and from the "working face" of the mines. The War Labor Board had approved wage and hour contracts that followed employer's refusal to pay for travel from "portal to portal." At stake were millions of dollars in penalties and attorney's fees if the Court should suddenly construe FLSA on behalf of the miners.

Shaping the Court's approach to the FLSA controversy was the issue of disqualification. The tradition was that generally each member of the Court decided for himself whether or not some conflict of interest justified disqualification from a particular case. Against the background of a national coal strike, government seizure of the industry, and the War Labor Board's protracted negotiations, the Court reviewed Jewell Ridge Coal Corporation v. Local No. 6167, United Mine Workers of America (1945), which raised directly the question of portal-to-portal compensation. The Court split evenly, giving Black the deciding vote. The union's lawyer, however, was Crompton Harris, who twenty years before had been Black's law partner. In conference Jackson vehemently contended that the attorney's presence required

Black's disqualification. The Alabaman just as stridently refused. Jackson was especially upset because initially a majority was prepared to uphold the interests of the employer, and Chief Justice Stone had selected Jackson to write the Court's opinion. But Stanley *Reed switched to the opposing side, leaving the entire case in Black's hands. As a result, Frank *Murphy wrote the majority opinion, which interpreted FLSA broadly in favor of the miners.

Jackson wrote an opinion for four dissenters that quoted out of context statements Black had made when he was in the Senate during the debate over the Fair Labor Standards Bill, which seemed to contradict the Jewel Ridge decision. Black was incensed. Because of the Black-Harris connection, the Jewel Ridge Company petitioned the Court for a rehearing. The Court denied the petition, but Jackson remained convinced that Black had acted improperly. Before long Congress enacted legislation that overturned the Court's decision, vindicating Jackson and the other dissenters on the issue of policy. Jackson's anger toward Black, however, did not abate.

The Jewel Ridge Company's rehearing petition engendered public debate concerning the question of the Court's impartiality. But the level of tension the disqualification issue caused within the Court remained confidential until the following year, when Stone died. President Harry Truman nominated Frederick M. *Vinson, a loyal friend and capable politician, as *chief justice. By then Jackson was serving as chief prosecutor at the Nuremberg war crimes trials. During the congressional review of Vinson's nomination, Black temporarily took over the duties of chief justice. Jackson reacted to the news with a bitter public statement from Nuremberg disclaiming any interest in the position of *chief justice himself. Furthermore, he revealed the Jewel Ridge controversy, publicizing his feud with Black.

The revelation was motivated partially by Justice Felix *Frankfurter's private intimation (not based on fact) that Black had influenced Truman to block Jackson's nomination as chief justice, perhaps to attain the office himself. When making Jackson's appointment as associate justice in 1941 Roosevelt had apparently implied that he would be a prime candidate for the chief justiceship if it opened up in the future. As Jackson's angry Nuremberg statement made headlines, Truman exclaimed that the "Supreme Court has really made a mess of itself." When the Senate confirmed Vinson, Truman expressed confidence in his nominee's "uncanny knack of placating opposing minds." Even so, Black was conciliatory when Jackson returned from Nuremberg and a relative calm once more characterized the Court's internal deliberations. The Jackson-Black feud suggested, however, the degree to which personal tensions shaped the Court's resolution of vital issues. It indicated, too, that the public image of impartiality upon which that role rested was often tenuous.

(See also EXTRAJUDICIAL ACTIVITIES; RECUSE.)

□ Tony Freyer, *Hugo L. Black and the Dilemma of American Liberalism* (1990).                                    Tony Freyer

**Jackson v. Metropolitan Edison Co.,** 419 U.S. 345 (1974), argued 15 Oct. 1974, decided 23 Dec. 1974 by vote of 6 to 3; Rehnquist for the Court, Douglas, Brennan, and Marshall in dissent. In *Metropolitan Edison* the Supreme Court considered the issue of when private action is sufficiently public in nature that it becomes bound by constitutional provisions limiting governmental conduct. The case was brought by a resident of York, Pennsylvania, who claimed that Metropolitan Edison, a privately owned utility, violated her due process rights by terminating electric service without adequate notice and the chance for a hearing. The Supreme Court rejected the argument on the ground that the utility was a private entity and hence not bound by the Due Process Clause, which applies only to actions by the state (see DUE PROCESS, PROCEDURAL).

The Court over the years has attempted unsuccessfully to develop a workable test to determine when private action is so public in nature, or so infused with public regulation and direction, that it amounts to state action within the meaning of the Due Process Clause. In *Metropolitan Edison* the plaintiff pointed to the partial monopoly granted by the state, the extensive state regulation, and the essential nature of utility operations as evidence of the state character of the utility's actions. The Court, however, deemed this evidence insufficient to label the utility's conduct as *state action.

*Metropolitan Edison* remains good law on the state action issue, although it is one of many decisions that, taken together, provide confused guidance on the issue. The decision's practical effect for utilities has been altered by legislative enactments.                                    Eric T. Freyfogle

**Japanese Relocation.** See HIRABAYASHI V. UNITED STATES; KOREMATSU V. UNITED STATES; WORLD WAR II.

**Jay, John** (b. New York City, 12 December 1745; d. Bedford, Westchester County, N.Y., 17 May 1829; interred at Jay family churchyard, Rye, N.Y.), chief justice, 1789–1795. The eldest son of Peter and Mary (Van Cortlandt) Jay, John Jay was educated privately until matriculation at King's College (Columbia University), from which he graduated in 1764. He read law with attorney Benjamin Kissam; four years later, he was admitted to the New York bar. His law practice prospered. In 1774, he married Sarah Van Brugh Livingston, the daughter of New York governor William Livingston.

*John Jay*

The American Revolution altered Jay's career. A member of New York's Committee of Correspondence, he served in the First and Second Continental Congresses. As colonists edged toward rebellion, Jay opposed war with Britain. He was instrumental in formulating the Olive Branch Petition and seriously considered expatriation; however, after adoption of the *Declaration of Independence, his ambivalence dissipated. In 1776, Jay helped draft New York's constitution; and, while his attendance was erratic, he sat until 1779 as the state's chief justice. After 1778, national affairs occupied ever-larger portions of Jay's calendar. In late 1778, New Yorkers again sent him to Congress, where he was elected president; less than a year later, he became minister plenipotentiary to Spain and in 1782 one of the commissioners in Paris to negotiate a peace treaty with England.

When Jay returned to New York in July 1784, his future as a diplomat was assured; yet, when offered positions as minister to Britain and then to France, he demurred in favor of law practice. Within weeks, Jay was drafted by Congress to be secretary of foreign affairs, a post he retained until 1789. His early misgivings about the impotence of the confederation solidified. By 1784–1785, he became a vocal advocate of a coercive, departmentalized federal government with vigorous executive and judicial branches and a Congress capable of securing economic stability. He took great satisfaction in the move toward a strong federation. While Jay was prevented by illness from writing more than three *Federalist* essays, he gladly accepted President George *Washington's 1789 nomination as *chief justice.

When the Court convened in the New York

City Stock Exchange, Jay expected that its original and exclusive jurisdictions might be exploited to ensure the supremacy of federal law and to force state compliance with key obligations such as the war debts addressed in the Treaty of Peace. (See TREATIES AND TREATY POWERS.) He was disappointed. Jay's Court lacked legitimacy. Antifederalist antipathy toward the federal judiciary still carried weight; the justices' *circuit-riding duties eroded morale.

Still, Jay's contributions were substantial. In a 1792 New York circuit court hearing of *Hayburn's Case, he defended the *separation of powers by refusing to allow federal courts to pass judgment, as an Act of Congress mandated, on the claims of invalid pensioners. He made creative use of grand jury charges to educate the citizenry on the rudiments of federal governance. On two occasions, Jay wielded federal judicial power in defense of both the Treaty of Paris and American sovereignty in relations with Europe. His dissent on circuit in *Ware v. Hylton (1796) paved the way for High Court insistence upon adherence to treaty provisions in a 1796 appeal of the same case; and in Glass v. The Sloop Betsy (1794), the Jay Court ruled against France's use of its American consul as a prize court.

Jay finally concluded that the Court was an ineffective instrument of domestic unification and diplomacy. When Georgia responded to the Court's ruling against the state's claim of *sovereign immunity in *Chisholm v. Georgia (1793) with defiance and the introduction of the *Eleventh Amendment in Congress, Jay abandoned the federal bench. In 1794, while still sitting as chief justice, he sailed to England as envoy extraordinaire to defuse tensions with Britain over unpaid debts, sequestration of Loyalist estates, and New World trading rights. The Jay Treaty established mixed commissions to resolve economic disputes, granted trade concessions to Britain, and shifted responsibility for payment of defaulted loans to Congress. While resistance to the treaty was formidable, the Senate ratified it in 1795.

Elected governor of New York in absentia, Jay resigned as chief justice in 1795. When President John Adams asked him to resume his duties as chief justice in 1800, he refused on the ground that the Court lacked "energy, weight and dignity." Nor could he abide Jeffersonian America. In 1801, Jay retired to his farm in Westchester County, New York; despite ill health, he devoted the next quarter century to the Episcopal church and antislavery causes.

□ Richard Morris, John Jay, the Nation and the Court (1967). Sandra VanBurkleo, " 'Honour, Justice and Interest': John Jay's Republican Politics and Statesmanship on the Federal Bench," Journal of the Early Republic 4 (Fall 1984): 239–274.　　　　　　　　　Sandra F. VanBurkleo

**Jefferson, Thomas** (b. Shadwell [now Albemarle County], Va., 13 April 1743; d. Monticello, Va., 4 July 1826), statesman and president of the United States, 1801–1809. Thomas Jefferson exerted a profound influence on the Supreme Court and the course of American constitutional development. As political leader and president, his thoughts on the role of judges and on the federal system provided a significant contrast to the nationalizing ideas of Alexander *Hamilton, John *Marshall, and Joseph *Story.

Jefferson and James *Madison produced the Kentucky and Virginia Resolutions of 1798–1799, which supported the compact theory of the Constitution and denied that the Supreme Court alone had authority to determine if the laws of Congress were constitutional. Jefferson argued that the Court was a creation of the Constitution and to give it the power of *judicial review would make "its discretion and not the Constitution the measure of its powers." He argued that when the federal government assumed a power not granted to it by the Constitution, each state, as a party to the constitutional compact, had a right to declare the law unconstitutional (see STATE SOVEREIGNTY AND STATES' RIGHTS). He also believed that each branch of the federal government had a coordinate right to resolve questions of constitutionality.

As president, Jefferson confronted Federalist judges of the Supreme and *lower federal courts who enjoyed tenure during good behavior. He did not support radicals in his party who wished to amend the Constitution to eliminate the federal judiciary and who favored a broad construction of the impeachment clause of Articles I, II, and III in order to remove judges for political reasons (see IMPEACHMENT). But he resisted Federalist attempts to broaden the powers of the national courts and to politicize them. He promoted repeal of the *Judiciary Act of 1801, which had increased the number of federal judgeships and expanded the jurisdiction of the circuit courts. Jefferson did not overreact to the Court's decision in *Marbury v. Madison (1803), although he found Chief Justice Marshall's reproof distasteful. Rather, he ignored the decision because he had gotten his way: the Court did not order the administration to deliver the commissions. Though Marshall claimed for the Court the power to interpret the Constitution, he did not explicitly claim that its power to do so was either exclusive or final. Jefferson helped initiate impeachment proceedings in 1803 against John Pickering, an alcoholic and insane district court judge, and worked behind the scenes for his conviction. But he did not support impeachment proceedings against Justice Samuel *Chase, who was eventually acquitted in 1805. In the treason trial of Aaron *Burr (1806), Jefferson refused to obey Marshall's subpoena to testify but accepted Burr's acquittal.

After his retirement in 1809, Jefferson criticized Marshall and the Supreme Court more directly. He opposed such nationalist decisions as *Martin

v. *Hunter's Lessee* (1816), \**McCulloch* v. *Maryland* (1819) and \**Cohens* v. *Virginia* (1821). He encouraged Spencer Roane and John Taylor to criticize the Court publicly. In private correspondence, Jefferson raised a number of important questions about the Supreme Court's power. Could the Court claim to be the final arbiter in conflicts between the states and the federal government, since this power was not explicitly granted in the Constitution? Could the Supreme Court arrogate this power to itself? What is the relationship of the Court to the will of the people, especially since its members are appointed during good behavior? Should the Court hold its discussions in secret and hide internal dissent by handing down unanimous decisions? Could the Court be an impartial arbiter in disputes between the federal government and the states, since it was a part of the federal government and its judges' salaries were paid by that government?

These questions do not lend themselves to easy answers, even today when we generally accept the idea of judicial supremacy on constitutional issues. As a consequence, Jefferson's criticism of the Supreme Court has resonated throughout American history and has formed the theoretical basis of the positions taken by presidents such as Andrew *Jackson and Franklin *Roosevelt, as well as other critics of an activist Court, who have attempted to confine the force of its decisions (see JUDICIAL SELF-RESTRAINT).

(See also HISTORY OF THE COURT: ESTABLISHMENT OF THE UNION.)

□ Richard Ellis, *The Jeffersonian Crisis: Courts and Politics in the Young Republic* (1971).　　　Richard E. Ellis

**Jenner-Butler Bill,** one of the several measures introduced in the Fifty-seventh Congress by right-wing senators seeking to retaliate against the Supreme Court for decisions protecting the constitutional rights of persons charged with subversive activities (see SUBVERSION). One provision would have restored full investigative authority to congressional committees, which had been subjected to some limitations by the Court's 1957 decision in *Watkins* v. *United States* (see CONGRESSIONAL POWER OF INVESTIGATION). Another section would have restored full enforceability of *state sedition laws, which had been limited in *Pennsylvania* v. *Nelson* (1956). A third would have rehabilitated the *Smith Act, which made advocating overthrow of the government unlawful. This statute had been narrowly interpreted by the Court in *Yates* v. *United States* (1957).

The most serious constitutional issue posed by the Jenner-Butler bill, however, was its assertion of congressional authority over the appellate jurisdiction of the Supreme Court. The bill specified five areas where the Court's rulings had been challenged by conservative legislators and would have barred the Court from accepting or deciding

such cases in the future. Arguably, constitutional support for such power may be found in *Article III, section 2 of the Constitution and in a post–Civil War decision, *Ex parte *McCardle* (1869).

Any such limits on the Court's appellate jurisdiction, however, would have severely challenged the Court's independent status, and the Senate was reluctant to subordinate the Court's appellate jurisdiction to control by Congress. Under the astute management of the Senate majority leader, Lyndon Johnson, all provisions of the bill were defeated, by a vote of 49 to 41, on 20 August 1958.

(See also APPELLATE JURISDICTION; COMMUNISM AND COLD WAR; REVERSALS OF COURT DECISIONS BY CONGRESS.)　　　C. Herman Pritchett

**Johnson, Thomas** (b. Calvert County, Md., 4 Nov. 1732; d. Frederick, Md., 26 Oct. 1819; interred Mount Olivet Cemetery, Frederick), associate justice, 1791–1793. The son of Thomas and Dorcas (Sedgwick) Johnson, the young Thomas Johnson received basic education at home, worked as a clerk of the Provincial Court, and read law with attorney Stephen Bordley. Johnson was admitted to the Frederick County and Baltimore bars in 1760; six years later, he married Ann Jennings. At age twenty-nine, he was elected to the provincial assembly. Johnson attended the Maryland convention of 1774 as well as the First and Second Continental Congresses; in June 1775 he nominated George *Washington for the post of supreme commander of American military forces. Upon return to Annapolis in August, he helped draft the Association of the Freemen of Maryland, a declaration of rights.

*Thomas Johnson*

Johnson was valued less for charisma than for prudence and impressive learning. He missed the signing of the *Declaration of Independence in Philadelphia, but he supported the Declaration of the Delegates of Maryland on 6 July 1776 and aided in the framing of the state constitution. In early 1777, shortly after Johnson was called to the state militia as first brigadier-general, he was elected governor of Maryland. He was inaugurated on 21 March 1777. After three one-year terms, he returned to the assembly; there, he supported adoption of the Articles of Confederation. After the Paris Peace, Johnson and Washington formed the Potomack Company to expand the river trade. Johnson sat again in the state legislature from 1786 to 1788; during the ratification convention of 1788, he urged Marylanders to join the new federation.

Johnson then tried to withdraw from public life to pursue business ventures, but privacy eluded him. Between April 1790 and October 1791, while serving as chief judge of the General Court of Maryland, he chaired the Board of Commissioners of the Federal City—a group authorized to buy land and erect government buildings for what became the District of Columbia. On 5 August 1791 Washington temporarily commissioned Johnson an associate justice of the United States Supreme Court to replace John *Rutledge; despite serious misgivings about *circuit riding, he accepted. The Senate confirmed Washington's recess appointment on 7 November 1791; Johnson took the oath of office on 6 August 1792.

On circuit, Johnson sat on the initial trial of *Ware v. Hylton (1796), a suit involving debtors' responsibility for repayment of revolutionary war debts. At virtually the same moment, he wrote the Court's first opinion in Georgia v. Brailsford (1792), a suit in equity testing the state's right to sequester Loyalist property (see STATE SOVEREIGNTY AND STATES' RIGHTS). A majority granted Georgia's motion for a permanent *injunction against Brailsford's claim; in dissent, Johnson and Justice William *Cushing argued that the bill did not support a motion for an injunction in federal court because legal remedies had not been exhausted.

Failing health prompted Johnson's resignation from the Court on 16 January 1793. In retirement, Johnson participated actively in Frederick County politics and church affairs; when Washington died in December 1799, his old friend delivered a poignant funeral oration in Frederick. Although Johnson fought a losing battle with physical infirmity, his mind remained sharp. He died in his sleep at Rose Hill mansion; days before his death, he told a relative that his fondest wish was to "meet Washington beyond the grave."

□ Edward S. Delaplaine, Life of Thomas Jefferson (1927). Maeva Marcus and James R. Perry, eds., Documentary History of the Supreme Court of the United States, 1789–1800, vol. 1 (1985).                    Sandra F. VanBurkleo

**Johnson, William** (b. near Charleston in St. James Goose Creek Parish, S.C., 27 December 1771; d. Brooklyn, N.Y., 4 August 1834, interred St. Philips churchyard, Charleston, S.C.), associate justice, 1805–1833. The son of blacksmith William Johnson and Sarah (Nightingale) Johnson, William Johnson attended grammar school in Charleston, graduated from Princeton in 1790, read law with Charles C. Pinckney, and was admitted to the bar in 1793. At age 22, he was elected to the state house of representatives; in March 1794, he married the well-born Sarah Bennett. During Johnson's three terms in the assembly, he joined the Jeffersonian Republican camp, served as Cashier of the House, and, in 1798, became Speaker of the House. In December 1799, the assembly elevated Johnson to the Constitutional Court; three years later, President Thomas *Jefferson appointed him to the United States Supreme Court.

The thirty-three-year-old Johnson attracted controversy. In 1807, he enraged Republicans by relying on Chief Justice John *Marshall's anti-Jeffersonian *Marbury v. Madison opinion to protest the Supreme Court's grant of *mandamus in the treason trial of two accomplices of Aaron *Burr. A year later, in Johnson's first major circuit court opinion, he denied presidential authority to remove the Collector of the Port of Charleston for refusing to implement the administration's embargo policies. Shortly afterward, Attorney General Caesar Rodney told Jefferson that the Carolinian had been infected with "leprosy of the Bench."

But Rodney's diagnosis was premature. After 1812, Johnson grappled constantly with Joseph *Story. In U.S. v. *Hudson and Goodwin (1812),

*William Johnson*

Johnson refused to extend federal jurisdiction to criminal cases; Story wrote a stinging *dissent and pointedly disregarded *Hudson* on circuit. (See JUDICIAL POWER AND JURISDICTION; FEDERAL COMMON LAW.) In *Ramsay* v. *Allegre* (1827) and elsewhere, Johnson challenged attempts to expand *admiralty jurisdiction to inland waterways without constitutional amendment. He also took a dim view of corporate power. On circuit in *Bank of the United States* v. *Deveaux* (1809), Johnson denied the Bank's right to sue in federal court. In *McCulloch* v. *Maryland* (1819) and *Osborn* v. *Bank of the United States* (1824), he agreed that the elastic clause permitted creation of a federal bank; but, in *Osborn*, he also blasted Marshall's grant of *privileges and immunities to artificial persons.

Although Johnson resisted the aggressive use of executive discretion, he encouraged broad readings of congressional power when it constructively supplemented state legislative authority. He therefore concurred in *Martin* v. *Hunter's Lessee* (1816) and *Cherokee Nation* v. *Georgia* (1831; see CHEROKEE CASES); repudiated President James Monroe's veto of the Cumberland Road Act in 1822; and sketched his cautiously nationalist, freetrading philosophy in a separate concurring *Gibbons* v. *Ogden* opinion (1824).

The slaveholding Johnson opposed abolitionism as well as inhumane treatment of Africans (see SLAVERY). Between 1822 and 1824, he jeopardized his reputation at home by denouncing both antifederal sentiment in South Carolina and state denial of *due process to slave rebel Denmark Vesey. In his circuit court opinion in *Elkison* v. *Deliesseline* (1823), he invalidated South Carolina's Negro Seamen Act, which excluded free African-American traders from state ports; later, he opposed state *nullification of the Tariff of Abominations.

In *contract disputes, Johnson walked a fine line between antifederalism and prounionism. Because Marshall initially had altered contract opinions to reflect dissent, Johnson endorsed the majority view in *Dartmouth College* v. *Woodward* (1819) and *Sturges* v. *Crowninshield* (1819); but in 1823, he broke silence over the Court's decision to wield the *Contract Clause against state exercise of ordinary remedial powers. Johnson reluctantly endorsed Bushrod *Washington's invalidation of Kentucky's occupying claimant laws in *Green* v. *Biddle* (1823); yet his concurring opinion pointed not to the federal clause but to abridgments of *property rights protected by the Kentucky constitution and to denial of the right to *trial by jury in federal courts. He also denounced the Court's use of the federal clause to support speculators and restrain legislatures. Johnson's fear of excessive deference to "money men" underlay his seriatim opinion in *Ogden* v. *Saunders* (1827) in which he supported state prohibition of unremitting creditors' claims (see BANKRUPTCY AND INSOLVENCY LEGISLATION); yet, in the same case, he promoted economic union by drawing the line at state discharge of debtors from obligations to out-of-state creditors.

During his twenty-nine years on the federal bench, Johnson wrote 112 majority opinions, twenty-one concurrences, thirty-four dissents, and five seriatim opinions; only Marshall and Story produced more opinions. He was regularly vilified—by Federalists for his devotion to legislative energy, and by Jeffersonians for attacks on executive power and radical states' rights theory. Johnson was indeed a loose cannon. He viewed written opinions as occasions for experimentation. He freely admitted that he was impetuous and easily distracted by nonjudicial activities—among them, land speculation and a two-volume biography of Nathaniel Greene.

Still, Johnson's legacy was substantial. After 1819, he experienced a principled sea change, away from abstract decisions rooted in political theory and *natural law toward a community-centered, systematic jurisprudence capable of accommodating disparate conceptions of fairness without devolving into mere relativism. He therefore was an unwitting harbinger of Chief Justice Roger *Taney's *"dual federalism" and economic pragmatism. Johnson's death was unexpected. In July 1834, he traveled to New York for jaw surgery; shortly after the painful procedure, he died, apparently of "exhaustion."

☐ Donald G. Morgan, *Justice William Johnson, the First Dissenter: The Career and Constitutional Philosophy of a Jeffersonian Judge* (1954). Sandra F. VanBurkleo

**Johnson and Graham's Lessee v. McIntosh,** 8 Wheat. (21 U.S.) 543 (1823), argued 17 Feb. 1823, decided 10 Mar. 1823 by vote of 7 to 0; Marshall for the Court. This was the first Supreme Court case to define the legal relationship of *Native Americans to the United States. It began in 1775 when the Piankeshaws ceded land in Illinois to a group of speculators, including William Johnson. However, Virginia in 1783 conveyed to the federal government its Illinois claims for the public domain.

In 1818 William McIntosh bought from the United States 11,560 acres of Illinois land that were part of Johnson's purchase. These same lands were claimed by Joshua Johnson and his son, Thomas J. Graham, and they brought an ejectment action against McIntosh. After losing in the lower courts, Johnson and Graham appealed.

The Supreme Court, in a unanimous decision written by Chief Justice John *Marshall, found for McIntosh. Marshall held that the principle of discovery gave European nations an absolute right to New World lands. Once established, Native Americans had only a lesser right of occupancy that could be abolished. Marshall also found that the United States acquired title to Native American lands through Great Britain's conquest. He mistakenly declared that a conquered people's rights to property could not be applied to Native Americans because Indians were "fierce nomadic savages" (p. 590).

Thus, Indians could not transfer lands to individuals, such as William Johnson, or to nations other than the United States. Subsequent decisions of the Supreme Court eroded *McIntosh*, although this decision has yet to be specifically overruled.                              John R. Wunder

**Johnson v. Louisiana,** 400 U.S. 356 (1972), argued 1 Mar. 1971, reargued 10 Jan. 1972, decided 22 May 1972 by vote of 5 to 4; White for the Court, Blackmun and Powell concurring, Douglas, Brennan, Marshall, and Stewart in dissent. The issues in *Johnson*, and its companion case *Apodaca* v. *Oregon* (1972), which had been left unresolved by *Duncan* v. *Louisiana* (1968), were whether the *Fourteenth Amendment due process and equal protection clauses required states to observe *jury unanimity in criminal cases, as is required in the federal courts. A jury had convicted Johnson of robbery by a 9-to-3 vote. Since Johnson's trial began before *Duncan* was decided, and that ruling had not been applied retroactively, its *Sixth Amendment protections were not available.

Johnson contended that he had been denied due process because a non-unanimous verdict meant the reasonable-doubt standard of guilt had not been met. The fact that three jurors disagreed with the verdict indicated doubt, and the nine-person majority could not have voted conscientiously in favor of guilt beyond a reasonable doubt.

Justice Byron *White responded that it was an unsupported assumption that the jury majority would not weigh carefully the arguments of dissenting jurors. Reasonable doubt was not ignored merely because three jurors disagreed. "[The] fact remains," wrote White, "that nine jurors—a substantial majority of the jury—were convinced by the evidence" (p. 362). The doubts of three jurors were simply not enough to impeach the jury's decision.

Because Louisiana required unanimity in twelve-person juries hearing capital cases and in five-person juries in other serious crimes, Johnson also argued that the less-then-unanimous verdict in his case was a denial of *equal protection of the law. The Court, however, found nothing invidious in the varying jury classifications. Requiring the number of jurors who must be convinced beyond a reasonable doubt to increase with the seriousness of the crime and the severity of the punishment was a reasonable legislative judgment.

The several dissenters argued that the Sixth Amendment unanimity rule should be incorporated into the Fourteenth Amendment. Alternatively, they claimed that it was a fundamental due process right.

(See also DUE PROCESS, PROCEDURAL; TRIAL BY JURY.)
                                    Charles H. Sheldon

**Johnson v. Santa Clara County,** 480 U.S. 616 (1987), argued 12 Nov. 1986, decided 25 Mar. 1987 by vote of 6 to 3; Brennan for the Court, O'Connor and Stevens concurring, White, Scalia, and Rehnquist in dissent. This was the first case in which the Court decided the legality of sex-based voluntary *affirmative action under Title VII of the *Civil Rights Act of 1964. In *United Steelworkers of America* v. *Weber* (1979), the Court had held that Title VII does not prohibit voluntary race-conscious affirmative action where it is necessary "to eliminate conspicuous racial imbalance in traditionally segregated job categories" (p. 209). In *Johnson*, the Court expanded this concept to include voluntary sex-conscious affirmative action where it is necessary to eliminate a "manifest imbalance that reflect[s] underrepresentation of women in 'traditionally segregated job categories' " (p. 631).

In 1978, the Santa Clara County (California) Transportation Agency adopted a temporary affirmative action plan designed to take into account the sex or race of qualified applicants with regard to promotion within traditionally segregated job classifications in which both women and members of racial minorities had been underrepresented. The agency acknowledged that although women constituted 36.4 percent of the area's labor market, they constituted only 22.4 percent of the agency's work force and were concentrated in classifications that traditionally employed women: women accounted for 76 percent of the agency's office and clerical employees but 0 percent of its skilled craft workers. The affirmative action program did not set aside a specific number of jobs for minority members and women but established annual goals as guidelines in hiring and promotion for a "statistically measurable yearly improvement" so as to attain, eventually, "a work force whose composition reflected the proportion of minorities and women in the labor force" (pp. 621–622).

In 1979, a vacancy for the job of road dispatcher was announced. Of the 238 positions in the skilled craft classifications, which included the road dispatcher's position, none had ever been held by a woman. The agency passed over Johnson, a male employee certified as eligible for promotion, and gave the job to Joyce, the female applicant, who was also certified as eligible but who had a slightly lower interview score. Both were rated as well qualified.

The Supreme Court affirmed the decision of the *Court of Appeals for the Ninth Circuit and held that, pursuant to Title VII, the affirmative action plan was appropriate in permitting the agency to remedy the imbalance of men and women in skilled job classifications. The plan established flexible promotional goals, not rigid quotas, and while recognizing *gender to be one of several factors to be considered, it required women to compete for promotion with other qualified applicants. The Court noted that because the plan authorized the agency to select any one of the qualified applicants, Johnson had no absolute entitlement to promotion. The Court concluded that the plan "unsettled no legitimate firmly rooted expectation on the part of the petitioner" (p. 638). The Court also found that the plan was a temporary measure designed to achieve a balanced work force, was not intended to maintain a permanent sexual or racial balance, and did not impose a complete ban on male employees' opportunities for advancement. It held that such a plan would further the statutory goal of Title VII by encouraging voluntary efforts to eliminate gender discrimination.

The majority limited its interpretation to Title VII prohibitions and did not clarify the relationship between statutory and constitutional standards. Justice Sandra Day *O'Connor, writing separately, found the constitutional and statutory standards to be identical. In a vigorous dissent, Justice Antonin *Scalia stated that the decision was an "enormous expansion" intended to alter social standards and not merely a decision to eliminate discrimination. He also argued that *Weber* should be overruled.

*Johnson* was the first case in which the Court held that voluntary affirmative action is permissible under Title VII to overcome the effects of societal discrimination. *Johnson* also established that the legality of voluntary affirmative action as approved in *Weber* applied to sex discrimination and to Title VII claims in public sector employment.

(See also EMPLOYMENT DISCRIMINATION.)

Herbert Hill

**Johnson v. Zerbst,** 304 U.S. 458 (1938), argued 4 Apr. 1938, decided 23 May 1938 by vote of 6 to 2; Black for the Court, Reed concurring, McReynolds and Butler in dissent, Cardozo not participating. Johnson was convicted in federal court of feloniously possessing, uttering, and passing counterfeit money. At the time of trial, he was indigent and unable to employ an attorney to represent him. While imprisoned, he filed for habeas corpus relief in a federal district court, arguing that he had been deprived of his Sixth Amendment right to counsel. The district court denied his claim and the court of appeals affirmed.

The Supreme Court held that under the Sixth Amendment, the federal courts have no jurisdiction to deprive an accused of his life or liberty unless he has the assistance of counsel or the trial court clearly determines, on the record, that he has intelligently and competently waived his right to counsel. In effect, the Court required that counsel be appointed for indigent defendants in all federal criminal cases. Six years earlier in *Powell* v. *Alabama* (1932), the Court had issued a more limited ruling applying to state courts, holding that the *Fourteenth Amendment's *Due Process Clause required that counsel be appointed in state courts when the defendant was charged with a capital offense and was incapable of making his own defense. The right to counsel in state courts was later expanded in *Gideon* v. *Wainwright* (1963) and *Argersinger* v. *Hamlin* (1972).

(See also COUNSEL, RIGHT TO; SIXTH AMENDMENT.)

Susan E. Lawrence

**Joint Anti-Fascist Refugee Committee v. McGrath,** 341 U.S. 123 (1951), argued 11 Oct. 1950, decided 30 Apr. 1951 by vote of 5 to 3; Burton for the Court; Vinson, Reed, and Minton in dissent; Clark not participating. The Court handed down this surprising ruling at the height of cold war hysteria over domestic communism. It ruled on *common law and constitutional grounds against the manner in which groups had been placed on the attorney general's list of subversive organizations. That list, created by President Harry S. Truman's Executive Order no. 9835 of 20 March 1948, included seventy-eight allegedly subversive organizations, falling into six categories. There was no requirement that the attorney general hold hearings before listing a group nor any provision for appeal from, or *judicial review of, his decisions. Public officials and private citizens used the list extensively to pillory, intimidate, and ostracize radicals and other dissidents. Three of the groups included on the list, the Joint Anti-Fascist Refugee Committee, the National Council of American-Soviet Friendship, and the International Workers Order, objected to being characterized as disloyal and filed suit seeking to have their names removed from the list. A federal district court dismissed their complaint; a divided court of appeals affirmed its ruling. The Supreme Court reversed, taking the position that listing the three organizations without affording them a hearing violated their constitutional rights. Because each member of the five-justice majority wrote his own opinion, the Court's decision lacked a coherent rationale.

(See also ASSEMBLY AND ASSOCIATION, FREEDOM OF; COMMUNISM AND COLD WAR.)

Michal R. Belknap

**Jones v. Alfred H. Mayer Co.,** 392 U.S. 409 (1968), argued 1–2 Apr. 1968, decided 17 June 1968 by vote of 7 to 2; Stewart for the Court, Harlan and White in dissent. This case established Congress's power under the *Thirteenth Amendment to legislate against private racial discrimination. It thus limited the *Civil Rights Cases* (1883) holding that Congress lacked the power to reach private racial discrimination and became an important influence on the modern era of civil rights legislation.

Jones alleged that private defendants refused to sell him a home because he was black. He brought an action under a surviving remnant of the Civil Rights Act of 1866 (now Title 42, section 1982 of the U.S. Code) that grants all citizens the same right to purchase property. Section 1982 plainly invalidated nineteenth-century southern states' black codes limiting blacks' power to own or lease property. The question in *Jones* was whether the statute also reached private individual discriminatory acts. Justice Potter *Stewart's opinion for the Court provided a questionable analysis of section 1982's text and legislative history and held that section 1982 reaches private behavior. Justice John M. *Harlan's dissent noted that the Court's interpretation of section 1982 made that statute a broad fair housing law, announced by the Court only months after Congress enacted the Civil Rights Act of 1968, which contained a more detailed fair housing law.

Congress's power to enact laws prohibiting private racial discrimination under the *Fourteenth Amendment is unclear, as suggested by the confusing array of opinions in *United States* v. *Guest* (1966). *Jones* avoided addressing the Fourteenth Amendment power question by finding congressional power under the Thirteenth Amendment. It thus supplied a powerful new basis for federal race discrimination legislation. In the *Civil Rights Cases*, the Court had indicated that, under the Thirteenth Amendment, Congress may outlaw not only *slavery itself but all badges or incidents of slavery as well. But it narrowly construed what those badges or incidents of slavery were and Congress's power to define them. It invalidated the Civil Rights Act of 1875, which prohibited discrimination in public accommodations, stating, "It would be running the slavery argument into the ground" (p. 24) to apply it to all private discriminatory acts in the area of public accommodations. In *Jones*, the Court more generously interpreted Congress's power to assess what social conditions might be badges or incidents of slavery and sustained applying section 1982 to private behavior.

*Jones* established the foundation for the later holding in *Runyon* v. *McCrary* (1976) that Title 42, section 1981 of the U.S. Code, a companion provision to section 1982, reaches private discrimination in *contracts. Together, *Jones* and *Runyon* establish sections 1981 and 1982 as broad federal antidiscrimination provisions covering most contractual and property relationships. *Jones's* questionable foundations reemerged in *Runyon*, when Justices *White, *Rehnquist, and *Stevens voiced doubts about its correctness, and again thirteen years later in *Patterson* v. *McLean Credit Union* (1989). By the time *Patterson* arose, President Ronald *Reagan's appointees to the Court had changed its receptivity to civil rights litigation. In *Patterson*, the Court took the unusual step of ordering the parties, on its own motion, to reargue the case and to address a question

neither party had raised—whether *Runyon* had been correctly decided. Following reargument, the Court's *Patterson* opinion left *Runyon* technically intact. But *Patterson* severely limited *Runyon* and section 1981 by holding that it protects only the initial decision to contract and not post-contractual behavior. The limiting interpretation probably is as attributable to lingering discontent with *Jones* as it is to doubts about *Runyon* itself.

Whatever doubts members of the Court have had about *Jones* and *Runyon*, Congress has never modified *Jones's* generous interpretation of section 1982 and *Runyon's* interpretation of section 1981. Congress's most important response to the Court was the *Civil Rights Act of 1991, which overruled *Patterson* by interpreting section 1981 to include post-contractual behavior.

(See also HOUSING DISCRIMINATION; PROPERTY RIGHTS; RACE AND RACISM.)

□ Charles Fairman, *History of the Supreme Court of the United States*, vol. 6, *Reconstruction and Reunion, 1864–88: Part One* (1971). Theodore Eisenberg

**Jones v. Van Zandt,** 5 How. (46 U.S.) 215 (1847), submitted on printed argument 1 Feb. 1847 and decided 5 Mar. 1847 by vote of 9 to 0; Woodbury for the Court. *Jones* v. *Van Zandt* presented abolitionists with their first opportunity to mount a direct legal challenge to the constitutionality of the Fugitive Slave Act of 1793. A conductor of the Underground Railroad was exposed to civil liability under the act for harboring a fugitive. Salmon P. *Chase, then in private practice, contended in argument that the statute was unconstitutional because: (1) the federal government lacked power to support *slavery; (2) slavery was incompatible with the *Declaration of Independence and contrary to "natural right"; (3) the statute violated various provisions of the *Bill of Rights, including the *Due Process Clause of the *Fifth Amendment; and (4) the Fugitive Slave Clause of Article IV, section 2 of the Constitution was merely an interstate compact giving no power of enforcement to Congress.

Justice Levi *Woodbury for the Court spurned these arguments. He stated that the legitimacy of slavery was a *political question for the states to resolve, and that the Fugitive Slave Clause was "one of [the] sacred compromises" of the Constitution (p. 231). Whatever a judge's views of the morality or policy of slavery, Woodbury went on, he was bound to uphold the Constitution and statutes as he found them and could not refuse to enforce them because of their conflict with moral obligation. As Justice Joseph *Story had before him in *Prigg* v. *Pennsylvania* (1842), Woodbury upheld the constitutionality of the 1793 statute. *Jones* therefore was one in an unbroken line of proslavery decisions of the antebellum Court.

(See also FUGITIVE SLAVES.)

William M. Wiecek

**Judicial Activism,** the charge that judges are going beyond their appropriate powers and engaging in making law and not merely interpreting it. Against this position is placed the ideal of judicial restraint, which counsels judges to resist the temptation to influence public policy through their decisions and decrees.

Judicial activism is not prisoner to any particular ideological or political viewpoint; it can be conservative as well as liberal. A long period of American history was characterized by conservative judicial activism, by a Supreme Court unwilling to allow the states or Congress to pass legislation that would regulate social or economic affairs. Typically such legislation—laws governing child *labor, workers' hours, and so forth—would be invalidated as violations of the Constitution's *Commerce Clause or *Contracts Clause or of the judicially created doctrine of "liberty of contract" under the Due Process Clause of the *Fourteenth Amendment (see CONTRACT, FREEDOM OF). The best-known example of conservative judicial activism is *Lochner v. New York (1905), a case in which the Court invalidated New York's law regulating the hours bakers could work as a violation of "liberty of contract," a part of the doctrine of substantive *due process under the Fourteenth Amendment.

More recently the Court has been subject to criticism that it is engaging in liberal activism. This has been especially the case since the advent of the Warren Court and the revolution that it wrought in civil liberties; but the charge has continued through the Burger Court and into the Rehnquist Court. The argument is that in the name of expanding the "rights" a majority of the justices find agreeable, the Court is twisting the Constitution by disregarding the original meaning of the due process and *equal protection clauses in order to reach desired results (see ORIGINAL INTENT). Probably the best-known example of liberal activism is *Roe v. Wade (1973), in which the Court struck down restrictive *abortion laws as violating the "right to *privacy" it had previously found inherent in the Due Process Clause of the Fourteenth Amendment.

What practitioners of liberal and conservative activism have in common is their willingness, at least as perceived by their opponents, to abandon the literal words of the Constitution in pursuit of what the Supreme Court considers to be the just or right or reasonable course of action, whether that be the right of employers to set whatever conditions they see fit for their employees or the right of a woman to abort a fetus. In both instances critics of judicial activism charge that such decisions are properly left under the Constitution to the legislative power of the states.

The distinction between judicial activism and judicial restraint is closely related to the distinction between *interpretivism and noninterpretivism and the question of whether it is ever appropriate for judges to import new meaning into the old words of the Constitution.

A campaign against judicial activism became a hallmark of presidencies as ideologically diverse as those of Franklin D. *Roosevelt, Richard M. *Nixon, and Ronald *Reagan.

(See also CONSTITUTIONAL INTERPRETATION; JUDICIAL SELF-RESTRAINT.)

□ Raoul Berger, *Government by Judiciary* (1977). Alexander M. Bickel, *The Least Dangerous Branch* (1962).
Gary McDowell

**Judicial Conference of the United States.** See ADMINISTRATION OF FEDERAL COURTS.

**Judicial Ethics.** Rules of judicial ethics address three aspects of judicial conduct. The first is a judge's conduct as a judge. The second is the circumstances in which a judge should refrain from participating in a case, the problem of *recusal. The third is the proper scope of a judge's nonjudicial activities. The rules and principles governing judicial ethics arise from custom and tradition; the constitutional guarantee of due process (see DUE PROCESS, PROCEDURAL); statutory provisions enacted by Congress; and rules adopted by the judiciary for its own governance. In general, justices of the Supreme Court are bound by the same principles of judicial ethics that govern judges of *lower federal courts and *state courts.

These basic principles are formulated as rules in the Code of Judicial Conduct, recommended by the American Bar Association and promulgated in 1972. Although the Code of Judicial Conduct does not govern the Supreme Court, its provisions reflect custom and the *common law and by implication are applicable to the members of the Supreme Court.

According to these principles, in performing official functions a judge should be diligent, attentive to the contentions made by the parties, intellectually honest, and courteous in dealings with litigants, attorneys, and fellow judges.

Another basic principle requires that a judge not participate in a case in which he has been personally involved, or has a financial interest, or with respect to which his impartiality might reasonably be questioned. This standard for recusal is codified in a federal statute that applies to Supreme Court justices as well as to other federal judges. In *Liljeberg* v. *Health Services Acquisition Corp* (1988) the Supreme Court held that a federal district judge should have disqualified himself when he was a trustee of a hospital that might have indirectly benefitted from his decision.

Constitutional decisions also establish that a judge should not participate in a case in which he has a direct interest. In *Aetna Life Insurance Co.* v. *Lavoie* (1986), the Court ruled that participation by a state supreme court justice in a case when he was a party to other pending litigation involving an identical legal issue violated the Due Process Clause of the *Fourteenth Amendment. This principle would apply to a Supreme Court justice as well. Direct interest includes a financial interest, prior involvement in the matter as a lawyer or other participant, and close family relationship to the litigants. The statute goes further and requires recusal when the federal judge has any relationship that reasonably indicates possible bias.

As for nonjudicial activities of judges, the understood principles have become much stricter since 1970. In earlier years various members of the Supreme Court participated behind the scenes in government and public affairs. For example, Chief Justice William Howard *Taft was actively involved in many controversial issues, not limited to those affecting the federal court system. Justice Felix *Frankfurter gave advice to President Franklin *Roosevelt and regularly discussed affairs of state with his friend Dean Acheson. Chief Justice Earl *Warren was chair of a commission that investigated the assassination of President John Kennedy, and Justice Abe *Fortas was a regular confidant of President Lyndon Johnson. Activities such as these are now regarded as improper. Justices of the Supreme Court may lecture and participate in discussions of legal topics of general interest and express views on matters affecting the federal courts. Otherwise they are expected to limit their nonjudicial activity to purely personal matters.

The unique aspect of judicial ethics of Supreme Court justices is not the substance of the governing principles but the manner of their enforcement. The conduct of judges of other courts may be challenged before a higher court. In contrast, the propriety of the conduct of a Supreme Court justice is regulated almost entirely by each justice individually. However, public criticism has been an effective influence toward conformity. Justice Fortas was induced to resign largely as a result of publicity given to his receipt of fee payments from a private client while on the bench (see FORTAS RESIGNATION).

The only written opinion in which a justice has addressed the propriety of his own conduct is by Justice William *Rehnquist in Laird v. Tatum (1972). Before his appointment to the Supreme Court, Justice Rehnquist had been in a position of responsibility in the Justice Department concerning the transaction that resulted in the Laird litigation. The sufficiency of Justice Rehnquist's decision that he could properly participate in the Supreme Court's decision was severely questioned in connection with his appointment as chief justice. In general, however, self-surveillance has proved adequate.

(See also EXTRAJUDICIAL ACTIVITIES; JACKSON-BLACK FEUD.)

□ John Leubsdorf, "Theories of Judging and Judicial Disqualification," New York University Law Review 62 (1987): 237–292.  Geoffrey C. Hazard, Jr.

**Judicial Immunity from Civil Damages.** The immunity of judges from civil damages for their official acts dates from the beginning of the sixteenth century and is well established in the *common law and in American precedents. The U.S. Supreme Court ruled in Randall v. Brigham (1869), that private persons may not sue judges for their judicial acts however injurious or deserving of condemnation those acts may be. Three years later, in Bradley v. Fisher (1872), the Court stated that immunity was a "general" principle of the "highest importance" (p. 347).

The Court that ruled in Bradley immunized malicious and corrupt actions unless they were done in the "clear absence of all jurisdiction" (p. 351). The court adopted this interpretation because judges' determinations about their jurisdiction are extremely difficult matters; therefore, jurisdiction should be broadly construed lest judges incur unfair liability. A modern case, Stump v. Sparkman (1978) graphically exemplifies the scope of judicial immunity today. Stump held that the signature of a judge of a state court of general jurisdiction on a mother's petition to sterilize her fifteen-year-old daughter was a judicial act, even though the petition received no docket number, was not filed in the clerk's office, and was approved in an *ex parte proceeding without notice to the minor or the appointment of a guardian ad litem. The Supreme Court majority conceded the absence of any state law or precedent authorizing the judge's act but held that the absence of any Indiana statute or case law prohibiting the judge's action immunized his obviously wrongful act. Stump also reaffirmed an earlier holding that judicial immunity applies to civil rights suits. Here the minor, who had been told she was operated on for appendicitis, found herself unable to become pregnant following her marriage and thereupon discovered that she had been sterilized.

In Pulliam v. Allen (1984), however, the Supreme Court ruled that judicial immunity neither bars prospective injunctive relief against judicial officers acting in their official capacity nor the award of attorneys' fees under the Civil Rights Attorney's Fees Awards Act. A Virginia magistrate had jailed two men—one for fourteen days, and the other four times for periods of two to six days—for failure to post bond following their arrest for abusive and insulting language and public drunkenness, for which they could not receive a jail sentence. The men brought a lawsuit against the judge and successfully obtained a federal court ruling that it was unconstitutional for a judge to require bail for nonjailable offenses. An injunction forbidding continuation of that practice was also granted. The same court

456 □ Judicial Improvements and Access to Justice Act

awarded them several thousand dollars in costs and attorneys' fees.

Efforts by the Conference of State Chief Justices, the Judicial Conference of the United States, and the American Bar Association to persuade Congress to overturn the *Pulliam* decision and restore full judicial immunity did not succeed during the 1980s. The *American Civil Liberties Union and the *Legal Defense Fund, Inc., have spearheaded opposition to such efforts.

(See also SOVEREIGN IMMUNITY.)

Harold J. Spaeth

**Judicial Improvements and Access to Justice Act.** Enacted in 1988, its major provision increases the jurisdictional amount for a federal court to hear a diversity of citizenship case from ten thousand to fifty thousand dollars. The provision effected a compromise between those who sought abolition of diversity jurisdiction and those content with the status quo. A secondary provision prevents plaintiffs from appointing nonresidents to represent decedents, infants, or incompetents. Such representatives will be deemed citizens of the state of the represented person.

Abolitionists have argued that reduction in burgeoning federal dockets may best be achieved by revoking the diversity jurisdiction of the federal courts. They allege that the framers' fear, when the Constitution was drafted, that *state courts would be biased against out-of-state litigants is no longer justified. Abolitionists have also argued that forum shopping by plaintiffs should not extend to the federal courts and that inasmuch as diversity disputes invariably concern matters—*tort, *contract, and commercial transactions—on which the state, but not the federal, courts are expert, they ought to be resolved there. Those supporting retention of diversity jurisdiction argue that parochialism continues to afflict the state courts and that justice is better served by providing litigants a choice of forums.

Whether the act will reduce federal caseloads remains a matter of dispute. Unless the amount in controversy is a sum certain, as when one is suing on a note, a skillfully drafted complaint should be able to allege credibly damages exceeding fifty thousand dollars in almost all diversity cases.

(See also DIVERSITY JURISDICTION; JUDICIAL POWER AND JURISDICTION.)

Harold J. Spaeth

**Judicial Power and Jurisdiction.** In a famous lecture delivered in 1942 Judge Learned *Hand said, "A constitution is primarily an instrument to distribute political power." In any system of government judicial power—the power to interpret and apply the law—is political power. American experience confirms this general proposition

in its strongest form. In addition to applying the law's generalities to particular cases, American judges exercise major responsibility for shaping substantive public policies and even the structures of government. The title of Hand's lecture, "The Contribution of an Independent Judiciary to Civilization," was only a mild exaggeration.

The framers of the Constitution gave political power to federal judges when they established the "judicial power of the United States" in *Article III. Today that phrase is a term of art, describing the outer boundaries of the jurisdiction—the power to decide—that Congress can confer on the Supreme Court and the *lower federal courts, which together comprise the core of the federal judiciary. For the framers, however, the crucial purpose of Article III was not limitation but empowerment: to ensure that the newly created judiciary would have a power of decision commensurate with the legislative powers of Congress. The framers did not mean to displace the *state courts, and they established limitations on the work federal judges would do. Mainly, though, they sought to provide a judicial mechanism for enforcing the laws that would emerge from the new national government.

Three ways of looking at the "judicial power of the United States" will aid understanding of the development of the legal doctrines governing the jurisdiction of the federal courts and of those courts' role in the system of government. All three perspectives are suggested in the language of the Constitution. First, the phrase describes a power assigned to courts, as opposed to other organs of government. Second, the term describes a power of the national government, as opposed to the states. Third, the power in question is one of the powers of governance allocated by the Constitution, a power to affect the substantive policies enforced in the name of the United States—in short, a political power.

*The Power of Judges.* Historians debate whether the Constitution's framers anticipated that the courts would exercise the power of *judicial review, that is, the power to hold laws and other governmental actions unconstitutional. Unquestionably, however, the framers were determined to assure the federal judiciary independence from the executive and legislative branches. The Constitution thus guarantees that the judges will hold their offices "during good Behaviour" (i.e., for life), and protects them against decreases in their salaries. Once the Supreme Court, under Chief Justice John *Marshall, had firmly established the power of judicial review, this independence from the other branches could be seen as a necessary condition of the American version of the rule of law. In the modern era this necessity came into bold relief after the Supreme Court decided *Brown v. Board of Education* (1954, 1955) and federal judges throughout the South carried out the constitutional imperative of desegregating public schools in the face of virulent political opposition (see also DESEGREGATION REMEDIES).

At the Constitutional Convention of 1787 the delegates were of one mind about the necessity of a Supreme Court. Such a court was needed, for example, to decide cases that might grow out of conflicts among the states. Furthermore, the legislative powers of the new national government would apply directly to the people, without any need to use the state governments as intermediaries. The Supreme Court was needed to maintain the uniformity and supremacy of federal law.

The delegates were divided, however, on the question whether the Constitution should create lower federal courts. They compromised, leaving that decision to Congress: Article III vests the judicial power in "one Supreme Court, and such inferior courts as the Congress may from time to time ordain and establish." When the First Congress met in 1789, it enacted the first Judiciary Act, establishing a system of federal trial courts. It gave the Supreme Court *appellate jurisdiction over those courts' decisions in civil cases and over state courts' decisions based on determinations of federal law (see JUDICIARY ACT OF 1789). Most commentators today agree that Congress retains the constitutional power to abolish the lower federal courts altogether—but no one has any idea how the government might carry on the business of governing without those courts to enforce its law. The judicial power of the United States has become an essential part of modern government, and the federal courts have become, in the words of Felix *Frankfurter, the nation's "primary and powerful reliances for vindicating every right given by the Constitution, the laws, and the treaties of the United States" (Frankfurter and Landis, 1927, p. 65).

In defining the judicial power, the Constitution specifies nine kinds of *cases and controversies that can be decided by the federal judiciary. These fall into two main categories: those defined according to their parties, and those defined according to their subject matter. The party-oriented category includes, most notably, controversies in which the United States is a party, in which the contending parties are different states, and in which the parties are citizens of different states (*"diversity of citizenship" jurisdiction). The subject-matter category includes cases arising under the Constitution or federal statutes or treaties (*"federal question" jurisdiction) as well as cases arising under *admiralty and maritime law. Within these limits, Congress may or may not choose to confer jurisdiction on the federal courts.

This constitutional framework offers two general ways in which the jurisdiction of the federal courts can be made to expand or contract. First, the Supreme Court itself may give a broadening or a narrowing interpretation to Article III's definition of the judicial power. Second, within the constitutional limits, Congress may by statute augment or diminish the courts' jurisdiction. Because judicial power is political power it is unsurprising that both the Supreme Court and Congress have expanded and contracted the federal courts' jurisdiction with substantive policies in mind.

The power to declare laws unconstitutional, and thus to refuse to enforce them, is not an obviously judicial function. When the Marshall Court asserted this power in *Marbury v. Madison (1803), however, the chief political opposition focused not on the principle of judicial review but on Marshall's intimations along other lines. Jeffersonians thought they saw in the Court's opinion a claim of broad judicial power to intrude into decisions that properly belonged within the executive branch. Marshall himself disclaimed any such ambitions and in so doing invented a principle that today is called the *political question doctrine. The essence of that doctrine is that some issues lie beyond the courts' jurisdiction because they fall within the exclusive domain of the political branches, that is, the president or Congress. The theoretical base for the political question doctrine is the specification, in Article III, of the cases and controversies that lie within the judicial power; a political question is one that the courts see as presenting something other than a judicial case or controversy.

In this century the territory reserved to the political branches has diminished somewhat, but the political question doctrine remains strong in fields such as *foreign affairs and Congress's control over the *constitutional amending process. Of far greater importance among the judicially created doctrines limiting the federal courts' jurisdiction are several other rules the Supreme Court has derived from Article III's references to cases and controversies: the doctrines of *standing, *ripeness, and *mootness. All these doctrines, the Court commonly says, are designed to ensure that the courts decide only issues whose resolution will affect the rights of persons in court and whose contours are well defined by facts that are concrete and by disputes that are real. The federal courts lack power to give *advisory opinions, that is, general statements about the law that are not attached to the decision of cases. Concrete facts and real harms illuminate a court's understanding of issues, and the doctrines of standing, ripeness, and mootness promote efficiency in judging, an efficiency that is especially valued when the courts are exercising the power of judicial review.

Just beneath the surface of this reasoning, however, lies a more important concern about the relation of the judiciary to the other branches. In the Marbury opinion Marshall defended judicial review by arguing that the essence of a court's function was to decide cases (and to do so according to law). The Court was ruling on the constitutionality of legislation not because it had a general commission to oversee Congress's legislative behavior but because the Constitution was law. By tying the courts' power of constitutional interpretation to their power to decide cases, Marshall founded the legitimacy of judicial review on its connection to that case-deciding function.

Ripeness and mootness are, in a sense, matters of timing. A federal court will dismiss a case for want of ripeness when the interests of the parties have not yet come into conflict in a way that gives the case sufficient concreteness to allow the court to understand the interests at stake or the legal issues raised. As the metaphor of ripening suggests, such a case may eventually be considered ready for decision, once additional facts have sharpened the contours of the dispute. A case becomes moot—and must be dismissed—when the decision of the case no longer can affect the parties' interests, the idea being that deciding a dispute that no longer exists would amount to giving an advisory opinion.

More important than the doctrines of ripeness and mootness in limiting the federal courts' jurisdiction is the other main branch of the cases and controversies requirement, the doctrine of standing. Here the concern is not the timing of the case but the identity of the parties seeking judicial relief. In general, when government officials act, only someone who is personally injured by those acts has standing to complain that they are unlawful. Generally a plaintiff does not satisfy the requirement of standing by alleging that governmental action was unconstitutional, if the only harm alleged has been caused to someone else or if the illegality in question is only a violation of some other person's legal right. Under the Supreme Court's present reading of the doctrine, there is no such thing as "citizen standing," that is, standing to challenge governmental action just because it is illegal.

Although the Supreme Court differentiates between requirements that flow from Article III and those that are matters of judicial prudence, all these doctrines have been made by judges. Still, the Court has made clear that Congress also has a role in defining their scope. In the Declaratory Judgments Act (1934), for example, Congress authorized suit in federal courts in a number of instances that would previously have failed the test of ripeness. The Supreme Court upheld the law, limiting its application to cases in which the dispute, even though not far advanced, was likely to generate a factual record concrete enough to inform the courts about the legal issues involved. In the Administrative Procedure Act (1946) Congress relaxed the law of standing by authorizing judicial review of actions of federal administrators at the behest of persons who were injured by those actions, even though the plaintiffs were asserting the legal rights of others who were not in court.

These two acts of Congress—one enacted in the early days of the *New Deal and the other

enacted in reaction to the New Deal—can be seen as efforts to adapt federal court jurisdiction to the complexity of modern social organization and the modern administrative state. The need to relax the rigors of the cases or controversies limitation became even more obvious during the years of Earl *Warren's chief justiceship (1953–1969), when the Court enlarged its interpretations of substantive constitutional rights in areas such as civil rights, criminal justice, freedom of expression, and legislative apportionment. These rulings not only increased the volume of constitutional litigation in the federal courts but also expanded the boundaries that had confined federal jurisdiction.

Most of these doctrinal changes occurred during the last six years of the Warren Court. Previously the question of standing, for example, tended to be asked in general terms: was the plaintiff asserting a legally protected interest? This formulation worked to the disadvantage of a plaintiff who was trying to get the courts to expand their definition of legal interests in order to recognize new claims. In such a case the natural inclination of a judge would be to deny standing on the ground that the plaintiff's claim did not fit into a category of legal interests already recognized. The jurisdictional issue of standing is normally raised at the outset of a lawsuit, and it would be awkward to recognize a new legal interest before the facts of the case had been explored. By 1970 the Supreme Court was beginning to say that the bedrock of standing—the showing needed to satisfy the cases and controversies requirement—was "injury in fact" to the plaintiff. For lawyers seeking to expand the reach of constitutional rights, this view had the advantage of divorcing the question of standing from the question of the plaintiff's legal rights.

In the 1970s the Court also began to relax the rigors of the mootness barrier. A *class action— for example, a school desegregation case brought by a few students on behalf of all the African-American children in a school district—would, in the traditional theory, become moot as the named plaintiffs were graduated from the school system. Nonetheless, the Court has held that such a case is not moot if it continues to present a live controversy between the school board and some members of the plaintiff class. Furthermore, the Court has held that a case, otherwise moot, will not be dismissed if the governmental action in question is capable of being repeated, but— owing to the time required to carry a lawsuit through all its stages, including appeals—might escape judicial review if the action were dismissed. On this theory the plaintiff in the *abortion case of *Roe v. Wade (1973) was allowed to continue litigating even though she had already had her baby by the time the Supreme Court heard her case.

These developments in jurisdictional doctrine are representative of the emergence of what

Abram Chayes has called "public law litigation." In the traditional *common-law model of a lawsuit there is one plaintiff and one defendant; the plaintiff personally initiates the lawsuit, and on both sides the parties control the conduct of the case; the parties' dispute concerns legal obligations founded on facts in the past; the remedies requested are closely fitted to the specific rights of the plaintiff; and the case culminates in a single trial and a single judgment. If, however, a class of plaintiffs sues a governmental institution such as a school board or the managers of a state hospital or prison, the lawsuit is likely to diverge from the common-law model. Public-interest lawyers may invent the lawsuit and then go out to find some plaintiffs. Under liberal rules allowing other parties to intervene, the dispute may become multisided, as where parents opposed to busing intervene as parties in a school desegregation case. The plaintiffs may be seeking remedies that will reform the structure of an institution. After the court initially decides the case, it may retain jurisdiction over a long period while this structural reform is going on—for example, while a hospital revises its methods of dealing with mentally ill patients. During this time, there may be more hearings and more fact-finding investigations, for example, to determine whether a school board is making sufficient progress toward desegregation. The whole process has a "legislative" or even "administrative" look. The interests of the particular parties in whose name the suit was filed seem secondary.

In view of these changes, Chief Justice William H. *Rehnquist suggested in 1988 that the Court abandon its pretense that the mootness doctrine was constitutionally compelled and recognize candidly that the doctrine was invoked as a matter of judicial prudence. Rehnquist has taken no such stance toward the doctrine of standing. He has, in fact, played a leading role in transforming the jurisdictional import of "injury in fact"; what began as a means of access to court is now a barrier to entry. Rehnquist has been a leader in the Court's recent restrictions on federal court jurisdiction and has also led the Court's efforts to contain and then contract a number of the substantive constitutional developments of the Warren era. These developments have greatly restricted the role of federal judges in the process of government—a result consistent with the explicit political agendas of Presidents Richard *Nixon, Ronald *Reagan, and George Bush, who have made all but one of the appointments to the Supreme Court since 1967.

*Federal Jurisdiction and National Power.* The theme of states' rights has also been a prominent feature of the agendas of Presidents Nixon, Reagan, and Bush. The assumption has been that limiting the jurisdiction of the federal courts is one way to limit the reach of the national government. In our national history this correlation has not always been present: during the early days of

the New Deal, for example, vigorous exercise of the federal judicial power restrained the president and Congress in their efforts to centralize regulation of the economy. Even so, for most of the nation's history the expansion of federal court jurisdiction has reflected an expanded power of the national government and, in turn, has served the ends of centralization.

The pattern was set early. The era of the Marshall Court (1801–1835) was, in every sense, a time of national expansion. The population was spilling over the Appalachians and into the heartland of the continent. A national economy was taking shape. No instrument of government was more important to this process than the federal judiciary. The Supreme Court gave the stamp of approval to a broad interpretation of the legislative powers of Congress, including not only the power to create substantive law but also the power to give jurisdiction to the federal courts. The Court's decision in *Osborn v. Bank of the United States (1824) was celebrated at the time mainly as a defense of an unloved federal institution against local populist attack, but its modern importance lies elsewhere. The Court gave a sweepingly broad interpretation of Congress's power to grant federal courts jurisdiction in federal question cases. For half a century Congress before 1875 declined to accept the Court's invitation to confer a broad federal-question jurisdiction on the federal courts. This reluctance paralleled Congress's unwillingness, until late in the nineteenth century, to adopt substantive legislation that gave effect to the Court's broad interpretation of its power to regulate interstate commerce (see COMMERCE POWER).

Despite this congressional disinclination to expand the reach of the national government, the Supreme Court's work during the first half of the nineteenth century contributed mightily to the making of a nation. Its decisions on both substantive law and federal court jurisdiction promoted this end. The Court was zealous to protect the growing national economy against local regulations that would stifle enterprise and inhibit interstate trade. Its doctrinal grounds for striking down state and local legislation were mainly the Commerce Clause and the *Contracts Clause. Every interpretation of the Constitution, of course, adds to a body of national law. Because Congress had not yet established a general federal-question jurisdiction in the lower federal courts, the Supreme Court itself was called on to rule on many of these constitutional challenges to state laws. In the first Judiciary Act (1789) Congress had given the Court appellate jurisdiction over judgments of the highest state courts in cases presenting issues of federal law, and the Court had upheld the constitutionality of this jurisdictional grant in *Martin v. Hunter's Lessee (1816).

Another substantive development added to federal judicial power at the local level. The heart of the jurisdiction of the federal district courts during this period was their power to decide diversity of citizenship cases (in Article III's language, controversies "between Citizens of different States"). In *Swift* v. *Tyson* (1842) the Supreme Court held that a federal court in such a case should apply principles of a general common law—that is, a *federal common law. The opinion's author, Justice Joseph *Story, surely hoped that the federal courts would take the lead in developing a uniform national body of law governing contracts and other commercial transactions, thus facilitating the smooth development of nationwide commerce. This arrangement had its problems; it led lawyers into "forum shopping," jockeying to locate cases in state or federal courts, depending on where the substantive law seemed more favorable to their clients. The Supreme Court did not abandon this system of federal common law until 1938, when it held in *Erie Railroad* v. *Tompkins* that a federal district court, in a diversity of citizenship case, must apply the common law of the state in which it sits. In a time when interregional hostility has dwindled, the federal courts' diversity of citizenship jurisdiction has lost much of its usefulness, and for a generation some justices and commentators have been suggesting its complete repeal. In response, Congress has narrowed that jurisdiction by various devices: increasing the requirement concerning the amount of money in controversy, for example, and adding to the number of states in which a corporation will be deemed a "citizen." Still, thanks to trial lawyers who want to retain the option of going to federal court, the much-criticized diversity jurisdiction clings to life.

Throughout the early nineteenth century the moral pestilence of *slavery was protected against eradication by much more than constitutional theory. Even so, such theory played its part. The doctrine of *dual federalism assumed that the national government and the states occupied separate spheres of sovereignty, with slavery largely assigned to the states' domain. As a general constitutional theory, dual federalism survived until the *New Deal, but its application to slavery perished in the *Civil War. The *Reconstruction era saw the adoption of three amendments to the Constitution and four major civil rights acts. This legislation promised equal *citizenship to freed slaves and established federal instrumentalities to enforce the rights of citizens. In addition, two acts of Congress—the Habeas Corpus Act of 1867 and the Judiciary Act of 1875—expanded the jurisdiction of the federal courts and have had enormous modern importance (see REMOVAL ACT OF 1875).

The 1867 act authorized federal circuit courts to grant the writ of *habeas corpus to persons held in custody in violation of the Constitution. The act's immediate purposes were to protect federal officers and their families from harassment by local officials in the southern states during the Union army's occupation and to release some freed slaves who were being held in unlawful captivity. The law has been amended from time to time and in its present version is extended to state prisoners who have been imprisoned in the ordinary criminal process. The law today allows a federal court to grant the writ, releasing any person held in custody by state authorities in violation of the federal Constitution. From the 1920s to the 1970s the Supreme Court gradually expanded the demands of the *Fourteenth Amendment's Due Process Clause in state criminal prosecutions (see DUE PROCESS, PROCEDURAL). Here, too, federal substantive law and federal court jurisdiction have interacted. Many of the Supreme Court's decisions recognizing new due process requirements for the states grew out of federal habeas corpus proceedings. As the substantive requirements of due process expanded, so did the numbers of state prisoners filing petitions for habeas corpus.

The 1875 Judiciary Act established the federal-question jurisdiction of the federal courts, limited only by the restriction that a controversy involve a certain amount of money; this statutory jurisdiction remains today in virtually the same form but no longer requires any jurisdictional amount. As a result, plaintiffs with federal constitutional challenges to state laws, or with claims based on federal statutes, have the option of suing in federal courts. Today a major portion of the lower federal courts' workload consists of such constitutional challenges.

Around the beginning of the twentieth century, the Supreme Court began to strike down a considerable number of state laws regulating economic activity; the preferred ground for these decisions was the Fourteenth Amendment's Due Process Clause, now in its substantive *due process mode. The *Eleventh Amendment, which had been interpreted as immunizing state governments from suit in federal court in a wide range of potential actions, seemed a serious jurisdictional obstacle to this substantive development. As a consequence, the Court in Ex parte *Young (1908) held that a state officer who was acting unconstitutionally was stripped of his official character, so that a suit to enjoin the officer's illegal conduct was not a suit against the state (see INJUNCTIONS AND EQUITABLE REMEDIES). In one perspective the ruling was a triumph of form over substance; but in the modern era it has provided the jurisdictional basis for federal judges to enjoin state officers from denying all manner of federal constitutional rights. A rigorous application of the Eleventh Amendment's immunity implies a drastic limitation of the power of the federal judiciary to enforce the Constitution. One observer's patent fiction is another's essential predicate for the rule of law.

The 1932 election of Franklin D. *Roosevelt brought a strong new political philosophy to power in the national government; his New Deal legislative program ran headlong into the Supreme Court's restrictive interpretations of the Commerce Clause and the Due Process Clause of the *Fifth Amendment. Given the Supreme Court's adamant refusal, for several years, to uphold the constitutionality of major New Deal statutes, one might have expected a move to limit the Court's jurisdiction. Instead, President Roosevelt asked Congress to authorize an increase in the Court's membership to a maximum of fifteen justices. The *court-packing plan died in the Senate, but the Court had already begun to uphold New Deal statutes, and, for a season, all talk of limiting the Court's jurisdiction ceased. The combination of the Great Depression and *World War II produced a wholesale transfer of political power from the states to the national government, and the federal courts retained ample jurisdiction to effectuate that shift of power (see FEDERALISM).

*Jurisdiction and Political Preferences.* During the New Deal years the Supreme Court's role in the governmental system generated an often impassioned, and sometimes fierce, debate. In those years no one could doubt that judicial power was political power. The Court's critics, echoing a famous dissent by Justice Oliver Wendell *Holmes in *Lochner v. New York (1905), said that the "nine old men" were simply writing their preferences for laissez-faire economics into the Constitution's two due process clauses (see LAISSEZ-FAIRE CONSTITUTIONALISM). By the 1950s critics of the Warren Court were complaining that a new generation of justices was writing its preferences for other kinds of liberty, and for racial equality, into the Constitution. The Brown v. Board of Education decisions of the mid-1950s not only served as catalysts for the *civil rights movement; Brown also introduced an era in which the federal judiciary, and the Supreme Court in particular, took on new responsibility for protecting outsiders, dissenters, subordinated groups, have-nots—in other words, constituencies dramatically different from those of the "nine old men."

The recognition of new substantive constitutional claims translates directly into new business for the federal judiciary, at least at the level of review by the Supreme Court. A good example from the Warren Court era is found in the law of defamation. Before 1964 the law of *libel and slander was part of the states' common law; normally a libel case raised no questions of federal law and thus came into federal court only if the plaintiff and defendant were citizens of different states. The common law of libel offered a defense of "privilege": a newspaper, for example, could defend itself against a libel action by a public official if the paper's allegedly libelous editorial constituted "fair comment" on the official's performance of public duties. A minority of states allowed this privilege even in cases of false

statements of fact (absent negligence concerning falsity), but the majority of states limited the privilege of fair comment to statements of opinion. In *New York Times Co. v. Sullivan (1964) the Supreme Court held that the *First Amendment demanded the broader form of privilege for libels of public officials and that the privilege could be defeated only by a showing that the defendant knew the libelous statement was false or was recklessly indifferent as to its falsity. Overnight, the former "minority" view became a uniform national rule governing libel actions by public officials in all states, and even actions brought in state courts were potentially reviewable by the Supreme Court.

For a federal court to offer protection of substantive constitutional rights, of course, the court must have jurisdiction over a case. When a challenged state law has been enforced in the state courts (for example, by criminal prosecution), a sympathetic Supreme Court can rule on the constitutional issues on appellate review. In some cases, however, jurisdictional limitations such as the political question doctrine or the rules of standing may make it difficult for anyone to raise the constitutional claims in question in any federal court. So it was with the problem of legislative apportionment until the 1960s, when the Warren Court dramatically broadened both substantive rights in this area and the federal courts' jurisdiction to protect those rights.

After a census, when it is time to draw new boundaries for legislative districts, every state legislature is disposed toward promoting the interests of the majority party. That purpose may counsel doing nothing at all, leaving the districting as it was before the latest census—or even as it has been for fifty years. Until 1962 the prevailing view of the Supreme Court was that the political questions doctrine (and arguably the law of standing as well) doomed any lawsuit challenging the constitutionality of a state's apportionment system, even a system that gave one representative each to a district with 100,000 voters and a district with 900,000 voters. These were roughly the figures in *Colegrove v. Green (1946), when the Supreme Court had refused to intervene in a congressional election in Illinois at the behest of a voter in the more populous district. Such facts, the Court said, raised a claim under Article IV's clause guaranteeing each state a republican form of government, and the Court had previously held that such claims raised questions lying within the domain of the political branches (see GUARANTEE CLAUSE). Congress, for example, might refuse to seat an Illinois delegation elected as a result of malapportionment, but it was no business of the federal courts to set things right.

In *Baker v. Carr (1962), however, the Court rejected this reasoning. The claim arose, said the Court, under the *Equal Protection Clause of the Fourteenth Amendment. Considering the "familiar" standards for applying that clause, the judiciary should be able to construct manageable doctrines and standards. Two years later, in *Reynolds* v. *Sims* (1964), the Court jettisoned those "familiar" standards and established a basic rule of population equality for legislative districts: absent some special reason for departing from equality, the rule was to be *one person, one vote. Constitutional amendments were proposed in Congress, with especially strong support from legislators who stood to lose seats that malapportionment had given them, but the American public saw the formula of one person, one vote as fair. These *reapportionment cases provide one of the best examples of the interconnection of judicial jurisdiction and substantive policies.

So, too, with the law of standing. Before the 1960s, the principle was well established that a federal taxpayer had no standing to challenge the constitutionality of the spending of money by Congress. One basis for this jurisdictional limitation was that an individual taxpayer had only a tiny personal stake in a federal appropriation; another was that a contrary rule would make the federal courts routinely available as "appellate legislatures" for congressional statutes, most of which require the spending of money in their execution. Then, in 1965, Congress adopted the first major program of federal subsidies for *education, including substantial subsidies for religious schools. This appropriation raised serious problems under the First Amendment's Establishment Clause; subsidies to churches were just the sort of thing the framers of the *Bill of Rights had in mind in prohibiting an act of Congress "respecting an establishment of religion." If a federal taxpayer lacked standing to challenge this subsidy, no other potential plaintiffs were in sight; the Establishment Clause would be a dead letter in such cases. In *Flast* v. *Cohen* (1968) the Supreme Court concluded that a federal taxpayer did have standing to raise an establishment clause challenge to federal spending. Along with *Baker* v. *Carr*, the *Flast* decision made clear the Warren Court's determination not to let restrictive precedents defeat its version of substantive justice.

The Warren Court's recognition of new federal constitutional rights in the area of criminal justice chiefly took the form of the selective *incorporation of the Bill of Rights into the Fourteenth Amendment's Due Process Clause. By that doctrinal means a number of guarantees—such as the privilege against *self-incrimination, *trial by jury, and the right to *counsel—were made applicable not only to the federal government but to the states as well. There was an immediate, dramatic increase in the number of instances in which persons caught up in the state criminal justice systems became potential claimants of federal constitutional rights. The traditional manner of bringing claims of this kind before a federal

court had been to seek appellate review in the Supreme Court. But the Supreme Court is only able to decide about 150 cases each year, and it was unimaginable that Supreme Court review would provide effective supervision of state court protection of the newly recognized rights.

The Supreme Court's solution to this problem was to rely on the federal district court as the federal forum in which those federal constitutional claims might be made, after state criminal processes had run their course. The Court found this solution in its interpretation of the modern habeas corpus statute, a descendant of the Habeas Corpus Act of 1867. In *Fay* v. *Noia* (1963) the Court authorized federal habeas corpus relief even when state prisoners had failed to raise their federal constitutional claims in a proper manner in the state courts, so long as these failures resulted from lawyers' errors and not from conscious strategic choices. The number of habeas corpus petitions increased greatly. So did the expression of outrage by state judges, who resented the idea that a conviction affirmed by a state supreme court could be overturned by the ruling of a single federal district judge.

A number of the Warren Court's politically controversial decisions, as well as some decisions of the Burger Court (1969–1986), have provoked serious efforts in Congress to restrict the Supreme Court's jurisdiction, the jurisdiction of the lower federal courts, or both. The usual bill of this type withdraws jurisdiction over cases involving a particular substantive area or even a particular substantive result. Various bills have proposed immunizing any number of areas from federal courts' intervention, including school busing, legislative apportionment, subversive activities, school prayers, and abortion. For several decades legal scholars have debated the constitutional validity of this sort of restriction on the federal courts' jurisdiction, and today the debate is no nearer authoritative resolution than it was in the 1950s. One reason for this lack of closure is that the Supreme Court has had no chance in the modern era to address the issue. Whatever effectiveness these bills may have in their authors' direct-mail solicitations of campaign funds, in Congress they fall on infertile ground. The idea of an independent judiciary has as strong a political constituency today as it did when Roosevelt sought to pack the Supreme Court.

Even so, some of the substantive goals of these congressional proposals have been accomplished without any restriction of the federal courts' jurisdiction, just as the constitutionality of the New Deal's program was consolidated in the 1940s wihtout any structural change. In both instances important doctrinal changes have followed changes in the Court's composition. The difference in the last two decades is that the Court's majority has not limited itself to a revision of substantive constitutional law. To complement this revision the recent anti-activist majority has undertaken a major program to restrict the federal courts' jurisdiction.

Consider the law of standing, which the Court has recently employed with some frequency to relieve government officials from responsibility for harms visited on members of racial minorities. In *Warth* v. *Seldin* (1975) a 5-to-4 majority held that low-income members of racial and ethnic minorities lacked standing to complain of the discriminatory effects of a *zoning law that effectively excluded low-income housing from a white suburban town. The town had rejected builders' applications for rezoning that would have permitted the construction of low-income housing. Yet, the majority said, the plaintiffs had not shown "injury in fact" directly caused by the town's actions. Plaintiffs had not proved that they would be able to afford housing in the planned buildings; rather, their allegations suggested that their inability to reside in the suburb was "the consequence of the economics of the area housing market," not the town's allegedly illegal acts (p. 506). But the town had played an important part in structuring the local housing market by maintaining its exclusionary zoning law. Another way to characterize the plaintiffs' injury would be to say that the town had denied them the chance to enter a housing market that had not been skewed by unconstitutional official action (see HOUSING DISCRIMINATION).

Similarly, in *Allen* v. *Wright* (1984) the Court held, 5 to 3, that African-American parents of children in school districts undergoing desegregation had no standing to complain that the Internal Revenue Service was failing to carry out its legal obligation to deny tax exemptions to private schools practicing racial discrimination. The Court said that the plaintiff parents had not proved a direct connection between the IRS's alleged failure to police the private schools and the departure of white children from the public schools. In the majority's view it was merely speculative to assume that the elimination of tax exemptions from "segregation academies" would, by making them more expensive, reduce the number of whites using them to avoid integrated education. Thus the plaintiffs were excluded from court before a trial could decide this question.

A parallel development in the law of standing was the extraordinary decision in *Valley Forge Christian College* v. *Americans United for Separation of Church and State, Inc.* (1982). The federal government disposed of surplus land and buildings worth half a million dollars by giving them, free of charge, to a church college that was training students for the ministry. A cash grant to the college would plainly have violated the Establishment Clause, and under *Flast* v. *Cohen* a taxpayer would have standing to seek an *injunction against payment of the money. A 5-to-4 majority said this case was different. The challenged action was not an act of Congress allowing for

disposition of surplus property but an administrative act of transfer. Furthermore, this transfer was not "spending" under Congress's power to spend money (see TAXING AND SPENDING CLAUSE) but an exercise of Congress's power to deal with federal property (see PUBLIC LANDS). Presumably, in the absence of some other potential recipient of the government property, no one at all has standing to challenge this direct federal subsidy-in-kind to a church, even assuming that the subsidy violates the Establishment Clause.

These decisions on the law of standing have had only a limited effect in preventing federal courts from hearing challenges to unconstitutional governmental action. Usually, some plaintiff will be able to satisfy even the Court's rigorous test of personal injury. But in the criminal justice area the reconstituted Supreme Court has succeeded in achieving a massive exclusion of petitioners from the federal courts. In the last two decades the Court has drastically limited federal jurisdiction in habeas corpus cases. First in *Stone* v. *Powell* (1976) the Court denied habeas corpus to petitioners who claimed that their state court convictions were infected by the introduction of evidence that had been obtained through unconstitutional searches and seizures, so long as they had been offered an opportunity for fair hearing on the search-and-seizure issue in the state courts (see FOURTH AMENDMENT). Then, in *Wainwright* v. *Sykes* (1977) the Court overruled the part of *Fay* v. *Noia* that had allowed federal habeas corpus as a backstop in cases in which trial attorneys had inadvertently failed to raise relevant constitutional issues in state court proceedings. Under the current regime, criminal defendants must live with their lawyers' mistakes unless those mistakes are truly horrendous, in which case the courts may conclude that the defendants have been denied the right to counsel.

The expansion of federal habeas corpus in the 1960s was founded on the premise that some federal forum should be provided for the protection of federal constitutional rights in the state criminal process. The justices who have recently cut back on federal habeas corpus jurisdiction make no pretense that the Supreme Court, on appellate review of state convictions, can hope to offer effective supervision of the state courts' protection of the guarantees in the Bill of Rights. In practical terms, the notion that a defendant in a state criminal case should be able to bring his or her federal constitutional claims before a federal forum has been abandoned. In this field of law, it is no longer true that the federal courts are, as Frankfurter put it, the "primary and powerful reliances for vindicating every right guaranteed by the Constitution."

These cases are merely illustrations of a broad range of jurisdictional doctrines that the Supreme Court's majority has recently used to shut the federal courthouse door to constitutional claims. One other doctrinal technique has been the

Eleventh Amendment, which has "constitutionalized" the common-law doctrine of *sovereign immunity, extending the doctrine not only to the states but also, in some cases, to state officials. Another technique has been the doctrine of "equitable restraint," which bars federal courts from giving injunctive relief against state criminal prosecutions (and some civil actions) even when those state proceedings may be based on unconstitutional state laws (see ABSTENTION DOCTRINE). The result of these doctrines is to stifle federal constitutional challenges altogether or to shunt them into state courts for decision by judges, many of whom must regularly run for reelection. Many more state judicial elections are contested today than were contested a generation ago. Three justices of the California Supreme Court were removed by voters in 1986 after a campaign prominently featuring charges that the justices were soft on crime and hostile to the death penalty. Another California justice, who had resigned before the 1986 campaign, remarked that it is about as easy for a judge to ignore such political considerations while judging as it is to ignore an alligator in the bathtub.

The wisdom of the framers of the Constitution in seeking to guarantee the independence of the federal courts from partisan politics is more apparent today than ever before. The wisdom of a wholesale transfer of the defense of federal constitutional rights away from those courts to elected state judges is less apparent (see STATE CONSTITUTIONS AND INDIVIDUAL RIGHTS). Today, as always, the allocation of judicial jurisdiction—especially the withdrawal of jurisdiction from courts that enjoy political independence—is an exercise of political power.

(See also SEPARATION OF POWERS; STATE SOVEREIGNTY AND STATES' RIGHTS.)

□ Jack Bass, Unlikely Heroes: The Dramatic Story of the Southern Judges Who Translated the Supreme Court's Brown Decision into a Revolution for Equality (1981). Paul M. Bator, Daniel J. Meltzer, Paul J. Mishkin, and David L. Shapiro, eds., Hart and Wechsler's The Federal Courts and the Federal System, 3d ed. (1988), with supplements. Abram Chayes, "The Supreme Court, 1981 Term—Foreword: Public Law Litigation and the Burger Court," Harvard Law Review 96 (1982): 4–60. Felix Frankfurter and James M. Landis, The Business of the Supreme Court: A Study in the Federal Judicial System (1927). Henry J. Friendly, Federal Jurisdiction: A General View (1973). Learned Hand, The Spirit of Liberty, edited by Irving Dilliard (1952). Richard A. Posner, The Federal Courts: Crisis and Reform (1985). Michael Wells, "The Impact of Substantive Interests on the Law of Federal Courts," William and Mary Law Review 30 (1989): 499–540.

Kenneth L. Karst

**Judicial Review** is a distinctive power associated with the Supreme Court that is nowhere specifically mentioned in the Constitution. Chief Justice John *Marshall in *Marbury v. Madison (1803) asserted the major principle on which it rests by observing: "[i]t is emphatically the province and duty of the judicial department to say what the law is" (p. 177). Through judicial review the Court most dramatically asserts its authority to determine what the Constitution means.

The power of the Court to review the law extends in two directions. The first involves decisions by other branches of the federal government. These cases include actions taken by the executive branch, like the decision by President Richard *Nixon to withhold taped records of conversations in the White House, and statutes passed by Congress, such as the Missouri Compromise, which excluded *slavery from northern portions of the Louisiana Purchase territory. Judicial review also expresses the authority of the federal courts over state laws and judicial decisions that involve the federal Constitution. Whether involving federal or state matters, the practice of judicial review has been marked by dynamic expansion and persistent controversy. Judicial power has been consolidated both in the superiority of the federal judiciary over the states and of the Supreme Court over the other branches of the federal government. The authority of the federal government that became centralized after the *Civil War is one of the pillars of judicial review and vice versa. Justice Thurgood *Marshall, in commenting on the constitutional bicentennial celebration of 1987, said that the Constitution did not survive the Civil War, but was remade following that conflict. Since the late nineteenth century, power has come to be increasingly centered in a Supreme Court that would be unrecognizable to the founding generation. Not only do the justices now have a home and no *circuit-riding responsibilities, but the power to subject the acts of other branches of the federal government and the states to judicial scrutiny is widely accepted. Thus, judicial review is a dynamic institution that expands with the federal authority over the nation.

*Origins.* Scholars trace the origins of judicial review to *Dr. Bonham's Case* (1610). Sir Edward Coke, of England's Court of Common Pleas, stated that "when an act of parliament is against common right and reason or repugnant, or impossible to be performed, the common law will control it, and adjudge such act to be void" (p. 118a). Coke believed that the common lawyer possessed "artificial reason of the law" and that this capacity elevated him to nearly equal footing with King and Parliament. According to Coke, special learning required to interpret the law placed it above politics.

In 1761 the first significant American elaboration of *Bonham's Case* occurred. James Otis, in the *Writs of Assistance Case* in Boston, argued that British officers had no power under the law to use search warrants that did not stipulate the object of the search. Otis based his challenge to the underlying act of Parliament on *Bonham's Case*, the English Constitution, and the principle of "natural equity." John Adams subsequently adopted this reasoning to defend the rights of Americans by appeal to a law superior to parliamentary enactment. Although colonial courts resisted such radical assertions, these claims nonetheless made the idea of judicial review an important feature of American constitutionalism (see FUNDAMENTAL RIGHTS).

After the Revolution, the framers of the Constitution debated, and then rejected, an aspect of judicial review, the judicial veto. Although they were concerned about consolidated power in the federal government and the authority of that government over the states, the framers approved the Supremacy Clause of Article VI resolving the latter issue and leaving the former to evolve over the years. They rejected explicit judicial authority over Congress as proposed in the Virginia Plan. James *Madison, for example, reiterated the authority of fundamental law, but he refused to acknowledge the authority of the judiciary over the other branches of government. Prominent leaders of the founding generation and future Supreme Court justices James *Wilson of Pennsylvania, Oliver *Ellsworth of Connecticut, and John Marshall of Virginia argued in their state ratifying conventions that the national government would be limited by the judicial check.

In *The Federalist Papers, Alexander *Hamilton endorsed the idea of judicial review and provided one of its most compelling ideological foundations. Hamilton wrote that "whoever attentively considers the different departments of power must perceive that, in a government in which they are separated from each other, the judiciary, from the nature of its functions, will always be the least dangerous to the political rights of the Constitution. . . . [T]he judiciary . . . has no influence over either the sword or purse; no direction either of the strength or of the wealth of the society; and can take no active resolution whatever. It may truly be said to have neither FORCE nor WILL but merely judgment" (no. 78). Thus, with such reassurances, Hamilton defended the practice of judicial review.

Since the origins of constitutional government in America, judicial review has followed Hamilton's thinking that judges have a special capacity and responsibility to expound the meaning of the Constitution. Attempts by *state courts in the 1780s to assert a power over other political institutions either were ignored or brought forth denunciations from the legislature, often with threats to remove the judges. Richard Dobbs Spaight of North Carolina asked "if the judiciary acted as a check on the legislature, then who was to act as a check on the judiciary?" Like the national judiciary, which was also hotly contested in the last years of the eighteenth century, the practice of judicial review was in its formative period.

As a Supreme Court justice, James *Iredell, who had been a proponent of judicial review

during the Constitutional Convention, developed an institutional foundation for judicial power in his seriatim opinion in *Calder v. Bull (1798). He argued against grounding decisions of the Court in the laws of nature. Instead, Iredell proposed that the only basis for invalidating a statute that had been erected by "the legislature of the Union, or the legislature of any member of the Union" was that it violated a provision of the written Constitution in a "clear and urgent case" (p. 399).

The Republican party of Thomas *Jefferson challenged Federalist dominance of the judiciary. Jefferson went so far as to predict in a letter to Abigail Adams of 1804 that "The efforts of Federalism to exalt the Judiciary over the Executive and Legislative and to give that favorite department a political character and influence . . . will probably terminate in the degradation and disgrace of the judiciary." Jefferson's prognostications proved faulty in several respects.

*Early Decisions.* "If Congress were to make a law not warranted by any of the powers enumerated, it would be considered by the judges as an infringement of the Constitution which they are to guard. . . . They would declare it void," insisted future chief justice John Marshall at the 1788 Virginia Ratifying Convention. Marshall supplied a practical meaning to these words in the classic case of Marbury v. Madison (1803), in which he securely rooted the modern doctrinal source of judicial review. Marshall himself contributed to the chain of events that culminated in Marbury. Shortly before his appointment to the Court in 1801, Marshall, as secretary of state, failed to deliver a commission as justice of the peace in the District of Columbia to William Marbury, a loyal Federalist. Marbury requested that James Madison, the secretary of state under newly elected president Thomas Jefferson, issue the commission. Madison refused, and Marbury went directly to the Supreme Court. He claimed that under section 13 of the *Judiciary Act of 1789 the Court had the original jurisdiction to issue writs of *mandamus. Marbury wanted the Federalist-dominated Supreme Court to order the Jeffersonian Republican-controlled executive branch to deliver his commission.

Marbury's case threatened to plunge the justices into a political thicket. They readily calculated the furor that a writ of mandamus issued against Jefferson's administration would stir at a time when more radical Republicans were bent on stripping the Court of its power. At best, the president might have simply ordered Madison to disregard the Court; at worst, he might have lent even more of his prestige to efforts already under way by the radical wing of his party in Congress to limit sharply the Court's power.

Marshall appreciated these exigencies. The first part of his opinion sustained Marbury's claim on the basis of the *vested-rights doctrine, an outgrowth of the natural-rights philosophy of the Revolution that held that certain rights were so fundamental that they were beyond government control. The Court, with its responsibility to preserve fundamental law, was obligated to protect such rights. Distinguishing between political and other rights, Marshall disallowed judicial concern with the former on the grounds that the protection of political rights belonged instead to the popularly accountable political branches. The Court, Marshall said, drew its authority from the well of popular sovereignty, but it could exercise that power only in settling controversies involving fundamental law rather than politics.

What Marshall gave to Marbury in the first half of the opinion he took away in the second. Although a writ of mandamus was in order, the Court could not issue it. The chief justice arrived at this conclusion through a close textual reading of section 13 of the 1789 act and also *Article III of the Constitution. Congress might subtract from the Court's original jurisdiction, but Congress could not add to it—as section 13 did—because Article III had already established the Court's jurisdiction fully. With arguments reminiscent of state court implementation of judicial review during the 1780s, Marshall worried that an expansion of the Court's jurisdiction would thrust the justices into political disputes that the political branches themselves could not settle. Such involvement, he concluded, would prevent the Court from acting primarily as the legal institution he believed the departmental theory required.

Because of judicial review the justices would not enforce an unconstitutional act. Through his opinion in Marbury, Marshall simultaneously limited and expanded the Court's power; less power became more. The chief justice accepted the inherent limitation placed on the scope of judicial power, but he boldly asserted that the Court had a responsibility to say what the Constitution meant.

Marbury was a problematic constitutional case in a difficult political setting. Marshall's opinion was defensive; it sought to keep the Court free of political pressures by limiting its role to clearly legal as opposed to political issues. Marshall did not exercise judicial discretion in the modern sense of the word. Interpreting law was not synonymous with making it. Marbury did not receive his commission, but Marshall used the occasion to pronounce the essential elements of judicial review.

Although some nineteenth-century state court decisions claimed no more for judicial authority than did Marbury, most later instances of judicial review asserted a broader scope of judicial power. Marshall's decisions involving the constitutionality of state legislation proved considerably more controversial in time than Marbury. In a series of major decisions between 1810 and 1824, Marshall resorted to *natural law, the *Contracts Clause, and the *commerce power, among oth-

ers, to void state statutes, while simultaneously narrowing the reach of the *Eleventh Amendment. In *Fletcher v. Peck (1810), Marshall relied both on natural-law formulations drawn from Calder and on the contracts clause of Article I, section 10 of the Constitution to strike down a state statute interfering with title to real *property.

But nine years later, in *Dartmouth College v. Woodward, Marshall abandoned the natural-law leg of his Fletcher reasoning and relied on the Contracts Clause alone to thwart a state's attempt to modify the charter of a *corporation. The Dartmouth College decision is regarded as an essential step in the emergence of the private, profit-making corporation as a legal entity in the United States (see PRIVATE CORPORATION CHARTERS).

Marshall limited a state's power to revoke a legislatively granted tax exemption in New Jersey v. Wilson (1812), a particularly controversial holding because it cut so close to sovereign state powers (see STATE SOVEREIGNTY AND STATES' RIGHTS). He extended the reach of judicial power over state taxation in *McCulloch v. Maryland (1819), arguably his greatest and most influential opinion, holding that a state could not tax the Bank of the United States or any other instrumentality of the federal government. McCulloch provoked a storm of controversy, most of it emanating from Virginia, but that did not deter Marshall from constricting the Eleventh Amendment in *Osborn v. Bank of the United States (1824) to prohibit the state of Ohio from taxing a branch of the Bank in violation of the McCulloch holding.

The decision that most antagonized the Virginians involved an assertion of the Court's authority not over state legislation but over a state supreme court. *Martin v. Hunter's Lessee (1816), an opinion written by Justice Joseph *Story after Marshall had to excuse himself for personal interest in the subject matter of the litigation, asserted the power of the United States Supreme Court over the politically sensitive subject of state confiscation of Loyalist property during the War for American Independence. Despite the fervid opposition of Chief Judge Spencer Roane of the Virginia Court of Appeals, who denounced Martin as a fatal incursion on state sovereignty, Marshall again reversed a Virginia holding in *Cohens v. Virginia (1821) in a ringing vindication of the Supremacy Clause of Article VI.

*Gibbons v. Ogden (1824) provided the Court its first opportunity to construe the Commerce Clause of Article I, section 8, which Marshall used to void a state monopoly of river transportation. Although the Contracts Clause remained the Court's most potent weapon of discipline over state legislation throughout the nineteenth century, the Commerce Clause was to emerge in the twentieth as the principal source of federal legislative authority, and Marshall's expansive reading set it off on its career as the basis of vast federal regulatory power over the economy.

President Thomas Jefferson, responding to

Marshall's opinion in *Marbury*, composed "Instructions to a Federal Prosecutory" in 1807, attempting to advance the prosecution of Aaron Burr for treason. Jefferson argued against citing *Marbury* and proposed "to have [the decision] denied to be law." He went on to hold "the three great branches of the government should be coordinate, and independent of each other." Jefferson believed each branch of the government had the right to decide for itself the constitutionality of matters before it and objected to a claim that the Court's judgment was superior to that of the other branches. His efforts on behalf of repeal of the *Judiciary Act of 1801 and the first judicial *impeachments supported the doctrine of "coordinate construction," whereby each branch of the federal government interprets the Constitution for itself.

The Pennsylvania case of *Eakin v. Raub* (1825) provided criticism of *Marbury* from the state's chief judge, John Gibson. His dissent in that case is viewed as the best exposition of legislative supremacy in early American history. The case dealt with judicial review in Pennsylvania state courts but also addressed questions of federal power raised in *Marbury*. Gibson argued that "[i]f the judiciary will inquire into anything besides the form of enactment, where shall it stop?" He went on to object, "That the judiciary is of superior rank, has never been pretended, although it has been said to be coordinate" (p. 330). Gibson's reading of the Constitution led him to observe, "[H]ad it been intended to interpose the judiciary as an additional barrier, the matter would surely not have been left in doubt" (p. 331). To Gibson, the written Constitution was accessible to the public and it was the public's ability to hold the legislature accountable to the text that provided the ultimate check on the excesses of government.

The Court's power of review over federal legislation lay dormant for a half century after *Marbury*, despite the Court's activism with respect to state legislation. Chief Justice Roger B. *Taney reassumed the power in *Scott v. Sandford* (1857) by invalidating the Missouri Compromise of 1820, a federal statute that prohibited the spread of slavery into the Louisiana Purchase territory north of Missouri. Taney's opinion would have been unpopular enough in the North even without the complication of expanded Supreme Court power over politically sensitive issues. Yet the violent northern political reaction to Taney's provocative decision did not produce a sustained assault on the Court as an institution, no matter how fervently northern political leaders assailed *Dred Scott* and its author. Late in his opinion, Taney also claimed that the slavery restriction violated the Due Process Clause of the *Fifth Amendment. But he did not pursue the point there, and *Dred Scott* was soon overtaken by events, so the potential of the dictum was not realized for over a generation.

President Abraham *Lincoln's first inaugural address (1861) indicates the continuing resistance to rule by the judiciary in the middle of the nineteenth century. In this address, Lincoln sought to reassure the southern states that they would continue to be governed by law rather than fiat. His discussion of the law upon assuming the office of the presidency included extended treatment of his role as interpreter. "I take the official oath today, with no mental reservations, and with no purpose to construe the Constitution or laws, by any hypercritical rules." Grounding his analysis on the concept of the perpetuity of the union, Lincoln engaged in a disquisition on the nature and interpretation of the Constitution. Union came first; the purpose of the Constitution was to form a more perfect one. Lincoln acknowledged that decisions of the Supreme Court were binding on the parties involved and that they were also "entitled to very high respect and consideration, in all parallel cases, by all other departments of the government." But he also insisted that "if the policy of the government, upon vital questions, affecting the whole people, is to be irrevocably fixed by decisions of the Supreme Court, the instant they are made, in ordinary litigation between parties, in personal actions, the people will have ceased, to be their own rulers, having, to that extent, practically resigned their government, into the hands of that eminent tribunal." Lincoln's concluding reaffirmation of popular sovereignty continues to influence the meaning of judicial review even today.

*Practice Emerges.* The Supreme Court of the late nineteenth century realized the full potential of judicial review over both federal and state legislation. Marshall had asserted it, but after 1824 he was reduced to seeing its reach weaken in the face of political assault on its use against state legislation. Taney's respect for state authority avoided that clash, but his resort to the power to overturn federal legislation proved abortive in the *Dred Scott* case. While the Supreme Court did not write on a clean slate after the Civil War, neither did its innovative decisions expanding judicial review occupy a crowded field of *precedent. Thus the Court's creation of the doctrines of substantive *due process and freedom of *contract were innovations far in advance of anything adopted by the justices in the antebellum era.

A five-justice majority of the Court relied on traditional notions of *police power to uphold state regulatory authority (in this case, the grant of a monopoly over butchering activity in New Orleans) in the *Slaughterhouse Cases* of 1873. Though the Court strongly reaffirmed the role of the police power just four years afterward in *Munn v. Illinois* (1877), the dissent of Justices Stephen J. *Field and Joseph P. *Bradley in *Slaughterhouse* laid the basis for the sweeping triumph of substantive due process within two decades. Each insisted that any individual had a right to enter into contracts (including employment and business relationships, such as slaughtering), and that this right was protected by the federal Constitution. Field found that right primarily in the *Privileges or Immunities Clause of the *Fourteenth Amendment, Bradley in the Due Process Clause of that amendment. Bradley's view prevailed in the 1890s, first somewhat obscurely in *Chicago, Milwaukee, and St. Paul Railway Co. v. Minnesota (1890) and then triumphantly in *Allgeyer v. Louisiana (1897), where the Due Process Clause protected business contracts from legislative regulation.

This trend culminated twice before the *New Deal, first in *Lochner v. New York (1905), where the Court by a 5-to-4 decision invalidated a New York statute prohibiting bakers from working more than sixty hours a week, and then after the war in *Adkins v. Children's Hospital (1923), when the Court, again by a 5-to-4 margin, struck down a state minimum-wage law for women. In both of these major decisions, the majority found in the Fourteenth Amendment's Due Process Clause a substantive restraint on state legislative policy making. The Court reached comparable results for federal legislative authority in *Adair v. United States (1908), which relied in part on the Fifth Amendment's Due Process Clause. Other decisions that curbed federal power to regulate the economy drew more on arguments based on concepts of *federalism than from substantive due process. The principal specimens of these were the two child-labor decisions: *Hammer v. Dagenhart (1918) (the Commerce Clause) and *Bailey v. Drexel Furniture (1922) (the Tax Clause).

Yet the Court was not consistent in its substantive due process approach, for it sustained far more legislation, state and federal, than it struck down. Major examples of decisions sustaining economic regulatory legislation included *Holden v. Hardy (1898), upholding a Utah maximum-hours law for men in mining and smelting industries; *Muller v. Oregon (1908), upholding maximum-hours legislation for women; and various decisions sustaining federal authority under the commerce and tax clauses. *World War I gave a short-lived impetus to such results, especially those involving federal power. Thus, by the 1930s the Court had created two inconsistent lines of precedent, the one sustaining, and the other rejecting, the exercise of legislative power at the state and federal levels.

This conflict came to a head in the New Deal. Between 1934 and 1937, the Court first accepted state and federal regulatory efforts to contend with the economic crises of the Depression, in such leading cases as *Home Building and Loan Association v. Blaisdell (1934) and *Nebbia v. New York (1934) (state authority) and *Ashwander v. TVA (1936) (federal). But the mind-set of substantive due process shortly triumphed, and in a series of decisions that shocked the Roosevelt administration, the Court overturned federal legislative initiatives (e.g., *Schechter Poultry v. United States, 1935, involving the National Recovery Act; and United States v. *Butler, 1936, involving regulation of agriculture), as well as state legislation: *Morehead v. New York ex rel. Tipaldo (1936, involving state minimum-wage legislation). By 1937, a five-justice majority of the Court seemed to have embraced the discredited Lochner and Adkins precedents in an effort to frustrate all legislative attempts to cope with the Depression.

President Franklin D. *Roosevelt responded with the *court-packing plan, an attempt to enlarge the Supreme Court and *lower federal courts with FDR appointees more sympathetic to an activist legislative program. Though he failed in this effort, he won the larger campaign of forcing the Court to reverse substantive economic due process precedents dating back to the Slaughterhouse dissents. The Court was now free to embark on a new period of judicial activism, liberated from the formalist mentality that produced Lochner and its progeny.

Though the Court abandoned substantive due process in questions of economic regulation, the concept itself was not defunct, nor had the Court forsaken activism. Rather, it diverted its concern over legislative power from economic matters to problems of civil liberties and civil rights. Justice Harlan Fiske *Stone enunciated this new direction obscurely, in *Footnote Four of United States v. Carolene Products Co. (1938) stating that the Court would now scrutinize three categories of issues: "where legislation appears on its face to be within a specific prohibition of the Constitution, such as those of the first ten amendments"; "legislation which restricts those political processes which can ordinarily be expected to bring about repeal of undesirable legislation", and "statutes directed at particular religious . . . or national . . . or racial minorities" (p. 153). The Court lost no time in putting that agenda into effect.

The two substantive doctrinal contributions that characterize the growth period for the modern Court are acceptance of economic regulation and the nationalization of civil liberties. Agency cases like those validating the National Labor Relations Board and social welfare decisions upholding Social Security solidified the federal administrative apparatus as the Court turned its attention elsewhere. Civil liberties protection was an extended consequence, a new preoccupation that represented, in the words of legal scholars, an "idea of progress."

The desegregation decision, *Brown v. Board of Education (1954), criminal procedure holdings like *Mapp v. Ohio (1961), and the *abortion decision in *Roe v. Wade (1973) epitomize the most recent period of *judicial activism. Brown was a bold restatement of the concept of equality, resulting from America's repudiation of racial discrimination. In Roe, the standard of equality applied to abortion accommodated women's expanded roles in the marketplace. All of these decisions mobilized the institutional authority of the Court and the authority of federal over state law to advance the political idea of equal treatment.

While the court-packing plan of the New Deal forced a major diversion in the Court's use of judicial review, United States v. *Nixon (1974) affirmed the Supreme Court's power to stand against the other branches of the government. This decision, in which the Court ordered the president to turn over politically damaging materials, came at the height of a dramatic confrontation between Congress and the presidency. The political context in which the decision was reached boosted the authority of the Court in American political culture, because the justices ordered the president to act against his own interests. The president obeyed. This decision was widely heralded as saving the country from executive tyranny and was accepted as an assertion of the authority of the Supreme Court as the "final arbiter" in constitutional matters.

*Modern Practice.* Mid-twentieth-century judicial review emphasizes the Supreme Court's predominance over the executive and the legislative branches of the federal government and the states in matters of constitutional interpretation. The power derives from the justices' expertise in interpreting the Constitution and its supremacy as law. The language of law is constitutive because the various communities that compose the American nation accept its conventions. In constitutional law, judicial review is a function of professional and seemingly apolitical practices dating to John Marshall's opinions. The lawyers who speak to the courts today and the lawyers who sit on the bench have developed a special way of speaking about the power of judges, so much so that some observers have concluded that the Constitution is "what the justices say it is."

On the occasion of the two hundredth anniversary of the Constitution, Americans had come to accept judicial review at the same time that the controversy over its origins persisted. Solicitor General Kenneth W. Starr observed that "by virtue of the status of the Constitution as supreme law" the American system would "include the power of judicial review." At the same time, the justices needed a power that brought them status in the present day far beyond what they ever had before. Chief Justice William H. *Rehnquist has noted that "We . . . must realize that our work has no more claim to infallibility than that of our predecessors." He pointed out that the statement "on the front of this building—Equal Justice Under Law—describes a quest, not an institution."

Recently the Court has shifted its attention away from civil liberties to *separation of powers, an area in which the authority of judges is grounded in the expectations of the founders and the canons of constitutional philosophy. The

erosion of the *political question doctrine and the political content of some recent decisions coexist with continued assertions that judges are not simply politicians behind the bench. Even as the Court attempts to establish the boundary of its legal authority, the justices continue to expand the bases of judicial review.

With regard to political questions, the evolution of the modern Supreme Court has been away from traditional legal forms associated with the judiciary in favor of informality and bureaucracy. National authority over the Constitution is based more on the Supreme Court's position at the helm of the national judiciary than any uniquely legal qualities. The political question doctrine is a device for transferring the responsibility for a question or decision to another branch of government, usually Congress. In the 1960s, the justices entered one of the last remaining spheres that had been closed off by the political question doctrine in the reapportionment decision *Baker v. Carr (1962). According to some scholars, questions became political simply because judges refused to decide them (see REAPPORTIONMENT CASES).

The Court continues to move in that direction, as indicated by *Davis v. Bandemer (1986), the political *gerrymandering case. Although the Court did not find political gerrymandering to be discriminatory, the clear implication was that the justices might soon make such a finding. Thus there is little in the way of substantive questions that separates judges from other actors in the political process.

Yet other cases, such as *Webster v. Reproductive Health Services (1989), provide evidence of the new limits of judicial review. In the matter of judicial authority, the dissenting opinion by Justice Antonin *Scalia portrayed vividly the need for the Court to protect itself from immersion in the political arena. "The outcome of today's case will doubtless be heralded as a triumph of judicial statesmanship. It is not that, unless it is statesmanlike needlessly to prolong this Court's self-awarded sovereignty over a field where it has little proper business since the answers to most of the cruel questions posed are political and not judicial" (p. 532).

Nomination hearings for appointment to the Supreme Court have highlighted the inevitable tension in judicial review between law and politics. Hearings on Sandra Day *O'Connor's nomination in 1981 attempted to draw out the nominee on the issue of abortion. She stated that it was facts, law, and constitutional principles that would guide her decisions, not her personal views. Extensive questioning of nominee Robert *Bork demonstrated that politics resides in the exercise of judicial power. In response to questions about his agenda, which often revolved around judicial review, Bork proposed a jurisprudence of *"original intent" that would affirm the importance of the constitutional text in guiding a justice. His failure to be confirmed was, in part, a failure to convince the Senate on this issue.

The current debate over the legitimacy of the Supreme Court's use of judicial review is only the most recent phase of a historical dialogue essential to the maintenance of the Constitution. The Court will continue to exercise judicial review; the constitutional order demands as much. In this sense, the lessons taught by the history of the Supreme Court and judicial review have nothing to do with the framers' intentions, either of implementation or scope. Rather, the past speaks to the present in another way. Americans can—and will—debate the legitimacy of judicial review, but they should know that dialogue nourishes their distinctive experiment in constitutionalism. Americans have never taken judicial review for granted, and they never can.

(See also IMPACT OF COURT DECISIONS; IMPLIED POWERS; JUDICIAL POWER AND JURISDICTION; JUDICIAL SELF-RESTRAINT.)

□ Alexander Bickel, *The Supreme Court and the Idea of Progress* (1970). John Brigham, *The Cult of the Court* (1987). Edward S. Corwin, *The "Higher Law" Backgrounds of American Constitutional Law* (1928). Richard E. Ellis, *The Jeffersonian Crisis: Courts and Politics in the Young Republic* (1971). Louis Fisher, *Constitutional Structures* (1990). Kermit L. Hall, *The Supreme Court and Judicial Review in American History* (1985). Catharine MacKinnon, *Toward a Feminist Theory of the State* (1989). Walter Murphy, William Harris, and James Fleming, *American Constitutional Interpretation* (1986). Elliot E. Slotnick, "The Place of Judicial Review in the American Tradition," *Judicature* (1987): 68–79. John Brigham

**Judicial Self-Restraint** is a general term for several distinct but associated ideas, each counseling the Court to confine its use of power, especially its power of judicial review, according to the principles of separation of powers and republican government. The various meanings of the term may be divided into technical and common branches. One technical branch of these ideas, rooted in *Article III of the Constitution, advises the Court to distinguish its function from that of the legislature or the executive by limiting itself to the resolution of concrete *cases and controversies according to standards of law. The Court should not decide a dispute if there is no concrete injury to be relieved by judicial decision (*standing), if the conflict between parties is a matter of contingency rather than actuality (*ripeness), if the conflict has already passed (*mootness), if there is no genuine case presented in an adversary proceeding, but a mere request for an opinion on a legal question (*advisory opinions). Nor should the Court resolve a dispute if no judicially manageable standard is to be found in the Constitution, nor if the matter has been committed by the Constitution to another branch of government (*political questions), impeachment being the clearest example of the latter.

A second technical branch of ideas stems less from *separation of powers than from the authority of republican government and the belief that the Court should avoid limiting that authority except when required by its judicial function. This branch includes several of the maxims articulated by Justice Louis D. *Brandeis in his famous concurrence in the case of *Ashwander v. TVA* (1936): "The Court will not 'anticipate a question of constitutional law in advance of the necessity of deciding it.' . . . The Court will not 'formulate a rule of constitutional law broader than is required by the precise facts to which it is to be applied.' . . . The Court will not pass upon a constitutional question . . . if there is also present some other ground upon which the case may be disposed of. . . . 'When the validity of an act of the Congress is drawn in question, and even if a serious doubt of constitutionality is raised, [the] Court will first ascertain whether a construction of the statute is fairly possible by which the question may be avoided' " (pp. 346–348).

These concerns with separation of powers and republican government that we find in the technical meanings of judicial self-restraint are paralleled in its more extended common usage. Echoing Montesquieu's dictum that judges are to be "only the mouth that pronounces the words of the law, inanimate beings who can moderate neither its force nor its rigor," perhaps the most widely used sense of judicial self-restraint stresses that justices are not to confuse their own ideas of right with the law; to enact new ideas is a legislative, not a judicial function. Often this emphasis on fidelity is allied with the theory that the true meaning of the Constitution is its original meaning and that the original meaning is the intention of the framers. Some critics of *original intent hold it defective on its own ground, arguing that the framers of the Constitution did not intend their own intentions to be authoritative, that they wished instead for the Constitution's meaning to evolve through political deliberation or even that they intended for the Supreme Court to play the leading role in the evolution of constitutional meaning. Others maintain that original intent is too ambiguous to be a useful source of law. Still others hold that original intent should be irrelevant to law. Without assessing the merits of these arguments, it is apparent that one might in good faith counsel constitutional fidelity and yet hold that the Constitution does not mean original intent. For that reason, controversies of constitutional meaning might be more fruitfully addressed without recourse to the term judicial self-restraint. Similarly, while some identify restraint with adherence to *precedent, this confuses precedent with law and masks the important question of what role precedent should play in determining constitutional meaning.

A less problematic common usage of judicial self-restraint identifies it with "deference" to republican authority. That is, justices should not declare a law unconstitutional when it merely violates their own idea of what the Constitution means, but only when the law clearly violates the Constitution. Essential to this idea of restraint is the notion that constitutional clauses do not have crisply defined meanings, that for most aspects of the Constitution there is a range of meaning within which reasonable persons might differ. When humility requires the Court to accept that the legislative opinion as to a law's constitutionality just might be right and its own opinion just might be wrong, the legislative opinion should prevail over that of the Court. Further support for this understanding of restraint derives from the belief that constitutional principles are secure in the long run only if the people and their representatives support them and understand their own responsibility for doing so. An easy recourse to judicial review and a casual exercise of it will tend, as Professor James Bradley *Thayer maintained in 1901, "to dwarf the political capacity of the people, and to deaden its sense of moral responsibility" (*John Marshall*, 1901, p. 107).

Although all of these meanings of judicial self-restraint share a concern for separation of powers and republican authority, they can diverge sharply, especially the two common meanings, on what will justify the Court in declaring a law unconstitutional. Consider, for example, the case of *Rochin* v. *California* (1952), where police obtained evidence of morphine possession by pummeling Rochin and then, against his will, having a physician pump his stomach. Justice Felix *Frankfurter, an advocate of restraint as "deference," held for the Court that the evidence could not be admitted. To admit this evidence, he acknowledged, would violate no specific provision of the Constitution, but it would flagrantly violate what an earlier opinion had referred to as principles "so rooted in the tradition and conscience of our people as to be ranked fundamental," or what is concisely stated as the principle of "ordered liberty" (p. 169). Justice Hugo L. *Black, a forceful exponent of restraint as "original intent," sharply criticized the majority's reasoning as "nebulous," totally wanting in authority for nullifying state acts, and ultimately a threat to the *Bill of Rights itself (p. 175). He found firmer authority in the *Fifth Amendment's command that "[n]o person . . . shall be compelled to be a witness against himself," though for the majority, equating testimony with vomitus and attributing this result to the framer's intent were rather far fetched.

In *Rochin,* the advocates of "deference" and "original intent" diverged in reasoning yet converged in result; elsewhere, as in *Griswold* v. *Connecticut* (1965), they would diverge in both reasoning and result. In that case, Justice Black dissented from the majority's decision to nullify Connecticut's rarely enforced ban on the use of contraception, arguing, "I like my privacy as well as the next one, but I am nevertheless compelled to admit that government has a right to invade it unless prohibited by some specific constitutional provision" (p. 510). Justice John M. *Harlan, by contrast, representing restraint as "deference" concurred in the result. He admitted that nothing specific in the Constitution covered this issue and urged a general posture of deference that acknowledged a broad range of state authority to deal with the morals of its citizens; yet as applied to married couples, he argued, this invasion of privacy constituted a gross violation of the principle of ordered liberty implicit in the Due Process Clause of the Fourteenth Amendment.

In *Griswold* "original intent" would uphold the law, while "deference" would allow its nullification. On the other hand, cases are numerous where "original intent" would void the law, and "deference" would uphold it. In several free speech cases of the 1950s and 1960s, for instance, often in the context of anticommunist legislation, Harlan or Frankfurter, weighing the claims of state authority against those of free speech, would find the balance struck by the legislature to be reasonable and therefore constitutional. Black, arguing that free speech was intended under the *First Amendment to be protected "absolutely," would find the law unconstitutional. By either school of thought, however, the majority opinion in the *abortion case of *Roe* v. *Wade* (1973) is "activist" for it both stretches beyond original intent and fails to defer (see JUDICIAL ACTIVISM).

The term "judicial self-restraint" was first used in Justice Harlan Fiske *Stone's dissent in *United States* v. *Butler* (1936), where he charged the majority with voiding *New Deal legislation because of its alleged lack of wisdom rather than its unconstitutionality. Each of the elements identified above, however, has been present in constitutional debates since the Court's first decades. Some of the earliest cases in the Court's history focused on what constitutes a case or controversy (e.g., *Hayburn's Case,* 1792) or what was the original intent. Deference is implied in Alexander *Hamilton's classic defense of judicial review in The *Federalist,* no. 78, where he argues that courts should declare acts void when they violate the "*manifest tenor* of the Constitution" (emphasis added), not simply when they seem unconstitutional.

As implied by the arguments supporting it, judicial self-restraint is widely regarded as a term of praise and judicial activism a term of criticism. Critics have attempted to attach more negative connotations to restraint by calling it "judicial timidity" or "judicial passivism." Proponents of restraint consider the failure of such terms to take hold in constitutional discourse as further evidence of the extent to which judicial self-restraint is rooted in fundamental principles of the Constitution.

(See also JUDICIAL REVIEW.)

☐ Alexander Bickel, *The Least Dangerous Branch* (1962). Robert Bork, *The Tempting of America* (1990). Ronald Dworkin, *Taking Rights Seriously* (1978).

Stanley C. Brubaker

**Judiciary Act of 1789.** The framers of the Constitution provided that the new national government would be divided into three branches. The third was to be a court system, an institution that did not exist in the previous national government under the Articles of Confederation. However, the Constitution set out only the barest of outlines for the new judiciary, unlike the legislative and executive branches that were extensively detailed and circumscribed. Thus the first Congress had to flesh out the Constitution by creating a court structure.

The Judiciary Act of 1789 ranks as one of the most important enactments Congress has ever undertaken, more akin to a constitutive act (like amendments to the Constitution) than to ordinary legislation. The task was arduous, given the weakness of the new government and the extreme political sensitivity of many features of the court system. Congress struggled with the problem during the whole of its long first session, and the act that finally emerged in September 1789 was thought by many to be a sound but temporary compromise. Yet, thanks to a combination of astute political foresight, hard work, and luck, most of the important features of the national judiciary established by the act are with us today.

*Structure.* The act's most enduring feature was also the aspect that most surprised contemporaries: a three-tiered hierarchical judicial structure. At the bottom were district courts, each with a single district judge, one in each state except Virginia and Massachusetts, which had two. (The remote Kentucky district of Virginia demanded its own court as the price of staying in the union, and the Maine portion of Massachusetts also received a court). At the top was a Supreme Court, staffed by five associate justices and one *chief justice. In between were three circuit courts, the Southern (consisting at the time of South Carolina and Georgia; North Carolina was added in 1790 after it joined the union), the Eastern (containing New York, Connecticut, Massachusetts, and New Hampshire; Rhode Island was added in 1790 and Vermont in 1791, when they joined the union), and the Middle (comprising Virginia, Maryland, Pennsylvania, Delaware, and New Jersey). In order to reduce expenses for the nation and for poor litigants, the circuit courts were not staffed with their own judges. Rather, each district judge sat in the circuit court when it convened in his state, and two itinerant Supreme Court judges joined them during each of three twice-yearly circuits. Since the broad trial jurisdiction of the circuit courts included the most sensitive and disputed kinds of federal cases, decisions there would be made by the most respected federal jurists, making costly appeals less likely. (The circuit courts are now known as the *Courts of Appeal, are solely appellate, and are staffed with their own judges, but the three-tiered arrangment has persisted.)

Both the hierarchy and the number of national courts surprised most Americans in 1789. All courts were trial courts at that time. No courts were confined to ruling on purely legal issues appealed from inferior courts, and an "appeal" might connote a new trial before a court containing more judges. However, opponents of the Constitution's ratification had feared that an "appellate" jury trial (or merely the Supreme Court sitting without a jury) might overturn facts found below by a local jury. To calm these fears and thus to reduce antagonism to the new centralized government, the Judiciary Act prohibited the Supreme Court from rehearing facts, thus limiting it to questions of law and coincidentally giving it hierarchical control over the lower federal courts in issues of law. Today all state and federal appellate courts follow this model, but it was a remarkable novelty in 1789.

If Americans had been polled in 1788, a large majority would probably have predicted that trials of cases coming within federal jurisdiction would take place in the various state supreme courts (see STATE COURTS). Many Americans anticipated that the only federal courts would consist of a few *admiralty judges scattered among seaports, dealing with maritime matters, and a single appellate Supreme Court. Such a scheme would have kept costs low while assuaging the fears of state judges and localistic opponents of the Constitution that federal courts would swallow up state court jurisdiction. Virginia Senator Richard Henry Lee and others supported this model in the first Congress, but nationalists led by Connecticut Senator (and later Chief Justice) Oliver *Ellsworth beat back the challenge. They desired a highly articulated court system so that crucial cases could be tried before national judges (rather than state judges susceptible to strong antinational pressure), and so that the majesty and power of an otherwise small and distant, distrusted new national government might be brought closer to everyone's doorstep.

A second alternative model was also rejected by the first Congress. This system, known as *nisi prius*, was patterned on the extant court systems in England, Massachusetts, and New York, among other jurisdictions. It would have entailed a large Supreme Court that would have traveled in groups of two or three to try federal cases in the hinterlands, then would have periodically returned to the capital to decide difficult issues of law as a group. There would have been no other federal courts. If either the Lee plan or the *nisi prius* plan had been adopted, our judicial landscape (and probably our constitutional history) would have been vastly different than it has been.

*Jurisdiction.* The fear widespread in 1787–1789 that the federal courts might swallow up state court jurisdiction was a rational one. The Constitution used quite broad, inclusive, and vague language to describe the jurisdiction that the federal judiciary would exercise. *Article III, section 2 states in pertinent part that "the judicial Power [of the United States] *shall* extend to *all* Cases" arising under the Constitution or federal law or treaties, and to controversies "between Citizens of different States . . . and between . . . the Citizens [of a State] and foreign . . . Citizens or Subjects" (emphasis added).

The political disputes that led James *Madison and others to demand a national court system in the first place involved state court refusal to enforce ordinary debt *contracts during the depression years of the 1780s. Hatred of the British impelled thousands of Americans to repudiate all or part of the debts that had been contracted with British merchants before the Revolution and that had remained unpaid when the courts closed on the eve of that bloody eight-year struggle. Despite prohibitions in the peace treaty with Great Britain, state legislatures continued to pass court-closing and debt-reducing acts that made collection of British debts difficult or impossible. They also enacted moratorium laws postponing, and legal tender laws allowing reductions in, the obligations Americans owed to domestic creditors, many of whom were speculators and many of whom, relative to the debtors, lived out of state. Many state courts respected the anticreditor message sent by the economically hard-pressed majority, enforcing this legislation and in some instances adding to its contract-repudiating effects.

Several provisions of the Constitution could bring ordinary contract cases involving such debts into the federal courts: such cases might be controversies between citizens of different states, or between a citizen and a foreigner; they might involve a statute contrary to the peace treaty, and thus "arise" under it; or they might involve a violation of the prohibitions in Article I, section 10 against a state's "mak[ing] any Thing but gold and silver Coin a Tender in Payment of Debts" or passing "Law[s] impairing the Obligation of Contracts," and thus "arise" under the Constitution. Many opponents of the Constitution did not want these cases taken away from the state courts. The Constitution's opponents also objected to the breadth and vagueness of the Constitution's jurisdictional language. The framers' avowed purpose of greatly strengthening the national government portended the possible sweep of many other ordinary cases into federal court. Especially upsetting was the possibility that ordinary cases between citizens of different states involving small amounts might allow out-of-state plaintiffs to win by default against poor and middling defendants unable to travel, or to bring their witnesses great distances to appear in federal court. The movement to amend the Constitution, which resulted in the adoption of the *Bill of Rights in 1791, had a strong component of support from these opponents of the Constitution, who wished to restrict federal court jurisdiction severely (although nothing in the Bill of Rights as enacted directly accomplished such an objective).

The fears of the Constitution's opponents were partially neutralized by the Judiciary Act of 1789, as Congress adopted restrictions on the jurisdiction that might have been allotted to the federal courts under a full and broad reading of the Constitution. The least controversial types of jurisdiction—admiralty, petty crimes, collection of revenue—were lodged in the single-judge district courts.

Much more controversial were cases involving citizens of two or more states ("diversity" suits) and those involving a United States citizen on one side and a foreigner on the other ("alienage" suits) (see DIVERSITY JURISDICTION). While debt contract cases were the primary reasons for these types of jurisdiction, nothing in Article III prevented many other kinds of suits from begin taken to federal court under them. Three judges, two of whom were members of the Supreme Court, would sit at the trial of such cases in the circuit courts, ensuring litigants more wisdom and care at their trials. Congress imposed an absolute amount-in-controversy limitation of $500—a large sum in 1789—on alienage and diversity cases, so that defendants involved in suits of less than that amount could not be taken to federal court by out-of-state or alien plaintiffs. Further, federal jurisdiction over diversity and *alienage suits was made concurrent, giving such plaintiffs their choice of state or federal court. If the state court were chosen, and the defendant decided at the beginning of the suit not to transfer the case to federal court, the case would remain in the state court, as no avenue of appeal to the Supreme Court from state courts in diversity or alienage cases was permitted. (These restrictions persist today, although the amount-in-controversy limitation now is $50,000.) A further amount-in-controversy limitation of $2,000 was placed upon appeal of alienage and diversity cases to the Supreme Court, lessening even further the likelihood that poor defendants would be twice subjected to expensive travel.

The most controversial type of jurisdiction was that over cases "arising" under the Constitution, treaties, or laws of the United States (*"federal question" suits). Today we have comprehensive federal regulatory legislation that gives rise to many federal question suits. However, such legislation was nonexistent in 1789. Modern readers have difficulty understanding the fears that such an open-ended jurisdiction raised in the minds of opponents of the Constitution. Might "laws of the United States" encompass the laws of all the states? What state control over its domestic affairs could be wrested away by the federal negotiation of a treaty with a foreign power?

On the other hand, proponents of the Constitution saw this as the most important type of federal jurisdiction. They believed that the courts could use it to repel attacks upon the new Constitution. The most significant restriction in the Judiciary Act of 1789 gave the trial of federal question suits to the state courts. Only upon appeal to the Supreme Court after a final decision was had in the highest court of a state might a federal question actually reach a federal court. (Except for a brief interlude in 1801–1802, federal courts did not obtain general trial jurisdiction over federal questions until 1875.)

The restrictions astutely placed in the Judiciary Act of 1789 were successful in preventing any jurisdictional limitations or restrictions from being adopted as amendments to the Constitution. Proponents of the new government grumbled about these restrictions and about the undignified and arduous *circuit riding that Supreme Court judges were forced to make, and planned to enact appropriate changes. They eventually did so in the *Judiciary Act of 1801, the famous "midnight judges' act," but Thomas *Jefferson and the Republicans repealed this new law in 1802 as their first action after coming to power. The Judiciary Act of 1789 attained hallowed status as the enduring blueprint for America's judicial structure.

(See also JUDICIAL POWER AND JURISDICTION; LOWER FEDERAL COURTS.)

□ Julius Goebel, Jr., *History of the Supreme Court of the United States*, vol. 1, *Antecedents and Beginnings to 1801* (1971). Wythe Holt, " 'To Establish Justice': Politics, The Judiciary Act of 1789, and the Invention of the Federal courts," *Duke Law Journal* (December 1989): 1421–1531. Wilfred J. Ritz, *Rewriting the History of the Judiciary Act of 1789: Exposing Myths, Challenging Premises, and Using New Evidence* (1990). Charles Warren, "New Light on the History of the Federal Judiciary Act of 1789," *Harvard Law Review* 37 (November 1923): 49–132.      Wythe Holt

**Judiciary Acts of 1801 and 1802.** Ratification of the Constitution provoked debate and conflict concerning the relationship of the federal judiciary to other branches of the national government and to the states. In 1799, the Federalists began efforts to expand both the organization and the jurisdiction of the national courts created by the *Judiciary Act of 1789. Before the Jeffersonian Republicans took office following their electoral triumph in 1800, the Federalist Congress passed the Judiciary Act of 1801.

The act responded both to complaints from Supreme Court justices and to those who sought a more centralized national government. It abolished the existing circuit courts and thereby freed Supreme Court justices from their duties as circuit judges (see CIRCUIT RIDING). It reduced the number of Supreme Court justices from six to five

(following the next vacancy) and created six new circuits, thereby enabling the outgoing Adams administration to appoint sixteen circuit judges, the so-called midnight judges. The scope of federal jurisdiction was radically increased. The 1801 act gave the circuit courts the *federal question jurisdiction that had been withheld in the 1789 act. It broadened diversity jurisdiction and expanded the removal jurisdiction. The act extended federal jurisdiction over all cases in which state-derived land titles were disputed, regardless of the value of the lands in question, and gave the circuit courts exclusive jurisdiction over litigation under the recent Bankruptcy Act of 1800 (see BANKRUPTCY AND INSOLVENCY LEGISLATION). The nationalizing potential of these provisions struck deeply at the powers of the states (see STATE SOVEREIGNTY AND STATES' RIGHTS). Because of the partisan support for the act and the appointment of Federalists to the new judgeships, the Republicans demanded its repeal as soon as they took control of Congress. The outgoing Congress also created new justices of the peace for the District of Columbia. In December 1801 four of them who had not actually received their commissions sought a writ of *mandamus from the Supreme Court in its original jurisdiction directing Secretary of State James *Madison to deliver their commissions, producing the landmark decision of *Marbury v. Madison (1803).

Extensive congressional debate in 1802 over repeal of the 1801 act raised many constitutional issues. Federalists maintained that abolishing the new federal courts constituted an unconstitutional attack on the independence of the judiciary. Republicans countered that because the Constitution gave Congress the power to establish inferior courts, it could abolish them. Federalists predicted that if the repeal bill passed, the Supreme Court would declare it unconstitutional. They insisted that *judicial review of acts of Congress by the Supreme Court was legitimate. Republicans did not agree that the judiciary could control the other departments of government; each department was free to interpret the Constitution as it saw fit. The ultimate check upon acts of Congress, Republicans asserted, was by the people themselves, through their elected legislators, state or federal, not through an appointed judiciary with tenure during good behavior. The Repeal Act, passed 8 March 1802, restored the former judicial system. Because the June 1802 term of the Supreme Court provided an opportunity for decisions on the constitutionality of the repeal as well as on the *Marbury* case, Congress also enacted the Judiciary Act of 1802, which postponed the Court's next term until February 1803. Efforts of the deposed circuit judges to retain their offices proved fruitless.

Despite the repeal of the Judiciary Act of 1801 and the passage of the 1802 act, the federal judiciary remained fundamentally unaltered.

The full jurisdiction authorized by the Constitution in federal question cases was not realized until 1875 (see REMOVAL ACT OF 1875). The profound constitutional questions embedded in the 1801–1802 debate were resolved by the Supreme Court in Marbury and in *Stuart v. Laird (1803), holding the 1802 repealer statute constitutional. But debates over the legitimacy of judicial review in a democratic society have continued into modern times.

(See also CIRCUIT COURTS OF APPEAL; JUDICIAL POWER AND JURISDICTION.)

□ Richard E. Ellis, *The Jeffersonian Crisis: Courts and Politics in the New Republic* (1974). Kathryn Turner, "Federalist Policy and the Judiciary Act of 1801." *William and Mary Quarterly* 22 (January 1965): 3–32.

Kathryn Preyer

**Judiciary Act of 1837.** The nine Mississippi Valley states added to the Union after 1802 clamored for representation on the Supreme Court. Eastern members of Congress, worried that the Court would become unwieldy and radical, supported only piecemeal measures that ignored western interests. *Circuit riding became more onerous. Justice Thomas *Todd, for example, had to travel 2,600 miles a year between Columbus, Ohio; Frankfort, Kentucky; Nashville and Knoxville, Tennessee; and Washington, D.C. Todd's circuit responsibilities contributed to his physical collapse. In other western states, district court judges served as circuit judges, forcing litigants to bear the additional time and costs required to appeal directly to the Supreme Court. Westerners also demanded a louder voice in constitutional matters, especially after the Marshall court struck a blow against their interests by upholding the Second Bank of the United States, (*McCulloch v. Maryland, 1819) and invalidating Kentucky's occupying claimant and stay laws (*Green v. Biddle, 1823).

By 1837 the West had sufficient votes in Congress to force the issue. The 1837 Judiciary Act raised the number of justices by two (to nine) and mapped out new circuits, including three for the Mississippi Valley. Ohio, Illinois, Michigan, and Indiana became the seventh circuit; Kentucky, Tennessee, and Missouri, the eighth; and Alabama, Louisiana, Mississippi, and Arkansas, the ninth. The two new justiceships went to John *Catron of Tennessee and John *McKinley of Alabama. The Mississippi Valley in 1837 claimed four of the nine justices (Catron, McKinley, John *McLean, and James *Wayne).

Kermit L. Hall

**Judiciary Act of 1866.** This statute set the number of justices at seven, reducing by three the then ten-member court. Congress had originally fixed the size of the court at six, then increased it to seven in 1807, nine in 1837, and ten in 1863. When Representative James Wilson of Iowa, Republican chairman of the Judiciary Committee,

introduced what became the Judiciary Act of 1866, he proposed to reduce the size of the Court by one, to nine, thereby creating an odd number of justices and making the Court more manageable. The Senate, however, urged a reduction by attrition to seven, to which the House ultimately agreed. The 1866 act effectively prevented President Andrew Johnson from making any appointments, although Johnson signed the legislation, suggesting his acquiescence in, if not outright support for, the measure. Moreover, Chief Justice Salmon P. *Chase had urged the reduction in an unsuccessful effort to persuade Congress to increase the salaries of the remaining justices. The Court's ranks dropped to eight in 1867, when Justice James Moore *Wayne died, but they were increased to nine again by the *Judiciary Act of 1869; since then the Court has remained at this number. The 1866 act retained the existing nine-circuit arrangement but reduced the number of southern circuits from three to two.

Kermit L. Hall

**Judiciary Act of 1869.** This statute fundamentally reformed the federal judicial system. Since the 1790s, the justices had regularly called for an end to *circuit riding and the establishment of a separate circuit court judiciary. Congress in 1801 had complied, but that measure was repealed a year later (see JUDICIARY ACTS OF 1801 AND 1802). By the 1860s such reform was urgent, in part because the Supreme Court's business had grown significantly because of the *Civil War and in part because the justices assigned to the more remote circuits could not fulfill their duties.

Like the *Judiciary Act of 1866, that of 1869 is often misinterpreted as a Republican assault on the Court. The evidence suggests, instead, that concerns about efficiency as much as politics spurred its passage. The 1869 act permanently fixed the size of the Court at nine, an increase of two over the number established in the 1866 act. Congress provided for a separate circuit court judiciary of nine members, having the same power and jurisdiction that Supreme Court justices had exercised while holding circuit court. A circuit court might be held by either of these judges or by a district judge, sitting together or alone. The 1869 statute still required the justices to attend circuit court in each of the districts, but they had to do so only once in every two years. Finally, the measure ameliorated the chronic problem of decrepit jurists by providing that after ten years of service and reaching the age of seventy, they could retire at full pay.

Kermit L. Hall

**Judiciary Act of 1875.** See REMOVAL ACT OF 1875.

**Judiciary Act of 1891.** By creating intermediate federal courts of appeal, this act constituted the first permanent and major alteration of the federal judiciary since 1789. The *Judiciary Act of

1789 created federal trial courts, called district and circuit courts. Except for a limited *appellate jurisdiction granted to the circuit courts, the United States Supreme Court was the only federal appeals court. In addition to their Supreme Court duties, justices were burdened with the arduous task of *circuit riding. The original idea that Supreme Court justices should be brought into contact with the people by riding circuit remained politically popular for most of the century. Although lessened in 1869 (see JUDICIARY ACT OF 1869), the circuit-riding burden remained until the Judiciary Act of 1891 eliminated it.

As the nation and its judicial business grew, Congress considered relieving the Supreme Court of its growing appellate burden as early as 1848. Concern for states' rights and the threat of an increased federal judicial presence scuttled the idea, but it was revived after the *Civil War (see STATE SOVEREIGNTY AND STATES' RIGHTS). Increases in *original and removal jurisdiction of *lower federal courts, together with the proliferation of litigation resulting from the rapid industrialization of the nation and the beginnings of a regulatory movement, increased the *workload of the Supreme Court. These phenomena are reflected in the number of cases coming to the Supreme Court for review: 1860 term, 310 cases; 1870 term, 636 cases; 1880 term, 1,212 cases; and 1890 term, 1,816 cases. Fears of federal-state judicial conflict were finally overcome by the mounting caseload and nearly unanimous sentiment of the legal community.

The Judiciary Act of 1891 established nine appellate courts staffed with new judges. Rather than merge the old circuit courts, whose limited appellate jurisdiction was now abolished, with the district courts, the 1891 act retained and even strengthened the circuit courts by providing for the appointment of an additional judge for each circuit court. Twenty years later, in 1911, they were finally eliminated and their work transferred to the district courts, thereby making a single tier of federal trial courts.

The new *Circuit Courts of Appeal, renamed *Courts of Appeal in 1948, were staffed with three judges each, two of whom would constitute a quorum. Their judgment was to be final in *diversity cases, that is, those suits in which the parties were from different states, and those involving federal *patent, revenue, and *admiralty laws. In these areas, the Circuit Courts of Appeal could certify a division of opinion to the Supreme Court. Congress anticipated that a considerable portion of the Supreme Court's docket would be shifted to new appellate courts. Although pending cases were not transferred to the new appellate tribunals, the docketing of new cases in the Supreme Court revealed the dramatic change: 1891 term, 379 cases; and 1892 term, 275 cases.

The docket of the Supreme Court had been substantially pruned, but the right of appeal was preserved in many cases, including those involving more than one thousand dollars. Even when circuit judgments were final, the Supreme Court had discretionary authority to review the decisions. Additionally, a right of review from the district and old circuit courts was extended or maintained in the following areas: jurisdictional questions; prize cases; convictions for capital or infamous crimes; and cases involving constitutional questions. Finally, the right of appeal to the Supreme Court was retained in cases coming from the highest courts of the states. Not until Congress enacted the *Judiciary Act of 1925 did the Supreme Court gain substantial control of its own docket.

Since 1891 the jurisdiction of the appellate courts has been changed and the original nine courts of appeal have become eleven, but the basic structure put in place by the 1891 act continues to characterize the federal judiciary today.

(See also JUDICIAL POWER AND JURISDICTION.)

☐ Edwin C. Surrency, *History of the Federal Courts* (1987).
John E. Semonche

**Judiciary Act of 1925.** Induced by a caseload crisis stimulated by *World War I, the "Judges' Bill," as the 1925 Judiciary Act was popularly known, aimed to scale back the Court's docket to fit its decision-making capacity. Chief Justice William Howard *Taft promoted the measure as an administrative-efficiency reform. But the 1925 act also entailed profound substantive consequences. Among them were radical changes in the Court's function and relationship to litigants, enhanced institutional separation from Congress, elevated power and status for the Courts of Appeals, and, as Taft proposed, assurance of national judicial supremacy in a federal system.

The bill provided for contraction of the Court's mandatory jurisdiction invoked through writs of *error or *appeal and expansion of its discretionary jurisdiction invoked by writs of *certiorari. These changes had the effect of diverting extensive final review responsibilities to the federal Courts of Appeals. The proposal emanated from a preexisting Court committee reconstituted by Taft after his accession to the *chief justiceship in 1921. The committee was composed of Justices William *Day (succeeded by George *Sutherland), James *McReynolds, and chairman Willis *Van Devanter, who drafted the bill. The chief justice energetically lobbied for congressional action beginning in 1922, mobilized American Bar Association support, and together with his colleagues, testified before congressional judiciary committees.

The original bill eliminated all obligatory review of decisions from federal courts of appeals, but retained mandatory oversight of cases decided by *state courts that raised *federal questions. Nationalistic impulses were to counter state legislation considered inimical to federally protected rights, especially that of private *property. A Senate amendment modified the measure to conform to *dual federalism tenets. The Bill as enacted required obligatory appeals for *state court decisions holding against the validity of a federal statute or treaty and required review of federal courts of appeals decisions denying the constitutionality or supremacy of state statutes. But the act retained discretionary certiorari review for state court decisions upholding the constitutionality of federal statutes and for those upholding or invalidating a state act allegedly repugnant to the national Constitution, laws, or treaties. Courts of Appeals decisions upholding or, until 1937, invalidating a federal statute and those affirming on federal grounds the validity of *state actions were subject to discretionary review by certiorari. Thus the 1925 act eliminated much of the Supreme Court's mandatory caseload flowing from courts of appeals and, with specific exceptions, from federal district courts.

The act enhanced the institutional status and power of the Supreme Court, which was no longer dependent on Congress for sporadic and fragmentary regulation of its appellate docket. The Supreme Court was transformed from a forum that primarily corrected errors arising in ordinary private litigation to a constitutional tribunal that resolved public policy issues of national importance. The Court's procedure for selecting cases thereafter became a critical step in the decision-making process, as certiorari petitions ballooned from an average of 737 in the 1920 to 4,468 in the 1988 term. Criteria for granting certiorari has been publicized in Court-drafted rules and in explanatory opinions such as *Singleton* v. *Commissioner of Internal Revenue* (1978). The discretionary writ is granted under the *"rule of four" (four justices must vote affirmatively for a "certworthy" appeal). Voting on petitions for certiorari, veiled in permanent secrecy, reflects varied considerations responsive to formal criteria and to often-unarticulated perceptions of the Court's role as a legal and political institution.

The 1925 act converted the Courts of Appeals from intermediate to final review tribunals for an estimated 98 percent of all appellate cases. Subject only to intermittent and selective Supreme Court supervision, the Courts of Appeals have become semiautonomous centers of judicial power. Their augmented status encouraged statutory separation in 1939 from executive and congressional control as well as administrative integration among federal courts.

Efforts in the 1970s to divert the Supreme Court's reputedly burdensome task of selecting cases to a "National Court of Appeals" provoked effective opposition. That opposition was grounded on the conviction that the screening function permitted the Court to control its own

agenda and thereby to play a vital role in American political life. The Court's remaining mandatory jurisdiction contracted, eroded by summary disposition strategies and statutory constriction, until its virtual elimination by the 1988 *Judicial Improvements and Access to Justice Act.

(See also COURTS OF APPEALS; JUDICIAL POWER AND JURISDICTION; WORKLOAD.)

□ Felix Frankfurter and James M. Landis, *The Business of the Supreme Court: A Study in the Federal Judicial System* (1927). Doris Marie Provine, *Case Selection in the United States Supreme Court* (1980).                   Peter G. Fish

**Juries.** See TRIAL BY JURY.

**Jurisdiction.** See APPELLATE JURISDICTION; DIVERSITY JURISDICTION; JUDICIAL POWER AND JURISDICTION.

**Just Compensation,** the amount government must pay the owner to take *property by exercise of the power of *eminent domain. The *Takings Clause of the *Fifth Amendment limits the use of eminent domain. Most important of these limitations is that "just compensation" must be given to the person from whom property is taken. Most state constitutions contain similar language. It seems to have been the customary, if not universal, practice for American colonial governments to award compensation when private property was taken for public purpose. The same practice can be traced back in England into the early fifteenth century.

Just compensation means the fair market value of what the owner has been compelled to transfer to the government. This amount is determined by a court. Fair market value is the sum of money that a willing buyer would pay a willing seller in a bargained-for sale upon the open market. That amount is a matter of opinion, upon which testimony is received from the owner and from expert appraisers. A recent sale price is strong evidence of value. In some cases, the owner is entitled to additional compensation for severance damages. This occurs when only part of a parcel of land is taken, but the taking of that part makes the remaining part less valuable. Also, in some cases when the project will confer special benefits on the owner, the value of those offsetting benefits may be credited against the award.

(See also PUBLIC USE DOCTRINE.)
William B. Stoebuck

**Justices, Number of.** The Constitution does not specify the size of the Supreme Court's membership. Consequently, administrative and political considerations have determined the varied number of positions on that bench. The *Judiciary Act of 1789 linked the court to organization of the *lower federal courts. It created three circuits wherein *circuit courts in each would be held by two Supreme Court justices and the resident district judge, thereby necessitating a Supreme Court of six. Although circuit courts required only a single justice beginning in 1793, court size remained at six until Congress in 1801 severed the justices from the circuit courts and pared the Court membership to five (see JUDICIARY ACTS OF 1801 AND 1802). Jeffersonian antipathy to the 1801 measure caused its repeal in 1802 and restoration of the circuit-linked court of six.

The number of justices thereafter increased when Congress, acknowledging the nation's westward expansion and the court's caseload exigencies, established additional circuits accompanied by requisite Supreme Court positions: the seventh in 1807; the eighth and ninth in 1837; the tenth on the Pacific Coast in 1863 (see JUDICIARY ACT OF 1837).

Politics influenced an increase to ten justices to secure a majority favorable to President Abraham *Lincoln's war policies. But antagonism toward President Andrew Johnson's *Reconstruction program combined with dissatisfaction over the unwieldy number of members resulted in an 1866 statute reducing court size by attrition to seven. This measure effectively deprived the president of vacancies to fill (see JUDICIARY ACT OF 1866). Congress in the *Judiciary Act of 1869 fixed the membership at nine, the number of circuits authorized by the 1866 act, creating a vacancy on the existing court then composed of eight justices. The number of positions has remained at nine notwithstanding the expansionistic potential of President Franklin D. *Roosevelt's *court-packing plan in 1937.                    Peter G. Fish

**Justiciability.** *Article III, section 2 of the Constitution defines the categories of federal jurisdiction in terms of *cases and controversies. This has led the Supreme Court to hold that federal courts may take jurisdiction only of "justiciable" disputes, that is, those "appropriate for judicial determination" (*Aetna Life Insurance Co.* v. *Haworth*, 1937, p. 240). In *Aetna*, Chief Justice Charles Evans *Hughes distinguished justiciable controversies from those merely hypothetical or moot. He stressed that there must be "a real and substantial controversy admitting of specific relief through a decree of a conclusive character" (p. 241). Justiciability is a conceptual umbrella covering several related doctrines or problems, including *standing, *mootness, and *ripeness. It prohibited federal courts from rendering *advisory opinions and, until the 1934 Declaratory Judgment Act (upheld in *Aetna*), *declaratory judgments as well. It excludes *collusive suits and *political questions from federal jurisdiction.

Conceptual problems of justiciability helped frame the issues in the leading reapportionment case of *Baker* v. *Carr* (1962). Justice William J. *Brennan for the majority held that the political question doctrine was mandated by the *separation of powers within the federal system and was not a doctrine of *federalism that prohib-

ited federal courts from taking jurisdiction of litigation involving the political structure of state government. Thus suits challenging malapportionment were not banned by the justiciability requirement or the political question doctrine. Justice Felix *Frankfurter in dissent insisted that apportionment litigation was innately nonjusticiable.

(See also JUDICIAL POWER AND JURISDICTION; REAPPORTIONMENT CASES.)

William M. Wiecek

**Juvenile Justice,** concept that originated at the end of the nineteenth century when Chicago established a separate juvenile court and Rhode Island, Massachusetts, and Indiana began to employ the *common-law doctrine of *parens patriae* to authorize their legislatures to protect children from themselves and their parents. Prior to this time, children under the state-mandated age of majority had been subject exclusively to the authority of their parents. The resulting system was paternalistic and reflected the middle-class biases of its reformist proponents. Safeguards accorded persons accused of crime and the taint of a criminal record were replaced by "child-saving" judges who supposedly tailored their decisions to the needs of neglected as well as delinquent minors.

Not until the Supreme Court's decision in *Kent* v. *United States* (1966) was the system constitutionalized. The Court ruled that juvenile courts may not waive their jurisdiction and authorize adult criminal prosecution without a hearing at which the minor has access to the records on which the juvenile court waived jurisdiction. Absent these safeguards, "the child"—here a sixteen-year-old confessed rapist and robber— may receive "the worst of both worlds: that he gets neither the protections accorded to adults nor the solicitous care and regenerative treatment postulated for children" (p. 556).

One year later, in the landmark case of *In re *Gault* (1967), the Court held that juvenile courts must provide the basic procedural protections that the *Bill of Rights guarantees to adults, including timely advance notice of the charges, the right to either retained or appointed *counsel, confrontation and cross-examination of adverse witnesses, *self-incrimination, and the right to remain silent. The opinion also rejected the basic premise of juvenile court actions: that the proceedings are civil in nature and that minors' rights are adequately protected by the judges acting as substitute parents.

Subsequent decisions held that when juveniles are charged with an act that would constitute a crime if committed by an adult, the charges must meet the adult standard of proof, "beyond a reasonable doubt," and not the less protective civil standard, "preponderance of the evidence" (*In re *Winship*, 1970); that the right to a trial by jury does not apply to juvenile delinquency proceedings (*McKeiver v. Pennsylvania, 1971); and that statutes authorizing pretrial detention up to seventeen days do not violate *due process when it is found that there is a "serious risk" that the juvenile may commit additional crimes (Schall v. Martin, 1984).

In Santosky v. Kramer (1982), the Court ruled that parental rights may be terminated only on a showing of "clear and convincing" evidence. The traditional standard, preponderance of the evidence, insufficiently protects parents' fundamental rights to the care, custody, and management of their children.

In decisions antithetical to children's rights, the Court held that parents may commit their children to mental hospitals, thus depriving them of their liberty, without a formal, trial-type hearing beforehand (Parham v. J.R., 1979). The law, the majority explained, has historically "recognized that natural bonds of affection lead parents to act in the best interests of their children" (p. 602). Absent such "bonds of affection," the failure of county social service agencies to protect children from parental abuse—in this case, severe brain damage that left a child retarded and institutionalized—does not violate their constitutional rights (DeShaney v. Winnebago County Department of Social Services, 1989). Although government may not deprive persons of life, liberty, or property without due process of law, the Constitution does not "impose an affirmative obligation on the State to ensure that those interests do not come to harm through other means" (p. 259). The most that can be said of the social service officials in this case "is that they stood by and did nothing when suspicious circumstances dictated a more active role for them" (p. 263).

Gault and its progeny have produced a legalistically constitutionalized system that has largely replaced the paternalistic authoritarianism that prevailed during the first eight decades of the twentieth century. Adversarial proceedings respectful of constitutionally mandated procedures and evidentiary standards have supplanted the informal conferences in which juvenile court judges did what they thought was in the best interest of the child. Such individualized treatment came to be viewed as unconfined discretion in which similarly situated children were treated vastly differently.

The post-Gault system differs from its predecessor by focusing more on punishment and prevention than on the treatment of errant children. Older, violence-prone juveniles are waived to the criminal courts, while status offenses—truancy, inappropriate deportment, and disobedience—are handled by community child specialists. Between these extremes, the juvenile courts still process delinquents in a manner more paternal and diagnostic than that afforded their adult criminal counterparts.

(See also DUE PROCESS, PROCEDURAL.)

Harold J. Spaeth

# K

Kagama, United States v., 118 U.S. 375 (1886), argued 2 Mar. 1886, decided 10 May 1886 by vote of 9 to 0; Miller for the Court. *Kagama* applied the broad principles governing Indian relations that Chief Justice John *Marshall had articulated in *Worcester* v. *Georgia* (1832) to the question of whether a federal criminal statute specifically applicable to Indians was constitutional. The Court upheld the statute and its application (see CHEROKEE CASES).

In *Ex parte *Crow Dog* (1883), the Court had held that tribal, not federal, law applied to criminal acts committed by an Indian in Indian country. In response, Congress enacted the "Major Crimes Act" as part of the Indian Appropriations Act of 1885, which extended the jurisdiction of federal courts to seven specified crimes, including murder and manslaughter committed by one Indian against another in Indian country. Applying *Worcester* in the *Kagama* case, the Court unanimously held that protection of Indians constituted a national obligation and thus sustained the power of Congress to legislate for Indians on reservations. In *obiter dictum, Justice Samuel F. *Miller added that *state courts lacked jurisdiction over crimes committed by Indians on reservations because federal power preempted state authority. He added that the states had historically been the Indians' "deadliest enemies" (p. 384).

The *Kagama* Court relied on Marshall's analogy to the *common-law guardian-ward relationship as a figure explaining federal authority over Indian affairs. But the federal-Indian relationship derives not from common law but from the Constitution's grant of power to the federal government over Indian relations. Although that power is broad, Indians may claim constitutional protection in their dealings with the federal government. Courts continue to affirm the *Worcester* principles of self government within tribal territory.

(See also NATIVE AMERICANS.)

Rennard J. Strickland

Kastigar v. United States, 406 U.S. 441 (1972), argued 11 Jan. 1972, decided 22 May 1972 by vote of 5 to 2; Powell for the Court, Douglas and Marshall in dissent, Brennan and Rehnquist not participating. In *Kastigar* the Court for the first time squarely confronted the question of whether witnesses can be compelled to testify before *grand juries under a grant of use immunity. In 1970, Congress had substituted use for transactional immunity in the federal immunity statute. *Use immunity* prevents the government from using compelled testimony or any information derived from such testimony against the witness in a subsequent criminal prosecution. It is not as broad as transactional immunity, which prevents any prosecution of a witness for offenses related to the compelled testimony. Kastigar argued that the *Fifth Amendment privilege against *self-incrimination prohibits the compulsion of testimony under a grant of use immunity but instead requires transactional immunity at the very least.

In rejecting that argument, the Court first noted that the power to compel testimony in court or before a grand jury is firmly established and essential to the effective functioning of government. That power, however, is not abso-

480

lute but is limited by the Fifth Amendment privilege against self-incrimination. The Fifth Amendment protects a person from being forced to give testimony that could be used against him or her in a subsequent criminal prosecution. Use immunity, the Court concluded, is compatible with the Fifth Amendment because it ensures that the compelled testimony cannot lead to prosecution. In a subsequent prosecution, an affirmative duty is placed on the government to prove that evidence it seeks to use is derived from a source wholly independent of the compelled testimony. As a result, use immunity removes the danger that testimony will be used against the witness and, thus, does not violate the privilege against self-incrimination.

(See also DUE PROCESS, PROCEDURAL.)

Daan Braveman

**Katzenbach v. McClung,** 379 U.S. 294 (1964), argued 5 Oct. 1964, decided 14 Dec. 1964 by vote of 9 to 0; Clark for the Court, Black, Douglas, and Goldberg in separate concurrences. This decision is the Supreme Court's most expansive reading of the constitutional grant of power to Congress to regulate interstate commerce (see COMMERCE POWER). The Court held that the Commerce Clause authorized Congress to regulate the racially discriminatory seating practices of Ollie's Barbecue, a small restaurant that purchased all of its food locally and served a local clientele. The discrimination was held to be subject to Congress's commerce power because some of the food that Ollie's purchased from its local supplier had originated out of state.

The Court stated that Congress need only demonstrate a "rational basis" for concluding that the local activity aggregated with other similar local activity would create a substantial economic effect on interstate commerce. The Court found that Congress could have rationally assumed that race discrimination by local restaurants would reduce the amount of food served in those restaurants and consequently reduce the amount of food purchased in interstate commerce by their suppliers. The Court suggested further that Congress could have reasonably concluded that race discrimination by local restaurants would deter individuals and industries from relocating through interstate commerce into areas where such practices prevailed.

The Court evidently accepted such an attenuated connection to interstate commerce, and thus assigned such pervasive legislative power to Congress under the Commerce Clause, because race discrimination demanded a national legislative solution. But nothing in the Court's opinion confines the Court's expansive reading of Congress's commerce power only to race discrimination cases. Thus, *Katzenbach* stands as authority for an apparently unlimited power in Congress to regulate any local activity if some aggregate

economic impact on interstate commerce can be plausibly posited.

(See also RACE AND RACISM.)

Thomas R. McCoy

**Katzenbach v. Morgan,** 384 U.S. 641 (1966), argued 18 Apr. 1966, decided 13 June 1966 by vote of 7 to 2; Brennan for the Court, Harlan and Stewart in dissent. A majority upheld a provision of the *Voting Rights Act of 1965 stipulating that no person who had successfully completed the sixth grade in an accredited Puerto Rican school was to be denied the right to vote because of an inability to read or write English. The Court in 1959 had upheld state power to impose a fairly administered literacy test. Speaking for the *Morgan* majority, however, Justice William *Brennan held that the earlier precedent was not the measure of congressional, as opposed to judicial, power to enforce the *Fourteenth Amendment's *equal protection guarantee. Congress, declared Brennan, need have only a rational basis for its laws; and Congress could reasonably have concluded that the challenged provision would help to eliminate discriminatory treatment in access to public services. Justice John M. *Harlan charged in dissent, however, that the Court had already decided that a literacy test did not violate the Constitution and that, while Congress had broad discretion in choosing the means for enforcing the equal protection clause, its substantive scope, like that of other constitutional guarantees, was ultimately a question for the courts, not the legislature. If Congress could expand on the Court's interpretations of constitutional rights, Harlan concluded, it could also restrict the content of such guarantees.

Tinsley E. Yarbrough

**Katz v. United States,** 389 U.S. 347 (1967), argued 17 Oct. 1967, decided 18 Dec. 1967 by vote of 7 to 1; Stewart for the Court, Harlan and White concurring, Black in dissent, Marshall not participating. *Katz* altered significantly the approach that courts must use in determining, under the *Fourth Amendment, whether certain police conduct constitutes a "search" that is subject to the amendment's warrant and *probable cause limitations. Illustrative of the pre-*Katz* approach is *Olmstead* v. *United States* (1928), where the Supreme Court held that it did not constitute a search for the authorities to place a tap on certain telephone wires and thereby eavesdrop on the defendant's telephone conversations. As the Court later put the matter in *Silverman* v. *United States* (1961), for there to be a Fourth Amendment search the police must have physically intruded into "a constitutionally protected area" (p. 682). *Katz* replaced the *Silverman* standard with a reasonable expectation of *privacy test.

At his trial for transmitting wagering information by phone, the government introduced over Katz's objection evidence of his end of telephone conversations, overheard by federal agents who had attached an electronic listening/recording device to the exterior of a public phone booth habitually used by Katz. The lower court concluded there was no search because the wall of the booth had not been physically penetrated. The Supreme Court reversed, holding that "[t]he Government's activities in electronically listening to and recording the petitioner's words violated the privacy upon which he justifiably relied while using the telephone booth and thus constituted a 'search and seizure' within the meaning of the Fourth Amendment" (p. 512). This proposition was elaborated in Justice John M. *Harlan's concurring opinion, later relied upon by lower courts and the Supreme Court itself in determining the meaning of Katz. Harlan stated that "there is a twofold requirement, first that a person have exhibited an actual (subjective) expectation of privacy and, second, that the expectation be one that society is prepared to recognize as 'reasonable' " (p. 516).

The first branch of the Harlan formulation should not be a part of any statement of what the Fourth Amendment protects. This is because the government could easily, either by edict or systematic practice, condition the expectations of the general public in such a way that there would be no hope of privacy. Harlan later appreciated this, stating in United States v. White (1971) that analysis under Katz must "transcend the search for subjective expectations" (p. 786). The Supreme Court has seldom addressed this point in more recent cases, though some of its statements are legitimate cause for concern. Illustrative is California v. Ciraolo (1986), holding that it is not a search to make an aerial observation of marijuana plants growing inside a fenced backyard, where it was intimated that defendant's ten-foot high solid wood fence would not provide a subjective expectation of privacy because the plants could be seen by "a policeman perched on the top of a truck or a two-level bus" (p. 211). A person is unlikely therefore to get by the first Katz hurdle unless he or she has taken steps to ensure against all conceivable efforts at scrutiny.

As for the second prong of the Harlan elaboration, he stressed in White that "those more extensive intrusions that significantly jeopardize the sense of security which is the paramount concern of Fourth Amendment liberties" are searches (p. 1143). Unfortunately, the Supreme Court has not interpreted Katz this way, as is evident from two cases: United States v. Miller (1976), holding that a person has no justified expectation of privacy in a bank's records of his financial transactions because those documents "contain only information voluntarily conveyed to the banks and exposed to their employees in the ordinary course of business" (p. 442); and Ciraolo, holding that it is not a search for police to look down from an airplane into one's solidly fenced yard because "any member of the public flying over this airspace who glanced down could

have seen everything that these officers observed" (pp. 213–214). In these and other cases the Court has failed to appreciate, as Justice Thurgood Marshall put it in his Smith v. Maryland (1979) dissent, that "privacy is not a discrete commodity, possessed absolutely or not at all" (p. 749).

□ Wayne R. LaFave, "The Forgotten Motto of Obsta Principiis in Fourth Amendment Jurisprudence," Arizona Law Review 28 (1986): 291–310. Wayne R. LaFave

**Kendall v. United States ex rel. Stokes,** 12 Pet. (37 U.S.) 524 (1838), argued 13, 19–24, 26–27 Feb. 1838, decided 12 Mar. 1838 by vote of 9 to 0; Thompson for the Court. The case originated when newly appointed postmaster general Amos Kendall refused to obey an order from the federal circuit court for the District of Columbia that he honor a contract negotiated by his predecessor with the firm of Stockton and Stokes. Kendall, appointed by President Andrew *Jackson to reform the Post Office, refused on the grounds that the contract was tainted with political favoritism, which it probably was. The matter was referred to Congress, which enacted a law requiring Kendall to follow the recommendations of the solicitor general of the treasury, Virgil Maxcy (who was a friend of the plaintiffs). Kendall refused again, arguing that the act of Congress was an unconstitutional infringement on the powers of the executive branch. This was the issue before the Supreme Court.

A unanimous decision, written by Justice Smith *Thompson, went against Kendall holding that (1) not every officer in the executive branch was under the exclusive control of the president; (2) Congress could assign ministerial duties to such officers, and (3) such duties could be enforced by a writ of *mandamus issuing from the federal circuit court. The case was significant because it resolved a conflict between the executive branch and Congress, while at the same time establishing a role for the courts in resolving such disputes. It clarified the mandamus-granting authority of federal circuit courts.

(See also LOWER FEDERAL COURTS; SEPARATION OF POWERS.)

R. Kent Newmyer

**Kennedy, Anthony McLeod** (b. Sacramento, Calif., 23 July 1936), associate justice, 1988–. Justice Anthony Kennedy's parents, Anthony and Gladys Kennedy, were an economically comfortable, middle-class professional family of the Roman Catholic faith. His undergraduate education combined work at Stanford University and the London School of Economics. After receiving his B.A. at Stanford in 1958, Kennedy studied at Harvard University Law School. Upon receiving his degree cum laude in 1961, he became an associate in the San Francisco law firm of Thelen, Marrin, John, and Bridges. He returned to Sacra-

*Anthony McLeod Kennedy*

mento to private practice as a partner in the firm of Evans, Jackson, and Kennedy. In 1965, Kennedy began a long and cherished association with the McGeorge School of Law of the University of the Pacific. He taught constitutional law from 1965 until his elevation to the Supreme Court of the United States in 1988.

In his years as a private practitioner in San Francisco and Sacramento, Kennedy was an able lawyer of conservative inclination and Republican party affiliation. After thirteen years in private practice, President Gerald Ford appointed Kennedy to the Ninth Circuit *Court of Appeals. Between 1975 and 1988, Judge Kennedy wrote over four hundred decisions, which the *Senate Judiciary Committee in its confirmation discussions in 1987–1988 subjected to sharp scrutiny as indicators of his views on *separation of powers and on minority and *gender discrimination.

Despite a solid career as an able lawyer and circuit judge, Anthony M. Kennedy's emergence as President Ronald *Reagan's successful nominee for the Supreme Court vacancy created by the resignation of Associate Justice Lewis *Powell was overshadowed by the events surrounding the nominations of Robert H. *Bork and Douglas *Ginsburg, both rejected for the same position. Comparisons between Bork and Kennedy enlivened Senate debate of the latter's qualifications. Kennedy received the highest evaluation of the *American Bar Association's Standing Committee on the Federal Judiciary—well qualified on the basis of his integrity, judicial temperament, and professional competence. In contrast this committee had disagreed over Bork with four of its members voting "not qualified" on the basis of his "extreme views respecting constitutional principles."

Since joining the Court, Justice Kennedy has contributed substantially to conservative majority coalitions. By the end of the October 1988–1989 term, he had voted with Chief Justice William *Rehnquist in 90 percent of the cases and with Justice Antonin *Scalia in 89 percent of the cases.                                    John R. Schmidhauser

**Kentucky v. Dennison,** 24 How. (65 U.S.) 66 (1861), argued 20 Feb. 1861, decided 14 Mar. 1861 by vote of 8 to 0; Taney for the Court. In 1859 Willis Lago, a free black from Ohio, helped a Kentucky slave named Charlotte escape to Ohio. Kentucky indicted Lago for theft and Governor Beriah Magoffin of Kentucky asked Ohio governor Salmon P. *Chase to extradite Lago. Chase, an antislavery advocate, refused to comply, arguing that Lago had not committed a crime recognized by Ohio law. Magoffin waited until Chase left office in 1860 and renewed the requisition with the new Ohio governor, William Dennison, who also refused to comply. Magoffin then sought a writ of *mandamus to force Dennison to act. Magoffin sued in the United States Supreme Court, under the court's *original jurisdiction for cases between two states.

The case presented Chief Justice Roger B. *Taney with a major dilemma. Taney was profoundly proslavery, deeply antagonistic toward the North, and desirous of settling all constitutional issues surrounding slavery in favor of the South. But with secession already in progress, Taney was loathe to rule that the Supreme Court or the federal government might have the power to force state governors to act. After chastising the Ohio governors for not cooperating with the criminal extradition clause of the Constitution, Taney ruled that the Court had no power to coerce a state to comply with its constitutional obligation. This decision remained good law until overturned by *Puerto Rico v. Branstad* (1987).

(See also FUGITIVE SLAVES; JUDICIAL POWER AND JURISDICTION; SLAVERY; STATE SOVEREIGNTY AND STATES' RIGHTS.)
                                                           Paul Finkelman

**Kent v. Dulles,** 357 U.S. 116 (1958), argued 10 Apr. 1958, decided 16 June 1958 by vote of 5 to 4; Douglas for the Court, Clark, joined by Burton, Harlan, and Whitaker, in dissent. The State Department denied Rockwell Kent a passport pursuant to its 1948 policy of refusing to issue passports to communists and their supporters, or to those whose foreign travel would be contrary to the interests of the United States. Kent argued that this abridged his *First Amendment rights and interfered with his right to travel. Justice William O. *Douglas for the majority acknowledged that the right to *travel was a liberty protected by the *Due Process Clause of the *Fifth Amendment. However, the majority ruled in favor of Kent on statutory grounds, holding that Congress had not given the secretary of state authority to withhold passports of citizens because of their beliefs or associations. The dissenters argued that the Immigration and Nationality Act of 1952 should be read as recognizing broad discretionary powers of the secretary of state in issuing passports.

The immediate decisional impact was that questions about Communist party membership were dropped from the passport application. Passports were promptly issued to Kent and others who had also contested the department on this matter. The broader legal impact was that the majority opinion recognized the right to travel abroad and dismantled barriers to its exercise. It is still good law.

The decision was criticized by some for not having fully addressed the First Amendment issues and for avoiding a ruling on constitutionality. However, a relatively narrow ruling was necessary to keep Justice Felix *Frankfurter's crucial fifth vote for the majority.

Sheldon Goldman

**Ker v. California,** 374 U.S. 23 (1963), argued 11 Dec. 1962, decided 10 June 1963 by vote of 5 to 4; Clark for the Court, Harlan concurring in the result, Brennan dissenting in part joined by Warren, Douglas, and Goldberg. When the Court decided in *Mapp v. Ohio* (1961) to impose the *exclusionary rule of the *Fourth Amendment on the states through the *Fourteenth Amendment, it was unclear to what extent federal standards of what constitutes unreasonable searches and seizures were applicable to the states. A case involving the marijuana dealings of George and Diane Ker resolved this issue. Reviewing their convictions, a consensus of eight justices agreed that the states were to be held to federal standards. The ninth justice, John M. *Harlan, argued that states should be judged by a more flexible concept of fundamental fairness. The consensus, however, broke down in applying the principle to the facts of the case. A plurality of four justices found that the actions of the California authorities who had entered the Kers' apartment with a passkey and without a warrant and who seized marijuana used to convict them met federal standards of *probable cause and reasonableness. Justice Harlan concurred only in affirming the convictions. The four justices in dissent argued that the arrests and subsequent seizure were illegal because in their view the unannounced entry into the apartment was unjustified.

*Ker* remains a very important component of the exclusionary rule. The doctrine that Fourth Amendment (i.e., federal) standards of reasonableness apply to the states through the Fourteenth Amendment is still controlling law. But the holding that an unannounced warrantless entry to a person's home is valid is inconsistent

with subsequent Court rulings such as *Payton* v. *New York* (1980).

(See also SEARCH WARRANT RULE, EXCEPTIONS TO.)

Sheldon Goldman

**Keyes v. Denver School District No. 1,** 413 U.S. 189 (1973), argued 12 Oct. 1972, decided 21 June 1973 by vote of 7 to 1; Brennan for the Court, Burger concurring in result without opinion, separate statement by Douglas, Powell concurring in judgment and dissenting in part, Rehnquist in dissent, White not participating. In the first nonsouthern school desegregation case to receive plenary consideration, the Supreme Court held that a school district that "racially or ethnically" segregated one part of a large urban district created an arguably rebuttable presumption that similar segregation throughout the district was not "adventitious" and implied that wholesale, districtwide relief under *Swann* v. *Charlotte-Mecklenburg* (1971) was not inappropriate (p. 208).

Although the opinion is tentative in tone and structured in terms of presumptions and future proceedings, *Keyes* was widely, and accurately, viewed as a green light for districtwide (if not necessarily interdistrict) desegregation of northern school districts. Justices William O. *Douglas and Lewis *Powell, in separate opinions, urged abandonment of the de jure/de facto distinction in school segregation cases, although Powell also suggested limits, and uniform guidelines, for *Swann*-type transportation decrees.

Justice William *Rehnquist's dissent objected to the majority's use of evidentiary presumptions to extend *Green* v. *County School Board* (1968) to northern schools and argued further that *Brown* v. *Board of Education* (1954, 1955) required elimination of racial standards, not *Green*'s achievement of an approved racial balance in public schools. The *Keyes* opinions ambiguously signaled *Green*'s application to de facto segregation in the North but also indicated growing fissures within the Court over the issue.

(See also DESEGREGATION REMEDIES; RACE AND RACISM; SEGREGATION, DE FACTO.)

Dennis J. Hutchinson

**Keyishian v. Board of Regents,** 385 U. S. 589 (1967), argued 17 Nov. 1966, decided 23 Jan. 1967 by vote of 5 to 4; Brennan for the Court, Clark, Harlan, Stewart, and White in dissent. In this case the Court declared unconstitutional New York statutes and administrative rules designed to prevent employment of "subversive" teachers and professors in state educational institutions and to dismiss them if found guilty of "treasonable or seditious" acts. The Board of Regents of New York had prepared a list of subversive organizations, including the Communist party, membership in which was sufficient reason for a teacher's disqualification. Originally there was also an oath requirement, but this was rescinded by the regents.

The Court held that the proscription of "treasonable or seditious" conduct and of "advocacy" of violent overthrow was unconstitutional for vagueness: a teacher could not foretell whether statements about abstract doctrine were prohibited or whether only speech intended to incite action was grounds for dismissal. The complexity of the New York plan aggravated the vice of vagueness. The Court also held that the statutes were unconstitutional because they did not require that the teacher have specific intent to further the illegal aims of a proscribed organization and hence were overly broad. The decision's importance lay in its rejection of a state's power to make public employment conditional on surrendering constitutional rights that could not otherwise be abridged by direct *state action as well as in its emphasis on *academic freedom.

(See also COMMUNISM AND COLD WAR; EDUCATION; FIRST AMENDMENT; SPEECH AND THE PRESS.)

Milton R. Konvitz

**Keystone Bituminous Coal Association v. DeBenedictis,** 480 U.S. 470 (1987), argued 10 Nov. 1986, decided 9 Mar. 1987 by vote of 5 to 4; Stevens for the Court, Rehnquist in dissent. In *Keystone*, a divided Court upheld a Pennsylvania mining-subsidence statute against a claim that the statute effected a taking of private property without payment of *just compensation. The challenged statute prohibited all underground mining that caused subsidence damage to surface structures, and it obligated mining companies to leave in place, for structural support, at least half of the coal that underlay a protected structure. The Court upheld the statute as a valid exercise of the state's *police power, noting that the statute substantially advanced public interests in health, safety, and welfare and did not render the mining companies unable to mine at a profit.

In *Keystone* the Court continued its prior refusal to divide property parcels into components when determining whether the state had taken property. The Court denied that the small amount of coal left in place for surface support was a discrete property interest that the Pennsylvania statute had, in effect, taken without compensation.

*Keystone* is remarkable because the facts of the case were virtually identical to those of *Pennsylvania Coal Co.* v. *Mahon* (1922), a landmark of takings jurisprudence. In *Mahon* a state statute prohibited an owner from engaging in underground mining if the mining caused structural subsidence. The Court in *Mahon* struck down this statute as a taking because the statute served private interests and denied the mining company all economically viable use of the underlying coal. In *Keystone*, the Court appreciated the public nature of the harms caused by land subsidence;

the Court viewed the new statute as one that furthered public interests, not private ones, and it saw land subsidence as a public nuisance.

(See also EMINENT DOMAIN; PROPERTY RIGHTS; TAKINGS CLAUSE.)

Eric T. Freyfogle

**Kidd v. Pearson,** 128 U.S. 1 (1888), argued 4 Apr. 1888, decided 22 Oct. 1888 by vote of 8 to 0; Lamar for the Court, Woods deceased. An Iowa statute prohibited the manufacture of liquor for shipment outside the state. The measure was challenged as an unconstitutional regulation of interstate commerce by a state. (See COMMERCE POWER.) The Supreme Court held that the statute did not interfere with federal commerce power and that it was a simple *police power regulation, well within a state's authority. At least when liquor, a putatively noxious product, was the subject, *Kidd* demonstrated the willingness of the Court to uphold the police powers of the states.

The real significance of the case lay in its definition of "commerce." The Court drew a distinction between commerce and manufacturing, holding that commerce did not begin until manufacture was completed. But if congressional power under the Commerce Clause did not encompass production, federal regulations could not be constitutionally applied to manufacturing, *agricultural, or extractive industries. The Court gradually deserted this holding over the years, broadening the permissible scope of federal regulation and correspondingly narrowing state power.

On the exact point of state liquor laws, however, *Kidd* is not good law today. To the extent that Congress wishes to exercise its powers under the Commerce Clause, it may undercut or negate state liquor laws.

Loren P. Beth

**Kilbourn v. Thompson,** 103 U.S. 168 (1881), decided by a vote of 9 to 0; Miller for the Court. The House of Representatives in 1876 appointed a special committee to examine the dealings of a real estate partnership in Washington, D.C. Hallett Kilbourn was ordered by the committee to appear and testify. He refused to answer a question or produce records. The committee declared Kilbourn to be in contempt of Congress and ordered him committed to jail (see CONTEMPT POWER.) He brought an action of false imprisonment against John Thompson, the sergeant-at-arms who had taken him into custody, and the members of the House committee.

The trial court held in favor of Thompson, but the Supreme Court reversed. The justices left open the question whether either house of Congress had power to punish for contempt, a question that was subsequently answered affirmatively. The Court invalidated the contempt order on the ground that it was rendered in pursuit of an unconstitutional objective. Congress may conduct investigations only for the purpose of gathering information relevant to contemplated future legislation. The proceedings at issue concerned debts owed by the real estate partnership to certain parties, including the United States. The Court viewed this as a judicial not as a legislative matter. Under these circumstances, the House exceeded its authority by investigating the private affairs of individuals. Consequently, it had no power to require Kilbourn to testify as a witness. Subsequently, however, the Supreme Court approved a broader investigative power, allowing Congress limited inquiry into private matters.

(See also CONGRESSIONAL POWER OF INVESTIGATION.)

Edgar Bodenheimer

**King, Edward** (b. Philadelphia, 31 Jan. 1794; d. Philadelphia, 8 May 1873), unconfirmed nominee to the Supreme Court. King studied law with Charles Chauncey and was admitted to the Pennsylvania bar in 1816. An active Democrat, he became clerk of the Philadelphia orphans' court in 1824 and in 1825 president judge of the Philadelphia Court of Common Pleas.

On 5 June 1844 President John *Tyler appointed King to the Supreme Court to fill a vacancy on the Third Circuit. On 15 June 1844 the Senate postponed consideration of the nomination by a vote of 29 to 18. Tyler reappointed King on 4 Dec. 1844 and the Senate again postponed consideration on 23 Jan. 1845. Tyler withdrew King's nomination on 7 Feb. 1845 and appointed instead John M. *Read, also of Pennsylvania. Both the King and Read nominations failed as a result of Tyler's lack of support from either the Whig or Democratic party.

While president judge of the Court of Common Pleas King was noted for decisions supporting equity jurisdiction. He retired from the bench in 1852 and was appointed in the same year to a commission that revised the criminal code of Pennsylvania.

(See also NOMINEES, REJECTION OF.)

Elizabeth B. Monroe

**Kirkpatrick v. Preisler,** 394 U.S. 526 (1969), argued 13 Jan. 1969, decided 7 April 1969 by vote of 6 to 3; Brennan for the Court, Fortas concurring, Harlan, Stewart, and White in dissent. In *Kirkpatrick* the Supreme Court affirmed a federal district court's rejection of Missouri's 1967 Congressional Redistricting Act. In the companion case of *Wells* v. *Rockefeller* the Court reversed a decision sustaining the validity of New York's 1968 congressional redistricting statute.

*Kirkpatrick* significantly narrowed the range of permissible population deviations among districts permitted by the 1964 reapportionment. Moreover, it reflected a split within the Warren Court over the meaning, in *Wesberry* v. *Sanders* (1964), of the phrase "as nearly equal as practicable" (p. 21). Missouri's districts entailed 1960

population disparities ranging from 3.13 percent above to 2.83 percent below a statewide average. For the Court, Justice William *Brennan insisted, "The 'as nearly as practicable' standard requires that the State make a good-faith effort to achieve precise mathematical equality. . . . Unless population variances among congressional districts are shown to have resulted despite such effort, the State must justify each variance, no matter how small" (pp. 530–531).

This standard drew strong criticism from four justices. Justice Abe *Fortas concurred in the result but decried the majority's quest for an illusory mathematical precision based on inexact, obsolete census data. Separate dissents by Justices John M. *Harlan and Byron *White additionally faulted judicial intrusion into legislative common sense while minimizing traditional constraints of local boundaries on gerrymandering.

Although *Kirkpatrick* and *Wells* were both congressional redistricting cases, the Court's broad language left an impression that state legislative districting might be similarly restricted. That question was resolved in several 1973 cases that reiterated the more flexible phraseology of *Reynolds* v. *Sims* (1964) for state legislatures (*Mahan* v. *Howell,* 1973) while maintaining *Kirkpatrick's* narrower approach for congressional constituencies (*White* v. *Weiser,* 1973).

A decade later, New Jersey's congressional districting, with a total population variance range of less than 0.7 percent, was invalidated in *Karcher* v. *Daggett* (1983). Although that holding was based on the *Kirkpatrick* precedent, five members of the Court (four dissenters plus Justice John Paul *Stevens, who concurred) questioned Brennan's quest for population precision, claiming that partisan gerrymandering was a greater threat to fair representation than were small population variances.

(See also GERRYMANDERING; REAPPORTIONMENT CASES.)

Gordon E. Baker

**Klopfer v. North Carolina** 386 U.S. 213 (1967), argued 8 Dec. 1966, decided 13 Mar. 1967 by vote of 6 to 3; Warren for the Court, Harlan and Stewart in dissent. Under North Carolina's "nolle prosequi with leave" law, challenged in this case, a prosecutor could indefinitely suspend prosecution on an indictment without having to provide a reason to the court. Frustrated by a prosecutor who after his inability to obtain a conviction at a first trial decided to reinstitute charges but suspend prosecution indefinitely, Klopfer, the defendant, pressed for a trial or dismissal of charges. When neither was forthcoming, he attacked the law and the prosecutor's decision on the grounds that his *Sixth Amendment guarantee of a *speedy trial had been denied.

In accepting Klopfer's arguments and extending the Sixth Amendment speedy trial guarantee to the states under the same standards that apply to the federal government, the Supreme Court also gave its first significant interpretation of the Sixth Amendment's right to a speedy trial. It held that the right was "as fundamental as any of the rights secured by the Sixth Amendment" and traced it back to "the very foundation of our English law heritage" (p. 223). Furthermore, the Court ruled, although the accused was neither being held in custody nor subject to restrictions on his movement, nevertheless the "anxiety and concern accompanying public accusation," as well as the possibility of public scorn, was injury enough to violate his right to a speedy trial (p. 222). Despite its sweeping language, in subsequent cases, such as *Barker* v. *Wingo* (1972), the Court has employed a balancing test to interpret this right and in so doing has almost always held for the prosecution.

(See also DUE PROCESS, PROCEDURAL.)

Malcolm M. Feeley

**Knaebel, Ernest** (b. Manhasset, N.Y., 14 June 1872; d. West Boxford, Mass., 19 Feb. 1947), reporter of decisions, 1916–1944. Knaebel received the A.B. (1894), LL.B. (1896), and LL.M. (1897) from Yale. He was admitted to the New Mexico and New York bars and practiced with Shearman & Sterling in New York City from 1897 to 1899. He moved to Colorado in 1898 and practiced with his father in Denver. Later becoming an attorney for the federal government, he prosecuted public land frauds in the West, and served as assistant U.S. attorney in Colorado from 1902 to 1907.

Knaebel came to Washington in 1907 as special assistant to the attorney general. He practiced in the Justice Department and in 1911 became assistant attorney general. He organized and directed the Public Lands Division of the Justice Department and directed litigation concerning public and Indian lands. In this capacity, he argued many cases before the Supreme Court. He succeeded Charles Henry *Butler as the Court's reporter of decisions in 1916, eventually editing volumes 242 through 321 of the *United States Reports*. Butler wrote that Knaebel had not known the position was vacant and that Knaebel was surprised by his appointment. Under Knaebel's tenure, the office of reporter was reorganized by statute and the printing and sale of the *U.S. Reports* exclusively by the government was begun. Knaebel resigned because of poor health in 1944.

(See also REPORTERS, SUPREME COURT.)

Francis Helminski

**Knox v. Lee.** See LEGAL TENDER CASES.

**Korean War.** See WAR; YOUNGSTOWN SHEET & TUBE CO. V. SAWYER.

**Korematsu v. United States,** 323 U.S. 214 (1944), argued 11 and 12 Oct. 1944, decided 18 Dec. 1944

by vote of 6 to 3; Black for the Court, Frankfurter concurring, Roberts, Murphy, and Jackson in dissent. Fred Korematsu, an American-born citizen of Japanese ancestry, grew up in the San Francisco Bay area. Rejected by the military for poor health, he obtained a defense industry job. In May 1942, when the Japanese internment began, Korematsu had a good job and a non-Japanese girlfriend. Rather than submit to incarceration, Korematsu moved to a nearby town, changed his name, had some facial surgery, and claimed to be Mexican-American. Korematsu ignored military orders prohibiting Japanese-Americans from either remaining on the California coast or moving from where they lived. As Justice Robert H. *Jackson noted in dissent, Korematsu was "convicted of an act not commonly a crime. It consists merely of being present in the state whereof he is a citizen, near the place where he was born, and where all his life he has lived" (p. 243). Justice Owen J. *Roberts, also dissenting, explained that Korematsu's only legal course of action was to enter a relocation center, which "was a euphemism for prison." Faced with the dilemma "that he dare not remain in his home, or voluntarily leave the area" and unwilling to be interned, Korematsu "did nothing" (p. 230). He was subsequently arrested, convicted, sentenced to five years in prison, paroled, and immediately interned at Topaz, Utah.

*Korematsu* is usually cited for Justice Hugo *Black's assertion that "all legal restrictions which curtail the civil rights of a single racial group are immediately suspect" and should be given "the most rigid scrutiny" (p. 216). Significantly, this is the only case in which the Supreme Court has applied the "rigid scrutiny" test to a racial restriction and upheld the restrictive law (see STRICT SCRUTINY).

As in *Hirabayashi* v. *U.S.* (1943), the Court majority never questioned the military's claim that Japanese-Americans threatened military security on the west coast (see NATIONAL SECURITY). Justice Black fully accepted "the finding of the military authorities that it was impossible to bring about an immediate segregation of the disloyal from the loyal. . . ." Black argued that this "temporary exclusion of the entire group" was based on a military judgment (p. 219).

Ignoring the fact that nearly all Japanese-Americans were shipped to an internment camp after entering an assembly center, Black asserted that "Had the petitioner here left the prohibited area and gone to an assembly center we cannot say either as a matter of fact or law . . . [this] would have resulted in his detention in a relocation center" (p. 219). Since Korematsu was charged with remaining in a restricted area and failing to report to the assembly center, Black would not examine the constitutionality of the military forcing people into relocation camps. Black thought "It will be time enough to decide the serious constitutional issues which the petitioner seeks to raise when an assembly or relocation order is applied or is certain to be applied to him . . ." (p. 220). In other words, Korematsu could only litigate the constitutionality of the internment after he had actually been incarcerated.

Black indignantly rejected the dissenters' claims that the internment was racist and that the "relocation centers" were "concentration camps." Black asserted that "Korematsu was not excluded from the Military Area because of hostility to him or his race. He *was* excluded because we are at war with the Japanese Empire, because the properly constituted military authorities feared an invasion of our West Coast" and because the military authorities believed the "military urgency" required "that all citizens of Japanese ancestry be segregated from the West Coast temporarily" (p. 223). Black never explained why segregating only people "of Japanese ancestry" was not racist.

In dissent Justices Roberts, Murphy, and Jackson distinguished the exclusion order and the order to report to an assembly center from the curfew approved in *Hirabayashi*. Roberts noted that "the two conflicting orders, one which commanded him to stay and the other which commanded him to go, were nothing but a cleverly devised trap to accomplish the real purpose of the military authority, which was to lock him up in a concentration camp" (p. 232).

Noting that the internment was justified "mainly upon questionable racial and sociological grounds not ordinarily within the realm of expert military judgment" (pp. 236–237), Justice Frank *Murphy challenged Black's blind support for military expertise. Finding no evidence tying Japanese-Americans to sabotage or espionage, Murphy argued the internment was based on "the misinformation, half-truths and insinuations that for years have been directed against Japanese Americans by people with racial and economic prejudices—the same people who have been among the foremost advocates of the evacuation" (p. 239) (see SUBVERSION). Murphy believed the Japanese-Americans should have been treated "on an individual basis" through "investigations and hearings to separate the loyal from the disloyal, as was done in the case of persons of German and Italian ancestry" (p. 241). He noted that the first exclusion order was not issued until "nearly four months elapsed after Pearl Harbor" and that "the last of these 'subversive' persons was not actually removed until almost eleven months had elapsed" (p. 241). Concluding such "leisure and deliberation" undermined the claim of military necessity, Murphy dissented "from this legalization of racism" (pp. 241–242).

Justice Jackson accepted that the military had the force to arrest citizens or that in the future this might happen again. He was not even willing to argue that "the courts should have attempted to

interfere with the Army in carrying out its task" (p. 248). But he feared that "a judicial construction" that would "sustain this order is a far more subtle blow to liberty than the promulgation of the order itself." He argued that "once judicial opinion rationalizes such an order to show that it conforms to the Constitution, or rather rationalizes the Constitution to show that the Constitution sanctions such an order, the Court for all time has validated the principle of racial discrimination in criminal procedure and of transplanting American citizens." He believed the precedent then "lies about like a loaded weapon ready for the hand of any authority that can bring forward a plausible claim to an urgent need" (pp. 245–246). Jackson urged reversal in order to preserve the integrity of the constitutional system.

(See also RACE AND RACISM; WORLD WAR II.)

☐ Roger Daniels, *Concentration Camps, North America* (1981). Roger Daniels, *The Decision to Relocate the Japanese-Americans (1986)*. Peter Irons, *Justice At War* (1983).
Paul Finkelman

**Kunz v. New York,** 340 U.S. 290 (1951), argued 17 Oct. 1950, decided 15 Jan. 1951 by vote of 8 to 1; Vinson for the Court, Black and Frankfurter concurring in the result only, Jackson in dissent. *Kunz* helped establish that government restrictions on speech must be narrowly tailored so that they do not inappropriately limit expression protected by the *First Amendment. In *Kunz*, the Court held that laws giving public officials broad discretion to restrain speech about religious issues in advance are an invalid *prior restraint in violation of the First Amendment. The Court reversed the 1948 conviction of Baptist minister Carl J. Kunz for violating a New York City ordinance that prohibited religious services on public streets without a permit from the police commissioner. Although the ordinance specified no grounds for refusing permission to speak, Kunz was denied permits in 1947 and 1948 after he was accused of "scurrilous attacks" on Catholics and Jews under a previous permit. Kunz's conviction for violating the ordinance was upheld by the Appellate Part of the Court of Special Sessions and by the New York Court of Appeals. The Supreme Court said that New York's ordinance was too broad because it provided no standards that an administrator could use to determine who ought to receive permits to speak about religious issues. In dissent, Justice Robert *Jackson said Kunz had used "fighting words" that were not protected by the First Amendment (see UNPROTECTED SPEECH). He also criticized the Court for striking down the permit scheme when it had, in *Feiner* v. *New York* (1951), allowed local officials the discretion to arrest volatile speakers during their presentations. (See also SPEECH AND THE PRESS.)

Bill F. Chamberlin

# L

**Labor.** Since the late nineteenth century, the U.S. Supreme Court has been the final arbiter of the place of trade unions in American life. During this century of conflict and accommodation, the Court has been an important actor in labor history, but labor, perhaps, has proved an even greater influence on the history of the Court. The relationship between organized labor and the Court has been a tumultuous one. Prior to the \*New Deal, the labor question came to the Court through two main routes: via judicial regulation of labor relations through \*injunctions and via Supreme Court scrutiny of reform legislation under the \*Fourteenth Amendment's Due Process Clause (see DUE PROCESS, SUBSTANTIVE). The crisis of the Great Depression as well as the reform coalition of the New Deal (in which labor played a key part) forced the Court to make room for trade unionism in its conception of American political economy. For a moment, it appeared that the Court might give some measure of constitutional protection to peaceful strikes and boycotts, but workers' traditional forms of protest and mutual aid soon lost the constitutional mantle that the Court had seemed about to bestow.

*Hostility to Class-based Reform.* From the 1880s through the 1920s, state and federal appellate judges were principal architects of the nation's industrial relations policies. In the 1890s the Supreme Court scrutinized maximum-hours laws and other protective labor legislation to determine whether such laws infringed on constitutional liberty of contract. In \*Holden v. Hardy (1898), the Court upheld a Utah law limiting the hours of miners. However, in \*Lochner v. New York (1905)—the decision that gave the era its name—

the Court voided a New York maximum-hours law for bakers. \*Muller v. Oregon (1908), in turn, upheld a maximum-hours law for women. Overall, the Court voided nearly two hundred statutes and upheld roughly half that number during these decades, leaving the exact borders of the states' \*police powers uncertain. But a general point appeared plain: although legislatures might protect "dependent" and "vulnerable" groups within the labor force, broader, class-based reforms would not pass constitutional muster. In *Coppage* v. *Kansas* (1915), the Court held that government could not temper the inequalities that sprang from the "fact that some men are possessed of industrial property and others are not" (p. 17). The Court's hostility toward class-based reform ambitions helped to shape the political perspective of the nation's labor movement, encouraging a majority of early twentieth-century trade unionists to embrace the anti-statist or "voluntarist" ideology associated with Samuel Gompers. Labor's dominant political outlook came, ironically, to resemble a trade-union version of the Court's own \*laissez-faire constitutionalism. By the same token, the Court's relative hospitality toward hours laws for women and children encouraged and ratified a \*gender-based division of the working class. Having once favored universal hours laws, the labor movement increasingly supported hours legislation solely for those "dependent" groups that could not "look after themselves" through collective self-help.

*Antilabor Injunctions.* As mainstream unions abandoned broad legislative ambitions in favor of self-help in the "private" realm of the economy, the nation's courts took an increasingly active role in policing workers' activities in that arena. With each decade, the number of labor injunctions multiplied; between 1880 and 1930, federal and *state courts issued roughly 4,300 antistrike decrees. The first appeared during the 1877 railroad strikes, issuing from several federal district courts holding bankrupt railroads in receivership. Irate at the reluctance of local and state officials to suppress the disruptions of the railroads caused by strikes, these federal judges took matters into their own hands, ordering their marshals to deputize volunteers or calling out federal troops to put down strikes. During the next great wave of railway strikes in the 1890s, federal courts enjoined strikes and boycotts against railroads that were not in receivership. For authority the courts relied chiefly on the new *Interstate Commerce Act (1887) and the *Sherman Antitrust Act (1890).

In 1895 the Supreme Court appraised this expansion of federal equity powers. The occasion was a far-flung national boycott of railway cars manufactured and owned by the Pullman corporation. Eugene Debs, president of the American Railway Union, led the boycott, which was condemned by federal courts in almost every large city west of the Alleghenies. Workers dubbed the court orders "Gatling gun injunctions," after the new weapon used by federal troops to enforce the bans. In *In re *Debs* (1895), a unanimous Court upheld the injunctions and the contempt convictions of Debs and other strike leaders; in bold strokes, it sanctioned the new use of equitable remedies in industrial conflicts.

By the time of the *Debs* decision, injunctions had been issued against strikes in many other industries besides the railroads. A key reason for this expansion of *judicial activism was labor's growing use of the boycott. Arraying national organizations or entire working-class communities against a single employer, boycotts often lent unions much greater power—and rubbed more abrasively against judges' individualism—than did an ordinary wage strike. Boycotts gave rise to the Court's next important injunction cases. In 1908, *Loewe* v. *Lawlor*, the "Danbury Hatters case," answered a question that *Debs* left open, holding, with the majority of *lower federal courts, that the Sherman Act applied to combinations of workers; the Court also ruled that activities of the defendant hatters' union in publicizing a consumer boycott of the goods of an "unfair" employer was illegal both under the Sherman Act and at *common law. *Gompers* v. *Buck's Stove & Range Co.* (1911) was a contempt case against Gompers and other national American Federation of Labor (AFL) officials for publicizing another consumer boycott in defiance of a trial-court injunction. Although it dismissed the contempt proceedings, the Supreme Court rejected Gompers's claim that the *First Amendment shielded such protest activities.

*Loewe* v. *Lawlor* and *Buck's Stove* proved crucial in prompting the AFL to turn in earnest to congressional lobbying and campaigning; its goal was statutory abolition of the labor injunction. Years of lobbying bore fruit in the labor provisions of the Clayton Act of 1914, which seemed to bar federal courts from enjoining peaceful picketing or any other communicative activities connected with strikes or boycotts. Gompers greeted the act as labor's "Magna Carta," but lower federal courts construed the (deliberately) ambiguous language of the act's anti-injunction provisions in so hostile a fashion that it worked no changes. In 1921 the Supreme Court announced that the key provisions merely codified the common law of the injunction as it already had existed (*Duplex Printing Press Co.* v. *Deering*), and another decade of broad injunctions and broken strikes followed before Congress again considered the matter.

**New Deal Reversals.** During that decade, organized labor staged massive protests against "government by injunction," and a growing portion of the nation's political elites became convinced that the repressive, judge-made rules of the game had to be changed. This conviction, combined with the broader depression-era decline in business legitimacy and Republican party fortunes, prompted passage of the Norris-LaGuardia Act in 1932. Compared to the earlier Clayton Act, Norris-LaGuardia was a less ambiguous, more lawyerly anti-injunction statute that circumscribed the labor injunction with procedural barriers and safeguards. It perfectly expressed the AFL's attitude toward the role of the courts in labor relations: that it should hardly exist. This time, the courts themselves seemed to agree.

Beginning in the late 1930s, the federal bench affirmed and extended the Norris-LaGuardia Act's protection of strike and boycott activities to embrace immunity not only from injunctions but also from civil actions for damages. Ironically, though, by the time the Supreme Court upheld the act in *Lauf* v. *E. G. Shinner and Co.* (1938) and the lower courts enacted their generous interpretations, Congress and the administration of Franklin D. *Roosevelt had rejected voluntarism as the basis for the government's industrial relations policy and put a system of administrative regulation and control in its place.

Labor law in the 1930s was the stage on which the Supreme Court performed the most dramatic about-face in its history, and a growing trade union movement played a critical role in convincing the Court to abandon its laissez-faire constitutionalism. At first, the Court seemed determined to defend the old regime. In *Schechter Poultry Corp.* v. *United States* (1935) the Court struck down the cornerstone of the Roosevelt administration's new federal labor-relations policy, the National Industrial Recovery Act, deeming it an unconstitutional delegation of legislative power as well as an expansion of federal authority unwarranted under the Commerce Clause because it reached working conditions in intrastate businesses (see COMMERCE POWER). Likewise, in 1936, the Court found a New York State minimum-wage law for women to be an unconstitutional interference with liberty of contract (*Morehead v. New York ex rel. Tipaldo*).

In the fall of 1936, however, President Roosevelt was reelected in a campaign conducted in significant part as a referendum on the Court. In early 1937, he introduced his *court-packing plan. In the spring came two landmark cases in which the Court pragmatically reversed course. *West Coast Hotel Co. v. Parrish* noted that the "Constitution does not speak of freedom of contract" (p. 391) and upheld the constitutionality of a Washington State law setting a minimum wage for women, a law indistinguishable from the New York statute struck down less than a year earlier. And in *National Labor Relations Board v. Jones & Laughlin Steel Corp.* the Court upheld the National Labor Relations Act (NLRA), which gave workers in private industry the right to organize and imposed on employers a duty to bargain with their employees' representatives. Roosevelt had signed the act into law in 1935, only two months after the *Schechter* decision, and employers relied on *Schechter* and earlier rulings to support their contention that the act was unconstitutional. Those precedents enabled employers' attorneys to tie the new National Labor Relations Board in knots in the lower federal courts for almost two years until the Supreme Court upheld the NLRA board's legitimacy.

*Jones & Laughlin* was the foundation of a new constitutional edifice extending federal power under the Commerce Clause and recognizing broad governmental authority to regulate the economy. The Court explicitly conceded that asymmetries of power rendered single employees helpless in dealing with employers, and it sanctioned state intervention in the interest of equality. But *Jones & Laughlin* also rested on other grounds with profoundly different implications for the legal status of unions, creating a tension that would haunt later rulings. On the one hand, the Court recognized workers' "fundamental right" to organize unions; on the other, the Court deemed unions and collective bargaining essential to "industrial peace" (pp. 33, 42). If fundamental, labor's new rights were arguably inviolable, but when conceived as promoting industrial peace, they could be trimmed to fit that purpose.

The doctrine that workers had a fundamental right to organize did not, however, simply constitute a platform for federal legislative protection of union activity. The confrontation between state repression and union organizing in the 1930s and early 1940s provoked a signal change in the Supreme Court's First Amendment jurisprudence, as the Court took its first steps toward extending the constitutional right to free expression to encompass union organizing.

*Hague v. Congress of Industrial Organizations* (1939) was the first case in which the Court endorsed use of the First Amendment as a sword to enjoin government suppression of expressive activity rather than as a shield from criminal prosecution. When organizers from the Congress of Industrial Organizations arrived in Jersey City, New Jersey, in 1937 to urge workers to exercise their rights under the new NLRA, city authorities denied their right to hold meetings or distribute leaflets and had them arrested and run out of town. Alleging a deprivation of First Amendment rights, the CIO's lawyers sought injunctive relief against Mayor Frank Hague. The Court's ruling in the organizers' favor brought labor organizing under the mantle of constitutional protection.

The Court soon extended the Constitution's protection of *speech and association to the most traditional expression of labor grievance—the picket line. Striking down an antipicketing ordinance as overbroad in *Thornhill v. Alabama* (1940), the Court found that free discussion of the labor question was integral to the "processes of popular government" that shaped the "destiny of modern industrial society" (p. 103). In *Thornhill*, the Court's focus on the public's First Amendment interest in open discussion of strikes emphasized one strain of its earlier reasoning in *Jones & Laughlin*. Notably, the Court did not dwell on the rights of strikers to communicate their grievances. Instead, it justified federal protection of labor's rights in the name of informed public regulation of industry. Such recognition of public interest in labor organization—as a means to an end—was a two-edged sword. It implied state authority to regulate and restrain collective action no less than to protect workers' freedoms.

**Labor Loses Ground.** Even as the Court upheld the NLRA, it moved to narrow its central provision protecting concerted activity. In a landmark 1939 ruling, *National Labor Relations Board v. Fansteel Metallurgical Corp.*, the Court refused to uphold a board order requiring reinstatement of workers fired after a sit-down strike. The ruling initiated a process, later adopted by the board, of denying protection where collective activity is considered either too potent a weapon in collective bargaining or an obstacle to the bargaining process. Thirty years after stripping sit-down strikes of protection, the Court, in *Boys Market, Inc. v. Retail Clerks' Local 770* (1970), also put federal courts back in the business of enjoining peaceful strikes and picketing when a strike violates a contractual no-strike pledge—despite the clear command of the Norris-LaGuardia Act. As the Court bluntly stated, federal policy had shifted from the "protection of the nascent labor movement to the encouragement of collective bargaining" (p. 251)—that is, from a theory of *fundamental rights to a theory of functional rights.

As the Court increasingly gave primacy to the public purpose furthered by endowing labor with rights rather than to workers' fundamental rights themselves, it allowed workers' statutory rights to be refashioned while also upholding state intervention into internal union affairs. These rulings undercut the principles established by *Hague* and *Thornhill*. With the passage of the Taft-Hartley Act in 1947, the Court confronted an array of measures curbing the labor movement's new legal freedoms. Taft-Hartley sharply restricted workers' right to select their own representatives, requiring union officers to swear they were not members of the Communist party on pain of disqualifying their unions from federal protection (see COMMUNISM AND COLD WAR). The Supreme Court upheld that requirement in *American Communications Association, CIO* v. *Douds* (1950). The Court acknowledged that Taft-Hartley inhibited lawful exercise of political freedoms, but, pushing the reasoning of *Jones & Laughlin* to its logical conclusion, the Court ruled that precisely because the NLRA rested on public interest in "the free flow of commerce," Congress could legislate against the threat to "that public interest" posed by Communists in positions of union leadership (pp. 387, 400).

In an equally significant line of rulings, the Court upheld Taft-Hartley restrictions on union picketing that urged consumers or fellow workers to pressure employers to cease doing business with an employer involved in a labor dispute. This ban on "secondary activity" aimed to check the spread of labor unrest. In *Electrical Workers* v. *National Labor Relations Board* (1951), the Court ruled that such restrictions did not unconstitutionally abridge free speech, a decision flowing from a body of precedent that had gradually eroded the expansive protection of labor expression promised in *Thornhill*. Just a few years later, in *Teamsters, Local 695* v. *Vogt, Inc.* (1957), the Court declared that this line of cases gave the states the broad prerogative to enforce public policy by "constitutionally enjoin[ing] peaceful picketing" (p. 293). By the late 1950s the Court thus had affirmed that the public's interest in labor peace could override even the rights that workers derived from the First Amendment. It again routinely upheld labor injunctions, much as it did in Samuel Gompers's day.

In the 1960s, legal advocates for African-American citizens stood on the precedents won by organized labor in urging the Supreme Court to expand First Amendment protections and federal legislative power to protect *civil rights. By then, however, the legal ground had shifted under the feet of the trade union movement. In 1982, three decades after the Supreme Court made clear that labor picketing was subject to close regulation, it held in *National Association for the Advancement of Colored People* v. *Clairborne*

*Hardware Co.* that the First Amendment shielded peaceful picketing by civil rights groups in support of a boycott of white merchants. Citing *Thornhill* as support, the Court nevertheless carefully distinguished secondary labor picketing from the protected civil rights advocacy. And, ironically, twenty years after the Court upheld the authority of Congress to guarantee civil rights in employment, public accommodations, and other areas, the union movement began to call for repeal of the NLRA—the very act that had precipitated the legal revolution of the New Deal, paving the constitutional way for the *Civil Rights Act of 1964. The Supreme Court's jurisprudence bears the indelible imprint of workers' collective activity. Nevertheless, while labor's legal legacy has advanced the rights of other citizens, it has left organized workers with scant protection.

(See CAPITALISM; CONTRACT, FREEDOM OF.)

☐ James B. Atleson, *Values and Assumptions in American Labor Law* (1983). John R. Commons, *Legal Foundations of Capitalism* (1924). William E. Forbath, *Law and the Shaping of the American Labor Movement* (1991). Christopher L. Tomlins, *The State and the Unions* (1985).
William E. Forbath and Craig Becker

**Laissez-Faire Constitutionalism.** The phrase "laissez-faire constitutionalism" refers to an ideological attitude that characterized some justices of the Supreme Court between the *Civil War and the *New Deal. The ideology reflected classical liberal economics, with its commitment to market control of the economy, a preference for entrepreneurial liberty, and a concomitant hostility to governmental regulation; social Darwinism, which extolled competition in the struggle for social existence and survival of the economically fittest; a formalist approach to adjudication, with a preference for abstractions and formal logic; traditional American values, including individualism, access to opportunity, and hostility to restraints on competition; and a fear of social unrest, spawned by immigration, industrialization, urbanization, and the struggles of organized labor.

The values of laissez-faire constitutionalism were first articulated on the Supreme Court in the dissents of Justices Stephen J. *Field and Joseph P. *Bradley in the *Slaughterhouse Cases* (1873). These values produced the doctrine of substantive *due process, which commanded a majority of the Court for the first time in *Chicago, Milwaukee & St. Paul Railway Co.* v. *Minnesota* (1890), and the derivative doctrine of freedom of *contract, which achieved its first triumph in *Allgeyer* v. *Louisiana* (1897). The Court during the chief justiceships of Melville W. *Fuller, Edward D. *White, and William Howard *Taft (1888–1930) was often receptive to these values, producing such specimens of laissez-faire constitutionalism as the *Income Tax Cases* (*Pollock* v. *Farmers' Loan &*

*Trust Co.*, 1895) and *\*Plessy* v. *Ferguson* (1896). Allied with traditional concepts of *federalism, the ideology led to decisions restrictive of federal regulatory power, including *United States* v. *\*E. C. Knight Co.* (1895) and the *Child Labor Cases* (*\*Hammer* v. *Dagenhart*, 1918, and *\*Bailey* v. *Drexel Furniture Co.*, 1922). Laissez-faire constitutionalism was marked by a virulent and unconcealed hostility to organized *labor, which resulted in such decisions as *In re \*Debs* (1895) and *\*Loewe* v. *Lawlor* (1908). The high points of laissez-faire constitutionalism's hold on the minds of Supreme Court jurists came in *\*Lochner* v. *New York* (1905) and *\*Adkins* v. *Children's Hospital* (1923). Various state supreme courts, including those of the leading industrial states, New York, Illinois, Pennsylvania, and Massachusetts, were receptive to laissez-faire premises, producing such monuments of conservative jurisprudence as *In re Jacobs* (New York, 1885) and *Ives* v. *South Buffalo Railway Co.* (New York, 1911). (See STATE COURTS.)

But the ideology never lacked for critics, foremost among them on the Court being Justice Oliver Wendell *Holmes, whose *Lochner* dissent trenchantly rejected its assumptions. Louis D. *Brandeis, then in private practice, struck a fatal blow at the doctrines of laissez-faire constitutionalism through the *"Brandeis brief," acknowledged as persuasive by a majority of the Court in *\*Muller* v. *Oregon* (1908)—but rejected by a later majority in *Adkins*. Off the Court, academic critics like Roscoe Pound of the Harvard Law School and political leaders, including Theodore Roosevelt in his Bull Moose campaign of 1912, condemned the results of the doctrines. Moreover, the ideology was only intermittently dominant; the Court sustained most regulatory legislation, as in *Muller* and *Holden* v. *Hardy* (1898).

Laisser-faire constitutionalism revived vigorously after World War I, dominating the Taft Court. Its grip weakened momentarily during the New Deal, enabling the Court to sustain some state and federal regulatory legislation. But its force recuperated powerfully in 1936 and 1937, producing the last great burst of antiregulatory decisions, including *\*Carter* v. *Carter Coal Co.* (1936) and *\*Morehead* v. *New York ex rel. Tipaldo* (1936). The constitutional revolution of 1937 swept it away completely, and the Court systematically repudiated its premises and the precedents that it had spawned (see COURT-PACKING PLAN).

Critics of the modern Court sometimes see a revival of laissez-faire doctrines in the Burger and Rehnquist Courts. But differences far outweigh similarities between the turn-of-the-century and the contemporary Court. Laissez-faire constitutionalism was profoundly suspicious of democracy, as evidenced by the writings of its foremost academic apologists, including Christopher Tiedeman, whereas modern conservatives extol the power of democratic majorities. Further, modern judicial conservatism shares few of the values of its ancestor. It is too sophisticated to accept the crudities of social Darwinism as extolled by Justice Rufus *Peckham. Nearly a century of experience has abated the visceral fears of organized labor and immigrants. Yet a preference for market control of the economy and private ordering by contract, rather than public ordering by regulation, display some continuities with the past.

(See also HISTORY OF THE COURT: RECONSTRUCTION, FEDERALISM, AND ECONOMIC RIGHTS.)

□ William F. Swindler, *Court and Constitution in the Twentieth Century: The Old Legality, 1889–1932* (1969).
William M. Wiecek

**Lamar, Joseph Rucker** (b. Ruckersville, Ga., 14 Oct. 1857; d. Washington, D.C., 2 Jan. 1916; interred Sand Hills Cemetery, Augusta, Ga.), associate justice, 1911–1916. Joseph Rucker Lamar followed a family legacy of involvement in civic affairs. The Lamars and Ruckers, among the social elite of their respective communities, had fashioned a reputation for public leadership. Two relatives on the paternal side, in fact, had achieved national prominence during the nineteenth century. Mirabeau Lamar served as president of the fledgling Republic of Texas (1838–1841) and L. Q. C. *Lamar enjoyed a distinguished career as a member of Congress, secretary of the interior, and associate justice of the United States Supreme Court (1888–1893). As a respected attorney and able jurist on the supreme courts of state and nation, Joseph R. Lamar kept alive that ancestral heritage.

*Joseph Rucker Lamar*

As a youth Lamar received the cultural and educational advantages derived from social affluence. Reared in the traditional graces of southern gentility, Lamar developed patrician values that continued to influence personal and professional actions throughout his life. He attended the University of Georgia and graduated in 1877 from Bethany College in West Virginia.

While Lamar served briefly in the Georgia legislature, his enduring public contributions as well as personal pleasure came in the realm of law, not politics. He studied law for one term at Washington and Lee University, then served as an apprentice before admission to the Georgia bar in 1878. Widespread recognition of his legal skills led to his appointment as one of three commissioners charged with the revision of the Georgia code. Lamar alone prepared the volume on civil law that the state legislature approved in 1895. A student of legal history, he also wrote several celebrated monographs on the evolution of law in Georgia. Appointed to the state supreme court in 1903, Lamar served two years before returning to private practice. He often represented corporations, mainly railroads, and on occasion argued cases before the United States Supreme Court.

Nomination to the Supreme Court in 1910 surprised the Georgia lawyer who had only the year before met President William Howard *Taft while the latter vacationed in Augusta. The Senate quickly and unanimously confirmed the appointment, and Lamar joined a Court confronted with issues, among others, of interstate commerce, state and national police power, and administrative discretion.

The tenure of Lamar was by and large unremarkable. On a highly consensual Court, he almost always voted with the majority. His noteworthy opinions were those that expanded administrative discretion for executive officials. In *United States v. Grimaud* (1911), for example, Lamar upheld the constitutionality of the Forest Reserve Act of 1891 against charges that it unlawfully delegated legislative power to the secretary of agriculture. This landmark decision allowed administrators the discretion to "fill in the details" when implementing laws. Similarly, in *United States v. Midwest Oil Company* (1915), Lamar expanded presidential power to withdraw land from public use without congressional authorization.

Lamar served in one noteworthy extrajudicial capacity. In 1914 President Woodrow Wilson, his childhood friend, dispatched Lamar to participate in sensitive diplomatic negotiations regarding Mexico at the Argentina, Brazil, Chile (A.B.C.) Conference. Lamar discharged that duty with the usual temperance that so characterized his public life.

□ Clarinda Pendleton Lamar, *The Life of Joseph Rucker Lamar* (1926). John W. Winkle III

**Lamar, Lucius Quintus Cincinnatus** (b. Eatonton, Ga., 17 Sep. 1825; d. Macon, Ga., 23 Jan. 1893; interred St. Peter's Cemetery, Oxford, Miss.), associate justice, 1888–1893. Few Americans have enjoyed as extensive and diverse a public career as L. Q. C. Lamar. During the latter half of the nineteenth century, he served in all three branches of the national government, first as a member of the House of Representatives and Senate, then as secretary of the interior, and finally as an associate justice of the United States Supreme Court.

Born into the plantation aristocracy of middle Georgia, Lamar developed a strong patrician code that emphasized tradition, region, and propriety. Those values especially influenced his decisions in public office. Law and politics dominated his career. Over time Lamar practiced, taught, wrote, enforced, and interpreted law. As a professor at the University of Mississippi, moreover, he pioneered the case method approach to legal education. Political influence came primarily from his father-in-law Augustus Longstreet, a college president and avowed separatist. Lamar authored the Mississippi ordinance of secession and resigned from Congress just before the onset of the Civil War. Yet years later the same Lamar stirred Congress with impassioned pleas for reunification, earning him the reputation as the "Great Pacificator." His eulogy of Massachusetts Senator Charles Sumner in 1874 is chronicled in *Profiles in Courage* by John F. Kennedy.

President Grover Cleveland in 1887 nominated his able interior secretary to fill the vacancy on the Court caused by the death of William B. *Woods. Senate confirmation did not come easily. Oppo-

*Lucius Quintus Cincinnatus Lamar*

nents attacked Lamar on grounds of legal inexperience and advanced age, issues that shrouded partisan Republican politics. By a narrow vote, 42 to 38, Lamar took a seat on the high bench as the first Southerner since his own cousin John A. *Campbell (1853) and the first Democrat since Stephen J. *Field (1862).

Lamar played a modest role on a Court faced with emergent issues of interstate commerce and state regulation of business. He almost always aligned with the majority, usually led by Chief Justice Melville W. *Fuller. Until failing health limited his participation, Lamar wrote his fair share of assigned opinions. For the most part, however, he received inconsequential cases involving patent rights, land claim disputes, mortgage foreclosures, personal injury suits, and municipal bonds.

Arguably the most salient theme in his judicial philosophy emerged in three notable dissents involving the scope of national authority. In the landmark case of *Chicago, Milwaukee, and St. Paul Railway Company v. Minnesota (1890), that ushered in a era of judicial activism, Lamar joined in a steadfast dissent that legislatures, not courts, should determine the reasonableness of public policy (see JUDICIAL SELF-RESTRAINT). Months later in what some scholars consider his finest opinion, In re *Neagle (1890), Lamar challenged the expansion of executive power. Without explicit statutory authorization, he reasoned, a United States marshal who had defended a federal judge by killing an assailant may not claim to have acted in an official capacity. And in Field v. Clark (1892), Lamar charged that Congress had unlawfully delegated to the president its legislative power to impose discretionary tariffs (see DELEGATION OF POWERS). In these and all cases, Lamar followed personal values refined by political experience.

□ James B. Murphy, L. Q. C. Lamar, Pragmatic Patriot (1973).          John W. Winkle III

**Land Grants.** From the beginning of European settlement in America, land was the principal basis of wealth. Successive governments assumed ownership and distributed much land for private settlement and development. In early cases, the Supreme Court implicitly accepted the premise that private property in land was a constitutionally protected element of the American political economy. In *Fletcher v. Peck (1810) the Supreme Court held that a state land grant was protected from legislative repeal by the *Contracts Clause of the Constitution (Art. I, sec. 10, cl. 1). Later cases similarly held that land became private property on conveyance by the Federal government to private persons.

The Property Clause of the Constitution (Art. IV, sec. 3, cl. 2) gives Congress the power to "dispose of" land owned by the federal government. Under this clause, Congress distributed most fed-

eral land through sales or grants to states, firms, or individuals. Many grants were made specifically to support education, the construction of railroads, or other beneficial activities.

The Court has consistently held that the power of disposing of public lands rests in Congress, not the courts. In general, the Court has construed congressional grants liberally in favor of the government. But whenever the government has sought to recover land for the failure of the grantee to comply with a condition stated in the grant, the Court has tended to construe the condition strictly and has insisted that the government follow proper forfeiture procedures.

(See also PROPERTY RIGHTS; PUBLIC LANDS.)
Bruce A. Campbell

**Lanza, United States v.** 260 U.S. 377 (1922), argued 23 Nov. 1922, decided 11 Dec. 1922 by vote of 9 to 0; Taft for the Court. Bootlegger Vito Lanza, convicted and fined in April 1920 for manufacturing, transporting, and possessing intoxicating liquor in violation of Washington state law, was subsequently charged with having violated the Volstead Act, the federal prohibition law, on the basis of the same evidence used in the state prosecution. A federal district court blocked the second prosecution as *double jeopardy, and the U.S. Department of Justice appealed. In sustaining the second conviction of Lanza, a unanimous Supreme Court held that state and federal governments each had independent sovereignty to punish offenses against their peace and dignity. In respect to liquor control, states had original authority. While the *Eighteenth Amendment established prohibition as national policy, its "concurrent power to enforce" clause preserved the right of each state to continue exercising an independent power as long as it was not inconsistent with federal statute. The *Fifth Amendment only barred repeated proceedings by the federal government and did not apply to a situation of this sort. Since nearly every state either had a prohibition law prior to the adoption of the Eighteenth Amendment or had passed one immediately after ratification, the Lanza decision meant that prohibition violators could be indicted and punished twice for almost every offense. While the Taft Court was clearly seeking, in this and other decisions, to buttress the new Eighteenth Amendment, the public perceived that traditional liberties were being restricted in the effort to enforce prohibition. (See also POLICE POWERS; STATE SOVEREIGNTY AND STATES' RIGHTS.)
David E. Kyvig

**Lassiter v. Northampton County Board of Elections,** 360 U.S. 45 (1959), argued 18–19 May 1959, decided 8 June 1959 by vote of 9 to 0; Douglas for the Court. Lassiter is an important case in the history of the federal protection of voting rights. The Court rejected a black citizen's challenge to a state literacy test, finding that states have broad powers to determine the conditions of suffrage. The literacy test applied to voters of all races, and the Court would not draw the inference that it was being used to facilitate racial discrimination.

*Lassiter* had to be addressed in assessing the constitutionality of the *Voting Rights Act of 1965. The act temporarily suspended literacy and other tests imposed as prerequisites to voting. In *South Carolina* v. *Katzenbach* (1966), the Court distinguished *Lassiter* on the ground that in most states covered by the 1965 act prerequisites to voting were instituted and administered in a discriminatory fashion for many years. In *Katzenbach* v. *Morgan* (1966), New York tested the 1965 act's effective prohibition of application of an English literacy requirement to persons who completed the sixth grade in a non-English-speaking American school. The act thus gave voting privileges to many former residents of Puerto Rico who had migrated to New York.

If the Court had adhered to its approach in *Lassiter* it would have struck down the literacy requirement only if a court would conclude that the requirement discriminated against non-English-speakers. But the Court refused to ask the *Lassiter*-like question whether the judiciary would find the English literacy requirement unconstitutional. Section 5 of the *Fourteenth Amendment required only that legislation be appropriate to enforce the Equal Protection Clause of the Fourteenth Amendment. It was Congress's decision to make. The challenged provision sought to secure for the New York Puerto Rican community nondiscriminatory treatment and was thus appropriate to enforce the Equal Protection Clause. Subsequent amendments to the Voting Rights Act prohibited all literacy tests as a prerequisite for voting.

(See also EQUAL PROTECTION; RACE AND RACISM; VOTE, RIGHT TO.)

Theodore Eisenberg

**Lawyers' Edition** is the popular designation of the *United States Supreme Court Reports, Lawyers' Edition*, an unofficial series of Supreme Court decisions published by the Lawyers Co-operative Publishing Company. It began publication in 1882 with a complete reprint of all Supreme Court decisions that had been issued up to that time. The initial publication contained many decisions not reported officially, including those in the appendixes to volumes 131 and 154 of *United States Reports*. Subsequent volumes contained a few decisions not officially reported. Volume numbering differs from that of the official reports, and a second numbering series was begun after volume 100. The bound volumes provide star paging to the official *U.S. Reports*.

Special features include summaries of counsel's briefs in selected cases and annotations to a few important cases in each volume. These now appear in an appendix at the back of each volume. Since volume 32 of *Lawyers' Edition*, 2d series, supplements in the back of the volumes contain updating of the annotations in that volume, a citator service summarizing relevant cases, and corrections made by the justices after the volume went to press.

Biweekly advance sheets with the same pagination as the bound volume provide current decisions, but not the annotations.     Morris L. Cohen

**Least Dangerous Branch.** Writing in *The *Federalist*, no. 78, Alexander *Hamilton prophesied that the judiciary would always be the "least dangerous branch" of the federal government, since it had "no influence over either the sword or the purse" and had "neither force nor will, but merely judgment." If Hamilton's readers thought he meant that the Supreme Court would never be a force in American government, they soon learned otherwise because of the rise of the Court under Chief Justice John *Marshall. But Hamilton was right about the Court's vulnerability. The president controls appointments, and the Court, as Hamilton said, "ultimately depend[s] upon the aid of the executive arm even for the efficacy of its judgments." Congress has control of all but the Supreme Court's *original jurisdiction and can often circumvent court decisions by simple legislation. The people can resist the Court and override unpopular decisions by constitutional amendment (see CONSTITUTIONAL AMENDING PROCESS). To function effectively, therefore, the Court must accommodate itself to the democratic process. The Court does best when it does what it best can do: exercise principled "judgment." As a legal institution it is uniquely equipped to do just this. Its distance from electoral politics, its deliberative tradition, the rational environment in which it hears arguments and renders opinions—all these elements invite a level of disinterested constitutional exposition not possible in the political branches. (See also JUDICIAL POWER AND JURISDICTION; SEPARATION OF POWERS.)

R. Kent Newmyer

**Least Restrictive Means Test.** Concern about the government's power to restrict speech is not limited to the end that is to be served. The manner in which restrictions are fashioned may be equally important. For at least a half century the Supreme Court has insisted that where any choice exists, government must use those means that least severely inhibit expression.

The doctrine had its origin in city laws that banned leafletting and distribution of other printed material. Such laws served the laudable civic purpose of keeping the streets and sidewalks clear of refuse. But they often did so in ways the justices found broader than necessary to ensure cleanliness. "There are," said the Court in *Schneider* v. *State* (1939), "obvious methods of preventing littering. Amongst these is the punishment of those who actually throw papers on the streets" (p. 162).

Later evidence of the force of this principle came in *Procunier* v. *Martinez* (1974), where the Supreme Court reviewed restrictions on prison correspondence: "The limitations of *First Amendment freedoms must be no greater than is necessary or essential to the protection of the particular governmental interest involved. Thus a restriction . . . that furthers an important or substantial interest . . . will nevertheless be invalid if its sweep is unnecessarily broad" (pp. 413–414).

This principle has been reaffirmed in recent years, even where the strength of the government's regulatory interest is beyond question. The burden now is more than simply showing that a proposed and less restrictive approach will not do what government needs done. Courts have increasingly rejected limits on speech or press because the public body advancing it has failed to negate all possible alternatives that might do less harm to free expression.

(See also SPEECH AND THE PRESS.)

Robert M. O'Neil

**Legal Counsel, Office of.** Created in 1972, the Office of Legal Counsel is a nonstatutory unit within the administrative infrastructure of the Supreme Court. The two attorneys who staff the office perform multiple functions, including preliminary research, analysis, and advice on petitions for extraordinary writs and cases invoking original jurisdiction. The office also acts as a general counsel for the Court, undertakes special projects at the request of the *chief justice, and may occasionally assist individual justices with their circuit work. Unlike law *clerks who serve in temporary capacities, this office provides a continuous and experienced service for the routine operations of the Court.

John W. Winkle III and Martha Swann

**Legal Defense Fund.** The *National Association for the Advancement of Colored People (NAACP) was founded in 1909 as an organization dedicated to lobbying, political education, and legal action to alter the status of African-Americans. In its early years the NAACP had a small paid staff that recruited members, published reports and a magazine, and lobbied government officials. The NAACP relied on volunteer attorneys to bring legal challenges to racial segregation, the most notable of which was *Buchanan* v. *Warley* (1917), which struck down residential segregation ordinances (see SEGREGATION, DE JURE).

In the 1920s the NAACP, aided by a grant from a liberal foundation, began to develop plans for a more systematic legal challenge to segregation. After Nathan Margold, a young white lawyer, outlined theories to challenge residential segregation (see HOUSING DISCRIMINATION) and segrega-

tion in public *education, the NAACP hired Charles Hamilton *Houston, the dean of the Howard Law School, as its first full-time legal staff member. Houston began lawsuits to compel southern universities to admit African-Americans to their graduate and professional schools and to equalize the salaries of black and white teachers in public schools. This campaign had its first success in *Missouri ex rel. Gaines* v. *Canada* (1938), which held that states either had to admit African-Americans to professional schools or create segregated professional schools, ordinarily a course that would be too expensive.

To preserve the NAACP's ability to obtain tax-exempt donations to support its legal and educational work while it continued to pursue political lobbying, the Legal Defense Fund (LDF) was incorporated as a separate group in 1939. Houston hired Thurgood *Marshall to assist him, and Marshall took over as director of the Legal Defense Fund in 1939. From 1945 to 1954 the LDF's legal campaign developed a sustained assault on segregation in education, initially expanding the *Gaines* decision by obtaining a decision from the Supreme Court that segregated professional facilities had to be equal to white ones in ways that were essentially impossible to reproduce (*Sweatt* v. *Painter,* 1950). Throughout this period, and until the 1960s, the legal staff was quite small, rarely exceeding seven attorneys.

After the success in *Sweatt,* the Legal Defense Fund turned its attention to segregation in elementary and secondary education and began the lawsuits that resulted in the desegregation decisions of 1954 (*Brown* v. *Board of Education; Bolling* v. *Sharpe*). For about a decade after *Brown* the Legal Defense Fund concentrated on efforts to defend itself against attempts by southern legislatures to keep it from operating, for example by charging it with unethical practices in soliciting clients, while attempting to compel school boards to comply with the desegregation decision. In 1963 the Supreme Court held that the Legal Defense Fund's activities in supporting litigation were protected by the *First Amendment (*NAACP* v. *Button,* 1963).

A further formal separation between the NAACP and the LDF occurred in 1954 when the boards of directors of the two groups became completely separate. For most of this period, however, the groups shared office space and maintained close working relations. In 1956, however, as a result of personality disagreements and policy differences over how to pursue desegregation, relations between the groups became strained. Ultimately the NAACP added its own legal staff, headed by Robert Carter, which aggressively pursued desegregation litigation in the North, while the Legal Defense Fund sought to implement desegregation in the South.

Thurgood Marshall left the Legal Defense Fund in 1961 to accept an appointment as a federal judge. He was replaced by Jack *Greenberg. In the 1960s the Legal Defense Fund provided legal support for African-Americans prosecuted during the *sit-in demonstrations. After enactment of the *Civil Rights Act of 1964, the LDF developed a substantial litigation campaign to eliminate racial discrimination in *employment. Motivated by concern that the death penalty was administered in ways that amounted to discrimination against African-Americans, the Legal Defense Fund also challenged *capital punishment. Although the death penalty campaign achieved a temporary victory in *Furman v. Georgia (1972) and a more permanent one with respect to the imposition of the death penalty for rape, which had been a particular concern for African-Americans (*Coker v. Georgia, 1977), changes in the composition of the Supreme Court ultimately led to the reinstitution of capital punishment. (See RACE DISCRIMINATION AND THE DEATH PENALTY.)

(See also CIVIL RIGHTS MOVEMENT; RACE AND RACISM.)

□ Richard Kluger, *Simple Justice* (1975). Mark Tushnet, *The NAACP's Legal Strategy against Segregated Education, 1925–1950* (1987).                    Mark V. Tushnet

**Legal Realism.** See HISTORY OF THE COURT: THE DEPRESSION AND THE RISE OF LEGAL LIBERALISM.

**Legal Tender Cases,** collective name for three cases of the 1870s: *Hepburn v. Griswold,* 75 U.S. 603 (1870), argued 10 Dec. 1869, decided 7 Feb. 1870 by vote of 4 to 3, Chase for the Court, Miller in dissent; and *Knox v. Lee* and *Parker v. Davis,* 79 U.S. 457 (1871), argued 23 Feb. and 18 Apr. 1871, decided 1 May 1871 by vote of 5 to 4, Strong for the Court, Chase, Clifford, and Field in dissent. The *Legal Tender Cases* stand for the proposition that the United States can compel creditors to receive its paper money in payment of debt. These cases also raised the issue of whether the Constitution is to be applied pursuant to the original understanding or judicially amended for unforeseen exigencies (see ORIGINAL INTENT). The cases also illustrate that whenever a Supreme Court decision is at odds with the Constitution, the result may well be irreversible and beyond judicial overruling, legislative recall, or possibly formal constitutional amendment (see CONSTITUTIONAL AMENDING PROCESS).

The legal tender controversy resulted from the decision of Secretary of Treasury (later Chief Justice) Salmon P. *Chase to help finance the *Civil War by issuing paper money not redeemable in species. Such money was popularly known as greenbacks. The bulk of subsequent monetary transactions—borrowing, lending, investment came to be conducted in paper currency rather than by gold coin, which also remained lawful money. To insure the acceptance of greenback dollars, it was proposed in Congress that they be made legal tender for debts and taxes.

This meant that creditors were compelled to accept greenbacks when offered or forfeit further interest on their debt, or possibly, the debt itself. Chase reluctantly went along, and Congress enacted the Legal Tender Act of 1862. Greenback dollars, however, rapidly depreciated in value.

Historically, legal tender had been the hallmark of an irredeemable, deteriorating paper money. The framers of the Constitution clearly intended to banish it from the American scene. Reflecting this view, Chief Justice John *Marshall excoriated legal tender. In 1862, the legal tender statute was seen as a temporary, if unfortunate, expedient.

The doctrine of *implied powers, derived from the war and borrowing authority, was repeatedly invoked in Congress to justify the legal tender quality of greenback dollars. The validity of the Legal Tender Act was challenged in *Hepburn v. Griswold.* Chief Justice Chase, with the support of three colleagues, reverted to his original reluctance and overturned the statute. Speaking for the Court, Chase found that the law was unconstitutional as applied to contracts made before its passage. He concluded that the act violated the *Due Process Clause of the *Fifth Amendment and impaired the obligation of contract contrary to the spirit of the Constitution.

Chase's judgment was flawed in two particulars. First was the sheer subjectivity of an appeal to an amorphous "spirit" of the Constitution, particularly when a substantial part of the Court, the Congress, and the presidency found that spirit quite compatible with what was done. Second, *Hepburn* was decided without a full bench. In 1863, the Court had been enlarged to ten, but sectional tension and reconstruction politics resulted in a fluctuating membership between seven (1866) and nine (1869). (See JUDICIARY ACT OF 1866; JUDICIARY ACT OF 1869.) In consequence *Hepburn* was decided by a narrow 4-to-3 margin. The one existing vacancy was enlarged to two by the resignation of the venerable Justice Robert C. *Grier between the decisional *conference and the formal entry of judgment.

President Ulysses S. Grant promptly appointed two Republican stalwarts to bring the Court to its reconstituted strength of nine. The new tribunal almost immediately heard reargument on the constitutionality of legal tender. Grant's action aroused controversy, but it does not appear that he consciously packed the Court. The Legal Tender Act had become a party-line issue, and *Hepburn* had been foredoomed by the obvious reaction of debtors, fearful of having to repay in gold what had been borrowed in paper.

The stark fact of practical irreversibility was evident in the opening lines of Justice William *Strong's opinion in *Knox v. Lee.* This case involved debts contracted after the passage of the Legal Tender Act. Such *ex post facto obligations, noted Strong, constituted the greater part of the indebtedness of the country. He observed that the injustice of voiding retroactive application alone would be compounded by holding the act invalid across the board. Accordingly, the Court by a vote of 5 to 4 overruled *Hepburn* and sustained the constitutionality of the Legal Tender Act. Although the Legal Tender Cases upheld broad congressional power over the currency, they impaired the Court's reputation for political independence and consistency.

(See also CONTRACT CLAUSE; JUDICIAL REVIEW; JUDICIAL POWER AND JURISDICTION.)

Gerald T. Dunne

**Legislative Standing** refers to the *standing of members of Congress to sue in their capacity as legislators. Although in the past such suits were rare, individual legislators have sought to sue executive agencies with greater frequency in recent years. Many factors have contributed to this trend, including the growth of federal programs, the decentralization of power in Congress, and a sharper sense of legislative-executive conflict since the Watergate scandal (and the resulting congressional investigations of 1973–1974) and the *Vietnam War.

If a member of Congress sues on behalf of a specific right identified by the Constitution, standing exists, as in *Powell v. McCormack* (1969), where a congressman sued to take the seat denied him. In other cases, a representative or senator must show that the executive's action effectively nullified his or her vote as a legislator.

The Supreme Court has not provided an authoritative opinion in this area. (*Coleman v. Miller*, 1939, dealt with *state* legislators' standing.) The most authoritative case on congressional standing is *Kennedy v. Sampson* (1974), decided by the U.S. *Court of Appeals for the District of Columbia Circuit, which held that a senator had standing to challenge a pocket veto of legislation for which the senator had voted. In *Goldwater v. Carter* (1979), the same court granted standing to senators challenging President Jimmy Carter's unilateral termination of a treaty on the grounds that his action prevented them from blocking termination by vote (see FOREIGN AFFAIRS AND FOREIGN POLICY).

In most cases, courts have dismissed legislators' suits for lack of standing or because of the presence of nonjusticiable *political questions. Courts have avoided creating incentives for legislators to sue rather than working through the legislative process. Even when injury-in-fact exists, the U.S. Court of Appeals for the District of Columbia Circuit, to which congressional standing suits are usually appealed, has used its discretion to dismiss suits out of deference to the dynamics of legislative-executive negotiation.

(See also JUSTICIABILITY; SEPARATION OF POWERS.)

Thomas O. Sargentich

**Legislative Veto.** In 1932 Congress and the administration of President Herbert Hoover agreed to a major new departure in the process of crafting legislation. Negotiators for the two branches prepared a statute with language that gave the president the power to reorganize the executive branch, while allowing Congress subsequently to override the chief executive if either the House or the Senate did not approve of the manner in which he accomplished that objective. Over the ensuing half century, Congress placed similar legislative veto provisions in more than two hundred laws.

The Supreme Court, in *Immigration and Naturalization Service v. Chadha* (1983), declared this practice a violation of the separation of powers doctrine. One house of Congress did not have the constitutional authority to veto a determination by the Immigration and Naturalization Service that a foreign student could remain in the United States after his visa had expired. More broadly, the Court held that while Congress has the power to pass laws, it may not participate in their execution. "Congress must abide by its delegation of authority until that delegation is legislatively altered or revoked" (pp. 954–955). All legislative vetoes, the Court held, violated the Presentment Clause (Art. I, sec. 7), and a one-house veto also violated the bicameral requirement (Art. I, secs. 1 and 7).

Despite the *Chadha* ruling, Congress and successive presidential administrations have continued to craft informal legislative understandings that require written approval of House and Senate appropriations committees before agencies may take specified actions. The executive has been willing to accept this after-the-fact congressional control as the price for obtaining a greater discretionary authority than Congress would otherwise have been likely to grant.

(See also SEPARATION OF POWERS.)

Richard Allan Baker

**Lemon Test,** a three-pronged test employed by the Supreme Court in deciding Establishment Clause disputes, such as state aid to parochial schools, public financing of religious displays, and *school prayers and Bible reading. It derives its name from its first use in Chief Justice *Burger's majority opinion in *Lemon v. Kurtzman* (1971). Under the Lemon Test, for a statute not to be a violation of the Establishment Clause, it must meet the following conditions: (1) it must have a secular legislative purpose, (2) its principle or primary effect must be one that neither advances nor inhibits religion, and (3) it must not foster an excessive entanglement with religion. The structure of the Lemon Test has now come under sustained attack by members of the Court. Chief Justice William *Rehnquist has challenged the test's historical and constitutional validity, most notably in his lengthy dissent in the school prayer case *Wallace v. Jaffree* (1985).

Scholars have differed in their commentary on the Lemon Test. Some have found it inconsistently applied, unprincipled, and too easily manipulable. Others view it as containing dichotomies too sharp (secular/religious, advance/decline of religious interests, excessive/acceptable entanglement) and thus too rigid to do justice to the complex nature of modern church-state relationships. Others find that the test undermines the value of religious autonomy, especially in public settings, as in *Lynch* v. *Donnelly* (1984), a case in which the Supreme Court allowed a crèche to be placed among less sectarian symbols of Christmas in a publicly funded holiday display. They see the Lemon Test when weakly applied as violating Establishment Clause principles by allowing majority religions to impose their beliefs on nonadherents.

Scholars also differ on the importance of the Lemon Test (and tests in general) as a guide to judicial choices. Leonard Levy, a leading critic, views it as merely lending the appearance of objectivity to judicial decisions that are necessarily subjective. Levy argues that there is no evidence that such a test actually guides the Court in reaching a decision that would not have been reached without it. He finds the excessive entanglement strand as carrying the seeds of its own misconstruction, because the term "excessive" is relative, and cannot possibly have a fixed or objectively ascertainable meaning (Levy, 1986, p. 129).

Levy argues further that the test has had little substantial restraining power upon the Court. Justices using the same test, Levy argues, often arrive at contradictory results—with Justice John Paul *Stevens and former justices William *Brennan and Thurgood *Marshall tending to find a violation of the Establishment Clause, and justices such as William *Rehnquist, Byron *White, Warren *Burger (and now Antonin *Scalia and Anthony *Kennedy) in most cases not finding a violation on the same facts. Levy argues that only centrist justices, such as Lewis *Powell, Potter *Stewart, and Harry *Blackmun, actually use the Lemon Test as a guide to their constitutional choices. Justice Sandra Day *O'Connor, while rejecting the Lemon Test, is a swing vote on religion cases.

Levy's approach to the Lemon Test obscures and undervalues justices' ongoing engagement with their long-held fundamental values (individual rights) and institutional norms (polity principles), as they decide on the proper relationship of church and state under the First Amendment. Rather than viewing the Lemon Test as a means to secure pragmatically policy wants, Ronald Kahn argues that all justices, even centrist justices, use the Lemon Test to conduct a highly motivated and highly competitive ideological jurisprudence, employing their own principles to make constitutional choices. In contrast to the Levy approach, Kahn argues that the Lemon Test adds to the coherence and discipline of Court choices by providing justices with important benchmarks or boundaries under which to determine whether a law or practice has violated the polity and rights principles that they view as central to the religion clauses of the First Amendment.

(See also FIRST AMENDMENT; RELIGION.)

□ Ronald Kahn, "Polity and Rights Values in Conflict: The Burger Court, Ideological Interests, and the Separation of Church and State," *Studies in American Political Development: An Annual* 3 (1989): 279–293. Leonard W. Levy, *The Establishment Clause: Religion and the First Amendment* (1986).                     Ronald Kahn

**Lemon v. Kurtzman,** 403 U.S. 602 (1971), argued 3 Mar. 1971, decided 28 June 1971 by vote of 7 to 0; Burger for the Court, Brennan and White concurring in part and dissenting in part, Marshall not participating. In this case, the Court considered the constitutionality of the Rhode Island Salary Supplement Act of 1969 and Pennsylvania's Non-Public Elementary and Secondary Education Act of 1968. Both laws allowed the state to support directly salaries of teachers of secular subjects in parochial and other nonpublic schools.

The issue was whether these laws violate the *First Amendment religion clauses, which prohibit laws that "respect" the establishment of religion or limit its free exercise. In this case the Court established what has come to be known as the "Lemon Test," which Chief Justice *Burger called "cumulative criteria developed by the Court over many years" (p. 642) to consider the constitutionality of statutes under the Establishment Clause. The Lemon test added a new "excessive entanglement" prong to the existing requirements that such laws be for a secular legislative purpose (*Abington School District* v. *Schempp*, 1963) and that their primary effect neither advance nor inhibit religion (*Board of Education* v. *Allen*, 1968).

The Court held that both statutes violated the excessive entanglement strand of the new test. The Court was particularly concerned that teachers in a parochial school setting, unlike the mere provision of secular books, may improperly involve faith and morals in the teaching of secular subjects; further, continuing surveillance by states to avoid this situation would nonetheless involve "excessive and enduring entanglement between state and church" (p. 619). Alluding to Thomas *Jefferson's famous metaphor of a "wall of separation between church and state," which the Court had previously employed to define the meaning of the Establishment Clause, Burger observed that "far from being a wall," it is a "blurred, indistinct, and a variable barrier depending on all the circumstances of a particular relationship" (p. 614).

To ensure the separation of church and state, the state would have to undertake a comprehensive, discriminating, and continuing surveillance of religious schools, including state audits and on-school visits. The Court also found that these laws foster a broader, yet different type of entanglement—the potential for divisive politics among those who support and those who oppose state aid to religious education. Although the Court has viewed political division along religious lines as one of the principal evils that the First Amendment was designed to prevent, it chose not to make fear of political divisiveness a separate and fourth tier of the test.

(See also LEMON TEST; RELIGION.)

Ronald Kahn

**Leon, United States v.,** 468 U.S. 897 (1984), argued 17 Jan. 1984, decided 5 July 1984 by vote of 6 to 3; White for the Court, Blackmun concurring, Brennan, Marshall, and Stevens in dissent. In *Leon*, the Court heard arguments regarding whether it should create a broad exception to the Fourth Amendment's exclusionary rule for good-faith police mistakes. The Court did create an exception to the rule that allows evidence seized in almost all searches conducted pursuant to unconstitutional warrants to be used without restriction in criminal prosecutions. Notwithstanding that it is frequently labeled as "the good-faith exception," however, the *Leon* exception is actually more limited in scope, and based on a different rationale, than the broad exception that had been proposed.

The idea for a good-faith exception came from critics of the exclusionary rule, who asserted that many unconstitutional searches were made simply because the police made honest mistakes about confusing search rules. These critics also argued, applying the deterrence rationale for the exclusionary rule adopted in *United States* v. *Calandra* (1974), that suppressing evidence that was seized unconstitutionally because of honest police mistakes served no purpose because the police could not be deterred from future unconstitutional searches if they had acted by mistake. Thus, the critics proposed that unconstitutionally seized evidence should be admissible in criminal trials whenever the police had acted because of a good-faith, albeit mistaken, belief that the search was constitutional.

Defenders of the exclusionary rule opposed the proposed exception on the ground that unconstitutionally seized evidence should be suppressed as a matter of principle to enforce Fourth Amendment rights and to protect the integrity of the courts. They also expressed doubt that honest mistakes are a frequent cause of illegal searches and argued that there is no reason to think that suppression of evidence would be less likely to deter future police misconduct just because the police had made a mistake. Defenders of the rule also questioned whether courts could reliably distinguish between mistaken and willful unconstitutional searches and, as a result, voiced concern that any good-faith mistake exception would

be so open-ended in practice that it would effectively end enforcement of Fourth Amendment search standards.

Although Justice Byron *White's majority opinion is clearly influenced by the proposal for a broad good-faith exception, the *Leon* exception is more limited in both its scope and its rationale. With regard to its scope, the *Leon* exception is explicitly limited to searches for which the police have obtained a search warrant that is later ruled to be invalid. Most police searches are, however, conducted without search warrants. Thus, as a practical matter, it is doubtful that the *Leon* exception will affect evidence in many cases, especially because search warrants were rarely found to be invalid even prior to *Leon*.

With regard to *Leon's* rationale, White did not discuss police "good faith" generally but justified the exception on the narrow premise that the police should not be asked to second guess the validity of a judge's decision to issue a search warrant. He asserted that the exclusionary rule was only designed to reach police misconduct, not judicial errors; hence, he concluded that the rule should not apply to an invalid search warrant that is the fault of a judge rather than the police. Because of this narrow rationale, it is questionable whether *Leon* should be viewed as precedent for a broad good-faith exception that would apply to unconstitutional warrantless searches. Nevertheless, *Leon* is a significant development because it is the first decision to find a Fourth Amendment violation but nevertheless allow unrestricted use of unconstitutionally seized evidence in criminal proceedings, including the prosecution's case-in-chief at trial. At least implicitly, *Leon* appears to embrace the proposition that there need not be any recourse or remedy available to victims of Fourth Amendment violations.

Justice William J. *Brennan's dissent, joined by Justice Thurgood *Marshall, rejected the entire approach of the majority opinion. It argued that suppression of unconstitutionally seized evidence is constitutionally required without regard to its deterrent effect. Hence, the reason the violation occurred should be legally irrelevant.

(See also EXCLUSIONARY RULE; FOURTH AMENDMENT; SEARCH WARRANT RULE, EXCEPTIONS TO.)

Thomas Y. Davies

**LEXIS** is the interactive computerized legal research service marketed nationally since 1973 by Mead Data Central, Inc. It contains the full text of all Supreme Court decisions from 1790 to the most recent rulings. Current opinions are transmitted electronically from the Court immediately after they are announced and are typically available for retrieval in LEXIS on the day of decision. The decisions are searchable in the GENFED library (General Federal Library) of LEXIS under the file designated US.

Through searching by key words, phrases, or

word combinations using Boolean connectors, users can retrieve either citations or the full text of relevant decisions and then print them out. The decisions can also be researched online in Shepard's citators or checked through a citation verification system called Auto-Cite. *United States Law Week, which provides comprehensive coverage of Supreme Court news and proceedings, is also available on LEXIS in the USLW file of the GENFED library.

LEXIS and its competitor, *WESTLAW, are now widely used by attorneys, judges, and scholars throughout the country, providing fast and sophisticated research access to Supreme Court decisions.                    Morris L. Cohen

**Libel.** The law of libel has a long, often bewildering, history. In almost any era, the legal literature contains numerous complaints about the irrationality, complexity, and venality of libel law. The Supreme Court's direct involvement with the law of libel, which began only in 1964 with *New York Times v. Sullivan, extended this legacy of confusion.

From the outset, the ambitious scope of libel law encouraged problems. According to an often-cited definition, common law libel covers all written communications that "tend to expose one to public hatred, shame, obloquy, contumely, odium, contempt, ridicule, aversion, ostracism, degradation, or disgrace, or to induce an evil opinion of one in the minds of right-thinking persons, and to deprive one of their confidence and friendly intercourse in society" (Kimmerle v. New York, N.Y., 1933). Including both civil suits for damages and criminal prosecutions, libel law also has a close (though little-used) relative, slander, which covers spoken defamation.

In theory, the law gave plaintiffs a favorable legal arena in which to confront detractors. *Common-law procedures allowed persons claiming injuries to reputation to take the offensive. Once it was established that a publication had been communicated and fell within the broad definition of libel, common law presumed damage to reputation. At this point, courts also required, in effect, that defendants "prove their innocence" by offering some type of legal justification for their libels. Evidence of truth became the most common defense, especially in civil suits, but courts gradually came to recognize a variety of "privileges," even for libelous falsehoods.

These common-law privileges acknowledged that libel laws, if strictly enforced, could seriously curtail public discussion. The most general privilege, "fair comment," permitted defendents to publish libelous opinions about matters of general interest, such as the quality of artistic works or the qualifications of political figures. It did not extend to false statements of libelous facts, and plaintiffs could defeat fair comment, and other "conditional" defenses, by showing that defen-

dants had exceeded their privilege by publishing with "malice."

During the nineteenth century, some state courts also recognized a broader, though still conditional, privilege in political libel cases. Under what came to be called the "minority rule," defendants could escape strict liability for libelous falsehoods when making nonmalicious criticisms of the "public" conduct of political officials and candidates for office. The citizenry's need to learn about corruption and its general interest in free speech, proponents of this rule argued, outweighed the reputational concerns of individual politicians.

Until 1964, however, most states confined the scope of these conditional privileges. During the early nineteenth century, some even limited the defense of truth by requiring that plaintiffs demonstrate they had published even libelous truths "with good motives and for justifiable ends." More typically, courts required defendants, including members of the press, to prove the truth of libelous political statements. And, as with fair comment for opinions, the conditional privilege for libelous poltiical falsehoods could be defeated by evidence of "malice," generally defined as ill will or hostility toward the persons defamed. Any wider privilege, it was argued, would threaten not only individual reputations but could discourage good people from entering or remaining in public life. Strict protection for the reputations of the "best" people, in short, was said to safeguard the public's interest as well.

Although doctrinal discussions invariably involved consideration of such general constitutional and public values, the actual impact of libel laws, over the course of American history, remains difficult to assess. Because of the time and expense that litigation required, wealthier citizens and political figures comprised the vast majority of plaintiffs. In spite of the pro-plaintiff tilt in libel law, even these people complained that the popular political culture encouraged more vituperation than black-letter law technically allowed. Except at specific times and in certain places, jurors generally seemed more sympathetic to defendants, especially newspaper publishers, than to plaintiffs. Still, publishing interests constantly complained about overly strict libel laws, arguing that even the occasional lawsuit (and rare criminal prosecution) dampened the critical tone of public discussion.

Despite numerous complaints, efforts to make dramatic changes gained little headway. Legal elites did tighten libel doctrines during the late nineteenth and early twentieth centuries, while simultaneously fighting back, in most states, efforts to adopt the minority rule on libelous political falsehoods. But stricter doctrines generally failed to make libel a commonly invoked restraint. In 1947, after studying the everyday operation of libel laws, the renowned libertarian Zechariah Chafee reported that, despite looking "bad on paper," libel laws worked fairly well in practice. For more than 150 years, the Supreme Court took a similar position. The law of libel, according to decisions such as *Chaplinsky* v. *New Hampshire* (1942) raised few, if any, First Amendment concerns.

In *New York Times* v. *Sullivan*, however, the Supreme Court constitutionalized libel law. Arising out of the civil rights struggle and involving a $500,000 judgment under Alabama's common-law rules, *Sullivan* clearly showed how a group, southern segregationists, could use libel laws to stifle political expression. In addition, by the early 1960s, a tide of large libel judgments, much higher than any handed down by juries in the past, seemed at hand. According to critics of libel law, the threat of costly litigation and expensive judgments might encourage journalists to avoid controversial issues, self-censor their publications, and thereby "chill" public discourse. Some libertarians, including Justices Hugo L. *Black and William O. *Douglas, consequently urged an end to actions by political figures and, eventually, to all libel suits involving subjects of general public interest.

The majority of the Supreme Court, led by Justice William *Brennan, mounted a less drastic, though still sweeping, revision of libel law. *Sullivan* and subsequent decisions brought a number of major changes. First, the Court held that *First Amendment requirements overrode the majority rule of strict liability for libelous political falsehoods. When sued by politicians, libel defendants enjoyed a new constitutional privilege that could be overcome only by evidence of *actual malice. Second, this new malice standard differed from the old common law one of ill will. Malice now meant publication with knowledge of falsehood or in "reckless disregard" of a statement's veracity. Third, *Sullivan* not only placed the burden of proving constitutional malice on plaintiffs but required them to offer "clear and convincing" evidence on the issue. Moreover, in order to assure adherence to *Sullivan*'s standards, the Supreme Court claimed power to review all aspects of any political libel case, including its factual basis, on the theory that judges, rather than jurors, could best safeguard free-speech values.

Post-*Sullivan* decisions—though handed down by a Court staffed with new, presumably "conservative" justices—introduced other innovations. After briefly applying the actual malice standard to any libel suit involving a subject of general public interest (*Rosenbloom* v. *Metromedia*, 1971), the Court took the more complex step of linking levels of constitutional protection to the status of different kinds of libel plaintiffs. Thus, after *Gertz* v. *Welch* (1974), public officials and "public figures," at least in libel suits against the media, had to meet *Sullivan*'s standards. But if individual states thought appropriate, purely private plaintiffs could recover under less stringent doctrines, as long as they showed some degree of fault, such as negligence, by libel defendants. In addition, the Court held that statements of pure "opinion," as opposed to libelous misstatements of "fact," were now absolutely privileged.

The resultant complexity pleased few people. Still confronting what they considered a flood of libel suits—especially by prominent figures from politics and mass culture—media executives helped to create the Libel Defense Resource Center as a clearinghouse for monitoring lawsuits and legislative changes. Although they lacked such organization, critics of the media countered with claims that libel law reforms were leaving public officials and ordinary citizens at the mercy of irresponsible journalism.

Meanwhile, commentary on the new doctrines, and proposals for further simplifying them, became a cottage industry. According to one tally, between 1973 and 1983 there were 718 reported lawsuits and nearly 450 law review articles about libel law. For their part, several academic studies suggested that the post-*Sullivan* years had not seen any dramatic reduction—and, perhaps, a slight increase—in libel suits; that defendants ultimately prevailed in the vast majority of suits; but that litigation costs and the amount of damages awarded in successful suits were both continuing to soar. Although this vast literature generally concluded that constitutionalization had helped protect First Amendment values, neither legal scholars nor directly interested parties could agree on how best to clarify the libel law muddle.

(See also SPEECH AND THE PRESS.)

□ Randall Bezanson, Gilbert Cranberg, and John Soloski, *Libel Law and the Press: Myth and Reality* (1987). Norman L. Rosenberg, *Protecting the Best Men: An Interpretive History of the Law of Libel* (1986). Rodney Smolla, *Suing the Press for Libel: The Media & Power* (1986).
Norman L. Rosenberg

**Library.** The Supreme Court Library has evolved into a significant collection of materials capable of supporting the most sophisticated legal research. The library was created by an act of 1832, providing that law books in the Library of Congress be separated from the others and that a law library be established for the Supreme Court justices. This statute also gave the justices power to promulgate rules for the use of the library. In 1832 the library contained 2,011 volumes.

The Supreme Court's librarian, Henry Deforest Clarke, was appointed in March 1887. A century later, the ninth librarian, Shelley L. Dowling, administers an institution that contains half a million volumes and has access to databases and other modern library technology. The library's collections are similar to those of a large law school library, including comprehensive coverage of the primary legal materials of the United States and each of the fifty states.

The librarian, who is appointed by the chief justice, has authority to choose assistants (the present staff numbers about twenty-five) and to acquire such books, pamphlets, periodicals, and microfilm required by the Court for its use and for the needs of its bar. The library is open to the personnel of the Court, members of the bar of the Court, members of Congress and attorneys of the federal government. The collection is noncirculating, except to justices and members of their legal staffs.

The present library facility dates from 1935, when the Court first occupied a building of its own. The library contains two distinct collections: one is for the bar of the Court and is located on the third floor of the Supreme Court building; the other, located on the second floor, is dedicated to the use of the justices. In practice, both bench and bar have access to each collection, but only the justices may use the reading room on the second floor.

The third-floor bar library consists of two reading rooms; the larger of these contains the card catalog and circulation and reference areas. The other reading room is the records and briefs room. It houses the most complete collection of the Court's records and briefs from 1832, when written briefs were first required, to the present.

Roy M. Mersky

**License Cases** (*Thurlow* v. *Massachusetts; Fletcher* v. *Rhode Island; Peirce* v. *New Hampshire*), 5 How. (46 U.S.) 504 (1847), argued 12, 14, 15, 20, 21 Jan. 1847, decided 6 Mar. 1847 by vote of 9 to 0; Taney, McLean, Catron, Daniel, Woodbury, and Grier delivered separate opinions. Establishing effective national authority to regulate interstate and foreign commerce was a primary reason for creating the Constitution of 1787. The Marshall Court asserted a broad national authority to regulate interstate commerce, though that power was limited by an extensive state *police power. Local business interests secured state legislation protecting their enterprises at the expense of merchants residing in other states. Meanwhile, after 1830 the antislavery movement made the states' control of *slavery the most explosive issue of the antebellum era.

The *License Cases* involved the legality of Massachusetts, Rhode Island, and New Hampshire statutes that taxed and otherwise regulated the sale of alcoholic beverages imported into those states. The statutes favored local retailers. The issue was whether the laws violated federal control of interstate commerce, or represented a lawful exercise of the state police power. The Court was unanimous in upholding the states' authority. Nine separate opinions written by six different justices revealed, however, that the slavery issue (raised by counsel in the Rhode

Island case) prevented agreement on the reasons governing the result.

The decision shaped the Taney Court's formulation of a compromise policy known as the doctrine of *selective exclusiveness, which influenced the application of the *commerce power until national power superseded state authority as a result of the constitutional revolution of the *New Deal era.

Tony Freyer

**Lincoln, Abraham** (b. Hardin County, Ky., 12 Feb. 1809; d. Washington, D.C. 15 Apr. 1865), lawyer, congressman, and president of the United States, 1861–1865.

As the newly inaugurated president of a divided nation, Abraham Lincoln anticipated working with a generally cooperative Congress. Though still viable, its Democratic ranks had been both diminished in size and deprived of some of its most forceful and experienced legislators owing to the departure of the seceded states' delegations. But of the southern justices of the Supreme Court, only Alabaman John A. *Campbell had resigned in 1860. As feared, the chief justice, Marylander Roger B. *Taney, did try to lead a bloc hostile to Union war objectives. His circuit opinion in *Ex parte Merryman* (1861) condemned Lincoln's "arbitrary arrests" of allegedly disloyal civilians as arrogations of Congress's sole authority to declare and wage war. Taney denounced the president's refusal to obey his order to produce the detainee John Merryman as a fatal blow to constitutional government. Like many other lawyers, however, Lincoln believed that the *Merryman* opinion violated Taney's own *political question doctrine counseling judicial restraint, as enunciated in *Luther* v. *Borden* (1849), which suggested that in civil strife the elective branches bore responsibility for making basic policy choices.

*Merryman* convinced no other justices and few lower federal judges. By stressing the obvious dangers to the Union, Lincoln stymied an antiwar bloc on the Court by disseminating the conclusions of legal scholars that previous crises had triggered comparable exercises of the nation's *war powers. Lincoln believed that the Constitution was adequate for both peace and war. Most northern lawyers accepted Lincoln's position that erroneous judicial opinions such as *Scott* v. *Sandford* (1857) and *Merryman* were ultimately reversible by political processes.

*Nature of the Lincoln Court.* While the war ground on, the Court's composition changed. Campbell's resignation in 1860, then Peter *Daniel's death in 1860, John *McLean's in 1861, and Taney's in 1864, permitted Lincoln to appoint Republicans Noah H. *Swayne of Ohio, David *Davis of Illinois, and Samuel *Miller of Iowa, plus antisecession Democrat Stephen J. *Field of California. For the post of chief justice, Lincoln named abolitionist veteran Salmon P. *Chase of Ohio, who since 1861 had served effectively as secretary of the treasury. Lincoln believed that these appointees concurred with administration civil-military policies and long-term postwar aims.

Lincoln supported statutes such as the 1862 Judicial Reorganization Act and the 1863 Habeas Corpus Act, which enlarged the federal courts' jurisdiction and increased the number of circuits and of justices and judges. These measures increased opportunities for antigovernment decisions and opinions on war governance from the highest bench.

Lincoln's desire for interbranch accord was apparent early in his administration. Meanwhile, the embittered Taney repeatedly violated judicial propriety by preparing opinions-without-cases declaring unconstitutional executive orders and statutes dealing with emancipation, conscription, and state *reconstruction. Lincoln ordered federal attorneys to avoid initiating prosecutions involving these policies, but he could not inhibit victims or other opponents from bringing suit. His gamble paid off because most justices also wished to emphasize shared constitutional responsibilities and to avoid confrontation, at least while the war continued.

*Prosecution of the War.* Despite Taney, throughout the war a narrow Court majority sustained presidential orders and statutes as constitutionally adequate. For example, Justice James M. *Wayne's opinion in *Ex parte Stevens* (1861) implicitly rejected *Merryman*. *Stevens* involved a Union soldier who had responded to Lincoln's call for ninety-day volunteers, then had his enlistment extended to three years by presidential order, an extension that Congress retroactively legitimized. The Court sustained the president's and Congress's actions.

Following a year-long interval, the Court heard arguments in the *Prize Cases* (1863). This challenge to Lincoln's proclamations of 1861 and 1862 imposing naval blockades on southern ports raised technical issues about when the Civil War began and basic questions about its legitimacy. The plaintiffs argued that no war, but rather a rebellion, existed. Blockades were appropriate only for formal international wars that only Congress could declare. Military necessities could not, they maintained, transcend the Constitution's provisions governing the declaration and conduct of war. Echoing arguments made earlier in *Stevens*, the *Prize Cases* claimants asserted that even if blockades were proper, all seizures of violators' property before Congress confirmed Lincoln's orders were illegal as, implicitly, were other executive initiatives. Government attorneys pleaded the adequacy of the Constitution's provisions for the nation's defense against foreign or domestic fees, the inappropriateness of excessively formal doctrines to the existing crisis, and the political-question precedent of *Luther*. By a bare 5-to-4 majority, the Court sustained the government, Justice Robert C. *Grier holding that the existence of the war was a political reality and

that the Confederacy's citizens were technically enemies whose property could be confiscated. For the minority, Justice Samuel *Nelson insisted that Lincoln's orders became legitimate only when Congress ratified them.

The justices similarly avoided constitutional confrontation in *Ex parte Vallandigham* (1864), which raised issued of military arrests and trials of civilians. Vallandigham, a former Ohio Democratic congressman, had encouraged antiwar activists in Ohio. General Ambrose Burnside had his charged with treason in 1863. An army court sentenced Vallandigham to prison for the duration of the war. Determined to make no martyrs, Lincoln commuted the sentence to exile to the Confederacy, from where Vallandigham slipped back into Ohio and resumed antiwar politicking. Lincoln ordered federal attorneys and the army to ignore him. Vallandigham petitioned the Supreme Court to void his earlier military arrest and trial as unlawful. Wayne's terse opinion skirted substantive civil-military questions, instead holding that the Court lacked jurisdiction over an appeal from a military tribunal (see MILITARY TRIALS AND MARTIAL LAW). The Court's majority again declined to hear an appeal on jurisdictional grounds in *Roosevelt* v. *Meyer* (1863), implicitly sustaining a wartime statute authorizing the issuance of paper money. By such cautious rulings and by avoiding challenges to executive orders on conscription, confiscation, and emancipation, the Court exercised *judicial review yet avoided confrontation with the president and Congress.

*Activist Wartime Court.* None of this suggests that the Court was supine, however. Instead, the justices vigorously established unprecedented authority over states' public policies and the judgments of states' supreme courts. The outstanding example is *Gelpcke* v. *Dubuque* (1864). Iowa municipalities defaulted on bonds issued to attract all rail lines and terminals. Successive elected Iowa Supreme Courts issued conflicting decisions on the validity of the bonds and of the repudiations. The bondholders appealed to *lower federal courts, which by statute and custom deferred to state supreme court rulings on state law. But the federal judges lacked guidance as to which of the multiple and contradictory state decisions prevailed. After federal judges in Iowa sustained repudiation, bondholders appealed to the U.S. Supreme Court. As recently as 1862, in *Leffingwell* v. *Warren*, the Court had ruled that the most recent state supreme court judgment construing state law should control. But in *Gelpcke*, Justice Swayne reverted to an earlier holding that a contract valid by state standards when made could not invalidated by subsequent state laws or state supreme court rulings. *Gelpcke* increased investors' confidence both in the stability of state bonds and in the role of the federal courts in supervising elected state judges, who allegedly bowed to their constituents' parochial interests. The Supreme Court's reporter, John W. *Wallace, extolled the justices for enforcing "high moral duties . . . upon a whole community, seeking apparently to violate them" (1 Wall. xiv).

Lincoln welcomed the Court's generally cooperative stance. Election results in 1862 and 1864 suggested that the northern public, including soldiers, believed that the Lincoln administration and the Supreme Court were sustaining constitutionalism and law. Republican congressmen sometimes expressed anti-Court views. Yet they and Lincoln applauded the Court's reviving credibility after *Dred Scott* and *Merryman*. Accordingly, Congress never transformed criticism into constraints on the Court that would have denied its appropriate role in evaluating public policies and protecting private rights.

*Emancipation, Citizenship, and Reconstruction.* Indeed, Lincoln deferred to the Court as the final legitimizer of one of his most sensitive war power orders, that of 8 December 1863 on the political reconstruction of the Confederate states. In this order, Lincoln reshaped the federal system by imposing standards for readmission and interim governance of the affected states, including the abolition of slavery in new constitutions and the reconstitution of the states' electorates. But Lincoln also feared that the Court might yet reverse his Reconstruction orders, a possibility that spurred Republican efforts to confirm emancipation in what became the *Thirteenth Amendment. Lincoln vigorously supported the amendment, seeing in the Constitution thus improved an appropriate guide for the post-Appomattox Supreme Court and for the reunited nation.

Lincoln believed that the Constitution was adequate for all purposes. His impressive educability and his innate instinct for interracial decency led him, on becoming president, to envisage an improved as well as reunified nation. In 1862 he requested Attorney General Edwin Bates to specify the rights adhering to national *citizenship. Bates's reply rested on Justice Bushrod *Washington's 1823 circuit opinion in *Corfield* v. *Coryell*. He stressed mobility, a right no slave enjoyed. Lincoln's catalog of federal citizens' rights grew much larger after his military emancipation order in 1862 and his 1863 orders to the army to recruit blacks, especially recent slaves.

In his address at Gettysburg, Pennsylvania, in late 1863, the president linked the *Declaration of Independence to the Constitution. Meanwhile, his administration was embodying equalitarian aspirations in recommended statutes, especially the Homestead, Morrill, and Jurisdiction laws of 1862 and 1863. These federal laws implicitly defined freedom as a cluster of national rights, including widened access to property (especially land), literacy (education), and legal remedies for both private and public wrongs. Having advocated in 1863 that the occupied states both constitutionalize abolition and educate their black residents, Lincoln expanded that idea to all states in 1865. He reported happily the numerous Homestead Act sales to smallholders, including Union Army veterans, among them many black soldiers. In April 1865, with total victory imminent and a new presidential term seemingly ahead, Lincoln defined his final objectives: suffrage for literate blacks and black veterans and state-supported education for all children, white and black.

*Postwar Era and the Johnson Administration.* Lincoln's perception of the Thirteenth Amendment was central to his postwar objectives. Abolition would help him and Congress implement individuals' rights derived from the national Constitution, rights paralleling and not displacing those derived from state citizenship. Lincoln's view of *federalism allowed for interstate diversity but required states' laws and customs to be race blind.

People who shared Lincoln's aspirations, like Chief Justice Chase, failed to convince his successor, Andrew Johnson, that the Thirteenth Amendment embraced civil and political rights and extended federal power over private as well as public wrongs. Johnson made no appointments to the Supreme Court, but he filled many lower federal judgeships and other court offices and the entire judiciary of all the southern states with whites, predominantly pardoned ex-Confederates. Though the Court after 1865 remained dominated by Lincoln's appointees, most justices shared only some of his views on the need for race-blind equality under state laws as a primary ingredient in federal rights. The Supreme Court began to lose its wartime sense of restraint and of enhanced national purpose.

In the *Test Oath* (see TEST OATHS) and *Ex parte *Milligan* decisions of 1866–1867, the Court, with Chase vainly dissenting, adopted increasingly ahistorical formalist views. The decision in the *Slaughterhouse Cases* (1873) limited the Thirteenth Amendment to formal abolition. Thereafter, victims of private wrongs, including those connived at by state authorities, enjoyed few practical federal remedies. Another retrograde decision in the pivotal 1873 Court term, *Osborn* v. *Nicholson*, validated a prewar contract for the sale of a slave. Another, *Bradwell* v. *Illinois*, excluded qualified women who sought access to state-licensed professions from Thirteenth and *Fourteenth Amendment protections. Nevertheless, the wartime Court had built enduring constitutional redoubts against a total return to official racism.

(See also CIVIL WAR; RACE AND RACISM.)

☐ Herman Belz, *Emancipation and Equal Rights: Politics and Constitutionalism in the Civil War Era* (1978). Harold M. Hyman and William M. Wiecek, *Equal Justice under Law: Constitutional Development, 1835–1875* (1982). James G. Randall, *Constitutional Problems under Lincoln*, rev. ed. (1951). David M. Silver, *Lincoln's Supreme Court* (1956).
Harold M. Hyman

**Lincoln, Levi** (b. Hingham, Mass., 15 May 1749; d. Worcester, Mass., 14 April 1820), lawyer, public official, and attorney general. Levi Lincoln was the son of Enoch and Rachel Fearing Lincoln. He graduated from Harvard College in 1772 and studied law in Newburyport and Northampton. After brief service in the Revolutionary War, he commenced a successful law practice in Worcester and a political career that saw him elected to the state legislature and then to Congress. President Thomas *Jefferson appointed Lincoln attorney general of the United States on 5 March 1801. Resigning in December 1804, he devoted the remainder of his life to occasional public duty in Massachusetts, serving as lieutenant governor, 1807–1808; and briefly as governor in 1808, completing an unexpired term.

Urged by Thomas Jefferson, who was anxious for a trusted Republican to be put on the Supreme Court to fill the vacancy created by the death of Justice William *Cushing, President James *Madison in November 1810 offered an associate justiceship to Lincoln. Pleading deteriorating health and poor eyesight, Lincoln declined the offer, but Madison, on 2 January 1811 submitted his name to the Senate, which confirmed him the next day. Lincoln repeated his refusal and Joseph *Story eventually filled the vacancy. Had Lincoln, not Story, taken the job it would have probably altered the course of the Supreme Court because Story proved to be a Federalist in sympathy.

Robert M. Ireland

**Lind, Henry Curtis** (b. 12 Oct. 1921, Cranston, R.I.), reporter of decisions, 1979–1987. Lind received his A.B. from Princeton in 1943. His military service began during World War II and continued afterward in the Counterintelligence Corps and in Military Intelligence. Lind graduated from Harvard Law School in 1949 and practiced law in Rhode Island until 1957.

From 1957 to 1973 Lind served in various editorial capacities for the Lawyers Co-operative Publishing Company of Rochester, New York. His responsibilities included editing the *Lawyers Edition of the U.S. *Supreme Court Reports, and the U.S. Supreme Court Digest. Lind became assistant reporter of decisions of the Supreme Court in 1973. While assistant reporter he prepared an updated style manual for the Court and helped select a computerized printing system for producing draft opinions and page proofs of the United States Reports, replacing the former "hot lead" system of printing.

During his tenure as reporter of decisions, Lind edited or coedited volumes 440–479 of the U.S. Reports. In 1982 he founded the Association of Reporters of Judicial Decisions, a group of appellate reporters from jurisdictions across North America. Upon Lind's retirement as reporter, Chief Justice William H. *Rehnquist paid tribute to him, noting that his editorial burden

was "not an enviable task" and that "Mr. Lind has performed his duties with great success."

After retiring as reporter, Lind was consultant for the University of Chicago Manual of Legal Citation (1989) and was a member of the committee sponsored by the American Bar Association that prepared the Judidial Opinion Writing Manual (1991). He also continued part-time editorial work for the Lawyers Co-operative Company and for the Supreme Court.

Francis Helminski

**Literacy Tests.** See FIFTEENTH AMENDMENT; VOTE, RIGHT TO.

**Livingston, Henry Brockholst** (b. New York City, 25 Nov. 1757; d. Washington, D.C., 18 Mar. 1823; interred Trinity Church churchyard, New York), associate justice, 1807–1823. Although born in New York City, this son of William Livingston and Susanna (French) Livingston grew up in New Jersey, where his father served as governor. Young Livingston attended the College of New Jersey (Princeton) with James *Madison. A patriot, he was commissioned captain in the Continental Army and served on the staffs of Generals Schuyler, St. Clair, and Arnold. He went to Spain as private secretary to John Jay, his brother-in-law, with whom he was often at odds. In 1782 he was captured by the British, paroled, and began the study of law.

Livingston practiced law in New York and dropped the "Henry," thereby avoiding confusion with several cousins. Active in politics, he served three terms in the state assembly. He delivered the first Independence Day address in the presence of George *Washington in 1789 and published Democracy: An Epic Poem under the pseudonym of Aquiline Nimble-Chops.

Livingston's legal activities were extensive. He assumed the leadership of the "Manor" branch of the family in its lawsuits with the "Clermont" side and aided Alexander *Hamilton in the Tory confiscation case of Rutgers v. Waddington (1784). By 1791 he emerged as a notable anti-Federalist, helping carry New York for Jefferson in 1800. His reward was appointment as a puisne judge on the New York Supreme Court in 1802.

In four years, Livingston wrote 149 opinions, attaining high judicial humor in the famous fox hunt case of Peirson v. Post (1805). Livingston wrote a powerful decision in Palmer v. Mulligan (1805), favoring the business use of water at the expense of agrarian interests. Although his commercial decisions supported emerging capitalism, Livingston held to the traditional view that the truth of an utterance and its good faith were irrelevant to a charge of seditious libel. In a rare constitutional case, Hitchcock v. Aicken (1803), he used the *full faith and credit clause to sustain an out-of-state judgment, a position he reaffirmed in Mills v. Duryee (1813). Livingston also served on the Council of Revision, where he voted against one bill because it altered charters of incorporation without the consent of the parties.

Livingston was considered for the United States Supreme Court in 1804 but had to wait until 1807. Those who expected him to be a pillar of opposition to Chief Justice John *Marshall were disappointed; Livingston reverted increasingly to the Federalism of his youth. Falling under the genial sway of Marshall, he produced only thirty-eight majority opinions, eight dissents, and six concurrences in sixteen years. Although Livingston had written a sweeping circuit court decision upholding New York's insolvency law (*Adams* v. *Storey*, 1817), he reluctantly followed the court in striking down the retrospective aspects in *Sturges* v. *Crowninshield* (1819). Justice Joseph *Story's private correspondence alone indicated his conflict with Marshall. More independent on circuit, in *United States* v. *Hoxie* (1808) he drew strictly the definition of treason to exclude the mere conveying of a raft of logs to the enemy.

Livingston was the Supreme Court's unofficial expert on commercial law until the arrival of Justice *Story and had great experience in prize law. His opinions were held in high regard by Story and subsequent legal critics.

Two acts of dubious judicial decorum involved Livingston (see JUDICIAL ETHICS). He informed John Quincy *Adams of the court's intended decision in *Fletcher* v. *Peck* (1810), and in the *Dartmouth College* case (1819) he reportedly was influenced by an extrajudicial communication from former colleague Chancellor Kent and accepted honorary degrees from Princeton and Harvard while the case was under advisement.

*Henry Brockholst Livingston*

Although lost under the shadow of John Marshall, Livingston was nevertheless a vigorous and forceful personality on and off the bar. He survived one assassination attempt in 1785 and killed a man in a duel in 1798. A persistent advocate of free public schools, he also served as treasurer and trustee of Columbia University. His death in 1823 marked the beginning of the breakup of Marshall's undisputed sway over the court.

□ Gerald T. Dunne, "Brockholst Livingston," in *The Justices of the United States Supreme Court, 1789–1969,* edited by Leon Friedman and Fred L. Israel, vol. 1 (1969), pp. 387–398. Charles Warren, *The Supreme Court in United States History,* 2 vols. (1928).          Michael B. Dougan

### Local 28 of Sheet Metal Workers International Association v. Equal Employment Opportunity Commission

478 U.S. 421 (1986), argued 25 Feb. 1986, decided 2 July 1986 by vote of 6 to 3; Brennan for the Court, White, Rehnquist, and Burger in dissent. The Supreme Court affirmed lower court orders requiring a sheet metal workers local union in New York City to establish a minority membership goal of 29 percent to be achieved by a specified date, and to maintain a fund to increase nonwhite participation in apprenticeship training and union membership. Six members of the Court rejected the argument of the Solicitor General that federal courts have no power to order numerical goals for training and promotion as a remedy for employment discrimination. A majority of the Court also rejected the argument that relief could be awarded only to identified victims of discrimination and held that judges may order race-conscious *affirmative action remedies in hiring, union membership and in other contexts to rectify "egregious" discrimination.

After years of futile action by state and municipal civil rights agencies, a federal district court had found the union guilty of violating Title VII of the *Civil Rights Act of 1964 by discriminating against nonwhite workers in recruitment, selection, training and in admission to the union. The union was ordered to cease its discriminatory practices and to establish a nonwhite membership goal based on the percentage of nonwhites in the relevant labor pool. Twice the Court of Appeals affirmed with modifications and twice the district court found the union guilty of civil contempt for disobeying court orders.

In affirming these decisions, the Supreme Court held that affirmative action requirements were appropriate remedies for job discrimination under Title VII, and within the context of such cases, this ruling remains intact.

(See also EMPLOYMENT DISCRIMINATION.)
                                                        Herbert Hill

### Lochner v. New York,

198 U.S. 45 (1905), argued 23–24 Feb. 1905, decided 17 Apr. 1905 by vote of 5

to 4; Peckham for the Court, Harlan and Holmes in dissent. In 1905 the Supreme Court invalidated a New York regulation limiting the hours of labor in bakeries to ten per day or sixty per week. At the turn of the century it was not uncommon for journeymen bakers to work more than one hundred hours per week. In cities, bakeries were usually located in the cellar of a tenement house. The combination of long hours exposed to flour dust, plus the dampness and extremes of hot and cold in tenement cellars, was thought to have an ill effect on workers' health. Because this unsanitary environment affected both the product and the workers, the state in 1895 enacted legislation to regulate sanitary conditions as well as reform working conditions and reduce the hours of labor prevalent in the industry.

Proponents of shorter hours statutes had for decades been arguing that such legislation was needed to promote citizenship, improve family life, and protect health and safety. But mostly shorter hours laws were seen as a means to assure fairness for workers who were in no position to bargain for equitable conditions of employment. Opponents based their arguments on theories of social Darwinism and laissez-faire economics. To them such legislation represented unwarranted governmental intrusion into the marketplace.

Political conditions in late nineteenth-century New York did not favor laws regulating business and industry. State government was dominated by a business oriented Republican political machine headed by boss Thomas Collier Platt. Large cities were controlled by Democratic machines like Tammany Hall. Organized *labor, the most likely proponent of such laws, represented only a small portion of the labor force. State regulation of the baking industry was made possible only when other reformers took an interest. Journalist Edward Marshall observed the squalor of New York City's cellar bakeries while serving on the Tenement House Committee of 1894. Beginning with an editorial in the *New York Press*, he led a crusade to clean up the industry and improve conditions of employment. Marshall was able to convince mainstream urban reformers that problems in the baking industry were linked to tenement reform and social reform generally. Meanwhile, Henry Weismann, an opportunistic leader of the Bakers' Union, seized the moment by getting his union behind the proposed law. Marshall's connection with urban mainstream reformers, however, provided the clout needed to push bakeshop regulation through the legislature. With their backing the Bakeshop Act unanimously passed both houses of the legislature and was signed by the governor on 2 May 1895.

The people hurt most by the new legislation were master bakers or "boss bakers." These were owners of the small shops that made up the bread baking industry. Most employed fewer than five workers and operated on a small margin of profit.

Joseph Lochner owned this type of shop in Utica, New York. In 1902 he was fined fifty dollars for allowing an employee to work more than sixty hours in one week. Lochner appealed his conviction to the Appellate Division of the New York Supreme Court, where he lost by a vote of 3 to 2. He then appealed to the New York Court of Appeals, where he lost again in a 4-to-3 ruling. Ironically, former labor leader Henry Weismann came to his aid. After a falling out with the Bakers' Union, Weismann had opened two bakeshops and become an active member of the Master Bakers' Association. He also studied law. With the help of attorney Frank Harvey Field, Weismann took Lochner's appeal to the Supreme Court of the United States.

Lochner claimed the Bakeshop Act violated the *Fourteenth Amendment by depriving him of life, liberty, or property without due process of law. Due process was originally thought of only as a guarantee that laws would be enforced through correct judicial procedure, but the concept changed drastically in the late nineteenth century. Under a theory called "substantive due process" courts assumed the power to examine the content of legislation as well as the means by which it was enforced. In the late 1880s the doctrine was employed successfully to overrule state attempts at regulating railroads. But it carried the broader implication that the Court could invalidate any type of state economic or reform legislation determined to be in conflict with a right protected by the Constitution.

In Lochner's case, the right arguably infringed by New York's workday ceiling was "liberty of contract" (see CONTRACT, FREEDOM OF). This was not a right written into the Constitution. Rather, like substantive due process, it evolved through judicial interpretation of the Fourteenth Amendment. Justice Stephen *Field, dissenting in the *Slaughterhouse Cases* (1873), first advanced the idea that the liberty protected by the Due Process Clause included "the right to pursue an ordinary trade or calling." With subsequent decisions expanding the idea, it became the means by which the judicial supervision envisioned by proponents of substantive due process could be applied to laws regulating the employer-employee relationship. Laws such as those requiring that wages be paid in cash rather than company scrip or setting standards for computing miners' pay were invalidated. By the 1880s this doctrine—liberty of contract—was being used by *state courts to suggest that the Constitution protected a right to enter into any agreement free from unreasonable governmental interference. However, the United States Supreme Court had applied the theory only once, in *Allgeyer* v. *Louisiana* (1897).

Justice Rufus *Peckham, who wrote *Allgeyer*, also wrote *Lochner*. He more firmly entrenched the doctrine of liberty of contract into constitutional law by ruling that New York's attempt to regulate hours of labor in bakeries "necessarily interfered with the right of contract between the employer and the employee." Peckham held that the liberty protected by the Fourteenth Amendment included the right to purchase and sell labor. Therefore, any statute interfering with it would be invalid "unless there are circumstances which exclude that right."

Liberty of contract was recognized, but it was not absolute. The protection it provided had to be balanced against the legitimate exercise of the state's power to govern. This authority was referred to as the *police powers of the states. As originally understood, the phrase was used to simply distinguish the function of state governments from that of the federal government. In the late nineteenth century, however, it was transformed into an ill-defined limit on the power of states to govern within their own sphere of authority. When interpreted broadly as the duty to enhance the general welfare, police power could accommodate most any type of law. But Peckham had a narrow conception of police power in mind when he wrote the *Lochner* decision. For him only legislation designed to protect public morals, health, safety, or peace and good order represented a legitimate exercise of a state's police power.

In the *Lochner* case this became a question of whether the Bakeshop Act was necessary to protect the public health or health of bakers. In *Holden* v. *Hardy* (1898) the Court upheld an eight-hour day for workers in mines and smelters. There the danger was obvious. But the claim that baking was an unhealthy trade was not so graphic. Reformers maintained that long hours of labor in bakeshops created a likelihood that workers would develop respiratory ailments such as "consumption." Peckham rejected this idea outright. Taking judicial notice of a "common understanding" that baking was never considered an unhealthy trade, he concluded that the Bakeshop Act was not a legitimate exercise of the police power and was therefore unconstitutional.

Dissenting, Justice John Marshall *Harlan argued that the majority started its reasoning from the wrong presumption. Harlan believed that, when the validity of a statute was questioned on constitutional grounds, a presumption ought to exist in favor of the legislature's determination. In his words, legislative enactments should be enforced "unless they are plainly and palpably beyond all question in violation of the fundamental law of the Constitution" (p. 68). Harlan did not disagree that liberty of contract applied to this situation. Nor did he disagree that concern for worker health and safety would be the only legitimate justification for the Bakeshop Act. Harlan was simply more willing than Peckham and the majority to recognize that there was evidence supporting that claim. The very fact that there was room for debate should have laid to rest all arguments that the law was unconstitutional.

The weighing of claims regarding health conditions in the industry was a matter of legislative discretion.

Taking a position similar to Harlan's, Justice Oliver Wendell *Holmes maintained that a state law should be upheld unless a rational person would necessarily admit that it would infringe upon fundamental principles of American laws and traditions (see FUNDAMENTAL RIGHTS). But Holmes's famous dissent also criticized the majority's decision to expand liberty of contract and its narrow view of the police power. Recognizing that these doctrines reflected the theories of social Darwinism and laissez-faire economics, Holmes directly attacked the underlying premise of the decision. "A constitution is not intended to embody a particular economic theory," he wrote. "It is made for people of fundamentally differing views" (p. 74). For Holmes, the opinion was dangerous because it represented the unwarranted infusion into the Constitution of a new fundamental right.

Peckham claimed his opinion did not substitute the judgment of the Court for that of the legislature on the matter of health in the baking industry. But many observers thought this was exactly what he had done. The Bakeshop Act had passed the state legislature unanimously. One hundred and nineteen elected representatives had voted in favor of the workday ceiling. Even seven of the twelve appellate judges who had previously ruled on Lochner's case voted to uphold the law. Critics maintained that the Court had no special knowledge of the industry and that it was in no better position than the state legislature to determine if the trade was unhealthy. And, although it was not irrefutable that the baking trade was unhealthy, ample statistical support for that contention was included in the record before the Supreme Court.

The usurpation of legislative authority and glaring subjectivity of Peckham's ruling brought the case into the limelight. In 1910, President Theodore Roosevelt pointed at *Lochner* when denouncing the judiciary for erecting insurmountable obstacles in the path of needed social reform (see JUDICIAL ACTIVISM). Critics found it frustrating that the opinion of one appointed judge could reverse the reforms adopted by elected legislatures. For the next three decades, *Lochner* symbolized judicial misuse of power.

The specific outcome was not the most important thing about the *Lochner* case. It was a setback, but not a fatal blow to the shorter hours movement. By 1912 collective bargaining gave the union bakers of New York the ten-hour day. In *Muller* v. *Oregon* (1908) the Court upheld a workday limit for women, and in *Bunting* v. *Oregon* (1917) it gave its blessing to a ten-hour ceiling for adult males as well as women and children working in most industries. (See GENDER.)

Of more lasting importance was the rationale adopted by the *Lochner* majority. It made the

Court the overseer of all kinds of state regulatory legislation. Between 1905 and 1937, when the Court rejected this rationale in *West Coast Hotel* v. *Parrish* (1937), countless subsequent attempts to reform social and economic conditions were challenged on the precedent of *Lochner.* Many of these state regulations were upheld. But state statutes such as minimum wage laws, child labor laws, regulations of the banking, insurance, and transportation industries were vetoed by the Court. Enough reform statutes were invalidated that the history of constitutional law during that time is commonly called "the *Lochner* era."

The Court is said to have made the mistake in *Lochner* of becoming involved in formulating policy rather than interpreting the law. As Holmes pointed out, it also embraced one theory of the function of government at the expense of all others. Judicial construction alone had imbedded that theory into the fundamental law of the land. For these reasons the case still stands as a symbol of unrestrained judicial activism.

(See also DUE PROCESS, SUBSTANTIVE.)

□ Felix Frankfurter, "Hours of Labor and Realism in Constitutional Law," *Harvard Law Review* 23 (1916): 353. Paul Kens, *Judicial Power and Reform Politics: The Anatomy of Lochner v. New York* (1990). Bernard H. Siegan, "Rehabilitating Lochner," *San Diego Law Review* 22 (1985): 453. Cass R. Sunstein, "Lochner's Legacy," *Columbia Law Review* 87 (1987): 873.                    Paul Kens

**Loewe v. Lawlor,** 208 U.S. 274 (1908), argued 4–5 Dec. 1907, decided 3 Feb. 1908 by vote of 9 to 0; Fuller for the Court. Popularly known as the Danbury Hatters' Case, *Loewe* v. *Lawlor* grew out of a unionization effort promoted by a secondary boycott sponsored by the American Federation of Labor, which had no direct interest in the dispute. Loewe, an employer, brought a treble-damage suit against individual members of the United Hatters of North America, including the resident union agent, Martin Lawlor. The union denied that it was a combination as defined by the *Sherman Antitrust Act.

For a unanimous Supreme Court, Chief Justice Melville W. *Fuller insisted that *every* combination in restraint of trade was illegal. Fuller stated that the Sherman Act required the Court to consider the union's actions as a whole, regardless of the intrastate character of particular actions. Fuller denied that Congress had intended to exempt unions from coverage by the act and maintained, therefore, that individual union members could be held liable for damages under section 7 of the act.

From a union perspective, *Loewe* provided a galling contrast to *United States* v. *E. C. Knight Co.* (1895), which had exempted local activities of the nationwide Sugar Trust from the Sherman Act's prohibitions, while *Loewe* extended the act's coverage to comparable union actions. This made *Loewe* the most threatening of the Court's labor decisions, raising the specter of dissolution and damage suits against unions. Unions therefore moved into the political sphere, seeking statutory exemption from Congress. The Clayton Act of 1914 failed to provide explicit exemption, but relief ultimately came within the changed labor-management context in the late 1930s.

(See also ANTITRUST; LABOR.)

Barbara C. Steidle

**Lone Wolf v. Hitchcock,** 187 U.S. 553 (1903), argued 23 Oct. 1902, decided 5 Jan. 1903 by vote of 9 to 0; White for the Court. In *Lone Wolf,* the Supreme Court recognized a near-absolute plenary congressional power over Indian affairs, virtually exempt from judicial oversight. This decision marked a decisive shift from the doctrines of the *Cherokee Cases* (1831–1832), which emphasized inherent tribal sovereignty and land rights. *Lone Wolf* has permitted the United States to appropriate tribal lands and resources under the guise of fulfilling federal trust responsibilities.

The litigation in *Lone Wolf* sought to block congressional ratification of an agreement alloting tribal lands, on the grounds that the allotment violated the 1867 Treaty of Medicine Lodge by failing to obtain the required consent of three-fourths of adult male tribal members to land cessions. (See TREATIES AND TREATY POWER.) Justice Edward D. *White rejected this claim, denying that the agreement violated property rights of tribal members or deprived them of due process of law. In conformity with the then-prevalent restrictive view of Indian tribal sovereignty, White held that Congress had plenary power over Indian property "by reason of its exercise of guardianship over their interests" (p. 565). He held this power to be political and not subject to judicial review. Under it, the United States could unilaterally abrogate provisions of treaties made with Indian nations, subject only to the requirement that actions of the United States toward its "wards" be guided by "perfect good faith" (p. 566).

Until recently, the *Lone Wolf* doctrine articulated an unreviewable congressional power and virtually standardless trust authority, which made it impossible for tribes to obtain judicial protection in disputes with the United States. Recent developments may suggest a narrower view of congressional power over Indian tribes as well as some constitutional limits on that power. In 1979 a federal judge called *Lone Wolf* "the Indian's *Dred Scott.*" But unlike that case, *Lone Wolf* has not yet been repudiated by political events or judicial decisions.

(See also JUDICIAL POWER AND JURISDICTION; NATIVE AMERICANS; PROPERTY RIGHTS.)

Jill Norgren

**Lottery Case.** See CHAMPION V. AMES.

**Louisiana ex rel. Francis v. Resweber,** 329 U.S. 459 (1947), argued 18 Nov. 1946, decided 13 Jan.

1947 by vote of 5 to 4; Reed for the Court, Burton in dissent. In November 1944, Andrew Thomas, a white St. Martinsville, Louisiana, druggist, was murdered, apparently by fifteen-year-old Willie Francis, who was black. With little help from his court appointed attorneys, Francis was quickly convicted and condemned to execution in the electric chair. But when Francis sat in it on 3 May 1946, it malfunctioned; the two-minute jolt of electricity failed to kill (or even disable) him. Reached by phone, the governor scheduled a new execution date for the next week.

But attorneys responding to the pleas of the inmate's father took the case to the Supreme Court. They argued that the attempt to execute Francis again would constitute *double jeopardy, and, more importantly, *cruel and unusual punishment under the *Eighth Amendment. The justices refused to block a second execution attempt. The swing vote was cast in a concurring opinion by Justice Felix *Frankfurter, usually a death penalty foe.

Petitions for rehearing and clemency were unsuccessful, and one year and six days after the original blunder, Willie Francis again sat in the electric chair. This time it worked.

(See also CAPITAL PUNISHMENT; RACE DISCRIMINATION AND THE DEATH PENALTY.)

Michael L. Radelet

**Louisville, New Orleans & Texas Railway Co. v. Mississippi,** 133 U.S. 587 (1890), argued 10 Jan. 1890, decided 3 Mar. 1890 by vote of 7 to 2; Brewer for the Court, Harlan in dissent. The Court upheld the constitutionality of a Mississippi statute that required railroads to provide "equal, but separate, accommodation for the white and colored races." The railroad argued that the statute was unconstitutional because its substantial effect on interstate commerce violated the Commerce Clause (see COMMERCE POWER). Unlike arguments that would mature in the twentieth century, the case did not involve the *Fourteenth Amendment.

The Mississippi statute, in its effect on interstate commerce, seemed identical to a Louisiana statute that had been declared unconstitutional in *Hall v. DeCuir (1878). Both statutes used race as the criterion for determining treatment of passengers. The Louisiana statute mandated that all parts of vehicles be open to passengers, regardless of race; the Mississippi statute required separation by race, into "equal" facilities. In spite of the apparent similarities, the Court upheld the Mississippi statute.

The inconsistency between the two decisions evidences the Court's struggle to define *federalism in the late nineteenth century. The Court had already so narrowed the scope of the Civil War Amendments that the national government had little role to play in protecting individual rights. Here, through interpretation of the Commerce Clause, the Court continued its efforts to preserve a major role for the states. Accordingly, Justice David J. *Brewer accepted without question the Supreme Court of Mississippi's view that the statute applied only to intrastate commerce. The Court saw no significant burden on interstate commerce from the requirement that railroads add an additional car upon entering the state. Justice John Marshall *Harlan dissented on the ground that the state statute was an unconstitutional regulation of interstate commerce.

Walter F. Pratt, Jr.

**Louisville Railroad Co. v. Letson,** 2 How. (43 U.S.) 497 (1844), argued 20 Feb. 1843, decided 7 Mar. 1844 by vote of 5 to 0; Wayne for the Court, Daniel, McKinley, and Taney not participating, Thompson had died. Letson, a New York resident, sued the Louisville Railroad Company, chartered by South Carolina, in federal circuit court under diversity of citizenship jurisdiction for breach of contract. The railroad argued that the federal circuit court had no jurisdiction because the U.S. Supreme Court had ruled, in *Bank of the United States v. Deveaux (1809), that the citizenship of a corporation for purposes of *diversity jurisdiction was that of its shareholders. The railroad maintained that there was no diversity since some of the its shareholders were citizens of New York.

On a writ of *error from a decision upholding jurisdiction, the Court overturned Deveaux and held that for purposes of diversity jurisdiction a corporation is a citizen of the state that chartered it. Because a corporation would thus be a citizen of a single state rather than a citizen of all of the states in which its shareholders resided, Letson increased the opportunities of corporations to sue or be sued in federal court under diversity jurisdiction and enhanced federal judicial power. For the next two decades corporations resisted federal diversity jurisdiction as often as they favored it, but following the Civil War many of them found the federal courts more hospitable than *state courts. In 1958 Congress somewhat limited the right of corporations to sue or be sued in federal court under diversity jurisdiction by providing that a corporation should be deemed a citizen of the state that incorporates it and of the state that is its principal place of business.

(See also JUDICIAL POWER AND JURISDICTION.)

Robert M. Ireland

**Lovell v. City of Griffin,** 303 U.S. 444 (1938), argued 4 Feb. 1938, decided 28 Mar. 1938 by vote of 8 to 0; Hughes for the Court, Cardozo not participating. Although the Supreme Court suggested in *Gitlow v. New York (1925) that the *First Amendment's guarantee of free speech was applicable to the states through the *Fourteenth Amendment, it was not until *Everson v. Board of Education (1947) that it so held with respect to both the religious establishment and free exercise clauses. During the intermediate period the Court developed a technique it still occasionally uses of treating *religion cases as if they were free speech cases. *Lovell* v. *Griffin* was an example of such treatment.

Alma Lovell, an adherent of the Jehovah's Witnesses, refused to abide by the city's ordinance that required the city manager's written permission for distribution or sale of circulars, magazines, pamphlets, or handbooks. She regarded herself as sent by "Jehovah to do His work," and that such an application would have been "an act of disobedience to His commandment."

The Court did not deal with the religious aspects of the case and did not even mention the Jehovah's Witnesses by name. Instead, it held the ordinance invalid as a violation of freedom of the press. The liberty of the press was not confined to newspapers and periodicals, the Court said; it necessarily embraced pamphlets and leaflets. Nor could the ordinance be saved because it related to distribution rather than publication; liberty of circulation was as essential as liberty of publication.

(See also SPEECH AND THE PRESS.)

Leo Pfeffer

**Lovett, United States v.,** 328 U.S. 303 (1946), argued 3 and 6 May 1946, decided 3 June 1946 by vote of 8 to 0; Black for the Court, Frankfurter, joined by Reed, concurring, Jackson not participating. The Bill of *Attainder Clauses of Article I of the Constitution have been interpreted broadly to prohibit any legislative act, by Congress or a state legislature, that inflicts punishment on a designated individual without a judicial trial. Historically, the English experience and abuses after the Revolution made this device unpopular. Functionally, such special acts reflect the general mistrust of retroactive legislation and violate *separation of powers.

The *Lovett* decision came during the cold war hysteria and McCarthy-era purges. Congress enacted a statute providing that no appropriated funds could be paid as salary to Lovett and two other named federal employees found to be disloyal. The Court ruled that this amounted to a bill of attainder.

The Court has struck down only three other statutes as forbidden bills of attainder: a state law that required clergy to take an oath that they had never aided the Confederacy; a congressional enactment that required a similar oath as a condition to practice law in federal courts; and a federal statute making it a crime for a member of the Communist party to serve as an officer of a *labor union.

In his autobiography *All Our Years* (1948), Robert Morss Lovett claimed for the three "a place in history in spite of ourselves" and described the outcome as an occasion when "government triumphed over hate" (pp. 308–309).

The decision stilled further congressional attempts to punish people by name in statutes.

(See also COMMUNISM AND COLD WAR).

Thomas E. Baker

**Loving v. Virginia,** 388 U.S. 1 (1967), argued 10 Apr. 1967, decided 12 June 1967 by vote of 9 to 0; Warren for the Court, Stewart concurring. In *Pace* v. *Alabama* (1883), the Court upheld an Alabama law that punished interracial fornication more severely than when the partners were of the same race. Since both partners were punished equally, it said, there was no violation of the *Equal Protection Clause of the *Fourteenth Amendment. This became known as the "equal discrimination" or "equal application" exception.

Later cases, such as *Shelley* v. *Kraemer* (1948), refused to apply it, however, and it was clearly inconsistent with the principle of racial nondiscrimination enunciated in *Brown* v. *Board of Education* (1954). But the Court was reluctant to address formally this very sensitive issue head on, recognizing that, coming on the heels of *Brown*, prohibiting laws against racial intermarriage would only further inflame southern resistance (*Naim* v. *Naim*, 1955). The doctrine was finally repudiated in the *Loving* case.

Loving, a white man who had married a black woman, challenged his conviction under the Virginia antimiscegenation law, which prohibited and punished racial intermarriage. Virginia was then one of sixteen southern states that had such laws. In the previous fifteen years, fourteen states had repealed laws outlawing interracial marriages. Chief Justice Earl *Warren, for a unanimous Court, invalidated the law as an invidious racial classification prohibited by the Equal Protection Clause of the Fourteenth Amendment. Warren held that: "Under our Constitution, the freedom to marry, or not marry, a person of another race resides with the individual and cannot be infringed by the State" (p. 12).

(See also MARRIAGE; RACE AND RACISM.)

Steven Puro

**Lower Federal Courts.** The structure of the federal courts was initially set by the *Judiciary Act of 1789 and has been basically unchanged since the end of the nineteenth century: a set of trial courts (courts of first instance) forms the base of the pyramid, above which are the intermediate *courts of appeal. At the apex sits the U.S. Supreme Court.

The trial courts in the federal system are the federal district courts. These courts have authority to hear and decide virtually all cases that the Constitution allows a federal court to resolve. The major exceptions are monetary claims against the United States, certain tax cases, duties imposed on imported goods, and matters initially heard by various federal regulatory commissions. Specialized trial courts handle these issues.

Historically, however, Congress did not authorize the federal district courts to hear those *"federal questions" that challenged the constitutionality of state governmental actions. Not until after the *Civil War did the district courts have general power to decide cases involving the Constitution, acts of Congress, and treaties of the United States—regardless of an alleged conflict with state law or state constitutional provisions (see REMOVAL ACT OF 1875). Prior to the Civil War, the state courts resolved these conflicts between state and federal law, with the losing litigant provided an opportunity to *appeal to the U.S. Supreme Court.

Each state has at least one federal district court within its boundaries and, with one exception, no district court's geographical reach extends beyond the boundary of a single state (the U.S. District Court for the District of Wyoming includes those portions of Idaho and Montana that are in Yellowstone National Park). In addition to the ninety district courts within the fifty states and the District of Columbia, Congress has established four others for *territories of the United States: Guam, Puerto Rico, the Northern Marianas, and the Virgin Islands.

Three states have four district courts (California, New York, and Texas); nine others—six in the South—have three. By contrast, such relatively populous states as Massachusetts, Connecticut, New Jersey, Minnesota, Arizona, and Oregon have only one. District courts bear the name of the state in which they are located, plus a geographical descriptor if the state has more than one district court: north, south, east, west, and central or middle.

The district courts are staffed by almost six hundred federal judges whom the president appoints with the consent of the Senate (see APPOINTMENT AND REMOVAL POWER). Assisting the judges are magistrates, who generally have responsibility for pretrial proceedings and the trial of misdemeanors, and referees in bankruptcy. The latter are now called bankruptcy judges. District court judges appoint the magistrates for terms of eight years, and circuit court judges appoint the bankruptcy judges for terms of fourteen years.

Unlike the courts of appeals and the Supreme Court, only a single judge hears cases in the district courts. At the beginning of the twentieth century, Congress required a few cases to be heard by a district court composed of three judges, one from the district and two from the court of appeals. The jurisdiction of these three-judge district courts was subsequently expanded so that by the mid-1970s, most three-judge courts were hearing cases alleging violations of civil rights. Congress, however, narrowly circumscribed the use of three-judge courts thereafter, with the result that their use almost disappeared by 1990.

Like the federal district courts, but unlike the Supreme Court, the U.S. courts of appeals are required to hear all cases that fall within their jurisdiction. As the general intermediate appellate courts for the federal system, they hear appeals from the federal district courts and the federal regulatory commissions.

The United States and its territories are divided into eleven numbered appellate circuits, plus the Court of Appeals for the District of Columbia. Except for the District of Columbia, which has jurisdiction over the D.C. district court and most of the decisions of the various federal regulatory agencies, the other courts of appeals are composed of regional state groupings. Three are in the East: the First, Second, and Third. The South also contains three: the Fourth, Fifth, and Eleventh. Until 1981, the Eleventh Circuit was part of the Fifth. In that year, Congress divided it in half. The Sixth Circuit is a midwest-southern hybrid, with the Seventh encompassing three Great Lakes' states. The other three circuits lie west of the Mississippi River.

Congress has created more than 150 judgeships to service these courts of appeals, with each court having at least six and as many as twenty-six judges assigned to it. The number in each circuit reflects the circuit's caseload. Judges sit in panels of three. Occasionally, all of the circuit's judges may sit *en banc* to decide an unusually divisive or important case. The circuit court judges are assisted by "senior" (i.e., semiretired) judges and by district court judges who temporarily sit on a circuit court "by designation."

A number of specialized courts of appeals also exist: the Court of Customs and Patent Appeals (see PATENT), renamed as the Court of Appeals for the Federal Circuit in 1982, the Court of International Trade (formerly the Customs Court), and the Court of Military Appeals (see MILITARY JUSTICE). Although decisions of these courts are important to those directly affected, they rarely have enough national or policy significance to warrant Supreme Court review.

(See also JUDICIAL POWER AND JURISDICTION.)

Harold J. Spaeth

**Lurton, Horace Harmon** (b. Newport, Ky., 26 Feb. 1844; d. Atlantic City, N.J., 12 July 1914; interred Greenwood Cemetery, Clarksville, Tenn.), associate justice, 1910–1914. Born in northern Kentucky, the son of a pious doctor who became an Episcopalian minister, Horace Harmon Lurton was taken by his parents while still a child to Clarksville, Tennessee, the town he ever after regarded as home. His college education at Douglas University in Chicago interrupted by the Civil War, the teenage Lurton proved himself an ardent Confederate soldier, reenlisting after a discharge for physical disability and after escape from a northern prisoner-of-war camp. Serving under General John Hunt Morgan during the raid into Ohio, Lurton was again captured, this time allegedly gaining parole by President Abraham

His opinions as an associate justice during his brief tenure were in accord with this opening statement, although he did prove willing to tolerate modest progressive reform; at his death even his eulogist confessed that he had rendered "no startling or sensational decisions." Perhaps his most significant contribution was in drafting the Federal Equity Rules of 1912, which remained in force until the abolition of federal equity practice in 1938.

A Cleveland Democrat who reached the Court during the era of Republican ascendancy, Lurton typified the consensus that underlay party differences. A sincere believer in the verities of small-town America, Lurton was one of a generation of judges who retarded needed reforms, not least by his transparent honesty and integrity.

□ James F. Watts, Jr., "Horace Harmon Lurton," in *The Justices of the United States Supreme Court, 1789–1969,* edited by Leon Friedman and Fred L. Israel, vol. 3 (1969), pp. 1847–1863.                                    John V. Orth

*Horace Harmon Lurton*

*Lincoln in response to his mother's appeal. After the war the young veteran entered law school at Cumberland University, from which he graduated in 1867. Married the same year to Mary Frances Owen, Lurton was admitted to the Tennessee bar and settled in Clarksville, where he practiced law until 1886, except for 1875–1878, when he served as one of the state's chancellors. Elected to the Tennessee Supreme Court on the Democratic ticket in 1886, the forty-two-year-old Lurton began a judicial career that lasted the rest of his life.

In January 1893 he became chief justice of Tennessee, only to resign a few months later when President Grover Cleveland appointed him to the United States Court of Appeals for the Sixth Circuit in Cincinnati. On the federal bench Lurton developed a warm friendship with William Howard *Taft, then presiding judge. Despite active judicial service, Lurton found time to teach law at Vanderbilt University from 1898 and was dean of the law school from 1905. In December 1909 President Taft named his friend to the Supreme Court. At age sixty-five Lurton was the oldest man ever appointed; as a southern Democrat and Confederate veteran, he was a surprising choice for a Republican president.

Soon after his appointment Lurton addressed a meeting of the Maryland and Virginia Bar Associations. His speech on the topic "A Government of Law or a Government of Men?" was an uninspired restatement of conservative judicial values, eschewing liberal construction of the Constitution, judicial lawmaking in the interests of social advancement, and infringements on states' rights, spiced by nativist fears of foreign immigrants (see JUDICIAL REVIEW; FEDERALISM).

**Luther v. Borden,** 7 How. (48 U.S.) 1 (1849), argued 24–28 Jan. 1848, decided 3 Jan. 1849 by vote of 8 to 1; Taney for the Court, Woodbury concurring in part and dissenting in part. The Constitution provides that the federal government shall guarantee to each state a "Republican Form of Government" (Art. IV, sec. 4), but does not specify how much popular participation in state government is required to retain the republican character, nor does it identify which branch of the federal government, if any, is responsible for enforcing the guarantee. Until the 1840s, this imprecision was of no practical significance. In the federal system, each state was as republican as its enfranchised citizens wanted it to be in matters of suffrage qualifications, apportionment, and tax burdens. But in 1842, the Dorr Rebellion implicated the *Guarantee Clause as a remedy for disfranchised Rhode Islanders, whose state officials ignored reformist demands to democratize the ossified state constitution.

Though foremost among American states in the Industrial Revolution, Rhode Island suffered from an unusually backward constitutional order derived from the 1663 royal charter, which continued to serve as the state constitution. Severe disfranchisement of the urban population, composed largely of displaced Yankees and recent immigrants drawn to Rhode Island's cities to work in textile mills, was compounded by malapportionment that preserved dominant political power in rural districts. This produced a political anomaly in the period of Jacksonian democracy.

The so-called Dorr Rebellion was precipitated when suffrage reformers, despairing of remedies for disfranchisement and malapportionment from the extant state government, invoked the principles of the *Declaration of Independence and attempted, in its words, to "alter or abolish" the oppressive government and "to institute [a] new government."

The reformers called an extralegal constitutional convention, drafted a new state constitution that substantially ameliorated disfranchisement and malapportionment, submitted the document for popular ratification, and held elections under it. A draft constitution submitted by the extant government failed of ratification, but the government refused to cede power, so for a few months in 1842, two opposing governments contended for legitimacy and possession of state offices.

The incumbent governor and legislators, covertly encouraged by President John *Tyler's promise of federal military aid should violence occur, declared martial law. State judges convicted the reform governor, Thomas Wilson Dorr, of treason. The U.S. Supreme Court refused Dorr's 1845 appeal (*Ex parte Dorr*) for release on *habeas corpus, because the federal writ did not reach state constitutions.

The Dorr supporter Martin Luther brought suit against a militiaman, Luther Borden, who had entered and searched Luther's home under authority of martial law. For Borden and the state, Daniel *Webster denied that the Rhode Island situation justified invoking the Constitution's Guarantee Clause. Luther's counsel claimed that the state's archaic constitutional arrangements prevented fair and peaceful redress of grievances through democratic procedures. Rhode Islanders had therefore exercised Americans' ultimate right inherent in popular sovereignty, that of replacing an oppressive government.

*Luther* v. *Borden* posed basic questions about the American constitutional order. Was the Supreme Court the appropriate institution to define the substantive content of republicanism? If frustrated in demands for orderly constitutional change, had Americans no alternatives to revolutionary violence? What was essential to a republican form of government?

The Supreme Court, speaking through Chief Justice Roger B. *Taney, skirted these difficult questions. Taney articulated the "political questions" doctrine, which diverts responsibility for resolving certain constitutional issues to the legislative and executive branches of government. "The sovereignty in every State resides in the people," he concluded—with an empty concession as to how and whether they had exercised it

in the Dorr cause—but "is a political question to be settled by the political power" (p. 47).

(See also POLITICAL QUESTIONS.)

□ George M. Dennison, *The Dorr War: Republicanism on Trial, 1831–1861* (1976).        Harold M. Hyman

**Lynch v. Donnelly,** 465 U.S. 668 (1984), argued 4 Oct. 1983, decided 5 Mar. 1984 by vote of 5 to 4; Burger for the Court; O'Connor concurring; Blackmun, Brennan, Marshall, and Stevens in dissent. The city of Pawtucket, Rhode Island, owned and annually erected a Christmas display in its downtown shopping district. The display included, among other things, a Santa's house, a Christmas tree, cut-out animal figures, colored lights, and a life-sized nativity scene. The plaintiffs, residents of Pawtucket, alleged that the presence of the nativity scene, or "crèche," in the display demonstrated official support for Christianity, violating the Establishment Clause.

By a five-justice majority, the Court denied the constitutional attack. It rejected the claim that the purpose or primary effect of the crèche's inclusion was to affiliate the city with the Christian beliefs associated with Christmas. Viewing the display within the context of the city's celebration of a national public holiday, the majority concluded that the crèche served the legitimate secular purpose of symbolically depicting the historical origins of the Christmas holiday. In contrast, five years later, in *Allegheny County* v. *American Civil Liberties Union* (1989), the Court found the display of the crèche in a public building, ungarnished by other holiday decorations, to violate the Establishment Clause.

Justice Sandra Day *O'Connor, supplying the crucial fifth vote, wrote a separate concurrence rejecting traditional Establishment Clause analysis and substituting the question whether government intends or is perceived to endorse religion. This position, introduced in *Lynch*, seemed to have gained majority support in *Allegheny County*, at least where the display of religious symbols is at issue.

*Lynch* generally signified a reduction in the separation of church and state, finding instead a constitutional mandate for religious accommodation.

(See also RELIGION.)

Stanley Ingber

**Madison, James** (b. Port Conway, Va., 16 Mar. 1751; d. Montpelier, Va., 28 June 1836), coauthor, with Alexander *Hamilton and John *Jay, of *The *Federalist;* often called the "father of the Constitution"; president of the United States, 1809–1817. Madison was not a lawyer, but he was a keen student of constitution-making and of Montesquieu's *Spirit of the Laws.* Madison perceived fundamental weaknesses in the Articles of Confederation, and as a Continental Congress delegate in 1786 he led the reform movement that culminated in the Constitutional Convention of 1787. There, Madison's "Virginia Plan" included a provision for a federal judiciary that would "consist of one or more supreme tribunals." Thus Madison was among the first advocates of a judicial system based on a supreme court. In the First Congress (1789), he opposed efforts that would have diluted the power of the federal courts by giving state jurists concurrent power to execute federal laws. "To make the federal laws dependent on them," he argued, "would throw us back into all the embarrassment which characterized our former situation."

When the Alien and *Sedition Acts passed in 1798, Madison agreed with Thomas *Jefferson that they were unconstitutional. Madison and Jefferson expected no relief from Federalist judges, however, and so they sought to nullify the laws through *interposition by state action. In his Virginia Resolutions, Madison urged state legislatures to declare the laws invalid, but the point became moot in 1801, when the laws expired.

As secretary of state under President Jefferson, Madison was the defendant in the landmark case of *Marbury v. Madison* (1803). Both he and Jefferson believed the decision was politically motivated and that it was aimed at curbing presidential power. Moreover, both considered Chief Justice John *Marshall's groundbreaking enunciation of *judicial review as contrary to the republican principle of majority rule. To allow courts to stamp legislation "with its final character," Madison observed, made "the Judiciary Dept. paramount in fact to the Legislature, which was never intended, and can never be proper."

As president Madison tried to deny Marshall further opportunities to entrench judicial review when he vetoed congressional grants of privileges to churches—laws he believed conflicted with the *First Amendment clause forbidding an establishment of *religion. Madison also sought to fortify the Republican, strict-constructionist position on the Supreme Court when two vacancies occurred. Despite Jefferson's warning, Madison appointed Joseph *Story, a New England attorney with Republican credentials, and was disappointed when Story became as much a Federalist as Marshall. Madison's second appointment, however, brought a staunch Republican, Gabriel *Duvall, to the bench.

In 1816 President Madison vetoed a bill creating a second Bank of the United States because he thought it stretched the chartering powers of Congress beyond constitutional limitations. Later he signed a revised law that adhered more closely to his ideas of strict constructionism. As an elder statesman, Madison equated the Union and the Constitution, and he denounced *nullification doctrines during the controversy of 1832–1833. Although Southerners criticized him for betraying his earlier states'-rights stance for a nationalist position, Madison maintained that only the courts could declare laws unconstitutional (see STATE SOVEREIGNTY AND STATES' RIGHTS).                                    Robert A. Rutland

**Magnet Schools.** See DESEGREGATION REMEDIES.

**Mahan v. Howell,** 410 U.S. 315 (1973), argued 12 Dec. 1972, decided 21 Feb. 1973 by vote of 5 to 3; Rehnquist for the court, Brennan, Douglas, and Marshall in dissent, Powell not participating. This was the first of four cases in 1973 that clarified the permissible range of population equality in designing state legislative and congressional districts. *Mahan* involved a challenge to a 1971 Virginia statute apportioning the lower house of one hundred delegates into a combination of single-member, multi-member, and floater districts. A three-judge federal district court had found the plan unconstitutional because district population deviations ranged from plus 9.6 to minus 6.8 percent. Virginia defended these variances as resulting from a consistently applied state policy of following county and city boundaries, excepting only populous Fairfax County, which was divided into two five-member districts.

In reversing the lower court the Supreme Court repeatedly emphasized the reasoning in *Reynolds* v. *Sims* (1964), which had recognized greater population flexibility for state legislative than for congressional districts. The Court reaffirmed that some deviations from the equal population standard, when based on legitimate considerations of state policy, are constitutionally permissible. The Court concluded that the 16.4 percent total variance range in Virginia "may well approach tolerable limits" but did not exceed them.

Some four months later, the Court handed down the three remaining districting cases of the term, two involving state legislative districts in Connecticut (*Gaffney* v. *Cummings*) and Texas (*White* v. *Regester*). Total population variances were smaller (7.8 and 9.9 percent, respectively) than in Virginia, but not justified as in that state by consistently following local boundaries. The Court shifted the burden of proof to those challenging redistricting acts not exceeding such *de minimis* variances. In *White* v. *Weiser*, a unanimous Court upheld stringent population standards for congressional districts in Texas, following the precedent of *Kirkpatrick* v. *Preisler* (1969).

(See also FAIR REPRESENTATION; REAPPORTIONMENT CASES.)

Gordon E. Baker

**Mallory v. United States,** 354 U.S. 449 (1957), argued 1 Apr. 1957, decided 24 June 1957 by vote of 9 to 0; Frankfurter for the Supreme Court. Although the power of the Supreme Court to overturn state convictions is limited to the enforcement of

*Fourteenth Amendment due process rights, the Court may formulate rules of evidence in the exercise of its "supervisory power" over the administration of federal criminal justice that go well beyond due process requirements. The best-known example is the McNabb-Mallory rule.

In *McNabb* v. *United States* (1943) the Court held, in the exercise of its supervisory power, that incriminating statements obtained from a suspect during his illegal detention (i.e., while held in violation of federal requirements that an arrestee be promptly brought before a committing magistrate) must be excluded in a federal trial whether or not the statements were made voluntarily. Although heavily criticized by law enforcement officials and members of Congress, the rule was reaffirmed in *Mallory* v. *United States* (1957). There, speaking for a unanimous Court, Justice Felix *Frankfurter (author of the original *McNabb* opinion) emphasized that the police should have *probable cause before they make an arrest and that it is not their function to arrest people "at large" and to question them later to determine whom they should charge. The decision provoked extreme outrage, particularly in Congress.

The *Mallory* rule offered an alternative to the "voluntariness" test for admitting confessions, but only in the federal courts. Nevertheless, many feared (and others hoped) that some day the Warren Court would impose the rule on the states as a matter of Fourteenth Amendment due process. The Supreme Court never did so. Instead it tackled the problem of confessions in a different way, increasingly resorting to the right to counsel and the privilege against *self-incrimination. These efforts culminated in the famous case of *Miranda* v. *Arizona* (1966).

Because the McNabb-Mallory rule was not a constitutional doctrine but only an exercise of the Court's supervisory power, it was always subject to congressional revision or repeal. In 1968, after numerous attempts to do so, Congress finally passed legislation that crippled the rule.

(See also COERCED CONFESSIONS; COUNSEL, RIGHT TO; DUE PROCESS, PROCEDURAL.)

Yale Kamisar

**Malloy v. Hogan,** 378 U.S. 1 (1964), argued 5 Mar. 1964, decided 15 June 1964 by vote of 5 to 4; Brennan for the Court, Harlan, Clark, Stewart, and White in dissent. Malloy pleaded guilty to taking part in an unlawful gambling operation. Connecticut's Superior Court sentenced him to a year in jail, but after ninety days his prison term was suspended and he was placed on probation for two years. While on probation he was called to testify in a state inquiry into gambling and other crimes. He refused to answer questions relating to his earlier arrest and conviction, citing his Fifth Amendment privilege against self-incrimination. Adjudged in contempt he was imprisoned until he was willing to answer. The Supreme Court agreed to review the case after *state courts had denied the defendant's application for a writ of *habeas corpus on federal constitutional grounds.

The Fifth Amendment provides that "no person shall be compelled in any criminal case to be a witness against himself." The privilege was designed originally to protect the individual against the federal government. For decades the Supreme Court refused to impose it on the states. The Court had long adhered to the view that the Due Process Clause of the *Fourteenth Amendment, which binds the states, requires only *fundamental fairness—meaning the avoidance of cruel or arbitrary procedures—and that a state could try persons fairly and justly without according them a privilege sanctioned by little more than age and tradition.

*Malloy*'s significance lies in the Court's sudden rejection of this older view; seven justices held that the states, through the Fourteenth Amendment, were indeed now bound by the Fifth Amendment's privilege against self-incrimination. *Malloy* thus effectively overruled *Twining* v. *New Jersey* (1908) and *Adamson* v. *California* (1947), cases seemingly reinforced as late as 1961 by *Cohen* v. *Hurley*. In these cases a prosecutor's comment on the failure of an accused to testify in a state proceeding was allowed to stand. The Court was unwilling to require the states to follow the harsh "no comment" rule it had derived from the Fifth Amendment privilege. But now, after *Malloy*, if a person invokes the privilege, all the Fifth Amendment standards that apply in a federal proceeding apply to the states.

This "incorporation" of the Self-Incrimination Clause of the Fifth Amendment into the Fourteenth was foreshadowed by the Court's increasing resolve to overturn state convictions based on confessions elicited by improper methods of influence. The time had come, the Court said, to recognize "that the American system of criminal prosecution is accusatorial, not inquisitorial, and that the Fifth Amendment privilege is its essential mainstay" (p. 7). The Court thus vindicated the right of a witness to remain silent. Unless a person freely chooses to testify the entire burden of producing evidence to establish guilt shifts to the government.

Justices John M. *Harlan and Tom *Clark, dissenting, rejected the Court's decision to bind the states to the Fifth Amendment's self-incrimination clause. They would have adhered to the rationale of *Twining* and *Adamson* under which state practices were to be judged in terms of basic principles of justice implicit in the Fourteenth Amendment's Due Process Clause, apart from and independent of the specific—and historically determined—privileges and safeguards laid down in the *Bill of Rights. In their view, the Due Process Clause is in its own right an exacting standard of justice whose meaning can and should be derived from accepted and evolving notions of decency in a civilized society. They

argued that a discriminatory approach of this kind, which allows the states a good measure of flexibility in meeting the problems of local law enforcement, contributes "to the sound working of our federal system in the field of criminal law" (p. 27).

Justices Byron *White and Potter *Stewart concurred with the majority's view that the Fourteenth Amendment incorporated the privilege against self-incrimination. They dissented, however, because in their view the facts of the case did not warrant the application of the privilege. Given the inquiry's focus and the nature of the questions asked they felt that the defendant was in no danger of incriminating himself.

(See also FIFTH AMENDMENT; INCORPORATION DOCTRINE; SELF-INCRIMINATION.)

Donald P. Kommers

**Mandamus, Writ of.** Along with the writs of *prohibition and *certiorari, the writ of mandamus was a prerogative writ in English *common law. A writ of mandamus issued from the court of King's Bench, directed to some officer, corporation, or inferior court and required that a duty prescribed by law, and not subject to discretion, be performed. Because of the extraordinary nature of mandamus, it was awarded only when other remedies had been exhausted.

In *Marbury* v. *Madison* (1803), Chief Justice John *Marshall held that in authorizing the Supreme Court to issue a writ of mandamus in an *original jurisdiction case, Congress had exceeded its constitutional powers. The Constitution made no provision for such a grant of power. However, Marshall indicated that mandamus would be available to support the *appellate jurisdiction of the Supreme Court, which by the Constitution was subject to legislative regulation.

The writ of mandamus is rarely used in current Supreme Court practice. It does not replace *appeals as a method of correcting judicial error, nor is it available when judicial discretion is involved. Only ministerial acts on the part of inferior courts, public officers, and corporations are subject to control by the writ of mandamus. Normally, mandamus is available only against federal officials or courts. However, in support of its appellate jurisdiction, the Supreme Court may issue a mandamus to the highest court of a state.

Herbert A. Johnson

**Mann Act.** Early twentieth-century *Progressivism witnessed the passage of a spate of legislation designed to raise the moral tone of the United States. One such law was the 1910 Mann Act, also known as the "White Slave Traffic Act." The act was passed in the wake of sensational—and largely exaggerated—stories of national vice rings.

The Mann Act made it a felony to transport or aid in the transportation of a woman in interstate or foreign commerce "for the purpose of prostitution or debauchery, or for any other immoral purpose, or with the intent and purpose to induce, entice, or compel such woman or girl" to immoral acts. One section of the law was indicative of the nativism that preoccupied the Progressives. It authorized immigration officials to gather and maintain information concerning the procuring of "alien women and girls" for immoral purposes. The proprietors of brothels who complied with the demands for information on foreign prostitutes were exempted from prosecution under the act.

The Mann Act was ruled constitutional by the Supreme Court in *Hoke* v. *U.S.* (1913). The appellant had been convicted under the act for enticing two veteran New Orleans prostitutes to travel to Beaumont, Texas, to ply their trade. Writing for a unanimous Court, Justice Joseph *McKenna dismissed the argument that prostitution should be left to the states to regulate and agreed with the drafters of the Mann Act that the regulation of interstate prostitution fell under the federal *commerce power.

(See also GENDER; POLICE POWER.)

John W. Johnson

**Mapp v. Ohio,** 367 U.S. 643 (1961), argued 29 Mar. 1961, decided 19 June 1961, by vote of 5 to 3 to 1; Clark for the Court, Black and Douglas concurring, Harlan, Frankfurter, and Whittaker in dissent, Stewart writing separately. *Mapp* finalized the "incorporation" of Fourth Amendment protections into the Due Process Clause of the Fourteenth Amendment. It required state officers to comply with Fourth Amendment standards when making searches and also extended the Fourth Amendment exclusionary rule to prosecutions in state courts.

In *Wolf* v. *Colorado* (1949), the Court had unanimously expanded the protections afforded by the Due Process Clause of the *Fourteenth Amendment by concluding that it did prohibit "arbitrary intrusion" by state police. The Court divided 5 to 4, however, on the exact scope of such protection. Four justices read the Fourteenth Amendment as incorporating all the protections of the Fourth Amendment, thus requiring state officials to comply with Fourth Amendment standards. Justice Felix *Frankfurter's majority opinion did not, however, go that far. Although he wrote that due process includes the "core of the Fourth Amendment," he declined to spell out the exact scope of due process protections applicable to searches (p. 27). He did conclude, however, that the Fourth Amendment exclusionary rule that had been created in *Weeks* v. *United States* (1914) need not be applied in state court proceedings. (The exclusionary rule vote was 6 to 3; Justice Hugo *Black joined the majority because he did not think the Fourth Amendment required exclusion.)

*Wolf's* refusal to apply the exclusionary rule to the states was undermined eleven years later in *Elkins* v. *United States* (1960), in which a 5-to-4 majority concluded that the protections regarding searches afforded by the Due Process Clause were equivalent to those in the Fourth Amendment. (Justice Potter *Stewart's majority opinion claimed *Wolf* had reached that conclusion; Frankfurter insisted in dissent that it had not.) Because *Elkins* was not a state prosecution itself, however, it did not provide a vehicle for overturning *Wolf's* refusal to apply the exclusionary rule to the state. The very next year, however, *Mapp* provided such an opportunity.

Seven police officers had broken into and searched Dolly Mapp's home in Cleveland, Ohio. The police claimed they had a warrant but never produced it. They said an informant had told them that a person wanted for a recent bombing was hiding in Mapp's home and also that gambling paraphernalia was being hidden there. In fact, the police found neither during an extensive search. Instead, they found several allegedly obscene books and pictures; Mapp was convicted of possession of obscene literature and imprisoned. In affirming her conviction, the Ohio Supreme Court concluded that, although the search had been "unlawful," *Wolf* nonetheless allowed the admission of the evidence.

In the Supreme Court, Mapp's attorney briefed and argued the case primarily on the *obscenity issue. An amicus brief filed by the *American Civil Liberties Union also argued, however, that the patently abusive search of Mapp's home by state officers also presented an opportunity to reconsider *Wolf.* Five justices seized that chance.

The voting in *Mapp,* however, was not a simple projection of the lineup a year earlier in *Elkins.* The opinion of the Court was written by Justice Tom *Clark, who had dissented in *Elkins.* Clark had adopted the unusual posture of a provocateur with regard to *Wolf*—voting in several pre-*Mapp* cases to press *Wolf* to its logical outcomes while hoping that (as he wrote in *Irvine* v. *California,* 1954) "strict adherence to the tenor of [*Wolf*] may produce needed converts for its extinction" (p. 139). On the other hand, Justice Stewart, who authored *Elkins* (and who later wrote that *Elkins* made it inevitable that the exclusionary rule would be applied to the states), refused to join the Court's opinion in *Mapp* because the exclusionary rule issue had not been properly briefed and argued. (During the oral argument, Mapp's attorney had stated that he was not asking the Court to overrule *Wolf.*)

As a result, the deciding vote in *Mapp* fell to Justice Black. Black was a staunch advocate of "incorporation," but his view of the exclusionary rule itself was highly idiosyncratic—in *Wolf* he alone had questioned whether the Fourth Amendment required the *Weeks* exclusionary rule; in *Mapp* he alone concluded that the rule was required only by the Fourth and *Fifth Amendments in combination. As a result, the opinion of the Court represented the views of only a four-justice plurality regarding the basis for the exclusionary rule, but a five-justice majority for its application to the states. Thus, although the extension of the exclusionary rule clearly should have been expected to generate political controversy, the prevailing justices apparently paid scant attention to judicial statecraft in deciding the issue in *Mapp*.

Justice Clark offered both "principled" and pragmatic reasons for extending the *Weeks* rule to the states. Although at one point he called the rule a "deterrent safeguard," Clark's opinion largely paralleled the principled rationale offered for the rule in *Weeks*. He described the rule as being required by the Fourth Amendment and stressed that without the rule the Fourth Amendment would be reduced, in Justice Oliver Wendell Holmes's phrase, "to a form of words" (p. 648). Clark noted Justice (then Judge) Cardozo's complaint about the exclusionary rule that "the criminal is to go free because the constable has blundered." He answered, "The criminal goes free if he must, but it is the law that sets him free" (p. 659).

Clark also argued that the pragmatic policy considerations in *Wolf* had proved to be unsound. He noted that the states without exclusionary rules had not developed any effective alternative means of dealing with unreasonable police searches; in fact, several additional state supreme courts had adopted state exclusionary rules in the years since *Wolf*, including the especially influential decision of the California Supreme Court in *People v. Cahan* (1955).

The three *Mapp* dissenters (who all had dissented in *Elkins*) continued to reject the *incorporation doctrine and, largely for that reason, also rejected the extension of the *Weeks* exclusionary rule to the "soverign judicial system[s]" of the states.

(See also EXCLUSIONARY RULE; FOURTH AMENDMENT.)

Thomas Y. Davies

**Marbury v. Madison,** 1 Cranch (5 U.S.) 137 (1803), argued 11 Feb. 1803, decided 24 Feb. 1803 by vote of 5 to 0; Marshall for the Court. *Marbury* was the first Supreme Court case to apply the emergent doctrine of judicial review to a congressional statute. William Marbury had been appointed a justice of the peace in the District of Columbia late in the administration of Federalist President John Adams. Along with a number of other Federalist partisans appointed to federal judgeships, Marbury fell within the group of "midnight judges" targeted for political attack by the incoming Republican administration of Thomas *Jefferson. Marbury's signed and sealed commission remained undelivered when the new secretary of state, James *Madison, took office. Madison refused to deliver the commission to Marbury, who then in-

voked the *original jurisdiction of the United States Supreme Court, asking that the Court issue a writ of *mandamus to Madison, ordering him to deliver the commission.

Congress altered the date of Supreme Court terms, thereby delaying hearing Marbury's case until February 1803. In the interval, the Federalist-sponsored Judiciary Act of 1801 was repealed and circuit judges appointed under its provisions were dismissed. (See JUDICIARY ACTS OF 1801 AND 1802.) *Stuart v. Laird* (1803), a challenge to the discharge of the circuit court judges, was argued on the date *Marbury* was decided. Justice William *Paterson upheld the constitutionality of the dismissals. Newly elected Republican legislatures, at both the state and federal levels, were contemplating or bringing *impeachment proceedings against Federalist judges. Republicans, including Jefferson himself, believed that, having lost at the polls, the Federalist party intended to frustrate Jeffersonian legislative programs through the power of the judiciary. This charged political atmosphere was aggravated by special circumstances present in Marbury's case. Chief Justice John *Marshall had been appointed during the last months of the Adams administration and thus was virtually a "midnight judge" himself. (Ironically, Marshall was also the outgoing Federalist secretary of state who, probably because of an oversight, failed to deliver Marbury's commission.)

In his opinion for the Court, Marshall held that Marbury was entitled to his commission and that Madison had withheld it from him wrongfully. Mandamus was the appropriate remedy at common law, but the question presented was whether it was available under *Article III's grant of *original jurisdiction to the Supreme Court. To decide that question, Marshall was required to compare the text of Article III with section 13 of the Judiciary Act of 1789, by which Congress authorized the mandamus writ. Finding that the statute conflicted with the Federal Constitution, Marshall considered it "the essence of judicial duty" (p. 178) to follow the Constitution. He concluded that "the particular phraseology of the Constitution of the United States confirms and strengthens the principle, supposed to be essential to all written constitutions, that a law repugnant to the constitution is void; and that *courts*, as well as other departments, are bound by that instrument" (p. 180).

Since affirming relief was denied, the decree in *Marbury* was self-executing, and notable as an example of self-restraint in the face of what Marshall described as an arbitrary denial of Marbury's *property rights. The opinion also seemed to preach respect for those rights to Jefferson and his subordinates, and it provided the judiciary, both state and federal, with a potent weapon for protecting individual rights against the actions of legislative majorities. At the time, it was attacked in newspaper articles by Judge

Spencer Roane of Virginia and Judge John Bannister Gibson of Pennsylvania in *Eakin* v. *Raub* (Pa., 1825). Critics contended then (as now) that the judiciary should not arrogate to itself the right to pass upon the validity of a legislative act. Such thinking, coupled with his personal animosity to Marshall, moved President Jefferson to encourage members of the House of Representatives to begin impeachment proceedings against Justice Samuel *Chase during the summer of 1803.

*Marbury* was not the first case to enunciate the principle of judicial review. Precedents existed in the *state courts and in the *lower federal courts where judges had refrained from following a law they considered contrary to the provisions of the state or federal constitution. Marshall's was the first statement of the doctrine by the United States Supreme Court. Marshall delineated a comprehensive rationale for the practice of judicial review. He justified it by the concepts of limited government, the written constitution, and the rule of law. Colonial lawyers, most notably James Otis arguing the Writs of Assistance Case in Massachusetts (1761), had drawn upon Sir Edward Coke's statement in *Dr. Bonham's Case* (1610) that parliamentary statutes contrary to custom and right reason were invalid. In *The Federalist*, no. 78 (1788) Alexander *Hamilton argued that limited government required that courts of justice be empowered to "declare all acts contrary to the manifest tenor of the Constitution void," and Marshall's opinion in *Marbury* reflected much of Hamilton's reasoning (See FEDERALIST, THE).

Marshall stressed the duty of judges to apply the law to cases before them. Carried to its logical conclusion, this meant that the life, liberty, and property of citizens depended upon the exercise of judicial review as a constitutional check on legislative discretion.

*Marbury* stands as the classic expression of judicial review in American constitutional law. It embodied what might be called "coordinate branch" judicial review. The more common form of judicial review in the federal system involves the statutes and judicial decisions of the states and the degree to which they conflict with the federal Constitution and thus violate the Supremacy Clause of Article VI. This subordination of state laws to the federal Constitution is what Professor Edward S. *Corwin called the "linchpin of the Constitution," without which the federal union would falter.

Marshall's opinion conceded that the federal government has only the limited authority conferred upon it by the terms of the Constitution; all other political power and sovereignty is reserved either to the states or to the people by the *Tenth Amendment. Thus concepts of limited government most vigorously circumscribed the powers of the federal government at least before the *Civil War. In *Marbury*, Marshall was asked to expand the meaning of the Constitution to permit Congress to grant a mandamus power not expressly given under Article III. But paradoxically, the authority to exercise judicial review was itself not conferred by any explicit constitutional provision or any act of Congress. The decision asserted one power even as it rejected the proffer of another.

The Court did not again exercise its power of "coordinate branch" judicial review until 1857 when it held the 1820 Missouri Compromise unconstitutional in the case of *Dred *Scott* v. *Sandford*. After 1868, judicial review of state statutes and decisions has become more frequent in Supreme Court jurisprudence owing to the expanded functions of the federal government and the creation of American *citizenship, with attendant rights under the *Fourteenth Amendment. *Dred Scott* undermined a political compromise over *slavery's expansion into the territories. It also dealt with the issue of federal jurisdiction—that is, whether diversity of citizenship conferred jurisdiction on the lower federal court over slavery's freedom suits. Chief Justice Roger B. *Taney invoked a "higher law" than the Constitution in an effort to defend owners' property rights in slaves, just as antislavery publicists urged moral and *natural law principles in support of federal power to abolish or restrict slavery. By 1900, the federal judiciary, led by the Supreme Court, evolved the principle of substantive *due process to restrict state and federal legislative power to regulate economic enterprise. This required a broader concept of judicial review than had been provided in *Marbury*.

The Supreme Court's decision in *Cooper* v. *Aaron* (1958) marked the high tide of expanded judicial review. Citing *Marbury*, the unanimous Court declared that "the federal judiciary is supreme in the exposition of the law of the Constitution, and that principle has ever since [*Marbury*] been . . . a permanent and indispensible feature of our constitutional system" (p. 18). *Cooper* v. *Aaron* slighted the fact that presidents have vetoed legislation on constitutional grounds (Andrew *Jackson's veto of the Maysville Road bill in 1830 being one example), and that Chief Justice Marshall had always been careful to defer to the political branches—Congress and the president—when important matters of domestic and foreign policy were involved.

Although the significance of *Marbury* has been enlarged over time, the case remains one of the fundamental judicial opinions in American constitutional history. It correctly assessed the role of the judiciary in maintaining constitutional limitations on legislative action; it provided a rationale for subjecting statutes to constitutional examination; it commanded judges to abide by constitutional norms, and it recognized the limited jurisdiction of all federal courts.

(See also JUDICIAL POWER AND JURISDICTION; JUDICIAL REVIEW.)

□ Robert L. Clinton, *Marbury v. Madison and Judicial Review* (1989). Edward S. Corwin, *John Marshall and the Constitution: A Chronicle of the Supreme Court* (1921). Charles Grove Haines, *The American Doctrine of Judicial Supremacy*, 2d ed. (1959). George L. Haskins and Herbert A. Johnson, *History of the Supreme Court of the United States*, vol. 2, *Foundations of Power: John Marshall, 1801–15* (1981).                             Herbert A. Johnson

**Maritime Law.** See ADMIRALTY AND MARITIME LAW.

**Marriage.** The Supreme Court has affirmed the right of the states to prescribe most of the conditions of marriage. Before the twentieth century, the most contentious issue was *comity. The Court generally held that states had to recognize the legitimacy of marriage entered into in other states. However, with *Reynolds v. United States* (1879), in which the justices refused to recognize polygamy as protected by the *First Amendment, the Court began to create a national standard of marital rights.

Beginning in the 1960s, the Court limited state marital regulation significantly by protecting rights of individuals to wed. Justice William O. *Douglas declared in dicta in *Griswold v. Connecticut* (1965) that marriage was a "noble" and "sacred" relationship, into whose *privacy the state could not intrude without compelling reasons. In *Loving v. Virginia* (1967), the Court affirmed that marriage was a *fundamental right and accordingly invalidated a state ban on interracial marriage. *Zablocki v. Redhail* (1978) voided a Wisconsin law prohibiting the remarriage of a noncustodial parent who failed to pay court-ordered child support. All these challenged restrictions violated the right to wed that the Court found implicitly guaranteed by the *Fourteenth Amendment. However, most kinds of state regulation of marriage have survived judicial scrutiny.

Tensions between individual choice and state regulation continue to dominate the law. The Court has recently refused to recognize marital status and related rights of individuals involved in homosexual unions (see HOMOSEXUALITY) or other cohabitation arrangements because, the Court maintains, such nontraditional unions do not serve the same social ends as matrimony.

                             Michael Grossberg

**Marshall, John** (b. Germantown [now Midland], Va., 24 Sept. 1755; d. Philadelphia, Pa., 6 July 1835; interred New Burying Ground, Richmond, Va.), chief justice, 1801–1835. By common acclaim, John Marshall is "the great Chief Justice," the single best representative of American constitutional law. His greatness, as Oliver Wendell Holmes noted in 1901, consisted partly in his "being there" during the formative period of the Court's history. But Marshall's conservative-national ideology fit the formative age perfectly,

just as his personality and legal genius exactly suited the duties of chief justice.

President John Adams appointed Marshall to the Court on 20 January 1801, to save the Constitution from the Jeffersonian Republicans. The well-settled values Marshall brought to his duties were the product of the revolutionary age as refracted through family and place. He was born and grew up in Fauquier County on the northwestern frontier of Virginia, the eldest of fifteen children. Frontier life imparted to Marshall an easy going, democratic demeanor that was balanced by the conservative values of the privileged class to which he belonged. Marshall's marriage to Betsy Ambler in 1783 further consolidated his membership in polite society and gave him a useful entree into politics and law. They had ten children, six of whom lived to maturity.

The strong love of union that infused his jurisprudence was due mainly to his father's influence and his own experience in the Revolutionary War. Young Marshall received only two years of formal education. Beyond that, his father taught him rudimentary math, deepened his love of English literature, introduced him to Blackstone's *Commentaries on the Laws of England* (1765) and most importantly perhaps, kept him abreast of political developments in pre-Revolutionary Virginia. Father and son were among the first to enlist. As an officer in the Culpepper Minutemen and later in the continental line, Marshall saw action at the battles of Great Bridge, Brandywine, Germantown, and Monmouth Courthouse. Wintering at Valley Forge instilled in him a lifelong hatred of state provincialism and feckless national government. While serving as deputy judge advocate, he met several members of General George *Washington's staff who would later become champions of national union. Marshall's intense patriotism and admiration of Washington can be gleaned from his *Life of George Washington* (1805–1807).

Marshall resumed his legal studies in 1780 by briefly attending the law lectures of George Wythe at William and Mary. With little more formal training than that he began legal practice, first in Fauquier County and then in Richmond, where he settled with his wife and family. Neither as lawyer nor as judge was he inclined to blackletter scholarship. He did possess, however, in rare combination, those qualities essential to legal greatness: a capacious, retentive, and quick mind; sharp analytical skills; and a logical prose style that bordered on eloquence. He rose rapidly to the top of the highly competitive Richmond bar, specializing in noncriminal appellate cases. The staple of his practice was British debt cases, but he litigated a wide range of cases in law and equity in state and federal courts. His only case before the Supreme Court, which he lost, was *Ware v. Hylton* (1796), which, ironically, he argued on states' rights grounds.

To be a nationalist in Virginia was to be a

Federalist and Marshall was both. Serving in Virginia's Council of State (1782–1784) and in the House of Delegates (1782, 1784–1785, 1787–1788, 1795) convinced him as it had James *Madison that state legislators were parochial and incompetent. He made his debut as a nationalist in the Virginia ratifying convention of 1788, where he spoke effectively in defense of federal judicial authority. As a prominent Federalist, he defended Washington's foreign policy and Alexander *Hamilton's domestic program. Proven ability, well-placed connections, and service to party brought him offers to serve as U.S. attorney general, minister to France, and associate justice of the Supreme Court. He rejected these offers for financial reasons, but he did agree to serve on the so-called XYZ mission to France, where he distinguished himself for his nationalism, his diplomatic skills, and the effectiveness of his written dispatches to President John Adams. At Washington's behest, he agreed to serve in Congress (1799–1800), where he became the leading spokesman for the moderate Federalism of President Adams. He served briefly but effectively as secretary of state before assuming his duties as chief justice on 5 March 1801.

As chief justice he immediately set out to strengthen the Court by unifying it—a chore made easier by the threats posed by President Thomas Jefferson and his party who controlled congress. His most important innovation was to persuade his colleagues to abandon seriatim opinions, thus making it possible for the Court to speak authoritatively in a single voice. Most often in important constitutional questions that voice belonged to Marshall, who sensed intuitively that the function of the Court was to legitimate and educate a people as yet unschooled in constitutional law. His great opinions were expansive constitutional state papers written with grace, eloquence, and authority and rooted in the republican principles of a written and supreme Constitution emanating from a sovereign people.

His first great effort as spokesman for the whole Court was *Marbury v. Madison (1803), which was the opening battle in the struggle for judicial review over acts of Congress. For a unanimous Court, Marshall ruled that section 13 of the *Judiciary Act of 1789 was void, so far as it extended *original jurisdiction not authorized by *Article III of the Constitution. Contrary to what is often written about the opinion, Marshall did not explicitly claim that the Court was the sole or final interpreter of the Constitution. In fact, not until Dred *Scott v. Sandford (1857) did the Court strike down another act of Congress. Marbury was not cited by the Supreme Court itself as the definitive statement on *judicial review until the late nineteenth century. Marshall did, however, successfully nullify an act of Congress and in the process grounded judicial authority in the supremacy of a written constitution. By lecturing President Jefferson on the rule of law, he implic-

*John Marshall*

itly put forth the Court as the special guardian of that sacred republican principle. Given the political vulnerability of the Court, it was a brilliant victory and a timely one as well. But the real meaning of judicial review—as the power of the Court to expound the text of the Constitution as law—became clear only in cases like *McCulloch v. Maryland (1819) where Marshall upheld the federal statute in question.

If McCulloch is the best example of Marshall's use of judicial review, *Cohens v. Virginia (1821) was his most elaborate defense of it. The case arose when Virginia challenged the appellate authority of the Supreme Court under section 25 of the Judiciary Act of 1789, which gave the Court the right to review federal questions decided by *state courts. Marshall's opinion demonstrated by logic and recourse to fundamental principles that the supremacy of the Constitution and the appellate authority of the Court are inseparable. By ruling that the *Eleventh Amendment was no bar to appellate jurisdiction, he further limited that amendment as a states' rights curb on judicial authority (see STATE SOVEREIGNTY AND STATES' RIGHTS). The importance of Cohens is suggested by the fact that John C. Calhoun, who initially supported the decision, developed his theory of nullification in direction refutation of Marshall's argument.

Another theme running through Marshall's constitutional opinions was *vested rights. As an extensive land speculator he learned first hand the Lockean principle that property and individual liberty were connected. Experience in state government taught him that the greatest threat to both was state legislation. *Fletcher v. Peck (1810) gave him a chance to address that problem. The question was whether an act passed by the Georgia legislature in 1796 repealing a previous act selling state land to private speculators violated Article 1, section 10, which prohibited states from passing laws impairing the obligation of contracts (see CONTRACTS CLAUSE). Georgia defended the repeal on the grounds that the original grant was induced by bribery and fraud—which it was. But if states could repeal their own grants, innocent buyers could lose their property and massive insecurity would be introduced into the land market. It was a judgment call for Marshall on constitutional as well as policy grounds, because available evidence pointed to the fact that Article 1, section 10 seemed intended by the framers to apply to private contracts but not public contracts to which the state itself was a party. In voiding the Georgia rescinding act—the first time a state law had been held in violation of the Constitution—Marshall opted for property rights and market stability. He also chose the Lockean spirit of the age over the letter of the Constitution

In Fletcher, Marshall made the Contract Clause the constitutional shield of property rights against state action; in *Dartmouth College v. Woodward (1819) he closed the circle of protection. In 1816 New Hampshire altered the charter of Dartmouth College, in effect making the private college into a state university. The question was whether the Contract Clause prevented it from doing so. Marshall ruled that state charters as well as state grants were contracts within the meaning of Article 1, section 10. The state could not alter the terms of charters unless, as Justice Joseph *Story pointed out in his concurrence, it had reserved the right to do so in the charter. The decision not only secured private education in America but also promoted the growth of business corporations by providing a stable climate for investment. *Corporations, which had been justified because of their public function and which accordingly had been subject to state control, now became private entities protected by the Constitution.

The chief justice was less successful in his effort to prohibit state bankruptcy legislation via the Contract Clause. The unsettled constitutional issue was whether the federal authority to pass uniform bankruptcy laws, granted in Article 1, section 8, automatically prohibited state action and whether state authority, if it existed, was valid only when applied to future contracts. Marshall's opinion in *Sturges v. Crowninshield (1819), which confronted the issue for the first time, struck down a New York bankruptcy law that applied to contracts made before the law was passed, but it did not resolve the questions of exclusivity and prospective contracts. When in *Ogden v. Saunders (1827) the Court upheld a state bankruptcy law governing prospective contracts,

Marshall entered a passionate dissent, denying the prospective-retrospective distinction altogether. Scholars have concluded that the justices were badly divided in Sturges and that Marshall had fashioned his opinion to avoid an open split.

Marshall's thinking about the relationship of law and *capitalism was shaped by an age where agriculture and commerce dominated, where large scale manufacturing was in its infancy, and the business cycle yet unknown. Yet his view of law and economics was progressive as his quest for the creation of a national market in McCulloch v. Maryland (1819) and *Gibbons v. Ogden (1824) indicates. The former construed implied powers to uphold a congressional act creating the Second Bank of the United States; the latter's broad construction of the federal commerce clause prohibited states from passing laws interfering with interstate transportation and the free flow of goods across state lines (see COMMERCE POWER). Taken with Marshall's effort in Fletcher and Dartmouth to provide a stable environment for investment in land and corporate stock, these opinions show the entrepreneurial cast of Marshall's jurisprudence. Jefferson and others accused him of having transformed the Constitution, yet Marshall followed the spirit if not the literal intent of the framers.

The central and most controversial theme in Marshall's decisions concerned *federalism and involved the Court in the effort to brighten the line between state and nation that was so indistinctly drawn in the Constitution. All his leading constitutional opinions, except Marbury, address this issue, either directly or indirectly, and all of them curb state power: in Cohens he demolished state judicial claims of finality in constitutional cases; in Fletcher and Dartmouth, state legislatures were kept from repudiating their own grants and charters; in McCulloch states were prohibited from taxing federally chartered corporations; in Gibbons from interfering with interstate commerce. In the process of curbing the states, Marshall created a vast reservoir of congressional power. Thus in McCulloch he read the "necessary and proper" clause of Article 1, section 8, so as to establish *implied powers. By his expansive definition of the Commerce Clause in Gibbons, he established the principle that Congress was supreme within its enumerated powers (though he drew back from the proposition that the mere grant of a power to Congress excluded the states from acting). These opinions not only settled the constitutional question at hand but repudiated the emerging political doctrine of state sovereignty. Here Marshall emphasized the Federalist insistence that the people, not the states, were sovereign, that they established an enduring nation with all the powers necessary to nationhood, and that the Supreme Court was mandated by the people themselves to preserve those powers.

Because Marshall's opinions have been cited

so frequently in the nineteenth and twentieth centuries as justifications of federal power, it is tempting to conclude that he was the unrelenting consolidationist that southern states' rights critics accused him of being. In evaluating Marshall's jurisprudence, it must be remembered that the federal regulatory state was a century away. Congress did legislate on tariff, banking, public lands, and internal improvements, and Marshall's opinions authorized congressional action in these areas. But there was almost no federal regulatory legislation in his day. Measured by the governmental practice of his own age, Marshall's theoretical assertions of national authority came mainly as a response to states' rights radicals who wanted to undo the concessions to national authority that believed had been unwisely agreed to in 1787.

Marshall's constitutional opinions taken as a whole stand as a comprehensive exposition of the Constitution on a par with the *Federalist Papers*, on which he drew heavily (see FEDERALIST, THE). Unlike those famous essays, however, Marshall's opinions were the law of the land. They were persuasive because they drew effectively on Revolutionary history, on the political theory of the founders, and on widely accepted sources of legal authority: *natural law, the law of nations, and English *common law. As befit a Court that was making precedents rather than following them, they were written in stately language that was logical, eloquent, and authoritative.

Indeed, because Marshall's constitutional opinions appear so authoritative, it is easy to overestimate their actual impact. In fact, they did not always control events or sometimes even the parties in the suit. Some of Marshall's contract decisions (*New Jersey* v. *Wilson* 1812, for example) went unenforced. Those in the Georgia Indian cases were resisted outright, with the support of the president. More threatening and disheartening to Marshall, however, was the fact that new appointments after 1823 brought states' rights ideology onto the bench itself. Beleaguered from outside by the rising tide of states' rights, challenged from the inside, Marshall was forced to retreat from his doctrinal preferences. In *Willson* v. *Blackbird Creek Marsh Company* (1829), for example, Marshall drew back from the broad view of congressional power over interstate commerce set forth in *Gibbons*. In *Providence Bank* v. *Billings* (1830), he retreated from the spirit if not the letter of *Dartmouth*, ruling that the state's power to tax corporations cannot be restricted by implications from the charter but must be specifically stated. There is considerable evidence, too, that he resisted implied charter rights in the *Charles River Bridge* case (1837) when it was first argued in 1831.

Occasionally he was able to hold the line, as in his opinion in *Craig* v. *Missouri* (1830) where, in the old nationalist spirit, he invalidated a Missouri law that indirectly legalized state paper money. In *Cherokee Nation* v. *Georgia* (1831) and *Worcester* v. *Georgia* (1832) (see CHEROKEE CASES), he struck a blow against states' rights and Jacksonian democracy and for the Indians. But here, as in some of his contract cases, the Court's opponents had the final word. Ironically, Marshall's last constitutional opinion was *Barron* v. *Baltimore* (1833), which conceded control over civil liberties to the states by ruling that the *Bill of Rights applied only to the federal government.

Where the chief justice stood on the *slavery issue is not clear, since no legal challenge to the institution was presented him. As an officer in the American Colonization Society, he was in favor of gradual emancipation. But his support of the proslavery forces at the Virginia Constitutional Convention of 1829–1830, his own experience as a small slaveholder, and his willingness to make pragmatic concessions to states' rights in the period after 1825 suggest that he would have been reluctant to unsettle the institution by judicial decision. It remained a possibility, however, and one readily perceived by Marshall's southern critics, that the broad power he gave Congress might do just that.

Marshall defined for all time the nature of the chief justiceship (see CHIEF JUSTICE, OFFICE OF), but his own role in the office varied according to circumstances. His greatest dominance came in the period from 1801 to 1811. From 1811 to 1823, during the Court's most stable and productive period, he increasingly shared power with strong-minded colleagues like Joseph Story and William *Johnson, sometimes compromising his doctrinal preferences to maintain unity. During his last decade on the Court, he further moderated his style of leadership to fit the new age and the new justices who represented it. He never surrendered his position as leader of the court, however, even after the onset of illness in 1831. But neither, to his great distress, could he quell the "revolutionary spirit" on the Court, and he died fearing that both it and the Constitution were gone. Modest man that he was, it never occurred to him that he would become the symbol of the living Constitution and the personal embodiment of the Court he loved.

(See also JUDICIAL POWER AND JURISDICTION; JUDICIAL REVIEW.)

□ Albert J. Beveridge, *The Life of John Marshall*, 4 vols. (1916–1919). Robert K. Faulkner, *The Jurisprudence of John Marshall* (1968). George L. Haskins and Herbert A. Johnson, *History of the Supreme Court of the United States*, vol. 2, *Foundations of Power: John Marshall, 1801–15* (1981). Charles F. Hobson, ed., *The Papers of John Marshall*, 6 vols. (1974–). G. Edward White, "John Marshall and the Genesis of the Tradition," in his *The American Judicial Tradition* (1976). G. Edward White, *History of the Supreme Court of the United States*, vols. 3–4, *The Marshall Court and Cultural Change, 1815–35* (1988). R. Kent Newmyer

**Marshall, Thurgood** (b. Baltimore, Md., 2 July 1908), associate justice, 1967–1991. Marshall, the

*Thurgood Marshall*

great-grandson of a slave and the son of a dining car waiter and a school teacher, became the first African-American justice of the U.S. Supreme Court. Marshall earned his bachelor's degree from Lincoln University in 1930, then entered Howard University Law School, where he studied under Charles Hamilton *Houston, the dean credited with transforming Howard into a laboratory for civil rights litigation.

After Marshall graduated first in his class from Howard in 1933, Houston enlisted him to help with the civil rights battles being waged by the *National Association for the Advancement of Colored People (NAACP). Working full time, first as special counsel for the NAACP and then as director of the NAACP *Legal Defense and Educational Fund, Marshall masterminded the litigation strategy that challenged racial oppression in *education, housing, transportation, electoral politics, and criminal justice. Ultimately, Marshall was responsible for achieving twenty-nine Supreme Court victories, including numerous landmark cases such as *Smith v. Allwright (1944), Shelley v. Kraemer (1948), and *Brown v. Board of Education (1954), in which the Court finally concluded that the doctrine of *separate but equal was inherently unequal and unconstitutional.

In 1961, President John F. Kennedy nominated Marshall to be circuit judge on the U.S. Court of Appeals for the Second Circuit. After a lengthy, hostile battle waged by southern senators, Marshall was finally confirmed. In his four years on the circuit, Marshall wrote several important opinions, including one applying the *Double Jeopardy Clause to the states, a position the Supreme Court later adopted in *Benton v. Mary-

land (1969), with Marshall writing for the Court. In 1965, President Lyndon Johnson named Marshall to be the first African-American *solicitor general of the United States.

Two years later, Johnson appointed Marshall to be associate justice of the U.S. Supreme Court, to occupy the seat vacated by Tom C. *Clark. During his long tenure, Marshall wrote many significant decisions in a wide variety of fields, including federal jurisdiction, federal preemption, *antitrust, and the rights of *Native Americans. But Marshall's most significant contributions were in constitutional law, where he made his mark with powerful majority opinions as well as passionate dissents.

Among Marshall's most-noted *First Amendment opinions were *Stanley v. Georgia (1969), which held that individuals have a right to possess obscene materials in their own homes; Police Department of Chicago v. Mosley (1972), which established the important principle that government may not constitutionally favor some types of speech over others; and Linmark Associates, Inc. v. Township of Willingboro (1977), which held that a municipality could not constitutionally ban the use of "for sale" signs simply because it feared their use might contribute to "blockbusting" and "white flight."

Marshall's contributions in matters of *equal protection came primarily through dissenting opinions. Two powerful dissents, in Dandridge v. Williams (1970) and *San Antonio Independent School District v. Rodriguez (1973), criticized the rigidity of the two-tiered equal protection analysis in which classifications based on race and other suspect categories were subjected to *strict scrutiny while all other classifications had to be merely "rational." Marshall proposed a more flexible, "sliding scale" theory under which courts would examine the nature of the group, the extent to which it previously had been subjected to discrimination, and the importance of the interests affected by the legislation. While the Court did not adopt Marshall's theory, his consistent criticism seems to have prodded the Court to somewhat greater flexibility. In addition, Marshall's views on *affirmative action—that it is necessary today because the Constitution was not colorblind in the past—may have influenced a majority of the Court to conclude, in *Regents of the University of California v. Bakke (1978), that it is constitutionally permissible to consider race in designing affirmative action programs.

Probably the most personally agonizing subject for Marshall was *capital punishment. When the Court upheld revised death-penalty statutes in *Gregg v. Georgia (1976), Marshall began the practice of dissenting in every death penalty case, including each time the Court denied a petition for *certiorari in a case involving the death penalty.

Marshall's life experiences enabled him to make sure his colleagues always knew whose ox was being gored. He was never reticent to make his views known. When the country was enthusiastically celebrating the bicentennial of the Constitution in 1989, Marshall noted that, with its acceptance of slavery, the Constitution was initially defective. Credit for its present stature belongs, he observed in the *Harvard Law Review* in 1987, not to the framers but "to those present who refused to acquiesce in outdated notions of 'liberty,' 'justice,' and 'equality,' and who strived to better them. The true miracle of the Constitution," observed Marshall, "was not the birth of the Constitution, but its life" (p. 5).

□ Richard A. Kluger, *Simple Justice* (1976). Thurgood Marshall, "Reflections on the Bicentennial of the United States Constitution," *Harvard Law Review* 101 (1987): 1–5. "A Tribute to Justice Marshall," symposium in *Harvard Blackletter Journal* 6 (1989): 1–140.          Susan Low Bloch

**Marshall Statue.** In 1882 Congress commissioned the acclaimed sculptor William Wetmore Story to execute a monumental statue of John *Marshall. Story depicted the chief justice in middle age as an authoritative interpreter of the Constitution. The colossal bronze figure, seated in judicial robes, clasps the Constitution tightly in one hand, while extending the other in a gesture of benevolent appeal. On the marble base of the statue, Story celebrated the nationalistic constitutional tradition with two symbolic friezes. Unveiled in 1884 on the west front of the Capitol, the Marshall statue was moved to the ground floor of the Supreme Court Building in 1982.

(See also SCULPTURE IN THE SUPREME COURT BUILDING.)

Maxwell Bloomfield

**Marshall v. Barlow's, Inc.,** 436 U.S. 307 (1978), argued 9 Jan. 1978, decided 23 May 1978 by vote of 5 to 3; White for the Court, Blackmun and Stevens in dissent joined by Rehnquist, Brennan not participating. This case involved the constitutionality of a provision in the Occupational Safety and Health Act (OSHA) that permitted inspectors to enter premises without a warrant to inspect for safety hazards and violation of OSHA regulations. The Court held that this provision violated the *Fourth Amendment.

One issue was whether a warrant was required. The Court had previously held that no warrant was required to inspect either the premises of a liquor licensee or a licensed gun dealer's storeroom. Distinguishing these earlier cases because each concerned a closely regulated industry, the Court in *Barlow's* concluded that requiring warrants in the OSHA context would not "impose serious burdens on the inspection system or the courts" (p. 316).

As for the grounds to obtain an inspection warrant, *Barlow's* follows the rule in *Camara* v. *Municipal Court* (1967) that traditional *probable cause is unnecessary if the authorities can show

that the contemplated inspection conforms to "reasonable legislative or administrative standards" (p. 538). Thus the Court in *Barlow's* concluded that a warrant "showing that a specific business has been chosen for an OSHA search on the basis of a general administrative plan for the enforcement of the Act derived from neutral sources" (p. 321) would suffice, for it would ensure against arbitrary selection of employers.

Wayne R. LaFave

**Marshals of the Court.** U.S. marshals date to the *Judiciary Act of 1789, under which President George *Washington appointed the first thirteen. Marshals protect judges and other participants in federal trials and may also serve warrants, make arrests, and enforce court orders and federal laws. Marshals helped collect the taxes that led to the Whiskey Rebellion, capture *fugitive slaves, protect the rights of freed slaves after the *Civil War, enforce law on the western frontier, seize alcohol during Prohibition, accompany freedom riders, and escort African-American students integrating schools. The exploits of frontier marshals and deputies like Bat Masterson, Doc Holliday, Wyatt Earp, and Wild Bill Hickok have often overshadowed routine functions, some of which have been assumed by more specialized agencies like the Secret Service and the Federal Bureau of Investigation. Current functions of marshals include transporting and assigning federal prisoners and operating a Witness Protection Program.

The Supreme Court affirmed broad authority for marshals in *In re *Neagle* (1890) by ordering the release of a marshal who had killed a man while defending Justice Stephen *Field. The Court cited the president's broad powers under Article II, section 3 to "take Care that the Laws be faithfully executed"—even absent specific statutory authority for marshals to protect justices.

The president appoints marshals, subject to senate confirmation, to four-year terms. The attorney general supervises marshals, thus making executive resistance to judicial orders possible. Today there is one U.S. marshal for each of the ninety-four judicial districts and about 2,100 career deputies.

(See also STAFF OF THE COURT, NONJUDICIAL.)

John R. Vile

**Martial Law.** See MILITARY TRIALS AND MARTIAL LAW.

**Martin, Luther** (b. Piscataway, N.J., ca. 20 Feb. 1748; d. New York, N.Y., 10 July 1826), lawyer and statesman. Of humble origins, Martin graduated from the College of New Jersey (later Princeton University) in 1766. After studying law, he established a flourishing law practice on the eastern shore of Maryland and Virginia. In 1778 he was appointed state attorney general, a post he held (with interruptions) for the next forty years. As a delegate to the Federal Convention in 1787,

Martin championed the cause of the small states and opposed extensive federal powers. A supporter of *judicial review, he proposed what became the supremacy clause of the Constitution, without however intending it to be an instrument of national supremacy. Unhappy with the results of the Convention, Martin became an outspoken opponent of the Constitution during the ratification contest.

Aside from his role in the making of the Constitution, Martin is remembered chiefly as an advocate in a number of celebrated judicial cases. Between 1801 and 1813 he frequently appeared in the Supreme Court, arguing mainly *admiralty, prize, and marine insurance cases and also the great constitutional case of *Fletcher v. Peck (1810). One of his notable performances was as counsel for Justice Samuel *Chase in the latter's 1805 impeachment trial. Two years later Martin helped successfully defend Aaron *Burr, on trial for treason before Chief Justice John *Marshall in the U.S. Circuit Court at Richmond. Martin's last appearance in a major case occurred in 1819, when, as Maryland attorney general, he represented the state in the great bank case *McCulloch v. Maryland (1819). In an exhaustive three-day argument, Martin denied that Congress had power to grant charters of incorporation and insisted, admitting such a power, that the states retained the right to tax federally charted corporations. Shortly after this argument, Martin suffered an incapacitating stroke that rendered him a helpless derelict for his remaining years. In 1823 he was taken in by Aaron Burr, with whom Martin lived until his death three years later.

Highly regarded as a formidable advocate, Martin was renowned for his legal learning. He managed to stay at the top of his profession for many years (though unable to stay out of debt) despite habitual drunkenness and careless personal appearance. A characteristic tendency of his advocacy was to inject personal and partisan feelings. This was particularly evident at the Burr trial, when Martin went out of his way to turn the defense of his client into an indictment of the Jefferson administration.          Charles F. Hobson

**Martin v. Hunter's Lessee,** 1 Wheat. (14 U.S.) 304 (1816), argued 12 Mar. 1816, decided 20 Mar. 1816 by vote of 6 to 0; Story for the Court, Marshall not participating. This case involved the constitutionality of section 25 of the 1789 *Judiciary Act, which empowered the Supreme Court to review the final judgments of the highest *state courts where federal statutes or treaties were involved, or when a state statute or common law rule had been upheld, though challenged under the federal Constitution. Several states, most notably Virginia, condemned section 25 as an unconstitutional authorization for the federal judiciary to usurp state power. States' rights advocates believed that the Union rested on a compact among the states that granted the central government

only limited and enumerated powers (see STATE SOVEREIGNTY AND STATES' RIGHTS).

During the War for American Independence, Virginia enacted legislation confiscating Loyalists' property. Thomas Lord Fairfax, a Loyalist, subsequently devised his vast holdings in the Northern Neck to a British subject, but the property had passed into private hands because of the confiscatory statute. The Fairfax interests challenged the Virginia legislation as inconsistent with the state's obligations under the Treaty of Paris (1783) and Jay's Treaty (1794), which protected Loyalist holdings. In *Fairfax's Devisee v. Hunter's Lessee (1813), Justice Joseph *Story sustained the Fairfax interests. (Chief Justice John *Marshall did not participate because of pecuniary interest and prior involvement as counsel.) Story's decision fueled already intense criticism of the Court. States' rights advocates, such as Spencer Roane and Thomas Ritchie, claimed that Story had reduced the states to mere administrative units lacking real sovereignty. The Virginia judiciary refused to enter judgment in favor of Fairfax, effectively denying the validity of section 25 of the 1789 Judiciary Act. The Virginia judges stated that they were under no obligation to obey the Supreme Court.

Virginia's intransigence brought the dispute back to the Supreme Court, this time as *Martin v. Hunter's Lessee.* Marshall again recused himself, although he played an important behind-the-scenes role. The Chief Justice framed the writ of *error that brought the case to the Court and consulted extensively with Joseph Story, who again wrote the Court's opinion.

Story's opinion, the most important of his thirty-four years on the Court, rebuked Virginia for failing to comply with the Court's previous order. Story rejected the compact theory and Virginia's claim that it was equally sovereign with the United States. The American people, Story argued, had created the nation and lodged the national judicial power exclusively in the federal courts. Story sustained section 25 of the 1789 act and insisted that the power to interpret the Constitution had to rest with one ultimate source of authority, which was the United States Supreme Court. He also noted that the national government possessed certain *implied powers, a position that Marshall adopted three years later in upholding the Bank of the United States in *McCulloch v. Maryland (1819).

Story's opinion was a landmark in the history of federal judicial supremacy. More than even Marshall, Story upheld federal judicial supremacy over the states. Without Story's decision, the Supreme Clause of the federal Constitution would have lost much of its salience, since the states would not have been bound to conform their laws to a national constitutional standard.

(See also JUDICIAL POWER AND JURISDICTION; JUDICIAL REVIEW.)

□ G. Edward White, *History of the Supreme Court of the United States*, vols. 3–4, *The Marshall Court and Cultural Change, 1815–35* (1988). Kermit L. Hall

**Martin v. Mott,** 12 Wheat. (25 U.S.) 19 (1827), argued 17 Jan. 1827, decided 2 Feb. 1827 by vote of 7 to 0; Story for the Court.

During the War of 1812, President James *Madison ordered some of the states to call out their militias because of the imminent danger of a British invasion. The president acted pursuant to the Enforcement Act of 1795, which Congress had enacted soon after the Whiskey Rebellion in western Pennsylvania in 1795. In compliance with the president's order, Governor Daniel Tompkins of New York ordered certain militia companies to assemble in New York City. Jacob Mott, a private in one of those companies, refused to obey the order. A court martial subsequently imposed a fine of ninety-six dollars for disobedience, which Mott refused to pay. Martin, the United States *marshal, seized Mott's goods, whereupon Mott filed a civil suit to recover his property. The New York state courts gave judgment to Mott, and Martin appealed to the U.S. Supreme Court. In a landmark decision that defined the scope of the president's military power, the Supreme Court unanimously overturned the decisions of the *state courts. Justice Joseph *Story declared that since the president had acted pursuant to a valid exercise of Congress's power under Article I, section 8 (to call out the militia and to regulate its service), the president, as commander in chief, had the sole authority to determine whether the exigency that necessitated his use of statutory authority actually existed. *Martin* v. *Mott* was a major precedent supporting President Abraham *Lincoln's decision to act decisively in the early days of the *Civil War. The case gave substantive authority to the president as the commander in chief and was the earliest decision in a long line of cases broadly defining the executive power.

(See also PRESIDENTIAL EMERGENCY POWERS.)

George Dargo

**Martin v. Wilks,** 490 U.S. 755 (1989), argued 18 Jan. 1989, decided 12 June 1989 by vote of 5 to 4; Rehnquist for the Court, Stevens, joined by Brennan, Marshall, and Blackmun, in dissent. A group of African-American firefighters alleged racial discrimination in hiring and promoting by Birmingham, Alabama, and a county personnel board. Before finally approving *consent decrees providing for long-term and interim annual goals for the hiring and promotion of African-American firefighters, a federal district court ordered public notice of a hearing on the fairness of the decrees. The Birmingham Firefighters Association (BFA) appeared at the hearing, objected to the decrees, and sought to intervene. The court denied their motions as untimely. Some other white firefighters, also members of the BFA, then brought a reverse discrimination action against the city and the personnel board. They argued that the consent decree made them victims of racial discrimination because they were being denied promotions in favor of less-qualified blacks.

The Supreme Court posed the issue as being a choice between whether the African-American plaintiffs should have joined all possibly affected parties before entry of the consent decree or whether possibly affected parties should have to seek to intervene in the lawsuit resulting in the consent decree. The Court held that the white firefighters, not having been parties to the original litigation, were not bound by the consent decree. The Court indicated that plaintiffs who seek to alter employment practices are best able to bear the burden of identifying those who might be adversely affected if plaintiffs prevail. Plaintiffs should join such parties to their lawsuit. Such parties need not seek to intervene. The Civil Rights Act of 1991 limited the scope of *Martin* v. *Wilks* and made it marginally more difficult for third parties to attack hiring and promotion decisions based on employment discrimination consent decrees.

(See also EMPLOYMENT DISCRIMINATION; RACE AND RACISM.)

Theodore Eisenberg

**Maryland v. Buie,** 494 U.S. 325 (1990), argued 4 Dec. 1989, decided 28 Feb. 1990 by vote of 7 to 2; White for the Court, Stevens and Kennedy concurring, Brennan and Marshall in dissent. In *Buie* the Supreme Court considered the level of justification required by the *Fourth Amendment before police, while effecting the arrest of a suspect in his home pursuant to an arrest warrant, can conduct a warrantless "protective sweep" of those premises to protect the safety of police officers or others. The Court adopted a two-pronged approach. First, police may always search closets and spaces immediately adjoining the place of arrest from which an attack could be launched. Second, a sweep of other places where a person may be found may be made only under circumstances that would warrant a reasonably prudent officer in believing that the area to be searched harbors an individual posing a danger to arresting officers and others.

(See also SEARCH WARRANT RULE, EXCEPTIONS TO.)

Wayne R. LaFave

**Maryland v. Craig** 110 S.Ct. 3157 (1990), argued 18 Apr. 1990, decided 27 June 1990 by vote of 5 to 4; O'Connor for the Court, Scalia, joined by Brennan, Marshall, and Stevens, in dissent. Craig was convicted of child abuse after a trial where the victim testified by one-way closed circuit television, a procedure permitted by state law. The judge, jury, and defendant remained in the courtroom and the child was examined and cross-examined outside of the defendant's presence. On appeal the state court of appeals sided with Craig and questioned the constitutionality of the statute and challenged the procedures. On *certiorari to the U.S. Supreme Court, Craig argued that the *Sixth Amendment did not permit one-way closed circuit television testimony because it deprived her of an opportunity to confront her accuser.

For the Court, Justice Sandra Day *O'Connor held that the Maryland statute did not violate the Sixth Amendment Confrontation Clause because its central purposes were realized in this novel procedure. These included efforts to insure the reliability of evidence, the opportunity to cross-examine witnesses, the taking of an oath, and observation of the witness's demeanor during testimony. Although O'Connor accepted the importance of face-to-face confrontation in criminal trials, she argued that it was not an indispensable element of criminal procedure, especially given the state's interest in protecting child witnesses from the trauma of direct confrontation with the accused. On this point O'Connor maintained that face-to-face confrontation was not an absolute right although the Court had held in Coy v. Iowa (1988) that "the Confrontation Clause guarantees the defendant a face-to-face meeting with witnesses appearing before the trier of fact" (p. 1016).

In dissent, Justice Antonin *Scalia argued that the majority was conspicuously failing to sustain a categorical guarantee of the Constitution. He charged that the Court was ignoring explicit constitutional text and substituting "currently favored public policy" in its place (p. 3172). Conceding that society may well favor the use of one-way closed circuit televised testimony for child victims, and even implying that such a procedure may not necessarily be unfair, Scalia nonetheless stressed that it was not one that was permitted by the Constitution. Procedures that realize the intrinsic objectives of the Sixth Amendment's Confrontation Clause, he said, do not compensate for the failure to respect the Constitution's explicitly worded protection.

The controversy generated by the Craig decision will not quickly abate. In a companion case, Idaho v. Wright (1990), the Court ruled, also 5 to 4, that a physician's account of statements offered by an alleged child victim of sexual abuse was not reliable and therefore inadmissible unless such an account fell within a firmly rooted exception to the hearsay rule or was supported by a showing of "particularized guarantees of trustworthiness."

(See also DUE PROCESS, PROCEDURAL.)

Susette M. Talarico

**Massachusetts v. Mellon,** 262 U.S. 447 (1923), argued 3 and 4 May 1923, decided 4 June 1923 by vote of 9 to o; Sutherland for the Court. In 1921 Congress passed the Sheppard-Towner Act, which provided federal grants to promote state infant and maternity care programs. Congress had passed its first grant program, the Weeks Act, in 1911 to encourage state forest fire prevention programs, but there had been no constitutional challenge until Massachusetts attacked the Maternity Act in an original suit, charging that the law and its grants induced states to yield sovereign rights reserved to them and that the burden of taxation fell unequally on its citizens. The Court heard this case in conjunction with *Frothingham v. Mellon, a taxpayer suit challenging the use of tax revenues for such programs.

Speaking for a unanimous Court, Justice George *Sutherland held that the offer of grants did not force the states to do anything or to yield any rights, except if they voluntarily chose to participate in the program. Nor could he find any right of the states that had been threatened by the act that fell within judicial cognizance, and without some specific issue, the Court "is without authority to pass abstract opinions upon the constitutionality of acts of Congress" (p. 485). He found no burden other than that of taxation, which fell not on the states but on their inhabitants, who, as citizens of the United States, were properly subject to federal taxes (see TAXING AND SPENDING CLAUSE). Perhaps most important, the Court held that a state could not, in its role of parens patriae, institute judicial proceedings to protect its citizens from operation of otherwise valid federal laws.

(See also STATE SOVEREIGNTY AND STATES' RIGHTS; TENTH AMENDMENT.)

Melvin I. Urofsky

**Massiah v. United States,** 377 U.S. 201 (1964), argued 3 Mar. 1964, decided 18 May 1964 by vote of 6 to 3; Stewart for the Court, White in dissent. Massiah was decided at a time when the Warren Court's "revolution in American criminal procedure" was accelerating. According to Massiah, after the initiation of adversary judicial proceedings (by indictment, as in Massiah's case, or by information, preliminary hearing or arraignment), the *Sixth Amendment guarantees a defendant the right to rely on counsel as the "medium" between himself and the government. Thus, once adversary proceedings have begun, the government cannot bypass the defendant's lawyer and deliberately elicit statements from the defendant himself.

The Burger Court revived and even expanded the Massiah doctrine in Brewer v. Williams (1977) and United States v. Henry (1980). As a result, the doctrine has become a more potent force than it had ever been during the Warren Court years.

After he had been indicted for federal narcotics violations, Winston Massiah retained a lawyer, pled not guilty, and was released on bail. Jesse Colson, a codefendant who had also pled not guilty and been released on bail, invited Massiah to discuss the pending case in Colson's car.

Unknown to Massiah, his codefendant had become a government agent and had hidden a radio transmitter in his car. The Massiah-Colson conversation was broadcast to a nearby federal agent. As expected, Massiah made several incriminating statements.

The *Massiah* facts are a far cry from a typical confession case. *Massiah* was neither in "custody" nor subjected to "police interrogation" as that term is normally used. Indeed, Massiah thought he was simply talking to a friend and a partner in crime. Nevertheless, a 6-to-3 majority held that the defendant's statements could not be used against him at his trial. The decisive feature of the case was that after adversary proceedings had commenced against the defendant, and therefore at a time when he was entitled to a lawyer's help, the government had deliberately set out to elicit incriminating statements from him in the absence of counsel. This constituted a violation of the defendant's Sixth Amendment right to counsel (see COUNSEL, RIGHT TO).

The government argued that there was reason to think that Massiah was part of a large, well-organized drug ring and that therefore it was entirely proper for federal agents to continue their investigation of him and his alleged confederates even though he had already been indicted. The Supreme Court responded that, even though the police were justified in investigating other crimes when they obtained Massiah's statements, the defendant's own incriminating statements *pertaining to charges pending against him* could not be used at the trial of those charges. On the other hand, evidence pertaining to new crimes as to which the Sixth Amendment right to counsel had not attached at the time the evidence was obtained would be admissible even though other charges against the defendant were pending at the time. This approach was reaffirmed in *Maine* v. *Moulton* (1985).

Although overshadowed by, and often confused with *Miranda* v. *Arizona* (1966), the *Massiah* doctrine is a separate and distinct rule, and it supplements *Miranda* in important respects. *Miranda* is based on the privilege against compelled self-incrimination and the now-familiar *Miranda* warnings are required when a suspect is subjected to custodial police interrogation, which the Warren Court deemed inherently coercive. *Massiah* is based on the right to counsel. Its application turns not on the conditions surrounding police questioning, but on whether, at the time the government attempts to elicit incriminating statements from an individual, the criminal proceedings against that individual have reached the point at which the Sixth Amendment right to counsel attaches.

The difference between *Massiah* and *Miranda* is underscored by the "jail plant" situation, the case where a secret government agent is placed in the same cell with a person and instructed to induce him to implicate himself in the crime for which he has been incarcerated. *Miranda* does not apply, for the inherent coercion generated by custodial police interrogation is not present when a prisoner speaks freely to a person he believes to be a fellow inmate. Coercion is determined from the perspective of the suspect. Therefore, unless a person realizes he is dealing with a government agent, the government's efforts to elicit damaging admissions from him do not constitute "police interrogation" within the meaning of *Miranda*.

However, the *Massiah* doctrine would prohibit the government from using such tactics if adversary proceedings had already been initiated against the person, as the Court held in *United States* v. *Henry* (1980). But the secret government agent was not completely passive in that case; he stimulated conversations about the crime charged. The Court, however, has permitted the government to place a completely "passive listener" in a person's cell and use the statements acquired by such an agent even though adversary proceedings have commenced against the person. The line between "active" and "passive" agents—between eliciting incriminating statements and merely listening—is an exceedingly difficult one to draw.

(See also COERCED CONFESSIONS; DUE PROCESS, PROCEDURAL.)

□ Yale Kamisar, *Police Interrogation and Confessions* (1980). Welsh White, "Interrogation without Questions: *Rhode Island v. Innis* and *United States v. Henry*," *Michigan Law Review* 78 (August 1980): 1209–1251.

Yale Kamisar

**Masson v. New Yorker Magazine, Inc.,** 111 S.Ct. 2419 (1991), argued 14 Jan. 1991, decided 20 June 1991 by vote of 7 to 2; Kennedy for the Court, White, joined by Scalia, in partial dissent. In *Masson* the Supreme Court had to decide an unusual issue for the first time: the extent to which a journalist's "deliberate alteration" of an interviewee's words is protected by the *First Amendment. Janet Malcolm had altered the words of a psychiatrist in an allegedly libelous manner. One of the six passages considered by the Court mistakenly quoted Dr. Jeffrey Masson describing himself as an "intellectual gigolo." The district court rendered summary judgment in favor of the *New Yorker* with respect to all of the contested alterations. The Court of Appeals for the Ninth Circuit affirmed, ruling in the *New Yorker*'s favor by applying a "substantial truth" test to the alterations: they were protected by the First Amendment so long as they were "rational interpretations" of the actual statements. The Supreme Court reversed.

Under the prevailing First Amendment standards established in *New York Times* v. *Sullivan* (1964), libelous remarks about public figures are not actionable unless they are made with "knowledge of falsity" or "reckless disregard" of the truth (pp. 279–280). After acknowledging that alterations of quotations could harm reputation, Justice Anthony *Kennedy rejected Masson's argument that any alteration other than grammatical or syntactical changes constitutes knowledge of falsity; such "technical distinctions" are "unworkable" (p. 2432). He also rejected the Court of Appeals' standard for encouraging journalistic irresponsibility.

Instead, the Court ruled that a deliberate alteration constituted knowledge of falsity if it "results in a material change in the meaning conveyed by the statement" (p. 2433). Applying this test, the majority held that most of the contested passages created issues of fact for the jury as to truth or falsity, and remanded the case.

In partial dissent, Justice Byron *White agreed with the reversal, but argued that the majority's test permitted irresponsibility. Malcolm's alterations, in his judgment, amounted to falsehood "by any definition of the term" (p. 2437).

(See also LIBEL; SPEECH AND THE PRESS.).

Donald A. Downs

**Maternity Leave.** See PREGNANCY, DISABILITY, AND MATERNITY LEAVES.

**Matthews, Thomas Stanley** (b. Cincinnati, Ohio, 21 July 1824; d. Washington, D.C., 22 Mar. 1889; interred Spring Grove Cemetery, Cincinnati), associate justice, 1881–1889. Thomas Stanley Matthews was the first child of Thomas Johnson Matthews, a professor of mathematics and natural history at Sylvania University in Lexington, Kentucky, and Isabella Brown. He preferred to be called Stanley and dropped his first name as an adult. Matthews entered Kenyon College as a

*Thomas Stanley Matthews*

junior and graduated in 1840. He read law for two years and then moved to Maury County, Tennessee, where he began a law practice and edited a newspaper. In 1844 he married Mary Ann Black and after her death in 1885 he wed Mary Theaker of Washington, D.C.

Matthews was originally nominated to the Supreme Court on 26 January 1881 by President Rutherford B. Hayes to replace retiring Justice Noah H. *Swayne. President Hayes, a fellow Ohioan, lifelong friend, and political colleague of his nominee, met Matthews when the two men were undergraduates at Kenyon College. Matthews served under Hayes in the Twenty-third Ohio Volunteer Infantry during the Civil War, and in the disputed presidential election of 1876, Matthews argued the case for the Hayes-Republican electors against the Tilden-Democrats in the electoral commission inquiry in Louisiana.

Matthews met bitter opposition and the Senate took no action on the nomination. It was only after Hayes's successor, President James A. Garfield (also from Ohio), renominated him on 14 March 1881 that Matthews was confirmed on 12 May 1881 by a vote of 24 to 23. Opposition to Matthews's nomination was rooted in his work as legal counsel to railroad and corporate interests and several political controversies in which he reluctantly had taken part. One of these, apparently distorted by opponents at his confirmation, was his prosecution as U.S. attorney for the Southern District of Ohio (1858–1861) in 1859 of a newspaper reporter for aiding in the escape of two *fugitive slaves. Some critics suggested that Matthews, who had embraced abolitionism, had sold his conscience for political favor. The specter of this case had been revived earlier to help defeat Matthews in his bid for a congressional seat in 1876, though he won a Senate seat the following year (1877–1879).

Justice Matthews served only seven years and ten months, yet in that short period he authored an impressive 232 opinions and five dissents. Matthews was a craftsman and realist rather than an ideologue. His two most famous opinions, undisturbed as precedent after more than a century, are *Hurtado v. California* (1884) and *Yick Wo v. Hopkins* (1886). Both illustrate Matthews's progressive and pragmatic approach to constitutional law.

In *Hurtado*, Matthews rejected the argument that the *Fifth and *Fourteenth Amendments' *"due process of law" provision required states to seek *grand jury indictments or presentments in prosecuting felonies. Against the argument promoted by Hurtado's counsel that grand jury indictments were an ancient requirement of English *common law, Matthews argued that this "would be to deny every quality of the law but its age, and to render it incapable of progress or improvement" (p. 529). Instead of looking at the form of the requirement of due process, Matthews concluded that if the defendant was given fair notice of the charge and sufficient time to prepare a defense, then the purposes of due process protection was satisfied.

Matthews's *Yick Wo* opinion stands as one of the few minority rights opinions in the post-*Reconstruction era and is a marvel of realistic jurisprudence. He looked beyond the neutral language of San Francisco's ordinance regulating the operation of public laundries to the statistically disparate application of the ordinance against Chinese laundry proprietors to find a violation of the Fourteenth Amendment's Equal Protection Clause. His classic statement stands as the basis of all twentieth-century public civil rights disparate impact cases: "Though the law itself be fair on its face and impartial in appearance, yet, if it is applied and administered by public authority with an evil eye and an unequal hand, so as practically to make unjust and illegal discrimination between persons in similar circumstances, material to their rights, and denial of equal justice is still within the prohibition of the Constitution" (pp. 373–374).

□ Charles T. Greve, "Stanley Matthews," in *Great American Lawyers: A History of the Legal Profession in America*, edited by William Draper Lewis, vol. 7 (1909), pp. 393–427.                                                N. E. H. Hull

**Maxwell v. Dow,** 176 U.S. 581 (1900), argued 4 Dec. 1899, decided 26 Feb. 1900 by vote of 8 to 1; Peckham for the Court, Harlan in dissent. Charles L. Maxwell challenged his conviction for robbery on two grounds: use of an information rather than indictment by a *grand jury to initiate a prosecution; and trial before a jury of eight, not twelve. Both grounds, according to Maxwell, violated his *privileges and immunities as protected by the *Fifth and *Fourteenth Amendments. He also argued that conviction by an eight-member jury violated the *due process guaranteed by the Fourteenth Amendment.

Justice Rufus W. *Peckham brusquely dismissed Maxwell's arguments and upheld the conviction, noting that the issues had been resolved in prior decisions. With that assertion, the Court continued to minimize the scope of the Privileges and Immunities Clause, a process begun in the *Slaughterhouse Cases (1873). Any other approach, Peckham reasoned, relying on the pre–Civil War case of *Corfield* v. *Coryell* (Pa., 1823), would so "fetter and degrade the state governments by subjecting them to the control of Congress" as to violate "the structure and spirit of our institutions" (p. 590). Thus, in the Court's view, the states remained the primary protectors of most rights.

Justice John Marshall *Harlan's dissent was a paean to the jury. He emphasized that at a minimum the *Bill of Rights identified the privileges and immunities that the Fourteenth Amendment protected. Harlan therefore concluded that the states could not avoid the *Sixth Amend-

ment's guarantee of a *trial by a jury of twelve members. He reached the same conclusion about due process, foreshadowing the Court's gradual *incorporation of the Bill of Rights into the Fourteenth Amendment after World War II.

                                                Walter F. Pratt, Jr.

**McCardle, Ex parte,** 74 U.S. 506 (1869), argued 2–4 and 9 Mar. 1868, decided 12 Apr. 1869 by vote of 8 to 0; Chase for the Court, Wayne had died. A product of the often-strained relations between the Supreme Court and Congress during Reconstruction, the *McCardle* case posed fundamental questions concerning Congress's ability to use its authority over the Court's *appellate jurisdiction to curb judicial independence.

In late 1867, army officials responsible for administering *Reconstruction in Mississippi arrested William McCardle, a Vicksburg editor, charging him with publishing libelous editorials that incited insurrection. Invoking the authority conferred by the Reconstruction Act (1867), they ordered McCardle tried by military commission. The editor challenged the government's action, asserting that Ex parte *Milligan (1866) precluded military trial of civilians when the civil courts were open and that the Reconstruction Act was therefore unconstitutional (see MILITARY TRIALS AND MARTIAL LAW). Relying on the Habeas Corpus Act of 1867, which directed federal courts to issue writs of *habeas corpus in cases involving persons who were confined in violation of their constitutional rights, he sought relief in the United States circuit court. When that tribunal rejected his argument, McCardle invoked a provision of the Habeas Corpus Act allowing the Supreme Court to hear appeals in habeas corpus, bringing the politically explosive question of the Reconstruction Act's constitutionality before the high court.

Republican leaders in Congress feared that the Court might strike down the act and destroy the party's Reconstruction program. Consequently, in March 1868, after the Court had heard arguments but before it had rendered a decision, Congress struck at the Court's jurisdiction by repealing the provision of the Habeas Corpus Act allowing appeals to the Supreme Court. Although Justices Robert C. *Grier and Stephen J. *Field wished to decide the case before Congress enacted the repeal, the majority rejected such a course. With the end of the Court's term approaching, the justices agreed to hold the case over until the next term.

When the Court issued its opinion, it bowed to Congress, dismissing the case for want of jurisdiction without passing judgment on the Reconstruction Act. Chief Justice Salmon P. *Chase pointed out that the Constitution provided that the Court was to exercise its appellate jurisdiction "with such exceptions, and under such regulations as the Congress shall make." Because Congress possessed express authority to make exceptions to the Court's appellate jurisdiction, he continued, the 1868 repeal measure was constitutional, regardless of Congress's motive. Consequently, the Court had no jurisdiction to hear McCardle's appeal and must dismiss the case.

Although sometimes viewed as an example of the Reconstruction Court's supineness, *McCardle* actually suggests its resiliency. In concluding his opinion, Chase pointedly noted that while Congress had repealed the provision of the Habeas Corpus Act on which McCardle had relied, this did not affect the jurisdiction that the Court possessed under other statutes. This was a thinly veiled reference to the *Judiciary Act of 1789, which authorized the Court to issue writs of habeas corpus to persons held under federal authority. Several months later, in *Ex parte Yerger* (1869), the Court agreed to hear a challenge to the Reconstruction Act brought under the 1789 statute by a Mississippi civilian who was charged with the murder of an army officer and held for trial by a military court. Although the Court again failed to reach the merits, its willingness to accept jurisdiction suggests that it had not been overawed.

*McCardle* has never been repudiated by the Court and has been read by some authorities to suggest unlimited congressional authority over the Court's jurisdiction. Indeed, some politicians have used it to support legislation prohibiting the Court from rendering unpopular decisions on controversial matters such as school prayer and busing. Others disagree, arguing that the case should not be read to permit Congress to use its authority to regulate the Court's jurisdiction to shield government policies from *judicial review. They point out that in *McCardle*, because the avenue provided by the Judiciary Act remained open, the Court did not accept congressional action denying the federal courts authority to hear challenges to the Reconstruction Act. Moreover, they note that in *U.S.* v. *Klein* (1872), the Court limited Congress's authority, holding that it may not limit the Court's jurisdiction to control the results of a particular case.

(See also JUDICIAL POWER AND JURISDICTION.)

□ Charles Fairman, *History of the Supreme Court of the United States*, vol. 6, *Reconstruction and Reunion, 1868–88. Part I* (1971). Donald G. Nieman

**McCarran Act.** Officially the Internal Security Act of 1950, the McCarran Act reflected America's exaggerated fear of communist subversion. Adopted over President Harry Truman's stern veto, the measure was aimed at lifting the veil of secrecy from the Communist party and its fronts. Title I created a Subversive Activities Control Board with authority to require communist-dominated organizations to register with the attorney general and make public the names of officers and members, sources of income, and expenditures. Designated organizations would

also have to label all publications and public broadcasts as disseminated by or sponsored by "a Communist organization." Their members were denied the use of passports and were excluded from employment by the federal government, labor unions, and defense facilities. The measure also imposed prohibitive limits on the immigration of aliens with communist affiliations.

Title II authorized the president, in the event of an invasion, insurrection, or war, to declare an "internal security emergency," during which the attorney general could order the detention without *due process of anyone deemed a potential spy or saboteur. His orders could be challenged before a nine-member Board of Detention Review whose decisions could be appealed to the federal courts.

While Congress appropriated moneys for the erection of "detention centers," the emergency detention provisions of the McCarran Act were never used and were finally repealed in 1971. Successive attorneys general attempted to force the registration of the Communist party under Title I of the act, but their efforts were ultimately frustrated by the federal courts in a series of rulings culminating in *Albertson* v. *SACB* (1965).

(See also COMMUNISM AND COLD WAR; SUBVERSION.)

Jerold L. Simmons

**McCleskey v. Kemp,** 481 U.S. 279 (1987), argued 15 Oct. 1986, decided 22 Apr. 1987 by vote of 5 to 4; Powell for the Court, Brennan in dissent joined by Marshall, Blackmun, and Stevens; Blackmun in dissent joined by Marshall, Stevens, and Brennan; Stevens in dissent joined by Blackmun. Warren McCleskey, a black man, was convicted and sentenced to death for the 1978 murder of a white Atlanta police officer. On appeal, attorneys for the *Legal Defense Fund argued that the Georgia death penalty statute was being implemented in a racially discriminatory fashion in violation of the *Eighth and *Fourteenth Amendments.

McCleskey's claim rested on a sophisticated study of Georgia death sentencing patterns conducted by Professor David Baldus. The study examined more than two thousand Georgia murders from the 1970s. Some 230 variables were analyzed for their ability to predict death sentencing. Other factors being equal, Baldus found the odds of a death sentence for those accused of killing whites were 4.3 times higher than the odds of a death sentence for those charged with killing blacks.

Justice Lewis *Powell's majority opinion rejected McCleskey's claim. He suggested that the Baldus data should be presented to legislative bodies, rather than to the courts. To prevail under the *Equal Protection Clause of the Fourteenth Amendment, McCleskey needed to prove that either the Georgia Legislature or the decision makers in his specific case acted with a discriminatory purpose. Nor could McCleskey prevail under the *Cruel and Unusual Punishment Clause of the Eighth Amendment, Powell said, since the disparities in the treatment of homicide cases revealed in the Baldus study did not offend "evolving standards of decency."

The dissenting justices relied primarily on the Eighth Amendment, arguing that demonstration of a significant risk of discrimination, rather than definitive proof of its existence, is all that is needed to show a constitutional violation.

The Court rejected a second *habeas corpus petition filed by McCleskey four years later in *McCleskey v. Zant (1991).

(See also CAPITAL PUNISHMENT; RACE DISCRIMINATION AND THE DEATH PENALTY.)

Michael L. Radelet

**McCleskey v. Zant,** 111 S.Ct. 1454 (1991), argued 30 Oct. 1990, decided 16 Apr. 1991 by vote of 6 to 3; Kennedy for the Court; Marshall in dissent, joined by Blackmun and Stevens. Warren McCleskey's first challenge to his death sentence for murder was rejected by the Supreme Court in *McCleskey v. Kemp (1987). Four years later he filed a second habeas corpus petition alleging that before his trial the state of Georgia had improperly induced him to make incriminating statements without the assistance of counsel (see COUNSEL, RIGHT TO). These statements (conversations with a fellow prisoner) were used against him at trial. The Court's decision, rejecting this claim, clarifies the standard for determining "abuse of the writ" and substantially narrows the possibility of habeas corpus relief in death penalty cases.

Claims deliberately abandoned in earlier petitions for a writ and included in a subsequent petition clearly constitute abuse of the writ, as do those omitted through inexcusable neglect. To avoid this, in second and later petitions the defendant must show cause, that is, he must show that his failure to raise the claim earlier was impeded by factors beyond his control. He must also show that the errors of which he complains resulted in actual prejudice. The only exception to this "cause and prejudice" standard is when the presented claim reveals an error so fundamental that the conviction came despite the petitioner's factual innocence.

McCleskey supported his allegation of the state's involvement in eliciting his harmful statements only after his first petition for habeas corpus, but the Supreme Court held that the facts of the trial should have put him on notice that the claim should have been pursued immediately. Nor did McCleskey show that the alleged violation resulted in the conviction of an innocent defendant. Hence, relief was denied. McCleskey was executed on 25 September 1991.

(See also CAPITAL PUNISHMENT; HABEAS CORPUS.)

Michael L. Radelet

**McCray v. United States,** 195 U.S. 27 (1904), argued 2 Dec. 1903, decided 31 May 1904 by vote of 6 to 3; White for the Court, Fuller, Peckham, and Brown in dissent. In 1886, Congress passed legislation based on the taxing power to regulate the production of oleomargarine (see TAXING AND SPENDING CLAUSE). Enacted to prevent product adulteration, the law also reflected industrial competition. McCray was fined fifty dollars for violating the law by purchasing for resale artificially colored oleo at the lower tax rate applied to the uncolored variety. The significant constitutional challenges claimed inappropriate use of the taxing power for regulation rather than for revenue; violation of the *due process and *taking of property clauses of the *Fifth Amendment; and violation of states' rights to regulate business under the *Tenth Amendment (see STATE SOVEREIGNTY AND STATES' RIGHTS).

Justice Edward D. *White argued vigorously against judicial interference with the powers of Congress, especially since an excise tax violated no expressed constitutional limitations on the taxing power. Nor did the Fifth and Tenth Amendments vitiate the original grant of the tax power. Due process was not violated when Congress categorized and taxed products to prevent fraud. Citing *McCulloch v. Maryland (1819), White declined to hold the tax unconstitutional because of its potential negative impact on production of oleomargarine. Reserving the right to inquire into abuses, the Court sustained broad use of the taxing power for purposes beyond revenue raising.

*McCray* established the taxing power as an additional base for exercise of a federal *police power. Constricted in the 1920s, the tax power was nevertheless reclaimed by the *New Deal as a basis for *general welfare legislation.

Barbara C. Steidle

**McCulloch v. Maryland,** 4 Wheat. (17 U.S.) 316 (1819), argued 22 Feb.–3 Mar. 1819, decided 6 Mar. 1819 by vote of 7 to 0; Marshall for the Court. *McCulloch* was one of Chief Justice John *Marshall's most important decisions, and among his most eloquent. It settled the meaning of the Necessary and Proper Clause of the United States Constitution and determined the distribution of powers between the federal government and the states. The specific issues involved were Congress's power to incorporate the Second Bank of the United States and the right of a state to tax an instrument of the federal government.

*Background.* The constitutionality of the power of Congress to charter a *corporation had been the source of debate ever since Alexander *Hamilton proposed the creation of the First Bank of the United States in 1791. James *Madison in Congress and Thomas *Jefferson in George *Washington's cabinet opposed the measure as unauthorized by the Constitution. But Congress and Washington sided with Hamilton, who justified it by a loose construction of the Constitution, and Congress chartered the Bank for a twenty-year period. In 1811 a Jeffersonian-dominated Congress refused to renew the charter, primarily on constitutional grounds, and the First Bank quietly expired. However, following five years of inflation and economic chaos that coincided with the War of 1812, Congress, though still under Jeffersonian control, reversed itself and chartered the Second Bank of the United States in 1816. Despite this, many Jeffersonians continued to oppose the Bank. They viewed it as unconstitutional and denied its economic necessity. Several states, including Ohio, Kentucky, Pennsylvania, Maryland, North Carolina, and Georgia, adopted laws taxing its branches. An 1818 Maryland statute imposed a tax on all banks operating in the state "not chartered by the legislature." The Baltimore branch of the Bank, headed by its cashier, James McCulloch, refused to pay the tax. The Baltimore County Court upheld the state law. This judgment was quickly affirmed by the Court of Appeals of Maryland and was appealed to the United States Supreme Court, on a writ of *error. The Supreme Court declared the Maryland tax unconstitutional and void.

*Opinion of the Court.* In rendering his opinion for the entire Supreme Court, Marshall first considered the question "has Congress power to incorporate a bank?" (p. 401). To answer this, he looked to the origins and nature of the federal union. The Constitution had been submitted to the people and ratified by specially elected conventions. As a consequence, "the government proceeds directly from the people; is 'ordained and established' in the name of the people" (p. 403). By asserting this, Marshall offered a nationalist alternative to the theory of the origins of the union propounded by Jeffersonians in the Kentucky and Virginia Resolutions of 1798–1799, which claimed that the federal government was a product of a compact of the states and had only specifically granted and limited power (see STATE SOVEREIGNTY AND STATES' RIGHTS). "The government of the Union," Marshall argued in clear and strong terms, ". . . is, emphatically, and truly, a government of the people. In form and in substance it emanates from them. Its powers are granted by them, and are to be exercised directly on them, and for their benefit" (pp. 404–405).

Like Hamilton before him, Marshall resorted to a loose interpretation of the Constitution to justify Congress's authority to create the Second Bank of the United States. Marshall admitted that the federal government was one of enumerated powers and could only exercise those powers granted to it. But, he added, there could be no doubt "that the government of the Union, though limited in its powers, is supreme within its sphere of action" (p. 405). He observed that although the power to charter a corporation is not a specifically enumerated power, there is nothing in the Constitution that excludes it. This included the *Tenth Amendment, which, unlike a predecessor provision in the Articles of Confederation, did not include the word "expressly" and therefore allowed "incidental or implied powers." Marshall further observed that the federal government was not established by a complex legal code, excessively detailed in a vain attempt to meet every exigency. Rather, the Constitution contained only a general outline of the federal government's structure and powers, in which only its most important objects were designated while the rest of its powers were to "be deduced from the nature of the objects themselves" (p. 407). He concluded, "we must never forget that it is a constitution we are expounding" (p. 407).

From these premises about the origins and nature of the Constitution, Marshall proceeded to justify the creation of the Bank of the United States. The Constitution had delegated certain specified powers to the federal government: to lay and collect taxes (see TAXING AND SPENDING CLAUSE), to borrow money, to regulate commerce, to declare and conduct war (see WAR POWERS), and to raise and support armies and navies. It was in the best interests of the nation, the chief justice observed, that Congress should have the means to exercise these delegated powers. In particular, the Bank was a convenient, useful, and essential instrument in the implementation of the nation's fiscal policies. Since the Constitution had given Congress the power to "make all Laws which shall be necessary and proper for carrying into execution the forgoing Powers," the Bank of the United States was constitutional.

Marshall elaborated on the need for a loose and expansive interpretation of the powers of the federal government. He rejected the idea of a strict interpretation of the Constitution then espoused by states' rights Jeffersonians. Such a reading of the Constitution would make it unworkable. Marshall argued that the Necessary and Proper Clause had been included among the powers of Congress, not among its limitations, and was meant to enlarge, not reduce, the ability of Congress to execute its enumerated powers. Marshall declared:

Let the end be legitimate, let it be within the scope of the constitution, and all means which are appropriate, which are plainly adapted to that end, which are not prohibited, but consist with the letter and spirit of the constitution, are constitutional. (p. 421)

Marshall next addressed the issue "whether the state of Maryland may, without violating the Constitution," tax a branch of the Bank of the United States (p. 425). Since the Constitution and federal law were supreme under the *Supremacy Clause of Article VI, they took precedence over the laws of the states. The state power to tax, important and vital as it was, is subordinate to the Constitution. A state cannot tax those subjects to which its sovereign powers do not extend. Marshall pointed out "that the power to tax involves the power to destroy" (p. 431). If a state had power to tax the bank, it could also tax other agencies of the federal government: the mail, the mint, patents, the customs houses, and the federal courts. In this manner the states could totally defeat "all the ends of government" determined by the people when they created the United States Constitution (p. 432). "This," Marshall observed, "was not intended by the American people. They did not design to make their government dependent on the states" (p. 432).

***Impact and Reaction.*** The decision was controversial. Opponents of the Bank remained irreconcilable. They did not view the Bank primarily as an agency of the federal government. To them it was a profit-making corporation that performed a few government services. The Second Bank had been capitalized at $35 million. Eighty percent of its stock (on which substantial dividends were paid) was in private hands, and shareholders appointed four-fifths of the board of directors.

Critics of the decision also denounced Marshall's ringing endorsement of a broad interpretation of the power of the federal government. Most proponents of states' rights in Virginia had doubts about the bank's constitutionality, but in 1816 they had accepted the argument that it was needed to restore financial stability. Unlike the Bank's opponents in several other states, the advocates of local government in Virginia never tried to tax the Bank out of existence. They were troubled not that the court had upheld the constitutionality of the Bank, but that it had justified loose and expansive interpretation of the Constitution. Thomas Jefferson privately encouraged public opposition to the decision. John Taylor published an important book, *Construction Construed* (1820), denouncing the decision, and Virginia jurists Spencer Roane and William Brockenbrough wrote a series of essays for the *Richmond Enquirer* condemning the broad implications of the Court's ruling. Marshall personally responded to Roane in a series of anonymous newspaper articles upholding his own handiwork.

Critics of the decision also included James Madison, who as president of the United States (1809–1817) had signed the bill creating the Second Bank of the United States into law, and who generally supported most of the Supreme Court's nationalist rulings during the second decade of the nineteenth century. Despite this, he believed "that the occasion did not call for the general and abstract doctrine interwoven with the decision of the particular case." The real danger of Marshall's decision, Madison believed, was "the high sanction given to a latitude in expounding the Constitution which seems to break down the landmarks intended by a specification of the powers of Congress, and to substitute for a definite connection between means and ends, a legislative discretion as to the former to

which no practical limit can be assigned." Among other things, the decision seemed to sanction a federal program of internal improvements. Such a program would have involved not only the building of roads, canals, and bridges, but also an assortment of educational, scientific, and literary institutions throughout the country. Both Jefferson and Madison favored such a program on policy grounds, but believed the jurisdictional problems raised by it were so complex and controversial that they could only be clarified through an amendment to the Constitution. In his *McCulloch* v. *Maryland* decision, Marshall aligned the U.S. Supreme Court with those aggressive nationalists like Henry Clay, John C. Calhoun, and John Quincy Adams, who argued that a constitutional amendment was not necessary since Congress already had power to enact such a program.

The Bank's victory in *McCulloch* v. *Maryland* turned out to be short-lived. In 1828 states' rights as a political movement triumphed with the election of Andrew *Jackson to the presidency. Rejecting the binding quality of *McCulloch* v. *Maryland* and building on the lingering resentment that continued toward the Bank, Jackson in 1832 vetoed a bill to recharter it, on constitutional grounds. In a series of other vetoes, Jackson also effectively finished off any hope for a federal program of internal improvements. Despite this, Marshall's broad interpretation of the Necessary and Proper Clause as well as his view of the origins and nature of the federal union were ultimately to triumph on a more significant level. The *Civil War brought an end to Jacksonian hegemony and discredited states' rights. The constitutional revolution that followed took the country in a strong nationalist direction. In the twentieth century *McCulloch* v. *Maryland* quickly became the virtually undisputed constitutional cornerstone for the federal government's broad involvement in the economy, for the *New Deal and the Welfare State, and for various other social, scientific, and educational programs.

(See also COMMERCE POWER; IMPLIED POWERS; JUDICIAL REVIEW.)

□ Gerald Gunther, ed., *John Marshall's Defense of McCulloch v. Maryland* (1969). Bray Hammond, *Banks and Politics in America from the Revolution to the Civil War* (1957). Harold J. Plous and Gordon E. Baker, "McCulloch v. Maryland: Right Principle, Wrong Case," *Stanford Law Review* 9 (1957): 710–739. G. Edward White, *History of the Supreme Court of the United States*, vols. 3–4, *The Marshall Court and Cultural Change, 1815–35* (1988).
Richard E. Ellis

**McKeiver v. Pennsylvania,** 403 U.S. 528 (1971), argued 9–10 Dec. 1970, decided 21 June 1971 by vote of 6 to 3; Blackmun for the Court, White and Harlan concurring separately, Brennan concurring in part and dissenting in part, Douglas, Black, and Marshall in dissent. When the Supreme Court decided *In re *Gault* (1967) and applied criminal *due process guarantees to state juvenile proceedings, the *Sixth Amendment's right to trial by jury had not yet been "incorporated" into the *Fourteenth Amendment (see INCORPORATION DOCTRINE). *Duncan v. Louisiana (1968) accomplished that for adult criminal defendants but left open the question of whether juvenile defendants also had this right. McKeiver, actually several cases involving juvenile procedures in North Carolina and Pennsylvania, answered this question in the negative.

Justice Harry *Blackmun, writing for a plurality of four justices, narrowly interpreted Gault and the previous term's In re *Winship (1970) as establishing only a standard of "fundamental fairness" to define due process in juvenile proceedings. Accordingly, the importance of the right to trial by jury in juvenile adjudications was to be balanced against its impact on the distinctively informal and flexible nature of juvenile justice. Blackmun then asserted that both Gault and Winship imposed due process guarantees primarily to improve the accuracy of fact finding in the juvenile process. An equally narrow interpretation of Duncan led Blackmun to conclude that the primary purpose of trial by jury is to prevent government oppression in adjudication, not to assure accurate fact finding. Thus, injection of the jury into juvenile adjudication would fundamentally disturb its character by making it more fully adversarial without necessarily enhancing its fact-finding accuracy. Blackmun's narrow reading of precedent, though frequently criticized, remains the prevailing interpretation. States are free to require juries in juvenile cases, but none has done so.

(See also JUVENILE JUSTICE; TRIAL BY JURY.)

Albert R. Matheny

**McKenna, Joseph** (b. Philadelphia, Pa., 10 Aug., 1843; d. Washington, D.C., 21 Nov., 1926; interred Mount Olivet Cemetery, Washington, D.C.), associate justice, 1898–1925. Joseph McKenna, son of an Irish immigrant baker, John McKenna and his wife, Mary (Johnson), was the living embodiment of the Horatio Alger myth, rising from poverty to a seat on the U.S. Supreme Court. His forbears reached Philadelphia with the famine migration of 1848. In 1855 his father moved the family to Benicia, California, where, for the few years remaining to him, his lot improved steadily. Joseph, educated in parochial schools, initially planned to enter the Catholic priesthood, but turned instead to the law.

After admission to the California bar in 1865, he practiced in Solano County, serving two terms as district attorney (1866–1870), and one in the state legislature (1875–1876). In 1869 he married Amanda F. Borneman of San Francisco, the mother of a son and three daughters.

McKenna used the legal profession as a stepping stone to a career in politics. In 1885 he won

*Joseph McKenna*

election, as a Republican, to the U.S. House of Representatives, serving four terms from California's third district. On 28 March 1892 he resigned his seat when President Benjamin Harrison appointed him to the Court of Appeals for the Ninth Circuit on the recommendation of his friend, California Senator Leland Stanford.

President William McKinley in 1897 appointed him attorney general. He held that office a few months until 16 December 1897, when he was elevated to the seat on the U.S. Supreme Court vacated by Justice Stephen *Field. Senate confirmation was delayed for weeks as the result of opposition from rival Pacific railway systems feuding with the Stanford network.

McKenna's Supreme Court opinions number 633. He adopted a distinctive style easily read and recognized by those familiar with the U.S. Reports. They are marked by grace and aptness of phrase. He did not write many majority opinions, but the few he wrote decided some exceedingly important cases.

By the turn of the century the Court was giving support to the growing body of what is now called the federal *police power legislation with such laws as the Pure Food and Drug Act (1906) and the *Mann Act (1910). In the case sustaining the former, Hipolite Egg Co. v. U.S. (1911), Justice McKenna, for a unanimous Court, reminded appellants (who had had several cases of preserved eggs seized by federal agents) that there were very few limits to the reach of the federal *commerce power. The opinion said nothing of the intent or purpose of Congress in enacting the Pure Food and Drug Act, but in a later case, Hoke v. U.S. (1913), testing the constitutionality of the

Mann Act, which prohibited the transportation of women in interstate or foreign commerce for immoral purposes, he argued that the powers reserved to the states and those conferred on the nation were intended to promote the general welfare, material and moral.

As he advanced in age, McKenna's mental processes slowed and, according to his critics, became confused. At his peak, however, his opinions reveal a strong nationalism, practicality, and sound social judgment with relation to developing federal power and its impact on the states. He served twenty-seven years on the Supreme Court. Under considerable prodding from Chief Justice William Howard *Taft, McKenna finally resigned in January, 1925. After an illness of several months, he died on 21 November 1926.

□ Brother Matthew McDevitt, *Joseph McKenna: Associate Justice of the United States* (1946). James F. Watts, "Joseph McKenna," in *The Justices of the U.S. Supreme Court, 1789–1969,* edited by Leon Friedman and Fred Israel, vol. 2 (1969), pp. 1719–1736. Marian C. McKenna

**McKinley, John** (b. Culpepper County, Va., 1 May 1780; d. Lexington, Ky., 19 July 1852; interred Cave Hill Cemetery, Louisville, Ky.), associate justice, 1837–1852. Soon after McKinley's birth, his family moved from Virginia to Kentucky, where he studied law and was admitted to the Kentucky bar in 1800. He practiced in Frankfort and Louisville before settling in Huntsville, Alabama.

After winning a seat in the Alabama legislature in 1822, he was elected to the U.S. Senate in 1826. He began as a follower of Henry Clay, but when that became politically untenable in Alabama, he switched to the camp of Andrew *Jackson. His concerns in the Senate included cheaper land for settlers, bankruptcy relief for all categories of debtors, and states' rights. In 1830, McKinley was defeated in his effort to keep the Senate seat, but he won later elections, including another Senate term in 1837, which he declined in order to accept appointment by President Martin Van Buren to the U.S. Supreme Court.

McKinley served on the Supreme Court until 1852, but his career was marked by absences from the Court and little contact with the major legal issues of the day. He wrote only twenty opinions and two concurrences in his fifteen years, and commentators and historians have disparaged his work as lacking any legal significance.

McKinley is best known for his dissent in *Bank of Augusta* v. *Earle* (1839), in which he insisted that Alabama, as a sovereign state, could limit business activity to corporations chartered in Alabama. He saw the United States as a federation of sovereign states and rejected the concept of national legal comity between the states (see STATE SOVEREIGNTY AND STATES' RIGHTS). Justice Joseph *Story and others desiring a national

*John McKinley*

economy prevailed, and McKinley was alone in his dissent.

McKinley argued for states' rights in three other cases. He was joined by Story in a dissent in *Groves* v. *Slaughter* (1841), in which he maintained that a Mississippi constitutional restriction of the importation of slaves was valid. In *Pollard* v. *Hagan* (1845), he wrote for the majority of the Court in holding that submerged land belonged to the states and not the federal government.

Throughout his Supreme Court service he complained bitterly about the extensive circuit duty he was required to fulfill. His circuit, the ninth, was the largest and included parts of Alabama, Louisiana, and Mississippi and all of Arkansas. There were years when he did not get to the last of these districts. McKinley petitioned Congress in 1838 and 1842 for relief, explaining the difficulty and expense of the circuit travel and the threat of yellow fever. He did not gain any relief from *circuit riding, however, and his many absences from the courts induced complaints from the public and other circuit judges.

McKinley lived in Louisville, Kentucky, during his Supreme Court tenure to take advantage of the water transportation between Washington and the Ninth Circuit. During the last years of his life, McKinley's poor health meant that he contributed little to the Court's work.

R. Michael McReynolds

**McLaurin v. Oklahoma State Regents for Higher Education,** 339 U.S. 637 (1950), argued 3–4 Apr. 1950, decided 5 June 1950 by vote of 9 to 0. Vinson for the Court. *McLaurin* was a companion case to

*Sweatt* v. *Painter* (1950), which defined the separate but equal standard in graduate education in such a way as to be unattainable. George W. McLaurin was an Oklahoma citizen and an African-American. Hoping to earn a doctorate in education, he applied for admission to graduate study at Oklahoma's all-white university at Norman. Initially denied admission on the basis of race, McLaurin was ordered admitted by a federal district court. But because Oklahoma law required that graduate instruction must be "upon a segregated basis," McLaurin found himself enshrouded in the segregationist equivalent of a plastic bubble: in class, he sat in a separate row "reserved for Negroes"; in the library he studied at a separate desk; in the cafeteria he ate at a separate table. McLaurin sought relief from these measures by returning to the district court, and eventually appealing to the Supreme Court. The case was argued and decided simultaneously with the *Sweatt* case in which applicant Heman Sweatt was seeking admission to the University of Texas's all-white law school.

In a brief and blunt ruling, Chief Justice Fred *Vinson ordered an end to McLaurin's separate treatment. Such practices, Vinson observed, denied McLaurin "his personal and present rights to the equal protection of the laws" (p. 642) as required by the *Fourteenth Amendment. McLaurin, Vinson wrote, "must receive the same treatment . . . as students of other races" (p. 642).

(See also EDUCATION; RACE AND RACISM; SEGREGATION, DE JURE; SEPARATE BUT EQUAL DOCTRINE.)
Augustus M. Burns III

**McLean, John** (b. Morris County, N.J., 11 Mar. 1785; d. Cincinnati, Ohio, 4 Apr. 1861; interred Spring Grove Cemetery, Cincinnati), associate justice, 1830–1861. The son of Ulsterman Fergus McLean (originally McLain) and Sophia Blackford, McLean grew up in a succession of frontier communities before settling in Warren County, Ohio, in 1797. Despite highly irregular schooling, he studied law with John S. Gano and Arthur St. Clair in Cincinnati in 1804. He established a Democratic newspaper at Lebanon, Ohio, after admission to the bar, and by 1811 was examiner in the United States Land Office in Cincinnati.

Elected as a War Hawk to the United States House of Representatives in 1812 and reelected in 1814, he actively promoted the presidential candidacy of James Monroe. He returned to Ohio and served on the state supreme court until 1822 when President Monroe appointed him commissioner of the General Land Office. Made postmaster general in 1823, he oversaw a tremendous expansion in westward routes and the elevation of the office to cabinet status. McLean remained in office under President John Quincy *Adams.

Although an early supporter of John C. Calhoun, he adroitly courted Andrew *Jackson but kept Adams from finding grounds to dismiss

*John McLean*

him. After Jackson's victory in 1828, McLean's reward was appointment to the Supreme Court.

Known as the "Politician on the Supreme Court" during his thirty-year coquettish quest for the presidency, McLean flirted successively with Jackson Democrats, anti-Jackson Democrats, Antimasons, Whigs, Free Soilers, and Republicans (see EXTRAJUDICIAL ACTIVITIES). McLean saw nothing injudicious in his quest, or as a devout Methodist, any conflict between politics and religion. He did not participate in *Smith* v. *Swormstedt* (1853), occasioned by the sectional division of the Methodist church, but agreed that Stephen Girard lawfully could ban clergy from his academy (*Vidal et al* v. *Philadelphia,* 1844).

McLean began his judicial career as a nationalist, concurring with Marshall in *Cherokee Nation* v. *Georgia* (1831) and *Worcester* v. *Georgia* (1832) (see CHEROKEE CASES). He favored state banking, dissented in *Craig* v. *Missouri* (1830) and convinced the court that state bank notes were not bills of credit in *Briscoe* v. *Commonwealth Bank of Kentucky* (1837). Another states' rights opinion was *Ex parte Dorr* (1845), where the court refused a writ of habeas corpus for the captured leader of Rhode Island's Dorr Rebellion. McLean wanted to be chief justice, but his pro-Indian decisions and opposition to Peggy Eaton severed his friendly relations with Jackson.

States' rights commercial issues bothered McLean. He supported the rulings of *New York* v. *Miln* (1837), the *License Cases* (1847), and the *Passenger Cases* (1849), but he rejected the doctrine of "selective exclusiveness" announced in *Cooley* v. *Board of Wardens* (1852). His claim for exclusive federal authority led Justice Curtis to label Justices McLean and Wayne "the most high-toned federalists on the bench." Federalism marked McLean's decision in *Piqua Branch of State Bank of Ohio* v. *Knoop* (1854), where he protected a bank charter from state modification. But McLean disallowed claims for a federal common law of *copyright in *Wheaton* v. *Peters* (1834).

McLean declined President John *Tyler's offer of secretary of war, and began looking first to the Whigs and then the Free Soilers. His abhorrence of *slavery was deeply rooted, and in an 1848 open letter he proclaimed that slavery existed only where established by law. He was outvoted in *Prigg* v. *Pennsylvania* (1842), where the Court permitted the kidnapping from a free state of an alleged runaway, but he rejected the claim of attorney William H. Seward in *Jones* v. *Van Zandt* (1847) that a *"higher law" permitted a man to harbor fugitive slaves.

McLean has been blamed, perhaps unfairly, for precipitating the Dred Scott decision (see *Scott* v. *Sandford*, 1857). After Justices McLean and Benjamin R. *Curtis announced plans to file dissents to Justice Samuel *Nelson's initial hands-off decision, the majority changed its mind and agreed to tackle the controverted issues. McLean's dissent read well, although in research and argument Justice Curtis's had the edge.

The case made McLean a possible presidential contender despite his advancing age. His name was mentioned in 1860 at the Constitutional Union convention, and he received twelve votes on the first ballot at the Republican convention. In early 1861 his health failed, and he died in Cincinnati on 4 April 1861.

McLean's persistent quest for the presidency prejudiced both contemporary and historical opinion against him. In 1848 Senator Henry S. Foote charged McLean violated *judicial ethics, but there is little to suggest that partisan considerations influenced McLean's decisions. Forcing Chief Justice Roger B. *Taney to commit the court's worst "self-inflicted wound" may have been his greatest contribution to American history.

□ Don E. Fehrenbacher, *The Dred Scott Case: Its Significance in American Law and Politics* (1978). Frank Otto Gatel, "John McLean," in *The Justices of the United States Supreme Court, 1789–1969*, edited by Leon Friedman and Fred L. Israel, vol. 1 (1969), pp. 535–570.

Michael B. Dougan

**McReynolds, James Clark** (b. Elkton, Ky., 3 Feb. 1862; d. Washington, D.C., 24 Aug., 1946; interred Elkton Cemetery), associate justice, 1914–1941. The son of a noted surgeon, McReynolds attended Vanderbilt University, where he graduated as valedictorian of the class of 1882. Although his early intellectual leanings were toward the natural sciences, McReynolds developed keen interests in both law and politics, which led him to study law at the University of Virginia. At Virginia, McReynolds was greatly

*James Clark McReynolds*

influenced by Professor John B. Minor, a man of stern morality and firm conservative convictions. McReynolds graduated from the law department at Virginia in 1884.

After a brief stint as personal secretary to United States Senator (and later Supreme Court Justice) Howell E. *Jackson, McReynolds established a law practice in Nashville. Within a very few years, McReynolds achieved notoriety as a lawyer, especially as an adviser to business interests. In 1900 he was appointed professor of commercial law, insurance, and corporations at Vanderbilt University.

McReynolds's first foray into public life came in 1886 when he mounted an unsuccessful campaign for a seat in Congress, running as a "Gold Democrat" with substantial Republican support. Despite his affiliation with the Democratic party, McReynolds was appointed assistant attorney general in 1903 by President Theodore Roosevelt. Four years later McReynolds left the Department of Justice and associated with a prestigious law firm in New York City. In 1913 President Woodrow Wilson made McReynolds his attorney general. The following year Wilson nominated him to succeed Supreme Court Justice Horace *Lurton.

As a Supreme Court justice, McReynolds was a staunch conservative whose participation in numerous constitutional decisions had a profound effect on both law and public policy, especially in relation to the *First Amendment, the civil rights of minorities, and the rights of the accused. Above all, McReynolds opposed the growing social and economic regulatory power of government and believed that the Constitution fairly committed the nation to a policy of laissez-faire capitalism (see LAISSEZ-FAIRE CONSTITUTIONALISM).

McReynolds is probably best remembered as one of the Four Horsemen (along with Justices George *Sutherland, Willis *Van Devanter and Pierce *Butler), so called because they consistently voted as a bloc against *New Deal legislation such as the National Industrial Recovery Act of 1933 (*Schechter Poultry Corporation v. United States, 1935), the Agricultural Adjustment Act of 1933 (United States v. *Butler, 1936), and the Bituminous Coal Act of 1935 (*Carter v. Carter Coal Co., 1936).

Prior to 1937 the Four Horsemen were joined in their opposition to New Deal legislation by moderate members of the Court. Suddenly, in 1937, the moderates (Chief Justice Charles Evans *Hughes and Justice Owen *Roberts) shifted their positions and joined the liberals on the Court (Justices Louis *Brandeis, Benjamin *Cardozo, and Harlan F. *Stone) to create a pro–New Deal majority. After this "constitutional revolution" and until his retirement in 1941, McReynolds became a dissenting voice on the Court, protesting what he considered to be unconstitutional exercises of power by the federal government. For example, in *Steward Machine Co. v. Davis (1937), McReynolds dissented from a decision of the Court upholding the Social Security Act, saying, "I can not find any authority in the Constitution for making the Federal Government the great almoner of public charity throughout the United States" (p. 603).

As a person, McReynolds was often rude, impatient, and sarcastic. He detested tobacco and prohibited others from smoking in his presence. His attitudes toward women, especially female attorneys, were likewise intolerant. Perhaps one of his least endearing characteristics was his thoroughgoing anti-Semitism, which prevented him from being civil to his Jewish brethren Brandeis and Cardozo. Yet McReynolds was known to be kind to the pages who worked at the Court and was especially sympathetic to children. Perhaps nothing illustrated McReynolds's charity toward children as much as his generous support of thirty-three young victims of the German bombardment of England in 1941.

Despite his love of children, McReynolds remained a lifelong bachelor. After his retirement in 1941, he continued to live in Washington until he died of pneumonia. He left his entire estate to charity.

(See also HISTORY OF THE COURT: THE DEPRESSION AND THE RISE OF LEGAL LIBERALISM.)

John M. Scheb II

**Metro Broadcasting v. Federal Communications Commission,** 110 S.Ct. 2997 (1990) argued 28 Mar. 1990, decided 27 June 1990 by vote of 5 to 4;

Brennan for the Court, O'Connor, Kennedy, Scalia and Rehnquist in dissent. In affirming the power of Congress to enact policies that favor African-Americans and other minorities, the Court upheld two federal *affirmative action programs intended to increase minority ownership of broadcast licenses. One of the major issues in contention was whether the FCC's desire to promote diversification in programming is served by its policy to integrate broadcast ownership. The majority held that congressional and FCC findings supported a sufficiently strong likelihood that diversity will be promoted by enlarging the numbers of underrepresented groups among owners. The specific groups named by the FCC were persons of "black, Hispanic surnamed, American Eskimo, Aluet, American Indian and Asiatic American extraction."

For the majority, congressional findings were persuasive not alone because of their authority but because the legislature acts as the expression of the common national interest. The Court's opinion also gave consideration to the historical context in which issues relating to affirmative action arise. The dissents doubted the sufficiency of the expression of legislative intent and questioned the assumption that an individual minority station owner would structure programming differently than a nonminority owner.

Beyond upholding the two affirmative action programs in question, the ruling was significant because it declared following *Fullilove v. Klutznick (1980) and rejecting the contrary implications of *Richmond v. J. A. Croson Co. (1989), that the federal government had greater authority than state and local governments to require affirmative action measures in the granting of licenses and other privileges. With this opinion the Court for the first time sustained an affirmative action program not intended as a remedy for past or present unlawful discrimination but as a means of promoting a policy for the future.

(See also RACE AND RACISM.)

Herbert Hill

**Meyer v. Nebraska,** 262 U.S. 390 (1923), argued 3 Feb. 1923, decided 4 June 1923 by vote of 7 to 2; McReynolds for the Court, Holmes, joined by Sutherland, in dissent. The Supreme Court as early as 1923 recognized the right of citizens to conduct their own lives, when it struck down a Nebraska law prohibiting the teaching of modern languages other than English to children who had not passed the eighth grade. Meyer taught in a parochial school and used a German bible history as a text for reading. The Court defined the issue as whether the 1919 statute was a violation of the liberty protected by the Due Process Clause of the *Fourteenth Amendment. Seven Justices maintained that it was. Dissenting on the basis of judicial restraint, Justice Oliver W. Holmes, contending that all citizens in the United States should speak a common tongue, argued that the Nebraska "experiment" was reasonable and not an infringement upon Fourteenth Amendment liberty. "That liberty," McReynolds argued for the Court, denotes the right of the individual "to contract, to engage in . . . common occupations, to acquire useful knowledge, to marry, to establish a home and bring up children, to worship God according to the dictates of his own conscience, and generally to enjoy privileges, essential to the orderly pursuit of happiness by free men" (p. 399). Such a view marked the emergence of a new branch of substantive *due process.

Although *Meyer* languished in doctrinal obscurity for forty years, it resurfaced in the 1960s as an important precedent for a constitutional right of *privacy.

(See also EDUCATION.)

Paul L. Murphy

**Miami Herald Publishing Co. v. Tornillo,** 418 U.S. 241 (1974), argued 17 Apr. 1974, decided 25 June 1974 by vote of 9 to 0; Burger for the Court, Brennan, Rehnquist, and White concurring. In this case, the Supreme Court took up the issue of whether a Florida statute that granted a political candidate the right to equal space to reply to newspaper attacks on his personal character or official record violated the *First Amendment guarantee of a free press.

In 1972, the *Miami Herald* had twice printed editorials critical of Pat Tornillo, a local teachers' union leader and candidate for the state house of representatives. In response to the newspaper's criticism and in accordance with Florida's 1913 "right to reply" statute, Tornillo demanded that the *Herald* print verbatim his replies to the negative editorials. When the newspaper refused to comply, Tornillo filed suit. After a circuit court declared the statute unconstitutional, the Florida Supreme Court, in *Tornillo* v. *Miami Herald Publishing Company* (1973), reversed the decision on appeal, upholding the right to reply law as furthering the "broad societal interest in the free flow of information to the public" (p. 82).

On appeal to the Supreme Court, the justices reversed the judgment of the state court by holding that the statute was a clear violation of the First Amendment guarantee of a free press. "The choice of material to go into a newspaper, and the decisions made as to limitations on the size and content of the paper," wrote Chief Justice Warren *Burger, "and treatment of public issues and public officials—whether fair or unfair—constitute the exercise of editorial control and judgment" (p. 258). Government regulation of this crucial process, the Court believed, violated the constitutional guarantees of a free press. In striking down the law, the Court applied precedents that rejected government-enforced access to newspapers beginning with *Associated Press* v. *United States* (1945) but overlooked past decisions that upheld "right of reply" regulations

in news broadcasting, particularly the Court's opinion in *Red Lion Broadcasting Co.* v. *Federal Communications Commission* (1969).

(See also LIBEL; REPLY, RIGHT OF; SPEECH AND THE PRESS.)

Timothy S. Huebner

**Michael M. v. Superior Court of Sonoma County,** 450 U.S. 464 (1981), argued 4 Nov. 1980, decided 23 Mar. 1981 by vote of 5 to 4; Rehnquist for plurality including Burger, Stewart, and Powell; Stewart concurring, Blackmun concurring in judgment; Brennan (with White and Marshall) and Stevens dissenting. This case presented an *equal protection challenge to the statutory rape law of California. Under that law, when two people between the ages fourteen and seventeen engaged in heterosexual intercourse, the male was guilty of statutory rape but the female was not. The California Supreme Court, applying *strict scrutiny, had nonetheless upheld the law.

The U.S. Supreme Court plurality applied the *Craig* v. *Boren* (1976) test of *intermediate scrutiny and upheld the law. The prevention of teenage pregnancy, said the plurality, was an important governmental interest. This interest was "substantially furthered" by this statute, since females and males were not (especially without the "equaling" effects of this law) similarly situated with regard to the burdens of pregnancy. Moreover, the plurality accepted California's convincing argument that a statutory rape law that was neutral with regard to *gender would be unenforceable because both culpable parties would be afraid to report the offense. In concurrence Justice Potter *Stewart asserted that a law may reasonably treat the sexes differently where, as here, they are not similarly situated.

Justice Harry *Blackmun's decisive fifth vote endorsed the plurality's *Craig* reasoning but complained about the Court majority's earlier insensitivity to pregnant women when it had refused to require Medicaid coverage for *abortions. He added lengthy excerpts from the trial testimony that seemed to show that this case involved a forcible, but difficult to prove, rape.

The dissents, too, applied *Craig* but found that this statute failed the test. Justice William J. *Brennan argued that California had not proved that its law was a greater deterrent to teenage pregnancy than a gender-neutral law would be. Justice John Paul *Stevens suggested that a law might punish whichever sex partner was the aggressor, or the more willing, but that to punish only one of two equally willing participants was irrational.

Leslie Friedman Goldstein

**Michigan Department of State Police v. Sitz,** 496 U.S. 444 (1990), argued 27 Feb. 1990, decided 14 June 1990 by vote of 6 to 3; Rehnquist for the Court, Blackmun concurring, Brennan, Marshall, and Stevens in dissent. Michigan had established a highway sobriety checkpoint program with specific guidelines regarding operation of the checkpoints, site selection, and publicity. In its first operation, state police arrested two persons out of 126 vehicles for driving under the influence of alcohol. Before the program could continue, a group of licensed Michigan drivers sued on the grounds that the checkpoint operation violated the *Fourth Amendment, in that it constituted a warrantless and unreasonable search and seizure. The drivers won their case in the lower courts, with the state tribunals ruling that although the state had a legitimate interest in curbing drunken driving, the checkpoint program constituted a substantial intrusion on individual liberties.

The Supreme Court reversed and ruled that the state courts had erred in interpreting the balancing test for administrative searches established in *United States* v. *Martinez-Fuerte* (1976; administrative search at borders for illegal aliens) and *Brown* v. *Texas* (1979; requirements for identification after a lawful stop). Chief Justice William Rehnquist agreed with the lower courts and the state that Michigan had a substantial and legitimate interest in curbing drunken driving.

The lower courts had erred, however, in applying the criteria of fear engendered in administrative searches. For Fourth Amendment purposes, the "fear and surprise" to be considered are not those of drunken drivers apprehensive of arrest but that engendered in law-abiding drivers confronting an administrative search. The majority therefore found the sobriety checkpoint program consistent with Fourth Amendment safeguards.

(See also SEARCH WARRANT RULE, EXCEPTIONS TO.)

Melvin I. Urofsky

**Michigan v. Long,** 463 U.S. 1032 (1983), argued 23 Feb. 1983, decided 6 July 1983 by vote of 6 to 3; O'Connor for the Court, Blackmun concurring, Brennan, Marshall, and Stevens in dissent. The Supreme Court's most recent development of the *"independent and adequate state grounds" doctrine arose from a Michigan Supreme Court case holding that both the federal Constitution's *Fourth Amendment and the state constitution's counterpart proscribed the search of an automobile. State court opinions like *Long* are often ambiguous about which constitutional provision forms the foundation of their holding. In *Long*, the Supreme Court announced a new presumption of state dependence on federal law, declaring that it will assume the state court relied on federal law when the state court decision "fairly appears to rest primarily on federal law, or to be interwoven with federal law and when the adequacy and independence of any possible state law ground is not clear from the face of the opinion" (pp. 1040–1041). Only when a state court's opinion or judgment incorporates a "plain statement" that "the federal cases are being used only for the

purpose of guidance, and do not themselves compel the result that the court has reached" and that the decision rests on "bona fide separate, adequate, and independent" state grounds will the Supreme Court decline to undertake direct review of the decision (p. 1041).

The *Long* decision has generated substantial debate. Some contend that it preserves the integrity and uniformity of federal law by enabling the Supreme Court to review state decisions arguably interpreting the federal Constitution, avoids the potential for issuing *advisory opinions, shows respect for the independence of the state courts by abandoning the Court's prior "ad hoc" approach to state court decisions, and provides an opportunity for state courts to develop state law. Others argue that *Long* reflects the Supreme Court's animosity to expansion of individual rights, noting that presumptive jurisdiction extends only to those cases in which a state court affirms rights but not to those in which it rejects rights claims.

(See also STATE CONSTITUTION AND INDIVIDUAL RIGHTS; STATE COURTS.)

Shirley S. Abrahamson and Charles G. Curtis, Jr.

**Micou, William Chatfield** (b. 1806; d. New Orleans, La., 1854), unconfirmed nominee to the Supreme Court. Micou was a prominent New Orleans attorney. On 24 Feb. 1853 Whig President Millard Fillmore appointed Micou to fill the vacancy caused by the death of Justice John *McKinley. Fillmore had already unsuccessfully nominated Edward A. *Bradford (a New Orleans lawyer) and George E. *Badger, senator from North Carolina, to the seat. On the failure of the Badger nomination, Fillmore offered the position to Judah P. Benjamin, newly elected Whig senator from Louisiana. Benjamin declined the offer but suggested his law partner Micou. The Democratic majority in the Senate, however, failed to confirm the appointment. Within a month the new Democratic president, Franklin Pierce, had appointed John A. *Campbell.

(See also NOMINEES, REJECTION OF.)

Elizabeth B. Monroe

**Midnight Judges.** See JUDICIARY ACTS OF 1801 AND 1802.

**Military Justice** is the system of legal policies, procedures, and penalties applicable to persons under the jurisdiction of the armed services. Congressional rules for American military justice, first adopted in 1775, drew heavily upon the British Articles of War. Although there have been some minor modifications at varying times in our history, from 1775 until 1951 administration of American military justice remained virtually the same. Intended to be rapid in executions, real in example, and rigorous in application, the principles of military justice have been designed for a military environment rather than administration in local courthouses before civilian judges. Moreover, unlike its civilian counterpart, military justice remains inextricably connected to military discipline.

Responsibility for the administration of military justice rests primarily with Congress, with one of its mandates under Article I of the Constitution being to make rules for the governance of the armed services. The president's role as commander in chief also can apply in this area, however. Generally, these two sources of constitutional authority complement rather than collide with each other. Congress has established general regulations for military justice, the latest complete revision being the Uniform Code of Military Justice (UCMJ), adopted in 1950, while the source for more specific provisons is the Manual for Courts Martial, which has traditionally been issued in the name of the president.

Before 1950, the army and navy each had independent institutions of military justice. A single military justice system applicable to all branches of the service was a logical corollary to the unification of the armed services in 1948. Such a statute was drafted in 1948–1949 by the office of Secretary of Defense James Forrestal, and President Harry S. Truman signed this Uniform Code of Military Justice into law in 1950. Although the code makes extensive use of federal rules of evidence, it is the basis of a separate body of jurisprudence, even having its own national reporting system. While military-justice procedures are similar in many ways to civilian criminal law, there are some important differences. Contrary to popular assumption, in certain instances military justice has been more solicitous of the rights of defendants than its civilian counterpart.

The Uniform Code provides for a pretrial investigation that is considerably fairer than the *grand jury proceedings common to civilian criminal law. The military also required appointment of *counsel and banned compulsory *self-incrimination long before the Supreme Court undertook these same actions. On the other hand, military justice has long had the potential for abuse in a matter unique to itself—the role of the commander. Today, however, the commander's authority is much more restricted than it was prior to 1950. Still, the commander—also known as the convening authority—has the authority to select the members of a court-martial, a procedure very different from that of civilian criminal trials. While the commander must approve the sentence, he or she may not increase—but can decrease—the penalty meted out by the court. The trial judge, trial counsel (the equivalent of the prosecutor in civilian court), and defense counsel are all appointed independently of the commander. Because military policy holds a commander responsible for his or her command, it is not surprising that military justice

grants the commander a dominant voice in initiating the trial process and in approving or rejecting the outcome, unless, of course, it is an acquittal.

On a formal level, the military has three kinds of courts-material: summary, special, and general. The uniform code also provides for a more informal and less stringent disciplinary proceeding known as nonjudicial punishment. Still called "captain's mast" in the navy, this type of process is usually held before the commanding officer alone. The code establishes an extensive appellate review system within the armed services: every branch has its own court of review, and above them is the U.S. Court of Military Appeals, which is composed of five judges drawn from civil life and appointed by the president for fifteen-year terms. The U.S. Supreme Court can hear certain cases on appeal from the Court of Military Appeals, but for the most part military justice and the courts that dispense it remain free from intervention by their civilian counterparts.

(See also MILITARY TRIALS AND MARTIAL LAW.)

☐ Joseph W. Bishop, Jr., *Justice under Fire* (1974). Robinson O. Everett, *Military Justice in the Armed Forces of the United States* (1956).              Jonathan Lurie

**Military Trials and Martial Law.** Although these two kinds of legal procedure are often conceptually linked, they are in fact separate and widely disparate. Military trials, usually referred to as courts-martial, are judicial proceedings conducted under the control of military, rather than civilian, authorities. Martial law, more difficult to define, can be described as simply the will of the commanding general.

Courts-martial are the oldest federal tribunals in American legal history. Rules for their operation were enacted by the Continental Congress in 1775, a year before the *Declaration of Independence and twelve years before the Constitution was written. Historically, the U.S. Supreme Court has, with few exceptions, declined to accept *appeals from or to enjoin military trials. The Court states its rationale for this position in *Dynes* v. *Hoover* (1858), in which it ruled that, where a military trial has been duly authorized and has exercised lawful jurisdiction, its findings cannot be altered by civilian courts. The Court based its conclusion on Article I of the Constitution, which specifically grants Congress the authority to make rules and regulations for the governance of the armed forces, including military trials. This authority has usually been held to be independent of the *judicial power conferred by *Article III. Further, the *Fifth Amendment specifically exempts courts-martial from *grand jury proceedings.

This virtual independence of military courts from supervision by civilian courts has posed difficulties for litigants seeking relief from improper verdicts. They have had to attack the military judicial process collaterally by, for example, challenging the jurisdiction of the military court to try them in the first place. The Supreme Court has been sympathetic to this tactic only on rare occasion. The case of *Ex parte \*Milligan* (1866) held that military courts could not try a civilian when civilian courts were open and outside the theater of war, and civil government in control of the community. In *O'Callahan v. Parker* (1969), a divided Court held that in order for a military trial to be lawful, the offense for which the defendant is tried must be "service connected": that is, it must be directly related to the functions of the military. Less than twenty years later, however, the court overruled *O'Callahan* and substituted service status as the criterion for military trial. In recent years the Court has made it clear that military appellate procedures are to be the primary, and often the only, route available to litigants involved in military trials.

American legal scholars have had difficulty in defining martial law. A slightly more elegant definition than the "will of the commanding general" might be that martial law is simply whatever it takes to preserve governmental authority within an area and protect it from enemy attack. In the American context, martial law is the rare exception. It presumes a breakdown in normal civilian governmental operations, and it has always been conceived of as a strictly temporary substitute for civil public law and administration. Its imposition is not authorized by specific constitutional provision, and because martial law has usually been imposed during a time of crisis, the Supreme Court has tried to avoid placing itself in conflict with the military.

The *Milligan* case might appear to be an exception to this tendency. In actuality, the dispute concerned a civilian, not a member of the military, and the decision was handed down long after *Civil War hostilities had ended, when its implementation could do no harm to the war effort. Indeed, in the earlier case of *Ex parte Vallandigham* (1864), involving much the same question, the Court refused to intervene. This preference was again reflected during *World War II, when the Court refused to entertain a challenge to military actions leading to the internment of Japanese-Americans in concentration camps. Thus, to some extent, martial law and judicial tolerance for military-trial procedures remain difficult to reconcile with traditional conceptions of American civil rights. Historically, the demands of "military necessity," especially when raised in time of war, have been and probably will continue to be inhibiting factors in the Supreme Court's decisions.

(See also MILITARY JUSTICE.)

□ Charles A. Shanor and Timothy P. Terrell, *Military Law* (1980).                          Jonathan Lurie

**Milkovich v. Lorain Journal Co.** 110 S.Ct. 2695 (1990), argued 24 Apr. 1990, decided 21 June 1990

by vote of 7 to 2. Rehnquist for the Court, Brennan, joined by Marshall, in dissent. This case demonstrated the complexity of late twentieth-century defamation law. In 1975 a high school coach sued a sports columnist for suggesting that the coach had lied during an investigation of a post-meet brawl. For nearly fifteen years, the case bounced, back and forth, through Ohio's courts until the Lorain *Journal* finally secured a summary judgment on the grounds that the sports column was a constitutionally protected opinion.

The Supreme Court overturned this holding and sent the case back for trial on the merits. According to Chief Justice William *Rehnquist, some courts, such as those in Ohio, mistakenly believed *Gertz v. Welch* (1974) created special, *First Amendment protection for any libelous statement that might be labeled an "opinion." Nothing in *Gertz*, according to Rehnquist, justified such a constitutionally based defense. Columns that implied any defamatory assertions, statements that could be proved to be true or false, might provide the basis for a *libel suit, even by public officials. Plaintiffs, of course, still had to meet all of the strict constitutional protections set forth in other cases, and Rehnquist thus used *Milkovich* to restate the constitutionallly based defense available in defamation cases.

Justice William *Brennan also rejected claims of a separate privilege for "opinion" but dissented from the holding that the sports column implied any factual claims; it simply offered the writer's "conjecture" about the coach's behavior, not any implications of fact, and was a constitutionally protected publication.

                                        Norman L. Rosenberg

**Miller, Samuel Freeman** (b. Richmond, Ky., 5 April 1816; d. Washington, D.C., 13 Oct. 1890; interred Oakland Cemetery, Kelkuka, Iowa), associate justice, 1862–1890. Samuel Miller, appointed by President Abraham Lincoln in 1862, helped shape the Supreme Court's early interpretation of the Civil War Amendments, particularly the *Fourteenth. A product of antebellum midwestern antislavery politics, Justice Miller developed a moderately conservative jurisprudence of the Fourteenth Amendment as the author of the Court's majority opinion in the *Slaughterhouse Cases* (1873). He served on the Court until his death 1890.

Miller was the son of Frederick Miller, a farmer, and Patsy Freeman. The future justice initially trained as a physician, earning a medical degree in 1838 from Transylvania University. He married Lucy Ballinger in 1839 (d. 1854) and Elizabeth Winter Reeves in 1857. After a decade-long medical practice, Miller taught himself the law. He was admitted to the bar in 1847. Active in antebellum politics, Miller's early sympathies lay with antislavery Whig candidates. As proslavery sentiment increased in Kentucky in the late

1840s, Miller moved to Iowa, a state considerably more hospitable to his emancipationist views (see SLAVERY). Miller was active in Iowa Republican politics and supported Lincoln's presidential candidacy in 1860. Lincoln in July 1862 appointed Miller to the Court.

Miller's early voting reflected his strong commitment to the Union. During the *Civil War, Justice Miller voted to sustain Lincoln's decisions to suspend *habeas corpus and to try civilians by courts-martial. After the war, Miller voted to uphold the constitutionality of loyalty oaths required of former Confederates seeking to hold office.

Miller left his most enduring mark on the Court's constitutional jurisprudence through his reading of the Fourteenth Amendment. As the author of the majority opinion in the *Slaughterhouse Cases*, Miller limited the effectiveness of the amendment's *"privileges or immunities" clause as a vehicle to protect individuals against state deprivations of rights. In the opinion, Miller articulated the view that the Fourteenth Amendment was meant to provide former slaves a measure of equality before the law with whites, not to expand the liberties of the general population.

Like the majority of the Court in the 1870s and 1880s, Miller steered a middle course in interpreting the Fourteenth Amendment. He viewed the amendment as prohibiting state-sponsored racial discrimination, but he generally refused to recognize its other guarantees. Miller voted with majorities in *United States* v. *Cruikshank* (1876) and the *Civil Rights Cases* (1883) to curtail federal efforts to combat private discrimination under the Fourteenth Amendment. Miller took a somewhat broader view of the *Fifteenth Amendment, concluding for a unanimous Court in *Ex parte* *Yarbrough* (1884) that that amendment gave Congress the power to protect black voting rights against private interference.

Consistent with his limited view of the Fourteenth Amendment, Miller favored granting states wide latitudes in the regulation of business. He also saw the necessity for greater use of the Commerce Clause to achieve uniformity in federal regulation, a position reflected in his opinion in *Wabash* v. *Illinois* (1886) that held that and Illinois statute on rate discrimination interfered with interstate commerce (see COMMERCE POWER).

Miller did not completely abandon politics while on the Court. He, along with Justices Nathan *Clifford, Stephen J. *Field, Noah *Swayne, and Joseph *Bradley, served on the electoral commission that counted the electoral votes in the disputed Hayes-Tilden election (see EXTRAJUDICIAL ACTIVITIES). President Ulysses Grant considered elevating Miller to *chief justice before turning instead to Morrison R. *Waite. In the 1880s Miller was considered by some Republican party leaders as a potential presidential candidate.

*Samuel Freeman Miller*

Throughout his tenure on the Court, Justice Miller's jurisprudence was characterized by a pragmatic concern for preserving what he viewed as necessary governmental powers.

□ Charles Fairman, *Mr. Justice Miller and the Supreme Court: 1862–1890* (1939). Robert J. Cottrol

**Miller v. California,** 413 U.S. 15 (1973), argued 18–19 Jan. and 7 Nov. 1972; **Paris Adult Theatre v. Slaton,** 413 U.S. 49 (1973), argued 19 Oct. 1972, both decided 21 June 1973 by vote of 5 to 4; Burger for the Court, Douglas, Brennan, Stewart, and Marshall in dissent. *Miller* v. *California* articulates the test for obscenity that resolved the dilemma of *First Amendment protection for allegedly obscene materials first identified in *Roth* v. *United States* (1957). Chief Justice Warren *Burger's majority opinion stated that material could be obscene only if "(a) the average person, applying contemporary community standards, would find that the work, taken as a whole, appeals to the prurient interest; [and] (b) the work depicts or describes, in a patently offensive way, sexual conduct specifically defined by the applicable state law; and (c) the work, taken as a whole, lacks serious literary, artistic, political, or scientific value" (p. 25). Burger went on to say that under this test "no one will be subject to prosecution for the sale or exposure of obscene materials unless those materials depict or describe patently offensive 'hard core' sexual conduct" (p. 27).

One of the most significant contributions of *Miller* was its identification of the geographic criterion of the contemporary community standards against which obscenity was to be measured. Burger held that both prurient interest and patent offensiveness could constitutionally be measured by local rather than national standards. Many persons assumed at the time that the definition of obscenity and thus the coverage of obscenity statutes could vary significantly from place to place. Subsequent cases revealed that this reading of *Miller* was unjustified.

The Court first indicated that the scope of local variation in the identification of prurient interest or patent offensiveness was much narrower than supposed. In *Jenkins* v. *Georgia* (1974) Justice William H. *Rehnquist stated that the film "Carnal Knowledge" could not, in light of the First Amendment, be found to appeal to the prurient interest, or be found patently offensive, regardless of the views of the Georgia courts and Georgia's community standards. This established a quite narrow range for permissible variance in local community standards. Moreover, in *Smith* v. *United States* (1977) and in *Pope* v. *Illinois* (1987) the Court required that the third prong of the *Miller* test, lack of serious literary, artistic, political, or scientific value, was to be measured against national standards. A work considered nationally to have literary, artistic, political, or scientific value could not constitutionally be found to be obscene regardless of whether it appealed to prurient interest or was patently offensive, and regardless of the standards of any community smaller than the nation as a whole.

*Miller* nevertheless remains controversial, in part because of continuing doubts about the extent to which any obscenity regulation can be squared with the First Amendment and in part because the factors identified by *Miller* may not be appropriate for issues of violence against or degradation of women. Feminists' attacks on pornography as a form inciting violence directed at women provide the background for antipornography ordinances such as that struck down by the Seventh Circuit Court of Appeals in *American Booksellers Association, Inc.* v. *Hudnut* (1985) (see also GENDER).

Miller's companion case, *Paris Adult Theatre* v. *Slaton*, reaffirmed the *Roth* holding that obscenity was outside the coverage of the First Amendment. Thus its regulation may be tested only against the minimal scrutiny of the rational basis test that the Court uses for regulation not restricting specific constitutional rights. This reaffirmation of *Roth* came as a surprise partly because the development of the right to *privacy since 1957 had suggested that state interference with the sexual activities of consenting adults, including watching highly sexually explicit films, was constitutionally suspect. But Chief Justice Burger's majority opinion in *Paris Adult Theatre* rejected the argument, and started a process of restricting the protections for privacy identified in cases such as *Griswold* v. *Connecticut* (1965) and *Roe* v. *Wade* (1973) to matters dealing with *marriage, *family, and procreation. In dissent, Justice William J. *Brennan, the author of the majority

opinion in *Roth*, maintained that the Court's inability since 1957 to come up with a workable test for obscenity made the whole enterprise impermissibly vague, especially since that vagueness inhibited the availability of nonobscene materials clearly protected by the First Amendment. Nevertheless, the majority in these two cases reaffirmed the view that, whatever the philosophical permissibility of the regulation of morals and private sexual conduct, the arguments in favor of some regulation were at least plausible enough to satisfy the minimal scrutiny of the rational basis standard.

(See also OBSCENITY AND PORNOGRAPHY.)

□ Frederick Schauer, "Speech and 'Speech'—Obscenity and 'Obscenity': An Exercise in the Interpretation of Constitutional Language," *Georgetown Law Journal* 67 (1979): 899–933.                                    Frederick Schauer

**Milligan, Ex parte,** 71 U.S. 2 (1866), argued 5–13 Mar. 1866, decided 3 Apr. 1866 by vote of 9 to 0; opinions released 17 Dec. 1866; Davis for the Court, Chase, joined by Miller, Swayne, and Wayne, concurring. The *Milligan* case grew out of restrictions on civil liberties in the North during the *Civil War and presented the Court with fundamental questions concerning military authority over civilians and the government's emergency powers in time of war.

In late 1864, United States army officials in Indiana arrested Lambdin P. Milligan and several other prominent antiwar Democrats, charging them with conspiracy to seize munitions at federal arsenals and to liberate Confederate prisoners held in several northern prison camps. Indiana was not in the theater of military operations, and the defendants could have been tried in federal court for treason. Nevertheless, army officials doubted the reliability of Indiana juries and elected to try the defendants by military commission. This tribunal found Milligan and two other defendants guilty and sentenced them to hang. When Milligan challenged the conviction in the United States Circuit Court in Indianapolis, the two judges disagreed, sending the case to the Supreme Court.

Although the Court announced its decision in April 1866, opinions were not released until December. All nine justices agreed that the military court lacked jurisdiction and that Milligan and the other two prisoners must be released. There was sharp disagreement among the justices, however, on the grounds for the decision.

Writing for the Court, Justice David *Davis emphasized that the Constitution was not suspended in time of emergency, eloquently noting that it was "a law for rulers and people, equally in time of war and peace" (pp. 120–121). Therefore, he concluded that military trial of civilians—which violated constitutional guarantees of indictment by *grand jury and public trial by an impartial jury (see TRIAL BY JURY)—was impermissible where the civil courts remained open. Although the court that had tried Milligan had been established by executive authority, Davis asserted that neither the president nor the Congress could authorize the trial of civilians by military commission as long as the civil courts were open.

A concurrence by Chief Justice Salmon P. *Chase, joined by three other justices, agreed that Milligan should be released. Chase, however, rested his conclusion on statutory grounds, arguing that the Habeas Corpus Act of 1863 (which stipulated that civilians detained by the military must be released if grand juries failed to indict them) had been intended to guarantee trial of civilians in the civil courts. Moreover, Chase disagreed with Davis's assertion that Congress could not authorize military trial of civilians if the civil courts were functioning. Under the war power, Chase argued, Congress could enact legislation necessary for prosecution of the war. If it concluded that the civil courts were incapable of punishing treason, Congress could authorize the military to try offenders.

The Court's opinion was controversial. By late 1866, when the opinions were released, violence against southern African-Americans was growing, and most Republicans believed that military courts were essential to afford the slaves security. Consequently, when President Andrew Johnson used Milligan as justification to reduce military authority in the occupied states, Republicans denounced the Court. Moreover, Davis's opinion led many Republicans to fear that the Court would declare unconstitutional the Reconstruction Act of 1867, which authorized military trial of civilians in the rebel states.

In the twentieth century many commentators have viewed Milligan as a constitutional landmark, and the Court has not repudiated it. Nevertheless, some have criticized Milligan, arguing that by categorically prohibiting imposition of martial law when the civil courts are open, it unduly limited the government's ability to protect national security. The Court itself has not always followed Milligan. In *Duncan v. Kahanamoku (1946), a case challenging the imposition of martial law in Hawaii during *World War II, the Court ruled against the government. The majority, however, rested its decision on congressional legislation governing Hawaii rather than on the constitutional principles established in Milligan. Moreover, in acquiescing in the government's internment of Japanese-Americans during World War II, the Court ignored the limits on the government's emergency powers suggested by Milligan.

(See also HABEAS CORPUS; MILITARY TRIALS AND MARTIAL LAW; WAR POWERS.)

□ Harold M. Hyman and William M. Wiecek, *Equal Justice under Law: Constitutional Development, 1835–1875* (1982). Donald G. Nieman

**Milliken v. Bradley,** 418 U.S. 717 (1974), argued 27 Feb. 1974, decided 25 July 1974, by vote of 5 to 4; Burger for the Court, Stewart concurring, Douglas, White, Marshall, and Brennan in dissent. In *School Board of Richmond* v. *State Board of Education* (1973), an equally divided Court—with Justice Lewis *Powell not participating—was unable to decide whether a district court could require the merger of three school districts in order to eliminate racial segregation in one. A year later, in *Milliken* v. *Bradley*, a bitterly divided Court ruled 5 to 4 that segregative practices in one district did not warrant relief that included another nonsegregating district. Thus, the Court that had implicitly extended *Green* v. *County Board* (1968) integration to the North only thirteen months before in *Keyes* v. *School District No. 1* (1973) drew the remedial line at the offending school district's boundary. For the first time since even before *Brown* v. *Board of Education* (1954), the Court refused to endorse a desegregation remedy sought by the *National Association for the Advancement of Colored People (NAACP), which had developed the litigation strategy attacking the constitutionality of Jim Crow schools beginning in the mid-1930s.

The Detroit school district, then fifth largest in the nation, covered 140 square miles; at the time of the suit in 1970, its school population of almost 290,000 was 65 percent black and 35 percent white—a substantial recent growth in black population owing to white flight to nearby suburbs; for the metropolitan area, the proportion of black to white student population was 19 to 81 percent. The district court found that the Detroit school district had engaged in segregative practices and concluded that the only way to achieve Green-mandated establishment of a unitary school system was to order busing that included some of the surrounding suburban districts. The court of appeals affirmed, fearing that not to do so would "nullify Brown v. Board of Education (1954)" and restore the "*separate but equal doctrine" of Plessy v. Ferguson (1896) (p. 249).

Chief Justice *Burger, who wrote the *Swann v. Charlotte-Mecklenburg County Board of Education (1971) opinion and affirmed the lower courts on the basis of the fit between constitutional violation and corresponding remedy, wrote for the narrow majority. His statement of the issues in Milliken signaled its outcome: "[may a federal court] impose a multi-district, area-wide remedy to a single-district de jure segregation problem absent any finding that the other included school districts have failed to operate unitary school systems within their districts, absent any claim or finding that boundary lines of any affected school district were established with the purpose of fostering racial segregation [and] absent any finding that the included districts committed acts which affected segregation within the other districts" (p. 721).

Since the suburban districts had not caused

or contributed to the violation, they logically could not be part of the remedy without a "drastic expansion of the constitutional right itself, an expansion without support in either constitutional principle or precedent" (p. 747). The chief justice may have been right but the difficulty was that the same thing could have been said of the nature of the desegregation cases from the beginning.

The dissenters echoed the anxieties of the court of appeals, but to no avail. The dissent by Justice Thurgood *Marshall, who had argued *Brown I* and *II* for the NAACP, bitterly complained that the Court was now turning back the clock in response "to a perceived public mood that we have gone far enough in enforcing the Constitution's guarantee of equal justice" (p. 814).

The gradual ratcheting out of remedies to implement *Brown I* ended as abruptly and as conclusorily as it began, twenty years and two months earlier. Subsequent cases fine-tuned the grounds for identifying constitutional violations and added minor remedial weapons, but *Milliken* v. *Bradley,* by rejecting so-called interdistrict remedies, established the new outer limit of constitutional remedies.

(See also DESEGREGATION REMEDIES; EDUCATION; RACE AND RACISM; SEGREGATION, DE FACTO; SEGREGATION, DE JURE.)

□ J. Harvie Wilkinson, *From Brown to Bakke* (1979).
                                    Dennis J. Hutchinson

**Minersville School District v. Gobitis,** 310 U.S. 586 (1940), argued 25 Apr. 1940, decided 3 June 1940 by vote of 8 to 1; Frankfurter for the Court; Stone in dissent. The first Flag Salute case, *Minersville School District* v. *Gobitis,* revealed the limits the Supreme Court of the liberal Roosevelt pre–World War II era still put on the religion clauses of the *First Amendment (see RELIGION). The Court held that a Jehovah's Witness's child could constitutionally be expelled from public school for refusing to participate in the daily ceremony of saluting the American flag and pledging allegiance to it, even though saluting the flag or reciting the pledge violated the child's religious beliefs against serving gods other than the Almighty.

Admittedly, said Justice Felix *Frankfurter for the majority, it is only when felt necessities of society compel it that the Constitution's free exercise provision can be overridden. But to say that freedom to follow religious conscience has no limits cannot be reconciled with American history.

National unity, he said, is the basis of national security. True enough, the flag is a symbol, but we live by symbols. To salute it is therefore a constitutionally allowable part of a school program, which may be made mandatory. A claim for exceptional immunity may be refused simply because granting it might weaken the effect of the exercise.

Although only Justice Harlan F. *Stone dissented, three years later the decision was reversed, primarily on free speech grounds, in *West Virginia State Board of Education v. Barnette.*
                                    Leo Pfeffer

**Minnesota Rate Cases.** See INTERSTATE COMMERCE COMMISSION.

**Minnesota Twins.** This name of a major-league baseball team was applied by journalists to Chief Justice Warren E. *Burger and Justice Harry A. *Blackmun, both nominated by President Richard M. *Nixon within a year of each other. Both jurists were Minnesotans as well as personal friends.
                                    William M. Wiecek

**Minor v. Happersett,** 21 Wall. (88 U.S.) 162 (1875), argued 9 Feb. 1875, decided 9 Mar. 1875 by vote of 9 to 0; Waite for the Court. The Supreme Court held that a state could constitutionally forbid a woman citizen to vote, despite her invocation of the *citizenship and *privileges or immunities clauses of the *Fourteenth Amendment, the Guarantee Clause (Art. IV, sec. 4); the *Due Process Clause of the *Fifth Amendment, and the prohibition against bills of *attainder (Art. I, sec. 9). Noticeably absent from this list, to a modern eye, are the equal protection and due process clauses of the Fourteenth Amendment.

The case is important as near-contemporary interpretation of the Fourteenth Amendment's *original intent. It is notable for its narrow definition of citizenship "as conveying the idea of membership of a nation, nothing more" (p. 166) and for its firm, unanimous rejection of the Fourteenth Amendment as a source either of a substantive federal suffrage right or of a federal limit on state control of the franchise. Otherwise, neither section 2 of the Fourteenth Amendment nor, later, the *Fifteenth, *Nineteenth, *Twenty-Fourth, and *Twenty-Sixth Amendments would have been necessary. "Certainly," the Court declared, "if the courts can consider any question settled, it is this one. . . . The Constitution, when it conferred citizenship, did not necessarily confer the right of suffrage" (p. 177). This interpretation was substantially, albeit tacitly, abandoned in *Reynolds* v. *Sims* (1964) and *Harper* v. *Virginia State Board of Elections* (1966).

(See also GENDER; VOTE, RIGHT TO.)
                                    Ward E. Y. Elliott

**Minton, Sherman** (b. Georgetown, Ind., 20 Oct. 1890; d. New Albany, Ind., 9 Apr. 1965; interred Holy Trinity Cemetery, New Albany), associate justice, 1949–1956. President Harry S. Truman on 15 September 1949 nominated Minton to be associate justice to replace Wiley B. Rutledge, who had died. Truman and Minton had become friends in the Senate. The *Senate Judiciary

Committee asked Minton to testify before it at his nomination hearings, but he refused, citing the impropriety of asking a sitting judge—he was then serving on the Seventh Circuit Court of Appeals—to testify. The committee acceded to Minton's objections and reported his nomination favorably (9 to 2) without his testimony. After prominent Republicans failed on the Senate floor to have Minton's nomination recommitted, Minton was easily confirmed on 4 October 1949 by a 48-to-16 vote.

Minton was the son of John Evan Minton and Emma Lyvers. After graduating at the top of his law class at Indiana University, Minton took a year of graduate study at Yale Law School. He entered public life as an Indiana public counselor in 1933, nominated for the position by his former law school classmate, Governor Paul V. McNutt. A strong supporter of the *New Deal, Minton successfully ran for the Senate in 1934. Minton's career in the Senate (1935–1941) ended when another former law school classmate and Indianian, Republican Wendell L. Wilkie, swept the state in his 1940 presidential bid and carried Minton's Republican rival into the Senate. In 1941, after Minton's defeat, Franklin D. *Roosevelt appointed Minton an adviser in charge of coordinating military agencies. Later that year the president appointed him to the U.S. Court of Appeals for the Seventh Circuit.

During his term in the Senate, Minton had loyally supported all of President Franklin Roosevelt's legislative initiatives to halt the effects of the Great Depression, including an endorsement of Roosevelt's plan to "pack" the Supreme Court (see COURT-PACKING PLAN). Minton's views about the role of the Supreme Court were shaped in the New Deal: he firmly believed that the judiciary should allow the executive and legislative branches the greatest freedom to create policy and programs with the minimum of interference from the judiciary. In the New Deal era, when the president and Congress were trying to establish administrative agencies and social welfare programs to assist the unemployed against conservative opposition from the Court, Minton appeared a liberal. In the post–World War II "cold war" context, in which anticommunist hysteria inspired governmental repression of free speech and association, Minton's continued, unwavering support of governmental policies made him a conservative (see COMMUNISM AND COLD WAR). Actually, Minton was totally consistent in his views of the relationship between the judiciary and the other branches of government, only the context had changed. In 1952 Minton wrote the majority opinion in Adler v. Board of Education upholding New York's Feinberg Law that barred members of subversive organizations from teaching in public schools and voted with the majority in Carlson v. Landon to allow alien communists to be held without bail if the attorney general thought them a danger to national security. In the

*Sherman Minton*

same year, he was the lone dissenter in the *Youngstown Sheet and Tube Co. v. Sawyer, in which his colleagues invalidated President Truman's seizure of the steel industry (see PRESIDENTIAL EMERGENCY POWERS).

Justice Minton, who had long suffered from pernicious anemia and had circulatory troubles in his legs, retired from the Supreme Court on 15 October 1956 owing to ill health.

□ Catherine A. Barnes, *Men of the Supreme Court: Profiles of the Justices* (1978), pp. 111–113.    N. E. H. Hull

**Miranda v. Arizona,** 384 U.S. 436 (1966), argued 28 Feb. 1966, decided 13 June 1966 by vote of 5 to 4; Warren for the Court, Clark, Harlan, White, and Stewart in dissent. The Warren Court's revolution in American criminal procedure reached its high point (or, depending upon one's perspective, its low point) on 13 June 1966. That day the Court handed down its opinion in *Miranda,* the most famous, and most bitterly criticized, confession case in the nation's history. To some, *Miranda* symbolized the legal system's determination to treat even the lowliest and most despicable criminal suspect with dignity and respect. But to others, especially those who attributed rising crime rates to the softness of judges, the case became a target of abuse.

*Background.* Prior to the decision in *Miranda,* the admissibility of a confession in a state criminal case was governed by the due process "voluntariness" or "totality of the circumstances" test. Under this approach, the courts decided on a case-by-case basis whether the will of the person who confessed had been "broken" or "overborne" or whether the confession had been "voluntary." But it soon became clear that these terms were not being used as tools of analysis, but as mere conclusions. When a court concluded that the "totality" of a suspect's treatment had not been too bad (e.g., although the police had exerted considerable pressure and used some trickery, they had given the suspect a sandwich and permitted him to have a normal night's sleep), it called the resulting confession "voluntary." On the other hand, when a court concluded that the police methods were too offensive or too heavy-handed (considering such factors as the suspect's youth, poor education, or low intelligence), it labeled the resulting confession "involuntary" or "coerced" (see COERCED CONFESSIONS).

The vagueness and unpredictability of the "voluntariness" test, its application (or manipulation) by lower courts so as to validate confessions of doubtful constitutionality, and the inability of the Supreme Court, because of its heavy workload, to review more than one or two state confession cases a year, led a growing number of the justices to search for a more meaningful and more manageable alternative approach. *Miranda* was the culmination of these efforts.

***Facts of the Case.*** Ernesto Miranda, an indigent twenty-three-year-old who had not completed the ninth grade, was arrested at his home and taken directly to a Phoenix, Arizona, police station. There, after being identified by the victim of a rape-kidnapping, he was taken to an "interrogation room," where he was questioned about the crimes. At first, Miranda maintained his innocence, but after two hours of questioning, the police emerged from the room with a signed written confession of guilt. At his trial, the written confession was admitted into evidence and Miranda was found guilty of kidnapping and rape.

Whether Miranda had been told that anything he said could be used against him was unclear. But the police admitted—and this was to prove fatal for the prosecution—that neither before nor during the questioning had Miranda been advised of his right to consult with an attorney before answering any questions or his right to have an attorney present during the interrogation (see COUNSEL, RIGHT TO).

Miranda's confession plainly would have been admissible under the "voluntariness" test. His questioning had been quite mild compared to the objectionable police methods that had rendered a resulting confession "involuntary" or "coerced" in previous cases. But the confession was obtained from Miranda under circumstances that did not satisfy the new constitutional standards the Court was to promulgate in this very case.

A remarkable feature of the American history of confessions law is that until the mid-1960s the privilege against *self-incrimination (the *Fifth Amendment provision that no person "shall be compelled . . . to be a witness against himself") did not apply to the proceedings in the interrogation room or to in-custody police interrogation.

One reason for this situation was that the privilege was not deemed applicable to the states until 1964 and by that time a large body of law pertaining to "involuntary" or "coerced" state confessions had developed (see INCORPORATION DOCTRINE). Moreover, and more important, the prevailing pre-*Miranda* view was that "compelling" someone to testify against himself meant *legal* compulsion. Since a suspect was threatened neither with perjury for testifying falsely nor contempt for refusing to testify at all, it could not be said, ran the argument, that a person undergoing police interrogation was being "compelled" to be "a witness against himself" within the meaning of the privilege—even though under such circumstances a person is likely to assume or to be led by the police to believe that there are legal (or extralegal) sanctions for "refusing to cooperate." Since the police had no lawful authority to make a suspect answer their questions (although, prior to *Miranda*, the police did not have to tell a person that), there was no legal obligation to answer to which a privilege in the technical sense could apply.

Although this reasoning seems quite strained, it prevailed as long as it did probably because of a widely held view that questioning a suspect without advising him of his rights was "indispensable" to law enforcement work. Moreover, the invisibility of police interrogation made it easy for society to be complacent about what really took place in the interrogation room.

On the eve of *Miranda*, however, there was reason to think that the self-incrimination clause would finally apply to the police station. In *Malloy* v. *Hogan* (1964), which did not involve a confession, the Court not only held the privilege against self-incrimination fully applicable to the states but stated by way of dictum (see OBITER DICTUM) that the admissibility of a confession in a state or federal court should be controlled by the Fifth Amendment privilege. The confession rules and the privilege had become intertwined in *Malloy*—and they would be fused in *Miranda*.

***Decision.*** There are three parts to the *Miranda* decision:

1. The Fifth Amendment privilege is available outside of court proceedings and other formal proceedings and serves to protect persons in all settings from being compelled to incriminate themselves. Thus, the privilege applies to informal compulsion exerted by law enforcement officers during "custodial interrogation," that is, questioning initiated by the police after a person has been taken into custody.

2. "An individual swept from familiar surroundings into police custody, surrounded by antagonistic forces, and subjected to the techniques of persuasion described in the [standard police interrogation manuals] cannot be otherwise than under compulsion to speak" (p. 461). Because the custodial interrogation environment "carries its own badge of intimidation" that is "at

odds" with the privilege, "[u]nless adequate protective devices are employed to dispel the compulsion inherent in custodial surroundings," no statement obtained from a person under these circumstances is admissible (pp. 457–458).

**3.** The Constitution does not require adherence to any particular system for dispelling the coercion of custodial interrogation. However, unless the government utilizes other procedures that are at least as effective, in order for a statement to be admissible a suspect must be given the now familiar four-fold *Miranda warning (set forth below) before being subjected to custodial interrogation and must effectively waive his rights before any questioning.

According to *Miranda*, advising a suspect that he has a right to remain silent and that anything he says can be used against him is not sufficient to assure that the suspect's right to choose between silence and speech will remain unfettered throughout the interrogation process. Therefore, a suspect must also be told of his right to counsel, either retained or (if he is indigent) appointed.

Although the warnings need not be given in the exact form described in the *Miranda* opinion—indeed, they are not described exactly the same way throughout the opinion—the substance of each of the following four warnings must be effectively given: (1) you have the right to remain silent; (2) anything you say can and will be used against you; (3) you have the right to talk to a lawyer before being questioned and to have him present when you are being questioned; and (4) if you cannot afford a lawyer, one will be provided for you before any questioning if you so desire.

*Miranda* has been widely criticized as a case that tilted the balance heavily in favor of criminal suspects. However, as the Court recently noted in *Moran* v. *Burbine* (1986), the decision "embodies a carefully crafted balance designed to fully protect *both* the defendant's and society's interests" (p. 433, n. 4).

*Miranda* does not require that a person taken into custody first consult with a lawyer or actually have a lawyer present in order for his waiver of constitutional rights to be valid. The decision's weakness (or saving grace, depending upon one's viewpoint) is that it permits someone subjected to the inherent pressures of police custody to "waive" his rights without actually obtaining the guidance of counsel. That waiver, at least in theory, must be "knowing" and "voluntary."

*Miranda* allows the police to conduct "general-on-the-scene questioning" without providing the warnings. It also allows the police to interview a suspect in his home or office without advising him of his rights, provided the questioning takes place in a context that does not restrict the person's freedom to terminate the meeting.

Moreover, *Miranda* leaves the police free to hear and act upon "volunteered" statements even though the "volunteer" has been taken into custody and neither knows nor is informed of his rights. "Custody" alone does not call for the *Miranda* warnings. It is the impact on the suspect of the interplay between police interrogation and police custody that makes "custodial police interrogation" so corrosive and calls for "adequate protective devices" (*Illinois* v. *Perkins,* 1990).

Even when warnings and the waiver of rights are required, *Miranda* permits the police to give the warnings and to obtain waivers without the presence of any disinterested observer and without any tape recording of the proceedings. (This is so even when a tape recording is readily available.)

Whether the promptings of conscience or the desire to get the matter over with usually override the impact of the warnings, or whether the police too often mumble or undermine the warnings, almost all empirical studies indicate that in the quarter century since *Miranda* was decided custodial suspects have continued to make incriminating statements with great frequency. This might not have been the case if a tape recording of police warnings and the suspect's response were required whenever feasible. There is little doubt that it would not have been the case if *Miranda* had required that a suspect first consult with a lawyer or actually have a lawyer present in order for his waiver of rights to be effective.

***Future of Miranda.*** For supporters of *Miranda*, an ominous note was struck in *Michigan* v. *Tucker* (1974), where the Court, speaking through Justice William *Rehnquist, viewed the *Miranda* warnings as "not themselves rights protected by the Constitution," but only "prophylactic standards" designed to "safeguard" or to "provide practical reinforcement" for the privilege against self-incrimination (p. 444). A decade later, first in *New York* v. *Quarles* (1984), recognizing a "public safety" exception to *Miranda*, and then in *Oregon* v. *Elstad* (1985), indicating that the prosecution may make considerable derivative use of *Miranda* violations, the Court reiterated *Tucker's* way of looking at, and thinking about, *Miranda*. Both *Quarles* and *Elstad* underscored the distinction between statements that are actually "coerced" or "compelled" and those obtained merely in violation of *Miranda's* "prophylactic rules."

Since the Supreme Court has no supervisory power over state criminal justice and if *Miranda* violations are not constitutional violations, where did the Warren Court get the authority to impose the new confession doctrine on the states? If a confession obtained in violation of *Miranda* does not violate the self-incrimination clause unless "actually coerced," why are the states not free to admit all confessions not the product of actual coercion? *Tucker* and its progeny thus may have prepared the way for the eventual overruling of *Miranda*.

Nevertheless, it would be surprising if the Court did overrule *Miranda*. The Court is well aware of *Miranda*'s rather limited scope—indeed, a number of commentators have forcefully argued that it does not go far enough. The Court is also cognizant of the many studies indicating that the decision has had no significant adverse impact on law enforcement. Despite their initial reaction of dismay, the police seem to have adjusted to *Miranda* fairly well. Under these circumstances, the Court is probably willing to "live with" a case that has become part of the American culture, especially if it continues to view it as a serious effort to strike a proper balance between the need for police questioning and the need to protect a suspect against impermissible police pressure.

□ Liva Baker, *Miranda: Crime, Law and Politics* (1983). Gerald Caplan, "Questioning *Miranda*," *Vanderbilt Law Review* 38 (November 1985): 1417–1476. Yale Kamisar, *Police Interrogation and Confessions* (1980). Stephen Schulhofer, "Reconsidering *Miranda*," *University of Chicago Law Review* 54 (Spring 1987): 435–461.

Yale Kamisar

**Miranda Warnings.** In one of its most famous decisions, *\*Miranda v. Arizona* (1966), the Warren Court required police to advise criminal suspects of particular constitutional rights prior to interrogation. These Miranda warnings consisted of four items: (1) the right to remain silent; (2) the reminder that anything said could be used against the suspect; (3) the right to \*counsel; and (4) the related reminder that counsel would be provided for indigents.

Miranda warnings apply when suspects are in police custody and under interrogation. In decisions subsequent to *Miranda*, the Court has emphasized that custody consists of the restriction of freedom of movement by police. This can occur in one's home (*Orozco v. Texas*, 1969) or in jail on an unrelated offense (*Mathis v. United States*, 1968). Public safety concerns, however, constitute an exemption to this requirement as the Court emphasized in *New York v. Quarles* (1984) when it ruled that emergency circumstances (e.g., the officer's immediate protection) do not require Miranda warnings, even if these situations could be described as interrogations.

Under *Miranda*, an interrogation exists whenever police reasonably expect that a suspect is likely to offer incriminating information (*Rhode Island v. Innis*, 1980). Although most interrogations are carried out by law enforcement officers, some psychiatric examinations (e.g., those related to competency to stand trial) constitute interrogations (*Estelle v. Smith*, 1981). \*Grand jury proceedings, however, are not included (*United States v. Wong*, 1977). Witnesses in grand jury proceedings may, of course, assert their \*Fifth Amendment privilege against \*self-incrimination, but they do not need to be advised of these rights in Miranda fashion. Some lower courts have applied Miranda to grand jury proceedings

in a departure from this pattern, but the majority do not, citing *U.S. v. Dionisio* (1973), where the Court argued that grand jury subpoenas are not unreasonable searches and seizures in the context of the \*Fourth Amendment and, therefore, not custodial in Fifth Amendment terms.

Related to the scope of interrogation are more subtle means of eliciting incriminating information. In 1977 the Supreme Court concluded that police comments to each other in the presence of a suspect could be designed to elicit incriminating evidence (*Brewer v. Williams*, 1977). In this decision, however, the Court relied more on the \*Sixth Amendment right to counsel protection than the Fifth Amendment privilege against self-incrimination. Several states filed \*amicus briefs in the *Brewer* case and explicitly asked the Court to overrule its decision in *Miranda*. A similar issue was raised in a 1987 case in which the Court accepted a tape recorded conversation between a couple suspected of murdering their son where the husband had been advised of his Miranda rights but the wife initiated the conversation (*Arizona v. Mauro*, 1987).

Related to the question of interrogation strategies is the admissibility of evidence obtained in involuntary physical tests. In *Schmerber v. California* (1966), the Court distinguished testimonial evidence that required Fifth Amendment protection and physical evidence that did not, thereby accepting the admissibility of an involuntary blood test.

Another question related to *Miranda* is the degree to which incomplete warnings violate the Court's standard. In *Michigan v. Tucker* (1974), the Court upheld a conviction where police failed to advise the suspect that counsel would be provided if he were indigent. This reluctance to require police to warn suspects in an unequivocal manner has been upheld in other decisions. In *Duckworth v. Eagan* (1989), the Court accepted a confession where police indicated that they did not have any way of providing a lawyer but did assure the defendant that one would be provided if and when he went to court. Although Eagan argued that this set of warnings did not conform to the Court's own precedent (*California v. Prysock*, 1981), the Court concluded that *Miranda* warnings did not have to be issued in an exact form and that police were not obligated to produce defense lawyers "on call."

In *Miranda*, the Court acknowledged that criminal defendants could waive their rights and talk to police. Questions remained related to police judgments that a defendant voluntarily offered information. In a series of cases the Court has ruled that a written waiver form is not essential (*North Carolina v. Butler*, 1979), that a waiver cannot be presumed from the suspect's failure to complain after warning (*Tague v. Louisiana*, 1980), that the suspect does not have to be notified of the specific offense under investigation (*Colorado v. Spring*, 1987), that a postwarning waiver is not invalidated by a prewarning confession (*Oregon v. Elstad*, 1985), and that all the ramifications of a waiver need to be appreciated by the suspect for constitutional validity (*Moran* v. *Burbine*, 1986). So general are the Court's waiver standards that suspects who explicitly refuse to offer a written statement without counsel may be regarded as having waived their Miranda rights (*Connecticut* v. *Barrett*, 1987).

One of the most important questions related to the continued vitality of *Miranda* is the indirect use of information obtained in violation of the warning requirement. In 1971 the Burger Court concluded that statements made in violation of *Miranda* could be used to impeach the credibility of the defendant if he took the stand in his own defense. This decision in *Harris* v. *New York* (1971) has been described as a "back-door" reversal of the famous 1966 precedent. Whether that is a fair characterization or not, it does illustrate the Court's continuing preoccupation with the warnings requirement.

Susette M. Talarico

**Mississippi University for Women v. Hogan,** 458 U.S. 718 (1982), argued 22 Mar. 1982, decided 1 July 1982 by vote of 5 to 4; O'Connor for the Court, Burger, Blackmun, Powell, and Rehnquist in dissent. Hogan, a male resident of Mississippi, challenged as a violation of *equal protection the women-only admission policy of the state-supported Mississippi University for Women nursing school. Justice Sandra Day *O'Connor, in her first opinion for the Court, applied the *Craig* v. *Boren* (1976) test of *intermediate scrutiny. As its "important interest," the state claimed that this policy compensated for discrimination against women. O'Connor reasoned that the exclusion of men from a nursing college did nothing to compensate women for discriminatory barriers faced by them. Moreover, the state failed to show that the policy "substantially furthered" the alleged objective since men were permitted to attend classes as auditors.

Chief Justice Warren *Burger's dissent expressed general agreement with Justice Lewis *Powell's but emphasized that the holding applied specifically to a nursing college. Justice Harry *Blackmun argued that Hogan had a choice of coed nursing schools elsewhere in the state, that it was valuable to offer women the choice of an all-female school, and that, while the holding applied specifically to nursing colleges, there would be inevitable spillover from the reasoning to other single-sex schools.

Powell (with Justice William *Rehnquist) asserted that, in effect, the Court was banning state-provided women-only colleges. He elaborated on Blackmun's educational-choice arguments by focusing on the educational benefits for women of single-sex colleges and claimed that because this was not a case of sex discrimination the *Craig* test was inappropriate, but he maintained that the *Craig* test was nonetheless satis-

fied. The dissenters argued further that this would lead to the eventual demise of publicly supported colleges exlusively for women, which it did.

(See also EDUCATION; GENDER.)

Leslie Friedman Goldstein

**Mississippi v. Johnson,** 71 U.S. 475 (1867), argued 12 Apr. 1867, decided 15 Apr. 1867 by vote of 9 to 0; Chase for the Court. In March 1867 Congress enacted the Reconstruction Act over the veto of President Andrew Johnson. The act gave military commanders appointed by the president political authority in the ten unrestored states of the old Confederacy and required these states to adopt new constitutions granting former slaves the right to vote. Mississippi filed a motion in the Supreme Court, challenging the constitutionality of the act and seeking to enjoin the president from enforcing it. Although Johnson had bitterly opposed the Reconstruction Act, he viewed Mississippi's action as a threat to presidential power and ordered his attorney general to oppose the motion.

Writing for a unanimous Court, Chief Justice Salmon P. *Chase held that the judiciary could not enjoin the president from enforcing an allegedly unconstitutional statute. Chase admitted that in *Marbury* v. *Madison* (1803) the Court had asserted its authority to command executive officials to fulfill their legal obligations. He ruled, however, that this extended only to ministerial duties, which involved no discretion, and not to executive duties, which involved broad discretion and the exercise of political judgment. Chase asserted that the president's unique position gave him a constitutional responsibility to execute the laws. The courts could not restrain him from carrying out this responsibility, although once he did so, his actions were subject to challenge in the courts.

The decision was not an indication of judicial timidity. Rather it rested on the widely shared belief that enjoining enforcement of a statute threatened separation of powers.

(See also JUDICIAL POWER AND JURISDICTIONS; RECONSTRUCTION.)

Donald G. Nieman

**Missouri ex rel. Gaines v. Canada,** 305 U.S. 337 (1938), argued 9 Nov. 1938, decided 12 Dec. 1938 by vote of 6 to 2; Hughes for the Court, McReynolds, joined by Butler, in dissent, Cardozo had died.

This case provided an early test in the campaign, launched by the *National Association for the Advancement of Colored People in 1930, to challenge the *separate but equal principle that required racial segregation in public educational institutions. Lloyd L. Gaines, an African-American resident, sought admission to Missouri's all-white law school in the absence of a facility for blacks. Predictably, the University of

Missouri denied Gaines's application on racial grounds and *state courts upheld the denial. Gaines's attorney, Charles H. *Houston, then sought from the U.S. Supreme Court a writ of *mandamus to compel Gaines's admission to the all-white law school, and the Supreme Court granted *certiorari.

Chief Justice Charles Evans *Hughes, for the majority, ordered Gaines admitted to the all-white facility, dismissing the state's offer to pay Gaines's tuition to an out of state law school as inadequate to the requirements of the Equal Protection Clause of the *Fourteenth Amendment. Nor was Hughes persuaded that Missouri's stated intention to develop a law school for blacks at state-supported Lincoln University would meet the separate but equal test.

The Gaines case thus became a pivotal event in the NAACP's campaign to overturn the separate but equal standard. While the Court did not repudiate *segregation, the case signaled a new urgency in evaluating the standard. As for Lloyd Gaines, he never enrolled in law school. Shortly after the Court rendered its opinion, he disappeared, never to be heard from again.

(See also RACE AND RACISM.)

Augustus M. Burns III

**Missouri v. Holland,** 252 U.S. 416 (1920), argued 2 Mar. 1920, decided 19 Apr. 1920 by vote of 7 to 2; Holmes for the Court, Van Devanter and Pitney in dissent. The state of Missouri sought to enjoin a United States game warden from enforcing federal regulations enacted pursuant to the Migratory Bird Treaty Act of 1918 on the grounds that the statute unconstitutionally interfered with rights reserved to the States under the *Tenth Amendment. (See STATE SOVEREIGNTY AND STATES' RIGHTS.) The Bird Treaty Act had been passed to fulfill United States obligations under a treaty with Great Britain to protect migratory birds. (See TREATIES AND TREATY POWERS.) Missouri appealed from lower court decisions upholding the statute's constitutionality. An earlier federal statute to regulate the taking of migratory birds, not passed pursuant to an international treaty, had been held unconstitutional in lower courts on the grounds that the birds were owned by the states in their sovereign capacity and were therefore immune from federal regulation under the Tenth Amendment.

Justice Oliver Wendell *Holmes concluded that the statute was a "necessary and proper" means of executing the powers of the federal government, valid under Article I, section 8, because the United States had the authority to implement treaty obligations.

The Court held that since the treaty was valid it superseded state authority as the supreme law of the land under Article VI of the Constitution. This was so, Holmes wrote, because migratory birds did not respect national boundaries and were therefore appropriate subjects for regula-

tion by agreement with other countries. Even if the states of the United States were capable of effectively regulating the subject, the Court found nothing in the Constitution to prohibit the federal government from acting by means of a treaty to deal with a "national interest of very nearly the first magnitude . . . [that] can be protected only by national action in concert with another power" (p. 435).

Holmes's analysis has been criticized as a bootstrap method to create new federal power by means of international treaty. Fears of an expansive application of this principle were instrumental in encouraging popular support for the "Bricker Amendment" in 1953, which would have amended the constitution to provide that "[a] treaty shall become effective as internal law in the United States only through legislation which would be valid in the absence of treaty." In 1957, the Supreme Court relieved much of this public concern in *Reid* v. *Covert*, when it held that status of forces agreements between the United States and foreign countries could not deprive U.S. civilian dependants of the right to a jury trial by making them subject to military courts martial while they were stationed abroad. Citing *Missouri* v. *Holland*, the Court wrote, "To the extent that the United States can validly make treaties, the people and the States have delegated their power to the National Government and the Tenth Amendment is no barrier" (p. 18).

The *Holland* opinion has become largely irrelevant because of the greatly expanded scope of national power today over all matters touching interstate or foreign commerce. But the case has continuing importance. First, the opinion contains what has come to be regarded as the classic statement of the "living document" approach to constitutional interpretation in which historic practice, rather than the intent of the framers, is given primary emphasis (see ORIGINAL INTENT). Second, even though the controversy in this case concerned the scope of the treaty power, rather than treaty supremacy, the theory of the case has provided support for later Court decisions such as *United States* v. *Belmont* (1937) and *United States* v. *Pink* (1942) establishing the supremacy of federal executive agreements over state law.

Last, Holmes's emphasis on the proposition that matters of international concern necessarily give rise to federal power has provided support for later holdings where the Court found that state law may be preempted, even by *federal common law, whenever the state rule may interfere with the conduct of *foreign affairs by the national government.

Harold G. Maier

**Missouri v. Jenkins,** 495 U.S. 33 (1990), argued 30 Oct. 1989, decided 18 Apr. 1990 by vote of 9 to 0; White for the Court, Kennedy, joined by Rehnquist, O'Connor, and Scalia, concurring. As a remedy for segregation in the Kansas City, Missouri, school district, the district court ordered a "magnet school" plan to attract suburban students back to the inner city schools— complete with a planetarium, a twenty-five-acre farm, a model United Nations, an art gallery, and swimming pools—at a cost of more than one-half billion dollars. The state had to pay 75 percent and the district 25 percent, but because the district's portion exceeded state law limits the court also ordered a doubling of the district's property tax.

Declining to review the plan, the Supreme Court unanimously disapproved the order directly raising the property tax. Reasoning from principles of equity and *comity and thus avoiding a constitutional holding, Justice Byron *White and four other justices approved an indirect remedy to set aside the state law tax limits and allow the district itself to raise the necessary future taxes. Justice Anthony *Kennedy and three other justices saw this as a distinction without a difference and would have held that a federal court could not impose a state tax, directly or indirectly.

Given seemingly intractable social segregation, school desegregation remedies today are strained to enforce civil rights and respect local political autonomy.

(See also DESEGREGATION REMEDIES; INJUNCTIONS AND EQUITABLE REMEDIES; LOWER FEDERAL COURTS; SEGREGATION, DE FACTO.)

Thomas E. Baker

**Mistretta v. United States,** 488 U.S. 361 (1989), argued 5 Oct. 1988, decided 18 Jan. 1989 by vote of 8 to 1; Blackmun for the Court, Scalia in dissent. Federal judges have traditionally exercised considerable discretion in fixing the terms of sentences for convicted offenders. Convinced of a need for more uniformity in sentencing practices, Congress passed the Sentencing Reform Act of 1984, creating the United States Sentencing Commission and giving it authority to establish ranges of sentences for all categories of federal offenses. The commission was established as an independent body within the judicial branch to consist of seven members appointed by the president and removable by him. At least three were required to be federal judges, selected by the president from a list of six judges recommended by the Judicial Conference of the United States.

This statutory challenge to judicial autonomy, plus the unusual provisions for appointment and removal of commission members, raised *separation of powers issues. However, in *Mistretta* the Supreme Court upheld the sentencing law in all respects. Though admitting that the commission was "an unusual hybrid in structure and authority," Justice Harry A. *Blackmun ruled that locating the commission within the judicial branch did not violate the separation of powers doctrine (p. 412). The commission was not a court nor controlled by the judiciary. Requiring three federal

judges to serve on the commission along with nonjudges did not affect the integrity or independence of the judicial branch. Giving the president power to remove commission members had no effect on the tenure or compensation of *Article III judges. The development of sentencing rules was an "essentially neutral endeavor" in which judicial participation was "peculiarly appropriate" (p. 407).

Justice Antonin *Scalia, dissenting, challenged the constitutionality of the commission. He concluded that it was a violation of *Article III of the Constitution to have federal judges serve in policy-making positions in the executive branch.

(See also APPOINTMENT AND REMOVAL POWER.)

C. Herman Pritchett

**Mobile v. Bolden,** 446 U.S. 55 (1980), argued 19 Mar. 1979, reargued 29 Oct. 1979, decided 22 Apr. 1980 by vote of 6 to 3; Stewart for the Court, Blackmun concurring in the result, Stevens concurring in the judgment, Brennan, White, and Marshall in dissent. This case was brought on behalf of the black residents of Mobile, Alabama. They alleged that the all-white Mobile City Commission, elected at large, diluted the voting strength of blacks in violation of section 2 of the *Voting Rights Act of 1965, and the *Fourteenth and *Fifteenth Amendments. No black had ever served on the five-member commission since its inception in 1911. The district court found constitutional violations and the court of appeals affirmed. In the Supreme Court the United States argued for the black parties.

The plurality opinion focused on the standard necessary to make out a claim of racial discrimination under the Fourteenth and Fifteenth Amendments where state action, on its face, is racially neutral. Examining the Fifteenth Amendment and reviewing numerous voting rights cases, the Court rejected a discriminatory result standard and concluded that a showing of a discriminatory purpose was required. Similarly, the Court relied on *Washington v. Davis (1976), *Arlington Heights v. Metropolitan Housing Development Corp. (1977), and *Personnel Administrator v. Feeney (1979) for the proposition that a showing of *discriminatory intent was necessary under the Fourteenth Amendment. Applying this discriminatory intent standard to Mobile, the Court found no constitutional violation. Mobile's black citizens could register and *vote without hindrance, and there were not official obstacles hindering blacks in seeking elective office. Finally, the Court strongly criticized the notion that the Fourteenth Amendment requires or guarantees proportional representation.

Justice Thurgood *Marshall, in a lengthy and angry dissent, labeled the Court an accessory to the perpetuation of racial discrimination. He rejected the necessity of finding a discriminatory intent and argued for a discriminatory effects test.

Critics of the decision maintain that the Court's discriminatory purpose test is too burdensome. *Mobile* caused a firestorm of protest. Congress, in its 1982 extension of the Voting Rights Act, incorporated a modified effects test into the act.

(See also RACE AND RACISM; STATE ACTION.)

Gerald N. Rosenberg

**Moment of Silence.** See RELIGION; SCHOOL PRAYER AND BIBLE READING.

**Monell v. Department of Social Services,** 436 U.S. 658 (1978), argued 2 Nov. 1977, decided 6 June 1978 by vote of 7 to 2; Brennan for the Court, Powell and Stevens concurring, Rehnquist, joined by Burger, in dissent. In *Monell,* the Court held that New York City's policy of requiring pregnant female city employees to take leave that was not medically necessary subjected the city to liability. It overruled the Court's seventeen-year-old holding, in *Monroe* v. *Pape* (1961), that local governments were wholly immune from suit under Title 42, section 1983 of the U.S. Code. *Monell* enabled civil rights plaintiffs to seek monetary recovery from local governments for constitutional violations.

While overruling *Monroe,* the Court limited the circumstances under which local governments are liable. It rejected imposing municipal liability simply because the municipality employed the person who violated the plaintiff's rights, so-called *respondeat superior* liability. Municipal liability instead depended on finding that the wrong resulted from the "official policy" of the municipality. The "official policy" test, as developed in later cases, requires that the wrongful policy be one made by someone in final policymaking authority. Mere egregious misbehavior by the police, for example, will not support municipal liability.

The Court's reasoning in rejecting *respondeat superior* liability is questionable in light of that doctrine's widespread acceptance in *tort law. It relied on congressional rejection of proposed amendments to section 1983 that would have made cities liable for wrongful acts by private persons. The proposed amendments did not, however, address the question of whether cities might be liable for their own employees' wrongful acts.

(See also GENDER; PREGNANCY, DISABILITY, AND MATERNITY LEAVES; SOVEREIGN IMMUNITY.)

Theodore Eisenberg

**Monetary Powers.** See FISCAL AND MONETARY POWERS.

**Monopoly.** See ANTITRUST.

**Moody, William Henry** (b. Newbury, Mass., 23 Dec. 1853; d. Haverhill, Mass., 2 July 1917; interred Newburyport Cemetery, Newburyport, Mass.), associate justice, 1906–1910. Born to

*William Henry Moody*

Henry L. and Melissa A. (Emerson) Moody on a two-hundred-year-old homestead, William came to embody the strong sense of duty and moral rectitude associated with his Puritan forebearers. Graduating from Phillips Andover Academy in 1872, Moody received a B.A. in history from Harvard College in 1876 but stayed only four months at its law school before reading law in Boston for eighteen months under lawyer and author Richard H. Dana, Jr. Despite this abbreviated study, Moody was admitted to the bar after making a legendary impression on his oral examiners.

Moving to Essex County and into law partnerships, Moody became a member of the Haverhill school board, a city solicitor (1888–1889), and a member of the city water board before being chosen in 1890 as attorney for the Eastern District of Massachusetts. In this capacity, he helped in the brilliant but unsuccessful murder prosecution of Lizzie Borden. Moody in 1895 won election to Congress as a Republican and was subsequently reelected three times.

Theodore Roosevelt first met Moody in 1895 and quickly came to admire a man with a similar physical build, athletic interests, and a progressive Republican perspective. In 1902, Roosevelt appointed Moody as secretary of the navy.

When Philander C. Knox resigned in 1904, Roosevelt chose Moody for attorney general. He became known for vigorous prosecutions under the *Sherman Antitrust Act, particularly in the *Beef Trust Case* of *Swift and Co.* v. *United States* (1905), which Moody argued personally. Moody also took a case of African-American *peonage to the Supreme Court and initiated contempt proceedings against a Tennessee sheriff who had permitted the lynching of a black rape suspect.

Roosevelt nominated Moody in 1906 to replace retiring Justice Henry B. *Brown. Despite some misgivings that Moody's *antitrust stance had been somewhat radical, the Senate quickly approved him. Moody's judicial career showed great promise, but it was effectively ended in 1908 when he developed crippling rheumatism. Moody spent his declining years in his house at Haverhill with his sister who, like himself, was unmarried. In 1910, Moody resigned after Congress passed legislation extending special retirement benefits to him.

While on the Court, Moody wrote sixty-seven opinions, of which five were dissents. Writing his most important dissent in the *Employers' Liability Cases* (1908), Moody voted to uphold federal legislation protecting employees in interstate commerce, a stance indicative of a broad view of governmental powers. Moody's most famous opinion was in *Twining* v. *New Jersey* (1908), where he refused to apply the privilege against *self-incrimination to the states. Though since overturned, *Twining* is still recognized as a model of legal reasoning and of deference to *federalism.

☐ Frederick B. Wiener, "The Life and Judicial Career of William Henry Moody" (Thesis, Harvard Law School, 1930).                                        John R. Vile

**Moore, Alfred** (b. New Hanover County, N.C., 21 May 1755; d. Bladen County, N.C., 15 Oct. 1810; interred St. Philip's Churchyard, Old Brunswick, N.C.), associate justice, 1799–1804. Born into a prominent family, the son of Maurice Moore, one of three colonial judges of North Carolina, Alfred Moore was sent to Boston for his early education. He then returned home to read law under the direction of his father and was admitted to the bar in 1775. A strong supporter of the movement for independence he served in the First North Carolina Regiment with distinction. He suffered heavy personal losses during the war as his father, brother, and uncle were killed, his plantation sacked, and his home destroyed. After the war he became a leading member of the bar and engaged in local politics; he married Suzanne Eagles. He served in the North Carolina General Assembly and in 1782 that body elected him attorney general, a post he held for almost nine years.

It was in this capacity that he argued the state's side in the case *Bayard* v. *Singleton* (1787). The case involved a North Carolina law that confiscated the property of Tories who had fled from the state. Although Moore eventually won on a technical point, the case is important because it involved one of the earliest and fullest discussions of the doctrine of *judicial review.

During the 1780s Moore also supported the movement to create a stronger central govern-

*Alfred Moore*

ment and in 1788 he played an important role in North Carolina's ratification of the United States Constitution. In the decade that followed he continued to practice law while remaining active in state and national politics. In December 1798 the North Carolina General Assembly elected him to the state's superior court; less than a year later President John Adams appointed him to the United States Supreme Court to replace fellow North Carolinian James *Iredell.

Moore left only one recorded opinion as a Supreme Court justice: *Bas* v. *Tingy* (1800). His decision upheld the view that France during the undeclared naval war of 1798 and 1799 was an "enemy" nation. Moore's opinion enforced a 1799 law that allowed the recaptor of an American merchant ship seized by the French one half the value of the ship and its goods as salvage, provided it took place ninety-six hours after the original capture. Although a member of the court at the time of *Marbury* v. *Madison* (1803), he did not participate in the decision and he acquiesced in *Stuart* v. *Laird* (1803). Moore's career made scarcely a ripple in American judicial history. Owing to ill health, Moore resigned from the Supreme Court in 1804 and returned to his home, where he helped establish the University of North Carolina.

☐ Leon Friedman, "Alfred Moore," in *The Justices of the United States Supreme Court, 1789–1969*, edited by Leon Friedman and Fred L. Israel, vol. 1 (1969), pp. 269–279.
                                        Richard E. Ellis

**Moore v. Dempsey,** 261 U.S. 86 (1923), argued 9 Jan. 1923, decided 19 Feb. 1923 by vote of 6 to 2;

Holmes for the Court, McReynolds and Sutherland in dissent, Clarke not participating. *Moore* resulted from a racial clash in Phillips County, Arkansas, in the fall of 1919, in which as many as two hundred blacks and five whites died. The *Moore* case involved six blacks sentenced to death for the murder of whites following the incident. They had petitioned the federal courts for a writ of *habeas corpus, contending that their trials had been mob dominated and that witnesses were tortured to force testimony against them. The federal district court, however, dismissed the habeas corpus petition.

On appeal sponsored by the *National Association for the Advancement of Colored People, the Supreme Court reversed the district court and ordered that a habeas corpus hearing be held. Speaking for the Court, Justice Oliver Wendell *Holmes held that a mob-dominated trial violated the *Due Process Clause of the *Fourteenth Amendment and that, upon being petitioned for a writ of habeas corpus, the federal courts were duty bound to review claims of mob domination of state trials and to order the release of defendants convicted in mob-dominated trials. In dissent, Justices James *McReynolds and George *Sutherland contended the Court's decision would result in undue interference by the federal courts in state criminal trials.

*Moore* v. *Dempsey* marked the beginning of stricter scrutiny of state criminal trials by the Supreme Court and more liberalized use of federal writs of habeas corpus to attack state convictions obtained in violation of federal constitutional rights.

(See also DUE PROCESS, PROCEDURAL; RACE AND RACISM; SIXTH AMENDMENT.)

Richard C. Cortner

**Moose Lodge v. Irvis,** 407 U.S. 163 (1972), argued 28 Feb. 1972, decided 12 June 1972 by vote of 6 to 3; Rehnquist for the Court, Douglas, Brennan, and Marshall in dissent. Irvis, an African-American man, was refused service as the guest of a member of the Moose Lodge in Harrisburg, Pennsylvania. The Pennsylvania Liquor Control Board had issued the Moose Lodge a private club license to dispense liquor, and Irvis contended that this involvement of the state in the racially discriminatory policy of the lodge constituted discriminatory state action in violation of the *Equal Protection Clause of the *Fourteenth Amendment. Irvis successfully brought suit in federal court against the state liquor authority and the Moose Lodge, winning an injunction that required the liquor authority to suspend the lodge's liquor license as long it continued to discriminate in its guest policies.

On appeal the Supreme Court reversed, holding that there was insufficient governmental involvement by the state of Pennsylvania in the racially discriminatory policies of the Moose Lodge to constitute a violation of the Equal

Protection Clause. Justice William *Rehnquist noted that the Court had held in the *Civil Rights Cases* (1883) that the Equal Protection Clause prohibited only racial discrimination supported by state action. Under the state action doctrine, acts of racial discrimination resulting from the choices of private individuals and unsupported by any official sanction did not fall within the prohibition of the Equal Protection Clause. The mere licensing of the lodge to dispense liquor and the regulations of the liquor trade enforced by the state, the Court held, did not constitute the official support of the racial discrimination practiced by the lodge necessary to bring its racial policies within the prohibition of the Equal Protection Clause.

The Court additionally distinguished its earlier decision in *Burton* v. *Wilmington Parking Authority* (1961). In *Burton*, the Court had held that the Equal Protection Clause did apply to racial discrimination practiced by a private restaurant that leased its premises from a parking facility owned and financed by the city of Wilmington, Delaware. The circumstances in the *Moose Lodge* case differed from those in *Burton*, the Court pointed out, because the Moose Lodge was located on land and housed in a building owned by the lodge and not by any public authority. Furthermore, the Court held that the liquor license alone did not constitute the kind of "interdependence" between the state and the lodge that had characterized the relationship between the restaurant and the parking authority in *Burton*. Pennsylvania law required that liquor license recipients adhere to all the provisions of their own constitutions and bylaws. At the time Irvis was denied service as a guest, the Moose Lodge constitution only prohibited accepting African-Americans as members. Inexplicably, while the lawsuit was pending, the lodge amended its constitution to prohibit serving African-Americans as guests as well. This entitled Irvis to a decree enjoining the Liquor Control Board from enforcing its regulation requiring recipients to adhere to their own constitutions, Rehnquist held, but not to an injunction dissolving the license itself. Since the liquor board had made no effort to enforce its rule, however, this was a meaningless concession by the Court. So long as the state made no enforcement effort, the lodge, as a private club, was entitled to refuse service to whomever it pleased.

Justice William O. *Douglas, in a dissent joined by Justice Thurgood *Marshall, agreed that merely issuing a liquor license to a private club with racially discriminatory membership and guest policies might not be sufficient to make the lodge's discrimination unconstitutional. But, Douglas noted, liquor licenses in Pennsylvania were subject to a quota system, and the quota for Harrisburg had been filled for many years. The state-enforced scarcity of liquor licenses thus resulted in restricting the access of African-

Americans to liquor, since liquor was available only at private clubs for significant portions of each week. Douglas concluded that the state had in this way put the weight of its liquor licensing and regulatory practices in support of racial discrimination.

Justice William J. *Brennan, also joined by Marshall, additionally argued that the state's regulatory scheme for liquor was so intertwined with the racially discriminatory policies of the Moose Lodge as to justify a finding that there was state support for racial discrimination and thus a violation of the Equal Protection Clause.

*Moose Lodge* marked the end of an expansion of the state action doctrine, which had begun with *Shelley* v. *Kraemer* (1948) and continued with *Burton* and subsequent "sit-in" cases of the 1960s, designed to subject private discrimination to the prohibitions of the Fourteenth Amendment.

(See also RACE AND RACISM; STATE ACTION.)

Richard C. Cortner

**Mootness** is one of several problems created by *Article III's limitation of the jurisdiction of federal courts to "Cases" and "Controversies." The mootness problem arises when the issue that is being litigated has become resolved in one way or another, thus leaving the plaintiff with no current complaint. For example, in a leading mootness case, *DeFunis* v. *Odegaard* (1974), the petitioner complained that admissions procedures at the University of Washington Law School denied him (a white male) *equal protection. He was admitted to the school pending litigation, and his case was docketed for argument shortly before he was about to graduate. A 5-to-4 majority dismissed his action, holding that it would have become moot by the time the merits were reached.

An important exception to the mootness exclusion is for cases "capable of repetition, yet evading review" (*Southern Pacific Terminal Co.* v. *Interstate Commerce Commission,* 1911, p. 515). The exception has been applied in cases involving the constitutionality of government restrictions on *abortion. In such actions, a pregnant woman contesting state-imposed restrictions on her access to abortion would certainly carry her pregnancy to term before her challenge could be resolved (see *Roe* v. *Wade,* 1973).

(See also CASES AND CONTROVERSIES; JUSTICIABILITY.)

William M. Wiecek

**Morehead v. New York ex rel. Tipaldo,** 298 U.S. 587 (1936), argued 28–29 Apr. 1936, decided 1 June 1936 by vote of 5 to 4; Butler for the Court, Hughes, Stone, Brandeis, and Cardozo in dissent. Perhaps the most unpopular decision of the 1935–1936 Supreme Court term was *Morehead,* in which a narrow majority struck down a New York minimum-wage law for women and children.

Speaking for the five-member majority, Justice

Pierce *Butler maintained that the right to contract for wages in return for work "is part of the liberty protected by the due process clause [of the *Fourteenth Amendment]" (p. 610). He further argued that a state government should not be permitted to interfere with any contracts for labor. Justice Butler was joined in his *Morehead* majority by the three other conservative justices on the Court—James *McReynolds, George *Sutherland and Willis *Van Devanter—and by the quixotic Justice Owen J. *Roberts.

In response to Butler's bald assertion that a state was powerless to enact minimum wage legislation—even in the throes of the Great Depression—one of the dissenters, Justice Harlan Fiske *Stone, accused the majority of acting on the basis of their "personal economic predilections" (p. 587) and submitted that "there is grim irony in speaking of the freedom of contract of those who, because of their economic necessities, give their services for less than is needful to keep body and soul together" (p. 632).

All but 10 of the 344 newspaper editorials written in response to the *Morehead* decision attacked it. Even the Republican Party Platform of 1936 repudiated the decision, as did the Court in *West Coast Hotel* v. *Parrish* (1937).

(See also CONTRACT, FREEDOM OF; LABOR; POLICE POWER.)

John W. Johnson

**Morgan v. Virginia,** 328 U.S. 373 (1946), argued 27 Mar. 1946, decided 3 June 1946 by vote of 7 to 1. Reed for the Court, Rutledge, Black, and Frankfurter concurring, Burton in dissent, Jackson not participating. This case was one of the constellation of civil rights cases brought to the Supreme Court in the post–World War II years by the *National Association for the Advancement of Colored People that challenged the pattern of racial segregation in the American South. Irene Morgan, an African-American woman, boarded an interstate Greyhound bus in Gloucester County, Virginia, bound for Baltimore, Maryland. When ordered by the driver to sit at the rear of the bus, as required by Virginia law, Morgan refused. She was arrested and convicted in Virginia of a misdemeanor, and fined ten dollars. The Supreme Court of Virginia affirmed her conviction.

Attorneys William H. Hastie and Thurgood *Marshall carried an appeal to the U.S. Supreme Court, arguing that the Virginia statute which required segregation on interstate carriers, imposed an improper burden on interstate commerce. Citing *Hall* v. *DeCuir* (1878), in which the justices voided a Louisiana statute prohibiting racial segregation in interstate transportation, Marshall and Hastie urged the Court to reverse the Virginia court and invalidate the statute. Justice Stanley *Reed, in his opinion, found their argument convincing and struck down the law. In practice, segregation on southern buses continued on an informal basis, even though it was clear that such practices on interstate bus travel would not survive legal challenge.

(See also SEGREGATION, DE FACTO; SEGREGATION, DE JURE; RACE AND RACISM.)

Augustus M. Burns III

**Morrison v. Olson,** 487 U.S. 654 (1988), argued 26 Apr. 1988, decided 29 June 1988 by vote of 7 to 1; Rehnquist for the Court, Scalia in dissent, Kennedy not participating. In this decision, the Supreme Court upheld the statute providing for an independent counsel to investigate possible federal criminal violations by senior executive officials. The independent counsel statute resulted from the Watergate crisis, in which senior officials of the *Nixon administration, including the attorney general, were implicated in covering up a politically motivated burglary at the Watergate office complex in Washington, D.C., before the 1972 presidential election.

Adopted in 1978, Title VI of the Ethics of Government Act provides for appointment of an independent counsel by a special court upon the attorney general's application. An independent counsel has more independence from the attorney general than a regular federal prosecutor, in particular because an independent counsel is removable by the attorney general only for good cause, not at will.

The Court held that an independent counsel is an "inferior officer" who can be appointed by a court of law under the Appointments Clause of the Constitution (Art. II, sec. 2). The Court also concluded that the removal limitation did not impermissibly limit executive authority. The decision signaled a renewed willingness by the Court to accept statutory limitations on removal of officers performing executive functions, as it had in *Humphrey's Executor v. United States (1935).

The Court took account of the practical consequences of the statute's innovations without relying chiefly on abstract formulations of doctrine. In this regard, Morrison is widely seen as a less formalistic approach to *separation of powers than either *Immigration and Naturalization Service v. Chadha (1983) or *Bowsher v. Synar (1986).

(See also APPOINTMENT AND REMOVAL POWER.)

Thomas O. Sargentich

**Mugler v. Kansas,** 123 U.S. 623 (1887), argued 11 Oct. 1887, decided 5 Dec. 1887 by vote of 8 to 1; Harlan for the Court, Field concurring in part and dissenting in part. Mugler v. Kansas was an important step toward the Court's acceptance of economic due process under the *Fourteenth Amendment. Peter Mugler continued manufacturing beer after the Kansas legislature, pursuant to a new provision of the state constitution, enacted a prohibition law, forbidding the manufacture or sale of liquor without a license. For violating the statute the state fined and impris-

oned Mugler and seized his brewery and inventory of beer. On appeal to the Supreme Court, Mugler denied that the *police power was so broad to prohibit the manufacture of beer for Mugler's private consumption or for sale outside Kansas. The state law, therefore, deprived Mugler of property without due process. Kansas officials, however, defended their actions against Mugler as a valid exercise of the police power to regulate health and morals.

Under the state's police power the Supreme Court upheld the prohibition statute. Justice John Marshall *Harlan held, however, that courts may scrutinize the purpose behind state regulations in order to determine whether the regulation had any real relationsip to health, safety, or morals under the police power. Justice Stephen *Field's dissent argued that the seizure of the property and prohibition of beer manufactured for export were violations of the due process clause. Taken together Justice Harlan's opinion and Field's dissent helped to lay the foundation for the Court's acceptance of Field's broader *property rights theory after 1890.

(See also DUE PROCESS, SUBSTANTIVE.)

Tony Freyer

**Mulford v. Smith,** 307 U.S. 38 (1939), argued 8 Mar. 1939, decided 17 Apr. 1939 by vote of 7 to 2; Roberts for the Court, Butler and McReynolds in dissent. This case involved a challenge to the constitutionality of the Second Agricultural Adjustment Act (1938). In holding this important federal law constitutional, the Court said that its January 1936 decision in United States v. *Butler, which struck down the original Agricultural Adjustment Act (1933), was a mistake. The justice who wrote the majority opinion in Butler was Owen *Roberts, the same justice who wrote the decision in Mulford v. Smith.

Both Agricultural Adjustment acts were motivated by Congress's desire to boost the disastrously low prices for agricultural products during the Great Depression. In speaking for the six-member majority in Butler, Roberts had held that the Agricultural Adjustment Act's processing tax, which provided the revenue to underwrite crop subsidies and soil restrictions, was an unconstitutional infringement on the states' rights to regulate *agriculture.

Yet in Mulford, Roberts and the Court majority voted to uphold a tobacco quota on production that had been instituted by the Second Agricultural Adjustment Act. In this decision, Roberts concluded that Congress's Article I power "to regulate Commerce . . . among the several states" provided ample justification for the agricultural market restrictions set by the second act. Thus, in 1939 Roberts acknowledged what he had refused to recognize in 1936: that the problems confronting agriculture were national in scope and required national legislative attention.

(See also COMMERCE POWER; TENTH AMEND-
MENT.)

John W. Johnson

**Muller v. Oregon,** 208 U.S. 412 (1908), argued 15
Jan. 1908, decided 24 Feb. 1908 by vote of 9 to 0;
Brewer for the Court. In February 1903, Oregon
set a maximum of ten hours work a day for
women employed in factories and laundries. The
law differed little from other state statutes passed
during the *Progressive era and constituted part
of the reform drive to ameliorate the harsher
aspects of industrialization. The Supreme Court
had upheld a similar Utah law for miners in
*Holden v. Hardy (1898), but then by a 5-to-4 vote
had struck down a New York ten-hour limit for
bakery workers as a violation of freedom of
*contract in *Lochner v. New York (1905).

Shortly after that decision, Joe Haselbock, the
foreman of Curt Muller's Grand Laundry in
Portland, Oregon, required Mrs. Elmer Gotcher
to work more than ten hours on 4 September
1905. Two weeks later a local court found Muller
guilty of violating the state ten-hour law and
fined him ten dollars. Aware of Lochner, Muller
appealed the misdemeanor conviction. The Oregon Supreme Court upheld the statute's constitutionality in 1906, and the following year the
Supreme Court agreed to hear the case.

With the permission of the state's attorney
general, the National Consumers' League secured Louis D. *Brandeis to defend the law before
the Supreme Court. Brandeis decided upon a
highly innovative strategy yet one firmly
grounded in previous decisions of the high court.

In various cases testing protective legislation,
the Court had repeatedly upheld the state's
*police power to guard the health, safety, and
welfare of its citizens. The majority opinion by
Justice Rufus W. *Peckham in Lochner had asserted that no connection existed between the
legitimate goals of the police power and the ten-
hour bakery law; in his dissent in that case,
Justice John Marshall *Harlan had suggested that
if a valid reason could be found to justify the
regulation of hours, such laws could withstand
judicial scrutiny.

Brandeis, with the aid of Florence Kelley and
Josephine Goldmark of the Consumers' League,
set about amassing the evidence to demonstrate
the connection between women's health and
long hours worked in factories. The two women
gathered every medical and government report
remotely connected to this issue, and Brandeis
assembled the material in a highly unusual brief.

He covered the legal precedents in only two
pages, and instead of trying to overturn Lochner,
used its assertion that concerns directly related to
health, safety, and welfare could justify a state in
abridging freedom of contract through limitation
of hours. In the next fifteen pages he included
excerpts of other state and foreign statutes to
show that Oregon was not alone in its belief that

long hours endangered women's health. Part 2 of
the brief consisted of ninety-five pages of quotations from American and European factory and
medical reports, representing the best data available at the time, supporting the assertion that
long hours had a detrimental effect on women's
health.

In what observers described as a masterful
argument before the Court, Brandeis followed
the same strategy, assuming that the law would
be upheld if the justices recognized the relationship between the statute and the state's legitimate interest in women's health.

The technique worked, and Justice David J.
*Brewer, speaking for the Court, not only upheld
the law, but in an unusual aside, mentioned
Brandeis and the "very copious collection" of
data he had filed. The Court acknowledged that
"woman's physical structure and the performance of maternal functions place her at a
disadvantage in the struggle for subsistence."
Long hours of work took a toll on a woman, "and
as healthy mothers are essential to vigorous
offspring, the physical well-being of women
becomes an object of public interest and care" (p.
421).

Brewer took care to note that the decision in
Muller did not "in any respect" undermine the
earlier opinion in Lochner, although many people
at the time assumed that the Court had sub silentio
overruled Lochner. In the 1920s, however, the
conservative majority resurrected Lochner and its
doctrine of freedom of contract.

Muller became the paradigm for efforts to make
courts aware of social and economic conditions
underlying reform legislation. Brandeis created
an entry into legal argument for social facts; the
*"Brandeis brief" would now be the norm for
advocates defending reform legislation as well as
those attacking particular social conditions, such
as racial segregation in *Brown v. Board of Education (1954).

(See also DUE PROCESS, SUBSTANTIVE; GENDER;
STATE REGULATION OF COMMERCE.)

□ Alpheus T. Mason, "The Case of the Overworked
Laundress," in Quarrels that Have Shaped the Constitution,
edited by John Garraty (1975), pp. 176–190.

Melvin I. Urofsky

**Municipal Corporations.** Two traditional—and
inconsistent—attitudes toward cities coexist in
American thought. On the one hand, cities are
places to be feared. They are prime locations for
vice, crime, and alienation; they frequently advance their own parochial interests over the
welfare of the states and the nation as a whole;
they all too often allow an entrenched majority to
threaten the rights of minorities. Thus James
*Madison, in The *Federalist, no. 10, argued that
local democracies were "spectacles of turbulence
and contention . . . incompatible with personal
security and rights of property." Only by "extend-

[ing] the sphere" of political power to the nation, he contended, could the danger to liberty posed by localism be cured.

Cities, however, are also seen as a source of human vitality and as a vehicle for the exercise of freedom. The concentration of people within cities unleashes an unmatched amount of creative energy and innovation; city policies serve as laboratories for social and economic experiments that benefit the rest of the country; local governments alone are close enough to their constituents to permit popular participation in governmental decision making. Alexis de Tocqueville, in *Democracy in America* (1835), contended that "the strength of free nations resides in the local community. Local institutions are to liberty what primary schools are to science; they bring it within people's reach, they teach people how to use and enjoy it."

The legal status of American municipal corporations (a term describing the legal form adopted by cities) reflects both of these inconsistent attitudes, but the negative image of cities predominates. Apprehensions about the nature of city life, about city parochialism, and about city invasion of minority rights have led to a host of limitations on local governmental power. The most important of these is that cities cannot adopt policies simply because city residents favor them. Cities can only exercise powers that have been delegated to them by the states, and the scope of such a delegation has traditionally been narrowly construed. Since the late nineteenth century, a number of American cities, in an attempt to overcome restrictive interpretations of city power, have been given general authority to exercise local self-government under "home rule" charters. But even the power of home rule cities is limited. Home rule cities can usually legislate only on matters that are local in scope, and today fewer and fewer subjects are of only local concern. Home rule cities are also often prohibited from legislating in specific areas, such as enacting "private" or *"civil"* law.

Not only must city actions be undertaken pursuant to a power delegated by the state but any such action can be modified or reversed if the state or the federal government decides to do so. Cities have long sought federal constitutional protection from the exercise of this state and federal power to reverse city policies. But in 1907 the Supreme Court decisively rejected the attempt to impose constitutional limits on state power over cities in *Hunter* v. *Pittsburgh:*

Municipal corporations are political subdivisions of the State created as convenient agencies for exercising such of the governmental powers of the State as may be entrusted to them. . . . The State, therefore, at its pleasure may modify or withdraw all such powers, may take without compensation such property, hold it itself, or vest it in other agencies, expand or contract the territorial area, unite the whole or part with another municipality, repeal the charter and destroy the corpora-

tion. . . . In all these respects the State is supreme, and its legislative body, conforming its actions to the state constitution, may do as it will, unrestrained by any provision of the Constitution of the United States. (pp. 178–179)

For a few short years, cities did gain a modicum of protection from federal control under the Supreme Court's decision in *National League of Cities* v. *Usery* (1976). But *National League of Cities* was overruled in 1985 by *Garcia* v. *San Antonio Transportation Authority,* leaving cities, like states, with only the protection from the exercise of federal power that Congress chooses to provide them.

This extensive state and federal power over cities has resulted in a wide variety of controls on city activity. On the state level, the most important are state-imposed restrictions on cities' ability to raise revenue. Cities can only impose taxes that are authorized by the state, and even these taxes are subject to state-defined limits. Strict controls have also been placed on city borrowing and profit-making activities. Moreover, a host of other city policies, ranging from attempts to combat homelessness to efforts to control pollution, have at one time or another been preempted by contrary state decisions. Without effective state constitutional restrictions on state legislative power—which are rare—cities have no power to resist either state policies with which they disagree or state mandates that city money be spent for state purposes.

Cities, like states, have been subjected to a vast array of federal controls in recent years as well. Since the 1970s, both city and state officials have become liable to federal criminal prosecution under an expansive interpretation of federal laws dealing with bribery, mail fraud, and extortion. Even federal laws that are inapplicable to states have been applied to cities. Cities, unlike states, are subject to federal *antitrust laws. And although the *Fourteenth Amendment's prohibitions on the abuse of governmental power applies equally to cities and states, cities, unlike states, have no immunity under the *Eleventh Amendment from being sued in federal court and, unlike states, are liable for damages under Title 42, section 1983 of the U.S. Code for constitutional violations (see SOVEREIGN IMMUNITY).

Despite these pervasive limits on city power, the Supreme Court in recent years has often extolled the value of "local control." When faced with an *equal protection challenge to school financing systems that made the amount of money available for education depend on district wealth, the Court, in *San Antonio Independent School District* v. *Rodriguez* (1973), argued that the locally financed education systems were justified because of the importance of local control of education. "Local control," the Court said, "is not only vital to continued public support of the schools, but is of overriding importance from an educational standpoint as well" (p. 49). In refusing to permit an interdistrict remedy to desegregate Detroit's school system in *Milliken v. Bradley (1974), the Court again stressed the importance of the autonomy of suburban school systems, contending that "no single tradition in public education is more deeply rooted than local control over the operation of schools" (p. 741). (See SEGREGATION, DE FACTO.) Similarly, the Court has refused to invalidate locally imposed exclusionary *zoning ordinances despite their impact on the ability of low and moderate income people to find adequate housing, holding that the zoning ordinances are unconstitutional only if they are motivated by intentional racial discrimination (Village of *Arlington Heights v. Metropolitan Housing Development Corp, 1977; see also HOUSING DISCRIMINATION).

The Court's defense of local autonomy is also frequently expressed in cases upholding cities' attempts to preserve their character. Thus cities have been given considerable leeway to establish rules prohibiting unrelated adults from living together in a single house. "The police power," the Court said in Village of *Belle Terre v. Boraas (1974), "is ample to lay out zones where family values, youth values, and the blessings of quiet seclusion and clean air make the area a sanctuary for people" (p. 9). An equally deferential attitude has permitted cities to use zoning laws to concentrate or disperse "adult" movie theaters and book stores. "A city's interest in attempting to preserve the quality of urban life," the Court stated in City of Renton v. Playtime Theatres (1986), "is one that must be accorded high respect" (p. 50).

There are many possible explanations for the Supreme Court's defense of local control in the desegregation, school financing, exclusionary zoning, and community character contexts despite its rejection of similar arguments when cities have asserted a right of local self-government immune from state or federal control. One commentator has argued that the Supreme Court, like state legislatures, has deferred to local autonomy in cases in which suburban communities have sought to protect family values from problems associated with the inner city but has allowed strict controls over central cities' regulatory authority. Another commentator has suggested that Supreme Court cases defending local autonomy as well as legal doctrines subjecting cities to state and federal control are efforts to protect private *property rights. Deference to suburban autonomy is one way to protect the interests of private property owners, and invalidating city regulation of private business is another.

A third explanation of the divided attitude toward local authority is also possible. Judges, like most of us, are ambivalent about city power. They see much in cities that they fear and much that they admire. What is feared and what is admired, however, seem inextricable. Perhaps the explanation of the division within legal

thought about city power, then, lies in the division within the predominant vision of cities: cities embody both our fears and our hopes for the future of American democracy.

(See also POLICE POWER; TAKINGS CLAUSE.)

□ Richard Briffault, "Our Localism," Columbia Law Review 90 (1990): 1–115, 346–454. Gerald E. Frug, "The City as a Legal Concept," Harvard Law Review 93 (1980): 1057–1154. Joan Williams, "The Constitutional Vulnerability of American Local Government: The Politics of City Status in American Law," Wisconsin Law Review (1986): 83–153.                                    Gerald E. Frug

**Munn v. Illinois,** 94 U.S. 113 (1877), argued 14, 18 Jan. 1876, decided 1 Mar. 1877 by vote of 7 to 2; Waite for the Court, Field, joined by Strong, in dissent. Munn v. Illinois forms with the related Granger Cases a historic ruling that tests the constitutionality of state *police power, through legislation, to regulate private business. Coming in the industrial upheaval of the late nineteenth century, the case gave vitality to the recently enacted *Fourteenth Amendment.

In 1875, the Illinois legislature, dominated by representatives sympathetic to the Patrons of Husbandry (the Grange), enacted legislation setting the rates that Illinois grain elevator operators could charge their grain-producing customers—provided the operators did business in any Illinois city larger than 100,000 in population. The law therefore applied to only one Illinois city: Chicago, where farmers were agitated that elevator operators were fixing rates and gouging farmers. The operators argued that the Illinois statute was an unconstitutional infringement on the *commerce power of the Congress and that it was violative of the Fourteenth Amendment *Due Process Clause, intended to bar any state from depriving persons of property without due process of law.

For the majority, Chief Justice Morrison R. *Waite vindicated the Granger forces. He upheld the Illinois law, arguing that such a statute was clearly within the limits of the police power of the state of Illinois. Waite eloquently traced the regulatory principle from its origins in English common law, observing that "[W]hen private property is affected with a public interest," it ceased to be exclusively private (p. 126). He went on to ground his ruling in nineteenth-century American case law regarding bridges, ferries, railroads, and navigable waterways. Waite observed that when one devotes "property to a use in which the public has an interest, he, in effect, grants to the public an interest in that use, and must submit to be controlled by the public for the common good, to the extent of the interest he has created" (p. 126).

Waite next asked if the facts of the case justified the legislature's statutory action—a question he answered affirmatively: "For our purposes we must assume that if a state of facts could exist that would justify such legislation, it actually did exist when the statute under consideration was passed" (p. 132). Moreover, it was the proper function of the judiciary to determine if the legislative power exercised here was a legitimate constitutional power (see JUDICIAL REVIEW). If so, its exercise was a *political question: "For protection against abuses by legislatures, the people must resort to the polls, not to the courts" (p. 134)—Waite's classic statement of nineteenth-century judicial restraint. Finally, Waite noted that the effect of the Illinois statute on interstate commerce was incidental, a local regulation that would stand in the absence of congressional involvement.

Justice Stephen J. *Field entered a vigorous dissent in which Justice William *Strong concurred. Field found the Illinois statute constitutionally impermissible and argued for a position that would come to be called substantive *due process. Field drew a distinction between private rights and public power, basing his dissent in part on the Due Process Clause of the Fourteenth Amendment. Field dismissed the argument that by using their private property to engage in the business of grain storage the private owners had granted the public an interest in that use. "If this be sound law," Field admonished in a celebrated passage, "all property and all business in the state are held at the mercy of the Legislature" (p. 140), a right to property so fragile as to be clearly unacceptable within the property guarantees of the Fourteenth Amendment (see PROPERTY).

In arguing for a substantive conception of the Due Process Clause—that a hierarchy of rights was embodied in the Constitution that representative bodies could not abridge—Field in dissent announced a position that, over time, a Supreme Court majority would embrace. While Field did not condemn all governmental regulation of business activity, especially in the matter of regulating large corporations, he sought to limit the use of the state police power as an instrument for business regulation. His argument, in addition, foresaw a more activist and interventionist role for the federal judiciary in the economic life of the states—a harbinger of the modern role of federal courts in a broad array of policy questions.                    Augustus M. Burns III

**Murdock v. Memphis,** 20 Wall. (87 U.S.) 590 (1875), argued 21 Jan. and 2 Apr. 1873, decided 11 Jan. 1875 by vote of 5 to 3; Miller for the Court, Bradley, Clifford, and Swayne in dissent, Waite not participating. Section 25 of the 1789 *Judiciary Act, the original grant of appellate authority to the Supreme Court over *federal question cases from the *state courts, excluded questions of state law from review by the Court. This provision established a basic principle of judicial *federalism: state courts, not the Supreme Court, have final and unreviewable authority over the interpretation of the state consti-

tutions and laws. In an 1867 reenactment of section 25, Congress omitted the proviso containing this exclusion. *Murdock v. Memphis* presented questions of whether Congress thereby conferred *appellate jurisdiction on the Supreme Court over questions of state law, and, if it did, whether such a breach of the bulkheads of federalism was constitutional.

Justice Samuel F. *Miller did not reach the second question because he decided the first in the negative. Expressing annoyance at the opacity of congressional intent in the 1867 reenactment, Miller held that such a far-reaching revision of the federal system would require at least a clear statement of Congress's determination to do so. Such a "radical and hazardous change of a policy vital . . . to the independence of the State courts," wrote Miller, could not be inferred from the silences of Congress (p. 630). Thus *Murdock v. Memphis* confirmed the modern foundations of American judicial federalism.

(See also JUDICIAL POWER AND JURISDICTION.)
William M. Wiecek

**Murdock v. Pennsylvania,** 319 U.S. 105 (1943), argued 10–11 Mar. 1943, decided 3 May 1943 by vote of 5 to 4; Douglas for the Court, Reed, Frankfurter, Jackson, and Roberts in dissent. The *Murdock* decision was one of a group of World War II–era cases that contributed to the rapid and contentious development of *First Amendment doctrine respecting freedom of *religion. Justice William O. *Douglas, speaking for the majority, stressed that freedom of speech, press, and religion occupied a "preferred position" under the Constitution (p. 115).

*Lovell v. City of Griffin* (1938), the first of the so-called Jehovah's Witnesses cases establishing specific guidelines for regulating religious communication, struck down a licensing ordinance as applied to religious colporteurs. Thereafter, in a line of decisions the Supreme Court voided ordinances requiring a permit for door-to-door religious pamphleteering and prior approval by a public official for soliciting funds for religious use.

In this context the justices in *Murdock* struck down the application of a city ordinance requiring Jehovah's Witnesses and other religious proselytizers to pay a license tax. Douglas concluded that the license tax "restrains in advance those constitutional liberties of press and religion and inevitably tends to suppress their exercise" (p. 114). Justice Stanley *Reed, dissenting, maintained that localities could levy reasonable and nondiscriminatory taxes on the sale of religious literature.

(See also PREFERRED FREEDOMS DOCTRINE.)
William M. Wiecek

**Murphy, Frank** (b. William Francis Murphy, Sand [now Harbor] Beach, Mich., 13 Apr. 1890; d. Detroit, Mich, 19 Jul. 1949; interred Rock Falls

Cemetery, Harbor Beach), associate justice, 1940–1949. A leading *New Deal politician and libertarian jurist, Frank Murphy came from an Irish-Catholic, middle-class family in a small town by Lake Huron. His father, a lawyer, and especially his mother filled him with intense idealism, ambition, and religious faith. After earning a law degree from the University of Michigan and serving as an army captain in France during World War I, he made his mark in Detroit. He was a private practitioner and assistant U.S. attorney (1921–1922), liberal judge on Recorder's Court (1924–1930), and crusading mayor (1930–1933) who pioneered public relief for the unemployed.

In the depression he reached national prominence as a progressive reformer and lieutenant of President Franklin D. *Roosevelt. He was the last governor general and first high commissioner of the Philippine Islands (1933–1936). As governor of Michigan (1937–1938), he mediated without loss of life the great sit-down strikes in General Motors and other factories, a pivotal turn in unionization of mass-production industries. Defeated for reelection, he was U.S. attorney general (1939) until chosen to replace Pierce *Butler in the Supreme Court's "Catholic seat." The midwestern Democrat was confirmed easily as FDR's fifth and majority appointment, though many lawyers, judges, and Murphy himself felt he was miscast.

His record as a justice was mixed. Neither legal scholar nor craftsman, he was criticized for relying on heart over head, results over legal reasoning, clerks over hard work, and emotional solos over team play in what he called the Great Pulpit. His strengths were practical experience, moral courage, compassion, and devotion to human rights. He strongly supported the post-1937 legal revolution by which the Roosevelt Court legitimated vast public power to regulate economic affairs and shifted its attention to championing less material rights of individuals and politically impotent minorities. Though others led these historic shifts, Murphy wrote important majority opinions in *labor law, notably *Thornhill v. Alabama (1940), which included peaceful picketing as free speech. His *Chaplinsky v. New Hampshire (1942) opinion, by contrast, excluded fighting words and obscentiy. He spoke for the Court in internally divisive battles over deportation (Schneiderman v. United States, 1943) and portal-to-portal pay (Jewell Ridge v. Local No. 6167, U.M.W.A., 1945). Most memorable are his powerful dissents against "legalization of racism" in the Japanese relocation (*Korematsu v. United States, 1944) and for high standards of criminal procedure in war crime trials (In re Yamashita, 1946), state cases (*Adamson v. California, 1947), and searches and seizures (*Wolf v. Colorado, 1949).

A complex, narcissistic bachelor, he was a priestly jurist whose support of African-Americans, aliens, criminals, dissenters, Jehovah's Witnesses, Native Americans, women, workers,

*Frank Murphy*

and other outsiders evoked a pun: "tempering justice with Murphy." "The law knows no finer hour," he wrote in Falbo v. United States (1944), "than when it cuts through formal concepts and transitory emotions to protect unpopular citizens against discrimination and persecution" (p. 561). Aiding the poor and promoting industrial peace in the Great Depression were major achievements; his civil liberties views were often vindicated by later decisions of the Court.

□ Sidney Fine, *Frank Murphy*, 3 vols. (1975–1984). J. Woodford Howard, Jr., *Mr. Justice Murphy: A Political Biography* (1968). J. Woodford Howard, Jr.

**Murphy v. Waterfront Commission of New York,** 378 U.S. 52 (1964), argued 5 Mar. 1964, decided 15 June 1964 by vote of 9 to 0; Goldberg for the Court. The main question before the Court was whether a state may compel a witness to answer questions under an immunity statute when those answers might prove incriminating under federal law. *Malloy v. Hogan* (1964), decided on the same day, anticipated the Court's answer. *Malloy* held, for the first time, that the Fifth Amendment's protection against self-incrimination applies to the states through the *Due Process Clause of the *Fourteenth Amendment (see INCORPORATION DOCTRINE).

Having established that the states are now bound by the self-incrimination clause of the Fifth Amendment, the Court in *Murphy* went on to say that incriminating testimony compelled by one government may not be used by another. Thus federal prosecutors would be prohibited from making any use, direct or derivative, of state-compelled incriminating testimony. *Feldman* v. *United States* (1944), which had held to the contrary, was overruled.

The privilege against self-incrimination is, of course, not absolute. The effective administration of justice may require the production of incriminating testimony. Immunizing a witness against the use or derivative use of such testimony is one way of obtaining it. But such immunity, said the Court, must be as broad as the privilege itself. If there is any probability that a defendant's testimony, or the fruits thereof, will be used against him even by prosecutors in another jurisdiction, any such proceeding would be constitutionally invalid unless based on evidence obtained wholly independently of the earlier compelled testimony. This is known as "use" immunity.

Use immunity was an issue in *Kastigar* v. *United States* (1972) because it did not appear to guarantee absolute protection against a prosecution arising out of the event or transaction in which the witness may have been criminally involved and about which he was forced to testify. "Transactional immunity," which Kastigar claimed, is far broader than use immunity and would virtually amount to a grant of amnesty. This, said the Court in *Kastigar,* would exceed the requirements of the privilege against self-incrimination. Use immunity is sufficient and coextensive with the privilege because it places the witness and the prosecution in substantially the same position as if the witness had claimed the privilege.

(See also FIFTH AMENDMENT; SELF-INCRIMINA-TION.)

Donald P. Kommers

**Murray's Lessee v. Hoboken Land & Improvement Co.,** 18 How (59 U.S.) 272 (1856), argued 30, 31 Jan., 1, 4 Feb. 1856, decided 19 Feb. 1856 by vote of 9 to 0; Curtis for the Court. Justice Benjamin R. *Curtis's opinion in this case provided the Supreme Court's first analysis of the *Due Process Clause of the *Fifth Amendment. The notorious Samuel Swartwout had embezzled $1.5 million in customs receipts and used the monies to purchase land. The Treasury Department issued distress warrants (a nonjudicial procedure) to void the land sales and recover the funds. Swartwout and purchasers of the lands challenged the proceedings as a violation of due process and the *separation of powers.

For a unanimous Court, Curtis upheld the constitutionality of this process, holding that the federal government could resort to nonjudicial procedures to recover funds embezzled from it. He interpreted the Due Process Clause of the Fifth Amendment to be the equivalent of the "law of the land" provisions that first appeared in Magna Carta's clause thirty-nine (p. 276). His

interpretation of the Due Process Clause—"the article is a restraint on the legislative as well as on the executive and the judicial powers of the government, and cannot be construed as to leave Congress free to make any process 'due process of law' "—relied on traditional procedural conceptions of due process, but contained within it an ambiguous hint of the possibility of a substantive interpretation (p. 276). With the New York Court of Appeals' contemporaneous decision in *Wynehamer* v. *People, Murray's Lessee* indirectly presaged the late nineteenth-century doctrine of substantive due process. However, Chief Justice Roger B. *Taney ignored both opinions in his reliance on the Due Process Clause in his *Dred *Scott* dictum (see OBITER DICTUM), and Curtis's opinion proved to be a premature anticipation of later doctrinal developments.      Thomas C. Mackey

**Muskrat v. United States,** 219 U.S. 346 (1911), argued 30 Nov.–2 Dec. 1910, decided 23 Jan. 1911 by vote of 7 to 0; Day for the Court; Van Devanter and Lamar not participating. On 1 March 1907, Congress passed legislation providing that certain named Cherokee Indians, including David Muskrat, were permitted to bring suit against the United States in the Court of Claims, with an appeal to the Supreme Court, to test the constitutionality of previous acts of Congress regulating the lands possessed by the Cherokees. Congress also directed the attorney general to represent the United States in the litigation, and provided that counsel for the Cherokees authorized to initiate the litigation should be paid by the U.S. Treasury.

When litigation reached the Supreme Court, it became obvious that under *Article III of the Constitution the judicial power of the United States courts, including the Supreme Court, could only be exercised in the decision of *cases and controversies brought to the courts for resolution. The cases and controversies requirement of Article III, the Court noted, had from almost the beginning of the republic been thought to impose limitations upon the exercise of *judicial power by the federal courts. The 1907 act of Congress, the Court held, had created a friendly suit, lacking any adverse clash of legal interests between two parties, which a real case or controversy required. The *Muskrat* case was thus not within the Court's legitimate jurisdiction under Article III and was therefore dismissed. *Muskrat* v. *United States* remains a classic example of the limitations imposed by the cases and controversies requirement upon the exercise of federal judicial power.

(See also NATIVE AMERICANS.)

Richard C. Cortner

**Myers v. United States,** 272 U.S. 52 (1926), argued 5 Dec. 1924, reargued 13–14 Apr. 1925, decided 25 Oct. 1926 by vote of 6 to 3; Taft for the Court, Holmes, McReynolds, and Brandeis in dissent. When he was President, William Howard *Taft believed that the Constitution strictly limited the chief executive's power. Yet, as *chief justice, he penned one of the broadest readings of presidential power in Supreme Court history. Spawning one of the longest decisions in the Court reports, the *Myers* case involved a suit for back pay instituted by a postmaster summarily removed from office by President Woodrow Wilson. The enabling statute provided for removal during the four-year term only with the advice and consent of the Senate. Whether the unpaid salary could be recovered hinged on the Court's interpretation of the power of Congress to limit the president's authority to remove lesser officials appointed by him.

Despite clear congressional authority to establish post offices and provide for the appointment and pay of postal employees, Taft, for the Court, concluded that the statute was an invasion of executive power. Taft found, in the 1789 congressional debates over the office of secretary of state, a legislative understanding that the president inherently possessed an unqualified power to remove government officials he had appointed. Taft accepted this legislative determination because he agreed with the rationale behind the conclusion. Since the president was ultimately responsible for seeing that the laws were faithfully executed, he must have the full discretion to remove all subordinates. To this Taft added that the executive article should be interpreted to promote the *separation of powers; the constitutional requirement for Senate advice and consent upon appointment should not be widened by implication. Except for judges, who are appointed during good behavior, the president should have full removal discretion. That was so, Taft said, because political differences between the executive and legislative branches could well prevent the president from performing his constitutional duty of executing the laws.

The dissenters easily exposed the weakness of Taft's opinion. Justice James *McReynolds, in an uncharacteristically long and thorough dissent, ridiculed the notion of an inherent ex-

ecutive power to remove governmental employees. Since Congress has the constitutional authority to place the appointment of lesser governmental officials in other hands than the president's and to provide for their removal, McReynolds rejected the view that vesting the president with the authority to appoint inferior officials deprived Congress of the power to limit removal.

In his dissent, Justice Louis D. *Brandeis concluded that in dealing with lesser governmental officials the president must act under the authority of Congress and that the president possessed only the power the enabling act provided. Held in check by the entrenched spoils system, Congress began to address the question of the removal of governmental employees only after the Civil War. But Brandeis saw nothing in the earlier period that would contradict the consistent practice since that time. While Taft pushed the concept of separation of powers to its logical extreme, Brandeis emphasized the importance of checks and balances. Congress, Brandeis continued, was not only permitted but was obliged to protect not only government employees but also free government from arbitrary executive action.

The *Myers* decision was too broadly drawn. In a country where administrative agencies were proliferating, an unlimited right of presidential removal threatened the policy-making functions of Congress (see ADMINISTRATIVE STATE). The unanimous Court in *Humphrey's Executor* v. *United States* (1935) repudiated Taft's expansive words and ruled that where government officials performed quasi-legislative and/or quasi-judicial functions, those officials could be protected from arbitrary executive removal by Congress. In regard to officials performing strictly executive functions, however, *Myers* remains good law.

(See also APPOINTMENT AND REMOVAL POWER; INHERENT POWERS.)

□ Louis Fisher, *Constitutional Conflicts between Congress and The President* (1985).　　　　John E. Semonche

# N

**Nabrit, James M., Jr.** (b. Atlanta, Ga., 4 Sept. 1919), lawyer and educator. A graduate of Northwestern University Law School, James Nabrit moved to Houston, Texas, where he represented *Native Americans in oil and gas matters and practiced real estate law. He also developed an active civil rights practice and was one of the principal attorneys handling litigation against the *white primary. After moving to Washington to join the faculty of Howard Law School, Nabrit remained active as a civil rights lawyer. He helped develop the legal theory for challenging the constitutionality of racially *restrictive covenants and participated in the trial of *Sweatt v. Painter* (1950). Nabrit was the principal attorney for the trial of *Bolling* v. *Sharpe* (1954), the challenge to school segregation in the District of Columbia, and argued the case before the Supreme Court. He was president of Howard University from 1960 to 1969, when he retired.

Mark V. Tushnet

**National Association for the Advancement of Colored People,** commonly known by it acronym NAACP, is the largest civil rights organization in the United States. Founded in 1909, the NAACP during its first two decades participated in a number of Supreme Court cases that expanded the rights of African-Americans. It submitted an *amicus brief in *Guinn* v. *United States.* (1915), which overturned the use of the *"grandfather clause" to disfranchise black voters, and it successfully challenged residential segregation ordinances in *Buchanan* v. *Warley* (1917). In *Moore* v. *Dempsey* (1923), the Court ratified the associa-

tion's arguments that federal courts could intervene to protect the procedural rights of defendants who were tried in mob-dominated state proceedings.

The NAACP's failure to wrest control of the Scottsboro cases from the International Labor Defense in 1931, however, exposed the organization's lack of a comprehensive litigation strategy. In 1934 the association appointed Charles Hamilton *Houston, dean of Howard Law School, as the NAACP's first full-time counsel. Houston advocated a unified approach to resolving the disparate problems associated with discrimination, segregation, and racial violence. The creation of the NAACP Legal Defense Fund (LDF) in 1939 further enhanced the organization's ability to fashion a viable constitutional litigation strategy. Most of the association's most famous legal victories, such as *Brown* v. *Board of Education* (1954), were achieved by the LDF, but the NAACP retains its own legal staff and continues to pursue litigation, particularly through its coordinated system of state conferences and local branches.

The NAACP also seeks to influence the Supreme Court through political action. In 1930, the association played a pivotal role in defeating John J. *Parker's nomination to the Court after it discovered that Parker had criticized political participation of African-Americans during the 1920 North Carolina gubernatorial campaign. Subsequently, the NAACP has opposed the appointments of Clement *Haynsworth, Harrold *Carswell, Robert *Bork, and Clarence *Thomas because of their positions regarding civil rights. (See also LEGAL DEFENSE FUND.)

Eric W. Rise

**National Association for the Advancement of Colored People v. Alabama ex rel. Patterson,** 357 U.S. 449 (1958), argued 15–16 Jan. 1958, decided 30 June 1958 by vote of 9 to 0; Harlan for the Court. In this case the Supreme Court upheld the right to freedom of association as an integral part of the *First Amendment despite the absence of an explicit reference to association in the amendment's wording.

The case arose in the context of the *NAACP's noncompliance with Alabama corporate filing laws and its efforts to operate in the face of state legal action to oust it for activities (such as organizing a bus boycott and aiding students seeking to desegregate the state university) that were allegedly causing irreparable injury to the state's citizenry. The Alabama trial court sought to obtain numerous NAACP records and, after some delay, the NAACP produced all the required documentation except its membership list, asserting that to supply such a list would threaten its organizational integrity. Publicizing the names of its members would lead to economic and employment reprisals, harrassment, violence, and similar burdens on its members' associational and expressive freedom. A trial judge held the NAACP in contempt and fined it $100,000.

The Supreme Court held that the NAACP could assert the constitutional right of its members as a defense against the contempt charge. To require individual members to come forward and assert their associational rights would, in this instance, effectively negate them. More broadly, the Court found that the membership list was so related to the members' rights to pursue their lawful interests privately, and to associate freely, as to be constitutionally protected. Forced disclosure of the membership list would unduly burden the NAACP's First Amendment freedom of association. Nor had the state demonstrated an interest in the list sufficient to outweigh the NAACP's constitutional objection. The Alabama court's contempt judgment and fine were overturned.

(See also ASSEMBLY AND ASSOCIATION, FREEDOM OF; RACE AND RACISM.)

Elliot E. Slotnick

**National Association for the Advancement of Colored People v. Button,** 371 U.S. 415 (1963), argued 8 Nov. 1961, reargued 9 Oct. 1962, decided 14 Jan. 1963 by vote of 5 to 1 to 3; Brennan for the Court, White concurring in part and dissenting in part, Harlan, Clark, and Stewart in dissent. This case arose in the context of a Virginia "barratry" statute that challenged civil rights groups (such as the *NAACP) and their attorneys who utilized the courts to combat racial discrimination through sponsored litigation. Under the statute attorneys who represented organi-

zations having no "pecuniary interest" in such litigation were subject to disbarment.

The Supreme Court said that the NAACP could assert the rights of its members in defending against the claim that they had engaged in barratry, the illegal solicitation of legal business. Further, the NAACP's efforts to provide attorneys in suits challenging racial discrimination was protected by the *First and *Fourteenth Amendments. Writing in dissent, Justice John M. *Harlan argued that unlike other group activities such as association, discussion, and advocacy, litigation was primarily conduct and not expression. Thus, it was subject to reasonable state regulation. The majority disagreed, however, and held that sponsored litigation might be the only means through which some groups could express the grievances of their members and seek redress. Such group litigation was protected by the First Amendment and, indeed, statutes such as those at issue in this case posed "the gravest danger of smothering all discussion looking to the eventual institution of litigation on behalf of the rights of Negroes" (pp. 416–417). The *Button* decision represents a landmark ruling upholding interest group utilization of the judicial process as a prime component of their political activity.

(See ASSEMBLY AND ASSOCIATION, FREEDOM OF; RACE AND RACISM.)

Elliot E. Slotnick

**National Labor Relations Board v. Jones & Laughlin Steel Corp.,** 301 U.S. 1 (1937), argued 10–11 Feb. 1937, decided 12 Apr. 1937 by vote of 5 to 4; Hughes for the Court, Sutherland, Van Devanter, McReynolds, and Butler in dissent. The *Jones & Laughlin* case was one of the five cases decided on 12 April 1937 that sustained the constitutionality of the National Labor Relations Act (NLRA) and proved to be a crucial turning point in the *New Deal constitutional crisis. Passed by Congress in 1935, the NLRA guaranteed the right of workers to organize unions both in businesses operating in interstate commerce and in businesses whose activities affected interstate commerce and prohibited employers from dismissing or otherwise discriminating against their employees because of union membership or activites.

Commonly regarded as the most radical of the legislation enacted by Congress during President Franklin D. *Roosevelt's New Deal, the NLRA was regarded at its passage as being of dubious constitutionality. In previous cases, the Court had held that liberty of contract (see CONTRACT, FREEDOM OF) was protected by the *Due Process Clause of the *Fifth Amendment and that under liberty of contract employers and employees had the right to bargain free of governmental interference. The Court had also held that labor relations associated with manufacturing or production enterprises only affected interstate commerce indirectly and were thus beyond the legitimate scope of congressional power under the Commerce Clause. The NLRA had been applied to employer-employee relations at Jones & Laughlin's Aliquippa, Pennsylvania, plant, where steel and steel products were manufactured.

Frustrated by the Supreme Court's invalidation of much of the New Deal legislation passed by Congress from 1933 to 1936, President Roosevelt in early 1937 sought legislation authorizing him to appoint additional justices to the Court in order to obtain a pro–New Deal majority. The key issue that spurred the introduction of this so-called *court-packing plan was the disagreement between the Supreme Court and the president and Congress over the scope of national power to regulate the economy, with the Court construing such power narrowly, while the President and Congress construed it broadly (see DELEGATION OF POWERS). The issue was presented to the Court in the *Jones & Laughlin* case, which was argued less than a week after Roosevelt had proposed the court-packing plan.

Dissenting in the *Jones & Laughlin* cases, Justices George *Sutherland, Pierce *Butler, Willis *Van Devanter, and James *McReynolds called for invalidation of the NLRA on both liberty of contract and Commerce Clause grounds. Only a year previously, both Chief Justice Charles Evans *Hughes and Justice Owen *Roberts had also endorsed the view that labor relations associated with production enterprises were local in nature and affected interstate commerce only indirectly. Yet both Hughes and Roberts voted to uphold the NLRA in the *Jones & Laughlin,* case, and many observers felt that they had shifted their views because of the court-packing plan.

In his opinion for the Court, Hughes brushed aside the due process and liberty of contract objections to governmental protection of the right of workers to organize unions. Hughes additionally held that the national government could legitimately protect the right of workers in manufacturing and production enterprises to organize and join unions as a means of preventing strikes in those enterprises that would affect interstate commerce. In effect, the Court abandoned the indirect effects test of the validity of Commerce Clause measures and instead adopted what is still the accepted view that, under the Commerce Clause, Congress can reach and regulate not only interstate commerce itself but also any activity affecting commerce, whether directly or indirectly. By upholding the validity of the NLRA on this basis, the Court signaled that it would no longer veto the national government's attempts to regulate the economy, thereby removing the principal reason for the Roosevelt court-packing plan, which was eventually defeated in the Congress.

(See also COMMERCE POWER; HISTORY OF THE COURT: THE DEPRESSION AND THE RISE OF LEGAL LIBERALISM; LABOR.)

□ Richard C. Cortner, *The Wagner Act Cases* (1964).
Richard C. Cortner

**National League of Cities v. Usery,** 426 U.S. 833 (1976), argued 16 Apr. 1975, reargued 2 Mar. 1976, decided 24 June 1976 by vote of 5 to 4; Rehnquist for the Court, Blackmun concurring, Brennan, White, Marshall, and Stevens in dissent. *National League of Cities* struck down a 1974 federal statute that extended the maximum hours and minimum wage provisions of the Fair Labor Standards Act to most state and municipal employees. That the maximum hours and minimum wage provisions of the Fair Labor Standards Act were constitutional as applied to the employees of private corporations was a matter of settled law. However, the Court, seemingly breathing new life into the *Tenth Amendment, held that as applied to the "states as states," the provisions were an unconstitutional interference with an essential "attribute of sovereignty attaching to every state government" (p. 845), and thus violated the Tenth Amendment.

The significance of *National League of Cities* lay not so much in the actual impact of the decision itself, but in its symbolic blow in favor of federalism. By invoking the Tenth Amendment as a serious barrier to federal power, the Court revived a provision that had been dormant since the *New Deal. The Court struck down the statute in question not because Congress lacked the affirmative power to pass it—the regulation clearly fell under Congress's power to regulate interstate and foreign commerce—but because the act violated "traditional aspects of state sovereignty" and "impermissibly interfere[d] with the integral governmental functions" of the states (pp. 849, 851). For the first time since the New Deal, the Supreme Court had struck down a federal law on the grounds that Congress had transgressed the permissible boundaries of federalism.

*National League of Cities* did not challenge Congress's power to regulate private corporations or individuals involved in interstate commerce or in activities that had a substantial effect on interstate commerce. The decision affected only those cases in which the states themselves—that is, the state governments or their political subdivisions—were so engaged. The Court held that "the States as States stand on a quite different footing from an individual or a corporation when challenging the exercise of Congress'[s] power to regulate commerce" (p. 833). In so holding, the Court overruled *Maryland* v. *Wirtz* (1968) but left intact the long line of decisions granting broad congressional powers to regulate interstate and foreign commerce.

*National League of Cities* left unclear exactly where to draw the line between permissible and impermissible federal intrusions on the states. Justice William *Rehnquist's formulation of the test varied from "functions essential to separate and independent existence" to "traditional aspects of state sovereignty" to "integral governmental functions" and "traditional operations of state and local governments." As examples of traditional or integral governmental functions the Court listed fire prevention, police protection, sanitation, public health, and parks and recreation. Since *National League of Cities* itself involved a general challenge to the sweeping provisions of the 1974 act, specific determinations of what constituted a traditional governmental function were left to later cases involving more specific congressional actions.

In a brief concurrence, Justice Harry *Blackmun suggested that the opinion of the Court adopted "a balancing approach, and does not outlaw federal power in areas such as environmental protection, where the federal interest is demonstrably greater and where state facility compliance with imposed federal standards would be essential" (p. 856).

Four justices dissented. Justice William *Brennan pointed out the Court's longstanding deference to congressional regulation in the commerce area and cited its previous holdings that "the sovereign power of the states is necessarily diminished to the extent of the grants of power to the federal government in the Constitution" (p. 859). Brennan accused the majority of creating an "ill-conceived abstraction . . . as a transparent cover for invalidating a congressional judgment with which they disagree" (p. 867), and of violating the principles of judicial restraint and deference to the political branches (see JUDICIAL SELF-RESTRAINT). He called the majority's "essential-function" test "conceptually unworkable" and meaningless. The Court's decision, he concluded, "was a catastrophic judicial body blow at Congress'[s] power under the Commerce Clause" (p. 832).

*National League of Cities* had a brief lifespan. After a decade of drawing fine distinctions between state functions that were or were not "essential" or "traditional," the Court gave up. In *Garcia* v. *San Antonio Metropolitan Transit Authority* (1985), it overruled *National League of Cities* by the same 5-to-4 vote, with Blackmun—who had indicated in *National League of Cities* that he was "not untroubled by certain possible implications of the Court's opinion" (p. 865)—switching his vote (*O'Connor voted the same way as *Stewart, whom she had replaced in 1981).

(See also COMMERCE POWER; FEDERALISM; STATE SOVEREIGNTY AND STATES' RIGHTS.)

William Lasser

**National Organization for Women** (NOW) was created in 1966 when women activists became frustrated at the Equal Employment Opportunity Commission's refusal to investigate claims of employment discrimination filed under the *Civil Rights Act of 1964. NOW has been a leader in efforts to secure passage of the Equal Rights Amendment (ERA) and numerous pieces of legislation including the Equal Credit Opportunity Act and the Pregnancy Discrimination Act.

In 1971 NOW established the separate tax-exempt NOW Legal Defense and Education Fund to secure the elimination of sex discrimination through litigation and to assist women who were the victims of such discrimination. Modeled after the NAACP *Legal Defense Fund, NOW is now an active participant in Supreme Court litigation. It has filed *amicus briefs in almost every major case involving gender-based discrimination that has been decided by the Court.

NOW has played an active role in the debate about legislation that discriminates on the basis of pregnancy, believing that laws, such as the one at issue in *California Savings and Loan Association* v. *Guerra* (1987), discriminate against women when they force an employer to extend benefits to women that are unavailable to men.

NOW and its Legal Defense Fund have been major forces in the debate over *abortion. NOW was the first major women's rights organization to call for a total repeal of all restrictive state abortion laws and continues to believe that abortion is a woman's right.

(See also GENDER.)

Karen O'Connor

**National Police Power.** See POLICE POWER.

**National Security.** The Constitution distributes the power to "provide for the common defense" between the legislative and executive branches of the federal government. This distribution of authority over national defense has been characterized by Edward S. Corwin in *The President: Office and Powers 1787–1957* as "an invitation to struggle" (p. 171). Certainly there have been struggles, but it seems closer to the framers' intent to say that the effective use of the constitutional arrangements for national security requires cooperation between Congress and the president. The role of the judicial branch is to monitor the constitutional boundaries between the other two branches and to protect civil liberties when they are threatened by efforts to secure the national defense. In pursuing this role, only rarely have the courts had any significant impact on the decisions of the political branches.

The "judicial power," besides its general jurisdiction over cases arising under the Constitution, laws and treaties, is made explicitly responsible for certain matters touching on national security, such as cases affecting ambassadors and consuls, those involving admiralty and maritime jurisdiction, and those in which treason is alleged. The Constitution defines treason quite precisely, limiting it to "levying war" against the nation or giving "aid and comfort" to its enemies. For conviction, it requires testimony by two witnesses to the same overt act or confession in open court. Rarely, if ever, however, have cases falling under these definitions had a central bearing on the conduct of national security policy.

**Role of the Courts.** Instead, the Supreme Court has more typically determined whether each branch has played its proper constitutional role in the initiation and conduct of military conflict. In such cases, the Court has usually deferred to the political process.

During the *Civil War, for example, ship owners challenged President Abraham *Lincoln's blockade on grounds that, when their property was seized, Congress had not yet declared war or otherwise signaled its cooperation in the use of armed force. The Court, albeit by the narrowest of majorities, rejected this argument, noting that the president had responded to an armed attack and Congress had supported his action as soon as it could.

When confronted by a sharp disagreement between Congress and the president, however, the Court has shown less deference. In 1952, during the Korean War, President Harry S. Truman cited his responsibilities as commander in chief and his inherent powers as chief executive as the basis for his power to seize steel mills that were threatened by a strike. The Court responded, in *Youngstown Sheet and Tube v. Sawyer (1952), that the president's power must come either from a statute, which everyone agreed Congress had refused to provide in this case, or from the Constitution. Power to seize private property could not be inferred, said the Court, either from the Vesting Clause or from the president's designation as commander in chief; to do that would make his power boundless. The Court therefore ordered that the mills be returned to their owners.

In protecting civil liberties, the Court has been unwilling to insist upon an absolute interpretation of *First Amendment rights of free *speech and association against claims based on national security. During *World War I, Congress passed legislation making it a crime to circulate false statements intended to interfere with military success or to utter or publish words intended to bring into contempt the government, Constitution, or flag of the United States. Nearly a thousand people were convicted under these statutes. Applying the *"clear and present danger" test, the Court upheld convictions under these laws in *Schenck v. United States (1919). During the cold war, in such cases as *Dennis v. United States (1951), the Court upheld convictions of leaders of the Communist party for willfully conspiring to teach and advocate the overthrow of the government by force and violence (see COMMUNISM AND COLD WAR). In United States v. *Nixon, (1974), the Court implied that if President Richard *Nixon's claim of *executive privilege had been grounded on the "need to protect military, diplomatic or sensitive national security secrets," it might have succeeded.

On the other hand, the Court has occasionally shown a willingness to confront a president's claim of national security interests with powerful countervailing considerations based on First Amendment freedoms. In *New York Times Co. v. United States (1971), the Court refused to prevent the publication of the Pentagon Papers, invoking the rule against *"prior restraint." Because nine opinions accompanied the short *per curiam decision, from which three of the justices dissented, the case left no clear precedent.

Freedom of speech, association (see ASSEMBLY AND ASSOCIATION, FREEDOM OF), and the press are not the only civil liberties that suffer in the conflict with national security. During the Civil War, having at first challenged the president's power to suspend *habeas corpus, Chief Justice Roger B. *Taney did not pursue the matter in the face of Lincoln's apparent refusal to accept the writ (Ex parte Merryman, 1861). Nor did the Court effectively resist the policy by which the Lincoln administration subjected more than thirteen thousand persons to arrest without warrant, detention without trial, and release only after the danger had passed. Ultimately the Court produced a magisterial reaffirmation of the right of civilians to a fair trial, but not until the war was over (Ex parte *Milligan, 1866).

Similarly, during *World War II, the Supreme Court found no constitutional obstacle to the relocation and internment of Japanese-American citizens (*Hirabayashi v. United States, 1943; *Korematsu v. United States, 1944). Again, it was not until after the war that the Court sought to repair the damage (*Duncan v. Kahanamoku, 1946).

**Since 1950, a Shifting Balance.** Historically, from the founding until the middle of the twentieth century, the need for the branches to cooperate, as the framers intended, was reinforced by two deep-seated cultural traditions: resistance to the maintenance of a standing army in peacetime and reluctance to enter into "entangling alliances." Because of these commitments, political leaders in both branches approached each looming conflict on its own terms and had to persuade each other and the nation of the need to prepare for armed conflict and to send troops into battle. Small engagements required no major mobilization, and presidents were often able to begin and end them without much public debate, though consultation with congressional leaders routinely took place in such circumstances.

After World War II, the usual pattern of radical demobilization began, but soon the cold war settled in, and the nation reluctantly agreed to abandon these historic commitments. The Truman administration negotiated and the Senate ratified a set of mutual defense treaties and other agreements (the North Atlantic Treaty of 1949 was the most important), by which the United States agreed to join with other nations in resisting communist aggression. Some of these agreements stated that an attack on any of the nations in the alliance would be viewed as an attack on all of them, and each would respond in accordance with its own constitutional procedures. As debates during the Constitutional Convention of 1787 had made clear, the president alone, under the Constitution, has power "to repel sudden attacks."

Congress and the president decided that the nations's responsibilities for defense of the "free world" required a massive military establishment. These armed forces included nuclear weapons mounted on rockets capable of devastating a foreign nation in a matter of hours. Since both sides had such weapons, command over the American arsenal had to be in hands capable of acting quickly.

These new facts greatly affected the balance of constitutional war powers. No longer would leaders in Congress and the administration have to seek political support for a mobilization of armed forces to meet a specific threat; they were continually ready. No longer would the president need authorization to respond when he perceived a communist threat; it was already there, in the treaties and agreements of the cold war and in the consensus from which these agreements arose.

These arrangements fortified Presidents Harry Truman and Lyndon Johnson when they led the nation into war in Korea and *Vietnam, respectively. Both wars were entered into without a congressional declaration. But when they proved to be prolonged and deadly, they exacted high political costs.

As the Vietnam War dragged on, many people began to question whether the constitutional distribution of war powers was still capable of ensuring that the use of military force required the cooperation of the political branches. In due course, some of the questions were presented to the courts. Young men drafted into military service challenged the government's power to make them fight in an undeclared war (*DaCosta* v. *Laird*, 1973). Members of Congress challenged the president's power to wage war without a declaration (*Holtzman* v. *Schlesinger*, 1973). In each case, the courts refused to intervene, noting that former presidents had, on more than two hundred separate occasions, sent military forces into combat without a formal declaration of war, that control over the use of military forces was committed by the Constitution to the political branches, and that Congress had many ways of resisting a president's policy, if it chose.

Only near the end of the war, in a case brought by thirteen members of Congress (*Mitchell* v. *Laird*, 1973), did a federal court finally acknowledge that appropriations ought not to be taken as indication of congressional support for the president's policy. "This court [the Court of Appeals for the District of Columbia] cannot be unmindful of what every schoolboy knows: that in voting to appropriate money or to draft men a Congress-

man is not necessarily approving of the continuation of a war" (p. 615). In the same opinion, however, Judge Charles Wyzanski, noting that President Nixon's stated policy was to bring the war to an end, held that the courts could not second-guess his strategy, and he refused to grant the congressmen's plea that the president be enjoined from prosecuting the war.

Frustration with the operation of the system during the war in Vietnam led Congress to enact, over President Nixon's veto, the *War Powers Resolution of 1973. Presented in its preamble as a fulfillment of the framers' intent, it enjoined the president to "consult" with "Congress" (neither term was defined in the legislation) before introducing armed forces into hostilities and to report to Congress within forty-eight hours whenever he did so. It further required him to remove the troops, unless Congress specifically affirmed the engagement, within sixty days and gave him an additional thirty days to accomplish the evacuation.

Every president since Nixon has regarded the War Powers Resolution as an unconstitutional invasion of powers provided by the Constitution. On the other hand, presidents have generally sought to abide by its requirements. In the Lebanon crisis (1983–1984), Congress finally agreed to a resolution authorizing the commitment of troops for eighteen months (they were in fact removed before that deadline), while in the Persian Gulf (1987), Congress was unable to pass a resolution forcing the president's hand.

Lawsuits seeking court enforcement of the resolution have been unsuccessful. In cases such as *Crockett* v. *Reagan* (1982), the federal courts have rejected claims by members of Congress on grounds that the facts are ambiguous and that the controversy had best be pursued by congressional majorities, acting through legislation, rather than by individuals or groups of members bringing suit.

Justice Robert *Jackson summed up the jurisprudence of national security in his eloquent dissent from the Supreme Court's acceptance of the internment of Japanese-Americans in *Korematsu* v. *United States:* If the people ever let command of the war power fall into irresponsible and unscrupulous hands, the courts wield no power equal to its restraint. The chief restraint upon those who command the physical forces of the country . . . must be their responsibility to the political judgments of their contemporaries and to the moral judgments of history" (p. 248).

(See also FOREIGN AFFAIRS AND FOREIGN POLICY; SEPARATION OF POWERS.)

☐ David Adler, "The Constitution and Presidential Warmaking," *Political Science Quarterly* 103 (Spring 1988): 1–36. Charles A. Lofgren, "*Government from Reflection and Choice": Constitutional Essays on War, Foreign Relations, and Federalism* (1986). Clinton Rossiter, *The Supreme Court and the Commander in Chief* (1951). Abraham D. Sofaer, *War, Foreign Affairs and Constitutional Powers: The Origins* (1976).                                    Donald L. Robinson

**National Treasury Employees Union v. Von Raab,** 489 U.S. 656 (1989), argued 2 Nov. 1988, decided 21 Mar. 1989 by vote of 5 to 4, Kennedy for the Court, Marshall, Brennan, Scalia, and Stevens in dissent. At issue in the case, decided along with *Skinner v. Railway Labor Executives Association* (1989), was the constitutionality of the United States Custom Service's drug-testing program that analyzed urine samples of employees who sought promotions to positions involving the interdiction of drugs, the carrying of firearms, or access to classified materials.

The program was challenged as violative of the *Fourth Amendment by a union of federal employees. A federal district court agreed and enjoined the service from continuing it. The court of appeals vacated the *injunction.

The Supreme Court held that the Fourth Amendment's prohibition of unreasonable searches and seizures applied to the program. Balancing the individual's privacy expectations against the government's special needs, the Court acknowledged that such needs can justify a departure from the Fourth Amendment's ordinary warrant, individualized suspicion, and *probable cause requirements. In this case, it stressed that the program only applied to those seeking promotions and that it was carefully designed to protect *privacy. Given the epidemic of drug abuse, the danger that service personnel using drugs could be bribed and the danger inherent in drug-using service agents misusing their firearms, the Court held that the government had demonstrated a compelling interest in safeguarding the borders and the public safety sufficient to out weigh the privacy expectations of those employees who sought promotions. The classified material issue was remanded to the lower court for further development of the record.

In dissent, Justices Thurgood *Marshall and William *Brennan, briefly summarizing their dissent in *Skinner,* found the Court's dismissal of the Fourth Amendment's probable cause requirement unprincipled and unjustifiable. Justices Antonin *Scalia and Anthony *Kennedy chastised the Court for accepting the service's program based solely on speculation without any showing of actual harm or its likelihood.

(See also SEARCH WARRANT RULE, EXCEPTIONS TO.)

Gerald N. Rosenberg

**Native Americans.** Native American constitutionalism is based on the recognition that Indian law is founded upon an established legal and historical relationship between the United States and Native American tribes or nations. This government-to-government relationship distinguishes the Supreme Court's approach to Native American questions from those of other ethnic or racial groups. The rights and obligations of Native Americans, unique to Indian law, derive from a legal status as members or descendants of an Indian tribe, not from their race.

Indian law is extraordinarily complex, rich, controversial, and diverse. Native American cases derive from elements of international law, American constitutionalism, federal jurisdiction, conflicts of law, *corporations, *torts, domestic relations, procedure, trust law, intergovernmental immunity, and taxation. No area of constitutional litigation has more severely tested the United States' commitment to the rule of law.

For Native Americans, law and the courts have provided both examples of balanced justice and instruments of a conquering empire. In the nineteenth century Alexis de Tocqueville noted in *Democracy in America* that the "conduct of the Americans of the United States towards the aborigines is characterized . . . by a singular attachment to the formalities of law." The United States, he observed, accomplished an extermination of much of its Indian race through law "with singular felicity, tranquility legally, philanthropically . . . without violating a single great principle of morality in the eyes of the world." De Tocqueville concluded: "It is impossible to destroy men with more respect for the laws of humanity."

Constitutional and historical scholarship in recent years affirms de Tocqueville's observations that courts manipulated Indian law to promote the expansionist objectives of the United States. American Indian policy has been characterized as "genocide-at-law" promoting both land acquisition and cultural extermination. Others have seen law and the courts as ineffective but not malevolently motivated. Francis Paul Prucha instead views the legal treatment of the American Indian as failed paternalism. Angie Debo expresses the prevailing view: "[b]ecause of the magnitude of the plunder and the rapidity of the spoliation . . . [s]uch treatment of an independent people by a great imperial power [should] have aroused international condemnation . . . but the Indians . . . were despoiled individually under the form of existing law." Robert Williams, Jr., finds much of the rationalization and legal justification for genocidal policy in Supreme Court decisions. He argues, for example, that Chief Justice John *Marshall provided a court-sanctioned blueprint for the destruction of the Indian land claims in *Johnson* v. *McIntosh* (1823). Vine Deloria, Jr., and Clifford M. Lytle note that Marshall in *Johnson* v. *McIntosh* "created a landlord-tenant relationship" under which the United States "could materially affect lives of Indians through its control and regulation of land use." Early in the nineteenth century the Shawnee leader Tecumseh stated that Native Americans "have vanished before the avarice and the oppression of the white man, as snow before a summer sun."

***Native American Law.*** Law, as conceived by Native Americans, was different from the European concept, designed to serve other purposes. Yet lawyers and scholars tend to be unaware of the sophistication of traditional tribal law and define Native American law as Federal Indian Law imposed by the national government, which is limited to statutes and regulations promulgated to govern land claims and jurisdictional conflicts with Indian tribes. The traditional law of Indian people is still too often dismissed as primitive custom or religious superstition, as when the Supreme Court in *Duro* v. *Reina* (1990) barely acknowledged long-standing tribal court systems with jurisdiction over nonmember Indians.

In Native American law, a command from the spirit world can have greater force as law than the most elaborate decision devised by the highest and most honored of court judges. In 1990, Oren Lyons, the Faithkeeper of the Turtle Clan of the Onondaga Nation, when asked "what law are you living under?" replied: "United States government law? That's Man's law. You break Man's law and you pay a fine or go to jail—maybe. That's the way it is with Man's law. You can break it and still get around it. Maybe you won't get punished at all. . . . But they forget there's another law, the Creator's law. We call it Natural law. . . . natural law prevails everywhere. It supersedes Man's law."

Law in Native American society cannot be separated from the life and customs of Indian people. Law to Native Americans is an organic part of a larger worldview, embodying a relationship between Earth and her people, disclosed in commands from the spirit world. This understanding guides Indians' lives in both formal and informal ways, setting values that run more deeply than the secular laws of the Republic and the decisions of the Supreme Court.

Federal Indian laws and policies adopted by Congress and interpreted by the courts dominate the lives of Native Americans. Constitutional law and public policy pervade Indian cultural, economic, and political life. More than four thousand statutes and treaties concern Native Americans. Tribal laws and some state statutes dealing with Indians further complicate Indian law. Thousands of court decisions interpreting these treaties, statutes, regulations, and policies plus innumerable Department of Justice opinions and administrative rulings as well as Bureau of Indian Affairs directives add to the legal maze. To understand "the intricacies and peculiarities of Indian law" Justice Felix *Frankfurter noted, requires "an appreciation of history and understanding of the economic, social, political and moral problems in which the more immediate problems of that law are entwined."

The historic principles of tribal self-govern-

ment predate European contact and form the basis of modern constitutional powers. The Court has consistently recognized that the rights of Native Americans and of American Indian tribes flow from a preexisting sovereignty, limited but not abolished by their inclusion within the territorial bounds of the United States. Tribal self-government today is recognized by the Constitution, legislation, treaties, judicial decisions, and administrative practice. Federal courts attempt to ensure continued viability of Indian self-government and to preempt competing assertions of state authority. No apparent assimilation of the Indians diminishes a tribe's status as a self-governing entity.

***The Constitution and Native Americans.*** The most basic principle of Indian law is that powers lawfully vested in an Indian tribe are not delegated powers granted by express acts, but rather "inherent powers of a limited sovereignty" that have never been extinguished. The Supreme Court in 1831 held that Indian tribes are "domestic dependent nations" that possess those aspects of sovereignty not surrendered or withdrawn by treaty or statute. The tribes began their relationships with the federal government with the sovereign powers of independent nations. The United States has protected the tribes in their internal government. In so doing, the United States applied a general principle of international law to the unique situation of the Indians. The Supreme Court has upheld tribal independence within a tribe's territory despite the admission of new states, citizenship of Indians, and dramatic changes in Native American life.

Indians are expressly mentioned only three times in the U.S. Constitution. "Indians not taxed" are excluded by both Article I and the *Fourteenth Amendment for the purpose of apportioning taxes and representatives to Congress among the states, and the Commerce Clause authorizes Congress to "regulate commerce with foreign nations and among the several states, and with the Indian Tribes" (see COMMERCE POWER). Other constitutional powers have affected federal management of Indian affairs. The Treaty Clause has been a principal foundation for federal powers over Indian affairs (see TREATIES AND TREATY POWER). Prior to the Civil War, the treaty power saw extensive use in the negotiations with Indian tribes, because Indian affairs were more an aspect of military and foreign policy than of domestic laws.

Although Indian treaties remain in force, Congress discontinued treaty-making with Indian tribes in 1871. As a result, recent decisions of the Supreme Court have referred to the Indian Commerce Clause as the primary constitutional provision supporting modern exercises of federal power over Indians. The power of Congress to regulate and dispose of "the Territory or other Property belonging to the United States" is an additional source of authority over Indian affairs.

The Necessary and Proper Clause gives Congress broad authority to execute its enumerated powers. In addition, federal constitutional power over Indian affairs is the "Supreme Law of the Land" and supersedes conflicting state laws or state constitutional provisions.

In most cases an amalgam of the several specific constitutional provisions taken together constitute a single power over Indian affairs. The court's recognition of a broad federal power over Indian affairs, coupled with the Supremacy Clause when state powers are involved is the constitutional basis for protection of Native American tribal government. The Court's interpretations of Indian law, like Congress's enactment of Indian legislation, follow the mainstream of American thought. Therefore Indian legal policy is in constant flow. Indian law and policy has been marked by idealistic periods, such as the early years of the Republic, when Congress pledged that "the utmost good faith shall be observed toward the Indian," and the 1930s, when a commitment was made to revive tribal governments. Other eras were more damaging: the Jacksonian period of removal, when hundreds of tribes were evicted forcibly from their ancestral homelands; the allotment era during the late nineteenth century, which resulted in the loss of more than ninety million acres of tribal lands; and the termination period in the 1950s, when more than one hundred tribes were stripped of their special relationship with the federal government and, in most cases, of their land. This history can be divided into five periods, as follows: (1) the formative or treaty era (1789–1871); (2) the period of assimilation and allotment (1871–1928); (3) the time of reorganization and reestablishment (1928–1942); (4) the termination movement (1943–1961); and (5) the self-determination and tribal revitalization era (1961–present). The content of Indian law depends upon white society's definition at any time of what it calls the "Indian problem," which in turn defines its legal dimensions.

*Indian Law and the Court.* Just as in the past the nation turned to traders, missionaries, soldiers, and teachers to administer Indian affairs, in recent years Indians themselves have turned to lawyers and to the courts. A significant source of this redefinition of the Indian question as a legal one has been the emergence of Native Americans trained as lawyers. These new Indian lawyers, many attracted to the American Indian Law Center at the University of New Mexico, numbered more than a thousand by the early 1990s. From the mid-1960s through the 1980s, the Supreme Court was the forum of choice for Indian tribes and their members. In the 1990s, the Court has been replaced by Congress as the public forum in which Native peoples prefer to submit their claims and resolve their conflicts.

In reviewing the court cases developing the principles of Indian law, it is impossible to under-

stand the treatment of Native Americans without reference to the varying times in which particular doctrines or statutory provisions were developed. Without this historical perspective, Indian law and the treatment of Native peoples seem a mystifying collection of inconsistencies and anachronisms. At every session of the Supreme Court, cases arise in which the validity of present claims of Native Americans depend upon what the law was at a particular point in some earlier period. In determining the rights of Native Americans, the Court continually interprets statutes that have created rights, duties, and obligations that can be understood only by reference to repealed legislation. The treaty-making experience demonstrates how history is crucial to understanding the Court's doctrinal development of Indian law. Treaty-making involved matters of immense scope, including land transfers of more then two billion acres. Out of the felt needs of the parties to treaty negotiations, comprehensive principles evolved: the sanctity of Indian title, the exclusion of state jurisdiction, the sovereign status of Indian tribes, and the special trust relationship between Indian tribes and the United States. The original treaties continue in force and provide the basis for the late twentieth-century protection of Indian lands and such reserved rights as hunting, fishing, and gathering.

Recent Supreme Court cases have upheld the preservation of hunting and fishing rights reserved by Indian treaties. In the State of Washington, for example, fish harvest is reserved for use in common by Indians as well as non-Indian fishers. Rights to fish, hunt, and gather, reserved in treaties, have similarly been recognized for the Chippewa and Menominee in Wisconsin. Use of reserved water rights, tribal rights of self-government, recognition of land claims, child-welfare protection, freedom of Indian religion, and powers of tribal taxation have similarly been protected. But such tribal victories, beginning with *Williams* v. *Lee* (1959), are vulnerable as the Court shifts with the changing economic and political viewpoints. These shifts are particularly notable in areas such as religious freedom, where tribal spiritual practices have come under state restrictive controls in *Oregon* v. *Smith* (1990) limiting use of peyote by Native Americans, and where tribal religious practices clash with the ease of timber harvesting as in *Lyng* v. *Northwest Cemetery Protective Association* (1988); and in the protection of the *environment, where tribal rights to zone are limited in *Brendale* v. *Yakima Nation* (1989).

Indian law, as interpreted by the Court, developed from legal concepts and precedents established by European colonists in their relations with Native Americans. For example, the colonial principle that land can be acquired from Indians only with their consent through treaties involved three assumptions that still form the basis of contemporary Court decisions: (1) that both parties to treaties were sovereign powers; (2) that Indian tribes had some form of transferrable title to land; and (3) that acquisition of Indian lands was solely a governmental matter, not to be left to individuals. In theory, if not in practice, these tenets determined the earliest dealings between European settlers and Indians, and provided Chief Justice John Marshall with the basis of Indian law in the famous trilogy of cases beginning with *Johnson* v. *McIntosh* (1823) and then *Cherokee Nation* v. *Georgia* (1831) and *Worcester* v. *Georgia* (1832) (see CHEROKEE CASES).

Chief Justice Marshall is the major figure in the development of Native American jurisprudence. His decision in *Worcester* v. *Georgia* remains one of the five most frequently cited Supreme Court cases of the pre–Civil War era. The *Worcester* decision was based on two principles: first, that the Constitution delegated to the federal government broad legislative authority over Indian matters; and second, that the Cherokee treaties reserved to the Cherokees tribal self-government within Cherokee territory free of interference from the state. The Court later grafted onto Indian law a concept known as "the trust doctrine," which sets the high standard of the trustee in federal relationships with Native Americans.

But the Cherokee removal controversy illustrates the inability of the Court as an institution to protect effectively the rights of the Native Americans—rights that the Court had announced in its decisions. In *Worcester*, the Court declared a series of Georgia actions void as repugnant to the Constitution, laws, and treaties of the United States. These included seizing tribal lands, executing Indian citizens who were precluded from testifying in court, and requiring the minister Samuel Worcester to have a Georgia permit to live in Cherokee Country. But President Andrew *Jackson's failure to enforce the Court mandate in *Worcester* left the Cherokees with a decision in their favor but with no effective remedy. Whether or not Jackson actually said, "John Marshall has made his ruling, now let him enforce it," the result was the same. Georgians remained on Cherokee soil enforcing Georgia law while Samuel Worcester languished in a Milledgeville prison for violation of a Georgia statute the Court had held unconstitutional. Despite Court decisions upholding Cherokee rights, Cherokee land was lotteried away and troops drove the Indians into prison stockades to wait the forced marches from Georgia.

In the winter of 1838–1839, sixteen thousand Cherokees were driven at gunpoint from their ancestral homeland over what has come to be known as "the Trail of Tears." More than four thousand of their number died on the way. "In truth," the Cherokees wrote in an 1835 memorial to Congress, "our cause is your own." The shared fate of all Americans under law has rarely been more poignantly evoked. "It is the cause of liberty and justice," they asserted. "It

is based upon your own principles, which we have learned from yourself; for we have gloried to count your Washington and your Jefferson our great teachers."

**Conclusion.** The experience of Native Americans over the last two hundred years suggests institutional impotence of the Supreme Court. The bitter irony of the Cherokee Nation's judicial victories in both the nineteenth and the twentieth century illustrate the truth of de Tocqueville's observation that in the United States respect for law did not prevent, indeed may have justified, the destruction of native peoples. More than 150 years have passed since the Court decided in favor of the Cherokees in *Worcester* v. *Georgia*. The Cherokees have returned to the Court several times since this ill-fated victory. Two instances involved the Arkansas Riverbed, in *Choctaw Nation* v. *Oklahoma* (1970) and *United States* v. *Cherokee Nation of Oklahoma* (1987). Again, the original decision was in their favor, but the results have been no more effective than those of the Marshall court. The Court held in the Riverbed cases that the Cherokees, Choctaws, and Chickasaws were the owners of a portion of the bed of the Arkansas River and were entitled to the income from the sand, the gravel, and leases for oil under the river. Subsequently, the riverbed was taken for the federally funded Arkansas Navigation Project. The taking totaled a value of $177 million. Despite a decision in their favor by the Court, the Cherokee Nation has not received compensation for the riverbed taking, which the Court had found to have been theirs under the terms of the 1835 Treaty of New Echota—ironically, the treaty forced on the tribe after Jackson's failure to execute the mandate of the Supreme Court in *Worcester* v. *Georgia* (see JUST COMPENSATION)..

For most of the more than two hundred years of American constitutionalism, Native Americans have suffered from a prevailing national view that the Indian as "savage" stood on the wrong end of the scale of progress. Native Americans were to some Europeans part of a hostile environment that had to be overcome if the white man was to fulfill his destiny to conquer and "civilize" this new world. Whites had pity for the plight of Native Americans and their "problem." But Native Americans and their culture were the inevitable victims of progress. For most of its history, the Court has created a "jurisprudence of justification" that rationalized legal grounds for conquest. Nonetheless, the Court has attempted to create a constitutionally recognized system of law protecting Indian rights as long as those rights are defined within the Western progressive tradition.

In the late eighteenth century, Sagowah, a Cherokee warrior, was asked by a missionary about changes being wrought by Europeans. He answered, "I do not understand, for I was born in another world. Your people and my people speak a different language. . . . We have our land, and your people want it." Law, Sagowah understood, is indeed a language. As an abettor in the task of conquering the continent, the Court, despite its constitutional humanitarianism and commitment to "the rule of law," spoke not the language of the Native American but the language of the European.

□ Robert Clinton, Nell Jessup Newton, and Monroe Price, *American Indian Law*, 3d ed. (1991). Angie Debo, *A History of the Indians of the United States* (1970). Vine Deloria, Jr., and Clifford M. Lytle, *American Indians, American Justice* (1983). Francis Paul Prucha, *The Great Father: The United States Government and the American Indian* (1984). Rennard Strickland, ed., *Felix S. Cohen's Handbook of Federal Indian Law*, 3d rev. ed. (1982). Rennard Strickland, "Genocide-at-Law: An Historic and Contemporary View of the Native American Experience," *University of Kansas Law Review* 34 (1986): 713–755. Charles Wilkinson, *American Indians, Time and the Law* (1987). Robert Williams, Jr., *The American Indian in Western Legal Thought: The Discourses of Conquest* (1990). Rennard J. Strickland

**Naturalization.** See ALIENAGE AND NATURALIZATION.

**Natural Law** is a philosophic doctrine holding that there is a certain order in nature that provides norms for human conduct. This doctrine received its most renowned form in St. Thomas Aquinas's "Treatise on Law," a part of his *Summa Theologiae*. For Aquinas, natural law was humanity's "participation" in the comprehensive eternal law. People could grasp certain self-evident principles of practical reason, which corresponded to the various goods toward which human nature inclined. Natural law was a standard for human laws: unjust laws in principle did not bind in conscience.

Early modern political philosophers, especially Thomas Hobbes and John Locke, who successfully sought to displace the older teleological philosophy also employed the terms "natural law" or "law of nature," but in a new sense. According to them, the source of natural law was not a set of naturally ordered ends of human well-being and fulfillment, but an innate desire for self-preservation. On this foundation, these theorists erected a new doctrine properly described as "natural rights." The desire for self-preservation in a state of nature, which Hobbes described in his *Leviathan* (1651) as "the war of all against all," led to the establishment of a social contract, the foundation of civil society. The fundamental duty of government, according to Locke's *Two Treatises of Government* (1690), became the protection of rights to life, liberty, and property.

Modern natural rights theory was an important influence on the founders of American government, as evidenced by the principles of the *Declaration of Independence. Nonetheless, aspects of the older teaching continued to be embedded in American law and political thought, through various concepts on the *common law and through the teachings of the "civic republican" tradition.

Some early judicial opinions such as that of Justice Samuel *Chase in *Calder v. Bull* (1798) held out the possibility that courts enforce "principles of natural justice" independently of particular constitutional provisions, but this idea was submerged when concepts of natural justice were channeled into the Fourteenth Amendment's Due Process Clause after the *Civil War (see DUE PROCESS, SUBSTANTIVE). In the early nineteenth century, both sides in the debate over *slavery invoked natural law.

From the late nineteenth century until 1937, natural law was a weapon in the debate over government power to regulate economic affairs. Defenders of a laissez-faire theory of capitalism sometimes invoked natural rights concepts (see LAISSEZ-FAIRE CONSTITUTIONALISM). Critics of this trend, whose intellectual descendants came to dominate the Supreme Court after 1937, included Oliver Wendell *Holmes, who achieved prominence as a proponent of legal positivism even before his tenure on the Supreme Court (1902–1932). For Holmes, natural law theorists naively assumed that what is familiar to them must be accepted as true by all people everywhere. Holmes maintained that law was only a prediction of the rules that the sovereign power in society would enforce. Owing to the influence of these views, the dominant philosophical position in law became pragmatism, as represented in the writings of Roscoe Pound, which emphasized adaptation of law to social change.

From the 1940s through the early 1960s, Justices Felix *Frankfurter and Hugo *Black engaged in a famous debate on the meaning of due process of law. Frankfurter contended that due process was a concept of considerable generality and flexibility, which had to be given content by appealing to the "canons of decency and fairness which express the notions of English-speaking peoples" (concurring in *Adamson v. California*, 1947). Black responded by criticizing the subjectivity of Frankfurter's "natural law" position. He later argued that the doctrine of substantive due process, formerly used to justify laissez-faire economic decisions, was being resuscitated to justify a new right to *privacy, including personal autonomy in childbearing decisions, in his dissent in *Griswold v. Connecticut* (1965).

The dominant strains in contemporary legal thinking continue to reject natural law doctrine. John *Rawls's *A Theory of Justice* (1971) has been influential in presenting a social-contractarian theory. Other influential positions such as utilitarianism and critical legal studies are also hostile to natural law thinking. Some natural rights thinkers may be found among libertarian legal scholars, and a more classical natural law approach survives in writers such as John Finnis (*Natural Law and Natural Rights*, 1980).

(See also FUNDAMENTAL RIGHTS; HIGHER LAW.)

□ Charles Grove Haines, *The Revival of Natural Law Concepts* (1930). Benjamin F. Wright, *American Interpretations of Natural Law* (1931).    Christopher Wolfe

**Neagle, In re,** 135 U.S. 1 (1890), argued 4–5 Mar. 1890, decided 14 Apr. 1890 by vote of 6 to 2; Miller for the Court, Lamar in dissent, Field not participating. Justice Stephen J. *Field had provoked the hostility of David *Terry, a popular lawyer and the justice's former colleague on the California Supreme Court by a circuit court opinion invalidating the previous marriage of Terry's wife. When Field returned to California for circuit duty in 1889, he was accompanied by David Neagle, a federal marshal assigned to him. When Terry encountered Field and assaulted him, Neagle shot and killed the assailant. Charged with murder under California law, Neagle sought a writ of *habeas corpus from the federal circuit court. Judge Lorenzo Sawyer, who had participated with Field in the decision invalidating Mrs. Terry's marriage, granted the writ.

The Supreme Court had to decide whether a federal court could make a definitive determination of justifiable homicide and thereby preempt the operation of California law. Federal legislation authorized a writ of habeas corpus if the person was held in violation of federal law, which had been understood to mean a statute. To rescue Neagle from the uncertainties of California justice, the Court now defined "law" to include acts done under the authority of the United States. The dissenters condemned this expansion of federal power for its intrusion into the domain of state criminal law.

(See also FEDERALISM.)

John E. Semonche

**Near v. Minnesota,** 283 U.S. 697 (1931), argued 30 Jan. 1931, decided 1 June 1931 by vote of 5 to 4; Hughes for the Court, Butler, Van Devanter, Sutherland, and McReynolds in dissent. Responding to the 1920s burgeoning of yellow journalism, the 1925 Minnesota legislature passed a Public Nuisance Abatement Law, subsequently dubbed the Minnesota Gag Law. It permitted a judge, acting without a jury, to stop the publication of a newspaper if the judge found it "obscene, lewd, and lascivious" or "malicious, scandalous, and defamatory." Periodicals could be abated and publishers enjoined for future violations. Further, the punishment of *contempt was available for disobeying an injunction. Minnesota's experiment drew warm national approval as a desirable remedy for these evils.

The first use of the law was against the *Saturday Press,* a hard-hitting weekly newspaper, which focused largely upon corruption and racketeering in Minneapolis. Flamboyant, but still reasonably accurate, its revelations outraged public officals, especially those targeted such as the mayor and police chief. As a result, the local attorney, Floyd B. Olson, successfully sought an *injunction to close down this publication. Although the publisher, J. M. Near, was an unsavory character—anti-Catholic, anti-Semitic, anti-black, and anti-labor, the action alarmed many as a form of *prior restraint. The *American Civil Liberties Union offered to support Near and to challenge the law but was quickly elbowed aside by the conservative Chicago publisher, Col. Robert R. McCormick, who put his legal staff on the case for its appeal to the U.S. Supreme Court. This proved an important test of the *First Amendment and an occasion for applying the traditional, historic concept of "no prior restraint" to state laws inhibiting the dispersal of information that a large part of the journalistic world felt the public had a right to know.

Chief Justice Charles Evans *Hughes, for the Court, held the law unconstitutional in a decision that firmly established the freedom of the press against censorship. But Hughes went further to say that "this statute . . . raises questions of grave importance, transcending the local interests involved in the particular action. It is no longer open to doubt that the liberty of the press . . . is within the liberty safeguarded by the *due process clause of the *Fourteenth Amendment from invasion by *state action" (p. 706). He also made clear that hostility to prior restraint is at the very core of the First Amendment. Only in exceptional circumstances could the possibility of turning to prior restraint be considered. Thus the "Gag Law" was struck down in its totality.

The *Four Horsemen, speaking through Justice Pierce *Butler, dissented. Charging that the decision gave to freedom of the press a meaning and scope not heretofore recognized and deploring the fact that the decision put upon the states "a federal restriction that is without precedent," Butler argued strongly that the Minnesota law did not constitute prior restraint (p. 723). The malice, once it was established by reading the published writing, was perfectly susceptible to control through the exertion of the state's *police power, a power that the justice viewed as constituting broad authority to prohibit a full range of questionable expression. But his position failed, and freedom of the press was now "incorporated" along with free speech, against the states (see INCORPORATION DOCTRINE).

The immediate reaction to the decision was overwhelmingly positive. The nation's press was gratified and relieved. Many newspapers quoted Col. McCormick's statement that "the decision of Chief Justice Hughes will go down in history as one of the great triumphs of free thought."

*Near* set forth a general principle that came to define freedom of the American press. Possibly, more importantly, the ruling stiffened the backbone of countless editors and publishers and helped stave off periodic attempts by politicians, judges, and prosecutors to muzzle the journalistic watch dog. It further represented an important development in the area of deregulation and decriminalization. It was a form of decontrol, striking at the use of state police power and informal local controls to curtail public information, essential to an informed citizenry.

(See also SPEECH AND THE PRESS.)

Paul L. Murphy

**Nebbia v. New York,** 291 U.S. 502 (1934), argued 4–5 Dec. 1933, decided 5 Mar. 1934 by vote of 5 to 4; Roberts for the Court, McReynolds, Butler, Sutherland, and Van Devanter in dissent. *Nebbia* involved emergency legislation passed by New York State to ease some of the economic hardships brought on by the Great Depression. Leo Nebbia, a grocer in Rochester, New York, broke the Milk Control Act of 1933 by selling a quart of milk for more than the fixed maximum price of nine cents a quart. On appeal to the Supreme Court, Nebbia's conviction was sustained and the New York law was ruled constitutional.

In the majority opinion, Justice Owen *Roberts abandoned the "affected with public interest" doctrine that the Court had adhered to since the late nineteenth century and concluded that a state "may regulate a business in any of its aspects, including the prices to be charged for the products or commodities it sells." He added that "a state is free to adopt whatever economic policy may reasonably be deemed to promote public welfare, and to enforce that policy by legislation adapted to its purpose" (pp. 502, 537).

In dissent, Justice James *McReynolds voiced the slippery substantive *due process argument, maintaining that the Due Process Clause of the *Fourteenth Amendment gave the justices license to sustain economic legislation they found reasonable and strike down laws they believed to be unreasonable.

John W. Johnson

**Nebraska Press Association v. Stuart,** 427 U.S. 539 (1976), argued 19 Apr. 1976, decided 30 June 1976 by vote of 9 to 0; Burger for the Court, Brennan and Stevens concurring. In *Nebraska Press Association* the Court considered for the first time the permissibility of a gag order on the press to protect a criminal defendant's right to a fair trial. The case involved the murder of six members of one family and the subsequent commission of necrophilia. The trial court prohibited publication of the confession of the accused as well as the contents of a note written by him on the night of the crime. In overturning the gag order, the Supreme Court reiterated its longstanding opposition to *prior restraints. It refused to erode established *First Amendment press freedoms in order to combat speculative dangers to an accused's fair trial rights.

The Court primarily viewed the gag order from the perspective of the First Amendment and presumptively treated it as unconstitutional. It concluded that most adverse publicity presented few threats to important *Sixth Amendment rights. Moreover, the Court observed that the

press often guards against miscarriages of justice by subjecting criminal trials to extensive public scrutiny. By employing a version of the *clear and present danger test, the Court articulated a First Amendment limit on the means available to trial judges to combat prejudicial publicity.

(See also PRETRIAL PUBLICITY AND THE GAG RULE; SPEECH AND THE PRESS.)

Patrick M. Garry

**Necessary and Proper Clause.** See IMPLIED POWERS.

**Nelson, Samuel** (b. Hebron, N.Y., 10 Nov. 1792; d. Cooperstown, N.Y., 13 Dec. 1873; interred Lakewood Cemetery, Cooperstown), associate justice, 1845–1872. Nelson was raised on the farm of his immigrant Scotch-Irish parents and educated at a common school, private academies, and Middlebury College in Vermont. After the required legal apprenticeship in upstate New York, he was admitted to the bar (1817) and developed a successful practice that emphasized litigation and real estate and commercial law. Nelson was married twice, first to Pamela Woods in 1819 and then, after Pamela's death, to Catharine Ann Russell in 1825.

He was elected the youngest delegate to the New York State Constitutional Convention (1821) and actively supported efforts to liberalize the state government, particularly by extending the franchise and restructuring the judiciary. He was appointed a New York circuit court judge in 1823, associate justice of the New York Supreme Court in 1831, and chief justice of the state supreme court in 1836. In 1845, President John *Tyler, after failing several times to fill a vacancy on the U.S.

*Samuel Nelson*

Supreme Court, nominated Nelson, a Jacksonian Democrat, who was quickly confirmed by the Senate.

Nelson was an expert in admiralty and patent law. His significant admiralty opinions included *New Jersey Steam Navigation Co.* v. *Merchants' Bank* (1848) and *Hough* v. *Western Transportation Co.* (1866), dealing with admiralty jurisdiction of the federal courts. In *patent law, his opinion in *Hotchkiss* v. *Greenwood* (1850) was a leading application of the doctrine of nonobviousness of subject matter, still one of the three conditions for patentability.

Nelson's decisions characteristically reached practical, common-sense results while adhering to established law. In *Knox County* v. *Aspinwall* (1859) he held county bonds enforceable though issued without full compliance with statutory requirements. The decision removed a potential obstacle to public acceptance and marketability of municipal bonds.

Nelson gave deference to the legislative branch. In *Pennsylvania* v. *Wheeling and Belmont Bridge Co.* (1856), he upheld a congressional act that legalized a bridge the Court itself had declared illegal under prior law. He emphasized states' rights against delegated powers of the federal government. In *Williamson* v. *Berry* (1850), his dissent argued that state law should govern matters relating to real property, thus anticipating by many years the Court's decision in *Erie Railroad* v. *Tompkins* (1938).

*Slavery and the *Civil War heightened the significance of his work. His concurring opinion in *Scott* v. *Sandford* (1857) would have affirmed the judgment of the lower court, deferring to state law on Dred Scott's citizenship and thus avoiding the inflammatory issue of the constitutionality of the Missouri Compromise, which mired the Court in the slavery debate. In the *Prize Cases* (1863), his minority opinion contended that an armed conflict did not become a war until it was declared by the Congress, not the president. Nelson's philosophy of *judicial self-restraint also informed his opinion for the Court in *Georgia* v. *Stanton* (1868), which dismissed efforts of two southern states to attack *Reconstruction. Nelson held that the case presented a *political question and hence was not justiciable.

In 1871 President Ulysses S. Grant named Nelson as one of the U.S. representatives to the Alabama Claims Commission, which satisfactorily resolved serious differences with Great Britain arising out of its actions supporting the South's prosecution of the Civil War. Thereafter, because of age and declining health, he resigned his seat on the Court.          Howard T. Sprow

**New Deal.** The phrase "New Deal" refers to the domestic program of President Franklin D. *Roosevelt, or in a more general sense, to his first two terms of office (1933–1941). The Supreme Court

had a great impact on the New Deal—and vice versa.

Roosevelt's approach to the crisis of the depression was characterized by an attitude of experimentation and a confidence that sufficient constitutional power already existed to enable the states and the nation to surmount economic difficulties. The Constitution was "so simple and practical," Roosevelt averred in a fireside chat, "that it can always meet extraordinary needs." The first hundred days of Roosevelt's administration produced a freshet of federal regulatory agencies and legislation, including the Agricultural Adjustment Act of 1933 (AAA) and the National Industrial Recovery Act of 1933 (NIRA).

Despite the presence of a conservative bloc dubbed by journalists the Four Horsemen (from *Revelation* 6:2–8)—Justices Willis *Van Devanter, James C. *McReynolds, Pierce *Butler, and George *Sutherland—the Court at first accepted some New Deal initiatives as well as important state regulatory legislation (*Home Building and Loan Association* v. *Blaisdell,* 1934; *Nebbia* v. *New York,* 1934). Federal measures included Congress's action voiding contractual clauses providing for payment in specie, upheld for private contracts in the so-called *Gold Clause Cases* of 1935, and creation of the Tennessee Valley Authority, sustained in *Ashwander* v. *T.V.A.* (1936).

But the conservative bloc, with the accession of Justice Owen *Roberts, and joined sometimes by Chief Justice Charles Evans *Hughes, struck powerful blows at the New Deal program in *Schechter* v. *United States* (1935), voiding the NIRA, and *United States* v. *Butler* (1936), voiding the AAA. *Carter* v. *Carter Coal Co.* (1936) exhumed the discredited *United States* v. *E. C. Knight Co.* (1895) to strike down an exercise of the *commerce power. Together with decisions negating state regulatory efforts (e.g. *Morehead* v. *New York ex rel. Tipaldo,* 1936), these decisions justified reasonable observers in concluding that the Court was likely to be blindly obstructive to all efforts to cope with the depression and to be wedded to the obsolete and regressive precedents of the *Lochner era.

Roosevelt responded with the ill-conceived *court-packing plan of 1937, which, though a tactical failure, was strategically successful in forcing a turnabout in the Court's judicial direction. Beginning with *West Coast Hotel Co.* v. *Parrish* (1937), the Court accepted state and federal regulatory legislation. It systematically dismantled the entire structure of *laissez-faire constitutionalism (including *Lochner* and *Knight*), and with it the dogmas of substantive *due process and freedom of *contract. The members of the conservative bloc (as well as Justices Benjamin N. *Cardozo, Louis D. *Brandeis, and Chief Justice Hughes) retired, enabling Roosevelt to make a string of judicial appointments that solidified the triumph of New Deal experimentation: Hugo L. *Black, Felix *Frankurter, William O. *Douglas,

Frank *Murphy, Stanley F. *Reed, and Robert H. *Jackson.
                                    William M. Wiecek

**Newsroom Searches.** Media emphasis on investigative reporting during the 1960s and 1970s intensified law enforcement interest in obtaining reporters' files and raised questions regarding the protection of the confidentiality of their sources. Protectors of newsroom materials argue that freedom of the press was designed to promote public access to information. Consequently, any interference in the newsroom harms the public.

Constitutionally, the issue focuses on the *Fourth Amendment question of the relative merits of search warrants and subpoenas. Authorities prefer warrants, which are *ex parte court orders, because they are faster and easier to obtain and execute. Journalists counter that searches increase the likelihood that investigators will see materials not specified in the warrant and thereby violate the confidentiality of sources.

Since most searched newsrooms are not under suspicion of criminal activity, additional issues of *privacy are raised. The Supreme Court ruling in Warden v. Hayden (1967) extended police search power beyond seeking instrumentalities of crime to include additional evidence within "plain sight." The opinion left unanswered the issue of whether writings obtained this way might be included within the range of court-accepted evidence.

The Supreme Court confronted the newsroom issue directly in *Zurcher v. The Stanford Daily (1978) and concluded that the First and Fourth Amendments did not provide additional protection for journalists, and that they were not entitled to any special exemption from the rules of search and seizure. As a result many media organizations revised their storage policies and destroyed photographs, notes, and other materials. In 1980, however, Congress passed the Privacy Protection Act, which limited newsroom searches to circumstances where subpoenas have been ineffective or where there is *probable cause to suspect a journalist of criminal involvement.

(See also FIRST AMENDMENT; SPEECH AND THE PRESS.)

                                    Carol E. Jenson

**New State Ice Co. v. Liebmann,** 285 U.S. 262 (1932), argued 19 Feb. 1932, decided 21 Mar. 1932 by vote of 6 to 2; Sutherland for the Court, Brandeis in dissent; Cardozo not participating. In New State Ice the Supreme Court demonstrated its commitment to the protection of entrepreneurial liberty under the Due Process Clause of the *Fourteenth Amendment. At issue was a 1925 Oklahoma statute that declared that the manufacture and sale of ice was a public business and forbade the grant of new licenses to sell ice except upon a showing of a necessity for ice in the desired community. The practical effect of the

regulation was to shut out new enterprises and thus confer a monopoly on the existing businesses. Under this statute New State Ice Company brought suit to enjoin Liebmann from selling ice in Oklahoma City without a license.

Concluding that the Oklahoma law unreasonably curtailed the common right to engage in a lawful business, Justice George *Sutherland held that the license requirement violated the Due Process Clause. Sutherland insisted that a state legislature could not impose economic regulations simply by declaring that a line of ordinary business was affected with a public use. In a lengthy dissenting opinion, Justice Louis D. *Brandeis argued that the need to eliminate destructive competition was primarily a matter for legislative determination. He maintained that federal and state governments must have the power "to remould, through experimentation, our economic practices and institutions to meet changing social and economic needs" (p. 311).

Although New State Ice has never been overruled, it has been effectively superseded by decisions that recognize broad legislative authority to regulate business enterprise. Some scholars, however, have defended New State Ice on grounds that the Oklahoma statute was classic special interest legislation designed to burden consumers in order to benefit established ice companies.

(See also DUE PROCESS, SUBSTANTIVE.)
                                    James W. Ely, Jr.

**New States.** See TERRITORIES AND NEW STATES.

**New York State Club Association v. City of New York,** 487 U.S. 1 (1988), argued 23 Feb. 1988, decided 20 June 1988 by vote of 9 to 0; White for the Court, O'Connor, joined by Kennedy and Scalia, concurring. Following the Supreme Court's decision in *Roberts v. U.S. Jaycees (1984), New York's city council sought to define clubs that were "not strictly private" and thus subject to the city's human rights law. A club with at least four hundred members, which regularly served meals and regularly received "payment for dues, fees, use of space, facilities, services, meals or beverages directly or indirectly from or on behalf of non-members for the furtherance of trade or business" was covered and thus prohibited from discriminating on account of race or sex. Benevolent orders and religious corporations were excluded.

The New York State Club Association challenged the law on its face as an unconstitutional restriction on the *First Amendment rights of intimate and expressive association of its members and also on *equal protection grounds (see ASSEMBLY AND ASSOCIATION, FREEDOM OF). A unanimous Court rejected this claim, ruling that the private associational rights of each and every club member would not be infringed by the law

## 586 □ New York Times Co. v. Sullivan

because many, if not all, had public characteristics. The Court noted that the clubs could still exclude members on the ground of nonshared views but simply could not exclude them on the basis of race or sex. The exemption for benevolent orders and religious corporations was not an equal protection violation because they uniquely exist for the benefit of their members and are not open to commercial activity.

As a result of this decision, many "males only" clubs across the country decided to admit women; these included the Cosmos Club in Washington, D.C., which counted among its members Justices Harry *Blackmun and Antonin *Scalia.

(See also GENDER.)

Inez Smith Reid

**New York Times Co. v. Sullivan,** 376 U.S. 254 (1964), argued 6 Jan. 1964, decided 9 Mar. 1964 by vote of 9 to 0; Brennan for the Court, Black, Douglas and Goldberg concurring. In this case, the Supreme Court for the first time considered the extent to which the constitutional guarantee of freedom of *speech and the press limits the award of damages in the *libel action brought by public officials against critics of their official conduct. Sullivan, an elected commissioner of the city of Montgomery, Alabama, brought a civil libel action against four black clergymen and The New York Times alleging that he had been libeled by statements in a full-page advertisement that was carried in the Times. The advertisement, which was entitled "Heed Their Rising Voices," described the *civil rights movement in the South and concluded with an appeal for funds.

It was uncontroverted that several statements contained in the text of the advertisement were inaccurate. For example, the advertisement stated that students protesting racial segregation sang "My Country, 'Tis of Thee" on the steps of the Alabama State Capitol, but they had actually sung "The Star-Spangled Banner"; it also said that several students were expelled from school for leading that protest, but they were actually expelled for demanding service at a segregated lunch counter in the Montgomery County Courthouse on another day; finally, the advertisement claimed that "the entire student body" of Alabama State College protested the expulsions, but only a majority of the students, not the "entire" student body, had protested the expulsions.

The trial judge submitted the case to the jury under instructions that these statements were libelous per se, that falsity and malice were presumed, and that general and punitive damages could be awarded without direct proof of pecuniary loss. Under these instructions, the jury returned a judgment for Sullivan in the amount of $500,000 against each of the defendants.

The Supreme Court reversed, holding that the rule of law applied by the Alabama court violated the *First Amendment. At the outset, the Court

confronted its own past declarations to the effect that libelous utterances are no essential part of any exposition of ideas (*Chaplinsky v. New Hampshire, 1942) and that they are not constitutionally protected speech (Beauharnais v. Illinois, 1952). In rejecting these prior declarations, the Court explained that, like "the various other formulae for the repression of expression that have been challenged in this Court, libel can claim no talismanic immunity from constitutional limitations"; to the contrary, libel "must be measured by standards that satisfy the First Amendment" (p. 269).

Turning to the task of articulating these standards, Justice William J. *Brennan observed in an oft-quoted passage that "we consider this case against the background of a profound national commitment to the principle that debate on public issues should be uninhibited, robust, and wide-open, and that it may well include vehement, caustic, and sometimes unpleasantly sharp attacks on government and public officials" (p. 270). Drawing upon history, the Court analogized the *civil law of libel, as applied by the Alabama court, to the *Sedition Act of 1798, which had been invalidated "in the court of history" because of the restraint it "imposed upon criticism of government and public officials" (p. 276).

The essential difficulty, Brennan explained, was that "erroneous statement is inevitable in free debate," and even false statements must therefore "be protected if the freedoms of expression are to have the 'breathing space' that they 'need . . . to survive' " (pp. 271–72). Thus, the Alabama rule of law could not be "saved by its allowance of the defense of truth," for a "rule compelling the critic of official conduct to guarantee the truth of all his factual assertions" would lead to intolerable "self-censorship." Indeed, under such a rule, "would-be critics of official conduct may be deterred from voicing their criticism, even though it is believed to be true and even though it is in fact true, because of doubt whether it can be proved in court or fear of the expense of having to do so." Such a rule, the Court concluded, "dampens the vigor and limits the variety of public debate" (pp. 278–279).

With these considerations in mind, the Court held that public officals may not recover damages for defamatory falsehood relating to their official conduct unless they can prove *actual malice; "that the statement was made with . . . knowledge that it was false or with reckless disregard of whether it was false or not" (pp. 279–280).

New York Times revolutionized the law of libel and, equally importantly, it signaled a critical shift in our general First Amendment jurisprudence. New York Times abandoned the traditional approach, which concentrated solely on whether libel was "protected" or "unprotected" speech, and embraced a more speech-protective analysis, which focused on the danger that actions for libel might deter expression that lies at the very heart of First Amendment concern. By fashioning its First Amendment standards in light of these "chilling" effects, the Court took an important step toward a more sensitive, less formulaic mode of analysis, a mode of analysis that is the hallmark of contemporary First Amendment jurisprudence.

Perhaps the most important question remaining after *New York Times* was whether the privilege it recognized governed only libel actions involving the official conduct of public officials or whether it extended to other persons. In *Curtis Publishing Co.* v. *Butts* (1967) and *Associated Press* v. *Walker* (1967), the Court, in a sharply divided set of opinions, extended the *New York Times* holding from public officials to figures such as movie stars, athletes, industrialists, and other individuals who, though they are not officials, are nonetheless well known to the public. In reaching this result, the Court rejected the argument that *New York Times* was premised on, and thus limited by, the analogy to seditious libel. Rather, the Court reasoned that *New York Times* rested on a profound national commitment to ininhibited, robust, and wide-open debate on public issues. The Court therefore concluded that libelous utterances concerning public figures, like libelous utterances concerning public officials, must be governed by the *New York Times* privilege.

Several years later, however, in *\*Gertz* v. *Robert Welch, Inc.* (1974), the Court, again sharply divided, recognized an important limitation on the scope of *New York Times*, holding that it did not extend to libel actions brought by private individuals, even where the defamatory statement concerned a matter of "public concern." The Court explained that, unlike public officials and public figures, private individuals are usually unable to rebut the libel effectively and they usually have not gone out of their way to seek the public's attention. The Court reasoned that, because private individuals are more vulnerable to injury and more deserving of recovery than either public officials or public figures, they may recover damages for libel merely by showing that the publisher or broadcaster had acted negligently in disseminating the defamatory material.

*New York Times* and its progeny have been criticized as both overprotective and underprotective of free expression. Some critics maintain that *New York Times* failed adequately to protect the press because its "reckless disregard" standard implicitly authorized highly intrusive inquiries into the thought processes of reporters and editors and because it failed to preclude large and potentially "chilling" damage awards whenever a jury would find that the press has acted with "reckless disregard." These critics, echoing the views expressed by Justices Hugo \*Black, William O. \*Douglas and Arthur \*Goldberg in their concurring opinions in *New York Times*, argue that the press should have absolute protec-

tion against actions for libel. Other critics maintain that *New York Times* gave too much protection to the press and failed to protect the innocent victims of libel. These critics fault *New York Times* for denying innocent victims reasonable compensation for the harm they suffer and for preventing such victims from obtaining a judicial declaration of falsity, which would at least set the record straight.

Several proposals have been offered in recent years in an effort to "cure" these "deficiencies." The most intriguing of these proposals calls for the creation of a new civil action in which the alleged victim of a defamatory falsehood could sue for a judicial declaration of falsity upon waiving the right to sue for damages. The theory is that such an action would reduce litigation costs and enable the victims of libel to vindicate their reputations without intruding into the editorial process or threatening the press with potentially devastating damage awards. Although this approach would avoid some of the problems identified with *New York Times*, it would effectively empower the judiciary to decide on a case-by-case basis whether specific statements made by the press are "true" or "false." It is questionable whether such a relationship between the judiciary and the press would comport with the underlying theory and assumptions of the First Amendment.

*New York Times* cannot be fully understood without recognizing that it was driven not only by concerns about free expression but also by the unique historical circumstances in which it arose. *New York Times* was, in short, a product of the civil rights movement of the 1950s and 1960s. Like other devices designed to obstruct the civil rights movement, the libel judgment against the *New York Times* and the African-American clergymen named in the advertisement was designed to dampen the drive for civil rights. After all, if this Alabama jury's massive damage award could be sustained on the basis of such minor inaccuracies, then no person or institution would be free to challenge racial segregation in the South. *New York Times*, one of most important decisions in the history of the First Amendment, was thus not only a triumph for free expression, it was a triumph for civil rights and racial equality as well.

□ David A. Barrett, "Declaratory Judgments for Libel," *California Law Review* 74 (1986): 847–888. Harry Kalven, Jr., "The New York Times Case: A Note on 'The Central Meaning of the First Amendment,' " *Supreme Court Review* (1964): 191–221. Rodney A. Smolla, *Suing the Press* (1986).                    Geoffrey R. Stone

**New York Times Co. v. United States,** 403 U.S. 713 (1971), argued 26 June 1971, decided 30 June 1971 by vote of 6 to 3; Douglas, Stewart, White, Marshall, Black, and Brennan writing separately, Burger, Blackmun, and Harlan in dissent. On 13 June 1971, the *New York Times* published the first installment of the "Pentagon Papers," a classified, seven thousand page document commissioned by President Lyndon Johnson's secretary of defense, Robert McNamara. It revealed that secrecy had been the handmaiden of deception. Other newspapers quickly serialized the documents, leaked by Daniel Ellsberg, a dissident former bureaucrat in the national security apparatus.

Nixon administration officials initially regarded the documents as embarrassing only to previous administrations. President Richard *Nixon himself thought that the "opposition" had an interest in forgetting the papers, but "ours is to play it up." But with National Security Adviser Henry Kissinger, Nixon also realized that publication imperiled his own policies, his patterns of secrecy, and his credibility. Most important, Nixon feared that future presidents would lose control over classified documents and thus potentially embarrass their predecessors.

The administration secured a lower court order on 15 June temporarily restraining publication. Three days later, the judge denied a permanent *injunction, but a circuit judge blocked further publication pending the government's appeal. On 25 June the Supreme Court agreed to take an expedited appeal, bypassing the intermediate court, yet did not lift the restraining order. Justices Hugo *Black, William *Brennan, William O. *Douglas, and Thurgood *Marshall protested the maintenance of the *prior restraint. Arguments were heard the next day, and in conference, the justices voted 6 to 3 to deny the government's request for a permanent order. The Court issued a brief *per curiam decision on 30 June, stating that the government had not met the burden of proving a need for prior restraint.

The government had contended that publication would endanger lives, the release of prisoners of war, and the peace process—arguments that most of the justices readily dismissed as transparent. *Solicitor General Erwin Griswold himself had serious doubts about the argument the Administration insisted on making; later, he said that the decision "came out exactly as it should."

The haste of hearing arguments and deciding inevitably led to fragmentation among the justices. Black, Brennan, and Douglas insisted that any injunction constituted prior restraint, and the Court never should have allowed any halt to publication. Justices Byron *White, Marshall, and Potter *Stewart agreed that prior restraint was unnecessary in this case but rejected the absolutist position of their majority colleagues. Chief Justice Warren *Burger and Justices Harry *Blackmun and John M. *Harlan dissented, each objecting to the rush of the proceedings. Burger also emphasized his belief that publishers could be prosecuted for criminal violations of security statutes for printing classified information, but only after publication.

The Court, however divided, largely agreed that prior restraint was extraordinary. Nevertheless, the Burger Court soon allowed the Central Intelligence Agency to require former employees to submit proposed writings to review (*Marchetti v. United States*, 1968; *Snepp* v. *United States*, 1980). Criminal statutes abounded for dealing with security breaches; indeed Daniel Ellsberg, who had leaked the documents, eventually was indicted and tried for his role in the case. Ironically, the administration's own illegal behavior resulted in a mistrial and, eventually, the dropping of the indictment.

The Supreme Court's decision legitimated the media's assaults against governmental secrecy and its self-assumed status as the people's paladin against official wrongdoing. The incident intensified an already sharpened adversarial relationship between the press and the administration, a relationship that was to deteriorate even more, and with devastating results for Nixon.

(See also FIRST AMENDMENT; SPEECH AND THE PRESS; VIETNAM WAR.)

Stanley I. Kutler

**New York v. Belton,** 453 U.S. 454 (1981), argued 27 Apr. 1981, decided 1 July 1981 by vote of 6 to 3; Stewart for the Court, Brennan and White in dissent. In this case six members of the Supreme Court agreed to expand the constitutionally permissible scope of a warrantless automobile search incident to a lawful custodial arrest. The circumstances here are similar to many *automobile search cases. After the car was stopped for speeding, the occupants were removed and arrested when the police detected the odor of marijuana. A policeman searched the back seat of the car, found a jacket belonging to Belton, unzipped one of the pockets and discovered cocaine. At his trial, Belton moved to suppress admission of the cocaine, arguing that it had been seized in violation of the *Fourth and *Fourteenth Amendments. Writing for the majority, Justice Potter *Stewart argued that to guide police officers it was necessary to adopt the "single familiar standard" articulated in *Chimel* v. *California* (1969). In *Chimel*, the Court said that a lawful custodial arrest justifies a search of the immediate surrounding areas without a warrant. Justice Stewart reasoned that because the jacket was located inside the car where Belton had been just before his arrest, the jacket was "within the arrestee's immediate control" (even though Belton and his companions were no longer in or near the automobile.

The dissenting justices disputed this interpretation of *Chimel*, arguing that its policy justifications for a warrantless search (i.e., to insure the safety of the arresting officer and to prevent evidence from being concealed or destroyed) were deliberately narrow and did not justify the latitude given police officers in this case. The issue in *Chimel*, they concluded, was not whether the arrestee could ever have reached the area that was searched, but whether he could have reached it at the time of the arrest and search.

(See also SEARCH WARRANT RULE, EXCEPTIONS TO.)

Christine B. Harrington

**New York v. Miln,** 11 Pet. (36 U.S.) 102 (1837), argued 27–28 Jan. 1837, decided 16 Feb. 1837 by vote of 6 to 1; Barbour for the Court, Thompson concurring, Story in dissent. *Miln* was the first major Commerce Clause case to come before the Taney Court. It involved an ordinance requiring ships' masters to provide a passenger manifest, to post security for indigent passengers, and to remove undesirable aliens. Because this ordinance involved the states' powers to control the ingress of persons, the ordinance raised delicate and explosive questions implicating the interstate transit of slaves, free blacks, abolitionists, and antislavery propaganda. The recent precedent of *Gibbons* v. *Ogden* (1824) might have suggested the unconstitutionality of such state regulation, but the hidden presence of *slavery questions skewed constitutional doctrine.

Justice Philip P. *Barbour avoided the dangerous question of concurrent federal-state commerce powers, suggesting only that the Commerce Clause probably encompassed trade in "goods" rather than "persons" (p. 136). For the first time in its history, the Court then invoked state *police powers as a constitutionally permissible ground for regulating the contents of vessels plying interstate waterways. Barbour's reading of state police powers alarmed antislavery groups. The statute, he said, was a "regulation, not of commerce, but of police" (p. 132); a state's right to protect the health and welfare of its citizens, unlike the right to regulate interstate commerce, had not been "surrendered or restrained," but was "complete, unqualified, and exclusive" (p. 139). In dissent, Justice Joseph *Story insisted that the law infringed federal powers under the Commerce Clause. *Miln* remained good authority until 1941, when the Court ruled that *Miln* erroneously permitted legislators to use economic status as a criterion for limiting personal mobility (*Edwards* v. *California*).

Sandra F. VanBurkleo

**Nine Old Men.** As the Supreme Court resisted *New Deal efforts to cope with the economic crisis of the depression in 1935–1937, many persons criticized the justices, often in ad hominen terms. President Franklin D. *Roosevelt's *court-packing plan of 1937, which drew attention to the elderly justices, encouraged a perception that the Court was composed of "Nine Old Men," the title of a critical book published in 1936 by journalists Drew Pearson and Robert Allen.

William M. Wiecek

**Nineteenth Amendment.** A women's suffrage amendment was first introduced in Congress in 1868. Ten years later, suffrage supporters proposed the so-called Anthony Amendment, named for Susan B. Anthony, which was modeled after the *Fifteenth Amendment. It provided that "the right of citizens of the United States to vote shall not be denied or abridged by the United States or by any State on account of sex." This was to become the language of section 1 of the Nineteenth Amendment, but forty-two years were to go by before it became part of the Constitution.

Unsure of the prospects of a constitutional amendment, suffragists simultaneously resorted to litigation, with no success. Anthony was prosecuted for attempting to vote when she had no "lawful right" to do so (*United States* v. *Anthony*, 1873). Virginia Minor brought a civil suit in an attempt to enforce her right to vote in national elections as a *privilege or immunity of national citizenship. The Supreme court rejected this argument, holding that the Fourteenth Amendment did not confer the right to vote on women any more than it conferred such a right on children, the insane, or criminals (*Minor* v. *Happersett*, 1875). This result conformed to the Court's restrictive interpretation of the clause in the *Slaughterhouse Cases* of 1873.

Impelled by women's activism in the temperance, social work, and other reform crusades, and taking advantage of the changing social environment wrought by *World War I, the suffragist movement succeeded in persuading Congress to enact the Nineteenth Amendment in 1919. It was ratified on 26 August 1920.

(See also CONSTITUTIONAL AMENDMENTS; GENDER.)

Nancy S. Erickson

**Ninth Amendment** provides that "[t]he enumeration in the Constitution, of certain rights, shall not be construed to deny or disparage others retained by the people." On its face, this provision seems to mean that a right is worthy of judicial protection even if it is not listed in the Constitution. To fail to protect these "other" unenumerated rights "retained by the people" in the same manner that we protect the enumerated rights would surely be to "disparage" them if not to "deny" their existence altogether.

Others doubt that this is what the Ninth Amendment means. Some have argued that it expresses a mere "truism" that the government should not do what it is not supposed to do. Some have thought that the "retained" rights refer only to state *common-law rights and state constitutional rights existing at the time of the framing. Unlike enumerated "constitutional" rights, these retained rights could be modified by simple legislation or state constitutional amendment without violating the Constitution.

*Background.* The Ninth Amendment was conceived after the heated debate surrounding the ratification of the Constitution. Antifederalist opponents of the Constitution emphasized its lack of a bill of rights securing the liberty of the people. Federalist proponents of ratification responded by questioning the wisdom of including a bill of rights in the Constitution. In *The *Federalist,* no. 84, for example, Alexander *Hamilton argued that "bills of rights . . . are not only unnecessary in the proposed Constitution, but would even be dangerous."

To appreciate the source of the perceived danger we must remember that the framers believed in natural rights—the idea that people by their nature have certain basic rights that precede the establishment of any government (see NATURAL LAW). As Representative Roger Sherman wrote in his proposed draft of a bill of rights: "The people have certain natural rights which are retained by them when they enter into Society." Sherman's words reflect the sentiments expressed by several state ratification conventions. According to John Locke, the English natural rights theorist who greatly influenced the founders' generation, the principal justification for founding a government is to make these rights more secure than they would be in a state of nature—that is, in a society without any government.

In this view, natural rights define a bounded domain of liberty for each person within which one may do as one pleases. Exactly how this liberty may be exercised is limited only by one's imagination, so it is impossible to enumerate specifically all of one's natural rights. As framer and bill of rights opponent James *Wilson stated: "Enumerate all the rights of men! I am sure, sirs, that no gentleman in the late Convention would have attempted such a thing."

The Antifederalists were defeated only when Federalists promised to propose and support a bill of rights in the First Congress. James *Madison and the committee of the House of Representatives charged with drafting a bill of rights had to sort through dozens of rights that state ratification conventions had officially recommended be included in the Constitution. The rights they eventually enumerated in the *Bill of Rights appear to be those that their experience suggested were the most in jeopardy. Some (but not all) of the rights they chose to enumerate—such as the right to freedom of speech—were considered by both Madison and Sherman to be natural rights that were "retained" by the people.

As for the Federalist warnings that later interpreters might assert that the people had surrendered any rights omitted from the enumeration, Madison proposed to guard against this possibility by adding the following amendment: "The exceptions here or elsewhere in the constitution, made in favor of particular rights, shall not be construed as to diminish the just importance of other rights retained by the people, or as to enlarge the powers delegated by the constitution; but either as actual limitations of such powers, or as inserted merely for greater caution." Eventually, this language was transformed into the words of the Ninth Amendment.

*Modern Interpretations.* For one and a half centuries following its ratification, the Ninth Amendment was largely ignored by the Supreme Court. Since *World War II, the Court has offered two different interpretations of the Ninth Amendment reflecting two views of constitutional rights. The first might be called the "rights-powers" interpretation. According to this view, retained rights and delegated powers are logically complementary. Retained rights are those left over after powers were delegated to the federal government. To interpret the Ninth Amendment, we simply look to see if the federal government has the power it claims; if so, any right that is logically inconsistent with this power could not be among those retained by the people.

Justice Stanley *Reed stated this view in *United Public Workers v. Mitchell (1947): "The powers granted by the Constitution to the Federal Government are subtracted from the totality of sovereignty originally in the states and the people. . . . If granted power is found, necessarily the objection of invasion of those rights, reserved by the Ninth and Tenth Amendment must fail" (p. 95). However, since the *Tenth Amendment clearly limits the exercise of federal power to powers delegated by the Constitution, this interpretation seems to render the Ninth Amendment without any practical function. Until recently, most scholars accepted this view.

The other approach may be called the "power-constraint" interpretation. According to this view, retained rights and delegated powers are functionally complementary. Even a power actually granted to the government can be constrained by a retained right. For example, when a retained right is infringed, the government might have to offer a more weighty justification for exercising its power than it would when no right is infringed. Moreover, although the Ninth Amendment, like the rest of the Bill of Rights, originally applied only to the federal government, this interpretation sees the passage of the *Fourteenth Amendment as extending federal protection against state infringement to both enumerated and unenumerated rights.

Justice Arthur *Goldberg took a power-constraint approach in his concurring opinion in *Griswold v. Connecticut (1965)—an opinion that did much to revive interest in the Ninth Amendment: "[W]here fundamental personal liberties are involved, they may not be abridged by the States simply on a showing that a regulatory statute has some rational relationship to the effectuation of a proper state purpose" (p. 497). Goldberg further argued that the Ninth Amendment justified protecting fundamental liberties that had not been included in the enumeration of rights. On this view, protecting both enumerated and unenumerated retained rights better safeguards the liberties of the people by reinforcing the scheme of limited delegated powers.

These two approaches are not mutually exclusive. Rather than view the set of retained rights as shrinking automatically as governmental powers are interpreted more expansively, we could reverse Justice Reed's rights-powers method of interpretation. Instead of limiting our inquiry to the expressed delegation of powers, we could examine the rights retained by the people to define the legitimate "ends" or powers of the government and thus provide an additional way of conceptualizing limits on government powers. An analysis of retained rights could also constrain the "means" by which governmental ends can be achieved.

Enumerated rights have long served a power-constraining function. For example, the *First Amendment has been interpreted as protecting the "retained" rights of free speech by constraining government from pursuing the end of regulating the content of one's speech. The *Fourth Amendment constrains government from pursuing its proper ends by means of unreasonable searches and seizures.

Similarly, the right to use birth control that was protected in *Griswold* exemplifies an unenumerated "ends constraint." If such activities are within the sphere of bounded liberty retained by the people, they are beyond the rightful power of government. The case of *Richmond Newspapers, Inc.,* v. *Virginia* (1980) provides an example of an unenumerated "means constraint." There, a plurality of the Court, relying in part on the Ninth Amendment, protected the rights of the press to attend a public trial. Although the government may have the power to prosecute and try a defendant, it cannot do so by means of excluding the press.

*Identifying Unenumerated Rights.* Some argue that, lacking an understanding of or belief in the framers' theory of natural rights, modern judges are simply unable to identify these "other" retained rights. As unsuccessful Supreme Court nominee Robert *Bork testified during his Senate confirmation hearings: "I do not think you can use the Ninth Amendment unless you know something of what it means. For example, if you had an amendment that says 'Congress shall make no' and then there is an inkblot, and you cannot read the rest of it, and that is the only copy you have, I do not think the court can make up what might be under the inkblot." On this view, empowering judges to protect rights where the Constitution is silent enables them illegitimately to "create" rights based only on their personal preferences and improperly obstruct the will of the people as expressed by their democratically elected representatives.

Ironically, this view is commonly advanced by constitutional theorists who profess a deep respect for the framer's intentions. Yet this skeptical view of unenumerated rights would have the practical effect of converting the original scheme of limited defined powers in a sea of individual rights into a scheme of limited enumerated rights in a sea of governmental powers.

There may, however, be a practical way to protect the bounded domain of individual liberty without engaging in an elaborate philosophical analysis of natural rights. We could adopt a constitutional "Presumption of liberty," by which people are presumed to be free to act in any way that did not violate the "common-law rights" of others. For example, actions that constituted a tort or a breach of contract could justly be prohibited. But actions that did not violate such rights could be regulated by government only upon a strong showing that such regulation was essential or necessary to achieve some proper governmental end.

Placing the burden on government to justify any action restricting a rightful exercise of liberty is precisely how the Court protects retained rights that are enumerated. For example, when legislation restricts the exercise of free speech, a serious burden is placed upon the government to justify such restrictions. A presumption of liberty would avoid "denying" or "disparaging" unenumerated rights by treating them on a par with enumerated rights.

A presumption of liberty would, however, be a departure from the prevailing attitude of the Supreme Court. In cases such as *Carolene Products Co.* v. *United States* (1944), the Court created the opposite: a presumption of constitutionality that upholds government action unless it violates an identifiable fundamental right. And, since using the unenumerated right to privacy to protect *abortion in *Roe* v. *Wade* (1973), the Court has become increasingly unwilling to deem any unenumerated right to be fundamental. In *Bowers* v. *Hardwick* (1986), for example, the Court majority belittled the idea that consensual *homosexual sodomy was protected by the right to privacy.

This attitude largely ignores or trivializes the Ninth Amendment as well as the Supreme Court's long tradition of protecting unenumerated rights. One early example is the right to *travel within the United States. Although such a right was explicit in the Articles of Confederation, it was omitted from the Constitution. Yet the Supreme Court protected this unenumerated right as early as 1867 in the case of *Crandall* v. *Nevada* (1867). And, after having greatly constricted its scrutiny of legislation in the 1930s and 1940s, the Court backed away from this stance after 1964 with a series of cases protecting *"fundamental rights" including an unenumerated right to privacy.

Protecting unenumerated rights as we protect those that are enumerated keeps a sphere of liberty "off limits" to government power and, at the same time, restricts the means by which government may use its delegated powers to restrict liberty. A power-constraining interpretation of the Ninth Amendment legitimizes the Court's tradition of protecting unenumerated rights and reinforces the original scheme of limited governmental powers.

☐ Randy E. Barnett, ed., "Symposium on Interpreting the Ninth Amendment," *Chicago-Kent Law Review* 64 (1988): 37–268. Randy E. Barnett, ed., *The Rights Retained by the People*, vol. 1, *The History and Meaning of the Ninth Amendment* (1989); vol. 2, *Constitutional Interpretation and the Ninth Amendment* (1992). Bennett B. Patterson, *The Forgotten Ninth Amendment* (1955).      Randy E. Barnett

**Nixon, Richard** (b. 9 Jan. 1913, Yorba Linda, Calif.), lawyer, statesman, and president of the United States, 1969–1974. President Nixon resigned in 1974 after five years in office because of his role in the Watergate scandal, the first chief executive in history to do so. The Supreme Court prominently figured in bringing about the resignation; it also loomed large throughout Nixon's presidency.

In the 1968 campaign, Nixon assailed the Warren Court's decisions, and he emphasized the need for new justices who favored the "peace forces" rather than criminals. Nixon ignored the social and economic bases for the increased crime and violence in the nation, but he undoubtedly appealed to a large bloc of voters who believed that the Supreme Court had fostered contempt for the law.

After Lyndon Johnson withdrew Abe *Fortas's nomination to succeed Earl *Warren as chief justice, Warren's resignation seemed in doubt. But Nixon promptly secured Warren's agreement to leave in June 1969. Nixon considered promoting Justice Potter *Stewart, but the president recognized the symbolic effect of the appointment. (See CHIEF JUSTICE, OFFICE OF THE.) Warren Earl *Burger of the D.C. Circuit Court of Appeals proved exactly that, for he consistently had been a lone dissenter on what was arguably the most liberal court in the nation. Burger regularly had criticized his colleagues, both on and off the bench, for their activism and excessive concern for the rights of the criminally accused. (See JUDICIAL ACTIVISM.)

After selecting Burger, Nixon promised more justices with "unquestioned integrity" and said he would have an "arm's length" relationship with Burger—both points clearly directed at Fortas, who had ethical problems and who regularly consulted with Johnson on policy matters. Nixon emphasized that he would appoint federal judges who shared his philosophy of "strict construction," a designated code for opposition to the Warren Court's rulings in areas of social policy. At one point, Nixon praised Chief Justice John *Marshall as a "strict constructionist"; at

another time, he denounced the Court's prayer ruling in 1962, because it "followed [the] usual pattern of interpreting the constitution rigidly."

When Fortas resigned in May 1969 because of new revelations questioning his ethical behavior, Nixon quickly decided to fulfill campaign obligations to his southern supporters. In August, he nominated Fourth Circuit Judge Clement F. *Haynsworth, from South Carolina, a choice that provoked intense opposition from labor and civil rights groups. Haynsworth's record also raised ethical issues, enough perhaps to justify opposition from liberals still resentful over the treatment of Fortas. Seventeen Republican senators joined northern Democrats in November 1969 to defeat Haynsworth's nomination, 55 to 45—the first time since 1930 that the Senate rejected a Supreme Court nomination. Haynsworth was victimized by political forces anxious to retaliate against Nixon, rather than by his own record. Nixon promptly nominated another southern conservative, Fifth Circuit Court Judge G. Harrold *Carswell, of Florida. Carswell's overtly racist record, and his mediocre legal and judicial record, struck many as a studied insult to the Court's standing as an institution. Again, Republicans broke ranks, and in April 1970, the Senate defeated the nomination, 51 to 45.

Furious, Nixon insisted that his choices had been turned down because they were "southern strict constructionists." The Senate, he charged, had denied him "the same right of choice" that had been "freely accorded" to others, a contention clearly at odds with the historical record. Nixon, however, understood his limitations, and he subsequently nominated Eighth Circuit Court Judge Harry *Blackmun, from Minnesota. Nixon peevishly let it be known that Blackmun was to the right of the candidates on law and order and only slightly to their left in civil rights. Ironically, Blackmun wrote the Court's pro-abortion ruling in 1973, easily the Burger-Nixon Court's most liberal opinion. (See ABORTION.)

In September 1971, Justices Hugo L. *Black and John M. *Harlan resigned because of ill health. Some presidential advisers wanted another confrontation with the Senate on civil rights; others cynically proposed nominating a southern Democratic senator who had a dubious record in the area. At one point, Attorney General John Mitchell asked the American Bar Association to approve California local judge Mildred Lillie, who would have been the first woman, and Herschel Friday, an Arkansas bond lawyer. (See AMERICAN BAR ASSOCIATION COMMITTEE ON FEDERAL JUDICIARY.) The ABA committee balked, but before its opposition became publicly known, the president nominated Virginian Lewis *Powell, a former ABA president, and Assistant Attorney General William *Rehnquist.

Powell's widely acclaimed selection gave the lie to Nixon's charge that the Senate would not accept a Southerner. Rehnquist, a man Nixon once called a "clown," however, proved trouble-some. An outspoken conservative, Rehnquist had antagonized congressmen because of his support for luxuriant claims for *executive privilege, but most of all because as Justice Robert H. *Jackson's clerk in 1953, he apparently had opposed reversing *Plessy v. Ferguson (1896). Rehnquist effectively defended himself and eventually was confirmed.

Powell and Rehnquist were Nixon's last appointments. But Nixon yearned for more opportunities to shape the Court in his own image. He asked Burger at one time to "nudge" Justices William O. *Douglas and Thurgood *Marshall to resign. With his knowledge, the Justice Department provided materials to Congressman Gerald Ford to assist him in the abortive effort to impeach Douglas. (See IMPEACHMENT.) Nixon considered asking Burger to step aside for a younger man. Nothing came of either idea.

Nixon's relationship with the Supreme Court also was distinguished by the policy and personal defeats he suffered at the hands of the Justices. In *United States v. United States District Court (1972), the Court unanimously rejected the administration's claim that it could order electronic surveillance without prior judicial approval. Most significant, of course, in United States v. *Nixon (1974), the Court, again in an 8-to-0 vote, ruled that notwithstanding Nixon's assertion of executive privilege, he must surrender certain tape recordings to the Watergate special prosecutor because of their links to criminal allegations. Those tapes clearly implicated the president in an obstruction of justice and led to congressional demands for Nixon's resignation.

The Court's role in resolving the tapes controversy was applauded throughout the nation. Ironically, the institution that Nixon had rather contemptuously regarded, but yet which he had significantly reshaped, unanimously contributed to his downfull.　　　　　Stanley I. Kutler

**Nixon, United States v.,** 418 U.S. 683 (1974), argued 8 July 1974, decided 24 July 1974 by vote of 8 to 0; Burger for the Court, Rehnquist not participating. A climactic incident in a dramatic event in U.S. history—the only case of a president being driven out of office in disgrace—the decision in United States v. Nixon was also a major constitutional landmark. It established the conditional nature of presidential immunity and in turn, may have affected the later decision, in *Butz v. Economou (1978), not to follow the plurality view in Barr v. Matteo (1959) of absolute administrative immunity. Above all, it reined in extravagant assertions of President Richard *Nixon's lawyers, who claimed presidential power to be unlimited, especially as to foreign and defense matters, and defined solely by a president's own judgment. In forcefully refuting such claims and proclaiming that no one is above the law, Chief Justice Warren *Burger's opinion

nevertheless twice quoted Chief Justice John *Marshall's words, in United States v. Burr (1807), to the effect that presidential accountability to the legal order does not mean courts may proceed with the president as with any other citizen. Burger also enunciated a strong presumption of executive immunity and privilege.

The background of the case is the stuff of which books, novels, and movies are (and were) made. In 1972, burglars were discovered breaking into the Democratic campaign headquarters in Washington's Watergate apartment/hotel complex. It gradually emerged that the burglars had CIA and White House connections. The legal (and illegal) efforts to protect the burglars eventually involved President Nixon, though it was never established with whom authority for the break-in ultimately rested nor why the act had been committed.

The effort to sweep matters under the rug generated complex further maneuvers, many involving payments of money to keep the arrested burglars from talking. The proliferation of illegal activity created new rumors and investigations. The courts, the Department of Justice, the FBI, and Congress all conducted investigations, and the media pursued the case thoroughly. Lower-level Nixon aides, many of whom ultimately went to jail, cooperated in order to minimize their sentences. There were flat discrepancies between their testimony and statements of the president. To quiet criticism, Nixon and Attorney General Eliot Richardson set up a special prosecutor's office with a promise of independence. Archibald Cox, who had been *solicitor general under President John F. Kennedy, agreed to serve.

Congressional hearings established that Nixon had installed a voice-activated tape recorder in his office, and, armed with this knowledge along with White House appointment records, the special prosecutor sought to obtain certain tapes that he thought would establish the truthfulness or falsity of the president's statements and the testimony of his aides, especially his legal counsel, John Dean.

The president ordered Cox to desist, and, when he refused, ordered the attorney general to remove him. The attorney general and his deputy resigned rather than obey, but on their advice Solicitor General Robert *Bork (who had not been a party to the original agreement) did the President's bidding as acting attorney general.

The public outcry was so great, however, that a new special prosecutor, Leon Jaworski, was appointed; Jaworski reinstated the request for tapes. Federal district court judge John Sirica then issued a subpoena to the president, demanding that he produce the tapes.

In the Supreme Court, Nixon's attorneys argued that the matter was nonjusticiable. They reasoned that it was a dispute among departments within the executive branch and that, as such, it was a matter to be resolved by the president, not by the courts; they compared the dispute to one between congressional committees, which would be resolved by Congress without judicial interference. The Court rejected this argument, noting that Bork's agreement with Jaworski had, in fact, included consultation with Congress. The decision also relied on cases such as *Peters* v. *Hobby* (1955) and *United States ex rel. Accardi* v. *Shaughnessy* (1953), which had made clear that executive regulations that were thoroughly repealable nonetheless had legal effect and created rights enforceable in court so long as they were still in effect. The Court's agreement with the special prosecutor thus gave him authority to proceed. The courts had assumed in prior decisions on congressional immunity that they, and not Congress, defined its boundaries, and were in parallel fashion the appropriate forum as to the executive's prerogatives.

On the basic questions of executive immunity and privilege the Supreme Court held that the president was entitled to great deference, especially in matters of defense and *national security, and that all presumptions were in his favor. But the prosecutor had particularized and precisely stated needs for specific tapes, both with respect to credibility of witnesses and for establishing the alleged crime. Too, Nixon's claim of confidentiality had already been weakened by his release of the partial contents of the subpoenaed tapes and others.

At odds, then, were the enfeebled and diffuse claims of the executive branch versus the specific claims of the justice system in prosecuting a criminal case.

Burger's opinion emphasized throughout the need for deference and accommodation and cautioned that courts must not take lightly the presumptions protecting the privilege and immunity of the president. Nonetheless, it unequivocably rendered such privileges conditional, dependent on circumstances. Nixon was ordered to give up the tapes, which, it turned out, contained the "smoking gun" linking him to the conspiracy to obstruct justice. Less than three weeks later, he resigned from office.

(See also EXECUTIVE IMMUNITY; EXECUTIVE PRIVILEGE; INHERENT POWERS.)

Samuel Krislov

**Nixon v. Administrator of General Services,** 433 U.S. 425 (1977), argued 20 Apr. 1977, decided 28 June 1977, by vote of 7 to 2; Brennan for the Court, White, Stevens, Blackmun, and Powell concurring, Rehnquist and Burger in dissent. Subsequent to President Richard *Nixon's resignation in 1974 to avoid *impeachment, he reached an agreement with the General Services Administration, by which they shared control of his presidential papers for three years after which they were to be at his disposal. The tapes of his White House meetings, which were a key element in

proving his complicity in the Watergate cover up, were to remain with the GSA. Except for those he requested destroyed after five years, all tapes were to be kept for ten years or until his death. Although ex-presidents had exercised full authority over their papers, Congress moved to protect those historically important papers and tapes by vesting complete control in the GSA subject to "any rights, defenses or privileges which the federal government or any person might invoke."

The day after the Presidential Recordings and Materials Act was signed into law, Nixon challenged the Act as violating the *separation of powers and his personal *privacy rights. Since presidents before had retained rights to their papers, he also claimed the act was a bill of *attainder. The district court and court of appeals sustained the act against those challenges.

Justice William *Brennan's opinion rejected the government's contention that since President Gerald Ford signed the act and President Jimmy Carter affirmed it, Nixon had no right to assert executive claims. On the merits, though, Nixon's claims were rejected. Reaffirming a flexible doctrine of separation of powers and qualified immunity and privilege, the Court noted the safeguards and opportunity for challenge by Nixon built into the statute. As to both privilege and privacy, archivists were to have access, but this was not more obtrusive than *in camera* inspection by judges, as in *United States* v. *Nixon* (1974).

Finally, the Court rejected the bill of attainder argument, finding it neither functionally nor in intent a punishment. Given the circumstances, Congress could reasonably infer a public need to know more and conclude that Nixon was an improper custodian of what historically have been regarded as public papers in ex-presidents' hands.

Justice Byron *White concurred but was troubled by the taking of what has in effect been treated as presidential property even though the act preserved Nixon's right to claim compensation. Justice John Paul *Stevens also concurred, specifically finding that Nixon constituted "a legitimate class of one."

Chief Justice Warren *Burger and Justice William *Rehnquist dissented separately. The chief justice emphasized that *U.S.* v. *Nixon* had authorized only narrow, need-to-know incursions on *executive privilege. The invasion of privacy here was almost untrammeled and the government seemed to him to have to bear a heavier burden to justify it. Finally he found the act in form and fact a bill of attainder. Rehnquist's opinion vigorously argued that the decision left all presidential papers available for seizure by future acts of congress, a policy that he opposed.

Samuel Krislov

**Nixon v. Condon,** 286 U.S. 73 (1932), argued 7 Jan. 1932, reargued 15 Mar. 1932, decided 2 May 1932 by vote of 5 to 4; Cardozo for the Court,

McReynolds in dissent. After *Reconstruction, the Democratic party dominated southern politics. A Democratic primary victory was tantamount to an election; therefore, state laws barring blacks from participation in primaries were an effective disfranchisement. In *Nixon v. Herndon (1927), the Supreme Court had held that a Texas statute prohibiting blacks from voting in primaries denied them *equal protection under the *Fourteenth Amendment. Texas responded by granting state party executive committees the power to determine qualifications. The state Democratic committee promptly limited primary participation to whites. When Nixon, a black, was denied a primary ballot he sued, alleging that the committee had acted under the authority of the state statute and violated the Fourteenth Amendment. The defendant election officials argued that the *political party was a private association and could define its own membership.

In his first opinion for the Court, Justice Benjamin N. *Cardozo held the arrangement unconstitutional. The power to determine membership qualifications rested with the annual state party convention, which had never delegated its authority to the executive committee; instead, the committee's authority was vested by the state statute. This narrow holding suggested the option—subsequently exercised by Texas—to repeal all primary election statutes thus allowing state party conventions to exclude blacks. This approach to black disfranchisement was permitted until *Smith v. Allwright (1944) established that primary elections were inherently *state action and subject to the Constitution.

(See also RACE AND RACISM; WHITE PRIMARY.)
Thomas E. Baker

**Nixon v. Herndon,** 273 U.S. 536 (1927), argued 4 Jan. 1927, decided 7 Mar. 1927 by vote of 9 to 0, Holmes for the Court. The collapse of the Republican party in the South after Reconstruction, and then, in 1896, of the Populist party, led to one-party government by the Democratic party in the region. This cut off southern blacks from the one election that counted: the Democratic primary. In the 1920s, Texas blacks sought to register and vote as Democrats. Texas countered with a law barring blacks from voting in the Democratic primary. Dr. L. A. Nixon, a black man from El Paso, attacked the law as a violation of the *Fourteenth and *Fifteenth Amendments. Though both sides had primarily argued the Fifteenth Amendment, the Court found it unnecessary to consider that issue because it found the Texas law a violation of the *Equal Protection Clause of the Fourteenth Amendment.

Whether, in fact, the law violated the Fourteenth Amendment is a harder question than one might have guessed from Justice Oliver Wendell *Holmes's brisk, epigrammatic opinion. None of the Fourteenth Amendment's sponsors thought it protected the right to vote; neither had the Supreme Court in *Minor v. Happersett (1875).

Nixon did not end the blacks' exclusion but merely induced Texas to shift that task to the Democratic party. Only in *Smith v. Allwright (1944) did the Court rely on the Fifteenth Amendment to outlaw *white primaries altogether and finally permit the integration of blacks into southern politics.
Ward E. Y. Elliott

**Nollan v. California Coastal Commission,** 483 U.S. 825 (1987), argued 30 Mar. 1987, decided 26 June 1987 by vote of 5 to 4; Scalia for the Court, Brennan, Blackmun, and Stevens in dissent. An important takings decision, Nollan involved a challenge to an effort by California to enhance the public's enjoyment of state beaches. California required the Nollans, owners of a small beachfront bungalow, to dedicate to the state a beach-access easement as a condition for obtaining a state permit to replace and expand their bungalow. The easement would have given the public a permanent right to walk along a narrow strip of the Nollan's beach. The Supreme Court invalidated the state's effort on the ground that California's demand for a public easement amounted to a taking of private property without the payment of *just compensation.

Nollan is significant because, in weighing the validity of California's action, the Court required a showing that the easement condition would substantially advance the state's interest in alleviating the congestion caused by beachfront construction. The principal effect of the Nollan's new home was to reduce the public's ability to see and enjoy the beach from the street. The easement that California demanded, however, would only have benefited persons already on the beach and would not have enhanced visual access from a distance. For the majority this connection or "nexus" between the harm (reduced visual access) and the remedy (enhanced physical access) was too tenuous. Several dissenting justices criticized the majority for requiring more than just a loose, rational connection between harm and remedy.

(See also EMINENT DOMAIN; PROPERTY RIGHTS; PUBLIC USE DOCTRINE; TAKINGS CLAUSE.)
Eric T. Freyfogle

**Nomination of Justices.** See APPOINTMENT AND REMOVAL POWER.

**Nominations, Controversial.** Article II, section 2 of the Constitution provides that the president, "shall nominate, and by and with the Advice and Consent of the Senate, shall appoint . . . Judges of the supreme Court." This textual division of power—the president's power to nominate and the Senate's power to confirm—is a crucial part of the system of checks and balances the framers created throughout the federal government. While the text establishes the formal require-

596 □ Nominees, Rejection of

ments for appointment, it does not specify the rules or factors either the president or the Senate are to consider in carrying out their respective roles. Since the Constitution's adoption, those roles have been determined by the political process, and it is that process that has produced both controversial nominations and the Senate's role in response to them. The late nineteenth century was characterized by a strong Congress and a weak presidency. That balance, however, changed at the beginning of the twentieth century as the executive branch grew in power and influence with the creation of regulatory agencies under the control of the executive branch. In addition, the *Seventeenth Amendment, which provided for the direct election of senators by the people (instead of the state legislatures), increased the power of the president, as the leader of his party, over the senators.

The Senate's role in confirmation is reactive. Presidents are motivated by three concerns in choosing a nominee: politics, policy, and professionalism. Political concerns reflect interest-group politics, with concessions to a geographical region, a particular racial or religious group, or a faction within the president's party. Policy considerations involve the political and judicial philosophy of a candidate. Professionalism includes the judicial abilities of a nominee. Professional criteria are those of the idealized common-law judge: the ability to reason from precedent and to write opinions that are well reasoned. These criteria allow for the law to change, but only gradually. They allow for predictability and limit the judicial role, while maintaining the judiciary as the ultimate arbiter of the pace of change.

Political concerns tend to dominate when presidents have limited policy objectives and do not perceive the courts as important policy makers. This occurred often in the late nineteenth century when presidents were relatively weak and when major issues, such as the tariff, were unlikely to come before the courts. Professionalism dominates when a president expects the Court to check the other branches. This occurred during the Taft, Hoover, Eisenhower, Nixon, and Ford administrations. Policy concerns dominate when presidents attempt to transform governmental structures or policies and perceive the Court as a necessary ally in accomplishing that agenda. Theodore Roosevelt, Franklin *Roosevelt, and Ronald *Reagan provide the clearest examples of this pattern.

Most justices have met all three concerns and have been confirmed by the Senate without controversy. There are occasions when an appointment sparks controversy, but the Senate plays only a limited role. Examples are the revelation that Hugo *Black had belonged to the Ku Klux Klan or that Douglas *Ginsburg had smoked marijuana. The Senate confirmed Black, a senator, with little debate, and Ginsburg's

nomination was withdrawn before the Senate acted. Occasionally, the nominee has aroused vigorous opposition, but has been confirmed nevertheless, as when Louis *Brandeis was nominated in 1916 and when William *Rehnquist was elevated from associate justice to chief justice in 1986. In both instances, the candidate's professionalism was at issue, but political differences between the president and a number of senators best explain the opposition. With the Brandeis nomination there was also some anti-Semitic feeling among his opponents. Judge Clarence *Thomas in 1991 withstood last-minute allegations of sexual harassment to win confirmation after a bruising battle before the *Senate Judiciary Committee.

The Senate has rejected or forced a president to withdraw a nomination twenty-five times since 1789—only five times in the twentieth century. During the eighteenth and nineteenth centuries when political issues dominated presidential selection, they also dominated Senate consideration. President John *Tyler, who had angered both Whigs and Democrats, failed to secure confirmation of five nominees. Republicans in the Senate forced the rejection of President Grant's nominee, Ebenezer *Hoar, in 1879 because they wanted one of their own faction to receive the appointment. When the presidency and the Senate were controlled by different parties, occasionally the Senate could muster the opposition to block a vulnerable candidate. The Senate rejected John J. *Parker in 1930 because of his perceived antilabor and anti-African-American judicial decisions while on the federal appellate bench. Similarly, Robert *Bork was rejected in 1987 because he was perceived as too conservative by the Senate.

Presidents determine a candidate's fitness and policy orientation by using the Justice Department to make inquiries. The Senate, since 1925, has held hearings by the Senate Judiciary Committee. Much scholarly and popular debate over the role the Senate should play revolves around the issue of whether senators should inquire into a nominee's policy orientation. Judging is not purely an act of craftsmanship; it also involves policy making. Since the Constitution does not bar the Senate from determining qualifications for the Supreme Court, a senator may inquire whether the nominee possesses the requisite professionalism and policy judgment to occupy a seat on the nation's highest court.

(See also APPOINTMENT AND REMOVAL POWER; NOMINEES, REJECTION OF; SELECTION OF JUSTICES.)

□ Laurence Tribe, *God Save This Honorable Court* (1985).
Rayman L. Solomon

**Nominees, Rejection of.** From 1789 to mid-1992 the U.S. Senate has rejected 28 of the 143 nominees forwarded to it by presidents. (Eleven were not rejected per se but were simply not acted upon.) Even counting the Senate's refusal to vote on President Lyndon B. Johnson's suggested promotion of Associate Justice Abe *Fortas to *chief justice in 1968, only five have been formally voted down in the twentieth century: Chief Judge John J. *Parker of the U.S. Fourth Circuit Court of Appeals (Hoover, 1930, by vote of 39 to 41); Chief Judge Clement F. *Haynsworth of the same tribunal as Parker (Nixon, 1969; 45 to 55); Judge G. Harrold *Carswell of the U.S. District Court of Florida (Nixon, 1970; 45 to 51); and Judge Robert H. *Bork of the U.S. Court of Appeals for the District of Columbia (Reagan, 1987; 42 to 58). Not counted are the 1968 Johnson nomination of Judge Homer *Thornberry of the U.S. Court of Appeals for the Fifth Circuit, which was never acted upon because of the failure of the Fortas promotion, and that by President Ronald *Reagan of Judge Douglas H. *Ginsburg of the U.S. Court of Appeals for the District of Columbia, whose nomination was never formally submitted to the Senate as a result of the instant controversy surrounding him.

An octet of fairly readily identifiable reasons for the Senate's negative actions in the twenty-eight instances may be listed: (1) opposition to the nominating president, not necessarily the nominee; (2) the nominee's involvement with one or more contentious issues of public policy or, simply, opposition to the nominee's perceived jurisprudential or sociopolitical philosophy (i.e., "politics"); (3) opposition to the record of the incumbent Court, which, rightly or wrongly, the nominee presumably supported; (4) *"senatorial courtesy," closely linked to the consultative nominating process; (5) a nominee's perceived "political unreliability" on the part of the party in power; (6) the evident lack of qualification or limited ability of the nominee; (7) concerted, sustained opposition by interest or pressure groups; and (8) fear that the nominee would dramatically alter the Court's jurisprudential lineup. Usually several of the above reasons, rather than one alone, play a role in a nominee's rejection. A number of specific illustrations may indicate the leading ones.

For example, in 1866 President Andrew Johnson's nomination of his gifted attorney general, Henry *Stanbery, fell only because of the Senate's antipathy to Lincoln's successor—indeed, the Senate rejected every nomination by the embattled president. In 1811, James *Madison's nomination of Alexander *Wolcott fell 9 to 24 because the Federalist senators opposed Wolcott's vigorous enforcement of the embargo and nonintercourse acts when he was U.S. collector of customs in Connecticut. Ulysses S. Grant's nomination of his eminently qualified and popular attorney general, Ebenezer R. *Hoar, fell 23 to 44 in 1870, chiefly because of Hoar's consistently "nonpolitical" stance on appointments to public office. President Herbert Hoover's nomination of John J. *Parker was defeated by two votes in 1930 largely

because he was deemed "unfriendly" to labor and to the burgeoning civil rights movement—both vast oversimplifications. The Nixon nominations of Judges *Haynsworth and *Carswell fell in 1969 and 1970 because of questions of the former's judicial ethics and the latter's obvious lack of fundamental qualifications. The Senate's refusal to accept closure in order to vote on the LBJ-sponsored promotion of Abe Fortas to the center chair was at least partly attributed to his "record" on the high bench in criminal justice cases; opposition to the Warren Court's advanced civil libertarianism; and the pending presidential 1968 elections, with Republicans predicting, accurately, that they would control the government as of that fall.

The 1987 rejection of Judge Robert H. Bork, whom the Senate had approved unanimously for the court of appeals just a few years earlier, was based on his widely articulated jurisprudence, the success of well-organized interest groups' opposition, his prickly performance during his confirmation hearings, the administration's faulty strategy, and the capture of the Senate by the Democrats in 1986. The best contemporary example of rejection because of the demonstrable lack of qualifications for the office of Supreme Court justice is that of the moribund Nixon nomination of Judge Carswell.

Recent rejections have given rise to the belief that the Senate might be inclined to assume an increasingly skeptical attitude vis-à-vis presidential nominations to the Supreme Court. In general, however, when the Senate and the presidency are controlled by the same political party, rejections are likely to be the rare exception, barring obvious lack of qualifications or a tainted personal or political background.

(See also NOMINATIONS, CONTROVERSIAL.)

□ Henry J. Abraham, *Justices & Presidents: A Political History of Appointments to the Supreme Court*, 3d ed. (1991).
Henry J. Abraham

**Nonverbal Expression.** Though we have curiously little guidance on the framers' intent, "speech" in the First Amendment must have been designed to protect more than words. Conduct was well understood in the eighteenth century as a medium of expression. Art, drama, and music served also to convey ideas, quite as much as they do today. A narrow confinement of the First Amendment to the written and spoken word would therefore seem at variance with its origins.

In fact, cases involving nonverbal expression have been major contributors to the expanding scope of protection for free expression. One of the earliest tests of the First Amendment involved a California law that forbade displaying a red flag. The Supreme Court struck down that law in *Stromberg* v. *California* (1931) and thereby conferred (though it did not define) protection for nonverbal expression. This was in fact one of the very earliest major First Amendment cases; it followed by less than a decade the Court's first insistence that, under the *Fourteenth Amendment, states must respect freedom of speech under the *Bill of Rights, despite the operative phrase "Congress shall make no law. . . ."

Soon the red flag precedent was joined by others involving nonverbal expression—or, as it has come increasingly to be known, *symbolic speech. The right to picket was specifically upheld in *Thornhill v. Alabama (1940), without reliance on the words that appeared on the signs and placards. The *civil rights movements brought to the Court a growing number of cases in which actions conveyed the views of protestors more prominently than did their words. While the status of lunch counter protests remained open, the right to march or demonstrate in support of equality received clear protection through *Edwards v. South Carolina (1963). Three years later, in Brown v. Louisiana (1966) the Court brought within the First Amendment's reach a peaceful *sit-in at a public library to protest racial segregation in its services (see RACE AND RACISM).

These early cases introduced an important caution that would persist. While recognizing that marches and demonstrations were a potentially protected medium, the Court warned against equating such expressive conduct with "pure speech." The stage was thus set for one of several major constitutional tests spawned by the war in Vietnam. Federal laws made it criminal for any registrant to destroy his draft card, and regulations required that such cards be carried at all times. Burning of draft cards became an increasingly visible and popular form of anti-Vietnam war protest (see CONSCRIPTION; VIETNAM WAR).

When the draft card issue reached the Supreme Court in United States v. *O'Brien (1968), the justices drew—between speech and conduct—a line with clear constitutional import: "When 'speech' and 'nonspeech' elements are combined in the same course of conduct, a sufficiently important governmental interest in regulating the nonspeech element can justify limitations of First Amendment freedoms" (p. 376).

In this case, that meant that destruction of draft cards, even in protest against an unpopular war, could be punished because of strong governmental interests in the Selective Service System. The decision evoked immediate alarm among civil libertarians. Professor Thomas I. Emerson objected: "The Court makes no attempt to determine whether the conduct of burning a draft card is to be classified as expression or 'action' " (p. 8).

The impact of the O'Brien case was soon tempered by several other Vietnam-era cases. In *Tinker v. Des Moines School District (1969), the justices held that a student suspended from public school for wearing a black armband in protest against the war in Southeast Asia was entitled to reinstatement, noting that students, too, have rights protected by the Constitution. While the armband display was clearly conduct rather than words, the Justices found it to be an expression of opinion "closely akin to pure speech" (p. 505) and thus entitled to First Amendment protection unless it disrupted the school or invaded the rights of others. The Tinker case thus reflected the clearest recognition to date of symbolic speech.

Soon the courts were deluged by cases involving flag burning and other forms of destruction. While the Court did not until 1989 rule on the basic constitutional issue, it did resolve a number of related questions in the 1970s—each time recognizing the essential ingredient of expression in conduct that involved much more than words, sometimes as remote from pure speech as the contemptuous wearing of a flag patch sewn into the seat of the protestor's pants.

One such case offers special insight into the Court's treatment of nonverbal expression. Reacting to the shooting of activist James Meredith, a protestor burned an American flag while declaiming bitterly against racial injustice. His conviction in a state court was reversed by the Supreme Court in Street v. New York (1969). In contrast to the recently decided O'Brien case, with its careful delineation of words and conduct, the justices warned that Street's conviction might rest upon his word alone. Clearly any citizen may express his or her views about the flag, however disrespectful (or hateful to others) those views may be. If a resulting conviction might reflect only the verbal expression of those views, there was not even any need to test the validity of the state's asserted interest in restricting conduct disrespectful of the flag.

These cases eventually set the stage for the Court's most significant pronouncement on nonverbal expression, in *Texas v. Johnson (1989). The Texas Court of Criminal Appeals had set aside a conviction under the state's rather typical flag desecration law. In reaching the same conclusion, a majority of the justices began by recalling their earlier "decisions recognizing the communicative nature of conduct relating to the flag." Given these precedents, it "should not be surprising . . . that we have had little difficulty identifying an expressive element in conduct relating to flags. . . ." Such nonverbal expression could, under the earlier cases, be proscribed only if government could prove a substantial interest "unconnected to expression" (p. 407).

Texas had shown no such interest, despite several claimed justifications for the law and its enforcement against flag burners. After a careful review of the cases, the majority (an unusual combination of liberal and conservative justices) found "nothing in our precedents [that] suggests that a State may foster its own view of the flag by prohibiting expressive conduct relating to it" (p.

415). Thus emerged the clearest and most substantial recognition of nonverbal expression as a major protected category of First Amendment speech. Soon after *Johnson,* Congress enacted a statute designed to reinstate penalties for flag desecration. The Court in *United States* v. *\*Eichman* (1990) declared it invalid.

All the cases to this point have involved political expression or ideas. While the terms of the First Amendment are not so confined, some scholars and judges argue that the free speech clause was meant not to go beyond the political arena. That claim had a more than superficial appeal in the early years.

Starting in the 1970s, however, the Supreme court has found protected expression in a number of contexts that were clearly not political. In *Southeastern Promotions, Ltd.* v. *Conrad* (1975), the justices voided a ban on performing the rock musical "Hair" in a city-owned theater. While the Court claimed it need not define the nature of the expression, its solicitude for procedure would have been most puzzling if the activity in question did not merit First Amendment protection.

Other forms of nonpolitical speech have received comparable recognition. Dancing, even topless or unclothed, has been viewed as nonverbal expression. Religious worship has been brought within the speech clause as well as the clause that protects free exercise of religion. Hair length and style have been found to be protected expression, as has style of dress and clothing. Art, sculpture, and music are surely protected speech without regard to words, unless one takes a narrow and grudging view of the First Amendment.

One other group of cases should be mentioned. In one of its most famous decisions, *\*West Virginia Board of Education* v. *Barnette* (1943), the Supreme Court held that a conscientious refusal to salute the flag by school children was a protected constitutional liberty. Government could not, declared the justices, compel a citizen to make an abhorrent declaration—not simply as a matter of free expression or worship, but as a matter of due process in the broadest sense. The Court reaffirmed that view in *Wooley* v. *Maynard* (1977), holding that New Hampshire could not force its citizens to display the motto "Live Free or Die" on their license plates. While neither case involves conventional nonverbal expression, both clearly recognize a comparable personal liberty of expression.

However broad and eclectic the meaning of "speech" may have become, protection for expressive conduct is not limitless. The essential core of communication thus requires both a message and an intention on the communicator's part to convey that message. Symbolic speech that is simply random, or lacks an intent to convey a message, would thus not be entitled to First Amendment protection despite a superficial resemblance. Not all forms of nonverbal expression can claim to be treated as constitutional "speech."

Other limitations are inherent in the First Amendment context. Even if symbolic speech is equated in constitutional stature with pure speech, it may be proscribed to the extent it creates a *\*clear and present danger. Constraints applicable to obscene and defamatory words presumably apply at least as forcefully to symbolic speech of like quality (see UNPROTECTED SPEECH). Nonverbal expression in a commercial setting presumably would be judged by the special and different standards that apply to words used in advertising. Most clearly applicable to symbolic speech are the same kinds of *\*time, place, and manner rules that govern pure speech.

The difference between verbal and nonverbal expression remains the one created by the *O'Brien* case. Symbolic speech by its nature involves more than words. However clearly those words enjoy constitutional protection by themselves, there are circumstances in which the link to behavior may jeopardize the entire communication, as in the draft card burning context. The two elements must be separable, and government must show a substantial regulatory interest "unconnected to expression."

If flag desecration does not meet those tests—and the Supreme Court has now made clear that it does not—then the scope of the *O'Brien* test seems quite limited beyond draft card burning as such. Whenever there exists a genuine risk that protected expression in a nonverbal form might be chilled by a law that is vague or comprehensive, the claim of free expression is likely to prevail. If government wishes to punish nonexpressive conduct, it must do so in ways that do not inhibit speech.

(See also FIRST AMENDMENT; SPEECH AND THE PRESS.)

□ Zechariah Chafee, Jr., *Free Speech in the United States* (1941). Thomas I. Emerson, *The System of Freedom of Expression* (1970). Kenneth L. Karst, ed., *The First Amendment* (1990). Melville B. Nimmer, *Nimmer on Freedom of Speech: A Treatise on the Theory of the First Amendment* (1984). Robert M. O'Neil

**Norris v. Alabama,** 294 U.S. 587 (1935), argued 15 and 18 Feb. 1935, decided 1 Apr. 1935 by vote of 8 to 0; Hughes for the Court, McReynolds not participating. This was the second decision of the Supreme Court in the Scottsboro rape cases. In *\*Powell* v. *Alabama* (1932), the Court reversed the convictions of African-American youths sentenced to death by the Alabama courts on the ground that the defendants, who lacked effective assistance of counsel, had not received a fair trial as mandated by the Due Process Clause of the *\*Fourteenth Amendment. The Scottsboro cases were then retried by the Alabama authorities, and one of the defendants, Clarence Norris, was again sentenced to death, although defense counsel alleged that African-Americans had been systematically excluded from the grand jury that indicted Norris and from the trial jury that convicted him.

On appeal from a decision of the Alabama Supreme Court affirming Norris's conviction, the U.S. Supreme Court reversed. Speaking for the Court, Chief Justice Charles Evans *Hughes held that the systematic exclusion of African-Americans from service on the grand and trial juries denied African-American defendants in the *state courts the *equal protection of law guaranteed by the Fourteenth Amendment. Since the defense had adduced convincing evidence that African-Americans had been systematically excluded from service on the grand jury that indicted Norris and from the trial jury that convicted him, the Court reversed the conviction.

(See also DUE PROCESS, PROCEDURAL; RACE AND RACISM; TRIAL BY JURY.)

Richard C. Cortner

**Norris v. Boston.** See PASSENGER CASES.

**Northern Securities Co. v. United States,** 193 U.S. 197 (1904), argued 14–15 Dec. 1903, decided 14 Mar. 1904 by vote of 5 to 4; Harlan for the Court, Brewer concurring, White and Holmes in dissent. At the end of the nineteenth century, the Court had begun to find some teeth in the *Sherman Antitrust Act. However, it was only when Theodore Roosevelt sought to dissolve the Northern Securities Company, which held the stock of three major railroads, that the question arose whether the statute reached stock ownership.

Reading both congressional power and the law broadly, Justice John Marshall *Harlan said that the Court could not properly concern itself with any adverse effects on the business community a decision to dissolve the company would have. A majority was formed when Justice David *Brewer, who believed that the Sherman Act should apply only to unreasonable restraints of trade, pronounced the restraint here unreasonable. All the dissenters agreed with Justice Edward *White's contentions that the restraint shown here was reasonable, that a broad interpretation of the act would unsettle business, and that congressional control over commerce could not embrace stock ownership. They also joined Justice Oliver Wendell *Holmes's opinion, which argued that the Sherman Act must be interpreted strictly to ensure its constitutionality; otherwise the most local of transactions would be brought within the ambit of Congress's control of interstate commerce (see COMMERCE POWER). In *Standard Oil Co. v. United States* (1911), Chief Justice White persuaded the Court to limit the Sherman Act's reach solely to unreasonable restraints of trade.

(See also ANTITRUST.)

John E. Semonche

**Northwest Ordinance.** Enacted by the Confederation Congress on 13 July 1787, the Northwest Ordinance established the basic framework of the American territorial system. After a period of direct rule by congressional appointees, the Northwest Territory—Ohio, Indiana, Illinois, Michigan, Wisconsin, and part of Minnesota—and its subsequent subdivisions would enjoy a limited measure of self-government until, when their populations reached sixty thousand, they were entitled to draft state constitutions and claim admission to the union on equal terms. The principle that the new states should become equal members of the union had been set forth in the states' western land cessions that created the national domain and it was preserved as a leading feature of the ordinance. Adoption of the Northwest Ordinance also reflected Congress's determination to implement its new land policy, outlined in the land ordinance of 20 May 1785, by guaranteeing secure titles and establishing law and order on the frontier. The ordinance's provisions for direct congressional rule in the first stage of territorial development were gradually modified and eventually superseded as frontier regions became more politically stable and less strategically vulnerable.

The six "Articles of Compact" in the second part of the ordinance—including the promise of statehood, boundary provisions for three to five new states, guarantees of basic individual rights (including *trial by jury and *habeas corpus), and a ban on *slavery—proved more durable, although constitutionally unenforceable (according to *obiter dictum by Chief Justice Roger B. *Taney in *Strader* v. *Graham,* 1851). What survived was a commitment to form new and equal states that was honored, if sometimes belatedly, throughout the original territory and in areas later added to the national domain.

(See also TERRITORIES AND NEW STATES.)

Peter S. Onuf

**Noto v. United States,** 367 U.S. 290 (1961), argued 10–11 Oct. 1960, decided 5 June 1961 by vote of 9 to 0; Harlan for the Court, Brennan, Warren, Black, and Douglas concurring. Like its companion case *Scales* v. *United States* (1961), *Noto* involved the constitutionality of the membership clause of the *Smith Act. In this case, however, the Court unanimously reversed the judgment of conviction. Five of the justices rested the decision on the ground that the evidence at the trial was insufficient to show that the Communist party, of which Noto was a member, engaged in advocacy of the doctrine of forcible overthrow of the government and in advocacy of action to that end, as distinguished from advocacy of mere abstract doctrine. There must be substantial evidence, direct or circumstantial, of a call to violence "now or in the future" that is both "sufficiently strong and sufficiently persuasive" to lend color to the "ambiguous theoretical material" regarding Communist party teaching (p. 298) and also substantial evidence to justify the reasonable inference that the call to violence may fairly be imputed to the party as a whole and not merely to a narrow segment of it.

Justice William *Brennan and Chief Justice Earl *Warren would have directed the trial court to dismiss the indictment under the terms of the Internal Security Act, which they interpreted as granting immunity from prosecution under the membership clause of the Smith Act—an immunity, they said, that extends to "active and purposive membership" no less than to membership that is merely passive or nominal. Justices Hugo Black and William O. Douglas found the conviction invalid as a violation of the *First Amendment.

(See also COMMUNISM AND COLD WAR; SPEECH AND THE PRESS.)

Milton R. Konvitz

**Nullification** is the doctrine by which states claimed power to declare a law of the federal government unconstitutional. It was the most important theoretical alternative to the idea that the U.S. Supreme Court is the final arbiter of constitutional controversies. In the Kentucky and Virginia Resolutions (1798–1800) Thomas *Jefferson and James *Madison briefly adverted to nullification. New England Federalists often ignored the authority of the national government, while other states, most notably Kentucky in *Green v. Biddle (1823) and Georgia in Worcester v.

Georgia (1832), refused to recognize the authority of the Supreme Court (see CHEROKEE CASES).

The most important and systematic development of nullification doctrine occurred in South Carolina. In the South Carolina Exposition and Protest (1828), John C. Calhoun, who was then vice president, argued that the Constitution was a compact among the sovereign states whereby they delegated limited and carefully specified powers to the federal government. If a state believed the federal government had overreached its authority, it could call a special convention to declare the law unconstitutional and nullify its operation. Should the federal government respond by adopting an amendment to the Constitution in order to legitimize its authority, the state could either acquiesce or secede from the Union.

Although Calhoun always stressed the peaceful and legal nature of nullification, President Andrew *Jackson viewed the doctrine as revolutionary and treasonous when South Carolina implemented it during the nullification controversy of 1832–1833. During the next three decades, nullification, with its emphasis on secession as a constitutional right, became increasingly intertwined with states' rights and the South's defense of *slavery.

(See also STATE SOVEREIGNTY AND STATES' RIGHTS.)

Richard E. Ellis

**Number of Justices.** See JUSTICES, NUMBER OF.

# O

**Obiter Dictum** (Lat., "said in passing"; often simply dictum [pl. dicta], occasionally obiter) is an assertion in an opinion that is not necessary to the result but is merely the gratuitous opinion of the judge. The distinction between holdings and dicta is often difficult to discern, especially in modern cases.                    William M. Wiecek

**O'Brien, United States v.,** 391 U.S. 367 (1968), argued 24 Jan. 1968, decided 27 May 1968 by vote of 7 to 1; Warren for the Court, Harlan concurring, Douglas in dissent, Marshall not participating. David O'Brien burnt his selective service registration certificate ("draft card") on the steps of the South Boston Courthouse to communicate his antiwar beliefs and was convicted under a federal statute prohibiting the knowing destruction or mutilation of such certificates. He argued that the statute was unconstitutional because it abridged his rights of free speech. The Court rejected O'Brien's claim and set out a test for determining when governmental regulation was justified in freedom of expression cases involving symbolic speech. This test required the government interest to be a valid and important one, and one unrelated to the suppression of free speech. Further, the restriction of First Amendment freedoms could be no greater than was essential to the furtherance of that interest.

The Court found that the statute here met all the requirements. First, the statute involved the broad and sweeping constitutional power to do what was necessary to raise and support an army. Second, the selective service certificate served a number of valid government interests, such as being proof of registration and facilitating com-

munication between the registrant and the local board. These were interests unrelated to the suppression of free speech. Finally, the Court held, the statute was limited to preventing harm to the smooth running of the Selective Service System and no alternative means would accomplish this. By his conduct O'Brien had frustrated the government's valid interest and it was because of this he was convicted.

The test in *O'Brien,* which focuses on whether the regulation is unrelated to content and narrowly tailored to achieve the government interest, is frequently invoked not only in symbolic speech cases, but also cases involving *time, place, and manner restrictions.

(See also CONSCRIPTION; FIRST AMENDMENT; SPEECH AND THE PRESS.)
                                        Keith C. Miller

**Obscenity and Pornography.** Virtually every society has struggled with the question of what to do about representations of sexual activity. Such material is prevalent because it manifests the tensions that arise between desire and social norms. Artful treatments of sex enhance our understanding of these tensions. But because societies are ambivalent about sexual freedom and are concerned about the impact of degrading sexual depictions on the quality of sexuality, they attempt by law to distinguish proper from improper display, or to prohibit display altogether.

This struggle is particularly acute in a liberal democracy, in which the values of liberty and democracy often conflict. Liberal principles hold that all forms of expression should be protected by the *First Amendment unless they cause direct, demonstrable harm to others. Though violent erotic materials have been shown in laboratory studies to make males more inclined to commit violence against women, such studies have not demonstrated direct, systematic harm. The liberal approach would limit regulation to protecting minors and the sensibilities of unconsenting adults. Democratic principles, however, endorse the right of majorities to restrain liberty in order to protect society from potential harm and to support communitarian norms of sexual virtue.

Though the Supreme Court has ratified the imposition of liberal principles in cases involving political or religious speech, it has allowed some measure of community control by holding that the First Amendment does not protect all forms of expression. Expression deemed to possess social value merits protection unless it causes substantial and demonstrable direct harm, while less valuable expression is "unprotected." It may be prohibited if the government simply shows a good reason to be concerned about its potential impact. In the seminal 1942 case of *Chaplinsky v. New Hampshire*, the Court established the rationale that distinguishes protected and unprotected speech. Obscenity and lewdness, *libel, and fighting words are not protected by the First Amendment because "such expressions are no essential part of any exposition of ideas, and are of such slight social value as a step to truth that any benefit that may be derived from them is clearly outweighed by the social interest in order and morality" (p. 572).

Traditionally, American law has used the concept of "obscenity" to draw the line between prohibited and permitted sexual representations. Obscenity is not the same thing as "pornography." Etymologically, obscenity refers to those things considered disgusting, foul, or morally unhealthy. Pornography is broader in meaning, pertaining to depictions of sexual lewdness or erotic behavior. Pornography may not be obscene.

*Chaplinsky's* rationale for First Amendment protection expressed a traditional notion of moral virtue and a conventional theory of truth as a purely cognitive process. But ensuing decades challenged these assumptions, as moral consensus concerning sexuality gave way to the experimental 1960s and 1970s, and the understandings of depth psychology and emotivist aesthetics supplemented traditional notions of knowledge.

Until 1957, obscenity cases simply dealt with the statutory meaning of obscenity. The absence of constitutional challenge reflected the strength of the moral consensus against obscenity. But as pornographic representations and literature became more available after *World War II, the Supreme Court was eventually confronted with a constitutional challenge to suppression of pornography. In *Roth v. United States* (1957), Justice William *Brennan held that obscenity is unpro-

tected because it is "utterly without redeeming social importance" (p. 484). Brennan confined obscenity to "material which deals with sex in a manner appealing to prurient interest." He defined prurient interest as either "[h]aving a tendency to excite lustful thoughts" or as a "shameful and morbid interest in sex" (p. 487). He then promulgated the following test for obscenity: "whether to the average person, applying contemporary community standards, the dominant theme of the material taken as a whole appeals to the prurient interest" (p. 489).

*Roth's* test focused on prurience. Yet prurience was never adequately defined, and the rest of the test provided little guidance as to what is obscene.

In *Jacobellis v. Ohio* (1964), the Court recognized that it had to make its own independent evaluation of the nature of allegedly obscene material in each case. This compelled the Court to create a decidedly more liberal three-part test in the 1966 Fanny Hill case, *A Book Named "John Cleland's Memoirs of a Woman of Pleasure" v. Attorney General of Massachusetts*. Justice Brennan declared that material is obscene if: its dominant theme is prurient; it is "patently offensive because it affronts contemporary community standards"; and it is "utterly without redeeming social value" (pp. 419–420). Only the most explicit material could meet the *Memoirs* test, which shifted emphasis from prurience (*Roth*) to patent offensiveness and the presence or absence of even minimal social value. The minimal social value test, in effect, required the prosecution to prove a negative—always a difficult task. Subsequently, the Court began to overturn virtually every obscenity prosecution it encountered unless the material was sold to minors or advertised salaciously (e.g., *Redrup v. New York*, 1967). Concurrently, the availability of progressively explicit materials mushroomed as publishers pushed the new standard to its limits. Antipornography activists reacted by turning pornography and the "permissive" Warren Court into major national issues.

In *Stanley v. Georgia* (1969), the Warren Court ruled that the constitutional right of *privacy prohibited punishing someone for using illegal obscenity in the home. But the Burger Court refused to carry out the logical implications of *Stanley*, and restored power to communities to control sexual materials. In *Miller v. California* (1973), the Court promulgated a revised test. Material is obscene if: its predominant theme is prurient according to the sensibilities of an average person of the community; it depicts sexual conduct in a patently offensive way; and taken as a whole, it "lacks serious literary, artistic, political, or scientific value" (p. 24).

*Miller's* reformulation of the social value test made it less likely that otherwise obscene works would slip over the threshold of protection by the spurious inclusion of minimal social commentary. But in another respect it simply reaffirmed *Memoirs'* implicit emphasis on hard-core pornography, because Chief Justice Warren *Burger stated that only hard-core depictions could be designated patently offensive. Burger presented some "plain examples" of such depictions, including "patently offensive representations or descriptions of ultimate sex acts," and "lewd exhibition of the genitals" (p. 25). Nudity alone, or pictures of sexual behavior short of "ultimate acts" are not obscene.

*Miller's* test is still the linchpin of obscenity doctrine. Courts have become fairly adept at distinguishing hard-core from non-hard-core pornography. Literary works that deal with sexuality are strongly protected, and magazines like *Playboy* and *Penthouse* are substantially secure from constitutional attack.

Problems persist, however. While *Miller* has resulted in fairly objective adjudication, decisions at the margin are unavoidably subjective. Only a direct-harm approach would alleviate this problem. But the Supreme Court has been unwilling to forsake completely nonliberal values in this area of expression. On the other side of the issue, some conservatives and feminists contend that *Miller* conceded too much to liberalism, crippling the community's ability to curb the spread of all but the most explicit forms of pornography. Obscenity law often delivers less than it modestly promises.

In reaction to these problems, some feminists in the early 1980s advocated making pornography a new exception to First Amendment freedoms (see GENDER). They defined pornography broadly, as the sexually explicit subordination of women, and provided no provision for redeeming artistic or social value. *Lower federal courts held this approach unconstitutional (*American Booksellers Association* v. *Hudnut*, 1984). But the Supreme Court has allowed some hedging of *Miller's* quasi-liberal approach in specific areas. It has allowed zoning control of nonobscene pornography (*City of Renton* v. *Playtime Theatres, Inc.*, 1986) and upheld the Federal Communications Commission's decision to limit (not ban) the availability of nonobscene "indecent" expression in broadcasting (*F.C.C.* v. *Pacifica Foundation*, 1978). In addition, the Court ruled that states may ban knowing distribution of nonobscene pornography made with minors as subjects (*New York* v. *Ferber*, 1982).

These measures have enhanced the power of democratic controls but (with the exception of child pornography in *Ferber*) have not expanded the domain of the prohibitable. In general, obscenity law maintains a balance between liberal and democratic values that favors liberalism. The Supreme Court could make application of the law easier by adopting a fully liberal standard that reconciled sexual expression with most other expression, but such a reconciliation would be tantamount to the abandonment of democratic control in this highly charged issue.

(See also SPEECH AND THE PRESS; UNPROTECTED SPEECH.)

□ Donald A. Downs, *The New Politics of Pornography* (1989). Catherine MacKinnon, "Pornography, Civil Rights, and Speech," *Harvard Civil Rights-Civil Liberties Law Review* 20 (1985): 1–70. Richard S. Randall, *Freedom and Taboo: Pornography and the Politics of a Self Divided* (1989).                                                Donald A. Downs

**O'Connor, Sandra Day** (b. El Paso, Tex., 26 Mar. 1930), associate justice, 1981–. Sandra Day O'Connor joined the Supreme Court in 1981 as its first female justice. She received both her degrees—undergraduate and law degrees (1952)—from Stanford University. In 1952 she married John O'Connor. Unable as a female attorney to find employment with a private firm, she began working as a deputy county attorney in Arizona. Thereafter she entered private practice, served as an assistant attorney general, was elected to the Arizona state senate, and finally, in 1974, joined the state judiciary, first as a trial judge and later as a judge of the state's intermediate court of appeals.

Since her appointment, O'Connor, with a few notable exceptions, has joined the conservative wing of the Supreme Court. Her conservative tendencies are most pronounced in criminal procedure cases and those involving issues of *federalism. Perhaps influenced by her experiences in state government, she consistently opposes federal attempts to regulate what she views as state matters or to interfere with state procedures.

Despite O'Connor's general support for her conservative colleagues, she has proved at times to be independent both in style and substance. Her opinions tend to demand fact-specific decision making, leading to narrow, limited holdings. Consequently she often writes separate concurring decisions designed to "clarify" the majority's opinion, to suggest alternative narrower grounds upon which the Court could have reached the same results, or to minimize the distance between the majority and the dissent.

O'Connor's influence on the Court is revealed in her decisions concerning *religion, *affirmative action, and *abortion. Early in her tenure, O'Connor rejected the traditional Establishment Clause test emanating from *Lemon* v. *Kurtzman* (1971), under which a statute is invalid if it has a primary purpose or effect of advancing or inhibiting religion, or if it causes excessive government entanglement with religion (see LEMON TEST). Preferring state neutrality toward religion over strict separation, starting with *Lynch* v. *Donnelly* (1984), O'Connor substituted the question of whether government intends or is perceived to

*Sandra Day O'Connor*

endorse religion. Five years later, in *Allegheny County v. ACLU* (1989), this position seemed to have gained majority support.

O'Connor may also have fashioned the majority test for constitutional challenges to state *affirmative action programs. In a number of separate opinions, beginning with *Wygant* v. *Jackson Board of Education* (1986), O'Connor argued that such programs should be tested under strict scrutiny to show a remedial need for the program to rectify prior governmental (rather than simply societal) discrimination. This position gained majority support in *Richmond* v. *J. A. Croson Co.* (1989).

Finally, prior to Justice William *Brennan's retirement, O'Connor's vote determined the continued vitality of *Roe* v. *Wade* (1973) and the extent of abortion rights. Although writing in *Akron* v. *Akron Center for Reproductive Health* (1983) that *Roe's* trimester approach needed to be reevaluated, she refused to join Chief Justice William *Rehnquist's plurality opinion in *Webster* v. *Reproductive Health Services* (1989), which rejected just that approach. She appears unwilling explicitly to overrule *Roe*, preferring to narrow its scope by upholding state regulations not "unduly burdensome" to the woman. Under this standard O'Connor has upheld all but one abortion regulation considered by the Court during her tenure.

□ Suzanna Sherry, "Civic Virtue and the Feminine Voice in Constitutional Adjudication," *Virginia Law Review* 72 (1986): 543–616.                                    Stanley Ingber

**Ogden v. Saunders,** 12 Wheat. (25 U.S.) 213 (1827), argued 18–20 Jan. 1827, decided 19 Feb. 1827 by vote of 4 to 3; majority justices by seriatim opinions, Marshall, Story, and Duvall in dissent. In this decision, a divided Supreme Court held that a New York insolvency law did not impair the obligation of contracts entered into after enactment of the statute, a question that had been left open in *Sturges* v. *Crowninshield* (1819), which had struck down a retroactive insolvency act. The majority justices agreed that contract rights were not absolute, that commerce required some kind of *bankruptcy legislation, that the bankruptcy power conferred on Congress by Article I, section 8 of the Constitution was not exclusive, and that therefore the states had concurrent powers in the area. In dissent, Chief Justice John *Marshall contended that the statute violated not only the *Contracts Clause but also various nontextual *vested rights of individuals. *Ogden* v. *Saunders* removed the Contracts Clause as an absolute bar to state insolvency legislation, an important achievement because Congress was unable to enact permanent bankruptcy legislation until 1898. *Ogden* was the only case where Chief Justice Marshall dissented in an important constitutional decision. On reargument, Justice William *Johnson joined the original dissenters to make a new majority for the holding that a state insolvency statute could not be applied to an out-of-state creditor who had no contract with the forum state other than the original contract.          Richard E. Ellis

**O'Gorman and Young v. Hartford Fire Insurance Co.,** 282 U.S. 251 (1930), argued 30 Apr. 1930, reargued 30 Oct. 1930, decided 5 Jan. 1931 by vote of 5 to 4; Brandeis for the Court, Van Devanter, McReynolds, Sutherland, and Butler in dissent. *O'Gorman* is a turning point case in the field of economic due process. One of the last liberty of contract cases, it involved a New Jersey statute regulating the fees paid to local agents by insurance companies. The statute was challenged as a violation of the *Fourteenth Amendment's Due Process Clause. Contending that the facts surrounding its origins and operation should be determinative, Justice Louis *Brandeis sustained the statute. He found that the presumption of constitutionality must prevail in the absence of some factual foundation of record for overthrowing the statute" (p. 258). Further, legislative judgment must prevail unless it could be demonstrated that the measure was utterly arbitrary. No such demonstration had been made. The business of insurance, he argued further, is so far affected with a public interest that the state may regulate the rates as a subject clearly within the scope of the police power. He further contended that the Court should cease using the Due Process Clause in a "substantive" manner to second guess the legislature (see DUE PROCESS, SUBSTANTIVE).

The four dissenters vigorously propounded freedom of *contract, restrictive alteration of the public interest doctrine, and the pressing obligation to check any legislative interference with property. They particularly objected to the idea that the right to regulate business implied the power to trespass on the duties of private management. The majority opinion, however, made clear that the constitutionality of state regulation of the economy should no longer turn on the question of its unreasonableness.

(See also POLICE POWER; STATE REGULATION OF COMMERCE.)

Paul L. Murphy

**Ohio v. Akron Center for Reproductive Health,** 110 S.Ct. 2972 (1990), argued 29 Nov. 1989, decided 25 June 1990 by vote of 6 to 3; Kennedy for the Court, Scalia and Stevens concurring, Blackmun, joined by Brennan and Marshall, in dissent. Relying on *Bellotti* v. *Baird* (1979), the Court upheld a statute that required minors seeking *abortions either to notify one parent or obtain approval of a court. Less important than other cases indicating that the holding in *Roe* v. *Wade* (1973) was less robust than its supporters wished, the decision turned on whether the state's system of providing judicial approval placed too many burdens on the applicants. There was always a chance that approval would be delayed for more than three weeks because the woman had to prove her maturity or that the abortion was in her best interests by clear and convincing evidence, or because the procedure was unnecessarily complicated. The Court rejected these arguments, finding that the time limits would almost always be much shorter than three weeks, that the burden of proof was permissible, and that the procedures were not overly confusing. The dissenters characterized the procedure as an "obstacle course" and a "labyrinth" and contended that the procedure did place unacceptable burdens on minors desiring abortions.

(See also PRIVACY.)

Mark V. Tushnet

**Oklahoma City Board of Education v. Dowell,** 111 S.Ct. 630 (1991), argued 2 Oct. 1990, decided 15 Jan. 1991 by vote of 5 to 3; Rehnquist for the Court, Marshall, joined by Blackmun and Stevens, in dissent, Souter not participating. African-American parents and their children brought this suit in 1961 to challenge the racial segregation in Oklahoma City's public schools. The federal district court terminated the case in 1977, declaring that the previously "dual" (intentionally segregated) school district had achieved "unitary" status. In 1985, claiming demographic changes, the school district curtailed busing and reassigned students to neighborhood schools. As a result, thirty-three of the district's sixty-four elementary schools became racially identifiable, with more than 90 percent of their student body

of one race. The plaintiffs sought to reopen the case.

The Supreme Court emphasized that court-ordered remedies were always intended to be temporary and not meant to operate in perpetuity. Calling for greater deference to local authorities, the Court held that a desegregation remedy should be terminated when the school district had complied in good faith with all court orders for a reasonable time and when vestiges of past discrimination had been eliminated to the extent practicable. This determination must consider every facet of operation of the schools, including student assignments, faculty, staff, transportation, extracurricular activities, and facilities.

There are more than five hundred school desegregation cases pending in federal courts nationwide, some for more than thirty years. This decision thus could signal a whole new body of case law establishing procedures for ending these lawsuits and the federal judiciary's involvement in school desegregation issues.

(See also DESEGREGATION REMEDIES; RACE AND RACISM; SEGREGATION, DE JURE.)

Thomas E. Baker

**Old City Hall, Philadelphia.** See BUILDINGS, SUPREME COURT.

**Olmstead v. United States,** 277 U.S. 438 (1928), argued 20–21 Feb. 1928, decided 4 June 1928 by vote of 5 to 4; Taft for the Court, Holmes, Brandeis, Butler, and Stone in dissent. Olmstead was convicted of unlawfully transporting and selling liquor under the National Prohibition Act. His petition from the court of appeals provided the Supreme Court with its first opportunity to consider whether the use of evidence obtained by an illegal wiretap in a federal court criminal trial violated the defendant's *Fourth and *Fifth Amendment rights. Chief Justice William H. *Taft held that it did not, finding that conversations are not protected by the Fourth Amendment and that no invasion of the defendant's house was involved in the wiretapping. In dissent, Justice Louis D. *Brandeis argued that the Fourth and Fifth Amendments confer a general right to individual *privacy rather than mere protection of material things and that allowing the introduction of evidence illegally acquired by federal officers makes government a lawbreaker. In the 1934 Federal Communications Act, Congress prohibited the interception of any communication and the divulgence of the contents of intercepted communications. The Court extended the *exclusionary rule to wiretapping in federal prosecutions in *Nardone* v. *United States* (1937); it overruled *Olmstead* in *Berger* v. *New York* (1967) and *Katz* v. *United States* (1967). In Title III of the Crime Control and Safe Street Act of 1968, Congress prohibited wiretapping for domestic purposes except when authorized by a federal judge following the specific requirements of the act.                                                   Susan E. Lawrence

**Olney, Richard** (b. Oxford, Mass., 15 Sept. 1835; d. 8 Apr. 1917) lawyer and statesman. A noted New England railroad lawyer, Richard Olney served from 1893 to 1895 as U.S. attorney general, and as secretary of state from 1895 to 1897. In *In re *Debs* (1895), the Supreme Court upheld an *injunction that Olney had sought to break the 1894 Pullman Strike. Because of his sympathy to big business, Olney failed to employ the 1890 *Sherman Antitrust Act aggressively to break up the sugar trust (*United States* v. *E.C. Knight*, 1895). Olney argued the government's position in the income tax cases, *Pollock* v. *Farmers' Loan & Trust Company* (1895).                John W. Johnson

**One Person, One Vote.** See BAKER V. CARR; FAIR REPRESENTATION.

**Opinions, Assignment and Writing of.** Opinions announce the decision(s) reached by the Supreme Court and explain the reasons for those results. Initially the Court prepared *seriatim opinions in which each member of the Court wrote a separate opinion. The result was that the Court spoke with multiple voices, none the controlling one.

When John *Marshall became *chief justice in 1801, the Court began to render a single opinion that announced its decision. Although the practice was not immediate, it became standard by the end of Marshall's tenure on the Court in 1835. When the chief justice is in the majority he can assign the opinion to himself or assign the task of writing to another member of the majority. When the chief justice is not in the majority, the assignment of opinions is done by the most senior associate justice in the majority. Numerous considerations influence the choice of opinion writers.

The first consideration of the assigner may be to distribute the work of opinion preparation among all the justices evenly. With minor variations, from term to term, the distribution of opinions does reflect a fairly even amount of work. The exceptions are when a justice has not served for the entire term or has been ill. Unavailability is the most likely reason for a lack of equitable distribution.

Another factor that the assigner might consider is whether the decision is an important one or is one that will be significant in the future. In such cases, the assigner may assign himself, as Chief Justice Earl *Warren did in *Brown* v. *Board of Education* (1954) and *Reynolds* v. *Sims* (1964) and Chief Justice Warren E. *Burger did in U.S. v. *Nixon* (1974). Short of that, the assigner may select a colleague who shares the assigner's views on the subject and who will prepare an opinion that reflects those views.

An additional set of tactical calculations may enter the assigner's mind in selecting the opinion writer. The writing of any opinion usually requires some adjustment of views and wording on the part of the writer. If the majority is small, the preparation of the opinion can be crucial to holding the majority together or attracting a justice who initially voted the other way. Since votes in cases are subject to change, the opinion can be designed to get a dissenting justice to switch his or her vote and join the majority. Thus, the ideological position of the writer within the majority block becomes significant. The assigning justice may give the task of writing up the opinion to a justice whose vote is not secure. Once assigned the majority opinion, the wavering justice obtains a permanent stake in seeing that position prevail and is thus less likely to switch sides and change the result.

The negotiating abilities of the opinion writer may also influence the assigner's choice, particularly if the majority is fragile and will require careful persuasion or negotiation to hold or build the majority. Cementing the majority coalition or building it by attracting a vote can be important in selecting the opinion writer.

The writing of the opinion may be done by the individual justice or by a law *clerk. When the justice is satisfied with the opinion, it is distributed to the other eight members of the Court. This means each of the other justices has the opportunity to join that opinion. Justices can withhold joining until the writer has modified the opinion slightly or drastically. When the writer has heard from all the justices who are willing to join the majority opinion, and any concurring and *dissenting opinions have been prepared, the decision is ready to announce.

Particularly in controversial or complicated cases, where there is a good deal of disagreement among the justices, the preparation of the Court's majority opinion may take months. Often, those cases are announced in the last days of the Court's term, in late June or early July. When there is no more time for negotiating and the term is ending, there is pressure to complete the opinions.

□ Alexander Bickel, *The Unpublished Opinions of Mr. Justice Brandeis: The Supreme Court at Work* (1957).
                                          William P. McLauchlan

**Opinions, Style of.** A cloistered branch of government, the Supreme Court communicates with the rest of the nation primarily through written opinions. Whether they come to us through newspaper synopses, straight from the papers of the *United States Reports* or from some intermediate source, it is almost exclusively by these opinions that we know the Court. If the opinions explaining the Court's decisions make sense to us, then all is well; if they confuse or strike us as false or unjust, then our sense of the fairness of our society is weakened. The words of the Court, then, must be well chosen—its use of language skillful and clear—or else we all, to one degree or another, suffer. To preserve our faith in it, the Court must write well.

*Period-Styles.* The form of Supreme Court opinions has changed greatly over the past two hundred years. There is no evident apex or nadir, but it is possible to generalize about what Karl Llewellyn called "period-styles." In the first half of the nineteenth century, the "grand style" was common in American courts, as exemplified by Chief Justice John *Marshall and Justice Joseph *Story, and on state appellate courts by John Bannister Gibson of Pennsylvania and Lemuel Shaw of Massachusetts. Judges spoke as the "mouthpieces of divinity" in polished, spartan opinions. The quality of judicial writing declined after 1850, when the "formal style," stressing logic and *precedent, emerged. Opinions became much less readable: turgid, obscure, jargonistic, repetitious, and full of string citations and careless English. At the turn of the twentieth century, Justice Oliver Wendell *Holmes's brilliant writing shone brightly amid this dreary gray. Perhaps as a result of his influence, the better Supreme Court opinions in the twentieth century have become, rhetorically speaking, increasingly powerful and persuasive. But the grand style has been dead since 1900, and the formal style, though mostly moribund since the rise of legal realism, lives on in the form of newly elaborated constitutional doctrines with layered sets of "tests" and "prongs" and "standards" and "hurdles."

This broadly conceived evolution of Supreme Court opinions is explainable partly on pragmatic grounds. In Marshall's day, the Court had more time to perfect its work product than in Chief Justice Melville *Fuller's day, when dockets had become more and more crowded and judges more and more rushed. Further, the judges of 1900, according to some commentators, were not as well educated than those of 1800, and therefore less likely to have a command of the language. In the latter half of the twentieth century, the justices have been cast more in the role of editors than of authors of their opinions; increasingly, law *clerks have been delegated the task of putting into words what the justices have decided and why— hence the pervasive "law-review style" so often decried by Court observers.

From a literary perspective, the gems in the *United States Reports* are well hidden. That exalted set of books has been called "a great literary wasteland (Frank, 1958, p. 130). A collection of first-rate writings might be gleaned from its nearly five hundred volumes, but it would account for less than half a percent of the whole. Likewise, from a substantial legal perspective the opinions may be said to be wanting. Few of the Court's opinions genuinely illuminate the area of law with which they deal.

Whatever its inadequacies, the Supreme Court opinion is one of the most powerful tools of law and of rhetoric in American life. The practice of issuing written opinions has added immensely to the power and prestige of the Court. Justice William *Brennan spoke in 1979 of the "fundamental . . . interdependence of the Court and the press," for it is through the press that the majority of Americans—probably the majority even of lawyers—learn what they know of the Court's activities. More important, though, is the role of opinion writing in coming to a just resolution of any given case. Chief Justice Charles Evans *Hughes said that "there is no better precaution against judicial mistakes than the setting out accurately and adequately the material facts as well as the points to be decided" (Hughes, 1928, p. 64). As anyone who has set out to write a judicial opinion well knows, the writing hones the thinking and sometimes exposes weaknesses in a tentative determination that was ill conceived. As judges often say, "Some opinions just won't write."

*Reduction to Writing.* Nothing in the federal Constitution, of course, requires that opinions be reduced to writing. In fact, during the Court's first decade, most were not; during the 1790s, the Court reduced its opinions to writing in only the most important cases. Justice James *Iredell's draft opinion in *Chisholm* v. *Georgia* (1793) is the earliest known manuscript and just about the only one of that decade. We do not know just how much of the early reports is the product of justices and how much is the handiwork of the unofficial reporter, Alexander James *Dallas, who reported only sixty cases in the first sixteen terms after 1790.

William *Cranch, the first official reporter (appointed in 1801), expressed relief at "the practice which the court had adopted of reducing their opinions to writing in all cases of difficulty or importance." By Cranch's time, written opinions were the rule, but it was not until 1834 that an order required all opinions to be filed with the *clerk.

*Opinion of the Court.* The justices' own great uncertainty in the early nineteenth century was not whether to reduce opinions to writing, but whether to deliver *seriatim opinions. During the 1790s, the justices delivered opinions in turn, after the manner of the King's Bench, except that the justices spoke inverse order of seniority. For example, in *Ware* v. *Hylton*, the most important case of 1796, Justice Samuel *Chase delivered a long opinion and then every other justice gave his separate opinion.

This practice changed abruptly when John *Marshall became *chief justice in 1801. Marshall instituted what we now know as the "opinion of the court," that is, an opinion attributed to a single justice but speaking for the entire court or a majority of its members. In Marshall's day, almost all the opinions were attributed to Marshall himself, though some of these were written by his colleagues. By means of the univocal opinion, Marshall was able to increase not only his own authority as chief justice but also the Court's authority within the American polity.

President Thomas *Jefferson, in well-known correspondence, protested against judicial opinions that were "huddled up in a conclave, perhaps by a majority of one, delivered as if unanimous, and with the silent acquiescence of lazy or timid associates, by a crafty chief judge, who sophisticates the law to his mind by the turn of his own reasoning" (Letter to Thomas Ritchie, 25 Dec. 1820, in *Works of Thomas Jefferson*, 1905, vol. 12, pp. 177–178). Jefferson wanted a rule requiring judges to announce their opinions seriatim and thus to take their positions publicly. Although he urged his own appointee Justice William *Johnson, known as the "First Dissenter," to write separately so as to attack Marshall's dominance, Johnson did so only sporadically. Had he done so more frequently, Johnson might have weakened his influence on the Marshall Court.

From Marshall's time until the death of Chief Justice Charles Evans Hughes—for well over a century—the Court spoke generally in single opinions, with occasional concurrences and dissents in matters of great importance. In his thirty-five-year tenure on the Court, Marshall dissented only nine times, less often in a long career than most of today's justices dissent in a single year. From Chief Justice Harlan Fiske *Stone's time (1941–1946) to the present day, both *concurring and dissenting opinions have been commonplace. Some commentators have called the modern fragmentation a return to seriatim opinions.

Scholars who follow the Court seem to agree—without dissent—that the proliferation of separate opinions is an undesirable trend. John P. Frank writes that "no single thing has more depreciated the standing of the institution since the time of Hughes than the impression that it is overtalkative" (Frank, p. 129). Other Court watchers agree that separate opinions have become excessive.

***Proliferation of Dissents.*** At its best, a dissent in the high court is, as Chief Justice Hughes termed it, "an appeal to the brooding spirit of the law, to the intelligence of a future day, when a later decision may possibly correct the error into which the dissenting judge believes the court to have been betrayed" (Hughes, p. 68). That description applies nicely to what Justice Holmes and Justice Louis D. *Brandeis did in giving dignity to dissenting opinions; indeed, Holmes was known as "the Great Dissenter" and was paid the honor of having an anthology of his dissents published. But as often as not, nowadays, dissents express disagreements over matters once considered too inconsequential to merit a separate opinion, and, in Justice Lewis F. *Powell's words, they are not "a model of temperate discourse." Thus popularizers of the Court's

activities are prone to speak of personal enmities on the Court, basing their inferences on nothing more than the language used in this or that justice's separate opinion.

Whereas the rhetoric of separate opinions may have become less restrained than yesteryear merely because of the gradual change of mores, the frequency of such opinions probably reflects something deeper than a mere loss of restraint. Justice William H. *Rehnquist attributed the rise of concurrences and dissents to the sharp jump in recent years in the percentage of cases in which a constitutional claim is raised and, more to the point, in which a constitutional claim is sustained. Constitutional adjudication may well invite more separate opinions than does adjudication in other areas of law.

Justice William *Brennan's philosophy of dissenting illustrates just how different the modern view is from Chief Justice Hughes's. In an essay entitled "In Defense of Dissents," Brennan noted a justice's duty to dissent when in disagreement with the majority. As he wrote in the *Hastings Law Journal* 37 (1986), "Each justice must be an active participant, and, when necessary, must write separately to record his or her thinking. Writing, then, is not an egoistic art—it is duty. Saying, 'listen to me, see it my way, change your mind,' is not self-indulgence—it is very hard work that we cannot shirk" (p. 427).

Thomas Jefferson might relish with this near-return to his ideal, but it robs the Court's opinions of the oracular quality they once had. Multiplicity of opinions may also impair the work of the Court. John P. Frank studied the separate opinions of Justice Felix *Frankfurter—the "concurringest" member of the Court during his time—and showed that they were almost never cited by anyone. Thus the conclusion that Frankfurter "consumed a large portion of his energy and talent in essays which, for all practical purposes, might as well have been written on paper airplanes and thrown out a Supreme Court window" (Frank, p. 126).

***Law Clerks and Verbosity.*** The crush of work at the Court is undoubtedly the single greatest influence on the style of modern opinions. Justice Harry *Blackmun was perhaps being delicate when he used the future tense to forecast a "breaking point" at which "one's work becomes second-rate" (see WORKLOAD OF THE SUPREME COURT). Opinion writing is the most time-consuming of the justices' work. Today, justices average more than twenty-five signed opinions apiece each year.

Traditionally, opinion writing has been viewed as that aspect of the justices' work in which law clerks are least competent to help. Yet federal judges at all levels are being transformed from writers into editors of their law clerks' work; the process is all but complete at the Supreme Court. The transformation is a recent one. Chief Justice Fred *Vinson was anomalous in "writing with his hands in his pockets," telling his clerks generally what he wanted and then criticizing drafts and suggesting revisions. In the 1990s, the anomaly would be to find a justice regularly writing his or her own opinions.

Ghostwriting does not present the problem most often raised by those unfamiliar with the practice; it does not empower inexperienced law clerks to participate in the decision-making. It does, however, gravely affect the deliverances of the Court. They are longer and more diffuse, loaded with footnotes, impersonal in tone, and unimaginative in presentation. Drafted by clerks who are former law-review editors, the opinions partake of most of the negative traits of law-review articles. As the number of clerks almost doubled between 1969 and 1979 (to a total of thirty-two), so these qualities associated with their work on opinions also increased.

Very likely, the clerks increase verbosity rather than productivity. In 1889, the Court produced 265 signed opinions with no help from law clerks. (Granted, this period did not mark the high point of the Court's judging or of its literary style.) In 1973, when each associate justice had three clerks and the chief justice had four, the Court produced only about 130 signed opinions, but their length vastly outstripped the length of nineteenth-century opinions. Indeed, just in the fifty years from 1936 to 1986, the average opinion doubled in length. In the flurry of concern over the length of the Court's opinions, Joseph W. Little half-mockingly suggested a constitutional amendment limiting opinions to five pages. That would be a far cry indeed from the 243 pages—50,000 words, all told—in which the Court expressed its nine separate opinions in *Furman* v. *Georgia* (1972). The effect of such editorial competition can only be to drive the reader to the opinion's summary preface and away from the text.

Not alone have law clerks been blamed for the Court's blossoming wordiness. Some commentators have cited the increasingly complex and ideologically heated issues generated by our ever-growing *administrative state and our heightened notions of personal rights. As Justice William O. *Douglas once observed, "the decision-making process is not getting any easier." Others maintain that the issues are no more difficult than in Justice Holmes's day, that it is patronizing to suggest that they are, and that the real problems are instinctive verbosity and lack of time to hew the clerks' work down to proper size.

The modern style of judging is no doubt also responsible. It was not just Holmes's habit of standing at a drafting table that helped him achieve brevity—"Nothing conduces to brevity like the caving in of the knees," he once said. It was also his elliptical treatment of legal issues, a treatment that most judges and scholars today would find unacceptable. In one of his most famous sententious formulations, in *Buck* v. *Bell*

(1927)—"Three generations of imbeciles are enough" (p. 207)—Holmes justified a vote that he might not have been able to sustain if he had had to detail his eugenic reasoning. Judges in the latter half of the twentieth century value an explicitness and a painstaking process of working through every step of the reasoning. Holmes would have been impatient with all that.

As a result of the prevailing legal ethos, we have lost much that is subtle and suggestive, and we have gained longer opinions and bulkier volumes. But not all that bulk is justified by a modern yearning for greater specificity. Generally, it is no trick at all to do what law professors regularly do in producing their casebooks: excise large chunks of the Court's opinions to expose the factual and analytical discussions that are of true importance in deciding a given case.

The exceptions often delight readers. In the shortest opinion in recent memory, Justice John Paul *Stevens—the only justice who, in the 1990s, writes his own first drafts of opinions—dispensed with *McLaughlin* v. *United States* (1986) in five short paragraphs. The opinion harks back to the pithy style of Holmes.

*Evaluating the Justices.* In the history of the Supreme Court, Marshall and Holmes and Robert H. *Jackson are at the first rank of judicial stylists. Marshall's grand style, of course, is distinctly rooted in the nineteenth century: orotund, divine-sounding, inerrantly lawgiving. Holmes and Jackson, as twentieth-century judges, are more nearly our contemporaries. Whereas other modern judges have usually made adventurous ideas dull, Holmes and Jackson could make the very dullest case a literary adventure.

Holmes habitually used rhetorical devices such as alliteration, metaphor, and periodic sentences to emphasize his points. His antitheses are legion. For example: "If a business is unsuccessful it means that the public does not care enough for it to make it pay. If it is successful the public pays its expenses and something more" (*Arizona Copper Co.* v. *Hammer*, 1919, p. 433). The literary critic Edmund Wilson went so far as to call Holmes's style "perfect."

Legal commentators have not been quite so kind to Holmes's style. Judge Richard A. Posner suggests that the power of Holmes's famous dissent in *Lochner* v. *New York* derives more from rhetorical devices than from close reasoning. Judge Abner Mikva says that purely Holmesian approach is now untenable, inasmuch as Holmes was "not above shaping or neglecting certain facts to preserve the force of a narrow analysis." Professor Jan Deutsch finds Holmes's persuasive power in sketching the selective vignette, not by detailing the "murky and confusing truth of how things are, but by confirming our felt certainties about how we know they should be."

These criticisms say as much about the critics as they do about Holmes. Holmes was no doubt conscious of his omissions: "the eternal effort of art, even the writing of legal decisions, is to omit all but the essentials." If Holmes had written so as to remedy the vices that his critics perceive, he would have introduced many others, including prolixity. The considerable virtues in his almost laconic style may necessarily have entailed a few vices.

Nor has Jackson been without detractors. But when it came to phrasing a thought aphoristically, memorably, pungently, Jackson was without equal. Like Holmes, Jackson was masterly with antithesis: "Very many are the interests which the state may protect against the practice of an occupation, very few are those it may assume to protect against the practice of propagandizing by speech or press" (*Thomas* v. *Collins*, 1945, p. 545). His wordplay was never merely playful; it was usually telling: "We can afford no liberties with liberty itself" (*United States* v. *Spector*, 1952, p. 180). His famous example of chiasmus expressed an insight about the Court incomparably well: "We are not final because we are infallible, but we are infallible only because we are final" (*Brown* v. *Allen*, 1953, p. 540). Justice Frankfurter wrote of Jackson that his writing "mirrored the man in him" more completely than any other "who ever sat on the Supreme Court," and that Jackson belonged to "the naturalistic school [of opinion writers]. He wrote as he talked, and he talked as he felt."

But talented writers on the Court have been rare. Justice William O. Douglas was the only justice in the history of the Court who inarguably could have made his living as a professional writer on nonlegal subjects. The Court has had more justices of the ilk of Justice James Moore *Wayne, whose style was criticized in about 1850 as being "overloaded with words; scarcely any of his sentences convey a distinct idea; and some of them are quite beyond the pale of criticism." That description fits much of what Justice George *Shiras, Samuel *Blatchford, or Chief Justice Edward D. *White wrote, as well as the early opinions of Justice Harold M. *Burton or the work of any number of others. In recent years, Chief Justice Warren *Burger received more criticism than his colleagues for incoherent footnotes and artless opinions.

Among the highly regarded judicial writers are Holmes, Jackson, and Douglas, but also Justices Louis *Brandeis, Benjamin *Cardozo, Felix Frankfurter, and Hugo *Black. Brandeis, who had great rhetorical skill, brought to the bench his penchant for the *"Brandeis brief," which took tirelessly thorough account of sociological as well as case-specific facts. Holmes is said to have remarked of Brandeis, "He believed in footnotes, and I didn't."

Cardozo would take a page to say what Holmes could say in a sentence, and on occasion his quest for exalted eloquence made his writing vacuous. In *Welch* v. *Helvering* (1933), involving the question whether a person who paid his employers' debts could take a tax deduction, Justice Cardozo said: "Life in all its fullness must supply the answer to the riddle" (p. 115). As Dean Erwin Griswold once pointed out, these are nice words, but essentially meaningless. On the whole, Cardozo's writing as a state judge—as a common-law judge—ranks more highly than his writing on the Supreme Court.

Frankfurter is a special case. English was his second language; his feel for words has been compared to Nabokov's. That comparison is extravagant, however, unless it merely stresses Frankfurter's fascination with ornate words, such as *adumbrate, excogitate, quixotism,* and *sub silentio.* Frankfurter often lapsed into "abstractitis": "The problems that are the respective preoccupations of anthropology, economics, law, psychology, sociology and related areas of scholarship are merely departmentalized dealing, by way of manageable division of analysis, with interpenetrating aspects of holistic perplexities" (*Sweezy* v. *New Hampshire*, 1957, pp. 261–262).

Both Black and Douglas had bold, nononsense styles. Their broad strokes of the pen to resolve constitutional uncertainties met with scorn from law professors. Both Black and Douglas might have been called technically deficient, result oriented, and unscholarly, but part of the reason is that they were the only justices of their time whose opinions displayed a concern that nonlawyers might ever read the reports.

On the Court today, Antonin *Scalia and William H. *Rehnquist are among the strongest writers. Their opinions delight in metaphor; they are piquant, witty, and sometimes biting. From all that one gathers, though, these qualities emerge when the justices have the time to edit and rewrite the work of their clerks. What is more usual are the tendencies that all the modern justices' opinions show: a plodding, pedantic style that unnecessarily emphasizes minor points and does not stop when the job is done.

Unfortunately, the Court's opinions rarely receive the literary scrutiny that might gradually lead to better opinions. Perhaps this failure on the part of academics, lawyers, and judges is due to the mistaken notion that the writing is merely incidental to the judging, not the greater part of its essence.

(See also BRIEFS; OPINIONS, ASSIGNMENT AND WRITING OF; REPORTING OF OPINIONS; REPORTERS, SUPREME COURT.)

□ John P. Frank, *Marble Palace: The Supreme Court in American Life* (1958). Charles Evans Hughes, *The Supreme Court of the United States* (1928). Karl Llewellyn, *The Common Law Tradition: Deciding Appeals* (1960). Robert F. Nagel, *Constitutional Cultures: The Mentality and Consequences of Judicial Review* (1989). Richard A. Posner, *Law and Literature: A Misunderstood Relation* (1988).

Bryan A. Garner

**Oral Argument.** Daniel *Webster, in his 1818 argument to the Court in *Dartmouth College* v. *Woodward*, which dealt with a state's power to alter Dartmouth's charter, ended with the words "It is a small college . . . and yet there are those who love it." Contemporaries reported that many in the room were in tears. Chief Justice John *Marshall himself was moved, and Webster won a decision in favor of the college. Before the *Civil War arguments before the Court might go on for days. Today, except for rare cases of extraordinary importance, each side is limited to thirty minutes. Occasionally the Court reverses a decision summarily without any argument at all. And the chief justice is very strict about the time limits. A red light shows on the lectern after thirty minutes and the chief will notify the advocate that his time is up, sometimes in mid-sentence.

Because every case argued to the Court has been fully briefed and the justices come to the argument with a thorough knowledge of the briefs and record, it is often said that oral argument never changes any minds and is therefore useless. This is not true. A good oral argument will never consist of a set speech—advocates, by a rule of the Court, may not read their arguments—and will generally avoid the kind of oratorical flourishes that made Court sessions a popular event in Webster's day. Rather, an able advocate will encourage questions from the bench and her skill will consist in the ability to make points as answers to questions. A skillful advocate will also discern from the justices' questions what concerns each of them may have and will use the occasion to address those particular concerns. Thus a successful oral argument is more like a compelling conversation than a lecture—this is aided by the fact that the lawyer's lectern in the Supreme Court is quite close to the bench, and the contact with the justices seems more intimate than in many other courts.

It is only in the oral argument that the lawyer must answer questions. In his brief a lawyer can avoid or try to obscure weaknesses in his case. While an opposing brief may seek to point out such evasions, it is during oral argument that there is no avoiding a direct question by one of the justices. Thus, though it is true that few cases have been won in oral argument, many have been lost. Under what can be relentless and sometimes even sadistic questioning by the justices, a quite plausible case may fall apart entirely. Thus oral argument provides a useful test of the soundness of an argument. Of great symbolic importance too is the fact that this test is one where the public may see that the justices do indeed attend to the cases before them and that no argument will prevail that is not submitted to an open challenge.

The questioning by the justices at oral argument also allows them a means of convincing, or at least arguing with, each other before their vote on a case is reached in their private *conference.

Such public duels, between Justices Hugo *Black and Felix *Frankfurter, for instance, across the person of the hapless advocate, have produced some legendary exchanges.

At times in the Court's history there has existed a small group of lawyers who specialized in arguing to the Supreme Court. Daniel Webster was perhaps the most famous advocate to appear before the Court. John W. *Davis was the best known in the twentieth century. Such specialization is much less common now, and most arguments are presented by advocates who will appear before the Court only once in their lives. The result is a greater variability in the quality and helpfulness of oral argument than is warranted by the importance of the Court's business.

(See also BRIEFS; DECISION-MAKING DYNAMICS.)

□ William H. Rehnquist, *The Supreme Court—How It Was, How It Is* (1987). G. Edward White, *The Marshall Court and Cultural Change, 1815–1835* (1988).

Charles Fried

**Orders List.** Found near the end of volumes of the *United States Reports*, order lists are prepared by the *clerk of the Supreme Court and summarize its actions in cases under review. Each list is dated and cites cases by docket number and title. The Court may choose to affirm a *writ of *appeal or refuse to accept such appeals for want of substantial *federal question or for lack of jurisdiction. The Court may accept, dismiss, vacate, and remand a case for consideration in light of a specified precedent or deny petition for a writ of *certiorari, adhering to the custom that four justices must agree to hear a case before it is accepted for review. Miscellaneous orders may deal with such matters as the disbarment of attorneys, stays of execution, appointment of special masters, the scheduling of *oral arguments during a particular month, the appointment of counsel, and invitations or permissions to file *amicus curiae briefs. Orders are usually succinct statements with no written justifications. Occasionally, justices will enter short explanations of why they voted to grant or deny a petition for certiorari. Justices William *Brennan and Thurgood *Marshall, for example, routinely cited their view that *capital punishment is unconstitutional per se when dissenting from denials of certiorari in death penalty cases. Sometimes, too, a justice's failure to participate in a hearing, perhaps because of possible conflicts of interest, will be noted.

John R. Vile

**Ordinary Scrutiny.** See STRICT SCRUTINY.

**Oregon v. Mitchell; Texas v. Mitchell; United States v. Arizona,** 400 U.S. 112 (1970), argued 19 Oct. 1970, decided 21 Dec. 1970 by vote of 5 to 4; Black for the Court, Douglas, Harlan, Stewart, Brennan, White, Marshall, Burger, and Blackmun concurring in part and dissenting in part. In

1970 Congress passed amendments to the 1965 *Voting Rights Act that extended the provisions of the original act for another five years. The amendments also standardized residency requirements for participation in national elections and, dramatically, lowered the voting age to eighteen years for national, state, and local elections. Congress based its action on the enforcement language of the *Fifteenth Amendment. The legislation raised the issue of federalism anew because national legislators were attempting to regulate the time and manner of conducting state and local elections, a traditional prerogative of the states. When the issue came to the Supreme Court, the major question was whether Congress had the constitutional authority to lower the national minimum voting age.

In a decision with five opinions and no clearcut majority, the Court ruled that Congress did not have the power to so act with respect to state elections but did have the authority to set the voting age at eighteen in federal elections for Congress and the presidency. Four of the justices believed that Congress had total power to regulate the voting age in any election, while four others believed that Congress had no such absolute power; Justice Hugo *Black cast the deciding vote, concluding that Congress could regulate the voting age in national but not in state elections.

To bring the confusion that followed the Court's ruling to a quick end, Congress immediately adopted the *Twenty-Sixth Amendment, which was ratified in short order. Reversing the Court's holding regarding voting age in state elections, the amendment states that "the rights of citizens of the United States, who are eighteen years of age or older, to vote shall not be abridged by the United States of any state on account of age."

(See also FEDERALISM; VOTE, RIGHT TO.)

Howard Ball

**Original Intent** is a method of constitutional and legal interpretation that seeks to discern the original meaning of the words being construed as that meaning is revealed in the intentions of those who created the law or the constitutional provision in question. In the American tradition, original intent is often referred to as the "framers' intentions," "original meaning," or "original understanding."

To those who advocate this approach, the search for original intention in interpretation is the very essence of the idea of the rule of law; it is the line that separates the act of judging from the act of legislating. Judges are obligated to determine what the lawgiver intended by the words chosen—no more, no less.

The idea of judges being bound to original intent as they seek to say what the law means is not an American innovation. Indeed, recourse to original intent as the guide to judging has ancient

roots. One sees evidence of it as early as Aristotle's writings on law and it is present among the earliest legal writings in England that sought to give definition to the unwritten *common law and the unwritten constitution.

Yet the greatest controversies over original intent have come to surround the power of the Supreme Court under the written Constitution of the United States. In deciding the constitutional cases that come before it, should the Court be bound to original intent or should it engage in an effort to keep the Constitution in tune with the times? Was original intent, in fact, the "original intent" of the framers themselves?

Critics of the original intent doctrine argue emphatically that it was not. Further, they hold that with respect to many of the Constitution's most important commands, written in what they consider to be majestic but open-ended language, the search for literal meaning is both impossible and undesirable.

Those who defend original intent believe that unless judges are bound to original intent, they are freed from the restraint of the law and become, in effect, lawmakers themselves. In this view, it is the obligation of the judges to keep the times in tune with the Constitution, not to keep the Constitution in tune with the times.

(See also CONSTITUTIONAL INTERPRETATION; INTERPRETIVISM AND NONINTERPRETIVISM.)

Gary L. McDowell

**Original Jurisdiction** is the jurisdiction exercised by the court that initially hears a lawsuit. As a court of first instance, this tribunal must conduct a trial or similar proceeding in order to determine the facts in the dispute and then settle the case by applying the law to those factual findings. Congress created the U.S. district courts as the primary courts of original jurisdiction for the federal judiciary.

*Article III of the Constitution confers original jurisdiction on the U.S. Supreme Court over cases involving ambassadors and suits involving states as parties. This grant, however, does not preclude Congress from granting concurrent original jurisdiction to other courts. Recognizing that the Supreme Court is better suited to exercise appellate review than to conduct trials, Congress has granted concurrent original jurisdiction to the federal district courts in all controversies except those between states. While the Supreme Court has not abdicated its original jurisdiction, the justices clearly support statutes that authorize cases to be heard first by the federal trial courts. Consequently, the Supreme Court hears very few original jurisdiction cases, with most involving a state suing another state over contested borders. When such cases are filed, the justices normally appoint a special master (frequently a former judge) to determine the facts and recommend an outcome. The Court then treats the report of the special master in much the same way as an appealed lower court ruling and issues a final opinion accepting, modifying, or rejecting the recommendations.

(See also JUDICIAL POWER AND JURISDICTION; LOWER FEDERAL COURTS.)

Thomas G. Walker

**Original Package Doctrine.** See BROWN V. MARYLAND.

**Orr v. Orr,** 440 U.S. 268 (1979), argued 27 Nov. 1978, decided 5 Mar. 1979 by vote of 6 to 3; Brennan for the Court, Blackmun and Stevens concurring, Rehnquist (with Burger) and Powell in dissent. Orr, a divorced male, challenged the alimony statutes of Alabama. He argued that because the statutory scheme allowed alimony orders only against males, it amounted to unconstitutional sex discrimination in violation of the *Equal Protection Clause.

The dissenters focused strictly on the standing question (see STANDING TO SUE), pointing out that Mr. Orr probably had nothing to gain from winning this case: his wife was the needy spouse and he was the spouse able to pay support. The possibility that Alabama would abolish alimony in order to render the laws neutral with regard to *gender was, they said, merely fanciful.

The Court majority addressed the standing question by insisting that any person who bears a gender-based financial burden must have standing to challenge it. Justice John Paul *Stevens's separate concurring opinion was devoted entirely to elaboration of this point.

The majority applied the *Craig v. Boren (1976) test to invalidate this statutory scheme. The state proffered three goals of the law: to structure family life, with wife at home and husband providing support; to cushion the cost of divorce for needy wives; and to compensate needy wives for economic discrimination attendant upon the traditional marital role. The Court declared the first goal invalid in this era but said that the second two were valid and important. The law, however, failed the second half of the *Craig* test: it was not "substantially related" to these goals. There was no need for blanket gender discrimination, since every alimony award came out of individualized hearings in which any needy spouse could be identified. Thus, both valid goals could be satisfied by a gender-neutral law.

(See also MARRIAGE.)

Leslie Friedman Goldstein

**Osborne v. Ohio,** 495 U.S. 103 (1990), argued 5 Dec. 1989, decided 18 Apr. 1990 by vote of 6 to 3; White for the Court, Blackmun concurring, Brennan, joined by Marshall and Stevens, in dissent. *Osborne* upheld a statute making it illegal to possess child pornography. An earlier case, *Stanley* v. *Georgia* (1969), had invalidated a statute prohibiting the private possession of obscene materials because the government's sole interest in prohibiting such possession, controlling the private thoughts of the owner, was not an interest the government was entitled to advance. The Court in *Osborne* said that banning the possession of child pornography protected the different interest of avoiding the exploitation of children against the harms of being used in pornography. Making private possession of child pornography illegal would reduce demand by destroying the market for exploitative use. The Court also held that the statute did not cover a substantial amount of constitutionally protected conduct because it had been construed to be limited to lewd depictions.

The dissenters argued that the statute remained unconstitutionally overbroad in its scope even after the narrowing construction. *Osborne* reflects the modern Court's discomfort with the prevalence of sexually explicit materials in American society, but its impact is limited because of the obvious importance of controlling the production of child pornography.

(See also OBSCENITY AND PORNOGRAPHY.)

Mark V. Tushnet

**Osborn v. Bank of the United States,** 9 Wheat. (22 U.S.) 738 (1824), argued 10–11 March 1824, decided 19 March 1824 by vote of 6 to 1; Marshall for the Court, Johnson in dissent. Originating in a challenge to the constitutionality of the Bank of the United States, *Osborn* produced an elaborate statement by Chief Justice John *Marshall concerning the jurisdiction of federal courts. In 1819 Ohio imposed a prohibitive tax on branches of the Bank of the United States. Defying a federal injunction against its collection (see INJUNCTIONS AND EQUITABLE REMEDIES), Ralph Osborn, the state auditor, ordered his agents to seize the money and deposit it in the state treasury. The bank sued Osborn in federal circuit court for return of the money and prevailed. On appeal by Osborn, the Supreme Court affirmed the judgment; its decision in *McCulloch v. Maryland (1819) had upheld the constitutionality of the bank and inhibited the states' power to tax federal instrumentalities.

At issue in *Osborn* was an unconstitutional state tax levied on a federal corporation. The Constitution extends federal judicial power to all cases "arising under" the Constitution, laws, and treaties of the United States. Marshall, however, used the case to proclaim federal jurisdiction over every case involving the bank, even those seemingly raising only questions of state law. Basing federal jurisdiction on the bare possibility of federal question, Marshall generously construed congressional power to confer jurisdiction, a proposition that Justice William *Johnson, writing in dissent, thought risked federalizing too many questions. A further jurisdictional issue concerned the *Eleventh Amendment, which restricted suits against states. Although Osborn was acting on behalf of his state, the Court held that he could not assert its immunity from suit, a proposition later reaffirmed in Ex parte *Young (1908).

(See also FEDERAL QUESTIONS; JUDICIAL POWER AND JURISDICTION; LOWER FEDERAL COURTS; STATE SOVEREIGNTY AND STATES' RIGHTS.)

John V. Orth

**Otto, William Tod** (b. Philadelphia, Pa., 19 Jan. 1816; d. Philadelphia, 7 Nov. 1905), reporter of decisions, 1875–1883. Otto, who authored the first series of nonnominative Supreme Court reports, received his A.B. in 1833 and A.M. in 1836 from the University of Pennsylvania. After studying law, he moved to Brownstown, Indiana, to practice. Otto became judge of the Second Circuit Court in Indiana in 1844 and served until his defeat in the 1852 election. He was an able, austere judge but a pleasant and good-humored man away from official life. Otto taught law at Indiana University during his last five years on

the bench, after which the university awarded him an LL.D.

Otto lost the 1858 election for attorney general of Indiana but was a Lincoln delegate at the 1860 Republican national convention. President Abraham *Lincoln rewarded Otto with appointment as assistant secretary of the interior in 1863, in which post Otto took a keen interest in Indian affairs. He left the Interior Department in 1871 to serve as arbitrator for claims against Spain from U.S. citizens in Cuba. Otto successfully argued before the U.S. Supreme Court in *Murdock v. Memphis (1875) that the *Judiciary Act of 1867 conferred no more power on the Court than had the *Judiciary Act of 1789.

Otto succeeded John William *Wallace as the Court's reporter of decisions in 1875 and served until 1883, publishing seventeen volumes (91–107 United States Reports). After leaving the Court, Otto returned to law practice, and in 1885 he served as a U.S. representative to the Universal Postal Congress in Lisbon.

(See also REPORTERS, SUPREME COURT.)

Francis Helminski

# P

**Pacific Mutual Life Insurance Company v. Haslip,** 111 S.Ct. 1032 (1991), argued 3 Oct. 1990, decided 4 Mar. 1991 by vote of 7 to 1; Blackmun for the Court, Scalia and Kennedy concurring, O'Connor in dissent, Souter not participating. Concerned about the marked increase in the frequency and size of punitive damage awards by trial juries, the business community in the late 1980s pressed several constitutional challenges to punitive damages. In *Browning-Ferris* v. *Kelco Disposal* (1989), the Supreme Court rejected an *Eighth Amendment challenge. In *Pacific Mutual,* an insurance company attacked an Alabama punitive damage award on *due process grounds, arguing that the award bore no rational relationship to the plaintiff's actual injuries and that juries had unlimited discretion to assess punitive damages. Stressing that juries have historically determined the imposition and amount of punitive damages, Justice Harry A. *Blackmun rebuffed this challenge. He reasoned that the *common-law method was not so inherently unfair as to deny due process under the *Fourteenth Amendment. Blackmun further concluded that the Alabama procedures at issue reasonably accommodated rational decision making and provided for adequate checks on jury discretion. He did recognize, however, that in some situations unbridled jury discretion in assessing punitive damages might violate due process norms.

Justice Antonin *Scalia, in a *concurring opinion, maintained that since juries historically had discretion to award punitive damages this traditional practice was not violative of due process.

Dissenting, Justice Sandra Day *O'Connor argued that the Alabama procedures were "so fraught with uncertainty that they defy rational implementation" (p. 1056) and encouraged inconsistent results. Since the justices left open the possibility that some punitive damage procedures might transcend constitutional limits, it seems likely that *Pacific Mutual* will not be the Supreme Court's last word on the validity of punitive damages.                James W. Ely, Jr.

**Pacific States Telephone & Telegraph Co. v. Oregon,** 223 U.S. 118 (1912), argued 3 Nov. 1911, decided 19 Feb. 1912 by vote of 9 to 0; White for the Court. Early in the twentieth century, reformers wanted to make government more responsive to the people. In 1902, Oregon led the way by enacting the initiative and referendum, devices that gave citizens the opportunity to directly propose and/or vote on the laws that would govern them. In 1906 Oregonians proposed and passed a tax of 2 percent on the gross revenues of telephone and telegraph companies in the state. Deprived of its lobbying strength in the legislature, one such company refused to pay the tax and was sued by the state. The company lost in the Oregon courts and appealed, arguing that the Constitution's guarantee to the states of a republican government meant that lawmaking was the exclusive responsibility of the legislature (see GUARANTEE CLAUSE).

That the company could really have expected the Supreme Court to invalidate the initiative procedure and throw Oregon into legal chaos stretched the credulity of the justices. They refused jurisdiction, saying that the matter was political and not judicial. Chief Justice Edward D. *White quoted heavily from *Luther v. Borden (1848) in concluding that only Congress could provide a remedy.

(See also POLITICAL QUESTIONS.)

John E. Semonche

**Paid Docket.** The Supreme Court receives well over four thousand petitions a year from litigants who want their cases reviewed by the nation's highest court. These petitions for review come from individuals who are unable to pay the court costs as well as from those who can afford to pay the filing fee and printing costs. The Court recognizes this distinction by classifying petitions filed as *"in forma pauperis" and "paid cases." Paid petitions are generally of higher quality than are unpaid ones because indigent defendants often draft their own petitions.

Nearly half of the increase in cases filed with the Court in the 1970s was because of a rise in petitions from indigent defendants, but the Court still accepts more paid petitions for review. In the 1988 term it accepted 10 percent of the paid cases for review, while it granted review to only 1 percent of the petitions from indigent defendants. However, the Court accepts few paid petitions when they are from criminal defendants. In cases involving criminal appeals, the Court tends to accept more paid petitions for review that come from state courts than it does paid petitions from federal criminal defendants. When the Court accepts a paid petition for review from a state criminal defendant, it usually does so in cases that involve the vindication of a federal right. However, the Court usually grants review to paid petitions from federal criminal defendants so that it can resolve an intercircuit conflict.

(See also WORKLOAD.)

Karen Maschke

**Paintings in the Supreme Court Building.** The only paintings on public display in the Supreme Court Building are oil portraits of the justices. The East Conference Room contains portraits of the *chief justices from John *Jay to Melville W. *Fuller. Until the late nineteenth century Congress did not authorize the expenditure of public funds for such portraits. The Court thus depended upon private donors for paintings of early chief justices. On 2 October 1888, Congress initiated a policy of government purchase, appropriating fifteen hundred dollars for the acquisition of portraits of Morrison R. *Waite, then recently deceased, and two chief justices of the 1790s, Oliver *Ellsworth and John *Rutledge. These commissions enabled the Court to complete its portrait collection; Congress has continued to subsidize portraits of later chief justices.

The portrait of John Jay is the most colorful. Copied from a 1794 painting by Gilbert Stuart, it suggests the patrician style of leadership that characterized the founding period. Jay, wearing a handsome black gown trimmed in scarlet, sits thoughtfully at a desk, one hand resting on a large lawbook. Behind him a white marble column and billowing drapery recall the classical foundations of American republicanism. Jay's resplendent gown does not appear in any other judicial portrait; the justices soon adopted a plain black robe as more appropriate garb for the servants of a nominally classless society.

Classical symbolism also contributed to Rembrandt Peale's famous "porthole" portrait of John *Marshall. In this painting within a painting, Peale dispensed with the customary background props. An oval portrait bust of the chief justice in his later years appears against a plain white backdrop. The portrait in turn is embedded in a larger imagined setting. Enclosed in a wreath of sculptured laurel leaves, it forms the center of an impressive monument, with a pedestal inscribed "Fiat Justitia" and a marble head of Solon at the apex. The classical analogue is explicit: Marshall the American jurist will be remembered as a peer of the greatest lawgiver of antiquity.

With the rise of a more democratic constitutional order in the middle decades of the nineteenth century, classical allusions disappeared from judicial portraits. Some early motifs have remained constant, however, and are discernible in the paintings of twentieth-century chief justices found in the West Conference Room. The portrait of Earl *Warren, for example, recalls in some striking ways Stuart's study of John Jay. Like Jay, Warren sits at a desk, with one hand resting on a lawbook; but behind him stands no antique column, but a modern bookcase filled with other lawbooks. The image suggests the complexity of modern jurisprudence, while reaffirming the eighteenth-century view of law as a prestigious intellectual pursuit. Warren's portrait is the most recent; by custom, a painting of retired Chief Justice Warren *Burger will not be hung until after his death.

Portraits of associate justices, contributed by family, friends, or former law clerks, are on display on the ground floor. The building also contains paintings of Court clerks and reporters; but these are in administrative offices not open to the public.

(See also BUILDINGS, SUPREME COURT; SCULPTURE IN THE SUPREME COURT BUILDING.)

□ Charles E. Fairman, *Art and Artists of the Capitol of the United States* (1927). Maxwell Bloomfield

**Palko v. Connecticut,** 302 U.S. 319 (1937), argued 12 Nov. 1937, decided 6 Dec. 1937 by vote of 8 to 1; Cardozo for the Court, Butler in dissent. Palko was tried for first-degree murder, but a jury found him guilty of the lesser crime of second-degree murder and sentenced him to life imprisonment. The state appealed this conviction under a Connecticut statute that permitted the prosecution to appeal the judgment of the trial court in certain criminal cases. The state won a new trial, which resulted in Palko being convicted of the greater charge and sentenced to death. Arguing that this chain of events placed him twice in jeopardy for the same offense, Palko appealed the second conviction.

The *Fifth Amendment, which provides immunity from *double jeopardy, applies only to the federal government, not to the states. Palko's appeal did not rely on the Fifth Amendment alone, however. He claimed the execution of his sentence would violate the *Fourteenth Amendment guarantee that no state shall deprive a person of life, liberty, or property without due process of law. The theory of his case was borrowed from Justice John *Harlan's dissents in *Twining v. New Jersey (1908) and *Hurtado v. California (1884). Harlan believed that whatever would be a violation of the original *Bill of Rights if done by the federal government was equally unlawful under the Fourteenth Amendment if done by the states. In Twining, a case involving the Fifth Amendment protection against *self-incrimination, the Court rejected this theory, but it later applied other parts of the Bill of Rights to the states. *First Amendment freedoms of *speech, *assembly, and *religion had been applied in this manner, as was the *Sixth Amendment guarantee of the right to *counsel.

While recognizing this trend, the Court pointedly rejected Palko's thesis. Justice Benjamin *Cardozo noted that cases holding the opposite existed as well. Parts of the Bill of Rights had surely been applied to the states, he admitted, but not as the automatic consequence of the first eight amendments being incorporated into the due process guarantee of the Fourteenth Amendment. Rather, some select protections were absorbed into the concept of due process only because they are fundamental to our notions of liberty and justice. In Cardozo's words, these rights imposed limits on the states because "they represented the very essence of a scheme of ordered liberty, . . . principles of justice so rooted in the traditions and conscience of our people as to be ranked fundamental" (p. 325). He concluded that the Connecticut statute did not fall into this category. The state had done no more than seek a trial free of substantial error. It had not subjected the accused to acute and shocking hardships nor attempted to wear him down by multiple trials.

*Palko* represents the beginning of a struggle to find a test for applying the Due Process Clause of the Fourteenth Amendment as a limit on state power. For more than thirty years the Court had used the doctrine of substantive *due process to exercise virtual veto power over all forms of state economic regulation. In 1937 most justices accepted the idea that the Due Process Clause gave the Court authority to review the substance of state legislation as well as the procedure by which

laws were enforced. However, in *West Coast Hotel v. Parrish (1937), decided in the same term as Palko, they rejected the uninhibited use of this power and the *judicial activism it represented. Now the Court was faced with the problem of replacing an open-ended standard with one that was more restrictive. In this respect, Cardozo's opinion was a precursor of the "incorporation debate" that became so evident later in *Adamson v. California (1947). His rationale for upholding the Connecticut law developed into the "fundamental fairness" test later championed by Justice Felix *Frankfurter, while the theory he rejected became known as the *incorporation doctrine favored by Justice Hugo *Black. A variation of the incorporation doctrine won out, as many of the protections of the Bill of Rights eventually were applied directly to the states. In 1969 Palko was overruled by *Benton v. Maryland, and double jeopardy became one of those provisions of the Bill of Rights selectively incorporated into the Fourteenth Amendment.

(See also DUE PROCESS, PROCEDURAL; FUNDAMENTAL RIGHTS.)

Paul Kens

**Palmer v. Thompson,** 403 U.S. 217 (1971), argued 14 Dec. 1970, decided 14 June 1971 by vote of 5 to 4; Black for the Court, Burger concurring, Douglas, White, Marshall, and Brennan in dissent. African-American citizens of Jackson, Mississippi, claimed that the city engaged in unlawful racial discrimination in violation of the Equal Protection Clause of the *Fourteenth Amendment when it closed public swimming pools rather than operating them on an integrated basis. The swimming pools were closed when lower courts invalidated racial segregation rules. The city contended that it was closing the pools to preserve public peace and because the pools could not be operated economically on an integrated basis, but black citizens challenged the action as unlawful discrimination on the theory that the decision to close the pools was based on discriminatory intentions, despite the publicly stated reasons. The Supreme Court turned aside the claim, largely on the ground that a legislative act does not violate the Equal Protection Clause simply because the act is adopted by government officials with discriminatory aims, at least when the officials put forth a valid, plausible reason for their actions.

The Palmer ruling is significant as an expression of the Court's strong unwillingness at the time to look beyond the surface of a seemingly neutral government act to search for discriminatory intent. Subsequent rulings have diminished the impact of Palmer by placing greater emphasis on *discriminatory intent in determining *equal protection violations. The decision remains important, however, as an indicator of the Court's general reluctance to examine the motives behind legislative acts.

Eric T. Freyfogle

**Panama Refining Co. v. Ryan,** 293 U.S. 388 (1935), argued 10–11 Dec. 1934, decided 7 Jan. 1935 by vote of 8 to 1; Hughes for the Court, Cardozo in dissent. During the Great Depression of the 1930s, oil prices collapsed because of overproduction and the general economic slowdown. The oil-producing states, unable individually to raise prices by limiting production, demanded congressional controls. The National Industrial Recovery Act (NIRA) of 1934, a wideranging effort by the administration of President Franklin *Roosevelt to deal with the depression, authorized the president to prohibit the shipment in interstate commerce of petroleum produced in excess of quotas fixed by the states (popularly referred to as "hot oil"). Precedents existed for federal assistance to state law enforcement. For example, the Webb-Kenyon Act of 1913 had prohibited the interstate transportation of liquor into states banning liquor imports.

The "hot oil" program was only one of the many provisions of the NIRA, but it was the first *New Deal initiative to be tested before the Supreme Court. *Panama Refining Co. v. Ryan* (1935), a decision widely perceived as a threat to the entire New Deal program, held the "hot oil" provision to be an unconstitutional delegation of legislative power to the president.

*Separation of powers is a basic principle of the Constitution, but up to 1935 the Supreme Court had never held that Congress had violated this principle by delegating its power to the executive. The reasons for legislative delegation are well understood. When adopting a legislative program, Congress cannot foresee all the problems that those administering the program will encounter or the adjustments that will be needed as the program develops. As early as 1825 Chief Justice John *Marshall, in *Wayman* v. *Southard*, held that officials administering a general statutory program must be permitted to "fill up the details" (p. 43). In previous delegation situations, the Court had insisted that Congress set "standards" to guide administrative discretion, but the justices had typically accepted broad general statements as meeting this requirement. Consequently, that a ruling in the *Panama Refining* case would be based on the delegation issue was so unanticipated by the Roosevelt administration that the government's brief of 427 pages devoted only 13 pages to it.

But in the *Panama* decision, Chief Justice Charles Evans *Hughes held the statute invalid because Congress had established no "primary standard," leaving the matter to the president without direction or rule, "to be dealt with as he pleased." The statute, wrote Hughes, established "no criteria to govern the President's course. It does not require any finding by the President as a condition of his action. The Congress . . . thus declares no policy as to the transportation of the excess production" (p. 430).

Justice Benjamin N. *Cardozo was the sole dissenter. He approved the statute because it was framed to meet a "national disaster," presenting problems that only the president could deal with on a day-to-day basis (p. 443). In fact, congressional intention to control the production and transportation of "hot oil" was fairly clear in the statute, and delegations of equal scope in earlier legislation had encountered no judicial ban.

Shortly after the "hot oil" decision, the Supreme Court in *Schechter Poultry Corp. v. U.S.* (1935) declared unconstitutional another major feature of NIRA—industry codes of fair competition—also on grounds of unconstitutional delegation of legislative power. The following year legislation regulating prices and labor relations in the bituminous coal industry was ruled unconstitutional on the same grounds in *Carter v. Carter Coal Co.* (1936).

After the defeat of Roosevelt's *court-packing plan by Congress in 1937, the Court made its peace with the New Deal, and on no subsequent occasion did the justices strike down a statutory program on a charge of unconstitutional delegation of legislative power to the president.

The *Panama* and *Schechter* decisions have never been overruled. In fact, *Panama* (nearly always paired with *Schechter*) has been cited in more than forty subsequent Supreme Court decisions, typically where administrative exercise of delegated power was involved. But in none of these cases was the congressional delegation held invalid. As Justice William H. *Rehnquist said in *Hampton* v. *Mow Sun Wong* (1976): "The Court has not seen fit during the forty years following these decisions to enlarge in the slightest their relatively narrow holdings" (p. 122). *Panama* and *Schechter* remain museum pieces from a period of troubled relations between the executive and judicial branches.

(See also COMMERCE POWER; DELEGATION OF POWERS.)

C. Herman Pritchett

**Pardon Power.** Vested in the president by Article II, section 2, the pardon power extends to "Offenses against the United States, except in Cases of Impeachment." Granting the power entailed a theoretical problem for the framers of the Constitution in 1787. It was vested in the Crown in England, for crimes there were reckoned as offenses against the Crown, but in a republic crimes are offenses against the people. Accordingly, it was widely held that only the people could forgive the offense. Most of the Revolutionary state constitutions provided for an executive pardon, but none did so unconditionally, and several gave the legislatures the final word. The framers of the federal Constitution saw the matter in a fresh light, less as a means of granting mercy than as an instrument for punishing or preventing crimes—pardoning a criminal to obtain his or her testimony against confederates, for instance, or granting general pardons to quell insurrections. It was on the latter ground that Alexander *Hamilton, in The *Federalist, no. 74, rejected the criticism of some Antifederalists that the pardoning power should not extend to cases of treason. No other serious objections were made to the executive pardon during the debates over the ratification of the Constitution.

Presidents exercised the power from the beginning. George *Washington pardoned two persons who had been convicted of treason in connection with the 1794 Whiskey Rebellion in Pennsylvania. John Adams pardoned John Fries, who was convicted of treason after an abortive uprising in Northampton County, Pennsylvania, in 1799. Thomas *Jefferson pardoned ten newspaper printers who had been convicted under the *Sedition Act of 1798. Along with those pardons, Congress voted to remit the printers' fines, suggesting that the original understanding of the president's power did not extend that far.

General pardons were also the norm, as Hamilton had suggested. James *Madison in 1815, Abraham *Lincoln in 1863, and Andrew Johnson in 1865 all granted such pardons. One of Johnson's pardons was challenged, giving the Supreme Court occasion to issue its definitive pronouncement on the subject. Under the Test Act of 1865, Congress required that persons seeking to practice law in federal court had to take an oath swearing that they had never given aid or comfort to enemies of the United States. An Arkansas attorney, Alexander Hamilton Garland, was unable to take the oath because he had been a Confederate sympathizer. He had, however, been pardoned, without having been tried, by President Johnson for any offenses he might have committed during the Civil War. In Ex parte Garland (1867) the Court ruled in Garland's favor, holding that a pardon "extends to every offense known to the law, and may be exercised at any time after its commission, either before legal proceedings are taken, or during their pendency, or after conviction and judgment" (p. 380) and that it makes the offender retroactively "innocent" in the eyes of the law.

The most publicized pardons in recent decades were those granted by Presidents Gerald Ford and Jimmy Carter. In 1974 Ford bestowed upon former president Richard *Nixon, "a full, free, and absolute pardon . . . for all offenses against the United States which he had committed or may have committed or taken part in." Ford justified his action by paraphrasing Hamilton's language in The Federalist: to "restore the tranquility of the commonwealth." In 1977 Carter issued a blanket amnesty proclamation—amnesty being a species of pardon—to all persons who had unlawfully evaded the military draft during the *Vietnam War. His justification was essentially the same as Ford's.

President Ronald *Reagan, following his convictions about crime as well as a trend that was already under way, normally refused to consider applications for pardons until five to seven years after offenders had served their full sentences. Then the pardon attorney, an officer in the Justice Department, supervised a thorough investigation to determine whether the offender had been a law-abiding and constructive citizen since leaving prison. Few measured up: only 9 percent of the more than three thousand applicants received pardons. Barring an unforeseen major decline in the crime rate in America, it seems probable that Reagan's hard-line policy will be followed by his successors in the presidency.

(See also INHERENT POWERS.)

□ William F. Duker, "The President's Power to Pardon: A Constitutional History," William and Mary Law Review 18 (Spring 1977): 475–538.          Forrest McDonald

**Parker, John Johnston** (b. Monroe, N.C., 20 November 1885; d. Washington, D.C., 17 March 1958), federal appellate judge and unconfirmed nominee to the U.S. Supreme Court. After practicing law for several years in North Carolina, Parker was appointed to the U.S. Court of Appeals, Fourth Circuit, by President Calvin Coolidge in 1925. On 21 March 1930, President Herbert Hoover nominated Parker to replace Edward *Sanford on the U.S. Supreme Court. The Senate rejected Parker's nomination, 39 to 41, on 7 May 1930. He then continued to serve with distinction as a Fourth Circuit judge until his death in 1958. He was considered again for the Supreme Court by later presidents, but was never nominated.

Parker's defeat is an early example of the influence of interest groups on judicial nominations. An opinion affirming a decision upholding *yellow dog contracts earned Parker the opposition of the American Federation of Labor. The *National Association for the Advancement of Colored People also opposed him, noting a statement he made in his 1920 gubernatorial campaign rejecting Negro participation in politics. Although Parker's defenders pointed out that he was merely responding to allegations that he intended to encourage such participation, the charges especially hurt Parker because his nomination followed by only a few months the controversial confirmation of Charles Evans *Hughes, whom some senators had also opposed as too conservative. He continued to try to be a moderate on racial matters. In his decision for the Fourth Circuit implementing *Brown v. Board of Education, he rejected "massive resistance" but narrowly construed the Supreme Court's decision: "The Constitution does not require integration . . . [but] merely forbids the use of governmental power to enforce segregation" (Briggs v. Elliott, 1954).

(See also NOMINATIONS, CONTROVERSIAL; NOMINEES, REJECTION OF.)

Susan M. Olson

**Parker v. Davis.** See LEGAL TENDER CASES.

**Party System.** Long periods of great stability, in which one party dominates the institutions of government and exercises control over the broad outlines of public policy, have marked the history of American politics. These stable periods are separated by brief but intense periods of realignment, in which the old party system collapses and a new one is ushered in. The Supreme Court has both shaped and been shaped by these periods of realignment.

Political scientists and historians recognize that realignments of the party system occurred during the late 1820s; the 1850s; the 1890s; and the 1930s. These periods of upheaval brought about the decline of old parties and the emergence of new ones; or saw major changes in the leadership, constituency, and policy orientation of the existing major parties. During these periods of realignment extraordinary controversy swirled around the Supreme Court, and these periods demarcate the major transition points in Supreme Court history.

Critical realignments were caused by the American political system's inability to respond to long-term demands for change on the part of large numbers of citizens. Such demands usually centered on government economic policy and typically cut across the existing lines of partisan division. The leadership of both parties had an incentive to suppress the building unrest or seek compromise solutions. If such pressures continued to build, however, moderates of both parties came under attack from the political extremes. Under the pressure of a series of triggering events—the *slavery crisis in Kansas, the Panic of 1893, or the Great Depression of 1929, for example—the forces seeking change eventually overwhelmed the existing system, capturing one or both political parties, or bringing forth new parties. There followed a "critical election," in which the stakes were particularly high; turnout and involvement was intense; the differences between the parties on issues were great; and the outcome was clear and decisive. The result was a realignment of the party system around new (or transformed) parties and the implementation of a new set of public policies by the newly elected coalition.

The key step in the realignment process was the capture of one of the major parties by extremist elements and a polarization of the party system. This polarization of the party system was followed within a short period by the critical election itself. Once the polarization began, realignment followed quickly.

In this polarization process, the Supreme Court played a major role. As the critical issue built in intensity, one or both sides expressed the issue in constitutional terms. In the slavery crisis, for example, both sides appealed to the Constitution to support their position on slavery in the *territories. The Republicans suggested that the Constitution required the abolition of slavery in the territories; southern Democrats took the opposite view and argued that the Constitution made it impossible for Congress to ban slavery in territories. Similarly, in the *New Deal period, the Republican party claimed that Franklin *Roosevelt's policies violated the Constitution. Once the issue became infused with a constitutional dimension, both sides turned to the Supreme Court; win or lose, a high court decision on the issue made the moderate compromise positions less and less tenable.

Typically the Supreme Court was reluctant to take on the constitutional issue, preferring to accept moderate, compromise solutions and to defer to Congress. The reason is clear: the justices, appointed by the major parties over the decades before the realignment, themselves reflected the moderate political leadership of those parties (see SELECTION OF JUSTICES). For decades before *Dred *Scott v. Sandford* (1857), for example, the Court simply ducked the slavery issue. In the same way, the justices in the pre–New Deal party system found ways of sustaining most, if not all, federal economic legislation. The justices, however, were under the same pressures as their counterparts in the political system; the same triggering events that begin to polarize the parties prompted one or more of the justices to shift from the center to a more radical position. The result was a constitutional decision on the critical issue that vindicated the position of one or the other of the extremist groups. More importantly, such a decision made compromise on the critical issue impossible, since centrist positions were in effect declared unconstitutional as well. The *Dred Scott* decision, for example, declared unconstitutional not only the Republican position on slavery, but also Stephen Douglas's compromise concept of popular sovereignty. Abraham *Lincoln masterfully exploited the weakness of Douglas's position after *Dred Scott*.

The Court's decision set in motion a process by which the extremist forces dominated the field, producing a critical election. The Supreme Court's decisions striking down New Deal legislation in 1935 and 1936, for example, resulted in both the strengthening of the anti–New Deal forces in the Republican party and the clear shift to the left by Roosevelt prior to the 1936 election. The critical election of that year settled the issue (or, in the 1850s case, made it clear that the issue could not be settled politically); the resulting partisan alignment then persisted for another generation or more, until the cycle repeated itself.

Critical issues are, by definition, issues of such magnitude or intensity that they cannot be resolved by the judicial branch. The Court's attempt to resolve the slavery issue in *Dred Scott*, like its attempt to block the New Deal, was in vain. The voice of the people, expressed in a critical election, eventually pulled the Supreme

Court along with it. The Supreme Court, for example, switched immediately after the election of 1936 and placed its stamp of approval on the New Deal (see COURT-PACKING PLAN).

These realignment scenarios may lead to the conclusion that the Supreme Court follows the election returns. In these exceedingly rare critical realignments, this old adage has merit. It is, however, just as important to remember that few presidential elections center around an issue that involves the Supreme Court; most of the time, there are no election returns for the Supreme Court to follow. Thus, in general the Court is remarkably free to decide as it wishes. Of course, since the Court is recruited from and appointed by the dominant political parties, they are unlikely to oppose major policies of the national government. Still, only rarely do the people directly impose their views on the Court.

The relationship between the Court and the party system is no longer as clear as it once was. With major changes in the American political system since the New Deal, the pattern of stability and change inherent in the critical realignment model no longer seems to characterize American politics. The tremendous growth in the federal government and its activist role in economic and social policy have made it far more responsive to demands for change than it once was and have perhaps transformed the underlying basis of the realignment model. The result is a weakened party system given to gradual rather than dramatic transformations and an indirect relationship between the party system and the Court.

(See also POLITICAL PARTIES.)

□ Walter Dean Burnham, *Critical Elections and the Mainsprings of American Politics* (1970). William Lasser, "The Supreme Court in Periods of Critical Realignment," *Journal of Politics* 47 (1985): 1174–1187. James L. Sundquist, *Dynamics of the Party System: Alignment and Realignment of Political Parties in the United States*, rev. ed. (1983).
William Lasser

**Pasadena Board of Education v. Spangler,** 427 U.S. 424 (1976), argued 27–28 Apr. 1976, decided 28 June 1976 by vote of 6 to 2; Rehnquist for the Court, Marshall and Brennan in dissent, Stevens not participating. Whatever doubts remained after *Milliken* v. *Bradley* (1974) that the Supreme Court would exercise a more lenient overview of school desegregation remedies were put to rest two years later in *Pasadena Board of Education* v. *Spangler*. Under a 1970 school desegregation plan, the trial court ordered that pupil assignments guarantee that no school in the district have a majority of minority students. Within four years, five schools were in violation of that provision of the plan. The trial court held that the system was not yet desegregated and that annual reassignments to avoid the prohibited outcome were necessary.

The Supreme Court disagreed, holding that annual reassignments exceeded the district court's authority and emphasizing that the changes in racial proportions were not chargeable to intentional segregative actions by the district. Quoting *Swann* v. *Charlotte-Mecklenburg* (1971), the Court found no constitutional requirement to make annual adjustments "once the affirmative duty to desegregate had been accomplished and racial discrimination through official action [has been] eliminated from the system" (p. 425).

The issue was narrow, but, as Justice Thurgood *Marshall's dissent indicated, prior to *Milliken* one might have expected that the district court's ruling would have been sustained as an exercise of sound *Swann*-like discretion.

(See also DESEGREGATION REMEDIES; RACE AND RACISM.)
Dennis J. Hutchinson

**Passenger Cases** (*Smith* v. *Turner, Norris* v. *Boston*), 7 How. (48 U.S.) 283 (1849), argued 19–22 Dec. 1848, decided 7 Feb. 1849 by vote of 5 to 4; no opinion for the Court (McLean, Wayne, Catron, McKinley, and Grier comprised the majority), Daniel, Woodbury, Taney, and Nelson in dissent. *Smith* v. *Turner* and *Norris* v. *Boston* had each been argued twice separately before being combined as the *Passenger Cases*, by which name they are commonly known. At issue were New York and Massachusetts taxes on incoming passengers, including immigrants, with the proceeds being used to finance hospitals for ships' passengers. The Court's majority invalidated the laws, but the decision produced no useful doctrine. It merely demonstrated the subsurface divisions on the Court caused by the problem of the states' control over *slavery, free African-Americans, abolitionists, and antislavery propaganda. The plethora of opinions (eight in all) demonstrated that in the charged atmosphere of the slavery controversy, the Court was unable to deal effectively with issues raised by the Commerce Clause. This problem had manifested itself in Chief Justice Roger B. *Taney's maiden term in *New York* v. *Miln* (1837) and would persist until a partial resolution was achieved in *Cooley* v. *Board of Wardens* (1852). (See also COMMERCE POWER.)
Donald M. Roper

**Patent.** Authorized by Article I, section 8 of the Constitution "to promote the progress of science and useful arts" by granting exclusive rights to authors and inventors "for limited times," Congress made patents broadly available to "whosoever invents or discovers any new and useful process, machine, manufacture or composition of matter." In practice, however, the Supreme Court in *Graham* v. *John Deere Co.* (1966) denied Congress the power "to remove existent knowledge from the public domain, or to restrict free access to materials already available" (p. 6); while the Court's decisions in the recent past so limited the enforcement of patent rights that Justice Robert *Jackson stated in a dissent his belief that "the only patent that is valid is one this Court hasn't been able to get its hands on" (*Jungersen* v. *Ostby*, 1949). In this way, echoes of the nineteenth-century controversy concerning the social utility of a patent system influenced the Supreme Court's thinking well into the twentieth century, particularly its belief that the useful arts prospered best when free market competition was unhindered by legal monopolies.

Beginning in the 1970s, however, both the executive and legislative branches reevaluated the role of the nation's intellectual property system in a drive for greater international competitiveness and for an improved balance of trade. In the spirit of reform, Congress conferred exclusive jurisdiction over patent appeals upon a newly created and specialized tribunal, the Court of Appeals for the Federal Circuit, which has revitalized the domestic patent law since its inception in 1982. Responding to this more protectionist ethos, the Supreme Court handed down several ground-breaking decisions in the 1980s that appeared to have expanded patent protection. Nevertheless, unresolved judicial tensions between the Court's traditional free-market bias and current protectionist sentiments continue to haunt every major branch of patent jurisprudence, and the extent to which the Supreme Court has made a lasting commitment to a stronger patent system remains uncertain.

Most of the rules judicially crafted during the nineteenth century derived from the Supreme Court's characterization of patents as the product of a social bargain in which inventors were rewarded for the benefit of society at large. The Court obliged patentees to distinguish their inventions from the prior art and to limit their claims accordingly. It required full disclosure of how to make and use the patented inventions. Prior public use or knowledge usually destroyed the element of novelty.

In the 1980s, the Court broadened its reading of the statute to permit the patenting of biogenetically engineered organisms (*Diamond* v. *Chakrabarty*, 1980) and of computer program-related inventions insofar as they partook of processes or mechanical devices otherwise eligible for protection (*Diamond* v. *Diehr*, 1981). In these decisions, the Court leaned toward greater emphasis on the role of patents in stimulating technological innovation.

Although the patent statute of 1793 had already set down the substantive prerequisites of novelty and utility, the Supreme Court derived a third requirement of "invention" (i.e., inventiveness) from the language of the Constitution. It was this controversial standard of invention, first articulated in *Hotchkiss* v. *Greenwood* (1850), that had enabled the Supreme Court to invalidate patents in twenty significant cases between 1930

and 1950, a period in which the Court upheld only five patents. Typically excluded were so-called combination patents that incorporated previously known elements in a new way. In contrast, "pioneer" inventions, such as Bell's telephone or Edison's electric lamp, received liberal treatment under the prevailing reward philosophy even in the face of doubtful evidence.

In 1952, Congress codified the nonobviousness test of invention, but it was not until the Supreme Court's landmark decision in *Graham* v. *John Deere Co.* that this codified test fully matured. According to *Graham*, courts evaluating nonobviousness were obliged to determine the scope and content of the prior art, the extent to which the candidate invention differed from the prior art, and the level of ordinary skill in the trade. The invention became patentable if it would not have been obvious to one reasonably skilled in the art at the time it was discovered. The *Graham* opinion also permitted these "subjective" indicia of nonobviousness to be corroborated by a fourth set of subtests, known as the secondary considerations, which look to such allegedly "objective" factors as commercial success, copying, long-felt but unsolved needs, failure of others, and acquiescence of the trade. The *Graham* test did not appreciably lessen the difficulties of applying the standard of invention until the Court of Appeals for the Federal Circuit, beginning in 1982, made the secondary considerations a crucial subtest in evaluating the nonobviousness of issued patents in all relevant cases. As a result, the likelihood of judicial invalidation has declined precipitously in recent years, as regards both utility patents and design patents, without provoking a negative response from the Supreme Court.

The patentee's right to make, use, or sell the patented invention is broad and domestic patent owners cannot be compelled to practice or license their patents. On the whole, the Supreme Court has tended to construe the scope of issued patents strictly, in keeping with its historical preference for free competition over private rewards and incentives. Despite this conservative record, the Supreme Court accepted and developed the doctrine of equivalents, which limits the ability of a competitor to take the substance of a patented invention while deviating from the literal language of the claims (*Winans* v. *Denmead*, 1853; *Graver Tank & Mfg. Co.* v. *Linde Air Products Co.*, 1950).

The restrictive view of patents espoused by the Supreme Court throughout much of the twentieth century logically inclined it to take a dim view of state action impinging on the patent system because that system "is one in which uniform federal standards are carefully used to promote invention while at the same time preserving free competition" (*Sears, Roebuck & Co.* v. *Stiffel Co.*, 1964; *Compco Corp.* v. *Day-Brite Lighting, Inc.*, 1964). In 1989, the Supreme Court reaffirmed this view in *Bonito Boats, Inc.* v. *Thunder Craft Boats,*

*Inc.* (1989), a unanimous opinion that struck down state statutes that encroached on the design patent law by prohibiting competitors from duplicating certain unpatented boat designs. This decision appeared to invest a competitor's right to reverse engineer unpatented products with Constitutional underpinnings.

(See also CAPITALISM.)

☐ Donald Chisum, *Patents: A Treatise on the Law of Patentability, Validity and Infringement* (1990). Edmund Kitch, "*Graham v. John Deere Co.*: New Standards for Patents," *Supreme Court Review* (1966): 293–316. Philip Kurland, ed., *The Supreme Court and Patents and Monopolies* (1975). J. H. Reichman, "Design Protection and the New Technologies: The United States Experience in a Transnational Perspective," *University of Baltimore Law Review* 19 (Winter 1990): 6–153.          J. H. Reichman

**Paternalism.** See GENDER; MULLER V. OREGON.

**Paterson, William** (b. County Antrium, Ireland, 24 Dec. 1745; d. Albany, N.Y., 9 Sept. 1806; interrred Albany Rural Cemetery, Menands, N.Y.), associate justice, 1793–1806. William Paterson played a significant role in the framing of the United States Constitution in the summer of 1787, helped write the *Judiciary Act of 1789, and was an important and active member of the Supreme Court during the 1790s and the early years of the Marshall Court.

*William Paterson*

Though born in Ireland, Paterson was brought to New Jersey at an early age. He did his undergraduate work at Princeton University, studied law, and was admitted to the bar in 1768. A vigorous advocate of independence, he quickly became a prominent member of New Jersey's revolutionary generation. He helped draft the state's first constitution and became its first attorney general. He also developed a lucrative law practice during the 1780s by defending wealthy landowners and creditors.

Paterson strongly supported the movement, in the 1780s, to create a more energetic national government. As a member of the Constitutional Convention he opposed the Virginia Plan's proposal that representation in both houses of Congress be apportioned according to population. Fearing that such a provision would give too much power to states with a large number of inhabitants and place smaller states like New Jersey, Delaware, and Connecticut at a disadvantage, he proposed as an alternative, the New Jersey Plan of Government, which, in its most important feature, provided for a continuance of the single house legislature of the Articles of Confederation in which each state, regardless of the number of its representatives, had only one vote. The proposal eventuated in the Great Compromise that arranged for the creation of a bicameral Congress where representation in the lower house would be by population and equal representation (two senators for each state) was

provided in the upper house. The plan also created a Supreme Court with broad powers and made the laws and treaties of the federal government the supreme law of the land, with *state courts bound to obey them. This arrangement probably was the source of the *Supremacy Clause of the United States Constitution (Art. VI, cl. II).

Elected to the first United States Senate, Paterson was one of the authors of the *Judiciary Act of 1789. This law implemented *Article III of the United States Constitution by providing that the United States Supreme Court consist of a *chief justice and five associate justices and a system of district and circuit courts at the lower level (see LOWER FEDERAL COURTS). It also created the office of attorney general. And in section 25, which was to be the foundation of some of the Supreme Court's most important decisions, it gave that Court appellate jurisdiction over final decisions of state courts when the Constitution, federal laws, and treaties were involved (see JUDICIAL POWER AND JURISDICTION).

Appointed to the Supreme Court by George *Washington in 1793, Paterson played a key role in almost all the important decisions of the 1790s. In them he always argued for the supremacy of the federal government over the states. His decision in *Penhallow v. Doane's Administration* (1795) articulated a strongly nationalist interpretation of the origins and nature of the Union. In *Ware v. Hylton* (1796), he rendered invalid a Virginia statute that had permitted the sequestration of debts owed to British citizens before the Revolution, on the grounds that the treaty of peace with Great Britain had specifically provided that there should be no legal obstacles placed in the way of the recovery of debts owed by Americans to English creditors and that it was the "supreme law of the land." Paterson also favored a strong and independent judiciary. His decision on circuit in *Van Horne's Lessee* v. *Dorrance* (1795) espoused the doctrine of *judicial review. Paterson's opinions are also important because as a member of the federal convention that framed the United States Constitution, he was able to speak with authority on what the *"original intention" of the framers was on a number of issues. Particularly important in this regard are his decisions in *Hylton* v. *United States* (1796) and *Calder* v. *Bull* (1798).

While riding circuit during the 1798–1800 period, Paterson enthusiastically enforced the *Sedition Act. He presided over the trials that led to the conviction of a number of Democratic-Republican critics of President John Adams's administration, including Congressman Matthew Lyon. Following the Jeffersonian victory in the election of 1800 and the appointment of John *Marshall as chief justice in 1801, Paterson became more cautious and moderate. His new attitude manifested itself most clearly in *Stuart* v. *Laird* (1803) when Paterson, speaking for a unanimous Supreme Court, declared the Jeffersonian sponsored repeal of the *Judiciary Act of 1801 constitutional.

In 1804, while riding circuit, Paterson suffered an injury from which he never recovered. He died in 1806.

□ John E. O'Connor, *William Paterson, Lawyer and Statesman, 1745–1806* (1979).                    Richard E. Ellis

**Patterson v. McLean Credit Union,** 491 U.S. 164 (1989), argued 29 Feb. 1988, reargued 12 Oct. 1988, decided 15 June 1989 by votes of 9 to 0 on one major issue and 5 to 4 on another; Kennedy for the Court; Brennan, Marshall, and Blackmun concurring in the judgment in part and joining in part in a dissent by Brennan; Stevens concurring in the judgment in part and dissenting in part. *Patterson* formally involved the question whether an African-American woman's claim of racial harassment in employment stated a cause of action under Title 42, section 1981 of the U.S. Code, a surviving portion of the Civil Rights Act of 1866. In *Runyon* v. *McCrary* (1976) and *Jones* v. *Alfred H. Mayer Co.* (1968), section 1981 and a companion provision had been interpreted to reach private racial discrimination in contractual and property relations. After the initial argument, the Court, on its own motion, ordered a reargument and requested that the parties address the question whether *Runyon's* interpretation of section 1981 should be overruled. *Patterson* thus seemed on the verge of becoming a landmark case reversing the prior twenty years' practice of applying the 1866 act's modern counterparts to cases involving private discrimination.

Few procedural orders in the Supreme Court's history have caused such a volatile reaction. Within the Court, the reargument order itself prompted sharp dissents from Justices Harry *Blackmun and John Paul *Stevens, both joined by Justices William *Brennan and Thurgood *Marshall. These dissents moved the majority to take the unusual steps of defending a reargument order in writing. The civil rights community, the press, and scholarly journals focused intense attention on the pending case.

After the second argument, relying on the doctrine of *stare decisis* (see PRECEDENT), the Court unanimously declined to overrule *Runyon*. But, in an unprecedented interpretation of section 1981 that prompted four dissents, the Court held that the right to make contracts does not extend to conduct by an employer after establishment of the contractual relation, including Patterson's claim of posthiring racial harassment. Congress reacted to *Patterson* and other decisions by passing the *Civil Rights Act of 1991, which overruled *Patterson's* narrow reading of section 1981.

(See also EMPLOYMENT DISCRIMINATION; RACE AND RACISM.)

Theodore Eisenberg

**Paul v. Virginia,** 8 Wall. (75 U.S.) 168 (1869), argued 12 Oct. 1869, decided 1 Nov. 1869 by vote of 8 to 0; Field for the Court. During the nineteenth century, fire and life insurance companies were among the first corporations to market products on a national basis. To encourage the development of local enterprise, many states levied discriminatory taxes and license fees against nonresident, or "foreign," insurance companies chartered in other states. Such protectionist legislation was directed chiefly against large corporations in the Northeast. *Paul* v. *Virginia* was a *test case financed by the National Board of Fire Underwriters to challenge these discriminatory practices. The case arose when Paul, an agent for a number of New York fire insurance companies, was convicted under a Virginia law for selling insurance without a license.

Company lawyers argued that corporations were "citizens" as defined in the Privileges and Immunities Clause of Article IV and that insurance sales were transactions in interstate commerce under Article I, section 8. A victory on the Commerce Clause issue would have preempted the states from regulating or taxing any aspects of interstate insurance sales.

A unanimous Supreme Court held against the insurance industry on both questions, thereby allowing state protectionist legislation to continue. The decision reflected the nineteenth-century view that corporations were not citizens for purposes of the Privileges and Immunities Clause. The Court ultimately held, in *United States* v. *South-Eastern Underwriters Association* (1944), that the insurance business affected interstate commerce, but by then state regulatory systems were well entrenched. Congress recognized this fact by authorizing the continuation of state insurance regulation through the McCarran-Ferguson Act of 1945.

(See also CITIZENSHIP; COMMERCE POWER; PRIVILEGES AND IMMUNITIES.)

Philip L. Merkel

**Payne v. Tennessee,** 111 S.Ct. 2597 (1991), argued 24 Apr. 1991, decided 27 June 1991 by vote of 6 to 3; Rehnquist for the Court, O'Connor, joined by White and Kennedy, concurring; Scalia, joined in part by O'Connor and Kennedy, concurring; Souter, joined by Kennedy, concurring; Marshall, joined by Blackmun, and Stevens, also joined by Blackmun, in dissent.

During the penalty phase of Payne's capital trial, the state presented the grandmother of a surviving victim, who stated that her grandson missed his mother and sister—both of whom were killed in Payne's attack. The prosecutor also referred to the effects of the crimes on the victims' family in his closing argument. Payne was sentenced to death. The Court held that the *Eighth Amendment does not prohibit a capital-sentencing jury from considering "victim impact" evidence, even though the defense may often find it prudent not to attempt a rebuttal. In so-doing, the Court overruled *Booth* v. *Maryland* (1987), which had disallowed victim-impact testimony, and *South Carolina* v. *Gathers* (1989), which had prohibited a prosecutor from even referring to victim impact.

(See also CAPITAL PUNISHMENT.)

Michael L. Radelet

**Payton v. New York,** 445 U.S. 573 (1980), argued 26 Mar. 1979, reargued 9 Oct. 1979, decided 15 Apr. 1980 by vote of 6 to 3; Stevens for the Court, Blackmun concurring, Burger, Rehnquist, and White in dissent. *Payton* resolved a longstanding open question: whether the *Fourth Amendment prohibits the police from making a warrantless nonconsensual entry into a suspect's home in order to accomplish a routine felony arrest. Noting the well-established rule that a nonconsensual warrantless entry of private premises to search for evidence is presumptively unreasonable, the Court concluded the same should be true of an arrest entry, for both types of entries "implicate the same interest in preserving the *privacy and the sanctity of the home" (p. 588). Thus a warrant is needed for an arrest entry unless there are "exigent circumstances."

Though some have argued that a search warrant should be necessary for an arrest entry because it would require a judicial officer to focus on the question of whether the wanted person was probably in the specific premises to be entered, the Court in *Payton* required only an arrest warrant (and thus only an advance judicial determination of grounds to arrest). But in *Steagald* v. *United States* (1981), the Court ruled

that in the case of entry of premises to arrest a guest a search warrant would be necessary absent exigent circumstances, for in such circumstances it is important to protect the resident's privacy by a preentry judicial determination that the person to be arrested is probably there.

One "exigent circumstance" is where the police are in hot pursuit of the person to be arrested. Beyond that, lower courts often use a difficult-to-apply test that takes into account the magnitude of the crime, the likelihood that the person is armed, the strength of the probable cause to arrest, the likelihood that the person is within, the likelihood of escape absent immediate arrest, whether the entry is peaceable, and whether the entry is at night. In *Welsh* v. *Wisconsin* (1984), the Court declined to give express approval to all these factors but, stressing the absence of the first, held that police could not enter a home without a warrant to arrest a person who had minutes earlier been engaged in the civil forfeiture offense of driving while intoxicated. The Court seems to have given insufficient attention to another reason why immediate warrantless entry to arrest is sometimes necessary: to prevent the loss of evidence (in *Welsh*, the defendant's blood-alcohol level).

(See also DUE PROCESS, PROCEDURAL; SEARCH WARRANT RULE, EXCEPTIONS TO.)

Wayne R. LaFave

**Peckham, Rufus Wheeler** (b. Albany, N.Y., 8 Nov. 1838; d. Altamont, N.Y., 24 Oct. 1909; interred Rural Cemetery, Albany), associate justice, 1895–1909. Rufus Peckham came from a prominent New York family of lawyers and judges. He was educated at Albany Boys Academy, studied abroad, and received an honorary degree from Columbia University in 1866. Peckham read law in his father's Albany office and was admitted to the bar in 1859. In private practice he represented mostly corporate clients and established himself as an influential member of the community and Democratic party. He served as district attorney for Albany County from 1869 to 1872. In 1883 he won election to the New York Supreme Court (the state's lower court). In 1886, Peckham was elected to the state's highest tribunal, the Court of Appeals, where he stayed until President Grover Cleveland nominated him to the United States Supreme Court in 1895.

Cleveland's nomination of Peckham followed an attempt to place his brother, Wheeler *Peckham, on the high court. Both brothers were connected with the upstate faction of the New York Democratic party, supporters of Grover Cleveland, and often in conflict with the New York Democratic machine led by U.S. Senator David Hill. Even though Cleveland won the presidency in 1892, the Hill faction remained strong in state politics. They claimed success in placing a Democrat in the governor's office and

*Rufus Wheeler Peckham*

taking over both houses of the state legislature. In 1893, when Cleveland had the opportunity to fill a place on the Court, he selected William B. *Hornblower. Hill invoked *senatorial courtesy and Hornblower's nomination was defeated. Cleveland's next choice was Wheeler Peckham, whose nomination was also defeated. Finally the president and Senate agreed on Louisiana Senator Edward *White. In 1895 Cleveland had a second opportunity to make an appointment to the Supreme Court and, on 3 December he nominated Rufus Peckham. By this time New York Democrats had suffered major defeats in the previous state elections. Less confident of his strength, Hill acquiesced to the nomination. Rufus Peckham was confirmed on 12 December 1895 and kept his seat on the United States Supreme Court until his death in 1909.

During his thirteen years on the bench, Peckham wrote 315 opinions. Few of them were of lasting importance. Although not as visible as some of his colleagues, Peckham was one of the Court's most consistent advocates of *laissez-faire constitutionalism. His disdain for government regulation was apparent even while he sat on the New York bench. Dissenting in *People v. Walsh* (1889), for example, he called a law that regulated grain elevators "vicious in its nature and communistic in its tendency" (p. 695).

In an era of conservative *judicial activism Peckham soon became a mainstay of the Court's conservatives. His first opinion of note was *Allgeyer v. Louisiana* (1897), in which the Supreme Court adopted "liberty of contract" as a limit on state regulatory authority (see CON-

TRACT, FREEDOM OF). This doctrine provided a rather open-ended standard against which the court could test the validity of legislation. Peckham refined its application in his most well-known opinion, *Lochner v. New York* (1905). There he ruled that a state law limiting the length of the workday for bakers violated the liberty of contract of both the employee and employer. Peckham emphasized that the state's *police power— the source of its authority to interfere with individual liberty—was limited to protecting public morals, health, safety, and welfare. He held that the workday limitation could not reasonably be considered a health law and was therefore invalid. Peckham believed federal authority to legislate economic regulations should be limited in the same manner. In *Champion v. Ames* (1903) he joined a dissent that urged that Congress could not prohibit sale of lottery tickets through the mail.

Shortly before Peckham came to the Court the *Sherman Antitrust Act was significantly weakened by judicial interpretation in the Sugar Trust Case, *U.S. v. *E.C. Knight* (1895). In a series of his early opinions, *U.S. v. Trans-Missouri Freight Association* (1897), *U.S. v. Joint Traffic Association* (1898), and *Addyston Pipe and Steel v. U.S.* (1899), Peckham restored some of the federal government's power to combat monopoly. These decisions indicate that, while Peckham's record undoubtedly reflects a business orientation, focus of his concern was individual economic liberty.

(See also DUE PROCESS, SUBSTANTIVE.)

□ Skolnik, Richard, "Rufus Peckham," in *Justices of the Supreme Court of the United States*, edited by Leon Friedman and Fred L. Israel, vol. 3 (1969), pp. 1685–1703.
Paul Kens

**Peckham, Wheeler Hazard** (b. Albany, N.Y., 1 Jan. 1833; d. New York City, 27 Sept. 1905), lawyer, unconfirmed nominee to the Supreme Court. Wheeler H. Peckham was one of Albany Law School's first graduates in 1855. After being admitted to the New York bar, Peckham joined his father's law firm. After an absence of eight years between 1856 and 1864, during which Peckham traveled because of ill health, he returned to New York, and entered into a law partnership with a large general practice firm. In 1868 he appeared before the United States Supreme Court in several cases involving the power of a state to tax "greenback" dollars; the Court upheld his argument that states had no such power. The opposing counsel was so impressed with Peckham's abilities that he asked him to assist in the prosecution of New York political boss William M. Tweed and his associates. Tweed was convicted in 1873, largely a result of Peckham's efforts.

Although he was not a politician, Peckham was an advocate of legal reform. He was a

628 □ Peirce v. New Hampshire

founder of the Association of the Bar of the City of New York in 1869 and its president from 1892 to 1894. President Grover Cleveland nominated Peckham to fill a vacancy on the Supreme Court on 23 January 1894. Peckham was opposed by Senator David B. Hill of New York because Peckham had become involved in a patronage squabble between Cleveland and Hill, in which Hill was the loser. Hill invoked *senatorial courtesy, and the Senate voted 41 to 32 against confirmation on 16 February 1894. Peckham continued in private law practice until 1905, when he died unexpectedly in his New York City law office.                                    Judith K. Schafer

**Peirce v. New Hampshire.** See LICENSE CASES.

**Penn Central Transportation Co. v. City of New York,** 438 U.S. 104 (1978), argued 17 Apr. 1978, decided 26 Jun. 1978 by vote of 6 to 3; Brennan for the Court, Rehnquist in dissent. This key decision on the *regulatory taking doctrine originated several important principles. New York City's Landmarks Preservation Committee designated Grand Central Terminal a landmark. Consequently, the plaintiff was denied permission to build a fifty-story office building (supported by arches) above the terminal. However, the city allowed "transferable development rights," by which the plaintiff or an assignee could make excess development on certain nearby "transfer" sites. Penn Central challenged the restriction as a denial of *due process and a taking.

In a wide-ranging opinion, the Court held that the development restriction was not a taking because it did not impede existing uses or prevent a reasonable return on investment. The opinion emphasized that the restriction did not unduly "frustrate distinct investment-backed expectations" (p. 127), a phrase that appears in subsequent takings decisions. While the Court did not consider the mitigating effect of the transferable development rights, it was suggested that such transferable rights might mitigate loss to prevent a taking or might, if there were a taking, provide a form of compensation. The Court also rejected the argument that airspace be considered a separate parcel of property for taking purposes. Underlying the opinion is the notion that aesthetic values, particularly historic preservation, are important public interests that justify restrictions on private land.

(See also EMINENT DOMAIN; FIFTH AMENDMENT; JUST COMPENSATION; TAKINGS CLAUSE.)
                                    William B. Stoebuck

**Pennoyer v. Neff,** 95 U.S. 714 (1878), argued 28 Nov. 1877, decided 21 Jan. 1878 by vote of 8 to 1; Field for the Court, Hunt in dissent. *Pennoyer* v. *Neff* provided the Court's earliest consideration of the constitutional and procedural bases for a state's exercise of jurisdiction over an individual who is neither a resident nor a citizen of the state and who is not physically present there. The case involved title to real property located in Oregon owned by a nonresident defendant. To secure judgment in a contract suit against him, the plaintiff attached the property and provided "constructive service" on the defendant by publication of a legal notice in a local newspaper.

For the Court, Justice Stephen J. *Field found that this combination of attachment and constructive service was insufficient to give the state jurisdiction over an out-of-state defendant. He laid down two complementary rules: "every State possess exclusive jurisdiction and sovereignty over persons and property within its territory"; and "no State can exercise direct jurisdiction and authority over persons or property without its territory" (p. 722). His opinion was based both on physical notions of jurisdiction (i.e., physical presence) and concepts of state sovereignty derived from the *Tenth Amendment.

*Pennoyer* proved increasingly inadequate as a comprehensive statement of *in personam jurisdiction in the twentieth century, especially because of the revolutions in transportation and communications, and because the idea of physical presence was irrelevant to explain jurisdiction over *corporations. The Court articulated a supplemental theory of in personam jurisdiction in *International Shoe Co.* v. *Washington* (1945), based on traditional notions of fair play and substantial justice. But *Burnham* v. *Superior Court* (1990) demonstrated that if the Tenth Amendment basis of *Pennoyer* is obsolete, the concept of physical presence is not, and can still furnish the basis for so-called tag service on a defendant temporarily present in the forum state.

(See also JUDICIAL POWER AND JURISDICTION.)
                                    William M. Wiecek

**Pennsylvania Coal Co. v. Mahon,** 260 U.S. 393 (1922), argued 14 Nov. 1922, decided 11 Dec. 1922 by vote of 8 to 1; Holmes for the Court, Brandeis in dissent. This decision is the origin of the doctrine that a regulation on the use of land may cause a taking of property. (See TAKINGS CLAUSE.) The coal company owned underground strata of coal but no surface rights. A Pennsylvania statute, designed to prevent subsidence, had the effect of prohibiting mining the coal strata. The Supreme Court invalidated the statute, because it constituted a taking of property without compensation, as required by the *Fifth Amendment. The Court said that a land-use regulation became a taking if it went "too far" in restricting use of land and diminishing its value (p. 415). It remains unclear when a regulation constitutes a taking of property for which compensation is required.

The concept of a *regulatory taking is binding upon both the federal government and states. It is the subject of a number of Supreme Court decisions. In *Keystone Bituminous Coal Association* v. *DeBenedictis* (1987) the Court upheld a Pennsylvania statute that bore some similarity to the statute that *Mahon* struck down, and appeared to limit the taking doctrine to regulations that almost totally prevent use of the regulated land. With the increasing number of land-use and environmental regulations, the taking issue has become the most celebrated question concerning such controls.

(See also PROPERTY RIGHTS.)

William B. Stoebuck

**Pennsylvania v. Nelson,** 350 U.S. 497 (1956), argued 15–16 Nov. 1955, decided 2 Apr. 1956 by vote of 6 to 3; Warren for the Court, Reed, joined by Burton and Minton, in dissent. During its 1955 term the Supreme Court began to withdraw from its previous cold war practice of sustaining state and federal anticommunist legislation. Until hostile congressional reaction led a majority to return to self-restraint in internal security matters for the remainder of the 1950s, the Court relied on procedural or statutory grounds to offer some judicial protection to radical dissenters.

In what was probably the most prominent cold war decision of that term, the Court affirmed a judgment of the Pennsylvania Supreme Court that had reversed the conviction of Steve Nelson, a Communist party leader, under the state's antisedition law. Like the state court, the U.S. Supreme Court held that federal legislation (including the *Smith Act of 1940) had occupied the field of preventing overthrow of the national government. Thus, state laws on this subject were excluded, the Court said, even though Congress had never expressed any such intention. The Court concluded that Congress had implicitly occupied the field because of the volume and pervasiveness of federal antisubversive legislation, because of the dominant interest of the federal government in protecting itself against overthrow, and because enforcement of state laws could undercut the effectiveness of federal legislation. A powerful congressional effort to overturn this decision ultimately failed when it became tied to proposed general legislation completely barring implied federal exclusion of state laws, a proposal that generated strong political opposition.

(See also COMMUNISM AND COLD WAR; STATE SEDITION LAWS.)

Dean Alfange, Jr.

**Pennsylvania v. Wheeling and Belmont Bridge Co.,** 13 How. (54 U.S.) 518 (1852), argued 1 Dec. 1851, decided 6 Feb. 1852 by vote of 7 to 2; McLean for the Court, Taney and Daniel in dissent. To provide access from Wheeling (now in West Virginia) to the western states, the Virginia legislature in 1847 chartered the Wheeling and Belmont Bridge Company to build a suspension bridge across the Ohio River. Pennsylvania brought suit based on the Supreme Court's

*original jurisdiction to abate the bridge as a public nuisance because it obstructed passage of large steamboats and thus constituted an impediment to interstate commerce and a violation of interstate compacts. At a more basic policy level, the litigation reflected the struggle between older waterborne transportation technology and the newer railroads.

Justice John *McLean's majority opinion held that Pennsylvania had *standing to sue because of financial losses to its state-owned internal improvements (the Main Line). The Court ordered abatement of the bridge by either removal or elevation to 111 feet. Chief Justice Roger B. *Taney and Justice Peter V. *Daniel argued in dissent that in the absence of a federal statute declaring an obstruction of the Ohio River to be a public nuisance, the Court lacked jurisdiction (see JUDICIAL POWER AND JURISDICTION).

Six months later Congress designated the bridge lawful at its extant height. In a later suit of the same name in 1856, a divided Court held that because of the federal statute, the bridge did not constitute an obstruction of interstate commerce. The dimensions of the Wheeling bridge were used throughout the nineteenth century to determine clearances of bridges across navigable rivers.

(See also COMMERCE POWER.)

Elizabeth B. Monroe

**Penry v. Lynaugh,** 492 U.S. 302 (1989), argued 11 Jan. 1989, decided 26 June 1989; O'Connor announced the judgment of the Court and delivered the opinion of the Court, which was joined in part and dissented to in part by the other justices. *Penry* held that the application of the death penalty to persons who are mentally retarded but not legally insane does not violate the *Eighth Amendment prohibition against *cruel and unusual punishments. The Court also held, however, that jurors in a capital case must be given the opportunity to consider mitigating evidence and to provide a "reasoned moral response" to that evidence in rendering its sentencing decision.

Penry was mildly to moderately mentally retarded, probably from birth but possibly as a result of childhood beatings. Though but a child in mental age and maturity, he was found legally sane and competent to stand trial and was sentenced to death for rape and murder.

Because the Texas jury was not specifically instructed that it could consider mitigating circumstances in deciding whether or not to apply the death penalty, the Supreme Court reversed. The Court, per Justice Sandra Day *O'Connor, held that "the jury must be able to consider and give effect to any mitigating evidence relevant to a defendant's background, character, or the circumstances of the crime" (p. 328).

The Court held, however, that the execution of a mildly or moderately retarded person was not automatically barred by the Eighth Amendment, whether viewed in light of the attitudes of its framers or interpreted in accordance with society's evolving attitudes toward crime and punishment. The Court's decision did not affect its previous decision, in Ford v. Wainwright (1986), that execution of an insane person was prohibited by the Eighth Amendment.

(See also CAPITAL PUNISHMENT.)

William Lasser

**Pentagon Papers Case.** See NEW YORK TIMES CO. V. UNITED STATES.

**Peonage** lay at the juncture of race and economic arrangements that fixed the distinctive character of the South during the *Progressive era. The *Peonage Cases—Bailey* v. *Alabama* (1911) and *United States* v. *Reynolds* (1914)—were the most lasting of the Supreme Court's contributions to justice for African-Americans during the tenure of Chief Justice Edward Douglass *White. The decisions gave realistic scope to the *Thirteenth Amendment's protection against involuntary servitude as they peeled back a corner of the system of forced labor that continued in the South into the twentieth century.

Peonage existed in many southern states and was a component of a system of state laws and customs, including statutes dealing with contract fraud, criminal surety, vagrancy, and other openended laws that permitted prosecution of laborers who sought to abandon their jobs. The laws and their enforcement contributed to what the Supreme Court called "a wheel of servitude" (*Reynolds*, pp. 146–147).

Peonage first became a serious concern to the Justice Department and in the federal and state courts after 1900. The first major peonage prosecution began in 1901 in Florida, with the prosecution of Samuel Clyatt of Georgia. *Clyatt* v. *United States* (1905) tested the legality of forced labor by persons under contract and in debt. On appeal, the Supreme Court affirmed the validity of the Peonage Abolition Act of 1867, which declared unlawful "the holding of any person to service or labor under the system known as peonage" and which nullified "all acts, laws, resolutions, or usages" by which peonage was maintained (p. 546). However, the Court defined peonage rather narrowly, restricting the federal statute's coverage to forced servitude for debt.

More than a hundred other peonage cases were prosecuted by the federal government between Clyatt's conviction in 1901 and the Supreme Court's 1905 decision in the *Clyatt* case. These other cases arose from the multiple prosecutions known as the *Alabama Peonage Cases*, conducted by U.S. District Judge Thomas Goode Jones in 1903. During the course of those prosecutions, Jones struck down several coercive Alabama statutes and affirmed the rights of individuals to work where they pleased subject only to

civil liability for breach of contractual obligations. By his efforts, Jones created a momentum against peonage that reached into the White House, stirred the Justice Department, galvanized public interest, and led directly to the great peonage decisions of the Supreme Court.

The first of these, *Bailey* v. *Alabama*, altered the legal relations of African-American and immigrant laborers to their employers in the South. Avoiding both sectional recrimination and the quagmire of race relations, the opinion of the Court extended federal protection to America's most wretched workers under the general rubric of freedom to labor, a progressive variation on the central laissez-faire abstraction of freedom of *contract. *Bailey* struck down criminal penalties for the breach of labor contracts. The second great decision, *United States* v. *Reynolds*, struck down criminal-surety laws under which indigent convicts avoided the chain gang by contracting themselves into servitude for employers who would put up their fines. The Court observed that the criminal-surety system stood as a major support of involuntary servitude. The *Bailey* and *Reynolds* decisions were reassuring symbols of the progressive tendencies of constitutional law in the Progressive era. They demonstrated the Court's willingness to apply general principles of liberty to achieve justice for African-Americans.

*Bailey* and *Reynolds* knocked out the main props from the peculiar system of laws prevailing in the South that were intended to compel labor from African-Americans, but the Court left vagrancy and other laws that permitted prosecution of discretion largely untouched. Entirely beyond the Court's reach were the lawless supports for peonage: the violence and intimidation that infected race relations; the cycle of poverty and debt that bound tenants, sharecroppers, and field hands to the land and the landlords; and the apathy of powerless, exhausted people. In the end, it was the wave of African-American migration northward and to the cities, more than judicial decisions or law enforcement efforts, that broke the wheel of black servitude in the South, but the *Peonage Cases* remain landmarks in the slow process of exorcising the vestiges of slavery from American law.

(See also LABOR; RACE AND RACISM.)

□ Alexander M. Bickel and Benno C. Schmidt, Jr., *The Judiciary and Responsible Government, 1910–21* (1984).

Benno C. Schmidt, Jr.

**Pepper, George Wharton** (b. Philadelphia, Pa., 16 Mar. 1867; d. Devon, Pa., 24 May 1961), lawyer. A statesman and Supreme Court practitioner, George Wharton Pepper received his A.B. and LL.B. from the University of Pennsylvania, where early in his career he became Biddle Professor of Law. Pepper taught and practiced law for seventeen years until the dual duties became too onerous and he resigned his professorship. Appointed to fill a vacancy, Pepper represented Pennsylvania in the United States Senate from 1922 to 1927. The Supreme Court asked Pepper to represent Congress as *amicus curiae in *Myers v. United States (1926), where he unsuccessfully contested the president's right to remove postmasters without congressional approval. He prevailed in arguing the invalidity of the New Deal's Agricultural Adjustment Act in United States v. *Butler (1936). A capable and much-honored counselor, Pepper authored works ranging from Pennsylvania law digests to an analytical index to the Episcopal Book of Common Prayer. His 1944 autobiography bears the appropriate title Philadelphia Lawyer.

Francis Helminski

**Per Curiam** (Lat., "by the court"), an opinion rendered by the whole court or a majority of it, rather than being attributed to an individual judge. Originally used for summary dispositions of cases, the per curiam has sometimes been the vehicle for major opinions, for example, *Brandenburg v. Ohio (1969).

William M. Wiecek

**Peremptory Challenge.** See DUE PROCESS, PROCEDURAL.

**Perry v. United States.** See GOLD CLAUSE CASES.

**Personnel Administrator of Massachusetts v. Feeney,** 442 U.S. 256 (1979), argued 26 Feb. 1979, decided 5 June 1979 by vote of 7 to 2; Stewart for the Court, Marshall and Brennan in dissent. The issue in Feeney was whether a Massachusetts statute granting an absolute lifetime preference to veterans in public employment discriminated against women in violation of the Equal Protection Clause of the *Fourteenth Amendment.

The case was brought in 1975 by a female civil servant who, despite achieving higher grades on civil service examinations than male veterans, was repeatedly passed over for employment and promotion in favor of those veterans. The federal district court twice found the statute unconstitutional. The state appealed, supported in the Supreme Court by the *solicitor general of the United States.

It was undisputed that more than 98 percent of the veterans in Massachusetts were male, that the veterans preference applied to approximately 60 percent of the public jobs in the state, and that its impact on public employment opportunities for women was severe. Relying on *Washington v. Davis (1976) and *Arlington Heights v. Metropolitan Housing Development Corp. (1977), however, the Court made clear that the constitutional standard required showing a discriminatory purpose, not merely a disproportionate impact.

Making a twofold inquiry into the legislative purpose, the Court held first that the statute was neutral and not based on *gender because it drew a distinction between veterans and nonveterans, not men and women, and thus also burdened significant numbers of male nonveterans. Second, looking at the totality of legislative actions establishing and extending the statute, the Court held that its enactment did not reflect intentional gender-based discrimination. Announcing a tough test for determining discriminatory purpose, the Court held that even if discriminatory results were forseeable, the constitutional standard required a finding that the legislature acted because of them, not merely in spite of them.

Justices Thurgood *Marshall and William *Brennan dissented, arguing that because the impact on women was both extreme and foreseeable, the state had the burden of establishing that gender considerations played no role in the legislation, a burden it failed to meet.

(See also DISCRIMINATORY INTENT; EQUAL PROTECTION.)

Gerald N. Rosenberg

**Peters, Richard, Jr.** (b. Belmont, Pa., 17 Aug. 1780; d. Belmont, Pa. 2 May 1848), fourth Supreme Court reporter, 1828–1843; also reported Justice Bushrod Washington's circuit opinions, 1826–1829. Peters is best remembered for his part in Wheaton v. Peters, the Supreme Court's first *copyright case. Peters's Condensed Reports (1830–1834) republished the reports of Alexander *Dallas, William *Cranch, and Henry *Wheaton. By paring concurring and dissenting opinions, arguments of counsel, and annotations, Peters was able to cut prices by 75 percent, thereby making the Court's opinions widely affordable but also destroying Wheaton's market. Wheaton sued. The Court's 1834 decision required copyright claimants to show punctilious compliance with the Copyright Act's statutory formalities and held even such compliance incapable of affording copyright in the Court's opinions. Practically speaking, Peters won.

Apart from Wheaton, Peters was less successful. He conceived an early headnote reference system but botched its execution; Congress complained generally about the "accuracy and fidelity" of his Reports; and he offended several justices politically. The Court dismissed him in 1843.

(See also REPORTERS, SUPREME COURT.)

Craig Joyce

**Petition, Right of.** The *First Amendment guarantees the right "to petition the government for redress of grievances." It has its roots, as do many of our constitutional safeguards, in the constitutional development of England, with the idea of "redress" suggested by Edgar the Peaceful as early as between 959 and 963 CE. It had a significant role in the burgeoning rise of parliamentary power with the Magna Carta of 1215 (chapter 61). The House of Commons commenced a formal practice of petitioning the king on behalf of individual citizens as well as corporations during the latter part of the thirteenth century, thus introducing formal attempts to bargain with him.

Some three centuries later, after the Glorious Revolution of 1688, Parliament enacted the Declaration of Rights of 1689, affirmed as the Bill of Rights in the same year, which endeavored to enshrine the right of petition, that is, access to an authority empowered to redress a grievance, or sanction a demand, as a basic constitutional entitlement. It became logically one of the cornerstones of America's *Declaration of Independence of 1776 and, ultimately, of the *Bill of Rights in 1791. Thomas *Jefferson's roster of grievances contained in the former catalogued the flouting of "petitions for redress" as one of the cardinal grievances against King George III. It was only natural that the Bill of Rights would also embrace the right of petition. Most *state constitutions included a similar guarantee.

The right to petition has received far less judicial attention than have the other four rights spelled out in the First Amendment, and is often taken for granted. It has frequently been subsumed under the collateral rights of *assembly and association in decisions such as *United States* v. *Cruikshank* (1876), *Twining* v. *New Jersey* (1908), *DeJonge* v. *Oregon* (1937), *Hague* v. *Congress of Industrial Organizations* (1939), and *Brown* v. *Glines* (1980). But it is nonetheless secure and employed with predictable alacrity by a petition-prone and litigious American citizenry.

The right of petitions takes two forms: one is the direct petitioning of legislators—and sometimes members of the executive branch, including administrative bodies—for the redress of whatever genuine or imaginary grievances an individual constituent (or, for that matter, a nonconstituent) or a group may have or fancy. It is here that members of legislative bodies, most prominently members of Congress, play a favorite role, that of errand running for those whom they represent, those who helped to select them, and also those who did not. Closely related to the other hallowed rights under the First Amendment, the American public demonstrably views the right of petition as a basic prerogative.

The second form is the popular practice of circulating petitions to be signed by individuals (and/or groups and business and professional organizations) so as to create visible pressure on individual players in the governmental process. Such petitions have become a major tool in that process and are frequently directly responsible for action by governmental bodies. This generation of massive pressuring runs the gamut from handwritten formats to sophisticated, mass-produced modes of appeal, often utilizing the media, especially in the form of paid newspaper advertisements, in which long lists of supplicants contribute to the costs involved and permit their names to be used.

Only once in the two centuries of the existence of the Constitution of the United States has there been a formal attempt to curb the right to petition for the redress of grievances. It occurred in 1836, when the House of Representatives—but not the Senate—enacted what became quickly known as the "gag rule" against the receipt of petitions from abolitionists who opposed the institution of slavery. The "gag rule" came under immediate fire, with opposition spearheaded by antislavery Whigs under the leadership of Congressman (and former President) John Quincy *Adams; it was repealed eight years later.

□ Don L. Smith, *The Right to Petition for Redress of Grievances: Constitutional Development and Interpretations* (1971).
Henry J. Abraham

**Petitioner and Respondent.** A petitioner is the party who initiates proceedings in equity by presenting a bill or petition; the opponent is referred to as the respondent. In appellate practice, the terms are often loosely used as equivalents of appellant and appellee.
William M. Wiecek

**Petit Juries.** Trial by jury is the main form of lay participation in the administration of justice in the United States—the *grand jury and the remnants of the justice-of-the-peace system being the minor forms. Together with judge-made law and adversarial proceedings, large-scale employment of the jury differentiates the American legal system from all others. Petit juries are used elsewhere, but not to the same extent as in the United States. Even in England jury trials have become infrequent. About 95 percent of all jury trials now take place in the United States.

Most criminal prosecutions and civil suits do not, however, lead to a jury trial. Only about 5 to 10 percent of all lawsuits in the United States are tried to a jury. On the criminal side, this reflects *plea bargaining and a rate of about 90 percent guilty pleas. On the civil side, the small proportion of jury trials mirror high settlement rates as well as mandated bench trials.

The 5- to 10-percent figure underestimates the true importance and influence of the jury. For example, in *Duncan* v. *Louisiana* (1968) the Supreme Court declared:

Those who wrote our constitutions knew from history and experience that it was necessary to protect against unfounded criminal charges brought to eliminate enemies and against judges too responsive to the voice of higher authority. . . . Providing an accused with the right to be tried by a jury of his peers gave him an inestimable safeguard against the corrupt or overzealous prosecutor and against the compliant, biased, or eccentric judge. (p. 156)

The jury provides a check on the power of the judiciary. Jury verdicts bring to bear on the legal system the community's sense of justice. Juries shape and temper all aspects of adjudication—from the prosecutor's decision to charge, to the defendant's willingness to plea-bargain and the civil parties' disposition to settle, to the judge's sentencing decisions.

The significance of the jury is not fully stated by a tally of its legal functions. In *Democracy in America*, Alexis de Tocqueville gives an account of the American jury that appreciates its political and educational functions:

The jury, and more specially the civil jury, serves to communicate the spirit of the judges to the minds of all citizens; and this spirit with the habits which attend it is the soundest preparation for free institutions.

The jury contributes powerfully to form the judgment, and to increase the natural intelligence of a people; and this is, in my opinion, its greatest advantage. It may be regarded as a gratuitous public school ever open. (pp. 295–296)

Trial by jury also serves to generate support for the the country's legal system, not least by increasing appreciation for the difficult task of the judges.

Trial by jury has its ultimate roots in the popular assemblies of the Germanic tribes—Anglo-Saxon as well as Norman. The earliest English assembly of lay persons chosen to perform legal tasks was the Clarendon jury of inquest in 1166, established by Henry II in each community as an accusatory body of twelve "good and lawful men." It served the interest of the Crown by reporting all offenses that had been (or were said to have been) committed in the venue. These reports became the key instrument for initiating prosecutions. In modern terms, the jury of inquest was a grand jury. The subsequent "trial" most often took the the form of battle or ordeal. These forms of dispute resolution became unavailable when in 1215 the Fourth Lateran Council prohibited the participation of priests. Trial by jury emerged shortly thereafter, substituting the voice of the community for the voice of God.

For about two hundred years trial jurors were drawn from among the jurors of inquest, some of the grand jurors reconstituting themselves as trial jurors. Since these trial jurors had sworn as grand jurors that certain persons were known to have committed certain crimes, and since the evidence to be considered by the trial jury was the same as at the initial inquest, few trials ended in acquittals. It was not until the middle of the fourteenth century that grand and trial juries became fully distinct. It took additional centuries to distinguish jurors and witnesses and for juries to cease being mere instruments of the royal will.

Trial by jury came to the American colonies as part of English law. When conflicts developed between England and the colonies, the Crown sought to use the jury to further its interests. But the colonists soon came to appreciate that the

jury's strength and authority could be used for the preservation of their privileges and liberties. The *Declaration of Independence set forth a series of grievances against the King, important among them the complaint of "depriving us in many cases, of the benefits of Trial by jury." And three of the ten articles of the *Bill of Rights dealt with grand and petit juries.

The U.S. Constitution guarantees trial by jury only in federal criminal cases (Art. III, sec. 3; and the Sixth Amendment) and civil litigations (Seventh Amendment). In *Duncan* v. *Louisiana*, however, the Supreme Court extended to the states, via the *Fourteenth Amendment, the right to trial by jury in criminal prosecutions (see INCORPORATION DOCTRINE). The Court has failed, so far, to extend likewise the right to a civil jury trial. Instead, beginning only two years after *Duncan*, the Court authored a series of jury-diminishing opinions. For example, *Baldwin* v. *New York* (1970) restricted the right to a criminal jury trial by making use of a distinction (not found in the Sixth Amendment) between petty and nonpetty crimes and by applying the Sixth (and Fourteenth) Amendment only to nonpetty offenses—defined as prosecutions that provide for a maximum possible confinement of more than six months.

In *Williams* v. *Florida* (1970) the Court approved the use of six-person juries in state criminal cases; and eventually approved small juries for civil cases in both state and federal courts. Having constitutionalized the "beyond a reasonable doubt" standard as the required proof in criminal cases, the Court, in *Johnson* v. *Louisiana* (1972) and *Apodaca* v. *Oregon* (1972), held that a state criminal jury could convict (in a noncapital case) by a 10-to-2 or 9-to-3 vote. More recently, *Batson* v. *Kentucky* (1986) restricted the prosecution's use of peremptory challenges.

Though trial by jury enjoys widespread support, the trend of Supreme Court decisions has been toward reduction of the employment, powers, and effectiveness of the jury. Perhaps the earliest instance of judicial jury slicing was the invention of the "directed verdict," that is, if the judge thought that the evidence was insufficient for conviction he could instruct the jury to return a verdict of "not guilty" (*Commonwealth* v. *Merrill*, 1860).

One of the most important examples of judicial ascendancy at the expense of the jury is the latter's loss of the right to decide questions of law (*Sparf & Hansen* v. *United States*, 1896). The law-deciding right of juries, it is true, had a customary rather than a constitutional base, but the custom was well established by the 1770s and most of the Founding Fathers strongly supported it. American juries, typically, were instructed that they had the right to decide the facts of the case and to interpret (e.g., to apply or not apply) the law. Except for Maryland and Indiana, today's jurors are instructed that they must take the law from the judge. A potential juror's stated unwillingness to accept the law from the judge is sufficient cause for exclusion from jury service.

The loss of the jury's law function is particularly surprising because it is contrary to the lessons of some well-remembered cases as well as to previous rulings, such as *Georgia* v. *Brailsford* (1792), which held that jurors not only had the right but the duty to set aside instructions on the law if they thought them to be erroneous or to create an injustice. Perhaps the most famous of these cases occurred when jurors refused to apply the existing law of *libel and declined to convict the publisher John Peter Zenger in 1735. The early American jury could make law as well as break it. Until about the middle of the nineteenth century, legal commentaries uniformly recognized that the jury had legislative powers.

What is at stake is not only the nonapplication of obviously unjust laws, but the introduction of a much needed element of flexibility in the application of all laws. Formal law making necessarily lags behind social and cultural developments. Statutes cannot anticipate all possible situations. The inflexible application even of a generally just law can create an injustice in particular circumstances. It is one of the virtues of the jury that it is not bound to the uniform administration of the laws. Judges, by contrast, are bound to uniformity and have much more limited discretionary powers.

Contemporary jurors still have the power not to apply the law as given to them ("nullification"). The right to do so, however, has largely been lost. Indeed, even the fact-finding right of the jury is not entirely safe. There is an argument that judges should be free to comment to the jury on the facts of the case, including which witnesses should be believed. Most state statutes and decisions now prohibit such commentary.

An important new form of jury diminution is the denial of jury trials in civil cases thought to be "too complex" for jurors. Encouraged by the Supreme Court's opinion in *Ross* v. *Bernhard* (1970), several lower courts have issued such denials. Further reducing the power of the civil jury, the Court recently held in *Tull* v. *United States* (1987) that it does not violate the Seventh Amendment for the judge rather than the jury to set civil penalties.

Since *Strauder* v. *West Virginia* (1880), however, the Court has consistently protected the right of all citizens to participate as jurors in the administration of justice. Through a long series of cases, it has prohibited *de jure* and *de facto* discrimination against racial (and other) groups in the selection of jury venires. These decisions have been codified by the Federal Jury Selection and Service Act of 1968. In *Batson* v. *Kentucky* the Court extended the prohibition of racial discrimination to the selection of the actual jury.

In spite of the formal guarantees of the Bill of Rights, trial by jury has an uncertain future. It seems unlikely that the Court's jury diminutions have reached their peak. Attacks on trial by jury continue inside and outside the judiciary. The main accusations are that jurors are incompetent, unfair, and lawless. The consensus of scholarly experts is different. Various investigations have found that most jurors take their task seriously, execute it competently, and strive earnestly to be fair to all parties. Furthermore, most juries follow the law as given to them by the court. The occasional "lawless" jury, in any case, brings flexibility to the system and should be regarded as a positive occurrence—as even the Court acknowledged in *Duncan* (p. 157).

Of course, there are occasional failures in jury comprehension and fairness. The same, however, can also be said about bench trials. The reasonable response to inadequacies is not jury abolition but improving the conditions under which jurors must work. As long as, for example, evidence continues to be presented in a disjointed fashion while jurors are refused access to the transcripts and, in many courts, may not even take notes, arguments for the abolition of trial by jury must be regarded as ill considered and premature.

(See also SEVENTH AMENDMENT; SIXTH AMENDMENT; TRIAL BY JURY.)

□ Reid Hastie, et al., *Inside the Jury* (1983). Harry Kalven and Hans Zeisel, *The American Jury* (1971). Peter W. Sperlich, "And Then There Were Six: The Decline of the American Jury," *Judicature* 63 (1980): 262–279. Lawrence S. Wrightsman, et al., *In the Jury Box* (1987).
Peter W. Sperlich

**Picketing.** See ASSEMBLY AND ASSOCIATION, FREEDOM OF; THORNHILL V. ALABAMA.

**Pierce v. Society of Sisters,** 268 U.S. 510 (1925), argued 16–17 Mar. 1925, decided 1 June 1925 by vote of 9 to 0; McReynolds for the Court. In 1922, the voters of Oregon adopted an initiative requiring nearly every parent to send a child between the ages of eight and sixteen to public school. The statute was unique, and the initiative campaign was organized primarily by the Ku Klux Klan and the Oregon Scottish Rite Masons. It was the product of post–World War I fears about Bolshevism and the influx of aliens. Supporters urged that the separation of children of different religions in private schools would cause dissension and discord. Anti-Catholicism also played a major role in the campaign.

A three-judge federal district court declared that the Oregon initiative violated the *Due Process Clause of the *Fourteenth Amendment and issued an interlocutory injunction restraining the defendants from enforcing the law. The Supreme Court affirmed. Relying on principles of substantive *due process, the Court held that under the doctrine of *Meyer* v. *Nebraska* (1925) the Oregon initiative unreasonably interfered with the liberty of parents and guardians to direct the education and upbringing of their children and that this interference with the schools threatened the destruction of the plaintiffs' businesses and property. The Court indicated, however, that the states have the power to require attendance at "some school" and to regulate all schools to ensure that "certain studies plainly essential to good citizenship . . . be taught . . . and that nothing be taught which is manifestly inimical to the public welfare" (p. 534).

The *Pierce* Court could have adopted any of three standards. First, it could simply have upheld the power of the states to compel attendance at public schools. Second, it might have determined that any compulsory education law violates the liberty of parents to control the education of their children. The standard actually adopted by the Court—the third choice—is that the states may compel attendance at some school, but the parents have a constitutional right to choose between public and private schools. This "Pierce compromise" recognizes that the state has a legitimate interest in socializing the young to *citizenship and other virtues, but it denies the state a monopoly over education: "The fundamental theory of liberty . . . excludes any general power of the State to standardize its children by forcing them to accept instruction from public teachers only" (p. 535).

Despite its reliance on now-repudiated doctrines of substantive due process in the economic sphere, *Pierce* has never been overruled and is in fact frequently cited with favor. The modern constitutional basis for the decision is sharply debated. *Board of Education* v. *Allen* (1968) treated *Pierce* as a decision based on the free exercise of religion. This position poses difficulties because one of the petitioners in *Pierce* was not a sectarian school, and because the religion clauses of the First Amendment were not made applicable to the states until *Cantwell* v. *Connecticut* (1940). Others see *Pierce* as involving the *fundamental right of parents (not explicitly protected by the Constitution) to raise their children, or as a check on the power of government to indoctrinate children, thereby protecting the personal autonomy essential to freedom of expression. But whatever its rationale, *Pierce* appears to be a permanent feature of American constitutional culture.

The *Pierce* decision has profoundly affected the evolution of civil liberties for more than seventy-five years. In its emphasis on fundamental rights not expressly articulated in the Constitution and on family autonomy, it presaged later *privacy decisions protecting, for example, *abortion rights (*Roe* v. *Wade,* 1973) and access to *contraceptives (*Griswold* v. *Connecticut,* 1965). If, as some scholars have asserted, America has an "unwritten constitution," *Pierce* is a critical example of its invocation. From this perspective, the modern debate over *original intent and *constitu-

tional interpretation, best exemplified by the Senate's rejection of Judge Robert *Bork for the Supreme Court in 1987, is but a continuation of the debate over the premises and implications of *Pierce.*

(See also EDUCATION; FAMILY AND CHILDREN.)

□ Mark G. Yudof, "When Governments Speak: Toward a Theory of Government Expression and the First Amendment," *Texas Law Review* 57 (1979): 863–918.

Mark G. Yudof

**Pinkney, William** (b. Annapolis, Md., 17 Mar. 1764; d. Washington, D.C., 25 Feb. 1822), lawyer and statesman. Distinguished in public affairs and law, William Pinkney was a member of the Maryland legislature and council (1788–1795), United States attorney general (1811–1815), and United States senator (1819–1822). As commissioner to England under the Jay Treaty (1796–1804), then American minister there (1807–1811), he grappled with maritime issues and mastered admiralty law. In his later years he became the leading member of the Supreme Court bar: superb oratory, thorough preparation, supreme confidence, even his dandified appearance enhanced his reputation. His most noteworthy Supreme Court argument was in *McCulloch* v. *Maryland* (1819), defining a strong union created by the American people and upholding the constitutionality of the Bank of the United States.

Maurice Baxter

**Pitney, Mahlon** (b. Morristown, N.J., 5 Feb. 1858; d. Washington, D.C., 9 Dec. 1924; interred Evergreen Cemetery, Morristown), associate justice, 1912–1922. Mahlon Pitney was the second son of Henry Cooper Pitney and his wife Sarah Louisa (Halsted) Pitney. After graduating from the College of New Jersey in 1879, Mahlon "read" for the New Jersey bar without attending law school, then managed the family law practice. He was elected to Congress in 1894, serving two terms. A Republican leader in northern New Jersey, he won election to the state senate in 1898, becoming its president in 1901. Appointed associate justice of the state supreme court in 1901, he was elevated to chancellor, New Jersey's highest judicial post, in 1908, serving until 1912.

President William Howard *Taft in 1912 appointed Pitney to the U.S. Supreme Court. He was confirmed 50 to 26, supported by Republican regulars and opposed by Democrats and progressive Republicans.

Justice Pitney wrote 274 opinions, 252 of them as spokesman for the Court; several of his opinions commanded national attention. His primary values were individualism and a belief in equality of opportunity unfettered by government meddling.

Pitney viewed the *due process clauses of the *Fifth and *Fourteenth Amendments as means by which the spirit of individualism, and vested *property rights, could be preserved. Illustrative was his dissenting opinion in *Wilson* v. *New* (1917), where he would have struck down on due process grounds an effort by Congress to fix an eight-hour workday and temporary wage scale for interstate railway employees. However, he supported restraints on individual liberty when necessary to further its ultimate interests. Thus, in *Pierce* v. *United States* (1920), he rejected a claim to freedom of expression under the *First Amendment presented by defendants prosecuted under the Espionage Act of 1917 (see ESPIONAGE ACTS). Because he perceived that individuality was often clearly subsumed by corporate activity, he supported the application of state and federal *antitrust statutes, although in *Eisner* v. *Macomber* (1920), he held that the *Sixteenth Amendment did not permit Congress to tax stock dividends as income.

Pitney believed that the right to contract was the essential expression of individual liberty. He read into the due process clauses a "liberty of contract" and he laid great stress on the *Contracts Clause of Article I (see CONTRACT, FREEDOM OF). He worried that organized labor posed a menace to the individual, and he ruled against union interests in such cases as *Coppage* v. *Kansas* (1915). But Pitney generally supported state prerogatives within America's federal system, upon which was also based his single expression of support for organized *labor in his dissenting opinion in *Truax* v. *Corrigan* (1921). He was also sensitive to the vagaries of the industrial workplace, and his most enduring contribution to the development of American constitutional law was his support for state workmen's compensation

*Mahlon Pitney*

statutes. In a series of cases beginning with *New York Central Railroad Co.* v. *White* (1917), he sustained several state laws holding employers liable to compensate individual employees for injuries suffered in the course of their employment. Justice Louis *Brandeis declared, "But for Pitney we would have had no workmen's compensation laws."

Pitney resigned from the Court in December 1922 after suffering a stroke the previous August. He died two years later.

□ Alan Ryder Breed, "Mahlon Pitney" (B.A. thesis, Princeton University, 1932).          Robert David Stenzel

**Plea Bargaining** is a process whereby persons accused of crime plead guilty to specified charges in return for an agreed-upon sentence, a sentence recommendation to the judge, or the dismissal or reduction of other charges. Typically, defense counsel and the prosecutor negotiate the charges to be brought. If the bargain pertains to the sentence to be meted out, a judge may also participate unless barred from doing so.

Specific aspects of the process vary greatly from one jurisdiction to another: from a highly adversarial setting to one in which the participants cooperatively seek "substantive justice" and from a court where only charges may be bargained because of mandatory sentencing policies to one that focuses on sentences because they are authorized to be indeterminate for most, if not all, offenses. In other courts, the emphasis is on the contestability of cases. If the facts are undisputed, a guilty plea becomes a foregone conclusion, and only a disposition needs to be negotiated. Within a given court or jurisdiction, the process may vary from case to case depending on the proclivities and the degree of involvement by the major actors: prosecutor, defense attorney, judge, and defendant.

The origins of plea bargaining are obscure. There is evidence by that it existed by the middle of the nineteenth century. Although heavy caseloads and overly crowded prisons are often cited as causes, a more likely explanation is the bureaucratization of the criminal justice system. It conveniently settles cases where guilt is obvious as well as those where proof of all elements of the charge is problematic, thereby lessening risk to both defendant and prosecution. Because nineteenth-century trials were fast-paced affairs that disproportionately ended in a guilty verdict, plea bargains were an attractive alternative especially to guilty defendants. By "copping a plea" they could determine their own fate, rather than leaving it to the not so tender mercies of judge and jury.

Although the frequency of plea bargains in rural areas belies its origin in backlogged courtrooms, today's criminal justice system would certainly collapse without the rapid disposition of most cases. Trials are slow, cumbersome, and long. Prosecutors and defense counsel would require much more time to prepare their cases. Scheduling witnesses would become guesswork. The time between arrest and trial would lengthen greatly. Conviction rates would fall. Court-appointed attorneys would refuse to serve because fee schedules would be inadequate to compensate them for their time.

Because defendants who plead guilty waive three important constitutional rights—self-incrimination, jury trial, and the right to confront and cross-examine one's accusers—the Supreme Court has been called upon to determine the constitutionality of plea bargaining. In *Boykin* v. *Alabama* (1969), the Court held that the record must disclose that the defendant voluntarily and understandingly pled guilty. In *Brady* v. *United States* (1970), it ruled that the voluntariness of a guilty plea was not vitiated by fear of a heavier sentence following trial, even though that fear was death under a statute that the Court declared unconstitutional subsequent to Brady's guilty plea. And in *Santobello* v. *New York* (1971), the Court described plea bargaining as "an essential component of the administration of justice. Properly administered, it is to be encouraged" (p. 260). The Supreme Court has defined the *Sixth Amendment's guarantee of "Assistance of Counsel" to mean effective assistance, which seems to entail a modicum of bargaining and negotiation, as suggested in *Strickland* v. *Washington* (1984) and *Nix* v. *Whiteside* (1986).

The Supreme Court's stamp of approval has overcome some concerns about *due process violations. But others remain: coercion, false pleas, and injustice, on the one hand, and excessive leniency, reduction of deterrence, and the value of the rule of law as a symbol, on the other. Although plea bargaining prevents the criminal courts from becoming submerged in a sea of cases, it does produce effects that deviate markedly from those of a formal adversarial system in which *trial by jury is the norm rather than the infrequent exception. Tasks that theoretically are the responsibility of judges and jurors—the determination of innocence and guilt, and the imposition of sentences—are performed instead by prosecutors and defense attorneys. Because the latters' primary role is that of advocate rather than decision maker, extraneous considerations may affect the process. Thus, a prosecutor may offer the accused an especially attractive plea in order to avoid disclosure of an undercover witness or where the evidence is weak or tainted, perhaps as the result of an illegal search or an involuntarily induced confession.

On the other side, experienced defendants and attorneys who have learned how to drive sharp bargains will fare better than those with lesser negotiating ability. Unskilled defendants may become chagrined or embittered to learn that their sentences are markedly more severe than those of similarly situated convicts.

The result is a system in which bargaining replaces evidence as the paramount determinant of guilt or innocence. Although plea agreements generally appear on the record, ambiguity clouds the extent to which judges require a factual basis to support them. Administrative pressure on the prosecutor and the economic orientation of the defense attorney drive the system. Guilt is presumed rather than innocence. Features of an assembly line characterize the process rather than those that typify a model of due process. (See also DUE PROCESS, PROCEDURAL.)

□ William F. McDonald and James Cramer, eds. *Plea Bargaining* (1980). William M. Rhodes, *Plea Bargaining: Who Gains? Who Loses?* (1978). Harold J. Spaeth

**Plessy v. Ferguson,** 163 U.S. 537 (1896), argued 13 Apr. 1896, decided 18 May 1896 by vote of 7 to 1; Brown for the Court, Harlan in dissent, Brewer not participating. In this case the Supreme Court upheld the constitutionality of a Louisiana statute (1890) that required railroads to provide "equal but separate accommodations for the white and colored races" and barred persons from occupying rail cars other than those to which their race had been assigned. The opinion is one of arresting contrasts: between its relative insignificance at the time and the symbolic importance it would attain during the next six decades, between the petty rationalization of the majority opinion and the abiding appeal of the dissent, and between the begrudging interpretation of the Civil War Amendments as applied to African-Americans and the expansive interpretation of the same amendments as applied to claims of economic right.

The dispute arose as a *test case to challenge a statute, an example of the Jim Crow laws then being passed in the South as whites sought to embellish their control of state governments. A New Orleans group of Creoles and blacks organized themselves as the Citizens' Committee to Test the Constitutionality of the Separate Car Law. Their challenge enjoyed some support from the railroads, who objected to the additional costs of providing separate cars. Plessy agreed to initiate the challenge on behalf of the committee. Although he appeared to be white, Plessy was classified as "colored" under the Louisiana code because he was one-eighth black.

A previous decision by the Louisiana Supreme Court had held that the statute could not apply to interstate commerce. Plessy was therefore careful to purchase a ticket for a journey entirely within the state of Louisiana, having insured in advance that the railroad and the conductor knew of his mixed race. He was arrested when he refused to move to the "colored only" section of the coach. Plessy attempted to halt the trial, arguing that the statute was unconstitutional under both the *Thirteenth and *Fourteenth Amendments to the Constitution. After the Louisiana courts rejected his arguments, he sought review by the Supreme Court.

Writing for the Court, Justice Henry Billings *Brown rejected both of Plessy's arguments. He continued the Court's practice of construing the Thirteenth Amendment to apply only to actions whose purpose was to reintroduce *slavery itself. It did not, he reasoned, reach all distinctions based on color.

He likewise held that the statute did not violate the Fourteenth Amendment's requirement that all citizens be afforded *equal protection of the laws. His cardinal postulate was that laws requiring separation of the races did not suggest that one race was inferior. Inferiority, according to Brown, arose only because one race chose to perceive the laws in such a way. It was equally fundamental to Brown that laws could not alter the long-established customs of society. For the Court to mandate that the races be mixed would be futile in the face of strong public sentiment as manifested by statutes requiring separation of the races in educational facilities. To support that proposition Brown pointed to a line of cases beginning with an opinion by Chief Justice Lemuel Shaw of Massachusetts in *Roberts* v. *City of Boston* (1849).

By linking racial separation on trains with that in *education, Brown touched one of the most sensitive parts of the efforts to maintain separation of the races. Education was a bugbear for anyone who suggested legislation mandating racial equality. Brown therefore sought to support his conclusion by implying that transportation was like education. The enduring effect of Brown's analogy was to place the Court's imprimatur on a considerably expanded field in which segregation was justified.

Justice John Marshall *Harlan's isolated *dissent would later support eloquent rejections of the *separate but equal doctrine, especially as applied to education. Harlan refused to restrict the Thirteenth Amendment to slavery itself, preferring to see the amendment as barring all "badge[s] of servitude" (p. 555). In one of the ringing phrases for which he is best known, Harlan argued that the "Constitution is colorblind, and neither knows nor tolerates classes among citizens" (p. 559). The epigram had been suggested in the brief field on behalf of Plessy by Albion Tourgée, a white attorney who was a leader in the campaign for equal rights.

(See also RACE AND RACISM; SEGREGATION, DE JURE.)

□ Charles A. Lofgren, *The Plessy Case* (1987). Otto H. Olsen, *The Thin Disguise: Turning Point in Negro History; Plessy v. Ferguson: A Documentary Presentation (1864–1896)* (1967).                    Walter F. Pratt, Jr.

**Plurality Opinion,** one that announces the judgment of the Court but that has been unable to secure the assent of a majority of the participating justices. Plurality opinions have become more numerous since 1970 as the Court has tended to fragment on doctrinal lines.

William M. Wiecek

**Plyler v. Doe,** 457 U.S. 202 (1982), argued 1 Dec. 1981, decided 15 June 1982 by a vote of 5 to 4; Brennan for the Court, Burger, White, Rehnquist, and O'Connor in dissent. Texas refused to finance the education of undocumented children and authorized local districts to exclude these children from enrollment in free public schools. The Supreme Court held this practice to be repugnant to the *Fourteenth Amendment's Equal Protection Clause, which guarantees that "no State shall . . . deny to any person *within its jurisdiction* the equal protection of the laws" [emphasis added]. Texas argued that the phrase "within its jurisdiction" excluded illegal aliens from *equal protection guarantees. The Court disagreed, holding that these guarantees extended to each person, regardless of citizenship or immigration status, inside the state's perimeter and subject to state laws.

The Court, however, refused to apply *strict scrutiny since *education was not a fundamental right and undocumented aliens did not constitute a suspect class because their own conscious actions caused their illegal status. The Court majority, however, did apply an escalated standard of protection ("heightened scrutiny"), appropriate because of education's special and lasting importance relative to other social welfare benefits and because undocumented children, unlike adults, lacked responsibility for their illegal situation. State denial of this especially important benefit to a discrete class of innocents violated equal protection, the Court stated, unless the policy furthered some substantial governmental interest.

Criticizing the majority for employing a result-oriented jurisprudence, flawed reasoning, and an inappropriate standard of review, Chief Justice Warren *Burger argued that Texas' exclusionary law was constitutionally valid because it rationally furthered legitimate state interests. Later, many of these children, undocumented in 1982, acquired legal residency under the federal government's amnesty program. The propriety of the majority's jurisprudence, however, is still debated.

(See also ALIENAGE AND NATURALIZATION.)

Richard A. Gambitta

**Pointer v. Texas,** 380 U.S. 400 (1965), argued 15 Mar. 1965, decided 5 Apr. 1965 by vote of 9 to 0; Black for the Court, Harlan, Stewart, and Goldberg concurring. The *Sixth Amendment provides in part that "[i]n all criminal prosecutions, the accused shall enjoy the right . . . to be confronted with the witness against him." Although the right to confrontation had long been recognized in state law, in this case the Supreme Court ruled that the Sixth Amendment guarantee was applicable to the states via the Due Process Clause of the *Fourteenth Amendment (see DUE PROCESS, PROCEDURAL; INCORPORATION DOCTRINE).

The case arose when a defendant's attorney objected to the introduction of a transcript of testimony of a robbery victim who had moved out of state between the time he had testified at a preliminary hearing and the trial. In this transcribed testimony the victim identified Pointer as the offender, and Pointer was convicted largely upon the basis of this testimony. In overturning his conviction the Supreme Court held that introduction of such testimony, which had been taken at a proceeding at which Pointer had been present but unrepresented by counsel, constituted a denial of his Sixth Amendment rights to confront witnesses and to cross-examine them by counsel.

In overturning the conviction and extending the right to confrontation to the states, the Court also ruled that this right must be determined by the same standards that hold in federal proceedings. In so doing, the Court also reiterated the underlying reason for the rule, which is to give defendants charged with crimes an opportunity to cross-examine witnesses against them. However, even as the Court embraced a sweeping interpretation of the right, it acknowledged some practical limits, noting for instance that declarations of dying persons and testimony of deceased witnesses who had testified at former trials could still be admissible despite the impossibility of confrontation.　　　　　　　Malcolm M. Feeley

**Police Power.** For two centuries, judges and scholars alike have repeatedly affirmed that the concept of the "police power" resists a clear definition. Indeed, it seems that the leading characteristic of the police power is that its definition changes with shifting social economic realities and with changing political conceptions of the legitimate reach of governmental authority. "An attempt to define its reach or trace its outer limits is fruitless," Justice William O. *Douglas asserted in *Berman v. Parker* (1954), "for each case must turn on its own facts. . . . The definition is essentially the product of legislative determinations" (p. 32).

*Early History.* In the eighteenth century, Anglo-American jurists treated police power as being virtually the entire authority, civil and criminal, exercised by government in the domestic affairs of the polity. On the few occasions when precise definitions were attempted, they tended to be either open-ended and vague; or else they were cast in homiletic terms that were of modest usefulness in forming principles of adjudication. For example, William Blackstone's *Commentaries* described the police power as "the due regulation and domestic order of the kingdom, whereby the individuals of the state, like members of a well-governed family, are bound to conform their general behaviour to the rules of propriety, good neighbourhood, and good manners: and to be decent, industrious, and inoffensive in their respective stations." Other jurists commonly equated exercise of the police power with the entire scope of "municipal law."

Several of the first American state charters of rights and constitutions, adopted amidst the Revolutionary crisis, explicitly mentioned the police power (see STATE CONSTITUTIONS AND INDIVIDUAL RIGHTS). Thus, the 1776 declarations of rights in Pennsylvania, Vermont, and Delaware asserted that the people had "the sole, exclusive, and inherent right of governing and regulating the internal police" of the state. The Maryland declaration of 1776 similarly stated that "all government of right originates from the people, is founded in compact only, and [is] instituted solely for the good of the whole. . . . The people of this State ought to have the sole and exclusive right of regulating the internal government and police thereof"—language also found in North Carolina's declaration.

These statements clearly were intended to proclaim the legitimacy of the transfer of sovereignty—from the king in Parliament, now repudiated, to the newly erected state governments. Given the explicit underlying theory in the American constitutions that all power is derived from the people—and given that these charters were revolutionary documents, intended not only to provide for orderly transfer of authority but also to justify the renunciation of former loyalty to Great Britain—the references to the police power were regarded as positive, comprehensive grants of authority from the people to the new governments.

This is not to say, however, that there was a shared sense in Revolutionary America that the new authority of the state governments was to be plenary and unrestrained. On the contrary, the constitutional assertions of the police power were juxtaposed with specific provisions in the charters and constitutions that were designed to constrain and limit state governmental operations. Scores of specific limitations were spelled out in the bills of rights or other provisions of the new constitutions—the provisions that defined the great liberties (speech, press, religion) and dealt with due process in the traditional categories (jury *trial, *habeas corpus, security of property against uncompensated *takings). Such provisions gave to *state courts explicit guidance for purposes of judicial review of legislation or administrative acts. Typically, the state judges in their constitutional cases applied both these provisions and also the principles of *natural law with respect to basic rights.

It became one of the most challenging and politically sensitive tasks of the state appellate courts in the nation's early period, however, to develop specific working doctrines that limited legislative power and executive authority. This process was slow because state judges were reticent to assert the power of judicial review in light of the eighteenth-century heritage of legislative supremacy, now given new claims to legitimacy by its populistic reformulation in the new republics. To substitute judicial judgment for the legislature's was, in effect, to frustrate the will of the sovereign—that is, of the people. Indeed, it was not until the 1850s that a well-developed set of standards for review of police regulations began to emerge in the state courts.

**The Supreme Court and Emerging Police Power Doctrines.** Meanwhile, it became necessary for the Supreme Court to develop a body of law bearing on the police powers of American government. This process had three distinctive elements.

First, the Court had to decide whether the national *Bill of Rights applied to the states. The Court managed for four decades to avoid confronting this issue directly, mainly because it relied upon other provisions of the Constitution, especially the *Contract Clause, to invalidate state legislation that trenched on private *vested rights. Finally, however, in the decision of *Barron v. Baltimore (1833), despite the prevailing nationalist bent of the Marshall Court's decisions, the justices ruled that the national Bill of Rights was not applicable to the states. This interpretation stood until the adoption of the *Fourteenth Amendment.

The second great doctrinal question was more complex and became the linchpin of the Court's entire jurisprudence on principles of *federalism until 1861. The issue was: to what extent was the state police power, or *state sovereignty, curbed by specific provisions of the federal Constitution limiting state action? The Court needed to develop a set of standards by which the Commerce Clause, the Contract Clause, the Supremacy Clause, and the guarantee of republican government in the states could be applied to determining the constitutionality of state legislation and common-law rules (see COMMERCE POWER; GUARANTEE CLAUSE). The Court's changing definitions of interstate commerce, of the obligation of contract, and of the reach of the Supremacy Clause all served to define the boundaries between state authority and national power.

The position of the Court on these issues changed, over time, with shifting majorities. The Court's basic orientation, however, was consistent: it was to concern itself with drawing the boundary line rather than bothering much with the doctrinal content of the police power. Thus, in *Gibbons v. Ogden (1824), Chief Justice John *Marshall referred to the police power of the states as "that immense mass of legislation, which embraces every thing within the territory of a State, not surrendered to the general government" (p. 202). Chief Justice Roger B. *Taney in *Charles River Bridge v. Warren Bridge (1837) and in

a series of Commerce Clause cases tended to speak even more broadly of the states' police power. Thus, in the *License Cases (1847), he defined it as "nothing more or less than the powers of government inherent in every sovereignty to the extent of its dominions" (p. 582).

In several taxation and *eminent domain decisions, without specifically distinguishing these powers from the police power, the Court also ruled on the question of inalienability of state sovereign powers. Beyond that, however, the antebellum Court left the major issues of definition, including the issue of basic constitutional limitations, to the state courts.

Over time, a third important constitutional issue emerged before the Supreme Court. It concerned the proper reach of the national government's own police power. The phrase "police power" does not appear in the Constitution. Yet the Constitution not only vests in the Congress the specific enumerated powers of section 8 but also refers in the Preamble to the basic purposes of the Union, "to . . . promote the general Welfare, and secure the Blessings of Liberty to ourselves and our Posterity." Over the course of its history, the Court has handled this third question with strong attention to interpretation of the Commerce Clause—by inquiring how far the federal regulatory power can reach, as being justified by the power to regulate interstate commerce. But the Court has also been much concerned, of course, with interpreting the Bill of Rights limitations on the procedures of the national government. In more recent times, the Court's interpretation of limits on the operations of a federal police power has depended critically upon its interpretation of Fourteenth Amendment requirements of "due process" and "equal protection."

**State Courts and Police Power.** In the antebellum state courts, judges gave more attention than did the Supreme Court to developing a legal view of the police power as being more than the residual of state powers that remained beyond the reach of federal preemption or judicial censorship. The leadership was taken by the Massachusetts high court under Chief Justice Lemuel Shaw, whose opinion in Commonwealth v. Alger (1851) became the lodestone of police power adjudication in subsequent years. Although Shaw conceded that it was "not easy to mark its boundaries, or prescribe limits to its exercise" (p. 85), the police power must be subject to some clear constraints if the principles of "well-ordered civil society" and the rights of private property were to be given due protection. Shaw isolated several complementary standards for judging the legitimacy of economic and social regulations. First, there was the foundation in common-law rules of property use, especially the rule sic utere tu ut alienum non laedas ("use your own property so as not to injure that of another"). Second, the Alger opinion reasserted "rights of the public" as a positive consideration, fully as legitimate an interest as private rights in any calculus of constitutionality. And third, when regulatory legislation went beyond what common-law nuisance doctrines would have validated, the legislature must have authority to act upon what they deemed "necessary and expedient"—but the regulations must also be "reasonable," and it was the function of the judicial branch to determine whether the reasonableness standard had been met (see also PUBLIC USE DOCTRINE).

Other state courts offered standards by which state police powers should be judged. For the Vermont Supreme Court in *Thorpe* v. *Rutland and Burlington Railroad Co.* (1855), it was "the general comfort, health, and prosperity of the State"—a capacious definition indeed (p. 150). A judge of the Michigan Supreme Court, however, provided a narrower definition: a regulation could only be justified under the police power if it was "clearly necessary to the safety, comfort and well being of society" (*People* v. *Jackson and Michigan Plank Road*, 1861, p. 307). Other courts and legal scholars took positions along the spectrum of opinion between these two views.

*The Conservative Era.* Adoption of the Fourteenth Amendment gave an entirely new context to police power cases before the Supreme Court. At first, the Court resisted efforts to invoke the "due process" provision of the amendment as a source for substantive review of the content of state regulatory legislation. In the *\*Slaughterhouse Cases* (1873) and *\*Munn* v. *Illinois* (1877), the Court's majority upheld far-reaching state laws that affected the operations of important private economic interests.

Even Justice Stephen J. \*Field, exemplar of the rising conservative jurisprudence, maintained in *Barbier* v. *Connolly* (1885) that neither the Fourteenth Amendment nor any other provision of the Constitution "was designed to interfere with the power of the State, sometimes termed its police power, to prescribe regulations to promote the health, peace, morals, education, and good order of the people, and to legislate so as to increase the industries of the State, develop its resources, and to add to its wealth and prosperity" (p. 31).

For Field—and, by the late 1880s, for the Court's majority—this statement of the powers of state legislatures was meant to be a statement of limits, rather than a charter of plenary discretion. Thus what Field termed "the ordinary avocations of life" (businesses and occupations outside the protected sphere of those "affected with a public interest") should be immune from the reach of the state police power; and the power should not be upheld when used to establish monopolies, or to restrict "freedom to pursue an occupation."

In the period from the 1880s to the \*New Deal, the Court increasingly assumed the role of judicial censor of the state legislatures' uses of the police power in important aspects of social and economic regulation. It did so by developing a set of doctrines that upheld vested private rights against the state's regulatory authority—that is, by going beyond scrutiny of the procedural aspects of "due process" to apply a standard of constitutionality based on the justices' scrutiny of legislative purpose and their assessment of the nature of private interests affected.

"Affectation with a public interest," which the Court first embraced in *Munn* v. *Illinois,* was one of these key doctrines. It was designed to differentiate "ordinary" businesses (not regulable at all as to prices they might charge, or as to availability of services to the general public) from businesses of a more public character (hence regulable in all aspects). Applied on a case-by-case basis, the "affectation" doctrine produced inconsistent results, but clearly it had a dampening effect on states' authority to bring business firms under regulatory regimes.

The Court also expanded the traditional doctrine of "reasonableness," far beyond what Shaw's opinion in *Commonwealth* v. *Alger* had invoked (see RULE OF REASON). Thus in *\*Mugler* v. *Kansas* (1887), the Court declared, first, that a regulation must be "for an end which is in fact public;" and, second, that

the means adopted for its enforcement must be reasonably adapted to the accomplishment of that end. . . . If, therefore, a statute purporting to have been enacted to protect the public health, the public morals, or the public safety, has no real or substantial relation to those objects, or is a palpable invasion of rights secured by the fundamental law, it is the duty of the courts to so adjudge, and thereby give effect to the Constitution. (p. 661)

In this doctrinal development, the Court's move toward a censorial role was encouraged by the views of such respected treatise writers as Thomas \*Cooley and Christopher G. Tiedeman, who urged that a robust theory of "constitutional limitations" was needed in the face of modern political demands for expansion of the regulatory state.

The most radical departure from earlier jurisprudence of the police power, however, was the acceptance by the Court of the "liberty of contract" doctrine as yet another limitation upon the states' police power (see CONTRACT, FREEDOM OF). This came to full flower in the decision of *\*Lochner* v. *New York* (1905), in which a divided Court overturned a statute restricting hours of work in bakeries. The *Lochner* majority acknowledged in the abstract the state's authority to protect health, safety, and morality through legislation that abridged personal and property rights; but it concluded that the challenged statute in fact failed to address any of these valid ends. The statute thus was deemed "an illegal interference" with the rights of workers and their employers to contract freely with one another in the marketplace—rights protected under the Due Process Clause of the Fourteenth Amendment.

Meanwhile the Court developed important distinctions between the states' police power (now increasingly defined solely in terms of the power to regulate economic and social relationships) and the powers of taxation and eminent domain (see STATE TAXATION). Even the conservative Court of the 1880s–1930s period was generally more supportive of expansive state taxing and eminent domain power than it was of the police power.

One of the continuing themes in the jurisprudence of the police power, in both state and national courts, has been the concern with *inverse condemnation—that is to say, with the question of when a "regulation" is of such character as to constitute, in fact and in law, a "taking." This issue, regularly advanced by parties suffering loss from the imposition of regulations on their interests, is a vital one because takings, under terms of the *Fifth Amendment—decided by the Supreme Court in 1897 to be incorporated by the Fourteenth, and so applicable to *state action—require that the imposed losses of property be for a public use and that compensation be paid (see REGULATORY TAKING). The Court's first effort at systematic line-drawing came in *Pennsylvania Coal Co. v. Mahon (1922), when it found unconstitutional a Pennsylvania statute that harmed the property claims of mining companies in the interest of saving urban structures from being undermined by mining digs. "While property may be regulated to a certain extent," Justice Oliver Wendell *Holmes wrote for the majority, "if regulation goes too far it will be recognized as a taking"—that is, as an *inverse condemnation (p. 415). The Court has struggled ever since to produce a definition of what "too far" means, and adjudication in this area until the late 1980s uniformly upheld the discretion of the state legislature and such administrative authorities as *zoning boards.

This is not to say that all regulatory legislation affecting important social or economic interests was overturned. In fact, the Court made a mixed record on this score. Thus its decision in *Muller v. Oregon (1908) upheld a state law establishing maximum hours of women workers; and other decisions validated tenement-inspection statutes and other laws affecting public health and safety. State laws establishing minimum wages, however, were uniformly rejected by the Court.

Contrary to the oft-repeated assertion that the Lochner doctrine uniformly prevailed, the Court thus pursued a varying and unpredictable course. Indicative of this development was the opinion for a unanimous Court by Justice Holmes in Noble State Bank v. Haskell (1911), upholding the state of Oklahoma's authority to compel banks to contribute to a state depositors' insurance fund; the case was decided only five years after Holmes filed a powerful and angry dissent in Lochner.

"With regard to the police power as elsewhere in the law," Holmes declared in Noble Bank, "lines are pricked out by the gradual approach and contact of decisions on the opposing sides" (p. 112). The hazards of the subjective element in the process by which the justices "pricked out" those lines, case by case, became a highly prominent feature of the Court's history in the era of conservative ascendency, to the early 1930s.

**Federal Police Power Doctrine.** The post–Civil War Court also undertook to develop a doctrine of the federal police power. As in earlier years, it remained based heavily in the Court's evolving view of congressional authority to regulate interstate commerce. The pivotal decision was *Champion v. Ames (1903), in which the Court in a 5-to-4 decision upheld an act of Congress regulating lottery traffic. The Court viewed such traffic as an element of commerce that Congress clearly regarded as immoral. Chief Justice Melville W. *Fuller, writing for the minority, condemned the decision because it served to "defeat the operation of the Tenth Amendment" and improperly permitted Congress to invade the domain of the state's sovereign police powers (p. 365).

In subsequent years, the Court had a mixed record in regard to the regulatory powers of Congress (see ADMINISTRATIVE STATE). Many important measures of the late nineteenth century and Progressive Era were in fact upheld, among them those providing for regulation of interstate railroad rates and operating practices, oversight of food and drug processing, inspection of meat packing, and tighter regulation of banking (see PROGRESSIVISM). But other acts of Congress were struck down on the reasoning of Fuller's minority opinion in Ames: that in light of the Commerce Clause and the *Tenth Amendment, certain areas of economic and social life lay beyond the legitimate reach of Congress and were within the exclusive domain of the state police power. Perhaps the most dramatic instances of the Court's rejection of congressional authority under the police power were in decisions overturning statutes seeking to outlaw *labor practices and to curb the use of child labor.

The states' police power, however, was itself also being severely curbed by the Supreme Court's conservative majority at that time, as the Court applied "liberty of contract" and other limiting doctrines. The result, therefore, was judicial creation of important enclaves of policy in which regulation at neither the state nor federal level could pass judicial muster.

**The Modern Era.** The *New Deal constitutional "revolution" in the 1930s brought with it a nearly complete overturning of the Court's prevailing doctrines on the police power. Two important props of the conservative position on state police authority were knocked down in 1934. The first came down in *Nebbia v. New York, in which the Court abandoned the "affection with a public interest" doctrine that had so long distinguished between "ordinary" businesses that were not regulable and the more public businesses that were. Now the Court left economic enterprises of every type open to regulations that were procedurally constitutional. The second 1934 decision was in *Home Building and Loan Association v. Blaisdell*, in which Chief Justice Charles Evans *Hughes, writing for the majority, declared that the police power must be viewed as justifying action in extreme economic emergencies. Because this decision affected the terms of existing mortgage contracts, it represented a dramatic repudiation of long-established Contract Clause and due process limitations.

The doctrinal legacy of *Lochner* and the earlier wage-and-hour cases were also set definitively to rest when, in *West Coast Hotel v. Parrish* (1937), the Court by a 5-to-4 vote upheld a state minimum wage law for women. In *Olsen v. Nebraska* (1941), the Court declared that it was not concerned "with the wisdom, need or appropriateness of the legislation;" it was for legislatures to decide upon these matters of policy (p. 246). This posture was reaffirmed in *Berman v. Parker* (1954), when, as noted earlier, the Court stated in very broad terms that legislative bodies must enjoy a wide latitude to define public needs; and that the authority to act followed where need was found to exist.

Similarly, the Commerce Clause and Tenth Amendment barriers to congressional regulatory measures fell in a series of cases after 1935. Thus in *American Power & Light Co. v. Securities and Exchange Commission* (1946), the Court declared that congressional authority to regulate must be "as broad as the economic needs of the nation" (p. 141). Throughout most of the post–World War II era, the Court has continued to uphold nearly plenary congressional authority to control economic institutions and behavior: and state legislatures and administrative agencies have been given wide latitude with respect to regulation of property rights. In *Nollan v. California Coastal Commission* (1987) and other recent decisions, however, the Court has partially reversed direction as to state powers; it has revived protection for vested interests in property by requiring that the state show a clear "nexus" between the regulation and a reasonable legislative purpose. In effect, the Court has thus broadened the grounds on which plaintiffs can successfully claim that land-use regulations constitute inverse condemnation, requiring the state to pay compensation for any economic losses incurred by private owners.

The police power issues before the Court do not, of course, relate exclusively to economic interests and their regulation. For personal and group claims to the constitutional protection of life and liberty, to equal protection guarantees, and to due process have also been at the core of modern-day challenges to the police power of the states. This fact is reflected in the complexities of recent controversies concerning the criminal justice system, the right to *privacy, *abortion rights, racial *desegregation and *affirmative action, and state legislation seeking to control the liberties specified in the federal Bill of Rights such as freedom of *speech and press or church-state separation. Hence, there remains today a wide range of vitally important questions as to the constitutional boundaries of governmental action under the police power.

(See also DUE PROCESS, SUBSTANTIVE; JUDICIAL REVIEW; PROPERTY RIGHTS.)

□ Ernst Freund, *The Police Power: Public Policy and Constitutional Rights* (1940). W. A. Hastings, "The Development of the Law as Illustrated by the Decisions Relating to the Police Power of the State," *Proceedings of the American Philosophical Society* 39 (1900): 359–554. Clyde Jacobs, *Law Writers and the Courts: The Influence of Thomas M. Cooley, Christopher G. Tiedeman, and John F. Dillon* (1954). Alfred H. Kelly, Winfred A. Harbison, and Herman Belz, *The American Constitution: Its Origin and Development*, 7th ed. (1991). Harry N. Scheiber, "Public Rights and the Rule of Law in American Legal History," *California Law Review* 72 (1984): 217–251. William E. Swindler, *Court and Constitution in the 20th Century*, vol. 1, *The Old Legality, 1889–1932* (1969); vol. 2, *The New Legality, 1932–1968* (1970). Melvin Urofsky, "Myth and Reality: The Supreme Court and Protective Legislation in the Progressive Era," *Yearbook of the Supreme Court Historical Society* (1983), pp. 53–72.

Harry N. Scheiber

**Political Parties** have an ambiguous status in American constitutional law. On the one hand, they are essentially voluntary associations of citizens organized to seek elective offices and share the political process. On the other hand, the Supreme Court has recognized the central and semi-official role played by the political parties in the American system of government.

The former description of parties—as voluntary organizations—has led the Court to avoid undue interference with their activities and to strike down state laws that would have a similar effect. Thus the Court in *O'Brien v. Brown* (1972) refused to interfere with the seating of convention delegates at the 1972 Democratic convention, citing the *political question doctrine and the desirability of avoiding judicial interference with the electoral process. Similarly, the Court has struck down state laws interfering with party rules for the selection and seating of delegates.

The justices, however, have protected the interests of third parties who are disadvantaged by state laws favoring the major parties. In *Anderson v. Celebrezze* (1983), for example, the Court struck down an early filing deadline that restricted third-party opportunities to challenge existing candidates. In general, the Court has signaled its determination to examine ballot access requirements with strict scrutiny, and it upheld in *Jenness v. Fortson* (1971) state laws that do not "freeze the political status quo" or that merely require a "preliminary modicum of support before printing the name of a political organization and its candidates on the ballot" (pp. 439, 442).

The Court has taken a more vigilant stance when political parties have acted in a racially discriminatory fashion. In *Smith* v. *Allright* (1944), the Court overturned an all-white Democratic party primary in Texas, holding that "when primaries become a part of the machinery for choosing officials . . . the same tests to determine the character of discrimination . . . should be applied to the primary as are applied to the general election" (p. 664). (See WHITE PRIMARY.) In *Terry* v. *Adams* (1953), the Supreme Court went even further, striking down the exclusion of blacks from a "preprimary" held by an all-white private group known as the "Jaybird Democratic Association" whose candidates generally went on to victory in the primary and general elections. The case produced no opinion of the Court, but a majority did agree that, for whatever reason, "the combined Jaybird-Democratic-general election machinery" added up to *state action in violation of the *Fifteenth Amendment (p. 470).

At the federal level, the Supreme Court has sustained campaign finance laws that provide financial assistance to political parties, along with laws restricting campaign contributions to political parties and requiring disclosure of such contributions. The Court in *Buckley* v. *Valeo* (1976) was unmoved by arguments that the financial assistance provisions would have the effect of reinforcing the dominant position of the two major parties. In the same case, however, the Court struck down limitations on independent expenditures by individuals, along with limitations on the amount a candidate can spend on his or her own campaign.

The Court has also taken a strong stand against state laws that seek to apportion seats in the state or federal legislature in order to benefit a particular party. In 1986, the Court in *Davis* v. *Bandemer* held that party gerrymandering—in which state legislative seats are apportioned so as to benefit one political party over the other—presents justiciable questions and poses potential *Fourteenth Amendment problems. Most recently, the Court in *Rutan* v. *Republican Party of Illinois* (1990) invalidated a state law that gave members of one political party an advantage in public employment. The Court was quick to point out that such discrimination was permissible when party affiliation or support was an "appropriate requirement" for the position involved.

(See also FINANCING POLITICAL SPEECH; POLITICAL PROCESS; VOTE, RIGHT TO.)

William Lasser

**Political Process.** The role of the Supreme Court in American government must be understood with reference to the larger political system. The unique features of the American political system

make it possible for the Court to play a vital role in the settlement of political issues. In turn, the Court is profoundly influenced by the political process, which guides and shapes its decisions and which can, at times, set clear limits to the Court's political independence.

**Nature of American Politics.** The political power of the Supreme Court is a product of the constitutional structure. In *Marbury* v. *Madison* (1803) and *Fletcher* v. *Peck* (1810), the Court established its power to interpret and enforce the Constitution against the encroachments of the federal and state governments. This power, known as *judicial review, derives in part from a limited, written constitution. Such a constitution, as Alexander *Hamilton stated in the The *Federalist*, no. 78, "can be preserved in practice no other way than through the medium of courts of justice, whose duty it must be to declare all acts contrary to the manifest tenor of the Constitution void."

The theoretical rationale for judicial review does not, however, explain sufficiently the Court's historical success in exercising that power. A full explanation of the Court's extraordinary political power must probe more deeply into the nature of the American political system.

The Court's power of judicial review is exercised against the backdrop of a broad liberal tradition in America, exemplified by widespread acceptance of what the political scientist Louis Hartz called the "Lockian creed." The existence of a political consensus accepting almost without question the doctrines of *capitalism, individualism, religious toleration, and, in some form at least, equality, makes it possible for the American political system to redirect major political issues to the courts. Judicial review, as Louis Hartz pointed out, would have been impossible in the United States without this foundation of agreement, since "the removal of high policy to the realm of adjudication implies a prior recognition of the principles to be legally interpreted" (*The Liberal Tradition in America*, 1955, p. 9).

This insight, of course, does not deny the existence of conflict, intolerance, discrimination, and disagreement in American history, though the level of agreement on fundamental issues has probably been greater in the United States than in European nations. The dynamics of American politics have tended to suppress such conflicts. For example, the structure of the American two-party system discourages the formation of third parties expressing views contrary to the prevailing consensus, by providing such parties no representation in Congress unless they obtain a plurality in any given congressional district (see PARTY SYSTEM; POLITICAL PARTIES). Similarly, the rules governing presidential elections encourage the selection of candidates with broad appeal to the center of American politics, while virtually freezing out fringe interests from any sort of coalition-building role.

The emergence of truly serious conflicts over the nature of the American regime—as, for example, in the *Civil War, or during the *New Deal period—has resulted in serious disruptions to the normal patterns of American politics. During such periods—known as "critical realignments"—American political debate has been unusually intense; the divisions between the major parties have increased; third parties have arisen and gained power; and there have been fundamental changes in public policy. When the Lockian consensus is itself called into question and political debate revolves around fundamental questions, the power of the Supreme Court has been greatly limited. Thus the Court was unable either to settle the Civil War crisis through its decision in Dred *Scott v. Sandford (1857) or to halt the New Deal in 1935 and 1936.

Under normal circumstances, however, the Court has great latitude on a wide range of public-policy issues. This freedom of action can be traced to three factors. First, the Court enjoys widespread public legitimacy. Second, it operates within a system of separated powers, as one of the three coequal branches of the federal government rather than as a subordinate branch (see SEPARATION OF POWERS). Finally, the Court benefits from the doctrine of *federalism, which divides power between the national government—of which the Court is a part—and the states.

No Court could exercise significant political power without widespread political legitimacy. And, whatever their views on particular Court decisions, Americans seem to have accepted the idea of judicial review as a legitimate power of the Supreme Court. Even the most notorious and unpopular Supreme Court decisions have not altered this basic acceptance of the idea of judicial review. Abraham *Lincoln, for example, though a vehement critic of the Dred Scott decision, never challenged the idea of judicial review in the abstract; nor did Franklin D. *Roosevelt, who also faced strong judicial opposition. Even the extraordinary controversies of the modern era—over such Supreme Court decisions as *abortion, *school prayer, and busing (see DESEGREGATION REMEDIES)—have not shaken the Court's political legitimacy. Public confidence in the Court remains high, and the Court ranks near the top when compared with other institutions. Researchers have found a high degree of support for the Court not only among those who disagree vehemently with particular decisions; but also among Americans who pay little or no attention to its work.

The separation of powers also contributes to the Supreme Court's effectiveness. Any attempt to "curb" the Court—whether by *constitutional amendment or statute—requires, at a minimum, cooperation between the executive and legislative branches (in theory, of course, Congress can act alone by overriding a presidential veto, but such action requires two-thirds of each house and, practically speaking, occurs only under extraordinary circumstances). In the modern era, where the White House has generally been held by the Republican party and the Congress by the Democratic party, such cooperation is especially unlikely. Even if the president and a majority of both Houses of Congress are opposed to a particular Court decision, it is usually possible for the minority to kill anti-Court legislation—by filibustering, holding up bills in committee, or other parliamentary maneuvers. (See COURT CURBING.)

Finally, the Court's power is heightened by the federal system, which divides power between the national and state governments. The Court, of course, is a constituent part of the national government; historically, many of its most important decisions have been directed toward the states, and have enjoyed the full support of the other branches of the national government. Certainly this is true of most of the civil rights decisions of the 1950s and 1960s, in which the Court's decisions were backed up by such federal legislation as the *Civil Rights Act of 1964 and the *Voting Rights Act of 1965. It is no coincidence that, historically, the most vehement critics of the Supreme Court have been those associated with support for states' rights or with opposition to the broad powers of the national government.

*Supreme Court and Federal Supremacy.* The overwhelming fact of the Supreme Court's political role over the past two hundred years has been its commitment to increasing and validating the power of the national government. This commitment has not been absolute; at key moments in American history the Court has turned its back on the federal government and sided with the states. Examples include some of the most important and dramatic episodes in American history—most notably, the Dred Scott case and the conflict between the Court and Franklin D. Roosevelt in the New Deal. Still, these events (and a few others) have been the exceptions; the bulk of the Court's energy has promoted and upheld the constitutional powers of the federal government.

The reasons for the Supreme Court's historical deference to the exercise of federal power are clear. The justices are appointed by a political process that involves nomination by the president and confirmation by the Senate; they tend to reflect, therefore, the political views of those who control those institutions. Since for the major part of American history Congress and the White House have been controlled by the same political party and have shared a common view of the appropriate role of the federal government in American life, the Supreme Court has usually expressed substantially different points of view. When, on occasion, significant disagreements have arisen between the Court and the political branches, the political process has provided a quick corrective. By the appointment of new justices, or on rare occasions through constitutional amendment, any serious disagreements between the Court and the political branches have been rapidly resolved (see REVERSALS OF COURT DECISIONS BY CONGRESS).

The appointments process, of course, does not ensure a direct match between the policy views of the justices and those of the political branches. For one thing, the best a president can hope for is that the justices he appoints agree in general with his political philosophy; it would be impossible to find an appointee whose views on every issue before the Court were acceptable to the president. For another, the justices typically serve far longer than the politicians who appoint them, and they are required to make decisions on issues never contemplated during the appointments process (see SELECTION OF JUSTICES). Justices Hugo *Black and William O. *Douglas, for example, were appointed by Franklin D. Roosevelt but served into the 1970s. Moreover, as many presidents have discovered, justices once appointed often take on a certain degree of independence: "Packing the Supreme Court simply can't be done," Harry Truman once said. "I've tried it and it won't work." The problem, Truman declared, is that "whenever you put a man on the Supreme Court he ceases to be your friend" (quoted in David M. O'Brien, *Storm Center: The Supreme Court in American Politics,* 1986, p. 81). Finally, many presidents have been relatively unconcerned with finding an exact fit between themselves and their judicial appointments; Herbert Hoover, for example, placed on the Court such diverse jurists as Owen *Roberts, Charles Evans *Hughes, and Benjamin *Cardozo.

Nevertheless, when fundamental differences between the Court and the political branches do arise, they can be resolved through the appointments process. A president determined to influence the Court's decisions on a particular issue or on a set of closely related issues can usually succeed. Whatever their views on other matters, for example, all of Franklin Roosevelt's appointees were committed New Dealers. The Roosevelt Court was divided over civil liberties and civil rights issues, but on the key question of the federal government's role in supervising the national economy they spoke as one with the president.

On the fundamental issues that shape a particular era of American politics, therefore, the Supreme Court is rarely out of sync with the legislative and executive branches. The Court has seldom been able to frustrate a federal policy of overriding importance in the long run. In resolving struggles for power between the states and the national government, the Court has sided consistently with the national government.

The Marshall Court decisions like *McCulloch v. Maryland* (1819) and *Gibbons v. Ogden* (1824) established the foundations of broad congressional authority under the Constitution, especially in the area of interstate and foreign commerce. Furthermore, the Court also made clear that any valid federal legislation would be given effect even if in direct conflict with the *police powers of the states. Even the Taney Court, though best known for *Dred Scott,* did its part to advance the interests of the national government. Though it did sustain a variety of state regulations of interstate commerce in the absence of relevant federal legislation, it did not waver from the Marshall Court's broad definition of the federal *commerce power. Even on *slavery matters the Taney Court generally stayed on the sidelines, deferring to Congress's attempts to forge a compromise—until, of course, *Dred Scott.*

After 1860, the Court reaffirmed national power. The *Prize Cases,* decided in 1863, provided critical support for Lincoln's war policies. Though *Reconstruction brought its share of conflicts between the Court and Congress, by 1870 the Court was again at work creating a constitutional environment favorable to the national government. Although it did invalidate a number of key federal laws in the 1870–1930 period and did weaken others through interpretation, it would be a mistake to characterize the Court in this period as hostile to the exercise of federal power. Such a view results from reading the Court's opposition to the New Deal back into the prior decades, emphasizing those cases that struck down federal authority and neglecting those that sustained that power. Though the Court held that the federal government could not regulate child labor, for example, it also upheld virtually every piece of federal railroad legislation brought before it; and while it at times prohibited Congress from regulating local manufacturing, it also permitted regulation of slaughterhouses, which were considered to be a part of the *"stream" of commerce. The Court also advanced national power by overturning many state laws that interfered with congressional regulations of interstate commerce. Taken together these decisions expanded greatly the federal government's role in American economic life.

The New Deal cases, to be sure, are a critical exception. In 1935 and 1936 the Court made a stand against Roosevelt's programs, striking down no fewer than fourteen pieces of federal legislation. The Court's opposition to the New Deal, however vehement, did not last long; by 1937, the Court capitulated and ratified Roosevelt's broad expansion of federal power.

The modern Court continues to be supportive of federal power. It has virtually abandoned its review of federal power under the Commerce Clause, permitting widespread federal regulation of banking, industry, *labor relations, working conditions, civil rights, the *environment, and public health. It has refused to interfere in *foreign policy even when substantial constitutional questions have arisen. It has permitted broad congressional interpretations of the enforcement provisions of the *Thirteenth, *Fourteenth, and *Fifteenth Amendments. Although the modern Court has not been reluctant to exercise its power of judicial review against specific provisions of federal law, it has rarely if ever attempted to interfere with the policy agendas of the political branches, or backed the states in a major policy dispute with the federal government.

*Supreme Court and National Policy.* That the Supreme Court rarely challenges the broad outlines of national policy does not mean, of course, that its role in national politics is unimportant. Because of separation of powers and the decentralized federal policy-making process, the Court has played a vital role in shaping government policies. The Court has achieved its influence not so much by umpiring institutional disputes between the legislative and executive branches, but by seizing the initiative and aligning itself with one branch against the other on specific policy questions.

Throughout its history, the Supreme Court has shied away from attempts to resolve institutional struggles between Congress and the executive branch. Instead, the Court has permitted the other branches to resolve such disputes between themselves. Not since the New Deal, for example, has the Court interfered with congressional *delegation of power to the president or the administrative bureaucracy. Nor, in general, has the Court objected to the evolution of various techniques of congressional oversight of the executive branch.

In the 1980s, the Court moved briefly away from this policy of noninterference. In *Immigration and Naturalization Service v. Chadha* (1983), it invalidated the so-called *legislative veto, a device by which Congress delegates power to the executive branch but reserves to itself the opportunity to review and veto the subsequent exercise of that power. The *Chadha* decision called into question more than two hundred different laws and portended a major shift in the relationship between Congress and the president. In fact, however, Congress and the White House have largely ignored the implications of *Chadha* and have continued to enact and apply the legislative veto in a wide variety of contexts. In later cases the Court tried to limit congressional attempts to delegate power to officials under its direct or indirect control, holding unconstitutional the enforcement provisions of the Gramm-Rudman-Hollings Act, which delegated executive power to the controller general, an official who could be fired, the Court said, only by Congress.

More recent cases seem to have restored the older pattern of judicial noninterference in separation of powers matters. In the past few years the Court appears to have once again adopted a laissez-faire approach to such questions, upholding the constitutionality of the Independent Counsel Act and permitting broad delegation of power over criminal sentencing policy to the federal judiciary. There is little sign that the Court will take seriously the implications of some of the language in its earlier cases and adopt a rigid, uncompromising attitude toward the separation of powers.

However, the separation of powers has contributed indirectly to the broad expansion of the Court's power over the past several decades. First, the Court has taken advantage of the struggles between the Democratic Congress and the Republican White House to increase its freedom of action. Disagreement between the legislative and executive branches has led at times to stalemate, and the Court has been more than willing to step into the void. At other times, the Court has taken its cues from Congress or the president and has made decisions that remained in force because one or the other of the branches refused to cooperate in overturning them.

The importance of divided government to the Court's political effectiveness should not be underestimated. For practical reasons, it is virtually impossible to reverse or modify a Supreme Court decision—especially on a constitutional question—without a clear consensus in both of the other branches. A constitutional amendment requires the initial approval only of Congress, of course; but it requires overwhelming support in both houses and the approval of three-fourths of the states (see REVERSALS OF COURT DECISIONS BY AMENDMENT). These steep hurdles have made constitutional amendments impractical except on the rarest of occasions; specific Supreme Court decisions have been overturned by amendment only four times in American history. Other methods of curbing the Court—including *court packing, removal of the Court's *appellate jurisdiction, or even the passage of ordinary statutes—require either cooperation of the two branches or extraordinary majorities in both Houses of Congress.

Little wonder, then, that attempts to reverse the various controversial Supreme Court decisions of the past forty years have all failed. When presidents have supported such measures, Congress has balked; when one house of Congress has given its approval, the other has objected. In 1990, Congress attempted to reverse several conservative civil rights decisions through the Civil Rights Act of 1990; the bill was vetoed by President George Bush, however, and Congress could not sustain the veto. Congress did succeed in passing similar legislation a year later, as the *Civil Rights Act of 1991. The handful of Court decisions that have been reversed include the 1978 *Zurcher v. Stanford Daily* decision permitting searches of newsroom files under a specific warrant.

Frequently, in fact, the Court's decisions have succeeded precisely because the Court allied itself with one of the other branches to accomplish an objective opposed by the third branch.

The Reagan and Bush administrations' semi-successful attempts to limit civil rights laws passed by Congress stand as one example. More commonly, Congress has "ducked" controversial issues to the Court, allowing the Court to make a decision that, though backed privately by congressmen, would be politically difficult to support in public. One recent example involves Congress's attempt to reverse the Court's 1989 decision in *Texas* v. *Johnson* prohibiting restrictions on flagburning. Congress denounced the decision and voted to reverse it by statute, but when that action was itself declared unconstitutional no further action was taken.

Private litigants too have discovered that they can frequently use the Supreme Court to accomplish objectives that would be impossible to achieve otherwise, usually because the political branches are unwilling to act. The *civil rights movement set the standard in this regard, but a similar strategy has since been pursued by countless interest groups on both sides of the political spectrum, including prochoice and prolife groups, business interests, and environmental groups. Interest group strategies include direct sponsorship of cases and participation as friends of the Court. Again the pattern is familiar: once the Court acts, its decision can usually be sustained against attack by the other side, usually because one of the branches will stand at least tacitly on the side of the Court.

*Supreme Court and the States.* To the extent that constitutional conflicts have arisen between the states and the federal government, the Supreme Court has usually sided with the federal government. Throughout most of American history, however, the Court left the states relatively free to manage their internal affairs. Between 1890 and 1930 the Court did apply the *Due Process Clause of the Fourteenth Amendment to nullify a number of state economic regulations, but even here the magnitude of the Court's interference is easily exaggerated (see DUE PROCESS, SUBSTANTIVE). Beginning in 1937, in any event, the Court abandoned its efforts to restrict the states' authority to regulate their internal economies, provided there was no substantial interference with interstate commerce. "The day is gone," as Justice William O. *Douglas wrote in *Williamson* v. *Lee Optical* (1955), "when this Court uses the Due Process Clause . . . [to] strike down state laws, regulatory of business and industrial conditions, because they may be unwise, improvident, or out of harmony with a particular school of thought" (p. 488).

Historically, three factors have limited the Court's interference with the internal affairs of the states. First, and most important, the Court did not apply the *Bill of Rights to the states until the early years of the twentieth century. Until then the state regulation of the public health, welfare, safety, and morals was relatively free from federal interference (see POLICE POWER).

Second, while the Supreme Court did at times enforce the Fourteenth Amendment's protections against racial discrimination, it did so with little enthusiasm. Such decisions, moreover, were far overshadowed by the Court's 1896 decision in *Plessy* v. *Ferguson,* which upheld racial segregation under the law. Finally, the Court's ability to supervise state activities, even had it been willing to do so, was hampered by a variety of technical constraints. The *Eleventh Amendment limited the power of the federal courts to entertain suits against the states by individuals; other restrictions, imposed by the Court itself or by Congress, served to limit access to the federal courts.

Many of these circumstances changed in the twentieth century. Beginning in 1908, the Supreme Court began to apply the provisions of the Bill of Rights, one by one, to the states (see INCORPORATION DOCTRINE). The first such case was *Gitlow* v. *New York* (1925), in which the Court applied the *First Amendment's protection of freedom of speech. In the years that followed, virtually all the important elements of the Bill of Rights were enforced against the states. In addition, the Court began actively to push for an end to racial segregation and discrimination. Over the years, a variety of technical devices facilitated federal review of claims against the states and expanded the nature and efficacy of the remedies that could be applied by the courts.

The modern Court has firmly established its primary role as the protection of individual civil rights and civil liberties against state encroachment. The justices have invalidated state laws concerning *contraception and *abortion, *obscenity, *libel, school prayer, and criminal procedure. Federal courts have taken active roles in the management of school systems, prisons, and mental hospitals in an effort to preserve and protect constitutional rights. The Supreme Court has steadfastly enforced the *Equal Protection Clause, and has extended its coverage to cases involving *gender, *alienage, and illegitimacy (see INHERITANCE AND ILLEGITIMACY). The redirection of the Court's activities to the protection of individual rights was the great accomplishment of the Warren Court and was pursued no less vigrously by the Burger Court as well.

There have been a number of attempts in recent years to overturn controversial Supreme Court decisions. Most of these have failed because success would require either a constitutional amendment or action by both Congress and the White House. Both courses of action face formidable obstacles. Most importantly, Congress has shown little enthusiasm for reversing liberal Court decisions, while a succession of Republican presidents have blocked most attempts to reverse conservative decisions.

In the past few years, the appointment of more conservative justices by the Reagan and Bush administrations has resulted in some contraction in the Supreme Court's interpretation of the various provisions of the Bill of Rights. In general, however, the Supreme Court continues to play a vigorous role in the supervision of state and local activities. Modifications in existing Warren and Burger Court decisions have been incremental and piecemeal; only rarely has the Court reversed outright a key Warren or Burger Court decision, and never on a case of central importance.

**Court and the Political Process, Writ Small.** Besides its role in shaping American politics at the highest levels, the Supreme Court has also taken on many cases important to the working of the political system. The Court's involvement in such cases has increased greatly since its 1938 decision in United States v. Carolene Products; *footnote four of that case declared explicitly that "legislation which restricts those political processes which can ordinarily be expected to bring about repeal of undesirable legislation" might be "subjected to more exacting judicial scrutiny than are most other types of legislation" (p. 152).

In 1944, for example, the Court in *Smith v. Allwright overturned an all-white primary rule adopted by the Texas Democratic convention itself. That decision overruled *Grovey v. Townsend (1935), which had held that a political convention was a private, voluntary association and not an organ of the state. Relying on the Fourteenth Amendment, the Court now held that primary elections were part of a unitary electoral process authorized under the laws of the state and that the "statutory system for the selection of party nominees for inclusion on the general election ballot makes the party which is required to follow these legislative directions an agency of the State in so far as it determines the participants in a primary election" (p. 663).

In the modern period the Court has extended its protection of the political process. In *Harper v. Virginia Board of Elections (1966), for example, the Court nullified a Virginia *poll tax of $1.50 per person, to be paid as a precondition of voting. Justice Douglas, writing for the Court, held that such a tax violated the Equal Protection Clause because "wealth, like race, creed, or color, is not germane to one's ability to participate intelligently in the political process" (p. 668). In 1969, the Court struck down a New York statute restricting participation in school district elections only to those persons who either owned or leased real property in the district or who were the parents of children enrolled in the local public schools. Chief Justice Earl *Warren held that the state's interest in restricting the franchise only to those "primarily interested" in school district elections was insufficient to override the constitutional presumption against ballot access restrictions. In the 1950s, the Court rejected a challenge to state literacy tests, though more recently it has outlawed obviously discriminatory practices in

this area and has upheld congressional action banning literacy tests under the Voting Rights Act.

Other decisions involving the political process include a number of cases dealing with third-party access to the ballot. The Court has steered a middle ground. In Williams v. Rhodes (1968), it rejected state schemes that virtually deny third-party access, but in Jenness v. Fortson (1971), it permitted those that simply require "some preliminary showing of a significant modicum of support before printing the name of a political organization and its candidates on the ballot" (p. 442). The Court has refused to allow states to require candidates to pay ballot-access fees but has sustained laws limiting current holders of state offices from running for other elective offices.

At the same time, the Court has upheld congressional attempts to preserve and extend voting rights under the Fourteenth and Fifteenth Amendments. In two 1966 cases, *South Carolina v. Katzenbach and *Katzenbach v. Morgan, the justices sustained the Voting Rights Act of 1965, holding that Congress could use broad discretion in enforcing the Fifteenth Amendment, including the suspension of literacy tests. In 1970, the Court sustained two key provisions of the Voting Rights Act amendments of 1970, including the nationwide suspension of literacy tests; a maximum thirty-day residency requirement in presidential elections; and the expansion of the franchise to eighteen-year-olds in federal elections. It balked, however, at a provision of the law granting eighteen-year-olds the right to vote in state elections. The latter holding was overruled by the adoption of the *Twenty-sixth Amendment in 1971.

Another key federal statute upheld in part and struck down in part by the Supreme Court was the Federal Election Campaign Act of 1971, as amended in 1974. In *Buckley v. Valeo (1976), the Court sustained federal limitations on campaign contributions (a maximum of one thousand dollars per candidate per election, with an overall limit of twenty-five thousand dollars by any contributor), along with provisions requiring disclosure of contributions by political campaigns and setting up a voluntary system of public financing for presidential elections. The Court objected to limitations on independent expenditures by individuals unrelated to the campaign, however, along with restrictions on the amount of his or her own money a candidate could contribute to a campaign and on the amount of money that could be spent, in total, by a campaign for political office.

The Court, in summary, has greatly expanded both the franchise and ballot access in state and federal elections, directly through its own decisions and indirectly by sanctioning broad exercises of congressional power. Moreover, the Court's role in enlarging and opening up the political process includes a wide range of cases expanding the rights of free *speech, free press, and free association (see ASSEMBLY AND ASSOCIATION, FREEDOM OF), and expanding the rights of African-Americans, women, and other minorities in *education and commerce. The effect of these decisions on the political process in the United States, while impossible to measure, has been significant.

*Political Questions.* The Court has traditionally shied away from so-called political question cases. These involve issues that, for some reason, the Court feels are more appropriately decided by the political branches of either the federal or state governments. The political question doctrine suffers from intellectual confusion and practical uncertainty and has been applied to several disparate types of cases. Nonetheless, the Supreme Court in the modern era has been increasingly willing to ignore it.

The classic statement of the political question doctrine appears in *Baker* v. *Carr* (1962), the reapportionment case. Ironically, Justice William J. *Brennan's summary of the political question doctrine appears in the case most responsible for the doctrine's relative decline in the modern era. The doctrine, wrote Brennan, is essentially a "function of the separation of powers"; such cases involve "a textually demonstrable constitutional commitment of the issue to a coordinate political department; or a lack of judicially discoverable and manageable standards for resolving it" (p. 217). Brennan also suggested that the political question doctrine might apply in cases that required the Court to make policy decisions which were inappropriate for judicial resolution or that might cause embarrassment or endanger the national interest.

The political question doctrine discouraged the Court from involving itself in many foreign policy issues and in disputes concerning the legitimate government of states in periods of rebellion. It also figured into the Court's reluctance to deal with a number of cases of direct importance to the political process, including those involving constitutional amendments, political party conventions, and, most of all, legislative reapportionment (see GERRYMANDERING).

The Court's reluctance to enter into what Justice Felix *Frankfurter called the *"political thicket" was expressed, for example, in *Coleman* v. *Miller*, a 1939 case concerning the proposed Child Labor Amendment. The amendment had been passed by Congress in 1924 and sent to the states; after more than a decade, its opponents sought to prevent further state ratifications on the grounds that too much time had passed (see CONSTITUTIONAL AMENDING PROCESS). The Court refused to get involved in the case, reasoning that the Constitution had lodged full authority over the amending process in the Congress. A similar episode occurred in 1972, when the Court refused to decide a dispute over the seating of the California and Illinois delegations to the Democratic National Convention. The Court has also refused to become involved in cases that, for prudential reasons, have seemed inappropriate for judicial involvement. One such case was *Mora* v. *McNamara* (1967), which presented a direct challenge to the constitutionality of the *Vietnam War.

It was in the reapportionment area, however, that the political question doctrine was given its fullest play. The 1946 case of *Colegrove* v. *Green* rejected a challenge to the Illinois congressional apportionment scheme. Justice Felix *Frankfurter cited the Court's lack of competence in determining whether such a policy violated the Constitution and expressed the view that the issue involved was "of a peculiarly political nature and therefore not meant for judicial determination" (p. 552). Participation in the apportionment controversy, Frankfurter warned, would bring the Court "into immediate and active relations with party contests" and would be "hostile to a democratic system" (pp. 553, 554).

Frankfurter's reasoning was rejected in *Baker* v. *Carr* (1962). Justice Brennan held that the Court's many Fourteenth Amendment equal protection cases provided an appropriate and manageable judicial standard; instead of involving a political question, the case simply involved the consistency of state action with the Constitution. In subsequent cases, including *Reynolds* v. *Sims* (1964), the Court created the *"one person, one vote" rule and applied it to every legislative body in the United States except the U.S. Senate, which, under the explicit command of the Constitution, consists of two senators from each state. Though certainly far more bounded than in the past, the political question doctrine remains a viable, self-imposed limitation on judicial power, particularly in the areas of constitutional amendments and foreign policy.

*Supreme Court and Modern American Politics.* Two features characterize the modern Supreme Court's relationship to the political process. First, the Court is extraordinarily deferential to the federal government on broad matters of public policy, especially foreign affairs and economic regulation. Since these areas comprehend the most critical activities of the modern federal government, the Court's deferential attitude makes full-scale confrontations with Congress— on the order of *Dred Scott* or the New Deal cases— unlikely.

As it has withdrawn from the issues most central to political controversy at the national level, however, the modern Supreme Court has increasingly applied the provisions of the Constitution to the states. This activism toward the states remains exceptionally high in historical terms despite a tendency toward *judicial self-restraint over the past decade. The Court's high profile on matters of central importance to the lives of individuals and communities practically guarantees that its decisions will continue to generate controversy.

For the modern Supreme Court, therefore, an ongoing atmosphere of intense controversy has become routine. Such controversy is likely to continue into the future despite (or perhaps because of) changes in the Supreme Court's interpretation of particular constitutional provisions. Elimination of this controversy as a staple of national political life would require a dramatic change in the role of the Supreme Court in American politics—a change as fundamental as the tranformation produced by the Court's adoption of the *Carolene Products* footnote. There is no indication that such a transformation will occur soon.

Despite the current atmosphere of nearly continual controversy, the Court operates with more freedom from direct restraint by the political system than ever before. Historically, the political branches of the federal government have been successful in overturning noxious Supreme Court decisions only under exceptional circumstances. Given the Court's deference to Congress in the key areas of foreign and economic policy, such a confrontation is unlikely.

□ Henry J. Abraham, *Justices and Presidents: A Political History of Appointments to the Supreme Court*, 3d ed. (1991). Alexander M. Bickel, *The Least Dangerous Branch: The Supreme Court at the Bar of Politics* (1962). Robert A. Dahl, "Decision-Making in a Democracy: The Supreme Court as a National Policy-Maker," *Journal of Public Law* 6 (1957): 279–95. Lee Epstein, "Courts and Interest Groups," in *The American Courts: A Critical Assessment*, edited by John B. Gates and Charles A. Johnson (1991), pp. 335–371. William Lasser, *The Limits of Judicial Power: The Supreme Court in American Politics* (1988). Robert McCloskey, *The American Supreme Court* (1960). David M. O'Brien, *Storm Center: The Supreme Court in American Politics*, 2d ed. (1990). Laurence H. Tribe, *American Constitutional Law*, 2d ed. (1988). Charles Warren, *The Supreme Court in United States History, 1836–1918*, 2 vols. (1926).
William Lasser

**Political Questions** are controversies that the U.S. Supreme Court has historically regarded as nonjusticiable and inappropriate for judicial resolution (see JUSTICIABILITY). Although the Court may have jurisdiction over cases involving such questions, it has often chosen not to decide them, preferring instead to allow them to be resolved by the "political" branches of government.

*First Attempts at Definition.* Chief Justice John *Marshall contended that when a case within the Supreme Court's jurisdiction qualifies for review by constitutional standards (for example, it meets the *cases and controversies requirement, presents a *federal question, etc.), the Court is obligated to decide the case on its merits. In *Cohens* v. *Virginia* (1821), he stated in dicta, "[W]e find this tribunal invested with appellate jurisdiction in all cases arising under the constitution and laws of the United States. We find no

exception to this grant, and we cannot insert one" (p. 109).

But at the same time the Court realized the impracticality of so rigid an interpretation of the Constitution, especially when a case threatened to propel it into uncharted political waters. Marshall perceived this in *Marbury* v. *Madison* (1803), where he wrote, "The province of the court is, solely, to decide on the rights of individuals. . . . Questions in their nature political . . . can never be made in this court" (p. 168). It was not long before a new category of cases that involved "nonjusticiable" political questions.

The first major attempt by the Court to define a political question came in *Luther* v. *Borden* (1849). Luther had sued Borden for an admitted trespass, arising out of the period of political turmoil in Rhode Island known as the Dorr Rebellion (1842). A group of citizens long dissatisfied with malapportionment and disfranchisement under the existing "charter" government of that state, sought to replace it (see FAIR REPRESENTATION). They called an extralegal constitutional convention, held elections, and proclaimed the formation of a new, more democratic, government with Thomas W. Dorr as governor. The charter government rejected the validity of the Dorr government and sought to retain political control of the state by force. Martial law was declared, and many of the leaders of the rebellion, including Dorr, were arrested. The Dorr forces used an otherwise inconsequential trespass case arising out of martial law activities in an attempt to have the charter government declared unconstitutional under the Guaranty Clause of Article IV. Under that provision, the United States must guarantee to each state a "republican form of government."

Chief Justice Roger B. *Taney's opinion in *Luther* listed various reasons why the Supreme Court should not decide the case. He noted that chaos that would follow a judicial replacement of the existing government with a new one. But primarily he found that this was an issue for which the Court had no standards to govern its decision; it was a controversy committed by the Constitution to the other branches of government. Article IV's guarantee of republican government was not the sort that the Supreme Court could enforce, hence it was a nonjusticiable political question.

The irony of this "political question doctrine" (a misnomer to the extent that it suggests that the Court *never* decides political issues), is that its operation demonstrates beyond any reasonable doubt the inherently political nature of the judicial process. That the justices should consider, implicitly or explicitly, questions of power and influence, questions affecting the Court's prestige and status, the judiciary's relationship to the other branches of the government, and the pragmatic problem of the Court's ability to decide a particular case effectively, belie any implication that it decides only "nonpolitical" questions.

Thus the political question doctrine is not a clearly conceptualized dividing line between appropriate issues but rather a discretionary device to permit the courts to avoid deciding certain inconvenient questions, and its precise scope and application are difficult to ascertain. Indeed, it was not until more than a century after *Luther* that the Supreme Court provided any formula for determining what is and is not a political question.

***Reapportionment Cases.*** Political pressure to bring *reapportionment cases to courts prompted the Supreme Court's modern reassessment of the political question doctrine. In *Colegrove* v. *Green* (1946), a challenge to the malapportionment of Illinois' congressional districts, Justice Felix *Frankfurter's plurality opinion announcing the Court's refusal to intervene implied that all reapportionment issues were nonjusticiable. Later decisions respected that admonition as if it had been the majority opinion of the Court. By 1960, however, it had become clear that only judicial intervention could break the logjam of state legislative malapportionment. The Court actually decided a malapportionment issue in *Gomillion* v. *Lightfoot* (1960). Ironically, the opinion was written by Frankfurter, but since the question in *Gomillion* was one of racial *gerrymandering, Frankfurter skirted the reapportionment issue—his *Colegrove* precedent—by contending that this was a right-to-vote case under the *Fifteenth Amendment (see VOTE, RIGHT TO).

The issue would not go away, however, and the appointments to the Court of Byron *White and Arthur *Goldberg in 1961 and 1962 provided the votes needed to bypass *Colegrove.* In *Baker* v. *Carr* (1962), a case challenging the apportionment of the Tennessee legislature, Justice William J. *Brennan, writing for a 6-to-2 majority, reviewed the political question doctrine and articulated a new formula for identifying political questions:

Prominent on the surface of any case held to involve a political question is found a textually demonstrable constitutional commitment of the issue to a coordinate political department; or a lack of judicially discoverable and manageable standards for resolving it; or the impossibility of deciding without an initial policy determination of a kind clearly for nonjudicial discretion; or the impossibility of a court's undertaking independent resolution without expressing lack of the respect due coordinate branches of government; or an unusual need for unquestioning adherence to a political decision already made; or the potentiality of embarrassment from multifarious pronouncements by various departments on one question. (p. 217)

Brennan conceded that Guaranty Clause questions were nonjusticiable (and they remain so). But he noted that *Baker* had also been brought under the *Equal Protection Clause, that it involved no separation of powers issues, and that it met his newly formulated test of justiciability. Reapportionment cases were now justiciable. Frankfurter's bitter dissent—his last—repeated

his *Colegrove* arguments that it was unwise for courts to enter this *political thicket of reapportionment and that to do so was a violation of the principles of *judicial self-restraint. *Baker* was a landmark decision, not only for narrowing the political question doctrine but also more generally as a symbol of the Warren Court's activist philosophy.

The Court in *Powell* v. *McCormack* (1969) further demonstrated its determination to relax the political question doctrine. In November 1966, Adam Clayton Powell, Jr., a flamboyant black preacher and political leader, was reelected to Congress by the Harlem constituency he had served since 1942. Because of allegations about improper use of congressional funds and other political misbehavior, the House of Representatives did not permit Powell to take his seat at the beginning of the Ninetieth Congress in January 1967. The House eventually voted to exclude him. Powell and some of his supporters filed suit in a federal district court, claiming that the House could exclude him only if he failed to meet the requirements of age, citizenship, and residence described in Article I, section 2 of the Constitution, which he clearly met. On appeal the Supreme Court held that exclusion for reasons other than those prescribed in the Constitution did not present a nonjusticiable political question. The Court then held that Powell had been unlawfully excluded.

After *Baker* and *Powell*, many legal scholars contended that there was little force left in the political questions doctrine. For example, in his well-known book *Impeachment* (1973), Raoul Berger argued forcefully that these two cases undermined the political questions doctrine to such an extent that the hypothetical question of judicial review of Senate conviction on *impeachment charges, long thought to have been settled in the negative, would have to be reopened. Berger claimed that the Article II categories of exclusion from Congress are much clearer than those defining impeachment (treason, bribery, and high crimes and misdemeanors—especially the last); and thus that impeachment could no longer be considered a nonjusticiable political question under the first *Baker* test. Furthermore, he argued that it is factual questions, such as those in *Luther* v. *Borden*, that properly implicate the political questions doctrine, not just determining "constitutional boundaries."

*Powell*, Berger argued, stands for the proposition that the Supreme Court may inquire into any governmental action in excess of jurisdiction or any alleged usurpation of power. He claimed that the Constitution implies the general principle that all arbitrary power must be condemned and therefore that all constitutional limits are subject to judicial enforcement. The resignation of President Richard M. *Nixon in 1974 foreclosed any immediate opportunity for the Supreme Court to review a presidential conviction by the Senate on impeachment charges. But if such a case had arisen, would the Court have found the issue to be a nonjusticiable political question?

Subsequent cases lent some support to the idea that the Court might have found such a question justiciable. For example, in *Immigration and Naturalization Service* v. *Chadha* (1983), which invalidated the legislative veto, the Court held that a *separation of powers issue was sometimes nonjusticiable. Similarly, in *Goldwater* v. *Carter* (1979) only four justices were calling to hold that unilateral presidential termination of a treaty was a political question, even though prior to *Baker* and *Powell* the President's foreign affairs authority would also have been as nonjusticiable (see FOREIGN AFFAIRS AND FOREIGN POLICY).

*War Powers Cases.* Nevertheless, the political question doctrine appears to have played a continuing role in judicial avoidance of certain kinds of cases since 1970, particularly in the *lower federal courts. The *Vietnam War, for example, created many opportunities for the courts to consider constitutional questions raised by the conduct of that war. In *Holtzman* v. *Schlesinger* (1973), *Orlando* v. *Laird* (1971), and *Mora* v. *McNamara* (1967), however, the lower courts refused to address the constitutionality of the war by determining that such issues were nonjusticiable or inappropriate for other reasons. The Supreme Court avoided these cases by not granting *certiorari, even though, as in *Mora* and later in *Massachusetts* v. *Laird* (1970), some justices dissented on the grounds that the Court should at least have openly faced the technical question of justiciability and the broader one of judicial responsibility.

Similarly, a number of cases involving the constitutionality of U.S. military involvement in Latin America have been dismissed by lower courts as nonjusticiable. For example, in *Crockett* v. *Reagan* (1982), the U.S. Court of Appeals for the District of Columbia affirmed the dismissal of a suit by twenty-nine members of Congress that challenged the legality of the American presence in El Salvador. They claimed that introduction of military personnel into a situation likely to involve imminent hostilities, as well as the President's failure to report to Congress, were violations both of the War Powers Act (1973) and the War Powers Clause of Article I the Constitution. The plaintiffs asked the court to order the withdrawal of American forces. The court refused, grounding its dismissal on the political question doctrine, and the appeals court affirmed. The Supreme Court denied certiorari.

In 1990, fifty-three representatives and one senator filed a lawsuit to enjoin President George Bush from using military force in the Persian Gulf without prior authorization from Congress. The administration responded that such action, if it occurred, would not be a "war" requiring a declaration of war or some other supporting act of Congress and claimed that this was in any case

not a matter for the courts (see PRESIDENTIAL EMERGENCY POWERS). The court rejected this latter argument, saying that it "put Congress' constitutional authority at the mercy of a semantic decision by the President" and that judicial deference would evade the plain language of the Constitution that only Congress can declare war. But Judge Harold Greene also refused to issue the requested injunction. The case, he said, did not possess the *ripeness required for judicial decision; it would become so only if and when a majority of both houses of Congress made clear—either by a joint resolution or by joining the the lawsuit—that Congress was asking the federal courts to prohibit the president's actions.

All these cases demonstrate the reluctance of courts to intervene in such momentous issues, either because they are regarded as political questions or for other, essentially similar, reasons. Though the Supreme Court's complete authority over certiorari may be its principal tool for case avoidance, the political question doctrine may now be the primary strategy open to the lower federal courts.

Not only does the doctrine appear still to have some life left in it, but some students of constitutional law contend that it is not merely an unprincipled means of avoiding controversies. There have always been restrictions on access to the judiciary, such as the case or controversy requirement of *Article III and Congress's authority to limit federal courts' jurisdiction. All branches share authority and responsibility in interpreting constitutional meaning.

At the least, the political question doctrine survives as a subjective caution against inappropriate judicial participation in certain kinds of policy issues. These issues often implicate the separation of powers, but all separation of powers issues do not necessarily present political questions. The doctrine's resilience is also a continuing reminder that the Supreme Court operates in a political environment and that there are occasions when its intervention in essentially political controversies between the other branches of government or in their internal operations, may be imprudent.

(See also JUDICIAL POWER AND JURISDICTION.)

□ Raoul Berger, *Impeachment: The Constitutional Problems* (1973). J. Peter Mulhern, "In Defense of the Political Questions Doctrine," *University of Pennsylvania Law Review* 137 (1988): 97–176. Martin Redish, "Judicial Review and the Political Question," *Northwestern University Law Review* 79 (1985): 1031–1061.

Joel B. Grossman

**Political Thicket,** phrase that originated in Justice Felix *Frankfurter's opinion for the Court, although he spoke only for two other justices, in *Colegrove* v. *Green* (1946), in which he argued that federal courts should not hear legislative reapportionment disputes. His precise words were: "To sustain this action [a *declaratory judgment that the Illinois statutes apportioning congressional districts were unconstitutional] would cut very deep into the very being of Congress. Courts ought not to enter this political thicket" (p. 556).

Justice Frankfurter's words took on a life of their own, became widely quoted, and are instantly recognized as the warning against *judicial review of questions relating to the nature of representation in governmental bodies. He was giving voice to the *political questions doctrine first announced by Chief Justice Roger B. *Taney in *Luther v. Borden (1849). Yet it is hard to support the contention that many justiciable issues, such as the constitutionality of governmentally imposed racial segregation, are any less likely to involve courts in political thickets (see JUSTICIABILITY). Questions of how best to secure "fair and effective representation" do, however, involve clashes between *political parties somewhat more sharply than most other constitutional issues (see FAIR REPRESENTATION). It was perhaps to this aspect that Justice Frankfurter's phrase drew attention.

Some sixteen years later in *Baker v. Carr (1962), the Supreme Court ignored Frankfurter's warning and opened the federal courts to reapportionment lawsuits. Two years later, in *Reynolds v. Sims (1964), the Court adopted the simplistic but easy-to-apply standard of mathematical equality among districts (see REAPPORTIONMENT CASES). In *Davis v. Bandemer, (1986), the Court ventured further into the political thicket by ruling justiciable claims of partisan *gerrymandering, even though it could muster no majority behind any formula for determining when such gerrymandering is unconstitutional.                J. W. Peltason

**Pollak, Walter Heilprin** (b. Summit, N.J., 4 June 1887; d. New York, N.Y., 2 Oct. 1940), lawyer and civil libertarian. Pollak used persuasive Supreme Court briefs to lead the movement to establish uniform national constitutional standards in the free expression and criminal areas by "incorporating" federal *Bill of Rights protections against the states (see INCORPORATION DOCTRINE). Starting with the 1925 *Gitlow case, the Supreme Court embraced this process as a proper interpretation of the Fourteenth Amendment, agreeing that freedom of *speech and press are part of the "liberty" that the *Fourteenth Amendment forbids the states to take away arbitrarily. This action laid the foundation for subsequent application of most of the Bill of Rights to the states. While Pollak did not succeed in persuading the Court to void the restrictive New York law under which Gitlow was convicted, or the California *criminal syndicalism law in the 1927 *Whitney case, his "incorporation" principle subsequently served to upset the California red flag law and the Minnesota gag law in 1931 and Mayor Frank Hague's suppression of open-air meetings in Jersey City in 1939.

Pollak was also committed to fair procedure, reflected in his work on the Wickersham Commission investigating lawless methods of law enforcement and prosecutions. He persuaded the Court to quash two separate death sentences upon the "Scottsboro boys," first because they were not fairly represented by counsel at their initial trial (*Powell v. Alabama, 1932), and later because blacks had been excluded from the jury list (*Norris v. Alabama, 1935). His work has been called "an awesome personal achievement" and a monument in the history of civil liberties.

Paul L. Murphy

**Pollock v. Farmers' Loan & Trust Co.** (1) 157 U.S. 429 (1895), argued 7–13 Mar. 1895, decided in three parts on 8 Apr. 1895 by votes of 8 to 0, 6 to 2, and 4 to 4; Fuller for the Court, Field concurring, White, Harlan, Brown, and Shiras in dissent, Jackson not participating. (2) 158 U.S. 601 (1895), rehearing argued 6–8 May 1895, decided 20 May 1895 by vote of 5 to 4; Fuller for the Court, Harlan, Brown, Jackson, and White in dissent. *Pollock* is not important as a precedent, since it was negated by the *Sixteenth Amendment and was probably on the way to reversal by the Supreme Court even before that amendment's adoption. Nevertheless, the decision stands as one of the most notorious examples—according to progressive historians—of judicial adherence to *laissez-faire constitutionalism (see PROGRESSIVISM).

At issue was the *income tax law of 1894, the nation's first peacetime attempt to tax incomes, including those from securities and corporate profits. The tax was itself miniscule—a flat 2 percent on all incomes above four thousand dollars—but the principle was of great significance. On one side, the national government needed additional revenue to support its burgeoning activities. Social reformers also argued that some action was needed to reduce the great disparities of wealth resulting from the rapidly industrializing American economy. On the other side, private individuals and businesses claimed constitutional protection against such measures to redistribute wealth.

*Pollock* was a contrived case in which a stockholder sued to enjoin his bank from paying a tax that the bank did not wish to pay anyway. The Court agreed to expedite hearings for the case, reflecting the need to have the question settled rapidly.

Lawyers opposing the tax, headed by Joseph H. *Choate of New York, argued that the income tax violated the principle of uniformity and that it was a "direct" tax that could be constitutional only if apportioned according to the populations of the several states. Neither argument had any support in precedent; the meaning of direct tax had long been given a narrow interpretation. Moreover, the Supreme Court, in *Springer v. United States (1881), had sustained the temporary *Civil War income tax, holding that an income tax was not a direct tax. Partly for this reason the lawyers freely resorted to hortatory claims that such taxation was an attack on private *property rights and the first step on the road to communism.

In the initial decision, the Supreme Court separated the law into three parts, deciding each by a different vote. First, the Court held unanimously that a tax on income from state and municipal bonds was essentially a tax on the state itself, violating the principle of *state sovereignty. Next, the Court, in an opinion by Chief Justice Melville *Fuller, ruled that a tax on income from real property was a direct tax. The Court split 6 to 2, with Justices Edward D. White and John Marshall *Harlan dissenting. Third, the Court divided equally, Justice Howell *Jackson being absent, on the question whether the general tax on private and corporate incomes was also a direct tax. Evidence suggests that Justices Henry B. *Brown and George *Shiras joined White and Harlan in believing the tax constitutional. Thus, a major part of the tax law was left standing.

This situation pleased no one, and the Court immediately agreed to a rehearing on the issue of taxing general income. The terminally ill Jackson struggled to Washington undoubtedly hoping that his vote would settle the question in favor of the tax's validity. But though Jackson voted to support the tax, another justice (probably Shiras) changed position, producing a 5-to-4 vote invalidating the entire tax law because it was a direct tax that had to be apportioned among the states according to their populations.

This barebones description of *Pollock* gives no adequate impression of its emotion-laden context. Both lawyers and judges departed far from constitutional argument; newspapers reported it fully and editorialized acidly. Harlan wrote privately that Justice Stephen J. *Field acted like a "madman" throughout the case, but the dissenters' own opinions were similarly emotional. It was doubtless the most controversial case of its era.

Only one part of the decision stood after the adoption of the Sixteenth Amendment in 1913: the ban on the taxation of income from state and municipal bonds. Although Congress has never enacted such a tax, the Court reversed its 1895 objection to such action in *South Carolina* v. *Baker* (1988).                                    Loren P. Beth

**Poll Taxes** are head taxes usually levied by local governments on adults within their jurisdiction. Compulsory poll taxes were employed in the United States from the colonial era until the early nineteenth century and a racially motivated poll tax came into use in the late nineteenth century. The *Twenty-fourth Amendment to the Constitution, ratified in 1964, outlawed poll tax payments in federal elections.

Commonly used in colonial America though occasionally resisted by local populations, poll taxes aroused little concern. In fact, the United States Constitution provides for the raising of monies through such a tax but only if the tax is proportioned among the states (Art. I, sec. 9). Congress has never used this taxing power to raise money.

Under democratizing pressures demanding universal white male suffrage in the early nineteenth century, poll tax requirements dramatically declined. But southern states resurrected their use as one of many ways to limit black political participation in the late nineteenth century. In *Breedlove* v. *Suttles* (1937), Justice Pierce *Butler for a unanimous Court upheld state poll taxes as valid state controls over elections. Congressmen routinely proposed *constitutional amendments to ban poll taxes in federal elections but none passed Congress until 1962, when only four states still retained the tax. The states ratified this amendment in 1964. In 1966, the Supreme Court declared state poll tax requirements for voting in state elections unconstitutional in *Harper* v. *Virginia Board of Elections,* overruling *Breedlove.* This decision, based on the *Equal Protection Clause, cleared the way for greater federal judicial oversight of suspect state action inhibiting the franchise. Poll taxes disappeared in the late 1960s and currently no such burden exists upon the citizens' right to vote.

(See also RACE AND RACISM; VOTE, RIGHT TO.)
                                    Thomas C. Mackey

**Popular Images of the Court.** The American public received its earliest impressions of the Supreme Court from the newspaper debates that preceded ratification of the Constitution. Proponents of a strong national government assured readers that the new federal judiciary would be the *"least dangerous branch" of the government, since the Court would have no control over the nation's finances or military forces. In The *Federalist Papers* (1787–1788) Alexander *Hamilton further defended the life-tenure and salary provisions of the Constitution as essential devices to protect a body of skilled jurists from the encroachments of Congress and the Executive (no. 78). Opponents of the Court, on the other hand, charged that, with its independence of popular control, it might easily become a despotic agency bent upon its own aggrandizement. Pennsylvania judge George Bryan, the reputed author of the widely circulated letters of "Centinel" (1787–1788), predicted that the Court would collaborate with Congress to establish a dangerously consolidated government, in which citizens might have to travel hundreds of miles to prosecute a lawsuit (letter no. 2). These archetypal images of the Court—a group of Platonic guardians versus a conspiratorial political cabal—have persisted, and continue to provide a point of departure for creative writers.

Early novelists and playwrights made only fleeting references to the Court in their works. To the average American in the decades before the Civil War, Washington seemed a distant—almost a foreign—capital, whose agents seldom intruded in any dramatic fashion upon the daily lives of citizens. Republican government, as practiced in a decentralized and sparsely populated country, implied strong local and regional loyalties as well as a permissive legal environment that encouraged private entrepreneurial activity and capital accumulation. In such a context the Court made little appeal to the literary imagination, especially since most writers believed that the justices were merely passive oracles of the law and had no hand in shaping important public policies.

Some early satirists introduced a Court scene into their plots as part of a larger commentary on the manners and mores of the Washington community. Typically, one character would escort a guest around the Capitol at some point in the story, and they would drop by the courtroom while an argument was in progress. The author would describe the justices in some detail, picturing them as physical embodiments of republican virtue: aged, learned, and impartial. A reverential mystique of the robe thus pervades the Court sections of such otherwise humorous works as Charles Jared Ingersoll's *Inchiquin, the Jesuit's Letters, During a Late Residence in the United States of America* (1810) and George Watterston's *The L. . . . Family at Washington* (1822). A rare political cartoon of 1834 likewise emphasizes the Court's moral authority by representing it as a statue of Justice atop a pedestal inscribed "Constitution."

Contradicting these images of judicial rectitude were several works in which justices conspire with ambitious presidents to destroy republican government. J. Horatio Nichols's play *Jefferson and Liberty* (1801), indicts the Adams administration for attempting to create a privileged aristocracy in America, with the help of a corrupt federal judiciary. According to Nichols, a "reign of terror" accompanied the Court's partisan enforcement of the unpopular *Sedition Act; and he identifies Associate Justice Samuel *Chase as the president's chief accomplice in the illegal suppression of political dissent.

A generation later Nathaniel Beverley Tucker described a comparable abuse of judicial power in his cautionary tale *The Partisan Leader* (1836). The story opens in 1849, by which time fourth-term president Martin Van Buren's centralizing policies have driven most southern states to form an independent confederacy. To maintain his tyrannical control of the North and West, Van Buren relies upon an inner circle of trusted advisers, including the servile Judge Baker of the Supreme Court. Out of self-interest Baker supports the aggrandizement of presidential power, and even agrees to convene an extraconstitutional court at Washington for the treason trials of those who resist Van Buren's decrees.

Judicial plots against the central government

also figured in imaginative literature by the time of the *Civil War. In 1861 a New York publisher reprinted *The Partisan Leader* as evidence that a southern conspiracy to dismember the Union had long existed. Antislavery writers linked the Court to such a conspiracy, especially after the notorious *Dred *Scott decision of 1857. Martin R. Delany's serialized novel *Blake; or, The Huts of America* (1861–1862) portrays the Court as a nest of slaveholders and northern racists, who twist the law to promote the political agenda of the Cotton Kingdom. Through his protagonist, Blake, Delany contrasts Chief Justice Roger *Taney ("the puppet figure . . . of the American Supreme Court") with Lord Mansfield of England, a jurist of "colossal stature," who had ruled in *Somerset's Case* (1772) that any slave brought to England was automatically entitled to freedom. James Russell Lowell's popular series of wartime poems *The Biglow Papers* (1862–1866) likewise denounced the Court for its southern sympathies and for its legalistic obstruction of the early war effort.

None of these writers described the Court as a working institution, or attempted to dramatize a justice's personal life. Nor did the federal judiciary make any stronger impression upon the fiction of the late nineteenth century. Albert Gallatin Riddle did devote one chapter of his Washington novel *Alice Brand* (1875) to a reception hosted by Chief Justice Salmon P. *Chase at his home, thereby suggesting the social prominence enjoyed by members of the Court. Typically, however, this was the only reference to the Court in a long book that otherwise dealt with corruption in Congress and the executive branch.

The cartoonists of the Gilded Age in fact offered readers more revealing glimpses of the Court than did novelists and playwrights. Thomas Nast denounced the presidential ambitions of Justices Chase and David *Davis in a biting cartoon of 1872. To illustrate the evils of a politicized bench, Nast pictured the two men in judicial robes, seated before a statue labeled "Justice (?)," whose blindfold reads "Politics" and whose scales are tilting dangerously to one side. From a different perspective, Joseph Keppler satirized the Waite Court's old-fashioned methods of dealing with an increasing workload in "Our Overworked Supreme Court," a memorable 1885 cartoon. Set in the judicial conference room, Keppler's drawing showed the justices vainly attacking a mass of undecided cases with quill pens, as messengers dump boxes of new petitions and appeals on the table and floor.

By the 1890s, as Keppler suggests, the leisurely agrarian republic of the Founding Fathers had long ceased to exist. In its place had arisen an industrial democracy, whose bloody labor conflicts threatened at times to overwhelm a political system still wedded to laissez-faire values. Turn-of-the-century reformers, fearing a successful socialist revolution, attempted to protect workers and consumers from the worst abuses of giant corporations. With the passage of the Interstate Commerce Act in 1887, Congress launched the modern regulatory state; and the Court, through its review of such national legislation, soon came to occupy a more prominent place in the public consciousness (see INTERSTATE COMMERCE COMMISSION; ADMINISTRATIVE STATE).

A series of controversial early decisions helped to shape popular perceptions of the Court through the first forty years of the twentieth century. In 1895 the justices struck down a progressive income tax law, refused to apply the *Sherman Antitrust Act against the hated Sugar Trust, and approved the issuance by federal judges of sweeping *injunctions against workers in labor disputes. A predictable outcry followed these actions and inspired several Utopian novels that called for a "peaceful" or "legal" revolution to restore political power to the people. Since, according to the authors, each branch of the government was controlled by corporate interests, fundamental change could only be brought about through the assembling of a "people's convention" to rewrite the Constitution. The new charter invariably borrowed planks from the Populist program and granted to the federal government regulatory power that had recently been denied by the Court.

Henry O. Morris, whose Waiting for the Signal (1897) went through several printings, dramatized the people's case against the Court more effectively than other Utopian novelists. Morris mixed living persons with his fictional characters and appropriately permitted Eugene Debs to deliver the principal attack on the high bench:

The money power now dominates every department of justice, even to the Supreme bench [Debs asserts]. It is not possible for a poor man to get into the Supreme Court. It is omnipotent and answerable to nobody. A short time ago Congress passed a law taxing the rich of the country, and this court adjudged it unconstitutional. If this law had been a tax on the poor, it would have been all right. Under the laws of the land the rich are always right, the poor are always wrong. (p. 228)

In Morris's tale the Court, prodded by the "multimillionaires," unwittingly starts a revolution by declaring all labor organizations illegal under the Sherman Act. Thereupon the workers go underground, form secret revolutionary lodges, ally with other discontented social groups, and take over the government through generally bloodless coups launched on 1 May (see LABOR). Once order is restored, a popularly elected convention drafts a "people's constitution" that guarantees employment to every person, revives the income tax, toughens the antitrust law, and nationalizes the railroads and telegraph companies. Under the new system the justices will be chosen by Congress for a single term of eight years, after which they will be ineligible for other political appointments.

The image of the Court as the guardian of economic privilege recurred often in the fiction of the early twentieth century. Some writers described a direct link between the justices and an "invisible government" whose interests they served. In Reginald Wright Kauffman's socialist novel The Spider's Web (1913), the justices are little more than hired employees of a sinister "Money Power;" while a "Napoleon of finance" in Charles Klein's long-running Broadway play The Lion and the Mouse (1906), engineers the *impeachment of Judge Rossmore, the only member of the Court he cannot bribe.

Other writers absolved the justices of personal corruption and explained their conservative decisions in terms of socioeconomic conditioning. When the Court strikes down a federal child labor law in Isaac K. Friedman's The Radical (1907), the author comments that the justices were "human, therefore fallible too, swayed by the prejudgments and the class consciousness of those to whom they owe birth, education and power" (p. 337). And Robert Herrick's A Life for a Life (1910) portrayed the justices as ancient logic machines, programmed to respond only to the legal formulas of a preindustrial age. When a government lawyer in an important antitrust case urges public policy considerations upon the Court, one justice inquires irritably: "Is it law or equity you are discussing?" (p. 222). The defendant corporation wins the case, because its counsel avoids all mention of justice or morality and argues instead from "irreproachable logic." Herrick's scene effectively captures the formalism of American jurisprudence at the turn of the century, when law was widely regarded as an objective science whose progress depended upon a strict adherence to established precedents.

Cartoonists of the early twentieth century commented more frequently on specific decisions than their predecessors had done. When the justices approved federal regulation of the meat-packing industry in *Swift and Company v. United States (1905), a Washington Post cartoon pictured the Court as a cowboy lassoing a mad bull (the "Meat Trust"). Conversely, judicial invalidation of an important child labor law in *Hammer v. Dagenhart (1918) provoked a sharply negative cartoon response in the Liberator magazine. The drawing showed a portly, cigar-smoking boss herding a crowd of undernourished children into a factory yard, with the caption: "Now, children, all together, three cheers for the Supreme Court." Such pointed cartoon criticism, which often appeared in syndicated newspapers or mass circulation magazines, attests to the public's heightened awareness of the Court as a powerful national institution.

While the Court's response to economic regulation shaped its popular image for most Americans down to World War II, some creative writers also considered the impact of its civil rights decisions. Sutton E. Griggs, whose privately printed novels circulated widely within the African-American community, portrayed the Court as a bastion of Anglo-Saxon racism. "The Supreme Court of the United States," comments a charismatic black leader in Grigg's *Imperium in Imperio* (1899), "may be relied upon to sustain any law born of prejudice against the Negro, and to demolish any law constructed in his interest" (p. 237). Unable to obtain justice from the white establishment, the "Imperium"—a black nationalist organization—creates a parallel shadow government in Texas and prepares to wage a race war against white America. Other works, including Charles W. Chesnutt's *The Colonel's Dream* (1905) and Walter F. White's *The Fire in the Flint* (1924), described the vicious caste system that the Court had legitimized in *Plessy* v. *Ferguson* (1896).

During the Great Depression of the 1930s, Americans reassessed their attitudes toward the judiciary in light of Franklin D. *Roosevelt's unprecedented recovery programs. Conservatives applauded the Court's opposition to early New Deal measures and pictured the justices as the last defenders of responsible republican government. "The Supreme Court is our Gibraltar," exulted David Milton Proctor in *Payday* (1936), a satirical attack upon the Roosevelt administration. "The people who prepared this New Deal legislation never read the Constitution, I am sure. If the New Dealers ever studied it, it was through some kind of a correspondence course" (pp. 102–103).

To liberals, on the other hand, the justices seemed willful obstructionists, who placed their ideological preferences and outmoded norms of constitutional intepretation ahead of the public welfare. The "Living Newspaper" productions commissioned by the Federal Theatre Project offered the most striking demonstrations of the Court's power to affect the future well-being of average Americans. Designed for popular audiences of limited means, the "Living Newspapers" dramatized contemporary social problems by combining imaginary characters and incidents with re-creations of real-life events, as reported in the daily press.

In *Power* (1937), playwright Arthur Arent argued the case for public ownership and distribution of electrical power, and brought the Court into his script as a kind of deus ex machina. Using a stylized representation of the high bench surmounted by nine illuminated facial masks, he quoted directly from the majority and minority opinions in *Ashwander* v. *Tennessee Valley Authority* (1936), a decision that upheld the constitutionality of TVA legislation within narrowly defined limits. As the decision is announced, a character shouts: "TVA has won!" and a crowd of people pours onstage for an impromptu victory celebration. But the Voice of the "Living Newspaper" interrupts them to report that the power companies are bringing a new test case to the Court. It will decide the ultimate fate of TVA and "other

projects through which the people seek to control their water power, to save their soil, and to obtain cheap energy" (p. 88). At this news, the people on stage all move one step forward, and ask: "What will the Supreme Court do?" A huge question mark then appears on the scrim, and the curtain falls.

Several weeks before the premiere of Arent's play, the president announced his plan to "reform" the Court by appointing six additional justices. The unsuccessful *Court-packing fight that ensued gave cartoonists a chance to employ a new symbol of judicial authority: the "marble palace" to which the justices had moved in October 1935. One of the best anti-Roosevelt cartoons shows the Court building with a giant target painted across its front, while the president, holding a paint brush, calls: " 'Fire' when you are ready, Congress!" Supporters of the administration, on the other hand, pictured the Court as a ball and chain restraining "Public Welfare;" or as massive boulders obstructing the passage of a "New Deal Emergency Ambulance."

In contrast to the cartoonists, no novelist took up the Court fight for another quarter century. Nor did it inspire any stage productions, with the single exception of George S. Kaufman and Moss Hart's musical comedy, *I'd Rather Be Right* (1937). In this zany farce Franklin Roosevelt wanders around Central Park trying to think up ways to balance the budget, so that a young couple, Phil and Peggy, can get married. Every time he comes up with a new idea for a law, however, the Supreme Court justices—all looking like clones of Charles Evans *Hughes—pop up from behind rocks and bushes, to warn: "Oh no! No, you don't!" Eventually Roosevelt learns that the justices are mad at him mainly because he once called them "old fogies." To prove that they are not, they give a shrill whistle, summoning nine shapely chorus girls who join them in a strenuous song-and-dance number titled "Having a Little Constitutional Fun." After this, they all disappear again into the bushes. Roosevelt, looking after them, muses: "You know, if I'd suggested putting six new *girls* on the Bench, I'll bet they'd have said, 'All right' " (p. 63). While the image of the justices as foxy grandpas did nothing to improve popular understanding of the Court, it provided at least a welcome respite from the customary solemnity associated with the high bench.

In the 1940s and 1950s several new trends, both jurisprudential and literary, coalesced to make the Court a more attractive and accessible subject for creative writers. First in importance was a major change in the kinds of cases that came before the Court. After 1937 the justices accepted the legitimacy of federal and state economic regulation and turned their attention increasingly to civil rights issues. Through the *Due Process Clause of the *Fourteenth Amendment they gradually applied the guarantees of the *Bill of Rights for the first time to the states. This trend, which was accelerated during the era of the Warren Court (1953–1969), brought up for decision a whole new range of problems that were at once controversial and inherently dramatic, such as the rights of suspects in state criminal proceedings.

Certain advances in the art of judicial biography also increased the attractiveness of the Court as a literary subject. The spectacular success of Catherine Drinker Bowen's A Yankee from Olympus (1944)—which was in turn a best-selling book, a play, a movie, and a television drama—emphasized that there was a definite market for gossipy stories about the private life of a colorful judicial personality. Mrs. Bowen's sentimental, and somewhat cloying, portrait of Oliver Wendell *Holmes, harked back in some ways to the tearjerkers of the nineteenth century; but none could deny that the public loved it.

Quite different in design and execution was Alpheus Thomas Mason's Harlan Fiske Stone: Pillar of the Law (1956), a massive award-winning study that illuminated the inner workings of the Court as no previous book had done. Mason made extensive use of *Stone's personal papers, which included draft opinions circulated among the justices for their individual comments. This evidence exposed the bickering and bargaining that went on among the justices in important cases, and some reviewers charged that Mason had violated the privacy of the Court. His book nevertheless provided invaluable insights into the Court's deliberations and served as a model for later judicial biographies. Its legacy also includes Bob Woodward and Scott Armstrong's bestseller, The Brethren: Inside the Supreme Court (1979), which relied heavily upon interviews with the justices' law clerks.

As popular nonfiction studies of the Court multiplied, writers began to produce the first full-dress treatments of the high bench in American literature. Nine works of fiction have appeared since 1963 that examine at length the internal and external pressures operating upon the Court. Seven of these are novels: Andrew Tully's Supreme Court (1963); William Woolfolk's Opinion of the Court (1966); Henry Denker's A Place for the Mighty (1973); Walter F. Murphy's The Vicar of Christ (1979); William J. Coughlin's No More Dreams (1982); Margaret Truman's Murder in the Supreme Court (1982); and Allen Drury's Decision (1983). Two plays complete the list: Jay Broad's A Conflict of Interest (1972) and Jerome Lawrence and Robert E. Lee's First Monday in October (1978), which enjoyed a second life as a 1981 movie.

Collectively, these works tend to follow a common format: A new justice is appointed to the Court. He (or she) meets the brethren, each of whom expresses a clearly articulated juristic philosophy and displays some distinguishing personal eccentricity. The physical and intellectual traits of living justices are carefully scrambled, so that recognizable liberals come out sounding like conservatives, and vice-versa. The new appointee finds himself/herself immersed at once in a series of dramatic cases. These generally involve recent civil rights issues that have been widely discussed in the media. After hearing oral argument, the justices deliberate gravely, even portentously, with one another. They are well aware of the historic dimensions of their work. As one character in The Vicar of Christ puts it, "One could look at a finished opinion and know that it would shape the future course of the law and perhaps even western civilization" (p. 138). Often tempers flare; brawls break out in the *robing room and acrimonious debate resounds at the conference table. But at some point institutional loyalties prevail over personal differences, as the justices join in a common effort to save the Court from some external danger, usually provided by a new court-packing plan or a threatened impeachment.

To balance these professional tensions, most authors add a generous share of painful domestic problems. The central judicial character in many cases turns out to be a man of early middle age, whose romantic involvements threaten to impair the moral influence of the Court. A few examples: Shall debonair bachelor Francis Dalton, forty-three, the youngest justice on the Court, go through with his plans to marry a beautiful actress, knowing that her scandal-ridden past will shock the public and trouble some of the brethren? (Supreme Court). Or, shall Associate Justice Paul Lowe, forty-six, a rugged Nebraskan, divorce his wife of twenty-five years, whom he has never really loved, to marry an exciting newspaperwoman who is secretly dying of leukemia? (Opinion of the Court). Such situations suggest the major weakness of these books: Despite their well-researched backgrounds, even the most ambitious do not rise above the level of soap operas.

Yet they do attest to the important place which the Court now occupies in the American imagination as the protector of minority rights. Innumerable television crime dramas, including the hit series Dragnet (1967–1970), have familiarized audiences with the rights of suspects, as defined in the *Miranda decision of 1966; and many other television and movie scripts have explored the impact of the Court's desegregation rulings. The Warren Court in particular has become a potent symbol of egalitarianism, as in Gideon's Trumpet (1980), a made-for-television docudrama in which the justices seem almost as wise and Olympian as their counterparts in the fiction of the early Republic.

Other writers, to be sure, have condemned the Court's activism, especially in the area of criminal justice. Drury's Decision presents a sympathetic view of the victims' rights movement, and reaches a climax when his protagonist—a liberal justice—joins four colleagues in weakening drastically the restraints imposed on the police by *Miranda*. Behind such assaults on the Warren Court's legacy lies the image of an imperial judiciary that has usurped power from the more representative branches of the government (see JUDICIAL ACTIVISM). "In recent times Federal court judges have taken unto themselves the right to ignore all past precedents, and indeed pursue their own sociological and political beliefs," complains Judge Harry Spencer, the old-fashioned hero of Henry Denker's polemical novel *Judge Spencer Dissents* (1986). "The right of the Federal courts to make the law as well as interpret it has become part of our judicial function" (p. 274).

Whether viewed as benevolent or threatening, the Court remains something of a mystery to most Americans. Creative writers from Watterston to the present have often characterized the justices as a priestly class, referring to their duty to expound the ambiguous language of the Constitution. On a superficial level, the black judicial gown reinforces the image. "People assume," remarks a character in Broad's play, *A Conflict of Interest*, "that when a man becomes a member of the Court, he is beatified and from that day hence, like a saint, he does not even have to go to the bathroom" (p. 38). But in a more meaningful sense, the justices do function as the keepers of the national conscience. They are called upon daily to choose between competing social policies in the light of democratic values, and thus to shape the changing national character. The process is tentative, neverending, and rich in literary potential.

☐ Bernard W. Bell, *The Afro-American Novel and Its Tradition* (1987). Maxwell Bloomfield, "The Supreme Court in American Popular Culture," *Journal of American Culture* 4 (Winter 1981): 1–13. Robert A. Ferguson, *Law and Letters in American Culture* (1984). Michael Kammen, *A Machine That Would Go Of Itself: The Constitution in American Culture* (1986). John D. Lewis, ed., *Anti-Federalists versus Federalists: Selected Documents* (1967). Gordon Milne, *The American Political Novel* (1966). Caspar H. Nannes, *Politics in the American Drama* (1960). Pierre de Rohan, ed., *Federal Theatre Plays* (1938).

Maxwell Bloomfield

**Pornography.** See OBSCENITY AND PORNOGRAPHY.

**Postal Power.** In Article I, section 8 of the Constitution, Congress is given the power "To establish Post Offices and post Roads." The postal power has been construed as an explicit authority to designate mail routes and post offices and as an implied authority to carry the mail and to regulate its prompt and secure delivery. Postal statutes and regulations protect the public welfare by delcaring certain matters to be nonmailable: obscene material, fraudulent mail, and material that poses a danger to personnel and equipment.

Applicable constitutional limitations are exem-

plified by the *First Amendment. Beginning with the 1873 Comstock Act, federal statutes have prohibited the knowing use of the mails to deliver obscene material, and the Supreme Court has consistently upheld such restrictions, most recently in *United States* v. *Reidel* (1971). In *Lamont* v. *Postmaster General* (1965), however, the Court invalidated restrictions on foreign mailings of "communist political propaganda." The Court has also held that state regulations that directly and immediately burden the postal function are invalid.

During the early years of the republic, building postal roads presented a common congressional pork-barrel opportunity. Until 1970, the U.S. Post Office was an executive-branch department and the postmaster general a member of the president's cabinet. The accumulation of political inefficiencies and economic losses led to the Postal Reorganization Act of 1970, which created the U.S. Postal Service as a public corporation removed from the cabinet, diminishing the control of appointments by the political branches and guaranteeing significant autonomy.

Thomas E. Baker

**Poverty.** See INDIGENCY.

**Powell, Lewis Franklin, Jr.** (b. Suffolk, Va., 19 Nov. 1907), associate justice, 1972–1987. Universally respected, admired, and indeed loved, Powell was a reluctant nominee to the Court. He had repeatedly declined President Richard *Nixon's entreaties to let him be designated for membership on the tribunal, at last relenting in October 1971. To the manner born and educated, Powell was one of America's most renowned and most principled attorneys and a descendant of distinguished old Virginia families. (The first Powell, one of the original Jamestown colonists, arrived on Virginia's soil in 1607.) A native of Suffolk in Virginia's Tidewater region, the future justice attended Washington and Lee College in Lexington, Virginia, where he became president of the student government; was graduated first in his class, with a Phi Beta Kappa key, in 1929; received his basic law degree there in 1931 (completing the course in two instead of the usual three years); and received his LL.M. one year later at Harvard, where he studied under Felix *Frankfurter and Dean Roscoe Pound.

Powell then joined the Richmond law firm of Christian, Barton, and Parker (at fifty dollars a month) but after two years commenced a long and happy association with the law firm of Hunton, Williams, Anderson, and Moore (later to become the powerful and large firm of Hunton and Williams). It was interrupted for three years by his service as a much-decorated air force intelligence officer in World War II. On his return he soon rose to influential positions in the community as well as the profession, including such prestigious plums as the chairmanship or presiden-

*Lewis Franklin Powell, Jr.*

He quickly became the Court's most revered and popular member. Cautious and basically conservative, yet moderate and utterly non-doctrinaire, he was comfortable in the Court's center, often casting the crucial decisive vote in such closely contested cases as those in the realm of the separation of church and state, for one, where he was on the winning side in some thirty major decisions, more than any other member of the Court. Because he frequently cast decisive "pro–civil rights" votes as the tribunal's "swing person" on the issue, the fear of a different jurisprudential philosophy by his would-be successor, Judge Robert H. *Bork contributed significantly to the latter's defeat (see also NOMINEES, REJECTION OF). Powell will probably be best remembered for his opinions for the Court in *Regents of the University of California* v. *Bakke* (1978), where he struck down (5 to 4) rigid racial quotas in university admissions but, concurrently, upheld (5 to 4) the principle of "affirmative action."

□ Henry J. Abraham, *Justices & Presidents: A Political History of Appointments to the Supreme Court*, 3d ed. (1991).
Henry J. Abraham

cies of the American Bar Association, the American College of Trial Lawyers, the Richmond School Board, the Virginia State Board of Education, the Richmond Family Services Society, the Richmond Citizens Association, the Colonial Williamsburg Foundation, the Virginia State Library Board, the Virginia Constitutional Revision Commission, and the American Bar Association.

Although an honored member of Virginia's conservative "establishment," he was no segregationist, and he denounced the Byrd organization's antidesegregation policy of "interposition," in what was for him uncharacteristic language, as "a lot of rot." Indeed, it was Powell who led the opposition to, and ultimately defeated, the state's "massive resistance policy." As early as 1959, while serving as chairman of Richmond's public school board (from 1952 to 1961), he presided over the successful, disturbance-free integration of the city's schools—a delicate and difficult task a mere four years after *Brown* v. *Board of Education II* (1955).

On his nomination to the Supreme Court, the American Bar Association's Committee on Judiciary termed him "the best person available" and Virginia's NAACP promptly endorsed him. Confirmed by a vote of 89 to 1, Powell took the oath of office on 7 January 1972. With predictable modesty, the new justice, comparing being named to the Court to "being struck by lightning," expressed his gratitude to Congress for "the generous margin of approval," and added: "I am too conscious of my own limitations to take it at face value. I am afraid I cannot live up to such high expectations." But, of course, he did until he retired fifteen years later.

**Powell v. Alabama,** 287 U.S. 45 (1932), argued 10 Oct. 1932, decided 7 Nov. 1932 by vote of 7 to 2; Sutherland for the Court, Butler and McReynolds in dissent. *Powell* v. *Alabama* was the first of the notorious Scottsboro cases decided by the Supreme Court. Nine black youths were arrested near Scottsboro, Alabama, and charged with having raped two white women riding on a freight train in March 1931. The accused youths were hastily indicted and tried for the crime of rape. On the day of the trials, an attorney appeared on behalf of the defendants, but indicated he would not formally represent them. The trial judge then stated that all members of the local bar present in the courtroom should represent the accused. Most of the local bar nevertheless withdrew from the case. Two attorneys did appear on behalf on the accused but had no opportunity to investigate the case and consulted with the defendants for only thirty minutes prior to the trials. Eight of the defendants were convicted and sentenced to death after brief trials, while there was a hung jury in the case of the remaining defendant.

Over the dissent of Chief Justice John C. Anderson, the Alabama Supreme Court affirmed the convictions of seven of the defendants, while reversing the conviction of one of the Scottsboro youths because he was a juvenile. Following a bitter struggle between the *National Association for the Advancement of Colored People and the International Labor Defense, the Communist-dominated International Labor Defense won control of the Scottsboro cases, and it was under the sponsorship of that group that *Powell* v. *Alabama* was appealed to the Supreme Court.

Speaking for the Court, Justice George *Sutherland held that the convictions of the Scottsboro defendants must be reversed under the Due Process Clause of the *Fourteenth Amendment. Under the Due Process Clause, the states were required to afford criminal defendants fair trials, and the right to *counsel was an integral part of due process. Hence, at least under the circumstances existing in the Scottsboro cases, the failure of the trial court to appoint counsel for indigent defendants denied them the right to a fair trial. Dissenting from the Court's reversal of the Scottsboro convictions, Justice Pierce *Butler, joined by Justice James *McReynolds, argued that the defendants had received the effective assistance of counsel. They contended that the Court, by reversing the convictions, was engaging in an unwarranted interference with the administration of justice in the state courts.

The *Powell* case was the first occasion in which the Supreme Court had held that the Due Proess Clause required the appointment of counsel by state courts for indigent defendants in those cases in which lack of representation by counsel would result in an unfair trial. The Court did not rule in *Powell,* however, that the assistance of counsel clause of the *Sixth Amendment was applicable to the states. Rather, the Court held only that the Fourteenth Amendment's Due Process Clause required fair trials for state criminal defendants, and that in some cases a fair trial could not be obtained unless the accused was represented by counsel. After the *Powell* decision, the Court thus followed the rule that the Due Process Clause required the state courts to appoint counsel for indigent defendants in all capital cases but that appointed counsel for indigent defendants in noncapital state cases was required only if an unfair trial would result for a defendant unrepresented by counsel. In contrast, the rule the Court enforced under the assistance of counsel clause of the Sixth Amendment, applicable in the federal courts, required the federal courts to appoint counsel for indigent defendants facing serious criminal charges in all cases, capital or noncapital.

In *Gideon v. Wainwright* (1963), however, the Court held that the Fourteenth Amendment's Due Process Clause required the appointment of counsel for indigent defendants facing serious criminal charges in all state cases, capital or noncapital. This brought the rule governing the right to counsel in state courts into conformity with the rule applicable in the federal courts under the Sixth Amendment. The *Gideon* case is regarded as having incorporated the assistance of counsel clause of the Sixth Amendment into the Fourteenth Amendment, making it applicable to the states, an expansion of the constitutional right to counsel that began with the Court's decision in *Powell v. Alabama* in 1932.

(See also DUE PROCESS, PROCEDURAL.)

□ Dan T. Carter, *Scottsboro: A Tragedy of the American South,* rev. ed. (1979).          Richard C. Cortner

**Powell v. McCormack,** 395 U.S. 486, argued 21 Apr. 1969, decided 16 June 1969 by vote of 8 to 1; Warren for the Court, Douglas concurring, Stewart in dissent. In 1966 the flamboyant black congressman, Adam Clayton Powell, Jr., was reelected by the Harlem constituency he had served since 1942. Because of allegations about improper use of congressional funds (and because, his supporters contended, he was about to become chairman of the House Labor and Education Committee) the House of Representatives refused to permit Powell to take his seat at the beginning of the Ninetieth Congress. A select committee reported that he met the qualifications of age, residency, and citizenship specified in Article I, section 2, but concluded that he was guilty of various improprieties. It recommended that he be sworn in and seated but fined forty thousand dollars and deprived of his seniority (and thus his chairmanship). This was rejected by the House, which then voted, 307 to 116, to exclude him from the Ninetieth Congress and declare his seat vacant.

Powell and some of his supporters then filed suit in federal court, seeking a *declaratory judgment that he had been improperly excluded, an *injunction prohibiting the House from excluding him, and back pay. While the suit was pending, Powell was reelected to the Ninety-first Congress. He was permitted to take his seat but fined twenty-five thousand dollars and stripped of his seniority and chairmanship.

The Supreme Court held that a lawsuit against members of Congress, including House Speaker John McCormack, violated the legislative immunity protected by the *Speech and Debate Clause of Article I, section 6, and removed them as defendants. But it ruled that the suit could be maintained against employees of the House such as the doorkeeper and sergeant-at-arms.

The government argued that Powell's lawsuit should be dismissed because Congress's decision to exclude one of its members constituted a nonjusticiable political question. Under the doctrine of *Baker v. Carr* (1962), *political questions that courts should not decide include those where the Constitution has made a "textually demonstrable commitment" to another branch of government to exercise a particular power (p. 518). Congress, the Court said, had only the exclusive authority to judge the qualificiations of its members as specified in Article I, section 2. Powell met those qualifications and thus exclusion for any other reason was reviewable—and, at least in this case, unconstitutional.

The Court also considered whether the vote to exclude could also be taken as a vote to expel, since the two-thirds requirement for expulsion had been met. It observed, however, that the

House had been advised by the speaker that it was voting to exclude and that only a majority vote was needed. Furthermore the rules of the House disfavored expulsion for misbehavior in a prior Congress. Thus a vote to exclude could not be transformed retroactively into a vote to expel; expulsion and exclusion are not equivalents.

If Powell had actually been expelled for misconduct, could the Supreme Court have reviewed the case or would this also have constituted a nonjusticiable political question? The Court gave no formal answer, although Justice William O. *Douglas suggested in a footnote that an expulsion would not be reviewable. Also left unanswered was whether a decision to exclude a member because of a disputed finding that he or she was not a citizen or properly a resident of the district would be subject to judicial review.

*Powell*, following closely on the heels of *Baker* v. *Carr*, seemed to have placed significant limits on the political questions doctrine, thus inviting greater judicial intrusion into the internal processes of the other branches of government. It does not, however, appear to have had that effect. In the many cases in which federal courts declined to address the legality of the war in *Vietnam, for example, the political questions doctrine, contrary to the implications in *Baker*, was employed to support judicial restraint.

(See also CONGRESS, QUALIFICATIONS OF MEMBERS OF.)

Joel B. Grossman

**Powers v. Ohio,** 111 S.Ct. 1364 (1991), argued 9 Oct. 1990, decided 1 Apr. 1991 by vote of 7 to 2; Kennedy for the Court, Scalia in dissent. Clarifying the basis of its decision in *Batson* v. *Kentucky* (1986), the Court ruled that the prosecution in a criminal trial cannot use peremptory challenges to exclude potential jurors on the basis of race, whether or not the defendant and the excluded potential juror are of the same race. Racial discrimination in jury selection, wrote Justice Anthony *Kennedy, violates not only the defendant's right to a fair trial but also the potential juror's right "to participate in the administration of justice" (p. 1368). Moreover, the Court held that "a criminal defendant has standing to raise the *equal protection rights of a potential juror excluded from service in violation of these principles" (p. 1370).

In dissent, Justice Antonin *Scalia argued that the Court's prior holdings sought only to protect criminal defendants from the exclusion of members of their own race from juries and to guarantee that no citizen could be excluded from jury lists on the basis of race. "The sum and substance of the Court's lengthy analysis," he wrote, "is that, since a denial of equal protection to other people occurred at the defendant's trial, though it did not affect the fairness of that trial, the defendant must go free" (p. 1381).

(See also DUE PROCESS, PROCEDURAL; RACE AND RACISM; TRIAL BY JURY.)

William Lasser

**Prayer in Public Schools.** See RELIGION; SCHOOL PRAYER AND BIBLE READING.

**Precedent.** Courts following Anglo-American legal traditions generally adhere to the principle of *stare decisis* ("let the decision stand"). This doctrine holds that judges should look to past decisions for guidance and answer questions of law consistent with precedent. Consequently, when a court decides an issue, the ruling sets precedent for future cases presenting identical or similar questions.

Following precedent gives consistency and predictability to the law. For example, when the Supreme Court ruled in *Brown* v. *Board of Education* (1954) that racially segregated public schools were in violation of the Constitution, the nation could reasonably expect that subsequent cases presenting issues of racial *segregation would be decided consistent with the *Brown* precedent. Decisions by the Supreme Court are not only binding on the future decisions of the justices themselves, but also on every inferior court in the land. This imposes a degree of national uniformity. By adhering to precedent, therefore, the courts allow the people to order their personal, business, and civic affairs with confidence in the stability of the law.

The doctrine of *stare decisis* is not inviolable. Judicial decisions are often based on historical conditions that may change as the nation develops and occasionally it becomes clear that a legal interpretation of the past was made in error. Consequently, the system recognizes that new precedents may need to replace old. The *Brown* decision itself replaced the *"separate but equal" precedent set in *Plessy* v. *Ferguson* (1896). Following precedent, therefore, promotes stability in the law without precluding opportunities for reasonable legal change.

Thomas G. Walker

**Preferred Freedoms Doctrine.** This doctrine holds that some constitutional freedoms, principally those guaranteed by the First Amendment, are fundamental in a free society and consequently are entitled to more judicial protection than other constitutional values. Justice Oliver Wendell *Holmes was the first to make this distinction. In *Lochner* v. *New York* (1905) and *Abrams* v. *United States* (1919), he contended that economic legislation needed simply a rational basis to establish its constitutionality, whereas limitations on freedom of speech could be justified only by "a *clear and present danger."

In *Palko* v. *Connecticut* (1937), Justice Benjamin *Cardozo justified preference for those "fundamental principles of liberty and justice which lie at the base of all our civil and political institutions." They are "the matrix, the indispensable condition, of nearly every other form of freedom" (pp. 327–328). In *Footnote Four to his opinion in *United States* v. *Carolene Products* (1938), Justice Harlan *Stone argued that legislation restricting the political processes or hostile to "discrete and insular minorities" must be subjected to "more exacting judicial scrutiny" (p. 153).

On the Roosevelt Court a majority of justices strongly affirmed this doctrine. Justice William O. *Douglas wrote in *Murdock* v. *Pennsylvania* (1943): "Freedom of the press, freedom of speech, freedom of religion are in a preferred position" (p. 115). Justice Hugo *Black spoke of the First Amendment as the heart of government. But Justice Felix *Frankfurter in *Kovacs* v. *Cooper* (1949) regarded such ranking as "mischievous" (p. 90). In fact the Court did subsequently find it possible to maintain a rigorous commitment to First Amendment values without specifically using a "preferred freedom" rationale. As Leonard Levy says, "the substance of the doctrine has been absorbed in the concepts of *strict scrutiny, *fundamental rights, and selective incorporation" (see INCORPORATION DOCTRINE).

(See also BILL OF RIGHTS.)

C. Herman Pritchett

**Pregnancy, Disability, and Maternity Leaves.** The first time the Supreme Court spoke about motherhood and gainful employment, it suggested a certain incompatibility between the two roles. *Muller* v. *Oregon* (1908) emphasized woman's "maternal functions" while upholding the state's power to limit her working hours "for her protection" (pp. 422–423). Then, only one-fifth of American women worked outside the home. Now, in the 1990s, more than half the mothers of preschool-age children are employed. But society, and the courts, still have difficulty reconciling these tensions.

Women still bear children, of course. But social sex roles have changed dramatically in the twentieth century. When it began, the old-fashioned family was the norm: husbands were breadwinners, wives homemakers. As the century ends, men and women share economic responsibility. But women's increased duties outside the home have not been matched by increases in men's responsibilities within it. Today, most men have one job—but most women have two.

Traditionally, government and business have not been eager to help women manage their double burden. Employers once fired pregnant workers or imposed mandatory maternity leaves—until *Cleveland Board of Education* v. *LaFleur* (1974) held that such leaves were arbitrary policies serving no rational purpose. But mandatory leaves are not the only policies that make work and motherhood a difficult mix. Despite *LaFleur*, the Court ruled in *Geduldig* v. *Aiello* (1974) and *General Electric* v. *Gilbert* (1976), respectively, that employee health insurance plans that excluded cov-

erage for pregnancy violated neither the Constitution nor the civil rights laws. The justices insisted that these policies did not discriminate against women but merely distinguished between pregnant and nonpregnant persons; since pregnancy was a "voluntary" condition, it was not like most disabilities.

Congress was several steps ahead of the Court in this area. The Pregnancy Discrimination Act (PDA) of 1978 rejected the reasoning of *Geduldig* and *Gilbert*. Employers must now treat pregnancy like any other physical condition. The PDA has not settled all the difficulties involved. While pregnancy may reasonably be viewed as one of many conditions that temporarily disable workers, childbirth has a crucial dimension that absolutely distinguishes it from other conditions: it produces a baby. The mother experiences physical changes after childbirth that foster emotional bonding with the baby. She alone can breast-feed the baby, and she is the primary provider of the continuous care that a newborn infant requires. At this point, families may be best served by policies that do *not* treat childbirth like any other condition. Childbirth is a sociopsychological as well as a medical phenomenon.

Some states have been ahead of the federal government in this area. California's Fair Employment and Housing Act, also passed in 1978, requires employers to grant up to four months' unpaid "pregnancy disability leave." The California Federal Savings and Loan Association (Cal Fed) refused to comply, maintaining that the law was preempted by Title VII of the *Civil Rights Act of 1964. *California Federal Savings and Loan Association* v. *Guerra* (1987), which tested the California law, was a case that generated considerable dispute even before it was decided. Many feminists argued that this kind of single-sex policy would reinforce women's disproportionate responsibility for child care. But not all feminists agree; some see this burden not only as a social reality but as both natural and desirable. Other critics feared that laws like California's would deter employers from hiring women of childbearing age, in violation of Title VII.

These complex issues were only superficially addressed in the *Guerra* case. Justice Thurgood *Marshall, for a 6-to-3 majority, found the state law compatible with the purpose of the PDA "to guarantee women the basic right to participate fully and equally in the workforce, without denying them the fundamental right to full participation in family life" (p. 289). Although sex-neutral parental leaves might be better policy, the *Guerra* result appears sensible. To the extent that pregnancy and childbirth are conditions that temporarily disable workers, they must be treated like all such conditions. To the extent childbirth creates unique social relations and responsibilities, it may be treated differently from physical conditions which do not. If the Court cannot force society to accommodate women's two roles, at least it has not frustrated these efforts.

(See also EMPLOYMENT DISCRIMINATION; GENDER.)

□ Sylvia Ann Hewlett, *A Lesser Life: The Myth of Women's Liberation in America* (1986).           Judith A. Baer

**Presidential Emergency Powers.** Presidential emergency powers should be distinguished into two categories, even though the boundary between them is sometimes obscure: the power to act in a crisis based entirely on the president's own prerogative; and the power to act in accordance with laws that give the executive special powers in a declared emergency. The latter is a long-standing feature of American law; the former is, from the standpoint of constitutional theory, more problematic.

There is no provision in the text of the Constitution that the president has special power to act on his own discretion in an emergency. It is sometimes argued that such power can be inferred from the Vesting Clause ("the executive Power shall be vested in a President of the United States of America") and from the president's oath of office ("I will faithfully execute the Office of President of the United States, and will to the best of my Ability, preserve, protect and defend the Constitution of the United States")—the only oath that is constitutionally prescribed.

According to Clinton Rossiter, in his *Constitutional Dictatorship* (2d ed., 1963), however, the framers seem never to have considered that public officials in some future crisis might have to go outside the regular procedures for lawmaking and enforcement established by the Constitution. Indeed, the commitment always to govern in accordance with the laws is underlined by the admonition in Article II, section 3, that the president "shall take Care that the Laws be faithfully executed." The view that the Constitution is equal to any emergency is set forth in *The *Federalist*, nos. 23 and 28, among others.

On the other hand, the philosophical tradition behind the idea of government by consent and by law has acknowledged that republican executives must have power to act in an emergency. In his *Discourses on the First Ten Books of Titus Livius*, Machiavelli wrote, "Those republics which in time of danger cannot resort to a dictatorship will generally be ruined when grave occasions occur" (book 1, chap. 34). In *The Second Treatise of Government* (1690), John Locke noted that, because it is "impossible to foresee, and so by laws to provide for, all accidents and necessities, . . . therefore there is a latitude left to the executive power, to do many things . . . which the laws do not prescribe." This power Locke called "prerogative"; it is the power "to act according to discretion, for the public good, without the prescription of the law, and sometimes even against it" (Laslett, ed., 1988, p. 375).

By Locke's definiton (that is, executive action in the absence of law or against the law), prerogative has become a pattern of presidential action, even for limited periods of time, only rarely. Rossiter regarded only Abraham *Lincoln, Woodrow Wilson, and Franklin *Roosevelt as "constitutional dictators," presidents who acted on their own discretion during crises for which the laws did not provide adequate authority.

Lincoln was the prime example. To meet the challenge of secession, he acted, before Congress convened in a special session, to suspend *habeas corpus, impose a naval blockade, and provide unappropriated funds for the purchase of military equipment. Chief Justice Roger B. *Taney, sitting alone on circuit, declared in *Ex parte Merryman* (1861) that only Congress had power to provide for the suspension of habeas corpus, but his decision was not enforced. In the *Prize Cases* (1863), the Supreme Court by a 5-to-4 margin upheld the blockade and supported the president's determination to preserve the Constitution, if necessary by the use of armed force and without lawful authorization, against citizens engaging in rebellion.

Once the *Civil War was over, the Supreme Court sought to restore the notion that the Constitution was "perfect," that is, able on its own terms to meet any emergency. In *Ex parte *Milligan* (1866), the Court unanimously voided the conviction of a civilian by a military tribunal. In his opinion (representing the views of five justices), Justice David *Davis wrote, "The Constitution of the United States is a law for rulers and people, equally in war and in peace. . . . [T]he government, within the Constitution, has all the powers granted to it which are necessary to preserve its existence" (p. 295). In the twentieth century *Duncan* v. *Kahanamoku* (1946), holding the wartime imposition of martial law in Hawaii unconstitutional, was a similar effort to restore constitutional protections after fighting stopped (see MILITARY TRIALS AND MARTIAL LAW). The same view was expressed even more emphatically by Chief Justice Charles Evans *Hughes, in *Home Building and Loan Association* v. *Blaisdell* (1934): "The Constitution was adopted in a period of grave emergency. Its grants of power to the federal government . . . were determined in the light of emergency and they are not altered by emergency" (p. 425).

The "perfection" of the Constitution was again sorely tested during the Great Depression of the 1930s. On the day following his inauguration, President Franklin Delano Roosevelt declared a national emergency, decreed a "bank holiday" (thereby preventing people from withdrawing deposits or cashing checks), forbade the export of gold and silver, and prohibited transactions in foreign exchange. For authority he cited the Trading with the Enemy Act of 1917, empowering the president to "investigate, regulate, or prohibit, under such rules and regulations as he may prescribe, . . . any transactions in foreign exchange and the export, hoarding, melting, or earmarkings of gold or silver coin or bullion or currency." This statute had been passed as a wartime measure. On the advice of his attorney general–designate Thomas Walsh, Roosevelt based his actions on this dormant statute, rather than on his constitutional office and oath. Either way, the president's actions went beyond any precedent save Lincoln's and took the government, for the first time in peacetime, into the realm where constitutional legitimacy is maintained, if at all, by statutes that delegate discretion to the executive.

Another severe test of the constitutional basis of presidential emergency powers came in 1952 when President Harry S Truman seized the steel mills. The Court, finding no basis for the president's action either in the Constitution or in statutes, ordered him to return the mills to their owners (*Youngstown Sheet & Tube Co.* v. *Sawyer,* 1952).

In a concurring opinion, Justice Robert *Jackson classified the constitutional authority of the president in a situation he deems to be an emergency. If he can find legislation authorizing his action, his powers are virtually unassailable. If he acts in the absence of a statute, he must rely on his own independent powers. In that event, his authority "is likely to depend on the imperatives of events and contemporary imponderables rather than abstract theories of law" (p. 637). But if he takes action incompatible with the expressed or implied will of Congress, "his power is at its lowest ebb," wrote Jackson. The Court could sustain his action "only by disabling the Congress from acting upon the subject" (pp. 637–638).

Jackson thought Truman's seizure of the steel mills fell into the third category, and he concurred in the Court's decision not to permit it. He went on to note, however, that the preservation of the balance ordained by the Constitution depended in part on the willingess of Congress to meet the challenges presented by events. Control over emergency powers ought to be lodged elsewhere than in the executive who exercises them, he wrote, but if Congress refuses to respond adequately to crises, government by law cannot survive. Quoting a maxim attributed to Napoleon ("The tools belong to the man who can use them"), Jackson warned that "only Congress itself can prevent power from slipping through its fingers" (p. 654).

The seizure of the mills "represents an exercise of authority without law," wrote Jackson, and "men have discovered no technique for long preserving free government except that the Executive be under the law, and that the law be made by parliamentary deliberations" (p. 655).

The other sources of presidential emergency powers are statutes that grant power to be exercised in the event of a declared emergency.

Normally it is the executive who discerns and declares an emergency. When he does, he quickens many powers. According to a report issued by the Senate Special Committee on National Emergencies and Delegated Emergency Powers in 1973, there were at that time 470 provisions of federal law that delegated powers to the president in the event of a declared emergency. (Some of them contained *legislative vetoes, a device declared unconstitutional in *Immigration and Naturalization Service [INS]* v. *Chadha,* 1983. The status of powers linked to legislative vetoes is not clear in the wake of this decision.)

In the mid-1970s, Congress became concerned about the possible abuse of these powers, especially because some declarations of emergency contain no termination date. In fact, the Senate study found that the nation had legally been in a continuous state of emergency since Roosevelt's declaration of 1933.

To correct this situation, Congress in 1976 passed the National Emergencies Act, which declared that any and all existing states of emergency would be terminated two years from the bill's enactment and that future presidential declarations would be subject to congressional review every six months. An example of the use of presidential emergency powers since the enactment of this statute came when President Jimmy Carter in November 1979 declared that the taking of American hostages in Iran created a national emergency and froze Iranian assets held in America. In January 1980, at the end of his term, he reached an agreement with the government of Iran to release the hostages in exchange for the transfer of the frozen assets to Iran and the extinguishing of any American claims to those assets. The Supreme Court, in *Dames & Moore* v. *Regan* (1981), found statutory authority for the transfer of the assets, but for the extinguishing of claims, the Court relied on "the general tenor of Congress' legislation in this area," which, it said, could be viewed as an invitation to exercise independent presidential authority (p. 678).

(See also FOREIGN AFFAIRS AND FOREIGN POLICY; INHERENT POWERS; SEPARATION OF POWERS; WAR POWERS.)

□ Louis Fisher, *Constitutional Conflicts between Congress and the President* (1985). Christopher H. Pyle and Richard Pious, *The President, Congress, and the Constitution* (1984). U.S. Congress, *The National Emergencies Act (Public Law 94-412). Source Book: Legislative History, Texts, and Other Documents* (1976).  Donald L. Robinson

**Press, Freedom of.** See SPEECH AND THE PRESS.

**Press Confidentiality.** See NEWSROOM SEARCHES; ZURCHER V. STANFORD DAILY.

**Press Coverage.** The Supreme Court is a paradox for journalists, at once one of the most open and one of the least accessible of the major institutions of government. Its openness derives from the public availability of nearly all documents filed with the Court; from public *oral argument sessions; and the fact that it decides cases by written opinions in which the justices explain their reasoning (see OPINIONS, ASSIGNMENT AND WRITING OF).

At the same time, the actual process of deciding cases is not open to public view. Only the final product emerges from behind the closed doors of the conference room and the justices' chambers (see CONFERENCE). Justices are typically not available for interviews and, for the most part, shun personal publicity.

These polarities define life for journalists who cover the Court. Petitions, *briefs, and opinions—the public record—form the basis of nearly all news coverage. The new "leaks" and "scoops" so common to the executive and legislative branches are rare, as are personal glimpses of life at the Court behind the scenes.

The other distinguishing feature of news coverage of the Court is the exclusion of radio and television from the courtroom. The public does not hear the justices' voices. Viewers see the courtroom through the eyes of the five courtroom artists, employed by the networks and accredited to the Court, who are masters of the quick impression in pastel or marking pen. Television correspondents themselves give their reports while standing on the plaza in front of the Court.

In August 1991, twenty-nine reporters for print and electronic media have permanent press credentials to cover the Court. By contrast, there are some two thousand reporters for daily newspapers alone accredited to the congressional press galleries. Unlike Congress, the Court limits it press credentials to those who cover the institution on a regular basis. Unaccredited reporters who need to hear a particular argument receive press passes on a day-by-day basis.

In the courtroom itself, two wooden benches, perpendicular to the justices' bench, accommodate nineteen reporters and are usually adequate for the demand. When press demand is great, the *Public Information Office can add several dozen more seats in an adjoining hallway, where occupants can hear the argument over a loudspeaker but can catch only a glimpse of the courtroom activity. Reporters can take notes in the courtroom but may not use tape recorders. The record of 119 press seats was set 26 April 1989, when the Court heard argument in an *abortion case, *Webster v. Reproductive Health Services.

Reporters receive copies of the justices' weekly conference list noting the petitions for *certiorari under current consideration. This list enables reporters to prepare for the Monday order lists, on which the Court announces grants and denials of certiorari. The conference lists distributed in the press room are marked "For Press Convenience Only—Not for Publication," and journalists are instructed not to report that the justices are considering a particular petition at a particular conference.

All petitions and briefs for the current term are kept on file for use by reporters in a room near the press room. Journalists with permanent press passes may also use the Supreme Court *Library.

The Public Information Office distributes all opinions and orders of the Court as they are announced from the bench. Some reporters choose to go to the courtroom to hear the justices announce their opinions, while others wait in the press room in order to receive the printed opinions as quickly as possible. On a typical day, the Public Information Office distributes to journalists about one hundred copies of each opinion. These are in the form of bench opinions, which are simply duplicated pages stapled together.

In contrast to the press operations for other government institutions, the Court's Public Information Office makes no effort to interpret the actions of the institution to which it is attached, or to explain anything beyond the purely procedural aspects of the Court's work. Reporters who ask for help in understanding an opinion are referred to the headnotes and the body of the opinion itself.

(See also PRESS ROOM.)

Linda Greenhouse

**Presser v. Illinois,** 116 U.S. 252 (1886), argued 23–24 Nov. 1885, decided 4 Jan. 1886 by vote of 9 to 0; Woods for the Court. In *Presser* v. *Illinois,* the Court sustained an Illinois state statute prohibiting parading with arms by groups other than the organized militia. Herman Presser, who had been convicted of leading armed members of a fraternal organization in a parade, challenged the statute on the grounds that it violated the *Second and *Fourteenth Amendments. The Court's opinion, written by Justice William B. *Woods, rejected Presser's claims holding that the Second Amendment's guarantee of the right to keep and bear arms only applied to the federal government.

Although the opinion in *Presser* is often discussed within the context of the Second Amendment debate, it is probably better viewed as an example of the Court's initial tendency to reject the view that the Fourteenth Amendment applied the *Bill of Rights to the states. The Woods opinion noted that the Illinois statute did not interfere with the right to keep and bear arms and that state governments could not disarm their populations because that would interefere with the federal government's ability to raise a militia from the population at large. Despite this the opinion stressed that the Second Amendment only limited action by the federal government.

The modern validity of the holding *Presser* is unclear in light of the Court's application of most provisions of the Bill of Rights to the states through the Fourteenth Amendment in the twentieth century. It has been relied on by *lower federal courts but has not been revisited by the Supreme Court, which has generally not looked at Second Amendment claims in recent times.

(See also INCORPORATION DOCTRINE.)

Robert J. Cottrol

**Press Room.** Since the Supreme Court building opened in 1935, there has been a press room in roughly the same ground floor location. But the room has expanded and changed over the years as press coverage of the Court has increased and as computer screens have replaced manual typewriters for many of the journalists who work there.

The press room's current appearance dates to a major renovation in 1982, when two rooms were combined to produce an enlarged rectangular space. Seventeen news organizations, including the *New York Times*, the *Wall Street Journal*, the *Washington Post*, and the major television networks, have permanently assigned desks. Fifteen of these are in small carrels defined by movable partitions and furnished with desks and bookcases built in the Court's carpentry shop. In addition, the Associated Press, with two reporters, has its own room with additional filing space. The correspondents for United Press International and the *Baltimore Sun* share a second separate work area.

Reporters without assigned spaces use the two long tables that take up the middle of the room. These reporters usually spend most of their time in their downtown offices, coming to the Court only to listen to an *oral argument or pick up an opinion. In adjoining rooms, a complete set of *briefs and petitions for the current term is available for reporters' use, as is a set of *United States Reports and other basic research materials.

(See also BUILDINGS, SUPREME COURT; PRESS COVERAGE.)

Linda Greenhouse

**Pretrial Publicity and the Gag Rule.** *First Amendment case law has encouraged a vigorous press in American public life. However, a vigorous press may also pose dangers to a criminal defendant's *Sixth Amendment rights to fair trial. Under the Sixth Amendment, a fair trial requires that the judge and jury make their judgment solely on the basis of the evidence introduced in the courtroom. Yet in trials receiving great publicity, "trial by newspaper" may be so complete that the task of securing a jury that has not prejudged the case becomes very difficult. When such publicity clearly threatens the conduct of a fair trial, a fundamental conflict occurs between two constitutional rights—a fair trial and a free press.

Traditionally, the Supreme Court had been reluctant to attempt any control of pretrial publicity. But *Irvin v. Dowd* (1961), and *Sheppard v. Maxwell* (1966)—where the Court reversed criminal convictions because of prejudicial publicity—

contributed to a heightened judicial awareness of the potential dangers of pervasive publicity. This awareness in turn led many trial courts to impose certain controls on the press's reporting of criminal proceedings.

The issuance of "gag orders" restricting the press from reporting certain facts regarding trials constituted one such control. In the wake of *Sheppard*, some trial courts faced with criminal trials attracting much publicity resorted to gag orders against the press. By the mid-1970s, however, gag orders themselves had become a glaring problem and threatened the hard-won freedoms previously secured by the press.

Although the use of gag orders became more frequent after *Sheppard*, the issue of their constitutionality was not addressed by the Supreme Court until *Nebraska Press Association v. Stuart* (1976), where it invalidated a gag order on the grounds that it was an unconstitutional prior restraint on the press. The Court held that such a prior restraint could only be sustained if the prohibited publicity constituted a clear and present danger to the defendant's right to a fair trial. As a result of that decision, gag orders must now be regarded as presumptively unconstitutional.

In *Oklahoma Publishing Co. v. District Court of Oklahoma County* (1977), the Court struck down a gag order restricting the press from publishing the name or picture of a juvenile involved in a delinquency proceeding. The Court held that the press could not be restricted from publishing what it lawfully obtained in open court, even if the courtroom could have been initially closed. Thus, *Nebraska Press* and *Oklahoma Publishing Co.* sounded the death knell for orders restraining publication of information concerning judicial proceedings legally obtained by the press.

Despite the *Nebraska Press* ban, however, trial judges continue to do indirectly what they cannot do directly and have attempted to control prejudicial publicity by curtailing the flow of information to the press. One means of curtailment is the restriction of information divulged by trial participants to the press, a course of action suggested in *Sheppard*. Blocking the flow of certain information to the press received qualified approval in *Seattle Times v. Rhinehart* (1984).

Another means of controlling the media subsequent to *Nebraska Press* was the closure of trial proceedings to the public and press. However, in *Richmond Newspapers, Inc. v. Virginia* (1980), the Court greatly narrowed a judge's ability to close trials and held that the paramount right of public and press to attend criminal trials was guaranteed by the First and *Fourteenth Amendments. *Globe Newspaper Co. v. Superior Court* (1982) made it clear that open trials were the rule, and excluding the public and press from even a portion of a trial the rare exception.

Thus, while the Supreme Court has allowed certain limited and indirect, restrictions on the press and its freedom to report on pending criminal trials—that is, closure of proceedings to be justified on a case-by-case basis, and restrictions on the broadcasting of judicial proceedings—gag orders, now categorized as *prior restraints, are to all intents and purposes prohibited. *First Amendment interests have thus prevailed over fair trial concerns (cf. *Capitol Cities Media, Inc. v. Toole*, 1983).

(See also SPEECH AND THE PRESS.)

Patrick M. Garry

**Prigg v. Pennsylvania,** 16 Pet. (41 U.S.) 539 (1842), argued and decided Jan. 1842 by vote of 8 to 1; Story for the Court, Taney, Thompson, Baldwin, Wayne, and Daniel concurring, McLean in dissent. In 1837, Edward Prigg, a professional slave catcher, seized Margaret Morgan, a runaway slave living in Pennsylvania. Prigg applied to a justice of the peace for certificates of removal under the federal Fugitive Slave Act of 1793 and Pennsylvania's 1826 personal liberty law. The federal law authorized state magistrates to hear cases involving *fugitive slaves. The justice of the peace refused Prigg's request for a certificate of removal. Without any legal authority, Prigg then removed to Maryland Morgan and her children, including one conceived and born in Pennsylvania. Pennsylvania then indicted Prigg for kidnapping under the 1826 state law.

After protracted negotiations, Maryland agreed to extradite Prigg for trial, and Pennsylvania agreed to expedite proceedings so that the case could quickly go to the U.S. Supreme Court so that it might define the power of the states to legislate on the rendition of fugitive slaves.

Speaking for the Court, Justice Joseph *Story held (1) that the federal Fugitive Slave Law of 1793 was constitutional; (2) that Pennsylvania's personal liberty law of 1826 (and by extension all similar laws) unconstitutionally added new requirements to the rendition process; (3), that the Constitution's Fugitive Slave Clause (Art. IV, sec. 2, cl. 3) implied a right of recaption, so that under the clause any slaveowner or his agent could capture a fugitive slave without complying with the federal law of 1793 if such a capture could be done without a breach of the peace; and (4) that all state judges and other officials ought to enforce the federal law but that the national government could not force them to do so because the federal government had no power to require state officials to act.

Story held that all state laws that interfered with the enforcement of the Fugitive Slave Act were unconstitutional. Story based much of his decision on an inaccurate analysis of the intentions of the Philadelphia framers, asserting "that it cannot be doubted that it [the Constitution's Fugitive Slave Clause] constituted a fundamental article, without the adoption of which the Union could not have been formed" (p. 611). In fact, the clause was added quite late in the Constitutional Convention, with almost no debate and little thought.

Chief Justice Roger B. *Taney concurred in the result in *Prigg*, but objected to Story's conclusion that state judges did not have to enforce the Fugitive Slave Act. In his concurrence (which read more like a dissent), Taney misrepresented Story's opinion by claiming that it prohibited state officials from enforcing the Fugitive Slave Act, when in fact Story actually urged state officials to enforce the law but conceded that the federal government had no power to require them to do so. Taney also complained, again erroneously, that Story's opinion prohibited all supplemental legislation on the rendition of fugitive slaves. Story's opinion actually allowed states to enact legislation aiding the rendition process as long as they did not add requirements beyond what the federal law mandated. Taney complained that under Story's opinion fugitive slave rendition would be virtually impossible, because at the time there were so few federal judges to enforce the federal statute. Taney's complaint became a self-fulfilling prophecy, as some northern judges used his characterization of Story's opinion as a justification for not hearing fugitive slave cases, and some state legislatures also prohibited the use of state facilities for fugitive slave rendition.

Story's son claimed that his father's opinion was an antislavery decision because it allowed the free states to withdraw their support for fugitive rendition. In private correspondence, however, Story urged Congress to create federal commissioners to enforce various federal laws, including the 1793 act. In the Fugitive Slave Act of 1850 Congress adopted Story's recommendation. Rather than being an antislavery opinion, Story's effort was actually an attempt to nationalize law, consistent with his opinion from the same term in *Swift v. Tyson* (1842).

(See also COMITY; FEDERALISM; SLAVERY.)

□ Paul Finkelman, "*Prigg v. Pennsylvania* and Northern State Courts: Anti-Slavery Use of a Pro-Slavery Decision," *Civil War History* 25 (March 1979): 5–35.

Paul Finkelman

**Prior Restraint.** The prohibition on prior restraints on speech or press lies at the very core of the *First Amendment. In the American view, prior restraint has been equated with *censorship. Classically, prior restraint constituted a system in which publication of a newspaper or book was illegal unless approved by the government in advance. A further vice of prior restraints was that a government official simply by inaction could prevent publication.

Constitutional historians are nearly unanimous in their conclusion that the framers of the First Amendment intended to codify the English common law as taught by Sir William Blackstone, which banned all prior restraints such as licensing or censorship. In *Near v. Minnesota (1931), the Court ruled that regardless of the nature of speech at issue, and with only limited exceptions an *injunction against publication constitutes an unconstitutional prior restraint. The Court reasoned that as between prior restraints and subsequent sanctions, the former posed a far greater danger because it altogether prevented the speech from entering the "marketplace of ideas."

The Supreme Court again struck down prior restraints in *New York Times Co. v. United States (1971), when it refused to permit the government to enjoin publication of the Pentagon Papers. By resorting to the rule against prior restraint, the Court avoided the issue of whether the classified material qualified as protected speech under the First Amendment. Thus, the Court did not rule that the newspapers could not be prosecuted or sanctioned subsequent to publication.

Despite the Court's longstanding ban on prior restraint, it has carved out a very narrow exception to that ban in the form of *"time, place or manner" regulations of public expression. These regulations govern the type of public expression that interferes with and jeopardizes other valid social interests, such as traffic and crowd control (e.g., *Cox v. New Hampshire, 1941, which upheld a narrowly drawn parade permit statute). However, they cannot be used as a device to censor expression based upon content.

(See also PRETRIAL PUBLICITY AND THE GAG RULE; SPEECH AND THE PRESS.)

Patrick M. Garry

**Prisoners' Rights of Speech.** The U.S. Supreme Court has decided a number of cases involving the free-speech rights of prison inmates to communicate with those on the outside. In *Procunier v. Martinez* (1974), the Court held that the attenuated *First Amendment rights of inmates, coupled with the full free-speech rights of those outside prison who wished to communicate with them, restricted the sort of mail *censorship prison authorities could impose. The Court ruled that censorship would be sustained if it furthered "an important or substantial governmental interst unrelated to the suppression of expression" (p. 413). The Court also held that the regulation must involve an infringement of First Amendment rights "no greater than is necessary or essential to the protection of the particular governmental interest involved" (p. 413). In light of these standards, the California regulations at issue in *Procunier*—which were aimed at suppressing inmate complaints, inflammatory political and other opinions, and obscene materials— were overly broad and thus unconstitutional.

More recently, the Court ruled in *Turner* v. *Safley* (1987) that Missouri prison regulations that prohibited correspondence between inmates at different state prisons were valid. In this case the Court used a lesser standard for review: whether the regulations were "reasonably related to legitimate penological interests" (p. 89).

In *Bell v. Wolfish* (1979), the Court upheld a regulation at the Metropolitan Correction Center in New York City that forbade inmates from receiving hardbound books from sources other that publishers, book clubs, and bookstores. The Court found this rule to be a rational response to the prison security threat posed by hardbound books, which may be used more easily than paperbacks and magazines for smuggling money, drugs, or weapons into prisons.

*Thornburg* v. *Abbott* (1989) sustained Federal Bureau of Prisons regulations allowing inmates to subscribe to or receive periodicals or books without prior approval but also permitting wardens to reject incoming items deemed detrimental to institutional security, order, or discipline on the basis of a nonexhaustive list of criteria contained in the regulations. Procedural safeguards were established in the regulations, but any item excluded was excluded entirely (the "all-or-nothing" rule). These regulations were upheld as being reasonably related to legitimate penological interests; the all-or-nothing rule was not found to be unduly harsh, and the bureau did not have to adopt a less restrictive alternative.

In *Jones v. North Carolina Prisoners' Labor Union* (1977), the Court sustained actions by prison officials that "prohibited inmates from soliciting other inmates to join . . . the North Carolina Prisoners' Labor Union . . . , barred all meetings of the Union, and refused to deliver packets of union publications that had been mailed in bulk to several inmates for redistribution among other prisoners" (p. 121). The Court held that the regulations on which these actions were based were reasonable and therefore constitutional.

In *Pell* v. *Procunier* (1974) the Court upheld a state regulation prohibiting personal interviews between media personnel and individual, named inmates. The Court held that because they had alternative ways of communicating with the media, inmates had no right to face-to-face interviews. The Court held further that the regulation did not abridge the rights of the media because it did not place reporters and other media personnel under greater restrictions than those imposed on the general public. This holding was extended to federal prisons by *Saxbe* v. *Washington Post* (1974).

The principle of *Pell* v. *Procunier* was reaffirmed by *Houchins* v. *KQED* (1978), in which both the public and the press were initially excluded entirely from a prison involved in controversy over conditions in its maximum-security area (the prison later allowed limited public tours of its facility except for the maximum-security area). Thus, despite the First Amendment rights of people on the outside to communicate with inmates (*Procunier v. Martinez*), all that prison officials seem to need to do to exclude the media from contact with inmates is to prohibit contact between inmates and the general public. Under the new standard enunciated by the Court in *Turner* and *Thornburg*, regulations restricting prisoners' contact with the general public need only be reasonably related to a legitimate penological interest.

*Procunier* has been substantially eroded as a precedent, but not because of changes in membership on the Court. After *Procunier*, Justices Warren *Burger, William H. *Rehnquist, Byron *White, and Potter *Stewart (as well as Burger's successor, Antonin *Scalia, and Stewart's replacement, Sandra Day *O'Connor) never again voted favorably on a prisoners' free-speech claim, with the exception of minor portions of cases that basically rejected such claims. Justices Lewis *Powell and Harry *Blackmun provided the swing votes resulting in prisoners losing all their Supreme Court free-speech cases since *Procunier.* (See also SPEECH AND THE PRESS.)

□ Emily Calhoun, "The First Amendment Rights of Prisoners," in *Prisoners' Rights Sourcebook: Theory Litigation Practice,* vol. 2 (1980), pp. 43–65. Ila Jeanne Sensenich, *Compendium of the Law on Prisoners' Rights* (1979). Daryl R. Fair

**Privacy.** As Justice Hugo *Black wrote, " 'Privacy' is a broad, abstract and ambiguous concept" (*Griswold* v. *Connecticut,* 1965, p. 509). Any commentary on the approach taken by the Supreme Court in regard to the notion of "privacy" must begin by acknowledging the truth of Black's insight. There is no simple grouping of cases that allows one to discern a particular doctrine of "privacy" that has been adopted by the justices or that can be easily conveyed. Instead, one discovers that "privacy" and associated words, such as "private," refer to a variety of notions, only loosely linked together, that have proved to be an enduring source of controversy in regard to the degree of constitutional protection afforded them.

*Definitional Dilemmas.* Perhaps the easiest way to demonstrate the protean qualities of the notion of privacy is through reference to some of the standard ways words like "private" and "privacy" are used in ordinary language. Contrast, for example, the quite different implications of the terms "private property" and "invasion of privacy." To be sure, they are related to one another; but they nonetheless point in substantially different directions and have elicited quite different reactions from the Court.

*Privacy and Political Liberalism.* Though the notion of private *property clearly goes back to ancient times, it is especially resonant in the liberal tradition out of which so much American political thought has developed, and it is appropriate to begin by looking at it more closely. The first thing one might notice is that "private" is an adjective. The word "property" is not always preceded by that adjective. The standard contrasting term to "private" is "public," and we often use the term "public property" to refer to property owned by the state, such as roads, parks, and government buildings. The sharp division between "public" and "private" is central to the liberal political tradition, especially as represented in the thought of someone like John Locke, and the term "private property" is central to the maintenance of this division.

What is "public" is, almost by definition, within the realm of government regulation; one of the purposes of governments is to regulate the conditions of public life. Further, one of the central roles of the Constitution is to place limits on what the state can do in the name of the public. Thus the *First Amendment prevents the state from offering public property only to political groups whose views it supports, even though the owner of a private auditorium is free to use political criteria when renting the hall.

The point of terming something "private" is to suggest that it is, in important ways, protected against governmental interference. The strongest defense of government, especially in the more libertarian versions of the Lockean heritage, is to establish certain mechanisms, including police forces and courts for the enforcement of contracts, that will serve to safeguard the basic natural rights of "life, liberty, and property." The basic value underlying the protection of such rights, according to most contemporary political theorists, especially those who come out of one or another version of the Kantian tradition, is *autonomy,* that is, individuals' ability to choose for themselves how to live their lives.

According to those who emphasize individual autonomy, the state should, as much as possible, serve only to facilitate the choices made by private citizens, at least so long as those choices do not conflict with the rights of other individuals. Indeed, many contemporary theorists who reject any Lockean notion of a "natural right" to private property nonetheless support recognition of a legal right to private property on the grounds, as argued by Aristotle nearly twenty-five hundred years ago, that its possession is necessary in order to allow the practical realization of freedom and autonomous choice. Egalitarians might object to a particular distribution of property within which too many poor people are without property and thus without effective means to realize their autonomy, but this distributional critique does not in the least entail a rejection of the basic importance of a realm of "private" rights protected against state negation.

*Defending Minorities.* Emphasis on a protected "private" realm can serve as a way of defending unpopular minorities against the power of a majority tempted to use the apparatus of the state to regulate those it dislikes. Examples are legion, and each probably generates a different emotional resonance in the reader. On the one hand, there are those parents who wish to send their children to a "private" school that teaches the tenets of their religion, against the effort by the state to outlaw such schooling and require every child to attend a "public" school that inculcates in the child the state-mandated way of looking at the world. (Just such an effort was made in the 1920s by the state of Oregon, then under the sway of the Ku Klux Klan, only to be rebuffed by the Supreme Court in *Pierce v. Society of Sisters, 1925.) Or one can think, for example, of a privately owned restaurant that chooses to serve only whites; although a traditional notion of "private property" included the right to exclude anyone from one's property on whatever basis one wished, the Supreme Court had little trouble, in *Heart of Atlanta Motel v. U.S. (1964) and *Katzenbach v. McClung (1964), unanimously upholding the *Civil Rights Act of 1964 and its prohibition of such exclusionary practices (see SEGREGATION, DE JURE). At the very least, these two examples should illustrate not only the complexities attached to notions such as "minority rights" and "majority imposition" but also the varying reactions of the Supreme Court to such claims.

*Privacy versus Secrecy.* One must recognize that there is nothing at all "secretive" about "private" property and many other autonomy-enhancing rights that have been judicially placed within a notion of "privacy." Thus, a property owner often announces his or her status to the world. One can find similar examples in other realms. Most religious people, for example, are proud to proclaim their allegiance to their faiths' tenets. No one reads the Free Exercise Clause of the *First Amendment as protecting only "out-of-sight" religious practices. To be sure, even such limited protection would be better than the totalitarian denial of all freedom of religion, but the basic cases in the constitutional canon treating freedom of religion all deal with "public" practices, such as handing out religious literature or even vigorously attacking the "false doctrines" of another church deemed to represent the forces of evil (see also RELIGION).

In this context, it is useful to consider the institution of *marriage. Even though many might consider marriage to be the most obvious symbol of private life, most people who marry proclaim their status publicly. As shall be discussed further in this essay's conclusion, problems arise when one tries to define notions such as property or marriage as "private" rather than "public," but it should at least be clear that there is no necessary linkage between assigning a particular activity—whether it has to do with land development or love—to the realm of the "private" and viewing that activity as something to be kept out of the public eye.

This element of secrecy, however, is precisely what is important in the concept of "invasion of privacy." To be sure, one cannot make sense even of this notion without recourse both to the value of autonomy and to some version of the public-private distinction noted above. The "privacy" protected against invasion, however, relies for its force not so much on the formal distinction between the domains of the individual and of the state but rather on a widely shared perception that some aspects of life should be protected not only against public regulation but, far more importantly, against uninvited public observation. The definition of a secret suggests that one should be able to disclose it only to those one trusts. A standard example is the release of what is often termed "intimate" information about oneself. Thus the marital partners who invite the public to observe their exchange of vows certainly do not invite the guests to witness the sexual consummation of those vows.

These are not meant to be hard-and-fast distinctions. But they are intended to aid the understanding of the very different meanings attached to the overall concept of privacy and, as well, to the understanding of why the cases decided by the Supreme Court under that rubric often seem so confusing. The Court, over the last twenty years, has used the notion of privacy especially, but not exclusively, in cases involving *contraception, *abortion, and *homosexuality. If one realizes that such cases much more often involve privacy-as-autonomy—a realm of conduct protected against invasive state regulation—rather than privacy-as-secrecy—a realm of life that should be protected against the intrusive observation of others—then at least some of the confusion can be dissolved. The remainder of this essay will therefore be organized by reference to these two quite different conceptions of privacy.

*Autonomous Choice.* Although it is commonly argued that the Constitution lacks any specific textual reference to "privacy," that argument overlooks the text of the *Fifth Amendment, which states that "private property [shall not] be taken for public use, without just compensation." The text makes no sense unless the framers of the Constitution believed, first, that the institution of private property already existed and, second, that there was something important about this institution worth protecting. That is, private property had a purpose, the most plausible purpose being that possessing private property helps one to become the master of one's own fate.

It is within this context that one should understand "The New Property," an influential 1965 article by then–Yale professor Charles Reich, which argues that the same kinds of constitutional protections accorded "old property," such as land, should be accorded "new property," such as social security, because of the latter's equally vital role in preserving individual autonomy. The deep paradox of Reich's article, however, lies precisely in the fact that the Supreme Court, throughout the twentieth century but especially following the so-called constitutional revolution of 1937, has been increasingly disinclined to give strong protection to the "old property" against state regulation. Among the seminal cases in this regard is *Euclid v. Ambler Realty Co. (1926), in which the conservative Justice George *Sutherland, speaking for the Court, upheld a local *zoning ordinance that severely restricted the development opportunities available to landowners. Although such zoning significantly reduced the practical market value of the land in question, it was deemed not to be a *taking requiring compensation under the Fifth Amendment, which had been applied to the states through the *Fourteenth Amendment.

*Regulation of Private Property.* Certainly one of the central characteristics of what has come to be called the modern regulatory, or *administrative, state is its propensity to regulate the use of "private" property. The post-1937 Court has expressed almost no concern about the constitutionality of such regulation. Only a few, exceptional cases have found regulations to constitute takings that require compensation (see REGULATORY TAKING). For better or worse, the protection of private property and the values attached to its ownership has increasingly been left to the vagaries of the ordinary political process, with judicial scrutiny limited to a bare minimum.

Post-1937 constitutional theorists, then, were left with the task of explaining the withdrawal of any strong judicial regard for private property. Did it result from a general notion that the Court, as an arguably undemocratic (or at least antimajoritarian) institution, should defer to legislative decisions? Or, on the other hand, was it the consequence of a more limited notion—that the protection of private property, far from enhancing individual autonomy, tended to lessen it insofar as it served to prevent the redistribution of economic resources from those who had a great deal (and thus maximum autonomy) to those who had too little (and thus little, if any, practical autonomy)? Post–New Deal constitutional theorists could be divided broadly into two camps, depending on which of these two rationales were emphasized to justify the diminution of protection given to traditional rights attached to the ownership of private property. These camps faced-off when "privacy" reemerged as a major topic of litigation in the 1960s.

*Contraception.* The modern debate about the constitutional protection accorded privacy derives from *Griswold v. Connecticut (1965). In *Griswold* the Court declared unconstitutional a Connecticut law that both prohibited the use of contraceptives and prevented anyone from encouraging the use of contraceptives through, for example, medical counseling. Connecticut prosecuted the executive director of the Planned Parenthood League for giving information to married persons about contraception. The Supreme Court, in an opinion by Justice William O. *Douglas, reversed Mrs. Griswold's conviction

on the basis that it violated her (and her clinic's patients') rights of privacy. Ignoring the Private Property Clause of the Fifth Amendment, Douglas noted that a general right of privacy is nowhere explicitly set out in the constitutional text, in contrast, say, to the right to free exercise of religion acknowledged in the First Amendment or the right against *self-incrimination set out in the Fifth Amendment. But, said Douglas, the real point of many of the "various guarantees" of the Constitution was precisely to "create zones of privacy" protected against state interference (p. 484).

Douglas pointed to cases interpreting the First Amendment, which had recognized the "freedom to associate and privacy in one's association"; to the *Third Amendment, which prohibits the quartering of soldiers "in any house" in time of peace without the owner's consent; to the *Fourth Amendment and its explicit affirmation of the "right of the people to be secure in their persons, houses, papers, and effects, against unreasonable searches and seizures"; and to the Fifth Amendment's Self-Incrimination Clause (p. 483). Douglas also took note of several cases from the 1920s involving private *education. In 1923 the Court, in *Meyer v. Nebraska, had invalidated a state ban (sparked by anti-German feeling during *World War I) on teaching German in private schools. Two years later, in *Pierce v. Society of Sisters,* the Court struck down Oregon's Klan-inspired attempt to prohibit private schooling entirely.

Similarly, Douglas said, Connecticut's law could not survive, for it "concern[ed] a relationship lying within the zone of privacy created by several fundamental constitutional guarantees" (p. 485). In particular, it attempted to regulate one of the most intimate aspects of marriage—the circumstances under which the partners would relate to one another sexually. To prosecute someone for violating Connecticut's "use" prohibition would require extraordinary state intrusiveness. "Would we allow the police," Douglas asked rhetorically, "to search the sacred precincts of marital bedrooms for telltale signs of the use of contraceptives?" He responded, "The very idea is repulsive to the notions of privacy surrounding the marriage relationship" (pp. 485–486).

*Griswold* was a surprisingly controversial decision, though not, certainly, because of any judicial sympathy with what one dissenter, Justice Potter *Stewart, called "an uncommonly silly law." Instead, for the dissenters, Hugo Black especially, the decision recalled an earlier era of the Court in which it used similar concepts, though denominated "freedom of *contract" rather than "privacy," to carve out a protected realm of conduct against almost any regulation by the state. This earlier era was symbolized by the decision in *Lochner v. New York (1905), in which the Court interpreted the Due Process

Clause of the Fourteenth Amendment to hold unconstitutional a New York state law that attempted to limit to sixty the hours that a baker could work each week. According to the five-justice majority in *Lochner*, this statute unconstitutionally interfered with the autonomy rights of the baker *and* his employee to negotiate as equals over the terms of employment.

*Lochner* occasioned perhaps the most-quoted dissenting opinion in American judicial history, by Justice Oliver Wendell *Holmes:

I think that the Fourteenth Amendment is perverted when it is held to prevent the natural outcome of a dominant opinion, unless it can be said that a rational and fair man necessarily would admit that the statute proposed would infringe fundamental principles as they have been understood by the traditions of our people and our law. (p. 76)

An entire generation of scholars and lawyers used Holmes's opinion almost as an anthem in behalf of judicial deference to majority rule and as a rejection of the doctrine of substantive *due process. To be sure, Justice Black, who dissented in *Griswold*, vigorously opposed state regulation of *speech, but he based this philosophy of judicial overruling of majority will on the specific text of the First Amendment, as applied to the states through the Fourteenth Amendment (see INCORPORATION DOCTRINE). "I like my privacy as well as the next one," wrote Black, "but I am nevertheless compelled to admit that government has a right to invade it unless prohibited by some specific constitutional provision" (p. 510). Black was squarely in the camp of those who viewed the message of 1937 as counseling general deference to legislative enactments unless explicitly prohibited by the constitutional text. *Griswold* was in his judgment as pernicious a decision as *Lochner*.

That *Griswold* and successor cases were written using the language of "privacy" was due primarily to the desire to avoid direct comparison with *Lochner*. These cases could have been decided using a different rhetoric, one more self-consciously libertarian and focusing on the centrality of such decisions in achieving one's own life plans. What prevented the use of such a neolibertarian rhetoric was much less its intellectual deficiency than its evocation of the earlier era of *Lochner*, based as that case was on a highly libertarian conception of the limits of government. Thus Holmes had reminded his colleagues that the "Fourteenth Amendment does not enact Mr. Herbert Spencer's Social Statics" (p. 75); Spencer's book was one of the most libertarian tracts of the nineteenth century. Given the bad repute of such overtly libertarian rhetoric, the Court was attracted to the purportedly different rhetoric of privacy. Because of the way legal argument operates, "privacy" became the catchword for a host of cases that would be better understood had they been analyzed under a more frankly libertarian, autonomy-oriented theory.

Regardless of this rhetorical point, it is fair to say that if the "right to privacy" had been confined to the circumstances of the Connecticut contraceptive ban, it is unlikely that the notion would have become particularly important, except among specialists in constitutional law: Connecticut was in fact the last state to ban contraceptives. Moreover, *Griswold* could have been fit within what were termed above the "invasion of privacy" cases designed to protect certain conduct, in this instance the use of contraceptives, from public gaze. The issue in *Griswold* could have been confined either to the prohibition of the "use" of contraceptives or to use plus the giving of relevant medical advice, in order to protect institutions like Planned Parenthood. Moreover, one could have maintained the emphasis on the particular circumstances under which contraceptives are in fact used, thus accounting for the power of Douglas's reference to the "sacred" marital bedroom.

It is worth noting, however, that no one seriously argues that the police are without power, assuming they have the *probable cause required by the Fourth Amendment to obtain a search warrant, to search "sacred" bedrooms for evidence of ordinary crime. A thief would not purchase immunity from search, for example, by hiding the loot under the sacred marital mattress! The fact that most of Douglas's examples are open to this kind of attack has led many observers to criticize his opinion, as least insofar as he attempted to derive the "right of privacy" from what he called the "penumbras and emanations" of the text of the *Bill of Rights.

Although Douglas's opinion was joined by a majority of the Court, two important separate concurring opinions, written by Justices Arthur *Goldberg and John M. *Harlan, attempted to sketch out other bases for the "right to privacy." Harlan alluded to an opinion he had written in an earlier case, *Poe v. Ullman* (1961), in which the Court had refused to address the legitimacy of the Connecticut law it struck down in *Griswold*. In *Poe*, Harlan had emphasized that the Due Process Clause of the Fourteenth Amendment legitimizes the Court's attempt to discern "the balance which our Nation, built upon postulates of respect for the liberty of the individual, has struck between that liberty and the demands of organized society" (p. 542). Examining the American (and, indeed, English-speaking) past, Harlan concluded that the Connecticut law "involves what, by common understanding throughout the English-speaking world, must be granted to a most fundamental aspect of [liberty,] the privacy of the home in its most basic sense" (p. 548). Goldberg focused attention on the *Ninth Amendment, with its reminder that the specification of certain enumerated rights in the Bill of Rights should not be interpreted as "disparaging" the existence of additional, unenumerated rights. Privacy, Goldberg argued, was just such a right—one that should be understood as being protected by the Constitution even though unenumerated.

In any event, *Griswold* did not remain an isolated case, and its import soon extended far beyond Harlan's "privacy of the home" or the particularity of the "sacred" marital relationship. The Court, in *Eisenstadt* v. *Baird* (1972), struck down a variety of state prohibitions on the sale or distribution of contraceptives first to single adults and then, five years later, invalidated, in *Carey* v. *Population Services International*, a New York law prohibiting the sale of contraceptives to minors under sixteen and forbidding anyone not a licensed pharmacist from selling even nonprescription contraceptives to persons of any age. As suggested above in the discussion about "private property," there is nothing secret about offering contraceptives for sale, much less advertising them. Once again, it is crucial that one separate the kind of privacy interest that is being protected in access-to-contraception cases—enhancement of individual autonomy—from the different aspect of privacy organized around the notion of secrecy. But even the liberation of contraceptives from state control would scarcely have caused significant public controversy, given the great changes that were taking place in sexual behavior and the use of contraceptives by a majority of the American public.

*Abortion.* The case that brought "privacy" to the forefront of national consciousness was *Roe* v. *Wade* (1973), which struck down laws in all fifty states that prohibited most (and in some cases all) abortions. "The right of privacy," Justice Harry *Blackmun wrote in behalf of the Court, "whether it be founded in the Fourteenth Amendment's concept of personal liberty . . . or . . . in the Ninth Amendment's reservation of rights to the people, is broad enough to encompass a woman's decision whether or not to terminate her pregnancy" (p. 153). To be sure, even this important "right of personal privacy" could be curbed by the state if it presented a "compelling interest," but the import of *Roe*, with some exceptions, has been to limit such state power. *Roe* is surely on anyone's list of most-important opinions, both in terms of the changes it brought to American life and the controversy it stirred up. Although it did not, as *Dred *Scott* v. *Sandford* (1857) was alleged to have done, spark a civil war, it almost certainly contributed, because of the identification of the antiabortion position with right-wing politics, to the defeat of many Democratic senators in 1976 and 1978, the capture of the presidency and the Senate by the Republican party two years later, and to the ultimate defeat of the Equal Rights Amendment.

Once again, it should be clear that abortion is centrally linked with autonomy concerning the conditions of one's life—thus the adoption of the term "prochoice" by its adherents. Many persons read the sequence of cases from *Griswold* to *Roe* as supporting, under the rubric of "privacy," a general right to what might be termed "sexual autonomy," that is, freedom of choice in regard to one's sexual identity, including its reproductive aspects.

*Homosexuality.* This claim of a right of sexual autonomy was most dramatically tested in the 1986 case *Bowers* v. *Hardwick*, which involved an attack by a gay Georgia man upon a state law that criminalized sodomy. A bitterly divided Court upheld, by a 5-to-4 vote, the constitutionality of the law. Justice Byron *White, who wrote the majority opinion, declared that the right to privacy encompassed by the Constitution did not include a right to engage in "homosexual sodomy." (His opinion ostentatiously refused to indicate whether the Constitution would tolerate the criminalization of heterosexual sodomy— with sodomy defined as including oral sex— which is apparently practiced by many Americans, including married couples.)

Although *Bowers* concerned bedroom conduct, what was ultimately at stake in the case was the integration of gays and lesbians into all aspects of American public life. Thus, had the decision gone the other way, it might have been increasingly difficult to maintain the prohibition of gay and lesbian marriage, for example, and other "public" acts that would signify the true emergence of gays and lesbians from the closets to which the American legal order has tended to condemn them. Although Justice Lewis *Powell, who provided the crucial fifth vote upholding the Georgia law, declared after his retirement that he regarded the decision as a mistake, it is highly unlikely, given the appointees to the Supreme Court following the resignations of Justices Powell, William J. *Brennan, and Thurgood *Marshall, that *Bowers* will be overruled. The issue, however, continues to percolate in a variety of contexts. These include debate over the ban by the armed forces on service by gays and lesbians in spite of Pentagon studies indicating that homosexuals often have service records better than those of heterosexuals.

Moreover, it is certainly not unthinkable that *Roe* itself will be overruled, though there appears to be no serious support for overruling *Griswold*. As has already been suggested, however, limiting the constitutionally protected right to privacy (as autonomy) to the use of contraceptives would scarcely be of any great significance so far as the general public is concerned. In any event, in the early 1990s it is hard to imagine that there will be any great extensions of this branch of the right to privacy in the foreseeable future.

*Information Control.* In a highly influential 1968 article, Harvard professor (and later solicitor general) Charles Fried offered the definition of privacy as "the *control* we have over information about ourselves." Fried related such control to central aspects of our lives as flourishing human beings, including "love and friendship." Although a rich philosophical literature on privacy exists and not everyone accepts Fried's specific views, there is certainly general agreement—and not only among philosophers—that a central component of privacy is precisely the capacity to maintain aspects of one's life apart from public awareness.

*Lack of Constitutional Foundation.* Although there may be widespread agreement that a decent society is one in which individuals possess significant control over the release of information about themselves, it is difficult to find much protection for such a right in the Constitution, at least as it has been interpreted by the Supreme Court. As Lucas Powe has written, "Privacy has never done as well in the courts as in the legal journals."

Consider in this context the constitutional tests most often cited by proponents of privacy, the Fourth and Fifth Amendments. Recall the Fourth Amendment's protection of the "right of the people to be secure in their persons, houses, papers, and effects," and the Fifth Amendment's prohibition of any person's being "compelled in any criminal case to be a witness against himself," both of which were quoted by Douglas in his *Griswold* opinion. As suggested above, though, these texts can as easily cut against proponents of privacy as work in their favor.

The Fourth Amendment, for all its evocation of the privacy of the home, nonetheless clearly allows searches of the home and the seizure of private papers so long as a search warrant has been issued, based on probable cause to believe that the search will provide evidence relevant to a criminal investigation. And warrants can serve as the predicate not only for invasions of marital bedrooms but also for tapping telephones or emplacing other hearing devices that allow the investigator to overhear the most intimate of conversations.

*Limits on Privacy.* In a series of cases during the mid-1960s, the most important of which, *Hoffa v. United States* (1966), involved a prosecution of Teamsters' Union leader Jimmy Hoffa, the Court refused even to require a warrant for the infiltration of "private space" by undercover investigators (see SEARCH WARRANT RULE, EXCEPTIONS TO). Thus it is perfectly constitutional for the state, without the slightest showing of probable cause, to use agents to insinuate themselves into the "private lives" of targets such as Hoffa. According to the Court, we are all at risk that those we choose to welcome into our private domain will later prove untrustworthy, and therefore we deserve no special protection against the possibility that a new "friend" might in fact be a member of the secret police. It should thus come as no surprise that the Court, in *United States* v. *Miller* (1976), refused to place any Fourth Amendment barriers in the way of state investigators who wished access to the "private" bank records of persons they were investigating.

Similarly, in *Ullman* v. *United States* (1956) and *Kastigar* v. *United States* (1972), the Court read the Fifth Amendment guarantee against self-incrimination as being limited to the prohibition of compelled testimony that could later be used as evidence in a prosecution of the witness being compelled to testify. The Court ruled that this did not limit the right of a state to confer an often unwanted "immunity" on a witness—an immunity that promises that nothing said by the witness will later be used against him or her. A beneficiary of such immunity will receive no judicial support for the claim that this violation of his or her ability to control the release of information constitutes a violation of whatever "privacy" rights are implied in the Fifth Amendment. Thus witnesses can be asked the most embarrassing and intrusive questions, so long as they are relevant to the case at hand, and can be punished for contempt of court if they refuse to answer. (The best-known examples of such immunity grants have arisen in congressional investigations, where refusal to testify has led to citation for contempt of Congress; see CONGRESSIONAL POWER OF INVESTIGATION).

Many critics of "immunity baths" adopt Douglas's view that they violate the right to privacy ostensibly protected by the Fifth Amendment, but these critics have not prevailed. Instead, the Court has defined the purpose of the Fifth Amendment as safeguarding individual autonomy by limiting the state's incentive to "solve" crimes not through independent investigation but through the far easier means of forcing, through torture or other mistreatment, accused defendants to confess to crimes that they may not have committed. Since, by definition, testimony given under immunity cannot lead to convictions, the state must still pursue its own investigations and gather independent evidence in order to convict those who have received immunity.

Close associates of criminal defendants, including, on occasion, close family members, are common sources of independent evidence. Although the state often recognizes certain "testimonial privileges" by which specific confidential communications can be protected against disclosure, it is highly debatable whether these privileges are constitutionally required or are instead simply granted by the state (perhaps in recognition of the moral claims articulated by Fried). Probably the most common examples of such privileges are those between lawyer and client and between spouses. In most contexts, a client does control the release of information and can prohibit his or her attorney from disclosing even information crucial to the interests of third parties. Similarly, many states still allow a defendant to prevent the introduction of testimony offered by even a willing spouse (or, often, ex-spouse) that refers to confidential communications made during the course of the marriage. But no such protection extends to close friends or other family members, although some judges have read *Griswold* as protecting a child who does not wish to testify against a parent, or vice versa.

*News Media.* The examples above involve the state's attempts to elicit information, but what about the equally common circumstance in which a private party investigates someone or discloses conduct that that other person would wish to keep secret? Does the Constitution allow strong protection against such invasions of privacy?

Given the complexities of the American legal system, it is hard to offer any summary answer, but it can be said that the Supreme Court has offered scant comfort to those who have brought suit claiming such "invasions." The most common cases have involved newspapers that have published truthful, albeit highly intrusive, information about the suing party. (The publication of false information would constitute not invasion of privacy but "defamation" and would be handled through the law of *libel.)

Standard issues in cases involving claimed invasions of privacy include printing the names of victims of sexual assaults or of juvenile offenders who, some think, are more likely to reform if not publicly stigmatized as delinquents. No matter how much sympathy such claimants may elicit, they have consistently lost before the Supreme Court, which has repeatedly declared that the First Amendment prevents sanctioning newspapers who publish such information. Thus, in *Florida Star* v. *B.J.F.* (1989), the Court set aside an award of monetary damages for the publication of the name of a rape victim because the newspaper had obtained the information by looking at government records. (The Court has refused to accept the argument that there is a difference between making information available to members of the public who are able to travel to a specific locale—such as City Hall—and publishing identical information in a newspaper read by many thousands of readers.)

Newspapers have been awarded protection not simply because of the text of the First Amendment but, more importantly, because of the recognition that it is often impossible to draw any clear lines between those secrets that one should be entitled to keep and those that are of legitimate interest to the public. Consider in this context the *Miami Herald*'s trailing, in 1987, of then–presidential candidate Gary Hart, a married man who had recently denied that he was a "womanizer," to his Georgetown townhouse in the company of Donna Rice, a woman who was not his wife. Though debate raged concerning the ethics of the *Herald*'s conduct in placing one of its reporters in the bushes outside Hart's home, few people argued that the information gained thereby was irrelevant to the public interest, or that it spoke merely to the public's prurient interest, or that the newspaper had no right to publish it.

It is clear that the Constitution protects newspapers that publish truthful information, however "private," about "public figures"—including candidates for office. Whether or not such figures entirely surrender any "right to privacy" they might otherwise have, as a practical matter newspapers and other media need not worry that they will face legal sanctions if they reveal indelicate truths. No Supreme Court decision supports privacy claims of public figures seeking political office who object to the disclosure of information that some voter might find relevant to their fitness to serve in office. Recognition of any such privacy rights would disserve the democratic process itself by depriving the public of salient information. "[T]he candidate who vaunts his spotless record and sterling integrity," Chief Justice William H. *Rehnquist has reiterated, "cannot convincingly cry 'Foul' when an opponent or an industrious reporter attempts to demonstrate the contrary," even if the demonstration involves scrutiny of what might be regarded as one's "private" life (*Hustler Magazine* v. *Falwell*, 1988, pp. 46, 51, quoting from *Monitor Patriot Co.* v. *Roy*, 1971).

The practical loss of privacy rights by public officials turns out also to extend, by and large, to ordinary people, at least if one looks at most of the decided case law. A famous case from half a century ago is exemplary: *The New Yorker* profiled a former child prodigy in a manner described by a state court as "merciless in its dissection of intimate details of subject's personal life" and a "ruthless exposure of a once public character who has since sought . . . the seclusion of private life" (*Sidis* v. *F-R Publishing Co.*, 2d Circuit, 1940, pp. 806–807). It would be hard to imagine a more sympathetic setting for recognition of a right against invasion of privacy, but even here the magazine was protected because of the "newsworthiness" of the subject. "Newsworthiness" is largely a circular term, standing for public curiosity that may itself be provoked by the newspaper's dredging up material from the past. (It is unlikely, for example, that any of *The New Yorker*'s readers had been curious about Mr. Sidis, the ex-prodigy, or had written demanding that the magazine find out what had happened to him.)

That there seems to be little constitutional protection of privacy-as-information-control does not, obviously, negate the force of Fried's argument. It simply points out the Constitution's limited scope. Privacy could be protected in many ways through legislative enactments (though such laws might run into constitutional problems if they attempted to limit the power of the press), but the point is that such privacy rights have come to be viewed as matters for legislative decision-making rather than judicial determination.

*Privacy as a Public Matter.* It is tempting to believe, and the discussion of property began by assuming, that there is a clear demarcation between the realms of "public" and "private." But even the brief discussion of the constitutional revolution of 1937 should illustrate how much the two are intertwined. As pointed out by theorists identified with "legal realism" or "critical legal studies," such as Morris R. Cohen and Robert Hale in the past or Gary Peller in the present, what is conceptualized as "private" is the result of an essentially public decision. Even to think of "private property," for example, requires one to think at the same time of a completely public realm of law that recognizes (and some would say establishes) an assignment of legal rights, to be protected by public force if need be, to certain people who will be called the "owners" of private property. And one of the central meanings of "1937" as a crucial event in American constitutional law is that these assignments are subject to significant changes, as the owners of private businesses discover that they can legitimately be forced, under certain circumstances, to bargain with trade unions or to sell to customers they would prefer not to deal with. To put it mildly, contemporary expectations as to the meaning of private property differ radically from those likely to have been held by property owners a hundred years ago, and there is no reason to believe that private property will have the same social meaning a hundred years from now.

This point can perhaps be made most clearly by reference to a case that explicitly turns on the notion of "expectations." In *Katz* v. *United States* (1967), the Court extended the Fourth Amendment's warrant requirement to wiretaps of telephone conversations; American citizens, the majority declared, had a "legitimate expectation" that their conversations would remain private, and violation of this expectation would require the demonstration of probable cause necessary to get a search warrant. As many commentators noted then and since, the Court was not entirely clear about the foundation of the "expectations" that were so important to its decision. Could the government, for example, defeat any such expectations by announcing that no one should, as a practical matter, expect a telephone conversation to be free of being overheard by third parties? Perhaps "expectation" refers instead to what most people believe ought to be the case about their privacy rights, so that the hypothetical government announcement could be defeated by showing that most people do have the expectation suggested and would be outraged if the government began promiscuously to listen to its citizen's telephone conversations. But what if public opinion changes? Consider the widespread calls for drug tests and tests for the HIV (AIDS) virus, which many view as significant invasions of privacy and presumptively unconstitutional without some showing of specific probable cause. The Court, in two 1989 cases (*National Treasury Employees Union* v. *Von Raab*, which dealt with customs agents, and *Skinner* v. *Railway Labor Executives Association*, which involved railroad engineers), upheld drug tests even without such probable cause. In both cases the Court focused on specific reasons to be especially concerned about the use of drugs by persons in such occupations.

If, however, the public in general comes to believe that the "war on drugs" requires, say, the frequent submission of urine samples, by America's more than fifteen million public employees, could one then speak of an "expectation" against such governmental intrusion? No one believes that an individual's idiosyncratic expectation should automatically be recognized. Inevitably, one discovers that the individual's right of privacy depends on a complex set of social interactions that defeat any easy separation of the public and the private. To the extent that "the public" continues to expect a strong recognition of a "private" realm cut off from ordinary public gaze, that realm will be protected; to the extent that, as with the "traditional" indices of private property, recognition of the claimed privacy right is thought to be too socially costly, then "privacy" will in all likelihood be redefined to exclude the too socially burdensome aspect.

American constitutional jurisprudence is deeply embedded in the liberal political tradition. This assures that the public-private distinction will continue to be a central part of our constitutional schema. There will always be a constitutional "right to privacy," whoever the members of the Supreme Court might be or whatever the particular intellectual trends of a given political moment. But its meaning and scope will always be in flux.

(See also FUNDAMENTAL RIGHTS; NATURAL LAW.)

□ Ruth Gavison, "Privacy and the Limits of Law," *Yale Law Journal* 89 (1980): 421–471. Jennifer Nedelsky, *Private Property and American Constitutionalism* (1990). Ellen Frankel Paul and Howard Dickman, eds., *Liberty, Property, and Government: Constitutional Interpretation Before the New Deal* (1989). J. Roland Pennock and John W. Chapman, eds., *Nomos XIII: Privacy* (1971). Alan Ryan, *Property and Political Theory* (1984). Ferdinand Schoeman, ed., *Philosophical Dimensions of Privacy* (1984). William B. Scott, *In Pursuit of Happiness: American Conceptions of Property from the Seventeenth to the Twentieth Century* (1977). Alan Westin, *Privacy and Freedom* (1967).

Sanford Levinson

**Private Corporation Charters.** A corporate charter, issued by a state or the federal government, authorizes a group of persons to be treated as a single entity for the purpose of operating a business, church, school, hospital, or municipality. In the nineteenth century, some charters also granted tax exemptions, the power of *eminent domain, limited liability for stockholders, *public land, or other assistance.

During the nineteenth century, the authority of state legislatures to regulate corporations was much debated. In *Dartmouth College v. Woodward (1819), the Supreme Court declared that the charter of a private corporation was protected by the *Contracts Clause of the Constitution (Art. I, sec. 10, cl. 1) from arbitrary state legislative amendment or repeal. The Dartmouth College doctrine limited state legislative control of both business and private nonprofit corporations.

The protection afforded private corporations by the Dartmouth College doctrine was never complete. In *Charles River Bridge v. Warren Bridge (1837), the Court held that the charter of a private corporation should be construed strictly against the corporation. The Court further declared that states retained substantial authority to protect the public health, safety, and welfare (see POLICE POWER). Finally, some states expressly reserved power to alter or repeal corporate charters, although the scope of the reserved power was never fully decided.

In the twentieth century, the charter has not been central to the constitutional law of private corporations. Rather, the Supreme Court has addressed issues of state governmental control of private institutions principally through substantive *due process doctrines under the *Fourteenth Amendment.

(See also CAPITALISM; CORPORATIONS.)

Bruce A. Campbell

**Private Discriminatory Associations.** In *Shelley v. Kraemer (1948) the Supreme Court ruled that state judicial enforcement of private restrictive housing covenants based on race or color was impermissible *state action in violation of the *Fourteenth Amendment (see RESTRICTIVE COVENANTS). In 1972, well after the dawn of the *civil rights movement, the scope of Shelley was limited in *Moose Lodge No. 107 v. Irvis. The Court held that Pennsylvania's licensing of the sale of liquor in a private club was insufficient "state action" to trigger Fourteenth Amendment review. The Court did, however, recognize that the line between conduct that is wholly private and conduct that may implicate the "state action" doctrine is often difficult to draw.

For many years, civil rights activists viewed Moose Lodge as an impenetrable barrier to attacks on private discriminatory associations and clubs. But as more and more women began to enter the work force, they began to view their exclusion from such clubs and associations as discrimination interfering with career advancement. This was particularly true of exclusion from associations that were routinely used by men as a means of promoting business opportunities.

The first kind of private discriminatory associations that came under judicial attack were large, all-male groups like the Rotary Clubs of America

and the United States Jaycees, both of which had African-American members. *Roberts v. United States Jaycees (1984) was the first of these cases to reach the high court. In 1978, the U.S. Jaycees notified two Minnesota chapters that had admitted women as members in violation of national policy that their charters would be revoked. The chapters then filed charges of discrimination with the Minnesota Department of Human Rights, alleging that the exclusion of women violated the Minnesota Human Rights Act. The Minnesota law prohibits discrimination on the basis of sex by businesses offering goods or services to the public.

The national Jaycees attempted to redefine the issue as one of freedom of association protected by the *First Amendment (see ASSEMBLY AND ASSOCIATION, FREEDOM OF). In weighing the nature of the First Amendment rights asserted against a state's right to prevent gender-based discrimination against its residents, the Supreme Court ruled that the state could bar certain private clubs from discriminating. Although the First Amendment clearly protects family relationships and small groups, which the Court labeled "intimate associational freedom," "large business enterprises" like the Jaycees were considered "remote . . . from this constitutional protection" because they involved only "expressive" associations (p. 620). The large and unselective nature of the Jaycees was held to bar its reliance on First Amendment grounds to rationalize its discrimination against women.

This standard was reiterated in Board of Directors of Rotary International v. Rotary Club of Duarte (1987). There the Court held that the Rotary's exclusion of female members did not warrant protection "in light of the potentially large size of local clubs, the high turnover rate among club members, the inclusive nature of each club's membership, the public purposes behind clubs' service activities, and the fact that the clubs encourage the participation of strangers in, and welcome media coverage of, many of their central activities" (pp. 537–538).

The Court again addressed this issue in *New York State Club Association v. City of New York (1988). New York City's Human Rights Law prohibited discrimination based on race, creed, sex and other grounds in any place of public accommodation, but specifically exempted private organization. A 1984 amendment, however, provided that a club was not to be considered private if it had more than four hundred members and provided regular meal service. Fraternal and religious organizations were excluded. A consortium of 125 private clubs sued on First and Fourteenth Amendment grounds. Again, the Court rejected the First Amendment claim.

These decisions have encouraged a growing number of states and local governments to ban discrimination in private clubs that meet the Rotary standard. Pressure on discriminatory clubs also has come from other sources. As early as 1984 the American Bar Association revised its Code of Judicial Ethics to state that it was inappropriate for a judge to belong to any organization that practices discrimination on account of race, sex, religion, or national origin. In 1990, the United States Senate began hearings on a nonbinding resolution that membership in such clubs would be "inappropriate" for prospective nominees to the federal judiciary and the Justice Department. Even more potentially potent in the arsenal against the tradition of discriminatory private clubs are the plethora of recently proposed or adopted municipal ordinances that are aimed to force more selective private clubs to admit women and African-Americans or lose their liquor licenses, an approach not required but also not foreclosed by *Moose Lodge*.

(See also GENDER.)

Karen O'Connor

**Privileges and Immunities.** Two provisions in the Constitution protect the "privileges and immunities" of American citizens. The first is Article IV, section 2, which provides that "[t]he Citizens of each State shall be entitled to all Privileges and Immunities of Citizens in the several states." While "privileges and immunities" are not defined, the idea that states could not discriminate against citizens of other states was regarded by Alexander *Hamilton as "the basis of the Union" (*The *Federalist*, no. 78).

The earliest interpretation of this provision was given by Justice Bushrod *Washington on circuit in *Corfield* v. *Coryell* (1823). A New Jersey statute prohibited any person not a resident of the state from gathering oysters in the state's waters. Washington asserted that the statute did not violate privileges and immunities because that clause protected only those privileges and immunities "which are, in their nature, fundamental; which belong, of right, to the citizens of all free governments"—for example, "the right to institute and maintain court actions." Oyster gathering was not such a right (see FUNDAMENTAL RIGHTS).

The Supreme Court, however, has rejected this "natural rights" conception of the Privileges and Immunities Clause (see NATURAL LAW). The Court has interpreted it simply to require substantial justification for state laws discriminating against persons from other states. Thus in *Toomer* v. *Witsell* (1948) the Court struck down discriminatory license fees for out-of-state shrimp fishermen in South Carolina waters. Justice William J. *Brennan wrote: "A state's unequal treatment of nonresidents [must] be reasoned and suitably tailored." A Georgia law that allowed only residents of the state to obtain *abortions in Georgia was struck down in *Doe* v. *Bolton* (1973). *Hicklin* v. *Orbeck* (1978) invalidated an Alaska law giving preference to Alaska residents for jobs on construction of the Alaska pipeline. *Supreme Court of New Hampshire* v. *Piper* (1985) ruled that states may not exclude nonresidents from admission to the practice of law.

The present-day significance of the Article IV Privileges and Immunities Clause is not great, however. The goal of interstate *comity can be served as well or better by the *Equal Protection and Interstate Commerce Clauses (see COMMERCE POWER).

The second privileges and immunities provision appears in the Fourteenth Amendment, and reads: "No state shall make or enforce any law which shall abridge the privileges or immunities of citizens of the United States." While pre–Civil War experience with the concept of privileges and immunities had not been significant, Justice Washington's interpretation of the provision was well known. It appealed to dominant Republican nationalists in the post–Civil War Congress. Senator Jacob M. Howard, a major figure in the drafting of the Fourteenth Amendment, admitted that the privileges and immunities protected by Article IV were vague and agreed that it would be "a somewhat barren discussion" to determine what they were. "But it is certain," he added, "the clause was inserted in the Constitution for some good purpose."

It was not at first clear to the Supreme Court what that purpose, as restated in the Fourteenth Amendment, was. In the first major litigation implicating the new clause, the *Slaughterhouse Cases* (1873), counsel contended that legislation granting a slaughtering monopoly to certain butchers in New Orleans violated the privileges or immunities of competitors. Justice Samuel F. *Miller for the Court majority held that the privileges or immunities of state citizens were not properly a national concern but rather "are left to the State governments for security and protection" (p. 78). Justice Stephen J. *Field, *dissenting, charged that this interpretation made the Privileges or Immunities Clause "a vain and idle enactment" (p. 96).

In *Slaughterhouse* the Court also rejected enforcement of the Fourteenth Amendment's Due Process Clause against the monopoly. Subsequently, however, due process was given a stunning substantive interpretation by the Court, but the Privileges or Immunities Clause has never achieved a significant role of its own (see DUE PROCESS, SUBSTANTIVE). In *Colgate* v. *Harvey* (1935) the Court briefly suggested that the clause was a limitation on state taxing power, but that holding was quickly reversed in *Madden* v. *Kentucky* (1940) (see STATE TAXATION). In *Edwards* v. *California* (1941) three justices ruled that the right to *travel from state to state was guaranteed by the Privileges or Immunities Clause, but the majority invoked the Commerce Clause to achieve the same result.

(See also CITIZENSHIP; FOURTEENTH AMENDMENT.)

C. Herman Pritchett

**Prize Cases,** 2 Black (67 U.S.) 635 (1863), argued 10–13, 16–20, 23–25 Feb. 1863, decided 10 Mar. 1863 by vote of 5 to 4; Grier for the Court, Nelson, joined by Catron, Clifford, and Taney, in dissent. On 19 April 1861 President Abraham *Lincoln ordered a blockade of Confederate ports, and later that month he extended the blockade to the recently seceded states of Virginia and North Carolina. On 13 July Congress authorized Lincoln to declare that a state of insurrection existed, and on 6 August Congress retroactively ratified all of Lincoln's previous military actions.

The *Prize Cases* involved libels against four different ships and their cargoes seized before 13 July. The *Amy Warwick* contained coffee and was en route to Richmond. The Court upheld its seizure as "that of enemies' property" (p. 675). The *Hiawatha* was a British ship caught in Richmond when the Civil War began. The ship's captain was on notice that all neutral ships had to leave Richmond within fifteen days after the blockade began. Because of the failure to obtain a tow the ship was unable to leave port until a few days after the blockade became effective, although its cargo was loaded within the fifteen-day period. The Court affirmed the condemnation of both the ship and its cargo. The *Brilliante* was a Mexican ship that entered New Orleans more than a month after the blockade was established. The ship was captured after leaving New Orleans, and the Court upheld the condemnation. The *Crenshaw,* owned by citizens of Richmond, was captured taking tobacco to England. This ship presented a straightforward question of enemy property. The Court upheld the libel against both the ship and its cargo.

While involving many different technical issues, the cases all turned on one key question: did the president have the power to impose the blockade without Congressional authorization? Lincoln argued that a state of insurrection existed after the firing on Fort Sumter and that he was empowered to take unilateral action against this situation. In supporting Lincoln on this issue the Supreme Court upheld his theory of the *Civil War as an insurrection against the United States government that could be suppressed according to the rules of war. In this way the United States was able to fight the war as if it were an international war, without actually having to recognize the *de jure* existence of the Confederate government.

In the *Prize Cases* Justice Robert *Grier held that "a blockade *de facto* existed" after Lincoln's proclamations and that as "Executive Chief of the Government and Commander-in-Chief of the Army and Navy" Lincoln "was the proper person to make such notifications" (p. 666). Grier argued that a war could exist even if one party did not recognize the sovereignty of another. He noted that, as "civil war is never publicly proclaimed, *eo nomine* against insurgents, its actual existence is a fact in our domestic history which the court is

bound to notice and to know" (p. 667). Here the Court took notice of the war and Lincoln's response to it.

In dissent Justice Samuel *Nelson argued that "no civil war existed between this Government and the State in insurrection till recognized by the Act of Congress" on 13 July and that the president did not have the power, under the Constitution, to either declare war "or recognize its existence within the meaning of the law of nations, which carries with it belligerent rights, and thus change the country and all its citizens from a state of peace to a state of war" (p. 698). Nelson believed that only Congress possessed such powers and thus that the seizures under the blockade were illegal.

In the *Prize Cases* the Court narrowly approved Lincoln's theory of the Civil War as a domestic insurrection with the attributes of an international war. For domestic constitutional purposes the Court affirmed the power of the president to act as if he were merely suppressing an insurrection, while for purposes of international relations, the Court held out to the world that the South was a belligerent and could be legally blockaded. The theory of the war accepted in this case implied that other actions by the president, including the Emancipation Proclamation and the suspension of *habeas corpus, were also constitutionally permissible, especially when supported by subsequent congressional approval.

(See also PRESIDENTIAL EMERGENCY POWERS.)

□ Stewart L. Bernath, *Squall across the Atlantic: American Civil War Prize Cases and Diplomacy* (1970).
Paul Finkelman

**Probable Cause.** The *Fourth Amendment to the U.S. Constitution stipulates that "no [search or arrest] warrants shall issue, but upon probable cause." The amendment stemmed from colonial objections to the British abuse of general warrants and writs of assistance, legal documents that allowed officers to search and arrest individuals on mere suspicion of smuggling. The framers did not define the meaning of this phrase, although they clearly intended it to prevent the central government from arbitrarily intruding upon personal *privacy.

The Fourth Amendment has been among the most heavily litigated of all the *Bill of Rights, but the Supreme Court has considered the probable cause requirement in a relatively small number of cases. The Court measures probable cause by the test of reasonableness, a necessarily subjective standard that falls between mere suspicion and certain knowledge. Facts and circumstances leading to an arrest or seizure must be sufficient to persuade a reasonable person that an illegal act has been or is being committed. Always the test involves the consideration of a particular suspicion and a specific set of facts. Hunches or generalized suspicions are not reasonable grounds for concluding that probable cause exists. Judges, not law officers, must determine if probable cause exists, and thus if a warrant should be issued.

In 1968 the Court modified this standard to allow police officers to *stop and frisk suspects in order to protect themselves, even without probable cause for arrest (*Terry v. Ohio). More recently, the Court has accepted a law officer's experience, a suspect's reputation, and even anonymous tips, when buttressed by other facts, to weigh in the test of reasonableness when determining probable cause.

(See also SEARCH WARRANT RULE, EXCEPTIONS TO.)

David J. Bodenhamer

**Procedural Due Process.** See DUE PROCESS, PROCEDURAL.

**Progressivism,** spanning roughly the first two decades of the twentieth century, was a reform movement through which Americans struggled to cope with a wide range of social, economic, and cultural changes. Progressives differed in their perceptions of the nature of the nation's problems and of how best to resolve them, but most shared the conviction that government at all levels must play an active role in reform. They sought legislation to broaden the state's power to curb the excesses of large-scale corporate *capitalism and to address the host of inequities that had resulted from rapid and unprecedented economic and social change. Since their vision of the function of government was somewhat unorthodox by traditional American standards, reformers had not only to secure the passage of new legislation but also to persuade the judicial system that such laws were both warranted and constitutional.

While contemporary social activists sometimes perceived the judiciary as a barrier to change, the Supreme Court actually upheld most of the legislation passed during the Progressive Era, in particular supporting reformers' efforts to expand the federal government's power to regulate commerce and to curb the growth of monopolies. The Hepburn Act of 1906 broadened the scope and authority of the *Interstate Commerce Commission, giving it genuine power for the first time. The Court sustained the invigoration of the ICC, and affirmed the constitutionality of administrative regulation.

Initially, the Court rendered the *Sherman Antitrust Act (1890) virtually ineffectual when in United States v. *E. C. Knight Co. (1895) it drew a sharp distinction between commerce and manufacturing, thus limiting the government's regulatory power over the latter. For several years thereafter the law was of value primarily to conservative judges who employed it as a weapon in the struggle to curb the power of organized *labor.

During the first decade of the twentieth century, however, the Supreme Court revived the Sherman Act in several important cases. In *Northern Securities Co. v. United States (1904), the Court resurrected the antitrust statute when it found a railroad holding company to be an illegal combination in restraint of trade. The following year in *Swift and Co. v. United States (1905) Justice Oliver Wendell *Holmes, writing the majority opinion, circumvented the commerce versus manufacturing distinction by espousing the doctrine of "stream of commerce," which stressed the impact of manufacturing upon commerce (see COMMERCE POWER). Like many progressive reformers, the justices of the Supreme Court believed that a large company's size, business practices, and substantial market share were not necessarily detrimental to the economic or social progress of the nation. In *Standard Oil Co. v. United States (1911), the Court adopted the *"rule of reason," indicating that it would interpret the Sherman Act in such a way as to break up only those companies whose existence constituted as unreasonable restraint of trade.

The *police power, the authority to protect the public's health, safety, and morals, was traditionally reserved to the states. Progressive legislators interpreted this power broadly and passed a variety of economic and social measures at the state level, including child labor, minimum wage, maximum hour, factory safety, employer liability, and workmen's compensation statutes. In several famous decisions, most notably *Lochner v. New York (1905), the Court overturned some of these laws. However, in *Muller v. Oregon (1908) and other cases, the Court sustained much of this legislation on the grounds that the statutes represented valid exercises of the states' police power.

When state government proved incapable of dealing effectively with economic and social problems, progressives sometimes turned to Washington for help. Between 1906 and 1916 Congress passed several significant pieces of social justice legislation such as the Pure Food and Drug, Meat Inspection, Mann, Adamson, and Keating-Owen Acts. When challenged, most of these laws, which were based on the commerce or taxing power of the federal government, were upheld by the Supreme Court. On several occasions, however, the justices concluded that Congress had overstepped constitutional bounds in its efforts to exercise federal police power. In 1908, in the first Employer Liability Case, the Court found that a 1906 employer's liability law represented a misuse of the commerce power since it affected workers not directly engaged in interstate commerce. In *Adair v. United States (1908), the Court ruled that the Erdman Act (1898) prohibiting yellow-dog contracts violated the liberty of contract under the Due Process Clause of the Fifth Amendment. In *Hammer v. Dagenhart (1918), the Court found that the Keating-Owen Child Labor Act (1916) was not a legitimate regulation of commerce and intruded upon the police power of the states.

As the Supreme Court considered the constitutionality of the progressive legislative agenda, the justices sometimes construed *judicial review narrowly, ruling only on the question of whether there was a clearly constitutional basis for the statute in question. On other occasions the Court interpreted its power broadly, assuming the right to examine the substance of state legislation. In the 1890s an activist conception of judicial review had often been used to protect *property rights, but in the early twentieth century progressive judges and lawyers such as Louis D. *Brandeis often successfully marshaled it to the cause of social change.

Although sometimes labeled reactionary by reform-minded critics, the Supreme Court during the Progressive Era was generally sensitive to the massive changes occurring within American life and struggled to reconcile legal tradition with the demands of modernity. While it sometimes obstructed reform in the name of individual liberty, property rights, or *federalism, the Court ultimately sanctioned an expansion of both state and federal power in order that government at both levels might cope more effectively with the unprecedented problems of the age.

(See also CAPITALISM; CONTRACT, FREEDOM OF; DUE PROCESS, SUBSTANTIVE.).

□ John W. Johnson, *American Legal Culture, 1908–1940* (1981). Melvin I. Urofsky, "State Courts and Protective Legislation During the Progressive Era: A Reevaluation," *Journal of American History* 72 (June 1985): 63–91.
—Robert F. Martin

**Prohibition, Writ of,** the negative counterpart of *mandamus, is an extraordinary writ issued by a superior court to an inferior court commanding it to abandon a cause pending before it over which it lacks jurisdiction. Use of the writ today is governed by the All Writs Act, Title 28, section 1651 of the U.S. Code, and by rule 21 of the Federal Rules of Appellate Procedure.
—William M. Wiecek

**Property Rights.** Throughout much of American history the Supreme Court has defended property rights against legislative interference. In assuming this role the justices have mirrored the values of the framers of the Constitution, who were strongly influenced by the natural law philosophy of John Locke. According to Locke, private property existed under *natural law before the creation of political authority. Building on natural law theory, the eighteenth-century Whig political tradition stressed the rights of property owners as a bulwark of freedom against arbitrary government. The framers also emphasized the economic utility of private property. They believed that security of property and contractual arrangements facilitated the development of in-

vestment capital and the emergence of a strong national economy. Although some state constitutions contained provisions to protect property rights, in the years immediately following the Revolution many became convinced that state governments could not be trusted to respect property ownership. Accordingly, the delegates to the Constitutional Convention were vitally concerned with the need to safeguard economic interests.

Numerous provisions of the Constitution pertain to economic interests. For instance, the Constitution prohibits Congress or the states from confiscating property through bills of *attainder and limits the power of Congress to impose direct taxes (see TAXING AND SPENDING CLAUSE). The Constitution also contained several clauses that protected property in slaves (see SLAVERY). Foremost among the constitutional restrictions on state authority was the *Contracts Clause, forbidding the states from enacting any law "impairing the Obligation of Contracts." Even more important was the *Fifth Amendment, which provided that no person should be "deprived of life, liberty, or property, without due process of law; nor shall private property be taken for public use, without just compensation." The Fifth Amendment in effect incorporated into the Constitution, the Lockean idea that protection of property was a chief aim of government.

From the outset, federal courts signaled their intention to safeguard existing economic arrangements and to curtail state legislative interference with property rights. In *Champion* v. *Casey* (1792), one of the first exercises of federal *judicial review, a circuit court held that a Rhode Island statute granting an individual debtor exemption from attachments for a period of time was an unconstitutional impairment of contract.

*Property Rights and Natural Law.* Looking to the precepts of natural law rather than any specific clause of the Constitution, some federal judges adopted the doctrine of *vested rights to protect established property rights from legislative impairment. According to this doctrine, property was a *fundamental right. Laws that disturbed such rights were void because they violated the principles limiting all constitutional governments. Justice William *Paterson articulated this view in the significant circuit court case *Van Horne's Lessee* v. *Dorrance* (1795). Observing that "the right of acquiring and possessing property, and having it protected, is one of the natural, inherent and inalienable rights of man" (p. 310), Paterson implicitly linked the doctrine of natural rights with the Contracts Clause.

Writing a separate opinion in *Calder* v. *Bull* (1798), Justice Samuel *Chase reiterated the vested rights doctrine. "There are certain vital principles in our free republican governments," he observed, "which will determine and overrule an apparent and flagrant abuse of legislative power" (p. 388). Chase maintained that the legislature could not "violate the right of an antecedent lawful private contract; or the right of private property" (p. 388).

**The Marshall and Taney Courts.** John *Marshall, who became chief justice 1801, dominated the Supreme Court for three decades. As a Federalist, Marshall was sympathetic to property interests and business enterprise. He believed that property ownership both preserved individual liberty and encouraged productive use of resources. The Contracts Clause emerged as the centerpiece of Marshall Court jurisprudence. Drawing upon the doctrine of vested rights, Marshall fashioned the clause into a powerful bulwark to property interests. His initial step was to broaden the definition of contracts that were entitled to protection under the Constitution. In the landmark case of *Fletcher v. Peck (1810), Marshall held that a state was constitutionally barred from breaching its contracts. At issue was an attempt by the Georgia legislature to rescind the huge Yazoo land grant. Marshall noted that the terms of the Contracts Clause "are general, and are applicable to contracts of every description" (p. 137). Likewise, in New Jersey v. Wilson (1812) the Marshall Court determined that a tax exemption was a contractual right and hence a state could not revoke such preferred treatment.

A more far-reaching application of the Contracts Clause occurred in *Dartmouth College v. Woodward (1819), which held that a corporate charter was a constitutionally protected contract. As corporations grew more numerous and powerful during the nineteenth century, public control of corporations became a major concern. The power of the state to repeal or alter the charter of incorporation suggested one avenue by which regulations might be imposed. The Dartmouth College ruling aided corporate enterprise by erecting a constitutional barrier against legislative infringement of existing charters. In a concurring opinion, however, Justice Joseph *Story suggested that state legislatures could reserve the right to modify corporate charters when they were issued. The exercise of such a reserved power would not constitute the impairment of contract. (See also PRIVATE CORPORATION CHARTERS.).

The Contracts Clause was also a major force in shaping debtor-creditor relations. After ratification of the Constitution, many states continued the practice of enacting debtor-relief measures (see BANKRUPTCY AND INSOLVENCY LEGISLATION). Creditors vigorously attacked such laws, arguing that state debtor-relief measures represented an unconstitutional impairment of contract. A challenge to New York's Bankruptcy Act of 1811 came before the Supreme Court in *Sturges v. Crowninshield (1819). Marshall concluded that New York's law was void because it relieved debtors of the obligation to pay debts contracted before the measure was passed. States could not retroactively discharge contractual obligations. Spurred by economic distress in wake of the Panic of 1819, many states passed new bankruptcy laws covering only debts incurred *after* the date of enactment. By a narrow, 4-to-3 margin, the Supreme Court sustained New York's revised statute in *Ogden v. Saunders (1827). The justices held that a law in effect when a contract was made formed part of the agreement. Consequently, the application of bankruptcy laws to posterior obligations did not impair any contract.

The Ogden decision marked a watershed in the history of the Contracts Clause's interpretation. Without retreating from early decisions, the Court was henceforth guided by a more cautious spirit in Contracts Clause cases. In *Providence Bank v. Billings (1830), Marshall declared that surrender of a state's power of taxation could not be implied from the grant of a charter incorporating a bank. This ruling established the principle that grants of privileges to corporations must be expressly set forth in their charters.

Reflecting his commitment to economic nationalism, Marshall labored for broad protection of contracts in order to encourage investment capital. By any standard he achieved considerable success—indeed, the Contracts Clause figured in more Supreme Court decisions than any other section of the Constitution during the nineteenth century. Despite criticism of some rulings, there was little hostility to Marshall's core belief that the federal courts should safeguard established economic rights.

The political triumph of Jacksonian Democracy brought new attitudes to the Supreme Court. On Marshall's death, President Andrew *Jackson named Roger B. *Taney as chief justice in 1837. Under Taney's leadership the Court shaped constitutional law to harmonize with the Jacksonian tenets of states' rights (see STATE SOVEREIGNTY AND STATES' RIGHTS), hostility to special privilege, and strict construction of the Constitution. Despite a shift of emphasis, however, the Court did not fundamentally depart from the constitutional principles of the Marshall era. Taney shared Marshall's economic values, especially the need to protect private property and to promote economic growth. To be sure, there were differences between the judicial approach of Taney and Marshall. Taney limited the reach of the Contracts Clause and allowed the states greater flexibility to fashion economic policy. This was illustrated by *Charles River Bridge v. Warren Bridge (1837), in which Taney rejected the notion of implied corporate privilege. He emphasized the principle that corporate grants must be strictly construed, a doctrine that affirmed legislative control over economic policy. Sensitive to the relationship between law and technology, Taney further asserted that recognition of implied corporate privileges would stymie economic progress.

To Taney's mind, existing property rights could sometimes be destroyed to make room for innovations and improvements.

The power of *eminent domain constituted another limit on the scope of the Contracts Clause. In *West River Bridge Co. v. Dix (1848) the Court held that the Contracts Clause did not protect a corporation against the exercise of eminent domain. The justices reasoned that all contracts were subject to the state's paramount power of eminent domain.

The justices, however, enforced the Contracts Clause in cases involving debtor-relief laws, exemptions from taxation, and banking regulations. In *Bronson v. Kinzie (1843) the Court heard a challenge to two Illinois statutes that retroactively limited mortgage foreclosure sales and gave mortgagors broad rights to redeem foreclosed property. Writing for the Court, Taney found the Illinois statutes to be an unconstitutional abrogation of contract.

The use of eminent domain to take private property did not receive much attention from the federal courts before the *Civil War. The Constitution makes no direct reference to the power of eminent domain, but the Fifth Amendment requires that private property be taken only for public use and upon payment of *just compensation. In Van Horne's Lessee, Justice Paterson had concluded that the "despotic power" of taking private property "exists in every government" and that "government could not subsist without it" (p. 311). He stressed, however, that compensation must be paid to landowners and that determination of land value was a judicial, not a legislative, function.

In practice, the *Takings Clause of the Fifth Amendment did not bulk large during the antebellum era. The most significant Supreme Court takings decision in this period was *Barron v. Baltimore (1833), in which the city of Baltimore sought to increase the access of shippers by undertaking harbor improvements. The city diverted water from the plaintiff's wharf, greatly reducing its value, and the plaintiff claimed compensation for his loss under the Fifth Amendment. Rejecting this contention, the Court held that the Fifth Amendment restricted the federal government but did not apply to the states.

Like the Takings Clause, the Due Process Clause of the Fifth Amendment played almost no role in the constitutional protection of economic interests before the Civil War. By the mid-nineteenth century, however, federal courts began to wrestle with substantive interpretations of due process. Substantive *due process first appeared in federal jurisprudence in the controversial 1857 *Scott v. Sandford decision. Chief Justice Taney interpreted the Due Process Clause as placing a limitation on the power of Congress to exclude slave property from the territories. The Dred Scott ruling was effectively superseded by the Civil War and the *Fourteenth Amendment,

but the concept of substantive due process was destined for a robust rebirth in a later generation. Hence, the property-conscious jurisprudence of the antebellum era was a precursor of laissez-faire constitutionalism later in the century.

**Civil War and Reconstruction.** The Civil War compelled the federal government to play an active role in managing the economy. Congress experimented with new methods of public finance. In 1861 it levied the first income tax, a flat tax of 3 percent on income over $800 a year. In addition, the government issued large amounts of paper money irredeemable in gold or silver, popularly known as greenbacks. The Legal Tender Act of 1862 declared such paper money to be lawful tender for all debts and the payment of taxes. The greenback dollars rapidly depreciated in value, and creditors resisted attempts to discharge debts with such currency. Further, in 1864 Congress organized the national banking system and established a uniform currency of national banknotes. A year later Congress placed a heavy tax on state banknotes, effectively driving them out of circulation as currency.

The Supreme Court sustained these fledgling moves toward national regulation of the economy. In *Springer v. United States (1881) the Court upheld the Civil War income tax as applied to professional earnings. Also significant was the decision in *Veazie Bank v. Fenno (1869), in which the Court affirmed the power of Congress to tax the notes of state banks (see TAX IMMUNITIES). Stressing the importance of securing a uniform currency, the Court refused to scrutinize the motives of Congress in levying such a prohibitive tax. Thus, Veazie Bank established that Congress could use the taxing power to regulate or even eliminate particular economic activities.

Far more controversial was the Court's handling of constitutional challenges to the legal tender legislation. In Hepburn v. Griswold (1870) the Supreme Court, by a vote of 4 to 3, declared the Legal Tender Act invalid as applied to contracts made before its passage. Speaking for the Court, Chief Justice Salmon P. *Chase concluded that the act violated the Due Process Clause of the Fifth Amendment and impaired the obligation of contract in a manner inconsistent with the spirit of the Constitution. Many in business and government feared economic chaos as a result of this ruling. After reargument the Court, in Knox v. Lee (1871), overruled Hepburn and upheld the constitutionality of the Legal Tender Act with respect to both preexisting and subsequent contracts. The upshot of these *Legal Tender Cases was judicial recognition of broad congressional power over currency and monetary policy.

Following the Civil War, America experienced an era of enormous economic growth. Spearheaded by the railroads, industrial development and technological innovation proceeded rapidly. Rapid industrialization, however, produced economic dislocation, and not all segments of society benefited from unbridled operation of the market economy. Corporations and property owners looked to the judiciary for protection against governmental regulations. They sought to utilize the Fourteenth Amendment as a shield against state legislation that in their view represented arbitrary and unreasonable interference with economic rights.

The first interpretation of the Fourteenth Amendment came in the *Slaughterhouse Cases (1873). During *Reconstruction, the Louisiana legislature created a monopoly of the slaughterhouse business in New Orleans. Some New Orleans butchers challenged the Louisiana statute, arguing that the monopoly deprived them of the property right to pursue a trade in violation of both the *Privileges or Immunities and Due Process Clauses of the Fourteenth Amendment. By a 5-to-4 vote, the Supreme Court rejected this contention and placed a narrow construction on the scope of the Privileges or Immunities Clause. According to the Court, no federally protected right to be free of monopoly existed. In sharp contrast, the dissenting justices saw the amendment as a substantive restraint on state power to regulate the rights of property owners. Attacking monopolies as an encroachment on the right to acquire property, Justice Stephen J. *Field argued that the right to pursue a lawful occupation was protected by the Fourteenth Amendment.

The Supreme Court next considered the authority of the states to control private property in *Munn v. Illinois (1877). At issue in Munn was an Illinois statute that set the rate for storing grain in Chicago elevators. The elevator managers assailed this measure as a deprivation of property without due process of law. Upholding the Illinois law, the Supreme Court again adopted a deferential attitude toward state authority to control the use of private property. Speaking for the Court, Chief Justice Morrison R. *Waite ruled that "when private property is devoted to a public use, it is subject to public regulation" (p. 130). Whether this public-interest doctrine applied to a particular enterprise was considered a matter for legislative judgment. Although recognizing that the owner of property "clothed with a public interest" was entitled to reasonable compensation, Waite declared that the determination of such compensation was a legislative, not a judicial, task (see RULE OF REASON). The only protection of property owners against legislative abuse was resort to the political process. Field vigorously dissented, warning that under the Munn rationale "all property and all business in the State are held at the mercy of a majority of its legislature" (p. 140).

During the 1880s the Supreme Court adopted a more skeptical posture toward state regulation of property and business. In Stone v. Farmers' Loan & Trust Co. (1886) the Court upheld a Mississippi statute that empowered a commission to regulate railroad rates, but it cautioned that such authority was not unlimited. Chief Justice Waite added that "the State cannot require a railroad corporation to carry persons or property without reward; neither can it do that which in law amounts to a taking of private property for public use without just compensation, or without due process of law" (p. 331). In addition, the Court strengthened the legal position of corporations. The justices ruled in *Santa Clara County v. Southern Pacific Railroad (1886), that corporations were persons within the meaning of the Fourteenth Amendment, and thus entitled to protection under the Due Process Clause.

**Economic Due Process.** In *Mugler v. Kansas (1887) the Supreme Court went a step further, moving toward a substantive interpretation of the Due Process Clause to safeguard fundamental property rights. This step laid the foundation for the doctrine of economic due process. Although the Court sustained a state measure prohibiting the manufacture and sale of alcoholic beverages as a valid use of the *police power to protect health and morals, Justice John Marshall *Harlan emphasized that courts could scrutinize the purpose behind state regulation as well as the means employed to achieve the stated ends. Moreover, Harlan insisted that there were "limits beyond which legislation cannot rightfully go" (p. 661).

Economic due process soon became the most important judicial instrument safeguarding property rights and vindicating the principles of *laissez-faire constitutionalism. In the 1890s, the Court ruled that utilities were constitutionally entitled to charge reasonable rates and that the determination of reasonableness was a judicial question. This line of development culminated in *Smyth v. Ames (1898), in which the Court unanimously held that a utility must be allowed a "fair return upon the value of that which it employs for public convenience" (p. 547). The Smyth formula required that rates be based on a company's present value and promulgated a complex text to ascertain such value.

In *Allgeyer v. Louisiana (1897) the Supreme Court also developed an important corollary of economic due process, the liberty of contract doctrine. The Court reasoned that liberty, as protected by the Fourteenth Amendment, encompassed the right to "enter into all contracts which may be proper" to pursue an occupation or acquire property (p. 589). States could not interfere with this contractual freedom, a position that cast a deep shadow over legislative attempts to regulate the terms of employment.

Although laissez-faire constitutionalism became predominant during the 1890s, the Court also recognized that states could lawfully restrict property and contractual rights in appropriate situations under the police power. The justices were usually sympathetic to laws that protected the health, safety, and morals of society. In *Holden v. Hardy (1898), for instance, the Supreme Court by a vote of 7 to 2 upheld a Utah statute limiting work in mines to eight hours a day. Rejecting a challenge based on the liberty of contract doctrine, the Court stressed the unhealthy conditions of mine work and noted that mine owners and their employees did not have equal bargaining power (see CONTRACT, FREEDOM OF).

*Takings.* In addition to fashioning the doctrine of economic due process, the Supreme Court enlarged the protection available to property owners under the Takings Clause of the Fifth Amendment. The Court broadened the definition of a taking in *Pumpelly* v. *Green Bay Company* (1871), holding that a physical invasion that destroyed the usefulness of land was a taking even though title technically remained with the owner. Further, the Court gave an expansive reading to the *just compensation requirement in *Monongahela Navigation Company* v. *United States* (1893), reiterating that the assessment of an indemnity payment was a judicial, not a legislative, task. Speaking for the Court, Justice David J. *Brewer ruled that the owner must receive "a full and exact equivalent" (p. 325), and that the value of property was determined by its profitableness. Even more important, in *Chicago, Burlington & Quincy Railroad Co.* v. *Chicago* (1897) the justices unanimously held that the just compensation requirement constituted an essential element of due process as guaranteed by the Fourteenth Amendment. Accordingly, the just compensation rule became in effect the first provision of the *Bill of Rights to be applied to the states.

At the same time, the Court was cool toward the claim that regulations limiting the use of property represented an unconstitutional taking without compensation. A Kansas law prohibited the manufacture or sale of liquor and ordered the destruction of liquor already in stock. By preventing the use of breweries for their intended purpose the statute drastically reduced the value of land and equipment to the owners. Stressing that this legislation did not disturb the owner's use of property for lawful activities, the Court in *Mugler* v. *Kansas* (1887) stated that a restriction on the use of property could not be deemed a taking.

*Declining Importance of Contracts Clause.* After the Civil War, the Contracts Clause continued to figure in constitutional policy. Indeed, the Supreme Court expanded the reach of the Contracts Clause to encompass arrangements made in reliance on judicial intepretation of state law. In *Gelpcke* v. *Dubuque* (1864) the Supreme Court sustained the validity of a municipal bond issue as a contract that could not be impaired by a changed interpretation of state law. Nonetheless, the Supreme Court contributed to the decline of the Contracts Clause by diluting the protection afforded by this provision. In *Stone* v. *Mississippi* (1880), for example, the Court held that a state could forbid the sale of lottery tickets despite the fact that a previous charter granted the right to operate lotteries. This concept of inalienable

police power opened the door for state legislatures to interfere with contracts in order to protect public health and morals.

*Income Tax.* The Supreme Court narrowly construed congressional taxing authority. Desiring to reduce concentrations of wealth and to enhance federal revenue, Congress in 1894 enacted a second income tax, placing a levy of 2 percent on individual and corporate income over $4,000 a year. Conservatives promptly arranged a challenge to the newly enacted levy in *Pollock* v. *Farmers Loan & Trust Co.* (1895). Writing for a 6-to-2 majority, Chief Justice Melville W. *Fuller held that the tax on income from land was a direct tax not apportioned among the states according to population as required by the Constitution. In addition, the Court unanimously found that the tax on income from municipal bonds was unconstitutional because the federal government could not tax state bonds. The Court was divided 4 to 4 on the validity of the tax on general incomes, and the case was reargued when the absent justice could be present. In the second *Pollock* decision, a 5-to-4 majority overturned the entire income tax as an unconstitutional direct tax.

The income tax controversy sharply divided both the Court and the nation. As Justice Field's concurring opinion demonstrates, the majority was moved to safeguard property interests against perceived spoliation by the political majority. Field darkly warned of class struggle: "The present assault upon capital is but the beginning. It will be but the stepping-stone to others, larger and more sweeping, till our political contests will become a war of the poor against the rich" (p. 607). The dissenters denied that the income tax discriminated against the wealthy and charged that the majority was frustrating political democracy.

(The authority of Congress to tax incomes was expressly established by adoption of the *Sixteenth Amendment in 1913. Seeking to defeat a direct challenge to the *Pollock* decision, Senate conservatives in 1909 proposed a constitutional amendment enabling Congress to tax incomes. They mistakenly calculated that the proposal would fail to win ratification by the states. The Sixteenth Amendment voided the *Pollock* decision [see REVERSALS OF COURT DECISIONS BY AMENDMENT].)

*Laissez Faire and Social Legislation.* By 1900 a new industrial and urban society increasingly supplanted the older America of rural communities. Although many Americans prospered during the early decades of the twentieth century, the tremendous economic expansion caused social dislocation. The progressives worked to correct the imbalance of economic power associated with the new industrial order (see PROGRESSIVISM). At the heart of the reform program lay the progressive insistence upon a more active role for both state and federal governments in regulating the economy and meeting social problems.

Influenced by laissez-faire values, the majority of Supreme Court justices remained leery of economic regulations that altered free-market ordering or infringed on property rights. In the seminal case of *Lochner* v. *New York* (1905), the Court gave sharp teeth to economic due process by invalidating a statute that restricted working hours in bakeries. Speaking for a 5-to-4 majority, Justice Rufus W. *Peckham held that the law violated the liberty of contract as protected by the Fourteenth Amendment (see CONTRACT, FREEDOM OF). He concluded that the statute exceeded the permissible bounds of state police power. Peckham also expressed broad disapproval of legislation protective of *labor. Two dissenters attacked the majority's position from different perspectives. Justice Harlan accepted the legitimacy of the liberty of contract doctrine but argued that the Court misapplied it in this case. Emphasizing that contracts were subject to health and safety regulations, he maintained that long hours of work in bakeries endangered the health of employees. Justice Oliver Wendell *Holmes went a step further and rejected the laissez-faire interpretation of the Constitution. Holmes articulated a philosophy of *judicial self-restraint under which the Court should defer to the right of a political majority to govern.

The *Lochner* decision firmly established the authority of the Supreme Court to review the substance of economic regulations under the Due Process Clause. For the next thirty years the Court closely scrutinized the reasonableness of numerous statutes affecting property rights, treating liberty of contract as the general rule governing economic affairs. State interference with this right under the police power could only be justified in exceptional circumstances, and such restraint could not be arbitrary. To the discomfort of the progressives, the *Lochner* decision became a symbol of the Supreme Court's commitment to property rights.

Despite the triumph of laissez-faire constitutionalism, the Supreme Court was receptive to laws dealing with obvious health and safety risks even when such regulations imposed heavy costs on property owners or businesses. For instance, the justices upheld the regulation of safety in mines and workmen's compensation statutes that provided for a financial award to employees injured by industrial accidents. The Court also took a deferential view with respect to state supervision of public morals, readily approving laws restricting the operation of lotteries and pool halls and prohibiting the manufacture and sale of alcoholic beverages. Nor did the Supreme Court see any constitutional infirmity with laws to prevent fraudulent business practices.

In *Muller* v. *Oregon* (1908) the Supreme Court sustained a state law that limited working hours for women in factories and laundries. The Court stressed the special health needs of women and their dependent status as justifying disparate treatment under law. The justices did not see women as equal competitors with men in the marketplace and thus accepted the necessity for protective legislation. Although a qualified victory for reform, *Muller* did not challenge the dominance of economic due process. Moreover, the paternalistic assumptions behind legislation designed to protect women appear suspect to modern eyes (see GENDER).

Notwithstanding this willingness to accommodate some regulation of economic life, the Supreme Court increasingly relied upon the doctrines of economic due process and liberty of contract to safeguard property rights. In general terms, the Court rejected those regulations that it deemed excessive or unwarranted. The contours of such review were imprecise, but the Court tended to look with disfavor on several types of economic legislation: labor laws, anticompetitive measures, and statutes fixing wages and prices.

A majority of the Court believed that government should not intervene in labor-management relations. This attitude was illustrated by a line of cases that struck down both federal and state laws prohibiting so-called *yellow dog contracts, which made it a term of employment that employees not belong to labor unions. Although the justices may have held unrealistic notions about the bargaining position of individual employees, allegations of systematic favoritism to business are difficult to demonstrate. In actuality the Supreme Court was committed to the laissez-faire norm of an unregulated market economy. Thus, the justices also invalidated laws that restricted the right to engage in business or that imposed barriers to new enterprises.

The decision in *New State Ice Co.* v. *Liebmann* (1932), confirmed the Supreme Court's devotion to free-market competition. Oklahoma required a certificate to enter the ice business. The Court emphasized that the practical effect of the certificate provision was to shut out new enterprises and thus foster a monopoly in the existing ice companies. Accordingly, the Court found by a margin of 6 to 2 that the Oklahoma statute unreasonably curtailed the right to engage in a lawful private business in violation of Due Process Clause.

Legislative attempts to set minimum wages raised novel issues. The justices were loath to accept wage regulation or to expand the category of businesses in which wage or price fixing was constitutional. In *Adkins* v. *Children's Hospital* (1923) the Supreme Court by a 5-to-3 margin overruled a District of Columbia statute that established a minimum wage for women as an infringement of the liberty of contract. Speaking for the Court, Justice George *Sutherland stressed that "freedom of contract is . . . the general rule and restraint the exception" (p. 546). He reasoned that the minimum-wage law arbitrarily cast upon employers a welfare function that belonged to society at large.

The Supreme Court sometimes treated economic rights and other liberties as interdependent. For instance, judicial protection of property rights was instrumental in a successful assault on residential segregation laws (see HOUSING DISCRIMINATION). The Supreme Court in *Buchanan v. Warley* (1917) held that such an ordinance restricted the right to alienate property and constituted a deprivation of property without due process.

Congressional taxing powers were also strengthened in the early twentieth century. The Supreme Court approved the use of taxation to regulate or prohibit economic activity that could not be reached directly by Congress under the Commerce Clause. In *McCray v. United States* (1904) the Court upheld the imposition of a prohibitory tax on yellow oleomargarine. Since the taxing power was not limited to interstate commerce, the *McCray* decision seemingly permitted Congress to regulate all aspects of the economy.

Any expectations for the broad use of tax authority to achieve regulatory ends were soon dashed. To halt the use of child labor Congress placed a 10-percent tax on the profits of companies employing children. In *Bailey v. Drexel Furniture Co.* (1922) the Court scrutinized the purpose behind the tax measure, and held by an 8-to-1 margin that child-labor tax was an unconstitutional infringement on state authority to regulate manufacturing. The result of the *Bailey* ruling was to curtail the use of the taxing power for regulatory purposes.

Further, the Court faced novel questions concerning the protection of property rights under the Takings Clause of the Fifth Amendment. Urbanization and industrialization created serious land-use problems in the years after 1900. Both the federal government and the states began more vigorously to control the use of land. In *Pennsylvania Coal Co. v. Mahon* (1922) the Court recognized the concept of a *regulatory taking* where the value of private property was unduly diminished by governmental action. A transfer of title or a physical incursion was unnecessary for a taking to occur. Justice Holmes formulated the crucial inquiry in *Mahon*: "The general rule at least is, that while property may be regulated to a certain extent, if regulation goes too far it will be recognized as a taking" (p. 415).

Another vexing issue was raised by the emergence of *zoning as a land-control technique. When traditional nuisance law proved inadequate to cope with urban land-use problems, localities began to enact specific restrictions to safeguard public health and safety. But such regulations restricted an owner's dominion over his land and often impaired its value. Critics argued that zoning represented an unconstitutional interference with the right of owners to make use of their property.

In *Euclid v. Ambler Realty Co.* (1926) the Court, by a 6-to-3 vote, upheld the constitutionality of a comprehensive zoning ordinance that divided a locality into residential and commercial districts, restricting the type of building construction in each district. Reasoning that such limitations served the health, safety, and morals of the public, Justice Sutherland ruled that state police power included the authority to classify land and prevent the erection of commercial buildings in residential areas. The Court stressed, however, that zoning power was not unfettered. In *Nectow v. Cambridge* (1928) the Supreme Court struck down a particular application of a zoning ordinance as a deprivation of property without due process.

The regulation of rental practices was also a source of controversy. Citing emergency housing conditions growing out of World War I, a congressional measure established a commission to determine reasonable rents in the District of Columbia and protected a tenant's right of occupancy. In *Block v. Hirsh* (1921) the Supreme Court upheld the validity of the statute by a vote of 5 to 4. Justice Holmes concluded that under the circumstances of a wartime housing shortage, the rental business in the District was cloaked with a public interest justifying temporary regulation.

***The New Deal and "Constitutional Revolution."*** Despite the Great Depression of the 1930s, the Supreme Court remained skeptical about regulation of the economy, particularly about attempts to adjust employment relationships or significantly alter the operations of the free market. Yet President Franklin D. *Roosevelt's *New Deal program was grounded on the notion that government had an affirmative duty to promote the general social welfare. New Deal liberals worked to remedy economic distress, manage the national economy, control corporate behavior, encourage labor unions, and actively promote the economic interests of the disadvantaged. This social-welfare approach flatly contradicted the insistence on limited governmental activity, marketplace competition, and respect for property rights that were at the heart of laissez-faire constitutionalism.

Among the problems spawned by the depression was the wholesale loss of homes and farms through foreclosure of delinquent mortgages. At issue in *Home Building & Loan Association v. Blaisdell* (1934) was a Minnesota act imposing a limited moratorium on the foreclosure of mortgages. By a 5-to-4 margin the Supreme Court held that the moratorium did not violate the Contracts Clause. Chief Justice Charles Evans *Hughes ruled that contracts were subject to the reasonable exercise of the state police power, which encompassed the authority to give temporary relief for extraordinary economic distress.

In *Nebbia v. New York* (1934), the justices by a 5-to-4 vote sustained a milk control law as a reasonable means of stabilizing milk prices. The *Nebbia* ruling signaled an important shift away from economic due process and judicial supervision of state regulatory legislation. Speaking for the Court, Justice Owen J. *Roberts emphasized that a state could validly "adopt whatever economic policy may reasonably be deemed to promote public welfare" (p. 537). He added, "The Constitution does not guarantee the unrestricted privilege to engage in a business or to conduct it as one pleases" (pp. 527–528).

In 1935 and 1936 the Supreme Court struck down a series of important New Deal measures. In *Schechter Poultry Corp.* v. *United States* (1935) the justices unanimously overturned the National Industrial Recovery Act as an unconstitutional delegation of lawmaking power to the executive branch (see DELEGATION OF POWERS). In *Carter* v. *Carter Coal Co.* (1936) the Court by a vote of 6 to 3 invalidated the Bituminous Coal Conservation Act on grounds that the legislation exceeded the authority of the federal government under the Commerce Clause.

The Supreme Court also took a restrictive view of congressional power to levy taxes and appropriate money. The Agricultural Adjustment Act authorized the payment of subsidies to farmers in exchange for reducing the amount of their crops. To raise revenue for this scheme Congress placed a "processing tax" on the first processor of such commodities. In *United States* v. *Butler* (1936) the justices struck down the processing tax. Writing for the Court, Justice Roberts concluded that the ostensible tax was in actuality a means of regulating agricultural production, a matter reserved for the states under the *Tenth Amendment.

Yet another objection to the New Deal centered on the Takings Clause of the Fifth Amendment. To assist indebted farmers, the Frazier-Lemke Act of 1934 compelled the holders of existing mortgages to relinquish farm property to mortgagors without full payment of the mortgage debt. In *Louisville Bank* v. *Radford* (1935) a unanimous Supreme Court found the act to constitute an unconstitutional taking of property without compensation.

Never before had the Supreme Court struck down so many acts of Congress in such a short period of time. These judicial setbacks dealt a blow to the New Deal program of economic revival and social reform. In their dogged adherence to laissez-faire constitutionalism, however, the justices were unmindful of the constraints imposed on the Court by political realities. The Court's stubborn defense of property rights precipitated a constitutional crisis. The political climate, combined with the threat of President Roosevelt's *court-packing plan, dictated a judicial retreat. In the process, the Court undertook a wholesale reversal of landmark decisions. This abrupt change in the Court's thinking, known as the constitutional revolution of 1937, is best understood within a larger political context.

In *West Coast Hotel Co.* v. *Parrish* (1937) the justices sustained a Washington State minimum-wage law for women and minors. Speaking for a 5-to-4 majority, Chief Justice Hughes overruled the *Adkins* precedent and effectively repudiated the liberty of contract doctrine. The decision in *West Coast Hotel* marked the virtual end of economic due process as a constitutional norm. Since 1937 the Supreme Court has not overturned any economic or social legislation on due process grounds.

The New Deal judicial revolution also had important implications for governmental regulation of utility rates. In *Federal Power Commission* v. *Hope Natural Gas Co.* (1944) the Supreme Court abandoned the fair-value standard of *Smyth* v. *Ames*, ruling that rate-making bodies were not bound to follow any single formula for determining charges. Judicial inquiry was directed only to the impact of the rate order on the regulated industry, not the method of calculation.

The lacerating struggle over the validity of the New Deal program engendered lasting hostility against judicial protection of property rights and had a profound impact on the course of American constitutional history. Once the Supreme Court accepted the New Deal, the justices abruptly withdrew from the field of economic regulation. This reflected a monumental change in the Court's attitude toward property rights and entrepreneurial liberty. The cornerstone of this new constitutional direction was a judicially created dichotomy between property rights and personal liberties articulated in 1938 in *United States* v. *Carolene Products Co.* (see FOOTNOTE FOUR). Henceforth, economic regulations would be found to violate the Due Process Clause only when such legislation did not rest "upon some rational basis within the knowledge and experience of the legislators" (p. 152). As a consequence, the Supreme Court virtually eliminated property rights from the constitutional agenda for several decades.

*Recent Developments.* Judicial concern for the protection of economic rights, however, never entirely disappeared. By 1970 a more conservative Supreme Court gradually began to revitalize constitution protection of economic rights. This shift became apparent in the late 1970s, when the Supreme Court reinvigorated the long-neglected Contracts Clause. In *United States Trust Co.* v. *New Jersey* (1977) the justices, for the first time in nearly forty years, applied the clause to strike down a state law. One year later, in *Allied Structural Steel Co.* v. *Spannaus* (1978) the Court relied on the Contracts Clause to void state interference with a private contractual arrangement. During the 1980s the Court seemed to revert to a more restrictive view of the Contracts Clause. In *Keystone Bituminous Coal Association* v. *DeBenedictis* (1987) the Court rejected a Contracts Clause challenge to a Pennsylvania law that prevented enforcement of contractual waivers of liability for surface damage caused by mining. Speaking for a 5-to-4 majority, Justice John Paul *Stevens observed that "the prohibition against impairing the obligation of contracts is not to be read literally" (p. 502).

The Takings Clause of the Fifth Amendment has emerged as the principal bulwark of property rights in contemporary constitutional law. The Supreme Court has virtually eliminated the "public use" requirement as a check on the power of government to appropriate private property by eminent domain. In *Berman* v. *Parker* (1954) the Court equated the "public use" clause with the police power. The justices insisted that the "concept of the public welfare is broad and inclusive" (p. 33) and concluded that the judiciary should defer to legislative determinations of the need to use eminent domain.

The justices have protected landowners against physical intrusion onto their property by the government. In *United States* v. *Causby* (1946), for instance, the Court held that regular military flights at low altitude over private land destroyed its value as a farm and in effect appropriated the property. The justices went a step further in *Loretto* v. *Teleprompter Manhattan CATV Corp.* (1982), ruling that any permanent physical occupation of property, no matter how slight, amounted to a taking.

The justices have been reluctant to invoke the doctrine of regulatory taking and have allowed Congress and the states wide latitude to impose conditions on the use of land. The Court has permitted cities to enact land-use regulations that enhance the aesthetic features of municipal life. In *Penn Central Transportation Co.* v. *New York City* (1978), the Court, by a 6-to-3 vote, sustained the designation of Grand Central Terminal as a historic landmark despite the fact that such action prevented the landowner from modifying the building without municipal permission, thereby causing a drastic reduction in its value.

Nonetheless, the Supreme Court took a fresh look at the question of regulatory taking in 1987 and strengthened the position of property owners against governmental authority to reduce the value of their property by regulation. In *Nollan* v. *California Coastal Commission* (1987) the Supreme Court struck down a land use regulation for the first time since the 1920s. The case arose when a state agency issued a permit to rebuild a beach house on the condition of the landowner's grant of a public easement across the beachfront. The Court held by a margin of 5 to 4 that the imposition of such a condition constituted a taking because the requirement was unrelated to any problem caused by the development. The *Nollan* decision signaled a heightened degree of judicial supervision of land-use controls. Moreover, in *First English Evangelical Lutheran Church of Glendale* v. *County of Los Angeles* (1987) the justices ruled that a property owner may be entitled to compensation for the temporary loss of land use when controls are later invalidated. This decision raised the prospect of damage awards against excessive regulations.

This resurgent interest in property rights was also manifest in renewed judicial review of utility rate-making under the Takings Clause. In *Duquesne Light Co.* v. *Barasch* (1989) the justices upheld a Pennsylvania rate order and reaffirmed that no particular rate-making method was mandated by the Constitution. Yet the Court emphasized that "the Constitution protects utilities from being limited to a charge for their property serving the public which is so 'unjust' as to be confiscatory" (p. 307).

For a brief period in the 1970s, the Supreme Court flirted with the protection of various government benefits as a type of "new property." The basic question was whether social security, welfare benefits, and public employment should be viewed as rights or as privileges subject to withdrawal. Critics charged that the "new property" notion was simply a subterfuge to constitutionalize the welfare state and protect the economic interests of political liberals. In *Goldberg* v. *Kelly* (1970) the justices, by a vote of 5 to 4, edged toward acceptance of the new property concept. They held that New York City violated due process procedural guarantees by terminating welfare benefits without a prior hearing. Ultimately, however, the Court declined to treat most entitlements under government programs as traditional property rights for the purpose of due process. Instead, the Court preserved a large measure of legislative authority to manage and even eliminate benefit schemes.

By the early 1990s it was apparent that the Supreme Court continued to play a major role in safeguarding economic rights. A return to laissez-faire constitutionalism, however, appears problematic. The Court will more likely strike a balance between popular democracy and the constitutional protection of private property ownership.

(See also CAPITALISM.)

□ James W. Ely, Jr., *The Guardian of Every Other Right: A Constitutional History of Property Rights* (1991). Kermit L. Hall, *The Magic Mirror: Law in American History* (1989). Herbert Hovenkamp, "The Political Economy of Substantive Due Process," *Stanford Law Review* 40 (1988): 379–447. Alfred H. Kelly, Winfred A. Harbison, and Herman J. Belz, *The American Constitution: Its Origins and Development*, 7th ed. (1991). Paul Kens, *Judicial Power and Reform Politics: The Anatomy of Lochner v. New York* (1990). R. Kent Newmyer, *Supreme Court Justice Joseph Story: Statesman of the Old Republic* (1985). Joel Francis Paschal, *Mr. Justice Sutherland: A Man Against the State* (1951). Benjamin Fletcher Wright, *The Contract Clause of the Constitution* (1938).                    James W. Ely, Jr.

**Pro Se Petition,** a written application submitted to a court by a litigant in his or her own behalf, rather than by legal counsel.                    Elaine J. Grant

**Providence Bank v. Billings,** 4 Pet. (29 U.S.) 514 (1830), argued 11 Feb. 1830, decided 22 Mar. 1830

by vote of 7 to 0; Marshall for the Court. Influenced by the currents of Jacksonian democracy and states' rights sentiment, the Supreme Court in *Providence Bank* limited the amount of protection accorded corporation charters under the *Contracts Clause. In 1791 the Rhode Island legislature granted a charter to Providence Bank to conduct a banking business. In 1822 the lawmakers sought to tax the capital stock of every bank in the state. Providence Bank argued that its charter impliedly conferred an exemption from state taxation and that the tax law thus impaired the obligation of contract.

Rejecting this contention, Chief Justice John *Marshall stressed that taxing authority "is essential to the existence of government" (p. 560) and could not be relinquished by implication. Only an express grant of immunity from taxation would bind the state (see TAX IMMUNITIES). Marshall added that the Constitution "was not intended to furnish the corrective for every abuse of power which may be committed by the state governments" (p. 563). The ruling in *Providence Bank* established the principle that corporate privilege must be expressly set forth in the charter in order to receive constitutional protection. The Court later built upon this doctrine in *Charles River Bridge* v. *Warren Bridge* (1837) to emphasize that corporate grants must be strictly construed.

(See also PRIVATE CORPORATION CHARTERS.)

James W. Ely, Jr.

**Prudential Insurance Co. v. Benjamin,** 328 U.S. 408 (1946), argued 8 and 11 Mar. 1946, decided 3 June 1946 by vote of 8 to 0; Rutledge for the Court, Black concurring in result without opinion, Jackson not participating. South Carolina imposed a 3 percent tax on the premiums received by out-of-state insurance companies from policies written in the state but did not impose a similar tax on South Carolina corporations. The Prudential, a New Jersey corporation, argued that in light of the Court's decision in *United States* v. *South-Eastern Underwriters Association* (1944), such a discriminatory tax imposed a burden upon interstate commerce and therefore exceeded the powers of the state. Congress, however, had reversed the *South-Eastern* decision in the *McCarran Act of 1945 and explicitly delegated to the states the power to regulate and tax insurance companies.

Justice Wiley *Rutledge's opinion assumed that a tax discriminating between in-state and foreign corporations constituted a violation of the Commerce Clause, but the Court upheld the tax in this case because Congress had "consented" to state regulation of insurance even if such regulation impinged on interstate commerce. Where earlier cases had held that states could act if Congress had failed to exercise its authority (e.g., *Cooley* v. *Board of Wardens of the Port of Philadelphia*, 1852), here the Court approved a "consent" authority for states to do what they would

otherwise be barred from doing, namely regulating some aspect of interstate commerce.

(See also COMMERCE POWER.)

Melvin I. Urofsky

**Public Forum Doctrine.** The Supreme Court established the doctrine of the public forum in 1939, when it ruled in *Hague* v. *Congress of Industrial Organizations* that government may not prohibit speech-related activities such as demonstrations, leafletting, and speaking in public areas traditionally provided for speech. Such places have historically served as essential vehicles of communication, especially for groups who lack power or access to alternative channels of communication.

The public forum doctrine matured during the social movements of the 1960s, as vociferous civil rights and other protesters pressed for social change. In striving to balance the *First Amendment interests at stake with the social need for order and domestic tranquility, the Supreme Court has had to address two major issues. First, assuming that a public forum exists, government may still regulate access to it and control harmful incidental effects of expression such as noise, congestion, litter, and disorder, so long as such regulation does not discriminate on grounds of viewpoint and does not substantially restrict the exchange of communication (*U.S.* v. *Grace*, 1983). This is the *"time, place, and manner" doctrine. Second, the Court has had to determine which areas are subject to public forum standards in the first place. This question is the central issue in modern public forum adjudication.

In *Perry Education Association* v. *Perry Local Educators' Association* (1983), the Court ruled that the level of First Amendment protection depended upon one of three types of forum being used. "Traditional" public forums are those established by historical practice or government fiat. Governments may not close these forums and must provide reasonable access to all speakers regardless of the viewpoint they express. Controversial speech in such forums may not be restricted because of the reactions of the audience ("hecklers' vetoes") unless police reasonably anticipate imminent disorder (*Gregory* v. *City of Chicago*, 1969). Areas the Court has designated traditional public forums (before and after *Perry*) include: streets or sidewalks adjoining such public buildings as state capitols (*Edwards* v. *South Carolina*, 1963), courthouses (*U.S.* v. *Grace*), schools (*Police Department of Chicago* v. *Mosley*, 1972), parks (*Niemotko* v. *Maryland*, 1951), and residential neighborhoods (*Frisby* v. *Schultz*, 1988). Government may prohibit access to a traditional public forum only if the prohibition is narrowly tailored and necessary to achieve a compelling social or governmental interest. For example, in *Frisby* the Court held that a city may protect residential privacy by prohibiting "focused picketing taking place solely in front of [and directed at] a particular residence" (p. 483).

A second type of forum is one created by governmental "designation." Government may shut these forums down in a viewpoint neutral manner but must adhere to neutral standards while such forums remain open. In *Widmar* v. *Vincent* (1981) the Court ruled that once a state university opens its facilities to student groups, it may not exclude religious groups without a compelling reason.

The third type is known as "off-limits" public property. Property that serves a specific government purpose and is not a public forum by tradition or designation is significantly less protected by the First Amendment. Government may even engage in viewpoint discrimination in these domains by showing that the disparate treatment is reasonably related to the property's function. For example, in *Perry* the Court ruled that a rival union could be excluded from access to a public interschool mailing system (only the duly elected union representative was granted access by the education association pursuant to a bargaining agreement), even though the Boy Scouts and related groups had been granted access. In the 1980s this category has included: mailboxes to deposit nonstamped mailable matter (*U.S. Postal Service* v. *Greenburgh Civic Association*, 1981); public lightposts for campaign signs (*Los Angeles* v. *Taxpayers for Vincent*, 1984); military bases (*U.S.* v. *Albertini*, 1985); and participation by advocacy groups in government charitable fund campaigns (*Cornelius* v. *NAACP Legal Defense and Educational Fund*, 1985).

The Court's reasons for placing public property in category three rather than categories one or two have not always been self-evident (e.g., *Perry; Vincent*). This suggests that the public forum doctrine may be less important to the actual disposition of the case than the Court's evaluation of the merits of the speech claim and the competing government interests. In addition, the expansion of government power to declare its property "off limits" has coincided with the Court's refusal to bestow public forum status upon such public-oriented private property as shopping centers (*Hudgens* v. *NLRB*, 1976). Consequently, the doctrine of the public forum has become less formidable as government asserts its property rights, and demographic trends favor the use of malls over traditional downtown streets, sidewalks, and parks for commerce and association.

(See also SPEECH AND THE PRESS.)

□ John Nowak and Dan Farber, "The Misleading Nature of Public Forum Analysis: Content and Context in First Amendment Adjudication," *Virginia Law Review* 70 (1984): 1219–1266. Donald A. Downs

**Public Information Office.** The office's origins trace to enhanced public visibility attained by the Court during 1935 in moving into its new building, to the reviewing of the constitutionality of New Deal programs, and to the misreporting of the *Gold Clause decisions by the Associated Press. Appointment of a nonstatutory "press contact man" emerged in December 1935 from discussions among the chief justice, court *clerk, and Washington correspondents. All were anxious to satisfy the increased demand for news of the Court and to improve the timely flow of information, especially printed opinions then disseminated only after oral delivery in open court. Located from its inception on the building's ground floor, the office by 1990 accommodated five employees, a *press room with assigned carrels accommodating seventeen major news organizations and tables for visiting reporters, and a documents resource room.

Nelson A. Potter, a "minute clerk" on the Court staff, became the first "press clerk." He was succeeded in 1947 by Banning Whittington, a United Press reporter, who served until 1973 when the position was retitled "public information officer." Appointed in 1973 by Chief Justice Warren *Burger, Barrett McGurn held the position until 1982. Burger in 1982 named Toni House, a former *Washington Star* reporter and editor.

The office provides information, but not interpretations of judicial decisions, to the media, the public, and to other Court offices. Its most visible function involves distribution of bench copies of opinions. Each set of 175 copies is released to reporters upon notification of the opinion's traditional announcement in the courtroom above. Opinions are also electronically disseminated through the Publications Unit.

(See also STAFF OF THE COURT, NONJUDICIAL.)
Peter G. Fish

**Public Lands.** Nearly all of the territory in the United States outside the original thirteen states once comprised public lands of the federal government, acquired from foreign powers or from states through cession, and from natives. Some public lands have been purchased by the federal government from private persons or states for governmental operations.

The federal government's authority over its lands is defined principally in the Constitution's enumerated powers of Congress and in the Property Clause (Art. IV, sec. 3, cl. 2), which provides, "The Congress shall have power to dispose of and to make all needful Rules and Regulations respecting Territory and other Property belonging to the United States." The Supreme Court has read the Property Clause expansively, stating that the clause gives Congress both a general legislative power and the power of a proprietor over federal lands. In light of the comprehensive authority granted to Congress, the Court has usually deferred to Congress, and confined itself largely to interpreting congressional statutes and administrative regulations controlling or disposing of public lands.

The Supreme Court must reconcile federal and state jurisdiction over federal public lands located within state borders. Under the Constitution's Supremacy Clause (Art. VI, sec. 2), federal provisions override conflicting state laws, and states may not interfere with federal ownership of public lands. Hence, states may not tax federal lands. However, the states have a residual jurisdiction to enforce their criminal laws on federal public lands within their borders, except where a state has ceded its jurisdiction or consented to the federal government's acquisition of land in the state under the Enclave Clause (Art. I, sec. 8, cl. 17).

(See also, LAND GRANTS; TERRITORIES AND NEW STATES.)

Bruce A. Campbell

**Public Opinion.** None of the major political institutions of the United States was designed to be more unaccountable to the public than the Supreme Court. Beyond the indirect method of selecting justices for the Court, granting the incumbents what amounts to life tenure is an exceptional structure in a polity that purports to be democratic. By the design of the framers of the U.S. Constitution, the justices of the Supreme Court are remarkably well insulated from the public.

Institutional designs, however, frequently portray a misleading picture of the actual operation of politics. To what degree has the Supreme Court actually been insulated from public opinion? To what degree has Court policy been inconsistent with the preferences of ordinary citizens? Despite life terms for the members of the Court, have individual justices been responsive? Is there variability across courts, across justices? What factors increase the likelihood of judicial responsiveness? What factors impede it? These are questions that have captured the attention of scholars for some time.

There has always been a tension among political thinkers about the role of public opinion in politics, and this tension is quite important for understanding the responsiveness of the Supreme Court. On one hand, satisfying the will of the public is one of the highest aims of democratic government. Democracy is a system that, by majority rule and political accountability, is meant to ensure that public officials act to implement the preferences of the people.

There is a less salutary view of the public that also has some currency. The public is often thought to be ill informed, and, worse, self-interested. This means that the public can rarely be trusted to act out of a broader sense of what is good for the polity as a whole. Consequently, at least some political institutions must be protected from the ill-considered and frequently selfish and short-sighted schemes of the majority.

The Supreme Court is meant to be that protected institution. The role of the Court in American politics is often conceptualized so as to minimize the influence of public opinion. For justices to "pander" to public opinion is often thought to base decisions on emotional and irrational considerations and to impair the Court's function as an "umpire" for the political game. The Founding Fathers, many of whom were deeply wary about the majority, sought to develop an institution that, though not completely disconnected from the political process, would nonetheless be shielded from the public in ways quite unlike the other so-called "political" branches. The Supreme Court, as the institution charged with the "minority rights" half of the democratic equation (rather than the "majority rule" part of democracy), was meant to fulfill this purpose.

The consequences of this institutional structure are that justices have long made public pronouncements about the importance of judges remaining independent of public opinion, and scholars have long assumed that it was not useful to investigate possible linkages between the public and the Court. Thus, the traditional view of public influence on the Court is that the public knows little about the institution and the issues it addresses, that the justices work outside the eye of the public, largely impervious to public policy preferences, and that this state is desirable.

Thus, any effort to assess the role of public opinion on the Supreme Court must be sensitive to indirect and subtle pathways of influence. Nearly all justices reject that view that the "mob" should rule in instant cases. Yet available evidence suggests that the institution is far from perfectly insulated from the preferences of the people. This evidence requires some attention.

There is ample research to suggest that over the course of American history the Supreme Court has often reflected the views of the broader public. Robert Dahl broadly surveyed the relationship between the Court policy and majority preferences (at least as reflected in the actions of the representatives of the people) and concluded that the Supreme Court is rarely long out-of-step with the wishes of the people. Though this research does not speak to the precise mechanisms through which the Court and the public coincide, it is impressive evidence of the congruence between public opinion and Court policy.

In the most comprehensive analysis to date, Thomas R. Marshall has assessed the degree of congruence between the policies of the Court and public opinion as measured by scientific opinion polls. Marshall concludes that in a clear majority of the instances in which relevant polls exist, Court decisions are consistent with public opinion. Perhaps most interesting, his and other analyses suggest that the level of public opinion influence on the Supreme Court is roughly comparable to the level of opinion influence on other policy-making institutions.

There is also evidence of the connection between the Court and the public from more detailed studies of Court policy during periods of political crisis. The most famous such incident occurred during the 1930s as the Supreme Court sought to thwart Franklin D. *Roosevelt's efforts to rescue the United States from the hard grip of economic depression. During FDR's first term, the Supreme Court consistently invalidated many of the recovery schemes. Following the electoral landslide of 1936, however, the Court altered its position, finding constitutional sanction for the New Deal policies. Many have interpreted this as evidence that the Supreme Court cannot long withstand intense political pressure to conform to the wishes of the majority (see COURT-PACKING PLAN).

Even the most deeply conventional observers concede that the Court as an institution changes over time and that often the change places the institution in closer alignment with the preferences of the people. Because there has been a fair amount of turnover on the bench, presidents have historically had ample opportunity to appoint justices with contemporary policy views, thereby keeping the Court in step with current political thinking. Thus, changes in public opinion are ultimately reflected in changes in Court composition and policy, but with a lag period. In this sense, the Court follows the election returns, even if belatedly, and even if individual justices act with complete oblivion to the preferences of their fellow citizens (see SELECTION OF JUSTICES).

The Court can also maintain consonance with public opinion to the extent that the values of justices change just as the values of ordinary citizens change. For instance, what the justices of the high bench view as "cruel punishment" has no doubt evolved over the last two centuries, just as public opinion on the meaning of cruelty has changed. This process may even occur in the short-term—for instance, as opinions change on the legitimacy of a lengthy war. Once more, these are mechanisms by which the Court is kept in contact with the wishes of the public, even without any conscious effort to do so.

Similarly, norms such as *judicial self-restraint—the belief that judges ought to restrain their own preferences and defer to the popularly elected branches—may actually work to make Court policy more consistent with the preferences of the majority. To the extent that the Congress and the president are attuned to the public and to the extent that legislation therefore reflects public views, Court deference to the elected branches serves to make for more responsive Court policy. Once more, Court policy can reflect opinion without any direct motives to represent on the part of individual justices.

There are also specific areas of law in which the Court openly and explicitly defers to public opinion. For instance, current policy on *obscenity makes direct reference to prevailing community views of what is and what is not obscene (e.g., *Miller v. California, 1973). Similarly, there is probably no area of modern law that has directed the justices to try to understand public opinion more than *Eighth Amendment death-penalty litigation. To the extent that Court policy recognizes an important role for public opinion, there will be at least some degree of congruence between what the public wants and what it gets in Court decisions (see CAPITAL PUNISHMENT).

At the same time, however, it must be acknowledged that there are important areas of law in which most modern Courts have resisted even stable and strong public opinion. Attitudes toward prayer in public schools is just one such example (see SCHOOL PRAYER AND BIBLE READING). To the extent that public opinion takes on the tint of majority tyranny, the justices are quite unlikely to defer.

But do individual justices respond to public opinion? Few of the conventional mechanisms for insuring individual responsiveness are available for members of the Court. The electoral sword is unavailable, and even the perhaps more powerful pull of individual ambition is often weak since many justices view a position on the Supreme Court as the ultimate career achievement. Absent fear of electoral retaliation and ambition for higher office, and with only very weak normative expectations that justices *should* respond to the public, it would be unlikely that the predominant pattern would be justices who adhere slavishly to the preferences of the public.

Evidence of the levels of individual justice responsiveness to public opinion has recently been adduced. For instance, Thomas Marshall discovered substantial variability in the degree to which the votes of individual justices were congruent with public opinion (p. 106). In recent history, the justices who seem to have been the most sensitive to public opinion include Charles Evans *Hughes and Fred *Vinson; the least sensitive justice was Wiley *Rutledge. On balance, it is unlikely that most justices of the Supreme Court have viewed their positions as that of being "instructed delegates" of the people, but at the same time most have been in relatively close step with the views of ordinary people.

Even those justices who are motivated to incorporate public opinion into their decisional calculus face some important difficulties. Indeed, perhaps the single greatest impediment to public influence on the Court lies not with the individual justices but is instead related to the public itself. There are many steps in the process of influencing Court policies, but all of these are dependent upon ordinary citizens having opinions on pressing legal issues and making an effort to communicate those opinions to the justices. There are quite obvious examples in which citizens have actively pressed their views on the Supreme Court—*abortion is a most salient example—but it is generally remarkable that citizens exert so little effort to try to influence the Court. For much of the history of that institution, public influence over public policy has been weakened simply by the fact that there has been little public effort to influence the Court.

How is the level of influence of public opinion on the Supreme Court likely to change in the near future? Over the longer course of time, the Court has generally not deviated too far from the views of the majority. The driving process here has been the tendency to have relatively frequent turnover of justices. To the extent that justices remain on the bench for longer periods of time, as is increasingly the case, the primary process through which the Court and the public remain consistent is weakening.

At the same time, however, individual justices have occasionally been motivated to represent public opinion. This linkage is not particularly strong, owing to well-grounded arguments in favor of judicial unaccountability; in addition, as justices are increasingly drawn from among legal careerists rather than legal politicos, the tendency to find this sort of individual on the high bench is declining as well. Indeed, it is reasonable to predict that while public opinion influence on the Court has never been particularly strong, public preferences will play a diminishing role for the foreseeable future.

In the final analysis, it is unlikely that justices of the Supreme Court are swayed by public opinion in specific disputes. Norms discouraging such responsiveness are quite strong. Yet it is also likely that broader currents in public opinion do receive some attention from the justices. It would be difficult, if not impossible, to ignore the changes in fundamental attitudes toward the role of women, family, marriage, and sex that have occurred over the course of the last several decades, for instance. But beyond the broad changes in cultural values it appears that the Supreme Court will become increasingly impervious to the views of ordinary citizens.

(See also DECISION-MAKING DYNAMICS.)

□ Robert Dahl, "Decision-making in a Democracy: The Supreme Court as a National Policy-maker," *Journal of Public Law* 6 (1957): 279–295. Thomas R. Marshall, *Public Opinion and the Supreme Court* (1989).

James L. Gibson

**Public Use Doctrine.** The public use doctrine suggests that there may be a limitation on the purposes for which the government can exercise the power of *eminent domain. The *Fifth Amendment to the Constitution reads, "nor shall private property be taken for public use without just compensation." Most state constitutions contain similar language.

In one form, as seen in some early state court decisions, and still in the interpretation of several state constitutions, the public use doctrine means that eminent domain may be used only when the public will make physical use of the land. However, modern Supreme Court decisions make it clear that under the Fifth Amendment, property may be taken if such action will aid government to attain some appropriate governmental objective. Thus, the phrase "public use" does not impose any special limitations on eminent domain. This view was established in *Berman v. Parker* (1954) and reinforced by *Hawaii Housing Authority v. Midkiff* (1984). *State courts are free to interpret their state taking clauses more restrictively, and, as suggested, several do so. Most states, however, interpret their own *taking clauses much as the Supreme Court interprets the public use langauge of the Fifth Amendment.

William B. Stoebuck

**Pure Speech.** See SPEECH AND THE PRESS.

**Putzel, Henry, Jr.,** (b. Denver, Colo., 8 Oct. 1913), reporter of decisions, 1964–1979. Putzel graduated from Yale College (1935) and Yale Law School (1938). After practicing law in St. Louis from 1938 to 1941, he held a succession of federal positions in Washington, D.C. These were attorney for the Office of Price Administration (1942–1945); for the Foreign Agents Registration Section of the Justice Department (1945–1948); and for the Civil Rights Section of the Justice Department's Criminal Division (1948–1957). Within the Civil Rights Section, Putzel's activities included school desegregation cases and prosecutions against persons who had denied civil rights under color of law.

In 1957 the Justice Department created a separate Civil Rights Division, and Putzel became chief of its Voting and Elections Section. There he was concerned with matters such as racially discriminatory voting practices, and later, with federal election frauds. On 17 February 1964 he was sworn as the Supreme Court's thirteenth reporter of decisions. Putzel edited or coedited volumes 376 through 440 of the *United States Reports*. An important change in reporting procedure occurred during his term: the Court ordered headnotes prepared before announcement of an opinion, rather than after announcement, as had been the case.

Putzel once described three characteristics necessary for a reporter of decisions: being a lawyer, a "word nut," and a "double revolving peripatetic nit-picker." When Putzel retired on 24 February 1979, Chief Justice Warren *Burger said that he had "performed the exacting duties of that important office with great distinction and in keeping with the tradition of the twelve men who preceded him in that position."

Francis Helminski

**Quirin, Ex Parte,** 317 U.S. 1 (1942), argued 29–30 July 1942, decided 31 July 1942 by vote of 8 to 0; per curiam, Murphy not participating; full opinion filed 29 Oct. 1942; Stone for the Court. In early July 1942, President Franklin D. *Roosevelt established a military commission to try eight recently captured German saboteurs for alleged violations of the uncodified international law of *war and the congressionally enacted Articles of War. During the trial, seven of the accused sought leave to file petitions for *habeas corpus. At a special session in late July, the Supreme Court summarily rejected the prisoners' applications, paving the way for the execution of six of the prisoners little more than a week later.

The Court's unanimous full opinion, issued in late October, upheld the prisoners' right to *judicial review. The Court declared, however, that a *military trial was justified by a combination of the president's power as commander in chief and valid congressional legislation authorizing military trials of those accused of committing offenses against the law of war. The Court upheld congressional adoption of the international *common law of war and declared that Congress need not specifically define all the acts that violate that law. The Court further found that the accused had been sufficiently charged with unlawful

belligerency and that this offense was within the commission's jurisdiction.

The justices declared that the prisoners were not entitled to *grand jury process or a *trial by jury. They distinguished *Ex parte *Milligan* (1866), which barred military trials of violations of the law of war when local state courts are in operation, on the ground that Milligan had not been deemed an enemy belligerent.

(See also SUBVERSION.)

□ Michal R. Belknap, "The Supreme Court Goes to War: The Meaning and Implications of the Nazi Saboteur Case," *Military Law Review* 89 (1980): 59–95.

James May

**Quo Warranto.** An extraordinary writ of medieval origin, quo warranto (Lat., "by what warrant") evolved over time into a proceeding either criminal or civil to contest a party's occupation or use of an office or franchise. In the United States, the Supreme Court has described it in *Johnson v. Manhattan Railway Co.* (1933) as "addressed to preventing a continued exercise of authority unlawfully asserted," brought by the state or federal government against any person alleged to "exercise an office or authority without lawful right" (p. 502).

William M. Wiecek

# R

**Race and Racism.** Problems of race and race relations—particularly issues concerning the status of African-Americans—have played a prominent role in American political life since the colonial era. Given the place of the Supreme Court in the political structure, it was almost inevitable that the Court would be called upon to take an active role in resolving these problems. Thus it is not surprising that the Court has often been a significant participant in controversies over race relations.

The response of the Court has been shaped by a variety of factors. The most obvious is the attitudes of the individual justices toward the race problem itself. These attitudes typically reflect the attitudes of white society as a whole toward blacks. As the position of white society as a whole on racial issues changed over time, so too has the position of the Court. Further, where there has been no consensus in society on a particular issue, the justices themselves have often been split.

The approach of the Court to racial questions has also been complicated by questions of *federalism. Where federal action on racial matters has been challenged, the justices have been forced to consider whether the challenged action was within the powers granted to the states or the federal government by the Constitution. The doctrine of states' rights has also had a significant impact on the resolution of challenges to state governmental action (see STATE SOVEREIGNTY AND STATES' RIGHTS). The attitude of the Court toward these issues has changed substantially in recent years, contributing to a change in the pattern of decisions on racial issues.

*Antebellum Era.* Federal law played only a relatively limited role in debates over the status of blacks prior to the *Civil War. The general primacy of state law was a function of both the basic philosophy of the Constitution and specific provisions relating to the *slavery issue. First, the general theory of federalism underlying the antebellum Constitution left to each state almost complete power to regulate the relationships among its inhabitants and purely domestic affairs generally. Moreover, the Constitution contains a number of specific provisions—most notably the Fugitive Slave Clause, Slave Trade Clause, and the three-fifths compromise—which plainly recognize the existence of the institution of slavery. In the face of such evidence, it is not surprising that only a small group of the most radical abolitionists—well out of the political mainstream—argued that Congress had the power and duty to attack directly slavery in the states.

Nonetheless, federal law became important in a number of contexts. One group of problems involved the interstate movement of slaves or free blacks generally. Such cases involved the sovereign interests of the nation (or at least those of more than one state) and thus provided an arguable basis for federal control. Thus, for example, federal constitutional arguments appeared in discussions of the obligation of free states to admit free Negroes and to respect the *property rights of slaveholders in transit. In both of those situations, however, nonfederal considerations remained the central force (see COMITY). By contrast, with respect to the problem of *fugitive slaves, the federal law became dominant.

In response to the demands of the representatives of southern states, the drafters of the Constitution had specifically included a provision dealing with the problem of fugitive slaves. Article IV, section two provided that

[n]o person held to Service or Labour in one State, under the Laws thereof, escaping into another, shall, in consequence of any Law or Regulation therein, be discharged from such Service or Labour, but shall be delivered up on claim of the Party to whom such Service or Labour may be due.

Clearly, this provision constitutionalized the *common-law right of "recaption"—the right of the master to retrieve his slave through self-help. But by its terms, the Fugitive Slave Clause does not define the respective roles of the state and federal governments in implementing and regulating this right.

The potential conflicts between state and federal authority in this area emerged soon after the adoption of the Constitution. The federal government passed the first Fugitive Slave Act in 1793. A few northern states responded by adopting personal liberty and antikidnapping laws, which significantly restricted the right of recaption. The issue of the constitutionality of these laws reached the Supreme Court in *Prigg v. Pennsylvania (1842).

Justice Joseph *Story's majority opinion took a middle ground between the antislavery position, which denied federal power to pass legislation to enforce the Fugitive Slave Clause, and the proslavery position, which posited both a federal and a state duty to adopt enforcement legislation. Story recognized the owner's right to resort to self-help and the unconstitutionality of any state law that interfered with that right; the authority of Congress to enact legislation that aided the owner; and the lack of any power in the states to enact additional enforcement legislation. Story also suggested that Congress could not constitutionally require state officials to assist in the enforcement process.

As intersectional tensions over the issue of slavery escalated sharply in the 1850s, the issue of fugitive slaves returned to the Court in *Ableman v. Booth (1859). The abolitionist Sherman Booth was a Wisconsin resident who had been arrested and charged under the Fugitive Slave Act of 1850 for obstructing the return of a fugitive slave. While in federal custody, but before his trial, Booth applied to the Wisconsin Supreme Court for a writ of *habeas corpus. A justice of the Wisconsin court freed Booth on the grounds that the Fugitive Slave Act was unconstitutional, and this judgment was affirmed by the entire state supreme court. While an appeal from this judgment to the United States Supreme Court was pending, Booth was rearrested and convicted in federal district court. Once more, the Wisconsin Supreme Court issued a writ of habeas corpus ordering his release from federal custody. In one

of Chief Justice Roger B. *Taney's most famous and well-respected decisions, he overturned the writs and forcefully asserted the principle of federal judicial supremacy. Although it clearly had implications for the struggle over slavery, Taney's opinion might be viewed as a simple defense of the supremacy of federal law.

Problems of federalism were also involved in Dred *Scott v. Sandford (1857). In Dred Scott, however, issues of race relations were more clearly at the center of the case. Scott had been held as a slave in Missouri, a slave state. His master brought him into a portion of the federal territories in which slavery was forbidden by the Missouri Compromise and into a free state. Scott brought a diversity action in federal court, arguing that he should be considered a free man by virtue of having been brought into a free territory and state. The case raised two critical issues of race relations. The first was whether Scott could be considered a citizen of the United States for purposes of determining diversity of *citizenship. The second was whether Congress could constitutionally prohibit slavery in the *territories.

Rejecting Scott's claim, Chief Justice Taney answered both questions in the negative, although whether he spoke for a majority of the Court on every issue raised in the case is questionable. Taney first concluded that the federal courts lacked jurisdiction over the case because, under the Constitution, descendants of slaves could never become citizens of the United States. He then argued that, in any event, the portion of the Missouri Compromise banning slavery in the northern territories was unconstitutional. Primarily, this contention was based on the theory of enumerated powers; in Taney's view the congressional power to "make all needful Rules and Regulations respecting the Territory . . . belonging to the United States" (Art. IV, sec. 3) did not include the authority to outlaw slavery. In addition, Taney made a substantive *due process argument, concluding that the prohibition on slavery in some of the territories deprived slaveholders of their property without due process of law.

While it cannot be considered a primary cause of the Civil War, the Dred Scott decision did exacerbate sectional tensions over the institution of slavery. On one hand, the decision reinforced Republican claims that the federal government was dominated by a "slave power" committed to the advancement of southern interests at the expense of the values held by northern society. It also raised fears that the Court might require free states to allow Southerners to bring slaves into their jurisdiction. At the same time, Dred Scott bolstered the proslavery contentions that the extension of slavery to the territories was not only just but also mandated by the Constitution itself. But in any event, the doctrinal framework of Dred Scott did not survive the constitutional changes wrought by the Civil War and the *Reconstruction period.

**Reconstruction Amendments and Their Aftermath.** The constitutional changes that took place following the Civil War substantially changed the role of the federal courts in defining the terms of race relations in the United States. Concerned about the conditions of blacks in the defeated southern states, Congress adopted three constitutional amendments and essentially forced their ratification. The *Thirteenth Amendment outlawed slavery. Section one of the *Fourteenth Amendment conferred both national and state citizenship on blacks. In addition, section one required that the states confer on all citizens the *privileges and immunities of national citizenship and required that the life, liberty and property of all persons be protected by due process of law, and that all persons be granted *equal protection of the laws. Finally, the *Fifteenth Amendment prohibited racial discrimination in voting rights. Each of the amendments contained a clause granting Congress enforcement authority. Purporting to act pursuant to this authority, Congress enacted a series of civil rights statutes intended to protect the newly freed slaves from racial discrimination.

In the last third of the nineteenth century, the Supreme Court faced a variety of issues related to the interpretation of the Reconstruction amendments and the statutes adopted under their enforcement authority. The difficulty was that, at the margins at least, the intentions of those who drafted the Reconstruction amendments were unclear. Clearly, the members of the Reconstruction Congresses intended to prohibit certain specific abuses and to arm Congress with the authority to reach those abuses. Beyond those specific problems, the intended impact of the constitutional changes on the states and the powers of Congress was controversial and remains so today.

Occasionally, the Court took a fairly broad view of the scope of the amendments. For example, in *Strauder v. West Virginia (1880), the Court found a statute limiting jury service to whites inconsistent with the Fourteenth Amendment, although a plausible historical argument could be made in favor of a contrary result. In a variety of other circumstances, however, the Court gave a relatively narrow construction to the Reconstruction enactments.

Once again, consideration of federalism played an important role in many of the Court's decisions. The concept of states' rights and its corollary, limited national government, were critical to the Court's approach to civil rights issues. Focusing on these principles, the Court often imposed strict limitations on the scope of both the Reconstruction amendments themselves and the civil rights statutes adopted by Congress.

United States v. *Cruikshank (1876) exemplified this trend. Cruikshank arose from an incident in which several hundred armed whites surrounded a courthouse in which blacks were holding a public assembly, burned the building, and murdered about one hundred people. They were indicted under a statute derived from the Force Act of 1870, which makes it a federal crime for two or more people to conspire "to injure, oppress, threaten, or intimidate any person in the free exercise of any right or privilege secured to him by the Constitution or laws of the United States."

The Cruikshank Court dismissed the indictment. Following the analysis of the *Slaughterhouse Cases (1873), Chief Justice Morrison R. *Waite closely circumscribed the definition of rights secured to persons by the Constitution. He argued that all of the rights described in the indictment, including the right to assemble peaceably and the right to bear arms, derived from state citizenship and thus were beyond the ambit of federal protection. The scope of congressional authority to protect blacks was thus sharply curtailed.

The Court's treatment of the *state action problem during this period reflects a similar attitude. The *Civil Rights Cases (1883) provide a particularly striking example. These cases involved the Civil Rights Act of 1875, which outlawed racial discrimination by operators of public accommodations and public conveyances. Such facilities had traditionally been held to be quasi-public in nature; even prior to the adoption of the Reconstruction amendments, a number of courts had held that the common law prohibited operators of public conveyances from segregating their passengers on the basis of race. Moreover, during the Reconstruction era Congress had specifically banned segregation on street railways in the District of Columbia. Nonetheless, the Court in the Civil Rights Cases held that neither the Thirteenth nor the Fourteenth Amendment granted Congress the authority to pass statutes such as the Civil Rights Act of 1875. Congressional power could control only the actions of states, not of individuals. Together with similar decisions in cases such as United States v. Harris (1883) and United States v. *Reese (1876), the Civil Rights Cases effectively curtailed the ability of Congress to improve the condition of the newly freed slaves.

The problem of discrimination in public conveyances returned to the Court in *Plessy v. Ferguson (1896). In Plessy, the Court was faced with a Fourteenth Amendment challenge to a state statute that required railways to maintain separate carriages for white and black patrons. The Court conceded that the object of the Fourteenth Amendment was to enforce "the absolute equality of the races before the law"; at the same time, however, the majority reasoned that the amendment "could not have been intended to abolish distinctions based on color, or to enforce social, as distinguished from political, equality" (p. 544). The Plessy majority also rejected the claim that the statute by its nature stamped blacks with "a badge of inferiority," arguing that "[i]f this be so, it is not by reason of anything found in the act, but solely because [the black person] chooses to put that construction upon it" (p. 551). (See SEPARATE BUT EQUAL DOCTRINE.)

Underlying the *Plessy* decision was an unstated belief that blacks were inherently inferior to whites. This belief was widely shared among whites in the late nineteenth century; indeed, even Justice John Marshall *Harlan's dissent in *Plessy* explicitly noted that "[t]he white race deems itself to be the dominant race in this country. . . . So, I doubt not, it will continue to be for all time, if it remains true to its great heritage, and holds fast to the principles of constitutional liberty" (p. 559). So long as the Court was dominated by men with such attitudes, constitutional law would be of little use to those seeking racial equality.

**Early Twentieth Century: From Plessy to Brown.** During the early twentieth century, the Supreme Court's record on race relations issues was uneven. In egregious cases, the Court did at times intervene actively to protect the rights of racial minorities; for example, in *Guinn* v. *United States* (1915), it struck down so-called *grandfather clauses—voting requirements that were clearly crafted with a view to restricting the right of blacks to *vote, while leaving the voting rights of whites unaffected. By contrast, in *Gong Lum* v. *Rice* (1927), the Court not only refused to require a state to allow a Chinese-American to attend school with whites, but also cited with apparent approval lower court cases that applied the separate but equal doctrine to public *education generally.

The Court was particularly hostile to wartime challenges to government actions aimed at Japanese-Americans during *World War II, Military authorities issued a number of orders placing severe restrictions on this group of citizens, including curfews, exclusions, and forced relocation. Congress adopted legislation criminalizing violations of these orders. In *Hirabayashi v. United States* (1943) and *Korematsu v. United States* (1944), the Court rejected claims that these orders violated constitutional norms. Speaking for the majority in *Korematsu*, Justice Hugo *Black declared that "[a]ll restrictions that curtail the civil rights of a single racial group are immediately suspect" and subject to "the most rigid scrutiny" (p. 216). (See SUSPECT CLASSIFICATIONS.) Nonetheless, he concluded that the exigencies of the wartime situation provided sufficient justification for imposing restrictions on those of Japanese ancestry.

Despite cases such as these, as the twentieth century progressed the Court showed signs of becoming more sensitive to the plight of minority races. For example, it soon became clear that cases such as *Hirabayashi* and *Korematsu* would not be extended to peace-time race-relations

issues. In *Oyama* v. *California* (1948) and *Takahashi* v. *Fish and Game Commission* (1948), the Court made clear that the states could not impose special disabilities on those of Asian descent.

The Court's decisions also expanded the concept of state action. In one of the most significant cases—*Screws* v. *United States* (1945)—the Court gave a broad interpretation to a federal statute that provides for the criminal prosecution of those who deprive persons of civil rights "under color of law." It held that state officials who wielded government power acted under color of law even when the specific actions for which they were being prosecuted were illegal under state law.

State action was also the central problem in *Shelley* v. *Kraemer* (1948) and *Barrows* v. *Jackson* (1953). In those cases the Court was asked to determine the constitutionality of judicial enforcement of private agreements not to sell real estate to blacks. Having held in *Buchanan* v. *Warley* (1917) and *Harmon* v. *Tyler* (1927) that the state could not directly restrict the right of blacks to live in particular neighborhoods, the Court in *Shelley* and *Barrows* had little difficulty in determining that courts could not constitutionally enforce private racially *restrictive covenants, finding such judicial involvement to be state action (see HOUSING DISCRIMINATION).

State action again was a key issue in challenges to political party rules that restricted party membership and political participation to whites. Such rules were particularly important in southern states, where nomination by the then all-white Democratic party was tantamount to election. After initially holding in *Grovey* v. *Townsend* (1935) that such rules were not state action and thus not inconsistent with the Reconstruction amendments, the Court reversed itself in *Smith* v. *Allwright* (1944), reasoning that by guaranteeing ballot access to the winner of the party primary, the state had in effect endorsed the exclusionary policy. The rule of *Smith* was expanded in *Terry* v. *Adams* (1953) to cover the preprimary election of an association of Democrats whose endorsement was functionally equivalent to selection as the party candidate (see WHITE PRIMARY).

Finally, during the latter part of this period, the Court began to ease the rigors of the principles underlying *Plessy* v. *Ferguson*. Ironically, the only direct assault on the separate but equal doctrine did not involve the Reconstruction amendments at all. In *Morgan* v. *Virginia* (1946), the Court held that a Virginia statute requiring interstate buses to maintain racial segregation was unconstitutional because it imposed an undue burden on interstate commerce (see COMMERCE POWER).

By contrast, during this era the Court consistently declined invitations to reconsider the application of the separate but equal doctrine to public education. At the same time, however, it viewed with increasing skepticism claims that states were in fact providing members of racial minorities with equal educational opportunity. In *Missouri ex rel. Gaines* v. *Canada* (1938), the Court held that a state could not discharge its obligations under the Equal Protection Clause by providing blacks with tuition to attend law schools in other states excluding them from its own. In *Sweatt* v. *Painter* (1950), it concluded that a law school for blacks was not functionally equivalent to a school for whites because by its nature it excluded most of those with whom graduates would inevitably have to deal during their professional lives. And in *McLaurin* v. *Oklahoma State Regents for Higher Education* (1950), the Court found insufficient a regime under which blacks were allowed to attend the same graduate schools as whites but were kept physically separated from their white counterparts.

In short, the early twentieth century Supreme Court was significantly more active than its predecessors in protecting the rights of minority races. The importance of the Court's shift should not be overstated, however; changes in basic constitutional doctrine took place only at the margins. Revolutionary changes did not come about until the advent of the Warren Court in 1953.

*Warren Era.* Under the leadership of Chief Justice Earl *Warren, after 1954 the Supreme Court mounted an increasingly aggressive campaign to ameliorate the condition of racial minorities in the United States. The campaign began with the landmark decisions in *Brown* v. *Board of Education* (1954) and its companion case, *Bolling* v. *Sharpe* (1954). Unlike the earlier cases dealing with segregated education, *Brown* focused directly on the applicability of the separate but equal doctrine to education. Focusing on the importance of education, the Court held that the maintenance of government-mandated segregated schools was inconsistent with the Equal Protection Clause of the Fourteenth Amendment. In sharp contrast to *Plessy*, the Court also relied heavily on the stigma imposed on blacks by segregation. Some of the language in *Brown* suggested that decision might have rested on the special place of public education in American society; it soon became clear, however, that the Court would invalidate all state-imposed racial segregation (see SEGREGATION, DE JURE).

The Court's approach to the state-action problem also reflected its growing concern with the issue of racial equality. While not rejecting the basic proposition that the Equal Protection Clause placed constraints only on governmental action, cases such as *Burton* v. *Wilmington Parking Authority* (1961) and *Evans* v. *Newton* (1966) held that a variety of seemingly private activities such as operating a restaurant in a public building would be considered state action for constitutional purposes. Thus the Warren Court's decisions expanded the scope of Fourteenth Amendment protections.

During the same period Congress also demonstrated a renewed commitment to the concept of racial equality, adopting a variety of landmark laws designed to deal with the problem of racial discrimination. The most important of the new statutes were the *Civil Rights Act of 1964 and the *Voting Rights Act of 1965. Not surprisingly, opponents of both statutes argued that Congress had exceeded the authority granted to it under the Constitution. The Supreme Court uniformly rejected these challenges.

The earliest attack on the Civil Rights Act focused on Title II, which prohibited discrimination in the provision of public accommodations. In upholding the statute, the Court did not rely on any specific constitutional grant of power to prohibit racial discrimination. Instead, *Heart of Atlanta Motel, Inc.* v. *United States* (1964) and *Katzenbach* v. *McClung* (1964) focused on Congress's power to regulate interstate commerce, reasoning that Congress could have plausibly determined that racial discrimination had an adverse effect on the free movement of goods and people.

In some respects the voting rights litigation was even more significant. The Voting Rights Act not only prohibited racial discrimination in voting rights but also provided that federal officials should register voters in areas where conditions indicated that racial discrimination was prevalent; required federal preclearance for suffrage-related changes in such areas in order to ensure that such changes did not have either the purpose or effect of diluting minority voting rights; and limited the use of literacy tests in some circumstances. By any standard, this legislation intruded deeply into areas that historically had been under state control. Nonetheless, the Court rejected all constitutional challenges to the power of Congress to adopt the Voting Rights Act. Upholding the preclearance provisions in *South Carolina* v. *Katzenbach* (1966), the Court declared that "Congress [is] chiefly responsible for implementing the rights created [by the Fifteenth Amendment]" and had broad discretion in devising remedies for perceived violations of voting rights (p. 326). *Katzenbach* v. *Morgan* (1966) went even further, holding that in some circumstances Congress could rely on its enforcement authority to prohibit even some practices that the Court had specifically found to be constitutionally unobjectionable.

The Warren Court not only took an expansive view of congressional authority to remedy perceived racial discrimination but also gave expansive interpretations to hitherto dormant federal statutes in this area. The most prominent example was *Jones* v. *Alfred H. Mayer Co.* (1968), in which the Court not only reaffirmed its view that Congress had the power to reach private racial discrimination but also reinterpreted the Civil Rights Act of 1866 to prohibit such discrimination.

In short, during the Warren era the Court consistently took an expansive view of Constitutional and statutory prohibitions on racial discrimination as well as congressional power to address such discrimination. The Court's experience with the school desegregation problem, however, reflected the difficulties that can arise when the judiciary attempts to impose its will on a recalcitrant populace. At the conclusion of the first *Brown* opinion, the Court requested briefing and argument on the question of what remedial action should be taken to dismantle segregated school systems. The following year, in its second *Brown* v. *Board of Education* (1955) opinion, the Court recognized the primacy of local officials in formulating educational policy but directed the district courts to ensure that the transition to a unitary school system was accomplished "with *all deliberate speed" (see DESEGREGATION REMEDIES).

Obviously, the *Brown II* Court hoped for cooperation between the federal courts and local authorities in the desegregation process. Such cooperation was not forthcoming. The judiciary was faced with southern school boards and state governments that were typically committed to the philosophy of "massive resistance" to desegregation. Even when forced by the courts to alter their pupil assignment practices to some degree, local school authorities often adopted policies that might be neutral on their face but were in fact designed to minimize racial integration in the schools. In the most extreme example, the school board of Prince Edward County, Virginia, attempted to close its public schools and provide tuition grants to students attending private schools, with the expectation that these schools would maintain racial segregation. In *Griffin* v. *County School Board* (1964), the Court ordered the public schools reopened, declaring that "[t]here has been entirely too much deliberation and not enough speed" in the desegregation process. The Court's frustration became even more evident in *Green* v. *County School Board* (1968). There, rejecting a "freedom of choice" plan for public school students, the Court declared that "[t]he burden on a school board today is to come forward with a plan that realistically promises to work . . . *now* . . . to convert to a unitary system in which racial discrimination would be eliminated root and branch" (pp. 439, 438). Despite such strong statements, the struggle over the proper scope of desegregation orders would continue well beyond the Warren era.

**Burger and Rehnquist Courts.** During the post-Warren era, the pattern of Supreme Court decisions on race relations issues has defied easy characterization. In part, the lack of a clear pattern derives from the diversity among the justices themselves. The Warren Court was dominated by liberal activists, and its record on race relations issues reflected this dominance (see JUDICIAL ACTIVISM). By contrast, the Burger and Rehnquist Courts were more ideologically balanced, a factor that has often been evidenced by close divisions on controversial questions. The increased influence of conservatives on the Court has been evident in cases such as *Patterson* v. *McLean Credit Union* (1989), which limited the scope of the previous holding in *Jones* v. *Alfred H. Mayer Co.*

The nature of the issues faced by the Court has also changed substantially. The legality of deliberate state-imposed segregation and private discrimination against minority races presented the easiest questions for persons committed to the basic principle of racial equality. Unlike their predecessor, the Burger and Rehnquist Courts have been presented with cases that raised more difficult questions about both the nature of racial equality and the proper role of the federal courts in promoting such equality.

*School Desegregation.* The influence of all of these factors has been apparent in the continued evolution of the law of school desegregation in the post-Warren era. The period began with the decision in *Swann* v. *Charlotte-Mecklenburg Board of Education* (1971). In *Swann*, the Court unanimously upheld a district court order that mandated wide-scale restructuring of a southern, urban school district in an effort to achieve racial balance by busing. While denying that there was any constitutional right to attend a school whose student body reflected the racial composition of the district as a whole, the opinion concluded that "[a]wareness of the racial composition of the entire school system is likely to be a useful starting point in shaping a remedy to correct past constitutional violations."

The problem became more complex as desegregation litigation moved to the North. Typically, the laws governing northern school systems did not explicitly mandate the type of racial segregation involved in the cases from *Brown* through *Swann;* instead, the systems were generally based on the principle of neighborhood schools. At the same time, however, these schools were often racially unbalanced. The imbalance resulted from two factors. First, demographic factors not directly related to school policies led to the geographic concentration of minority races. Second, boundaries were often subtly adjusted to minimize the mixing of the races in schools. Given *Swann's* statement that the constitution did not guarantee to students the right to attend racially balanced schools, distinguishing between the effects of deliberate segregative acts and other factors became an important and difficult consideration (see SEGREGATION, DE FACTO).

*Keyes* v. *Denver School District No. 1* (1973) provided the basis for widespread judicial intervention in northern school systems. In *Keyes*, the Court held that where a "meaningful portion" of a school system was found to be intentionally segregated, other racial imbalance in the system would be almost irrefutably presumed to also be the result of deliberate segregative acts. *Keyes* and subsequent cases such as *\*Columbus Board of Education* v. *Penick* (1979) and *Dayton Board of Education* v. *Brinkman* (1979) opened the way for *Swann*-type orders to be applied to many northern, urban school systems. *Milliken* v. *Bradley* (1977) expanded the scope of permissible orders even further, holding that the federal courts could order previously segregated school districts to adopt measures not directly related to racial balance. *\*Missouri* v. *Jenkins* (1990) held that a federal district court judge could order local property taxes raised to pay for such measures.

The power of the federal courts to deal with the problem of segregated schools is not unlimited, however. In the first *\*Milliken* v. *Bradley* (1974), the Court held that in the absence of a showing of segregative acts with intersystem effects, the courts could not impose intersystem desegregation orders. Given that the student population of many city school systems has become increasingly dominated by members of minority races, *Milliken* was an important limitation on the ability of the federal courts to achieve actual racial balance in the schools.

*Discriminatory Impact.* The Warren Court had generally been preoccupied with problems of deliberate discrimination against minority races. In the post-Warren era, by contrast, race-neutral actions with discriminatory impact came under increasing attack. Some argued such actions should be closely scrutinized in order to ensure that members of minority racial groups were not arbitrarily denied access to opportunities. Others contended that only deliberate racial discrimination should be proscribed. The issue had both statutory and constitutional dimensions (see DIS-CRIMINATORY INTENT).

In *\*Griggs* v. *Duke Power Co.* (1971), the Court held unanimously that discriminatory impact was an important element to be considered under Title VII of the Civil Rights Act of 1964. Under *Griggs*, employment practices with a *\*disparate impact* were held illegal unless justified by a "business necessity." The scope of the business necessity defense became a much-debated issue. Cases such as *\*Albemarle Paper Co.* v. *Moody* (1975) and *Dothard* v. *Rawlinson* (1977) suggested that the business necessity criterion would be difficult to satisfy. *\*Washington* v. *Davis* (1976) and *New York City Transit Authority* v. *Beazer* (1979) conveyed a quite different impression. Ultimately, in *\*Ward's Cove Packing Co.* v. *Atonio* (1989), the Court modified disparate impact analysis, holding that those challenging an employment practice were required to prove that an employer's proffered justification was in fact illusory (see EMPLOYMENT DISCRIMINATION). The *\*Civil Rights Act of 1991*, however, curtailed the full impact of *Ward's Cove.*

The Court's treatment of the constitutional status of discriminatory impact showed a similar ambivalence. In *Washington* v. *Davis* (1976) and *\*Mobile* v. *Bolden* (1980), the Court held that a simple showing of discriminatory impact was insufficient to raise the level of scrutiny under the Fourteenth and Fifteenth Amendments, respectively (see STRICT SCRUTINY). At the same time, however, in *\*Arlington Heights* v. *Metropolitan Housing Development Corp.* (1977), the Court indicated that discriminatory impact could in some cases raise an inference of discriminatory intent and in *Rogers* v. *Lodge* (1982) held that impact was particularly important to the evaluation of voting rights claims.

*Affirmative Action.* The most controversial race-related issue of the post-Warren era has been the status of *\*affirmative action* programs, described by their critics as "reverse racial discrimination." The details of these programs vary widely, but all involve the principle of preferential treatment for members of minority racial groups. Opponents claim that affirmative action programs violate the moral imperative that a person's race should not be taken into account in the decision-making process. Proponents, by contrast, argue that because the long history of racial discrimination in America has a continuing, negative effect on members of minority racial groups, preferential treatment is necessary to provide them with their fair share of benefits and privileges.

The split in society as a whole on this issue has been mirrored in the reactions of the Court when programs granting preferential treatment to minority races have faced legal challenges. Some justices have voted to reject all such challenges. Others have consistently voted to strike down preferential treatment programs. Still others have taken some middle ground. Until quite recently, the middle group seemed to hold the balance of power on the issue. The Court struck down a medical school's reservation of a certain number of places for members of minority groups in *\*Regents of University of California* v. *Bakke* (1978). It also found unconstitutional a modification of seniority rights to ensure minority representation among teachers in *Wygant* v. *Jackson Board of Education* (1986). During the same period, however, the Court rejected a statutory challenge to a private party's affirmative action plan in *\*United Steelworkers of America* v. *Weber* (1979); a constitutional challenge to a set-aside program mandating minority participation in federal public works projects in *\*Fullilove* v. *Klutznick* (1980); and constitutional challenges to racial quotas imposed by courts as remedies for past discrimination in *\*Local 28 of Sheet Metal Workers International Association* v. *Equal Employment Opportunity Commission* (1986) and *United States* v. *Paradise* (1987).

Recent personnel changes have shifted the balance on the Court against preferential treatment programs. *\*Richmond* v. *J. A. Croson Co.* (1989), the Court held unconstitutional a city-adopted minority set-aside program virtually identical to the federal program that had been upheld in *Fullilove.* Even more importantly,

*Croson* was the first case in which a majority of the Court clearly committed itself to very stringent scrutiny of affirmative action programs.

*Croson*, however, did not sound the death knell for all affirmative action programs. In *Metro Broadcasting, Inc.* v. *FCC* (1990), the Court rejected constitutional challenges to regulations of the Federal Communications Commission that gave preferential treatment to minority-owned stations in licensing proceedings. The regulations were adopted pursuant to a statutory directive requiring the commission to promote diversification of programming in the broadcasting industry, and had been explicitly approved by Congress. Rather than applying strict scrutiny, the majority held that the regulations were constitutionally permissible because they served important government objectives and were substantially related to those objectives.

In practical terms, *Metro Broadcasting* probably does not suggest that the Court will accept a wide range of affirmative action programs. The constitutional attack on the plan was only rejected by a narrow 5-to-4 margin, and one of the members of the majority emphasized that in his view use of racial and ethnic classifications was acceptable in "extremely rare circumstances." Further, Justices William J. *Brennan and Thurgood *Marshall, the most persistent judicial champions of preferential treatment, retired from the Court soon after the case was decided. Finally, like the plurality opinion in *Fullilove*, the majority opinion in *Metro Broadcasting* emphasized that a federal program was being challenged and emphasized the deference due to the decisions of coordinate branches of the federal government. Thus the case seems likely to have little significance for legal challenges to programs adopted by state governments or private parties.

On a theoretical level, however, *Metro Broadcasting* has far more significance. It reflects the profound changes in the theory of federalism that have taken place in the latter part of the twentieth century. For most of the history of the United States, private parties and state governments have been given great flexibility in dealing with social problems. The role of the federal government has been limited by the doctrine of enumerated powers. Prior to the Warren years, the approach of the Court to racial issues was largely shaped by this conception of federalism.

Since the constitutional revolution of 1937, however, the role of the federal government in dealing with social problems has grown exponentially, and the Court has generally acquiesced in the expansion of federal power. *Metro Broadcasting* reflects this trend; indeed, the juxtaposition of *Metro Broadcasting* and *Croson* essentially turns the traditional theory of federalism on its head. Henceforth, the federal government is apparently to be granted more authority than the states in crafting responses to the fundamental issues raised by the history of racial injustice in the United States. Whatever one's view of the desirability of preferential treatment generally, this surely is a significant development in constitutional theory.

**Conclusion.** It is quite difficult to evaluate the overall impact of the Supreme Court on race relations in America. One point does emerge clearly, however. In many respects, the evolution of the Supreme Court's approach to issues of race relations mirrors that of American society as a whole. Overall, whites in 1990 almost certainly view racial minorities more benignly than did their predecessors of 1850 or even 1950. At the same time, however, there are limits to the price that most white Americans are willing to pay in order to ameliorate the conditions of racial minorities, and this factor is also reflected in contemporary decisions.

Changes in perceptions of state-federal relations have also had a strong impact on the Court's decisions. The movement from *Cruikshank* to *Katzenbach* v. *McClung* to *Metro Broadcasting* is not only a function of the evolution of social attitudes toward race. It also reflects the degree to which large segments of American society have come to look to the federal government rather than the state governments as the proper agent to solve social problems.

In short, the Supreme Court's experience with race relations provides an excellent illustration of the interaction between the Court and society as a whole. The range of actions likely to be considered by the Court will be determined by the overall political culture in which it operates. The choice among those actions will be determined by a variety of factors, not the least of which are the specific predilections of the serving justices. These considerations define both the possibilities and limits of the Court's potential for dealing with major social problems such as race relations.

□ Derrick A. Bell, Jr., *Race, Racism and American Law* (1980). Harold M. Hyman and William M. Wiecek, *Equal Justice under Law: Constitutional Development 1835–1875* (1982). Richard Kluger, *Simple Justice: The History of Brown v. Board of Education and Black America's Struggle for Equality* (1975). Charles A. Lofgren, *The Plessy Case: A Legal-Historical Interpretation* (1987). J. Harvie Wilkinson, *From Brown to Bakke: The Supreme Court and School Integration: 1954–1978* (1979). Earl M. Maltz

**Race Discrimination and the Death Penalty.** The Supreme Court did not directly address a constitutional claim that the death penalty is administered in a racially discriminatory pattern until it decided *McCleskey* v. *Kemp* (1987). The justices have, however, been aware of the issue for decades. In fact, many of the procedural protections that the Court has established in criminal cases since the 1930s were announced in capital cases involving African-American defendants from the South. Moreover, several early empirical studies were suggestive of racially discriminatory patterns, especially in southern states. But the Court has demonstrated a persistent reluctance to confront the race question directly. In a number of capital cases between 1962 and 1986, the Court either declined requests to hear issues of racial discrimination by denying *certiorari or has resolved the case on other grounds.

A noteworthy example of the Court's diffidence on this issue is *Maxwell v. Bishop* (1970). Maxwell, a black male, received a death sentence from an Arkansas jury for the nonfatal rape of a white woman. The case received particular attention because Maxwell's attorneys supported with statistical evidence their claim that Maxwell's death sentence was part of a racially discriminatory pattern. They first offered data showing that, nationwide, 89 percent of the defendants who were executed for the crime of rape between 1930 and 1962 were black.

Maxwell's attorneys also offered the results of a detailed empirical study of sentencing patterns commissioned by the NAACP *Legal Defense Fund (LDF). The results of this study showed that, between 1945 and 1965, the probability that a black male convicted of raping a white woman would receive the death sentence in Arkansas was about 50 percent, while the death-sentencing rate for cases involving a conviction for intraracial rape was only 14 percent. Maxwell's experts further established that this disparity could not be explained by nonracial factors, such as the level of violence involved or the defendant's prior criminal record. Despite this evidence, the Court of Appeals for the Eighth Circuit ruled that Maxwell's statistics were insufficient to invalidate his death sentence on *equal protection grounds. The Supreme Court agreed to review, and ultimately vacated, the Eighth Circuit's decision on another constitutional ground; but the Court pointedly declined to review Maxwell's statistically based, equal protection claim.

Two years after it decided *Maxwell v. Bishop*, the Supreme Court again confronted claims of racial discrimination in a major capital case, *Furman v. Georgia* (1972). The Court ruled, 5 to 4, that the essentially standardless procedures under which juries in Georgia and in many other states were permitted to impose capital sentences violated the *Cruel and Unusual Punishments Clause of the *Eighth Amendment. The brief, per curiam opinion of the Court did not directly address the claims of racial discrimination asserted both by Furman and another petitioner in a companion case, both of whom were African-American. However, three concurring justices and one dissenting justice expressed in separate opinions their concern that the jury sentencing practices under scrutiny created a dangerous opportunity for racial discrimination. Justice Thurgood *Marshall's concurring opinion gave the question of racially discriminatory death sentences the greatest attention. He recited the same national statistics for rape cases previously presented in *Maxwell v. Bishop* and also reviewed comparable

national statistics for murder cases, which indicated that, although African-Americans constitute just over 10 percent of the nation's population, 49 percent of the 3,334 persons executed between 1930 and 1968 for the crime of murder were African-American.

Although *Furman* invalidated all death-sentencing systems that were in place in 1972, it implied that capital punishment was not absolutely unconstitutional, so long as death sentences were imposed in a nonarbitrary manner. In response to this ruling, the legislatures of more than thirty states amended their laws to comply with *Furman* by creating new sentencing standards—including lists of aggravating and mitigating factors for the jury's consideration—with the aim of limiting the exercise of discretion by sentencing juries. In 1976, the Supreme Court affirmed the constitutionality of all of the new death-sentencing systems except those that made death a mandatory sentence for certain prescribed crimes.

The question remained, however, whether the new systems, which still allowed prosecutors and juries much room for the exercise of discretion, were being applied in a racially discriminatory manner. During the next decade, more than two dozen empirical studies, primarily in southern jurisdictions, tested the discrimination hypothesis in murder cases (the death penalty for rape having been banned by the Supreme Court in 1977). These studies showed mixed and generally inconclusive results with respect to race-of-defendant discrimination. However, the great majority of the studies showed that defendants who murdered whites were more likely to receive a death sentence than those who murdered blacks.

One of the largest of these studies was commissioned by the NAACP Legal Defense Fund in the early 1980s. This study, conducted by David Baldus, George Woodworth, and Charles Pulaski, Jr., analyzed the relationship between sentencing outcomes and racial characteristics in 2,484 homicide cases charged and sentenced in Georgia from 1973 to 1979. The following tabulation, from what the courts have described as "the Baldus study," indicates how death-sentencing outcomes correlated with the defendant/victim racial combination:

| | | |
|---|---|---|
| Black Defendant/White Victim: | 21% | (50/233) |
| White Defendant/White Victim: | 8% | (58/748) |
| Black Defendant/Black Victim: | 1% | (18/1443) |
| White Defendant/Black Victim: | 3% | (2/60) |

These data suggested strong race-of-victim discrimination as well as more punitive treatment of black offenders in white-victim cases. The study further subjected these data to extensive multivariate statistical analysis, designed to estimate racial disparities after adjustment for a large variety of legitimate case characteristics, such as the number of victims, contemporaneous offenses such as rape or robbery, and the defendant's prior record.

Those results provided no evidence of systematic, statewide discrimination against black defendants. They did indicate, however, that the average defendant's odds of receiving a death sentence were 4.3 times higher if the homicide victim in the case was white. The study also showed that the race-of-victim disparities were largest in cases involving a moderate degree of aggravation, that is, among the cases in which the circumstances were neither so heinous as virtually to assure a death sentence nor so extenuated as to assure a life sentence. These "midrange" cases, which gave prosecutors and sentencing juries the largest degree of discretion, were the principal source of the overall race-of-victim effects that emerged in the study. Finally, the study showed that the observed disparities in sentencing were primarily the product of prosecutorial rather than jury decision making.

LDF's Georgia study provided the basis for *McCleskey v. Kemp (1987), a federal habeas corpus proceeding commenced in 1982. McCleskey was a black male whom a jury had sentenced to death for killing a white police officer in Atlanta. In the case, LDF attorneys alleged that the Georgia study of death sentencing demonstrated a pattern of purposeful and intentional discrimination, and that McCleskey's sentence consequently violated the Equal Protection Clause of the *Fourteenth Amendment. McCleskey's lawyers also claimed that the Georgia study demonstrated a sufficient showing of arbitrariness and caprice in Georgia's administration of its capital statute to violate the cruel and unusual punishment prohibition of the Eighth Amendment, as interpreted by Furman.

The Supreme Court rejected both of these constitutional claims by a vote of 5 to 4. The majority opinion, written by Justice Lewis *Powell, declared that, because the Baldus study did not prove "that the decisionmakers in his case acted with discriminatory purpose," no equal protection violation had been established (p. 292). One surprising effect of this Fourteenth Amendment holding is that equal protection claims of purposeful race discrimination in death-sentence cases will now be subjected to a far heavier burden of proof than is applied in ordinary jury discrimination and *employment discrimination cases.

In response to McCleskey's Eighth Amendment arbitrariness claim, the Supreme Court majority acknowledged that proof of racially discriminatory sentencing patterns in capital cases would establish a constitutional violation. However, Justice Powell's opinion rejected McCleskey's claim on the ground that the statistical evidence he offered failed to establish "a constitutionally significant risk" that racial factors had, indeed, infected Georgia's death-sentencing process (p. 313).

The Supreme Court's decision in McCleskey seems to have put a practical end to statistical challenges to the administration of the death penalty for the foreseeable future. Instead, researchers and litigants working in the early 1990s on issues of arbitrariness and discrimination in the administration of the death penalty have shifted their focus to nonquantitative approaches for documenting the underlying sources of race-of-victim and race-of-defendant discrimination.

Another consequence of McCleskey has been an effort by civil rights advocates to invoke the legislative process. As Justice Powell himself suggested in his opinion, efforts are being made in Congress to pass federal legislation to regularize state capital-sentencing procedures. Two such proposals, the "Racial Justice Act" and the "Fairness in Death Sentencing Act," seek to give condemned prisoners a federal right, analogous to Title VII rights in the employment context, to challenge any death sentence that "furthers a racially discriminatory pattern," based on the race of either the defendant or the victim. Moreover, the proposed acts would give condemned prisoners the right to support such challenges with ordinary methods of statistical proof and without the necessity of showing "discriminatory motive, intent or purpose on the part of any individual or institution." If enacted, such legislation might provide a suitable vehicle for addressing concerns about the administration of *capital punishment. A federal legislative solution has the additional advantage of permitting a comprehensive evaluation of the methods and procedures to be employed, as opposed to the case-by-case, issue-by-issue approach that courts must necessarily employ.

(See also RACE AND RACISM.)

□ David C. Baldus, George Woodworth, and Charles A. Pulaski, Jr., Equal Justice and the Death Penalty: Legal and Empirical Analysis (1990). General Accounting Office, Death Penalty Sentencing: Research Indicates Patterns of Racial Disparities, GGD-90-57 (1990). Samuel R. Gross and Robert Mauro, Death and Discrimination: Racial Disparities in Capital Sentencing (1989). Barry Nakell and Kenneth A. Hardy, The Arbitrariness of the Death Penalty (1987).

David C. Baldus, Charles A. Pulaski, Jr., and George Woodworth

**Railroads.** See COMMERCE POWER; INTERSTATE COMMERCE COMMISSION.

**Ranking of the Justices.** Over the past half-century, a number of individual scholars and one panel of academic experts have attempted to evaluate the judicial performance of the justices who have sat on the nation's highest bench. Despite the lack of specified and accepted criteria for such evaluations, some consensus emerges as to the few justices who may be considered "great." This essay summarizes the evaluations published to date, offers some speculative conclusions about their findings, and suggests a potentially fruitful avenue for further inquiry.

In 1938 Roscoe Pound, a distinguished Harvard legal scholar, provided his personal list of the ten judges who must be ranked first in American judicial history. Pound's list, covering both federal and state judges, included four men whose judicial careers included service on the Supreme Court bench: John *Marshall, Joseph *Story, Oliver Wendell *Holmes, and Benjamin N. *Cardozo.

More than two decades later, George R. Currie, then chief justice of the Wisconsin Supreme Court, adopted a baseball metaphor to select an "all-time, all-star United States Supreme Court." In comparison to Pound, Currie in 1964 omitted Cardozo; agreed on Marshall, Story, and Holmes; and added six more names: William *Johnson, Roger B. *Taney, Samuel F. *Miller, Joseph *Bradley, Louis D. *Brandeis, and Charles Evans *Hughes.

The next effort to rank the justices was the first to reflect more than one individual's opinion. Based on a poll of sixty-five academic experts, this list compiled by law professors Albert Blaustein and Roy Mersky in 1972 added eight names to the four identified by Pound: Hugo *Black, Brandeis, Felix *Frankfurter, John *Harlan I, Hughes, Harlan F. *Stone, Taney, and Earl *Warren. Although undertaken as an academic parlor game without pretension of being a definitive study, the Blaustein and Mersky list became the subject of doctoral dissertations and of debate in scholarly journals.

More recent studies, most of which were inspired by Blaustein and Mersky, were summarized by Jim Hambleton in 1983. Hambleton limited his selections to nine justices from the Blaustein and Mersky list, omitting Frankfurter, Harlan, and Stone.

Even including the sixty-five academics polled by Blaustein and Mersky, these studies recorded the opinions of only a handful of Court observers. While some consensus is evident, any confidence in the rankings is eroded by the small number of voices being heard. Moreover, the published studies lack consistency in methodology and in application of standards. Of course, any assessment of judicial performance is subjective and dependent on individual value preferences. Even a survey of a broad range of scholars, practitioners, and journalists—undertaken with modern polling techniques—would merely lend a veneer of "scientific" respectability to what remains a matter of individual opinion.

Some of the biases inherent in any opinion survey are reflected in the evaluations we have summarized. Foremost is the academic orientation of the evaluators; law professors admire brilliance, education, and a professorial writing style—traits obviously shared by the consensus great justices. Time bias is also apparent, as most of the great justices served during the twentieth century. Finally, it is unarguable that the ratings show a liberal tilt. The latter point may be best illustrated by the example of Harlan, famed for his dissents in *Plessy v. Ferguson (1896) and the *Civil Rights Cases (1883), who is ranked higher than the second Justice Harlan, a demonstrably finer legal craftsman.

The performance of an appellate judge, especially of a Supreme Court justice, could be more objectively gauged by examining the long-term influence of that judge's written opinions (see OPINIONS, STYLE OF). Given the Supreme Court's precedential power, an effective justice can literally mold the law for decades. Citation patterns in subsequent decisions accurately reflect the extent to which an opinion—whether majority or dissenting—has had a lasting impact. The process remains tedious and exacting, but computerized legal databases now make comprehensive citation studies feasible (see WESTLAW; LEXIS). The potential exists for quantitative studies of judicial influence and achievement.

☐ Albert P. Blaustein and Roy Martin Mersky, *The First One Hundred Justices: Statistical Studies on the Supreme Court of the United States* (1978).

Roy M. Mersky and Gary R. Hartman

**Rawls, John** (b. Baltimore, Md., 21 Feb. 1921), moral philosopher and academician. John Rawls is one of the most influential contemporary moral philosophers. Educated at Princeton, he has taught primarily at Cornell and Harvard, where he has been for over twenty-five years.

Rawls is best known for *A Theory of Justice* (1971), a book that rejects the utilitarian claim that justice is that which will produce the greatest good for the greatest number. Rawls states that justice is found in those acts that treat individuals fairly. He sets forth as principles of justice those precepts that free and rational persons would accept in an initial position of equality. In this hypothetical situation, agreement is reached in circumstances such that no one knows either what position each will occupy in the social structure or what his own talents or psychological propensities will be. Thus, deliberating behind a "veil of ignorance," individuals determine their rights and duties. Rawls concludes that in such a contingency, people will choose, out of self-interest, a societal structure that safeguards the least well-off class.

Although Rawls has never been specifically discussed by the Supreme Court, he has influenced constitutional scholarship, fostering constitutional perspectives consistent with affirmative action programs, election spending reforms, and greater media access. Additionally, Rawls has validated the idea that through judicial review the Constitution should embody national aspirations for social justice, brotherhood, and human dignity.

Stanley Ingber

**Read, John Meredith** (b. Philadelphia, 21 July 1797; d. 29 Nov. 1874), unconfirmed nominee to the Supreme Court. Read graduated from the University of Pennsylvania in 1812 and was admitted to the bar on 7 Sept. 1818. From 1837 to 1841 he served as U.S. attorney for the eastern district of Pennsylvania. On 7 Feb. 1845 President John *Tyler appointed Read to the Supreme Court to fill a vacancy on the third circuit. Read's nomination followed the withdrawal of the nomination of Edward *King. Both nominations suffered from Tyler's lack of support from either Whigs or Democrats. Read's nomination died without action at the end of the Twenty-eighth Congress.

In 1846 Read was appointed attorney general of Pennsylvania but soon returned to private practice. In the mid-1850s Read became an active member of the new Republican party; as a result of that party's victory in Pennsylvania in 1858, he was elected to the Pennsylvania Supreme Court, where he served for fifteen years, becoming chief justice in 1872. During the Civil War he was one of the bare majority on that court who sustained federal legislation, and his opinions supporting the constitutionality of the national draft and legal tender acts received wide national circulation.

(See also NOMINEES, REJECTION OF.)

Elizabeth B. Monroe

**Reagan, Ronald** (b. Tampico, Ill., 6 Feb. 1911), governor of California, 1967–1974, and president of the United States, 1981–1989. Ronald Reagan was inaugurated fortieth president of the United States in January 1981 and was reelected in November 1984. He was the first president to serve two complete terms since Dwight Eisenhower. During his tenure, Reagan pulled together a coalition of conservatives and libertarians who were dedicated to promoting what they dubbed the Reagan Revolution, an attempt to restructure American politics, law, and economics. The core of this effort was Reagan's oft-repeated desire to reduce the role of government in American life.

When Reagan won the presidency, he promised to effect great change in many areas. One of the most important was that of changing the direction of the federal courts generally and the Supreme Court in particular. To Reagan's way of thinking, the judiciary, inspired by the liberalism of the Supreme Court under Chief Justice Earl *Warren, had moved beyond exercising merely judgment and had begun to make policy. Part of Reagan's pledge to get the government off the backs of the people included returning the courts to what he deemed their proper and limited constitutional roles.

The means to this end lay in the power of the president to nominate, and by and with the advice and consent of the Senate, to appoint federal judges. Reagan took this power seriously

and set about to appoint to the federal courts only those who shared his philosophy of judicial restraint (see SELECTION OF JUSTICES). By the time he finished his second term Reagan had, to a great extent, delivered on his campaign promise to redirect the courts.

During his two terms President Reagan appointed 372 of the 736 *Article III judges on the federal courts. This included 290 judges on the district courts; 78 on the *courts of appeal; and four justices to the Supreme Court. At the end of his tenure 346—some 47 percent of the federal judiciary—were still in active service.

Reagan's effort to transform the federal judiciary through his appointments began to draw heavy political fire. The Department of Justice became the focus of attention for Reagan's critics on the issue of the courts. Under his first attorney general, William French Smith, and especially later during the second term under Smith's replacement, Edwin Meese III, the Department of Justice went about the business of picking judges with a precision never before seen. The newly created Office of Legal Policy screened potential nominees with great care in an effort to fulfill the president's wish to have on the bench those who shared his views on the nature and extent of judicial power.

As Reagan's tenure wore on, the politics of judicial selection became more heated. While there were controversies over particular nominees at all levels, the primary concern was over the Supreme Court. When Justice Potter *Stewart retired in 1982, the politically shrewd Reagan sidestepped any real controversy by nominating a largely unknown state judge from Arizona, Sandra Day *O'Connor, making her the first woman ever to sit on the Supreme Court.

In 1985, when Chief Justice Warren *Burger announced his retirement, the political path to the Court had become tougher to traverse. Reagan's nomination of Justice William *Rehnquist, the most outspoken judicial conservative then on the Court, drew a great deal of political opposition. Ironically, the more conservative Antonin *Scalia, then a judge on the United States Court of Appeals for the District of Columbia Circuit, who was named to replace Rehnquist as associate justice, was overwhelmingly approved by the Senate. Much was made of the fact that he was the first Italian-American ever to sit on the high court.

With three nominees in place it was inevitable that any other vacancies would generate ever more heated opposition. This was made clear when the centrist Justice Lewis *Powell resigned in 1987 and Reagan nominated Judge Robert H. *Bork to take his seat. Bork was the best-known conservative judge then sitting on the federal courts. Despite his public service as both a federal judge and *solicitor general of the United States, his distinguished career as a professor at the Yale Law School, and his experience in private practice, he was decisively denied confirmation after a bruising confirmation hearing.

After Reagan's next nominee, Judge Douglas *Ginsburg, withdrew following disclosures that as a Harvard law professor he had smoked marijuana, Reagan finally replaced Powell with Judge Anthony *Kennedy, then sitting on the Ninth Circuit Court of Appeals. By the end of Justice Kennedy's second term on the Court, it seemed clear that Reagan had indeed succeeded in shifting the direction of the Supreme Court. Although the shift was not as pronounced as the President might have wished, there was a difference with the Reagan justices in place.

Reagan had the greatest influence on the Supreme Court—both as to the actions of the Court and its place in the broader political context—of any president since Franklin D. *Roosevelt. Not only because of his appointments to the Supreme Court but because of his lower court appointments as well, the contours of American law have been changed. The kinds of cases and their attendant opinions that now go before the Supreme Court on appeal also bear the mark of judges who share Reagan's vision of judicial power under the Constitution. As had President Roosevelt a half-century earlier, President Reagan dramatically demonstrated that a president's most powerful legacy can be the judges he appoints to the federal courts.

(See also JUDICIAL ACTIVISM; JUDICIAL SELF-RESTRAINT; NOMINATIONS, CONTROVERSIAL.)

□ Robert H. Bork, *The Tempting of America; The Political Seduction of the Law* (1989). Terry Eastland, *Taking the Presidency Seriously* (1991).           Gary L. McDowell

**Reapportionment Cases,** collective name of six cases argued 13 November 1963 and decided 15 June 1964: involving Alabama—*Reynolds* v. *Sims,* 377 U.S. 533 (1964), decided by vote of 8 to 1, Warren for the Court, Harlan in dissent; involving New York—*WMCA* v. *Lomenzo,* 377 U.S. 633 (1964), decided by vote of 6 to 3, Clark and Stewart joining Harlan in dissent; involving Maryland—*Maryland Committee for Fair Representation* v. *Tawes,* 377 U.S. 656 (1964), decided by vote of 7 to 2, Clark concurring, Harlan in dissent, Stewart, refusing either to affirm or reverse, would nonetheless vacate the judgment of the court; involving Virginia—*Davis* v. *Mann,* 377 U.S. 656 (1964), decided by vote of 8 to 1, Warren for the Court, Clark, and Stewart concurring, Harlan in dissent; involving Delaware—*Roman* v. *Sincock,* 377 U.S. 695 (1964), decided by vote of 8 to 1, Warren for the Court, Clark and Stewart concurring, Harlan in dissent; and involving Colorado—*Lucas* v. *Forty-Fourth General Assembly of Colorado,* 377 U.S. 713 (1964), decided by vote of 6 to 3, Warren for the Court, Harlan, Clark and Stewart in dissent.

These cases effectively declared the apportionment of every state legislature unconstitutional.

They were prompted by *Baker* v. *Carr* (1962), which opened federal courts to cases in which state legislatures were challenged for failing to provide equitable legislative districts and thereby depriving citizens of *equal protection of the laws. Earlier in its 1963 term, in *Wesberry* v. *Sanders* (1964) the Supreme Court had extended the requirement of population equality (i.e., that districts must be as nearly equal as is practicable) to electoral districts for seats in the House of Representatives; that decision had been based on its reading of Article I, section 2.

Chief Justice Earl *Warren's opinion in *Reynolds* v. *Sims,* which along with *Lucas* was the leading case, reemphasized the "one man, one vote" principle announced the year before in *Gray* v. *Sanders* (1963), a case setting aside Georgia's gubernatorial county unit system. "Legislators represent people," wrote Warren "not trees or acres. Legislators are elected by voters, not farms or cities or economic interests" (p. 562). The Court also rejected the "federal analogy" argument that the states, like Congress, could base only one house on population. As the Court repeatedly stated throughout the opinion, "The Equal Protection Clause requires that the seats in both Houses of a bicameral state legislature must be apportioned on a population basis." Each state legislative district should be "as nearly of equal population as is practicable," as based on the most recent decennial census (p. 577). The Court, however, noted, "Somewhat more flexibility may . . . be constitutionally permissible with respect to state legislative apportionment than in congressional districting" (p. 578).

Warren, responding to Justice John M. *Harlan's *dissent and to the earlier warnings of Justice Felix *Frankfurter, commented: "We are cautioned about the dangers of entering into political thickets and mathematical quagmires. Our answer is this: a denial of constitutional protected rights demands judicial protection" (p. 567).

The other cases applied the doctrines of *Reynolds* to the facts of the involved states, except in *Lucas* v. *Forty-Fourth General Assembly of Colorado,* where the Court held that the fact that the Colorado apportionment plan had been incorporated into the state's Constitution via the initiative process did not protect it from federal constitutional challenge.

Justices Tom *Clark and Potter *Stewart concurred in *Reynolds* and dissented in *Lucas.* They objected to the mathematical nicety of *Reynolds* and to extending the requirement of population equality to both chambers of a bicameral legislature. In *Lucas,* Stewart wrote, "The Court's draconian pronouncement . . . finds no support in the words of the Constitution, in any prior decision of this Court, or in the 175-year political history of our Federal Union" (p. 746). Clark would have required only that the legislature avoid "invidious discrimination." As long as one house was based on population, he would have permitted some departure from it in the other chamber "so as to take into account, on a rational basis, other factors in order to afford some representation to the various elements of the State" (p. 588).

Harlan dissented in all the cases, protesting what he characterized as this "placing basic aspects of state political systems under the pervasive overlordship of the federal judiciary" (p. 589). By 1964, he was the lone justice to take the view that federal courts should refuse to review any apportionment issues.

Following these cases, Senator Everett Dirksen of Illinois led a charge for a constitutional amendment to override the holding that both chambers of a state legislature must be based on equal population districts. He came close to securing the necessary petitions from two-thirds of the state legislatures to require Congress to call a convention to consider such an amendment, but by the early 1970s enough state legislatures had been reapportioned to undermine this effort (see REVERSALS OF COURT DECISIONS BY AMENDMENT). The newly reapportioned legislatures, after all, had no desire to return to the status quo ante the *Reapportionment Cases*.

(See also FAIR REPRESENTATION.)

J. W. Peltason

**Reconstruction.** The process of reconstructing the Union began with the outbreak of the *Civil War and lasted through the presidential election of 1876. It presented two challenges to the Union: the status of the seceded states and the future of African-Americans. President Abraham *Lincoln issued an executive order in 1863 that dealt with both by requiring that the constitutions of the seceded states undergoing Reconstruction had to abolish *slavery as a condition of readmission to the Union. By 1865, Union military and civil authorities had begun a thorough reorganization of the South's political and social systems.

Lincoln appointed his secretary of the treasury, Salmon P. *Chase, to replace Roger S. *Taney as chief justice of the United States. Chase joined previous Lincoln appointees David *Davis, Stephen J. *Field, Samuel F. *Miller, and Noah *Swayne, but though the Court was dominated by Republican appointees, it split over questions involving executive power, *federalism, and individual liberty. In the *Prize Cases (1863), the Court sustained the president's powers to blockade Confederate ports. Though both cases presented Lincoln with political embarrassments, Ex parte Merryman (1861) and Ex parte Vallandigham (1864) upheld the national government's authority to arrest and detain civilians who posed security risks in states that had not seceded. In *Gelpcke v. Dubuque (1864), the Court condemned state repudiation of public debts. On the whole, the Court moved circumspectly in the war years.

After Appomattox, however, the Court resolved constitutional issues in a more assertive spirit. In the *Test Oath Cases of 1867 (Ex parte Garland and *Cummings v. Missouri), the Court struck down federal and state requirements that individuals swear loyalty to the Union as a condition of practicing professions. This process had the effect of returning former secessionists to political power in the South. The 1866 decision in Ex parte *Milligan raised again the Vallandigham question of the Supreme Court's jurisdiction to hear civilians' appeals from the decisions of courts martial and implicitly challenged the entire structure of military authority in areas removed from the theater of war (see MILITARY TRIALS AND MARTIAL LAW). These early Reconstruction decisions, combined with President Andrew Johnson's obstructive policies (such as his veto of all civil rights legislation and his amnesties and pardons for former Confederates), hobbled implementation of the Freedmen's Bureau Act, the Civil Rights Act of 1866, and the Military Reconstruction Acts of 1867–1868. As a result federal efforts to aid the freed slaves became a politicized constitutional debate.

After these early confrontations, the Supreme Court sidestepped direct contests with Congress over Reconstruction policies. In *Mississippi v. Johnson (1867) and Georgia v. Stanton (1868), the Court declined an invitation by counsel representing anti-Reconstruction interests to hold the Military Reconstruction Acts unconstitutional. In Ex parte *McCardle (1869), the justices accepted the constitutionality of a statute that excised their jurisdiction in some *habeas corpus appeals (though in Ex parte Yerger, decided the same year as McCardle, the Court reaffirmed the original reach of its *appellate jurisdiction over habeas appeals conferred by the *Judiciary Act of 1789.) Chief Justice Chase invoked the *political-question doctrine to uphold congressional authority over Reconstruction policy.

In a variety of cases that challenged the evasion of the *Thirteenth Amendment by "apprenticeship" agreements (In re Turner, 1867), violation of the Civil Rights Act (United States v. Rhodes, 1866) and the *Fourteenth Amendment's inhibitions on the states (Blyew v. United States, 1872 and United States v. Hall, 1871), *lower federal court judges or justices of the Supreme Court on circuit suggested that the Reconstruction amendments and statutes that implemented them created the power and perhaps the obligation of the federal government to protect the full spectrum of civil rights against the acts of individuals.

The Supreme Court, however, quashed these initiatives. Asserting the values of traditional federalism over individual rights, the Court affirmed the power of a state to deny a female attorney admission to the bar in *Bradwell v. Illinois (1873). Despite the ratification of the Thirteenth Amendment, the Court upheld the validity of a contract made before the war for the sale of a slave in Osborn v. Nicholson (1873). In the

*Slaughterhouse Cases* of 1873, the first decision that directly construed and defined the scope of the Reconstruction amendments, a 5-to-4 majority of the Court determined that the Constitution (including its recent amendments) created few federal civil rights and left most slaves at the mercy of the southern states for both the definition and the enforcement of their rights—cold comfort in view of the fact that the southern state governments were falling under the control of racist Democrats. The Court also rejected claims that the *Fourteenth Amendment prohibited the states from denying women the right to *vote (*Minor v. Happersett*, 1875).

The Supreme Court was determined to protect economic interests, especially when states attempted to repudiate debt obligations (*Gelpcke v. Dubuque*, 1864). The effect of *Gelpcke* was to limit the states' capacity to control public indebtedness and to inhibit cities' efforts to build roads and bridges. In the *License Tax Cases* (1867), the Court, by upholding a federal statute licensing and taxing lotteries, rejected state claims that the federal government improperly intruded into local affairs and condoned immorality. The Court similarly upheld federal power in *Veazie Bank v. Fenno* (1869), sustaining a wartime tax that had the purpose and effect of abolishing banknotes issued by state-chartered banks as a circulating medium.

The Court at first denied the federal government's power to issue paper notes as legal tender (*Hepburn v. Griswold*, 1871) but reversed itself that same year in *Knox v. Lee* (see LEGAL TENDER CASES). At the same time, the Court also sustained a federal wartime *income tax that presented problems of intergovernmental *tax immunities (*Collector v. Day*, 1871).

Throughout Reconstruction, the Court usually deferred to congressional determinations of policy while reasserting its coordinate constitutional status. Still, the Chase Court held ten federal statutes unconstitutional, as compared with two such decisions between 1789 and 1864. Just as *Gelpcke* curtailed state control over state and local finance, the *Test Oath Cases*, *Bradwell*, and *Slaughterhouse* obstructed the cause of racial and gender equality.

(See also HISTORY OF THE COURT: RECONSTRUCTION, FEDERALISM, AND ECONOMIC RIGHTS.)

☐ Harold M. Hyman and William M. Wiecek, *Equal Justice under Law: Constitutional Development, 1835–1875* (1982). Robert J. Kaczorowski, *The Nationalization of Civil Rights: Constitutional Theory and Practice in a Racist Society, 1866–1883* (1987).                    Harold M. Hyman

**Recuse.** A judge may be recused (from Lat., *recusare*, "to refuse") from participating in the hearing or decision of a case because of interest or bias in the matter. For example, Chief Justice John *Marshall recused himself in *Martin v. Hunter's Lessee* (1816) because he had appeared as counsel in an earlier phase of the case and had a financial interest in the property in question.

William M. Wiecek

**Red Lion Broadcasting Co., Inc., v. Federal Communications Commission,** 395 U.S. 367 (1969), argued 2–3 April 1969, decided 9 June 1969 by vote of 8 to 0; White for the Court; Douglas not participating. In *Red Lion* the Court upheld the *fairness doctrine of the Federal Communications Commission (FCC), which requires broadcast licensees to allow reply time to individuals subjected to personal attacks or political editorials. In this instance, radio station WGCB refused to allow Fred Cook, the author of a book critical of Arizona senator Barry Goldwater, time to respond to an attack by the Rev. Billy James Hargis. The Court utilized the case to explore the different contexts of broadcast and print journalism that result in different *First Amendment considerations. The finite number of broadcast frequencies meant it was "idle to posit an unabridgeable First Amendment right to broadcast comparable to the right of every individual to speak, write, or publish" (p. 388).

The Court asserted that the interests of the listening and viewing public must prevail over those of broadcast licensees when allocating scarce airwaves. This scarcity rationale has met with considerable criticism since cable television (and public access to the airwaves) have proliferated while countless outlets for the printed word have been silenced by mergers and commercial failures. Further, the decision was widely criticized for its possible "chilling effect" on broadcasters who had to censor themselves to avoid controversy and the allowance of response time. Indeed, after President Ronald Reagan vetoed legislation codifying the fairness doctrine, the FCC responded to long-term criticism by eliminating the rule in 1987. In other contexts, however, the Court continues to maintain that critical differences between broadcast and print journalism bring different First Amendment considerations into play.

(See also SPEECH AND THE PRESS.)

Elliot E. Slotnick

**Reed, Stanley Forman** (b. Minerva, Ky., 31 Dec. 1884; d. Huntington, N.Y., 2 April 1980, interred Maysville Cemetery, Maysville, Ky.), associate justice, 1938–1957. As the seventy-seventh justice, Reed served during a period of major change brought by the rise of the *administrative state, the civil rights movement, and controversies over international communism. He was an economic liberal who was generally conservative on civil rights and liberties.

Born in a small town in Mason County, Kentucky, Reed was the only child of John A. Reed and Frances Forman Reed. After attending local private schools, he went to Kentucky Wesleyan

*Stanley Forman Reed*

College. Following graduation, he then earned a second bachelor's degree at Yale University.

Reed did not graduate from law school. However, he attended the University of Virginia Law School for a year and spent another at Columbia University. In 1908, Reed married Winifred Elgin. They combined their honeymoon with another year of studying law in Paris, at the Sorbonne. On returning from Europe, Reed settled in Mason County, was admitted to the bar in 1910, and began practicing law.

Reed's legal and political careers were intertwined. After nine years as a solo practioner, he became a partner in Worthinton, Browning and Reed. Also active in local Democratic politics, Reed served two terms in the state General Assembly, before serving in the army until the end of World War I.

Reed's rise in national politics began in 1929, when Republican president Herbert Hoover appointed him counsel to the Federal Farm Board. Although a Democrat, he was later promoted to general counsel for the Reconstruction Finance Corporation, where he remained after Democratic president Franklin D. *Roosevelt came into office. In 1935, as a special assistant to the attorney general, he successfully defended before the Supreme Court the administration's elimination of the gold standard. Immediately after the Court's ruling in the *Gold Clause Cases (1935), Reed was named *solicitor general.

In that position, Reed had mixed success defending New Deal programs. He persuaded the Court to uphold the Tennessee Valley Authority Act in *Ashwander v. TVA (1936), but he

suffered major defeats when the justices struck down the National Industrial Recovery Act, in *Schechter Poultry Corporation v. United States (1935), and the Agricultural Adjustment Act, in United States v. *Butler (1936). Angered by those decisions, in 1937 Roosevelt proposed his ill-fated *court-packing plan. Although the plan failed, Roosevelt eventually rewarded Reed with an appointment to the Court.

On the bench, Reed wrote 228 opinions for the Court, 21 concurring opinions, and 79 dissenting opinions; he also concurred without an opinion 34 other times, and dissented without an opinion from another 125 rulings. As an economic liberal, Reed supported Congress's broad powers under the Commerce Clause. Although joining the landmark school desegregation decision in *Brown v. Board of Education (1954) and writing the opinion in *Smith v. Allwright (1944) striking down "white primaries," Reed was generally conservative when reviewing claims of civil rights and liberties. In one of his most notable opinions, *Adamson v. California (1947), he opposed the application of the *Fifth Amendment's guarantee against *self-incrimination to the states. As a legal technician inclined toward *judicial self-restraint, Reed was a moderating influence on the Court.

□ F. William O'Brien, *Justice Reed and the First Amendment* (1958).
David O'Brien

**Reed v. Reed,** 404 U.S. 71 (1971), argued 19 Oct. 1971, decided 22 Nov. 1971 by vote of 7 to 0; Burger for the Court, two seats (to be occupied by Rehnquist and Powell) were vacant. This was the first decision in a century of *Fourteenth Amendment litigation to rule that statutory *gender discrimination violated the Equal Protection Clause. Earlier cases had established that the clause did not forbid group-based discrimination as long as the legislature might have some reason for believing the statutory distinction promoted some aspect of the public good. Under this "rational basis test" the Supreme Court had upheld flat bans on the practice of law by women (*Bradwell v. Illinois, 1873), prohibitions on women's tending bar (Goesaert v. Cleary, 1948), and blanket exclusions of women from jury service (*Hoyt v. Florida, 1961). In Reed the Court ignored this unbroken line of precedents and explained in an extraordinarily short opinion that this case of gender discrimination presented "the very kind of arbitrary legislative choice forbidden by the Equal Protection Clause" (p. 76).

The law in question had distinguished categories of preference for selecting administrators of the estates of people deceased intestate. Part of the law preferred spouses to offspring, offspring to parents, parents to siblings, and so on; another preferred males to females within each category. The Reeds were the separated parents of a deceased son. Sally, challenging the statutory gender preference, sued Cecil for the right to administer an estate valued at less than one thousand dollars. After striking down this law in *Reed*, the Court often used the *Reed* precedent during the following decade to strike down many other statutes that discriminated on the basis of gender.

(See also EQUAL PROTECTION.)

Leslie Friedman Goldstein

**Reese, United States v.,** 92 U.S. 214 (1876), argued 13–14 Jan. 1875, decided 27 Mar. 1876 by vote of 8 to 1; Waite for the Court, Clifford concurring, Hunt in dissent. This was the Supreme Court's first voting rights case under the *Fifteenth Amendment and the Enforcement Act of 1870. A Kentucky electoral official had refused to register an African-American's vote in a municipal election and was indicted under two sections of the 1870 act: section 2 required that administrative preliminaries to elections be conducted without regard to race, color, or previous condition of servitude; section 3 forbade wrongful refusal to register votes where a prerequisite step "required as aforesaid" had been omitted. The Court held that the Fifteenth Amendment did not confer the right of suffrage but prohibited exclusion on racial grounds. The justices invalidated the operative section 3 since it did not repeat the words about race, color, and servitude and thus exceeded the scope of the Fifteenth Amendment.

In this case involving local elections the Court, dominated by Lincoln and Grant Republicans, chose not to set an expansive, national stamp on the Constitution. Though the Court was willing to uphold the Enforcement Acts in cases involving federal elections, its cramped, technical treatment of state and local cases crippled the acts for practical purposes. This left southern states free to disfranchise African-Americans during the 1890s with literacy, character, and other tests that, while not based on race, were disproportionately exclusive of African-Americans.

(See also GRANDFATHER CLAUSE; POLL TAXES; RACE AND RACISM; RECONSTRUCTION; UNDERSTANDING TEST; VOTE, RIGHT TO.)

Ward E. Y. Elliott

**Regents of the University of California v. Bakke,** 438 U.S. 265 (1978), argued 12 Oct. 1977, decided 28 June 1978 by vote of 5 to 4; Powell for the Court, Brennan, White, Marshall, and Blackmun concurring in part and dissenting in part, Stevens, Burger, Stewart, and Rehnquist concurring in part and dissenting in part. Bakke wanted to be a physician. The University of California Medical School at Davis sought greater racial and ethnic diversity in its student body. The conflict between these two goals produced the first major constitutional test of *affirmative action. It also posed an intractable conundrum: how to overcome the tension between an individual's claim to equal treatment by a state, and that state's responsibility to foster some degree of equality among its citizens.

Bakke was one of 2,664 applicants for one hundred entering positions at the Davis medical school in 1972. Eighty-four slots were filled through the regular admissions program; sixteen were filled through a special admissions program—a distinct and separate process established in 1970 to address the faculty's concern over the paucity of African-American, Asian, Latino, and Native American students. Grade-point average and standard test score requirements were not as stringent as for students admitted under the regular program.

Rejected twice by the university, Bakke filed a lawsuit alleging that the Davis program violated Title VI of the *Civil Rights Act of 1964, forbidding racial or ethnic preferences in programs supported by federal funds, and that the university's practice of setting aside positions for minorities denied him *equal protection of the law under the *Fourteenth Amendment.

The university agreed that racial classifications are disfavored because racial characteristics are generally irrelevant to permissible state objectives. However, the meritocratic promise of non-discrimination was offset by the state's equally compelling concern for the victims of past and continuing racial injustice. The university also stressed the program's practical benefits: enriched medical education through a diverse student body, successful role models for minority youth, and improved medical services to minority communities.

Both the state trial court and supreme court ruled that racially exclusionary preferences constituted a quota and that such quotas, absent a finding of prior discrimination by the university itself, were a denial of equal protection.

The U.S. Supreme Court held that a university may consider racial criteria as part of a competitive admissions process so long as "fixed quotas" were not used. But the holding masked a sharply divided Court, with six separate opinions. Four justices (John Paul *Stevens, Warren *Burger, Potter *Stewart, and William *Rehnquist) preferred to address the statutory rather than the constitutional issue. The "plain meaning" of Title VI and its "broad prohibition against the exclusion of any individual" (pp. 412–413) on racial grounds from a publicly funded program were sufficient grounds, in their judgment, to order Bakke admitted.

A second group (William J. *Brennan, Thurgood *Marshall, Byron *White, and Harry *Blackmun) saw no difference between the commands of the Equal Protection Clause and Title VI. Absent a stigmatizing intent or effect, one "drawn on the presumption that one race is inferior to another" or one that places "the weight of government behind racial hatred and separation" (pp. 357–358), there was no reason to trigger the strictest equal protection test. However, the "mere rationality" test deployed in cases not affecting *fundamental rights or *suspect classifications was too lenient. Instead, Brennan opted for the middle test of *heightened scrutiny. So long as the state can demonstrate an important purpose and the means do not unduly burden "those least well represented in the political process" (pp. 361), race-conscious remedies to help members of groups that had suffered racially motivated injuries were constitutional (see STRICT SCRUTINY).

Justice Lewis *Powell cast the deciding vote, joining with Stevens's plurality on the illegality of the racial quota and in ordering Bakke admitted, while agreeing with Brennan's plurality on the permissibility of racial considerations in admissions. The decisive factor for Powell was the exclusionary nature of the Davis program. Since Bakke had been "totally foreclosed" (p. 305) from competing for the sixteen special positions, he had been denied equal protection. Racial quotas are allowed only when there was a past constitutional or legal violation identified by a properly authorized governmental body. Powell did find justification for less exclusionary affirmative action programs in the *First Amendment's guarantee of *academic freedom. In a truly competitive process, racial considerations could be taken into account as part of the university's interest in promoting a "diverse student body" (p. 312).

Despite predictions that the decision would exert a chilling effect on minority admissions to graduate and professional schools, it had little impact. Rather than providing a definitive answer on affirmative action, Bakke nibbled at the question, settling only the narrower issue of racial quotas in admissions to state supported schools and leaving later cases to test the propriety of affirmative action in other realms.

(See also EDUCATION; RACE AND RACISM.)

□ Timothy J. O'Neill, Bakke and the Politics of Equality (1985). Susan Welch and John Gruhl, "The Impact of the Bakke Decision on Black and Hispanic Enrollment in Medical and Law Schools," Social Science Quarterly 71 (Sept. 1990): 458–473. J. Harvie Wilkinson, From Brown to Bakke: The Supreme Court and School Integration (1979).
Timothy J. O'Neill

**Regulatory Taking.** A regulatory taking occurs when land use restrictions substantially interfere with an owner's beneficial enjoyment of property even though the owner's title is undisturbed. Such a regulation constitutes a taking of property requiring the payment of *just compensation under the *Takings Clause of the *Fifth Amendment. Although the doctrine of a regulatory taking was recognized by the Supreme Court in *Pennsylvania Coal Co. v. Mahon (1922), the justices have found it difficult to distinguish between appropriate land use controls and regulations that effect a taking.
James W. Ely, Jr.

**Rehnquist, William Hubbs** (b. Milwaukee, Wis., 1 Oct. 1924), associate justice, 1972–1986; chief justice, 1986–. Appointed by President Richard *Nixon, who selected him for his views on criminal justice and his endorsement of a more modest role for the Court, Rehnquist was the most conservative member of the Burger Court; he was also often identified as the justice with the most impressive intellectual ability. Later, when Chief Justice Warren *Burger announced his retirement, President Ronald *Reagan, impressed by Rehnquist's conservative views and exceptional mind, elevated him to the position of chief justice.

Rehnquist graduated from Stanford Law School in December 1951 after having earned two masters degrees in political science, one from Stanford, in 1949, and one from Harvard, in 1950. He served as clerk to Justice Robert H. *Jackson in 1952 and 1953. In that capacity he wrote a memorandum to help the justice prepare for the Court's discussion of the constitutional challenge to officially segregated schools. Rehnquist's memorandum argued in favor of upholding the *separate but equal doctrine of *Plessy v. Ferguson (1896). He then moved to Phoenix, Arizona, where for sixteen years he was an outspoken conservative lawyer, participating in a variety of local political activities. He appeared as a witness before the Phoenix City Council in opposition to a political accommodations ordinance and took part in a program of challenging voters at the polls. From 1969 until 1971 Rehnquist served as assistant attorney general for the Office of *Legal Counsel. In that position, he supported executive authority to order wiretapping and surveillance without a court order, no-knock entry by the police, preventive detention, and abolishing the *exclusionary rule.

As a member of the Burger Court, Rehnquist played a crucial role in reviving the debate regarding the relationship between the federal government and the states. His decision making manifested a strong commitment to shifting power away from the federal government toward more extensive, independent authority for the states. He urged his colleagues to limit Congress's power under the Commerce Clause (e.g., *National League of Cities v. Usery, 1976), to constrain the power of the federal courts (e.g., *Edelman v. Jordan, 1974; Rizzo v. Goode, 1976), and to construe broadly the power of the states (e.g., Philadelphia v. New Jersey, 1978). As chief justice he retained his steadfast commitment to state power (see TENTH AMENDMENT).

The consequences of Rehnquist's state-centered *federalism surfaced dramatically in the area of individual rights. Since the 1960s, the Court had held that nearly every provision in the *Bill of Rights applies to the states through the Due Process Clause of the *Fourteenth Amendment (see DUE PROCESS, SUBSTANTIVE; INCORPORATION DOCTRINE). In cases such as Carter

v. *Kentucky* (1981) and *Richmond Newspapers* v. *Virginia* (1980), Rehnquist voiced his disagreement with such a method of determining the constitutional requirements of state action, particularly in the context of criminal proceedings, urging a return to an earlier approach whereby the states were not required to comply with the Bill of Rights but only to treat individuals with "fundamental fairness."

Rehnquist consistently supported law enforcement in cases that involved the rights of the accused. In *Rakas* v. *Illinois* (1970) and *Rawlings* v. *Kentucky* (1980), he wrote opinions for the majority restricting a defendant's ability to challenge police searches. In *Illinois* v. *Gates* (1983), he formulated a new rule that made it easier for police to obtain a warrant on the basis of an informant's tip. In 1984, he wrote for the majority endorsing a "public safety" exception to the *Miranda* rules in *New York* v. *Quarles* (see MIRANDA WARNINGS). He endorsed diluting the exclusionary rule with an exception based on the "good faith" of the police in *United States* v. *Leon* (1984), and he wrote the opinion for the majority upholding pretrial detention in *United States* v. *Salerno* (1987). He urged the Court to retain the death penalty against the charge that it violated the *Eighth Amendment (in *Furman* v. *Georgia*, (1972), and he joined the majority in decisions upholding the imposition of the death penalty on minors who commit murder (*Penry* v. *Lynaugh*, 1989) and on mentally retarded murderers (*Stanford* v. *Kentucky*, 1989).

Rehnquist's interpretation of the Due Process Clause minimized constraints on the states in their treatment of those accused of crimes (see DUE PROCESS, PROCEDURAL). Similarly, when a majority held in *Roe* v. *Wade* (1973) that there was a constitutional right to *privacy that prohibited the states from making *abortion illegal during the first six months of pregnancy, he disagreed. In 1989 he wrote for a five-member majority when the Court upheld several state provisions restricting abortion rights but stopped just short of overruling *Roe* v. *Wade*.

Likewise, Rehnquist narrowly construed the Fourteenth Amendment's mandate to the states not to deny any person the *equal protection of the laws. He contended that all that the framers of the Fourteenth Amendment hoped to achieve with the Equal Protection Clause was to prevent the states from treating black and white citizens differently. Consequently, according to Rehnquist, that clause should not apply when the state has not intentionally discriminated (*Columbus* v. *Penick*, 1979) nor when the state has not participated in discrimination (*Moose Lodge* v. *Irvis*, 1972); nor should the Equal Protection Clause be construed to prohibit disparate treatment based on gender (*Craig* v. *Boren*, 1976; *Michael M.* v. *Superior Court of Sonoma County*, 1981). Although Rehnquist declined to reach the constitutional issue in *affirmative action cases, he maintained

*William Hubbs Rehnquist*

that the provisions in federal *civil rights laws condemning racial discrimination in *education and employment incontrovertibly prohibit preferential treatment for members of disadvantaged groups (e.g., *United Steelworkers* v. *Weber*, 1979). In 1989 Rehnquist joined the majority in *Richmond* v. *J. A. Croson Co.* to invalidate a minority set-aside program. Finally, he was a member of the majority in the Court's spate of decisions restricting the use of civil rights laws to challenge discrimination (*Ward's Cove* v. *Atonio*, 1989; *Patterson* v. *McLean Credit Union*, 1989; Will v. *Michigan*, 1989).

Scholars have explained his record in a variety of ways. Early assessments identified *judicial self-restraint as the driving force behind his decision-making. By his own account, Rehnquist favored judicial deference to legislative decisions. In cases in which the Court was called on to resolve a conflict between the power of government and an individual, Rehnquist favored restraint, but when the conflict was between the federal government and a state, he was willing to use judicial power to invalidate federal laws in favor of state autonomy, as in *National League of Cities* v. *Usery*.

Such apparent inconsistencies promoted the view that Rehnquist was unprincipled and result oriented and that he was using his position on the Court to achieve the goals of his own conservative political agenda. Yet Rehnquist's decision making can also be understood as the product of a judicial philosophy with legal positivism at its core and a particular ordering of judicial values. The most important value for Rehnquist was his state-centered federalism, followed by private *property and individual rights. Federalism was so central to Rehnquist's decision making that it abrogated any prescription for a minimal role of the Court, which accounted for his failure to support judicial restraint faithfully. Moreover, the consequences of state autonomy were usually consistent with such political objectives as facilitating the punishment of criminals.

Whether a judicial philosophy of legal positivism or simply a conservative political agenda provides a better explanation of Rehnquist's decision making, he will be remembered as the member of the Burger Court who was least supportive of civil liberties. He was often in the minority during his tenure as associate justice, but by his third term as chief justice a solid conservative majority had emerged with views that coincided with his.

(See also CHIEF JUSTICE, OFFICE OF THE.)

□ Sue Davis, *Justice Rehnquist and the Constitution* (1989). Jeff Powell, "The Compleat Jeffersonian: Justice Rehnquist and Federalism," *Yale Law Journal* 91 (1982): 1317–1370. John R. Rydell. "Mr. Justice Rehnquist and Judicial Self-Restraint," *Hastings Law Journal* 26 (1975); 875–915.
Sue Davis

**Released Time,** the practice of permitting public school students to receive religious instruction during school hours. A Champaign, Illinois, program was declared invalid as an establishment of religion in *Illinois ex rel. McCollum* v. *Board of Education* (1948). The board allowed sectarian teachers nominated by a council of churches and approved by the superintendent of schools to conduct religious instruction in public school classrooms. Attendance at the religion classes was required for participating students; other students received secular instruction in alternate classrooms. The Court held that the superintendent's approval of the teachers, the use of public school classrooms, and the assistance given by compulsory attendance laws breached the separation of church and state.

However, in *Zorach* v. *Clauson* (1952), the Court approved a New York City practice of releasing students from school to attend the religious center of their choice to receive instruction. Absences from the religious classes were reported but not acted upon. Nonparticipating students remained in school. There was no school approval of the teachers, public school classrooms were not used, and no public funds were expended in this program.

*Zorach* modified the strict separationist approach of *McCollum* to allow some accommodation of church and state. The line between the acceptable and the forbidden is drawn according to the degree of interaction required between religious and governmental institutions. These two holdings anticipate the "excessive entanglement" test enunciated in 1971 in *Lemon* v. *Kurtzman* (see LEMON TEST). *Zorach* opened up the possibility that some government aid to religious educational institutions might be constitutionally permissible.

(See also EDUCATION; FIRST AMENDMENT; RELIGION; SCHOOL PRAYER AND BIBLE READING.)
Robert H. Birkby

**Religion.** The development of the constitutional law of religion by the Supreme Court came at the end of a decisive shift in public values in the United States from Protestantism to secularism. From the founding era at the end of the eighteenth century until well into the twentieth century, Protestant religion was thought to be a significant and legitimate component of American public life. By the 1940s, however, American public life had become largely secular, although large numbers of Americans remained committed to traditional religious beliefs and practices in their private lives. The constitutional doctrines developed by the Court under the free exercise and establishment clauses can best be understood as the product of the Court's struggle to define appropriate relationships between religion and government within the context of a secular public culture that considers religion a predominantly private activity of no unique social significance.

*Historical Origins of the Religion Clauses.* The evidence bearing on precisely what the First Congress intended to accomplish with the religion clauses of the *First Amendment is ambiguous. At a minimum, the Establishment Clause was directed at preventing the newly created federal government from granting to any denomination the political and governmental privileges enjoyed in England by the established Anglican church. On the other hand, it is clear that the clause was not intended to do away with religious establishments then existing among the new American states. It is likely that most of the framers meant only to outlaw national religious establishments while leaving the question of state religious establishments to the political judgment of the states.

Similar historical ambiguities exist with respect to the origins of the Free Exercise Clause. Many of the framers hoped that the clause would prevent the governmental persecution of dissenting religions that was permitted in England under the Anglican establishment. Some framers also understood the clause to require that religious believers be released from the obligation to obey federal laws that violated their religious beliefs. Yet, even after ratification of the First Amendment, federal laws were consistently applied to believers without regard to the burden this placed on their religious beliefs and activities, and state governments commonly imposed civil disabilities on non-Protestants and atheists. Again, it is likely that most of the framers probably intended the Free Exercise Clause to prevent the federal government from imposing serious civil disabilities on religious dissenters, while still permitting recognition of the preeminent status of Protestantism as the foundation of American cultural and social life.

*De Facto Establishment.* State religious establishments died a natural political death early in the nineteenth century. Even when combined with the Establishment Clause's prohibition on national establishments, however, the elimination of state establishments did not lead to a separation of religion from public life. Nineteenth-century Americans understood the Constitution to require separation of church and state only at the institutional level. This meant that constitutionally prohibited establishments of religion were created when the government coerced funding of or participation in a particular denomination or sect. However, it did not require that government or politics be secular. On the contrary, nineteenth-century Americans generally believed that Protestant values formed an important part of the foundation on which society was built.

Accordingly, from shortly after the founding era until early in the twentieth century, church-state relations in the United States were governed by what legal historian Mark De Wolfe Howe called the "de facto Protestant establishment." Public schools had a distinctly Protestant flavor, with teachers leading prayers and scripture readings from the King James Bible in their lessons. Customs like legislative prayer became widespread among the states, Thanksgiving, Christmas, and Easter were officially recognized as holidays, and political rhetoric made frequent reference to the Almighty. States enforced prohibitions on blasphemy, levied civil penalties on atheists, enforced the Christian Sabbath, and continued to visit civil disabilities upon the heads of non-Protestants and nonbelievers. Toward the end of the nineteenth century, Protestant fundamentalists rallied to invoke government authority to enforce temperance and antievolution laws (see EVOLUTION AND CREATION SCIENCE). Building on opposition to Mormon polygamy, these fundamentalists also were instrumental in building political support for the federal government's efforts in the latter part of the century to eradicate this practice.

The inapplicability of the *Bill of Rights to the states and the relatively small role played by the federal government in American life prior to the 1930s minimized the religion clauses as a source of constitutional challenge to the practices of the de facto establishment. Consequently, this era of constitutional history generated virtually no religion clause doctrine. Between the Court's decision in *Barron v. Baltimore* (1833) that the Bill of Rights did not bind the states, and its abandonment of that holding with respect to the Free Exercise Clause in *Cantwell v. Connecticut* (1940) and the Establishment Clause in *Everson v. Board of Education* (1947), the Court decided only two establishment clause cases and no free exercise

cases other than the *Mormon Polygamy Cases.* *Reynolds v. United States* (1879) is the only religion clause decision from the era of the de facto establishment that retains any significance in contemporary constitutional law.

In summary, the de facto establishment was a curious meld of religion and government. Religious and governmental authority were aligned in a variety of ways, but always in a diffuse and generally nonsectarian sense. Because the de jure Anglican establishment of England exemplified for Americans the kind of establishment that was prohibited by the Constitution, the possibility that the more subtle alignments of religion and government under the de facto establishment were also constitutionally prohibited was never taken seriously. In the minds of nineteenth-century Americans, the separation of church and state demanded by the Establishment Clause was merely institutional. They honored that separation not only by refraining from establishing a national church but also by having abandoned their state religious establishments. Beyond these measures, however, nineteenth-century Americans saw no need to cabin the public influence of religion. On the contrary, they saw that influence as being critical to the creation and maintenance of civilized society.

*From Protestantism to Secularism.* The assumptions of the de facto establishment about the legitimacy and importance of public religious influence came under serious pressure early in the twentieth century. Exactly how and why this secularization came about is a complex issue. The growth of naturalistic approaches to science spawned by Charles Darwin's *On the Origin of the Species* (1859) undoubtedly pushed public culture away from orthodox Protestant theology. In the early twentieth century, this cultural trend was reinforced by the professionalization of American higher education that saw theologians and clergymen replaced by secular degree-holders as university faculty and administrators. Law itself was significantly influenced by the legal realists, who rejected theologically resonant *natural law as the source of optimal legal rules for a society, believing instead that such rules could be discovered by pragmatic reasoning and careful empirical investigation.

The 1930s also saw elaboration of the "secularization hypothesis" by intellectuals in both the United States and Europe. Under this hypothesis, progressive secularization of society was seen as an inevitable and positive long-term trend that would eventually end in the elimination of religion as a public influence. Although this hypothesis remains controversial, it can at least be said that since the end of World War II, the creation of a "secular society" in the United States has been a genuine political and social option.

For whatever reasons, the de facto establishment had become problematic by the 1940s. In *The Crisis of Democratic Theory* (1972), intellectual historian Edward Purcell, Jr., describes how in the twentieth century, religion "emerged as the preeminent symbol of everything that was bad in human society," whereas science "was inextricably tied up in the minds of most intellectuals with everything that was best in human society" (p. 61). Rather than an indispensable foundation of civilized society, as presupposed by the de facto establishment, religion had come to be seen as a reactionary obstacle to secular progress.

This shift in the perception of religion is evident in the Court's first establishment clause decision in the modern era, *Everson v. Board of Education* (1947). In *Everson*, the Supreme Court considered whether a city could pay for the bus transportation of school-aged children to parochial as well as to public schools. Holding that such funding was constitutionally permissible, the Court summarized the principal force behind the drafting of the Establishment Clause as the desire of the framers to eliminate the civil disorder and violent persecution that historically had accompanied the establishment of a single sect. Observing that early American colonials had brought with them the European tradition of the established church, the Court stressed the indignity of the fact that religious dissenters in America were compelled to support government churches whose principal aim was "to strengthen and consolidate the established faith by generating a burning hatred against dissenters" (p. 16). After a review of Virginia's 1785 rejection of general taxation for the support of ministers and churches (in which Madison and Jefferson are portrayed as having played the decisive roles), the Court stated in unequivocal terms that the Establishment Clause required an absolute neutrality on the part of government, both as between particular religions and as between religion and nonreligion. The decision closed with a flourish, quoting the now-famous phrase from Jefferson's letter to the Danbury Baptists to the effect that the Establishment Clause "was intended to erect a 'wall of separation' between Church and State" (p. 16).

With *Everson*, the Supreme Court clearly signaled that the de facto establishment would not be abandoned as a guide to church-state relations. Although governmental neutrality among particular Protestant sects was consistent with the de facto establishment, governmental neutrality between Protestants and non-Protestants and between believers and atheists was antithetical to it. Likewise, although the institutional separation of church and state was consistent with the de facto establishment, the more decisive division implied by the "wall of separation" was not.

Perhaps most important, neutrality and separation both bespeak a conception of religion that is private and unconnected to government and other institutions of public life. The de facto establishment was built on the premise that religion is essential to civilized society. By contrast, the modern requirement that government remain neutral with respect to the religious choices of its citizens suggests that a wholly secular society is possible and perhaps even preferable. In any event, government in the contemporary era can safely remain indifferent about how religious choice is exercised.

***Establishment Clause.*** For more than twenty years after *Everson*, the Supreme Court measured the constitutionality of governmental action under the Establishment Clause by analyzing whether such action was secular in its purpose and primary impact. The Court later added a third consideration, whether governmental action required or implied a constitutionally dangerous relationship between religion and government. In *Lemon v. Kurtzman* (1971), the Court synthesized its prior decisions into a three-pronged test that centered around the concept of neutrality first articulated in *Everson*. To escape constitutional invalidation under the Establishment Clause, governmental action must (1) have a secular purpose that neither endorses nor disapproves of religion, (2) have an effect that neither advances nor inhibits religion, and (3) avoid creating a relationship between religion and government that entangles either in the internal affairs of the other.

The Court has been widely criticized for its establishment clause decisions under *Lemon*. Indeed, ideological and political opponents who seem unable to agree on anything else are united in their criticism of the contradictory and arbitrary results generated by the Court's application of the three-pronged *Lemon* test. These criticisms are largely misdirected, however. Certainly the *Lemon* test is indeterminate since, like most constitutional tests, it does not specify the general level of scrutiny that governmental actors are to employ in applying its parts to particular cases. Thus, when applied with particular rigor, the test yields one result, yet when applied in a less-exacting way to the same set of facts, the test can be made to yield an equally plausible, but contradictory result.

The source of the controversy surrounding the Court's establishment clause doctrine is not so much in the *Lemon* test as in the unrealistic expectations placed upon it by judges, lawyers, and scholars. Constitutional interpretation is an inherently indeterminate enterprise, and no amount of doctrinal refinement is likely to remedy that. The best one can do is to try to distinguish those situations in which the Court tends to apply the *Lemon* test with particular rigor from those in which it tends to apply a more deferential standard of review.

***Financial Aid to Religion.*** Since direct financial support of churches by government was characteristic of the Anglican establishment, government grants of financial or other tangible aid to churches and other religious groups have always been among the most suspect of government actions under the Establishment Clause. In modern establishment clause jurisprudence, direct financial aid by government to religion has most often come before the Supreme Court in the form of state grants to private religious schools, especially Roman Catholic parochial schools. The state can usually articulate plausible social welfare purposes for such grants. Thus, litigation over the constitutionality of these grants under the Establishment Clause has centered on whether their primary effect is one that advances religion and on whether they create an entangling relationship between the government and the religious recipient of the grant.

Virtually every Supreme Court decision involving financial aid granted directly to a private religious educational organization has found that such aid violates the Establishment Clause. The sole exception relates to religious institutions of higher education. The Court has permitted states to provide financial and "in-kind" aid directly to religious colleges and universities, when the purpose for which the aid is given is clearly secular, carefully monitored, and unlikely to generate a perception that the state has endorsed the religious beliefs of the institutional recipients. However, the Court has never approved direct aid in any form to private religious secondary and elementary schools, even when similar controls are implemented.

*Aid to Religious Schools.* The Court has relied on two separate arguments to invalidate financial aid to religious schools, one directed at the effect prong of *Lemon* and the other directed at the entanglement prong. The premise of the first argument is that private religious elementary and secondary schools exist principally to inculcate their students with the religious beliefs and values of the sponsoring religion. Such schools are "pervasively sectarian," in the words of the decisions, and direct aid to them constitutes direct aid to the school's efforts to proselytize religious values among its students. Thus, financial aid to parochial schools generates a primary effect that advances religion in violation of the effects prong of *Lemon.*

In response to this argument, many states narrowly tailored their financial grants to religious schools so that the money could be used only for specific educational purposes unrelated to the school's principal mission of teaching religious values. One program, for example, sought to reimburse private religious schools for the costs of administering standardized tests mandated by the state for both public and private school students. These grants were accompanied by affirmative monitoring and other controls designed to ensure that the financial aid was not diverted by the school to fund its religious mission.

The Court might have held these grant programs unconstitutional as financial aid to pervasively sectarian organizations. Without the

grants, religious schools would have to pay for state mandated services with privately raised funds. With the grants, more private funds are available for religious education. Thus, the grants free funds for religious education that otherwise would be used to pay for state-mandated services, thereby causing a primary effect of advancing religion.

The Court, however, chose a different tack. It observed that the usual effect of the spending controls built into these grant programs was to impede the religious recipients' ability to carry out their primary religious mission as well as to require secular state authorities regularly to monitor how such schools spend their funds and implement their religious mission on a day-to-day basis. The Court has consistently held that this is an unacceptable entanglement of the state in the affairs of the church, in violation of the third *Lemon* prong.

The Court's application of the entanglement prong of *Lemon* ensnares religious elementary and secondary schools in a constitutional trap with respect to financial grants. If the grants come without strings attached, to avoid entangling the state in the affairs of the religious school, the Court finds them unconstitutional because they have the primary effect of advancing religion. If strings are attached to prevent use of the funds to advance the school's religious mission, the Court finds them unconstitutional because the controls represent an unacceptable intrusion of the state into the religious school's affairs. The Court simply will not permit direct financial or other tangible assistance to religious elementary and secondary schools.

The Court has been considerably more lenient in cases involving state aid given directly to private religious school students and their parents, rather than to the schools themselves. In *Mueller* v. *Allen* (1983), for example, the Court reviewed a state tax law that permitted taxpayers to deduct from their state taxable income up to seven hundred dollars per child for tuition, textbook, and transportation expenses incurred in educating their children. Parents of both public and private schoolchildren were equally eligible for the deduction. However, those challenging the constitutionality of the deduction introduced statistical evidence showing that public school children did not pay tuition, and that their book and transportation expenses fell well below the upper limits of the deduction. Since this evidence showed that the bulk of the tax benefit from the deduction was realized by parents of children in private schools, 95 percent of which were religiously sponsored, the challengers argued that the primary effect of the deduction was religious.

The state responded by challenging the validity of the statistical evidence. However, the Court found the evidence unimportant and declined to examine arguments about it in any detail. In the words of the majority opinion, "the historic purposes of the clause simply do not encompass the sort of attenuated financial benefit, ultimately controlled by the private choices of individual parents, that eventually flows to parochial schools from the neutrally available tax benefit at issue in this case" (p. 400). Because the financial aid represented by the deduction was funnelled to parents rather than to schools, the Court did not strictly scrutinize the effect of the deduction under *Lemon*.

Similar rationales explain other decisions of the Court upholding the constitutionality of in-kind aid to religion, such as free bus transportation and textbooks for parochial school students. Since such aid is provided on a nondiscriminatory basis directly to students, regardless of their status as public school or religious school students, the Court considers its effect to be religiously neutral for purposes of the Establishment Clause, even though the aid clearly makes the operation of religious schools less expensive.

Likewise, the provision to religious school students of educational testing and counselling services, which are provided to public school students on their school campuses as a matter of course, has been upheld under certain circumstances. To avoid establishment clause difficulties, these services are provided to religious school students in a manner that is geographically and administratively separated from the religious school itself, usually by setting up a location adjacent to the religious school campus. This has enabled the Court to view the services as being delivered directly to students rather than to schools. Again, religious aid to individuals does not generate a religious effect that is "primary" under the second prong of *Lemon*.

*Identifying Departures from Neutrality.* The parochial school aid cases provide a particular example of a general problem that haunts decisions under the Establishment Clause: How does one identify the baseline measure of religious neutrality? In a world in which no individuals or organizations receive any governmental aid whatsoever, any aid to religion, whether to religious individuals or to religious organizations, would depart from the baseline of no aid and violate *Everson*'s neutrality principle. In a modern welfare state, however, government aid to both individuals and organizations is widespread. Religious neutrality in a world in which every person and entity is entitled to some kind of government financial aid demands that similar aid be granted to religion.

The parochial school aid cases suggest that the Court does not consistently use the same baseline when it measures religious neutrality under the *Lemon* test. It uses a baseline of pervasive aid when it measures the neutrality of financial aid to religious individuals, which leads to the conclusion that such individuals and institutions must be granted access to such aid if religious neutrality is to be maintained. When measuring direct financial aid to religious elementary and secondary schools, however, the Court assumes a baseline of no aid, which leads in the opposite direction, to the conclusion that religious schools must be denied access to preserve religious neutrality. Thus, the apparent inconsistency of results stems less from any deficiencies of the *Lemon* test than from slippage in the conceptual baseline that anchors the substantive definition of religious neutrality.

Other Supreme Court decisions suggest that outside of the context of religious elementary and secondary schools, the governing neutrality baseline in cases of financial aid to religion is one of pervasive aid even when the assistance in question flows directly to religious organizations. For example, the Court has upheld numerous programs of direct financial grants to religiously sponsored colleges and universities. The Court has assumed that, in contrast to religious elementary and secondary schools, religious colleges and universities have as part of their mission the teaching of critical thinking skills in addition to (if not instead of) the inculcation of religious values. Moreover, college students are older and more mature than elementary and secondary school students, so there is considerably less likelihood that college students will be coerced into adopting and conforming to particular religious beliefs and practices. For both of these reasons, the Court has concluded that religious colleges and universities are not "pervasively sectarian," so that state aid to such institutions does not assist the teaching of religious values in the way that such aid does when granted to religious elementary and secondary education.

Thus, in all of the decisions of the Supreme Court that have upheld the constitutionality of tangible aid to religious schools under the Establishment Clause, the aid has been directly granted either to a religious college or university or to students enrolled at religious elementary or secondary schools (or their parents). Accordingly, the strongest case for the constitutionality of tangible aid by government to religion would appear to be one in which the aid was provided directly to an individual student at a religiously sponsored college or university. In just such a case, *Witters* v. *Washington Department of Services for the Blind* (1986), the Court agreed unanimously that the tangible governmental aid at issue did not violate the Establishment Clause.

There are indications that the pervasive aid baseline remains in place even outside the context of religious higher education. In *Bowen* v. *Kendrick* (1988), the Court considered an establishment clause challenge to the Adolescent Family Life Act (1982), which mandated federal grants-in-aid to social service organizations, including religiously sponsored ones, that performed research or provided services aimed at reducing teenage pregnancy. In an opinion that echoed its prior analyses of direct financial aid to religious higher education, the Court held that giving grants directly to religious social service organizations under the act did not violate the Establishment Clause so long as the organizational recipients were not "pervasively sectarian" (p. 590).

*Nonfinancial Aid to Religion.* Although the United States has largely avoided direct financial support of churches because of its association of that practice with the abuses of the Anglican establishment, American government has sometimes employed its power directly to coerce conformity with majoritarian religious practices even when it refused to aid religion financially. It was not until *Everson's* articulation of religious neutrality as the governing norm of establishment clause jurisprudence that the Court began to scrutinize such uses of governmental power. By then, however, most of the overtly coercive practices of the de facto establishment had ceased, so that relatively few cases of actual coercion have reached the Supreme Court. The Court did rebuff a constitutional challenge to state laws that prohibited businesses from operating on Sunday in 1961, reasoning that, after the passage of time, neither the purpose nor the primary effect of such laws was religious. A generation later, in *Larkin v. Grendel's Den* (1982), the Court struck down on establishment clause grounds an ordinance that granted churches the power to veto the issuance of liquor licenses to applicants located within five hundred feet of their premises, on the theory that it was an unconstitutional delegation of government authority to religious bodies.

*Government Endorsement of Religion.* The principal argument relied on by the Court to invalidate nonfinancial government aid to religion is the official endorsement of religion that is implied by such aid. The nature of the harm caused by endorsement is different from that caused by actual government coercion. Whereas coercion results in a deprivation of physical liberty—for example, the right to conduct business on Sunday, the right to obtain a liquor license in the vicinity of a church—the harm caused by government endorsement is completely psychological. In an influential concurring opinion in *Lynch v. Donnelly* (1984), Justice Sandra Day *O'Connor described the harm as follows: "Endorsement sends a message to nonadherents that they are outsiders, not full members of the political community, and an accompanying message to adherents that they are insiders, favored members of the political community" (p. 688). The knowledge that government endorses particular religious groups alienates members of unendorsed religions as well as those of no religion; even though endorsement does not by itself result in direct physical or economic harm to such people, it constitutes official disapproval of their beliefs and makes them feel less worthy than those who belong to the endorsed group.

Government endorsement of religion thus vio-

lates *Everson's* neutrality principle as it is measured by *Lemon*. A government that subjectively intends to endorse religion by its actions violates the first prong of *Lemon*, which requires a secular governmental purpose that advances nor inhibits religion. A government that does not subjectively intend to endorse religion by its actions but whose actions nevertheless have the objective effect of endorsement, violates the second prong of *Lemon*, which requires a primary secular effect that neither advances nor inhibits religion.

As with questions of financial aid to religion, a principal battleground for questions of the constitutionality of religious endorsements by government has been the public schools. Whenever public schools have institutionally sponsored a religious presence on their campuses through organized classroom prayers and Bible reading, school-mandated moments of silence during the school day to encourage personal prayers, posting religious texts like the Ten Commandments, and teaching religious precepts, the Court has found that they placed the power of the state behind those who believe in the validity of such activities (see SCHOOL PRAYER AND BIBLE READING). Allowing such activities in public schools is an implicit endorsement of them, thereby making those students and parents with no religious beliefs or with beliefs at odds with the institutionally sponsored activities feel separated and excluded from the school that they support with their tax dollars. Accordingly, the Supreme Court has found a violation of the Establishment Clause in every case involving institutional sponsorship of religious activities by public elementary or secondary schools.

*Endorsement and Public Schools.* The decisions involving endorsement of religion reflect a structure similar to that of the financial aid cases. In endorsement cases, the Court's scrutiny level increases when a public school institutionally endorses religious activities by sponsoring them as part of the school day, and decreases when such activities are the result of individual choices by students and their parents.

For example, in *Illinois ex. rel. McCollum v. Board of Education* (1948), the Court considered a program under which priests, ministers, and rabbis came into public school classrooms each week to give religious instruction to students affiliated with their congregations. Students who did not wish to receive the instruction were permitted to attend a study hall instead. The Court found that formal integration of on-campus religious instruction into the public schools curriculum constituted unacceptable aid to religion in violation of the Establishment Clause. Just four years later in *Zorach v. Clauson* (1952), however, the Court approved a program under which public school students were released from their normal classes once each week to travel to religious instruction classes held off of the public school campus (see RELEASED TIME).

The most obvious distinction between the two cases is the on- or off-campus location of the religious instruction. However, this approach ignores that in both cases the state endorses religious instruction to some significant extent, and consequently it has been widely criticized.

A more promising approach focuses on the different way in which each religious instruction program structured the individual choices of students and their parents about whether to participate. Although in *McCollum* students had the right not to participate, they had to act affirmatively to be excused from the instruction, leaving the decisional inertia on the side of participation. By contrast, in *Zorach* students had the right to participate in the instruction only if they acted affirmatively to attend; otherwise, they simply remained in class for their normal school-day activities. Thus, the decisional inertia was shifted onto the side of nonattendance. Whereas in *McCollum* the public school was implicated directly in the effort of churches and synagogues to provide religious instruction, in *Zorach* the school merely cooperated with students and parents to give effect to individual choices to receive religious instruction made outside and independent of the public school environment.

The Court recently confirmed that the difference between *McCollum* and *Zorach* was the degree of public school involvement in influencing student participation in religious instruction, rather than the location of the instruction. In *Board of Education* v. *Mergens* (1990), the Court considered the constitutionality of prayer meetings organized and held in a public high school classroom by Christian students during a twice-weekly "activity period." During the period, students were free to engage in a wide variety of secular cocurricular activities besides the prayer meetings, including intramural sports, music, academic, and social clubs, career counseling, and independent study. The prayer meetings were student organized and administered; a faculty adviser was present only for the limited purpose of ensuring that school property was not misused and took no active part. Although no single opinion commanded a majority of the Court, the justices held by an 8-to-1 margin that the prayer meetings did not violate the Establishment Clause. An important factor was the structuring of the activity period so that participation in the prayer meetings was entirely the decision of the students, who had many other nonreligious options. This enabled six justices to conclude that any perception of religious endorsement was the result of individual student choice rather than any action by the public school. Accordingly, the cooperation of the high school with Christian students who wished to pray did not constitute an endorsement of their prayer meetings in violation of the Establishment Clause.

It is noteworthy that *McCollum* found a violation of the Establishment Clause even though students who did not wish to receive religious instruction were excused from attending. The psychological harm stemming from government endorsement of religion helps to explain why permitting students to be excused from participation in school-sponsored religious activities does not avoid a violation of the Establishment Clause. The endorsement argument assumes that the Establishment Clause guards not only against physical or economic harm that might be imposed by government upon a person because of her religion, but also against the psychological harm that one suffers when her religion is disapproved by government. This psychological harm is present even if the government refrains from using its power of coercion to force conformity with the approved religious belief or practice, in the form of implicit disapproval of the beliefs of those who affiliate with nonendorsed religions or with no religion at all.

Again paralleling cases involving financial aid to religious schools, the age and maturity of students have a bearing on the level of scrutiny employed by the Court in reviewing endorsements of religion in the public school context. In *Widmar* v. *Vincent* (1981), one of its least controversial establishment clause decisions, the Court held by an eight to one margin that religiously oriented student organizations at a state university were entitled to the same access to university funds and facilities as were secular student organizations. *Mergens* effectively applied the *Widmar* holding to high school students, suggesting that higher levels of scrutiny in cases of religious endorsement are not triggered by age until one reaches public middle and elementary schools. *Weisman* v. *Lee* (1st Cir., 1990), a case to be reviewed by the Court in 1992 involving junior high school graduation prayers, may give some insight into whether the youth and immaturity of middle school students relative to high school and college students will trigger heightened scrutiny under the Establishment Clause.

*Endorsement in Other Contexts.* Outside of public schools, the Court has been considerably more lenient in permitting government actions that endorse religion, so long as the actions take place in a context which suggests no denominational preference. For example, in *Lynch*, the Court found that the Establishment Clause was not violated by display of a city-owned nativity scene on city property near a display of Santa and his reindeer. Similarly, in *Allegheny County* v. *American Civil Liberties Union* (1989), the Court held that a Menorah displayed next to a forty-five-foot Christmas tree outside a county office building did not violate the Establishment Clause. However, the Court in *Allegheny* found that the isolated display of a nativity scene inside the county courthouse one block away violated the Establishment Clause because its implicit endorsement of Christianity was not mitigated by comparable endorsements of other religious denominations or of secular celebrations of Christmas in the immediate vicinity.

The problem of setting the baseline from which to measure religious neutrality also exists with respect to endorsement of religion. In a world in which wholly secular government is the norm and religion is considered a purely private activity of no public significance, as posited by the secularization hypothesis, any cooperation by government with religion gives to religion a public status and departs from the baseline of public secularism, thereby violating the neutrality principle. In a world in which religion is considered a legitimate public influence, however, like that of nineteenth-century America under the de facto establishment, neutrality demands that government cooperate with religion to the same extent that it cooperates with secular organizations.

The Court's endorsement cases suggest that it uses a public secularism baseline whenever there is institutional sponsorship of religious activities by public schools. Thus, sponsorship of such activities by the school itself constitutes a violation of religious neutrality, whereas facilitation by the school of private individual choice about participation in religious activities does not violate neutrality. On the other hand, when the Court considers the constitutionality of endorsements of religion outside of the public school context, it assumes a baseline of public religious influence. There is no departure from neutrality as measured by this baseline so long as the belief or activity endorsed is only recognized as one influence on public life together with many other religious and secular influences.

*Free Exercise Clause.* Constitutional litigation under the Free Exercise Clause has largely centered on whether the clause requires that a person be excused from complying with laws that contradict that person's religious beliefs. Hence, the Supreme Court has considered whether the Free Exercise Clause permits believers to ignore any law that requires them to perform an act that is prohibited by their religious beliefs, or prohibits them from performing any act that is required by their religious beliefs.

In *Reynolds v. United States* (1879), the Supreme Court refused to find a constitutionally compelled exemption for Mormon polygamists. Under the so-called belief-action doctrine that the *Reynolds* Court articulated, government is without constitutional authority to punish a person for his or her religious *beliefs* but has full authority to regulate religiously motivated *actions* so long as it has a rational basis for doing so. Since the government can always meet this relatively light burden of justification, the belief-action doctrine effectively forecloses the possibility of constitutionally compelled exemptions.

*Reynold's* belief-action doctrine was apparently dismantled by two more recent decisions. In *Sherbert v. Verner* (1963), the Court ordered a state to pay unemployment benefits to a Seventh-Day Adventist even though she would not make herself available for work on Saturday (her Sabbath) as required by the state's unemployment compensation law. The state argued that protecting the integrity of the unemployment insurance fund against depletion by those who were not really looking for work was a sufficient reason to deny the benefits. However, the Court in *Sherbert* held that government could burden a fundamental right like the free exercise of religion only if it was protecting a compelling interest by the least intrusive means possible, and found the state's interest insufficient to justify the infringement. The Court has expressly reaffirmed this holding on numerous subsequent occasions.

In the second case, *Wisconsin v. Yoder* (1972), the Court held that the Amish were not required to send their children to public schools past the eighth grade in violation of their religious beliefs, because the state could not show that its compelling interest would be significantly undermined by granting the Amish an exemption from compulsory attendance laws. Whereas *Sherbert* required only that the state justify the law that burdened free exercise by a compelling interest, *Yoder* required that the state justify its denial of an exemption to religious objectors by a compelling interest. Thus, the effect of *Yoder* was to raise substantially the government's burden of justifying any law that incidentally burdened the free exercise of religion.

When combined with other holdings of the Court, the extraordinary protection of religious exercise afforded by the *Sherbert-Yoder* doctrine may have created a serious problem. Religious objectors usually constitute a very small minority whose disobedience of general legislation would rarely undermine its general effectiveness. Moreover, in *United States v. Ballard* (1944), the Court had foreclosed judicial inquiry into the sincerity and reasonableness of religious beliefs. When read with *Ballard,* the *Sherbert-Yoder* doctrine appeared to require that a constitutional exemption from compliance with the law be granted to any religious objector who asked for one.

The mandate of free exercise exemptions that followed from the *Sherbert-Yoder* doctrine did not pose a serious difficulty when the benefit to be gained from exemption was something few people would want, like receipt of unemployment benefits despite being unavailable for work on Saturday, or freedom from prosecution under compulsory school attendance laws. In *United States v. Lee* (1982), however, the Amish asked the Court to grant them a free exercise exemption from paying social security taxes. Perhaps fearing a tidal wave of exemption lawsuits by people claiming that their religious beliefs prevented them from paying any kind of tax at all, the Court found the government's interest in denying the Amish an exemption to be compelling.

*Lee* marked the beginning of the end of the *Sherbert-Yoder* doctrine. In quick succession after *Lee*, the Court denied free exercise relief to a *Native American who sought to prevent the government from assigning his daughter a social security number, an Orthodox Jew who sought to wear a yarmulke in violation of Air Force uniform regulations, and a Native American tribe that sought to prevent construction of a federal highway that would prevent them from worshiping. In *Red, White and Blue* (1988) law professor Mark Tushnet concluded that the Court was willing to protect religious exercise only when doing so was either relatively inexpensive or consistent with secular constitutional norms like freedom of expression or *due process of law.

In *Employment Division* v. *Smith* (1990), the Court brought free exercise jurisprudence full circle by reaffirming the belief-action doctrine of *Reynolds*. In *Smith*, a state denied two Native Americans unemployment compensation after they were dismissed from their jobs for smoking peyote as part of tribal religious rituals. Because use of peyote was a criminal offense under state law, the state ruled that the Native Americans had been dismissed for "work-related misconduct" that permitted benefits to be withheld. The Native Americans sued for the benefits, arguing that the Free Exercise Clause prevented the state from applying the misconduct provision to them.

The Court in *Smith* effectively abandoned the *Sherbert-Yoder* doctrine. Noting that denial of unemployment compensation in *Sherbert* was not based on the plaintiff's commission of an illegal act, the Court held in *Smith* that the state's interest in ensuring the integrity of the unemployment insurance fund was sufficiently important to justify its refusal to pay benefits to claimants who were guilty of unlawful conduct. The majority opinion by Justice Antonin *Scalia strictly confined *Sherbert* and its progeny to their facts and recast *Yoder* from a free exercise opinion that protected freedom of religion into a substantive *due process opinion that protected parental and family autonomy. The opinion expressly stated that the only independent protection offered by the Free Exercise Clause lay in its prohibition of laws motivated by a desire to disadvantage religion, on the theory that such laws impose an intentional burden, rather than a merely incidental one, on religious exercise. Even this protection is redundant of other parts of the Constitution, however, since the Court had already held in *Larson* v. *Valente* (1982) that legislation demonstrably intended to disadvantage particular religious denominations violates the Establishment Clause.

*Smith* did approve the legislative practice of writing religious exemptions into laws, a practice that the Court had upheld against an establishment clause challenge in *Corporation of the Presiding Bishop* v. *Amos* (1987). Thus, although there is no longer any constitutionally compelled exemption under the Free Exercise Clause, it still remains constitutionally permissible for lawmakers to grant exemptions. What this means is that politically powerful religions will be able to lobby successfully for exemptions from burdensome legislation in Congress and the state legislatures, while the free exercise of politically powerless religions—those most in need of constitutional protection from the majoritarian political process—will be wholly dependent upon the goodwill of political majorities. *Reynolds* and *Smith* themselves are evidence that politically powerless religions will often fail to obtain legislative exemptions for their religious practices.

A final area of free exercise doctrine relates to adjudication by secular courts of religious disputes. In a typical case, a hierarchy or congregation divides itself into two or more theologically opposed factions that then argue over which faction is entitled to control the property and offices of the preexisting church.

The Court has developed a free exercise analogue to the *political question doctrine that disposes of most of these cases. To the extent that resolution of a hierarchical or congregational dispute depends upon interpretation of religious doctrine, the secular court must defer to the interpretation advanced by the church's governing structure. If no interpretation is forthcoming, the court must abstain from adjudicating the case rather than offer the interpretation itself, on the theory that ecclesiastical and theological questions are not *justiciable.

The Court has recognized one important exception to this rule of abstention from deciding religious questions. In *Jones* v. *Wolf* (1979), the Court held that if a court can resolve a religious dispute under secular legal principles without resort to interpretation of religious doctrine, it may do so, even if the secular resolution ignores or contradicts the result that would have been indicated by deference to church polity.

The rationale of the church property cases is that judicial resolution of ecclesiastical or theological disputes impermissibly entangles government in the affairs of religion. Accordingly, the decisions frequently advert to the constitutional value of church autonomy.

□ Frederick Mark Gedicks, "Toward a Constitutional Jurisprudence of Religious Group Rights," *Wisconsin Law Review* 1989: 99–169. Donald A. Gianella, "Religious Liberty, Nonestablishment, and Doctrinal Development" *Harvard Law Review* 80 (1967): 1381–1431; 81 (1968): 513–590. Mark DeWolfe Howe, *The Garden and the Wilderness: Religion and Government in American Constitutional History* (1965). Philip B. Kurland, *Religion and the Law: Of Church and State and the Supreme Court* (1961). William Marshall, "The Case Against the Constitutionally Compelled Free Exercise Exemption." *Case Western Reserve Law Review* 40 (1990): 357–412. Michael W. McConnell, "The Origins and Historical Understanding of Free Exercise of Religion," *Harvard Law Review* 103

(1990): 1410–1517. Stephen Pepper, "Taking the Free Exercise Clause Seriously." *Brigham Young University Law Review* 1986: 299–336. Steven Douglas Smith, "Reconstructing the Disestablishment Decision," *Texas Law Review* 67 (1989): 955–1031.     Frederick Mark Gedicks

**Removal Act of 1875.** Sometimes known as the Judiciary Act of 1875 in recognition of its sweeping importance, this statute for the first time conferred on federal courts both *original and removal jurisdiction that was coextensive with the constitutional grant over *federal questions. *Article III conveys jurisdiction over "all Cases, in Law and Equity, arising under this Constitution, the Laws of the United States, and Treaties." The First Congress chose, however, to vest federal question jurisdiction primarily in the state courts and permitted only limited *appeal of federal questions from *state courts to the Supreme Court. It also created a narrow right of pretrial removal from state to federal courts.

Expansion of federal question and removal jurisdiction went hand-in-hand throughout the nineteenth century. The growth of national power during the *Civil War included an expansion of the jurisdiction of federal courts as a necessary concomitant to the increase in federal substantive powers created by the Reconstruction Amendments. This trend culminated in the Removal Act of 1875, which empowered federal courts to take concurrent jurisdiction of civil suits "arising under the Constitution or laws of the United States, or treaties." The statute also greatly expanded removal jurisdiction, extending it to plaintiffs as well as defendants. The Judiciary Act of 1887 completed the work of the 1875 act by unifying the requirements of removal and original federal jurisdiction. Because of these statutes, federal courts became for the first time the primary forums for vindicating rights secured by the United States Constitution.

(See also JUDICIAL POWER AND JURISDICTION.)

William M. Wiecek

**Removal of Cases.** A feature of American *federalism is the existence of a dual judicial system. Each state has its own court system, typically consisting of trial courts, intermediate appellate courts, and a supreme court. The federal system has a similarly structured judicial system. Generally, it is the plaintiff who decides whether to bring a case in state or federal courts and the plaintiff's decision is undisturbed so long as the selected court has jurisdiction over that kind of case and over the defendant.

Removal is an exception to this general rule, allowing a defendant to remove a case from a state court to the federal court in the district where the case is pending. Removal thus enables the defendant to defeat the plaintiff's choice of state court. After a case is removed, the state court loses power over it and the federal court assumes power to decide all aspects of the case.

Although removal jurisdiction is not mentioned in the Constitution, it has been statutorily authorized in some form since the *Judiciary Act of 1789 established the *lower federal court system. Under current statutes, removal is allowed only if the case falls within the jurisdiction of the federal courts and could have been brought in the federal forum by the plaintiff. As a further limit, removal of cases involving citizens of different states is allowed only if the defendant is not a citizen of the state in which the action is pending. Because removal is inconsistent with the general policy of allowing the plaintiff to choose the forum, the Supreme Court has construed removal statutes narrowly, limiting somewhat the defendant's ability to defeat plaintiff's choice.

(See also JUDICIAL POWER AND JURISDICTION; STATE COURTS.)

Daan Braveman

**Removal Power.** See APPOINTMENT AND REMOVAL POWER.

**Reply, Right of.** The question arises whether the government, consistent with the *First Amendment, can require the media to provide space or time to people wishing to respond to views expressed in the same media. Some legal scholars have argued that the First Amendment forbids only abridgment of expression, not its enhancement. Just as scarcity of frequencies limits the number of broadcast outlets, they argue, economic concentration has drastically reduced the number of newspapers. Thus, to foster the exchange of diverse ideas in the media marketplace, it is reasonable to require newspapers and electronic media to provide some right of access to those who do not own newspapers, hold broadcast licenses, or operate cable television systems.

In the leading case of *Miami Herald Publishing Co. v. Tornillo* (1974), the Supreme Court rejected a state-imposed right of reply. Pat Tornillo, a candidate for the Florida legislature, was criticized in editorials by the *Miami Herald*. Tornillo demanded space under a Florida statute that required a newspaper to provide free reply space to any candidate whose personal character or official record the newspaper assailed. The *Herald* refused. The Court unanimously declared the law unconstitutional as an infringement of the First Amendment guarantee of freedom of the press. A "responsible press is an undoubtedly desirable goal," the Court remarked, "but press responsibility is not mandated by the Constitution and like many other virtues it cannot be legislated" (p. 256). The Court concluded that a right of reply could impose intolerable financial costs, force newspapers to omit material they wished to publish in order to make room for replies, lead newspapers to avoid publishing anything that might trigger a reply, and constitute an unwarranted intrusion into the editorial process.

Only five years earlier, in *Red Lion Broadcasting Co. Inc.* v. *FCC* (1969), the Court unanimously upheld a strikingly similar right of reply applicable to the broadcast media. *Red Lion* upheld the Fairness Doctrine and the personal attack and political editorial rules imposed by the Federal Communications Commission. By implication, the decision also affirmed the constitutionality of the so-called equal opportunity section of the Federal Communications Act. The Federal Communications Commission in 1987 repealed the Fairness Doctrine, but the personal attack rule, political editorial rule, and Equal Opportunity Law remain in place. The FCC rules, with certain exceptions, require broadcasters to provide free reply time to people or groups whose personal integrity is impugned and to political candidates who are editorially opposed by a station. The Equal Opportunity Law, again with certain exceptions, requires broadcasters who provide legally qualified candidates with free or paid air time to make similar time available to all other qualified candidates for the same office.

In *Red Lion*, the Court found the First Amendment right of viewers and listeners to have access to diverse ideas to be more important than any First Amendment rights enjoyed by broadcasters. The Court also upheld in *CBS* v. *FCC* (1981) a federal statute requiring broadcasters to provide "reasonable access" to federal candidates. But it refused to recognize in *CBS* v. *Democratic National Committee* (1973) any First Amendment right to purchase air time for editorial advertising. Thus, any right of reply applicable to the broadcast media exists only in the narrow realm of certain personal attacks and in the context of political campaigns.

The Fairness Doctrine never required broadcasters to provide reply time to specific individuals or groups. It required only that broadcasters cover controversial issues of public importance in a fair manner. Nevertheless, the FCC's rationale for repeal of the doctrine included concern that it discouraged broadcasters from bold public affairs coverage, intruded on their editorial judgment, and gave *censorship power to the FCC. The personal attack and political editorial rules as well as the Equal Opportunity Law appear highly vulnerable to similar attack. The question may only be how long a right of reply can survive in the electronic media.

(See also SPEECH AND THE PRESS.)

□ Jerome A. Barron, *Freedom of the Press for Whom?: The Right of Access to Mass Media* (1973).

Robert E. Drechsel

**Reporters, Supreme Court.** The first reporter of decisions was an unappointed Pennsylvanian who took commercial advantage of the Supreme Court's move to his state in 1791. Reporters now hold a statutory office whose occupants have consistently been public officials of high distinction.

Alexander *Dallas, a journalist, editor, and future secretary of the treasury, had already begun the business of publishing Pennsylvania opinions for private sale when the Supreme Court moved from New York City to Philadelphia. His first volume, entitled "1 Dallas" in the tradition of English nominative reports, has become volume 1 of the *United States Reports*, yet contains only Pennsylvania state opinions. His second volume included some decisions of the United States Supreme Court, and Dallas continued, sometimes belatedly, to publish the Court's decisions through 1800. The Court moved to Washington, D.C., that year, and William *Cranch assumed the reporter's job. For fifty-four years a judge in the District of Columbia, Cranch reported the Court's decisions until 1815. Cranch's judicial duties strained his time, however, and his reports were increasingly tardy toward the end of his tenure.

Congress formally recognized the reporter's office by statute in 1816, and for the first time the reporter was modestly remunerated after the Judiciary Act of 1817. Henry *Wheaton, the first reporter appointed by the Court, was a close friend of Justice Joseph *Story, and in part with Story's assistance promptly published accurate, annotated decisions. His verbose volumes, however, also included "long, baroque disquisitions on arcane branches of law." After Wheaton's appointment as minister to Denmark in 1827, his successor, Richard *Peters, produced more concise and less expensive reports, even publishing cases that had been in Wheaton's volumes. This action by Peters threatened the market for Wheaton's own reports. Accordingly Wheaton brought suit against Peters, alleging violation of his common-law *copyright. In *Wheaton* v. *Peters* (1834), the Court held that its opinions were in the public domain, and that the reporter's notes and commentary alone were subject to copyright.

Former congressman Benjamin Chew *Howard was reporter from 1843 to 1861, producing highly praised volumes. His successor, Jeremiah *Black, published but two volumes during his brief term as reporter. James Buchanan's attorney general and secretary of state, the fiery Black had alienated so many senators that his nomination as associate justice of the Court was rejected in 1861, and he became its reporter instead. An "advocate of surpassing power," Black resigned after two years and became a leader of the post–Civil War Supreme Court bar.

Nominative reports ended with John William *Wallace. The judiciary appropriation of 1874 for the first time included a sum for publishing the Court's opinions under government auspices, and Wallace's twenty-third volume was the last to bear a reporter's name on its spine. Relieved of tedious publishing and distribution tasks, late nineteenth-century reporters faced a less demanding job.

William Tod *Otto was the first of the "anonymous" reporters, although his name continued to appear prominently on each volume's title page. Otto's successor, John Chandler Bancroft *Davis, was perhaps the most prolific officeholder ever to occupy the position. Davis was a member of the New York assembly, assistant secretary of state, American secretary to the Joint High Commission with Great Britain, arbitrator between Britain and Portugal in an African dispute, minister to Germany, judge of the court of claims, and finally reporter of the Supreme Court. Davis exemplifies the typically distinguished qualifications of the reporters. They have often held numerous positions of high responsibility before appointment as reporter although some, such as Charles Henry *Butler, have perhaps consequently found the reporter's office monotonous and obscure.

Recent reporters have had equally full careers. Ernest *Knaebel organized and directed the Public Lands Division of the Justice Department. Walter *Wyatt rose to become general counsel of the Board of Governors of the Federal Reserve System. Henry *Putzel was first chief of the voting and elections section of the Justice Department's Civil Rights Division. Henry *Lind was an editor at the Lawyers Co-Operative Publishing Company, responsible for editing its *U.S. Supreme Court Reports and Digest* and then served as the Court's assistant reporter of decisions.

Supreme Court reporters are unknown to the public but make possible expeditious and wide dissemination of the nation's highest judicial decisions. Although the position now calls for progressive expertise ranging from computers to systems of citation, reporters quietly continue their overlooked role as heralds of the Supreme Court.

(See also REPORTING OF OPINIONS.)

□ Gerald T. Dunne, "Early Court Reporters," *Yearbook of the Supreme Court Historical Society* (1976): 61–72. Craig Joyce, "The Rise of the Supreme Court Reporter: An Institutional Perspective on Marshall Court Ascendancy," *Michigan Law Review* 83 (1985): 1291–1391.

Francis Helminski

**Reporting of Opinions.** Cases in the English royal courts were first reported through the official clerk's record, showing particular pleas and judgments, although omitting instructive legal argument between counsel and the court. In the late thirteenth century case arguments first circulated, in Law French. In the fourteenth century chronological "Year Book" reports appeared. Anonymously authored, they had little precedential value but preserved for academic purposes the arguments of counsel. The Year Book series extended to the reign of Henry VIII, after which various practitioners authored nominative reports and opinions with inconsistent accuracy.

Few early American judicial decisions were systematically published. Ephraim Kirby published the first volume of state law reports in America, and soon afterward Alexander *Dallas published his reports of the Supreme Court of Pennsylvania. Dallas's first Pennsylvania Supreme Court volume, published in 1790, became "1 Dallas," first volume of the series that became the *United States Reports*. Dallas, while continuing to publish the Pennsylvania cases in another series, filled a parallel line of volumes starting with "2 Dallas" with opinions of the United States Supreme Court. His successors up to 1874, William *Cranch, Henry *Wheaton, Richard *Peters, Benjamin *Howard, Jeremiah *Black, and John *Wallace, also edited Supreme Court reports bearing their names.

The initial volumes were purely commercial ventures, and the reporter received no government compensation. Editing and publishing the reports were a demanding private enterprise. There were sometimes long lapses between the announcement of a decision by the Court and its publication. Prices for the books were high, the market was limited, and many of the court's early decisions were not published at all, or were published inaccurately.

In 1816 Congress officially created the office of reporter and in 1817 established a one-thousand-dollar annual salary for the position. This salary supplemented whatever revenue the reporter already received from sales of the published volumes. In a letter of 7 February 1817, Chief Justice John *Marshall said that the Court's justices all concurred "that the object of the bill is in a high degree desirable." Marshall thought that accurate and prompt reporting of cases was "essential to correctness and uniformity of decision in all the courts of the United States." The justices' experience had been that "the publication of decisions of the Supreme Court will remain on a very precarious footing if the reporter is to depend solely on the sales of his work for a reimbursement of the expenses which must be incurred in preparing it, and for his own compensation. The patronage of the Government is believed to be necessary to the secure and certain attainment of the object."

Under Henry Wheaton, reporter from 1816 to 1827, annotated Supreme Court decisions first appeared, and volumes were published more promptly. Wheaton sued his successor, Richard Peters, for infringement of copyright when Peters published a less expensive set of reports, impairing the market for Wheaton's volumes. The Court decided in *Wheaton v. Peters* (1834), however, that the reporter held no copyright in the Court's decisions. This permitted competing versions of Supreme Court reports.

The judiciary appropriation of 1874 for the first time allocated twenty-five thousand dollars for the purpose of official reporting, and starting with volume 91 the *United States Reports* no longer carried the name of the current reporter of decisions. Until 1921, the government authorized private publishers to publish the Reports, but since 1921 they have been published only by the Government Printing Office.

The West Publishing Company began its *Supreme Court Reporter* series in 1883, starting with cases decided in the October 1882 term. Its reports continue today. The Lawyers Co-Operative Publishing Company began its *Lawyers Edition* of Supreme Court reports in 1901. The first series, one hundred volumes, contains decisions from the first term of the Court through the October 1955 term. Its second series begins with the October 1956 term, and still continues. The Bureau of National Affairs from 1931 has published *United States Law Week*. This periodical delivers the full text of the most recent Supreme Court decisions within days of their announcement. Supreme Court decisions also appear on such on-line computer services as *WESTLAW and LEXIS. Fast and accurate availability of the Court's decisions has helped realize the hope of William Cranch, the second reporter, for an American "code of common law."

(See also REPORTERS, SUPREME COURT.)

□ Gerald T. Dunne, "Early Court Reporters," *Yearbook of the Supreme Court Historical Society* (1976): 61–72. Craig Joyce, "The Rise of the Supreme Court Reporter: An Institutional Perspective on Marshall Court Ascendancy," *Michigan Law Review* 83 (1985): 1291–1391.
Francis Helminski

**Reserved Powers.** See STATE SOVEREIGNTY AND STATES' RIGHTS; TENTH AMENDMENT.

**Resignation and Retirement.** Tenure during good behavior provides a crucial guarantee of judicial independence in the American constitutional system. It also assures the justices discretion in making decisions about whether to remain on the Supreme Court, to resign, or to retire.

Prior to 1869 there was no financial inducement to retire because no retirement compensation was available to the justices. The judiciary act of that year provided full salary for justices who had served at least ten years and had not reached the age of seventy (see JUDICIARY ACT OF 1869). But its passage did not persuade Nathan *Clifford, the only appointee of President James Buchanan. Clifford was determined to remain on the Court until a Democratic president could appoint his replacement. Justice Samuel F. *Miller felt that Clifford's mental failure was obvious, but Clifford died in office three years short of Grover Cleveland's election in 1884.

There were three instances in the mid-nineteenth century when financial considerations had a bearing on retirement or resignation. The only resignation from the Supreme Court clearly traced to financial causes is that of Associate Justice Benjamin R. *Curtis in 1857, although

the distrust of some prosouthern colleagues was also an important factor. Ward *Hunt, though he had been unable actually to serve for five years, would not resign until Congress passed a special pension bill for him in 1882. Salmon P. *Chase died in office in 1873, three years after he suffered a debilitating paralytic stroke. He was ineligible for retirement benefits and inaccurately deemed himself indispensable.

David N. Atkinson made a detailed examination of the deaths, health problems, and resignation and retirement decisions of members of the Supreme Court. His data for the periods of 1789–1864, 1865–1890, and 1937–1975 provide important information for comparison. The first period indicated that advanced age was not necessarily associated with infirmity nor was poor health associated with inclination to resign. Chief Justice Roger B. *Taney was described as "frail" for all of his twenty-eight years on the Court but by determination and careful use of his waning physical resources he remained on the Court until his death at age eighty-eight. Three major factors have accounted for departure from the Supreme Court. One, death, was involuntary. Most voluntary departures were related to ill health or politics. In many instances, especially in the nineteenth century, a deliberate decision to remain on the Court as long as physical and mental capability permitted was determined by a combination of partisan or ideological factors and personal commitment. After 1838 the average age at which members of the Supreme Court have been selected has been well over fifty years. Age and career status generally combined to reinforce the tendency of justices to view appointment as their final career advancement. Hence, there was little incentive to invoke the statutory options for retirement or resignation until health considerations made it imperative.

There are some characteristics of the historic periods that are distinguishable. Party and ideology contributed to a tendency in the nineteenth century to remain on the Court as long as possible. This tendency was undoubtedly strengthened by the absence, until 1870, of monetary inducements for retirement plus the absence of an informal Court peer group tradition to encourage resignation or retirement because of perceived incapacity. Such a tradition has since developed, but it has not always been successful. For example, Justice Stephen *Field initially refused to resign as urged by some of his colleagues in 1897.

There is little evidence that more generous retirement provisions have had much impact upon the retirement choices of members of the Supreme Court. Conversely, *extrajudicial activities have led to several resignations in modern times, reflecting greater media, professional, and public insistence on heretofore lightly observed institutional proprieties. Rarely have Court members resigned in order to pursue other political objectives. Charles Evans *Hughes, a major exception, resigned to run for president in 1916 and had the rare good fortune to return to the Court as chief justice. Arthur *Goldberg was persuaded by President Lyndon B. Johnson to step down to become ambassador to the United Nations. In modern times media attention has become a new factor, but its consequences are largely speculative regarding the encouragement of retirement or resignation. Threatened by *impeachment in the late 1960s William O. *Douglas was determined to stay on the bench. Later weakened by physical and occasional mental disability, Douglas initially planned to remain on the Court, hoping for recovery. Only after receiving two separate doctors' negative opinions did Douglas resign in 1975. Douglas resisted media and peer pressures until he realized that recovery was impossible. Conversely, media and partisan political pressure combined with Justice Abe *Fortas's own serious violation of institutional proprieties led to his resignation in 1969. While Fortas did consult some of his colleagues and former chief justice Earl *Warren, the prospect of impeachment was the underlying determinant of his resignation.

Ultimately, the partisan or ideological inclination to remain on the Court, buttressed by a powerful sense of professional and institutional achievement, have been of most significance throughout the Court's history.

(See also APPOINTMENT AND REMOVAL POWER.)

□ David N. Atkinson, "Retirement and Death on the United States Supreme Court: From Van Devanter to Douglas," *University of Missouri Kansas City Law Review* 45 (1976): 1–27.                  John R. Schmidhauser

**Res Judicata** (Lat., "the matter adjudged") is a principle of the common law, holding that a final judgment on the merits by a jurisdictionally competent court is conclusive of the rights of the parties in all subsequent litigation on the issues resolved.                  William M. Wiecek

**Respondent.** See PETITIONER AND RESPONDENT.

**Restrictive Covenants.** In urban centers restrictive convenants, which first became popular in the late nineteenth century, created segregated neighborhoods. Such covenants took the form of *contracts between home owners, prohibiting the sale of real estate to nonwhites and often to Jews and other ethnic groups. Because these covenants were private agreements, there appeared to be no direct *state action in creating segregated neighborhoods, and thus no violation of the *Fourteenth Amendment. Such covenants were especially common in the North, where segregation was often illegal. For example, both Michigan and Illinois prohibited segregation, but in Detroit and Chicago, restrictive covenants

created neighborhoods segregated by race and ethnicity.

The United States Supreme Court inhibited the use of restrictive convenants in *Shelley v. Kraemer* (1948). The Court conceded that the convenants themselves constituted private action and therefore did not violate the Fourteenth Amendment. However, because *state courts enforced the covenants, the Court found unconstitutional state action.

In *Jones v. Alfred H. Mayer, Co.* (1968), the Court agreed that the 1866 Civil Rights Act prohibited "all discrimination against Negroes in the sale or rental of property—discrimination by private owners as well as discrimination by public authorities." The Court found that the Enforcement Clause (section 2) of the *Thirteenth Amendment empowered Congress to prohibit housing discrimination by private individuals.

(See also HOUSING DISCRIMINATION; RACE AND RACISM; SEGREGATION, DE JURE.)

Paul Finkelman

**Retirement.** See RESIGNATION AND RETIREMENT.

**Reversals of Court Decisions by Amendment.** Supreme Court decisions that interpret provisions of the Constitution can be overturned directly only by amendment. Article V of the Constitution provides that amendments can be proposed by two-thirds majorities of both houses of Congress or by a convention that Congress calls at the request of two-thirds of the state legislatures; amendments must be ratified by three-quarters of the states, either by their legislatures or by special conventions. All successful amendments thus far have been proposed by Congress, and all but one (the *Twenty-first, ending Prohibition) have been ratified by state legislature.

Of the twenty-six amendments to the Constitution, as many as seven can be interpreted as overturning Supreme Court decisions. The first such amendment was the *Eleventh, adopted in 1795, which overturned *Chisholm v. Georgia* (1793) by restating the immunity of states from lawsuits in federal court. The *Thirteenth Amendment (1865), which prohibited slavery, and the *Fourteenth (1868), which ensured that blacks had the right of citizenship, in effect overturned the Court's most infamous decision, *Scott v. Sandford* (1857). The *Sixteenth Amendment (1913) gave Congress the power to levy an *income tax and therefore negated *Pollock v. Farmers' Loan and Trust Co.* (1895). In the most recent instance, the *Twenty-sixth Amendment, adopted in 1971, overturned the portion of *Oregon v. Mitchell* (1970) that held that Congress could not require the states to set the voting age at eighteen in elections to state offices: the amendment itself lowered the voting age to 18. The *Nineteenth Amendment (1920), which prohibited the denial of the vote to women, and the *Twenty-fourth Amendment (1964), which prohibited the imposition of a *poll tax as a requirement to vote in federal elections, superseded decisions that had upheld these practices under the Constitution. A great many efforts to overturn other decisions through amendments have failed.

Although no amendments have yet been proposed by convention, in a few instances several state legislatures have petitioned for such a convention to overcome a Supreme Court decision. After the Court's decisions of the 1960s requiring that state legislative districts be reapportioned on a "one person, one vote" basis, the number of petitions for a convention to consider overturning those rulings fell only one short of the thirty-four that were required.

(See also CONSTITUTIONAL AMENDING PROCESS; CONSTITUTIONAL AMENDMENTS.)

Lawrence Baum

**Reversals of Court Decisions by Congress.** When the Supreme Court interprets the meaning of a provision in the Constitution, its decision can be overturned directly only by a constitutional amendment. But decisions interpreting a federal statute can be overturned simply through the enactment of a new statute, so that Congress has a relatively easy means to reject the Court's reading of statutes.

This congressional power is important, because the Court devotes a large share of its efforts to statutory interpretation. In the 1988 term, according to data presented in *Harvard Law Review* (November 1989, p. 401), in only 44 percent of the Court's decisions was the major issue one of constitutional law. The Court's work in such fields as *labor law, *antitrust, and taxation is concentrated on the interpretation of federal statutes. Thus Congress stands in a stronger position vis-à-vis the Court in these fields than in fields where constitutional law plays a more prominent role, such as civil liberties.

A substantial majority of the Court's statutory decisions attract little attention in Congress. But bills are introduced to overturn or modify a significant number of them. The impetus for such bills can come from several sources. Individual members may be unhappy with the Court's reading of a statute in a policy area that is of special concern to them. More often, interest groups will press for legislation to overcome decisions that run counter to their interests. In fields in which strong groups exist on both sides, such as labor law, Court decisions that favor one side significantly often attract reversal efforts by groups that represent the opposing interest.

Occasionally, the Court itself invites Congress to overturn a decision by suggesting in an opinion that its reading of a statute requires it to reach an unfortunate result. In *Westfall* v. *Irwin* (1988),

for instance, the Court limited the immunity of federal employees from lawsuits. Justice Thurgood *Marshall's opinion for a unanimous Court strongly suggested that Congress rewrite the law, and within a year a new statute was adopted to supersede the *Westfall* decision.

Most bills that are introduced to overturn statutory decisions fail to become law. Indeed, in some instances opponents of a Court decision introduce bills to overturn the decision several times without achieving success. This has been the case thus far with legislation directed against *Feres* v. *United States* (1950), which limited the right of military personnel to sue the federal government for medical malpractice. The fact that only a small proportion of Court-reversing legislation is adopted does not result from a consensus that it is inappropriate to reject Supreme Court rulings on statutes. Unlike amending the Constitution, rewriting of a statute often is viewed as a routine matter rather than a confrontation between two branches. Rather, these failures reflect primarily the difficulties involved in enacting legislation.

These difficulties notwithstanding, it is not uncommon for Congress to adopt legislation that reverses a statutory decision altogether or in part. During the 1980s, reversal legislation was adopted on such issues as the allocation of military retirement pay in divorce settlements, the damages that foriegn governments can collect in *antitrust cases, alteration of labor contracts by companies that have filed *bankruptcy cases, and overtime pay for employees of state and local governments.

The routine character of most such actions is reflected in the lack of attention given to them. This is particularly true of obscure fields of law; in 1984, a successful bill to overturn a 1972 decision concerning rules for *patent infringement went almost unnoticed outside of Congress and the patent community. A striking exception to the general pattern was the campaign to overturn *Grove City College* v. *Bell* (1984), a decision that had applied a narrow interpretation to laws prohibiting discrimination by business and other institutions that receive funds from the federal government; the Court held that only the part of the institution that discriminated was prohibited from receiving federal money. Acting at the behest of civil rights groups, Congress in 1988 overrode a veto by President Ronald *Reagan and overturned the decision after a long and well-publicized battle.

This battle underlines both the significance of the Supreme Court's statutory decisions and the importance of the congressional power to overturn them. Through use of that power, Congress helps to maintain for itself a continuing role in the development of the law on statutory matters.

(See also REVERSALS OF COURT DECISIONS BY AMENDMENT.)

Lawrence Baum

**Reverse Discrimination.** See AFFIRMATIVE ACTION.

**Review, Process of.** In the last two hundred years, the mechanisms by which cases come to the Supreme Court have changed substantially. The Court has evolved from a court of obligatory appellate jurisdiction to a court of virtually complete discretionary jurisdiction. No longer can we speak of taking a case all the way to the Supreme Court; few cases fit within the Court's obligatory jurisdiction. Indeed, the Court's obligatory jurisdiction has been shrinking since the end of the nineteenth century.

From 1789 through 1891, virtually all cases came to the Court by a writ of *error. The writ of error permitted the Court to review questions of law but not of fact. It was available to all parties whose cases fell within appellate jurisdiction of the Court. By the middle 1880s, as a result of the open-ended character of the writ of error, the caseload of the Court had grown at an alarming pace; the justices faced a large and growing backlog. To deal with this crisis, Congress in 1891 created the *circuit courts of appeals and added a discretionary writ of *certiorari in certain cases. Thereafter, Congress incrementally expanded the Court's certiorari jurisdiction.

Despite these legislative actions, the caseload of the Court continued to mount, so Congress enacted the *Judiciary Act of 1925, which eliminated most, but not all, obligatory jurisdiction. Subsequently, about 95 percent of the Court's cases came up on a writ of certiorari. In the 1970s, once again under the pressure of growing caseloads, Congress chipped away at the Court's remaining obligatory jurisdiction and eliminated most of the remaining direct *appeals from the lower courts. In 1988, after nearly two decades of debate over the Court's caseload, Congress removed virtually all of the Court's obligatory *appellate jurisdiction (see JUDICIAL IMPROVEMENTS AND ACCESS TO JUSTICE ACT).

Gregory A. Caldeira

**Reynolds v. Sims,** 377 U.S. 533 (1964), argued 13 Nov. 1963, decided 15 June 1964 by vote of 8 to 1; Warren for the Court, Stewart and Clark concurring, Harlan in dissent. In June 1964, the Supreme Court handed down a group of decisions—collectively known as the *Reapportionment Cases—that won immediate recognition as historical landmarks. In cases from six different states, the Court declared that representation in state legislatures must be based substantially on population. One week later, the Court handed down similar rulings (without opinions) for nine additional states. The controlling philosophy for all of these decisions is articulated in the Alabama case of Reynolds v. Sims, with the opinion written by Chief Justice Earl *Warren.

The 1964 decisions marked the culmination of a two-year period of accelerating litigation involv-

ing most states in the wake of the decision in *Baker v. Carr (1962), which affirmed the *justiciability of apportionment suits. While Baker furnished no guidelines for lower courts, most of them assertively fashioned decrees mandating more equipopulous legislative districts. In 1963, *Gray v. Sanders had invalidated Georgia's county unit system and given currency to the phrase "one person, one vote." Then, in *Wesberry v. Sanders (1964), the Supreme Court invalidated Georgia's grossly unequal congressional districts. While based on Article I rather than the *Fourteenth Amendment, Wesberry articulated the fundamental constitutional principle of equal representation for equal numbers of people.

The Supreme Court's decisions in Reynolds and other 1964 apportionment cases were thus not entirely unexpected. Yet the sweeping nature of the rulings and their forthright language surprised many on both sides of the controversy. As a result of the decisions and their underlying rationale, at least one house in nearly all state legislatures was considered invalid, and both houses in most. The decision portended a vast institutional revolution.

The basis for the 1964 decisions was the holding that the Fourteenth Amendment's Equal Protection Clause guarantees to each citizen an equal weight in the election of state legislators. Speaking for the Court, Warren declared, "Legislators represent people, not trees or acres. Legislators are elected by voters, not farms or cities or economic interests" (p. 562). The opinion went on to reason that any substantial disparity in the populations of legislative districts has the same effect as allotting a different number of votes to different individuals. Hence the Court regarded inequality of representation as a suffrage issue, citing various franchise cases that had invalidated the "dilution" or "debasement" of a citizen's fundamental right to vote.

The Court stated that mathematical exactness or precision is hardly a workable constitutional requirement and declined to suggest any numerical or percentage guidelines. Some deviations from an equal population plan in either or both houses of a state legislature would be constitutionally permissible "so long as the divergences from a strict equal population standard are based on legitimate considerations incident to the effectuation of a rational state policy" (p. 579). There could be some recognition of political subdivisions and community interests, but "population is, of necessity, the starting point for consideration and the controlling criterion for judgment in legislative apportionment controversies" (p. 567).

The Court specifically rejected the "federal analogy," the contention that states may base one legislative house, as in the national Congress, on the equal representation of units of government rather than of people. The opinion dismissed as inapposite the suggested parallel between states in the federal union and local units such as counties or towns within a unitary state. The Court was persuaded by evidence that the original constitutions of nearly three-fourths of the states provided that both legislative houses be based entirely or predominantly on population, with most recent support for the federal analogy merely a rationalization of malapportionment.

Dissenting in *Reynolds* as well as the remaining reapportionment cases, Justice John M. *Harlan reiterated his view, expressed in *Baker*, that the judiciary was intruding needlessly and dangerously into the political process and that the subject matter was not suitable for the development of judicial standards. A detailed analysis of the history, drafting, language, and ratification of the Fourteenth Amendment convinced Harlan that the Equal Protection Clause was not intended to inhibit states from choosing any democratic method desired in constructing legislative bodies. Thus the decisions, he felt, cut deeply into the fabric of American *federalism. Cautioning against *judicial activism to cure perceived social ills, Harlan declared, "The Constitution is not a panacea for every blot upon the public welfare, nor should this Court, ordained as a judicial body, be thought of as a general haven for reform movements" (pp. 624–625).

The Supreme Court's choice of *Reynolds* as the lead reapportionment case in 1964 is understandable. Alabama's pattern of legislative representation was among the nation's most egregious departures from the concept of meaningful voter equality. Neither house reflected a population basis, with approximately one-fourth of the state's voters theoretically in a position to elect majorities in both. Population variance ratios in the Alabama senate were 41 to 1, in the house, 16 to 1. Within a few months of the *Baker* decision, litigation brought swift action by a federal district court, the first judicially ordered apportionment in the nation. The court had fashioned what it considered the best of available legislative plans, drawn from a judicially prompted special session. The district court had ordered the plans into effect temporarily, pending further legislative and state constitutional action. The appeal from this judicial order became *Reynolds v. Sims*.

Although the Supreme Court decided *Reynolds* (and several other 1964 reapportionment cases) by an overwhelming vote of 8 to 1, the majority was split on the reasoning, best illustrated by its 6-to-3 decision invalidating Colorado's apportionment. The result of an initiative ballot measure overwhelmingly ratified in 1962 by a statewide popular vote that carried all counties, the new state constitutional amendment established a lower house based on population and a senate with population as a prime factor but modified by geographic considerations. Invalidating this apportionment in *Lucas v. the Forty-Fourth General Assembly of the State of Colorado*, the court relied on its newly expressed philosophy that legislatures must reflect the right of individuals to cast an equally weighted vote, a right that cannot be infringed by popular majorities. In response, Justice Potter *Stewart's opinion (joined by Justice Tom C. *Clark) rejected the position that the apportionment cases involved the right to vote or the "dilution" or "debasement" of that vote. The Stewart-Clark approach held that the Equal Protection Clause permits states considerable latitude in designing legislative constituencies, provided only that (1) they are rational in the light of each state's own characteristics and needs and (2) they do not systematically prevent "ultimate effective majority rule." Yet Stewart and Clark were unable to agree when applying these guidelines in some other cases.

The Supreme Court majority in *Reynolds* made its own attempt to reconcile the population principle and divergent state interests with various assurances that absolute uniformity was not mandated. While the same basic constitutional logic applied to all states, flexibility to accommodate diverse circumstances was indicated, with the expressed confidence that lower courts could work out specific and appropriate standards on a case-by-case basis.

Such optimism was not borne out by events. Lower courts tended to seek standards that could be applied to apportionment plans, usually in quantifiable ways. The most commonly accepted index was a population deviance range of plus-15 to minus-15 percent of the average population per district, a rule perhaps borrowed from a recommendation made by a committee of the American Political Science Association in 1951, long before judicial entry into apportionment disputes. Furthermore, acceptable ranges of population variances kept shrinking as courts handling apportionment disputes found it difficult to reject plaintiffs' alternative plans that were "more equal" in population.

In *Kirkpatrick v. Preisler* (1969) a Supreme Court majority of five, speaking through Justice William J. *Brennan, set forth a new population standard requiring states to make a good-faith effort to achieve precise mathematical equality among districts. While this and the companion case of *Wells v. Rockefeller* involved congressional districts, presumably controlled by Article I following *Wesberry v. Sanders*, the line between that and the Fourteenth Amendment's Equal Protection Clause was increasingly blurred. The 1969 cases found the Court's majority, as well as the concurring and dissenting opinions, all citing *Reynolds v. Sims*.

In 1973, the Supreme Court shifted back to the more flexible guidelines of *Reynolds* to govern state redistricting. In *Mahan v. Howell*, Virginia's state legislative apportionment, with a total plus-to-minus variance of 16.4 percent, was upheld because state policy consistently followed town and county boundaries. In three subsequent

# 734 □ Reynolds v. United States

decisions that term, the Court (1) upheld smaller variance ranges of under 10 percent (plus-to-minus) as *de minimis,* needing no state justification, and with the burden of proof shifting to plaintiffs; and (2) emphasized the far more narrow population range expected for congressional districts.

In *Reynolds* Warren had cautioned, "Indiscriminate districting, without any regard for political subdivision or natural or historical boundary lines, may be little more than an open invitation to partisan gerrymandering (pp. 578–579). This warning was recalled by several observers who suggested that boundary manipulation had been encouraged by increasing judicial preoccupation with equipopulous districts at the expense of various territorial checks (compactness, contiguity, integrity of local boundaries).

Similar judicial concerns have been raised periodically since 1969. In *Karcher* v. *Daggett* (1983) the Court invalidated New Jersey's congressional districting because it lacked a good-faith effort to achieve absolute population equality (the variance percentage from most- to least-populous district was less than 0.7 percent). Five justices (one concurring, four dissenting) objected that partisan *gerrymandering posed a greater threat to fair representation than minor population deviations.

The question whether claims of political gerrymandering were justiciable was answered affirmatively by the Supreme Court in *Davis* v. *Bandemer* (1986). But the Court's plurality opinion confined judicial scrutiny only to boundary manipulations that consistently degraded a voter's, or group of voters', influence on the political process as a whole. The plurality seemed loathe to sanction judicial interference in those instances of partisan advantage subject to correction by genuine electoral competition.

Few Supreme Court decisions have had the impact of *Reynolds* v. *Sims.* Within a period of scarcely two years, the constituency maps of virtually all state legislatures had changed, often dramatically. Patterns of rural and small-town domination in several largely urban states had disappeared. Moreover, the principle of equal representation was soon extended to the local level of county boards and city councils.

In spite of this rapid restructuring, problems and litigation persisted. The question of how precisely equal in population districts must be led to mechanistic approaches maximizing equipopulous districts at the expense of other dimensions of representation and very likely encouraged the proliferation of sophisticated partisan gerrymandering. Ironically, as a result, events appeared to prod the Supreme Court to advance, step by step, further into the *political thicket.

In *Reynolds,* Warren asserted that "the achieving of fair and effective representation for all citizens is concededly the basic aim of legislative apportionment" (pp. 565–566). That goal may be

elusive and incapable of complete attainment, but it serves as a continuing challenge to courts and others.

(See also EQUAL PROTECTION; FAIR REPRESENTATION; VOTE, RIGHT TO.)

□ Gordon E. Baker, *The Reapportionment Revolution* (1966). Richard C. Cortner, *The Apportionment Cases* (1970). Robert G. Dixon, Jr., *Democratic Representation* (1968). Bernard Grofman, ed., *Political Gerrymandering and the Courts* (1990). Gordon E. Baker

**Reynolds v. United States,** 98 U.S. 145 (1879), argued 14–15 Nov. 1878 decided 5 May 1879 by vote of 9 to 0; Waite for the Court, Field concurring. This case grew out of the Grant administration's campaign to stamp out Mormon polygamy. Grant appointed James B. McKean, chief justice of the Utah Territorial Supreme Court, and General J. Wilson Shaffer, territorial governor, with orders to end Mormon polygamy. McKean's United States Marshalls rounded up hundreds of Mormons under a federal antibigamy statute. To test federal law, the Mormon church hierarchy prepared George Reynolds, secretary to Brigham Young, for a test case. Following conviction in territorial district court and appeal to the Utah Territorial Supreme Court, Reynolds appealed before the U.S. Supreme Court.

Anti-Mormon arguments termed polygamy socially destructive and accused the Mormons of constituting a moral menace to the country. Mormons argued that the *First Amendment protected religious freedom and that plural marriage was part of religious practice. In the alternative, they argued that polygamy was not bigamy and that it was supportive of mainstream American values such as family and spiritual growth, was not destructive of the social fabric, and clearly did not threaten the public peace.

Chief Justice Morrison R. *Waite, for a unanimous court, declared that federal statute constitutionally could punish criminal activity regardless of religious beliefs. Simply, religious practices that impaired the public interest did not fall under the protection of the First Amendment.

In analyzing the original position of the founders on the First Amendment's language on religion, Waite relied heavily upon history and in particular upon Thomas *Jefferson (see HISTORY, COURT USES OF). In the process, Waite observed that "a wall of separation between church and state" existed, thus using a metaphor that would trouble the courts for the next century (p. 164).

(See also MARRIAGE; RELIGION.)

Gordon Morris Bakken

**Richardson, United States v.,** 418 U.S. 166 (1974), argued 10 Oct. 1973, decided 25 June 1974 by vote of 5 to 4; Burger for the Court, Powell concurring, Douglas, Brennan, Stewart, and Marshall in dissent. Seeking to apply and expand the doctrine of taxpayer standing of *Flast v. Cohen* (1968),

Richardson challenged the law that prohibited disclosure of CIA expenditures. He claimed a violation of Article I, section 9, which requires publication of *all* public expenditures. The trial court held that Richardson lacked standing under *Flast* because he was not challenging an appropriations act under the *Taxing and Spending Clause. The court of appeals reversed, holding that he could first sue to obtain information about the CIA's appropriations that he needed in order to bring suit under the *Flast* doctrine.

The Supreme Court, giving *Flast* the narrowest possible reading, reversed again. It held that Richardson lacked standing because he was not directly alleging the unconstitutionality of an appropriations act and did not allege a specific violation of Congress's taxing and spending power. Chief Justice Warren *Burger's opinion reaffirmed a basic principle of *Frothingham* v. *Mellon* (1923), which scholars thought *Flast* had modified: a taxpayer cannot use federal courts "as a forum to air his general grievances about the conduct of government or the allocation of power in the federal system" (p. 175). Richardson had suffered no personal injury from the government's failure to disclose the CIA's budget; the issue, Burger said, was clearly not one for the courts to resolve. In dissent, Justices Potter *Stewart and Thurgood *Marshall insisted that a citizen ought to be able to challenge the failure of the government to carry out an affirmative constitutional duty without any showing of personal harm.

(See also STANDING TO SUE.)

Joel B. Grossman

**Richmond Newspapers, Inc. v. Virginia,** 448 U.S. 555 (1980), argued 19 Feb. 1980, decided 2 July 1980 by vote of 7 to 1; Burger for the Court, Rehnquist in dissent, Powell not participating. After a series of inconclusive and confusing earlier decisions on the right of access to criminal trials, *Richmond Newspapers, Inc. v. Virginia* announced that the public and the press have a *First Amendment right to attend criminal trials. This landmark 1980 Supreme Court decision left other issues open, however, some of which have since been resolved.

In a number of cases during the 1970s the Supreme Court supported the media's right, under the First Amendment, to publish whatever information they had in their possession— whether classified and obtained surreptitiously (*New York Times Co.* v. *United States*, 1971), or whether obtained in open court (*Nebraska Press Association* v. *Stuart*, 1976). Having established that the press could publish what they knew, the Supreme Court then faced the question of whether the press was constitutionally entitled to access to criminal court proceedings.

In *Gannett* v. *DePasquale* (1979), a newspaper reporter challenged the court-ordered closure of a pretrial hearing on suppression of evidence in a

murder case. The closure resulted from the defendants' concern (shared by the prosecutor) that *pretrial publicity would jeopardize their right to a fair trial. On appeal, the Supreme Court upheld the exclusion of press and public from pretrial hearings on the grounds that only the accused has a *Sixth Amendment right to demand an open trial. In contrast, several dissenters in *Gannett* saw the Sixth Amendment as protecting not only the defendant's but also the public's right of access.

The *Gannett* decision was close (5 to 4), fragmented (five separate opinions), and ambiguous in its scope (whether this ruling on pretrials would extend to trials) over the application of the First Amendment to the issue of access (which the Court did not decide) and over the findings needed to justify closure. Despite this uncertainty, *Gannett* gave new power to trial judges who increasingly granted motions to close all types of criminal proceedings. Representatives of the news media protested *Gannett* and urged the Court to reconsider and affirm a public right to access to court.

The Court did so the next year. In *Richmond Newspapers Inc.* v. *Virginia*, it severely limited the defendant's right to a closed courtroom by holding that the First and *Fourteenth Amendments guarantee the right of the public (including the press) to attend criminal trials. This case began with the fourth murder trial of a defendant whose earlier trials had been reversed or declared mistrials. Out of concern for pretrial publicity and relying on a Virginia statute, the trial court granted the defendant's motion to exclude the press. Richmond Newspapers challenged the order and sued for access to the trial. The Supreme Court affirmed the First Amendment right of access in its 7-to-1 decision.

The majority view in *Richmond Newspapers* was expressed in six different opinions. Chief Justice Warren *Burger wrote for the Court, emphasizing the long history of criminal trials at *common law and their presumption of openness. Burger concluded that the press exclusion must be overturned since the trial judge had not pursued alternatives to courtroom closure nor had he made specific findings to support the order. Justices Byron *White and John Paul *Stevens joined Burger's opinion but also wrote separately. Justice White, a dissenter in *Gannett*, simply noted that this case would have been unnecessary had the Court found a Sixth Amendment right to courtroom access in the earlier decision. Justice Stevens, in his concurrence, extended the principle to prohibit arbitrary governmental restrictions on access to other important and newsworthy information.

In a separate opinion Justice William *Brennan (joined by Justice Thurgood *Marshall) developed a different First Amendment theory to balance the important right of public access with opposing interests. He proposed two principles to determine the right of access: the history and tradition of openness of a given proceeding, and the specific structural value or function of the proceeding. Applying these principles to the criminal trial, Brennan found a public right of access and agreed that the Virginia statute was in violation of the First and Fourteenth Amendments.

Justice Potter *Stewart concurred in the Court's judgment and, in his separate opinion, stressed limits that could be placed on the right of access, noting that the right is not absolute. Justice Harry *Blackmun also wrote separately to reiterate his preference for a Sixth Amendment right of access, but accepted the First Amendment protections as well. In dissent, Justice William *Rehnquist argued against Supreme Court intervention in the matter, preferring to let the access issues be resolved by the fifty states without additional constitutional review.

*Richmond Newspapers Inc. v. Virginia* left open key questions. Does the First Amendment right of access to trials extend to pretrial hearings and to civil as well as criminal trials? Does it extend to other governmental proceedings besides the courtroom? What restrictions will be allowed on the right of access? What is the underlying First Amendment theory for the right of access and what standards will be used to guide further cases?

In *Globe Newspaper Co. v. Superior Court* (1982), the Court held unconstitutional a Massachusetts statute that required closed trials during testimony of minors who were victims of sexual abuse. For the majority, Justice Brennan emphasized the general functions for self-governance to be served by an open trial and held that a trial might be closed only in specific cases where there was a documented or reasonable fear of harm to such minors. Chief Justice Burger, in dissent, pointed instead to the historical evidence supporting closure of this particular type of trial. The split between these two approaches from *Richmond Newspapers* was also evident in *Press-Enterprise Co. v. Superior Court* (1984). Here the Court extended the First Amendment right of access to *voir dire* proceedings.

In *Waller v. Georgia* (1984) the Court found that a defendant's Sixth Amendment right to a public trial precluded a trial court from closing a pretrial suppression hearing over the objections of the accused. The question of a public First Amendment right of access to pretrial hearings, left open in *Waller* and in *Richmond Newspapers*, was resolved in *Press-Enterprise Co. v. Superior Court* (1986) in favor of allowing public access to preliminary hearings. In this case the Court also reiterated the principle of *Globe Newspaper* that only an overriding governmental interest can justify denial of access. The Court has not yet ruled on the right of access to civil trials, but it is likely that eventually they will also be included.

(See also SPEECH AND THE PRESS.)

Lynn Mather

**Richmond v. J. A. Croson Co.,** 488 U.S. 469 (1989), argued 5 Oct. 1988, decided 23 Jan. 1989 by vote of 6 to 3; O'Connor for the Court, Stevens, Kennedy, and Scalia concurring, Marshall, Brennan, and Blackmun in dissent. In *Croson*, a majority of the Supreme Court was finally assembled in support of the application of the *strict scrutiny standard to determine the constitutionality of *affirmative action plans based on race. However, it is still not possible to determine specifically the content of this standard as applied to affirmative action.

In 1983, the Richmond, Virginia, City Council enacted the Minority Business Utilization Plan requiring prime contractors to subcontract at least 30 percent of the dollar amount of the contract to minority business enterprises. The plan was to remain in effect for five years and contained waiver provisions for cases where every feasible attempt to comply failed.

The Supreme Court found the plan in violation of the Equal Protection Clause of the *Fourteenth Amendment. It rejected Richmond's argument that it was legitimately copying an earlier federal minority business set-aside law that had been upheld in *Fullilove v. Klutznick* (1980). *Fullilove* was distinguishable, Justice Sandra Day *O'Connor wrote, because section 5 of the Fourteenth Amendment granted Congress a unique mandate to enforce its dictates. States, however, are not equally empowered by the Constitution. Justice Antonin *Scalia's dissent went even further, declaring that the Constitution is colorblind and that race-conscious plans, presumably even federal ones, are unacceptable.

Because of *Croson* most state or local affirmative action plans will now be judged by the strict scrutiny standard. When combined with two earlier cases, *Wygant v. Jackson Board of Education* (1986) and *United States v. Paradise* (1987), *Croson* seems to require that these plans demonstrate a compelling interest that requires a showing of past discrimination, not mere reliance on societal discrimination for their justification. They must also choose means that are narrowly tailored to vindicate that interest and must take into account factors such as the necessity of the relief and the efficiency of alternative remedies, the duration of the remedy, the flexibility of the remedy and/or the availability of waivers, the relationship of the numerical goals to minorities within the relevant labor market, and the likely effect on innocent parties. It is uncertain how many of these factors, and in what combination and circumstances, a majority of the Court will require in future cases.

(See also EQUAL PROTECTION.)

James E. Jones, Jr.

**Right to_____.** See under latter part of term.

**Right to Bear Arms.** See SECOND AMENDMENT.

**Ripeness and Immediacy.** A family of jurisdictional problems lumped together under the category of *justiciability raise the question whether the challenged litigation can be resolved by federal courts, which are limited to deciding only *cases and controversies by *Article III, section 2 of the Constitution. Among these are questions of *mootness, ripeness, *standing, *collusive suits, and *advisory opinions. Most of these problems have both constitutional and prudential dimensions. Ripeness is the "front-end" counterpart to mootness. When a case has become moot, it has ceased to exist as a live controversy, whereas if a case has not "ripened," it has not yet matured into a threat to an individual's property, liberty, or other rights.

The classic ripeness precedent, *United Public Workers* v. *Mitchell* (1947), illustrates the sort of problems ripeness poses as a matter of Article III justiciability. The appellants were federal employees who sought an *injunction against enforcement of the Hatch Act, alleging that they feared prosecution if they engaged in political activities they believed were protected by the *First Amendment. They had not yet participated in any of the activities they feared would subject them to prosecution. The Court refused to enjoin a merely "hypothetical threat" because it presented no actual case or controversy.

Ripeness problems have also complicated litigation involving state antisubversive statutes (*Adler* v. *Board of Education*, 1952), the Federal Election Campaign Act (*Buckley* v. *Valeo*, 1976), *abortion restrictions (one of the would-be petitioners in *Roe* v. *Wade*, 1973), and criminal prosecutions (e.g., *Erznoznik* v. *Jacksonville*, 1975).
James B. Stoneking

**Robel, United States v.,** 389 U.S. 258 (1967), argued 14 Nov. 1966, reargued 9 Oct. 1967, decided 11 Dec. 1967 by vote of 6 to 2; Warren for the Court, White and Harlan in dissent; Marshall not participating. The Court in this case, for only the second time in history, struck down an act of Congress as an infringement of the *First Amendment. In *Communist Party* v. *Subversive Activities Control Board* (1961), the Court upheld an order of the Subversive Activities Control Board requiring the Communist party to register as a communist-action organization under the Subversive Activities Control Act of 1950. Robel, a member of the party, was employed at a shipyard that had been officially designated as a defense facility. He was indicted for unlawfully and willfully engaging in employment at the shipyard with knowledge of the order against the party and notice of the shipyard's designation as a defense facility.

The Court held that the relevant section of the act was an unconstitutional abridgment of the right of association protected by the First Amendment. The statute established guilt by association without proof that defendant's association posed

a threat to national defense, which includes values and ideals enshrined in the Constitution. The statute was overbroad for proscribing activities that can be punished and membership that cannot be proscribed. The statute disregarded the fact that a person may be a passive or an active member of a registered organization and may be unaware of the party's unlawful aims or may disagree with those aims; or the member may occupy a nonsensitive position in a defense facility.

(See also ASSEMBLY AND ASSOCIATION, FREEDOM OF; COMMUNISM AND COLD WAR.)
Milton R. Konvitz

**Roberts, Owen Josephus** (b. Germantown, Pa., 2 May 1875; d. West Vincent Township, Chester County, Pa., 17 May 1955; interred St. Andrews Cemetery, West Vincent Township), associate justice, 1930–1945. Educated at the University of Pennsylvania, where he received his law degree in 1898, Owen Roberts worked first as a private attorney and then as assistant district attorney in Philadelphia. He taught law part time at the University of Pennsylvania until 1919. In 1924 President Calvin Coolidge named Roberts a special U.S. attorney in the Teapot Dome Scandals. When Herbert Hoover's initial choice for a 1930 Supreme Court vacancy, John J. *Parker of North Carolina, failed to get Senate confirmation (see NOMINEES, REJECTION OF), Hoover nominated Roberts, who took the seat in June.

Roberts joined a conservative depression-era Court identifed with entrepreneurial liberty and skeptical of government regulation of business. On a Court deeply divided by new appointments (Charles Evans *Hughes and Benjamin *Cardozo), Roberts's vote was pivotal in the struggle between Franklin *Roosevelt and the Court.

Roberts's opinions reviewed the constitutional challenges of the *New Deal in a way that puzzled Court critics, who could find no consistent jurisprudential principle in his rulings. In *Nebbia* v. *New York* (1934), Roberts upheld state regulation of business—in this case a New York statute regulating milk prices (see STATE REGULATION OF COMMERCE). As conservative opposition to New Deal legislation intensified, the Court's attitude toward federal economic regulation hardened. Roberts joined the majority in *Panama Refining Co.* v. *Ryan* (1935) to invalidate section 9c of the National Industrial Recovery Act; his opinion in *Retirement Board* v. *Alton Railroad Co.* (1935) struck down the Railroad Retirement Pension Act; a unanimous Court held the entire National Industrial Recovery Act unconstitutional in *Schechter Poultry Corp.* v. *United States* (1935); *Louisville Bank* v. *Radford* (1935) voided the Federal Farm Bankruptcy Act of 1934. One of Roberts's most far-reaching opinions came in a 6-to-3 ruling that overturned the first Agricultural Adjustment Act (*U.S.* v. *Butler*, 1936). In *Carter* v. *Carter Coal Co.*

(1936), Roberts joined the majority that invalidated the Bituminous Coal Act of 1935 as a federal intrusion upon matters reserved to the states.

The Court's persistent opposition to New Deal legislation led to the 1937 battle over Roosevelt's *court-packing plan. Partly as a response to the criticism directed at the Court, Roberts softened his attitude toward the New Deal. In 1937 Roberts joined the majority in *West Coast Hotel v. Parrish in upholding a state minimum wage law (a conclusion Roberts reached before the Court reorganization was announced). The Court also sustained the Farm Mortgage Act of 1935, the National Labor Relations Act of 1935, and the Social Security Act of 1935. In each case Roberts voted with the majority to sustain New Deal legislation.

As the Court in the 1930s increasingly turned its attention to civil liberties, Roberts again walked an unpredictable path. He wrote the Court's unanimous opinions that upheld the constitutionality of the *white primary (*Grovey v. Townsend, 1935) and dissented in 1944 when that holding was overturned 8 to 1 in *Smith v. Allwright. Roberts's 1940 opinion in *Cantwell v. Connecticut reversed a Jehovah's Witness's conviction for soliciting contributions without a permit. He also voted with the majority to uphold a flag-salute requirement in *Minersville School District v. Gobitis (1940). Three years later, the Court reversed itself in *West Virginia Board of Education v. Barnette, but Roberts adhered to Gobitis. In *Missouri ex rel. Gaines v. Canada (1938), the Court invalidated exclusion of African-American students from the state's law school as a violation of the Equal Protection Clause of the *Fourteenth Amendment, and Roberts voted with the majority. Finally, in *Korematsu v. United States (1944), Roberts dissented powerfully in the constitutional test of the forced relocation of Japanese-Americans during World War II. He insisted that the West Coast exclusion orders were a "case of convicting a citizen as punishment for not submitting to imprisonment in a concentration camp, . . . solely because of his ancestry" (p. 226).

While a sitting justice, Roberts chaired an inquiry into the Japanese attack on Pearl Harbor (see EXTRAJUDICIAL ACTIVITIES). The committee exonerated the Roosevelt administration and placed responsibility on the military commanders at Pearl Harbor. After his retirement from the Court in 1945, Roberts served as dean of the University of Pennsylvania Law School (1948–1951) and chaired the Security Board of the Atomic Energy Commission. He died of a heart attack in 1955, shortly after his eightieth birthday.

☐ G. Edward White, *The American Judicial Tradition: Profiles of Leading American Judges* (1976). Elder Witt, *Congressional Quarterly's Guide to the U.S. Supreme Court,* 2d ed. (1990).                Augustus M. Burns III

**Roberts v. United States Jaycees,** 468 U.S. 609 (1984), argued 18 Apr. 1984, decided 3 July 1984 by vote of 7 to 0; Brennan for the Court, Rehnquist and O'Connor concurring, Burger and Blackmun not participating. The Supreme Court held that the application of the Minnesota Human Rights Act to the Minnesota Junior Chamber of Commerce (Jaycees), requiring the Jaycees to admit women as members, did not violate the *First and *Fourteenth Amendments' guarantee of freedom of association, and that the Human Rights Act was not void on account of vagueness.

For the Court William J. *Brennan recognized two types of associational freedom deserving constitutional protection: freedom of association related to *marriage, procreation, *contraception, and *family and children, and freedom of association related to expressive activities. The Jaycees' freedom of association, the Court held, fell outside the first category of associational freedom because of the large, unselective nature of the group. If there was any constitutional claim here, it was the freedom of association related to the expression of collective views and interests. That right of association was not absolute, however, the Court noted. It could be overridden by a compelling governmental interest and Minnesota's interest in prohibiting *gender discrimination was such a compelling governmental interest and, as such, was sufficient to override the expressive associational interests of male Jaycee members.

Justice Sandra Day *O'Connor concurred, stating that associations could be rationally divided into expressive and nonexpressive associations. The Jaycees were essentially a nonexpressive, commercial association in relation to which

*Owen Josephus Roberts*

greater governmental regulatory power had long been recognized, and the application of the Minnesota Human Rights Act to the Jaycees was thus justified because of the predominantly commercial, nonexpressive nature of the group.

(See also ASSEMBLY AND ASSOCIATION, FREEDOM OF.)

Richard C. Cortner

**Robing Room,** an oak-paneled room located on the main floor of the Supreme Court building next to the Conference Room. It contains nine adjacent closets that hold the judicial robes of the justices. Each closet door has a brass nameplate for its justice. The closets are arranged in order of the justices' seniority. The room's dark maroon carpeting bears a design of laurel wreaths and five-pointed stars. Here, the justices come before sessions to robe. The room also holds a copying machine and a desk for the Court's messenger.

Francis Helminski

**Robinson v. California,** 370 U.S. 660 (1962), argued 17 Apr. 1962, decided 25 June 1962 by vote of 7 to 2; Stewart for the Court, White and Clark in dissent. In *Robinson* v. *California* a California law making it a crime to be a drug addict was held to be unconstitutional as *cruel and unusual punishment in violation of the *Eighth and *Fourteenth Amendments. The statute did not require proof that the defendant bought or used drugs or had any in his or her possession. The mere status of being an addict, which could be established, for example, by needle marks on the offender's arm, was sufficient. The U.S. Supreme Court held that addiction is an illness rather than a crime and thought that ninety days in jail for being ill constituted cruel and unusual punishment. Justices Byron *White and Tom *Clark argued in dissent that detention was a feature of "a comprehensive and enlightened program for the control of narcotism" (p. 679).

The *Robinson* decision was not followed in a 1968 ruling, *Powell* v. *Texas*, where the Court, by a 5-to-4 vote, rejected the contention that criminal conviction for chronic alcoholism was cruel and unusual. The Court majority thought that knowledge about alcoholism and the record in this case were inadequate for a wide-ranging new constitutional principle. Justice Abe *Fortas, writing for the minority in the *Powell* case, insisted that the *Robinson* rule should be followed, and that "criminal penalties may not be inflicted upon a person for being in a condition he is powerless to change" (p. 533).

Controversy has continued concerning whether addiction-related conduct is involuntary and entitled to be regarded as a disease, but the *Robinson* case did establish that the Cruel and Unusual Punishment Clause of the Eighth Amendment applies to the states in appropriate cases by reason of the Due Process Clause of the Fourteenth Amendment.

C. Herman Pritchett

**Robinson v. Memphis and Charleston Railroad Co.** See CIVIL RIGHTS CASES.

**Rochin v. California,** 342 U.S. 165 (1952), argued 16 Oct. 1951, decided 2 Jan. 1952 by vote of 8 to 0; Frankfurter for the Court, Minton not participating. Rochin was convicted in a California superior court for possession of a "preparation of morphine," which doctors pumped from his stomach against his will and on the direction of law enforcement officers. Rochin appealed and charged that the manner of extracting the evidence violated the Due Process Clause of the *Fourteenth Amendment. Rochin lost his appeal, the California Supreme Court declined to review his case, but the U.S. Supreme Court granted *certiorari. The Court reversed Rochin's conviction, holding that stomach-pumping did constitute a method of obtaining evidence that violated the Due Process Clause of the Fourteenth Amendment.

In his opinion for the Court, Justice Felix *Frankfurter emphasized that there was no distinction between a "verbal confession extracted by physical abuse and evidence forced from the petitioner's lips, evidence that consisted of real objects" (p. 167). Frankfurter stressed that the Due Process Clause required that the Court review and challenge state procedures when decency and fairness were suspect, but he indicated that this responsibility did not leave judges free to apply their own personal and private conceptions of due process. In Rochin's case, Frankfurter concluded that the use of stomach-pumping to obtain evidence when conducted without the accused's consent "shocks the conscience" and constitutes "methods too close to the rack and the screw to permit constitutional differentiation" (p. 172).

In separate concurring opinions, Justices Hugo *Black and William O. *Douglas argued that the conviction should have been reversed with reference to the *Fifth Amendment privilege against *self-incrimination and not the "nebulous standard" employed by Frankfurter (p. 175).

The Supreme Court's eventual incorporation of the Fifth Amendment privilege against self-incrimination in *Malloy* v. *Hogan,* (1964) and the application of the exclusionary rule to the states in *Mapp* v. *Ohio,* (1961) have rendered moot the majority and minority differences in Rochin, as state criminal procedures can now be reviewed against most provisions of the *Bill of Rights.

(See also DUE PROCESS, PROCEDURAL.)

Susette M. Talarico

**Roe v. Wade,** 410 U.S. 113 (1973), argued 13 Dec. 1971, reargued 11 Oct. 1972, decided 22 Jan. 1973 by vote of 7 to 2; Blackmun for the Court, Douglas, Stewart, and Burger concurring, White and Rehnquist in dissent. After the middle of the nineteenth century most states, under the prodding of physicians wishing to establish the scientific stature of their activities, adopted laws severely restricting the availability of *abortion. The so-called sexual revolution of the 1950s and 1960s, which fostered increased access to contraceptives and the development of contraceptive drugs, also resulted in an increasing number of situations in which women desired abortions. In the 1960s and early 1970s the discovery that thalidomide, a drug that many women had used in early stages of pregnancy to relieve morning sickness, occasionally caused birth defects, as well as the highly publicized case of Sherry Finkbine, an Arizona broadcasting figure who went to Sweden to obtain an abortion when she feared her baby would be severely handicapped, increased public pressure to relax the abortion laws. Illegal abortions were widespread, though their exact number is impossible to determine, and some women died because of the unsanitary conditions in which illegal abortions were sometimes performed. The revitalized women's movement made change in the abortion laws one of its priority goals.

Abortion reform took two forms. State legislatures began to make it easier to obtain abortions, usually by allowing abortion to protect a woman's health, broadly defined, but also requiring approval of the abortion by a committee of doctors in addition to the woman's own physician. Once some states had begun to relax abortion restrictions, any woman who could afford it found it relatively easy to travel to a state with an unrestrictive law or to find a doctor who would certify that the abortion was necessary to preserve her health.

Court attacks on restrictive abortion laws focused initially on the most restrictive of the traditional laws; challengers argued that such laws, which permitted abortions only to save a woman's life, were so vague that doctors could not know when they were committing an illegal act. The California Supreme Court agreed with such a challenge in *People* v. *Belous* (1969), and the United States Supreme Court in *United States* v. *Vuitch* (1971) avoided a decision on the constitutional question by construing a federal abortion law, applicable in the District of Columbia, to allow abortions when the woman's health, broadly defined, was in danger.

At the time these challenges were being brought, the Court was also developing a law of personal *privacy in sexual matters, holding, for example, that a severe restriction on the availability of contraceptives was a violation of a constitutional right to privacy in *Griswold* v. *Connecticut*, 1965. Challenges to restrictive abortion laws relied on *Griswold* as the basis for arguing that such laws violated the right to privacy.

*Roe* v. *Wade* involved a challenge to a traditional, severely restrictive abortion law (from Texas) as well as a challenge to a more modern abortion law (from Georgia) that allowed abortions to be performed in hospitals, when ap-

proved by a hospital committee, to avoid danger to a woman's health. The action was brought in the name of Jane Roe, a procedure adopted to ensure that the plaintiff would not have to reveal the facts surrounding her pregnancy to the Court. Although those facts were irrelevant in light of the Court's analysis of the legal issues, shortly after the case was decided the plaintiff was identified as Norma McCorvey. At first McCorvey stated that her pregnancy had resulted from a gang rape; later she revealed that it resulted from a failed relationship.

***Blackmun's Analysis.*** When the case was first argued, Justice Harry *Blackmun, who had once served as counsel to the Mayo Clinic in Rochester, Minnesota, drafted an opinion that would have held both statutes unconstitutionally vague. In part because his analysis was clearly unpersuasive and in part because some justices believed that the case had been improperly assigned to Blackmun to write, the case was set for reargument. During the summer preceding the reargument, Blackmun engaged in an extensive study of medical material relating to abortion.

After reargument, Blackmun circulated an opinion finding both statutes unconstitutional on the ground that they violated the woman's right to privacy, which the opinion located in the Due Process Clause of the *Fourteenth Amendment. Justice Potter *Stewart's concurring opinion properly pointed out that this invocation of substantive *due process meant that the Court was enforcing a right not specifically spelled out in the Constitution.

After finding that the case was not moot despite the fact that there had been no time to secure a decision before the opportunity for obtaining an abortion had passed, Blackmun's opinion acknowledged that states had some valid interests in regulating abortion. The opinion divided pregnancy into three periods, or trimesters. During the first trimester the woman had an essentially unrestricted right to choose abortion in consultation with her physician; thus, Blackmun held, the hospitalization and committee requirements of the more "liberal" state laws were unconstitutional. During the second trimester, when according to medical experts abortion posed a greater threat to a woman's health, states could regulate abortion to protect her health. Only in the third trimester was the state's interest in protecting the potential life of the fetus great enough to warrant severe restrictions on abortion, and even then, the Court held, states must permit abortions to save a woman's life. In the course of this analysis, Blackmun's opinion stated that because of uncertainty about the medical and moral status of the fetus, the states could not adopt a particular theory of when life begins—they could not decide, for example, that because life begins at conception fetuses have the same rights as newborn infants.

Although Chief Justice Warren *Burger's concurring opinion denied that *Roe* had established a right to abortion on demand, that was its practical effect. Justices Byron *White and William *Rehnquist, in separate dissents, criticized the Court for enforcing a right not specified in the Constitution to overturn statutes that were no more restrictive than those widely in force when the Fourteenth Amendment was adopted. In addition, they criticized the Court for the trimester framework, which, in their view, was arbitrary. If the state had an interest in protecting the potential life of the fetus, that interest existed, and was equally strong, through the entire pregnancy. Further, they said, the Court's balancing of competing interests and careful laying out of what doctors could do in various circumstances resembled a statute.

Three justices appointed by President Richard *Nixon joined the majority in *Roe*, whose outcome appears to be inconsistent with the sort of "strict construction" of the Constitution that they were said to support. In political terms, *Roe* is probably best understood as part of the Court's attempt to respond to and develop support within an important emerging constituency, the organized women's movement. Although the opinion did not treat the issue as one of *gender discrimination, there were plainly questions of gender at stake in the abortion controversy, for it was widely understood that the burdens of undesired pregnancy fell exclusively on women. Restrictive abortion laws have typically been enacted by legislatures dominated by men. This practice could have been treated as raising questions of gender discrimination. The Court's failure to present its opinion on these grounds may have been a serious tactical error, for the flaws of Blackmun's privacy analysis, employing a newly discovered constitutional "right," were widely noted after *Roe* was decided.

***Criticism and Aftermath of* Roe.** Academic critics of *Roe* argued that invalidating legislation where there was no constitutional text or history to indicate that the legislation contravened fundamental values protected by the Constitution was reminiscent of the *Lochner* v. *New York* era, when the Court invalidated many statutes aimed at improving the economic conditions of workers on the ground that the statutes violated a "liberty of contract" nowhere spelled out in the Constitution (see CONTRACT, FREEDOM OF). Critics also pointed out that, given the acknowledged impact of abortion on the fetus and the medical dimensions of the technique, it was silly to treat the case as one involving "privacy" in the way that *Griswold*, which was about the use of contraceptives, involved actions performed in the privacy of the home.

Academic defenders of *Roe* offered two lines of argument. Some suggested that the case should be reconceptualized as a case of gender discrimination, which, they argued, was indeed barred by the Equal Protection Clause of the Fourteenth

Amendment. Others agreed that *Roe* resembled *Lochner* but argued that the vice of *Lochner* was not that it enforced values not found in the constitutional text but that it enforced values that were not fundamental according to any well-developed theory of rights, whereas the right to privacy, or to personal autonomy in sexual matters, was fundamental under many uncontroversial versions of liberal political theory.

*Roe* was even more controversial among the public. It generated a substantial "right to life" movement that lobbied legislatures to adopt regulations that went as far as possible within the *Roe* framework to restrict the availability of abortions and was particularly influential in gaining power within the Republican party, whose presidential candidates in the 1980s agreed not to appoint judges who were sympathetic to the constitutional analysis adopted in *Roe*.

The Court adhered to the *Roe* analysis for the next decade, but in several important cases it upheld legislative attempts to restrict a woman's right to choose an abortion. Perhaps the most important early such decision was *Harris* v. *McRae* (1980), which held that Congress did not violate the Constitution when it prohibited the use of Medicaid funds to pay for nontherapeutic abortions. In an earlier decision, *Maher* v. *Roe* (1977), the Court had held, similarly, that the states were not required to fund abortions for indigent women. (Most states do not fund nontherapeutic abortions, but some do.)

A predicted likely effect of these decisions was the return to the situation that prevailed before *Roe*, in which women who could afford them secured abortions relatively easily, while women without means were forced to rely on illegal abortions or, like Jane Roe, left to carry their unwanted pregnancies to term. The actual impact of *Harris*, however, is uncertain, since despite the absence of public funding legal abortions rose steadily until reaching the present (1991) plateau of about 1.6 million abortions annually. Private charitable sources now fund a majority of those abortions.

Other restrictions the Court upheld were requirements regarding record-keeping about abortions and regulations requiring the notification of the parents of a minor woman seeking an abortion unless the woman could show a court that notifying the parents was inappropriate. The Court, however, did strike down requirements of parental and spousal consent as well as a variety of regulations designed to make the decision to have an abortion more difficult (e.g., *Akron* v. *Akron Center for Reproductive Health*, 1983; *Thornburgh* v. *American College of Obstetricians & Gynecologists*, 1986).

The retirements of Burger and Stewart, both of whom were in the majority in *Roe*, gave President Ronald *Reagan the opportunity to begin to reshape the Court's position on the abortion issue, but it was the retirement of Justice Lewis

*Powell in 1987 that provided the greatest opportunity for change. Reagan nominated Judge Robert *Bork to succeed Powell, in part because of Bork's vigorous and well-known opposition to *Roe*. That opposition was a source of great concern to supporters of *Roe*, who formed an important part of the political coalition that defeated Bork's nomination.

In 1989 the Court, with Justice Anthony *Kennedy sitting in an abortion case of the first time, came close to overruling *Roe* in *Webster* v. *Reproductive Services*, but in the end a majority of the justices held only that two additional restrictions on abortions were relatively minor extensions of what *Roe* itself allowed. Partisans on both sides of the abortion issue, however, took *Webster* as a signal that further political action was appropriate. Abortion-rights activists, in particular, realized that the right to choose abortion might no longer be adequately protected in the courts, and they revived the sort of political lobbying in which they had engaged prior to *Roe*. Immediately after *Webster* two gubernatorial elections suggested that the threat to abortion rights was an important factor in the election of two Democratic governors, but as the *Webster* decision became part of the overall political landscape the implications for the long term were less clear.

□ Marian Faux, *Roe v. Wade* (1988). Laurence Tribe, *Abortion: The Clash of Absolutes* (1990).

Mark V. Tushnet

**Roman Law.** American law has developed apart from both other *common-law jurisdictions and from *civil-law countries. Yet other legal systems have influenced American law. Among those, Roman law is one of the most significant.

The role played by Roman law in shaping the thinking of American jurists and in the development of substantive law in the United States can be easily exaggerated. There was never any possibility that Roman law might displace common law in the United States as a whole, though in those territories once under civil-law systems, such as Florida and Texas, Roman law did play a dominant role for a time. In the Supreme Court, however, Roman law was always peripheral and served, at most, as a backdrop or counterpoint to American common law. Some specific characteristics of the influence exerted by Roman law are clear and consistent. First, Roman and civil law provided a model of systematic legal structure, especially in their organizational and conceptual framework. Second, Roman law provided a wealth of precise terminology to express complex legal concepts. Third, and most importantly, Roman law provided a source for comparative materials by which to judge American rules, as well as the historical substrata upon which many American and English rules used in the United States rested. Many Supreme Court opinions attempted to provide not only a theoretical justifi-

cation for legal rules laid down, but also a historical rationale for these rules. Citations to Roman law are common in this context.

Finally, Roman law citations found their way into Supreme Court opinions because individual justices were interested in Roman law. The greatest of the Romanist justices were Joseph *Story and Oliver Wendell *Holmes, though no Supreme Court justice, including Story and Holmes, was a true scholar of Roman law.

M. H. Hoeflich

**Roosevelt, Franklin Delano** (b. Hyde Park, N.Y., 30 Jan. 1882; d. Warm Springs, Ga., 12 Apr. 1945), president of the United States, 1933–1945. Franklin D. Roosevelt's presidency was the longest and one of the most acclaimed in United States history. During his twelve years in office the New Deal helped to transform the structure of American government by expanding the scope and reach of federal power, by modernizing the federal bureaucracy, and by bringing into government many bright reformers who were committed to making government work to solve the social, political, and economic problems that confronted the country.

Roosevelt attended Columbia Law School for three years after his graduation from Harvard. Following admission to the New York bar, he briefly practiced in a Wall Street firm (1907–1910). He again was a member of a firm during the 1920s, but he served mainly as a name to attract clients, not as a practitioner. Roosevelt relished politics; he was a superb politician with a genius for public communication and building coalitions. He was a patrician who could trace his roots in the United States to the seventeenth century (Theodore Roosevelt was his fifth cousin), yet he was perhaps the most loved national politician of this century, easily winning four presidential elections—one of record-setting landslide proportions. At the age of twenty-eight he was elected as a Democrat to the New York senate. He served in President Woodrow Wilson's cabinet as assistant secretary of the navy and lost as the Democratic vice presidential candidate in James Cox's defeat by Warren G. Harding in 1920. FDR twice won election as governor of New York, and in 1932 he secured the Democratic nomination for president. In his convincing electoral triumph over President Herbert Hoover, he forged a coalition of Progressives, northern urban liberals, conservative southern Democrats, labor unions, farmers, middle- and lower-class white ethnic groups, and African-Americans that survived almost intact for fifty years.

Roosevelt held to no fixed political vision. Rather he had a commitment to using the federal government to accomplish tasks that he and his advisers believed were necessary to move America forward—first out of the Great Depression, and then toward victory over Axis powers in World War II. During the first hundred days (the "first New Deal"), he launched federal efforts to reform banking laws and relieve the plight of farmers, and later to regulate securities. The centerpiece of his economic recovery measure was the National Recovery Administration, which was a cooperative effort between business, labor, and government. After the Supreme Court struck down the NRA, and after his overwhelming electoral victory in 1936 (which also created enormous Democratic margins in Congress), FDR switched from cooperation to confrontation with business and the wealthy. His "second New Deal" included the passage of the Wagner Act (guaranteeing unions the right to organize and bargain collectively), a large increase in the tax rate of the most wealthy, the Social Security Act, further banking reform, and the most massive public works program undertaken in American history. As he lost support for his more radical reform efforts, and as World War II began, he switched back to the more cooperative politics of the first New Deal.

Unlike another lawyer-president, William Howard *Taft, FDR had little reverence for the traditions of the Supreme Court as an institution, nor did he worship constitutional precedents. He perceived the Constitution as a document that must change to accommodate modern economic and social conditions of the country. These views led Roosevelt to the most strident and direct clash between the executive branch and the judiciary in the twentieth century: the court-packing struggle of 1937.

Fearing that the Supreme Court—dominated in 1936–1937 by its conservative bloc joined by Justice Owen *Roberts and often by Chief Justice Charles Evan *Hughes—would stymie New Deal efforts to cope with the Depression, FDR proposed a bill that would permit him to name additional justices to the Court and judges to the *lower federal courts equal in number to jurists with ten years' service who had attained the age of seventy and refused to retire. The proposal encountered immediate and powerful opposition. Meanwhile, the Court handed down its decision in *West Coast Hotel Co. v. Parrish (1937), which by a 5-to-4 margin upheld a state minimum-wage law for women and minors, thus signaling a reversal of its hostility to federal and state legislation that regulated the economy. When Justice Willis *Van Devanter announced his retirement, it became apparent that the president would soon be able to nominate enough justices to assure the permanence of this turn-around. When the *Senate Judiciary Committee reported the bill out negatively, FDR lost the legislative battle but won the war for the soul of the Supreme Court.

Roosevelt named nine justices to the court, second only to the number of justices appointed by George *Washington. The only seat on the Court not filled by FDR at the time of his death was that of Owen Roberts. He nominated the populist senator Hugo *Black to replace Willis Van Devanter. Solicitor General Stanley *Reed, who had argued many important agency cases, filled the vacancy caused by George *Sutherland's resignation. Felix *Frankfurter, Harvard Law School professor and a crucial member of FDR's brain trust, was named to Benjamin N. *Cardozo's seat. Former Yale Law School professor and chairman of the Security and Exchange Commission, William O. *Douglas, succeeded Louis D. *Brandeis. Attorney General Frank *Murphy replaced Pierce *Butler, and his replacement as attorney general, Robert H. *Jackson, filled Harlan F. *Stone's seat when Stone replaced Chief Justice Charles Evans Hughes. FDR named Senator James *Byrnes to James *McReynolds' seat. Byrnes resigned after only one year to take a place in the president's war cabinet and was replaced by Wiley *Rutledge, a federal appellate judge who had supported court packing while dean of the University of Iowa law school. Eight of the nine men named had directly served in the New Deal, and Rutledge in writings before and on the bench had shown himself to be supportive of New Deal measures. All were selected in large part because they agreed with the issues that mattered most to FDR; that is, they were certain to take an expansive view of the power of Congress to regulate the economic life of the nation under the Interstate Commerce Clause of the Constitution. After 1938 no New Deal legislation was declared unconstitutional, and the doctrine of substantive *due process rapidly withered in areas of economic regulation. FDR had no integrated constitutional philosophy that his appointees fit. They were diverse, and as the issue before the Court shifted from the scope of federal regulatory power to issues of social justice and the protection of civil rights and civil liberties in an expanded governmental state, they differed, often quite sharply, about the nature of government and judicial power.

Franklin Roosevelt had the most profound influence on the Supreme Court of any president in the twentieth century, partly because of the longevity of the justices he appointed; Douglas served thirty-six years, Black thirty-three years, Frankfurter twenty-three years, and Reed nineteen years. Five of the justices deciding the most famous twentieth-century case, *Brown v. Board of Education (1954), were Roosevelt appointees. Additionally, other justices appointed later were in some measure New Dealers. Justice Abe *Fortas had served in the Roosevelt administration, and others such as Justices Arthur *Goldberg, William *Brennan, and Thurgood *Marshall were profoundly influenced by the New Deal. Perhaps Roosevelt's most enduring legacy is that the issues with which the Supreme Court dealt during the last half of the twentieth century were framed and shaped by the transformation of federal power and the federal government that FDR had created.

(See also COURT-PACKING PLAN; HISTORY OF THE COURT: THE DEPRESSION AND THE RISE OF LEGAL LIBERALISM; NEW DEAL.)

□ William E. Leuchtenburg, *Franklin D. Roosevelt and the New Deal 1932–1940* (1963). Paul L. Murphy, *The Constitution in Crisis Times, 1918–1969* (1972).

Rayman L. Solomon

**Rosenberg v. United States,** 346 U.S. 273 (1953), argued 18 June 1953, decided 19 June 1953 by a vote of 6 to 3; Vinson for the Court, Black, Douglas, and Frankfurter in dissent. In 1951, Julius and Ethel Rosenberg were convicted of conspiring to violate the Espionage Act of 1917 by transmitting secret atomic and other military information to the Soviet Union. The Rosenbergs' actions relating to atomic secrets occurred before enactment of the Atomic Energy Act of 1946, but other aspects of the conspiracy continued until 1950. The Rosenbergs were sentenced to death. The court of appeals affirmed the judgment, and the U.S. Supreme Court denied *certiorari. Several subsequent collateral attacks on the judgment were unsuccessful.

In 1953, counsel for a "next friend" of the Rosenbergs, without their authorization, argued that the Atomic Energy Act of 1946 had superseded the Espionage Act of 1917 and rendered the district court powerless to impose a death sentence without recommendation by a jury. Holding that this claim presented a substantial question of law, Justice William O. *Douglas granted a stay of execution. Two days later, the Court vacated the stay on the ground that the Atomic Energy Act did not displace the penalties of the Espionage Act. The Court further concluded that, since most of the activities forming the basis of the conviction had been committed prior to the passage of the Atomic Energy Act, the alleged inconsistency of its penalty provisions with those of the Espionage Act was irrelevant. The dissenting justices maintained that the stay should not be vacated without a full review of the substantive issue. The Rosenbergs were executed on the day of this decision.

(See also CAPITAL PUNISHMENT; COMMUNISM AND COLD WAR.)

Edgar Bodenheimer

**Rose's Notes on the United States Reports** (1899–1901), thirteen volumes, was a popular annotated citator from its initial publication until the mid-1930s. Walter Malins Rose (1872–1908), the young California lawyer who developed the publication, arranged chronologically the legal principles found in the Supreme Court decisions from 2 Dallas to 172 *United States Reports* and appended to them citations to all subsequent cases that had cited each principle. The citing

cases were from the Supreme Court, intermediate, and *lower federal courts, and courts of last resort in all the states (see STATE COURTS). These subsequent decisions were analyzed to show the points of law to which they referred as well as the application of the cited principle. Rose's annotated citator offered analytical discussions that were lacking in the bare listings of citings in Shepard's citators. Although, during the period of their greatest popularity, *Rose's Notes* were often cited by the courts, there have been no references to the *Notes* in appellate decisions for more than a decade. A revised edition (1917–1920) by Charles L. Thompson enlarged the *Notes* to twenty volumes and two supplements (1925 and 1932) and extended the citing cases through 283 *United States Reports.*

Morris L. Cohen

**Ross, United States v.,** 456 U.S. 798 (1982), argued 1 Mar. 1982, decided 1 June 1982 by vote of 6 to 3; Stevens for the Court, White and Marshalli, joined by Brennan, in dissent. To what extent can the "automobile exception" to the warrant requirement of the *Fourth Amendment justify warrantless searches of containers that are placed in automobiles? The Supreme Court first addressed this issue in *United States* v. *Chadwick* (1977). Speaking for a unanimous court, Chief Justice Warren *Burger said in that decision that the mere fact that a footlocker, which police officers had *probable cause to believe contained narcotics, was placed in the trunk of a car did not render the automobile exception applicable. The Court reaffirmed the general principle that closed packages and containers may not be searched without warrant because a person's expectation of *privacy in personal luggage is substantially greater than in an automobile.

Not all police suspicions are directed at a specific container, however. In *Robbins* v. *California* (1981), a companion case to *New York* v. *Belton* (1981), a plurality of the Court invalidated the warrantless search of a closed package found in a car trunk. Only after Robbins, the driver of the automobile, was placed in the police car did the officers search the trunk and discover two packages wrapped in green plastic. The police unwrapped the packages and found marijuana inside. Justice Potter *Stewart said that unless the contents of such a package are in plain view, it could not be searched without a warrant.

The rationale of *Robbins* was abandoned a year later in *Ross.* Acting on a tip from a reliable informant that a person known as "Bandit" was selling drugs from the trunk of his car, District of Columbia police stopped the car and arrested the driver. In the trunk they found a closed brown paper bag that contained a white powder later determined to be heroin. At headquarters another search of the trunk revealed a zippered red leather pouch containing cash. Ross's motion to suppress the evidence was denied and he was convicted of possession of heroin with intent to distribute.

Justices John Paul *Stevens, writing for six members of the Court, held that police may search compartments and containers within a vehicle even though the contents are not in plain view, so long as the search is based on probable cause, the same standard needed to obtain a search warrant. Stevens said that the "practical consequences of the automobile exception would be largely nullified if the permissible scope of a warrantless search of an automobile did not include containers and packages found inside the vehicle" (p. 820). The Court's holding in *Ross* broadened the automobile exception established in *Carroll* v. *United States* (1925). *Ross* not only held the automobile exception to the minimum probable cause standard for searching containers but effectively placed the power to determine probable cause in the hands of the police rather than a magistrate.

Some observers maintained that with the retirement of Justice Stewart, who wrote the majority opinions in both *Belton* and *Robbins*, and the appointment of Justice Sandra Day *O'Connor to the Court, the controversy about warrantless container searches may have ended. The subsequent appointments of Justices Antonin *Scalia and Anthony *Kennedy will no doubt confirm that result. Police may now conduct warrantless searches incident to an arrest of containers discovered in an automobile and must only demonstrate that they had probable cause to believe contraband was located somewhere in the car. Since police have been granted the power to carry out warrantless searches of automobiles and containers therein so long as they meet the probable cause standard, it is unlikely that they would find it necessary to get a warrant to search a particular container located in an automobile.

Justice Thurgood *Marshall's dissent in *Ross*, joined by Justice William J. *Brennan and agreed to by Justice Byron *White, takes issue with the idea that a police officer should have the same power as a magistrate to determine probable cause. He argued that the majority's position "takes a first step toward an unprecedented 'probable cause' exception to the warrant requirement" (p. 828).

(See also SEARCH WARRANT RULE, EXCEPTIONS TO.)

□ Michael A. Jeter, "Constitutional Law—*United States* v. *Ross:* Final Obliteration of Fourth Amendment Protection From Warrantless Searches of Cars and Their Contents," *Black Law Journal* 8 (1983): 306–332.

Christine Harrington

**Rostker v. Goldberg,** 453 U.S. 57 (1981), argued 24 Mar. 1981, decided 25 June 1981 by vote of 6 to 3; Rehnquist for the Court, White (joined by Brennan) and Marshall (joined by Brennan) in dissent. In 1971, several men facing the draft for the *Vietnam War, challenged male-only conscription on the basis of the *equal protection principle contained in the *Fifth Amendment's Due Process Clause. The draft was discontinued and the case entered legal limbo for several years until 1980, when President Jimmy Carter reinstituted registration (although not actual conscription). The lawsuit was then revived, with Goldberg litigating on behalf of himself and all situated similarly males against Rostker, head of the Selective Service. On 18 July 1980, three days before the new draft registration was to begin, a federal district court declared the act unconstitutional and enjoined the government from requiring registration. Rostker immediately requested a stay pending *appeal, and Justice William J. *Brennan granted it. Registration began on time.

Rejecting Goldberg's claims, the majority argued that judicial deference is at its peak when the Court, as here, is considering the combined executive-legislative power over *national security. The majority further held that the test of *"heightened scrutiny" articulated in *Craig* v. *Boren* (1976) for measuring the constitutionality of *gender discrimination was satisfied because military flexibility was an important government goal. The exclusion of females from registration for a potential draft substantially furthered that goal, since women, unlike men, could not be rotated from combat into noncombat positions. The Court did not consider the possibility that women could occupy combat roles.

Justice Byron *White's dissent read the legislative record differently, and, he urged a remand for hearings on the relation between registering women and military flexibility. Justice Thurgood *Marshall's dissent emphasized the distinction between registration for the draft and *conscription itself, insisting that the government had failed to demonstrate that excluding women from registration substantially furthered any important governmental interest. Neither dissent challenged the rule of excluding women from combat.

Leslie Friedman Goldstein

**Roth v. United States; Alberts v. California,** 354 U.S. 476 (1957), argued 22 Apr. 1957, decided 24 June 1957 by vote of 6 to 3; Brennan for the Court, Douglas and Black in dissent, Harlan in dissent in *Roth* only. Laws prohibiting the sale or distribution of obscene literature have existed in the United States since the early part of the nineteenth century. Until 1957, however, neither those laws nor their enforcement was taken to implicate the concerns of freedom of *speech or freedom of the press. Obscenity laws were considered to be beyond the province of the *First Amendment; the Supreme Court's passing statements to that effect in cases such as *Ex parte Jackson* (1878) and *Near* v. *Minnesota* (1931) were merely restatements of settled understandings. As a result, criminal obscenity convictions based even on works of obvious literary value, such as Theodore Dreiser's *An American Tragedy* (*Commonwealth* v. *Friede*, 1930) and Arthur Schnitzler's *Casanova's Homecoming* (*People* v. *Seltzer*, 1924), were beyond the bounds of constitutional intervention.

After dealing with the issue tangentially in several cases in the late 1940s and early 1950s, the Supreme Court finally turned to the obscenity question in 1957. In *Roth* v. *United States* and its companion case *Alberts* v. *California*, the Court reaffirmed the longstanding view that obscenity was not covered by the First Amendment and that both state and federal obscenity laws were therefore constitutionally permissible. Justice William J. *Brennan's majority opinion based this conclusion not only on history and *precedent but also on the view that, although the First Amendment protects all ideas with even the slightest social importance no matter how hateful they may be, it does not even cover obscenity because obscenity is "utterly without redeeming social importance" (p. 484).

This conclusion, which both remains the law and remains controversial, likened obscenity to those various other utterances whose regulation need not be measured against a First Amendment standard. By holding that obscenity was to be treated as constitutionally equivalent to conduct rather than speech, the Court allowed obscenity regulation to proceed without the necessity of the kind of showing of particular harm normally required for restrictions on the kinds of speech covered by the First Amendment. Consequently, although there have long been debates on the effect of sexually explicit material on human conduct, the doctrinal exclusion of obscenity from First Amendment coverage made it unnecessary for the Court then (or since) to look at these debates critically.

Although the Court ratified the historical exclusion of obscenity from First Amendment coverage and thus put obscenity into the category of verbal or linguistic activities (such as perjury and price fixing) that lie outside the First Amendment, it also made clear that, unlike in the past, the test for obscenity would have to be tailored to First Amendment concerns in order to ensure that material that did have First Amendment value would not be subject to restriction.

If obscenity was unprotected by the First Amendment because it did not involve the conveyance of ideas, then the test of obscenity would have to guarantee that only material not conveying ideas would be determined to be obscene. The Court did not specify the exact test that would satisfy constitutional standards, but it did specifically rule that the traditional American test, taken from the English case of *Regina* v. *Hicklin* (1868), allowing prosecutions based on the tendency of selected excerpts of the work to "deprave and corrupt" the most susceptible part of an audience, would no longer be tolerated. Henceforth a work could be obscene only if

"taken as a whole" it appealed to the "prurient interest" of "the average person" (p. 489).

All of these terms were to cause enormous definitional problems in years to come, but the substitution of "taken as a whole" for the selected-excerpts approach and the substitution of "the average person" for the most susceptible segment of an audience (usually taken to be children) were designed to, and did in fact, remove from the threat of the obscenity laws most works, even those dealing quite explicitly with sex, whose goal was to convey ideas rather than provide sexual stimulation.

*Roth* accordingly remains important both for having established the doctrinal foundations for the exclusion of obscenity from the coverage of the First Amendment and for providing the constitutional basis for the conclusion that the definition of obscenity must be established primarily on a First Amendment basis rather than that of the *common law.

(See also OBSCENITY AND PORNOGRAPHY.)

Frederick Schauer

**Royal Exchange in New York City.** See BUILDINGS, SUPREME COURT.

**Rule-making Power** is the power of agencies of the executive branch of the federal government to issue rules and regulations. A large portion of American law takes the form of agency rules. This has occurred because of the growth in the number and responsibilities of federal agencies during the twentieth century, especially during the *New Deal era. Another period of growth was the 1970s, when new programs were created in the areas of the environment, occupational health and safety, and consumer safety, among others.

The basic definition of a rule is found in the Administrative Procedure Act (1946), still the central charter of agency procedure: a rule implements, interprets, or prescribes law or policy for the future. For practical purposes, rules are like laws because they bind individuals and companies in the future by laying down norms that must be obeyed. Rules should be distinguished from adjudications. A rule is a general, prospective norm, while an adjudication resolves a concrete case involving certain facts under governing law. The Supreme Court has played a limited role in defining these terms. In *National Labor Relations Board* v. *Wyman-Gordon* (1969), the majority concluded that a new, prospective policy is a rule. In *Georgetown University Hospital* v. *Bowen* (1988), the Court reaffirmed the principle that a rule has future effect.

In the early twentieth century, the Supreme Court grappled with the constitutional question of how agencies could adopt binding rules, which have the effect of laws, since Article I of the Constitution grants legislative power to Congress. The Court defined the question as one of *delegation of powers. In, for example, *Schechter Poultry Corp.* v. *United States* (1935), the Court struck down key New Deal legislation that contained broad, unrestricted delegations of legislative power to administrative agencies. In 1937, however, a momentous shift in the Supreme Court's views produced a more relaxed delegation doctrine. Soon, the Court upheld broad delegations to agencies as in *Yakus* v. *United States* (1944), which upheld wartime price control statutes. Today, agencies can issue rules if the governing statute contains an intelligible principle to guide the agency and the courts.

The scope of rule-making power depends largely on the governing statutes of each particular agency. A rule must be authorized by the governing statutes. It cannot conflict with them and must confine itself within their limits. The Supreme Court and other courts are often called on to interpret statutes. When construing them, courts look first at the relevant language of the statute. They also consult the legislative history to see why the provision in question was written and to discern the statute's purposes as reflected in its history, as in *American Textile Manufacturers' Institute* v. *Donovan* (1981).

Judges and commentators have debated the extent to which courts should defer to an agency's interpretation of its statute. The rationale for deference is that an agency is the presumed expert about its law, since it has most experience in interpreting it. The Court's decision in *Chevron* v. *Natural Resources Defense Council* (1984) intensified this debate by suggesting that when a statute's language is not clear, a court should inquire whether an agency's interpretation is reasonable, thereby giving considerable deference to the agency. In practice, the degree of judicial deference to an agency continues to vary depending on the subject area, the purpose of the agency's governing statute, the nature of the issue at stake, and the scope and purposes of the rule itself.

(See also ADMINISTRATIVE STATE.)

Thomas O. Sargentich

**Rule of Four,** term that describes the Supreme Court's long-standing practice of reviewing a case if four justices favor granting the petition for *certiorari. The rule was apparently developed by the justices as a procedural device after the Courts of Appeals Act of 1891 enlarged the Supreme Court's discretionary jurisdiction (see JUDICIARY ACT OF 1891). The rule, which became public knowledge in 1924, assures that the Court will hear cases that a substantial minority of justices regards as important.     James W. Ely, Jr.

**Rule of Reason** is a standard courts use in testing the legality of business conduct under section 1 of the *Sherman Antitrust Act (1890), which prohib-

its "every contract, combination . . . or conspiracy, in restraint of trade."

At first, the Supreme Court read the act as condemning every restraint of trade. The Court then began moving away from literalness, and in 1911 Chief Justice Edward D. *White, writing for the majority in *Standard Oil Co. of New Jersey* v. *United States* and *United States* v. *American Tobacco Co.,* explained that the act condemned only those practices "which operated to the prejudice of the public interests" by unduly restraining trade (p. 179). He stated that Congress intended that the courts apply the "standard of reason" in determining whether the Act had been violated (p. 60). Although the Court ordered the oil trust dissolved, the rule of reason's factual evaluation of business practices on a case-by-case basis was widely viewed as "protrust."

In *Chicago Board of Trade* v. *United States* (1918), Justice Louis D. *Brandeis listed some factors to be considered in applying the rule of reason: "the facts peculiar to the business to which the restraint is applied; its condition before and after the restraint was imposed; the nature of the restraint, and its effect, actual or probable. The history of the restraint, the evil believed to exist, the reason for adopting the particular remedy, the purpose or end sought to be attained, are all relevant facts" (p. 238).

The rule of reason was the dominant approach in antitrust cases for about two decades. After 1937, as the the power of the national government expanded, the Court increasingly declared that various business agreements or practices were conclusively presumed to be unreasonable without elaborate inquiry about the harm caused or the business justification. These activities were per se illegal "because of their pernicious effect on competition and lack of any redeeming virtue" (*Northern Pacific Railway Co.* v. *United States*, 1958, p. 5). The per se approach dominated antitrust litigation from the 1940s through the 1960s. Per se rules proscribed a range of restrictive agreements that included price fixing and market allocations.

With an increasing emphasis on deregulation and a free market in the 1970s and 1980s, the Court began to abolish or modify per se rules, returning to the rule of reason as the prevailing standard to test many business practices (e.g., *Continental T.V., Inc.* v. *GTE Sylvania, Inc.,* 1977). Per se rules retain some vitality, however, particularly when applied to restraints among competitors. In 1978 the Court declared in *National Society of Professional Engineers* v. *United States* that "the inquiry mandated by the Rule of Reason is whether the challenged agreement is one that promotes competition or one that suppresses competition. . . . [The] purpose of the analysis is to form a judgment about the competitive significance of the restraint" (pp. 691–692).

Although the rule of reason and the per se illegality rule are sometimes viewed as dichotomous, they can also be viewed as complementary categories and converging methods of antitrust analysis. Several Court cases in the 1980s reflect a methodological overlap between the two standards, with some justices advocating a quick threshold examination of a business practice for competitive impact before applying a per se or rule of reason approach.

Debate over the rule of reason remains lively. Some commentators view the Court's renewed emphasis on the rule of reason as part of a free market, probusiness, antigovernment philosophy and as fostering increased economic concentration. Others welcome the diminishing influence of per se rules they consider to be based on unsound economic theory. Several commentators criticize the rule of reason as lacking substantive content, asserting that it establishes a lengthy list of unweighted factors, allowing an unlimited, free-wheeling, high-cost judicial inquiry without providing sufficient guidance to trial courts or businesses. Others propose that the Court adopt "per se rules of legality," declaring lawful certain business practices that are probably beneficial, with the rule of reason applying only to practices with significant risk of competitive injury.

In the first century of antitrust law, the courts have given shape to the Sherman Act's broad mandate. The interpretation and application of the act have varied over the years, and the rule of reason has provided the means for accommodating changes in economic theory with changing political and social concerns about business practices and the concentration of economic power. (See also ANTITRUST.)

□ Phillip E. Areeda, *Antitrust Law*, vols. 7 and 8 (1986).
   Shirley S. Abrahamson and Charles G. Curtis, Jr.

**Rules of the Court.** The Supreme Court first adopted rules to govern its activities in 1790. Since then, the Court has made numerous revisions, of which the latest set became effective on 1 January 1990. The Court's power to establish these rules is provided under Title 28, section 2071 of the U.S. Code. Rule changes may be requested by members of the bar, by committees that the Court occasionally creates expressly for that purpose, or simply at the initiative of one or more of the justices. Traditionally, the justices agree upon the rules by consensus rather than by a strict majority-rule vote. The Court publishes revisions of the rules in the United States Reports. Attorneys practicing before the Court should obtain the most recent version because revisions change rule numbers and contents.

Currently, forty-eight rules, some long and complicated, govern the Court's operations. They range from expressions of broad principles (e.g., who may file an *amicus curiae brief [rule 37] and how to apply for a writ of *certiorari [rule 12]) to specific details (e.g., the days and hours when the Court will hear oral argument [rule 4],

and the color-coding of petitions, briefs, and other Court documents [rule 33]). The rules discuss court officers (rules 1–9), the Court's jurisdiction (rules 10–20), forms and procedures for attorneys to follow (rules 20–40), and finally the actions that the Court and litigants may take once a case has been decided (rules 41–46).

The first group of rules guides the conduct of Court officers. For example, rules 1 and 2 describe the duties and responsibilities of two of the Court's statutory officers, the *clerk and the librarian. Rule 5 stipulates that in order to be admitted to the Supreme Court Bar an attorney must have been licensed to practice before the highest court in his or her state for at least three years (see ADMISSION TO PRACTICE BEFORE THE BAR OF THE COURT).

Another set of rules addresses the circumstances under which the Court may assume jurisdiction. Rule 10 describes the considerations governing review on a writ of certiorari. These writs, the most common type of review of lower court decisions, are granted entirely at the Court's discretion. Rule 17 explains *original jurisdiction, those few cases in which the Supreme Court must act as a trial court, as delineated in *Article III of the United States Constitution. Rule 18 addresses the other commonly invoked jurisdiction, direct appeal, an appeal that the Court is required to consider (see APPELLATE JURISDICTION). Direct appeal can be made only in cases involving federal laws that specifically provide for it. Rule 20 explains extraordinary writs by which one justice or the entire Court may issue temporary restraining orders to prevent damage to litigants while appeals are pending.

The rules also explain the procedures to be followed by attorneys in Court proceedings. For every type of document, they specify the required format and contents as well as deadlines, page limitations, and fees for each filing (rules 33, 38). Rule 39 waives fees and certain other requirements in cases involving indigent litigants. Many rules address important procedural details, including the steps for translating documents in foreign languages, the proper use of diagrams, and technical specifications for typesetting briefs (rules 31–33).

Other rules give attorneys advice and suggestions rather than requirements. For example, rule 37 contains an emphatic caution that amicus curiae briefs be submitted only when they add relevant material not already brought to the Court's attention. Rule 10 explains that the Court will be more inclined to grant requests for certiorari when a decision will resolve conflicting rulings from different circuit courts of appeals or involves an "important question of federal law" not yet addressed by the Court.

A final group of rules discusses what happens after the Court decides a case. Rules 42 and 43 explain the calculation of interest payments on damage awards and the allocation of Court costs to the losing party. Rule 44 describes the procedure to petition for rehearing after a decision, a request seldom granted by the Court.

□ Bennett Boskey and Eugene Gressman, "The Supreme Court's New Rules for the Nineties" *Federal Rules Decisions* 128 (1990): 295–319.          Lawrence H. Averill

**Runyon v. McCrary,** 427 U.S. 160 (1976), argued 26 Apr. 1976, decided 25 June 1976 by vote of 7 to 2; Stewart for the Court, Powell and Stevens concurring, White and Rehnquist in dissent. A surviving remnant of the Civil Rights Act of 1866, Title 42, section 1981 of the U.S. Code provides that all persons shall have the same right to make and enforce contracts. In *Jones* v. *Alfred H. Mayer Co.* (1968), the Supreme Court held that a closely related portion of the 1866 act, section 1982, applied to private racial discrimination in housing. *Runyon* extended *Jones's* reasoning to section 1981. It held that section 1981 prohibits private, nonsectarian schools from denying admission to African-Americans because of their race. Justices Byron *White and William H. *Rehnquist dissented on the ground that *Jones* had been wrongly decided. Justice John Paul *Stevens's concurrence agreed that *Jones* may have been incorrect but viewed overruling *Jones* as too much of a step backward in overcoming race discrimination.

*Runyon's* application of section 1981's right-to-contract provision to private discrimination has had substantial implications for the scope of federal civil rights law. Section 1981, on its face, applies to all contracts. Armed with *Runyon's* holding, lower federal courts applied it to a broad range of behavior, including race-based behavior in security deposit requirements, in admissionss to barber school, in banking services, in supply contracts, in amusement park admissions policy, in sales of insurance, and in dealings with mortuaries. Since, as interpreted in *Runyon,* section 1981 outlaws discrimination in many contexts not reached by other federal laws, it, as much as any other statute, supports the generalization that racial discrimination in the United States is unlawful. Even as interpreted in *Runyon,* however, there are limits to section 1981's reach. In close personal relationships such as *marriage, for example, few believe that section 1981 prohibits race-conscious behavior.

Because it covers most contracts, section 1981 prohibits racial discrimination in employment and therefore overlaps with Title VII of the *Civil Rights Act of 1964. This overlap and continuing concern about *Runyon's* interpretation of the statute led the Court to the brink of overruling it. After oral argument in *Patterson* v. *McLean Credit Union* (1989), the Supreme Court, on its own motion, requested that the parties brief and argue whether *Runyon's* interpretation of section 1981 should be overruled. *Patterson* did not overrule

*Runyon* but held that the right to make contracts does not extend to conduct by an employer after the contractual relation has been established, including breach of the terms of the contract or imposition of discriminatory working conditions. *Patterson* thus severely restricted *Runyon.* Two years later, however, Congress passed the *Civil Rights Act of 1991, which overruled *Patterson's* narrow interpretation of section 1981.

(See also CONTRACT; RACE AND RACISM.)

□ Theodore Eisenberg and Stewart J. Schwab, "The Importance of Section 1981," *Cornell Law Review* 73 (March 1988): 596–604.          Theodore Eisenberg

**Rust v. Sullivan,** 111 S.Ct. 1759 (1991), argued 30 Oct. 1990, decided 23 May 1991 by vote of 5 to 4; Rehnquist for the Court, Blackmun, Marshall, Stevens, and O'Connor in dissent. In 1970 Congress passed a statute providing federal funds to support family-planning services. The statute said that no appropriated funds could be used in programs where abortion was a method of family planning. From 1971 to 1986 the government's regulations barred family-planning clinics that received federal assistance from providing abortions. In 1986 it changed the regulations to ensure a stricter separation between abortion providers and family-planning clinics. In 1988, at the end of the Reagan administration, the regulations were tightened even more to impose the so-called gag rule at issue in this case. Under the rule, clinics receiving federal funds may not counsel pregnant women about the availability of abortions; if they refer pregnant women for other services, they may not mention abortion, and if a pregnant woman asks about abortion, the services are directed to say something like, "We do not consider abortion an appropriate method of family planning."

Family-planning services argued that the rule was not authorized by Congress and that it violated their rights under the First Amendment and their clients' rights under *Roe v. Wade (1973). The Court rejected both arguments and found that the statute was ambiguous. By funding family-planning services but prohibiting assistance for abortion, Congress left the precise definition of family-planning services open. The 1988 regulation was, the Court said, a permissible interpretation of the statute by the agency charged with administering it, to which the courts should defer. The four dissenters emphasized that the 1988 regulations were a sharp departure from those originally in force. They also argued that the gag rule raised serious constitutional questions, which the Court could avoid by finding that the rule was unauthorized.

The Court rejected the free speech challenge to the gag rule. In an important discussion of the doctrine of unconstitutional conditions, sometimes known as the doctrine of conditional spending, the Court held that the government could impose conditions on fund recipients designed to assure that the funds were used for the program's purposes. The Court held that this condition did not force clinic doctors to give up their free speech rights; the doctors could continue to advise women about the availability of abortions outside the confines of the program receiving federal funds. The Court suggested that conditions limiting what professionals receiving government money could say to their clients might be unconstitutional, but said that the relationship between a doctor in a family-planning clinic and the clinic's clients was so narrow that limiting the advice the doctor could give did not impair the doctor's free speech rights.

The Court also found that the rules did not impermissibly burden the right to choose to have an abortion. Acknowledging that it would be easier for women to obtain abortions if they could receive information about them from family-planning services, the Court concluded that the right to choose guaranteed by the Constitution did not require the government to "distort the scope of its mandated program" of providing family-planning services (p. 1777).

Justice Harry *Blackmun, joined by Justices Thurgood *Marshall and John Paul *Stevens, argued in dissent that the government could not impose spending conditions that discriminated against a particular viewpoint and that the gag rule distorted the professional relation between doctor and client. Finally, he argued that because many poor pregnant women receive their only information about family planning from federally funded clinics, restricting the information those clinics can provide does significantly impair their ability to choose to have an abortion.

*Rust* is important as an indicator of the Court's shifting views on abortion; it was the first abortion-related case in which Justice David *Souter cast a vote. In addition, it provided some shape to the doctrine of unconstitutional conditions, which is likely to become increasingly important as government funding of controversial activities expands.

(See also ABORTION; PRIVACY; SPEECH AND THE PRESS.)

Mark V. Tushnet

**Rutan v. Republican Party of Illinois,** 110 S.Ct. 2729 (1990), argued 16 Jan. 1990, decided 21 June 1990 by vote of 5 to 4; Brennan for the Court; Stevens concurring, Scalia, Rehnquist, Kennedy, and O'Connor in dissent. Following its earlier decisions against dismissals for party-patronage reasons of non–policy-making government employees in *Elrod* v. *Burns* (1976) and *Branti* v. *Finkel* (1980), a sharply divided Court now extended *First Amendment protection against party tests covering promotions, transfers, recalls from layoffs, and even hiring itself. The tests, plaintiffs asserted, had been applied in Illinois under a Republican governor's order

prohibiting state hiring without his express permission. Speaking for a bare majority Justice William J. *Brennan held that denying low-level government jobs on partisan grounds would abridge First Amendment rights and that such infringement served no vital government interests that could not be secured by defining work standards for non–policy makers and choosing or dismissing only certain high-level employees on the basis of political views. Nor, Brennan added, was patronage necessary to preserve the democratic process since, in his view, *political parties prosper by other means.

Justice Antonin *Scalia's dissent, longer than the Court's opinion, was especially blunt. He described the party-enhancing benefits claimed for traditional patronage and, without endorsing the system, argued that a legislative body, not the Court, should be allowed to weigh such benefits against other values. Scalia's dissent was not merely against extending *Elrod* and *Branti;* he would have overruled them. Supported by three other justices, and written just before Brennan's resignation from the Court, Scalia's dissent commands attention. Justice John Paul *Stevens's opinion, concurring with the Court, responds specifically to Scalia's arguments.

(See also ASSEMBLY AND ASSOCIATION, FREEDOM OF.)

Leon D. Epstein

**Rutledge, John** (b. Charleston, S.C., ca. Sep. 1739; d. Charleston, 21 June 1800; interred St. Michael's churchyard, Charleston); associate justice, 1789–1791; chief justice (unconfirmed), 1795. Born into wealth and privilege, John Rutledge was one of seven children born to Dr. John

*John Rutledge*

Rutledge and Sarah Hext. Rutledge studied law between 1755 and 1760, first with his uncle, Andrew Rutledge, and James Parson, and then in London at the Middle Temple. Upon his return to South Carolina in 1761 he enjoyed immediate and continuing success as a lawyer and politician, becoming a leader of the bar and an influential member of the general assembly. He also served as a delegate to the Stamp Act Congress, the Continental Congresses, and as governor of the newly constituted state of South Carolina. He helped write the U.S. Constitution in 1787 and supported its ratification.

Washington seriously considered appointing Rutledge, whom he had known and admired since 1775, as the first *chief justice of the United States but instead appointed him as an associate justice on 24 September 1789; the Senate confirmed him two days later. Apparently somewhat miffed at not being named chief justice, exhausted by the duties of riding his federal circuit, and bored by the Court's inactivity, Rutledge resigned his justiceship on 5 March 1791 in order to accept appointment as chief justice of the South Carolina Court of Common Pleas. His initial service on the U.S. Supreme Court essentially had amounted to nothing since the Court had heard no cases during his brief tenure.

In June 1795, upon notice of John *Jay's election as governor of New York, Rutledge solicited Washington for the office of chief justice of the Supreme Court. On 1 July Washington replied that he would happily appoint Rutledge to his desired post and that a commission to that office awaited his arrival in Philadelphia. Rutledge arrived in the temporary capital in time to preside over the Court at its August term. He participated in two cases, the first being *United States* v. *Peters* (1795) in which the Court issued a writ of *prohibition forbidding a federal district judge from hearing a prize case involving a ship owned by the French republic on the grounds that the property of a sovereign nation was immune from such judicial proceedings. In *Talbot* v. *Janson* (1795), Rutledge, in his only opinion delivered as a member of the Supreme Court, joined in the Court's decision that restored a captured Dutch ship to its owners because the capturing privateer had been illegally commissioned.

Rutledge's nomination as chief justice was in extreme jeopardy even before Washington submitted it to the Senate. On 16 July 1795 Rutledge presided over a meeting in Charleston protesting the Senate's ratification of Jay's Treaty. Not content simply to lead the meeting, Rutledge delivered a lengthy harangue against the treaty and urged the president not to sign it. Outraged by his opposition to Jay's Treaty, a cornerstone of the administration's diplomacy, and concerned by the reports of his insanity, the Federalist majority in the Senate voted against Rutledge's nomination on 15 December 1795 by a vote of 14 to 10 (see NOMINATIONS, CONTROVERSIAL). Shortly after his

rejection, Rutledge, who had been depressed since the death of his wife in 1792, attempted suicide by jumping off a wharf into Charleston Bay. He spent most of the remainder of his life as a recluse.

(See also NOMINEES, REJECTION OF.)

Robert M. Ireland

**Rutledge, Wiley Blount, Jr.** (b. Cloverport, Ky., 20 July 1894; d. York, Maine, 10 Sep. 1949; interred Green Mountain Cemetery, Boulder, Colo.), associate justice, 1943–1949. Wiley Rutledge, the last of Franklin D. *Roosevelt's Court appointments, received his B.A. from the University of Wisconsin in 1914 and spent his early years as a high school teacher in Indiana, New Mexico, and Colorado. A law degree from the University of Colorado in 1922 was followed by two years of private practice. For the next fifteen years, he taught law as an associate professor at the University of Colorado and as professor and dean first at Washington University in St. Louis and then at the State University of Iowa.

Rutledge's vocal criticism of anti–New Deal Supreme Court decisions and his support for FDR's *court-packing plan brought him national attention. In 1939, he was suggested for two Supreme Court vacancies, but the president chose William O. *Douglas and Felix *Frankfurter and then appointed Rutledge to the prestigious District of Columbia circuit. As an appellate court judge, his opinions consistently reflected New Deal constitutional legal perspectives. When James F. *Byrnes retired from the Court in 1942, FDR, in spite of Frankfurter's energetic support of Learned *Hand, chose Rutledge.

During his six-year tenure, Rutledge wrote

*Wiley Blount Rutledge, Jr.*

significant opinions in the areas of administrative law, *National Labor Relations Board* v. *Hearst Publications* (1944); civil procedure, *Guaranty Trust* v. *York* (1945); labor law, *Elgin, Joliet & Eastern Railway* v. *Burley* (1946) and *United States* v. *\*United Mine Workers* (1947); and tax law, *United States* v. *Massachusetts* (1948). Yet his most enduring contribution was his participation in the development of constitutional doctrine in the areas of freedom of speech and religion.

When Rutledge joined the court, it had begun to recognize a constitutional double standard. In *United States* v. *Carolene Products* (1938), Justice Stone had suggested that restrictions on First Amendment freedoms would be subject to more exacting judicial scrutiny than government economic regulation (see FOOTNOTE FOUR). Then in his *Jones* v. *Opelika* (1942) dissent, joined by Justices Black, Douglas, and Frank Murphy, Stone, by then chief justice, explicitly embraced this position. When Rutledge joined the court, he provided the fifth vote for Douglas's opinion in *\*Murdock* v. *Pennsylvania* (1943), which overruled *Opelika* and struck down on preferred freedom grounds a license fee imposed on the peddlars of religious materials.

Rutledge's contribution to fundamental rights analysis came in *Thomas* v. *Collins* (1945). His opinion for the court provided the clearest exposition of the preferred position doctrine in condemning a state license requirement as a violation of labor organizers' First Amendment rights. In *Kovacs* v. *Cooper* (1949), he defended the doctrine against Frankfurter's claim that it was an exercise in mechanical jurisprudence that automatically condemned government regulation. Rutledge knew otherwise. When he joined Black's opinion in *\*Korematsu* v. *United States* (1944) and authored the court's opinion in *Prince* v. *Massachusetts* (1944), he had acknowledged that preferred freedoms were not beyond the reach of government when its interests in national security and the general welfare were compelling.

□ "Mr. Justice Rutledge," symposium in *Iowa Law Review* 35 (Summer 1950): 541–699.

William Crawford Green

# S

**Salaries of the Justices.** To fortify judicial independence, the Constitution forbids diminution of judicial compensation. Unmentioned are salary increases, a subject entangled in economics and politics. The *Judiciary Act of 1789 pegged the *chief justice's pay at $4,000 and the associates' at $3,500, thereby creating a $500 differential that persisted until 1969. Thereafter the difference grew to reflect the chief justice's disproportionate administrative responsibilities.

Congress increased court salaries at long intervals during the nineteenth and twentieth centuries. After 1955 raises occurred more frequently. The 1989 Ethics Reform Act set the chief justice's 1990 salary at $124,000 and the associates' at $118,600.

Increased salaries for the justices have faced several obstacles: linkage of congressional and judicial salaries, politically induced legislative inertia, the setting of court salaries comparable to those of the speaker of the House and vice-president but not to incomes derived from lucrative law practices, and inflation. The justices have lobbied for higher salaries, an endeavor aided since the 1950s by a bipartisan interbranch salary commission.

The congressional compensation power was wielded in 1964 to express displeasure with the Warren Court's decisions. Congress then increased judicial pay but reduced the prevailing salary differential between Supreme Court justices and *lower federal court judges. In *United States* v. *Will* (1980), the Supreme Court held unconstitutional statutes freezing automatic increased cost of living salary adjustments that had previously vested. However, in *O'Malley* v.

*Woodrough* (1939), the Court held that federal judges enjoyed no immunity from tax burdens shared by all citizens and consequently judicial salaries were subject to general tax laws.

Peter G. Fish

**San Antonio Independent School District v. Rodriguez,** 411 U.S. 1 (1973), argued 12 Oct. 1972, decided 21 Mar. 1973 by vote of 5 to 4; Powell for the Court, Stewart concurring; Douglas, Brennan, White, and Marshall in dissent. In 1968, Demetrio Rodriguez and other parents residing in Texas' property-poor Edgewood school district filed a *class-action suit in federal district court contending that their state's school finance law violated the *Equal Protection Clause of the *Fourteenth Amendment. Under Texas law, the state appropriated funds to provide each child with a minimum education; local school districts then enriched that basic education with funds derived from locally levied ad valorem property taxes. Because the value of taxable property as well as the number of school-aged children differed greatly among the state's more than one thousand districts, significant interdistrict disparities existed in available enhancement revenues, per-pupil expenditures, and tax rates.

In 1971, the district court found that the Texas statute operated for property-poor school districts as a spend-less, tax-more system of school finance, and for rich ones as a spend-more, tax-less system. Education, the three-judge panel held unanimously, was a fundamental constitutional right (see FUNDAMENTAL RIGHTS); wealth-based classifications, as Texas had created here, were constitutionally suspect. Applying the test of *strict scrutiny, the lower court held that the Texas method of school finance deprived plaintiffs of their equal protection guarantees. It ordered the state to finance its schools so that the amount spent on a child's education did not depend upon the wealth of the neighborhood in which the child resided.

In 1973, a divided Supreme Court reversed the lower court decision and sustained the school finance policy operating in Texas and, in effect, forty-eight other states. Justice Lewis *Powell's majority opinion held that education was not a fundamental right, since it was guaranteed neither explicitly nor implicitly in the Constitution. Texas did not, in any case, deprive any class or anyone of an education, but rather assured that each child in the state received a free minimum education. Moreover, no discrete, wealth-based class existed against which the state discriminated, since, among other things, some school children from poor families resided in property-rich school districts expending high per-pupil amounts on their education. Acknowledging its traditional reluctance to meddle in local fiscal affairs, the Court applied the rational basis (or minimal scrutiny) test. It found that the state's method of school finance, incorporating local choice over tax rates and degree of educational enrichment, furthered the state's legitimate interest in fostering local participation in public education while simultaneously providing every child in the state with a free basic education.

Vigorous dissents registered a spectrum of interpretations and objections. Justice Byron *White, also applying the minimal scrutiny test, argued that the statute bore no rational relationship to the state's purported goal of local control, since property-poor districts had no meaningful enhancement options available to them. Justice William *Brennan argued that a fundamental right to education did exist because of education's importance to the enjoyment of rights that are guaranteed explicitly or implicitly in the Constitution. Hence, strict scrutiny should apply. Justice Thurgood *Marshall argued for the adoption of a variable equal protection standard, one that assessed the characteristics of the class and the importance of the governmental benefits to that class, relative to the government's interest in retaining the classification.

During the decade following the *Rodriguez* decision, Texas and numerous other states enacted a series of "equalization" reforms but failed to reduce effectively the interdistrict inequities in access to resources, per-pupil expenditures, and tax rates. In 1984, with federal court pathways foreclosed, the Mexican American Legal Defense and Education Fund, on behalf of the Edgewood district, Rodriguez, and other plaintiffs, filed suit in a lower *state court alleging that Texas school finance policy violated the Texas constitution.

In October 1989 the Texas Supreme Court held unanimously for the petitioners in *Edgewood* v. *Kirby* (1989). It declared that the legislature had failed "to establish and make suitable provision for . . . an efficient system of public free schools" throughout the state, as mandated by Article VII of the Texas constitution (p. 500). Existent inequality among the districts, the justices held, affronted the constitutional vision of efficiency. The court ordered the legislature to redesign its school finance system by 1 May 1990, so that districts would have access to relatively equal revenues per pupil when making equal tax efforts. With this decision, Texas became the tenth state to have its state supreme court declare a school finance law in violation of the state constitution.

(See also EDUCATION; RACE AND RACISM.)

Richard A. Gambitta

**Sanford, Edward Terry** (b. Knoxville, Tenn., 23 July 1865; d. Washington, D.C., 8 Mar. 1930; interred Greenwood Cemetery, Knoxville), associate justice, 1923–1930. Born in the last days of the Civil War, Edward Terry Sanford was influenced during his formative years by his wealthy southern family and its close New England ties. Sanford was educated extensively at both southern and northern schools, earning undergraduate and graduate degrees from the University of Tennessee and from Harvard. This background enhanced a significant personality trait in Sanford—that of balancing interests. Following completion of his law degree at Harvard, Sanford studied abroad before returning to Tennessee to practice law.

Sanford's pre-Court career included private law practice in Tennessee (1890–1907), lecturer in law at the University of Tennessee (1898–1907), special assistant to the attorney general of the United States (1906), assistant attorney general (1907), and federal district judge for eastern and middle Tennessee (1908–1923). His nomination to the United States Supreme Court in 1923 was secured by the lobbying efforts of Chief Justice William H. *Taft and Attorney General Harry Daugherty who urged President Warren G. Harding to select Sanford because of his *lower federal court experience and his cosmopolitan education. As a southern Republican Sanford was acceptable to Harding, who had received political support in the South.

Sanford's greatest impact on American constitutional law came in the area of civil liberties and involved the establishment of the *incorporation doctrine. Originally the guarantees to the *Bill of Rights applied only at the federal level. The controversy leading to the Civil War demonstrated that all states did not guarantee personal, fundamental liberties. The *Fourteenth Amendment purported to do this. The extent of this guarantee was tested during the early twentieth century when state and federal authorities reacted to political unrest with repressive laws. In a series of cases the Supreme Court had to balance

*Edward Terry Sanford*

both state and national *police power against individual rights.

In this setting Justice Sanford articulated this incorporation doctrine in two major cases. In *Gitlow v. New York* (1925) Sanford, writing for the Court, included dicta stating that the First Amendment's freedom of speech and press clauses were fundamental to personal liberty and protected from state infringement. Although the holding sustained the conviction of a publisher whose pamphlets urged violent overthrow of government, Sanford's dicta had major significance. The incorporation doctrine would use the liberty guaranteed by the Fourteenth Amendment against state action to extend the rights listed in the Bill of Rights. Sanford further enunciated the doctrine two years later in *Fiske v. Kansas* (1927), where, in speaking for the Court, he upheld a defense invoking the Fourteenth Amendment to guarantee the federal right of free speech against a state criminal anarchy statute. (See SPEECH AND THE PRESS.)

More highly visible justices like Holmes and Brandeis overshadowed Sanford in life, while the fact that he died on the same day as Chief Justice Taft obscured him in death.

Alice Fleetwood Bartee

**Santa Clara County v. Southern Pacific Railroad Co.,** 118 U.S. 394 (1886), argued 26–29 Jan. 1886, decided 10 May 1886 by vote of 9 to 0; Harlan for the Court. This was one of the legion of cases involving railroads and government agencies (at every level) that inundated the courts in the late nineteenth century. The State of California and certain affected counties sought to collect taxes

that they claimed were owed by both the Southern Pacific and Central Pacific railroads. Argument focused almost entirely on whether the taxes were barred by the Due Process Clause of the *Fourteenth Amendment.

The U.S. Supreme Court did not address the constitutional issues posed by counsel. Instead, it based its ruling on a narrower issue: whether the fences on the railroads' property should have been assessed by either county or state taxing authorities. Justice John Marshall *Harlan held that such fences could not be taxed as property subject to taxation under California statute; the Court's ruling upheld that of the California court.

Despite the Court's narrow holding, the case was not without constitutional consequence. In an unusual preface, entered before argument, Chief Justice Morrison R. *Waite observed that the Court would not consider the question "whether the provision in the Fourteenth Amendment to the Constitution which forbade a state to deny to any person within its jurisdiction the equal protection of the Constitution, applied to these corporations. We are all of the opinion that it does" (p. 396). It followed that *corporations enjoyed the same rights under the Fourteenth Amendment as did natural persons.

(See also DUE PROCESS, SUBSTANTIVE; PRIVATE CORPORATION CHARTERS.)

Augustus M. Burns III

**Santa Clara Pueblo v. Martinez,** 436 U.S. 49 (1978), argued 29 Nov. 1977, decided 15 May 1978 by vote of 7 to 1; Marshall for the Court, White in dissent, Blackmun not participating. The 1968 Indian Civil Rights Act applied most of the guarantees of the federal *Bill of Rights to *Native American tribal governments. It initially provided only a *habeas corpus remedy in criminal cases. But *lower federal courts developed a series of "implied" civil remedies—actions for declaratory or injunctive relief or *mandamus—so that federal courts came to review matters central to tribal self-government, including election procedures, reapportionment cases, the right to *vote and hold public office, and proper qualifications for tribal membership. (See INDIAN BILL OF RIGHTS.)

Martinez was a membership case, filed under the Indian Civil Rights Act on a *gender discrimination charge. The case claimed that a tribal rule allowing tribal membership to children of male members who married outside the tribe but not to women who did the same violated the equal protection clause of the act. Justice Thurgood *Marshall, writing for the Court, denied the claim and eviscerated the law. Contending that a federal cause of action was not required to extend constitutional norms to tribal governments, he urged that grieving Indians sue in their tribal courts so as to preserve tribal self-determination. Justice Byron *White, in his dissent, wrote, "I cannot believe that Congress desired the enforcement of these acts to be left up to the very tribal authorities alleged to have violated them. Extension of constitutional rights to individual citizens is intended to intrude upon the authority of government" (p. 69).

The outcome was that the decision strengthened tribal self-determination, but an Indian with a complaint against a tribal government had little opportunity for relief. Few tribal court decisions were subsequently appealed.

(See also EQUAL PROTECTION.)

Paul L. Murphy

**Scales v. United States,** 367 U.S. 203 (1961), reargued 10 Oct. 1960, decided 5 June 1961 by vote of 5 to 4; Harlan for the Court, Brennan, Warren, Douglas, and Black in dissent. The Supreme Court had dealt with the conspiracy provisions of the *Smith Act in two previous cases: *Dennis* v. *United States* (1951) and *Yates* v. *United States* (1957). In *Scales*, as well as in *Noto* v. *United States* (1961), the Court considered the Smith Act's membership clause. The Court upheld Scales's conviction by interpreting the membership clause as requiring proof of "active" as distinguished from merely "nominal" or "passive" membership in the Communist party.

The Court found in the language of the statute clear warrant for requiring "not only knowing membership, but active and purposive membership, purposive that is as to the organization's criminal ends" (p. 210). As thus construed, it held that the membership clause did not violate the Due Process Clause of the *Fifth Amendment nor the free speech guarantee of the *First Amendment. Since the Communist party was considered an organization that engaged in criminal activity, the Court saw no constitutional obstacle to the prosecution of a person who actively and knowingly works in its ranks with intent to contribute to the success of its illegal objectives. Even though the evidence disclosed no advocacy for immediate overthrow of the government, the Court held that present advocacy of future action satisfied statutory and constitutional requirements no less than advocacy of immediate action.

(See also COMMUNISM AND COLD WAR; SPEECH AND THE PRESS.)

Milton R. Konvitz

**Scalia, Antonin** (b. Trenton, N.J., 11 Mar. 1936), associate justice, 1986–. The second of the three associate justices nominated by President Reagan that the Senate confirmed, Antonin Scalia replaced Justice William *Rehnquist, whom Reagan elevated to the chief justiceship upon the retirement of Warren *Burger.

The son of an Italian immigrant who taught Romance languages at Brooklyn College, Scalia became the first Roman Catholic to sit on the Court since Justice William J. *Brennan in 1957. After graduating from Georgetown University, he spent a year in Europe as a student at the

*Antonin Scalia*

University of Fribourg in Switzerland. He earned his law degree at Harvard, from which he graduated magna cum laude in 1960.

He joined a leading Cleveland law firm, resigning in 1967 to teach at the University of Virginia Law School. From 1971 to 1977 he served the Nixon and Ford administrations in various legal capacities. He then went to the University of Chicago Law School where he remained until President Ronald *Reagan nominated him in 1982 for the U.S. Court of Appeals for the District of Columbia. The father of nine children, he became the first academic to sit on the Supreme Court since Justice Felix *Frankfurter (1939–1962).

On taking his seat, Scalia quickly established a solidly conservative voting record, one that has made him the Court's most conservative member on many issues. His opinions—notably his dissents and concurrences—display a vigor and an incisiveness that is far removed from the turgidity of most judicial prose. Although reputed to be jovial and gregarious, he is not above acerbic attacks on his fellow justices (for example, his scathing criticism of Justice Sandra Day *O'Connor's opinion in the 1989 abortion case, *Webster* v. *Reproductive Health Services*).

Scalia's early Court years also produced noteworthy legal contributions. He has regularly voiced strong disapproval of divining constitutional and statutory meaning by reference to the "intention" of framers or legislators. As he explained in *Pennsylvania* v. *Union Gas Co.* (1989): "It is our task . . . not to enter the minds of the Members of Congress—who need have nothing in mind in order for their votes to be both lawful and effective" (p. 34). Additionally, Scalia has displayed a lack of respect for precedents of youthful vintage, candidly recognizing in *South Carolina* v. *Gathers* (1989) that "Overrulings of precedent rarely occur without a change in the Court's personnel," and that he would think it a violation of his oath to adhere to a precedent so that the Court "might save face" (pp. 891, 892).

The candor of Scalia's opinions also characterizes his frequent off-the-bench statements. He has, for example, asserted that the federal courts are being swamped by a flood of trivial cases that special tribunals should hear so that the "continuing deterioration" of the federal courts may be reversed. Scalia has also criticized the Court's conferences because the justices fail to debate the correctness of the votes they cast.

Harold J. Spaeth

**Schechter Poultry Corp. v. United States,** 295 U.S. 495 (1935), argued 2–3 May 1935, decided 27 May 1935 by vote of 9 to 0; Chief Justice Hughes for the Court. The National Industrial Recovery Act (NIRA), adopted by Congress on 16 June 1933, was the Roosevelt administration's first and major instrument for dealing with the Great Depression. Intended to curb unemployment and stimulate business recovery, the statute was wide ranging. But its principal reliance was upon codes of fair competition, which all industry groups were directed to draw up. Within two years more than 750 NIRA codes had been adopted, covering some twenty-three million people. The act declared a national emergency and justified congressional action under the *Commerce and *General Welfare Clauses of the Constitution.

The codes had some positive effects in raising wages, banning unfair practices, and encouraging business morale. But they were hastily drawn, favored big businesses, and encouraged cartels. The drafting of the codes was done by industry groups, and the role of the president was simply to sign them.

The Department of Justice had recognized from the beginning that the regulatory program's constitutionality might well be difficult to establish before the Supreme Court and made a considerable effort to find an appropriate case to take up to the Court for review. These efforts failed, however, and the commercial activity involved in *Schechter*, considering the issues at stake, was absurdly minor. Certain Brooklyn slaughterhouse operators had been found guilty of violating the wage and hour provisions of their industry's code and, among other offenses, selling an "unfit chicken." While the poultry was brought in from outside the state, the Schechters were only local operators selling in their immediate area.

The Supreme Court was unanimous in rejecting the government's case for the program. First, Chief Justice Charles Evans *Hughes disposed of the contention that the legislation was justified by the national economic emergency. Although the Court had recently accepted the claim that the agricultural emergency had justified mortgage relief for Minnesota farmers in *Home Building & Loan Assn.* v. *Blaisdell* (1934), Hughes now held that "extraordinary conditions do not create or enlarge constitutional power" (p. 398).

Hughes's most telling argument, however, was that the statute had unconstitutionally delegated legislative power to the president. Only a few months earlier, in *Panama Refining Co.* v. *Ryan* (1935), the Court had declared unconstitutional another section of the NIRA that authorized the president to ban shipment in interstate commerce of oil produced in excess of state quotas. That decision was by vote of 8 to 1; Justice Benjamin N. *Cardozo, dissenting, contended that the law was justified by the economic emergency. But here the statute had given industry groups, with the cooperation of the president, authority to draft regulations covering the entire economic life of the country. "This," said Cardozo, "is delegation run riot" (p. 553).

Hughes's third count against the statute was that the poultry code involved regulation of local transactions, not interstate commerce properly subject to congressional control. The Court had agreed in earlier cases that local commerce could be regulated by Congress if it had a "direct" effect upon interstate commerce. Though the distinction between "direct" and "indirect" effects had always been difficult to draw. Hughes believed that the difference was "clear in principle" and that the effects here were clearly "indirect." Cardozo thought that the distinction was less clear but agreed that the connection of Schechters' business with interstate commerce was remote. If a local poultry dealer could be regarded as engaged in interstate commerce, then all limitations on congressional control would disappear.

By 1988 the *Schechter* decision had been cited in more than seventy Supreme Court cases, nearly always along with *Panama Refining* on the now discredited delegation issue. As Justice Byron R. *White noted in *Immigration and Naturalization Service* v. *Chadha* (1983), "restrictions on the scope of the power that could be delegated [have] diminished and all but disappeared" (p. 985). The decision has retained more relevance for its interpretation of the commerce power.

President Franklin D. *Roosevelt attacked the Court after the *Schechter* decision for its "horse and buggy" interpretation of the Constitution, but in fact the National Recovery Administration (NRA) program was collapsing, and the Supreme Court's unanimous ruling rescued the administration from an embarassing failure. However, the lessons of the NRA were of value in the drafting of later *New Deal measures such as the National Labor Relations Act and the Fair Labor Standards Act.

(See also ADMINISTRATIVE STATE; CAPITALISM.)

C. Herman Pritchett

**Schenck v. United States,** 249 U. S. 47 (1919), argued 9–10 Jan. 1919, decided 3 Mar. 1919 by vote of 9 to 0; Holmes for the Court. Differences of opinion regarding U.S. involvement in *World War I provided the opportunity for the initial Supreme Court consideration of a *First Amendment free speech case based on federal law. At issue was whether Charles Schenck and other Socialist party members had violated the 1917 Espionage Act that prohibited obstruction of military recruiting.

Schenck, who served as general secretary of the Socialist party, directed the printing of fifteen thousand antidraft leaflets that were to be mailed to those Philadelphia men who were in the midst of the *conscription process. The pamphlets argued that conscripts were victims of the intimidation of war zealots and that young men should assert their individual rights in opposition to the war in Europe. The pamphlets urged people to visit the Socialist party headquarters to sign an anticonscription petition to Congress.

Several recipients of letters complained to Philadelphia postal inspectors, and on 28 August 1917 federal agents searched the Socialist offices, seized files and the party minute book, and arrested Schenck. The defendant pleaded "not guilty" in a trial before Judge J. Whitaker Thompson in the U. S. District Court for the Eastern District of Pennsylvania.

After Schenck's conviction on 20 December 1917, he appealed to the U. S. Supreme Court, questioning the constitutionality of the Espionage Act on First Amendment grounds. He argued that the act prevented full public discussion of the war issue. Schenck's attorneys contended that the law was out of step with Anglo-American legal tradition that in their view distinguished between speech that communicated honest opinion and speech that involved incitement of illegal action. Attorneys for the government contended that the case did not involve the First Amendment but rather congressional draft policy, a question that the Court had settled in favor of the United States in 1918. Therefore, the Supreme Court should refuse to consider the case.

In the Schenck appeal the Court ruled unanimously to uphold the Espionage Act (see ESPIONAGE ACTS). In his opinion Justice Oliver Wendell *Holmes laid out what would become his famous *clear and present danger test to determine the limits of First Amendment protection of political speech. Holmes's analysis considered the context of the speech as well as the intent of the persons who sent the leaflets. "The question in every case is whether the words used are used in such circumstances and are of such a nature as to create a clear and present danger that they will bring about the substantive evils that Congress has a right to prevent" (p. 52). Holmes distinguished wartime and peacetime contexts and concluded that Schenck's words constituted such

an evil since the statute applied to conspiracies as well as actual obstruction of the military. Under the statute the action did not have to be successful in order to violate the law. His analysis did not, however, explain why Congress could outlaw a conspiracy of words in the first place.

The issues raised in *Schenck* underscored the conflict over the war in the nation at large. American Socialists continued their opposition even after U.S. entry. Other reform groups continued to insist upon their right to criticize the war effort. A number of German-Americans suffered the abuse of superpatriots who feared immigrant ties to the fatherland. Other Americans, including many politicians at all levels of government, insisted upon one hundred percent patriotism and demanded the discontinuance of reform programs in order to maintain full support of the war effort.

Holmes's clear and present danger test attempted to draw a line between protected and *unprotected speech in a field of constitutional law where he was pioneering new territory—First Amendment interpretation. Later, in November 1919, Holmes along with Justice Louis D. *Brandeis dissented in another free speech case, *Abrams v. United States. In this dissent Holmes appeared to have modified his earlier view by insisting that a present danger must relate to some immediate evil and specific action. Through the decade of the 1920s, Holmes developed his clear and present danger doctrine in a series of dissents. By the 1930s his persistence had convinced a Court majority to support his thinking, and many aspects of the doctrine remain in First Amendment constitutional interpretation today.

□ Fred Ragan, "Justice Oliver Wendell Holmes, Jr., Zechariah Chafee, Jr. and the Clear and Present Danger Test for Free Speech: The First Year, 1919," *Journal of History* 58 (June 1971): 24–45.                    Carol E. Jenson

**School Attendance.** See EDUCATION; WISCONSIN V. YODER.

**School Prayer and Bible Reading.** For generations, organized *education in America was religious education, with prayer and devotional reading of scripture a part of daily school activities. With the creation of public schools, this tradition was widely continued. The Establishment Clause of the *First Amendment, initially interpreted by the Supreme Court to restrict only the federal government, was perceived as irrelevant to religious activities in state-run schools.

Immigration at the beginning of the twentieth century added to the nation's religious diversity. Complaints were increasingly directed at the Protestant orientation of public school religious instruction. These complaints strengthened when the Supreme Court, in *Everson v. Board of Education* (1947), applied the Establishment

Clause to the states through the *Fourteenth Amendment's *Due Process Clause.

Since many early commentators understood the Establishment Clause to prohibit not governmental support of religion generally but merely support of one religious sect over others, public school officials in New York formulated a "nonsectarian" prayer. Despite its denominational neutrality, the Supreme Court held in *Engel v. Vitale (1962) that the state could not compose an official prayer and that aid to all religions was as impermissible as aid to any one religion. The voluntary nature of student observance was also found immaterial. Compulsion was not a necessary component of an Establishment Clause violation.

The Court in *Abington School District v. Schempp (1963) prohibited the common practice of commencing the school day with a prayer or devotional Bible reading. According to the Court, the defect in Engel was not simply who authored the prayer but that its purpose and primary effect was to advance religion. The Court rejected the argument that recitation of the Lord's Prayer and Bible reading fulfilled the secular purposes of promoting moral values and diminishing materialism. The Court emphasized, however, that the Bible could be studied as part of a secular program of education.

Over the years the Court has remained adamant that school-sponsored prayer and devotional Bible reading are unacceptable. Kentucky's effort to post the Ten Commandments in public school rooms was condemned in Stone v. Graham (1980). Nonetheless, surveys show a significant portion of the American populace favors school prayer and that many schools continue such practices.

The school-prayer controversy plays an ongoing role in American politics. Repeated unsuccessful efforts have been made to amend the Constitution to allow school prayer. Two other developments have proven more significant. First, many state legislatures have mandated a moment's silence at the start of the school day during which students may meditate or pray. Alabama's moment-of-silence statute was found invalid by the Supreme Court in *Wallace v. Jaffree (1985). The Court, however, emphasized that the statute had initially allocated time only "for meditation." The legislation was later amended to include "voluntary prayer." This addition, concluded the Court, signified a governmental effort to endorse prayer. Justice Sandra Day *O'Connor's concurrence suggested a willingness to accept a statute permitting silent meditation or prayer whose history conveyed a message of religious neutrality rather than endorsement.

Consistent with an insistence on neutrality, the Court in Widmar v. Vincent (1981) held that, where state university facilities were available to student groups of all kinds, the predisposition against content-based restrictions on free *speech required equal access for student organizations wishing to participate in religious expression. Congress then passed The Equal Access Act of 1984, extending the Widmar analysis to public secondary schools. Under the act, any school receiving federal financial assistance that allows non–curriculum-related student groups to meet on campus outside regular school hours has created a "limited open forum" and cannot deny equal access to other student groups on the basis of the religious, political, or philosophical content of their speech. In Board of Education v. Mergens (1990), the Court upheld the statute, permitting formation of a student group wishing to read and discuss the Bible, share Christian fellowship, and pray together. The Court found that the equal access principle neither endorsed nor disapproved of religion. Essentially, the Court distinguished between "government speech endorsing religion, which the Establishment Clause forbids, and private speech endorsing religion, which the Free Speech and Free Exercise Clauses protect" (p. 2372).

□ Rodney K. Smith, Public Prayer and the Constitution (1987). Stanley Ingber

**Scottsboro Cases.** See NORRIS V. ALABAMA; POWELL V. ALABAMA.

**Scott v. Sandford,** 19 How. (60 U.S.) 393 (1857), argued 11–14 Feb. 1856 and 15–18 Dec. 1856, decided 6–7 Mar. 1857 by vote of 7 to 2; Taney for the Court, Curtis and McLean in dissent. Scott v. Sandford (1857) stands as one of the most important cases in American constitutional history. It played a major role in precipitating the *Civil War; it provided a basis for far-reaching interpretations of substantive *due process; and it stirred deep-seated emotions in the saga of race relations in the United States.

*Background.* The Dred Scott Case began unobtrusively in 1846 in the lower *state courts of Missouri. Born in Virginia, the slave Dred Scott moved with his master to St. Louis, where in 1833 he was sold to Dr. John Emerson, an army surgeon. Emerson's military career subsequently took them both, among other places, to the free state of Illinois and to free Wisconsin Territory. While in Wisconsin, Scott married Harriet Robinson, whose ownership was transferred to Emerson. Meanwhile, during a tour of duty in western Louisiana in 1838, Emerson married Eliza Irene Sanford, whose family lived in St. Louis.

In 1842 the army posted Dr. Emerson to Florida, where the Seminole War was being fought. Mrs. Emerson and the family's slaves remained in St. Louis. In 1843, with hostilities winding down, Emerson rejoined his family, but he died shortly thereafter. The slaves continued to work for Mrs. Emerson, and, occasionally, as was common in urban servitude, they were hired out to others.

On 6 Apr. 1846, Dred and Harriet Scott instituted a suit for freedom against Irene Emerson in the Circuit Court of St. Louis County, under Missouri law. (Two separate but similar suits were filed. In 1850, to avoid costly duplication, only Dred Scott's case was pursued, with an agreement that its resolution would apply also to Harriet.) Although some details of the litigation's beginnings remain fuzzy, overwhelming evidence indicates that the slaves sued only for freedom and not, as some charged later, to challenge slavery-oriented political issues. Indeed, based on numerous precedents in Missouri case law—the principal precedent being *Rachael v. Walker* (1837)—if a slave returned to Missouri, as Dred Scott had done, after having sojourned in a free state or territory, that slave was entitled to freedom by virtue of residence in the free state or territory. The established legal principle in Missouri was "once free, always free." In fact, when the suit came to trial in 1847, Scott could have been emancipated had not a problem of hearsay evidence resulted in the judge ordering a mistrial. When the case was retried in 1850 and the problem corrected, the court unhesitatingly ordered Scott freed.

The three-year delay before the second trial proved, however, to be fateful. Pending that trial, Scott's wages were held in escrow until the court determined whether he was free or slave. Meanwhile, Mrs. Emerson remarried, moved to New England with her new husband, and left her affairs in St. Louis in the hands of her businessman brother, John F. A. Sanford. When the court declared Scott free, the possible loss of his accumulated wages led Sanford, acting for his sister, to appeal to the Missouri Supreme Court seeking a reversal.

While the appeal was before the Missouri high court, events associated with the increasingly troublesome *slavery issue transformed the litigation from a routine freedom suit to a *cause célèbre*. Asserting that "times now are not as they were" and defiantly exclaiming that Missouri law would not be dictated by antislavery outsiders, the Missouri Supreme Court in 1852 reversed the lower court, overturned numerous legal precedents, and in a manifestly partisan decision proclaimed controversial proslavery rhetoric as the law of Missouri, replacing the principle of "once free, always free" (*Scott v. Emerson*, 1852, p. 586).

**The Federal Suit.** To enable the U.S. Supreme Court to clarify to what degree, if at all, a state court could reverse the "once free, always free" principle, Scott's lawyers began a new suit, *Dred Scott v. John F. A. Sandford*, in the federal courts. (Through a clerical error, Sanford's name was misspelled in the court records.) Scott could have appealed directly from the Missouri Supreme Court to the U.S. Supreme Court, but the recent precedent of *Strader v. Graham* (1851) might have enabled the U.S. Supreme Court to endorse the state court decision without considering its mer-

its. Mrs. Emerson's brother was named defendant because his New York residency made a federal diversity-of-citizenship case possible.

Sanford's attorneys injected additional issues into the federal litigation, including Scott's ability to sue in a federal court, raising the issue of a black person's claim to be a citizen of the United States. Equally troublesome was their proslavery challenge to the constitutionality of the 1820 Missouri Compromise. The power of Congress to forbid slavery in the territories had been long established but Sanford's attorneys now argued the extreme proslavery doctrine that slaves were private property protected by the United States Constitution and, therefore, that Congress could not abolish slavery in the territories. The issue was no longer whether Missouri could remand Dred Scott to slavery, but rather whether he had ever been free at all. So controversial and delicate were the issues that the Supreme Court requested parties to argue twice, a most unusual procedure, in February 1856 and again the following December.

At first it appeared that judicial restraint would prevail (see JUDICIAL SELF-RESTRAINT). With *Strader v. Graham* as a precedent, the Court was prepared to confirm the Missouri high court as having the final word on its own state law, with no need for the United States court to explore the merits separately. Justice Samuel *Nelson was designated to write a Court opinion that would thus avoid any controversial, substantive slavery questions.

But the momentous forces of the time pressured the Court to resolve judicially what political institutions had been unable to do. Justice James M. *Wayne of Georgia proposed that a new Court opinion deal with the issues that had until then been sidestepped. Though Wayne made the specific proposal, responsibility falls also on Chief Justice Roger B. *Taney and Associate Justices *John McLean, Benjamin R. *Curtis, and Peter V. *Daniel. In conference a bare majority of five justices, all from slave states, approved the Wayne proposal, and Taney wrote a new opinion for the Court. Delivered on 6 March 1857, it became famous (or infamous) as the *Dred Scott* decision.

In its decision the Court divided 7 to 2 along ideological lines. Taney's opinion for the Court declared Scott to be still a slave for several reasons. First, although blacks could be citizens of a given state, they were not citizens of the United States having the concomitant right to sue in federal courts. Scott's suit was therefore dismissed because the Court lacked jurisdiction. Second, aside from not having the right to sue, Scott was still a slave because he had never been free in the first place. Congress exceeded its authority when it forbade or abolished slavery in territories because no such power could be inferred from the Constitution. Furthermore, slaves were property protected by the Constitution. The Missouri Compromise was accordingly declared invalid. Finally, whatever the status of an erstwhile slave might have been in a free state or territory, if the slave voluntarily returned to a slave state, his or her status there depended upon the law of that state as interpreted by its own courts. Since Missouri's high court had declared Scott to be a slave, that was the law that the U.S. Supreme Court would recognize.

*Aftermath.* The Supreme Court's decision triggered violent reaction, unleashing irreconcilable partisan passions that merged with other forces already building toward the coming national calamity. The press, the pulpit, the political stump, and the halls of Congress reverberated with scathing condemnations and vigorous defenses of the Court's action. Antislavery forces feared the next step, which might be to legalize slavery everywhere. They instituted a furious assault on the Court, charging that Taney's opinion was mostly *obiter dictum, attacking the personal integrity of individual justices, and even suggesting a judicial proslavery conspiracy. The decision undermined the prestige of the Court just at the time when the stabilizing influence of a respected national judiciary might have provided the sound guidance so desperately needed. With the intrusion of the Court into the slavery issue, many felt that any compromise over slavery was now impossible, and the North and the South moved inexorably toward civil war.

American legal and constitutional scholars consider the *Dred Scott* decision to be the worst ever rendered by the Supreme Court. Historians have abundantly documented its role in crystalizing attitudes that led to war. Taney's opinion stands as a model of censurable judicial craft and failed judicial statesmanship. It took the Civil War and the Civil War Amendments to overturn the *Dred Scott* decision. The *Thirteenth Amendment abolished slavery, and all persons born in the United States, regardless of color or previous condition of servitude, were declared citizens of the United States by the *Fourteenth Amendment. Unfortunately Dred Scott himself died in 1858, too soon to reap the benefits of those changes.

(See also CITIZENSHIP; COMITY; JUDICIAL POWER AND JURISDICTION; PROPERTY RIGHTS; RACE AND RACISM; TERRITORIES AND NEW STATES.)

□ Walter Ehrlich, *They Have No Rights: Dred Scott's Struggle for Freedom* (1979). Don E. Fehrenbacher, *The Dred Scott Case: Its Significance in American Law and Politics* (1978). David M. Potter, *The Impending Crisis, 1848–1861* (1976). Walter Ehrlich

**Sculpture in the Supreme Court Building.** In keeping with the neoclassical design of the Supreme Court Building, sculptor John Donnelly depicted the sources of the Western legal tradition on its massive bronze entrance doors. Four panels on the left trace the contributions of

Greece and Rome: two litigants argue their claims before a council of elders, as described in the *Iliad*; a Roman praetor hands down a judicial edict; the jurist Julian instructs a pupil; and the emperor Justinian proclaims his famous *Code* (see ROMAN LAW). Complementary panels on the right portray major developments in Anglo-American jurisprudence: King John signs the Magna Carta; Edward I expands *common-law remedies in the Statute of Westminster; Chief Justice Coke defies James I by asserting judicial independence and the rule of law; and John *Marshall establishes *judicial review in *Marbury v. Madison. Together these scenes celebrate the enduring quest for justice and the growth of modern judicial power.

Appeals to tradition and authority similarly characterize the sculpture in the Great Hall, originally called Memorial Hall. White marble busts of deceased chief justices line the side walls, either in niches or on alternating marble pedestals. They are the work of many hands, and reflect changing standards of public taste. The earliest justices, such as John *Jay and Oliver *Ellsworth, are swathed in classic drapery; later figures appear in ordinary judicial gowns or coats. Congress has regularly appropriated funds for the purchase of busts of *chief justices since 1874; it has made no provision for memorializing associate justices, however. Private donors, including family, friends, and former law clerks, have contributed busts of some associate justices; these are displayed on the ground floor.

The courtroom contains four marble friezes along the upper walls. Adolph A. Weinman sculpted these group panels, which employ heroic images and classical symbols to suggest the grandeur and necessity of law. Two male figures, seated in regal dignity, dominate the frieze on the east wall, above the justices' bench. Clothed in drapery from the waist down, they represent, respectively, the "Majesty of Law" and the "Power of Government." Between them stands a tablet, symbolizing the earliest written laws. On either side two smaller figures, "Wisdom" and "Justice," hold protective shields, while at the ends of the panel representatives of "the People" look to Law and Government for the protection of their rights and liberties.

Facing the justices on the opposite wall is a frieze that commemorates the religious foundations of law. In the center, "Justice," a male figure, rests on a sheathed sword, his face turned toward "Divine Inspiration," a winged female figure that holds aloft a pair of scales in balance. Beside Justice sits "Wisdom," with its ancient symbol, an owl; while "Truth" sits beside Divine Inspiration. Allegorical figures, the "Powers of Good" and the "Powers of Evil," stand at opposite ends of the panel, awaiting judgment.

The frieze on the south wall features a procession of "Ancient Lawgivers," from Menes to Augustus; their modern counterparts, including Blackstone, Marshall, and Napoleon, appear on the north wall. Such sculpture contributes to a general atmosphere of quasi-religious veneration appropriate for Chief Justice William Howard *Taft's vision of a "temple" of justice.

(See also PAINTINGS IN THE SUPREME COURT; SUPREME COURT BUILDINGS.)

□ Federal Writers' Project, *Washington: City and Capital* (1937). Maxwell Bloomfield

**Seamstress's Room,** a small, plain room on the ground floor of the Supreme Court building, which contains a sewing machine, ironing board, and space for fabric repair. There, the Court's seamstress repairs employee uniforms or any other fabric items that need attention.

Francis Helminski

**Search Warrant Rule, Exceptions to.** The *Fourth Amendment protects against unreasonable searches, and the Supreme Court has concluded that warrantless searches, even if *probable cause is present, "are *per se* unreasonable" (*Katz v. United States,* 1967). Exceptions occur when it is impractical to secure a warrant or when there is explicit or implied consent to the search. Also, warrants may not be required when facts and circumstances preclude any reasonable expectation of *privacy. Exceptions to the warrant rule include but are not limited to: searches incident to a lawful arrest or required to ensure safety, such as "stop and frisk" procedures; inspections by customs, border, and airport officials; searches made with the suspect's consent; searches made in compliance with lawful government actions, such as health inspections; searches of items in plain view; and searches of student belongings. The same probable cause standard applies to all searches, under warrant or not (*Brinegar v. United States,* 1949).

A long standing exception permits warrantless searches incident to a lawful arrest. Circumstances may not permit an arresting officer to obtain a warrant. But only the person under arrest and the immediately surrounding area are subject to search (*Chimel v. California,* 1969), although a cursory visual inspection of adjacent hiding places may be conducted as a protective measure (*Maryland v. Buie,* 1990). Unusual circumstances may justify a warrantless search even though no arrest is made. These exceptions rest on the need of law officers to protect themselves and others. Courts will judge after the fact whether "exigent circumstances" justified the exception, including the officer's reasonable suspicions based on his experience, the suspect's conduct and reputation, and other relevant factors (*Terry v. Ohio,* 1968). Not all police actions incident to a arrest are permitted. For example, police may not conduct a warrantless search of a private home in order to make a felony arrest (*Payton v. New York,* 1980), nor may they search without probable cause other parties who hap-

pen to be in a place also occupied by a suspect (*Ybarra v. Illinois,* 1979). (See STOP AND FRISK RULE.)

Prior to the 1960s, administrative inspections for violations of municipal codes and other government regulations fell outside the restrictions of the Fourth Amendment. In *Camara v. Municipal Court* (1967), however, the Supreme Court extended warrant protection to a homeowner who refused to permit a warrantless code-enforcement inspection of his personal residence. But in *James v. Valtierra* (1971), the Court held that home visitations for welfare programs did not require a warrant because, unlike a code violation, refusal subjected a person to loss of governmental support only, not criminal prosecution. The Court also has generally deferred to congressional determinations as to when a warrant is not required, such as in a warrantless search of a gun dealer's locked storeroom during business hours, an action explicitly authorized under the Gun Control Act of 1968. Heavily regulated industries, such as guns or liquor, have no reasonable expectation of privacy and thus are subject to warrantless searches.

New technology often has persuaded the Court to carve exceptions from the search warrant rule. In *Carroll v. United States* (1925), the justices upheld a warrantless search of an automobile used by suspected bootleggers. Probable cause existed, and there was no time to secure a warrant because the car and its illegal cargo could escape. The automobile exception still exists, with the Court generally giving police broad latitude in this area. Evidence from these warrantless searches is acceptable so long as there was probable cause for stopping the car, even if the evidence is concealed from view (*United States v. *Ross,* 1982). The interior of an automobile is not subject to the same expectation of privacy that exists in a home (*New York v. Class,* 1986). (See AUTOMOBILE SEARCHES.)

Another exception, no longer applicable, appeared with wiretapping. In *Olmstead v. United States* (1928), the Court concluded that this new technology was only an enhanced sense of hearing, not a warrantless invasion of one's premises. The opinion brought a famous dissent from Justice Louis *Brandeis, who warned that the government was breaking the law by illegally invading a person's privacy, which was at the heart of the Fourth Amendment guarantee. Congress in 1934 prohibited wiretap evidence in federal courts, but not until 1967, in *Berger v. New York* and *Katz v. United States,* did the Court extend Fourth Amendment requirements to electronic surveillance.

Two other exceptions are worthy of note. School officials, on reasonable suspicion, may search student belongings or lockers for proscribed articles, such as guns and drugs (*New Jersey v. T.L.O.,* 1985). And aerial surveillance of a person's backyard does not constitute a search, even if it reveals illegal activity that leads to a warrant and arrest (*California* v. *Ciraolo*, 1986).

David J. Bodenhamer

**Second Amendment.** With its reference to "the right of the people to keep and bear Arms," the Second Amendment is currently the subject of considerable attention in the debate over gun control. Proponents of stricter controls generally contend that the amendment was meant to protect the collective right of states to maintain militia units. Their opponents respond that the amendment was intended to protect an individual right, noting that in the eighteenth century, the militia was composed of the entire free white male population, who were expected to muster bearing their own arms.

This lively debate notwithstanding, the Supreme Court has only considered Second Amendment claims in a handful of cases. One reason for this is that for much of American history there were few regulations concerning firearms ownership. The settlers of colonial America were heirs to the English tradition of distrust of standing armies and professional police forces as dangerous to individual liberty. The English tradition of relying on the armed yeomanry to both enforce laws and protect the realm from external enemies was reinforced in the colonial era. The need to defend settlements against the Native American populations and the settlements of other European powers led to the deputization of the entire white population. Colonial statutes required all white men, with few exceptions, to both keep arms and bear them in militia formations. The American Revolution strengthened the traditional suspicion of standing armies and reinforced the view that militias composed of the armed citizenry were the best way to guarantee both security and liberty.

Like the rest of the *Bill of Rights, the Second Amendment was an attempt to answer the objections of Antifederalists who charged that the new Constitution could be used to deprive the people of rights traditionally considered among the rights of Englishmen. Statements by the amendment's principal author, James *Madison, indicate that he saw the amendment as protecting the arms of the population at large.

The antebellum era brought no Second Amendment cases before the Supreme Court. The few firearms regulations that existed were primarily statutes in the slave states, severely limiting or prohibiting African-Americans from possessing firearms. Some antebellum state statutes prohibited the carrying of concealed weapons, but those laws were not the subject of Supreme Court scrutiny. The Court's holding in *Barron v. Baltimore* (1833) that the *Bill of Rights only limited congressional action effectively precluded Supreme Court review of state restrictions. Although the Court did not rule on the amendment before the *Civil War, statements by Justice Jo-

seph *Story and Chief Justice Roger *Taney expressed the then prevailing view. Story in his *Commentaries on the Constitution of the United States* (1833) offered the opinion that the right to keep and bear arms provided a "strong moral check against the usurpation and arbitrary power of rulers" (pp. 746–747). Taney in *Dred *Scott* v. *Sandford* (1857) listed the right to own and carry arms as one of the rights of citizenship.

The aftermath of the Civil War brought a new dimension to the history of the amendment. The Black Codes, enacted in southern states immediately after the war, limited the civil rights of the newly freed slaves, including the right to own firearms. These codes helped spur the passage of the *Fourteenth Amendment. A number of the framers expressed the view that the new amendment would require the states to honor the Bill of Rights, including the Second Amendment.

Despite this, the Court continued to adhere to the holding in *Barron*. The two principal postbellum cases involving Second Amendment claims, United States v. *Cruikshank* (1876) and *Presser* v. *Illinois* (1886) tell us at least as much about the Court's early reaction to the Fourteenth Amendment as they do about the the Second Amendment. In *Cruikshank*, the Court, in an opinion authored by Justice Joseph P. *Bradley, held that the Second and Fourteenth Amendments did not give Congress the authority to legislate against private interference with the right to bear arms. The Court in *Presser* declared that the Second Amendment only protected individuals from federal not state infringement.

The Court thus entered the twentieth century adhering to the view that the Second Amendment only limited federal power. That view, coupled with the virtual absence of federal firearms regulation left the Court with little to say on the topic. That changed with the violence generated during Prohibition. Responding to the increase in organized crime in the 1920s and 1930s, Congress passed the National Firearms Act of 1934. The act, which provided for taxation and registration of automatic weapons and sawed-off shotguns, generated the principal Second Amendment case, United States v. Miller (1939). The unanimous opinion, authored by Justice James C. *McReynolds, noted that the Second Amendment protected the citizen's right to own those firearms that were ordinary militia weapons. As the defendant in *Miller* had been charged with possession of an unregistered sawed-off shotgun, the Court noted that it had no evidence that such a weapon constituted ordinary militia equipment.

Since *Miller*, the Supreme Court has declined to directly address the issue. *Lower federal courts have upheld firearms regulations against Second Amendment claims, sometimes applying the collective rights theory, at other times on the grounds that the amendment has not been applied to the states. The cases that have arisen since *Miller* have generally not presented clear Second Amendment issues. Most have either involved restrictions on possession of weapons by criminals or licensing schemes, not outright prohibitions. One exception to this was the case of *Quilici* v. *Village of Morton Grove* (1983) in which the Court declined to review a lower court's finding that an ordinance banning handgun possession was not repugnant to the Second Amendment.

The Court's institutional reticence stems in part from the relative absence of firearms prohibition in the United States and partly because of what appears to be the policy preferences of a number of modern justices. Several justices have indicated a desire to see the Second Amendment narrowly construed. Despite these preferences, the Court has not fully embraced the collective rights theory, perhaps because history gives little support for that view and because the individual rights interpretation enjoys considerable public support. Widespread firearms ownership coupled with strong demands for stricter gun controls ensure that the debate over the Second Amendment will remain lively.

□ D. B. Kates, Jr., "Handgun Prohibition and the Original Meaning of the Second Amendment," *Michigan Law Review* 82 (1983): 204–273. S. L. Levinson, "The Embarassing Second Amendment," *Yale Law Journal* 99 (1989): 637–659. Robert J. Cottrol

**Sedition Act of 1798.** Passed 14 July 1798 at the height of anti-French sentiment following the embarrassing XYZ affair, the Sedition Act of 1798 was an attempt by the administration of John Adams to quiet *subversion and dissent, which it believed to be caused in large part by unscrupulous English, Irish, and French immigrants to America. This act, which provided for the punishment of persons conspiring to oppose or obstruct measures of the federal government and for the punishment of some writings critical of the government, is usually portrayed in standard American histories as an outrageous infringement on free speech and comparable to the roughly contemporary French Terror. In retrospect it does appear that the act was the product of paranoia on the part of the Federalists, but the statute was not without the provocation of some mendacious publications, and, viewed in its proper historical context, the act was not really an illiberal measure. The act reflected fear that the sort of instability of life and liberty that prevailed in revolutionary France might be brought to the shores of America, and the prevalence of frankly francophiliac Democratic societies all over the new American states gave some substance to the fear, as did reports that some of the participants in the Whiskey Rebellion, who stymied the collection of federal revenues in 1794, wore the French tricolor.

The most important provision of the act codified the English *common law of *seditious libel and made it a crime punishable by fine or imprisonment to speak disparagingly of the national government or government officials in a manner intending to hold them up to public ridicule and erode their authority. Still, the act liberalized the English common law insofar as it allowed evidence of the truth of a charge against the government to be entered into the defense at a trial and insofar as it allowed the jury to be the judge not only of the fact of publication, but also of the allegedly seditious character of the published matter. Both of these reforms were also part of the roughly contemporaneous English Fox's Libel Act of 1792, widely viewed as a triumph for English liberals.

The act resulted in several important trials for seditious libel in the late 1790s, most notably those of Matthew Lyon, Thomas Cooper, and James Thompson Callender. Lyon was a feisty Irish Vermont congressman who had made intemperate remarks about the unnecessary pomp displayed by President Adams. An unsympathetic Federalist judge, William *Paterson, presided over his trial (*U.S.* v. *Matthew Lyon*, 1798), and although Paterson instructed the jury that they must find Lyon guilty of having made his seditiously libelous statements beyond a reasonable doubt, he was still convicted, fined one thousand dollars and costs, and sentenced to imprisonment for four months.

Thomas Cooper was a transplanted British social critic who allied himself with Thomas *Jefferson against John Adams in the presidential election of 1800. Cooper had published remarks critical of Adams, notably that he had borrowed money at too high a rate during peacetime, that he had maintained a standing army and navy, and that he had interfered with the independence of the judiciary in a matter involving extradition of a British murder suspect. Cooper's statements were probably matters of opinion rather than fact, and though they were arguably more false than true, the presiding justice, Samuel *Chase, in his jury instructions, required Cooper to prove the truth of his assertions "beyond a marrow" before he could be acquitted (*U.S.* v. *Thomas Cooper*, 1800). This was in stark contrast to Paterson's standards in the *Lyon* trial, and probably flowed from some understandable confusion in Chase's mind over whether he should apply the standards from English private libel law (which he did), or liberalize the standards in keeping with emerging American ideas about the value of free speech (which he did not). Cooper was found guilty and sentenced to pay a fine of four hundred dollars and to be imprisoned for six months. Like the other seditious libel defendants he was later pardoned by Thomas Jefferson, but he refused his pardon, with what one historian later called "commendable perversity," and insisted on serving out his sentence.

The most famous seditious libel trial, however, was probably that of James Thompson Callender (*U.S.* v. *James Thompson Callender*, 1800), a particularly rebarbative Scottish immigrant and Jeffersonian party scribbler, who published a whole book of calumny about Adams. Callender was once ejected from the Virginia House of Representatives for being covered with lice and filth, and he later turned on Jefferson and proceeded to publish scurrilous gossip about him.

Justice Chase presided over the Callender trial, and appears to have been convinced that the author of Callender's book ought to have been punished, having read the book on the way to the trial on the Virginia circuit. Callender's counsel, however, made almost no effort to defend their client, preferring instead to goad Justice Chase into some of the outbursts for which he was already becoming famous and to score political and rhetorical points against the Adams administration. Callender's lawyers unsuccessfully sought to argue that the jury should be allowed to reject the Sedition Act as unconstitutional and to enter partial evidence in order to demonstrate the truth of only one of the nineteen libelous statements charged against their client. As their defense collapsed in the face of adverse and incredulous rulings from Chase, Callender's counsel gave up the argument, and Callender was then convicted, fined two hundred dollars, and sentenced to an imprisonment of nine months.

Chase's actions, which were probably not unreasonable given the obviously political nature of Callender's defense, were severely and unfairly excoriated in the Republican press and were magnified into more spectacular charges that the Federalist judiciary was bent on silencing all dissenters and depriving hapless Republican defendants of their rights to speech and jury trials (see TRIAL BY JURY). Chase's conduct in the *Callender* trial was later made the centerpiece of the impeachment trial against him.

Jefferson or his party appear to have paid Cooper's and Callender's fines, and as, indicated, the new president, shortly after his inauguration, pardoned all defendants convicted under the Sedition Act, which had, by its terms, already expired.

While the act was at odds with emerging Jeffersonian and Madisonian thought on free expression, it was meliorative of the common law. While the act appears to have enjoyed popular support when it was passed in 1798, when the threat of French invasion collapsed with Napoleon's defeat in Egypt in late 1798, public sympathy shifted away from the Federalists. Eventual public revulsion, fostered by the Jeffersonian press, at the act's enforcement in the Lyons, Cooper, and Callender trials, and Justice Chase's conduct in particular, accounted in large part for the loss of the presidency and the Congress by the Federalists in 1800.

(See also SPEECH AND THE PRESS.)

□ Stephen Presser and Jamil Zainaldin, *Law and Jurisprudence in American History: Cases and Materials*, 2d ed. (1989). James Morton Smith, *Freedom's Fetters: The Alien and Sedition Laws and American Civil Liberties* (1956).
                                                    Stephen B. Presser

**Seditious Libel.** Slowly taking shape in seventeenth-century England, the crime of seditious libel encompassed any political criticism that threatened to diminish respect for the government, its laws, or public officials. Developed in Star Chamber and refined in *common-law courts, the law initially empowered judges, rather than jurors, to determine whether or not criticism was libelous, and it prohibited defendants from pleading truth as a defense. According to the orthodox view, "the greater the truth, the greater the libel."

Especially in colonial North America, seditious libel prosecutions seemed more effective in stimulating controversy than in stiffling dissent. A significant body of opinion, popularly associated with the 1732 prosecution of John Peter Zenger, challenged the orthodox view. Libertarians of the mid-eighteenth century argued that jurors (not judges) should decide the libelous nature of expression and that defendants could plead truth as a defense. As late as 1791, when the *First Amendment's guarantees of free speech and freedom of press were adopted, these "Zengerian principles" generally marked the limits of articulated opposition to the theory that public officials could, under certain legal safeguards, prosecute seditious expression. Popular political culture, however, tolerated a much broader range of criticism than any theory of seditious libel allowed.

Enacted by Federalists prior to the elections of 1800, the *Sedition Act of 1798 both renewed controversy over theory and underscored the dubious value of prosecutions for seditious libel. Although the law did incorporate the Zengerian principles, Federalist judges used procedures highly unfavorable to Jeffersonian defendants. With every trial ending in conviction, Jeffersonian libertarians broadened the theoretical case against seditious libel, contending that the Zengerian principles offered insufficient protection for political expression. Some even urged an end to all seditious libel prosecutions. Although several justices had presided over sedition trials, the act expired before the full Court ever considered this new libertarianism. Meanwhile, though, popular opinion generally condemned the Sedition Act, and Congress repaid the fines of persons convicted under it.

Between the Sedition Act and *World War I, constitutional theorists continued to debate the status of seditious libel, and after 1919 the Supreme Court began to hear appeals, involving successful prosecutions against political expression, that touched upon the issue. In his famous dissent in *Abrams* v. *United States* (1919), for example, Justice Oliver Wendell *Holmes argued that the First Amendment had wiped out the common law of seditious libel and that the government could prosecute political speech only under his *clear and present danger doctrine. And during the cold-war era, in response to prosecutions of political radicals, some influential First Amendment scholars insisted that seditious libel violated fundamental understandings of free expression. As one of these cold-war libertarians, Harry Kalven, Jr., later wrote, no society that recognized seditious libel, whatever its other qualities, could be a free one (see COMMUNISM AND COLD WAR).

Finally, more than 160 years after its expiration, the Supreme Court belatedly confronted the Sedition Act of 1798. In *New York Times v. Sullivan (1964), a lawsuit that grew out of civil rights activities in Alabama, Justice William *Brennan compared civil libel suits by public officials with seditious-libel prosecutions on behalf of government itself. Opposition to seditious libel, "which first crystalized" with the new libertarianism of the 1790s, had grown into "a profound national commitment to the principle that debate on public issues should be uninhibited, robust and wide open" (p. 270). Even in its Zengerian form, seditious libel violated First Amendment guarantees. Later, the Court reaffirmed this position, overturning a criminal libel conviction in Garrison v. Louisiana (1964). Only "clear and convincing" evidence of *"actual malice"—proof that defendants knew their statements to be false or that they had published in "reckless disregard" of their veracity—might sustain any political libel action, criminal or civil.

What, then, was left of seditious libel? In both Sullivan and Garrison, libel cases involving the reputations of individual public officials, a majority of the Court refused to repudiate seditious libel altogether. But in these cases and *Brandenburg v. Ohio (1969)—which overturned a *criminal syndicalist law on the theory that even extremist political speech could not, by itself, be punished—the Court seemed to have finally dismantled the theoretical and constitutional scaffolding for any seditious-libel prosecution for general criticism of governments or their laws.
(See also LIBEL; SPEECH AND THE PRESS.)

☐ Leonard W. Levy, Emergence of A Free Press (1985). Norman L. Rosenberg, Protecting the Best Men: An Interpretive History of the Law of Libel (1986).
Norman L. Rosenberg

**Segregation, De Facto.** Racial segregation that exists in fact but was neither created by specific statutes nor enforced by statutes or judicial decrees is known as de facto segregation. Such segregation is typically a result of housing patterns and economic conditions, combined with governmental policies that were not specifically

designed to segregate the races but that had that effect (see HOUSING DISCRIMINATION).

The Supreme Court first used the term "de facto segregation" in *Swann v. Charlotte-Mecklenburg Board of Education (1971), but that case, involving court-ordered busing in a district that had once been segregated by law, turned on other issues (see SEGREGATION, DE JURE). In *Keyes v. Denver School District No. 1 (1973) Justices William O. *Douglas and Lewis *Powell, concurring, urged the Court to abandon the distinction between de facto and de jure segregation. Douglas cited past *state action, *restrictive covenants, public funds used "by urban development agencies to build racial ghettoes," the assignment of teachers, and the building or closing of schools as ways in which de facto segregation was a function of state action. In *Milliken v. Bradley (1974) the Court rejected this analysis, effectively holding that courts could not remedy de facto segregation that was not caused by explicit government policies. In *Washington v. Davis (1976) the Court held that, to be unconstitutional, de facto segregation had to be the result of a "racially discriminatory purpose" by the state (see DISCRIMINATORY INTENT). In Washington v. Seattle School District No. 1 (1982), the Court upheld the power of school boards and state agencies to take voluntary remedial measures to end de facto segregation. On the other hand, Crawford v. Board of Education of Los Angeles (1982) upheld the right of California to amend its constitution to prohibit state officials from instituting busing to end de facto segregation.
(See also RACE AND RACISM.)

Paul Finkelman

**Segregation, De Jure.** Racial separation that is required by law is known as de jure segregation. The Supreme Court first approved of de jure segregation in *Plessy v. Ferguson (1896), holding that legislatively mandated segregation in transportation did not violate the *Equal Protection Clause of the *Fourteenth Amendment as long as the facilities were *separate but equal. After Plessy, the fifteen former slave states, along with West Virginia and Oklahoma, mandated segregation in most public facilities, while other states allowed, but did not require, localities or state agencies to create de jure segregation (see SEGREGATION, DE FACTO).

The Court also upheld segregation that did not purport to be "separate but equal." In *Cumming v. Richmond County Board of Education (1899) the Court refused to interfere with a county school system that provided high school education for whites but not blacks, and in Berea College v. Kentucky (1908) the Court sustained a statute requiring private colleges to exclude blacks. In Gong Lum v. Rice (1927) the Court affirmed the right of Mississippi to segregate Chinese-Americans from public schools set up for whites.

Throughout the South, statutes segregated court-rooms, jails and prisons, restaurants, hotels, bars, trains and train stations, buses, streetcars, elevators, lunch counters, swimming pools, beaches, baseball fields, fishing holes, telephone booths, prizefights, pool halls, factories, public toilets, hospitals, cemeteries, and virtually all other places where blacks and whites might meet. In *Buchanan v. Warley* (1917), one rare case that went against the trend of legitimizing segregation, the Court struck down a statute requiring segregation in residential neighborhoods (see HOUSING DISCRIMINATION).

Starting with *Missouri ex rel. Gaines v. Canada* (1938), the Court began to require the integration of graduate and professional schools, on the theory that separate schools for blacks could never be equal. In *Henderson v. United States* (1950) the United States government joined black plaintiffs in convincing the Supreme Court that de jure segregation on interstate railroad dining cars was unconstitutional. This case, along with others forcing the integration of graduate and law schools, set the stage for *Brown v. Board of Education* (1954). There the Court held that in "the field of public education the doctrine of 'separate but equal' has no place" (p. 495). In *Gayle v. Browder* (1956) the Court silently overturned *Plessy* by upholding a *declaratory judgment invalidating statutes requiring segregation on public transportation in Montgomery, Alabama. This case stemmed from the Montgomery Bus Boycott, which catapulted the Rev. Dr. Martin Luther King, Jr. to national fame. Within a decade the Court had applied this doctrine to all forms of statutorily mandated segregation. The last case to reach this result was *Loving v. Virginia* (1967), which struck down Virginia's antimiscegenation statute.

(See also RACE AND RACISM.)

Paul Finkelman

**Selection of Justices.** The selection of Supreme Court justices is of enormous importance since the behavior of the Court, a relatively unconstrained institution, largely reflects its membership. Judicial selection is a political process with few formal requirements. The Constitution (Art. II) simply states that the president "shall nominate . . . and with the Advice and Consent of the Senate . . . appoint . . . judges of the Supreme Court." The process of presidential nomination, senatorial confirmation, and presidential appointment does not even include the formal requirement that the nominee be a lawyer, although surely no president would nominate nor Senate confirm someone lacking legal training.

Creating a judicial selection process was a major concern at the Constitutional Convention. Early proposals sought either Senate appointment or joint House-Senate action. The Federalists, however, wanted the national perspective of a strong executive role. Late during the Conven-

tion, a compromise was reached. The executive and legislative branch would play a selection role, and tenure during good behavior would insulate justices from political pressures.

While Article II, the Constitution's "presidential power" blueprint, set the terms for judicial selection, the framers never clarified the exact meaning of "advice and consent," and periodic efforts to amend the Constitution suggested including the House of Representatives in the process or electoral selection. If Alexander *Hamilton and the Federalists thought they won a process with a perfunctory Senate approval role, that has certainly not transpired. Historically, about 20 percent of Supreme Court nominees have not been confirmed, with rejection rates running disproportionately high during the nineteenth century and the last three decades. Prior to the withdrawal of Abe *Fortas, Lyndon Johnson's nominee to the chief justiceship in 1968, the only rejected twentieth-century nomination was that of John *Parker in 1930. Since Fortas, two of Richard *Nixon's nominees (Clement *Haynsworth in 1969 and G. Harrold *Carswell in 1970) were defeated. The Senate in 1987 also rejected Ronald *Reagan's nomination of Robert *Bork in one of the greatest judicial selection battles in American history. Reagan's subsequent candidate, Douglas *Ginsburg, withdrew from consideration before his formal nomination (see NOMINEES, REJECTION OF).

Vacancies on the Court march to the tune of an irregular drummer. None, for example, occurred during Franklin *Roosevelt's first term, yet FDR enjoyed five appointments during his second term. Nixon was able to remake the liberal Warren Court in his own more conservative image with four appointments during his first term. Gerald Ford had the opportunity to appoint a Supreme Court justice despite his short tenure. Jimmy Carter, on the other hand, was the first president in more than a century not to have the opportunity to appoint a justice. During his eight-year presidency Reagan filled four vacancies.

*Actors in the Selection of Justices.* The president is the only individual constitutionally empowered to nominate a justice, yet he must consult widely. Supreme Court nominees are more likely to be known personally by the president and to be his own choice than are nominees to the *lower federal courts. Nevertheless, presidents will rely heavily on Justice Department personnel (particularly the attorney general) and White House staff members for assistance in generating candidates and choosing among them. Occasionally, such "assistance" makes the president's decision more difficult. Thus, in the wake of Reagan's Bork defeat, White House staff members desired a more moderate nominee while hard line Justice Department conservatives continued seeking an ideological appointment.

In addition to advice from within their own administrations, presidents are inundated with unsolicited suggestions from interested groups and individuals. Prospective nominees may pursue their own candidacy, and sitting justices attempt to influence nominations. Thus, for example, Justice Harlan *Stone actively supported the choice of Benjamin *Cardozo, even offering to resign to facilitate his fellow New Yorker's chances. As chief justice, William Howard *Taft attempted to influence several appointments, and Warren *Burger acted on behalf of nominees Haynsworth, Carswell, and Bork as well as Justices Harry *Blackmun and Sandra Day *O'Connor.

Supreme Court appointments are national in scope and of critical importance. Consequently, all senators believe they have a watchdog role to play. Controversy exists over what criteria are appropriate in exercising advice and consent: whether senators must limit their assessment only to the ethics and professional competence of a nominee or, alternatively, whether ideological and/or philosophical considerations are more important. Bork's defeat clearly suggests that senators may consider any factors during confirmation that the president considered in making a nomination (see SENATE JUDICIARY COMMITTEE).

Another important actor in the selection of justices is the *American Bar Association Standing Committee on Federal Judiciary. The role of the committee, established in 1946, has varied with its influence generally greatest when a Republican occupies the presidency. The committee rates Supreme Court candidates "well qualified," "not opposed," or "not qualified." A unanimous finding of "well qualified" clearly facilitates confirmation; a more ambiguous evaluation foreshadows trouble for a nominee.

Finally, it should be noted, numerous interest groups may be activated to support a nominee or fan the flames of opposition during the confirmation process. In the protracted Senate battle over Robert Bork among those opposing the nomination were the *ACLU, the *NAACP, *NOW, the AFL-CIO, Common Cause, and the Sierra Club. Bork's supporters included the American Conservative Union, NCPAC, the Fraternal Order of Police, and the National Right to Work Committee. While the scope of mobilization over the Bork nomination may have been unprecedented, the tradition of group involvement in the appointment process is a long one. Conservative groups were quite active in the effort to deny a justiceship to Brandeis in 1916. Similarly, labor organizations and the NAACP were critical elements in the Parker, Haynsworth, and Carswell defeats (see NOMINATIONS, CONTROVERSIAL).

**Criteria for the Selection of Justices.** Numerous criteria operate in the selection process including representational, partisan and political, personal, professional, and ideological concerns. Presidents utilize vacancies to reward identifiable

constituencies. They seek to balance geographical, religious, ethnic, and, most recently, gender concerns. Geographical balance has always been sought on the Court and, indeed, almost served to disqualify Cardozo from consideration since sitting justices Stone and Charles Evans *Hughes were also from New York. Nixon's "southern strategy" was, in large measure, politically motivated and attempted to satisfy elements of his electoral coalition and influential supporter South Carolina senator Strom Thurmond.

The quest for religious balance has also shaped recruitment. From Louis *Brandeis's 1916 appointment through Fortas's 1969 resignation, a Jewish justice sat on the Court; indeed, Justices Cardozo, Felix *Frankfurter, Arthur *Goldberg, and Fortas actually occupied the same "Jewish seat" in succession. Similarly, a Catholic has sat on the Court since 1894 except for the brief period between Frank *Murphy's death (1949) and William *Brennan's appointment (1956). Lyndon Johnson's appointment of Thurgood *Marshall created a "black seat," continued by George Bush's nomination of Clarence *Thomas to succeed him. Sandra Day O'Connor's historic appointment by President Reagan augers well for women.

Political and partisan motives often complement representational concerns. Nixon's southern strategy sought representation and votes. Much was to be gained politically by Gerald Ford, after Watergate, through the seemingly nonpolitical appointment of respected moderate John Paul *Stevens. Eisenhower, facing reelection, made a statesmanlike appointment (and bowed to the opposition) choosing Democrat William Brennan. Well over 90 percent of nominees are members of the president's party, while the rare exceptions (such as Nixon's nomination of conservative Democrat Lewis *Powell) are readily understood. Personal motivations may also play a role in some nominations. Truman's appointees included close friends Harold *Burton, Sherman *Minton, Fred *Vinson and Tom *Clark. Kennedy appointed a top campaign aide, Byron *White, while Johnson designated his close adviser and confidant Abe Fortas.

The emphasis a president places on partisan and political motivations as well as his reliance on personal relationships suggests the role that ideology may play in recruitment. This does not mean a president expects his nominees to agree with him on each and every case. Rather, a president may be concerned that his nominees share his broad views about the nature and meaning of American constitutionalism and the Court's policy-making role. Nixon sought to appoint "strict constructionists," although some would argue that this was shorthand for seeking nominees with narrow conceptions of personal rights and hard line "law and order" stances. The amount of controversy over a candidate's ideology will be commensurate with how "extreme" an ideological commitment appears to be as well as how pivotal a given vacancy is on the Court. Thus, Antonin *Scalia, perhaps even more of a "mainstream" conservative than Robert Bork, was easily confirmed prior to Bork's ill-fated nomination since Scalia's public persona seemed less ideologically extreme and his seating would not fundamentally alter the Court's ideological balance.

There is no widespread agreement about what qualities a jurist should possess, and attacks on a candidate's credentials may be a smokescreen for ideological opposition. It is axiomatic that a president wishes to appoint well-qualified and respected justices and, at times, inherent quality may rise above all of the factors arrayed against it. Such was the case when Republican president Hoover appointed Cardozo when all of the representational criteria were "wrong." Cardozo was a Democrat, a Jew (with Jewish justice Brandeis already on the Court), and a New Yorker (on a Court including New Yorkers Stone and Hughes). Debate over professional qualifications of a nominee reached its nadir when Nebraska senator Hruska, floor manager for the Carswell nomination, struck a chord for mediocrity by asserting, "Even if he is mediocre there are a lot of mediocre judges and people and lawyers. They are entitled to a little representation aren't they, and a little chance? We can't have all Brandeises, Cardozos and Frankfurters and stuff like that there."

Another issue that surfaces when considering professional qualifications is whether a justice needs prior judicial experience. Historically, Republican presidents have been most concerned about such experience. Clearly, many renowned justices including Oliver Wendell *Holmes, Taft, Cardozo, Burger, and Brennan served on the Court only after lengthy apprenticeships on state or lower federal tribunals. A long list of equally renowned justices lacking prior judicial experience exists as well, including Justices Brandeis, Frankfurter, William O. *Douglas, and Powell and Chief Justices John *Marshall and Earl *Warren.

*Looking Ahead.* Today, there has been an explicit politicization of the appointment process and a blatant ideologizing of the Court by presidents. When FDR sought to alter a Court blocking his *New Deal policies he felt compelled to justify *court packing as an effort to aid overworked elderly jurists. By 1968, Nixon was openly utilizing judicial vacancies as a campaign issue and in 1972 he boasted about successfully changing the direction of judicial policies. Subsequent presidential campaigns have utilized prospective judicial appointments as an issue.

Presidential actions have corresponded with a public increasingly concerned with the policy views of its members. As the Court continues to focus on issues such as *abortion and *affirmative action, and as the public continues to see these issues resolved with great divisiveness, concern over appointments will only increase.

Appointment transactions will generally run smoothly when the objective quality of the nominee is clear, ethical problems are not raised, and ideological extremism is not feared. Defeat of a nominee appears to be quite possible, however, when questions of competency are credible (Carswell), ethical considerations are raised (Fortas, Haynsworth, Thomas), or fears of ideological extremism are widespread (Bork). Presidents are generally more successful in gaining confirmation earlier, rather than later in their administrations. Similarly, the partisan makeup of the Senate will affect the president's success rate and appointment discretion with greater presidential freedom when the Senate is controlled by his party.

(See also APPOINTMENT AND REMOVAL POWER.)

□ Henry J. Abraham, *Justices and Presidents*, 2d ed. (1985). Harold W. Chase, *Federal Judges: The Appointing Process* (1972). David J. Danelski, *A Supreme Court Justice is Appointed* (1964). Joel B. Grossman, *Lawyers and Judges* (1965). Elliot E. Slotnick

**Selective Draft Law Cases.** 245 U.S. 366 (1918), argued 13–14 Dec. 1917, decided 7 Jan. 1918 by vote of 9 to 0, White for the Court. Not until after the passage of the Selective Service Act of 1917 was the authority of the federal government to draft citizens for military duty tested. Convicted violators of the act appealed to the Supreme Court on grounds that the draft was incompatible with free government and individual liberty, that congressional authority to raise armies was limited by the scope and purposes of the constitutional clause providing for calling the state militia into national service, and that the draft was in conflict with the *Thirteenth Amendment's prohibition of involuntary servitude and the *First Amendment's religion clauses. Chief Justice Edward D. *White, citing Anglo-American history and the common practice of nations, ruled that *citizenship carried with it a clear obligation to perform the "supreme and noble duty of contributing to the defense of the rights and honor of the nation" (p. 390). How such service could be characterized as involuntary servitude or how the act with its religious exemption for conscientious objectors could be viewed as establishing religion, White was at a loss to understand. Most of the opinion was addressed to a refutation of the claims that the militia clause imposed limitations on the broad authority of Congress to raise and support armies. Neither in 1918 nor later would the Court challenge congressional authority to institute a draft. (See also CONSCIENTIOUS OBJECTION; CONSCRIPTION; RELIGION.)

John E. Semonche

**Selective Exclusiveness.** In *Cooley* v. *Board of Wardens* (1852), a case involving a Pennsylvania pilotage law, the Court held that the power to regulate interstate commerce was not granted exclusively to the national government. In the Court's view, although some aspects of commerce necessitated uniform national rules established by Congress, other areas compelled diversity among the states and required *state regulation. The Court, Justice Benjamin R. *Curtis stated, needed to assess *state regulations of commerce on a case-by-case basis, in order to decide whether the issue in question required uniformity or diversity.

This notion of the "selective exclusiveness" of congressional power under the Commerce Clause did not definitively solve the problem of allocating state and federal power over commerce. It did, however, mark a shift in the Court's approach to the issue, away from arguments over the relative sovereignty of the federal and state governments (see STATE SOVEREIGNTY AND STATES' RIGHTS) and toward a more pragmatic and economically realistic view of commercial regulation.

(See also COMMERCE POWER.)

Timothy S. Huebner

**Self-Incrimination.** The *Fifth Amendment provides that no person "shall be compelled in any criminal case to be a witness against himself." The right applies to investigatory processes, pretrial disclosures, and trials themselves, as well as to testimony in civil, administrative, and legislative proceedings. Built on the *common-law right to silence, the self-incrimination protection has to be asserted to be realized.

Contemporary Supreme Court interpretation of this Fifth Amendment provision dates from *Twining v. New Jersey (1908), where the Court argued that protection from compulsory self-incrimination is not a fundamental right but an important rule of evidence. Current interpretation builds on the Court's rejection of Twining in *Malloy v. Hogan (1964), which applied the protection against compulsory self-incrimination to the states (see INCORPORATION DOCTRINE). The Warren Court reinforced this incorporation of the Fifth Amendment when it ruled in *Miranda v. Arizona (1966) that protection from compulsory self-incrimination required police to remind criminal suspects of this procedural guarantee.

Generally, the Supreme Court has expanded the protection provided by the constitutional guarantee of a right to remain silent. This is especially obvious in the Court's application of the privilege against self-incrimination to pretrial and noncriminal proceedings and the affirmative obligations included in the famous Miranda decision. These affirmative obligations are important because they cover almost all police interrogations of criminal suspects and because they specify procedures to protect the privilege against self-incrimination.

These twentieth-century developments are rooted in part in British legal history. For example, prior to the sixteenth century, forced oaths and confessions were excluded from trials, while by the late eighteenth century, confessions forced before trial were also excluded. As these rules of evidence took hold in American law, the Supreme Court relied on the voluntariness test to judge whether undue pressure to waive Fifth Amendment protections had been brought to bear on criminal defendants. The Supreme Court's Miranda decision added a new dimension to these efforts to insure that defendants were not compelled to waive the privilege against self-incrimination.

The Court's decision in Miranda called considerable attention to the privilege against self-incrimination, attention that earlier was engendered when Senator Joseph McCarthy conducted congressional hearings on Communists in the United States. Several witnesses at the McCarthy hearings refused to testify on grounds that they were likely to incriminate themselves. These assertions were frequently interpreted as admissions of guilt and the witnesses labeled "Fifth Amendment Communists" (see COMMUNISM AND COLD WAR).

When the state wants or needs the testimony of individuals who assert their privilege against self-incrimination, particular inducements can be exercised. These include two grants of immunity, transactional and use. The former guarantees that the witness will not be prosecuted for anything that transacts from his or her testimony, while the latter protects the witness against prosecutorial use of any evidence drawn from his or her testimony (see FIFTH AMENDMENT IMMUNITY).

Regardless of the controversies that have surrounded the privilege against self-incrimination, it remains an important right in criminal due process. The right builds on common-law rules of evidence, reflects our reluctance to compel anyone to incriminate himself, and remains an integral part of our adversarial system of justice.

(See also DUE PROCESS, PROCEDURAL.)

Susette M. Talarico

**Senate Judiciary Committee.** Established in 1816 as one of the Senate's original eleven standing committees, the Judiciary Committee quickly became a powerful influence on national legislation and, before the *Civil War, played a role in spurring the adoption of the Compromise of 1850. The committee's power was later felt during the post–Civil War era when it shared jurisdiction over federal Reconstruction efforts.

Despite the committee's broad impact on national government, it is most popularly known for investigating nominees to the federal bench (see SELECTION OF JUSTICES). While the Constitution requires the advice and consent of the full Senate on presidential nominees, in 1868 the Senate directed that all nominations would first be referred to an appropriate committee for review. Customarily, then, the Judiciary Committee receives the president's judicial nominations from the full Senate for investigation. Afterward, the committee reports its findings and recommendations (if any) to the full Senate for a vote on the nominee.

The committee's handling of nominations has been a subject of controversy almost from the origins of that practice. Early assessments of the committee leveled the same charges that were brought against the full Senate's treatment of nominations, that it was a system rife with patronage and secrecy. Recent attention has been drawn, however, to the committee's superficial inquiry into a nominee's qualifications and the dangers posed by that practice for a competent and independent judiciary. On closer examination, the sheer number of nominees currently referred to the committee makes it improbable that a detailed inquiry may readily occur. For example, in the year 1989–1990, President George Bush nominated forty-eight district court and eighteen appellate court judges, and in 1990 Congress created eighty-five new federal judgeships. Under such constraints, it is not unusual for committee chairmen to further delegate responsibilities to subcommittees for reviewing lower court nominees.

In the case of Supreme Court nominees, however, the full committee normally conducts a hearing. The present dispute in this setting is not the shallowness of the committee's questioning, but rather the depth and extent of its probing into the nominee's background. The furor surrounding Justice Clarence *Thomas's nomination suggests to some the need to remove a nominee's personal qualities and political affiliation from the committee's scrutiny. However, the history of Supreme Court nominations show that personal and political characteristics play a considerable role in the committee's deliberations. Of the twenty-six persons whose nominations to the Court have been rejected or withdrawn, only five are currently seen as judicially unqualified. Indeed, vigorous opposition during hearings was brought to bear even on the nomination of such luminaries as Justice Louis *Brandeis (the first Jewish nominee), Justice Hugo *Black (a former Ku Klux Klan member), and Justice Felix *Frankfurter (a foreign-born, Jewish liberal). (See NOMINEES, REJECTION OF.)

But not all struggles within the committee's hearing end in triumph for the nominee. Six nominees out of forty have been rejected or withdrawn in the last sixty years. Most memorable among these is Justice Abe *Fortas, President Lyndon Johnson's nominee for *chief justice, who resigned from the bench amid allegations of financial misconduct. In another example, Judge Douglas *Ginsburg withdrew his name after accusations surfaced of former illegal drug use. Finally, Judge Robert *Bork was cast by some committee

members as a rigid intellectual, and after his name was recommended unfavorably to the full Senate, President Ronald *Reagan's nominee was defeated (see NOMINATIONS, CONTROVERSIAL).

While committee hearings concerning Supreme Court nominees have historically delved into political and personal qualifications, little precedent exists for the current state of the hearings as a national *cause célèbre*. For the nation's first 140 years, the nominees were rarely invited to appear before the Senate, and if they were invited, the nominees declined out of a sense of decorum. However, to answer questions regarding his actions as attorney general, Harlan *Stone, in 1925, became the first nominee to appear before the Committee. Next, Felix Frankfurter addressed the committee in 1939 when slanderous accusations surfaced following his nomination. Only one other justice appeared at the committee's hearing until John *Harlan's testimony in 1955. The subsequent nineteen nominees have all made statements during the Committee's investigation. Because only twenty-two of the 147 Supreme Court nominees have ben interrogated by the committee, those calling for the committee's reform in the post-Thomas era find support in the relatively high quality of the justices approved by the Senate without personal appearances. Perhaps, after all, the committee's recent practice of inviting testimony by the nominee is not necessary for ensuring a competent and independent Supreme Court.

Whatever may be the place occupied by presidential nominees, the future of the Judiciary Committee will remain unique within American political life. Operating constitutionally as a screen on executive nominations, the committee is a fulcrum balancing the powers exerted by the coordinate branches. By nomination, presidents seek to leave a mark on a judicial institution that will far outlive their administration. The Senate's power of advice and consent acts as a veto of presidential designs. Unlike the check of legislative override, the ability to reject a judicial nominee has more than a political background. Instead, the Senate is composing a supreme and independent judicial body that itself exercises *judicial review over Congress's activities. The forces at play in the Judiciary Committee, then, touch the foundation of American constitutionalism and will continue to make the committee's work, in any form, a worthy object of public attention.

□ Henry J. Abraham. *Justices and Presidents*, 3d ed. (1991). Robert C. Byrd. *The Senate (1789–1989): Addresses on the History of the United States Senate*, edited by Wendy Wolf (1989).       Kermit L. Hall and Mitchell S. Ritchie

**Senatorial Courtesy** requires that care be taken by the president that, above all, the nominee to a high-level federal position is not personally obnoxious to a home-state senator (or other significant political personage) on pain of having him or her invoke that age-old, almost invariably honored, custom—an almost certain death knell to confirmation by the Senate. The custom or practice is based on the assumption that a president will, as a matter of political patronage, practice, and courtesy, ipso facto engage in consultation prior to the nominee's designation, provided usually that the senator, or other pertinent political power, is a member of the president's political party.

Senatorial courtesy dates back to the first years of the Republic, when the Senate recognized the need for solidarity to prevent a president from appointing a senator's political adversary to high office. Actually, the practice commenced in the very first session of Congress in 1789, when President George *Washington nominated Benjamin Fisbourn as a naval officer in the port of Savannah, Georgia. Although apparently well qualified, Fishbourn was opposed by Georgia's two United States senators, and Washington withdrew his nomination when it was apparent that the Senate would side with its Georgia colleagues. Washington subsequently nominated someone favored by the two legislators, thereby enshrining the concept of senatorial courtesy perpetually. Ensuing events have made amply clear that if a president fails to adhere to this custom, the aggrieved senator's or senators' colleagues will almost certainly be supportive of the latter on their call for the nominee's defeat as a matter of courtesy, of a fraternal quid pro quo.

An appropriate application of senatorial courtesy in a specific area of the realm of presidential nominations is that of the chief executive's selections for the federal bench. In view of the fact that federal judges are appointed for "good behavior,"—that is, in effect for life—a judicial post represents one of the plums available to a president. Not only is it a lifetime appointment, it enables the president at the very least to endeavor to single out candidates who generally seem to agree with his own constitutional cum jurisprudential-political philosophy. No wonder, then, that senatorial courtesy enters here more pronouncedly and more predictably than for any other post over which the president has appointive authority. Consequently, chairpersons of the Senate Committee on the Judiciary, which is charged with the approval of all candidates for the federal bench, developed through the years a system of concurrence by home state senators that has become part and parcel of the senatorial courtesy practice. Thus, until Senator Edward M. Kennedy, the incoming chairman of the *Senate Judiciary Committee, announced early in 1979 that he would not unilaterally table a nomination simply because a "blue slip" is not returned by a colleague concerned by and interested in a nominee, the so-called blue slip system had institutionalized senatorial courtesy. It proceeded as follows: once the president formally nominated a candidate for the judiciary, the Senate Judiciary Committee would send to each of the nominee's home-state senators a blue sheet of paper, asking his or her "opinion and information concerning the nomination." In fact, the blue slip asked whether the chief executive's formal choice was either the person the home-state senator(s) wanted or at least could agree to. If a senator approved, he or she returned the blue slip to the committee; if not, the senator retained the slip. If the senator was from the president's own party, a withheld blue slip amounted to a one-person veto, terminating the nominee's chances.

Senator Kennedy's bold effort to end this system met with considerable condemnation by a number of his committee colleagues, and when Senator Strom Thurmond succeeded to the chair of the committee in 1981, he was at first inclined to reinstitute it but evidently decided to handle matters more informally. His 1987 successor, Senator Joseph R. Biden, announced a new policy under which failure to consult with the home-state senator, combined with a negative blue slip, would automatically kill a nomination.

(See also APPOINTMENT AND REMOVAL POWER; SELECTION OF JUSTICES.)

□ Henry J. Abraham, *The Judicial Process: An Introductory Analysis of the Courts of the United States, England, and France,* 6th ed. (1992).                    Henry J. Abraham

**Seniority.** Supreme Court justices have traditionally employed seniority to resolve a variety of issues. Generally, seniority is determined by the length of time a justice has held a seat on the Supreme Court. The *chief justice alone is exempt from the considerations related to seniority.

Some of the consequences of the seniority tradition involve matters of etiquette. The senior justices may choose to occupy the four larger office suites in the Court's building. They are also given the more spacious spots around the Court's conference table, with the four junior justices crowded along one side. The newer justices are seated on the ends of the dais in the courtroom. The most junior justice functions as the gatekeeper, receiving and sending messages during the Court's private conferences; he or she also speaks first when the Court publicly announces the decision in a case.

Seniority controls more important procedural matters. In conference, the justices speak in descending order of seniority. This sequence allows the long-term members to frame the issues, shape deliberations, and exhaust discussion of relevant perspectives on a case, often to the frustration of the more junior justices. And when the chief justice, normally responsible for the important task of assigning the job of drafting the opinion in a case, is not part of the majority, the senior associate justice who is part of the majority coalition assumes the task (see OPINIONS, ASSIGNMENT AND WRITING OF).

In most instances, seniority provides a simple and efficient method for resolving questions of etiquette and procedure. However, there have been a number of instances in which the seniority of particular justices has been unclear. When two or more vacancies arise simultaneously, confusion may occur. Scholars disagree as to the line of succession for several nineteenth- and early twentieth-century justices.

□ George A. Christensen, "Supreme Court Succession, or, Who Succeeded Whom," *The Supreme Court Historical Society Quarterly* 4 (Summer 1982): 2–7.

Robert J. Janosik

**Separability of Statutes.** The problem of the separability of statutes arises when courts construe the constitutionality of a statute that contains more than one provision. The question arises: what is the effect of a judicial decision that rules that one part of a statute is invalid with respect to the other parts? The first decision of a *state court holding that the invalidity of a part of a statute might nullify the remainder was *Warren v. City of Charlestown*, rendered by the highest court of Massachusetts in 1854.

The Supreme Court of the United States began to apply this doctrine after about 1870, in effect ruling that the presumption is against the multilation of a statute. For example, when the Court held in 1895 that the federal income tax act of 1894 was invalid as it applied to incomes derived from property, it went on to rule that those portions of the statute that levied taxes on incomes derived from professions, trades, and employments were also invalid, on the grounds that the parts of the statute were inseparable. In other words, the Court decided that Congress did not intend to put the whole burden of this tax on incomes derived from professions, trades and employments. While a statute may be valid in part, and invalid in part, this is so only if the parts are independent of each other; the rule is otherwise when the parts are inseparable (*Pollock v. Farmers' Loan & Trust Co.*, 1895).

The problem of separability became more complicated when legislatures began to add separability or "savings" clauses to statutes. A savings clause declares that it is the legislature's intent that a judicial declaration of invalidity of a part of a statute shall not affect the validity of the rest of the statute. On the whole, courts have read such savings clauses to mean that only separable provisions survive. For example, in the leading case of *Williams v. Standard Oil Co. of Louisiana* (1929), the Supreme Court ruled invalid a portion of a Tennessee statute regulating the retail price of gasoline and then ruled unconstitutional other parts of the statute dealing with such matters as record keeping, investigations, the gathering of data, and the issuance of permits, even though the legislature had written a savings clause into the statute. A savings clause, the Court declared,

is not an inexorable command, but only an aid to construction; it merely establishes a presumption that, like all presumptions, may be overcome. This particular statute, the Court held, was indivisible; the information and licensing provisions were designed, in its judgment, to facilitate the regulation of prices. Similar reasoning was applied to invalidate the Guffey-Snyder Coal Act in *Carter v. Carter Coal Co.* (1936).

David Fellman

**Separate But Equal Doctrine** derived from the Supreme Court's decision in *Plessy v. Ferguson* (1896) that state-mandated separation of the races in public transportation did not violate the *Thirteenth Amendment's ban on involuntary servitude or the *Fourteenth Amendment's *Equal Protection and *Due Process Clauses so long as the facilities provided for the segregated races were equal.

In *Plessy*, all the justices save John Marshall *Harlan assumed that the custom of segregation was so well established in the South and so beneficial to both races that it created no stigma in and of itself (see SEGREGATION, DE JURE). Citing rulings in interstate transportation cases in which the Court found that Louisiana could not prevent segregation by race in interstate travel (*Hall v. DeCuir*, 1878) but Mississippi could segregate by race in intrastate carriers (*Louisville, New Orleans & Texas Railway Co. v. Mississippi*, 1890), Justice Henry B. *Brown held that "Laws permitting, and even requiring . . . separation [of the races], in places where they are liable to be brought into contact, do not necessarily imply the inferiority of either race to the other, and have been generally, if not universally, recognized as within the competency of the state legislatures in the exercise of their police power" (p. 544).

In a series of cases commencing in 1898, the Court extended the separate but equal doctrine from public transportation to public education. Racial segregation of schools predated racial segregation in public transportation, and Justice Brown cited state school-segregation rulings in *Plessy*. The first and most noteworthy of these rulings was *Roberts v. City of Boston* (1849), in which Massachusetts Chief Justice Lemuel Shaw decided that segregation of black schoolchildren did not violate the equality clause of the Massachusetts State Constitution. The Supreme Court followed *Roberts* in *Cumming v. Richmond County Board of Education* (1899) and *Gong Lum v. Rice* (1927). Under Jim Crow education laws, black schools were woefully financed, staffed, and maintained compared to white schools. Even when black students were provided with their own schools, they often had to go many miles past the "whites only" school in their neighborhood to reach the "colored" school. Moreover, they had to provide their own transportation while whites were bused to their schools.

From 1938 to 1950, the separate but equal

doctrine was hobbled by a series of Court decisions requiring *professional schools at state universities in Missouri, Oklahoma, and Texas to desegregate, and crippled in *Brown v. Board of Education (1954). Chief Justice Earl *Warren, writing for a unanimous court, held that the separate but equal rationale in elementary school education violated the Equal Protection Clause of the Fourteenth Amendment. In a series of *per curiam decisions thereafter, the Court extended the Brown doctrine to other public facilities. The *Civil Rights Act of 1964 gave separate but equal doctrine its death blow, and the court upheld the constitutionality of the act in *Heart of Atlanta Motel v. United States (1964). The separate but equal doctrine was formally interred in *Green v. School Board of New Kent County (1968), in which Justice William J. *Brennan announced that the Fourteenth Amendment could not be satisfied by anything less than unitary school systems.

(See also RACE AND RACISM.)

□ Richard A. Kluger, Simple Justice: The History of Brown v. Board of Education and Black America's Struggle for Equality (1976).　　　　　　　　Peter Charles Hoffer

**Separation of Powers.** In American discourse separation of powers is more a name than a description. None of the three branches (legislative, executive, or judicial) of the national government are clearly separate from one another. Congress, for example, has an impeachment club to check the others; the president's *veto power is plainly legislative in nature. No wonder James *Madison in The *Federalist, no. 47, undertook to answer the Anti-Federalist charge that "The several departments of power are [not separated but] blended in such a manner as at once to destroy all symmetry and beauty of form, and to expose some of the essential parts of the edifice to the danger of being crushed by the disproportionate weight of other parts." Madison's answer was that Montesquieu—the "oracle" of separation—did not mean that "departments ought to have no partial agency in, or control over, the acts of each other." He meant rather that "the whole power of one department [should not be] exercised by the same hands which possess the whole power of another department." The merit of "blending," according to Madison, was that along with bicameralism and *federalism it produced a safety net of "checks and balances."

A crucial problem is that split power inevitably entails split accountability. No wonder then that so many difficulties in American government spring ultimately from our divided power system. In contrast, the parliamentary system seeks safety in clear, direct lines of electoral accountability—and less in a mechanistic clash of sundered agencies of government. Concentrating power for effective action in a prime minister, it makes that person directly amenable to parliament while the latter is directly amenable to the

electorate. This scheme largely eliminates what for us is a persistent quandary: which of several shells hide the peas of power and responsibility. That quandary partially accounts for the sense of frustration that is so widespread in the American electorate.

*Historical Background.* What was the evil that checks and balances were designed to cure? The founders presumably were haunted by monarchy and, in particular, George III. Perhaps, as some progressive historians insist, they feared the untutored masses. In this view the Constitution was foisted upon the country as an antidote against "the evils of democracy." The prime purpose allegedly was to protect vested interests by such curbs upon the masses as checks and balances—especially judicial review—and a central government in which only the House of Representatives was to be popularly elected.

Madison suggested in The Federalist that what most moved the founders was neither monarchy nor the masses but human nature, as they understood it. In their view mankind is moved less by reason than by passion, less by benevolence than by self-interest. As Alexander *Hamilton put it: "Why has government been instituted at all? Because the passions of men will not conform to the dictates of reason and justice without constraint" (Federalist, no. 15). Separated powers along with checks and balances are prominent among the several "interior" and "exterior" constraints described in The Federalist, nos. 10, 47, 51. It is crucial that these essays are concerned with checking both minority and majority "factions" that spring from man's self-interest, whereas the progressives seem to have thought majorities could do no wrong.

But if majority as well as minority factions were to be constrained, how could government be expected to function efficiently? The answer must be that the founders favored inefficient government checked and balanced against itself because it seemed safer than the greater risk of tyranny in a more efficient system. The choice was relatively easy given the simple, static society of 1787 that required, by modern standards, very little government. Surely the founders might reasonably have supposed that the modest needs of their day could be met by machinery that at best would work slowly and, perhaps, only when supported by a consensus of opinion so great as to neutralize the built-in impediments. While the simple community the founders knew has long since passed away, their basic plan of government lives on.

*Separation and the Party System.* The need for coordination of the separated branches helps to explain the extraconstitutional rise of our political party system that began in President George *Washington's administration. Former members of the Constitutional Convention moved into all branches of the new government. Indeed, the convention's Federalist values prevailed throughout the Washington administration and in the Supreme Court as well. That is why, despite checks and balances, Hamilton was able to achieve speedily his famous, if controversial, legislative program. The key to his success was a kind of embryonic one-party system that bridged and neutralized checks and balances. The lesson was not lost on Thomas *Jefferson. Recognizing that opposition from within was futile, he resigned from Washington's cabinet to build and lead an opposing party. What he achieved was an informal constitutional amendment that made political parties a vital element of American government.

Strong parties promote strong government because they cultivate cooperation at the expense of friction among the separated organs. Thus in the long view the history of American government seems a history of spasms. In weak party eras when the founders' system prevails, Congress and the president are apt to be at odds. In strong-party eras the built-in friction is ameliorated. Then we are apt to have vigorous legislative programs in response to accumulated problems. President Woodrow Wilson's crucial reforms were the fruit of the high tide of the progressive movement, which for a brief time reinvigorated both major parties (See PROGRESSIVISM). Later the Great Depression gave Franklin D. *Roosevelt the leverage to build a potent new Democratic party; a massive *New Deal program followed. By the 1950s that party had lost its zest as had the Republican party much earlier. Even the bright new Kennedy administration was frustrated in Congress. Then the shock of the assassination along with huge Democratic congressional majorities—thanks to Barry Goldwater's unsuccessful 1964 campaign—enabled President Lyndon B. Johnson to push a major reform program through Congress. Given the *Vietnam War, the period of harmony and vigorous legislative reform was brief. Then separation of powers produced another period of stagnation.

Those who like clear, logical lines of power and responsibility find all this at best discouraging. Others, perhaps more sensitive to mankind's long, unhappy experience with government, find that among the world's few free nations the United States does not suffer by comparison; that history portends enough congressional-presidential cooperation to meet pressing needs; that the gaps between these periods of creative harmony are in fact periods of gestation; that checks and balances have not prevented, but only delayed, innovation—thus promoting substantial consensus behind public policy. Of course, almost any determined and not insignificant minority generally can erect multiple constitutional or extraconstitutional barriers to frustrate virtually any proposal it finds seriously objectional.

*Judicial Independence in a Check and Balance System.* The Constitution contemplates both judicial independence and checks and balances.

It follows that the judiciary, particularly the Supreme Court, is the most separated and least checked of all the branches of government. When, in *Hammer v. Dagenhart* (1918), for example, it held unconstitutional federal restraints on child labor no more was required than the concurrence of five of its own members. Nothing more was required when in *Roe v. Wade* (1973) it killed virtually all existing restraints on *abortion. Yet to impose such edicts by *legislation* would require the approval of the Senate, the House of Representatives, and the president. A veto could be overriden only by a two-thirds majority in both houses of Congress. Moreover, unlike the nine Supreme Court justices, the members of Congress and the president are accountable to the votes in an election, which for most of them would be less than two years away. If, notwithstanding all these checks and balances the measures in question were adopted, they would face yet another hurdle; namely, judicial review.

Free of elections and fortified by tenure "during good behavior" with pay that may "not be diminished," no Supreme Court justice has ever been removed from office by the *impeachment process. Indeed, impeachment charges have been brought against a Supreme Court judge only once—almost two hundred years ago. That case against Justice Samuel *Chase seems to have established the principle that impeachment lies only for criminal conduct, not as reprisal against judicial points of view.

Supreme Court decisions have been overridden by constitutional amendment in only four instances (see REVERSAL OF COURT DECISIONS BY AMENDMENT). The *Eleventh, *Fourteenth, *Sixteenth, and *Twenty-sixth Amendments nullify, respectively, *Chisholm v. Georgia* (1793), Dred *Scott v. Sandford* (1857), *Pollock v. Farmers' Loan and Trust Co.* (1895), and *Oregon v. Mitchell* (1970). Numerous other *proposed* amendments aimed at court decisions relating, for example, to school busing, school prayers, equal rights for women, and abortion, have failed. In the end, of course, judges determine the meaning of amendments as they do with respect to other parts of the Constitution. This is to say the "checkee" determines the meaning and application—and thus the impact—of the check!

If these court-control devices may properly be called checks and balances, they have been rarely used. Yet the judiciary does not live in a political vacuum. It may not follow the election returns, but it is not entirely unresponsive to the social forces that determine election results. The strength or weakness of the political party system in any given era seems to affect the functioning not only of the president and Congress but of the Supreme Court as well. In eras when a strong party coordinates the efforts of the two political branches there seems to be little room for *judicial activism. Surely it is not by chance that each of our three outbursts of wholesale national policy-making by judges came when the party system was at peculiarly low ebb. Perhaps judges feel duty-bound to intervene when other branches falter, or maybe only then are they willing to risk wholesale intrusion upon the political processes. Large-scale court intrusion upon national policy did not begin until the Kansas-Nebraska Act (1854) had wrecked both major political parties. The disrupting issue was whether slavery should be allowed in the new territories. Congress being deadlocked (read "checked and balanced"), the Supreme Court undertook in *Dred Scott* v. *Sandford* (1857) to settle the matter. The result was a moral and legal disaster.

With the lingering death of the old sectional party system the Supreme Court again became a major policy maker. In a matter of months it killed the federal income tax in *Pollock* v. *Farmers' Loan and Trust Co.* (1895), emasculated the *Sherman Antitrust Act in *United States* v. *E. C. Knight Co.* (1895) and the Interstate Commerce Commission in *ICC* v. *Alabama Midland Railway Co.* (1897). So too it sanctioned the labor *injunction in *In re *Debs* (1895) along with racial segregation in *Plessy* v. *Ferguson* (1896). Later it struck down two federal efforts to restrict child labor as well as a host of state regulatory measures symbolized by *Lochner* v. *New York* (1905). With a brief respite in the Progressive Era this economic activism continued until 1937, devastating virtually the whole early New Deal legislative program.

The aggressive role that judges had played in the era of moribund sectional politics could not be maintained in the face of a potent new urban party system led by Franklin Roosevelt. The "old" Supreme Court surrendered early in 1937. In short order the New Deal Court repudiated most of the activist innovations of the years from 1890 through 1936.

The decisions in *Mapp* v. *Ohio* (1961) and *Baker* v. *Carr* (1962) seem to mark the beginning of a new judicial era. By the late 1960s Americans seem to have lost their capacity for self-government. Reasoned argument, compromise, and accommodation were increasingly replaced by polarization and violence in word and deed. There was no party coalition in command of a sufficiently stable majority to advance coherent policies. The decline of Franklin Roosevelt's dynamic urban party system seems to have invited another outburst of judicial activism—supposedly led by Chief Justice Earl *Warren.

*Judicial Enforcement of Separation.* By virtue of their power of judicial review, judges have the last word short of constitutional amendment on the allocation of authority among the three branches of the federal government. It is worth special notice that this includes power to set the bounds of their own authority—as well as their own immunity from outside checks and balances. This power, a part of the classic problem of judicial review, reinforces what was suggested above on other grounds; namely, that the judi-

ciary is at best only marginally within the checks-and-balances system. Virtually immune itself, it has enormous checking power with respect to all other organs of American government. Its decisions define the nature of congressional-presidential separation.

*Scope of Presidential Authority.* The Supreme Court ruled in *United States* v. *Curtiss-Wright Export Corporation* (1936) that the "investment of the Federal government with the powers of external sovereignty did not depend upon the affirmative grants of the Constitution [rather these powers] vested in the Federal government as a necessary concomitant of nationality" (p. 318). In a word, they are extraconstitutional in origin. Moreover, these "inherent" and "plenary" powers belong to "the President as the sole organ of the federal government in the field of international relations" (see INHERENT POWERS; PRESIDENTIAL EMERGENCY POWERS). On that basis the Supreme Court upheld a quasi-legislative presidential decree that forbade the sale in this country of war materials to those engaged in armed conflict in the Chaco. The purpose was to promote peace between Bolivia and Paraguay. The *Curtiss-Wright* decision has never been judicially qualified.

The Constitution authorizes the president to make treaties, subject to ratification by a two-thirds vote of the Senate. May the chief executive by virtue of his inherent foreign affairs power bypass the senatorial concurrence requirement by means of executive agreement? In *United States* v. *Belmont* (1937), affirming the Litvinov Agreement, the Supreme Court responded affirmatively though the Court's opinion rests in part on the "express" power of the president to recognize foreign nations. In the Litvinov accord President Roosevelt recognized the Soviet Union and accepted in satisfaction of Soviet debts property located in the United States that the Soviet Union had confiscated from Russian citizens. Presidential policy prevailed without approval of the Senate, and despite the law of the state in which the confiscated property was located. Thus, like a treaty, the Litvinov Agreement became the "supreme law of the land" under Article VI of the Constitution. Decisions of this type, especially *Missouri* v. *Holland* (1920), led eventually to the proposed Bricker Amendment (1954). Failing by only one vote in the Senate, the Bricker Amendment would have provided: "An international agreement other than a treaty shall become effective as internal law in the United States only by an act of Congress." While this proposed amendment was not adopted, the forces behind it seem to have softened the Court's language, though not its decisions. In *Dames and Moore* v. *Regan* (1981), the Court upheld President Jimmy Carter's executive agreement with Iran concerning the American hostages and private claims against Iranian assets in this country. Emphasizing the "narrowness" of its decision, confined to a claims settlement, the Court took care to observe this was not a situation "in which Congress has in some way resisted the exercise of Presidential authority" (p. 688).

*Goldwater* v. *Carter* (1979) raised the issue whether the president may terminate a treaty without the consent of Congress or the Senate. A court of appeals *en banc* decided in favor of President Carter, who, in conjunction with the recognition of China, had abrogated a treaty with Taiwan. The Supreme Court dismissed the case without decision on the merits. The net effect was a victory for presidential authority.

The Constitution authorizes Congress "to declare War," and makes the president commander in chief of the armed forces (see WAR POWERS). Moreover, the president plays, and was intended to play, a major role in the conduct of *foreign affairs. The classic and constant problem is to what extent, if any, may the presidential commander in chief properly use the military forces without a congressional declaration of war? This problem came before the Supreme Court when President Abraham *Lincoln instituted a naval blockade of the southern ports—clearly an act of war though Congress had not declared war. In the *Prize Cases* (1863), the justices upheld the president's action in the face of objections by those whose ships had been seized for trying to run the blockade. Four justices dissented powerfully. The problem of warlike measures in undeclared "wars," including the sending of draftees into combat, came before the judiciary repeatedly with respect to the Vietnam conflict. Ever since the *Prize Cases* the Supreme Court has left such issues to be resolved by Congress, the president, and the electorate. Obviously Congress acquiesced in the Vietnam and Civil wars in the sense that it provided the troops and money without which war would have been impossible. Moreover, Congress did not do with respect to either of these wars what it eventually did with respect to the "invasion" of Cambodia: cut off funding.

To avert an industrywide strike during the Korean conflict, President Harry S. Truman seized the privately owned steel mills. Congress had provided quite different ways for dealing with such crises. Government lawyers argued that the president had acted within his constitutional powers as chief executive and commander in chief. In *Youngstown Sheet & Tube Co.* v. *Sawyer* (1952), Justice Hugo *Black wrote a brief "opinion of the Court." The seizure, he said, could not be justified as an exercise of military power. Then, noting Congress's refusal to authorize what the president had done, the justice found it forbidden by separation of powers doctrine: "In the framework of our constitution, the President's power to see that the laws are faithfully executed refutes the idea that he is to be a lawmaker. . . . And the Constitution is neither silent nor equivocal about who shall make laws which the President is to execute" (p. 587). All of the other judges

found the problem more complex than did Justice Black. Even the five *concurring judges wrote separate opinions. The trouble was a premise that Justice Black ignored: both the Constitution and history reject strictly separated powers. While we have three quite distinct branches, each of them has some traces of legislative, executive, and judicial power. Moreover, what remains of the separation of powers has been qualified by history. The three dissenters noted an impressive array of presidential lawmaking. Without waiting for Congress, George Washington proclaimed neutrality; Thomas Jefferson bought Louisiana; James Monroe issued his famous doctrine; Andrew *Jackson removed federal deposits from the Bank of the United States; Lincoln emancipated the Confederacy slaves. This pattern continued through Roosevelt's Bank Holiday proclamation and his numerous war-effort edicts. The five justices who concurred in Black's judgment quite clearly could not accept the part of his opinion that would outlaw all presidential lawmaking and a large part of American history as well.

***Congress vis-à-vis the Executive.*** A corollary of the separation of powers doctrine holds that Congress may not delegate legislative power to the executive branch. Yet the Supreme Court in *J. W. Hampton* v. *United States* (1928) upheld an act of Congress giving the president authority to raise or lower tariffs within prescribed limits when he found such revision necessary to equalize the costs of production in the United States and other nations. This authorization was sustained on the ground that "If Congress shall lay down by legislative act an intelligible principle to which the ["delegee"] is directed to conform, such legislative action is not a forbidden delegation of legislative power" (p. 409).

*Delegation of Power.* Congress has often made such grants of authority to various executive and administrative agencies. Usually these grants are extremely broad and the guidelines so vague as to be essentially meaningless. For example, the *Interstate Commerce Commission is authorized to order "just and reasonable" railroad freight rates, and the Federal Communications Commission to license radio stations in accordance with "public convenience, interest or necessity." Similarly Congress provided for the renegotiation of *World War II procurement contracts and authorized the recovery from contractors of profits that administrative officials found "excessive." Save two instances, *Panama Refining Co.* v. *Ryan* (1935) and *Schechter Poultry Corp.* v. *United States* (1935), no congressional delegation of lawmaking power has been held invalid no matter how vague the purported guidelines. The two exceptions perhaps are best explained as part of the old laissez-faire judicial activism that virtually destroyed the early New Deal (see LAISSEZ-FAIRE CONSTITUTIONALISM). In effect, it is now enough both in law and practice for Congress merely to identify problems and leave solutions to administrative specialists. It is worth noticing that in *Mistretta v. United States* (1989) the Supreme Court found no improper delegation and no separation of powers problems in an act of Congress that gave an independent agency within the judicial branch the power to promulgate mandatory sentencing guidelines for federal courts.

An open-ended delegation may be an irresponsible passing of the buck. Sometimes, however, legislators resort to abstract public interest guides simply because they cannot foresee many of the mundane problems that necessarily attend implementation of their general policy objectives. Hence, the contemporary judicial approach is not to invalidate statutory delegations of power but to assure that they are accompanied by adequate controls. Many such controls are built into the administrative process itself; our concern here is presidential and congressional oversight. Until the *Chadha* case (1983; see below), Congress often retained a "legislative veto" with respect to the use by administrative agencies of delegated power.

*Administrative Personnel.* At issue in *Myers v. United States* (1926) was an act of Congress providing that postmasters could be appointed and removed by the president with Senate consent (see APPOINTMENT AND REMOVAL POWER). The Supreme Court held that the requirement of senatorial consent for removal was inconsistent with the constitutional grant of "the executive power" to the president and also with his duty to "take care that the laws be faithfully executed" (pp. 163–164). Without the power to control via unfettered removal authority the president would not be the *chief* executive.

The presidential victory in *Myers* was soon qualified. *Humphrey's Executor v. United States* (1935) arose under a statute providing that members of the Federal Trade Commission could be removed from their seven-year terms of office only "for inefficiency, neglect of duty, or malfeasance in office." President Roosevelt sought to remove Humphrey from office not on any of the statutory grounds but on the basis of *Myers*. A unanimous Court found the removal invalid. The Court distinguished between officials who perform purely executive functions as in *Myers* and those who perform quasi-judicial functions as in *Humphrey*. This is a classic example of promoting freedom through governmental inefficiency that springs from checks and balances. Mr. Humphrey was a holdover from the Hoover administration, which the electorate had rejected in 1932 by electing Roosevelt. Yet the *Humphrey* case means that a new administration must live with a person in high office whose policy views are clearly at odds with those of the new regime. Securing the independence of the regulatory commissions, *Humphrey* provided the foundation for a "headless fourth branch of government."

Just as the Supreme Court in *Myers* held Congress cannot limit the president's authority to remove from office those who perform "purely" executive functions, in *Buckley v. Valeo* (1976) the justices held Congress cannot appoint such officers. Nor, according to *Bowsher v. Synar* (1986), can Congress remove them.

*Policy Differences.* Recognizing that it has been delegating away dangerously broad powers, Congress since 1932 had frequently reserved for one or both houses power to "veto" what are deemed improper or unwise exercises of delegated authority (see LEGISLATIVE VETO). The Supreme Court in *Immigration and Naturalization Service v. Chadha* (1983) held invalid a one-house veto of a deportation exemption granted (pursuant to delegated authority) by the INS. Such a veto, the Supreme Court said, was legislation that only Congress, subject to the president's veto, can enact. True to eighteenth-century dogma, the Court declared the "fact that a given law or procedure is efficient, convenient, and useful in facilitating functions of the government, standing alone, will not save it, if it is contrary to the Constitution" (p. 944). In *U.S. Senate v. Federal Trade Commission* (1983), the justices extended the *Chadha* principle to a veto that is effective upon approval by both houses of Congress. Of course, Congress may influence the independent regulatory commissions through its investigation and its budget powers, but this is quite different from day-to-day oversight.

The Ethics in Government Act of 1978 provided for the appointment of "independent counsel" to investigate and, when appropriate, prosecute certain high-ranking officials for violations of federal criminal laws. The purpose of the measure was to bypass a regular function of the Department of Justice lest *inter alia* an administration find itself in the role of investigating and prosecuting itself. In *Morrison v. Olson* (1988), the Court held that Congress had not violated separation of powers principles because under the act the president can at any time remove from office an "independent counsel"—but only for "good cause." In the Supreme Court's view the latter proviso did not substantially impede the president's law-enforcing function. Unless the justices are prepared to undercut *Myers*, it seems likely they will not find much of an impediment in the "good cause" limitation.

Since Jefferson's day presidents have used military force from time to time without formal declarations of war. Jefferson fought pirates in Tripoli; Lincoln battled the Confederacy; Truman fought the North Koreans; Kennedy, Johnson, and Richard M. *Nixon used the military in Vietnam. Widely felt dissatisfaction with the Vietnam venture led to congressional adoption—over President Nixon's veto—of the *War Powers Resolution of 1973. Its purpose was to "insure that the collective judgment of both Congress and the President will apply to the introduction of United States armed forces into hostilities, or into situations where imminent involvement in hostilities is clearly indicated by the circumstances." To achieve this objective the resolution requires consultation between Congress and the president before any military venture. It requires the president to report to Congress within forty-eight hours any such action that he has undertaken and the reasons therefor. It also compels him to end any military involvement after sixty (or ninety) days unless Congress approves or is unable to meet. Moreover the president must "remove" armed forces engaged in hostilities outside American territory and possessions if Congress so directs by a concurrent resolution that is not subject to a presidential veto.

At least three presidents since 1973 have insisted the resolution violates long-settled traditions as well as presidential authority granted by the Constitution. Other commentators have been critical because in their view Congress has given its advance blessing to any sixty- or ninety-day military venture by the president. Another difficulty with the War Powers Resolution is the subsequent *Chadha* restraint on legislative vetoes.

One cannot ascertain to what extent, if any, the War Powers Resolution has in fact restrained presidential action. Presidents Gerald Ford, Carter, and Ronald *Reagan reported seventeen military ventures to Congress—sometimes not strictly within the forty-eight hour deadlines. Among those reported late was President Carter's effort to rescue the hostages in Iran and President Reagan's involvement in Granada. Congress has never rebuked a president for violating the War Powers Resolution nor has the judiciary found that it raises any justiciable as distinct from political questions. However, differences between President Reagan and Congress with respect to what started as a peacekeeping mission in Lebanon led to a compromise whereby the marines would be withdrawn within eighteen months.

*Summary and Conclusion.* America's peculiar institution of judicial review gives courts enormous supervisory power with respect to the other branches of government. It also permits courts to define whatever powers of self-defense the other branches have against the judiciary. The upshot is that separation of powers means largely what the Supreme Court says it means.

As a matter of history the political branches have rarely tried to use their formal weapons (impeachment, constitutional amendment, and jurisdiction control) against the Supreme Court. Thus, political parties seem—when robust—our most effective, if indirect, check against otherwise independent judges.

Few Supreme Court decisions confine the presidency. *Humphrey* was a severe and perhaps debatable blow. The *Steel Seizure Case* recognizes significant presidential lawmaking power provided it does not collide with prior congressional measures. While *United States* v. *Nixon* (1974) was an unmitigated defeat for President Nixon, it

was a victory for the presidency because the Court recognized a need for confidentiality in the conduct of presidential affairs. In many other cases, whether relating to foreign or domestic matters, the Supreme Court has either withheld its hand or supported the president in the face of separation of powers challenges. This judicial leniency along with the habitual willingness of Congress to delegate to the executive branch vast discretionary power helps to explain the rise since the Great Depression of what Arthur Schlesinger, Jr., calls the "imperial presidency." Expansive delegation may be largely a symptom.

As though recognizing its own carelessness with respect to delegation, Congress has provided repeatedly for that after-the-fact remedy called the legislative veto. The *Chadha* ruling ended that approach, which may have been less important as a remedy than as a recognition by Congress that it had been giving away too much authority and had not been performing adequately. Such a confession seems implicit in the Gramm-Rudman Act, in which Congress sought by a kind of automatic pilot device to make good its own lack of discipline with respect the budget. The *Chadha* decision and Congress's farcical maneuvering to avoid Gramm-Rudman strictures may yet bring real reform.

In his famous *Myers* dissent Justice Louis D. *Brandeis said: "The doctrine of the separation of powers was adopted by the convention of 1787, not to promote efficiency but to preclude the exercise of arbitrary power. The purpose was, not to avoid friction, but, by means of the inevitable friction incident to the distribution of the governmental powers among three department, to save the people from autocracy" (p. 293). This is a classic expression of the eighteenth-century hope that freedom could be secured by calculated inefficiency in government. A more modern hope is that freedom would be better served with more efficiency and more democratic accountability. We are still haunted by an ancient riddle: How far can we build up effective government before it topples over into despotism? How much inefficiency can we afford without slipping into disaster?

(See also DELEGATION OF POWERS; JUDICIAL POWER AND JURISDICTION; JUDICIAL REVIEW; PARTY SYSTEM; POLITICAL PARTIES.)

□ Benjamin Ginsberg and Martin Shefter, *Politics by Other Means* (1990). Louis Henkin, *Foreign Affairs and the Constitution* (1972). Philip B. Kurland, *Watergate and the Constitution* (1978). Theodore Lowi, *The End of Liberalism* (1980). M. J. C. Vile, *Constitutionalism and the Separation of Powers* (1967). Martin Wattenberg, *The Decline of American Political Parties* (1986). Christopher Wolfe, *The Rise of Modern Judicial Review* (1986). Gordon Wood, *The Creation of the American Republic* (1969).      Wallace Mendelson

**Seriatim Opinions.** Under the English legal traditions in effect at the time of American indepen-

dence, appellate courts announced case outcomes through the separate opinions of each
participating judge. This practice of issuing separate or "seriatim" opinions remains common in
England today.

Consistent with its legal ancestry, the Supreme
Court initially adopted seriatim opinions as an
accepted way of announcing decisions. Chief
Justice John *Marshall ended the practice. When
Marshall took command of the Court in 1801, the
judiciary was the weakest of the three branches of
government, and because of the *Jeffersonian
electoral victories of 1800, it was the only branch
remaining under Federalist control. Marshall was
committed to building the Court into a coequal
institution. He saw the termination of seriatim
opinions as one step toward achieving that goal.
Marshall reasoned that for the Court to grow in
stature, it must speak with one voice rather than
many. He, therefore, adopted the practice of
issuing a single opinion announcing the ruling of
the Court, a change vigorously criticized by
Thomas *Jefferson.

Some contemporary observers see an erosion
in the majority opinion procedure. Since the mid-
1940s there has been a dramatic increase in
*concurring and *dissenting opinions and occa-
sionally the Court has almost reverted back to the
days of seriatim opinions. For example, in the
important Pentagon Papers case of *New York
Times v. United States (1971) and the capital
punishment case of *Furman v. Georgia (1972),
each of the nine justices issued individual opinions.

(See also OPINIONS, ASSIGNMENT AND WRITING
OF.)

Thomas G. Walker

**Seventeenth Amendment.** Article I, section 3 of
the Constitution provided for election of senators
by the state legislatures, apparently in the hope
that the Senate would represent a different constituency than the House of Representatives. By
1900 the evolving ideal of democracy had made
this scheme seem inappropriate, and some states
had evaded the provision by requiring the legislature to name the candidate already approved by a
popular vote. There was much pressure on
Congress—including the threat of calling a constitutional convention—to amend the clause. In
response, Congress proposed an amendment,
ratified by the states in 1913, providing that
senators be elected directly by those citizens
qualified to vote for the "most numerous branch"
of the state legislature.

The amendment has not often been subjected
to *judicial review, because states seemingly had
little reason to evade or minimize its effects.
Politically, it probably helped to break up the
party oligarchy in the Senate, since state political
bosses found it more difficult to get their candidates elected by the voters. Otherwise the amendment has had little perceptible effect on the

nature of the Senate. But like much of the
progressive agenda of the period, such as the
direct primary, it has tended to undercut party
power by bypassing the political mechanisms
through which that power was exercised.

(See also CONSTITUTIONAL AMENDMENTS; ELEC-
TIONS; PROGRESSIVISM.)

Loren P. Beth

**Seventh Amendment.** An issue that divided
supporters and opponents of the original Constitution was the document's silence on the guarantee of right to *trial by jury in civil cases. This
question was debated during the Constitutional
Convention of 1787, but a proposal to delineate
the right in *Article III was defeated. Antifederalists seized on this perceived deficiency in their
campaign against ratification. Alexander *Hamilton responded in The *Federalist Papers by denying
that the Constitution would limit the right to civil
jury trial as it existed at *common law. The
Seventh Amendment, which was ratified in 1791,
resolved the controversy by guaranteeing the
right in suits at common law in federal courts
where the amount in controversy exceeds twenty
dollars.

The Supreme Court has had several recent
occasions to interpret the Seventh Amendment.
In Colegrove v. Battin (1973), it held that a six-
member jury, as opposed to the traditional
twelve-person panel, does not violate the amendment. The Court has required jury trials when
Congress created new causes of action analogous
to actions at common law. Since there has been a
merger of law and equity in the federal courts, the
parties can insist on their right to jury trial on
facts relating to the legal aspects of the case. For
instance, actions for money damages are usually
within the province of the jury. The Supreme
Court has refused to hold that the Seventh
Amendment is applicable to civil trials in *state
courts.

Philip L. Merkel

**Sex Discrimination.** See GENDER.

**Shapiro v. Thompson,** 394 U.S. 618 (1969), argued 29 Apr. 1968, reargued 23–24 Oct. 1968,
decided 21 Apr. 1969 by vote of 6 to 3; Brennan for
the Court, Stewart concurring, Warren, joined by
Black, and Harlan in dissent. This landmark
decision considered three separate appeals involving the Connecticut, Pennsylvania, and District of Columbia one-year durational residency
requirement for eligibility for welfare benefits.
The lead case concerned Vivian M. Thompson,
who, at the age of nineteen, was a single mother
of one child and pregnant with another. She
moved from her residence in Massachusetts to
Connecticut to be with her mother and applied
for but was denied welfare because she had not
lived in Connecticut for one year prior to her
application. A three-judge federal district court
struck down the requirement as an unconstitu-

tional burden on the right to *travel and a violation of the *Equal Protection Clause of the *Fourteenth Amendment. The two other lower courts decided similarly.

The Supreme Court agreed with the lower courts and emphasized that among fundamental personal liberties is the freedom to travel "throughout the length and breadth of our land uninhibited by statutes, rules, or regulations which unreasonably burden or restrict this movement" (p. 629). It held that the right to travel was a "fundamental" right that required the application of *strict scrutiny. The state, however, could not demonstrate a "compelling state interest" in such a restrictive law, or that it had chosen the least restrictive alternative to achieve its legitimate ends. Chief Justice Earl *Warren and Justice Hugo *Black dissented, seeing no restriction on the right to travel. Justice John M. *Harlan viewed the durational residency requirement as only an indirect and insubstantial inhibition on that right.

This decision provided a *precedent for successful attacks on other residency requirements such as those for voting and for practicing law. The impact of the decision on the poor was considerable and as a result, many thousands received welfare assistance who otherwise would not have received it.            Sheldon Goldman

**Shelley v. Kraemer,** 334 U.S. 1 (1948), argued 15–16 Jan. 1948, decided 3 May 1948 by vote of 6 to 0; Vinson for the Court, Reed, Jackson, and Rutledge not participating. *Shelley* is one of four cases known collectively as the *Restrictive Covenant Cases,* the others being *McGhee* v. *Sipes, Hurd* v. *Hodge,* and *Urciolo* v. *Hodge.* In its decision in these cases, the Court held that state judicial enforcement of agreements barring persons from ownership or occupancy of real property on racial grounds is forbidden by the *Equal Protection Clause of the *Fourteenth Amendment. The Court also determined that enforcement of racial covenants by federal courts violated the *Due Process Clause of the *Fifth Amendment.

Agreements to impose restrictions of various sorts on the uses of land are a familiar device in real estate law. Racial covenants, however, sought not to bar specific uses of land but, rather, certain classes of persons from its ownership and occupancy. It was not until municipal *zoning laws requiring racial segregation in urban residential housing were invalidated by the Court in *Buchanan* v. *Warley* (1917), that persons promoting housing segregation turned in significant numbers to the use of racial covenants. By the time that *Shelley* v. *Kraemer* reached the Supreme Court, racial restrictive agreements were being enforced in many northern cities, and the prospects for the spread of the racial covenant system to other parts of the country were very strong.

In reaching its decision the Supreme Court largely ignored the massive collection of social data submitted by the parties attacking the racial covenants. Instead, the Court's opinion focussed on traditional concepts of *"state action" in Fourteenth Amendment law. A sharp distinction was drawn between the creation of the restrictive agreements and their enforcement by courts of equity. According to the Court, those entering into the agreements engaged in merely private behavior, activity not regulated or restricted by constitutional provisions. The judicial enforcement of the covenants, however, was seen as constituting official action violative of rights to equal protection of the laws of minority persons excluded from from occupancy of the land by the covenants. Among the factors cited by the Court to support its result were that in enforcing the covenants the courts applied *common-law rules of the jurisdiction in question, that equitable powers were applied directly against minority members subjected to discrimination on racial grounds, and that the transactions being invalidated were those between willing sellers and willing buyers, thus frustrating efforts of sellers to ignore racial criteria in the sale of their land.

The opinion of the Court has been frequently criticized. Ordinarily it is not assumed that the state when enforcing private agreements adopts or is accountable for the various and often conflicting purposes of the contracting parties. Rather, the state is seen as simply providing the means through which a system of private contract can be administered. The facts surrounding the covenant cases, however, suggest that in enforcing the racial covenants the states did more than provide neutral enforcement of private contracts, but had, in fact, adopted policies of racial residential segregation in the supposed interests of protecting property values, suppressing crime, and promoting racial purity (see HOUSING DISCRIMINATION). Unfortunately, these matters were not fully canvassed in the Court's opinion, nor were adequate indicia suggested to determine the point at which enforcement of private agreements becomes transmuted into state action to advance public policies.

*Shelley* v. *Kraemer* has not exerted great influence in subsequent civil rights cases. In *Barrows* v. *Jackson* (1953), the *Shelley* holding was expanded to deny the right of a party to a restrictive agreement to recover damages in a suit at law from one who in violation of the agreement sold his property to a black purchaser. In a number of other cases *Shelley* v. *Kraemer* has been discussed or cited, but it rarely has appeared dispositive of the outcomes (*Moose Lodge* v. *Irvis,* 1972; *Black* v. *Cutter Laboratories,* 1956; *Rice* v. *Sioux City Memorial Park Cemetery,* 1955). One reason for the comparative neglect of *Shelley* may be the enactment of state and federal civil rights legislation in the 1960s (see CIVIL RIGHTS ACT OF 1964), which provided statutory answers to questions that might otherwise have called *Shelley* v. *Kraemer* into consideration.

Despite its infrequent citation, the decision constitutes an important event in modern constitutional history. By invalidating enforcement of racial covenants, it destroyed one of the most formidable instruments yet devised to effectuate racial discrimination. The decision provided impetus for further efforts in the civil rights struggle. Finally, by raising the problem of housing segregation to a constitutional level it clothed the issues with greater seriousness and moral concern.

(See also RACE AND RACISM; RESTRICTIVE COVENANTS.)

□ Francis A. Allen, "Remembering *Shelley v. Kraemer,*" *Washington University Law Quarterly* 67 (1989): 709–735.
Francis A. Allen

**Sheppard v. Maxwell,** 384 U.S. 333 (1966), argued 28 Feb. 1966, decided 6 June 1966 by vote of 8 to 1; Clark for the Court, Black in dissent. The threat of prejudicial publicity to a criminal defendant's constitutional rights is as old as the media itself. Traditionally, the Court had placed few constraints on the press in reporting on criminal trials. However, in the 1960s, during a decade of expanding constitutional rights for defendants in criminal actions, the courts reassessed this problem.

In *Estes* v. *Texas* (1965), the Court reversed the conviction of a defendant whose trial proceedings had been televised. A plurality of the Court held that the televised proceedings had deprived the accused of his due process rights and that televising of a trial was inherently prejudicial.

In *Sheppard* the Court reversed the conviction of Dr. Sam Sheppard for the murder of his wife. His case attracted extensive media coverage; after his conviction he served several years in prison before seeking *habeas corpus relief in the federal courts. The Supreme Court granted the writ and ordered Sheppard released. It held that Sheppard had been deprived of a fair trial because of the "Roman Holiday" atmosphere surrounding the trial and because the judge failed to minimize the prejudicial impact of massive publicity.

In reversing the conviction, the Court gave heightened consideration to *Sixth Amendment interests. Noting that prejudicial news comment on pending trials had become prevalent, it warned trial judges that, when faced with a reasonable likelihood that publicity would prevent a fair trial, they should take certain narrowly tailored measures, such as juror sequestration, to diminish the likelihood of prejudice. Despite the potential dangers of prejudicial publicity recognized in *Sheppard,* the Supreme Court has continued to give the press substantial freedom in reporting.

(See also PRETRIAL PUBLICITY AND THE GAG RULE; SPEECH AND THE PRESS.)
Patrick M. Garry

**Sherman Antitrust Act.** The oldest and most important federal antitrust law, the Sherman Antitrust Act has provided the primary statutory basis for American antitrust enforcement and case law over the last one hundred years. Like the other antitrust laws, the Sherman Act targets activities restricting marketplace competition. The act's sweeping prohibition of "[e]very contract, combination . . . or conspiracy" in restraint of interstate or foreign trade or commerce, set forth in its first section, addresses collusive or exclusionary group behavior. Section 2, prohibiting monopolization and attempted monopolization, primarily addresses single-firm conduct, although it also condemns conspiracies to monopolize. Violations of the act currently are punishable by fines of up to $350,000 for individuals and up to $10 million for corporations, as well as by imprisonment of up to three years. Both the United States and private parties can seek federal court *injunctions against threatened breaches of the act and are entitled to collect three times the amount of any injury they have sustained because of its violation. In addition, individual states are authorized to sue for treble damages on behalf of injured natural persons residing in the state.

The nearly unanimous congressional adoption of the act in 1890 responded to mounting public concerns generated by dramatic late nineteenth-century increases in cartelization, consolidation, and apparent predatory business behavior. The congressional deliberations reflected traditional American concerns that anticompetitive conduct potentially imperils distributional fairness, productive efficiency, individual economic opportunity, and political liberty. Ever since 1890, however, scholars have disagreed with regard to specific congressional aims. Recently, scholars, judges, and enforcement officials increasingly have posited an exclusive congressional desire to promote economic efficiency. A prominent alternative view has suggested that Congress primarily sought to prevent unfair wealth transfers resulting from noncompetitive pricing. These interpretations reflect a modern perception that the various economic, political, and moral goals reflected in the debates are in substantial tension. In late nineteenth-century thinking, however, they largely were deemed to be complementary, so that most congressmen may well have sought to further all of these ends.

Rather than specifying the act's application in any detail, Congress left the task of further doctrinal development to the federal courts. Congress intended to incorporate in a general way the existing common-law restraint of trade approaches of the state courts. The Sherman Act's enforcement provisions, however, went substantially beyond traditional common-law doctrines that merely denied legal enforcement to restrictive agreements.

Despite the Supreme Court's initial limitation

of the act's reach in *United States* v. *\*E. C. Knight Co.* (1895), the Court found for the government in a series of early cases culminating in its landmark decisions in *\*Standard Oil Co.* v. *United States* (1911) and *United States* v. *American Tobacco Co.* (1911). The Court's ambiguous new embrace of a generalized *\*"rule of reason"* standard for Sherman Act interpretation in those cases sparked new political debate and ultimately prompted Congress to pass the Clayton and Federal Trade Commission Acts in 1914 to supplement the Sherman Act.

*World War I and the prosperous 1920s saw only limited Sherman Act enforcement. Federal antitrust enforcement activity dramatically expanded, however, in the later \*New Deal and since then has remained at a much higher level than at any time prior to the 1930s.

Over time, judicial interpretation of the act also has changed substantially. Sherman Act interpretation, scholarship, and enforcement have changed particularly dramatically since the middle 1970s. In recent cases, for example, the Court greatly has reduced, although not entirely eliminated, its use of "per se" rules to condemn summarily particular agreements among competitors or among firms in a supplier-purchaser relationship. Simultaneously, the Court has given increasing weight to new economic perspectives suggesting that various collaborative arrangements beneficially may increase output and efficiency. The Supreme Court and lower courts similarly have shown growing tolerance for potentially efficient conduct that furthers the market position of dominant firms, even while continuing to condemn exclusionary behavior by such firms in the absence of such an efficiency justification.

Numerous special exceptions limit or preclude the normal application of the Sherman Act in particular circumstances. Some of the more important of these relate to *labor activities, conduct within particular regulated industries, activities attributable to state rather than private decision making, and *First Amendment protected activities.

(See also ANTITRUST; CAPITALISM.)

□ E. Thomas Sullivan and Jeffrey L. Harrison, *Understanding Antitrust and Its Economic Implications* (1988).
James May

**Shiras, George, Jr.** (b. Pittsburgh, Pa. 26 January 1832; d. Pittsburg, Pa., 2 August 1924; interred Allegheny Cemetery, Pittsburgh), associate justice, 1892–1903. George Shiras, Jr., was an obscure but nonetheless important justice in determining winning blocs on the Court and designating accepted constitutional interpretations. His career demonstrated the impact that background variables of family position, educational experience, and pre-Court career can have on judicial attitudes.

*George Shiras, Jr.*

The son of a wealthy, retired brewery merchant turned gentleman farmer, Shiras was raised to respect property and business entrepreneurship. Educated at Yale College, Shiras also spent a short time at the law school there. Throughout the Civil War he left military service to his brothers, concentrating instead on his expanding, lucrative corporate law practice. He refused positions in public service, rejecting a senatorial nomination in 1881 on the grounds that it would make him a pawn of Pennsylvania's Republican party machine.

Although Shiras lacked both judicial and public service experience, he was nevertheless nominated to the bench of the United States Supreme Court in July 1892 by President Benjamin Harrison. Two factors were critical in his selection: first, he was from the same geographic section as his predecessor on the Court; and second, he had demonstrated independence of the anti-Harrison faction of the Pennsylvania Republican party.

Shiras brought to the Court a professional style and a social and economic ideology that shaped his and the Court's constitutional positions from 1892 to 1903. During this time the Court expanded *judicial review of socio-economic legislation through the *Due Process Clause of the *Fourteenth Amendment. Shiras's lawyerly approach to case facts and precedent meant that he did not always agree with the bloc of ultraconservative justices dedicated to the establishment of laissez-faire economics through strict judicial review of state and national progressive reform laws (see LAISSEZ-FAIRE CONSTITUTIONALISM). Thus in *Brass* v. *North Dakota* (1894) Shiras produced a liberal opinion upholding state *police power to regulate business. Shiras's social and economic background, however, appeared directly in a long line of conservative decisions from *United States* v. \**E. C. Knight* (1895) to \**Allegeyer* v. *Louisiana* (1897) that struck down national and state regulatory laws. In these cases Shiras voted to restrict the \*Sherman Antitrust Act of 1890 and to use the \*freedom of contract doctrine to annul \*labor and other social legislation.

Identified by history as the justice who made the \*Sixteenth Amendment necessary, Shiras's legal reputation has suffered undeservedly. He was accused of having "Shirased," that is, torpedoed, the most promising reform measure of the 1890s, the \*income tax. While it was true that he was one of the five justices voting to strike down the income tax in \**Pollock* v. *Farmers' Loan and Trust Company* (1895), Shiras himself was not apparently the pivotal vote. And this focus has obscured Shiras's liberal civil liberties decisions where he adopted a consistent due process approach and, as in *Wong Wing* v. *United States* (1896), protested denial of basic rights to individuals.          Alice Fleetwood Bartee

**Shreveport Rate Cases** (*Houston, East and West Texas Railway Co.* v. *United States, Texas and Pacific Railway Co.* v. *United States*), 234 U.S. 342 (1914), argued 28–29 Oct. 1913, decided 8 June 1914 by vote of 7 to 2; Hughes for the Court, Lurton and Pitney in dissent (without opinion). These cases are among many that reveal the Supreme Court's willingness to accept the revitalization of the \*Interstate Commerce Commission (ICC) during the \*Progressive era. Following mandates of the state railroad commission, Texas railroads imposed rates that discriminated against out-of-state shippers who were located the same distance from markets in Texas as shippers within the state. The intrastate rates were set significantly lower than the federal interstate rates. Thus, freight costs from Shreveport, Louisiana, to points in east Texas were much higher than those from Dallas or Houston to the same locations. The ICC found that the lower intrastate rate had an injurious effect on interstate commerce and ordered it superseded by the higher interstate rates. The Texas railroads made an appeal on the grounds that Congress, through the ICC, lacked the power to control intrastate rates of interstate carriers. The Court sustained the ICC order that set intrastate rates of interstate carriers and asserted that such regulation was within the scope of federal \*commerce power. Recognizing the interconnected nature of local and interstate commerce, the Court held that the lower, intra-Texas rate had a negative impact on interstate commerce.          Richard F. Hamm

**Siebold, Ex parte,** 100 U.S. 371 (1880), argued 24 Oct. 1879, decided 8 Mar. 1880 by vote of 7 to 2; Bradley for the Court, Field and Clifford in dissent. Siebold, a Baltimore election judge, was convicted under the Enforcement Acts of 1870–1871 of ballot-box stuffing in a federal congressional election. The Enforcement Acts made it a federal crime for a state official to neglect his duties under state or federal law in a federal election.

Petitioning for a writ of \*habeas corpus, Siebold argued that, while the federal government was competent to make and enforce its own election laws, it could not adopt existing state laws by reference, far less prospectively adopt state laws not yet in existence, and that it could not punish state officials for neglect of a state duty. Justice Joseph P. \*Bradley and the majority rejected this invocation of dual sovereignty, holding that a violation of a mixed state and national duty was "an offense against the United States, for which the offender is justly amenable to that government" (p. 388). The Court, however, limited its spacious reading of national powers to federal congressional elections and disavowed federal power over purely state and local elections.

Only Justice Stephen J. \*Field, in his dissenting opinion, accepted Siebold's arguments. Field reasoned that the federal government had no power to impose duties on a state officer.

(See also DUAL FEDERALISM; FIFTEENTH AMENDMENT; VOTE, RIGHT TO.)

          Ward E. Y. Elliott

**Silver Platter Doctrine.** This exception to the \*exclusionary rule, valid until 1960, permitted federal courts to accept evidence seized illegally by state officers in searches that involved neither federal participation nor federal direction. First applied to federal trials in \**Weeks* v. *United States* (1914), the exclusionary rule prevented the use in trials of evidence seized in an illegal search. This decision did not apply to \*state courts, however, many of which continued to follow the \*common-law practice of admitting such evidence.

In 1927, the Supreme Court developed the so-callled silver platter doctrine in two cases involving enforcement of the \*Eighteenth (Prohibition) Amendment, *Byars* v. *United States* and *Gambino* v. *United States*. State law enforcement officials, often at the secret instigation of federal agents, violated search and seizure procedures and turned evidence from illegal searches over to federal prosecutors, evoking the image of a gift on a silver platter to describe this ploy to evade the federal exclusionary rule.

The extension to state courts of the Fourth Amendment prohibition of illegal searches in \**Wolf* v. *Colorado* (1949) cast doubt on the continued viability of the silver platter doctrine. In *Elkins* v. *United States* (1960), the Supreme Court finally abandoned it. The doctrine undermined \*federalism, the justices concluded. Almost half of the states had by then adopted the exclusionary rule, so admitting illegally seized evidence in federal courts defeated state court efforts to uphold \*Fourth Amendment standards. The next year, in *Mapp v. Ohio (1961), the Supreme Court made the exclusionary rule binding on all state courts, thus ending completely the tactics prompted by the silver platter doctrine.

David J. Bodenhamer

**Sit-In Demonstrations,** which occurred throughout the South in the early 1960s, were at the core of efforts to overthrow racial discrimination in public accommodations. Acting under its authority to enforce the *Thirteenth and *Fourteenth Amendments, Congress had banned such discrimination in the Civil Rights Act of 1875. But the law was overturned by the Supreme Court in the *Civil Rights Cases (1883). The Court held that the Thirteenth Amendment's ban against *slavery or involuntary servitude did not extend to discrimination in public accommodations; and it decided that the Fourteenth Amendment did not empower Congress to prohibit directly private discrimination but only discriminatory *"state action." Following this decision and *Plessy v. Ferguson (1896), which constitutionalized the doctrine of *"separate but equal" as an acceptable interpretation of the *Equal Protection Clause, the southern states rewrote their constitutions to require separate facilities and accommodations. The "equal" component of the formula was, for the most part, ignored.

Opposition to discrimination in public accommodations began to grow after *World War II. In 1947, President Harry S. Truman's Committee on Civil Rights recommended the "enactment by the states of laws guaranteeing equal access to places of public accommodation, broadly defined, for persons of all races, colors, creeds, and national origins" (p. 170). By 1962 there were twenty-eight states with such laws, but none in the South. There was also discrimination in the North, but it was only the southern and some border states that required segregated facilities.

The first sit-in demonstration was in Greensboro, North Carolina, on 1 February 1960. Four Negro college students protested the refusal of service at a campus luncheonette by "sitting-in" for several days. They were joined by other students and heckled by white protesters. This particular demonstration ended in negotiations, and no arrests were made. But it lit a spark that burned throughout the nation. About seventy thousand black and white students, many from the North, participated in the spiraling demonstrations; an estimated thirty-six hundred were arrested and convicted on a variety of charges such as breach of the peace, trespass, loitering, vagrancy, and failing to obey a police officer's order to disperse. Violence, brutality, and economic sanctions were also directed against the demonstrators and their families.

Sit-in cases soon began coming to the Supreme Court in large numbers—most seeking reversal of convictions in *state courts. The Court granted *certiorari to an exceptionally large number of these cases and sided with the demonstrators in all but a few. The basic issue was whether there had been sufficient "state action" to convert private discriminatory decisions, which do not violate the Constitution, to state-aided discrimination that is prohibited by the Fourteenth Amendment. In Peterson v. Greenville (1963), where a group of demonstrators at a lunch counter were asked to leave (and then arrested) "because it was contrary to local customs" and because a city ordinance prohibited integrated lunch counters, the Court held that the ordinance involved the state to a significant extent in the discrimination and reversed the conviction. But it often had to strain to find such a linkage. In Lombard v. Louisiana (1963), for example, New Orleans had no such ordinance. But city officials had publicly condemned sit-in demonstrations and privately pressured lunch counter owners not to give in to the demonstrator's demands. The Court reversed these convictions too, holding that the statements of city officials were state action no less than a city ordinance.

In Bell v. Maryland (1964), a badly divided Court refused to hold that, where there was no other state involvement, the mere "neutral" arrest of demonstrators on trespass charges was sufficient to overthrow their convictions. A majority of the justices was reluctant to convert the Fourteenth Amendment into a public accommodations statute, especially since Congress was on the verge of passing a national public accommodations law, albeit one grounded in the Commerce Clause rather than the Fourteenth Amendment (see COMMERCE POWER). That law, Title II of the *Civil Rights Act of 1964, was unanimously sustained in *Heart of Atlanta Motel v. United States (1964).

The law did more than prohibit discrimination in public accommodations. It also prohibited the punishment of any person attempting to exercise rights secured by the act, for example, demanding nondiscriminatory service in a place of public accommodations. In Hamm v. Rock Hill (1964), the Court not only upheld this ban on state prosecutions but applied it retroactively to wipe out all nonfinal convictions pending appeal. Thus, Congress had vindicated both the aims and tactics of the sit-in demonstrators.

(See also CIVIL RIGHTS MOVEMENT; RACE AND RACISM; SEGREGATION, DE JURE.)

□ President's Committee on Civil Rights, To Secure These Rights (1947). Joel B. Grossman

**Sixteenth Amendment.** This amendment was a response to the Supreme Court's decision in *Pollock v. Farmers' Loan (1895), which had declared the federal income tax law of 1894 unconstitutional. The burgeoning size of the federal government rendered traditional revenue sources increasingly inadequate, while there was great public criticism of the growing disparities of wealth produced by industrialization. Some conservatives in Congress supported the amendment as part of a scheme to defeat a pending income tax law in 1909. They mistakenly believed that the states would fail to approve it.

Ratified in 1913, the Sixteenth Amendment specifically empowered Congress to levy an income tax "upon any source whatever without apportionment among the several states," a power that Congress immediately exercised. The graduated income tax soon became the major source of revenue and has remained such ever since.

The Supreme Court has largely confined itself to interpretation of the increasingly complex income tax laws and the regulations of the Internal Revenue Service. The amendment itself has infrequently been a subject of constitutional litigation. Nevertheless, the Court has held that incomes from illegal sources may be taxed and that corporations may be taxed at a different rate than individuals. The Supreme Court has also ruled in *South Carolina* v. *Baker* (1988) that income from state and municipal bonds may be taxed, although Congress has not seen fit to do so.

While the fact of income tax is now beyond constitutional challenge, Congress has great discretion over how to use its power. Political battles are frequently waged over tax questions and the related issue of reform.

(See also INCOME TAX; REVERSALS OF COURT DECISIONS BY AMENDMENT.)

Loren P. Beth

**Sixth Amendment** was adopted as part of the *Bill of Rights in 1791. Some states had made their ratification of the Constitution contingent upon such adoption, reflecting a perceived need to limit the federal government's power to investigate, prosecute, and punish crime. The original Constitution had few provisions relating to the criminal process, but of the twenty-six separate rights specified in the first eight amendments, fifteen are aimed specifically at that process. The Sixth Amendment itself specifies seven rights applicable "in all criminal prosecutions": (1) *speedy trial; (2) public trial; (3) *trial by jury; (4) notice of the accusation; (5) confrontation of opposing witnesses; (6) compulsory process for obtaining favorable witnesses; and (7) the assistance of counsel (see COUNSEL, RIGHT TO). Although the Sixth Amendment guarantees these rights only with respect to the federal government, the adoption of the *Fourteenth Amendment in 1868 began a process of selective incorporation of the Bill of Rights provisions into its Due Process Clause. All Sixth Amendment rights have been incorporated and thus are also applicable to the states (see INCORPORATION DOCTRINE).

*Speedy Trial.* The right to speedy trial protects three basic demands of our criminal justice system: "to prevent undue and oppressive incarceration prior to trial, to minimize anxiety and concern accompanying public accusation, and to limit the possibilities that long delay will impair the ability of an accused to defend himself" (*Smith* v. *Hooey*, 1969, p. 378). A defendant's right to speedy trial, which can be forfeited by failure to invoke it before trial or guilty plea, attaches at the time of arrest or formal charge, whichever comes first (see PLEA BARGAINING). If the right has been violated, dismissal of the charges is the only possible remedy.

In *Barker* v. *Wingo* (1972), the Supreme Court elaborated how courts should determine whether a denial of the right has occurred. The Court first rejected two rigid approaches: the notion that the Constitution requires a trial within a specified time was rightly rejected on the ground that it would require the Court to engage in legislative or rulemaking activity; and the so-called demand-waiver rule, under which the right would be deemed waived for any period as to which trial had not been demanded, was rejected because it would be inconsistent with prior decisions on what it takes to waive a constitutional right. The Court then adopted a balancing test in which the conduct of both the prosecution and the defendant are weighed. The first factor of this test is the length of delay, which the Court seemed to treat mainly as a triggering mechanism. After a certain time (somewhere between six and eight months, the lower courts generally assume), the delay is presumptively prejudicial, so that further inquiry is necessary. The second factor is the reason for delay. The Court in *Barker* identified three categories: (1) a "deliberate attempt to delay the trial in order to hamper the defense," which "should be weighted heavily against the government"; (2) a "more neutral reason such as negligence or overcrowded courts," which "should be weighed less heavily but nevertheless should be considered since the ultimate responsibility for such circumstances must rest with the government"; and (3) "a valid reason such as a missing witness," which "should serve to justify appropriate delay" (p. 531). The third factor is whether and when the defendant asserted his right to speedy trial. The final *Barker* factor is prejudice to any of the three interests noted above, which, as with the previous factors, is alone neither a necessary nor a sufficient condition to finding a deprivation of the right to speedy trial.

*Public Trial.* The Sixth Amendment right to a public trial, which belongs to the defendant rather than the public, covers the entire trial and also certain pretrial proceedings, such as a suppression hearing, which bear a resemblance to a criminal trial. The right is adequately protected so long as there is freedom of access by the public to the trial; it is not necessary that everyone who wants to attend be accommodated. To show a violation of the right, the defendant need not show he was prejudiced in any specific way.

Exercise of the right serves as a restraint on

possible abuse of judicial power, helps ensure testimonial trustworthiness, and sometimes causes material witnesses to come forward. But the right is not absolute, and thus those benefits must be balanced against interests that might justify closing the trial. A party seeking to close a trial "must advance an overriding interest that is likely to be prejudiced, the closure must be no broader than necessary to protect that interest, the trial court must consider reasonable alternatives to closing the proceeding, and it must make findings adequate to support the closure" (*Waller* v. *Georgia*, 1984, p. 48).

*Jury Trial.* The right to jury trial reflects "a profound judgment about the way in which law should be enforced and justice administered. A right to jury trial is granted to criminal defendants in order to prevent oppression by the Government. . . . Providing an accused with the right to be tried by a jury of his peers gave him an inestimable safeguard against the corrupt or overzealous prosecutor and against the compliant, biased, or eccentric judge" (*Duncan* v. *Louisiana*, 1968, p. 156). This right has to do with a jury's determination of guilt or innocence and does not extend to the matter of sentencing.

The right does not apply to the trial of petty offenses, and any offense punishable by six months or less is presumably petty. Although the Court once viewed the traditional number of twelve jurors as a part of the right, six-person juries have been upheld on the ground that this number is "large enough to promote group deliberation, free from outside attempts at intimidation, and to provide a fair possibility for obtaining a representative cross-section of the community" (*Williams* v. *Florida*, 1970, p. 100). On similar reasoning the Court has held that the traditional requirement of unanimity is not a part of the constitutional right. Because of the cross-section requirement, there is a constitutional violation if "the jury pool is made up of only segments of the populace or if large, distinctive groups are excluded from the pool" (*Taylor* v. *Louisiana*, 1975, p. 530). In *Taylor*, the right was violated because women were selected for jury service only when they filed a written declaration of a desire to serve (see PETIT JURIES).

*Notice of the Accusation.* The Sixth Amendment also affords to a criminal defendant a right "to be informed of the nature and cause of the accusation" against him. This means that a defendant may not be convicted of one crime on an indictment charging a quite different crime. It also means that a defendant is entitled to a fair degree of specificity in the charge. Illustrative of a constitutionally defective charge is an indictment charging the defendants, in the language of the applicable statute, with having hindered certain citizens in their "free exercise and enjoyment . . . of the several rights and privileges granted and secured to them by the constitution." The Court in *United States* v. *Cruikshank* (1876) held that when a statute uses such generic terms the charge must be more particular, for example, in this case it must indicate which constitutional rights were allegedly hindered.

*Confrontation of Opposing Witnesses.* A part of this Sixth Amendment right is that the defendant is entitled to be present at his trial. This right can be waived, but it takes more than absence to establish a waiver, as when the defendant "had been expressly warned by the trial court not only that he had a right to be present but also that the trial would continue in his absence" (*Taylor* v. *United States*, 1973, p. 19). The right can also be forfeited, as when a defendant engages in disruptive behavior.

Another aspect of this right of confrontation is that the defendant is entitled to cross-examine the witnesses against him. This right, like the right to be present, can be overcome only for compelling reasons. In *Smith* v. *Illinois* (1968), the Court held that a desire to maintain the confidential status of a police informant was insufficient reason to permit the informant to testify without revealing his true name and address. The right of confrontation also affords the defendant protection against the use of hearsay when the trier of fact would lack "a satisfactory basis for evaluating the truth of a prior statement" (*California* v. *Green*, 1970, p. 161).

*Compulsory Process for Obtaining Favorable Witnesses.* One aspect of this right is that the defendant may testify on his own behalf. This right may be restricted to accommodate other legitimate interests in the criminal trial process, but those restrictions may not be arbitrary or disproportionate to the purposes they are designed to serve; thus a per se exclusion of a defendant's hypnotically refreshed testimony is unconstitutional. Another aspect of the compulsory process right is that the defendant is entitled to *subpoena witnesses. This provides that the government may not undermine the defendant's use of the subpoena authority, as when a trial judge drives a defense witness off the stand by unnecessarily strong warnings against perjury. Yet another part of the right is the right to put the witness on the stand, which is violated, for example, by a statutory provision making accomplices incompetent to testify for one another. But testimonial privileges, such as the privilege against *self-incrimination, are constitutional even though they might make a certain person unavailable as a defense witness.

*Assistance of Counsel.* The Sixth Amendment right of a defendant "to have the assistance of counsel for his defense" quite obviously guarantees a right to representation by privately retained counsel. That it also includes a right to state-provided counsel to indigent defendants was for many years less than clear. The Court first recognized a due process right to appointed counsel in special circumstances, as in *Powell* v. *Alabama* (1932)—the Scottsboro Boys case—

where illiterate defendants were facing the death penalty. This special circumstances rule prevailed as to state cases until *Gideon v. Wainwright (1963), holding the Sixth Amendment right to counsel applicable to the states, where the Court reasoned that "in our adversary system of criminal justice, any person hauled into court, who is too poor to hire a lawyer cannot be assured a fair trial unless counsel is provided for him" (p. 344). Counsel need not be provided to indigent defendants in cases not resulting in imprisonment.

This right can be waived, but courts are typically quite demanding with respect to what will suffice to constitute a knowing and intelligent waiver. A court cannot simply resolve all doubts against waiver, for often the "waiver" may actually involve the invocation of another constitutional right. In *Faretta v. California* (1975), the Court interpreted the Sixth Amendment as making "counsel, like the other defense tools guaranteed, . . . an aid to a willing defendant—not an organ of the State interposed between an unwilling defendant and his right to defend himself personally" (p. 820). Thus the Court held that a defendant also has a constitutional right to proceed *pro se, that is, to represent himself in a criminal trial.

What the defendant is entitled to under the Sixth Amendment is the effective assistance of counsel. This means, for one thing, that the government may not unreasonably restrict defense counsel's performance, as when a trial judge ordered a defendant not to consult with his attorney during an overnight recess. It also means that the defendant is entitled to undivided loyalty from his lawyer; a defendant has shown a violation of this right if he establishes an actual conflict of interest that adversely affected his lawyer's performance, without regard to whether the defendant was prejudiced thereby. Finally, it means that the defendant is entitled to have an attorney whose performance is not defective. To show a constitutional violation, it must appear that "in light of all the circumstances, the identified acts or omissions [of counsel] were outside the range of professionally competent assistance," and "there is a reasonable probability that, but for counsel's unprofessional errors, the result of the proceeding would have been different" (*Strickland v. Washington,* 1984, pp. 690, 694).

(See also DUE PROCESS, PROCEDURAL.)

□ Joseph G. Cook, *Constitutional Rights of the Accused,* 2 vols. (1972). David Fellman, *The Defendant's Rights Today* (1976). Wayne R. LaFave and Jerold H. Israel, *Criminal Procedure* (1984). Charles H. Whitebread and Christopher Slobogin, *Criminal Procedure,* 2d ed. (1986).

Wayne R. LaFave

**Skinner v. Oklahoma,** 316 U.S. 535 (1942), argued 6 May 1942, decided 1 June 1942 by vote of 9 to 0; Douglas for the Court, Stone and Jackson concur-

ring. In 1942 most states authorized sterilization of the "feeble-minded" or habitual criminals. Such laws were justified under theories of eugenics, but critics of compulsory sterilization argued that it was not certain that criminality and mental illness were inheritable. Skinner, convicted once for stealing chickens and twice for armed robbery, was ordered to submit to a vasectomy under the Oklahoma Criminal Sterilization Act.

In deciding Skinner's case, the Court recognized the right to have offspring as a *fundamental right but did not declare compulsory sterilization laws totally invalid. Instead, Douglas's majority opinion focused upon an exemption in the Oklahoma law for persons convicted of embezzlement or political crimes. *Douglas reasoned that, where a basic right is involved, *strict scrutiny of such classifications is essential. He saw no rational basis to conclude that the tendency to commit larceny was inheritable, thus exposing repeat offenders to sterilization, while the tendency to embezzle was not. Therefore, the Oklahoma statute violated the requirements of the *Equal Protection Clause of the *Fourteenth Amendment and was unconstitutional.

Concurring, Chief Justice Harlan F. *Stone argued that the statute violated the Due Process Clause because it did not require a hearing specifically on the question of whether Skinner's criminal traits were inheritable. Justice Robert *Jackson, also concurring, recognized that there are limits to the extent to which the state may conduct biological experiments at the expense of the dignity of a minority.

(See also BUCK V. BELL.)

Paul Kens

**Skinner v. Railway Labor Executives Association,** 489 U.S. 602 (1989), argued 2 Nov. 1988, decided 21 Mar. 1989 by vote of 7 to 2; Kennedy for the Court, Stevens concurring in the judgment, Marshall and Brennan in dissent. At issue in this case, decided along with *National Treasury Employees Union v. Von Raab (1989), was the constitutionality of the drug testing of railroad employees. The case began when the Federal Railroad Administration promulgated regulations requiring blood and urine tests of railroad employees involved in certain major train accidents or incidents and permitting breath or urine tests where employees violated certain safety rules. Railroad *labor unions challenged the regulations, arguing that they violated the *Fourth Amendment's prohibition of unreasonable searches and seizures.

The Supreme Court held that although the covered workers were employed by private companies, the level of government involvement was such, and the program was intrusive enough, to implicate the Fourth Amendment. As to whether the program was unreasonable under the Fourth Amendment, the Court pointed to the surrounding circumstances. Focusing on the loss of life and property in train accidents, the Court held that the government's interest in ensuring safety presented a special need that made the program reasonable. Further, finding that the employees' expectations of *privacy were minimal and that there was little discretion involved, and again stressing the safety aspect, the Court held that the usual Fourth Amendment requirements of a warrant, probable cause, and suspicion of individual wrongdoing were unnecessary.

Dissenting, Justices Thurgood *Marshall and William J. *Brennan warned that the Court had allowed basic constitutional protections to wither because of hysteria over drugs. They found the Court's special needs approach unprincipled and dangerous, with a resulting cavalier disregard for the constitutional text.

(See also SEARCH WARRANT RULE, EXCEPTIONS TO.)

Gerald N. Rosenberg

**Slaughterhouse Cases,** 16 Wall. (83 U.S.) 36 (1873), argued 3–5 Feb. 1873, decided 14 Apr. 1873 by vote of 5 to 4; Miller for the Court, Field, Bradley, Chase, Swayne in dissent. The *Slaughterhouse Cases* consisted of three suits precipitated by a Louisiana law that incorporated the Crescent City Live-Stock Landing and Slaughtering Company and required that all butchering of animals in New Orleans be done in its facilities. The cases provided the first important opportunity for the Supreme Court to interpret the meaning of the *Fourteenth Amendment, ratified in 1870. In an opinion that remains controversial but has never been overruled, the majority of the justices severely limited the meaning of the Privileges or Immunities Clause of the first section of the Fourteenth Amendment.

Louisiana passed the law at issue at a time when many state and local governments were enacting health reforms. Regulations to control the slaughtering of animals were enacted in many localities, because it was a business entailing grave health risks to surrounding neighborhoods in an age before modern refrigeration technology and insect control. Centralizing slaughterhouse operations was one means of regulation.

Although it was conceivable that a state itself might build and operate a new central slaughterhouse, it had been a common practice for states to incorporate privately owned businesses to assume the expense of providing needed public facilities in return for a government-regulated monopoly. Financially strapped after the *Civil War, Louisiana chose this alternative. However, this decision presented the problem of choosing who would have the privilege of incorporating the new slaughterhouse company and earning the tidy profit likely to accrue. As was usual in nineteenth-century America, the privilege went to a group of wealthy and politically influential

individuals, who brought leading politicians into the concern. Naturally, when governments chose this method to provide public services or facilities, they opened themselves to charges of corruption. Dissatisfied citizens perceived such transactions to confer illicit special privileges on the influential few at the expense of the rest of the people.

This was especially the case in Louisiana. That state was governed by Republicans, elected primarily by black voters enfranchised as part of *Reconstruction. Most white Louisianans believed that the white leaders of the Louisiana Republican party were "carpetbaggers" and "scalawags," interested solely in plunder. Democrats charged that the slaughterhouse law was another example of Republican corruption, even though both Democrats and Republicans were among the incorporators of the Crescent City Company.

The slaughterhouse laws imposed by the states seriously inconvenienced butchers. Some of them were accustomed to slaughtering animals on their own property. Others, like those in New Orleans, had formed trade associations that operated slaughterhouses. Now they were required to undertake their business at a distance from the city and often at a single center where they were required to pay fees. In many places affected butchers filed lawsuits challenging the constitutionality of the laws. However, few litigants or counsel in the late 1860s and early 1870s perceived the potential of the Fourteenth Amendment to protect the ordinary rights of white citizens; it had been discussed almost entirely in terms of the *slavery controversy. Therefore the butchers brought their suits in state courts, alleging violation of state constitutions. Everywhere they lost, with *state courts holding the laws to be legitimate exercises of the *police power—the power to make laws to promote the health, safety, and morals of the community.

However, the Louisiana butchers were blessed with outstanding counsel, among them John A. *Campbell, former associate justice of the Supreme Court, who had resigned when his state seceded from the Union. Campbell filed a petition in the local state court for an *injunction on behalf of the Butchers' Benevolent Association, which operated a slaughterhouse for its members. He asked the court to bar the Crescent City Company from interfering with the association's slaughterhouse business or that of its members. Although Campbell presented arguments similar to those made by butchers in other states, he added the novel claim that the law contravened the Fourteenth Amendment. The new amendment forbade states from enforcing "any law which shall abridge the privileges or immunities of citizens of the United States," among which, Campbell argued, was the right to labor freely in an honest avocation.

The issue was taken to the Louisiana Supreme Court in 1870. The butchers' lawyers argued that the law went beyond the inherent powers of legislation and violated both the state constitution and the Fourteenth Amendment, because it deprived them of property rights, not for the good of the community, but for the private gain of monopolists. With only one dissent, the judges rejected the butchers' contention that the law worked such a redistribution of property rights.

The butchers appealed to the Supreme Court, based on their Fourteenth Amendment argument. But in the meantime the Crescent City Company secured state court injunctions against the operation of the association slaughterhouse. Campbell petitioned the United States circuit court to issue an injunction forbidding any interference with butchers' activities until the Supreme Court announced its decision. Supreme Court Justice Joseph P. *Bradley, sitting on circuit, seized the opportunity to offer his view of the Fourteenth Amendment.

Convinced by the legal and business leaders of New Orleans that the law was designed to enrich the incorporators of the Crescent City Company, he ruled that the law was not a legitimate exercise of the police power in Live-Stock Dealers and Butchers' Association v. Crescent City Live-Stock Landing and Slaughter-House Company (1870). In reality the law was designed to confer "a monopoly of a very odious character" (p. 653). Such a law violated the Fourteenth Amendment. Although the framers of the amendment may not have understood the far-reaching character of the amendment, it nonetheless worked a revolutionary change in the federal system, giving the national government the power to intervene to prevent such deprivations of basic rights. Among the privileges and immunities of citizens of the United States was a right to *labor, which the Louisiana slaughterhouse law invaded.

Bradley's opinion was important for its articulation of the Fourteenth Amendment rather than for its practical effect. Federal law forbade United States courts from enjoining the action of state courts. Therefore he could only enjoin the Crescent City Company and state officials from bringing new legal actions against the butchers and their association. The state courts enforced the injunctions the company had already obtained.

When the Slaughterhouse Cases reached the Supreme Court in 1873, the justices faced a major dilemma. The Republican party, sustained by the people of the North, had framed the *Thirteenth, Fourteenth, and *Fifteenth Amendments in a political struggle that turned primarily upon the future place of African-Americans in American society (see RACE AND RACISM). By ratifying the amendments and sustaining the Republican party, the people had indicated that black Americans should be entitled to the same civil and political rights as white Americans. Moreover, the rhetoric of the debates suggested a vague but general belief that all Americans, white and black, had certain *fundamental rights that had been violated in the interest of *slavery and that should henceforth be secured against infringement. Yet at the same time Republicans were committed to maintaining the essentials of the federal system. The primary responsibility for governing relationships among Americans and for protecting their rights from infringement by others would remain with the states, they had insisted.

Republicans tried to reconcile the two commitments by framing laws and *constitutional amendments that authorized the national government to intervene when the states themselves infringed rights or failed to protect them. Furthermore, those laws and amendments carefully avoided making black Americans the special object of protection. They guaranteed the rights of all Americans equally. But in fact Republicans had not solved the problem, and the Slaughterhouse Cases made the failure clear. It was not an infringement of black people's civil rights or white unionists' freedom of speech that was at issue, but a health regulation not dissimilar from many passed around the nation. If the Supreme Court agreed that the Fourteenth Amendment authorized it to review such legislation, it could expect similar appeals whenever any person believed a police regulation denied basic rights. Moreover, the Court would in effect be recognizing Congress's power to intervene as well, because the fifth section of the Fourteenth Amendment authorized it to pass legislation appropriate for enforcing the other sections. Yet if the Court declined to review such appeals, how could it avoid undermining the guarantees the Fourteenth Amendment was designed to secure?

The court divided dramatically on the issue. A bare majority ruled that the Privileges or Immunities Clause did not protect such fundamental rights as the right to labor, while four justices trenchantly dissented. Justice Samuel F. *Miller delivered the majority opinion. He concluded that "the one pervading purpose" behind the Civil War Amendments was to secure the freedom of black Americans, not to expand or add protections for the rights of whites (p. 71).

In interpreting the Privileges or Immunities Clause, Miller stressed that it barred states from abridging only the "privileges or immunities of citizens of the United States." Even after the Civil War most Americans continued to make a rigid distinction between those areas where the states had jurisdiction and those areas within the jurisdiction of the national government (see DUAL FEDERALISM). Miller turned to this distinction to limit the scope of the Fourteenth Amendment. The term "privileges or immunities of citizens of the United States" was meant to differentiate between those rights associated with state citizenship and those associated with United States citizenship, he insisted. The Fourteenth Amendment forbade states only from abridging the latter.

Since the foundation of the Union the states had been conceded to have final authority over such basic rights as the right to labor, Miller said. With that right, the Fourteenth Amendment had nothing to do. To hold otherwise, Miller explained, would make "this court a perpetual censor upon all legislation of the states, on the civil rights of their own citizens," authorized to nullify any law it believed violated those rights (p. 78). Moreover, Congress would have the same right to intervene. With some justification, Miller argued that the American people had no such understanding of the amendment when they discussed and ratified it.

The four dissenting justices wrote three different opinions, although they all joined in that prepared by Justice Stephen J. *Field. They denied that the Fourteenth Amendment was designed to secure the rights of black Americans alone. They insisted that the right to labor was among the privileges and immunities of citizens of the United States. Justices Bradley and Noah *Swayne also insisted that Louisiana's regulation deprived the butchers of property without due process of law, another of the Fourteenth Amendment's prohibitions.

The *Slaughterhouse Cases* are generally assessed within the context of Reconstruction and the efforts to secure national protection for citizens' rights. They have been heavily criticized by scholars, who argue that Miller artificially narrowed the scope of the Privileges or Immunities Clause. Not only did he impose a distinction between the rights of state and national *citizenship that had not been in the minds of the framers, but the language of the opinion implied that the rights of national citizenship were few. Some scholars and twentieth-century Supreme Court justices have argued that the privileges and immunities of the citizens of the United States included at least those listed in the *Bill of Rights.

Critics complain that the *Slaughterhouse* decision severely undermined the ability of the government to protect the rights of the freedmen. There is ample evidence indicating that the decisions did in fact have that effect. Those who opposed national action to protect the rights of African-American citizens in the 1870s pointed to it to justify their position.

On the other hand, the cases did not involve the rights of black Louisianans. The points at issue were more similar to property rights cases of later years than to the noneconomic civil liberty cases of Reconstruction. From that perspective Miller's opinion may be seen as an articulation of judicial restraint in economic cases rather than an abdication of responsibility to protect human rights. Ultimately the Supreme Court did overturn state regulations affecting the rights Miller placed within state jurisdiction, by holding them among the liberties and property rights that

states could not infringe "without due process of law." Many scholars have perceived a direct line of descent between these decisions and the *Slaughterhouse* dissents.

(See also DUE PROCESS, SUBSTANTIVE; FEDERALISM; PRIVILEGES AND IMMUNITIES; PROPERTY RIGHTS; STATE SOVEREIGNTY AND STATES' RIGHTS.)

□ Michael Les Benedict, "Preserving Federalism: Reconstruction and the Waite Court," *Supreme Court Review* 1978: 39–79. Loren Beth, "The Slaughter-House Cases—Revisited," *Louisiana Law Review* 23 (April 1963): 587–605. Charles Fairman, *History of the Supreme Court*, vol. 6, *Reconstruction and Reunion, 1864–1888, Part One* (1971). Robert Kaczorowski, *The Politics of Judicial Interpretation: The Federal Courts, Department of Justice and Civil Rights, 1866–1876* (1985).　　　　Michael Les Benedict

**Slavery** was the most divisive constitutional issue in pre–Civil War America. The problem stemmed from a federal republic that was in Abraham *Lincoln's words, "half slave and half free." Slavery led to the Supreme Court's most infamous decision—Dred *Scott v. Sandford (1857)—a case characterized as a "self-inflicted wound" by Charles Evans *Hughes. This case became a political issue in 1858 and 1860, helping to elect Lincoln president in the latter year. But *Dred Scott* was not the only controversial slavery case to come before the high court. A full understanding of Supreme Court jurisprudence on slavery begins with an examination of the Constitution and its slavery-related clauses.

***Constitutional Structure and Slavery.*** The word *slavery* did not appear in the Constitution until the *Thirteenth Amendment abolished human bondage in 1865. Nevertheless, the Constitution explicitly protected slavery in five clauses. The three-fifths clause (Art. I, sec. 2) gave slave states representation in Congress based on 60 percent of their slaves; the same clause and the capitation tax clause (Art. I, sec. 9) limited the potential taxation of slaves; the migration and importation clause (Art. I, sec. 9) prohibited Congress from ending the African slave trade before 1808; amendment provisions (Art. V) gave added protection to the slave trade by prohibiting any amendment of the migration and importation clause before 1808; finally, the fugitives from labor clause (Art. IV, sec. 2) provided for the return of fugitive slaves (see CONSTITUTIONAL AMENDING PROCESS). Other clauses strengthened slavery by guaranteeing that federal troops would be used to suppress slave rebellions, prohibiting taxes on exports (which would have allowed for the indirect taxation of slaves), and giving the slave states extra votes in the electoral college under the three-fifths clause. The requirement that three-fourths of the states assent to any constitutional amendment guaranteed that the South could always block any proposed amendments. With good reason William Lloyd Garrison, America's most celebrated abolitionist, believed the Constitution's many compromises over slavery created a "covenant with death" and "an agreement with Hell."

Under generally accepted nineteenth-century interpretations of the Constitution, the national government had no power to interfere with slavery in the states where it existed. During the ratification struggle (1787–1789), South Carolina's Charles Cotesworth Pinckney articulated this understanding of the limitations on the national government. Pinckney, who had been one of the most forceful proslavery advocates at the Philadelphia Convention, told the South Carolina legislature "we have a security that the general government can never emancipate them [slaves], for no such authority is granted, and it is admitted on all hands, that the general government has no powers but what are expressly granted by the constitution; and that all rights not expressed were reserved by the several states."

Major Supreme Court cases involving slavery arose over five areas where slavery came under federal jurisdiction: (1) the African slave trade, (2) interstate commerce and slaves, (3) the return of fugitive slaves, (4) slavery in the federal territories, and (5) the interstate transit or sojourn of slaves through or in free states. In addition to these issues, slavery came before the Supreme Court in a number of cases as a result of the normal civil and criminal litigation that arose in the District of Columbia, which was a slaveholding jurisdiction. Though those cases are of little importance to the Court's slavery jurisprudence, they reaffirmed the proslavery leanings of the Marshall and Taney courts.

From 1790 to 1861 (with the exception of a few years in the early 1830s), the majority of Supreme Court justices were Southerners. In addition, most of the Northerners on the Court were Democrats who voted with their proslavery southern colleagues. Most prominent among these Northerners—known as "doughfaces" because they were shaped by southern interests—were Justices Henry *Baldwin (Pa.), Robert *Grier (Pa.), Samuel *Nelson (N.Y.) and Levi *Woodbury (N.H.). Except for early cases involving the slave trade, all important slavery-related cases came before a Court headed by Chief Justice Roger B. *Taney, a Southerner who, by the end of his long career on the bench, became fanatically proslavery. The Court's decisions from 1837 until the Civil War reflected Taney's passionate support for slavery and the South.

**African Slave Trade and the Supreme Court.** At the time of the Revolution, the African slave trade was viewed as an abomination, even by many who favored the continued existence of slavery itself. In his original draft of the *Declaration of Independence, Thomas *Jefferson condemned George III for maintaining the African slave trade. His abhorrence for the slave trade, a view shared by many other slave owners, did not prevent the author of the Declaration of Independence from continuing to own a large number of slaves throughout his life. Jefferson illustrates well the possibility of supporting slavery while opposing the slave trade.

Similarly, at the Constitutional Convention slaveowners like James *Madison and George Mason attacked the slave trade without opposing slavery itself. A majority of the Convention delegates favored giving Congress the power to end the African slave trade immediately. However, delegates from South Carolina persuaded the Convention to allow the trade to continue for at least twenty years. In 1807 Congress passed legislation ending the trade the following year and in 1818 adopted tougher legislation against traders.

After 1808 the federal courts heard numerous cases involving the importation of slaves from Africa. Out of these cases the Supreme Court defined two quite different jurisprudential theories. In The *Antelope (1825), Chief Justice John *Marshall asserted that the African slave trade was "contrary to the law of nature" but that it was "consistent with the law of nations" and "cannot in itself be piracy" (pp. 120, 122). The Court recognized the right of foreigners to engage in the slave trade, if their own nations allowed them to do so. Thus Marshall wrote: "If it be neither repugnant to the law of nations, nor piracy, it is almost superfluous to say in this Court, that the right of bringing in for adjudication in time of peace, even where the vessel belongs to a nation which has prohibited the trade, cannot exist" (pp. 122–123). This allowed the Court to uphold prosecutions against American traders while also protecting the property rights in enslaved Africans owned by nationals where the trade was legal. The Antelope was a Spanish vessel seized on the high seas by pirates. By the time the ship was captured by an American revenue cutter and taken to Savannah, the Antelope held more than 280 slaves taken from numerous ships owned by citizens of various countries, including Spain and the United States. The Court ruled that some of the slaves on this ship were to be given to the Spanish government because they were lawfully owned by a Spanish subject at the time the ship was captured in American waters. The rest of the Africans, however, were to be turned over to the United States government as the fruit of the illegal trade. Cases between 1820 and 1860 illustrate how the Court dealt with the trade. In United States v. Gooding (1827), the Court, continuing its opposition to the African trade, upheld an interpretation of the 1818 act that allowed prosecution of secret owners of vessels illegally participating in the trade.

United States v. The Amistad (1841) involved a Spanish ship that had drifted into American waters after a mutiny of slaves left most of the crew dead. All of the mutinous slaves had been recently imported from Africa in violation of Spanish law. The case became a major abolitionist

*cause célèbre*, with former president John Quincy
*Adams and the future Connecticut senator
Roger S. Baldwin arguing before the Supreme
Court on behalf of the slaves. The Court rejected
attempts by the United States government to
prosecute the Africans for murder or to allow
their extradition to Spain for either criminal trials
or enslavement. The Supreme Court ruled that
because the African trade was illegal under
Spanish law, all of the Africans were legally free
and should be returned to Africa. Somewhat
gratuitously, the Court also held that the United
States government was under no obligation to
pay for their passage back to Africa. Eventually
private funds enabled the Africans to return to
their homeland.

In *Ex parte Gordon* (1861), the Supreme Court
sustained the conviction and death sentence of
an American slave trader. In a series of cases
known as *The Slavers* (1864), the Court upheld
condemnation proceedings against vessels outfit-
ted in the United States for slave trading activities. The Court consistently condemned the trade
as a violation of *natural law and morality. But in
all slave trading cases, the Court enforced concepts of international law. Thus Justice Joseph
*Story noted in a circuit court opinion, *La Jeune
Eugenie* (1822), "I am bound to consider the trade
an offence against the universal law of society,
and in all cases, where it is not protected by a
foreign government, to deal with it as an offence
carrying with it the penalty of confiscation . . ."
(p. 847). The Constitution prohibited any federal
interference with African slave trade before 1808.
In that year a federal ban went into effect.
Although in the 1850s some proslavery advocates
demanded reopening the slave trade, even most
Southerners rejected the idea. In 1861 the Confederate Constitution banned the African trade in
that new nation.

**Slavery and Interstate Commerce.** After the
adoption of the Constitution, the nation reached
an unstated political consensus on the question
of slavery and interstate commerce. Although
most lawyers would have conceded that after
1808 Congress had the power to regulate the
interstate slave trade, the consensus held that
such regulation would be impossible to get
through Congress and would threaten the
Union. Arguments of counsel and the opinions of
the justices in commerce clause cases, such as
*Gibbons v. Ogden (1824), *New York v. Miln (1837),
The *License Cases (1847), and the *Passenger Cases
(1849), recognized the special status of slaves in
the general regulation of commerce. Indeed,
slavery directly or indirectly influenced almost
every antebellum Commerce Clause case.

*Groves v. Slaughter* (1841) was the only major
slavery case to come before the Supreme Court
that directly raised commerce clause issues. The
Mississippi Constitution of 1832 prohibited the
importation of slaves for sale. This was not an
antislavery provision, but an attempt to reduce

the flow of capital out of the state. In violation of
this provision, Slaughter, a slave trader, sold
slaves in Mississippi and received notes signed
by Groves and others. Groves later defaulted on
the notes, arguing that the sales of slaves in
Mississippi were void. The Court ruled that the
notes were not void because Mississippi's constitutional prohibition on the importation of slaves
was not self-executing. Thus, absent legislation
implementing the prohibition, the Mississippi
constitutional clause was inoperative. In separate
concurrences northern and southern justices
agreed that a state might legally ban the importation of slaves. This principle supported Northerners who wanted to keep slaves out of their states
and the Southerners who wanted to make sure
that the federal courts could not interfere with
slavery on the local level.

**Slavery and Extraterritoriality: Fugitive
Slaves.** The jurisprudence surrounding fugitive
slaves was the most divisive constitutional issue
in antebellum America. The Supreme Court
heard four major cases involving fugitive slaves:
*Prigg v. Pennsylvania (1842), *Jones v. Van Zandt
(1847), *Ableman v. Booth (1859), and *Kentucky v.
Dennison (1861). While settling legal issues, none
of the these cases satisfactorily dealt with the
moral and political questions raised when human
beings escaped to freedom. These cases only exacerbated the sectional crisis. Ultimately, these issues were decided not by constitutional arguments and ballots, but by war.

Late in the Constitutional Convention Pierce
Butler of South Carolina proposed that the Constitution "require fugitive slaves and servants to be
delivered up like criminals." Pennsylvania's
James Wilson complained that this would oblige
"the Executive of the State to do it, at the public
expense." Connecticut's Roger Sherman added,
perhaps sarcastically, that there was "no more
propriety in the public seizing and surrendering a
slave or servant, than a horse." In the face of this
opposition, Butler withdrew his proposal. The
next day, without any further debate or a recorded vote, the Convention accepted what became the Fugitive Slave Clause of the Constitution. In the first Supreme Court case interpreting
the clause, *Prigg v. Pennsylvania* (1842), Justice
Story erroneously characterized the clause as "a
fundamental article without the adoption of
which the Union could not have been formed" (p.
611).

The wording of this clause and its juxtaposition with the other clauses of Article IV suggest
that the Convention did not anticipate any federal enforcement of the law. However, in 1793
Congress passed the first fugitive slave law,
which spelled out procedures for the return of
runaway slaves. The law allowed masters or their
agents to capture runaways and bring them to
any magistrate, state or federal, to request a
certificate of removal. Armed with such a certificate, the claimant was then free to take the

runaway slave out of the state where he or she was found and back to the claimant's state.

At the time this law was passed, all the New England states and Pennsylvania had either abolished slavery outright or were in the process of eliminating it through gradual emancipation. In 1799 and 1804 New York and New Jersey joined this first emancipation. These changes in northern law and public policy meant that in half the nation a racially based presumption of enslavement no longer existed. With its arbitrary procedures and resultant lax evidentiary standards for the return of fugitive slaves, the 1793 law presented a grave threat to the many free blacks in the North. To prevent the kidnapping of free blacks, many northern states passed personal liberty laws, which placed burdens on claimants beyond what the federal law required. These laws were a good faith effort by the northern states to protect free blacks from enslavement through kidnapping or mistaken identity and to provide some procedures by which state officials could also aid in the rendition of actual fugitives. Before the 1830s the northern states generally tried to balance their desire to protect the freedom of their free black population with their desire to comply with the obligations of the Constitution to return runaway slaves.

While the *lower federal courts and some state courts enforced the federal law of 1793, its constitutionality was not tested in the Supreme Court until Prigg v. Pennsylvania. The facts of the case and Story's opinion reveal the constitutional difficulties raised by fugitive slave rendition. Justice Story upheld the 1793 law and struck down state laws that interfered with the rendition process. Story urged state officials to continue to enforce the 1793 law but concluded that they could not be required to do so. In 1837 Edward Prigg, a professional slave catcher, seized Margaret Morgan, a runaway slave living in Pennsylvania. Prigg applied to a justice of the peace for certificates of removal under the federal law of 1793 and Pennsylvania's 1826 personal liberty law, which had higher evidentiary requirements than the federal law. The magistrate refused Prigg's request. Without any legal authority Prigg then removed to Maryland Morgan and her children, including one born in Pennsylvania. Prigg was later convicted of kidnapping under the 1826 law and he appealed to the U.S. Supreme Court. At issue was the constitutionality of both the federal law of 1793 and the Pennsylvania law of 1826.

Speaking for the Court, Story held that: (1) the Fugitive Slave Law of 1793 was constitutional; (2) Pennsylvania's personal liberty law of 1826 (and by extension all similar laws) unconstitutionally added new requirements to the rendition process; (3) the United States Constitution's Fugitive Slave Clause implied a *common-law right of recaption, and so any slaveowner or his agent could remove a fugitive slave without complying

with the federal law of 1793, if such a capture could be done without a breach of the peace; and (4) all state judges and other officials should enforce the federal law, but that the national government could not require them to do so.

Chief Justice Taney concurred with the result in Prigg but objected to Story's assertion that state judges did not have to enforce the federal law. Taney correctly predicted that the states would use Story's opinion to undermine the effectiveness of the 1793 law.

It is not clear that Taney's criticisms of Story's opinion were fair or well founded. Story's opinion in fact allowed laws that aided the rendition process, which the Court accepted in Moore v. Illinois (1852). Nevertheless, Taney's impassioned misstatement of Story's opinion was apparently read more frequently than the majority opinion, thus ironically enhancing its antislavery potential. The result was that in the 1840s a number of state jurists refused to hear cases involving fugitive slaves, claiming that the Supreme Court's decision precluded them from taking jurisdiction. Some states adopted legislation that actually prohibited state officials from participating in fugitive slave cases. In 1843, for example, in response to the attempted removal of a fugitive slave named George Latimer, Massachusetts passed the "Latimer Law," which prohibited any sheriff or other civil officer from arresting an alleged fugitive slave, prohibited the use of public facilities including jails to incarcerate fugitives, and prohibited any state judge from hearing a case under the law of 1793 (see STATE SOVEREIGNTY AND STATES' RIGHTS).

Further stimulating northern opposition to fugitive slave rendition was the Supreme Court's harsh interpretation of the 1793 statute in Jones v. Van Zandt (1847). This was a civil suit for the value of slaves who had escaped from Kentucky to Ohio, where Van Zandt offered them a ride in his wagon. His attorneys, Salmon P. *Chase and William H. Seward, unsuccessfully argued that in Ohio all people were presumed free, and thus he had no reason to know he was transporting runaway slaves. Chase's printed brief thrust its author into the national spotlight, and he soon became known as the "Attorney General for Fugitive Slaves."

In response to the "Latimer Law" and other personal liberty laws, as well as the rise of an antislavery bar led by men like Chase, the South demanded a new and more stringent fugitive slave law. This was achieved in 1850. The new Fugitive Slave Act authorized the appointment of a federal commissioner in every county of the United States. The commissioners could issue certificates of removal for fugitive slaves and were empowered to call on federal marshals, the military, and "bystanders, or posse comitatus" to enforce the law. People interfering in the enforcement of the law could be jailed for up to six months and fined up to one thousand dollars.

Procedures under the law failed to provide even a semblance of due process to its victims. Alleged fugitives could be remanded on minimal evidence, or mere affidavit; seized blacks were not allowed to testify on their own behalf, and no jury trial was allowed to determine the status of the alleged fugitive. Worst of all federal commissioners received a fee of ten dollars if they found on behalf of the claimant, but only five dollars if they decided the alleged fugitive was in fact a free person. Congress justified this differential on the ground that the commissioner would have to do more paperwork if he found in favor of the claimant, but, for many Northerners, this seemed like a blatant attempt at bribery.

The Fugitive Slave Act quickly became imbedded in American culture, in part through Harriet Beecher Stowe's instant bestseller, *Uncle Tom's Cabin* (1852). About half the novel focused on the plight of the slave Eliza and her son, who escaped across the Ohio River to freedom. This book struck a responsive chord with Northerners. Equally important was the open hostility to the law throughout the North and the sporadic instances of violent opposition to it. Most seizures ended in the peaceful return of the alleged fugitive. But riots and rescues in Boston, Massachusetts (1851, 1854); Christiana, Pennsylvania (1851); Syracuse, New York (1851); Racine, Wisconsin (1854); Oberlin, Ohio (1858); Ottawa, Illinois (1859); and Iberia, Ohio (1860) made national headlines, as alleged fugitive slaves sometimes avoided the clutches of federal officers, while an occasional slaveowner or local policeman lost his life.

Most cases under the 1850 law never reached the Supreme Court. The trials of abolitionists and rescuers were usually decided in the district and circuit courts. The most dramatic lower federal case, *United States* v. *Hanway* (1851), stemmed out of the Christiana riot, in which a fugitive slave killed his former owner and then escaped to Canada. In response more than forty men were indicted for treason. Supreme Court Justice Robert Grier, on circuit at the time, ruled that opposition to the fugitive slave law did not constitute *treason. Although he was a proslavery doughface who despised abolitionists, Grier did not believe their actions constituted levying war on the national government.

*Ableman* v. *Booth* (1859) stemmed from the 1854 Racine rescue. After being arrested by a federal marshal for helping rescue a fugitive slave who had been seized, Sherman Booth, a prominent Republican editor, obtained a writ of habeas corpus from a state judge to secure his release from federal custody. The Wisconsin Supreme Court declared the Fugitive Slave Act unconstitutional and refused to send a record of the case to the Supreme Court. Speaking for a unanimous Court, Chief Justice Taney wrote a powerful opinion upholding federal judicial power at the expense of the states. Taney found that every

state was pledged *"to support this Constitution"* and that "no power is more clearly conferred than the power of this court to decide ultimately and finally, all cases arising under" the federal "Constitution and laws" (p. 525). (See JUDICIAL POWER AND JURISDICTION). *Ableman* is still cited for the proposition that the federal government "should be supreme, and strong enough to execute its laws by its own tribunals, without interruption from a State or from State authorities" and that "the supremacy thus conferred on this Government could not peacefully be maintained unless it was clothed with judicial power, equally paramount in authority to carry it into execution" (p. 517). Ironically, the Supreme Court used this century-old proslavery decision in the 1950s to bolster its affirmation of desegregation decrees.

*Kentucky* v. *Dennison* (1861), decided after secession had begun, was the Court's last major decision on slavery. Willis Lago, a free black living in Ohio, had helped a Kentucky slave escape to Ohio. Kentucky asked the governor of Ohio to extradite Lago so that he could stand trial for helping a slave escape. Governor Dennison, like his predecessor Salmon P. Chase, refused to order the extradition. Thus, Kentucky asked the Supreme Court to intervene. Chief Justice Taney faced a difficult dilemma. If he ordered Dennison to extradite Lago, he would be setting a precedent that the federal government could force state officials to act. With the Confederacy already formed, and *Civil War on the horizon, Taney did not want to give authority to the federal government to compel the actions of a state governor. Thus, in an opinion reminiscent of Marshall's in *Marbury* v. *Madison* (1803), Taney castigated Dennison for his refusal to act, but ultimately refused to issue a *mandamus against Dennison. Taney ruled that interstate extradition was a matter of gubernatorial discretion, to be performed out of *comity and good citizenship. This precedent remained good law until 1987.

**Slaves in Transit and Slavery in the Territories.** In two monumental acts, the *Northwest Ordinance (1787) and the Missouri Compromise (1820), Congress prohibited slavery in most of the territories owned by the United States. These acts led to some of the most important, controversial, and complicated cases that ever reached the Supreme Court.

Even before the Constitution was written, the United States Congress, acting under the old Articles of Confederation, regulated slavery in the western territories. Article VI of the Northwest Ordinance (1787) prohibited slavery north and west of the Ohio River. Eventually the free states of Ohio, Indiana, Illinois, Michigan, Wisconsin, and part of Minnesota would be carved out of this territory. The meaning of the slavery prohibition came before the Supreme Court in *LaGrange* v. *Chouteau* (1830), *Menard* v. *Aspasia* (1831), and *Strader* v. *Graham* (1851). Each case involved the status of slaves that had lived or worked in the old Northwest; in each case the court dismissed the appeal for lack of jurisdiction. In *Strader* the Court held that the slavery prohibition ceased to be in force when the territories became states (see TERRITORIES AND NEW STATES). Thus it was up to each state to determine for itself the status of persons within its jurisdiction, and this was not subject to review by the Supreme Court. *Strader* left it for each state, and an issue of interstate comity, to decide if a slave gained freedom through residence or sojourn in a free state.

*Dred Scott Case.* Along with *Marbury* v. *Madison* (1803), *Dred Scott* v. *Sandford* (1857) is the most famous nineteenth-century U.S. Supreme Court case. Besides *Marbury*, it is the only antebellum case in which the Supreme Court held a federal law unconstitutional.

The Missouri Compromise of 1820 admitted the state of Missouri into the Union as a slave state and prohibited slavery in the territory north of the new state, which was called the Missouri territory. As the slave of army surgeon Dr. John Emerson, Scott lived on a military base in the free state of Illinois and at Fort Snelling, in what was then the Missouri territory and later became Minnesota. After Dr. Emerson died, Scott sued for his freedom, and in 1850 a state court in St. Louis declared him free, under the principle that he had become free in Fort Snelling, and once free, he remained free, despite his return to the state of Missouri. This decision followed Missouri precedents dating from 1824. In *Scott* v. *Emerson* (1852), the Missouri Supreme Court, reflecting the growing proslavery ideology of the South, reversed this long standing rule. The Missouri court declared:

Times are not as they were when the former decisions on this subject were made. Since then not only individuals but States have been possessed of a dark and fell spirit in relation to slavery, whose gratification is sought in the pursuit of measures, whose inevitable consequence must be the overthrow and destruction of our government. Under such circumstances it does not behoove the State of Missouri to show the least countenance to any measure which might gratify this spirit. (p. 586)

By this time Scott was technically under the control of John F. A. Sanford, a New Yorker who was the executor of Dr. Emerson's estate. This allowed Scott to sue Sanford in federal court under diversity jurisdiction. In the United States district court, Sanford argued, in a plea in abatement, that Scott could not be a citizen of the United States for diversity purposes because he was a Negro. District Judge Robert W. Wells denied this plea, ruling that if Scott was free, then he was a citizen, for purposes of diversity jurisdiction, and could sue. If he was not free, then of course whether he could sue or not became moot (see MOOTNESS). Wells then held a trial on the merits of the case, and ruled that Scott's status was legitimately determined by the Missouri

Supreme Court, and he was in fact a slave. At this point, Scott's attorneys appealed to the United States Supreme Court. By the time the case reached Chief Justice Taney's court, the question of slavery in the territories had become the central political issue of the decade. Taney's decision must be seen in the context of this background.

From 1820 until 1850 the issue of slavery in the territories had been governed by the Missouri Compromise, which prohibited slavery in almost all of the West. However, with the acquisition of new lands in the Mexican War, and the acceptance throughout the South of a "positive good" view of slavery, Southerners were no longer content to see slavery shut out of the western territories. In 1854 Congress repealed the Missouri Compromise, by opening Kansas and Nebraska to slavery in 1854, under a theory of popular sovereignty. Under the theory of popular sovereignty, the settlers of a territory would decide for themselves whether to admit slavery or not. Rather than democratizing the West, popular sovereignty led to a mini–civil war known as "Bleeding Kansas," in which free state and slave state settlers fought for control of the territorial government. Meanwhile, in the North the newly organized Republican party gained enormous support by campaigning against the spread of slavery into the territories. In the 1856 presidential election this party, which was less than two years old, carried all but five northern states.

*Taney's Decision.* The avidly proslavery Chief Justice Taney used *Dred Scott* to decide pressing political issues in favor of the South. Taney's two most controversial points dealt with the constitutionality of the Missouri Compromise and the rights of free blacks under the federal Constitution.

By strained logic Taney argued that the territories clause of Article IV of the Constitution only applied to the territories owned by the United States in 1787 and did not apply to territories acquired after that date. This led him to conclude that the Missouri Compromise was unconstitutional. In addition, Taney argued that freeing slaves in the territories constituted a *taking of property without due process, which violated the *Fifth Amendment. This was the Supreme Court's first use of the concept of substantive *due process. Thus, under Taney's theory of the Constitution Dred Scott had not been entitled to freedom, even while he lived in Minnesota. More importantly, Taney's theory meant that all congressional limitation on slavery in federal jurisdictions was unconstitutional. This was a direct assault on Northerners who had been working to make the territories free.

Taney compounded this attack on northern attitudes with a stunning and gratuitous denial of the rights of free blacks in the United States. Although unnecessary for the outcome of the case, Taney examined whether Scott had *standing to sue in federal court, even if he were free. Taney asked: "Can a negro, whose ancestors were imported into this country, and sold as slaves, become a member of the political community formed and brought into existence by the Constitution of the United States, and as such become entitled to all the rights, privileges, and immunities guaranteed by that instrument to the citizens?" Rigorously applying a jurisprudence of *original intent, Taney answered his own question with a resounding no. Taney concluded that even those free blacks living in the North with full state citizenship could never be citizens of the United States. Taney argued that blacks

are not included, and were not intended to be included, under the word "citizens" in the Constitution, and can therefore claim none of the rights and privileges which that instrument provides and secures to citizens of the United States. On the contrary, they were at that time [1787] considered as a subordinate and inferior class of beings who had been subjugated by the dominant race, and, whether emancipated or not, yet remained subject to their authority, and had no rights or privilege but such as those who held the power and the Government might choose to grant them. (pp. 404–405)

In an analysis that was historically incorrect and shocking to the North, Taney asserted that at the time the Constitution was adopted blacks were universally considered "beings of an inferior order, and altogether unfit to associate with the white race, either in social or political relations; and so far inferior, that they had no rights which the white man was bound to respect; and that the negro might justly and lawfully be reduced to slavery for his [white people's] benefit" (p. 407). Taney gave examples of colonial laws discriminating against blacks, which were "still in force when the Revolution began" (p. 409), to show that blacks were not citizens in those states. He then cited sources from "the States where slavery had worn out, or measures taken for its speedy abolition," to prove that from the Revolution onward blacks were degraded and unequal throughout New England (p. 413). He argued that these precedents illustrated "the entire repudiation of the African Race" (p. 415). What Taney ignored, of course, was that at the time of the Revolution free blacks in fact voted in a number of states, including Massachusetts, Pennsylvania, and North Carolina, and were clearly constituent members of the society that adopted the Constitution.

Finally, Taney discussed how Scott's status was affected by his residence in Illinois. Here he relied on *Strader* v. *Graham*, where the Court had ruled that each state had a right to decide for itself the status of persons under its jurisdiction. Thus, if Scott had sued in Illinois, that state could have freed him. But Scott sued in Missouri, whose supreme court had refused to free Scott based on his residence in Illinois, a ruling binding on Federal courts.

*Curtis's Dissent.* All nine justices wrote opin-

ions in *Dred Scott*. Six concurred with Taney, including two northern doughfaces, Robert Grier and Samuel Nelson. Justices John *McLean of Ohio and Benjamin R. *Curtis of Massachusetts dissented. Curtis refuted Taney at almost every point. Curtis asserted that United States citizenship preceded the Constitution, and that under the Articles of Confederation state *citizenship qualified one for national citizenship. Curtis noted that free blacks were citizens of at least five states before 1787 and thus they were also citizens of the United States at the time the Constitution was adopted. In answer to Taney's argument that Congress could not regulate slavery in the territories, Curtis noted that everyone, including Taney, admitted "Congress has some power to institute temporary Governments over the territory" (p. 609). Curtis believed this power came from the territories clause of Article IV, because that was a "reasonable interpretation of the language of the Constitution" (p. 610) and made much greater sense than Taney's unpersuasive attempt to show that the clause only applied to the federal territories existing in 1787. Curtis demonstrated that if Congress has a power, it is a broad power, and not the narrow and constricted one that Taney found. Curtis reasoned that the words "needful regulation" in the territories clause was a grant of such power. Could a "needful regulation" reach slavery? Curtis noted that

while no other clause of the Constitution can be shown, which requires the insertion of an exception respecting slavery, and while the practical construction for a period of upwards of fifty years forbids such an exception, it would, in my opinion violate every sound rule of interpretation to force that exception into the Constitution upon the strength of abstract political reasoning which we are bound to believe the people of the United States thought insufficient to induce them to limit the power of Congress, because what they have said contains no such limitation. (p. 623)

*Political Reaction to Dred Scott.* Curtis's dissent heartened Northerners like Horace Greeley, the editor of the *New York Tribune*, who wrote that Taney's decision was an "atrocious," "wicked," "abominable," "false," opinion. It was a "collection of false statements and shallow sophistries," a "detestable hypocrisy" and a "mean and skulking cowardice." The *Chicago Tribune* expressed the reaction of many Northerners: "We scarcely know how to express our detestation of its inhuman dicta, or to fathom the wicked consequences which may flow from it."

The *Dred Scott* case gave Taney an opportunity to try to settle the issue of slavery, once and for all, in favor of the South. Taney hoped that his magisterial decision would end the controversy over slavery in the territories and in the process destroy the new Republican party, which so threatened slavery. Yet his decision had just the opposite affect, in part because, as historian Don Fehrenbacher has written in his *The Dred Scott*

*Case* (1978): "Taney's opinion, carefully read, proves to be a work of unmitigated partisanship, polemical in spirit though judicial in its language, and more like an ultimatum than a formula for sectional accommodation. Peace on Taney's terms resembled the peace implicit in a demand for unconditional surrender." The decision was, as political scientist Harry Jaffa has written, "nothing less than a summons to the Republicans to disband" (p. 3).

Instead of disbanding, Republicans successfully made Taney and the decision the focus of their 1858 and 1860 campaigns. In his "House Divided" speech (1858), Abraham Lincoln argued that Taney's opinion was part of a proslavery conspiracy to nationalize slavery and a prelude to future proslavery jurisprudence. He warned of "another Supreme Court decision, declaring that the Constitution of the United States does not permit a *state* to exclude slavery from its limits." He told the voters in Ilinois, and by extension the entire North, that "We shall *lie down* pleasantly dreaming that the people of Missouri are on the verge of making their state *free;* and we shall *awake* to the *reality,* instead, that the Supreme Court has made *Illinois a slave* state." Lincoln feared such a decision because of language in a concurring opinion in *Dred Scott* by Justice Samuel Nelson, a New York doughface, and because of a slave case that was then making its way through the New York courts.

Justice Nelson noted that "except as restrained by the Federal Constitution" the states had "complete and absolute power over the subject of slavery." Nelson may have only been referring to the Fugitive Slave Clause's limitation on the states. But Republicans, such as Governor Salmon P. Chase of Ohio and Abraham Lincoln, saw a darker side to Nelson's opinion, especially because Nelson concluded by observing:

A question has been alluded to . . . namely: the right of the master with his slave of transit into or through a free State, on business or commercial pursuits, or in the exercise of a federal right, or the discharge of a federal duty, being a citizen of the United States, which is not before us. This question depends upon different considerations and principles from the one in hand, and turns upon the rights and privileges secured to a common citizen of the republic, under the Constitution of the United States. When that question arises, we shall be prepared to decide it. (p. 468)

In the Illinois senate race of 1858 Abraham Lincoln condemned the "wicked consequences" of the *Dred Scott* decision and expressed the fear that the Supreme Court might soon force slavery on the North through what he called "the next Dred Scott Case." He noted that "In what cases" the states were restrained was "left an open question." Lincoln warned the North that the "next Dred Scott Case" would legalize slavery throughout the nation.

Lincoln's fears were far from paranoid. In 1852 the New York Supreme Court ruled that eight slaves were properly liberated when their owner brought them into New York while changing ships for a voyage to New Orleans. After the *Dred Scott* decision the New York Court of Appeals, that state's highest court, upheld this result in *Lemmon* v. *The People* (1860). Had that case gone to the Supreme Court it is likely that Taney and his proslavery colleagues would have ruled that New York did not have the power to free slaves in transit. The election of Lincoln, secession, and the Civil War, mooted that issue.

*Summary.* From 1790 to 1861 the Supreme Court's slavery jurisprudence reflected American politics. In the end the Court tried to solve the American dilemma over slavery with decisions that entirely protected slavery and thoroughly repudiated the dominant ideology of the North. Such a solution was bound to fail. The solution of the Taney Court was consistent with the makeup of that court. Dominated by Southerners and northern Democrats, the Court supported slavery at almost every turn. Slaveowners and the institution of slavery almost always won before the high court. The only exceptions to this general rule involved the African slave trade, *Kentucky* v. *Dennison,* which turned on critical political issues, and a few minor cases, which were decided on strictly technical grounds. Blacks seeking freedom could find no sympathy on the nation's highest court until the chief justice from Maryland died and was succeeded by abolitionist Salmon P. Chase. Less than two years after this change on the Court, slavery itself disappeared, and the Court was left with the difficult task of building a new jurisprudence, based on concepts of freedom and racial equality. Saddled with formidable proslavery precedents, the postwar Court was not as successful in protecting freedom as the prewar Court had been in protecting slavery.

(See also COMMERCE POWER; FUGITIVE SLAVES.)

□ Robert M. Cover, *Justice Accused: Anti-Slavery and the Judicial Process* (1975). Paul Finkelman, "*Prigg* v. *Pennsylvania* and Northern State Courts: Antislavery Use of a Proslavery Decision," *Civil War History* 25 (1979): 5–35. Paul Finkelman, *An Imperfect Union: Slavery, Federalism, and Comity* (1981). Paul Finkelman, "Slavery and the Constitutional Convention: Making a Covenant with Death," in *Beyond Confederation: Origins of the Constitution and American National Identity,* edited by Richard Beeman, et al. (1987), pp. 188–225. Harold M. Hyman and William M. Wiecek, *Equal Justice under Law: Constitutional Development, 1835–1875* (1982). Thomas D. Morris, *Free Men All: The Personal Liberty Laws of the North, 1780–1861* (1974). William M. Wiecek, *The Sources of Antislavery Constitutionalism in America, 1760–1848* (1977). William M. Wiecek, "Slavery and Abolition before the United States Supreme Court, 1820–1860," *Journal of American History* 65 (1978): 34–59. Paul Finkelman

**Slip Opinion.** Initial publication of Supreme Court opinions occurs in two stages: bench copies available on the day of the decision and slip opinions that circulate within three days of decisions. The four thousand slip opinion copies are distributed free of charge to attorneys and the public. Fee-paying subscribers may receive advance unofficial copies from commercial services or, beginning in 1990, official copies from the Court's electronic information system.

Slip opinions are a single sheet or center-stapled sheets issued in booklet form. Consecutively paginated, the headnote or syllabus includes the title, originating court, docket number, dates of arguments and decision, summary of the facts, holdings, reasoning and judgment of the Court, and the justices' voting line-up. Following is the consecutively paginated text of the Court's opinion and that of each separate opinion. Modern slip opinions evolved from page proofs once obtainable only from the Court-selected private printer or from a justice. Their circulation became routinized, initially for the benefit of journalists, during William Howard *Taft's chief justiceship.

Proofreading and headnote-drafting responsibilities fall to the reporter's office (see REPORTERS, SUPREME COURT). The Court in 1970 authorized inclusion of headnotes in slip opinions as an aid to the press. All such headnotes are prefaced by a disclaimer of authority derived from *United States v. Detroit Lumber Co.* (1905). Following the headnote is an invitation to notify the reporter of errors to be corrected prior to publication of the preliminary print.

Technological innovation expedited production of slip opinions during Chief Justice Warren *Burger's tenure. But security against premature disclosures of opinions continued to be of concern after a 1979 "leak" of the Court's ruling in *Herbert v. Lando.*

(See also ADVANCE SHEETS; OPINIONS, ASSIGNMENT AND WRITING OF.)

Peter G. Fish

## Slochower v. Board of Education of New York City, 350 U. S. 551 (1956), argued 18–19 Oct. 1955, decided 9 Apr. 1956, by vote of 5 to 4; Clark for the Court, Reed, Burton, Minton, and Harlan in dissent. At a hearing of a congressional committee investigating subversion in education, a tenured faculty member at Brooklyn College stated that he was not a communist, that he was willing to testify about his associations since 1941, but claimed the self-incrimination privilege about inquiries concerning activities in 1940–1941. The New York City Charter provided that if an employee of the city used the privilege against self-incrimination to avoid answering a question relating to his official conduct, his tenure of employment would terminate. Acting under this provision, the Board of Education discharged Slochower without affording him the usual hearing for tenured faculty members.

The Supreme Court held the provision of the charter was unconstitutional, and that the summary dismissal violated the *Due Process Clause. The provision of the charter, as applied in the case, had converted the constitutional privilege into a conclusive presumption of guilt; there was no inquiry into the faculty member's fitness; his dismissal was based solely on events occurring before a congressional committee. The Court held that the action of the Board of Education fell squarely within the prohibition of *Wieman* v. *Updegraff* (1952). The dissenters contended that a state may justifiably conclude that teachers who refuse to answer questions concerning their official conduct are no longer qualified to teach. The case has been limited by *Lerner* v. *Casey* (1958) and *Nelson* v. *County of Los Angeles* (1960), which in turn may have been limited by *Gardner* v. *Broderick* (1968).

(See also COMMUNISM AND COLD WAR; SELF-INCRIMINATION.)

Milton R. Konvitz

**Smith, William** (b. North Carolina, ca. 1762; d. 26 June 1840, at family estate near Huntsville, Ala.), lawyer and jurist. Reared and educated in York County, South Carolina, William Smith knew Andrew *Jackson and William H. Crawford as boyhood friends. He became a successful lawyer in York County and served in the state senate from 1802 until 1808, when he was elected to the state court of appeals. He resigned from the bench in 1816 when he was elected by the legislature to the United States Senate. Smith served in the Senate until 1823 and again from 1826 to 1831. As a senator he defended states' rights and opposed banks, internal improvements, the tariff, and John C. Calhoun. In 1832 Smith moved to Louisiana and then to Huntsville, Alabama, where he prospered through shrewd investments in land and served in the lower house of the legislature.

President Jackson offered twice to nominate Smith to the Supreme Court, once in 1829 and again in 1837. Smith declined each time, declaring on the latter occasion that he desired to maintain the right to comment freely on public affairs. Had Smith served on the Court and adhered to his oft-expressed political creed, he would have espoused an extreme states' rights position and one of strict construction that severely limited the powers of the federal government.

Robert M. Ireland

**Smith Act.** The Smith Act was a product of America's prewar anxieties. Proposed by Representative Howard W. Smith of Virginia, the measure was one of several antisubversive bills introduced in Congress during 1939. A modified version was adopted by both houses on 22 June 1940, as Title I of the Alien Registration Act.

Section I provided a fine of up to ten thousand dollars and ten years in prison for attempting to undermine the morale of the armed forces. Sections II and III provided the same penalties for anyone who "advocates, abets, advises, or teaches" the violent overthrow of the government; publishes or distributes printed matter that advocates the violent overthrow; organizes any society with such a purpose; knowingly joins such a society; or conspires to do any of the above.

The Smith Act was initially invoked in 1941 against eighteen members of the Socialist Workers party in Minnesota but was rarely used during *World War II. After the war, it became a primary weapon in the government's war on domestic communists. In 1948 the Justice Department brought charges against twelve members of the Communist party's Central Committee, and after the Supreme Court upheld those convictions and affirmed the validity of the act in *Dennis v. United States (1951), indictments were secured against state party leaders throughout the country. In all, 141 persons were indicted for violating the Smith Act, but, because of the more liberal standards applied by the Court in *Yates v. United States (1957) and *Scales v. United States (1961), only twenty-nine of those indicted served jail terms.

(See also COMMUNISM AND COLD WAR; SUBVERSION.)

Jerold L. Simmons

**Smith v. Allwright,** 321 U.S. 649 (1944), argued 10 and 12 Nov. 1943, reargued 12 Jan. 1944, decided 3 Apr. 1944 by vote of 8 to 1; Reed for the Court, Roberts in dissent. The history of the "white primary" was a game of constitutional chess waged against blacks and the Supreme Court by whites and the Texas legislature. After *Reconstruction, a Democratic primary victory assured success in the general election in Texas and throughout the one-party South. Therefore, exclusion of African-Americans from primary participation had the practical effect of disfranchisement.

Initially, in Newberry v. United States (1921), the Court concluded that party primary elections were unknown to the framers and therefore were beyond the reach of the Constitution. Two years later, the Texas legislature enacted a statute expressly barring African-Americans from voting in a Democratic primary. The Court in *Nixon v. Herndon (1927) held this measure invalid under the *Fourteenth Amendment. The Texas legislature then enacted another statute that authorized the state party executive committee to determine membership qualifications, including race, and again the Court held the statute invalid in *Nixon v. Condon (1932). Next the Texas legislature repealed all state primary election statutes, anticipating that the Democratic state convention would exclude African-Americans, which the Court upheld, in *Grovey v. Townsend (1935), as "private" discrimination beyond the Constitution.

African-American voters were checked until the *NAACP saw an opening in United States v. *Classic (1941), which held that Congress could regulate primary as well as general elections for federal office. The NAACP sponsored Smith, who brought suit against Texas Democratic party election officials in a direct challenge on the Grovey holding, alleging that he had been unconstitutionally denied a primary ballot because of his race.

Justice Stanley *Reed applied the Classic reasoning to overrule Grovey, and the white primary was checkmated. Since the primary system was an integral part of the state's election procedures, citizens had the right under the *Fifteenth Amendment to vote in party primaries free of racial discrimination. The discrimination was not merely "private." First, since state law authorized primary elections and regulated the party's procedures, the party in convention acted as an agent of the state in excluding African-Americans. Second, conducting elections was a state function; therefore, the state was responsible for allowing the private racial discrimination.

Justice Owen J. *Roberts, who had written for a unanimous Court only nine years before in Grovey, dissented on the grounds that the overruling promoted disrespect for the Court and instability in the law. Justice Reed replied that the Court's decision only required correcting a misapplication of settled principles. Neither opinion noted that seven of the justices had been appointed by President Franklin D. *Roosevelt in that interim.

Constitutional scholars cite Allwright as one of the seminal cases in the development of the "public function" concept. Certain activities traditionally performed by the government—such as elections—are deemed to be state action under the Constitution even when performed by private actors. This doctrine was extended in *Terry v. Adams (1953) in which the Court invalidated an unofficial primary held by a private, all-white "club" despite the lack of state regulation of the club.

After Allwright, the available methods for reducing African-American participation in elections were limited to those directed at individuals rather than groups, such as literacy tests and poll taxes. These methods proved less effective with time. The federal legislative response came in the *Civil Rights Acts of 1957, 1960, and 1964, followed by the *Twenty-Fourth Amendment, which banned poll taxes in federal elections, and especially in the *Voting Rights Act of 1965 with subsequent amendments.

The broader significance of this decision lies in the Court's focus on substance over form in determining voting rights. This approach became the conceptual foundation for later landmark civil rights cases involving such matters as racially restrictive covenants, school segregation, and political reapportionment.

(See also RACE AND RACISM; REAPPORTIONMENT CASES; WHITE PRIMARY.)

□ Ward E. Y. Elliot, *The Rise of Guardian Democracy—The Supreme Court's Role in Voting Rights Disputes, 1845–1969* (1974). Darlene Clark Hine, *Black Victory—The Rise and Fall of the White Primary in Texas* (1979).

Thomas E. Baker

**Smyth v. Ames,** 169 U.S. 466, argued 5–7 Apr. 1897, decided 7 Mar. 1898 by vote of 9 to 0; Harlan for the Court. In *Smyth* v. *Ames*, the Supreme Court voided a schedule of railroad tariffs enacted by Nebraska and defined the constitutional limits of governmental power to set railroad and utility rates. The Court held that regulated industries were constitutionally entitled to earn a "fair return" on the "fair value" of the enterprise. Under the *fair value rule a governmental authority was required to determine a "rate base," which was the present value of the enterprise's assets, and to allow the enterprise to charge rates sufficient to earn a normal return on that value.

*Smyth* v. *Ames* was emblematic of the Court's protection of the free market economy in the late nineteenth century. Over time, the decision was criticized by jurists who objected to *laissez-faire constitutionalism. Critics claimed that the fair value rule was impractical because of the complex administrative proceedings required to determine the current value of utility assets as the rate base. *Smyth*'s critics also claimed that the case was illogical because a utility's value is determined by its rates. Rates could not be set according to an enterprise's value since that value cannot be known until the rates are determined.

Despite these criticisms, the conservative Court steadfastly adhered to *Smyth* v. *Ames*, which set the constitutional limits of rate regulation until it was overruled in *Federal Power Commission* v. *Hope Natural Gas Co.* (1944).

Stephen A. Siegel

**Social Background of the Justices.** The personal attributes of the justices of the Supreme Court have, since the Court's beginning in 1790, been the center of intense political interest. Serious scholarly analysis of such attributes has largely been a twentieth-century endeavor. Selection to the Court has reflected, in successive historic eras, the extent to which groups have been denied or have achieved access to major national political elite positions. From this broad perspective, Supreme Court appointments generally have been gained later than election to Congress, but earlier than election to the presidency for those historically denied equality and/or political participation, such as African-Americans and women. Thus Roger Brooke *Taney, the first Catholic justice, was chosen in 1836; Louis D. *Brandeis, the first Jewish appointee, became a member in 1916; Thurgood *Marshall, the first African-American, was chosen in 1967; and the

first woman, Sandra Day *O'Connor, was selected in 1981.

The background of an individual is important or, in some instances, essential to selection to the Court. Background includes an individual's social status, paternal occupation, patterns of occupational "heredity," ethnicity, religion, and education. With exceedingly few exceptions, Supreme Court justices have been white males chosen past middle age from socially and economically advantaged families: Protestant by religion and high status by denomination, descendants of natives of the British Isles, and recipients of undergraduate education in schools of national reputation. Upper-class bias has lessened, but by no means disappeared, in the late twentieth century. Career characteristics such as political party affiliation, legal and political philosophy, political involvement, previous judicial experience, interest group affinity (for example, Stephen J. *Field's relationship with railroad magnates), membership and leadership in important bar groups (for example, William Howard *Taft's presidency of the American Bar Association or Thurgood *Marshall's role as counsel for the *NAACP *Legal Defense Fund) also have been factors in selection to the Court.

Perhaps the most intensely debated aspect of the significance of background and career characteristics is whether such attributes bear any relationship to the justices' decision making. One persistently argued position is that background and career factors are neutralized by or virtually eliminated by the judicial role itself. Justice Felix *Frankfurter provided one of the clearest statements of this position in recusing himself in the so-called *Captive Audience Case*. Frankfurter asserted in *Public Utilities Commission* v. *Pollak* (1952) that

> There is a good deal of shallow talk that the judicial role does not change the man within it. It does. The fact is that on the whole judges do lay aside private views in discharging their judicial functions. This is achieved through training, professional habits, self-discipline, and that fortunate alchemy by which men are loyal to the obligation with which they are entrusted. (pp. 466–467)

Several generations of scholars, however, have found a good deal of evidence confirming the significance of party and other background variables, including Rodney Mott in the 1930s, Herman Pritchett in the 1940s, and an increasingly larger number of scholars thereafter. A scholarly reappraisal occurred in the 1960s when Bowen and Grossman, among others, raised questions about the behavioral conceptualization of background variables in relation to judicial voting behavior and the extent to which such variables actually explain judicial voting behavior. On the other hand, summing up the empirical evidence obtained by the end of the 1980s, C. Neal Tate concluded that background attributes explained significant voting differences in cases involving civil rights and liberties as well as economic issues.

☐ Donald R. Bowen, "The Explanation of Judicial Voting Behavior from Sociological Characteristics of Judges" (Ph.D. diss., Yale University, 1965). Joel B. Grossman, "Social Backgrounds and Judicial Decision-making," *Harvard Law Review* 79 (1966): 1551–1564. C. Neal Tate, "Personal Attributes as Explanations of Supreme Court Justices' Decision Making," in *Courts in American Politics,* edited by Henry M. Glick (1990), pp. 261–275.

John R. Schmidhauser

**Social Science.** The increasing role of the courts in law and policy making has significant implications for the interaction of law and science. Even trial courts often require the assistance of science to decide a particular case. This need for science is still greater when litigation involving policy issues reaches the appellate level. Law and science, however, are rather unequal partners in the forensic enterprise. While law needs science considerably more than science needs the law, law controls the terms of the relationship. Science can participate in formal dispute resolution only at the invitation of the law and the interaction of the two disciplines takes place in legal territory and is conducted according to the principles and rules of the law. The only real choice scientists have is to participate or not.

Adjudication requires legal and factual determinations. The former is the province of the law; the latter is not. Through the testimony of lay (direct) or expert witnesses, litigants present evidence regarding the factual issues of the case. Lay witnesses testify on the basis of their personal knowledge of the relevant facts. Expert witnesses testify on the basis of their command of a general body of knowledge and/or the conduct of case-oriented, special-purpose inquiries.

Scientists, as expert witnesses, provide two types of testimony, one regarding case facts (adjudicative facts), the other scientific generalizations (legislative facts). Giving evidence about a defendant's blood type in a contested paternity case is an example of the former. Testifying about the differential application of the death penalty is an example of the latter (see RACE DISCRIMINATION AND THE DEATH PENALTY).

Many scientists are willing to assist the courts, but their testimony is not always welcome or well used. The record of the U.S. Supreme Court and other appellate courts shows nonuse and misuse of scientific evidence at least as often as proper utilization. The fault does not always lie with the courts. Sometimes the evidence is flawed or incoherent; sometimes no evidence is available. Sometimes neither the litigants nor the court know where to find the relevant evidence. They may not even realize that it is available or, even, that it is needed.

Often the adversarial process gets in the way of a clear and full presentation of the best available scientific evidence. The tactics of cross-examination—ad hominem attacks, witness bullying, cutting answers short, deliberate deception and setting traps—are designed to confuse, discredit, and embarrass witnesses (who, of course, are unable to fight back), when their testimony cannot be otherwise refuted. Adversarial procedures do not seek truth but partisan advantage.

Scientists tend to misunderstand the primary purpose of the law. The objective is to resolve disputes, not to establish the truth. Scientists are committed to objective fact finding. Objectivity consists of neutrality and autonomy. Neutrality means that the scholar's own preferences will not influence the results of his work. Autonomy means that the preferences of outside agencies will not have such an influence. Of course, objectivity is a goal that is not always reached. In the forensic context, the greater threat is to autonomy. Attorneys want to win. Understandably, they tend to nudge their experts towards partisanship.

A number of procedural and structural reforms have been suggested to improve the interaction of law and science and to make scientific findings more correctly and more readily available to the courts—beginning, perhaps, with the *"Brandeis brief." These range from "science clerks" to panels of experts to assist judges and to special masters and monitors to supervise the development of scientific evidence and testimony. A greater use of courts of special jurisdiction and, even, "science courts" has also been advocated. Few such reforms have yet been tried or adopted, though some of them are authorized under current rules, for example, the appointment of special masters. In any case, judges should consider taking a more active role in assuring complete and accurate presentation of relevant evidence. The courts should also consider developing new (nonadversarial) procedures to test the validity of scientific evidence.

The special characteristics of social science deserves attention. The law's failure to use the findings of the social sciences has often been rationalized by pointing to the "softness" of these disciplines—in contrast to the "hardness" of the physical sciences and the "certainty" of the law. Both comparisons are less persuasive than might appear at first.

As regards scientific "hardness," all scientific generalizations are probabilistic. No scientific discipline generates "absolutes." It is a serious error to confuse the deductive certainties of mathematics with the inductive probabilities of science—as did Justice Felix *Frankfurter, when he refused to accept psychological evidence because such evidence lacked "mathematical certainty" (*Brown* v. *Board of Education,* 1954).

As regards the "certainty" of the law, a reasonably close inspection exposes the fictitious nature of this claim. To believe that judges simply can deduce decisions from case law, statutes, and general principles—that two equally competent judges would necessarily arrive at the same decision—requires considerable blindness to the realities of the law: 5-to-4 decisions, reversals, overrulings, judge-shopping, and the politics of judicial appointments.

The real problem is not the "softness" or the "uncertainty" of social science evidence. Rather, it is the way in which such evidence is introduced, processed, and tested. At the bottom of it all may well be the law's great reluctance to deal with the unaccustomed and unfamiliar.

□ Saul M. Kassin and Lawrence S. Wrightsman, eds., *The Psychology of Evidence and Trial Procedure* (1985). Richard Lempert and Joseph Sanders, *An Invitation to Law and Social Science* (1986). Peter W. Sperlich, "Social Science Evidence in the Courts: Reaching Beyond the Adversary Process," *Judicature* 63 (1980): 280–289.
Peter W. Sperlich

**Sociological Jurisprudence.** In a series of law review articles published between 1905 and 1923, Roscoe Pound of the Harvard Law School criticized the prevailing assumptions of what he called "mechanical jurisprudence." He denied that just legal results would be produced by logical deductions from axiomatic premises about the laws of economics or the structure of society and pointed out that such axioms reflected more a judge's individual biases than they did universal truths. In this criticism, Pound echoed the skepticism of Justice Oliver Wendell *Holmes, especially as expressed in his dissent in *Lochner v. New York* (1905).

In place of this discredited formalism that masked conservative political prejudices, Pound called for what he termed a "sociological jurisprudence." Such a judicial outlook would recognize that law is not an autonomous collection of self-contained and self-referential rules. Instead, the judge would seek enlightenment from disciplines outside law, including the political and social sciences. Judges would become more sensitive to the actual impact of legal doctrine. They would strive for an equitable application of law to reach just results in particular cases. The *"Brandeis brief," introduced by Louis D. Brandeis in *Muller* v. *Oregon* (1908), exemplified the approach advocated by Pound.

Sociological jurisprudence is often regarded as an early expression of the movement known as Legal Realism, but there were significant differences between the two. Realists like Karl Llewellyn, while acknowledging their debt to sociological jurisprudence, found themselves engaged in mutual criticism with Pound, who was skeptical of the premises of Realism.
William M. Wiecek

**Solicitor General.** Of all the nation's officials, the solicitor general is the only one required by statute to be "learned in the law." He is the chief courtroom lawyer for the executive branch and serves in the Justice Department, but he also has chambers at the Supreme Court. The fact that he keeps offices at these two institutions underscores his special role, which is summed up in his informal title as the "tenth justice."

The post of solicitor general was established in 1870, when Congress created the Department of Justice. Congress intended that the solicitor would assist the attorney general by representing the United States wherever the government had an interest in litigation. Early solicitors tried occasional cases. Benjamin Bristow, the first solicitor general, made his reputation prosecuting the Ku Klux Klan. However, for many years solicitors have concentrated on the government's appeals, especially to the Supreme Court.

Within the executive branch, the solicitor general has filled an almost judicial function. For every petition for a writ of *certiorari that the solicitor general sends to the Supreme Court, he rejects five from federal agencies with grievances they want the justices to settle. The solicitor's restraint in petitioning pays off in credibility with the Court. The justices rely heavily on the solicitor general to help choose and present the most pressing cases for review. The Court grants approximately 80 percent of the certiorari petitions submitted by the solicitor general, as opposed to only 3 percent submitted by other lawyers across the country.

The justices also turn to the solicitor general for help on legal problems that appear especially vexing and regularly invite him to submit briefs in cases where the executive branch is not a party. The justices expect him to look beyond the government's narrow interests, to take a long view about the development of legal doctrine.

Clearly, there is a special relationship between the solicitor's office and the Supreme Court. When a member of the Court dies, the solicitor general is asked to call a meeting of the Supreme Court bar to honor the justice. The justices also give the solicitor general dispensations in Court. In the Supreme Court's rules, the solicitor general is the only *amicus curiae regularly given time to argue.

There is also a practice called "lodging" not mentioned in the Court's rules that is rarely used except by the solicitor's office. Lodging occurs when the solicitor finds an official document (e.g., an annual report from Congress) that, while not in the trial record, sheds new light on the government's argument in a pending case. The lawyers "lodge" the document with the *clerk of the Court, and inform the justices that the materials are there in case they want to examine the papers.

The solicitor general reciprocates to such dispensations with a number of distinctive practices. One is known as "confessing error." If a private attorney wins a case he thinks he should have lost in a *lower federal court, he is likely to accept his victory in diplomatic silence. But when the government wins on terms that strike the solicitor general as unjust, he may "confess error" and recommend that the Supreme Court overturn the flawed decision.

Chief Justice William *Rehnquist and Justice Byron *White have criticized the practice from the bench and in opinions, on the ground that the solicitor is playing a role properly left to the Court. But former solicitor general Archibald Cox expressed faith in the practice of confessing error. In his view, it tests the conviction that the office has a special responsibility to the Court. If the solicitor takes a disinterested position even when it means surrendering a victory, then the government's other cases are more likely to be presented with restraint, candor, and a long view.

The tradition of restraint practiced by Cox and other solicitors in both Democratic and Republican administrations since the early years of this century was challenged by the Reagan administration. Rex Lee, the first Reagan solicitor, was forced from office after he refused to press the administration's social policies at every turn. The administration turned the solicitor's post into that of a partisan spokesman for the policies of the president, rather than the legal conscience of the government, and for a vision of the roles of the three branches of government largely at odds with the view that had evolved in the American mainstream during the previous fifty years.

When Robert H. *Jackson was solicitor for the administration of Franklin D. *Roosevelt, by contrast, he argued for *New Deal constitutionalism to an anti–New Deal court, yet maintained the traditional role of his office. A key difference between the use of the solicitor's office by the Roosevelt and Reagan administrations, although both asked the Court to overturn established doctrine, was their view about the roles of the executive and judicial branches in interpreting the Constitution.

The Roosevelt administration urged the Court to uphold social legislation that it had struck down, but deferred to the Court as the final arbiter of constitutional law. The Reagan administration attacked *judicial review, on the ground that the Supreme Court had misapplied this principle for a quarter of a century, making social policy instead of interpreting the law. This challenge led to a controversy about the relationship between the solicitor's office and the Supreme Court, for, once the administration elevated the executive branch to the Court's level as an interpreter of the Constitution, there was no reason for the solicitor to maintain traditional deference to the Court.

Many solicitors general have enjoyed successful subsequent careers. John W. *Davis ran for president in 1924 and pursued a distinguished career at the private bar. Robert Jackson, William Howard *Taft, Stanley *Reed, and Thurgood *Marshall later served on the Supreme Court.

Archibald Cox served as a Watergate special prosecutor.

The recent debate about the solicitor's role drew wide attention to the solicitor general in his own right for the first time and led to fresh theorizing about his role. In the wake of controversy, there remains wide agreement that the solicitor general plays a unique role in American law, but no view about how the role should be defined commands a clear consensus among scholars or practitioners.

□ Lincoln Caplan, *The Tenth Justice: The Solicitor General and the Rule of Law* (1987). "The Role and Function of the United States Solicitor General," symposium in *Loyola Law Review* 21 (June 1988): 1047–1271.

Lincoln Caplan

**Souter, David** (b. Melrose, Mass., 17 Sept 1939), associate justice, 1990–. On 25 July 1990 President George Bush nominated David H. Souter to replace retiring Justice William *Brennan. Although Souter had served for a short time as a federal appellate judge, his legal experience was primarily in state government. He was the attorney general of New Hampshire, a New Hampshire superior judge, and a justice of the Supreme Court of New Hampshire.

Having replaced the liberal Justice Brennan, much of the speculation surrounding Souter's appointment centered on whether he would provide a fifth vote for an emerging conservative majority. Predicting a justice's voting pattern over an entire career from a single term is hazardous. Nonetheless, in a number of 5-to-4 decisions during his first term Justice Souter joined the conservative majority and signaled that he would actively participate in changing the Court's direction. In *Rust* v. *Sullivan* (1991), he voted to uphold federal regulations prohibiting doctors from advising patients of *abortion as an available procedure. In *Barnes* v. *Glen Theatre, Inc.* (1991), he voted to uphold a state ban on nude dancing. In *Payne* v. *Tennessee* (1991), he voted to overrule recent decisions excluding from death penalty determinations evidence on the impact of the crime on the victim's family (see CAPITAL PUNISHMENT).

Statistics also demonstrate the shift in direction with Justice Souter's appointment. He voted with Chief Justice William H. *Rehnquist in 86 percent of cases. In 1989 Justice Brennan had voted with Chief Justice Rehnquist in only 38 percent of cases. Justice Souter voted least often with liberal Justice Thurgood *Marshall (58 percent).

An assessment of Justice Souter must await further development. He has yet to stake out a position on *judicial review of economic regulations of property. His votes in *Parker* v. *Dugger* (1991), invalidating a death sentence imposed by the trial court over a jury's recommendation of life imprisonment, and *Cohen* v. *Cowles Media Co.*

*David Souter*

(1991), where he dissented from the majority's refusal to give *First Amendment protection to a newspaper's publication of a confidential source, suggest some degree of flexibility in his views.

Nicholas S. Zeppos

**South Carolina v. Katzenbach**, 383 U.S. 301 (1966), argued 17–18 Jan. 1966, decided 17 Mar. 1966 by vote of 8 to 1; Warren for the Court, Black dissenting in part. This case, which sustained the constitutionality of the *Voting Rights Act of 1965, is a milestone in the development of congressional power to enforce the *Civil War Amendments. It established Congress's power to proscribe a class of suspect practices without finding that in every instance the practices would be held by the judiciary to be unconstitutional. In sustaining the 1965 act, *South Carolina* v. *Katzenbach* contributed to the enfranchisement of millions on nonwhite Americans.

In the Voting Rights Act, Congress relied on its powers under section 2 of the *Fifteenth Amendment, which authorizes it by appropriate measures to enforce the amendment's prohibition on racial discrimination in voting. The act prescribed a formula defining the state and political subdivisions to which its novel remedies applied. The remedies applied to a state that maintained a "test or device" as a prerequisite to voting, *and* that had low voter registration or voting rates in the 1964 presidential election. South Carolina was covered by the act and thus was temporarily barred from enforcing a literacy test and a property ownership requirement. New voting re-

quirements could be imposed only if submitted to the attorney general and not disapproved by him. Coverage by the act also authorized federal appointment of voting examiners to place on the state and local voting rolls voters who might otherwise not be listed because of their race.

In an *original jurisdiction suit, South Carolina challenged the act's coverage formula, the suspension of voting requirements, the requirement of federal review of new voting requirements, and the authorization of appointment of federal voting examiners. It also asserted that Congress's section 2 power authorized nothing more than legislation forbidding violations of the Fifteenth Amendment in general terms, with remedies necessarily left entirely to the courts. Chief Justice Earl *Warren's opinion rejected all these challenges. His opinion addressed both the general power of Congress to enforce the Fifteenth Amendment and each of the challenged provisions.

With respect to the general scope of Congress's section 2 power, the Court relied on the classic statement of congressional legislative power in *McCulloch* v. *Maryland* (1819). Legitimate ends not banned by the Constitution may be pursued through all appropriate means. Congress's findings that case-by-case litigation proved ineffective in dealing with widespread discriminatory voting practices warranted a sweeping measure not dependent for application on findings of specific discrimination. As Warren wrote, "Congress might well decide to shift the inertia from the perpetrators of the evil to its victims" (p. 328). The Voting Rights Act's selective geographic coverage was permissible because voting discrimination, Congress found, occurred primarily in certain areas of the country. Congress could limit its attention to the most troublesome geographic areas.

In attacking the suspension of existing voting requirements, South Carolina relied on the statement in *Lassiter* v. *Northampton County Board of Elections* (1959) that literacy tests and related devices themselves violate the Fifteenth Amendment. The Court distinguished *Lassiter* on the ground that the Voting Rights Act addressed discriminatory use of tests, a use *Lassiter* itself questioned.

The Court acknowledged that suspension of new voting regulations pending review by federal authorities was an uncommon exercise of congressional power. But Congress knew of past elaborate strategies employed by states to perpetuate voting discrimination despite federal court decrees prohibiting such practices. Congress reasonably feared similar maneuvers in response to the 1965 act and was thus authorized to attack the problem in a decisive manner. The use of federal voting examiners to list qualified voters appropriately countered procedural tactics used to deny African-Americans the franchise.

*South Carolina* v. *Katzenbach* served as an important precedent in *Katzenbach* v. *Morgan* (1966). The breadth of legislative discretion granted Congress in enforcing the Fifteenth Amendment paved the way for similar treatment of Congress's power under the *Fourteenth Amendment. In *Morgan*, the Court rejected New York's argument that Congress may abrogate state laws only if they conflict with the Fourteenth Amendment. These cases, along with *Jones* v. *Alfred H. Mayer Co.* (1968), contributed to a major revitalization of Congress's power to enforce the Civil War Amendments against racial discrimination.

(See also RACE AND RACISM; VOTE, RIGHT TO.)

□ Ward E. Y. Elliott, *The Supreme Court's Role in Voting Rights Disputes* (1974).          Theodore Eisenberg

**South Dakota v. Dole,** 483 U.S. 203 (1987), argued 28 Apr. 1987, decided 23 June 1987 by vote of 7 to 2; Rehnquist for the Court, Brennan and O'Connor in dissent. In this case the Supreme Court upheld congressional legislation that required states to raise their legal drinking age to twenty-one as a condition of receiving their full allotment of federal highway funds. The Court rejected South Dakota's arguments that such a requirement violated congressional power under the spending clause (see TAXING AND SPENDING CLAUSE) and also under the *Twenty-first Amendment, which repealed prohibition and gave to the states authority over alcoholic beverages.

Congressional restrictions on grants to the states are constitutional, the Supreme Courts held, if they meet four requirements. First, the spending must be in the "general Welfare," although "courts should defer substantially to the judgment of Congress" in this regard (p. 207). Second, Congress's conditions on a state's receipt of funds must be "unambiguous." Third, conditions on federal grants must not be unrelated to "the federal interest in particular national projects or programs." Finally, the conditions placed on a grant must not run afoul of "other constitutional provisions . . . [that] provide an independent bar" to Congress's restrictions (p. 207). The last condition, the Court explained, means only that Congress cannot use a conditional grant to induce states to engage in unconstitutional activities.

The Court held that all four conditions had been met. Only the last produced even a serious argument from the Court. O'Connor, in dissent, suggested that Congress's interest in setting a minimum drinking age of twenty-one was insufficiently related to its interest in highway construction under the third part of the test.

(See also FEDERALISM; STATE SOVEREIGNTY AND STATES' RIGHTS.)

William Lasser

**South-Eastern Underwriters Association, United States v.,** 322 U.S. 533 (1944), argued 11 Jan. 1944, decided 5 June 1944 by vote of 4 to 3;

Black for the Court, Stone and Frankfurter in dissent, Jackson dissenting in part, Roberts and Reed not participating. Ever since *Paul* v. *Virginia* (1869), the issuance of insurance policies had not been considered a transaction of commerce, and the Court had consistently ruled that, since insurance did not constitute interstate commerce, states could regulate even out-of-state insurance companies doing business within their borders.

Then the Justice Department filed a suit against the South-Eastern Underwriters Association, charging it with collusive price-fixing of premiums for fire insurance in violation of the *Sherman Antitrust Act. Despite the long string of cases holding to the contrary, a plurality of the Court agreed that fire insurance companies that conducted substantial parts of their business across state lines were engaged in interstate commerce. Justice Hugo *Black explained away previous court decisions on the grounds that all of them had involved state laws; this was the first instance in which a federal law had been applied to insurance, and "Congress wanted to go to the utmost extent of its Constitutional power in restraining trust and monopoly agreements" (p. 558).

Congress immediately responded by passing the McCarran Act of 1945, which explicitly declared that the continued regulation and taxation of insurance companies should remain under state jurisdiction and that no act of Congress, unless specifically addressed to the insurance business, should be interpreted as superseding the states' authority over insurance.

(See also ANTITRUST; COMMERCE POWER; REVERSALS OF COURT DECISIONS BY CONGRESS; STATE REGULATION OF COMMERCE.)

Melvin I. Urofsky

**Sovereign Immunity,** a principle with origins in early English common law, declared that the king was immune from suit by his subjects. The rationale for the rule was that since law emanated from the sovereign, he could not be held accountable in courts of his own creation. In practice, however, numerous exceptions to this rule afforded aggrieved parties the opportunity to sue the crown, especially where the sovereign expressly consented to suit.

In the Unites States, sovereign immunity was used during the nineteenth century to limit suits by individuals against both state and federal governments. The *Eleventh Amendment, which was ratified in 1795, prohibited suits against states in federal courts. The highest courts of the states also recognized the doctrine. In *Gibbons* v. *United States* (1868), the Supreme Court held that the federal government could not be sued without the consent of Congress.

Today, the concept of sovereign immunity is in disfavor. Many states have narrowed the immunity through statutes and judicial decisions. With the adoption of the *Federal Tort Claims Act (1946), Congress expressly authorized individuals to sue the federal government for specified claims, subject to various exceptions. This trend evinces a belief that governments should be accountable for losses they occasion.

Sovereign immunity has been eroded in an indirect fashion as well. Even where the principle of sovereign immunity bars suit against the government, the injured party may seek damages from individual officials who are personally liable for the judgment.       Philip L. Merkel

**Spallone v. United States,** 493 U.S. 265 (1990), argued 2 Oct. 1989, decided 10 Jan. 1990 by vote of 5 to 4; Rehnquist for the Court, Brennan, in dissent. After finding that the City of Yonkers, New York, deliberately concentrated public housing in minority neighborhoods, effectively funneling minorities into one quarter, a federal district court ordered that future public housing be dispersed. After losing on appeal, the city accepted a *consent decree that included the necessary ordinance, but the defiant city council reneged and failed to enact the ordinance. The district court held the city and the recalcitrant councilmembers in contempt and imposed escalating daily fines. After months of political posturing, the council finally passed the ordinance when the city's daily fines reached nearly one million dollars.

By a 5-to-4 vote, the Court, speaking through Chief Justice William H. *Rehnquist, held that the district court abused its discretion under traditional equitable principles by fining the individual councilmembers without first allowing a reasonable time for sanctions against the city alone to obtain compliance. In dissent, Justice William J. *Brennan would have deferred to the discretion of the district judge, who was more familiar with local political realities.

Two important issues went undecided: whether the order against the councilmembers violated their freedom of speech to vote in a particular manner and whether they were protected against sanctions by the absolute legislative immunity that applies to state legislators.

(See also DESEGREGATION REMEDIES; INJUNCTIONS AND EQUITABLE REMEDIES; LOWER FEDERAL COURTS; SEGREGATION, DE JURE.)

Thomas E. Baker

**Speech and Debate Clause.** The Constitution provides that members of Congress "for any Speech or Debate in either House . . . shall not be questioned in any other Place" (Art, I, sec. 6). This protection, which grew out of centuries of struggle between the English parliament and throne, grants immunity to members against civil or criminal action stemming from the performance of their legislative duties.

During the sixteenth- and seventeenth-

century reigns of the Tudor and Stuart monarchs, the Crown had sought to intimidate unsympathetic legislators through legal action. The English Bill of Rights in 1689 sharply limited this practice by providing that "the Freedom of Speech, and Debates or Proceedings in Parliament, ought not to be impeached or questioned in any Court or Place out of Parliament."

In the American Constitution, the Speech and Debate Clause, which protects legislators from punitive executive or judicial action, reinforced the *separation of powers among the government's three branches. Interpretation of this clause has centered on a definition of "legitimate legislative activity." Such activity had been commonly held to extend beyond debate on the floor of the respective chambers to include views expressed in committee deliberations and reports and to encompass the act of voting as well. In *Kilbourn v. Thompson (1881), the Supreme Court gave this clause its broadest interpretation, defining protected actions as "things generally done in a session of [Congress] by one of its members in relation to the business before it" (p. 204).

During the 1970s the Supreme Court considered several cases aimed at narrowing this reading. In Doe v. McMillan (1973), the Court limited protection for the views expressed within congressional reports only to those documents disseminated within Congress. Allowing a suit against the Government Printing Office for publishing a committee report that allegedly contained defamatory material, the Court ruled somewhat ambiguously that dissemination in normal channels outside Congress was not protected. Under a related subsequent decision, *Hutchinson v. Proxmire (1979), members became liable for their views as expressed through press releases and newsletters. The Court found that although these means of communication are valuable and desirable, neither forms an integral part of Congress's deliberative process. Here the Court distinguished between the indispensable "informing function," under which Congress informs itself in an effort to produce better legislation, and the less vital "informing function" of reporting its activities to the public.

In United States v. Brewster (1972), the Court significantly reduced the Speech or Debate Clause's protection. Former U.S. senator Daniel Brewster had been indicted for allegedly taking a bribe to influence the performance of his official legislative duties. Brewster sought protection under the clause to declare the indictment invalid. In upholding the indictment, the Court ruled that "Taking a bribe is, obviously, no part of the legislative process or function" (p. 526). The clause was read as prohibiting an inquiry into the motivation for performing specific legislative acts, but it provides no restraint against an inquiry into taking a bribe for specific legislative actions. The subject of the inquiry against Senator Brewster was the bribe, rather than the legislative objective the bribe was intended to promote.

In that same year, the Court issued a ruling in a second case involving a United States senator. In *Gravel* v. *United States*, it upheld the right of a *grand jury to inquire into the circumstances under which a member obtained security classified government documents and arranged for their private republication. "While the Speech or Debate Clause recognizes speech, voting and other legislative acts as exempt from liability that otherwise might attach, it does not privilege either Senator or aide to violate an otherwise valid criminal law in preparing for or implementing legislative acts" (p. 626).

The *Gravel* case also explicitly brought congressional staff under the clause's protection. During the 1960s, the number of legislative aides increased at a rate greater than in any previous decade. Recognizing the expanding role of staff, counsel for the Senate successfully argued that "the day-to-day work of such aides is so critical to the Member's performance that they must be treated as the latters' alter ego; and that if they are not so recognized, the central role of the Speech or Debate Clause . . . will inevitably be diminished and frustrated" (pp. 616–617). It is not surprising that the expanded speed and power of modern mass communication media has resulted in significant expansion of congressional immunities under the Speech and Debate Clause.

Richard Allan Baker

**Speech and the Press.** The *First Amendment to the Constitution declares that "Congress shall make no law . . . abridging freedom of speech, or of the press." The Speech and Press Clauses of the Constitution have gradually come to mean that government officials cannot restrict the public debate about public affairs. Free expression has become both the foundation and the symbol of the policy-making process in the United States.

The framers of the First Amendment recognized that a press free of government control is a vital part of a political system based on the will of the people. The press needs the freedom to report abuses of power by public officials. The people must be able to receive news critical of the government and exchange information and opinions about public affairs without interference by government officials. The lack of government censorship is also considered vital to the search for knowledge, including the advancement of science. In addition, the lack of government supervision over expression allows individuals to search for their own self-fulfillment through art, literature, and music, as well as public debate.

Although the First Amendment was adopted as part of the *Bill of Rights in 1791, almost all of the Supreme Court cases interpreting its language have been decided since *World War I. Not until 1925 did the Court decide that state governments, as well as the federal government, are

prohibited from restricting free expression under the Constitution. In *Gitlow* v. *New York*, the Supreme Court declared that First Amendment rights such as the Speech and Press Clauses were protected from infringement by state governments through the *Due Process Clause of the *Fourteenth Amendment, which prohibits states from depriving citizens of liberty without due process of law (see INCORPORATION DOCTRINE).

Even *Gitlow* is an ancient case compared to most of the Supreme Court opinions affecting the media. Only since 1960 has the Court decided the most significant cases in the law of *libel, *privacy, prejudicial *pretrial publicity, access to court, *cameras in court, rights of *reply to comments in the print and broadcast media, *commercial speech, and confidential news sources. The Court continues to consider speech and press cases annually, thereby adding to its interpretation of the Speech and Press Clauses of the First Amendment.

The Supreme Court's treatment of free speech and press issues is not only dynamic, but also to some degree unpredictable. The Court relies on a wide variety of legal concepts and tests to decide the speech and press cases it hears. Frequently the Court places a heavy burden of proof on a government institution trying to restrict expression, assuming the effort to be unconstitutional unless the government can show a substantial or compelling government interest. In some circumstances, however, the Court has balanced the interests in free expression against other social values without seeming to give favored treatment to individual speech or the press.

Some consistent themes can be identified, however. For example, the Court ordinarily makes every effort to prohibit governmental interference in the content of a message. The government cannot control the thoughts, ideas, and facts that enter into the public debate. In contrast, the Court permits government to establish content-neutral restrictions on the *time, place, and manner of speech if those restrictions serve a substantial government interest such as a litter-free environment.

The Court has also ruled unconstitutional laws that are so vague that citizens would be tempted to keep quiet out of fear, not knowing whether what they said was illegal. In *Smith* v. *Goguen* (1974), the Court ruled unconstitutional a statute that punished anyone who treated the United States flag "contemptuously." The Court reasoned that what is "contemptuous to one man may be a work of art to another," declaring that the wording of the act left enforcement authorities with too much discretion (p. 573). The Court has also frequently struck down laws that appear to be so broadly written that they would restrict protected speech as well as unprotected speech. In *Los Angeles* v. *Jews for Jesus* (1987), the Court declared unconstitutional an airport regulation that banned all First Amendment activities, such as discussing politics, reading newspapers, and wearing campaign buttons.

The Supreme Court has declared that government efforts to exercise *prior restraint of speech and publication are almost always unconstitutional. Similarly, the Court has said that government can only prosecute political dissidents or socially disruptive speech when the expression is intended to incite imminent lawless activity and is likely to do so. In civil cases, the justices have required persons complaining about expression to show at least negligence or harm before they can collect damages.

The press, in spite of its separate mention in the First Amendment, usually has no greater privileges than any member of the public. However, the Court has established a hierarchy of speech that provides the most protection for political messages and substantially less protection for commercial expression. Some kinds of speech, such as *obscenity, have been excluded from First Amendment protection altogether. Further, the Court applies the First Amendment to different media in different ways, permitting greater regulation of the content of broadcasting than of the news columns in the print media, for example.

The meaning of the Speech and Press Clauses of the First Amendment has changed rapidly since *World War II at least in part because of increased litigation, new scholarship, changes in technology, and the increasing importance of long distance communication. The words "freedom of speech, or of the press" mean significantly more today than they meant in 1791.

*Words of the First Amendment.* When the founding fathers adopted the First Amendment in 1791 they certainly intended to prohibit government licensing of books and periodicals and other forms of prior restraint on publication. Laws requiring that officials approve books and newspapers prior to publication had been abandoned in England, and never worked effectively in the colonies.

Scholars are less certain that the founders were ready to abandon the English tradition of punishing writers for criticizing public officials. The *common law of *seditious libel, alive in both Britain and the colonies in the eighteenth century, provided for fines and incarceration of anyone who criticized government officials, laws, or policies in a way that could lead to a loss of reputation or disturbance of the peace. Truth was not a defense. In fact, officials believed truth was more damaging because it would more likely lead to social instability.

The famous trial of John Peter Zenger in 1734 demonstrated the impatience of colonial juries with libel prosecutions brought by English officials, but the jury's verdict did not change the law. Zenger, publisher of the *New-York Weekly Journal*, was tried for seditious libel after he printed criticism of New York governor William Cosby. Under the law of the time, the jury only had to decide whether Zenger had printed the material. Zenger admitted printing the remarks but argued that citizens should have the right to speak the truth about public officials. Although a colonial jury found Zenger innocent of defaming an English official, the verdict did not change the law limiting the role of juries or establish that truth could be a defense in libel cases.

In fact, legal historian Leonard Levy said the generation that adopted the First Amendment largely believed in the right of government to punish the criticism of official conduct. Levy argued that at the time the First Amendment was adopted the universal understanding of the words "freedom of the press" came from the renowned compiler of English law, William Blackstone. Blackstone asserted that liberty of the press meant that anyone could print anything they wanted to, but publishing "what is improper, mischievous, or illegal" was a crime that could be punished. While most states adopted constitutions with provisions protecting freedom of the press, they also passed statutes punishing persons critical of the government. In addition, most states adopted the English common law, which included seditious libel provisions.

Yet, newspapers in the 1790s were usually political party organs dominated by heated rhetoric in essays and letters to the editor. Newspapers commonly ridiculed public officials. In addition, many scholars claim, the founders believed that freedom of the press was necessary for a government chosen by the public. Both Federalists and Antifederalists, legal scholar David Anderson contends, believed the public needed an independent press as a necessary restraint on the natural tendency of government to be tyrannical and despotic. A press that risked punishment under seditious libel laws when it published criticism of government could hardly be expected to inform the public effectively, scholars argue.

The historical record does not provide enough evidence for twentieth-century Americans to know what the framers meant when they adopted the First Amendment. No persuasive explanations surface in the congressional debates or the public discussions over ratification of the Bill of Rights. Levy suggests that few of the drafters gave much thought to what the Speech and Press Clauses meant, and that they probably did not agree on a single definition.

By 1798, however, there was much less ambiguity. Within seven years of the time the Bill of Rights was approved, the Federalist majority in Congress passed legislation designed to stop the rhetoric of the opposition Republicans. The Federalists were afraid that the Republicans would destroy the young American republic by fostering the radical French ideas that led to the French Revolution. The Federalists adopted the *Sedition Act, making it a crime to "write, print, utter or publish . . . any false, scandalous and malicious" writing against the government, Congress, or the president with the intent to defame them. Persons found guilty could be fined up to two thousand dollars and be jailed up to two years. At least ten persons were successfully prosecuted and three newspapers were forced to stop publishing. The law expired when Republican Thomas *Jefferson succeeded the Federalists in office in 1801.

The 1798 Sedition Act included two important reforms that survived the act itself. The statute provided that juries could decide both whether a defendant had published allegedly defamatory language and whether the language was defamatory. Juries, rather than politically appointed judges, could determine what was defamatory. In addition, the act specified that defendants could win libel cases by proving that what they said was true. Although the common-law interpretation after 1800 limited the defense of truth by requiring "good motives," the courts began to protect truthful criticism of government, a significant step toward open discussion of public affairs.

The end of the Sedition Act did not mark the end of attempts to punish criticism of government. The Jeffersonians, while defending themselves against the Sedition Act, argued that punishing criticism of government amounted to an abridgement of speech, contrary to the First Amendment. Once Jefferson was president, the Jeffersonians filed several libel suits of their own. In 1812, however, the Supreme Court repudiated a federal common law of seditious libel. Slowly, libel law shifted from a matter of criminal law to *civil law. Instead of government bringing prosecutions for libel, individuals sued to protect their own reputations. During the nineteenth century, in addition to the protection of truth, privileges developed for reporting defamatory information that was contained in the public record and for statements expressing opinion rather than assertions of fact.

*Speech versus Press.* The Supreme Court has not specifically distinguished between the words "press" and "speech" in the First Amendment. Rather, the Court ordinarily provides the same kind of protection for both "speech" and "press." The Court has often said that a journalist has no more rights under the Constitution than does any member of the public. Therefore, the Court does not usually accord writers who publish in newspapers any more freedom under the First Amendment than any citizen who chooses to become a speaker. Only a minority of justices have argued that the institutional press should be allowed privileges not available to the average citizen. Only a minority have contended that the press, if no one else, should have access to such places as prisons, so that the media can act as a surrogate when members of the public must be excluded.

Only a few exceptions to the general rule that the terms "speech" and "press" are treated equally can be found. The Supreme Court has suggested that some of the constitutional protections afforded libel defendants may apply only to the media. Journalists are also sometimes granted the special privilege of refusing to disclose confidential sources in court, a privilege developed largely in the lower courts.

The Supreme Court has not clearly differentiated the terms "speech" and "press" at least in part because of the practical difficulty of distinguishing which of the two protections might apply to a given circumstance. Should the pamphleteer be considered a speaker or a member of the press? Should the pamphleteer be treated differently than the soapbox orator? Are book authors protected by the speech clause or the press clause, or both? Or, should a television news reporter be treated differently than a reporter for the print media? The Supreme Court has raised some of the questions without providing the answers.

*No Prior Restraint or Compelled Publication.* The Supreme Court has yet to find a permanent government restraint on publication that was not unconstitutional. The justices have said repeatedly that government cannot suppress an idea because society considers it repugnant or offensive, and therefore have made it all but impossible to stop an idea from entering the intellectual marketplace.

The Court has struck down government efforts to stop publication in cases involving libel, *national security risks, and prejudicial *pretrial publicity. It has indicated that prior restraint might be tolerated in cases of obscenity and incitement to violence and national security if the government demonstrates a sufficient risk of harm.

The Court first declared prior restraint to be unconstitutional in *Near v. Minnesota* (1931), when it struck down a Minnesota state law that allowed officials to prevent the publication of a "malicious, scandalous and defamatory" magazine or newspaper. Five justices backed an opinion declaring that the most widely accepted understanding of the First Amendment is that liberty of the press means a prohibition of prior restraints on publication. "The fact that the liberty of the press may be abused," wrote Chief Justice Charles Evans *Hughes, "does not make any less necessary the immunity of the press from previous restraint in dealing with official misconduct" (pp. 719–720). The Court said that public officials who are defamed can sue for libel, but they cannot constitutionally stop the reporting about their behavior. The First Amendment, the Court said, rests on the belief that even if charges of official crimes and blunders disturb the peace, "a more serious public evil" would result if officials could determine which stories were published by the media (p. 722).

The ban against prior restraints has been such an accepted interpretation of the First Amendment that it has only infrequently been challenged. Therefore, no one can be sure under what circumstances a prior restraint might be acceptable. In *Nebraska Press Association v. Stuart (1976), the Court established that criminal defendants trying to stop the publication of potentially prejudicial pretrial publicity face perhaps an insurmountable burden of proof. The Court said that even though prejudicial pretrial publicity may require a conviction to be set aside on appeal, a prior restraint is an irreversible sanction on expression, the "most serious and least tolerable infringement on First Amendment rights" (p. 558). The Court said that a threat of sanctions after publication may "chill" speech, but the law ensures that sanctions are applied only after careful judicial scrutiny. Prior restraints, by their nature, the Court implied, are not exhaustingly evaluated and prevent speech from occurring, possibly destroying its value in the case of reports about rapidly developing current events.

The Court in *Nebraska Press Association* said that a defendant, in order to obtain an *injunction on the media, would have to establish that the threat to a fair trial was serious and highly probable. A defendant would have to show that restraining the press would eliminate the threat to a fair trial caused by prejudicial publicity and that no other alternatives available to a judge, such as moving the trial, would adequately protect the defendant.

The Court has said even less about what the government would have to prove to convince justices to allow a prior restraint on national security grounds. In the only case decided so far, *New York Times v. United States (1971), the Court prohibited the federal government from stopping the printing of news stories about a classified Defense Department report about the *Vietnam War commonly known as the "Pentagon Papers." The Court split so badly that the only agreement among the six justices in the majority was that the government had not met the heavy burden of proof required to restrain publication. However, a majority of justices would have required the government to prove at a minimum that disclosure of the imformation would "surely" result in "direct, immediate, and irreparable damage" to the national security interests of the nation. The ambiguous nature of the *New York Times* decision is heightened by the fact that only three of the justices deciding the case remain on the bench, only one of whom voted with the majority.

If the government cannot prohibit a newspaper from publishing a specific story, neither can the government require a newspaper to publish a story it would not otherwise run. In *Miami Herald Publishing Co. v. Tornillo (1974), the Court struck down a Florida statute that required newspapers to publish replies to criticism about political candidates. The Court said that requiring a paper to print one story as opposed to another unconstitutionally interfered with the rights of editors to determine the content of newspapers.

A unanimous Court said that the First Amendment protected against government control of a newspaper's treatment of public issues and public officials. A statute compelling a newspaper to use its space to print a reply could encourage newspapers to curb their coverage of public affairs.

*Licensing and Regulation of Speech.* The Court has never suggested that its heavy presumption against prior restraint meant that all speech would be tolerated under all conditions. The Court said in *Cornelius v. NAACP Legal Defense & Educational Fund, Inc.* (1985), for example, that "even protected speech is not equally permissible in all places and at all times" (p. 799). In fact, the Supreme Court tolerates significant regulation of both person-to-person expression and the mass media.

Since the Constitution was adopted long before the invention of telephones, moving pictures, radio, cable television, and satellite communications, the founders could have only envisioned the First Amendment in light of person-to-person speech and the printing press. The newer methods of delivering messages do not generally receive as much First Amendment protection from the Supreme Court as face-to-face communication and the printed word. In *Burstyn v. Wilson* (1951), in a case involving motion picture censorship, the Supreme Court announced that special characteristics of some media require different treatment under the First Amendment. The Court said the basic principles of freedom of speech and press do not vary, but "each method tends to present its own peculiar problems" (p. 503). Thus no one medium will necessarily be subject "to the precise rules" governing other modes of expression.

The most striking example of a different First Amendment standard is the Court's toleration of a licensing system for broadcasters. In fact, the Court has allowed the government to consider radio and television programming content, including speech about public affairs, when making licensing decisions.

The government began licensing broadcasters who would pledge to serve the "public interest, convenience, or necessity" in 1927. Congress passed the 1927 Radio Act so that a government agency could regulate the time and frequency of radio broadcasts, cutting down on signal interference and making the most efficient use of broadcast frequencies. In the Radio Act, and subsequently in the 1934 Communications Act, Congress adopted such program regulations as a requirement that, if broadcasters provide air time to a political candidate, they must provide equal opportunities to opponents. Congress also prohibited indecent, obscene, and profane speech on the air waves.

In *Red Lion Broadcasting Co. v. FCC (1969), the Supreme Court upheld the constitutionality of at least one broadcast programming regulation. The

Court permitted the Federal Communications Commission to require broadcasters to provide time to reply to persons attacked during the discussion of a controversial issue, a regulation similar to the one the Court struck down for newspapers in *Miami Herald Publishing Co.* v. *Tornillo.* In *Red Lion,* the Court said that no person could have a constitutional right to communicate through broadcasting since the electromagnetic spectrum could not accommodate everyone. Therefore, those chosen by the government to receive broadcast licenses must act as fiduciaries for the public, and permit diverse views on public issues. The public has a right, the Court maintained, to have broadcasters "function consistently with the ends and purposes of the First Amendment." The Court continued, that "it is the right of the viewers and listeners, not the right of the broadcasters, which is paramount" (p. 390).

In *FCC* v. *Pacifica Foundation* (1978), the Supreme Court permitted the regulation of broadcast indecency under a different rationale. The Court said the Federal Communications Commission could regulate the depiction or description of sexual and excretory activities in a manner patently offensive to the broadcast audience when there is a reasonable risk that children may be watching or listening. The Court said broadcast indecency such as the repetitious use of so-called dirty words could be regulated, but not banned, because broadcast signals intrude into the privacy of the home. In addition, children too young to read might inadvertently be exposed to indecent broadcast programming.

The Court has yet to decide the degree of First Amendment protection cable television operators will receive. While cable operators do not use the broadcast spectrum, they are licensed by local communities and transmit the same kind of video programming as broadcasters licensed by the Federal Communications Commission. The Court said in *Los Angeles* v. *Preferred Communications* (1986) that cable operators perform many of the First Amendment activities undertaken by newspapers, book publishers, public speakers, and pamphleteers. But when a cable company said its First Amendment rights were violated because Los Angeles refused to issue a permit, the Supreme Court held the First Amendment rights of cable operators must be balanced against the space available on public utility poles for cable and the disruption caused by the laying of cable under city streets.

If the Court has different First Amendment models for different technologies, it also treats various kinds of content differently under the First Amendment. The Supreme Court gives the most deference to political speech, including debates and reports about public policy and criticism of public officials. The Court has often said that a primary purpose of the First Amendment was to protect an intense and wide-ranging debate about public issues, the kind of speech "indispensable" to the decision-making process in a democracy. The Court usually gives close scrutiny to the regulation of any political speech and often requires that the government substantiate a compelling state interest before regulating. The protections for political speech generally extend to social and economic speech as well.

*Commercial speech receives less First Amendment protection, in part because the motivation to market goods and services is believed sufficient to overcome any "chill" that might occur because of regulation. The Court has also said that commercial speech about a specific product or service is easier to verify than political commentary. In *Central Hudson Gas & Electric Corporation* v. *Public Service Commission* (1980), the Court ruled that only the truthful advertising of legal products is protected by the First Amendment interest of consumers to receive commercial information. In order for the government to regulate protected commercial expression, it must restrict speech only as much as necessary to effectively protect a substantial governmental interest.

In contrast, speech defined as obscene has been ruled as outside the boundaries of First Amendment protection. Obscenity, the Court said in *Miller* v. *California* (1973), is speech that (1) the average person, applying contemporary community standards, would find, taken as a whole, to appeal to the prurient interest; (2) depicts or describes in a patently offensive way sexual conduct specifically defined by state law; and (3) lacks serious literary, artistic, politcal, or scientific value.

Another kind of expression falling outside the protection of the First Amendment is what are called "fighting words," words that the Court has said in *Chaplinsky* v. *New Hampshire* (1942) are "likely to provoke the average person to retaliation, and thereby cause a breach of the peace" (p. 574). The Court concluded that "fighting words," which "by their very utterance inflict injury or tend to incite an immediate breach of peace" (p. 572), have no important role in the debate of public issues.

Even in the case of protected speech, the Court will permit narrowly tailored content-neutral regulation of speech. The Court will permit the regulation of time, place, or manner of speech that does not interfere with the message being delivered and leaves adequate channels of communication available. The Court allows the regulation of speech that will facilitate traffic safety or protect the environment from litter, or fulfill another substantial government interest. However, a law regulating speech cannot give a public official broad discretion that can be used to discriminate on the basis of the content of the expression.

The Court will also allow the regulation of conduct that incidentally restricts expression as long as the regulation furthers a substantial government interest unrelated to the suppression of speech. In *United States* v. *\*O'Brien* (1968), the Court permitted the federal government to punish the burning of a draft card to protest the *Vietnam War because the act infringed on the government interest in efficient military mobilization. The Court said restriction on First Amendment freedoms must be no greater than necessary to further the governmental concern.

*Access and News Gathering.* If the Court has usually protected the ability of journalists to publish any information in their possession, it has not protected the ability of the media to gather information for publication with the same tenacity. The Court has generally refused to declare that the news media have a right to attend governmental proceedings, observe government officials at work, see government records, or protect confidential news sources. The Supreme Court has largely left questions of access by the public and press to government proceedings and information up to the determination of Congress and the state legislatures.

In the one major exception to the rule, the Court has said, in a series of cases in the 1980s, that both the public and the press have a qualified right to observe criminal trials, jury selection, and pretrial hearings. Beginning with *Richmond Newspapers* v. *Virginia* (1980), the Court said open judicial proceedings were implicit in the First Amendment guarantee of the freedom of the press, designed to ensure open communications about government. Criminal proceedings ought to be open to the public and the press, the Court said, because of the tradition of openness in the American judicial system and because of the critical role open proceedings play in encouraging accurate testimony, discouraging corrupt judges, and giving the public confidence in the court system. In order to close judicial proceedings, the Court said in *Press-Enterprise Co.* v. *Riverside County Superior Court* (1984), a judge must have evidence of an overriding interest, such as a defendant's right to a fair trial, that cannot be effectively protected except by closing the courtroom. Even then, closure can only be for as long as necessary to protect the specifically documented need.

The qualified right to observe the courts does not include a First Amendment right to use cameras and tape recorders in court. However, the Court said in *Chandler* v. *Florida* (1981) that individual states may permit cameras in state courts as long as cameras do not interfere with the *Sixth Amendment right of a criminal defendant to a fair trial.

In order for the courts to protect the rights of defendants to a fair trial while preserving the rights of the press under the First Amendment, the Supreme Court has encouraged judges to use such devices as the questioning of potential jurors about their impartiality during the jury selection process, moving the trial, delaying the trial, and sequestering jurors from trial publicity. In *\*Sheppard* v. *Maxwell* (1966), the Court also encouraged judges to restrain lawyers, witnesses, and jurors from talking to the media. The Court has said restrictions on the media to gather news do not constitute a prior restraint on the publication of information already in the media's possession.

The Supreme Court has required reporters to reveal their confidential news sources to *grand juries. The Court, in *Branzburg* v. *Hayes* (1972), decided 5 to 4 that reporters did not have a First Amendment right to refuse to testify before grand juries. The Court said that reporters who witness drug use and talk to persons suspected of crimes have the same responsibilities to testify in court as other citizens. The Court said the critical need for citizens to contribute to solving crimes overcame the "uncertain" impact that testifying would have on news gathering. However, concurring and dissenting opinions in *Branzburg* argued for a qualified privilege under the First Amendment for reporters to refuse to reveal confidential news sources. Because of the split in the Supreme Court, lower courts have often protected journalists from testifying unless persons seeking information can prove there is a compelling need for the testimony that overrides First Amendment interests, the information sought is relevant to the proceedings, and there is no alternative source for the information. In *\*Cohen* v. *Cowles Media* (1991), the Court held that the First Amendment does not bar a state from enforcing state laws punishing reporters who break their promises of confidentiality to sources.

The fact that the Court has found only a limited First Amendment right to gather news may be due in part to the nature of the cases reviewed by the Court. In three cases involving a government interest in prison security, the Court has denied a First Amendment right of access to prisons and prisoners. The Court's majority refused to acknowledge even a qualified right of access for the public. The Court acknowledged that the First Amendment prevents government from interfering with a journalist's efforts to seek information. However, the Court concluded that the Constitution does not impose on the government an "affirmative duty" to provide information not available to the public generally.

The unwillingness of the Court to grant a First Amendment right to the gathering—as well as to the publishing—of news can at least partially be explained by the Court's unwillingness to give a distinct meaning to the word "press" in the First Amendment. Since the Court treats the press and the public the same, the Court is reluctant to give the press a constitutional right to go places where the public cannot routinely be present. However, in refusing to let the press act as a surrogate for the public, the Court has limited the constitutional rights of access to government information under the First Amendment.

***Civil and Criminal Liability.*** The Court has said often that First Amendment protections for freedom of speech and press do not prohibit the punishment of some expression or prohibit civil suits asserting that expression caused personal injury. One of the most quoted passages in Supreme Court history is Justice Oliver Wendell *Holmes's comment in *Schenck v. *United States* (1919) that the First Amendment does not protect from prosecution a person who created panic by falsely shouting "fire" in a crowded theater.

However, the Court ruled in *Brandenburg v. Ohio* (1969) that the government cannot punish a speaker unless it can demonstrate the speech "is directed to inciting or producing imminent lawless action and is likely to incite or produce such action" (p. 447). The Court overturned the conviction of a Ku Klux Klan member for advocating an illegal act at an indefinite time in the future. The Court's language in *Brandenburg* reformulated a test the Court often used in sedition cases in the twentieth century. Beginning in 1919, in a case based on World War I sedition acts, the Court said speakers could not be punished unless their speech constituted a clear and present danger to the security of the nation. However, the test was used more often to punish speech than to protect it in large part because the Court seldom required more than a bare assertion from the government that a danger was "clear and present."

Yet in the early 1940s, the *clear and present danger test was used to protect journalists writing about the criminal justice system. The Supreme Court held that judges could not cite the news media for contempt of court for comments critical of the judicial process absent a clear and present danger to the administration of justice.

The Court has also ruled unconstitutional laws punishing defamation that disturbs the peace. The Court has said that laws criminalizing words for disrupting civil order punish a speaker because the listeners become violent. The criminal law of libel focuses more on the reaction of the listener than the content of the message, the Court said in *Ashton* v. *Kentucky* (1966). Indeed in *Terminiello* v. *Chicago* (1949), the Court noted that free speech may best serve its purpose when it "induces a condition of unrest, creates dissatisfaction with conditions as they are, or even stirs people to anger" (p. 4).

The Court is also reluctant to tolerate criminal prosecution of the media for publishing truthful information about public issues that has been lawfully obtained, even when a newspaper or broadcast station disseminates the information contrary to a state law. In *Smith* v. *Daily Mail Publishing Co.* (1979), for example, the Court said that the government must demonstrate an interest of the highest order before punishing journalists for accurate stories including the names of juveniles charged with crimes.

The Court has so far also refused to tolerate civil liability for truthful speech without at least a showing of media negligence. The Court has not ruled out the possibility of permitting civil damages when the media reveal sensitive information involving an individual's private life. However, it ruled in *Florida Star* v. *B.J.F.* (1989) that civil liability for the publication of lawfully obtained, truthful information about rape victims is unconstitutional without a narrowly tailored remedy protecting an important state interest. In *Florida Star,* while the Court acknowledged that protecting the identity of rape victims may be a significant government interest, it said that a newspaper could not be held automatically liable when the information was obtained through law enforcement officials and could have been disseminated by other means such as office gossip. In addition, the Supreme Court has determined that the First Amendment requires that plaintiffs suing for libel must prove a defamatory story is false and, at a minimum, was published or broadcast with negligence.

Public officials and public figures must prove that information was published with knowing falsity or reckless disregard for the truth. In *New York Times Co.* v. *Sullivan* (1964), the Court constitutionalized the law of libel, reasoning that the First Amendment was designed to ensure an unfettered exchange of ideas in order to facilitate social and political change. The Court said the common law of libel, which assumed a defamatory story was false, did not provide enough protection for a wide open, robust debate about government and public officials that "may well include vehement, caustic, and sometimes unpleasantly sharp attacks" (p. 270). The justices declared that political expression does not lose its constitutional protection if it is false because "erroneous statement is inevitable in free debate, and must be protected if the freedoms of expression are to have the 'breathing space' that they 'need . . . to survive' " (pp. 271–272). The Court said that officials should not be able to intimidate critics by threatening to sue for huge civil damage awards any more than they can by the criminal punishment of libel. In order to protect the citizen-critic adequately, the First Amendment requires that public officials prove *actual malice, knowing falsity, or reckless disregard for the truth.

In *St. Amant* v. *Thompson* (1968), the Court said proof of actual malice requires evidence that a defendant entertained serious doubts about the truth of a publication. The Court has subsequently ruled that criteria for determining actual malice can include a combination of factors such as thoroughness of an investigation, the reliability of sources, the believability of a story, deadline pressures, and motivation for publication. Fabricating a story constitutes actual malice.

In *Gertz* v. *Robert I. Welch* (1974), the Court established that the First Amendment required that public figures—persons with widespread fame or notoriety and persons who had injected themselves into the debate about a public controversy for the purpose of influencing the resolution of the issue involved—also had to prove knowing falsehood or reckless disregard to win their libel suits. The Court's decisions requiring public officials and public figures to prove knowing falsehood or reckless disregard for the truth has created a barrier to winning libel suits that few have been able to surmount.

The Court in *Gertz* also said that states could establish their own liability standard for persons who are not public figures as long as every libel plaintiff has to prove that a news medium did not exercise a reasonable amount of care during story preparation. In *Philadelphia Newspapers* v. *Hepps* (1986), the Court said that private persons trying to sue for defamation for stories about matters of public interest must prove the stories are false in addition to proving they are defamatory.

In *Milkovich* v. *Lorain Journal Co.* (1990), the Court said that the requirement that plaintiffs prove a story is false is a major protection against libel suits for opinion critical of government, restaurants, and art. The Court said that *Philadelphia Newspapers* v. *Hepps* ensures that statements of personal opinion about public affairs that do not contain a false factual assertion are constitutionally protected. The Court also pointed to previous decisions that said that publications and broadcast stations cannot be held liable for using loose, figurative language or rhetorical hyperbole that cannot reasonably be mistaken as statements of fact. In addition, in *Milkovich* the Court rejected a movement in lower courts to declare all opinion constitutionally protected. The Court said that decisions such as *Hepps* and those protecting hyperbole provided adequate "breathing space" to allow freedom of expression "to survive" without constitutionally distinguishing between statements of opinion and statements of fact.

In a related issue, the Court has said that the First Amendment substantially protects the media when public-figure plaintiffs contend that publications or broadcasts intentionally expose persons to emotional distress. In *Hustler Magazine* v. *Falwell* (1987), the Court concluded that the First Amendment prohibits media liability based on the motivation of expression since opinions about public figures spoken out of hatred, but honestly believed, can contribute to an open discussion of ideas and issues. The Court also refused to permit liability for "outrageous" speech, a requirement for establishing intentional infliction of emotional distress. The Court said that "outrageousness" in the discussion of political and social issues is so subjective that juries could impose liability merely on the basis of their dislike of the expression. The Court held that at least public officials and public figures will have to prove actual malice in suits for intentional infliction of emotional distress in order to avoid unduly restricting the debate about public affairs. Likewise, in *Time, Inc.* v. *Hill* (1967), the Court

declared that people who are newsworthy must also prove actual malice to win damages in a privacy suit for a story that is false but not defamatory.

**Conclusion.** The Court has developed a sizable body of law in the less than seventy years that it has been interpreting the Free Speech and Press Clauses of the First Amendment. While the Court has certainly not protected all expression under the umbrella of the First Amendment, it has ordinarily protected political speech, including ideas well outside of the mainstream of political thought, from governmental interference. The Court has been less protective of nonpolitical speech and speech transmitted through media other than print.

While the Court has protected speaking and writing from government control, it has been less willing to view the First Amendment as a tool to enhance the information gathering process. Still, by a strong majority, the Court has mandated access to the courts.

The Court has provided significant protection for speech and press without a coherent theoretical framework. Although the Court has often stressed the importance of unrestricted expression about public issues, its decisions do not fit into a single cohesive paradigm. The lack of a systematic framework for viewing speech and press will be noticed as the Court tries to fit the regulation of the emerging electronic technologies into the patchwork quilt it has already fashioned. The cases of the past will not provide adequate solutions to conflicts arising from the development of cable television, the fight over the control of the video information systems soon to be available through strands of glass fiber, and the growth of satellite communications.

The Court's interpretation of the First Amendment has, of course, changed over time and there is evidence of another shift under way. With Justices William J. *Brennan and Thurgood *Marshall retiring in 1990 and 1991, none of the justices at the forefront of interpreting the press clause of the First Amendment in the past thirty years remains. There are already signs in the First Amendment cases of the 1990s that the Supreme Court under Chief Justice William H. *Rehnquist is less prepared to scrutinize rigorously restrictions on expression and more willing to approve of new forms of regulation.

□ David A. Anderson, "The Origins of the Press Clause," *UCLA Law Review* 30 (1983): 456–541. Walter Berns, *The First Amendment and the Future of American Democracy* (1976). Margaret A. Blanchard, "Filling in the Void: Speech and Press in State Courts prior to Gitlow" in *The First Amendment Reconsidered: New Perspectives on the Meaning of Freedom of Speech and Press*, edited by Bill F. Chamberlin and Charlene J. Brown (1982), pp. 14–59. Vincent Blasi, "The Checking Value in First Amendment Theory," *American Bar Association Research Journal* (1977): 521–649. Ithiel de Sola Pool, *Technologies of Freedom* (1983). Leonard Levy, *Emergence of a Free Press* (1985).

Norman L. Rosenberg, *Protecting the Best Men; An Interpretive History of the Law of Libel* (1986). William W. Van Alstyne, *Interpretations of the First Amendment* (1984).
Bill F. Chamberlin

**Speedy Trial.** The Sixth Amendment provides in part that "In all criminal cases the accused shall enjoy the right . . . to a speedy trial." It was one of several provisions included in the *Bill of Rights to reject explicitly earlier English practice that had permitted the accused to languish in prison for extended periods of time prior to indictment and the commencement of *trial.

The *Sixth Amendment speedy trial guarantee has been before the Supreme Court a number of times. The Court has spoken eloquently about its importance as a fundamental right and in *Klopfer v. North Carolina* (1967) incorporated it into the *Fourteenth Amendment's Due Process Clause. Despite the applicability of the speedy trial doctrine to notoriously overcrowded state courts, the Court has rarely found the right to have been violated. For instance, in *Barker* v. *Wingo* (1972), it held that despite a five-year delay between indictment and trial, there was no violation of the right. Observing that circumstances vary in each case, the Court rejected a hard and fast time-limit rule in favor of a balancing test that considers length of delay, reason for delay, prejudice to the defendant, and the defendant's timely assertion of rights. However, when balancing these factors, the Court almost invariably has ruled in favor of the prosecution.

There are at least two reasons why the Court has not been eager to breathe much meaning into the speedy trial right. First, although framed as a right of the accused, it is in fact defense lawyers who have the greatest incentive to delay a trial. Second, the Court has encouraged courts, through their rule-making powers, and legislatures to address the problems of delay by adopting their own rules for reducing delay. Still, the constitutional right to a speedy trial serves to protect against the most egregious abuses of prosecutorial discretion to delay cases.

(See also DUE PROCESS, PROCEDURAL.)
Malcolm M. Feeley

**Spencer, John C.** (b. Hudson, N.Y., 8 Jan. 1788; d. Albany, N.Y., 17 May 1855), lawyer, public official, and unconfirmed nominee to the Supreme Court. Spencer, the son of Ambrose and Laura Canfield Spencer, was reared and educated in Albany, New York. He also received instruction at Williams College and Union College. In 1809, after being admitted to the bar and marrying Elizabeth Scott Smith, he moved to Canandaigua, New York, where he established a flourishing law practice. After service as assistant attorney general and district attorney, Spencer was elected to Congress in 1817. Defeated for reelection, he served terms in both the New York assembly and the state senate. Spencer moved to

Albany in 1837, where he became a member of the Whig party and secretary of state of New York in 1839.

In 1841 President John *Tyler appointed Spencer secretary of war, an office he held until 3 March 1843, when he became secretary of the treasury. On 9 January 1844 Tyler nominated Spencer to the Supreme Court, but on 31 January 1844 the Senate rejected him by a vote of 21 to 26, owing largely to the opposition of those Whigs who distrusted any friend of Tyler and to Spencer's fierce temper. Spencer resigned from the Treasury Department on 2 May 1844 to resume the practice of law in Albany. Colleagues praised his skills as a lawyer but noted that his excessive attention to detail prevented him from understanding larger public questions.

(See also NOMINEES, REJECTION OF.)
Robert M. Ireland

**Spite Nominations.** Among considerations entering into Supreme Court nominations is that of presidential revenge. Judicial or Senate attacks on the president's policies with resultant damage to the chief executive's political power have induced White House retaliation. Interbranch retribution may take the form of spite nominations to the Court. Appointments so motivated span a continuum reflecting at one pole generalized or implicit presidential antipathy toward the Court or the Senate. Richard *Nixon's appointment of Warren *Burger to succeed Earl *Warren as chief justice seemed a rebuke to Warren's perception of the Court as a social and political superlegislature. The nomination of Roger *Taney as *chief justice by Andrew *Jackson reflected presidential dissatisfaction with the Senate's previous treatment of the loyal political ally. Franklin D. *Roosevelt's selection of Hugo *Black reflected presidential retribution against the Senate for its defeat of his *court-packing bill, which Black had supported, and against the Court for its anti–*New Deal judicial record.

At the opposite pole are nominations intended as explicit expressions of presidential wrath. Occurring against an existing or prospective changing constitutional tide, such vindictive appointments emerge in the wake of senatorial defeats administered to the president's initial choice for the vacant Court seat. A thwarted chief executive predictably emits public or private expressions of resentment over the treatment accorded his nominee by the recalcitrant Senate. He resolves to stay the course, to stand by his loyalists in the Senate, and to name a second choice whose political-judicial profile broadly resembles that of his predecessor. By means of such strategy, the president seeks to recover lost political capital, and cause the Senate to capitulate and confirm the second choice.

Three times in the twentieth century the Senate has wielded its constitutional prerogative by rejecting the president's most favored Court nominee: Robert *Bork (1987), Clement *Haynsworth (1969), and John J. *Parker (1930). Perceived political and ideological attributes of these federal courts of appeals judges ignited fatal Senate opposition. Southerners Parker and Haynsworth were demonized as antilabor and anti–civil rights while Bork was deemed to be unsympathetic to prevailing fundamental rights jurisprudence. In defeat, Presidents Ronald *Reagan and Richard Nixon voiced public indignation and openly promised a nominee whose credentials would be no more satisfactory to the Senate than those possessed by the initial choice. But Reagan's nomination of youthful jurist Douglas *Ginsburg dissolved amid news of prior marijuana use while Nixon's second choice, circuit judge George Harrold *Carswell, met Senate defeat based on the aspirant's perceived racism and professional mediocrity. Their explicit spite nominations destroyed, Reagan and Nixon both acted as political pragmatists. They selected substitute nominees with different regional affiliations and possessed of impeccable professional and seemingly moderate ideological credentials: Anthony M. *Kennedy and Harry A. *Blackmun, respectively.

Only Herbert Hoover easily won confirmation for his second-choice nominee, Owen Josephus *Roberts. Although Hoover made no public protest, he fulminated in private against the Senate's treatment of Parker while finding the perfect foil for his antagonists in the Senate. Corporate lawyer Roberts had publicly proclaimed himself an apostle of economic laissez faire, prosecuted seditious speech cases during *World War I, espoused an internationalist foreign policy, and opposed national prohibition. All were attributes anathema to elements of the anti-Parker Senate coalition. But personable Roberts could be presented as a liberal. It was an image cultivated as a crusading special prosecutor in the Senate's "Teapot Dome" oil scandal investigations and by his philanthropic association with Lincoln University, an African-American institution. His putative liberalism turned out to be largely in the eyes of the exhausted and credulous Senate, a fact apparent in Roberts's subsequent Supreme Court record.

Eschewing overt vindictiveness, emotion, and cursory background investigation of his replacement candidate, Hoover succeeded where Nixon failed in his spite nomination of Carswell and where Reagan fell short with his emotive and hasty Ginsburg appointment. With Roberts, Hoover offered a pragmatic second-choice candidate whose public image belied intensely held attitudes on major public policies, wholly incongruent with those held by the president's Senate opponents who unanimously confirmed his nominee.

(See also NOMINEES, REJECTION OF; POLITICAL PROCESS; SENATORIAL COURTESY.)

□ Peter G. Fish, "Spite Nominations to the United States Supreme Court: Herbert Hoover, Owen J. Roberts, and the Politics of Presidential Vengeance in Retrospect," *Kentucky Law Journal* 77 (1988–1989): 545–576.

Peter G. Fish

**Springer v. United States,** 102 U.S. 586 (1881), argued 8–9 Apr. 1880, decided 24 Jan. 1881 by vote of 7 to 0; Swayne for the Court, Hunt and Clifford not participating. At issue in *Springer* was the constitutionality of the 1862 *income tax, enacted to help finance the *Civil War. William M. Springer refused to pay the income tax on his professional earnings as an attorney. The federal government taxed land belonging to Springer, and the property was eventually sold to the United States for the amount of the unpaid tax. The government brought an action of ejectment against Springer, who argued that the income tax was an invalid direct tax not apportioned among the states according to population as prescribed by the Constitution.

Relying on historical evidence, Justice Noah H. *Swayne determined that Congress had only treated taxes on real property and slaves as direct taxes. He accorded great weight to this "uniform practical construction of the Constitution" by Congress (p. 599). Swayne also emphasized the Supreme Court's decision in *Hylton* v. *United States* (1796), upholding a tax on carriages. He concluded that direct taxes included only capitation taxes and taxes on land, and hence the income tax was constitutional. The Civil War income tax remained in force until 1872.

The *Springer* decision was narrowly construed and distinguished by the Court in *Pollock* v. *Farmers' Loan & Trust Co.* (1895), in which justices invalidated the 1894 income tax as a direct tax not apportioned among the states. The authority of Congress to levy an income tax was not settled until the adoption of the *Sixteenth Amendment in 1913.

James W. Ely, Jr.

**Staff of the Court, Nonjudicial.** The staff of the United States Supreme Court has traditionally been long tenured, low profile, and reliable in supporting the *chief justice and associate justices. Employees have fed upon, and in turn strengthened the Court's mystique of independence, mystery, and power. The movement of the Court to its own building in 1935 saw its institutionalization. Previously, the nine justices functioned out of their homes, with almost no staff, and came to the Capitol to hear *oral arguments and hold *conferences.

The most recent, 1990 personnel budget of $17.5 million supports up to 319 permanent staff, as compared with the 221 positions in 1970. During the last two decades, the demands of an expanded caseload and increased security requirements, as well as the addition of the new legal counsel, curatorial, data systems, and public information offices, have caused the increase (see WORKLOAD OF THE COURT). The Court staff continues to be small, however, compared to the 22,000 congressional staff.

Most Court employees work under one of the five statutory Court officers. With a staff of three and several interns, the *administrative assistant to the chief justice (created 1972) assists the chief justice in nonadjudicatory responsibilities including the internal management of the Court, the coordination of the Court's relatively independent offices, the Judicial Conference of the United States, the Federal Judicial Center, the Administrative Office of the U.S. Courts (see ADMINISTRATION OF FEDERAL COURTS). The administrative assistant also serves as liaison with the executive and legislative branches, state and private organizations and the Smithsonian Institution, and assists in the preparation of addresses and publications. The personnel and budget functions of the Court are supervised by this office.

The *clerk of court (created 1790) supervises 25 employees, who administer dockets and calendars, record petitions and briefs, prepare order lists and journals, notify of judgments, collect fees, admit attorneys to the Supreme Court Bar, and advise lawyers on procedure. The initiation of a computerized information system in 1976 has enabled the office to handle the growing caseload more efficiently.

The *reporter of decisions (a volunteer from 1790 to 1816, when Congress set the reporter's salary) supervises nine people who are responsible for editing and printing the opinions of the Court.

The *marshal (created 1867) supervises 180 Court employees, in addition to 33 maintenance employees from the office of the architect of the Capitol. The marshal's staff handles payroll, procurement, security, and physical facilities.

The librarian (created 1887) supervises a staff of 25, including 6 professional research librarians, who manage almost half a million volumes, a multitude of databases, interlibrary loans, and research (see LIBRARY).

Other Court staff work for relatively new or expanded offices under the direction of the chief justice. The legal office (created 1973) is comprised of two attorneys, who typically serve several years, and a secretary. In contrast to the annually rotating law clerks, this office provides continuity with unusual procedural issues and serves as in-house counsel. These attorneys prepare memoranda for all justices on original cases, reapplications, and motions for extraordinary relief. On request, these attorneys assist with circuit work and special research.

The *public information officer (created in 1935) supervises a staff of four, distributes *slip opinions, maintains a *press room and broadcast booths, and responds to queries other than interpretation of opinions and orders.

The curator's office (created in 1974) with four assistants plus interns, supervises the Court's historical papers and collections, develops exhibits, and provides tours.

The data systems office (created in 1985) provides technological support, including several word processing systems and electronic typesetting of all Court opinions, for the justices' *chambers and other Court offices. In 1990, through the direction of the data systems office, the Court began a two-year pilot project for distributing its opinions electronically to organizations outside the Court.                                    Mark W. Cannon

**Stanbery, Henry** (b. New York, N.Y., 20 Feb. 1803; d. New York, N.Y., 26 June 1881), U.S. attorney general, 1866–1868; unconfirmed nominee to the Supreme Court. Henry Stanbery's nomination fell victim to the bitter conflict between President Andrew Johnson and Republican leaders in Congress. Like Johnson, Stanbery, who served as Johnson's attorney general, advocated a conservative approach to *Reconstruction.

Stanbery spent his early years in Ohio, where he was admitted to the bar at the age of twenty-one. Elected Ohio attorney general in 1846, he practiced in that state until 1866.

Stanbery came to Johnson's attention while representing the government in Ex parte *Milligan (1866). Johnson nominated him for the Supreme Court in 1866. The Senate never acted upon his nomination. Congressional Republicans, fearful that a Johnson nominee would support the president's conservative policies, reduced the number of justices from ten to seven. This deprived Johnson of an opportunity to place a justice on the Court.

After the failed nomination, Stanbery served as attorney general. He supported Johnson's policies and helped influence him to veto congressional Reconstruction measures. During the Johnson impeachment in 1868 Stanbery resigned as attorney general in order to represent the president. After that he resumed private practice in Ohio.

(See also NOMINEES, REJECTION OF.)
                                             Robert J. Cottrol

**Standard Oil v. United States,** 221 U.S. 1 (1911), argued 14–16 Mar. 1910, reargued 12–17 Jan. 1911, decided 15 May 1911 by vote of 9 to 0; White for the Court, Harlan concurring. The *Standard Oil* case was decided at a time when the *Sherman Antitrust Act was being increasingly challenged by big business. The Supreme Court remained divided over the appropriate approach to construing the statute; Congress repeatedly considered (and sometimes enacted) amendments; executive enforcement alternated between trust-busting and regulation.

Responding to a lower court's decree dissolving it under the Sherman Act, Standard Oil appealed to the Supreme Court. Chief Justice Edward D. *White resorted to common law and statutory construction to define "restraints of trade" and "monopoly." Emphasizing Congress's intent to protect the right to contract (see CONTRACT, FREEDOM OF) and freedom of commerce, White concluded that the law covered only "unreasonable" restraints of trade and that a common-law standard of reasonableness should be used to identify the actions that the act prohibited. Justice John Marshall *Harlan concurred, but he denounced the new "rule of reason" as judicial legislation, imposing on the statute a construction rejected by Congress.

The Court upheld the order to dissolve the Oil Trust, but though its decision was popular, the Court was criticized by progressives for emasculating the law and by business leaders for generating new uncertainties for businesses. The debate over *antitrust policy continued through the presidential campaign of 1912, leading to the Clayton Antitrust Act and the Federal Trade Commission Act. The *rule of reason, however, remained the judicial standard for interpreting antitrust statutes, allowing considerable flexibility in later cases. — Barbara C. Steidle

**Standing to Sue** is one of the doctrines of *justiciability derived from the "case or controversy" requirement of *Article III (see CASES AND CONTROVERSIES). In its simplest form, standing identifies *who* may bring claims that some government action violates the Constitution. Other justiciability doctrines identify *what* claims may be brought (the *political questions doctrine) and *when* they may be brought (doctrines of *mootness and *ripeness).

Stated generally, people have standing to challenge a government action only if they are injured by the action. Ordinarily the injury is apparent, as when a plaintiff claims that police conducted an illegal search, and in most constitutional cases no serious question of standing arises. Occasionally the government action inflicts no tangible harm on any particular individual, as when Congress fails to disclose the budget of the Central Intelligence Agency in arguable violation of the payments and accounts clause of Article I, section 9 (United States v. *Richardson, 1974). In these cases plaintiffs sue in their capacity as citizens or taxpayers, claiming not that they have suffered any individualized injury but that the government's alleged violation of the Constitution inflicts an injury on every citizen or taxpayer.

*Origins.* The doctrine of standing's origins are unclear. The *common-law system of *writs appears to have supplied some writ sufficient to challenge any government action. Assuming no bar of *sovereign immunity, ordinary *tort claims could be brought if individuals suffered obvious injury. Writs of *mandamus or *quo warranto could challenge actions as beyond the authority of the government even if they did not harm anyone in the usual sense. As government expanded, practical and conceptual difficulties arose in using traditional common-law writs.

Under the writ system, people could sue where their rights were invaded. The concept of an invasion of rights was clear enough in cases such as those involving police misconduct, which could result in physical injuries. With the rise of activist government in the twentieth century, the concept of rights became more diffuse. Governments enacted statutes conferring benefits on a group, but some members of the group might allege that the statutes were not being implemented properly. Were these plaintiffs injured? Only if their rights were invaded. But, it seemed, their rights were invaded only if the statute was not being implemented properly. Thus, the concept of injury, and the associated concept of standing, seemed to collapse into the merits of the claim the plaintiffs made.

Activist government also generated political opposition. Having lost in legislatures, opponents of activist government sought to transfer their battles to the courts by bringing lawsuits alleging that the activist statutes were beyond the power of the government to enact. The plaintiffs claimed standing as taxpayers, arguing that the statutes unlawfully wasted their money. These lawsuits were efforts to use the federal courts to limit the power of Congress and were associated with substantive theories of constitutional limitation associated with the ideas of *dual federalism and substantive *due process that prevailed during the "Lochner era" from the 1890s to 1937 (see *Lochner v. New York, 1905).

As the Supreme Court confronted challenges to the activist state, it began to develop the law of standing beyond its common-law origins. The Court substantially eliminated the possibility of taxpayer standing, at least in cases claiming only that Congress's action intruded on domains reserved to the states (*Frothingham v. Mellon, 1923). It also began to pry the concept of standing apart from the merits by developing the idea that people should have standing if Congress wanted to let them challenge government action, even if they were not injured by a denial of their common-law or statutory rights.

By the 1960s the doctrine of standing placed few restrictions on plaintiffs. Two cases in this period attempted to define the doctrine. In *Flast v. Cohen (1968) the Court allowed taxpayer standing to challenge expenditures alleged to violate the *First Amendment's ban on an establishment of *religion, such as arguably occurs in certain forms of public support of parochial *education. According to Flast, taxpayer standing should be allowed where the Constitution places specific limitations on the power of Congress to spend money. In Association of Data Processing Services v. Camp (1970) the Court allowed standing to anyone arguably within the zone of interests that Congress sought to protect. These decisions appeared to authorize more substantial judicial supervision of government action than earlier versions of the standing doctrine. Just as restrictive notions of standing were associated with efforts to limit the power of courts in the *Lochner* era, expansive notions were associated with the more activist era of the 1960s.

*Injury-in-Fact.* When the Supreme Court began to limit its own activism, it used the doctrine of standing as one of its vehicles (see JUDICIAL ACTIVISM). It did not, however, alter the rules regarding standing in cases challenging actions by administrative agencies, and it continued to affirm that Congress had power to confer standing. But in constitutional cases, the Court identified two aspects of the standing doctrine: "injury-in-fact" and a showing of actual government causation of that injury. According to the Court, the traditional requirement of injury-in-fact, derived from ideas of common-law injuries, was always required. Doctrines of causation and remedies were associated with the injury-in-fact requirement: the challenged government action must have caused the injury, and the court must be able to order a remedy that will eliminate the injury. *Simon v. Eastern Kentucky Welfare Rights Organization* (1976) demonstrated the force of the causation requirment. It involved a challenge to an Internal Revenue Service decision that made it easier for hospitals to retain their tax-exempt status even if they restricted services to poor people. Describing the injury as the denial of hospital services to the poor, the Court said that this injury resulted from the hospitals' decisions, not the allegedly unlawful change in the IRS position, and that there was no assurance that, were the courts to invalidate the IRS position, indigents would receive increased hospital services.

*Prudential Limitations.* In addition, the Court identified "prudential" limitations on standing. The Court has not clarified the precise dimensions of these prudential limitations, but it has said that they are designed to ensure that the courts will not intervene in cases where it would be better to let the political process address the claimed constitutional violation or where judicial intervention might provoke a congressional response adverse to the courts. The Court has said that, though Congress may eliminate the prudential restrictions on standing, Article III itself requires injury-in-fact; Congress therefore cannot authorize the courts to decide cases unless there is an injury-in-fact.

*Criticisms.* Both the prudential and the injury-in-fact requirements have been widely criticized. The prudential requirements are so ill-defined, critics claim, that they essentially allow the Court to use the doctrine of standing as a surrogate for a decision on the merits. If the Court believes that it will be criticized for ducking a hard constitutional question, it will find no prudential standing barrier; if it believes that it will be more severely criticized for resolving a constitutional question than for ducking it, it can invoke the prudential dimensions of standing to avoid deciding the merits. Most defenders of this aspect of the doctrine acknowledge that the critics have accurately described the Court's practices but argue that it is valuable for the Court to have available flexible doctrines of this sort so that it can more smoothly play its role in the nation's overall system of constitutional politics.

The injury-in-fact requirement has been criticized for reviving the problem that standing and the merits tend to collapse into each other. *Allen v. Wright* (1984) illustrates the problem. African-American taxpayers whose children attended public schools in districts under judicial orders to desegregate challenged the Internal Revenue Service's system of investigating claims that private schools discriminated on the basis of race. Federal law clearly prohibited the granting of tax-exempt status to racially discriminatory private schools, and the plaintiffs claimed that they were injured by the IRS practice in two ways: first, the government's failure to investigate claims of private racial discrimination aggressively itself sent a message supporting discrimination and, second, the government's inadequate system of investigation meant that discriminatory schools could continue to operate in ways that interfered with the ongoing process of desegregation (see RACE AND RACISM).

The Court held that the plaintiffs did not have standing, contending that they had not shown that the IRS practices actually made it more difficult for their school districts to desegregate. The second alleged injury-in-fact, the Court said, was not caused by the IRS practice and could not be remedied by judicial intervention. The first injury, the stigma caused by the government's inadequate system, was not, according to the Court, the kind of injury that the Constitution addressed.

Both aspects of the analysis have been questioned. The causation analysis seems to deny that prices affect purchases—that is, the seemingly undeniable facts that a more adequate system of investigation would increase the cost of private education at schools denied tax-exempt status because they were racially discriminatory, that the higher cost would mean that fewer white parents could afford to send their children to these schools, and that having fewer white children in private schools would make it easier to desegregate the public schools. The Court's denial that the government's failure to regard the interests of African-Americans seriously is an injury-in-fact seems to be a determination about the scope of the Constitution, that is, a decision on the merits rather than a decision about standing. *Allen v. Wright* is perhaps best understood as an expression of the Court's discomfort with the remedy the plaintiffs proposed, which would have required more intrusive judicial supervision of the daily operation of the IRS than the Court believed appropriate. Thus the Court may in fact have been discussing the remedies or causation prongs in the guise of interpreting injury-in-fact.

Such confusion is not unusual in recent standing cases.

*Other Issues.* Although the Court has said that Congress may create new rights the invasion of which will confer standing, it is unclear how broadly Congress may act. Under the Freedom of Information Act of 1967, anyone may demand government documents, without giving any reason, and may sue to challenge a withholding of the documents. Here, Congress created a right, held by everyone, of access to documents, and anyone has standing to sue if that right is invaded. Reconciling this result with a restrictive interpretation of the injury-in-fact requirement is difficult. To push this situation to its logical extreme, could Congress enact a statute creating a right, held by every citizen, to live in a society whose government complies with the Constitution, and could Congress then authorize everyone to sue to enforce this statutory right?

The Court has said that the constitutional dimensions of standing are related to the *separation of powers. Allowing the courts to act without requiring some form of standing, on this view, would substantially alter the balance of power between the political branches and the courts. Congressional action conferring standing can be understood, according to this view, as a statement by the political branches that they invite judicial determination of the constitutionality of their action. Confrontation between the courts and the political branches would not occur, although an alteration of their power relations would; that alteration might itself violate separation of powers even if Congress wanted the alteration to occur.

The doctrine of standing is important as part of the theory of *judicial review. Analyzing standing has provided the Court with opportunities to periodically revisit and redefine its conception of the role of judicial review in the constitutional system. As a practical matter, the situations in which no one has standing to challenge government action are few, though often important.

□ Henry P. Monaghan, "Constitutional Adjudication: The Who and When," *Yale Law Journal* 82 (1973): 1363–1397. Gene R. Nichol, "Injury and the Disintegration of Article III," *California Law Review* 74 (1986): 1915–1950. Kenneth E. Scott, "Standing in the Supreme Court–A Functional Analysis," *Harvard Law Review* 86 (1973): 645–692. Mark V. Tushnet, "The New Law of Standing: A Plea for Abandonment," *Cornell Law Review* 62 (1977): 663–700.                      Mark V. Tushnet

**Stanford v. Kentucky,** 492 U.S. 361 (1989), argued 27 Mar. 1989, decided 26 June 1989 by vote of 5 to 4; Scalia for the Court, joined in whole by Rehnquist, White, and Kennedy and in part by O'Connor, who concurred in the judgment and concurred in part in the opinion; Brennan, Marshall, Blackmun, and Stevens in dissent. *Stanford* rejected the contention that the *Eighth Amendment's prohibition of *cruel and unusual punish-

ments forbids the execution of those who were juveniles when they committed the crimes for which they were convicted. The Court held that such a practice was not one of "those modes of punishment that had been considered cruel and unusual at the time that the Bill of Rights was adopted" (p. 361) and that it did not violate the "evolving standards of decency that mark the progress of a maturing society" (p. 369). By implication, however, the Court seemed to indicate that it would be unconstitutional for the state to impose the death penalty on a person who was under sixteen at the time of his or her offense.

The Court rejected the first prong of the two-part test outright, since the *common law at the time of the *Bill of Rights set the minimum age for the application of *capital punishment in theory at seven and in practice at fourteen. The Court found that at least 281 offenders under the age of eighteen, including at least 126 under the age of seventeen, had been executed in the United States.

The Court's rejection of the second argument—that evolving standards of decency were violated—was more involved. Considering the laws of the several states, both as enacted and as applied, Justice Antonin *Scalia found that a majority of states allow capital punishment for those above the age of sixteen and rejected as irrelevant the defendants' contention that prosecutors rarely seek and juries rarely apply the death penalty to juveniles.

In dissent, Justice William J. *Brennan argued that the evidence from the laws and practices of the states, properly interpreted, suggests that the imposition of the death penalty on juveniles violates "contemporary standards of decency" (p. 388).

(See also CAPITAL PUNISHMENT; JUVENILE JUSTICE.)

William Lasser

**Stanley, United States v.** See CIVIL RIGHTS CASES.

**Stanley v. Georgia,** 394 U.S. 557 (1969), argued 14–15 Jan. 1969, decided 7 Apr. 1969 by vote of 9 to 0; Marshall for the Court. From 1957, when the Supreme Court decided *Roth v. United States, to 1973, when it decided *Paris Adult Theatre I v. Slaton and *Miller v. California, obscenity doctrine was in disarray. Different pluralities of the Court used different definitions and employed widely divergent views about the permissibility and scope of obscenity law in light of *First Amendment limitations. In *Stanley v. Georgia,* the Court decided that the purely private possession in the home of even legally obscene material could not be punished. Justice Thurgood *Marshall's opinion is unclear about the basis for this conclusion, subject under one interpretation as being based primarily on *Fourth Amendment restrictions on search and seizure, under another as based on freedom of *speech and the press, and under still another as based on a more broadly premised right of *privacy that makes it impermissible for the state to restrict conduct affecting no one except the actor.

In part because of this uncertainty, question remains about the vitality of *Stanley* as good law. Insofar as it is based on a right of privacy, its holding has been undercut by subsequent decisions, particularly *Bowers* v. *Hardwick* (1986), which allowed state regulation of private sexual conduct. Insofar as the decision is about the limits of obscenity law, there is some question whether the 1973 decisions in *Miller* and *Paris* have rendered it obsolete. In any event the Court is clearly disinclined to extend its implications. In *Osborne* v. *Ohio* (1990) Justice Byron *White for the Court held *Stanley* inapplicable to private possession of child pornography and warned that "*Stanley* should not be read too broadly."

(See also OBSCENITY AND PORNOGRAPHY.)

Frederick Schauer

**Stanton, Edwin M.** (b. Steubenville, Ohio, 19 Dec. 1814; d. Washington, D.C., 24 Dec. 1869), nominee for associate justice. Before the Civil War, Stanton enjoyed a successful legal practice in Ohio, Pittsburgh, and Washington, D.C. He served energetically as secretary of war from 1862 through 1868. Alienated from President Andrew Johnson and his *Reconstruction policies, Stanton refused to submit his resignation when Johnson demanded it. He resigned only when the Senate failed to convict Johnson in *impeachment proceedings. Despite declining health, Stanton accepted President Ulysses S. Grant's nomination to the Supreme Court on 20 December 1869. The Senate, where Stanton was popular, confirmed him on the same day, but he died four days later, before he could take his seat.

William M. Wiecek

**Stanton v. Stanton,** 421 U.S. 7 (1975), argued 19 Feb. 1975, decided 15 Apr. 1975 by vote of 8 to 1; Blackmun for the Court, Rehnquist in dissent. *Stanton* was one of several sex discrimination cases decided in the period between *Reed* v. *Reed* (1971) and *Craig* v. *Boren* (1976) in which the Court majority purported to be applying a rational basis test but declared void a statute that legislators and other judges had nonetheless found rational. The statute here declared unconstitutional, as a violation of the *Fourteenth Amendment's *Equal Protection Clause, had mandated a twenty-one-year age of majority for males and an eighteen-year age of majority for females.

Thelma Stanton, ex-wife of James Stanton, had brought suit when he ceased child support payments for their daughter Sherri upon the latter's eighteenth birthday. The Supreme Court of Utah had rejected her claim on the grounds that the statute had a reasonable basis: girls tend to mature physically, mentally, and emotionally before boys, and also, since men must provide for their families, they need time to acquire an education for that responsibility.

Justice Harry *Blackmun, for the Court, denied that the statute was rational. He insisted that coeducation is a fact and that women are increasingly present in business and the professions. He said that the court failed to perceive the "unquestioned truth" of females' tendency to earlier maturity or its relevance to the need for child support (p. 15).

Justice William *Rehnquist's dissent argued that Thelma Stanton's claim arose out of a voluntary property settlement at divorce, which could have specified any age whatever to terminate support payments, and therefore the issue of the constitutionality of the age of majority law was not properly before the Court.

(See also EQUAL PROTECTION; GENDER.)

Leslie Friedman Goldstein

**Stare Decisis.** See PRECEDENT.

**State Action.** The Fourteenth and *Fifteenth Amendments were principally intended to protect former slaves and to guarantee *due process of law, the *equal protection of the laws, and the right to *vote against state infringement. In the *Civil Rights Cases* (1883), the Supreme Court held that the Fourteenth Amendment applies only to action directly authorized or sanctioned by state law. This narrow interpretation of the state action requirement excluded any private, nongovernmental act of racial discrimination from the reach of federal power, thus inhibiting the potential scope of the Reconstruction Amendments. One consequence of this approach was *Grovey* v. *Townsend* (1935), which sustained the *white primary, a device employed to circumvent the Fifteenth Amendment's guarantee of nondiscriminatory access to the ballot.

Between 1944 and 1972, the Court took a less liberal view of state action. Reversing *Grovey* in *Smith* v. *Allwright* (1944), the Court held that since primaries play an integral role in governmental processes, they must be considered as officially sanctioned by the state. *Marsh* v. *Alabama* (1946) ruled that a town owned by a private company performed traditional public functions. Less obvious connections between private and state action were discerned in cases involving housing and public accommodations. *Shelley* v. *Kraemer* (1948) held that while racially *restrictive covenants were private *contracts, state court enforcement rendered them unconstitutional. *Burton* v. *Wilmington Parking Authority* (1961) determined that the discriminatory practices of a restaurant located on premises leased from a municipal parking facility constituted state action.

Expansion of the concept of state action paralleled a series of federal court decisions that struck down state segregation laws. It also reflected political realities: until state and federal legislatures prohibited racial discrimination in access to housing, goods, and services, the federal judiciary provided an alternative recourse. The *Sit-In Cases* (1964) were illustrative. They stemmed from the arrest and conviction for trespass of African-Americans who refused to leave segregated lunch counters (see SIT-IN DEMONSTRATIONS). The Supreme Court reversed the convictions because the restaurant operators' deference to public policy and police enforcement of their discriminatory conduct were tantamount to state denial of the equal protection of the laws. Passage of the *Civil Rights Act of 1964 transferred responsibility for assuring equal access from the Court to Congress.

State tolerance of discrimination may constitute state action. In *Terry* v. *Adams* (1953), a privately conducted, unofficial, whites-only pre-primary election was deemed state action. *Reitman* v. *Mulkey* (1967) invalidated a voter-initiated and -ratified state constitutional amendment that secured freedom of choice in sales and rentals of residential property. Since the amendment's intended effect was the repeal of an open occupancy law, voters had authorized discrimination. Four dissenting justices asserted that the amendment's neutral wording did not condone discrimination (see HOUSING DISCRIMINATION).

Subsequent cases drew distinctions, which some justices and commentators feared earlier cases had blurred, between the private and public realms and between tacit state approval of private conduct and neutrality toward it. In *Moose Lodge* v. *Irvis* (1972), the Court did not regard the discriminatory conduct of a private club that held a routinely issued liquor license as state action. The three dissenters argued that the limited number of licenses, one of which the club held, restricted the availability of access for African-Americans, thereby denying them equality of treatment under the law (see PRIVATE DISCRIMINATORY ASSOCIATIONS).

*Moose Lodge* marked a significant contraction of the state action doctrine. The Supreme Court has consistently rejected invitations to jettison the doctrine by overruling the *Civil Rights Cases* and has insisted that state action is present only when private parties perform customary governmental functions, or when the state has required or actively encouraged the challenged private conduct, or when that conduct may be attributed to a state official or to a party acting in concert with state officials. *Jackson* v. *Metropolitan Edison Co.* (1974), for example, found no violation of due process in the termination of service without prior hearing by a public utility possessing a government-granted monopoly.

Expansion of the state action doctrine comprised a crucial element of the Court's overall response to racial discrimination. Some commentators believe that enactment of federal public accommodations and fair housing legislation diminishes the need for state action jurisprudence

manifested in *Wilmington Parking, Shelley,* and *Reitman.* Nonetheless, critics of the current approach argue that private parties who are substantially related to government, such as state-sanctioned regulated monopolies that provide the sole source of service available to consumers, should be held to the same obligations that the Fourteenth Amendment imposes on the states.

(See also FOURTEENTH AMENDMENT; RACE AND RACISM.)

□ Maimon Schwarzchild, "Value Pluralism and the Constitution: In Defense of the State Action Doctrine," *Supreme Court Review* (1988), pp. 129–161.
Mary Cornelia Aldis Porter

**State Constitutions and Individual Rights.** In 1951 a law professor wrote that "if our liberties are not protected in Des Moines the only hope is in Washington" (Paulsen, "State Constitutions, State Courts and First Amendment Freedoms," *Vanderbilt Law Review* 4 [Apr. 1951]: 620, 642). In 1988 the quip was revised to read that "if our liberties are not protected in Washington, the only hope is in Des Moines" (Giudicessi, "Independent State Grounds for Freedom of Speech and of the Press: Article 1, Section 7 of the Iowa Constitution," *Drake Law Review* 38 [1988–1989]: 9, 29). The last quarter of the twentieth century has witnessed a revival of state constitutional law in the area of individual rights. Some observers extol a "new judicial federalism" in which state and federal courts use state constitutions to protect the rights of individuals, subject, of course, to the Supremacy Clause of Article VI.

Although the Supreme Court is widely considered to be uniquely responsible for protecting individual rights through its interpretation of the federal *Bill of Rights, the Court's role in guarding individual rights against encroachment by *state action is of relatively recent origin. In 1789 Congress rejected a proposed constitutional amendment that would have barred the states from infringing the right of *trial by jury in criminal cases, the right of conscience, and the freedom of *speech and of the press. In 1833 the Supreme Court held that the federal Bill of Rights did not apply to the states (*Barron v. Baltimore*). Thus for more than a century after the adoption of the Bill of Rights, state bills of rights—not the federal Bill of Rights—protected individual liberties from encroachment by state governments. By way of illustration, the Wisconsin Supreme Court in 1859 interpreted the Wisconsin constitution as guaranteeing indigent felony defendants the right to counsel at public expense (*Carpenter* v. *County of Dane*). It was not until 104 years later that the U.S. Supreme Court enunciated a similar right to counsel in state felony cases under the *Fourteenth Amendment to the United States Constitution (*Gideon* v. *Wainwright,* 1963).

The application of the Bill of Rights to state action followed the ratification of the Fourteenth

Amendment in 1868. Beginning in 1925 the U.S. Supreme Court selectively incorporated many provisions of the first eight amendments into the Fourteenth Amendment and thus declared these provisions of the Bill of Rights applicable to the states (*Gitlow v. New York*). By the end of the 1960s, the Supreme Court was perceived as the preeminent court protecting individual rights against encroachment by the federal and state governments (see HISTORY OF THE COURT: RIGHTS CONSCIOUSNESS IN CONTEMPORARY SOCIETY.) The Court established a "floor" of protection, that is, minimum federally protected rights that states were bound to honor. For many states, the federal "floor" was above the state "ceiling" of protection. While a state may not provide a claimant less favorable treatment than the federal Constitution, a state may enforce a state-granted right above the federal "floor" of protection unless the extended right bumps into the "floor" of protection of another federal right.

As federal constitutional guarantees expanded, the bench, bar, and public apparently came to regard state bills of rights as adding little to their federal counterpart, and state courts' reliance on state bills of rights diminished. The 1950s and 1960s saw an atrophy of the use of state constitutional protections for individual liberties. In the 1970s and 1980s, the political winds shifted, bringing an emphasis on the states in the American federal system. Some believed that the Supreme Court was retreating from its rulings protecting individual rights. Others viewed procedural changes as limiting the ability of federal courts to hear federal constitutional claims against state action. At the end of the 1970s, many commentators, judges, and lawyers increasingly advocated reliance on state constitutional law, as well as federal constitutional law, to protect the rights of Americans.

When a judgment of a state court rests on a state ground independent of a federal ground and adequate to support the state court judgment and no *federal question is in issue, the U.S. Supreme Court declines to review the state judgment. Thus the federal system recognizes the state as an independent legal entity capable of endowing persons within its jurisdiction with rights independent of federal law and insulated from federal judicial review (*Michigan v. Long, 1983).

In many cases, however, state courts continue to ignore their state constitutions or cite them only in passing and rely instead on the federal Constitution. When a state court turns to its own constitution to decide a case, more often than not it adopts the U.S. Supreme Court's interpretation of a similar provision in the Bill of Rights. Nevertheless by 1990 in more than five hundred cases state courts had declared that state constitutional rights surpass the protections of the federal Constitution.

Cases interpreting state constitutional rights may be divided into two broad categories. One category involves state courts' reliance on state constitutional provisions that have no federal analog. For example, while the Supreme Court finds a right to *privacy implicit in the Bill of Rights and the Fourteenth Amendment (*Griswold v. Connecticut, 1965), several state constitutions contain explicit guarantees of privacy. A few state constitutions protect environmental values or collective bargaining rights. Several provide for open courts and a remedy in law for all injuries or wrongs. State courts have applied state constitutional guarantees of the right of access to the courts, as well as other constitutional provisions, to statutory innovations in *tort law, such as limiting compensatory damages, with a variety of results.

Although the states failed to ratify the proposed federal Equal Rights Amendment, by 1990 a significant number of state constitutions expressly provided for *gender equality. Furthermore, even without an express *equal protection guarantee, state courts have interpreted various state constitutional provisions as guaranteeing equal protection of the laws. Some commentators predict that state courts will depart from the standard the Supreme Court uses to scrutinize alleged violations of equal protection and will take a more expansive view of gender equality and equal protection guarantees.

All state constitutions contain provisions relating to *education, and some state courts have viewed these as creating a fundamental right to education. States have divided on the question whether their educational-funding statutes are unconstitutional under state education and equal protection provisions. In contrast, in *San Antonio Independent School District v. Rodriguez (1973), the U.S. Supreme Court rejected arguments that education is a fundamental right and that financing schools through the property tax constitutes a classification based on poverty that is constitutionally suspect under the Fourteenth Amendment.

The second category of cases interpreting state constitutional rights involves state courts' reliance on state constitutional provisions that are similar or identical to provisions in the Bill of Rights. For example, more state constitutions contain criminal procedural protections similar to those in the *Fourth, *Fifth, *Sixth, and *Eighth Amendments, as well as guarantees of freedom of expression and religion comparable to those in the *First Amendment.

State courts frequently adopt the Supreme Court's analysis and interpretation of the federal Constitution as a guide to interpreting their own parallel state constitutional guarantees. Nevertheless many state courts have chosen not to apply federal constitutional rulings when interpreting their own state constitutional provisions. In the area of criminal procedure, state courts are divided, for example, on accepting the good faith exception to the *exclusionary rule recognized in *United States* v. *Leon* (1984) and on accepting the test for evaluating search warrants established in *Illinois* v. *Gates* (1983). (See SEARCH WARRANT RULE, EXCEPTIONS TO.) State courts have similarly divided on whether a warrantless police roadblock to apprehend drunk drivers is unconstitutional and whether a right to *counsel attaches prior to the administration of a breath test to a suspected drunk driver. Some state courts have invalidated laws allowing drug testing programs without *probable cause and curtailed the power of law enforcement officers to conduct *automobile searches.

The U.S. Supreme Court has concluded that a state may interpret its constitutional guarantee of free speech as limiting private as well as state action (*PruneYard Shopping Center* v. *Robins*, 1980). A few state courts have read their state constitutional provisions of free speech (which often are worded more broadly than the First Amendment) as granting citizens free speech rights on the premises of private shopping malls and college campuses. Most state courts deciding this issue have, however, refused to extend their state constitutional free speech provisions to private property.

While the Supreme Court has held that *obscenity is without federal constitutional protection (*Miller* v. *California*, 1973), state courts have divided on the question whether their state constitutions afford greater protection to obscenity than the federal courts afford under the First Amendment.

Some scholars and judges maintain that a state court may reject a Supreme Court interpretation of a federal guarantee of individual rights in interpreting a parallel state constitutional provision simply on the grounds that it lacks analytical soundness. Others assert that a state court's mere disagreement with a particular Supreme Court decision does not justify the court's interpreting the state constitution differently from the federal Constitution. They believe that only a "state-specific" reason supports divergence. Some state courts have attempted to enunciate criteria for following or departing from Supreme Court decisions. These criteria commonly include the wording of the state constitution and the comparable federal provision, structural differences between the state and federal constitutions, state constitutional history, and local traditions. Thus, for example, several state judges have examined the history of their constitutions and determined that constitutional delegates intended their freedom of speech provisions, stated as an affirmative right rather than as a prohibition, to be broader than the First Amendment, and not to require state action.

The proponents of state courts' interpreting state constitutional provisions independently of the U.S. Supreme Court's interpretation of similar federal constitutional provisions assert that

the "new judicial federalism" is a process-oriented approach that comports with the historical relationship between the national and state governments. They claim that the approach offers diversity and the opportunity to experiment.

Opponents view the renewed emphasis on state constitutional law as a result-oriented liberal ploy, a way of getting around the Burger and Rehnquist Courts' retreat from the rights-expanding decisions of the Warren Court. They contend that the "new judicial federalism" creates a confusing multiplicity of rules, subverts the idea of America as one nation, thwarts *judicial review by the U.S. Supreme Court, and undermines the public's confidence in the Supreme Court and the rule of law.

Despite these criticisms, state constitutions have been and likely will continue to be, in Justice William J. *Brennan's words, "a font of individual liberties." Nevertheless a cautionary note must be sounded. State constitutions are easier to amend than is the federal Constitution. Thus individual rights protected solely by state constitutions are more readily subject to change. In 1982 the voters of Florida amended their constitution to prohibit divergence from U.S. Supreme Court rulings on the exclusionary rule. Furthermore, many state judges, unlike the life-tenured federal judiciary, are subject to popular election. In 1984 California voters ousted three state Supreme Court justices reputed to be willing to extend protections guaranteed by the state constitution beyond the scope of the federal Constitution.

These occurrences underscore the critical importance of the dual constitutional protection of individual rights in the American federal system. The federal Constitution is not the only American constitution. State constitutions cannot, however, substitute for the federal Constitution. The U.S. Supreme Court is not the only court protecting constitutional guarantees of individual rights against state encroachment. Rather, both the federal and state courts, through dialogue and disagreement, can best guard American liberties.

(see also FEDERALISM; INCORPORATION DOCTRINE; STATE COURTS; STATE SOVEREIGNTY AND STATES' RIGHTS.)

□ William J. Brennan, "State Constitutions and the Protection of Individual Rights," *Harvard Law Review* 90 (Jan. 1977): 489–504. Columbia University Legislative Drafting Research Fund, *Constitutions of the United States: National and State*, 2d ed. (1991). "Developments in the Law—The Interpretation of State Constitutional Rights," *Harvard Law Review* 95 (April 1982): 1324–1502. Bradley D. McGraw, ed., *Developments in State Constitutional Law* (1985).

Shirley S. Abrahamson and Charles G. Curtis, Jr.

**State Courts.** State cases come to the United States Supreme Court from the highest appellate courts of the states. Under its discretionary authority to accept or reject cases, and in keeping with its own rules of *standing to sue, the Court accepts less than 10 percent of all state appeals. State cases also come to the Court from *lower federal court rulings on cases originating in state courts. Included in this category are disputes removed from a state to a federal court, federal court *injunctions halting state court proceedings, and federal court issuance of *habeas corpus writs to state prisoners claiming violation of federal rights (see REMOVAL OF CASES).

Relations between federal and state courts are referred to as "judicial federalism." As legally established and commonly understood, judicial federalism denotes a hierarchical arrangement. The federal Constitution establishes a national court system and stipulates that inconsistencies between federal and state law are to be resolved in favor of the former and that state judges are bound by this principle. Thus state courts must give precedence to federal over state law and interpret federal law in line with current rulings of the Supreme Court. Federal statutes that authorize Supreme Court review of state supreme court decisions on federal law as well as statutes that vest lower federal courts with jurisdiction over federal questions formerly adjudicated in state courts are intended to ensure the supremacy of federal law. Under the leadership of Chief Justice John *Marshall (1801–1835), the Court, against strong state court opposition, successfully reserved for itself the final authority to determine whether state law comported with the federal Constitution, laws, and treaties.

Despite its dominant role in the system of judicial federalism, the Supreme Court has instituted practices that preserve the integrity and autonomy of state law and state courts. The observance of *comity assures respectful recognition of the laws and judicial decisions of the states. The *"independent and adequate state ground" doctrine requires Supreme Court acceptance of state court interpretation of state constitutions and statutes provided state law does not violate the federal Constitution, the state court's judgment is solidly based in state law, and its reasoning does not rely on federal judicial precedent.

Further, the Court will not review state court judgments unless *federal questions have been raised early in the proceedings, thereby allowing their full consideration at all state court levels; nor will the Court consider appeals when those raising federal claims have failed to comply with state court procedures. It has also held that habeas corpus petitions may not be considered until a prisoner has exhausted all state remedies. Finally, the principle of "equitable abstention" encourages the Court to stay its hand until a state court has had an opportunity to rule in a manner that might preclude Court review (see ABSTENTION DOCTRINE).

The Constitution and federal statutes indicate a command-obedience relationship between the highest federal and state courts, and state court autonomy could be viewed as existing at the sufferance of the Supreme Court. In reality, the interactions between the Supreme Court and state high courts are shifting and multifarious, reflecting the Court's perspectives on its role in the federal system, its policy preferences, and state court response to its mandates. Nowhere is this better illustrated than by federal and state high court management of civil liberties questions during the twentieth century.

Until shortly after *World War I, a division of labor characterized the relationship between the two judicial systems. State guarantees were enforced in state courts; federal guarantees (namely, the first ten amendments to the Constitution, or the *Bill of Rights) were enforced in federal courts. In effect, federal and state courts went their separate ways.

In the subsequent three decades, the Court cautiously extended its supervisory authority over state courts. Typically it invalidated state decisions involving individual rights on *Fourteenth Amendment *due process and *equal protection grounds. On the rare occasion that it based a holding on the applicability of the Bill of Rights to the states it was because the constitutional guarantees in question, notably freedom of the press, speech, and religion, were, as the Court explained, "implicit in the concept of ordered liberty." During these years, the Court resisted arguments that state criminal defendants enjoy the same protections as the *Fourth, *Fifth, *Sixth, *Seventh, and *Eighth Amendments provided federal defendants. Instead, in order to determine the constitutionality of treatment accorded the accused, the Court relied upon judicially established Fourteenth Amendment due process standards such as the "fair trial rule" for defendants unrepresented by counsel and the "shock the conscience test" for defendants subjected to egregious searches and seizures.

The Court's fundamental fairness and due process precepts, enunciated to provide state courts with the leeway to develop acceptable protections of the accused, were considered vague and subjective. Some state judges made conscientious efforts to apply *precedent; others took advantage of the lack of precise guidelines.

During Chief Justice Earl *Warren's tenure (1954–1969), a Court strongly committed to the protection of civil liberties furthered the process commenced in the 1930s and 1940s of applying the Bill of Rights to the states. As a result, many state high court holdings, especially those pertaining to the rights of criminal defendants, were overturned.

Justices in virtually all states expressed resentment over what they regarded as the Court's insensitivity to judicial relationships in a federal system and its assumption that state courts lacked the will and capability to protect civil rights. Tensions between state supreme courts and their federal counterpart were further exacerbated by Court holdings that sustained *lower federal court grants of habeas corpus petitions to prisoners seeking to vindicate rights enunciated by the Warren Court and allegedly disregarded by state courts.

Under the leadership of Chief Justices Warren *Burger (1969–1986) and William H. *Rehnquist (1986–), the Court has significantly curtailed the reach of the Warren Court's numerous civil liberties rulings. In response to the Court's retrenchment, a number of state high courts, some more enthusiastically and consistently than others, have relied on state constitutions to extend protections greater than those accorded by the Supreme Court.

Initially, the Court applauded what is referred to as "the new judicial federalism." Within a few years, however, the Court paid closer attention to the independent and adequate state ground strictures and a number of civil libertarian state court rulings were reversed or remanded to the states for further consideration. Critics have argued that the Court's increasingly stringent approach pertained less to independent and adequate state ground considerations and more to its restrictive view of civil rights and liberties in general and its distaste for civil libertarian judicial activism in particular.

The Burger and Rehnquist Courts have accompanied this retrenchment process with disapproval of lower federal court grants or habeas corpus petitions in search and seizure and death penalty appeals (see CAPITAL PUNISHMENT; SEARCH WARRANT RULE, EXCEPTIONS TO). Since the Supreme Court hears so few of the appeals coming from state courts, denial of state prisoner access to federal courts results in augmenting the authority of state courts to make final decisions in these areas.

While noncompliance with Supreme Court decisions is the exception rather than the rule, state courts have historically contrived means of distinguishing, limiting, or eroding federal precedent and of evading the Supreme Court's jurisdiction. The Court has the power to exercise its will over all lower state and federal courts, but it must determine how much of its time, its institutional capacities and prestige it is willing to expend in order to assure compliance with its mandates.

In different historical periods and according to different issues, the Court has faced down, mollified, accommodated, and on rare occasions, capitulated to state courts that either defy the Court's direct mandates or fail to observe precedents that enunciate applicable constitutional principles. Examples include the tug-of-war between the Virginia judiciary and the Marshall Court over the final determination of federal constitutional questions; the Court's willingness to give state courts more than ample time to follow directives in race relations cases, to clarify ambiguous right to counsel rulings, to overlook or ignore state court manipulation of *self-incrimination precedent, and by default to permit a state supreme court, after protracted litigation in the highest state and federal courts, to have its way in a capital punishment case that involved complicated procedural questions.

The interaction of the Supreme Court and state courts is complex. It is misleading simply to depict the Supreme Court as prime mover, state courts as responders, and the Supreme Court as the institution that selectively and loftily considers the state responses. The Supreme Court is not the only initiator; it also has been receptive to substantive state court influence.

In the first place, as Justice William *Brennan acknowledged in a 1964 law review article, state high courts have provided the Supreme Court with guidance in deciding federal constitutional questions in areas such as *reapportionment, *obscenity, freedom of *religion, and defendants' rights. Second, state courts, expanding on recently enunciated Supreme Court principles, have charted the way for further Supreme Court evolution of its new doctrines. The California high court, for example, employing techniques developed by the Supreme Court for deciding Fourteenth Amendment equal protection cases, ruled in *Purdy and Fitzpatrick* v. *State* (1969) that special treatment for aliens constituted impermissible discrimination. In *Graham* v. *Richardson* (1971), the Supreme Court followed suit.

In the third place, the process of state court response to Supreme Court holdings and Supreme Court response to the state court responses has over time produced a "hybrid federal-state constitutional law" covering a wide spectrum of issues. For instance, in the seven years that followed a Supreme Court holding concerning right to *counsel for indigents at probation revocation hearings, state courts decided hundreds of similar cases. When the Court again reviewed the issue, its ruling took account of state court problems with and objections to the earlier mandate. Similarly, New York's highest court so impressed a Warren Court majority with its *People* v. *Rivera* (1964) that admitted holding evidence obtained from a police *stop and frisk search and seizure, that the Court in *Terry* v. *Ohio* (1968) essentially agreed that such procedures were exempt from what had been its increasingly expansive interpretation of *Fourth Amendment protections.

The Supreme Court is in control of its relations with state courts. But how it chooses to exercise that control is another matter. In some periods, as illustrated by the Warren Court, the Court has come close to adhering to a hierarchical model. In others, as illustrated by pre-Warren and the Burger and Rehnquist courts, it has allowed state courts considerable leeway. Traditional considerations for state court autonomy may be overridden by the Court's concern for preserving its own precepts, but the Court has been willing to shift authority from federal to state courts in order to reduce substantially what the Court regards as excessive appeals concerning issues that do not elicit the Court's sympathy.

Finally, if past trends portend the future, relations between federal and state supreme courts will continue to fluctuate. No matter how persuasive or consistent state courts may be, the Supreme Court will continue to establish the terms of judicial federalism.

(see also FEDERALISM; INCORPORATION DOCTRINE; STATE CONSTITUTIONS AND INDIVIDUAL RIGHTS.)

□ William J. Brennan, Jr., "Some Aspects of Federalism." *New York University Law Review* 39 (1964): 945–961. Robert M. Cover and T. Alexander Aleinikoff, "Dialectical Federalism: Habeas Corpus and the Court," *Yale Law Journal* 86 (1977): 1035–1102. Stanley H. Friedelbaum, ed., *Human Rights in the States* (1988), chaps. 1, 2, and 6. Mary Cornelia Porter and G. Alan Tarr, eds., *State Supreme Courts: Policymakers in the Federal System* (1982), intro. and chaps. 1, 2, 7, and 8. G. Alan Tarr and Mary Cornelia Aldis Porter, *State Supreme Courts in State and Nation* (1988). Mary Cornelia Aldis Porter

**State Police Power.** See POLICE POWER.

**State Regulation of Commerce.** Today's economy is one of enormous complexity and interdependence. Even the smallest businesses may be tied to interstate markets by such commonplace items as the mailbox, the telephone, and the computer. Goods and services routinely cross state lines. Major corporations may have offices, factories, and distribution centers located in dozens of states. Mass media such as radio and television make it possible for businesses to reach a nationwide audience. It is apparent, then, that the modern business world is oblivious to state lines.

Expansion of businesses into interstate markets was not accomplished without some risk. One of these was the risk of multiple tax liability (see TAX IMMUNITIES). An inescapable fact of life is that states are quick to tax successful businesses. They are inclined to tax out-of-state businesses more readily and more severely. This is so for a simple reason: taxes are passed by politicians, and politicians prefer to tax those who cannot vote. A tax imposed on an out-of-state business is a politician's dream. Not only does it ensure an influx of tax money into the state's coffers, it does so with few adverse political consequences.

Exposure to multiple taxation is a harsh reality for businesses with multistate ties. Were the states' tax power unchecked, they could collectively tax out-of-state businesses to the point of extinction. Sadly, the drain on the assets of nonresident businesses and the welfare of communities hundreds of miles distant do not command the states' attention. Their only immediate concern is the tax dollar. The Commerce Clause, however, is an important historic check on the taxing power.

To understand fully the purposes that underlie the Commerce Clause, it is useful to sketch some of our country's earliest history. In the days of the American Confederation, there was no national control over commerce. Every state was free to regulate and tax all commerce that crossed it borders. It is therefore no surprise that taxes were laid on commodities as they were transported into and out of each state. Goods were even banned and subject to forfeiture. This practice tended to snuff out the development of a truly interstate commerce and drew a wave of criticism from merchants who wished to exploit out-of-state markets.

*Early Cases.* The framers of the Constitution resolved to promote interstate commerce by centralizing the power to control commerce. They first imposed certain limits on the states' power. Henceforth, states were forbidden to lay taxes on imports and exports, to enter into trade pacts, to coin their own money, or to alter retroactively commercial contracts by law. Beyond these specific limits, Congress was vested with a largely undefined power to "regulate Commerce . . . among the several States" (see COMMERCE POWER). In the decades to come, this clause would lay the foundation for national control over commerce and become the source of a body of law that closely circumscribed the states' tax powers.

Early federal cases charted the development of this body of law. One of the country's earliest and most famous tax cases was *McCulloch* v. *Maryland* (1819). *McCulloch* did not discuss the Commerce Clause, but it sounded the same themes that would be repeated in subsequent commerce cases. It is, therefore, an appropriate point to start our inquiry. In the aftermath of the War of 1812, Congress formed the Second Bank of the United States as a depository for federal money. Maryland passed a law that taxed certain operations of the bank's Baltimore branch. The bank's cashier declined to pay the tax, and the battle lines were drawn.

Chief Justice John *Marshall's opinion in the case is considered by some to be his greatest state paper. Mashall, in an oft-quoted phrase, commented that "the power to tax involves the power to destroy" (p. 430). While the states possessed the power to tax, that power could not be used to weaken or destroy the purpose of a federal law. Congress was authorized to form the bank and the states were powerless to interfere with its lawful operations. Marshall concluded forcefully,

[T]he states have no power, by taxation or otherwise, to retard, impede, burden, or in any manner control the operation of the constitutional laws enacted by Congress to carry into execution the powers vested in the general government. (p. 36)

*McCulloch* was followed by *\*Brown* v. *Maryland* (1827). A Maryland statute required all importers of foreign goods to secure a license for fifty dollars. To sell imported goods without a license was made a criminal offense. A Maryland importer, Brown, attacked the statute as a violation of the Commerce Clause. Marshall's opinion in *Brown* recognized the states' power to tax but stated that it must yield to the federal commerce power. The purpose of that power was to insure a robust and unfettered flow of commerce. Marshall posed a simple question: Why would one import goods except to enter them into commerce? Maryland's statute was in effect a penalty on importers who wished to profit from commerce and was thus hostile to federal law.

A question asked in *Brown*, but not authoritatively answered, was whether a tax on sales of goods in interstate commerce would suffer the same fate. The Supreme Court in *\*Woodruff* v. *Parham* (1869) answered that question in the negative. The tax involved in *Woodruff* was imposed on all auction sales within the city of Mobile, Alabama. Distinguishing *Brown*, the Court stressed that Mobile's tax was one on sales and was not hostile per se to commerce. Added to that was the fact the tax applied equally to all goods, whether in-state or out-of-state. This focus on discrimination between in-state and interstate commerce foreshadowed future Commerce Clause analysis.

One of the principles that developed from these early cases was that a tax on interstate commerce was an undue burden on commerce and was void. This proved to be the catalyst for an economic explosion. New industries blossomed. East and West became linked by railroads, waterways, and early telecommunication systems. But this "tax exempt" status was short-lived. States were anxious to ride the wave of economic boom, and they undertook efforts to require interstate commerce to "pay its way." They soon laid taxes based on receipts that a business derived from interstate activity, but they proportioned these taxes to the activity that was actually carried on within the state. These efforts were fueled by the fact that states lend valuable services to out-of-state businesses. Consider a simple example. A trucker that hauls commodities in interstate commerce will have substantial ties to its home state. It will employ workers there, it will use that state's roads, it will own or lease real property, and it will receive the protection of the state's laws. These kinds of ties, the states contended, were sufficient to justify a tax. By the early twentieth century the federal courts were convinced of such taxes' validity.

One further principle, an anomaly of sorts, persisted. If a business was involved *solely* in interstate commerce, it was immune from taxation by any state. This led to some absurd results. In cases decided over a thirty-year span, taxes were struck down for the sole reason that no in-state business was carried on. There was widespread unhappiness with these cases and the courts quietly retreated. Taxes were upheld despite the lack of in-state business where states did not purport to tax interstate commerce. And thus the law remained until the 1970s.

*Recent Law.* Possibly the most important state taxation case in recent history was *Complete Auto Transit, Inc.* v. *Brady* (1977), overruling cases that immunized interstate commerce from taxation. Little contained in that decision was new. Its importance lay instead in the fact that it synthesized strands of law from earlier cases. For the first time a reader could find, in one place, the questions that must be asked and answered for a tax to survive a Commerce Clause attack. These questions may be summarized as follows:

1. *Nexus.* Is the business activity "sufficiently connected" to the state to support the tax?
2. *Impact.* Does the tax discriminate against interstate commerce?
3. *Fairness.* Is the tax fairly related to the services provided by the state and is it fairly apportioned?

These questions mark the threefold inquiry that characterizes modern state taxation analysis. Each is traceable to the historic purposes of the Commerce Clause. Each is in search of balance. To justify a tax on commerce, a state must show that it has a sufficient connection to the business activity that is to be taxed. There are no absolutes, and courts must examine the facts on a case-by-case basis. A tax must also be evenhanded, so that it applies alike to in-state and interstate commerce. States must draft their tax laws to ensure that interstate commerce is taxed equitably. Finally, a tax on commerce must fairly relate to the state's nexus with the business activity. Only when these factors are in proper balance will businesses be fully protected from the evils of multiple taxation.

Recent state taxation cases have attempted to refine these concepts, particularly the concept of nexus. It has not been an easy task. Many cases explore the kind of nexus that an out-of-state business must have before it may properly be taxed. The line they draw is, however, blurry. Does it suffice that the business has an in-state office or facility or that it solicits customers within the state? Must the tax relate to the business's actual nexus with the state, or is it sufficient that the business has *some* nexus? Does the analysis of nexus depend, in part, on the kind of tax involved? These questions will continue to shape the future of the Commerce Clause as a limit on state taxation. In its state taxation cases, the Court has attempted to work a division of national and state responsibility in a way that furthers the framers' vision of the Commerce Clause.

(See also CAPITALISM; STATE TAXATION.)

□ Merrill Jensen, *The New Nation* (1950). John E. Nowak, Ronald D. Rotunda, and J. Nelson Young, *Treatise on Constitutional Law: Substance and Procedure* (1986). Laurence H. Tribe, *American Constitutional Law*, 2d ed. (1988).

James B. Stoneking

**State Sedition Laws** developed historically from the same apprehensions that divided the United States during and immediately following *World War I: fear of foreign influence and concern over the effect of the Bolshevik revolution in Russia. In an attempt to quell concerns about alleged disloyal activity, a number of states passed laws punishing *speech and print that might discourage support for the war effort or undermine the state or federal government.

The first Supreme Court challenge of a state sedition statute came in *Gilbert v. Minnesota* (1920) and involved allegedly disloyal remarks made by an organizer for the Nonpartisan League, a farmers' group seeking political and economic reform. A seven-justice majority accepted the state defense that such legislation was an example of cooperative *federalism and that a state *police power, based on the *Tenth Amendment, could be exercised to protect the health and welfare of the people in this manner.

In dissent, Chief Justice Edward *White rejected the concept of state sedition statutes on grounds that the subject was exclusively within the power of Congress. Dissenter Louis D. *Brandeis suggested the application of the *Due Process Clause of the *Fourteenth Amendment to protect freedom of speech from state encroachment.

State sedition laws encountered few successful court challenges until the Supreme Court in *Pennsylvania v. Nelson* (1956) accepted the congressional preemption argument and voided the Pennsylvania law. Nevertheless, many state sedition statutes, as well as similar restrictive laws, remained on the books. They were sometimes revived by authorities in later generations to arrest civil rights and antiwar demonstrators.

(See also COMMUNISM AND COLD WAR; SUBVERSION.)

Carol E. Jenson

**State Sovereignty and States' Rights** doctrines emphasized ambiguities in the Constitution's distribution of national and state powers in order to oppose strong federal government. As political arguments they peaked between the Constitution's ratification and the *Civil War. Although their ultimate claim—the right to secede—died at Appomattox, both doctrines maintained juridical vitality until 1937. They were shadows of their former selves from then until the 1970s, when conservative Supreme Court justices began reinvigorating them.

States' rights doctrine's main constitutional embodiment is the *Tenth Amendment. State sovereignty doctrine held that as a result of the American Revolution the Crown's American sovereignty was transferred to individual states. The states could act much as independent nations except respecting powers vested exclusively in the federal government.

These doctrines were represented as a geometric metaphor—the "two separate spheres of dual sovereignty." Each government was sovereign and hence supreme in its respective sphere. The metaphor aided two views of intergovernmental relations favorable to the states. The first was that the two spheres had *mutually exclusive powers.* If one sphere could regulate something, the other could not. The second was the *concurrent powers* view. If a state's *"police power" and Congress's Commerce Clause power legitimately reached the same object, each sphere could regulate though the results be chaotic (see COMMERCE POWER).

Two bold states' rights and sovereignty assertions, *interposition and *nullification, were first advanced in the 1798 Virginia and 1799 Kentucky legislative resolutions drafted, respectively, by James *Madison and Thomas *Jefferson. These resolutions attempted to render inoperative in each state the 1798 Alien and *Sedition Acts passed by anti–French Revolution Federalists. Sedition Act prosecutions of Jeffersonian newspaper editors aided Jefferson's 1800 defeat of incumbent president John Adams. Considering the acts unconstitutional, Jefferson refused to enforce convictions. The acts soon expired. The Supreme Court had no opportunity to rule on the constitutionality of either the acts or the Virginia and Kentucky resolutions' chief assertions. These were Madison's contention that where the federal government exceeded its powers the states "have the right and are in duty bound to *interpose* for arresting the progress of the evil," and Jefferson's proposition that *"nullification . . . of all unauthorized acts . . . is the rightful remedy"* (emphasis added).

Although also uninvolved in other major peaceably settled antebellum states' rights crises (New England's opposition to the 1812 War and South Carolina's opposition to high tariffs in the 1830s), the Supreme Court has played over the years an important role at the "subcrisis" level. Three broad questions have been adjudicated. First, how much do state sovereignty and states' rights considerations limit federal judicial power to hear and determine *cases and controversies? Second, how much do similar considerations limit congressional powers? Third, how much do national government powers limit the rights of states to act?

Limits on federal judicial power have largely involved four more specific issues. One gave the Court little difficulty before the Civil War. Each state supreme court was assumed the final arbiter as to state legislation's consonance with state constitution.

A second issue arose because English *common law had been "received" colony by colony. Was there also a *federal common law? If not, absent a congressional statute, an activity most would have thought punishable (e.g., murder in the District of Columbia) would not be. If *Article III's extending federal judicial power to "all Cases . . . arising under . . . the Laws of the United States" included the common law among the "Laws," many a common-law controversy involving a national question would be open to federal judicial inquiry. Arch-Federalists thought that fine. In 1812, *United States* v. *Hudson and Goodwin* took the opposite, Jeffersonian, position. In 1842, however, *Swift* v. *Tyson* created a 'Federalist exception' by holding that the common law of the state where a contract was made between two states' citizens would not necessarily govern. Rather, the Court would apply "general principles and doctrines of commercial jurisprudence." *New Deal justices overruled *Swift* in *Erie Railroad Co.* v. *Tompkins* (1938).

The most recurrently troublesome issue in states' rights and sovereignty litigation arose because, becoming states, the thirteen colonies inherited the British sovereign's immunity from suit. He, however, always granted to his subjects a petition of right to secure redress. Here was an irony of independence. Out with the bathwater of the monarch's American power went the baby of the petition of right. What then did Article III's list of cases and and controversies over which the federal judiciary had jurisdiction mean by the phrase "Controversies . . . between a State and Citizens of another State"?

Could, as in *Chisholm* v. *Georgia* (1793), a South Carolinian sue Georgia in federal court over a debt? Did Article III abrogate *sovereign immunity in a *"diversity jurisdiction" situation? So argued Attorney General Edmund Randolph, prominent at the Constitutional Convention and retained as Chisholm's private counsel. All but one justice read the article literally and agreed. The upshots were irate Georgia legislation ordering the hanging of any federal official entering Georgia to enforce *Chisholm*, and the *Eleventh Amendment, which stated: "The Judicial Power of the United States shall not be construed to extend to any suit . . . commenced or prosecuted against one of the United States by Citizens of another State, or . . . of any Foreign State."

Thus rebuffed, the justices could have been expected to treat the Eleventh Amendment gingerly. However, in 1821 Chief Justice John *Marshall (1801–1835) outraged states' rights supporters by accepting jurisdiction over an appeal from Virginia's conviction of a lottery ticket seller operating under a congressional licensing statute and hence claiming immunity from prosecution for violating Virginia's prohibition of such sales. Though reading the congressional statute as not authorizing sales contravening state law, *Cohens* v. *Virginia* held that the Eleventh Amendment barred federal jurisdiction only if the individual

began proceedings. In 1824 *Osborn* v. *Bank of the United States* pruned the amendment further. It declared a suit begun by an individual against Ohio's state auditor not a suit against the state itself.

The Marshall Court resolved the fourth judicial powers and "dual sovereignties" issue in *Martin* v. *Hunter's Lessee* (1816). Virginia's Court of Appeals, having interpreted post-Revolutionary treaties with Britain as *not* overriding wartime Virginia statutes confiscating Tory lands, denied that the U.S. Supreme Court had jurisdiction to reverse. Virginia Judge William Cabell's opinion embodied the era's "moderate" states' rights position. Unlike Jefferson's Kentucky Resolutions, Cabell claimed no unconditional state right to nullify federal laws or treaties. Instead, Cabell viewed dual sovereignty as turning control over the outcome on whether highest state court or U.S. Supreme Court first heard the case. "The constitution . . . regards the *residuary* sovereignty of the states, as not less inviolable, than the *delegated* sovereignty of the United States." If Virginia's judges heeded Supreme Court "instructions" overruling them, they would be acting as "State Judges" since they held no federal commissions. The U.S. Supreme Court would "bear . . . the relation of an appellate Court" to the Virginia Court. The word "appellate . . . includes the idea of *superiority.* But one Court cannot be . . . superior to another, unless both . . . belong to the same sovereignty. . . . The Courts of the United States . . . belonging to one sovereignty, cannot be appellate Courts in relation to the State Courts, which belong to a different sovereignty." The section 25 of the *Judiciary Act of 1789 unconstitutionally "attempt[ed] . . . to make the State Courts *Inferior Federal Courts.*" The argument favoring the section turned jurisdiction erroneously on the "case," not on the "tribunals" and "would give appellate jurisdiction, as well over the courts of . . . France. . . ."

Justice Joseph *Story—whose expansive nationalism prompted the states' rights jibe that he would claim federal admiralty jurisdiction over a corncob floating in a water pail—wrote for the Supreme Court because of Marshall's financial interest in the lands. Story employed four main arguments to rebut Cabell. The Constitution: (1) turned jurisdiction on the case, not the court; (2) was "crowded with provisions which restrain or annul the sovereignty of the states" (p. 343); (3) foresaw that "state jealousies . . . might . . . obstruct justice" (p. 347), and hence provided that respecting "powers granted to the United States," state judges "are not independent"; and (4) anticipated the "necessity of *uniformity* of decisions throughout the whole United States." If "judges of equal learning . . . in different states . . . differently interpret, . . . laws . . . treaties and . . . constitution . . . might . . . never have precisely the same construction . . . in any two states." The public mischief "would be truly deplorable; and it cannot be believed . . . the enlightened convention which formed the constitution" intended such mischief (p. 348). This argument is often thought Story's strongest. But it did not logically demolish Cabell's point that one could just as well suppose the framers had intended "foreseen controversies would sometimes arise . . ." but had deliberately "provided no umpire . . . no tribunal by which they shall be settled . . . from the belief, that such a tribunal would produce evils greater than those of the occasional collisions . . . it would be designed to remedy. . . ." The Supreme Court prevailed as a matter of political power.

Marshall's Court rejected Eleventh Amendment arguments in ten of eleven cases raising them. The Court under Chief Justice Roger *Taney (1836–1864) did so in five of five. Occasionally that Court struck down state legislation on the dual sovereignty grounds of interfering with a federal instrumentality, but never vice versa. For example, using Marshall precedents—*McCulloch v. Maryland (1819) and *Weston v. Charleston (1829)—*Dobbins v. Erie County (1842) voided a $3.58 nondiscriminatory county tax on a U.S. revenue cutter captain's post valued at $500.

In 1859 Taney ruled against Wisconsin judges who outdid the Martin judges. In *Ableman v. Booth Wisconsin high court judges, thinking the 1850 Fugitive Slave Act unconstitutional, issued *habeas corpus writs to free a Wisconsan held as federal prisoner during federal prosecution for aiding a *fugitive slave's escape. The literalism of Taney's separate spheres trope aided a nationalist result: "the sphere of . . . the United States is as far beyond the reach of the judicial process issued by a . . . state court, as if the line of division was traced by landmarks and monuments visible to the eye" (p. 516). Of Supreme Court power, he said; "[N]o power is more clearly conferred by the Constitution . . . than the power . . . to decide ultimately and finally, all cases arising under the Constitution and laws" (p. 525).

However, confronted in 1861 with an Ohio governor's refusal to extradite someone Kentucky sought for violating its fugitive slave statute, Taney dwelt on the Ohio governor's moral duty to fulfill his Constitutional obligations but concluded in *Kentucky v. Dennison: "there is no power delegated to the general government . . . to use . . . coercive means to compel him" (pp. 109–110).

Ableman remains law today. Dennison lasted 126 years. But in 1987, in Puerto Rico v. Branstad, Justice Thurgood *Marshall stated for the Court that Dennison's "conception of the relation between the States and the Federal Government is fundamentally incompatible with more than a century of constitutional development. . . . [T]he world of which it was a part has passed away. We conclude that it may stand no longer" (p. 230).

The Union's Civil War victory and Abraham

*Lincoln's appointing the nation's first Republican chief justice, Salmon *Chase (1864–1873), by no means ended dual sovereignty. *Texas v. White (1869) and the *Slaughterhouse Cases (1873) illustrate this well. Justice Samuel *Miller's 5-to-4 majority Slaughterhouse opinion read the Civil War Amendments narrowly and in deft, if not convincing, fashion. But Chase's Texas v. White opinion assumed what ought to have been proved, that correct was the abolitionist Republican theory about what happened to seceding states and their financial obligations. Its oft-quoted sonorous sentence—"The Constitution, in all its provisions, looks to an indestructible Union, composed of indestructible States" (p. 725)—explains little and strictly speaking is false. Most Constitutional provisions "look" neither to, nor away from, either indestructibility or destructibility.

Two Chase opinions of the same term indicated the constitutional balance was not greatly altered against nonseceding states. In United States v. DeWitt (1869) Chase's Court did what no antebellum Court had done—voided a congressional statute as intruding unconstitutionally into the "sphere" of state *police power. Today the intrusion—outlawing sale of dangerously inflammable lamplight oil igniting below 110 degrees—looks modest. Attorney General Ebenezer R. *Hoar's Commerce Clause defense—that the law was permissible to protect employees of companies transporting the product interstate—seems unexceptionable. But in those pre-electricity days the law had important everyday-life effects. DeWitt makes much-critiqued turn-of-the-century cases limiting Congress's *commerce powers (e.g., United States v. *E. C. Knight, 1895) appear less discontinuous with their doctrinal past. DeWitt's sticklishness about constitutional balance also renders more intelligible a set of "equal footing of newly admitted states" cases posing issues now remote, but hotly contested in the era of westward expansion. The set began with Pollard v. Hagan (1845; ruling that Alabama was entitled by 1819 admission to as favorable allocations as those of the original thirteen states respecting ownership of lands below navigable waters) and reached the Progressive era (e.g., *Coyle v. Smith, 1911; ruling that Congress could not condition Oklahoma's admission on locating the state capital where Congress wanted).

"Dual government" pervaded Lane County v. Oregon (1869). Chief Justice Chase made explicit that: "In this court the construction given by the state courts to the laws of a State, relating to local affairs, is . . . received as the true construction" (p. 74). However, *Murdock v. Memphis (1875) broke with the past in a states' rights direction. The Court twice heard argument whether an 1867 congressional act's omission of certain words in modifying the 1789 Judiciary Act expanded Supreme Court jurisdiction over appeals from state courts. The omitted 1789 words had limited the Court to scrutinizing "questions of validity or construction of . . . Constitution, treaties, statutes . . . in dispute . . . *on the face of the record"* (p. 617, emphasis added). Did the 1867 omission mean that, when a case came up on such ground, the Supreme Court was no longer restricted to questions on the record's face but could look for other errors as well, including state law interpretations? Yes, argued retired Justice Benjamin *Curtis (author of the chief *Dred* *Scott* dissent) from whom the perplexed Court sought *amicus* advice. Chase died between the argument and the decision. His successor, moderate Republican Morrison *Waite (1874–1888), did not participate. As in *Slaughterhouse*, Samuel Miller carried a slim majority in rejecting the jurisdiction-expanding opportunity—one which, almost certainly, Marshall and Story would have grasped.

Between the Civil War and the New Deal the Supreme Court developed states' rights along two other lines. First, beginning with *Collector* v. *Day* (1871) it developed the mirror-image of antebellum rulings that states could not tax federal "instrumentalities." *Day*, voiding federal taxation of state judges' salaries, was the *taximmunity converse of the *Dobbins* ruling regarding the federal cutter captain. By the 1930s this "reciprocal tax immunities" doctrine had blossomed wondrously. States could not levy sales taxes on gasoline used by federal vehicles (*Panhandle Oil* v. *Mississippi*, 1928). The federal government could not apply its sales tax to city police motorcycles (*Indian Motorcycle Co.* v. *U.S.*, 1931). In 1938, New Deal justices summarily uprooted the "reciprocal tax immunities" plant (*Helvering* v. *Gerhardt*).

Second, *sovereign immunity issues resurfaced because some "big spender" *Reconstruction governments profligately sold state bonds. Post-Reconstruction successors repudiated them. During the 1870s the Court continued the Marshallian enterprise of limiting the Eleventh Amendment but changed course in the 1880s. Despite holding that counties did not enjoy sovereign immunity (e.g., *Lincoln County* v. *Luning*, 1890), the Court rejected even the two strongest cases against states themselves. New Hampshire and New York tried to overcome southern Eleventh Amendment defenses against northern holders of defaulted Dixie bonds by authorizing the states' attorneys general to receive assignments of bonds from resident bondholders, sue defaulting states in the names of New Hampshire and New York, and return any proceeds to the bondholders.

Marshall and Story would surely have read *New Hampshire* v. *Louisiana* and *New York* v. *Louisiana* as State v. State suits authorized by Article III. The 1883 Court majority, however, held: (1) that by ratifying the Constitution, states surrendered independent nations' sovereign rights to sue another sovereign nation on behalf of their citizens; (2) that during the nine years between ratification of the Constitution (1789)

and the Eleventh Amendment (1798), citizens had possessed such right as individuals; and (3) that the Eleventh Amendment had nullified such right of citizen without restoring the earlier right of the state. To top this off, in 1890 *Hans* v. *Louisiana* decided that, even if the Eleventh Amendment didn't foreclose suit by a citizen against his own state, general principles of sovereign immunity did. So to conclude, the Court had to dismiss as dictum one of Marshall's *Cohens* arguments—the Eleventh Amendment *had not* in such a case displaced Article III's grant of federal judicial power "to all cases arising under the constitution . . . without respect to parties" *whereas* the Article III grant *had* displaced states' sovereign immunity from suit by their own citizens. Said the 1890 Court, although "highest demands of natural and political law" require a state "to hold inviolate . . . public obligations," federal interference with state failure to observe "this rule . . . would be attended with greater evils than such failure can cause" (p. 21).

In 1908, however, probusiness justices fashioned a Marshallian exception in *Ex parte* *Young*. To strengthen the Minnesota Railway Commission's rate-reducing powers, the state legislature enacted heavy day-by-day penalties for violations. Asserting that challenging rates in the usual manner (ignoring them and awaiting state prosecution) would be ruinous, railroads sought a federal *injunction barring Minnesota's attorney general from enforcing the rates. Agreeing, the Court created a legal fiction for vindicating federal constitutional rights. If the law was unconstitutional, the state was not acting. The state official was (mis)using the state's name to enforce a legal nullity. Sovereign immunity was irrelevant.

The fortunes of states' rights and state sovereignty reached bottom during the middle of the twentieth century, casualties of two factors. One was Roosevelt-era justices' conviction that modern society and economy required strong national government. A 1941 comment by Justice Harlan *Stone expressed the attitude well. Ruling the Fair Labor Standards Act constitutional in *United States* v. *Darby*, Stone observed that the Tenth Amendment "states but a truism that all is retained which has not been surrendered" (p. 124).

The other factor was that midcentury white supremacist use of states' rights arguments in resisting desegregation rendered the doctrine morally suspect. To force compliance, the justices limited it more than they otherwise likely would have. *Heart of Atlanta Motel* v. *United States* (1964), *Katzenbach* v. *McClung* (1964), and *South Carolina* v. *Katzenbach* (1966) illustrate the point. The *Civil Rights Act of 1964 forbade segregation in interstate commerce. Upholding its applicability to Heart of Atlanta Motel, which mainly served travelers using Interstate 85, was easy. However, McClung's barbecue restaurant in Birmingham, eleven blocks from a federal highway, almost exclusively served Birmingham residents. The Court held McClung's eatery covered on the tenuous ground that meat McClung served had once been cow in another state and his refusal to serve blacks lessened the numbers of interstate cow and burger trips. *McClung* nearly extinguished any state's power over local commerce independent of congressional will.

Two years later in *South Carolina* v. *Katzenbach,* all justices agreed Congress had *Fifteenth Amendment power to suspend state-prescribed voter literacy tests and authorize the attorney general to appoint voting examiners in low turnout states. The majority also upheld the requirement that before such states amended voting laws they persuade the U.S. attorney general or the federal district court for the District of Columbia that the changes involved no racially discriminatory purpose or effect. Dissenting, Justice Hugo *Black stated that the requirement so "distort[ed] . . . constitutional structure . . . as to render any distinction . . . between state and federal power almost meaningless" (p. 358).

To those doubting then that states rights had any future, post-1970 trends in two areas—state sovereign immunity and states' rights limits on congressional power—have come as an ongoing surprise. Three aspects of state sovereign immunity have been reconsidered. First, what demonstrates congressional intention to remove the immunity? In *Parden* v. *Terminal Railway* (1964) the Warren Court had held the Federal Employers Liability Act's general declaration that employees could bring federal court suits for work-related injury overrode any opposite Alabama provision with respect to employees of a state-owned railroad. However, in *Atascadero State Hospital* v. *Scanlon* (1985) the Burger court (1969–1986) held that bringing federally aided California programs within a Rehabilitation Act's opening of federal courts to handicapped persons experiencing discrimination required "unmistakable language in the statute itself" (p. 243).

Second, post-1970 decisions lessened individuals' abilities to secure federal injunctions against adverse *state action and federal court transfers of state litigation involving federal rights. The Burger Court was only two years old when *Younger* v. *Harris* (1971) blunted *Ex parte Young,* holding that, once state criminal proceedings are initiated, federal courts will not grant injunctive relief before demonstration of the infeasibility of fair state court determination of any federal issue at stake. By 1991 divided justices had curtailed both injunctive and declaratory federal relief regarding both ongoing criminal and civil state court proceedings. They even aborted relief when, though federal litigation began first, state proceedings commenced before the federal courts reached the merits of the federal rights claim. Occasionally liberal justices condemned conservative justices, as did Harry *Blackmun in

*Pennzoil* v. *Texaco* (1987), for "expand[ing] . . . Younger to an unprecedented extent . . . no matter how attenuated the State's interests . . . and what abuses . . . plaintiff might be sustaining" (pp. 27–28).

Third, conservative majorities' customary close linguistic attention to the text of the Eleventh Amendment when attention aided states' rights lapsed suddenly in *Welch* v. *State Dept. of Highways* (1987). In *Welch,* other justices pointed out that the amendment did not cover, and urged overruling, *Hans*'s 1890 conclusion about citizens' suits against their own states.

If the Burger and Rehnquist Courts' sovereign immunity jurisprudence seems murky, their jurisprudence concerning states' rights as a limit on Congress is clear: it is whatever any five justices agree makes for a nice day. In *National League of Cities* v. *Usery* (1976), a 6-to-3 majority voided a 1974 amendment to the Fair Labor Standards Act expanding federal maximum hours and minimum wage provisions to state and local government employees because, explained Justice William *Rehnquist, those provisions made more expensive those governments' basic and traditional functions—for example, police protection. *Hodel* v. *Virginia Surface Mining* (1981) decided that Congress could require states either to formulate strip-mining standards conforming to federal standards or to let strip-mining be governed by federal regulatory programs. It also fashioned a constitutional test. Did congressional legislation regulate states as states, indisputably impinge on an attribute of state sovereignty, and directly impact integral operations in areas of traditional governmental functions? If any part of the answer was negative, the legislation was sustained.

Applying the test produced conflict. Extending the Railway Labor Acts to disputes between a New York–owned railroad and a labor union was unanimously held constitutional (*United Transportation Union* v. *Long Island R.R.,* 1982). The 1978 Public Utility Regulatory Policies Act's requirement that states "consider" a group of Federal Energy Regulatory Commission guidelines produced five justices upholding the statute in whole, and four justices concurring in part and dissenting in part (*FERC* v. *Mississippi,* 1982). Applying the federal Age Discrimination in Employment Act to Wyoming government employees yielded five affirmatives and four out and out dissents (*Equal Employment Opportunity Commission* v. *Wyoming,* 1983). Then in 1985 came *Garcia* v. *San Antonio Transit Authority.* A 5-to-4 majority, asked whether employees of a city-owned bus line were excluded from *National League*'s veto of congressional authority, overruled *National League* itself. Rehnquist, about to become chief justice, was not happy at this reversal of his 1976 states' rights victory. He wrote a one-paragraph dissent. He did not think it necessary for the dissenters "to spell out further . . . a principle that will, I am confident, in time again command the support of a majority of this Court" (p. 580). Chief Justice Rehnquist may prove Associate Justice Rehnquist correct.

(See also FEDERALISM.)

□ Laurence H. Tribe, *American Constitutional Law,* 2d ed. (1988). Melvin I. Urofsky, *A March of Liberty: A Constitutional History of the United States* (1988).

A. E. Keir Nash

**State Taxation.** History has shown that, to govern effectively, a sovereign must possess the power to lay and collect taxes. The lack of a tax power was one of the main reasons for the failure of the Articles of Confederation. The Constitution established a national tax power in Congress and, in the *Tenth Amendment, reserved that same power to the states (see TAXING AND SPENDING CLAUSE).

Federal restraints on state taxation are limited. When a federal court is called on to review a state tax, it may not consider the wisdom of the tax, its overall fairness, or its potential for hardship. All these judgments must be left to the elected officials of the states. The federal courts must focus on one question only: Does the tax violate any provision of the Constitution?

The Constitution itself contains only two express limitations on the states' power to tax. The first concerns imports and exports. A state may not lay taxes on foreign trade that leaves or enters its ports, nor may it tax the use of its ports. A state is also forbidden from imposing a *poll tax that applies to any federal election. Neither of these provisions has generated a substantial amount of litigation. Instead, the contours of state tax power have been defined by the Constitution's *implied* limitations. The Constitution has numerous clauses that have some application to state taxation, including the commerce, equal protection, and privileges and immunities clauses.

Congress has the sole power "to regulate commerce . . . among the several states" (see COMMERCE POWER). One of the historic concerns that underlay the Commerce Clause was the need to promote a healthy and robust free trade. An unrestrained power to tax interstate commerce would have disastrous consequences, for states are naturally inclined to tax out-of-state businesses more heavily. In its commerce cases, the Court has shown sensitivity to this threat and has carefully circumscribed the states' tax power.

Modern commerce cases reveal a threefold focus. First, does the taxpayer have sufficient "nexus," or connection, with the state to justify imposition of a tax? Second, does the tax apply equally to in-state and interstate commerce? Finally, is the tax "fair" in the sense that it relates to the services the state renders to the taxpayer? These factors were summarized in *Complete Auto Transit, Inc.* v. *Brady* (1977) and have been applied

aggressively to strike down any state tax that imperils the free flow of commerce.

The *Fourteenth Amendment ensures *equal protection of the laws for all citizens. The amendment's Equal Protection Clause, intended to secure civil liberties for emancipated blacks, soon became the source of a broader jurisprudence of equality and evenhandedness in the law. Equal protection has been applied as a minimum restraint on the states' tax power.

It would be unwise, and perhaps even impossible, to insist on strict equality in taxation. Taxes frequently have built-in inequities. Graduated tax rates and tax exemptions are but two common examples. This is not to say that the Equal Protection Clause is entirely impotent. The clause has been the source of some fundamental principles: property must be assessed uniformly for tax purposes; like property must be taxed equally to the extent possible; and distinctions made between like properties must be fair and reasonable. Thus, in *Allegheny Pittsburgh Coal Co.* v. *Webster County* (1989) the Supreme Court ruled that systematic undervaluation of some property in the same tax class denied other taxpayers equal protection.

Two clauses in the Constitution ensure the *privileges and immunities of American citizenship. These clauses prohibit discrimination against nonresidents. A tax must therefore apply equally to in-state and out-of-state residents. In *Toomer* v. *Witsell* (1948), for instance, the Court invalidated a state requirement that nonresidents pay a much larger license fee to engage in commercial shrimping. These examples dramatically illustrate the diversity of federal restraints on the states' tax power.

(See also FEDERALISM; STATE REGULATION OF COMMERCE; TAX IMMUNITIES.)

James B. Stoneking

**Statutory Construction** refers to techniques and guidelines followed by courts when they give effect to a statutory command. The guidelines include such obvious rules as: when two statutes conflict, the later in time controls. But more difficult and subtle problems arise when legislators use vague or ambiguous language (e.g., *Sherman Antitrust Act of 1890: "contract, combination . . . or conspiracy, in restraint of trade"). In such instances, courts seek to discern legislative intent, which is often a frustrating task.

William M. Wiecek

**Stay,** the order to arrest or suspend a judicial proceeding or the execution of a judgment resulting from that proceeding. Stays may be authorized by statute, the decision of a court, or agreement of the parties.    William M. Wiecek

**St. Clair, James** (b. Akron, Ohio, 14 April 1920), lawyer. In *United States* v. *Nixon,* presidential attorney St. Clair unsuccessfully argued that *executive privilege allowed President Richard M. *Nixon to withhold tape recordings; he also defended the president in the *impeachment inquiry. Nixon's tight personal control of his defense strategy and tactics unquestionably hampered St. Clair.                    Stanley I. Kutler

**Steel Seizure Case.** See YOUNGSTOWN SHEET & TUBE CO. V. SAWYER.

**Stevens, John Paul** (b. Chicago, Ill. 20 Apr. 1920), associate justice, 1975–. President Gerald Ford's only nominee to the Supreme Court, Justice John Paul Stevens has established a reputation for independence and moderation. Not easily associated with any particular voting bloc, Justice Stevens was, thus, cast in a centrist, mediating role on an increasingly polarized Rehnquist Court. Born to a prominent Chicago family, Stevens served in the navy during World War II. At Northwestern University he had a distinguished academic career as a law student; he then clerked for Supreme Court Justice Wiley *Rutledge before entering private practice. In that practice he developed a specialization in *antitrust law, which he also taught as an adjunct professor at both Northwestern and the University of Chicago law schools.

Appointed to the United States Court of Appeals for the Seventh Circuit in 1970, Stevens came to the Supreme Court with five years' federal appellate experience and a reputation for craftsmanlike opinions. This commitment to craftsmanship, coupled with a penchant for brevity, has led Stevens to produce a number of extraordinarily frank, plain-spoken, even pithy opinions often issued as separate concurrences or dissents. Indeed, during his first term on the Court, Stevens appears to have set a record for solo dissents by a freshman member. This manifest self-confidence, together with his independence of spirit, has meant that Stevens has apparently moved more easily than some of his colleagues from the concerns with civil rights and liberties of the 1960s and 1970s to the consideration of other, more contemporary issues. Ironically, for Justice Stevens this has meant a return to the framers' concerns with the constitutional structure of American government.

Having joined the opinion in *Immigration and Naturalization Service v. Chadha (1983), striking down the *legislative veto, in *Bowsher v. Synar (1986) Justice Stevens authored a thoughtful separate concurrence in support of the proposition that the Gramm-Rudman Act violated the constitutional concept of *separation of powers. Similarly, in a separate concurrence in Karcher v. Daggett (1983), Justice Stevens pointed out the potential for unconstitutional vote dilution in legislative districting contrived for partisan advantage, even though such districting might strictly comply with the simple-minded arithmetic requirements of "one person, one vote." Three

*John Paul Stevens*

years later, in *Davis v. Bandemer (1986), the Court agreed, holding claims of political *gerrymandering to be *justiciable. Justice Stevens' concern for maintaining the integrity of the electoral process was also evidenced in Anderson v. Celebrezze (1983), in which he authored the majority opinion opening ballot access to independent presidential candidates (see POLITICAL PROCESS).

On civil liberties questions Justice Stevens has demonstrated a reappearing concern for the less fortunate, siding with the claims of welfare recipients and aliens. He has also tended to adopt a broad construction of the *Fourth Amendment, and he has been particularly receptive to allegations of discrimination on the basis of sex (see GENDER). His record on these issues, however, has been mixed, as his opinion in *Rostker v. Goldberg (1981), upholding the all-male draft, and Washington County v. Gunther (1981), denying consideration to the theory of "comparable worth," suggest.

A concern for governmental process has characterized Justice Stevens's service on the Court. It is too early, however, to assess confidently his overall contribution to the development of American jurisprudence.

□ John Paul Stevens, "Judicial Restraint," *San Diego Law Review* 22 (1985): 437–457.            Richard Y. Funston

**Steward Machine Co. v. Davis,** 301 U.S. 548 (1937), argued 8–9 Apr. 1937, decided 24 May 1937 by vote of 5 to 4; Cardozo for the Court, Butler, McReynolds, Sutherland, and Van Devanter in dissent. One of the centerpieces of the *New Deal was the Social Security Act of 1935.

Among other things, this law established mechanisms to provide for unemployment compensation and old age benefits.

In *Steward Machine Company* v. *Davis* the unemployment compensation feature of the law was upheld 5 to 4, and in the companion case of *Helvering* v. *Davis* the old age benefits provisions were sustained by a more comfortable 7-to-2 majority. Justice Benjamin *Cardozo wrote both opinions.

In *Steward,* the Court held that the payroll tax on employers that generated the revenue to fund Social Security's unemployment compensation was constitutionally permissable under Article I, section 8, which grants Congress the power "to lay and collect taxes . . . to . . . provide . . . for the General Welfare of the United States." In contrast to the majority opinion in *United States* v. *Butler* (1936)—decided prior to Justice Owen *Roberts's switch to the liberal side—Cardozo and the Court's majority in *Steward* refused to read the *Tenth Amendment as a restriction on Congress's taxing and spending power.

(See also TAXING AND SPENDING CLAUSE.)

John W. Johnson

**Stewart, Potter** (b. Cincinnati, Ohio, 23 Jan. 1915; d. Hanover, N.H., 7 Dec. 1985; interred Arlington National Cemetery), associate justice, 1958–1981. Stewart was born into an old, affluent family in Cincinnati, the son of James Garfield Stewart. His father served as mayor of Cincinnati and as a justice of the Ohio Supreme Court. Potter Stewart attended University School, Hotchkiss, and then Yale University, after which he spent a year at Cambridge on a fellowship. Then in 1938 he entered Yale Law School, a hotbed of legal

*Potter Stewart*

realism and criticism of formalistic approaches to law and public policy. Stewart received a law degree from Yale in 1941 and joined a firm on Wall Street, but following the attack on Pearl Harbor he joined the navy as an officer. He received three battle stars for his service aboard oil tankers in the Atlantic and Mediterranean. He married Mary Ann Bertles on 24 April 1943.

After the end of the war, Stewart returned to Wall Street, but he soon left to join a large firm in Cincinnati as a litigator. Law led to politics; Stewart was elected to the city council twice and as vice-mayor once. For Stewart, though, politics was an avocation. He devoted most of his effort to building a practice. When a seat on the sixth Circuit Court of Appeals opened in 1954, President Eisenhower appointed Stewart based on his eminence as a member of the bar.

On the Sixth Circuit, Stewart compiled a record as a clearheaded and technically competent appellate judge, one of the leaders of the federal bench. President Eisenhower had made a habit of appointing lower court judges to the Supreme Court, and, when Justice Harold H. *Burton retired in 1958, the administration turned to the Sixth Circuit. On 14 October 1958, President Eisenhower announced Stewart's nomination as an associate justice. Oddly, several southern senators opposed him as a "northern integrationist" because one of his few constitutional opinions had involved school desegregation. He was, however, easily confirmed.

Justice Stewart's record on the Court defies easy characterization as either liberal or conservative. He joined a divided Court, and on many significant issues he became the swing vote. Recently, a commentator referred to him as a conservative on a liberal court and a liberal on a conservative court. Stewart charted a moderate course. In the hundreds of cases on civil liberties decided during his tenure, Stewart voted to support the claimant fifty-two percent of the time, somewhat more than Justices *Blackmun and *Frankfurter and slightly less than Justices *Stevens and *Black.

A number of Stewart's phrases have become part of the lode of quotable quotes in American law. Admitting his inability to formulate a coherent test for *obscenity in *Jacobellis* v. *Ohio* (1964), Stewart claimed "I know it when I see it" (p. 197). He explained his vote to invalidate the death penalty in *Furman* v. *Georgia* (1972) as a response to its quirky implementation: "These death sentences are cruel and unusual in the same way that being struck by lightning is cruel and unusual" (p. 309) (see CAPITAL PUNISHMENT).

Stewart wrote several notable opinions. *Jones* v. *Mayer Co.* (1968), a civil rights case, is surely one of the most important, since his opinion for the Court revived long-dormant legislative protections for African-Americans against discrimination in housing. When the Court in *Ginzburg* v. *United States* (1966) upheld a publisher's conviction on obscenity, Stewart dissented: "The *First Amendment protects us all with an even hand. It applies to Ralph Ginzburg with no less completeness and force than to G. P. Putnam's Sons" (p. 501). In *Roe v. Wade (1973), he concurred in an expansion of the right of *privacy but called upon the Court to admit its revival of the much-reviled "substantive due process" (p. 167). He had voiced concern over the constitutionalization of a right to privacy in the first place, despite his distate for invasions of personal affairs; yet in *Griswold v. Connecticut (1965) he referred to one state's law against contraception as "uncommonly silly" but nevertheless constitutional (p. 527).

Unlike many of the justices, such as Black and *Douglas, Stewart left no readily identifiable mark on the Court's doctrines or policies. Instead, he bequeathed a distinctive approach to and style of resolving legal issues. He is, as a result, best remembered as a lawyer.

□ Jerald H. Israel, "Potter Stewart," in *The Justices of the United States Supreme Court, 1789–1969,* edited by Leon Friedman and Fred Israel, vol. 4 (1969), 2919–2947. John P. Mackenzie, "Potter Stewart is Dead at 70," *New York Times,* 8 Dec. 1985.                    Gregory A. Caldeira

**Stone, Harlan Fiske** (b. Chesterfield, N.H., 11 Oct. 1872; d. Washington, D.C., 22 Apr. 1946; interred Rock Creek Park, Washington, D.C.), associate justice, 1925–1941, chief justice, 1941–1946. Republican Harlan Fiske Stone was the single university professor ever to serve as chief justice and, like Democrat Edward Douglass

*Harlan Fiske Stone*

*White (chief justice, 1910–1921), one of only two chief justices appointed by a president from a different political party. Stone is one of three promoted directly from an associate justiceship (White again, and William *Rehnquist, chief justice, 1986–). The only other chief justice with any prior Supreme Court service was his predecessor, Charles Evans *Hughes (associate justice, 1910–1916, and chief justice, 1930–1941), with whom he worked closely for eleven years.

Stone, like White, was promoted in part because of support from fellow justices, including Hughes. Of the five Republican justices during Franklin D. *Roosevelt's early presidency, Stone most frequently voted to uphold *New Deal legislation against constitutional challenge—more frequently indeed than two of the Court's four Democrats (Justices Pierce *Butler and James *McReynolds). Like Hughes, Stone first experienced being the runner-up choice. Hughes quite happily remained secretary of state after President Harding appointed William Howard *Taft to the chief justiceship. Stone, having served five years under Taft, continued under Hughes. Stone became on his 1941 promotion by Roosevelt the only chief justice potentially to profit from experiencing the leadership styles of two predecessors.

Stone's leadership little resembled either predecessor's. Where Taft used the illusion of amiable bumbling and much politicking to secure prevalence of his constitutional views and Hughes was said to play his colleagues adroitly like stops on a cathedral organ, Stone favored reasoning cases out at length (see CHIEF JUSTICE, OFFICE OF THE). The unintended accompaniment was an upsurge of strident dissents and public backbiting among the associate justices. Scholarly appraisals have debated the relative causal importance to two factors: an unusual number of very bright but very prickly personalities among the associate justices; and Stone's reluctance to alleviate conflict. However, some rise in antagonism among the justices was probably inevitable as the Court during the early 1940s moved away from issues of *federalism and economic regulation and toward civil liberties and civil rights. Later chief justices have experienced at least as much intra-Court disagreement.

Born in rural New Hampshire in 1872, Stone was the son of Frederick Lawson Stone, a farmer, and Ann Sophia Butler. Later Stone identified New England's hard-to-work granite soil as a prime source of the Yankee virtues of diligence, civic responsibility, and independence, which he both prized and exemplified. However, it was the burly teenaged Stone's specific dislike of work on the family's farm in Amherst, Massachusetts, that led him to attend college. Expelled from Massachusetts Agricultural College for accidentally assaulting the college chaplain during a freshman-sophomore chapel melee, Stone went through Amherst College playing varsity football, editing the college newspaper, being thrice elected class president, and graduating in 1894. He financed his Columbia Law School education by teaching high school and received his law degree in 1898. A few months later, he accepted a Columbia law faculty position. In 1899 he married Agnes Harvey, whom he had known from childhood summer visits to his New Hampshire birthplace. Very close through almost forty-seven years of marriage, they had two sons, one a prominent New York lawyer and the other a Harvard mathematics professor elected to the National Academy of Sciences. Enthusiastically encouraged by Stone, Agnes Harvey Stone reached sufficient excellence as a painter for the Corcoran Gallery twice to exhibit her landscapes.

Stone's legal career developed along two paths—the primary one in academia, which climaxed with his deanship of Columbia Law School (1910–1923), and a secondary one in corporate practice that peaked with his appointment as head of the Sullivan and Cromwell litigation department in 1923. His writings—especially "reformist" law review articles on rights of trust beneficiaries, bankers' duties, and specific performance of contracts—widely influenced judges. His activities in building a research-oriented faculty and defending free speech rights of professors and socialists became known throughout the legal community. In 1924 President Calvin Coolidge named Stone attorney general to clear the Justice Department of scandals inherited from the Harding administration.

Although some western senators feared that Stone's Wall Street links would make him excessively probusiness, corruption-investigating activism dominated his short term as attorney general. Nonetheless, there was Senate opposition when Coolidge in January 1925 nominated Stone to the Supreme Court. Always the straightforward rationalist, Stone proposed what was then a novelty, that he answer questions in person before the *Senate Judiciary Committee—thus inventing the current practice. So disarmingly intelligent was his testimony that the final Senate vote for confirmation was 71 to 6.

Between 1925 and 1936 Stone's most significant role was dissenting (often with Louis *Brandeis, and Oliver W. *Holmes or Benjamin *Cardozo) against Taft and his strongest allies, Democrats Butler and McReynolds and Republicans George *Sutherland and Willis *Van Devanter. Continuing past Taft's retirement, they became known as "the four horsemen" (of the Apocalypse) opposing New Deal economic legislation. Even before the New Deal, Stone thought they were advancing outlandish positions that made the laissez faire of their turn-of-the-century predecessors seem moderate. For example, Di Santo v. Pennsylvania (1927) involved a Pennsylvania fraud statute based on a 1910 New York statute signed by Charles Evans Hughes, then New York governor. To protect semiliterate immi-

grant men from swindlers selling fake cheap tickets for transporting families left behind, both states required licenses and bonds of steamship ticket sellers. Hughes had seen no constitutional barrier. Yet Taft and the "horsemen" found an unconstitutional "direct burden" on Congress's Commerce Clause power, despite congressional silence on the matter (see COMMERCE POWER). As Brandeis pointed out, Pennsylvania's statute affected the flow of commerce far less than many state regulations that earlier Courts had sustained—for example, compelling a railroad to eliminate grade crossings even if the expense threatened its solvency. In Stone's view, the majority was applying a test "too mechanical, too . . . remote from actualities, to be of value" (p. 44).

Three years into the New Deal, the "four horsemen," often joined by Owen *Roberts (1930–1945), and occasionally by Hughes, having told the states they could not regulate much because of Congress's commerce power, were telling Congress it could not regulate much either because of the states' police power. Thus in Railroad Retirement Board v. Alton R.R. Co. (1935) a 5-to-4 majority barred Congress from requiring interstate railroads to provide pensions for railway workers. Though not convinced New Deal legislation was wise, Stone ridiculed the 6-to-3 majority reasoning of Owen Roberts's opinion in U.S. v. *Butler (1936) as having absurd consequences. "The government may give seeds to farmers, but may not condition the gift upon their being planted . . . may give money to the unemployed, but may not ask . . . those who get it . . . to support their families . . ." (p. 85).

In *Morehead v. New York ex rel. Tipaldo (1936) the "four horsemen" and Owen Roberts not merely rejected Hughes's centrist Republican constitutionalism. They underlined that they were to the right even of Taft by reiterating the doctrine of a 1923 women's minimum wage case, *Adkins v. Children's Hospital; in Adkins the D.C. regulation forbade employers paying women below what the cost of living required for health. Though Taft had seen nothing wrong with that, the "four horsemen" and one other justice had asserted that the *Fourteenth Amendment's Due Process Clause required striking it down. The employer could be prosecuted even if the "health standard" required him to pay more than the value of the services rendered. The New York statute sought to cure that defect by forbidding only wages both below the health standard and below the value of the services rendered. Hughes vainly argued for upholding the New York law by distinguishing Adkins; Stone vainly urged overruling Adkins.

Stone's dissents proceeded from three basic principles he thought should control constitutional interpretation respecting government regulation of the economy. First, the Constitution gives the appropriate level of government the power to govern. Second, as he observed in *Morehead*, the power to govern changes to meet changing conditions: "problems of poverty, subsistence, health . . . a generation ago . . . were for the individual to solve; today they are the burden of the nation" (p. 635). Third, "It is not for the courts to resolve doubts whether the remedy . . . is . . . efficacious . . . or is better even than the blind operation of uncontrolled economic forces" (p. 635). Less than a year later, in the aftermath of Roosevelt's *court-packing threat, changed voting behavior (chiefly by Roberts), and retirements, Stone's dissenting constitutional views were fast becoming the law of the land.

Most scholarly appraisals of Stone, written in the mid-twentieth century, lauded his jurisprudence in other areas—particularly executive power and civil liberties. To a later generation, witness to the growth both of an imperial presidency and of civil rights, two qualifications may be in order. First, Stone's occasional qualms about the Court's expansions of presidential power were of little consequence. He later regretted having said nothing when Sutherland, in *U.S.* v. *Curtiss-Wright* (1936), allowed the president almost unconfined foreign policy powers. In 1942 Stone carried only the other remaining pre-Roosevelt justice (Roberts) with him when dissenting from *U.S.* v. *Pink*, which permitted the president to override state law and circumvent the Senate treaty-making power in order to make executive agreements with other countries (see TREATIES AND TREATY POWER).

Second, when executive powers collided with civil liberties during *World War II, Stone was sometimes but not always a stout defender of the latter. Least satisfactory today seems his upholding punishment of Americans of Japanese ancestry for disobeying curfew laws (*Hirabayashi* v. *U.S.*, 1943) and sending them to concentration camps (*Korematsu* v. *U.S.*, 1944) without prior inquiry as to their individual loyalty. Irony, at least, attaches to one of his justifications: "[S]ocial, economic and political conditions since the close of the last century . . . have intensified their solidarity and in large measure prevented their assimilation as an integral part of the white population" (*Hirabayashi*, p. 96).

However, much of the Court's history since Stone's death in 1946, which ended the briefest chief justiceship since 1801, is the history of working out affirmatively the implications of one of the Court's most quoted passages. That is *footnote four of Stone's opinion in *U.S.* v. *Carolene Products* (1938).

Stone was important in beginning the history of drawing out the implications of civil rights. More than any other justice he was responsible for maneuvering the Court over nine years from holding the so-called *white primary constitutional (*Grovey* v. *Townsend*, 1935), through declaring that having one's vote in a primary counted

fairly was a federally enforceable right (*U.S.* v. *Classic*, 1941), to ruling the white primary unconstitutional, (*Smith* v. *Allwright*, 1944). Stone's views prevailed in the *First Amendment free exercise of *religion issue concerning whether Jehovah's Witness schoolchildren could constitutionally be forced to salute the flag. In 1940 he lost 8 to 1 to Frankfurter who thought in *Minersville* v. *Gobitis* they could; in 1943, Stone won 6 to 3, assigning (as he frequently did when his earlier minority position came to prevail) another justice (Robert Jackson) to write the court's opinion in *West Virginia* v. *Barnette*.

Few who came to maturity steeped in the mores of nineteenth century America did as much as Stone to adapt Court and Constitution to the problems of the twentieth century. Among the most important sources of his achievements was a deep-running psychological trait of anticipatory prudence. It was most evident doctrinally in adjudicating New Deal legislative efforts to cope with the aftermath of the great October 1929 stock market crash. But it operated on a practical level too. In spring 1929 Stone decided that the market was getting dangerously high. He converted his considerable stock holdings into cash. While the "four Horsemen" bucked, Stone rode through Depression and New Deal financially secure as well as jurisprudentially victorious.

□ Alpheus Thomas Mason, *Harlan Fiske Stone: Pillar of the Law* (1956). Charles Herman Pritchett, *The Roosevelt Court: A Study in Judicial Politics and Values, 1937–1947* (1948). Merlo J. Pusey, *Charles Evans Hughes*, 2 vols. (1963). Herbert Wechsler, "Mr. Justice Stone and the Constitution," *Columbia Law Review* 46 (1946): 764.

A. E. Keir Nash

**Stone v. Mississippi,** 101 U.S. 814 (1880), argued 4–5 Mar. 1880, decided 10 May 1880 by vote of 8 to 0; Waite for the Court; Hunt not participating. Chief Justice John *Marshall and the early Supreme Court brought both public and private contracts within the scope of the Contract Clause. The dilemma posed by the undifferentiated inclusion of all contracts, public or private, within the clause came before the Court in *Stone*. In 1867, the provisional, post–Civil War government of Mississippi had granted to a corporation, with which John B. Stone was associated, a twenty-five year charter to conduct a lottery. The following year, the state adopted a new Constitution that prospectively and retrospectively prohibited all lottery activity. Stone ignored the new state constitutional provision and the state attorney general obtained an order precluding the lottery, which the Mississippi Supreme Court upheld.

Affirming the judgment, the U.S. Supreme Court stated that it was "too late" to contend that public contracts were not within the prohibition of contractual impairments (p. 816). Instead, the Court held that the state legislature could not bargain away by contract the inalienable *police power. Admitting difficulty defining the extent of this reservation the Court concluded that the police power included the prohibition of a lottery that presented a grave injury to public morals. The Court further ruled that persons who ran lotteries pursuant to a state charter, had merely a license or privilege, not a contract. Thus, the effect of *Stone* was a narrowing, but not an abandonment, of the application of the clause to public contracts.

Douglas Kmiec

**Stone v. Powell,** 428 U.S. 465 (1976), argued 24 Feb. 1976, decided 6 July 1976 by vote of 6 to 3; Powell for the Court, Burger concurring, Brennan, joined by Marshall, and White in dissent. By an act of Congress (Title 28, sec. 2254 of the U.S. Code), state prisoners may petition a federal court for a writ of *habeas corpus and challenge the constitutionality of their state convictions. Generally, a party may not relitigate a matter already presented to or decided by a court. In *Brown* v. *Allen* (1953), however, the Court had held that under section 2254 a state prisoner was entitled to a federal court hearing on all federal constitutional issues.

Writing for the majority in *Stone* v. *Powell,* Justice Lewis *Powell reevaluated this interpretation of the statute and held that *Fourth Amendment claims once raised and decided in state court could not be heard again in the federal habeas corpus proceeding when the state had provided an opportunity for a full and fair hearing. Applying a cost/benefit analysis, Powell argued that the marginal additional deterrence against police misconduct was insufficient to justify excluding evidence and allowing a guilty defendant to go free. This would only undermine respect for the criminal justice system. Concerns for finality and *federalism buttressed his conclusion.

The dissenters disagreed. Habeas corpus, they maintained, protects rights of all persons, including the guilty. Lifetime-tenured federal judges are better situated than state judges to vindicate constitutional rights. Finally, *separation of powers considerations weighed against reinterpreting the long-standing statutory language.

Proving wrong commentators who predicted a "*Stone*-age" for the writ of habeas corpus, the Court has squarely refused to add other grounds to the *Stone* exception for Fourth Amendment claims.

Thomas E. Baker

**Stop and Frisk Rule.** The phrase "stop and frisk" refers to the authority of a police officer to stop and search a person for concealed weapons without a warrant. The search may take place with less than the *probable cause otherwise required by the *Fourth Amendment.

In 1942 the Uniform Arrest Act allowed an officer to search a person stopped or detained for questioning if the officer had "reasonable ground" to suspect a concealed weapon. Only

three states adopted the Uniform Arrest Act, but in 1964 New York adopted what became known as a "stop and frisk" law. Several studies of police behavior indicated that when officers suspected a person they were talking to had a concealed weapon, they frisked that person ("frisking" being defined as running hands on the outside of the suspect's clothing to feel for a weapon, and not intruding inside the garment unless the officer felt something suspicious).

The Supreme Court gave its imprimatur in *Terry* v. *Ohio* (1968). Chief Justice Earl *Warren described the practice as one a reasonably prudent police officer should take for both personal and public safety if the circumstances warranted it. In subsequent cases during Chief Justice Warren *Burger's tenure, the Court expanded the *Terry* holding to allow warrantless searches for weapons, narcotics, and illegal aliens on "reasonable" suspicion of their concealment.

(See also SEARCH WARRANT RULE, EXCEPTIONS TO.)

Melvin I. Urofsky

**Story, Joseph** (b. Marblehead, Mass., 18 Sep. 1779; d. Cambridge, Mass., 10 Sep. 1845; interred Mt. Auburn Cemetery, Cambridge), associate justice, 1811–1845. No justice embodied the symbiotic relationship between national and regional jurisprudence more fully than Joseph Story. To the New England circuit he brought national law; to the full Court in Washington he brought an expertise in the commercial law of New England. Like Justice Felix *Frankfurter, he used his legal learning to leverage the Court, sometimes to the distress of his colleagues. Chief Justice John *Marshall welcomed the young scholar, and their working relationship was one of the most productive in the history of the Court. While performing a disproportionately large share of the Court's duties, Story also served as Dane Professor at Harvard Law School, where he pioneered the development of national, university-based legal education. From his teaching came a dozen volumes of legal commentary on public and private law. Through his multiple roles as judge, teacher, and publicist, Story was the most commanding legal figure of his age.

New England culture defined the basic themes of Story's jurisprudence: republicanism, nationalism, and Lockean liberalism. He grew up in the fishing village of Marblehead, Massachusetts. His family was deeply religious and, though Story would later shift from Congregationalism to Unitarianism, he retained a deep faith in God and the social utility of Christian ethics. From his mother he got a restless energy and a gift of gab. From his father, a physician who served in George Washington's army, Story inherited an abiding love of country and the idea that public service was a noble virtue. This message was confirmed at Harvard University, where Story graduated with second honors in 1798, already determined to achieve personal success and republican fame through the practice of law.

After graduation Story was admitted to the Essex County bar in 1801 and settled in Salem. After the death of his first wife, he married Sarah Wetmore, who, in a long and happy marriage, bore seven children, two of whom survived to adulthood. He rose rapidly in the growing Jeffersonian Democratic-Republican party. He served with distinction in the Massachusetts House from 1805 to 1811 and represented Essex South in Congress in 1808–1809, long enough to incur President Thomas *Jefferson's wrath for his vote to repeal the embargo. Increasingly suspect as a defector from party ranks, Story turned to lawyering in his quest for distinction. He argued mainly in the state courts in Essex County, in the federal courts in Boston, and once before the Surpreme Court as counsel for the land speculators in *Fletcher v. Peck (1810). His service to the Republican party and his position as New England's rising legal star made him the logical candidate to fill the vacancy left by Justice William *Cushing's death in 1810. Only after being turned down by his first three choices, however, did President James *Madison offer Story the position, and then over the objections of Jefferson, who thought him—correctly as it turned out—to be a "pseudo-republican."

In Story's scheme of republican government, judges, armed with objective legal science, protect the Constitution from the corrosive forces of self-interest operating through political parties in state legislatures. His opinions were carefully crafted state papers full of scholarly references intended to clarify constitutional ambiguity and put public law beyond political manipulation. He was most inclined to ground constitutional opinions in *common-law principles, but he also drew on *natural law, *civil law, comparative law, history, and sometimes on the practice of New England businessmen.

True to his theory of judging, Story was the Court's most aggressive champion of federal jurisdiction. Indeed, one of his first acts as a new justice was to pressure his colleagues to reconsider their repudiation of a federal criminal common law jurisdiction (see FEDERAL COMMON LAW). When his reasoning, set forth on circuit in *United States v. Coolidge* (1813), was rejected by the Court in 1816, he urged Congress to legislate a criminal code and in fact drafted the one enacted in 1825 with the help of Daniel *Webster. It was the beginning of an alliance between the two men, in which Story drafted legislation, wrote speeches for Webster, gave him political advice and occasionally (as in the *Dartmouth College case) offered hints about legal strategy.

Story was most successful in expanding federal jurisdiction in the areas of maritime and commercial law. On circuit in *De Lovio v. Boit* (1816), for example, he took off on a technical question of marine insurance and boldly reinter-

*Joseph Story*

preted several centuries of English legal history in order to reach an expansive definition of federal *admiralty and maritime jurisdiction in *Article III. *Swift v. Tyson* (1842) was another telling blow for federal jurisdiction and uniform commercial law. In a unanimous decision, Story held that the Supreme Court, in section 34 diversity cases, was not bound by state court commercial law holdings, but could consult general principles of commercial law. The decision paved the way for a revolutionary expansion of federal jurisdiction until it was reversed in *Erie Railroad v. Tompkins* (1938).

Story's most important and most controverted jurisdictional opinion was *Martin v. Hunter's Lessee* (1816). At issue was the constitutionality of section 25 of the *Judiciary Act of 1789, which allowed the Court to review state judicial decisions interpreting the Constitution and federal laws. Not only was section 25 constitutional, ruled Story, but it was mandated by the Constitution. While his bold opinion sparked an anti-Court movement in Virginia, it also supplied a definitive answer to future challenges to the Court's appellate jurisdiction.

Story took an expansive view of executive authority in *United States v. Sears* (1812) and in his dissent in *Brown v. United States* (1814). He also went beyond most of his colleagues in expanding the powers of Congress. In upholding the authority of Congress over enlistment in the navy, on circuit in *United States v. Bainbridge* (1816), for example, Story had recourse to implied powers reasoning that anticipated Marshall in *McCulloch v. Maryland* (1819), an opinion that he heartily endorsed. He also supported the chief justice in *Gibbons* v. *Ogden* (1824) and there is inferential evidence (in his dissent in *New York* v. *Miln*, 1837, and his majority opinion in *Prigg* v. *Pennsylvania*, 1842) that he argued in conference for an exclusivist interpretation of congressional commerce power, that is, that the mere grant of power to Congress by the Constitution eliminated concurrent state authority. On this point he never captured a majority.

Story's legal nationalism was economic as well as political. As his speech at the Massachusetts Constitutional Convention of 1820–1821 clearly shows, private property was basic to his theory of republican government. Unleashing its creative energies would, in his Federalist-Whig view, also strengthen the bonds of constitutional union. As a champion of New England capitalism, he strongly favored the creation of an arena of enterprise secure from state interference. Thus in *Terrett* v. *Taylor* (1815) and *Town of Pawlet* v. *Clark* (1815), he fused natural-law principles with the *Contracts Clause to void state acts confiscating land. He was eager to restrict state control over the rising business corporation. Marshall led the way in the *Dartmouth College* case (1819) by bringing the charters of private corporations (see PRIVATE CORPORATION CHARTERS) under the protection of the Contract Clause. But it was Story's concurrence that defined private corporations by reference to their capitalization, not their function, thus assuring that business corporations as well as educational ones would be the beneficiaries of constitutional protection. Story was a pioneer in establishing the fiduciary responsibilities of corporations. He also put his circuit court on the side of the common seamen in interpreting maritime contracts.

The economic dimension of Story's jurisprudence was apparent in his work on the New England circuit, where he worked closely with the business community, and in his teaching and scholarship. His objective in all three areas was to counter localist tendencies by creating a body of "scientific" legal principles governing commercial activities that would be rational and uniform. He rejected comprehensive codification as a means of doing this because he distrusted state legislatures and turned instead to writing legal treatises on commercial law that would clarify principle and practice. These became standard fare for the students at Harvard Law School, whom Story counted on to carry correct law to all parts of the country.

Story wanted to put reformed law at the service of dynamic entrepreneurs; as a conservative he also wanted to preserve absolute rights of property as guaranteed by republican principles and what he called the "old law." The difficulty in balancing the two is apparent in the riparian rights case of *Tyler* v. *Wilkinson* (1827). The issue was whether upstream mill dams illegally interfered with the right to the natural flow claimed by the downstream owners. To rule for the latter according to established common-law principles would retard economic progress; to rule for the former would undercut *property rights. In an opinion that illustrated the creative leeway of the common law as well as the transitional nature of his jurisprudence, Story created the doctrine of "reasonable use"—reserving for the judges the right to determine what that meant.

Story's plans for a national system of law created by judicial statesmen like himself came on hard times in the Age of Jackson as the forces of democracy and states' rights gained ground on and off the Court. It was to exorcise these twin evils that he wrote his *Commentaries on the Constitution* (3 vols., 1833). His strategy on the Court was to hold the line for nationalism and doctrinal purity. This he did in the first term of the Taney Court, in three passionate dissents. In *New York* v. *Miln* he relied on his theory of exclusivism to repudiate the doctrine of *police power used by the new majority to uphold New York's regulation of immigrants. In *Briscoe* v. *Commonwealth Bank of Kentucky* (1837), he summoned the spirit of Marshall to berate the Court for upholding the constitutionality of legal tender notes issued by a state-owned bank, which were tantamount to paper money prohibited by Article I, section 10. In *Charles River Bridge Co.* v. *Warren Bridge Co.* (1837) he mobilized all his learning to protect corporate property from state confiscation. The question was whether the imprecise wording of the 1785 charter of the Charles River Bridge Company implicitly conferred a monopoly to collect tolls that the charter of a new free bridge destroyed, in violation of the Contract Clause as interpreted in *Dartmouth College*. Chief Justice Roger B. *Taney said no, arguing that implied monopolies would unduly curb the right of states to legislate in the public interest, and at the same time, curtail progress in transportation by entrenching static capital. For Story economic progress could come only if states were held to a strict performance of charter promises. His dissent was a brilliant defense of "the old law," the morality of contract, and republican values as he saw them.

Story remained a force on the Taney Court, but he was distressed by its fragmentation and its increasingly ad hoc concessions to states' rights. (See STATE SOVEREIGNTY AND STATES' RIGHTS.) Especially traumatic was the appearance of cases involving the constitutional status of slavery. He was opposed to the institution on moral as well as policy grounds; he was also firmly convinced that the Constitution sanctioned it. His solution was to strike a blow for freedom where the law gave him leeway and uphold the constitutional compromise on slavery when he had no choice. Thus on circuit in *Le Jeune Eugenie* (1822) he read broad principles of natural justice into international law to outlaw the international slave trade—a construction that was repudiated by Marshall in *The *Antelope* (1825). In *The Amistad* (1841), he freed the Africans who had been sold into slavery by a narrow reading of the treaty with Spain. His effort to accommodate morality to objective law failed tragically in *Prigg* v. *Pennsylvania* (1841). There his concept of judicial duty obliged him to rule that state personal liberty laws violated federal statutory and constitutional law providing for the return of fugitives (see FUGITIVE SLAVES). He tried to salvage something for freedom by ruling that states were not required to participate in the rendition process, but in fact his opinion gave slavery a national constitutional standing that it had not previously had.

Attacks by abolitionist constitutional theorists on the decision and against him personally confirmed his decision to resign from the Court and devote his energies to teaching and scholarship. He died in 1845, before he was able to do so, believing that his labors had been largely in vain.

(See also JUDICIAL POWER AND JURISDICTION; SLAVERY.)

☐ Gerald T. Dunne, *Justice Joseph Story and the Rise of the Supreme Court* (1970). James McCellan, *Joseph Story and the American Constitution: A Study in Political and Legal Thought* (1971). R. Kent Newmyer, *Supreme Court Justice Joseph Story: Statesman of the Old Republic* (1985). W. W. Story, ed., *The Miscellaneous Writings of Joseph Story* (1852).                                      R. Kent Newmyer

**Strauder v. West Virginia,** 100 U.S. 303 (1880), argued 21 Oct. 1879, decided 1 Mar. 1880 by vote of 7 to 2; Strong for the Court, Clifford and Field in dissent. *Strauder* was one of four cases decided in 1880 involving exclusion of African-Americans from jury service that provided guidelines enabling the southern states to evade the *Fourteenth Amendment's equal-protection mandate in jury selection. *Strauder* was the easiest of the four to resolve, because it involved a state statute that expressly limited jury service to "all white male persons." The Court had no difficulty in finding that this violated the equal protection clause. In *Ex parte Virginia* and *Neal* v. *Delaware,* the Court held that deliberate exclusion in practice, even if not mandated by express constitutional or statutory provision, also violated the Fourteenth Amendment, thus anticipating its scrutiny of nonfacial discrimination in *Yick Wo* v. *Hopkins* six years later. However, the Court negated any advantages these cases might have held out to African-Americans by holding in *Virginia* v. *Rives* (1880) that their mere absence from juries, no matter how complete, systematic, or obvious, was not in itself a violation of the Fourteenth Amendment. Southern officials took advantage of this concession to create exclusionary systems that did not run afoul of *Strauder's* ban on facial discrimination. In modern times, the Court has held the right of access to jury service a function of the *Sixth Amendment's guarantee of civil juries (*Taylor* v. *Louisiana,*

1975), but the *Strauder* rule remains good law. (See also EQUAL PROTECTION; TRIAL BY JURY.)
                                      William M. Wiecek

**Strawbridge v. Curtiss,** 3 Cranch (7 U.S.) 267 (1806), argued 12 Feb. 1806, decided 13 Feb. 1806 by vote of 6 to 0; Marshall for the Court. *Article III of the Constitution provides that federal judicial authority extends to controversies "between Citizens of different States." The *Strawbridge* case raised for the first time the knotty problem of *diversity jurisdiction involving multiple parties and produced what is known today as the rule of "complete diversity." Construing section 11 of the *Judiciary Act of 1789 (the original grant of diversity jurisdiction) rather than the Constitution itself, Chief Justice John *Marshall held that, where multiple parties assert different "interests," each party must have an adequate jurisdictional basis for being in federal court. The practical effect of this holding was to require that all parties on one side must be diverse from all parties on the other. This requirement remains law today, but only as a matter of statutory construction, not as a mandate of the Constitution itself. (See also JUDICIAL POWER AND JURISDICTION.)                        William M. Wiecek

**Stream of Commerce.** Variously known as "current of commerce" or "flow theory," the "stream of commerce" concept had its origin in the case of *Swift & Co.* v. *United States* (1905). A conservative Supreme Court had erected a strong constitutional barrier to federal regulation of the economy in *United States* v. *E. C. Knight Co.* (1895), when it blocked the government's attempt to break up a sugar monopoly allegedly in violation of the *Sherman Antitrust Act of 1890. The Court maintained a distinction between manufacturing and commerce, adopting a restrictive view of congressional power under the Commerce Clause.

Ten years later, however, the Court in the *Swift* case fashioned the "stream of commerce" doctrine, a judicial formula that would in time obliterate the distinction between manufacturing and commerce across state lines. In upholding an *injunction against a group of meatpacking houses that had allegedly combined to control prices in the stockyards, the Court, while admitting that sales were local, emphasized the recurring movement of live animals into and the shipment of meat out of the area. Writing for the Court, Justice Oliver Wendell *Holmes characterized the transaction as a "current of commerce among the States" (p. 399). Thus, the local monopolistic activities restrained the "current" or "flow" of interstate commerce and were subject to congressional regulation. In *Stafford* v. *Wallace* (1922), Chief Justice William Howard *Taft reinforced the principle in his opinion upholding the Packers and Stockyards Act of 1921. Eventually the doctrine became the basis for upholding the economic legislation of the late *New Deal years.

(See also COMMERCE POWER.)

Robert J. Steamer

**Strict Scrutiny** is the standard under the *Equal Protection Clause that federal courts use to assess the constitutionality of governmental classifications based on race as well as those that impinge on *fundamental constitutional rights. Until the mid-1970s, strict scrutiny also applied to classifications based on *alienage (see *Graham v. Richardson, 1971).

To pass muster, a challenged governmental action must be "closely" related to a "compelling" governmental interest. As such, strict scrutiny is the most rigorous of the three levels of scrutiny that courts have formulated. Ordinary (minimum) scrutiny applies to most bases on which government classifies people and their activities—for example, economic and social considerations such as wealth (or the lack of it). This test merely requires government to show that the classificatory scheme "reasonably" relates to a "legitimate" governmental interest. An intermediate level, called "heightened scrutiny," applies to classifications based on *gender and illegitimacy. Here, the governmental action must be "substantially" related to an "important" governmental interest (see INTERMEDIATE SCRUTINY).

In contrast to ordinary scrutiny, where courts presume that the legislation or challenged governmental activity is constitutional and the plaintiff has the burden of showing a constitutional violation, strict scrutiny assumes that it is unconstitutional and the government has the burden of demonstrating its compelling interest. Courts must focus on government's purpose rather than merely on the effect of governmental action to determine the validity of a challenged law or regulation. The Court held in *Washington v. Davis (1976) that, to be unconstitutional under the *Fourteenth Amendment, discrimination must be intentional.

The difference between a "close" and a "substantial" relationship and the difference between a "compelling" and a "substantial" governmental interest are not delineated by a bright line. The Court has indicated, however, that a close relationship is one that adheres to the "least restrictive" or "least intrusive" means of regulation, and the likelihood that an interest is compelling is greater if it pertains to public health or safety than if it concerns mere administrative convenience or fiscal considerations. There are few cases in which a challenged statute has passed the test of strict scrutiny.

(See also BILL OF RIGHTS; PREFERRED FREEDOMS DOCTRINE.)

Harold J. Spaeth

**Stromberg v. California,** 283 U. S. 359 (1931), argued 15 April 1931, decided 18 May 1931 by vote of 7 to 2; Hughes for the Court, Butler and McReynolds in dissent. Yetta Stromberg's summer job teaching at a youth camp for working-class children in rural California led to a court challenge of the previously unenforced 1919 state law that prohibited public use or display of a red flag. The legislature had determined that the presence of red fabric demonstrated opposition to organized government and invited anarchy and sedition.

During the summer of 1929, the Pioneer Summer Camp, maintained by a conference of organizations, some of them communist in ideology, became the target of the Better American Federation (BAF), a group determined to rid California of "dangerous" dissent. The BAF convinced the San Bernardino County sheriff to search the camp, where his men discovered the red flag and arrested Stromberg and other staff members.

After Stromberg's conviction she appealed to the Supreme Court where her attorneys argued that the California statutes prohibited a symbol of a legally constituted party that had received fifty thousand votes in the previous election. Stromberg's lawyers based much of their argument on Justice Oliver Wendell *Holmes's *clear and present danger test that maintained that the circumstances of the act must be considered in testing the law.

Seven members of the Court voted to overturn Stromberg's conviction. In the majority opinion Chief Justice Charles Evans *Hughes followed the reasoning of the Holmes's doctrine and concluded that the red flag ban was too vague and could be used to interfere with constitutionally based political and partisan opposition to those in power. Therefore, the majority declared the California Red Flag Law unconstitutional because it violated the liberty protected by the *Fourteenth Amendment. The legislature repealed the statute in 1933.

Hughes's Stromberg opinion is considered a milestone in First Amendment constituional law, for it was the first ruling in which a Court majority extended the Fourteenth Amendment to include a protection of First Amendment substance—in this case *symbolic speech—from state encroachment.

(See also FIRST AMENDMENT; SPEECH AND THE PRESS.)

Carol E. Jenson

**Strong, William** (b. 6 May 1808, Somers, Conn.; d. 19 Aug. 1895, Lake Minnewaska, N.Y.; interred Charles Evans Cemetery, Reading, Pa.), associate justice, 1870–1880. William Strong was the eldest son of Rev. William Lighthouse Strong and Marriet Deming Strong. Rev. Strong was a Somers' Congregational ("Standing Order") minister. Young Strong attended local schools and graduated from Yale College. He taught briefly but returned to Yale to study law. Although admitted to the Connecticut bar, he eventually moved to Reading, Pennsylvania, where he mastered German and built a successful practice.

In 1846 Strong was elected to the Thirtieth Congress as a "Locofoco" Democrat and served two terms. He remained out of politics until elected to the state supreme court in 1857, serving until 1868. Strong became a Republican during the 1860s and may have been considered by Abraham *Lincoln for the chief justiceship in 1864.

In February 1870 even as the Court announced its decision in *Hepburn* v. *Griswold* (see LEGAL TENDER CASES), striking down the legal tender law, President Ulysses S. Grant nominated Strong and Joseph P. *Bradley to fill vacancies. Previously Strong upheld the law in *Shollenberger* v. *Brinton* (1866). The "packed" Court reversed *Hepburn* in 1871 with Strong writing the opinion.

In *Reconstruction cases, Justice Strong wrote the opinion for a unanimous Supreme Court emasculating the confiscation laws (*Bigelow* v. *Forrest*, 1870) and in *Blyew* v. *United States* (1872) stopped the government's prosecution of an alleged murderer because his black victims, being dead, no longer had rights to lose. Strong supported jury rights for blacks in *Strauder* v. *West Virginia* (1880) and *Ex parte Virginia* (1880), but in *Virginia* v. *Rives* (1880), he refused to require that blacks be on juries.

Strong's expertise was in *patent and business law where he often sided with Justice Stephen J. *Field, notably in *Munn* v. *Illinois* (1877). He wrote the *State Freight Tax Case* (1873), prohibiting Pennsylvania from taxing interstate commerce (see COMMERCE POWER).

Strong figured in two other controversies. A reluctant member of the Electoral Commission in 1877, he voted to seat disputed president-elect Rutherford B. Hayes. (See EXTRAJUDICIAL ACTIVITIES.) In 1880, at age seventy-two, his abrupt resignation surprised Court observers.

An ardent churchgoer since 1846 and active in Presbyterian affairs, Strong held offices in the American Tract Society, the American Sunday-School Union, the American Bible Society, and the American Board of Commissioners of Foreign Missions. Convinced that secularization threatened America's heritage, he headed the National Reform Association that wanted an amended Constitution establishing "Lord Jesus Christ as the Governor among nations, and His revealed will as of supreme authority. . . ." At Union Theological Seminary, Strong disclaimed wanting a national church, but insisted that Christian principles be enforced on marriage, Sabbath observances, blasphemy, and so forth. Strong voted his principles against the Mormons in *Reynolds* v. *United States* (1879), but it was Justice David J. *Brewer who inserted Strong's "Christian nation" conviction into *Church of the Holy Trinity* v. *United States* (1891).

*William Strong*

Strong typified Americans during the age of industrialization. As a lawyer, he worked to facilitate capitalism; as a moralist, he deplored the social consequences without seeing accurately the causal factors.

□ Stanley I. Kutler, "William Strong," in *The Justices of the United States Supreme Court, 1789–1969*, edited by Leon Friedman and Fred L. Israel, vol. 2 (1969), pp. 1153–1180. Jon C. Teaford, "Toward a Christian Nation: Religion, Law and Justice Strong," *Journal of Presbyterian History* 54 (Winter 1976): 422–437.

Michael B. Dougan

**Stuart v. Laird,** 1 Cranch (5 U.S.) 299 (1803), argued 23–24 Feb. 1803, decided 2 Mar. 1803 by vote of 5 to 0; Paterson for the Court, Marshall not participating. *Stuart* v. *Laird* presented two constitutional questions raised by the repeal of the *Judiciary Act of 1801. First, could Congress abolish the *circuit courts created by the 1801 statute and thereby, in effect, deprive the judges appointed to them of their positions despite the good-behaviour provision of *Article III, section 1? Second, could Congress require justices of the Supreme Court to sit as circuit judges? Justice William *Paterson's brief opinion answered both questions in the affirmative, but on narrow and technical grounds that avoided rather than resolved the constitutional challenges. Paterson narrowed the first question to the validity of transfer of a pending case from a court existing under the 1801 act to one created under the 1802 repealer and held that Congress had power to require the transfer. As to *circuit riding, he stated that the Court had acquiesced in the duty since its inception, so that it was too late in the day to challenge the practice. Implicitly, however, only six days after it had handed down its opinion in *Marbury* v. *Madison* (1803), the Court upheld the 1802 repeal act and thereby avoided a confrontation with the Republican-dominated Congress and executive.                    William M. Wiecek

**Sturges v. Crowninshield,** 4 Wheat. (17 U.S.) 122 (1819), argued 8 Feb. 1819, decided 17 Feb. 1819 by vote of 7 to 0; Marshall for the Court. This case provided the first test of the constitutionality of state insolvency laws, in this instance an 1811 New York statute that freed debtors from imprisonment for debt and discharged their debt if they assigned their property for the benefit of their creditors.

Chief Justice John *Marshall rejected a challenge to the state act based on the argument that federal power over bankruptcy was exclusive but warned in dictum that a federal statute would preempt conflicting state legislation (see OBITER DICTUM). He voided the statute because it discharged a preexisting debt and thus ran afoul of the *Contracts Clause (Article I, section 10). Marshall did, however, concede that a state could modify remedies that enforced an obligation (thus the constitutionality of that section of the statute that liberated an insolvent from debtors' prison), provided that it not revise the underlying obligation itself.

The constitutionality of state relief laws remained unsettled until 1827, when the Court ruled in *Ogden* v. *Saunders* that states could discharge debts, provided they did not impair contracts made before the statute was enacted.

Even so, the policy question relating to *bankruptcy and insolvency remained unresolved throughout the nineteenth century. Some states, mostly in the North, did create debtor relief systems, but legislators had difficulties in balancing the interests of both debtors and creditors. They wanted to ease the plight of "unfortunate" defaulters, especially during periods of economic hardship, but at the same time they did not want to discourage lenders, whose role they prized as essential to business well being and economic growth. This conflict was largely resolved by enactment of national bankruptcy legislation in 1898.                    Peter J. Coleman

**Subpoena** (Lat., "under penalty"), an order of a court to a person commanding him or her to appear as a witness or to produce documents in his or her possession (*subpoena duces tecum*). The use of subpoenas in civil proceedings in federal courts is regulated by rule 45 of the Federal Rules of Civil Procedure.                    William M. Wiecek

**Substantive Due Process.** See DUE PROCESS, SUBSTANTIVE.

**Subversion.** Since the late eighteenth century, federal and state governments have attempted to use legal methods, including statutory prohibition, legislative investigation, and criminal prosecution, to suppress what political majorities of the time deemed to be efforts to overthrow or undermine existing systems and policies of governance. The Supreme Court has seldom found such measures unconstitutional.

The Court's encounters with antisubversive legislation have included some of its most significant First Amendment cases, such as *Schenck* v. *United States* (1919) and *Abrams* v. *United States* (1919), in which Justice Oliver Wendell *Holmes first articulated, then refined, the *clear and present danger test; *Gitlow* v. *New York* (1925), which upheld a state *criminal syndicalism statute but which also began the process of incorporating *Bill of Rights guarantees as limitations on the states (see INCORPORATION DOCTRINE); *Dennis* v. *United States* (1951), where the Court gave the clear and present danger test a speech-repressive interpretation based on the *bad-tendency doctrine of *common law; *Pennsylvania* v. *Nelson* (1956), a rare instance of the Court striking down state antisubversive legislation, on grounds of federal preemption (see STATE SEDITION LAWS); and *Communist Party* v. *Subversive Activities Control Board* (1961), which upheld the constitutionality of the federal Internal Security Act of 1950 (see McCARRAN ACT). The *Dennis* and *Subversive Activities Control Board* cases typify constants in the Court's approach to antisubversive legislation: deference to legislative judgments about the existence of a subversive conspiracy, minimal rationality standards for review of the means chosen to suppress subversion, and a balancing of the rights of individuals to freedom of political expression versus the state's interest in maintaining its power (see FIRST AMENDMENT BALANCING). With the thawing of the cold war, the Court has been somewhat more forward in protecting political speech, as, for example, in *Brandenburg* v. *Ohio* (1969), where the Court gave the clear and present danger test the libertarian emphasis demanded by Holmes in *Abrams*.

(See also COMMUNISM AND COLD WAR; FIRST AMENDMENT; SPEECH AND THE PRESS.)
                    William M. Wiecek

**Suffrage.** See FIFTEENTH AMENDMENT; NINETEENTH AMENDMENT; TWENTY-SIXTH AMENDMENT; VOTE, RIGHT TO.

**Sugar Trust Case.** See E. C. KNIGHT CO. V. UNITED STATES.

**Sunday Closing Laws,** state or local laws requiring all but the most essential businesses to be closed on Sunday, commonly known as blue laws from the color of the paper on which the early ones were printed. They originated in the colonial period, when their religious purpose was expressly stated, and *state courts in the nineteenth century generally upheld them.

In *McGowan v. Maryland* (1961) the Supreme Court considered the broad issue of whether the laws were an establishment of *religion. Claimants contended that Sunday was selected for closing to recognize the Christian sabbath and to encourage church attendance. The Court held that while these laws had a sectarian purpose at one time, their contemporary purpose was secular: to provide a common day of rest for the entire community. Since there was a valid secular purpose and only an indirect effect on religion, the laws were not an establishment of religion.

*Braunfeld v. Brown* (1961) posed the issue whether Orthodox Jews who shut their businesses on Saturday for religious reasons could be forced to close on Sunday as well. Closing both days would impose an economic hardship on them. The Court ruled that there was no interference with their free exercise of religion. Sabbatarians were free to close on Saturday, and their religion did not command Sunday opening. Sunday closing imposed only an indirect burden on religious observance and was valid.

Despite the legitimization of these laws, suburbanization, the growth of shopping malls, and police reluctance to enforce them induced many communities to repeal Sunday closing laws. Except for bans on beer and liquor sales, there are few localities today that have Sunday laws.

(See also FIRST AMENDMENT.)

Robert H. Birkby

**Supreme Court Reporter,** the West Publishing Company's unofficial edition of Supreme Court decisions, began publication in 1883, printing decisions of the October 1882 term. *Advance sheets are issued semimonthly, with final page-numbering. Only the bound volume, however, offers star paging to the official reports and parallel citations to both the official reports and to *Lawyer's Edition. The text of decisions is the same as in the official edition. Case summaries and headnotes are prepared by West, and the headnotes are classified by West's key-number system. Through their assigned topics and key numbers, abstracts of the legal points in *Supreme Court Reporter* decisions appear in the various digests published by West. Both advance sheets and bound volumes contain the usual features of West reporters, including tables of cases, a key-number digest, and tables of words, phrases, statutes, and rules judicially construed. In addition to advance sheets, West since 1986 has been publishing a temporary "interim edition" of the bound cumulation, in two or three physical volumes, to offset the delay in publication of the final volumes.

Morris L. Cohen

**Suspect Classfications.** The *Due Process Clause of the *Fifth Amendment and the *Equal Protection Clause of the *Fourteenth Amendment pro-

hibit federal and state governments from engaging in certain forms of discriminatory behavior. Not all government discrimination is unconstitutional, however. It is legitimate for the law to treat individuals differently if such classification is reasonable and designed to accomplish a compelling government interest. A state, for example, may discriminate on the basis of age in treating youthful and adult offenders differently even if they have committed the same illegal act. The Constitution only prohibits discrimination that is invidious, arbitrary, or irrational. The validity of the government action depends largely on the criterion on which the discrimination is based.

The Supreme Court has determined certain classifications to be constitutionally suspect. Discrimination based on any characteristic that the Court has declared suspect is presumed to be irrational and constitutionally invalid. When such discrimination is constitutionally challenged, the courts proceed with *strict scrutiny and the government carries a difficult burden of proof to justify the legitimacy of its actions. The Supreme Court, for example, has declared *race and *religion suspect. Therefore, government discrimination against racial minorities or religious groups is unlikely to be upheld. The Court has occasionally conferred suspect class status on other characteristics, such as poverty and illegitimacy, especially when the discrimination has impinged on the exercise of *fundamental rights (see INDIGENCY; INHERITANCE AND ILLEGITIMACY). Women's groups have long fought to have *gender elevated to a suspect class, but the Supreme Court has yet to endorse that position.

Thomas G. Walker

**Sutherland, George** (b. Buckinghamshire, England, 15 March 1862; d. Stockbridge, Mass., 18 July 1942; interred Cedar Hill Cemetery, Washington, D.C.), associate justice, 1922–1938. George Sutherland's appointment to the Supreme Court by President Warren G. Harding on 5 September 1922 was expected, since his name had been mentioned for the position as early as 1910. A strong conservative, he remained on the Court long enough to witness the demise of substantive *due process, a doctrine that had become almost synonymous with his name. In his last years on the Court, his detractors castigated him as one of the *Four Horsemen who repeatedly struck down *New Deal social legislation. After the defeat of President Franklin *Roosevelt's "court-packing scheme," Sutherland resigned from the Court, where his beliefs had become unfashionable (see COURT-PACKING PLAN).

Sutherland's values were forged in the Utah frontier where his Scottish father, Alexander, and his English mother, Frances, brought him as a toddler from England. The Mormon church, which had attracted Alexander to Utah, soon proved uncongenial, and the elder Sutherland went on to pursue a variety of careers, including

*George Sutherland*

the law. His son Geroge at the age of twelve entered Brigham Young Academy (later University), where he studied under the Mormon scholar Karl G. Maeser. Maeser impressed on him that the framers of the Constitution had been divinely inspired. Both Maeser and Judge Thomas M. *Cooley, who instructed Sutherland at the University of Michigan Law School, passed along to the young man such notions as the existence of individual rights antecedent to the state, limited government dedicated to protecting these rights, and evolution toward social betterment.

After admission to the bars of Michigan and Utah in 1883, Sutherland briefly joined his father's law firm in Provo, and after another partnership there, moved to a prestigious firm in Salt Lake City. Active in Utah politics, first in the Liberal party (or Gentile party, opposed to Mormon polygamy) and after statehood in the newly founded Republican party, Sutherland served in the territorial legislature and as a state senator (1896–1900). In the latter capacity, he sponsored legislation extending *eminent domain powers to mining and irrigation industries and advocated a bill for an eight-hour day for miners. As a member of the United States House of Representatives (1901–1903), he championed protective tariffs for Utah's sugar crop, a commitment to protectionism that he maintained throughout his subsequent career in the United States Senate (1905–1917).

His two terms in the Senate were marked by the advocacy of many positions that defy the conventional image of him as a staunch conservative. He supported the Postal Savings Banks bill

(1910), arguing that government had a duty to provide banking where none was available; the *Nineteenth Amendment for women's suffrage; workmen's conpensation legislation for the railroads, arguing that the Due Process Clause did not stand in the way of what the "enlightened minds of mankind" now regard as just; and legislation to improve the working condition of seamen.

Justice Sutherland's record on the Court likewise defies facile ideological categorization. His name is most often associated with liberty of contract cases such as *Adkins v. Children's Hospital (1923). (See CONTRACT, FREEDOM OF.) He wrote the majority opinion holding unconstitutional minimum wage legislation for women as an interference with a woman's right to contract and a step backward from the movement toward equality between the sexes. His laissez-faire faith also surfaced in *Home Building & Loan Association v. Blaisdell (1934), where he invoked the *Contract Clause in dissent against the Court's affirmation of a Minnesota debt moratorium plan.

Yet, Sutherland was as zealous in defense of liberty rights as *property rights. In *Powell v. Alabama (1932), the famous case of the Scotsboro black youths condemned to death for an assault on a white girl, he wrote the Court's opinion overturning their conviction on the grounds that a criminal defendant has a right to *counsel, including a reasonable opportunity for consultation. *Grosjean v. American Press Co. (1936) was the occasion for his majority opinion declaring unconstitutional, as a *prior restraint of the press, a state license tax on newspaper advertising. Even in property rights cases, Sutherland was not opposed to reasonable and necessary regulation. Thus, he upheld as constitutional: *zoning, a ban on women working in restaurants after 10 P.M., the Illinois Fair Trade Act, and a statute regulating motor carriers' use of the streets and highways, among other regulatory acts.

The meaning of constitutional guarantees never varies, Sutherland argued in *Euclid v. Ambler Realty Co. (1926), but "the scope of their application must expand or contract to meet the new and different conditions" (p. 387). This elasticity of application of constitutional principles gave him sufficient leeway to view as unconstitutional minimum wage legislation but as permissible regulation of the hours of work, especially in dangerous occupations. This distinction the Court would ultimately find untenable as it abandoned strict oversight of government economic regulations and embraced the New Deal.

(See also HISTORY OF THE COURT: THE DEPRESSION AND THE RISE OF LEGAL LIBERALISM.)

Ellen Frankel Paul

**Swann v. Charlotte-Mecklenburg Board of Education,** 402 U.S. 1, argued 12 Oct. 1970, decided 20 Apr. 1971 by vote of 9 to 0; Burger for the

Court. A logical extension of *Green* v. *County School Board of New Kent County* (1968), *Swann* nonetheless represented a further—and highly controversial—milestone in the Supreme Court's effort, following *Brown* v. *Board of Education II* (1955), to effectuate the desegregation of southern public schools. *Swann* is best known for its approval of busing as a tool to achieve desegregation. But in thirty pages—the longest school desegregation opinion then to date—the Court, still unanimous, supplied broad guidelines to federal district judges still faced with dual school systems fifteen years after *Brown II*.

Unlike many previous important school desegregation cases involving small rural districts, *Swann* arose from a sprawling, part-urban, part-rural district covering 550 square miles and serving 84,000 pupils in 101 schools. The school population was 29 percent black, and those pupils were concentrated in one quadrant of Charlotte. The district operated under a court-ordered desegregation plan that focused on geographic zoning and free transfers, but even then more than half of the black pupils attended schools without any white students or teachers. After *Green*, the federal district court announced that the rules of the game had changed and adopted a sweeping plan to disperse the highly concentrated black-student population under a program that would transport an additional 13,000 children in more than 100 new buses at an annual operating cost of more than $500,000 and a startup cost of more than $1 million.

The Supreme Court approved the plan in a disarmingly simple opinion. After deploring "deliberate resistance" to *Brown II* and other "dilatory tactics," the Court announced that new guidelines were necessary in light of *Green* (p. 13). Once a constitutional violation was found, the question of the scope of the remedy became a routine issue of the appropriate use of remedial powers in equity. Chief Justice Warren *Burger's opinion, which recent evidence has shown to have been the product of desperate and extensive negotiation among the justices, is important mainly for two features: its treatment of "mathematical ratios" for school composition and its approval of the trial court's transportation method for effectuating pupil transfers between schools.

In upholding the trial court's order that efforts be made to reach a 71:29 (white-to-black) ratio in the various schools, the Supreme Court observed that the "constitutional command to desegregate schools does not mean that every school in every community must always reflect the racial composition of the school system as a whole" but only that "the very limited use of mathematical ratios was within the equitable remedial discretion of the District Court" (pp. 24–25). Burger did not explain whether there were any limitations on the use of ratios aimed to achieve racial balance in the schools—absent, hypothetically, the eventual achievement of a unitary system.

The opinion was even more elliptical on the focal point of the case: busing. After noting that 39 percent of public school children nationally are bused to school, Burger declared that freedom of choice would not eliminate the dual system and that busing and other remedial techniques, such as redrawing attendance zones, were within the district court's power to provide equitable relief: "Desegregation plans cannot be limited to the walk-in school" (p. 30). Finally, Burger construed Title VI of the *Civil Rights Act of 1964, which appeared to reaffirm *Brown* but seemed inconsistent with *Green*, as not disturbing the Court's rulings and thus as not circumscribing the district court's plan. In a companion case, *North Carolina State Board of Education* v. *Swann* (1971), Burger held that a state could not prohibit racially explicit transportation or assignment of schoolchildren without violating *Brown*.

Despite *Swann's* frank approval of wholesale, districtwide supervision of affected public schools by federal district courts, the opinion did contain two limitations on equitable discretion that would quickly loom large. Burger stated several times, in different words, that the scope of the constitutional violation determined the scope of the remedy. He also declared that the district court's jurisdiction ended when remediation had been achieved to the point where the system was once again "unitary." The former point shaped the decision in *Milliken* v. *Bradley* (1974); the latter presaged *Pasadena Board of Education* v. *Spangler* (1976).

(See also DESEGREGATION REMEDIES; RACE AND RACISM; SEGREGATION, DE JURE.)

□ Bernard Schwartz, *Swann's Way* (1986).

Dennis J. Hutchinson

**Swayne, Noah Haynes** (b. Frederick County, Va., 7 Dec. 1804; d. New York City, 8 June 1884; interred Oak Hill Cemetery, Washington, D.C.), associate justice, 1862–1881. Born in Virginia in 1804, Noah Swayne read law in the offices of two Virginia lawyers and was admitted to the bar at the age of nineteen. By this time, however, his antislavery views induced him to move west into Ohio, a free state. He began a practice of law and was an active Jacksonian Democrat. Indeed in 1830, President Andrew *Jackson appointed Swayne U.S. attorney, a post he occupied until 1841. He built up a successful law practice, including involvement as counsel in several Ohio *fugitive slave cases.

His continued opposition to *slavery led Swayne to join the Republican party and to support the presidential candidacy of John Fremont in 1856. When his friend Justice John *McLean suddenly died in April 1861, Swayne quickly enlisted the support of his friends ranging from the entire Ohio congressional delegation including Senators John Sherman and Benjamin Wade, to New York attorney Samuel Tilden. He even traveled to Washington and helped to

*Noah Haynes Swayne*

orchestrate a campaign aimed at educating President Abraham *Lincoln about his suitability for the post. Lincoln was convinced; he nominated Swayne on 22 January 1862. Senate confirmation followed two days later with only one dissent.

Unfortunately, Swayne's potential greatness as a jurist did not materialize. He was in fact both the first and the weakest of Lincoln's five appointments to the Court. His only major claim to any sort of distinction was his staunch judicial support of Lincoln's war measures. These included the Union blockade, issuance of paper money (greenbacks), and the legitimacy of martial law. On the other hand, in *Gelpcke v. Dubuque* (1864) he supported with equal vigor the contractual rights of railroad bond holders, even in the face of repudiation sanctioned both by the Iowa state legislature and state supreme court. Obligations sacred to law are not to be destroyed simply because "a state tribunal has erected the altar and decreed the sacrifice."

As a justice, Swayne had no inclination to withdraw from politics. He eagerly schemed to replace Roger *Taney as chief justice in 1864. And when Lincoln's ultimate choice, Salmon *Chase, died in 1873, Swayne willingly joined the resulting scramble for the post again—even though he was almost sixty-nine years old. Passed over for the appointment, Swayne lingered on the bench until 1881. Only after pressure from his fellow Ohioan President Rutherford B. Hayes and the presidential promise that a close friend, Stanley *Mathews, would be appointed in his place did he finally resign, ending a judicial career that had promised much, but produced little.

Jonathan Lurie

**Sweatt v. Painter,** 339 U.S. 629 (1950), argued 4 Apr. 1950, decided 5 June 1950 by vote of 9 to 0; Vinson for the unanimous Court. *Sweatt v. Painter* is a landmark decision in the history of United States race relations. Although the ruling was a more narrow holding than the decision of *Brown v. Board of Education of Topeka* (1954), it nonetheless made clear that the *separate but equal standard established by *Plessy v. Ferguson* (1896) was unattainable—at least in state-supported higher education. By implication, the principle was not achievable in any area of public life.

Heman Marion Sweatt was a Houston, Texas, mail carrier intent on becoming a lawyer. Having been denied admission to the University of Texas law school in 1946 because he was an African-American, Sweatt sought the assistance of the *National Association for the Advancement of Colored People and its chief legal counsel, Thurgood *Marshall. An involved legal battle ensued while Texas scrambled to establish an accredited law school for African-Americans within the state, as required by the Supreme Court in *Missouri ex rel. Gaines v. Canada* (1938).

Speaking for a unanimous Court, Chief Justice Fred M. *Vinson concluded that a newly created state law school for African-Americans in Texas was in no objective way equal to the University of Texas Law School. Even if it were, Vinson wrote, it would still lack the nonmeasurable elements that made a distinguished law school, among which were faculty reputation, alumni prestige, tradition, and history, a test no recent school could meet. The *Equal Protection Clause of the *Fourteenth Amendment thus required Sweatt's admission to the previously all-white state university law school. The decision made clear that statutory *segregation was doomed, whether by piecemeal dismemberment or one sweeping judicial thrust.

(See also RACE AND RACISM.)

Augustus M. Burns III

**Swift & Co. v. United States,** 196 U.S. 375 (1905), argued 6–7 Jan. 1905, decided 30 Jan. 1905 by vote of 9 to 0; Holmes for the Court. In *Swift,* the most prominent antitrust action against the Beef Trust, the Court abandoned the restrictive interpretations of its earliest antitrust holdings and accepted a broader definition of the federal *commerce power. Enjoined under the *Sherman Antitrust Act, Swift contended that the statute was vague and that the company's activities were wholly intrastate, thus being outside the reach of federal commerce power under the doctrine of *United States v. *E. C. Knight Co.* (1895). A unanimous Court rejected Swift's argument, holding that a combination that excluded competitors with intent to monopolize interstate commerce violated the Sherman Act. Justice Oliver Wendell *Holmes framed the *stream of commerce doctrine to produce a "practical," rather than a "technical, legal conception" of commerce (p.

398). The recurring series of acts by which the Beef Trust operated, from shipping to sale of cattle and with only temporary interruptions in the flow, amounted to a current of commerce among the states, however intrastate the nature of the independent acts. Moreover, Swift's anti-competitive impact on commerce was a direct restraint of trade. Noting that intent might render unlawful even independently lawful components of a scheme, Holmes elevated the importance of intent in defining corporate restraints of trade and attempts to monopolize commerce.

As the administration of President Theodore Roosevelt shifted from trust-busting to regulation, the *Swift* decision attracted little notice. The "stream of commerce" doctrine remained an untapped resource until the 1930s, when the *New Deal Court restored expansive readings of the commerce power.                    Barbara C. Steidle

**Swift v. Tyson,** 16 Pet. (41 U.S.) 1 (1842), argued 14 Jan. 1842, decided 25 Jan. 1842 by vote of 9 to 0; Story for the Court. In *Swift* v. *Tyson*, the Supreme Court established the freedom of the federal courts to follow principles of general commercial law, even if those principles were contrary to judicial decisions of the state in which the federal court sat. In *Swift*, New York defendants were sued in a New York federal district court on a bill of exchange made by them and transferred to a nonresident. The defendants invoked New York decisions under which the instrument was defective, but the plaintiffs argued that the general interstate commercial law would uphold the instrument.

The conflict between the New York cases and commercial decisions elsewhere implicated section 34 of the *Judiciary Act of 1789, which required federal courts to follow state "laws" whenever they were applicable. Thus the Court had to decide whether New York decisions were "laws" that federal courts were required to follow. Justice Joseph *Story wrote:

In the ordinary use of language, it will hardly be contended that the decisions of courts constitute laws.

[Section 34 does not] . . . apply to questions of a more general nature, not at all dependant local statutes or local usages. . . . As for example, to the construction of ordinary contracts of other written instruments, and especially to questions of general commercial law, where the state tribunals are called upon to perform the like functions as ourselves, that is, to ascertain upon general reasoning and legal analogies, what is the true exposition of the contract or instrument or what is the just rule furnished by the principles of commercial law to govern the case. (pp. 18–19)

*Swift* was a case falling within the diversity jurisdiction of the federal courts. It did not fall within the exclusive lawmaking authority of New York. The New York decisions cited by the defendants were themselves based upon "general commercial law," that is, the common commercial custom and jurisprudence applicable to

multistate business transactions. Thus Story determined that the New York decisions were not "laws" in the sense of being some fixed and definite pronouncement by the sovereign state of New York but were rather attempts by New York courts to articulate the content of commercial custom common to all the states and, as such, were wrong.

A federal court had no reason to regard as a matter of constitutional law the New York decisions as the sole and exclusive governing rule in an interstate commercial transaction. New York opinions addressed multistate general commercial law, as defined by judicially recognized commercial custom. Story compared the New York decisions to the general body of multistate commercial law and found them to be wrong.

Therefore, the *Swift* opinion was not meant to determine the substantive content of New York commercial law but rather was intended to vindicate plaintiff's reliance on the general and accepted commercial rule. By his skillful handling of the federalism issue, Story limited the ability of local precedent to upset the reasonable expectations of parties in interstate commercial dealings. He affirmed the power of the federal courts as independent tribunals to invoke established general commercial rules already embodied in judicial precedent. He thereby freed interstate commercial transactions from disruptive local aberrations. At a critical time in the nation's commercial development, Story encouraged independent federal courts to nationalize commercial rules and established the law merchant and its mature body of predictable and efficient rules in national and international commerce. The *Swift* decision was thus critical in preventing the balkanization of the commercial law that might have otherwise occurred.

In 1938, the Supreme Court in *Erie Railroad Co.* v. *Tompkins* repudiated *Swift*. Story's theory of adjudication as the resolution of disputes under customary standards evolved from private conduct was incompatible with Justice Louis D. *Brandeis's scientific positivism, under which an applicable legal rule could come only from the command of the state. His rejection of *Swift* thus represented a transition from nineteenth-century liberalism, concerned with a self-ordering society operating within a federal legal system composed of coequal sovereign states subject to traditional choice-of-law rules, to the modern state as exclusive lawgiver.

(See also CAPITALISM; FEDERAL COMMON LAW; FEDERALISM; JUDICIAL POWER AND JURISDICTION; LOWER FEDERAL COURTS.)

□ Tony A. Freyer, *Harmony and Discourse: The Swift and Erie Cases in American Federalism* (1981).
                                        Robert Randall Bridwell

**Symbolic Speech.** The Supreme Court has determined that the *First Amendment protects *nonverbal expression. In *Stromberg* v. *California* (1931), for example, the Court struck down a statute that prohibited the display of a red flag as a symbol of opposition to the government. The court has always attempted, however, to balance the protection of symbolic speech against the governmental interest in preventing harmful conduct. In evaluating regulations of symbolic expression the Court's primary consideration is whether the regulation suppresses the communicative content of the expression or simply regulates the accompanying conduct. In *United States* v. *O'Brien* (1968), the Court upheld a federal law prohibiting the mutilation of draft registration cards because the law was not intended to infringe the free speech rights of antiwar protestors, but rather served a legitimate governmental interest in effectively administering national conscription. By contrast, in *Tinker* v. *Des Moines School District* (1969), the Court ruled that the suspension of students who wore black arm-

bands to protest the *Vietnam War violated the students' First Amendment rights because school officials intended to suppress the antiwar message of the protest, not any disruptive conduct the students might cause.

Most recently, the Court has confronted statutes that attempt to punish individuals who burn the American flag to express dissent. In *Texas* v. *Johnson* (1989) and *United States* v. *Eichman* (1990), the Court invalidated state and federal laws prohibiting flag desecration because such laws served no governmental interest except to create a specific class of political orthodoxy—adoration of the flag—with which no one could express disagreement. The decisions demonstrated the persistence of First Amendment libertarianism even on a conservative court, but they also led to calls for a constitutional amendment that would prohibit flag burning.

(See also SPEECH AND THE PRESS.)

Eric W. Rise

# T

**Taft, William Howard** (b. Cincinnati, Ohio, 15 Sep. 1857; d. Washington, D.C., 8 Mar. 1930; interred Arlington National Cemetery), president of the United States, 1909–1913; chief justice, 1921–1930. William Howard Taft, the only figure in American history to serve both as president of the United States and chief justice of its highest court, was born in Cincinnati on 15 September 1857, the son and grandson of judges. Ample in girth as well as intellect, he possessed amiability rather than political ambition. Taft was attracted not to politics, but to law in general, and judging in particular, throughout his long and varied career. Though capable as a lawyer, he achieved his greatest fulfillment as a judge. He served in a number of political capacities, including the highest political office in this country, but his calling remained the judiciary. "I love judges, and I love courts. They are my ideals, that typify on earth what we shall meet hereafter in heaven under a just God." And toward the end of his life, when, after losing reelection to the presidency, he ultimately attained his lifelong goal of the chief justice's seat on the Court, an observer described him on the bench "as one of the high gods of the world, a smiling Buddha, placid, wise, gentle, sweet" (J. Anderson, *William Howard Taft*, 1981, p. 259).

Taft graduated from Yale in 1878, and after attending the University of Cincinnati law school, was admitted to the Ohio bar two years later. But his private practice was a short one. The son of a family well known in Ohio politics, he was appointed to the Ohio Superior Court in 1887. Within two years, he tried to have his name submitted to President Benjamin Harrison for a

vacancy on the United States Supreme Court. Although he did not receive the appointment, the influence exercised on his behalf was sufficient for Harrison to name the thirty-two-year-old Ohio judge as *solicitor general. The required relocation to Washington afforded Taft the opportunity to meet lawyers and political figures on the national scene. Taft was not an eloquent advocate, but his performance as solicitor general was more than competent; he won sixteen out of the eighteen cases that he argued before the Court. In 1892, Harrison appointed him a federal judge for the Sixth Circuit.

Taft served on the circuit bench for eight years. Many of the cases before him concerned organized *labor. Throughout his later career, especially during his presidential term, Taft would be severely criticized for his hostility to the working man. In fact, examination of his federal judicial career indicates ambivalence rather than outright antagonism toward labor. He had no doubt, for example, that workers had the right to organize into unions and strike when they considered it necessary. Moreover, he ruled in one case that it was unlawful for owners to force their workers to accept nonliability clauses as a condition of employment, a device popular among employers for avoiding liability for accidents. Taft's ruling was later reversed by the Supreme Court.

On the other hand, a strike was not the same thing as a boycott; Taft regularly enjoined the latter. While he occasionally supported the workers' position in a particular case, he remained staunchly conservative in his attitudes toward *property rights. And, like many conservatives, he reacted with outrage to violence resulting

*William Howard Taft*

from conflict between labor and management. During the Pullman strike in 1894, Taft wrote to his wife that "it will be necessary for the military to kill some of the mob. . . . They have only killed six . . . as yet. This is hardly enough to make an impression."

Taft found his years as a federal judge extremely fulfilling. There was always the possibility of advancement to the high court, a goal not shared by Taft's wife, who consistently urged her husband to venture into fields with greater potential for political rewards. When in 1900 President William McKinley named him chair of the Philippine Commission, pressure from Helen Taft, rather than his own preference, proved persuasive. He remained in the islands for four years, ultimately serving as civil governor, a position that he considered similar to his earlier judicial functions. So absorbing did he find his island responsibilities that on at least two separate occasions between 1901 and 1904, Taft declined appointments to the Supreme Court, choosing instead to remain in the Philippines. Finally in 1904, President Theodore Roosevelt recalled him to Washington as secretary of war. His close association with the president, together with Helen Taft's vigorous encouragement and Roosevelt's stated determination not to seek reelection in 1908, all combined to propel a reluctant Taft into the White House.

Had Roosevelt been able to offer Taft the position of chief justice, subsequent events might have been very different. Neither interested in politics nor astute in the ways of politicians, Taft found his four years as chief executive a frustrat-

ing and unrewarding experience. He was, however, able to make six appointments to the Supreme Court, more than any other one-term president in American history. He even named a new chief justice in place of Melville *Fuller, commenting with real regret that "the one place in the government which I would have liked to fill myself I am forced to give to another." Indeed, Taft's self-interest in this matter colored his conduct.

Ultimately faced with two choices, both justices currently on the Court, either Edward D. *White or Charles Evans *Hughes, Taft ultimately named White, even though White was a Democrat, and though Taft respected Hughes more as a judge. But White was a dozen years older than Taft, and seventeen years older than Hughes. Refusing to abandon his goal of ultimately serving as chief justice, Taft realized that given the vicissitudes of time, he might yet have a chance of succeeding White. Actuarial considerations may thus have been the dominant factor in White's ultimate selection.

Taft expected defeat in the bitter three-way 1912 presidential campaign and left the presidency to Woodrow Wilson with relief. Offered the Kent Chair in Constitutional Law at Yale Law School, Taft commented jocularly that a chair would not be adequate, but perhaps "a sofa of law" might suffice. He adjusted to the life of an academician with an extensive and, for the time, lucrative lecture schedule. He remained interested in national affairs and strongly endorsed Wilson's League of Nations, even as he severely criticized the embattled president's political intransigence. Always a loyal Republican, he supported Warren G. Harding with consistency if not enthusiasm. After Harding's triumphant election, the new chief executive offered to place Taft on the bench, but the former president replied that he would only accept the position of chief justice.

With an eagerness to succeed his own nominee as chief justice that was understandable if not unseemly, Taft might have pondered Thomas *Jefferson's famous lament about justices on the high court: "few die and none resign." Although he had a few anxious months owing to Chief Justice White's seeming longevity, ultimately Taft's calculations concerning the length of the chief's term were correct. To some extent in 1908, but even more so in 1921, Taft happened to be in the right place for the right position with the right president at the right time. Nominated chief justice by Harding on 30 June 1921, the former president was confirmed later that same day by the Senate, which did not even bother to refer the matter to committee.

As chief justice, Taft was distinguished less by doctrinal than by departmental innovation. Especially in the first half of his nine-year term, while he remained in relatively sound health, he was the most active chief justice in court administrative matters thus far in the history of that tribunal. Taft did not hesitate to use many of his old presidential and congressional contacts to further his goals for the Court. His skillful combination of informal lobbying, matched with a sound understanding of the needs of the federal judicial system, led to congressional enactment of the *Judiciary Act of 1925, which gave the justices almost total discretion over their docket. This discretionary flexibility continues to the present, allowing the Court, with very few exceptions, to decide what cases need to be resolved and in what context. Later, Taft employed these same skillful techniques to insure congressional support for the construction of a building appropriate to the Court's role in American constitutional adjudication. He did not live to see it completed, but the structure remains one fitting tribute to Taft's vision of the Court.

As chief justice, Taft emphasized teamwork among his associates. He did not appreciate frequent dissents (especially those replete with lengthy footnotes that seemed to emanate too often from Justice Louis *Brandeis) because he thought they lessened the effectiveness of the Court's work. His reluctance to see disagreement within the Court made public is reflected in the fact that in his eight full terms he dissented about twenty times and submitted written dissents in only four cases. Yet he wrote 249 opinions on behalf of the Court.

Taft's conservative tendencies demonstrated during his first judicial career were very much in evidence during his second. In 1921, speaking for a bare majority of the Court, he struck down an Arizona statute that limited use of injunctions during labor disputes. Conduct that strikers claimed to be sanctioned by the statute was, according to Taft in *Truax v. Corrigan (1921), "moral coercion by illegal annoyance and obstruction, and it thus was plainly a conspiracy" (p. 328). Less than six months later, he held a federal statute dealing with child labor unconstitutional. Earlier, Congress had enacted a similar law, based upon its power to regulate commerce, only to see it struck down by the Court (see COMMERCE POWER). Its second attempt was based not on the Commerce Clause, but rather on the taxing power; yet Taft saw no difference worth discussing (see TAXING AND SPENDING CLAUSE). In reality, the act was a penalty, Taft concluded in *Bailey v. Drexel Furniture Co. (1922), because in seeking "to do the same thing, and the effort must be equally futile" (p. 39).

Taft was nevertheless capable of unusual doctrinal flexibility. In one of his rare dissents, he criticized the majority's rejection of a minimum wage for women. Sounding more like Justice *Holmes than himself, Taft wrote in *Adkins v. Children's Hospital (1923), "it is not the function of this Court to hold congressional acts invalid simply because they are passed to carry out economic views which the Court believes to be

unwise or unsound" (p. 562). When the Court unanimously rejected a congressional attempt to regulate commodity futures trading through the taxing power, in the course of his opinion, Taft advised Congress to reenact the measure based on its plenary authority to regulate commerce. Congress did so, and with the sections regulating futures trading still intact, Taft upheld the law. Indeed, Taft's opinions for the Court dealing with the national commerce power tended to be sweeping in their endorsement of congressional authority. If they represented a conservative viewpoint, it was a dynamic conservatism—restricted only by Taft's insistence that the "sanctity and inviolability of judicial decisions" from his court be unimpaired.

By 1928, Taft's health was failing. Although he sat in his accustomed chair for the opening of the 1929 October term, illness forced him to resign in February 1930. He died barely a month later and was the first president to be buried in Arlington National Cemetery. If not a distinguished judge in his doctrines and opinions, Taft was an outstanding judicial administrator. Especially in the first half of his term, no chief justice thus far in our history matched his active role in court administration, and his leadership in bringing about legislation gave needed judicial discretion to the Court to control its docket. Taft's leadership helped modernize a tribunal badly in need of such change. In retrospect, however, too often his decisions reflected a fear of change rather than its necessary facilitation.

(See also CHIEF JUSTICE, OFFICE OF THE).

□ Alpheus Thomas Mason, *The Supreme Court from Taft to Warren* (1958). Alpheus Thomas Mason, *William Howard Taft: Chief Justice* (1964). Walter F. Murphy, "In His Own Image: Mr. Chief Justice Taft and Supreme Court Appointments," in *The Supreme Court and the Constitution,* edited by Philip Kurland (1965). Hentry F. Pringle, *The Life and Times of William Howard Taft,* 2 vols. (reprint, 1964).                    Jonathan Lurie

**Takings Clause.** More accurately called the *Eminent Domain Clause, the Takings Clause is part of the *Fifth Amendment to the Constitution. Property is taken, or condemned, when a governmental entity compels the owner to transfer ownership of, or property rights in, real or personal property to the government. Private individuals may not compel other individuals to transfer property to them. The Constitution does not expressly grant eminent domain power, which is regarded as an inherent power of government. Instead, the Takings Clause imposes limitations on exercise of power, most importantly by the requirement that *just compensation be paid the owner. The purpose of the Takings Clause is to ensure that the financial burdens of public policy should be shared by the entire public and not unfairly placed on individual property owners.

The Takings Clause expressly limits exercise of

the power of eminent domain by the federal government. Moreover, the Supreme Court in *Chicago, Burlington & Quincy Railroad Co.* v. *Chicago* (1897) said that the Takings Clause applied to state governments through the *Due Process Clause of the *Fourteenth Amendment. The concept is that it would be a denial of due process to compel owners to give up property without compensation. In addition, nearly all state constitutions contain takings clauses, usually in language like that of the Fifth Amendment. Thus, persons are protected against uncompensated seizures of property by the federal government by the Fifth Amendment and against such seizures by state governments by both the Fifth Amendment and state constitutions.        William B. Stoebuck

**Talton v. Mayes,** 163 U.S. 376 (1896), argued 16–17 Apr. 1896, decided 18 May 1896 by vote of 8 to 1; White for the Court, Harlan in dissent. *Talton* v. *Mayes* was an appeal by a Cherokee from a homicide conviction by a Cherokee Nation court. He contended that his trial violated the *Fifth Amendment because the *grand jury that indicted him consisted of only five members, as permitted by Cherokee law. The Supreme Court held that the Fifth Amendment did not apply to legislation of the Cherokee Nation. The Indian tribes have retained the sovereign power to make their own laws, which is binding on tribal members unless in conflict with some provision of federal law specifically applicable to tribal governments.

*Talton* v. *Mayes* has been interpreted to hold that constitutional limitations on the federal and state governments do not of their own force limit Indian tribes, which are not "states" of the union within the meaning of the Constitution. The *Indian Bill of Rights of 1968 modified the *Talton* holding by imposing on tribes certain specified securities for personal liberty copied (sometimes in modified form) from the United States Constitution.

(See also NATIVE AMERICANS.)
        Rennard J. Strickland

**Taney, Roger Brooke** (b. Calvert County, Md., 17 Mar. 1777; d. Washington, D. C., 12 Dec. 1864; interred St. John the Evangelist Cemetery, Frederick, Md.), chief justice, 1836–1854. Roger B. Taney is best known as the author of one of the most infamous opinions ever written for the Supreme Court, the majority opinion in *Dred *Scott* v. *John F. A. Sandford* (1857). It is perhaps no surprise, then, that many students of American constitutional and legal history have a passionate, almost instinctive, negative reaction to the mention of Taney's name. Yet when the American Bar Association asked professors of law, history, and political science to evaluate Supreme Court justices, they ranked Taney in the "great" category along with giants John *Marshall, Oliver

*Roger Brooke Taney*

Wendell *Holmes, and Louis D. *Brandeis. Obviously many people associate Taney with only a narrow phase of his career—indeed, with a single case—while overlooking virtually everything else.

Roger Brooke Taney was descended from a prominent and aristocratic tobacco-growing family. The family tradition was conservative agrarian; its politics during Taney's formative years were pro-Constitution, pro-Federalist, and strongly supportive of the rights of private property. Being a second son (the eldest inherited the family plantation), Roger was educated and trained for the law. He practiced briefly in Annapolis and then in Frederick, where he developed into one of Maryland's foremost attorneys. That inevitably led to election to the state legislature, first as a member of the House of Delegates and then as a state senator. In short order he became a leader in Maryland's Federalist party.

In 1806 Taney married Anne Key, daughter of wealthy farmer John Ross Key. (Her brother, Francis Scott Key, achieved everlasting fame when he authored "The Star Spangled Banner" during the dramatic bombardment of Baltimore's Fort McHenry in the War of 1812.) Taney was Roman Catholic, his wife Episcopalian. They reconciled religious differences by agreeing that sons would be raised as Catholics, daughters as Episcopalians. The Taneys had six children who survived, all girls.

*Early Career.* During his years in the Maryland legislature, Taney found himself often involved in matters of finance and banking. Representing a rural agrarian constituency, he viewed with misgivings monopolistic tendencies of Baltimore banks, though he supported others that dealt more favorably with farmers. Like many of his fellow Federalists, Taney's politics were somewhat erratic. Early a supporter of the national bank (he would turn against it after becoming a staunch Jacksonian), Taney nevertheless essentially endorsed states' rights. This showed especially in his views toward *slavery. He freed his own slaves (whom he inherited), but he opposed giving the federal government authority to limit the institution, holding that that power rested in the individual states. These early-held tenets would remain with him throughout his later judicial career.

By the time Taney's term in the Maryland senate expired in 1821, the Federalist party had fallen into disarray, both nationally and in the individual states. Taney soon found a new political home: the Democratic party of Andrew *Jackson. By 1826 he emerged among his state's Democratic leaders, and he was elected Maryland's attorney general, a post he held for five years. Along with a creditable legal performance, Taney's handling of patronage earned him a reputation as a loyal Jacksonian. Accordingly, when the Peggy Eaton affair forced a reorganization of President Jackson's cabinet in 1831, Taney was summoned to Washington as attorney general of the United States.

As attorney general (1831–1833), Taney rendered opinions that comported with his earlier constitutional views and that presaged his later judicial tenets. A steadfast Jacksonian, he viewed moneyed and monopoly-protected interests as threats to economic democracy, concepts starkly expressed in Jackson's famous bank veto message, which Taney helped draft. Taney believed unwaveringly in a divided state-federal sovereignty and in the power of the Supreme Court to decide on the locus of undetermined *concurrent powers. As to slavery, however, he authored an opinion that asserted unequivocally that except where the Constitution expressly granted power to the national authority, control over slavery rested exclusively with the states.

Taney's elevation to the Supreme Court climaxed a unique scenario of partisan Jacksonian politics. Having vetoed the recharter of the Second Bank of the United States, President Jackson sought to speed the "monster's" demise by transferring federal deposits into state banks. However, statutory authority to move those funds rested in the secretary of the treasury. Two secretaries resigned rather than acquiesce in Jackson's tactics. Finally, in 1833, the president shifted a more compliant Taney from Justice to Treasury, and he removed the funds. Taney's new post was on an interim appointment; when Congress convened and the president requested the appointment be made permanent, the Senate rejected it. Taney thereupon returned to private practice in Baltimore. In the next two years, however, several vacancies opened on the Supreme Court, and Jackson sought to fill them

with suitable nominees. He proposed Taney to replace Associate Justice Gabriel *Duvall, but Jackson's opponents in the Senate mustered enough votes to reject the nomination. When Chief Justice John Marshall died in 1835, Jackson again submitted Taney's name, this time to be chief justice, along with the nomination of Philip P. *Barbour to fill Duvall's still-vacant seat. On 15 March 1836, after an executive session in which no records were kept, the Senate confirmed both nominations. Anti-Jacksonians lamented that the Supreme Court had been sullied with a "political hack."

*Service on the Court.*    Taney succeeded a remarkable jurist, John Marshall, who left an extraordinary legacy that scholars have labeled "constitutional nationalism" and "national capitalism." Taney's philosophy differed. He was a consummate Jacksonian. Though an aristocrat who inherited conservative tidewater traditions, he believed like Jackson in the new West and its agrarianism. He was dedicated also to Jacksonian economic principles, especially to the processes of economic growth and competition. (It is worth noting that where Marshall affected knee breeches, Taney wore long trousers—"sans coulottes"—symbolic of democratization.) Taney's devotion to the Union, like Marshall's, was unequivocal; yet, unlike Marshall, he saw much merit in states' rights. After all, Taney grew up after the American Revolution and was not affected by the same driving nationalism that influenced Marshall.

Taney's appointment to the Supreme Court coincided with a general turnover of the Court's personnel, and within a few years Jacksonians dominated. This development alarmed those who feared that *property rights would be at the mercy of state legislatures, but Taney proved to be a skillful and shrewd tactician who knew how to exercise *judicial self-restraint. He led the Court along pathways of pragmatism and compromise, virtually devoid of dogmatism—except on the issue of slavery. In the end, Taney proved as vigilant as his predecessor in maintaining federal authority over American economic development.

The new chief justice did not have long to wait before making his mark on American jurisprudence. In *Charles River Bridge Company v. Warren Bridge Company* (1837), the Court faced the unremitting dilemma of American democratic capitalism: the conflict between the rights of private property and those of society. Taney asserted a basic premise of American constitutional thought: "The object and end of all government is to promote the happiness and prosperity of the community. . . . While the rights of private property are sacredly guarded, we must not forget that the community also have rights, and that the happiness and well-being of every citizen depends on their faithful preservation" (p. 420). The problem was where to draw the line.

Moderating Marshall's categorical primacy of vested rights, Taney stressed process over doctrine and purposefully adapted the rule of law to the historical realities of change and progress. Later jurists (with some notable exceptions) would reason in the same vein as commercial expansion and technology transformed American society from rural agricultural to urban industrial. Building on Taney's Jacksonian tenets, they would gradually formulate a philosophy that emphasized the social responsibilities of private property.

The Court's adaptation of process in *Charles River Bridge* paved the way for further assessments of Marshall's nation-centered views of the *Contract and Commerce Clauses. In a series of momentous decisions—which included *New York* v. *Miln* (1837), *Bank of Augusta* v. *Earle* (1839), *Swift* v. *Tyson* (1842), the *License Cases* (1847), the *Passenger Cases* (1849), *Genesee Chief* v. *Fitzhugh* (1852), and *Cooley* v. *Board of Wardens of the Port of Philadelphia* (1852), among others—the Taney Court asserted a concurrent federal-state relationship that warranted state supervision as long as it did not interfere with a federal statute. That freed the new technology from monopolistic restraints of established *corporations and outmoded charters. Without weakening federal regulative powers, except for negating exclusivity, these cases broadened the sphere of *laissez faire* and competition and raised the status of state involvement in contract and corporate affairs, thereby allowing the burgeoning West and the new technology to lead the nation reasonably untrammeled into the future (see COMMERCE POWER).

Contrary to considerable popular misconception, then, Taney did not reverse the Marshall trend and institute radical agrarian egalitarianism and state sovereignty. On the contrary, he preserved and refined the main lines of Marshall's constitutional law, opened economic opportunities for many Americans, and retained a strong national power redefined to accommodate a judicious dual sovereignty.

Nevertheless, Taney is remembered most for *Dred Scott*. Yet that decision comported with his earlier constitutional record on slavery, including opinions rendered as attorney general. In several cases preceding *Dred Scott*, Taney and his colleagues cautiously refrained from passing on the fundamental issue of slavery, exercising a modified judicial restraint by stressing process. In *Groves* v. *Slaughter* (1841) and in *Strader* v. *Graham* (1851), for instance, the Court evaded major substantive issues while striking a blow for state determination of the status of slavery. (Yet in *Prigg* v. *Pennsylvania*, 1842, Taney supported federal supremacy when state law interfered with Congressional fugitive-slave legislation.)

By 1857, however, the slavery issue had reached explosive proportions. Even though he saw nothing positive about the institution of slavery itself, Taney withal was a southern gentle-man imbued with southern values, and here was an opportunity to settle the issue. Furthermore, the majority of the Court was southern and proslavery. The result was *Dred Scott:* (1) blacks could not be citizens of the United States; (2) slaves were property protected by the Constitution; and (3) a state could decide for itself if someone formerly emancipated should revert to slavery within that state's boundaries. Coming when forces already were setting the stage for civil war, Taney's inflammatory opinion of the Court added enough fuel to the fire that it became unextinguishable.

Taney lived for seven years after *Dred Scott*, but the rancor engendered by that decision dogged him for the rest of his life. Even though he remained a loyal Unionist in the *Civil War and sought to protect constitutional rights precariously stretched during that conflict, his effectiveness on the Court waned, just as did that of the Court itself, both casualties of *Dred Scott*. Taney died a weary octogenarian whose final years suffered from anger, bitterness, and frustration.

Taney brought infamy upon himself because he viewed the alleged inferiority of blacks as an axiom of both law and the Constitution, a legal discrimination that he saw sanctioned even in the *Declaration of Independence. No wonder so many react negatively to his constitutionalism. Yet when scholars evaluate Taney's overall contributions to American jurisprudence, they rank him, in spite of *Dred Scott*, among the greats.

(See also STATE SOVEREIGNTY AND STATES' RIGHTS.)

□ Frank Otto Gatell, "Roger B. Taney," in *The Justices of the United States Supreme Court 1789–1969*, edited by Leon Friedman and Fred L. Israel, vol. 1, (1969) pp. 635–655. Walker Lewis, *Without Fear or Favor: A Biography of Chief Justice Roger Brooke Taney* (1965). Carl Brent Swisher, *Roger B. Taney* (1935). Samuel Tyler, *Memoir of Roger Brooke Taney, LL.D.* (1872).          Walter Ehrlich

**Tax Immunities.** The doctrine of intergovernmental tax immunity arises from concerns about the viability of the federal system if a state or the federal government can tax the operations of the other. Chief Justice John *Marshall in *McCulloch* v. *Maryland* (1819) contended that "the power to tax involves the power to destroy" (p. 431). The doctrine of tax immunity he articulated in that case has been seen as critical to the preservation of the constitutional system. Expansion of the doctrine and the notion of correlative state and federal immunities grew until the 1930s, when governmental financial needs placed pressure on the doctrine and the Supreme Court responded with decisions narrowing its scope.

In *McCulloch*, the Supreme Court reviewed the constitutionality of a Maryland statute that required banks operating without a charter from that state's legislature either to issue notes on state-furnished stamped paper or to pay an annual fee to the state. Marshall's decision, which found the Bank of the United States immune from these imposts, raised issues that were critical to the development of intergovernmental tax immunity—the sources of such immunities, the asymmetry of state and federal immunities, and the characteristics of an offending tax. In *McCulloch,* the source of the federal government's immunity from state taxation was not found in any express provision of the Constitution but rather in the structure of the document, which posited the supremacy of the federal constitution and laws.

In *Collector v. Day* (1871), a case holding that the federal government could not tax the salary of a state judge, the constitutional structure and the *Tenth Amendment were invoked as the bases of a reciprocal state immunity from federal taxation. Because of the different sources of immunity and the structure of the federal government, however, the immunity of the federal government differs from state immunity from federal taxation. The Supremacy Clause of Article VI and the representation of the states' interests in Congress have led the Court to conclude that the two types of intergovernmental immunities are asymmetrical.

The number and variety of taxes that ran afoul of the doctrine of intergovernmental tax immunities grew until the 1930s, when Court decisions began to retreat from the previous broad application of the doctrine. In the years following *McCulloch,* the doctrine of intergovernmental immunities came to shield employees, lessees, vendors to the government, *patent and *copyright holders, and governmental bondholders from various federal and state taxes. These immunities were based on the idea that taxation of third parties would increase the economic burden on the government contracting with them and that such economic burdens violated constitutional principles.

In the 1930s, the Court rejected the economic burden test, adopting instead a legal incidence test to identify unconstitutional taxes. During the 1930s and 1940s most third-party tax exemptions were overturned, although the exemption for recipients of governmental bond interest remained intact during this period. The administration of Franklin D. *Roosevelt reversed previous federal government positions by accepting state taxation of federal contractors in 1937 and sought to collect federal *income tax from state lessees and employees in 1938. Justice Felix *Frankfurter, in his concurrence in *Graves v. New York ex rel. O'Keefe* (1939), rejected the previous expansion of the doctrine as being "without regard to the actual workings of our federalism" at a time "when the financial needs of all governments began to steadily mount" (p. 490). Much later, in *South Carolina v. Baker* (1988), the Supreme Court upheld federal taxation of interest on unregistered state bonds in an opinion that rejected constitutional immunity for state bondholders.

Justice William J. *Brennan in *Baker* summarized what was left of the doctrine of intergovernmental immunities: "the States can never tax the United States directly but can tax any private parties with whom it does business . . . as long as the tax does not discriminate against the United States or those with whom it deals" (p. 523). The opinion indicated that "some nondiscriminatory federal taxes can be collected directly from the States, even though a parallel state tax could not be collected directly from the Federal Government" (p. 523), reiterating the asymmetry of the doctrine.

The doctrine of intergovernmental tax immunities has changed as fears about taxation's potential for destroying *federalism have waned and as demands for increasing government services and revenues have increased at both the state and federal level.

(See also STATE TAXATION.)

☐ Thomas Reed Powell, "The Waning of Intergovernmental Tax Immunities," *Harvard Law Review* 58 (1945): 633–674. Thomas Reed Powell, "The Remnant of Intergovernmental Tax Immunities," *Harvard Law Review* 58 (1945): 757–805.                    Carolyn C. Jones

**Taxing and Spending Clause.** Congress's power to "lay and collect Taxes, Duties, Imposts, and Excises, to pay the Debts and provide for the common Defence and general Welfare of the United States" (Art. I, sec. 8) is extraordinarily important and controversial.

The precise meaning of the clause has never been clear. Its peculiar wording and placement in the Constitution have contributed to the problem. One interpretation was that it granted to Congress the broad power to provide for the *general welfare. This interpretation assumes that the clause is the first of Congress's enumerated powers (it does immediately precede the long list of enumerated powers in Article I, section 8) and is consistent with a literal reading (see also IMPLIED POWERS). Still, this interpretation was inconsistent with the premise that the federal government is one of limted powers and would have rendered the list of enumerated powers redundant. It was never authoritatively accepted and was rejected officially by the Supreme Court in *United States v. *Butler* (1936).

At the other extreme, James *Madison and Thomas *Jefferson argued that the Taxing and Spending Clause conferred on Congress no additional power whatsoever—that it was merely a summary or general description of the specific powers. Under this view, the clause simply gives to Congress the power to tax and spend to carry out its enumerated powers, which follow immediately afterwards. This interpretation was also rejected by the Court in *Butler.*

A third view was offered by Alexander *Hamilton in his 1792 *Report on Manufactures.* Hamilton argued that the Taxing and Spending Clause conferred on Congress a separate and distinct power and was therefore in addition to, and not limited by, other grants of power under the Constitution. Such a view gives Congress the substantive power to tax and spend for the general welfare over and above its power to tax and spend to carry out its other enumerated powers.

In the *Butler* case the Supreme Court accepted Hamilton's position. But Justice Owen *Roberts made it clear that "the powers of taxation and appropriation extend only to matters of national, as distinguished from local, welfare" (p. 67), and that, in the final analysis, the Supreme Court has the power to determine what constitutes the national welfare. Whether the federal program at issue in *Butler* did or did not serve the general welfare, however, was never decided, because the Court struck down the statute on *Tenth Amendment grounds.

Less than a year later, however, the Court abandoned *Butler*. In *Helvering* v. *Davis* (1937), it held that although Congress's power to tax and spend was limited by the General Welfare Clause, "discretion belongs to Congress, unless the choice is clearly wrong, a display of arbitrary power" (p. 640). No Taxing and Spending Clause statute has ever been invalidated because it did not serve the general welfare, and none is likely to be.

The spending power has raised other constitutional issues as well. Congress is reasonably free to place "noncoercive" restrictions on its expenditures of funds, including requirements that recipients of federal moneys act or refrain from acting in certain ways. This is true whether the recipient is a state government (as, for example, in *South Dakota* v. *Dole*, 1987, which required the states to adopt a minimum drinking age of twenty-one years or forfeit a small portion of their federal highway funds) or a private individual. Congress's power to spend is also limited, of course, by various provisions of the *Bill of Rights.

The taxing aspects of the clause have also produced controversy. Prior to the adoption of the *Sixteenth Amendment, Congress was required to "apportion" all direct taxes (head taxes, for example). Excises, however, need only be "uniform," which, the Supreme Court decided in 1900, required only geographic uniformity (*Knowlton* v. *Moore*). Thus there was an advantage to having certain taxes classified as excises, in which case they would not be considered direct taxes. The Sixteenth Amendment, in 1913, ended most of this controversy. It granted Congress the power to levy taxes on incomes "from whatever source derived" and "without apportionment."

The Taxing Clause, like the Spending Clause, gives Congress a separate power in addition to its other powers. If a tax were for regulatory as opposed to revenue purposes, however, it is possible that it would not be justified under the taxing power and would have to be justified under some other congressional power, such as the *commerce power. Since the *New Deal, however, the Court has interpreted the taxing power generously, and, in any event, its recent broad view of congressional power under the Commerce Clause makes the distinctions at this point purely academic.　　William Lasser

**Taylor v. Louisiana,** 419 U.S. 522 (1975), argued 16 Oct. 1974, decided 21 Jan. 1975 by vote of 8 to 1; White for the Court, Burger concurring, Rehnquist in dissent. *Taylor* was brought by a man charged with rape who had argued unsuccessfully in the Louisiana state courts that its "volunteers only" jury service provision violated his *Sixth Amendment right to a jury drawn from a representative cross-section of the community. In *Hoyt* v. *Florida* (1961) the Supreme Court had upheld the conviction of a female defendant who had argued that a similar Florida provision violated her rights to *equal protection of the law and to a trial by a jury of her peers. The Florida registration provision had yielded only ten females in a pool of 9,900 jurors, and none of the women were called for her venire.

In *Taylor*, the Court held, first, that the systematic exclusion of women from jury panels violated any defendant's (male or female) *fundamental right to a jury trial drawn from a representative cross-section of the community and, second, that women as a class cannot be excluded from jury service or given automatic exemptions if the result is that panels are almost all male. Thus, the Court effectively overruled *Hoyt* v. *Florida*, although it was distinguished as not resting on the Sixth Amendment grounds. Four years later, in *Duren* v. *Missouri* (1979), the Court extended *Taylor* to invalidate a Missouri statute that allowed for the exemption of women from jury service, which had produced juries that generally were at least 85 percent male.

(See also GENDER; TRIAL BY JURY.)
　　Karen O'Connor

**Tenth Amendment.** Ratified in 1791 as part of the *Bill of Rights, the Tenth Amendment specifies that "the powers not delegated to the United States by the Constitution, nor prohibited by it to the States, are reserved to the States respectively, or to the people." Of all the amendments demanded by anti-Federalists in the state conventions that ratified the Constitution, one calling for a reserved powers clause was the most common. A number of Federalist spokesmen, including Alexander *Hamilton, James *Madison, and James *Wilson, argued that no such clause was necessary. As Wilson said in a public address delivered in Philadelphia on 7 October 1787, "The congressional authority is . . . from the positive grant expressed in the instrument of union. Hence it is evident, that . . . everything which is not given, is reserved." But fear of central authority was widespread and support for an explicit guarantee that the states should retain control over their internal affairs reached irresistable proportions. Few Federalists thought the amendment would be harmful, and thus it came as no surprise when Madison included a reserved powers clause among the amendment he proposed in 1789.

Discussion of the proposal was brief but significant. Elbridge Gerry of Massachusetts, an erstwhile member of the Philadelphia Convention who had been elected to Congress as an anti-Federalist, led a group in the House of Representatives who sought to add the word "expressly" to the amendment, so as to make it read "powers not expressly delegated." That had been the language of a clause in the defunct Articles of Confederation, and it had prevented the old Congress from carrying into effect the few powers with which it had been entrusted. Remembering that, the House voted down Gerry's proposition by a margin of 32 to 17.

Nonetheless, early in 1791 Thomas *Jefferson invoked the as-yet unratified Tenth Amendment in opposition to an act of Congress and did so as if the word "expressly" were in it. President George *Washington asked Secretary of State Jefferson for his opinion on the constitutionality of a bill to incorporate the Bank of the United States. Jefferson described the Tenth Amendment as "the foundation of the Constitution" and added, "To take a single step beyond the boundaries thus specially drawn . . . is to take possession of a boundless field of power, no longer susceptible of any definition." Jefferson's formulation of this doctrine of "strict construction" was echoed by champions of state sovereignty for many decades.

The opposite, "loose construction" point of view, formulated on the same occasion by Secretary of the Treasury Hamilton, became the model for advocates of extended congressional power; but Hamilton's opinion did not conflict with the substance of the Tenth Amendment. Indeed, he dismissed Jefferson's reference to it as irrelevant: to him the Reserved Powers Clause was tautological, expressing a principle that inheres in any republican government. Since Hamilton specifically rejected any claim that Congress could interfere in the internal affairs of a state—such concerns as the governance of the health, morality, education, and welfare of the people—his stand was not an argument against the Tenth Amendment, but against its necessity.

Early pronouncements on the subject by the Supreme Court adhered to the proposition that the *police power had been reserved exclusively to the states. Even Chief Justice John *Marshall, whose decision upholding the constitutionality of the Second Bank of the United States in *McCulloch v. Maryland (1819) closely reflected the reasoning in Hamilton's 1791 opinion, vehemently denied afterward that he had thereby contributed to "any extension by construction of the powers of Congress" and insisted that he had ruled only upon the legitimacy of the "means" of carrying out a power that had been constitutionally delegated. Justice Joseph *Story, despite his ardent nationalism, wrote in his celebrated Commentaries on the Constitution of the United States (1833) that inspection laws and health laws, even when they affected interstate or foreign commerce, were "purely internal" and not subject to congressional regulation. The Court under Chief Justice Roger Brooke *Taney can be said almost to have gone to extremes in its protection of the reserved powers of the states.

Thus, from the presidency of Jefferson to that of Abraham *Lincoln, the consensus was that Jefferson had been right in calling the Tenth Amendment the foundation of the constitutional union. Indeed, at one time or another state governments in all parts of the country defied the authority of the national government. New Englanders threatened secession after the Louisiana Purchase (1803) and again during the War of 1812 and blocked federal action during the Mexican War (1846–1848). Illinois, Ohio, and Wisconsin thwarted federal laws on several occasions. Southern states attempted to prevent the enforcement of federal laws in 1799 and the 1830s, and then in 1860–1861 eleven of them seceded. The relative impotence of the federal government is indicated by the fact that as of 1861 it had only six thousand civilian employees, apart from the thirty thousand in the post office department.

Everything changed—temporarily—during the *Civil War and the *Reconstruction that followed. The powers of the federal government were enormously increased during the war, and though there was considerable shrinkage afterward, the government never returned to its minuscule prewar proportions. More to the point, the Tenth Amendment was virtually suspended for several years after the war, as far as the defeated and discredited southern states were concerned. Through armies of occupation, Congress governed those states directly, and the congressionally created Freedmen's Bureaus exercised the full range of police powers in regard to the former slaves. Of greater long-range significance, the *Fourteenth Amendment opened the door for congressional action in areas that would earlier have been regarded as reserved to the states.

But the constitutional revolution was transitory. In 1883 the Supreme Court, having already limited the Fourteenth Amendment's protections of the rights of freedmen, declared the Civil Rights Act of 1875 unconstitutional on the ground that is was "repugnant to the Tenth Amendment" (*Civil Rights Cases, p. 15). During the next generation the Court did strike down a number of state exercises of the police power—in keeping with the Tenth Amendment's "prohibited by it to the states" clause—yet it never once allowed Congress to exercise a *police power itself.

Erosion of the Tenth Amendment began early in the twentieth century. In 1895 Congress passed an act forbidding the shipment of lottery tickets in interstate commerce. The purpose was only nominally a regulation of commerce: its real purpose was to restrict gambling, a matter that had always been the exclusive domain of the states. In *Champion v. Ames* (1903), by a 5-to-4 vote, the Supreme Court upheld the act. The next year the Court in *McCray v. United States* upheld a congressional act imposing a prohibitive excise tax on oleomargarine, which amounted to an exercise of a police power to protect the health of the citizenry, under the guise of a constitutional exercise of the power to levy taxes for the *"general welfare," as provided in Article I, section 8.

The Supreme Court was not, however, consistent in its rulings, and the justices were sorely, even angrily, divided during the next three decades. The tension, throughout the period, was between the Tenth Amendment on one side and the powers of Congress to regulate interstate commerce and to levy taxes on the other. The most important police power actions justified under the Commerce Clause were the Pure Food and Drug Act (1906), the Meat Inspection Acts (1906 and 1907), and the White Slave Traffic Act (1910); the Supreme Court upheld all of these, even though it had ruled in *Keller v. United States* (1909) that an act protecting alien women from immoral trafficking was an unconstitutional violation of the Tenth Amendment. The most important police power actions justified under the taxing power were the Phosphorous Match Act (1912) and the Harrison Anti-Narcotics Act (1914), both of which were approved by the Supreme Court despite arguments that they violated the Tenth Amendment.

Then in 1918 the Court dropped a bombshell. Congress, in keeping with the reform spirit of the times and with recent Court decisions, had in 1916 passed an act prohibiting the shipment in interstate commerce of the products of mines or factories that employed children under the age of fourteen. Two years later, in *Hammer v. Dagenhart*, the Court ruled that the act was unconstitutional. In the majority opinion, Justice William R. *Day inserted the word "expressly" into the Tenth: "It must never be forgotten that the nation is made up of states, to which are entrusted the powers of local government. And to them and to the people the powers not expressly delegated to the national government are reserved" (p. 275). The next year the Court did uphold a prohibitive tax on the use of narcotics, but in *Bailey v. Drexel Furniture Company* (1922) it held unconstitutional a second child labor law based upon the government's taxing power. In sum, the Supreme Court was sending mixed and confused signals to the Congress.

A new complication soon arose. Congress began to vote grants-in-aid to the states for various purposes, ranging from the prevention of forest fires to providing medical care for expectant mothers. In 1923 one such grant was challenged on the ground that it undermined the Tenth Amendment. In *Massachusetts v. Mellon* (1923) the Court rejected the argument, declaring that "the statute imposes no obligation, but simply extends an option which the state is free to accept or reject" (p. 480). Ultimately, and especially from the 1950s onward, grants-in-aid or "revenue sharing" would grow so large as to make the states, in many ways, mere appendages of federal administrative agencies.

In the meantime, the whole subject had come to a head—and the Tenth Amendment was becoming a nullity—in the wake of the Great Depression and *World War II. Between 1934 and 1935 the Supreme Court declared unconstitutional a number of emergency economic recovery measures that formed part of Franklin *Roosevelt's *New Deal program. Among the most far-reaching was the National Industrial Recovery Act, which had authorized the president to negotiate with industry to draw up "codes of fair practices" that would have the force of law. Writing for a unanimous Court in *Schechter Poultry Corp. v. United States* (1935), Chief Justice Charles Evans *Hughes gave three reasons for striking down the law, the first being that it flew directly in the face of the Tenth Amendment. However, the composition and direction of the Court changed radically in the face of political attacks, and soon a majority of the justices were Roosevelt appointees. That was the end for the Tenth Amendment. In *Mulford v. Smith* (1939) the Court completely rejected the Tenth Amendment opinions it had laid down in the child labor cases. In United States v. *Darby (1941), Chief Justice Harlan Fiske *Stone reduced the amendment to rubble, describing it as merely declaratory of intergovernmental relationships and as having no substantive meaning.

Only in one major case since then has the Court seriously invoked the Tenth Amendment. In *National League of Cities v. Usery (1976), it held that application of the Fair Labor Standards Act to state and local government employees was a violation of the amendment. That decision opened so many problems, however, that the Court found it expedient to reverse itself explicitly in *Garcia v. San Antonio Metropolitan Transit Authority (1985). And yet, inasmuch as the states continue to exist as distinct political and legal entities and the Tenth Amendment remains a part of the Constitution, the tensions arising from dual and divided sovereignty remain.

(See also DUAL FEDERALISM; FEDERALISM; STATE SOVEREIGNTY AND STATES' RIGHTS.)

□ Raoul Berger, *Federalism: The Founders' Design* (1987). E. S. Corwin, *The Commerce Power Versus States Rights* (1936). Charles A. Lofgren, "The Origins of the Tenth Amendment: History, Sovereignty, and the Problem of

Constitutional Intention," in *Constitutional Government in America*, edited by Ronald K. L. Collins (1980), pp. 331–357. Ruth Locke Roettinger, *The Supreme Court and State Police Power* (1957). Forrest McDonald

**Terminiello v. Chicago,** 337 U.S. 1 (1949), argued 1 Feb. 1949, decided 16 May 1949 by vote of 5 to 4; rehearing denied 13 June 1949; Douglas for the Court, Frankfurter, Vinson, Jackson in dissent. While Terminiello, a priest, was addressing a sympathetic audience inside a packed auditorium, a hostile crowd, which denounced him as anti-Semitic and pro-Fascist, gathered outside. Fearing violence, police arrested him for disorderly conduct. The Illinois courts upheld the conviction under the "fighting words" doctrine of *Chaplinsky v. New Hampshire* (1942), but a bare majority of the Supreme Court reversed.

Admittedly deciding the case on a "preliminary question," Justice William O. *Douglas held that the trial judge allowed a conviction upon the mere finding that Terminiello's speech had provoked anger and controversy. This violated the *First Amendment standard requiring evidence of a *clear and present danger of substantial violence and disorder.

All of the dissenters criticized Douglas's opinion for not directly confronting the constitutional status of emotionally charged political expression. Chief Justice Fred *Vinson argued that use of "fighting words" in the proximity of a hostile audience could certainly sustain a conviction. In his lengthy dissent, Justice Robert H. *Jackson emphasized that the explosive context of the case, a crowded auditorium of sympathizers and a group of angry protestors outside, made Terminiello's speech akin to the deliberate incitement of violence.

*Terminiello* remains a classic example of the difficulties of applying abstract First Amendment values to situations in which speakers run some risk of inflaming an unfriendly audience.

(See also SPEECH AND THE PRESS.)

Norman L. Rosenberg

**Terms.** The time during which the Supreme Court is in session is referred to as a *term* of the Court. The *Judiciary Act of 1789 stipulated terms commencing on the first Mondays in February and August, thereby enabling the justices to undertake *circuit riding in temperate spring and autumn weather. Political strife over the scope of federal judicial power caused the 1802 repeal of the *Judiciary Act of 1801, which, in freeing the justices from circuit duties, had fixed terms beginning on the first Mondays in June and December. To forestall constitutional challenges to the 1802 act, Congress reestablished only the former February term, enforcing a recess from December 1801 to February 1803.

Subsequent term changes responded to rising case backlogs. To avoid interference with spring circuit-riding as sitting days increased, Congress

in 1826 advanced the opening day to the second Monday in January and in 1844 to the first Monday in December. Empowered by an 1866 statute to hold special terms, the Court expanded its sitting time by convening in October. Congress in 1873 formally set the first day for the second Monday in October. In 1917 Congress advanced term time to the *first Monday in October because of continued docket congestion.

Infrequent special terms vanished when the Court began holding continuous terms in 1979, a practice formalized by rule in 1989. Cases heard in special terms included *Ex parte *Quirin* (1942), *Rosenberg v. United States* (1953), *Cooper v. Aaron* (1958), and *O'Brien v. Brown* (1972).

Peter G. Fish

**Territories and New States.** Article IV, section 3 of the Constitution empowered Congress to make appropriate "Rules and Regulations" for federal territory and provided that new states "may be admitted by the Congress into this Union." The permissive character of the latter clause was the source of considerable controversy: despite the promises of the *Northwest Ordinance (1787), Congress was apparently under no constitutional obligation to create new states. Advocates of territorial rights resisted this implication, insisting that Congress governed the territories as trustee for the future new states. In *American Insurance Co. v. Canter* (1828), the Supreme Court sought to avoid such issues, however, and deferred to Congress's "general right of sovereignty" over the territories (p. 545).

Until the *Civil War, debate over the status of slavery in the territories tended to subvert congressional authority. Efforts by antislavery congressmen to block Missouri's admission as a slave state (1819–1820) precipitated the first great intersectional crisis. The resulting Missouri Compromise preserved the sectional balance in the Senate by linking Missouri's admission as a slave state to that of Maine as a free state. By excluding slavery in federal territory above 36° 30', the compromise was meant to preempt controversy over the status of subsequent new states. But the annexation of extensive territory south of the compromise line as a result of the Mexican War (1846–1848) jeopardized this tenuous intersectional accord. In July 1848 the Senate adopted the Clayton Compromise, inviting the Supreme Court to decide the status of slavery in California and New Mexico on appeal from territorial courts. Although the House rejected the Clayton formula at this time, Congress's unwillingness to take responsibility for the slavery issue was apparent in its reliance on "popular sovereignty" in organizing territorial governments for Utah and New Mexico in 1850 and Kansas and Nebraska in 1854. By repealing the Missouri Compromise and establishing the principle of congressional nonintervention, the Kansas-Nebraska Act invited the Supreme Court to take a decisive role in determining the future of slavery in the territories. In *Dred *Scott v. Sandford* (1857), Chief Justice Roger B. *Taney declared the Missouri Compromise unconstitutional and guaranteed slave "property" throughout the territories.

Taney's challenge to congressional authority ran counter to the long-term development of the territorial system. The crucial mechanism for extending the union was the congressional enabling act, authorizing a state constitutional convention and setting forth terms of admission. The subsequent negotiations over conditions of admission were "political" transactions, the Court affirmed, and therefore beyond its purview (*Scott v. Jones*, 1847). The most important conditions were designed to protect federal property interests. Although the public-land states resented a continuing federal presence after statehood, generous land grants and the rapid distribution of federal lands muted complaints about their supposedly unequal condition. Of course, all states were interested in preserving the principle of state equality, and this was the most significant limitation on congressional authority over new state creation.

After the Civil War the Supreme Court significantly expanded its authority over territorial government and the process of new state formation. The principle of new state equality finally achieved constitutional standing in 1911 when, in *Coyle v. Smith*, the Court overturned a condition in the congressional enabling act prohibiting the new state of Oklahoma from moving its capital city before 1913.

Over the course of the nineteenth century citizens of the territories gained the full range of constitutional guarantees, thus effectively limiting congressional "sovereignty." At the same time, Congress relaxed its control over territorial politics and extended the scope of self-government; the Wisconsin organic act (1836) replaced the Northwest Ordinance as the basic model for congressional rule.

The growth of federal power made possible the recognition of territorial rights and limitations on congressional authority. Significantly, however, the Constitution did not necessarily follow the flag to new overseas territories, and even "incorporated" territories that could claim the full range of constitutional rights could not look forward to statehood and membership in the union (*Insular Cases*, 1901–1904).

(See also POLITICAL QUESTIONS.)

□ Peter S. Onuf, "Territories and Statehood," in *Encyclopedia of American Political History*, edited by Jack P. Greene, vol. 3 (1984), pp. 1283–1304.

Peter S. Onuf

**Terry, David Smith** (b. Todd County, Ky., 8 Mar. 1823; d. Lathrop, Calif., 13 Aug. 1889), lawyer, jurist. David Smith Terry, a Texas lawyer and justice of the California Supreme Court, was a political opportunist with a violent history. Raised on the Texas frontier, Terry had numerous scrapes with the law. Elected to the California court in 1855 and serving as its chief justice, 1857–1859, Terry exhibited religious toleration, but was generally unsympathetic to aliens and minorities. In 1879 he was elected to the California Constitutional Convention. Exhibiting characteristic personal violence, Terry died assaulting Associate Justice Stephen J. *Field.

Gordon Morris Bakken

**Terry v. Adams,** 345 U.S. 461 (1953), argued 16 Jan. 1953, decided 4 May 1953 by vote of 8 to 1; Black announced the judgment for the Court, Minton in dissent. This was the last of the so-called *white primary cases. Beginning in 1889 in Fort Bend County, Texas, the Jaybird Democratic Association, or Jaybird party, held an unofficial primary election to select candidates for county offices. These candidates entered the Democratic party primary and were invariably nominated and then elected in a usually uncontested general election. White voters automatically became members; blacks were excluded. This "self-governing, voluntary, club" thus was purposefully organized to disfranchise blacks and circumvent the *Fifteenth Amendment (p. 463).

There was no majority opinion. Justice Hugo *Black said that the state could not countenance the exclusion of blacks from the only election that mattered. Justice Felix *Frankfurter emphasized the participation of state election officials in the discrimination. Justice Tom *Clark maintained that the Jaybird party was an auxiliary of the state-regulated Democratic party. Eight justices seemed to agree that the Jaybird party was performing a public function and was therefore violating the Fifteenth Amendment. Only Justice Sherman *Minton dissented, saying that the Jaybird party constitutionally was nothing more than another "pressure group" (p. 494).

Besides marking the last hurrah of the southern white primary, this decision provided a precedent for Congressional proscription of private racial discrimination under the Fifteenth Amendment in later federal legislation such as the *Voting Rights Act of 1965.

(See also RACE AND RACISM.)

Thomas E. Baker

**Terry v. Ohio,** 392 U.S. 1 (1968), argued 12 Dec. 1967, decided 10 June 1968 by vote of 8 to 1; Warren for the Court, Harlan, Black, and White concurring, Douglas in dissent. For years police have engaged in an investigative practice commonly referred to as *stop and frisk, involving the stopping of a suspicious person or vehicle for purposes of interrogation or other brief investigation, sometimes accompanied by a patting down of the clothing of the suspect to ensure that the person was not armed. *Terry* was the first in a now-substantial line of Supreme Court cases recognizing stop and frisk as a valid practice.

In *Terry*, a policeman became suspicious of two men when one of them walked up the street, peered into a store, walked on, started back, looked into the same store, and then conferred with his companion. The other suspect repeated this ritual, and between them the two men went through this performance about a dozen times before following a third man up the street. The officer, thinking they were "casing" a stickup and might be armed, confronted the men, asked their names and patted them down, thereby discovering pistols on Terry and his companion. In affirming Terry's conviction for carrying a concealed weapon, the Supreme Court concluded that "where a police officer observes unusual conduct which leads him reasonably to conclude in light of his experience that criminal activity may be afoot and that the person with whom he is dealing may be armed and presently dangerous, where in the course of investigating this behavior he identifies himself as a policeman and makes reasonable inquiries, . . . he is entitled for the protection of himself and others in the area to conduct a carefully limited search of the outer clothing of such persons in an attempt to discover weapons which might be used to assault him" (p. 30).

This rather cautious holding fell short of resolving all the important legal issues surrounding this practice; many were ultimately answered in subsequent decisions. But *Terry* did settle two fundamental points: stop and frisk neither falls outside the *Fourth Amendment nor is subject to the usual Fourth Amendment restraints. In rejecting "the notions that the Fourth Amendment does not come into play at all as a limitation upon police conduct if the officers stop short of something called a 'technical arrest' or a 'full-blown search' " (p. 19), the Court wisely concluded that the protections of the Fourth Amendment are not subject to verbal manipulation. It is the reasonableness of the officer's conduct, not what the state chooses to call it, that counts.

In concluding that a stop and frisk does not require *probable cause, the Court in *Terry* explained that because the policeman had acted without a warrant his conduct was not to be judged by the Fourth Amendment's Warrant Clause (which contains an express "probable cause" requirement) but rather "by the Fourth Amendment's general proscription against unreasonable searches and seizures" (p. 20). Dissenting Justice William O. *Douglas objected that the majority had held, contrary to earlier rulings of the Court, "that the police have greater authority to make a 'seizure' and conduct a 'search' than a judge has to authorize such action" (p. 36). Douglas was correct in this, but his point casts into question only some of the reasoning in *Terry*, not the result.

The *Terry* result is grounded in the balancing test of *Camara* v. *Municipal Court* (1967), which the Court quoted and specifically relied upon. *Camara*, which concerned the grounds needed to obtain a warrant to conduct a housing inspection, quite clearly involved the Warrant Clause of the Fourth Amendment and its probable cause requirement. Yet the Court adopted a significantly lower probable cause standard for such warrants than is typically required to satisfy the Fourth Amendment, and it did so by "balancing the need to search against the invasion which the search entails" (p. 537). It thus makes sense to view *Terry* as a case in which probable cause is required, albeit a lesser quantum of probable cause than is ordinarily needed to justify Fourth Amendment activity because the intrusion into *privacy and freedom is quite limited and the law enforcement interest being served is substantial.

Under the search part of the *Terry* doctrine, policy may pat down the detained suspect on reasonable suspicion that the suspect is armed and may then remove any object from the suspect's clothing that by its size or density might be a weapon. An object so discovered is admissible in evidence whether it turns out to be a gun or something else seizable as contraband or evidence; in *Michigan* v. *Long* (1983), the Court rejected the notion that to ensure against pretext frisks only weapons should be admissible. (*Long* also holds, by rather strained logic, that the protective search allowed by *Terry* may extend to the passenger compartment of a vehicle to which the suspect has access.)

□ George E. Dix, "Nonarrest Investigatory Detention in Search and Seizure Law," *Duke Law Journal* 85 (1985): 849–959.                                    Wayne R. LaFave

**Test Cases.** A test case has usually been thought of as one in which an individual, but more likely an interest group, initiates a case in order to challenge the constitutionality, or perhaps a particular disliked intepretation, of a statute. There are other situations that, although somewhat different from this traditional sense of "test case," can also be loosely called "test case." Some people challenge laws, not necessarily with the thought of "going to the Supreme Court," but simply because the laws are thought improper, but their cases end up in the Supreme Court; examples are provided by civil rights demonstrators who sat in at restaurants in the South in the 1950s and 1960s. Their convictions on a variety of misdemeanor charges provided convenient opportunities for the federal courts to speak out against racial discrimination. Others might specifically provoke arrest under a statute, with the intention that the case reach the high court, as occurred after Congress in 1989 passed a statute against flag burning. In still other situations, when individuals run afoul of a law they did not specifically seek to break, a lawyer taking their case may challenge the statute's validity rather than try to avoid a conviction.

The examples just noted are relatively recent civil liberties or civil rights situations. Instances of test cases are also found in economic regulation: many challenges to *New Deal regulatory legislation were intentionally brought by businesses, their trade associations, or conservative interest groups like the Liberty Lobby. Test cases can be found much earlier as well. One example is the famous *"separate but equal" case, *Plessy v. Ferguson (1896), which resulted from a concerted effort by some lawyers, joined by railroads, to invalidate Jim Crow statutes; another was an effort by conservatives to challenge the federal income tax through action masked in a collusive suit, *Pollock v. Farmers' Loan and Trust Company (1895).

Interest groups engaging in litigation are now more likely to undertake immediate focused challenges to objectionable laws almost before the ink is dry, rather than waiting for individual cases to arise when the laws are implemented and someone is adversely affected by them.

There are several reasons for frequent contemporary use of test cases. The Supreme Court has broadened access to the courts by those seeking to challenge laws. Judges are also more willing to entertain actions for *declaratory judgments, that is, declarations of a party's rights before the person is charged with violation of a law; to entertain attacks on a statute "on its face," that is, on the statute as written, not as applied; to issue *injunctions against enforcement of a law; and to grant summary judgments, that is, to rule on the basis of affidavits rather than waiting until extensive testimony has been taken about contested facts. As a result, few new controversial statutes last long before being tested.

Test cases serve to move political issues quickly into a legal setting and to accelerate their arrival at the Supreme Court. Because the Supreme Court is a major political actor likely to confront any major current controversy in due course, test cases are to be expected and are consonant with this view of the Court's role. However, some test cases leave the justices without the benefit of seeing how a statute is applied and, however it may appear "on its face," whether it might have been applied in a constitutional manner. To the extent our adversary legal system is associated with cases heavily anchored in particular facts, the greater use of facial statutory challenges is a departure from that tradition. The Court itself could make it harder to bring test cases lacking a thorough factual development. One way would be to alter rulings on procedure, as the Burger Court did by tightening rules on access to the courts, for example, limiting who had *standing to challenge *zoning rules (Warth v. Selden, 1975). Another would be simply not to grant review in cases where a thorough factual record had not been developed.                         Stephen L. Wasby

**Test Oaths.** Coercive and exclusionary test oaths commonly require foreswearing *past* associates, conduct, or beliefs, but mandatory commitments about *future* behavior, such as the Mayflower Compact and the *Declaration of Independence, have also served informally as the basis for test oaths. The Articles of Confederation left anti-Tory exclusionary oaths to the states. Skeptical about oaths, the Constitution's framers forbade religious tests for office but, seeking unity, specified an oath for the president (Art. II, sec. 1) and required all federal and state officers to swear an unspecified oath to support the new Constitution (Art. VI). In the 1832–1833 *nullification controversy, South Carolina obliged its officials to swear primary loyalty to the state, not the nation.

Test oaths proliferated during the *Civil War and *Reconstruction. Initially, the Union used oaths to identify security risks. An 1861 statute required an oath of future loyalty from federal officials. Then, the 1862 "ironclad test oath" act demanded past loyalty, and in 1865 Congress extended it to lawyers in federal courts, contractors, and pensioners. With approval from Abraham *Lincoln and most congressmen, the Union army applied this form in the occupied South to would-be officials and licensed professionals—a policy that was capable of wholly redefining civil leadership. In 1865–1866 President Andrew Johnson ignored the 1862 act. The Supreme Court's 1867 decisions in Ex parte Garland and *Cummings v. Missouri blunted the oaths' potential to broaden access to political and professional leadership by blacks and Unionist whites. The Court's majority denounced the federal and Missouri oaths as *ex post facto laws and bills of *attainder prohibited by Article I, section 9, as substantive denials of *property rights in professions, and as infringements on the president's *pardoning power. Arguing that loyalty was a legitimate requirement for office, the dissenting justices insisted that pardons did not erase guilt and that the majority was aggrandizing judicial power by voiding the Missouri constitution's oath requirement. Military Reconstruction failed to deny ex-rebels political and professional dominance, in part because of the Test Oath decisions.

*World War I inspired few official oaths but many concerns about the loyalty of "hyphenated Americans" and labor unionists. During the war and the ensuing first "red scare," test-oath requirements infused federal naturalization proceedings for aliens (upheld in United States v. Schwimmer, 1929) and states' professional licensing procedures and *criminal syndicalist laws. During *World War II, President Franklin D. *Roosevelt concluded that security was weakened by numerous, local, unaccountable loyalty-enforcers. Except for the Japanese-American relocations, few excesses marred the homefront. This resulted in part because private groups such as the *American Civil Liberties Union monitored abuses of the *Bill of Rights and in part because the Court's decisions on flag-salute laws (*West Virginia Board of Education* v. *Barnette*, 1943), on denaturalizing pro-Nazi citizens (*Baumgartner* v. *United States*, 1944), and on implementing the 1917 *Espionage* Act (*Hartzel* v. *United States*, 1944), gave new meaning to some Bill of Rights guarantees.

The cold war's red scare eroded these gains (see COMMUNISM AND COLD WAR). Federal and state legislative investigations, as well as private "superpatriots," exaggerated security threats posed by the few communists in government, classrooms, and unions. Public employees (especially teachers) and labor union officers were faced with having to sign disclaimers stating that they were not communists. The Supreme Court, while condemning congressional excesses in *United States* v. *Lovett* (1946), sustained loyalty policies in *Wieman* v. *Updegraff* (1952). But the Warren Court forced security policies to conform to Bill of Rights standards. In *Pennsylvania* v. *Nelson* (1956), the Court reaffirmed federal primacy in loyalty matters, thereby invalidating criminal statutes in more than forty states. The Court in *United States* v. *Brown* (1965), *Keyishian* v. *Board of Regents* (1967), and *Brandenburg* v. *Ohio* (1969), held state loyalty statutes to the bills of *attainder and so vague as to violate the *First Amendment, thus defending Americans' liberty more effectively than had the 1867 Test Oath decisions.

Neither the post–World War II "Second Reconstruction" in race relations nor the *Vietnam War resurrected claims that test oaths are essential to America's internal or external security. As the 1990s open, a diminished cold war makes revival of test oaths unlikely but, as suggested by history and by revived proposals for a constitutional amendment to punish flag desecrations, not impossible.

□ Harold M. Hyman, *To Try Men's Souls: Loyalty Tests in American History* (1959).          Harold M. Hyman

**Texas and Pacific Railway Co. v. United States.**
See SHREVEPORT RATE CASES.

**Texas v. Johnson,** 491 U.S. 397 (1989), argued 21 Mar. 1989, decided 21 June 1989 by vote of 5 to 4; Brennan for the Court, Rehnquist, White, O'Connor, and Stevens in dissent. In *Texas* v. *Johnson* a majority of the Supreme Court considered for the first time whether the *First Amendment protects desecration of the United States flag as a form of symbolic speech. A sharply divided Court had previously dealt with symbolic speech cases that involved alleged misuses of the flag. While the Court had ruled in favor of the defendants in those cases (*Street* v. *New York*, 1969; *Smith* v. *Goguen*, 1974; *Spence* v. *Washington*, 1974), it had done so on narrow grounds, refusing to confront the ultimate question of the constitutional status of flag desecration.

Johnson had burned a flag in front of a building while protesting policies of the administration of President Ronald *Reagan during the 1984 Republican national convention in Dallas. Johnson's act seriously offended several onlookers. He was arrested for violating a Texas statute that made it a crime to intentionally or knowingly desecrate a state or national flag. He was convicted and sentenced to a year in prison and a fine of two thousand dollars. The Texas Court of Criminal Appeals reversed, holding that Johnson's actions were symbolic speech protected by the First Amendment.

Texas asserted two justifications for Johnson's conviction: preventing breaches of the peace triggered by the offense that desecration inflicts and preserving the integrity of the flag as a symbol of national unity. In order to assess the validity of these claims, Justice William J. *Brennan had to weigh them against the First Amendment values at stake. Because government has more license to prohibit harmful "conduct" than harmful "speech," the Court first had to decide whether Johnson's desecration was "conduct" or "speech." Brennan ruled that the desecration was "expressive conduct" because it was an attempt to "convey a particularized message" (p. 404).

But First Amendment doctrine also grants the government more power to regulate "expressive conduct" than "pure expression" because, as the Court said in the draft-card burning case *United States* v. *O'Brien* (1968), where " 'speech' and 'nonspeech' elements are combined in the same course of conduct, a sufficiently important governmental interest in regulating the nonspeech element can justify incidental limitations of First Amendment freedoms (p. 376). Texas claimed that Johnson's flag burning was a harmful nonspeech element and that he could have made his criticisms of America without resorting to desecration. The state, however, may not use such "incidental" regulation as a pretext for restricting speech because of its controversial content or because it simply causes offense. If the law is ultimately directed at the content of speech itself, it must pass the most stringent First Amendment standards (*Boos* v. *Barry*, 1988, p. 321). Only speech that incites others to imminent lawless or violent conduct may be subject to abridgment on these grounds (*Brandenburg* v. *Ohio*, 1969).

Applying these standards, Brennan concluded that Texas's conviction of Johnson was impermissible. There was no evidence that Johnson's expression threatened an imminent disturbance of the peace, and the statute's protection of the integrity of the flag as a symbol was improperly directed at the communicative message entailed in flag burning. "If there is a bedrock principle underlying the First Amendment," Brennan wrote, "it is that Government may not prohibit the expression of an idea simply because society finds the idea itself offensive or disagreeable" (p. 414).

The majority's opinion reaffirmed central First Amendment doctrine. Nonetheless, four members of the Court dissented because of the special nature of the flag as a symbol. Chief Justice William *Rehnquist issued a poetic dissent that celebrated the history of the flag in America. The reaction to *Johnson* spilled into the national political arena. Within a few months Congress passed the Flag Protection Act of 1989, which attempted to challenge legislatively the Supreme Court's ruling in *Johnson*. Following *Johnson*, the Supreme Court declared this act unconstitutional in *United States* v. *Eichman* (1990).

(See also SPEECH AND THE PRESS; SYMBOLIC SPEECH.)

Donald A. Downs

**Texas v. White,** 74 U.S. 700 (1869), argued 5, 8, and 9 Feb. 1869, decided 12 Apr. 1869 by vote of 5 to 3; Chase for the Court, Grier in dissent. Following the *Civil War, the presidentially reconstructed government of Texas brought suit to recover state-owned securities that had been sold by the state's Confederate government. Defendants argued that Texas, which had seceded and had not yet been restored to the Union, was not a state and therefore could not sue in federal courts. Hence the case presented fundamental questions concerning secession, *Reconstruction, and the nature of the Union.

Asserting that the Constitution created "an indestructible Union, composed of indestructible States" (p. 725), Chief Justice Salmon P. *Chase held that secession was illegal and that Texas had never left the Union. He admitted that participation in the rebellion had left the state without a lawful government and had suspended its rights as a member of the Union. Consequently, under the *Guarantee Clause, Congress had authority to reestablish state government. Although Texas had not been restored to its normal position in the Union, Chase noted that Congress had recognized the presidentially reconstructed government as provisional, entitling it to sue in the federal courts. Turning to the merits of the case, Chase ruled that the state's Confederate government had been unlawful, that its acts in support of the rebellion were null and void, and that the state was entitled to recover the securities.

The decision endorsed the Republican position that the Union was perpetual and that Reconstruction was a political problem that lay within the scope of congressional power.

(See also STATE SOVEREIGNTY AND STATES' RIGHTS.)

Donald G. Nieman

**Thayer, James Bradley** (b. Haverhill, Mass., 15 Jan. 1831; d. Cambridge, Mass., 14 Feb. 1902), scholarly authority on constitutional law. After nearly two decades of successful legal practice in Boston, Thayer became a member of the faculty of law at Harvard and one of a quadrumvirate there (the others being Christopher C. Langdell, James Barr Ames, and John Chipman Gray), who created the modern system of legal education known generally as the "case method." Thayer was an authority on the law of evidence and on constitutional law. He is best remembered for his call for *judicial self-restraint in "The Origin and Scope of the American Doctrine of Constitutional Law," published in the *Harvard Law Review* 7 (1893), which was one of the first scholarly reconsiderations of *judicial review.

William M. Wiecek

**Third Amendment.** The Constitution's Third Amendment, which forbids nonconsensual quartering of soldiers in private homes during peacetime, lies almost forgotten among the *Bill of Rights. It has been neither the source of much judicial concern nor the object of extensive academic or political controversy. Yet its subject was of great importance to the framers of the Constitution, and it has recently received a modest new lease on life as one of the foundations of the modern constitutional right to *privacy.

The English Bill of Rights of 1689, the result of the seventeenth-century struggle against Stuart authoritarianism, listed the forced quartering of troops among the worst abuses committed by King James II. The increased British military presence prior to and during the American Revolution revived these fears, and contributed to the view of American colonists that they were being deprived of the traditional rights of Englishmen. This sense of deprivation led to the ratification of the Third Amendment in 1791.

The Supreme Court has never decided a case dealing directly with the issue of forced quartering of troops, although the Court of Appeals for the Second Circuit in *Engblom* v. *Carey* (1982) did hold that the Third Amendment applied to the National Guard while on state duty. The Amendment remains one of the few provisions of the Bill of Rights that the Supreme Court has not incorporated into the *Fourteenth Amendment and thus made directly applicable to the states (see INCORPORATION DOCTRINE). The philosophy of the amendment was an important component of Justice William O. *Douglas's opinion in *Griswold* v. *Connecticut* (1965) that a constitutional right of privacy could be constructed from the commitment to personal autonomy found in the penumbras of the Bill of Rights.

Robert J. Cottrol

**Thirteenth Amendment.** Slavery in the United States was abolished by the Thirteenth Amendment. Its adoption was made possible by the confluence of a variety of forces. One necessary element was the precipitate decline of slave-state influence in Congress. The secession of most slave states in 1860 gave the free states almost complete control of the Union government. In the early 1860s, most members of Congress from the loyal states belonged to either the Republican or Union party, whose policies were influenced by the antislavery movement.

A second critical factor was the *Civil War's impact on the American concept of *federalism. Before 1861, the belief in states' rights sharply limited the potential scope of federal action on *slavery; only the most radical abolitionists advocated removing the authority of each state over slavery within its borders. Although idea of states' rights remained a strong ideological influence even after the Civil War, by the end of the war Republicans were more receptive to an expanded federal role.

Nonetheless, Congressional approval of the amendment in 1865 came only after a protracted political struggle. Although the amendment passed easily in the Senate in 1864, during the Thirty-eighth Congress Republicans lacked the required two-thirds majority in the House of Representatives. When the House first considered the amendment in 1864, proponents were unable to attract the necessary Democratic votes. The Republican victory in the elections of 1864 changed the political dynamic, however. After that election, an intensive lobbying effort by the White House changed enough Democratic votes to allow the amendment to pass the House on reconsideration in 1865. In the same year, the Thirteenth Amendment became part of the Constitution after approval by the requisite number of state legislatures. Some of the ratifications came under duress; Congressional Republicans made clear to the legislatures of the ex-Confederate states that ratification was necessary before readmission to full participation in the Union (see CONSTITUTIONAL AMENDING PROCESS).

Section 1 of the amendment specifically prohibits slavery and involuntary servitude, except as a punishment for crime. Section 2 grants Congress the authority to enforce the provisions of section 1. Even under the narrowest possible interpretation, the adoption of the Thirteenth Amendment was a major change in the American political structure. For the first time, federal law imposed a significant constraint on the power of the states to define the status of their own residents.

The precise scope of the change intended by the drafters was a matter of some debate during the *Reconstruction era and continues to be an issue on which scholars differ. Some contend that the drafters intended only to dissolve the master-slave relationship per se, leaving all other state prerogatives untouched. Others argue for a broader reading, asserting that section 1 constitutionalizes an open-ended, evolving concept of freedom or, at the very least, that section 2 grants Congress the authority to prescribe and protect the rights that differentiate a slave from a free person.

The Supreme Court's decision in the *Civil Rights Cases (1883) suggested that section 2 gave Congress the authority to outlaw "badges and incidents" of slavery as well as the institution itself. At the same time, however, the Court defined badges and incidents quite narrowly, holding that the Thirteenth Amendment gave Congress no power to reach private action generally (United States v. Harris, 1883) or to prohibit racial discrimination in public accomodations (Civil Rights Cases). Thus it is not surprising that for much of the twentieth century civil rights litigation focused almost entirely on section 1 of the *Fourteenth Amendment, which was adopted in 1868.

The Thirteenth Amendment made a dramatic reappearance in *Jones v. Alfred H. Mayer Co. (1968). Jones dealt with the interpretation of a statute that granted to all citizens the same property rights "as [are] enjoyed by white citizens." The question was whether this prohibition—derived from the *Civil Rights Act of 1866—prohibited private racial discrimination and whether Congress had authority to reach private action under the Thirteenth Amendment. The Court held that the statute did prohibit private discrimination, and that section 2 of the amendment granted Congress the necessary authority. Thus the Thirteenth Amendment re-emerged as an important element of contemporary civil rights jurisprudence.

(See also CONSTITUTIONAL AMENDMENTS; STATE SOVEREIGNTY AND STATES' RIGHTS.)

□ Earl M. Maltz, Civil Rights, The Constitution and Congress, 1863–1869 (1990).                    Earl M. Maltz

**Thomas, Clarence** (b. Savannah, Georgia, 23 June 1948), associate justice, 1991–. On 1 July 1991 President George Bush nominated Clarence Thomas to become the 106th justice of the Supreme Court. He assumed office after an unusual confirmation process where senators pursued questions of constitutional interpretation and allegations of sexual harassment by a former aide.

A graduate of Yale Law School, Thomas had extensive experience in the federal government. He served as the assistant secretary of education and the chairman of the Equal Employment Opportunity Commission under President Ronald *Reagan. At the EEOC he took positions at odds with those of established civil rights groups, thus marking him as a prominent black conservative and potential nominee for the Court. In 1990 he was appointed to the District of Columbia Circuit, and after approximately one year there he was selected to replace Justice Thurgood *Marshall.

At Justice Thomas's confirmation hearings senators tried to draw out his views on many controversial issues. He carefully avoided any statement on how he might vote as a justice.

Shortly before the Senate confirmation vote the media reported that during Thomas's back-

*Clarence Thomas*

ground investigation a former employee of his named Anita Hill had accused him of sexual harassment. Thomas's supporters brushed aside the charge as a last ditch effort by opponents. But it became clear that crucial senators would oppose Thomas if the charges were not fully reviewed.

The *Senate Judiciary Committee reconvened, calling Thomas, Hill (a law professor), and a number of other witnesses. Professor Hill detailed her charges of harassment. Justice Thomas denied all the allegations. With the hearings televised and widely reported in the media, the public—as well as the committee—debated the veracity of the charges. The committee, however, made no further recommendation to the Senate. On 15 October 1991, the Senate voted 52 to 48 to confirm Justice Thomas, the smallest margin of approval in more than one hundred years.

With many controversial matters pending, Justice Thomas's first term will provide ample opportunity to gauge his constitutional philosophy. If, as expected, he does solidify the Court's conservative majority, his judicial tenure may eventually overshadow his controversial confirmation. In the near future, however, the Thomas confirmation is likely to trigger debate over the appropriate role for the Senate in exercising its power to advise and consent to judicial nominations. (See also NOMINATIONS, CONTROVERSIAL.)

Nicholas S. Zeppos

**Thompson, Smith** (b. Amenia, N.Y., 17 Jan. 1768; d. Poughkeepsie, N.Y., 19 Dec. 1843; interred Poughkeepsie Rural Cemetery), associate justice,

1823–1843. Thompson was a resident of Dutchess County for most of his life. A 1788 graduate of the College of New Jersey (Princeton), he served his legal apprenticeship with Gilbert Livingston and James Kent. His political views coincided with those of the Antifederalist Livingston, but he received most of his legal education from the conservative Kent. In 1795, Thompson replaced Kent as Livingston's partner and married the latter's daughter, Elisha. Livingston was a relatively poor relation of the "manor" Livingstons but enjoyed sufficient political clout to enable Thompson's appointment to the state supreme court (after a term in the assembly) in 1802. He remained there until 1818, serving as chief justice from 1814 to 1818. Thompson was the candidate of Martin Van Buren's Bucktail faction when President James Monroe sought a New Yorker for secretary of the navy in 1818. Monroe apparently was comfortable with Thompson's political views, and when Justice Brockholst *Livingston died in March 1823, Monroe literally refused to appoint anyone else.

Thompson's twenty years on the Court mark him as a transitional figure between the Marshall and Taney eras. More inclined to express his differences with his brethren than Livingston, Thompson was one of a 4-to-3 majority that forced Chief Justice John *Marshall into his sole constitutional dissent in *Ogden* v. *Saunders* (1827). The case involved a New York insolvency law, which Marshall felt violated the Constitution's *Contract Clause, but which Thompson

*Smith Thompson*

believed was not only part of any contract negotiated but was essential for any commercial society.

Thompson's major role was in interpreting the Commerce Clause (see COMMERCE POWER). Consistent with his position taken on the New York court, and subsequently taken on the Supreme Court, there is no doubt that Thompson would have dissented in *Gibbons* v. *Ogden* (1824), had he sat on the case. Thompson believed that states could regulate commerce unless such acts directly conflicted with congressional laws. For example, in his concurring opinion in *New York* v. *Miln* (1837), Thompson agreed with the result but refused to distinguish a New York tax on immigrants as a valid exercise of *police powers. Thompson's concurrent position contrasted with the exclusive theory of Marshall and Joseph *Story, and later James Moore *Wayne and John *McLean.

Thompson's position on *Native Americans also reflected his New York background, as his dissent in *Cherokee Nation* v. *Georgia* (1831), relied upon his former mentor and colleague, James Kent (see CHEROKEE CASES). Arguably Thompson's finest opinion, his *Cherokee* dissent set forth the concept that Indian tribes are separate sovereigns despite their conquered position.

□ Donald M. Roper, *Mr. Justice Thompson and the Constitution* (1987).                    Donald M. Roper

**Thornberry, William Homer** (b. Austin, Tex., 9 Jan. 1909), federal judge and unconfirmed nominee to the Supreme Court. After a lengthy career in Texas politics, including service in state and local legislatures and eight terms in the U.S. House of Representatives (1949–1963), Thornberry was appointed to the U.S. District Court for the Western District of Texas by President Lyndon Johnson in 1963. Two years later Johnson elevated Thornberry to the Fifth Circuit Court of Appeals. On 26 June 1968, Johnson announced that he would nominate him for the U.S. Supreme Court vacancy that would be created by Johnson's planned elevation of Justice Abe *Fortas to the chief justiceship to replace Earl *Warren. His "nomination" died on 2 October 1968, when President Johnson withdrew Fortas's nomination, eliminating the vacancy that Thornberry would have filled. Although Thornberry was not implicated by the concerns about Fortas's liberal decisions and alleged ethical improprieties, he, like Fortas, was viewed as a Johnson "crony." In his book *Justices and Presidents* (1985), Henry J. Abraham describes Thornberry as "a decent and experienced public servant of moderate ability, but he was hardly of the caliber that would have prompted a basically hostile Senate to overlook political factors" (p. 286). Thornberry continues to serve on the Fifth Circuit Court of Appeals, since 1979 as a senior judge.

(See also NOMINEES, REJECTION OF.)

Susan M. Olson

**Thornburgh v. American College of Obstetricians and Gynecologists,** 476 U.S. 747 (1986), argued 5 Nov. 1985, decided 11 June 1986 by vote of 5 to 4; Blackmun for the Court, Burger, White, and Rehnquist, joined by O'Connor, in dissent. The Court invalidated several Pennsylvania *abortion regulations, including a requirement that women seeking abortions be given detailed information (much like the information required by the ordinance invalidated three years earlier in *Akron* v. *Akron Center for Reproductive Health*, 1983), detailed record-keeping requirements, a requirement that the physician use the technique most likely to protect the fetus in postviability abortions, and a requirement that a second physician be present at such abortions.

As in the law invalidated in *Akron*, the information requirement was viewed as an effort to discourage the woman from having an abortion; furthermore, the Court said, the requirement intruded on the private relationship between the woman and her physician. The record-keeping requirements were invalid because they were too detailed and because they would be available to the public in a way that would make it possible to identify some women who had abortions. The requirements regarding medical care were invalid because they forced the physician to "trade off" the woman's health against that of the fetus and because the statute made no exception to the two-doctor rule for cases in which the woman's life or health would be endangered by waiting for the second doctor to arrive.

The Court expressed impatience at what it regarded as repeated efforts by states to evade the requirements of *Roe* v. *Wade* (1973), and it reasserted the justification for the abortion decision in the face of an argument presented by the *solicitor general that *Roe* should be overruled. Chief Justice Warren *Burger's dissent stated that because *Roe* had come to stand for a requirement that abortions be available on demand, he was prepared to overrule it.

Justice Byron *White's dissent also urged that *Roe* be overruled because it was misguided. His opinion acknowledged that the right to choose an abortion was an aspect of liberty protected by the Due Process Clause of the *Fourteenth Amendment but argued that it, like other liberties not specifically identified in the Constitution, could nonetheless be restricted quite substantially. Because states could permissably regard the interest of the fetus as important, a women's liberty to choose abortion was not fundamental and did not require *strict scrutiny.

*Thornburgh* was to be the last case in which a firm majority of the Court adhered to the reasoning of *Roe* v. *Wade*. The retirement of Justice Lewis *Powell, who had consistently supported *Roe*, and the appointment of Justice Anthony *Kennedy led to a substantial assault on the framework established by *Roe* in *Webster* v. *Reproductive Services* (1989).

(See also DUE PROCESS, SUBSTANTIVE; GENDER; PRIVACY.)

Mark V. Tushnet

**Thornhill v. Alabama,** 310 U.S. 88 (1940), argued 29 Feb. 1940, decided 22 Apr. 1940 by vote of 8 to 1; Murphy for the Court, McReynolds in dissent. *Thornhill* v. *Alabama* explicitly placed peaceful labor picketing under the protection of the Free Speech Clause of the *First Amendment. In an opinion by Justice Frank *Murphy, who had served as governor of Michigan during the 1937 General Motors sit-down strike, the Court struck down an Alabama statute that prohibited all manner of picketing. The Court overturned the statute because it did not regulate specific elements of labor demonstrations, such as the number of pickets, but rather proscribed "every practicable method whereby the facts of a labor dispute may be publicized" (p. 100). Murphy denied, however, that the First Amendment guaranteed an absolute right to picket. The value of picketing lay in its educational function, because public labor demonstrations could inform citizens about economic matters that were "indispensable to the effective and intelligent use of the processes of popular government to shape the destiny of modern industrial society" (p. 103). Thus, the government could properly regulate picketing that interfered with the public's ability to evaluate labor disputes.

*Thornhill* acknowledged that *New Deal reforms had absorbed organized labor into the industrial polity. Protecting labor's freedom of expression served to incorporate the interests of the working class into the formulation of public policy. At the same time, the decision permitted courts to curtail picketing when the activities of picketers went beyond publicizing the issues of a labor dispute. In subsequent cases, the Court specifically invoked the *Thornhill* rationale to limit labor activism that threatened economic production. The *Thornhill* decision, therefore, reflected a balance between the protection of the constitutional rights of workers and the maintenance of economic stability in a changing industrial order.

(See also LABOR; SPEECH AND THE PRESS.)

Eric W. Rise

**Thurlow v. Massachusetts.** See LICENSE CASES.

**Tidelands Oil Controversy.** Until World War II, jurisdiction and control over a three-mile band of "tidelands" adjacent to ocean coasts was exercised by the states and not the federal government. States authorized offshore fishing and imposed limited regulation over other coastal activity. Then in the 1920s and 1930s, California, Louisiana, and Texas offered offshore oil leases and scientists indicated that the oceans might be a major source of oil and gas. State and federal officials saw the potential for revenues from leasing mineral rights to coastal tidelands and began the debate over who should control the resources in these tidelands.

In 1945, President Harry S. Truman issued the Continental Shelf Proclamation, asserting federal jurisdiction over all the mineral resources in the lands beneath the oceans, out to the end of the United States' continental shelf. Immediately after the proclamation, the United States commenced litigation against the states, claiming sovereignty over all offshore resources, including those historically controlled by the states. In *United States* v. *California* (1947) and later cases the Supreme Court held that the federal government had "paramount rights" over the area three miles seaward from the normal low-water mark. States had no title to, nor property interest in, the waters and submerged lands off their coasts. The state-federal "tidelands" dispute became a campaign issue in the presidential election of 1952. Congress passed bills seeking to overrule the Supreme Court and affirm state coastal rights, but Truman vetoed them. As a result of campaign promises made by Dwight Eisenhower, who won the 1952 election, Congress in 1953 enacted the Submerged Lands Act, which gave coastal states title to offshore lands within their historic boundaries and exclusive rights to the resources in those areas. In most cases, this meant the three-mile territorial sea.

Coastal states and the United States continue Supreme Court litigation over claims of historic states' rights to coastal waters beyond three miles (up to three marine leagues or 10.5 miles). In almost all cases such claims were rejected, but as recently as 1986, the Supreme Court was continuing to resolve these claims on a case-by-case basis.

Beginning in the 1970s, the states shifted the issue from control of resources to control of activity. Concerned about federal oil and gas leasing, fishing regulation, and pollution, they sought state control over all federal offshore activities that affected their coasts and coastal waters. They secured funding for management of these zones and a right to policy input.

In December 1988, President Ronald Reagan, following the new international law rule, declared a twelve-mile territorial sea for the United States. But he stated that this new claim only related to U.S. rights against other nations and was not to affect the present state-federal division of jurisdiction. States, opposed by the federal government, are now urging Congress to apply the philosophy of the original Submerged Lands Act, which adopted the territorial sea zone as the basis for state control, and expand their jurisdiction out to twelve miles. The "tidelands controversy" continues.

(See also DUAL FEDERALISM; FEDERALISM.)

Martin H. Belsky

**Time, Inc. v. Hill,** 385 U.S. 374 (1967), argued 27 Apr. 1966, reargued 18–19 Oct. 1966, decided 9

Jan. 1967 by vote of 5 to 4; Brennan for the Court, Black and Douglas concurring, Harlan concurring in part and dissenting in part, Fortas, joined by Warren and Clarke, in dissent. This case concerned a *Life* magazine article describing a Broadway play about the ordeal of a family trapped in their own house by escaped convicts. *Life* claimed that the play described events that had actually happened to the Hill family, which had in fact been held hostage several years before by escaped prisoners. The article was inaccurate in several nondefamatory but nevertheless deeply disturbing respects. Members of the Hill family sued for invasion of *privacy under a New York statute.

The Supreme Court's opinion in *Hill* built upon the 1964 decision of *New York Times Co. v. Sullivan*, in which the Court had held that plaintiffs who were public officials could not recover damages for defamation unless they could demonstrate that the defamation had been published with *actual malice, "that is, with knowledge that it was false or with reckless disregard of whether it was false or not" (pp. 279–280). In *Time, Inc. v. Hill* the Court extended the application of the actual malice rule to actions alleging that a plaintiff's privacy had been invaded by "false reports of matters of public interest" (p. 388). In 1974 the Court held in *Gertz v. Robert I. Welch, Inc.* that private plaintiffs did not have to prove actual malice to recover damages in defamation suits, even if the publication at issue concerned matters of public interest. Since then, the courts have divided over the question of whether *Gertz* put limits on the holding in *Time* or whether defendants in false-light privacy actions should receive greater constitutional protection than defendants in defamation actions.

(See also LIBEL; SPEECH AND THE PRESS.)

Robert C. Post

**Time, Place, and Manner Rule,** a doctrine holding that government may protect society by controlling the harmful incidental effects of *speech so long as such regulation meets certain requirements: first, it must be neutral concerning the content of expression, and, second, it may not even incidentally burden the flow of ideas to a substantial extent. The most important time, place, and manner regulations include licensing schemes controlling the entry and use of public forums; regulations designed to ameliorate the undesirable side-effects of expression, such as noise, litter, obstruction of traffic, and invasions of *privacy; rules governing the conditions under which groups may solicit funds in order to protect the public from fraud or misrepresentation; and *zoning laws that limit access to certain expressive materials.

The doctrine assumes that distinctions can be made between the substantive message of speech and its medium and between outright *censorship and the regulation of speech's incidental manifestations. However, the form and the substance of a message are not always readily separable. Furthermore, governments may deploy ostensibly neutral time, place, and manner regulations as a pretext to inhibit unpopular expression, as in the zoning of pornographic establishments (see OBSCENITY AND PORNOGRAPHY).

The first question the Supreme Court asks in addressing a time, place, and manner dispute is whether the challenged regulation actually is neutral. If it is not, the Court will apply the test of *strict scrutiny and the measure will survive only if it is narrowly tailored ("necessary") to protect a "compelling" state interest. Accordingly, the Court has consistently struck down laws that prohibit demonstrations in neighborhoods or by schools, but provide exceptions for particular groups, such as *labor demonstrators (*Police Department of Chicago v. Mosley*, 1972). But the Court did uphold an ordinance that prohibited all demonstrations targeted at private residences; the ordinance was viewpoint-neutral and specifically tailored to protect the interest in residential privacy (*Frisby v. Schultz*, 1988). The Court has also consistently invalidated licensing and antinoise regulations that are vague or bestow too much discretion on administrative officials, for such laws often have been applied in a discriminatory fashion (*Lakewood v. Plain Dealer Publishing Co.*, 1988).

If a regulation is truly viewpoint-neutral the Court must then balance several additional factors. When the incidental impact on speech is not deemed substantial, the regulation will usually be upheld. Laws that reasonably control noise levels are examples (*Kovacs v. Cooper*, 1949). But when the incidental impact on expression is substantial, the regulation must be "narrowly tailored to serve a significant government interest, and leave open ample alternative channels of communication" (*United States v. Grace*, 1983, p. 177). This approach is applied with special rigor in instances of speech in the "public forum," where *First Amendment interests are high, especially for groups that lack access to other forums of communication. Laws that prohibit methods of communications employed by less-powerful groups (leafleting, anonymous pamphleteering, and soliciting) have foundered on this basis (e.g., *Schneider v. Irvington*, 1939). Antifraud regulations that broadly prohibit solicitation by groups that spend less than a specified percentage of their receipts on charitable purposes have also fallen because they impact too harshly on speech (*Village of Schaumburg v. Citizens for a Better Environment*, 1980).

The case in which the largely Jewish village of Skokie, Illinois, attempted to prevent a Nazi demonstration in 1977 by erecting a complex licensing scheme is a famous example of time, place, and manner doctrine in operation. In ruling in favor of the Nazis' right to demonstrate in Skokie, the Illinois and *lower federal courts had to address most major time, place, and manner issues, including licensing, crowd control, the nature of the public forum, and viewpoint discrimination (*Smith* v. *Collin*, 1978; *Village of Skokie* v. *National Socialist Party of America*, 1978).

In recent years the Supreme Court has given governments more leeway to regulate the "incidental" effects of expression. First, the Court has narrowed its interpretation of what constitutes a public forum, reducing the types of public property subject to the most rigorous First Amendment standards (*Perry Educational Association* v. *Perry Local Educators' Association*, 1983). Second, the Court has been more willing to find significance in the social interests served by restrictive regulations, to minimize their harmful impact on speech interests, and to discern ample alternative channels of communication for affected groups. For example, the Court has allowed extensive zoning of pornographic establishments for these reasons (*City of Renton* v. *Playtime Theatres, Inc.*, 1986). And it upheld Los Angeles' prohibition on placing campaign signs on street lightposts because the posts were not considered public forums and because the measure was deemed to serve a significant social interest in environmental quality (*City Council of Los Angeles* v. *Taxpayers for Vincent*, 1984).

Thus, while the Supreme Court has maintained strong suspicion of regulations that overtly discriminate among viewpoints or otherwise facilitate discrimination through suspect licensing schemes, it has increasingly tolerated regulations that affect expression only incidentally.

□ Donald Alexander Downs, *Nazis in Skokie: Freedom, Community, and the First Amendment* (1985).

Donald A. Downs

## Tinker v. Des Moines Independent Community School District, 393 U.S. 503 (1969),

argued 12 Nov. 1968, decided 24 Feb. 1969 by vote of 7 to 2; Fortas for the Court, Stewart and White concurring, Black and Harlan in dissent. Some Des Moines, Iowa, high school and junior high school students protested the *Vietnam War by wearing black armbands in school. School officials had adopted a policy banning the wearing of armbands two days before the students' action. When the students wore the armbands to school they were sent home and suspended until they returned without them. The students claimed that their *First Amendment rights were violated by the schools' action.

The Court's opinion noted that school officials had comprehensive authority to set rules in the schools but that this had to be done consistent with the First Amendment rights of students and teachers, who did not "shed their constitutional rights to freedom of speech or expression at the schoolhouse gate" (p. 506). Wearing an armband as a silent form of expressing an opinion was,

according to the Court, "akin to pure speech" and involved "primary First Amendment rights" (p. 508).

Two aspects of the Court's opinion are especially significant. First, the expression of the students who wore the armbands caused no disruption and did not, in the Court's opinion, intrude on the work of the school or the rights of other students. Of the eighteen thousand students in the school system, only a few wore the armbands and only five were suspended. A few students made hostile remarks to the students wearing the armbands, but no acts of violence or threats occurred on school premises. The school officials' actions could not, said the Court, be based merely on an undifferentiated fear of a disturbance, for all unpopular views may create some unpleasantness and discomfort. Such is the price we pay for living in an open and often disputatious society.

Second, the Court stressed the fact that school officials had permitted other political symbols to be worn. For example, some students wore political campaign buttons, and others wore the Iron Cross, a symbol of Nazism. But only the black armbands protesting American involvement in Vietnam were singled out. Thus the regulation was directly related to the suppression of a specific view on a given subject, and the Court struck it down as not constitutionally permissible. As the Court put it, "state-operated schools may not be enclaves of totalitarianism," and "students may not be regarded as closed-circuit recipients of only that which the State chooses to communicate" (p. 511).

Justice Hugo *Black, in a notable and bitter dissenting opinion, argued that local officials should be permitted to determine the extent to which freedom of expression should be allowed in their public schools. These officials, Black asserted, knew better than federal judges how to run the schools, and their judgment was also to be preferred to that of the students. Moreover, he disagreed with the majority's finding that there were no disruptions resulting from the students' wearing the armbands. According to Black, there were comments and warnings to the students wearing the armbands, and one mathematics teacher had his lesson period "wrecked" as a result of a dispute with one of the petitioners regarding her armband.

*Tinker* stands as one of the most significant cases dealing with the constitutional rights of public school students. In stating that the classroom should be a "marketplace of ideas," *Tinker* represents the Court's concern over the role school officials play in indoctrinating students. In other cases (such as *Hazelwood School District* v. *Kuhlmeier*, 1988, and *Bethel School District No. 403* v. *Fraser*, 1986), however, the Court has spoken approvingly of value inculcation in the public schools and has noted the central role schools play in, for example, promoting civic virtues. The tension between these two strains of thought has produced a great deal of inconsistency in Supreme Court and lower court rulings concerning claims of constitutional protection by public school students. The Court has given school officials more extensive powers of regulation where curricular matters are involved or where student expression takes place in a school-sponsored setting such as a school newspaper or assembly.

(See also EDUCATION; SPEECH AND THE PRESS.)
Keith C. Miller

**Todd, Thomas** (b. King and Queen County, Va., 23 Jan. 1765; d. 7 Feb. 1826; interred Frankfort Cemetery, Frankfort, Ky.), associate justice, 1807–1826. Thomas Todd, whose ancestor of the same name settled in Norfolk County in 1669, was the youngest of five children of Elizabeth Richards and Robert Todd. His father died when he was eighteen months old; his mother before he reached maturity. After two short enlistments during the War for Independence when he was fourteen and sixteen, Todd graduated from Liberty Hall (later Washington and Lee University). He then lived with his older first cousin, Harry Innes, tutored the Innes children, and studied surveying. When Innes was appointed a judge of the Supreme Court of Judicature for the Kentucky District in 1783, Todd accompanied the family on its emigration to Danville. The two men were among the founding members of the Political Club, a small but influential organization that included the leadership of the commonwealth.

Todd is said to have begun practicing law in 1788 with only a horse, a bridle, and three shillings in his pockets. (He enjoyed breeding horses, but unlike many contemporaries in Kentucky with his education and training, he never acquired a fortune in land.) Meanwhile, he had established a minor career as the official recorder for almost every official body in Kentucky, thus earning the gratitude of generations of historians for his uniquely legible handwriting. He was clerk for all of the ten conventions (1784–1792) called to arrange separation from Virginia; clerk of the federal district court (of which Innes was judge), 1789–1792; clerk of the Kentucky Court of Appeals, 1792–1801; clerk of the Kentucky constitutional conventions in 1792 and 1799; sometime clerk of the House of Representatives; and in 1793–1794, clerk of the Lexington Democratic Society.

Todd also earned a reputation for untangling the conflicting land claims resulting from the complicated Virginia law that the commonwealth inherited. He was appointed a judge of Kentucky's highest court in 1801 and its chief judge in 1806. When a seventh seat was created on the United States Supreme Court in 1807, Todd was the first or second choice of the senators and representatives from Kentucky, Tennessee, and Ohio, the states to be served by the new Seventh

*Thomas Todd*

Circuit Court. After his unanimous confirmation, he received President Thomas *Jefferson's commission in March and took his seat at the February 1808 session.

Todd served on the Supreme Court until 1826, but probably had greater judicial impact through his work on the Seventh Circuit. In Kentucky, for example, where as circuit judge he was Innes's superior until his death in 1816, the court ceased adjudicating cases below the jurisdictional minimum and certified eight cases to the higher court because of disagreement between the judges. Fortunately, the judges' professional differences did not disrupt their close familial relationship, which was reinforced when one of Todd's sons married one of Innes's daughters.

Because of illness, family affairs, and the hardships of traveling to Washington, Todd was absent from half a dozen terms of the Supreme Court. Although he was a Jeffersonian, he accepted Chief Justice John *Marshall's leadership and wrote only fourteen opinions of his own: eleven for the majority (of which ten involved land claims), two concurring opinions, and one in dissent.
Mary K. Bonsteel Tachau

**Tort,** a harmful wrong (other than a breach of contract) for which courts will provide a remedy, usually damages, to a private party. Torts include injuries to persons, such as injuries caused by negligent automobile accidents, medical malpractice, or product defects; injuries to property, such as nuisances and trespasses; and injuires to reputation. Courts allow recovery when a defendant breaches a legal duty to a plaintiff and this breach proximately causes an injury recognized under the law.

Under the federal system, *state courts and legislatures are primarily responsible for developing the law of torts. The Supreme Court sometimes finds that state law conflicts with the Constitution or is preempted by federal statutes. For example, since 1964 the Supreme Court has substantially altered the torts of defamation and invasion of *privacy, holding that state tort law may violate constitutional protections of free *speech. Moreover, the Court has considered several attempts to establish constitutional limits on the award of punitive damages. In another area, the Supreme Court frequently concludes that federal environmental statutes preempt state *common-law actions for nuisance (see ENVIRONMENT).

The Court also applies state tort law in federal cases. For example, state tort law is followed in diversity of citizenship cases and in suits brought against the United States under the *Federal Tort Claims Act.

In a few cases, the Supreme Court finds the creation of a federal tort authorized, expressly or implicitly, by statute or under the Constitution. Civil damage remedies for violations of constitutional rights are recognized both under section 1983 of the *Civil Rights Act of 1964 and under a cause of action implied in the Constitution.

Donald G. Gifford

**Travel, Right to.** The right freely to leave the political and geographic entity in which one resides as well as to move about within its internal borders has deep historical roots. When Moses entreated Pharaoh to "let my people go," he was invoking the right to travel. Article 42 of the Magna Carta (1215) recognized a right to foreign travel. The concept was implicitly considered a right during the founding and settling of the American colonies and later during the westward expansion. Although the Constitution does not explicitly acknowledge a right to travel, it is assumed to reside in Article IV, section 2, which guarantees that "the Citizens of each State shall be entitled to all Privileges and Immunities of Citizens in the several States." Furthermore, Article IV, section 2 contains explicit restrictions on the right to travel by providing that a criminal suspect who flees to another state shall be returned to the state having jurisdiction of the crime and also that persons "held to Service or Labour" (the Constitution's euphemism for *slavery) who escape to another state shall be returned by that state's authorities to the persons "to whom such Service or Labour may be due," that is, the slaveowners (see FUGITIVE SLAVES).

For much of American history, issues surrounding the right to travel were linked with oppression of African-Americans. Before the *Civil War, slaveowners claimed the right to travel with their slaves to states and territories where slavery was prohibited and yet retain full title to their slaves. This was upheld in the infamous Dred *Scott decision in 1857. White citizens could obtain

passports for foreign travel, but African-Americans ordinarily could not. In 1875, Congress enacted legislation prohibiting racial discrimination in public accommodations, including modes of transportation. This was declared unconstitutional by the Supreme Court in the *Civil Rights Cases (1883). Subsequently, southern and border states enacted laws requiring the separation of the races in all aspects of life, including public transportation. The Supreme Court in *Plessy v. Ferguson (1896) upheld racial segregation in a case concerning railroad travel (see SEPARATE BUT EQUAL). As the Court was to recognize some sixty-eight years later, in a decision upholding the public accommodations provision of the *Civil Rights Act of 1964 (*Heart of Atlanta Motel v. United States, 1964), segregated public accommodations and transportation greatly impeded the right of black Americans to travel.

The right to travel abroad is dependent upon obtaining a passport. The State Department in 1948 began refusing to issue passports to communists and others for their political beliefs and associations (see COMMUNISM AND COLD WAR). This was challenged in the courts, and in 1955 a *lower federal court recognized the right to travel as "a natural right" protected by the *Due Process Clause of the *Fifth Amendment. The Supreme Court, in *Kent v. Dulles (1958), came to the same conclusion and invalidated the State Department restrictions. Legislation forbidding members of a communist organization who were ordered to register with the Subversive Activities Control Board from applying for or using passports was invalidated in *Aptheker v. Secretary of State (1964). The right to travel abroad, however, is subject to some restrictions. Passports can be (and are) required. In Regan v. Wald (1984), the Court upheld the president's restriction on tourist travel to Cuba as a reasonable exercise of presidential power under statutory law.

The right to travel within the United States was first acknowledged in the 1868 decision of Crandall v. Nevada, which struck down a Nevada tax on every person leaving the state by public transportation. The Court ruled that the right to travel from state to state was a right of national *citizenship. This right was strengthened by the *privileges and immunities guarantee of the *Fourteenth Amendment and reaffirmed in the *Slaughterhouse Cases (1873). In the twentieth century, the right to domestic travel was furthered by the invalidation (albeit under the Commerce Clause) of a California law aimed at keeping out nonresident poor people from entering the state (*Edwards v. California, 1941). In later years the Court has struck down as impediments to the right to travel durational residency requirements for governmental services (e.g., *Shapiro v. Thompson, 1969) and voting (e.g., Dunn v. Blumstein, 1972), and residency as a requirement for the practice of law (e.g., Supreme Court of New Hampshire v. Piper, 1985; and Barnard v. Thorstenn, 1989). However, some durational residency requirements have been allowed (as in *Vlandis* v. *Kline*, 1973; and *Sosna* v. *Iowa*, 1975).

The concept of a constitutional right to travel is recognized as a *fundamental right deeply embedded in American constitutional law.

Sheldon Goldman

**Treaties and Treaty Power.** In one sense, the Supreme Court has played a minor role in charting the contours of the treaty power and in interpreting treaty terms. No part of any treaty has been held unconstitutional by the Supreme Court, and only a few have been subject to constitutional attack before the Court. Moreover, through its reluctance to become involved in disputes between the political branches concerning the treaty power, the Court has nurtured the understanding that the political branches should shape the nation's foreign policy largely free from judicial supervision (see FOREIGN AFFAIRS AND FOREIGN POLICY). This reticence has contributed to the growth of presidential power over foreign affairs, but the federal judiciary has contributed to the evolution of the treaty power. On a few important occasions, the Court has determined the place of treaties in the hierarchy of federal and state law, and it has ruled that treaties are, like other exercises of federal power, subject to constitutional limitations.

The framers of the Constitution required that the president make treaties, but only with the advice and consent of the Senate. It forbade treaty making by the states and declared in the Supremacy Clause of Article VI that treaties, like the Constitution and laws of the United States, shall be the supreme law of the land and therefore binding on the states. While it is clear that there must be joint participation in treaty making, the framers did not otherwise prescribe limits on treaties or offer a rule for deciding a conflict between treaties and the Constitution or the laws.

Before *World War I, the major debates about the treaty power concerned the supremacy of treaties to state law. The framers had required that those who made treaties—the president (elected by state electors) and the Senate—be especially representative of state interests (see STATE SOVEREIGNTY AND STATES' RIGHTS). Nonetheless, states often contended that treaties could not deal with matters reserved to them by the *Tenth Amendment. Although the Court early held that treaties override inconsistent state law, not until 1920 did the Supreme Court definitely establish the scope of the treaty power relative to the states.

*Missouri* v. *Holland* (1920) involved the validity of a Canadian-American treaty regulating the hunting of migratory birds. The state of Missouri, locus of a principal midcontinent flyway of migrating waterfowl, challenged the treaty as an invasion of powers reserved to the states by the Tenth Amendment. In rejecting Missouri's challenge, the Court, speaking through Justice Oliver Wendell *Holmes, said in *obiter dictum, "There may be matters of the sharpest exigency for the national well being that an act of Congress could not deal with but that a treaty followed by such an act could" (p. 433). Holmes seemed to suggest that the constitutional restraints on the treaty power were feebler than those on the other enumerated powers of Congress. But state power is not an inherent limitation on the treaty power.

The language of the Supremacy Clause of Article VI, which identifies treaties together with the Constitution and the laws of the United States as "the supreme Law of the Land," was held to mean in *Foster* v. *Neilson* (1829) that a treaty must "be regarded in courts . . . as equivalent to an act of the legislature" (p. 254) and thus that a treaty is not valid if it contravenes the Constitution. The controversy engendered by the Bricker Amendment in the early 1950s resurrected fears generated by *Missouri* v. *Holland* that the treaty power might somehow be superior to constitutional restraint. In *Reid* v. *Covert* (1957), the Court held that civilian dependents of American military personnel overseas are entitled to a civilian trial, notwithstanding a contrary statute, and a plurality stated that no treaty or executive agreement "can confer power on the Congress, or on any other branch of Government, which is free from the restraints of the Constitution" (p. 16).

The Supremacy Clause has had an additional effect on the status and consequences of treaties. As the supreme law of the land, equivalent to an act of Congress, a treaty "operates of itself without the aid of any legislative provision [unless] the terms of the stipulation import a contract [in which case] the legislature must execute the contract before it can become a rule for the Court" (p. 254). On the other hand, if a treaty and a law of Congress are inconsistent, the Court has held that the most recent prevails. Viewing the text of the Supremacy Clause, the Court's is one reasonable interpretation of the relationship between treaties and statutes, but it is not necessarily the one that was in the minds of the framers. The Supremacy Clause says that treaties and statutes are supreme over state law, not that they are equal to each other. The Court's interpretation is nonetheless well settled and has rendered academic all arguments that Congress or the treaty makers should prevail where there is a conflict.

The Court has had little to say about the process of making, interpreting, or terminating treaties, but its silence has had important ramifications. In 1979, the Court ordered the dismissal of Senator Barry Goldwater's challenge to President Jimmy Carter's action terminating a mutual defense treaty with Taiwan without seeking the Senate's prior approval. Only Justice William J. *Brennan voted to uphold the president's decision on the merits in *Goldwater* v. *Carter,* and his opinion was based on what he viewed as the president's plenary power regarding recognition of foreign governments. Justice William H. *Rehnquist's plurality opinion stated that the role of the Senate in treaty termination was a nonjusticiable *political question in light of the silence of the constitutional text on the question and because termination processes may vary in different situations (see also JUSTICIABILITY). Justice Lewis *Powell supplied the fifth vote for dismissal, although he disagreed with Rehnquist's political question analysis. For Powell, the case was not *ripe for decision because the Senate as a whole had not acted to express opposition to the president's termination decision.

As a result of the Court's decision not to resolve the *Goldwater* case, the *Reagan administration terminated, modified, and "reinterpreted" many treaties without seeking the advice and consent of the Senate. Whether or not *Goldwater* can be read as allowing so much, the effect of the Court's reticence has been to tip the locus of foreign affairs power further in the direction of the president and away from Congress.

Before and since *Goldwater*, however, presidents have conducted foreign relations unilaterally by making international agreements that concern subjects properly within the domain of treaty making but that, because of the form they take, are not subject to the procedural requirement of obtaining the support of two-thirds of the Senate. While the Supreme Court has not explicitly defined the scope of the president's power to make international executive agreements without the Senate's participation, dicta from a few decisions of the Court suggest that such agreements may concern the same matters as treaties. The possibility that this unilateral agreement making may negate the check on presidential discretion supplied by the Senate has not as yet produced a justiciable controversy. Instead, the Court has validated executive agreements in various contexts where the Senate has not objected to the president's action.

(See also SEPARATION OF POWERS.)

□ Louis Henkin, *Foreign Affairs and the Constitution* (1972). Laurence Tribe, *American Constitutional Law*, 2d ed. (1988).                    William C. Banks

**Trial by Jury.** The seeds of the jury system were sowed in *common-law England. From England, the jury migrated to America. While the jury has taken root and prospered in American soil, it has withered in its original home.

In the United States, the right to jury trial is guaranteed by *Article III and the *Sixth, *Seventh, and *Fourteenth amendments to the Constitution. As a result, the jury is largely immune from legislative abolition. In England, no such constitutional protection is available; Parliament is free to abolish jury trials at any time, and it has. In English civil trials a jury is now available only

in actions for fraud, *libel, slander, malicious prosecution, and false imprisonment—trials that, though high in notoriety, tend to be low in frequency. The picture in criminal law is not much brighter. In Magistrate's Court, where the overwhelming bulk of cases are disposed of, there is no right to a jury trial.

By comparison, in the United States a jury trial is constitutionally available in any nonjuvenile criminal prosecution where the potential penalty is in excess of six months (*Baldwin* v. *New York*, 1970) and in a federal civil case where more than twenty dollars are in controversy (Seventh Amendment). State constitutional provisions provide comparable protection. In fact, most criminal and civil cases are disposed of by guilty pleas and settlements (see PLEA BARGAINING).

Why has the right to trial by jury taken such disparate paths in England and the United States? The answer may lie in common ground, for aspects of the jury that are seen as strengths in the United States are viewed as weaknesses in England. The abolition of the jury in civil trials in England was attributable to several factors. There was concern, for example, that juries were time-consuming and costly. There was also dissatisfaction with the vagaries of damage awards. A mathematical formula was substituted for the jury's deliberations on damages—a formula with multipliers, multiplicands, and resulting awards far less than would be expected from a jury.

In the United States, on the other hand, the ability of a jury to individualize damages, to take pain and suffering into account, to adjust for local living conditions, and to award punitive damages in some instances are seen as virtues. One Oklahoma court, in holding that a prospective juror who had for years been suffering from the results of an accident had been improperly excused from a jury, opined that a juror who had "experienced a good deal of pain" would help the jury reach a just result and, indeed, conceivably could be "the only one to fully understand and properly evaluate the pain element of plaintiff's damages" (*Brown* v. *Oklahoma Transportation Co.*, 1978, p. 598). Similarly, a jury, because it is drawn from the community, can take into account the costs of living in a particular area, something that the English mathematical formula cannot adequately capture.

In criminal cases a concern for certainty has also led to calls for the jury's abolition in England. A criticism made of English juries is that they too often reach "perverse" verdicts. The term "perverse" is apparently used to signify a verdict with which the speaker, usually a government official, does not agree. The assumption of the critics seems to be that the sole function of the jury is to determine factual guilt. But this cannot be so. Otherwise, cases in which there were no disputed facts would not reach the jury. A judge may direct a verdict of acquittal, but in neither England nor America can a judge direct a jury to return a verdict of guilty, no matter how strong the evidence of factual guilt.

A jury in a criminal case does far more than decide issues of fact. It has the power to extend mercy where mercy is called for, and to mete out individualized justice. It has the power, although not necessarily the right, to nullify—that is, to return a verdict of not guilty even though a strict application of controlling legal principles to the facts would seem to require a verdict of guilty. It may decide, as in the case of a mercy killing, that the law was not intended to apply to such a state of facts and that to return a verdict of guilty would be unjust. Or it may decide that the law itself is unjust. Thus it might acquit where a defendant is charged with violating a law requiring enforced *segregation of the races. It may also decide to acquit where the prosecution or the police have behaved in a reprehensible manner, as where the defendant has been beaten by the police or where the police have unfairly, in the jury's eyes, entrapped a defendant into committing a crime.

The strength of the jury lies in the fact that it is not totally circumscribed by legal rules; and that it has the practical power to do what is right, and not just what is technically required by law. While this power may on occasion have been abused, its proper exercise presents the jury in its finest light. The potential for abuse can and should be corrected by greater care in the selection and instruction of juries, but such potential may be an acceptable price for providing the jury the freedom to do justice in the individual case.

(See also GRAND JURIES; PETIT JURIES.)

□ James J. Gobert, *The Jury on Trial: A Political, Philosophical, and Psychological Examination of the Jury* (1993). Harry Kalven and Hans Zeisel, *The American Jury* (1966).

James J. Gobert

**Trimble, Robert** (b. Berkeley County, Va. [now W. Va.], 17 Nov. 1776; d. Paris, Ky., 25 Aug. 1828; interred Paris, Ky.), associate justice, 1826–1828. Robert Trimble was the oldest of seven children of Mary McMillan and William Trimble. The family moved to central Kentucky, perhaps as early as 1780. Information about Trimble's early schooling is conjectural, but it seems certain that he read law under George Nicholas, the principal author of the first Kentucky constitution, and James Brown, minister to France. Trimble in 1800 began what became a prosperous legal practice in Paris, Kentucky, and two years later served a single term in the commonwealth's House of Representatives.

His judicial career began with his appointment to the Kentucky Court of Appeals in April 1807. Citing financial sacrifice, he resigned in December 1808, but served briefly as chief justice in 1810. Trimble succeeded Harry Innes, Kentucky's first federal district judge, in 1817. Other public service included his 1820 appointment to the

*Robert Trimble*

commission that finally resolved a boundary dispute with Tennessee and membership on the Board of Trustees of Transylvania University during the turbulent presidency of Horace Holley.

When President John Quincy *Adams nominated Trimble in 1826, be became the first lower federal court judge to become a justice of the Supreme Court. He served only in 1827 and 1828 before his sudden death from a "malignant bilious fever." During those two years, he wrote sixteen opinions. Of those, by far the most important was a concurring opinion in *Ogden v. Saunders* (1827), in which the Court decided by a vote of 4 to 3, with Chief Justice John *Marshall dissenting, that a New York *bankruptcy act applying to debts incurred after passage of the statute did not violate the *Contracts Clause in Article I.

Mary K. Bonsteel Tachau

**Trop v. Dulles,** 356 U.S. 86 (1958), argued 2 May and 28–29 Oct. 1957, decided 31 Mar. 1958 by vote of 5 to 4; Warren, joined by Black, Douglas, and Whittaker, for the plurality, Brennan concurring, Frankfurter, Burton, Clark, and Harlan in dissent. This case was decided on the same day as *Perez v. Brownell,* in which a majority of 5 to 4 affirmed Congress's power to take away the American *citizenship of a person who had voted in a foreign election. With Justice William *Brennan, who had been in the majority in the *Perez* case, changing sides, the Court in *Trop* held that Congress had no power to withdraw an individual's citizenship for wartime desertion from the military. Chief Justice Earl *Warren, who had dissented in *Perez* on the ground that Congress was entirely without power to denationalize anyone without consent, wrote for the plurality in *Trop*, which consisted of the four *Perez* dissenters. Warren reiterated the broad constitutional argument he made in *Perez* and further contended that Congress could not impose expatriation as punishment without violating the *Cruel and Unusual Punishments Clause of the *Eighth Amendment. Involuntary expatriation, wrote Warren, was cruel and unusual punishment because it constituted "the total destruction of the individual's status in organized society" (p. 101). Brennan, concurring separately, merely concluded that expatriation for wartime desertion was not a rational exercise of the *war power. The Eighth Amendment argument, therefore, was not embraced by a majority. Although that argument had no further development in this area of law, its core idea, that the Eighth Amendment "must draw its meaning from the evolving standards of decency that mark the progress of a maturing society" (p. 101), has been accepted as a critical element of constitutional law relating to capital punishment (e.g., *Gregg v. Georgia*, 1976).

In *Afroyim* v. *Rusk* (1967), the Court overruled *Perez* and adopted Warren's broad argument that citizenship could only be voluntarily relinquished.                                Dean Alfange, Jr.

**Truax v. Corrigan,** 257 U.S. 312 (1921), argued 29–30 Apr. 1920, reargued 5–6 Oct. 1921, decided 19 Dec. 1921 by vote of 5 to 4; Taft for the Court, Holmes, Pitney (joined by Clarke), and Brandeis in dissent. In the late nineteenth and early twentieth century, courts often ended labor disputes by issuing *injunctions against strikers. To redress this judicial favoritism, some states, including Arizona, passed statutes seeking to insulate strikers from labor injunctions. Such statutes did not preclude suits for damages. The Arizona courts upheld a peaceful-picketing, no-injunction law when it was challenged by a local restaurant owner who saw his business decline more than 50 percent when strikers picketed his establishment.

A bare majority of the Supreme Court said that the picketing, despite an absence of violence, invalidated the law. Chief Justice William Howard *Taft found that the law abridged the *Due Process Clause of the *Fourteenth Amendment by depriving the owner of his property and violated the *Equal Protection Clause of that same amendment by singling out disputes between an employer and his former employees for special treatment. The probusiness, antiunion bias of the majority was exposed in three dissenting opinions. Justice Oliver Wendell *Holmes protested the Court's continuing use of the Fourteenth Amendment to cut off state experimentation; Justice Mahlon *Pitney challenged all of Taft's conclusions; and Justice Louis D. *Brandeis provided historical and legal justification for the Arizona statute.

The decision in *Truax* v. *Corrigan* is representative of the Taft Court, but its reading of the Due Process and Equal Protection Clauses would not long survive. Specifically, in *Senn* v. *Tile Layers Union* (1937), a similar Wisconsin law was upheld.

(See also LABOR.)

                                John E. Semonche

**Twelfth Amendment.** The Twelfth Amendment provides that presidential electors vote separately for president and for vice president. Article II of the Constitution had provided for one ballot: whoever received the largest number of votes, if more than half, became president, and whoever received the next highest total, vice president. Under this system, John Adams defeated Thomas *Jefferson for president in 1796 but Jefferson served as vice president under President Adams. In 1800, Democratic-Republicans Jefferson and Burr defeated Federalists Adams and Pinckney, but, with identical totals, the election was thrown into the House of Representatives under Article II. It took the House of Representatives thirty-five ballots to resolve the election. In response, Congress passed the Twelfth Amendment in 1803. It was ratified in 1804. By requiring separate ballots for president and vice president, the Twelfth Amendment took into account the rise of national party voting (see POLITICAL PARTIES).

The Supreme Court has treated the Twelfth Amendment as evidence of the decentralization of the presidential election process. The Constitution permits electors selected at large or in districts (*MacPherson* v. *Blacker,* 1892), and pledged by party to its national ticket (*Ray* v. *Blair,* 1952). The latter case was decided in the wake of the Dixiecrat challenge to the national Democratic party ticket.

The Twelfth Amendment nearly unraveled the compromise setting up the Federal Election Commission when the Court held that Congress had no power under the Twelfth Amendment ballot counting provisions to appoint members of the commission except by Senate ratification of presidential nominations (*Buckley* v. *Valeo,* 1976).

(See also CONSTITUTIONAL AMENDMENTS.)

                                Stephen E. Gottlieb

**Twentieth Amendment.** The 1933 "Norris Lame Duck" Amendment, as it was popularly known at the time of its ratification, eliminates the December to March Congressional "lame duck" short sessions that resulted from constitutionally and legislatively established dates for the beginning (December) and close (March in odd numbered years) of congressional sessions. The March date reflected the time required to journey to Washington before railroads shortened travel time. Sessions beginning in December of the even years lasted only three months. Congressmen elected in those years did not take office for thirteen months, and those whom they had defeated continued service in the short session. The sessions, marked by obstructionist filibusters, were unproductive, and in light of change in travel and communications, became obsolete. Their potential for troublemaking was confirmed during and after "Secession Winter" (1860–1861).

Since altering the term commencement from December and March to January shortened the constitutionally mandated terms of those in office, a constitutional amendment rather than legislation was required to effectuate the reform. The amendment's author, Senator George Norris, concerned with congressional efficiency and accountability, regarded it as one of his greatest achievements.

The amendment also moves the inauguration date for president and vice president from March to January, clarifies the status of the vice president–elect should the president-elect die before taking office (vice president–elect becomes president-elect), and enables Congress to legislate concerning other stipulated exigencies regarding presidential succession.

(See also CONSTITUTIONAL AMENDMENTS.)

Mary Cornelia Aldis Porter

**Twenty-fifth Amendment.** Article II of the U.S. Constitution provided that the vice president shall "discharge the Powers and Duties" of the president in the case of the president's "Death, Resignation, or Inability." It left Congress to legislate for the incapacity of both. It did not resolve how to determine inability or return powers to the president.

President James Garfield lay in a coma nearly two months after being shot in 1881. President Woodrow Wilson was disabled by a stroke in 1919–1921. Many presidents have suffered shorter periods of disability. In no instance were the disability provisions invoked.

The Twenty-fifth Amendment establishes procedures by which the vice president becomes "Acting President" in the event of disability and the president may resume the powers of the office on the termination of the disability: by the president's written declaration or the vice president's together with a majority of top executive officials. A finding of disability may be made over the president's objection, subject to review in Congress—a two-thirds vote of both houses within twenty-one days is necessary for the vice president to continue as acting president. By contrast, the House, acting without the two-thirds requirement, may present the Senate with articles of *impeachment. Apparently the vice president may act as president during the twenty-one day maximum period for resolving the dispute.

Following precedent set by John *Tyler in 1841, under the Twenty-fifth Amendment the vice president becomes president on the president's death or resignation, and does not merely "discharge" the president's duties. The Twenty-fifth Amendment also provides for filling the office of vice president when it becomes vacant.

The amendment was proposed in 1965 and ratified in 1967. Vice President Spiro Agnew resigned on 10 October 1973 in the face of criminal charges focusing on alleged bribery in prior office. Gerald R. Ford became vice president on 6 December 1973. Richard M. *Nixon resigned the presidency on 9 August 1974 in the face of impeachment procedures stemming from the Watergate coverup. Ford became president and Nelson A. Rockefeller became vice president on 19 December 1974. The disability procedures of the amendment were invoked for seven hours on 13 July 1985 when President Reagan underwent surgery for cancer and Vice President Bush temporarily assumed the powers of the office. (See also CONSTITUTIONAL AMENDMENTS.)

Stephen E. Gottlieb

**Twenty-first Amendment.** The only constitutional amendment ratified by the electorate rather than legislators, the Twenty-first was also the only amendment to repeal another, the *Eighteenth. Not quite fourteen years elapsed between the adoption of the national prohibition amendment on 16 January 1919, and the ratification of the Twenty-first Amendment on 5 December 1933.

National prohibition sharply reduced but did not altogether eliminate the use of alcoholic beverages in the United States. Neither state and local law enforcement officials nor the small federal Prohibition Bureau authorized by the 1919 Volstead Act could cope with the variety and volume of prohibition violations. The longer sentences and larger fines imposed by the 1929 federal Jones "Five-and Ten" Act had little effect. Nor did a series of Supreme Court decisions upholding concurrent powers of state and federal enforcement, U.S. v. *Lanza (1922); warrantless automobile searches, *Carroll v. U.S. (1925); restrictions on medicinal liquor prescriptions, *Lambert v. Yellowley (1926); and wiretap telephone surveillance *Olmstead v. U.S. (1928).

Opposition to prohibition came from politically active groups of recent immigrants who saw prohibition as a slap at their cultures and antiprohibition organizations, which argued that the liquor ban encouraged crime and disrespect for all law, while simultaneously giving the federal government too much power over people's personal lives. The economic collapse of the early 1930s brought arguments that prohibition took away jobs and liquor taxes.

The Democratic party endorsed prohibition repeal in 1932, and its sweeping November victory brought quick congressional action. On 20 February 1933, Congress adopted, by more than the required two-thirds, an amendment resolution that would repeal the Eighteenth Amendment and prohibit transportation of intoxicating beverages into any U.S. state, territory, or possession in violation of its laws. The resolution also called for ratification of the proposed amendment by state conventions rather than legislatures. The Supreme Court in *Hawke* v. *Smith* (1920), overturning a 1919 Ohio referendum on the Eighteenth Amendment, had stirred demands that this never-employed alternative Article V procedure be used so that convention delegate elections would provide a direct expression of popular opinion on the proposed constitutional amendment. During 1933 thirty-eight states held delegate elections: 73 percent of 21 million voters cast ballots for candidates who favored an end to national prohibition, and only South Carolina voters rejected repeal. Ratification conventions quickly certified the results, and on 5 December 1933, when Pennsylvania, Ohio, and finally Utah acted, national prohibition came to an end. Despite the fact that alcohol consumption rates remained below pre-1920 levels for forty years after national prohibition, the federal effort to forbid adult use of alcohol has been generally perceived as a failure, a futile policy, and a misapplication of the *constitutional amending process.

(See also CONSTITUTIONAL AMENDMENTS.)

David E. Kyvig

**Twenty-fourth Amendment** forbids states and the federal government to deny or abridge the right of a citizen of the United States to vote in a federal election because of failure to pay a *poll tax or other assessment. Passed by Congress on 27 August 1962 and ratified on 23 January 1964, its target was the poll tax, a per capita levy long employed by southern states to prevent African-Americans from voting.

By 1964 only five states still required would-be voters to pay such an assessment, and even many Southerners favored its abolition. The principal sponsor of the Twenty-fourth Amendment was Spessard Holland, a conservative Florida Democrat. Bills to abolish the poll tax were repeatedly introduced in Congress from 1939 onward; Holland himself took up the cause in 1949. By 1960 the idea was no longer particularly controversial. The only real disagreement was over whether the poll tax could be abolished by ordinary legislation or whether a constitutional amendment was required. Many liberals favored enactment of a statute, but Holland, who believed Congress lacked the authority to pass such a law, insisted on amending the Constitution (see CONSTITUTIONAL AMENDING PROCESS).

The Twenty-fourth Amendment encountered resistance from Virginia, which imposed a special federal registration requirement on voters who did not pay the poll tax in state elections. In *Harman* v. *Forssenius* (1965) the Supreme Court held this tactic unconstitutional. Although the new amendment did not prohibit requiring poll taxes in state elections, in *Harper* v. *Virginia Board of Elections* (1966), the Court invalidated that practice too, holding it violated the *Equal Protection Clause of the *Fourteenth Amendment.

(See also VOTE, RIGHT TO.)

Michal R. Belknap

**Twenty-second Amendment.** George *Washington declined a third term as president for "the shade of retirement." Thomas *Jefferson, citing Washington's example, declined a third term to make the two-term limit a principle. No president before Franklin D. *Roosevelt served more than two terms. Roosevelt, in the shadow of World War II, sought and was elected to third and fourth terms in 1940 and 1944. He died in April 1945 and was succeeded by Harry S. Truman, a Democrat who shortly presided over a Republican Congress.

The Constitutional Convention had discussed at length a limited presidential term coupled with selection by the Congress in the manner of the British Parliament. After extensive discussion centering largely on the relationship of the president and the Congress, the Constitutional Convention had coupled unlimited reeligibility with four-year terms and an electoral college in Article II.

The Twenty-second Amendment was proposed by Congress in 1947 and adopted in 1951. It limited presidents to two elected terms, one if the president had served more than half of the term of a previously elected president. President Truman was excepted from its provisions by an exemption for the current president but did not seek a second elected term in 1952. Since the adoption of the amendment, only Presidents Dwight D. Eisenhower and Ronald *Reagan have served two full terms.

Although the Twenty-second Amendment overrules the convention's decision to permit unlimited reeligibility, it may restore some of the balance between presidents and Congress.

(See also CONSTITUTIONAL AMENDMENTS.)

Stephen E. Gottlieb

**Twenty-sixth Amendment.** In the Voting Rights Act of 1970, Congress provided that the voting age in federal, state, and local elections should be eighteen years, whereas the previous voting age had commonly been twenty-one under state law. In *Oregon* v. *Mitchell* (1970), four members of the Supreme Court held that Congress could not set the voting age at eighteen for either federal or state and local elections, while four other members of the Court held that Congress possessed the power to set the age of eighteen as the voting age in federal as well as state and local elections. The deciding vote was cast by Justice Hugo *Black, who held that Congress could set eighteen as the age for voting in federal elections but could not do so for state and local elections, for which the voting qualifications could only be set by the states.

As a result of this decision, eighteen-year-olds could vote for president and vice president and members of Congress, but they could not participate in state and local elections unless permitted to do so under state law. The impending 1972 elections were thus threatened with serious complications. Responding to this situation, on 23 March 1971, Congress proposed the Twenty-sixth Amendment to the Constitution, providing that the voting age in all federal, state, and local elections should be prescribed at eighteen. Within 107 days of its proposal by Congress, the amendment was ratified by the requisite three-fourths of the states and became a part of the Constitution, having been ratified in the shortest period of time of any constitutional amendment in United States history.

(See also CONSTITUTIONAL AMENDING PROCESS; CONSTITUTIONAL AMENDMENTS; ELECTIONS; VOTE, RIGHT TO.)

Richard C. Cortner

**Twenty-third Amendment.** Article I of the U.S. Constitution provided for congressional power to accept land from the states and administer it as the seat of government. The District of Columbia was organized under this power on land ceded by the states of Maryland and Virginia. Congress legislated for the district.

As the House report accompanying the proposal noted, "District citizens have all the obligations of citizenship, including the payment of Federal taxes, of local taxes, and service in our Armed Forces." Although taxed and drafted, citizens of the district were not represented. Representation in Congress and electors for president are all apportioned by the Constitution to states. Hence the Constitution made no provision for representation of citizens of the district.

The Twenty-third Amendment was proposed by Congress in 1960 and ratified in 1961. It granted the district electors not to exceed in number the amount allocated to the smallest state—in practice three electoral votes though its population would have entitled it to more.

The Supreme Court has treated the amendment as another in a long series of amendments expanding suffrage in the United States (cf. *Reynolds* v. *Sims*, 1964) and therefore precedent by analogy for its one person per vote rulings.

(See also CONSTITUTIONAL AMENDMENTS; VOTE, RIGHT TO.)

Stephen E. Gottlieb

**Twining v. New Jersey,** 211 U.S. 78 (1908), argued 19–20 Mar. 1908, decided 9 Nov. 1908 by vote of 8 to 1; Moody for the Court, Harlan in dissent. Twining and Cornell were convicted of intentionally deceiving a New Jersey state banking examiner. At issue in their appeal was the trial judge's charge to the jury that the defendant's refusal to testify in their own behalf could be considered in determining guilt. New Jersey was among a minority of states that permitted trial judges to make such charges.

The Supreme Court weighed whether the trial judge's instructions violated the *Fifth Amend-

ment privilege against *self-incrimination and, if so, whether that provision was incorporated by the *Fourteenth Amendment against *state action. Justice William H. *Moody, writing for the majority, rejected the incorporation argument and declined to consider the specific dimensions of Twining's complaint. Moody acknowledged that, for purposes of discussion, the trial court's comment on the defendants' refusal to take the stand in their own defense constituted an "infringement of the privilege against self-incrimination" (p. 114), but he emphasized that the New Jersey courts did not violate their own interpretation of that privilege and, consequently, the "exemption from compulsory self-incrimination in the courts of the States is not secured by any part of the Federal Constitution" (p. 114).

In dissent, Justice John Marshall *Harlan argued that the Court should first have considered whether the trial court's action constituted a violation of the privilege against self-incrimination. If so, then the Court had to consider the applicability of federal constitutional provisions to the states. Harlan concluded that the trial court violated the privilege against self-incrimination and that that privilege applied to all citizens as guaranteed by the Fourteenth Amendment.

Although the Court has never explicitly contested Twining's rejection of total incorporation, the process of selective incorporation has been applied to most of the *Bill of Rights. *Twining* v. *New Jersey* was reversed in *Malloy* v. *Hogan* (1964).

(See also INCORPORATION DOCTRINE.)

Susette M. Talarico

**Tyler, John** (b. Charles City County, Va., 29 Mar. 1790; d. Richmond, Va., 18 Jan. 1862), statesman, and president of the United States, 1841–1845. After assuming the nation's highest office upon the death of President William Henry Harrison in 1841, John Tyler found himself locked in a political struggle with his own Whig party. Tyler's unexpected ascension to the presidency horrified Senate Whigs led by Kentucky's Henry Clay, who fundamentally opposed the Virginian's states' rights political philosophy (see STATE SOVEREIGNTY AND STATES' RIGHTS). As a result of this party split, Tyler was the least successful of all presidents in securing confirmation of his nominees to the Supreme Court.

When Justice Smith *Thompson died in December 1843, Tyler nominated his secretary of the treasury, John C. *Spencer, a lawyer from New York. A political enemy of Clay, Spencer failed to gain Senate confirmation; subsequently, Tyler nominated another capable New York attorney, Reuben H. *Walworth. Before the Senate could act, however, Justice Henry *Baldwin died in April 1844, creating a second vacancy on the Court. To this seat, Tyler hoped to appoint Pennsylvania's James Buchanan, but, in keeping with the president's luck, Buchanan declined the position. Tyler then nominated Philadelphia lawyer Edward *King. Senate Whigs, however, sensing a victory in the fall presidential election, postponed in June the nominations of both Walworth and King.

Although the Whig Party failed to capture the presidency, Tyler's political position continued to wane in the final months of his term. He withdrew both of his nominations in January 1845 and instead proposed Samuel *Nelson, chief justice of New York. After the Senate speedily confirmed this choice, Tyler attempted to fill the second vacancy with Philadelphia lawyer John Meredith *Read. Political success, however, did not come easy to Tyler. Dealing the president a final defeat, the Senate adjourned without acting on the nomination, leaving the seat to the choice of Tyler's successor, James K. Polk.

(See also NOMINEES, REJECTION OF.)

Timothy S. Huebner

**Tyson v. Banton,** 273 U.S. 418 (1927), argued 6–7 Oct. 1926, decided 28 Feb. 1927 by vote of 5 to 4; Sutherland for the Court, Holmes, Brandeis, Stone, and Sanford in dissent. New York sought to protect theatergoers against the excessive charges demanded by licensed brokers who trafficked in ticket resale. The Court disagreed in this renowned and widely criticized opinion. Theaters were not public utilities or affected with a public interest, the Court ruled. Theaters served only a small percentage of the public and neither they nor that limited public could enjoy special governmental protection or privilege. Writing for the majority, Justice George *Sutherland pointed out that a ticket agency did not fall into any of the three categories Chief Justice William H. *Taft had listed in *Wolff Packing* v. *Court of Industrial Relations* (1923), and thereby held the law unconstitutional as a violation of freedom of *contract.

There were four dissents. Justice Oliver Wendell *Holmes objected strongly to the use of the public interest doctrine in curtailing legitimate social control. The legislature, he argued, when it had sufficient force of public opinion behind it, should have the power to forbid or restrict any business without legal apology. He urged, more broadly, that legislatures should do what they saw fit to do unless restrained by some express prohibition in the Constitution. The concept of public interest, he made clear, was an artificial one, little more than a fiction intended to "beautify what is disagreeable to the sufferers" (p. 446). Justice Louis *Brandeis concurred. Justice Harlan F. *Stone, in a separate dissent, deplored how far the Court had progressed in destroying the various criteria of social control formerly accepted as valid. In substance, the minority judges were all demanding that the entire concept of public interest be abandoned and replaced by a recognition of the general right of any state legislature to regulate private business whenever it thought the public welfare demanded it.

(See also STATE REGULATION OF COMMERCE.)

Paul L. Murphy

# U

**Ullman v. United States,** 350 U.S. 422 (1956), argued 6 Dec. 1955, decided 26 Mar. 1956 by vote of 7 to 2; Frankfurter for the Court, Douglas and Black in dissent. A federal district court issued an order under the Immunity Act requiring Ullman to testify before a *grand jury that was investigating attempts to endanger the *national security. Under the act, a witness could not refuse to testify on the ground that the testimony may have tended to incriminate him. The Immunity Act, however, gave the witness transactional immunity, which prevented state or federal prosecutions for any transactions or matters concerning the compelled testimony. Despite the immunity, Ullman refused to testify and was sentenced to six months imprisonment for contempt.

On appeal to the Supreme Court, Ullman argued that the Immunity Act violated the *Fifth Amendment privilege against *self-incrimination. He argued that the act did not give him complete immunity because his testimony might lead to practical disabilities, such as loss of job, expulsion from a labor union, and public opprobrium.

The Supreme Court rejected this argument, holding that the act did not violate the Fifth Amendment. It observed that the privilege against self-incrimination protected a witness not from the disabilities described by Ullman but only from giving testimony that might lead to a criminal prosecution. By granting transactional immunity, the act removed exposure to a criminal charge. As a result, the reason for the privilege no longer existed and petitioner could not refuse to answer questions.

(See also DUE PROCESS, PROCEDURAL.)

Daan Braveman

**Understanding Tests** were imposed by state statutes and constitutions after the *Reconstruction era and required prospective voters to "understand and explain" selected laws to the satisfaction of local registrars before being allowed to cast their ballots. Such tests were part of a broad array of subterfuges used in southern states from the 1890s through the mid-1960s in an avowed attempt to evade constitutional prohibitions against race discrimination in voting. In their actual administration, understanding tests were applied laxly if at all to whites while being invoked to disfranchise many blacks for their failure to comprehend arcane legal language. As Gunnar Myrdal reported in *An American Dilemma* (1944), one southern official boasted, "I can keep the President of the United States from registering, if I want to. God, Himself, couldn't understand that sentence. I, myself, am the judge" (p. 1325, n. 34).

Although the Supreme Court in 1949 summarily affirmed a federal district court's invalidation of Alabama's understanding test, several other southern states persisted in using the contrivance into the 1960s. It was not until *Louisiana* v. *United States* (1965) that the Court issued a full opinion striking down the practice as "not a test but a trap" turning upon the unchecked "whim or impulse" of individual registrars (p. 153). Although the Court held open the possibility that standardized, fairly administered "citizenship tests" might be constitutional, Congress in the *Voting Rights Act of 1965 and later amendments subsequently restricted the use of all literacy, "understanding," and other educational tests in determining voter eligibility. The

Court upheld these broad bans in *South Carolina v. Katzenbach* (1966) and *Oregon v. Mitchell* (1970).

(See also FIFTEENTH AMENDMENT; RACE AND RACISM; VOTE, RIGHT TO.)

Charles G. Curtis, Jr., and Shirley S. Abrahamson

## United Jewish Organizations of Williamsburgh v. Carey, 430 U.S. 144 (1977), argued 6 Oct. 1976, decided 1 Mar. 1977 by vote of 7 to 1; White for the Court, Burger in dissent, Marshall not participating.

In this case, the Supreme Court held constitutional a New York State reapportionment plan that was based upon a fixed racial quota. In 1972, the State of New York reapportioned three counties for congressional, state senate and state assembly seats. Pursuant to provisions of the *Voting Rights Act of 1965, New York was required to seek approval of the plan by the United States attorney general. The attorney general found that the state had failed to demonstrate that the plan had neither the purpose nor the effect of abridging the right to vote by reason of race or color with respect to state assembly and senate districts in the Bedford-Stuyvesant area of Kings County (Brooklyn).

The plan for Kings County included the Williamsburgh area, a community whose population included approximately 30,000 Hasidic Jews. Previously, and again in the 1972 plan, the Hasidic community was located entirely in one district for representation in both the state assembly and senate. Based on representations that only a 65 percent nonwhite assembly district would be acceptable to the attorney general, the State of New York submitted a revised plan that split the Hasidic community into two state assembly and senate districts.

Before the attorney general gave his approval to the revised reapportionment proposal, the Hasidic community brought suit for injunctive and declaratory relief in district court, alleging that the new plan was discriminatory under the *Fourteenth and *Fifteenth Amendments (see INJUNCTIONS AND EQUITABLE REMEDIES). The district court granted motions to dismiss the suit on grounds that Hasidic Jews enjoyed no constitutional right to recognition as a separate community; in reapportionment, that Hasidic Jews had not been and were not disfranchised, and that under the Voting Rights Act racial considerations could legitimately be invoked in order to correct past discrimination.

The Court of Appeals for the Second Circuit held that the plan did not discriminate against the plaintiffs as white voters, finding no intent by the State of New York to eliminate or to minimize white voting power in Kings County. Because the New York legislature had previously violated the Voting Rights Act, the majority did not consider the constitutional question whether a state legislature could draw district lines on the basis of race in order to achieve a proportional or equal representation of white and nonwhite voters. Relying on the Voting Rights Act and *Allen* v. *Board of Elections* (1969), the appeals court found that consideration of race was proper in reapportionment cases to correct invidious discrimination against nonwhites.

The Supreme Court held that under the Voting Rights Act the state's action was clearly constitutional. Four members of the Court agreed with the Second Circuit that (1) the use of racial criteria in drawing district lines may be required by section 5 of the Voting Rights Act, (2) under the act, the use of racial criteria is not limited to remedies of explicit prior discrimination, and (3) the use of numerical racial quotas in establishing certain black majority districts does not automatically violate the Fourteenth and Fifteenth Amendments. Writing for the plurality, Justice Byron *White agreed with the lower court's interpretation of the Voting Rights Act and its interpretation of the decisions upholding the act's constitutionality. Given the proper conditions for invoking the act, the use of explicitly racial criteria is appropriate whether or not there is a finding of prior discrimination. Justice Potter *Stewart's separate concurring opinion, in which Justice Lewis *Powell joined, emphasized the lack of any showing of purposeful discrimination in the New York redistricting.

Chief Justice Warren *Burger's dissent opposed any use of quotas or "racial gerrymandering." He also argued that *state action not otherwise acceptable is not made constitutionally permissable by attempts to comply with the Voting Rights Act.

In *United Jewish Organizations* the Court moved beyond earlier cases to uphold the use of explicitly numerical racial goals to obtain the attorney general's approval for redistricting under the Voting Rights Act. This approach continues as law, but it applies only to those states or subdivisions covered by the act.

(See also RACE AND RACISM; VOTE, RIGHT TO.)

Herbert Hill

## United Mine Workers, United States v., 330 U.S. 258 (1947), argued 14 Jan. 1947, decided 6 Mar. 1947 by vote of 7 to 2; Vinson for the Court, Frankfurter and Jackson concurring in the judgment, Black and Douglas concurring in part and dissenting in part, Murphy and Rutledge in dissent.

After contract negotiations broke down between the miners union and coal operators in the spring of 1946, the federal government determined that the resulting shortage of coal had created a national emergency. President Harry S. Truman seized the mines on 21 May 1946, claiming coal production to be essential to both the war effort and to sustaining the domestic economy in the transition from war to peace. The union, with the silent approval of its president, John L. Lewis, refused to work in government-held mines until a contract had been signed. The government in turn secured an *injunction against further work stoppages, and when the workers refused to return to the pits, the district court fined the union $3.5 million and Lewis $10,000 for contempt of court.

The union appealed on the grounds that the Norris-LaGuardia Act of 1932 prohibited federal courts from issuing injunctions against labor during a strike. The government responded that the War Labor Disputes Act of 1942 superseded the Norris-LaGuardia Act in situations in which the president, as commander-in-chief, issued an executive order pursuant to the declaration of a national emergency (see PRESIDENTIAL EMERGENCY POWERS).

The Court held that the Norris-LaGuardia Act did not apply when the government was the employer and that the district court therefore had jurisdiction in the case. General public approval of this decision led Congress to pass the Taft-Hartley Act later in the year, cutting back some of the privileges *labor had been granted during the *New Deal, especially by the Wagner Labor Relations Act of 1935.

(See also LOWER FEDERAL COURTS.)

Melvin I. Urofsky

**United Public Workers v. Mitchell,** 330 U.S. 75 (1947), argued 3 Dec. 1945, reargued 17 Oct. 1946, decided 10 Feb. 1947 by vote of 4 to 3; Reed for the Court, Frankfurter concurring, Rutledge and Douglas concurring in part and dissenting in part, Black in dissent, Murphy and Jackson not participating. The Hatch Act of 1940 forbade officers and employees of the executive branch, with certain exceptions, from "taking any active part in political management or in political campaigning." Executive-branch employees now came under the same restrictions concerning political activities as had applied to civil service employees, and violation of those rules required dismissal from their positions. Several members of executive agencies sought a *declaratory judgment, claiming that the law unconstitutionally restricted their freedom of speech as protected by the *First Amendment.

Justice Stanley *Reed pointed out that the Court, in a series of cases going back to *Ex parte Curtis* (1882), had upheld similar restrictions on civil service employees, and he balanced individual speech rights against Congress's decision that the public interest required that government employees be barred from active political participation. "It is accepted constitutional doctrine that these fundamental human rights are not absolute. . . . The essential rights of the First Amendment in some instances are subject to the elemental need for order without which the grandeur of civil rights to others would be a mockery" (p. 95).

In his partial dissent, Justice William O. *Douglas described the statute as too broadly drawn. He did not deny that Congress could restrict the political activity of government workers, but to do so, said Douglas, it had to fashion a more narrowly drawn law aimed at the specific conduct it deemed a *clear and present danger. In his dissent, Justice Hugo *Black bitterly attacked the Hatch Act as depriving several million people of their constitutional rights to free speech and political participation.

(See also SPEECH AND THE PRESS; UNPROTECTED SPEECH.)

Melvin I. Urofsky

**United States District Court, United States v.,** 407 U.S. 297 (1972), argued 24 Feb. 1972, decided 19 June 1972 by vote of 8 to 0; Powell for the Court, Burger, Douglas and White concurring, Rehnquist not participating. In the early 1970s, the nation was in a state of civil unrest. Various groups were accused of bombing buildings and plotting against the government. In the name of *national security, the administration of President Richard *Nixon claimed authority to use electronic surveillance to monitor American citizens allegedly involved in subversive activities without, as customarily required by the *Fourth Amendment, first obtaining a warrant from a magistrate on a showing of *probable cause (see SEARCH WARRANT RULE, EXCEPTIONS TO).

The government argued that the vesting of executive power in the president in Article II of the Constitution implied authority to use electronic surveillance to secure information necessary to protect the government from destruction. A judicial warrant requirement would interfere with the executive's responsibility by increasing the risk that sensitive information would be disclosed. Moreover, judges would not be able to evaluate domestic intelligence involving issues beyond judicial expertise.

A unanimous Court rejected the administration's claim. The Court emphasized that the case involved *First Amendment as well as Fourth Amendment values because political organizations antagonistic to prevailing policies are the organizations most likely to be suspected by government of raising domestic national-security dangers. In light of these First Amendment values and the vagueness of the concept of national security, the Court concluded that to permit official surveillance of domestic groups on the basis of a presidential decision without prior judicial warrant would create undue dangers of abuse.

Two days before this opinion was rendered, five men were arrested for attempting to plant electronic surveillance devices in the Democratic National Committee Headquarters in Washington, D.C., an event that initiated the Watergate affair.

(See also POLITICAL PROCESS; PRESIDENTIAL EMERGENCY POWERS.)

Stanley Ingber

**United States Law Week** is a two-volume looseleaf service, devoted in part to Supreme Court decisions and news and published commercially, on a weekly basis, by the Bureau of National Affairs, Inc., of Washington, D.C. Like its competitor, the *U.S. Supreme Court Bulletin*, published by Commerce Clearing House, the "Supreme Court" volume of *U.S. Law Week* issues the full text of all decisions of the Supreme Court of the United States, alone with Court dockets, calendars, related Court news, and brief summaries of the cases docketed. Typically, issues of *U.S. Law Week* are mailed to their respective subscribers on each decision day of the Court. Until the advent of the computer services *LEXIS and *WESTLAW, these two services provided the fastest access to Supreme Court decisions.

In addition to the "Supreme Court" volume of *U.S. Law Week*, a second volume called "General Law" covers other legal news and summaries of important decisions from the *lower federal courts and from *state courts. It also includes legislative and administrative law highlights.

*U.S. Law Week* is available online through both LEXIS and WESTLAW. A "Daily Edition," containing Supreme Court actions and other new developments throughout the legal system, only appears online through both electronic services.

(See also REPORTING OF OPINIONS.)

Morris L. Cohen

**United States Reports,** the official edition of the decisions of the Supreme Court of the United States, began with a volume of decisions prepared and published by Alexander J. *Dallas, a Philadelphia lawyer and occasional journalist and editor. The volume, entitled *Reports of Cases Ruled and Adjudged in the Courts of Pennsylvania, Before and Since the Revolution*, was printed in Philadelphia by Thomas Bradford in 1790. Paradoxically, the volume contained only Pennsylvania decisions since the federal Supreme Court had not yet decided any cases. The next three volumes of reports by Dallas (in 1798, 1799, and 1807, respectively) included decisions of the Supreme Court as well as of the *lower federal courts and Pennsylvania courts. The 1790 volume has long been treated as the first of a series that later became known as the *U.S. Reports*.

Although the position of *reporter of the Supreme Court was not authorized until an 1817 act of Congress provided for the post with an annual salary, the earlier reports were issued with the Court's approval. Since the early reports, following English tradition, were known and cited by the names of their respective reporters, they are called nominative or nominate reports. Court-appointed reporters have continued to prepare the decisions for publication, although only the first ninety volumes of the series are still designated by the reporter's name, as listed in Table 1.

The *U.S. Reports* were issued by private pub-

TABLE 1. Nominative Reports.

| Reporter | Nominative Volumes | U.S. Reports Volumes | Coverage |
|---|---|---|---|
| Alexander J. *Dallas | 1–4 | 1–4 | 1790–1800 |
| William *Cranch | 1–9 | 5–13 | 1801–1815 |
| Henry *Wheaton | 1–12 | 14–25 | 1816–1827 |
| Richard *Peters | 1–16 | 26–41 | 1828–1842 |
| Benjamin C. *Howard | 1–24 | 42–65 | 1843–1860 |
| Jeremiah S. *Black | 1–2 | 66–67 | 1861–1862 |
| John W. *Wallace | 1–23 | 68–90 | 1863–1874 |

lishers until 1922 when the U.S. Government Printing Office assumed publication, beginning with volume 257 covering the October term, 1921.

Prior to the issuance of each bound volume of the *United States Reports*, the court's decisions appear in two temporary, official forms: the *slip decision, in which each decision appears separately in an individually paginated pamphlet, and the preliminary print, an *advance sheet format that groups a number of decisions in pamphlets with continuous (and permanent) pagination through the three pamphlets that currently make up each bound volume. In 1990, through an experimental program called, "Project Hermes," the Court began providing electronic access to its decisions to a variety of organizations and publishers on the same day the decision is issued.

Virtually all of the commerical forms of publication of the Court's decisions (e.g., *Lawyers' Edition; *LEXIS; *Supreme Court Reporter; *United States Law Week;* and *WESTLAW) offer faster and more sophisticated access than the *U.S. Reports*. Nevertheless, the official report must be cited in briefs and memoranda to the Court and is traditionally given first in citations to decisions.

(See also REPORTING OF OPINIONS.)

Morris L. Cohen

**United States v. _____.** See under latter part of case name.

**United Steelworkers of America v. Weber,** 443 U.S. 193 (1979), argued 28 Mar. 1979, decided 27 June 1979 by vote of 5 to 2; Brennan for the Court, Burger and Rehnquist in dissent, Powell and Stevens not participating. Despite earlier opportunities, *Weber* was the first case in which the Supreme Court specifically addressed *affirmative action in employment.

The master collective bargaining agreement for the Kaiser Aluminum Company had been adapted from a settlement of employment discrimination claims in the steel industry. Craft hiring goals for blacks were set at each Kaiser plant equal to the percentage of blacks in the respective local labor forces. On the job training programs were established for unskilled production workers, both black and white. Admission to the programs was based on seniority, with 50 percent of the openings in these newly created in-plant training jobs available for whites.

Weber, an unskilled white employee at the Kaiser plant in Gramercy, Louisiana, had more service than some of the black employees selected for the program but less than any of the successful white applicants. He sued the company and the union, alleging that the program's racial classification for admission violated TItle VII of the *Civil Rights Act of 1964.

Acknowledging that Weber's literal interpretation of the act was not without force, Justice William J. *Brennan, for the majority, emphasized the significance of the fact that the program was voluntarily adopted by private parties to eliminate traditional patterns of racial *segregation. He noted that judicial findings of exclusion from crafts on racial grounds are so numerous as to make such exclusion a proper subject for judicial notice.

The court rejected Weber's argument that Title VII specifically prohibited *any* grant of preferential treatment to racial minorities. It held that Title VII's prohibitions against racial discrimination do not condemn all private, voluntary, race-conscious affirmative action plans.

The Court declined to define in detail the line of demarcation between permissible and impermissible affirmative action plans. But this plan did not unnecessarily trammel the interests of white employees, did not require the discharge of whites to make room for blacks, and did not permanently bar the advancement of white employees. The plan was temporary, and it was not intended to maintain racial balance but simply to eliminate a manifest racial imbalance. Therefore, it fell within the area of discretion left by Title VII to the private sector voluntarily to adopt affirmative action plans designed to eliminate conspicuous racial imbalance in traditionally segregated job categories.

(See also EMPLOYMENT DISCRIMINATION; LABOR; RACE AND RACISM.)

James E. Jones, Jr.

**Unprotected Speech.** One of the Supreme Court's most difficult tasks in free-speech adjudication has been to distinguish "protected" from "unprotected" expression. The Court has heeded Justice Benjamin *Cardozo's remark in *Palko* v. *Connecticut* (1937) that "freedom of thought and speech" is "the matrix, the indispensable condition, of every other form of freedom" and has provided substantial constitutional protection for freedom of expression (p. 327). Some expression,

however, such as direct incitements to unlawful behavior, is "performative" and harmful by its very utterance. And other nonperformative forms of expression may possess such low social value that they merit less constitutional support than expression that is deemed more valuable. The Supreme Court has been more tolerant of government restriction in these areas.

*Free-Speech Principle.* The Court has fashioned *First Amendment doctrine around a "free-speech principle." This principle has two fundamental tenets: (1) that free speech serves special and significant constitutional purposes, and (2) that the First Amendment should not protect all speech but only speech of a certain quality. The free-speech principle reflects a tension between two cardinal values in our constitutional system: liberalism and democracy. Liberal values stress individual liberty and beckon the Court to protect expression that does not constitute substantial direct harm to society, while democratic norms endorse the right of the majority to enact value judgments that limit liberty. The Supreme Court's free-speech principle applies liberal standards to "protected" expression but is more tolerant of democratic controls in the regulation of "unprotected" expression.

Defenders argue that free speech furthers the search for objective truth, buttresses an open "marketplace of ideas" that assists temporary majorities in defining (subjective) truth for themselves, promotes individual self-realization, contributes to the practice of self-government, and helps check government abuse.

Though each of these theories has influenced the Supreme Court, it has relied mainly on the rationale developed in *Chaplinsky* v. *New Hampshire* (1942). *Chaplinsky* involved the constitutionality of punishing *fighting words, performative epithets designed to harm emotionally or to trigger a hostile reaction. In upholding Chaplinsky's conviction for swearing at a police officer, Justice Frank *Murphy wrote that lewdness, *obscenity, *libel, and fighting words are unprotected expression because "such utterances are no essential part of any exposition of ideas, and are of such slight social value as a step to truth that any benefit that may be derived from them is clearly outweighed by the social interest in order and morality" (p. 572).

On the one hand, speech that falls within *Chaplinsky's* category of protected expression is protected by the liberal content-neutrality rule, which stipulates that "government has no power to restrict expression because of its message, its ideas, its subject matter, or its content" (*Police Department of Chicago* v. *Mosely*, 1972, pp. 95–96). Nor may government restrict speech because of a fear that the speech might have undesirable long-range consequences. Only direct and substantial harm to vital social interests may justify abridgment. In constitutional terms, abridgment is permissible only if it satisfies the test of *strict scrutiny: that is, it must be necessary to achieve a "compelling" state interest. On the other hand, government may prohibit unprotected expression simply by showing that the restriction is reasonably related to a legitimate government objective. Immediate harm need not be demonstrated.

The most important illustration of the liberal standards governing protected expression is the Supreme Court's treatment of political speech that advocates lawless action. The 1969 case of *Brandenburg v. Ohio held that such advocacy is punishable only if it "is directed to inciting or producing imminent lawless action and is likely to incite or produce such action" (p. 447). This direct incitement test is clearer and more objective than the *clear and present danger test that preceded it in determining the boundaries of advocacy speech (*Schenck v. United States, 1919).

Brandenburg's liberal standard does not apply to unprotected speech such as libel, obscenity, and fighting words. The Court's treatment of these exceptions, however, has become more liberal in recent decades. Chaplinsky's two-level speech theory favored rational, civil discourse over indecent or highly provocative expression. It assumed that sufficient social consensus existed concerning the nature of the moral order. These tenets and assumptions were challenged when the Court got down to the business of applying the two-level test in an environment of rapid political and cultural transformation in the 1960s.

**Fighting Words.** The fare of the fighting-words exception signifies the modern liberalization of free-speech doctrine. In the 1960s, when authorities suppressed civil rights protests by pointing to the disorder threatened by angry counterdemonstrators, the Supreme Court responded by enhancing the protection of politically disputatious speech in the public forum. Free speech may not be held hostage to the mere threats of "hecklers' vetoes" (*Edwards v. South Carolina, 1963). The "heckler's veto" doctrine challenged the fighting-words rationale, which had made intentionally provocative speech blameworthy. The Court carried this challenge a step further in *Cohen v. California (1971), which involved a young man being convicted of disturbance of the peace for wearing a jacket that had "Fuck the Draft" emblazoned on its back in a courthouse. In overturning the conviction, the Court made the fighting-words doctrine subject to the Brandenburg test by limiting the doctrine's applicability to instances of imminent hostile reaction. The Court has since applied this relatively objective and determinate test consistently, striking down all fighting-words convictions it has considered since Cohen (e.g., Hess v. Indiana, 1973). Furthermore, the Cohen Court broadened the theoretical definition of protected speech established in Chaplinsky by espousing a theory of moral relativism and by recognizing the

noncognitive, emotive aspects of communication. (Cohen, pp. 25–26).

**Obscenity.** Not surprisingly, similar currents affected the constitutional approach to *obscenity. The first explicit constitutional test for obscenity arose in *Roth v. U.S. (1957). The Court ruled that the First Amendment does not protect material that is predominantly "prurient" (lascivious or impure) according to community standards because such material harms moral values concerning sexuality and is not conducive to the rational exposition of ideas (p. 484). Roth endorsed a traditional conservative view of sexuality, but it also had a liberal implication in its rejection of the nonliberal standard of an old English case, Regina v. Hicklin (1868), which had prevailed in many American states. Under Hicklin, material was obscene if it merely had a tendency to corrupt the sexual morality of depraved or vulnerable individuals.

The Court developed an even more liberal test in the context of changes in sexual mores in the 1960s. Materials some considered obscene merited constitutional protection if they possessed any plausible redeeming social value (A Book Named John Cleland's "Memoirs of a Woman of Pleasure" v. Massachusetts, 1966) or was not "patently offensive" to community standards. After this ruling the Court began to reverse virtually every obscenity conviction it encountered unless the purveyor sold the material to minors or advertised it salaciously. Obscenity remained "unprotected speech" under the First Amendment, but little was held to be obscene.

As the market in sexually explicit materials exploded after Memoirs, a divided Burger Court ostensibly attempted to provide more leeway for obscenity prosecutions in *Miller v. California (1973). Under Miller, prurient (according to local community standards) and "patently offensive" sexual material is obscene unless it possesses "serious literary, artistic, political, or scientific value" (p. 24). The "utterly without redeeming social importance" test was discarded. But Miller was no major counterrevolution: its obscenity test boiled down to "hard core" pornography. The Court provided some examples of what would constitute obscenity: "[p]atently offensive representations or descriptions of ultimate sexual acts, . . . [p]atently offensive representations or descriptions of masturbation, excretory functions, and lewd exhibition of the genitals" (p. 25). Under this standard, only extremely explicit works have been found obscene. In this sense, Miller represented only a minor defeat for liberal values. The Miller test, however, is still inherently vague or subjective, at least in comparison to the more objective imminent-danger test of Brandenburg. But the Court refused to adopt the danger test in a companion case to Miller (Paris Adult Theatre I v. Slaton), because under this test the community would lose the right to control obscenity except in very unusual cases. The Court has tolerated this state of uncertainty because it considers obscenity a significant social problem.

**Libel.** Although it distorts the "expositions of ideas," *libel may also be the unintended byproduct of an honest inquiry. Consequently, in *New York Times Co. v. Sullivan* (1964), a case involving a suit brought by the Montgomery, Alabama, police commissioner against the *Times* for publishing a libelous advertisement by a civil rights groups, the Supreme Court extended unprecedented constitutional protection to libelous speech. Alabama law embodied the traditional approach to libel: if the material was defamatory, strict liability prevailed, truth being the only defense. But the Court unanimously ruled that the First Amendment shields the press from liability for defaming a "public official" unless the victim can show by "convincing clarity" that the libel was made with actual malice, that is, "knowledge" of falsehood or "reckless disregard of whether it was false or not" (p. 280). Few plaintiffs can meet this standard. *Sullivan* thus safeguarded the "breathing space" that facilitates honest but erroneous criticism of the government, the essence of the self-government function of speech (p. 278).

Libel doctrine has followed a self-government logic: the more public the issue or the person libeled, the greater the leeway and protection accorded the press. The *Sullivan* test applies to libels of "public officials"; to government employees who possess "substantial control over governmental affairs" (*Rosenblatt v. Baer*, 1966, p.85); and to "public figures," those who enjoy positions of "persuasive power and influence" (*Gertz v. Robert Welch, Inc.*, 1974, p. 345). Private figures may recover damages more easily (*Gertz*), especially if the matter at issue is "not a matter of public concern" (*Dun and Bradstreet v. Greenmoss Builders, Inc.*, 1985).

Because a balance must be struck between the community's protection of individual reputation and First Amendment values, these distinctions appear to make analytical sense. But uncertainties similar to those of obscenity law have arisen. First, the Court has not adequately defined what constitutes a "matter of public concern," and its treatment of "public figures" has become somewhat arbitrary, suggesting a desire to restrict the domain covered by *Sullivan* (e.g., *Time, Inc. v. Firestone*, 1976). Second, excessive fine-tuning of libel law creates the "chilling effect" of uncertainty that the *Sullivan* Court strove to avoid. Finally, the skyrocketing costs of libel defenses have made *Sullivan*'s protections somewhat less meaningful, as the mere threat of a lawsuit now looms as ominously as the remote possibility of an unfavorable jury decision. At some point in the future the Court may have to refashion libel doctrine and make a more definitive choice between liberal and democratic values.

**Quasi-Protected Speech and New Categories.** The complex fine-tuning of libel law has been repeated in the creation of an intermediate level of "quasi-protected" speech and in the creation of a new "unprotected" category of speech. Perhaps uncomfortable with the liberal implications of its obscenity and offensive-speech doctrines, the Supreme Court upheld the Federal Communications Commission's decision to restrict (but not ban) "indecent but not obscene" radio performances to time slots when children would be least likely to hear them (*FCC v. Pacifica Foundation, 1978*). The Court has allowed communities to limit substantially the availability of nonobscene but offensive sexual materials under the pretext of protections against environmental harm through zoning (*Renton v. Playtime Theatres, Inc.*, 1986). And in *New York v. Ferber* (1982) the Court unanimously upheld a New York law that prohibited the knowing distribution of pornography made with minors as actors or models. The Court extended *Ferber's* logic when it ruled that a state may make it illegal to view or possess child pornography, even in the home (*Osborne v. Ohio*, 1990). This decision carved an exception to the rule of *Stanley v. Georgia* (1969), in which the Supreme Court held that the constitutional right to *privacy prohibited states from criminalizing the use of obscene materials in the home.

On the other side of the coin, the Court accorded First Amendment protection to *commercial speech for the first time during the 1970s because such speech sometimes conveys useful information and contributes to the exposition of ideas. Yet because it is associated with economic inducements, not just ideas, commercial speech is not fully protected. Government may ban advertisting shown to be untruthful, misleading, or coercive. And it may ban even truthful, nonmisleading advertising if the restriction directly advances a substantial government interest without unduly burdening overall freedom of expression, (*Central Hudson Gas & Electric Corp. v. Public Service Commission*, 1980, p. 566). On this relatively permissive ground the Court upheld Puerto Rico's ban against casino advertising, holding that government may ban the advertising of any activity that it could prohibit outright (*Posadas de Puerto Rico Associates v. Tourism Co. of Puerto Rico*, 1986).

Unless the Court applies *Brandenburg's* liberty principle to all forms of expression, it must assume the difficult burden of distinguishing protected from unprotected speech. The modern Court has balanced liberalism and democracy by deciding that only expression that contributes to the exposition of ideas in cognitive, emotional, or aesthetic senses merits First Amendment protection in the absence of imminent harm. This balance, which presently favors liberalism, reflects the sound view that the constitutional order embraces both democratic and liberal principles. But as the subtleties and complexity of constitutional doctrine proliferate, the balance between these principles becomes increasingly indeterminate, and the quality of the free-speech principle grows less distinct. Regardless, the Supreme Court is unlikely to abandon its commitment to a free-speech principle that distinguishes protected from unprotected expression.

(See also SPEECH AND THE PRESS.)

□ Kent Greenawalt, *Speech, Crime, and the Uses of Language* (1989). Frederick Schauer, *Free Speech: A Philosophical Inquiry* (1982). Steven Shiffrin, "The First Amendment and Economic Regulation: Away from a General Theory of the First Amendment," *Northwestern Law Review* 78 (1983): 1212–1283. Geoffrey Stone, "Content Regulation and the First Amendment," *William and Mary Law Review* 25 (1983): 189–252.　　Donald A. Downs

**Vacate.** In legal procedure, to vacate an order or judgment is to declare it void and of no legal effect. "Vacate" in that context is thus synonymous with "annul, rescind, cancel." "Vacate" has the additional meaning of leaving, abandoning, or surrendering occupancy of real property.

William M. Wiecek

**Van Devanter, Willis** (b. Marion, Ind., 17 Apr. 1859; d. Washington, D.C., 8 Feb. 1941; interred Rock Creek Cemetery, Washington, D.C.), associate justice, 1910–1937. Willis Van Devanter, one of the *Four Horsemen, graduated from the University of Cincinnati Law School in 1881. After three years in his father's Marion, Indiana, law firm, he moved to Wyoming where he quickly became involved in public life, first as city attorney of Cheyenne and as a territorial legislator and then as chief justice of the territorial court. When Wyoming became a state, he returned to private practice, counting the Union Pacific Railroad among his clients. Van Devanter's involvement in Republican party politics led to his appointment as assistant attorney general in the Department of Interior in 1897. President Theodore Roosevelt appointed him to the Eighth Circuit Court of Appeals in 1903 and seven years later President William Howard *Taft chose him to replace retiring Supreme Court Justice William *Moody.

Van Devanter was considered the foremost intellectual conservative on the court during his twenty-six-year tenure. His service was distinguished primarily by his performance in the *conference and as a critic of his colleague's opinions. His knowledge of jurisdictional matters also led Chief Justice Taft to choose him to play a leading role in drafting the *Judiciary Act of 1925 and testifying before Congress on its behalf.

Never a prolific writer, Van Denvanter made his legal contributions in obscure areas of the court's docket: public land claims, water rights issues, Indian controversies, corporate law, jurisdictional issues, and admiralty law. His most important majority opinion was *McGrain* v. *Daugherty* (1927), in which he broadly interpreted the *implied power of Congress to conduct investigations. Congress, he said, had the power to investigate and to issue subpoenas even without an explicitly stated legislative purpose. Aside from *McGrain,* Van Devanter is known primarily for the opinions he wrote or joined that subscribed to the principles of limited government. His opinion for the court in *Mondou* v. *New York, New Haven, and Hartford Railroad* (1912) upheld the Employees' Liability Act of 1908, because it was restricted to the Court's prevailing view that congressional power was limited to interstate commerce itself and to actions that directly affected that commerce. Van Devanter was, however, fiercely opposed to the use of the *commerce power, along with the taxing power (see TAXING AND SPENDING CLAUSE) and the Due Process Clause to regulate industry and labor-management relations. He joined Justice William *Day in *Hammer* v. *Dagenhart* (1918), Chief Justice Taft in *Bailey* v. *Drexel Furniture Co.* (1922), and Justice George *Sutherland in *Adkins* v. *Children's Hospital* (1923) in striking down federal child labor and state minimum wage legislation on commerce, tax, and due process grounds.

The Great Depression provided a clear test of

*Willis Van Devanter*

Van Devanter's commitment to limited government principles. *Hammer, Bailey*, and *Adkins* suggested his response. Along with three conservative justices—James *McReynolds, Sutherland, and Pierce *Butler—he consistently opposed *New Deal economic and social programs. These Four Horsemen, as they became known, joined by Justice Owen *Roberts, overturned the Railway Pension Act in *Railroad Retirement Board v. Alton Railroad* (1935), voided the Agricultural Adjustment Act's processing tax in *United States v. *Butler* (1936), and struck down the New York State minimum wage law in *Morehead v. New York ex rel. Tipaldo* (1936) as commerce, tax, and due process clause violations.

These decisions and *Schechter Poultry v. United States* (1935), which condemned the National Industrial Recovery Act, precipitated a constitutional crisis. In response to FDR's *"court-packing" plan, the court retreated. Chief Justice Charles Evans *Hughes and Justice Roberts joined Justices Louis *Brandeis, Harlan Fiske *Stone, and Benjamin *Cardozo to uphold federal and state legislation over dissents by the Four Horsemen. In his dissent in *National Labor Relations Board v. Jones and Laughlin Steel Corporation* (1937), Van Devanter, joined by Sutherland and Butler, argued that federal regulation of labor-management relations violated the Commerce Clause, because the effect on interstate commerce was indirect and remote. In *Steward Machine Co. v. Davis* (1937), Van Devanter agreed with Sutherland that the Social Security Act of 1935 exceeded the congressional taxing power. Sutherland's opinion for all Four Horsemen in

*West Coast Hotel v. Parrish* (1937) also expressed Van Devanter's firm conviction that the state minimum wage statute offended the Due Process Clause. In subsequent cases, Van Devanter's fellow conservative justices continued to resist the Roosevelt revolution, but these three decisions and his retirement at the end of the 1936 term resolved the Court's confrontation with the New Deal.

□ James O'Brien Howard, *Constitutional Doctrines of Mr. Justice Van Devanter* (1937).       William Crawford Green

**Veazie Bank v. Fenno,** 8 Wall. (75 U.S.) 533 (1869), argued 18 Oct. 1869, decided 13 Dec. 1869 by vote of 7 to 2; Chase for the Court, Nelson, joined by Davis, in dissent. This important case arose out of the need for revenue to finance the Union effort in the *Civil War. In 1866, Congress enacted a statute that increased a 1 percent tax on state bank notes to a rate of 10 percent. The Veazie Bank of Maine refused to pay the increased tax, and a case ensued between the bank and Fenno, a collector of internal revenue. The bank contended that the 10-percent levy was excessive and threatened it with extinction. Congress, the bank argued, could not use its taxing power to destroy the bank. Such an action was an unconstitutional use of Congress's power to tax because the levy was a direct tax forbidden by the Constitution and because the levy was a tax on a state agency, as Veazie Bank had been chartered by the State of Maine (see TAX IMMUNITIES).

Justice Salmon P. *Chase held that, consistent with *Hylton v. United States* (1796), the tax on bank notes did not constitute a direct tax within the meaning of the Constitution. Nor was the levy a tax on a state instrumentality. Finally, he ruled that the tax was not unconstitutional simply because Veazie Bank thought the tax excessive. Congress's authority in this matter was clear, Chase concluded, and the remedy for excessive taxes was through the political process, not the courts. Indeed, Chase concluded that the act could be viewed not as a tax but as an action to control the national currency, clearly a congressional function. Chase's explanation of the power to tax would prove to be an important landmark in the years ahead, as the taxing power became a powerful instrument of public policy.

In dissent, Justice Samuel *Nelson insisted that Congress had overreached its authority. Nelson thought that the statute impaired the authority of the states, as constitutionally sovereign bodies, to incorporate and control the banks that operated within their borders.

(See also TAXING AND SPENDING POWER.)

Augustus M. Burns III

**Vested Rights.** The phrase "vested rights" is today more a slogan for both admirers and detractors than a concept of determinate meaning. In a general way it connotes a legal regime that protects *property rights both from private interference and from taking by government without compensation. It derives its force from more specific, analogous concepts of property law, such as vested estates or vested interests, and is an extrapolation of their content into the realm of public law, where it is associated with the more tangible doctrine of *eminent domain and substantive *due process.                                     William M. Wiecek

**Veto Power.** The Constitution's framers agreed that a presidential veto could limit legislative encroachments, but they had difficulty agreeing on the form that the veto power would take. Ultimately, they drafted Article I, section 7, which gives the president the power to veto every bill or vote to which both House and Senate concurrence is necessary, except a vote of adjournment. Congressional resolutions proposing amendments to the Constitution are not subject to presidential veto power. The presidential veto is not absolute, but Congress needs a two-thirds vote of both houses to override it—that is, two-thirds of a quorum present, not two-thirds of all the members.

The veto power gives the president an important role in shaping legislation. Congress overrides vetoes only about 3 percent of the time. Given this limited success rate, the mere threat of a presidential veto provides the president with power to mold proposed legislation to his liking.

If the president fails to sign a bill within ten days (Sundays excepted) after it is presented to him, it becomes law without his signature unless "Congress by their Adjournment prevent its Return, in which Case it shall not be a Law" (Art. I, sec. 7). This is called a pocket veto. In the *Pocket Veto Case* (1929) the Supreme Court held that "adjournment" means any time during a session that Congress adjourns and is not limited to the final adjournment of a session.

(See also SEPARATION OF POWERS.)
                                        Ronald D. Rotunda

**Vietnam War.** The Vietnam conflict triggered constitutional controversies that split the nation and confronted the Supreme Court with some of the most difficult issues that it faced between 1965 and 1975. The Court ducked the toughest of these questions: the constitutionality of the war itself. While declining to order an end to the fighting, however, it provided a surprising degree of protection to antiwar protestors. The Court also expanded significantly the number of men who could gain exemption from military service as conscientious objectors.

Although benefitted by many of its decisions, opponents of the war were deeply disappointed in the Supreme Court because of its persistent refusal to rule that American military involvement was unlawful. Article I, section 8 of the Constitution provides that "Congress shall have Power . . . [t]o declare war . . . ," but no congres-

sional declaration preceded President Lyndon Johnson's commitment of half a million men to combat in Southeast Asia. Johnson and his successor, Richard *Nixon, insisted that the August 1964 Tonkin Gulf Resolution, in which Congress urged the commander in chief to "take all necessary measures to repel any armed attack against the forces of the United States and to prevent further aggression" and the many appropriations acts in which the legislature provided funds for the armed forces gave them whatever congressional authorization they needed to conduct combat operations in Vietnam. Critics of their policies countered that because Congress had not declared war, they were behaving unconstitutionally. Some also accused the United States of waging a war of aggression in Vietnam and argued that anyone who participated in this conflict would be subject to punishment under principles established at the Nuremberg war crime trials.

The Supreme Court evaded these issues. Beginning with the cases of *Mora* v. *McNamara* (1967) and *Mitchell* v. *United States* (1967), the Court persistently employed its discretionary authority to determine what cases it would hear to exclude from consideration all constitutional challenges to the war and all cases raising the Nuremberg defense. In *Massachusetts* v. *Laird* (1970) it even spurned what amounted to a request from the Massachusetts legislature to decide the constitutionality of the war. Outraged by his colleagues' refusal to confront this issue, Justice William O. *Douglas (joined sometimes by Justices Potter *Stewart and John M. *Harlan) took the unusual step of filing lengthy written dissents from his colleagues' denials of writs of *certiorari, but his protests did no good. The Supreme Court would not even allow a federal district judge to halt the bombing of Vietnam's neutral neighbor, Cambodia, which Nixon initiated without any authorization from Congress. Unwilling to precipitate a conflict with the Executive, the Court protected its institutional interests by leaving the question of the legality of the war to be resolved in the political arena.

But the Court did assist those struggling in that realm to bring American involvement in Southeast Asia to an end. In 1971 Daniel Ellsberg, a "think tank" employee who had formerly worked at the Pentagon, turned against the war. He set out to discredit it by handing over to several newspapers photocopies of a documentary history, prepared by the Defense Department itself, that revealed a number of embarrassing facts concerning the origins of the Vietnam conflict. The Justice Department immediately sought *injunctions, forbidding the press to publish what came to be known as the "Pentagon Papers." The Supreme Court prevented the government from suppressing this official history by ruling in *New York Times Co.* v. *United States* (1971) that the government had failed to meet the heavy burden necessary to justify *prior restraint. In a related case, *Gravel* v. *United States* (1972), the Court held that the *Speech and Debate Clause protected a senator who read the purloined papers at a congressional committee hearing and an aide who had helped him prepare for this exposé.

While willing to safeguard those who made the Pentagon Papers public, the Supreme Court proved reluctant to shield dissidents from the military. In *Laird* v. *Tatum* (1972) it affirmed a district judge's dismissal of a suit brought by antiwar activists, who alleged that army surveillance of civilian protesters was chilling the exercise of *First Amendment rights, announcing that the case raised issues that were not justiciable (see JUSTICIABILITY). The justices also joined the military legal system and lower civilian courts in withholding meaningful constitutional protection from members of the armed forces who wished to protest the war. In *Parker* v. *Levy* (1974) it ruled that the army had violated neither the First Amendment nor the *Fifth when it convicted a dissident captain of conduct prejudicial to the discipline and good order of the service and conduct unbecoming an officer and a gentleman for urging enlisted men not to serve in Vietnam. The Court, however, was not totally insensitive to the interests of citizen-soldiers. In *O'Callahan* v. *Parker* (1969) it held that members of the armed forces, many of whom were conscripts or draft-induced volunteers, could not be tried by courts martial for ordinary crimes that were not service connected (see MILITARY JUSTICE; MILITARY TRIALS AND MARTIAL LAW).

And while unwilling to undermine military discipline by sanctioning protest in the ranks, the Supreme Court did provide constitutional shelter to civilian critics of American involvement in Vietnam. Initially, the Court appeared to be no more protective of dissent than it had been during *World War I. In *United States* v. *O'Brien* (1968) the Warren Court held that a federal statute that criminalized one of the most popular means of expressing opposition to the war, draft card burning, did not violate the First Amendment. *O'Brien* proved to be quite unrepresentative. Even before that highly controversial decision came down, the Warren Court had held in *Bond* v. *Floyd* (1966) that the First Amendment precluded the Georgia legislature from denying an African-American man the seat to which he had been elected because of his affiliation with an organization that had issued a statement condemning the war and endorsing draft resistance. After *O'Brien* Warren and his colleagues held in *Tinker* v. *Des Moines School District* (1969) that it was unconstitutional for a pubic school to expel students who wore black armbands to class to protest American involvement in Vietnam.

When Warren *Burger became chief justice the Court continued to protect dissent. Although holding in *Lloyd Corp.* v. *Tanner* (1972) that the

management of a shopping mall might exclude demonstrators who wanted to hand out antiwar leaflets from its property without violating the First Amendment, in another case it ruled that the Constitution protected from punishment a man who wore a real military uniform in a protest skit. In *Flower* v. *United States* (1972) the Burger Court took the position that the armed services could not exclude antiwar activists from bases or parts of bases that were otherwise open to the public. Such rulings reflected the mood of an American public growing increasingly disaffected with the Vietnam conflict. The Supreme Court joined the rest of the federal judiciary in using the First Amendment to protect agitation aimed at bringing an end to the fighting.

The Court also made it easier for young men who did not wish to participate in the war to gain exemption from military service as conscientious objectors. Section 6(j) of the Universal Military Training and Service Act exempted from combatant duty in the armed forces anyone who, by reason of religious training and belief, conscientiously opposed participation in war. The statute defined religious training and belief as "an individual's belief in relation to a Supreme Being. . . ." The defendants in *United States* v. *Seeger* (1965) and *Welsh* v. *United States* (1970) were both denied classification as conscientious objectors because they were agnostics. Although neither man appeared to meet the requirements of section 6(j), the Supreme Court held that both Welsh and Seeger were entitled to be classified as conscientious objectors. Apparently convinced that if the statute were read literally, it would have to be invalidated as a violation of the First Amendment's prohibition against the establishment of religion, the Court interpreted religious beliefs as including moral and philosophical tenets held with the strength of traditional religious convictions. While *Seeger* and *Welsh* blatantly distorted the intent of Congress, they did preserve the exemption for those to whom the legislature had wanted to give it. These rulings also increased the number of men who could avoid serving in an increasingly unpopular war. The Court refused, however, to allow those opposed only to fighting in Vietnam to claim conscientious objector status. In *Gillette* v. *United States* (1971), it held that denying the exemption to those, such as Catholics, whose religious views precluded only participation in unjust military conflicts, did not violate the First Amendment's Establishment Clause. The Court feared selective conscientious objection could not be administered fairly and might "corrode the spirit of public service and the values of willing performance of citizen's duties that are the very heart of free government" (p. 460).

Yet, the war itself ate away at all those things. By using the First Amendment to prevent suppression of antiwar protest, the Court legitimated the expressions of disillusionment, anger, and alienation that eventually pressured the political branches into withdrawing from Southeast Asia.

(See also CONSCIENTIOUS OBJECTION; SPEECH AND THE PRESS; WAR; WAR POWERS.)

□ W. Taylor Reveley, *War Powers of the President and Congress: Who Holds the Arrows and Olive Branch* (1981). Arthur Schlesinger, Jr., *The Imperial Presidency* (1973). Bob Woodward and Scott Armstrong, *The Brethren* (1979).                          Michal R. Belknap

**Vinson, Frederick Moore** (b. Louisa, Ky., 22 Jan. 1890; d. Washington, D.C., 8 Sept. 1953; interred Louisa, Ky.), chief justice, 1946–1953. The thirteenth chief justice was the son of a small-town Kentucky jailer. He achieved the highest academic record in the history of Centre College in Danville, Kentucky, earning his LL.B. degree. He soon became city attorney in his hometown. In 1921, he was elected district attorney and three years later, was elected to Congress. After being defeated in the Republican landslide of 1928, Vinson was sent back to Congress in 1930, where he served four more terms, and on the Committee on Appropriations and the powerful Ways and Means Committee proved a staunch supporter of President Franklin *Roosevelt's *New Deal.

His legislative skill and collegiality garnered Vinson strong congressional goodwill for later confirmations. President Roosevelt nominated Vinson for the United States Court of Appeals for the District of Columbia in 1937. Vinson resigned from the court in May 1943 to become director of Economic Stabilization in the Roosevelt administration. His executive branch experience continued in a brief succession of positions of increasing responsibility (Federal Loan Administrator, director of War Mobilization and Reconversion) culminating with President Harry S. Truman's appointment to be secretary of the treasury in July 1945.

A flurry of speculation and political maneuvering followed the death of Chief Justice Harlan F. *Stone in April 1946 over whether President Truman should elevate a sitting justice and appoint a new associate justice, or simply select a new chief from outside the Court. The infighting intensified when two different justices threatened Truman with their resignations to keep Justice Robert H. *Jackson from being elevated. These bitter disagreements among the justices became personal and public. Truman apparently chose his longtime friend because of Vinson's experience in each of the three branches of government, because Vinson could be expected to support strong governmental action by the executive and because he thought Vinson had the ability and personality to calm the Court.

That the public rancor dissipated somewhat may have been to Vinson's credit. Ideologically, Vinson usually voted with the conservative justices (Jackson, Felix *Frankfurter, Harold *Burton, and Stanley *Reed) against the liberals (Wil-

*Frederick Moore Vinson*

liam O. *Douglas, Wiley *Rutledge, Frank *Murphy, and Hugo *Black). The conservative wing began to dominate the Court with the 1949 appointments of Justices Tom C. *Clark and Sherman *Minton.

Vinson was not a philosopher. He never undertook to formulate a broad or systematic view of the Constitution. He was a pragmatic man, guided by a few generalities: democracy is the ideal form of government by the informed judgment of the people; a strong government is essential to preserve individual liberty; and the president ought to lead the government.

During his tenure, the number of cases heard by the Court declined, and he assigned relatively few important cases to himself. One rumored criticism then, which since has become a Supreme Court norm, was that Vinson did all his "writing" with his hands in his pockets, outlining the general approach to his clerk and then suggesting but few revisions in the draft. His most famous opinion was his dissent in *Youngstown Sheet and Tube Co.* v. *Sawyer* (1952), known as the *Steel Seizure Case*. When the Court held by a 6-to-3 vote that President Truman's seizure of the steel mills during the Korean War was unconstitutional, Vinson sided with the president. Vinson's cold war worries (see COMMUNISM AND COLD WAR) were best exemplified in *Dennis* v. *United States* (1951), which affirmed criminal convictions against leaders of the American Communist party. Setting the stage for the successor Warren Court, he agreed with challenges brought by African-Americans against various discriminatory state actions.

A 1970 poll of "experts" rated Vinson as one of eight "failures," the only chief justice to be so categorized. Other scholars have labeled this characterization unfair. Vinson's tenure on the Court was shorter than most of his counterparts (seven years), and he presided over a Court divided by ideology and personality. His opinions were conservative, except in the area of civil rights, but not poorly reasoned.

☐ C. Herman Pritchett, *Civil Liberties and the Vinson Court* (1954). Symposium, "In Memoriam: Chief Justice Fred M. Vinson," *Northwestern University Law Review* 49 (1954): 1–75.                    Thomas E. Baker

**Virginia v. Tennessee,** 148 U.S. 503 (1893), argued 8–9 Mar. 1893, decided 3 Apr. 1893 by vote of 8 to 0; Field for the Court, Harlan not participating. Virginia invoked the *original jurisdiction of the Supreme Court, asking it to set aside a survey that both Virginia and Tennessee had recognized in 1803 as correctly marking their boundary. Virginia argued that the joint recognition was unenforceable because it had not received the approval of Congress as required by the Compact Clause of Article I, section 10, which states that "no state shall, without the consent of Congress, . . . enter into any agreement or compact with another state, or with a foreign power." The "compact" was said to arise from each state's ratification of the line in consideration of the ratification by the other.

Justice Stephen J. *Field rejected Virginia's argument. In Field's pragmatic view, the clause did not require congressional approval of every compact. Instead, Congress need approve only those that threatened to increase the powers of the states at the expense of the national government. Furthermore, Field reasoned that the approval need not be explicit; approval could be found, as it was here, in successive Congressional acts recognizing the result of the pact.

Field's opinion had two obvious advantages: it fit well within the Court's continuing effort to preserve a place for the states in the federal scheme, and it rid Congress of the burden of considering every joint action taken by two or more states. The interpretation is still followed and continues to allow states considerable freedom to contract with each other to deal with regional problems.

(See also STATE SOVEREIGNTY AND STATES' RIGHTS.)

                    Walter F. Pratt, Jr.

**Virginia v. West Virginia,** 206 U.S. 290 (1907), argued 11–12 Mar. 1907, decided 27 May 1907 by vote of 9 to 0; Fuller for the Court. The first of nine cases concerning the division of fiscal responsibilities between one state and another formed from its territory, *Virginia* v. *West Virginia* sorely tested the power of the Supreme Court to enforce decrees against a state. When West Virginia separated from Virginia in 1863 during the Civil War, no settlement was made concerning its

respective share of its parent's prewar state debt. Delayed by Virginia's disputes with the state bondholders even as to the share it concededly owed, negotiation on West Virginia's portion did not begin until 1894. Virginia attributed one-third of its debt to West Virginia since the latter had succeeded to one-third of its territory, while West Virginia offered to pay a much smaller share, based on the proportion of the borrowed money actually expended within its borders. Negotiation proved fruitless, and in 1906 Virginia commenced an original action in the Supreme Court on behalf of the bondholders. After fact-finding by a court-appointed master, a decree was issued in 1911 apportioning West Virginia's share on the basis of property values (exclusive of slaves) at the time of separation; by this reckoning West Virginia owed less than a quarter of the original debt, plus accrued interest. When West Virginia failed to pay, Virginia—in marked contrast to its usual states' rights position—asked the Court to consider means of coercion. The possibility was raised that the Supreme Court might order the West Virginia legislature to levy a tax, or even that the Court might levy the tax itself. In 1919 West Virginia admitted liability and began payment on its share of the debt, which was completed in 1939.

(See also STATE SOVEREIGNTY AND STATES' RIGHTS.)

                    John V. Orth

**Vote, Right to.** Even the most arbitrary and tyrannical governments often feel compelled to hold elections in order to create the appearance of popular legitimacy. But in such states citizens who vote are nonetheless disfranchised. The right to vote means the right to choose among a range of candidates with competing views. Periodic elections in which opposing candidates vie for office are the foundation upon which democracies are built.

It may seem remarkable, then, that nowhere in the United States Constitution is there an explicit declaration of the right to vote. But that right is certainly implicit—in the guarantee that every state will have a republican form of government (Art. IV, sec. 6; see GUARANTEE CLAUSE), in the description of the House of Representatives as "chosen . . . by the People of the several States" (Art. 1 sec. 2), and in the references to the election of senators and the president. In addition, the matter of who will qualify to vote in elections for the House is mentioned, with the clear implication that there will indeed be voters whose qualifications will need to be set.

Setting voter qualifications in both state and national elections was a task initially left entirely to the states, which excluded all men without property and all women from electoral participation. Beginning in the nineteenth century, however, states gradually opened the door to wider participation. In part, amendments to the Constitution forced them to do so. The *Fifteenth Amendment (1870) prohibited states from denying the right to vote on account of "race, color, or previous condition of servitude." The *Nineteenth Amendment (1920) enfranchised women (see GENDER). The *Twenty-fourth (1964) banned *poll taxes, although only for federal elections. The *Twenty-sixth (1971) directed states to allow qualified citizens who were age eighteen or older to vote. Finally, the *Equal Protection and *Due Process Clauses of the *Fourteenth Amendment (1868) came to be read as preventing states from enacting suffrage laws that conflict with fundamental principles of fairness, liberty, and self-government.

*Enfranchisement of African-Americans.* Some amendments have required no judicial interpretation: the Nineteenth, Twenty-fourth, and Twenty-sixth contain clear directives. But the Due Process and Equal Protection Clauses are open to a variety of readings. The Fifteenth Amendment is in a class by itself: seemingly unambiguous, it was interpreted in ways that all but ignored its plain purpose. Ninety-five years after its passage most southern blacks still could not vote.

From the late nineteenth century until 1965, most southern blacks were disfranchised by poll taxes, fradulently administered literacy tests, *white primaries, intimidation, and violence. The Supreme Court initially upheld literacy tests and poll taxes as constitutionally permissible means by which to maintain a responsible and informed electorate, but in the 1920s Democratic party primaries in which participation was restricted to whites began to crumble under judicial attack. And in 1953 the Supreme Court in *Terry v. Adams dealt the last of what had been a series of blows to that exclusionary practice.

*An Egalitarian Message.* Those decisions vindicated the basic, indisputable right of access to the ballot for African-Americans. But 1953 was also the year in which Earl *Warren became chief justice, and when the high Court turned again to the question of suffrage its decisions were bold and adventurous. In a radical break with precedent, the Court took on the issue of legislative apportionment (*Baker v. Carr, 1962) and embraced the principle of equal representation for equal numbers of people—one person, one vote (*Reynolds v. Sims, 1964). The Court's traditional deference to state legislatures on franchise matters gave way to a new concern with equality. Wading into what Justice Felix *Frankfurter had once called a *political thicket (*Colegrove v. Green, 1946), the Court was now prepared to redraw the nation's political map (see REAPPORTIONMENT CASES).

The Court also extended its egalitarian message to other electoral matters. For instance, in *Harper v. Virginia State Board of Elections (1966) the Court outlawed the imposition of a poll tax in state elections, although the tax met traditional constitutional standards: it was neither racially discriminatory nor indefensible as rational policy, but the court found that it unconstitutionally signaled out the poor.

*Group Rights.* A more radical extension of the egalitarian principle came when the Court addressed an issue that lay just beneath the surface of the "one person, one vote" decisions: group voting rights. From the outset, reapportionment decisions had clearly involved more than the individual's right to vote, as Justices Frankfurter and John M. *Harlan, had suggested in dissents in *Baker* and *Reynolds,* respectively, had understood. The Court had upheld the right of the individual, autonomous voter to cast a ballot of no less weight than that of his neighbor—as measured by the standard of a uniform ratio between residents and respresentatives throughout the jurisdiction. But *Reynolds* and other decisions had spoken as well of the unconstitutionality of electoral arrangements that diluted or debased the weight of a citizen's vote, and in directing states simply to create equal population districts (to ensure mathematical parity) while promising "full and effective participation," the decisions had clearly promised more than they delivered. Citizens were, in fact, politically effective only as members of groups. The Court had spoken of "full and effective participation" and an "equally effective voice," but the promised equality was not one that individuals, as individuals, could attain. Thus there were bound to be demands by groups whose appetites had been whetted by the rhetoric and who felt their interests to be improperly represented and their ballots to be of insufficient weight.

*Constitutional Implications.* The neglected question of group rights has been explored in a series of constitutional and statutory decisions involving the weight of ballots cast by African-American and Latino voters. In 1965 and 1966 two constitutional cases involving group rights (*Fortson v. Dorsey* and *Burns v. Richardson*) virtually invited civil rights groups to initiate further litigation challenging potentially discriminatory electoral arrangements. Multimember districts, at-large voting, and districting plans fragment minority voting strength and thus decrease the likelihood of minority officeholding. (The level of minority *representation* is a separate question, since whites can represent minority voters.) Divide a white-majority city into wards, create some heavily African-American (and/or Latino) districts, and the election of minorities to office will usually be assured.

The invitation to civil rights litigants was readily accepted, and in a series of constitutional cases from 1971 to 1982 the Supreme Court struggled unsuccessfully with the meaning of electoral exclusion. In *Whitcomb v. Chavis* (1971) the Court noted that black candidates can lose elections for reasons unrelated to race. They can be Democrats, say, in a Republican district. Electoral defeat alone does not suggest inadequate electoral opportunity, and opportunity *is* the Fourteenth Amendment question. It was a clear message, made murky by subsequent rulings. In 1973, in *White* v. *Regester,* the Court held for minority plaintiffs in a decision that contained no coherent definition of electoral exclusion. In *\*Mobile* v. *Bolden* (1980), the Court made racist intention the test of electoral exclusion and thus brought voting rights cases into line with other Fourteenth Amendment holdings. That amendment, it suggested, was about racism; only racists can create or sustain a racist electoral system; and racists, by definition, have bad intentions. Invidious purpose was thus the Fourteenth Amendment test. But two years later (*Rogers* v. *Lodge,* 1982) the Court ignored its own rule. The intent test had metamorphosed into one that relied on evidence of discriminatory effect.

The Court never adequately defined electoral discrimination in these constitutional cases. In part, its failure reflected the magnitude of the task it faced. These cases posed large and perhaps judicially unmanageable questions about the meaning of political equality and the "normal" relationship between racial and ethnic groups in the political sphere.

*Statutory Implications.* These questions became no more manageable in the statutory context. Similar problems have plagued the Court's rulings interpreting the *\*Voting Rights Act, enacted in 1965 and amended in 1970, 1975, and 1982. The statute requires federal approval ("preclearance") of all changes in the method of election in "covered" jurisdictions—those identified as having a record of minority disfranchisement by an arguably questionable formula. (Black disfranchisement was the sole concern in 1965, but the 1975 amendment extended special emergency protection to Latinos, Asian-Americans, and Native Americans and expanded the definition of disfranchising devices to include the use of English-only ballots.) The statutory decisions dealt, first, with the question of what constitutes a change in the method of voting (necessitating preclearance) and, second, with the circumstances in which an electoral change can be labeled discriminatory.

In 1965 the preclearance provision had been regarded as merely a hedge against inventive schemes that denied southern blacks access to the polls. In 1969, however, in *Allen* v. *Board of Elections,* the Supreme Court enlarged the meaning of a "voting" change to include new districting lines, the institution of at-large elections or of multimember districts, the relocation of a polling place, and even urban annexations of adjacent suburban or rural areas.

The preliminary definitional question had been settled, but a further one remained: When was a districting plan, annexation or other change in a covered jurisdiction without discriminatory purpose or effect? For instance, what sort of change in the location of a polling place or jurisdictional lines was discriminatory?

Different standards came to be applied to different sorts of cases. The strength of the African-American vote may be diminished when a city annexes suburban territory that contains more whites than blacks. If elections are at-large, the Court has said (e.g., *Richmond* v. *United States,* 1975), a city must compensate its African-American residents by switching to ward voting and creating as many "safe" minority districts as it can.

With redistricting and other changes, however, backsliding became the issue. The proper question, the Court held, was whether a new districting plan had left black voters less able to elect black representatives—that is, whether they had become *relatively* worse off. This approach made sense for two reasons. It squared with the initial point of the preclearance provision, which was to guard against attempts to pull African-Americans back from the gains other provisions had enabled them to make. And it established an administratively viable framework. Preclearance became primarily a Justice Department job, and the question of backsliding became one that federal attorneys remote from the scene could answer. Had the Court hinged preclearance on a showing that the new electoral rules were fair in some *absolute* sense, federal attorneys would have been forced either to address complex questions of electoral equality appropriate only for a court, or, alternatively, to fall back on a statistical rule of thumb—that of proportionate racial and ethnic representation on all legislative bodies.

Different standards for different sorts of cases never made much sense, and in 1980 the Court resolved the tension by implicitly reinterpreting the purpose of the statute. In *Rome* v. *United States* it suggested that the point of the Voting Rights Act was to promote black officeholding and that only African-Americans could represent African-Americans. And in *Thornburg* v. *Gingles* (1986), interpreting a 1982 amendment to the act, the justices again came very close to equating proportionate electoral success with minority inclusion in the political process. If a state is 30 percent black, the Court seemed to imply, then the state legislature should be 30 percent black; African-Americans have a right to electoral arrangements that promote proportionate officeholding by African-Americans.

The notion of group rights to proportionate representation has never been embraced, however. The traditional political consensus has been that, in the American system, legislators represent individual voters whose political identity has been a matter of personal choice. Whites can represent blacks because not all blacks "vote black." Some see themselves, for political purposes, as primarily Republican or pro-life or urban or anticrime. Moreover, when the state categorizes individuals for political purposes along lines of race and sanctions group membership as a qualification for office, it inhibits political integration; the commitment to the group is heightened at the expense of the sense of common citizenship.

In true democracies, citizens cast ballots that are meaningful. That is their distinguishing characteristic. But the meaning of a meaningful ballot has radically altered over time. The minority-vote-dilution decisions are but the latest chapter in an extended tale.

(See also FAIR REPRESENTATION; RACE AND RACISM.)

□ Ward E. Y. Elliott, *The Rise of Guardian Democracy: The Supreme Court's Role in Voting Rights Disputes, 1845–1869* (1974). William Gillette, *The Right to Vote: Politics and the Passage of the Fifteenth Amendment* (1969). Frank R. Parker, *Black Votes Count: Political Empowerment in Mississippi after 1965* (1990). Abigail M. Thernstrom, *Whose Votes Count?: Affirmative Action and Minority Voting Rights* (1987).

Abigail M. Thernstrom

**Voting Rights Act of 1965.** Prior to passage of the Voting Rights Act of 1965, the national government responded to racial discrimination in voting in the South in a tepid, haphazard way that relied on litigation. This was due in part to restrictive Supreme Court decisions, such as the *\*Civil Rights Cases* (1883), which limited the reach of congressional authority to enforce the Civil War Amendments. But it was also due to the South's disproportionate influence in Congress, and particularly in the Senate, where southern Democrats could successfully filibuster.

Prior to *\*World War II, minority voter registration in the deep South was virtually nonexistent. In 1940 about 150,000 blacks, representing about 3 percent of the five million southern blacks of voting age, were registered to vote. Various tactics and devices, such as literacy tests (often discriminatorily applied), economic and physical coercion, and the *\*white primary, combined to keep blacks from effective voting participation. The demise of the white primary, banned by the Supreme Court in *\*Smith* v. *Allwright* (1944) and the return from World War II of many black soldiers no longer willing to accept the Jim Crow system, resulted in some increases in voter registration. But the hostile southern resistance to *\*Brown* v. *Board of Education* (1954) temporarily ended those gains.

*Civil Rights Movement. Brown* was about school desegregation, but it soon became a symbol of the drive for complete racial equality. It was extended to prohibit all forms of public *\*segregation, and it energized a *\*civil rights movement of theretofore unimaginable proportions. Beginning late in the 1950s, black civil rights organizations such as the Southern Christian Leadership

Conference (SCLC), the Student Nonviolent Coordinating Committee (SNCC), and the Council on Racial Equality (CORE) organized and implemented various sit-ins, boycotts, voter registration drives, freedom rides, and "freedom summers" in order to end racial discrimination of all kinds. Enfranchising African-Americans was a major goal.

During this time Congress also responded to the new call for racial equality. The southern filibuster was broken and civil rights bills were passed in 1957 and 1960—the first civil rights legislation since 1875. But these acts, though symbolically important, were modest in scope and lacking in enforcement power; they relied heavily on a passive, litigation-oriented strategy. The attorney general was empowered to file suit in federal court seeking injunctive relief against violations of the *\*Fifteenth Amendment (see INJUNCTIONS AND EQUITABLE REMEDIES). The 1957 act did, however, create the office of assistant attorney general for civil rights, and it upgraded the civil rights unit to a division in the Department of Justice. The U.S. Commission on Civil Rights was also created.

Both acts enabled the Justice Department to go into three-judge federal district courts on behalf of African-American citizens who had been disfranchised without first exhausting remedies in *\*state courts. But the burden of challenging local voting practices fell disproportionately on a few black citizens who had to initiate legal proceedings in an extremely hostile environment before generally unsympathetic federal judges. By 1961 there were fewer than five cases in the federal courts challenging southern voter discrimination. The 1963 report of the Civil Rights Commission pointed to the inadequacies of a litigative strategy in both a Republican (Eisenhower) and Democratic (Kennedy) administration, and it called for more direct action by the national government to implement meaningful voter-registration plans.

Civil rights, however, was not initially a major agenda item for the Kennedy administration. Its passive strategy eschewed comprehensive litigation and a strong federal presence in the southern states. In the words of Assistant Attorney General Burke Marshall, "We must realize the constitutional rights of Negroes in states where they are denied but we must do so with the smallest possible federal intrusion into the conduct of state affairs" (Garrow, pp. 21–22). Inexorably the Kennedy administration's concern increased and its response became more forceful with the escalation of the protest movement, the need to protect the freedom riders, the 1963 march on Washington, and resistance to integrating the universities of Mississippi and Alabama.

More confrontational strategies to combat voting discrimination increased pressure on Congress to pass meaningful legislation. The 1965 SCLC march to Selma, Alabama, was designed to create a scenario that would force the federal government to pass a more aggressive, interventionist voting-rights bill. The (expected and hoped for) harsh reaction of Selma sheriff Jim Clark to the protesters and the murder of several of them, carried around the world by television, engendered a dramatic reaction to the indiscriminate use of police dogs, firehoses, and excessive force and violence against the nonviolent civil-rights protesters.

Walter Mondale, then a Democratic senator from Minnesota, expressed the view of many when he said that the "outrage in Selma, Alabama, makes passage of legislation to guarantee southern Negroes the right to vote an absolute imperative for Congress this year." Shortly thereafter, the Johnson administration introduced the Voting Rights Act.

Less then five months later the Voting Rights Act was the law of the land. The draft law had actually been written several months before the Selma protests. Lyndon Johnson, according to his autobiography *Vantage Point*, instructed Attorney General Nicholas Katzenbach to "write the god-damnedest, toughest voting rights act that you can devise" (p. 161). The result was, in fact, a deliberate effort to enforce voting rights directly, avoiding litigation and bypassing hostile southern federal judges.

*Direct Federal Intervention.* The Voting Rights Act, based on Congress's power to enforce the Fifteenth Amendment, broadly restated the amendment's prohibitions against voting discrimination. But it was specially directed toward seven southern states that had relied on literacy tests, spurious educational achievement norms, and good moral character tests to obstruct black voter registration. The "covered" states (or subdivisions) were those that employed a "test or device" to determine voter qualifications *and* in which less than 50 percent of the voting age population was registered to vote for president on 1 November 1964: Alabama, Georgia, Louisiana, Mississippi, North Carolina (parts), South Carolina, Virginia, and, additionally, Alaska. The act suspended for five years the use of all such tests and devices in the covered states. Arkansas, Texas, and Florida were not covered because they did not employ literacy tests, although they too had large nonvoting African-American populations. A covered state could "bail out" by demonstrating to a federal district court in Washington, D.C., that no test or device had been used for racial discrimination in the preceding five years. Alaska, which was initially covered although not an intended target of the act, was permitted to bail out in 1969. No other covered state has been permitted to do so.

Under the act, U.S. marshals and other federal officers could be used as examiners to ensure that African-Americans and members of other minority groups could register to vote without delay or harassment by local white registrars. Indeed, they were authorized to register qualified voters directly.

Most controversial was section 5, the "preclearance" section. In order to insure that covered states did not pass new legislation to obstruct black voter registration or to dilute the expected emergent voting strength of blacks, the states were prohibited from enacting any change in "voting qualifications or prerequisites to voting, or standard, practice or procedures with respect to voting" without first obtaining clearance from the attorney general or a federal district court in Washington, D.C. Thus these states had an affirmative burden to secure federal permission to change their voting laws. (Section 5 was not formally implemented until 1971; the vast majority of all changes submitted have been precleared by the attorney general.)

The Voting Rights Act shifted the burden from the victims of discrimination to the perpetrators; it was the latter who now had to demonstrate that they did not discriminate. This was an unprecedented use of federal power and limit on the powers of the covered states to set and enforce voter qualifications (see FEDERALISM), but the Supreme Court upheld its constitutionality in *South Carolina v. Katzenbach* (1966), in which it held, "As against the reserved powers of the states, Congress may use any rational means to effectuate the constitutional prohibition of racial discrimination in voting" (p. 324). The decision was unanimous except for Justice Hugo *Black's objection to section 5 as a violation of the *Tenth Amendment. A special provision of the law, which was inserted to enfranchise a large group of voters in the Puerto Rican community in New York City, provided that English-language literacy tests could not be used to deny the vote to persons with at least a sixth-grade education in another language in an "American flag" school. This was upheld as an appropriate congressional enforcement of the *Fourteenth Amendment in *Katzenbach v. Morgan* (1966).

*Extensions of the Act.* In 1970 the Voting Rights act was extended for five years. The ban on literacy tests was made nationwide, the coverage formula was amended to include additional jurisdictions, and extended durational residency requirements to vote for president were prohibited. These changes were upheld in *Oregon v. Mitchell* (1970). In 1975 the act was extended for an additional seven years. The ban on literacy tests was made permanent, and bilingual assistance and federal enforcement efforts for language-minority voters (Native Americans, Alaskan natives, and Spanish-heritage citizens) was required in twenty-four states.

The act was extended once again in 1982, but only after extensive debate and initial opposition from the *Reagan administration, which claimed that it had achieved its purposes and should be allowed to expire. Section 5 was extended for twenty-five years, and the bail-out procedure for covered states was amended. Now a state may bail out of the preclearance requirement if it can show that it has not discriminated for ten years and has made efforts to promote minority voting.

A very heated controversy in the 1982 debates concerned section 2, which had been the focus of the Supreme Court's decision in *Mobile v. Bolden* (1980). In that case the Court overturned a federal-court order that the city of Mobile, Alabama, revamp its at-large electoral system to ensure that its 40-percent African-American minority had a fair opportunity to elect some representatives. Under the existing system, dating back to 1911, no black had ever been elected to the three-member city commission. The Court held that there was no violation of either section 2 of the act or of the Fifteenth Amendment because blacks could both register and vote and there was no evidence that the Mobile electoral system was motivated by a *discriminatory intent. As revised in 1982, section 2 (which now applies nationwide) allows a voter to challenge a voting practice or procedure by showing that the results of such a practice or procedure, based on a totality of the evidence presented, are racially discriminatory. Plaintiffs are forbidden, however, to use section 2 to establish racial quotas, and a system of proportional representation designed to protect a particular minority from electoral defeat cannot be required. The revision of section 2 has led to much litigation—and to dozens of cases won by minority plaintiffs (or successfully settled).

The Voting Rights Act has been the most successful civil rights act ever passed by Congress. It resulted in substantial increases in minority-voter registration and (to a lesser extent) voting, and there have been significant derivative increases in the number of African-American elected officials. But there are still some who are opposed to full political participation by racial minorities. The focus of their efforts has been on vote dilution rather than vote denial. Efforts at vote dilution focus on *reapportionment, *gerrymandering, and the misuse of multimember districts and at-large elections (see FAIR REPRESENTATION). Covered states are still monitored by the attorney general under section 5, and vote-dilution efforts in other states have increasingly been challenged under section 2. Thus, more than a quarter of a century after its passage, the Voting Rights Act is alive and well.

(See also RACE AND RACISM; VOTE, RIGHT TO.)

□ Howard Ball, Dale Krane, and Thomas P. Lauth, *Compromised Compliance: Implementation of the 1965 Voting Rights Act* (1982). Numan V. Bartley and Hugh Graham, *Southern Politics and the Second Reconstruction* (1975). David J. Garrow, *Protest at Selma: Martin Luther King, Jr., and the Voting Rights Act of 1965* (1978). Stephen Lawson, *Black Ballots: Voting Rights in the South, 1944–1969* (1976).

Howard Ball

# W

**Wabash, St. Louis & Pacific Railway Co. v. Illinois,** 118 U.S. 557 (1886), argued 14–15 Apr. 1886, decided 25 Oct. 1886 by vote of 6 to 3; Miller for the Court, Bradley, Waite, and Gray in dissent. In *Wabash*, the Supreme Court held that the states have no power to regulate railroad rates for interstate shipments. Substantially modifying the standard employed since *Cooley v. Board of Wardens* (1852), the Court said the Commerce Clause allows the states to enact "indirect" but not "direct" burdens on interstate commerce. State rate regulations were "direct" burdens on commerce and therefore could not govern interstate transportation.

*Wabash* did not deny the states all power over interstate railroading. The Court, for example, upheld state safety regulations as permissible "indirect" burdens. Yet *Wabash* created an important regulatory void by making rate regulation of interstate shipments an exclusive federal power. Prior to *Wabash*, the federal government had left the subject of railroad regulation almost entirely to the states. In response to the decision, Congress established the *Interstate Commerce Commission (1887). Thus, *Wabash* precipitated the advent of the modern independent regulatory agency and initiated the shift of governmental responsibility for economic affairs from the states to the national government. *Wabash* remains a landmark even though the "direct" versus "indirect" test it propounded to define the domain of exclusive federal power over interstate commerce was abandoned in the 1930s in favor of a functional balancing approach.

(See also ADMINISTRATIVE STATE; COMMERCE POWER; FEDERALISM.)

Stephen A. Siegel

**Wade, United States v.,** 388 U.S. 218 (1967), argued 16 Feb. 1967, decided 12 June 1967 by vote of 5 to 4; Brennan for the Court; White, joined by Harlan and Stewart, dissented from the second part of the holding (see below) and would have upheld the conviction; Black dissented from the first part of the holding but would have upheld the conviction; Fortas, joined by Warren and Douglas, concurred in overturning the conviction, but dissented from the first part of the holding. Wade was indicted for bank robbery, and the FBI put him in a lineup without notifying his attorney. Everyone in the lineup was required to wear a mask and say "put the money in the bag." The Supreme Court held that (1) putting defendants in a lineup and having them wear certain items and utter words used in the crime is not compelled *self-incrimination because it is not testimonial evidence, but also that (2) lineups are a "critical stage" of the prosecution and defendants are entitled to have counsel present. The Court thought that prejudicial conditions, perhaps created unintentionally, existed at lineups for unrepresented defendants. Wade's conviction was overturned on that basis. This holding enlarged the right to *counsel, already greatly expanded in *Miranda v. Arizona* (1966).

Many saw *Wade* as epitomizing the Warren Court's "softness" on crime. In the Crime Control and Safe Streets Act of 1968, Congress allowed use of lineup identification evidence obtained without counsel present in the federal courts. The Burger Court undermined *Wade* in *Kirby* v. *Illinois* (1972) by ruling that the right to counsel at lineups did not take effect until after indictment or its equivalent. In *United States* v. *Ash* (1973), it ruled that counsel was unnecessary when witnesses were shown photographs of the defendant.

(See also SIXTH AMENDMENT.)

Bradley C. Canon

**Waite, Morrison Remick** (b. Lyme, Conn., 29 Nov. 1816; d. Washington, D.C., 23 March 1888; interred Forest Cemetery, Toledo, Ohio), chief justice, 1874–1888. The eldest son of a lawyer who became chief justice of Connecticut, Morrison Remick Waite was destined for a career in law. After graduating from Yale in 1837, he read law with his father for a year, then joined the westward migration of enterprising Yankees, settling in Maumee, Ohio. After a further apprenticeship with a local lawyer, Waite was admitted to the Ohio bar in 1839, promptly entering into partnership with his former mentor. In 1840 Waite married his second cousin, Amelia C. Warner, also of Lyme, Connecticut, who trekked west to join him. Active in the Whig party, Waite was elected to the Ohio legislature in 1849. In 1850 he moved his family to Toledo, where he opened a branch office of his law firm. On the retirement of his senior partner in 1856, Waite established a firm with his younger brother Richard. At the same time the future chief justice abandoned the dying Whig party and helped organize the Republican party in Ohio.

Prosperous and respected in Ohio, Waite first attained national prominence in 1871 when he was appointed one of three United States counsel at the Geneva Arbitration Tribunal, convened to settle the *Alabama* claims. So unexpected was the appointment that Waite at first regarded the telegrams from Washington as a practical joke. When the tribunal ruled in favor of the Americans and awarded $15 million in damages, the counsellors returned home covered in glory. On Chief Justice Salmon *Chase's unexpected death in 1873, President Ulysses S. Grant cast about for a nominee, at first among his unscrupulous political cronies. When one after another refused or withdrew, the president was persuaded to reward a Geneva counsellor, associated with one of the administration's few triumphs. Waite, who had never once argued before the Supreme Court, was suddenly raised to its head.

On first taking his seat, the new chief justice faced a restive and powerful set of associate justices, some of whom had actively sought the appointment for themselves. Rather unexpectedly, Waite took decisive control of the Court, thereafter showing himself a competent judicial administrator. (See CHIEF JUSTICE, OFFICE OF THE.) On the major constitutional issues of the day the

*Morrison Remick Waite*

new chief justice was a disciple of Roger *Taney rather than John *Marshall. While recording a few notable nationalizing opinions—such as in the *Sinking-Fund Cases* (1879), permitting Congress to amend corporate charters in the public interest—Waite favored the states in the key areas of civil rights and economic regulation. In *Minor* v. *Happersett* (1875) he held that denying votes to women was no violation of the *Fourteenth Amendment because suffrage was not a right of *citizenship. The next year in *United States* v. *Cruikshank* (1876) and *United States* v. *Reese* (1876), he wrote opinions that narrowed national protection of the newly freed slaves. At the same time, in *Reynolds* v. *United States* (1879), the first church-state case to reach the Supreme Court, Waite upheld the conviction of a Mormon in a polygamous marriage. (See RELIGION.)

On the issue of regulation of the economy, Waite's leadership in favor of states' rights was vigorously challenged by Justice Stephen J. *Field. The leading case was *Munn* v. *Illinois* (1877), one of a set of related cases known collectively as the *Granger Cases*. Apparently taking his cue from Justice Joseph P. *Bradley, Waite upheld state power to regulate businesses "affected with a public interest," drawing the wrath of railroads and monied men. Waite's pedestrian writing style deprived *Munn* and much else that he wrote of public and scholarly recognition; as Felix *Frankfurter later put it, "Even in his most famous opinion Waite lacked art." In a later case, *Stone* v. *Farmers' Loan and Trust Co.* (1886), also upholding state power, he made a feeble attempt to improve on Chief Justice Marshall's famous dictum in *McCulloch v. Maryland* (1819): "This power to regulate is not a power to destroy, and limitation is not the equivalent of confiscation" (p. 331).

The author of civil rights opinions unpopular in the late twentieth century, underrated for his defense of state power to regulate the economy, and unfairly associated with judicial restraints on national regulation that properly belong to a later generation, Waite lacks an outstanding judicial reputation.

☐ C. Peter Magrath, *Morrison R. Waite* (1963).

John V. Orth

**Wallace, John William** (b. Philadelphia, Pa., 17 Feb. 1815; d. Philadelphia, Pa., 12 Jan. 1884), reporter of decisions, 1863–1875. Last author of a nominative series of Supreme Court reports, Wallace was the son of a distinguished Philadelphia lawyer. He graduated from the University of Pennsylvania in 1833 and studied law in his father's office. Wallace soon turned to the discipline of law librarianship, becoming librarian and treasurer of the Law Association of Philadelphia in 1841. In 1849 he published the first of three volumes of decisions of the United States Court for the Third Circuit.

Wallace's most important publication before coming to the Supreme Court was the 1844 work *The Reporters, Chronologically Arranged: with Occasional Remarks upon their Reporting Merits*. This commentary on the English reporters was revised and republished several times. A work of great scholarship, it established Wallace's reputation in the national bar. He also wrote notes on American cases for the third volume of the series known as *British Crown Cases Reserved* (6 vols., 1839–1853).

When Jeremiah *Black resigned as Supreme Court reporter in 1863, Wallace succeeded him as the seventh reporter. Before his own resignation in 1875, Wallace authored twenty-three volumes of reports (1–23 Wallace and 68–90 U.S. Reports), often praised for their quality. After the judiciary appropriation of 1874, in which Congress allocated twenty-five thousand dollars toward reporting decisions of the Court, 23 Wallace became the last official nominative volume.

After leaving the Court, Wallace continued to write works of literary quality and became president of the Historical Society of Pennsylvania. A devout Roman Catholic, Wallace was known as a reserved man of old-fashioned courtesy.

(See also REPORTERS, SUPREME COURT.)

Francis Helminski

**Wallace v. Jaffree,** 472 U.S. 38 (1985), argued 4 Dec. 1984, decided 4 June 1985 by vote of 6 to 3; Stevens for the Court, Powell concurring, O'Connor concurring in the judgment, Burger, White, and Rehnquist in dissent. Public opinion has never endorsed the Supreme Court's school prayer decisions. Since 1961, more than 75 percent of those questioned by the Gallup Poll have consistently supported reintroduction of formal prayer into the public schools. *Constitutional amendments to this end were periodically but unsuccessfully introduced in Congress. The constitutional doctrine of *Engel* v. *Vitale* (1962) and *Abington* v. *Schempp* (1963) remained in force. *Wallace* was the first serious test of its continuing vitality.

The Alabama statute at issue in *Wallace*, as initially enacted in 1978, authorized schools to provide a minute of silence for "meditation." A 1981 amendment provided a similar period for "meditation or voluntary prayer," and in 1982 the law was changed to allow teachers to lead "willing students" in a specified prayer to "Almighty God." Upon challenge by Ishmael Jaffree and various separationist groups, a federal district court held that *Engel* and *Schempp* were wrong; states did have the authority to establish religion. A court of appeals reversed, and the Supreme Court granted *certiorari to decide the constitutionality of only the 1981 amendment: Can a state provide a moment of silence at the beginning of a school day for the express purpose of facilitating "meditation or prayer?"

There were reasons to believe that the Court would be amenable to opening a crack in the "wall of separation" on this question. The public's support for school prayer was translated by various state legislatures into statutes aiding religious schools and practices. The election of Ronald *Reagan and the legal mobilization of accommodationist forces—seven groups, including the Moral Majority, the Christian Legal Society, and the Legal Foundation of America, filed *amicus curiae briefs in *Wallace*—also augured ill for separationist precedents. The Administration was dedicated to an interpretation of the Establishment Clause that would lower or abandon the "wall." It filed numerous amicus briefs before the Court and split oral argument with states sympathetic to its view (as in *Wallace*) to advance this argument.

There were also signs from the Court that it was ready to reject its earlier approach. Even before Reagan's election, it adopted an accommodationist posture in affirming, for the first time, direct payment of public funds to religious schools (*Committee for Public Education and Religious Liberty* v. *Regan,* 1980). In subsequent cases, it upheld tax credits and deductions to parents of all school children (*Mueller* v. *Allen,* 1983), state-paid legislative chaplains (*Marsh* v. *Chambers,* 1983), and a publicly sponsored nativity creche (*Lynch* v. *Donnelly,* 1984). The time seemed ripe for a reconsideration of *Engel/Schempp*. However, it proved not to be.

Justice John Paul *Stevens's majority opinion striking down the law was short, to the point, and girded by separationist precedents. Applying the *Schempp* test as it had been reworked in

*Lemon* v. *Kurtzman* (1971), he found the practices sanctioned by the statute to lack a "secular purpose"—one not grounded in a desire to "advance" religion. Although the meditation and prayer statute failed constitutional scrutiny, the Court left open the possibility that one confined to an undefined moment of silence might pass muster; Powell's concurrence emphasized that point. Justice Sandra Day *O'Connor concurred separately to reiterate her "endorsement" standard, first articulated in her *Lynch* concurrence, and to note that a neutral moment of silence law would not be controlled by the doctrine of *Engel* and *Schempp*.

The dissents of Chief Justice Warren *Burger and Justice Byron *White held that the Alabama act was an example of "benevolent neutrality" and was thus constitutional under the Court's accommodationist precedents (p. 89). Justice William *Rehnquist's dissent was more pointed. He contended that any decision based on *Everson* v. *Board of Education* (1947) was wrong; the Constitution does not impose a "wall of separation" between church and state. After an extended analysis of the intent of the framers of the First Amendment, he concluded that the Establishment Clause merely forbids state establishment of a national church or preference of one sect over others and most certainly does not require a state to be neutral between religion and "irreligion."

(See also RELIGION.)

Joseph F. Kobylka

**Walworth, Reuben Hyde** (b. Bozrah, Conn., 26 Oct. 1788; d. Saratoga Springs, N.Y., 27 Nov. 1867) unconfirmed appointee to the Supreme Court. Walworth studied law with John Russell of Troy, New York, and was admitted to the bar in 1809. In 1817 he was appointed circuit judge of the Supreme Court for the Fourth District of New York; he concurrently served in the U.S. House of Representatives from 1821 to 1823.

In 1828 Walworth was appointed chancellor of New York state, where he contributed significantly to equity jurisprudence, producing important decisions on evidence, pleading, injunctions and arbitration. On 13 March 1844 President John *Tyler nominated Walworth to the Supreme Court to fill the vacancy on the Second Circuit. Walworth's nomination suffered from Tyler's lack of support from either Whigs or Democrats. The Senate postponed action on 15 January 1844, and on 17 June 1844 Tyler withdrew Walworth's name and proposed instead John C. *Spencer. Later Tyler removed Spencer's name and resubmitted Walworth, who again failed to be confirmed.

Walworth retired as chancellor in 1848 but in 1850 was asked by the Supreme Court to serve as special master in *Pennsylvania* v. *Wheeling and Belmont Bridge Company* (1852). The Court published his extensive report in 1851.

(See also NOMINEES, REJECTION OF.)

Elizabeth B. Monroe

**War** presents special problems for all governmental institutions, but especially for the Supreme Court. During war, tensions of the moment make it difficult for the Court to range beyond the narrow facts of a case or even to decide issues when decisions may have direct consequences for the war's conduct.

The dominant pattern of the use of power during wartime has been one of presidential initiative, often without advance legislative authorization, followed by congressional approval or acquiescence. This pattern became clear in the early days of the *Civil War, when President Abraham *Lincoln took dramatic action during the ten weeks between the fall of Fort Sumter and the convening of Congress in special session on 4 July 1861. Among other things, Lincoln consolidated state militias into one force, summoned volunteers for active service, increased the size of the army and navy without legislative authorization, paid money from the Treasury without an appropriation, closed the Post Office to "treasonable correspondence," and suspended the writ of *habeas corpus. Only some of these actions were later specifically approved by Congress.

The pattern repeated itself during *World War I, when President Woodrow Wilson closed German wireless stations and created a host of administrative boards before the declaration of war. During *World War II, the pattern occurred yet again. Before America's entry into the war, President Franklin D. *Roosevelt agreed with Britain to exchange overage destroyers for leases of British ports in the Caribbean. Roosevelt also created several presidential offices, exercised considerable control over labor relations, and employed broad powers under statutory delegations (see PRESIDENTIAL EMERGENCY POWERS).

From a few leading cases where the Supreme Court has been called on to decide the legality of presidential conduct, two main themes have emerged. First, the Court has tended not to interfere with major policies of the political branches of government even when constitutional issues have been presented. Second, in a few instances, the Court has laid down limits, although these often have been after the fact. These opposing tendencies have prompted the comment that, in the crucible of war, constitutional principles can become "highly malleable" (Corwin, 1984, p. 271).

*Civil War Period.* In the *Prize Cases* (1863) the Court rebuffed a challenge to President Lincoln's blockade of southern ports, which led to the capture of ships as prizes of war. The Court, divided 5 to 4, upheld Lincoln's action as a defensive use of his power as commander in chief, even though there was no declaration of war or other legislative authorization.

*Ex parte *Milligan* (1866) resulted from Lincoln's suspension of the writ of habeas corpus. Lincoln acted without advance legislative approval, although Congress passed a statute in

1863 retroactively authorizing the writ's suspension. During the war, military authorities arrested persons suspected of treason or espionage, placed them in prison, and tried them before military tribunals; if convicted, they were unable to petition a civilian court for a writ of habeas corpus. This scenario led to conflict between the president and Chief Justice Roger B. *Taney, who questioned the president's power to suspend the writ in *Ex parte Merryman* (1861). The chief justice, acting as a circuit judge in Baltimore, ordered a prisoner's release. The local military commander refused, and President Lincoln continued to direct suspension of the writ. *Merryman* reaffirmed the practical limits of the justices' authority.

In *Milligan*, the Court reviewed the legality of trying civilians before military tribunals. It ruled that so long as regular courts are open and functioning, civilians must be tried there, where they receive procedural protections such as *trial by jury. *Milligan*'s apparently bold result should be considered in light of the fact that the Court acted after the war was over and hostilities had ceased. The same happened in *Duncan* v. *Kahanamoku* (1946), where after World War II the Court reaffirmed *Milligan*.

*World War I.* Numerous statutes delegated broad administrative authority to the president during World War I. While many such statutes were never challenged, the Court in 1918 upheld the Selective Service Act in *Arver* v. *United States* (see SELECTIVE DRAFT LAW CASES) and in 1919 sustained a prohibition statute in *Hamilton* v. *Kentucky Distilleries & Warehouse Co.*

The Court failed to protect freedom of speech during and after World War I, when legislatures attempted to control seditious expression (see SPEECH AND THE PRESS; STATE SEDITION LAWS; SUBVERSION). In *Schenck* v. *United States* (1919), defendants had been convicted under the 1917 *Espionage Act of conspiracy to cause insubordination in the armed forces, and of obstructing recruiting, by circulating to draftees a leaflet criticizing the draft. The Court affirmed the conviction. In his majority opinion, Justice Oliver Wendell *Holmes wrote, "When a nation is at war many things that might be said in time of peace are such a hindrance to its effort that their utterance will not be endured" (p. 52). The Court affirmed another conviction under the Espionage Act in *Debs* v. *United States* (1919). These decisions came under heavy criticism in ensuing decades. In cases such as *Brandenburg* v. *Ohio* (1969), the Supreme Court eventually developed an approach that is more protective of speech. Yet *Schenck* and *Debs* are reminders of the pressures that war imposes on civil liberties.

*World War II.* The pattern of broad presidential assertions of power, with legislative approval or acquiescence, recurred during World War II. The Lend Lease Act of 1941, passed before the attack on Pearl Harbor, gave the president authority to order or procure articles of war for transfer to any country that the president deemed vital to the nation's defense. The Emergency Price Control Act of 1942 authorized the Office of Price Administration (OPA) to regulate consumer prices. The Supreme Court upheld this statute in *Yakus* v. *United States* (1944). It also upheld the sanctions power of the OPA in *Steuart & Bros.* v. *Bowles* (1944), which dealt with the claim of a fuel-oil dealer charged with violating an OPA order. Congress had not enacted the penalty provision under which the OPA proceeded against the retailer, but the Court nonetheless held the executive had authority to penalize suppliers for violating rules on fuel-oil distribution.

The Court upheld other economic controls during World War II. These included a statute authorizing recovery of excess profits under the Renegotiation Act (*Lichter* v. *United States*, 1948) as well as rent controls (*Bowles* v. *Willingham*, 1944). In *Woods* v. *Miller Co.* (1948) the Court sustained the continuation of rent controls after the war, on the theory they were necessary to cope with condition caused by the war.

Civil liberties came to the fore during World War II in leading decisions in which the Court—as in earlier conflicts—tended to defer to executive determinations. A key action was President Roosevelt's order in February 1942, giving the secretary of war power to establish military areas from which persons could be excluded to prevent espionage and sabotage. Through a series of subsequent military orders and a 1942 statute ratifying the President's order, tens of thousands of persons of Japanese descent were made to leave their homes in the western states and report to a central staging area, from which they were taken to camps hundreds or thousands of miles away from their homes and workplaces.

In *Hirabayashi* v. *United States* (1943), the Court upheld a curfew restriction imposed by military order. The Court relied on the president's power as commander in chief of the armed forces and noted that Congress had enacted a statute ratifying the president's initial order. In *Korematsu* v. *United States* (1944), the Court determined that the exclusion program did not unconstitutionally burden Japanese persons because of their race. Three justices dissented, including Justice Frank *Murphy, who concluded that the exclusion program reflected racism. In subsequent years, the *Korematsu* decision has come under sharp criticism; the conviction was finally set aside in 1984. In the 1980s, Congress enacted legislation providing compensation to families that suffered from the exclusion program.

*Korea, Vietnam, and After.* The first large-scale conflict fought without a declaration of war was the Korean War (1950–1953). In *Youngstown Sheet & Tube Co.* v. *Sawyer* (1952), the Supreme Court struck down President Harry S. Truman's order seizing the steel mills to prevent a steel shortage during the Korean conflict. *Youngstown* has been hailed as a leading statement of the need for checks on the president in foreign affairs. The majority stressed that Congress had specifically denied the president seizure power to prevent strikes. Justice Robert H. *Jackson's concurrence presented a conceptual framework for judging presidential action. In category 1, when the president acts with the express or implied authority of Congress, his actions enjoy the highest degree of legitimacy. In category 2, when the president acts in the context of legislative silence, a "zone of twilight" requires the Court to consider the scope of the president's constitutional authority in light of "imponderables" of the moment. In category 3, when the president acts contrary to the express or implied will of Congress, his authority is at its lowest ebb. Jackson contended that the Court cannot uphold the president's action in category 3 without disabling Congress from acting, which should not be done except in unusual circumstances because it would threaten the equilibrium between the branches.

Many commentators have praised Jackson's effort to clarify limits on presidential power. In practical reality, the president can initiate action more swiftly than Congress. Given its size, the diversity of its membership, and its generally reactive posture, Congress takes time to formulate a position. But when a negative congressional reaction occurs, *Youngstown* suggests that it should be taken seriously.

Congress was slow to mobilize against the *Vietnam War. But by 1973 and 1974, Congress imposed specific restrictions on further warmaking in Vietnam. Although American military involvement was a presidential initiative, Congress ultimately played a key role in bringing that involvement to an end.

Since Vietnam, American military engagements have tended to be brief. As the Iran-Contra episode during the presidency of Ronald *Reagan indicated, much of the country's involvement in foreign conflicts is covert. These changes in the use of American power reflect new international conditions, including the fear of major conflicts that might escalate into nuclear confrontations.

While the technology and scope of military engagements have changed, underlying constitutional themes endure. *Youngstown* taught that presidential actions are of most doubtful legitimacy when Congress has expressed its disapproval of executive action. Because civil liberties are endangered during war, we must be especially sensitive to their protection during peacetime.

(See also MILITARY TRIALS AND MARTIAL LAW; SEPARATION OF POWERS; WAR POWERS.)

□ Edwin S. Corwin, *The President: Office and Powers,* 5th ed. (1984). Harold H. Koh, *The National Security Constitution* (1990). Clinton Rossiter, *The Supreme Court and the Commander in Chief* (1976). J. Malcolm Smith and Stephen Jurika, *The President and National Security: His Role as Commander-in-Chief* (1972).          Thomas O. Sargentich

**Ward's Cove Packing Co. v. Atonio,** 490 U.S. 642 (1989), argued 18 Jan. 1989, decided 5 June 1989 by vote of 5 to 4; White for the Court, Stevens (joined by Brennan, Marshall, and Blackmun) and Blackmun (joined by Brennan and Marshall) in dissent. Plaintiffs alleging *employment discrimination in Alaskan salmon canneries showed a high percentage of nonwhite workers in low-paying jobs and a low percentage of nonwhite workers in high-paying jobs. The nonwhite workers relied on this disproportion in the workforce to help establish a violation of Title VII of the *Civil Rights Act of 1964. The Supreme Court held that the comparison between the racial composition of the high- and low-paying jobs was flawed because the data failed to take into account the pool of qualified job applicants.

Three additional rulings in *Ward's Cove* overshadowed this holding and arguably shifted legal standards in favor of Title VII defendants. First, building on *Watson* v. *Fort Worth Bank and Trust* (1988), the Court held that, in Title VII *disparate-impact cases, plaintiffs must show which specific employment practice led to the statistical disparity. Second, even if plaintiffs make a satisfactory statistical showing, if defendants supply a business justification for the practice, the ultimate burden of persuading the decision maker that discrimination occurred rests with the plaintiffs. Third, the business justification offered by the defendants must show that the "challenged practice serves, in a significant way, the legitimate employment goals of the employer" (p. 659). *Ward's Cove* was overturned by the *Civil Rights Act of 1991, which shifted the burden of proof back to the employers, thereby making it easier for plaintiffs to win employment discrimination suits.

(See also RACE AND RACISM.)

Theodore Eisenberg

**Ware v. Hylton,** 3 Dall. (3 U.S.) 199 (1796), argued 6–12 Feb. 1796, decided 7 March 1796 by vote of 4 to 0; Chase, Paterson, Wilson, and Cushing delivered seriatim opinions; Ellsworth and Iredell not participating (Iredell later submitted an opinion for the record). *Ware* established the supremacy of national treaties over conflicting state laws. It was representative of numerous cases brought by British creditors to recover pre-Revolutionary War debts owed them by Americans. The Treaty of Paris (1783) provided that creditors should meet with no legal impediment to the recovery of such debts. Virginia, however, enacted legislation enabling its citizens to pay debts owed to British subjects into the state treasury in depreciated currency and thereby obtain a certificate of discharge.

In losing the only case he argued before the Supreme Court, future Chief Justice John *Marshall, then an attorney representing a Virginia debtor, contended that the state had a "sovereign right" to confiscate British debts during the war, that the debtor's payment into the state treasury was a lawful discharge of the debt, and that the peace treaty could not revive the debt without violating the "plighted" faith of the state and destroying *vested rights accruing under state law. The Supreme Court rejected his arguments, holding that the treaty nullified the inconsistent state statute. Justice Samuel *Chase set forth a sweeping nationalist interpretation of the Supremacy Clause of Article VI as operating retrospectively to "prostrate" all state laws in conflict with national treaties.

(See also STATE SOVEREIGNTY AND STATES' RIGHTS; TREATIES AND TREATY POWER.)

Charles F. Hobson

**War Powers** involve the power to deploy U.S. troops abroad in hostile situations. Two constitutional provisions are central: Article I, section 8, clause 11, which gives Congress the power to "declare war"; and Article II, section 2, clause 1, which designates the president as commander in chief of the armed forces.

United States troops have been deployed abroad in five declared wars: the War of 1812, the Mexican War (1846–1848), the Spanish-American War (1898), *World War I (1917–1918), and *World War II (1941–1945). In addition to these, more than 150 military actions of varying dimensions have been undertaken without a declaration of war. In *Bas v. Tingy* (1800) the Supreme Court accepted that Congress can authorize limited hostile engagements without a congressional declaration of war. Later precedent supports presidential use of troops for defensive purposes. In the *Prize Cases* (1863), a sharply divided Court upheld President Abraham *Lincoln's blockade of southern ports at the start of the *Civil War. Moreover, presidents have successfully asserted power to deploy troops to protect Americans' lives and property.

In the twentieth century, the principal question has become the extent to which the president, without a declaration of war, can use troops in a nondefensive situation to further the nation's interests. In several instances, presidents have used troops without advance legislative authorization, including the Korean War (1950); the American incursion into the Dominican Republic (1965); the *Vietnam War (the 1960s), the rescue of the crew of an American vessel, the *Mayaguez* (1975); the attempted rescue of hostages in Iran (1980); actions in Lebanon (1983) and Grenada (1983); the bombing of targets in Libya (1986); actions to protect oil tankers in the Persian Gulf from attack (1987); the overthrow of General Manuel Noriega in Panama (1989); and the buildup of American forces in Saudi Arabia (1990) leading to war with Iraq (1991). In the war with Iraq, President George Bush secured prior congressional approval before commencing hostilities.

The chief legislative initiative in this area is the

*War Powers Act of 1973, which was passed over President Richard *Nixon's veto. It requires the president to consult with Congress about possible troop deployment, and it limits use of troops to sixty days without specific legislative authorization. No president has conceded the validity of the act, and in many circumstances presidents since Nixon have argued that the act's requirements do not apply to specific situations.

Increasingly, this area is dominated by a struggle between a vision of presidential dominance and an insistence on checks and balances involving Congress as a key actor. Courts have tended to avoid the issue, treating the question as inappropriate for judicial resolution under the *political question doctrine.

(See also INHERENT POWERS; PRESIDENTIAL EMERGENCY POWERS; SEPARATION OF POWERS; WAR.)

Thomas O. Sargentich

**War Powers Act of 1973.** Passed over President Richard *Nixon's *veto during the Watergate crisis, the War Powers Act (more properly, War Powers Resolution) of 1973 provided a framework for "collective judgment" of Congress and the president regarding introduction of American armed forces into combat or imminent hostilities abroad. Reflecting increasing frustration over unilateral executive warmaking and covert actions abroad since the Korean War (1950), the joint resolution was one of several measures intended to help Congress restore its constitutional roles of declaring *war and overseeing *national security policies.

The act prescribes procedures for consulting, reporting, and terminating deployment of armed forces unauthorized by Congress. The president is required to: (1) consult Congress "in every possible instance" before deploying forces abroad; (2) report to both houses within forty-eight hours and periodically about the circumstances and estimated duration of a deployment; and (3) terminate deployment within sixty days of the initial report unless Congress specifically approves or the president requests a thirty-day extension to protect safety of personnel. Congress is authorized to direct withdrawal at any time by concurrent resolution, which presidents cannot veto. To guide interpretation, the act disclaims inferences from statutes, appropriations, or treaties that presidents may commit forces without specific authorization; it also disclaims intentions to alter constitutional powers of the two branches.

Supporters hoped that these guidelines would improve both legislative capacity and executive accountability without crimping American leadership in international affairs. Critics of the act's legality and wisdom abound. Champions of Congress contend that the prior consultation clause is toothless. Far from curbing presidents, they argue, the reporting and termination provisions unconstitutionally delegate legislative *war powers for up to ninety days and give presidents a dangerous blank check to start wars without congressional consent (see DELEGATION OF POWERS).

Champions of executive supremacy, including all presidents except Jimmy Carter, claim that the act unconstitutionally invades independent foreign policy and war powers of the president. Law aside, pragmatists criticize automatic deadlines as inflexible and formalistic. Congress, they say, should act overtly, not by inaction; and channels of consultation are less problematic than balancing practical needs for speed and secrecy with Congress's inability to organize itself for more effective participation.

The consensus is that the guidelines have not worked well. Since 1973, they have been used most when needed least—quick rescue missions rather than open-ended commitments of armed forces. Though President Gerald Ford sought Congress's approval before evacuating refugees from Vietnam (1975), presidents have mostly ignored prior consultation. "Act now, inform later" was the style during the invasions of Grenada in 1983 and Panama in 1989 as well as the deployments after Iraq invaded Kuwait in 1990.

Reporting also has been grudging. President Ford tardily reported the rescue of the *Mayaguez* crew in 1976. President Ronald *Reagan refused to report sending military advisers to El Salvador in 1981 on the grounds that hostilities were not imminent. He said the same on sending Marines to Lebanon in 1982, thus avoiding the clock until bloodshed prompted a negotiated extension of eighteen months. Separate intelligence and neutrality laws ostensibly covered the mining of Nicaraguan harbors in 1984 and the bombing of Libya in 1986. Sharply criticized for destroying Iranian oil rigs in the Persian Gulf without consultation in 1987, Reagan garnered support for similar attacks the following year by consulting legislative leaders and promising to report. Still, presidents have typically asserted that reports were merely "consistent with" rather than pursuant to the War Powers Act. They continue to base deployments on their autonomous powers as chief executive and commander in chief. The act hardly figured in the Persian Gulf crisis of 1990–1991, the most massive engagement of armed forces since the *Vietnam War. President George Bush, reporting by a letter "consistent with" the act, avoided the clock by claiming that hostilities were not imminent. Congress acquiesced until it passed a joint resolution, at the president's request, approving the use of force against Iraq under United Nations mandates.

Enforcement of the act is clearly weak. The Supreme Court's invalidation of *legislative vetoes in *Immigration and Naturalization Service* v. *Chadha* (1983) probably nullifies Congress's power to end deployments by concurrent resolu-

tion. While the justices have yet to rule on the issue, *lower federal courts declined to review as *political questions alleged violations of the act in the *Mayaguez*, El Salvador, Grenada, Nicaragua, and Iranian oil rig episodes, at least until Congress exhausted political remedies. Self-enforcement having failed, effective enforcement depends on mobilizing Congress politically. The dilemma thus remains: it takes two-thirds of both houses to stop a presidential war but only "one-third plus one" in either house to sustain one.

As a framework for executive-legislative relations in a government of shared authority, the War Powers Act may condition interbranch negotiation, as in Lebanon. Experience suggests, however, that the joint consensus essential to sustain effective warmaking depends less on formal machinery than on *comity and the political will of both branches in any situation.

(See also PRESIDENTIAL EMERGENCY POWERS.)

□ Louis Fisher, *Constitutional Conflicts between Congress and the President* (1985). Michael J. Glennon, *Constitutional Diplomacy* (1990). J. Woodford Howard, Jr.

**Warren, Charles** (b. Boston, Mass., 9 Mar. 1868; d. Washington, D.C., 16 Aug. 1954), lawyer, authority on American constitutional law and history. Warren graduated from Harvard Law School and served as assistant attorney general in the Department of Justice during World War I. In that office he helped draft the Espionage Act of 1917 and the Trading With the Enemy Act of 1917 (see ESPIONAGE ACTS). He retained an interest in international law throughout his career.

Warren's most lasting contribution was as a historian. His three-volume book, *The Supreme Court in the History of the United States* (1922), won the Pulitzer Prize for History in 1923 and established him as a preeminent authority on the Court. A strong nationalist and conservative, Warren rejected Charles *Beard's economic interpretation of the formation of the Constitution as well as Beard's critical analysis of the Supreme Court. He agreed with Beard, however, that *judicial review was so well known and normal a function of courts in 1787 that the Framers took it for granted. In *Congress, the Constitution, and the Supreme Court* (1925), Warren urged, however, that Congress free itself from the constitutional straitjacket the justices had imposed on it. Justice Louis *Brandeis, a close friend of Warren's, cited an article Warren published in 1923 on the *Judiciary Act of 1789 as authority for the decision in *Erie Railroad* v. *Tompkins* (1938), which overruled almost a century of decisions based on *Swift* v. *Tyson* (1842).

(See also HISTORY, COURT USES OF.)

Kermit L. Hall

**Warren, Earl** (b. Los Angeles, Calif., 19 Mar. 1891; d. Washington, D.C., 9 July 1974; interred Arlington National Cemetery), chief justice,

*Earl Warren*

1953–1969. Earl Warren presided as chief justice of the United States during one of the most turbulent times in our nation's history, during which the Court forged new doctrines regarding civil rights and civil liberties and the nature of the political system.

Warren was born in Los Angeles but grew up in Bakersfield, where his father worked as a railroad car repairman on the Southern Pacific Railroad. Bakersfield was then a rough, semifrontier town with more than its share of saloons and brothels. In his *Memoirs* (1977), Warren recalled that he witnessed "crime and vice of all kinds countenanced by a corrupt government" (p. 31), and that left an indelible impression on him. Summer work on the railroads also left him with knowledge about working people and their problems, as well as with the anti-Asian racism then rampant on the West Coast.

Warren attended the University of California at Berkeley and its law school, served a brief stint in the army during World War I, and then joined the district attorney's office in Alameda County for what he thought would be a brief stint. But he stayed for eighteen years, thirteen as district attorney. During that time Warren proved an effective, tough prosecutor. But Warren also proved sensitive to the rights of the accused and personally fought to secure a public defender for indigents. A 1931 survey concluded that Earl Warren was the best district attorney in the United States, a fact often ignored by critics who claimed he had little trial experience and was "soft" on criminals.

In 1938 Warren successfully ran for attorney general of California, a post he held until 1942,

when he was elected governor. In his one term as attorney general, Warren modernized the office but is remembered primarily for his role in demanding the evacuation of Japanese from the West Coast. Throughout his life Warren maintained that at the time, it seemed the right and necessary thing to do, and not until his memoirs were published posthumously did he acknowledge that it had been an error. (See WORLD WAR II.)

A popular three-term governor, Warren seemed headed for some national office. He ran as the Republican vice-presidential candidate with Thomas Dewey in 1948 and played a key role in securing Dwight Eisenhower's nomination in 1952. For that, Eisenhower promised him the first appointment to the Supreme Court. Warren had, in fact, already accepted an offer to become the solicitor general when Chief Justice Fred *Vinson unexpectedly died on 8 September 1953. Although Eisenhower seemed reluctant to name Warren to head the Court, the Californian reminded Attorney General Herbert Brownell of the earlier promise.

Although some people questioned whether Warren had either the ability or stature to be *chief justice, his record shows a sure-footed instinct in mastering the mechanics of the institution and in what Chief Justice William Howard *Taft described as "massing the Court." Unfamiliar with the Court's procedures, Warren asked Hugo *Black, as the senior associate justice, to preside over the conferences until he could familiarize himself with his duties, a task that took him only a few weeks. His political experience also proved invaluable. Warren took over a Court deeply divided between the judicial activists, led by Hugo Black and William O. *Douglas, and strong advocates of judicial restraint, led by Felix *Frankfurter and Robert H. *Jackson (see JUDICIAL ACTIVISM; JUDICIAL SELF-RESTRAINT). Among the four Truman appointees, only Tom *Clark displayed any mental acuity. Within a short time Warren had established himself as the Court's leader, a man who, according to Potter *Stewart, "was an instinctive leader whom you respected and for whom you had affection" (Schwartz, p. 31).

Warren took the *center chair at the opening of the October 1953 term with the Court confronting one of the most significant issues in its history, the constitutionality of racial segregation. Cases challenging school segregation had been argued the preceding term and then set for reargument with counsel asked to address specifically the applicability of the *Fourteenth Amendment's *Equal Protection Clause. Within the Court the justices stood divided; even some of those who personally opposed racial segregation doubted if the Court had the authority under the Constitution to overturn it. Warren, moreover, had to trod carefully; he held only an interim appointment until Congress convened in January 1954; at that time the *Senate Judiciary Committee, with powerful southern members, would have to confirm him.

In *Brown* v. *Board of Education* (1954), Warren displayed all of the skills that would earn him the reputation as one of the great chief justices in the nation's history. He personally made up his mind on the issue quickly and announced in the first conference following the oral argument that one could not sustain racial segregation unless one assumed blacks to be inferior to whites, and he did not accept that premise. But he also recognized the political volatility of the issue, and that how the Court framed its opinion would be as important as what that decision held.

Throughout the winter and early spring of 1953–1954 Warren kept the issue open, letting the justices talk it out and review the options. Gradually all but one member of the Court, Stanley *Reed, came to agree on reversing *Plessy* v. *Ferguson* (1896), and confronted by that situation, *Reed signed on. Warren then circulated drafts of his opinion that carefully distinguished between the principle that racial segregation violated the Equal Protection Clause and that remedies to this situation would be determined in the future (see RACE AND RACISM). He wanted to give the southern states a chance to digest the fact that segregation would end, give moderates a chance to calm the inevitable passions that the decision would arouse, and then invite the southern states to join in framing an equitable decree to implement the decision.

The decision in *Brown*, announced on 17 May 1954, held racial segregation unconstitutional and triggered the massive civil rights revolution of the 1950s and 1960s. But aside from its immediate holding, *Brown* can also be seen as a major shift in the role of the Supreme Court in American life. For the previous century, the major issues before the Court had been economic, questions concerning the rights of *property, and the Court, in defending property, had for the most part told Congress and the states that they could not take certain actions.

The chief issues before the Court since World War II have concerned individual rights, and in defending and expanding those rights, the Court has often told the states and Congress that they would have to change their practices, that they would have to act differently in the future than in the past. Rather than a barrier to legislation, the Court became an active partner in the governing process. This is in essence the "activism" of the Warren Court that upset so many conservatives, but Earl Warren at all times considered the defense and enforcement of individual rights a proper role for the courts; he never saw the role of the judiciary as passive, or as somehow inferior to that of the other branches.

Warren's opinion in *Brown* has been criticized for its lack of rigorous constitutional analysis, and this too is a reflection of the man. Warren never claimed to have a great legal mind, but he believed common sense, justice, and fairness to be more important than doctrinal hairsplitting. In *Brown* the key finding is based not on appeal to precedent or even to the history of the Fourteenth Amendment, but on the belief that racially segregated facilities were not equal, could never be equal, and had a detrimental effect on African-American children. Warren based his conclusions on contemporary social perceptions rather than on doctrine, which also damned him in the eyes of critics.

As one of Warren's biographers has noted, Warren intended to fuse constitutional interpretation with a search for justice, finding in provisions such as the Equal Protection and *Due Process Clauses the basis for squaring the Constitution with the contemporary demand for increased individual rights. *Brown* thus previewed the Warren Court's "activism," its commitment to social justice and protection of the individual against the power of the state. The case did not, of course, turn the Court around all at once; it would take several terms before the "Warren Court" emerged with its activist commitment to social justice.

Not all members of the Court agreed with this approach, and Felix Frankfurter energetically fought any departure from what he considered the strictures of judicial restraint. Although Frankfurter had supported Warren in the desegregation cases, he and the chief justice soon parted company. Frankfurter considered Warren a mere politician, who should be grateful for the instruction in the law and in the proper role of the Court that Frankfurter stood ready to provide. Warren, however, had been a successful district attorney, state attorney general, and governor, and although he tried to be polite to Frankfurter, the chief justice soon chafed at the incessant barrage of memos and words from his colleague, a situation that the pedantic Frankfurter exacerbated.

Two members of the Court, Black and Douglas, had already moved to the position that Warren would take, namely, that the Constitution gave the Court sufficient authority to remedy injustice. Although he would get on well with both of them, the man who became Warren's closest confidant and chief ally would be William J. *Brennan, Jr., whom Eisenhower appointed to the Court in 1956. In many ways, Brennan served as Warren's theoretician and technician, framing the judicial arguments to carry out Warren's strategy. Frankfurter, who had welcomed his one-time pupil onto the Court, was soon in despair at his seeming apostasy, especially since Brennan, unlike Warren, could parse a constitutional argument with the best. Before long Brennan and Warren began the practice of meeting together before the conference, to frame out judicial argument and political strategy.

The Warren-led activists became dominant

with the appointment of the open-minded Potter Stewart in 1958 and the openly liberal Arthur *Goldberg in 1962, and before long, the barriers that Frankfurter and the conservatives had erected began to tumble. A key set of cases involved the justiciability of challenges to state legislative apportionment. In 1946 Frankfurter had declared that a *"political question" and warned the courts to stay out of the *"political thicket."

In 1962, with Brennan writing the majority opinion in *Baker v. Carr, the Court held that it did have jurisdiction, and two years later Chief Justice Warren delivered the Court's opinion in a series of cases that, taken together, required a complete overhaul of the nation's state legislative apportionment schemes based on the criterion of one person, one vote (see REAPPORTIONMENT CASES). In response to Justice John M. *Harlan's dissent that the Court ignored history and precedent, Warren made clear that the Constitution mandated democracy and justice. "Citizens, not history or economic interests cast votes," he declared in *Reynolds v. Sims (1964). "People, not land or trees or pastures vote" (p. 579).

This commitment to democratic procedures, to justice and to individual liberties, marks the core of Earl Warren's jurisprudence, and also its weakness. He believed that in the Constitution and the *Bill of Rights, the Founders had erected barriers against majoritarian rule to protect the individual, whether in the exercise of political rights or the expression of unpopular opinions or as a shield against vengeance in criminal prosecutions. The will of the majority expressed itself in the laws of the Congress and the actions of the Executive; the Court, in turn, had been assigned the critical role of ensuring that the elective branches did not ride roughshod over individual liberties. When Governor Orville Faubus challenged the Court's authority to bind the states to its interpretation of the Constitution, Warren massed the Court behind Brennan's opinion in *Cooper v. Aaron (1958), one of the strongest statements in the Court's history affirming its role as the final arbiter of what the Constitution means.

Whether one looks at the Court's record in matters of free speech, separation of church and state, apportionment, racial discrimination, or criminal procedure, Warren and his Court essentially asked the same questions: Is this fair? Does this protect the individual, especially the one with unpopular views? Does this impose the power of the state where it does not belong? Warren was not antigovernment or anti–law enforcement, but he believed that the Constitution prohibited the government from acting unfairly against the individual. This can be clearly seen in two cases involving criminal procedure. In 1963, to general approbation from state attorneys general, the Court extended the *Sixth Amendment right to counsel to the states in the landmark decision of *Gideon v. Wainright. Three years later, in one of the most criticized of all the decisions during his tenure, Warren attempted to set up clear rules governing police procedures. His opinion in *Miranda v. Arizona required that at minimum, a person accused of a crime would be informed of his or her rights (see COUNSEL, RIGHT TO). Warren recognized, and empirical studies have since confirmed, that the Miranda warnings do not hamper effective police work; they serve as a prophylactic to make sure both the state and the individual are treated fairly.

Warren also had no trouble supporting the activist bloc when it read bold new rights into the Constitution, such as in the landmark case of *Griswold v. Connecticut (1965), which proclaimed a right to *privacy.

Warren predictably came under criticism from conservatives who opposed judicial activism and his broad interpretation of the Bill of Rights, but even some of his admirers questioned his judgment in 1963 when he accepted the chairmanship of the special commission to investigate the assassination of John F. Kennedy (see EXTRAJUDICIAL ACTIVITIES). The chief justice did not want to take the assignment, believing that extrajudicial assignments tended to undermine the work of the Court and violated *separation of powers. But he found himself no match against Lyndon Johnson's powers of persuasion and the president's appeal to Warren's patriotism. Although Warren did not participate actively in the commission's work, he kept himself apprised of its progress, and took a hand in shaping its final report.

As several scholars have noted, it was not a happy experience for the chief justice, whose instincts for candor and justice collided with his recognition of the political implications of the report and his desire, for reasons similar to that in Brown, to have the report endorsed unanimously. The commission and its report have been under continuous criticism from one group or another ever since; while there can be little question that a man of Warren's integrity would not participate in a blatant coverup, evidence does suggest that even if the commission's ultimate findings are correct, it did not have access to important FBI and CIA files. Warren should have followed his initial instincts to turn the assignment down.

In June 1968, Earl Warren went to the White House to inform the president that he intended to retire, but left the date open until the confirmation of his successor. Johnson named Abe *Fortas, whose views coincided closely with those of Warren, but the Republicans smelled victory in 1968, and determined to deny Johnson the chance to name the next chief justice. Then came revelations of alleged financial misconduct by Fortas, and in October Fortas asked Johnson to withdraw the nomination. Warren agreed to stay on until the next president, his old political foe, Richard M. *Nixon, named his successor.

In his last term, however, Warren still had one more civics lesson to deliver. Warren's valedictory came on 16 June 1969 in *Powell v. McCormack;* the chief justice ruled that the House of Representatives had exceeded its authority in denying a seat to the flamboyant African-American representative from Harlem, Adam Clayton Powell, Jr. Although a "textually demonstrable constitutional commitment" gave each house the power to judge its members' qualifications, Warren read this clause narrowly. "The Constitution leaves the House without authority," he declared, "to *exclude* any person duly elected by his constituents, who meets all the requirements for membership expressly prescribed by the Constitution." Any other rule, he held, would deprive the people of their right to elect their own representative (p. 522).

The *Powell* opinion, like that in the apportionment cases, reaffirmed Warren's faith in the democratic process; but it also, like the opinion he had helped to craft in *Cooper,* reasserted the Court's primacy in interpreting the Constitution. One week later, he stepped down after sixteen terms as chief justice. In his retirement he worked on his memoirs (which tell very little about the Court years) and opposed the proposal to create a new intermediate appeals court to reduce the Supreme Court's jurisdiction, a proposal he believed aimed at minimizing the Court's ability to remedy injustices. He maintained a fairly active schedule until he began to suffer from congestive heart failure in early 1974, a condition from which he died on 9 July of that year.

In evaluating Warren, scholars are in general agreement that as a jurisprude he does not rank alongside *Brandeis, Louis Black, or even Frankfurter. The chief justice's opinions were not always clear, and they rarely involved complex or sophisticated legal analysis. Warren's strengths, however, lay in his belief that the Constitution embodied certain natural rights that the Court had the power to articulate and that in doing so it was always under the obligation to protect individual liberties and to ensure justice.

Conservatives believed this an inappropriate philosophy and called for a restricted view of judicial activity. Yet the fact remains that Warren's ideas struck a responsive chord in the minds of many Americans. Shortly after Warren's retirement, Professor Joseph Bishop of Yale remarked that nothing would have made the Court's major decisions in such sensitive areas as race relations and criminal procedure "palatable to a large segment of the population, including a great many highly vocal politicians. . . . But in these areas it is my judgment . . . that (1) the Court was right, and (2) most people knew it was right" (M. I. Urofsky, *A March of Liberty,* 1987, p. 852). This sense of law as morality, often derided as an anachronism, showed, in Earl Warren's hands, that it could still be a powerful tool in forging public policy.

□ Jack Harrison Pollack, *Earl Warren: The Judge Who Changed America* (1979). Bernard Schwartz, *Super Chief: Earl Warren and His Supreme Court—A Judicial Biography* (1983). Earl Warren, *The Memoirs of Earl Warren* (1977). John D. Weaver, *Warren: The Man, The Court, the Era* (1967). G. Edward White, *Earl Warren: A Public Life* (1982).                                              Melvin I. Urofsky

**Wartime Seizure Power** involves the U.S. government's power to seize the *property of enemy aliens and citizens during time of *war. The authority of Congress to pass seizure statutes derives from Article I, section 8, clause 11, of the Constitution, which gives Congress power, among others, to "declare war" and "make rules concerning capture on land and water."

The power of Congress to authorize seizure of enemy property in the United States has long been recognized. During the *Civil War, Congress enacted two confiscation acts directed at the property of Confederate supporters. In *Stoehr v. Wallace* (1921) the Supreme Court upheld the seizure of the property of a German corporation under the Trading with the Enemy Act of 1917. The Court sustained the act's mechanism for executive determinations of the government's title in alien enemy property, specifically concluding that prior judicial determination of enemy status was not required.

Seizures of German property in the United States also occurred during *World War II, when Congress passed the first War Powers Act (1941). In *Silesian-American Corp. v. Clark* (1947), the Court declared, "Unquestionably to wage war successfully, the United States may confiscate enemy property" (p. 475). The Court later confirmed in *Uebersee Finanz-Korp. v. McGrath* (1952) that the government can take alien property in the United States without having proved or asserted actual use of the property for economic warfare against the United States.

Governments have also temporarily seized domestic property during wartime. At the beginning of the Civil War, President Abraham *Lincoln ordered the seizure of railroad and telegraph lines between Washington, D.C., and Annapolis, Maryland, without advance legislative authorization. He did so in order to restore communications between the capital and the North, which had been interrupted by southern sympathizers who destroyed railway and telegraph facilities. The seizure was later ratified by the Railroad and Telegraph Act of 1862. The Supreme Court in *Miller v. United States* (1871) confirmed the constitutionality of the seizures.

During *World War I, Congress authorized seizure of domestic transportation systems in the Army Appropriations Act of 1916 as well as the seizure of plants that manufactured necessary military supplies (or that could be readily transformed to such use) in the National Defense Act of 1916. Under such authorization, the government seized railroads, telegraph lines, and various companies that failed to perform contracts with the government.

During World War II, the scope of domestic seizures expanded enormously. There were some sixty seizures of industrial plants or other facilities in response to labor disputes, including several before the Japanese attack on Pearl Harbor on 7 December 1941. Such actions were based on World War I–vintage statutes, on presidential powers in general (see INHERENT POWERS), or on new seizure statutes. These new laws included the Selective Training and Service Act of 1940, which authorized the president to take immediate possession of any plant equipped for or readily transformable for manufacture of necessary war supplies when the plant's owner refused to give a government order precedence or to fill it. Another important statute was the War Labor Disputes Act of 1943. It authorized the president to take immediate possession of a facility for producing articles required or useful for the war effort when there was an interruption from labor disturbance.

The leading case involving limitations on presidential power to seize domestic property during wartime is *Youngstown Sheet & Tube Co. v. Sawyer (1952), in which the Court struck down President Harry S. Truman's order seizing the steel mills during the Korean War (see PRESIDENTIAL EMERGENCY POWERS). The majority concluded that Congress had specifically established mechanisms of seizure—which required certain procedures that the president had not followed—and had declined to extend further power to the executive. In this situation, the Court held there was no general presidential seizure power.

Although *Youngstown* remains the law, its spirit of restraining presidential power has not always predominated. In *Dames & Moore v. Regan (1981) the Court upheld President Jimmy Carter's executive orders suspending Americans' claims against Iran for payment of debts, essentially authorizing presidential actions involving property even when the statutes did not grant explicit authority to do so.

(See also WAR POWERS.)

Thomas O. Sargentich

**Washington, Bushrod** (b. Virginia, 5 June 1762; d. Philadelphia, 26 Nov. 1829; interred family vault, Mount Vernon, Va.), associate justice, 1798–1829. Bushrod Washington was born into one of Virginia's leading families. He was George *Washington's favorite nephew, eventually inheriting Mount Vernon and becoming executor of his uncle's estate, including his public and private papers, which he loaned out to Chief Justice John *Marshall for his celebratory *Life of George Washington*.

Bushrod graduated from the College of William and Mary in 1778 and studied law under George Wythe. He joined the Continental Army in 1781. After the end of the revolutionary war he

*Bushrod Washington*

returned to Virginia and was admitted to the bar in 1784. As a practicing attorney he developed a reputation for being hard working and learned in the law. He then entered politics and was elected a delegate to the Virginia ratifying convention, where he favored the adoption of the United States Constitution. During the 1790s he supported the Federalist party and in 1798 John Adams appointed him to the United States Supreme Court.

Although he served on the Supreme Court for thirty-one years, Washington is not really known for handing down any important decisions. Rather, he tended to go along with the opinions of John Marshall and Justice Joseph *Story, which increased the powers of the federal government, protected private property rights, and encouraged economic development. In fact, so closely allied was he with Marshall that another member of the Court observed that they "are commonly estimated as a single judge."

Washington's great strength was the patience, tact, and fairness he demonstrated while riding *circuit, especially in politically charged jury trials. For example, he managed to enforce the *Sedition Act of 1798 without arousing the strong partisan feelings that made Samuel *Chase and William *Paterson so controversial. Washington also presided over the important treason case *United States v. Bright (1809). The case involved Michael Bright, a brigadier general of the Pennsylvania State Militia who had been officially ordered to prevent the enforcement of the United States Supreme Court's decision in *United States v. Peters (1809). When President James *Madison threatened to use force, the state backed down, and Bright and a number of other officers were arrested, convicted, and fined. The trial took place amid a great deal of political tension, but Washington maintained order throughout it while upholding the power of the national government. Upon sentencing Bright, Washington warned that a state simply did not have the right "to employ force to resist the execution of a decree of a federal court." Satisfied that the authority of the federal government had been vindicated, Madison proceeded to pardon the officers on humanitarian grounds.

Washington handed down another important circuit court decision in *Golden* v. *Prince* (1814), when he ruled that the power to pass bankruptcy laws belonged exclusively to the federal government. He abandoned this position in *Ogden* v. *Saunders* (1827), which also was one of the few times he broke with Marshall. Two other Supreme Court decisions of note are a concurring opinion in *Dartmouth College* v. *Woodward* (1819), where he tried to limit the more sweeping implications of the majority opinion, and *Green* v. *Biddle* (1823), where he delivered what eventually proved an unenforceable decision declaring various Kentucky laws, passed to protect actual settlers from absentee landlords, unconstitutional.

□ Albert P. Blaustein and Roy M. Mersky, "Bushrod Washington," in *The Justices of the United States Supreme Court 1789–1969*, edited by Leon Friedman and Fred L. Israel, vol. 1 (1969), pp. 243–257.      Richard E. Ellis

**Washington, George** (b. Pope's Creek [now Wakefield], Westmoreland County, Va., 22 Feb. 1732; d. Mt. Vernon, Va., 14 Dec. 1799), commander in chief of Continental Army, president (1789–1797). Washington's most enduring legacy to the Supreme Court was the precedent he established in his selection criteria for the nomination of justices. During his two terms of office he made fourteen nominations to the high court—a record that still stands and is unlikely to be surpassed.

Of Washington's fourteen Supreme Court nominations, only ten individuals served. The Senate confirmed twelve, but Robert H. *Harrison and William Cushing (as chief justice) declined their appointments. Washington's recess appointment of John Rutledge for chief justice was ultimately rejected. Washington withdrew his selection of William Paterson but later successfully appointed him. Thus, the fourteen nominations involved eleven different men. The ten who served on the Court include the following with their dates of tenure: John *Jay (chief justice, 1789–1795), John *Rutledge (1789–1791), William *Cushing (1789–1810), James *Wilson (1789–1798), John *Blair, Jr. (1789–1796), James *Iredell (1790–1799), Thomas *Johnson (1791–1793), William *Paterson (1793–1806), Samuel *Chase (1796–1811), and Oliver *Ellsworth (chief justice, 1796–1800).

President Washington's considerations in naming Supreme Court justices are readily identifiable. First, he insisted that his nominees be political and ideological soul mates. A number of Washington's choices for the high court had established their loyalty to the nation through distinguished service during the Revolutionary War. Washington was particularly impressed with Thomas Johnson's war record, which included recruiting a force of 1,800 soldiers while governor of Maryland and personally leading them to the commander in chief's headquarters. Moreover, the first president insisted that future justices demonstrate support for and advocacy of the new U.S. Constitution. Indeed, all but three of the justices that Washington placed on the Court (Jay, Cushing, and Iredell) had participated in the Constitutional Convention. The first chief executive also established the precedent of choosing judicial nominees solely from his own political party, the Federalists.

Washington's second criterion for Supreme Court service was merit. In addition to having a distinguished record during the Revolutionary War, a Washington nominee had to display a "favorable reputation with his fellows." For example, James Wilson, who had signed the Declaration of Independence and contributed his abundant talents to the Philadelphia Convention, was considered among the outstanding lawyers and legal scholars of his day.

Third, Washington usually chose justices with whom he had forged personal ties. John Blair, for instance, was a fellow Virginian, who had joined Washington and James Madison as the only members of their state delegation to support the entire Constitution.

Fourth, America's first president established the tradition of balancing the nation's highest court along representational lines. Although his predecessors would expand the list of representative criteria to include religious affiliation, race, and gender, Washington focused on the Court's geographic balance. In appointing James Iredell, the president commented: "He is of a State [North Carolina] of some importance in the Union that has given no character to a federal office."

Finally, he searched for nominees who had political experience at the state or local level or judicial experience on the lower courts. Oliver Ellsworth of Connecticut was an illustrative appointee with his previous service as a state judge and as a member of Congress.

(See also HISTORY OF THE COURT: ESTABLISHMENT OF THE UNION; SELECTION OF JUSTICES.)

□ Henry J. Abraham, *Justices and Presidents: A Political History of Appointments to the Supreme Court*, 3d ed. (1991).
Barbara A. Perry

**Washington v. Davis,** 426 U.S. 229 (1976), argued 1 Mar. 1976, decided 7 June 1976 by vote of 7 to 2;

White for the Court, Brennan and Marshall in dissent. This case involved the standard required to show unconstitutional racial discrimination, specifically the distinction between laws having a racially disproportionate impact and laws adopted with a racially discriminatory purpose or intent.

The case originated in 1970 as a suit by African-American police officers and unsuccessful applicants against the District of Columbia's Metropolitan Police Department. The suit alleged that the department's promotion and hiring policies were racially discriminatory. The rejected applicants contended that the department's use of a written personnel test (Test 21), which a disproportionately high number of African-American applicants failed, violated the *equal protection component of the Due Process Clause of the *Fifth Amendment as well as several federal and District of Columbia statutes.

The district court held for the police department. On appeal, the decision was reversed. The court of appeals, in examining whether Test 21 unconstitutionally discriminated against African-Americans, relied on an earlier Supreme Court decision, *Griggs v. Duke Power Co. (1971). Under Griggs, which developed standards for interpreting the prohibition on employment discrimination in Title VII of the 1964 *Civil Rights Act, a showing of disproportionate impact was sufficient to make out a rebuttable case of unconstitutional race discrimination. Applying the Griggs standard, the court of appeals held that because four times as many blacks as whites failed Test 21 and because the test had not been shown to be an adequate measure of job performance, the Constitution had been violated. It found that Test 21 had a racially discriminatory impact with no adequate justification for its use (see DISPARATE IMPACT).

The Supreme Court reversed the court of appeals' decision, finding that it had erroneously applied standards developed for Title VII to the Constitution. It flatly rejected the disproportionate impact claim as sufficient to make out a case of unconstitutional racial discrimination. Rather, the Court held that an intent or purpose to discriminate had to be present for there to be a constitutional violation. The Court cited numerous opinions in jury discrimination, legislative apportionment, and school desegregation cases to show that its decisions had always required a showing of racially *discriminatory intent or purpose for a holding of unconstitutional discrimination. Thus, the Title VII requirement for a showing of unlawful race discrimination differed from the showing required to make such a case under the Constitution.

The Court also addressed the question of what might count as proof of a racially discriminatory purpose or intent. It held that a racially discriminatory purpose could be inferred from the totality of relevant facts, including disproportionate impact. This relatively weak test was considerably strengthened, to the disadvantage of civil rights litigants, in *Personnel Administrator v. Feeney (1979).

Focusing on Test 21, the Court argued that the fact that many more blacks failed the test than whites did not demonstrate that the original plaintiffs were being denied equal protection. It found the test neutral on its face and rationally related to a legitimate government purpose, the modest upgrading of the communicative skills of government employees. The Court took note of the efforts of the department to recruit black officers and the changing racial composition of the recruit classes. Putting the totality of the circumstances together, no constitutional violation was found.

In their dissenting opinion, Justices William J. *Brennan and Thurgood *Marshall argued that the department failed to show that Test 21 was sufficiently related to the job of a police officer.

While the case remains good law, it has been criticized on several grounds. First, the Court gave little indication of how discriminatory purpose or intent is to be shown. Aside from the very few cases where statutes or policies discriminate on their face or are administered in a racially discriminatory fashion, what serves as proof? Second, as Justice John Paul *Stevens suggested in his concurring opinion, the distinction between discriminatory purpose and discriminatory impact is not always clear. Indeed, if racially discriminatory impact is evidence of racially discriminatory intent, as the Court states, the two standards collapse toward each other. Third, as is often argued, the decision ignores the fact that a statute or policy lacking discriminatory intent or purpose can build on the present effects of past discrimination to produce identical results. For example, if Test 21 was intended to discriminate, and four times as many blacks failed it as whites, it would be unconstitutional, but if there were no such intent, and the result were identical because of a history of school segregation that was still being felt, no constitutional violation would occur.

(See also DUE PROCESS, SUBSTANTIVE; EMPLOYMENT DISCRIMINATION; RACE AND RACISM.)

Gerald N. Rosenberg

**Watergate Affair.** See EXECUTIVE PRIVILEGE; NIXON, RICHARD; NIXON, UNITED STATES V.

**Watkins v. United States,** 354 U.S. 178 (1957), argued 7 Mar. 1957, decided 17 June 1957 by vote of 6 to 1; Warren for the Court, Clark in dissent, Burton and Whittaker not participating. Watkins, a labor union officer, appeared as a witness before a subcommittee of the Un-American Activities Committee of the House of Representatives. He was willing to answer any questions about himself and also about others whom he knew to be members of the Communist party, but he refused to answer questions about persons who may in the past have been, but were no longer, members of the party.

Watkins's conviction for contempt of Congress was set aside. Though the rationale for the decision may have been limited to the subcommittee as failure to state the subject under inquiry or to show the pertinence of the questions to the investigation, *Watkins* is especially important for its articulation of broad constitutional principles that place limits on the *congressional power of investigation. The power of inquiry is not unlimited; there is no authority to expose the private affairs of individuals unless justified by a function of Congress; and it is not a function of Congress to engage in law enforcement (an executive function) nor to act as a trial agency (a judicial function). An inquiry may not be an end in itself but it must be in furtherance of a legitimate task of Congress. The *Bill of Rights, said the Court, is applicable to congressional investigations. The public is entitled to be informed as to the workings of government, but this does not mean that Congress has the power to invade the private lives of individuals.

(See also COMMUNISM AND COLD WAR.)

Milton R. Konvitz

*James Moore Wayne*

**Wayne, James Moore** (b. Savannah, Ga., 1790; d. Washington, D.C., 7 July 1867; interred Laurel Grove Cemetery, Savannah), associate justice, 1835–1867. James Moore Wayne was the son of Richard Wayne and Elizabeth Clifford, members of Georgia's aristocracy. Educated in the northeast, he was a local politician with a national perspective, and a slaveholder who during the Civil War supported the cause of union.

Wayne graduated from the College of New Jersey, later Princeton University, in 1808. He studied law in Connecticut under Judge Charles Chauncey of New Haven and in 1810 returned to Georgia where he was admitted to the bar and entered private practice a year later.

Though he saw no action, Wayne interrupted his legal career to serve as a captain with a Georgia militia unit during the War of 1812. After the war, he reentered private practice and embarked upon a peripatetic political career. Between 1815 and 1819, Wayne served as a member of the legislature, a member of Savannah's Board of Aldermen, and then mayor. In 1819 the state legislature elected him judge of the Savannah Court of Common Pleas, which handled misdemeanors and small civil claims. In 1822 Wayne became a judge of the superior court, the trial court of general jurisdiction. In 1828 he was elected to the U.S. House of Representatives. A loyal supporter of President Andrew *Jackson, Wayne was reelected three times. When Associate Justice William *Johnson of South Carolina died in 1834, President Jackson rewarded Wayne's loyalty with Johnson's seat.

Justice Wayne's particular expertise was *admiralty, and in this area he adopted an expansive

view of federal power. In *Waring* v. *Clarke* (1847), for example, he ruled that the federal admiralty power extended to sea waters flowing by tide or otherwise into ports and rivers.

In Commerce Clause cases, Justice Wayne tracked a course mindful of the states' police powers but nonetheless jealous of federal power. In *City of *New York* v. *Miln* (1837), Wayne concurred in a decision forcing ship captains to report on and to post bond for immigrant passengers who might become public charges. Wayne concurred without opinion in the *License Cases* (1847), involving taxes levied upon ship captains for each immigrant carried, but in the *Passenger Cases* (1849), he delivered a concurring opinion that the *commerce power was vested exclusively in Congress. In *Cooley* v. *Board of Wardens* (1852), involving a local pilotage law, Wayne restated his view of the exclusivity of federal power over interstate and foreign commerce and dissented from Justice Benjamin R. *Curtis's formula recognizing state power to regulate those aspects of commerce that were essentially local and not demanding of national uniformity.

As a Southerner and slaveholder, Justice Wayne regularly ruled in favor of slave interests (see SLAVERY). Consistent with his vision of the supremacy and the expansiveness of federal power, in *Ableman* v. *Booth* (1859), Wayne was part of a unanimous Court that turned back Wisconsin's effort to interpose the power of its state courts between a federal court and those arrested for violations of the federal Fugitive Slave Act. Similarly, in *Prigg* v. *Pennsylvania* (1842), Wayne concurred that federal power regarding the subject of *fugitive slaves was exclusive.

It was in *Scott v. Sandford (1857) that the conflict between Justice Wayne's view of the expansiveness of federal power over slavery and his desire to conserve the institution came to judicial fruition. The only justice to concur in Chief Justice Roger B. *Taney's opinion, Justice Wayne agreed foursquare with the position that under the Due Process Clause of the *Fifth Amendment, Congress had no power to prohibit the introduction of slavery into the territories, nor to declare as free those slaves brought into the territories (see DUE PROCESS, SUBSTANTIVE).

Unlike many other southern federal officeholders, including Justice John A. *Campbell of Alabama, Justice Wayne did not resign to join the South during the *Civil War. The Confederacy branded him a traitor and confiscated his property in Georgia. Wayne voted to uphold President Abraham *Lincoln's declaration of a naval blockade of Southern ports during the war, in the *Prize Cases (1863), but after the war, he voted in *Cummings v. Missouri (1867) and Ex parte Garland (1867) to strike down the *test oaths.

□ Alexander A. Lawrence, James Moore Wayne, Southern Unionist (1943).                    Raymond T. Diamond

**Webster, Daniel** (b. Salisbury, N.H., 18 Jan. 1782; d. Marshfield, Mass., 24 Oct. 1852), lawyer and statesman. At fifteen, Daniel Webster left his family's farm to attend Dartmouth College; after graduation he taught school, read law, and was admitted to the bar. He practiced in New Hampshire from 1805 until 1816, when he moved to Boston and to greater professional opportunities.

Webster had a remarkable career in politics and law. He was a conservative nationalist and Federalist-Whig, serving as congressman (1813–1817 from New Hampshire and 1823–1827 from Massachusetts), senator (1827–1841, 1845–1850), and secretary of state (1841–1843, 1850–1852). He espoused policies to encourage economic growth and to preserve the Union, but sectionalism and slavery undermined those objectives and denied him the presidency as well. As a lawyer, he drew upon his political experience, particularly on constitutional questions.

Webster made many eloquent arguments before the Supreme Court, where he argued 249 cases. In *Gibbons v. Ogden (1824), he supported a broad congressional *commerce power. In *Dartmouth College v. Woodward (1819), he defended his alma mater against state regulation by bringing corporate charters within the Constitution's *Contract Clause (Article I, section 10). Frequently successful in the Marshall Court before 1835, he was less so in the Taney Court, as it shifted toward greater state power and less judicial protection of *vested rights. In *Charles River Bridge v. Warren Bridge (1837), Chief Justice

Roger B. *Taney rejected Webster's argument for an implied monopoly in a corporate charter.

Maurice Baxter

**Webster v. Reproductive Health Services,** 492 U.S. 490 (1989), argued 29 Apr. 1989, decided 3 July 1989 by vote of 5 to 4; Rehnquist for the plurality, concurrences by Scalia and O'Connor, Blackmun, joined by Brennan and Marshall, and Stevens in dissent. Webster upheld various restrictions on the availability of *abortion, but, more importantly, the decision was taken by partisans in the political battles over abortion as a signal that the Court was willing to accept substantially more restrictive regulation than it had earlier. As a result, interest groups, especially those supporting the abortion rights, began to mobilize more vigorously for political action in state legislatures and election campaigns.

Webster involved several restrictions imposed on abortions by Missouri. A preamble to the statute stated that life begins at conception; a majority of the Court held that this statement had no operative legal effect and therefore did not conflict with the statement in *Roe v. Wade (1973) that a state may not adopt a particular theory of when human life begins. Another provision barred the use of state property for abortions; as a result, no public hospital in the state could perform an abortion even if the patient paid for it herself. The provision, if read broadly, might have barred private hospitals located on land leased from the state from performing abortions. A majority of the Court did not decide whether this provision would be constitutional if read broadly, holding that in its core application the provision was indistinguishable from the ban on public funding of abortions whose constitutionality had been upheld in *Harris v. McRae (1980).

The third provision at issue required physicians to perform medically appropriate tests to determine the viability of the fetus in cases where, in the doctor's judgment, the fetus was twenty or more weeks of gestational age. In the framework established by Roe v. Wade, twenty weeks falls within the second trimester and, under Roe, regulation was permissible only to assure the health of the woman. Justice Sandra Day *O'Connor, who agreed that the medical test provision was constitutional, noted that there was roughly a four-week margin of error in determining gestational age. Thus, when a doctor believes a fetus to be twenty weeks old, it might be twenty-four weeks old, which would place the pregnancy in its third trimester. Because, under Roe, states can regulate third-trimester abortions to protect fetuses if they are viable, O'Connor argued that the medical testing provision was consistent with Roe.

The plurality opinion by Chief Justice William *Rehnquist argued, in contrast, that the provision was a second-trimester regulation and therefore could not be upheld unless *Roe* were modified. The opinion would have modified *Roe*. It acknowledged that the woman's interest in choosing abortion or not was a "liberty" interest protected by the *Due Process Clause. But, the plurality said, that interest could be affected, consistent with the Constitution, whenever the state had a sufficient countervailing interest. *Roe* had said that the state's interest in protecting potential life increased in weight as the pregnancy advanced. The plurality rejected that analysis and insisted that the state's interest in protecting potential life was of equal weight throughout the pregnancy. Because the medical test requirement promoted the state's interest, it was constitutional.

The plurality opinion did not explicitly overrule *Roe* v. *Wade*, although the analytic framework it established appears to authorize states to adopt any regulations they desire to promote the interest in protecting potential life, including criminal bans on performing or obtaining abortions. The plurality disclaimed that it envisioned such an outcome, saying that it had confidence that state legislatures would not return to the "dark ages" of such severe restrictions on the availability of abortions. Justice Antonin *Scalia concurred in the result but chastised the plurality and particularly O'Connor for failing to take the step of overruling *Roe*.

Justice Harry *Blackmun, the author of *Roe*, wrote a vigorous dissent, whose tone indicates that the Court had come close to overruling *Roe*. Like the plurality, he took the medical test provision to be a second-trimester regulation that was not designed to protect the health of the woman, and he would have held that it was therefore unconstitutional.

As a matter of legal analysis, *Webster* might have been treated as unexceptional. Blackmun indicated that he agreed with the main lines of O'Connor's analysis of the medical test requirement if it was treated as a requirement to find out whether the pregnancy was in the second or third trimester. The ban on the use of public facilities was not significantly different in law, and probably not in practical impact, from the ban on the use of public funds to pay for abortions that the Court had upheld almost a decade earlier.

Interest groups organized around the abortion issue, however, interpreted *Webster* as a major assault on *Roe*. Both sides in the abortion controversy saw political advantage to be gained by representing it as a major change in the law. Proponents of increased restrictions on the availability of abortions used the decision to prod state legislatures into doing more than they had already done; some state legislatures enacted laws that were clearly unconstitutional under *Roe*. Opponents found that they could mobilize a good deal of latent support for their position by presenting the decision as a major threat to the right to choose abortion; courts could no longer be relied on to block restrictions on the availability of abortions.

(See also GENDER; PRIVACY.)

Mark V. Tushnet

**Weeks v. United States,** 232 U.S. 383 (1914), argued 2–3 Dec. 1913, decided 24 Feb. 1914 by vote of 9 to 0; Day for the Court. *Weeks* marked the birth of the federal *exclusionary rule. Prior to *Weeks*, courts admitted illegally seized evidence on the premise that the individual's right of possession was secondary to the needs of justice. Subjected to warrantless arrest and searches by state officers and a federal marshal, Weeks was convicted on charges of using the mails to transport lottery tickets. His pretrial petition for return of his effects and subsequent objection to their introduction at trial laid the grounds for challenges in the Supreme Court based on the *Fourth and *Fifth amendments.

Narrowing the issue, Justice William R. *Day emphasized the obligation of federal courts and officers to effectuate the guarantees of the Fourth Amendment. Drawing upon *Boyd* v. *United States* (1886), he suggested that the essential violation was the invasion of Weeks's right of personal security, personal liberty, and private property. The original warrantless search by the federal marshal and the trial court's subsequent refusal to return the materials violated the plaintiff's constitutional rights. Day relied exclusively on Fourth Amendment grounds to order the judgment reversed.

*Weeks* attracted little attention until the enforcement of prohibition compounded issues of search and seizure.

Barbara C. Steidle

**Weems v. United States,** 217 U.S. 349 (1910), argued 30 Nov.–1 Dec. 1909, decided 2 May 1910 by vote of 4 to 2; McKenna for the Court, White in dissent, Lurton and Moody not participating, Brewer's seat vacant. American control of the Philippines gave the Court a rare opportunity to define the protections the *Bill of Rights afforded individuals. This was so because the Philippine Bill of Rights contained much of the wording of its American model.

Under Philippine law, an American disbursing officer was convicted of falsifying official documents. He was sentenced to a heavy fine and to fifteen years of hard labor while in chains. Confronted with this graphic example of Philippine justice, the Court seized on an argument first made in the defendant's brief—that the punishment was cruel and unusual. Realizing that any interpretation of the Philippine protection against such punishment would also interpret the *Eighth Amendment to the American Constitution, the majority did not flinch. What was cruel and unusual, Justice Joseph *McKenna said, should be determined by current sensibilities and not fixed by "impotent and lifeless formulas" (p. 373). Because the penalty was disproportionate when compared to that levied for more serious crimes, the Court ordered Weems freed because the Philippine law, which prescribed the harsh penalties, violated the ban on *cruel and unusual punishment. Justice Edward *White, joined by Justice Oliver Wendell *Holmes, protested against judicial interference with the legislative function and against the expansive reading of constitutional protections.

John E. Semonche

**Weinberger v. Wiesenfeld,** 420 U.S. 636 (1975), argued 20 Jan. 1975, decided 19 Mar. 1975 by vote of 8 to 0; Brennan for the Court, Powell, joined by Burger, and Rehnquist concurring; Douglas not participating. Following its initial decision to void a *gender classification as a denial of *equal protection in *Reed v. Reed (1971), the Supreme Court faced a dilemma. Many sex-based classifications benefited women but not men. Should the justices consider these "benign" classifications to be equivalent to those that disfavored women? Such laws could be said to foster stereotypes ultimately harmful to women, not to mention their discrimination against men. In Kahn v. Shevin (1974), the Court had badly splintered on this question in sustaining an old Florida law that granted a property tax exemption to widows but not to widowers.

In Weinberger, though, a unanimous eight-member Court overturned a provision of the federal Social Security Act that awarded survivor's benefits to widows but not to widowers. The Court achieved unanimity for two reasons. First, it treated the statute not as a benevolent aid for widows, as the government had urged, but rather as a denial of equality to the deceased wife: the *Fifth Amendment's equal protection principle no more allowed Congress now "to deprive women of protection for their families which men receive as a result of their employment" (p. 645) than it had in the statute voided by *Frontiero v. Richardson (1973). Second, no justice believed the classification satisfied even the minimum "rational basis" test for equal protection. The clear purpose of the benefits was to help the surviving parent to raise a child. For this goal, the law's gender distinction was "entirely irrational."

G. Roger McDonald

**Wesberry v. Sanders,** 376 U.S. 1 (1964), argued 18–19 Nov. 1963, decided 17 Feb. 1964 by vote of 7 to 2; Black for the Court, Clark concurring in part and dissenting in part, Harlan in dissent. This is the second of the "reapportionment decisions" of the 1960s, which established that federal courts have jurisdiction to enforce the constitutional requirement that representation in governmental bodies be based on equal-population districts. The first, *Baker v. Carr (1962), was not a ruling on the merits but a holding that the question of the apportionment of a state legislature is a *justiciable question.

Wesberry dealt with the apportionment of congressional districts in Georgia, which were challenged under Article I, section 2, which provides that "The House of Representatives shall be composed of Members chosen every second Year by the People of the several states," and the part of section 2 of the *Fourteenth Amendment that provides that "Representatives shall be apportioned among the several states according to their respective numbers."

In Baker, Justice William J. *Brennan had argued for the Court that since the question of whether the Tennessee legislature's reapportionment of its own legislative districts did not present the Court with the possibility of a conflict with a coordinate branch of the national government, the Court could handle the matter as a justiciable issue. In Wesberry, however, the Court was faced with such a conflict. Congress had made a deliberate decision in 1929, reaffirmed after each decennial apportionment, to drop any requirement that state legislatures create congressional districts that were compact, contiguous, and equal in population.

Wesberry involved a challenge by voters in Georgia's Fifth Congressional District, the population of which was two to three times greater than that of other congressional districts. Claiming that their vote had been debased by the Georgia legislature's failure to realign congressional districts on a population basis, they brought a *class action asking that the apportionment statute be declared unconstitutional and that the Georgia officials be enjoined from conducting elections under it. A three-judge district court, although recognizing a constitutional issue, dismissed the complaint for "want of equity," primarily relying on Justice Felix *Frankfurter's opinion in *Colegrove v. Green (1946).

Justice Hugo *Black promptly disposed of the *political question issue on the grounds that the "right to vote is too important in our free society to be stripped of judicial protection" (p. 7). He also completely ignored prior actions of Congress and construed Article I, section 2, as commanding that "as nearly as is practicable one man's vote in a congressional election is to be worth as much as another's." Hence, "[w]hile it may not be possible to draw congressional districts with mathematical precision," the "Constitution's plain objective" is that "equal representation for equal numbers of people" is a fundamental goal for the House of Representatives (p. 18).

Justice John M. *Harlan, in *dissent, rather persuasively pointed out that such a conclusion could hardly be drawn from the intent of the framers—as Black had argued—or from Congressional actions that had, rather pointedly in the 1929 reapportionment act, deleted the requirement of five previous acts that congressional districts be equal in population.

With the coming of computers it became possible, contrary to Black's observation, to draw congressional districts with mathematical precision, and, in *Kirkpatrick* v. *Preisler* (1969), that quickly became the Court's constitutional standard for congressional apportionment. State legislatures and other governmental bodies were held to a less rigidly precise mathematical standard in *Mahan* v. *Howell* (1973). Later cases have made it clear that the Supreme Court will now tolerate substantial deviations (of as much as 20 percent or more) in state districting. The Court has, however, maintained the "near precision" requirement for congressional districts.

(See also FAIR REPRESENTATION.)

J. W. Peltason

**West Coast Hotel Co. v. Parrish,** 300 U.S. 379 (1937), argued 16–17 Dec. 1936, decided 29 Mar. 1937 by vote of 5 to 4; Hughes for the Court, Sutherland in dissent. In *West Coast Hotel Co.* v. *Parrish*, the Supreme Court supposedly made "the switch in time that saved nine." The decision was handed down less than two months after President Franklin D. *Roosevelt announced his plan to pack the Supreme Court with justices supportive of New Deal economic regulation. Yet the circumstances surrounding the *Parrish* decision have made it seem more of a direct reaction to the *court-packing plan than it probably was.

*Parrish* heralded greater Supreme Court deference to economic regulation by upholding a Washington State minimum wage law for women. In doing so, the Court ratified a policy that many argued was desperately needed by underpaid women workers. However, because the minimum wage for women rested on a theory of women's inequality, and because labor restrictions based on *gender interfered with women's employment opportunities, many feminists opposed minimum wage laws.

In *Lochner* v. *New York* (1905), the Court had struck down a statute restricting the number of hours bakers could work on the basis that it violated the *due process rights of employers and employees to freedom of *contract. In *Muller* v. *Oregon* (1908), however, the Court had upehld a statute limiting the number of hours women could work under the theory that states had a greater interest in regulating the employment of women because their central role as childbearers meant that women's health was essential to the well-being of future generations. The Court distinguished maximum hours legislation from minimum wage legislation, and ruled in *Adkins* v. *Children's Hospital* (1923) that a minimum wage law for women and children violated freedom of contract. Just one year before *Parrish* was decided, the Court had applied *Adkins* and struck down a minimum wage for women in *Morehead* v. *New York ex rel. Tipaldo* (1936).

In *Parrish*, the Court overturned the *Adkins* decision. Chief Justice Charles Evans *Hughes, writing for a majority of five, argued that the concept of freedom of contract was not unlim-

ited. "What is this freedom?" Hughes asked. "The Constitution does not speak of freedom of contract" (p. 391). The Constitution protected liberty, but subject to reasonable regulation in the interest of the community. Hughes found that state power to restrict freedom of contract was especially evident in the area of protective labor legislation for women. Relying on *Muller*, he argued that women's physical structure and their role as mothers required that the state protect them in order to "preserve the strength and vigor of the race" (p. 394). Hughes could find no relevant difference between laws regulating hours and those regulating wages, and suggested that state legislatures could address the abuses of unconscionable employers who paid their workers less than a living wage. Hughes adopted a posture of deference to legislative judgment, suggesting that even if the wisdom of a policy was debatable, the legislature was entitled to enact it as long as it was not arbitrary or capricious.

Justice George *Sutherland wrote a vigorous dissent. He argued, in part, that women and men were equal under the law and that, consequently, legislation that treated them differently with respect to the right to contract constituted arbitrary discrimination.

Because Justice Owen *Roberts, who voted with the majority in *Morehead*, provided the fifth vote in *Parrish*, his role in the decision has received much attention. There has been much speculation as to whether Roberts switched his vote in response to President Roosevelt's pressure. Two factors militate against such a conclusion. First, because the *Morehead* majority rested on very narrow grounds, Roberts could argue that he had not changed his position because he had never expressed an opinion on the substantive issue in *Adkins*. More importantly, a vote on *Parrish* was taken in December 1936, before the court-packing plan, and Roberts voted to sustain the minimum wage law. Consequently, the court-packing plan seems not to have directly affected Roberts's vote. Harsh criticism of the Court preceded the court-packing plan, however, so it remains likely that Roberts's vote in *Parrish* was to some degree responsive to the concerns and pressures of the times.

(See also DUE PROCESS, SUBSTANTIVE.)

☐ Charles A. Leonard, *A Search for a Judicial Philosophy: Mr. Justice Roberts and the Constitutional Revolution of 1937* (1971).

Mary L. Dudziak

**WESTLAW,** West Publishing Company's computerized legal-research service, contains all Supreme Court decisions from 1790 to the present. Current decisions are transmitted electronically from the Court and are usually retrievable on the same day that they are decided. The system allows searching by key words, phrases, or word combinations using Boolean connectors. One advantage of Supreme Court research on WESTLAW, as against the competing LEXIS system, is the ability to research post–1915 cases by West topics and key numbers, either as the primary search method or as an added search element. The Court's decisions from 1945 to the present are in the WESTLAW database designated SCT; those from 1790 to 1944 are in the SCT-OLD database.

Decisions can be researched through Shepard's citators, Shepard's PreView and QuickCite, on WESTLAW or checked through a citation verification system called Insta-Cite, similar to Auto-Cite on LEXIS. *United States Law Week* is also available under the database designations BNA-USLW (1986–) and BNA-USLWD (for *U.S. Law Week–Daily Edition* from March 1987 to date). Another feature is *WESTLAW Bulletin–U.S. Supreme Court* (database designation WLB-SCT), which contains documents summarizing recent decisions and other developments such as rule changes and orders.                    Morris L. Cohen

**Weston v. Charleston,** 2 Pet. (27 U.S.) 449 (1829), argued 28 Feb. and 10 Mar. 1829, decided 18 Mar. 1829 by vote of 4 to 2; Marshall for the Court, Johnson and Thompson in dissent, Trimble deceased. *Weston* involved an attempt by the city of Charleston (a political subdivision of the state of South Carolina), to tax "stock of the United States," that is, debt certificates held by creditors of the federal government. The Court struck down the tax as an interference with the Article I, section 8 power "To borrow Money on the credit of the United States." Chief Justice John *Marshall reaffirmed *McCulloch* v. *Maryland* (1819), which had vigilantly guarded federal powers against state encroachment by invoking the maxim "the power to tax involves the power to destroy." (See also TAX IMMUNITIES.)
                               William M. Wiecek

**West River Bridge Co. v. Dix,** 6 How. (47 U.S.) 507 (1848), argued 5–7 Jan. 1848, decided 31 Jan. 1848 by vote of 7 to 1. Daniel for the Court, McLean and Woodbury concurring, Wayne in dissent, McKinley not participating. In *West River Bridge Co.* the Supreme Court established that the exercise of *eminent domain power to extinguish a franchise did not violate the *Contract Clause. In 1795 the Vermont legislature invested a *corporation with the exclusive privilege of maintaining a toll bridge over West River for one hundred years. The state subsequently decided to lay out a free public highway over the toll bridge. The bridge company was awarded compensation for the appropriation of its property and franchise. The bridge company, however, objected that the state proceeding violated the Contract Clause. Daniel *Webster, appearing for the bridge company, contended that the state's action constituted an impairment of the grant to erect a toll bridge. He also argued that unrestrained use of

eminent domain would allow the states despotic authority over private property.

Rejecting Webster's arguments, Justice Peter V. *Daniel reasoned that all private property rights were subordinate to the paramount power of eminent domain. He emphasized that a franchise was simply a form of property. Daniel concluded that the exercise of eminent domain power did not abrogate any contractual rights protected by the Contract Clause. This decision established the principle that a grant or franchise does not divest a state of eminent domain authority and pointed the way for later rulings that a state cannot contract away certain *police powers. As a result, states could use eminent domain broadly to promote public welfare.

(See also PROPERTY RIGHTS.)
                               James W. Ely, Jr.

**West Virginia State Board of Education v. Barnette,** 319 U.S. 624 (1943), argued 11 Mar. 1943, decided 14 June 1943 by vote of 6 to 3; Jackson for the Court, Black, Douglas, and Murphy concurring, Frankfurter, Roberts, and Reed in dissent. In 1940, in *Minersville School District* v. *Gobitis*, the Supreme Court had upheld a law mandating flag salute and recitation of the Pledge of Allegiance in public schools, rejecting a challenge brought on grounds of religious conscience by a member of the Jehovah's Witnesses. Only one dissent, that of Justice Harlan *Stone, had been registered in the *Gobitis* decision. Only three years later, the Court ruled to the contrary. The majority opinion in *West Virginia State Board of Education* v. *Barnette*, written by Justice Robert *Jackson, became one of the great statements in American constitutional law and history.

The Court's opinion in *Gobitis* had been taken as a signal by many that further attacks on flag salute and the pledge by Jehovah's Witnesses would now be futile. The onset of *World War II made refusal to pledge loyalty to the flag even more suspect. In one week alone the Justice Department received reports of hundreds of physical assaults on Jehovah's Witnesses. Officials threatened to send nonconformist Witnesses' children to reformatories for juvenile delinquents. Witnesses' meeting places were burned and their leaders driven out of town.

In turn, these actions aroused a backlash. The *Gobitis* decision was widely criticized by scholars, and even organizations as staunchly patriotic as the American Legion supported enactment of a 1942 law making flag observance voluntary at the federal level. When Walter Barnette and other Jehovah's Witnesses brought suit challenging a compulsory flag-salute law in the schools of West Virginia, a law patterned directly on the rationale of the Supreme Court's opinion in *Gobitis*, the lower court simply rejected the *Gobitis* holding and ruled for the parents.

None of this was lost on the Supreme Court,

which overruled *Gobitis* and held the West Virginia statute unconstitutional. But it did so by invoking the broad Free Speech Clause of the *First Amendment rather than relying primarily on the Religion Clause.

The flag salute, said the Court, was a form of speech. The government could not compel citizens to express beliefs without violating freedom of speech. Hence, regardless of whether objections to saluting the flag were religiously based or not, that freedom had to be respected.

In a sense, the *Barnette* decision marked the end of an era. Not only was it the last of the major Supreme Court victories of the Jehovah's Witnesses, it was also the last case for many years to subsume claims for religious liberty under the free speech clause. Indeed, beginning with *Sherbert* v. *Verner* (1963), the Court began carving out constitutional exemptions exclusively for religious believers. This trend has continued, although the Court still resorts on occasion to dealing with religious issues in terms of free speech.

The true legacy of *Barnette* is less its jurisprudence than its defense of the principles of freedom. The opinion's eloquent closing has been cited in both religious and secular contexts. Thus, it said, in part: "The very purpose of a Bill of Rights was to withdraw certain subjects from the vicissitudes of political controversy, to place them beyond the reach of majorities and officials and to establish them as legal principles to be applied by the courts (p. 1185).

(See also NATIONAL SECURITY; RELIGION; SPEECH AND THE PRESS.)

Leo Pfeffer

**Wheaton, Henry** (b. Providence, R.I., 27 Nov. 1785; d. Dorchester, Mass., 11 Mar. 1848), third reporter of decisions, 1816–1827. The ablest of the early reporters, Wheaton redefined the office and greatly improved the quality of the product. His service spanned the epochal years from *Martin* v. *Hunter's Lessee* (1816) to *Ogden* v. *Saunders* (1827). Upon Wheaton's death, a German obituary proclaimed his twelve volumes "the golden book of American national law"—owing in significant part to the reporter's contributions.

Unlike his self-appointed predecessors, Wheaton became reporter through selection by the Supreme Court, held an office recognized by law (as of 1816), and received a modest salary. His sponsor was Justice Joseph *Story, a fellow scholar and perfectionist who valued Wheaton's learning and determination. The two roomed together in Washington and sought to create a comprehensive, coherent body of national law, relying where appropriate on British and continental analogues.

Wheaton attended court sessions faithfully, reported arguments and opinions accurately, and published each volume within the year, thereby enabling bench and bar to know promptly the rulings of the nation's highest court. In addition, aided occasionally (but anonymously) by Story, Wheaton enhanced his *Reports* with unprecedented annotations, elucidating particular points in opinions or exploring entire areas of developing law, apropos the business of the term.

Wheaton's career following the reportership was equally notable. He engaged in lengthy litigation with his successor, Richard *Peters, Jr., concerning Wheaton's rights in his *Reports*. This case, *Wheaton* v. *Peters* (1834), established the major contours of American *copyright law. As a diplomat, Wheaton served with distinction under six presidents. As an expounder and historian of international law, he achieved renown on both sides of the Atlantic, publishing *Elements of International Law* (1836) and *History of the Law of Nations* (1845). Subsequent editions of *Elements* extended Wheaton's influence on international law well into the twentieth century.

Of Wheaton's contributions to American jurisprudence, his contemporary William Pinkney's observation, occasioned by publication of Wheaton's first volume of *Reports,* is apt: "The Profession [is] infinitely indebted to you. . . ."

(See also REPORTERS, SUPREME COURT.)

Craig Joyce

**White, Byron Raymond** (b. Fort Collins, Colo., 8 June 1917), associate justice, 1962–. Byron White was born into a family of modest means in Fort Collins, Colorado. He spent his childhood in Wellington, a small agricultural community in northern Colorado, where his father worked in the lumber industry. The future justice attended the University of Colorado on scholarship, graduating in 1938 as valedictorian of his class. White excelled in athletics, being voted All American in football and earning the nickname "Whizzer" for his talent as a running back. Following graduation, White played one season for the Pittsburgh Steelers and led the league in rushing. In 1939, he accepted a Rhodes Scholarship to study at Oxford University. When war erupted in Europe, White returned to the United States to study law at Yale and during the 1940–1941 season resumed his professional football career with the Detroit Lions. He joined the navy shortly after the United States entered the war and served in the Pacific. Upon cessation of hostilities, he married his college sweetheart, Marion Stearns, and completed law school at Yale with high honors in 1946. White clerked for Chief Justice Fred M. *Vinson in 1946–1947, after which he returned to his native Colorado to practice law with a Denver firm.

When John Kennedy mounted his campaign for the Presidency in 1960, White became an active supporter. The two had crossed paths three previous times—first when White studied in England and Kennedy's father was ambassador to Great Britain, then again when both were

*Byron Raymond White*

naval officers in World War II, and finally in Washington when White's clerkship at the Supreme Court coincided with Kennedy's first term in Congress. White first headed the Kennedy forces in Colorado and then chaired "Citizens for Kennedy," a national organization devoted to recruiting Republican and Independent voters. The new president rewarded White's efforts by naming him deputy attorney general, a position in which he focused on the selection of lower court judges and on civil rights issues.

In 1962, Justice Charles *Whittaker announced his resignation, giving President Kennedy his first Supreme Court appointment. With the encouragement of Attorney General Robert Kennedy, the president selected White, who was judged both extremely qualified and a supporter of New Frontier policies. White's 3 April 1962 nomination was confirmed in the Senate by voice vote on 11 April. On 16 April at the age of forty-four, Byron White was sworn in as the ninety-third justice of the Supreme Court.

White's performance on the Court has been one of nondoctrinaire pragmatism, avoiding expansive interpretations of the Constitution. His voting record, while consistent within specific policy areas, has varied from liberal to quite conservative across a broad range of issues.

White's most liberal positions have been on discrimination questions. During the Warren Court era he steadfastly supported the constitutionality and enforcement of the *Civil Rights Act of 1964 and the *Voting Rights Act of 1965, and he advocated an expanded definition of state action in *equal protection cases. He has taken similarly liberal positions on issues of sex and economic discrimination. In the 1980s, however, White often parted company with the Court's liberal wing on questions of *affirmative action and "set aside" programs designed to eliminate the effects of past discrimination.

On personal liberty issues, White has generally taken a conservative stance. He supported the Burger Court's restrictive position on obscenity (see OBSCENITY AND PORNOGRAPHY), rejected the notion of a newsman's privilege, voted to enforce laws against flag burning by political protesters, and approved government aid to sectarian schools. Although White voted to recognize the right to *privacy in 1965, he was one of only two dissenters in *Roe v. Wade (1973) and has consistently voted to uphold state regulation of *abortions. Additionally, White wrote the majority opinion in *Bowers v. Hardwick (1986) upholding state sodomy statutes against privacy right challenges.

Justice White's most consistently conservative rulings have occurred in criminal rights cases. He dissented from the Court's liberal rulings in *Escobedo v. Illinois (1964) and *Miranda v. Arizona (1966) and has voted to uphold *capital punishment against a number of constitutional challenges. White has also been a critic of the *exclusionary rule in search and seizure cases and authored the 1984 majority opinions limiting that rule.

□ Fred L. Israel, "Byron R. White," in *The Justices of the United States Supreme Court, 1789–1969*, edited by Leon Friedman and Fred L. Israel, vol. 4 (1969), pp. 2951–2974.　　　　　　　　　　　　　Thomas G. Walker

**White, Edward Douglass** (b. LaFourche Parish, La., 3 Nov. 1845; d. 19 May 1921, Washington, D.C.; interred Oak Hill Cemetery, Washington, D.C.), associate justice, 1894–1910; chief justice, 1910–1921. Edward Douglass White was the scion of a wealthy Louisiana sugar-planting family. His father was a prosperous farmer, New Orleans judge, governor, and five-term member of the U.S. House of Representatives. The younger White was educated in Jesuit schools, Mount St. Mary's College, and Georgetown University. During the Civil War, he was captured by Union forces and held as a prisoner. After the war he read law with Edward Bermudez in New Orleans and became a political lieutenant of Governor Francis T. Nicholls, leader of the "Redeemer" cause in Louisiana. White was rewarded in 1878 with an appointment to the state supreme court. However, following Nicholls' electoral defeat in 1880, White was removed from a position that had appeared to be permanent. In political exile, White retired to a lucrative law practice in New Orleans. In 1888, Governor Nicholls returned to office and shortly thereafter appointed White to fill a vacancy as the junior senator from Louisiana.

During his three-year term in the Senate, the corpulent, thick-maned White presented almost a caricature of the nineteenth-century southern senator. His position on virtually every public policy issue appears to have been guided by a basic premise: What is good for Louisiana sugar is good for America. Indeed, even following his appointment to the Supreme Court in 1894, White refused for several weeks to accept his robe, in order to lead the fight for the protection of domestic sugar in the Wilson-Gorman Tariff Act. The same year he married Virginia Montgomery Kent.

Once on the bench, White found no impropriety in sitting on the cases that challenged the income tax provisions of the Wilson-Gorman Act. Not surprisingly, the justice who as senator had voted for the tariff act also supported the constitutionality of its income tax provision in *Pollock v. Farmers' Loan and Trust Co.* (1895). White, however, was in the minority. A 5-to-4 majority declared federal income taxation to be unconstitutional. Similarly, in *DeLima v. Bidwell* (1901), the first of the so-called *Insular Cases*, Justice White joined a four-man minority opposed to the idea that, given the acquisition of Puerto Rico after the Spanish-American War, sugar imported from that island was no longer subject to American tariff duties. The dissent in *DeLima*, however, marked the first expression of the doctrine of "incorporation" that White himself would later champion in a concurrence in *Downes v. Bidwell* (1901). This doctrine answered the question, Does the Constitution follow the flag? with a resounding, Sometimes. The doctrine postulated that the extent to which constitutional guarantees were extended to the inhabitants of American territories depended upon the extent to which the territory had been "incorporated" into the American political community. The greater the incorporation, the greater the degree of constitutional protection for the territory's citizens. How such incorporation was accomplished, however, was vague and ambiguous, allowing for judicial subjectivism.

Judicial subjectivity was the one consistent theme during White's tenure. During those twenty-seven years the principal constitutional issue involved governmental power to regulate the economy. The Court's response, whether in the interpretation of the Due Process Clauses, the Commerce Clause, or the taxing power, was erratic (see COMMERCE POWER). For example, in *McCray v. United States* (1904), the Court, speaking through Justice White, recognized a federal *police power under the power to tax. Congress's motive in enacting the tax was not, White declared, a fit subject for judicial inquiry. Yet, fifteen years later, White himself repudiated this position in *United States v. Doremus* (1919).

Justice White's single greatest legal contribution, however, lay in the area of statutory, not constitutional construction. He introduced the

*Edward Douglass White*

*rule of reason into the interpretation of the *Sherman Antitrust Act. Despite the fact that the Sherman Act outlawed all combinations in restraint of trade, White from the time of his appointment to the Court objected to a literal reading of the statute. Only "unreasonable" restraints, he contended, were prohibited. This idea, initially rejected by the Court, gained adherents the longer White remained on the bench until in *Standard Oil v. United States* (1911), perhaps White's most famous opinion for the Court, it garnered a majority. From that day onward the Sherman Act, whatever its words may say, has been read to permit "reasonable" monopolies. Of course, what is "reasonable" is for the Court to say; and, once again, the theme of unbridled judicial power appears in White's handiwork. White was the first associate justice elevated to the position of *chief justice.

□ James F. Watts, Jr., "Edward Douglass White," in *The Justices of the Supreme Court, 1789–1970,* edited by Leonard M. Friedman and Fred L. Israel, vol. 3 (1980), pp. 1633–1657.
　　　　　　　　　　　　　　　　　Richard Y. Funston

**White Primary.** The *Fifteenth Amendment prohibited racial discrimination in voting, but in *United States v. *Reese* (1876) the Supreme Court severely limited Congress's enforcement power, holding that the "Fifteenth Amendment does not confer the right of suffrage upon any one" (p. 217). After this, states used various methods, including literacy tests and *poll taxes, to disfranchise blacks. However, these methods also prevented many whites from voting.

In 1923 Texas prohibited blacks from voting in

the Democratic primary, effectively barring blacks from political participation in local and state elections in what was then a one-party state. In *Nixon v. Herndon* (1927), a unanimous Supreme Court found this law violated the *Equal Protection Clause of the *Fourteenth Amendment. The Texas legislature responded with a new law giving political party officials the power to set their own rules in primary elections. The executive committee of the Texas Democratic party immediately prohibited black participation in its primaries. In *Nixon v. Condon* (1932), the Court ruled, 5 to 4, that the party's executive committee was in effect a creation of the state legislature and therefore that the prohibition of black voters amounted to unconstitutional *state action. The Texas Democratic party then called a state convention and on its own passed a resolution limiting participation in Democratic primaries to "white citizens." In *Grovey v. Townsend* (1935) the Court unanimously upheld this version of the white primary. However, in *Smith v. Allwright* (1944) a Court made up almost entirely of new justices ruled, 8 to 1, that white primaries violated the Fifteenth Amendment.

(See also VOTE, RIGHT TO.)

Paul Finkelman

**Whitney v. California,** 274 U.S. 357 (1927), argued 18 Mar. 1926, decided 26 May 1927 by vote of 9 to 0; Sanford for the Court, Brandeis and Holmes concurring. In 1919, California passed a *criminal syndicalism law designed to restrict the activities of the Industrial Workers of the World (IWW), a union long active in the state's agricultural fields and lumber camps. The statute prohibited advocacy of changes in the system of industrial ownership or political control.

The first significant prosecution under the law involved Charlotte Anita Whitney, social activist and prominent member of the Socialist party. In late 1919 authorities arrested her for participating in a November convention of the Communist Labor party (CLP), an organization from which she had recently resigned. At Whitney's trial, the prosecution introduced considerable IWW literature in an attempt to tie the organization to the CLP, which had generally endorsed IWW objectives. Whitney did not deny her short-lived CLP membership, and the jury convicted her solely on that count—a classic example of guilt by association.

Subsequently, the U. S. Supreme Court unanimously upheld the California statute on the basis of the state's power to protect the public from violent political action. However, in his concurrence, Justice Louis *Brandeis, joined by Justice Oliver Wendell *Holmes, contended that Whitney's attorneys should have argued for a *clear and present danger test to distinguish between membership and dangerous action. They reasoned that the liberty protection of the *Fourteenth Amendment Due Process Clause joined with the *First Amendment to protect freedom of assembly from state regulation (see INCORPORATION DOCTRINE).

The Brandeis concurrence became an important step in the Court's eventual acceptance of the clear and present danger test. In *Brandenburg v. Ohio* (1969), the Supreme Court overturned *Whitney,* but a modified version of the law remains in force.

(See also ASSEMBLY AND ASSOCIATION, FREEDOM OF; DUE PROCESS, SUBSTANTIVE; SPEECH AND THE PRESS.)

Carol E. Jenson

**Whittaker, Charles Evans** (b. Troy, Kans., 22 Feb. 1901; d. Kansas City, Mo., 26 Nov. 1973; interred Calvary Cemetery, Kansas City), associate justice, 1957–1962. Charles E. Whittaker grew up on a farm, the son of Charles and Ida Miller Whittaker. In 1920, before completing high school, he enrolled at the University of Kansas City Law School. He joined the bar in 1923 while still in school and was graduated the next year. While in law school he began working for a law firm, Watson, Gage & Ess; he continued to practice with that firm until his appointment to the federal bench in 1954. Whittaker was primarily a litigator although he also did corporate work, and his firm's clients included Kansas City as well as national corporations. Except for his Missouri state bar activities, Justice Whittaker was largely uninvolved in social or political work.

In 1954 Whittaker's position as a leader of the corporate bar in Kansas City brought him to the attention of U.S. Attorney General Herbert Brownell, who was looking for a nominee for the U.S. District Court in Missouri. Ordinarily such

*Charles Evans Whittaker*

an appointment would have been made on the recommendation of a senator of the same party as the president. Both senators from Missouri were Democrats, however, which accounted for the heightened participation of the Republican White House in filling the judgeship. Whittaker served on the district court from 6 July 1954 until 22 July 1956, when the Senate confirmed him judge of the United States Court of Appeals for the Eighth Circuit.

Early in 1957, Justice Stanley Reed retired. President Dwight Eisenhower, who had a predilection for appointing justices from among the ranks of sitting judges, nominated Justice Whittaker, apparently on the strong urging of Herbert Brownell.

During Justice Whittaker's brief tenure on the Court, he joined the majority in a large number of 5-to-4 decisions. Whittaker was usually a conservative, although occasionally he would join in an opinion protecting a particularized individual right against government encroachment. His own opinions were undistinguished and they failed to reflect a consistent judicial philosophy. Perhaps his most notable opinion was *Staub* v. *City of Baxley* (1958), in which the Court held (7 to 2) that a city ordinance requiring a permit for union soliciting was unconstitutional because of the discretion given to the city officials.

Physically exhausted, he retired on the advice of his physician effective 1 April 1962. Unlike other retired justices, he devoted himself to private legal interests rather than to judicial or public service. Eric A. Chiappinelli

**Wickard v. Filburn,** 317 U.S. 111 (1942), argued 4 May 1942, decided 9 Nov. 1942 by vote of 9 to 0; Jackson for the Court. Perhaps the decision that best indicated how completely the Supreme Court had come in acquiescing to the nationalist economic philosophy of President Franklin *Roosevelt and the Democratic majorities in both houses of Congress was *Wickard* v. *Filburn*. In this case, a unanimous court, speaking through Justice Robert *Jackson, upheld important features of the Second Agricultural Adjustment Act (1938).

Previously, in *Mulford* v. *Smith* (1939), the Supreme Court had upheld the tobacco quotas set by the Second Agricultural Adjustment Act. Now the Court was asked to examine problems involving a more commonly grown crop—wheat. The specific question presented in *Wickard* was whether wheat that never left the farm should be subject to the marketing quotas established by the act.

The man who challenged the act's wheat quotas was Roscoe C. Filburn, a small Ohio farmer. Filburn maintained a herd of dairy cattle, raised poultry, and sold milk, poultry, and eggs in the open market. He planted a small acreage of winter wheat that he fed to his chickens and cattle, ground into flour for his family's consump-

tion, and saved for the following year's seed. Filburn did not sell a single bushel of wheat in the open market. In 1941, Filburn sowed twelve acres of wheat more than he was permitted by Second Agricultural Adjustment Act's regulations. This unauthorized planting yielded 239 bushels of wheat, on which the federal government imposed a penalty of 49 cents a bushel. Filburn contested the government's assessment, arguing that the federal power to regulate commerce did not extend to the production and consumption of wheat that was never marketed (see COMMERCE POWER).

When Filburn's challenge reached the Supreme Court in 1942, the tribunal had been dramatically refashioned by the appointments of President Roosevelt. The only justice whom Roosevelt had no hand in appointing to the Court that reviewed Filburn's case was Owen *Roberts, the individual who had undergone the famous "switch in time that saved nine" in 1937. So, by 1942 the Supreme Court was very much "the Roosevelt Court."

Following the logic of the important Commerce Clause case of *United States* v. *Darby Lumber Co.* (1941), Jackson held for the Court in *Wickard* that the quota on wheat authorized by the Second Agricultural Adjustment Act was constitutional under Article I, section 8 of the Constitution, which permitted Congress to "regulate Commerce . . . among the several States." Jackson maintained that wheat consumed but not marketed still had an effect upon interstate commerce and thus could be regulated. Filburn's 239 bushels of home-consumed wheat might by itself have seemed trivial, but it was part of a much larger story. In the early 1940s more than 20 percent of all the wheat grown in the country never left the farm. By consuming their own grain, Filburn and thousands of farmers like him cut the overall demand and depressed the market price of wheat. Their actions clearly affected interstate commerce and were, Jackson concluded, subject to federal regulation.

In several previous Commerce Clause cases, the Supreme Court had struggled to find an appropriate standard to determine what could be constitutionally regulated. In one line of cases, the Court held production could not be regulated. In another, it determined that intrastate commerce could be regulated only if it placed a direct burden on interstate commerce. Jackson's ruling in *Wickard* further extended the federal commerce power and, more importantly, stipulated that economic realities—not deceptive terminology like "direct" and "indirect"—should henceforth determine what matters would fall within the ambit of the Commerce Clause.

(See also AGRICULTURE.)

John W. Johnson

**Wiener v. United States,** 357 U.S. 349 (1958), argued 18 Nov. 1957, decided 30 June 1958 by vote of 9 to 0; Frankfurter for the Court. The Constitution is silent on the removal powers of the president. In *Myers v. United States* (1926), the Supreme Court had held that a president had the absolute right, without concurrence by the Senate, to remove executive-branch officers whom he had appointed and that Congress had no authority to limit this removal power. In dicta (see OBITER DICTUM), Chief Justice William Howard *Taft also claimed that the president had constitutional authority to remove administrators "who perform duties of a quasi-judicial character" (p. 352). In *Humphrey's Executor v. United States* (1935) this far-reaching claim of inherent presidential power was curtailed; the Court held that Congress could protect the independence of agencies that exercised "quasi-legislative" and "quasi-judicial" functions by prohibiting the president from removing commissioners "except for cause" (p. 629).

The facts in *Wiener* were strikingly similar to those in *Humphrey's Executor,* and so was the result. Wiener was appointed to the War Claims Commission by President Harry Truman. Under the War Claims Act, commissioners were to serve for the life of the commission; there was no provision made for removal. In 1953 President Dwight Eisenhower asked Wiener to step down. Wiener declined, and Eisenhower removed him. Wiener then filed suit with the Court of Claims for back pay from the date of his removal to the end of the life of the commission. The Court of Claims dismissed his suit, but the Supreme Court unanimously reversed.

Writing for the Court, Justice Felix *Frankfurter solidly endorsed both the philosophy and the holding of *Humphrey's Executor.* The War Claims Commission, like the Federal Trade Commission in the earlier case, was a quasi-judicial body whose officials were protected from removal by the president without good cause.

Joel B. Grossman

**Williams, George Henry** (b. New Lebanon, N.Y., 26 Mar. 1820; d. Portland, Oreg., 4 Apr. 1910), U.S. Senator from Oregon, U.S. attorney general, unsuccessful nominee for chief justice of the United States. President Ulysses S. Grant's 1873 nomination of George Williams for the position of *chief justice met with considerable controversy, arousing opposition in the Senate and among the organized bar that viewed Williams as too undistinguished for the nation's chief legal position. At Williams's request Grant withdrew the nomination.

Williams's early years were spent in New York, where he was admitted to the bar in 1844. He was a district judge in Iowa and in 1853 became chief justice of the Oregon territory. Williams gained a seat in the United States Senate in 1864. While in the Senate, Williams generally supported Radical Republican policies. After losing his Senate seat,

Williams was appointed attorney general by Grant in 1871.

Grant's attempt to place Williams on the Court met with opposition on the part of the bar. Part of that opposition included some sentiment that a lawyer from frontier Oregon would be ill-suited to deciding some of the Court's more complex commercial cases. In the face of this opposition, Grant withdrew the nomination.

Williams continued as attorney general until 1875. In later life he resumed law practice and public service in Oregon.

(See also NOMINEES, REJECTION OF.)

Robert J. Cottrol

**Williams v. Florida,** 399 U.S. 78 (1970), argued 4 Mar. 1970, decided 22 June 1970 by vote of 7 to 1; White for the Court, Marshall in dissent, Blackmun not participating. Pursuant to state law, Williams was tried and convicted of a felony by a jury of six persons—the six-person jury having been adopted by Florida for all but capital cases in 1967. Williams had filed a pretrial motion to impanel a jury of twelve, arguing that the smaller jury would deprive him of his *Sixth Amendment right to *trial by jury. Williams was sentenced to life imprisonment. The Supreme Court approved the use of six-person juries in state criminal cases and affirmed the judgment.

*Williams* was the first in a series of cases decided by the Court during the 1970s that overturned centuries of legal tradition, namely, the long-established universal practice and common understanding that the constitutionally required trial jury consisted of twelve persons who decided unanimously: *Landry v. Hoepfner* (1988), *Colgrove v. Battin* (1973), *Ballew v. Georgia* (1978), *Johnson v. Louisiana* (1972), *Apodaca v. Oregon* (1972), and *Burch v. Louisiana* (1979). *Williams* held that six-person state criminal juries were constitutionally adequate because they were functionally equivalent to twelve-person juries. The ruling was particularly unexpected because only two years earlier the Court had extended the Sixth Amendment right to trial by jury to the states in *Duncan v. Louisiana* (1968).

Nearly all commentators on *Williams* regarded the Court's reasoning and sense of evidence as bizarre. A close reading of Justice Byron *White's opinion made it clear that there was no constitutional or factual support for the ruling. The Court cited several items of "evidence" to support its assertion of functional equivalence—ranging from a statement that "it could be argued that there would be no differences," to a trial judge's thought on the economies of smaller juries. None of the items were competent evidence and most of them were not even relevant to the issue at hand.

The reviews of *Williams* were scathing. The only difference in opinion was whether the Court had been willfully or naively ignorant. Three years later in *Colegrove v. Battin* (1973), which authorized six-person civil juries for the federal courts, the Court answered the question in favor of willfulness. It boldly reasserted the *Williams* "proofs," added further flawed materials to the evidentiary array, and rebuked the critics of *Williams* as unpersuasive. For whatever reasons, the Court wanted smaller juries and got them.

Peter W. Sperlich

**Williams v. Mississippi,** 170 U.S. 213 (1898), argued 18 Mar. 1898, decided 25 Apr. 1898 by vote of 9 to 0; McKenna for the Court. An all-white *grand jury indicted Williams, a Mississippi black man, for murder. An all-white *petit jury convicted him and sentenced him to be hanged. Williams attacked the indictment and trial for violating the Equal Protection Clause of the *Fourteenth Amendment because blacks had been excluded from jury service. Only qualified voters could serve on juries, and a Mississippi constitutional convention in 1890 had adopted literacy and *poll-tax qualifications for voting, drastically reducing the number of registered black voters and effectively eliminating blacks from jury rolls after 1892. Nevertheless, the U.S. Supreme Court unanimously rejected Williams's contention, distinguishing the principle of *Yick Wo v. Hopkins, (1886) that a law fair on its face would be voided if it was administered by public authorities in an unequal manner. Williams had not shown that the actual administration of the Mississippi suffrage provisions was discriminatory.

Other southern states followed Mississippi's lead, and the new laws, together with *white primary elections, effectively disfranchised southern blacks until the white primaries were ended in the 1940s. *Williams* was, for practical purposes, superseded by the *Civil Rights Act of 1964 and the *Voting Rights Act of 1965, which banned exclusionary tests and devices in states and areas where minority turnout was unusually low.

(See also EQUAL PROTECTION; TRIAL BY JURY; VOTE, RIGHT TO.)

Ward E. Y. Elliott

**Willson v. Blackbird Creek Marsh Co.,** 2 Pet. (27 U.S.) 245 (1829), argued 17 Mar. 1829, decided 20 Mar. 1829 by vote of 6 to 0; Marshall for the Court; Trimble had died. The *Willson* decision had a double significance: it suggested what has since come to be known as the doctrine of the dormant *commerce power; and it was one of several post-1824 cases that constituted Chief Justice John *Marshall's retreat from the uncompromising nationalism that characterized the earlier period of his Court.

In *Gibbons v. Ogden (1824), Marshall had upheld expansive congressional power under the Commerce Clause and given a broad reading of a federal coastal licensing statute. The Delaware statute challenged in *Willson,* which permitted a company to erect a dam across a minor navigable stream to drain a swamp, might have been invalidated on the same grounds. Marshall, however, upheld it. He observed in passing that Congress had not enacted any directly pertinent legislation. Hence, Marshall suggested that when Congress chose to allow its *commerce power to lie dormant, states could exercise a concurrent power to regulate commerce. This indirectly repudiated an ambiguous hint in Marshall's *Gibbons* opinion that congressional power over interstate commerce was always exclusive, even when unexercised. The difference in result between the two cases may be explained in several ways. The waterway in *Willson* was insignificant, the doctrine of state *police power was emergent, and the Delaware statute was defensible as a public health measure.

William M. Wiecek

**Wilson, James** (b. Fifeshire, Scotland, 14 Sept. 1742; d. Edenton, N.C., 21 Aug. 1798; originally interred Hayes Plantation, Edenton, N.C.; remains removed to Christ Church, Philadelphia, Pa., Nov. 1906), associate justice, 1789–1798. Born into humble circumstances in rural Scotland, James Wilson became a poignant example of the "lad o'parts": after university study during the heyday of the eighteenth-century Scottish Enlightenment, he emigrated to America, at age twenty-three, and achieved fame and fortune, largely through his intellect and industry. In Pennsylvania and on the national scene, he became a noted lawyer, pamphleteer, politician, financier, and framer and theorist of American constitutionalism. Yet ultimately he failed to realize the promise of his talents and achievements; his tenure on the Court proved largely but the anticlimax of his public career.

After settling in Philadelphia in 1765, Wilson read law under John Dickinson, one of the best-educated American lawyers of the day. Like Dickinson, Wilson made the legal profession a vehicle to political prominence. In 1767 he launched a successful law practice in western Pennsylvania; but by 1768 his aspiration to become a voice in American politics was already evident. In that year he composed (although he did not revise and publish it until 1774) his *Considerations on the Nature and Extent of the Legislative Authority of the British Parliament,* widely recognized as an important contribution to the pre-Revolutionary pamphlet literature.

During the early 1770s Wilson expanded his law practice and began his public career. In 1775 he was elected to the Second Continental Congress. Although not an early advocate of independence, he signed the Declaration, and during the Revolution and its aftermath he continued to make his way in national and Pennsylvania politics. Aligning himself with the leading conservatives in his home state, he was an inveterate critic both of the 1776 Pennsylvania constitution and of the Articles of Confederation. Having moved to Philadelphia in 1778, and become

*James Wilson*

widely identified both as lawyer and investor with the interest of Robert Morris and the financial establishment there, Wilson produced in 1785 yet another important political pamphlet, his *Considerations on the Bank of North America*.

In that pamphlet, and otherwise as a delegate to Congress in the 1780s, Wilson promoted his strongly nationalist persuasion. His nationalism eventually brought him to the climax of his public career: his work in helping to frame and secure the federal Constitution. At the 1787 Convention, where he played a part second only to James *Madison's, and during the ratification campaign he led in Pennsylvania, Wilson contributed at least as much as any other founder to promoting several of the signal features of American constitutionalism, especially the theory of the *separation of powers, the importance of the presidency, and, above all, the fundamental significance of "the sovereignty of the People." In 1790 he also successfully led a movement to replace the 1776 Pennsylvania constitution with a document that embodied his distinctive constitutional theory even more notably than the federal Constitution did. Wilson's most comprehensive exposition of his constitutional theory came in his *Lectures on Law*, composed for delivery during 1790–1791, upon his appointment as professor of law at the College of Philadelphia.

In 1789, on President George Washington's nomination, Wilson was also appointed an associate justice of the first Court. Although suggested by himself and others for the office of *chief justice, he was passed over not only in 1789 but again in 1795 and 1796. Moreover, Wilson's cumulative accomplishments as associate justice

fell short of fulfilling his earlier promise. His few written opinions were brief, except for his much-remarked opinion in *Chisholm v. Georgia* (1793). There, in disposing of a state's claim of sovereign immunity from suit in the federal courts, Wilson elaborated a conception of popular sovereignty that, while grounded on leading principles of contemporary philosophical thought, was nevertheless out of tune with the politics of the times. Yet, in eschewing the legal positivism associated with Sir William Blackstone, and in exalting and interrelating the authority of national government and of popular democracy, Wilson's *Chisholm* opinion prefigured future American jurisprudence.

Increasingly during the 1790s Wilson became overextended in his investments and overwhelmed by financial distresses. Twice he was jailed for debt. Eventually, to escape creditors he went into hiding in North Carolina. Isolated and disgraced, he died there, a great legal mind and constitutional theorist arguably undone by the visionary tendencies that have distinguished his legacy as a founder.

□ Stephen A. Conrad, "Metaphor and Imagination in James Wilson's Theory of Federal Union," *Law & Social Inquiry* 13 (1988): 1–70. Robert Green McCloskey, ed., *The Works of James Wilson*, 2 vols. (1967).

Stephen A. Conrad

**Winship, In re,** 397 U.S. 358 (1970), argued 20 Jan. 1970, decided 31 Mar. 1970 by vote of 6 to 3; Brennan for the Court, Harlan concurring, Burger, Stewart, and Black in dissent. The Supreme Court's extension of criminal defendants' rights to juveniles faced with possible incarceration revealed the inconsistencies between existing juvenile procedures in the states and the adversary standards implied by In re *Gault (1967). *Winship* addressed one of these and, in the process, raised significant jurisprudential questions about the nature of due process in a constitutional system.

At issue was the standard of proof necessary to commit a twelve-year-old boy to a training school for an act that would have constituted larceny if committed by an adult. Under New York juvenile law at the time, a family court judge needed only a "preponderance of the evidence" to justify juvenile detention, rather than the criminal standard of proof "beyond a reasonable doubt."

On appeal, the Court ventured beyond the explicit guarantees of the Constitution (since the reasonable doubt standard is nowhere specified) to assert that such a standard, accepted at common law and historically by the Court for determining guilt, was essential for due process and the fair treatment of juveniles facing incarceration; furthermore, it would not disturb the distinctiveness and flexibility of juvenile adjudication. The Court thus "constitutionalized" the reasonable doubt standard for adult criminal defendants as well as juveniles.

Significantly, Chief Justice Warren *Burger's dissent foreshadowed the emergence of a more conservative attitude toward the procedural protections afforded minors. A year later, the Court sharply curtailed the expansion of due process. In *McKeiver* v. *Pennsylvania* (1971) it narrowly interpreted *Gault* and *Winship* and denied juveniles the right to trial by jury.

(See also DUE PROCESS, PROCEDURAL; JUVENILE JUSTICE.)

Albert R. Matheny

**Wiretapping.** See KATZ V. UNITED STATES; OLMSTEAD V. UNITED STATES; SEARCH WARRANT RULE, EXCEPTIONS TO.

**Wirt, William,** (b. Bladensburg, Md., 8 Nov. 1772; d. Washington, D.C., 18 Feb. 1834), lawyer and statesman. A prominent lawyer in the early republic, William Wirt helped shape its legal system. Though Wirt was inclined toward a scholar's life, he never escaped the financial necessity of frequently arguing in court. As United States attorney general (1817–1829) in cabinets confronted with controversial issues, he seemed uninterested in politics. When nominated for president by the Antimasons in 1832, he wished to withdraw in favor of Whig candidate Henry Clay but did not. Originally a states' righter, he moved toward constitutional nationalism under the influence of Chief Justice John *Marshall. Still, he seemed not to understand the connections between law and politics.

Wirt argued 174 cases in the Supreme Court, some as attorney general for the government and more as counsel for private clients. (He and his contemporaries saw no impropriety in a mixture of the two roles.) In his long tenure as attorney general, he strengthened that office, which before his term had been quite weak. His advocacy of state power over a chartered *corporation was unsuccessful in *Dartmouth College* v. *Woodward* (1819). But in *Gibbons* v. *Ogden* (1824), the Court's first Commerce Clause case, he assisted Daniel *Webster in breaking New York's steamboat monopoly. His argument for the constitutionality of the Bank of the United States in *McCulloch* v. *Maryland* (1819) was strong, though overshadowed by William *Pinkney's powerful exposition of nationalism. In a valiant effort near the end of his life, he won the case of *Worcester* v. *Georgia* (1832), yet found that Indian removal to the West was unavoidable (see CHEROKEE CASES).

Maurice Baxter

**Wisconsin v. Yoder,** 406 U.S. 205 (1972), argued 8 Dec. 1971, decided 15 May 1972 by vote of 6 to 1; Burger for the Court, Douglas in dissent, Powell and Rehnquist not participating. In this case the Supreme Court decided that the application of Wisconsin's compulsory high school attendance law to children of members of the Conservative Amish Mennonite Church violated the parents'

rights under the Free Exercise Clause of the *First Amendment.

The Court decided that a state's interest in universal *education is not totally free from a balancing process when it impinges on other fundamental rights, such as those specifically protected by the Free Exercise Clause and the traditional liberty interests of the parents with respect to the upbringing of their children. The Amish had argued that enforcement of this law after the eighth grade would gravely endanger if not destroy their religious beliefs. They pointed to their long history as a self-sufficient religious community, the sincerity of their beliefs, and the interrelationship of those beliefs with a unique way of life, and the need to continue that interplay for the survival of the sect.

The majority concluded that the Amish met the difficult burden of demonstrating that their alternative mode of informal vocational education did not violate the objectives and important state interests upon which the Wisconsin Supreme Court had relied in sustaining the state's program of compulsory high school attendance. The Amish demonstrated that forgoing one or two additional years of compulsory education would not impair the physical or mental health of their children or their ability to become self-supporting and productive citizens. Moreover, the Amish argued that high school attendance emphasizes intellectual and scientific accomplishments, self-distinction, and competitiveness—all values opposed to Amish concerns for learning through doing, a life of goodness, support for community welfare, and separation rather than integration into worldly society.

The Court decided that genuine religious beliefs, not mere personal preference or philosophical wants, were behind the Amish claims. Also important to the Court was the breadth and historical constancy of Amish religious culture; the Court acknowledged that secondary school life would present a far greater threat to their religious community than grammar school. Compulsory high school attendance, the Court found, would undermine the Amish religious community by forcing young adherents to abandon the free exercise of their religion or move to more tolerant environs.

The Court rejected the State's claims that only religious beliefs, not actions, even though religiously grounded, are within the protection of the First Amendment. The Court drew on *Sherbert* v. *Verner* (1963) to argue that a regulation neutral on its face may in its application offend the constitutional requirement for government neutrality if it unduly burdens the free exercise of religion. Where parents' interests in their children's religious upbringing are combined with a valid free exercise claim, more than the usual reasonableness basis test is needed to sustain the law.

The Court repeatedly emphasized the historical uniqueness and self-sufficiency of the Amish community. Indeed, it went out of its way to suggest that without such a long history, courts should not grant the exemption from compulsory school attendance laws. Few other groups, the Court said, will be able to carry the burden of showing that informal vocational education or other training will meet valid state interests in compulsory school attendance.

Justice William O. *Douglas's dissent focused on the narrowness of the Court's framework, which encompassed only the interests of the parents and the state. He argued that the child must first be heard as to his or her desire for a high school education and emancipation from the Amish religion and community. In addition, he questioned whether only formal religious communities can seek an exemption from compulsory high school for their adherents.

Many scholars believe, as Douglas did, that the Court made a content-based choice in violation of a cardinal principle of the *First Amendment. They question the Court's reasoning in choosing to grant exemptions from attending high school to those with prescribed religious beliefs and long-standing membership in religious communities, while apparently withholding such opportunities from citizens and groups whose independent and individualistic moral choices are based on secular grounds. In addition, many scholars agree with Douglas that children have constitutional rights of religious beliefs and liberty interests that may be different from those of their parents and that they need a neutral legal forum for their protection.

(See also RELIGION.)

□ Jesse H. Choper, "Defining 'Religion' in the First Amendment," *University of Illinois Law Review* (1984): 579–613. Ronald Kahn

**Witnesses, Confrontation of.** The adversary system of law is premised upon the ability of each party to offer proofs and counterarguments. By its very nature it implies the ability of each side to challenge the arguments of the other. This general principle has been reinforced in the criminal process by the *Sixth Amendment, which provides in part that in all criminal prosecutions, "the accused shall enjoy the right . . . to be confronted with the witnesses against him." This provision was inserted in the *Bill of Rights in reaction to eighteenth-century English practices that did not always permit such an opportunity. Although states have long had their own confrontation guarantees as well as prohibitions against hearsay evidence, in *Pointer* v. *Texas* (1965) this constitutional guarantee was made applicable to the states via the *Fourteenth Amendment (see INCORPORATION DOCTRINE).

The theory of the Confrontation Clause is to ensure that testimony relied on in a criminal proceeding is presented in open court and that

the accused not only has a right to hear adverse witnesses but a right as well to confront those witnesses through cross-examination. Although this general principle is well established and widely accepted, there continue to be debates about how broadly it should be interpreted. For instance, in order to protect especially vulnerable witnesses—for example, children in sexual abuse cases—some states modify traditional cross-examination practices in ways that have led to complaints that defendants are being denied their right of confrontation. Furthermore, as a practical matter courts have allowed use of some testimony in the absence of an opportunity to confront, as in proceedings allowing the introduction of the declarations of dying persons and of testimony of deceased witnesses who had testified at former trials. Malcolm M. Feeley

**Wolcott, Alexander** (b. Windsor, Conn., 15 Sept. 1758; d. Middletown, Conn., 26 June 1828), lawyer, public official, and unconfirmed nominee for associate justice. The son of Dr. Alexander and Mary Richards Wolcott, Wolcott attended Yale College and thereafter studied law. He commenced law practice in Windsor, Connecticut and then in Springfield, Massachusetts, where he married Frances Burbank in September 1785. He returned with his wife to Connecticut, where he became a leader of the Republican party and served as collector of the Port of Middletown.

On 4 February 1811, President James Madison nominated Wolcott for an associate justiceship of the Supreme Court. Spurred on by Wolcott's vigorous and unpopular enforcement of the Embargo, a federal statute of 1807 that prohibited all naval commerce to foreign countries, Federalists greeted his nomination with contempt, describing him as a man of mediocre legal talent. Despite the partisanship of these attacks, they were not far off the mark and even Republicans found it difficult to defend Wolcott. The extreme doubts within both parties about his judicial abilities caused the Senate to reject his nomination by a vote of 9 to 24.

Wolcott's rejection by the Senate did not discourage his political activities. He assumed a prominent role in the Connecticut State Constitutional Convention of 1818, where he argued that any judge who declared a legislative act unconstitutional should be expelled. He further contended that the Supreme Court's exercise of *judicial review was a usurpation of power.

(See also NOMINEES, REJECTION OF.)
Robert M. Ireland

**Wolff Packing Co. v. Court of Industrial Relations,** 262 U.S. 522 (1923), argued 27 Apr. 1923, decided 11 June 1923 by vote of 9 to 0; Taft for the Court. Kansas startled the nation in 1920 by enacting the Industrial Relations Act, which provided for the compulsory arbitration of all disputes in key industries—food, clothing, fuel—through a specially appointed court. This court had the right to restrict strikes and employer lockouts, and also had the power to fix wages and oversee working conditions. The measure proved to be unpopular with both management and *labor.

Ruling the law unconstitutional, Chief Justice William Howard *Taft used the occasion to formulate definitive guidelines for freedom of *contract and to settle precisely which businesses could be regulated on the basis of being "affected with a public interest." These included businesses carried on under the authority of a public grant (i.e., public utilities that rendered public services; occupations traditionally recognized as vested with a public service dimension, such as inns, cabs, grist mills; and businesses where natural economic laws did not operate, such as monopolies or businesses whose operations had changed toward public service so as to warrant some governmental regulation.

The ruling negated a half-century of legal development since *Munn v. Illinois (1877) by putting the majority of businesses outside the reach of state regulation. Economic freedom became the rule, and restraint the exception. Affording the legal rationale for even more vigorous assaults upon statutes directly regulating business behavior, the case led to the voiding of a series of state measures enacted to impose social controls upon a variety of private businesses.

(See also STATE REGULATION OF COMMERCE.)

Paul L. Murphy

**Wolf v. Colorado,** 338 U.S. 25 (1949), argued 19 Oct. 1948, decided 27 June 1949 by vote of 6 to 3; Frankfurter for the Court, Douglas and Murphy in dissent. Wolf was convicted of conspiracy to commit *abortion in Colorado. The Colorado Supreme Court affirmed the conviction against Wolf's challenge to the constitutionality of the seizure and the use of evidence in criminal proceedings. Granting *certiorari, the U. S. Supreme Court considered whether the *Fourth Amendment search and seizure protection was incorporated by the *Fourteenth Amendment's Equal Protection Clause and thereby applicable to the states as well as the federal government. The Court also considered whether incorporation required the application of the *exclusionary rule as defined and applied to federal courts in *Weeks v. United States (1914). The Court responded in the affirmative to the first question but rejected the extension of the exclusionary rule to state courts.

Writing for the majority, Justice Felix *Frankfurter argued that protection from arbitrary intrusion by law enforcement is implied in the "concept of ordered liberty" and thereby incorporated by the Fourteenth Amendment and applicable to the states (p. 27). He rejected, however, the claim that illegally or unconstitutionally obtained evidence had to be excluded in state criminal proceedings. Frankfurter acknowledged that such a rule could deter police from unreasonable searches but stressed that there were other means of enforcing such a basic right and that state courts were resistant to the rule defined in the Weeks decision. Much the same arguments were offered by Justice Hugo *Black in a concurring opinion in which he emphasized that incorporation did not require the application of a "judicially created rule of evidence" (p. 40).

Two dissenting opinions were filed in the case: one by Justice William O. *Douglas and one by Justice Frank *Murphy with Wiley B. *Rutledge in agreement. Douglas observed that the Fourth Amendment protection is rendered ineffective without the exclusion of evidence seized in an unconstitutional fashion, while Murphy stressed that few states would devise practically efficient means of redressing Fourth Amendment violations.

Wolf has since been overruled by *Mapp v. Ohio, (1961). The Supreme Court accepted the minority position in Wolf and required states not only to abide by Fourth Amendment provisions but to exclude evidence seized in violation of such protections.

(See also INCORPORATION DOCTRINE; SILVER PLATTER DOCTRINE.)

Susette M. Talarico

**Women.** See GENDER.

**Wong Kim Ark, United States v.,** 169 U.S. 649 (1898), argued 5–8 Mar. 1897, decided 28 Mar. 1898 by vote of 6 to 2; Gray for the Court, Fuller and Harlan in dissent, McKenna not participating. This case arose out of the debate over the exclusion of Chinese from the Unites States in the late nineteenth century. At issue was the *citizenship status of persons of Chinese descent born in the United States. Chinese had already been denied the privilege of becoming naturalized citizens under an 1882 act. Exclusionists urged that persons of Chinese descent should be denied birthright citizenship as well and pushed for a definition of citizenship based upon the nationality of the parents ("jus sanguinis") rather than upon place of birth ("jus soli").

The issue came before the Supreme Court when Wong Kim Ark, born to Chinese parents in San Francisco in 1873, was denied admission to the United States after traveling to China for a visit. The decision hinged upon the interpretation of the first clause of the *Fourteenth Amendment, which provided that "all persons born or naturalized in the United States, and subject to the jurisdiction thereof, are citizens of the United States." The government argued that Wong Kim Ark was not a citizen because his Chinese parentage made him subject to the emperor of China. The Supreme Court, however, ruled in favor of Wong Kim Ark, holding that the common law and the *Fourteenth Amendment guaranteed citizenship to all persons born in the United States, regardless of their ethnic heritage. The case proved to be an important legal victory for Chinese-Americans as well as other persons of Asian descent during a period of intense anti-Asian sentiment.

(See also CHINESE EXCLUSION CASES; CITIZEN-SHIP.)

Lucy E. Salyer

**Woodbury, Levi** (b. Francestown, N.H., 22 Dec. 1789; d. Portsmouth, N.H., 4 Sept. 1851; interred Harmony Grove Cemetery, Portsmouth), associate justice, 1845–1851. Levi Woodbury, son of Peter and Mary Woodbury, studied law with Judge Jeremiah Smith and at the Litchfield Law School. He was admitted to the bar and began practicing in Francestown, New Hampshire, in 1812. An ardent Jeffersonian Republican, Woodbury in 1817 was appointed associate justice of the state superior court, where in the same year he joined in a decision favoring the Republican takeover of his alma mater, Dartmouth College. In June 1819 he married Elizabeth Williams Clapp, daughter of a wealthy Republican merchant of Portsmouth, who would help him politically. In 1823 a faction of independent Republicans, with help from Federalists, elected Woodbury governor of New Hampshire.

Factional infighting accounted for Woodbury's unsuccessful bid for reelection, but in 1825 he was first elected to the legislature and then to the United States Senate. He began his senatorial career as a supporter of John Quincy Adams but rather quickly switched to the Jacksonians. In

*Levi Woodbury*

1831, having chosen not to seek another term in the Senate, Woodbury was appointed secretary of the navy by President Andrew *Jackson. In 1834 Jackson appointed Woodbury secretary of the treasury, a position he held, despite complaints about his competence, until 1841, Martin Van Buren having carried him over into his term as president. Woodbury returned to the United States Senate in 1841, having been elected by the New Hampshire legislature as a Democrat. President James K. Polk indicated on 20 September 1845 he would appoint Woodbury to the United States Supreme Court to fill the vacancy created by the death of Justice Joseph *Story. On 23 December 1845, Polk submitted the nomination to the Senate, which confirmed Woodbury on 3 January 1846.

For the most part, Woodbury joined the mainstream of the Taney Court, although occasionally his penchant for states' rights prompted a dissenting opinion. For example in *Waring* v. *Clarke* (1847), he dissented from the Court's ruling that federal admiralty jurisdiction (see ADMIRALTY AND MARITIME LAW) extended to waters ninety-five miles north of New Orleans. He likewise disagreed with the Court's decision in the *Passenger Cases* (1849), which ruled that state head taxes on incoming immigrants violated the federal Commerce Clause (see COMMERCE POWER). His dissenting opinions expressed his fear that the majority's decision might lead to a future ruling that a state could not exclude emancipated slaves, a result that would outrage the South and disrupt the union. Earlier, Woodbury had made clear his proslavery views when he wrote the opinion for the Court in *Jones* v. *Van Zandt* (1847), which ruled in favor of a slaveowner who sued a Northerner for illegally harboring a *fugitive slave. He generally supported the Taney Court's decisions on the *contracts clause, writing for the majority in *Planters' Bank* v. *Sharp* (1848), which held that a state could not revoke a bank's right to transfer bills and notes that had been granted to it in its charter, and concurring in *Cook* v. *Moffat* (1847), which ruled that a state *bankruptcy law could not discharge a resident's obligations under a contract made out of state.

All in all, Woodbury possessed an acute legal mind, but his brief tenure and his tendency to write overly long, convoluted opinions compromised his sojourn on the Supreme Court.

Robert M. Ireland

**Woodruff v. Parham,** 8 Wall. (75 U.S.) 123 (1869), argued 13 Oct. 1869, decided 8 Nov. 1869 by vote of 8 to 1; Miller for the Court, Nelson in dissent. The plaintiffs refused to pay the Mobile, Alabama, tax on sales of goods at auction, contending that, since their goods were brought in from other states and sold in original packages they were exempt from taxation. They invoked the Constitution's prohibition against state taxation of imports and the Commerce Clause, stressing

the original package doctrine established in
*Brown* v. *Maryland* (1827). In *Brown,* the Court
held that state power over commerce attached
when a commodity lost its character as an import.
While in its original package it remained a part of
interstate commerce. In *Woodruff* the Court read
the *Brown* precedent narrowly, holding that the
Constitution did not prohibit one state from
taxing articles imported from another providing
the taxing state did not discriminate against such
goods. As this case concerned a tax imposed on
all sales made in Mobile, it did not discriminate
against interstate commerce. Conversely, the
opinion underscored the limitations of state
power. States could not tax products of other
states so as to drive them out of the jurisdiction or
interfere with commerce between the states; a tax
that attempted to fetter interstate commerce
would be unconstitutional. Thus, the *Woodruff*
decision helped to establish the principle that
state discrimination against interstate commerce
violated the Commerce Clause. (See COMMERCE
POWER.)
Richard F. Hamm

*William Burnham Woods*

**Woods, William Burnham** (b. Newark, Ohio, 3
August 1824; d. Washington, D.C., 14 May 1887;
interred Cedar Hill Cemetery, Newark), associate
justice, 1881–1887. Appointed to the Court by
President Rutherford B. Hayes in 1880, Justice
William B. Woods served until his death in 1887.
During his brief tenure, Woods was part of the
Court's mainstream that gave a narrow reading
to the Civil War Amendments, particularly the
Fourteenth. His most important opinions restricted congressional ability to protect individuals from private infringement of civil rights and
rejected the applicability of the Bill of Rights to
the states.

William B. Woods was the son of Ezekiel S.
Woods, a farmer and merchant, and Sarah Burnham. He graduated from Yale College and
clerked with S. D. King, an Ohio attorney; in 1847
he was admitted to Ohio's bar. Active in the
state's Democratic party before the Civil War, he
served in the state legislature on the eve of the
conflict. During the war he served in an Ohio
volunteer regiment and rose to the rank of brevet
major general.

After the war, Woods settled in Alabama and
switched his political allegiances to the Republican party. He served in that state's chancery court
system, developing an expertise in equity for
which he would later be noted in the federal
courts. In 1869 President Ulysses S. Grant appointed him to the Fifth Circuit Court, where he
initially took a more expansive view of the
guarantees provided by the Fourteenth Amendment than he would later on the Supreme Court.
While on the Fifth Circuit he voted to strike down
government mandated monopoly as violative of
the Fourteenth Amendment's Privileges or Immunities Clause. He also interpreted that clause as

allowing the federal government to punish private violations of civil rights.

After his appointment to the Supreme Court in
1881, Woods' view of the Fourteenth Amendment grew more conservative. He joined with the
majority in the *Civil Rights Cases* to strike down
the Civil Rights Act of 1875 as exceeding federal
power.

His two most significant opinions involved the
Fourteenth Amendment. In *United States* v. *Harris*
(1883) he struck down the Ku Klux Klan Act of
1871 on the grounds that protection of individuals from private conspiracies was a state not a
federal function. In another opinion, *Presser* v.
*Illinois* (1886), Woods limited the possibilities of
applying the *Bill of Rights to the states through
the *Fourteenth Amendment. In *Presser,* which
involved an Illinois statute that prohibited private citizens from parading while armed, Woods
held that the *Second Amendment limited federal but not state action.

Justice Woods' jurisprudence reflected a concern with maintaining state prerogative and limiting federal power. That concern played a significant role in helping to limit the ability of the
Fourteenth Amendment to act as a vehicle to
protect individual rights.

☐ L. Filler, "William B. Woods," in *The Justices of the
Supreme Court of the United States, 1789–1969,* edited by
Leon M. Friedman and Fred L. Israel, vol. 2 (1969), pp.
1327–1336.
Robert J. Cottrol

**Woodson v. North Carolina,** 428 U.S. 280 (1976),
argued 31 Mar. 1976, decided 2 July 1976 by vote
of 5 to 4; Stewart for the Court, Brennan and

Marshall concurring, White, Burger, Blackmun, and Rehnquist in dissent. Woodson, an accomplice in a robbery/murder, had been convicted of first-degree murder. Under North Carolina law, he received a mandatory death sentence. Following *Furman* v. *Georgia* (1972), North Carolina had replaced its discretionary sentencing system with a mandatory death sentence for first-degree murder. This case, decided on the same day as *Gregg* v. *Georgia* (1976), reversed the lower court's approval of mandatory sentencing on *Eighth Amendment grounds.

Justice Potter *Stewart's opinion held that the constitutional proscription of *cruel and unusual punishments required the state to exercise its power to punish within the limits of civilized standards. Stewart insisted that evolving standards of decency have moved away from mandatory sentencing and that most death penalty laws reenacted after *Furman* did not provide for automatic death sentences. Those that did treated people not as unique individuals but as part of a faceless and inhuman mass, in violation of the Eighth Amendment. Stewart also noted that, in light of evidence that juries will tailor the death penalty to individual circumstances, the North Carolina statute might encourage juries to find a defendant innocent only to avoid mandatory *capital punishment. Such choices would necessarily be made without specific statutory guidance and would thus violate the requirements set out in *Gregg*. William J. *Brennan and Thurgood *Marshall concurred by reiterating their view that the death penalty violated the Eighth Amendment per se. The dissenters questioned the Court's capacity to determine that mandatory sentencing was less evenhanded than a system of statutory guides to discretionary sentencing.

Lief H. Carter

**Woodward, George W.** (b. Bethany, Penn., 26 Mar. 1809; d. Rome, Italy, 10 May 1875), judge, congressman, and unconfirmed nominee to the Supreme Court. After being admitted to the bar in 1830, George W. Woodward practiced law in his home state of Pennsylvania, served as a delegate to the state constitutional convention in 1837, and assumed the position of president judge of Pennsylvania's fourth judicial district in 1841. Four years later, after making an unsuccessful bid for the U.S. Senate, Woodward received an appointment on 23 December 1845 from President James K. Polk to fill the Supreme Court vacancy created by the death of Justice Henry *Baldwin.

Although a loyal Democrat from a distinguished family, Woodward failed to gain Senate confirmation. Divisions within the Democratic party—especially the opposition of a senator from Woodward's home state—caused the Senate on 22 January 1846 to reject Woodward's nomination by a vote of 20 to 29. Woodward later served as associate justice and chief justice of the

Pennsylvania Supreme Court and eventually won election the U.S. House of Represenatatives.

Timothy S. Huebner

**Worcester v. Georgia.** See CHEROKEE CASES.

**Workload.** Since the end of *World War II, the number of cases filed with the Supreme Court has grown significantly, mushrooming from 1,295 in 1947 to 3,939 in 1989. Filings are the cases presented to the Court for its consideration each term. Since, however, the Court's discretionary power permits it to deny substantive review to more than 90 percent of the cases filed, the number of filings alone cannot constitute a precise indicator of the Court's workload. Other factors must also be considered, including the time allotted to each case decided on the merits; the number, length, and complexity of opinions; and the amount of work delegated to law *clerks.

Nevertheless, the upward trend in case filings has generated wide concern. As former Chief Justice Warren *Burger and others have observed, the increase in filings has magnified the sheer volume of cases that require some action. More petitions require more time, although there is little empirical evidence that more filings require substantially more screening time. While the justices have not taken commensurately greater numbers of cases to review on the merits, there is at least mixed evidence that the time required for the Court to render a decision on the merits has increased. But this may be due more to the increasing complexity of cases decided than to the initial number of cases filed.

Much of the concern about the Court's workload focuses not on time or level of effort but on the quality of attention devoted to individual cases. Particular concern has been expressed about the justices' seeming inability to agree on major opinions and about the clarity of their reasoning and decisions. In a 1983 article Philip Kurland and Dennis Hutchinson charge that an overloaded docket leads to "sleazy" opinions on the merits. Whether the Court's product has in fact deteriorated cannot be assessed fully or even objectively. There is no agreed-on basis for judgment or comparison, and, even if such standards could be developed, the causes of alleged deterioration would be difficult to identify. How much could be attributed to workload and how much to clashing ideological and attitudinal preferences of the justices?

There are also those, including a number of the justices, who simply deny that there is a workload problem of any consequence—certainly not one that requires corrective action beyond a little more concentrated effort and/or greater reliance on law clerks. No justice claims that he or she personally reads all *certiorari petitions. There is also widespread agreement among the justices that *in forma pauperis cases, which comprise nearly half the initial filings, are largely frivolous and can be disposed of quickly. In fact, fewer than 1 percent of these cases are granted review. Nevertheless, these petitions do require some attention and thus must be factored into any calculation of just what the Court's workload is and whether or not it constitutes a problem.

If the nature of the Court's workload is clouded by disagreement about causes, consequences, and significance, there is no paucity of proposed solutions to the alleged problem. Some of these involve statutory changes in jurisdiction, such as the *Judicial Improvements and Access to Justice Act of 1988, which eliminated the mandatory appeal route of access to the Court in all but a few cases. Others have called for limiting or expediting the consideration of certain categories of cases that are particularly time consuming, such as *habeas corpus in *capital punishment cases. But these are also cases with high political content; proposals to limit them are at least as responsive to ideological as to workload considerations.

Still other critics have called for the creation of new courts, or the modification of the jurisdiction of existing courts, to siphon off certiorari petitions, or other cases referred by the Court itself, from its docket. But such "solutions" might add to the problem rather than solving it. They would create another tier of federal appellate courts, thus inevitably increasing problems of delay and policy confusion. And, more important to many, they would necessarily detract from, and thus reduce, the Court's policy impact. Of course, weakening the Court is (or was) high on the agenda of its conservative critics. Now that the Court has taken a distinctly rightward turn, these suggested "reforms" have become much less prominent.

The Court has itself attempted to address the workload issue. The justices rely on their law clerks to screen certiorari petitions. Seven of the nine justices now participate in a clerk *cert pool established by former Justice Lewis *Powell. One clerk from each justice's chambers is assigned to review petitions and distribute a "pool memo" to each participating justice's chambers—where they may be taken at face value or reviewed again by another clerk. In theory this reduces the number of clerks and the amount of individual judicial attention devoted to certiorari petitions. How much time it actually saves is, at best, debatable.

Beyond screening certiorari petitions, there has been an increased delegation to clerks of additional duties in the writing of *opinions. The number of clerks assigned to each justice (though not always utilized) has increased to four. Whether increasing the clerks' workload and responsibilities also eases the workload on individual justices is unclear. Relying more heavily on clerks to draft opinions has also resulted in opinions of much greater length, with vastly more footnotes, and probably in a reduced receptivity to a genuinely collegial product.

The Court can also dispose of some cases by summary procedures that do not require the same level of intense and individualized attention as full opinion cases. It has, in the past decade, increased the number of petitions in which, without additional *briefs or *oral argument, it has *vacated the judgment of a lower court and remanded for decision "not inconsistent with" a recently decided case. The Court has also decided more cases with only a *per curiam opinion. While these opinions may contain some legal reasoning, they are usually too brief to provide lower courts or future litigants with much guidance. In either instance the charge could be made that the litigants—and the law—are receiving treatment that is below par.

Finally, the Court can adjust to its workload by lengthening the deliberative process, for example, in extending the time frame between certiorari and oral argument and again between argument and the announcement of its decision. But this simply increases the wait or queue for decision and leads to a growing backlog—something that, except for a few recent terms, the modern Court has been able to avoid. Some cases are inevitably carried over until the next term: those filed late in the term, those selected for decision late in a term, and a few that have been argued but cannot be resolved in time to announce by the term's end (or which are set over for reargument). This allows the Court to maintain its traditional deliberative practices.

When the Court's normal rhythm is disturbed, however, litigants have to wait longer to learn if the Court will decide their case and longer again for the case to be decided. While a few months extra delay, if uniform and expected, would not be severely consequential for the litigants or the society, it would certainly diminish the Court's image as perhaps the only governmental body in Washington that keeps more or less abreast of its work.

Assuming that the Supreme Court will not (and should not) alter its traditional deliberative practices for those cases that it does decide "on the merits," it has probably instituted most of the marginal, internal changes that might expedite processing of cases. There is little support, and probably no authority, for more radical changes designed to ease its workload (such as a division of the Court into panels) or for delegating some opinion-writing functions to a central staff. Thus unless and until American society redirects its increasing reliance on judicial decisions, the Court's workload is likely to continue to grow. Only when the justices themselves cry for help is some major restructuring likely to occur.

□ Gerhard Casper and Richard Posner, *The Workload of the Supreme Court* (1976). Philip Kurland and Dennis Hutchinson, "The Business of the Supreme Court, O.T.

1982," *University of Chicago Law Review* 50 (1983): 628–651. "Of High Designs: A Compendium of Proposals to Reduce the Workload of the Supreme Court," note in *Harvard Law Review* 97 (1983): 307–325.

William P. McLauchlan

**World War I** is considered the first modern war because it involved the mobilization of entire populations. For the United States, it also represented a break with tradition because, for the first time, American armies were sent to fight on European soil. Believing the nation faced a crisis of unprecedented proportion, President Woodrow Wilson and Congress acted swiftly to extend the authority of the federal government after war was declared in April 1917. In May, the Selective Service Act instituted a wartime military draft. In June, the Wilson administration proposed the Lever Food Control Bill, which subjected fuel and food to federal regulation and which gave the president the power in an "extreme" emergency to dictate price schedules in any industry. Although congressional critics charged the measure gave the president dictatorial powers and violated the *Tenth Amendment, it became law in August 1917. In November 1918, the War Prohibition Act banned the making and sale of alcoholic beverages during the war. Other statutes empowered the president to compel preferential treatment for government war contracts, to seize and run plants needed for the war effort, to operate the water and rail transport systems, and to regulate exports.

Through a combination of executive orders and federal statutes, the government was able to curtail sharply freedom of *speech and the press. In April 1917, Wilson issued two executive orders, one creating the first large-scale government propaganda agency, the Committee on Public Information, the other giving the government control of land and cable telegraph lines out of the country. In June 1917, the *Espionage Act made it a felony to cause insubordination, interfere with enlistments, and transmit false statements that obstructed the military (see SUBVERSION). It also established postal censorship and gave the postmaster general, Albert S. Burleson, power (which he often used capriciously) to ban material deemed seditious or treasonable from the mails (see POSTAL POWER). In October, the Trading with the Enemy Act created a Censorship Board to coordinate and make recommendations about *censorship. It allowed censorship of mail or any other kind of communication with foreign countries. The Sedition Act of May 1918 (an amendment to the Espionage Act) sought to repress anarchists, socialists, pacifists, and certain labor leaders. The law made it a felony to disrupt recruiting or enlistments, to encourage either support for Germany and its allies or disrespect for the American cause, or otherwise to bring the United States government, its leaders, or its symbols into disrepute.

Critics charged that virtually every right guaranteed to Americans under the Constitution was nullified or abridged during the war. The Supreme Court, however, was not asked to pass judgment on the constitutionality of many of these statutes. Those cases that did reach the Court did so, with a few exceptions, only after the war had ended.

Chief Justice Edward D. *White, a one-time Confederate soldier from Louisiana and the president of a sugar company, led the Court during the war years and after. Joining White on the bench were Justices Joseph *McKenna, a California lawyer appointed by President William McKinley; two Theodore Roosevelt appointees, William R. *Day and Oliver Wendell *Holmes; Willis *Van Devanter and Mahlon *Pitney, both appointees of William Howard *Taft and two of the Court's most conservative members; and three Wilson appointees, Louis D. *Brandeis (whose Judaism and advocacy for social causes made him anathema to conservatives), John H. *Clarke, a progressive-minded railroad attorney, and James C. *McReynolds from Tennessee, who as Wilson's first attorney general had vigorously prosecuted *antitrust cases. As a Supreme Court justice, McReynolds became a champion of *property rights against the expansion of government regulation and thus proved far less liberal than Wilson had hoped.

***Enlargement of Federal Power.*** Despite his *Civil War record, White was strongly nationalistic on issues relating to states rights and the war. Under his leadership the Court did little to challenge the expansion of federal power. It upheld the Selective Service Act in January 1918 in *Arver* v. *United States,* known as the *Selective Draft Law Cases.* Writing for a unanimous Court, White said Congress had the power to "raise and support armies" and that the draft was not "involuntary servitude" as defined by the *Thirteenth Amendment (p. 367). A few months later, in *Cox* v. *Wood* (1918), the Court refused relief to a man who sought discharge from the armed forces on grounds that the draft could not be used to force military service abroad. In *Ruthenberg* v. *United States* (1918), the Court rejected a claim by socialists that their constitutional rights had been violated. (The socialists had argued that at their trial for not registering for the draft, the grand jury and trial jury had been made up entirely of people from other political parties.)

A similar pattern of approving the enlargement of federal power appeared in other cases. Although the War Prohibition Act was passed after the armistice, the Court sustained its validity in the *War Prohibition Cases* of late 1919. Brandeis accepted the measure's legality under the federal war power and held that federal regulatory authority continued even after the armistice. The Court again upheld prohibition a few months later in *Rupert* v. *Caffey* (1920), rejecting the argument that the act encroached on the *police powers of the states. In *Northern Pacific Railway Co.* v. *North Dakota* (1919), a unanimous Court endorsed a section of the Army Appropriation Act of August 1916 that empowered the president to take over and run railroads during wartime. White noted that "the complete and undivided character of the war power of the United States is not disputable" and said that the federal government could override state rate controls that would be binding during peacetime (p. 135). The Court also turned back challenges to the Trading with the Enemy Act (*Rumely* v. *McCarthy*, 1919; *Central Union Trust Co.* v. *Carvin*, 1921; *Stoehr* v. *Wallace*, 1921), to government takeover of telegraph and telephone lines (*Dakota Central Telephone* v. *South Dakota*, 1919), and to federal-government use of cable property during the war (*Commercial Cable* v. *Burleson*, 1919). The Court invalidated a section of the Lever Act dealing with unfair charges for food in *United States* v. *L. Cohen Grocery Co.* (1921), but it did not deny the federal government's right to fix prices during war. Rather, it contended that the Lever Act had not set clear standards for what constituted unreasonable prices.

**Limits on Dissent.** Not since the Alien and *Sedition Act of 1798 had the national government limited dissent so severely as during World War I. The government prosecuted almost twenty-two hundred people under the Espionage and Sedition Acts, and more than a thousand were convicted. No cases involving the constitutionality of these statutes came before the Supreme Court during the war, although *lower federal courts upheld and interpreted the measures in several instances.

Several cases involving civil liberties came before the Supreme Court after the war. The Court upheld government security legislation, relying on the *bad tendency test, which held that the prosecution did not have to establish a cause-and-effect relationship between an utterance and an illegal act. The mere intent of the speaker or writer was sufficient to establish guilt. *Schenck* v. *United States* (1919) involved a prosecution under the Espionage Act for distributing antidraft leaflets to American military personnel. The appellant, Schenck, argued that the Espionage Act violated the *First Amendment, but the Court unanimously upheld the constitutionality of the law. Justice Holmes, who wrote the opinion, argued that free speech was not an absolute right (it would not, for example, "protect a man in falsely shouting fire in a theatre, and causing a panic," he said) and that during war the government could limit some utterances that might be acceptable during times of peace (p. 52). Holmes set forth the *clear and present danger test to determine whether the words used in a given situation "caused" someone to violate the law. Although the phrase "clear and present danger" would later be used to shield some types of dissent, in *Schenk* Holmes employed it in a way

that was consistent with the bad tendency doctrine. He believed that Schenck had intended to interfere with the draft in publishing the leaflets.

The Court sustained convictions under the Espionage Act in two other cases: in *Frohwerk* v. *U.S.* (1919), the editor of a German-language newspaper was convicted for publishing articles that criticized the war and questioned the legality of the draft; in *Debs* v. *United States* (1919), the socialist leader Eugene V. Debs was prosecuted for a speech in which he had praised people convicted for hindering enlistments. The Court sustained the conviction on grounds that Debs had intended to hinder recruiting. In writing the opinions in *Frohwerk* and *Debs*, Holmes made no mention of the clear and present danger principle. Before the year ended, however, he changed his position, thanks in part to the influence of Zechariah *Chafee. When he dissented in subsequent cases, he interpreted clear and present danger in a way that broadened protection for dissent.

In *Abrams* v. *United States* (1919), the Court upheld the Sedition Act of 1918. Abrams and others were charged with publishing leaflets condemning the American expeditionary force in Russia and called for a general strike. Justice Clarke, writing for the majority, contended that the pamphlets sought to "excite, at the supreme crisis of the war, disaffection, sedition, riots, and . . . revolution" and were not protected by the First Amendment (p. 623). Holmes, joined by Brandeis, argued in dissent that the prosecution failed to demonstrate that the leaflets had any impact on the war effort. Publishing a "silly leaflet by an unknown man" was unlikely to present "any immediate danger" of obstructing, or even have a tendency to interfere with, the success of the government's armed forces. Holmes relied on the notion of a "marketplace of ideas" to justify his stand (p. 628).

Four months later Clarke joined Holmes and Brandeis in dissenting from the Court's majority in *Schaefer* v. *United States* (1920). The case involved a German-language paper in Philadelphia that had published articles favorable to the German war effort that were generally unpatriotic in tone. Brandeis, in writing for the minority, thought the publications in question were relatively harmless and that their suppression imperiled free press as well as freedom of thought not only during the war but also in peacetime.

*Pierce* v. *United States* (1920) grew out of the government's wartime security legislation. Three socialists had been prosecuted for distributing an antiwar pamphlet. Justice Pitney, speaking for the majority, attacked one of the publication's arguments—that the war had economic roots—and contended that such material could only hurt the war effort. Once again, Holmes and Brandeis dissented, arguing that if statements of judgment and opinion could be prosecuted, then freedom of expression was imperiled especially during national emergencies. In *United States ex rel. Milwaukee Social Democratic Publishing Co.* v. *Burleson* (1921), the Court upheld the postmaster general's decision to exclude a socialist newspaper, the *Milwaukee Leader,* from the mails. In *Gilbert* v. *Minnesota* (1920) the Court upheld a Minnesota statute similar to the Espionage Act. While Holmes concurred with the majority in this case, White dissented, arguing that only Congress had power to legislate in this area. Brandeis also dissented, but on the grounds that the state law invaded civil liberties.

World War I accelerated the growth of nationalism in the United States, enhancing the authority of the federal government at the expense of the states and the power of the president relative to Congress. Through its decisions the Supreme Court endorsed these developments. One legacy from this period was the example that expanded federal authority provided for later national emergencies. Americans were more willing during the Great Depression and World War II to accept the idea that the national government and the president could deal with problems more effectively than could the individual states and Congress. World War I also initiated controversies about the meaning of the First Amendment. While the Court upheld the government's security legislation, the idea of clear and present danger, as applied in the *Abrams* case, opened the door—if only slightly—to stronger safeguards for dissent.

(See also PRESIDENTIAL EMERGENCY POWERS; WAR.)

□ David P. Currie, "The Constitution and the Supreme Court: 1910–1921," *Duke Law Journal* (Dec. 1985): 1111–1162. Paul L. Murphy, *The Constitution in Crisis Times, 1918–1969* (1972). Richard Polenberg, *Fighting Faiths: The Abrams Case, the Supreme Court, and Free Speech* (1987). Fred D. Ragan, "Justice Oliver Wendell Holmes, Jr., Zechariah Chaffee, Jr., and the Clear and Present Danger Test for Free Speech: The First Year, 1919," *Journal of American History* 58 (1971): 24–45.
—Stephen Vaughn

**World War II.** During the period 1941–1945 the United States waged total *war against Germany and Japan, fully mobilizing both its population and its economy in a struggle to defeat the Axis enemy. The Supreme Court enlisted in this national crusade, giving constitutional sanction to the steps taken by the president and Congress to achieve military victory. Although protecting freedom of expression, it rejected all challenges to the economic controls adopted by the federal government and repeatedly subordinated other constitutional rights to the supposed demands of military necessity.

Complicating the Court's efforts to deal with the legal issues raised by total war were personal and philosophical conflicts among the justices. Chief Justice Harlan *Stone (1941–1946), who seemed utterly unable to control his frac-

tious colleagues, once compared them to a team of wild horses. They disagreed, for example, over the extent to which judges should defer to legislative determinations. All subscribed to *judicial self-restraint in cases challenging the constitutionality of economic regulatory legislation, but while Justice Felix *Frankfurter thought this same approach should be followed when civil liberties were at issue, a number of his colleagues insisted that individual rights should be accorded a preferred position and that governmental actions impinging on them should be subjected to rigorous judicial scrutiny (see PREFERRED FREEDOMS DOCTRINE). World War II also revealed disagreements within the Stone Court over the appropriateness of subjecting actions of the commander in chief and the armed forces to judicial examination.

The Court did not have to wrestle with that issue until well after the United States formally declared war in December 1941. Franklin D. *Roosevelt took a number of constitutionally questionable actions between the outbreak of hostilities in Europe in September 1939 and the Japanese attack on Pearl Harbor on 7 December 1941. These included initiating an undeclared naval war with Germany in the North Atlantic and seizing several defense plants threatened with strikes. None of these presidential actions ever came before the Supreme Court.

*Economic Regulation.* The Court did pass judgment on one of Roosevelt's creations, the Office of Price Administration (OPA). Originally established by Roosevelt in the exercise of his inherent emergency powers, OPA received congressional sanction in the Emergency Price Control Act of 1942, which empowered it to set prices. In *Yakus* v. *United States* (1944) the Supreme Court rejected the contention that this statute delegated too much legislative authority to an administrative agency. While technically the Court did not rule on the issue of whether federal *war powers gave Congress itself the authority to fix prices, Stone's opinion left little doubt that the six members of the majority believed it did. In a companion case, *Bowles* v. *Willingham* (1944), the justices rejected a procedural *due process challenge to a requirement that OPA rent controls had to go into effect before their validity might be litigated. The Court even upheld the right of OPA to suspend, without benefit of any judicial process, fuel-oil deliveries to a retail dealer who sold oil in violation of the agency's coupon-rationing system. In *Steuart and Bros.* v. *Bowles* (1944) the Court reasoned somewhat implausibly that no judicial process was required because OPA's suspension order did not constitute punishment but was merely a means of promoting the efficient distribution of fuel oil. So tolerant were the justices of governmental actions in the economic realm that they upheld as a valid exercise of the war power the Housing and Rent Act of 1947, which was not even enacted until after the fighting was over and the president had proclaimed hostilities to be at an end.

*Freedom of Expression.* The Court's willingness to uphold almost any economic regulation based on wartime necessity resembled the its posture during *World War I. In the area of freedom of *speech, though, the Supreme Court's performance during this war contrasted sharply with its response to World War I. The federal government had vigorously repressed dissent during the first war, prosecuting socialists, German-Americans, and other criticis of government policy under the *Espionage and Sedition Acts. The Court affirmed the convictions the government obtained, consistently rejecting arguments that these violated the *First Amendment. American liberals came to regret the repression of those years, and, during World War II, Attorney General Francis Biddle sought to prevent another wholesale assault on freedom of expression. The liberal Stone Court shared his commitment. In *Hartzel* v. *United States* (1944) it overturned the Espionage Act conviction of a fascist sympathizer who had mailed to army officers and Selective Service registrants literature urging the occupation of the United States by foreign troops. The same day, in *Baumgartner* v. *United States* (1944), the Court unanimously set aside the denaturalization of a German-born citizen accused of continued loyalty to Adolf Hitler's Third Reich, and in *Keegan* v. *United States* (1945) it ruled that the evidence against twenty-four members of the German-American Bund was insufficient to support convictions for conspiracy to counsel resistance to the draft. Although decided on narrow grounds and without declaring any legislation unconstitutional, these decisions afforded considerable protection to the exercise of First Amendment rights.

The Court's most important defense of freedom of expression came in *West Virginia State Board of Education* v. *Barnette* (1943). Three years earlier, in *Minersville School District* v. *Gobitis* (1940), it had upheld a Pennsylvania school board's expulsion of Jehovah's Witnesses' children for refusing to salute the flag, with Frankfurter emphasizing in his majority opinion that the flag salute served to build national unity and that national unity was the basis of *national security (see RELIGION). Now, in the midst of a war, the Court reversed *Gobitis.* Frankfurter dissented, arguing that the justices should not substitute their policy views for those of the legislators who had adopted the flag-salute law. Rejecting his pleas for judicial restraint, the majority emphasized that the First Amendment permitted *censorship of expression only when the expression in question presented a *clear and present danger of an evil the state was empowered to prevent and that it demanded an even more urgent and immediate reason for compelling affirmation.

Although the Supreme Court rigorously protected freedom of expression, it proved to be an unreliable guardian of other constitutional values. It is true that its ruling in *Cramer* v. *United States* (1945), expansively intepreting the Constitution's requirement that treason be proved by the testimony of two witnesses to the same overt act, provided a remarkable degree of protection against the overuse of one of the most serious and abused charges in criminal law. But Justice William O. *Douglas pointed out in dissent that this decision went so far as to make future treason prosecutions virtually impossible. Apparently concerned about that, the Court in *Haupt* v. *United States* (1947) voted 8 to 1 to sustain a conviction based on evidence that did not really satisfy the requirements of *Cramer.* That ruling facilitated numerous treason prosecutions of American nationals, such as "Tokyo Rose," for allegedly assisting the Germans and Japanese during the war.

The Court's decision in *Duncan* v. *Kahanamoku* (1946) also did little to protect civil liberties. At issue was the imposition of martial law in the Territory of Hawaii. The Supreme Court ruled that establishing military tribunals to try civilians there had been illegal, but it based its decision on the failure of the armed forces to comply with the provisions of the Hawaiian Organic Act rather than on the constitutional provision governing suspension of the writ of *habeas corpus. Furthermore, the Court did not decide *Duncan* until two years after the termination of military government in Hawaii and one year after the war ended (see MILITARY TRIALS AND MARTIAL LAW).

It likewise extended protection to *conscientious objectors only after the fighting ended. In *Girouard* v. *United States* (1946) the Court overruled three earlier decisions holding that they were ineligible for naturalization. Earlier, however, in *In re Summers* (1945), the Court had held it was constitutional for Illinois to refuse to permit a conscientious objector to practice law.

*Japanese-Americans.* While the fighting raged, the Court would do nothing that might interfere with the quest for victory. Convinced that protection of individual rights should not hamper the nation's ability to wage total war, the Court upheld as constitutional any governmental action that the executive branch insisted was required by military necessity. It even allowed 112,000 Japanese-Americans living on the West Coast, 70,000 of whom were United States citizens, to be punished without indictment or trial and blatantly discriminated against on the basis of *race. They were subjected to a curfew, then banned from coastal areas, and subsequently shipped to inland detention camps, known euphemistically as "relocation centers." In *Hirabayashi* v. *United States* (1943) the Court ruled unanimously that the curfew order was constitutional. In *Korematsu* v. *United States* (1944) it upheld the validity of the exclusion order. Speaking for the Court, Justice Hugo *Black acknowledged that in the absence of a war, this sort of curtailment of the civil rights of a single racial group would have been unconstitutional. He observed, however, that hardships are part of war and argued that the Japanese-Americans could be required to bear this one because national security required it. In fact, War Department officials and even government lawyers (who willfully deceived the Court about this matter) knew there was no military necessity for the exclusion and confinement of the Japanese Americans. Justice Frank *Murphy, who dissented, characterized *Korematsu* as a plunge into the ugly abyss of racism. In *Ex parte Endo* (1944), the Court ruled that a Japanese-American girl whose loyalty to the United States had been clearly established was entitled to a writ of habeas corpus, freeing her from a relocation center. In neither this case nor *Korematsu*, though, was the Court willing to examine the constitutionality of the relocation program itself.

**Military Trials.** As these Japanese-American cases reveal, during World War II the Supreme Court succumbed to a constitutional relativism that made the security of individual rights dependent on the extent to which their exercise might interfere with the fight against Germany and Japan. The justices did not want to impede prosecution of the war, and they deferred completely to the president and the armed forces on the question of what military necessity required. They practiced such deference even when it required ignoring judicial *precedent. Relying on the *Fifth Amendment's requirement of a *grand jury indictment and the *Sixth Amendment's guarantee of a *trial by jury, the Court had ruled in *Ex parte *Milligan* (1866) that military trials were unconstitutional where the civilian courts were open and functioning. The World War II Justice Department regarded *Milligan* as an inconvenient relic, and in *Ex parte *Quirin* (1942) it persuaded the Supreme Court to disregard it. The president had determined that military necessity required trying eight captured Nazi saboteurs before a secret military commission. Although *Milligan* required that at least some of them be granted civilian trials, the Supreme Court upheld a presidential order creating the commission that failed even to comply with applicable statutes.

At least in *Quirin* the Court started from the assumption that the Constitution applied, stoutly maintaining that, even in wartime, judges might examine the legality of executive actions. When the defeated Japanese commander in the Philippines sought review of his military conviction for war crimes, it refused even to consider his case. In *In re Yamashita* (1946) the Court took the position that an enemy general could have no constitutional rights. What that meant, of course,

as the dissenters recognized, was that in dealing with some people the government was not constrained by the Constitution from which it derived its authority.

The idea that the enemy had no rights was to have enormous appeal amid the anticommunist hysteria associated with the early years of the cold war between the United States and the Soviet Union (see COMMUNISM AND COLD WAR). So would the sort of constitutional relativism that authorized the sacrifice of individual rights to the perceived demands of national security. These lines of reasoning were an unfortunate legacy of a wartime Court that, though committed to the protection of civil liberties, was so determined to advance the war effort that it often subverted them.

(See also FOREIGN AFFAIRS AND FOREIGN POLICY; PRESIDENTIAL EMERGENCY POWERS.)

□ Michal R. Belknap, "The Supreme Court Goes to War: The Meaning and Implications of the Nazi Saboteur Case," *Military Law Review* 89 (1980): 59–96. J. Woodford Howard, *Mr. Justice Murphy* (1968). Peter Irons, *Justice at War: The Story of the Japanese American Internment Cases* (1983). Richard Polenberg, *War and Society: The United States 1941–1945* (1972).                          Michal R. Belknap

**Writ.** In modern practice, a writ is a formal written order of a court commanding someone to do something or refrain from doing something.
                                              William M. Wiecek

**Wyatt, Walter** (b. Savannah, Ga., 20 July 1893; d. Washington, D.C., 26 Feb. 1978), reporter of decisions, 1946–1963. Wyatt received his legal education at the University of Virginia, where he was editor in chief of the *Virginia Law Review*. Awarded the LL.B. in 1917, he began a long tenure at the Federal Reserve Board, rising from law clerk, to assistant to counsel, to general counsel of the Board of Governors of the Federal Reserve System from 1922 to 1946. During World War I, Wyatt was an associate member of the Legal Advisory Board of the Selective Service. Wyatt was also general counsel to the Federal Open Market Commission from 1936 to 1946.

Wyatt was appointed the Supreme Court's reporter of decisions on 1 March 1946, after the position had been vacant for more than two years. Serving until 1963, he edited or coedited volumes 322 through 376 of the *United States Reports*. Wyatt edited volumes 322–325 retroactively; they contained decisions of the Court announced during the reporter's vacancy and had been supervised by Assistant Reporter Philip U. Gayaut. During his career, Wyatt published a number of works about banking law.
                                              Francis Helminski

# Y

**Yakus v. United States,** 321 U.S. 414 (1944), argued 7 Jan. 1944, decided 27 Mar. 1944 by vote of 6 to 3, Stone for the Court, Roberts, Rutledge, and Murphy in dissent. The Court upheld congressional power to fetter *judicial review and to delegate broad and flexible lawmaking power to an administrative agency in this constitutional challenge to the Emergency Price Control Act of 1942. The wartime anti-inflation measure, intended to expedite price control enforcement, conferred on the lower federal courts jurisdiction over violations of Office of Price Administration (OPA) regulations made under the act. But judicial power to consider the validity of such regulations was excepted. Congress specified that challenges to them be initially reviewed under stringent time limitations by the OPA and on appeal exclusively by a special *Article III tribunal in the District of Columbia—the Emergency Court of Appeals and thereafter by the Supreme Court. Massachusetts meat dealer Albert Yakus, criminally prosecuted for violating the wholesale beef price ceiling, had failed to launch a procedurally difficult preenforcement attack on the regulation's constitutionality. The Court affirmed his conviction, holding that "so long as there is an opportunity . . . for judicial review which satisfies the demands of due process," the bifurcated enforcement and constitutional proceedings were permissible (p. 444).

In dissent, Wiley *Rutledge, with Frank *Murphy, asserted that once Congress conferred jurisdiction, it could not compel the justices to ignore *Marbury v. Madison nor to violate the Constitution by criminally enforcing unconstitutional regulations. A *Yakus*-like incontestability provi-

sion reached the Court in *Adamo Wrecking Co. v. United States* (1978). Statutory construction facilitated evasion of the constitutional issue, but Lewis *Powell, concurring, questioned the validity of *Yakus*.

Owen *Roberts's dissent in *Yakus* contended that the OPA had exercised unconstitutionally delegated congressional powers. The *New Deal Court majority reacted by stipulating that statutory standards need only be sufficiently defined to permit ascertainment of the administrative agency's obedience to the congressional will.

(See DELEGATION OF POWERS; JUDICIAL POWER AND JURISDICTION.)

Peter G. Fish

**Yarbrough, Ex parte,** 110 U.S. 651 (1884), argued 23–24 Jan. 1884, decided 3 Mar. 1884 by vote of 9 to 0; Miller for the Court. The *Yarbrough* decision is the one instance during *Reconstruction in which the Supreme Court upheld federal power to punish private obstruction of someone's voting rights. Yarbrough and a band of Ku Klux Klansmen were convicted of beating and wounding Saunders, a Georgia black man, to prevent him from voting in a federal congressional election. The Court unanimously upheld the conviction against claims that there was no constitutional provision authorizing the pertinent statute, which forbade conspiring to injure or intimidate any citizen in the exercise of a federal right.

Justice Samuel F. *Miller considered *implied powers and the "times, places, and manner clause" (Art. I, sec. 4), and observed that the *Fifteenth Amendment "does, *proprio vigore,* substantially confer on the negro the right to vote" (p. 665). He justified his extremely broad interpretation of these clauses on practical grounds. Otherwise, he argued, the country would be "at the mercy of the combinations of those who respect no right but brute force" (p. 667).

This broad interpretation, however, proved to be exceptional in its time. In a similar case, *James v. Bowman* (1903), the Court ignored *Yarbrough* and voided the federal act for attempting to control private action.

(See also RACE AND RACISM; VOTE, RIGHT TO.)
Ward E. Y. Elliott

**Yates v. United States,** 354 U.S. 298 (1957), argued 8–9 Oct. 1956, decided 17 June 1957 by vote of 6 to 1; Harlan for the Court, Clark in dissent, Burton, Black, and Douglas dissenting in part, Brennan and Whittaker not participating. Fourteen Communist party leaders had been convicted under the conspiracy provisions of the *Smith Act just as were the eleven defendants in *Dennis v. United States* (1951). But in this case the Court found two decisive differences and reversed the convictions of all defendants; however, the cases of nine of the defendants were sent back for new trials.

One of the charges was that the defendants had conspired to organize the Communist party to advocate and teach the duty and necessity of overthrowing the Government of the United States by force and violence as speedily as circumstances would permit. Although the American Communist Party was first organized in 1919, the conspiracy was alleged to have originated in 1940, when the Smith Act was enacted, and continued down to the date of the indictment in 1951. The government's contention was that the term "organize" meant a continuing process that went on throughout the life of an organization and included recruitment of new members, forming new units, organizing clubs and classes. The defense, however, contended that the party had disbanded and was reformed in 1945 and that "to organize" means to establish, to found, to bring into existence, and that under this meaning of the term the prosecutions were barred by the three-year statute of limitations.

The Court, conceding that the term "organize" was ambiguous, held that the statute was defective for lack of precision in its definition of a crime. It held that the term "organize" as used in the Smith Act referred only to acts involving the creation of a new organization and did not connote a continuing process.

The indictment also charged the defendants with conspiring to advocate and teach the duty and necessity of overthrowing the government of the United States by force and violence. The Court found that the charge to the jury with respect to advocacy was constitutionally defective because it failed to distinguish between advocacy of forcible overthrow as an abstract doctrine and advocacy of action to that end. The Court said that *Dennis* did not obliterate that distinction. There may be advocacy of violent action to be taken immediately or at some future date. The latter case must involve the establishment of a seditious group that is maintained in readiness for action at a propitious time. Interpreting *Dennis*, the Court now said,

[T]hat indoctrination of a group in preparation for future violent action, as well as exhortation to immediate action, by advocacy found to be directed to "action for the accomplishment" of forcible overthrow, [directed] to violence "as a rule or principle of action," and employing "language of incitement,". . . is not constitutionally protected when the group is of sufficient size and cohesiveness, is sufficiently oriented towards action, and other circumstances are such as reasonably to justify apprehension that action will occur. (p. 321)

The trial court had not read *Dennis* as having this meaning. In the view of the trial court, mere doctrinal justification of forcible overthrow, if engaged in with the intent to accomplish overthrow, was punishable per se under the Smith Act. The charge to the jury—at best ambiguous or equivocal—thus blurred the essential distinction between the advocacy or teaching of abstract doctrine and the advocacy or teaching of action. The advocacy to act, however, the Court held, again interpreting *Dennis*, did not need to be incitement to take immediate action. It could have been advocacy to do something in the future, as having a group in readiness for action at an appropriate time—a time to strike when the leaders feel the circumstances permit.

The case is chiefly important as a gloss on *Dennis*. The opinion for the Court clarifies the distinction between advocacy of action and advocacy of doctrine or belief, a distinction, the Court said, that can be found in the free speech and free press cases of the 1920s, especially in *Gitlow v. New York* (1925). The case also elucidates the point that was so essential to the decision in *Dennis*, namely, advocacy of action in the future when circumstances will permit the action that the Smith Act proscribes.

Justices Hugo *Black and William O. *Douglas would have directed that all defendants be acquitted and argued that the Court should hold the Smith Act unconstitutional as a violation of the First Amendment. As a practical matter, its interpretation of *Dennis* rendered the Smith Act's conspiracy provisions virtually unusable, and no futher prosecutions were ever brought under them.

(See also COMMUNISM AND COLD WAR; FIRST AMENDMENT; SPEECH AND THE PRESS.)

□ Milton R. Konvitz, *Expanding Liberties: Freedom's Gains in Postwar America* (1966), chap. 4. Laurence H. Tribe, *American Constitutional Law*, 2d ed. (1988), chap. 12.
Milton R. Konvitz

**Yellow Dog Contracts** were used by employers during the late nineteenth and early twentieth centuries to keep their employees from joining *labor unions. Such contracts made it a condition of employment that the worker not belong to any union. Under such agreements, union membership was grounds for dismissal. In operation, yellow dog contracts coerced workers into staying out of unions; a prospective employee contracted on this condition or lost the chance to work. Labor organizers deeply resented these agreements and labeled them "yellow dog" (i.e., contemptible) contracts. To assist the union movement, Congress and many state legislatures outlawed yellow dog contracts, but in *Adair* v. *United States* (1908) and *Coppage* v. *Kansas* (1915) the Supreme Court, relying on the freedom of *contract doctrine, struck down both state and federal bans on the contracts. During the *New Deal era, Congress and state legislatures revived the prohibitions. The Norris-LaGuardia Anti-Injunction Act of 1932 declared such agreements contrary to public policy and unenforceable in federal courts. By adopting "little Norris-LaGuardia acts," various industrial states copied this restriction on yellow dog contracts. In 1935 the National Labor Relations Act, which forms the basis of modern labor law, recognized an employee's right to join a union. It also labeled interference with this right as an unfair labor practice. Today, therefore, yellow dog contracts are implicitly outlawed.          Richard F. Hamm

**Yick Wo v. Hopkins,** 118 U.S. 356 (1886), argued 14 Apr. 1886, decided 10 May 1886 by vote of 9 to 0; Matthews for the Court. During the summer of 1885, many Chinese in San Francisco, including Yick Wo, violated a municipal laundry ordinance to test its validity. This local law allowed only the city's Board of Supervisors to approve laundry operating licenses. Failure to secure a license and continuing to do business could result in a misdemeanor conviction, a thousand-dollar fine, and a jail term of up to six months. The ordinance did not apply to laundries located in brick buildings.

This ordinance was clearly aimed at Chinese businesses since Chinese laundries were invariably located in wooden buildings. The law followed several other attempts by San Francisco to discourage Chinese settlement. In 1870 the Cubic Air Ordinance restricted the number of occupants in Chinese apartment buildings based upon certain space requirements. The Queue Ordinance of 1876 stipulated that all Chinese prisoners had to have their hair cut, and the No Special Police for Chinese Quarter Ordinance of 1878 denied Chinatown police protection. In addition, Chinese laundries had to pay a special fee if they used horse-drawn delivery vehicles.

The laundry ordinance was also drafted with white Californians' concern about the Chinese presence in mind. From 1820 up to 1882, the year the first Chinese Exclusion Act was passed by Congress, open immigration brought many Chinese to California. In 1880 approximately 75,000 Chinese lived in California, amounting to 10 percent of that state's population. Nearly half of California's Chinese were concentrated in the San Francisco area.

According to an 1881–1882 labor census taken in San Francisco, Chinese were primarily employed in four businesses: making cigars, shoes, and clothes, and operating laundries. Most laundries in San Francisco were owned by Chinese. Yick Wo had lived in California since 1861 and had been in the laundry business for twenty-two years. His laundry had been inspected by local authorities as late as 1884 and found safe. But in 1885 the Board of Supervisors denied him and two hundred other Chinese laundry owners their licenses. Only one Chinese laundry owner was given a license, and she had probably not been identified as Chinese. The Board was obviously seeking to wipe out the Chinese laundry business.

After Yick Wo was denied his license, he continued to operate and was arrested. In police court Yick Wo was found guilty, and fined ten dollars. He refused to pay and was ordered to jail for ten days. Yick Wo then petitioned the California Supreme Court for a writ of *habeas corpus. The petition was denied, and he appealed to the U.S. Supreme Court, naming the sheriff, a man named Hopkins, in the suit.

Yick Wo claimed that the ordinance abrogated his *Fourteenth Amendment rights because of the blatant discriminatory results of its implementation. He presented statistical evidence showing the discrimination to San Francisco's Chinese community. Only 25 percent of San Francisco laundries could operate under the Board of Supervisors' licensing requirements, seventy-nine of them owned by non-Chinese and only one owned by a Chinese. His attorneys also contended that the ordinance violated China's 1880 treaty with the United States. San Francisco argued that the Fourteenth Amendment could not infringe upon the *police powers granted to cities and states.

In a unanimous opinion, the Supreme Court found for Yick Wo and directed his discharge. Justice Stanley *Matthews wrote that the ordinances as enforced conferred an authority broader than the traditional police power to regulate the use of property. This power was discriminatory and constituted class legislation prohibited by the Fourteenth Amendment. Matthews held that the Fourteenth Amendment applied to all persons, citizens and aliens alike. For Matthews, legitimate police power had to regulate safety and health practices with specificity, and the power had to be applied in good faith. Such was not the circumstance for the Chinese in San Francisco.

The Court had clearly expanded the meaning

of the Fourteenth Amendment. State police powers had been limited and the Due Process Clause was now available to apply to local governmental discriminatory actions. Although the *Yick Wo* decision was potentially sweeping, it did not achieve instant recognition. After 1886 the Supreme Court's composition changed, and the Court did not build upon this precedent until the mid-twentieth century.

(See also ALIENAGE AND NATURALIZATION; DUE PROCESS, SUBSTANTIVE; EQUAL PROTECTION; RACE AND RACISM.)

□ William L. Tang, "The Legal Status of the Chinese in America," in *The Chinese in America*, edited by Paul K. T. Sih and Leonard B. Allen (1976), pp. 3–15.
John R. Wunder

**Young, Ex parte,** 209 U.S. 123 (1908), argued 2–3 Dec. 1907, decided 23 Mar. 1908 by vote of 8 to 1; Peckham for the Court, Harlan in dissent. One incident in the long contest over state legislation to control the power of railroads, *Ex parte Young* became a landmark in federal jurisdiction over state officers. A 1907 Minnesota law reduced railroad rates and imposed Draconian penalties on violators. Illustrating Oliver Wendell Holmes's maxim that "people who no longer hope to control the legislatures . . . look to the courts," railroad shareholders brought a derivative action in federal court seeking to enjoin their companies from complying with the law and state officers from enforcing it. The reduced rates were alleged to be confiscatory, depriving the companies of their property without due process of law in violation of the *Fourteenth Amendment. The petitioners claimed that an injunction was needed because the penalties were so severe that the companies could not afford to violate the law in order to test its constitutionality directly. Although a temporary injunction was granted, Young, the Minnesota attorney general, violated it by seeking to enforce the new rates in state court. Jailed for contempt, he petitioned the Supreme Court for a writ of *habeas corpus.

Holding against Young, the Court, in an opinion by Justice Rufus *Peckham, completed the jurisdictional circle. Although the *Eleventh Amendment restricts the power of federal courts to hear suits against states, Peckham wrote that a state officer seeking to enforce an unconstitutional statute is "in that case stripped of his official or representative character and is subjected in his person to the consequences of his individual conduct" (p. 160). Peckham left unanswered the question how, if "stripped of his official or representative character," the officer was threatening state action for purposes of the Fourteenth Amendment (p. 160). In *In re Ayers* (1887), a procedurally similar case, the Court had discharged another state attorney general who had been imprisoned for seeking to enforce state law in violation of a federal injunction. Peckham

put to rest the embarrassment by limiting *Ayers*, a state bond repudiation case, to cases involving an attempt to compel a state to perform its contract.

In a lengthy dissent Justice John Marshall *Harlan argued that the Court's decision would "practically obliterate the Eleventh Amendment" (p. 204). He too was embarrassed since he had dissented in *Ayers*. "I propose," Harlan wrote, "to adhere to former decisions of the court, whatever may have been once my opinion as to certain aspects of this general question" (p. 169). In a final irony the Court subsequently determined, in *Simpson* v. *Shepard* (1913), that the Minnesota railroad rates were not unconstitutional, so Young had not committed a wrong after all.

In its day, *Ex parte Young* was an unpopular decision. The same Court and the same justice who decided *Lochner* v. *New York* (1905), invalidating a state regulation of the hours of labor, had again sided with the monied interests against the public. "Government by injunction" was condemned, and Congress, fending off bills to curtail the power of federal courts, responded with the cumbersome and inefficient Three-Judge Court Act of 1910, which created a special court of three judges and a direct appeal to the Supreme Court to handle suits for injunctions against state officers. (The act was largely repealed in 1976, long after it had outlived it usefulness.) Among legal scholars, especially in recent years, the case of *Ex parte Young* has been widely criticized and its illogicality regularly demonstrated. The Supreme Court, too, had been loath to extend the case, refusing in *Pennhurst State School and Hospital* v. *Halderman* (1984) to apply "the fiction of *Young*" to official violations of state law (p. 105). Notwithstanding its illogicality, *Ex parte Young* has long survived *Lochner* and substantive *due process because of its indispensability to the federal scheme of government. As Holmes (who joined the majority in *Young*) elsewhere observed, "the Union would be imperiled" if the Supreme Court could not declare unconstitutional the laws of the several states. The power to enjoin state officers from violating federal law seems a necessary adjunct to that ability. Ironically, this power, forged by corporate shareholders and a conservative Court, is today regularly exercised on behalf of private (and otherwise powerless) parties in conflict with state governments.

(See also JUDICIAL POWER AND JURISDICTION; LOWER FEDERAL COURTS.)

□ William F. Duker, "Mr. Justice Rufus W. Peckham and the Case of *Ex parte Young*: Lochnerizing *Munn* v. *Illinois*," *Brigham Young University Law Review* (1980): 539–558.
John V. Orth

**Younger v. Harris,** 401 U.S. 37 (1971), argued 1 Apr. 1969, reargued 29 Apr. and 6 Nov. 1970, decided 23 Feb. 1971 by vote of 8 to 1; Black for the Court, Stewart, Harlan, Brennan, White, and

Marshall, concurring, Douglas in dissent. Harris was indicted in a California court for violation of the state's *criminal syndicalism act. The U.S. Supreme Court had held the act valid in *Whitney v. California (1927), but an identical statute had been found unconstitutional in *Brandenburg v. Ohio (1969), and Whitney was overruled. Harris therefore sought an *injunction in the federal courts to prohibit his prosecution under an almost certainly unconstitutional statute. He claimed that both the prosecution and the act violated his rights under the *First and *Fourteenth Amendments and that *Dombrowski v. Pfister (1965) permitted federal intervention.

Without discussing the implications of Brandenberg, and despite the alleged threat to freedom of expression, the Supreme Court reversed the federal district court and lifted the federal *injunction.

For Justice Hugo *Black, the issue turned on the nature of *federalism. Long-established policy prohibited federal courts from intervening in state court proceedings except (1) when authorized by Congress, (2) when necessary to "aid in its jurisdiction," (3) when necessary "to protect or effectuate its judgments," and (4) when those being prosecuted by states will "suffer irreparable damages" (p. 43).

The policy was designed to protect the principle of *comity. The legitimate concerns of both state and federal governments must be carefully balanced. Consequently, federal courts should interfere with pending state prosecutions only under extraordinary circumstances, when the danger of irreparable injury is both substantial and imminent. Even then, intervention is warranted only if the threat to protected federal rights could not be resolved at the state criminal trial. According to Black, none of these reasons for intervention was present in Harris.

Unlike Dombrowski, Harris was not threatened with continued bad-faith prosecutions or harassment that created a "chilling effect" on freedom of expression. Neither was any irreparable injury to Harris, beyond the ordinary consequences of a criminal trial, foreseen. And, according to Black, the validity of the threat to Harris's federally protected rights could well be determined in his state trial.

Black admitted that the First Amendment issues involved in Dombrowski suggested that even absent bad faith and harassment, a "chilling effect" might result from the enforcement of statutes that are on their face unconstitutional. Such a suggestion, however, was not directly relevant to the earlier decision and a possible "chilling effect" by itself was not enough to justify federal injunctive intervention here. Black also maintained that injunctive intervention in pending prosecutions involving constitutional issues places the federal judiciary in an inappropriate role. Federal courts ought not to pass judgment on state statutes without benefit of *state court interpretation. Such judgment would constitute a form of *advisory opinion and would fail to meet requirements of true *cases and controversies under *Article III.

In separate concurring opinions, Justice Potter *Stewart carefully outlined the limited reach of the decision, and Justice William *Brennan emphasized those factors that distinguished the case from Dombrowski.

Justice William O. *Douglas, however, praised the wisdom of Dombrowski in his dissent. During times of repression, Douglas wrote, the federal judiciary has a special obligation to protect constitutional rights, and the circumstances in Harris called for such protection. A threatened prosecution under an unconstitutionally overbroad and vague state criminal statute created a "chilling effect" on the exercise of federal rights and thus required the exercise of federal equity power. Otherwise, when "criminal prosecution can be leveled against [persons] because they express unpopular views, the society of the dialogue is in danger" (p. 65).

(See also ABSTENTION DOCTRINE; JUDICIAL POWER AND JURISDICTION; LOWER FEDERAL COURTS.)

Charles H. Sheldon

**Youngstown Sheet & Tube Co. v. Sawyer,** 343 U.S. 579 (1952), argued 12 and 13 May 1952, decided 2 June 1952 by vote of 6 to 3; Black for the Court, Frankfurter, Douglas, Jackson, Burton, and Clark concurring, Vinson, Reed, and Minton in dissent. This decision rejected the argument that President Harry Truman had inherent constitutional authority to issue an executive order seizing private steel mills in 1952.

Apprehensive that an impending strike by steelworkers would harm the country's participation in the United Nations' police action in Korea, President Truman issued an executive order instructing Secretary of Commerce Charles Sawyer to seize and operate the nation's steel mills. Secretary Sawyer directed the companies' presidents to operate the facilities in compliance with government regulations. The president immediately gave Congress formal notice of his action, but Congress took no action. Although the seizure lacked statutory authority, Truman took the view that his action was valid under the powers invested in him as president and commander in chief. He relied upon the many historical precedents of executive seizure without the consent of Congress.

The steel industry argued that the purpose of the Labor Management Relations Act of 1947 (Taft-Hartley Act) was to allow the parties to arrive at a settlement and to permit Congress to become involved if collective bargaining was unsuccessful. The fact that Congress had specifically rejected a seizure provision during the debate of this act could only be interpreted as a prohibition against executive seizure.

The opinions of the justices reflected the two polar interpretations of the first clause of Article II of the Constitution—"The executive Power shall be vested in a President of the United States."

Justice Hugo *Black, writing for the Court, held that inasmuch as Congress could have directed the seizure of the steel mills, the president had no power to do so without an express prior congressional authorization. Black insisted that each of the popular branches must be left to carry out its duties according to the original constitutional understanding. The power exercised by Truman clearly was a lawmaking task that properly belonged only to Congress.

Concurring, Justice Felix *Frankfurter suggested that long-standing executive practices, with the silent acquiescence of Congress, might provide an additional gloss on the executive powers. Justice William O. *Douglas concurred, observing that Congress has the power to pay compensation and is the only branch able to authorize a lawful seizure.

Justice Robert *Jackson also concurred and distinguished constitutional situations in which presidential powers fluctuate: strongest with a congressional authorization, weakest against a congressional prohibition, and uncertain alongside a congressional silence. Jackson concluded that the president acted unconstitutionally because Congress had refused to authorize the seizure.

Justice Harold *Burton concurred because Congress had prescribed specific procedures exclusive of seizure. Justice Tom *Clark, who as attorney general had earlier advised Truman, concurred because the president's authority to act in times of national emergency was subject to the limitations expressly prescribed by Congress.

Chief Justice Fred *Vinson dissented, joined by Justices Stanley *Reed and Sherman *Minton, and surveyed the elements of the emergency: the Korean military involvement, the importance of steel as a war material, and the impasse in the labor negotiation. Presidential emergency action had been allowed in the past and the dissent concluded that the president acted constitutionally.

This decision, especially Justice Jackson's concurring opinion, has provided an important precedent for resisting subsequent claims of presidential inherent authority in areas such as impoundment, executive privilege, electronic surveillance, and national security. The holding has come to be generally understood as an interpretive effort to restrain the executive branch within a proper separation of power.

(See also INHERENT POWERS; LABOR; PRESIDEN-TIAL EMERGENCY POWERS; SEPARATION OF POWERS; WAR POWERS.)

□ Maeva Marcus, *Truman and the Steel Seizure Case—the Limits of Presidential Power* (1977). Alan F. Westin, *The Anatomy of A Constitutional Law Case* (1958).

Thomas E. Baker

**Young v. American Mini Theatres, Inc.,** 427 U.S. 50 (1976), argued 24 Mar. 1976, decided 24 June 1976 by vote of 5 to 4; Stevens for a plurality of the Court, Powell concurring, Stewart, Brennan, Marshall, and Blackmun in dissent. Although most legal questions about the control of sexually explicit material turn into questions about criminal prosecution and obscenity law, *Young* v. *American Mini Theatres* is the most important case on the issue of zoning of "adult" establishments, that is, businesses specializing in the sale of sexually oriented films, magazines, and other items sold only to adults. The case arose when the city of Detroit attempted, through *zoning, to prevent concentrations of such businesses, although other constitutionally indistinguishable zoning approaches focus on concentration rather than dispersal of adult establishments.

The case's importance lies in the fact that the Detroit ordinance did not require a finding that the establishment dealt in legally obscene materials as a prerequisite to legal action. Under the then-existing doctrine of *Erznoznik* v. *City of Jacksonville* (1975), this would seem to have rendered the restriction impermissible, for all sexually oriented material not legally obscene was thought to be entitled to complete *First Amendment protection. But Justice John Paul *Stevens's plurality opinion held that some degree of content regulation within the First Amendment was permissible and that the regulation here was constitutional for three reasons. First, the material was so sexually explicit as to be entitled to less protection than other speech more central to the First Amendment; as Stevens wrote, "[F]ew of us would march our sons and daughters off to war to preserve the citizen's right to see 'Specified Sexual Activities' exhibited in the theaters of our choice" (p. 70). Second, the zoning restriction was not a total prohibition on the availability of the material. Third, the material would be considered highly offensive by many people.

These conclusions, which represent current law (as in *City of Renton* v. *Playtime Theatres, Inc.,* 1986), remain especially important because they have been the basis for a number of other restrictions that fall short of outright prohibition of sexually explicit but nonobscene communication, such as *Federal Communications Commission* v. *Pacifica Foundation* (1978), and because they represent the beginnings of the increasingly influential First Amendment approach of Justice Stevens, in which distinctions among forms of constitutionally protected speech are permissible depending on the offensiveness of the material and the form of the restriction.

(See also OBSCENITY AND PORNOGRAPHY.)

Frederick Schauer

# Z

Zoning is the process by which a local government regulates the use of privately owned land within its jurisdiction. A municipality or county derives authority to engage in zoning from an enabling statute adopted by the state legislature. The enabling statute constitutes a delegation of the state's *police power to regulate land use to promote the public welfare. Under this authority, the local legislative body, such as the city council, enacts a comprehensive zoning scheme by which the entire community is carved into discrete sections or zones. Certain uses are allowed in each zone. For example, only residences may be permitted in one area, while factories may be authorized elsewhere.

Predicated on traditional principles of *common-law nuisance, zoning became popular early in the twentieth century. Nonetheless, the notion of zoning was not uncritically embraced by the judiciary. *State courts initially disagreed as to whether zoning ordinances were constitutional, and the decisions conflicted regarding the validity of excluding certain uses from certain areas. Debate centered on questions of *due process, *equal protection, and *taking private *property without *just compensation. Ultimately, the constitutionality of zoning as a land-control device was sustained by the Supreme Court in the seminal case of *Euclid v. Ambler Realty Co. (1926).

Notwithstanding the Euclid decision, many aspects of zoning required refinement and further judicial scrutiny. The fundamental problem was that, although a zoning scheme might be reasonable in general terms, it could have an inappropriately harsh impact on certain parcels of land. The Supreme Court recognized this

possibility in Euclid and in the subsequent case, Nectow v. City of Cambridge (1928), actually found a zoning ordinance unconstitutional as it applied to a specific tract. Nectow was the forerunner of much of our modern zoning litigation; today, landowners frequently assert that a local zoning ordinance is invalid with respect to a particular parcel of property.

A local legislative body may rezone to correct deficiencies in its original zoning scheme. Furthermore, zoning ordinances contain administrative mechanisms designed to fine-tune the general scheme and thereby avoid disparate impact on landowners in the community. An administrative agency, such as a board of zoning appeals, is generally authorized to grant variances when the zoning scheme produces "unnecessary hardship" on individual landowners. The same body also has the power to grant conditional permits for which provision has been made in the ordinance itself. Moreover, nonconforming uses that antedated the zoning ordinance are permitted to continue.

During the latter half of this century, the zoning concept has been utilized in novel ways to address various urban problems. Regulating land use to promote aesthetic values, to preserve landmarks or historical districts, and to manage growth are a few examples. These modern adaptations have often been challenged, and after 1970 several land-use regulation cases have reached the Supreme Court.

During this period the Court has frequently considered whether certain zoning or related action by a local government exceeded its regulatory authority and constituted taking property without compensation. In *Penn Central Transportation Co. v. New York City (1978), the city employed a landmark preservation ordinance to prevent construction of an office building over Grand Central Terminal. The Supreme Court upheld the constitutionality of this action, noting that under the ordinance the landowner could still make reasonable use of the premises and could transfer development rights to other parcels. Conversely, in *Nollan v. California Coastal Commission (1987), the Court held that an uncompensated taking occurred when a state commission conditioned issuance of a beachfront building permit on the landowner's grant of a public beach-access easement. The Court concluded that the condition was unrelated to the commission's avowed purposes for imposing it.

The Court also addressed a vexing question regarding remedies available to an aggrieved landowner. In *First English Evangelical Lutheran Church of Glendale v. County of Los Angeles (1987), the Court recognized the right of a landowner to obtain compensation for the temporary taking of property that may result from the adverse impact of an ordinance ultimately declared invalid.

Notwithstanding recent Supreme Court decisions, it remains difficult to formulate rules for determining when a land-use regulation constitutes a permanent or temporary taking. Hence, the regulation/taking controversy continues.

□ Daniel R. Mandelker, Land Use Law, 2d ed. (1988; supp., 1991). Jon W. Bruce

**Zorach v. Clauson,** 343 U.S. 306 (1952), argued 31 Jan.–1 Feb. 1952, decided 28 Apr. 1952 by vote of 6 to 3; Douglas for the Court, Black, Frankfurter, and Jackson in dissent. Zorach v. Clauson was the Supreme Court's second decision on "released time" plans that allow religious instruction for public school students during the school week. In *Illinois ex rel. McCollum v. Board of Education, (1948), a plan, including instruction within school buildings, had been held to violate the *First Amendment's Establishment Clause. In Zorach, the Court, stressing the desirability of accommodation to religious needs, approved New York City's program for religious instruction taking place outside the public schools.

According to Justice William O. *Douglas's opinion for the Court, the result in McCollum was to be explained by the use of school buildings for religious instruction. New York, by contrast, had not violated separation of church and state. In language often quoted by those who oppose strict separationist approaches to the Establishment Clause, Justice Douglas wrote, "We are a religious people whose institutions presuppose a Supreme Being" (p. 313).

The three justices who had written in favor of the result in McCollum dissented in Zorach. Justice Hugo *Black protested that his opinion for the Court in McCollum had not emphasized the location of the religious instruction. He contended, as did Justices Felix *Frankfurter and Robert *Jackson, that New York, like Illinois, had impermissibly placed the coercive apparatus of the public school laws behind religious instruction, receiving attendance reports for those released and treating as truants students who failed to go to religious instruction.

The Court's language in Zorach does not comport comfortably with its language in McCollum. Some justices who did not write in McCollum may have thought the school location of the religious instruction mattered more than the opinions reflected, or they may have come to that view on further reflection, perhaps partly in response to criticism of the Court's "hostility" to *religion. In subsequent cases, Zorach has been used to advocate permissible accommodation to religion; ironically, Douglas later adopted strictly separationist positions and disavowed the result his language eloquently justifies.

(See also EDUCATION.)

Kent Greenawalt

**Zurcher v. The Stanford Daily,** 436 U.S. 547 (1978), argued 17 Jan. 1978, decided 31 May 1978 by vote of 5 to 3; White for the Court, Stewart, Marshall, and Stevens in dissent, Brennan not participating. In April 1971, violence and injuries resulted when police from Palo Alto, California, confronted demonstrators at Stanford University Hospital. Subsequently, officers obtained a warrant and searched the offices of the student newspaper, which had printed a photograph of the incident. Police found no additional pictures, but in the process they read a number of confidential files. The Stanford Daily brought civil charges against the police, contending that the search violated the *First Amendment's guarantee of freedom of the press and the *Fourth Amendment's protection against unreasonable searches.

The U.S. District Court for the Northern District of California ruled that a warrant was not appropriate for searching press offices unless a *subpoena was shown to be impractical and the Ninth Circuit Court of Appeals affirmed. In the Supreme Court Justice Byron *White argued that the Fourth Amendment did not provide special search provisions for press offices. He rejected the argument that the search interfered with the Daily's sources and created a chilling atmosphere that would contribute to self-censorship. He held that requiring a subpoena prior to authorization of a search warrant would undermine law enforcement efforts.

Justice Potter *Stewart, dissenting for himself and Justice Thurgood *Marshall, concluded that, under these circumstances, the warrant impermissibly burdened freedom of the press because it threatened physical disruption of newspaper operations and might force disclosure of confidential sources essential to news gathering. Justice John Paul *Stevens argued that the search did not meet the Fourth Amendment's standards for reasonableness because the newspaper was not itself under suspicion.

The *Zurcher* ruling caused a furor in the press community and led to congressional passage of a provision in the Privacy Protection Act of 1980 limiting the use of search warrants in newsrooms where neither the organization nor its members were suspected of wrongdoing.

(See also SPEECH AND THE PRESS.)

Carol E. Jenson

# The Constitution of the United States

WE THE PEOPLE OF THE UNITED STATES, in order to form a more perfect Union, establish Justice, insure domestic Tranquility, provide for the common defence, promote the general Welfare, and secure the Blessings of Liberty to ourselves and our Posterity, do ordain and establish this Constitution for the United States of America.

ARTICLE. I.

*Section 1.* All legislative Powers herein granted shall be vested in a Congress of the United States, which shall consist of a Senate and House of Representatives.

*Section 2.* The House of Representatives shall be composed of Members chosen every second Year by the People of the several States, and the Electors in each State shall have the Qualifications requisite for Electors of the most numerous Branch of the State Legislature.

No Person shall be a Representative who shall not have attained to the Age of twenty five Years, and been seven Years a Citizen of the United States, and who shall not, when elected, be an Inhabitant of that State in which he shall be chosen.

Representatives and direct Taxes shall be apportioned among the several States which may be included within this Union, according to their respective Numbers, which shall be determined by adding to the whole Number of free Persons, including those bound to Service for a Term of Years, and excluding Indians not taxed, three fifths of all other Persons. The actual Enumeration shall be made within three Years after the first Meeting of the Congress of the United States, and within every subsequent Term of ten Years, in such Manner as they shall by Law direct. The Number of Representatives shall not exceed one for every thirty Thousand, but each State shall have at Least one Representative; and until such enumeration shall be made, the State of New Hampshire shall be entitled to chuse three, Massachusetts eight, Rhode-Island and Providence Plantations one, Connecticut five, New-York six, New Jersey four, Pennsylvania eight, Delaware one, Maryland six, Virginia ten, North Carolina five, South Carolina five, and Georgia three.

When vacancies happen in the Representation from any State, the Executive Authority thereof shall issue Writs of Election to fill such Vacancies.

The House of Representatives shall chuse their Speaker and other Officers; and shall have the sole Power of Impeachment.

*Section 3.* The Senate of the United States shall be composed of two Senators from each State, chosen by the Legislature thereof, for six Years; and each Senator shall have one Vote.

Immediately after they shall be assembled in Consequence of the first Election, they shall be divided as equally as may be into three Classes. The Seats of the Senators of the first Class shall be vacated at the Expiration of the second Year, of the second Class at the Expiration of the fourth Year, and of the third Class at the Expiration of the sixth Year, so that one third may be chosen every second Year; and if Vacancies happen by Resignation, or otherwise, during the Recess of the Legislature of any State, the Executive thereof may make temporary Appointments until the next Meeting of the Legislature, which shall then fill such Vacancies.

No Person shall be a Senator who shall not have attained to the Age of thirty Years, and been nine Years a Citizen of the United States, and who shall not, when elected, be an Inhabitant of that State for which he shall be chosen.

The Vice President of the United States shall be President of the Senate, but shall have no Vote, unless they be equally divided.

The Senate shall chuse their other Officers, and also a President pro tempore, in the Absence of the Vice President, or when he shall exercise the Office of President of the United States.

The Senate shall have the sole Power to try all Impeachments. When sitting for that Purpose, they shall be on Oath or Affirmation. When the President of the United States is tried, the Chief Justice shall preside: And no Person shall be convicted without the Concurrence of two thirds of the Members present.

Judgment in Cases of Impeachment shall not extend further than to removal from Office, and disqualification to hold and enjoy any Office of honor, Trust or Profit under the United States: but the Party convicted shall nevertheless be liable and subject to Indictment, Trial, Judgment and Punishment, according to Law.

*Section 4* The Times, Places and Manner of holding Elections for Senators and Representatives, shall be prescribed in each State by the Legislature thereof, but the Congress may at any time by Law make or alter such Regulations, except as to the Places of chusing Senators.

The Congress shall assemble at least once in every Year, and such Meeting shall be on the first Monday in December, unless they shall by Law appoint a different Day.

*Section 5.* Each House shall be the Judge of the Elections, Returns and Qualifications of its own Members, and a Majority of each shall constitute a Quorum to do Business; but a smaller Number may adjourn from day to day, and may be authorized to compel the Attendance of absent Members, in such Manner, and under such Penalties as each House may provide.

Each House may determine the Rule of its Proceedings, punish its Members for disorderly Behaviour, and, with the Concurrence of two thirds, expel a Member.

Each House shall keep a Journal of its Proceedings, and from time to time publish the same, excepting such Parts as may in their Judgment require Secrecy; and the Yeas and Nays of the Members of either House on any question shall, at the Desire of one fifth of those Present, be entered on the Journal.

Neither House, during the Session of Congress, shall, without the Consent of the other, adjourn for more than three days, nor to any other Place than that in which the two Houses shall be sitting.

*Section 6.* The Senators and Representatives shall receive a Compensation for their Services, to be ascertained by Law, and paid out of the Treasury of the United States. They shall in all Cases, except Treason, Felony and Breach of the Peace, be privileged from Arrest during their Attendance at the Session of their respective Houses, and in going to and returning from the same; and for any Speech or Debate in either House, they shall not be questioned in any other Place.

No Senator or Representative shall, during Time for which he was elected, be appointed to any civil Office under the Authority of the United States, which shall have been created, or the Emoluments whereof shall have been encreased during such time; and no Person holding any Office under the United States, shall be a Member of either House during his Continuance in Office.

*Section 7.* All Bills for raising Revenue shall originate in the House of Representatives; but the Senate may propose or concur with Amendments as on other Bills.

Every Bill which shall have passed the House of Representatives and the Senate shall, before it become a Law, be presented to the President of the United States; if he approve he shall sign it, but if not he shall return it, with his Objections to that House in which it shall have originated, who shall enter the Objections at large on their Journal, and proceed to reconsider it. If after such Reconsideration two thirds of the House shall agree to pass the Bill, it shall be sent, together with the Objections, to the other House, by which it shall likewise be reconsidered, and if approved by two thirds of that House, it shall become a Law. But in all such Cases the Votes of both Houses shall be determined by yeas and Nays, and the Names of the Persons voting for and against the Bill shall be entered on the Journal of each House respectively. If any Bill shall not be returned by the President within ten Days (Sundays excepted) after it shall have been presented to him, the Same shall be a Law, in like Manner as if he had signed it, unless the Congress by their Adjournment prevent its Return, in which Case it shall not be a Law.

Every Order, Resolution, or Vote to which the Concurrence of the Senate and House of Representatives may be necessary (except on a question of Adjournment) shall be presented to the President of the United States; and before the Same shall take Effect, shall be approved by him, or being disapproved by him, shall be repassed by two thirds of the Senate and House of Representatives, according to the Rules and Limitations prescribed in the Case of a Bill.

*Section 8.* The Congress shall have Power To lay and collect Taxes, Duties, Imposts and Excises, to pay the Debts and provide for the common Defence and general Welfare of the United States; but all Duties, Imposts and Excises shall be uniform throughout the United States.

To borrow Money on the credit of the United States;

To regulate Commerce with foreign Nations, and among the several States, and with the Indian Tribes;

To establish an uniform Rule of Naturalization, and uniform Laws on the subject of Bankruptcies throughout the United States;

To coin Money, regulate the Value thereof, and of foreign Coin, and fix the Standard of Weights and Measures;

To provide for the Punishment of counterfeiting the Securities and current Coin of the United States;

To establish Post Offices and Post Roads;

To promote the Progress of Science and useful Arts, by securing for limited Times to Authors and Inventors the exclusive Right to their respective Writings and Discoveries;

To constitute Tribunals inferior to the supreme Court;

To define and punish Piracies and Felonies

committed on the high Seas, and Offences against the Law of Nations;

To declare War, grant Letters of Marque and Reprisal, and make Rules concerning Captures on Land and Water;

To raise and support Armies, but no Appropriation of Money to that Use shall be for a longer Term than two Years;

To provide and maintain a Navy;

To make Rules for the Government and Regulation of the land and naval Forces;

To provide for calling forth the Militia to execute the Laws of the Union, suppress Insurrections and repel Invasions;

To provide for organizing, arming, and disciplining, the Militia, and for governing such Part of them as may be employed in the Service of the United States, reserving to the States respectively, the Appointment of the Officers, and the Authority of training the Militia according to the discipline prescribed by Congress;

To exercise exclusive Legislation in all Cases whatsoever, over such District (not exceeding ten Miles square) as may, by Cession of particular States, and the Acceptance of Congress, become the Seat of the Goverment of the United States, and to exercise like Authority over all Places purchased by the Consent of the Legislature of the State in which the Same shall be, for the Erection of Forts, Magazines, Arsenals, dock-Yards, and other needful Buildings;—And

To make all Laws which shall be necessary and proper for carrying into Execution the foregoing Powers, and all other Powers vested by this Constitution in the Government of the United States, or in any Department or Officer thereof.

*Section 9.* The Migration or Importation of such Persons as any of the States now existing shall think proper to admit, shall not be prohibited by the Congress prior to the Year one thousand eight hundred and eight, but a Tax or duty may be imposed on such Importation, not exceeding ten dollars for each Person.

The Privilege of the Writ of Habeas Corpus shall not be suspended, unless when in Cases of Rebellion or Invasion the public Safety may require it.

No Bill of Attainder or ex post facto Law shall be passed.

No Capitation, or other direct, Tax shall be laid, unless in Proportion to the Census or Enumeration herein before directed to be taken.

No Tax or Duty shall be laid on Articles exported from any State.

No Preference shall be given by any Regulation of Commerce or Revenue to the Ports of one State over those of another: nor shall Vessels bound to, or from, one State, be obliged to enter, clear, or pay Duties in another.

No Money shall be drawn from the Treasury, but in Consequence of Appropriations made by Law, and a regular Statement and Account of the Receipts and Expenditures of all public Money shall be published from time to time.

No Title of Nobility shall be granted by the United States: And no Person holding any Office of Profit or trust under them, shall, without the Consent of the Congress, accept of any present, Emolument, Office, or Title, of any kind whatever, from any King, Prince, or foreign State.

*Section 10.* No State shall enter into any Treaty, Alliance, or Confederation; grant Letters of Marque and Reprisal; coin Money; emit Bills of Credit; make any Thing but gold and silver Coin a Tender in Payment of Debts; pass any Bill of Attainder, ex post facto Law, or Law impairing the Obligation of Contracts, or grant any Title of Nobility.

No State shall, without the Consent of the Congress, lay any Imposts or Duties on Imports or Exports, except what may be absolutely necessary for executing it's inspection Laws: and the net Produce of all Duties and Imposts, laid by any State on Imports or Exports, shall be for the Use of the Treasury of the United States; and all such Laws shall be subject to the Revision and Controul of the Congress.

No State shall, without the Consent of Congress, lay any Duty of Tonnage, keep Troops, or Ships of War in time of Peace, enter into any Agreement or Compact with another State, or with a foreign Power, or engage in War, unless actually invaded, or in such imminent Danger as will not admit of delay.

ARTICLE. II.

*Section 1.* The executive Power shall be vested in a President of the United States of America. He shall hold his Office during the term of four Years, and, together with the Vice President, chosen for the same Term, be elected, as follows

Each State shall appoint, in such Manner as the Legislature thereof may direct, a Number of Electors, equal to the whole Number of Senators and Representatives to which the State may be entitled in the Congress: but no Senator or Representative, or Person holding an Office of Trust or Profit under the United States, shall be appointed an Elector.

The Electors shall meet in their respective States, and vote by Ballot for two Persons, of whom one at least shall not be an Inhabitant of the same State with themselves. And they shall make a List of all the Persons voted for, and of the Number of Votes for each; which List they shall sign and certify, and transmit sealed to the Seat of the Government of the United States, directed to the President of the Senate. The President of the Senate shall, in the Presence of the Senate and House of Representatives, open all the Certificates, and the Votes shall then be counted. The

Person having the greatest Number of Votes shall be the President, if such Number be a Majority of the whole Number of Electors appointed; and if there be more than one who have such Majority, and have an equal Number of Votes, then the House of Representatives shall immediately chuse by Ballot one of them for President; and if no Person have a Majority, then from the five highest on the List the said House shall in like Manner chuse the President. But in chusing the President, the Votes shall be taken by States, the Representation from each State having one Vote; A quorum for this Purpose shall consist of a Member or Members from two thirds of the States, and a Majority all the States shall be necessary to a Choice. In every Case, after the Choice of the President, the Person having the greatest Number of Votes of the Electors shall be the Vice President. But if there should remain two or more who have equal Votes, the Senate shall chuse from them by Ballot the Vice President.

The Congress may determine the Time of chusing the Electors, and the Day on which they shall give their Votes; which Day shall be the same throughout the United States.

No Person except a natural born Citizen, or a Citizen of the United States, at the time of the Adoption of this Constitution, shall be eligible to the Office of President, neither shall any Person be eligible to that Office who shall not have attained to the Age of thirty-five Years, and been fourteen Years a Resident within the United States.

In Case of the Removal of the President from Office, or of his Death, Resignation, or Inability to discharge the Powers and Duties of the said Office, the Same shall devolve on the Vice President, and the Congress may by Law provide for the Case of Removal, Death, Resignation or Inability, both of the President and Vice President, declaring what Officer shall then act as President, and such Officer shall act accordingly, until the Disability be removed, or a President shall be elected.

The President shall, at stated Times, receive for his Services, a Compensation, which shall neither be encreased or diminished during the Period for which he shall have been elected, and he shall not receive within that Period any other Emolument from the United States, or any of them.

Before he enters on the Execution of his Office, he shall take the following Oath or Affirmation:—"I do solemnly swear (or affirm) that I will faithfully execute the Office of President of the United States, and will to the best of my Ability, preserve, protect and defend the Constitution of the United States."

*Section 2.* The President shall be Commander in Chief of the Army and Navy of the United States, and of the Militia of the several States, when called into the actual Service of the United States; he may require the Opinion, in writing, of the principal Officer in each of the executive Departments, upon any Subject relating to the Duties of their respective Offices, and he shall have Power to grant Reprieves and Pardons for Offences against the United States, except in Cases of Impeachment.

He shall have Power, by and with the Advice and Consent of the Senate, to make Treaties, provided two thirds of the Senators present concur; and he shall nominate, and by and with the Advice and Consent of the Senate, shall appoint Ambassadors, other public Ministers and Consuls, Judges of the supreme Court, and all other Officers of the United States, whose Appointments are not herein otherwise provided for, and which shall be established by Law; but the Congress may by Law vest the Appointment of such inferior Officers, as they think proper, in the President alone, in the Courts of Law, or in the Heads of Departments.

The President shall have Power to fill up all Vacancies that may happen during the Recess of the Senate, by granting Commissions which shall expire at the End of their next Session.

*Section 3.* He shall from time to time give to the Congress Information of the State of the Union, and recommend to their Consideration such Measures as he shall judge necessary and expedient; he may, on extraordinary Occasions, convene both Houses, or either of them, and in Case of Disagreement between them with Respect to the Time of Adjournment, he may adjourn them to such Time as he shall think proper; he shall receive Ambassadors and other public Ministers; he shall take Care that the Laws be faithfully executed, and shall Commission all the Officers of the United States.

*Section 4.* The President, Vice President and all civil Officers of the United States, shall be removed from Office on Impeachment for, and Conviction of, Treason, Bribery, or other high Crimes and Misdemeanors.

ARTICLE. III.

*Section 1.* The judicial Power of the United States, shall be vested in one supreme Court, and in such inferior Courts as the Congress may from time to time ordain and establish. The Judges, both of the supreme and inferior Courts, shall hold their Offices during good Behaviour, and shall, at stated Times, receive for their Services, a Compensation, which shall not be diminished during their Continuance in Office.

*Section 2.* The judicial Power shall extend to all Cases, in Law and Equity, arising under this Constitution, the Laws of the United States, and Treaties made, or which shall be made, under their

Authority;—to all Cases affecting Ambassadors, other public Ministers and Consuls;—to all Cases of admiralty and maritime Jurisdiction;—to Controversies to which the United States shall be a Party;—to Controversies between two or more States;—between a State and Citizens of another State;—between Citizens of different States;—between Citizens of the same State claiming Lands under Grants of different States, and between a State, or the Citizens thereof, and foreign States, Citizens or Subjects.

In all cases affecting Ambassadors, other public Ministers and Consuls, and those in which a State shall be Party, the supreme Court shall have original Jurisdiction. In all the other Cases before mentioned, the supreme Court shall have appellate Jurisdiction, both as to Law and Fact, with such Exceptions, and under such Regulations as the Congress shall make.

The Trial of all Crimes, except in Cases of Impeachment, shall be by Jury; and such Trial shall be held in the State where the said Crimes shall have been committed; but when not committed within any State, the Trial shall be at such Place or Places as the Congress may by Law have directed.

*Section 3.* Treason against the United States, shall consist only in levying War against them, or in adhering to their Enemies, giving them Aid and Comfort. No Person shall be convicted of Treason unless on the Testimony of two Witnesses to the same overt Act, or on Confession in open Court.

The Congress shall have Power to declare the Punishment of Treason, but no Attainder of Treason shall work Corruption of Blood, or Forfeiture except during the Life of the Person attainted.

## ARTICLE. IV.

*Section 1.* Full Faith and Credit shall be given in each State to the public Acts, Records, and judicial Proceedings of every other State. And the Congress may by general Laws prescribe the Manner in which such Acts, Records, and Proceedings shall be proved, and the Effect thereof.

*Section 2.* The Citizens of each State shall be entitled to all Privileges and Immunities of Citizens in the several States.

A person charged in any State with Treason, Felony, or other Crime, who shall flee from Justice, and be found in another State, shall on Demand of the executive Attorney of the State from which he fled, be delivered up, to be removed to the State having Jurisdiction of the Crime.

No Person held to Service or Labour in one State, under the Laws thereof, escaping into another, shall, in Consequence of any Law or Regulation therein, be discharged from such Service or Labour, but shall be delivered up on Claim of the Party to whom such Service or Labour may be due.

*Section 3.* New States may be admitted by the Congress into this Union; but no new State shall be formed or erected within the Jurisdiction of any other State; nor any State be formed by the Junction of two or more States, or Parts of States, without the consent of the Legislatures of the States concerned as well as of the Congress.

The Congress shall have Power to dispose of and make all needful Rules and Regulations respecting the Territory or other Property belonging to the United States; and nothing in this Constitution shall be so construed as to Prejudice any Claims of the United States, or of any particular States.

*Section 4.* The United States shall guarantee to every State in this Union a Republican Form of Government, and shall protect each of them against Invasion; and on Application of the Legislature, or of the Executive (when the Legislature cannot be convened) against domestic Violence.

## ARTICLE. V.

The Congress, whenever two thirds of both Houses shall deem it necessary, shall propose Amendments to this Constitution, or, on the Application of the Legislatures of two thirds of the several States shall call a Convention for proposing Amendments, which, in either Case, shall be valid to all Intents and Purposes, as Part of this Constitution, when ratified by the Legislatures of three fourths of the several States, or by Conventions in three fourths thereof, as the one or the other Mode of Ratification may be proposed by the Congress; Provided that no Amendment which may be made prior to the Year One thousand eight hundred and eight shall in any Manner affect the first and fourth Clauses in the Ninth Section of the first Article; and that no State, without its Consent, shall be deprived of it's equal Suffrage in the Senate.

## ARTICLE. VI.

All Debts contracted and Engagements entered into, before the Adoption of this Constitution, shall be as valid against the United States under this Constitution, as under the Confederation.

This Constitution, and the Laws of the United States which shall be made in Pursuance thereof; and all Treaties made, or which shall be made, under the Authority of the United States, shall be the supreme Law of the Land; and the Judges in every State shall be bound thereby, any Thing in the Constitution or Laws of any State to the Contrary notwithstanding.

The Senators and Representatives before mentioned, and the Members of the several State Legislatures, and all executive and judicial Officers, both of the United States and of the several States, shall be bound by Oath or Affirmation, to support this Constitution; but no religious Test shall ever be required as a Qualification to any Office or public Trust under the United States.

## ARTICLE. VII.

The Ratification of the Conventions of nine States, shall be sufficient for the Establishment of this Constitution between the States so ratifying the Same.

Done in Convention by the Unanimous Consent of the States present the Seventeenth Day of September in the Year of our Lord one thousand seven hundred and Eighty seven and of the Independence of the United States of America the Twelfth. In witness thereof We have hereunto subscribed our Names,

G°: Washington
*Presidᵗ and deputy from Virginia*

New Hampshire { John Langdon / Nicholas Gilman

Massachusetts { Nathaniel Gorham / Rufus King

Connecticut { Wᵐ Samˡ Johnson / Roger Sherman

New York { Alexander Hamilton

New Jersey { Wil: Livingston / David A. Brearley. / Wᵐ Paterson. / Jona: Dayton

Pennsylvania { B. Franklin / Thomas Mifflin / Robᵗ Morris / Geo. Clymer / Thoˢ. FitzSimons / Jared Ingersoll / James Wilson / Gouv Morris

Delaware { Geo: Read / Gunning Bedford jun / John Dickinson / Richard Bassett / Jaco: Broom

Maryland { James McHenry / Dan of Sᵗ Thoˢ Jenifer / Danˡ Carroll

Virginia { John Blair- / James Madison Jr.

North Carolina { Wᵐ. Blount / Richᵈ Dobbs Spaight. / Hu Williamson

South Carolina { J. Rutledge / Charles Cotesworth Pinckney / Charles Pinckney / Pierce Butler.

Georgia { William Few / Abr Baldwin

## AMENDMENT I.

Congress shall make no law respecting an establishment of religion, or prohibiting the free exercise thereof; or abriding the freedom of speech, or of the press; or the right of the people peaceably to assemble, and to petition the Government for a redress of grievances.

## AMENDMENT II.

A well regulated Militia, being necessary to the security of a free State, the right of the people to keep and bear Arms, shall not be infringed.

## AMENDMENT III.

No Soldier shall, in time of peace be quartered in any house, without the consent of the Owner,

nor in time of war, but in a manner to be prescribed by law.

## AMENDMENT IV.

The right of the people to be secure in their persons, houses, papers, and effects, against unreasonable searches and seizures, shall not be violated, and no Warrants shall issue, but upon probable cause, supported by Oath or affirmation, and particularly describing the place to be searched, and the persons or things to be seized.

## AMENDMENT V.

No persons shall be held to answer for a capital, or otherwise infamous crime, unless on a presentment or indictment of a Grand Jury, except in cases arising in the land or naval forces, or in the Militia, when in actual service in time of War or public danger; nor shall any person be subject for the same offence to be twice put in jeopardy of life or limb; nor shall be compelled in any criminal case to be a witness against himself, nor be deprived of life, liberty, or property, without due process of law; nor shall private property be taken for public use, without just compensation.

## AMENDMENT VI.

In all criminal prosecutions, the accused shall enjoy the right to a speedy and public trial, by an impartial jury of the State and district wherein the crime shall have been committed, which district shall have been previously ascertained by law, and to be informed of the nature and cause of the accusation; to be confronted with the witnesses against him; to have compulsory process for obtaining witnesses in his favor, and to have the Assistance of Counsel for his defence.

## AMENDMENT VII.

In Suits at common law, where the value in controversy shall exceed twenty dollars, the right of trial by jury shall be preserved, and no fact tried by a jury, shall be otherwise re-examined in any Court of the United States, than according to the rules of the common law.

## AMENDMENT VIII.

Excessive bail shall not be required, nor excessive fines imposed, nor cruel and unusual punishments inflicted.

## AMENDMENT IX.

In

The enumeration in the Constitution, of certain rights, shall not be construed to deny or disparage others retained by the people.

## AMENDMENT X.

The powers not delegated to the United States by the Constitution, nor prohibited by it to the States, are reserved to the States respectively, or to the people.

## AMENDMENT XI.

The Judicial power of the United States shall not be construed to extend to any suit in law or equity, commenced or prosecuted against one of the United States by Citizens of another State, or by Citizens or Subjects of any Foreign State.

## AMENDMENT XII.

The Electors shall meet in their respective states, and vote by ballot for President and Vice-

President, one of whom, at least, shall not be an inhabitant of the same state with themselves; they shall name in their ballots the person voted for as President, and in distinct ballots the person voted for as Vice-President, and they shall make distinct lists of all persons voted for as President, and of all persons voted for as Vice-President, and of the number of votes for each, which lists they shall sign and certify, and transmit sealed to the seat of the government of the United States, directed to the President of the Senate;—The President of the Senate shall, in the presence of the Senate and House of Representatives, open all the certificates and the votes shall then be counted;—The person having the greatest number of votes for President, shall be the President, if such number be a majority of the whole number of Electors appointed; and if no person have such majority, then from the persons having the highest numbers not exceeding three on the list of those voted for as President, the House of Representatives shall choose immediately, by ballot, the President. But in choosing the President, the votes shall be taken by states, the representation from each state having one vote; a quorum for this purpose shall consist of a member or members from two-thirds of the states, and a majority of all the states shall be necessary to a choice. And if the House of Representatives shall not choose a President whenever the right of choice shall devolve upon them, before the fourth day of March next following, then the Vice-President shall act as President, as in the case of the death or other constitutional disability of the President.— The person having the greatest number of votes as Vice-President, shall be the Vice-President, if such number be a majority of the whole number of Electors appointed, and if no person have a majority, then from the two highest numbers on the list, the Senate shall choose the Vice-President; a quorum for the purpose shall consist of two-thirds of the whole number of Senators, and a majority of the whole number shall be necessary to a choice. But no person constitutionally ineligible to the office of President shall be eligible to that of Vice-President of the United States.

## AMENDMENT XIII.

*Section 1.* Neither slavery nor involuntary servitude, except as a punishment for crime whereof the party shall have been duly convicted, shall exist within the United States, or any place subject to their jurisdiction.

*Section 2.* Congress shall have power to enforce this article by appropriate legislation.

## AMENDMENT XIV.

*Section 1.* All persons born or naturalized in the United States, and subject to the jurisdiction thereof, are citizens of the United States and of the State wherein they reside. No State shall make or enforce any law which shall abridge the privileges or immunities of citizens of the United States; nor shall any State deprive any person of life, liberty, or property, without due process of law; nor deny to any person within its jurisdiction the equal protection of the laws.

*Section 2.* Representatives shall be apportioned among the several States according to their respective numbers, counting the whole number of persons in each State, excluding Indians not taxed. But when the right to vote at any election for the choice of electors for President and Vice President of the United States, Representatives in Congress, the Executive and Judicial officers of a State, or the members of the Legislature thereof, is denied to any of the male inhabitants of such State, being twenty-one years of age, and citizens of the United States, or in any way abridged, except for participation in rebellion, or other crime, the basis of representation therein shall be reduced in the proportion which the number of such male citizens shall bear to the whole number of male citizens twenty-one years of age in such State.

*Section 3.* No person shall be a Senator or Representative in Congress, or elector of President and Vice President, or hold any office, civil or military, under the United States, or under any State, who, having previously taken an oath, as a member of Congress, or as an officer of the United States, or as a member of any State legislature, or as an executive or judicial officer of any State, to support the Constitution of the United States, shall have engaged in insurrection or rebellion against the same, or given aid or comfort to the enemies thereof. But Congress may be a vote of two-thirds of each House, remove such disability.

*Section 4.* The validity of the public debt of the United States, authorized by law, including debts incurred for payment of pensions and bounties for services in suppressing insurrection or rebellion, shall not be questioned. But neither the United States nor any State shall assume or pay any debt or obligation incurred in aid of insurrection or rebellion against the United States, or any claim for the loss or emancipation of any slave; but all such debts, obligations and claims shall be held illegal and void.

*Section 5.* The Congress shall have power to enforce, by appropriate legislation, the provisions of this article.

## AMENDMENT XV.

*Section 1.* The right of citizens of the United States to vote shall not be denied or abridged by the United States or by any State on account of race, color, or previous condition of servitude.

*Section 2.* The Congress shall have power to enforce this article by appropriate legislation.

## AMENDMENT XVI.

The Congress shall have power to lay and collect taxes on incomes, from whatever source derived, without apportionment among the several States, and without regard to any census or enumeration.

## AMENDMENT XVII.

The Senate of the United States shall be composed of two senators from each State, elected by the people thereof, for six years; and each Senator shall have one vote. The electors in each State shall have the qualifications requisite for electors of the most numerous branch of the State legislature.

When vacancies happen in the representation of any State in the Senate, the executive authority of such State shall issue writs of election to fill such vacancies: *Provided,* That the legislature of any State may empower the executive thereof to make temporary appointments until the people fill the vacancies by election as the legislature may direct.

This amendment shall not be so construed as to affect the election or term of any senator chosen before it becomes valid as part of the Constitution.

## AMENDMENT XVIII.

After one year from the ratification of this article, the manufacture, sale, or transportation of intoxicating liquors within, the importation thereof into, or the exportation thereof from the United States and all territory subject to the jurisdiction thereof for beverage purposes is hereby prohibited.

The Congress and the several States shall have concurrent power to enforce this article by appropriate legislation.

This article shall be inoperative unless it shall have been ratified as an amendment to the Constitution by the legislatures of the several States, as provided in the Constitution, within seven years from the date of the submission thereof to the States by Congress.

## AMENDMENT XIX.

The right of citizens of the United States to vote shall not be denied or abridged by the United States or by any State on account of sex.

The Congress shall have power by appropriate legislation to enforce the provisions of this article.

## AMENDMENT XX.

*Section 1.* The terms of the President and Vice-President shall end at noon on the twentieth day of January, and the terms of Senators and Representatives at noon on the third day of January, of the years in which such terms would have ended if this article had not been ratified; and the terms of their successors shall then begin.

*Section 2.* The Congress shall assemble at least once in every year, and such meeting shall begin at noon on the third day of January, unless they shall by law appoint a different day.

*Section 3.* If, at the time fixed for the beginning of the term of the President, the President-elect shall have died, the Vice-President-elect shall become President. If a President shall not have been chosen before the time fixed for the beginning of his term, or if the President-elect shall have failed to qualify, then the Vice-President-elect shall act as President until a President shall have qualified; and the Congress may by law provide for the case wherein neither a President-elect nor a Vice-President-elect shall have qualified, declaring who shall then act as President, or the manner in which one who is to act shall be selected, and such person shall act accordingly until a President or Vice-President shall have qualified.

*Section 4.* The Congress may by law provide for the case of the death of any of the persons from whom the House of Representatives may choose a President whenever the right of choice shall have devolved upon them, and for the case of the death of any of the persons from whom the Senate may choose a Vice-President whenever the right of choice shall have devolved upon them.

*Section 5.* Sections 1 and 2 shall take effect on the 15th day of October following the ratification of this article.

*Section 6.* This article shall be inoperative unless it shall have been ratified as an amendment to the Constitution by the legislatures of three-fourths of the several States within seven years from the date of its submission.

## AMENDMENT XXI.

*Section 1.* The eighteenth article of amendment to the Constitution of the United States is hereby repealed.

*Section 2.* The transportation or importation into any State, Territory or possession of the United States for delivery or use therein of intoxicating liquors, in violation of the laws thereof, is hereby prohibited.

*Section 3.* This article shall be inoperative unless it shall have been ratified as an amendment to the Constitution by convention in the several States, as provided in the Constitution, within seven years from the date of the submission thereof to the States by the Congress.

## AMENDMENT XXII.

*Section 1.* No person shall be elected to the office of the President more than twice, and no person who has held the office of President, or acted as President, for more than two years of a term to which some other person was elected President shall be elected to the office of the President more than once. But this Article shall not apply to any person holding the office of President when this Article was proposed by the Congress, and shall not prevent any person who may be holding the office of President, or acting as President, during the term within which this Article becomes operative from holding the office of President or acting as President during the remainder of such term.

*Section 2.* This article shall be inoperative unless it shall have been ratified as an amendment to the Constitution by the legislatures of three-fourths of the several States within seven years from the date of its submission to the States by the Congress.

## AMENDMENT XXIII.

*Section 1.* The District constituting the seat of government of the United States shall appoint in such manner as the Congress may direct:

A number of electors of President and Vice-President equal to the whole number of Senators and Representatives in Congress to which the District would be entitled if it were a State, but in no event more than the least populous State; they shall be in addition to those appointed by the States, but they shall be considered, for the purposes of the election of President and Vice-President, to be electors appointed by a State; and they shall meet in the District and perform such duties as provided by the twelfth article of amendment.

*Section 2.* The Congress shall have the power to enforce this article by appropriate legislation.

## AMENDMENT XXIV.

*Section 1.* The right of citizens of the United States to vote in any primary or other election for President or Vice President, for electors for President or Vice President, or for Senator or Representative in Congress, shall not be denied or abridged by the United States or any State by reason of failure to pay any poll tax or other tax.

*Section 2.* The Congress shall have power to enforce this article by appropriate legislation.

### AMENDMENT XXV.

*Section 1.* In case of the removal of the President from office or of his death or resignation, the Vice President shall become President.

*Section 2.* Whenever there is a vacancy in the office of Vice President, the President shall nominate a Vice President who shall take office upon confirmation by a majority vote of both Houses of Congress.

*Section 3.* Whenever the President transmits to the President pro tempore of the Senate and the Speaker of the House of Representatives his written declaration that he is unable to discharge the powers and duties of his office, and until he transmits to them a written declaration to the contrary, such powers and duties shall be discharged by the Vice President as Acting President.

*Section 4.* Whenever the Vice President and a majority of either the principal officers of the executive departments or of such other body as Congress may by law provide, transmit to the President pro tempore of the Senate and the Speaker of the House of Representatives their written declaration that the President is unable to discharge the powers and duties of his office, the Vice President shall immediately assume the powers and duties of the office as Acting President.

Thereafter, when the President transmits to the President pro tempore of the Senate and the Speaker of the House of Representatives his written declaration that no inability exists, he shall resume the powers and duties of his office unless the Vice President and a majority of either the principal officers of the executive departments or of such other body as Congress may by law provide, transmit within four days to the President pro tempore of the Senate and the Speaker of the House of Representatives their written declaration that the President is unable to discharge the powers and duties of his office. Thereupon Congress shall decide the issue, assembling within forty-eight hours for that purpose if not in session. If the Congress, within twenty-one days after receipt of the latter written declaration, or, if Congress is not in session, within twenty-one days after Congress is required to assemble, determines by two-thirds vote of both Houses that the President is unable to discharge the power and duties of his office, the Vice President shall continue to discharge the same as Acting President; otherwise, the President shall resume the powers and duties of his office.

### AMENDMENT XXVI.

*Section 1.* The right of citizens of the United States, who are eighteen years of age or older, to vote shall not be denied or abridged by the United States or by any State on account of age.

*Section 2.* The Congress shall have power to enforce this article by appropriate legislation.

### AMENDMENT XXVII.

No law, varying the compensation for the services of the Senators and Representatives, shall take effect, until an election of Representatives shall have intervened.

# APPENDIX TWO

# Nominations and Succession of the Justices

## Supreme Court Nominations, 1789–1991

| 1<br>President/<br>Nominee | 2<br>Appointed | 3<br>Action (vote) | 4<br>Oath Taken | 5<br>Term End | 6<br>Yrs. of<br>Service |
|---|---|---|---|---|---|
| *Washington* | | | | | |
| John Jay* | 24 Sep. 1789 | C  26 Sep. 1789 | 19 Oct. 1789 | R  29 June 1795 | 6 |
| John Rutledge | 24 Sep. 1789 | C  26 Sep. 1789 | 15 Feb. 1790 | R  5 Mar. 1791 | 1 |
| William Cushing | 24 Sep. 1789 | C  26 Sep. 1789 | 2 Feb. 1790 | D  13 Sep. 1810 | 21 |
| Robert Harrison | 24 Sep. 1789 | D  26 Sep. 1789 | | | |
| James Wilson | 24 Sep. 1789 | C  26 Sep. 1789 | 5 Oct. 1789 | D 21 Aug. 1798 | 9 |
| John Blair, Jr. | 24 Sep. 1789 | C  26 Sep. 1789 | 2 Feb. 1790 | R  25 Oct. 1795 | 6 |
| James Iredell | 8 Feb. 1790 | C  10 Feb. 1790 | 12 May 1790 | D  20 Oct. 1799 | 9 |
| Thomas Johnson* | R  5 Aug. 1791 | | 19 Sep. 1791 | | |
| | 31 Oct. 1791 | C  7 Nov. 1791 | 6 Aug. 1792 | R  16 Jan. 1793 | 1 |
| William Paterson | 27 Feb. 1793 | W  28 Feb. 1793 | | | |
| William Paterson | 4 Mar. 1793 | C  4 Mar. 1793 | 11 Mar. 1793 | D  9 Sep. 1806 | 13 |
| John Rutledge*† | R  1 July 1795 | | 12 Aug. 1795 | | |
| | | R  15 Dec. 1795<br>(10-14) | | | |
| William Cushing* | 26 Jan. 1796 | D  27 Jan. 1796 | | | |
| Samuel Chase | 26 Jan. 1796 | C  27 Jan. 1796 | 4 Feb. 1796 | D  19 June 1811 | 15 |
| Oliver Ellsworth | 3 Mar. 1796 | C  4 Mar. 1796<br>(21–1) | 8 Mar. 1796 | R  15 Dec. 1800 | 4 |
| | | | | | |
| *Adams* | | | | | |
| Bushrod Washington | R  29 Sep. 1798 | | 9 Nov. 1798 | | |
| | 19 Dec. 1798 | C  20 Dec. 1798 | 4 Feb. 1799 | D 26 Nov. 1829 | 31 |
| Alfred Moore | 4 Dec. 1799 | C  10 Dec. 1799 | 21 Apr. 1800 | R  26 Jan. 1804 | 4 |
| John Jay | 18 Dec. 1800 | D  19 Dec. 1800 | | | |
| John Marshall* | 20 Jan. 1801 | C  27 Jan. 1801 | 4 Feb. 1801 | D  6 July 1835 | 34 |
| *Jefferson* | | | | | |
| William Johnson | 22 Mar. 1804 | C  24 Mar. 1804 | 8 May 1804 | D  4 Aug. 1834 | 30 |
| Brockholst Livingston | R 10 Nov. 1806 | | 20 Jan. 1807 | | |
| | 13 Dec. 1806 | C  17 Dec. 1806 | 2 Feb. 1807 | D  18 Mar. 1823 | 16 |
| Thomas Todd | 28 Feb. 1807 | C  3 Mar. 1807 | 4 May 1807 | D  7 Feb. 1826 | 19 |

*Column 1.* * = chief justice. † = nomination for promotion to chief justice; years of service, where applicable, are as chief justice only; see prior listing for nomination and service as associate justice. *Column 2.* R = recess appointment. *Column 3.* C = confirmed. D = declined. P = postponed. R = rejected. W = withdrawn. *Column 5.* D = died. P = promoted to chief justice (see separate listing for service as chief justice). R = retirement/resignation.

| 1 President/ Nominee | 2 Appointed | 3 Action (vote) | 4 Oath Taken | 5 Term End | 6 Yrs. of Service |
|---|---|---|---|---|---|
| *Madison* | | | | | |
| Levi Lincoln | 2 Jan. 1811 | D 3 Jan. 1811 | | | |
| Alexander Wolcott | 4 Feb. 1811 | R 13 Feb. 1811 (9-24) | | | |
| John Quincy Adams | 21 Feb. 1811 | D 22 Feb. 1811 | | | |
| Joseph Story | 15 Nov. 1811 | C 18 Nov. 1811 | 3 Feb. 1812 | D 10 Sep. 1845 | 34 |
| Gabriel Duvall | 15 Nov. 1811 | C 18 Nov. 1811 | 23 Nov. 1811 | R 14 Jan. 1835 | 23 |
| *Monroe* | | | | | |
| Smith Thompson | R 1 Sep. 1823 | | | | |
| | 8 Dec. 1823 | C 19 Dec. 1823 | 10 Feb. 1824 | D 18 Dec. 1843 | 20 |
| *J. Q. Adams* | | | | | |
| Robert Trimble | 11 Apr. 1826 | C 9 May 1826 (27-5) | 16 June 1826 | D 25 Aug. 1828 | 2 |
| John Crittenden | 17 Dec. 1828 | P 12 Feb. 1829 | | | |
| *Jackson* | | | | | |
| John McLean | 6 Mar. 1829 | C 7 Mar. 1829 | 11 Jan. 1830 | D 4 Apr. 1861 | 32 |
| Henry Baldwin | 4 Jan. 1830 | C 6 Jan. 1830 (41-2) | 18 Jan. 1830 | D 21 Apr. 1844 | 14 |
| James M. Wayne | 6 Jan. 1835 | C 9 Jan. 1835 | 14 Jan. 1835 | D 5 July 1867 | 32 |
| Roger B. Taney* | 15 Jan. 1835 | P 3 Mar. 1835 | | | |
| | 28 Dec. 1835 | C 15 Mar. 1836 (29-15) | 28 Mar. 1836 | D 12 Oct. 1864 | 28 |
| Philip P. Barbour | 28 Dec. 1835 | C 15 Mar. 1836 (30-11) | ·12 May 1836 | D 25 Feb. 1841 | 5 |
| William Smith | 3 Mar. 1837 | D 8 Mar. 1837 (23-18) | | | |
| John Catron | 3 Mar. 1837 | C 8 Mar. 1837 | 1 May 1837 | D 30 May 1865 | 28 |
| *Van Buren* | | | | | |
| John McKinley | R 22 Apr. 1837 | | | | |
| | 18 Sep. 1837 | C 25 Sep. 1837 | 9 Jan. 1838 | D 19 July 1852 | 15 |
| Peter V. Daniel | 26 Feb. 1841 | C 2 Mar. 1841 (22-5) | 10 Jan. 1842 | D 31 May 1860 | 19 |
| *Tyler* | | | | | |
| John C. Spencer | 9 Jan. 1844 | R 31 Jan. 1844 (21-26) | | | |
| Reuben H. Walworth | 13 Mar. 1844 | W 17 June 1844 | | | |
| Edward King | 5 June 1844 | P 15 June 1844 (29-18) | | | |
| | 4 Dec. 1844 | W 7 Feb. 1845 | | | |

*Column 1.* * = chief justice. † = nomination for promotion to chief justice; years of service, where applicable, are as chief justice only; see prior listing for nomination and service as associate justice. *Column 2.* R = recess appointment. *Column 3.* C = confirmed. D = declined. P = postponed. R = rejected. W = withdrawn. *Column 5.* D = died. P = promoted to chief justice (see separate listing for service as chief justice). R = retirement/resignation.

| 1 | 2 | 3 | 4 | 5 | 6 |
|---|---|---|---|---|---|
| President/ Nominee | Appointed | Action (vote) | Oath Taken | Term End | Yrs. of Service |
| Samuel Nelson | 4 Feb. 1845 | C 14 Feb. 1845 | 27 Feb. 1845 | R 28 Nov. 1872 | 27 |
| John M. Read | 7 Feb. 1845 | No action | | | |
| *Polk* | | | | | |
| George W. Woodward | 23 Dec. 1845 | R 22 Jan. 1846 (20-29) | | | |
| Levi Woodbury | R 20 Sep. 1845 23 Dec. 1845 | C 3 Jan. 1846 | 23 Sep. 1845 3 Jan. 1846 | D 4 Sep. 1851 | 5 |
| Robert C. Grier | 3 Aug. 1846 | C 4 Aug. 1846 | 10 Aug. 1846 | R 31 Jan. 1870 | 23 |
| *Fillmore* | | | | | |
| Benjamin R. Curtis | R 22 Sep. 1851 11 Dec. 1851 | C 20 Dec. 1851 | 10 Oct. 1851 | R 30 Sep. 1857 | 5 |
| Edward A. Bradford | 16 Aug. 1852 | No action | | | |
| George E. Badger | 10 Jan. 1853 | P 11 Feb. 1853 | | | |
| William C. Micou | 24 Feb. 1853 | No action | | | |
| *Pierce* | | | | | |
| John A. Campbell | 22 Mar. 1853 | C 25 Mar. 1853 | 11 Apr. 1853 | R 30 Apr. 1861 | 8 |
| *Buchanan* | | | | | |
| Nathan Clifford | 9 Dec. 1857 | C 12 Jan. 1858 (26-23) | 21 Jan. 1858 | D 25 July 1881 | 23 |
| Jeremiah S. Black | 5 Feb. 1861 | R 21 Feb. 1861 (25-26) | | | |
| *Lincoln* | | | | | |
| Noah H. Swayne | 22 Jan. 1862 | C 24 Jan. 1862 (38-1) | 27 Jan. 1862 | R 24 Jan. 1881 | 19 |
| Samuel F. Miller | 16 July 1862 | C 16 July 1862 | 21 July 1862 | D 13 Oct. 1890 | 28 |
| David Davis | R 17 Oct. 1862 1 Dec. 1862 | C 8 Dec. 1862 | 10 Dec. 1862 | R 4 Mar. 1877 | 14 |
| Stephen J. Field | 6 Mar. 1863 | C 10 Mar. 1863 | 20 May 1863 | R 1 Dec. 1897 | 34 |
| Salmon P. Chase* | 6 Dec. 1864 | C 6 Dec. 1864 | 15 Dec. 1864 | D 7 May 1873 | 8 |
| *A. Johnson* | | | | | |
| Henry Stanbery | 16 Apr. 1866 | No action | | | |
| *Grant* | | | | | |
| Ebenezer R. Hoar | 15 Dec. 1869 | R 3 Feb. 1870 (24-33) | | | |
| Edwin M. Stanton | 20 Dec. 1869 | C 20 Dec. 1869 (46-11) | (Died 24 Dec. 1869) | | |
| William Strong | 7 Feb. 1870 | C 18 Feb. 1870 | 14 Mar. 1870 | R 14 Dec. 1880 | 10 |
| Joseph P. Bradley | 7 Feb. 1870 | C 21 Mar. 1870 (46-9) | 23 Mar. 1870 | D 22 Jan. 1892 | 21 |
| Ward Hunt | 3 Dec. 1872 | C 11 Dec. 1872 | 9 Jan. 1873 | R 27 Jan. 1882 | 9 |
| George H. Williams | 1 Dec. 1873 | W 8 Jan. 1874 | | | |
| Caleb Cushing | 9 Jan. 1874 | W 13 Jan. 1874 | | | |
| Morrison R. Waite* | 19 Jan. 1874 | C 21 Jan. 1874 (63-0) | 4 Mar. 1874 | D 23 Mar. 1888 | 14 |

| 1 | 2 | 3 | 4 | 5 | 6 |
|---|---|---|---|---|---|
| President/ Nominee | Appointed | Action (vote) | Oath Taken | Term End | Yrs. of Service |

**Hayes**

| President/ Nominee | Appointed | Action (vote) | Oath Taken | Term End | Yrs. of Service |
|---|---|---|---|---|---|
| John Marshall Harlan | 16 Oct. 1877 | C  29 Nov. 1877 | 10 Dec. 1877 | D  14 Oct. 1911 | 34 |
| William B. Woods | 15 Dec. 1880 | C  21 Dec. 1880 (39-8) | 5 Jan. 1881 | D  14 May 1887 | 6 |

**Garfield**

| | | | | | |
|---|---|---|---|---|---|
| Stanley Matthews | 26 Jan. 1881 14 Mar. 1881 | No action 12 May 1881 (24-23) | 17 May 1881 | D  22 Mar. 1889 | 7 |

**Arthur**

| | | | | | |
|---|---|---|---|---|---|
| Horace Gray | 19 Dec. 1881 | C  20 Dec. 1881 (51-5) | 9 Jan. 1882 | D  15 Sep. 1902 | 20 |
| Roscoe Conkling | 24 Feb. 1882 | D  2 Mar. 1882 (39-12) | | | |
| Samuel Blatchford | 13 Mar. 1882 | C  27 Mar. 1882 | 3 Apr. 1882 | D  7 July 1893 | 11 |

**Cleveland**

| | | | | | |
|---|---|---|---|---|---|
| Lucius Q. C. Lamar | 6 Dec. 1887 | C  16 Jan. 1888 (32-28) | 18 Jan. 1888 | D  23 Jan. 1893 | 5 |
| Melville W. Fuller* | 30 Apr. 1888 | C  20 July 1888 (41-20) | 8 Oct. 1888 | D  4 July 1910 | 22 |

**Harrison**

| | | | | | |
|---|---|---|---|---|---|
| David J. Brewer | 4 Dec. 1889 | C  18 Dec. 1889 (53-11) | 6 Jan. 1890 | D  28 Mar. 1910 | 20 |
| Henry B. Brown | 23 Dec. 1890 | C  29 Dec. 1890 | 5 Jan. 1891 | R  28 May 1906 | 15 |
| George Shiras | 19 July 1892 | C  26 July 1892 | 10 Oct. 1892 | R  23 Feb. 1903 | 10 |
| Howell E. Jackson | 2 Feb. 1893 | C  18 Feb. 1893 | 4 Mar. 1893 | D  8 Aug. 1895 | 2 |

**Cleveland**

| | | | | | |
|---|---|---|---|---|---|
| William B. Hornblower | 19 Sep. 1893 | R  15 Jan. 1894 (24-30) | | | |
| Wheeler H. Peckham | 23 Jan. 1894 | R  16 Feb. 1894 (32-41) | | | |
| Edward D. White | 19 Feb. 1894 | C  19 Feb. 1894 | 12 Mar. 1894 | P  18 Dec. 1910 | 17 |
| Rufus W. Peckham | 3 Dec. 1895 | 9 Dec. 1895 | 6 Jan. 1896 | D  24 Oct. 1909 | 13 |

**McKinley**

| | | | | | |
|---|---|---|---|---|---|
| Joseph McKenna | 16 Dec. 1897 | C  21 Jan. 1898 | 26 Jan. 1898 | R  5 Jan. 1925 | 26 |

**T. Roosevelt**

| | | | | | |
|---|---|---|---|---|---|
| Oliver Wendell Holmes | R 11 Aug. 1902 2 Dec. 1902 | C  2 Dec. 1902 | 8 Dec. 1902 | R  12 Jan. 1932 | 29 |
| William R. Day | 2 Mar. 1903 | C  23 Feb. 1903 | 2 Mar. 1903 | R  13 Nov. 1922 | 19 |
| William H. Moody | 3 Dec. 1906 | C  12 Dec. 1906 | 17 Dec.1906 | R  20 Nov. 1910 | 3 |

*Column 1.* * = chief justice. † = nomination for promotion to chief justice; years of service, where applicable, are as chief justice only; see prior listing for nomination and servic as associate justice. *Column 2.* R = recess appointment. *Column 3.* C = confirmed. D = declined. P = postponed. R = rejected. W = withdrawn. *Column 5.* D = died. P = promoted to chief justice (see separate listing for service as chief justice). R = retirement/resignation.

| 1<br>President/<br>Nominee | 2<br><br>Appointed | 3<br><br>Action (vote) | 4<br><br>Oath Taken | 5<br><br>Term End | 6<br>Yrs. of<br>Service |
|---|---|---|---|---|---|
| *Taft* | | | | | |
| Horace H. Lurton | 13 Dec. 1909 | C 20 Dec. 1909 | 3 Jan. 1910 | D 12 July 1914 | 4 |
| Charles E. Hughes | 25 Apr. 1910 | C 2 May 1910 | 10 Oct. 1910 | R 10 June 1916 | 6 |
| Edward D. White*† | 12 Dec. 1910 | C 12 Dec. 1910 | 19 Dec. 1910 | D 19 May 1921 | 10 |
| Willis Van Devanter | 12 Dec. 1910 | C 15 Dec. 1910 | 3 Jan. 1911 | R 2 June 1937 | 26 |
| Joseph R. Lamar | 12 Dec. 1910 | C 15 Dec. 1910 | 3 Jan. 1911 | D 2 Jan. 1916 | 5 |
| Mahlon Pitney | 19 Feb. 1912 | C 13 Mar. 1912<br>(50-26) | 18 Mar. 1912 | R 31 Dec. 1922 | 10 |
| *Wilson* | | | | | |
| James C. McReynolds | 19 Aug. 1914 | C 29 Aug. 1914<br>(44-6) | 5 Sep. 1914 | R 1 Feb. 1941 | 26 |
| Louis D. Brandeis | 28 Jan. 1916 | C 1 June 1916<br>(47-22) | 5 June 1916 | R 13 Feb. 1939 | 22 |
| John H. Clarke | 14 July 1916 | C 24 July 1916 | 1 Aug. 1916 | R 18 Sep. 1922 | 6 |
| *Harding* | | | | | |
| William H. Taft* | 30 June 1921 | C 30 June 1921 | 11 July 1921 | R 3 Feb. 1930 | 8 |
| George Sutherland | 5 Sep. 1922 | C 5 Sep. 1922 | 2 Oct. 1922 | R 17 Jan. 1938 | 15 |
| Pierce Butler | 23 Nov. 1922<br>5 Dec. 1922 | No action<br>C 21 Dec. 1922<br>(61-8) | 2 Jan. 1923 | D 16 Nov. 1939 | 17 |
| Edward T. Sanford | 24 Jan. 1923 | C 29 Jan. 1923 | 5 Feb. 1923 | D 8 Mar. 1930 | 7 |
| *Coolidge* | | | | | |
| Harlan F. Stone | 5 Jan. 1925 | C 5 Feb. 1925<br>(71-6) | 2 Mar. 1925 | P 2 July 1941 | 16 |
| *Hoover* | | | | | |
| Charles E. Hughes*† | 3 Feb. 1930 | C 13 Feb. 1930<br>(52-26) | 24 Feb. 1930 | R 1 July 1941 | 11 |
| John J. Parker | 21 Mar. 1930 | R 7 May 1930<br>(39-41) | | | |
| Owen J. Roberts | 9 May 1930 | C 20 May 1930 | 2 June 1930 | R 31 July 1945 | 15 |
| Benjamin N. Cardozo | 15 Feb. 1932 | C 24 Feb. 1932 | 14 Mar. 1932 | D 9 July 1938 | 6 |
| *F. D. Roosevelt* | | | | | |
| Hugo L. Black | 12 Aug. 1937 | C 17 Aug. 1937<br>(63-16) | 19 Aug. 1937 | R 17 Sep. 1971 | 34 |
| Stanley F. Reed | 15 Jan. 1938 | C 25 Jan. 1938 | 31 Jan. 1938 | R 25 Feb. 1957 | 19 |
| Felix Frankfurter | 5 Jan. 1939 | C 17 Jan. 1939 | 30 Jan. 1939 | R 28 Aug. 1962 | 23 |
| William O. Douglas | 20 Mar. 1939 | C 4 Apr. 1939<br>(62-4) | 17 Apr. 1939 | R 12 Nov. 1975 | 36 |
| Frank Murphy | 4 Jan. 1940 | C 16 Jan. 1940 | 18 Jan. 1940 | D 19 July 1949 | 9 |
| Harlan F. Stone*† | 12 June 1941 | C 27 June 1941 | 3 July 1941 | D 22 Apr. 1946 | 5 |
| James F. Byrnes | 12 June 1941 | C 12 June 1941 | 8 July 1941 | R 3 Oct. 1942 | 1 |
| Robert H. Jackson | 12 June 1941 | C 7 July 1941 | 11 July 1941 | D 9 Oct. 1954 | 13 |
| Wiley B. Rutledge | 11 Jan. 1943 | C 8 Feb. 1943 | 15 Feb. 1943 | D 10 Sep. 1949 | 6 |
| *Truman* | | | | | |
| Harold H. Burton | 18 Sep. 1945 | C 19 Sep. 1945 | 1 Oct. 1945 | R 13 Oct. 1958 | 13 |

| 1 President/ Nominee | 2 Appointed | 3 Action (vote) | 4 Oath Taken | 5 Term End | 6 Yrs. of Service |
|---|---|---|---|---|---|
| Fred M. Vinson* | 6 June 1946 | C 20 June 1946 | 24 June 1946 | D 8 Sep. 1953 | 7 |
| Tom C. Clark | 2 Aug. 1949 | C 18 Aug. 1949 (73-8) | 24 Aug. 1949 | R 12 June 1967 | 18 |
| Sherman Minton | 15 Sep. 1949 | C 4 Oct. 1949 (48-16) | 12 Oct. 1949 | R 15 Oct. 1956 | 7 |
| *Eisenhower* | | | | | |
| Earl Warren* | R 2 Oct. 1953 11 Jan. 1954 | C 1 Mar. 1954 | 5 Oct. 1953 2 Mar. 1954 | R 23 June 1969 | 15 |
| John M. Harlan II | 9 Nov. 1954 10 Jan. 1955 | No action C 16 Mar. 1955 (71-11) | 28 Mar. 1955 | R 23 Sep. 1971 | 16 |
| William J. Brennan, Jr. | R 15 Oct. 1956 14 Jan. 1957 | C 19 Mar. 1957 | 16 Oct. 1956 22 Mar. 1957 | R 20 July 1990 | 33 |
| Charles E. Whittaker | 2 Mar. 1957 | C 19 Mar. 1957 | 25 Mar. 1957 | R 1 Apr. 1962 | 5 |
| Potter Stewart | R 14 Oct. 1958 17 Jan. 1959 | C 5 May 1959 (70-17) | 14 Oct. 1958 15 May 1959 | R 3 July 1981 | 22 |
| *Kennedy* | | | | | |
| Byron R. White | 3 Apr. 1962 | C 11 Apr. 1962 | 16 Apr. 1962 | | |
| Arthur J. Goldberg | 31 Aug. 1962 | C 25 Sep. 1962 | 1 Oct. 1962 | R 25 July 1965 | 3 |
| *L. B. Johnson* | | | | | |
| Abe Fortas | 28 July 1965 | C 11 Aug. 1965 | 4 Oct. 1965 | R 14 May 1969 | 4 |
| Thurgood Marshall | 13 June 1967 | C 30 Aug. 1967 (69-11) | 2 Oct. 1967 | R 27 June 1991 | 24 |
| Abe Fortas† | 26 June 1968 | W 4 Oct. 1968 | | | |
| Homer Thornberry | 26 June 1968 | W 2 Oct. 1968 | | | |
| *Nixon* | | | | | |
| Warren E. Burger* | 21 May 1969 | C 9 June 1969 (74-3) | 23 June 1969 | R 26 Sep. 1986 | 17 |
| Clement Haynsworth, Jr. | 18 Aug. 1969 | R 21 Nov. 1969 (45-55) | | | |
| G. Harrold Carswell | 19 Jan. 1970 | R 8 Apr. 1970 (45-51) | | | |
| Harry A. Blackmun | 15 Apr. 1970 | C 12 May 1970 (94-0) | 9 June 1970 | | |
| Lewis F. Powell, Jr. | 22 Oct. 1971 | C 6 Dec. 1971 (89-1) | 7 Jan. 1972 | R 26 June 1987 | 16 |
| William H. Rehnquist | 22 Oct. 1971 | C 10 Dec. 1971 (68-26) | 7 Jan. 1972 | P 26 Sep. 1986 | 15 |

*Column 1.* * = chief justice. † = nomination for promotion to chief justice; years of service, where applicable, are as chief justice only; see prior listing for nomination and service as associate justice. *Column 2.* R = recess appointment. *Column 3.* C = confirmed. D = declined. P = postponed. R = rejected. W = withdrawn. *Column 5.* D = died. P = promoted to chief justice (see separate listing for service as chief justice). R = retirement/resignation.

| 1 | 2 | 3 | 4 | 5 | 6 |
|---|---|---|---|---|---|
| **President/ Nominee** | **Appointed** | **Action (vote)** | **Oath Taken** | **Term End** | **Yrs. of Service** |
| *Ford* | | | | | |
| John Paul Stevens | 28 Nov. 1975 | C 17 Dec. 1975 (98-0) | 19 Dec. 1975 | | |
| *Reagan* | | | | | |
| Sandra Day O'Connor | 7 July 1981 | C 21 Sep. 1981 (99-0) | 25 Sep. 1981 | | |
| William H. Rehnquist*† | 17 June 1986 | C 17 Sep. 1986 (65-33) | 26 Sep. 1986 | | |
| Antonin Scalia | 17 June 1986 | C 17 Sep. 1986 (98-0) | 26 Sep. 1986 | | |
| Robert H. Bork | 1 July 1987 | R 23 Oct. 1987 (42-58) | | | |
| Douglas Ginsburg | 29 Oct. 1987 | W 7 Nov. 1987 | | | |
| Anthony M. Kennedy | 24 Nov. 1987 | C 3 Feb. 1988 (97-0) | 18 Feb. 1988 | | |
| *Bush* | | | | | |
| David H. Souter | 25 July 1990 | C 2 Oct. 1990 (90-9) | 9 Oct. 1990 | | |
| Clarence Thomas | 1 July 1991 | C 15 Oct. 1991 (52-48) | 1 Nov. 1991 | | |

# Appointments, by Presidential Term

*In this chart, arrows pointing out from presidents indicate appointments of justices;*
*arrows pointing in from chief justices indicate administration of presidential oath of office.*

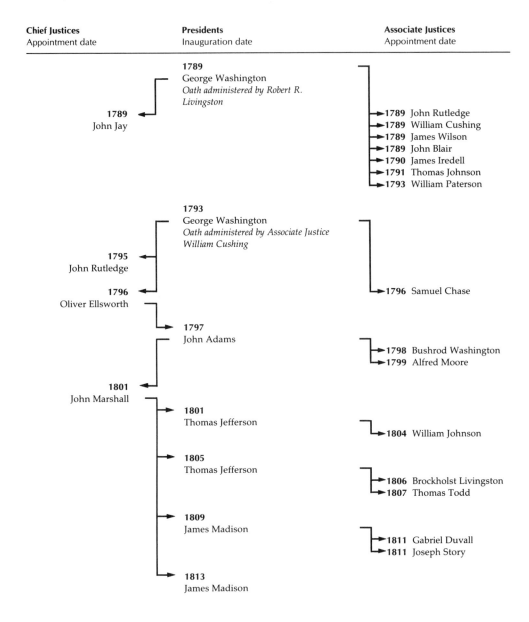

| Chief Justices<br>Appointment date | Presidents<br>Inauguration date | Associate Justices<br>Appointment date |
|---|---|---|
| | **1789**<br>George Washington<br>*Oath administered by Robert R.*<br>*Livingston* | |
| **1789**<br>John Jay | | **1789**  John Rutledge<br>**1789**  William Cushing<br>**1789**  James Wilson<br>**1789**  John Blair<br>**1790**  James Iredell<br>**1791**  Thomas Johnson<br>**1793**  William Paterson |
| | **1793**<br>George Washington<br>*Oath administered by Associate Justice*<br>*William Cushing* | |
| **1795**<br>John Rutledge | | |
| **1796**<br>Oliver Ellsworth | | **1796**  Samuel Chase |
| | **1797**<br>John Adams | **1798**  Bushrod Washington<br>**1799**  Alfred Moore |
| **1801**<br>John Marshall | **1801**<br>Thomas Jefferson | **1804**  William Johnson |
| | **1805**<br>Thomas Jefferson | **1806**  Brockholst Livingston<br>**1807**  Thomas Todd |
| | **1809**<br>James Madison | **1811**  Gabriel Duvall<br>**1811**  Joseph Story |
| | **1813**<br>James Madison | |

| **Chief Justices** | **Presidents** | **Associate Justices** |
|---|---|---|
| Appointment date | Inauguration date | Appointment date |

John Marshall

**1817**
James Monroe

**1821**
James Monroe

**1823** Smith Thompson

**1825**
John Quincy Adams

**1826** Robert Trimble

**1829**
Andrew Jackson

**1829** John McLean
**1830** Henry Baldwin

**1833**
Andrew Jackson

**1835** James M. Waynecr
**1836** Philip P. Barbourcr

**1836**
Roger Brooke Taney

**1837**
Martin Van Buren

**1837** John Catron
**1837** John McKinley
**1841** Peter V. Daniel

**1841**
William H. Harrison

**1841**
John Tyler
*Oath administered by William Cranch*

**1845** Samuel Nelson

**1845**
James K. Polk

**1845** Levi Woodbury
**1846** Robert C. Grier

**1849**
Zachary Taylor

**1850**
Millard Fillmore
*Oath administered by William Cranch*

**1851** Benjamin R. Curtis

**1853**
Franklin Pierce

**1853** John A. Campbell

**1857**
James Buchanan

**1858** Nathan Clifford

| Chief Justices<br>Appointment date | Presidents<br>Inauguration date | Associate Justices<br>Appointment date |
|---|---|---|
| Roger Brooke Taney | | |
| | **1861**<br>Abraham Lincoln | |
| | | **1862** Noah H. Swayne |
| | | **1862** Samuel F. Miller |
| | | **1862** David Davis |
| | | **1863** Stephen J. Field |
| **1864**<br>Salmon P. Chase | | |
| | **1865**<br>Abraham Lincoln | |
| | **1865**<br>Andrew Johnson | |
| | **1869**<br>Ulysses S. Grant | |
| | | **1870** William Strong |
| | | **1870** Joseph P. Bradley |
| | | **1872** Ward Hunt |
| | **1873**<br>Ulysses S. Grant | |
| **1874**<br>Morrison R. Waite | | |
| | **1877**<br>Rutherford B. Hayes | |
| | | **1877** John Marshall Harlan |
| | | **1880** William B. Woods |
| | **1881**<br>James A. Garfield | |
| | | **1881** Stanley Matthews |
| | **1881**<br>Chester A. Arthur | |
| | | **1881** Horace Gray |
| | | **1882** Samuel Blatchford |
| | **1885**<br>Grover Cleveland | |
| **1888**<br>Melville W. Fuller | | **1888** Lucius Q. C. Lamar |
| | **1889**<br>Benjamin Harrison | |
| | | **1889** David J. Brewer |
| | | **1890** Henry B. Brown |
| | | **1892** George Shiras, Jr. |
| | | **1893** Howell Jackson |
| | **1893**<br>Grover Cleveland | |
| | | **1894** Edward Douglass White |
| | | **1895** Rufus W. Peckham |

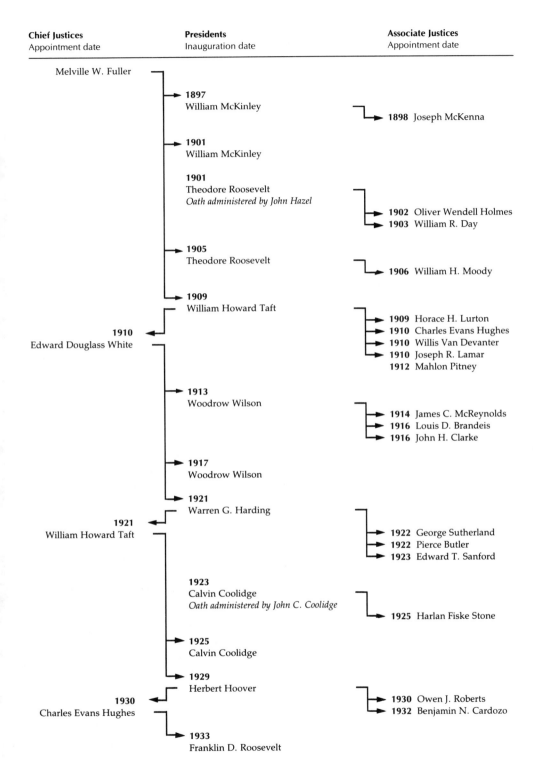

| Chief Justices<br>Appointment date | Presidents<br>Inauguration date | Associate Justices<br>Appointment date |
| --- | --- | --- |

Melville W. Fuller

**1897**
William McKinley

1898 Joseph McKenna

**1901**
William McKinley

**1901**
Theodore Roosevelt
*Oath administered by John Hazel*

1902 Oliver Wendell Holmes
1903 William R. Day

**1905**
Theodore Roosevelt

1906 William H. Moody

**1909**
William Howard Taft

**1910**
Edward Douglass White

1909 Horace H. Lurton
1910 Charles Evans Hughes
1910 Willis Van Devanter
1910 Joseph R. Lamar
1912 Mahlon Pitney

**1913**
Woodrow Wilson

1914 James C. McReynolds
1916 Louis D. Brandeis
1916 John H. Clarke

**1917**
Woodrow Wilson

**1921**
Warren G. Harding

**1921**
William Howard Taft

1922 George Sutherland
1922 Pierce Butler
1923 Edward T. Sanford

**1923**
Calvin Coolidge
*Oath administered by John C. Coolidge*

1925 Harlan Fiske Stone

**1925**
Calvin Coolidge

**1929**
Herbert Hoover

**1930**
Charles Evans Hughes

1930 Owen J. Roberts
1932 Benjamin N. Cardozo

**1933**
Franklin D. Roosevelt

| Chief Justices<br>Appointment date | Presidents<br>Inauguration date | Associate Justices<br>Appointment date |
|---|---|---|
| Charles Evans Hughes | | |
| | **1937**<br>Franklin D. Roosevelt | **1937** Hugo L. Black<br>**1938** Stanley Forman Reed<br>**1939** Felix Frankfurter<br>**1939** William O. Douglas<br>**1940** Frank Murphy |
| | **1941**<br>Franklin D. Roosevelt | |
| **1941**<br>Harlan Fiske Stone | | **1941** James F. Byrnes<br>**1941** Robert H. Jackson<br>**1943** Wiley B. Rutledge |
| | **1945**<br>Franklin D. Roosevelt | |
| | **1945**<br>Harry S. Truman | |
| **1946**<br>Fred M. Vinson | | **1945** Harold H. Burton |
| | **1949**<br>Harry S. Truman | **1949** Thomas C. Clark<br>**1949** Sherman Minton |
| | **1953**<br>Dwight D. Eisenhower | |
| **1953**<br>Earl Warren | | **1955** John Marshall Harlan<br>**1956** William J. Brennan, Jr. |
| | **1957**<br>Dwight D. Eisenhower | **1957** Charles E. Whittaker<br>**1958** Potter Stewart |
| | **1961**<br>John F. Kennedy | **1962** Byron R. White<br>**1962** Arthur J. Goldberg |
| | **1963**<br>Lyndon B. Johnson<br>*Oath administered by<br>Judge Sarah Hughes* | |
| | **1965**<br>Lyndon B. Johnson | **1965** Abe Fortas<br>**1967** Thurgood Marshall |

**Chief Justices**
Appointment date

**Presidents**
Inauguration date

**Associate Justices**
Appointment date

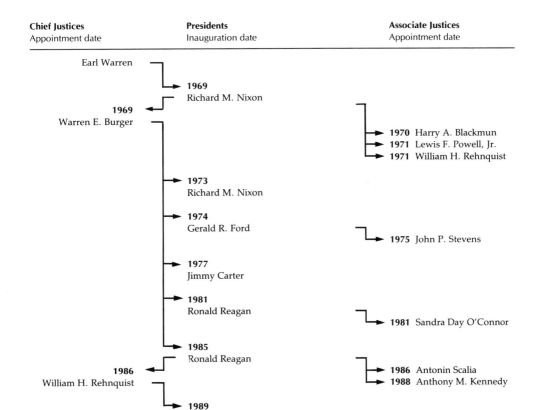

Earl Warren

**1969**
Richard M. Nixon

**1969**
Warren E. Burger

**1970** Harry A. Blackmun
**1971** Lewis F. Powell, Jr.
**1971** William H. Rehnquist

**1973**
Richard M. Nixon

**1974**
Gerald R. Ford

**1975** John P. Stevens

**1977**
Jimmy Carter

**1981**
Ronald Reagan

**1981** Sandra Day O'Connor

**1985**
Ronald Reagan

**1986**
William H. Rehnquist

**1986** Antonin Scalia
**1988** Anthony M. Kennedy

**1989**
George Bush

**1990** David H. Souter
**1991** Clarence Thomas

# Chronology of the Justices' Succession

| Date[1] | Justice | Action |
|---|---|---|
| 5 Oct. 1789 | James Wilson | Oath of Office |
| 19 Oct. 1789 | John Jay* | Oath of Office |
| 2 Feb. 1790 | William Cushing | Oath of Office |
| 2 Feb. 1790 | John Blair | Oath of Office |
| 15 Feb. 1790 | John Rutledge | Oath of Office |
| 12 May 1790 | James Iredell | Oath of Office |
| 5 Mar. 1791 | John Rutledge | Resigned |
| 6 Aug. 1792 | Thomas Johnson | Oath of Office |
| 16 Jan. 1793 | Thomas Johnson | Resigned |
| 11 Mar. 1793 | William Paterson | Oath of Office |
| 29 June 1795 | John Jay* | Resigned |
| 12 Aug. 1795 | John Rutledge* | Oath of Office |
| 25 Oct. 1795 | John Blair | Resigned |
| 15 Dec. 1795 | John Rutledge* | Rejected |
| 4 Feb. 1796 | Samuel Chase | Oath of Office |
| 8 Mar. 1796 | Oliver Ellsworth* | Oath of Office |
| 21 Aug. 1798 | James Wilson | Death |
| 4 Feb. 1799 | Bushrod Washington | Oath of Office |
| 20 Oct. 1799 | James Iredell | Death |
| 21 Apr. 1800 | Alfred Moore | Oath of Office |
| 15 Dec. 1800 | Oliver Ellsworth* | Resigned |
| 4 Feb. 1801 | John Marshall* | Oath of Office |
| 26 Jan. 1804 | Alfred Moore | Resigned |
| 8 May 1804 | William Johnson | Oath of Office |
| 9 Sep. 1806 | William Paterson | Death |
| 20 Jan. 1807 | Brockholst Livingston | Oath of Office |
| 4 May 1807 | Thomas Todd | Oath of Office |
| 13 Sep. 1810 | William Cushing | Death |
| 19 June 1811 | Samuel Chase | Death |
| 23 Nov. 1811 | Gabriel Duvall | Oath of Office |
| 3 Feb. 1812 | Joseph Story | Oath of Office |
| 18 Mar. 1823 | Brockholst Livingston | Death |
| 10 Feb. 1824 | Smith Thompson | Oath of Office |

---

*Denotes chief justice*

[1]In some instances, justices were appointed to the Court while the Senate was not in session, and a handful of these "recess appointees" took their judicial oaths before their names had been formally submitted to the Senate. The dates of oaths listed in this table refer to oaths taken *after* Senate confirmation. For other information regarding recess appointees, see the table of nominations, above.

| Date[1] | Justice | Action |
|---|---|---|
| 7 Feb. 1826 | Thomas Todd | Death |
| 16 June 1826 | Robert Trimble | Oath of Office |
| 25 Aug. 1828 | Robert Trimble | Death |
| 26 Nov. 1829 | Bushrod Washington | Death |
| 11 Jan. 1830 | John McLean | Oath of Office |
| 18 Jan. 1830 | Henry Baldwin | Oath of Office |
| 4 Aug. 1834 | William Johnson | Death |
| 14 Jan. 1835 | Gabriel Duvall | Resigned |
| 14 Jan. 1835 | James Moore Wayne | Oath of Office |
| 6 July 1835 | John Marshall* | Death |
| 28 Mar. 1836 | Roger Brooke Taney* | Oath of Office |
| 12 May 1836 | Philip Pendleton Barbour | Oath of Office |
| 1 May 1937 | John Catron | Oath of Office |
| 9 Jan. 1838 | John McKinley | Oath of Office |
| 25 Feb. 1841 | Philip Pendleton Barbour | Death |
| 10 Jan. 1842 | Peter Vivian Daniel | Oath of Office |
| 18 Dec. 1843 | Smith Thompson | Death |
| 21 Apr. 1844 | Henry Baldwin | Death |
| 27 Feb. 1845 | Samuel Nelson | Oath of Office |
| 10 Sep. 1845 | Joseph Story | Death |
| 3 Jan. 1846 | Levi Woodbury | Oath of Office |
| 10 Aug. 1846 | Robert Cooper Grier | Oath of Office |
| 4 Sep. 1851 | Levi Woodbury | Death |
| 10 Oct. 1851 | Benjamin Robbins Curtis | Oath of Office |
| 19 July 1852 | John McKinley | Death |
| 11 Apr. 1853 | John Archibald Campbell | Oath of Office |
| 30 Sep. 1857 | Benjamin Robbins Curtis | Resigned |
| 21 Jan. 1858 | Nathan Clifford | Oath of Office |
| 31 May 1860 | Peter Vivian Daniel | Death |
| 4 Apr. 1861 | John McLean | Death |
| 30 Apr. 1861 | John Archibald Campbell | Resigned |
| 27 Jan. 1862 | Noah Haynes Swayne | Oath of Office |
| 21 July 1862 | Samuel Freeman Miller | Oath of Office |
| 10 Dec. 1862 | David Davis | Oath of Office |
| 20 May 1863 | Stephen Johnson Field | Oath of Office |
| 12 Oct. 1864 | Roger Brooke Taney* | Death |
| 15 Dec. 1864 | Salmon Portland Chase* | Oath of Office |
| 30 May 1865 | John Catron | Death |
| 5 July 1867 | James Moore Wayne | Death |
| 31 Jan. 1870 | Robert Cooper Grier | Retired |
| 14 Mar. 1870 | William Strong | Oath of Office |
| 23 Mar. 1870 | Joseph P. Bradley | Oath of Office |
| 28 Nov. 1872 | Samuel Nelson | Retired |
| 9 Jan. 1873 | Ward Hunt | Oath of Office |
| 7 May 1873 | Salmon Portland Chase* | Death |
| 4 Mar. 1874 | Morrison Remick Waite* | Oath of Office |
| 4 Mar. 1877 | David Davis | Resigned |
| 10 Dec. 1877 | John Marshall Harlan | Oath of Office |

| Date [1] | Justice | Action |
|---|---|---|
| 14 Dec. 1880 | William Strong | Retired |
| 5 Jan. 1881 | William Burnham Woods | Oath of Office |
| 24 Jan. 1881 | Noah Haynes Swayne | Retired |
| 17 May 1881 | Stanley Matthews | Oath of Office |
| 25 July 1881 | Nathan Clifford | Death |
| 9 Jan. 1882 | Horace Gray | Oath of Office |
| 27 Jan. 1882 | Ward Hunt | Disabled |
| 3 Apr. 1882 | Samuel Blatchford | Oath of Office |
| 14 May 1887 | William Burnham Woods | Death |
| 18 Jan. 1888 | Lucius Quintus C. Lamar | Oath of Office |
| 23 Mar. 1888 | Morrison Remick Waite* | Death |
| 8 Oct. 1888 | Melville Weston Fuller* | Oath of Office |
| 22 Mar. 1889 | Stanley Matthews | Death |
| 6 Jan. 1890 | David Josiah Brewer | Oath of Office |
| 13 Oct. 1890 | Samuel Freeman Miller | Death |
| 5 Jan. 1891 | Henry Billings Brown | Oath of Office |
| 22 Jan. 1892 | Joseph P. Bradley | Death |
| 10 Oct. 1892 | George Shiras, Jr. | Oath of Office |
| 23 Jan. 1893 | Lucius Quintus C. Lamar | Death |
| 4 Mar. 1893 | Howell Edmunds Jackson | Oath of Office |
| 7 July 1893 | Samuel Blatchford | Death |
| 12 Mar. 1894 | Edward Douglass White | Oath of Office |
| 8 Aug. 1895 | Howell Edmunds Jackson | Death |
| 6 Jan. 1896 | Rufus Wheeler Peckham | Oath of Office |
| 1 Dec. 1897 | Stephen Johnson Field | Retired |
| 26 Jan. 1898 | Joseph McKenna | Oath of Office |
| 15 Sep. 1902 | Horace Gray | Death |
| 8 Dec. 1902 | Oliver Wendell Holmes | Oath of Office |
| 23 Feb. 1903 | George Shiras, Jr. | Retired |
| 2 Mar. 1903 | William Rufus Day | Oath of Office |
| 28 May 1906 | Henry Billings Brown | Retired |
| 17 Dec. 1906 | William Henry Moody | Oath of Office |
| 24 Oct. 1909 | Rufus Wheeler Peckham | Death |
| 3 Jan. 1910 | Horace Harmon Lurton | Oath of Office |
| 28 Mar. 1910 | David Josiah Brewer | Death |
| 4 July 1910 | Melville Weston Fuller* | Death |
| 10 Oct. 1910 | Charles Evans Hughes | Oath of Office |
| 20 Nov. 1910 | William Henry Moody | Disabled |
| 18 Dec. 1910 | Edward Douglass White | Promoted |
| 19 Dec. 1910 | Edward Douglass White* | Oath of Office |
| 3 Jan. 1911 | Willis Van Devanter | Oath of Office |
| 3 Jan. 1911 | Joseph Rucker Lamar | Oath of Office |
| 14 Oct. 1911 | John Marshall Harlan | Death |
| 18 Mar. 1912 | Mahlon Pitney | Oath of Office |
| 12 July 1914 | Horace Harmon Lurton | Death |
| 5 Sep. 1914 | James Clark McReynolds | Oath of Office |
| 2 Jan. 1916 | Joseph Rucker Lamar | Death |
| 5 June 1916 | Louis Dembitz Brandeis | Oath of Office |

| Date[1] | Justice | Action |
|---|---|---|
| 10 June 1916 | Charles Evans Hughes | Resigned |
| 1 Aug. 1916 | John Hessin Clarke | Oath of Office |
| 19 May 1921 | Edward Douglass White* | Death |
| 11 July 1921 | William Howard Taft* | Oath of Office |
| 18 Sep. 1922 | John Hessin Clarke | Resigned |
| 2 Oct. 1922 | George Sutherland | Oath of Office |
| 13 Nov. 1922 | William Rufus Day | Retired |
| 31 Dec. 1922 | Mahlon Pitney | Disabled |
| 2 Jan. 1923 | Pierce Butler | Oath of Office |
| 5 Feb. 1923 | Edward Terry Sanford | Oath of Office |
| 5 Jan. 1925 | Joseph McKenna | Retired |
| 2 Mar. 1925 | Harlan Fiske Stone | Oath of Office |
| 3 Feb. 1930 | William Howard Taft* | Retired |
| 24 Feb. 1930 | Charles Evans Hughes* | Oath of Office |
| 8 Mar. 1930 | Edward Terry Sanford | Death |
| 2 June 1930 | Owen Josephus Roberts | Oath of Office |
| 12 Jan. 1932 | Oliver Wendell Holmes | Retired |
| 14 Mar. 1932 | Benjamin Nathan Cardozo | Oath of Office |
| 2 June 1937 | Willis Van Devanter | Retired |
| 19 Aug. 1937 | Hugo Lafayette Black | Oath of Office |
| 17 Jan. 1938 | George Sutherland | Retired |
| 31 Jan. 1938 | Stanley Forman Reed | Oath of Office |
| 9 July 1938 | Benjamin Nathan Cardozo | Death |
| 30 Jan. 1939 | Felix Frankfurter | Oath of Office |
| 13 Feb. 1939 | Louis Dembitz Brandeis | Retired |
| 17 Apr. 1939 | William Orville Douglas | Oath of Office |
| 16 Nov. 1939 | Pierce Butler | Death |
| 18 Jan. 1940 | Frank Murphy | Oath of Office |
| 1 Feb. 1941 | James Clark McReynolds | Retired |
| 1 July 1941 | Charles Evans Hughes* | Retired |
| 2 July 1941 | Harlan Fiske Stone | Promoted |
| 3 July 1941 | Harlan Fiske Stone* | Oath of Office |
| 8 July 1941 | James Francis Byrnes | Oath of Office |
| 11 July 1941 | Robert Houghwout Jackson | Oath of Office |
| 3 Oct. 1942 | James Francis Byrnes | Resigned |
| 15 Feb. 1943 | Wiley Blount Rutledge | Oath of Office |
| 31 July 1945 | Owen Josephus Roberts | Resigned |
| 1 Oct. 1945 | Harold Hitz Burton | Oath of Office |
| 22 Apr. 1946 | Harlan Fiske Stone* | Death |
| 24 June 1946 | Fred Moore Vinson* | Oath of Office |
| 19 July 1949 | Frank Murphy | Death |
| 24 Aug. 1949 | Thomas Campbell Clark | Oath of Office |
| 10 Sep. 1949 | Wiley Blount Rutledge | Death |
| 12 Oct. 1949 | Sherman Minton | Oath of Office |
| 8 Sep. 1953 | Fred Moore Vinson* | Death |
| 5 Oct. 1953 | Earl Warren* | Oath of Office |
| 9 Oct. 1954 | Robert Houghwout Jackson | Death |
| 28 Mar. 1955 | John Marshall Harlan II | Oath of Office |

| Date[1] | Justice | Action |
|---|---|---|
| 15 Oct. 1956 | Sherman Minton | Retired |
| 25 Feb. 1957 | Stanley Forman Reed | Retired |
| 22 Mar. 1957 | William J. Brennan, Jr. | Oath of Office |
| 25 Mar. 1957 | Charles Evans Whittaker | Oath of Office |
| 13 Oct. 1958 | Harold Hitz Burton | Retired |
| 14 Oct. 1958 | Potter Stewart | Oath of Office |
| 1 Apr. 1962 | Charles Evans Whittaker | Disabled |
| 16 Apr. 1962 | Byron Raymond White | Oath of Office |
| 28 Aug. 1962 | Felix Frankfurter | Retired |
| 1 Oct. 1962 | Arthur Joseph Goldberg | Oath of Office |
| 25 July 1965 | Arthur Joseph Goldberg | Resigned |
| 4 Oct. 1965 | Abe Fortas | Oath of Office |
| 12 June 1967 | Thomas Campbell Clark | Retired |
| 2 Oct. 1967 | Thurgood Marshall | Oath of Office |
| 14 May 1969 | Abe Fortas | Resigned |
| 23 June 1969 | Earl Warren* | Resigned |
| 23 June 1969 | Warren Earl Burger* | Oath of Office |
| 9 June 1970 | Harry A. Blackmun | Oath of Office |
| 17 Sep. 1971 | Hugo Lafayette Black | Retired |
| 23 Sep. 1971 | John Marshall Harlan II | Retired |
| 7 Jan. 1972 | Lewis F. Powell, Jr. | Oath of Office |
| 7 Jan. 1972 | William H. Rehnquist | Oath of Office |
| 12 Nov. 1975 | William Orville Douglas | Retired |
| 19 Dec. 1975 | John Paul Stevens | Oath of Office |
| 3 July 1981 | Potter Stewart | Retired |
| 25 Sep. 1981 | Sandra Day O'Connor | Oath of Office |
| 26 Sep. 1986 | Warren Earl Burger | Retired |
| 26 Sep. 1986 | William H. Rehnquist | Promoted |
| 26 Sep. 1986 | William H. Rehnquist* | Oath of Office |
| 26 Sep. 1986 | Antonin Scalia | Oath of Office |
| 26 June 1987 | Lewis F. Powell, Jr. | Retired |
| 18 Feb. 1988 | Anthony M. Kennedy | Oath of Office |
| 20 July 1990 | William J. Brennan, Jr. | Retired |
| 9 Oct. 1990 | David H. Souter | Oath of Office |
| 27 June 1991 | Thurgood Marshall | Retired |
| 1 Nov. 1991 | Clarence Thomas | Oath of Office |

# Succession of the Justices

| Departing Justice/<br>Date of Vacancy | Replacement Justice/<br>Date of Arrival[1] | Days without<br>Full Court[1] |
|---|---|---|
| John Rutledge<br>5 Mar. 1791 | Thomas Johnson<br>6 Aug. 1792 | 519 |
| Thomas Johnson<br>16 Jan. 1793 | William Paterson<br>11 Mar. 1793 | 54 |
| John Jay*<br>29 June 1795 | John Rutledge*<br>12 Aug. 1795 | 44 |
| John Rutledge*<br>15 Dec. 1795 | Oliver Ellsworth*<br>8 Mar. 1796 | 83 |
| John Blair<br>25 Oct. 1795 | Samuel Chase<br>4 Feb. 1796 | 102 |
| James Wilson<br>21 Aug. 1798 | Bushrod Washington<br>4 Feb. 1799 | 167 |
| James Iredell<br>20 Oct. 1799 | Alfred Moore<br>21 Apr. 1800 | 183 |
| Oliver Ellsworth*<br>15 Dec. 1800 | John Marshall*<br>4 Feb. 1801 | 51 |
| Alfred Moore<br>26 Jan. 1804 | William Johnson<br>8 May 1804 | 102 |
| William Paterson<br>9 Sep. 1806 | Brockholst Livingston<br>20 Jan. 1807 | 133 |
| William Cushing<br>13 Sep. 1810 | Joseph Story<br>3 Feb. 1812 | 508<br>(between Cushing's<br>departure and<br>Story's arrival)[2] |
| Samuel Chase<br>19 June 1811 | Gabriel Duvall<br>23 Nov. 1811 | |
| Brockholst Livingston<br>18 Mar. 1823 | Smith Thompson<br>10 Feb. 1824 | 330 |
| Thomas Todd<br>7 Feb. 1826 | Robert Trimble<br>16 June 1826 | 129 |
| Robert Trimble<br>25 Aug. 1828 | John McLean<br>11 Jan. 1830 | 505<br>(between Trimble's<br>departure and<br>Baldwin's arrival) |
| Bushrod Washington<br>26 Nov. 1829 | Henry Baldwin<br>18 Jan. 1830 | |

---

*Denoted chief justice

[1]In some instances, justices were appointed to the Court while the Senate was not in session, and a handful of these "recess appointees" took their judicial oaths before their names had been formally submitted to the Senate. The dates and numbers of days listed in this table refer to the official arrival of a justice on the Supreme Court, that is, the date of oath *after* Senate confirmation, even though the justice may already have taken his or her seat and participated in decisions. For further information regarding recess appointees, see the table of nominations, above.

[2]Braces indicate periods when a new vacancy occurred before all existing vacancies were filled. Thus, the number of days without a full court continues to increase until all vacancies are filled, although the succession was not broken. In this instance, before Justice Cushing could be replaced, Justice Chase retired and was replaced by Justice Duvall. Justice Story finally took Justice Cushing's seat 508 days after it had been vacated.

| Departing Justice/ Date of Vacancy | Replacement Justice/ Date of Arrival[1] | Days without Full Court[1] |
|---|---|---|
| William Johnson 4 Aug. 1834 | James Moore Wayne 14 Jan. 1835 | 646 (between Johnson's departure and Taney's arrival) |
| Gabriel Duvall 14 Jan. 1835 | Philip P. Barbour 12 May 1836 | |
| John Marshall* 6 July 1835 | Roger Brooke Taney* 28 Mar. 1836 | |
| Philip P. Barbour 25 Feb. 1841 | Peter Vivian Daniel 10 Jan. 1842 | 319 |
| Smith Thompson 18 Dec. 1843 | Samuel Nelson 27 Feb. 1845 | 965 (between Thompson's departure and Grier's arrival)[3] |
| Henry Baldwin 21 Apr. 1844 | Robert Cooper Grier 10 Aug. 1846 | |
| Joseph Story 10 Sep. 1845 | Levi Woodbury 3 Jan. 1846 | |
| Levi Woodbury 4 Sep. 1851 | Benjamin Robbins Curtis 10 Oct. 1851 | 36 |
| John McKinley 19 July 1852 | John Archibald Campbell 11 Apr. 1853 | 266 |
| Benjamin Robbins Curtis 30 Sep. 1857 | Nathan Clifford 21 Jan. 1858 | 113 |
| Peter Vivian Daniel 31 May 1860 | Samuel Freeman Miller 21 July 1862 | 923 (between Daniel's departure and Davis's arrival) |
| John McLean 4 Apr. 1861 | Noah Haynes Swayne 27 Jan. 1862 | |
| John Archibald Campbell 30 Apr. 1861 | David Davis 10 Dec. 1862 | |
| Roger Brooke Taney* 12 Oct. 1864 | Salmon Portland Chase* 15 Dec. 1864 | 64 |
| John Catron 30 May 1865 | No Replacement[4] | |
| James Moore Wayne 5 July 1867 | No Replacement[4] | |
| Robert Cooper Grier 31 Jan. 1870 | William Strong 14 Mar. 1870 | 42 |
| Samuel Nelson 28 Nov. 1872 | Ward Hunt 9 Jan. 1873 | 42 |
| Salmon Portland Chase* 7 May 1873 | Morrison Remick Waite* 4 Mar. 1874 | 301 |
| David Davis 4 Mar. 1877 | John Marshall Harlan 10 Dec. 1877 | 281 |
| William Strong 14 Dec. 1880 | William Burnham Woods 5 Jan. 1881 | 22 |

[3]Although Justice Baldwin left the bench before Justice Story, his replacement, Justice Grier, did not arrive until after Justice Story's replacement did. Therefore, at least one seat was vacant for 965 days, from Justice Thompson's departure to Justice Grier's arrival.

[4]Under the provisions of the Judiciary Act of 1866, the size of the Court was to decrease from ten to seven by attrition; the Judiciary Act of 1869 reestablished the number of justices at nine.

| Departing Justice/ Date of Vacancy | Replacement Justice/ Date of Arrival[1] | Days without Full Court[1] |
|---|---|---|
| Noah Haynes Swayne 24 Jan. 1881 | Stanley Matthews 17 May 1881 | 113 |
| Nathan Clifford 25 July 1881 | Horace Gray 9 Jan. 1882 | 168 |
| Ward Hunt 27 Jan. 1882 | Samuel Blatchford 3 Apr. 1882 | 66 |
| William Burnham Woods 14 May 1887 | Lucius Quintus C. Lamar 18 Jan. 1888 | 249 |
| Morrison Remick Waite* 23 Mar. 1888 | Melville Weston Fuller* 8 Oct. 1888 | 199 |
| Stanley Matthews 22 Mar. 1889 | David Josiah Brewer 6 Jan. 1890 | 290 |
| Samuel Freeman Miller 13 Oct. 1890 | Henry Billings Brown 5 Jan. 1891 | 84 |
| Joseph P. Bradley 22 Jan. 1892 | George Shiras, Jr. 10 Oct. 1892 | 261 |
| Lucius Quintus C. Lamar 23 Jan. 1893 | Howell Edmunds Jackson 4 Mar. 1893 | 40 |
| Samuel Blatchford 7 July 1893 | Edward Douglass White 12 Mar. 1894 | 248 |
| Howell Edmunds Jackson 8 Aug. 1895 | Rufus Wheeler Peckham 6 Jan. 1896 | 151 |
| Stephen Johnson Field 1 Dec. 1897 | Joseph McKenna 26 Jan. 1898 | 56 |
| Horace Gray 15 Sep. 1902 | Oliver Wendell Holmes 8 Dec. 1902 | 84 |
| George Shiras, Jr. 23 Feb. 1903 | William Rufus Day 2 Mar. 1903 | 7 |
| Henry Billings Brown 28 May 1906 | William Henry Moody 17 Dec. 1906 | 203 |
| Rufus Wheeler Peckham 24 Oct. 1909 | Horace Harmon Lurton 3 Jan. 1910 | 71 |
| David Josiah Brewer 28 Mar. 1910 | Charles Evans Hughes 10 Oct. 1910 | |
| Melville Weston Fuller* 4 July 1910 | Edward Douglass White* 19 Dec. 1910 | 281 (between Brewer's departure and Lamar's arrival) |
| William Henry Moody 20 Nov. 1910 | Willis Van Devanter 3 Jan. 1911 | |
| Edward Douglass White[5] 18 Dec. 1910 | Joseph Rucker Lamar 3 Jan. 1911 | |
| John Marshall Harlan 14 Oct. 1911 | Mahlon Pitney 18 Mar. 1912 | 155 |
| Horace Harmon Lurton 12 July 1914 | James Clark McReynolds 5 Sep. 1914 | 55 |
| Joseph Rucker Lamar 2 Jan. 1916 | Louis Dembitz Brandeis 5 June 1916 | 154 |

[5]Note that in these instances the vacancy was created by elevation of a sitting associate justice to the position of chief justice, not as a result of the justice's departure from the Court.

| Departing Justice/<br>Date of Vacancy | Replacement Justice/<br>Date of Arrival[1] | Days without<br>Full Court[1] |
|---|---|---|
| Charles Evans Hughes<br>10 June 1916 | John Hessin Clarke<br>1 Aug. 1916 | 51 |
| Edward Douglass White*<br>19 May 1921 | William Howard Taft*<br>11 July 1921 | 53 |
| John Hessin Clarke<br>18 Sep. 1922 | George Sutherland<br>2 Oct. 1922 | 14 |
| William Rufus Day<br>13 Nov. 1922 | Pierce Butler<br>2 Jan. 1923 | 84<br>(between Day's<br>departure and<br>Sanford's arrival) |
| Mahlon Pitney<br>31 Dec. 1922 | Edward Terry Sanford<br>5 Feb. 1923 | |
| Joseph McKenna<br>5 Jan. 1925 | Harlan Fiske Stone<br>2 Mar. 1925 | 56 |
| William Howard Taft*<br>3 Feb. 1930 | Charles Evans Hughes*<br>24 Feb. 1930 | 21 |
| Edward Terry Sanford<br>8 Mar. 1930 | Owen Josephus Roberts<br>2 June 1930 | 86 |
| Oliver Wendell Holmes<br>12 Jan. 1932 | Benjamin Nathan Cardozo<br>14 Mar. 1932 | 61 |
| Willis Van Devanter<br>2 June 1937 | Hugo Lafayette Black<br>19 Aug. 1937 | 78 |
| George Sutherland<br>17 Jan. 1938 | Stanley Forman Reed<br>31 Jan. 1938 | 14 |
| Benjamin Nathan Cardozo<br>9 July 1938 | Felix Frankfurter<br>30 Jan. 1939 | 205 |
| Louis Dembitz Brandeis<br>13 Feb. 1939 | William Orville Douglas<br>17 Apr. 1939 | 63 |
| Pierce Butler<br>16 Nov. 1939 | Frank Murphy<br>18 Jan. 1940 | 61 |
| James Clark McReynolds<br>1 Feb. 1941 | James Francis Byrnes<br>8 July 1941 | 160<br>(between McReynolds's<br>departure and<br>Jackson's arrival) |
| Charles Evans Hughes*<br>1 July 1941 | Harlan Fiske Stone*<br>3 July 1941 | |
| Harlan Fiske Stone[5]<br>2 July 1941 | Robert H. Jackson<br>11 July 1941 | |
| James Francis Byrnes<br>3 Oct. 1942 | Wiley Blount Rutledge<br>15 Feb. 1943 | 135 |
| Owen Josephus Roberts<br>31 July 1945 | Harold Hitz Burton<br>1 Oct. 1945 | 62 |
| Harlan Fiske Stone*<br>22 Apr. 1946 | Fred Moore Vinson*<br>24 June 1946 | 63 |
| Frank Murphy<br>19 July 1949 | Thomas Campbell Clark<br>24 Aug. 1949 | 36 |
| Wiley Blount Rutledge<br>10 Sep. 1949 | Sherman Minton<br>12 Oct. 1949 | 32 |
| Fred Moore Vinson*<br>8 Sep. 1953 | Earl Warren*<br>2 Mar. 1953 | 174 |
| Robert H. Jackson<br>9 Oct. 1954 | John Marshall Harlan II<br>28 Mar. 1955 | 170 |
| Sherman Minton<br>15 Oct. 1956 | William J. Brennan, Jr.<br>22 Mar. 1957 | 161<br>(between Minton's<br>departure and<br>Whittaker's arrival) |
| Stanley Forman Reed<br>25 Feb. 1957 | Charles Evans Whittaker<br>25 Mar. 1957 | |

| Departing Justice/ Date of Vacancy | Replacement Justice/ Date of Arrival[1] | Days without Full Court[1] |
|---|---|---|
| Harold Hitz Burton 13 Oct. 1958 | Potter Stewart 15 May 1959 | 213 |
| Charles Evans Whittaker 1 Apr. 1963 | Byron Raymond White 16 Apr. 1962 | 45 |
| Felix Frankfurter 28 Aug. 1962 | Arthur Joseph Goldberg 1 Oct. 1962 | 34 |
| Arthur Joseph Goldberg 25 July 1965 | Abe Fortas 4 Oct. 1965 | 71 |
| Thomas Campbell Clark 12 June 1967 | Thurgood Marshall 2 Oct. 1967 | 112 |
| Abe Fortas 14 May 1969 | Harry A. Blackmun 9 June 1970 | 391 |
| Earl Warren* 23 June 1969 | Warren Earl Burger* 23 June 1969 | 0 |
| Hugo Lafayette Black 17 Sep. 1971 | Lewis F. Powell, Jr. 7 Jan. 1972 | 112 (between Black's departure and Rehnquist's arrival) |
| John Marshall Harlan II 23 Sep. 1971 | William H. Rehnquist 7 Jan. 1972 | |
| William Orville Douglas 12 Nov. 1975 | John Paul Stevens 19 Dec. 1975 | 37 |
| Potter Stewart 3 July 1981 | Sandra Day O'Connor 25 Sep. 1981 | 84 |
| Warren Earl Burger* 26 Sep. 1986 | William H. Rehnquist* 26 Sep. 1986 | 0 |
| William H. Rehnquist[5] 26 Sep. 1986 | Antonin Scalia 26 Sep. 1986 | 0 |
| Lewis F. Powell, Jr. 26 June 1987 | Anthony M. Kennedy 18 Feb. 1988 | 237 |
| William J. Brennan, Jr. 20 July 1990 | David H. Souter 9 Oct. 1990 | 81 |
| Thurgood Marshall 27 June 1991 | Clarence Thomas 1 Nov. 1991 | 127 |

# Trivia and Traditions of the Court

**Firsts and Trivia**
*From the Research Files of the
Curator's Office in the
Supreme Court of the United States*

## FIRSTS

■ The first session of the Supreme Court was on 2 February 1790, in the Royal Exchange building in New York City.

■ The first session in the new Supreme Court building was on 7 October 1935. There were no cases argued in that first session.

■ The first case argued in the new building was *Douglas* v. *Willcuts,* argued on 14 October 1935.

■ The first Supreme Court bar member was Elias Boudinot, sworn in on 5 February 1790.

■ The first black Supreme Court bar member was John S. Rock, admitted on 5 February 1865.

■ The first woman Supreme Court bar member was Belva Ann Lockwood of the District of Columbia, admitted on 3 March 1879.

■ The first deaf attorney to argue a case before the Court was Michael A. Chatoff, who argued *Board of Education* v. *Rowley* on 23 March 1982.

■ The first woman law clerk was Lucile Loman, who clerked for Justice Douglas from 22 October 1944 to 30 September 1945.

■ The first black law clerk was William T. Coleman, who clerked for Justice Frankfurter from 1 September 1948 to 31 August 1949.

■ The first woman Court officer was Helen Newman, who was the Court's first female librarian.

■ The Court's first female police sargeant was Eileen F. Cincotta, appointed on 18 August 1985.

■ The first president and vice president elect to visit the Court were Ronald Reagan and George Bush on 11 November 1980.

■ The first woman justice to issue the oath of office in a presidential inauguration was Justice O'Connor, who issued the oath of office to Vice President elect Dan Quayle on Friday, 20 January 1989.

## TRIVIA

■ The youngest Supreme Court appointee was Joseph Story, who was appointed on 3 February 1812, at the age of 32.

■ The longest living justice was Stanley F. Reed, who lived to be 95 years old. He retired on 25 February 1957, at the age of 72.

■ The only foreign-born justices were James Wilson, born in Scotland in 1742; James Iredell, born in England in 1751; David Brewer, born in Asia Minor in 1837; George Sutherland, born in England in 1862; and Felix Frankfurter, born in Austria in 1882.

■ There have been sixteen chief justices in the history of the Court.

■ George Washington appointed the most justices to the Court: 11. President Franklin D. Roosevelt appointed 9.

■ Jimmy Carter was the only president to serve a full term in office without appointing any justices to the Court. Only four presidents—William H. Harrison, Zachary Taylor, Andrew Johnson, and Jimmy Carter—never appointed a justice.

■ Chief Justice Roger B. Taney swore in the most presidents (7), but Chief Justice John Marshall administered the oath of office the most times (9 times to 5 presidents).

■ There have been three family connections on the high court:

1. John Marshall Harlan (1877–1911) and his grandson John Marshall Harlan (1955–1971).

2. Stephen J. Field (1863–1897) and his nephew David J. Brewer (1890–1910).

3. Lucius Q. C. Lamar (1883–1893) was a distant relative of Joseph R. Lamar (1911–1916).

■ Five justices have been associate justices before becoming chief justices: John Rutledge, Edward D. White, Charles E. Hughes, Harlan F. Stone, and William H. Rehnquist.

■ Harlan F. Stone was the only justice to sit in every chair on the bench. He progressed from most junior to most senior associate justice before he was appointed chief justice.

■ Oliver W. Holmes, at the age of 90, was the oldest justice ever to sit on the Supreme Court.

■ William O. Douglas served the longest term on the Court: 36 years and almost 7 months.

■ John Rutledge served the shortest term on the Court: 1 year as an associate justice and 4 months as chief justice.

■ William H. Taft was the only justice also to serve as president of the United States.

■ The most justices have come from New York (13) and Ohio (9).

■ Samuel Chase was the only justice to be impeached. He was not convicted, however.

■ Salmon P. Chase is the only justice whose likeness ever appeared on U.S. currency. He was on the $10,000 bill, which is no longer printed.

■ Justices Byron White, John Paul Stevens, and William H. Rehnquist are the only justices who served as Supreme Court law clerks after graduating from law school. White worked for Justice Fred M. Vinson in 1946–1947; Stevens worked for Justice Wiley B. Rutledge in 1947–1948; Rehnquist worked for Justice Robert H. Jackson in 1952–1953.

## Traditions of the Court

■ Since at least 1800, it has been traditional for justices to wear black robes while in Court. During the Court's earliest years, under Chief Justice John Jay, the justices wore robes with a red facing, somewhat like those worn by English judges.

■ Seniority has always been an important part of the institutional practices of the Court. Seniority is determined by length of service, except in the case of the chief justice, who is always considered the most senior justice.

■ On the bench, seniority determines seating. The chief justice sits in the center of the Supreme Court bench, while the senior associate justice sits to his right. The next senior justice sits to the chief justice's left, the next to his right, and so forth, alternating right to left by degree of seniority. The most junior justice, therefore, sits in the farthest seat to the left of the chief justice.

■ Seniority also determines seating in the conference room. The chief justice sits at one end of the table, while the senior associate justice sits at the other. The junior justice sits closest to the door and, because no one besides the justices is present during conferences, must serve as the doorkeeper. While in conference, the Court discusses and votes on cases in order of seniority.

■ In the 1880s, Chief Justice Melville Fuller instituted the tradition of the judicial handshake. When the justices gather to meet in conference or to go on the bench, each justice shakes the hands of the other eight justices. Fuller initiated the practice to remind the justices that, despite their differences, all members of the Court shared a unity of purpose.

■ New justices take their oaths of office in a formal investiture ceremony in the courtroom. The new justice, seated below the bench in a chair that belonged to John Marshall, listens as the attorney general reads the letters patent nominating the justice to the Court. The chief justice then administers the oath to the new justice and seats him/her on the bench with the others.

■ On state occasions, such as presidential inaugurations, the justices attend together, wearing their robes. The justices formerly wore top hats at outdoor ceremonies, but, beginning at the inauguration of Woodrow Wilson, justices began to wear black brimless hats known as skullcaps. At President George Bush's inauguration, Chief Justice Rehnquist and Justice O'Connor wore skullcaps.

■ The titles affixed to the names of the justices have changed over time. Traditionally, a justice's title had been "Mr. Justice," as in "Mr. Justice Blackmun." In November 1980, however, the justices dropped the prefix and began signing their opinions simply "Justice Blackmun." When orally addressing a member of the Court, one refers to the justice as simply "Justice Blackmun," but one still addresses the chief justice as "Mr. Chief Justice."

■ Traditionally all attorneys practicing before the Supreme Court were required to wear formal "morning clothes." Today, only members of the Department of Justice and other advocates of the United States government adhere to the tradition of formal dress. Most private attorneys wear dark business suits, although some still follow the more formal custom.

■ Quill pens remain an important part of the courtroom, as they did in the Court's earliest days. The staff of the Court places twenty ten-inch white quills on counsel tables each day that the Court is in session.

■ The Court has a traditional seal, much like the Great Seal of the United States but with a single star beneath the eagle's claws. The clerk of the Court keeps the seal of the Supreme Court and uses it to certify official documents, such as certificates given to attorneys newly admitted to practice before the Court. The seal the Court presently uses is the fifth in the institution's history.

■ When a new justice is appointed to the Court, one of the justices will host a dinner to welcome him/her. These dinners are open only to the justices (including former justices) and their spouses.

■ Upon the retirement of a justice, the rest of the Court will purchase either his bench chair or his conference room chair and present it to the justice. After retiring, a justice retains an office and a small staff in the Court building until his death.

■ The justices throw a Christmas party each year for the entire staff of the Supreme Court. Moreover, in recent years the justices have instituted a new tradition: giving welcome and farewell parties to law clerks as they arrive and depart.

■ Another new tradition at the Court are law clerk reunions, in which former clerks of a specific justice host a dinner for that justice at the Supreme Court courtroom.

■ Although the Constitution prescribes that the president take the oath of office, it is only a tradition that the chief justice administer the oath. Indeed, on seven occasions, an official other than the chief justice administered the oath of office (see chart of appointments by presidential term, Appendix 2, pp. 972–977).

# Case Index

# Topical Index